British Dramatists

FROM

DRYDEN TO SHERIDAN

EDITED BY

GEORGE H. NETTLETON, *Yale University*

and

ARTHUR E. CASE, *Northwestern University*

HOUGHTON MIFFLIN COMPANY

BOSTON

The Riverside Press Cambridge

The Riverside Press

CAMBRIDGE · MASSACHUSETTS

PRINTED IN THE U.S.A.

PREFACE

THIS collection of plays seeks to illustrate significant periods and types of English drama from 1660 to 1780. Characteristic works of dramatists from Dryden to Sheridan are accordingly grouped and discussed in broad relation to their times and tendencies. For further background, some salient passages are quoted from contemporary commentators like Dryden, Jeremy Collier, Fielding, and Goldsmith, who variously reflect different periods and aspects of critical controversy in the theatre. The choice of representative plays freely includes familiar masterpieces and examples. Thus the historic trio of eighteenth-century comedies, *She Stoops to Conquer*, *The Rivals*, and *The School for Scandal*, and the outstanding trio of dramatic burlesques, *The Rehearsal*, *Tom Thumb*, and *The Critic*, are maintained in the full force of their firm associations in dramatic history and stage tradition. Other interrelations within a given period, as in the close connection of *The Rehearsal* with *The Conquest of Granada*, or between different periods, as in the case of Restoration and eighteenth-century comedies of manners, or of early and late sentimental comedies, are considerably exemplified. In the rich field of Restoration comedy, the choice of representative dramatists includes the four grouped by Leigh Hunt in 1840, together with Etherege, their predecessor, whom Gosse may be said to have prefixed to the canon. Most of the plays in this volume were promptly established as typical stage favorites, and many of them long outlived on the stage the immediate periods and fashions which they represent in the historic development of English drama.

In printing these plays, explanatory notes for the general reader are distinctly separated from textual variants that need concern only the special student. For similar convenience, an appendix entitled TEXTUAL NOTES (pp. 913–957) segregates detailed bibliographical and textual information concerning each play, and indicates the preferred text, the specific copies of different editions collated, and the location in various libraries, British and American, of many other early and rare editions. The general method has been first to study, with especial heed to the author's sanctions and revisions, the successive editions published in his lifetime, and then to consider later reprints and critical editions. To clarify the details of factual evidence, there is supplied for each play a general history of the printed text, together with interpretation of significant collations. Bibliographical and textual data, though often sufficiently extensive to serve other purposes, are here considered less as ends in themselves than as means to establish and illustrate the main critical conclusions. In turn, these similar studies of so many representative plays will, it is hoped, combine to fuller understanding of the varying practices of Restoration and eighteenth-century playwrights and publishers, and of the methods and findings of later editors of their texts.

The bibliographical and critical sections of this volume attest our constant obligations to many libraries and scholars at home and abroad. Our debts to the officers and staffs of the British and American libraries where this work has been mainly accomplished have multiplied beyond the possibilities of individual acknowledgment. It seems, however, peculiarly fitting in a work so directly dependent on their united resources and generosity to express to them undivided gratitude. To the body of scholars whose manifold contributions to the common field are later specified, we here return like gratitude.

The editors have closely collaborated in developing this work both as a general anthology of plays and as a critical study of their printed texts. In the sections individually contributed, indicated by the editor's initials at the end of general introductions or special textual studies, some freedom of method and interpretation has seemed preferable to insistent rule. The early habit of fitting a Latin motto to a printed play might perhaps suggest for this anthology: *In necessariis unitas, in dubiis libertas, in omnibus caritas.*

Main texts and collations of plays have regularly been based on editions definitely located and freely accessible in libraries listed in the bibliographies in the appendix. Special collections and privately owned copies of rare editions have appreciably aided textual investigation, but its essential processes and results have been habitually presented in terms of more convenient reference. Some exceptions to this practice, however, permit individual acknowledgment. The special editor of *The London Merchant* is directly and deeply indebted to Professor R. H. Griffith of the University of Texas for the use of his apparently unique copy of the fifth edition, representing Lillo's final draft of his most important play, as basic text in this anthology. The special editor of *The School for Scandal* is primarily and lastingly indebted to the gracious aid and sanctions of the late Mrs. William J. B. Macaulay for the recovery and use as basic text of Sheridan's presentation copy of his play to Mrs. Crewe. Father Parsons, Librarian of the Georgetown University Library, to which Mrs. Macaulay (then Mrs. Nicholas F. Brady) presented the Crewe copy, has very considerately continued and confirmed privileges which, as owner, she had previously accorded with characteristic generosity. This 'MS. copy of the play finely bound' which, according to Sheridan's own account, accompanied the gift of 'verses of mine to Mrs. (now Lady) Crewe,' was early established by Thomas Moore as of unique authority. Subsequent biographers and editors of Sheridan regretfully regarded it as 'missing,' but the late R. Crompton Rhodes, though lacking the original text, made his endeavor to approximate it, through secondary means, the central and most extensive study of his three-volume critical edition of Sheridan in 1928. The present and related studies of Sheridan's texts have been generously advanced by the friendly encouragement and courtesies of Mrs. Clare Sheridan, Mr. Barton Currie, owner of the Frampton Court manuscript of *The School for Scandal*, Mr. V. Valta Parma, of the Library of Congress, and the officers of the Yale University Library, who have liberally enlarged the materials and the means of textual investigation.

The illustrative pages which precede each play are, unless otherwise indicated, reproduced from early editions in the Yale University Library. They include different specimens of title-pages (printed or specially engraved), and of initial or other significant pages of main text, dedication, prefatory essay, and the like, which reflect some salient features of Restoration and eighteenth-century printing of contemporary plays. To the authorities of the Yale, Harvard, and Georgetown University Libraries, and of the Victoria and Albert Museum, South Kensington, London, the editors are especially indebted for permission to include the illustrations that accompany the plays. The music of *The Beggar's Opera* is reproduced through like courtesies of the Huntington Library at San Marino, California. With the kind consent of the editors of *Modern Language Notes*, the textual note on *The Conquest of Granada, Part I*, largely embodies essential material that the writer had presented in June, 1935, in an article on 'Author's Changes' in that play. For these and for other generous aids that have mounted past measure in the long course of years, the editors of this anthology have sought to make some tangible return in correlating widespread materials and interpreting results that may serve students of Restoration and eighteenth-century drama.

CONTENTS

RESTORATION DRAMA
(1660–1700)

I. HEROIC DRAMA

II. BLANK-VERSE TRAGEDY

III. COMEDY OF MANNERS

IV. JEREMY COLLIER'S ATTACK ON THE STAGE

EIGHTEENTH–CENTURY DRAMA
(1700–1780)

EARLY EIGHTEENTH–CENTURY DRAMA
(1700–1730)

I. SENTIMENTAL COMEDY

II. SENTIMENTAL COMEDY

III. DRAMATIC SATIRE

TEXTUAL NOTES

Restoration Drama

HEROIC DRAMA

Elizabethan drama may be said to end with the formal closing of the theatres in 1642, when Parliament, by ordinance of September 2, decreed that 'public stage-plays shall cease, and be forborne.' *Restoration drama* may be said to begin with the reopening of the theatres in 1660, when Charles II, by letters patent of August 21, authorized Thomas Killigrew and Sir William D'Avenant to 'erect' two companies of players, later housed in the two 'Patent Theatres,' in London. The interval between 1642 and 1660 may be called the *dramatic interregnum*. Though the official ban upon the theatres during this period failed to suppress fully theatrical activity, English drama languished in times of civil war and Puritan constraint. Fortunately, in spite of adverse conditions, the earlier stage tradition was partly sustained throughout the interregnum by surreptitious revivals of old plays, by frequent adaptation of their comic scenes into 'drolls,' or short farces, and finally by the bolder innovations of D'Avenant's 'operas.'

Sir WILLIAM D'AVENANT (1606–1668) best personifies the continuity of dramatic tradition in the transition from Elizabethan to Restoration drama. He links with the Elizabethans as Ben Jonson's successor in the poet-laureateship and as author of early plays that antedate the closing of the theatres. *Love and Honor* (1634) is in its very title prophetic of his later drama and influence on the school of love-and-honor dramatists. During the closing years of the interregnum he emerges as leader in the reawakening of dramatic impulse. *The Siege of Rhodes* (1656), produced with politic emphasis on its musical and scenic adornment to veil its essentially dramatic character, directly foreshadows the *heroic drama* of the Restoration. It blends elements of music and scenery already familiar in the English masque with elements of drama that derive from Elizabethan hero-plays like Marlowe's *Tamburlaine* and the heroic romances of Beaumont and Fletcher — for D'Avenant is an inheritor of earlier tradition. It reflects likewise the foreign influences of Italian opera and of French drama. But *The Siege of Rhodes*, in rekindling the spent fires of dramatic energy, despite the curfew law that still smothered them, is in itself a new and vital force. It has thus often been regarded as the first English opera and the immediate ancestor of Restoration heroic drama — for D'Avenant is a true pioneer. The general heroic and operatic features of *The Siege of Rhodes* are maintained by D'Avenant in *The Cruelty of the Spaniards in Peru* (1658) and in *The History of Sir Francis Drake* (1659). Detailed stage directions as to scenery and appropriate costume foreshadow his significant influence on the pictorial setting of the Restoration stage.

With the restoration of monarchy to the throne in 1660, D'Avenant becomes a conspicuous leader of the Restoration stage. As patentee of the new theatre in Lincoln's Inn Fields, where his company of actors — known as the Duke of York's — was soon housed, D'Avenant enlarges as manager his influence already acquired as playwright. In reviving on the Restoration stage various plays of Shakespeare, Jonson, and Beaumont and Fletcher, and in reverting largely to Elizabethan drama for materials for his own new plays and adaptations, he again emphasizes the continuity of the earlier dramatic tradition. From the Elizabethan period onward, through the dramatic interregnum, and into the Restoration period, D'Avenant maintains unbroken the sorely strained thread of English drama. His place in the history of drama is doubly assured, as conservator of the old stage tradition and as prophet of the coming drama.

The Siege of Rhodes holds its chief historical significance as precursor of Restoration *heroic drama*. In its themes of love and honor, and their personification in martial hero and angelic heroine, in its choice of foreign setting and of semi-historical atmosphere, in its preference for exalted characters and stirring scenes, and in its victory of virtue over the vicissitudes of war, *The Siege of Rhodes* largely fixed the formula for heroic drama. Among the varied verse forms employed is the heroic couplet, which later became the regular requirement of rhymed heroic drama. D'Avenant's address 'To the Reader' shows that neither his conception of heroic drama nor his freedom in versification was accidental. 'The story represented is *heroical*' and aims 'to advance the characters of virtue in the shapes of valor and conjugal love.' Though recognizing that 'a continuation of the usual length of English verse would appear more *heroical* in reading,' he insists that 'frequent alterations of measure . . . are necessary to recitative music for variation of airs.' This distinct reminder that *The Siege of Rhodes* is, in form, an opera does not lessen its vital influence on the content and character of heroic drama. Dryden, chief of the heroic dramatists, and foremost advocate and exponent of the heroic couplet, generously recognized that 'for Heroic Plays . . . the first light we had of them, on the English theatre, was from the late Sir William D'Avenant.'

With like generosity, Dryden recognized Roger Boyle, Earl of Orrery, as his predecessor in 'the new way of writing scenes in verse,' though his further remark that the use of couplets in serious drama was 'not so much a new way amongst us, as an old way new revived' admits some precedents in pre-Restoration drama. It was, nevertheless, Dryden's own adoption and development of the *heroic couplet* that established its supremacy in Restoration *heroic drama*, during the brief period of its fullest authority, 1664–1677. The use of rhyme in these decades was not confined to heroic drama, for its partial employment in comedy and tragi-comedy, as in early plays of Dryden and Etherege, indicates wider influence on the Restoration stage; but the vogue of the heroic couplet is directly linked with heroic drama. Not until Dryden himself finally abandoned heroic verse did rhymed heroic drama become a lost cause.

JOHN DRYDEN (1631–1700) early established himself as leader of the heroic dramatists. After collaborating with his brother-in-law, Sir Robert Howard, in *The Indian Queen* (1664), he added independently its sequel, *The Indian Emperor* (1665). In these plays the heroic features of D'Avenant's dramatic operas are heightened by increased intricacy of plot and violence of action, and by exaggeration of characters and bombastic speech. Battle, murder, and sudden death are so prevalent that Dryden confessed the paucity of materials for his sequel, 'there remaining but two of the considerable characters alive.' The frequent term *heroic tragedy* is, however, somewhat misleading since the final emphasis of heroic drama is ordinarily on the 'happy ending' for triumphant hero and heroine. Historically considered, English heroic drama is the resultant of component forces, English and French. But the influence of French classical drama and precept did not curb scenes of bloodshed and violent death on the English stage, nor did the inheritance of the Elizabethan 'tragedy of blood' prevail to sweep the later English heroic drama to the full tragic conclusion. The stress is on the superhuman hero; the deaths of his victims serve but to point his prowess and to assure the ultimate triumph of valor. Virtue incarnate in the heroine becomes likewise virtue rewarded in the final triumph of love. The 'happy ending' thus habitually differentiates heroic drama from regular tragedy.

The fashion of rhyme largely set by Dryden's early heroic plays did not continue without challenge. Howard, his collaborator, soon turned to engage him in protracted critical controversy (1665–1668), the successive stages of which are tersely recalled in the final paragraph of Dryden's *Defence of an Essay of Dramatic Poesy*. Dryden then proceeded to exemplify his critical theories in the typical heroic dramas of his middle period — *Tyrannic Love* (1669) and *The Conquest of Granada* (1670). In the latter, heroic drama found its fullest and most striking expression. In two parts, like Marlowe's *Tamburlaine*, it doubles the usual measure of five-act drama, and magnifies to heroic proportions the hero, Almanzor — a hero, confesses Dryden, 'not absolutely perfect, but of an excessive and over-boiling courage; but Homer and Tasso are my precedents.' For materials of plot Dryden drew largely on several French heroic romances of Madeleine de Scudéry, but masculine vigor and violence sustain and surcharge the dramatic action. Dryden's obvious excesses are stressed in Dr. Johnson's dictum that the two parts of the play 'are written with a seeming determination to glut the public with dramatic wonders; to exhibit in its highest elevation a theatrical meteor of incredible love and to leave no room for a wilder flight to the extravagance of posterity.' Neither play nor author was suffered to await unchallenged the verdict of posterity. Their high heroics were immediately exposed to the merciless mockery of contemporary burlesque.

GEORGE VILLIERS (1628-1687), Duke of Buckingham, the 'graceless wit' and favorite of the Merry Monarch, led a coterie of literary and political adherents in joint authorship of *The Rehearsal*, finally produced December 7, 1671. Thomas Sprat, the Duke's chaplain, Martin Clifford, Master of the Charterhouse, and probably 'Hudibras' Butler and others shared variously in the scheme of concerted satire upon serious contemporary dramatists. Begun in 1663, delayed by the temporary closing of the theatres on account of the plague, and gradually diverted in aim from D'Avenant and Sir Robert Howard, its chief early targets, *The Rehearsal* eventually levelled its main shafts against the author of *The Conquest of Granada*. The hero Almanzor is travestied in the character of Drawcansir, while Dryden himself, as Mr. Bayes, becomes the mock-heroic author of the tragedy that is rehearsed. Many of Dryden's heroic couplets are directly parodied, while the 'grand manner' of heroic drama is burlesqued in plot and characters as well as in bombastic speech. Almost a score of contemporary plays, including several comedies, are so specifically parodied that a bookseller's *Key*, published in 1704, attests later effort to whet again the point of 'local hits' no longer palpable. The satire of *The Rehearsal*, though conspicuously aimed at Dryden, ranges widely. The 'local hits' exceed verbal burlesque, for Bayes's broken nose, plastered with a 'wet bit of brown paper,' retains, even after D'Avenant's death, its pointed allusion to his notorious personal disfigurement. But beyond the parodies and personalities pointed to the quick comprehension of its immediate audience, *The Rehearsal* ridicules perennial absurdities of the drama. Burlesque does not readily outlive the subject of its momentary ridicule. *The Rehearsal*, however, by the mordant wit and vitality of its general satire, continued to hold the English stage long after heroic drama had disappeared.

The mockery of Buckingham and his followers did not, indeed, laugh the heroic drama immediately off the boards. Dryden, stubborn defender of the faith, remains unshaken in *An Essay of Heroic Plays* (1672), which opens aggressively: 'Whether Heroic Verse ought to be admitted into serious plays, is not now to be disputed: 'tis already in possession of the stage; and I dare confidently affirm that very few tragedies, in this age, shall be received without it.' Equally confident is his assertion that 'an heroic play ought to be an imitation, in little, of an heroic poem; and consequently, that Love and Valor ought to be the subject of it.' Equally dogmatic is his creed that 'an heroic poet is not tied to a bare representation of what is true, or exceedingly probable.' Twenty years later, in 1692, Dryden declared: 'I answered not *The Rehearsal*, because I knew the author sat to himself when he drew the picture, and was the very Bayes of his own farce.' But, if free from personal retaliation, the *Essay of Heroic Plays* in devoting its closing pages to a defence of Almanzor betrays immediate sensitiveness to criticism, and Dryden's later portrait of Buckingham as Zimri feeds fat the ancient grudge.

Though Dryden and his followers maintained for the time being a bold front against the attacks of *The Rehearsal*, other forces soon combined to undermine confidence within their own camp. Dryden, their leader, was provoked to a war of pamphlets with the young dramatist, Elkanah Settle, in which Settle's attacks on *The Conquest of Granada* were countered by Dryden's exposure of Settle's play, *The Empress of Morocco*, as a 'rhapsody of nonsense.' Their mutual charges of extravagant action and bombastic dialogue doubtless helped Dryden to realize the dangers of exposing himself in subsequent plays to fresh attacks. Furthermore, the publication in France, in 1674, of two significant critical works of Boileau and Rapin enhanced the chastening influence of classical and Continental standards. The effect is evident in Dryden's final rhymed heroic drama, *Aureng-Zebe* (1675). Plot and dialogue are handled with greater restraint, with increased respect for the dictates and decorum of the French theatre. If, however, *Aureng-Zebe* marks the turn of the tide of heroic drama from bombast towards simplicity and sobriety, it is accompanied with clear evidences of Dryden's increasing regard for the freer practices of the earlier English stage. His dedication of his play supports the confession of his prologue that he 'grows weary of his long-loved mistress, Rhyme.' In the epilogue to the Second Part of *The Conquest of Granada* he had boasted the supremacy of his own age over that of the Elizabethan dramatists. Now,

> 'spite of all his pride, a secret shame
> Invades his breast at Shakespeare's sacred name:
> Awed when he hears his god-like Romans rage,
> He, in a just despair, would quit the stage;
> And to an age less polished, more unskilled,
> Does, with disdain, the foremost honors yield.'

Though Dryden was too confirmed a dramatist to 'quit the stage,' the main portents of his prophecy were largely fulfilled. In *All for Love* (1677) he turned from the heroic couplet and happy ending of heroic drama to 'a tragedy written in imitation of Shakespeare's style,' alike in the adoption of blank verse and in the choice of *Antony and Cleopatra* as his tragic theme. With the final defection of its leader, the cause of rhymed heroic drama was virtually lost.

G. H. N.

REFERENCE WORKS

1903. Chase, Lewis N. *The English Heroic Play.* New York.

1910. Noyes, George R. *Selected Dramas of John Dryden with The Rehearsal.* Chicago and New York. [*Introduction.*]

1914. Nettleton, George H. *English Drama of the Restoration and Eighteenth Century.* New York and London. [Chapters II, III, IV, with Bibliographical Notes.]

1923. Nicoll, Allardyce. *A History of Restoration Drama, 1660–1700.* Cambridge [England]. [Chapter Two, section III.] (Second edition revised, 1928.)

1929. Dobrée, Bonamy. *Restoration Tragedy, 1660–1720.* Oxford.

1931. Deane, Cecil V. *Dramatic Theory and the Rhymed Heroic Play.*

The Conquest of Granada
by the Spaniards

Part I

(Almanzor and Almahide; or,

The Conquest of Granada)

BY JOHN DRYDEN

OF
HEROIQUE PLAYES.

An Essay.

Hether Heroique *verse ought to be admitted into serious Playes, is not
now to be disputed:* 'tis already *in
possession of the Stage: and I dare
confidently affirm, that very few
Tragedies, in this Age, shall be re-
ceiv'd without it. All the arguments, which are form'd against it,*
can amount to no more than this, that it is not so near conversation as Prose; and therefore not so natural. But it
is very clear to all, who understand Poetry, that serious
Playes ought not to imitate Conversation too nearly. If nothing were to be rais'd above that level, the foundation of
Poetry would be destroy'd. and, if you once admit of a Lati-
tude, that thoughts may be exalted, and that Images and
Actions may be rais'd above the life, and describ'd in measure without Rhyme, that leads you insensibly, from your own
Principles to mine: You are already so far onward of your way,
that you have forsaken the imitation of ordinary converse.
You are gone beyond it; and, to continue where you are, is
to lodge in the open field, betwixt two Inns. You have lost
that which you call natural, and have not acquir'd the last
perfection of Art. But it was onely custome which cozen'd*

a 2   *us*

EMBELLISHED PAGE FROM DRYDEN'S PREFATORY ESSAY IN THE FIRST QUARTO,
1672, OF *THE CONQUEST OF GRANADA*

PROLOGUE TO THE FIRST PART

Spoken by Mrs. Ellen Gwyn, in a broad-brimmed hat, and waist-belt.[1]

This jest was first of t'other house's making,
And, five times tried, has never failed of taking.
For 'twere a shame a poet should be killed
Under the shelter of so broad a shield.
This is that hat whose very sight did win ye   5
To laugh and clap as though the devil were in ye.
As then, for Nokes, so now, I hope, you'll be
So dull, to laugh, once more, for love of me.
'I'll write a play,' says one, 'for I have got
A broad-brimmed hat, and waist-belt, towards a plot.'   10
Says t'other, 'I have one more large than that.'
Thus they out-write each other with a hat.
The brims still grew with every play they writ;
And grew so large, they covered all the wit.
Hat was the play: 'twas language, wit, and tale: 15
Like them that find meat, drink, and cloth, in ale.
What dulness do these mongrel wits confess,
When all their hope is acting of a dress!
Thus, two the best comedians of the age
Must be worn out, with being blocks o' th' stage;   20
Like a young girl, who better things has known,
Beneath their poet's impotence they groan.
See now, what charity it was to save!
They thought you liked, what only you forgave:
And brought you more dull sense, dull sense much worse   25
Than brisk gay nonsense, and the heavier curse.
They bring old ir'n and glass upon the stage,
To barter with the Indians of our age.
Still they write on, and like great authors show: ⎫
But 'tis as rollers in wet gardens grow   ⎬   30
Heavy with dirt, and gath'ring as they go.   ⎭
May none who have so little understood
To like [2] such trash, presume to praise what's good!
And may those drudges of the stage, whose fate
Is damned dull farce more dully to translate,   35
Fall under that excise the state thinks fit
To set on all French wares, whose worst is wit.
French farce, worn out at home, is sent abroad;
And, patched up here, is made our English mode.
Henceforth, let poets, ere allowed to write,   40
Be searched, like duellists, before they fight,
For wheel-broad hats, dull humor, all that chaff,
Which makes you mourn, and makes the vulgar laugh:
For these, in plays, are as unlawful arms,
As, in a combat, coats of mail, and charms.   45

---

[1] Nell Gwyn's costume borrowed its idea from the comedian Nokes at the rival Patent Theatre. Nokes is said to have taken the visit of the Duchess of Orleans to England, in May, 1670, as occasion for caricaturing, on the English stage, French fashions.
[2] As to like.

PERSONS REPRESENTED

MEN

MAHOMET BOABDELIN, *the last King of Granada.*

PRINCE ABDALLA, *his brother.*

ABDELMELECH, *chief of the Abencerrages.*

ZULEMA, *chief of the Zegrys.*

ABENAMAR, *an old Abencerrago.*

SELIN, *an old Zegry.*

OZMYN, *a brave young Abencerrago, son to Abenamar.*

HAMET, *brother to Zulema, a Zegry.*

GOMEL, *a Zegry.*

ALMANZOR.

FERDINAND, *King of Spain.*

DUKE OF ARCOS, *his General.*

DON ALONZO D'AGUILAR, *a Spanish Captain.*

WOMEN

ALMAHIDE, *Queen of Granada.*

LYNDARAXA, *sister to* ZULEMA; *a Zegry lady.*

BENZAYDA, *daughter to* SELIN.

ESPERANZA, *slave to the Queen.*

HALYMA, *slave to* LYNDARAXA.

ISABELLA, *Queen of Spain.*

Messengers, Guards, Attendants, Men and Women.

THE SCENE, IN GRANADA, AND THE CHRISTIAN CAMP BESIEGING IT.

[TIME, 1491.]

THE CONQUEST OF GRANADA
BY THE SPANIARDS

By JOHN DRYDEN

THE FIRST PART

Major rerum mihi nascitur ordo;
Majus opus moveo.[1]   VIRGIL, *Æneid*, vii [44, 45].

ACT I

[SCENE I]

BOABDELIN, ABENAMAR, ABDELMELECH, *Guards.*

BOAB. Thus, in the triumphs of soft peace, I
    reign;
And, from my walls, defy the pow'rs of Spain:
With pomp and sports my love I celebrate,
While they keep distance, and attend my state. —
                (*To* ABENAMAR.)
Parent to her, whose eyes my soul enthral,   5
Whom I, in hope, already father call,
Abenamar, thy youth these sports has known,
Of which thy age is now spectator grown:
Judge-like thou sit'st, to praise, or to arraign
The flying skirmish of the darted cane:[2]   10
But, when fierce bulls run loose upon the place,
And our bold Moors their loves with danger grace,
Then heat new-bends thy slackened nerves again,
And a short youth runs warm through every vein.

ABEN. I must confess th' encounters of this day 15
Warmed me indeed, but quite another way:
Not with the fire of youth, but gen'rous rage,
To see the glories of my youthful age
So far outdone.

ABDELM. Castile could never boast, in all its
    pride,   20
A pomp so splendid, when the lists, set wide,
Gave room to the fierce bulls, which wildly ran
In Sierra Ronda, ere the war began:
Who, with high nostrils snuffing up the wind,
Now stood the champions of the savage kind.   25
Just opposite, within the circled place,
Ten of our bold Abencerrages' race

[1] Dryden freely translated the Latin motto thus:
    'A larger scene of action is displayed;
    And, rising hence, a greater work is weighed.'
[2] A contest in which horsemen contended with blunt javelins.

(Each brandishing his bull-spear in his hand)
Did their proud jennets[3] gracefully command.
On their steeled heads their demi-lances wore   30
Small pennons, which their ladies' colors bore.
Before this troop did warlike Ozmyn go;
Each lady, as he rode, saluting low;
At the chief stands, with reverence more profound,
His well-taught courser, kneeling, touched the
    ground;   35
Thence raised, he sidelong bore his rider on,
Still facing, till he out of sight was gone.

BOAB. You praise him like a friend, and I confess
His brave deportment merited no less.

ABDELM. Nine bulls were launched[4] by his victori-
    ous arm,   40
Whose wary jennet, shunning still the harm,
Seemed to attend the shock, and then leaped wide:
Meanwhile, his dext'rous rider, when he spied
The beast just stooping, 'twixt the neck and head
His lance, with never-erring fury, sped.   45

ABEN. My son did well, and so did Hamet too;
Yet did no more than we were wont to do;
But what the stranger did was more than man: —

ABDELM. He finished all those triumphs we began.
One bull, with curled black head, beyond the rest,   50
And dew-laps hanging from his brawny chest,
With nodding front a while did daring stand,
And with his jetty hoof spurned back the sand:
Then, leaping forth, he bellowed out aloud:
Th' amazed assistants back each other crow'd,   55
While monarch-like he ranged the listed field:
Some tossed, some gored, some trampling down he
    killed.
Th' ignobler Moors, from far, his rage provoke,
With woods of darts, which from his sides he shook.
Meantime your valiant son, who had before   60

[3] Small Spanish horses.
[4] Lanced.

TITLE] QQ give main title as above, but head actual text (p. 1) thus: *Almanzor and Almahide, or, The Conquest of Granada. The First Part.* This latter form is maintained in *The Second Part* both in title-page and in text-heading.
24] Q5 *snuflng;* F *snuffling.* (F detects misprint in Q5, but ignores the correct reading in Q1-Q4.)
25] Q1Q4 *champions;* Q2Q3Q5F *champion.* 29] Q1-Q4 *ginnets;* Q5F *gennets.*
47] Q1Q2 *then;* Q3Q4Q5F *than.* (Like variants occur *passim.*)
55] Q1 *crow'd* (i.e. 'crowded'); Q2-Q5 *croud* (i.e. 'crowd').

Gained fame, rode round to every mirador; [1]
Beneath each lady's stand a stop he made,
And, bowing, took th' applauses which they paid.
Just in that point of time, the brave unknown }
Approached the lists.
    BOAB.   I marked him, when alone } 65
(Observed by all, himself observing none)
He entered first, and with a graceful pride
His fiery Arab dext'rously did guide,
Who, while his rider every stand surveyed,
Sprung loose, and flew into an escapade: [2]   70
Not moving forward, yet, with every bound,
Pressing, and seeming still to quit his ground.
What after passed ——
Was far from the ventanna [3] where I sate,
But you were near, and can the truth relate.   75
                (To ABDELMELECH.)
    ABDELM. Thus while he stood, the bull, who saw
      this foe,
His easier conquests proudly did forego;
And, making at him with a furious bound,
From his bent forehead aimed a double wound.
A rising murmur ran through all the field,   80
And every lady's blood with fear was chilled.
Some shrieked, while others, with more helpful care,
Cried out aloud, 'Beware, brave youth, beware!'
At this he turned, and, as the bull drew near,
Shunned, and received him on his pointed spear. 85
The lance broke short: the beast then bellowed loud,
And his strong neck to a new onset bowed.
Th' undaunted youth ——
Then drew; and from his saddle bending low, }
Just where the neck did to the shoulders grow, } 90
With his full force discharged a deadly blow. }
Not heads of poppies (when they reap the grain)
Fall with more ease before the lab'ring swain,
Than fell this head: —
It fell so quick, it did even death prevent, [4]   95
And made imperfect bellowings as it went.
Then all the trumpets victory did sound:
And yet their clangors in our shouts were drowned.
            (A confused noise within.)
    BOAB. Th' alarm-bell rings from our Alhambra
    walls,
And, from the streets, sound drums and atabals. [5] 100
     (Within, a bell, drums, and trumpets.)

To them a Messenger.

How now? from whence proceed these new alarms?
    MESS. The two fierce factions are again in arms:
And, changing into blood the day's delight,
The Zegrys with th' Abencerrages fight;
On each side their allies and friends appear;   105

    [1] Balcony, spectators' gallery.   [2] Rearing and plunging.
    [3] Window.   [4] Anticipate.   [5] Kettledrums.

    104] Q1Q4Q5F *the Abencerrages*; Q2Q3 *th' Abencerrages*.

The Maças here, the Alabezes there:
The Gazuls with the Bencerrages join,
And, with the Zegrys, all great Gomel's line.
    BOAB. Draw up behind the Vivarambla place;
Double my guards! these factions I will face;   110
And try if all the fury they can bring,
Be proof against the presence of their king.
                Exit BOABDELIN.

The Factions appear: At the head of the Abencerrages,
    OZMYN; *at the head of the Zegrys,* ZULEMA,
    HAMET, GOMEL, *and* SELIN: ABENAMAR *and*
    ABDELMELECH *joined with the Abencerrages.*

    ZUL. The faint Abencerrages quit their ground:
Press 'em; put home your thrusts to every wound.
    ABDELM. Zegry, on manly force our line
    relies;   115
Thine poorly takes th' advantage of surprise.
Unarmed and much out-numbered we retreat;
You gain no fame, when basely you defeat:
If thou art brave, seek nobler victory;   }
Save Moorish blood; and, while our bands }
    stand by,   } 120
Let two to two an equal combat try.   }
    HAM. 'Tis not for fear the combat we refuse;
But we our gained advantage will not lose.
    ZUL. In combating, but two of you will fall;
And we resolve we will dispatch you all.   125
    OZM. We'll double yet th' exchange before we die;
And each of ours two lives of yours shall buy.

ALMANZOR *enters betwixt them, as they stand ready to*
    engage.

    ALMANZ. I cannot stay to ask which cause is best;
But this is so to me, because opprest.
            (Goes to the Abencerrages.)

To them BOABDELIN *and his Guards, going betwixt*
    them.

    BOAB. On your allegiance, I command you stay; 130
Who passes here, through me must make his way;
My life's the Isthmus; through this narrow line
You first must cut, before those seas can join.
What fury, Zegrys, has possessed your minds?
What rage the brave Abencerrages blinds?   135
If of your courage you new proofs would show,
Without much travel you may find a foe.
Those foes are neither so remote nor few,
That you should need each other to pursue.
Lean times and foreign wars should minds unite; 140
When poor, men mutter, but they seldom fight.
O holy Allah! that I live to see
Thy Granadins assist their enemy!
You fight the Christians' battles; every life
You lavish thus, in this intestine strife,   145

Does from our weak foundations take one prop
Which helped to hold our sinking country up.

Ozm. 'Tis fit our private enmity should cease;
Though injured first, yet I will first seek peace.

Zul.[1] No, murd'rer, no; I never will be won   150
To peace with him, whose hand has slain my son.

Ozm. Our prophet's curse
On me, and all th' Abencerrages light,
If unprovoked I with your son did fight.

Abdelm. A band of Zegrys ran within the
place,   155
Matched with a troop of thirty of our race.
Your son and Ozmyn the first squadrons led,
Which, ten by ten, like Parthians, charged and
fled.
The ground was strowed with canes, where we did
meet,
Which crackled underneath our coursers' feet: 160
When Tarifa (I saw him ride apart)
Changed his blunt cane for a steel-pointed dart,
And meeting Ozmyn next,
Who wanted time for treason to provide,
He basely threw it at him, undefied.   165

Ozm. (showing his arm).   Witness this blood —
which when by treason sought,
That followed, sir, which to myself I ought.[2]

Zul. His hate to thee was grounded on a grudge,
Which all our generous Zegrys just did judge;
Thy villain[3] blood thou openly didst place   170
Above the purple of our kingly race.

Boab. From equal stems their blood both houses
draw,
They from Morocco, you from Cordova.

Ham. Their mongrel race is mixed with Christian
breed;
Hence 'tis that they those dogs in prisons feed.   175

Abdelm. Our holy prophet wills, that charity
Should ev'n to birds and beasts extended be:
None knows what fate is for himself designed;
The thought of human chance should make us kind.

Gom. We waste that time we to revenge should
give: 180
Fall on! let no Abencerrago live.

(Advancing before the rest of his party. Almanzor, advancing on the other side, and
describing a line with his sword.)

Almanz. Upon thy life pass not this middle space;
Sure death stands guarding the forbidden place.

Gom. To dare that death, I will approach yet
nigher.

[1] M ingeniously assigns this speech to Selin, citing II, 242,
and III, 285, as references to 'Selin's thirst to avenge the
murder of his son Tarifa by Ozmyn.' M errs, however, as to
textual variants. QQF give alike the speech to Zulema.
[2] Owed.   [3] Ignoble.

Thus — wert thou compassed in with circling fire.
(They fight.)   185

Boab. Disarm 'em both; if they resist you, kill.
(Almanzor, in the midst of the Guards, kills
Gomel, and then is disarmed.)

Almanz. Now, you have but the leavings of my
will.

Boab. Kill him! this insolent unknown[4] shall fall,
And be the victim to atone you all.

Ozm. If he must die, not one of us will live: 190
That life he gave for us, for him we give.

Boab. It was a traitor's voice that spoke those
words;
So are you all, who do not sheathe your swords.

Zul. Outrage unpunished, when a prince is by,
Forfeits to scorn the rights of majesty: 195
No subject his protection can expect,
Who what he owes himself does first neglect.

Aben. This stranger, sir, is he,
Who lately in the Vivarambla place
Did, with so loud applause, your triumphs grace.   200

Boab. The word which I have giv'n, I'll not
revoke;
If he be brave, he's ready for the stroke.

Almanz. No man has more contempt than I, of
breath,
But whence hast thou the right to give me death?
Obeyed as sovereign by thy subjects be,   205
But know, that I alone am king of me.
I am as free as nature first made man,
Ere the base laws of servitude began,
When wild in woods the noble savage ran. ⎭

Boab. Since, then, no pow'r above your own you
know,   210
Mankind should use you like a common foe;
You should be hunted like a beast of prey;
By your own law I take your life away.

Almanz. My laws are made but only for my sake;
No king against himself a law can make.   215
If thou pretend'st to be a prince like me,
Blame not an act which should thy pattern be.
I saw th' opprest and thought it did belong
To a king's office to redress the wrong:
I brought that succor which thou ought'st to
bring,   220
And so, in nature, am thy subjects' king.

Boab. I do not want your counsel to direct,
Or aid to help me punish or protect.

Almanz. Thou want'st 'em both, or better thou
wouldst know,
Than to let factions in thy kingdom grow.   225
Divided int'rests, while thou think'st to sway,
Draw, like two brooks, thy middle stream away:

[4] Early quartos, by capitalizing 'Unknown,' indicate the
noun.

161] Tarifa or Tariffa (variants in QQ).   166] Q2Q3 omit stage direction, but assign ll. 166–167 to Ozmyn.
220] F needlessly alters that (QQ) to the.

For though they band and jar, yet both combine
To make their greatness by the fall of thine.
Thus, like a buckler, thou art held in sight,   230
While they behind thee with each other fight.

BOAB. Away, and execute him instantly!
                              (*To his Guards.*)

ALMANZ. Stand off; I have not leisure yet to die.

To them ABDALLA, *hastily.*

ABDAL. Hold, sir! for heav'n sake hold!
Defer this noble stranger's punishment,   235
Or your rash orders you will soon repent.

BOAB. Brother, you know not yet his insolence.

ABDAL. Upon yourself you punish his offence:
If we treat gallant strangers in this sort,
Mankind will shun th' inhospitable court;   240
And who, henceforth, to our defence will come,
If death must be the brave Almanzor's doom?
From Africa I drew him to your aid,
And for his succor have his life betrayed.

BOAB. Is this th' Almanzor whom at Fez you
        knew,   245
When first their swords the Xeriff [1] brothers drew?

ABDAL. This, sir, is he, who for the elder fought,
And to the juster cause the conquest brought;
Till the proud Santo, seated in the throne,
Disdained the service he had done to own: 250
Then, to the vanquished part, his fate he led:
The vanquished triumphed, and the victor fled.
Vast is his courage, boundless is his mind,
Rough as a storm, and humorous as wind;
Honor's the only idol of his eyes: 255
The charms of beauty like a pest he flies;
And, raised by valor from a birth unknown,
Acknowledges no pow'r above his own.

                    (BOABDELIN *coming to* ALMANZOR.)

BOAB. Impute your danger to our ignorance;
The bravest men are subject most to chance: 260
Granada much does to your kindness owe: ⎫
But towns, expecting sieges, cannot show ⎬
More honor, than t' invite you to a foe. ⎭

ALMANZ. I do not doubt but I have been to blame:
But, to pursue the end for which I came,   265
Unite your subjects first; then let us go,
And pour their common rage upon the foe.

BOAB. (*to the Factions*). Lay down your arms; and
        let me beg you cease
Your enmities.

ZUL.   We will not hear of peace,
Till we by force have first revenged our slain.   270

ABDELM. The action we have done we will maintain.

SELIN. Then let the king depart, and we will try
Our cause by arms.

---
[1] Moroccan royal family.

234] Q3 *heav'ns.*

ZUL.   For us and victory!

BOAB. A king entreats you.

ALMANZ. What subjects will precarious [2] kings
        regard?   275
A beggar speaks too softly to be heard:
Lay down your arms! 'tis I command you now.
Do it — or, by our prophet's soul I vow,
My hands shall right your king on him I seize.
Now, let me see whose look but disobeys.   280

OMNES. Long live king Mahomet Boabdelin!

ALMANZ. No more; but hushed as midnight
        silence go:
He will not have your acclamations now.
Hence, you unthinking crowd! —
                    (*The common people go off on both parties.*)
Empire, thou poor and despicable thing,   285
When such as these unmake or make a king!

ABDAL. How much of virtue lies in one great
        soul,   (*Embracing him.*)
Whose single force can multitudes control!
                              (*A trumpet within.*)

Enter a Messenger.

MESSEN. The Duke of Arcos, sir,
Does with a trumpet from the foe appear.   290

BOAB. Attend him; he shall have his audience here.

Enter the DUKE OF ARCOS.

D. ARCOS. The monarchs of Castile and Aragon ⎫
Have sent me to you, to demand this town: ⎬
To which their just and rightful claim is known. ⎭

BOAB. Tell Ferdinand, my right to it appears   295
By long possession of eight hundred years.
When first my ancestors from Afric sailed,
In Rodrique's death your Gothic title failed. [3]

D. ARCOS. The successors of Rodrique still remain,
And ever since have held some part of Spain.   300
Ev'n in the midst of your victorious pow'rs,
Th' Asturias, and all Portugal, were ours.
You have no right, except you force allow;
And if yours then was just, so ours is now.

BOAB. 'Tis true, from force the noblest title
        springs;   305
I therefore hold from that, which first made
        kings.

D. ARCOS. Since then by force you prove your
        title true,
Ours must be just, because we claim from you.
When with your father you did jointly reign,
Invading with your Moors the south of Spain,   310
I, who that day the Christians did command,
Then took, and brought you bound to Ferdinand.

---
[2] Supplicating.
[3] The defeat of Roderic, last King of the Visigoths, by the invading Arabs in 711, established Moorish rule in Spain.

BOAB. I'll hear no more; defer what you would
    say:
In private we'll discourse some other day.
    D. ARCOS. Sir, you shall hear, however you are
        loath,   315
That, like a perjured prince, you broke your oath:
To gain your freedom you a contract signed,
By which your crown you to my king resigned,
From thenceforth as his vassal holding it,
And paying tribute such as he thought fit;   320
Contracting, when your father came to die,
To lay aside all marks of royalty,
And at Purchena [1] privately to live,
Which, in exchange, King Ferdinand did give.
    BOAB. The force used on me made that contract
        void.   325
    D. ARCOS. Why have you then its benefits en-
        joyed?
By it you had not only freedom then,
But, since, had aid of money and of men;
And, when Granada for your uncle held,
You were by us restored, and he expelled.   330
Since that, in peace we let you reap your grain,
Recalled our troops, that used to beat your plain;
And more——
    ALMANZ. Yes, yes, you did with wondrous care,
Against his rebels prosecute the war,
While he secure in your protection slept;   335
For him you took, but for yourselves you kept.
Thus, as some fawning usurer does feed,
With present sums, th' unwary unthrift's need,
You sold your kindness at a boundless rate,
And then o'erpaid the debt from his estate;   340
Which, mould'ring piecemeal, in your hands did fall,
Till now at last you came to swoop it all.
    D. ARCOS. The wrong you do my king I cannot
        bear;
Whose kindness you would odiously compare.
Th' estate was his; which yet, since you deny, 345
He's now content, in his own wrong, to buy.
    ALMANZ. And he shall buy it dear what his he
        calls——
We will not give one stone from out these walls.
    BOAB. Take this for answer, then——
Whate'er your arms have conquered of my land, 350
I will, for peace, resign to Ferdinand:
To harder terms my mind I cannot bring;
But, as I still have lived, will die a king.
    D. ARCOS. Since thus you have resolved, hence-
        forth prepare
For all the last extremities of war: 355
My king his hope from heav'n's assistance draws.
    ALMANZ. The Moors have heav'n, and me, t'
        assist their cause.   Exit ARCOS.

[1] A town in southeastern Spain.

Enter ESPERANZA.

ESPER. Fair Almahide,
(Who did with weeping eyes these discords see,
And fears the omen may unlucky be)   360
Prepares a zambra [2] to be danced this night,
In hope soft pleasures may your minds unite.
    BOAB. My mistress gently chides the fault ⎫
        I made: ⎬
But tedious business has my love delayed —
Business, which dares the joys of kings in-
    vade.   365
    ALMANZ. First let us sally out, and meet the
        foe.
    ABDAL. Led on by you, we [on] to triumph go.
    BOAB. Then with the day let war and tumult
        cease;
The night be sacred to our love and peace:
'Tis just some joys on weary kings should wait; 370
'Tis all we gain by being slaves of state.
                                    Exeunt omnes.

ACT II

[SCENE I]

ABDALLA, ABDELMELECH, OZMYN, ZULEMA, HAMET,
    as returning from the sally.

    ABDAL. This happy day does to Granada bring
A lasting peace, and triumphs to the king:
The two fierce factions will no longer jar,
Since they have now been brothers in the war:
Those who, apart, in emulation fought,   5
The common danger to one body brought;
And, to his cost, the proud Castilian finds
Our Moorish courage in united minds.
    ABDELM. Since to each other's aid our lives we
        owe,
Lose we the name of faction, and of foe,   10
Which I to Zulema can bear no more,
Since Lyndaraxa's beauty I adore.
    ZUL. I am obliged to Lyndaraxa's charms,
Which gain the conquest I should lose by arms;
And wish my sister may continue fair,   15
That I may keep a good,
Of whose possession I should else despair.
    OZM. While we indulge our common happiness,
He is forgot, by whom we all possess;
The brave Almanzor, to whose arms we owe   20
All that we did, and all that we shall do;
Who, like a tempest that outrides the wind,
Made a just battle ere the bodies joined.
    ABDAL. His victories we scarce could keep in
        view,
Or polish 'em so fast as he rough-drew.   25

[2] A Moorish festival with dancing and music (as in Act III).

317] Q1Q2Q3 *your*; Q4Q5F *you.*   336] Q5F *self* for *selves.*   367] Q1Q2 *to*; Q3 *unto*; Q4Q5F *on to.*   371] Q5F *to state.*

ABDELM. Fate, after him, below with pain did
    move,
And victory could scarce keep pace above.
Death did at length so many slain forget,
And lost the tale, and took 'em by the great.[1]

To them ALMANZOR *with the* DUKE OF ARCOS *prisoner.*

HAMET. See, here he comes,   30
And leads in triumph him who did command
The vanquished army of King Ferdinand.

ALMANZ. (*to the* DUKE OF ARCOS). Thus far your
    master's arms a fortune find
Below the swelled ambition of his mind;
And Allah shuts a misbeliever's reign   35
From out the best and goodliest part of Spain.
Let Ferdinand Calabrian conquests make,
And from the French contested Milan take;
Let him new worlds discover to the old,
And break up shining mountains big with gold; 40
Yet he shall find this small domestic foe
Still sharp, and pointed to his bosom grow.

D. ARCOS. Of small advantages too much you
    boast;
You beat the out-guards of my master's host:
This little loss, in our vast body, shows   45
So small, that half have never heard the news.
Fame's out of breath, ere she can fly so far
To tell 'em all that you have e'er made war.

ALMANZ. It pleases me your army is so great:
For now I know there's more to conquer yet.   50
By heav'n, I'll see what troops you have behind:
I'll face this storm that thickens in the wind:
And, with bent forehead, full against it go,
Till I have found the last and utmost foe.

D. ARCOS. Believe, you shall not long attend in
    vain;   55
Tomorrow's dawn shall cover all your plain.
Bright arms shall flash upon you from afar,
A wood of lances, and a moving war.
But I, unhappy, in my bands,[2] must yet
Be only pleased to hear of your defeat: 60
And with a slave's inglorious ease remain,
Till conquering Ferdinand has broke my chain.

ALMANZ. Vain man, thy hopes of Ferdinand are
    weak!
I hold thy chain too fast for him to break.
But, since thou threaten'st us, I'll set thee free, 65
That I again may fight, and conquer thee.

D. ARCOS. Old as I am, I take thee at thy word,
And will tomorrow thank thee with my sword.

ALMANZ. I'll go, and instantly acquaint the king,
And sudden orders for thy freedom bring.   70
Thou canst not be so pleased at liberty
As I shall be to find thou dar'st be free.

    Exeunt ALMANZOR, ARCOS, *and the rest; ex-*
    cepting only ABDALLA *and* ZULEMA.

[1] Lost count and took them *en masse.*   [2] Bonds.

ABDAL. Of all those Christians who infest this
    town,
This Duke of Arcos is of most renown.

ZUL. Oft have I heard that, in your father's
    reign,   75
His bold advent'rers beat the neighb'ring plain;
Then under Ponce Leon's[3] name he fought,
And from our triumphs[4] many prizes brought;
Till in disgrace from Spain at length he went,
And since continued long in banishment.   80

ABDAL. But see, your beauteous sister does
    appear.

To them LYNDARAXA.

ZUL. By my desire she came to find me here.
    (ZULEMA *and* LYNDARAXA *whisper; then*
    ZULEMA *goes out, and* LYNDARAXA *is going*
    after.)

ABDAL. Why, fairest Lyndaraxa, do you fly
                                (*staying her*)
A prince, who at your feet is proud to die?

LYNDAR. Sir, I should blush to own so rude a
    thing,   (*staying*) 85
As 'tis to shun the brother of my king.

ABDAL. In my hard fortune I some ease should
    find,
Did your disdain extend to all mankind.
But give me leave to grieve, and to complain,
That you give others what I beg in vain.   90

LYNDAR. Take my esteem, if you on that can live;
For, frankly, sir, 'tis all I have to give.
If from my heart you ask or hope for more,
I grieve the place is taken up before.

ABDAL. My rival merits you.   95
To Abdelmelech I will justice do,
For he wants worth, who dares not praise a foe.

LYNDAR. That for his virtue, sir, you make de-
    fence,
Shows in your own a noble confidence:
But him defending, and excusing me,   100
I know not what can your advantage be.

ABDAL. I fain would ask, ere I proceed in this,
If, as by choice, you are by promise his?

LYNDAR. Th' engagement only in my love does
    lie;
But that's a knot which you can ne'er untie.   105

ABDAL. When cities are besieged, and treat to
    yield,
If there appear relievers from the field,
The flag of parley may be taken down,
Till the success of those without be known.

LYNDAR. Though Abdelmelech has not yet pos-
    sessed,   110
Yet I have sealed the treaty for my breast.

ABDAL. Your treaty has not tied you to a day;
Some chance might break it, would you but delay:

[3] Spanish leader against the Moors.   [4] Triumphs over us.

If I can judge the secrets of your heart,
Ambition in it has the greatest part;   115
And wisdom, then, will show some difference
Betwixt a private person and a prince.

LYNDAR. Princes are subjects still —
Subject and subject can small diff'rence bring:
The diff'rence is 'twixt subjects and a king.   120
And since, sir, you are none, your hopes remove;
For less than empire I'll not change my love.

ABDAL. Had I a crown, all I should prize in it,
Should be the pow'r to lay it at your feet.

LYNDAR. Had you that crown which you but
     wish, not hope,   125
Then I, perhaps, might stoop and take it up.
But till your wishes and your hopes agree,
You shall be still a private man with me.

ABDAL. If I am king, and if my brother die ——

LYNDAR. Two *if's* scarce make one possibil-
     ity.   130

ABDAL. The rule of happiness by reason scan;
You may be happy with a private man.

LYNDAR. That happiness I may enjoy, 'tis true;
But then that private man must not be you.
Where'er I love, I'm happy in my choice;   135
If I make you so, you shall pay my price.

ABDAL. Why would you be so great?

LYNDAR.   Because I've seen,
This day, what 'tis to hope to be a queen.
Heav'n, how y'all watched each motion of ⎤
     her eye!   ⎟
None could be seen while Almahide was by, ⎟ 140
Because she is to be Her Majesty! —   ⎦
Why would I be a queen? Because my face
Would wear the title with a better grace.
If I became it not, yet it would be
Part of your duty, then, to flatter me.   145
These are not half the charms of being great:
I would be somewhat — that I know not yet:
Yes! I avow th' ambition of my soul,
To be that one, to live without control:
And that's another happiness to me,   150
To be so happy as but one can be.

ABDAL. Madam, — because I would all doubts
     remove, —
Would you, were I a king, accept my love?

LYNDAR. I would accept it; and, to show 'tis
     true,
From any other man as soon as you.   155

ABDAL. Your sharp replies make me not love
     you less;
But make me seek new paths to happiness.
What I design, by time will best be seen:
You may be mine, and yet may be a queen:
When you are so, your word your love assures.   160

LYNDAR. Perhaps not love you — but I will be
     yours.   (*He offers to take her hand, and kiss it.*)
Stay, sir, that grace I cannot yet allow,
Before you set the crown upon my brow.
That favor which you seek,
Or Abdelmelech, or a king, must have;   165
When you are so, then you may be my slave.
          Exit; but looks smiling back on him.

ABDAL. Howe'er imperious in her words she were,
Her parting looks had nothing of severe;
A glancing smile allured me to command,
And her soft fingers gently pressed my hand: 170
I felt the pleasure glide through every part;
Her hand went through me to my very heart.
For such another pleasure, did he live,
I could my father of a crown deprive.
What did I say?   175
Father! — That impious thought has shocked my
     mind:
How bold our passions are, and yet how blind! —
She's gone; and now,
Methinks there is less glory in a crown;
My boiling passions settle, and go down.   180
Like amber chafed, when she is near, she acts;
When farther off, inclines, but not attracts.

To him ZULEMA

Assist me, Zulema, if thou wouldst be
That friend thou seem'st, assist me against me.
Betwixt my love and virtue I am tossed;   185
This must be forfeited, or that be lost.
I could do much to merit thy applause;
Help me to fortify the better cause.
My honor is not wholly put to flight,
But would, if seconded, renew the fight.   190

ZUL. I met my sister, but I do not see
What difficulty in your choice can be:
She told me all; and 'tis so plain a case,
You need not ask what counsel to embrace.

ABDAL. I stand reproved, that I did doubt at
     all;   195
My waiting virtue stayed but for thy call:
'Tis plain that she, who, for a kingdom, now
Would sacrifice her love, and break her vow,
Not out of love, but int'rest, acts alone,
And would, ev'n in my arms, lie thinking of a
     throne.   200

ZUL. Add to the rest this one reflection more:
When she is married, and you still adore,
Think then — and think what comfort it will
     bring —
She had been mine,
Had I but only dared to be a king!   205

ABDAL. I hope you only would my honor try;
I'm loath to think you virtue's enemy.

ZUL. If, when a crown and mistress are in
     place,
Virtue intrudes, with her lean holy face,
Virtue's then mine, and not I virtue's foe.   210
Why does she come where she has nought to do?

Let her with anchorites, not with lovers, lie;
Statesmen and they keep better company.

ABDAL. Reason was giv'n to curb our headstrong will.

ZUL. Reason but shows a weak physician's skill: 215
Gives nothing, while the raging fit does last,
But stays to cure it, when the worst is past.
Reason's a staff for age, when nature's gone;
But youth is strong enough to walk alone.

ABDAL. In curst ambition I no rest should find, 220
But must for ever lose my peace of mind.

ZUL. Methinks that peace of mind were bravely lost.
A crown, whate'er we give, is worth the cost.

ABDAL. Justice distributes to each man his right;
But what she gives not, should I take by might? 225

ZUL. If justice will take all, and nothing give,
Justice, methinks, is not distributive.

ABDAL. Had fate so pleased, I had been eldest born,
And then, without a crime, the crown had worn.

ZUL. Would you so please, fate yet a way would find; 230
Man makes his fate according to his mind.
The weak low spirit fortune makes her slave;
But she's a drudge when hectored by the brave:
If fate weaves common thread, he'll change the doom,
And with new purple spread a nobler loom. 235

ABDAL. No more! — I will usurp the royal seat;
Thou, who has made me wicked, make me great.

ZUL. Your way is plain: the death of Tarifa
Does on the king our Zegrys' hatred draw;
Though with our enemies in show we close, 240
'Tis but while we to purpose can be foes.
Selin, who heads us, would revenge his son;
But favor hinders justice to be done.
Proud Ozmyn with the king his pow'r maintains,
And in him each Abencerrago reigns. 245

ABDAL. What face of any title can I bring?

ZUL. The right an eldest son has to be king.
Your father was at first a private man,
And got your brother ere his reign began;
When, by his valor, he the crown had won, 250
Then you were born, a monarch's eldest son.

ABDAL. To sharp-eyed reason this would seem untrue;
But reason I through love's false optics view.

ZUL. Love's mighty pow'r has led me captive too:
I am in it unfortunate as you. 255

ABDAL. Our loves and fortunes shall together go;
Thou shalt be happy, when I first am so.

ZUL. The Zegrys at old Selin's house are met,
Where, in close council, for revenge they sit:

There we our common int'rest will unite; 260
You their revenge shall own, and they your right.
One thing I had forgot which may import:
I met Almanzor coming back from court,
But with a discomposed and speedy pace,
A fiery color kindling all his face: 265
The king his pris'ner's freedom has denied,
And that refusal has provoked his pride.

ABDAL. Would he were ours! —
I'll try to gild th' injustice of the cause,
And court his valor with a vast applause. 270

ZUL. The bold are but the instruments o' th' wise;
They undertake the dangers we advise:
And, while our fabric with their pains we raise,
We take the profit, and pay them with praise.

Exeunt.

ACT III

[SCENE I]

ALMANZOR, ABDALLA.

ALMANZ. That he should dare to do me this disgrace!
Is fool or coward writ upon my face?
Refuse my pris'ner! — I such means will use,
He shall not have a pris'ner to refuse.

ABDAL. He said you were not by your promise tied; 5
That he absolved your word, when he denied.

ALMANZ. He break my promise and absolve my vow!
'Tis more than Mahomet himself can do!
The word which I have giv'n shall stand like fate;
Not like the king's, that weathercock of state. 10
He stands so high, with so unfixed a mind,
Two factions turn him with each blast of wind.
But now, he shall not veer: my word is passed;
I'll take his heart by th' roots, and hold it fast.

ABDAL. You have your vengeance in your hand this hour; 15
Make me the humble creature of your pow'r:
The Granadins will gladly me obey,
Tired with so base and impotent a sway;
And, when I show my title, you shall see
I have a better right to reign than he. 20

ALMANZ. It is sufficient that you make the claim:
You wrong our friendship when your right you name.
When for myself I fight, I weigh the cause,
But friendship will admit of no such laws:
That weighs by th' lump; and, when the cause is light, 25
Puts kindness in to set the balance right.
True, I would wish my friend the juster side;

212] Q1Q2Q3 *anchorit's*; Q4 *anchorite's*; Q5 *anchorites* (progressive changes in orthography).
234] Q1Q2Q3 *thrid*; Q4Q5 *thread*.   241] N (p. 436) suggests emending *while* to *till* to better the sense.
269] Q5F *his cause* (F relies on Q5).

But, in th' unjust, my kindness more is tried.
And all the opposition I can bring,
Is that I fear to make you such a king.   30
  ABDAL. The majesty of kings we should not
    blame,
When royal minds adorn the royal name:
The vulgar, greatness too much idolize,
But haughty subjects it too much despise.
  ALMANZ. I only speak of him,   35
Whom pomp and greatness sit so loose about,
That he wants majesty to fill 'em out.
  ABDAL. Haste, then, and lose no time! —
The business must be enterprised this night:
We must surprise the court in its delight.   40
  ALMANZ. For you to will, for me 'tis to obey;
But I would give a crown in open day:
And, when the Spaniards their assault begin,
At once beat those without, and these within.
                    Exit ALMANZOR.

        Enter ABDELMELECH.

  ABDELM. Abdalla, hold! — there's somewhat I
    intend   45
To speak, not as your rival, but your friend.
  ABDAL. If as a friend, I am obliged to hear;
And what a rival says I cannot fear.
  ABDELM. Think, brave Abdalla, what it is ⎫
    you do: ⎪
Your quiet, honor, and our friendship too, ⎬ 50
All for a fickle beauty you forego.   ⎭
Think, and turn back, before it be too late.
Behold in me th' example of your fate:
I am your sea-mark; and, though wracked and lost,
My ruins stand to warn you from the coast.   55
  ABDAL. Your counsels, noble Abdelmelech, move
My reason to accept 'em, not my love.
Ah, why did heav'n leave man so weak defence,
To trust frail reason with the rule of sense!
'Tis overpoised and kicked up in the air,   60
While sense weighs down the scale, and keeps it
    there;
Or, like a captive king, 'tis borne away,
And forced to count'nance its own rebel's sway.
  ABDELM. No, no; our reason was not vainly lent;
Nor is a slave, but by its own consent: 65
If reason on his subject's triumph wait,
An easy king deserves no better fate.
  ABDAL. You speak too late; my empire's lost too
    far:
I cannot fight.
  ABDELM.   Then make a flying war;
Dislodge betimes before you are beset.   70
  ABDAL. Her tears, her smiles, her every look's a
    net.
Her voice is like a siren's of the land;
And bloody hearts lie panting in her hand.

  ABDELM. This do you know, and tempt the dan-
    ger still?
  ABDAL. Love, like a lethargy, has seized my
    will.   75
I'm not myself, since from her sight I went;
I lean my trunk that way, and there stand bent.
As one who, in some frightful dream, would shun
His pressing foe, labors in vain to run;
And his own slowness in his sleep bemoans,   80
With thick short sighs, weak cries, and tender
    groans,
So I ——
  ABDELM. Some friend, in charity, should shake,
And rouse, and call you loudly till you wake.
Too well I know her blandishments to gain,
Usurper-like, till settled in her reign;   85
Then proudly she insults, and gives you cares
And jealousies, short hopes and long despairs.
To this hard yoke you must hereafter bow,
Howe'er she shines all golden to you now.
  ABDAL. Like him, who on the ice   90
Slides swiftly on, and sees the water near,
Yet cannot stop himself in his career,
So am I carried. This enchanted place,
Like Circe's isle, is peopled with a race
Of dogs and swine; yet, though their fate I
    know,   95
I look with pleasure, and am turning too.

    LYNDARAXA *passes over the stage.*

  ABDELM. Fly, fly, before th' allurements of her ⎫
    face,   ⎪
Ere she return with some resistless grace,   ⎬
And with new magic covers all the place.   ⎭
  ABDAL. I cannot, will not—nay, I would not fly: 100
I'll love, be blind, be cozened till I die;
And you, who bid me wiser counsel take,
I'll hate, and, if I can, I'll kill you for her sake.
  ABDELM. Ev'n I, that counselled you, that choice
    approve:
I'll hate you blindly, and her blindly love.   105
Prudence, that stemmed the stream, is out of breath;
And to go down it is the easier death.

  LYNDARAXA *re-enters, and smiles on* ABDALLA.
                      Exit ABDALLA.

  ABDELM. That smile on Prince Abdalla seems to
    say,
You are not in your killing mood today:
Men brand, indeed, your sex with cruelty,   110
But you're too good to see poor lovers die.
This godlike pity in you I extol;
And more, because, like heav'n's, 'tis general.
  LYNDAR. My smile implies not that I grant his
    suit:
'Twas but a bare return of his salute.   115

ABDELM. It said, you were engaged, and I in place:
But, to please both, you would divide the grace.
LYNDAR. You've cause to be contented with your part,
When he has but the look, and you the heart.
ABDELM. In giving but that look, you give what's mine: 120
I'll not one corner of a glance resign.
All's mine; and I am cov'tous of my store:
I have not love enough; I'll tax you more.
LYNDAR. I gave not love; 'twas but civility:
He is a prince; that's due to his degree. 125
ABDELM. That prince you smiled on is my rival still,
And should, if me you loved, be treated ill.
LYNDAR. I know not how to show so rude a spite.
ABDELM. That is, you know not how to love aright;
Or, if you did, you would more difference see 130
Betwixt our souls, than 'twixt our quality.
Mark, if his birth makes any difference,
If to his words it adds one grain of sense.
That duty which his birth can make his due
I'll pay, but it shall not be paid by you. 135
For, if a prince courts her whom I adore,
He is my rival, and a prince no more.
LYNDAR. And when did I my pow'r so far resign,
That you should regulate each look of mine?
ABDELM. Then, when you gave your love, you gave that pow'r. 140
LYNDAR. 'Twas during pleasure, 'tis revoked this hour.
Now call me false, and rail on womankind —
'Tis all the remedy you're like to find.
ABDELM. Yes, there's one more;
I'll hate you, and this visit is my last. 145
LYNDAR. Do't, if you can; you know I hold you fast:
Yet, for your quiet, would you could resign
Your love, as easily as I do mine.
ABDELM. Furies and hell, how unconcerned she speaks!
With what indifference all her vows she breaks! 150
Curse on me, but she smiles!
LYNDAR. That smile's a part of love, and all's your due:
I take it from the prince, and give it you.
ABDELM. Just heav'n, must my poor heart your May-game prove,
To bandy, and make children's play in love? 155
(Half crying.)
Ah! how have I this cruelty deserved?
I, who so truly and so long have served!
And left so easily! oh, cruel maid!

So easily! 'Twas too unkindly said.
That heart which could so easily remove 160
Was never fixed, nor rooted deep in love.
LYNDAR. You lodged it so uneasy in your breast,
I thought you had been weary of the guest.
First, I was treated like a stranger there;
But, when a household friend I did appear, } 165
You thought, it seems, I could not live else-where.
Then, by degrees, your feigned respect withdrew;
You marked my actions, and my guardian grew.
But I am not concerned your acts to blame;
My heart to yours but upon liking [1] came; 170
And, like a bird whom prying boys molest,
Stays not to breed where she had built her nest.
ABDELM. I have done ill —
And dare not ask you to be less displeased:
Be but more angry, and my pain is eased. 175
LYNDAR. If I should be so kind a fool, to take
This little satisfaction which you make,
I know you would presume some other time
Upon my goodness, and repeat your crime.
ABDELM. Oh never, never! upon no pretence! 180
My life's too short to expiate this offence.
LYNDAR. No, now I think on't, 'tis in vain to try;
'Tis in your nature, and past remedy.
You'll still disquiet my too loving heart:
Now we are friends, 'tis best for both to part. 185
ABDELM. (taking her hand). By this — will you not give me leave to swear?
LYNDAR. You would be perjured if you should, I fear:
And, when I talk with Prince Abdalla next,
I with your fond suspicions shall be vexed.
ABDELM. I cannot say I'll conquer jealousy; 190
But, if you'll freely pardon me, I'll try.
LYNDAR. And, till you that submissive servant prove,
I never can conclude you truly love.

To them the KING, ALMAHIDE, ABENAMAR,
ESPERANZA, *Guards, Attendants.*

BOAB. Approach, my Almahide, my charming fair,
Blessing of peace, and recompence of war. 195
This night is yours; and may your life still be
The same in joy, though not solemnity.

SONG

I

Beneath a myrtle shade,
Which love for none but happy lovers made,
I slept; and straight my love before me brought 200

[1] On approval.

SONG] Printed in Q1 after Epilogue with this heading: 'Misplac'd. Sung at the dance, or Zambra in the third Act.' Q2Q3 insert here; Q4Q5 put 'THE ZAMBRA DANCE' before SONG.

Phyllis, the object of my waking thought;
Undressed she came my flames to meet,
While Love strowed flow'rs beneath her feet;
Flow'rs which, so pressed by her, became more
    sweet.

II

From the bright vision's head   205
A careless veil of lawn was loosely spread:
From her white temples fell her shaded hair,
Like cloudy sunshine, not too brown nor fair:
Her hands, her lips, did love inspire;
Her every grace my heart did fire: 210
But most her eyes, which languished with desire.

III

'Ah, charming fair,' said I,
'How long can you my bliss and yours deny?
By nature and by love this lonely shade
Was for revenge of suff'ring lovers made.   215
Silence and shades with love agree:
Both shelter you and favor me;
You cannot blush, because I cannot see.'

IV

'No, let me die,' she said,
'Rather than lose the spotless name of maid!'   220
Faintly, methought, she spoke; for all the while
She bid me not believe her, with a smile.
'Then die,' said I: she still denied:
'And is it thus, thus, thus,' she cried,
'You use a harmless maid?' — and so she died!   225

V

I waked, and straight I knew
I loved so well, it made my dream prove true:
Fancy, the kinder mistress of the two,
Fancy had done what Phyllis would not do!
Ah, cruel nymph, cease your disdain;   230
While I can dream, you scorn in vain —
Asleep or waking, you must ease my pain.

THE ZAMBRA DANCE

*(After the dance, a tumultuous noise of drums
and trumpets.)*

To them OZMYN, *his sword drawn.*

OZM. Arm, quickly, arm; yet all, I fear, too late:
The enemy's already at the gate.

BOAB. The Christians are dislodged; what foe
    is near?   235

OZM. The Zegrys are in arms, and almost here:
The streets with torches shine, with shoutings ring,
And Prince Abdalla is proclaimed the king.
What man could do, I have already done,
But bold Almanzor fiercely leads 'em on.   240

ABEN. Th' Alhambra yet is safe in my command;
    (To the KING.)
Retreat you thither, while their shock we stand.

BOAB. I cannot meanly for my life provide:
I'll either perish in't, or stem this tide.
To guard the palace, Ozmyn, be your care.   245
If they o'ercome, no sword will hurt the fair.

OZM. I'll either die, or I'll make good the place.

ABDELM. And I with these will bold Almanzor face.
    Exeunt all but the Ladies.   An alarm within.

ALMAH. What dismal planet did my triumphs
    light!
Discord the day, and death does rule the night: 250
The noise my soul does through my senses wound.

LYNDAR. Methinks it is a noble, sprightly sound,
The trumpet's clangor, and the clash of arms!
This noise may chill your blood, but mine it warms.
    (Shouting and clashing of swords within.)
We have already passed the Rubicon.   255
The dice are mine: now, fortune, for a throne!
    (A shout within, and clashing of swords afar off.)
The sound goes farther off, and faintly dies;
Curse of this going back, these ebbing cries!
Ye winds, waft hither sounds more strong and quick:
Beat faster, drums, and mingle deaths more
    thick.   260
I'll to the turrets of the palace go,
And add new fire to those that fight below.
Thence, Hero-like, with torches by my side
(Far be the omen, though) my love I'll guide.
No; like his better fortune I'll appear,   265
With open arms, loose veil, and flowing hair,
Just flying forward from my rolling sphere.
My smiles shall make Abdalla more than man;
Let him look up, and perish if he can.   *Exit.*

An alarm nearer: then enter ALMANZOR *and* SELIN
in the head of the Zegrys; OZYMN, *prisoner.*

ALMANZ. We have not fought enough; they fly too
    soon: 270
And I am grieved the noble sport is done.
This only man, of all whom chance did bring
    (pointing to OZYMN)
To meet my arms, was worth the conquering.
His brave resistance did my fortune grace;
So slow, so threat'ning forward, he gave place.   275
His chains be easy, and his usage fair.

SELIN. I beg you would commit him to my care.

ALMANZ. Next, the brave Spaniard free without
    delay;
And with a convoy send him safe away.
    Exit a Guard.

To them HAMET *and others.*

HAMET. The king by me salutes you; and, to
    show   280

THE ZAMBRA DANCE] Stage direction as in Q2Q3.   241] QQ *Th'*; F *The.*

That to your valor he his crown does owe,
Would from your mouth I should the word receive;
And that to these you would your orders give.

    ALMANZ. He much o'errates the little I have done.
    (ALMANZOR *goes to the door, and there seems to
    give out orders, by sending people several
    ways.*)

    SELIN (*to* OZMYN). Now, to revenge the murder
      of my son,   285
Tomorrow for thy certain death prepare:
This night I only leave thee to despair.

    OZMYN. Thy idle menaces I do not fear:
My business was to die or conquer here.
Sister, for you I grieve I could no more: 290
My present state betrays my want of pow'r;
But, when true courage is of force bereft,
Patience, the noblest fortitude, is left.

                  Exit cum SELIN.

    ALMAH. Ah, Esperanza, what for me remains
But death, or, worse than death, inglorious
    chains!   295

    ESPER. Madam, you must not to despair give
    place;
Heav'n never meant misfortune to that face.
Suppose there were no justice in your cause,
Beauty's a bribe that gives her judges laws.
That you are brought to this deplored estate,   300
Is but th' ingenious flatt'ry of your fate;
Fate fears her succor like an alms to give;
And would you, God-like, from yourself should live.

    ALMAH. Mark but how terrible his eyes appear!
And yet there's something roughly noble there,   305
Which, in unfashioned nature, looks divine,
And, like a gem, does in the quarry shine.

    (ALMANZOR *returns; she falls at his feet, being
    veiled.*)

    ALMAH. Turn, mighty conqu'ror, turn your face
    this way,
Do not refuse to hear the wretched pray!

    ALMANZ. What business can this woman have
    with me?   310

    ALMAH. That of th' afflicted to the Deity.
So may your arms success in battles find;
So may the mistress of your vows be kind,
If you have any; or, if you have none,
So may your liberty be still your own!   315

    ALMANZ. Yes, I will turn my face, but not my
    mind:
You bane and soft destruction of mankind,
What would you have with me?

    ALMAH.   I beg the grace   (*Unveiling.*)
You would lay by those terrors of your face.
Till calmness to your eyes you first restore,   320
I am afraid, and I can beg no more.

    ALMANZ. (*looking fixedly on her*). Well; my fierce
    visage shall not murder you.

Speak quickly, woman; I have much to do.

    ALMAH. Where should I find the heart to speak
    one word?
Your voice, sir, is as killing as your sword.   325
As you have left the lightning of your eye,
So would you please to lay your thunder by!

    ALMANZ. I'm pleased and pained, since first her
    eyes I saw,
As I were stung with some tarantula.
Arms, and the dusty field, I less admire,   330
And soften strangely in some new desire;
Honor burns in me not so fiercely bright,
But pale as fires when mastered by the light:
Ev'n while I speak and look, I change yet more,
And now am nothing that I was before.   335
I'm numbed, and fixed, and scarce my eyeballs
    move;
I fear it is the lethargy of love!
'Tis he; I feel him now in every part:
Like a new lord he vaunts about my heart;
Surveys, in state, each corner of my breast,   340
While poor fierce I, that was, am dispossessed.
I'm bound; but I will rouse my rage again; ⎫
And, though no hope of liberty remain,   ⎬
I'll fright my keeper when I shake my chain. ⎭
You are ——   (*Angrily.*)

    ALMAH.   I know I am your captive, sir. 345

    ALMANZ. You are — You shall — And I can
    scarce forbear ——

    ALMAH. Alas!

    ALMANZ. (*aside*). 'Tis all in vain; it will not do:
I cannot now a seeming anger show:
My tongue against my heart no aid affords;
For love still rises up, and chokes my words.   350

    ALMAH. In half this time a tempest would be still.

    ALMANZ. 'Tis you have raised that tempest in
    my will.
I wonnot love you; give me back my heart;
But give it, as you had it, fierce and brave.
It was not made to be a woman's slave: 355
But, lion-like, has been in deserts bred,
And, used to range, will ne'er be tamely led.
Restore its freedom to my fettered will,
And then I shall have pow'r to use you ill.

    ALMAH. My sad condition may your pity
    move;   360
But look not on me with the eyes of love. —
I must be brief, though I have much to say.

    ALMANZ. No, speak; for I can hear you now all
    day.   (*Softly.*)
(*Aside.*) Her suing soothes me with a secret pride:
A suppliant beauty cannot be denied: 365
Ev'n while I frown, her charms the furrows seize;
And I'm corrupted with the pow'r to please.

    ALMAH. Though in your worth no cause of fear
    I see,

293] Q1–Q4 *noblest*; Q5F *only*.   336] Q1–Q4 *numm'd*; Q5F *mum'd* (F follows Q5).

I fear the insolence of victory;
As you are noble, sir, protect me then   370
From the rude outrage of insulting men.
   ALMANZ. Who dares touch her I love? I'm all
     o'er love:
Nay, I am Love; Love shot, and shot so fast,
He shot himself into my breast at last.
   ALMAH. You see before you her who should be
     queen,   375
Since she is promised to Boabdelin.
   ALMANZ. Are you beloved by him? O wretched
     fate,
First, that I love at all; then, love too late!
Yet, I must love!
   ALMAH.   Alas, it is in vain;
Fate for each other did not us ordain.   380
The chances of this day too clearly show
That heav'n took care that it should not be so.
   ALMANZ. Would heav'n had quite forgot me this
     one day!
But fate's yet hot ——
I'll make it take a bent another way.   385
    (*He walks swiftly and discomposedly, studying.*)
I bring a claim which does his right remove:
You're his by promise, but you're mine by love.
'Tis all but ceremony which is past;
The knot's to tie which is to make you fast.
Fate gave not to Boabdelin that pow'r;   390
He wooed you but as my ambassador.
   ALMAH. Our souls are tied by holy vows above.
   ALMANZ. He signed but his; but I will seal my love.
I love you better, with more zeal than he.
   ALMAH. This day   395
I gave my faith to him, he his to me.
   ALMANZ. Good heav'n, thy book of fate before
     me lay,
But to tear out the journal of this day:
Or, if the order of the world below
Will not the gap of one whole day allow,   400
Give me that minute when she made her
     vow!
'That minute, ev'n the happy from their bliss
     might give:
'And those, who live in grief, a shorter time would
     live.'
So small a link, if broke, th' eternal chain
Would, like divided waters, join again. ——   405
It wonnot be; the fugitive is gone,
Pressed by the crowd of following minutes on:
That precious moment's out of nature fled,
And in the heap of common rubbish laid,
Of things that once have been, and are decayed.   410
   ALMAH. Your passion, like a fright, suspends my
     pain:

It meets, o'erpowers, and bears mine back again:
But as, when tides against the current flow,
The native stream runs its own course below,
So, though your griefs possess the upper part,   415
My own have deeper channels in my heart.
   ALMANZ. Forgive that fury which my soul does
     move;
'Tis the essay of an untaught first love.
Yet rude, unfashioned truth it does express:
'Tis love just peeping in a hasty dress.   420
Retire, fair creature, to your needful rest;
There's something noble lab'ring in my breast:
This raging fire which through the mass does move
Shall purge my dross, and shall refine my love.
     Exeunt ALMAHIDE *and* ESPERANZA.
She goes, and I like my own ghost appear: 425
It is not living when she is not here.

     To him ABDALLA *as King, attended.*
   ABDAL. My first acknowledgments to heav'n are
     due;
My next, Almanzor, let me pay to you.
   ALMANZ. A poor surprise, and on a naked foe,
Whatever you confess, is all you owe;   430
And I no merit own, or understand
That fortune did you justice by my hand.
Yet, if you will that little service pay
With a great favor, I can show the way.
   ABDAL. I have a favor to demand of you;   435
That is, to take the thing for which you sue.
   ALMANZ. Then, briefly, thus: when I th' Albayzin
     won,
I found the beauteous Almahide alone,
Whose sad condition did my pity move;
And that compassion did produce my love.   440
   ABDAL. This needs no suit; in justice, I declare,
She is your captive by the right of war.
   ALMANZ. She is no captive then; I set her
     free;
And, rather than I will her jailer be,
I'll nobly lose her in her liberty.   445
   ABDAL. Your generosity I much approve;
But your excess of that shows want of love.
   ALMANZ. No, 'tis th' excess of love which mounts
     so high
That, seen far off, it lessens to the eye.
Had I not loved her, and had set her free,   450
That, sir, had been my generosity:
But 'tis exalted passion, when I show
I dare be wretched, not to make her so.
And, while another passion fills her breast,
I'll be all wretched rather than half blest.   455
   ABDAL. May your heroic act so prosperous be,
That Almahide may sigh you set her free.

378] Q4Q5 *loved* (F *lov'd) too late.*
402, 403] QQF print this couplet in quotation-marks probably to mark it for special emphasis or quotation. (See N, p. 437.)
412] Q4Q5F *beats.*   445] Q1Q5F *loose*; Q2Q3Q4 *lose.* (See also V. iii. 295.)

Enter ZULEMA.

ZUL. Of five tall tow'rs which fortify this town,
All but th' Alhambra your dominion own.
Now, therefore, boldly I confess a flame,   460
Which is excused in Almahida's name.
If you the merit of this night regard,
In her possession I have my reward.

ALMANZ. She your reward! why, she's a gift so
     great,
That I myself have not deserved her yet;   465
And therefore, though I won her with my sword,
I have, with awe, my sacrilege restored.

ZUL. What you deserve —
I'll not dispute because I do not know;
This only I will say, she shall not go.   470

ALMANZ. Thou, single, art not worth my answer-
     ing:
But take what friends, what armies thou canst
     bring;
What worlds; and, when you are united all,
Then I will thunder in your ears: 'She shall!'

ZUL. I'll not one tittle of my right resign.   475
Sir, your implicit promise made her mine;
When I in general terms my love did show,
You swore our fortunes should together go.

ABDAL. The merits of the cause I'll not decide,
But, like my love, I would my gift divide.   480
Your equal titles, then, no longer plead;
But one of you, for love of me, recede.

ALMANZ. I have receded to the utmost line,
When, by my free consent, she is not mine:
Then let him equally recede with me,   485
And both of us will join to set her free.

ZUL. If you will free your part of her, you may;
But, sir, I love not your romantic way.
Dream on, enjoy her soul, and set that free;
I'm pleased her person should be left for me.   490

ALMANZ. Thou shalt not wish her thine; thou
     shalt not dare
To be so impudent as to despair.

ZUL. The Zegrys, sir, are all concerned to see
How much their merit you neglect in me.

HAMET. Your slighting Zulema this very
     hour   495
Will take ten thousand subjects from your pow'r.

ALMANZ. What are ten thousand subjects such
     as they?
If I am scorned — I'll take myself away.

ABDAL. Since both cannot possess what both
     pursue,
I grieve, my friend, the chance should fall on
     you.   500
But when you hear what reasons I can urge ——

ALMANZ. None, none that your ingratitude can
     purge.

Reason's a trick, when it no grant affords;
It stamps the face of majesty on words.

ABDAL. Your boldness to your services I give: 505
Now take it, as your full reward — to live.

ALMANZ. To live!
If from thy hands alone my death can be,
I am immortal, and a god, to thee.
If I would kill thee now, thy fate's so low,   510
That I must stoop ere I can give the blow.
But mine is fixed so far above thy crown,
That all thy men,
Piled on thy back, can never pull it down.
But at my ease thy destiny I send,   515
By ceasing from this hour to be thy friend.
Like heav'n, I need but only to stand still,
And, not concurring to thy life, I kill.
Thou canst no title to my duty bring:
I'm not thy subject, and my soul's thy king.   520
Farewell. When I am gone,
There's not a star of thine dare stay with thee:
I'll whistle thy tame fortune after me;
And whirl fate with me wheresoe'er I fly,
As winds drive storms before 'em in the sky.   525
         Exit.

ZUL. Let not this insolent unpunished go;
Give your commands; your justice is too slow.
    (ZULEMA, HAMET, *and others are going after
     him.*)

ABDAL. Stay! and what part he pleases let him
     take;
I know my throne's too strong for him to shake.
But my fair mistress I too long forget: 530
The crown I promised is not offered yet.
Without her presence all my joys are vain,
Empire a curse, and life itself a pain.
         Exeunt.

ACT IV

[SCENE I]

BOABDELIN, ABENAMAR, *Guards.*

BOAB. Advise, or aid, but do not pity me;
No monarch born can fall to that degree.
Pity descends from kings to all below;
But can, no more than fountains, upward flow.
Witness, just heav'n, my greatest grief has been,   5
I could not make your Almahide a queen.

ABEN. I have too long th' effects of fortune
     known,
Either to trust her smiles, or fear her frown.
Since in their first attempt you were not slain,
Your safety bodes you yet a second reign.   10
The people like a headlong torrent go,
And every dam they break, or overflow;
But, unopposed, they either lose their force,

Or wind in volumes to their former course.

BOAB. In walls we meanly must our hopes en-
    close,   15
To wait our friends, and weary out our foes,
While Almahide
To lawless rebels is exposed a prey,
And forced the lustful victor to obey.

ABEN. One of my blood, in rules of virtue bred! 20
Think better of her, and believe she's dead.

To them ALMANZOR.

BOAB. We are betrayed, the enemy is here;
We have no farther room to hope or fear.

ALMANZ. It is indeed Almanzor whom you see,
But he no longer is your enemy.   25
You were ungrateful, but your foes were more;
What your injustice lost you, theirs restore.
Make profit of my vengeance while you may;
My two-edged sword can cut the other way.
I am your fortune, but am swift like her,   30
And turn my hairy front if you defer:
That hour when you delib'rate, is too late;
I point you the white [1] moment of your fate.

ABEN. Believe him sent as Prince Abdalla's spy;
He would betray us to the enemy.   35

ALMANZ. Were I, like thee, in cheats of ⎫
    state grown old   ⎬
(Those public markets, where for foreign gold ⎭
The poorer prince is to the richer sold),
Then thou mightst think me fit for that low part:
But I am yet to learn the statesman's art.   40
My kindness and my hate unmasked I wear;
For friends to trust, and enemies to fear.
My heart's so plain
That men on every passing thought may look,
Like fishes gliding in a crystal brook;   45
When troubled most, it does the bottom show;
'Tis weedless all above, and rockless all below.

ABEN. Ere he be trusted, let him first be tried;
He may be false, who once has changed his side.

ALMANZ. In that you more accuse yourselves
    than me: 50
None who are injured can unconstant be.
You were unconstant, you, who did the wrong;
To do me justice does to me belong.
Great souls by kindness only can be tied;
Injured again, again I'll leave your side.   55
Honor is what myself, and friends, I owe;
And none can lose it who forsake a foe.
Since, then, your foes now happen to be mine,
Though not in friendship, we'll in int'rest join:

[1] Propitious.

So while my loved revenge is full and high,   60
I'll give you back your kingdom by the by.

BOAB. (*embracing him*). That I so long delayed
    what you desire,
Was not to doubt your worth, but to admire.

ALMANZ. This counsellor an old man's cau- ⎫
    tion shows,   ⎪
Who fears that little he has left, to lose: ⎬ 65
Age sets to fortune; while youth boldly   ⎪
    throws.[2]   ⎭
But let us first your drooping soldiers cheer:
Then seek out danger, ere it dare appear.
This hour I fix your crown upon your brow;
Next hour fate gives it, but I give it now.   70
                                        Exeunt.

SCENE II

LYNDARAXA *alone*.

LYNDAR. O could I read the dark decrees of fate,
That I might once know whom to love, or hate!
For I myself scarce my own thoughts can guess,
So much I find 'em varied by success.
As in some weather-glass, my love I hold;   5
Which falls or rises with the heat or cold.
I will be constant yet, if fortune can;
I love the king: — let her but name the man.

To her HALYMA.

HAL. Madam, a gentleman, to me unknown,
Desires that he may speak with you alone.   10

LYNDAR. Some message from the king.   Let him
    appear.

To her ABDELMELECH; *who, entering, throws off his
    disguise. She starts.*

ABDELM. I see you are amazed that I am here:
But let at once your fear and wonder end.
In the usurper's guard I found a friend,
Who led me to you safe in this disguise.   15

LYNDAR. Your danger brings this trouble in my
    eyes.
But what affair this vent'rous visit drew?

ABDELM. The greatest in the world — the seeing
    you.

LYNDAR. The courage of your love I so admire
That, to preserve you, you shall straight retire. 20
                        (*She leads him to the door.*)
Go, dear! each minute does new dangers bring;
You will be taken; I expect the king.

[2] 'Age encounters fortune's hazards warily, while youth
boldly stakes all on one throw.'

21] Q1Q2 *and I believe*; Q3 *I believe*; Q4Q5F *and believe* (showing successive metrical amendments).
37] Q3Q4F *where*; Q1Q2Q5 misprint *were*.   38] Q1–Q4 *poorer | richer*; Q5F *poorest | richest.*
44] Q1Q2Q3 *thought*; Q4Q5 *though*; F *through* (F detects misprint but emends without consulting the correct early quartos).
48] Q1–Q4 *first*; Q5F *then.*   66] Q1Q2Q3 *sets to*; Q4 errs in dropping *to* before *fortune*; Q5F follow blindly.
SCENE II. 4] Q1–Q4 *'em*; Q5F *them.*

ABDELM. The king! — the poor usurper of an
   hour:
His empire's but a dream of kingly pow'r. —
I warn you, as a lover and a friend,   25
To leave him ere his short dominion end.
The soldier I suborned will wait at night,
And shall alone be conscious of your flight.
   LYNDAR. I thank you that you so much care
   bestow;
But, if his reign be short, I need not go.   30
For why should I expose my life and yours
For what, you say, a little time assures?
   ABDELM. My danger in th' attempt is very small:
And, if he loves you, yours is none at all.
But, though his ruin be as sure as fate,   35
Your proof of love to me would come too late.
This trial I in kindness would allow;
'Tis easy; if you love me, show it now.
   LYNDAR. It is because I love you, I refuse:
For all the world my conduct would accuse,   40
If I should go with him I love away:
And, therefore, in strict virtue, I will stay.
   ABDELM. You would in vain dissemble love to
   me:
Through that thin veil your artifice I see.
You would expect th' event,[1] and then declare;   45
But do not, do not drive me to despair:
For, if you now refuse with me to fly,
Rather than love you after this, I'll die.
And therefore weigh it well before you speak;
My king is safe, his force within not weak.   50
   LYNDAR. The counsel you have giv'n me may be
   wise;
But, since th' affair is great, I will advise.[2]
   ABDELM. Then that delay I for denial take.
                            (Is going.)
   LYNDAR. Stay! you too swift an exposition make.
If I should go, since Zulema will stay,   55
I should my brother to the king betray.
   ABDELM. There is no fear: but, if there were, I see
You value still your brother more than me.
Farewell! some ease I in your falsehood find;
It lets a beam in that will clear my mind.   60
My former weakness I with shame confess,
And, when I see you next, shall love you less.
                     (Is going again.)
   LYNDAR. Your faithless dealing you may blush
   to tell.   (Weeping.)
This is a maid's reward, who loves too well. —
                    (He looks back.)
Remember that I drew my latest breath   65
In charging your unkindness with my death.
   ABDELM. (coming back). Have I not answered all
   you can invent,
Ev'n the least shadow of an argument?

[1] 'Wait to see the outcome.'   [2] Reflect.

   LYNDAR. You want not cunning what you please
   to prove,
But my poor heart knows only how to love;   70
And, finding this, you tyrannize the more:
'Tis plain, some other mistress you adore;
And now, with studied tricks of subtilty,
You come prepared to lay the fault on me.
                (Wringing her hands.)
But oh, that I should love so false a man!   75
   ABDELM. Hear me, and then disprove it, if you
   can.
   LYNDAR. I'll hear no more; your breach of faith
   is plain:
You would with wit your want of love maintain.
But, by my own experience, I can tell,
They who love truly cannot argue well.   80
Go, faithless man!
Leave me alone to mourn my misery:
I cannot cease to love you, but I'll die.
            (Leans her head on his arm.)
   ABDELM. (weeping). What man but I so long un-
   moved could hear
Such tender passion, and refuse a tear!   85
But do not talk of dying any more,
Unless you mean that I should die before.
   LYNDAR. I fear your feigned repentance comes
   too late:
I die, to see you still thus obstinate.
But yet, in death, my truth of love to show,   90
Lead me; if I have strength enough, I'll go.
   ABDELM. By heav'n, you shall not go! I will not
   be
O'ercome in love or generosity.
All I desire, to end th' unlucky strife,
Is but a vow that you will be my wife.   95
   LYNDAR. To tie me to you by a vow is hard;
It shows my love you as no tie regard.
Name anything but that, and I'll agree.
   ABDELM. Swear, then, you never will my rival's
   be.
   LYNDAR. Nay, prithee, this is harder than be-
   fore.   100
Name anything, good dear, but that thing more.
   ABDELM. Now I too late perceive I am undone:
Living and seeing, to my death I run.
I know you false, yet in your snares I fall;
You grant me nothing, and I grant you all.   105
   LYNDAR. I would grant all; but I must curb my
   will,
Because I love to keep you jealous still.
In your suspicion I your passion find;
But I will take a time to cure your mind.
   HALYMA. Oh, madam, the new king is drawing
   near!   110
   LYNDAR. Haste quickly hence, lest he should
   find you here!

63] Q4Q5F dealings.

ABDELM. How much more wretched than I
    came, I go!
I more my weakness and your falsehood know;
And now must leave you with my greatest foe!

Exit ABDELMELECH.

LYNDAR. Go! — How I love thee, heav'n can
    only tell: 115
And yet I love thee, for a subject, well. —
Yet, whatsoever charms a crown can bring,
A subject's greater than a little king.
I will attend till time this throne secure;
And, when I climb, my footing shall be sure. —   120
    (*Music without.*)
Music! and, I believe, addressed to me.

SONG

I

Wherever I am, and whatever I do,
  My Phyllis is still in my mind;
When angry, I mean not to Phyllis to go,
  My feet, of themselves, the way find: 125
Unknown to myself I am just at her door,
And, when I would rail, I can bring out no more
  Than, 'Phyllis too fair and unkind!'

II

When Phyllis I see, my heart bounds in my breast,
  And the love I would stifle is shown: 130
But asleep, or awake, I am never at rest,
  When from my eyes Phyllis is gone.
Sometimes a sad dream does delude my sad mind,
But, alas! when I wake, and no Phyllis I find,
  How I sigh to myself all alone!   135

III

Should a king be my rival in her I adore,
  He should offer his treasure in vain:
O let me alone to be happy and poor,
  And give me my Phyllis again!
Let Phyllis be mine, and but ever be kind,   140
I could to a desert with her be confined,
  And envy no monarch his reign.

IV

Alas! I discover too much of my love,
  And she too well knows her own power!
She makes me each day a new martyrdom prove,   145
  And makes me grow jealous each hour:
But let her each minute torment my poor mind,
I had rather love Phyllis, both false and unkind,
  Than ever be freed from her pow'r.

ABDALLA *enters with Guards.*

ABDAL. Now, madam, at your feet a king you
    see;   150
Or, rather, if you please, a sceptred slave;

'Tis just you should possess the pow'r you gave.
Had love not made me yours, I yet had been
But the first subject to Boabdelin.
Thus heav'n declares the crown I bring your
    due;   155
And had forgot my title, but for you.
    LYNDAR. Heav'n to your merits will, I hope, be
    kind;
But, sir, it has not yet declared its mind.
'Tis true, it holds the crown above your head;
But does not fix it till your brother's dead.   160
    ABDAL. All but th' Alhambra is within my pow'r;
And that, my forces go to take this hour.
    LYNDAR. When, with its keys, your brother's
    head you bring,
I shall believe you are indeed a king.
    ABDAL. But since th' events of all things doubt-
    ful are,   165
And, of events, most doubtful those of war,
I beg to know before, if fortune frown,
Must I then lose your favor with my crown?
    LYNDAR. You'll soon return a conqueror again;
And, therefore, sir, your question is in vain.   170
    ABDAL. I think to certain victory I move;
But you may more assure it by your love.
That grant will make my arms invincible.
    LYNDAR. My pray'rs and wishes your success
    foretell. —
Go then, and fight, and think you fight for me;   175
I wait but to reward your victory.
    ABDAL. But if I lose it, must I lose you too?
    LYNDAR. You are too curious, if you more would
    know.
I know not what my future thoughts will be:
Poor women's thoughts are all *extempore*.   180
Wise men, indeed,
Beforehand a long chain of thoughts produce;
But ours are only for our present use.
    ABDAL. Those thoughts you will not know, too
    well declare
You mean to wait the final doom of war.   185
    LYNDAR. I find you come to quarrel with me now;
Would you know more of me than I allow?
Whence are you grown that great divinity
That with such ease into my thoughts can pry?
Indulgence does not with some tempers suit;   190
I see I must become more absolute.
    ABDAL. I must submit,
On what hard terms soe'er my peace be bought.
    LYNDAR. Submit! — you speak as you were not
    in fault.
'Tis evident the injury is mine;   195
For why should you my secret thoughts divine?
    ABDAL. Yet if we might be judged by reason's
    laws!
    LYNDAR. Then you would have your reason
    judge my cause!

Either confess your fault, or hold your tongue;
For I am sure I'm never in the wrong.   200
ABDAL. Then I acknowledge it.
LYNDAR.   Then I forgive.
ABDAL. (*aside*). Under how hard a law poor lovers
        live!
Who, like the vanquished, must their right release,
And with the loss of reason buy their peace. —
Madam, to show that you my pow'r command,   205
I put my life and safety in your hand:
Dispose of the Albayzin as you please:
To your fair hands I here resign the keys.
    LYNDAR. I take your gift, because your love it
        shows;
And faithful Selin for alcalde [1] choose.   210
    ABDAL. Selin, from her alone your orders take.
This one request, yet, madam, let me make,
That from those turrets you th' assault will see;
And crown, once more, my arms with victory.
                                Leads her out.

SELIN *remains with* GAZUL *and* REDUAN, *his servants.*

    SELIN. Gazul, go tell my daughter that I
        wait.   215
You, Reduan, bring the pris'ner to his fate.
                    Exeunt GAZUL *and* REDUAN.
Ere of my charge I will possession take,
A bloody sacrifice I mean to make:
The manes of my son shall smile this day,
While I, in blood, my vows of vengeance pay.   220

Enter at one door BENZAYDA, *with* GAZUL; *at the
    other,* OZMYN *bound, with* REDUAN.

    SELIN. I sent, Benzayda, to glad your eyes:
These rites we owe your brother's obsequies. —
You two (*to* GAZUL *and* REDUAN) th' accurst Aben-
        cerrago bind:
You need no more t' instruct you in my mind.
        (*They bind him to one corner of the stage.*)
    BENZ. In what sad object am I called to
        share?   225
Tell me, what is it, sir, you here prepare?
    SELIN. 'Tis what your dying brother did bequeath,
A scene of vengeance, and a pomp of death!
    BENZ. The horrid spectacle my soul does fright;
I want the heart to see the dismal sight.   230
    SELIN. You are my principal invited guest,
Whose eyes I would not only feed, but feast:
You are to smile at his last groaning breath,
And laugh to see his eyeballs roll in death;
To judge the ling'ring soul's convulsive strife,   235
When thick short breath catches at parting life.
    BENZ. And of what marble do you think me made?
    SELIN. What! can you be of just revenge afraid?
    BENZ. He killed my brother in his own defence.
[1] Ruler.

Pity his youth, and spare his innocence.   240
    SELIN. Art thou so soon to pardon murder won?
Can he be innocent, who killed my son?
Abenamar shall mourn as well as I;
His Ozmyn, for my Tarifa, shall die.
But since thou plead'st so boldly, I will see   245
That justice thou wouldst hinder done by thee.
Here — (*gives her his sword*) — take the sword, and
        do a sister's part:
Pierce his, fond girl, or I will pierce thy heart.
    OZM. To his commands I join my own request;
All wounds from you are welcome to my breast: 250
Think only, when your hand this act has done,
It has but finished what your eyes begun.
I thought with silence to have scorned my doom;
But now your noble pity has o'ercome;
Which I acknowledge with my latest breath —   255
The first whoe'er began a love in death.
    BENZ. (*to* SELIN). Alas, what aid can my weak
        hand afford?
You see I tremble when I touch a sword:
The brightness dazzles me, and turns my sight:
Or, if I look, 'tis but to aim less right.   260
    OZM. I'll guide the hand which must my death
        convey;
My leaping heart shall meet it half the way.
    SELIN (*to* BENZAYDA). Waste not the precious
        time in idle breath.
    BENZ. Let me resign this instrument of death.
        (*Giving the sword to her father, and then pulling
        it back.*)
Ah, no! I was too hasty to resign: 265
'Tis in your hand more mortal than in mine.

To them HAMET.

    HAMET. The king is from th' Alhambra beaten back,
And now preparing for a new attack;
To favor which, he wills that instantly
You reinforce him with a new supply.   270
    SELIN (*to* BENZAYDA). Think not, although my
        duty calls me hence,
That with the breach of yours I will dispense.
Ere my return see my commands you do:
Let me find Ozmyn dead, and killed by you. —
Gazul and Reduan, attend her still;   275
And, if she dares to fail, perform my will.
                        Exeunt SELIN *and* HAMET.
        (BENZAYDA *looks languishing on him, with
            her sword down;* GAZUL *and* REDUAN
            standing with drawn swords by her.)
    OZM. Defer not, fair Benzayda, my death;
Looking on you,
I should but live to sigh away my breath.
My eyes have done the work they had to do;   ⎫ 280
I take your image with me, which they drew;   ⎬
And, when they close, I shall die full of you. ⎭

BENZ. When parents their commands unjustly
　　lay,
Children are privileged to disobey;
Yet from that breach of duty I am clear,　　285
Since I submit the penalty to bear.
To die, or kill you, is th' alternative;
Rather than take your life, I will not live.
　　OZM. This shows th' excess of generosity;
But, madam, you have no pretence to die.　　290
I should defame th' Abencerrages' race,
To let a lady suffer in my place.
But neither could that life you would bestow ⎫
Save mine; nor do you so much pity owe　　⎬
To me, a stranger, and your house's foe.　　⎭　295
　　BENZ. From whencesoe'er their hate our houses
　　drew,
I blush to tell you, I have none for you.
'Tis a confession which I should not make,
Had I more time to give, or you to take:
But, since death's near, and runs with so much
　　force,　　300
We must meet first, and intercept his course.
　　OZM. Oh, how unkind a comfort do you give!
Now I fear death again, and wish to live.
Life were worth taking, could I have it now; ⎫
But 'tis more good than heav'n can e'er allow ⎬ 305
To one man's portion, to have life and you. ⎭
　　BENZ. Sure, at our births,
Death with our meeting planets danced above,
Or we were wounded by a mourning love!
　　　　　　　　　　　(Shouts within.)
　　RED. The noise returns, and doubles from
　　behind;　　310
It seems as if two adverse armies joined:
Time presses us.
　　GAZ.　　　If longer you delay,
We must, though loath, your father's will obey.
　　OZM. Haste, madam, to fulfil his hard commands,
And rescue me from their ignoble hands.　　315
Let me kiss yours, when you my wound begin,
Then easy death will slide with pleasure in.
　　BENZ. (to GAZUL and REDUAN). Ah, gentle sol-
　　diers, some short time allow!
My father has repented him ere now;
Or will repent him, when he finds me dead.　　320
My clue of life is twined with Ozmyn's thread.
　　RED. 'Tis fatal to refuse her, or obey!
But where is our excuse? what can we say?
　　BENZ. Say; anything—
Say that to kill the guiltless you were loath;　　325
Or if you did, say I would kill you both.
　　GAZ. To disobey our orders is to die.—
I'll do't: who dare oppose it?
　　RED.　　　　　　That dare I.
　　(REDUAN stands before OZMYN, and fights
　　with GAZUL. BENZAYDA unbinds OZMYN,
　　and gives him her sword.)

BENZ. Stay not to see the issue of the fight;
　　　　　　　　　(REDUAN kills GAZUL.)
But haste to save yourself by speedy flight.　　330
　　OZM. (kneeling to kiss her hand). Did all mankind
　　against my life conspire,
Without this blessing I would not retire.
But, madam, can I go and leave you here?
Your father's anger now for you I fear:
Consider you have done too much to stay.　　335
　　BENZ. Think not of me, but fly yourself away.
　　RED. Haste quickly hence; the enemies are nigh!
From every part I see our soldiers fly.
The foes not only our assailants beat,
But fiercely sally out on their retreat,　　340
And, like a sea broke loose, come on amain.

*To them ABENAMAR, and a party with their swords
drawn, driving in some of the enemies.*

　　ABEN. Traitors, you hope to save yourselves in
　　vain!
Your forfeit lives shall for your treason pay;
And Ozmyn's blood shall be revenged this day.
　　OZM. (kneeling to his father). No, sir, your Ozmyn
　　lives; and lives to own　　345
A father's piety to free his son.
　　ABEN. (embracing him). My Ozmyn!—O thou
　　blessing of my age!
And art thou safe from their deluded rage!—
Whom must I praise for thy deliverance?
Was it thy valor, or the work of chance?　　350
　　OZM. Nor chance, nor valor, could deliver me;
But 'twas a noble pity set me free.
My liberty, and life,
And what your happiness you're pleased to call,
We to this charming beauty owe it all.　　355
　　ABEN. (to her). Instruct me, visible divinity!
Instruct me by what name to worship thee!
For to thy virtue I would altars raise,
Since thou art much above all human praise.
But see——　　360

*Enter ALMANZOR, his sword bloody, leading in
ALMAHIDE, attended by ESPERANZA.*

My other blessing, Almahide, is here!
I'll to the king, and tell him she is near:
You, Ozmyn, on your fair deliverer wait,
And with your private joys the public celebrate.
　　　　　　　　　　　　　Exeunt.

ALMANZOR, ALMAHIDE, ESPERANZA.

　　ALMANZ. The work is done; now, madam, you are
　　free:　　365
At least, if I can give you liberty.
But you have chains which you yourself have chose;
And O that I could free you too from those!
But you are free from force, and have full pow'r
To go, and kill my hopes and me, this hour.　　370

I see, then, you will go; but yet my toil
May be rewarded with a looking-while.

ALMAH. Almanzor can from every subject raise
New matter for our wonder and his praise.
You bound and freed me; but the difference is,   375
That showed your valor; but your virtue this.

ALMANZ. Madam, you praise a fun'ral victory,
At whose sad pomp the conqueror must die.

ALMAH. Conquest attends Almanzor everywhere;
I am too small a foe for him to fear: 380
But heroes still must be opposed by some,
Or they would want occasion to o'ercome.

ALMANZ. Madam, I cannot on bare praises live:
Those who abound in praises seldom give.

ALMAH. While I to all the world your worth make
          known,   385
May heav'n reward the pity you have shown!

ALMANZ. My love is languishing, and starved to
          death;
And would you give me charity — in breath?
Pray'rs are the alms of churchmen to the poor:
They send to heaven's, but drive us from their
          door.   390

ALMAH. Cease, cease a suit
So vain to you, and troublesome to me,
If you will have me think that I am free.
If I am yet a slave, my bonds I'll bear;
But what I cannot grant, I will not hear.   395

ALMANZ. You wonnot hear! You must both hear
          and grant;
For, madam, there's an impudence in want.

ALMAH. Your way is somewhat strange to ask
          relief;
You ask with threat'ning, like a begging thief.
Once more, Almanzor, tell me, am I free?   400

ALMANZ. Madam, you are, from all the world —
          but me!
But as a pirate, when he frees the prize ⎫
He took from friends, sees the rich merchandise, ⎬
And, after he has freed it, justly buys; ⎭
So, when I have restored your liberty —   405
But then, alas, I am too poor to buy!

ALMAH. Nay, now you use me just as pirates do:
You free me; but expect a ransom too.

ALMANZ. You've all the freedom that a prince can
          have;
But greatness cannot be without a slave.   410
A monarch never can in private move,
But still is haunted with officious love.
So small an inconvenience you may bear;
'Tis all the fine Fate sets upon the fair.

ALMAH. Yet princes may retire whene'er they
          please,   415
And breathe free air from out ¹ their palaces:

¹ From outside.

They go sometimes unknown, to shun their state;
And then 'tis manners not to know or wait.

ALMANZ. If not a subject, then a ghost I'll be;
And from a ghost, you know, no place is free.   420
Asleep, awake, I'll haunt you everywhere;
From my white shroud groan love into your ear:
When in your lover's arms you sleep at night,
I'll glide in cold betwixt, and seize my right.
And is't not better, in your nuptial bed,   425
To have a living lover than a dead?

ALMAH. I can no longer bear to be accused,
As if, what I could grant you, I refused.
My father's choice I never will dispute;
And he has chosen ere you moved your suit.   430
You know my case; if equal ² you can be,
Plead for yourself, and answer it for me.

ALMANZ. Then, madam, in that hope you bid me
          live;
I ask no more than you may justly give:
But in strict justice there may favor be,   435
And may I hope that you have that for me?

ALMAH. Why do you thus my secret thoughts
          pursue,
Which, known, hurt me, and cannot profit you?
Your knowledge but new troubles does prepare,
Like theirs who curious in their fortunes are.   440
To say, I could with more content be yours,
Tempts you to hope; but not that hope assures.
For since the king has right,
And favored by my father in his suit,
It is a blossom which can bear no fruit.   445
Yet, if you dare attempt so hard a task,
May you succeed; you have my leave to ask.

ALMANZ. I can with courage now my hopes pursue,
Since I no longer have to combat you.
That did the greatest difficulty bring;   450
The rest are small, a father and a king!

ALMAH. Great souls discern not when the leap's
          too wide,
Because they only view the farther side.
Whatever you desire, you think is near;
But, with more reason, the event I fear.   455

ALMANZ. No; there is a necessity in fate,
Why still the brave bold man is fortunate:
He keeps his object ever full in sight,
And that assurance holds him firm and right.
True, 'tis a narrow path that leads to bliss, ⎫   460
But right before there is no precipice: ⎬
Fear makes men look aside, and then their ⎪
          footing miss. ⎭

ALMAH. I do your merit all the right I can;
Admiring virtue in a private man:
I only wish the king may grateful be,   465
And that my father with my eyes may see.

² Impartial.

455] Q1Q4Q5F *event*; Q2Q3 *success* (Q2 indicates a definite change which Q3 follows and Q4 ignores, as usual).

Might I not make it as my last request,
(Since humble carriage suits a suppliant best)
That you would somewhat of your fierceness hide —
That inborn fire — I do not call it pride? 　　470

ALMANZ. Born, as I am, still to command, not sue,
Yet you shall see that I can beg for you;
And if your father will require a crown,
Let him but name the kingdom, 'tis his own.
I am, but while I please, a private man; 　　475
I have that soul which empires first began.
From the dull crowd, which every king does lead,
I will pick out whom I will choose to head:
The best and bravest souls I can select,
And on their conquered necks my throne erect. 480
　　　　　　　　　　　　　　　　　　Exeunt.

ACT V

[SCENE I]

ABDALLA *alone, under the walls of the Albayzin.*

ABDAL. While she is mine, I have not yet lost all,
But in her arms shall have a gentle fall:
Blest in my love, although in war o'ercome,
I fly, like Antony from Actium,
To meet a better Cleopatra here. — 　　5
You of the watch! you of the watch! appear.

SOLDIER (*above*). Who calls below? What's your
　　demand?

ABDAL. 　　　'Tis I:
Open the gate with speed; the foe is nigh.

SOLDIER. What orders for admittance do you bring?

ABDAL. Slave, my own orders; look, and know
　　the king. 　　10

SOLDIER. I know you; but my charge is so severe
That none, without exception, enter here.

ABDAL. Traitor, and rebel! thou shalt shortly see
Thy orders are not to extend to me.

LYNDAR. (*above*). What saucy slave so rudely
　　does exclaim, 　　15
And brands my subject with a rebel's name?

ABDAL. Dear Lyndaraxa, haste; the foes pursue.

LYNDAR. My lord, the Prince Abdalla, is it you?
I scarcely can believe the words I hear;
Could you so coarsely treat my officer? 　　20

ABDAL. He forced me; but the danger nearer
　　draws:
When I am entered, you shall know the cause.

LYNDAR. Entered! Why, have you any business
　　here?

ABDAL. I am pursued, the enemy is near.

LYNDAR. Are you pursued, and do you thus de-
　　lay 　　25
To save yourself? Make haste, my lord, away.

ABDAL. Give me not cause to think you mock my
　　grief:

What place have I, but this, for my relief?

LYNDAR. This favor does your handmaid much
　　oblige,
But we are not provided for a siege: 　　30
My subjects few, and their provision thin;
The foe is strong without, we weak within.
This to my noble lord may seem unkind,
But he will weigh it in his princely mind;
And pardon her, who does assurance want 　　35
So much, she blushes when she cannot grant.

ABDAL. Yes, you may blush; and you have cause
　　to weep.
Is this the faith you promised me to keep?
Ah yet, if to a lover you will bring
No succor, give your succor to a king. 　　40

LYNDAR. A king is he, whom nothing can with-
　　stand;
Who men and money can with ease command:
A king is he, whom fortune still does bless:
He is a king, who does a crown possess.
If you would have me think that you are he, 　　45
Produce to view your marks of sovereignty;
But if yourself alone for proof you bring,
You're but a single person, not a king.

ABDAL. Ingrateful maid, did I for this rebel?
I say no more; but I have loved too well. 　　50

LYNDAR. Who but yourself did that rebellion
　　move?
Did I e'er promise to receive your love?
Is it my fault you are not fortunate?
I love a king, but a poor rebel hate.

ABDAL. Who follow fortune, still are in the
　　right. — 　　&
But let me be protected here this night.

LYNDAR. The place tomorrow will be circled round;
And then no way will for your flight be found.

ABDAL. I hear my enemies just coming on;
　　　　　　　　　　　　(*Trampling within.*)
Protect me but one hour, till they are gone. 　　60

LYNDAR. They'll know you have been here; it
　　cannot be;
That very hour you stay, will ruin me:
For if the foe behold our interview,
I shall be thought a rebel too, like you
Haste hence; and that your flight may prosperous
　　prove, 　　65
I'll recommend you to the pow'rs above.
　　　　　　　　　　　Exit LYNDARAXA *from above.*

ABDAL. She's gone! Ah, faithless and ingrateful
　　maid!
I hear some tread; and fear I am betrayed.
I'll to the Spanish king; and try if he,
To count'nance his own right, will succor me. 　　70
There is more faith in Christian dogs, than
　　thee.
　　　　　　　　　　　　　　　　　　　Exit.

68] Q3F *I hear*; Q1Q2Q4Q5 *I fear* (a misprint discussed in Textual Notes, p. 921).

[SCENE II]

OZMYN, BENZAYDA, ABENAMAR.

BENZ. I wish
(To merit all these thanks) I could have said ⎫
My pity only did his virtue aid: ⎬
'Twas pity, but 'twas of a love-sick maid.   ⎭
His manly suffering my esteem did move;   5
That bred compassion, and compassion love.
  OZM. O blessing sold me at too cheap a rate!
My danger was the benefit of fate. — (*To his father.*)
But that you may my fair deliverer know,
She was not only born our house's foe,   10
But to my death by pow'rful reasons led;
At least, in justice, she might wish me dead.
  ABEN. But why thus long do you her name
        conceal?
  OZM. To gain belief for what I now reveal:
Ev'n thus prepared, you scarce can think it ⎫
        true,   ⎬ 15
The saver of my life from Selin drew   ⎪
Her birth; and was his sister whom I slew.   ⎭
  ABEN. No more; it cannot, was not, must not be:
Upon my blessing, say not it was she.
The daughter of the only man I hate!   20
Two contradictions twisted in a fate!
  OZM. The mutual hate, which you and Selin bore,
Does but exalt her generous pity more.
Could she a brother's death forgive to me,
And cannot you forget her family?   25
Can you so ill requite the life I owe,
To reckon her, who gave it, still your foe?
It lends too great a lustre to her line,
To let her virtue ours so much outshine.
  ABEN. Thou giv'st her line th' advantage which
        they have,   30
By meanly taking of the life they gave.
Grant that it did in her a pity show;
But would my son be pitied by a foe?
She has the glory of thy act defaced:
Thou kill'dst her brother; but she triumphs last: 35
Poorly for us our enmity would cease;
When we are beaten, we receive a peace.
  BENZ. If that be all in which you disagree,
I must confess 'twas Ozmyn conquered me.
Had I beheld him basely beg his life,   40
I should not now submit to be his wife.
But when I saw his courage death control.
I paid a secret homage to his soul;
And thought my cruel father much to blame,
Since Ozmyn's virtue his revenge did shame.   45
  ABEN. What constancy canst thou e'er hope to
        find

In that unstable, and soon conquered mind?
What piety canst thou expect from her,
Who could forgive a brother's murderer?
Or, what obedience hop'st thou to be paid,   50
From one who first her father disobeyed?
  OZM. Nature, that bids us parents to obey,
Bids parents their commands by reason weigh.
And you her virtue by your praise did own,
Before you knew by whom the act was done.   55
  ABEN. Your reasons speak too much of insolence;
Her birth's a crime past pardon or defence.
Know, that as Selin was not won by thee,
Neither will I by Selin's daughter be.
Leave her, or cease henceforth to be my son: 60
This is my will: and this I will have done.
                              Exit ABENAMAR.
  OZM. It is a murd'ring will,
That whirls along with an impetuous sway,
And, like chain-shot, sweeps all things in its way.
He does my honor want of duty call;   65
To that, and love, he has no right at all.
  BENZ. No, Ozmyn, no; it is [a] much less ill
To leave me, than dispute a father's will:
If I had any title to your love,
Your father's greater right does mine remove: 70
Your vows and faith I give you back again,
Since neither can be kept without a sin.
  OZM. Nothing but death my vows can give me
        back:
They are not yours to give, nor mine to take.
  BENZ. Nay, think not, though I could your vows
        resign,   75
My love or virtue could dispense with mine.
I would extinguish your unlucky fire,
To make you happy in some new desire:
I can preserve enough for me and you,
And love, and be unfortunate, for two.   80
  OZM. In all that's good and great
You vanquish me so fast, that in the end
I shall have nothing left me to defend.
From every post you force me to remove;
But let me keep my last retrenchment,[1] love.   85
  BENZ. Love then, my Ozmyn; I will be content
                              (*giving her hand*)
To make you wretched by your own consent:
Live poor, despised, and banished for my sake,
And all the burden of my sorrows take.
For, as for me, in whatsoe'er estate,   90
While I have you, I must be fortunate.
  OZM. Thus then, secured of what we hold most
        dear,
(Each other's love) we'll go — I know not where.

  [1] Inner line of defense (military).

SCENE II] QQF give scene-divisions in Act IV, but not in Act V.   The present divisions follow N.
  30] Q1Q2Q3 *giv'st*; Q4Q5 *gavest* (Q5 depends solely on Q4).   35] Q5F *kill'st* (F depends solely on Q5).
  67] FC supply *a*, omitted in Q1Q4Q5.   Q2Q3 significantly alter the couplet (see Textual Notes, pp. 920–921).
  70] Q1Q4Q5F *Your father's*; Q2Q3 *A parent's*.   93] Q4Q5F *Earth* for *Each* (a persistent misprint).

For where, alas, should we our flight begin?
The foe's without; our parents are within.   95
   BENZ. I'll fly to you, and you shall fly to me:
Our flight but to each other's arms shall be.
To providence and chance permit the rest;
Let us but love enough, and we are blest.   *Exeunt.*

[SCENE III]

Enter BOABDELIN, ABENAMAR, ABDELMELECH,
   Guard; ZULEMA *and* HAMET, *prisoners.*

   ABDELM. They're Lyndaraxa's brothers; for her
    sake,
Their lives and pardon my request I make.
   BOAB. Then, Zulema and Hamet, live; but know,
Your lives to Abdelmelech's suit you owe.
   ZUL. The grace received so much my hope ex-
    ceeds   5
That words come weak and short to answer deeds.
You've made a venture, sir, and time must show
If this great mercy you did well bestow.
   BOAB. You, Abdelmelech, haste before 'tis night,
And close pursue my brother in his flight.   10
    Exeunt ABDELMELECH, ZULEMA, HAMET.

Enter ALMANZOR, ALMAHIDE, *and* ESPERANZA.

But see, with Almahide
The brave Almanzor comes, whose conquering
   sword
That crown, it once took from me, has restored.
How can I recompence so great desert!
   ALMANZ. I bring you, sir, performed in every
    part,   15
My promise made; your foes are fled or slain;
Without a rival, absolute you reign.
Yet though, in justice, this enough may be,
It is too little to be done by me:
I beg to go   20
Where my own courage and your fortune calls,
To chase these misbelievers from our walls.
I cannot breathe within this narrow space;
My heart's too big, and swells beyond the place.
   BOAB. You can perform, brave warrior, what you
    please;   25
Fate listens to your voice, and then decrees.
Now I no longer fear the Spanish pow'rs;
Already we are free, and conquerors.
   ALMANZ. Accept, great king, tomorrow, from my
    hand,
The captive head of conquered Ferdinand.   30
You shall not only what you lost regain,
But o'er the Biscayn mountains to the main,
Extend your sway, where never Moor did reign.
   ABEN. What, in another, vanity would seem,
Appears but noble confidence in him;   35

No haughty boasting, but a manly pride;
A soul too fiery, and too great a guide:
He moves eccentric, like a wand'ring star,
Whose motion's just, though 'tis not regular.
   BOAB. It is for you, brave man, and only you,   40
Greatly to speak, and yet more greatly do.
But, if your benefits too far extend,
I must be left ungrateful in the end:
Yet somewhat I would pay,
Before my debts above all reck'ning grow,   45
To keep me from the shame of what I owe.
But you —
Are conscious to yourself of such desert,
That of your gift I fear to offer part.
   ALMANZ. When I shall have declared my high
    request,   50
So much presumption there will be confessed,
That you will find your gifts I do not shun,
But rather much o'er-rate the service done.
   BOAB. Give wing to your desires, and let 'em fly,
Secure they cannot mount a pitch too high.   55
So bless me Allah both in peace and war,
As I accord whate'er your wishes are.
   ALMANZ. (*putting one knee on the ground*).   Em-
    boldened by the promise of a prince,
I ask this lady now with confidence.
   BOAB. You ask the only thing I cannot grant.   60
    (*The* KING *and* ABENAMAR *look amazedly on
    each other.*)
But, as a stranger, you are ignorant
Of what by public fame my subjects know;
She is my mistress.
   ABEN.   — And my daughter too.
   ALMANZ. Believe, old man, that I her father knew:
What else should make Almanzor kneel to you?   65
Nor doubt, sir, but your right to her was known: ⎫
For had you had no claim but love alone,   ⎬
I could produce a better of my own.   ⎭
   ALMAH. (*softly to him*). Almanzor, you forget my
    last request:
Your words have too much haughtiness ex-
    pressed.   70
Is this the humble way you were to move?
   ALMANZ. (*to her*). I was too far transported by my
    love.
Forgive me; for I had not learned to sue
To anything before, but heav'n and you.
Sir, at your feet, I make it my request —   75
    (*To the* KING. *First line kneeling: second,
    rising, and boldly.*)
Though, without boasting, I deserve her best;
For you her love with gaudy titles sought,
But I her heart with blood and dangers bought.
   BOAB. The blood which you have shed in her
    defence

Shall have in time a fitting recompence: 80
Or, if you think your services delayed,
Name but your price, and you shall soon be paid.

ALMANZ. My price! Why, king, you do not think
    you deal
With one who sets his services to sale?
Reserve your gifts for those who gifts regard;   85
And know, I think myself above reward.

BOAB. Then sure you are some godhead; and our
    care
Must be to come with incense and with pray'r.

ALMANZ. As little as you think yourself obliged,
You would be glad to do't, when next besieged.   90
But I am pleased there should be nothing due;
For what I did was for myself, not you.

BOAB. You with contempt on meaner gifts look
    down;
And, aiming at my queen, disdain my crown.
That crown, restored, deserves no recompence,   95
Since you would rob the fairest jewel thence.
Dare not henceforth ungrateful me to call;
Whate'er I owed you, this has cancelled all.

ALMANZ. I'll call thee thankless, king, and per-
    jured both:
Thou swor'st by Allah, and hast broke thy
    oath.   100
But thou dost well: thou tak'st the cheapest way;
Not to own services thou canst not pay.

BOAB. My patience more than pays thy service
    past;
But know this insolence shall be thy last.
Hence from my sight! and take it as a grace,   105
Thou liv'st, and art but banished from the place.

ALMANZ. Where'er I go, there can no exile be;
But from Almanzor's sight I banish thee:
I will not now, if thou wouldst beg me, stay;
But I will take my Almahide away.   110
Stay thou with all thy subjects here; but know,
We leave thy city empty when we go.

               (*Takes* ALMAHIDE'S *hand.*)

BOAB. Fall on; take; kill the traitor.

    (*The Guards fall on him; he makes at the*
    KING *through the midst of them, and falls*
    upon him; they disarm him, and rescue the
    KING.)

ALMANZ.   — Base and poor,
Blush that thou art Almanzor's conqueror.

    (ALMAHIDE *wrings her hands, then turns and*
    veils her face.)

Farewell, my Almahide!   115
Life of itself will go, now thou art gone,
Like flies in winter, when they lose the sun.

    (ABENAMAR *whispers the* KING *a little, then*
    speaks aloud.)

ABEN. Revenge, and taken so secure a way,
Are blessings which heav'n sends not every day.

BOAB. I will at leisure now revenge my
    wrong;   120
And, traitor, thou shalt feel my vengeance long:
Thou shalt not die just at thy own desire,
But see my nuptials, and with rage expire.

ALMANZ. Thou dar'st not marry her while I'm in
    sight:
With a bent brow thy priest and thee I'll fright,   125
And in that scene
Which all thy hopes and wishes should content,
The thought of me shall make thee impotent.

             He is led off by Guards.

BOAB. (*to* ALMAHIDE). As some fair tulip, by
    a storm oppressed,
Shrinks up, and folds its silken arms to rest;   130
And, bending to the blast, all pale and dead,
Hears from within the wind sing round its head;
So, shrouded up, your beauty disappears:
Unveil, my love, and lay aside your fears.
The storm that caused your fright is passed and
    done.   135

    (ALMAHIDE *unveiling, and looking round for*
    ALMANZOR.)

ALMAH. So flow'rs peep out too soon, and miss
    the sun.   (*Turning from him.*)

BOAB. What myst'ry in this strange behavior
    lies?

ALMAH. Let me for ever hide these guilty eyes
Which lighted my Almanzor to his tomb;
Or, let 'em blaze, to show me there a room.   140

BOAB. Heav'n lent their lustre for a nobler end:
A thousand torches must their light attend,
To lead you to a temple and a crown. —
Why does my fairest Almahida frown?
Am I less pleasing than I was before,   145
Or is the insolent Almanzor more?

ALMAH. I justly own that I some pity have,
Not for the insolent, but for the brave.

ABEN. Though to your king your duty you
    neglect,
Know, Almahide, I look for more respect: 150
And, if a parent's charge your mind can move,
Receive the blessing of a monarch's love.

ALMAH. Did he my freedom to his life prefer,
And shall I wed Almanzor's murderer?
No, sir; I cannot to your will submit: 155
Your way's too rugged for my tender feet.

ABEN. You must be driv'n where you refuse to go;

104] Q1–Q4 *know*; Q5F *now.* (F follows Q5's misprint.)   120] Q1Q4Q5F *leisure*; Q2Q3 *pleasure.*
131, 132] Q2, followed only by Q3, significantly revises the entire couplet:

    Bends to the blast, all pale, and almost dead,
    While the loud wind sings round its drooping head.

(See discussion of 'author's changes,' Textual Notes, p. 921.)

And taught, by force, your happiness to know.
   ALMAH. (*smiling scornfully*). To force me, sir, is
    much unworthy you,
And, when you would, impossible to do.   160
If force could bend me, you might think, with
    shame,
That I debased the blood from whence I came.
My soul is soft, which you may gently lay ⎤
In your loose palm; but, when 'tis pressed   ⎟
    to stay,   ⎬
Like water, it deludes your grasp and slips ⎟
    away.   165 ⎦
   BOAB. I find I must revoke what I decreed:
Almanzor's death my nuptials must precede.
Love is a magic which the lover ties;
But charms still ¹ end when the magician dies.
(*To his Guards.*) Go; let me hear my hated rival's
    dead;   170
And, to convince my eyes, bring back his head.
   ALMAH. Go on: I wish no other way to prove
That I am worthy of Almanzor's love.
We will in death, at least, united be:
I'll show you I can die as well as he.   175
   BOAB. What should I do! when equally I dread
Almanzor living and Almanzor dead! —
Yet, by your promise, you are mine alone.
   ALMAH. How dare you claim my faith, and break
    your own?
   ABEN. This for your virtue is a weak defence: 180
No second vows can with your first dispense.
Yet, since the king did to Almanzor swear,
And in his death ingrateful may appear,
He ought, in justice, first to spare his life,
And then to claim your promise as his wife.   185
   ALMAH. Whate'er my secret inclinations be,
To this, since honor ties me, I agree:
Yet I declare, and to the world will own,
That, far from seeking, I would shun the throne,
And with Almanzor lead an humble life: 190
There is a private greatness in his wife.
   BOAB. That little love I have, I hardly ² buy;
You give my rival all, while you deny.
Yet, Almahide, to let you see your pow'r,
Your loved Almanzor shall be free this hour.   195
You are obeyed; but 'tis so great a grace,
That I could wish me in my rival's place.
               Exeunt KING *and* ABENAMAR.
   ALMAH. How blest was I before this fatal day,
When all I knew of love, was to obey!
'Twas life becalmed, without a gentle breath;   200
Though not so cold, yet motionless as death.
A heavy, quiet state; but love, all strife,
All rapid, is the hurricane of life.
Had love not shown me, I had never seen

An excellence beyond Boabdelin.   205
I had not, aiming higher, lost my rest;
But with a vulgar good been dully blest:
But, in Almanzor, having seen what's rare,
Now I have learnt too sharply to compare;
And, like a fav'rite quickly in disgrace,   210
Just know the value ere I lose the place.

       To her ALMANZOR, *bound and guarded.*

   ALMANZ. I see the end for which I'm hither
    sent,   (*looking down*)
To double, by your sight,³ my punishment.
There is a shame in bonds I cannot bear;
Far more than death, to meet your eyes I fear.   215
   ALMAH. (*unbinding him*). That shame of long
    continuance shall not be:
The king, at my entreaty, sets you free.
   ALMANZ. The king! my wonder's greater than
    before;
How did he dare my freedom to restore?
He like some captive lion uses me;   220
He runs away before he sets me free,
And takes a sanctuary in his court:
I'll rather lose my life than thank him for 't.
   ALMAH. If any subject for your thanks there be,
The king expects 'em not; you owe 'em me   225
Our freedoms through each other's hands have
    passed;
You give me my revenge in winning last.
   ALMANZ. Then fate commodiously for me has
    done;
To lose mine there where I would have it won.
   ALMAH. Almanzor, you too soon will under-
    stand,   230
That what I win is on another's hand.⁴
The king (who doomed you to a cruel fate)
Gave to my pray'rs both his revenge and hate;
But at no other price would rate your life,
Than my consent and oath to be his wife.   235
   ALMANZ. Would you, to save my life, my love ⎤
    betray?   ⎬
Here; take me; bind me; carry me away;   ⎟
Kill me! I'll kill you if you disobey.   ⎦
                     (*To the Guards.*)
   ALMAH. That absolute command your love does
    give,
I take; and charge you, by that pow'r, to live.   240
   ALMANZ. When death, the last of comforts, you
    refuse,
Your pow'r, like heav'n upon the damned, you use;
You force me in my being to remain,
To make me last, and keep me fresh for pain.
When all my joys are gone,   245
What cause can I for living longer give,

---

¹ Always.   ² On hard terms.   ³ By seeing you.   ⁴ To another's profit.

But a dull, lazy habitude to live?

ALMAH. Rash men, like you, and impotent of will,
Give Chance no time to turn, but urge her still; [1]
She would repent; you push the quarrel on,   250
And once because she went, she must be gone.

ALMANZ. She shall not turn: what is it she can do,
To recompence me for the loss of you?

ALMAH. Heav'n will reward your worth some
        better way;
At least, for me, you have but lost one day.   255
Nor is't a real loss which you deplore;
You sought a heart that was engaged before.
'Twas a swift love which took you in his way;
Flew only through your heart, but made no stay.
'Twas but a dream, where truth had not a
        place;   260
A scene of fancy, moved so swift a pace,
And shifted, that you can but think it was;
Let, then, the short vexatious vision pass.

ALMANZ. My joys, indeed, are dreams; but not
        my pain:
'Twas a swift ruin, but the marks remain.   265
When some fierce fire lays goodly buildings waste,
Would you conclude
There had been none, because the burning's past?

ALMAH. It was your fault that fire seized all your
        breast;
You should have blown up some to save the
        rest: 270
But 'tis, at worst, but so consumed by fire,
As cities are, that by their falls rise high'r.
Build love a nobler temple in my place;
You'll find the fire has but enlarged your space.

ALMANZ. Love has undone me; I am grown ⎤
        so poor,   } 275
I sadly view the ground I had before,   ⎟
But want a stock, and ne'er can build it more. ⎦

AMAH. Then say what charity I can allow;
I would contribute, if I knew but how.
Take friendship; or, if that too small appear,   280
Take love which sisters may to brothers bear.

ALMANZ. A sister's love! that is so palled a thing,
What pleasure can it to a lover bring?
'Tis like thin food to men in fevers spent;
Just keeps alive, but gives no nourishment.   285
What hopes, what fears, what transports can it
        move?
'Tis but the ghost of a departed love.

ALMAH. You, like some greedy cormorant, devour
All my whole life can give you, in an hour.
What more I can do for you is to die,   290
And that must follow, if you this deny.
Since I gave up my love, that you might live,
You, in refusing life, my sentence give.

[1] Incessantly.

ALMANZ. Far from my breast be such an impious
        thought!
Your death would lose the quiet mine had
        sought.   295
I'll live for you, in spite of misery:
But you shall grant that I had rather die.
I'll be so wretched, filled with such despair,
That you shall see to live was more to dare.

ALMAH. Adieu, then, O my soul's far better'
        part!   300
Your image sticks so close,
That the blood follows from my rending heart.
A last farewell!
For, since a last must come, the rest are vain,
Like gasps in death, which but prolong our pain. 305
But, since the king is now a part of me,
Cease from henceforth to be his enemy.
Go now, for pity go! for, if you stay,
I fear I shall have something still to say.
Thus — I for ever shut you from my sight.   310
                        (Veils.)

ALMANZ. Like one thrust out in a cold winter's
        night,
Yet shivering underneath your gate I stay;
One look — I cannot go before 'tis day. —
                (She beckons him to be gone.)
Not one — Farewell: whate'er my sufferings ⎤
        be   ⎟
Within, I'll speak farewell as loud as she: } 315
I will not be outdone in constancy. —   ⎦
                (She turns her back.)
Then like a dying conqueror I go;
At least I have looked last upon my foe.
I go — but if too heavily I move,
I walk encumb'red with a weight of love.   320
Fain I would leave the thought of you behind,
But still, the more I cast you from my mind,
You dash, like water, back, when thrown against
        the wind.   Exit.
(As he goes off, the KING meets him with
ABENAMAR; they stare at each other without
saluting.)

BOAB. With him go all my fears.   A guard there
        wait,
And see him safe without the city gate.   325

                To them ABDELMELECH.

Now, Abdelmelech, is my brother dead?

ABDELM. Th' usurper to the Christian camp is
        fled;
Whom as Granada's lawful king they own,
And vow, by force, to seat him on the throne.
Meantime the rebels in th' Albayzin rest;   330
Which is in Lyndaraxa's name possessed.

BOAB. Haste, and reduce it instantly by force.

ABDELM. First give me leave to prove a milder
    course.
She will, perhaps, on summons yield the place.
  BOAB. We cannot to[1] your suit refuse her
    grace.   335

One enters hastily, and whispers ABENAMAR.

  ABEN. How fortune persecutes this hoary head!
My Ozmyn is with Selin's daughter fled,
But he's no more my son:
My hate shall like a Zegry him pursue,
Till I take back what blood from me he drew.   340
 [1] At.

  BOAB. Let war and vengeance be tomorrow's
    care;
But let us to the temple now repair.
A thousand torches make the mosque more bright:
This must be mine and Almahida's night.
Hence, ye importunate affairs of state;   345
You should not tyrannize on love, but wait.
Had life no love, none would for business live;
Yet still from love the largest part we give;
And must be forced, in empire's weary toil,
To live long wretched, to be pleased a while.   350
                          Exeunt.

EPILOGUE

Success, which can no more than beauty last,
Makes our sad poet mourn your favors past:
For, since without desert he got a name,
He fears to lose it now with greater shame.
Fame, like a little mistress of the town,　　　　　　5
Is gained with ease; but then she's lost as soon,
For, as those tawdry misses, soon or late,
Jilt such as keep 'em at the highest rate —
(And oft the lacquey, or the brawny clown,
Gets what is hid in the loose-bodied gown) —　　　10
So, Fame is false to all that keep her long;
And turns up to the fop that's brisk and young.
Some wiser poet now would leave Fame first:
But elder wits are, like old lovers, curst:
Who, when the vigor of their youth is spent,　　　15
Still grow more fond, as they grow impotent.
This, some years hence, our poet's case may prove;
But yet, he hopes, he's young enough to love.
When forty comes,[1] if e'er he live to see
That wretched, fumbling age of poetry,　　　　　　20
'Twill be high time to bid his Muse adieu:
Well he may please himself, but never you.
Till then, he'll do as well as he began,
And hopes you will not find him less a man.
Think him not duller for this year's delay;[2]　　25
He was prepared, the women were away;
And men, without their parts, can hardly play.
If they, through sickness, seldom did appear,
Pity the virgins of each theatre!
For, at both houses, 'twas a sickly year!　　　　　30
And pity us, your servants, to whose cost,
In one such sickness, nine whole months are lost.[3]
Their stay, he fears, has ruined what he writ:
Long waiting both disables love and wit.
They thought they gave him leisure to do well;　35
But, when they forced him to attend, he fell!
Yet, though he much has failed, he begs, today,
You will excuse his unperforming[4] play:
Weakness sometimes great passion does express;
He had pleased better, had he loved you less.　　40

[1] Next year, for Dryden was born in 1631.
[2] The interval since the production of Dryden's *Tyrannic Love*.
[3] Referring to Nell Gwyn's previous absence from the Drury Lane stage owing to the birth, on May 8, 1670, of Charles Beauclerk, her son by Charles II.
[4] Ineffective.

22] Q1Q4Q5F *Well he may*; Q2Q3 *Well, he may.*

The Rehearsal

BY GEORGE VILLIERS, DUKE OF BUCKINGHAM
AND OTHERS

THE
REHEARSAL,

As it is now Acted at the

Theatre-Royal.

The third Edition with Amendments and large Additions by the Author.

LONDON,

Printed for *Thomas Dring*, at the *Harrow* at the Corner of *Chancery-lane* in *Fleet-street*. 1 6 7 5.

PROLOGUE

We might well call this short mock-play of ours
A posy made of weeds instead of flowers;
Yet such have been presented to your noses,
And there are such, I fear, who thought 'em roses.
Would some of 'em were here, to see, this night,   5
What stuff it is in which they took delight.
Here, brisk, insipid rogues, for wit, let fall
Sometimes dull sense; but oft'ner, none at all:
There, strutting heroes, with a grim-faced train,
Shall brave the gods, in King Cambyses' vein.[1]   10
For (changing rules, of late, as if men writ
In spite of reason, nature, art, and wit)
Our poets make us laugh at tragedy,
And with their comedies they make us cry.
Now, critics, do your worst, that here are met;   15
For, like a rook, I have hedged in my bet.[2]
If you approve, I shall assume the state
Of those high-flyers whom I imitate:
And justly too, for I will show you more
Than ever they would let you know before: 20
I will not only show the feats they do,
But give you all their reasons for 'em too.
Some honor may to me from hence arise: ⎫
But if, by my endeavors, you grow wise,   ⎬
And what you once so praised shall now despise, ⎭   25
Then I'll cry out, swelled with poetic rage,
'Tis I, John Lacy,[3] have reformed your stage.

---

[1] Ranting tragedy fashion (an echo of Falstaff's phrase, *1 Henry IV*, II. iv.).   Successive editions of Elkanah Settle's popular heroic drama, *Cambyses, King of Persia* (acted in 1667), had appeared in 1671 and in 1672, and it was again reprinted in 1675.

[2] 'Like a sharper, I have played safe by wagering both ways' (i.e., he stands to win either way, whether the critics take his imitation of high-flown heroic drama seriously or not).

[3] Lacy created the part of Bayes.

7] Q1 *blades* for *rogues.*   21] Q1 *I will both represent the feats they do.*   23] Q1 *Some honor to me will from this arise.*

THE ACTORS' NAMES

[MEN]

BAYES	General	Players
JOHNSON	Lieutenant-General	Soldiers
SMITH	CORDELIO	[Stage-keeper]
Two Kings of Brentford	TOM THIMBLE	Two Heralds
PRINCE PRETTY-MAN	Fisherman	Four Cardinals
PRINCE VOLSCIUS	Sun [SOL]	Mayor
Gentleman-Usher	Thunder	Judges
Physician	[HARRY]	Sergeants at Arms
DRAWCANSIR	[SHIRLEY]	[Three Fiddlers]

} *Mutes*

WOMEN

AMARYLLIS	PALLAS	Moon [LUNA]
CLORIS	Lightning	Earth [ORBIS]
PARTHENOPE		

Attendants of Men and Women

SCENE — BRENTFORD

THE ACTORS' NAMES] Despite the heading, the list is of *Dramatis Personæ*, without the acting cast.

THE REHEARSAL

By GEORGE VILLIERS, DUKE OF BUCKINGHAM, AND OTHERS

ACT I

SCENE I

JOHNSON and SMITH.

JOHNSON. Honest Frank! I'm glad to see thee with all my heart: how long hast thou been in town?

SMITH. Faith, not above an hour: and, if I had not met you here, I had gone to look you out; for I long to talk with you freely, of all the strange 5 new things we have heard in the country.

JOHNSON. And, by my troth, I have longed as much to laugh with you, at all the impertinent, dull, fantastical things we are tired out with here.

SMITH. Dull and fantastical! that's an excel- 10 lent composition. Pray, what are our men of business doing?

JOHNSON. I ne'er enquire after 'em. Thou knowest my humor lies another way. I love to please myself as much, and to trouble others as little 15 as I can: and therefore do naturally avoid the company of those solemn fops who, being incapable of reason, and insensible of wit and pleasure, are always looking grave, and troubling one another, in hopes to be thought men of business. 20

SMITH. Indeed, I have ever observed that your grave lookers are the dullest of men.

JOHNSON. Aye, and of birds, and beasts too: your gravest bird is an owl, and your gravest beast is an ass. 25

SMITH. Well; but how dost thou pass thy time?

JOHNSON. Why, as I use to do — eat and drink as well as I can, have a she-friend to be private with in the afternoon, and sometimes see a play; where there are such things, Frank, — such hideous, 30 monstrous things, — that it has almost made me forswear the stage and resolve to apply myself to the solid nonsense of your men of business, as the more ingenious pastime.

SMITH. I have heard, indeed, you have had 35 lately many new plays; and our country wits commend 'em.

JOHNSON. Aye, so do some of our city wits, too; but they are of the new kind of wits.

SMITH. New kind! what kind is that? 40

JOHNSON. Why, your virtuosi, your civil persons, your drolls — fellows that scorn to imitate nature, but are given altogether to elevate and surprise.

SMITH. Elevate and surprise? Prithee, make me understand the meaning of that. 45

JOHNSON. Nay, by my troth, that's a hard matter: I don't understand that myself. 'Tis a phrase they have got among them, to express their no-meaning by. I'll tell you, as near as I can, what it is. Let me see; 'tis fighting, loving, sleeping, rhyming, 50 dying, dancing, singing, crying; and everything but thinking and sense.

Mr. BAYES[1] passes o'er the stage.

BAYES. Your most obsequious, and most observant, very servant, sir.

JOHNSON. Godso, this is an author! I'll fetch 55 him to you.

SMITH. No, prithee, let him alone.

JOHNSON. Nay, by the Lord, I'll have him. (*Goes after him.*) Here he is. I have caught him. — Pray, sir, now for my sake, will you do a favor 60 to this friend of mine?

BAYES. Sir, it is not within my small capacity to do favors, but receive 'em, especially from a person that does wear the honorable title you are pleased to impose, sir, upon this. — Sweet sir, your 65 servant.

SMITH. Your humble servant, sir.

JOHNSON. But wilt thou do me a favor, now?

BAYES. Aye, sir. What is't?

JOHNSON. Why, to tell him the meaning of 70 thy last play.[2]

BAYES. How, sir, the meaning? Do you mean the plot?

JOHNSON. Aye, aye — anything.

BAYES. Faith, sir, the intrigo's now quite 75 out of my head; but I have a new one in my pocket, that I may say is a virgin; 't has never yet been blown upon. I must tell you one thing, 'tis all new wit; and though I say it, a better than my last — and you know well enough how that took. In 80 fine, it shall read, and write, and act, and plot, and show — aye, and pit, box and gallery,[3] 'y gad, with any play in Europe. This morning is its last re-

---

[1] The name Bayes suits Dryden's appointment as Poet Laureate in August, 1670.

[2] Dryden's *Conquest of Granada.*

[3] A hit at the 'usual language' of Edward Howard 'at the rehearsal of his plays.' (Briscoe's *Key*, 1704.)

HEADING] QQ *Actus I. Scæna I.,* and so throughout the play.

41] QI *your blade, your frank persons.* 42] Q1Q2Q5 *scorn;* Q3Q4 *scorns* (Q4 follows misprint in Q3).

49] QI *well* for *near.* 57] QI *Nay* for *No.* 60] QI omits *now.* 82] QQ *I gad,* throughout.

33] QI *pretenders to business.*

hearsal, in their habits, and all that, as it is to be acted; and if you and your friend will do it but 85 the honor to see it in its virgin attire, though, perhaps, it may blush, I shall not be ashamed to discover its nakedness unto you. (*Puts his hand in his pocket.*) I think it is in this pocket.

JOHNSON. Sir, I confess I am not able to 90 answer you in this new way; but if you please to lead, I shall be glad to follow you; and I hope my friend will do so too.

SMITH. Sir, I have no business so considerable as should keep me from your company. 95

BAYES. Yes, here it is. — No, cry you mercy! this is my book of *Drama Commonplaces*, the mother of many other plays.

JOHNSON. *Drama Commonplaces!* pray, what's that? 100

BAYES. Why, sir, some certain helps that we men of art have found it convenient to make use of.

SMITH. How, sir, helps for wit?

BAYES. Aye, sir, that's my position. And I do here aver that no man yet the sun e'er shone 105 upon has parts sufficient to furnish out a stage, except it were by the help of these my rules.

JOHNSON. What are those rules, I pray?

BAYES. Why, sir, my first rule is the rule of transversion,[1] or *regula duplex* — changing verse 110 into prose, or prose into verse, *alternative* as you please.

SMITH. Well; but how is this done by a rule, sir?

BAYES. Why, thus, sir — nothing so easy when understood. I take a book in my hand, either 115 at home or elsewhere, for that's all one — if there be any wit in't, as there is no book but has some, I transverse it: that is, if it be prose, put it into verse (but that takes up some time), and if it be verse, put it into prose. 120

JOHNSON. Methinks, Mr. Bayes, that putting verse into prose should be called transprosing.

BAYES. By my troth, sir, 'tis a very good notion, and hereafter it shall be so.

SMITH. Well, sir, and what d'ye do with it 125 then?

BAYES. Make it my own. 'Tis so changed that no man can know it. My next rule is the rule of record, by way of table-book.[2] Pray, observe.

JOHNSON. We hear you, sir: go on. 130

BAYES. As thus. I come into a coffee-house, or some other place where witty men resort. I make as if I minded nothing (do you mark?), but as soon as any one speaks, pop! I slap it down, and make that, too, my own. 135

JOHNSON. But, Mr. Bayes, are you not sometimes in danger of their making you restore, by force, what you have gotten thus by art?

BAYES. No, sir; the world's unmindful; they never take notice of these things. 140

SMITH. But pray, Mr. Bayes, among all your other rules, have you no one rule for invention?

BAYES. Yes, sir, that's my third rule that I have here in my pocket.

SMITH. What rule can that be, I wonder. 145

BAYES. Why, sir, when I have anything to invent, I never trouble my head about it, as other men do; but presently turn over this book, and there I have, at one view, all that Perseus, Montaigne, Seneca's tragedies, Horace, Juvenal, Claudian, Pliny, 150 Plutarch's *Lives*, and the rest, have ever thought upon this subject; and so, in a trice, by leaving out a few words or putting in others of my own, the business is done.

JOHNSON. Indeed, Mr. Bayes, this is as sure 155 and compendious a way of wit as ever I heard of.

BAYES. Sirs, if you make the least scruple of the efficacy of these my rules, do but come to the playhouse and you shall judge of 'em by the effects.

SMITH. We'll follow you, sir. 160

Exeunt.

[SCENE II]

Enter three Players upon the stage.

1ST PLAYER. Have you your part perfect?

2D PLAYER. Yes, I have it without book; but I don't understand how it is to be spoken.

3D PLAYER. And mine is such a one as I can't guess for my life what humor I'm to be in — 5 whether angry, melancholy, merry, or in love. I don't know what to make on't.

1ST PLAYER. Phoo! the author will be here presently and he'll tell us all. You must know, this is the new way of writing; and these hard things 10 please forty times better than the old plain way. For, look you, sir, the grand design upon the stage is to keep the auditors in suspense; for to guess presently at the plot and the sense, tires 'em before the end of the first act. Now, here, every line 15 surprises you and brings in new matter. And, then, for scenes, clothes, and dances, we put 'em quite down, all that ever went before us; and those are the things, you know, that are essential to a play.

---

[1] Langbaine (1691) instanced Dryden's Prologue to *The Maiden Queen* as evidence of 'his making use of Bayes's art of transversing' in borrowing from an English translation of de Scudéry's prose romance *Ibrahim*.

[2] Pocket notebook.

89] Q1 *is o' this side.*   94] Q1 *I [Aye], sir.*   103] Q1 *help.*   107] Q1 *it be with.*
113] Q1 *Smi. How's that, sir, by a rule, I pray?*   114] Q1 *more for so.*   119] Q1 omits *and.*   123] Q1 omits *'tis.*
127] Q1 *altered* for *changed.*   130] Q1 *Well, we hear you: go on.*   136] Q1 *are not you.*   145] Q1 omits *I wonder.*
148] Q1 *o'er.*   157] Q1 *Aye, sirs, when you come to write yourselves, o' my word, you'll find it so. But, gentlemen, if,* etc.
SCENE II] QQ make no scene-division. N is here followed.   3] Q1 *do not.*   18] Q1 *these.*

2D PLAYER. Well, I am not of thy mind; but,   20
so it gets us money, 'tis no great matter.

Enter BAYES, JOHNSON, *and* SMITH.

BAYES. Come, come in, gentlemen. Y'are very
welcome, Mr.—a—. Ha' you your part ready?

1ST PLAYER. Yes, sir.

BAYES. But do you understand the true   25
humor of it?

1ST PLAYER. Aye, sir, pretty well.

BAYES. And Amaryllis, how does she do? Does
not her armor become her?

3D PLAYER. Oh, admirably!   30

BAYES. I'll tell you, now, a pretty conceit.
What do you think I'll make 'em call her anon, in
this play?

SMITH. What, I pray?

BAYES. Why, I'll make 'em call her Ar-   35
maryllis, because of her armor — ha, ha, ha!

JOHNSON. That will be very well, indeed.

BAYES. Aye, it's a pretty little rogue; I knew
her face would set off armor extremely, and, to tell
you true, I writ that part only for her. You   40
must know she is my mistress.[1]

*JOHNSON.[2] Then I know another thing, little
Bayes, that thou hast had her, 'y gad.

*BAYES. No, 'y gad, not yet; but I'm sure I shall,
for I have talked bawdy to her already.   45

*JOHNSON. Hast thou, faith? Prithee, how was
that?

*BAYES. Why, sir, there is, in the French tongue,
a certain criticism which, by the variation of the
masculine adjective instead of the feminine,   50
makes a quite different signification of the word:
as, for example, *Ma vie* is my life; but if before *vie*
you put *Mon* instead of *Ma*, you make it bawdy.[3]

*JOHNSON. Very true.

*BAYES. Now, sir, I, having observed this,   55
set a trap for her the other day in the tiring-room;[4]
for this said I: *Adieu, bel esperansa [5] de ma vie*
(which, 'y gad, is very pretty); to which she answered,
I vow, almost as prettily every jot. For, said she,
Songes à ma vie, Mounsieur; whereupon I pres-   60
ently snapped this upon her: *Non, non, Madam —*

---

[1] Mrs. Anne Reeve, who acted the part of Amaryllis, was
said to be Dryden's mistress (*Key*). Q3 significantly expands
the original allusions in Q1.

[2] Asterisks indicate speeches not included in the first edition
(Q1) but constituting the 'large additions' made in the amended
third edition (Q3) . See Textual Notes.

[3] Throughout the whole passage, Bayes takes gross liberties
with pure French.

[4] Dressing-room at theatre.

[5] Mrs. Reeve played the part of Esperanza in *The Conquest
of Granada.*

songes vous à mon, by gad, and named the thing
directly to her.

*SMITH. This is one of the richest stories, Mr.
Bayes, that ever I heard of.   65

*BAYES. Aye, let me alone, 'y gad, when I get to
'em; I'll nick 'em, I warrant you. But I'm a little
nice; [6] for you must know, at this time I am kept
by another woman in the city.

*SMITH. How kept? for what?   70

*BAYES. Why, for a *beau gerson.* I am, i'fackins.[7]

*SMITH. Nay, then, we shall never have done.

*BAYES. And the rogue is so fond of me, Mr.
Johnson, that I vow to gad, I know not what to do
with myself.   75

*JOHNSON. Do with thyself! No; I wonder how
thou canst make a shift to hold out at this rate.

*BAYES. O devil, I can toil like a horse; only some-
times it makes me melancholy; and then I vow to
gad, for a whole day together I am not able   80
to say you one good thing if it were to save my life.

*SMITH. That we do verily believe, Mr. Bayes.

*BAYES. And that's the only thing, 'y gad, which
mads me in my amours; for I'll tell you, as a friend,
Mr. Johnson, my acquaintants, I hear, begin   85
to give it out that I am dull. Now I am the far-
thest from it in the whole world, 'y gad; but only,
forsooth, they think I am so, because I can say
nothing.

*JOHNSON. Phoo! Pox! That's ill-naturedly   90
done of 'em.

BAYES. Aye, gad, there's no trusting o' these
rogues; but—a—Come, let's sit down. — Look you,
sirs, the chief hinge of this play, upon which the
whole plot moves and turns, and that causes   95
the variety of all the several accidents, which, you
know, are the things in nature that make up the
grand refinement of a play, is that I suppose two
kings to be of the same place — as, for example, at
Brentford,[8] for I love to write familiarly. Now   100
the people having the same relations to 'em both,
the same affections, the same duty, the same obedience, and all that, are divided among themselves in
point of *devoir* and interest, how to behave themselves equally between 'em: these kings differ-   105
ing sometimes in particular, though in the main
they agree. (I know not whether I make myself
well understood.)

JOHNSON. I did not observe you, sir; pray, say
that again.   110

---

[6] Fastidious, scrupulous.   [7] In faith.

[8] Near London. Bayes's two Kings of Brentford may have
been meant to mock the rival brothers who contest the throne
in *The Conquest of Granada.*

38] Q1 adds (after *rogue*) *she is my mistress.*   40] Q3 misprints *write* for *writ.*

40–41] Q1 substitutes for last sentence: *Well, gentlemen, I dare be bold to say, without vanity, I'll show you something here that's
very ridiculous, 'y gad. (Exeunt Players.)* JOHNS. *Sir, that we do not doubt of.* BAYES. *Pray, sir, let's sit down. Look you, sir,
the chief hinge,* etc. [See line 94.]   57] Q4Q5 *Esperance.*   97] Q1 *thing.*

BAYES. Why, look you, sir (nay, I beseech you, be a little curious [1] in taking notice of this, or else you'll never understand my notion of the thing), the people being embarrassed by their equal ties to both, and the sovereigns concerned in a re- 115 ciprocal regard, as well to their own interest as the good of the people, may make a certain kind of a — you understand me — upon which there does arise several disputes, turmoils, heart-burnings, and all that. In fine, you'll apprehend it better when 120 you see it.   *Exit, to call the Players.*

SMITH. I find the author will be very much obliged to the players, if they can make any sense out of this.

Enter BAYES.

BAYES. Now, gentlemen, I would fain 125 ask your opinion of one thing. I have made a prologue and an epilogue which may both serve for either (that is, the prologue for the epilogue, or the epilogue for the prologue) — do you mark? Nay, they may both serve too, 'y gad, for any other 130 play as well as this.

SMITH. Very well. That's, indeed, artificial. [2]

BAYES. And I would fain ask your judgments now, which of them would do best for the prologue. For you must know there is, in nature, but 135 two ways of making very good prologues. The one is by civility, by insinuation, good language, and all that, to — a — in a manner, steal your plaudit from the courtesy of the auditors: the other, by making use of some certain personal things, 140 which may keep a hank [3] upon such censuring persons as cannot otherways, a gad, in nature, be hindered from being too free with their tongues. To which end my first prologue is, that I come out in a long black veil, and a great, huge hangman 145 behind me, with a furred cap and his sword drawn; and there tell 'em plainly that if, out of good nature, they will not like my play, 'y gad, I'll e'en kneel down, and he shall cut my head off. Whereupon they all clapping — a —— 150

SMITH. Aye, but suppose they don't.

BAYES. Suppose! Sir, you may suppose what you please, I have nothing to do with your suppose, sir; nor am not at all mortified at it — not at all, sir; 'y gad, not one jot, sir. 'Suppose,' quoth 155 a! — ha, ha, ha!   (*Walks away.*)

JOHNSON. Phoo! prithee, Bayes, don't mind what he says. He is a fellow newly come out of the

[1] Careful.   [2] Contrived with art.
[3] Restraining hold.

country; he knows nothing of what's the relish, here, of the town.   160

BAYES. If I writ, sir, to please the country, I should have followed the old plain way; but I write for some persons of quality and peculiar friends of mine, that understand what flame and power in writing is; and they do me the right, sir, to ap- 165 prove of what I do.

JOHNSON. Aye, aye, they will clap, I warrant you; never fear it.

BAYES. I'm sure the design's good: that cannot be denied. And then, for language, 'y gad, I 170 defy 'em all, in nature, to mend it. Besides, sir, I have printed above a hundred sheets of paper, to insinuate the plot into the boxes: [4] and, withal, have appointed two or three dozen of my friends to be ready in the pit, who, I'm sure, will 175 clap, and so the rest, you know, must follow; and then pray, sir, what becomes of your suppose? — Ha, ha, ha!

JOHNSON. Nay, if the business be so well laid, it cannot miss.   180

BAYES. I think so, sir, and therefore would choose this to be the prologue. For, if I could engage 'em to clap before they see the play, you know 'twould be so much the better, because then they were engaged: for let a man write never 185 so well, there are, now-a-days, a sort of persons [5] they call critics, that, 'y gad, have no more wit in them than so many hobby-horses; but they'll laugh you, sir, and find fault, and censure things that, 'y gad, I'm sure they are not able to do them- 190 selves — a sort of envious persons that emulate the glories of persons of parts, and think to build their fame by calumniating of persons that, 'y gad, to my knowledge, of all persons in the world are, in nature, the persons that do as much despise all 195 that as — a — In fine, I'll say no more of 'em.

JOHNSON. Nay, you have said enough of 'em, in all conscience — I'm sure more than they'll e'er be able to answer.

BAYES. Why, I'll tell you, sir, sincerely, and 200 *bona fide*; were it not for the sake of some ingenious persons and choice female spirits that have a value for me, I would see 'em all hanged, 'y gad, before I would e'er more set pen to paper; but let 'em live in ignorance like ingrates.   205

[4] Referring to the 'printed papers given the audience before the acting of *The Indian Emperor*, telling them that it was the sequel of *The Indian Queen*.' (*Key.*)
[5] Many of Bayes's mannerisms of speech here and elsewhere are, as the *Key* suggests, in the 'constant style of Failer, in *The Wild Gallant*,' Dryden's first play.

124] Q1 omits *out*.
128–129] Q1 lacks and Q2 first introduces the interpolated phrase (*that is . . . prologue*). See Textual Notes.
148] Q1 adds *why* after *play*.   151] Q1 *But, suppose they do not*.   156] Q1 omits *ha, ha, ha*.
158] Q1 *He's*.   182] Q1 *for*; Q3 *to be*.   188] Q1 *'em* for *them*.   197] Q1 *Aye, aye*; Q3 *Nay*.
197–198] Q1 *in conscience*.

JOHNSON. Aye, marry! that were a way to be revenged of 'em, indeed; and, if I were in your place, now, I would do so.

BAYES. No, sir; there are certain ties upon me [1] that I cannot be disengaged from; otherwise, 210 I would. But pray, sir, how do you like my hangman?

SMITH. By my troth, sir, I should like him very well.

BAYES. But how do you like it, sir? (for, I 215 see, you can judge). Would you have it for the prologue, or the epilogue?

JOHNSON. Faith, sir, 'tis so good, let it e'en serve for both.

BAYES. No, no! that won't do. Besides, I 220 have made another.

JOHNSON. What other, sir?

BAYES. Why, sir, my other is Thunder and Lightning.

JOHNSON. That's greater. I'd rather stick 225 to that.

BAYES. Do you think so? I'll tell you then; though there have been many witty prologues written of late, yet I think you'll say this is a non pareillo. I'm sure nobody has hit upon it yet. 230 For here, sir, I make my prologue to be dialogue; [2] and as, in my first, you see I strive to oblige the auditors by civility, by good nature, good language, and all that, so, in this, by the other way, in terrorem, I choose for the persons Thunder 235 and Lightning. Do you apprehend the conceit?

JOHNSON. Phoo, pox! then you have it cocksure. They'll be hanged before they'll dare to affront an author that has 'em at that lock.[3]

BAYES. I have made, too, one of the most 240 delicate, dainty similes in the whole world, 'y gad, if I knew but how to apply it.

SMITH. Let's hear it, I pray you.

BAYES. 'Tis an allusion to love.

So boar and sow, when any storm is nigh,[4]   245
Snuff up, and smell it gath'ring in the sky;
Boar beckons sow to trot in chestnut groves,
And there consummate their unfinished loves:
Pensive, in mud, they wallow all alone,
And snort and gruntle to each other's moan.   250

How do you like it now, ha?

[1] Dryden failed to fulfil his contract to furnish annually three plays.   [2] As Dryden had done in various early prologues.
[3] Wrestling hold (cf. 'deadlock').
[4] A parody of The Conquest of Granada, Part II, I. ii:

So two kind turtles, when a storm is nigh,
Look up, and see it gath'ring in the sky;
Each calls his mate to shelter in the groves,
Leaving, in murmurs, their unfinished loves;
Perched on some drooping branch, they sit alone,
And coo, and hearken to each other's moan.

JOHNSON. Faith, 'tis extraordinary fine; and very applicable to Thunder and Lightning, methinks, because it speaks of a storm.

BAYES. 'Y gad, and so it does, now I think 255 on't. Mr. Johnson, I thank you, and I'll put it in profecto.[5] Come out, Thunder and Lightning.

Enter Thunder and Lightning.[6]

THUNDER. I am the bold Thunder.

BAYES. Mr. Cartwright,[7] prithee, speak that a little louder, and with a hoarse voice. 'I am 260 the bold Thunder!' Pshaw! speak it to me in a voice that thunders it out indeed: '*I am the bold Thunder!*'

THUNDER. I am the bold Thunder.
LIGHTNING. The brisk Lightning, I.

BAYES. Nay, you must be quick and nim- 265 ble.—'The brisk Lightning, I.'—That's my meaning.

THUNDER. I am the bravest Hector of the sky.
LIGHTNING. And I, fair Helen, that made Hector die.
THUNDER. I strike men down.
LIGHTNING. I fire the town.   270
THUNDER. Let the critics take heed how they grumble,
For then begin I for to rumble.
LIGHTNING. Let the ladies allow us their graces,
Or I'll blast all the paint on their faces,
And dry up their peter[8] to soot.   275
THUNDER. Let the critics look to't.
LIGHTNING. Let the ladies look to't.
THUNDER. For Thunder will do't.
LIGHTNING. For Lightning will shoot.
THUNDER. I'll give you dash for dash.   280
LIGHTNING. I'll give you flash for flash.
Gallants, I'll singe your feather.
THUNDER. I'll thunder you together.
BOTH. Look to't, look to't; we'll do't, we'll do't; look to't, we'll do't.   (*Twice or thrice repeated*)   285
Exeunt AMBO.

BAYES. There's no more. 'Tis but a flash of a prologue — a droll.[9]

SMITH. Yes, 'tis short, indeed, but very terrible.

BAYES. Aye, when the *simile's* in, it will do to a miracle, 'y gad. Come, come, begin the play. 290

Enter First Player.

1ST PLAYER. Sir, Mr. Ivory[10] is not come yet, but he'll be here presently; he's but two doors off.

BAYES. Come then, gentlemen, let's go out and take a pipe of tobacco.   *Exeunt.*

[5] Effect.
[6] This scene burlesques the lyrical dialogue, in Sir Robert Stapylton's The Slighted Maid (1663), between Evening and Jack-with-the-Lantern (Act III).
[7] William Cartwright, a robust actor with sonorous voice, created the part of Thunder.
[8] Rouge.   [9] Short farce.
[10] Abraham Ivory, a decayed actor, was retained out of charity as a messenger at Drury Lane.

208] Q1 *it* for *so.*   215] Q1 *Aye, but;* and omits *sir.*   216] Q1Q4Q5 *the prologue;* Q3 *a prologue.*
250] Q1 *snort;* Q3 *snore.*   259] Q1 omits *that.*   260] Q1 *hoarser.*   261] Q1 omits *to.*   286] Q1 *That's all.*
288] Q1 omits *Yes.*   289] Q1 *is in.*

ACT II

SCENE I

BAYES, JOHNSON, *and* SMITH.

BAYES. Now, sir, because I'll do nothing here that ever was done before, instead of beginning with a scene that discovers something of the plot, I begin this play with a whisper.[1]

SMITH. Umph! very new, indeed.   5

BAYES. Come, take your seats. Begin, sirs.

Enter Gentleman-Usher and Physician.

PHYSICIAN. Sir, by your habit, I should guess you to be the gentleman-usher of this sumptuous place.

USHER. And by your gate and fashion I should almost suspect you rule the healths of both our noble kings,   10
under the notion of physician.

PHYSICIAN. You hit my function right.

USHER. And you, mine.

PHYSICIAN. Then let's embrace.

USHER. Come.   15

PHYSICIAN. Come.

JOHNSON. Pray, sir, who are those so very civil persons?

BAYES. Why, sir, the gentleman-usher and physician of the two kings of Brentford.   20

JOHNSON. But, pray then, how comes it to pass that they know one another no better?

BAYES. Phoo! that's for the better carrying on of the plot.

JOHNSON. Very well.   25

PHYSICIAN. Sir, to conclude,

SMITH. What, before he begins?

BAYES. No, sir; you must know they had been talking of this a pretty while without.

SMITH. Where? In the tiring-room?   30

BAYES. Why, aye, sir. — He's so dull! — Come, speak again.

PHYSICIAN. Sir, to conclude, the place you fill has more than amply exacted the talents of a wary pilot, and all these threat'ning storms which, like impregnate   35
clouds, hover o'er our heads, will (when they once are grasped but by the eye of reason) melt into fruitful showers of blessings on the people.

BAYES. Pray, mark that allegory. Is not that good?   40

JOHNSON. Yes; that grasping of a storm with the eye is admirable.

PHYSICIAN. But yet some rumors great are stirring; and if Lorenzo should prove false (which none but the great gods can tell), you then perhaps would find   45
that —   (*Whispers.*)

[1] In Mrs. Aphra Behn's *The Amorous Prince* (1671) 'all the chief commands and directions are given in whispers.' (*Key*, 1704.) Summers notes various other similar passages.

BAYES. Now he whispers.

USHER. Alone, do you say?

PHYSICIAN. No; attended with the noble — (*Whispers.*)

BAYES. Again.   50

USHER. Who — he in gray?

PHYSICIAN. Yes; and at the head of —   (*Whispers.*)

BAYES. Pray, mark.

USHER. Then, sir, most certain, 'twill in time appear These are the reasons that have moved him to't: 55
First, he —   (*Whispers.*)

BAYES. Now the other whispers.

USHER. Secondly, they —   (*Whispers.*)

BAYES. At it still.

USHER. Thirdly, and lastly, both he and they —   60
                                              (*Whispers.*)

BAYES. Now they both whisper.
                                    Exeunt whispering.

— Now, gentlemen, pray tell me true, and without flattery, is not this a very odd beginning of a play?

JOHNSON. In troth, I think it is, sir. But why two kings of the same place?   65

BAYES. Why? because it's new, and that's it I aim at. I despise your Jonson[2] and Beaumont, that borrowed all they writ from nature. I am for fetching it purely out of my own fancy, I.

SMITH. But what think you, sir, of Sir John   70
Suckling?

BAYES. By gad, I am a better poet than he.

SMITH. Well, sir; but pray, why all this whispering?

BAYES. Why, sir (besides that it is new, as I   75
told you before), because they are supposed to be politicians; and matters of state ought not to be divulged.

SMITH. But then, sir, why —

BAYES. Sir, if you'll but respite your curi-   80
osity till the end of the fifth act, you'll find it a piece of patience not ill recompensed. (*Goes to the door.*)

JOHNSON. How dost thou like this, Frank? Is it not just as I told thee?

SMITH. Why, I did never, before this, see   85
anything in nature, and all that (as Mr. Bayes says), so foolish but I could give some guess at what moved the fop to do it; but this, I confess, does go beyond my reach.

JOHNSON. It is all alike. Mr. Wintershul[3]   90
has informed me of this play already. And I'll tell thee, Frank, thou shalt not see one scene here worth one farthing, or like anything thou canst imagine

[2] Dryden disparages Jonson in the Epilogue to *The Conquest of Granada, Part II.*

[3] William Wintershul (Wintersel, Wintershal, and other spellings), a celebrated veteran actor had played in *The Conquest of Granada* and many other plays of Dryden.

ACTS II–V] As in Act I, asterisks continue to indicate the 'large additions' of new material in Q3, but illustration of other textual variants between Q1 and Q3 is discontinued. (See Textual Notes.)

has ever been the practice of the world. And then, when he comes to what he calls 'good lan- 95 guage,' it is, as I told thee, very fantastical, most abominably dull, and not one word to the purpose.

SMITH. It does surprise me, I'm sure, very much.

JOHNSON. Aye, but it won't do so long: by that time thou hast seen a play or two that I'll show 100 thee, thou wilt be pretty well acquainted with this new kind of foppery.

*SMITH. Pox on't, but there's no pleasure in him: he's too gross a fool to be laughed at.

Enter BAYES.

*JOHNSON. I'll swear, Mr. Bayes, you have 105 done this scene most admirably; though, I must tell you, sir, it is a very difficult matter to pen a whisper well.

*BAYES. Aye, gentlemen, when you come to write yourselves, o' my word, you'll find it so. 110

*JOHNSON. Have a care of what you say, Mr. Bayes, for Mr. Smith there, I assure you, has written a great many fine things already.

*BAYES. Has he, i'fackins? Why, then, pray, sir, how do you do when you write? 115

*SMITH. Faith, sir, for the most part, I am in pretty good health.

*BAYES. Aye, but I mean, what do you do, when you write?

*SMITH. I take pen, ink, and paper, and sit 120 down.

*BAYES. Now I write standing; that's one thing: and then, another thing is, with what do you prepare yourself?

*SMITH. Prepare myself! What the devil 125 does the fool mean?

*BAYES. Why, I'll tell you, now, what I do. If I am to write familiar things, as sonnets to Armida,[1] and the like, I make use of stewed prunes only; but, when I have a grand design in hand, I ever take 130 physic, and let blood, for, when you would have pure swiftness of thought and fiery flights of fancy, you must have a care of the pensive part. In fine, you must purge the belly.

*SMITH. By my troth, sir, this is a most ad- 135 mirable receipt for writing.

*BAYES. Aye, 'tis my secret; and, in good earnest, I think, one of the best I have.

*SMITH. In good faith, sir, and that may very well be. 140

*BAYES. May be, sir? 'Y gad, I'm sure on't: *experto crede Roberto.*[2] But I must give you this caution by the way — be sure you never take snuff, when you write.

[1] Duchess of Richmond ('la belle Stuart'), celebrated in verses ascribed to Dryden — 'Farewell, fair Armida.' See also p. 53, ll. 113–114, and footnote.

[2] The 'expert Robert' may possibly be Dryden's brother-in-law, Robert Howard.

*SMITH. Why so, sir? 145

*BAYES. Why, it spoiled me once, 'y gad, one of the sparkishest plays in all England. But a friend of mine, at Gresham College,[3] has promised to help me to some spirit of brains, and, 'y gad, that shall do my business. 150

SCENE II

Enter the two Kings, hand in hand.[4]

BAYES. Oh, these now are the two kings of Brentford. Take notice of their style: 'twas never yet upon the stage; but, if you like it, I could make a shift, perhaps, to show you a whole play, writ all just so. 5

1ST KING. Did you observe their whisper, brother king?

2D KING. I did; and heard besides a grave bird sing That they intend, sweetheart, to play us pranks.

BAYES. This is now familiar, because they are both persons of the same quality. 10

SMITH. 'Sdeath, this would make a man spew.

1ST KING. If that design appears, I'll lug 'em by the ears Until I make 'em crack.

2D KING. And so will I, i'fack. 15

1ST KING. You must begin, *mon foy.*

2D KING. Sweet sir, *pardonnes moy.*

BAYES. Mark that: I makes 'em both speak French to show their breeding.

JOHNSON. Oh, 'tis extraordinary fine. 20

2D KING. Then, spite of Fate, we'll thus combinèd stand;
And, like true brothers, walk still hand in hand.

Exeunt Reges.

JOHNSON. This is a very majestic scene indeed.

BAYES. Aye, 'tis a crust, a lasting crust for your rogue critics, 'y gad: I would fain see the proud- 25 est of 'em all but dare to nibble at this; 'y gad, if they do, this shall rub their gums for 'em, I promise you. It was I, you must know, that have written a whole play just in this very same style; but 'twas never acted yet. 30

JOHNSON. How so?

BAYES. 'Y gad, I can hardly tell you for laughing (ha, ha, ha!). It is so pleasant a story — ha, ha, ha!

SMITH. What is't?

BAYES. 'Y gad, the players refused to act it. 35 Ha, ha, ha!

SMITH. That's impossible.

BAYES. 'Y gad, they did it, sir, point blank refused it, 'y gad. — Ha, ha, ha!

JOHNSON. Fie, that was rude. 40

BAYES. Rude! Aye, 'y gad, they are the rudest,

[3] The early London home of the Royal Society.

[4] Summers notes in this scene parodies of Orrery's *Mustapha* (1665) and, in 'the second King's endearment,' of Burr, in Dryden's *The Wild Gallant* (1663).

uncivilest persons, and all that, in the whole world, 'y gad: 'y gad, there's no living with 'em. I have written, Mr. Johnson, I do verily believe, a whole cart-load of things every whit as good as this; 45 and yet, I vow to gad, these insolent rascals have turned 'em all back upon my hands again.

JOHNSON. Strange fellows, indeed.

SMITH. But pray, Mr. Bayes, how came these two kings to know of this whisper? for, as I re- 50 member, they were not present at it.

BAYES. No, but that's the actors' fault, and not mine; for the two kings should (a pox take 'em) have popped both their heads in at the door, just as the other went off. 55

SMITH. That, indeed, would ha' done it.

BAYES. Done it! Aye, 'y gad, these fellows are able to spoil the best things in Christendom. I'll tell you, Mr. Johnson, I vow to gad, I have been so highly disobliged by the peremptoriness of 60 these fellows, that I'm resolved hereafter to bend my thoughts wholly for the service of the Nursery,[1] and mump[2] your proud players, 'y gad. So; now Prince Pretty-man comes in, and falls asleep making love to his mistress, which, you know, was a 65 grand intrigue in a late play[3] written by a very honest gentleman, a knight.

SCENE III

Enter PRINCE PRETTY-MAN.[4]

PRETTY-MAN. How strange a captive am I grown of late! Shall I accuse my love, or blame my fate? My love, I cannot; that is too divine: And against Fate what mortal dares repine?

Enter CLORIS.
— But here she comes. 5
Sure 'tis some blazing comet, is it not? (Lies down.)

BAYES. Blazing comet! mark that. 'Y gad, very fine.

PRETTY-MAN. But I am so surprised with sleep I cannot speak the rest. (Sleeps.) 10

BAYES. Does not that, now, surprise you, to fall asleep in the nick? His spirits exhale with the heat of his passion, and all that, and — swop! falls asleep, as you see. Now, here, she must make a simile. 15

SMITH. Where's the necessity of that, Mr. Bayes?

BAYES. Because she's surprised. That's a general rule — you must ever make a simile when you are surprised,[5] 'tis the new way of writing.

[1] Training-school for young actors. Both Patent Theatres used 'Nurseries' to recruit their companies.
[2] Overreach.
[3] Probably, as Bishop Percy suggested, a reference to Sir Richard Fanshawe's To Love Only for Love's Sake (printed 1671).
[4] In 1701, Q7 gives marginal references to the Prince in Dryden's Marriage à-la-Mode.
[5] A speech of Almeria in The Indian Emperor (IV. iv) cited by Bishop Percy, exemplifies the rule.

CLORIS. As some tall pine, which we, on Ætna, find 20 T'have stood the rage of many a boist'rous wind, Feeling without, that flames within do play Which would consume his root and sap away, He spreads his worsted arms unto the skies, Silently grieves, all pale, repines and dies: 25 So, shrouded up, your bright eye disappears. Break forth, bright scorching sun, and dry my tears.[6]
Exit.

*JOHNSON. Mr. Bayes, methinks this simile wants a little application, too.

*BAYES. No, faith; for it alludes to passion, to 30 consuming, to dying, and all that; which, you know, are the natural effects of an amour. But I'm afraid this scene has made you sad; for, I must confess, when I writ it, I wept myself.

SMITH. No, truly, sir, my spirits are almost 35 exhaled too, and I am likelier to fall asleep.

(PRINCE PRETTY-MAN starts up, and says)
PRETTY-MAN. It is resolved. Exit.

*BAYES. That's all.

SMITH. Mr. Bayes, may one be so bold as to ask you a question now, and you not be angry? 40

BAYES. O Lord, sir, you may ask me anything — what you please — I vow to gad, you do me a great deal of honor: you do not know me if you say that, sir.

SMITH. Then, pray, sir, what is it that this 45 prince here has resolved in his sleep?

BAYES. Why, I must confess, that question is well enough asked for one that is not acquainted with this new way of writing. But you must know, sir, that, to outdo all my fellow-writers, whereas 50 they keep their intrigo secret till the very last scene before the dance, I now, sir, (do you mark me) a —

SMITH. Begin the play and end it, without ever opening the plot at all?

BAYES. I do so; that's the very plain troth 55 on't. Ha, ha, ha! I do, 'y gad. If they cannot find it out themselves, e'en let 'em alone for Bayes, I warrant you. But here, now, is a scene of business. Pray observe it, for I dare say you'll think it no unwise discourse this, nor ill argued. To tell you 60 true, 'tis a discourse I overheard once betwixt two grand, sober, governing persons.

SCENE IV

Enter Gentleman-Usher and Physician.

USHER. Come, sir; let's state the matter of fact, and lay our heads together.

[6] A parody of The Conquest of Granada, Part I, V. iii. 129–134:

> As some fair tulip, by a storm oppressed,
> Shrinks up, and folds its silken arms to rest;
> And, bending to the blast, all pale and dead,
> Hears from within the wind sing round its head;
> So, shrouded up, your beauty disappears:
> Unveil, my love, and lay aside your fears.

PHYSICIAN. Right! lay our heads together.[1] I love to be merry sometimes; but when a knotty point comes, I lay my head close to it, with a snuff box in my 5 hand, and then I fegue [2] it away, i'faith.

BAYES. I do just so, gad, always.

USHER. The grand question is, whether they heard us whisper; which I divide thus —

*PHYSICIAN. Yes, it must be divided so indeed.   10

*SMITH. That's very complaisant, I swear, Mr. Bayes, to be of another man's opinion before he knows what it is.

*BAYES. Nay, I bring in none here but well-bred persons, I assure you.   15

USHER. I divided the question into when they heard, what they heard, and whether they heard or no.

JOHNSON. Most admirably divided, I swear.

USHER. As to the when; you say, just now: so that is answered. Then, as for what; why, what answers 20 itself; for what could they hear but what we talked of? So that naturally, and of necessity, we come to the last question, videlicet, whether they heard or no.

SMITH. This is a very wise scene, Mr. Bayes.

BAYES. Aye, you have it right: they are   25 both politicians.

*USHER. Pray, then, to proceed in method, let me ask you that question.

*PHYSICIAN. No, you'll answer better; pray let me ask it you.   30

*USHER. Your will must be a law.

*PHYSICIAN. Come then, what is it I must ask?

*SMITH. This politician, I perceive, Mr. Bayes, has somewhat a short memory.

*BAYES. Why, sir, you must know that   35 t'other is the main politician, and this is but his pupil.

*USHER. You must ask me whether they heard us whisper.

*PHYSICIAN. Well, I do so.   40

*USHER. Say it then.

*SMITH. Hey day! here's the bravest work that ever I saw.

*JOHNSON. This is mighty methodical!

*BAYES. Aye, sir; that's the way: 'tis the   45 way of art; there is no other way, 'y gad, in business.

*PHYSICIAN. Did they hear us whisper?

*USHER. Why, truly I can't tell; there's much to be said upon the word whisper. To whisper, in Latin, is susurrare, which is as much as to say, to speak softly; now, 50 if so they heard us speak softly, they heard us whisper: but then comes in the quomodo, the how: how did they hear us whisper? Why, as to that, there are two ways; the one, by chance or accident: the other, on purpose — that is, with design to hear us whisper.   55

*PHYSICIAN. Nay, if they heard us that way, I'll never give 'em physic more.

*USHER. Nor I e'er more will walk abroad before 'em.

*BAYES. Pray mark this; for a great deal depend[s] upon it, towards the latter end of the play.   60

*SMITH. I suppose that's the reason why you brought in this scene, Mr. Bayes?

*BAYES. Partly it was, sir; but, I confess, I was not unwilling, besides, to show the world a pattern here how men should talk of business.   65

JOHNSON. You have done it exceeding well indeed.

BAYES. Yes, I think this will do.

PHYSICIAN. Well, if they heard us whisper, they'll turn us out, and nobody else will take us.   70

SMITH. Not for politicians, I dare answer for it.

PHYSICIAN. Let's then no more ourselves in vain bemoan;
We are not safe until we them unthrone.

USHER. 'Tis right.
And, since occasion now seems debonair,   75
I'll seize on this, and you shall take that chair.

(They draw their swords, and sit down in the two great chairs upon the stage.)

BAYES. There's now an odd surprise; the whole state's turn'd quite topsy-turvy,[3] without any puther or stir in the whole world, 'y gad.

JOHNSON. A very silent change of govern-   80 ment, truly, as ever I heard of.

BAYES. It is so. And yet you shall see me bring 'em in again, by and by, in as odd a way every jot.

The Usurpers march out flourishing their swords.

Enter SHIRLEY.[4]

SHIRLEY. Hey ho, hey ho! what a change is here! 85 Hey day, hey day! I know not what to do, nor what to say.[5]   Exit.

*JOHNSON. Mr. Bayes, in my opinion now, that gentleman might have said a little more upon this occasion.   90

*BAYES. No, sir, not at all; for I under-writ his part on purpose to set off the rest.

*JOHNSON. Cry you mercy, sir.

SMITH. But pray, sir, how came they to depose the kings so easily?   95

BAYES. Why, sir, you must know, they long had a design to do it before; but never could put it in practice till now; and, to tell you true, that's one reason why I made 'em whisper so at first.

SMITH. Oh, very well: now I'm fully satisfied. 100

BAYES. And then, to show you, sir, it was not done so very easily neither, in this next scene you shall see some fighting.

---

[1] MS cites The Conquest of Granada, Part II, III. ii, among instances of 'Dryden's partiality for scholastic logic and argument in verse.'   [2] Drive.

[3] As in the last act of Dryden's Marriage à-la-Mode (1672), cited by the Key as evidence that he was 'not to be laughed out of his method.' His forthcoming play was doubtless already known in manuscript.   [4] A dancer in Killigrew's company.

[5] A close parody of passages in Killigrew's plays cited in the Key.

SMITH. Oh, ho! so then you make the struggle to be after the business is done? 105

BAYES. Aye.

SMITH. Oh, I conceive you. That, I swear, is very natural.

SCENE V [1]

Enter four men at one door, and four at another, with their swords drawn.

1ST SOLDIER. Stand! Who goes there?

2D SOLDIER. A friend.

1ST SOLDIER. What friend?

2D SOLDIER. A friend to the house.

1ST SOLDIER. Fall on! 5

(*They all kill one another. Music strikes.*)

BAYES (*to the music*). Hold, hold! (*It ceaseth.*) Now, here's an odd surprise: all these dead men you shall see rise up presently, at a certain note that I have made, in *Effaut* [2] *flat*, and fall a-dancing. Do you hear, dead men? (*To the music.*) Re- 10 member your note in *Effaut flat*. Play on. — Now, now, now.

(*The music plays his note, and the dead men rise; but cannot get in order.*)

O Lord, O Lord! — Out, out, out! — Did ever men spoil a good thing so? no figure, no ear, no time, nothing! Udzookers, you dance worse than 15 the angels in *Harry the Eight*, or the fat spirits in *The Tempest*, [3] 'y gad.

1ST SOLDIER. Why, sir, 'tis impossible to do anything in time, to this tune.

BAYES. O Lord, O Lord! Impossible? why, 20 gentlemen, if there be any faith in a person that's a Christian, I sate up two whole nights in composing this air and apting it for the business. For, if you observe, there are two several designs in this tune; it begins swift, and ends slow. You talk of 25 time, and time; you shall see me do't. Look you now. (*Lies down flat on his face.*) Here I am dead. Now mark my note in *Effaut flat*. — Strike up music. Now.

(*As he rises up hastily, he falls down again.*)

— Ah, gadsookers! I have broke my nose. [4] 30

JOHNSON. By my troth, Mr. Bayes, this is a very unfortunate note of yours, in *Effaut*.

BAYES. A plague of this damned stage, with your nails and your tenter-hooks, that a gentleman cannot come to teach you to act but he must break 35 his nose, and his face, and the devil and all. Pray, sir, can you help me to a wet piece of brown paper?

[1] The opening of this scene burlesques the opening of Act IV of Dryden's *The Maiden Queen* (1667).

[2] An obsolete term for the note F.

[3] D'Avenant's Restoration revival of *Henry VIII* and the D'Avenant-Dryden revision of *The Tempest* stressed spectacular features. Q7 has an early (1701) explanatory note.

[4] A palpable hit at D'Avenant's notorious facial disfigurement. (See Act III, opening stage direction.)

SMITH. No indeed, sir; I don't usually carry any about me.

2D SOLDIER. Sir, I'll go get you some within 40 presently.

BAYES. Go, go then; I follow you. Pray, dance out the dance, and I'll be with you in a moment. Remember you dance like horsemen. *Exit* BAYES.

*SMITH. Like horsemen! What a plague can 45 that be?

(*They dance the dance, but can make nothing of it.*)

1ST SOLDIER. A devil! let's try this no longer. Play my dance that Mr. Bayes found fault with so. *Dance, and exeunt.*

SMITH. What can this fool be doing all this while about his nose? 50

JOHNSON. Prithee, let's go see. *Exeunt.*

ACT III

SCENE I

BAYES with a paper on his nose, and the two Gentlemen.

BAYES. Now, sirs, this I do because my fancy, in this play, is to end every act with a dance. [5]

SMITH. Faith, that fancy is very good, but I should hardly have broke my nose for it, though.

JOHNSON. That fancy, I suppose, is new, too. 5

BAYES. Sir, all my fancies are so. I tread upon no man's heels, but make my flight upon my own wings, I assure you. Now, here comes in a scene of sheer wit, without any mixture in the whole world, 'y gad, between Prince Pretty-man and his 10 tailor. It might properly enough be called a prize of wit; for you shall see 'em come in upon one another snip snap, hit for hit, as fast as can be. First one speaks, then presently t'other's upon him slap, with a repartee; then he at him again, dash! 15 with a new conceit, and so eternally, eternally, 'y gad, till they go quite off the stage.

(*Goes to call the Players.*)

SMITH. What a plague does this fop mean by his snip snap, hit for hit, and dash?

JOHNSON. Mean? why, he never meant any- 20 thing in's life. What dost talk of meaning for?

Enter BAYES.

BAYES. Why don't you come in?

Enter PRINCE PRETTY-MAN *and* TOM THIMBLE.

BAYES. This scene will make you die with laughing, if it be well acted; for 'tis as full of drollery as ever it can hold: 'tis like an orange stuffed with 25 cloves, as for conceit.

[5] Briscoe's *Key* suggests that this scene parodies one between Failer and Bibber, his tailor, in the opening act of *The Wild Gallant*.

PRETTY-MAN. But prithee, Tom Thimble, why wilt thou needs marry? If nine tailors make but one man, and one woman cannot be satisfied with nine men, what work art thou cutting out here for thyself, trow?　30

BAYES. Good!

THIMBLE. Why, an't please your highness, if I can't make up all the work I cut out, I shan't want [1] journeymen to help me, I warrant you.

BAYES. Good again.　35

PRETTY-MAN. I am afraid thy journeymen, though, Tom, won't work by the day, but by the night.

BAYES. Good still.

THIMBLE. However, if my wife sits but crosslegged, as I do, there will be no great danger — not half so　40 much as when I trusted you, sir, for your coronation suit.

BAYES. Very good, i'faith.

PRETTY-MAN. Why, the times then lived upon trust; it was the fashion. You would not be out of time, at such a time as that, sure. A tailor, you know, must　45 never be out of fashion.

BAYES. Right.

THIMBLE. I'm sure, sir, I made your clothes in the Court fashion, for you never paid me yet.

BAYES. There's a bob [2] for the Court.　50

PRETTY-MAN. Why, Tom, thou art a sharp rogue when thou art angry, I see; thou pay'st me now, methinks.

*BAYES. There's pay upon pay! as good as ever was written, 'y gad!

THIMBLE. Aye, sir, in your own coin: you give　55 me nothing but words.

BAYES. Admirable, before gad!

PRETTY-MAN. Well, Tom, I hope shortly I shall have another coin for thee; for now the wars are coming on, I shall grow to be a man of mettle.　60

BAYES. Oh, you did not do that half enough.

JOHNSON. Methinks he does it admirably.

BAYES. Aye, pretty well; but he does not hit me in't. He does not top his part.[3]

THIMBLE. That's the way to be stamped your-　65 self, sir. I shall see you come home, like an angel [4] for the king's evil, with a hole bored through you. *Exeunt.*

BAYES. Ha, there he has hit it up to the hilts, 'y gad. How do you like it now, gentlemen? Is not this pure wit?　70

SMITH. 'Tis 'snip snap,' sir, as you say; but, methinks, not pleasant nor to the purpose, for the play does not go on.

BAYES. Play does not go on? I don't know what you mean; why, is not this part of the play?　75

SMITH. Yes, but the plot stands still.

BAYES. Plot stand still! why, what a devil is the plot good for but to bring in fine things?

SMITH. Oh, I did not know that before.

BAYES. No, I think you did not — nor many　80 things more that I am master of. Now, sir, 'y gad, this is the bane of all us writers: let us soar but never so little above the common pitch, 'y gad, all's spoiled; for the vulgar never understand it. They can never conceive you, sir, the excellency of　85 these things.

JOHNSON. 'Tis a sad fate, I must confess. But you write on still, for all that?

BAYES. Write on? Aye, 'y gad, I warrant you. 'Tis not their talk shall stop me: if they catch　90 me at that lock, I'll give 'em leave to hang me. As long as I know my things are good, what care I what they say? — What, are they gone without singing my last new song? *'Sbud,[5] would it were in their bellies! I'll tell you, Mr. Johnson, if I have　95 any skill in these matters, I vow to gad, this song is peremptorily the very best that ever yet was written. You must know it was made by Tom Thimble's first wife after she was dead.

*SMITH. How, sir? After she was dead?　100

*BAYES. Aye, sir, after she was dead. Why, what have you to say to that?

*JOHNSON. Say? Why, nothing: he were a devil that had anything to say to that!

*BAYES. Right.　105

*SMITH. How did she come to die, pray, sir?

*BAYES. Phoo! that's no matter — by a fall. But here's the conceit — that upon his knowing she was killed by an accident, he supposes, with a sigh, that she died for love of him.　110

*JOHNSON. Aye, aye, that's well enough. Let's hear it, Mr. Bayes.

*BAYES. 'Tis to the tune of 'Farewell, fair Armida,'[6] 'On seas and in battles, in bullets' and all that.　115

* Song

In swords, pikes, and bullets, 'tis safer to be
Than in a strong castle, remoted from thee:
My death's bruise pray think you gave me, though a fall
Did give it me more, from the top of a wall;
For then, if the moat on her mud would first lay,　120
And after, before you my body convey,
The blue on my breast when you happen to see,
You'll say, with a sigh, there's a true-blue for me.

Ha, rogues! when I am merry, I write these things as fast as hops, 'y gad; for, you must know, I am　125 as pleasant a debauchee as ever you saw — I am, i'faith.

*SMITH. But, Mr. Bayes, how comes this song in here? for, methinks, there is no great occasion for it.

---

[1] Lack.　　[2] Taunt.

[3] According to the *Key*, a favorite phrase of Edward Howard.

[4] The gold coin given by the King to those whom he 'touched' for scrofula.

[5] A corruption of 'God's bodikins,' used as a mild oath.

[6] 'Farewell, fair Armida,' is the title, and 'On seas,' etc., the first line of the second stanza of a poem ascribed to Dryden, on the death, in May, 1672, of Captain Digby, an ardent admirer of 'la belle Stuart.' (Included in Scott-Saintsbury *Dryden*, XI, 165–166.)

BAYES. Alack, sir, you know nothing. You 130 must ever interlard your plays with songs, ghosts, and dances if you mean to — a —

JOHNSON. Pit, box, and gallery, Mr. Bayes.

BAYES. 'Y gad and you have nicked it. Hark you, Mr. Johnson, you know I don't flatter; a 135 gad, you have a great deal of wit.

JOHNSON. O Lord, sir, you do me too much honor.

BAYES. Nay, nay, come, come, Mr. Johnson, i' faith this must not be said, amongst us that have it. I know you have wit by the judgment you 140 make of this play, for that's the measure I go by — my play is my touchstone. When a man tells me such a one is a person of parts, 'Is he so?' say I. What do I do but bring him presently to see this play. If he likes it, I know what to think of 145 him; if not, your most humble servant, sir, I'll no more of him upon my word; I thank you. I am *clara voyant*,[1] 'y gad. Now here we go on to our business.

SCENE II

Enter the two Usurpers, hand in hand.[2]

USHER. But what's become of Volscius the great? His presence has not graced our courts of late.

PHYSICIAN. I fear some ill, from emulation sprung, Has from us that illustrious hero wrung.

BAYES. Is not that majestical? 5

SMITH. Yes, but who a devil is that Volscius?

BAYES. Why, that's a prince I make in love with Parthenope.

SMITH. I thank you, sir.

Enter CORDELIO.

CORDELIO. My lieges, news from Volscius the Prince. 10

USHER. His news is welcome, whatsoe'er it be.

SMITH. How, sir, do you mean — whether it be good or bad?

BAYES. Nay, pray, sir, have a little patience! Godsookers, you'll spoil all my play! Why, 15 sir, 'tis impossible to answer every impertinent question you ask.

SMITH. Cry you mercy, sir.

CORDELIO. His highness, sirs, commanded me to tell you That the fair person whom you both do know, 20 Despairing of forgiveness for her fault, In a deep sorrow, twice she did attempt Upon her precious life; but, by the care Of standers-by, prevented was.

SMITH. 'Sheart, what stuff's here!

CORDELIO. At last, 25 Volscius the great this dire resolve embraced:

[1] Clairvoyant.

[2] Q7 (1701) gives here a marginal reference to 'the two Kings in Granada' (i.e., Dryden's *Conquest of Granada*).

His servants he into the country sent, And he himself to Piccadillé went; Where he's informed, by letters, that she's dead!

USHER. Dead! Is that possible? Dead!

PHYSICIAN. O ye gods! *Exeunt.* 30

BAYES. There's a smart expression of a passion — 'O ye gods!' That's one of my bold strokes, 'y gad.

SMITH. Yes, but who is the fair person that's dead? 35

BAYES. That you shall know anon, sir.

SMITH. Nay, if we know it at all, 'tis well enough.

BAYES. Perhaps you may find too, by and by, for all this, that she's not dead neither. 40

SMITH. Marry, that's good news indeed. I am glad of that with all my heart.

BAYES. Now, here's the man brought in that is supposed to have killed her. (*A great shout within.*)

SCENE III

Enter AMARYLLIS *with a book in her hand; and Attendants.*

AMARYLLIS. What shout triumphant's that?

Enter a Soldier.

SOLDIER. Shy maid, upon the river brink, Near Twick'nam Town, the false assassinate Is ta'en.

AMARYLLIS. Thanks to the powers above, for this deliverance! 5 I hope its slow beginning will portend A forward exit to all future end.

BAYES. Pish, there you are out! 'To all future end?' No, no — 'to all future *end*': you must lay 10 the accent upon 'end,' or else you lose the conceit.

SMITH. I see you are very perfect in these matters.

BAYES. Aye, sir; I have been long enough at it, one would think, to know something.

Enter Soldiers dragging in an old Fisherman.[3]

AMARYLLIS. Villain, what monster did corrupt thy mind 15 T'attack the noblest soul of human kind? Tell me who set thee on.

FISHERMAN. Prince Pretty-man.

AMARYLLIS. To kill whom?

FISHERMAN. Prince Pretty-man. 20

AMARYLLIS. What, did Prince Pretty-man hire you to kill Prince Pretty-man?

FISHERMAN. No; Prince Volscius.

AMARYLLIS. To kill whom?

FISHERMAN. Prince Volscius. 25

AMARYLLIS. What, did Prince Volscius hire you to kill Prince Volscius?

[3] N suggests Dryden's *Marriage à-la-Mode* (Act I) as the inspiration of this burlesque scene.

FISHERMAN. No; Prince Pretty-man.

AMARYLLIS. So! — drag him hence,

Till torture of the rack produce his sense. *Exeunt.* 30

BAYES. Mark how I make the horror of his guilt confound his intellects — for he's out at one and t'other; and that's the design of this scene.

SMITH. I see, sir, you have a several design for every scene. 35

BAYES. Aye, that's my way of writing, and so, sir, I can dispatch you a whole play, before another man, 'y gad, can make an end of his plot.

SCENE IV

BAYES. So, now enter Prince Pretty-man in a rage. — Where the devil is he? Why, Pretty-man! Why, when, I say? Oh, fie, fie, fie, fie! all's marred, I vow to gad, quite marred.

Enter PRETTY-MAN.

— Phoo, pox! you are come too late, sir; now 5 you may go out again, if you please. I vow to gad, Mr. — a — I would not give a button for my play, now you have done this.

PRETTY-MAN. What, sir?

BAYES. What, sir! 'Slife, sir, you should 10 have come out in choler, rous[1] upon the stage, just as the other went off. Must a man be eternally telling you of these things?

JOHNSON. Sure, this must be some very notable matter that he's so angry at. 15

SMITH. I am not of your opinion.

BAYES. Pish! come, let's hear your part, sir.

PRETTY-MAN.[2] Bring in my father; why d'ye keep
    him from me?
Although a fisherman, he is my father!
Was ever son yet brought to this distress, 20
To be, for being a son, made fatherless?
Ah, you just gods, rob me not of a father:
The being of a son take from me rather. *Exit.*

SMITH. Well, Ned, what think you now?

JOHNSON. A devil! this is worst of all. — Mr. 25 Bayes, pray what's the meaning of this scene?

BAYES. O, cry you mercy, sir; I purtest I forgot to tell you. Why, sir, you must know that, long before the beginning of this play, this prince was taken by a fisherman. 30

SMITH. How, sir — taken prisoner?

BAYES. Taken prisoner! O Lord, what a question's there! did ever any man ask such a question? Godsookers, he has put the plot quite out of my head with this damned question. What was I 35 going to say?

JOHNSON. Nay, the Lord knows; I cannot imagine.

---

[1] With a bounce.

[2] MS cites the opening scene of *Marriage à-la-Mode* for parallel.

BAYES. Stay, let me see — taken. O, 'tis true. Why, sir, as I was going to say, his highness 40 here, the Prince, was taken in a cradle by a fisherman and brought up as his child.

SMITH. Indeed?

BAYES. Nay, prithee, hold thy peace. — And so, sir, this murder being committed by the river- 45 side, the fisherman, upon suspicion, was seized; and thereupon the prince grew angry.

SMITH. So, so; now 'tis very plain.

JOHNSON. But, Mr. Bayes, is not this some disparagement to a prince to pass for a fisher- 50 man's son? Have a care of that, I pray.

BAYES. No, no, not at all; for 'tis but for a while: I shall fetch him off again presently, you shall see.

Enter PRETTY-MAN *and* THIMBLE.

PRETTY-MAN. By all the gods, I'll set the world on
    fire 55
Rather than let 'em ravish hence my sire.

THIMBLE. Brave Pretty-man, it is at length revealed
That he is not thy sire who thee concealed.

BAYES. Lo, you now; there he's off again.

JOHNSON. Admirably done, i' faith. 60

BAYES. Aye, now the plot thickens very much upon us.

PRETTY-MAN. What oracle this darkness can evince?
Sometimes a fisher's son, sometimes a prince.
It is a secret, great as is the world, 65
In which I, like the soul, am tossed and hurled.
The blackest ink of fate, sure, was my lot,
And, when she writ my name, she made a blot. *Exit.*

BAYES. There's a blust'ring verse for you now.

SMITH. Yes, sir, but why is he so mightily 70 troubled to find he is not a fisherman's son?

BAYES. Phoo! that is not because he has a mind to be his son, but for fear he should be thought to be nobody's son at all.

SMITH. Nay, that would trouble a man, in- 75 deed.

BAYES. So; let me see.

SCENE V[3]

[BAYES] (*reads*). 'Enter Prince Volscius going out of town.'

SMITH. I thought he had been gone to Piccadillé.

BAYES. Yes, he gave it out so; but that was only to cover his design. 5

JOHNSON. What design?

BAYES. Why, to head the army that lies concealed for him in Knightsbridge.

JOHNSON. I see here's a great deal of plot, Mr. Bayes. 10

BAYES. Yes, now it begins to break; but we shall have a world of more business anon.

---

[3] *Key* shows that this scene burlesques James Howard's *The English Monsieur* (1666), IV. ii.

Enter PRINCE VOLSCIUS, CLORIS, AMARYLLIS, *and*
HARRY *with a riding-cloak and boots.*

AMARYLLIS. Sir, you are cruel, thus to leave the town
And to retire to country solitude.

CLORIS. We hoped this summer that we should at
least   15
Have held the honor of your company.

BAYES. 'Held the honor of your company!'
prettily expressed! — 'Held the honor of your
company!' Godsookers, these fellows will never
take notice of anything.   20

JOHNSON. I assure you, sir, I admire it extremely; I don't know what he does.

BAYES. Aye, aye, he's a little envious; but 'tis
no great matter. — Come!

AMARYLLIS. Pray, let us two this single boon obtain, 25
That you will here with poor us [1] still remain.
Before your horses come, pronounce our fate;
For then, alas, I fear 'twill be too late.

BAYES. Sad!

VOLSCIUS. Harry, my boots; for I'll go rage among 30
My blades encamped, and quit this urban throng.

SMITH. But pray, Mr. Bayes, is not this a little
difficult, that you were saying e'en now, to keep
an army thus concealed in Knightsbridge?

BAYES. In Knightsbridge? — stay.   35

JOHNSON. No, not if the innkeepers be his
friends.

BAYES. His friends! Aye, sir, his intimate acquaintance; or else, indeed, I grant it could not be.

SMITH. Yes, faith, so it might be very easy.   40

BAYES. Nay, if I do not make all things easy,
'y gad, I'll give you leave to hang me. Now you
would think that he is going out of town, but you
shall see how prettily I have contrived to stop him
presently.   45

SMITH. By my troth, sir, you have so amazed me
that I know not what to think.

Enter PARTHENOPE.

VOLSCIUS. Bless me! how frail are all my best re-
solves!
How, in a moment, is my purpose changed!
Too soon I thought myself secure from love.   50
Fair madam, give me leave to ask her name
Who does so gently rob me of my fame:
For I should meet the army out of town,
And, if I fail, must hazard my renown.

PARTHENOPE. My mother, sir, sells ale by the town
walls,   55
And me her dear Parthenope she calls.

*BAYES. Now that's the Parthenope I told you of.

*JOHNSON. Aye, aye; 'y gad, you are very right.

[1] Cf. 'And leaves poor me defenceless here alone,' *The Indian
Emperor*, V. ii (N).

VOLSCIUS. Can vulgar vestments high-born beauty
shroud?
Thou bring'st the morning pictured in a cloud.[2]   60

BAYES. 'The morning pictured in a cloud!'
A, gadsookers, what a conceit is there!

PARTHENOPE. Give you good ev'n, sir.   *Exit.*

VOLSCIUS. O inauspicious stars! that I was born
To sudden love and to more sudden scorn!   65

AMARYLLIS. } — How! Prince Volscius in love?
CLORIS.   } Ha, ha, ha!   *Exeunt laughing.*

SMITH. Sure, Mr. Bayes, we have lost some
jest here that they laugh at so.

BAYES. Why did you not observe? He first   70
resolves to go out of town, and then, as he is pulling
on his boots, falls in love with her. Ha, ha, ha!

*SMITH. Well, and where lies the jest of that?

*BAYES. Ha?   (*Turns to* JOHNSON.)

JOHNSON. Why, in the boots: where should   75
the jest lie?

*BAYES. 'Y gad, you are in the right: it does (*turns
to* SMITH) lie in the boots. Your friend and I know
where a good jest lies, though you don't, sir.

*SMITH. Much good do't you, sir.   80

BAYES. Here, now, Mr. Johnson, you shall see
a combat betwixt love and honor.[3] An ancient
author has made a whole play on't,[4] but I have dispatched it all in this scene.

(VOLSCIUS *sits down to pull on his boots;*
BAYES *stands by and over acts the part as
he speaks it.*)

VOLSCIUS. How has my passion made me Cupid's
scoff!   85
This hasty boot is on, the other off,
And sullen lies, with amorous design
To quit loud fame and make that beauty mine.

SMITH. Prithee, mark what pains Mr. Bayes takes
to act this speech himself!   90

JOHNSON. Yes, the fool, I see, is mightily transported with it.

VOLSCIUS. My legs, the emblem of my various
thought,
Show to what sad distraction I am brought.
Sometimes with stubborn honor, like this boot,   95
My mind is guarded, and resolved to do't:
Sometimes, again, that very mind, by love
Disarmèd, like this other leg does prove.
Shall I to Honor or to Love give way?
'Go on,' cries Honor; tender Love says, 'Nay,'   100
Honor aloud commands, 'Pluck both boots on';
But softer Love does whisper, 'Put on none.'
What shall I do? what conduct shall I find

[2] A phrase from D'Avenant's *Siege of Rhodes, Part I*, cited
in the *Key*.
[3] For parallels, see Arber, pp. 86–88.
[4] D'Avenant's *Love and Honor* (printed 1649) was familiar to
Restoration audiences.

73–79] Q2 adds this passage (not in Q1) thus: *Smi.* But pray, sir, where lies the jest? *Johns.* In the boots. *Bayes.* Gad,
you're i'th' right, it does lie in the boots; your friend and I know where the jest lies, though you don't.

To lead me through this twilight of my mind?
For as bright day with black approach of night   105
Contending, makes a doubtful, puzzling light,
So does my honor and my love together
Puzzle me so, I can resolve for neither.
          (*Goes out hopping with one boot on, and the other off.*)

JOHNSON. By my troth, sir, this is as difficult a
combat as ever I saw, and as equal; for 'tis   110
determined on neither side.

BAYES. Aye, is't not now, 'y gad, ha? For to go
off hip hop, hip hop, upon this occasion, is a thousand times better than any conclusion in the world,
'y gad.   115

*JOHNSON. Indeed, Mr. Bayes, that hip hop in this
place, as you say, does a very great deal.

*BAYES. O, all in all, sir; they are these little things
that mar or set you off a play; as I remember once,
in a play of mine, I set off a scene,[1] 'y gad,   120
beyond expectation, only with a petticoat and the
belly-ache.

*SMITH. Pray, how was that, sir?

*BAYES. Why, sir, I contrived a petticoat to be
brought in upon a chair (nobody knew how)   125
into a prince's chamber, whose father was not to see
it, that came in by chance.

*JOHNSON. God's my life, that was a notable con-
trivance, indeed.

*SMITH. Aye; but, Mr. Bayes, how could you   130
contrive the belly-ache?

*BAYES. The easiest i'th' world, 'y gad: I'll tell
you how: I made the prince sit down upon the petticoat, no more than so, and pretended to his father
that he had just then got the belly-ache;   135
whereupon his father went out to call a physician,
and his man ran away with the petticoat.

*SMITH. Well, and what followed upon that?

*BAYES. Nothing, no earthly thing, I vow to gad.

*JOHNSON. O' my word, Mr. Bayes, there you   140
hit it.

*BAYES. Yes, it gave a world of content. And
then I paid 'em away besides, for I made 'em all
talk bawdy — ha, ha, ha! — beastly, downright bawdy upon the stage, 'y gad — ha, ha, ha! — but   145
with an infinite deal of wit, that I must say.

*JOHNSON. That, aye that, we know well enough,
can never fail you.

*BAYES. No, 'y gad, it can't. Come, bring in the
dance.   *Exit to call 'em.*   150

*SMITH. Now, the devil take thee for a silly, con-
fident, unnatural, fulsome rogue!

Enter BAYES *and Players.*

*BAYES. Pray dance well, before these gentlemen.
You are commonly so lazy, but you should be light
and easy, tah, tah, tah.   155

[1] The opening scene of Act IV of Dryden's *The Assignation;
or, Love in Nunnery* (1672). (*Key*)

(*All the while they dance, Bayes puts 'em out with
teaching 'em.*)

Well, gentlemen, you'll see this dance, if I am not
deceived, take very well upon the stage, when they
are perfect in their motions, and all that.

SMITH. I don't know how 'twill take, sir, but I
am sure you sweat hard for't.   160

BAYES. Aye, sir, it costs me more pains and
trouble to do these things than almost the things
are worth.

SMITH. By my troth, I think so, sir.

BAYES. Not for the things themselves, for I   165
could write you, sir, forty of 'em in a day; but, 'y
gad, these players are such dull persons that, if a man
be not by 'em upon every point and at every turn,
'y gad, they'll mistake you, sir, and spoil all.

Enter a Player.

What, is the funeral ready?   170

PLAYER. Yes, sir.

BAYES. And is the lance filled with wine?

PLAYER. Sir, 'tis just now a-doing.

BAYES. Stay, then, I'll do it myself.

SMITH. Come, let's go with him.   175

BAYES. A match! But, Mr. Johnson, 'y gad, I am
not like other persons; they care not what becomes
of their things, so they can but get money for 'em.
Now, 'y gad, when I write, if it be not just as it
should be in every circumstance, to every par-   180
ticular, 'y gad, I am no more able to endure it; I am
not myself, I'm out of my wits, and all that; I'm
the strangest person in the whole world. For what
care I for money? I write for reputation. *Exeunt.*

ACT IV

SCENE I

BAYES *and the two Gentlemen.*

BAYES. Gentlemen, because I would not have any
two things alike in this play, the last act beginning
with a witty scene of mirth, I make this to begin
with a funeral.[2]

SMITH. And is that all your reason for it, Mr.   5
Bayes?

BAYES. No, sir, I have a precedent for it besides.
A person of honor, and a scholar, brought in his funeral just so; and he was one (let me tell you) that
knew as well what belonged to a funeral as any   10
man in England, 'y gad.

JOHNSON. Nay, if that be so, you are safe.

BAYES. 'Y gad, but I have another device — a
frolic, which I think yet better than all this; not
for the plot or characters (for in my heroic plays,   15

[2] According to the *Key*, Colonel Henry Howard's unpublished
play *The United Kingdoms* 'began with a funeral; and had also
two kings in it.'

I make no difference as to these matters), but for another contrivance.

SMITH. What is that, I pray?

BAYES. Why, I have designed a conquest that cannot possibly, 'y gad, be acted in less than a 20 whole week;[1] and I'll speak a bold word, it shall drum, trumpet, shout, and battle,[2] 'y gad, with any the most warlike tragedy we have, either ancient or modern.

JOHNSON. Aye, marry, sir, there you say 25 something.

SMITH. And pray, sir, how have you ordered this same frolic of yours?

BAYES. Faith, sir, by the rule of romance. For example: they divided their things into three, 30 four, five, six, seven, eight, or as many tomes as they please: now I would very fain know what should hinder me from doing the same with my things, if I please?

JOHNSON. Nay, if you should not be master 35 of your own works, 'tis very hard.

BAYES. That is my sense. And then, sir, this contrivance of mine has something of the reason of a play in it, too; for as every one makes you five acts to one play, what do me I but make five 40 plays to one plot, by which means the auditors have every day a new thing.

JOHNSON. Most admirably good, i'faith! and must certainly take, because it is not tedious.

BAYES. Aye, sir, I know that; there's the 45 main point. And then, upon Saturday, to make a close of all (for I ever begin upon a Monday), I make you, sir, a sixth play, that sums up the whole matter to 'em, and all that, for fear they should have forgot it. 50

JOHNSON. That consideration, Mr. Bayes, indeed, I think, will be very necessary.

SMITH. And when comes in your share, pray, sir?

BAYES. The third week.[3]

JOHNSON. I vow, you'll get a world of money. 55

BAYES. Why, faith, a man must live; and if you don't thus pitch upon some new device, 'y gad, you'll never do it; for this age (take it o' my word) is somewhat hard to please. But there's one pretty odd passage, in the last of these plays, which 60 may be executed two several ways, wherein I'd have your opinion, gentlemen.

JOHNSON. What is't, sir?

BAYES. Why, sir, I make a male person to be in love with a female. 65

SMITH. Do you mean that, Mr. Bayes, for a new thing?

BAYES. Yes, sir, as I have ordered it. You shall hear. He having passionately loved her through my five whole plays, finding at last that she 70 consents to his love, just after that his mother had appeared to him like a ghost,[4] he kills himself. That's one way. The other is, that she coming at last to love him with as violent a passion as he loved her, she kills herself. Now my question 75 is, which of these two persons should suffer upon this occasion?

JOHNSON. By my troth, it is a very hard case to decide.

BAYES. The hardest in the world, 'y gad; and 80 has puzzled this pate very much. What say you, Mr. Smith?

SMITH. Why, truly, Mr. Bayes, if it might stand with your justice, I should now spare 'em both.

BAYES. 'Y gad, and I think—ha—why then, 85 I'll make him hinder her from killing herself. Aye, it shall be so. — Come, come, bring in the funeral.

Enter a Funeral, with the two Usurpers and Attendants.

Lay it down there — no, no, here, sir. — So; now speak.

KING USHER. Set down the funeral pile, and let our grief 90
Receive from its embraces some relief.

KING PHYSICIAN. Was't not unjust to ravish hence her breath,
And, in life's stead, to leave us nought but death?
The world discovers now its emptiness,
And by her loss demonstrates we have less. 95

BAYES. Is not that good language, now? is not that elevate? 'Tis my *non ultra*, 'y gad. You must know they were both in love with her.

SMITH. With her? — with whom?

BAYES. Why, this is Lardella's funeral. 100

SMITH. Lardella! Aye, who is she?

BAYES. Why, sir, the sister of Drawcansir—a lady that was drowned at sea and had a wave for her winding-sheet.[5]

KING USHER. Lardella, O Lardella, from above 105
Behold the tragic issues of our love.
Pity us sinking under grief and pain,
For thy being cast away upon the main.

BAYES. Look you now, you see I told you true.

SMITH. Aye, sir, and I thank you for it, very 110 kindly.

BAYES. Aye, 'y gad, but you will not have pa-

[1] This hit at the length of the two-part *Conquest of Granada* is presently enforced by comparison with the prolixity of the French heroic romances.

[2] A hit at Dryden's defence of his 'frequent use of drums and trumpets' and 'representations of battles.' (See his prefatory *Essay of Heroic Plays* in Q1 (1672) of *The Conquest of Granada*.)

[3] The third performance was often 'for the benefit of the author.'

[4] A hit at the appearance to Almanzor of his mother's Ghost to warn him from 'crimes of lawless love,' *The Conquest of Granada, Part II*, IV. iii.

[5] In the scene cited (ftn. to line 72) the Ghost says:

> On seas I bore thee, and on seas I died.
> I died; and for my winding-sheet a wave
> I had, and all the ocean for my grave.

tience; honest M — a — you will not have patience.

JOHNSON. Pray, Mr. Bayes, who is that 115
Drawcansir? [1]

BAYES. Why, sir, a fierce hero, that frights his
mistress, snubs up kings, baffles armies, and does
what he will, without regard to numbers, good manners, or justice. 120

JOHNSON. A very pretty character.

SMITH. But, Mr. Bayes, I thought your heroes had
ever been men of great humanity and justice.

BAYES. Yes, they have been so; but, for my part,
I prefer that one quality of singly beating of 125
whole armies above all your moral virtues put together, 'y gad. You shall see him come in presently.
(To the Players.) Zookers, why don't you read the
paper?

KING PHYSICIAN. Oh, cry you mercy. 130
(Goes to take the paper.)

BAYES. Pish! — nay, you are such a fumbler.
Come, I'll read it myself. (Takes a paper from off
the coffin.) — Stay, it's an ill hand; I must use my
spectacles. This, now, is a copy of verses which I
make Lardella compose just as she is dying, with 135
design to have it pinned upon her coffin, and so read
by one of the usurpers, who is her cousin.

SMITH. A very shrewd design that, upon my
word, Mr. Bayes.

BAYES. And what do you think I fancy her 140
to make love like, here, in the paper?

SMITH. Like a woman. What should she make
love like?

BAYES. O' my word you are out though, sir;
'y gad, you are. 145

SMITH. What then? like a man?

BAYES. No, sir, like a humble-bee.

SMITH. I confess, that I should not have fancied.

BAYES. It may be so, sir. But it is, though, in order to the opinion of some of your ancient phi- 150
losophers who held the transmigration of the soul.

SMITH. Very fine.

BAYES. I'll read the title: 'To my dear Couz,
King Phys.'

SMITH. That's a little too familiar with a 155
king though, sir, by your favor, for a humble-bee.

BAYES. Mr. Smith, in other things I grant your
knowledge may be above me; but, as for poetry,
give me leave to say, I understand that better. It
has been longer my practice; it has indeed, sir. 160

SMITH. Your servant, sir.

BAYES. Pray, mark it.   (Reads.)

'Since death my earthly part will thus remove,[2]
I'll come a humble-bee to your chaste love.

---

[1] Almanzor, Dryden's hero.
[2] A close parody, as Noyes shows, of 'a speech of Berenice,
the faithful wife of the tyrant Maximin, to her lover Por-
phyrius, in Dryden's *Tyrannic Love* (Act III):

With silent wings I'll follow you, dear couz; 165
Or else, before you, in the sun-beams buzz.
And when to melancholy groves you come,
An airy ghost, you'll know me by my hum;
For sound, being air, a ghost does well become.'

SMITH (after a pause). Admirable! 170

BAYES. 'At night into your bosom I will creep,
And buzz but softly if you chance to sleep:
Yet in your dreams I will pass sweeping by,
And then both hum and buzz before your eye.'

JOHNSON. By my troth, that's a very great 175
promise.

SMITH. Yes, and a most extraordinary comfort to
boot.

BAYES. 'Your bed of love from dangers I will free;
But most, from love of any future bee. 180
And when with pity your heart-strings shall crack,
With empty arms I'll bear you on my back.'

SMITH. A pick-a-pack, a pick-a-pack.

BAYES. Aye, 'y gad, but is not that *tuant* now,
ha? is it not *tuant*? Here's the end: 185

'Then, at your birth of immortality,
Like any wingèd archer, hence I'll fly,
And teach you your first flutt'ring in the sky.'

JOHNSON. Oh, rare! This is the most natural,
refined fancy that ever I heard, I'll swear. 190

BAYES. Yes, I think, for a dead person, it is a
good enough way of making love; for being divested of
her terrestrial part, and all that, she is only capable
of these little, pretty, amorous designs that are innocent, and yet passionate. — Come, draw your 195
swords.

KING PHYSICIAN. Come, sword, come sheathe thyself
within this breast,
Which only in Lardella's tomb can rest.

KING USHER. Come, dagger, come, and penetrate this
heart,
Which cannot from Lardella's love depart. 200

Enter PALLAS.

PALLAS. Hold! stop your murd'ring hands
At Pallas's commands!
For the supposèd dead, O kings,
Forbear to act such deadly things.

My earthy part —
Which is my tyrant's right, death will remove;
I'll come all soul and spirit to your love.
With silent steps I'll follow you all day;
Or else, before you, in the sunbeams play;
I'll lead you thence to melancholy groves,
And there repeat the scenes of our past loves.
At night I will within your curtains peep;
With empty arms embrace you while you sleep;
In gentle dreams I often will be by,
And sweep along before your closing eye.
All dangers from your bed I will remove,
But guard it most from any future love;
And when at last, in pity, you will die,
I'll watch your birth of immortality:
Then, turtle-like, I'll to my mate repair,
And teach you your first flight in open air.

Lardella lives: I did but try   205
If princes for their loves could die.
Such celestial constancy
Shall, by the gods, rewarded be:
And from these funeral obsequies
A nuptial banquet shall arise.   210
    (*The coffin opens, and a banquet is discovered.*)

BAYES. So, take away the coffin. Now it's out.
This is the very funeral of the fair person which
Volscius sent word was dead, and Pallas, you see, has
turned it into a banquet.

*SMITH. Well, but where is this banquet?   215

*BAYES. Nay, look you, sir, we must first have a
dance, for joy that Lardella is not dead. Pray, sir,
give me leave to bring in my things properly at least.

*SMITH. That, indeed, I had forgot. I ask your
pardon.   220

*BAYES. O, d'ye so, sir? I am glad you will confess
yourself once in an error, Mr. Smith.

    (*Dance.*)

KING USHER. Resplendent Pallas, we in thee do find
The fiercest beauty and a fiercer mind;
And since to thee Lardella's life we owe,   225
We'll supple statues in thy temple grow.

KING PHYSICIAN. Well, since alive Lardella's found,
Let, in full bowls, her health go round.
    (*The two Usurpers take each of them a bowl in their*
    hands.)

KING USHER. But where's the wine?

PALLAS. That shall be mine.   230
Lo, from this conquering lance,[1]
Does flow the purest wine of France;
    (*Fills the bowls out of her lance.*)
And, to appease your hunger, I
Have, in my helmet, brought a pie:
Lastly, to bear a part with these,   235
Behold a buckler made of cheese. (*Vanish* PALLAS.)

*BAYES. There's the banquet. Are you satisfied
now, sir?

JOHNSON. By my troth, now, that is new, and
more than I expected.   240

BAYES. Yes, I knew it would please you: for the
chief art in poetry is to elevate your expectation, and
then bring you off some extraordinary way.

    Enter DRAWCANSIR.

KING PHYSICIAN. What man is this that dares disturb our feast?

DRAWCANSIR. He that dares drink, and for that drink
dares die,[2]   245
And, knowing this, dares yet drink on, am I.

---

[1] A hit at a scene (III. v) in Thomas Porter's *The Villain*,
fully quoted in the *Key* (1704).

[2] A famous parody of Dryden's Almanzor:
    He who dares love, and for that love must die,
    And knowing this, dares yet love on, am I.
        (*The Conquest of Granada, Part II*, IV. iii.)

JOHNSON. That is, Mr. Bayes, as much as to say
that, though he would rather die than not drink,
yet he would fain drink for all that, too.

BAYES. Right; that's the conceit on't.   250

JOHNSON. 'Tis a marvellous good one, I swear.

*BAYES. Now there are some critics that have
advised me to put out the second *dare*, and print
must in the place on't; but, 'y gad, I think 'tis better
thus a great deal.   255

*JOHNSON. Whoo! a thousand times!

*BAYES. Go on, then.

KING USHER. Sir, if you please, we should be glad to
know
How long you here will stay, how soon you'll go.

BAYES. Is not that now like a well-bred per-   260
son, 'y gad? So modest, so gent![3]

SMITH. Oh, very like.

DRAWCANSIR. You shall not know how long I here
will stay;
But you shall know I'll take your bowls away.[4]
    (*Snatches the bowls out of the Kings' hands and*
    drinks 'em off.)

SMITH. But, Mr. Bayes, is that, too, modest 265
and gent?

BAYES. No, by gad, sir, but it's great.

KING USHER. Though, brother, this grum stranger
be a clown,
He'll leave us, sure, a little to gulp down.

DRAWCANSIR. Whoe'er to gulp one drop of this dares
think,   270
I'll stare away his very pow'r to drink.
    (*The two Kings sneak off the stage, with their*
    Attendants.)
I drink, I huff, I strut, look big and stare;
And all this I can do, because I dare.[5]   *Exit.*

SMITH. I suppose, Mr. Bayes, this is the fierce
hero you spoke of.   275

BAYES. Yes, but this is nothing: you shall see
him, in the last act, win above a dozen battles, one
after another, 'y gad, as fast as they can possibl[y]
come upon the stage.

JOHNSON. That will be a fight worth the   280
seeing, indeed.

SMITH. But pray, Mr. Bayes, why do you make
the kings let him use 'em so scurvily?

BAYES. Phoo! that is to raise the character of
Drawcansir.   285

JOHNSON. O' my word, that was well thought on.

---

[3] Genteel.

[4] This and the following couplet of Drawcansir parody
couplets in *The Conquest of Granada, Part I*, V. iii.

[5] A parody of Almanzor, in *The Conquest of Granada,
Part II*, II. iii:
    Spite of myself I'll stay, fight, love, despair;
    And I can do all this because I dare.

239–243] In Q1 these two speeches follow Bayes's earlier speech (lines 211–214). At that point Q3 inserts four new speeches
(lines 215–222), but retains the two speeches of Q1 by transfer to a later context.
278–279] Q3 *possible* (for *possibly*); Q1 *can possibly be represented.*

BAYES. Now, sirs, I'll show you a scene indeed; or rather, indeed, the scene of scenes. 'Tis an heroic scene.

SMITH. And pray, sir, what is your design in   290 this scene?

BAYES. Why, sir, my design is gilded truncheons,¹ forced conceit, smooth verse, and a rant: in fine, if this scene do not take, 'y gad, I'll write no more. Come, come in, Mr.—a—nay, come in   295 as many as you can. Gentlemen, I must desire you to remove a little, for I must fill the stage.

SMITH. Why fill the stage?

BAYES. Oh, sir, because your heroic verse never sounds well but when the stage is full.   300

SCENE II ²

Enter PRINCE PRETTY-MAN *and* PRINCE VOLSCIUS.

BAYES. Nay, hold, hold! pray, by your leave a little.—Look you, sir, the drift of this scene is somewhat more than ordinary; for I make 'em both fall out because they are not in love with the same woman.   5

SMITH. Not in love? You mean, I suppose, because they are in love, Mr. Bayes?

BAYES. No, sir; I say not in love. There's a new conceit for you. Now, speak.

PRETTY-MAN. Since fate, Prince Volscius, now has
    found the way   10
For our so longed-for meeting here this day,
Lend thy attention to my grand concern.

VOLSCIUS. I gladly would that story from thee learn;
But thou to love dost, Pretty-man, incline:
Yet love in thy breast is not love in mine.   15

BAYES. *Antithesis!*—thine and mine.

PRETTY-MAN. Since love itself's the same, why should
    it be
Diff'ring in you from what it is in me?

BAYES. Reasoning! 'y gad, I love reasoning in verse.

VOLSCIUS. Love takes, chameleon-like, a various dye   20
From every plant on which itself does lie.

BAYES. *Simile!*

PRETTY-MAN. Let not thy love the course of nature
    fright:
Nature does most in harmony delight.

VOLSCIUS. How weak a deity would nature prove   25
Contending with the pow'rful god of love?

BAYES. There's a great verse!

VOLSCIUS. If incense thou wilt offer at the shrine
Of mighty love, burn it to none but mine.
Her rosy lips external sweets exhale;   30
And her bright flames make all flames else look pale.

¹ MS annotates fully this reference to an elaborate revival of Jonson's *Cataline*, which Pepys attended in December, 1668. The early (Q1) text referred to 'Roman clothes' as well as 'gilded truncheons.'

² Summers finds in this scene reminiscences of Orrery's heroic dramas.

BAYES. 'Y gad, that is right.

PRETTY-MAN. Perhaps dull incense may thy love suf-
    fice;
But mine must be adored with sacrifice.
All hearts turn ashes which her eyes control: 35
The body they consume as well as soul.

VOLSCIUS. My love has yet a power more divine;
Victims her altars burn not, but refine:
Amidst the flames they ne'er give up the ghost,
But, with her looks, revive still as they roast.   40
In spite of pain and death, they're kept alive:
Her fiery eyes makes 'em in fire survive.

BAYES. That is as well, 'y gad, as I can do.

VOLSCIUS. Let my Parthenope at length prevail.

BAYES. Civil, 'y gad.   45

PRETTY-MAN. I'll sooner have a passion for a whale,
In whose vast bulk, though store of oil doth lie,
We find more shape, more beauty, in a fly.

SMITH. That's uncivil, 'y gad.

BAYES. Yes; but as far a fetched fancy   50
though, 'y gad, as ever you saw.

VOLSCIUS. Soft, Pretty-man, let not thy vain pretence
Of perfect love defame love's excellence.
Parthenope is sure as far above
All other loves as above all is love.   55

BAYES. Ah! 'y gad, that strikes me.

PRETTY-MAN. To blame my Cloris, gods would not
    pretend.

BAYES. Now mark.

VOLSCIUS. Were all gods joined, they could not hope
    to mend
My better choice; for fair Parthenope   60
Gods would, themselves, un-god themselves to see.

BAYES. Now the rant's a-coming.

PRETTY-MAN. Durst any of the gods be so uncivil,
I'd make that god subscribe himself a devil.³

BAYES. Ah, godsookers, that's well writ!   65
    (*Scratching his head, his peruke falls off.*)

VOLSCIUS. Couldst thou that god from heav'n to earth
    translate,
He could not fear to want a heav'nly state.
Parthenope, on earth, can heav'n create.

PRETTY-MAN. Cloris does heav'n itself so far excel,
She can transcend the joys of heav'n in hell.   70

BAYES. There's a bold flight for you now!— 'Sdeath, I have lost my peruke!—Well, gentlemen, this is that I never yet saw anyone could write but myself. Here's true spirit and flame all through, 'y gad. So, so; pray clear the stage.   75
    (*He puts 'em off the stage.*)

*JOHNSON. I wonder how the coxcomb has got the knack of writing smooth verse thus.

*SMITH. Why, there's no need of brain for this; 'tis but scanning; the labor's in the finger. But where's the sense of it?   80

³ Hits at the proverbial rant of Dryden's Maximin, in *Tyrannic Love.*

*JOHNSON. Oh, for that, he desires to be excused; he is too proud a man to creep servilely after sense, I assure you. — But pray, Mr. Bayes, why is this scene all in verse?

BAYES. O sir, the subject is too great for 85 prose.

SMITH. Well said, i'faith. I'll give thee a pot of ale for that answer; 'tis well worth it.

BAYES. Come, with all my heart.

'I'll make that god subscribe himself a devil.' 90 That single line, 'y gad, is worth all that my brother poets ever writ. Let down the curtain.   *Exeunt.*

ACT V
SCENE I

BAYES *and the two Gentlemen.*

BAYES. Now, gentlemen, I will be bold to say, I'll show you the greatest scene that ever England saw — I mean not for words, for those I do not value, but for state, show, and magnificence. In fine, I'll justify it to be as grand to the eye every 5 whit, 'y gad, as that great scene in *Harry the Eight* — and grander too, 'y gad; for, instead of two bishops, I bring in here four cardinals.

The Curtain is drawn up; the two usurping Kings appear in state, with the four Cardinals, PRINCE PRETTY-MAN, PRINCE VOLSCIUS, AMARYLLIS, CLORIS, PARTHENOPE, *&c.; before them, Heralds and Sergeants at Arms with maces.*

SMITH. Mr. Bayes, pray what is the reason that two of the cardinals are in hats and the other in 10 caps?

BAYES. Why, sir, because — by gad, I won't tell you. — Your country friend, sir, grows so troublesome.

KING USHER. Now, sir, to the business of the day. 15
KING PHYSICIAN. Speak, Volscius.

VOLSCIUS. Dread sovereign lords, my zeal to you must not invade my duty to your son. Let me entreat that great Prince Pretty-man first do speak, whose high pre-eminence, in all things that do bear the name of good, 20 may justly claim that privilege.

BAYES. Here it begins to unfold. You must perceive, now, that he is his son.

JOHNSON. Yes, sir; and we are very much beholding to you for that discovery.   25

PRETTY-MAN. Royal father, upon my knees I beg That the illustrious Volscius first be heard.

VOLSCIUS. That preference is only due to Amaryllis, sir.

BAYES. I'll make her speak very well, by and 30 by; you shall see.

AMARYLLIS. Invincible sovereigns —   (*Soft Music.*)

KING USHER. But stay, what sound is this invades our ears? [1]
KING PHYSICIAN. Sure 'tis the music of the moving spheres.
PRETTY-MAN. Behold, with wonder! yonder comes from far,   35
A god-like cloud and a triumphant car,
In which our two right kings sit one by one,
With virgin vests, and laurel garlands on.
KING USHER. Then, Brother Phys', 'tis time we should be gone.
     (*The two Usurpers steal out of the throne and go away.*)

BAYES. Look you now, did not I tell you that 40 this would be as easy a change as the other?

SMITH. Yes, faith, you did so; though I confess, I could not believe you; but you have brought it about, I see.

     (*The two right Kings of Brentford descend in the clouds,*[2] *singing in white garments; and three fiddlers sitting before them, in green.*)

BAYES. Now, because the two right kings 45 descend from above, I make 'em sing to the tune and style of our modern spirits.

1ST KING. Haste, brother king, we are sent from above.
2D KING. Let us move, let us move —
          Move to remove the fate   50
          Of Brentford's long united state.
1ST KING. Tara, tan tara, full east and by south,
2D KING. We sail with thunder in our mouth,
In scorching noon-day, whilst the traveller stays,
Busy, busy, busy, busy, we bustle along.   55
Mounted upon warm Phœbus his rays,
          Through the heavenly throng,
          Hasting to those
Who will feast us, at night, with a pig's pettitoes.
1ST KING. And we'll fall with our pate   60
          In an *olio* [3] of hate.
2D KING. But now supper's done, the servitors try,
Like soldiers, to storm a whole half-moon pie.
1ST KING. They gather, they gather hot custard in spoons;
But alas, I must leave these half-moons,   65
And repair to my trusty dragoons.
2D KING. Oh, stay, for you need not as yet go astray;
The tide, like a friend, has brought ships in our way,
And on their high ropes we will play.
Like maggots in filberts, we'll snug in our shell,   70
          We'll frisk in our shell,
          We'll firk in our shell,
          And farewell.
1ST KING. But the ladies have all inclination to dance,
And the green frogs croak out a coranto [4] of France.   75

BAYES. Is not that pretty, now? The fiddlers are all in green.

---

[1] A mock echo of a line in the opening scene of *The Indian Queen:*
          'What noise is this invades my ear?'
[2] In *Tyrannic Love* (Act IV) two spirits 'descend in clouds and sing.'
[3] Medley.   [4] Lively dance.

SMITH. Aye, but they play no coranto.

JOHNSON. No, but they play a tune, that's a great deal better.   80

BAYES. 'No coranto,' quoth a! — that's a good one, with all my heart. — Come, sing on.

2D KING.   Now mortals that hear
          How we tilt and career,
          With wonder will fear   85
The event of such things as shall never appear.

1ST KING. Stay you to fulfil what the gods have decreed.

2D KING. Then call me to help you if there shall be need.

1ST KING. So firmly resolved is a true Brentford king
To save the distressèd and help to 'em bring,   90
That ere a full pot of good ale you can swallow,
He's here with a whoop, and gone with a holla.

(BAYES *fillips his finger, and sings after 'em.*)

BAYES. 'He's here with a whoop, and gone with a holla.' This, sir, you must know, I thought once to have brought in with a conjurer.[1]   95

JOHNSON. Aye, that would have been better.

BAYES. No, faith, not when you consider it; for thus 'tis more compendious and does the thing every whit as well.

SMITH. Thing! — what thing?   100

BAYES. Why, bring 'em down again into the throne, sir. What thing would you have?

SMITH. Well; but methinks the sense of this song is not very plain.

BAYES. Plain? why, did you ever hear any   105 people in clouds speak plain? They must be all for flight of fancy, at its full range, without the least check or control upon it. When once you tie up spirits and people in clouds to speak plain, you spoil all.   110

SMITH. Bless me, what a monster's this!

(*The two Kings light out of the clouds and step into the throne.*)

1ST KING. Come, now to serious counsel we'll advance.

2D KING. I do agree; but first let's have a dance.

BAYES. Right. You did that very well, Mr. Cartwright. 'But first, let's have a dance.' Pray,   115 remember that; be sure you do it always just so, for it must be done as if it were the effect of thought and premeditation. — 'But first, let's have a dance.' Pray, remember that.

SMITH. Well, I can hold no longer; I must   120 gag this rogue; there's no enduring of him.

JOHNSON. No, prithee make use of thy patience a little longer; let's see the end of him now.

(*Dance a grand dance.*)

BAYES. This, now, is an ancient dance, of right belonging to the Kings of Brentford, but since   125 derived, with a little alteration, to the Inns of Court.

An Alarm.   Enter two Heralds.

1ST KING. What saucy groom molests our privacies?

1ST HERALD. The army's at the door, and, in disguise, Desires a word with both your Majesties:

2D HERALD. Having, from Knightsbridge, hither marched by stealth.   130

2D KING. Bid 'em attend a while and drink our health.

SMITH. How, Mr. Bayes — the army in disguise?

BAYES. Aye, sir, for fear the usurpers might discover them, that went out but just now.

SMITH. Why, what if they had discovered   135 them?

BAYES. Why, then they had broke the design.

1ST KING. Here, take five guineas for those warlike men.[2]

2D KING. And here's five more; that makes the sum just ten.

1ST HERALD. We have not seen so much the Lord knows when.   *Exeunt Heralds.*   140

1ST KING. Speak on, brave Amaryllis.

AMARYLLIS. Invincible sovereigns, blame not my modesty
If at this grand conjuncture —

(*Drum beat behind the stage.*)

1ST KING. What dreadful noise is this that comes and goes?

Enter a Soldier with his sword drawn.

SOLDIER. Haste hence, great sirs, your royal persons save,   145
For the event of war no mortal knows!
The army, wrangling for the gold you gave,
First fell to words, and then to handy-blows.   *Exit.*

*BAYES. Is not that now a pretty kind of a stanza, and a handsome come off?   150

2D KING. O dangerous estate of sovereign pow'r!
Obnoxious to the change of every hour.

1ST KING. Let us for shelter in our cabinet stay:
Perhaps these threat'ning storms may pass away.
          Exeunt.

JOHNSON. But, Mr. Bayes, did not you pro-   155 mise us, just now, to make Amaryllis speak very well?

BAYES. Aye, and so she would have done but that they hindered her.

SMITH. How, sir, whether you would or no?   160

BAYES. Aye, sir; the plot lay so that, I vow to gad, it was not to be avoided.

SMITH. Marry, that was hard.

JOHNSON. But, pray, who hindered her?

BAYES. Why, the battle, sir, that's just com-   165 ing in at door. And I'll tell you now a strange thing — though I don't pretend to do more than other men, 'y gad, I'll give you both a whole week to guess how I'll represent this battle.

SMITH. I had rather be bound to fight your   170 battle, I assure you, sir.

BAYES. Whoo! there's it now. Fight a battle?

---

[1] Summers cites, as instances in Dryden, *Tyrannic Love* (Act IV) and *The Indian Queen* (Act III).

[2] Summers points out that this scene parodies *The Conquest of Granada, Part II*, I. ii.

there's the common error. I knew presently where I should have you. Why, pray, sir, do but tell me this one thing — can you think it a decent 175 thing, in a battle before ladies, to have men run their swords through one another, and all that?

JOHNSON. No, faith, 'tis not civil.

BAYES. Right! On the other side — to have a long relation of squadrons here, and squad- 180 rons there — what is it but dull prolixity?

JOHNSON. Excellently reasoned, by my troth!

BAYES. Wherefore, sir, to avoid both those inde- corums, I sum up my whole battle [1] in the represen- tation of two persons only — no more — and 185 yet so lively that, I vow to gad, you would swear ten thousand men were at it, really engaged. Do you mark me?

SMITH. Yes, sir; but I think I should hardly swear, though, for all that. 190

BAYES. By my troth, sir, but you would, though, when you see it; for I make 'em both come out in armor, cap-a-pie, with their swords drawn, and hung with a scarlet ribbon at their wrists (which, you know, represents fighting enough). 195

*JOHNSON. Aye, aye; so much that, if I were in your place, I would make 'em go out again without ever speaking one word.

*BAYES. No; there you are out; for I make each of 'em hold a lute in his hand. 200

SMITH. How, sir — instead of a buckler?

BAYES. O Lord, O Lord! — instead of a buckler? Pray, sir, do you ask no more questions. I make 'em, sir, play the battle in *recitativo*. And here's the conceit — just at the very same instant that 205 one sings, the other, sir, recovers you his sword, and puts himself in a warlike posture, so that you have at once your ear entertained with music and good language, and your eye satisfied with the garb and accoutrements of war. 210

SMITH. I confess, sir, you stupefy me.

BAYES. You shall see.

JOHNSON. But, Mr. Bayes, might not we have a little fighting? — for I love those plays where they cut and slash one another, upon the stage, 215 for a whole hour together.

BAYES. Why, then, to tell you true, I have con- trived it both ways. But you shall have my *recita- tivo* first.

*JOHNSON. Aye, now you are right; there is 220 nothing then can be objected against it.

*BAYES. True; and so, 'y gad, I'll make it, too, a tragedy in a trice.

Enter, at several doors, the General and Lieutenant- General, armed cap-a-pie, with each of them a

lute in his hand, and his sword drawn, and hung with a scarlet ribbon at his wrist.

LIEUTENANT-GENERAL. Villain, thou liest!

GENERAL. Arm, arm, Gonsalvo, arm! What ho! 225
The lie no flesh can brook, I trow.

LIEUTENANT-GENERAL. Advance, from Acton, with the musketeers.

GENERAL. Draw down the Chelsea cuirassiers.

LIEUTENANT-GENERAL. The band you boast of, Chel- sea cuirassiers,
Shall, in my Putney pikes, now meet their peers. 230

GENERAL. Chiswickians agèd, and renowned in fight,
Join with the Hammersmith brigade.

LIEUTENANT-GENERAL. You'll find my Mortlake boys will do them right,
Unless by Fulham numbers overlaid.

GENERAL. Let the left wing of Twick'nam foot ad- vance 235
And line that eastern hedge.

LIEUTENANT-GENERAL. The horse I raised in Petty- France [2]
Shall try their chance,
And scour the meadows, overgrown with sedge.

GENERAL. Stand! give the word. 240

LIEUTENANT-GENERAL. Bright sword.

GENERAL. That may be thine,
But 'tis not mine.

LIEUTENANT-GENERAL. Give fire, give fire, at once give fire,
And let those recreant troops perceive mine ire. 245

GENERAL. Pursue, pursue! They fly
That first did give the lie. *Exeunt.*

BAYES. This, now, is not improper, I think, be- cause the spectators know all these towns, and may easily conceive them to be within the domin- 250 ions of the two kings of Brentford.

JOHNSON. Most exceeding well designed!

BAYES. How do you think I have contrived to give a stop to this battle?

SMITH. How? 255

BAYES. By an eclipse — which, let me tell you, is a kind of fancy that was yet never so much as thought of but by myself and one person more that shall be nameless.

Enter Lieutenant-General.

LIEUTENANT-GENERAL. What midnight darkness does invade the day, 260
And snatch the victor from his conquered prey?
Is the Sun weary of his bloody sight,
And winks upon us with his eye of light?
'Tis an eclipse. This was unkind, O Moon,
To clap between me and the Sun so soon. 265
Foolish eclipse! thou this in vain hast done;
My brighter honor had eclips'd the Sun.
But now behold eclipses two in one. *Exit.*

JOHNSON. This is [as] admirable representation of a battle as ever I saw. 270

[1] The *Key* cites D'Avenant's *The Siege of Rhodes, Part I*, as performed 'by seven persons only.'

[2] Beyond the London city wall.

269] QQ *an* for *as.*

BAYES. Aye, sir. But how would you fancy now to represent an eclipse?

SMITH. Why, that's to be supposed.

BAYES. Supposed! Aye, you are ever at your *suppose* — ha, ha, ha! Why, you may as well   275 suppose the whole play. No, it must come in upon the stage, that's certain; but in some odd way that may delight, amuse, and all that. I have a conceit for't that I am sure is new and, I believe, to the purpose.   280

JOHNSON. How's that?

BAYES. Why, the truth is, I took the first hint of this out of a dialogue between Phœbus and Aurora, in *The Slighted Maid*,[1] which, by my troth, was very pretty, but I think you'll confess this is a little   285 better.

JOHNSON. No doubt on't, Mr. Bayes. A great deal better.

(BAYES *hugs* JOHNSON, *then turns to* SMITH.)

BAYES. Ah, dear rogue! But — a — sir, you have heard, I suppose, that your eclipse of the moon   290 is nothing else but an interposition of the earth between the sun and moon: as likewise your eclipse of the sun is caused by an interlocation of the moon betwixt the earth and sun?

SMITH. I have heard some such thing, indeed.   295

BAYES. Well, sir, then what do me I but make the earth, sun, and moon come out upon the stage, and dance the Hey?[2] — hum! And, of necessity, by the very nature of this dance, the earth must be sometimes between the sun and the moon, and   300 the moon between the earth and sun; and there you have both your eclipses, by demonstration.

JOHNSON. That must needs be very fine, truly.

BAYES. Yes, it has fancy in't. And then, sir, that there may be something in't, too, of a joke,   305 I bring 'em in all singing, and make the moon sell the earth a bargain. — Come, come out, eclipse, to the tune of *Tom Tyler*.

Enter LUNA.

LUNA. Orbis, O Orbis!
Come to me, thou little rogue Orbis.   310

Enter the EARTH.

EARTH. Who calls Terra Firma, pray?
LUNA. Luna that ne'er shines by day.
EARTH. What means Luna in a veil?
LUNA. Luna means to show her tail.
*BAYES. There's the bargain.   315

Enter SOL, *to the tune of 'Robin Hood.'*

SOL. Fie, sister, fie! thou mak'st me muse,
      Derry, derry down,
   To see the[e] Orb abuse.

---

[1] A comedy by Sir Robert Stapylton produced in 1663.
[2] The hey (hay), a popular English folk dance.

LUNA. I hope his anger 'twill not move;
Since I showed it out of love.   320
      Hey down, dery down.
EARTH. Where shall I thy true love know,
      Thou pretty, pretty Moon?
LUNA. To-morrow soon, ere it be noon —   (*Bis.*)
      On Mount Vesuvio.   325
SOL. Then I will shine.
      (*To the tune of* 'Trenchmore.')
EARTH. And I will be fine.
LUNA. And we will drink nothing but Lipari wine.
ALL. And we, etc.

(*As they dance the Hey,* BAYES *speaks.*)

*BAYES. Now the earth's before the moon; now   330 the moon's before the sun; there's the eclipse again.

*SMITH. He's mightily taken with this, I see.

*JOHNSON. Aye, 'tis so extraordinary, how can he choose?

BAYES. So, now, vanish eclipse, and enter   335 t'other battle, and fight. Here now, if I am not mistaken, you will see fighting enough.

(*A battle is fought between foot and great hobby-horses. At last,* DRAWCANSIR *comes in, and kills 'em all on both sides. All this while the battle is fighting,* BAYES *is telling them when to shout, and shouts with 'em.*)

DRAWCANSIR. Others may boast a single man to kill;
But I the blood of thousands daily spill.
Let petty kings the names of parties know: 340
Where'er I come, I slay both friend and foe.
The swiftest horsemen my swift rage controls,
And from their bodies drives their trembling souls.
If they had wings and to the gods could fly,
I would pursue, and beat 'em through the sky: 345
And make proud Jove, with all his thunder, see
This single arm more dreadful is than he.   *Exit.*

BAYES. There's a brave fellow for you now, sirs. You may talk of your Hector, and Achilles, and I know not who; but I defy all your histories,   350 and your romances, too, to show me one such conqueror as this Drawcansir.

JOHNSON. I swear, I think you may.

SMITH. But, Mr. Bayes, how shall all these dead men go off? for I see none alive to help 'em.[3]   355

BAYES. Go off! why, as they came on — upon their legs. How should they go off? Why, do you think the people here don't know they are not dead? He is mighty ignorant, poor man; your friend here is very silly, Mr. Johnson, 'y gad, he is — ha, ha, ha!   360 Come, sir, I'll show you how they shall go off. — Rise, rise, sirs, and go about your business. There's 'go off' for you now — ha, ha, ha! Mr. Ivory, a word. — Gentlemen, I'll be with you presently.   *Exit.*

JOHNSON. Will you so? then we'll be gone.   365

SMITH. Aye, prithee, let's go, that we may pre-

---

[3] Bearers were needed to clear the stage when deaths had occurred on the 'apron' projecting in front of the curtain. See the famous epilogue to *Tyrannic Love*, spoken by Nell Gwyn 'when she was to be carried off dead by the bearers.' (Cf. Summers.)

serve our hearing. One battle more will take mine
quite away. *Exeunt.*

Enter BAYES *and Players.*

BAYES. Where are the gentlemen?

1ST PLAYER. They are gone, sir. 370

BAYES. Gone! 'Sdeath, this last act is best of
all. I'll go fetch 'em again. *Exit.*

*1ST PLAYER. What shall we do, now he is gone
away?

*2D PLAYER. Why, so much the better. 375
Then let's go to dinner.

3D PLAYER. Stay, here's a foul piece of paper of
his. Let's see what 'tis.

*3D OR 4TH PLAYER. Aye, aye, come, let's hear it.

3D PLAYER *reads:* ' *The Argument of the Fifth Act:* 380

'Cloris, at length, being sensible of Prince Pretty-man's
passion, consents to marry him; but just as they are
going to church, Prince Pretty-man meeting, by chance,
with old Joan the chandler's widow, and rememb'r-
ing it was she that first brought him acquainted 385
with Cloris, out of a high point of honor breaks
off his match with Cloris and marries old Joan. Upon
which, Cloris, in despair, drowns herself: and Prince
Pretty-man, discontentedly, walks by the river side.'

[3D PLAYER.] This will never do; 'tis just like 390
the rest. Come, let's be gone.

*MOST OF THE PLAYERS. Aye, pox on't, let's go
away. *Exeunt.*

Enter BAYES.

BAYES. A plague on 'em both for me! they have
made me sweat, to run after 'em. A couple 395
of senseless rascals that had rather go to dinner than
see this play out, with a pox to 'em! What comfort
has a man to write for such dull rogues? — (*Calls*)
Come Mr. — a — Where are you, sir? come away
quick — quick! 400

Enter Stage-keeper.

STAGE-KEEPER. Sir, they are gone to dinner.

BAYES. Yes, I know the gentlemen are gone; but
I ask for the players.

386] Q1 *breaks*; Q3 *brake.*

STAGE-KEEPER. Why, an't please your worship,
sir, the players are gone to dinner, too. 405

BAYES. How! are the players gone to dinner?
'Tis impossible: the players gone to dinner! 'Y gad,
if they are, I'll make 'em know what it is to injure
a person that does 'em the honor to write for 'em,
and all that. A company of proud, conceited, 410
humorous, cross-grained persons, and all that. 'Y
gad, I'll make 'em the most contemptible, despicable,
inconsiderable persons, and all that, in the whole
world for this trick. 'Y gad, I'll be revenged on 'em;
I'll sell this play to the other house. 415

STAGE-KEEPER. Nay, good sir, don't take away
the book; you'll disappoint the company that
comes to see it acted here this afternoon.

BAYES. That's all one. I must reserve this comfort to myself—my play and I shall go together; 420
we will not part, indeed, sir.

STAGE-KEEPER. But what will the town say, sir?

BAYES. The town! Why, what care I for the
town? 'Y gad, the town has used me as scurvily as the players have done. But I'll be re- 425
venged on them too; for I'll lampoon 'em all. And
since they will not admit of my plays, they shall
know what a satirist I am. And so farewell to this
stage, 'y gad, forever. *Exit.*

Enter Players.

1ST PLAYER. Come, then, let's set up bills for 430
another play.

2D PLAYER. Aye, aye; we shall lose nothing by
this, I warrant you.

1ST PLAYER. I am of your opinion. But before
we go, let's see Haynes [1] and Shirley practise 435
the last dance; for that may serve us another time.

2D PLAYER. I'll call 'em in; I think they are but
in the tiring-room. (*The dance done.*)

1ST PLAYER. Come, come; let's go away to dinner. *Exeunt omnes.* 440

[1] Joseph Haines (d. 1701), a favorite in broad farce and,
according to Pepys, 'an incomparable dancer.'

EPILOGUE

The play is at an end, but where's the plot?
That circumstance our poet Bayes forgot,
And we can boast, though 'tis a plotting age,
No place is freer from it than the stage.
The ancients plotted, though, and strove to please 5
With sense that might be understood with ease;
They every scene with so much wit did store
That who brought any in, went out with more:
But this new way of wit does so surprise,
Men lose their wits in wond'ring where it lies. 10
If it be true that monstrous births presage
The following mischiefs that afflict the age,
And sad disasters to the state proclaim,
Plays without head or tail may do the same.
Wherefore, for ours, and for the kingdom's peace, 15
May this prodigious way of writing cease.
Let's have, at least, once in our lives, a time
When we may hear some reason, not all rhyme:
We have these ten years felt its influence;
Pray let this prove a year of prose and sense. 20

BLANK-VERSE TRAGEDY
(1677-1700)

A NEW period in the history of serious Restoration drama begins in 1677 with the deliberate turn of Dryden and Lee from rhymed heroic drama to blank-verse tragedy. After three plays in heroic verse (1674-76), Nathaniel Lee, in *The Rival Queens, or The Death of Alexander the Great* (March, 1677), reinstated blank verse as the medium of tragedy. Some months later, Dryden fulfilled in *All for Love, or The World Well Lost* (*circ.* December, 1677) his long-threatened renunciation of rhyme. In reverting to the story of *Antony and Cleopatra*, he sought, indeed, Shakespeare's substance as well as style. So, too, did Thomas Otway, who turned from high success in his rhymed heroic drama, *Don Carlos* (1676), to borrow from *Romeo and Juliet* not merely the theme but largely the poetic diction of his Roman version, *The History and Fall of Caius Marius* (1679). Dryden had commanded and mainly controlled the period of rhymed heroic drama. In the succeeding era of blank-verse tragedy he was to share with Lee and Otway the powers of a dominant triumvirate.

Of the trio, NATHANIEL LEE (1648-49?-1692) alone gave himself unstintedly to tragedy. Dryden, as during his earlier period of heroic drama, deviated at will from strictly serious drama into comedy, tragi-comedy, and opera. Otway essayed comedy, and admitted into tragedy some comic appeal. But the nondescript *Princess of Cleve* (1681) — 'this Farce, Comedy, Tragedy, or mere Play,' as the dedication puts it — is the solitary exception to Lee's fixed tragic rule. *The Rival Queens*, his first and foremost blank-verse tragedy, exhibits both the swelling diction that made his name proverbial for rant and his characteristic sense of theatrical appeal. Lee knew his actors and his audience. He gave his public what it wanted — familiar ingredients of impulsive action and declamatory passion, of pictorial display and theatrical device, and novelty enough in his departures from the conventions of rhyme and the 'happy ending' of heroic drama, and from the formal frame of its love-and-honor conflicts. For his actors he created compelling situations and speeches — ranging from passages where 'Declamation roared,' to lines as arresting and familiar as, ''Tis beauty calls, and glory shows the way,' or 'When Greeks joined Greeks, then was the tug of war.' Compounding plot materials from French heroic romance and from classical history, and freely exploiting the spectacular, whether in the Elizabethan dramatic tradition of ghosts and omens, or in the Restoration theatrical fashion of scenic ornamentation and machinery, Lee surcharged the matter and manner of tragedy, but gratified the popular taste. Despite the 'furious fustian and turgid rants' which made the judicious Colley Cibber grieve and which lent themselves readily to Fielding's mockery in *Tom Thumb*, *The Rival Queens* remained a favorite with players and playgoers throughout the eighteenth century.

A succession of other tragedies intensified Lee's qualities and defects. Increasing excesses marked and marred his life and work. His collaboration with Dryden in *Œdipus* (1678) prompted a later Restoration writer, George Granville, to ascribe 'the noble and sublime thoughts' to Dryden, 'the rants and fustian' to Lee, and to deplore popular applause of the latter as proof that 'mad men are only fit to write, when nothing is esteemed great but what is non-intelligible.' Such criticism was itself intemperate, for though it admitted perforce Lee's theatrical appeal, it sensed only the perversion, and not the random inspiration, of his true poetic powers. The Goddess of Unreason, it is true, marked him for her own. Whom she would destroy, she first made mad. The 'ungoverned fancy' of Lee's later tragedies, tainted with morbid brooding on the inroads of insanity, had its literal counterpart in the growing disorders of the brain of 'the mad poet.' His poet's eye in a fine frenzy rolled, kindling at times with almost Elizabethan fire, but often con-

founding ecstasy with extravagance.   In his own person and in the personages of his mimic stage,
the drama of life distorted by excess moved inevitably to a tragic close.   That way madness lies,
as Lee found to his cost.   Doubtless, in the case of Lee, logic rests not with the disordered author,
but with the critics who have abundantly proved his transgressions.   But it is not irrational to
recognize, as did his contemporary Wycherley, that Lee had the qualities of his defects — 'high
flights, above all common sense,' as well as mere rant — method enough, in his madness, to lash
'the madder Age' — the ability to hold, as well as to bewilder, his 'staring audience' — and, in
his 'poetic rage,' the implication of poetic power, as well as of its tragic abuse.

In contrast with Lee, the Dryden of *All for Love* seems to restore sanity and order to drama.
In the last of his rhymed heroic dramas, *Aureng-Zebe* (1675), he had largely curbed his earlier
excesses.   Now, in *All for Love*, he deliberately put off the armor and the accent of the heroic
warrior.   'He fights this day unarmed,' as the Prologue heralds, 'without his rhyme'; and his
hero 'Bates of his mettle, and scarce rants at all . . . Weeps much; fights little; but is wondrous
kind.'   In substituting blank verse for rhyme, and Antony for Almanzor, Dryden openly imitated
Shakespeare, and rightly felt that he had thereby excelled himself.   In *All for Love*, the only play
he had written to please himself, Dryden found freedom from rhyme and rhetoric.   His self-
imposed restraint of language helped, in reality, to liberate his poetic utterance.   But the Restoration mind neither could nor would recapture the careless Elizabethan rapture.   Even Dryden,
whose instinctive love of Shakespeare often rose superior to the critical compunctions of his age,
was never free from its form and pressure.   Judging even the 'divine Shakespeare' of his adoption 'deficient in the mechanic beauties of plot,' Dryden imposed upon his drama the limitations
of pseudo-classical tragedy — observance of the dramatic unities and of due order and decorum.
In limiting the scene to Alexandria, the time to the fatal final day, and the action to a relatively
small group of characters, Dryden gained simplicity at the cost of Shakespeare's infinite variety,
and concentration at the cost of comprehensive vision.   Obviously, the world was not well lost
in exchanging Shakespeare's imperial empire for Dryden's narrowed circle.   But there is individuality, not mere imitation, in Dryden's treatment.   If he unhappily banished Shakespeare's
Enobarbus from the boards, he created his own Ventidius, and in the opening act gave to him
the memorable scene with Antony which particularly delighted the author, and has continued to
delight his critics.

All for Love invites inevitable Shakespearean comparisons, but its challenge was to the prevalent practices of Dryden's own age.   Many Restoration playwrights — Dryden himself among
them — had previously perverted and pilfered Shakespeare wantonly.   In *All for Love*, Dryden
approached the master as a disciple, and in a new spirit of ardent devotion and of sincere, though
partly uncomprehending, appreciation.   In a literal sense he did not restore to Shakespeare his
full rights on the English stage, since his own play replaced *Antony and Cleopatra* for a century
and more.   But he did restore to the Restoration theatre the conception of genuine tragedy which
his own heroic dramas had helped to obscure, and he restored to blank verse the traditional authority which his own heroic couplets had helped to discredit.   Once again, and this time in a better
cause, Dryden demonstrated to his own age his potent leadership in drama.

Of his later tragedies, the best is *Don Sebastian* (1690).   In individual scenes or passages of
dialogue and in some of its characterizations, it shows that Dryden had not exhausted his tragic
vein.   Walter Scott, Dryden's early editor, insistently pronounced it Dryden's dramatic masterpiece, but failed to shake the settled preference of critics, early and late, for *All for Love*.   In *Don
Sebastian* the partial use of prose and a lean admixture of comic element broaden the methods
without enlarging the effective powers of Restoration blank-verse tragedy.   In consistent strength
and totality of impression, the advantage lies with *All for Love*.   An intervening tragi-comedy,
The Spanish Friar (1681), shows firmer handling of the elements of comic contrast than Dryden

attained within his wavering definition of the scope of tragedy itself. The best of his comedies and tragi-comedies show more aptitude for comedy than he realized. But his own conviction of inferiority in that regard may account for his uneasiness when he tried to vary the straight pattern and stretch the close-knit fabric which, as *All for Love* attests, best suited him in tragedy. Like Lee, Dryden is best remembered by his first and foremost blank-verse tragedy.

THOMAS OTWAY (1652–1685), whose life and dramatic work run closely parallel with Lee's, followed the still prevalent fashion of rhyme in three early dramas (1675–77), and then the example of Lee and Dryden in the turn to blank-verse tragedy. More particularly he followed Dryden in selecting as his model a definite Shakespearean tragedy. Dryden's 'imitation' of *Antony and Cleopatra*, however, is far more independent than Otway's direct borrowing from *Romeo and Juliet* of much of the poetic dialogue as well as of the plot for *The History and Fall of Caius Marius* (1679). Otway's confession that he 'has rifled' Shakespeare 'of half a play' exaggerates the actual ratio of borrowed lines, but his fears that he 'has done him wrong' are well founded. Variations in the manipulation of plot, characters, and comic elements are many, and his touch is not masterful.

With *The Orphan* (1680), Otway found his true field and entered it as master. In this domestic tragedy he struck straight to the heart. His theme is simple, his emotion intense. Neglecting the customary trappings of aristocratic tragedy, he is wholly absorbed with the poignancy of human suffering. The misunderstandings of twin brothers, Castalio and Polydore, rivals for the love of the orphan Monimia, move with compelling power to their fatal end. In the pathos of the tragedy of the innocent victim, Monimia, the natural sympathies of 'tender Otway' find at last full expression.

Venice Preserved (1682), by common consent Otway's masterpiece, confirms his mastery of the appeal to pity. In outward appearance, the drama resumes aspects of aristocratic tragedy which had been set aside in *The Orphan*. The main subject is derived from the Abbé de St. Réal's historical romance, *La Conjuration des Espagnols contre la République de Venise en l'année 1618*, but the foreign setting and remote time fail to exclude intrusions of the local color of contemporary English politics. The Venetian conspiracy is brought home to Otway's London audience by thinly veiled allusions to the 'Popish Plot.' In name and in general semblance, the Antonio of *Venice Preserved* intentionally suggests Anthony Ashley Cooper, Earl of Shaftesbury, the Whig leader whose political agitations had fomented Tory resentment and had led in the previous year (1681) to his arrest and temporary imprisonment on the charge of high treason. Prologue and play pointedly refer to Shaftesbury's ambition to become King of Poland, to his exact age, sixty-one, and to his garrulity, and the farcical scenes of the sub-plot descend to gross personal and political caricature.

Other formative influences besides those of Venetian history and English politics are discernible in the structure and style of *Venice Preserved*. The classical influence is recalled in the general attitude towards the unities of time and place, but the animating spirit is not so much deference to dramatic precept as instinct for dramatic art. Within the brief compass of allotted time, events march breathlessly to the fatal catastrophe. Within the limits of Venice, the lesser shifts of scene give sufficient range and variety, without disturbing the close concentration of the unfolding tragedy. Again, the list of *Dramatis Personæ*, far more extensive than in *The Orphan*, points superficially to the resumption of the broader constituency of characters familiar in historical drama, while the title of the play accentuates the fate of the Venetian state rather than of its individual members. But, in deeper reality, action centers, as in *The Orphan*, in three characters and tragedy remains domestic. Still another formative influence on *Venice Preserved* is that of Shakespeare's tragedies, notably *Othello* and *Julius Cæsar*. Otway's drama opens on the Venetian scene and vividly recalls the relations of Brabantio, Desdemona, and Othello. In developing the theme of conspiracy it recalls as distinctly the individual relations and conflicts of Cassius, Brutus, and Portia. But Otway's inept Shakespearean borrowings and revisions in *Caius Marius* have given way to evidences of truer contagion with the master's spirit.

Beneath many changes in outward form, *Venice Preserved* retains the same fundamental appeal to simple human sympathies which allies *The Orphan* with domestic tragedy.   Above and beyond the general issues to the Venetian state and to the conspiracy against it, rise the issues of life and death that confront the irresolute Jaffeir, torn between the tender entreaties of his wife, Belvidera, and the stern admonitions of his friend, Pierre. The old conflict of love and honor is still supreme, but Otway's tragedy invokes neither the magniloquent accent nor the happy issue of heroic drama. His eloquence is from the heart, his appeal is to compassion. Belvidera is his own creation, his final incarnation alike of his characteristic type of heroine and of his own sensitive spirit. She is akin to the queen in *Don Carlos* and to Monimia, a new embodiment of Otway's compelling sense of sympathy. The Queen Anne dramatist Nicholas Rowe characterized his own dramas as 'She-Tragedies,' but Thomas Otway had already anticipated and interpreted with finer instinct and art the appeal to pity of the tragic heroine.

The half-decade (1677–1682) that had included Lee's *Rival Queens*, Dryden's *All for Love*, and Otway's *The Orphan* and *Venice Preserved* had turned the current decisively from rhymed heroic drama to blank-verse tragedy. In contrast, the following decades lack the initial impetus and the fresh vigor of the early leaders of the new period. Succeeding dramatists, like John Banks and Thomas Southerne, follow largely the stream of tendencies already set in motion in the emotional tragedy of Otway. If the main themes of Banks's tragedies are notably drawn from English history, their treatment accentuates the notes of pathos and sentiment. In the successive choice of Anna Bullen, Mary, Queen of Scotland, and Lady Jane Grey, as heroines, Banks continues Otway's dominant stress on the dire distresses and fatal catastrophes of woman. Southerne's outstanding serious dramas — *The Fatal Marriage, or The Innocent Adultery* (1694) and *Oroonoko* (1696) — are likewise akin to Otway's softened emotional tragedy in their insistent pathetic appeal. In enforcing the development of domestic tragedy, and in marshalling to its aid the rising forces of the drama of sentiment and sensibility, Southerne caught up and concentrated his inheritance from Otway and carried over well into the eighteenth century the impress of his own incessant dramatic productivity. He is thus a highly significant influence in the transition from Otway's tragedy of pity and pathos to the sentimental tragedy of the eighteenth century.

G. H. N.

REFERENCE WORKS

1914. Nettleton, George H. *English Drama of the Restoration and Eighteenth Century.* [Especially chapter VI.]

1923. Nicoll, Allardyce. *A History of Restoration Drama 1660–1700.* Cambridge. [Especially pp. 131–145, 152–158.] (Revised edition, 1928.)

1929. Dobrée, Bonamy. *Restoration Tragedy 1660–1720.* Oxford.

1931. Ham, Roswell G. *Otway and Lee; biography from a baroque age.* New Haven (Yale University Press).

1933. Dodds, John W. *Thomas Southerne, dramatist.* New Haven (Yale University Press).

All for Love; or, The World Well Lost

BY JOHN DRYDEN

ALL FOR LOVE:

OR, THE

World well Loſt.

A

TRAGEDY,

As it is Acted at the

THEATRE-ROYAL;

And Written in Imitation of *Shakeſpeare*'s Stile.

By *John Dryden*, Servant to His Majeſty.

Facile eſt verbum aliquod ardens (ut ita dicam) notare : idque reſtinctis animorum incendiis irridere. Cicero.

In the *SAVOY*:

Printed by *Tho. Newcomb*, for *Henry Herringman*, at the Blew Anchor in the Lower Walk of the *New-Exchange*. 1 6 7 8.

TITLE-PAGE OF THE FIRST QUARTO

PREFACE

THE death of Antony and Cleopatra is a subject which has been treated by the greatest wits of our nation,[1] after Shakespeare; and by all so variously, that their example has given me the confidence to try myself in this bow of Ulysses amongst the crowd of suitors; and, withal, to take my own measures, in aiming at the mark. I doubt not but the same motive has prevailed with all of us in this attempt; I mean the excellency of the moral: for the chief persons represented were famous patterns of unlawful love; and their end accordingly was unfortunate. All reasonable men have long since concluded, that the hero of the poem ought not to be a character of perfect virtue, for then he could not, without injustice, be made unhappy; nor yet altogether wicked, because he could not then be pitied. I have therefore steered the middle course; and have drawn the character of Antony as favorably as Plutarch, Appian, and Dion Cassius would give me leave; the like I have observed in Cleopatra. That which is wanting to work up the pity to a greater height was not afforded me by the story; for the crimes of love which they both committed were not occasioned by any necessity, or fatal ignorance, but were wholly voluntary; since our passions are, or ought to be, within our power. The fabric of the play is regular enough, as to the inferior parts of it; and the unities of time, place, and action, more exactly observed than, perhaps, the English theatre requires. Particularly, the action is so much one, that it is the only of the kind without episode, or underplot; every scene in the tragedy conducing to the main design, and every act concluding with a turn of it. The greatest error in the contrivance seems to be in the person of Octavia; for, though I might use the privilege of a poet, to introduce her into Alexandria, yet I had not enough considered that the compassion she moved to herself and children was destructive to that which I reserved for Antony and Cleopatra; whose mutual love being founded upon vice, must lessen the favor of the audience to them, when virtue and innocence were oppressed by it. And, though I justified Antony in some measure, by making Octavia's departure to proceed wholly from herself, yet the force of the first machine[2] still remained; and the dividing of pity, like the cutting of a river into many channels, abated the strength of the natural stream. But this is an objection which none of my critics have urged against me; and therefore I might have let it pass, if I could have resolved to have been partial to myself. The faults my enemies have found are rather cavils concerning little and not essential decencies; which a master of the ceremonies may decide betwixt us. The French poets, I confess, are strict observers of these punctilios. They would not, for example, have suffered Cleopatra and Octavia to have met; or, if they had met, there must only have passed betwixt them some cold civilities, but no eagerness of repartee, for fear of offending against the greatness of their characters, and the modesty of their sex. This objection I foresaw, and at the same time contemned; for I judged it both natural and probable that Octavia, proud of her new-gained conquest, would search out Cleopatra to triumph over her; and that Cleopatra, thus attacked, was not of a spirit to shun the encounter. And 'tis not unlikely that two exasperated rivals should use such satire as I have put into their mouths; for, after all, though the one were a Roman, and the other a queen, they were both women. 'Tis true, some actions, though natural, are not fit to be represented; and broad obscenities in words ought in good manners to be avoided: expressions therefore are a modest clothing of our thoughts, as breeches and petticoats are of our bodies. If I have kept myself within the bounds of modesty, all beyond it is but nicety and affectation; which is no more but modesty depraved into a vice. They betray themselves who are too quick of apprehension in such cases, and leave all reasonable men to imagine worse of them, than of the poet.

Honest Montaigne[3] goes yet farther: *Nous ne sommes que cérémonie; la cérémonie nous emporte, et laissons la substance des choses. Nous nous tenons aux branches, et abandonnons le tronc et le corps. Nous avons appris aux dames de rougir, oyans seulement nommer ce qu'elles ne craignent aucunement à faire: Nous n'osons appeller à droit nos membres, et ne craignons pas de les employer à toute sorte de débauche. La cérémonie nous défend d'exprimer par paroles les choses licites et naturelles, et nous l'en croyons; la raison nous défend de n'en faire point d'illicites et mauvaises, et personne ne l'en croit.*[4] My comfort is, that by this opinion my enemies are but sucking critics, who would fain be nibbling ere their teeth are come.

---

[1] Sir Charles Sedley's *Antony and Cleopatra* (Feb., 1677) had recently appeared. Various Elizabethan and Restoration versions attest the popularity of the dramatic subject.

[2] Dramatic contrivance.   [3] *Essais*, II, 17.

[4] 'We are naught but ceremony; ceremony sweeps us away and we let go the substance of things. We cling to the branches and abandon the trunk and body. We have taught ladies to blush at the mere mention of what they are not at all afraid to do. We dare not call our members by their right names, and yet we are not afraid to use them in all sorts of debauchery. Ceremony forbids us to express in words things lawful and natural, and to it we trust; reason forbids us to do anything illicit or bad, and yet nobody trusts to reason.'

Yet, in this nicety of manners does the excellency of French poetry consist; their heroes are the most civil people breathing; but their good breeding seldom extends to a word of sense. All their wit is in their ceremony; they want the genius which animates our stage; and therefore 'tis but necessary, when they cannot please, that they should take care not to offend. But as the civilest man in the company is commonly the dullest, so these authors, while they are afraid to make you laugh or cry, out of pure good manners make you sleep. They are so careful not to exasperate a critic, that they never leave him any work; so busy with the broom, and make so clean a riddance, that there is little left either for censure or for praise: for no part of a poem is worth our discommending, where the whole is insipid; as when we have once tasted of palled [1] wine, we stay not to examine it glass by glass. But while they affect to shine in trifles, they are often careless in essentials. Thus, their Hippolytus [2] is so scrupulous in point of decency, that he will rather expose himself to death, than accuse his stepmother to his father; and my critics I am sure will commend him for it: but we of grosser apprehensions are apt to think that this excess of generosity is not practicable but with fools and madmen. This was good manners with a vengeance; and the audience is like to be much concerned at the misfortunes of this admirable hero: but take Hippolytus out of his poetic fit, and I suppose he would think it a wiser part to set the saddle on the right horse, and choose rather to live with the reputation of a plain-spoken, honest man, than to die with the infamy of an incestuous villain. In the meantime we may take notice, that where the poet ought to have preserved the character as it was delivered to us by antiquity, when he should have given us the picture of a rough young man, of the Amazonian strain, a jolly huntsman, and both by his profession and his early rising a mortal enemy to love, he has chosen to give him the turn of gallantry, sent him to travel from Athens to Paris, taught him to make love, and transformed the Hippolytus of Euripides into Monsieur Hippolyte. I should not have troubled myself thus far with French poets, but that I find our *Chedreux* [3] critics wholly form their judgments by them. But for my part, I desire to be tried by the laws of my own country; for it seems unjust to me, that the French should prescribe here, till they have conquered. Our little sonneteers, who follow them, have too narrow souls to judge of poetry. Poets themselves are the most proper, though I conclude not the only critics. But till some genius as universal as Aristotle shall arise, one * who can penetrate into all arts and sciences, without the practice of them, I shall think it reasonable that the judgment of an artificer in his own art should be preferable to the opinion of another man; at least where he is not bribed by interest, or prejudiced by malice. And this, I suppose, is manifest by plain induction: for, first, the crowd cannot be presumed to have more than a gross instinct of what pleases or displeases them. Every man will grant me this; but then, by a particular kindness to himself, he draws his own stake first,[4] and will be distinguished from the multitude, of which other men may think him one. But, if I come closer to those who are allowed for witty men,[5] either by the advantage of their quality, or by common fame, and affirm that neither are they qualified to decide sovereignly concerning poetry, I shall yet have a strong party of my opinion; for most of them severally will exclude the rest, either from the number of witty men, or at least of able judges. But here again they are all indulgent to themselves; and every one who believes himself a wit, that is, every man, will pretend at the same time to a right of judging. But to press it yet further, there are many witty men, but few poets; neither have all poets a taste of tragedy. And this is the rock on which they are daily splitting. Poetry, which is a picture of nature, must generally please; but 'tis not to be understood that all parts of it must please every man; therefore is not tragedy to be judged by a witty man whose taste is only confined to comedy. Nor is every man who loves tragedy a sufficient judge of it: he must understand the excellencies of it too, or he will only prove a blind admirer, not a critic. From hence it comes that so many satires on poets, and censures of their writings, fly abroad. Men of pleasant conversation (at least esteemed so), and endued with a trifling kind of fancy, perhaps helped out with some smattering of Latin, are ambitious to distinguish themselves from the herd of gentlemen, by their poetry —

Rarus enim fermè sensus communis in illâ
Fortunâ.[6]

And is not this a wretched affectation, not to be contented with what fortune has done for them, and sit down quietly with their estates, but they must call their wits in question, and needlessly expose their nakedness to public view? Not considering that they are not to expect the same approbation from sober men, which they have found from their flatterers after the third bottle? If a little glittering in discourse

---

[1] Stale.   [2] Racine's *Phèdre* (1677) had just appeared.
[3] Fashionable periwig (hence 'modish' critics).   [4] Exempts himself (withdraws his own wager).
[5] Pointed especially at Rochester, Dryden's former patron, but subsequent satirist.
[6] 'For common sense is rare in that station of life.' Juvenal, *Satires*, VIII, 73–74.

* Q2Q3F omit *one* after *arise*.

has passed them on us for witty men, where was the necessity of undeceiving the world? Would a man who has an ill title to an estate, but yet is in possession of it, would he bring it of his own accord to be tried at Westminster? We who write, if we want the talent, yet have the excuse that we do it for a poor subsistence; but what can be urged in their defence, who, not having the vocation of poverty to scribble, out of mere wantonness take pains to make themselves ridiculous? Horace was certainly in the right where he said [1] that 'no man is satisfied with his own condition.' A poet is not pleased, because he is not rich; and the rich are discontented, because the poets will not admit them of their number. Thus the case is hard with writers: if they succeed not, they must starve; and if they do, some malicious satire is prepared to level them for daring to please without their leave. But while they are so eager to destroy the fame of others, their ambition is manifest in their concernment: some poem of their own is to be produced, and the slaves are to be laid flat with their faces on the ground, that the monarch may appear in the greater majesty.

Dionysius and Nero had the same longings, but with all their power they could never bring their business well about. 'Tis true, they proclaimed themselves poets by sound of trumpet; and poets they were, upon pain of death to any man who durst call them otherwise. The audience had a fine time on't, you may imagine; they sate in a bodily fear, and looked as demurely as they could: for 'twas a hanging matter to laugh unseasonably; and the tyrants were suspicious, as they had reason, that their subjects had 'em in the wind; so, every man, in his own defence, set as good a face upon the business as he could. 'Twas known beforehand that the monarchs were to be crowned laureates; but when the show was over, and an honest man was suffered to depart quietly, he took out his laughter which he had stifled, with a firm resolution never more to see an emperor's play, though he had been ten years a-making it. In the meantime the true poets were they who made the best markets, for they had wit enough to yield the prize with a good grace, and not contend with him who had thirty legions.[2] They were sure to be rewarded, if they confessed themselves bad writers, and that was somewhat better than to be martyrs for their reputation. Lucan's example was enough to teach them manners; and after he was put to death, for overcoming Nero, the emperor carried it without dispute for the best poet in his dominions. No man was ambitious of that grinning honor; for if he heard the malicious trumpeter proclaiming his name before his betters, he knew there was but one way with him. Mæcenas took another course, and we know he was more than a great man, for he was witty too: but finding himself far gone in poetry, which Seneca assures us was not his talent, he thought it his best way to be well with Virgil and with Horace; that at least he might be a poet at the second hand; and we see how happily it has succeeded with him; for his own bad poetry is forgotten, and their panegyrics of him still remain. But they who should be our patrons are for no such expensive ways to fame; they have much of the poetry of Mæcenas, but little of his liberality. They are for persecuting Horace and Virgil,* in the persons of their successors (for such is every man who has any part of their soul and fire, though in a less degree). Some of their little zanies [3] yet go farther; for they are persecutors even of Horace himself, as far as they are able, by their ignorant and vile imitations of him; [4] by making an unjust use of his authority, and turning his artillery against his friends. But how would he disdain to be copied by such hands! I dare answer for him, he would be more uneasy in their company, than he was with Crispinus, their forefather, in the Holy Way; [5] and would no more have allowed them a place amongst the critics, than he would Demetrius the mimic, and Tigellius the buffoon;

—— *Demetri, teque, Tigelli,*
Discipulorum inter jubeo plorare cathedras.[6]

With what scorn would he look down on such miserable translators, who make dogg'rel of his Latin, mistake his meaning, misapply his censures, and often contradict their own? He is fixed as a landmark to set out the bounds of poetry, —

—— *Saxum antiquum ingens,* —
Limes agro positus, litem ut discerneret arvis.[7]

---

[1] *Satires,* I, i, 1–3.
[2] Montaigne (*Essais*) and Bacon (*Apophthegms*) had made familiar the story found in Spartianus, *Life of Hadrian*, XV, of the philosopher who, when reproached for disputing but weakly with the Emperor, rejoined: 'Why, would you have me contend with him that commands thirty legions?'
[3] Attendant mimics.
[4] Dryden here retaliates for Rochester's ridicule in his *Allusion to the Tenth Satire of the First Book of Horace.*
[5] *Via Sacra,* in Rome.
[6] 'Demetrius, and you, Tigellius, I bid you whine in the midst of your pupils' easy chairs.' Dryden points his retort by quoting Horace's Tenth Satire (see preceding ftn. 4). He alters the feminine *discipularum* to the masculine.
[7] Dryden's translation of the *Æneid* (XII, 897–898) reads:
An antique stone he saw, the common bound
Of neighb'ring fields, and barrier of the ground.

---

* QQ *for* persecuting Horace and Virgil; F *for* procuring themselves reputation.

But other arms than theirs, and other sinews are required, to raise the weight of such an author; and when they would toss him against their enemies —

> *Genua labant, gelidus concrevit frigore sanguis.*
> *Tum lapis ipse viri vacuum per inane volutus,*
> *Nec spatium evasit totum, nec pertulit ictum.*[1]

For my part, I would wish no other revenge, either for myself, or the rest of the poets, from this rhyming judge of the twelve-penny gallery, this legitimate son of Sternhold,[2] than that he would subscribe his name to his censure, or (not to tax him beyond his learning) set his mark. For, should he own himself publicly, and come from behind the lion's skin, they whom he condemns would be thankful to him, they whom he praises would choose to be condemned; and the magistrates whom he has elected would modestly withdraw from their employment, to avoid the scandal of his nomination. The sharpness of his satire, next to himself, falls most heavily on his friends, and they ought never to forgive him for commending them perpetually the wrong way, and sometimes by contraries. If he have a friend whose hastiness in writing is his greatest fault, Horace would have taught him to have minced the matter, and to have called it readiness of thought, and a flowing fancy; for friendship will allow a man to christen an imperfection by the name of some neighbor virtue:

> *Vellem in amicitiâ sic erraremus; et isti*
> *Errori nomen virtus posuisset honestum.*[3]

But he would never have allowed him to have called a slow man hasty, or a hasty writer a slow [4] drudge, as Juvenal explains it:

> ——— *Canibus pigris, scabieque vetustâ*
> *Levibus,*[*] *et siccæ lambentibus ora lucernæ,*
> *Nomen erit Pardus, Tigris, Leo; si quid adhuc est*
> *Quod fremit in terris violentius.*[5]

Yet Lucretius laughs at a foolish lover, even for excusing the imperfections of his mistress:

> *Nigra μελίχροοs est, immunda et fœtida ἄκοσμοs.*
> *Balba loqui non quit, τραυλίζει; muta pudens est,* etc.[6]

But to drive it *ad Æthiopem cygnum* [7] is not to be endured. I leave him to interpret this by the benefit of his French version on the other side, and without farther considering him, than I have the rest of my illiterate censors, whom I have disdained to answer, because they are not qualified for judges. It remains that I acquaint the reader, that I have endeavored in this play to follow the practice of the ancients, who, as Mr. Rymer [8] has judiciously observed, are and ought to be our masters. Horace likewise gives it for a rule in his art of poetry,

> ——— *Vos exemplaria Græca*
> *Nocturnâ versate manu, versate diurnâ.*[9]

Yet, though their models are regular, they are too little for English tragedy; which requires to be built in a larger compass. I could give an instance in the *Œdipus Tyrannus*, which was the masterpiece of Sophocles;

---

[1] Dryden's translation of the *Æneid* (XII, 905–907) reads:

> His knocking knees are bent beneath the load,
> And shiv'ring cold congeals his vital blood.
> The stone drops from his arms, and, falling short
> For want of vigor, mocks his vain effort.

[2] Thomas Sternhold, who, with John Hopkins and others, made a popular metrical version of the *Psalms*, is held up to ridicule in Dryden's *Religio Laici* and *Absalom and Achitophel*.

[3] 'Would that in friendship we could make the like mistake, and that on such mistake good sense had conferred an honorable name.' Horace, *Satires*, I, iii, 41–42.

[4] Rochester in his *Allusion* speaks of 'hasty Shadwell and slow Wycherley.'

[5] 'Lazy curs, hairless from inveterate mange, and licking the edges of a dry lamp, shall be named Panther, Tiger, Lion, or whatever else roars more furiously in the world.' Juvenal, *Satires*, VIII, 34–37.

[6] In his *Second Poetical Miscellany*, Dryden freely renders these lines of Lucretius (*De Rerum Natura*, IV, 1160, 1164) thus:

> 'The sallow skin is for the swarthy put,
> And love can make a slattern of a slut.
> . . . .
> She stammers: O, what grace in lisping lies!
> If she says nothing, to be sure she's wise.'

[7] 'To the point of calling an Ethiopian a swan.' Adapted from Juvenal, *Satires*, VIII, 33.

[8] Thomas Rymer's *Tragedies of the Last Age Considered* appeared in 1678, the year when *All for Love* was first printed.

[9] 'Study, night and day, your Greek models.' Horace, *Ars Poetica*, 268–269.

[*] Qr *Lævibus;* Q2Q3 correct to *Levibus.*

but I reserve it for a more fit occasion, which I hope to have hereafter.[1] In my style, I have professed to imitate the divine Shakespeare; which that I might perform more freely, I have disencumbered myself from rhyme. Not that I condemn my former way, but that this is more proper to my present purpose. I hope I need not to explain myself, that I have not copied my author servilely: words and phrases must of necessity receive a change in succeeding ages: but 'tis almost a miracle that much of his language remains so pure; and that he who began dramatic poetry amongst us, untaught by any, and as Ben Jonson[2] tells us, without learning, should by the force of his own genius perform so much, that in a manner he has left no praise for any who come after him. The occasion is fair, and the subject would be pleasant to handle the difference of styles betwixt him and Fletcher, and wherein, and how far they are both to be imitated. But since I must not be over-confident of my own performance after him, it will be prudence in me to be silent. Yet I hope I may affirm, and without vanity, that, by imitating him, I have excelled myself throughout the play; and particularly, that I prefer the scene betwixt Antony and Ventidius in the first act, to anything which I have written in this kind.

[1] In 1678 Dryden collaborated with Lee in an English *Œdipus*, enlarged by an underplot.
[2] See Jonson's tribute *To the Memory of My Beloved Master William Shakespeare*.

PROLOGUE

What flocks of critics hover here today,
As vultures wait on armies for their prey,
All gaping for the carcass of a play!
With croaking notes they bode some dire event,
And follow dying poets by the scent.   5
Ours gives himself for gone; y' have watched your time!
He fights this day unarmed — without his rhyme; —[1]
And brings a tale which often has been told,
As sad as Dido's; and almost as old.
His hero, whom you wits his bully call,   10
Bates of his mettle, and scarce rants at all:[2]
He's somewhat lewd; but a well-meaning mind;
Weeps much; fights little; but is wondrous kind.
In short, a pattern, and companion fit,
For all the keeping Tonies[3] of the pit.   15
I could name more: a wife, and mistress too;
Both (to be plain) too good for most of you:
The wife well-natured, and the mistress true.
Now, poets, if your fame has been his care,
Allow him all the candor you can spare.   20
A brave man scorns to quarrel once a day;
Like Hectors[4] in at every petty fray.
Let those find fault whose wit's so very small,
They've need to show that they can think at all:
Errors like straws upon the surface flow;   25
He who would search for pearls must dive below.
Fops may have leave to level all they can,
As pigmies would be glad to lop a man.
Half-wits are fleas; so little and so light,
We scarce could know they live, but that they bite.   30
But, as the rich, when tired with daily feasts,
For change, become their next poor tenant's guests;
Drink hearty draughts of ale from plain brown bowls,
And snatch the homely rasher from the coals:
So you, retiring from much better cheer,   35
For once, may venture to do penance here.
And since that plenteous autumn now is past,
Whose grapes and peaches have indulged your taste,
Take in good part, from our poor poet's board,
Such rivelled[5] fruits as winter can afford.   40

---

[1] In *All for Love* Dryden abandons his 'long-loved mistress, Rhyme' for blank verse.
[2] Dryden's Antony abates the bombast of previous 'heroic drama.'
[3] Simpletons (with an added play on Antony's name).
[4] A current term for London street-brawlers, like the later 'Mohocks.'
[5] Shrivelled.

PERSONS REPRESENTED

MARK ANTONY.[1]
VENTIDIUS, *his general.*
DOLABELLA,[1] *his friend.*
ALEXAS, *the Queen's eunuch.*
SERAPION, *Priest of Isis.*
[MYRIS,] [2] *another priest.*
Servants to Antony.

CLEOPATRA, *Queen of Egypt.*
OCTAVIA, *Antony's wife.*
CHARMION, } *Cleopatra's maids.*
IRAS,
Antony's two little daughters.

SCENE — ALEXANDRIA.

[TIME, 30 B.C.]

[1] For variants in spelling see Textual Notes, pp. 925–927.
[2] Supplied from the opening stage direction, I. 1.

ALL FOR LOVE;

OR,

THE WORLD WELL LOST

By JOHN DRYDEN

ACT I

SCENE [I]

The Temple of Isis.

Enter SERAPION, MYRIS, *Priests of Isis.*

SERAP. Portents and prodigies are grown so fre-
quent,
That they have lost their name. Our fruitful Nile
Flowed ere the wonted season, with a torrent
So unexpected, and so wondrous fierce,
That the wild deluge overtook the haste   5
Ev'n of the hinds that watched it: men and beasts
Were borne above the tops of trees, that grew
On th' utmost margin of the water-mark.
Then, with so swift an ebb the flood drove back-
ward,
It slipt from underneath the scaly herd: 10
Here monstrous phocæ[1] panted on the shore;
Forsaken dolphins there, with their broad tails,
Lay lashing the departing waves: hard by 'em,
Sea-horses flound'ring in the slimy mud,
Tossed up their heads, and dashed the ooze about
'em.   15

Enter ALEXAS *behind them.*

MYR. Avert these omens, heav'n!
SERAP. Last night, between the hours of twelve
and one,
In a lone aisle o' th' temple while I walked,
A whirlwind rose, that, with a violent blast,
Shook all the dome: the doors around me clapt;   20
The iron wicket, that defends the vault,
Where the long race of Ptolemies is laid,
Burst open, and disclosed the mighty dead.
From out each monument, in order placed,
An armèd ghost start[2] up: the boy-king[3] last   25
Reared his inglorious head. A peal of groans
Then followed, and a lamentable voice
Cried, 'Egypt is no more!' My blood ran back,
My shaking knees against each other knocked;
On the cold pavement down I fell entranced,   30
And so unfinished left the horrid scene.

---

[1] Seals.   [2] Started (old form of preterite).
[3] Cleopatra's brother.

ALEX. (*showing himself*). And dreamed you this?
or did invent the story,
To frighten our Egyptian boys withal,
And train 'em up betimes in fear of priesthood?
SERAP. My lord, I saw you not,   35
Nor meant my words should reach your ears; but
what
I uttered was most true.
ALEX.   A foolish dream,
Bred from the fumes of indigested feasts,
And holy luxury.
SERAP.   I know my duty:
This goes no farther.
ALEX.   'Tis not fit it should;   40
Nor would the times now bear it, were it true.
All southern, from yon hills, the Roman camp
Hangs o'er us black and threat'ning, like a storm
Just breaking on our heads.
SERAP. Our faint Egyptians pray for Antony;   45
But in their servile hearts they own Octavius.
MYR. Why then does Antony dream out his hours,
And tempts not fortune for a noble day
Which might redeem what Actium[4] lost?
ALEX. He thinks 'tis past recovery.
SERAP.   Yet the foe   50
Seems not to press the siege.
ALEX.   Oh, there's the wonder.
Mæcenas and Agrippa, who can[5] most
With Cæsar, are his foes. His wife Octavia,
Driv'n from his house, solicits her revenge;
And Dolabella, who was once his friend,   55
Upon some private grudge now seeks his ruin:
Yet still war seems on either side to sleep.
SERAP. 'Tis strange that Antony, for some days
past,
Has not beheld the face of Cleopatra;
But here, in Isis' temple, lives retired,   60
And makes his heart a prey to black despair.
ALEX. 'Tis true; and we much fear he hopes by
absence
To cure his mind of love.
SERAP.   If he be vanquished,

---

[4] The scene of Antony's defeat, by Octavius, in 31 B.C.
[5] Can accomplish (archaic, absolute use of *can*).

1] S silently changes *are* to *have*.   25] QQ *start*; FS *starts* (violating the sequence of past tenses).

Or make his peace, Egypt is doomed to be
A Roman province; and our plenteous harvests   65
Must then redeem the scarceness of their soil.
While Antony stood firm, our Alexandria
Rivalled proud Rome (dominion's other seat),
And Fortune striding, like a vast Colossus,
Could fix an equal foot of empire here.   70
   ALEX. Had I my wish, these tyrants of all na-
    ture
Who lord it o'er mankind, should perish — perish,
Each by the other's sword; but, since our will
Is lamely followed by our pow'r, we must
Depend on one, with him to rise or fall.   75
   SERAP. How stands the queen affected?
   ALEX.   Oh, she dotes,
She dotes, Serapion, on this vanquished man,
And winds herself about his mighty ruins;
Whom would she yet forsake, yet yield him up,
This hunted prey, to his pursuers' hands,   80
She might preserve us all; but 'tis in vain —
This changes my designs, this blasts my counsels,
And makes me use all means to keep him here,
Whom I could wish divided from her arms
Far as the earth's deep center. Well, you know   85
The state of things; no more of your ill omens
And black prognostics; labor to confirm
The people's hearts.

Enter VENTIDIUS, *talking aside with a Gentleman of*
    ANTONY'S.
   SERAP.   These Romans will o'erhear us.
But, who's that stranger? By his warlike port,
His fierce demeanor, and erected look,   90
He's of no vulgar note.
   ALEX.   Oh, 'tis Ventidius,
Our emp'ror's great lieutenant in the East,
Who first showed Rome that Parthia could be con-
    quered.
When Antony returned from Syria last,
He left this man to guard the Roman frontiers.   95
   SERAP. You seem to know him well.
   ALEX. Too well. I saw him in Cilicia first,
When Cleopatra there met Antony:
A mortal foe he was to us, and Egypt.
But, let me witness to the worth I hate,   100
A braver Roman never drew a sword;
Firm to his prince, but as a friend, not slave.
He ne'er was of his pleasures; but presides
O'er all his cooler hours, and morning counsels:
In short, the plainness, fierceness, rugged virtue 105
Of an old true-stamped Roman lives in him.
His coming bodes I know not what of ill
To our affairs. Withdraw, to mark him better;
And I'll acquaint you why I sought you here,
And what's our present work.

(They withdraw to a corner of the stage; and
   VENTIDIUS, *with the other, comes forwards*
   to the front.)
   VENT.   Not see him, say you?   110
I say, I must, and will.
   GENT.   He has commanded,
On pain of death, none should approach his presence.
   VENT. I bring him news will raise his drooping
    spirits,
Give him new life.
   GENT.   He sees not Cleopatra.
   VENT. Would he had never seen her!   115
   GENT. He eats not, drinks not, sleeps not, has no
    use
Of anything, but thought; or, if he talks,
'Tis to himself, and then 'tis perfect raving:
Then he defies the world, and bids it pass;
Sometimes he gnaws his lip, and curses loud   120
The boy Octavius; then he draws his mouth
Into a scornful smile, and cries, 'Take all,
The world's not worth my care.'
   VENT.   Just, just his nature.
Virtue's his path; but sometimes 'tis too narrow
For his vast soul; and then he starts out wide,   125
And bounds into a vice that bears him far
From his first course, and plunges him in ills:
But, when his danger makes him find his fault,
Quick to observe, and full of sharp remorse,
He censures eagerly his own misdeeds,   130
Judging himself with malice to himself,
And not forgiving what as man he did,
Because his other parts are more than man.
He must not thus be lost.
   (ALEXAS *and the Priests come forward.)*
   ALEX. You have your full instructions, now ad-
    vance;   135
Proclaim your orders loudly.
   SERAP. Romans, Egyptians, hear the queen's com-
    mand.
Thus Cleopatra bids: 'Let labor cease,
To pomp and triumphs give this happy day,
That gave the world a lord: 'tis Antony's.'   140
Live, Antony; and Cleopatra live!
Be this the general voice sent up to heav'n,
And every public place repeat this echo.
   VENT. *(aside).* Fine pageantry!
   SERAP.   Set out before your doors
The images of all your sleeping fathers,   145
With laurels crowned; with laurels wreathe your posts,
And strow with flow'rs the pavement; let the priests
Do present [1] sacrifice; pour out the wine,
And call the gods to join with you in gladness.
   VENT. Curse on the tongue that bids this general
    joy!   150

[1] Instant.

134] Q3F *Priest* for *Priests* in stage directions.

Can they be friends of Antony, who revel
When Antony's in danger? Hide, for shame,
You Romans, your great grandsires' images,
For fear their souls should animate their marbles,
To blush at their degenerate progeny.   155
  ALEX. A love which knows no bounds to Antony,
Would mark the day with honors, when all heaven
Labored for him, when each propitious star
Stood wakeful in his orb, to watch that hour,
And shed his better influence. Her own birth-
    day   160
Our queen neglected, like a vulgar fate
That passed obscurely by.
  VENT.   Would it had slept,
Divided far from his; till some remote
And future age had called it out, to ruin
Some other prince, not him.
  ALEX.   Your emperor,   165
Though grown unkind, would be more gentle than
T' upbraid my queen for loving him too well.
  VENT. Does the mute sacrifice upbraid the priest?
He knows him not his executioner.
Oh, she has decked his ruin with her love,   170
Led him in golden bands to gaudy slaughter,
And made perdition pleasing; she has left him
The blank of what he was;
I tell thee, eunuch, she has quite unmanned him.
Can any Roman see, and know him now,   175
Thus altered from the lord of half mankind,
Unbent, unsinewed, made a woman's toy,
Shrunk from the vast extent of all his honors,
And cramped within a corner of the world?
O Antony!   180
Thou bravest soldier, and thou best of friends!
Bounteous as nature; next to nature's God!
Couldst thou but make new worlds, so wouldst thou
    give 'em,
As bounty were thy being: rough in battle,
As the first Romans when they went to war;   185
Yet, after victory, more pitiful
Than all their praying virgins left at home!
  ALEX. Would you could add, to those more shin-
    ing virtues,
His truth to her who loves him.
  VENT.   Would I could not!
But wherefore waste I precious hours with thee?   190
Thou art her darling mischief, her chief engine,
Antony's other fate. Go, tell thy queen,
Ventidius is arrived, to end her charms.
Let your Egyptian timbrels play alone;
Nor mix effeminate sounds with Roman trum-
    pets.   195
You dare not fight for Antony; go pray,

And keep your cowards' holiday in temples.
              Exeunt ALEXAS, SERAPION.

Enter [a second] Gentleman of M[ARK] ANTONY.
  2 GENT. The emperor approaches, and com-
    mands,
On pain of death, that none presume to stay.
  1 GENT. I dare not disobey him.
              Going out with the other.
  VENT.   Well, I dare.   200
But I'll observe him first unseen, and find
Which way his humor drives: the rest I'll venture.
              (*Withdraws.*)

Enter ANTONY, *walking with a disturbed motion before*
          he speaks.

  ANT. They tell me, 'tis my birthday, and I'll
    keep it
With double pomp of sadness.
'Tis what the day deserves, which gave me
    breath.   205
Why was I raised the meteor of the world,
Hung in the skies, and blazing as I travelled,
Till all my fires were spent; and then cast down-
    ward
To be trod out by Cæsar?
  VENT. (*aside*).   On my soul,
'Tis mournful, wondrous mournful!
  ANT.   Count thy gains.   210
Now, Antony, wouldst thou be born for this?
Glutton of fortune, thy devouring youth
Has starved thy wanting age.
  VENT. (*aside*).   How sorrow shakes him!
So, now the tempest tears him up by th' roots,
And on the ground extends the noble ruin.   215
  ANT. (*having thrown himself down*). Lie there, thou
    shadow of an emperor;
The place thou pressest on thy mother earth
Is all thy empire now: now it contains thee;
Some few days hence, and then 'twill be too large,
When thou'rt contracted in thy narrow urn,   220
Shrunk to a few cold ashes; then Octavia
(For Cleopatra will not live to see it),
Octavia then will have thee all her own,
And bear thee in her widowed hand to Cæsar;
Cæsar will weep, the crocodile will weep,   225
To see his rival of the universe
Lie still and peaceful there. I'll think no more on't.
Give me some music; look that it be sad:
I'll soothe my melancholy, till I swell,
And burst myself with sighing. — (*Soft music.*)   230
'Tis somewhat to my humor. Stay, I fancy
I'm now turned wild, a commoner of nature,

174] Q2Q3F omit *quite.*
197] Q1Q2 *Re-enter the Gentleman;* Q3F *Re-enter the Gentlemen.* The emendation here given follows N.
202] Q3F omit *the rest.*   216–227] FS wrongly give *Lie . . . on't* to Ventidius. (See Noyes, p. 244, ftn.) C corrects.
220] Q3F *the* for *thy.*

Of all forsaken, and forsaking all;
Live in a shady forest's sylvan scene;
Stretched at my length beneath some blasted oak, 235
I lean my head upon the mossy bark,
And look just of a piece as I grew from it:
My uncombed locks, matted like mistletoe,
Hang o'er my hoary face; a murm'ring brook
Runs at my foot.

VENT.   Methinks I fancy   240
Myself there too.

ANT.   The herd come jumping by me,
And, fearless, quench their thirst, while I look on,
And take me for their fellow-citizen.
More of this image, more; it lulls my thoughts.
                                (Soft music again.)

VENT. I must disturb him; I can hold no
    longer.   *(Stands before him.)* 245
ANT. *(starting up).* Art thou Ventidius?

VENT.   Are you Antony?
I'm liker what I was, than you to him
I left you last.

ANT.   I'm angry.

VENT.   So am I.

ANT. I would be private: leave me.

VENT.   Sir, I love you,
And therefore will not leave you.

ANT.   Will not leave me! 250
Where have you learnt that answer? Who am I?

VENT. My emperor; the man I love next heaven;
If I said more, I think 'twere scarce a sin;
Y'are all that's good, and good-like.

ANT.   All that's wretched.
You will not leave me then?

VENT.   'Twas too presuming 255
To say I would not; but I dare not leave you:
And, 'tis unkind in you to chide me hence
So soon, when I so far have come to see you.

ANT. Now thou hast seen me, art thou satisfied?
For, if a friend, thou hast beheld enough;   260
And, if a foe, too much.

VENT. *(weeping).* Look, emperor, this is no com-
    mon dew.
I have not wept this forty year; but now
My mother comes afresh into my eyes;
I cannot help her softness.   265

ANT. By heav'n, he weeps, poor good old man,
    he weeps!
The big round drops course one another down
The furrows of his cheeks. Stop 'em, Ventidius,
Or I shall blush to death: they set my shame,
That caused 'em, full before me.

VENT.   I'll do my best. 270
ANT. Sure there's contagion in the tears of friends:
See, I have caught it too. Believe me, 'tis not

For my own griefs, but thine. — Nay, father.

VENT.   Emperor.
ANT. Emperor! Why, that's the style of victory;
The conqu'ring soldier, red with unfelt wounds, 275
Salutes his general so: but never more
Shall that sound reach my ears.

VENT.   I warrant you.
ANT. Actium, Actium! Oh!——

VENT.   It sits too near you.
ANT. Here, here it lies; a lump of lead by day,
And, in my short, distracted, nightly slumbers, 280
The hag that rides my dreams.——

VENT.   Out with it; give it vent.
ANT.   Urge not my shame.
I lost a battle.

VENT.   So has Julius done.
ANT. Thou favor'st me, and speak'st not half thou
    think'st;
For Julius fought it out, and lost it fairly: 285
But Antony——

VENT.   Nay, stop not.
ANT.   Antony,
(Well, thou wilt have it) like a coward, fled,
Fled while his soldiers fought; fled first, Ventidius.
Thou long'st to curse me, and I give thee leave.
I know thou cam'st prepared to rail.

VENT.   I did. 290
ANT. I'll help thee. — I have been a man, Ven-
    tidius —

VENT. Yes, and a brave one; but——
ANT.   I know thy meaning.
But I have lost my reason, have disgraced
The name of soldier, with inglorious ease.
In the full vintage of my flowing honors,   295
Sat still, and saw it pressed by other hands.
Fortune came smiling to my youth, and wooed it,
And purple greatness met my ripened years.
When first I came to empire, I was borne
On tides of people, crowding to my triumphs,   300
The wish of nations; and the willing world
Received me as its pledge of future peace;
I was so great, so happy, so beloved,
Fate could not ruin me; till I took pains,
And worked against my fortune, chid her from
    me,   305
And turned her loose; yet still she came again.
My careless days, and my luxurious nights,
At length have wearied her, and now she's gone,
Gone, gone, divorced for ever. Help me, soldier,
To curse this madman, this industrious fool,   310
Who labored to be wretched: pr'ythee, curse me.

VENT. No.
ANT.   Why?

VENT.   You are too sensible already

244] Q3F omit *it.*   254] QQF *good-like*; CS *god-like*, a plausible, though needless, emendation.
259] Q3F omit *me.*   260] Q3F insert *seen me*, before *beheld* (another corruption of text).   263] Q2Q3F *years.*
289] Q2Q3F *com'st.*   298] QQCS *purple*; FM *purpl'd.* (M supports F, p. 72, ftn.)

Of what y'have done, too conscious of your failings;
And, like a scorpion, whipped by others first
To fury, sting yourself in mad revenge.   315
I would bring balm, and pour it in your wounds,
Cure your distempered mind, and heal your fortunes.

ANT. I know thou would'st.

VENT.   I will.

ANT.   Ha, ha, ha!

VENT. You laugh.

ANT.   I do, to see officious love
Give cordials to the dead.

VENT.   You would be lost, then?   320

ANT. I am.

VENT.   I say you are not.   Try your fortune.

ANT. I have, to th' utmost.   Dost thou think me
    desperate,
Without just cause?   No, when I found all lost
Beyond repair, I hid me from the world,
And learned to scorn it here; which now I do   325
So heartily, I think it is not worth
The cost of keeping.

VENT.   Cæsar thinks not so;
He'll thank you for the gift he could not take.
You would be killed like Tully,[1] would you?   Do,
Hold out your throat to Cæsar, and die tamely.   330

ANT. No, I can kill myself; and so resolve.

VENT. I can die with you too, when time shall
    serve;
But fortune calls upon us now to live,
To fight, to conquer.

ANT.   Sure thou dream'st, Ventidius.

VENT. No; 'tis you dream; you sleep away your
    hours   335
In desperate sloth, miscalled philosophy.
Up, up, for honor's sake; twelve legions wait you,
And long to call you chief; by painful journeys
I led 'em, patient both of heat and hunger,
Down from the Parthian marches[2] to the Nile.   340
'Twill do you good to see their sunburnt faces,
Their scarred cheeks, and chopped[3] hands; there's
    virtue in 'em.
They'll sell those mangled limbs at dearer rates
Than yon trim bands can buy.

ANT.   Where left you them?

VENT. I said in Lower Syria.

ANT.   Bring 'em hither;   345
There may be life in these.

VENT.   They will not come.

ANT. Why didst thou mock my hopes with pro-
    mised aids,
To double my despair?   They're mutinous.

VENT. Most firm and loyal.

---

[1] Marcus Tullius Cicero, when overtaken by pursuing soldiers, forbade his attendants to resist, and offered his neck to
the fatal sword.

[2] Frontiers.   [3] Chapped.

ANT.   Yet they will not march
To succor me.   O trifler!

VENT.   They petition   350
You would make haste to head 'em.

ANT.   I'm besieged.

VENT. There's but one way shut up: how came I
    hither?

ANT. I will not stir.

VENT.   They would perhaps desire
A better reason.

ANT.   I have never used[4]
My soldiers to demand a reason of   355
My actions.   Why did they refuse to march?

VENT. They said they would not fight for Cleo-
    patra.

ANT. What was't they said?

VENT. They said they would not fight for Cleo-
    patra.
Why should they fight indeed, to make her con-
    quer,   360
And make you more a slave? to gain you kingdoms,
Which, for a kiss, at your next midnight feast,
You'll sell to her?   Then she new-names her jewels,
And calls this diamond such or such a tax;
Each pendant in her ear shall be a province.   365

ANT. Ventidius, I allow your tongue free license
On all my other faults; but, on your life,
No word of Cleopatra: she deserves
More worlds than I can lose.

VENT.   Behold, you pow'rs,
To whom you have intrusted humankind;   370
See Europe, Afric, Asia, put in balance,
And all weighed down by one light, worthless wo-
    man!
I think the gods are Antonies, and give,
Like prodigals, this nether world away
To none but wasteful hands.

ANT.   You grow presumptuous.   375

VENT. I take the privilege of plain love to speak.

ANT. Plain love! plain arrogance, plain insolence!
Thy men are cowards; thou, an envious traitor,
Who, under seeming honesty, hast vented
The burden of thy rank, o'erflowing gall.   380
Oh, that thou wert my equal, great in arms
As the first Cæsar was, that I might kill thee
Without a stain to honor!

VENT.   You may kill me;
You have done more already, — called me traitor.

ANT. Art thou not one?

VENT.   For showing you yourself,   385
Which none else durst have done? but had I been
That name, which I disdain to speak again,
I needed not have sought your abject fortunes,
Come to partake your fate, to die with you.

---

[4] Accustomed.

What hindered me t' have led my conqu'ring
    eagles   390
To fill Octavius's bands? I could have been
A traitor then, a glorious, happy traitor,
And not have been so called.
  ANT.   Forgive me, soldier:
I've been too passionate.
  VENT.   You thought me false;
Thought my old age betrayed you. Kill me,
    sir;   395
Pray, kill me; yet you need not, your unkindness
Has left your sword no work.
  ANT.   I did not think so;
I said it in my rage: pr'ythee, forgive me.
Why didst thou tempt my anger, by discovery
Of what I would not hear?
  VENT.   No prince but you   400
Could merit that sincerity I used,
Nor durst another man have ventured it;
But you, ere love misled your wand'ring eyes,
Were sure the chief and best of human race,
Framed in the very pride and boast of nature; 405
So perfect, that the gods, who formed you, wondered
At their own skill, and cried, 'A lucky hit
Has mended our design.' Their envy hindered,
Else you had been immortal, and a pattern,
When heav'n would work for ostentation sake,   410
To copy out again.
  ANT.   But Cleopatra —
Go on; for I can bear it now.
  VENT.   No more.
  ANT. Thou dar'st not trust my passion, but thou
    may'st;
Thou only lov'st, the rest have flattered me.
  VENT. Heav'n's blessing on your heart for that
    kind word!   415
May I believe you love me? Speak again.
  ANT. Indeed I do. Speak this, and this, and this.
                     (Hugging him.)
Thy praises were unjust; but I'll deserve 'em,
And yet mend all. Do with me what thou wilt;
Lead me to victory, thou know'st the way.   420
  VENT. And, will you leave this ——
  ANT.   Pr'ythee, do not curse her,
And I will leave her; though, heav'n knows, I love
Beyond life, conquest, empire, all but honor;
But I will leave her.
  VENT.   That's my royal master;
And, shall we fight?
  ANT.   I warrant thee, old soldier,   425
Thou shalt behold me once again in iron;
And at the head of our old troops, that beat
The Parthians, cry aloud, 'Come, follow me!'
  VENT. Oh, now I hear my emperor! in that word
Octavius fell. Gods, let me see that day,   430

And, if I have ten years behind, take all;
I'll thank you for th' exchange.
  ANT.   O Cleopatra!
  VENT. Again?
  ANT.   I've done: in that last sigh, she went.
Cæsar shall know what 'tis to force a lover
From all he holds most dear.
  VENT.   Methinks you breathe 435
Another soul: your looks are more divine;
You speak a hero, and you move a god.
  ANT. Oh, thou hast fired me; my soul's up in arms,
And mans each part about me. Once again,
That noble eagerness of fight has seized me;   440
That eagerness with which I darted upward
To Cassius's camp; in vain the steepy hill
Opposed my way; in vain a war of spears
Sung round my head, and planted all my shield;
I won the trenches, while my foremost men   445
Lagged on the plain below.
  VENT.   Ye gods, ye gods,
For such another hour!
  ANT.   Come on, my soldier!
Our hearts and arms are still the same: I long
Once more to meet our foes, that thou and I,
Like Time and Death, marching before our
    troops,   450
May taste fate[1] to 'em; mow 'em out a passage,
And, ent'ring where the foremost squadrons yield,
Begin the noble harvest of the field.   Exeunt.

ACT II

[SCENE I]

CLEOPATRA, IRAS, and ALEXAS.

  CLEO. What shall I do, or whither shall I turn?
Ventidius has o'ercome, and he will go.
  ALEX. He goes to fight for you.
  CLEO. Then he would see me, ere he went to
    fight.
Flatter me not: if once he goes, he's lost,   5
And all my hopes destroyed.
  ALEX.   Does this weak passion
Become a mighty queen?
  CLEO.   I am no queen:
Is this to be a queen, to be besieged
By yon insulting Roman, and to wait
Each hour the victor's chain? These ills are
    small: 10
For Antony is lost, and I can mourn
For nothing else but him. Now come, Octavius,
I have no more to lose; prepare thy bands;
I'm fit to be a captive: Antony

   [1] Test, in advance, their coming fate (as the 'King's taster'
used to taste first the royal food to prevent poisoning).

391] QQF *Octavius's*, but doubtless scanned as a trisyllable. (Cf. *Cassius's*, line 442.)
410] S *ostentation's.*   447] Q3FS *honour* for *hour*, a misprint which betrays F's reliance on Q3, and S's on F.

Has taught my mind the fortune of a slave.   15
IRAS. Call reason to assist you.
CLEO.   I have none,
And none would have: my love's a noble madness,
Which shows the cause deserved it. Moderate sor-
     row
Fits vulgar love, and for a vulgar man:
But I have loved with such transcendent pas-
     sion,   20
I soared, at first, quite out of reason's view,
And now am lost above it.   No, I'm proud
'Tis thus; would Antony could see me now!
Think you he would not sigh?   Though he must
     leave me,
Sure he would sigh; for he is noble-natured,   25
And bears a tender heart: I know him well.
Ah, no, I know him not; I knew him once,
But now 'tis past.
IRAS.   Let it be past with you:
Forget him, madam.
CLEO.   Never, never, Iras.
He once was mine; and once, though now 'tis
     gone,   30
Leaves a faint image of possession still.
ALEX. Think him unconstant, cruel, and un-
     grateful.
CLEO. I cannot: if I could, those thoughts were
     vain.
Faithless, ungrateful, cruel, though he be,
I still must love him.

Enter CHARMION.

                    Now, what news, my Charmion? 35
Will he be kind? and will he not forsake me?
Am I to live, or die? — nay, do I live?
Or am I dead? for when he gave his answer,
Fate took the word, and then I lived or died.
CHAR. I found him, madam ——
CLEO.   A long speech preparing? 40
If thou bring'st comfort, haste, and give it me,
For never was more need.
IRAS.   I know he loves you.
CLEO. Had he been kind, her eyes had told me so,
Before her tongue could speak it: now she studies,
To soften what he said; but give me death,   45
Just as he sent it, Charmion, undisguised,
And in the words he spoke.
CHAR.   I found him, then,
Incompassed round, I think, with iron statues;
So mute, so motionless his soldiers stood,
While awfully he cast his eyes about,   50
And ev'ry leader's hopes or fears surveyed:
Methought he looked resolved, and yet not pleased.
When he beheld me struggling in the crowd,
He blushed, and bade make way.
ALEX.   There's comfort yet.

CHAR. Ventidius fixed his eyes upon my pas-
     sage   55
Severely, as he meant to frown me back,
And sullenly gave place: I told my message,
Just as you gave it, broken and disordered;
I numbered in it all your sighs and tears,
And while I moved your pitiful request,   60
That you but only begged a last farewell,
He fetched an inward groan, and ev'ry time
I named you, sighed, as if his heart were breaking,
But shunned my eyes, and guiltily looked down.
He seemed not now that awful Antony   65
Who shook an armed assembly with his nod;
But, making show as he would rub his eyes,
Disguised and blotted out a falling tear.
CLEO. Did he then weep?   And was I worth a
     tear?
If what thou hast to say be not as pleasing,   70
Tell me no more, but let me die contented.
CHAR. He bid me say, he knew himself so well,
He could deny you nothing, if he saw you;
And therefore ——
CLEO. Thou wouldst say, he would not see me?
CHAR. And therefore begged you not to use a
     power,   75
Which he could ill resist; yet he should ever
Respect you as he ought.
CLEO.   Is that a word
For Antony to use to Cleopatra?
O that faint word, *respect*! how I disdain it!
Disdain myself, for loving after it!   80
He should have kept that word for cold Octavia.
Respect is for a wife: am I that thing,
That dull, insipid lump, without desires,
And without pow'r to give 'em?
ALEX.   You misjudge;
You see through love, and that deludes your
     sight,   85
As, what is straight, seems crooked through the wa-
     ter;
But I, who bear my reason undisturbed,
Can see this Antony, this dreaded man,
A fearful slave, who fain would turn away,
And shuns his master's eyes: if you pursue him, 90
My life on't, he still drags a chain along,
That needs must clog his flight.
CLEO.   Could I believe thee! —
ALEX. By ev'ry circumstance I know he loves.
True, he's hard pressed, by int'rest and by honor;
Yet he but doubts, and parleys, and casts out 95
Many a long look for succor.
CLEO.   He sends word,
He fears to see my face.
ALEX.   And would you more?
He shows his weakness who declines the combat,
And you must urge your fortune.   Could he speak

More plainly?   To my ears, the message
   sounds —   100
'Come to my rescue, Cleopatra, come;
Come, free me from Ventidius, from my tyrant:
See me, and give me a pretence to leave him!' —
I hear his trumpets.   This way he must pass.
Please you, retire a while; I'll work him first,   105
That he may bend more easy.

   CLEO.   You shall rule me;
But all, I fear, in vain.

          Exit with CHARMION *and* IRAS.

   ALEX.   I fear so too;
Though I concealed my thoughts, to make her bold;
But 'tis our utmost means, and fate befriend it!
          Withdraws.

*Enter Lictors with fasces, one bearing the eagle: then
   enter* ANTONY *with* VENTIDIUS, *followed by other
   Commanders.*

   ANT.   Octavius is the minion of blind chance,   110
But holds from virtue nothing.

   VENT.   Has he courage?[1]

   ANT.   But just enough to season him from coward.
Oh, 'tis the coldest youth upon a charge,
The most deliberate fighter! if he ventures
(As in Illyria once they say he did,   115
To storm a town), 'tis when he cannot choose;
When all the world have fixed their eyes upon
   him;
And then he lives on that for seven years after;
But, at a close revenge he never fails.

   VENT.   I heard you challenged him.

   ANT.   I did, Ventidius.   120
What think'st thou was his answer?   'Twas so tame!
He said, he had more ways than one to die;
I had not.

   VENT.   Poor!

   ANT.   He has more ways than one;
But he would choose 'em all before that one.

   VENT.   He first would choose an ague, or a
   fever.   125

   ANT.   No; it must be an ague, not a fever;
He has not warmth enough to die by that.

   VENT.   Or old age and a bed.

   ANT.   Aye, there's his choice,
He would live, like a lamp, to the last wink,
And crawl upon the utmost verge of life.   130
O Hercules!   Why should a man like this,
Who dares not trust his fate for one great action,
Be all the care of heav'n?   Why should he lord it
O'er fourscore thousand men, of whom each one
Is braver than himself?

   VENT.   You conquered for him: 135

    [1] Antony's reply has been 'held to be a slur upon Louis XIV
for physical cowardice' (Stevens).

Philippi[2] knows it; there you shared with him
That empire, which your sword made all your own.

   ANT.   Fool that I was, upon my eagle's wings
I bore this wren, till I was tired with soaring,
And now he mounts above me.[3]   140
Good heav'ns, is this — is this the man who
   braves me?
Who bids my age make way, drives me before him,
To the world's ridge, and sweeps me off like rubbish?

   VENT.   Sir, we lose time; the troops are mounted
   all.

   ANT.   Then give the word to march: 145
I long to leave this prison of a town,
To join thy legions; and, in open field,
Once more to show my face.   Lead, my deliverer.

          Enter ALEXAS.

   ALEX.   Great emperor,
In mighty arms renowned above mankind,   150
But, in soft pity to th' oppressed, a god,
This message sends the mournful Cleopatra
To her departing lord.

   VENT.   Smooth sycophant!

   ALEX.   A thousand wishes, and ten thousand
   prayers,
Millions of blessings wait you to the wars;   155
Millions of sighs and tears she sends you too,
And would have sent
As many dear embraces to your arms,
As many parting kisses to your lips;
But those, she fears, have wearied you already.   160

   VENT. (*aside*).   False crocodile!

   ALEX.   And yet she begs not now, you would not
   leave her;
That were a wish too mighty for her hopes,
Too presuming
For her low fortune, and your ebbing love;   165
That were a wish for her more prosp'rous days,
Her blooming beauty, and your growing kindness.

   ANT. (*aside*).   Well, I must man it out! — What
   would the queen?

   ALEX.   First, to these noble warriors, who attend
Your daring courage in the chase of fame,   170
(Too daring, and too dang'rous for her quiet),
She humbly recommends all she holds dear,
All her own cares and fears, — the care of you.

   VENT.   Yes, witness Actium.

   ANT.   Let him speak, Ventidius.

   ALEX.   You, when his matchless valor bears him
   forward,   175
With ardor too heroic, on his foes,
Fall down, as she would do, before his feet;

    [2] In 42 B.C., Antony and Octavius defeated Brutus and
Cassius.
    [3] An allusion to the fable of the wren who surpassed the
eagle by first flying upwards hidden in the eagle's feathers.

122] Q3F omit *one*.   164–165] QQ print as one line.

Lie in his way, and stop the paths of death.
Tell him, this god is not invulnerable;
That absent Cleopatra bleeds in him;   180
And, that you may remember her petition,
She begs you wear these trifles, as a pawn,
Which, at your wished return, she will redeem
          (Gives jewels to the Commanders.)
With all the wealth of Egypt:
This to the great Ventidius she presents,   185
Whom she can never count her enemy,
Because he loves her lord.
    VENT.   Tell her, I'll none on't;
I'm not ashamed of honest poverty:
Not all the diamonds of the East can bribe
Ventidius from his faith. I hope to see   190
These, and the rest of all her sparkling store,
Where they shall more deservingly be placed.
    ANT. And who must wear 'em then?
    VENT.   The wronged Octavia.
    ANT. You might have spared that word.
    VENT.   And he that bribe.
    ANT. But have I no remembrance?
    ALEX.   Yes, a dear one: 195
Your slave the queen ——
    ANT.   My mistress.
    ALEX.   Then your mistress;
Your mistress would, she says, have sent her soul,
But that you had long since; she humbly begs
This ruby bracelet, set with bleeding hearts,
(The emblems of her own), may bind your arm. 200
          (Presenting a bracelet.)
    VENT. Now, my best lord, in honor's name, I
      ask you,
For manhood's sake, and for your own dear safety,
Touch not these poisoned gifts,
Infected by the sender; touch 'em not;
Myriads of bluest plagues lie underneath 'em, 205
And more than aconite has dipped the silk.
    ANT. Nay, now you grow too cynical, Ventidius:
A lady's favors may be worn with honor.
What, to refuse her bracelet! On my soul,
When I lie pensive in my tent alone,   210
'Twill pass the wakeful hours of winter nights,
To tell these pretty beads upon my arm,
To count for every one a soft embrace,
A melting kiss at such and such a time,
And now and then the fury of her love,   215
When —— And what harm's in this?
    ALEX.   None, none, my lord,
But what's to her, that now 'tis past for ever.
    ANT. *(going to tie it).* We soldiers are so awkward—
    help me tie it.
    ALEX. In faith, my lord, we courtiers too are
    awkward
In these affairs: so are all men indeed;   220
Ev'n I, who am not one. But shall I speak?

    ANT. Yes, freely.
    ALEX.   Then, my lord, fair hands alone
Are fit to tie it; she, who sent it, can.
    VENT. Hell, death! this eunuch pander ruins you.
You will not see her?
        ALEXAS whispers an Attendant, who goes out.
    ANT.   But to take my leave. 225
    VENT. Then I have washed an Æthiope. Y'are
    undone;
Y'are in the toils; y'are taken; y'are destroyed:
Her eyes do Cæsar's work.
    ANT.   You fear too soon.
I'm constant to myself; I know my strength;
And yet she shall not think me barbarous nei-
    ther,   230
Born in the depths of Afric: I'm a Roman,
Bred to the rules of soft humanity.
A guest, and kindly used, should bid farewell.
    VENT. You do not know
How weak you are to her, how much an infant: 235
You are not proof against a smile, or glance;
A sigh will quite disarm you.
    ANT.   See, she comes!
Now you shall find your error. Gods, I thank you:
I formed the danger greater than it was,
And now 'tis near, 'tis lessened.
    VENT.   Mark the end yet. 240

    Enter CLEOPATRA, CHARMION, and IRAS.

    ANT. Well, madam, we are met.
    CLEO.   Is this a meeting?
Then, we must part?
    ANT.   We must.
    CLEO.   Who says we must?
    ANT. Our own hard fates.
    CLEO.   We make those fates ourselves.
    ANT. Yes, we have made 'em; we have loved
    each other
Into our mutual ruin.   245
    CLEO. The gods have seen my joys with envious
    eyes;
I have no friends in heav'n; and all the world,
(As 'twere the bus'ness of mankind to part us)
Is armed against my love: ev'n you yourself
Join with the rest; you, you are armed against
    me.   250
    ANT. I will be justified in all I do
To late posterity, and therefore hear me.
If I mix a lie
With any truth, reproach me freely with it;
Else, favor me with silence.
    CLEO.   You command me, 255
And I am dumb.
    VENT. I like this well: he shows authority.
    ANT. That I derive my ruin
From you alone ——

215] QQF print period after *love.*   230] Q1Q2 print period after *neither;* Q3F emend with comma after *neither.*

CLEO.   O heav'ns! I ruin you!
ANT. You promised me your silence, and you
        break it   260
Ere I have scarce begun.
CLEO.   Well, I obey you.
ANT. When I beheld you first, it was in Egypt,
Ere Cæsar saw your eyes; you gave me love,
And were too young to know it; that I settled
Your father in his throne, was for your sake;   265
I left th' acknowledgment for time to ripen.
Cæsar stepped in, and with a greedy hand
Plucked the green fruit, ere the first blush of red,
Yet cleaving to the bough. He was my lord,
And was, beside, too great for me to rival;   270
But, I deserved you first, though he enjoyed you.
When, after, I beheld you in Cilicia,
An enemy to Rome, I pardoned you.
    CLEO. I cleared myself ——
ANT.   Again you break your promise.
I loved you still, and took your weak excuses,   275
Took you into my bosom, stained by Cæsar,
And not half mine: I went to Egypt with you,
And hid me from the bus'ness of the world,
Shut out enquiring nations from my sight,
To give whole years to you.   280
VENT. (aside). Yes, to your shame be't spoken.
ANT.   How I loved,
Witness, ye days and nights, and all your hours,
That danced away with down upon your feet,
As all your bus'ness were to count my passion!
One day passed by, and nothing saw but love;   285
Another came, and still 'twas only love:
The suns were wearied out with looking on,
And I untired with loving.
I saw you ev'ry day, and all the day;
And ev'ry day was still but as the first,   290
So eager was I still to see you more.
VENT. 'Tis all too true.
ANT.   Fulvia, my wife, grew jealous,
As she indeed had reason; raised a war
In Italy, to call me back.
VENT.   But yet
You went not.
ANT.   While within your arms I lay,   295
The world fell mould'ring from my hands each hour,
And left me scarce a grasp (I thank your love for't).
VENT. Well pushed: that last was home.
CLEO.   Yet may I speak?
ANT. If I have urged a falsehood, yes; else, not.
Your silence says I have not. Fulvia died,   300
(Pardon, you gods, with my unkindness died);
To set the world at peace, I took Octavia,
This Cæsar's sister; in her pride of youth
And flow'r of beauty did I wed that lady,

Whom blushing I must praise, because I left her.   305
You called; my love obeyed the fatal summons:
This raised the Roman arms; the cause was yours.
I would have fought by land, where I was stronger;
You hindered it: yet, when I fought at sea,
Forsook me fighting; and (O stain to honor!   310
O lasting shame!) I knew not that I fled;
But fled to follow you.
    VENT. What haste she made to hoist her purple
        sails!
And, to appear magnificent in flight,
Drew half our strength away.
ANT.   All this you caused.   315
And, would you multiply more ruins on me?
This honest man, my best, my only friend,
Has gathered up the shipwrack of my fortunes;
Twelve legions I have left, my last recruits,
And you have watched the news, and bring your
        eyes   320
To seize them too. If you have aught to answer,
Now speak, you have free leave.
    ALEX. (aside).   She stands confounded:
Despair is in her eyes.
    VENT. Now lay a sigh i' th' way to stop his pas-
        sage:
Prepare a tear, and bid it for his legions;   325
'Tis like they shall be sold.
    CLEO. How shall I plead my cause, when you,
        my judge,
Already have condemned me? Shall I bring
The love you bore me for my advocate?
That now is turned against me, that destroys
        me;   330
For love, once past, is, at the best, forgotten;
But oft'ner sours to hate: 'twill please my lord
To ruin me, and therefore I'll be guilty.
But, could I once have thought it would have
        pleased you,
That you would pry, with narrow searching
        eyes,   335
Into my faults, severe to my destruction,
And watching all advantages with care,
That serve to make me wretched? Speak, my lord,
For I end here. Though I deserve this usage,
Was it like you to give it?
    ANT.   Oh, you wrong me,   340
To think I sought this parting, or desired
To accuse you more than what will clear myself,
And justify this breach.
    CLEO.   Thus low I thank you.
And, since my innocence will not offend,
I shall not blush to own it.
    VENT.   After this,   345
I think she'll blush at nothing.

263] Q3F print comma after *eyes.* S, following F, adopted the comma, and was then led to put a period after *Egypt* (l. 262), thereby altering the original meaning.
282] QQF *your;* S *ye,* a change frequently adopted.   318] Q2Q3F *shipwreck.*

CLEO.   You seemed grieved
(And therein you are kind) that Cæsar first
Enjoyed my love, though you deserved it better;
I grieve for that, my lord, much more than you;
For, had I first been yours, it would have
    saved   350
My second choice: I never had been his,
And ne'er had been but yours. But Cæsar first,
You say, possessed my love. Not so, my lord:
He first possessed my person; you, my love:
Cæsar loved me; but I loved Antony.   355
If I endured him after, 'twas because
I judged it due to the first name of men;
And, half constrained, I gave, as to a tyrant,
What he would take by force.
VENT.   O siren! siren!
Yet grant that all the love she boasts were
    true,   360
Has she not ruined you? I still urge that,
The fatal consequence.
CLEO.   The consequence indeed,
For I dare challenge him, my greatest foe,
To say it was designed: 'tis true, I loved you,
And kept you far from an uneasy wife —   365
(Such Fulvia was).
Yes, but he'll say, you left Octavia for me; —
And, can you blame me to receive that love,
Which quitted such desert, for worthless me?
How often have I wished some other Cæsar,   370
Great as the first, and as the second young,
Would court my love, to be refused for you!
VENT. Words, words; but Actium, sir, remember
    Actium.
CLEO. Ev'n there, I dare his malice. True, I
    counselled
To fight at sea; but I betrayed you not.   375
I fled, but not to the enemy. 'Twas fear;
Would I had been a man, not to have feared!
For none would then have envied me your friend-
    ship,
Who envy me your love.
ANT.   We're both unhappy:
If nothing else, yet our ill fortune parts us.   380
Speak; would you have me perish by my stay?
CLEO. If as a friend you ask my judgment, go;
If as a lover, stay. If you must perish ——
'Tis a hard word — but stay.
VENT. See now th' effects of her so boasted
    love!   385
She strives to drag you down to ruin with her:
But, could she 'scape without you, oh, how soon
Would she let go her hold, and haste to shore,
And never look behind!
CLEO. Then judge my love by this.
                (*Giving* ANTONY *a writing.*)

                  Could I have borne   390
A life or death, a happiness or woe,
From yours divided, this had giv'n me means.
ANT. By Hercules, the writing of Octavius!
I know it well: 'tis that proscribing hand,
Young as it was, that led the way to mine,   395
And left me but the second place in murder. —
See, see, Ventidius! here he offers Egypt,
And joins all Syria to it, as a present,
So, in requital, she forsake my fortunes,
And join her arms with his.
CLEO.   And yet you leave me!   400
You leave me, Antony; and yet I love you,
Indeed I do: I have refused a kingdom;
That's a trifle:
For I could part with life, with anything,
But only you. Oh, let me die but with you!   405
Is that a hard request?
ANT.   Next living with you,
'Tis all that heav'n can give.
ALEX. (*aside*).   He melts; we conquer.
CLEO. No; you shall go; your int'rest calls you
    hence;
Yes; your dear interest pulls too strong, for these
Weak arms to hold you here. —   (*Takes his hand.*)
           Go; leave me, soldier   410
(For you're no more a lover); leave me dying:
Push me all pale and panting from your bosom,
And, when your march begins, let one run after,
Breathless almost for joy, and cry, 'She's dead.'
The soldiers shout; you then, perhaps, may sigh,   415
And muster all your Roman gravity:
Ventidius chides; and straight your brow clears up,
As I had never been.
ANT.   Gods, 'tis too much;
Too much for man to bear!
CLEO.   What is't for me then,
A weak, forsaken woman, and a lover? —   420
Here let me breathe my last: envy me not
This minute in your arms: I'll die apace,
As fast as e'er I can, and end your trouble.
ANT. Die! rather let me perish: loosened nature
Leap from its hinges! Sink the props of
    heav'n,   425
And fall the skies to crush the nether world!
My eyes, my soul, my all! —   (*Embraces her.*)
VENT.   And what's this toy,
In balance with your fortune, honor, fame?
ANT. What is't, Ventidius? — it outweighs 'em all;
Why, we have more than conquered Cæsar
    now: 430
My queen's not only innocent, but loves me.
This, this is she who drags me down to ruin!
'But, could she 'scape without me, with what haste
Would she let slip her hold, and make to shore,

365] Q3F misprint *will* for *wife*; C corrects.   394] Q2Q3F *prescribing*; CS restore *proscribing*.
418–419] QQF print Antony's speech as one full line.   419] Q3 *beard* for *bear*.

And never look behind!'   435
Down on thy knees, blasphemer as thou art,
And ask forgiveness of wronged innocence.
    VENT. I'll rather die, than take it. Will you go?
    ANT. Go! whither? Go from all that's excellent?
Faith, honor, virtue, all good things forbid   440
That I should go from her, who sets my love
Above the price of kingdoms. Give, you gods,
Give to your boy, your Cæsar,
This rattle of a globe to play withal,
This gewgaw world, and put him cheaply off: 445
I'll not be pleased with less than Cleopatra.
    CLEO. She['s] wholly yours. My heart's so full
        of joy,
That I shall do some wild extravagance
Of love, in public; and the foolish world,
Which knows not tenderness, will think me
        mad.   450
    VENT. O women! women! women! all the gods
Have not such pow'r of doing good to man,
As you of doing harm.   Exit.
    ANT.   Our men are armed.
Unbar the gate that looks to Cæsar's camp;
I would revenge the treachery he meant me;   455
And long security makes conquest easy.
I'm eager to return before I go;
For, all the pleasures I have known beat thick
On my remembrance. How I long for night!
    That both the sweets of mutual love may try,   460
And once triúmph o'er Cæsar [ere] we die.
                                         Exeunt.

ACT III

[SCENE I]

At one door, enter CLEOPATRA, CHARMION, IRAS, *and*
ALEXAS, *a train of Egyptians: at the other,*
ANTONY *and Romans. The entrance on both
sides is prepared by music, the trumpets first
sounding on* ANTONY'S *part, then answered by
timbrels, etc., on* CLEOPATRA'S. CHARMION *and*
IRAS *hold a laurel wreath betwixt them. A dance
of Egyptians. After the ceremony,* CLEOPATRA
crowns ANTONY.

    ANT. I thought how those white arms would fold
        me in,
And strain me close, and melt me into love;
So pleased with that sweet image, I sprung forwards,
And added all my strength to every blow.
    CLEO. Come to me, come, my soldier, to my
        arms!   5
You've been too long away from my embraces;
But, when I have you fast, and all my own,

With broken murmurs, and with amorous sighs,
I'll say, you were unkind, and punish you,
And mark you red with many an eager kiss.   10
    ANT. My brighter Venus!
    CLEO.   O my greater Mars!
    ANT. Thou join'st us well, my love!
Suppose me come from the Phlegræan plains,[1]
Where gasping giants lay, cleft by my sword,
And mountain-tops pared off each other blow,   15
To bury those I slew. Receive me, goddess!
Let Cæsar spread his subtile nets, like Vulcan;
In thy embraces I would be beheld
By heav'n and earth at once;
And make their envy what they meant their
        sport.   20
Let those who took us blush; I would love on
With awful state, regardless of their frowns,
As their superior god.
There's no satiety of love in thee;
Enjoyed, thou still art new; perpetual spring   25
Is in thy arms; the ripened fruit but falls,
And blossoms rise to fill its empty place;
And I grow rich by giving.

        Enter VENTIDIUS, *and stands apart.*

    ALEX. Oh, now the danger's past, your general
        comes!
He joins not in your joys, nor minds your tri-
        umphs;   30
But, with contracted brows, looks frowning on,
As envying your success.
    ANT. Now, on my soul, he loves me; truly loves
        me;
He never flattered me in any vice,
But awes me with his virtue: ev'n this minute,   35
Methinks, he has a right of chiding me.
Lead to the temple: I'll avoid his presence;
It checks too strong upon me.
        Exeunt the rest. As ANTONY *is going,* VEN-
            TIDIUS *pulls him by the robe.*
    VENT.   Emperor!
    ANT. (*looking back*). 'Tis the old argument; I
        pr'ythee, spare me.
    VENT. But this one hearing, emperor.
    ANT.   Let go   40
My robe; or, by my father Hercules[2] —
    VENT. By Hercules his father, that's yet greater,
I bring you somewhat you would wish to know.
    ANT. Thou see'st we are observed; attend me
        here,
And I'll return.   *Exit.*   45

[1] In Macedonia, where the gods subdued the Titans.
[2] Plutarch derives the name Antony from Anton, son of
Hercules.

447] QQ *she*; F *she's*, correcting an apparent misprint.
461] Q2Q3F supply *ere*, omitted in Q1. CS silently invert to *triumph once.*   ACT III. s.d.] Q3 *parts* for *part.*
17] Q2Q3F *subtile*   42] QQF *Hercules his*; S *Hercules'*, a modernization that mars the meter.

VENT. I'm waning in his favor, yet I love him;
I love this man, who runs to meet his ruin;
And sure the gods, like me, are fond of him:
His virtues lie so mingled with his crimes,
As would confound their choice to punish one, 50
And not reward the other.

Enter ANTONY.

ANT.   We can conquer,
You see, without your aid.
We have dislodged their troops;
They look on us at distance, and, like curs
'Scaped from the lion's paws, they bay far off, 55
And lick their wounds, and faintly threaten war.
Five thousand Romans, with their faces upward,
Lie breathless on the plain.

VENT.   'Tis well: and he,
Who lost 'em, could have spared ten thousand more.
Yet if, by this advantage, you could gain 60
An easier peace, while Cæsar doubts the chance
Of arms! ——

ANT.   Oh, think not on't, Ventidius!
The boy pursues my ruin, he'll no peace;
His malice is considerate in advantage;
Oh, he's the coolest murderer! so staunch, 65
He kills, and keeps his temper.

VENT.   Have you no friend
In all his army, who has power to move him?
Mæcenas, or Agrippa, might do much.

ANT. They're both too deep in Cæsar's interests.
We'll work it out by dint of sword, or perish. 70

VENT. Fain I would find some other.

ANT.   Thank thy love.
Some four or five such victories as this
Will save thy farther pains.

VENT. Expect no more; Cæsar is on his guard:
I know, sir, you have conquered against odds; 75
But still you draw supplies from one poor town,
And of Egyptians: he has all the world,
And, at his back, nations come pouring in,
To fill the gaps you make. Pray, think again.

ANT. Why dost thou drive me from myself, to
search   80
For foreign aids? — to hunt my memory,
And range all o'er a waste and barren place,
To find a friend? The wretched have no friends.——
Yet I had one, the bravest youth of Rome,
Whom Cæsar loves beyond the love of women; 85
He could resolve his mind, as fire does wax,
From that hard rugged image melt him down,
And mould him in what softer form he pleased.

VENT. Him would I see, that man of all the world;
Just such a one we want.

ANT.   He loved me too, 90
I was his soul; he lived not but in me;
We were so closed within each other's breasts,

The rivets were not found that joined us first.
That does not reach us yet: we were so mixed,
As meeting streams, both to ourselves were lost; 95
We were one mass; we could not give or take,
But from the same; for he was I, I he!

VENT. (*aside*). He moves as I would wish him.

ANT.   After this,
I need not tell his name — 'twas Dolabella.

VENT. He's now in Cæsar's camp.

ANT.   No matter where, 100
Since he's no longer mine. He took unkindly
That I forbade him Cleopatra's sight,
Because I feared he loved her: he confessed
He had a warmth, which, for my sake, he stifled;
For 'twere impossible that two, so one, 105
Should not have loved the same. When he departed,
He took no leave; and that confirmed my thoughts.

VENT. It argues that he loved you more than her,
Else he had stayed; but he perceived you jealous,
And would not grieve his friend: I know he loves
    you.   110

ANT. I should have seen him, then, ere now.

VENT.   Perhaps
He has thus long been lab'ring for your peace.

ANT. Would he were here!

VENT.   Would you believe he loved you?
I read your answer in your eyes; you would.
Not to conceal it longer, he has sent 115
A messenger from Cæsar's camp, with letters.

ANT. Let him appear.

VENT.   I'll bring him instantly.

Exit VENTIDIUS, *and re-enters immediately with*
DOLABELLA.

ANT. 'Tis he himself! himself, by holy friendship!
    (*Runs to embrace him.*)
Art thou returned at last, my better half?
Come, give me all myself! — Let me not live, 120
If the young bridegroom, longing for his night,
Was ever half so fond.

DOLA. I must be silent, for my soul is busy
About a nobler work: she's new come home,
Like a long-absent man, and wanders o'er 125
Each room, a stranger to her own, to look
If all be safe.

ANT.   Thou hast what's left of me;
For I am now so sunk from what I was,
Thou find'st me at my lowest water-mark.
The rivers that ran in, and raised my fortunes, 130
Are all dried up, or take another course.
What I have left is from my native spring;
I've still a heart that swells, in scorn of fate,
And lifts me to my banks.

DOLA. Still you are lord of all the world to me. 135

ANT. Why, then I yet am so; for thou art all.
If I had any joy when thou wert absent,

78] QQ *back*; FS *beck* (S relies on F). 120] QQF print as two separate lines. 124] Q2Q3F *noble.*

I grudged it to myself; methought I robbèd
Thee of thy part.   But, O my Dolabella!
Thou hast beheld me other than I am.   140
Hast thou not seen my morning chambers filled
With sceptered slaves, who waited to salute me?
With eastern monarchs, who forgot the sun,
To worship my uprising?   Menial kings
Ran coursing up and down my palace-yard,   145
Stood silent in my presence, watched my eyes,
And, at my least command, all started out,
Like racers to the goal.

DOLA.   Slaves to your fortune.

ANT.   Fortune is Cæsar's now; and what am I?

VENT.   What you have made yourself; I will not
flatter.   150

ANT.   Is this friendly done?

DOLA.   Yes, when his end is so, I must join with
him;
Indeed I must, and yet you must not chide:
Why am I else your friend?

ANT.   Take heed, young man,
How thou upbraid'st my love; the queen has
eyes,   155
And thou too hast a soul.   Canst thou remember,
When, swelled with hatred, thou beheld'st her first,
As accessary to thy brother's death?

DOLA.   Spare my remembrance; 'twas a guilty day,
And still the blush hangs here.

ANT.   To clear herself   160
For sending him no aid, she came from Egypt.
Her galley down the silver Cydnos rowed,
The tackling silk, the streamers waved with gold;
The gentle winds were lodged in purple sails;
Her nymphs, like Nereids, round her couch were
placed,   165
Where she, another sea-born Venus, lay.

DOLA.   No more: I would not hear it.

ANT.   Oh, you must!
She lay, and leant her cheek upon her hand,
And cast a look so languishingly sweet,
As if, secure of all beholders' hearts,   170
Neglecting, she could take 'em: boys, like Cupids,
Stood fanning with their painted wings the winds
That played about her face: but if she smiled,
A darting glory seemed to blaze abroad,
That men's desiring eyes were never wearied,   175
But hung upon the object.   To soft flutes
The silver oars kept time; and while they played,
The hearing gave new pleasure to the sight,
And both to thought.   'Twas heav'n, or somewhat
more;
For she so charmed all hearts, that gazing
crowds   180
Stood panting on the shore, and wanted breath

To give their welcome voice.
Then, Dolabella, where was then thy soul?
Was not thy fury quite disarmed with wonder?
Didst thou not shrink behind me from those
eyes,   185
And whisper in my ear, 'Oh, tell her not
That I accused her with my brother's death?'

DOLA.   And should my weakness be a plea for
yours?
Mine was an age when love might be excused,
When kindly warmth, and when my springing
youth   190
Made it a debt to nature.   Yours ——

VENT.   Speak boldly.
Yours, he would say, in your declining age,
When no more heat was left but what you forced,
When all the sap was needful for the trunk,
When it went down, then you constrained the
course,   195
And robbed from nature, to supply desire;
In you (I would not use so harsh a word)
But 'tis plain dotage.

ANT.   Ha!

DOLA.   'Twas urged too home.
But yet the loss was private that I made;
'Twas but myself I lost: I lost no legions;   200
I had no world to lose, no people's love.

ANT.   This from a friend?

DOLA.   Yes, Antony, a true one;
A friend so tender, that each word I speak
Stabs my own heart, before it reach your ear.
Oh, judge me not less kind, because I chide!   205
To Cæsar I excuse you.

ANT.   O ye gods!
Have I then lived to be excused to Cæsar?

DOLA.   As to your equal.

ANT.   Well, he's but my equal;
While I wear this, he never shall be more.

DOLA.   I bring conditions from him.

ANT.   Are they noble?   210
Methinks thou shouldst not bring 'em else; yet he
Is full of deep dissembling; knows no honor
Divided from his int'rest.   Fate mistook him;
For nature meant him for an usurer:
He's fit indeed to buy, not conquer, kingdoms.   215

VENT.   Then, granting this,
What pow'r was theirs who wrought so hard a tem-
per
To honorable terms?

ANT.   It was my Dolabella, or some god.

DOLA.   Nor I, nor yet Mæcenas, nor Agrippa: 220
They were your enemies; and I, a friend,
Too weak alone; yet 'twas a Roman's deed.

ANT.   'Twas like a Roman done: show me that man,

145] Q3F *run*.   186] Q2Q3F *ears*.   198] S silently inverts to *'Tis but*.
208] Q2Q3F drop by mistake the half line, ANT. *Well...equal*, thus transferring his speech to *Dola*.   CS correct to Q1.   See
Textual Note (p. 926).

Who has preserved my life, my love, my honor;
Let me but see his face.

VENT.   That task is mine,   225
And, heav'n, thou know'st how pleasing.

Exit VENTIDIUS.

DOLA.   You'll remember
To whom you stand obliged?

ANT.   When I forget it,
Be thou unkind, and that's my greatest curse.
My queen shall thank him too.

DOLA.   I fear she will not.

ANT. But she shall do't — the queen, my Dolabella!   230
Hast thou not still some grudgings of thy fever?

DOLA. I would not see her lost.

ANT.   When I forsake her,
Leave me, my better stars! for she has truth
Beyond her beauty. Cæsar tempted her,
At no less price than kingdoms, to betray me;   235
But she resisted all: and yet thou chid'st me
For loving her too well. Could I do so?

DOLA. Yes; there's my reason.

Re-enter VENTIDIUS, *with* OCTAVIA, *leading* ANTONY'S
two little daughters.

ANT. (*starting back*).   Where? — Octavia there!

VENT. What, is she poison to you? — a disease?
Look on her, view her well, and those she
          brings: 240
Are they all strangers to your eyes? has nature
No secret call, no whisper they are yours?

DOLA. For shame, my lord, if not for love, re-
ceive 'em
With kinder eyes. If you confess[1] a man,
Meet 'em, embrace 'em, bid 'em welcome to you.   245
Your arms should open, ev'n without your knowl-
          edge,
To clasp 'em in; your feet should turn to wings,
To bear you to 'em; and your eyes dart out
And aim a kiss, ere you could reach the lips.

ANT. I stood amazed to think how they came
          hither.   250

VENT. I sent for 'em; I brought 'em in, unknown
To Cleopatra's guards.

DOLA.   Yet are you cold?

OCTAV. Thus long I have attended for my wel-
come,
Which, as a stranger, sure I might expect.
Who am I?

ANT.   Cæsar's sister.

OCTAV.   That's unkind.   255
Had I been nothing more than Cæsar's sister,
Know, I had still remained in Cæsar's camp;
But your Octavia, your much injured wife,

[1] Confess yourself.

Though banished from your bed, driv'n from your
          house,
In spite of Cæsar's sister, still is yours.   260
'Tis true, I have a heart disdains your coldness,
And prompts me not to seek what you should offer;
But a wife's virtue still surmounts that pride:
I come to claim you as my own; to show
My duty first; to ask, nay beg, your kindness: 265
Your hand, my lord; 'tis mine, and I will have it.

(*Taking his hand.*)

VENT. Do, take it; thou deserv'st it.

DOLA.   On my soul,
And so she does: she's neither too submissive,
Nor yet too haughty; but so just a mean
Shows, as it ought, a wife and Roman too.   270

ANT. I fear, Octavia, you have begged my life.

OCTAV. Begged it, my lord?

ANT.   Yes, begged it, my ambassadress,
Poorly and basely begged it of your brother.

OCTAV. Poorly and basely I could never beg;
Nor could my brother grant.   275

ANT. Shall I, who, to my kneeling slave, could say,
'Rise up, and be a king,' shall I fall down
And cry, 'Forgive me, Cæsar'? Shall I set
A man, my equal, in the place of Jove,
As[2] he could give me being? No; that word,   280
'Forgive,' would choke me up,
And die upon my tongue.

DOLA.   You shall not need it.

ANT. I will not need it. Come, you've all be-
trayed me —
My friend too! — to receive some vile conditions.
My wife has bought me, with her prayers and
          tears;   285
And now I must become her branded slave:
In every peevish mood, she will upbraid
The life she gave: if I but look awry,
She cries, 'I'll tell my brother.'

OCTAV.   My hard fortune
Subjects me still to your unkind mistakes.   290
But the conditions I have brought are such
You need not blush to take: I love your honor,
Because 'tis mine; it never shall be said,
Octavia's husband was her brother's slave.
Sir, you are free — free, ev'n from her you
          loathe;   295
For, though my brother bargains for your love,
Makes me the price and cément of your peace,
I have a soul like yours; I cannot take
Your love as alms, nor beg what I deserve.
I'll tell my brother we are reconciled;   300
He shall draw back his troops, and you shall march
To rule the East: I may be dropped at Athens;
No matter where, I never will complain,

[2] As if.

But only keep the barren name of wife,
And rid you of the trouble.   305
   VENT. Was ever such a strife of sullen honor!
Both scorn to be obliged.
   DOLA. Oh, she has touched him in the tender'st
     part;
See how he reddens with despite and shame,
To be outdone in generosity!   310
   VENT. See how he winks! how he dries up a tear,
That fain would fall!
   ANT. Octavia, I have heard you, and must praise
The greatness of your soul;
But cannot yield to what you have proposed;   315
For I can ne'er be conquered but by love;
And you do all for duty.   You would free me,
And would be dropped at Athens; was't not so?
   OCTAV. It was, my lord.
   ANT.   Then I must be obliged
To one who loves me not, who, to herself,   320
May call me thankless and ungrateful man: —
I'll not endure it; no.
   VENT. [aside]. I'm glad it pinches there.
   OCTAV. Would you triúmph o'er poor Octavia's
     virtue?
That pride was all I had to bear me up;   325
That you might think you owed me for your life,
And owed it to my duty, not my love.
I have been injured, and my haughty soul
Could brook but ill the man who slights my bed.
   ANT. Therefore you love me not.
   OCTAV.   Therefore, my lord,   330
I should not love you.
   ANT.   Therefore you would leave me?
   OCTAV. And therefore I should leave you — if I
     could.
   DOLA. Her soul's too great, after such injuries,
To say she loves; and yet she lets you see it.
Her modesty and silence plead her cause.   335
   ANT. O Dolabella, which way shall I turn?
I find a secret yielding in my soul;
But Cleopatra, who would die with me,
Must she be left?   Pity pleads for Octavia;
But does it not plead more for Cleopatra?   340
   VENT. Justice and pity both plead for Octavia;
For Cleopatra, neither.
One would be ruined with you, but she first
Had ruined you: the other, you have ruined,
And yet she would preserve you.   345
In everything their merits are unequal.
   ANT. O my distracted soul!
   OCTAV.   Sweet heav'n compose it!
Come, come, my lord, if I can pardon you,
Methinks you should accept it.   Look on these;
Are they not yours?   Or stand they thus neg-
     lected,   350

As they are mine?   Go to him, children, go;
Kneel to him, take him by the hand, speak to him;
For you may speak, and he may own you too,
Without a blush; and so he cannot all
His children: go, I say, and pull him to me,   355
And pull him to yourselves, from that bad woman.
You, Agrippina, hang upon his arms;
And you, Antonia, clasp about his waist:
If he will shake you off, if he will dash you
Against the pavement, you must bear it, chil-
     dren;   360
For you are mine, and I was born to suffer.
       (Here the Children go to him, etc.)
   VENT. Was ever sight so moving? — Emperor!
   DOLA. Friend!
   OCTAV.   Husband!
   BOTH CHILD.   Father!
   ANT.   I am vanquished; take me,
Octavia; take me, children; share me all.
       (Embracing them.)
I've been a thriftless debtor to your loves,   365
And run out much, in riot,[1] from your stock;
But all shall be amended.
   OCTAV.   O blest hour!
   DOLA. O happy change!
   VENT.   My joy stops at my tongue:
But it has found two channels here for one,
And bubbles out above.   370
   ANT. (to OCTAVIA).   This is thy triumph; lead me
     where thou wilt;
Ev'n to thy brother's camp.
   OCTAV.   All there are yours.

      Enter ALEXAS hastily.

   ALEX. The queen, my mistress, sir, and yours —
   ANT.   'Tis past. —
Octavia, you shall stay this night; to-morrow,
Cæsar and we are one.   375
     Exit leading OCTAVIA; DOLABELLA and the
     Children follow.
   VENT. There's news for you; run, my officious
     eunuch,
Be sure to be the first; haste forward;
Haste, my dear eunuch, haste!   *Exit.*
   ALEX. This downright fighting fool, this thick-
     skulled hero,
This blunt, unthinking instrument of death,   380
With plain dull virtue has outgone my wit.
Pleasure forsook my earliest infancy;
The luxury of others robbed my cradle,
And ravished thence the promise of a man.
Cast out from nature, disinherited   385
Of what her meanest children claim by kind,
Yet greatness kept me from contempt: that's gone.

[1] Prodigally expended.

Had Cleopatra followed my advice,
Then he had been betrayed who now forsakes.
She dies for love; but she has known its joys: 390
Gods, is this just, that I, who know no joys,
Must die, because she loves?

Enter CLEOPATRA, CHARMION, IRAS, [*and*] *train.*

O madam, I have seen what blasts my eyes!
Octavia's here!
    CLEO.   Peace with that raven's note.
I know it too; and now am in   395
The pangs of death.
    ALEX.   You are no more a queen;
Egypt is lost.
    CLEO.   What tell'st thou me of Egypt?
My life, my soul is lost! Octavia has him!—
O fatal name to Cleopatra's love!
My kisses, my embraces now are hers;   400
While I —— But thou hast seen my rival; speak,
Does she deserve this blessing? Is she fair?
Bright as a goddess? And is all perfection
Confined to her? It is. Poor I was made
Of that coarse matter, which, when she was fin-
    ished,   405
The gods threw by, for rubbish.
    ALEX. She's indeed a very miracle.
    CLEO. Death to my hopes, a miracle!
    ALEX. (*bowing*).   A miracle;
I mean of goodness; for in beauty, madam,
You make all wonders cease.
    CLEO.   I was too rash: 410
Take this in part of recompense. But, oh!
                                (*Giving a ring.*)
I fear thou flatter'st me.
    CHAR. She comes! she's here!
    IRAS.   Fly, madam, Cæsar's sister!
    CLEO. Were she the sister of the thund'rer Jove,
And bore her brother's lightning in her eyes,   415
Thus would I face my rival.
    Meets OCTAVIA *with* VENTIDIUS. OCTAVIA
    *bears up to her. Their trains come up on
    either side.*
    OCTAV. I need not ask if you are Cleopatra;
Your haughty carriage ——
    CLEO.   Shows I am a queen:
Nor need I ask you who you are.
    OCTAV.   A Roman:
A name that makes and can unmake a queen.   420
    CLEO. Your lord, the man who serves me, is a
    Roman.
    OCTAV. He was a Roman, till he lost that name,
To be a slave in Egypt; but I come
To free him thence.
    CLEO.   Peace, peace, my lover's Juno.
When he grew weary of that household clog,   425

He chose my easier bonds.
    OCTAV.   I wonder not
Your bonds are easy; you have long been practised
In that lascivious art: he's not the first
For whom you spread your snares: let Cæsar witness.
    CLEO. I loved not Cæsar; 'twas but grati-
    tude   430
I paid his love. The worst your malice can,
Is but to say the greatest of mankind
Has been my slave. The next, but far above him
In my esteem, is he whom law calls yours,
But whom his love made mine.
    OCTAV. (*coming up close to her*). I would view
    nearer   435
That face which has so long usurped my right,
To find th' inevitable charms that catch
Mankind so sure, that ruined my dear lord.
    CLEO. Oh, you do well to search; for had you
    known
But half these charms, you had not lost his
    heart.   440
    OCTAV. Far be their knowledge from a Roman
    lady,
Far from a modest wife! Shame of our sex,
Dost thou not blush to own those black endearments
That make sin pleasing?
    CLEO.   You may blush, who want [1] 'em.
If bounteous nature, if indulgent heav'n   445
Have giv'n me charms to please the bravest man,
Should I not thank 'em? Should I be ashamed,
And not be proud? I am, that he has loved me;
And, when I love not him, heav'n change this face
For one like that.
    OCTAV.   Thou lov'st him not so well.   450
    CLEO. I love him better, and deserve him more.
    OCTAV. You do not — cannot: you have been his
    ruin.
Who made him cheap at Rome, but Cleopatra?
Who made him scorned abroad, but Cleopatra?
At Actium, who betrayed him? Cleopatra.   455
Who made his children orphans, and poor me
A wretched widow? only Cleopatra.
    CLEO. Yet she who loves him best is Cleopatra.
If you have suffered, I have suffered more.
You bear the specious title of a wife,   460
To gild your cause, and draw the pitying world
To favor it: the world contemns poor me,
For I have lost my honor, lost my fame,
And stained the glory of my royal house,
And all to bear the branded name of mistress.   465
There wants but life, and that too I would lose
For him I love.
    OCTAV.   Be't so, then; take thy wish.
                                Exit cum suis.

[1] Lack.

CLEO. And 'tis my wish,
Now he is lost for whom alone I lived.
My sight grows dim, and every object dances, 470
And swims before me, in the maze of death.
My spirits, while they were opposed, kept up;
They could not sink beneath a rival's scorn:
But now she's gone, they faint.

ALEX. Mine have had leisure
To recollect their strength, and furnish counsel, 475
To ruin her, who else must ruin you.

CLEO. Vain promiser!
Lead me, my Charmion; nay, your hand too, Iras:
My grief has weight enough to sink you both.
Conduct me to some solitary chamber,
And draw the curtains round; 480
Then leave me to myself, to take alone
My fill of grief.
There I till death will his unkindness weep;
As harmless infants moan themselves asleep.
Exeunt.

ACT IV

[SCENE I]

ANTONY, DOLABELLA.

DOLA. Why would you shift it from yourself on
me?
Can you not tell her you must part?

ANT. I cannot.
I could pull out an eye, and bid it go,
And t'other should not weep. O Dolabella,
How many deaths are in this word 'depart!' 5
I dare not trust my tongue to tell her so:
One look of hers would thaw me into tears,
And I should melt till I were lost again.

DOLA. Then let Ventidius;
He's rough by nature.

ANT. Oh, he'll speak too harshly; 10
He'll kill her with the news: thou, only thou.

DOLA. Nature has cast me in so soft a mould,
That but to hear a story feigned for pleasure
Of some sad lover's death, moistens my eyes,
And robs me of my manhood. I should speak 15
So faintly, with such fear to grieve her heart,
She'd not believe it earnest.

ANT. Therefore — therefore
Thou only, thou art fit; think thyself me,
And when thou speak'st (but let it first be long),
Take off the edge from every sharper sound, 20
And let our parting be as gently made
As other loves begin: wilt thou do this?

DOLA. What you have said so sinks into my soul,
That, if I must speak, I shall speak just so.

ANT. I leave you then to your sad task. Farewell! 25

I sent her word to meet you.
(*Goes to the door, and comes back.*)
I forgot;
Let her be told, I'll make her peace with mine:
Her crown and dignity shall be preserved,
If I have pow'r with Cæsar. —— Oh, be sure
To think on that.

DOLA. Fear not, I will remember. 30
(ANTONY *goes again to the door, and comes
back.*)

ANT. And tell her, too, how much I was constrained;
I did not this, but with extremest force:
Desire her not to hate my memory,
For I still cherish hers; —— insist on that.

DOLA. Trust me, I'll not forget it.

ANT. Then that's all. 35
(*Goes out, and returns again.*)
Wilt thou forgive my fondness this once more?
Tell her, though we shall never meet again,
If I should hear she took another love,
The news would break my heart. — Now I must go;
For every time I have returned, I feel 40
My soul more tender; and my next command
Would be to bid her stay, and ruin both. *Exit.*

DOLA. Men are but children of a larger growth;
Our appetites as apt to change as theirs,
And full as craving too, and full as vain; 45
And yet the soul, shut up in her dark room,
Viewing so clear abroad, at home sees nothing;
But, like a mole in earth, busy and blind,
Works all her folly up, and casts it outward
To the world's open view: thus I discovered, 50
And blamed the love of ruined Antony;
Yet wish that I were he, to be so ruined.

Enter VENTIDIUS *above.*

VENT. Alone? and talking to himself? concerned
too?
Perhaps my guess is right; he loved her once,
And may pursue it still.

DOLA. O friendship! friendship! 55
Ill canst thou answer this; and reason, worse:
Unfaithful in th' attempt; hopeless to win;
And if I win, undone: mere madness all.
And yet th' occasion's fair. What injury
To him, to wear the robe which he throws by? 60

VENT. None, none at all. This happens as I wish,
To ruin her yet more with Antony.

Enter CLEOPATRA, *talking with* ALEXAS; CHARMION,
IRAS, *on the other side.*

DOLA. She comes! What charms have sorrow
on that face!
Sorrow seems pleased to dwell with so much sweetness;
Yet, now and then, a melancholy smile 65

Breaks loose, like lightning in a winter's night,
And shows a moment's day.
   VENT. If she should love him too! her eunuch
     there!
That porc'pisce [1] bodes ill weather. Draw, draw
     nearer,
Sweet devil, that I may hear.
   ALEX.   Believe me; try 70
     (DOLABELLA *goes over to* CHARMION *and*
     IRAS; *seems to talk with them.*)
To make him jealous; jealousy is like
A polished glass held to the lips when life's in doubt:
If there be breath, 'twill catch the damp, and show it.
   CLEO. I grant you, jealousy's a proof of love,
But 'tis a weak and unavailing med'cine;   75
It puts out [2] the disease, and makes it show,
But has no pow'r to cure.
   ALEX. 'Tis your last remedy, and strongest too:
And then this Dolabella — who so fit
To practise on? He's handsome, valiant, young, 80
And looks as he were laid for nature's bait
To catch weak women's eyes.
He stands already more than half suspected
Of loving you: the least kind word or glance
You give this youth will kindle him with love: 85
Then, like a burning vessel set adrift,
You'll send him down amain before the wind,
To fire the heart of jealous Antony.
   CLEO. Can I do this? Ah, no; my love's so true
That I can neither hide it where it is, 90
Nor show it where it is not. Nature meant me
A wife, a silly, harmless, household dove,
Fond without art, and kind without deceit;
But Fortune, that has made a mistress of me,
[Has] thrust me out to the wide world, unfur-
     nished   95
Of falsehood to be happy.
   ALEX.   Force yourself.
Th' event [3] will be, your lover will return
Doubly desirous to possess the good
Which once he feared to lose.
   CLEO.   I must attempt it;
But oh, with what regret!   100
                       Exit ALEXAS.
     (*She comes up to* DOLABELLA.)
   VENT. So, now the scene draws near; they're in
     my reach.
   CLEO. (*to* DOLABELLA). Discoursing with my
     women! might not I
Share in your entertainment?
   CHAR.   You have been
The subject of it, madam.
   CLEO.   How! and how?
   IRAS. Such praises of your beauty!

[1] Porpoise (*porcus piscis*), the 'messenger of tempests.'
[2] Brings out.   [3] Outcome.

   CLEO.   Mere poetry. 105
Your Roman wits, your Gallus and Tibullus,
Have taught you this from Cytheris and Delia.
   DOLA. Those Roman wits have never been in
     Egypt;
Cytheris and Delia else had been unsung:
I, who have seen —— had I been born a poet, 110
Should choose a nobler name.
   CLEO.   You flatter me.
But, 'tis your nation's vice: all of your country
Are flatterers, and all false. Your friend's like you.
I'm sure he sent you not to speak these words.
   DOLA. No, madam; yet he sent me ——
   CLEO.   Well, he sent you —— 115
   DOLA. Of a less pleasing errand.
   CLEO.   How less pleasing?
Less to yourself, or me?
   DOLA.   Madam, to both;
For you must mourn, and I must grieve to cause it.
   CLEO. You, Charmion, and your fellow, stand
     at distance. ——
(*Aside.*) Hold up, my spirits. —— Well, now your
     mournful matter;   120
For I'm prepared, perhaps can guess it too.
   DOLA. I wish you would; for 'tis a thankless
     office
To tell ill news: and I, of all your sex,
Most fear displeasing you.
   CLEO.   Of all your sex,
I soonest could forgive you, if you should. 125
   VENT. Most delicate advances! Woman! Woman!
Dear, damned, inconstant sex!
   CLEO.   In the first place,
I am to be forsaken; is't not so?
   DOLA. I wish I could not answer to that question.
   CLEO. Then pass it o'er, because it troubles
     you: 130
I should have been more grieved another time.
Next, I'm to lose my kingdom. —— Farewell,
     Egypt!
Yet, is there any more?
   DOLA.   Madam, I fear
Your too deep sense of grief has turned your reason.
   CLEO. No, no, I'm not run mad; I can bear
     fortune: 135
And love may be expelled by other love,
As poisons are by poisons.
   DOLA.   You o'erjoy me, madam,
To find your griefs so moderately borne.
You've heard the worst; all are not false like
     him.   140
   CLEO. No; heav'n forbid they should.
   DOLA.   Some men are constant.
   CLEO. And constancy deserves reward, that's cer-
     tain.
   DOLA. Deserves it not; but give it leave to hope.

69] Q3F print as two short lines.   95] QQ *hast*; F *has*.

VENT. I'll swear thou hast my leave. I have
   enough.
But how to manage this! Well, I'll consider. 145
                                   Exit.
  DOLA. I came prepared
To tell you heavy news; news, which I thought
Would fright the blood from your pale cheeks to
   hear:
But you have met it with a cheerfulness
That makes my task more easy; and my
   tongue,   150
Which on another's message was employed,
Would gladly speak its own.
  CLEO.   Hold, Dolabella.
First tell me, were you chosen by my lord?
Or sought you this employment?
  DOLA. He picked me out; and, as his bosom
   friend,   155
He charged me with his words.
  CLEO.   The message then
I know was tender, and each accent smooth,
To mollify that rugged word 'depart.'
  DOLA. Oh, you mistake: he chose the harshest
   words;
With fiery eyes, and with contracted brows, 160
He coined his face in the severest stamp:
And fury shook his fabric, like an earthquake;
He heaved for vent, and burst like bellowing Ætna,
In sounds scarce human — 'Hence, away for ever:
Let her begone, the blot of my renown, 165
And bane of all my hopes!

    (*All the time of this speech,* CLEOPATRA *seems
    more and more concerned, till she sinks quite
    down.*)

Let her be driv'n as far as men can think
From man's commérce! She'll poison to the center.'
  CLEO. Oh, I can bear no more!
  DOLA. Help, help! — O wretch! O cursèd,
   cursèd wretch!   170
What have I done!
  CHAR.   Help, chafe her temples, Iras.
  IRAS. Bend, bend her forward quickly.
  CHAR.   Heav'n be praised,
She comes again.
  CLEO.   Oh, let him not approach me.
Why have you brought me back to this loathed being,
Th' abode of falsehood, violated vows, 175
And injured love? For pity, let me go;
For, if there be a place of long repose,
I'm sure I want it. My disdainful lord
Can never break that quiet; nor awake
The sleeping soul with hollowing in my tomb 180
Such words as fright her hence. — Unkind, unkind!
  DOLA. (*kneeling*). Believe me, 'tis against myself
   I speak;

That sure deserves belief; I injured him:
My friend ne'er spoke those words. Oh, had you seen
How often he came back, and every time 185
With something more obliging and more kind,
To add to what he said; what dear farewells;
How almost vanquished by his love he parted,
And leaned to what unwillingly he left!
I, traitor as I was, for love of you 190
(But what can you not do, who made me false!)
I forged that lie; for whose forgiveness kneels
This self-accused, self-punished criminal.
  CLEO. With how much ease believe we what we
   wish!
Rise, Dolabella; if you have been guilty, 195
I have contributed, and too much love
Has made me guilty too.
Th' advance of kindness which I made was feigned,
To call back fleeting love by jealousy;
But 'twould not last. Oh, rather let me lose, 200
Than so ignobly trifle with his heart.
  DOLA. I find your breast fenced round from hu-
   man reach,
Transparent as a rock of solid crystal,
Seen through, but never pierced. My friend, my
   friend!
What endless treasure hast thou thrown away, 205
And scattered, like an infant, in the ocean,
Vain sums of wealth, which none can gather thence!
  CLEO. Could you not beg
An hour's admittance to his private ear?
Like one who wanders through long barren wilds, 210
And yet foreknows no hospitable inn
Is near to succor hunger, eats his fill,
Before his painful march:
So would I feed a while my famished eyes
Before we part; for I have far to go, 215
If death be far, and never must return.

       VENTIDIUS *with* OCTAVIA, *behind.*

  VENT. From hence you may discover — oh,
   sweet, sweet!
Would you indeed? the pretty hand in earnest?
  DOLA. I will, for this reward. — (*Takes her hand.*)
   Draw it not back,
'Tis all I e'er will beg.   220
  VENT. They turn upon us.
  OCTAV.   What quick eyes has guilt!
  VENT. Seem not to have observed 'em, and go on.

    They [VENTIDIUS *and* OCTAVIA] *enter.*

  DOLA. Saw you the emperor, Ventidius?
  VENT.   No.
I sought him; but I heard that he was private,
None with him but Hipparchus, his freedman. 225
  DOLA. Know you his bus'ness?

183] S silently alters *deserves* to *desires*.   212–213] QQF print *eats . . . march* as one line.
219] QQF put the stage direction at end of l. 218.

VENT.   Giving him instructions,
And letters to his brother Cæsar.
DOLA.   Well,
He must be found.

Exeunt DOLABELLA *and* CLEOPATRA.

OCTAV.   Most glorious impudence!
VENT. She looked, methought,
As she would say, 'Take your old man, Octavia;   230
Thank you, I'm better here.' Well, but what use
Make we of this discovery?
OCTAV.   Let it die.
VENT. I pity Dolabella; but she's dangerous:
Her eyes have pow'r beyond Thessalian charms
To draw the moon from heav'n; for eloquence,   235
The sea-green Sirens taught her voice their flatt'ry;
And, while she speaks, night steals upon the day,
Unmarked of those that hear.   Then she's so charm-
    ing,
Age buds at sight of her, and swells to youth:
The holy priests gaze on her when she smiles;   240
And with heaved hands, forgetting gravity,
They bless her wanton eyes: even I, who hate her,
With a malignant joy behold such beauty;
And, while I curse, desire it.   Antony
Must needs have some remains of passion still,   245
Which may ferment into a worse relapse,
If now not fully cured.   I know, this minute,
With Cæsar he's endeavoring her peace.
OCTAV. You have prevailed: — but for a farther
    purpose   (*Walks off.*)
I'll prove how he will relish this discovery.   250
What, make a strumpet's peace! it swells my heart:
It must not, sha' not be.
VENT.   His guards appear.
Let me begin, and you shall second me.

Enter ANTONY.

ANT. Octavia, I was looking you, my love:
What, are your letters ready?   I have giv'n   255
My last instructions.
OCTAV.   Mine, my lord, are written.
ANT. Ventidius!   (*Drawing him aside.*)
VENT.   My lord?
ANT.   A word in private.
When saw you Dolabella?
VENT.   Now, my lord,
He parted hence; and Cleopatra with him.
ANT. Speak softly. — 'Twas by my command he
    went,   260
To bear my last farewell.
VENT. (*aloud*).   It looked indeed
Like your farewell.
ANT.   More softly. — My farewell?
What secret meaning have you in those words

Of 'my farewell'?   He did it by my order.
VENT. (*aloud*). Then he obeyed your order.   I
    suppose   265
You bid him do it with all gentleness,
All kindness, and all —— love.
ANT.   How she mourned,
The poor forsaken creature!
VENT. She took it as she ought; she bore your
    parting
As she did Cæsar's, as she would another's,   270
Were a new love to come.
ANT. (*aloud*).   Thou dost belie her;
Most basely, and maliciously belie her.
VENT. I thought not to displease you; I have done.
OCTAV. (*coming up*). You seemed disturbed, my
    lord.
ANT.   A very trifle.
Retire, my love.
VENT.   It was indeed a trifle.   275
He sent ——
ANT. (*angrily*). No more.   Look how thou dis-
    obey'st me;
Thy life shall answer it.
OCTAV.   Then 'tis no trifle.
VENT. (*to* OCTAVIA). 'Tis less, a very nothing;
    you too saw it,
As well as I, and therefore 'tis no secret.
ANT. She saw it!
VENT.   Yes: she saw young Dola-
    bella ——   280
ANT. Young Dolabella!
VENT.   Young, I think him young,
And handsome too; and so do others think him.
But what of that?   He went by your command,
Indeed 'tis probable, with some kind message;
For she received it graciously; she smiled;   285
And then he grew familiar with her hand,
Squeezed it, and worried it with ravenous kisses;
She blushed, and sighed, and smiled, and blushed
    again;
At last she took occasion to talk softly,
And brought her cheek up close, and leaned on
    his;   290
At which, he whispered kisses back on hers;
And then she cried aloud that constancy
Should be rewarded.
OCTAV.   This I saw and heard.
ANT. What woman was it, whom you heard and saw
So playful with my friend?   Not Cleopatra?   295
VENT. Ev'n she, my lord.
ANT.   My Cleopatra?
VENT. Your Cleopatra;
Dolabella's Cleopatra;
Every man's Cleopatra.

231] QQF print *Well . . . use* as a separate short line.   295] QQF print *Not Cleopatra?* as separate line.
297–299] QQF print as three short lines.   This echo of Shakespeare's prose, 'Leonato's Hero, your Hero, every man's Hero'
(*Much Ado About Nothing*), interrupts Dryden's regular verse.

ANT. Thou li'st.

VENT. I do not lie, my lord. 300
Is this so strange? Should mistresses be left,
And not provide against a time of change?
You know she's not much used to lonely nights.

ANT. I'll think no more on't.
I know 'tis false, and see the plot betwixt you. 305
You needed not have gone this way, Octavia.
What harms it you that Cleopatra's just?
She's mine no more. I see, and I forgive:
Urge it no farther, love.

OCTAV. Are you concerned,
That she's found false?

ANT. I should be, were it so; 310
For, though 'tis past, I would not that the world
Should tax my former choice, that I loved one
Of so light note; but I forgive you both.

VENT. What has my age deserved, that you
should think
I would abuse your ears with perjury? 315
If heav'n be true, she's false.

ANT. Though heav'n and earth
Should witness it, I'll not believe her tainted.

VENT. I'll bring you, then, a witness
From hell, to prove her so. (*Seeing* ALEXAS *just
ent'ring, and starting back.*) —Nay, go not
back;
For stay you must and shall.

ALEX. What means my lord? 320

VENT. To make you do what most you hate,—
speak truth.
You are of Cleopatra's private counsel,
Of her bed-counsel, her lascivious hours;
Are conscious of each nightly change she makes,
And watch her, as Chaldeans do the moon, 325
Can tell what signs she passes through, what day.

ALEX. My noble lord!

VENT. My most illustrious pander,
No fine set speech, no cadence, no turned periods,
But a plain homespun truth, is what I ask:
I did, myself, o'erhear your queen make love 330
To Dolabella. Speak; for I will know,
By your confession, what more passed betwixt 'em;
How near the bus'ness draws to your employment;
And when the happy hour.

ANT. Speak truth, Alexas; whether it offend 335
Or please Ventidius, care not: justify
Thy injured queen from malice: dare his worst.

OCTAV. (*aside*). See how he gives him courage!
how he fears
To find her false! and shuts his eyes to truth,
Willing to be misled! 340

ALEX. As far as love may plead for woman's
frailty,
Urged by desert and greatness of the lover,

So far, divine Octavia, may my queen
Stand ev'n excused to you for loving him
Who is your lord: so far, from brave Ventid-
ius, 345
May her past actions hope a fair report.

ANT. 'Tis well, and truly spoken: mark, Ventidius.

ALEX. To you, most noble emperor, her strong
passion
Stands not excused, but wholly justified.
Her beauty's charms alone, without her crown, 350
From Ind and Meroe drew the distant vows
Of sighing kings; and at her feet were laid
The sceptres of the earth, exposed on heaps,
To choose where she would reign:
She thought a Roman only could deserve her, 355
And, of all Romans, only Antony.
And, to be less than wife to you, disdained
Their lawful passion.

ANT. 'Tis but truth.

ALEX. And yet, though love, and your unmatched
desert,
Have drawn her from the due regard of honor, 360
At last heav'n opened her unwilling eyes
To see the wrongs she offered fair Octavia,
Whose holy bed she lawlessly usurped.
The sad effects of this improsperous war
Confirmed those pious thoughts.

VENT. (*aside*). Oh, wheel you there? 365
Observe him now; the man begins to mend,
And talk substantial reason. — Fear not, eunuch;
The emperor has giv'n thee leave to speak.

ALEX. Else had I never dared t'offend his ears
With what the last necessity has urged 370
On my forsaken mistress; yet I must not
Presume to say her heart is wholly altered.

ANT. No, dare not for thy life, I charge thee
dare not
Pronounce that fatal word!

OCTAV. (*aside*). Must I bear this? Good heav'n,
afford me patience. 375

VENT. On, sweet eunuch; my dear half-man,
proceed.

ALEX. Yet Dolabella
Has loved her long; he, next my god-like lord,
Deserves her best; and should she meet his passion,
Rejected, as she is, by him she loved —— 380

ANT. Hence, from my sight! for I can bear no
more:
Let Furies drag thee quick to hell; let all
The longer damned have rest; each torturing hand
Do thou employ, till Cleopatra comes;
Then join thou too, and help to torture her! 385

Exit ALEXAS, *thrust out by* ANTONY.

OCTAV. 'Tis not well,
Indeed, my lord, 'tis much unkind to me,

319] Q3F omit *not.*　　356] Q3F misprint *Roman.*　　363] Q2Q3F *lawfully,* a misprint that persists amusingly.
382-383] Q2Q3F omit *let all … rest.* CS restore Q1 fully.

To show this passion, this extreme concernment,
For an abandoned, faithless prostitute.

ANT. Octavia, leave me: I am much disor-
    dered.   390
Leave me, I say.

OCTAV.   My lord!

ANT.   I bid you leave me.

VENT. Obey him, madam: best withdraw a while,
And see how this will work.

OCTAV. Wherein have I offended you, my lord,
That I am bid to leave you?   Am I false,   395
Or infamous?   Am I a Cleopatra?
Were I she,
Base as she is, you would not bid me leave you;
But hang upon my neck, take slight excuses,
And fawn upon my falsehood.

ANT.   'Tis too much,   400
Too much, Octavia; I am pressed with sorrows
Too heavy to be borne; and you add more:
I would retire, and recollect what's left
Of man within, to aid me.

OCTAV.   You would mourn,
In private, for your love, who has betrayed you;   405
You did but half return to me: your kindness
Lingered behind with her.   I hear, my lord,
You make conditions for her,
And would include her treaty.   Wondrous proofs
Of love to me!

ANT.   Are you my friend, Ventidius?   410
Or are you turned a Dolabella too,
And let this Fury loose?

VENT.   Oh, be advised,
Sweet madam, and retire.

OCTAV. Yes, I will go; but never to return.
You shall no more be haunted with this Fury.   415
My lord, my lord, love will not always last,
When urged with long unkindness and disdain;
Take her again whom you prefer to me;
She stays but to be called.   Poor cozened man!
Let a feigned parting give her back your heart,   420
Which a feigned love first got; for injured me,
Though my just sense of wrongs forbid my stay,
My duty shall be yours.
To the dear pledges of our former love
My tenderness and care shall be transferred,   425
And they shall cheer, by turns, my widowed nights:
So, take my last farewell; for I despair
To have you whole, and scorn to take you half.
                              Exit.

VENT. I combat heav'n, which blasts my best de-
    signs:
My last attempt must be to win her back;   430
But oh! I fear, in vain.   *Exit.*

ANT. Why was I framed with this plain, honest
    heart,
Which knows not to disguise its griefs and weakness,
But bears its workings outward to the world?

I should have kept the mighty anguish in,   435
And forced a smile at Cleopatra's falsehood:
Octavia had believed it, and had stayed.
But I am made a shallow-forded stream,
Seen to the bottom, — all my clearness scorned,
And all my faults exposed! — See where he
    comes,   440

Enter DOLABELLA.

Who has profaned the sacred name of friend,
And worn it into vileness!
With how secure a brow, and specious form,
He gilds the secret villain!   Sure that face
Was meant for honesty; but heav'n mismatched
    it,   445
And furnished treason out with nature's pomp,
To make its work more easy.

DOLA.   O my friend!

ANT. Well, Dolabella, you performed my message?

DOLA. I did, unwillingly.

ANT.   Unwillingly?
Was it so hard for you to bear our parting?   450
You should have wished it.

DOLA.   Why?

ANT.   Because you love me.
And she received my message with as true,
With as unfeigned a sorrow as you brought it?

DOLA. She loves you, ev'n to madness.

ANT.   Oh, I know it.
You, Dolabella, do not better know   455
How much she loves me.   And should I
Forsake this beauty, this all-perfect creature?

DOLA. I could not, were she mine.

ANT.   And yet you first
Persuaded me: how come you altered since?

DOLA. I said at first I was not fit to go;   460
I could not hear her sighs, and see her tears,
But pity must prevail: and so, perhaps,
It may again with you; for I have promised,
That she should take her last farewell: and, see,
She comes to claim my word.

Enter CLEOPATRA.

ANT.   False Dolabella!   465

DOLA. What's false, my lord?

ANT.   Why, Dolabella's false,
And Cleopatra's false; both false and faithless.
Draw near, you well-joined wickedness, you ser-
    pents,
Whom I have in my kindly bosom warmed
Till I am stung to death.

DOLA.   My lord, have I   470
Deserved to be thus used?

CLEO.   Can heav'n prepare
A newer torment?   Can it find a curse
Beyond our separation?

ANT.   Yes, if fate

Be just, much greater: heav'n should be ingenious
In punishing such crimes.   The rolling stone,[1]   475
And gnawing vulture,[2] were slight pains, invented
When Jove was young, and no examples known
Of mighty ills; but you have ripened sin,
To such a monstrous growth, 'twill pose the gods
To find an equal torture.   Two, two such! —   480
Oh, there's no farther name, two such! — to me,
To me, who locked my soul within your breasts,
Had no desires, no joys, no life, but you;
When half the globe was mine, I gave it you
In dowry with my heart; I had no use,   485
No fruit of all, but you: a friend and mistress
Was what the world could give.   O Cleopatra!
O Dolabella! how could you betray
This tender heart, which with an infant fondness
Lay lulled betwixt your bosoms, and there
      slept,   490
Secure of injured faith?
DOLA.   If she has wronged you,
Heav'n, hell, and you revenge it.
ANT.   If she wronged me!
Thou wouldst evade thy part of guilt; but swear
Thou lov'st not her.
DOLA.   Not so as I love you.
ANT. Not so!   Swear, swear, I say; thou dost
      not love her.   495
DOLA. No more than friendship will allow.
ANT.   No more?
Friendship allows thee nothing: thou art perjured —
And yet thou didst not swear thou lov'dst her not;
But not so much, no more.   O trifling hypocrite,
Who dar'st not own to her, thou dost not love,   500
Nor own to me, thou dost!   Ventidius heard it;
Octavia saw it.
CLEO.   They are enemies.
ANT. Alexas is not so: he, he confessed it:
He, who, next hell, best knew it, he avowed it.
(To DOLABELLA.)   Why do I seek a proof beyond
      yourself?   505
You, whom I sent to bear my last farewell,
Returned to plead her stay.
DOLA.   What shall I answer?
If to have loved be guilt, then I have sinned;
But if to have repented of that love
Can wash away my crime, I have repented.   510
Yet, if I have offended past forgiveness,
Let not her suffer: she is innocent.
CLEO. Ah, what will not a woman do, who loves!
What means will she refuse, to keep that heart
Where all her joys are placed?   'Twas I encour-
      aged,   515

[1] Sisyphus, in Hades, had ceaselessly to roll uphill a stone
which always rolled back upon him just as he neared the top.
[2] Tityus, in Tartarus, was tortured by having vultures
continually gnaw his liver.

'Twas I blew up the fire that scorched his soul,
To make you jealous, and by that regain you.
But all in vain; I could not counterfeit.
In spite of all the dams my love broke o'er,
And drowned my heart again.   Fate took th' occa-
      sion;   520
And thus one minute's feigning has destroyed
My whole life's truth.
ANT.   Thin cobweb arts of falsehood,
Seen, and broke through at first.
DOLA.   Forgive your mistress.
CLEO. Forgive your friend.
ANT.   You have convinced [3] yourselves,
You plead each other's cause.   What witness have
      you,   525
That you but meant to raise my jealousy?
CLEO. Ourselves, and heav'n.
ANT. Guilt witnesses for guilt.   Hence, love and
      friendship!
You have no longer place in human breasts,
These two have driv'n you out.   Avoid my
      sight!   530
I would not kill the man whom I [have] loved,
And cannot hurt the woman; but avoid me, —
I do not know how long I can be tame.
For, if I stay one minute more to think
How I am wronged, my justice and revenge   535
Will cry so loud within me, that my pity
Will not be heard for either.
DOLA.   Heav'n has but
Our sorrow for our sins; and then delights
To pardon erring man: sweet mercy seems
Its darling attribute, which limits justice;   540
As if there were degrees in infinite,
And infinite would rather want perfection
Than punish to extent.
ANT.   I can forgive
A foe, but not a mistress and a friend.
Treason is there in its most horrid shape,   545
Where trust is greatest: and the soul resigned
Is stabbed by its own guards.   I'll hear no more;
Hence from my sight for ever!
CLEO.   How? for ever!
I cannot go one moment from your sight,
And must I go for ever?   550
My joys, my only joys, are centered here.
What place have I to go to?   My own kingdom?
That I have lost for you.   Or to the Romans?
They hate me for your sake.   Or must I wander
The wide world o'er, a helpless, banished wo-
      man,   555
Banished for love of you, banished from you?
Aye, there's the banishment!   Oh, hear me! hear me,
With strictest justice, for I beg no favor;

[3] Convicted.

492] S inserts has after she.   498] S alters lov'dst to lov'st.   531] QQF omit have; CS emend by supplying have.

And if I have offended you, then kill me,
But do not banish me.

ANT.   I must not hear you. 560
I have a fool within me takes your part;
But honor stops my ears.

CLEO.   For pity hear me!
Would you cast off a slave who followed you?
Who crouched beneath your spurn? — He has no
         pity!
See, if he gives one tear to my departure,   565
One look, one kind farewell: O iron heart!
Let all the gods look down, and judge betwixt us,
If he did ever love!

ANT.   No more. —— Alexas!

DOLA. A perjured villain!

ANT. (to CLEOPATRA).   Your Alexas, yours!

CLEO. Oh, 'twas his plot, his ruinous design,   570
T' engage you in my love by jealousy.
Hear him; confront him with me; let him speak.

ANT. I have; I have.

CLEO.   And if he clear me not ——

ANT. Your creature! one who hangs upon your
         smiles!
Watches your eye, to say or to unsay   575
Whate'er you please! I am not to be moved.

CLEO. Then must we part? Farewell, my cruel lord!
Th' appearance is against me; and I go,
Unjustified, for ever from your sight.
How I have loved, you know; how yet I love,   580
My only comfort is, I know myself:
I love you more, ev'n now you are unkind,
Than when you loved me most: so well, so truly,
I'll never strive against it; but die pleased,
To think you once were mine.   585

ANT. Good heav'n, they weep at parting!
Must I weep too? That calls 'em innocent.
I must not weep; and yet I must, to think
That I must not forgive. ——
Live, but live wretched; 'tis but just you
         should,   590
Who made me so. Live from each other's sight:
Let me not hear you meet: set all the earth,
And all the seas, betwixt your sundered loves:
View nothing common but the sun and skies.
Now, all take several ways;   595
     And each your own sad fate, with mine, deplore;
     That you were false, and I could trust no more.
                              Exeunt severally.

ACT V

[SCENE I]

CLEOPATRA, CHARMION, IRAS.

CHAR. Be juster, heav'n: such virtue punished thus,
Will make us think that chance rules all above,

And shuffles, with a random hand, the lots
Which man is forced to draw.

CLEO. I could tear out these eyes, that gained his
         heart,   5
And had not pow'r to keep it. O the curse
Of doting on, ev'n when I find it dotage!
Bear witness, gods, you heard him bid me go;
You, whom he mocked with imprecating vows
Of promised faith! —— I'll die; I will not bear it. 10
     (*She pulls out her dagger, and they hold her.*)
You may hold me ——
But I can keep my breath; I can die inward,
And choke this love.

Enter ALEXAS.

IRAS.   Help, O Alexas, help!
The queen grows desperate; her soul struggles in her
With all the agonies of love and rage,   15
And strives to force its passage.

CLEO.   Let me go.
Art thou there, traitor! — Oh!
Oh, for a little breath, to vent my rage!
Give, give me way, and let me loose upon him.

ALEX. Yes, I deserve it, for my ill-timed
         truth.   20
Was it for me to prop
The ruins of a falling majesty?
To place myself beneath the mighty flaw,
Thus to be crushed, and pounded into atoms,
By its o'erwhelming weight? 'Tis too presuming 25
For subjects to preserve that wilful pow'r
Which courts its own destruction.

CLEO.   I would reason
More calmly with you. Did not you o'errule,
And force my plain, direct, and open love
Into these crooked paths of jealousy?   30
Now, what's th' event? Octavia is removed;
But Cleopatra's banished. Thou, thou, villain,
Has[t] pushed my boat to open sea; to prove,
At my sad cost, if thou canst steer it back.
It cannot be; I'm lost too far; I'm ruined!   35
Hence, thou impostor, traitor, monster, devil! —
I can no more: thou, and my griefs, have sunk
Me down so low, that I want voice to curse thee.

ALEX. Suppose some shipwracked seaman near
         the shore,
Dropping and faint, with climbing up the cliff, 40
If, from above, some charitable hand
Pull him to safety, hazarding himself
To draw the other's weight; would he look back,
And curse him for his pains? The case is yours;
But one step more, and you have gained the
         height.   45

CLEO. Sunk, never more to rise.

ALEX. Octavia's gone, and Dolabella banished.
Believe me, madam, Antony is yours.

33] QQF *has.*   39] Q1 *some;* Q2Q3F *from.*

His heart was never lost, but started off
To jealousy, love's last retreat and covert;   50
Where it lies hid in shades, watchful in silence,
And list'ning for the sound that calls it back.
Some other, any man ('tis so advanced),
May perfect this unfinished work, which I
(Unhappy only to myself) have left   55
So easy to his hand.

    CLEO.   Look well thou do't; else ——
    ALEX.   Else, what your silence threatens. — Antony
Is mounted up the Pharos, from whose turret
He stands surveying our Egyptian galleys,
Engaged with Cæsar's fleet.   Now death or conquest!   60
If the first happen, fate acquits my promise;
If we o'ercome, the conqueror is yours.

    (*A distant shout within.*)

    CHAR. Have comfort, madam: did you mark that
    shout?   (*Second shout nearer.*)
    IRAS. Hark! they redouble it.
    ALEX.   'Tis from the port.
The loudness shows it near: good news, kind
    heavens!   65
    CLEO. Osiris make it so!

Enter SERAPION.

    SERAP.   Where, where's the queen?
    ALEX. How frightfully the holy coward stares!
As if not yet recovered of th' assault,
When all his gods, and, what's more dear to him,
His offerings, were at stake.

    SERAP.   O horror, horror!   70
Egypt has been; our latest hour is come:
The queen of nations, from her ancient seat,
Is sunk for ever in the dark abyss:
Time has unrolled her glories to the last,
And now closed up the volume.

    CLEO.   Be more plain: 75
Say, whence thou com'st (though fate is in thy face,
Which from thy haggard eyes looks wildly out,
And threatens ere thou speak'st).

    SERAP.   I came from Pharos;
From viewing (spare me, and imagine it)
Our land's last hope, your navy ——

    CLEO.   Vanquished?
    SERAP.   No.   80
They fought not.

    CLEO.   Then they fled?
    SERAP.   Nor that.   I saw,
With Antony, your well-appointed fleet
Row out; and thrice he waved his hand on high,
And thrice with cheerful cries they shouted back:
'Twas then false Fortune, like a fawning strumpet,   85
About to leave the bankrupt prodigal,

With a dissembled smile would kiss at parting,
And flatter to the last; the well-timed oars
Now dipped from every bank, now smoothly run
To meet the foe; and soon indeed they met,   90
But not as foes.   In few,[1] we saw their caps
On either side thrown up; th' Egyptian galleys
(Received like friends) passed through, and fell behind
The Roman rear; and now, they all come forward,
And ride within the port.

    CLEO.   Enough, Serapion: 95
I've heard my doom. — This needed not, you gods:
When I lost Antony, your work was done;
'Tis but superfluous malice. — Where's my lord?
How bears he this last blow?

    SERAP. His fury cannot be expressed by
    words: 100
Thrice he attempted headlong to have fall'n
Full on his foes, and aimed at Cæsar's galley:
Withheld, he raves on you; cries, he's betrayed.
Should he now find you —

    ALEX.   Shun him; seek your safety,
Till you can clear your innocence.

    CLEO.   I'll stay.   105
    ALEX. You must not; haste you to your monument,
While I make speed to Cæsar.

    CLEO.   Cæsar! No,
I have no business with him.

    ALEX.   I can work him
To spare your life, and let this madman perish.

    CLEO. Base fawning wretch! wouldst thou betray him too?   110
Hence from my sight!   I will not hear a traitor;
'Twas thy design brought all this ruin on us.
Serapion, thou are honest; counsel me:
But haste, each moment's precious.

    SERAP. Retire; you must not yet see Antony.   115
He who began this mischief,
'Tis just he tempt the danger: let him clear you;
And, since he offered you his servile tongue,
To gain a poor precarious life from Cæsar,
Let him expose that fawning eloquence,   120
And speak to Antony.

    ALEX.   O heavens! I dare not;
I meet my certain death.

    CLEO.   Slave, thou deserv'st it. —
Not that I fear my lord, will I avoid him;
I know him noble: when he banished me,
And thought me false, he scorned to take my
    life;   125
But I'll be justified, and then die with him.

    ALEX. O pity me, and let me follow you!

---

[1] In brief (in few words).

CLEO. **To death, if thou stir hence.** Speak, if
   thou canst,
Now for thy life, which basely thou wouldst save;
While mine I prize at — this! Come, good Sera-
   pion.   130
   Exeunt CLEOPATRA, SERAPION, CHARMION,
      IRAS.
ALEX. O that I less could fear to lose this being,
Which, like a snowball in my coward hand,
The more 'tis grasped, the faster melts away.
Poor reason! what a wretched aid art thou!
For still, in spite of thee,   135
These two long lovers, soul and body, dread
Their final separation. Let me think:
What can I say, to save myself from death?
No matter what becomes of Cleopatra.
ANT. (*within*). Which way? where?
VENT. (*within*).   This leads to th'
   monument.   140
ALEX. Ah me! I hear him; yet I'm unprepared:
My gift of lying's gone;
And this court-devil, which I so oft have raised,
Forsakes me at my need. I dare not stay;
Yet cannot far go hence.   *Exit.* 145

   Enter ANTONY *and* VENTIDIUS.

ANT. O happy Cæsar! thou hast men to lead:
Think not 'tis thou hast conquered Antony;
But Rome has conquered Egypt. I'm betrayed.
VENT. Curse on this treach'rous train!
Their soil and heav'n infect 'em all with base-
   ness: 150
And their young souls come tainted to the world
With the first breath they draw.
ANT. Th' original villain sure no god created;
He was a bastard of the sun, by Nile,
Aped into man; with all his mother's mud   155
Crusted about his soul.
VENT.   The nation is
One universal traitor; and their queen
The very spirit and extract of 'em all.
ANT. Is there yet left
A possibility of aid from valor?   160
Is there one god unsworn to my destruction?
The least unmortgaged hope? for, if there be,
Methinks I cannot fall beneath the fate
Of such a boy as Cæsar.
The world's one half is yet in Antony;   165
And from each limb of it that's hewed away,
The soul comes back to me.
VENT.   There yet remain
Three legions in the town — the last assault
Lopped off the rest. If death be your design
(As I must wish it now), these are sufficient 170
To make a heap about us of dead foes,
An honest pile for burial.

ANT.   They're enough.
We'll not divide our stars; but side by side
Fight emulous, and with malicious eyes
Survey each other's acts: so every death   175
Thou giv'st, I'll take on me, as a just debt,
And pay thee back a soul.
VENT. Now you shall see I love you. Not a word
Of chiding more. By my few hours of life,
I am so pleased with this brave Roman fate, 180
That I would not be Cæsar, to outlive you.
When we put off this flesh, and mount together,
I shall be shown to all th' ethereal crowd, —
'Lo, this is he who died with Antony!'
ANT. Who knows but we may pierce through all
   their troops,   185
And reach my veterans yet? 'Tis worth the tempt-
   ing,
T' o'erleap this gulf of fate,
And leave our wond'ring destinies behind.

   Enter ALEXAS, *trembling.*

VENT. See, see, that villain!
See Cleopatra stamped upon that face,   190
With all her cunning, all her arts of falsehood!
How she looks out through those dissembling eyes!
How he has set his count'nance for deceit,
And promises a lie, before he speaks!
Let me despatch him first.   (*Drawing.*)
ALEX.   O spare me, spare me! 195
ANT. Hold; he's not worth your killing. — On thy
   life
(Which thou may'st keep, because I scorn to take
   it),
No syllable to justify thy queen;
Save thy base tongue its office.
ALEX.   Sir, she's gone,
Where she shall never be molested more   200
By love, or you.
ANT.   Fled to her Dolabella!
Die, traitor! I revoke my promise! die!
      (*Going to kill him.*)
ALEX. O hold! she is not fled.
ANT.   She is: my eyes
Are open to her falsehood; my whole life
Has been a golden dream of love and friend-
   ship.   205
But, now I wake, I'm like a merchant, roused
From soft repose, to see his vessel sinking,
And all his wealth cast o'er. Ingrateful woman!
Who followed me, but as the swallow summer,
Hatching her young ones in my kindly beams, 210
Singing her flatt'ries to my morning wake;
But, now my winter comes, she spreads her wings,
And seeks the spring of Cæsar.
ALEX.   Think not so:
Her fortunes have, in all things, mixed with yours.

188] Q2Q3F *wand'ring.*   193] Q2Q3F *he sets.*

Had she betrayed her naval force to Rome,   215
How easily might she have gone to Cæsar,
Secure by such a bribe!

VENT.   She sent it first,
To be more welcome after.

ANT.   'Tis too plain;
Else would she have appeared, to clear herself.

ALEX. Too fatally she has; she could not
     bear   220
To be accused by you; but shut herself
Within her monument; looked down and sighed;
While, from her únchanged face, the silent tears
Dropped, as they had not leave, but stole their part-
     ing.
Some undistinguished words she inly mur-
     mured;   225
At last, she raised her eyes; and, with such looks
As dying Lucrece cast, ——

ANT.   My heart forebodes ——

VENT. All for the best; go on.

ALEX.   She snatched her poniard,
And, ere we could prevent the fatal blow,
Plunged it within her breast: then turned to me: 230
'Go, bear my lord,' said she, 'my last farewell;
And ask him if he yet suspect my faith.'
More she was saying, but death rushed betwixt.
She half pronounced your name with her last breath,
And buried half within her.

VENT.   Heav'n be praised!   235

ANT. Then art thou innocent, my poor dear love,
And art thou dead?
O those two words! their sound should be divided:
Hadst thou been false, and died; or hadst thou lived,
And hadst been true. — But innocence and
     death!   240
This shows not well above. Then what am I,
The murderer of this truth, this innocence!
Thoughts cannot form themselves in words so horrid
As can express my guilt!

VENT. Is't come to this? The gods have been
     too gracious: 245
And thus you thank 'em for't!

ANT. (to ALEXAS).   Why stay'st thou here?
Is it for thee to spy upon my soul,
And see its inward mourning? Get thee hence!
Thou art not worthy to behold what now
Becomes a Roman emperor to perform.   250

ALEX. (aside). He loves her still:
His grief betrays it. Good! The joy to find
She's yet alive, completes the reconcilement.
I've saved myself, and her. But, oh! the Romans!
Fate comes too fast upon my wit,   255
Hunts me too hard, and meets me at each double.
                                          Exit.

VENT. Would she had died a little sooner, though,
Before Octavia went; you might have treated:

Now 'twill look tame, and would not be received.
Come, rouse yourself, and let's die warm to-
     gether.   260

ANT. I will not fight: there's no more work for
     war.
The bus'ness of my angry hours is done.

VENT. Cæsar is at your gates.

ANT.   Why, let him enter;
He's welcome now.

VENT. What lethargy has crept into your
     soul?   265

ANT. 'Tis but a scorn of life, and just desire
To free myself from bondage.

VENT.   Do it bravely.

ANT. I will; but not by fighting. O Ventidius!
What should I fight for now? My queen is dead.
I was but great for her; my pow'r, my empire, 270
Were but my merchandise to buy her love;
And conquered kings, my factors. Now she's dead,
Let Cæsar take the world, —
An empty circle, since the jewel's gone
Which made it worth my strife: my being's nau-
     seous;   275
For all the bribes of life are gone away.

VENT. Would you be taken?

ANT.   Yes, I would be taken;
But, as a Roman ought, — dead, my Ventidius:
For I'll convey my soul from Cæsar's reach,
And lay down life myself.   'Tis time the world   280
Should have a lord, and know whom to obey.
We two have kept its homage in suspense,
And bent the globe, on whose each side we trod,
Till it was dinted inwards.   Let him walk
Alone upon't; I'm weary of my part.   285
My torch is out; and the world stands before me
Like a black desart at th' approach of night:
I'll lay me down, and stray no farther on.

VENT. I could be grieved,
But that I'll not outlive you: choose your death; 290
For, I have seen him in such various shapes,
I care not which I take: I'm only troubled,
The life I bear is worn to such a rag,
'Tis scarce worth giving. I could wish, indeed,
We threw it from us with a better grace;   295
That, like two lions taken in the toils,
We might at least thrust out our paws, and wound
The hunters that inclose us.

ANT.   I have thought on't.
Ventidius, you must live.

VENT.   I must not, sir.

ANT. Wilt thou not live, to speak some good of
     me?   300
To stand by my fair fame, and guard th' approaches
From the ill tongues of men?

VENT.   Who shall guard mine,
For living after you?

ANT.   Say, I command it.
VENT. If we die well, our deaths will speak them-
        selves
And need no living witness.
ANT.   Thou hast loved me, 305
And fain I would reward thee. I must die;
Kill me, and take the merit of my death
To make thee friends with Cæsar.
VENT.   Thank your kindness.
You said I loved you; and, in recompense,
You bid me turn a traitor. Did I think 310
You would have used me thus? — that I should die
With a hard thought of you?
ANT.   Forgive me, Roman.
Since I have heard of Cleopatra's death,
My reason bears no rule upon my tongue,
But lets my thoughts break all at random out. 315
I've thought better; do not deny me twice.
VENT. By heav'n, I will not.
Let it not be t' outlive you.
ANT.   Kill me first,
And then die thou; for 'tis but just thou serve
Thy friend, before thyself.
VENT.   Give me your hand. 320
We soon shall meet again. Now, farewell, em-
        peror! —   (*Embrace.*)
Methinks that word's too cold to be my last:
Since death sweeps all distinctions, farewell, friend!
That's all. ——
I will not make a bus'ness of a trifle; 325
And yet I cannot look on you, and kill you;
Pray turn your face.
ANT.   I do: strike home, be sure.
VENT. Home as my sword will reach.
                              (*Kills himself.*)
ANT.   Oh, thou mistak'st!
That wound was none of thine: give it me back:
Thou robb'st me of my death!
VENT.   — I do indeed; 330
But think 'tis the first time I e'er deceived you,
If that may plead my pardon. — And you, gods,
Forgive me, if you will; for I die perjured,
Rather than kill my friend.   (*Dies.*)
ANT. Farewell! Ever my leader, ev'n in
        death! 335
My queen and thou have got the start of me,
And I'm the lag of honor. — Gone so soon?
Is Death no more? He used him carelessly,
With a familiar kindness; ere he knocked,
Ran to the door, and took him in his arms, 340
As who should say, 'Y'are welcome at all hours,
A friend need give no warning.' Books had spoiled
        him;
For all the learn'd are cowards by profession.
'Tis not worth
My farther thought; for death, for aught I know, 345

Is but to think no more. Here's to be satisfied.
                              (*Falls on his sword.*)
I've missed my heart. O unperforming hand!
Thou never couldst have erred in a worse time.
My fortune jades me to the last; and Death,
Like a great man, takes state, and makes me
        wait 350
For my admittance. —— (*Trampling within.*)
Some, perhaps, from Cæsar:
If he should find me living, and suspect
That I played booty [1] with my life! I'll mend
My work, ere they can reach me.
                              (*Rises upon his knees.*)

Enter CLEOPATRA, CHARMION, IRAS.

CLEO. Where is my lord! where is he?
CHAR.   There he lies, 355
And dead Ventidius by him.
CLEO. My fears were prophets; I am come too
        late.
O that accurst Alexas!   (*Runs to him.*)
ANT.   Art thou living?
Or am I dead before I knew, and thou
The first kind ghost that meets me?
CLEO.   Help me seat him. 360
Send quickly, send for help!
                              (*They place him in a chair.*)
ANT.   I am answered.
We live both. Sit thee down, my Cleopatra:
I'll make the most I can of life, to stay
A moment more with thee.
CLEO. How is it with you?
ANT.   'Tis as with a man 365
Removing in a hurry; all packed up,
But one dear jewel that his haste forgot;
And he, for that, returns upon the spur:
So I come back, for thee.
CLEO. Too long, you heav'ns, you have been cruel
        to me; 370
Now show your mended faith, and give me back
His fleeting life!
ANT.   It will not be, my love.
I keep my soul by force.
Say but thou art not false.
CLEO.   'Tis now too late
To say I'm true: I'll prove it, and die with you. 375
Unknown to me, Alexas feigned my death:
Which, when I knew, I hasted to prevent
This fatal consequence. My fleet betrayed
Both you and me.
ANT.   And Dolabella ——
CLEO.   Scarce
Esteemed before he loved; but hated now. 380

[1] Played badly at first like a false gamester, in order to
swindle the victim eventually (shammed suicide to trick Cæsar
into pity).

ANT. Enough: my life's not long enough for more.
Thou say'st thou wilt come after: I believe thee;
For I can now believe whate'er thou say'st
That we may part more kindly.
CLEO.   I will come:
Doubt not, my life, I'll come, and quickly too: 385
Cæsar shall triumph o'er no part of thee.
ANT. But grieve not, while thou stay'st[,]
My last disastrous times:
Think we have had a clear and glorious day,
And heav'n did kindly to delay the storm,   390
Just till our close of ev'ning. Ten years' love,
And not a moment lost, but all improved
To th' utmost joys, — what ages have we lived!
And now to die each other's; and, so dying,
While hand in hand we walk in groves below, 395
Whole troops of lovers' ghosts shall flock about us,
And all the train be ours.
CLEO. Your words are like the notes of dying
    swans,
Too sweet to last. Were there so many hours
For your unkindness, and not one for love?   400
ANT. No, not a minute. — This one kiss — more
    worth
Than all I leave to Cæsar.   (Dies.)
CLEO. Oh, tell me so again,
And take ten thousand kisses for that word.
My lord, my lord! speak, if you yet have being; 405
Sigh to me, if you cannot speak; or cast
One look! Do anything that shows you live.
IRAS. He's gone too far to hear you;
And this you see, a lump of senseless clay,
The leavings of a soul.
CHAR.   Remember, madam,   410
He charged you not to grieve.
CLEO.   And I'll obey him.
I have not loved a Roman not to know
What should become his wife; his wife, my Charmion,
For 'tis to that high title I aspire,
And now I'll not die less! Let dull Octavia 415
Survive, to mourn him dead: my nobler fate
Shall knit our spousals with a tie too strong
For Roman laws to break.
IRAS.   Will you then die?
CLEO. Why shouldst thou make that question?
IRAS. Cæsar is merciful.
CLEO.   Let him be so   420
To those that want his mercy: my poor lord
Make no such cov'nant with him, to spare me
When he was dead. Yield me to Cæsar's pride?
What! to be led in triumph through the streets,
A spectacle to base plebeian eyes;   425
While some dejected friend of Antony's,
Close in a corner, shakes his head, and mutters
A secret curse on her who ruined him?

I'll none of that.
CHAR.   Whatever you resolve,
I'll follow, ev'n to death.
IRAS.   I only feared   430
For you; but more should fear to live without you.
CLEO. Why, now 'tis as it should be. Quick, my
    friends,
Dispatch; ere this, the town's in Cæsar's hands:
My lord looks down concerned, and fears my stay,
Lest I should be surprised;   435
Keep him not waiting for his love too long.
You, Charmion, bring my crown and richest jewels;
With 'em, the wreath of victory I made
(Vain augury!) for him who now lies dead.
You, Iras, bring the cure of all our ills.   440
IRAS. The aspics, madam?
CLEO.   Must I bid you twice?
            Exeunt CHARMION and IRAS.
'Tis sweet to die, when they would force life on me,
To rush into the dark abode of Death,
And seize him first; if he be like my love,
He is not frightful, sure.   445
We're now alone, in secrecy and silence;
And is not this like lovers? I may kiss
These pale, cold lips; Octavia does not see me;
And, oh! 'tis better far to have him thus,
Than see him in her arms. — Oh, welcome, wel-
    come!   450

        Enter CHARMION [and] IRAS.
CHAR. What must be done?
CLEO.   Short ceremony, friends;
But yet it must be decent. First, this laurel
Shall crown my hero's head: he fell not basely,
Nor left his shield behind him. — Only thou
Couldst triumph o'er thyself; and thou alone   455
Wert worthy so to triumph.
CHAR.   To what end
These ensigns of your pomp and royalty?
CLEO. Dull that thou art! why, 'tis to meet my
    love;
As when I saw him first, on Cydnos' bank,
All sparkling, like a goddess: so adorned,   460
I'll find him once again: my second spousals
Shall match my first in glory. Haste, haste, both,
And dress the bride of Antony.
CHAR.   'Tis done.
CLEO. Now seat me by my lord. I claim this
    place;
For I must conquer Cæsar too, like him,   465
And win my share o' th' world. — Hail, you dear
    relics
Of my immortal love!
Oh, let no impious hand remove you hence;
But rest for ever here! Let Egypt give

398] Q3F swan.   406] S alters sigh to sign.   413] Q1 become; Q2Q3F become of.
420] Q2Q3F most merciful.

His death that peace, which it denied his life. — 470
Reach me the casket.

IRAS.   Underneath the fruit
The aspic lies.

CLEO. (*putting aside the leaves*). Welcome, thou
    kind deceiver!
Thou best of thieves, who, with an easy key,
Dost open life, and, unperceived by us,
Ev'n steal us from ourselves; discharging so 475
Death's dreadful office, better than himself;
Touching our limbs so gently into slumber,
That Death stands by, deceived by his own image,
And thinks himself but Sleep.

SERAP. (*within*).   The queen, where is she?
The town is yielded, Cæsar's at the gates. 480

CLEO. He comes too late t' invade the rights of
    death.
Haste, bare my arm, and rouse the serpent's fury.
    (*Holds out her arm, and draws it back*.)
Coward flesh,
Wouldst thou conspire with Cæsar to betray me,
As thou wert none of mine? I'll force thee to't, 485
And not be sent by him,
But bring, myself, my soul to Antony.
    (*Turns aside, and then shows her arm bloody*.)
Take hence; the work is done.

SERAP. (*within*).   Break ope the door,
And guard the traitor well.

CHAR.   The next is ours.

IRAS. Now, Charmion, to be worthy 490
Of our great queen and mistress.
                    (*They apply the aspics*.)

CLEO. Already, death, I feel thee in my veins;
I go with such a will to find my lord,
That we shall quickly meet.
A heavy numbness creeps through every limb, 495

And now 'tis at my head: my eyelids fall,
And my dear love is vanished in a mist.
Where shall I find him, where? O turn me to him,
And lay me on his breast! — Cæsar, thy worst;
Now part us, if thou canst.   (*Dies*.)
    (IRAS *sinks down at her feet, and dies*; CHAR-
    MION *stands behind her chair, as dressing her
    head*.)

Enter SERAPION, *two Priests*, ALEXAS *bound,
    Egyptians*.

2 PRIESTS.   Behold, Serapion, 500
What havoc death has made!

SERAP.   'Twas what I feared. —
Charmion, is this well done?

CHAR. Yes, 'tis well done, and like a queen, the
    last
Of her great race: I follow her. (*Sinks down; dies*.)

ALEX.   'Tis true,
She has done well: much better thus to die, 505
Than live to make a holiday in Rome.

SERAP. See,
See how the lovers sit in state together,
As they were giving laws to half mankind!
Th' impression of a smile, left in her face, 510
Shows she died pleased with him for whom she lived,
And went to charm him in another world.
Cæsar's just ent'ring: grief has now no leisure.
Secure that villain, as our pledge of safety,
To grace th' imperial triumph. — Sleep, blest
    pair, 515
Secure from human chance, long ages out,
While all the storms of fate fly o'er your tomb;
    And fame to late posterity shall tell,
    No lovers lived so great, or died so well.

471–472] QQF *Underneath . . . lies* as one line.   481] Q2Q3F *to invade.*   500–501] QQF *Behold . . . made* as one line.
507–508] QQF *See, see . . . together* as one line.   S solves the metrical difficulty by deliberately omitting one *see*.

EPILOGUE

Poets, like disputants, when reasons fail,
Have one sure refuge left — and that's to rail.
Fop, coxcomb, fool, are thundered through the pit;
And this is all their equipage of wit.
We wonder how the devil this diff'rence grows, 5
Betwixt our fools in verse, and yours in prose:
For, 'faith, the quarrel rightly understood,
'Tis civil war with their own flesh and blood.
The threadbare author hates the gaudy coat;
And swears at the gilt coach, but swears afoot: 10
For 'tis observed of every scribbling man,
He grows a fop as fast as e'er he can;
Prunes up, and asks his oracle, the glass,
If pink or purple best become his face.
For our poor wretch, he neither rails nor prays; 15
Nor likes your wit just as you like his plays;
He has not yet so much of Mr. Bayes.[1]
He does his best; and if he cannot please,
Would quietly sue out his *writ of ease*.[2]
Yet, if he might his own grand jury call, 20
By the fair sex he begs to stand or fall.
Let Cæsar's pow'r the men's ambition move,
But grace you him who lost the world for love!
Yet if some antiquated lady say,
The last age is not copied in his play; 25
Heav'n help the man who for that face must drudge,
Which only has the wrinkles of a judge.
Let not the young and beauteous join with those;
For should you raise such numerous hosts of foes,
Young wits and sparks he to his aid must call; 30
'Tis more than one man's work to please you all.

[1] See *The Rehearsal*.   [2] Certificate of discharge from employment.

Venice Preserved; or, A Plot Discovered

BY THOMAS OTWAY

Venice Preserv'd,

OR,

A Plot Discover'd.

A

TRAGEDY.

As it is Acted at the

DUKE'S THEATR

Written by *THOMAS OTWAY*.

LONDON,

Printed for *Joſ. Hindmarſh* at the Sign of the
Black Bull, over againſt the Royal
Exchange in *Cornhill.* 1682.

TITLE-PAGE OF FIRST QUARTO, WITH CARELESS MISPRINT 'THEATR,' OF *VENICE PRESERVED*

PROLOGUE

In these distracted times, when each man dreads
The bloody stratagems of busy heads;
When we have feared three years [1] we know not what,
Till witnesses begin to die o' th' rot,
What made our poet meddle with a plot?
Was't that he fancied, for the very sake
And name of plot, his trifling play might take?
For there's not in't one inch-board [2] evidence,
But 'tis, he says, to reason plain and sense,
And that he thinks a plausible defence.   10
Were truth by sense and reason to be tried,
Sure all our swearers might be laid aside:
No, of such tools our author has no need,
To make his plot, or make his play succeed;
He, of black bills,[3] has no prodigious tales,   15
Or Spanish pilgrims [4] cast ashore in Wales;
Here's not one murdered magistrate at least,
Kept rank like ven'son for a city feast,
Grown four days stiff, the better to prepare
And fit his pliant limbs to ride in chair.[5]   20
Yet here's an army raised, though underground,
But no man seen, nor one commission found;
Here is a traitor [6] too, that's very old,
Turbulent, subtle, mischievous, and bold,
Bloody, revengeful, and to crown his part,   25
Loves fumbling with a wench, with all his heart;
Till after having many changes passed,
In spite of age (thanks heaven) is hanged at last.
Next is a senator that keeps a whore;
In Venice none a higher office bore;   30
To lewdness every night the lecher ran —
Show me, all London, such another man;
Match him at Mother Creswold's [7] if you can.
O Poland, Poland! [8] had it been thy lot,
T'have heard in time of this Venetian plot,   35
Thou surely chosen hadst one king from thence,
And honored them as thou hast England since.

---

[1] In 1679, the publication of Titus Oates's *True Narrative of the Horrid Plot and Conspiracy against the Life of his Sacred Majesty, the Government, and the Protestant Religion,* fomented fears.
[2] Hard-sworn (sworn through an inch-board).   [3] 'A kind of obsolete weapon like the halberd' (G).
[4] The Jesuits were accused of planning to land Irish soldiers disguised as Spanish pilgrims in Wales (G).
[5] Referring to the murderers' disposition of the body of Sir Edmund Godfrey, strangled on October 12, 1678.   [6] Renault.
[7] A notorious resort of London libertines.   [8] A hit at Shaftesbury's earlier aspirations to the Polish throne.

14] Q1Q2 *may his play;* Q3 *make his play* (correcting the misprint). The separately printed (1681) Prologue reads correctly *make.* See G, II, 485.   28] Q3 *(thanks t' Heav'n).*

PERSONÆ DRAMATIS

DUKE OF VENICE
PRIULI, *father to Belvidera, a senator*
ANTONIO, *a fine speaker in the Senate*
JAFFEIR
PIERRE
RENAULT
BEDAMAR, [*The Spanish ambassador*]
SPINOSA
THEODORE
ELIOT
REVILLIDO
DURAND   } *Conspirators*
MEZZANA
BRAINVEIL
TERNON
[RETROSI]
BRABE

BELVIDERA
AQUILINA

Two Women, *attendants on Belvidera*
Two Women, *servants to Aquilina*
The Council of Ten
Officer
Guards
Friar
Executioner and Rabble

[SCENE — VENICE.]

[TIME, 1618.]

PERS. DRAM.] Q3 supplies the bracketed description of Bedamar, and begins the list of Conspirators with BEDAMAR, JAFFEIR, PIERRE, RENAULT.   Variants in spelling of names occur: e.g., here (Q1 *Prinli*; Q2 *Revellido*; QQ *Bramveil*); and, at times, in main text (Q1 *Pierrè, Peirre*; Q1Q2 *Bedamore*).

VENICE PRESERVED;

OR,

A PLOT DISCOVERED

BY THOMAS OTWAY

ACT I

SCENE I

Enter PRIULI *and* JAFFEIR.

PRIULI. No more! I'll hear no more; begone and
    leave.

JAFFEIR. Not hear me! by my sufferings, but you
    shall!
My lord, my lord! I'm not that abject wretch
You think me. Patience! where's the distance throws
Me back so far, but I may boldly speak   5
In right, though proud oppression will not hear me!

    PRIU. Have you not wronged me?

    JAFF.   Could my nature e'er
Have brooked injustice or the doing wrongs,
I need not now thus low have bent myself,
To gain a hearing from a cruel father!   10
Wronged you?

    PRIU.   Yes! wronged me, in the nicest point,
The honor of my house; you have done me wrong.
You may remember (for I now will speak,
And urge its baseness) when you first came home
From travel, with such hopes as made you looked
    on   15
By all men's eyes, a youth of expectation;
Pleased with your growing virtue, I received you,
Courted, and sought to raise you to your merits:
My house, my table, nay, my fortune, too,
My very self, was yours; you might have used me   20
To your best service. Like an open friend,
I treated, trusted you, and thought you mine;
When in requital of my best endeavors,
You treacherously practised to undo me,
Seduced the weakness of my age's darling,   25
My only child, and stole her from my bosom.
O Belvidera!

    JAFF.   'Tis to me you owe her;
Childless you had been else, and in the grave,
Your name extinct, nor no more Priuli heard of.
You may remember, scarce five years are past   30
Since in your brigandine you sailed to see
The Adriatic wedded by our Duke,[1]

¹ With ancient ceremonial rites, the Doge of Venice annually celebrated the wedding of the city with the sea.

And I was with you: your unskilful pilot
Dashed us upon a rock; when to your boat
You made for safety, entrèd first yourself;   35
The affrighted Belvidera following next,
As she stood trembling on the vessel side,
Was by a wave washed off into the deep;
When instantly I plunged into the sea,
And buffeting the billows to her rescue,   40
Redeemed her life with half the loss of mine.
Like a rich conquest in one hand I bore her,
And with the other dashed the saucy waves
That thronged and pressed to rob me of my prize:
I brought her, gave her to your despairing arms.   45
Indeed you thanked me; but a nobler gratitude
Rose in her soul: for from that hour she loved me,
Till for her life she paid me with herself.

    PRIU. You stole her from me; like a thief you
        stole her,
At dead of night; that cursèd hour you chose   50
To rifle me of all my heart held dear.
May all your joys in her prove false like mine;
A sterile fortune and a barren bed
Attend you both: continual discord make
Your days and nights bitter and grievous: still   55
May the hard hand of a vexatious need
Oppress and grind you; till at last you find
The curse of disobedience all your portion.

    JAFF. Half of your curse you have bestowed in vain;
Heav'n has already crowned our faithful loves   60
With a young boy, sweet as his mother's beauty.
May he live to prove more gentle than his grandsire,
And happier than his father!

    PRIU.   Rather live
To bait ² thee for his bread, and din your ears
With hungry cries, whilst his unhappy mother   65
Sits down and weeps in bitterness of want.

    JAFF. You talk as if it would please you.

    PRIU.   'Twould, by heav'n!
Once she was dear indeed; the drops that fell
From my sad heart when she forgot her duty,
The fountain of my life was not so precious: 70
But she is gone, and if I am a man,
I will forget her.

² Torment.

1] Q3 *leave me.*   2] Q2Q3 *suffering.*   29] Q3 omits *nor.*   37] Q3 *vessel's.*
71–72] Q2 prints *But . . . her* as one line.

JAFF. Would I were in my grave.

PRIU.   And she, too, with thee;
For, living here, you're but my curs'd remembrancers
I once was happy.   75

JAFF. You use me thus because you know my soul
Is fond of Belvidera.   You perceive
My life feeds on her, therefore thus you treat me
Oh! could my soul ever have known satiety,
Were I that thief, the doer of such wrongs   80
As you upbraid me with, what hinders me
But I might send her back to you with contumely,
And court my fortune where she would be kinder!

PRIU. You dare not do't. —

JAFF.   Indeed, my lord, I dare not.
My heart, that awes me, is too much my master.   85
Three years are past since first our vows were
          plighted,
During which time, the world must bear me witness,
I have treated Belvidera like your daughter,
The daughter of a senator of Venice;
Distinction, place, attendance, and observance,   90
Due to her birth, she always has commanded;
Out of my little fortune I have done this,
Because (though hopeless e'er to win your nature)
The world might see I loved her for herself,
Not as the heiress of the great Priuli. —   95

PRIU. No more!

JAFF.   Yes! all, and then adieu forever!
There's not a wretch that lives on common charity
But's happier than me: for I have known
The luscious sweets of plenty; every night
Have slept with soft content about my head,   100
And never waked but to a joyful morning,
Yet now must fall like a full ear of corn,
Whose blossom 'scaped, yet's withered in the ripen-
          ing.

PRIU. Home, and be humble; study to retrench;
Discharge the lazy vermin of thy hall,   105
Those pageants of thy folly;
Reduce the glittering trappings of thy wife
To humble weeds, fit for thy little state;
Then to some suburb cottage both retire;
Drudge, to feed loathsome life; get brats, and
          starve —   110
Home, home, I say!   Exit PRIULI.

JAFF.   Yes, if my heart would let me —
This proud, this swelling heart.   Home I would go
But that my doors are hateful to my eyes,
Filled and dammed up with gaping creditors,
Watchful as fowlers when their game will
          spring;   115
I have now not fifty ducats in the world,
Yet still I am in love, and pleased with ruin.
O Belvidera! oh, she's my wife —
And we will bear our wayward fate together,
But ne'er know comfort more.

Enter PIERRE.

PIERRE.   My friend, good morrow!   120
How fares the honest partner of my heart?
What! melancholy? not a word to spare me?

JAFF. I'm thinking, Pierre, how that damned starv-
          ing quality
Called honesty, got footing in the world.

PIERRE. Why, pow'rful villainy first set it up,   125
For its own ease and safety: honest men
Are the soft, easy cushions on which knaves
Repose and fatten.   Were all mankind villains,
They'd starve each other; lawyers would want prac-
          tice,
Cut-throats rewards; each man would kill his bro-
          ther   130
Himself; none would be paid or hanged for murder.
Honesty was a cheat invented first
To bind the hands of bold deserving rogues,
That fools and cowards might sit safe in power,
And lord it uncontrolled above their betters.   135

JAFF. Then honesty is but a notion.

PIERRE.   Nothing else;
Like wit, much talked of, not to be defined:
He that pretends to most, too, has least share in't;
'Tis a ragged virtue.   Honesty! — no more on't.

JAFF. Sure, thou art honest?

PIERRE.   So indeed men think me.   140
But they're mistaken, Jaffeir; I am a rogue
As well as they —
A fine, gay, bold-faced villain, as thou seest me.
'Tis true, I pay my debts when they're contracted;
I steal from no man; would not cut a throat   145
To gain admission to a great man's purse,
Or a whore's bed; I'd not betray my friend,
To get his place or fortune; I scorn to flatter
A blown-up fool above me, or crush the wretch be-
          neath me;
Yet, Jaffeir, for all this, I am a villain!   150

JAFF. A villain —

PIERRE.   Yes, a most notorious villain:
To see the suff'rings of my fellow creatures,
And own myself a man; to see our senators
Cheat the deluded people with a show
Of liberty, which yet they ne'er must taste of;   155
They say by them our hands are free from fetters;
Yet whom they please they lay in basest bonds;
Bring whom they please to infamy and sorrow;
Drive us like wracks down the rough tide of power,
Whilst no hold's left to save us from destruc-
          tion.   160
All that bear this are villains; and I one,
Not to rouse up at the great call of nature,
And check the growth of these domestic spoilers,
That make us slaves and tell us 'tis our charter.

JAFF.   O Aquilina!   Friend, to lose such
          beauty,   165

116] Q3 *I've.*   132] Q1Q2 *Honesty was;* Q3 *Honesty! 'twas.*   164] Q1Q2 *makes|tells;* Q3 *make|tell.*

The dearest purchase of thy noble labors!
She was thy right by conquest, as by love.

PIERRE. O Jaffeir! I'd so fixed my heart upon her
That wheresoe'er I framed a scheme of life
For time to come, she was my only joy   170
With which I wished to sweeten future cares;
I fancied pleasures, none but one that loves
And dotes as I did, can imagine like 'em:
When in the extremity of all these hopes,
In the most charming hour of expectation,   175
Then when our eager wishes soar the highest,
Ready to stoop and grasp the lovely game,
A haggard owl, a worthless kite of prey,
With his foul wings sailed in and spoiled my quarry.

JAFF. I know the wretch, and scorn him as thou
    hat'st him.   180

PIERRE. Curse on the common good that's so pro-
    tected,
Where every slave that heaps up wealth enough
To do much wrong, becomes a lord of right!
I, who believed no ill could e'er come near me,
Found in the embraces of my Aquilina   185
A wretched, old, but itching senator;
A wealthy fool, that had bought out my title,
A rogue that uses beauty like a lambskin,
Barely to keep him warm. That filthy cuckoo, too,
Was in my absence crept into my nest,   190
And spoiling all my brood of noble pleasure.

JAFF. Didst thou not chase him thence?

PIERRE.   I did, and drove
The rank old bearded Hirco [1] stinking home.
The matter was complained of in the Senate;
I, summoned to appear, and censured basely,   195
For violating something they call *privilege* —
This was the recompense of my service.
Would I'd been rather beaten by a coward!
A soldier's mistress, Jaffeir, 's his religion;
When that's profaned, all other ties are broken;   200
That even dissolves all former bonds of service,
And from that hour I think myself as free
To be the foe as ere the friend of Venice —
Nay, dear Revenge, whene'er thou call'st I am ready.

JAFF. I think no safety can be here for virtue,   205
And grieve, my friend, as much as thou to live
In such a wretched state as this of Venice,
Where all agree to spoil the public good,
And villains fatten with the brave man's labors.

PIERRE. We have neither safety, unity, nor
    peace,   210
For the foundation's lost of common good;
Justice is lame as well as blind amongst us;
The laws (corrupted to their ends that make 'em)
Serve but for instruments of some new tyranny,
That every day starts up to enslave us deeper.   215

[1] Lecher (cf. *hircus*, a he-goat).

Now could this glorious cause but find out friends
To do it right!   O Jaffeir! then mightst thou
Not wear these seals of woe upon thy face;
The proud Priuli should be taught humanity,
And learn to value such a son as thou art.   220
I dare not speak! But my heart bleeds this moment.

JAFF. Curst be the cause, though I thy friend be
    part on't!
Let me partake the troubles of thy bosom,
For I am used to misery, and perhaps
May find a way to sweeten't to thy spirit.   225

PIERRE. Too soon it will reach thy knowledge —

JAFF.   Then from thee
Let it proceed.   There's virtue in thy friendship
Would make the saddest tale of sorrow pleasing,
Strengthen my constancy, and welcome ruin.

PIERRE. Then thou art ruined!

JAFF.   That I long since knew;   230
I and ill fortune have been long acquaintance.

PIERRE. I passed this very moment by thy doors,
And found them guarded by a troop of villains;
The sons of public rapine were destroying;
They told me, by the sentence of the law,   235
They had commission to seize all thy fortune —
Nay, more, Priuli's cruel hand hath signed it.
Here stood a ruffian with a horrid face
Lording it o'er a pile of massy plate
Tumbled into a heap for public sale.   240
There was another making villainous jests
At thy undoing; he had ta'en possession
Of all thy ancient, most domestic ornaments,
Rich hangings intermixed and wrought with gold;
The very bed which on thy wedding night   245
Received thee to the arms of Belvidera,
The scene of all thy joys, was violated
By the coarse hands of filthy dungeon villains,
And thrown amongst the common lumber.

JAFF. Now thanks, heav'n —   250

PIERRE. Thank heav'n! for what?

JAFF.   That I am not worth a ducat.

PIERRE. Curse thy dull stars and the worse fate
    of Venice!
Where brothers, friends, and fathers, all are false;
Where there's no trust, no truth; where innocence
Stoops under vile oppression, and vice lords it.   255
Hadst thou but seen, as I did, how at last
Thy beauteous Belvidera, like a wretch
That's doomed to banishment, came weeping forth,
Shining through tears, like April suns in showers
That labor to o'ercome the cloud that loads 'em;   260
Whilst two young virgins, on whose arms she
    leaned,
Kindly looked up, and at her grief grew sad,
As if they catched the sorrows that fell from her.
Even the lewd rabble that were gathered round

To see the sight, stood mute when they beheld
   her,   265
Governed their roaring throats, and grumbled pity.
I could have hugged the greasy rogues; they pleased
   me.
  JAFF. I thank thee for this story from my soul,
Since now I know the worst that can befall me.
Ah, Pierre!   I have a heart that could have
   borne   270
The roughest wrong my fortune could have done me;
But when I think what Belvidera feels,
The bitterness her tender spirit tastes of,
I own myself a coward.   Bear my weakness,
If throwing thus my arms about thy neck,   275
I play the boy and blubber in thy bosom.
Oh! I shall drown thee with my sorrows!
  PIERRE.   Burn!
First burn, and level Venice to thy ruin!
What! starve like beggar's brats in frosty weather
Under a hedge, and whine ourselves to death!   280
Thou, or thy cause, shall never want assistance
Whilst I have blood or fortune fit to serve thee;
Command my heart: thou art every way its master.
  JAFF. No! There's a secret pride in bravely dying.
  PIERRE. Rats die in holes and corners, dogs run
   mad;   285
Man knows a braver remedy for sorrow —
Revenge! the attribute of gods; they stamped it
With their great image on our natures.   Die!
Consider well the cause that calls upon thee,
And if thou art base enough, die then; remem-
   ber   290
Thy Belvidera suffers.   Belvidera!
Die — damn first!   What! be decently interred
In a church-yard, and mingle thy brave dust
With stinking rogues that rot in winding sheets —
Surfeit-slain fools, the common dung o'th' soil? 295
  JAFF. Oh!
  PIERRE. Well said! out with't; swear a little —
  JAFF.   Swear!
By sea and air! by earth, by heaven and hell,
I will revenge my Belvidera's tears!
Hark thee, my friend: Priuli — is — a senator!
  PIERRE. A dog!
  JAFF.   Agreed.
  PIERRE.   Shoot him.
  JAFF.   With all my heart.   300
No more.   Where shall we meet at night?
  PIERRE.   I'll tell thee:
On the Rialto every night at twelve
I take my evening's walk of meditation;
There we two will meet, and talk of precious
Mischief —
  JAFF. Farewell.
  PIERRE.   At twelve.
  JAFF.   At any hour; my plagues 305

Will keep me waking.   *Exit* PIERRE.
           Tell me why, good heav'n,
Thou mad'st me what I am, with all the spirit,
Aspiring thoughts, and elegant desires
That fill the happiest man?   Ah! rather why
Didst thou not form me sordid as my fate,   310
Base-minded, dull, and fit to carry burdens?
Why have I sense to know the curse that's on me?
Is this just dealing, Nature? — Belvidera!

      Enter BELVIDERA [*with Attendants*].

Poor Belvidera!
  BELV.   Lead me, lead me, my virgins,
To that kind voice! — My lord, my love, my ref-
   uge!   315
Happy my eyes when they behold thy face:
My heavy heart will leave its doleful beating
At sight of thee, and bound with sprightful joys.
Oh, smile, as when our loves were in their spring,
And cheer my fainting soul!
  JAFF.   As when our loves 320
Were in their spring? has then my fortune changed?
Art thou not Belvidera, still the same —
Kind, good, and tender, as my arms first found thee?
If thou art altered, where shall I have harbor?
Where ease my loaded heart? oh! where com-
   plain?   325
  BELV. Does this appear like change, or love de-
   caying,
When thus I throw myself into thy bosom
With all the resolution of a strong truth?
Beats not my heart as 'twould alarm thine
To a new charge of bliss?   I joy more in thee   330
Than did thy mother when she hugged thee first,
And blessed the gods for all her travail past.
  JAFF. Can there in woman be such glorious faith?
Sure, all ill stories of thy sex are false.
O woman! lovely woman!   Nature made thee   335
To temper man; we had been brutes without you.
Angels are painted fair, to look like you;
There's in you all that we believe of heav'n —
Amazing brightness, purity, and truth,
Eternal joy, and everlasting love.   340
  BELV. If love be treasure, we'll be wondrous rich:
I have so much, my heart will surely break with't.
Vows cannot express it: when I would declare
How great's my joy, I am dumb with the big thought:
I swell and sigh, and labor with my longing.   345
Oh, lead me to some desert wide and wild,
Barren as our misfortunes, where my soul
May have its vent; where I may tell aloud
To the high heavens and every list'ning planet,
With what a boundless stock my bosom's
   fraught;   350
Where I may throw my eager arms about thee,
Give loose to love with kisses, kindling joy,

283] Q3 *Thou'rt.*   290] Q3 *thou'rt.*   329] Q3 *alarum.*   343] Q3 *can't.*   344] Q3 *I'm.*

And let off all the fire that's in my heart.

JAFF. O Belvidera! double I am a beggar —
Undone by fortune, and in debt to thee. 355
Want! worldly want! that hungry, meager fiend
Is at my heels, and chases me in view.
Canst thou bear cold and hunger? Can these limbs,
Framed for the tender offices of love,
Endure the bitter gripes of smarting poverty? 360
When banished by our miseries abroad,
(As suddenly we shall be) to seek out
(In some far climate where our names are strangers)
For charitable succor; wilt thou then,
When in a bed of straw we shrink together, 365
And the bleak winds shall whistle round our heads,
Wilt thou then talk thus to me? Wilt thou then
Hush my cares thus, and shelter me with love?

BELV. Oh, I will love thee, even in madness love
thee.
Though my distracted senses should forsake me, 370
I'd find some intervals when my poor heart
Should 'suage itself, and be let loose to thine.
Though the bare earth be all our resting-place,
Its roots our food, some clift our habitation,
I'll make this arm a pillow for thy head; 375
As thou sighing li'st, and swelled with sorrow,
Creep to thy bosom, pour the balm of love
Into thy soul, and kiss thee to thy rest;
Then praise our God, and watch thee till the morn-
ing.

JAFF. Hear this, you heav'ns, and wonder how
you made her! 380
Reign, reign, ye monarchs that divide the world!
Busy rebellion ne'er will let you know
Tranquillity and happiness like mine.
Like gaudy ships, th'obsequious billows fall
And rise again, to lift you in your pride; 385
They wait but for a storm and then devour you:
I, in my private bark, already wrecked,
Like a poor merchant driven on unknown land,
That had by chance packed up his choicest treasure
In one dear casket, and saved only that, 390
Since I must wander further on the shore,
Thus hug my little, but my precious store;
Resolved to scorn, and trust my fate no more.
Exeunt.

ACT II

[SCENE I]

[AQUILINA'S *house.*]

Enter PIERRE *and* AQUILINA.

AQUIL. By all thy wrongs, thou art dearer to my
arms
Than all the wealth of Venice; prithee, stay,

And let us love tonight.

PIERRE.   No: there's fool,
There's fool about thee. When a woman sells
Her flesh to fools, her beauty's lost to me; 5
They leave a taint, a sully where th'ave passed;
There's such a baneful quality about 'em,
Even spoils complexions with their own nauseous-
ness;
They infect all they touch; I cannot think
Of tasting any thing a fool has palled. 10

AQUIL. I loathe and scorn that fool thou mean'st,
as much
Or more than thou canst; but the beast has gold
That makes him necessary; power too,
To qualify my character, and poise me
Equal with peevish virtue, that beholds 15
My liberty with envy. In their hearts,
Are loose as I am; but an ugly power
Sits in their faces, and frights pleasures from 'em.

PIERRE. Much good may't do you, madam, with
your senator.

AQUIL. My senator! why, canst thou think that
wretch 20
E'er filled thy Aquilina's arms with pleasure?
Think'st thou, because I sometimes give him leave
To foil [1] himself at what he is unfit for,
Because I force myself to endure and suffer him,
Think'st thou I love him? No, by all the joys 25
Thou ever gav'st me, his presence is my penance;
The worst thing an old man can be's a lover —
A mere *memento mori* to poor woman.
I never lay by his decrepit side
But all that night I pondered on my grave. 30

PIERRE. Would he were well sent thither!

AQUIL.   That's my wish, too:
For then, my Pierre, I might have cause with pleasure
To play the hypocrite. Oh! how I could weep
Over the dying dotard, and kiss him too,
In hopes to smother him quite; then, when the
time 35
Was come to pay my sorrows at his funeral,
(For he has already made me heir to treasures
Would make me out-act a real widow's whining)
How could I frame my face to fit my mourning!
With wringing hands attend him to his grave; 40
Fall swooning on his hearse; take mad possession
Even of the dismal vault where he lay buried;
There like the Ephesian matron [2] dwell, till thou,
My lovely soldier, comest to my deliverance;
Then throwing up my veil, with open arms 45
And laughing eyes, run to new dawning joy.

[1] Thrust.
[2] This story, given by Petronius in the *Satyricon*, had been
used by George Chapman in the plot of *The Widow's Tears*
(printed 1612).

354] Q3 *doubly I'm.*   372] Q1Q2 *swage;* Q3 *'swage.*   1] Q3 *thou'rt.*   8] Q3 *E'en,* and omits *own.*
17] Q3 *They're* for *Are.*

PIERRE. No more! I have friends to meet me here tonight,
And must be private. As you prize my friendship,
Keep up your coxcomb.[1] Let him not pry nor listen
Nor fisk[2] about the house as I have seen him,   50
Like a tame mumping[3] squirrel with a bell on.
Curs will be abroad to bite him, if you do.

AQUIL. What friends to meet? may I not be of your council?

PIERRE. How! a woman ask questions out of bed?
Go to your senator, ask him what passes   55
Amongst his brethren; he'll hide nothing from you.
But pump not me for politics. No more!
Give order that whoever in my name
Comes here, receive admittance; so, good night.

AQUIL. Must we ne'er meet again? Embrace no more?   60
Is love so soon and utterly forgotten?

PIERRE. As you henceforward treat your fool, I'll think on't.

AQUIL. [aside]. Curst be all fools, and doubly curst myself,
The worst of fools. — I die if he forsakes me;
And how to keep him, heav'n or hell instruct me.   65
                                        Exeunt.

SCENE [II]
The Rialto.

Enter JAFFEIR.

JAFFEIR. I am here; and thus, the shades of night around me,
I look as if all hell were in my heart,
And I in hell. Nay, surely, 'tis so with me;
For every step I tread methinks some fiend
Knocks at my breast, and bids it not be quiet.   5
I've heard how desperate wretches like myself
Have wandered out at this dead time of night
To meet the foe of mankind in his walk:
Sure, I'm so curst that, though of heav'n forsaken,
No minister of darkness cares to tempt me.   10
Hell! Hell! why sleepest thou?

Enter PIERRE.

PIERRE [aside]. Sure, I have stayed too long;
The clock has struck, and I may lose my proselyte.
— Speak, who goes there?

JAFF.   A dog that comes to howl
At yonder moon. What's he that asks the question?

PIERRE. A friend to dogs, for they are honest creatures,   15
And ne'er betray their masters; never fawn

On any that they love not. Well met, friend.
— Jaffeir!

JAFF. The same. O Pierre! thou art come in season:
I was just going to pray.

PIERRE.   Ah, that's mechanic: 20
Priests make a trade on't, and yet starve by't, too:
No praying; it spoils business, and time's precious.
Where's Belvidera?

JAFF.   For a day or two
I've lodged her privately, till I see farther
What fortune will do with me. Prithee, friend,   25
If thou wouldst have me fit to hear good counsel,
Speak not of Belvidera —

PIERRE.   Speak not of her?

JAFF. Oh, no!

PIERRE.   Nor name her? May be I wish her well.

JAFF. Who well?

PIERRE.   Thy wife, thy lovely Belvidera;
I hope a man may wish his friend's wife well,   30
And no harm done!

JAFF.   Y'are merry, Pierre!

PIERRE.   I am so.
Thou shalt smile too, and Belvidera smile;
We'll all rejoice.   [Gives him a purse.]
                    Here's something to buy pins;
Marriage is chargeable.[4]

JAFF. [aside].   I but half wished
To see the devil, and he's here already.   35
— Well!
What must this buy — rebellion, murder, treason?
Tell me which way I must be damned for this.

PIERRE. When last we parted, we had no qualms like these,
But entertained each other's thoughts like men   40
Whose souls were well acquainted. Is the world
Reformed since our last meeting? What new miracles
Have happened? Has Priuli's heart relented?
Can he be honest?

JAFF.   Kind heav'n! let heavy curses
Gall his old age! cramps, achès, rack his bones,   45
And bitterest disquiet wring his heart!
Oh, let him live till life become his burden;
Let him groan under't long, linger an age
In the worst agonies and pangs of death,
And find its ease but late!

PIERRE.   Nay, couldst thou not   50
As well, my friend, have stretched the curse to all
The Senate round, as to one single villain?

JAFF. But curses stick not. Could I kill with cursing,

---

[1] 'Keep your coxcomb shut up.'
[2] Scamper.   [3] Nibbling.
[4] Expensive.

53] Q3 mayn't I be.
SCENE II. 11] Q3 I've.   19] Q3 thou'rt.   27] Q3 Not of her?   29] Q3 Whom.
33] Q3 supplies stage direction.   39] Q1Q2 we had; Q3 we'd.

By heav'n, I know not thirty heads in Venice
Should not be blasted; senators should rot   55
Like dogs on dunghills, but their wives and daughters
Die of their own diseases. O for a curse
To kill with!
    PIERRE.   Daggers, daggers, are much better.
    JAFF. Ha!
    PIERRE.   Daggers.
    JAFF.   But where are they?
    PIERRE.   Oh, a thousand
May be disposed in honest hands in Venice.   60
    JAFF. Thou talk'st in clouds.
    PIERRE.   But yet a heart half wronged
As thine has been, would find the meaning, Jaffeir.
    JAFF. A thousand daggers, all in honest hands,
And have not I a friend will stick one here?
    PIERRE. Yes, if I thought thou were not to be
      cherished   65
To a nobler purpose, I'd be that friend.
But thou hast better friends — friends whom thy
      wrongs
Have made thy friends — friends worthy to be
      called so.
I'll trust thee with a secret: there are spirits
This hour at work. But as thou art a man   70
Whom I have picked and chosen from the world,
Swear that thou wilt be true to what I utter;
And when I have told thee that which only gods
And men like gods are privy to, then swear
No chance or change shall wrest it from thy
      bosom.   75
    JAFF. When thou wouldst bind me, is there need
    of oaths?
(Green-sickness girls lose maiden-heads with such
    counters!)
For thou art so near my heart that thou mayst see
Its bottom, sound its strength and firmness to thee.
Is coward, fool, or villain in my face?   80
If I seem none of these, I dare believe
Thou wouldst not use me in a little cause,
For I am fit for honor's toughest task,
Nor ever yet found fooling was my province;
And for a villainous, inglorious enterprise,   85
I know thy heart so well, I dare lay mine
Before thee, set it to what point thou wilt.
    PIERRE. Nay, it's a cause thou wilt be fond of,
    Jaffeir,
For it is founded on the noblest basis —
Our liberties, our natural inheritance.   90
There's no religion, no hypocrisy in't;
We'll do the business, and ne'er fast and pray for't;
Openly act a deed the world shall gaze
With wonder at, and envy when it is done.
    JAFF. For liberty!

    PIERRE.   For liberty, my friend!   95
Thou shalt be freed from base Priuli's tyranny,
And thy sequestred fortunes healed again.
I shall be freed from opprobrious wrongs
That press me now and bend my spirit downward:
All Venice free, and every growing merit   100
Succeed to its just right: fools shall be pulled
From wisdom's seat — those baleful, unclean birds,
Those lazy owls, who (perched near fortune's top)
Sit only watchful with their heavy wings
To cuff down new-fledged virtues, that would
    rise   105
To nobler heights, and make the grove harmonious.
    JAFF. What can I do?
    PIERRE.   Canst thou not kill a senator?
    JAFF. Were there one wise or honest, I could kill him
For herding with that nest of fools and knaves.
By all my wrongs, thou talk'st as if revenge   110
Were to be had, and the brave story warms me.
    PIERRE. Swear then!
    JAFF.   I do, by all those glittering stars
And yond great ruling planet of the night!
By all good pow'rs above, and ill below,
By love and friendship, dearer than my life,   115
No pow'r or death shall make me false to thee!
    PIERRE. Here we embrace, and I'll unlock my
    heart.
A council's held hard by, where the destruction
Of this great empire's hatching: there I'll lead thee!
But be a man, for thou art to mix with men   120
Fit to disturb the peace of all the world,
And rule it when it's wildest —
    JAFF.   I give thee thanks
For this kind warning. Yes, I will be a man,
And charge thee, Pierre, whene'er thou see'st my
    fears
Betray me less, to rip this heart of mine   125
Out of my breast, and show it for a coward's.
Come, let's begone, for from this hour I chase
All little thoughts, all tender human follies
Out of my bosom. Vengeance shall have room —
Revenge!
    PIERRE. And liberty!
    JAFF.   Revenge! Revenge —   130
                      Exeunt.

[SCENE III]

The scene changes to AQUILINA'S *house, the Greek
courtesan.*

Enter RENAULT.

RENAULT. Why was my choice ambition the first
    ground
A wretch can build on? It's indeed at distance

66] Q3 *T'a nobler purpose, I would be* ...   73] Q3 *I've.*   78] Q3 *thou'rt.*   94] Q3 *'tis.*
98] Q3 *those opprobrious.*   128] Q1Q2 *humane;* Q3 *human.*
SCENE III. 1] Q3 *worst* for *first.*

A good prospect, tempting to the view;
The height delights us, and the mountain top
Looks beautiful, because it's nigh to heav'n.   5
But we ne'er think how sandy's the foundation,
What storm will batter, and what tempest shake us!
— Who's there?

Enter SPINOSA.

SPINOSA.   Renault, good morrow! for by this time
I think the scale of night has turned the balance
And weighs up morning.   Has the clock struck
    twelve?   10
REN.   Yes, clocks will go as they are set.   But man,
Irregular man's ne'er constant, never certain.
I've spent at least three precious hours of darkness
In waiting dull attendance; 'tis the curse
Of diligent virtue to be mixed, like mine,   15
With giddy tempers, souls but half resolved.
SPIN. Hell seize that soul amongst us it can frighten.
REN.   What's then the cause that I am here alone?
Why are we not together?

Enter ELIOT.

— O sir, welcome!
You are an Englishman: when treason's hatching   20
One might have thought you'd not have been be-
    hindhand.
In what whore's lap have you been lolling?
Give but an Englishman his whore and ease,
Beef and a sea-coal[1] fire, he's yours forever.
ELIOT.   Frenchman, you are saucy.
RENAULT.   How!

Enter BEDAMAR *the ambassador*, THEODORE, BRAIN-
    VEIL, DURAND, BRABE, REVILLIDO, MEZZANA,
    TERNON, RETROSI, *Conspirators.*

BEDAMAR.   At difference? — fie!   25
Is this a time for quarrels?   Thieves and rogues
Fall out and brawl.   Should men of your high call-
    ing,
Men separated by the choice of Providence
From this gross heap of mankind, and set here
In this great assembly as in one great jewel,   30
T'adorn the bravest purpose it e'er smiled on —
Should you like boys wrangle for trifles?
REN.   Boys!
BEDA.   Renault, thy hand!
REN.   I thought I'd given my heart
Long since to every man that mingles here,
But grieve to find it trusted with such tempers,   35
That can't forgive my froward age its weakness.
BEDA.   Eliot, thou once hadst virtue; I have seen
Thy stubborn temper bend with godlike goodness,
Not half thus courted.   'Tis thy nation's glory,
To hug the foe that offers brave alliance.   40

[1] Mineral coal, as distinguished from charcoal.   (*N.E.D.*)

30] Q3 *this assembly.*   44] Q3 *'twere.*

Once more embrace, my friends — we'll all embrace.
United thus, we are the mighty engine
Must twist this rooted empire from its basis!
Totters it not already?
ELIOT.   Would it were tumbling.
BEDA.   Nay, it shall down: this night we seal its
    ruin.   45

Enter PIERRE.

— O Pierre! thou art welcome!
Come to my breast, for by its hopes thou look'st
Lovelily dreadful, and the fate of Venice
Seems on thy sword already.   O my Mars!
The poets that first feigned a god of war   50
Sure prophesied of thee.
PIERRE.   Friends! was not Brutus,
(I mean that Brutus who in open senate
Stabbed the first Cæsar that usurped the world)
A gallant man?
REN.   Yes, and Catiline too,
Though story wrong his fame: for he conspired   55
To prop the reeling glory of his country:
His cause was good.
BEDA.   And ours as much above it
As, Renault, thou art superior to Cethegus,[2]
Or Pierre to Cassius.
PIERRE.   Then to what we aim at.
When do we start? or must we talk forever?   60
BEDA.   No, Pierre, the deed's near birth: Fate
    seems to have set
The business up and given it to our care.
I hope there's not a heart nor hand amongst us
But is firm and ready.
ALL.   All!   We'll die with Bedamar.
BEDA.   O men,   65
Matchless as will your glory be hereafter!
The game is for a matchless prize, if won;
If lost, disgraceful ruin.
REN.   What can lose it?
The public stock's a beggar; one Venetian
Trusts not another.   Look into their stores   70
Of general safety: empty magazines,
A tattered fleet, a murmuring unpaid army,
Bankrupt nobility, a harassed commonalty,
A factious, giddy, and divided senate
Is all the strength of Venice.   Let's destroy it;   75
Let's fill their magazines with arms to awe them,
Man out their fleet, and make their trade maintain
    it;
Let loose the murmuring army on their masters,
To pay themselves with plunder; lop their nobles
To the base roots, whence most of 'em first
    sprung;   80
Enslave the rout, whom smarting will make humble;
Turn out their droning senate, and possess

[2] One of Catiline's leading conspirators.

That seat of empire which our souls were framed for.

PIERRE. Ten thousand men are armèd at your
　　nod,
Commanded all by leaders fit to guide   85
A battle for the freedom of the world;
This wretched state has starved them in its service,
And by your bounty quickened, they're resolved
To serve your glory, and revenge their own.
They've all their different quarters in this city, 90
Watch for th'alarm, and grumble 'tis so tardy.

BEDA. I doubt not, friend, but thy unwearied
　　diligence
Has still kept waking, and it shall have ease;
After this night it is resolved we meet
No more, till Venice own us for her lords.   95

PIERRE. How lovely the Adriatic whore,
Dressed in her flames, will shine! — devouring
　　flames,
Such as shall burn her to the watery bottom
And hiss in her foundation!

BEDA.　　　　　　　Now if any
Amongst us that owns this glorious cause   100
Have friends or interest he'd wish to save,
Let it be told. The general doom is sealed,
But I'd forgo the hopes of a world's empire,
Rather than wound the bowels of my friend.

PIERRE. I must confess you there have touched
　　my weakness.   105
I have a friend; hear it, such a friend!
My heart was ne'er shut to him. Nay, I'll tell you.
He knows the very business of this hour,
But he rejoices in the cause and loves it:
We've changed a vow to live and die together, 110
And he's at hand to ratify it here.

REN.　　　　　　　How! all betrayed?

PIERRE. No — I've dealt nobly with you.
I've brought my all into the public stock;
I had but one friend, and him I'll share amongst
　　you!
Receive and cherish him; or if, when seen   115
And searched, you find him worthless, as my tongue
Has lodged this secret in his faithful breast,
To ease your fears I wear a dagger here
Shall rip it out again, and give you rest.
— Come forth, thou only good I e'er could boast
　　of!   120

Enter JAFFEIR *with a dagger.*

BEDA. His presence bears the show of manly vir-
　　tue.

JAFF. I know you'll wonder all, that thus uncalled
I dare approach this place of fatal councils;
But I am amongst you, and by heav'n it glads me
To see so many virtues thus united   125
To restore justice and dethrone oppression.
Command this sword, if you would have it quiet,

Into this breast; but if you think it worthy
To cut the throats of reverend rogues in robes,
Send me into the curst, assembled Senate: 130
It shrinks not, though I meet a father there.
Would you behold this city flaming? Here's
A hand shall bear a lighted torch at noon
To the arsenal, and set its gates on fire.

REN. You talk this well, sir.

JAFF.　　　　　　　Nay — by heav'n, I'll do this! 135
Come, come, I read distrust in all your faces,
You fear me a villain, and indeed it's odd
To hear a stranger talk thus at first meeting,
Of matters that have been so well debated;
But I come ripe with wrongs as you with coun-
　　cils.   140
I hate this Senate, am a foe to Venice,
A friend to none but men resolved like me,
To push on mischief. Oh, did you but know me,
I need not talk thus!

BEDA.　　　　　　　Pierre! I must embrace him;
My heart beats to this man as if it knew him. 145

REN. [*aside*]. I never loved these huggers.

JAFF.　　　　　　　Still I see
The cause delights me not. Your friends survey
　　me
As I were dang'rous — but I come armed
Against all doubts, and to your trust will give
A pledge worth more than all the world can pay
　　for.   150
— My Belvidera! Ho! my Belvidera!

BEDA. What wonder next?

JAFF.　　　　　　　Let me entreat you,
As I have henceforth hopes to call ye friends,
That all but the ambassador, this
Grave guide of councils, with my friend that owns
　　me,   155
Withdraw awhile to spare a woman's blushes.

Exeunt all but BEDAMAR, RENAULT, JAFFEIR,
　　PIERRE.

BEDA. Pierre, whither will this ceremony lead us?

JAFF. My Belvidera! Belvidera!

Enter BELVIDERA.

BELV.　　　　　　　Who?
Who calls so loud at this late, peaceful hour?
That voice was wont to come in gentler whis-
　　pers,   160
And fill my ears with the soft breath of love.
Thou hourly image of my thoughts, where art thou?

JAFF. Indeed, 'tis late.

BELV.　　　　　　　Oh! I have slept, and dreamt,
And dreamt again. Where hast thou been, thou
　　loiterer?
Though my eyes closed, my arms have still been
　　opened,   165
Stretched every way betwixt my broken slumbers,

To search if thou wert come to crown my rest;
There's no repose without thee. Oh, the day
Too soon will break, and wake us to our sorrow;
Come, come to bed, and bid thy cares good
    night.   170
  JAFF. O Belvidera! we must change the scene
In which the past delights of life were tasted.
The poor sleep little; we must learn to watch
Our labors late, and early every morning,
Midst winter frosts, thin clad and fed with spar-
    ing,   175
Rise to our toils, and drudge away the day.
  BELV. Alas! where am I? whither is't you lead me?
Methinks I read distraction in your face,
Something less gentle than the fate you tell me!
You shake and tremble too! your blood runs
    cold!   180
Heavens, guard my love, and bless his heart with
  patience.
  JAFF. That I have patience, let our fate bear wit-
  ness,
Who has ordained it so that thou and I
(Thou the divinest good man e'er possessed,
And I the wretched'st of the race of man)   185
This very hour, without one tear, must part.
  BELV. Part! must we part? Oh! am I then for-
  saken?
Will my love cast me off? have my misfortunes
Offended him so highly that he'll leave me?
Why drag you from me? whither are you going? 190
My dear! my life! my love!
  JAFF.   Oh, friends!
  BELV. Speak to me.
  JAFF.   Take her from my heart,
She'll gain such hold else, I shall ne'er get loose.
I charge thee take her, but with tender'st care,
Relieve her troubles, and assuage her sorrows. 195
  REN. Rise, madam! and command amongst your
  servants.
  JAFF. To you, sirs, and your honors, I bequeath
  her,
And with her this. When I prove unworthy —
                (Gives a dagger)
You know the rest — then strike it to her heart;
And tell her, he who three whole happy years 200
Lay in her arms, and each kind night repeated
The passionate vows of still increasing love,
Sent that reward for all her truth and sufferings.
  BELV. Nay, take my life, since he has sold it
  cheaply;
Or send me to some distant clime your slave;   205
But let it be far off, lest my complainings
Should reach his guilty ears, and shake his peace.
  JAFF. No, Belvidera, I've contrived thy honor;
Trust to my faith, and be but Fortune kind
To me, as I'll preserve that faith unbroken,   210

When next we meet, I'll lift thee to a height
Shall gather all the gazing world about thee
To wonder what strange virtue placed thee there.
But if we ne'er meet more —
  BELV.   Oh, thou unkind one,
Never meet more! Have I deserved this from
  you?   215
Look on me, tell me, tell me, speak, thou dear de-
  ceiver,
Why am I separated from thy love?
If I am false, accuse me; but if true,
Don't, prithee, don't in poverty forsake me,
But pity the sad heart that's torn with parting. 220
Yet hear me! yet recall me —
    Exeunt RENAULT, BEDAMAR, *and* BELVIDERA.
  JAFF.   O my eyes,
Look not that way, but turn yourselves awhile
Into my heart, and be weaned altogether!
— My friend, where art thou?
  PIERRE.   Here, my honor's brother.
  JAFF. Is Belvidera gone?
  PIERRE.   Renault has led her 225
Back to her own apartment: but, by heav'n!
Thou must not see her more till our work's over.
  JAFF. No.
  PIERRE. Not for your life.
  JAFF.   O Pierre, wert thou but she,
How I could pull thee down into my heart,
Gaze on thee till my eye-strings cracked with
  love,   230
Till all my sinews with its fire extended,
Fixed me upon the rack of ardent longing;
Then swelling, sighing, raging to be blest,
Come like a panting turtle to thy breast;
On thy soft bosom, hovering, bill and play,   235
Confess the cause why last I fled away;
  Own 'twas a fault, but swear to give it o'er,
And never follow false ambition more.
                  Exeunt ambo.

ACT III

[SCENE I]

[AQUILINA'S *house.*]

Enter AQUILINA *and her Maid.*

  AQUILINA. Tell him I am gone to bed; tell him I
am not at home; tell him I've better company with
me, or anything; tell him in short I will not see him,
the eternal troublesome, vexatious fool! He's worse
company than an ignorant physician — I'll not   5
be disturbed at these unseasonable hours!
  MAID. But, madam, he's here already, just entered the doors.
  AQUIL. Turn him out again, you unnecessary,

useless, giddy-brained ass! If he will not be- 10
gone, set the house afire and burn us both. I had
rather meet a toad in my dish than that old hideous
animal in my chamber tonight.

Enter ANTONIO.[1]

ANT. Nacky, Nacky, Nacky — how dost do,
Nacky? Hurry durry. I am come, little 15
Nacky; past eleven a-clock, a late hour; time in all
conscience to go to bed, Nacky — Nacky, did I say?
Aye, Nacky; Aquilina, lina, lina, quilina, quilina,
quilina, Aquilina, Naquilina, Naquilina, Acky,
Acky, Nacky, Nacky, queen Nacky — come, 20
let's to bed — you fubbs, you pugg, you — you little
puss — purree tuzzey — I am a senator.

AQUIL. You are [a] fool, I am sure.

ANT. May be so, too, sweetheart. Never the
worse senator for all that. Come Nacky, 25
Nacky, let's have a game at rump, Nacky.

AQUIL. You would do well, signior, to be troublesome here no longer, but leave me to myself, be
sober, and go home, sir.

ANT. Home, Madonna! 30

AQUIL. Aye, home, sir. Who am I?

ANT. Madonna, as I take it you are my — you
are — thou art my little Nicky Nacky — that's all!

AQUIL. I find you are resolved to be troublesome;
and so to make short of the matter in few words, 35
I hate you, detest you, loathe you, I am weary of
you, sick of you — hang you, you are an old, silly,
impertinent, impotent, solicitous coxcomb, crazy in
your head and lazy in your body, love to be meddling with everything, and if you had not money, 40
you are good for nothing.

ANT. Good for nothing! Hurry durry, I'll try
that presently. Sixty-one years old,[2] and good for
nothing; that's brave! (*To the Maid.*) — Come,
come, come, Mistress Fiddle-faddle, turn you 45
out for a season. Go, turn out, I say, it is our will
and pleasure to be private some moments — out,
out when you are bid to! (*Puts her out and locks
the door.*) — 'Good for nothing,' you say.

AQUIL. Why, what are you good for? 50

ANT. In the first place, madam, I am old, and
consequently very wise, very wise, Madonna, d'e
mark that? In the second place, take notice, if
you please, that I am a senator, and when I think
fit can make speeches, Madonna. Hurry durry, 55
I can make a speech in the Senate-house now and
then — would make your hair stand on end, Madonna.

AQUIL. What care I for your speeches in the

Senate-house? If you would be silent here, I 60
should thank you.

ANT. Why, I can make speeches to thee, too, my
lovely Madonna; for example: 'My cruel fair one
(*takes out a purse of gold, and at every pause shakes it*),
since it is my fate that you should with your servant angry prove; though late at night — I hope 65
'tis not too late with this to gain reception for my
love.' — There's for thee, my little Nicky Nacky —
take it, here take it — I say take it, or I'll throw
it at your head. How now, rebel!

AQUIL. Truly, my illustrious senator, I must 70
confess your honor is at present most profoundly
eloquent, indeed.

ANT. Very well: come now, let's sit down and
think upon't a little. Come sit, I say — sit down
by me a little, my Nicky Nacky, hah — (*sits 75
down*) Hurry durry — 'good for nothing!'

AQUIL. No, sir; if you please, I can know my
distance, and stand.

ANT. Stand! How? Nacky up, and I down!
Nay, then, let me exclaim with the poet, 80

> Show me a case more pitiful who can,
> A standing woman, and a falling man.

Hurry durry — not sit down! — See this, ye gods.
— You won't sit down?

AQUIL. No, sir. 85

ANT. Then look you now, suppose me a bull, a
Basan-bull, the bull of bulls, or any bull. Thus up
I get and with my brows thus bent — I broo, I say
I broo, I broo, I broo. You won't sit down, will
you? — I broo — 90
(*Bellows like a bull, and drives her about.*)

AQUIL. Well, sir, I must endure this. (*She sits
down.*) Now your honor has been a bull, pray what
beast will your worship please to be next?

ANT. Now I'll be a senator again, and thy lover,
little Nicky Nacky! (*He sits by her.*) Ah, toad, 95
toad, toad, toad! spit in my face a little, Nacky —
spit in my face, prithee, spit in my face, never so
little. Spit but a little bit — spit, spit, spit, spit
when you are bid, I say; do, prithee, spit — now,
now, now, spit. What, you won't spit, will 100
you? Then I'll be a dog.

AQUIL. A dog, my lord?

ANT. Aye, a dog — and I'll give thee this t'other
purse to let me be a dog — and to use me like a dog
a little. Hurry durry — I will — here 'tis. 105
(*Gives the purse.*)

AQUIL. Well, with all my heart. But let me beseech your dogship to play your tricks over as fast
as you can, that you may come to stinking the sooner
and be turned out of doors as you deserve.

ANT. Aye, aye — no matter for that — that 110

---

[1] The name emphasizes the hit at Anthony Ashley Cooper,
Earl of Shaftesbury.

[2] A direct hit at Shaftesbury's age.

shan't move me. (*He gets under the table.*) Now, bough waugh waugh, bough waugh —
                              (*Barks like a dog.*)

AQUIL. Hold, hold, hold, sir, I beseech you: what is't you do? If curs bite, they must be kicked, sir. — Do you see, kicked thus?   115

ANT. Aye, with all my heart. Do kick, kick on; now I am under the table, kick again — kick harder — harder yet, bough waugh waugh, waugh, bough — 'odd, I'll have a snap at thy shins — bough waugh wough, waugh, bough! — 'Odd, she   120 kicks bravely. —

AQUIL. Nay, then, I'll go another way to work with you; and I think here's an instrument fit for the purpose. (*Fetches a whip and bell.*) — What, bite your mistress, sirrah! out, out of doors, you   125 dog, to kennel and be hanged — bite your mistress by the legs, you rogue!   (*She whips him.*)

ANT. Nay, prithee, Nacky, now thou art too loving! Hurry durry, 'odd! I'll be a dog no longer.

AQUIL. Nay, none of your fawning and   130 grinning, but begone, or here's the discipline! What, bite your mistress by the legs, you mongrel? Out of doors — hout hout, to kennel, sirrah! go!

ANT. This is very barbarous usage, Nacky, very barbarous. Look you, I will not go — I will   135 not stir from the door; that I resolve — hurry durry — what, shut me out?   (*She whips him out.*)

AQUIL. Aye, and if you come here any more tonight, I'll have my footmen lug you, you cur. What, bite your poor mistress Nacky, sirrah?   140

Enter Maid.

MAID. Heav'ns, madam! what's the matter?
                    (*He howls at the door like a dog.*)

AQUIL. Call my footmen hither presently.

Enter two Footmen.

MAID. They are here already, madam; the house is all alarmed with a strange noise that nobody knows what to make of.   145

AQUIL. Go, all of you, and turn that troublesome beast in the next room out of my house — If I ever see him within these walls again, without my leave for his admittance, you sneaking rogues — I'll have you poisoned all — poisoned like rats! Every   150 corner of the house shall stink of one of you; go! and learn hereafter to know my pleasure. So now for my Pierre:

Thus when godlike lover was displeased,
We sacrifice our fool and he's appeased.   155
                              Exeunt.

SCENE II

[*A Street.*]

Enter BELVIDERA.

BELV. I'm sacrificed! I am sold! betrayed to
        shame!
Inevitable ruin has inclosed me!
No sooner was I to my bed repaired,
To weigh, and (weeping) ponder my condition,
But the old hoary wretch to whose false care   5
My peace and honor was entrusted, came
(Like Tarquin) ghastly with infernal lust.
O thou Roman Lucrece! thou couldst find friends
        to vindicate thy wrong!
I never had but one, and he's proved false;
He that should guard my virtue has betrayed
        it —   10
Left me! undone me! Oh, that I could hate him!
Where shall I go? oh, whither, whither wander?

Enter JAFFEIR.

JAFF. Can Belvidera want a resting place
When these poor arms are open to receive her?
Oh, 'tis in vain to struggle with desires   15
Strong as my love to thee; for ever_._oment
I am from thy sight, the heart ·   . my bosom
Moans like a tender infant in   .adle,
Whose nurse had left it. Come, and with the songs
Of gentle love persuade it to its peace.   20

BELV. I fear the stubborn wanderer will not own
        me;
'Tis grown a rebel to be ruled no longer,
Scorns the indulgent bosom that first lulled it,
And like a disobedient child disdains
The soft authority of Belvidera.   25

JAFF. There was a time —

BELV.   Yes, yes, there was a time
When Belvidera's tears, her cries, and sorrows
Were not despised; when if she chanced to sigh,
Or look but sad — there was indeed a time
When Jaffeir would have ta'en her in his arms,   30
Eased her declining head upon his breast,
And never left her till he found the cause.
But let her now weep seas,
Cry till she rend the earth, sigh till she burst
Her heart asunder — still he bears it all,   35
Deaf as the wind, and as the rocks unshaken.

JAFF. Have I been deaf? am I that rock unmoved,
Against whose root tears beat and sighs are sent
In vain? have I beheld thy sorrows calmly?
Witness against me, heav'ns; have I done this?   40
Then bear me in a whirlwind back again,
And let that angry dear one ne'er forgive me!
Oh, thou too rashly censur'st of my love!

154] Q3 *the Godlike.*
SCENE II.   8] T emends the metrical arrangement by ending a half line with *Lucrece!* and printing *Thou ... wrong!* as separate line.   37–39] QI ends l. 37 with *?*, and ends ll. 38 and 39 with *!*; G suggests the punctuation adopted above.

Couldst thou but think how I have spent this night,
Dark and alone, no pillow to my head, 45
Rest in my eyes, nor quiet in my heart,
Thou wouldst not, Belvidera, sure thou wouldst not
Talk to me thus, but like a pitying angel
Spreading thy wings, come settle on my breast
And hatch warm comfort there ere sorrows freeze
    it. 50
  BELV. Why, then, poor mourner, in what baleful
    corner
Hast thou been talking with that witch, the Night?
On what cold stone hast thou been stretched along,
Gathering the grumbling winds about thy head,
To mix with theirs the accents of thy woes? 55
Oh, now I find the cause my love forsakes me!
I am no longer fit to bear a share
In his concernments: my weak, female virtue
Must not be trusted; 'tis too frail and tender.
  JAFF. O Portia! Portia! what a soul was thine! 60
  BELV. That Portia was a woman, and when
    Brutus,
Big with the fate of Rome (heav'n guard thy safety!),
Concealed from her the labors of his mind,
She let him see her blood was great as his,
Flowed from a spring as noble, and a heart 65
Fit to partake his troubles, as his love.
Fetch, fetch that dagger back, the dreadful dower
Thou gav'st last night in parting with me; strike it
Here to my heart, and as the blood flows from it,
Judge if it run not pure as Cato's daughter's. 70
  JAFF. Thou art too good, and I indeed un-
    worthy —
Unworthy so much virtue. Teach me how
I may deserve such matchless love as thine,
And see with what attention I'll obey thee.
  BELV. Do not despise me: that's the all I ask. 75
  JAFF. Despise thee! hear me —
  BELV.   Oh, thy charming tongue
Is but too well acquainted with my weakness;
Knows, let it name but love, my melting heart
Dissolves within my breast, till with closed eyes
I reel into thy arms, and all's forgotten. 80
  JAFF. What shall I do?
  BELV.   Tell me! be just, and tell me
Why dwells that busy cloud upon thy face?
Why am I made a stranger? why that sigh,
And I not know the cause? Why, when the world
Is wrapped in rest, why chooses then my love 85
To wander up and down in horrid darkness,
Loathing his bed and these desiring arms?
Why are these eyes bloodshot with tedious watching?
Why starts he now? and looks as if he wished
His fate were finished? Tell me, ease my fears; 90
Lest, when we next time meet, I want the power
To search into the sickness of thy mind,
But talk as wildly then as thou look'st now.

  JAFF. O Belvidera!
  BELV. Why was I last night delivered to a vil-
    lain? 95
  JAFF. Hah, a villain!
  BELV. Yes! to a villain! Why at such an hour
Meets that assembly all made up of wretches
That look as hell had drawn 'em into league?
Why, I in this hand, and in that a dagger, 100
Was I delivered with such dreadful ceremonies?
'To you, sirs, and to your honor I bequeath her,
And with her this: whene'er I prove unworthy —
You know the rest — then strike it to her heart?'
Oh! why's that *rest* concealed from me? Must I 105
Be made the hostage of a hellish trust?
For such I know I am; that's all my value!
But by the love and loyalty I owe thee,
I'll free thee from the bondage of these slaves;
Straight to the Senate, tell 'em all I know, 110
All that I think, all that my fears inform me.
  JAFF. Is this the Roman virtue? this the blood
That boasts its purity with Cato's daughter?
Would she have e'er betrayed her Brutus?
  BELV.   No,
For Brutus trusted her; wert thou so kind, 115
What would not Belvidera suffer for thee!
  JAFF. I shall undo myself and tell thee all.
  BELV. Look not upon me as I am, a woman,
But as a bone,[1] thy wife, thy friend, who long
Has had admission to thy heart, and there 120
Studied the virtues of thy gallant nature;
Thy constancy, thy courage, and thy truth
Have been my daily lesson: I have learnt them,
Am bold as thou, can suffer or despise
The worst of fates for thee, and with thee share
    them. 125
  JAFF. O you divinest powers! look down and hear
My prayers! instruct me to reward this virtue!
Yet think a little ere thou tempt me further:
Think I have a tale to tell will shake thy nature,
Melt all this boasted constancy thou talk'st of 130
Into vile tears and despicable sorrows:
Then if thou shouldst betray me —!
  BELV.   Shall I swear?
  JAFF. No: do not swear. I would not violate
Thy tender nature with so rude a bond;
But as thou hop'st to see me live my days 135
And love thee long, lock this within thy breast.
I've bound myself by all the strictest sacraments,
Divine and human —
  BELV.   Speak! —
  JAFF.   To kill thy father —
  BELV. My father!
  JAFF.   Nay, the throats of the whole
    Senate
Shall bleed, my Belvidera. He amongst us 140

[1] Cf. *Gen.* II. 23, 'bone of my bones, and flesh of my flesh.'

That spares his father, brother, or his friend,
Is damned.   How rich and beauteous will the face
Of ruin look, when these wide streets run blood;
I and the glorious partners of my fortune
Shouting, and striding o'er the prostrate dead,   145
Still to new waste; whilst thou, far off in safety
Smiling, shall see the wonders of our daring;
And when night comes, with praise and love receive
me.
BELV. Oh!
JAFF.   Have a care, and shrink not, even in
thought,
For if thou dost —
BELV.   I know it — thou wilt kill me.   150
Do, strike thy sword into this bosom. Lay me
Dead on the earth, and then thou wilt be safe.
Murder my father! though his cruel nature
Has persecuted me to my undoing,
Driven me to basest wants, can I behold him   155
With smiles of vengeance, butchered in his age?
The sacred fountain of my life destroyed?
And canst thou shed the blood that gave me being?
Nay, be a traitor too, and sell thy country?
Can thy great heart descend so vilely low,   160
Mix with hired slaves, bravoes, and common stab-
bers,
Nose-slitters, alley-lurking villains? join
With such a crew, and take a ruffian's wages,
To cut the throats of wretches as they sleep?
JAFF. Thou wrong'st me, Belvidera! I've en-
gaged   165
With men of souls, fit to reform the ills
Of all mankind. There's not a heart amongst them
But's as stout as death, yet honest as the nature
Of man first made, ere fraud and vice were fashions.
BELV. What's he to whose curst hands last night
thou gav'st me?   170
Was that well done? Oh! I could tell a story
Would rouse thy lion heart out of its den,
And make it rage with terrifying fury.
JAFF. Speak on, I charge thee!
BELV.   O my love! if e'er
Thy Belvidera's peace deserved thy care,   175
Remove me from this place! Last night, last night!
JAFF. Distract me not, but give me all the truth.
BELV. No sooner wert thou gone, and I alone,
Left in the pow'r of that old son of mischief;
No sooner was I lain on my sad bed,   180
But that vile wretch approached me; loose, unbut-
toned,
Ready for violation.   Then my heart
Throbbed with its fears. Oh, how I wept and sighed,
And shrunk and trembled; wished in vain for him
That should protect me. Thou, alas, wert gone!   185
JAFF. Patience, sweet heav'n! till I make venge-
ance sure.

BELV. He drew the hideous dagger forth thou
gav'st him,
And with upbraiding smiles he said, 'Behold it;
This is the pledge of a false husband's love.'
And in my arms then pressed, and would have
clasped me;   190
But with my cries I scared his coward heart,
Till he withdrew and muttered vows to hell.
These are thy friends! with these thy life, thy honor,
Thy love — all's staked, and all will go to ruin.
JAFF. No more. I charge thee keep this secret
close;   195
Clear up thy sorrows, look as if thy wrongs
Were all forgot, and treat him like a friend,
As no complaint were made. No more; retire,
Retire, my life, and doubt not of my honor;
I'll heal its failings and deserve thy love.   200
BELV. Oh, should I part with thee, I fear thou wilt
In anger leave me, and return no more.
JAFF. Return no more! I would not live without
thee
Another night, to purchase the creation.
BELV. When shall we meet again?
JAFF.   Anon at twelve!   205
I'll steal myself to thy expecting arms,
Come like a travelled dove and bring thee peace.
BELV. Indeed!
JAFF.   By all our loves!
BELV.   'Tis hard to part:
But sure, no falsehood e'er looked so fairly.
Farewell. — Remember twelve!
                    Exit BELVIDERA.
JAFF.   Let heav'n forget me   210
When I remember not thy truth, thy love.
How curst is my condition, tossed and jostled
From every corner; Fortune's common fool,
The jest of rogues, an instrumental ass
For villains to lay loads of shame upon,   215
And drive about just for their ease and scorn!

Enter PIERRE.

PIERRE. Jaffeir!
JAFF.   Who calls?
PIERRE.   A friend, that could have wished
T'have found thee otherwise employed. What, hunt
A wife on the dull foil![1] sure, a staunch husband
Of all hounds is the dullest! Wilt thou never,   220
Never be weaned from caudles[2] and confections?
What feminine tale hast thou been listening to,
Of unaired shirts, catarrhs, and tooth-ache got
By thin-soled shoes? Damnation! that a fellow
Chosen to be sharer in the destruction   225
Of a whole people, should sneak thus in corners
To ease his fulsome lusts and fool his mind.

[1] Track of a hunted animal.
[2] Warm drink fit for the sick.

JAFF. May not a man, then, trifle out an hour
With a kind woman and not wrong his calling?
   PIERRE. Not in a cause like ours.
   JAFF.   Then, friend, our cause 230
Is in a damned condition; for I'll tell thee,
That canker-worm called lechery has touched it;
'Tis tainted vilely. Wouldst thou think it? Renault
(That mortified, old, withered, winter rogue)
Loves simple fornication like a priest.   235
I found him out for watering at [1] my wife:
He visited her last night like a kind guardian.
Faith, she has some temptations, that's the truth
   on't.
   PIERRE. He durst not wrong his trust!
   JAFF.   'Twas something late, though,
To take the freedom of a lady's chamber.   240
   PIERRE. Was she in bed?
   JAFF.   Yes, faith, in virgin sheets
White as her bosom, Pierre, dished neatly up,
Might tempt a weaker appetite to taste.
Oh, how the old fox stunk, I warrant thee,
When the rank fit was on him!
   PIERRE.   Patience guide me! 245
He used no violence?
   JAFF.   No, no! out on't, violence!
Played with her neck, brushed her with his gray
   beard,
Struggled and towzed,[2] tickled her till she squeaked
   a little,
Maybe, or so — but not a jot of violence —
   PIERRE. Damn him!
   JAFF.   Aye, so say I; but hush, no
   more on't! 250
All hitherto is well, and I believe
Myself no monster [3] yet, though no man knows
What fate he's born to. Sure, 'tis near the hour
We all should meet for our concluding orders.
Will the ambassador be here in person?   255
   PIERRE. No: he has sent commission to that villain, Renault,
To give the executing charge.
I'd have thee be a man if possible,
And keep thy temper; for a brave revenge
Ne'er comes too late.
   JAFF.   Fear not; I am cool as patience. 260
Had he completed my dishonor, rather
Than hazard the success our hopes are ripe for,
I'd bear it all with mortifying [4] virtue.
   PIERRE. He's yonder, coming this way through
   the hall;
His thoughts seem full.
   JAFF.   Prithee retire, and leave me 265

---

[1] Lusting after.   [2] Tousled, pulled about.
[3] Cuckold.   [4] Self-denying.

289] Q3 *in* for *into*.

With him alone. I'll put him to some trial,
See how his rotten part will bear the touching.
   PIERRE. Be careful then.   *Exit* PIERRE.
   JAFF.   Nay, never doubt, but trust me.
What, be a devil? take a damning oath
For shedding native blood? can there be a sin 270
In merciful repentance? Oh, this villain!

Enter RENAULT.

   REN. [*aside*]. Perverse and peevish! What a slave
   is man!
To let his itching flesh thus get the better of him!
Dispatch the tool, her husband — that were well.
— Who's there?
   JAFF.   A man.
   REN.   My friend, my near ally! 275
The hostage of your faith, my beauteous charge,
Is very well.
   JAFF.   Sir, are you sure of that?
Stands she in perfect health? beats her pulse
   even?
Neither too hot nor cold?
   REN.   What means that question?
   JAFF. Oh, women have fantastic constitutions, 280
Inconstant as their wishes, always wavering,
And ne'er fixed. Was it not boldly done
Even at first sight to trust the thing I loved
(A tempting treasure too!) with youth so fierce
And vigorous as thine? But thou art honest. 285
   REN. Who dares accuse me?
   JAFF.   Curst be him that doubts
Thy virtue! I have tried it, and declare,
Were I to choose a guardian of my honor,
I'd put it into thy keeping; for I know thee.
   REN. Know me!
   JAFF.   Aye, know thee. There's no falsehood
   in thee. 290
Thou look'st just as thou art. Let us embrace.
Now wouldst thou cut my throat or I cut thine?
   REN. You dare not do't.
   JAFF.   You lie, sir.
   REN.   How!
   JAFF.   No more.
'Tis a base world, and must reform, that's all.

Enter SPINOSA, THEODORE, ELIOT, REVILLIDO, DURAND, BRAINVEIL, *and the rest of the Conspirators.*

   REN. Spinosa! Theodore!
   SPINOSA.   The same.
   REN.   You are welcome! 295
   SPIN. You are trembling, sir.
   REN.   'Tis a cold night, indeed; I am aged,
Full of decay and natural infirmities.
We shall be warm, my friend, I hope tomorrow.

PIERRE *re-enters.*

PIERRE (*aside*).   'Twas not well done; thou
shouldst have stroked him
And not have galled him.

JAFF. (*aside*). Damn him, let him chew on't.   300
Heav'n! where am I? beset with cursèd fiends,
That wait to damn me.   What a devil's man
When he forgets his nature — hush, my heart.

REN.   My friends, 'tis late; are we assembled
all?
Where's Theodore?

THEODORE.   At hand.

REN.   Spinosa.

SPIN.   Here.   305

REN. Brainveil.

BRAINVEIL.   I am ready.

REN.   Durand and Brabe.

DURAND.   Command us;
We are both prepared!

REN.   Mezzana, Revillido,
Ternon, Retrosi; oh, you are men, I find,
Fit to behold your fate and meet her summons.
Tomorrow's rising sun must see you all   310
Decked in your honors!   Are the soldiers ready?

OMNES. All, all.

REN. You, Durand, with your thousand must pos-
sess
St. Mark's.   You, captain, know your charge al-
ready;
'Tis to secure the Ducal Palace.   You,   315
Brabe, with a hundred more must gain the Secque: [1]
With the like number, Brainveil, to the Procuralle. [2]
Be all this done with the least tumult possible,
Till in each place you post sufficient guards:
Then sheathe your swords in every breast you
meet.   320

JAFF. (*aside*). Oh, reverend cruelty! damned,
bloody villian!

REN. During this execution, Durand, you
Must in the midst keep your battalia fast.
And, Theodore, be sure to plant the cannon
That may command the streets; whilst Revil-
lido,   325
Mezzana, Ternon and Retrosi, guard you.
This done, we'll give the general alarm,
Apply petards, and force the Ars'nal gates;
Then fire the city round in several places,
Or with our cannon (if it dare resist)   330
Batter't to ruin.   But above all I charge you,
Shed blood enough; spare neither sex nor age,
Name nor condition; if there live a senator
After tomorrow, though the dullest rogue
That e'er said nothing, we have lost our ends;   335
If possible, let's kill the very name
Of senator, and bury it in blood.

[1] The Mint (where *sequins* were coined).
[2] Where the nine Procurators of Venice lived.

JAFF. (*aside*). Merciless, horrid slave! — Aye,
blood enough!
Shed blood enough, old Renault: how thou charm'st
me!

REN. But one thing more, and then farewell till
fate   340
Join us again or separate us ever.
First, let's embrace; heav'n knows who next shall
thus
Wing ye together.   But let's all remember
We wear no common cause upon our swords:
Let each man think that on his single virtue   345
Depends the good and fame of all the rest —
Eternal honor or perpetual infamy.
Let's remember through what dreadful hazards
Propitious Fortune hitherto has led us,
How often on the brink of some discovery   350
Have we stood tottering, and yet still kept our
ground
So well, the busiest searchers ne'er could follow
Those subtle tracks which puzzled all suspicion.
— You droop, sir!

JAFF.   No: with a most profound attention
I've heard it all, and wonder at thy virtue.   355

REN. Though there be yet few hours 'twixt them
and ruin,
Are not the Senate lulled in full security,
Quiet and satisfied, as fools are always?
Never did so profound repose forerun
Calamity so great!   Nay, our good fortune   360
Has blinded the most piercing of mankind,
Strengthened the fearfull'st, charmed the most sus-
pectful,
Confounded the most subtle: for we live,
We live, my friends, and quickly shall our life
Prove fatal to these tyrants.   Let's consider   365
That we destroy oppression, avarice,
A people nursed up equally with vices
And loathsome lusts, which Nature most abhors,
And such as without shame she cannot suffer.

JAFF. (*aside*). O Belvidera, take me to thy
arms,   370
And show me where's my peace, for I've lost it.
Exit JAFFEIR.

REN. Without the least remorse, then, let's re-
solve
With fire and sword t'exterminate these tyrants;
And when we shall behold those curst tribunals,
Stained by the tears and sufferings of the inno-
cent,   375
Burning with flames rather from heav'n than ours,
The raging, furious, and unpitying soldier
Pulling his reeking dagger from the bosoms
Of gasping wretches; death in every quarter,
With all that sad disorder can produce,   380
To make a spectacle of horror — then,
Then let's call to mind, my dearest friends,

That there is nothing pure upon the earth;
That the most valued things have most allays;[1]
And that in change of all those vile enormities 385
Under whose weight this wretched country labors,
The means are only in our hands to crown them.

  PIERRE. And may those powers above that are
    propitious
To gallant minds record this cause and bless it.

  REN. Thus happy, thus secure of all we wish
    for, 390
Should there, my friends, be found amongst us one
False to this glorious enterprise, what fate,
What vengeance were enough for such a villain?

  ELIOT. Death here without repentance, hell here-
    after.

  REN. Let that be my lot, if as here I stand 395
Listed by fate amongst her darling sons,
Though I had one only brother, dear by all
The strictest ties of nature; though one hour
Had given us birth, one fortune fed our wants,
One only love, and that but of each other, 400
Still filled our minds: could I have such a friend
Joined in this cause, and had but ground to fear
Meant foul play, may this right hand drop from me,
If I'd not hazard all my future peace,
And stab him to the heart before you. Who 405
Would do less? wouldst not thou, Pierre, the same?

  PIERRE. You have singled me, sir, out for this
    hard question,
As if 'twere started only for my sake!
Am I the thing you fear? Here, here's my bosom;
Search it with all your swords! Am I a traitor? 410

  REN. No: but I fear your late commended friend
Is little less. Come, sirs, 'tis now no time
To trifle with our safety. Where's this Jaffeir?

  SPIN. He left the room just now in strange dis-
    order.

  REN. Nay, there is danger in him: I observed
    him 415
During the time I took for explanation;
He was transported from most deep attention
To a confusion which he could not smother.
His looks grew full of sadness and surprise,
All which betrayed a wavering spirit in him, 420
That labored with reluctancy and sorrow.
What's requisite for safety must be done
With speedy execution: he remains
Yet in our power. I for my own part wear
A dagger.

  PIERRE. Well.

  REN.   And I could wish it —

  PIERRE.   Where? 425

  REN. Buried in his heart.

  [1] Alloys.

  PIERRE.   Away! w'are yet all friends!
No more of this; 'twill breed ill blood amongst us!

  SPIN. Let us all draw our swords, and search the
    house,
Pull him from the dark hole where he sits brooding
O'er his cold fears, and each man kill his share of
    him. 430

  PIERRE. Who talks of killing? Who's he'll shed
    the blood
That's dear to me? — Is't you? — or you? — or you,
    sir?
What, not one speak? how you stand gaping all
On your grave oracle, your wooden god there;
Yet not a word? (To RENAULT.) Then, sir, I'll tell
    you a secret: 435
Suspicion's but at best a coward's virtue!

  REN. A coward —   (Handles his sword.)

  PIERRE.   Put, put up thy sword, old man,
Thy hand shakes at it; come, let's heal this breach,
I am too hot; we yet may live friends.

  SPIN. Till we are safe, our friendship cannot be
    so. 440

  PIERRE. Again! Who's that?

  SPIN.   'Twas I.

  THEO.   And I.

  REVILL.   And I.

  ELIOT.   And all.

  REN. Who are on my side?

  SPIN.   Every honest sword.
Let's die like men and not be sold like slaves.

  PIERRE. One such word more, by heav'n, I'll to
    the Senate
And hang ye all, like dogs in clusters! 445
Why peep your coward swords half out their shells?
Why do you not all brandish them like mine?
You fear to die, and yet dare talk of killing?

  REN. Go to the Senate and betray us! Hasten,
Secure thy wretched life; we fear to die 450
Less than thou dar'st be honest.

  PIERRE.   That's rank falsehood!
Fear'st not thou death? fie, there's a knavish itch
In that salt blood, an utter foe to smarting.
Had Jaffeir's wife proved kind, he had still been true.
Foh — how that stinks! 455
Thou die! thou kill my friend! — or thou — or thou
— Or thou, with that lean, withered, wretched face!
Away! disperse all to your several charges,
And meet tomorrow where your honor calls you;
I'll bring that man whose blood you so much thirst
    for, 460
And you shall see him venture for you fairly —
Hence, hence, I say!   Exit RENAULT angrily.

  SPIN.   I fear we have been to blame,
And done too much.

403] Q3 He meant.   405–406] Q1Q2 Who|Would not do less; Q3 Who?|Who would do less? (An attempt to clarify
the meaning without disturbing the scansion.)
407] Q3 You've.   439] Q3 all live.   449] Q3 haste.   462] Q3 we've.

THEO. 'Twas too far urged against the man you
loved.

REVILL. Here, take our swords and crush 'em with
your feet.   465

SPIN. Forgive us, gallant friend.

PIERRE.   Nay, now y'have found
The way to melt and cast me as you will,
I'll fetch this friend and give him to your mercy:
Nay, he shall die if you will take him from me;
For your repose I'll quit my heart's jewel,   470
But would not have him torn away by villains
And spiteful villainy.

SPIN.   No, may you both
Forever live and fill the world with fame!

PIERRE. Now you are too kind.   Whence rose all
this discord?
Oh, what a dangerous precipice have we
'scaped!   475
How near a fall was all we had long been building!
What an eternal blot had stained our glories,
If one, the bravest and the best of men,
Had fallen a sacrifice to rash suspicion,
Butchered by those whose cause he came to cher-
ish!   480
Oh, could you know him all as I have known him,
How good he is, how just, how true, how brave,
You would not leave this place till you had seen him;
Humbled yourselves before him, kissed his feet,
And gained remission for the worst of follies.   485
  Come but tomorrow, all your doubts shall ⎫
    end,   ⎪
  And to your loves me better recommend,   ⎬
  That I've preserved your fame, and saved   ⎪
    my friend.   ⎭

                              Exeunt omnes.

ACT IV

[SCENE I]

[*A street.*]

Enter JAFFEIR *and* BELVIDERA.

JAFF. Where dost thou lead me?   Every step I
move,
Methinks I tread upon some mangled limb
Of a racked friend.   O my dear charming ruin!
Where are we wand'ring?

BELV.   To eternal honor;
To do a deed shall chronicle thy name   5
Among the glorious legends of those few
That have saved sinking nations.   Thy renown
Shall be the future song of all the virgins
Who by thy piety have been preserved

From horrid violation.   Every street   10
Shall be adorned with statues to thy honor,
And at thy feet this great inscription written,
Remember him that propped the fall of Venice.

JAFF. Rather, remember him who after all
The sacred bonds of oaths and holier friendship 15
In fond compassion to a woman's tears,
Forgot his manhood, virtue, truth and honor,
To sacrifice the bosom that relieved him.
Why wilt thou damn me?

BELV.   O inconstant man!
How will you promise? how will you deceive?   20
Do, return back, replace me in my bondage,
Tell all thy friends how dangerously thou lov'st me,
And let thy dagger do its bloody office.
Oh, that kind dagger, Jaffeir, how 'twill look
Stuck through my heart, drenched in my blood to
th'hilts!   25
Whilst these poor dying eyes shall with their tears
No more torment thee, then thou wilt be free.
Or if thou think'st it nobler, let me live
Till I am a victim to the hateful lust
Of that infernal devil, that old fiend   30
That's damned himself and would undo mankind:
Last night, my love!

JAFF.   Name, name it not again.
It shows a beastly image to my fancy,
Will wake me into madness.   Oh, the villain!
That durst approach such purity as thine   35
On terms so vile!   Destruction, swift destruction
Fall on my coward head, and make my name
The common scorn of fools if I forgive him!
If I forgive him, if I not revenge
With utmost rage, and most unstaying fury,   40
Thy sufferings, thou dear darling of my life, love!

BELV. Delay no longer then, but to the Senate;
And tell the dismal'st story e'er was uttered:
Tell 'em what bloodshed, rapines, desolations,
Have been prepared — how near's the fatal hour! 45
Save thy poor country, save the reverend blood
Of all its nobles, which tomorrow's dawn
Must else see shed.   Save the poor, tender lives
Of all those little infants which the swords
Of murderers are whetting for this moment.   50
Think thou already hear'st their dying screams,
Think that thou seest their sad, distracted mothers
Kneeling before thy feet, and begging pity,
With torn, dishevelled hair and streaming eyes,
Their naked, mangled breasts besmeared with
blood,   55
And even the milk with which their fondled babes.
Softly they hushed, dropping in anguish from 'em.
Think thou seest this, and then consult thy heart.

JAFF. Oh!

474] Q3 *y'are.*
476] Q3 *we'd.*   (Hereafter, minor variants, such as Q3's elisions to better the scansion, are not generally listed.   See Textual
Notes.)

BELV. Think too, if thou lose this present min-
    ute,   60
What miseries the next day bring upon thee.
Imagine all the horrors of that night,
Murder and rapine, waste and desolation,
Confusedly ranging.   Think what then may prove
My lot!   The ravisher may then come safe, 65
And 'midst the terror of the public ruin
Do a damned deed — perhaps to lay a train
May catch thy life; then where will be revenge,
The dear revenge that's due to such a wrong?
    JAFF.   By all heaven's powers, prophetic truth
    dwells in thee;   70
For every word thou speak'st strikes through my
    heart
Like a new light, and shows it how 't has wandered.
Just what th'hast made me, take me, Belvidera,
And lead me to the place where I'm to say
This bitter lesson, where I must betray 75
My truth, my virtue, constancy, and friends.
Must I betray my friends?   Ah, take me quickly,
Secure me well before that thought's renewed;
If I relapse once more, all's lost forever.
    BELV.   Hast thou a friend more dear than Belvi-
    dera?   80
    JAFF.   No, th'art my soul itself; wealth, friendship,
    honor,
All present joys, and earnest of all future,
Are summed in thee: methinks, when in thy arms
Thus leaning on thy breast, one minute's more
Than a long thousand years of vulgar hours. 85
Why was such happiness not given me pure?
Why dashed with cruel wrongs, and bitter wantings?
Come, lead me forward now like a tame lamb
To sacrifice; thus in his fatal garlands,
Decked fine, and pleased, the wanton skips and
    plays,   90
    Trots by the enticing, flattering priestess' side,
    And much transported with his little pride,
    Forgets his dear companions of the plain
    Till by her, bound, he's on the altar lain;
    Yet then too hardly bleats, such pleasure's in
    the pain.   95

Enter Officer and Six Guards.

OFFICER.   Stand!   Who goes there?
    BELV.   Friends.
    JAFF.   Friends, Belvidera!   Hide me from my
    friends.
By heaven, I'd rather see the face of hell
Than meet the man I love.
    OFFIC.   But what friends are you?
    BELV.   Friends to the Senate and the state of
    Venice.   100
    OFFIC.   My orders are to seize on all I find
At this late hour, and bring 'em to the Council,
Who now are sitting.

    JAFF.   Sir, you shall be obeyed.
Hold, brutes, stand off! none of your paws upon me!
Now the lot's cast, and, Fate, do what thou
    wilt.   *Exeunt guarded.* 105

SCENE [II]

The Senate-house.

Where appear sitting, the DUKE OF VENICE, PRIULI,
    ANTONIO, *and eight other Senators.*

    DUKE.   Anthony, Priuli, senators of Venice,
Speak; why are we assembled here this night?
What have you to inform us of, concerns
The state of Venice, honor, or its safety?
    PRIU.   Could words express the story I have to
    tell you,   5
Fathers, these tears were useless — these sad tears
That fall from my old eyes; but there is cause
We all should weep, tear off these purple robes,
And wrap ourselves in sack-cloth, sitting down
On the sad earth, and cry aloud to heaven. 10
Heaven knows if yet there be an hour to come
Ere Venice be no more!
    ALL SENATORS.   How!
    PRIU.   Nay, we stand
Upon the very brink of gaping ruin.
Within this city's formed a dark conspiracy
To massacre us all, our wives and children, 15
Kindred and friends, our palaces and temples
To lay in ashes — nay, the hour, too, fixed;
The swords, for aught I know, drawn even this mo-
    ment,
And the wild waste begun.   From unknown hands
I had this warning: but if we are men, 20
Let's not be tamely butchered, but do something
That may inform the world in after ages,
Our virtue was not ruined, though we were.
    (*A noise without:* 'Room, room, make room for
    some prisoners!')
    2D SENATOR.   Let's raise the city!

Enter Officer and Guard.

    PRIU.   Speak there — what disturbance? 25
    OFFIC.   Two prisoners have the guard seized in
    the streets,
Who say they come to inform this reverend Senate
About the present danger.

Enter JAFFEIR *and* BELVIDERA, *guarded.*

    ALL.   Give 'em entrance —
Well, who are you?
    JAFF.   A villain.
    ANT.   Short and pithy.
The man speaks well.
    JAFF.   Would every man that hears me 30
Would deal so honestly, and own his title.

DUKE. 'Tis rumored that a plot has been contrived

Against this state; that you have a share in't, too.

If you are a villain, to redeem your honor,

Unfold the truth and be restored with mercy.   35

JAFF. Think not that I to save my life come
hither —

I know its value better — but in pity

To all those wretches whose unhappy dooms

Are fixed and sealed.   You see me here before
you,

The sworn and covenanted foe of Venice.   40

But use me as my dealings may deserve,

And I may prove a friend.

DUKE.   The slave capitulates.

Give him the tortures.

JAFF.   That you dare not do;

Your fears won't let you, nor the longing itch

To hear a story which you dread the truth of —   45

Truth which the fear of smart shall ne'er get from
me.

Cowards are scared with threat'nings.   Boys are
whipped

Into confessions: but a steady mind

Acts of itself, ne'er asks the body counsel.

'Give him the tortures!'   Name but such a thing   50

Again, by heaven, I'll shut these lips forever.

Not all your racks, your engines, or your wheels

Shall force a groan away — that you may guess at.

ANT. A bloody-minded fellow, I'll warrant;

A damned bloody-minded fellow.   55

DUKE. Name your conditions.

JAFF.   For myself, full pardon,

Besides the lives of two and twenty friends

(delivers a list)

Whose names are here enrolled.   Nay, let their
crimes

Be ne'er so monstrous, I must have the oaths

And sacred promise of this reverend Council,   60

That in a full assembly of the Senate

The thing I ask be ratified.   Swear this,

And I'll unfold the secrets of your danger.

ALL. We'll swear.

DUKE.   Propose the oath.

JAFF.   By all the hopes

Ye have of peace and happiness hereafter,   65

Swear!

ALL.   We all swear.

JAFF.   To grant me what I've asked,

Ye swear.

ALL.   We swear.

JAFF.   And as ye keep the oath,

May you and your posterity be blest

Or curst forever.

ALL.   Else be curst forever!

JAFF. (delivers another paper). Then here's the list,
and with't the full disclose   70

Of all that threatens you.

Now, Fate, thou hast caught me.

ANT. Why, what a dreadful catalogue of cut-
throats is here!   I'll warrant you not one of these
fellows but has a face like a lion.   I dare not so   75
much as read their names over.

DUKE. Give orders that all diligent search be
made

To seize these men; their characters are public.

The paper intimates their rendezvous

To be at the house of a famed Grecian courtesan   80

Called Aquilina; see that place secured.

ANT. What!   My Nicky Nacky, Hurry Durry,
Nicky Nacky in the plot?   I'll make a speech.
— Most noble senators,

What headlong apprehension drives you on,   85

Right noble, wise, and truly solid senators,

To violate the laws and right of nations?

The lady is a lady of renown.

'Tis true, she holds a house of fair reception,

And though I say't myself, as many more   90

Can say as well as I.

2D SEN.   My lord, long speeches

Are frivolous here when dangers are so near us.

We all well know your interest in that lady;

The world talks loud on't.

ANT.   Verily, I have done.

I say no more.

DUKE.   But, since he has declared   95

Himself concerned, pray, captain, take great caution

To treat the fair one as becomes her character,

And let her bed-chamber be searched with decency.

You, Jaffeir, must with patience bear till morning

To be our prisoner.

JAFF.   Would the chains of death   100

Had bound me fast ere I had known this minute!

I've done a deed will make my story hereafter

Quoted in competition with all ill ones:

The history of my wickedness shall run

Down through the low traditions of the vulgar,   105

And boys be taught to tell the tale of Jaffeir.

DUKE. Captain, withdraw your prisoner.

JAFF.   Sir, if possible,

Lead me where my own thoughts themselves may
lose me;

Where I may doze out what I've left of life,

Forget myself and this day's guilt and falsehood.   110

Cruel remembrance, how shall I appease thee!

Exit guarded.

(Noise without: 'More traitors; room, room,
make room there!')

DUKE. How's this?   Guards —

46] Q1 misprints with for which.   70–71] Q1 prints Then . . . you without metrical division.

77] Q3 order for orders.   99–100] The metrical division follows Q3.   106] Q3 taught; Q1Q2 thought.

Where are our guards? Shut up the gates; the treason's
Already at our doors!

Enter Officer.

OFFIC. My lords, more traitors —
Seized in the very act of consultation; 115
Furnished with arms and instruments of mischief.
Bring in the prisoners.

Enter PIERRE, RENAULT, THEODORE, ELIOT, REVIL-
LIDO, *and other Conspirators, in fetters, guarded.*

PIERRE. You, my lords and fathers
(As you are pleased to call yourselves) of Venice,
If you sit here to guide the course of justice,
Why these disgraceful chains upon my limbs 120
That have so often labored in your service?
Are these the wreaths of triumphs ye bestow
On those that bring you conquests home and honors?
DUKE. Go on; you shall be heard, sir.
ANT. And be hanged too, I hope. 125
PIERRE. Are these the trophies I've deserved for fighting
Your battles with confederated powers,
When winds and seas conspired to overthrow you,
And brought the fleets of Spain to your own harbors?
When you, great Duke, shrunk trembling in your palace, 130
And saw your wife, th'Adriatic, ploughed
Like a lewd whore by bolder prows than yours —
Stepped not I forth, and taught your loose Venetians
The task of honor and the way to greatness,
Raised you from your capitulating fears, 135
To stipulate the terms of sued-for peace —
And this my recompense! If I am a traitor,
Produce my charge; or show the wretch that's base enough
And brave enough to tell me I am a traitor.
DUKE. Know you one Jaffeir?
(*All the Conspirators murmur.*)
PIERRE. Yes, and know his virtue. 140
His justice, truth, his general worth and sufferings
From a hard father taught me first to love him.

Enter JAFFEIR, *guarded.*

DUKE. See him brought forth.
PIERRE. My friend, too, bound? nay, then
Our fate has conquered us, and we must fall.
— Why droops the man whose welfare's so much mine 145
They're but one thing? These reverend tyrants, Jaffeir,
Call us all traitors; art thou one, my brother?
JAFF. To thee I am the falsest, veriest slave
That e'er betrayed a generous, trusting friend,

And gave up honor to be sure of ruin. 150
All our fair hopes which morning was to have crowned,
Has this curst tongue o'erthrown.
PIERRE. So, then all's over.
Venice has lost her freedom; I, my life.
No more. Farewell!
DUKE. Say, will you make confession
Of your vile deeds and trust the Senate's mercy? 155
PIERRE. Curst be your Senate; curst your Constitution.
The curse of growing factions and division
Still vex your councils, shake your public safety,
And make the robes of government you wear
Hateful to you as these base chains to me! 160
DUKE. Pardon, or death?
PIERRE. Death — honorable death!
REN. Death's the best thing we ask or you can give.
ALL CONSPIR. No shameful bonds, but honorable death!
DUKE. Break up the council. Captain, guard your prisoners.
Jaffeir, y'are free, but these must wait for judgment. *Exeunt all the Senators.* 165
PIERRE. Come, where's my dungeon? Lead me to my straw.
It will not be the first time I've lodged hard
To do your Senate service.
JAFF. Hold one moment!
PIERRE. Who's he disputes the judgment of the Senate?
Presumptuous rebel — on — (*Strikes* JAFFEIR.)
JAFF. By heaven, you stir not. 170
I must be heard, I must have leave to speak:
Thou hast disgraced me, Pierre, by a vile blow.
Had not a dagger done thee nobler justice?
But use me as thou wilt, thou canst not wrong me,
For I am fallen beneath the basest injuries; 175
Yet look upon me with an eye of mercy,
With pity and with charity behold me;
Shut not thy heart against a friend's repentance,
But as there dwells a god-like nature in thee,
Listen with mildness to my supplications. 180
PIERRE. What whining monk art thou? what holy cheat
That wouldst encroach upon my credulous ears,
And cant'st thus vilely? Hence! I know thee not.
Dissemble and be nasty: leave me, hypocrite.
JAFF. Not know me, Pierre?
PIERRE. No, know thee not. What art thou? 185
JAFF. Jaffeir, thy friend, thy once loved, valued friend,
Though now deservedly scorned, and used most hardly.

114-115] The metrical division follows Q3.

PIERRE. Thou Jaffeir! thou my once loved, valued
  friend!
By heavens, thou li'st!   The man so called, my
  friend,
Was generous, honest, faithful, just and valiant,   190
Noble in mind, and in his person lovely,
Dear to my eyes and tender to my heart:
But thou, a wretched, base, false, worthless coward,
Poor even in soul, and loathsome in thy aspect,
All eyes must shun thee, and all hearts detest
  thee.   195
Prithee avoid, nor longer cling thus round me
Like something baneful, that my nature's chilled at.
  JAFF.   I have not wronged thee — by these tears I
    have not!
But still am honest, true, and hope, too, valiant;
My mind still full of thee; therefore, still noble.   200
Let not thy eyes then shun me, nor thy heart
Detest me utterly.   Oh, look upon me!
Look back and see my sad, sincere submission!
How my heart swells, as even 'twould burst my
  bosom,
Fond of its gaol,[1] and laboring to be at thee!   205
What shall I do, what say to make thee hear me?
  PIERRE. Hast thou not wronged me? dar'st thou
    call thyself
Jaffeir, that once loved, valued friend of mine,
And swear thou hast not wronged me?   Whence
  these chains?
Whence the vile death, which I may meet this mo-
  ment?   210
Whence this dishonor but from thee, thou false one?
  JAFF. — All's true; yet grant one thing, and I've
    done asking.
  PIERRE. What's that?
  JAFF.   To take thy life on such conditions
The Council have proposed.   Thou and thy friends
May yet live long, and to be better treated.   215
  PIERRE. Life! ask my life! confess! record myself
A villain for the privilege to breathe
And carry up and down this cursèd city
A discontented and repining spirit,
Burdensome to itself, a few years longer,   220
To lose, it may be, at last in a lewd quarrel
For some new friend, treacherous and false as thou
  art!
No, this vile world and I have long been jangling,
And cannot part on better terms than now,
When only men like thee are fit to live in't.   225
  JAFF. By all that's just —
  PIERRE.   Swear by some other powers,
For thou hast broke that sacred oath too lately.
  JAFF. Then by that hell I merit, I'll not leave thee
Till to thyself, at least, thou'rt reconciled,
However thy resentments deal with me.   230
  PIERRE. Not leave me!

  [1] Jail.

  JAFF.   No, thou shalt not force me from thee.
Use me reproachfully, and like a slave;
Tread on me, buffet me, heap wrongs on wrongs
On my poor head; I'll bear it all with patience
Shall weary out thy most unfriendly cruelty,   235
Lie at thy feet and kiss 'em though they spurn me,
Till, wounded by my sufferings, thou relent,
And raise me to thy arms with dear forgiveness.
  PIERRE. Art thou not —
  JAFF.   What?
  PIERRE.   A traitor?
  JAFF.   Yes.
  PIERRE.   A villain?
  JAFF. Granted.
  PIERRE.   A coward — a most scandalous
    coward,   240
Spiritless, void of honor, one who has sold
Thy everlasting fame for shameless life?
  JAFF. All, all, and more — much more.   My
    faults are numberless.
  PIERRE. And wouldst thou have me live on terms
    like thine?
Base as thou art false —
  JAFF.   No, 'tis to me that's granted;   245
The safety of thy life was all I aimed at,
In recompense for faith and trust so broken.
  PIERRE. I scorn it more because preserved by thee.
And as, when first my foolish heart took pity
On thy misfortunes, sought thee in thy miseries,   250
Relieved thy wants, and raised thee from thy state
Of wretchedness in which thy fate had plunged thee,
To rank thee in my list of noble friends,
All I received in surety for thy truth,
Were unregarded oaths; and this, this dagger,   255
Given with a worthless pledge, thou since hast stol'n;
So I restore it back to thee again,
Swearing by all those powers which thou hast vio-
  lated,
Never from this curst hour to hold communion,
Friendship, or interest with thee, though our
  years   260
Were to exceed those limited the world.
Take it — farewell — for now I owe thee nothing.
  JAFF. Say thou wilt live, then.
  PIERRE.   For my life, dispose it
Just as thou wilt, because 'tis what I'm tired with.
  JAFF. O Pierre!
  PIERRE.   No more.
  JAFF.   My eyes won't lose the sight
    of thee,   265
But languish after thine, and ache with gazing.
  PIERRE. Leave me. — Nay, then, thus, thus, I
    throw thee from me,
And curses, great as is thy falsehood, catch thee!
                                          [Exit.]
  JAFF. Amen. — He's gone, my father, friend, pre-
    server,

And here's the portion he has left me.   270
                    (*Holds the dagger up.*)
This dagger, well rememberèd — with this dagger
I gave a solemn vow of dire importance,
Parted with this and Belvidera together;
Have a care, Mem'ry, drive that thought no farther;
No, I'll esteem it as a friend's last legacy,   275
Treasure it up in this wretched bosom,
Where it may grow acquainted with my heart,
That when they meet, they start not from each other.
— So: now for thinking. A blow; called traitor, villain,
Coward, dishonorable coward — fogh!   280
Oh, for a long, sound sleep, and so forget it!
Down, busy devil —

            Enter BELVIDERA.

BELV.   Whither shall I fly?
Where hide me and my miseries together?
Where's now the Roman constancy I boasted?
Sunk into trembling fears and desperation!   285
Not daring to look up to that dear face
Which used to smile even on my faults, but down
Bending these miserable eyes to earth,
Must move in penance, and implore much mercy.
JAFF. Mercy! — Kind heaven has surely endless
            stores   290
Hoarded for thee of blessings yet untasted;
Let wretches loaded hard with guilt as I am,
Bow [with] the weight, and groan beneath the burden,
Creep with a remnant of that strength th'have left
Before the footstool of that heaven th'have injured.   295
O Belvidera! I'm the wretched'st creature
E'er crawled on earth! Now if thou hast virtue,
            help me;
Take me into thy arms, and speak the words of peace
To my divided soul that wars within me,
And raises every sense to my confusion.   300
By heav'n, I am tottering to the very brink
Of peace; and thou art all the hold I've left.
BELV. Alas! I know thy sorrows are most mighty.
I know th'hast cause to mourn — to mourn, my Jaffeir,
With endless cries, and never-ceasing wailings; 305
Th'hast lost —
JAFF.   Oh, I have lost what can't be counted!
My friend, too, Belvidera, that dear friend,
Who, next to thee, was all my health rejoiced in,
Has used me like a slave — shamefully used me.
'Twould break thy pitying heart to hear the
            story.   310
What shall I do? resentment, indignation,
Love, pity, fear, and mem'ry, how I've wronged him,
Distract my quiet with the very thought on't,

And tear my heart to pieces in my bosom.
BELV. What has he done?
JAFF.   Thou'dst hate me should I
            tell thee.   315
BELV. Why?
JAFF. Oh, he has used me! Yet, by heaven, I
            bear it!
He has used me, Belvidera — but first swear
That when I've told thee, thou'lt not loathe me
            utterly,
Though vilest blots and stains appear upon me; 320
But still at least with charitable goodness,
Be near me in the pangs of my affliction,
Not scorn me, Belvidera, as he has done.
BELV. Have I then e'er been false that now I am
            doubted?
Speak, what's the cause I'm grown into distrust?   325
Why thought unfit to hear my love's complainings?
JAFF. Oh!
BELV.   Tell me.
JAFF.   Bear my failings, for they are many.
O my dear angel! In that friend I've lost
All my soul's peace; for every thought of him
Strikes my sense hard, and deads in it my
            brains.   330
Wouldst thou believe it?
BELV.   Speak.
JAFF.   Before we parted,
Ere yet his guards had led him to his prison,
Full of severest sorrows for his suff'rings,
With eyes o'erflowing and a bleeding heart
Humbling myself almost beneath my nature,   335
As at his feet I kneeled and sued for mercy,
Forgetting all our friendship, all the dearness
In which w'have lived so many years together,
With a reproachful hand he dashed a blow —
He struck me, Belvidera, by heaven, he struck
            me,   340
Buffeted, called me traitor, villain, coward! —
Am I a coward? am I a villain? Tell me:
Th'art the best judge, and mad'st me, if I am so.
Damnation — coward!
BELV.   Oh! forgive him, Jaffeir.
And if his sufferings wound thy heart already, 345
What will they do tomorrow?
JAFF.   Hah!
BELV.   Tomorrow,
When thou shalt see him stretched in all the agonies
Of a tormenting and a shameful death,
His bleeding bowels, and his broken limbs,
Insulted o'er by a vile, butchering villain;   350
What will thy heart do then? Oh, sure 'twill stream
Like my eyes now.
JAFF.   What means thy dreadful story?
Death, and tomorrow? broken limbs and bowels?

293] Q3 supplies *with*; Q1Q2 omit.

Insulted o'er by a vile, butchering villain?
By all my fears, I shall start out to madness 355
With barely guessing if the truth's hid longer.

BELV. The faithless senators, 'tis they've decreed
    it:
They say, according to our friend's request,
They shall have death, and not ignoble bondage:
Declare their promised mercy all as forfeited, 360
False to their oaths, and deaf to intercession;
Warrants are passed for public death tomorrow.

JAFF. Death! doomed to die! condemned un-
    heard! unpleaded!

BELV. Nay, cruel'st racks and torments are pre-
    paring,
To force confessions from their dying pangs. 365
Oh, do not look so terribly upon me!
How your lips shake, and all your face disordered!
What means my love?

JAFF. Leave me! I charge thee, leave me —
    strong temptations
Wake in my heart.

BELV.   For what?

JAFF.   No more, but leave me. 370

BELV. Why?

JAFF. Oh! by heaven, I love thee with that fond-
    ness,
I would not have thee stay a moment longer
Near these curst hands. Are they not cold upon
    thee?
        (*Pulls the dagger half out of his bosom and puts
        it back again.*)

BELV. No, everlasting comfort's in thy arms;
To lean thus on thy breast is softer ease 375
Than downy pillows decked with leaves of roses.

JAFF. Alas, thou think'st not of the thorns 'tis
    filled with:
Fly ere they gall thee: there's a lurking serpent
Ready to leap and sting thee to thy heart;
Art thou not terrified?

BELV.   No.

JAFF.   Call to mind 380
What thou hast done, and whither thou hast brought
    me.

BELV. Hah!

JAFF.   Where's my friend? my friend, thou
    smiling mischief?
Nay, shrink not, now 'tis too late, thou shouldst have
    fled
When thy guilt first had cause, for dire revenge
Is up and raging for my friend. He groans — 385
Hark, how he groans! His screams are in my ears
Already; see, th'have fixed him on the wheel,
And now they tear him. — Murder! perjured Senate!
Murder — Oh! — hark thee, trait'ress, thou has done
    this;
Thanks to thy tears and false persuading love. 390

How her eyes speak! O thou bewitching creature!
        (*Fumbling for his dagger.*)
Madness cannot hurt thee. Come, thou little trem-
    bler,
Creep, even into my heart, and there lie safe:
'Tis thy own citadel. — Hah — yet stand off!
Heaven must have justice, and my broken vows 395
Will sink me else beneath its reaching mercy.
I'll wink and then 'tis done —

BELV.   What means the lord
Of me, my life and love? What's in thy bosom
Thou grasp'st at so? Nay, why am I thus treated?
        [JAFFEIR] *draws the dagger; offers to stab her.*
What wilt thou do? Ah, do not kill me, Jaffeir! 400
Pity these panting breasts, and trembling limbs,
That used to clasp thee when thy looks were
    milder —
That yet hang heavy on my unpurged soul;
And plunge it not into eternal darkness.

JAFF. No, Belvidera, when we parted last, 405
I gave this dagger with thee as in trust
To be thy portion if I e'er proved false.
On such condition was my truth believed;
But now 'tis forfeited and must be paid for.
        (*Offers to stab her again.*)

BELV. (*kneeling*). Oh, mercy!

JAFF.   Nay, no struggling.

BELV. (*leaps upon his neck and kisses him*). Now
    then kill me! 410
While thus I cling about thy cruel neck,
Kiss thy revengeful lips and die in joys
Greater than any I can guess hereafter.

JAFF. I am, I am a coward; witness't, heaven,
Witness it, earth, and every being, witness! 415
'Tis but one blow; yet — by immortal love,
I cannot longer bear a thought to harm thee!
        (*He throws away the dagger and embraces her.*)
The seal of Providence is sure upon thee,
And thou wert born for yet unheard-of wonders:
Oh, thou wert either born to save or damn me! 420
By all the power that's given thee o'er my soul,
By thy resistless tears and conquering smiles,
By the victorious love that still waits on thee,
Fly to thy cruel father: save my friend,
Or all our future quiet's lost forever: 425
Fall at his feet; cling round his reverend knees;
Speak to him with thy eyes, and with thy tears
Melt his hard heart, and wake dead nature in
    him.
Crush him in th' arms, and torture him with thy
    softness:
Nor, till thy prayers are granted, set him
    free, 430
But conquer him, as thou hast vanquished me.
        Exeunt ambo.

378] QQ *call* for *gall*.   392] Q3 *can't* for *cannot*.   428] Q1Q2 *thy* for *his*.

ACT V

[SCENE I]

[A street of the city.]

Enter PRIULI, *solus.*

PRIU. Why, cruel heaven, have my unhappy days
Been lengthened to this sad one? Oh! dishonor
And deathless infamy is fall'n upon me.
Was it my fault? Am I a traitor? No.
But then, my only child, my daughter, wedded;　5
There my best blood runs foul, and a disease
Incurable has seized upon my memory,
To make it rot and stink to after ages.
Curst be the fatal minute when I got her;
Or would that I'd been anything but man,　10
And raised an issue which would ne'er have wronged
　　me.
The miserablest creatures (man excepted)
Are not the less esteemed, though their posterity
Degenerate from the virtues of their fathers;
The vilest beasts are happy in their offsprings,　15
While only man gets traitors, whores, and villains.
Curst be the names, and some swift blow from fate
Lay his head deep, where mine may be forgotten!

Enter BELVIDERA *in a long mourning veil.*

BELV. He's there — my father, my inhuman fa-
　　ther,
That, for three years, has left an only child　20
Exposed to all the outrages of fate,
And cruel ruin. — Oh! —
PRIU. 　　　　　　　What child of sorrow
Art thou, that com'st thus wrapped in weeds of sad-
　　ness,
And mov'st as if thy steps were towards a grave?
BELV. A wretch who from the very top of happi-
　　ness　25
Am fallen into the lowest depths of misery,
And want your pitying hand to raise me up again.
PRIU. Indeed, thou talk'st as thou hadst tasted sor-
　　rows;
Would I could help thee!
BELV. 　　　　　　'Tis greatly in your power.
The world, too, speaks you charitable, and I,　30
Who ne'er asked alms before, in that dear hope
Am come a-begging to you, sir.
PRIU. 　　　　　　　For what?
BELV. Oh, well regard me! Is this voice a strange
　　one?
Consider, too, when beggars once pretend
A case like mine, no little will content 'em.　35
PRIU. What wouldst thou beg for?
BELV. 　　　　　　　Pity and forgiveness.
　　　　　　　　　　(Throws up her veil.)
By the kind tender names of child and father,

Hear my complaints, and take me to your love.
PRIU. My daughter?
BELV. 　　　　Yes, your daughter, by a mother
Virtuous and noble, faithful to your honor,　40
Obedient to your will, kind to your wishes,
Dear to your arms. By all the joys she gave you,
When in her blooming years she was your treasure,
Look kindly on me; in my face behold
The lineaments of hers y'have kissed so often,　45
Pleading the cause of your poor cast-off child.
PRIU. Thou art my daughter.
BELV. 　　　　　Yes — and y'have oft told me
With smiles of love and chaste, paternal kisses,
I'd much resemblance of my mother.
PRIU. 　　　　　　　　　Oh!
Hadst thou inherited her matchless virtues,　50
I'd been too blest. .
BELV. 　　　　Nay, do not call to memory
My disobedience, but let pity enter
Into your heart, and quite deface the impression;
For could you think how mine's perplexed, what sad-
　　ness,
Fears, and despairs distract the peace within me,　55
Oh, you would take me in your dear, dear arms,
Hover with strong compassion o'er your young one,
To shelter me with a protecting wing
From the black gathered storm that's just, just break-
　　ing!
PRIU. Don't talk thus.
BELV. 　　Yes, I must; and you must hear too.　60
I have a husband —
PRIU. 　　　Damn him!
BELV. 　　　　　　Oh, do not curse him!
He would not speak so hard a word towards you
On any terms, howe'er he deal with me.
PRIU. Hah! what means my child?
BELV. Oh, there's but this short moment　65
'Twixt me and fate. Yet send me not with curses
Down to my grave; afford me one kind blessing
Before we part: just take me in your arms
And recommend me with a prayer to heaven,
That I may die in peace; and when I'm dead —　70
PRIU. How my soul's catched!
BELV. 　　　　Lay me, I beg you, lay me
By the dear ashes of my tender mother.
She would have pitied me, had fate yet spared her.
PRIU. By heaven, my aching heart forebodes much
　　mischief.
Tell me thy story, for I'm still thy father.　75
BELV. No, I'm contented.
PRIU. 　　　Speak.
BELV. 　　　　　　No matter.
PRIU. 　　　　　　　　　Tell me.
By yon blest heaven, my heart runs o'er with fond-
　　ness.
BELV. Oh!

PRIU.   Utter't.

BELV.   Oh, my husband, my dear husband
Carries a dagger in his once kind bosom,
To pierce the heart of your poor Belvidera.   80
   PRIU.   Kill thee!

   BELV.   Yes, kill me.   When he passed his faith
And covenant against your state and Senate,
He gave me up as hostage for his truth,
With me a dagger and a dire commission,
Whene'er he failed, to plunge it through this bos-
      om.   85
I learnt the danger, chose the hour of love
T'attempt his heart, and bring it back to honor.
Great love prevailed and blessed me with success.
He came, confessed, betrayed his dearest friends
For promised mercy; now they're doomed to suf-
      fer,   90
Galled with remembrance of what then was sworn,
If they are lost, he vows t'appease the gods
With this poor life, and make my blood th'atone-
      ment.
   PRIU.   Heavens!

   BELV.   Think you saw what passed at our
      last parting;
Think you beheld him like a raging lion,   95
Pacing the earth, and tearing up his steps,
Fate in his eyes, and roaring with the pain
Of burning fury; think you saw his one hand
Fixed on my throat, while the extended other
Grasped a keen, threat'ning dagger.   Oh, 'twas
      thus   100
We last embraced; when, trembling with revenge,
He dragged me to the ground, and at my bosom
Presented horrid death, cried out, 'My friends —
Where are my friends?' swore, wept, raged, threat-
      ened, loved —
For he yet loved, and that dear love preserved
      me   105
To this last trial of a father's pity.
I fear not death, but cannot bear a thought
That that dear hand should do th' unfriendly office;
If I was ever then your care, now hear me;
Fly to the Senate, save the promised lives   110
Of his dear friends, ere mine be made the sacrifice.
   PRIU.   Oh, my heart's comfort!

   BELV.   Will you not, my father?
Weep not, but answer me.
   PRIU.   By heaven, I will!
Not one of 'em but what shall be immortal.
Canst thou forgive me all my follies past,   115
I'll henceforth be indeed a father; never,
Never more thus expose, but cherish thee,
Dear as the vital warmth that feeds my life,
Dear as these eyes that weep in fondness o'er thee.
Peace to thy heart!   Farewell.
   BELV.   Go, and remember,   120

'Tis Belvidera's life her father pleads for.

                              Exeunt severally.

                    Enter ANTONIO.

   ANT.   Hum, hum, hah.   Signior Priuli, my lord
Priuli, my lord, my lord, my lord. — How we lords
love to call one another by our titles. — My lord,
my lord, my lord — Pox on him, I am a lord as   125
well as he.   And so let him fiddle. — I'll warrant
him he's gone to the Senate-house, and I'll be there
too, soon enough for somebody.   Odd! — here's a
tickling speech about the plot.[1]   I'll prove there's a
plot with a vengeance — would I had it with-   130
out book.   Let me see — 'Most reverend senators,
That there is a plot, surely by this time, no man that
hath eyes or understanding in his head will presume
to doubt; 'tis as plain as the light in the cowcumber'
— no — hold there — cowcumber does not   135
come in yet — ''tis as plain as the light in the sun,
or as the man in the moon, even at noonday.   It is,
indeed, a pumpkin-plot, which, just as it was mellow, we have gathered; and now we have gathered
it, prepared and dressed it, shall we throw it   140
like a pickled cowcumber out at the window?   No!
That it is not only a bloody, horrid, execrable,
damnable, and audacious plot, but it is, as I may so
say, a saucy plot; and we all know, most reverend
fathers, that what is sauce for a goose is sauce   145
for a gander: therefore, I say, as those blood-thirsty
ganders of the conspiracy would have destroyed us
geese of the Senate, let us make haste to destroy
them.   So I humbly move for hanging' — Hah,
hurry durry — I think this will do — though I   150
was something out, at first, about the sun and the
cowcumber.

                    Enter AQUILINA.

   AQUIL.   Good morrow, senator.

   ANT.   Nacky, my dear Nacky, morrow, Nacky;
odd, I am very brisk, very merry, very pert,   155
very jovial — ha-a-a-a-a — kiss me, Nacky; how
dost thou do, my little Tory, rory strumpet?   Kiss
me, I say, hussy, kiss me.

   AQUIL.   'Kiss me, Nacky!'   Hang you, sir! —
coxcomb, hang you, sir!   160

   ANT.   Hayty tayty, is it so indeed, with all my
heart, faith — (*sings*) Hey then, up go we, faith —
hey then, up go we, dum dum derum dump.

   AQUIL.   Signior.

   ANT.   Madonna.   165

   AQUIL.   Do you intend to die in your bed? —

   ANT.   About threescore years hence, much may be
done, my dear.

   AQUIL.   You'll be hanged, signior.

[1] Antonio's speech hits at the fears aroused by the Polish
Plot.

99] Q1Q2 *while*; Q3 *whilst*.   123] Q3 *How*; Q1Q2 *Now.*

ANT. Hanged, sweetheart? Prithee, be 170
quiet. Hanged, quoth-a, that's a merry conceit,
with all my heart. Why, thou jok'st, Nacky; thou
art given to joking, I'll swear. Well, I protest,
Nacky — nay, I must protest, and will protest that
I love joking dearly, man. And I love thee for 175
joking, and I'll kiss thee for joking, and touse thee
for joking — and odd, I have a devilish mind to
take thee aside about that business for joking, too —
odd, I have! and (sings) *Hey then, up go we,* dum dum
derum dump.   180
  AQUIL. (*draws a dagger*). See you this, sir?
  ANT. O laud, a dagger! O laud! it is naturally
my aversion; I cannot endure the sight on't; hide it,
for heaven's sake! I cannot look that way till it be
gone — hide it, hide it, oh, oh, hide it!   185
  AQUIL. Yes, in your heart, I'll hide it.
  ANT. My heart! What, hide a dagger in my
    heart's blood!
  AQUIL. Yes, in thy heart — thy throat, thou pam-
    pered devil!
Thou hast helped to spoil my peace, and I'll have
    vengeance
On thy curst life for all the bloody Senate,   190
The perjured, faithless Senate. Where's my lord,
My happiness, my love, my god, my hero?
Doomed by thy accursèd tongue, amongst the rest,
T'a shameful wrack? By all the rage that's in me,
I'll be whole years in murdering thee!   195
  ANT. Why, Nacky, wherefore so passionate?
What have I done? What's the matter, my dear
Nacky? Am not I thy love, thy happiness, thy lord,
thy hero, thy senator, and everything in the world,
Nacky?   200
  AQUIL. Thou! Thinkst thou, thou art fit to meet
    my joys —
To bear the eager clasps of my embraces?
Give me my Pierre, or —
  ANT. Why, he's to be hanged, little Nacky —
trussed up for treason, and so forth, child.   205
  AQUIL. Thou li'st! stop down thy throat that
    hellish sentence,
Or 'tis thy last. Swear that my love shall live,
Or thou art dead.
  ANT.   Ah-h-h-h.
  AQUIL.   Swear to recall his doom —
Swear at my feet, and tremble at my fury.
  ANT. I do. [*Aside.*] Now, if she would but 210
kick a little bit — one kick now, ah-h-h-h.
  AQUIL. Swear, or —
  ANT. I do, by these dear fragrant foots and little
toes, sweet as — e-e-e-e, my Nacky, Nacky, Nacky.
  AQUIL. How!   215
  ANT. Nothing but untie thy shoestring, a little,
faith and troth; that's all — that's all, as I hope to
live, Nacky, that's all.

  AQUIL. Nay, then —
  ANT. Hold, hold! thy love, thy lord, thy hero 220
Shall be preserved and safe.
  AQUIL.   Or may this poniard
Rust in thy heart!
  ANT.   With all my soul.
  AQUIL.   Farewell —
                              Exit AQUILINA.
  ANT. Adieu. Why, what a bloody-minded, in-
veterate, termagant strumpet have I been plagued
with! Oh-h-h, yet more! nay, then, I die, I 225
die — I am dead already. (*Stretches himself out.*)

[SCENE II]

[*A street near* PRIULI's *house.*]

Enter JAFFEIR.

JAFF. Final destruction seize on all the world!
Bend down, ye heavens, and shutting round this
    earth,
Crush the vile globe into its first confusion;
Scorch it with elemental flames to one curst cinder,
And all us little creepers in't, called men,   5
Burn, burn to nothing: but let Venice burn
Hotter than all the rest: here kindle hell
Ne'er to extinguish, and let souls hereafter
Groan here, in all those pains which mine feels now.

Enter BELVIDERA.

BELV. (*meeting him*). My life —
JAFF. (*turning from her*).   My plague —
BELV.   Nay, then I see my ruin, 10
If I must die!
  JAFF.   No, Death's this day too busy;
Thy father's ill-timed mercy came too late.
I thank thee for thy labors, though, and him, too,
But all my poor, betrayed, unhappy friends
Have summons to prepare for fate's black hour; 15
And yet I live.
  BELV.   Then be the next my doom.
I see thou hast passed my sentence in thy heart,
And I'll no longer weep or plead against it,
But with the humblest, most obedient patience
Meet thy dear hands, and kiss 'em when they wound
    me;   20
Indeed I am willing, but I beg thee do it
With some remorse; and where thou giv'st the blow,
View me with eyes of a relenting love,
And show me pity, for 'twill sweeten justice.
  JAFF. Show pity to thee?
  BELV.   Yes, and when thy hands, 25
Charged with my fate, come trembling to the deed,
As thou hast done a thousand, thousand dear times
To this poor breast, when kinder rage has brought
    thee,

When our stinged hearts have leaped to meet each
    other,
And melting kisses sealed our lips together,   30
When joys have left me gasping in thy arms,
So let my death come now, and I'll not shrink from't.
   JAFF. Nay, Belvidera, do not fear my cruelty,
Nor let the thoughts of death perplex thy fancy,
But answer me to what I shall demand,   35
With a firm temper and unshaken spirit.
   BELV. I will when I've done weeping —
   JAFF.   Fie, no more on't!
How long is't since the miserable day
We wedded first —
   BELV.   Oh-h-h.
   JAFF.   Nay, keep in thy tears,
Lest they unman me, too.
   BELV.   Heaven knows I cannot;   40
The words you utter sound so very sadly
These streams will follow —
   JAFF.   Come, I'll kiss 'em dry, then.
   BELV. But was't a miserable day?
   JAFF.   A curst one.
   BELV. I thought it otherwise, and you've oft sworn
In the transporting hours of warmest love,   45
When sure you spoke the truth, you've sworn you
    blessed it.
   JAFF. 'Twas a rash oath.
   BELV.   Then why am I not curst too?
   JAFF. No, Belvidera; by th'eternal truth,
I dote with too much fondness.
   BELV.   Still so kind?
Still then do you love me?
   JAFF.   Nature, in her workings,   50
Inclines not with more ardor to creation
Than I do now towards thee; man ne'er was blest
Since the first pair first met, as I have been.
   BELV. Then sure you will not curse me.
   JAFF.   No, I'll bless thee;
I came on purpose, Belvidera, to bless thee.   55
'Tis now, I think, three years w'have lived together.
   BELV. And may no fatal minute ever part us
Till, reverend grown for age and love, we go
Down to one grave as our last bed, together;
There sleep in peace till an eternal morning.   60
   JAFF. (sighing). When will that be?
   BELV.   I hope long ages hence.
   JAFF. Have I not hitherto (I beg thee tell me
Thy very fears) used thee with tender'st love?
Did e'er my soul rise up in wrath against thee?
Did I e'er frown when Belvidera smiled,   65
Or, by the least unfriendly word, betray
A bating passion? Have I ever wronged thee?
   BELV. No.
   JAFF.   Has my heart, or have my eyes e'er
    wand'rèd
To any other woman?

   BELV.   Never, never —
I were the worst of false ones, should I accuse
    thee.   70
I own I've been too happy, blest above
My sex's charter.
   JAFF. Did I not say I came to bless thee?
   BELV. Yes.
   JAFF.   Then hear me, bounteous heaven!
Pour down your blessings on this beauteous
    head,   75
Where everlasting sweets are always springing.
With a continual giving hand, let peace,
Honor, and safety always hover round her;
Feed her with plenty; let her eyes ne'er see
A sight of sorrow, nor her heart know mourning;   80
Crown all her days with joy, her nights with rest,
Harmless as her own thoughts, and prop her virtue
To bear the loss of one that too much loved,
And comfort her with patience in our parting.
   BELV. How — parting, parting!
   JAFF.   Yes, forever parting.   85
I have sworn, Belvidera, by yon heaven,
That best can tell how much I lose to leave thee,
We part this hour forever.
   BELV.   Oh, call back
Your cruel blessings; stay with me and curse me!
   JAFF. No, 'tis resolved.
   BELV.   Then hear me, too, just heaven!   90
Pour down your curses on this wretched head
With never-ceasing vengeance; let despair,
Danger, or infamy — nay all, surround me;
Starve me with wantings; let my eyes ne'er see
A sight of comfort, nor my heart know peace,   95
But dash my days with sorrow, nights with horrors
Wild as my own thoughts now, and let loose fury
To make me mad enough for what I los ,
If I must lose him. — If I must! — I will not.
Oh, turn and hear me!
   JAFF.   Now hold, heart, or never!   100
   BELV. By all the tender days we have lived to-
    gether,
By all our charming nights, and joys that crowned
    'em,
Pity my sad condition — speak, but speak!
   JAFF. Oh-h-h!
   BELV.   By these arms that now cling round
    thy neck,
By this dear kiss and by ten thousand more,   105
By these poor streaming eyes —
   JAFF.   Murder! unhold me.
By th'immortal destiny that doomed me
               (draws his dagger)
To this curst minute, I'll not live one longer.
Resolve to let me go or see me fall —
   BELV. Hold, sir; be patient. (Passing-bell tolls.)
   JAFF.   Hark, the dismal bell   110

50] Q3 you; Q1Q2 you you.

Tolls out for death! I must attend its call, too;
For my poor friend, my dying Pierre, expects me:
He sent a message to require I'd see him
Before he died, and take his last forgiveness.
Farewell forever.   (*Going out, looks back at her.*)
BELV.   Leave thy dagger with me; 115
Bequeath me something. — Not one kiss at parting?
O my poor heart, when wilt thou break?
JAFF.   Yet stay!
We have a child, as yet a tender infant.
Be a kind mother to him when I am gone;
Breed him in virtue and the paths of honor, 120
But let him never know his father's story.
I charge thee guard him from the wrongs my fate
May do his future fortune or his name.
Now — nearer yet —   (*approaching each other*)
                      Oh, that my arms were riveted
Thus round thee ever! — But my friends, my
      oath!   (*Kisses her.*) 125
This and no more.
BELV.   Another, sure another,
For that poor little one you've ta'en such care of;
I'll give't him truly.
JAFF. [*kissing her*].   So! — now farewell.
BELV.   Forever?
JAFF. Heaven knows, forever; all good angels
      guard thee.   [*Exit.*]
BELV. All ill ones sure had charge of me this mo-
      ment.   130
Curst be my days, and doubly curst my nights,
Which I must now mourn out in widowed tears;
Blasted be every herb and fruit and tree;
Curst be the rain that falls upon the earth,
And may the general curse reach man and
      beast.   135
Oh, give me daggers, fire, or water!
How I could bleed, how burn, how drown, the waves
Huzzing and booming round my sinking head,
Till I descended to the peaceful bottom!
Oh, there's all quiet; here, all rage and fury: 140
The air's too thin, and pierces my weak brain:
I long for thick, substantial sleep. Hell, hell,
Burst from the center, rage and roar aloud
If thou art half so hot, so mad as I am.

Enter PRIULI *and Servants.*

Who's there?
PRIU.   Run, seize and bring her safely
      home.   (*They seize her.*) 145
Guard her as you would life. Alas, poor creature!
BELV. What? To my husband then conduct me
      quickly.
Are all things ready? Shall we die most gloriously?
Say not a word of this to my old father.
Murmuring streams, soft shades, and springing
      flowers,   150

Lutes, laurels, seas of milk, and ships of amber.
                                    Exeunt.

[SCENE III]

Scene opening, discovers a scaffold and a wheel pre-
pared for the executing of PIERRE; *then enter*
Officers, PIERRE, *and Guards, a Friar, Execu-*
tioner, and a great Rabble.

OFFIC. Room, room there! Stand all by; make
room for the prisoner.
PIERRE. My friend not come yet?
FATHER.   Why are you so obstinate?
PIERRE. Why you so troublesome, that a poor
wretch cannot die in peace,   5
But you, like ravens, will be croaking round him?
FATH. Yet, heaven —
PIERRE.   I tell thee, heaven and I are
      friends.
I ne'er broke peace with't yet by cruel murders,
Rapine, or perjury, or vile deceiving;
But lived in moral justice towards all men, 10
Nor am a foe to the most strong believers,
Howe'er my own short-sighted faith confine me.
FATH. But an all-seeing Judge —
PIERRE.   You say my conscience
Must be mine accuser: I have searched that con-
      science,
And finds no records there of crimes that scare
      me.   15
FATH. 'Tis strange you should want faith.
PIERRE.   You want to lead
My reason blindfold, like a hampered lion,
Checked of its nobler vigor; then, when baited
Down to obedient tameness, make it couch,
And show strange tricks which you call signs of
      faith.   20
So silly souls are gulled and you get money.
Away, no more! — Captain, I would hereafter
This fellow wrote no lies of my conversion,
Because he has crept upon my troubled hours.

Enter JAFFEIR.

JAFF. Hold. Eyes, be dry; heart, strengthen me
      to bear   25
This hideous sight, and humble me [to] take
The last forgiveness of a dying friend,
Betrayed by my vile falsehood to his ruin!
— O Pierre!
PIERRE.   Yet nearer.
JAFF.   Crawling on my knees,
And prostrate on the earth, let me approach thee. 30
How shall I look up to thy injured face,
That always used to smile with friendship on me?
It darts an air of so much manly virtue,
That I, methinks, look little in thy sight,
And stripes are fitter for me than embraces. 35

SCENE III. 22] Q1Q2 *I would;* Q3 *I'd have.*   26] 1727 ed. supplies *to,* an emendation frequently adopted.

PIERRE. Dear to my arms, though thou hast un-
    done my fame,
I cannot forget to love thee: prithee, Jaffeir,
Forgive that filthy blow my passion dealt thee;
I am now preparing for the land of peace,
And fain would have the charitable wishes   40
Of all good men, like thee, to bless my journey.
    JAFF. Good! I am the vilest creature, worse than
    e'er
Suffered the shameful fate thou art going to taste of.
Why was I sent for to be used thus kindly?
Call, call me villain, as I am, describe   45
The foul complexion of my hateful deeds;
Lead me to the rack, and stretch me in thy stead;
I've crimes enough to give it its full load,
And do it credit. Thou wilt but spoil the use on't,
And honest men hereafter bear its figure   50
About 'em as a charm from treacherous friendship.
    OFFIC. The time grows short; your friends are
    dead already.
    JAFF. Dead!
    PIERRE. Yes, dead, Jaffeir; they've all died like
    men too,
Worthy their character.
    JAFF.   And what must I do?   55
    PIERRE. O Jaffeir!
    JAFF.   Speak aloud thy burthened soul,
And tell thy troubles to thy tortured friend.
    PIERRE. Friend! Couldst thou yet be a friend, a
    generous friend,
I might hope comfort from thy noble sorrows.
Heav'n knows I want a friend.
    JAFF.   And I a kind one, 60
That would not thus scorn my repenting virtue,
Or think, when he is to die, my thoughts are idle.
    PIERRE. No! live, I charge thee, Jaffeir.
    JAFF.   Yes, I will live,
But it shall be to see thy fall revenged
At such a rate as Venice long shall groan for.   65
    PIERRE. Wilt thou?
    JAFF.   I will, by heav'n!
    PIERRE.   Then still thou'rt noble,
And I forgive thee. Oh — yet — shall I trust thee?
    JAFF. No: I've been false already.
    PIERRE.   Dost thou love me?
    JAFF. Rip up my heart, and satisfy thy doubtings.
    PIERRE. Curse on this weakness! (He weeps.)
    JAFF.   Tears! Amazement! Tears! 70
I never saw thee melted thus before;
And know there's something lab'ring in thy bosom
That must have vent: though I'm a villain, tell me.
    PIERRE (pointing to the wheel). Seest thou that en-
    gine?
    JAFF. Why?   75
    PIERRE. Is't fit a soldier who has lived with honor,
Fought nations' quarrels, and been crowned with con-
    quest,

Be exposed a common carcass on a wheel?
    JAFF. Hah!
    PIERRE.   Speak! is't fitting?
    JAFF.   Fitting?
    PIERRE.   Yes, is't fitting?
    JAFF. What's to be done?
    PIERRE.   I'd have thee undertake 80
Something that's noble, to preserve my memory
From the disgrace that's ready to attaint it.
    OFFIC. The day grows late, sir.
    PIERRE.   I'll make haste. — O Jaffeir,
Though thou'st betrayed me, do me some way jus-
    tice.
    JAFF. No more of that. Thy wishes shall be sat-
    isfied.   85
I have a wife, and she shall bleed; my child, too,
Yield up his little throat, and all t'appease thee —
          (Going away, PIERRE holds him.)
    PIERRE. No — this — no more!
          (He whispers JAFFEIR.)
    JAFF.   Hah! is't then so?
    PIERRE.   Most certainly.
    JAFF. I'll do't.
    PIERRE.   Remember!
    OFFIC.   Sir.
    PIERRE.   Come, now I'm ready.
          (He and JAFFEIR ascend the scaffold.)
Captain, you should be a gentleman of honor; 90
Keep off the rabble, that I may have room
To entertain my fate, and die with decency.
Come!
    (Takes off his gown. Executioner prepares to
    bind him.)
    FATHER.   Son!
    PIERRE.   Hence, tempter!
    OFFIC.   Stand off, priest!
    PIERRE. I thank you, sir.
    (To JAFFEIR.)   You'll think on't?
    JAFF. 'Twon't grow stale before tomorrow.   95
    PIERRE. Now, Jaffeir! now I am going. Now —
          (Executioner having bound him.)
    JAFF. Have at thee,
Thou honest heart, then — here —   (Stabs him.)
— And this is well, too.   (Then stabs himself.)
    FATHER.   Damnable deed!
    PIERRE. Now thou hast indeed been faithful. 100
This was done nobly. — We have deceived the Sen-
    ate.
    JAFF. Bravely.
    PIERRE. Ha, ha, ha — Oh, oh —   (Dies.)
    JAFF.   Now, ye curst rulers,
Thus of the blood y'have shed I make libation,
And sprinkle't mingling. May it rest upon you, 105
And all your race. Be henceforth peace a stranger
Within your walls; let plagues and famine waste
Your generations. — Oh, poor Belvidera!
Sir, I have a wife; bear this in safety to her —

A token that with my dying breath I blest her, 110
And the dear little infant left behind me.
I am sick — I am quiet — (JAFFEIR *dies.*)
  OFFIC. Bear this news to the Senate,
And guard their bodies till there's farther order.
Heav'n grant I die so well —
  (*Scene shuts upon them.*)

[SCENE IV]

[*A room in* PRIULI'S *house.*]

Soft music. Enter BELVIDERA *distracted, led by two of her Women,* PRIULI, *and Servants.*

  PRIU. Strengthen her heart with patience, pitying
    heav'n.
  BELV. Come, come, come, come, come! Nay, come
    to bed,
Prithee, my love. The winds! hark, how they whistle!
And the rain beats: oh, how the weather shrinks me!
You are angry now; who cares? pish, no indeed. 5
Choose then. I say you shall not go, you shall not!
Whip your ill nature; get you gone then! —
  (JAFFEIR'S *Ghost rises.*)
  Oh,
Are you returned? See, father, here he's come again!
Am I to blame to love him? Oh, thou dear one!
  (*Ghost sinks.*)
Why do you fly me? Are you angry still, then? 10
Jaffeir! where art thou? — Father, why do you do
    thus?
Stand off, don't hide him from me! He's here some-
    where.
Stand off, I say! — What, gone? Remember't, tyrant!
I may revenge myself for this trick one day.
I'll do't — I'll do't. Renault's a nasty fellow. 15
Hang him, hang him, hang him!

Enter Officer and others.

  PRIU. News — what news?
  (*Officer whispers* PRIULI.)
  OFFIC. Most sad, sir.
Jaffeir, upon the scaffold, to prevent
A shameful death, stabbed Pierre, and next himself:
Both fell together.
  PRIU. — Daughter —

(*The Ghosts of* JAFFEIR *and* PIERRE *rise together,
    both bloody.*)

  BELV. Hah, look there! 20
My husband bloody, and his friend, too! Murder!
Who has done this? Speak to me, thou sad vision;
On these poor trembling knees I beg it.
  (*Ghosts sink.*)
  Vanished —
Here they went down. Oh, I'll dig, dig the den up.
You shan't delude me thus. Hoa, Jaffeir, Jaffeir! 25
Peep up and give me but a look. — I have him!
I've got him, father; oh, now how I'll smuggle him!
My love! my dear! my blessing! help me, help me!
They have hold on me, and drag me to the bottom!
Nay — now they pull so hard — farewell —
  (*She dies.*)
  MAID. She's dead — 30
Breathless and dead.
  PRIU. Then guard me from the sight on't:
Lead me into some place that's fit for mourning;
Where the free air, light, and the cheerful sun
May never enter. Hang it round with black;
Set up one taper that may last a day — 35
As long as I've to live; and there all leave me,
  Sparing no tears when you this tale relate,
  But bid all cruel fathers dread my fate.
  Curtain falls. Exeunt omnes.

36] Q2Q3 omit *all.*

EPILOGUE

The text is done, and now for application,
And when that's ended, pass your approbation.
Though the conspiracy's prevented here,
Methinks I see another hatching there;
And there's a certain faction fain would sway, 5
If they had strength enough, and damn this play.
But this the author bade me boldly say:
If any take his plainness in ill part,
He's glad on't from the bottom of his heart;
Poets in honor of the truth should write, 10
With the same spirit brave men for it fight;
And though against him causeless hatreds rise, ⎫
And daily where he goes of late he spies   ⎬
The scowls of sullen and revengeful eyes,   ⎭
'Tis what he knows with much contempt to bear, 15
And serves a cause too good to let him fear:
He fears no poison from an incensed drab,
No ruffian's five-foot-sword, nor rascal's stab,
Nor any other snares of mischief laid,
Not a Rose-alley cudgel-ambuscade,[1] 20
From any private cause where malice reigns,
Or general pique all blockheads have to brains:
Nothing shall daunt his pen when truth does call,
No, not the picture-mangler[2] at Guildhall.
The rebel-tribe, of which that vermin's one, 25
Have now set forward and their course begun;
And while that prince's figure they deface,
  As they before had massacred his name,
Durst their base fears but look him in the face,
  They'd use his person as they've used his fame; 30
A face, in which such lineaments they read
Of that great martyr's[3] whose rich blood they shed,
That their rebellious hate they still retain,
And in his son would murder him again.
With indignation then, let each brave heart, 35
Rouse and unite to take his injured part;
Till royal love and goodness call him home,[4]
And songs of triumph meet him as he come;
Till heaven his honor and our peace restore,
And villains never wrong his virtue more. 40

---

[1] A reference to the attack upon Dryden, in December, 1679, by Rochester's hired ruffians.
[2] 'The rascal that cut the Duke of York's picture' [in Guildhall]. NOTE in QQ.
[3] Charles I.
[4] From Scotland, where the Duke of York was temporarily.

COMEDY OF MANNERS

THE term 'Restoration comedy' is somewhat loosely applied to English comedy written during the period which began with the return of Charles II in 1660 and which closed at an indeterminate date half a century or so later. Another more significant term for the same school of writing is 'the seventeenth-century comedy of manners.' This phrase serves to distinguish the *genre* from the comedy of humors, or character, which had flourished before the Commonwealth, and which had for its chief exponent Ben Jonson. The two schools had several things in common. Both of them relied upon ridicule of human failings; both of them assumed, but avoided stating, an ideal mode of life, with which they expected their audiences to agree; both (at their best) eschewed romance and sentiment. But the comedy of humors had greater depth, the comedy of manners greater polish. This was inevitably true, since Jonson and his contemporaries were more critical of lapses from wise living, and the Restoration writers were more concerned with breaches of the sophisticated code of manners which their times had erected. This code was principally the creation of the courtiers of Charles II who, during their exile in France, had observed the elegance and charm of life in the court of Louis XIV, and who endeavored to transplant that life in England, with some modifications. The ideal gentleman, according to the comic dramatists from Etherege to Farquhar, must fulfill certain definite requirements. He must be well born; he must dress well, but not ostentatiously; he must be poised and witty, so that he is never out of countenance; he must be skilled in making love, whether to women of the town, to married women, or to young ladies of his own rank, and he may conduct several love-affairs simultaneously, provided his head is always master of his heart. He must not boast of his amours, however, and he must be discreet: it is unpardonable to betray the confidence of any woman of his own class. If he is so weak as to entertain a serious passion he must conceal the fact by an affectation of indifference or by over-acted and conventional protestations of devotion. If he is married he must not show any jealousy of his wife, nor may he let it be seen that he is in love with her. The fashionable lady is his counterpart, except that she has somewhat less freedom in love. Ideally she should be perfectly familiar with the world of intrigue without allowing herself to become involved in it; if she is a widow, or is married to an uncongenial husband, she may indulge in illicit love, provided she is not found out. In any case she will not expect complete constancy in her husband.

Deviations from this code provide much of the laughter of the comedy of manners. Persons who do not attempt to conform to the code are laughable as a matter of course, whether they be merchants, country squires, members of the clergy, or men of learning. But those who profess the code and fall short of its requirements in some way are still dearer to the dramatist. The fop who is too careful of his dress and manner, the wit who strains too hard to gain a reputation, the coquette who publishes her triumphs too openly, are all fair game. It is a cardinal rule of Restoration society that the highest art lies in concealing art. A favorite situation is that in which the hero and the heroine, who have permitted themselves to fall unfashionably in love with each other, engage in a battle of wits in which each tries to force the other to make the first admission of affection.

All of this might have made for excellent high comedy, but for two things. The Restoration comic dramatists could not hope to persuade the world for very long that their fine ladies and gentlemen were really admirable. The laughter which they directed at those whom they regarded as ridiculous was sophisticated, rather than wise, and the public was bound, sooner or later, to enquire whether the laughers were in fact so superior to those by whom they were amused. The emptiness of the 'ideal life' of fashion is admirably, though perhaps not intentionally displayed in the depiction of old age. The old, even the middle-aged, are viewed as comic in themselves. They have spent their youth in following the art of elegant intrigue, and when youth departs there is nothing left. The elderly buck, the superannuated beauty, are stock figures from Etherege onward.

The other point of weakness in Restoration comedy was its lack of a sense of ethical values. Not infrequently it chastised folly by means of an agent who was definitely vicious, without any reprehension, express or implied, of that agent's conduct. This was a result of a conscious intention of the dramatists to set up the code of their own lax circle in opposition to 'middle-class morals.' The conflict between the two codes provided them with much material, but it also provoked a clash with general public opinion, which had always held a middle ground between Puritan strictness and Cavalier license, and which began to protest against the latter before the reign of Charles II was very old. The protest was not immediately effective in the theatrical world, where the court circle was in power, but as the stage began to rely on the whole of London for its support the movement for some kind of reform gathered way. There was even some recognition among the writers themselves of the need for improvement. In 1685 Dryden, in his ode to the memory of Mrs. Anne Killigrew, frankly confessed the faults of himself and his fellow-dramatists:

> O gracious God! how far have we
> Profaned thy heav'nly gift of poesy!
> Made prostitute and profligate the Muse,
> Debased to each obscene and impious use,
> Whose harmony was first ordained above
> For tongues of angels and for hymns of love!
> O wretched we! why were we hurried down
>   This lubric and adult'rate age
> (Nay, added fat pollutions of our own,)
>   T'increase the steaming ordures of the stage?

That the attitude displayed in these lines did not find expression more often during the reign of James II and the early part of the reign of William and Mary may have been due in part to the fact that the school of Etherege and Wycherley seemed to be dying of itself: those two authors had ceased to write for the theatre; Dryden and Shadwell were producing but little comedy, and that not of a kind to provoke much adverse criticism on the score of immorality; and none of the other comic writers was of any real importance. But the almost simultaneous rise of Congreve and Vanbrugh, in the 1690's, revived the old issue, and the opposition to the Restoration mode finally crystallized in Jeremy Collier's *Short View of the Profaneness and Immorality of the English Stage* (1698). This book became a rallying-point for the forces of reform, which were quickly seen to be so strong that some heed would have to be paid to them. There were, of course, several replies to Collier by the dramatists whom he attacked, but the effects of his strictures were almost immediately evident in the altered tone of the theatre. The ultimate result of all this was the emergence of moralized and sentimental comedy.

Of the five authors who, by common consent, are the best representatives of Restoration comedy two belong to the earlier and three to the later part of the period. The plays of Etherege and Wycherley appeared between 1664 and 1676: those of Congreve, Vanbrugh and Farquhar between 1693 and 1707. Sir GEORGE ETHEREGE (?1635–?1691), though by no means the first of the five in ability, is of especial importance because of his influence upon his successors. He was himself a member of the court of Charles II, and the moral code of that circle therefore sat quite naturally upon him. He wrote but three plays: *The Comical Revenge*, partly in rhyme (1664); *She Would if She Could* (1668); and *The Man of Mode* (1676). None of them is remarkable for depth or for structure, but they are all full of life and wit. Moreover, there is an unmistakable improvement visible in Etherege's art as he proceeds: if he had been willing to work more seriously over his compositions they might have been a great deal finer than they were. His most interesting characters are all to be found in his last play. Dorimant, who, it has been said, represents the Earl of

Rochester, is certainly Etherege's ideal of a fine gentleman, and, indeed, he became the accepted representative of the Restoration courtier-rake in the eyes of later generations. When Steele wished to attack this ideal he centered his attention upon Dorimant (*Spectator* No. 65). But Dorimant is, in fact, overshadowed by Harriet and Sir Fopling Flutter. The former comes near to perfection, from the point of view of 1676, and her wit, her charm, her worldly wisdom, as well as her masterly handling of Dorimant and of her affairs in general, are likely to win modern readers of the play to acquiescence in the verdict of the Restoration. As for Sir Fopling, he is the father of the whole tribe of dandies, and though Vanbrugh's Lord Foppington may surpass him, a good share of the credit for the later creation must go to the earlier character.

WILLIAM WYCHERLEY (1641–1715), like Etherege, was attached to the court of Charles II, although less securely. His four comedies were all written during the time of his dependence upon the favor of the king. The order of their composition is in some doubt, but it seems probable that it is the same as the order of their stage production, viz., *Love in a Wood* (1671); *The Gentleman Dancing-Master* (?1671); *The Country Wife* (?1673); *The Plain Dealer* (1676). At first Wycherley writes in a vein much like that of Etherege; the code of the courtier is taken for granted and the laughter is aimed at those persons who do not succeed in living up to it. As time goes on, however, a deeper satiric note is evident in Wycherley, so that some of the fine ladies and gentlemen come in for a share of the dramatist's criticism. It is noticeable, too, that it is these characters who suffer most at his hands; the merely foolish escape with ridicule. In his attack upon selfishness and treachery, in the persons of Vernish and Olivia, Wycherley is so savage as to pass out of the ordinary range of Restoration comedy. It is this honest indignation, coupled, perhaps, with the frankness of his dialogue, which earned for him the names of 'brawny' and 'manly' Wycherley.

WILLIAM CONGREVE (1670–1729), an Englishman brought up in Ireland, where he was a school- and college-mate of Swift, made his appearance in the world of the theatre nearly twenty years after Wycherley quitted it. His first comedy, *The Old Bachelor* (1693) owes an obvious debt to that predecessor: anyone who did not know of the gap in time might easily believe that the two men were exact contemporaries. But Congreve was to develop the old mode in his own fashion. In *The Double Dealer* (1693) and *Love for Love* (1695) he worked old veins with varying success. In 1697 he brought out his only tragedy — the only one, indeed, written by any one of the five great Restoration comic writers — *The Mourning Bride*. This was much admired throughout the eighteenth century: of one passage from it Dr. Johnson wrote that he knew not what he could prefer to it, if he were required to select from the whole mass of English poetry the most poetical paragraph, and in private conversation he said that he recollected none in Shakespeare equal to it. As a matter of fact, Congreve's blank verse, while not bad, is not comparable to that of Dryden or Otway. In 1700, after a five years' rest from comedy, Congreve brought out the last and best of his plays, *The Way of the World*. In wit, in polish, in brilliance of dialogue this is almost universally regarded as the finest of Restoration plays. The author has himself achieved that poise which was the goal of the Restoration gentleman. Mirabell is a refined Dorimant, and Millamant a more charming and somewhat more feminine Harriet. The intrigues are carried out with more finesse than those of Etherege or Wycherley, and sex does not hold the center of the stage so constantly as it was wont to do. Mirabell's gallantries, in fact, are all in the past, and one is given to understand that he will be constant to his wife after his marriage. Even the old theme of marital infidelity is modified, for although Mrs. Fainall has been Mirabell's mistress, the affair began and ended during the interval between her first and her second marriages. The play was a failure when it was first produced, for which some modern editors have blamed the alleged faults of its plot, especially complexity. Complex the play certainly is, but it may be said in its defence that it is intended as a satirical picture of an artificially complex society. Congreve, together with Steele, who wrote commendatory verses for the comedy, attributed its lack of success to the fact that the author's ridicule had been too fine for the taste of the town, and there is probably a good deal of truth in this. The portraits of Petulant and Witwoud are painted by strokes much more delicate than those with which Vanbrugh had caricatured Lord Foppington, and the play as a whole is much more quiet in tone than Vanbrugh's, or, indeed, than any of Congreve's earlier comedies.

Sir JOHN VANBRUGH (1664-1726) was a soldier and an architect as well as a dramatist. His theatrical interests belong to the central part of his career; they began with the writing of original plays, from which they proceeded to translations and adaptations from the French, and at length to a brief experiment in theatrical management. The two original plays with which he began (*The Relapse*, 1696; *The Provoked Wife*, 1697) are by far the most important: his other original play, *A Journey to London*, was left unfinished at his death. The last completed play in which it is certain that he had a hand was produced in 1705. He was a more breezy and less urbane writer than Congreve: his plays are full of action and gayety, but they are perhaps the most loosely constructed of the period. The two plots of *The Relapse* are connected by the slenderest of threads, and the main plot can hardly be said to have been brought to a conclusion. But the characters and the individual scenes of Vanbrugh were so amusing that his two original plays were very popular in their own day. The author's subject-matter and license of speech were probably the chief causes for the revival of the protests against the immorality of the stage. Moreover, Vanbrugh was given to baiting the clergy and religion, and this fact further aroused such opponents as Jeremy Collier. Vanbrugh's retort to criticism was coolly insolent: the tone of his preface to *The Relapse* is typical. When Collier's famous pamphlet appeared in the year following *The Provoked Wife*, Vanbrugh replied in much the same vein. His last comedy, *The Confederacy* (adapted from the French, but with considerable alteration) showed him still unrepentant.

GEORGE FARQUHAR (?1678-1707) took a different road to success. Born and educated in Ireland, he left Trinity College, Dublin, to become an actor in that city's theatre. When he was about twenty he accidentally wounded a fellow-actor, and as a consequence determined to quit the stage. Removing to London, he had his apprentice comedy, *Love and a Bottle*, produced in 1698. His natural bent was for the comedy of Etherege, although he was gayer and less sophisticated than his prototype: he had an irrepressible spirit and a youthful irresponsibility which forestall criticism. He sensed, however, the turn in public sentiment, and his later plays show an increasing tendency to placate the reformers, at the same time retaining as much of the old attitude toward life as possible. His method of 'moralizing' his comedies was to permit his characters to talk like Restoration rakes, but usually to prevent them from acting in accordance with their professions. A speech of Plume in *The Recruiting Officer* (1706) illustrates this: 'No, faith, I'm not that rake the world imagines; I have got an air of freedom, which people mistake for lewdness in me, as they mistake formality in others for religion. The world is all a cheat; only I take mine, which is undesigned, to be more excusable than theirs, which is hypocritical. I hurt nobody but myself, and they abuse all mankind.' The compromise shows that Farquhar's comic sense allied him to the older school, but it also points unmistakably to the eventual triumph of the sentimental comedy which was already being supported by Cibber and Steele.

A. E. C.

REFERENCE WORKS

1913. Palmer, John. *The Comedy of Manners.*

1914. Nettleton, George H. *English Drama of the Restoration and Eighteenth Century.* New York and London. [Chapters V, VIII, with Bibliographical Notes.]

1923. Nicoll, Allardyce. *A History of Restoration Drama, 1660-1700.* Cambridge [England]. [Chapter Three, section VI.]

1924. Dobrée, Bonamy. *Restoration Comedy, 1660-1720.* Oxford.

1924. Krutch, Joseph Wood. *Comedy and Conscience after the Restoration.* New York.

1925. Perry, Henry Ten Eyck. *The Comic Spirit in Restoration Drama.* New Haven.

The Man of Mode; or, Sir Fopling Flutter

BY SIR GEORGE ETHEREGE

THE
Man of Mode,
OR,
Sᴿ Fopling Flutter.

ACT I. SCENE I.

A Dreſſing Room, a Table Covered with a Toilet,
Cloaths laid ready.

Enter Dorimant *in his Gown and Slippers, with a Note in*
his hand made up, repeating Verſes.

Dor. **N**OW *for ſome Ages had the pride of* Spain,
Made the Sun ſhine on half the World in vain.
[*Then looking on the Note.*

For Mrs. Loveit.
What a dull inſipid thing is a Billet doux written in
Cold blood, after the heat of the buſineſs is over?
It is a Tax upon good nature which I have
Here been labouring to pay, and have done it,
Put with as much regret, as ever Fanatick paid
The Royal Aid, or Church Duties ; 'Twill
Have the ſame fate I know that all my notes
To her have had of late, 'Twill not be thought
Kind enough. Faith Women are i'the right
When they jealouſly examine our Letters, for in them

B   We

FIRST PAGE, FIRST QUARTO, 1676, OF *THE MAN OF MODE, OR, SIR FOPLING FLUTTER*
With main prose text set as if in verse

PROLOGUE

By Sir CAR SCROOPE, Baronet [1]

Like dancers on the ropes poor poets fare,
Most perish young, the rest in danger are;
This, one would think, should make our authors wary,
But, gamester-like, the giddy fools miscarry.
A lucky hand or two so tempts 'em on,   5
They cannot leave off play till they're undone.
With modest fears a muse does first begin,
Like a young wench newly enticed to sin;
But tickled once with praise, by her good will,
The wanton fool would never more lie still.   10
'Tis an old mistress you'll meet here tonight,
Whose charms you once have looked on with delight.
But now of late such dirty drabs have known ye,
A muse o'th' better sort's ashamed to own [ye].
Nature well drawn, and wit, must now give place   15
To gaudy nonsense and to dull grimace;
Nor is it strange that you should like so much
That kind of wit, for most of yours is such.
But I'm afraid that while to France we go,
To bring you home fine dresses, dance, and show,   20
The stage, like you, will but more foppish grow.
Of foreign wares, why should we fetch the scum,
When we can be so richly served at home?
For heav'n be thanked, 'tis not so wise an age
But your own follies may supply the stage.   25
Though often plowed, there's no great fear the soil
Should barren grow by the too frequent toil;
While at your doors are to be daily found
Such loads of dunghill to manure the ground.
'Tis by your follies that we players thrive,   30
As the physicians by diseases live;
And as each year some new distemper reigns,
Whose friendly poison helps to increase their gains,
So among you there starts up every day
Some new, unheard-of fool for us to play.   35
Then, for your own sakes be not too severe,
Nor what you all admire at home, damn here;
Since each is fond of his own ugly face,
Why should you, when we hold it, break the glass?

---

[1] One of the most popular of 'the mob of gentlemen who wrote with ease.'

The dedication, to the Duchess of York, is omitted.   14] Q1 *own you*; Q2 *own ye.*

DRAMATIS PERSONÆ

MR. DORIMANT,
MR. MEDLEY,
OLD [HARRY] BELLAIR,   } Gentlemen
YOUNG [HARRY] BELLAIR,
SIR FOPLING FLUTTER,

LADY TOWNLEY,
EMILIA,
MRS. LOVEIT,   } Gentlewomen
BELLINDA,
LADY WOODVILL, and
HARRIET, her daughter,

PERT,
and   } Waiting Women
BUSY,

[TOM,] a Shoemaker,
[NAN,] an Orange Woman,
Three Slovenly Bullies
Two Chairmen
MR. SMIRK, a Parson
HANDY, a *Valet-de-chambre*
Pages, Footmen. etc.

THE MAN OF MODE;

OR,

SIR FOPLING FLUTTER

BY SIR GEORGE ETHEREGE

ACT I

SCENE I

A dressing-room. A table covered with a toilet; clothes laid ready.

Enter DORIMANT in his gown and slippers, with a note in his hand, made up, repeating verses.

DOR.

Now for some ages had the pride of Spain
Made the sun shine on half the world in vain.[1]

(*Then looking on the note.*)

'For Mrs. Loveit.' — What a dull, insipid thing is a billet-doux written in cold blood, after the heat of the business is over! It is a tax upon good nature 5 which I have here been laboring to pay, and have done it, but with as much regret as ever fanatic paid the Royal Aid or church duties.[2] 'Twill have the same fate, I know, that all my notes to her have had of late; 'twill not be thought kind enough. 10 'Faith, women are i'the right when they jealously examine our letters, for in them we always first discover our decay of passion. — Hey! Who waits?

Enter HANDY.

HAND. Sir —

DOR. Call a footman.   15

HAND. None of 'em are come yet.

DOR. Dogs! Will they ever lie snoring abed till noon?

HAND. 'Tis all one, sir; if they're up, you indulge 'em so they're ever poaching after whores all the 20 morning.

DOR. Take notice henceforward who's wanting in his duty; the next clap he gets, he shall rot for an example. What vermin are those chattering without?

HAND. Foggy[3] Nan, the orange-woman, and 25 Swearing Tom, the shoemaker.

DOR. Go, call in that over-grown jade with the flasket[4] of guts before her; fruit is refreshing in a morning.   *Exit* HANDY.

It is not that I love you less   30
Than when before your feet I lay —[5]

---

[1] Waller, *Of a War with Spain*, ll. 1–2.

[2] Taxes levied in support of the civil and ecclesiastical governments.

[3] Bloated.   [4] A long shallow basket or tub.

[5] Waller, *The Self-banished*, ll. 1–2.

Enter Orange-Woman [and HANDY*].*

— How now, double tripe, what news do you bring?

OR. WOM. News! Here's the best fruit has come to town t'year; gad, I was up before four o'clock this morning and bought all the choice i'the market. 35

DOR. The nasty refuse of your shop.

OR. WOM. You need not make mouths at it; I assure you, 'tis all culled ware.

DOR. The citizens buy better on a holiday in their walk to Totnam.[6]   40

OR. WOM. Good or bad, 'tis all one; I never knew you commend anything. Lord! would the ladies had heard you talk of 'em as I have done! (*Sets down the fruit.*) Here, bid your man give me an angel.[7]   45

DOR. [*to* HANDY]. Give the bawd her fruit again.

OR. WOM. Well, on my conscience, there never was the like of you! — God's my life, I had almost forgot to tell you there is a young gentlewoman lately come to town with her mother, that is so taken with 50 you.

DOR. Is she handsome?

OR. WOM. Nay,[8] gad, there are few finer women, I tell you but so, and a hugeous fortune, they say. Here, eat this peach. It comes from the stone;[9] 55 'tis better than any Newington[10] y'have tasted.

DOR. (*taking the peach*). This fine woman, I'll lay my life, is some awkward, ill-fashioned country toad who, not having above four dozen of black hairs on her head, has adorned her baldness with a large, 60 white fruz,[11] that she may look sparkishly in the fore-front of the King's box at an old play.

OR. WOM. Gad, you'd change your note quickly if you did but see her.

DOR. How came she to know me?   65

OR. WOM. She saw you yesterday at the Change;[12] she told me you came and fooled with the woman at the next shop.

---

[6] Tottenham, a northern suburb of London.

[7] A gold coin worth ten shillings.

[8] A meaningless interjection equivalent to 'why!'

[9] The meaning of this phrase is not clear: it may be either that the fruit was sun-ripened upon a tree trained against a stone wall, or that it was a freestone peach.

[10] Newington is the center of a fruit-growing district in Kent.

[11] A frizzy arrangement of artificial hair.

[12] The New Exchange in the Strand.

Dor. I remember there was a mask observed me, indeed. Fooled, did she say?   70

Or. Wom. Ay; I vow she told me twenty things you said, too, and acted with [her] head and with her body so like you —

Enter Medley.

Med. Dorimant, my life, my joy, my darling sin! how dost thou?   [*Embraces* Dorimant.]   75

Or. Wom. Lord, what a filthy trick these men have got of kissing one another!   (*She spits.*)

Med. Why do you suffer this cartload of scandal to come near you and make your neighbors think you so improvident to need a bawd?   80

Or. Wom. [*to* Dorimant]. Good, now! we shall have it you did but want [1] him to help you! Come, pay me for my fruit.

Med. Make us thankful for it,[2] huswife, bawds are as much out of fashion as gentlemen-ushers;[3]   85 none but old formal ladies use the one, and none but foppish old stagers[4] employ the other. Go! You are an insignificant brandy bottle.

Dor. Nay, there you wrong her; three quarts of Canary is her business.   90

Or. Wom. What you please, gentlemen.

Dor. To him! give him as good as he brings.

Or. Wom. Hang him, there is not such another heathen in the town again, except it be the shoemaker without.   95

Med. I shall see you hold up your hand at the bar next sessions for murder, huswife; that shoemaker can take his oath you are in fee with the doctors to sell green fruit to the gentry, that the crudities may breed diseases.   100

Or. Wom. [*to* Dorimant]. Pray, give me my money.

Dor. Not a penny! When you bring the gentlewoman hither you spoke of, you shall be paid.

Or. Wom. The gentlewoman! the gentle-   105 woman may be as honest[5] as your sisters for aught I know. Pray, pay me, Mr. Dorimant, and do not abuse me so; I have an honester way of living — you know it.

Med. Was there ever such a resty[6] bawd!   110

Dor. Some jade's tricks she has, but she makes amends when she's in good humor. — Come, tell me the lady's name and Handy shall pay you.

Or. Wom. I must not; she forbid me.

Dor. That's a sure sign she would have you.[7]   115

Med. Where does she live?

Or. Wom. They lodge at my house.

[1] Need.   [2] I.e., God make us thankful for it.
[3] Male attendants upon a lady.   [4] Old hands.
[5] Chaste.   [6] Restive.
[7] I.e., have you tell me.

Med. Nay, then she's in a hopeful way.

Or. Wom. Good Mr. Medley, say your pleasure of me, but take heed how you affront my house!   120 God's my life! — 'in a hopeful way!'

Dor. Prithee, peace! What kind of woman's the mother?

Or. Wom. A goodly, grave gentlewoman. Lord, how she talks against the wild young men o' the   125 town! As for your part, she thinks you an arrant devil; should she see you, on my conscience she would look if you had not a cloven foot.

Dor. Does she know me?

Or. Wom. Only by hearsay; a thousand   130 horrid stories have been told her of you, and she believes 'em all.

Med. By the character this should be the famous Lady Woodvill and her daughter Harriet.

Or. Wom. The devil's in him for guessing, I   135 think.

Dor. Do you know 'em?

Med. Both very well; the mother's a great admirer of the forms and civility of the last age.

Dor. An antiquated beauty may be allowed   140 to be out of humor at the freedoms of the present. This is a good account of the mother; pray, what is the daughter?

Med. Why, first, she's an heiress — vastly rich.

Dor. And handsome?   145

Med. What alteration a twelvemonth may have bred in her I know not, but a year ago she was the beautifullest creature I ever saw: a fine, easy, clean shape; light brown hair in abundance; her features regular; her complexion clear and lively; large,   150 wanton eyes; but above all, a mouth that has made me kiss it a thousand times in imagination; teeth white and even, and pretty, pouting lips, with a little moisture ever hanging on them, that look like the [Provins][8] rose fresh on the bush, ere the morn-   155 ing sun has quite drawn up the dew.

Dor. Rapture! mere[9] rapture!

Or. Wom. Nay, gad, he tells you true; she's a delicate creature.

Dor. Has she wit?   160

Med. More than is usual in her sex, and as much malice. Then, she's as wild as you would wish her, and has a demureness in her looks that makes it so surprising.

Dor. Flesh and blood cannot hear this and   165 not long to know her.

Med. I wonder what makes her mother bring her up to town; an old doating keeper cannot be more jealous of his mistress.

[8] The town of Provins, some 50 miles E.S.E. of Paris, is still noted for its trade in roses.
[9] Pure.

93] Q2 *there's*.   139] Q2 *civilities*.   146] Q2 *What an*.
155] Q1Q2 *Province: Provins* is adopted from Morgan's explanatory note.   162] Q2 *you'd*.

OR. WOM. She made me laugh yesterday; 170
there was a judge came to visit 'em, and the old
man, she told me, did so stare upon her, and when he
saluted her smacked so heartily. Who would think
it of 'em?

MED. God-a-mercy, judge! [1]   175

DOR. Do 'em right; the gentlemen of the long
robe [2] have not been wanting by their good examples
to countenance the crying sin o' the nation.

MED. Come, on with your trappings; 'tis later than
you imagine.   180

DOR. Call in the shoemaker, Handy.

OR. WOM. Good Mr. Dorimant, pay me. Gad,
I had rather give you my fruit than stay to be abused
by that foul-mouthed rogue; what you gentlemen
say, it matters not much, but such a dirty fellow 185
does one more disgrace.

DOR. [to HANDY]. Give her ten shillings — [to
ORANGE-WOMAN] and be sure you tell the young
gentlewoman I must be acquainted with her.

OR. WOM. Now do you long to be tempting 190
this pretty creature. Well, heavens mend you!

MED. Farewell, bog! [3]

Exit ORANGE-WOMAN *and* HANDY.

— Dorimant, when did you see your *pisaller*, [4] as
you call her, Mrs. Loveit?

DOR. Not these two days.   195

MED. And how stand affairs between you?

DOR. There has been great patching of late, much
ado; we make a shift to hang together.

MED. I wonder how her mighty spirit bears it.

DOR. Ill enough, on all conscience; I never 200
knew so violent a creature.

MED. She's the most passionate in her love and
the most extravagant in her jealousy of any woman
I ever heard of. What note is that?

DOR. An excuse I am going to send her for 205
the neglect I am guilty of.

MED. Prithee, read it.

DOR. No; but if you will take the pains, you may.

MED. (*reads*).

I never was a lover of business, but now I have a 210
just reason to hate it, since it has kept me these two days
from seeing you. I intend to wait upon you in the afternoon, and in the pleasure of your conversation forget all I
have suffered during this tedious absence.

This business of yours, Dorimant, has been 215
with a vizard [5] at the playhouse; I have had an eye
on you. If some malicious body should betray you,
this kind note would hardly make your peace with
her.

DOR. I desire no better.   220

[1] An ironical exclamation of applause, equivalent to 'Well
done, judge!'
[2] Lawyers.   [3] Fat person.   [4] Makeshift.
[5] Mask: by metonymy, a masked person.

MED. Why, would her knowledge of it oblige you?

DOR. Most infinitely; next to the coming to a good
understanding with a new mistress, I love a quarrel
with an old one. But the devil's in't! there has been
such a calm in my affairs of late, I have not had 225
the pleasure of making a woman so much as break
her fan, to be sullen, or forswear herself, these three
days.

MED. A very great misfortune. Let me see; I
love mischief well enough to forward this busi- 230
ness myself. I'll about it presently, and though
I know the truth of what y'ave done will set her
a-raving, I'll heighten it a little with invention, leave
her in a fit o' the mother, [6] and be here again before
y'are ready.   235

DOR. Pray, stay; you may spare yourself the
labor. The business is undertaken already by one
who will manage it with as much address, and I think
with a little more malice than you can.

MED. Who i' the devil's name can this be!   240

DOR. Why, the vizard — that very vizard you
saw me with.

MED. Does she love mischief so well as to betray
herself to spite another?

DOR. Not so neither, Medley. I will make 245
you comprehend the mystery: this mask, for a
farther confirmation of what I have been these two
days swearing to her, made me yesterday at the
playhouse make her a promise before her face utterly
to break off with Loveit, and, because she 250
tenders [7] my reputation and would not have me do
a barbarous thing, has contrived a way to give me
a handsome occasion.

MED. Very good.

DOR. She intends about an hour before me, 255
this afternoon, to make Loveit a visit, and, having
the privilege, by reason of a professed friendship
between them, to talk of her concerns —

MED. Is she a friend?

DOR. Oh, an intimate friend!   260

MED. Better and better; pray, proceed.

DOR. She means insensibly to insinuate a discourse of me and artificially raise her jealousy to such
a height that, transported with the first motions of
her passion, she shall fly upon me with all the 265
fury imaginable as soon as ever I enter; the quarrel
being thus happily begun, I am to play my part,
confess and justify all my roguery, swear her impertinence and ill-humor makes her intolerable, tax
her with the next fop that comes into my head, 270
and in a huff march away, slight her, and leave her
to be taken by whosoever thinks it worth his time to
lie down before her.

MED. This vizard is a spark and has a genius that
makes her worthy of yourself, Dorimant.   275

[6] Hysteria.   [7] Cherishes.

Enter HANDY, *Shoemaker, and Footman.*

DOR. You rogue there, who sneak like a dog that
has flung down a dish! if you do not mend your
waiting, I'll uncase you [1] and turn you loose to the
wheel of fortune. — [*Giving* HANDY *the letter.*] Handy,
seal this and let him run with it presently.   280
                                    Exit Footman.
MED. Since y'are resolved on a quarrel, why do
you send her this kind note?

DOR. To keep her at home in order to the business. — (*To the Shoemaker.*) How now, you drunken
sot?   285

SHOEM. 'Zbud, you have no reason to talk; I have
not had a bottle of sack of yours in my belly this
fortnight.

MED. The orange-woman says your neighbors
take notice what a heathen you are, and design   290
to inform the bishop and have you burned for an
atheist.

SHOEM. Damn her, dunghill, if her husband does
not remove her, she stinks so, the parish intend to
indict him for a nuisance.   295

MED. I advise you like a friend; reform your life.
You have brought the envy of the world upon you
by living above yourself. Whoring and swearing
are vices too genteel for a shoemaker.

SHOEM. 'Zbud, I think you men of quality   300
will grow as unreasonable as the women. You
would ingross [2] the sins of the nation; poor folks can
no sooner be wicked but th'are railed at by their
betters.

DOR. Sirrah, I'll have you stand i'the pillory   305
for this libel!

SHOEM. Some of you deserve it, I'm sure; there
are so many of 'em, that our journeymen nowadays,
instead of harmless ballads, sing nothing but your
damned lampoons.   310

DOR. Our lampoons, you rogue!

SHOEM. Nay, good master, why should not you
write your own commentaries as well as Cæsar?

MED. The rascal's read, I perceive.

SHOEM. You know the old proverb — ale   315
and history.[3]

DOR. Draw on my shoes, sirrah.

SHOEM. Here's a shoe —!

DOR. — Sits with more wrinkles than there are
in an angry bully's forehead!   320

SHOEM. 'Zbud, as smooth as your mistress's skin
does upon her! So; strike your foot in home.
'Zbud, if e'er a monsieur of 'em all make more
fashionable ware, I'll be content to have my ears
whipped off with my own paring knife.   325

[1] Strip you (of your livery).   [2] Monopolize.
[3] The proverb has not been identified: it may have been a
vernacular equivalent of the Latin *in vino veritas*, referring to
the frankness of an intoxicated person.

MED. And served up in a ragout instead of coxcombs to a company of French shoemakers for
a collation.

SHOEM. Hold, hold! Damn 'em, caterpillars!
let 'em feed upon cabbage. — Come master,   330
your health this morning next my heart now!

DOR. Go, get you home and govern your family
better! Do not let your wife follow you to the alehouse, beat your whore, and lead you home in
triumph.   335

SHOEM. 'Zbud, there's never a man i'the town
lives more like a gentleman with his wife than I do.
I never mind her motions,[4] she never inquires into
mine; we speak to one another civilly, hate one
another heartily, and because 'tis vulgar to lie   340
and soak [5] together, we have each of us our several [6]
settle-bed.

DOR. [*to* HANDY]. Give him half a crown.

MED. Not without he will promise to be bloody
drunk.   345

SHOEM. 'Tope' 's the word i'the eye of the world.
[HANDY *gives him money: he invites* HANDY, *in dumb-
show, to join him in a drink.*] For my master's
honor, Robin!

DOR. Do not debauch my servants, sirrah.   350

SHOEM. I only tip him the wink; he knows an alehouse from a hovel.
                                    Exit Shoemaker.
DOR. [*to* HANDY]. My clothes, quickly.

MED. Where shall we dine today?

Enter YOUNG BELLAIR.

DOR. Where you will; here comes a good   355
third man.

Y. BELL. Your servant, gentlemen.

MED. Gentle sir, how will you answer this visit
to your honorable mistress? 'Tis not her interest
you should keep company with men of sense   360
who will be talking reason.

Y. BELL. I do not fear her pardon; do you but
grant me yours for my neglect of late.

MED. Though y'ave made us miserable by the
want of your good company, to show you I am   365
free from all resentment, may the beautiful cause
of our misfortune give you all the joys happy lovers
have shared ever since the world began.

Y. BELL. You wish me in heaven, but you believe
me on my journey to hell.   370

MED. You have a good strong faith, and that may
contribute much towards your salvation. I confess I am but of an untoward constitution, apt to have
doubts and scruples — and in love they are no less
distracting than in religion. Were I so near   375

[4] Actions.
[5] Get drunk.
[6] Individual.

marriage, I should cry out by fits as I ride in my coach, 'Cuckold, cuckold!' with no less fury than the mad fanatic does 'glory!' in Bethlem.[1]

Y. BELL. Because religion makes some run mad must I live an atheist?   380

MED. Is it not great indiscretion for a man of credit, who may have money enough on his word, to go and deal with Jews, who for little sums make men enter into bonds and give judgments?

Y. BELL. Preach no more on this text. I am   385 determined, and there is no hope of my conversion.

DOR. (to HANDY, who is fiddling about him). Leave your unnecessary fiddling; a wasp that's buzzing about a man's nose at dinner is not more troublesome than thou art.   390

HAND. You love to have your clothes hang just, sir.

DOR. I love to be well dressed, sir, and think it no scandal to my understanding.

HAND. Will you use the essence or orange   395 flower water?

DOR. I will smell as I do today, no offence to the ladies' noses.

HAND. Your pleasure, sir.   [Exit HANDY.]

DOR. That a man's excellency should lie in   400 neatly tying of a ribband or a cravat! How careful's nature in furnishing the world with necessary coxcombs!

Y. BELL. That's a mighty pretty suit of yours, Dorimant.   405

DOR. I am glad't has your approbation.

Y. BELL. No man in town has a better fancy in his clothes than you have.

DOR. You will make me have an opinion of my genius.   410

MED. There is a great critic, I hear, in these matters lately arrived piping hot from Paris.

Y. BELL. Sir Fopling Flutter, you mean.

MED. The same.

Y. BELL. He thinks himself the pattern of   415 modern gallantry.

DOR. He is indeed the pattern of modern foppery.

MED. He was yesterday at the play, with a pair of gloves up to his elbows, and a periwig more exactly curled than a lady's head newly dressed for a   420 ball.

Y. BELL. What a pretty lisp he has!

DOR. Ho! that he affects in imitation of the people of quality of France.

MED. His head stands, for the most part,   425 on one side, and his looks are more languishing than a lady's when she lolls at stretch in her coach or leans her head carelessly against the side of a box i'the playhouse.

DOR. He is a person indeed of great ac-   430 quired follies.

MED. He is like many others, beholding to his education for making him so eminent a coxcomb; many a fool had been lost to the world had their indulgent parents wisely bestowed neither learn-   435 ing nor good breeding on 'em.

Y. BELL. He has been, as the sparkish word is, 'brisk upon the ladies' already. He was yesterday at my Aunt Townley's and gave Mrs. Loveit a catalogue of his good qualities under the charac-   440 ter of a complete gentleman, who, according to Sir Fopling, ought to dress well, dance well, fence well, have a genius for love letters, an agreeable voice for a chamber, be very amorous, something discreet, but not overconstant.   445

MED. Pretty ingredients to make an accomplished person!

DOR. I am glad he pitched upon Loveit.

Y. BELL. How so?

DOR. I wanted a fop to lay to her charge,   450 and this is as pat as may be.

Y. BELL. I am confident she loves no man but you.

DOR. The good fortune were enough to make me vain, but that I am in my nature modest.   455

Y. BELL. Hark you, Dorimant. — With your leave, Mr. Medley; 'tis only a secret concerning a fair lady.

MED. Your good breeding, sir, gives you too much trouble; you might have whispered with-   460 out all this ceremony.

Y. BELL. (to DORIMANT). How stand your affairs with Bellinda of late?

DOR. She's a little jilting baggage.

Y. BELL. Nay, I believe her false enough,   465 but she's ne'er the worse for your purpose; she was with you yesterday in a disguise at the play.

DOR. There we fell out and resolved never to speak to one another more.

Y. BELL. The occasion?   470

DOR. Want of courage to meet me at the place appointed. These young women apprehend loving as much as the young men do fighting, at first; but once entered, like them too, they all turn bullies straight.   475

Enter HANDY.

HAND. (to YOUNG BELLAIR). Sir, your man without desires to speak with you.

Y. BELL. Gentlemen, I'll return immediately.

Exit YOUNG BELLAIR.

MED. A very pretty fellow this.

DOR. He's handsome, well bred, and by   480 much the most tolerable of all the young men that do not abound in wit.

MED. Ever well dressed, always complaisant, and

---

[1] Bethlehem Hospital, more commonly known as Bedlam, an asylum for the insane, in Moorfields. The fanatic referred to may have been Oliver Cromwell's mad porter.

seldom impertinent. You and he are grown very intimate, I see.   485

DOR. It is our mutual interest to be so: it makes
the women think the better of his understanding,
and judge more favorably of my reputation; it makes
him pass upon some for a man of very good sense,
and I upon others for a very civil person.   490

MED. What was that whisper?

DOR. A thing which he would fain have known,
but I did not think it fit to tell him; it might have
frighted him from his honorable intentions of marrying.   495

MED. Emilia — give her her due — has the best
reputation of any young woman about the town
who has beauty enough to provoke detraction; her
carriage is unaffected, her discourse modest— not
at all censorious nor pretending, like the   500
counterfeits of the age.

DOR. She's a discreet maid, and I believe nothing
can corrupt her but a husband.

MED. A husband?

DOR. Yes, a husband. I have known many   505
women make a difficulty of losing a maidenhead, who
have afterwards made none of making a cuckold.

MED. This prudent consideration, I am apt to
think, has made you confirm poor Bellair in the
desperate resolution he has taken.   510

DOR. Indeed, the little hope I found there was
of her, in the state she was in, has made me by my
advice contribute something towards the changing
of her condition.

Enter YOUNG BELLAIR.

— Dear Bellair, by heavens, I thought we had   515
lost thee! men in love are never to be reckoned on
when we would form a company.

Y. BELL. Dorimant, I am undone. My man has
brought the most surprising news i'the world.

DOR. Some strange misfortune is befallen   520
your love.

Y. BELL. My father came to town last night and
lodges i'the very house where Emilia lies.

MED. Does he know it is with her you are in
love?   525

Y. BELL. He knows I love, but knows not whom,
without some officious sot has betrayed me.

DOR. Your Aunt Townley is your confidant and
favors the business.

Y. BELL. I do not apprehend any ill office   530
from her. I have received a letter, in which I am
commanded by my father to meet him at my aunt's
this afternoon. He tells me farther he has made a
match for me and bids me resolve to be obedient to
his will or expect to be disinherited.   535

MED. Now's your time, Bellair; never had lover
such an opportunity of giving a generous proof of
his passion.

Y. BELL. As how, I pray?

MED. Why, hang an estate, marry Emilia   540
out of hand, and provoke your father to do what he
threatens; 'tis but despising a coach, humbling
yourself to a pair of goloshes,[1] being out of countenance when you meet your friends, pointed at and
pitied wherever you go by all the amorous fops   545
that know you, and your fame will be immortal.

Y. BELL. I could find in my heart to resolve not
to marry at all.

DOR. Fie, fie! That would spoil a good jest and
disappoint the well-natured town of an occa-   550
sion of laughing at you.

Y. BELL. The storm I have so long expected
hangs o'er my head and begins to pour down upon
me; I am on the rack and can have no rest till I'm
satisfied in what I fear. Where do you dine?   555

DOR. At Long's or Locket's.[2]

MED. At Long's let it be.

Y. BELL. I'll run and see Emilia and inform myself how matters stand. If my misfortunes are not so
great as to make me unfit for company, I'll be   560
with you.   *Exit* YOUNG BELLAIR.

Enter a Footman with a letter.

FOOT. (*to* DORIMANT). Here's a letter, sir.

DOR. The superscription's right: 'For Mr. Dorimant.'

MED. Let's see; the very scrawl and spell-   565
ing of a true-bred whore.

DOR. I know the hand; the style is admirable,
I assure you.

MED. Prithee, read it.

DOR. (*reads*).   570

I told a you you dud not love me, if you dud, you
wou'd have seen me again ere now. I have no money
and am very mallicolly; pray send me a guynie to see
the operies.

                 Your servant to command,   575
                                    Molly.

MED. Pray, let the whore have a favorable answer,
that she may spark it in a box and do honor to her
profession.

DOR. She shall, and perk up i'the face of   580
quality. [*To* HANDY.] Is the coach at the door?

HAND. You did not bid me send for it.

DOR. Eternal blockhead! (HANDY *offers to go out.*)
Hey, sot —

HAND. Did you call me, sir?   585

DOR. I hope you have no just exception to the
name, sir?

HAND. I have sense, sir.

DOR. Not so much as a fly in winter. — How did
you come, Medley?   590

[1] Pattens or clogs.
[2] Fashionable taverns, one in the Haymarket, the other in
Charing Cross.

565] Q1 (U. of Chicago copy) om. semi-colon.

MED. In a chair.

FOOT. [to DORIMANT]. You may have a hackney coach if you please, sir.

DOR. I may ride the elephant if I please, sir. Call another chair and let my coach follow 595 to Long's.

Be calm, ye great parents, etc.

Exeunt, singing.

ACT II

[SCENE I]

[LADY TOWNLEY'S *house.*]

Enter my LADY TOWNLEY *and* EMILIA.

L. TOWN. I was afraid, Emilia, all had been discovered.

EMIL. I tremble with the apprehension still.

L. TOWN. That my brother should take lodgings i'the very house where you lie! 5

EMIL. 'Twas lucky we had timely notice to warn the people to be secret. He seems to be a mighty good-humored old man.

L. TOWN. He ever had a notable smirking way with him. 10

EMIL. He calls me rogue, tells me he can't abide me, and does so bepat me.

L. TOWN. On my word, you are much in his favor then.

EMIL. He has been very inquisitive, I am 15 told, about my family, my reputation, and my fortune.

L. TOWN. I am confident he does not i'the least suspect you are the woman his son's in love with.

EMIL. What should make him, then, inform 20 himself so particularly of me?

L. TOWN. He was always of a very loving temper himself; it may be he has a doting fit upon him — who knows?

EMIL. It cannot be. 25

Enter YOUNG BELLAIR.

L. TOWN. Here comes my nephew. — Where did you leave your father?

Y. BELL. Writing a note within. Emilia, this early visit looks as if some kind jealousy would not let you rest at home. 30

EMIL. The knowledge I have of my rival gives me a little cause to fear your constancy.

Y. BELL. My constancy! I vow —

EMIL. Do not vow. Our love is frail as is our life and full as little in our power; and are you sure 35 you shall outlive this day?

Y. BELL. I am not; but when we are in perfect

health, 'twere an idle thing to fright ourselves with the thoughts of sudden death.

L. TOWN. Pray, what has passed between 40 you and your father i'the garden?

Y. BELL. He's firm in his resolution, tells me I must marry Mrs. Harriet, or swears he'll marry himself and disinherit me. When I saw I could not prevail with him to be more indulgent, I dis- 45 sembled an obedience to his will, which has composed his passion and will give us time — and, I hope, opportunity — to deceive him.

Enter OLD BELLAIR *with a note in his hand.*

L. TOWN. Peace, here he comes!

O. BELL. Harry, take this and let your man 50 carry it for me to Mr. Fourbe's[1] chamber, my lawyer i'the Temple.[2] [*Exit* YOUNG BELLAIR.] (*To* EMILIA.) Neighbor, a dod! I am glad to see thee here. — Make much of her, sister; she's one of the best of your acquaintance. I like her counte- 55 nance and her behavior well; she has a modesty that is not common i'this age, a dod, she has!

L. TOWN. I know her value, brother, and esteem her accordingly.

O. BELL. Advise her to wear a little more 60 mirth in her face; a dod, she's too serious.

L. TOWN. The fault is very excusable in a young woman.

O. BELL. Nay, a dod, I like her ne'er the worse. A melancholy beauty has her charms. I love 65 a pretty sadness in a face, which varies now and then, like changeable colors, into a smile.

L. TOWN. Methinks you speak very feelingly, brother.

O. BELL. I am but five and fifty, sister, you 70 know — an age not altogether unsensible. — (*To* EMILIA.) Cheer up, sweetheart! I have a secret to tell thee may chance to make thee merry. We three will make collation together anon; i'the meantime, mum, I can't abide you! go, I can't abide 75 you!

Enter YOUNG BELLAIR.

— Harry, come! you must along with me to my Lady Woodvill's. — I am going to slip the boy at[3] a mistress.

Y. BELL. At a wife, sir, you would say. 80

O. BELL. You need not look so glum, sir; a wife is no curse when she brings the blessing of a good estate with her; but an idle town flirt, with a painted face, a rotten reputation, and a crazy fortune, a dod!

---

[1] 'Fourbe' is a 'label' name, meaning a cheat.
[2] The center of the life of the legal profession in London, lying between Fleet Street and the Thames.
[3] Release the boy in pursuit of (a hunting term).

is the devil and all, and such a one I hear you   85
are in league with.

Y. BELL. I cannot help detraction, sir.

O. BELL. Out! 'A pize [1] o' their breeches, there
are keeping fools [2] enough for such flaunting bag-
gages, and they are e'en too good for 'em. —   90
(*To* EMILIA.) Remember 'night. Go, y'are a rogue,
y'are a rogue! Fare you well, fare you well! — [*To*
YOUNG BELLAIR.] Come, come, come along, sir!

Exeunt OLD *and* YOUNG BELLAIR.

L. TOWN. On my word, the old man comes on
apace; I'll lay my life he's smitten.   95

EMIL. This is nothing but the pleasantness of his
humor.

L. TOWN. I know him better than you. Let it
work; it may prove lucky.

Enter a Page.

PAGE. Madam, Mr. Medley has sent to   100
know whether a visit will not be troublesome this
afternoon.

L. TOWN. Send him word his visits never are so.
[*Exit Page.*]

EMIL. He's a very pleasant man.

L. TOWN. He's a very necessary man among   105
us women; he's not scandalous i'the least, perpetually
contriving to bring good company together, and
always ready to stop up a gap at ombre; then, he
knows all the little news o'the town.

EMIL. I love to hear him talk o'the intrigues;   110
let 'em be never so dull in themselves, he'll make 'em
pleasant i'the relation.

L. TOWN. But he improves things so much one
can take no measure of the truth from him. Mr.
Dorimant swears a flea or a maggot is not made   115
more monstrous by a magnifying glass than a story
is by his telling it.

Enter MEDLEY.

EMIL. Hold, here he comes.

L. TOWN. Mr. Medley.

MED. Your servant, madam.   120

L. TOWN. You have made yourself a stranger of
late.

EMIL. I believe you took a surfeit of ombre last
time you were here.

MED. Indeed, I had my belly full of that   125
termagant, Lady Dealer. There never was so
unsatiable a carder; [3] an old gleeker [4] never loved
to sit to't like her. I have played with her now at
least a dozen times till she 'as worn out all her fine

complexion and her tour [5] would keep in curl   130
no longer.

L. TOWN. Blame her not, poor woman; she loves
nothing so well as a black ace. [6]

MED. The pleasure I have seen her in when she
has had hope in drawing for a matadore!   135

EMIL. 'Tis as pretty sport to her as persuading
masks off is to you, to make discoveries.

L. TOWN. Pray, where's your friend Mr. Dorimant?

MED. Soliciting his affairs; he's a man of   140
great employment — has more mistresses now depending than the most eminent lawyer in England has
causes. [7]

EMIL. Here has been Mrs. Loveit so uneasy and
out of humor these two days.   145

L. TOWN. How strangely love and jealousy rage
in that poor woman!

MED. She could not have picked out a devil
upon earth so proper to torment her; [h'as] made her
break a dozen or two of fans already, tear half a   150
score points [8] in pieces, and destroy hoods and knots [9]
without number.

L. TOWN. We heard of a pleasant serenade he
gave her t'other night.

MED. A Danish serenade with kettle-drums   155
and trumpets.

EMIL. Oh, barbarous!

MED. What! You are of the number of the
ladies whose ears are grown so delicate since our
operas you can be charmed with nothing but   160
flûtes douces [10] and French hautboys? [11]

EMIL. Leave your raillery, and tell us, is there any
new wit come forth — songs or novels?

MED. A very pretty piece of gallantry, by an
eminent author, called *The Diversions of Brux-*   165
elles, [12] very necessary to be read by all old ladies who
are desirous to improve themselves at questions and
commands, blindman's buff, and the like fashionable
recreations.

EMIL. Oh, ridiculous!   170

MED. Then there is *The Art of Affectation*, written
by a late beauty of quality, teaching you how to
draw up your breasts, stretch up your neck, to thrust
out your breech, to play with your head, to toss up
your nose, to bite your lips, to turn up your   175
eyes, to speak in a silly, soft tone of a voice, and use
all the foolish French words that will infallibly make
your person and conversation charming; with a

---

[1] A meaningless imprecation of uncertain origin.
[2] I.e., keepers of mistresses.
[3] Card-player.
[4] Player of gleek (an old card game).

[5] A crescent-shaped front of false hair.
[6] In the game of ombre the black aces were two of the three
highest trumps, which were known as 'matadores.'
[7] Cases.   [8] Lace kerchiefs.   [9] Bows of ribbon.
[10] High-pitched flutes.   [11] Oboes.
[12] This book, and that named by Medley in his next speech,
appear to be the creations of his imagination.

---

short apology at the latter end in the behalf of young ladies who notoriously wash [1] and paint though 180 they have naturally good complexions.

EMIL. What a deal of stuff you tell us!

MED. Such as the town affords, madam. The Russians, hearing the great respect we have for foreign dancing, have lately sent over some of 185 their best balladines,[2] who are now practising a famous ballet which will be suddenly [3] danced at the Bear Garden.[4]

L. TOWN Pray, forbear your idle stories, and give us an account of the state of love as it now 190 stands.

MED. Truly, there has been some revolutions in those affairs — great chopping and changing among the old, and some new lovers whom malice, indiscretion, and misfortune have luckily brought into 195 play.

L. TOWN. What think you of walking into the next room and sitting down before you engage in this business?

MED. I wait upon you, and I hope (though 200 women are commonly unreasonable) by the plenty of scandal I shall discover, to give you very good content, ladies.   *Exeunt.*

SCENE II

[MRS. LOVEIT's *lodgings*.]

Enter MRS. LOVEIT *and* PERT. MRS. LOVEIT *putting up a letter, then pulling out her pocket-glass and looking in it.*

LOV. Pert.

PERT. Madam?

LOV. I hate myself, I look so ill today.

PERT. Hate the wicked cause on't, that base man Mr. Dorimant, who makes you torment and vex 5 yourself continually.

LOV. He is to blame, indeed.

PERT. To blame to be two days without sending, writing, or coming near you, contrary to his oath and covenant! 'Twas to much purpose to make 10 him swear! I'll lay my life there's not an article but he has broken — talked to the vizards i'the pit, waited upon the ladies from the boxes to their coaches, gone behind the scenes, and fawned upon those little insignificant creatures, the players. 15 'Tis impossible for a man of his inconstant temper to forbear, I'm sure.

LOV. I know he is a devil, but he has something of

the angel yet undefaced in him, which makes him so charming and agreeable that I must love him, 20 be he never so wicked.

PERT. I little thought, madam, to see your spirit tamed to this degree, who banished poor Mr. Lackwit but for taking up another lady's fan in your presence. 25

LOV. My knowing of such odious fools contributes to the making of me love Dorimant the better.

PERT. Your knowing of Mr. Dorimant, in my mind, should rather make you hate all man- 30 kind.

LOV. So it does, besides himself.

PERT. Pray, what excuse does he make in his letter?

LOV. He has had business. 35

PERT. Business in general terms would not have been a current excuse for another. A modish man is always very busy when he is in pursuit of a new mistress.

LOV. Some fop has bribed you to rail at him. 40 He had business; I will believe it, and will forgive him.

PERT. You may forgive him anything, but I shall never forgive him his turning me into ridicule, as I hear he does. 45

LOV. I perceive you are of the number of those fools his wit [has] made his enemies.

PERT. I am of the number of those he's pleased to rally, madam, and if we may believe Mr. Wagfan and Mr. Caperwell, he sometimes makes merry 50 with yourself too, among his laughing companions.

LOV. Blockheads are as malicious to witty men as ugly women are to the handsome; 'tis their interest, and they make it their business to defame 'em.

PERT. I wish Mr. Dorimant would not make 55 it his business to defame you.

LOV. Should he, I had rather be made infamous by him than owe my reputation to the dull discretion of those fops you talk of.

Enter BELLINDA.

— Bellinda!   (*Running to her.*) 60

BELL. My dear!

LOV. You have been unkind of late.

BELL. Do not say unkind — say unhappy.

LOV. I could chide you. Where have you been these two days? 65

BELL. Pity me rather, my dear; where I have been so tired with two or three country gentlewomen, whose conversation has been more unsufferable than a country fiddle.

LOV. Are they relations? 70

BELL. No; Welsh acquaintance I made when I

---

[1] Use cosmetic washes.   [2] Ballet dancers.
[3] Shortly.
[4] There were several bear-gardens, used not only for bear-baiting, but for other entertainments. It is not clear which one is referred to here.

18] Q2 *he's.*   38] Q2 *he's.*   47] Q1Q2 *had.*

was last year at St. Winifred's.[1] They have asked
me a thousand questions of the modes and intrigues
of the town, and I have told 'em almost as many
things for news that hardly were so when their   75
gowns were in fashion.

Lov. Provoking creatures! How could you endure 'em?

Bell. (aside). Now to carry on my plot. Nothing
but love could make me capable of so much   80
falsehood. 'Tis time to begin, lest Dorimant should
come before her jealousy has stung her. — (Laughs,
and then speaks on.) I was yesterday at a play with
'em, where I was fain to show 'em the living as the
man at Westminster does the dead:[2] 'That is   85
Mrs. Such-a-one, admired for her beauty; that is Mr.
Such-a-one, cried up for a wit; that is sparkish Mr.
Such-a-one, who keeps reverend Mrs. Such-a-one;
and there sits fine Mrs. Such-a-one who was lately
cast off by my Lord Such-a-one.'   90

Lov. Did you see Dorimant there?

Bell. I did, and imagine you were there with him
and have no mind to own it.

Lov. What should make you think so?

Bell. A lady masked in a pretty déshabillé,   95
whom Dorimant entertained with more respect than
the gallants do a common vizard.

Lov. (aside). Dorimant at the play entertaining
a mask! Oh, heavens!

Bell. (aside). Good!   100

Lov. Did he stay all the while?

Bell. Till the play was done, and then led her out,
which confirms me it was you.

Lov. Traitor!

Pert. Now you may believe he had busi-   105
ness, and you may forgive him too.

Lov. Ingrateful, perjured man!

Bell. You seem so much concerned, my dear, I
fear I have told you unawares what I had better have
concealed for your quiet.   110

Lov. What manner of shape had she?

Bell. Tall and slender. Her motions were very
genteel; certainly she must be some person of condition.

Lov. Shame and confusion be ever in her   115
face when she shows it!

Bell. I should blame your discretion for loving
that wild man, my dear, but they say he has a way so
bewitching that few can defend their hearts who
know him.   120

Lov. I will tear him from mine or die i'the attempt.

Bell. Be more moderate.

Lov. Would I had daggers, darts, or poisoned
arrows in my breast, so I could but remove   125
the thoughts of him from thence!

Bell. Fie, fie! your transports are too violent, my
dear; this may be but an accidental gallantry, and
'tis likely ended at her coach.

Pert. Should it proceed farther, let your com-   130
fort be, the conduct Mr. Dorimant affects will quickly make you know your rival, ten to one let you see
her ruined, her reputation exposed to the town — a
happiness none will envy her but yourself, madam.

Lov. Whoe'er she be, all the harm I wish   135
her is, may she love him as well as I do and may he
give her as much cause to hate him.

Pert. Never doubt the latter end of your curse,
madam.

Lov. May all the passions that are raised by   140
neglected love — jealousy, indignation, spite, and
thirst of revenge — eternally rage in her soul, as
they do now in mine.

(Walks up and down with a distracted air.)

Enter a Page.

Page. Madam, Master Dorimant —

Lov. I will not see him.   145

Page. I told him you were within, madam.

Lov. Say you lied — say I'm busy — shut the
door — say anything!

Page. He's here, madam.

Enter Dorimant.

Dor. They taste of death who do at heaven
          arrive;   150
But we this paradise approach alive.[3]

(To Mistress Loveit.) What, dancing The Galloping Nag[4] without a fiddle? (Offers to catch her by the
hand; she flings away and walks on. [He], pursuing
her.) I fear this restlessness of the body, madam,   155
proceeds from an unquietness of the mind. What unlucky accident puts you out of humor? A point ill
washed, knots spoiled i'the making up, hair shaded
awry, or some other little mistake in setting you in
order?   160

Pert. A trifle, in my opinion, sir, more inconsiderable than any you mention.

Dor. O Mrs. Pert! I never knew you sullen
enough to be silent; come, let me know the business.

Pert. The business, sir, is the business that   165
has taken you up these two days. How have I seen
you laugh at men of business, and now to become
a man of business yourself!

Dor. We are not masters of our affections; our
inclinations daily alter: now we love pleasure,   170
and anon we shall dote on business. Human frailty
will have it so, and who can help it?

---

[1] St. Winifred's Well, a famed miraculous spring in Flint-
shire, Wales, near the modern Holywell.
[2] For the flippant attitude of the guides in the Abbey see *A
Description of the Tombs in Westminster Abbey*, in the third
volume of Tonson's *Miscellany*.

[3] Waller, *Of her Chamber*, ll. 1–2.
[4] A country dance, the music of which may be found in John
Playford's *The Dancing Master*, 9th ed. (1695).

Lov. Faithless, inhuman, barbarous man —

Dor. [aside]. Good! Now the alarm strikes.

Lov. — Without sense of love, of honor, or 175 of gratitude, tell me, for I will know, what devil masked she was you were with at the play yesterday?

Dor. Faith, I resolved as much as you, but the devil was obstinate and would not tell me.

Lov. False in this as in your vows to me! — 180 you do know.

Dor. The truth is, I did all I could to know.

Lov. And dare you own it to my face? Hell and furies!   (Tears her fan in pieces.)

Dor. Spare your fan, madam; you are grow- 185 ing hot and will want it to cool you.

Lov. Horror and distraction seize you! Sorrow and remorse gnaw your soul, and punish all your perjuries to me!   (Weeps.)

Dor. (turning to Bellinda).   190

> So thunder breaks the cloud in twain
> And makes a passage for the rain.

(To Bellinda.) Bellinda, you are the devil that have raised this storm; you were at the play yesterday and have been making discoveries to your dear. 195

Bell. Y'are the most mistaken man i'the world.

Dor. It must be so, and here I vow revenge — resolve to pursue and persecute you more impertinently than ever any loving fop did his mistress, hunt you i'the Park,[1] trace you i'the Mail,[2] dog you 200 in every visit you make, haunt you at the plays and i'the drawing-room, hang my nose in your neck and talk to you whether you will or no, and ever look upon you with such dying eyes till your friends grow jealous of me, send you out of town, and 205 the world suspect your reputation. — (In a lower voice.) At my Lady Townley's when we go from hence.
(He looks kindly on Bellinda.)

Bell. I'll meet you there.

Dor. Enough.

Lov. (pushing Dorimant away). Stand off! 210 You sha' not stare upon her so.

Dor. Good; there's one made jealous already.

Lov. Is this the constancy you vowed?

Dor. Constancy at my years! 'Tis not a virtue in season; you might as well expect the fruit 215 the autumn ripens i'the spring.

Lov. Monstrous principle!

Dor. Youth has a long journey to go, madam; should I have set up my rest [3] at the first inn I lodged

at, I should never have arrived at the happi- 220 ness I now enjoy.

Lov. Dissembler, damned dissembler!

Dor. I am so, I confess: good nature and good manners corrupt me. I am honest in my inclinations, and would not, wer't not to avoid of- 225 fence, make a lady a little in years believe I think her young, willfully mistake art for nature, and seem as fond of a thing I am weary of as when I doted on't in earnest.

Lov. False man!   230

Dor. True woman!

Lov. Now you begin to show yourself.

Dor. Love gilds us over and makes us show fine things to one another for a time, but soon the gold wears off and then again the native brass ap- 235 pears.

Lov. Think on your oaths, your vows, and protestations, perjured man!

Dor. I made 'em when I was in love.

Lov. And therefore ought they not to bind? 240 Oh, impious!

Dor. What we swear at such a time may be a certain proof of a present passion, but to say truth, in love there is no security to be given for the future.

Lov. Horrid and ingrateful, begone, and 245 never see me more!

Dor. I am not one of those troublesome coxcombs who, because they were once well received, take the privilege to plague a woman with their love ever after. I shall obey you, madam, though 250 I do myself some violence.
(He offers to go and Mrs. Loveit pulls him back.)

Lov. Come back! You sha' not go! Could you have the ill-nature to offer it?

Dor. When love grows diseased, the best thing we can do is to put it to a violent death. I can- 255 not endure the torture of a ling'ring and consumptive passion.

Lov. Can you think mine sickly?

Dor. Oh, 'tis desperately ill. What worse symptoms are there than your being always uneasy 260 when I visit you, your picking quarrels with me on slight occasions, and in my absence kindly list'ning to the impertinences of every fashionable fool that talks to you?

Lov. What fashionable fool can you lay to 265 my charge?

Dor. Why, the very cock-fool of all those fools — Sir Fopling Flutter.

Lov. I never saw him in my life but once.

Dor. The worse woman you, at first sight 270 to put on all your charms, to entertain him with that softness in your voice, and all that wanton kindness in your eyes you so notoriously affect when you design a conquest.

---

[1] Probably referring to Hyde Park, which was more fashionable than St. James's Park at this time: see III. iii. 54 ff.

[2] The Mall (to use the more common spelling) was a long tract in St. James's Park originally laid out for playing the game of paille-maille (pall-mall): at this time, and for many years thereafter, a place of fashionable resort. Not to be confused with Pall Mall, some four hundred yards to the north, where the game was played earlier in the century.

[3] Taken up my permanent abode.

191] Q2 clouds.

Lov. So damned a lie did never malice yet in- 275
vent. Who told you this?

Dor. No matter. That ever I should love a woman that can dote on a senseless caper, a tawdry
French ribband, and a formal cravat!

Lov. You make me mad. 280

Dor. A guilty conscience may do much. Go on
— be the game-mistress o' the town, and enter [1] all
our young fops as fast as they come from travel.

Lov. Base and scurrilous!

Dor. A fine mortifying reputation 'twill be 285
for a woman of your pride, wit, and quality!

Lov. This jealousy's a mere pretence, a cursed
trick of your own devising. I know you.

Dor. Believe it and all the ill of me you can: I
would not have a woman have the least good 290
thought of me, that can think well of Fopling.
Farewell! Fall to, and much good may do you with
your coxcomb.

Lov. Stay, oh stay! and I will tell you all.

Dor. I have been told too much already. 295
Exit DORIMANT.

Lov. Call him again!

Pert. E'en let him go — a fair riddance.

Lov. Run, I say! call him again! I will have him
called!

Pert. The devil should carry him away first 300
were it my concern. *Exit* PERT.

Bell. H'as frighted me from the very thoughts
of loving men. For heaven's sake, my dear, do
not discover [2] what I told you! I dread his tongue
as much as you ought to have done his 305
friendship.

Enter PERT.

Pert. He's gone, madam.

Lov. Lightning blast him!

Pert. When I told him you desired him to come
back, he smiled, made a mouth at me, flung 310
into his coach, and said —

Lov. What did he say?

Pert. 'Drive away!' and then repeated verses.

Lov. Would I had made a contract to be a witch
when first I entertained this greater devil, mon- 315
ster, barbarian! I could tear myself in pieces. Revenge — nothing but revenge can ease me. Plague,
war, famine, fire — all that can bring universal ruin
and misery on mankind — with joy I'd perish to
have you in my power but this moment. 320
Exit MRS. LOVEIT.

Pert. Follow, madam; leave her not in this outrageous passion! (PERT *gathers up the things*.)

Bell. [*aside*]. H'as given me the proof which I desired of his love,

———
[1] Initiate.   [2] Disclose.

But 'tis a proof of his ill-nature too. 325
I wish I had not seen him use her so.
I sigh to think that Dorimant may be
One day as faithless and unkind to me.
Exeunt.

ACT III

[SCENE I]

[LADY WOODVILL'S *lodgings*.]

Enter HARRIET *and* BUSY, *her woman.*

Busy. Dear madam, let me set that curl in order.

Har. Let me alone; I will shake 'em all out of
order.

Busy. Will you never leave this wildness?

Har. Torment me not. 5

Busy. Look! There's a knot falling off.

Har. Let it drop.

Busy. But one pin, dear madam.

Har. How do I daily suffer under thy officious
fingers! 10

Busy. Ah, the difference that is between you and
my Lady Dapper! how uneasy she is if the least
thing be amiss about her!

Har. She is indeed most exact; nothing is ever
wanting to make her ugliness remarkable. 15

Busy. Jeering people say so.

Har. Her powdering, painting, and her patching
never fail in public to draw the tongues and eyes of
all the men upon her.

Busy. She is, indeed, a little too pretending. 20

Har. That women should set up for beauty as
much in spite of nature as some men have done for
wit!

Busy. I hope without offence one may endeavor
to make one's self agreeable. 25

Har. Not when 'tis impossible. Women then
ought to be no more fond of dressing than fools
should be of talking; hoods and modesty, masks and
silence, things that shadow and conceal — they
should think of nothing else. 30

Busy. Jesu! Madam, what will your mother
think is become of you? For heaven's sake go in
again!

Har. I won't.

Busy. This is the extravagant'st thing that 35
ever you did in your life, to leave her and a gentleman who is to be your husband.

Har. My husband! Hast thou so little wit to
think I spoke what I meant when I overjoyed her in
the country with a low curtsey and 'What you 40
please, madam; I shall ever be obedient'?

Busy. Nay, I know not, you have so many
fetches.[3]

———
[3] Tricks.

HAR. And this was one, to get her up to London. Nothing else, I assure thee. 45

BUSY. Well, the man, in my mind, is a fine man.

HAR. The man indeed wears his clothes fashionably and has a pretty, negligent way with him, very courtly and much affected; he bows, and talks, and smiles so agreeably, as he thinks. 50

BUSY. I never saw anything so genteel.

HAR. Varnished over with good breeding, many a blockhead makes a tolerable show.

BUSY. I wonder you do not like him.

HAR. I think I might be brought to endure 55 him, and that is all a reasonable woman should expect in a husband; but there is duty i'the case, and like the haughty Merab,[1] I

Find much aversion in my stubborn mind, Which 60

Is bred by being promised and designed.[2]

BUSY. I wish you do not design your own ruin. I partly guess your inclinations, madam — that Mr. Dorimant —

HAR. Leave your prating and sing some fool- 65 ish song or other.

BUSY. I will — the song you love so well ever since you saw Mr. Dorimant. [Sings.]

SONG

When first Amintas charmed my heart,
    My heedless sheep began to stray;
The wolves soon stole the greatest part, 70
    And all will now be made a prey.

Ah, let not love your thoughts possess,
    'Tis fatal to a shepherdess;
The dang'rous passion you must shun, 75
    Or else like me be quite undone.

HAR. Shall I be paid down by a covetous parent for a purchase? I need no land; no, I'll lay myself out all in love. It is decreed —

Enter YOUNG BELLAIR.

Y. BELL. What generous resolution are you 80 making, madam?

HAR. Only to be disobedient, sir.

Y. BELL. Let me join hands with you in that —

HAR. With all my heart; I never thought I should have given you mine so willingly. Here I, Har- 85 riet —

Y. BELL. And I, Harry —

HAR. Do solemnly protest —

Y. BELL. And vow —

HAR. That I with you — 90

Y. BELL. And I with you —

BOTH. Will never marry.

---

[1] The story of Merab is found in I Sam. 14.49 and 18.17–19.
[2] Altered from Cowley's *Davideis*, III, 705–06.

HAR. A match!

Y. BELL. And no match! How do you like this indifference now? 95

HAR. You expect I should take it ill, I see.

Y. BELL. 'Tis not unnatural for you women to be a little angry: you miss a conquest, though you would slight the poor man were he in your power.

HAR. There are some, it may be, have an eye 100 like Bart'lomew [3] — big enough for the whole fair; but I am not of the number, and you may keep your gingerbread. 'Twill be more acceptable to the lady whose dear image it wears, sir.

Y. BELL. I must confess, madam, you came 105 a day after the fair.

HAR. You own then you are in love?

Y. BELL. I do.

HAR. The confidence is generous, and in return I could almost find in my heart to let you know 110 my inclinations.

Y. BELL. Are you in love?

HAR. Yes, with this dear town, to that degree I can scarce endure the country in landscapes and in hangings. 115

Y. BELL. What a dreadful thing 'twould be to be hurried back to Hampshire!

HAR. Ah, name it not!

Y. BELL. As for us, I find we shall agree well enough. Would we could do something to de- 120 ceive the grave people!

HAR. Could we delay their quick proceeding, 'twere well. A reprieve is a good step towards the getting of a pardon.

Y. BELL. If we give over the game, we are 125 undone. What think you of playing it on booty?[4]

HAR. What do you mean?

Y. BELL. Pretend to be in love with one another; 'twill make some dilatory excuses we may feign pass the better. 130

HAR. Let us do't, if it be but for the dear pleasure of dissembling.

Y. BELL. Can you play your part?

HAR. I know not what it is to love, but I have made pretty remarks [5] by being now and then 135 where lovers meet. Where did you leave their gravities?

Y. BELL. I'th' next room. Your mother was censuring our modern gallant.

Enter OLD BELLAIR *and* LADY WOODVILL.

HAR. Peace! here they come. I will lean 140 against this wall and look bashfully down upon my

---

[3] Bartholomew Fair, held annually in Smithfield, in the eastern quarter of London, for several days about St. Bartholomew's Day (Aug. 24), was extensive and popular.
[4] Gamesters who joined together secretly to swindle a third player and divide the gains were said to be playing on booty.
[5] Observations.

---

fan, while you, like an amorous spark, modishly entertain me.

L. WOOD. [*to* OLD BELLAIR]. Never go about to excuse 'em; come, come, it was not so when I   145 was a young woman.

O. BELL. A dod, they're something disrespectful —

L. WOOD. Quality was then considered, and not rallied by every fleering [1] fellow.   150

O. BELL. Youth will have its jest — a dod, it will.

L. WOOD. 'Tis good breeding now to be civil to none but players and Exchange women; [2] they are treated by 'em as much above their condition as others are below theirs.   155

O. BELL. Out! a pize on 'em! talk no more. The rogues ha' got an ill habit of preferring beauty no matter where they find it.

L. WOOD. See your son and my daughter; they have improved their acquaintance since they   160 were within.

O. BELL. A dod, methinks they have! Let's keep back and observe.

Y. BELL. [*to* HARRIET]. Now for a look and gestures that may persuade 'em I am saying   165 all the passionate things imaginable —

HAR. Your head a little more on one side. Ease yourself on your left leg and play with your right hand.

Y. BELL. Thus, is it not?

HAR. Now set your right leg firm on the   170 ground, adjust your belt, then look about you.

Y. BELL. A little exercising will make me perfect.

HAR. Smile, and turn to me again very sparkish.

Y. BELL. Will you take your turn and be instructed?   175

HAR. With all my heart!

Y. BELL. At one motion play your fan, roll your eyes, and then settle a kind look upon me.

HAR. So!

Y. BELL. Now spread your fan, look down   180 upon it, and tell [3] the sticks with a finger.

HAR. Very modish!

Y. BELL. Clap your hand up to your bosom, hold down your gown. Shrug a little, draw up your breasts, and let 'em fall again gently, with a   185 sigh or two, etc.

HAR. By the good instructions you give, I suspect you for one of those malicious observers who watch people's eyes, and from innocent looks make scandalous conclusions.   190

Y. BELL. I know some, indeed, who out of mere love to mischief are as vigilant as jealousy itself, and will give you an account of every glance that passes at a play and i'th' Circle. [4]

---

[1] Grimacing.   [2] Shop-women in the New Exchange.
[3] Count.   [4] Perhaps the reference here is to the inner circle at Court; cf. IV. i. 157.

HAR. 'Twill not be amiss now to seem a   195 little pleasant.

Y. BELL. Clap your fan, then, in both your hands, snatch it to your mouth, smile, and with a lively motion fling your body a little forwards. So! Now spread it, fall back on the sudden, cover your   200 face with it and break out into a loud laughter — take up, look grave, and fall a-fanning of yourself. — Admirably well acted!

HAR. I think I am pretty apt at these matters.   205

O. BELL. [*to* LADY WOODVILL]. A dod, I like this well!

L. WOOD. This promises something.

O. BELL. Come! there is love i'th' case, a dod there is, or will be. What say you, young lady?   210

HAR. All in good time, sir; you expect we should fall to and love as game-cocks fight, as soon as we are set together. A dod, y'are unreasonable!

O. BELL. A dod, sirrah, I like thy wit well.

Enter a Servant.

SERV. The coach is at the door, madam.   215

O. BELL. Go, get you and take the air together.

L. WOOD. Will not you go with us?

O. BELL. Out! a pize! A dod, I ha' business and cannot. We shall meet at night at my sister Townley's.   220

Y. BELL. (*aside*). He's going to Emilia. I overheard him talk of a collation.   *Exeunt.*

SCENE II

[LADY TOWNLEY'S *drawing-room.*]

Enter LADY TOWNLEY, EMILIA, *and*
MR. MEDLEY.

L. TOWN. I pity the young lovers we last talked of, though to say truth their conduct has been so indiscreet they deserve to be unfortunate.

MED. Y'have had an exact account, from the great lady i'th' box down to the little orange   5 wench.

EMIL. Y'are a living libel, a breathing lampoon. I wonder you are not torn in pieces.

MED. What think you of setting up an office of intelligence for these matters? The project   10 may get money.

L. TOWN. You would have great dealings with country ladies.

MED. More than Muddiman [5] has with their husbands.   15

---

[5] Henry Muddiman (1629–1692), editor of the *London Gazette,* and also for some thirty years the author of handwritten news-letters which circulated widely among country gentlemen.

Enter BELLINDA.

L. TOWN. Bellinda, what has been become of you? We have not seen you here of late with your friend Mrs. Loveit.

BELL. Dear creature, I left her but now so sadly afflicted!   20

L. TOWN. With her old distemper, jealousy!

MED. Dorimant has played her some new prank.

BELL. Well, that Dorimant is certainly the worst man breathing.

EMIL. I once thought so.   25

BELL. And do you not think so still?

EMIL. No, indeed!

BELL. Oh, Jesu!

EMIL. The town does him a great deal of injury, and I will never believe what it says of a man I   30 do not know, again, for his sake.

BELL. You make me wonder.

L. TOWN. He's a very well-bred man.

BELL. But strangely ill-natured.

EMIL. Then he's a very witty man.   35

BELL. But a man of no principles.

MED. Your man of principles is a very fine thing, indeed.

BELL. To be preferred to men of parts by women who have regard to their reputation and quiet.   40 Well, were I minded to play the fool, he should be the last man I'd think of.

MED. He has been the first in many ladies' favors, though you are so severe, madam.

L. TOWN. What he may be for a lover, I know   45 not; but he's a very pleasant acquaintance, I am sure.

BELL. Had you seen him use Mrs. Loveit as I have done, you would never endure him more.

EMIL. What, he has quarreled with her again!   50

BELL. Upon the slightest occasion; he's jealous of Sir Fopling.

L. TOWN. She never saw him in her life but yesterday, and that was here.

EMIL. On my conscience, he's the only man   55 in town that's her aversion! How horribly out of humor she was all the while he talked to her!

BELL. And somebody has wickedly told him —

EMIL. Here he comes.

Enter DORIMANT.

MED. Dorimant! you are luckily come to   60 justify yourself: here's a lady —

BELL. — Has a word or two to say to you from a disconsolate person.

DOR. You tender your reputation too much, I know, madam, to whisper with me before this   65 good company.

BELL. To serve Mrs. Loveit I'll make a bold venture.

DOR. Here's Medley, the very spirit of scandal.

BELL. No matter!   70

EMIL. 'Tis something you are unwilling to hear, Mr. Dorimant.

L. TOWN. Tell him, Bellinda, whether he will or no.

BELL. (*aloud*). Mrs. Loveit —   75

DOR. Softly! these are laughers; you do not know 'em.

BELL. (*to* DORIMANT *apart*). In a word, y'ave made me hate you, which I thought you never could have done.   80

DOR. In obeying your commands.

BELL. 'Twas a cruel part you played. How could you act it?

DOR. Nothing is cruel to a man who could kill himself to please you. Remember five o'clock   85 tomorrow morning!

BELL. I tremble when you name it.

DOR. Be sure you come!

BELL. I sha'not.

DOR. Swear you will!   90

BELL. I dare not.

DOR. Swear, I say!

BELL. By my life — by all the happiness I hope for —

DOR. You will.   95

BELL. I will!

DOR. Kind!

BELL. I am glad I've sworn. I vow I think I should ha' failed you else!

DOR. Surprisingly kind! In what temper   100 did you leave Loveit?

BELL. Her raving was prettily over, and she began to be in a brave way of defying you and all your works. Where have you been since you went from thence?   105

DOR. I looked in at the play.

BELL. I have promised, and must return to her again.

DOR. Persuade her to walk in the Mail this evening.   110

BELL. She hates the place and will not come.

DOR. Do all you can to prevail with her.

BELL. For what purpose?

DOR. Sir Fopling will be here anon; I'll prepare him to set upon her there before me.   115

BELL. You persecute her too much, but I'll do all you'll ha' me.

DOR. (*aloud*). Tell her plainly 'tis grown so dull a business I can drudge on no longer.

EMIL. There are afflictions in love, Mr. Dori-   120 mant.

DOR. You women make 'em, who are commonly as unreasonable in that as you are at play — without the advantage be on your side, a man can never quietly give over when he's weary.   125

MED. If you would play without being obliged to

complaisance, Dorimant, you should play in public places.

DOR. Ordinaries [1] were a very good thing for that, but gentlemen do not of late frequent 'em.   130 The deep play is now in private houses.

(BELLINDA *offering to steal away*.)

L. TOWN. Bellinda, are you leaving us so soon?

BELL. I am to go to the Park with Mrs. Loveit, madam.   *Exit* BELLINDA.

L. TOWN. This confidence [2] will go nigh to   135 spoil this young creature.

MED. 'Twill do her good, madam. Young men who are brought up under practicing lawyers prove the abler counsel when they come to be called to the bar themselves.   140

DOR. The town has been very favorable to you this afternoon, my Lady Townley; you use to have an *embarras* [3] of chairs and coaches at your door, an uproar of footmen in your hall, and a noise of fools above here.   145

L. TOWN. Indeed, my house is the general rendez-vous, and next to the playhouse is the common refuge of all the young idle people.

EMIL. Company is a very good thing, madam, but I wonder you do not love it a little more chosen.   150

L. TOWN. 'Tis good to have an universal taste; we should love wit, but for variety be able to divert ourselves with the extravagancies of those who want it.

MED. Fools will make you laugh.   155

EMIL. For once or twice, but the repetition of their folly after a visit or two grows tedious and unsuffer-able.

L. TOWN. You are a little too delicate, Emilia.

Enter a Page.

PAGE. Sir Fopling Flutter, madam, desires   160 to know if you are to be seen.

L. TOWN. Here's the freshest fool in town, and one who has not cloyed you yet. — Page!

PAGE. Madam!

L. TOWN. Desire him to walk up. [*Exit Page*.]   165

DOR. Do not you fall on him, Medley, and snub him. Soothe him up in his extravagance; he will show the better.

MED. You know I have a natural indulgence for fools and need not this caution, sir.   170

Enter SIR FOPLING FLUTTER *with his Page after him.*

SIR FOP. Page, wait without. (*To* LADY TOWN-LEY.) Madam, I kiss your hands. I see yesterday was nothing of chance; the *belles assemblées* [4] form themselves here every day. (*To* EMILIA.) Lady, your servant. — Dorimant, let me embrace   175

thee! Without lying, I have not met with any of my acquaintance who retain so much of Paris as thou dost — the very air thou hadst when the marquise mistook thee i'th' Tuileries and cried, 'Hey, Che-valier!' and then begged thy pardon.   180

DOR. I would fain wear in fashion as long as I can, sir; 'tis a thing to be valued in men as well as baubles.

SIR FOP. Thou art a man of wit and understands the town. Prithee, let thee and I be intimate; there is no living without making some good man the   185 confidant of our pleasures.

DOR. 'Tis true! but there is no man so improper for such a business as I am.

SIR FOP. Prithee, why hast thou so modest an opinion of thyself?   190

DOR. Why, first, I could never keep a secret in my life; and then, there is no charm so infallibly makes me fall in love with a woman as my knowing a friend loves her. I deal honestly with you.

SIR FOP. Thy humor's very gallant, or let   195 me perish! I knew a French count so like thee!

L. TOWN. Wit, I perceive, has more power over you than beauty, Sir Fopling, else you would not have let this lady stand so long neglected.

SIR FOP. (*to* EMILIA). A thousand pardons,   200 madam; some [civility's] due of course upon the meeting a long absent friend. The *éclat* [5] of so much beauty, I confess, ought to have charmed me sooner.

EMIL. The *brillant* [6] of so much good language, sir, has much more power than the little beauty I   205 can boast.

SIR FOP. I never saw anything prettier than this high work on your *point d'Espagne*. [7]

EMIL. 'Tis not so rich as *point de Venise*.

SIR FOP. Not altogether, but looks cooler   210 and is more proper for the season. — Dorimant, is not that Medley?

DOR. The same, sir.

SIR FOP. Forgive me, sir; in this *embarras* [8] of civilities I could not come to have you in my   215 arms sooner. You understand an equipage [9] the best of any man in town, I hear.

MED. By my own you would not guess it.

SIR FOP. There are critics who do not write, sir.

MED. Our peevish poets will scarce allow it.   220

SIR FOP. Damn 'em, they'll allow no man wit who does not play the fool like themselves and show it! Have you taken notice of the *gallesh* [10] I brought over?

MED. Oh, yes! 't has quite another air than   225 th' English makes.

SIR FOP. 'Tis as easily known from an English

---

[1] Taverns.   [2] Intimacy.   [3] Blockade.
[4] Gatherings of fashionable people.
[5] Splendor.   [6] Brilliance.
[7] Point lace.   [8] Crush.
[9] Retinue of personal attendants.
[10] *Calèche*, an open carriage.

201] Q1 *civilities*; Q2 *civilitie's*.

tumbril [1] as an Inns of Court [2] man is from one of us.

DOR. True; there is a *bel air* [3] in galleshes as well as men.   230

MED. But there are few so delicate to observe it.

SIR FOP. The world is generally very *grossier* [4] here, indeed.

L. TOWN. [*to* EMILIA]. He's very fine.

EMIL. Extreme proper. [5]   235

SIR FOP. [*overhearing*]. A slight suit I made to appear in at my first arrival — not worthy your consideration, ladies.

DOR. The pantaloon is very well mounted.

SIR FOP. The tassels are new and pretty.   240

MED. I never saw a coat better cut.

SIR FOP. It makes me show long waisted, and, I think, slender.

DOR. That's the shape our ladies dote on.

MED. Your breech, though, is a handful too   245 high, in my eye, Sir Fopling.

SIR FOP. Peace, Medley! I have wished it lower a thousand times, but a pox on't! 'twill not be.

L. TOWN. His gloves are well fringed, large,   250 and graceful.

SIR FOP. I was always eminent for being *bien ganté*. [6]

EMIL. He wears nothing but what are originals of the most famous hands in Paris.   255

SIR FOP. You are in the right, madam.

L. TOWN. The suit!

SIR FOP. Barroy. [7]

EMIL. The garniture! [8]

SIR FOP. Le Gras.   260

MED. The shoes!

SIR FOP. Piccar.

DOR. The periwig!

SIR FOP. Chedreux.

L. TOWN. ⎱ The gloves!
EMIL. ⎰   265

SIR FOP. Orangerie — you know the smell, ladies. — Dorimant, I could find in my heart for an amusement to have a gallantry with some of our English ladies.

DOR. 'Tis a thing no less necessary to con-   270 firm the reputation of your wit than a duel will be to satisfy the town of your courage.

SIR FOP. Here was a woman yesterday —

DOR. Mistress Loveit.

SIR FOP. You have named her.   275

DOR. You cannot pitch on a better for your purpose.

SIR FOP. Prithee, what is she?

DOR. A person of quality, and one who has a rest [9] of reputation enough to make the con-   280 quest considerable; besides, I hear she likes you too.

SIR FOP. Methoughts she seemed, though, very reserved and uneasy all the time I entertained her.

DOR. Grimace and affectation! You will see her i' th' Mail tonight.   285

SIR FOP. Prithee, let thee and I take the air together.

DOR. I am engaged to Medley, but I'll meet you at Saint James's and give you some information upon the which you may regulate your pro-   290 ceedings.

SIR FOP. All the world will be in the Park tonight. Ladies, 'twere pity to keep so much beauty longer within doors and rob the Ring [10] of all those charms that should adorn it. — Hey, page!   295

Enter Page.

See that all my people be ready.

[*Page*] *goes out again.*

— Dorimant, *au revoir.*   [*Exit.*]

MED. A fine, mettled coxcomb.

DOR. Brisk and insipid.

MED. Pert and dull.   300

EMIL. However you despise him, gentlemen, I'll lay my life he passes for a wit with many.

DOR. That may very well be; Nature has her cheats, stums [11] a brain, and puts sophisticate dulness often on the tasteless multitude for true wit and   305 good humor. Medley, come!

MED. I must go a little way; I will meet you i' the Mail.

DOR. I'll walk through the garden thither. — (*To the women.*) We shall meet anon and bow.   310

L. TOWN. Not to-night. We are engaged about a business the knowledge of which may make you laugh hereafter.

MED. Your servant, ladies.

DOR. '*Au revoir*,' as Sir Fopling says.   315

Exeunt MEDLEY *and* DORIMANT.

L. TOWN. The old man will be here immediately.

EMIL. Let's expect [12] him i' th' garden.

L. TOWN. 'Go! you are a rogue.'

EMIL. 'I can't abide you.'   *Exeunt.*

---

[1] A heavy cart.
[2] Lawyer, or other professional man, resident in one of the 'Temples.'
[3] Fashionable mode.   [4] Coarse.
[5] Handsome, elegant.   [6] Well-gloved.
[7] This name and those which follow are those of fashionable Parisian tradesmen.
[8] Trimmings.

[9] Remnant.
[10] A circular course in Hyde Park, used for riding and driving.
[11] Revives (a term usually employed in connection with the reclamation of wine or ale).   [12] Await.

295] Q1Q2 Enter Page, and goes out again.

297 and 315] Q1Q2 *A revoir.* The errors in French spelling are not confined to Sir Fopling's speeches, and are probably not intentional.

SCENE III

[*The Mail.*]

Enter HARRIET *and* YOUNG BELLAIR, *she pulling him.*

HAR. Come along.

Y. BELL. And leave your mother!

HAR. Busy will be sent with a hue and cry after us, but that's no matter.

Y. BELL. 'Twill look strangely in me.   5

HAR. She'll believe it a freak of mine and never blame your manners.

Y. BELL. What reverend acquaintance is that she has met?

HAR. A fellow-beauty of the last king's time,[1]   10 though by the ruins you would hardly guess it.

Exeunt.

Enter DORIMANT *and crosses the stage.*

Enter YOUNG BELLAIR *and* HARRIET.

Y. BELL. By this time your mother is in a fine taking.

HAR. If your friend Mr. Dorimant were but here now, that she might find me talking with him!   15

Y. BELL. She does not know him, but dreads him, I hear, of all mankind.

HAR. She concludes if he does but speak to a woman, she's undone — is on her knees every day to pray heaven defend me from him.   20

Y. BELL. You do not apprehend him so much as she does?

HAR. I never saw anything in him that was frightful.

Y. BELL. On the contrary, have you not   25 observed something extreme delightful in his wit and person?

HAR. He's agreeable and pleasant, I must own, but he does so much affect being so, he displeases me.

Y. BELL. Lord, madam! all he does and says   30 is so easy and so natural.

HAR. Some men's verses seem so to the unskillful, but labor i'the one and affectation in the other to the judicious plainly appear.

Y. BELL. I never heard him accused of af-   35 fectation before.

Enter DORIMANT *and stares upon her.*

HAR. It passes on the easy town, who are favorably pleased in him to call it humor.

[*Exeunt* YOUNG BELLAIR *and* HARRIET.]

DOR. 'Tis she! it must be she — that lovely hair, that easy shape, those wanton eyes, and all   40 those melting charms about her mouth which Medley spoke of! I'll follow the lottery and put in for a prize with my friend Bellair.

Exit DORIMANT *repeating:*

[1] Of the reign of Charles I, which had ended more than a quarter of a century earlier.

In love the victors from the vanquished fly;
They fly that wound, and they pursue that die.[2]   45

Enter YOUNG BELLAIR *and* HARRIET *and after them* DORIMANT *standing at a distance.*

Y. BELL. Most people prefer High Park[3] to this place.

HAR. It has the better reputation, I confess; but I abominate the dull diversions there — the formal bows, the affected smiles, the silly by-words   50 and amorous tweers[4] in passing. Here one meets with a little conversation now and then.

Y. BELL. These conversations have been fatal to some of your sex, madam.

HAR. It may be so; because some who   55 want temper[5] have been undone by gaming, must others who have it wholly deny themselves the pleasure of play?

DOR. (*coming up gently and bowing to her*). Trust me, it were unreasonable, madam.   60

HAR. (*she starts and looks grave*). Lord, who's this?

Y. BELL. Dorimant!

DOR. Is this the woman your father would have you marry?

Y. BELL. It is.   65

DOR. Her name?

Y. BELL. Harriet.

DOR. I am not mistaken; she's handsome.

Y. BELL. Talk to her; her wit is better than her face. We were wishing for you but now.   70

DOR. (*to* HARRIET). Overcast with seriousness o'the sudden! A thousand smiles were shining in that face but now; I never saw so quick a change of weather.

HAR. (*aside*). I feel as great a change within,   75 but he shall never know it.

DOR. You were talking of play, madam. Pray, what may be your stint?[6]

HAR. A little harmless discourse in public walks, or at most an appointment in a box, barefaced,   80 at the playhouse: you are for masks and private meetings, where women engage for all they are worth, I hear.

DOR. I have been used to deep play, but I can make one at small game when I like my gamester   85 well.

HAR. And be so unconcerned you'll ha' no pleasure in't.

DOR. Where there is a considerable sum to be won, the hope of drawing people in makes every   90 trifle considerable.

HAR. The sordidness of men's natures, I know,

[2] Waller, *To a Friend, of the Different Success of their Loves,* ll. 27–28.

[3] An alternative name for Hyde Park.

[4] Leers.   [5] Self-control.

[6] Pre-determined amount, after the loss of which the gamester intends to cease playing.

makes 'em willing to flatter and comply with the rich, though they are sure never to be the better for 'em.   95

DOR. 'Tis in their power to do us good, and we despair not but at some time or other they may be willing.

HAR. To men who have fared in this town like you, 'twould be a great mortification to live on   100 hope. Could you keep a Lent for a mistress?

DOR. In expectation of a happy Easter and, though time be very precious, think forty days well lost to gain your favor.

HAR. Mr. Bellair, let us walk; 'tis time to   105 leave him. Men grow dull when they begin to be particular.

DOR. Y'are mistaken; flattery will not ensue, though I know y' are greedy of the praises of the whole Mail.   110

HAR. You do me wrong.

DOR. I do not. As I followed you, I observed how you were pleased when the fops cried, 'She's handsome, very handsome! by God she is!' and whispered aloud your name; the thousand sev-   115 eral forms you put your face into; then, to make yourself more agreeable, how wantonly you played with your head, flung back your locks, and looked smilingly over your shoulder at 'em!

HAR. I do not go begging the men's, as you do   120 the ladies', good liking, with a sly softness in your looks and a gentle slowness in your bows as you pass by 'em — as thus, sir. (*Acts him.*) Is not this like you?

Enter LADY WOODVILL *and* BUSY.

Y. BELL. Your mother, madam.   125
          (*Pulls* HARRIET; *she composes herself.*)

L. WOOD. Ah, my dear child Harriet!

BUSY [*aside*]. Now is she so pleased with finding her again she cannot chide her.

L. WOOD. Come away!

DOR. 'Tis now but high Mail,[1] madam — the   130 most entertaining time of all the evening.

HAR. I would fain see that Dorimant, mother, you so cry out of for a monster; he's in the Mail, I hear.

L. WOOD. Come away then! The plague is   135 here and you should dread the infection.

Y. BELL. You may be misinformed of the gentleman.

L. WOOD. Oh, no! I hope you do not know him. He is the prince of all the devils in the town   140 — delights in nothing but in rapes and riots!

DOR. If you did but hear him speak, madam!

L. WOOD. Oh, he has a tongue, they say, would tempt the angels to a second fall.

Enter SIR FOPLING *with his equipage, six Footmen and a Page.*

SIR FOP. Hey! Champagne, Norman, La   145 Rose, La Fleur, La Tour, La Verdure! — Dorimant —

L. WOOD. Here, here he is among this rout! He names him! Come away, Harriet; come away!

          Exeunt LADY WOODVILL, HARRIET, BUSY,
          and YOUNG BELLAIR.

DOR. This fool's coming has spoiled all.   150 She's gone, but she has left a pleasing image of herself behind that wanders in my soul — it must not settle there.

SIR FOP. What reverie is this? Speak, man!

DOR. Snatcht from myself, how far behind   155
     Already I behold the shore![2]

Enter MEDLEY.

MED. Dorimant, a discovery! I met with Bellair.

DOR. You can tell me no news, sir; I know all.

MED. How do you like the daughter?

DOR. You never came so near truth in your   160 life as you did in her description.

MED. What think you of the mother?

DOR. Whatever I think of her, she thinks very well of me, I find.

MED. Did she know you?   165

DOR. She did not; whether she does now or no, I know not. Here was a pleasant scene towards, when in came Sir Fopling, mustering up his equipage, and at the latter end named me and frighted her away.   170

MED. Loveit and Bellinda are not far off; I saw 'em alight at St. James's.

DOR. Sir Fopling! hark you, a word or two. (*Whispers.*) Look you do not want assurance.

SIR FOP. I never do on these occasions.   175

DOR. Walk on; we must not be seen together. Make your advantage of what I have told you. The next turn you will meet the lady.

SIR FOP. Hey! Follow me all!
          Exeunt SIR FOPLING *and his equipage.*

DOR. Medley, you shall see good sport anon   180 between Loveit and this Fopling.

MED. I thought there was something toward, by that whisper.

DOR. You know a worthy principle of hers?

MED. Not to be so much as civil to a man   185 who speaks to her in the presence of him she professes to love.

DOR. I have encouraged Fopling to talk to her tonight.

MED. Now you are here, she will go nigh to   190 beat him.

DOR. In the humor she's in, her love will make her do some very extravagant thing doubtless.

_____

[1] The busiest hour of the Mall's social activities.

[2] Waller, *Of Loving at First Sight*, ll. 3-4.

MED. What was Bellinda's business with you at my Lady Townley's?   195

DOR. To get me to meet Loveit here in order to an *éclaircissement*.[1] I made some difficulty of it and have prepared this rencounter to make good my jealousy.

MED. Here they come.   200

Enter MRS. LOVEIT, BELLINDA, *and* PERT.

DOR. I'll meet her and provoke her with a deal of dumb civility in passing by, then turn short and be behind her when Sir Fopling sets upon her —
          See how unregarded now
          That piece of beauty passes.[2]   205
          Exeunt DORIMANT *and* MEDLEY.

BELL. How wonderful respectfully he bowed!

PERT. He's always over-mannerly when he has done a mischief.

BELL. Methoughts, indeed, at the same time he had a strange, despising countenance.   210

PERT. The unlucky look he thinks becomes him.

BELL. I was afraid you would have spoke to him, my dear.

LOV. I would have died first; he shall no more find me the loving fool he has done.   215

BELL. You love him still?

LOV. No!

PERT. I wish you did not.

LOV. I do not, and I will have you think so. — What made you hale me to this odious place,   220 Bellinda?

BELL. I hate to be hulched up[3] in a coach; walking is much better.

LOV. Would we could meet Sir Fopling now!

BELL. Lord, would you not avoid him?   225

LOV. I would make him all the advances that may be.

BELL. That would confirm Dorimant's suspicion, my dear.

LOV. He is not jealous; but I will make him   230 so, and be revenged a way he little thinks on.

BELL. (*aside*). If she should make him jealous, that may make him fond of her again. I must dissuade her from it. — Lord, my dear, this will certainly make him hate you.   235

LOV. 'Twill make him uneasy, though he does not care for me. I know the effects of jealousy on men of his proud temper.

BELL. 'Tis a fantastic remedy; its operations are dangerous and uncertain.   240

LOV. 'Tis the strongest cordial we can give to dying love: it often brings it back when there's no

sign of life remaining. But I design not so much the reviving of his, as my revenge.

Enter SIR FOPLING *and his equipage.*

SIR FOP. Hey! Bid the coachman send   245 home four of his horses and bring the coach to Whitehall;[4] I'll walk over the Park. — [*To* MRS. LOVEIT.] Madam, the honor of kissing your fair hands is a happiness I missed this afternoon at my Lady Townley's.   250

LOV. You were very obliging, Sir Fopling, the last time I saw you there.

SIR FOP. The preference was due to your wit and beauty. [*To* BELLINDA.] Madam, your servant; there never was so sweet an evening.   255

BELL. 'T has drawn all the rabble of the town hither.

SIR FOP. 'Tis pity there's not an order made that none but the *beau monde* should walk here.

LOV. 'Twould add much to the beauty of   260 the place. See what a sort[5] of nasty fellows are coming!

Enter four ill-fashioned fellows, singing:

          'Tis not for kisses alone
          [So long I have made my address, —][6]

LOV. Fo! Their periwigs are scented with   265 tobacco so strong —

SIR FOP. It overcomes our pulvilio.[7] Methinks I smell the coffee-house they come from.

1 MAN. Dorimant's convenient,[8] Madam Loveit.

2 MAN. I like the oily buttock[9] with her.   270

3 MAN. What spruce prig[10] is that?

1 MAN. A caravan[11] lately come from Paris.

2 MAN. Peace! they smoke.[12]

          All of them coughing; exeunt singing:

          There's something else to be done,
          [Which you cannot choose but guess.]   275

Enter DORIMANT *and* MEDLEY.

DOR. They're engaged.

MED. She entertains him as if she liked him!

DOR. Let us go forward — seem earnest in discourse and show ourselves; then you shall see how she'll use him.   280

BELL. Yonder's Dorimant, my dear.

4 The palace on the east side of St. James's Park; at this time (and until its destruction by fire in 1698) the royal residence.
5 Group.
6 These two lines, with ll. 274, 275, are ll. 5–8 of an anonymous song beginning, 'Tell me no more you love,' to be found in *The Last and Best Edition of New Songs* (1677), from which the missing lines are supplied here.
7 Scented cosmetic powder.   8 Mistress.
9 Smooth-appearing prostitute.   10 Fop.
11 Gull, 'easy mark.'   12 Observe (us).

---

1 Understanding.
2 Suckling, *Sonnet I*, ll. 1–2, altered.
3 Huddled up like a hunchback.

Lov. (*aside* [*to* Bellinda]). I see him. He comes insulting, but I will disappoint him in his expectation. (*To* Sir Fopling.) I like this pretty, nice humor of yours, Sir Fopling. — [*To* Bellinda.] 285 With what a loathing eye he looked upon those fellows!

Sir Fop. I sat near one of 'em at a play today and was almost poisoned with a pair of cordovan gloves he wears. 290

Lov. Oh, filthy cordovan! How I hate the smell! (*Laughs in a loud, affected way.*)

Sir Fop. Did you observe, madam, how their cravats hung loose an inch from their neck and what a frightful air it gave 'em? 295

Lov. Oh, I took particular notice of one that is always spruced up with a deal of dirty sky-colored ribband.

Bell. That's one of the walking flageolets [1] who haunt the Mail o'nights. 300

Lov. Oh, I remember him; h'has a hollow tooth enough to spoil the sweetness of an evening.

Sir Fop. I have seen the tallest walk the streets with a dainty pair of boxes [2] neatly buckled on.

Lov. And a little foot-boy at his heels, 305 pocket-high, with a flat cap, a dirty face —

Sir Fop. And a snotty nose.

Lov. Oh, odious! — There's many of my own sex with that Holborn equipage [3] trig [4] to Gray's Inn [5] Walks and now and then travel hither on a 310 Sunday.

Med. [*to* Dorimant]. She takes no notice of you.

Dor. Damn her! I am jealous of a counterplot.

Lov. Your liveries are the finest, Sir Fopling 315 — oh, that page! that page is the prettily'st dressed — they are all Frenchmen.

Sir Fop. There's one damned English blockhead among 'em; you may know him by his mien.

Lov. Oh, that's he — that's he! What do 320 you call him?

Sir Fop. Hey — I know not what to call him —

Lov. What's your name?

Footm. John Trott, madam. 325

Sir Fop. Oh, unsufferable! Trott, Trott, Trott! There's nothing so barbarous as the names of our English servants. — What countryman are you, sirrah?

Footm. Hampshire, sir. 330

Sir Fop. Then Hampshire be your name. Hey, Hampshire!

Lov. Oh, that sound — that sound becomes the mouth of a man of quality!

Med. Dorimant, you look a little bashful 335 on the matter.

Dor. She dissembles better than I thought she could have done.

Med. You have tempted her with too luscious a bait. She bites at the coxcomb. 340

Dor. She cannot fall from loving me to that.

Med. You begin to be jealous in earnest.

Dor. Of one I do not love —

Med. You did love her.

Dor. The fit has long been over. 345

Med. But I have known men fall into dangerous relapses when they have found a woman inclining to another.

Dor. (*to himself*). He guesses the secret of my heart. I am concerned, but dare not show it, 350 lest Bellinda should mistrust all I have done to gain her.

Bell. (*aside*). I have watched his look and find no alteration there. Did he love her, some signs of jealousy would have appeared. 355

Dor. [*to* Mrs. Loveit]. I hope this happy evening, madam, has reconciled you to the scandalous Mail. We shall have you now hankering [6] here again —

Lov. Sir Fopling, will you walk? 360

Sir Fop. I am all obedience, madam.

Lov. Come along then, and let's agree to be malicious on all the ill-fashioned things we meet.

Sir Fop. We'll make a critique on the whole Mail, madam. 365

Lov. Bellinda, you shall engage [7] —

Bell. To the reserve of our friends,[8] my dear.

Lov. No! no exceptions!

Sir Fop. We'll sacrifice all to our diversion. 370

Lov. All — all.

Sir Fop. All.

Bell. All? Then let it be.

Exeunt Sir Fopling, Mrs. Loveit, Bellinda, *and* Pert, *laughing.*

Med. Would you had brought some more of your friends, Dorimant, to have been witnesses of 375 Sir Fopling's disgrace and your triumph.

Dor. 'Twere unreasonable to desire you not to laugh at me; but pray do not expose me to the town this day or two.

Med. By that time you hope to have re- 380 gained your credit.

Dor. I know she hates Fopling and only makes use of him in hope to work me on again; had

---

[1] ?Tall, thin men. Cf. Sir Fopling's next speech.
[2] Presumably pattens or clogs.
[3] Middle-class sort of attendance.   [4] Walk briskly.
[5] The gardens of this, one of the Inns of Court, were apparently the middle-class equivalent of the Mall.

[6] Loitering about.   [7] Take part.
[8] Exempting our friends.

it not been for some powerful considerations which will be removed tomorrow morning, I had 385 made her pluck off this mask and show the passion that lies panting under.

Enter a Footman.

MED. Here comes a man from Bellair with news of your last adventure.

DOR. I am glad he sent him; I long to 390 know the consequence of our parting.

FOOTM. Sir, my master desires you to come to my Lady Townley's presently [1] and bring Mr. Medley with you. My Lady Woodvill and her daughter are there. 395

MED. Then all's well, Dorimant.

FOOTM. They have sent for the fiddles and mean to dance. He bid me tell you, sir, the old lady does not know you, and would have you own yourself to be Mr. Courtage. They are all prepared to 400 receive you by that name.

DOR. That foppish admirer of quality, who flatters the very meat at honorable tables and never offers love to a woman below a lady-grandmother.

MED. You know the character you are to 405 act, I see.

DOR. This is Harriet's contrivance — wild, witty, lovesome, beautiful, and young! — Come along, Medley.

MED. This new woman would well supply 410 the loss of Loveit.

DOR. That business must not end so; before tomorrow sun is set I will revenge and clear it.

And you and Loveit, to her cost, shall find,
I fathom all the depths of womankind. *Exeunt.* 415

ACT IV

[SCENE I]

[LADY TOWNLEY'S *drawing-room.*]

The scene opens with the fiddles playing a country dance. Enter DORIMANT *and* LADY WOODVILL, YOUNG BELLAIR *and* MRS. HARRIET, OLD BELLAIR *and* EMILIA, MR. MEDLEY *and* LADY TOWNLEY, *as having just ended the dance.*

O. BELL. So, so, so! — a smart bout, a very smart bout, a dod!

L. TOWN. How do you like Emilia's dancing, brother?

O. BELL. Not at all — not at all! 5

L. TOWN. You speak not what you think, I am sure.

O. BELL. No matter for that; go, bid her dance no more. It don't become her — it don't become her. Tell her I say so. (*Aside.*) A dod, I love 10 her!

DOR. (*to* LADY WOODVILL). All people mingle nowadays, madam. And in public places women of quality have the least respect showed 'em.

L. WOOD. I protest you say the truth, Mr. 15 Courtage.

DOR. Forms and ceremonies, the only things that uphold quality and greatness, are now shamefully laid aside and neglected.

L. WOOD. Well, this is not the women's age, 20 let 'em think what they will. Lewdness is the business now; love was the business in my time.

DOR. The women, indeed, are little beholding to the young men of this age; they're generally only dull admirers of themselves, and make their 25 court to nothing but their periwigs and their cravats, and would be more concerned for the disordering of 'em, though on a good occasion, than a young maid would be for the tumbling of her head or handkercher.

L. WOOD. I protest you hit 'em. 30

DOR. They are very assiduous to show themselves at court, well dressed, to the women of quality, but their business is with the stale mistresses of the town, who are prepared to receive their lazy addresses by industrious old lovers who have cast 'em off and 35 made 'em easy.

HAR. [*to* MEDLEY]. He fits my mother's humor so well, a little more and she'll dance a kissing dance with him anon.

MED. Dutifully observed, madam. 40

DOR. [*to* LADY WOODVILL]. They pretend to be great critics in beauty. By their talk you would think they liked no face, and yet [they] can dote on an ill one if it belong to a laundress or a tailor's daughter. They cry, 'A woman's past her 45 prime at twenty, decayed at four-and-twenty, old and unsufferable at thirty.'

L. WOOD. Unsufferable at thirty! That they are in the wrong, Mr. Courtage, at five-and-thirty, there are living proofs enough to convince 'em. 50

DOR. Ay, madam. There's Mrs. Setlooks, Mrs. Droplip, and my Lady Lowd; show me among all our opening buds a face that promises so much beauty as the remains of theirs.

L. WOOD. The depraved appetite of this 55 vicious age tastes nothing but green fruit, and loathes it when 'tis kindly [2] ripened.

DOR. Else so many deserving women, madam, would not be so untimely neglected.

L. WOOD. I protest, Mr. Courtage, a dozen 60 such good men as you would be enough to atone for that wicked Dorimant and all the under [3] debauchees of the town. (HARRIET, EMILIA, YOUNG BELLAIR, MEDLEY, [*and*] LADY TOWNLEY *break out into a laughter.*) — What's the matter there? 65

MED. A pleasant mistake, madam, that a lady has made, occasions a little laughter.

---

[1] Immediately.   [2] Naturally.   [3] Lesser.

O. BELL. Come, come, you keep 'em idle! They are impatient till the fiddles play again.

DOR. You are not weary, madam? 70

L. WOOD. One dance more; I cannot refuse you, Mr. Courtage.

(They dance. After the dance OLD BELLAIR, singing and dancing up to EMILIA.)

EMILIA. You are very active, sir.

O. BELL. A dod, sirrah! when I was a young fellow I could ha' capered up to my woman's 75 gorget.[1]

DOR. [*to* LADY WOODVILL]. You are willing to rest yourself, madam —

L. TOWN. [*to* LADY WOODVILL]. We'll walk into my chamber and sit down. 80

MED. Leave us Mr. Courtage; he's a dancer, and the young ladies are not weary yet.

L. WOOD. We'll send him out again.

HAR. If you do not quickly, I know where to send for Mr. Dorimant. 85

L. WOOD. This girl's head, Mr. Courtage, is ever running on that wild fellow.

DOR. 'Tis well you have got her a good husband, madam; that will settle it.

Exeunt LADY TOWNLEY, LADY WOODVILL, *and* DORIMANT.

O. BELL. (*to* EMILIA). A dod, sweetheart, be 90 advised and do not throw thyself away on a young, idle fellow.

EMIL. I have no such intention, sir.

O. BELL. Have a little patience! Thou shalt have the man I spake of. A dod, he loves thee 95 and will make a good husband — but no words!

EMIL. But, sir —

O. BELL. No answer — out a pize! peace! and think on 't.

Enter DORIMANT.

DOR. Your company is desired within, sir. 100

O. BELL. I go, I go! Good Mr. Courtage, fare you well! — (*To* EMILIA.) Go, I'll see you no more!

EMIL. What have I done, sir?

O. BELL. You are ugly, you are ugly! — Is she not, Mr. Courtage? 105

EMIL. Better words or I shan't abide you.

O. BELL. Out a pize; a dod, what does she say? Hit her a pat for me there. *Exit* OLD BELLAIR.

MED. You have charms for the whole family.

DOR. You'll spoil all with some unseason- 110 able jest, Medley.

MED. You see I confine my tongue and am content to be a bare spectator, much contrary to my nature.

EMIL. Methinks, Mr. Dorimant, my Lady 115 Woodvill is a little fond of you.

DOR. Would her daughter were!

[1] Kicked as high as my partner's neck-piece.

MED. It may be you may find her so. Try her — you have an opportunity.

DOR. And I will not lose it. — Bellair, 120 here's a lady has something to say to you.

Y. BELL. I wait upon her. — Mr. Medley, we have both business with you.

DOR. Get you all together then. (*To* HARRIET.) That demure curtsey is not amiss in jest, but 125 do not think in earnest it becomes you.

HAR. Affectation is catching, I find; from your grave bow I got it.

DOR. Where had you all that scorn and coldness in your look? 130

HAR. From nature, sir; pardon my want of art. I have not learnt those softnesses and languishings which now in faces are so much in fashion.

DOR. You need 'em not; you have a sweetness of your own, if you would but calm your frowns 135 and let it settle.

HAR. My eyes are wild and wand'ring like my passions, and cannot yet be tied to rules of charming.

DOR. Women, indeed, have commonly a 140 method of managing those messengers of love. Now they will look as if they would kill, and anon they will look as if they were dying. They point and rebate[2] their glances, the better to invite us.

HAR. I like this variety well enough, but 145 hate the set face that always looks as if it would say, 'Come love me!' — a woman who at plays makes the *doux yeux*[3] to a whole audience and at home cannot forbear 'em to her monkey.

DOR. Put on a gentle smile and let me 150 see how well it will become you.

HAR. I am sorry my face does not please you as it is, but I shall not be complaisant and change it.

DOR. Though you are obstinate, I know 'tis capable of improvement, and shall do you jus- 155 tice, madam, if I chance to be at Court when the critics of the Circle[4] pass their judgment; for thither you must come.

HAR. And expect to be taken in pieces, have all my features examined, every motion censured, 160 and on the whole be condemned to be but pretty, or a beauty of the lowest rate. What think you?

DOR. The women — nay, the very lovers who belong to the drawing-room — will maliciously allow you more than that: they always grant what 165 is apparent, that they may the better be believed when they name concealed faults they cannot easily be disproved in.

HAR. Beauty runs as great a risk exposed at Court as wit does on the stage, where the ugly 170 and the foolish all are free to censure.

[2] Sharpen and blunt.
[3] Casts amorous glances.
[4] Cf. III. i. 194.

DOR. (aside). I love her and dare not let her know it; I fear sh'as an ascendant o'er me and may revenge the wrongs I have done her sex. (To her.) Think of making a party, madam; love will 175 engage.

HAR. You make me start! I did not think to have heard of love from you.

DOR. I never knew what 'twas to have a settled ague yet, but now and then have had ir- 180 regular fits.

HAR. Take heed! sickness after long health is commonly more violent and dangerous.

DOR. (aside). I have took the infection from her, and feel the disease now spreading in me. 185 (To her.) Is the name of love so frightful that you dare not stand it?

HAR. 'Twill do little execution out of your mouth on me, I am sure.

DOR. It has been fatal — 190

HAR. To some easy women, but we are not all born to one destiny. I was informed you use to laugh at love and not make it.

DOR. The time has been, but now I must speak —

HAR. If it be on that idle subject, I will put 195 on my serious look, turn my head carelessly from you, drop my lip, let my eyelids fall and hang half o'er my eyes — thus, while you buzz a speech of an hour long in my ear, and I answer never a word. Why do you not begin? 200

DOR. That the company may take notice how passionately I make advances of love, and how disdainfully you receive 'em!

HAR. When your love's grown strong enough to make you bear being laughed at, I'll give you 205 leave to trouble me with it. Till when pray forbear, sir.

Enter SIR FOPLING *and others in masks.*

DOR. What's here — masquerades?

HAR. I thought that foppery had been left off, and people might have been in private with a 210 fiddle.

DOR. 'Tis endeavored to be kept on foot still by some who find themselves the more acceptable the less they are known.

Y. BELL. This must be Sir Fopling. 215

MED. That extraordinary habit shows it.

Y. BELL. What are the rest?

MED. A company of French rascals whom he picked up in Paris and has brought over to be his dancing equipage on these occasions. Make 220 him own himself; a fool is very troublesome when he presumes he is incognito.

SIR FOP. (to HARRIET). Do you know me?

HAR. Ten to one but I guess at you.

SIR FOP. Are you women as fond of a viz- 225 ard as we men are?

HAR. I am very fond of a vizard that covers a face I do not like, sir.

Y BELL. Here are no masks, you see, sir, but those which came with you. This was intended a 230 private meeting; but because you look like a gentleman, if you will discover yourself and we know you to be such, you shall be welcome.

SIR FOP. (pulling off his mask). Dear Bellair!

MED. Sir Fopling! How came you hither? 235

SIR FOP. Faith, as I was coming late from Whitehall, after the King's *couchée*,[1] one of my people told me he had heard fiddles at my Lady Townley's, and —

DOR. You need not say any more, sir. 240

SIR FOP. Dorimant, let me kiss thee.

DOR. Hark you, Sir Fopling — (Whispers.)

SIR FOP. Enough, enough, Courtage. — A pretty kind of young woman that, Medley. I observed her in the Mail — more *éveillée*[2] than our Eng- 245 lish women commonly are. Prithee, what is she?

MED. The most noted coquette in town. Beware of her.

SIR FOP. Let her be what she will, I know how to take my measures. In Paris the mode is to 250 flatter the prude, laugh at the *faux-prude*, make serious love to the *demi-prude*, and only rally with the *coquette*. Medley, what think you?

MED. That for all this smattering of the mathematics, you may be out in your judgment at 255 tennis.

SIR FOP. What a *coq-à-l'âne*[3] is this? I talk of women and thou answer'st tennis.

MED. Mistakes will be for want of apprehension.

SIR FOP. I am very glad of the acquaintance 260 I have with this family.

MED. My lady truly is a good woman.

SIR FOP. Ah, Dorimant — Courtage, I would say — would thou hadst spent the last winter in Paris with me! When thou wert there, La Corneus and 265 Sallyes[4] were the only habitudes we had: a comedian would have been a *bonne fortune*.[5] No stranger ever passed his time so well as I did some months before I came over. I was well received in a dozen families where all the women of quality used to visit; 270 I have intrigues to tell thee more pleasant than ever thou read'st in a novel.

HAR. Write 'em, sir, and oblige us women. Our language wants such little stories.

[1] Evening reception.   [2] Vivacious.   [3] Nonsense.
[4] Verity's suggestion that the reference is to Mesdames Cornuel and Selles (two minor figures in fashionable Parisian literary circles), while not entirely convincing, is the best that has been made.   [5] Piece of good luck.

SIR FOP. Writing, madam, 's a mechanic 275
part of wit. A gentleman should never go beyond a
song or a billet.

HAR. Bussy[1] was a gentleman.

SIR FOP. Who, d'Ambois?[2]

MED. Was there ever such a brisk blockhead? 280

HAR. Not d'Ambois, sir, but Rabutin — he who
writ the loves of France.

SIR FOP. That may be, madam; many gentlemen
do things that are below 'em. Damn your authors,
Courtage; women are the prettiest things we 285
can fool away our time with.

HAR. I hope ye have wearied yourself to-night at
Court, sir, and will not think of fooling with anybody here.

SIR FOP. I cannot complain of my fortune 290
there, madam. — Dorimant —

DOR. Again!

SIR FOP. Courtage — a pox on't! — I have something to tell thee. When I had made my court within,
I came out and flung myself upon the mat un- 295
der the state[3] i'th' outward room, i'th' midst of half a
dozen beauties who were withdrawn to jeer among
themselves, as they called it.

DOR. Did you know 'em?

SIR FOP. Not one of 'em, by heavens! — not 300
I. But they were all your friends.

DOR. How are you sure of that?

SIR FOP. Why, we laughed at all the town — spared
nobody but yourself. They found me a man for
their purpose. 305

DOR. I know you are malicious, to your power.[4]

SIR FOP. And faith, I had occasion to show it, for
I never saw more gaping fools at a ball or on a birthday.[5]

DOR. You learned who the women were? 310

SIR FOP. No matter; they frequent the drawing-
room.

DOR. — And entertain themselves pleasantly at
the expense of all the fops who come there.

SIR FOP. That's their bus'ness. Faith, I 315
sifted 'em,[6] and find they have a sort of wit among
them. — Ah, filthy!   (Pinches a tallow candle.)

DOR. Look, he has been pinching the tallow
candle.

SIR FOP. How can you breathe in a room 320
where there's grease frying? — Dorimant, thou art

intimate with my lady; advise her, for her own sake
and the good company that comes hither, to burn
wax lights.

HAR. What are these masquerades who 325
stand so obsequiously at a distance?

SIR FOP. A set of balladines whom I picked out of
the best in France and brought over with a flute-
douce or two — my servants. They shall entertain you. 330

HAR. I had rather see you dance yourself, Sir
Fopling.

SIR FOP. And I had rather do it — all the company knows it — but, madam —

MED. Come, come, no excuses, Sir Fopling! 335

SIR FOP. By heavens, Medley —

MED. Like a woman I find you must be struggled with before one brings you [to] what you desire.   [They converse in dumb-show.]

HAR. (aside). Can he dance? 340

EMIL. And fence and sing too, if you'll believe
him.

DOR. He has no more excellence in his heels than
in his head. He went to Paris a plain, bashful English blockhead, and is returned a fine under- 345
taking[7] French fop.

MED. [to HARRIET]. I cannot prevail.

SIR FOP. Do not think it want of complaisance,
madam.

HAR. You are too well bred to want that, 350
Sir Fopling. I believe it want of power.

SIR FOP. By heavens, and so it is! I have sat up
so damned late and drunk so cursed hard since I came
to this lewd town, that I am fit for nothing but low
dancing now — a courante, a bourrée, or a men- 355
uet.[8] But St. André[9] tells me, if I will but be regular,
in one month I shall rise again. Pox on this debauchery!   (Endeavors at a caper.)

EMIL. I have heard your dancing much commended. 360

SIR FOP. It had the good fortune to please in
Paris. I was judged to rise within an inch as high
as the Basque[10] in an entry[11] I danced there.

HAR. [to EMILIA]. I am mightily taken with this
fool; let us sit. — Here's a seat, Sir Fopling. 365

SIR FOP. At your feet, madam; I can be nowhere
so much at ease. — By your leave, gown.

[Sits at HARRIET's feet.]

HAR. } Ah, you'll spoil it!
EMIL. }

---

[1] Roger de Rabutin, Comte de Bussy, author of the *Histoire amoureuse des Gaules*: still living at this time, despite the implication of Harriet's 'was.'

[2] Sir Fopling displays his actual ignorance of the fashionable
world of Paris by supposing Harriet refers to the sixteenth-
century French adventurer, who was well-known to the English
as the hero of Chapman's play of the same name.

[3] Canopy.   [4] To the extent of your power.

[5] At a celebration of the king's birthday.   [6] Examined.

[7] Enterprising, bold.

[8] Dances that did not require 'capers' (high kicks).

[9] A famous French dancing-master.

[10] Usually explained as the skirt of a coat — but this would
scarcely be a leap to boast of. Perhaps the reference is to a
contemporary Basque professional dancer.

[11] A dance performed as an interlude in an entertainment.

287] Q2 *you have.*   288] Q2 *and I will.*   336] Q2 om. *Medley.*
338] Q1Q2 *you what;* 1704 *you to what.*   361] Q2 *the fortune.*

SIR FOP. No matter; my clothes are my creatures.
I make 'em to make my court to you ladies. 370
[*To his servants.*] Hey! *Qu'on commence!* [1] (*Dance.*)
— To an English dancer, English motions. I was
forced to entertain [2] this fellow [*pointing to* JOHN
TROTT], one of my set miscarrying. — Oh, horrid!
Leave your damned manner of dancing and 375
put on the French air: have you not a pattern be-
fore you? — Pretty well! imitation in time may bring
him to something.

After the dance, enter OLD BELLAIR, LADY WOODVILL,
and LADY TOWNLEY.

O. BELL. Hey, a dod, what have we here — a
mumming? 380
L. WOOD. Where's my daughter? Harriet!
DOR. Here, here, madam! I know not but under
these disguises there may be dangerous sparks;
I gave the young lady warning.
L. WOOD. Lord! I am so obliged to you, 385
Mr. Courtage.
HAR. Lord, how you admire this man!
L. WOOD. What have you to except against
him?
HAR. He's a fop. 390
L. WOOD. He's not a Dorimant, a wild extrava-
gant fellow of the times.
HAR. He's a man made up of forms and common-
places sucked out of the remaining lees of the last
age. 395
L. WOOD. He's so good a man that, were you not
engaged —
L. TOWN. You'll have but little night to sleep
in.
L. WOOD. Lord, 'tis perfect day.[3] 400
DOR. (*aside*). The hour is almost come I ap-
pointed Bellinda, and I am not so foppishly in love
here to forget. I am flesh and blood yet.
L. TOWN. I am very sensible,[4] madam. [*Bowing.*]
L. WOOD. Lord, madam! [*Bowing.*] 405
HAR. Look! in what a struggle is my poor mother
yonder!
Y. BELL. She has much ado to bring out the com-
pliment.
DOR. She strains hard for it. 410
HAR. See, see! her head tottering, her eyes staring,
and her under lip trembling —
DOR. Now — now she's in the very convulsions
of her civility. (*Aside.*) 'Sdeath, I shall lose Bellin-
da! I must fright her hence; she'll be an hour 415
in this fit of good manners else. (*To* LADY WOOD-
VILL.) Do you not know Sir Fopling, madam?
L. WOOD. I have seen that face — oh, heaven!

[1] Begin!   [2] Engage, hire.
[3] Broad daylight.
[4] Aware (of your courtesy to me).

'tis the same we met in the Mail. How came he
here? 420
DOR. A fiddle, in this town, is a kind of fop-call;
no sooner it strikes up but the house is besieged
with an army of masquerades straight.
L. WOOD. Lord! I tremble, Mr. Courtage. For
certain, Dorimant is in the company. 425
DOR. I cannot confidently say he is not. You had
best be gone. I will wait upon you; your daughter
is in the hands of Mr. Bellair.
L. WOOD. I'll see her before me. — Harriet, come
away. 430
Y. BELL. Lights! lights!
L. TOWN. Light, down there!
O. BELL. A dod, it needs not —
DOR. [*calling to the Servants without*]. Call my Lady
Woodvill's coach to the door quickly. 435
[*Exeunt* YOUNG BELLAIR, HARRIET, LADY
TOWNLEY, DORIMANT, *and* LADY WOOD-
VILL.]
O. BELL. Stay, Mr. Medley: let the young fellows
do that duty; we will drink a glass of wine together.
'Tis good after dancing. [*Indicating* SIR FOPLING.]
What mumming [5] spark is that?
MED. He is not to be comprehended in few 440
words.
SIR FOP. Hey, La Tour!
MED. Whither away, Sir Fopling?
SIR FOP. I have business with Courtage.
MED. He'll but put the ladies into their 445
coach and come up again.
O. BELL. In the meantime I'll call for a bottle.
Exit OLD BELLAIR.

Enter YOUNG BELLAIR.

MED. Where's Dorimant?
Y. BELL. Stol'n home. He has had business waiting for him there all this night, I believe, by an 450
impatience I observed in him.
MED. Very likely; 'tis but dissembling drunkenness, railing at his friends, and the kind soul will embrace the blessing and forget the tedious expectation. 455
SIR FOP. I must speak with him before I sleep.
Y. BELL. [*to* MEDLEY]. Emilia and I are resolved
on that business.
MED. Peace! here's your father.

Enter OLD BELLAIR *and* [*a*] *Butler with a bottle of wine.*

O. BELL. The women are all gone to bed. 460
— Fill, boy! — Mr. Medley, begin a health.
MED. (*whispers*). To Emilia!
O. BELL. Out a pize! she's a rogue, and I'll not
pledge you.
MED. I know you [will]. 465

[5] Masquerading.

O. Bell. A dod, drink it, then!

Sir Fop. Let us have the new bacchic.

O. Bell. A dod, that is a hard word. What does it mean, sir?

Med. A catch or drinking-song. 470

O. Bell. Let us have it then.

Sir Fop. Fill the glasses round and draw up in a body. — Hey, music! (*They sing.*)

The pleasures of love and the joys of good wine
To perfect our happiness wisely we join. 475
We to beauty all day
Give the sovereign sway
And her favorite nymphs devoutly obey.
At the plays we are constantly making our court,
And when they are ended we follow the sport 480
To the Mall and the Park,
Where we love till 'tis dark.
Then sparkling champagne
Puts an end to their reign;
It quickly recovers 485
Poor languishing lovers;
Makes us frolic and gay, and drowns all our sorrow.
But alas! we relapse again on the morrow.
  Let every man stand
  With his glass in his hand, 490
And briskly discharge at the word of command:
  Here's a health to all those
  Whom to-night we depose!
Wine and beauty by turns great souls should inspire;
Present all together! and now, boys, give fire! 495
[*They drink.*]

O. Bell. A dod, a pretty business and very merry!

Sir Fop. Hark you; Medley, let you and I take the fiddles and go waken Dorimant.

Med. We shall do him a courtesy, if it be as I guess. For after the fatigue of this night he'll 500 quickly have his belly full and be glad of an occasion to cry, 'Take away, Handy!'

Y. Bell. I'll go with you, and there we'll consult about affairs, Medley.

O. Bell. (*looks on his watch*). A dod, 'tis 505 six o'clock!

Sir Fop. Let's away, then.

O. Bell. Mr. Medley, my sister tells me you are an honest man — and a dod, I love you. Few words and hearty — that's the way with old Harry, 510 old Harry.

Sir Fop. [*to his Servants*]. Light your flambeaux. Hey!

O. Bell. What does the man mean?

Med. 'Tis day, Sir Fopling. 515

Sir Fop. No matter; our serenade will look the greater. *Exeunt omnes.*

SCENE II

Dorimant's *lodging. A table, a candle, a toilet, etc.* Handy, *tying up linen.*

Enter Dorimant *in his gown, and* Bellinda.

Dor. Why will you be gone so soon?

Bell. Why did you stay out so late?

Dor. Call a chair, Handy. — What makes you tremble so?

Bell. I have a thousand fears about me. 5
Have I not been seen, think you?

Dor. By nobody but myself and trusty Handy.

Bell. Where are all your people?

Dor. I have dispersed 'em on sleeveless [1] errands. What does that sigh mean? 10

Bell. Can you be so unkind to ask me? Well — (*sighs*) — were it to do again —

Dor. We should do it, should we not?

Bell. I think we should — the wickeder man you to make me love so well. Will you be discreet 15 now?

Dor. I will.

Bell. You cannot.

Dor. Never doubt it.

Bell. I will not expect it. 20

Dor. You do me wrong.

Bell. You have no more power to keep the secret than I had not to trust you with it.

Dor. By all the joys I have had and those you keep in store — 25

Bell. — You'll do for my sake what you never did before.

Dor. By that truth thou hast spoken, a wife shall sooner betray herself to her husband.

Bell. Yet I had rather you should be false in 30 this than in another thing you promised me.

Dor. What's that?

Bell. That you would never see Loveit more but in public places — in the Park, at Court and plays.

Dor. 'Tis not likely a man should be fond of 35 seeing a damned old play when there is a new one acted.

Bell. I dare not trust your promise.

Dor. You may —

Bell. This does not satisfy me. You shall 40 swear you never will see her more.

Dor. I will, a thousand oaths. By all —

Bell. Hold! You shall not, now I think on't better.

Dor. I will swear! 45

Bell. I shall grow jealous of the oath and think I owe your truth to that, not to your love.

Dor. Then, by my love; no other oath I'll swear.

[1] Useless.

Enter HANDY.

HAND. Here's a chair.

BELL. Let me go.   50

DOR. I cannot.

BELL. Too willingly, I fear.

DOR. Too unkindly feared. When will you promise me again?

BELL. Not this fortnight.   55

DOR. You will be better than your word.

BELL. I think I shall. Will it not make you love me less? (*Starting.*) Hark! what fiddles are these?
(*Fiddles without.*)

DOR. Look out, Handy.

Exit HANDY *and returns.*

HAND. Mr. Medley, Mr. Bellair, and Sir Fop-   60
ling; they are coming up.

DOR. How got they in?

HAND. The door was open for the chair.

BELL. Lord, let me fly!

DOR. Here, here, down the back stairs! I'll   65
see you into your chair.

BELL. No, no! Stay and receive 'em. And be sure you keep your word and never see Loveit more. Let it be a proof of your kindness.

DOR. It shall. — Handy, direct her. — (*Kiss-*   70
ing her hand.) Everlasting love go along with thee.

Exeunt BELLINDA *and* HANDY.

Enter YOUNG BELLAIR, MEDLEY, *and* SIR FOPLING.

Y. BELL. Not abed yet?

MED. You have had an 'irregular fit,' Dorimant.

DOR. I have.

Y. BELL. And is it off already?   75

DOR. Nature has done her part, gentlemen; when she falls kindly to work, great cures are effected in little time, you know.

SIR FOP. We thought there was a wench in the case, by the chair that waited. Prithee, make   80
us a *confidence.*

DOR. Excuse me.

SIR FOP. *Le sage* Dorimant! Was she pretty?

DOR. So pretty she may come to keep her coach and pay parish duties if the good humor of the   85
age continue.

MED. And be of the number of the ladies kept by public-spirited men for the good of the whole town.

SIR FOP. (*dancing by himself*). Well said, Medley.

Y. BELL. See Sir Fopling dancing!   90

DOR. You are practising and have a mind to recover, I see.

SIR FOP. Prithee, Dorimant, why hast not thou a glass hung up here? A room is the dullest thing without one.   95

Y. BELL. Here is company to entertain you.

SIR FOP. But I mean in case of being alone. In a glass a man may entertain himself —

DOR. The shadow of himself, indeed.

SIR FOP. — Correct the errors of his motions   100
and his dress.

MED. I find, Sir Fopling, in your solitude you remember the saying of the wise man, and study yourself.[1]

SIR FOP. 'Tis the best diversion in our re-   105
tirements. Dorimant, thou art a pretty fellow and wear'st thy clothes well, but I never saw thee have a handsome cravat. Were they made up like mine, they'd give another air to thy face. Prithee, let me send my man to dress thee but one day; by   110
heavens, an Englishman cannot tie a ribbon.

DOR. They are something clumsy fisted —

SIR FOP. I have brought over the prettiest fellow that ever spread a toilet. He served some time under Merille,[2] the greatest *genie* in the world   115
for a *valet-de-chambre.*

DOR. What! he who formerly belonged to the Duke of Candale?

SIR FOP. The same, and got him his immortal reputation.   120

DOR. Y'have a very fine brandenburgh [3] on, Sir Fopling.

SIR FOP. It serves to wrap me up after the fatigue of a ball.

MED. I see you often in it, with your periwig   125
tied up.

SIR FOP. We should not always be in a set dress; 'tis more *en cavalier* [4] to appear now and then in a *deshabillé.*

MED. Pray, how goes your business with   130
Loveit?

SIR FOP. You might have answered yourself in the Mail last night. Dorimant, did you not see the advances she made me? I have been endeavoring at a song.   135

DOR. Already!

SIR FOP. 'Tis my *coup d'essai* [5] in English: I would fain have thy opinion of it.

DOR. Let's see it.

SIR FOP. Hey, page, give me my song. —   140
Bellair, here; thou hast a pretty voice — sing it.

Y. BELL. Sing it yourself, Sir Fopling.

SIR FOP. Excuse me.

Y. BELL. You learnt to sing in Paris.

SIR FOP. I did — of Lambert,[6] the greatest   145
master in the world. But I have his own fault, a weak voice, and care not to sing out of a *ruelle.*[7]

[1] This saying is attributed to several of the Seven Wise Men of Greece, most frequently to Thales.
[2] Subsequently valet to the Duke of Orleans, brother of Louis XIV and an even more eminent figure in French society than the Duke of Candale, whom Dorimant mentions in his next speech.
[3] Morning gown.   [4] Fashionable.
[5] First attempt.
[6] Michel Lambert, master of chamber music to Louis XIV.
[7] Except in a lady's bedchamber (sc. at a levee).

Dor. [*aside*]. A *ruelle* is a pretty cage for a singing fop, indeed.

Y. Bell. (*reads the song*). 150

> How charming Phillis is, how fair!
> Ah, that she were as willing
> To ease my wounded heart of care,
> And make her eyes less killing.
> I sigh, I sigh, I languish now, 155
> And love will not let me rest;
> I drive about the Park and bow,
> Still as I meet my dearest.

Sir Fop. Sing it! sing it, man; it goes to a pretty new tune which I am confident was made 160 by Baptiste.[1]

Med. Sing it yourself, Sir Fopling; he does not know the tune.

Sir Fop. I'll venture. (Sir Fopling *sings*.)

Dor. Ay, marry! now 'tis something. I shall 165 not flatter you, Sir Fopling; there is not much thought in't, but 'tis passionate and well turned.

Med. After the French way.

Sir Fop. That I aimed at. Does it not give you a lively image of the thing? Slap! down goes 170 the glass,[2] and thus we are at it.

[*He bows and grimaces.*]

Dor. It does, indeed, I perceive, Sir Fopling. You'll be the very head of the sparks who are lucky in compositions of this nature.

Enter Sir Fopling's *Footman*.

Sir Fop. La Tour, is the bath ready? 175

Footm. Yes, sir.

Sir Fop. *Adieu donc, mes chers.*

Exit Sir Fopling.

Med. When have you your revenge on Loveit, Dorimant?

Dor. I will but change my linen and about 180 it.

Med. The powerful considerations which hindered have been removed then?

Dor. Most luckily this morning. You must along with me; my reputation lies at stake 185 there.

Med. I am engaged to Bellair.

Dor. What's your business?

Med. Ma-tri-mony, an't like you.

Dor. It does not, sir. 190

Y. Bell. It may in time, Dorimant: what think you of Mrs. Harriet?

Dor. What does she think of me?

Y. Bell. I am confident she loves you.

Dor. How does it appear? 195

Y. Bell. Why, she's never well but when she's talking of you — but then, she finds all the faults in you she can. She laughs at all who commend you — but then, she speaks ill of all who do not.

Dor. Women of her temper betray them- 200 selves by their over-cunning. I had once a growing love with a lady who would always quarrel with me when I came to see her, and yet was never quiet if I stayed a day from her.

Y. Bell. My father is in love with Emilia. 205

Dor. That is a good warrant for your proceedings. Go on and prosper; I must to Loveit. Medley, I am sorry you cannot be a witness.

Med. Make her meet Sir Fopling again in the same place and use him ill before me. 210

Dor. That may be brought about, I think. I'll be at your aunt's anon and give you joy, Mr. Bellair.

Y. Bell. You had not best think of Mrs. Harriet too much; without church security there's no taking up[3] there. 215

Dor. I may fall into the snare too. But —
The wise will find a difference in our fate;
You wed a woman, I a good estate. *Exeunt.*

Scene III

[*The street before* Mrs. Loveit's *lodgings.*]

Enter the chair with Bellinda; *the men set it down and open it.* Bellinda *starting.*

Bell. (*surprised*). Lord, where am I? — in the Mail! Whither have you brought me?

1 Chairm. You gave us no directions, madam.

Bell. (*aside*). The fright I was in made me forget it. 5

1 Chairm. We use to carry a lady from the Squire's hither.

Bell. (*aside*). This is Loveit: I am undone if she sees me. — Quickly, carry me away!

1 Chairm. Whither, an't like your honor? 10

Bell. Ask no questions —

Enter Mrs. Loveit's *Footman.*

Footm. Have you seen my lady, madam?

Bell. I am just come to wait upon her.

Footm. She will be glad to see you, madam. She sent me to you this morning to desire your com- 15 pany, and I was told you went out by five o'clock.

Bell. (*aside*). More and more unlucky!

Footm. Will you walk in, madam?

Bell. I'll discharge my chair and follow. Tell your mistress I am here. *Exit Footman.* ([Bel- 20 linda] *gives the Chairmen money.*) Take this, and if ever you should be examined, be sure you say you took me up in the Strand over against the Exchange, as you will answer it to Mr. Dorimant.

---

[1] Jean Baptiste Lully, composer, and director of opera for Louis XIV.

[2] The glass window of the coach.

[3] Taking up quarters.

CHAIRM. We will, an't like your honor.   25
Exeunt Chairmen.

BELL. Now to come off, I must on —
In confidence and lies some hope is left;
'Twere hard to be found out in the first theft.
Exit.

ACT V

[SCENE I]

[MRS. LOVEIT'S *lodgings.*]

Enter MRS. LOVEIT *and* PERT, *her woman.*

PERT. Well! in my eyes Sir Fopling is no such despicable person.

LOV. You are an excellent judge!

PERT. He's as handsome a man as Mr. Dorimant, and as great a gallant.   5

LOV. Intolerable! Is't not enough I submit to his impertinences, but must I be plagued with yours too?

PERT. Indeed, madam —

LOV. 'Tis false, mercenary malice —

Enter her Footman.

FOOTM. Mrs. Bellinda, madam.   10

LOV. What of her?

FOOTM. She's below.

LOV. How came she?

FOOTM. In a chair; Ambling Harry brought her.

LOV. [*aside*]. He bring her! His chair stands   15
near Dorimant's door and always brings me from thence. [*To Footman.*] Run and ask him where he took her up. [*Exit Footman.*] Go! there is no truth in friendship neither. Women, as well as men, all are false — or all are so to me, at least.   20

PERT. You are jealous of her too?

LOV. You had best tell her I am. 'Twill become the liberty you take of late. This fellow's bringing of her, her going out by five o'clock — I know not what to think.   25

Enter BELLINDA.

— Bellinda, you are grown an early riser, I hear.

BELL. Do you not wonder, my dear, what made me abroad so soon?

LOV. You do not use to be so.

BELL. The country gentlewomen I told you   30
of (Lord, they have the oddest diversions!) would never let me rest till I promised to go with them to the markets this morning to eat fruit and buy nosegays.

LOV. Are they so fond of a filthy nosegay?   35

BELL. They complain of the stinks of the town, and are never well but when they have their noses in one.

LOV. There are essences and sweet waters.

BELL. Oh, they cry out upon perfumes, they   40
are unwholesome; one of 'em was falling into a fit with the smell of these *nerolii.*[1]

LOV. Methinks in complaisance you should have had a nosegay too.

BELL. Do you think, my dear, I could be so   45
loathsome, to trick myself up with carnations and stock-gillyflowers? I begged their pardon and told them I never wore anything but orange flowers and tuberose. That which made me willing to go, was a strange desire I had to eat some fresh nectarines.   50

LOV. And had you any?

BELL. The best I ever tasted.

LOV. Whence came you now?

BELL. From their lodgings, where I crowded   55
out of a coach and took a chair to come and see you, my dear.

LOV. Whither did you send for that chair?

BELL. 'Twas going by empty.

LOV. Where do these country gentlewomen   60
lodge, I pray?

BELL. In the Strand over against the Exchange.

PERT. That place is never without a nest of 'em. They are always, as one goes by, fleering in balconies or staring out of windows.   65

Enter Footman.

LOV. (*to the Footman*). Come hither! (*Whispers.*)

BELL. (*aside*). This fellow by her order has been questioning the chairmen. I threatened 'em with the name of Dorimant; if they should have told truth, I am lost forever.   70

LOV. In the Strand, said you?

FOOTM. Yes, madam; over against the Exchange.
Exit Footman.

LOV. [*aside*]. She's innocent, and I am much to blame.

BELL. (*aside*). I am so frighted, my coun-   75
tenance will betray me.

LOV. Bellinda, what makes you look so pale?

BELL. Want of my usual rest and jolting up and down so long in an odious hackney.

Footman returns.

FOOTM. Madam, Mr. Dorimant.   80

LOV. What makes him here?

BELL. (*aside*). Then I am betrayed, indeed. H'has broke his word, and I love a man that does not care for me!

LOV. Lord, you faint, Bellinda!   85

BELL. I think I shall — such an oppression here on the sudden.

---

[1] Essences of orange.

PERT. She has eaten too much fruit, I warrant you.

Lov. Not unlikely.

PERT. 'Tis that lies heavy on her stomach. 90

Lov. Have her into my chamber, give her some surfeit water,[1] and let her lie down a little.

PERT. Come, madam! I was a strange [2] devourer of fruit when I was young — so ravenous —

Exeunt BELLINDA, *and* PERT, *leading her off.*

Lov. Oh, that my love would be but calm 95 awhile, that I might receive this man with all the scorn and indignation he deserves!

Enter DORIMANT.

DOR. Now for a touch of Sir Fopling to begin with. — 'Hey, page, give positive order that none of my people stir. Let the *canaille* wait as they 100 should do.' Since noise and nonsense have such powerful charms,

I, that I may successful prove,
Transform myself to what you love.[3]

Lov. If that would do, you need not change 105 from what you are: you can be vain and loud enough.

DOR. But not with so good a grace as Sir Fopling. — 'Hey, Hampshire!' — 'Oh, that sound, that sound becomes the mouth of a man of quality!'

Lov. Is there a thing so hateful as a sense- 110 less mimic?

DOR. He's a great grievance indeed to all who, like yourself, madam, love to play the fool in quiet.

Lov. A ridiculous animal, who has more of the ape than the ape has of the man in him! 115

DOR. I have as mean an opinion of a sheer [4] mimic as yourself; yet were he all ape, I should prefer him to the gay, the giddy, brisk, insipid, noisy fool you dote on.

Lov. Those noisy fools, however you despise 120 'em, have good qualities which weigh more (or ought at least) with us women than all the pernicious wit you have to boast of.

DOR. That I may hereafter have a just value for their merit, pray do me the favor to name 'em. 125

Lov. You'll despise 'em as the dull effects of ignorance and vanity; yet I care not if I mention some. First, they really admire us, while you at best but flatter us well.

DOR. Take heed! Fools can dissemble too. 130

Lov. They may, but not so artificially [5] as you. There is no fear they should deceive us. Then, they are assiduous, sir; they are ever offering us their service, and always waiting on our will.

DOR. You owe that to their excessive idle- 135

ness. They know not how to entertain themselves at home, and find so little welcome abroad they are fain to fly to you who countenance 'em, as a refuge against the solitude they would be otherwise condemned to. 140

Lov. Their conversation, too, diverts us better.

DOR. Playing with your fan, smelling to your gloves, commending your hair, and taking notice how 'tis cut and shaded after the new way —

Lov. Were it sillier than you can make it, 145 you must allow 'tis pleasanter to laugh at others than to be laughed at ourselves, though never so wittily. Then, though they want skill to flatter us, they flatter themselves so well they save us the labor. We need not take that care and pains 150 to satisfy 'em of our love, which we so often lose on you.

DOR. They commonly, indeed, believe too well of themselves, and always better of you than you deserve. 155

Lov. You are in the right. They have an implicit faith in us which keeps 'em from prying narrowly into our secrets and saves us the vexatious trouble of clearing doubts which your subtle and causeless jealousies every moment raise. 160

DOR. There is an inbred falsehood in women which inclines 'em still to them whom they may most easily deceive.

Lov. The man who loves above his quality does not suffer more from the insolent impertinence 165 of his mistress than the woman who loves above her understanding does from the arrogant presumptions of her friend.

DOR. You mistake the use of fools; they are designed for properties, and not for friends. 170 You have an indifferent stock of reputation left yet. Lose it all like a frank gamester on the square; 'twill then be time enough to turn rook [6] and cheat it up again on a good, substantial bubble.[7]

Lov. The old and the ill-favored are only fit 175 for properties, indeed, but young and handsome fools have met with kinder fortunes.

DOR. They have, to the shame of your sex be it spoken! 'Twas this, the thought of this, made me by a timely jealousy endeavor to prevent the 180 good fortune you are providing for Sir Fopling. But against a woman's frailty all our care is vain.

Lov. Had I not with a dear experience bought the knowledge of your falsehood, you might have fooled me yet. This is not the first jealousy 185 you have feigned, to make a quarrel with me and get a week to throw away on some such unknown, inconsiderable slut as you have been lately lurking with at plays.

DOR. Women, when they would break off 190

[1] A medicine to counteract excessive eating.
[2] Notable, extraordinary.
[3] Waller, *To the Mutable Fair*, ll. 5–6, altered.
[4] Pure, mere.
[5] Artfully.

[6] Sharper, swindler.
[7] Dupe.

with a man, never want th' address to turn the fault on him.

Lov. You take a pride of late in using of me ill, that the town may know the power you have over me, which now (as unreasonably as yourself) 195 expects that I (do me all the injuries you can) must love you still.

Dor. I am so far from expecting that you should, I begin to think you never did love me.

Lov. Would the memory of it were so wholly 200 worn out in me, that I did doubt it too! What made you come to disturb my growing quiet?

Dor. To give you joy of your growing infamy.

Lov. Insupportable! Insulting devil! — this from you, the only author of my shame! This 205 from another had been but justice, but from you 'tis a hellish and inhumane outrage. What have I done?

Dor. A thing that puts you below my scorn, and makes my anger as ridiculous as you have made my love.   210

Lov. I walked last night with Sir Fopling.

Dor. You did, madam, and you talked and laughed aloud, 'Ha, ha, ha!' — Oh, that laugh! that laugh becomes the confidence of a woman of quality.   215

Lov. You who have more pleasure in the ruin of a woman's reputation than in the endearments of her love, reproach me not with yourself — and I defy you to name the man can lay a blemish on my fame.   220

Dor. To be seen publicly so transported with the vain follies of that notorious fop, to me is an infamy below the sin of prostitution with another man.

Lov. Rail on! I am satisfied in the justice of what I did; you had provoked me to't.   225

Dor. What I did was the effect of a passion whose extravagancies you have been willing to forgive.

Lov. And what I did was the effect of a passion you may forgive if you think fit.

Dor. Are you so indifferent grown?   230

Lov. I am.

Dor. Nay, then 'tis time to part. I'll send you back your letters you have so often asked for. I have two or three of 'em about me.

Lov. Give 'em me.   235

Dor. You snatch as if you thought I would not. There! [giving her the letters] and may the perjuries in 'em be mine if e'er I see you more!

(Offers to go; she catches him.)

Lov. Stay!

Dor. I will not.   240

Lov. You shall.

Dor. What have you to say?

Lov. I cannot speak it yet.

Dor. Something more in commendation of the fool. — Death, I want patience; let me go!   245

Lov. I cannot. (Aside.) I can sooner part with the limbs that hold him. — I hate that nauseous fool; you know I do.

Dor. Was it the scandal you were fond of then?

Lov. Y'had raised my anger equal to my 250 love — a thing you ne'er could do before, and in revenge I did — I know not what I did. Would you would not think on't any more!

Dor. Should I be willing to forget it, I shall be daily minded of it; 'twill be a commonplace for 255 all the town to laugh at me, and Medley, when he is rhetorically drunk, will ever be declaiming on it in my ears.

Lov. 'Twill be believed a jealous spite. Come, forget it.   260

Dor. Let me consult my reputation; you are too careless of it. (Pauses.) You shall meet Sir Fopling in the Mail again tonight.

Lov. What mean you?

Dor. I have thought on it, and you must. 265 'Tis necessary to justify my love to the world. You can handle a coxcomb as he deserves when you are not out of humor, madam.

Lov. Public satisfaction for the wrong I have done you! This is some new device to make me 270 more ridiculous.

Dor. Hear me!

Lov. I will not.

Dor. You will be persuaded.

Lov. Never!   275

Dor. Are you so obstinate?

Lov. Are you so base?

Dor. You will not satisfy my love?

Lov. I would die to satisfy that; but I will not, to save you from a thousand racks, do a shame- 280 less thing to please your vanity.

Dor. Farewell, false woman!

Lov. Do — go!

Dor. You will call me back again.

Lov. Exquisite fiend, I knew you came but 285 to torment me!

Enter BELLINDA and PERT.

Dor. (surprised). Bellinda here!

Bell. (aside). He starts and looks pale! The sight of me has touched his guilty soul.

Pert. 'Twas but a qualm, as I said — a little 290 indigestion; the surfeit water did it, madam, mixed with a little mirabilis.[1]

Dor. [aside]. I am confounded, and cannot guess how she came hither!

Lov. 'Tis your fortune, Bellinda, ever to be 295 here when I am abused by this prodigy of ill-nature.

---

[1] Aqua mirabilis, an old-fashioned restorative, made of spirits of wine and a variety of spices.

BELL. I am amazed to find him here. How has he the face to come near you?

DOR. (*aside*). Here is fine work towards! I never was at such a loss before.   300

BELL. One who makes a public profession of breach of faith and ingratitude — I loathe the sight of him.

DOR. [*aside*]. There is no remedy; I must submit to their tongues now, and some other time bring   305 myself off as well as I can.

BELL. Other men are wicked; but then, they have some sense of shame. He is never well but when he triumphs — nay, glories to a woman's face in his villainies.   310

LOV. You are in the right, Bellinda, but methinks your kindness for me makes you concern yourself too much with him.

BELL. It does indeed, my dear. His barbarous carriage[1] to you yesterday made me hope you   315 ne'er would see him more, and the very next day to find him here again, provokes me strangely. But because I know you love him, I have done.

DOR. You have reproached me handsomely, and I deserve it for coming hither; but —   320

PERT. You must expect it, sir. All women will hate you for my lady's sake.

DOR. (*aside to* BELLINDA). Nay, if she begins too, 'tis time to fly; I shall be scolded to death else. [*Aloud*.] I am to blame in some circumstances,   325 I confess; but as to the main, I am not so guilty as you imagine. I shall seek a more convenient time to clear myself.

LOV. Do it now. What impediments are here?

DOR. I want time, and you want temper.   330

LOV. These are weak pretenses.

DOR. You were never more mistaken in your life; and so farewell.   DORIMANT *flings off*.

LOV. Call a footman, Pert, quickly; I will have him dogged.   335

PERT. I wish you would not, for my quiet and your own.

LOV. I'll find out the infamous cause of all our quarrels, pluck her mask off, and expose her barefaced to the world!   [*Exit* PERT.] 340

BELL. (*aside*). Let me but escape this time, I'll never venture more.

LOV. Bellinda, you shall go with me.

BELL. I have such a heaviness hangs on me with what I did this morning, I would fain go home   345 and sleep, my dear.

LOV. Death and eternal darkness! I shall never sleep again. Raging fevers seize the world and make mankind as restless all as I am!

Exit MRS. LOVEIT.

BELL. I knew him false and helped to make   350

[1] Demeanor.

him so. Was not her ruin enough to fright me from the danger? It should have been, but love can take no warning.   *Exit* BELLINDA.

SCENE II
LADY TOWNLEY'S *house*.

Enter MEDLEY, YOUNG BELLAIR, LADY TOWNLEY, EMILIA, *and* [SMIRK, *a*] *Chaplain*.

MED. Bear up, Bellair, and do not let us see that repentance in thine we daily do in married faces.

L. TOWN. This wedding will strangely surprise my brother when he knows it.

MED. Your nephew ought to conceal it for   5 a time, madam; since marriage has lost its good name, prudent men seldom expose their own reputations till 'tis convenient to justify their wives.

O. BELL. (*without*). Where are you all there? Out, a dod! will nobody hear?   10

L. TOWN. My brother! Quickly, Mr. Smirk, into this closet! you must not be seen yet.

[SMIRK] *goes into the closet*.

Enter OLD BELLAIR *and* LADY TOWNLEY'S *Page*.

O. BELL. Desire Mr. Fourbe to walk into the lower parlor; I will be with him presently. (*To* YOUNG BELLAIR.) Where have you been, sir, you could   15 not wait on me to-day?

Y. BELL. About a business.

O. BELL. Are you so good at business? A dod, I have a business too, you shall dispatch out of hand, sir. — Send for a parson, sister; my   20 Lady Woodvill and her daughter are coming.

L. TOWN. What need you huddle up things thus?

O. BELL. Out a pize! youth is apt to play the fool, and 'tis not good it should be in their power.

L. TOWN. You need not fear your son.   25

O. BELL. H' has been idling this morning, and a dod, I do not like him. (*To* EMILIA.) How dost thou do, sweetheart?

EMIL. You are very severe, sir — married in such haste.   30

O. BELL. Go to, thou'rt a rogue, and I will talk with thee anon. Here's my Lady Woodvill come.

Enter LADY WOODVILL, HARRIET, *and* BUSY.

— Welcome, madam; Mr. Fourbe's below with the writings.

L. WOOD. Let us down and make an end then.   35

O. BELL. Sister, show the way. (*To* YOUNG BELLAIR, *who is talking to* HARRIET.) Harry, your business lies not there yet. — Excuse him till we have done, lady, and then, a dod, he shall be for thee. Mr. Medley, we must trouble you to be a wit-   40 ness.

MED. I luckily came for that purpose, sir.

Exeunt OLD BELLAIR, YOUNG BELLAIR, LADY
TOWNLEY, *and* LADY WOODVILL.

BUSY. What will you do, madam?

HAR. Be carried back and mewed up in the country again — run away here — anything rather 45
than be married to a man I do not care for! Dear
Emilia, do thou advise me.

EMIL. Mr. Bellair is engaged, you know.

HAR. I do, but know not what the fear of losing
an estate may fright him to. 50

EMIL. In the desperate condition you are in, you
should consult with some judicious man. What
think you of Mr. Dorimant?

HAR. I do not think of him at all.

BUSY [*aside*]. She thinks of nothing else, I am 55
sure.

EMIL. How fond your mother was of Mr. Courtage!

HAR. Because I contrived the mistake to make
a little mirth you believe I like the man. 60

EMIL. Mr. Bellair believes you love him.

HAR. Men are seldom in the right when they
guess at a woman's mind. Would she whom he
loves loved him no better!

BUSY (*aside*). That's e'en well enough, on all 65
conscience.

EMIL. Mr. Dorimant has a great deal of wit.

HAR. And takes a great deal of pains to show it.

EMIL. He's extremely well fashioned.

HAR. Affectedly grave, or ridiculously wild 70
and apish.

BUSY. You defend him still against your mother!

HAR. I would not were he justly rallied, but
I cannot hear anyone undeservedly railed at.

EMIL. Has your woman learnt the song you 75
were so taken with?

HAR. I was fond of a new thing; 'tis dull at a
second hearing.

EMIL. Mr. Dorimant made it.

BUSY. She knows it, madam, and has made 80
me sing it at least a dozen times this morning.

HAR. Thy tongue is as impertinent as thy fingers.

EMIL. You have provoked her.

BUSY. 'Tis but singing the song and I shall appease her. 85

EMILY. Prithee, do.

HAR. She has a voice will grate your ears worse
than a cat-call, and dresses so ill she's scarce fit to
trick up a yeoman's daughter on a holiday.

(BUSY *sings.*)

SONG

BY SIR C. S.[1]

As Amoret with Phyllis sat, 90
One evening on the plain,

And saw the charming Strephon wait
To tell the nymph his pain;

The threat'ning danger to remove,
She whispered in her ear, 95
'Ah, Phyllis, if you would not love,
This shepherd do not hear!

'None ever had so strange an art,
His passion to convey
Into a list'ning virgin's heart, 100
And steal her soul away.

'Fly, fly betimes, for fear you give
Occasion for your fate.'
'In vain,' said she; 'in vain I strive!
Alas, 'tis now too late.' 105

Enter DORIMANT.

DOR. Music so softens and disarms the mind —

HAR. That not one arrow does resistance find.[2]

DOR. Let us make use of the lucky minute, then.

HAR. (*aside, turning from* DORIMANT). My love
springs with my blood into my face; I dare not 110
look upon him yet.

DOR. What have we here? the picture of celebrated beauty giving audience in public to a declared
lover?

HAR. Play the dying fop and make the piece 115
complete, sir.

DOR. What think you if the hint were well improved — the whole mystery[3] of making love
pleasantly designed and wrought in a suit of hangings?[4] 120

HAR. 'Twere needless to execute fools in effigy
who suffer daily in their own persons.

DOR. (*to* EMILIA, *aside*). Mrs. Bride, for such I
know this happy day has made you —

EMIL. [*aside*]. Defer the formal joy you are 125
to give me, and mind your business with her.
(*Aloud.*) Here are dreadful preparations, Mr. Dorimant — writings sealing, and a parson sent for.

DOR. To marry this lady —

BUSY. Condemned she is, and what will be- 130
come of her I know not, without you generously
engage in a rescue.

DOR. In this sad condition, madam, I can do no
less than offer you my service.

HAR. The obligation is not great; you are 135
the common sanctuary for all young women who
run from their relations.

DOR. I have always my arms open to receive the

---

[1] Almost certainly Sir Car Scroope, who wrote the prologue.
[2] Waller, *On My Lady Isabella Playing on the Lute*, ll. 11–12,
altered.
[3] Art.
[4] Drawn and embroidered in a set of draperies.

90] Q2 *sate.*

distressed. But I will open my heart and receive you, where none yet did ever enter. You have   140 filled it with a secret, might I but let you know it —

HAR. Do not speak it if you would have me believe it; your tongue is so famed for falsehood, 'twill do the truth an injury.   (*Turns away her head.*)

DOR. Turn not away, then, but look on me   145 and guess it.

HAR. Did you not tell me there was no credit to be given to faces? — that women nowadays have their passions as much at will as they have their complexions, and put on joy and sadness, scorn   150 and kindness, with the same ease they do their paint and patches? Are they the only counterfeits?

DOR. You wrong your own while you suspect my eyes. By all the hope I have in you, the inimitable color in your cheeks is not more free from art   155 than are the sighs I offer.

HAR. In men who have been long hardened in sin we have reason to mistrust the first signs of repentance.

DOR. The prospect of such a heaven will   160 make me persevere and give you marks that are infallible.

HAR. What are those?

DOR. I will renounce all the joys I have in friendship and in wine, sacrifice to you all the interest   165 I have in other women —

HAR. Hold! Though I wish you devout, I would not have you turn fanatic. Could you neglect these a while and make a journey into the country?

DOR. To be with you, I could live there and   170 never send one thought to London.

HAR. Whate'er you say, I know all beyond High Park's a desert to you, and that no gallantry can draw you farther.

DOR. That has been the utmost limit of my   175 love; but now my passion knows no bounds, and there's no measure to be taken of what I'll do for you from anything I ever did before.

HAR. When I hear you talk thus in Hampshire I shall begin to think there may be some [little]   180 truth enlarged upon.

DOR. Is this all? Will you not promise me —?

HAR. I hate to promise; what we do then is expected from us and wants much of the welcome it finds when it surprises.   185

DOR. May I not hope?

HAR. That depends on you and not on me, and 'tis to no purpose to forbid it.   (*Turns to* BUSY.)

BUSY. Faith, madam, now I perceive the gentleman loves you too, e'en let him know your   190 mind, and torment yourselves no longer.

HAR. Dost think I have no sense of modesty?

BUSY. Think, if you lose this you may never have another opportunity.

HAR. May he hate me (a curse that frights   195 me when I speak it), if ever I do a thing against the rules of decency and honor.

DOR. (*to* EMILIA). I am beholding to you for your good intentions, madam.

EMIL. I thought the concealing of our mar-   200 riage from her might have done you better service.

DOR. Try her again.

EMIL. What have you resolved, madam? The time draws near.

HAR. To be obstinate and protest against   205 this marriage.

Enter LADY TOWNLEY *in haste.*

L. TOWN. (*to* EMILIA). Quickly, quickly! let Mr. Smirk out of the closet.

                           (SMIRK *comes out of the closet.*)

HAR. A parson! [*To* DORIMANT.] Had you laid him in here?   210

DOR. I knew nothing of him.

HAR. Should it appear you did, your opinion of my easiness may cost you dear.

Enter OLD BELLAIR, YOUNG BELLAIR, MEDLEY, *and* LADY WOODVILL.

O. BELL. Out a pize! the canonical hour [1] is almost past. Sister, is the man of God come?   215

L. TOWN. He waits your leisure.

O. BELL. [*to* SMIRK]. By your favor, sir. — A dod, a pretty spruce fellow. What may we call him?

L. TOWN. Mr. Smirk — my Lady Biggot's chaplain.   220

O. BELL. A wise woman! a dod, she is. The man will serve for the flesh as well as the spirit. [*To* SMIRK.] Please you, sir, to commission a young couple to go to bed together a God's name? — Harry!

Y. BELL. Here, sir.   225

O. BELL. Out a pize! Without your mistress in your hand!

SMIRK. Is this the gentleman?

O. BELL. Yes, sir.

SMIRK. Are you not mistaken, sir?   230

O. BELL. A dod, I think not, sir.

SMIRK. Sure, you are, sir!

O. BELL. You look as if you would forbid the banns, Mr. Smirk. I hope you have no pretension to the lady.   235

SMIRK. Wish him joy, sir; I have done him the good office to-day already.

O. BELL. Out a pize! What do I hear?

[1] The time (at this period from eight to twelve o'clock in the morning) during which a marriage could be legally performed.

180] Brett-Smith notes the presence of *little* after *some* in this line in several copies of Q1: it is not in any copies I have examined, or in Q2.

234] Q1Q2 *bains*.

L. Town. Never storm, brother; the truth is out.

O. Bell. How say you, sir? Is this your 240 wedding day?

Y. Bell. It is, sir.

O. Bell. And a dod, it shall be mine too. (*To* Emilia.) Give me thy hand, sweetheart. What dost thou mean? Give me thy hand, I say. 245

(Emilia *kneels and* Young Bellair.)

L. Town. Come, come! give her your blessing; this is the woman your son loved and is married to.

O. Bell. Ha! cheated! cozened! and by your contrivance, sister!

L. Town. What would you do with her? 250 She's a rogue and you can't abide her.

Med. Shall I hit her a pat for you, sir?

O. Bell. [*flinging away*]. A dod, you are all rogues, and I never will forgive you.

L. Town. Whither? Whither away? 255

Med. Let him go and cool awhile.

L. Wood. (*to* Dorimant). Here's a business broke out now, Mr. Courtage; I am made a fine fool of.

Dor. You see the old gentleman knew nothing of it. 260

L. Wood. I find he did not. I shall have some trick put upon me if I stay in this wicked town any longer. — Harriet, dear child, where art thou? I'll into the country straight.

O. Bell. A dod, madam, you shall hear me 265 first.

Enter Mrs. Loveit *and* Bellinda.

Lov. Hither my man dogged him.

Bell. Yonder he stands, my dear.

Lov. I see him (*aside*) and with him the face that has undone me. Oh, that I were but where I 270 might throw out the anguish of my heart! Here it must rage within and break it.

L. Town. Mrs. Loveit! Are you afraid to come forward?

Lov. I was amazed to see so much company 275 here in a morning. The occasion sure is extraordinary.

Dor. (*aside*). Loveit and Bellinda! The devil owes me a shame to-day and I think never will have done paying it. 280

Lov. Married! dear Emilia! How am I transported with the news!

Har. (*to* Dorimant). I little thought Emilia was the woman Mr. Bellair was in love with. I'll chide her for not trusting me with the secret. 285

Dor. How do you like Mrs. Loveit?

Har. She's a famed mistress of yours, I hear.

Dor. She has been, on occasion.

O. Bell. (*to* Lady Woodvill). A dod, madam, I cannot help it. 290

L. Wood. You need make no more apologies, sir.

Emil. (*to* Mrs. Loveit). The old gentleman's excusing himself to my Lady Woodvill.

Lov. Ha, ha, ha! I never heard of anything so pleasant! 295

Har. (*to* Dorimant). She's extremely overjoyed at something.

Dor. At nothing. She is one of those hoyting [1] ladies who gaily fling themselves about and force a laugh when their aching hearts are full of dis- 300 content and malice.

Lov. O heaven! I was never so near killing myself with laughing. — Mr. Dorimant, are you a brideman?

L. Wood. Mr. Dorimant! — Is this Mr. 305 Dorimant, madam?

Lov. If you doubt it, your daughter can resolve you, I suppose.

L. Wood. I am cheated too — basely cheated!

O. Bell. Out a pize! what's here? More 310 knavery yet?

L. Wood. Harriet, on my blessing come away, I charge you!

Har. Dear mother, do but stay and hear me.

L. Wood. I am betrayed and thou art un- 315 done, I fear.

Har. Do not fear it; I have not, nor never will, do anything against my duty — believe me, dear mother, do!

Dor. (*to* Mrs. Loveit). I had trusted you 320 with this secret but that I knew the violence of your nature would ruin my fortune, as now unluckily it has. I thank you, madam.

Lov. She's an heiress, I know, and very rich.

Dor. To satisfy you, I must give up my in- 325 terest wholly to my love. Had you been a reasonable woman, I might have secured 'em both and been happy.

Lov. You might have trusted me with anything of this kind — you know you might. Why did 330 you go under a wrong name?

Dor. The story is too long to tell you now. Be satisfied, this is the business; this is the mask has kept me from you.

Bell. (*aside*). He's tender of my honor 335 though he's cruel to my love.

Lov. Was it no idle mistress, then?

Dor. Believe me, a wife to repair the ruins of my estate, that needs it.

Lov. The knowledge of this makes my grief 340 hang lighter on my soul, but I shall never more be happy.

Dor. Bellinda!

Bell. Do not think of clearing yourself with me; it is impossible. Do all men break their words 345 thus?

Dor. Th'extravagant words they speak in love.

[1] Hoydenish, romping.

'Tis as unreasonable to expect we should perform all we promise then, as do all we threaten when we are angry. When I see you next — 350

BELL. Take no notice of me, and I shall not hate you.

DOR. How came you to Mrs. Loveit?

BELL. By a mistake the chairmen made for want of my giving them directions. 355

DOR. 'Twas a pleasant one. We must meet again.

BELL. Never.

DOR. Never!

BELL. When we do, may I be as infamous as you are false. 360

L. TOWN. [to LADY WOODVILL]. Men of Mr. Dorimant's character always suffer in the general opinion of the world.

MED. You can make no judgment of a witty man from common fame, considering the prevailing 365 faction, madam.

O. BELL. A dod, he's in the right.

MED. Besides, 'tis a common error among women to believe too well of them they know, and too ill of them they don't. 370

O. BELL. A dod, he observes well.

L. TOWN. Believe me, madam, you will find Mr. Dorimant as civil a gentleman as you thought Mr. Courtage.

HAR. If you would but know him better — 375

L. WOOD. You have a mind to know him better! Come away! You shall never see him more.

HAR. Dear mother, stay!

L. WOOD. I wo'not be consenting to your ruin.

HAR. Were my fortune in your power — 380

L. WOOD. Your person is.

HAR. Could I be disobedient, I might take it out of yours and put it into his.

L. WOOD. 'Tis that you would be at; you would marry this Dorimant. 385

HAR. I cannot deny it; I would, and never will marry any other man.

L. WOOD. Is this the duty that you promised?

HAR. But I will never marry him against your will.

L. WOOD. (aside). She knows the way to 390 melt my heart. — (To HARRIET.) Upon yourself light your undoing!

MED. (to OLD BELLAIR). Come, sir, you have not the heart any longer to refuse your blessing.

O. BELL. A dod, I ha' not. — Rise, and God 395 bless you both! Make much of her, Harry; she deserves thy kindness. (To EMILIA.) A dod, sirrah, I did not think it had been in thee

Enter SIR FOPLING *and's Page.*

SIR FOP. 'Tis a damned windy day. — Hey, page, is my periwig right? 400

PAGE. A little out of order, sir.

SIR FOP. Pox o' this apartment! It wants an antechamber to adjust oneself in. (*To* MRS. LOVEIT.) Madam, I came from your house, and your servants directed me hither. 405

LOV. I will give order hereafter they shall direct you better.

SIR FOP. The great satisfaction I had in the Mail last night has given me much disquiet since.

LOV. 'Tis likely to give me more than I 410 desire.

SIR FOP. [aside]. What the devil makes her so reserved? — Am I guilty of an indiscretion, madam?

LOV. You will be of a great one if you continue your mistake, sir. 415

SIR FOP. Something puts you out of humor.

LOV. The most foolish, inconsiderable thing that ever did.

SIR FOP. Is it in my power?

LOV. To hang or drown it. Do one of 'em 420 and trouble me no more.

SIR FOP. So *fière*? *Serviteur*, madam! [1] — Medley, where's Dorimant?

MED. Methinks the lady has not made you those advances today she did last night, Sir Fopling. 425

SIR FOP. Prithee, do not talk of her!

MED. She would be a *bonne fortune*.

SIR FOP. Not to me at present.

MED. How so?

SIR FOP. An intrigue now would be but a 430 temptation to me to throw away that vigor on one which I mean shall shortly make my court to the whole sex in a ballet.

MED. Wisely considered, Sir Fopling.

SIR FOP. No one woman is worth the loss of 435 a cut [2] in a caper.

MED. Not when 'tis so universally designed.

L. WOOD. Mr. Dorimant, everyone has spoke so much in your behalf that I can no longer doubt but I was in the wrong. 440

LOV. [to BELLINDA]. There's nothing but falsehood and impertinence in this world; all men are villains or fools. Take example from my misfortunes. Bellinda, if thou wouldst be happy, give thyself wholly up to goodness. 445

HAR. (to MRS. LOVEIT). Mr. Dorimant has been your God Almighty long enough; 'tis time to think of another.

LOV. Jeered by her! I will lock myself up in my house and never see the world again. 450

HAR. A nunnery is the more fashionable place for such a retreat, and has been the fatal consequence of many a *belle passion*.

[1] So fierce? Your servant, madam!
[2] A rapid 'twiddling' of the feet by a dancer whc has sprung in the air.

375] Q2 *If you have mind to know him better —*

Lov. [aside]. Hold, heart, till I get home! Should I answer, 'twould make her triumph greater. 455
(Is going out.)

Dor. Your hand, Sir Fopling —

Sir Fop. Shall I wait upon you, madam?

Lov. Legion of fools, as many devils take thee!
Exit Mrs. Loveit.

Med. Dorimant, I pronounce thy reputation clear; and henceforward when I would know 460 anything of woman, I will consult no other oracle.

Sir Fop. [gazing after Mrs. Loveit]. Stark mad, by all that's handsome! — Dorimant, thou hast engaged me in a pretty business.

Dor. I have not leisure now to talk about it. 465

O. Bell. [indicating Sir Fopling]. Out a pize! what does this man of mode do here again?

L. Town. He'll be an excellent entertainment within, brother, and is luckily come to raise the mirth of the company. 470

L. Wood. Madam, I take my leave of you.

L. Town. What do you mean, madam?

L. Wood. To go this afternoon part of my way to Hartly.[1]

O. Bell. A dod, you shall stay and dine first! 475 Come, we will all be good friends, and you shall give Mr. Dorimant leave to wait upon you and your daughter in the country.

L. Wood. If his occasions bring him that way,

[1] ?Hartley Row, Hampshire, about half-way between London and Salisbury.

I have now so good an opinion of him, he shall 480 be welcome.

Har. — To a great rambling, lone house that looks as it were not inhabited, the family's so small. There you'll find my mother, an old lame aunt, and myself, sir, perched up on chairs at a distance in 485 a large parlor, sitting moping like three or four melancholy birds in a spacious volary.[2] Does not this stagger your resolution?

Dor. Not at all, madam. The first time I saw you you left me with the pangs of love upon me, 490 and this day my soul has quite given up her liberty.

Har. This is more dismal than the country! Emilia, pity me, who am going to that sad place. Methinks I hear the hateful noise of rooks already — kaw, kaw, kaw! There's music in the worst 495 cry[3] in London — 'My dill and cowcumbers to pickle!'

O. Bell. Sister, knowing of this matter, I hope you have provided us some good cheer.

L. Town. I have, brother, and the fiddles 500 too.

O. Bell. Let 'em strike up, then; the young lady shall have a dance before she departs.   (Dance.)
(After the dance.) — So! now we'll in and make this an arrant wedding-day.   (To the pit.) 505

And if these honest gentlemen rejoice,
A dod, the boy has made a happy choice.
Exeunt omnes.

[2] Aviary.   [3] Street-vendor's cry.

EPILOGUE

By Mr. DRYDEN

Most modern wits such monstrous fools have shown,
They seemed not of heav'n's making, but their own.
Those nauseous harlequins in farce may pass,
But there goes more to a substantial ass.
Something of man must be exposed to view   5
That, gallants, they may more resemble you.
Sir Fopling is a fool so nicely writ,
The ladies would mistake him for a wit;
And when he sings, talks loud, and cocks,[1] would cry,
'I vow, methinks he's pretty company!   10
So brisk, so gay, so travelled, so refined,
As he took pains to graff upon his kind.'[2]
True fops help nature's work and go to school,
To file and finish God A'mighty's fool.
Yet none Sir Fopling him, or him, can call;   15
He's knight o'th' shire,[3] and represents ye all.
From each he meets, he culls whate'er he can;
Legion's his name, a people in a man.
His bulky folly gathers as it goes
And, rolling o'er you, like a snowball grows.   20
His various modes from various fathers follow;
One taught the toss,[4] and one the new French wallow.[5]
His sword-knot, this; his cravat, this designed;
And this, the yard-long snake [6] he twirls behind.
From one the sacred periwig he gained,   25
Which wind ne'er blew, nor touch of hat profaned.
Another's diving bow he did adore,
Which with a shog [7] casts all the hair before
Till he with full decorum brings it back,
And rises with a water spaniel shake.   30
As for his songs (the ladies' dear delight),
Those sure he took from most of you who write.
Yet every man is safe from what he feared,
For no one fool is hunted from the herd.

---

[1] Cocks his hat.   [2] As if he had taken pains to improve his natural talents.
[3] A representative (properly, in parliament).   [4] An upward jerk of the head.   [5] A rolling gait.
[6] A long curl or tail attached to a wig.   [7] A shake.

The Plain Dealer

BY WILLIAM WYCHERLEY

The Plain-Dealer.

ACT I. SCENE I.

Captain Manly's *Lodging.*

Enter Captain Manly, *surlily; and my Lord* Plausible *following him:
and two* Sailors *behind.*

Man. Ell not me (my good Lord *Plausible*) of your *Decorums*, supercilious Forms, and slavish Ceremonies; your little Tricks, which you the Spaniels of the World, do daily over and over, for, and to one another; not out of love or duty, but your servile fear.

L. Plauf. Nay, i'faith, i'faith, you are too passionate, and I must humbly beg your pardon and leave to tell you, they are the Arts, and Rules, the prudent of the World walk by.

Man. Let 'em. But I'll have no Leading-strings, I can walk alone; I hate a Harness, and will not tug on in a Faction, kissing my Leader behind, that another Slave may do the like to me.

L. Plauf. What will you be singular then, like no Body? follow Love, and esteem no Body?

Man. Rather than be general, like you; follow every Body, Court and kiss every Body; though, perhaps at the same time, you hate every Body.

L. Plauf. Why, seriously with your pardon, my dear Friend——

Man. With your pardon, my no Friend, I will not, as you do, whisper my hatred, or my scorn, call a man Fool or Knave, by signs, or mouths over his shoulder, whil'st you have him in your arms; for such as you, like common Whores and Pickpockets, are only dangerous to those you embrace.

L. Plauf. Such as I! Heav'ns defend me —upon my Honour——

Man. Upon your Title, my Lord, if you'd have me believe you.

L. Plauf. Well then, as I am a Person of Honour, I never attempted to abuse, or lessen any person, in my life.

Man. What, you were afraid?

L. Plauf. No; but seriously, I hate to do a rude thing: no, faith, I speak well of all Mankind.

Man. I thought so; but know that speaking well of all Mankind, is the worst kind of Detraction; for it takes away the Reputation of the few good

B   men

DEDICATION

To my Lady B —— [1]

Madam,

Though I never had the honor to receive a favor from you, or be known to you, I take the confidence of an author to write to you a *billet doux* dedicatory; which is no new thing, for by most dedications it appears that authors, though they praise their patrons from top to toe, and seem to turn 'em inside out, know 'em as little as sometimes their patrons their books, though they read them out; and if the poetical daubers did not write the name of the man or woman on top of the picture, 'twere impossible to guess whose it were. But you, madam, without the help of a poet, have made yourself known and famous in the world, and, because you do not want it, are therefore most worthy of an epistle dedicatory. And this play claims naturally your protection, since it has lost its reputation with the ladies of stricter lives in the playhouse; and (you know) when men's endeavors are discountenanced and refused by the nice, coy women of honor, they come to you, to you, the great and noble patroness of rejected and bashful men, of which number I profess myself to be one, though a poet, a dedicating poet — to you, I say, madam, who have as discerning a judgment in what's obscene or not as any quick-sighted, civil person of 'em all, and can make as much of a double-meaning saying as the best of 'em, yet would not, as some do, make nonsense of a poet's jest, rather than not make it bawdy: by which they show they as little value wit in a play as in a lover, provided they can bring t'other thing about. Their sense, indeed, lies all one way, and therefore are only for that in a poet which is moving, as they say; but what do they mean by that word 'moving'? Well, I must not put 'em to the blush, since I find I can do't. In short, madam, you would not be one of those who ravish a poet's innocent words, and make 'em guilty of their own naughtiness (as 'tis termed) in spite of his teeth; nay, nothing is secure from the power of their imaginations — no, not their husbands, whom they cuckold with themselves, by thinking of other men, and so make the lawful matrimonial embraces adultery — wrong husbands and poets in thought and word to keep their own reputations: but your ladyship's justice, I know, would think a woman's arraigning and damning a poet for her own obscenity like her crying out a rape and hanging a man for giving her pleasure, only that she might be thought not to consent to't; and so to vindicate her honor forfeits her modesty. But you, madam, have too much modesty to pretend to't, though you have as much to say for your modesty as many a nicer she; for you never were seen at this play, no, not the first day; and 'tis no matter what people's lives have been, they are unquestionably modest who frequent not this play: for, as Mr. Bayes says of his, that is the only touchstone of men's wit and understanding; [2] mine is, it seems, the only touchstone of women's virtue and modesty. But hold! — that touchstone is equivocal, and by the strength of a lady's imagination may become something that is not civil; but your ladyship, I know, scorns to misapply a touchstone. And, madam, though you have not seen this play, I hope (like other nice ladies) you will the rather read it; yet lest the chambermaid or page should not be trusted and their indulgence could gain no further admittance for it than to their ladies' lobbies or outward rooms, take it into your care and protection, for by your recommendation and procurement it may have the honor to get into their closets; for what they renounce in public often entertains 'em there, with your help especially. In fine, madam, for these and many other reasons you are the fittest patroness or judge of this play; for you show no partiality to this or that author; for from some many ladies will take a broad jest as cheerfully as from the watermen,[3] and sit at some downright filthy plays (as they call 'em) as well satisfied, and as still, as a poet could wish 'em elsewhere: therefore it must be the doubtful obscenity of my plays alone they take exceptions at, because it is too bashful for 'em; and indeed most women hate men for attempting to halves on their chastity; and bawdy, I find, like satire, should be home, not to have it taken notice of. But now I mention satire, some there are who say 'tis the plain dealing of the play, not the obscenity; 'tis taking off the ladies' masks, not offering at their petticoats, which offends 'em; and generally they are not the handsomest, or most innocent, who are the most angry at being discovered:

—————— Nihil est audacius illis
Deprehensis; iram, atque animos a crimine sumunt.[4]

—————

[1] 'Mother' (or 'Lady') Bennet, a well-known procuress.   [2] *The Rehearsal*, III. i. 142.
[3] The watermen who rowed boats on the Thames had an immemorial license of speech.
[4] 'Nothing is bolder than they when they are detected; they assume an attitude of indignation and arrogance when they are accused.' Juvenal, *Satires*, VI, 284, 285.

—————

5] Q1 *read 'em out.*   8] Q4Q6 om. *of.*   32] Q4Q6 *indulgences.*
33] Q6W1 *room.*   39] W1 *play.*   40] Q4 *must woman.*

Pardon, madam, the quotation, for a dedication can no more be without ends of Latin than flattery; and 'tis no matter whom it is writ to, for an author can as easily (I hope) suppose people to have more understanding and languages than they have, as well as more virtues. But why the devil should any of the few modest and handsome be alarmed? — for some there are who as well as any deserve those attributes, yet refrain not from seeing this play, nor think it any addition to their virtue to set up for it [1] in a playhouse, lest it should look too much like acting. But why, I say, should any at all of the truly virtuous be concerned, if those who are not so are distinguished from 'em? For by that mask of modesty which women wear promiscuously in public they are all alike, and you can no more know a kept wench from a woman of honor by her looks than by her dress; for those who are of quality without honor (if any such there are) they have their quality to set off their false modesty, as well as their false jewels, and you must no more suspect their countenances for counterfeit than their pendants, though, as the plain dealer Montaigne says, '*Elles envoyent leur conscience au bordel, et tiennent leur contenance en règle!*' [2] but those who act as they look ought not be scandalized at the reprehension of others' faults, lest they tax themselves with 'em, and by too delicate and quick an apprehension not only make that obscene which I meant innocent, but that satire on all, which was intended only on those who deserved it. But, madam, I beg your pardon for this digression to civil women and ladies of honor, since you and I shall never be the better for 'em; for a comic poet and a lady of your profession make most of the other sort, and the stage and your houses, like our plantations, are propagated by the least nice women; and as with ministers of justice, the vices of the age are our best business. But, now I mention public persons, I can no longer defer doing you the justice of a dedication and telling you your own, who are, of all public-spirited people, the most necessary, most communicative, most generous and hospitable; your house has been the house of the people, your sleep still disturbed for the public, and when you arose, 'twas that others might lie down, and you waked that others might rest. The good you have done is unspeakable: how many young, unexperienced heirs have you kept from rash, foolish marriages? and from being jilted for their lives by the worst sort of jilts, wives? how many unbewitched widowers' children have you preserved from the tyranny of stepmothers? how many old dotards from cuckoldage, and keeping other men's wenches and children? how many adulteries and unnatural sins have you prevented? In fine, you have been a constant scourge to the old lecher, and often a terror to the young; you have made concupiscence its own punishment, and extinguished lust with lust, like blowing up of houses to stop the fire.

> Nimirum propter continentiam, incontinentia
> Necessaria est, incendium ignibus extinguitur.[3]

There's Latin for you again, madam; I protest to you, as I am an author, I cannot help it; nay, I can hardly keep myself from quoting Aristotle and Horace, and talking to you of the rules of writing (like the French authors) to show you and my reader I understand 'em, in my epistle, lest neither of you should find it out by the play; and, according to the rules of dedications, 'tis no matter whether you understand or no what I quote or say to you of writing; for an author can as easily make any one a judge or critic, in an epistle, as an hero in his play: but, madam, that this may prove to the end a true epistle dedicatory, I'd have you know 'tis not without a design upon you, which is in the behalf of the fraternity of Parnassus, that songs and sonnets may go at your houses and in your liberties [4] for guineas and half-guineas, and that wit, at least with you, as of old, may be the price of beauty; and so you will prove a true encourager of poetry, for love is a better help to it than wine, and poets, like painters, draw better after the life than by fancy; nay, in justice, madam, I think a poet ought to be as free of your houses as of the playhouses, since he contributes to the support of both, and is as necessary to such as you as a ballad-singer to the pick-purse, in convening the cullies at the theatres, to be picked up and carried to supper and bed at your houses. And, madam, the reason of this motion of mine is because poor poets can get no favor in the tiring-rooms, for they are no keepers, you know; and folly and money, the old enemies of wit, are even too hard for it on its own dunghill; and for other ladies, a poet can least go to the price of them; besides, his wit, which ought to recommend him to 'em, is as much an obstruction to his love as to his wealth or preferment; for most women nowadays apprehend wit in a lover as much as in a husband: they hate a man that knows 'em: they must have a blind, easy fool whom they can lead by the nose, and as the Scythian women of old, must baffle [5] a man and put out his eyes ere they will

---

[1] Lay claim to it.

[2] *Essays*, III, 5: 'They send their conscience to the brothel, and keep their countenance in order.' Wycherley has altered '*Ils*' to '*Elles.*'

[3] Tertullian, *De Pudicitia*, chapter 1. The substance of the quotation is contained in the preceding sentence of the text. It is prose, not verse, in the original.

[4] Precincts.   [5] Hoodwink.

---

lie with him; and then too, like thieves, when they have plundered and stript a man, leave him.   But if there should be one of an hundred of those ladies generous enough to give herself to a man that has more wit than money, all things considered, he would think it cheaper coming to you for a mistress, though you made him pay his guinea, as a man in a journey, out of good husbandry, had better pay for what he has in an inn, than lie on free-cost at a gentleman's house.

In fine, madam, like a faithful dedicator, I hope I have done myself right in the first place, then you and your profession, which, in the wisest and most religious government of the world is honored with the public allowance, and in those that are thought the most uncivilized and barbarous is protected and supported by the ministers of justice; and of you, madam, I ought to say no more here, for your virtues deserve a poem rather than an epistle, or a volume entire to give the world your memoirs or life at large, and which (upon the word of an author that has a mind to make an end of his dedication) I promise to do, when I write the annals of our British love, which shall be dedicated to the ladies concerned, if they will not think them something too obscene too; when your life, compared with many that are thought innocent, I doubt not may vindicate you, and me, to the world, for the confidence I have taken in this address to you, which then may be thought neither impertinent nor immodest; and whatsoever your amorous misfortunes have been, none can charge you with that heinous and worst of women's crimes, hypocrisy; nay, in spite of misfortunes or age, you are the same woman still; though most of your sex grow Magdalens at fifty, and, as a solid French author [1] has it,

> Après le plaisir vient la peine,
> Après la peine, la vertu. [2]

But sure, an old sinner's continency is much like a gamester's forswearing play when he has lost all his money; and modesty is a kind of a youthful dress which, as it makes a young woman more amiable, makes an old one more nauseous; a bashful old woman is like an hopeful old man; and the affected chastity of antiquated beauties is rather a reproach than an honor to 'em, for it shows the men's virtue only, not theirs. But you, in fine, madam, are no more an hypocrite, than I am when I praise you; therefore I doubt not will be thought (even by yours and the play's enemies, the nicest ladies) to be the fittest patroness for,

Madam,
Your ladyship's most obedient,
Faithful, humble servant, and
The Plain Dealer.

[1] Not identified.   [2] 'After pleasure comes pain; after pain, virtue.'

102] W1 *in the world.*   116] Q4Q6W1 *had.*

PROLOGUE.

SPOKEN BY THE PLAIN DEALER.

I the Plain Dealer am to act today,
And my rough part begins before the play.
First, you who scribble, yet hate all that write,
And keep each other company in spite,
As rivals in your common mistress, Fame,   5
And with faint praises one another damn —
'Tis a good play, we know, you can't forgive,
But grudge yourselves the pleasure you receive:
Our scribbler therefore bluntly bid me say,
He would not have the wits pleased here today.   10
Next you, the fine, loud gentlemen o' th' pit,
Who damn all plays, yet, if y'ave any wit,
'Tis but what here you sponge and daily get —
Poets, like friends to whom you are in debt,
You hate; and so rooks laugh, to see undone   15
Those pushing gamesters whom they live upon.
Well, you are sparks, and still will be i' th' fashion;
Rail then at plays, to hide your obligation.
Now, you shrewd judges, who the boxes sway,
Leading the ladies' hearts and sense astray,   20
And, for their sakes, see all, and hear no play —
Correct your cravats, foretops, lock behind;
The dress and breeding of the play ne'er mind;
Plain dealing is, you'll say, quite out of fashion;
You'll hate it here, as in a dedication;   25
And your fair neighbors, in a limning poet [1]
No more than in a painter will allow it.
Pictures too like, the ladies will not please;
They must be drawn too here like goddesses.
You, as at Lely's [2] too, would truncheon [3] wield,   30
And look like heroes in a painted field;
But the coarse dauber of the coming scenes
To follow life and nature only means,
Displays you as you are: makes his fine woman
A mercenary jilt, and true to no man;   35
His men of wit and pleasure of the age
Are as dull rogues as ever cumbered stage:
He draws a friend only to custom just,
And makes him naturally break his trust.
I, only, act a part like none of you,   40
And yet, you'll say, it is a fool's part too:
An honest man who, like you, never winks
At faults, but, unlike you, speaks what he thinks:
The only fool who ne'er found patron yet,
For truth is now a fault as well as wit.   45
And where else but on stages do we see
Truth pleasing, or rewarded honesty?
Which our bold poet does this day in me.
If not to th' honest, be to th' prosp'rous kind:
Some friends at court let the Plain Dealer find.   50

---

[1] A poet who depicts life.   [2] Sir Peter Lely was the popular court-painter of the day.
[3] A military baton, carried by a high-ranking officer.

24] W1 *you'ld.*   32] Q1Q3Q4Q6W1 *course.*   33] W1 *life, and nature's only means.*

THE PERSONS

MANLY, of an honest, surly, nice humor, supposed first, in the time of the Dutch War,[1] to have procured the command of a ship, out of honor, not interest, and choosing a sea-life only to avoid the world.

FREEMAN, MANLY's lieutenant, a gentleman well educated, but of a broken fortune; a complier with the age.

VERNISH, MANLY's bosom and only friend.

NOVEL, a pert railing coxcomb, and an admirer of novelties; makes love to OLIVIA.

MAJOR OLDFOX,[2] an old impertinent fop, given to scribbling; makes love to the WIDOW BLACKACRE.

LORD PLAUSIBLE, a ceremonious, supple, commending coxcomb, in love with OLIVIA.

JERRY BLACKACRE, a true raw squire, under age, and his mother's government; bred to the law.

[SERJEANT PLODDON,
[QUAINT,
[BLUNDER,
[PETULANT,
[BUTTONGOWN,
[SPLITCAUSE, } lawyers]

OLIVIA, MANLY's mistress.

FIDELIA [GREY], in love with MANLY, and followed him to sea in man's clothes.

ELIZA, cousin to OLIVIA.

LETTICE, OLIVIA's woman.

The WIDOW BLACKACRE, a petulant, litigious widow, always in law, and mother to Squire JERRY.

Lawyers, Knights of the Post, Bailiffs, an Alderman, a Bookseller's 'Prentice, a Footboy, Sailors, Waiters, and Attendants.

THE SCENE: LONDON.

---

[1] Probably the war of 1664–1667, rather than that of 1672–1674, in which there was less opportunity for the trading by the sailors which is referred to in I. i. 130–137. If so, this fact lends color to the probability that the first draft of the play was written when Wycherley was twenty-five, in accordance with his statement to Pope.

[2] 'Fox,' in this compound name, signifies 'sword.' The meanings of the other 'label-names' are obvious, except 'Blackacre.' This last was a conventional name for a piece of land, which was used in stating hypothetical law-cases, as 'John Doe' and 'Richard Roe' are used to designate persons involved in a law suit.

20] Q4 *and Alderman;* Q6W1 *and Aldermen.*

THE PLAIN DEALER

By WILLIAM WYCHERLEY

— Ridiculum acri
Fortius et melius magnas plerumque secat res.[1]

ACT I

SCENE I

CAPTAIN MANLY'S *lodging.*

Enter CAPTAIN MANLY, *surlily, and my* LORD
PLAUSIBLE, *following him; and two Sailors
behind.*

MAN. Tell not me, my good Lord Plausible, of
your decorums, supercilious forms, and slavish
ceremonies! your little tricks, which you, the spaniels
of the world, do daily over and over, for and to one
another; not out of love or duty, but your servile   5
fear.

L. PLAUS. Nay, i' faith, i' faith, you are too passionate, and I must humbly beg your pardon and
leave to tell you, they are the arts and rules the
prudent of the world walk by.   10

MAN. Let 'em. But I'll have no leading-strings,
I can walk alone; I hate a harness, and will not tug
on in a faction, kissing my leader behind, that another slave may do the like to me.

L. PLAUS. What, will you be singular then,   15
like nobody? follow love, and esteem nobody?[2]

MAN. Rather than be general, like you, follow
everybody, court and kiss everybody; though perhaps at the same time you hate everybody.

L. PLAUS. Why, seriously, with your pardon,   20
my dear friend —

MAN. With your pardon, my no friend, I will
not, as you do, whisper my hatred or my scorn, call
a man fool or knave by signs or mouths over his
shoulder, whilst you have him in your arms; for   25
such as you, like common whores and pickpockets,
are only dangerous to those you embrace.

L. PLAUS. Such as I! Heavens defend me! —
upon my honor —

MAN. Upon your title. my lord, if you'd have   30
me believe you.

L. PLAUS. Well then, as I am a person of honor,

I never attempted to abuse or lessen any person
in my life.

MAN. What, you were afraid?   35

L. PLAUS. No; but seriously, I hate to do a rude
thing: no, faith, I speak well of all mankind.

MAN. I thought so: but know, that speaking well
of all mankind is the worst kind of detraction; for
it takes away the reputation of the few good   40
men in the world, by making all alike. Now, I
speak ill of most men, because they deserve it —
I that can do a rude thing, rather than an unjust
thing.

L. PLAUS. Well, tell not me, my dear friend,   45
what people deserve; I ne'er mind that. I, like an
author in a dedication, never speak well of a man
for his sake, but my own; I will not disparage any
man, to disparage myself; for to speak ill of people
behind their backs is not like a person of honor;   50
and, truly to speak ill of 'em to their faces, is not like
a complaisant person. But if I did say or do an ill
thing to any, it should be sure to be behind their
backs, out of pure good manners.

MAN. Very well; but I, that am an unman-   55
nerly sea-fellow, if I ever speak well of people (which
is very seldom indeed), it should be sure to be behind
their backs; and if I would say or do ill to any, it
should be to their faces. I would justle a proud, strutting, overlooking coxcomb, at the head of his   60
sycophants, rather than put out my tongue at him
when he were past me; would frown in the arrogant,
big, dull face of an overgrown knave of business,
rather than vent my spleen against him when his
back were turned; would give fawning slaves   65
the lie whilst they embrace or commend me; cowards
whilst they brag; call a rascal by no other title,
though his father had left him a duke's; laugh at
fools aloud before their mistresses; and must desire
people to leave me, when their visits grow at   70
last as troublesome as they were at first impertinent.

L. PLAUS. I would not have my visits troublesome.

MAN. The only way to be sure not to have 'em
troublesome, is to make 'em when people are   75
not at home; for your visits, like other good turns,
are most obliging when made or done to a man in

---

[1] 'Usually ridicule decides great affairs more forcefully and
effectually than severity.' Horace, *Satires*, I. x. 14, 15.

[2] Apparently referring to one of the many variations of an
old saying, probably suggested by Acts x. 34, that Love is
no respecter of persons. ('Love' is capitalized as a noun in
all the early editions.)

17] Q1 *then.*   38] Q6W1 *that the speaking.*   53] Q1 *any body, it.*

his absence. A pox! why should anyone, because he has nothing to do, go and disturb another man's business?   80

L. PLAUS. I beg your pardon, my dear friend. What, you have business?

MAN. If you have any, I would not detain your lordship.

L. PLAUS. Detain me, dear sir! I can never   85 have enough of your company.

MAN. I'm afraid I should be tiresome: I know not what you think.

L. PLAUS. Well, dear sir, I see you would have me gone.   90

MAN. (aside). But I see you won't.

L. PLAUS. Your most faithful —

MAN. God be w'ye, my lord.

L. PLAUS. Your most humble —

MAN. Farewell.   95

L. PLAUS. And eternally —

MAN. (aside). And eternally ceremony — then the devil take thee eternally!

L. PLAUS. You shall use no ceremony, by my life.

MAN. I do not intend it.   100

L. PLAUS. Why do you stir then?

MAN. Only to see you out of doors, that I may shut 'em against more welcomes.

L. PLAUS. Nay, faith, that shan't pass upon your most faithful, humble servant.   105

MAN. (aside). Nor this any more upon me.

L. PLAUS. Well, you are too strong for me.

MAN. (aside). I'd sooner be visited by the plague; for that only would keep a man from visits, and his doors shut.   110

Exit, thrusting out my LORD PLAUSIBLE.

Manent Sailors.

1ST SAIL. Here's a finical fellow, Jack! What a brave fair-weather captain of a ship he would make!

2ND SAIL. He a captain of a ship! it must be when she's in the dock, then; for he looks like one of those that get the king's commissions for hulls to sell 115 a king's ship, when a brave fellow has fought her almost to a longboat.

1ST SAIL. On my conscience then, Jack, that's the reason our bully tar sunk our ship: not only that the Dutch might not have her, but that the   120 courtiers, who laugh at wooden legs, might not make her prize.

2ND SAIL. A pox of his sinking, Tom! we have made a base, broken, short voyage of it.

1ST SAIL. Ay, your brisk dealers in honor al-   125 ways make quick returns with their ship to the dock and their men to the hospitals; 'tis, let me see, just a month since we set out of the river, and the wind was almost as cross to us as the Dutch.

2ND SAIL. Well, I forgive him sinking my   130 own poor truck,[1] if he would but have given me time and leave to have saved black Kate of Wapping's small venture.

1ST SAIL. Faith, I forgive him, since, as the purser told me, he sunk the value of five or six thou- 135 sand pound of his own, with which he was to settle himself somewhere in the Indies; for our merry lieutenant was to succeed him in his commission for the ship back; for he was resolved never to re-turn again for England.   140

2ND SAIL. So it seemed, by his fighting.

1ST SAIL. No; but he was a-weary of this side of the world here, they say.

2ND SAIL. Ay, or else he would not have bid so fair for a passage into t'other.   145

1ST SAIL. Jack, thou think'st thyself in the fore-castle, thou'rt so waggish; b.t I tell you then, he had a mind to go live and bask himself on the sunny side of the globe.

2ND SAIL. What, out of any discontent? for   150 he's always as dogged as an old tarpaulin, when hindered of a voyage by a young pantaloon captain.[2]

1ST SAIL. 'Tis true, I never saw him pleased but in the fight; and then he looked like one of us coming from the pay-table, with a new lining to our   155 hats under our arms.

2ND SAIL. A pox! he's like the Bay of Biscay, rough and angry, let the wind blow where 'twill.

1ST SAIL. Nay, there's no more dealing with him than with the land in a storm — no-   160 near! — [3]

2ND SAIL. 'Tis a hurry-durry [4] blade; dost thou remember, after we had tugged hard the old leaky longboat to save his life, when I welcomed him ashore, he gave me a box on the ear, and called 165 me fawning waterdog?

Enter MANLY *and* FREEMAN.

1ST SAIL. Hold thy peace, Jack, and stand by; the foul weather's coming.

MAN. You rascals! dogs! how could this tame thing get through you?   170

1ST SAIL. Faith, to tell your honor the truth, we were at hob [5] in the hall, and whilst my brother and I were quarrelling about a cast he slunk by us.

2ND SAIL. He's a sneaking fellow, I warrant for't.

MAN. Have more care for the future, you   175 slaves; go, and with drawn cutlasses stand at the

---

[1] Commodities for barter. Officers and seamen alike counted on making a profit for themselves and their friends by trading.
[2] Pantaloons were French in origin, and were considered foppish.
[3] Ordinarily a command not to sail too close to the wind; here, perhaps, it means not to sail too close to the shore.
[4] Tumultuous.   [5] Quoits.

stair-foot, and keep all that ask for me from coming up; suppose you were guarding the scuttle to the powder-room; let none enter here, at your and their peril.　　180

1ST SAIL. No, for the danger would be the same: you would blow them and us up, if we should.

2ND SAIL. Must no one come to you, sir?

MAN. No man, sir.

1ST SAIL. No man, sir; but a woman then,　185 an't like your honor —

MAN. No woman neither, you impertinent dog! Would you be pimping? a sea-pimp is the strangest monster she has.

2ND SAIL. Indeed, an't like your honor, 'twill　190 be hard for us to deny a woman anything, since we are so newly come on shore.

1ST SAIL. We'll let no old woman come up, though it were our trusting landlady at Wapping.

MAN. Would you be witty, you brandy casks,　195 you? you become a jest as ill as you do a horse. Begone, you dogs! I hear a noise on the stairs.

Exeunt Sailors.

FREE. Faith, I am sorry you would let the fop go; I intended to have had some sport with him.

MAN. Sport with him! A pox! then why did　200 you not stay? You should have enjoyed your coxcomb and had him to yourself, for me.

FREE. No, I should not have cared for him without you, neither; for the pleasure which fops afford is like that of drinking, only good when 'tis　205 shared; and a fool, like a bottle, which would make you merry in company, will make you dull alone. But how the devil could you turn a man of his quality down stairs? You use a lord with very little ceremony, it seems.　　210

MAN. A lord! What, thou art one of those who esteem men only by the marks and value fortune has set upon 'em, and never consider intrinsic worth; but counterfeit honor will not be current with me: I weigh the man, not his title; 'tis not the king's　215 stamp can make the metal better or heavier. Your lord is a leaden shilling, which you may bend every way, and debases the stamp he bears, instead of being raised by't. — Here again, you slaves?

Enter Sailors.

1ST SAIL. Only to receive farther instruc-　220 tions, an't like your honor. — What if a man should bring you money; should we turn him back?

MAN. All men, I say: must I be pestered with you too? You dogs, away!

2ND SAIL. Nay, I know one man your honor　225 would not have us hinder coming to you, I'm sure.

MAN. Who's that? speak quickly, slaves!

2ND SAIL. Why, a man that should bring you a challenge; for though you refuse money, I'm sure you love fighting too well to refuse that.　230

MAN. Rogue! rascal! dog!

Kicks the Sailors out.

FREE. Nay, let the poor rogues have their forecastle jests; they cannot help 'em in a fight, scarce when a ship's sinking.

MAN. Damn their untimely jests! a servant's　235 jest is more sauciness then his counsel.

FREE. But what! will you see nobody? not your friends?

MAN. Friends! I have but one, and he, I hear, is not in town; nay, can have but one friend, for　240 a true heart admits but of one friendship, as of one love; but in having that friend I have a thousand; for he has the courage of men in despair, yet the diffidency and caution of cowards; the secrecy of the revengeful, and the constancy of martyrs; one　245 fit to advise, to keep a secret, to fight and die for his friend. Such I think him, for I have trusted him with my mistress in my absence, and the trust of beauty is sure the greatest we can show.

FREE. Well, but all your good thoughts are　250 not for him alone, I hope? Pray, what d'ye think of me for a friend?

MAN. Of thee! Why, thou art a latitudinarian in friendship, that is no friend; thou dost side with all mankind, but wilt suffer for none. Thou art　255 indeed like your Lord Plausible, the pink of courtesy, therefore hast no friendship: for ceremony, and great professing, renders friendship as much suspected as it does religion.

FREE. And no professing, no ceremony at all　260 in friendship, were as unnatural and as undecent as in religion; and there is hardly such a thing as an honest hypocrite, who professes himself to be worse than he is, unless it be yourself; for, though I could never get you to say you were my friend, I　265 know you'll prove so.

MAN. I must confess, I am so much your friend, I would not deceive you; therefore must tell you, not only because my heart is taken up, but according to your rules of friendship, I cannot be your friend.　270

FREE. Why, pray?

MAN. Because he that is, you'll say, a true friend to a man, is a friend to all his friends; but you must pardon me, I cannot wish well to pimps, flatterers, detractors, and cowards, stiff nodding knaves,　275 and supple, pliant, kissing fools. Now, all these I have seen you use like the dearest friends in the world.

FREE. Ha, ha, ha! What, you observed me, I warrant, in the galleries at Whitehall,[1] doing　280 the business of the place? Pshaw! Court profes-

[1] The royal palace.

sions, like court promises, go for nothing, man. But, faith, could you think I was a friend to all those I hugged, kissed, flattered, bowed to? Ha! ha! —

MAN. You told 'em so, and swore it too; I 285 heard you.

FREE. Ay, but when their backs were turned, did I not tell you they were rogues, villains, rascals, whom I despised and hated?

MAN. Very fine! But what reason had I to 290 believe you spoke your heart to me, since you professed deceiving so many?

FREE. Why, don't you know, good captain, that telling truth is a quality as prejudicial to a man that would thrive in the world, as square play to a 295 cheat, or true love to a whore? Would you have a man speak truth to his ruin? You are severer than the law, which requires no man to swear against himself; you would have me speak truth against myself, I warrant, and tell my promising friend, 300 the courtier, he has a bad memory!

MAN. Yes.

FREE. And so make him remember to forget my business; and I should tell the great lawyer, too, that he takes oftener fees to hold his tongue, 305 than to speak!

MAN. No doubt on't.

FREE. Ay, and have him hang or ruin me, when he should come to be a judge, and I before him. And you would have me tell the new officer, 310 who bought his employment lately, that he is a coward!

MAN. Ay.

FREE. And so get myself cashiered, not him, he having the better friends, though I the better 315 sword. And I should tell the scribbler of honor, that heraldry were a prettier and fitter study for so fine a gentleman than poetry!

MAN. Certainly.

FREE. And so find myself mauled in his next 320 hired lampoon. And you would have me tell the holy lady, too, she lies with her chaplain!

MAN. No doubt on't.

FREE. And so draw the clergy upon my back, and want a good table to dine at sometimes. And 325 by the same reason too, I should tell you that the world thinks you a mad man, a brutal, and have you cut my throat, or worse, hate me. What other good success of all my plain dealing could I have, than what I've mentioned? 330

MAN. Why, first, your promising courtier would keep his word out of fear of more reproaches, or at least would give you no more vain hopes: your lawyer would serve you more faithfully, for he, having no honor but his interest, is truest still 335 to him he knows suspects him: the new officer would provoke thee to make him a coward, and so be

cashiered, that thou, or some other honest fellow who had more courage than money, might get his place: the noble sonneteer would trouble thee 340 no more with his madrigals: the praying lady would leave off railing at wenching before thee, and not turn away her chambermaid for her own known frailty with thee: and I, instead of hating thee, should love thee for thy plain dealing; and in lieu of 345 being mortified, am proud that the world and I think not well of one another.

FREE. Well, doctors differ. You are for plain dealing, I find; but against your particular notions, I have the practice of the whole world. Ob- 350 serve but any morning what people do when they get together on the Exchange, in Westminster Hall,[1] or the galleries in Whitehall.

MAN. I must confess, there they seem to rehearse Bayes's grand dance:[2] here you see a bishop 355 bowing low to a gaudy atheist; a judge to a doorkeeper; a great lord to a fishmonger, or a scrivener with a jack-chain[3] about his neck; a lawyer to a sergeant-at-arms; a velvet physician to a threadbare chemist; and a supple gentleman-usher to 360 a surly beefeater; and so tread round in a preposterous huddle of ceremony to each other, whilst they can hardly hold their solemn false countenances.

FREE. Well, they understand the world.

MAN. Which I do not, I confess. 365

FREE. But, sir, pray believe the friendship I promise you real, whatsoever I have professed to others: try me, at least.

MAN. Why, what would you do for me?

FREE. I would fight for you. 370

MAN. That you would do for your own honor: but what else?

FREE. I would lend you money, if I had it.

MAN. To borrow more of me another time. That were but putting your money to interest; a 375 usurer would be as good a friend. But what other piece of friendship?

FREE. I would speak well of you to your enemies.

MAN. To encourage others to be your friends, by a show of gratitude: but what else? 380

FREE. Nay, I would not hear you ill spoken of behind your back by my friend.

MAN. Nay, then, thou'rt a friend, indeed; but it were unreasonable to expect it from thee, as the world goes now, when new friends, like new 385 mistresses, are got by disparaging old ones.

Enter FIDELIA.

But here comes another, will say as much at least. —

---

[1] Two popular places for shopping and lounging, although the latter was at this time the location of the law courts.
[2] *The Rehearsal*, V. i. 123.
[3] An ornamental chain made of double loops of wire.

Dost not thou love me devilishly too, my little volunteer, as well as he or any man can?

FID. Better than any man can love you, my 390 dear captain.

MAN. Look you there, I told you so.

FID. As well as you do truth or honor, sir; as well.

MAN. Nay, good young gentleman, enough, for shame! thou hast been a page, by thy flattering 395 and lying, to one of those praying ladies who love flattery so well they are jealous of it; and wert turned away for saying the same things to the old housekeeper for sweetmeats, as you did to your lady; for thou flatterest everything and everybody 400 alike.

FID. You, dear sir, should not suspect the truth of what I say of you, though to you; Fame, the old liar, is believed when she speaks wonders of you; you cannot be flattered, sir, your merit is un- 405 speakable.

MAN. Hold, hold, sir, or I shall suspect worse of you, that you have been a cushion-bearer to some state hypocrite, and turned away by the chaplains, for out-flattering their probation-sermons for a 410 benefice.

FID. Suspect me for anything, sir, but the want of love, faith, and duty to you, the bravest, worthiest of mankind; believe me, I could die for you, sir.

MAN. Nay, there you lie, sir; did I not see 415 thee more afraid in the fight than the chaplain of the ship, or the purser that bought his place?

FID. Can he be said to be afraid, that ventures to sea with you?

MAN. Fie! fie! no more; I shall hate thy 420 flattery worse than thy cowardice, nay, than thy bragging.

FID. Well, I own then I was afraid, mightily afraid; yet for you I would be afraid again, an hundred times afraid: dying is ceasing to be 425 afraid; and that I could do sure for you, and you'll believe me one day. (Weeps.)

FREE. Poor youth! believe his eyes, if not his tongue: he seems to speak truth with them.

MAN. What, does he cry? A pox on't! a 430 maudlin flatterer is as nauseously troublesome as a maudlin drunkard. No more, you little milksop, do not cry, I'll never make thee afraid again; for of all men, if I had occasion, thou shouldst not be my second; and when I go to sea again, thou 435 shalt venture thy life no more with me.

FID. Why, will you leave me behind then? — (Aside.) If you would preserve my life, I'm sure you should not.

MAN. Leave thee behind! Ay, ay, thou art 440 a hopeful youth for the shore only; here thou wilt live to be cherished by fortune and the great ones; for thou mayst easily come to outflatter a dull poet,

outlie a coffee-house or gazette-writer, outswear a knight of the post,[1] outwatch a pimp, outfawn 445 a rook,[2] outpromise a lover, outrail a wit, and outbrag a sea-captain: all this thou canst do, because thou'rt a coward, a thing I hate; therefore thou'lt do better with the world than with me; and these are the good courses you must take in the world. 450 There's good advice, at least, at parting; go, and be happy with't.

FID. Parting, sir! Oh, let me not hear that dismal word!

MAN. If my words frighten thee, begone the 455 sooner; for, to be plain with thee, cowardice and I cannot dwell together.

FID. And cruelty and courage never dwelt together, sure, sir. Do not turn me off to shame and misery, for I am helpless and friendless. 460

MAN. Friendless! there are half a score friends for thee then; (offers her gold) I leave myself no more: they'll help thee a little. Begone! go! I must be cruel to thee (if thou call'st it so) out of pity.

FID. If you would be cruelly pitiful, sir, let 465 it be with your sword and not gold. Exit.

Enter first Sailor.

1ST SAIL. We have, with much ado, turned away two gentlemen, who told us, forty times over, their names were Mr. Novel and Major Oldfox.

MAN. Well, to your post again. 470
　　　　　　　　　　　　　　　　Exit Sailor.
But how come those puppies coupled always together?

FREE. Oh, the coxcombs keep each other company, to 'show' each other, as Novel calls it; or, as Oldfox says, like two knives, to whet one an- 475 other.

MAN. And set other people's teeth an edge.

Enter second Sailor.

2ND SAIL. Here is a woman, an't like your honor, scolds and bustles with us to come in, as much as a seaman's widow at the Navy Office: her name 480 is Mrs. Blackacre.

MAN. That fiend too!

FREE. The Widow Blackacre, is it not? that litigious she-pettifogger, who is at law and difference with all the world; but I wish I could make her 485 agree with me in the church: they say she has fifteen hundred pounds a year jointure, and the care of her son, that is, the destruction of his estate.

MAN. Her lawyers, attorneys, and solicitors have fifteen hundred pound a year, whilst she is 490 contented to be poor, to make other people so; for she is as vexatious as her father was, the great

---

[1] A corrupt hanger-on of the law-courts.
[2] Swindler.

attorney — nay, as a dozen Norfolk [1] attorneys, and as implacable an adversary as a wife suing for alimony, or a parson for his tithes; and she loves 495 an Easter term, or any term, not as other country ladies do, to come up to be fine, cuckold their husbands, and take their pleasure; for she has no pleasure but in vexing others, and is usually clothed and daggled like a bawd in disguise, pursued 500 through alleys by serjeants.[2] When she is in town she lodges in one of the Inns of Chancery,[3] where she breeds her son, and is herself his tutoress in law-French; and for her country abode, though she has no estate there, she chooses Norfolk. But, bid 505 her come in, with a pox to her! she is Olivia's kinswoman, and may make me amends for her visit by some discourse of that dear woman.

Exit Sailor.

Enter WIDOW BLACKACRE, *with a mantle and a green bag, and several papers in the other hand:* JERRY BLACKACRE, *her son, in a gown, laden with green bags, following her.*

WID. I never had so much to do with a judge's doorkeeper, as with yours; but — 510

MAN. But the incomparable Olivia, how does she since I went?

WID. Since you went, my suit —

MAN. Olivia, I say, is she well?

WID. My suit, if you had not returned — 515

MAN. Damn your suit! how does your cousin Olivia?

WID. My suit, I say, had been quite lost; but now —

MAN. But now, where is Olivia? in town? 520 for —

WID. For tomorrow we are to have a hearing.

MAN. Would you'd let me have a hearing today!

WID. But why won't you hear me?

MAN. I am no judge, and you talk of nothing 525 but suits; but, pray tell me, when did you see Olivia?

WID. I am no visitor, but a woman of business; or if I ever visit, 'tis only the Chancery Lane ladies, ladies towards the law, and not any of your lazy, good-for-nothing flirts, who cannot read law- 530 French, though a gallant writ it. But, as I was telling you, my suit —

MAN. Damn these impertinent, vexatious people of business, of all sexes! they are still troubling the world with the tedious recitals of their law- 535 suits: and one can no more stop their mouths than

a wit's, when he talks of himself, or an intelligencer's,[4] when he talks of other people.

WID. And a pox of all vexatious, impertinent lovers! they are still perplexing the world with 540 the tedious narrations of their love-suits, and discourses of their mistresses. You are as troublesome to a poor widow of business as a young coxcombly rithming[5] lover.

MAN. And thou art as troublesome to me as 545 a rook to a [losing] gamester, or a young putter of cases to his mistress and sempstress, who has love in her head for another.

WID. Nay, since you talk of putting of cases, and will not hear me speak, hear our Jerry a 550 little; let him put our case to you, for the trial's tomorrow; and since you are my chief witness, I would have your memory refreshed and your judgment informed, that you may not give your evidence improperly. — Speak out, child. 555

JER. Yes, forsooth. Hem! hem! John-a-Stiles — [6]

MAN. You may talk, young lawyer, but I shall no more mind you than a hungry judge does a cause after the clock has struck one.

FREE. Nay, you'll find him as peevish too. 560

WID. No matter. — Jerry, go on. — [*To* FREEMAN.] Do you observe it then, sir; for I think I have seen you in a gown once. Lord, I could hear our Jerry put cases all day long! Mark him, sir.

JER. John-a-Stiles — no — there are first, 565 Fitz, Pere, and Ayle, — no, no, Ayle, Pere, and Fitz; Ayle is seised in fee of Blackacre; John-a-Stiles disseises Ayle; Ayle makes claim, and the disseisor dies; then the Ayle — no, the Fitz —

WID. No, the Pere, sirrah. 570

JER. Oh, the Pere! ay, the Pere, sir, and the Fitz — no, the Ayle, — no, the Pere and the Fitz, sir, and —

MAN. Damn Pere, Mere, and Fitz, sir!

WID. No, you are out, child. — Hear me, 575 captain, then: there are Ayle, Pere, and Fitz; Ayle is seised in fee of Blackacre; and, being so seised, John-a-Stiles disseises the Ayle, Ayle makes claim, and the disseisor dies; and then the Pere re-enters — (*to* JERRY) the Pere, sirrah, the Pere — and 580 the Fitz enters upon the Pere, and the Ayle brings his writ of disseisin in the *post*; and the Pere brings his writ of disseisin in the *per*, and —

MAN. Canst thou hear this stuff, Freeman? I

---

[1] The people of Norfolk were reputed to be especially guileful, and also, apparently, litigious: cf. l. 505 below.
[2] Members of a superior order of barristers.
[3] Certain houses where students of the law resided; these houses were subordinate to the four Inns of Court, which controlled admission to the bar.

[4] Newsmonger's, gossip's.   [5] Rhyming.
[6] A fictitious name like 'John Doe.' It is not necessary to understand the complicated case that follows in detail: it is enough to say that, like most of the widow's law-cases, it concerns the title to real property. 'Ayle,' 'Pere,' and 'Fitz' are law-French terms for grandfather, father, and son. It might be added that in general the widow's knowledge of the law is sound and extensive.

---

could as soon suffer a whole noise of flatterers   585
at a great man's levee in a morning; but thou hast
servile complacency enough to listen to a quibbling
statesman in disgrace, nay, and be beforehand with
him, in laughing at his dull no-jest; but I —

(Offering to go out.)

WID. Nay, sir, hold! — Where's the subpœna,   590
Jerry? — I must serve you, sir.   You are required, by
this, to give your testimony —

MAN. I'll be forsworn, to be revenged on thee.

Exit MANLY, throwing away the subpœna.

WID. Get you gone, for a lawless companion! —
Come, Jerry, I had almost forgot, we were to   595
meet at the master's[1] at three: let us mind our
business still, child.

JER. Ay, forsooth, e'en so let's.

FREE. Nay, madam, now I would beg you to hear
me a little, a little of my business.   600

WID. I have business of my own calls me away, sir.

FREE. My business would prove yours too, dear
madam.

WID. Yours would be some sweet business, I
warrant.   What, 'tis no Westminster Hall   605
business?   Would you have my advice?

FREE. No, faith, 'tis a little Westminster Abbey
business: I would have your consent.

WID. Oh, fie, fie, sir! to me such discourse, before
my dear minor there!   610

JER. Ay, ay, mother, he would be taking livery
and seisin of your jointure, by digging the turf;[2]
but I'll watch your waters,[3] bully, i'fac.[4] — Come
away, mother. <i>Exit</i> JERRY, <i>haling away his Mother.</i>

Manet FREEMAN: enter to him FIDELIA.

FID. Dear sir, you have pity; beget but   615
some in our captain for me.

FREE. Where is he?

FID. Within, swearing as much as he did in the
great storm, and cursing you, and sometimes sinks
into calms and sighs, and talks of his Olivia.   620

FREE. He would never trust me to see her.   Is she
handsome?

FID. No, if you'll take my word; but I am not a
proper judge.

FREE. What is she?   625

FID. A gentlewoman, I suppose, but of as mean
a fortune as beauty; but her relations would not
suffer her to go with him to the Indies, and his
aversion to this side of the world, together with the
late opportunity of commanding the convoy,   630

[1] At the chambers of the master in chancery.

[2] The jointure is the widow's dower right in the real estate of
her husband.   Possession of land was anciently transferred by
livery of seisin — the delivery by the old owner to the new of
a piece of turf, dug from the land in question.

[3] I'll keep an eye upon you.   [4] In faith.

would not let him stay here longer, though to enjoy
her.

FREE. He loves her mightily then?

FID. Yes, so well, that the remainder of his fortune
(I hear about five or six thousand pounds) he   635
has left her, in case he had died by the way, or before
she could prevail with her friends to follow him,
which he expected she should do, and has left behind
him his great bosom friend to be her convoy to him.

FREE. What charms has she for him, if she   640
be not handsome?

FID. He fancies her, I suppose, the only woman of
truth and sincerity in the world.

FREE. No common beauty, I confess.

FID. Or else sure he would not have trusted   645
her with so great a share of his fortune, in his
absence; I suppose (since his late loss) all he has.

FREE. Why, has he left it in her own custody?

FID. I am told so.

FREE. Then he has showed love to her in-   650
deed, in leaving her, like an old husband that dies
as soon as he has made his wife a good jointure.
But I'll go in to him, and speak for you, and know
more from him of his Olivia.   <i>Exit.</i>

Manet FIDELIA sola.

FID. His Olivia, indeed, his happy Olivia!   655
Yet she was left behind, when I was with him:
But she was ne'er out of his mind or heart.
She has told him she loved him; I have showed it,
And durst not tell him so, till I had done,
Under this habit, such convincing acts   660
Of loving friendship for him, that through it
He first might find out both my sex and love;
And, when I'd had him from his fair Olivia,
And this bright world of artful beauties here,
Might then have hoped, he would have looked on
        me,   665
Amongst the sooty Indians; and I could
To choose there live his wife, where wives are forced
To live no longer, when their husbands die;
Nay, what's yet worse, to share 'em whilst they live
With many rival wives.   But here he comes,   670
And I must yet keep out of his sight, not
To lose it forever.   <i>Exit.</i>

Enter MANLY and FREEMAN.

FREE. But pray, what strange charms has she
that could make you love?

MAN. Strange charms indeed!   She has   675
beauty enough to call in question her wit or virtue,
and her form would make a starved hermit a ravisher; yet her virtue and conduct would preserve her
from the subtle lust of a pampered prelate.   She is
so perfect a beauty that art could not better it,   680

nor affectation deform it; yet all this is nothing. Her tongue as well as face ne'er knew artifice; nor ever did her words or looks contradict her heart. She is all truth, and hates the lying, masking, daubing world, as I do; for which I love her, and 685 for which I think she dislikes not me: for she has often shut out of her conversation, for mine, the gaudy, fluttering parrots of the town, apes and echoes of men only, and refused their commonplace pert chat, flattery, and submissions, to be 690 entertained with my sullen bluntness and honest love. And, last of all, swore to me, since her parents would not suffer her to go with me, she would stay behind for no other man, but follow me, without their leave, if not to be obtained. Which 695 oath —

FREE. Did you think she would keep?

MAN. Yes; for she is not, I tell you, like other women, but can keep her promise, though she has sworn to keep it; but, that she might the better 700 keep it, I left her the value of five or six thousand pound: for women's wants are generally their most importunate solicitors to love or marriage.

FREE. And money summons lovers more than beauty, and augments but their importunity 705 and their number; so makes it the harder for a woman to deny 'em. For my part, I am for the French maxim, 'If you would have your female subjects loyal, keep 'em poor.' But, in short, that your mistress may not marry, you have given her a 710 portion.

MAN. She had given me her heart first, and I am satisfied with the security; I can never doubt her truth and constancy.

FREE. It seems you do, since you are fain 715 to bribe it with money. But how come you to be so diffident of the man that says he loves you, and not doubt the woman that says it?

MAN. I should, I confess, doubt the love of any other woman but her, as I do the friendship of 720 any other man but him I have trusted; but I have such proofs of their faith as cannot deceive me.

FREE. Cannot!

MAN. Not but I know that generally no man can be a great enemy but under the name of friend; 725 and if you are a cuckold, it is your friend only that makes you so, for your enemy is not admitted to your house: if you are cheated in your fortune, 'tis your friend that does it, for your enemy is not made your trustee: if your honor or good name be in- 730 jured, 'tis your friend that does it still, because your enemy is not believed against you. Therefore, I rather choose to go where honest, downright barbarity is professed, where men devour one another like generous, hungry lions and tigers, not like 735 crocodiles; where they think the devil white, of our

complexion; and I am already so far an Indian. But if your weak faith doubts this miracle of a woman, come along with me, and believe; and thou wilt find her so handsome that thou, who art so much 740 my friend, wilt have a mind to lie with her, and so will not fail to discover what her faith and thine is to me.

When we're in love, the great adversity,
Our friends and mistresses at once we try. 745
[Exeunt.]

ACT II

SCENE I

OLIVIA's *lodging.*

Enter OLIVIA, ELIZA, LETTICE.

OLIV. Ah, cousin, what a world 'tis we live in! I am so weary of it.

ELIZA. Truly, cousin, I can find no fault with it, but that we cannot always live in't; for I can never be weary of it. 5

OLIV. Oh, hideous! you cannot be in earnest, sure, when you say you like the filthy world.

ELIZA. You cannot be in earnest, sure, when you say you dislike it.

OLIV. You are a very censorious creature, 10 I find.

ELIZA. I must confess, I think we women as often discover where we love, by railing, as men when they lie, by their swearing; and the world is but a constant keeping gallant, whom we fail not to quarrel 15 with when anything crosses us, yet cannot part with't for our hearts.

LET. A gallant indeed, madam, whom ladies first make jealous, and then quarrel with it for being so; for if, by her indiscretion, a lady be talked of for 20 a man, she cries presently, ''Tis a censorious world!'; if, by her vanity, the intrigue be found out, ''Tis a prying, malicious world!'; if, by her over-fondness, the gallant proves unconstant, ''Tis a false world!'; and if, by her niggardliness, the chambermaid 25 tells, ''Tis a perfidious world!' — but that, I'm sure, your ladyship cannot say of the world yet, as bad as 'tis.

OLIV. But I may say, ''Tis a very impertinent world!' Hold your peace! — And, cousin, if the 30 world be a gallant, 'tis such an one as is my aversion. Pray name it no more.

ELIZA. But is it possible the world, which has such variety of charms for other women, can have none for you? Let's see — first, what d'ye think of 35 dressing and fine clothes?

OLIV. Dressing! Fie, fie, 'tis my aversion. — [*To* LETTICE.] But come hither, you dowdy; me-

thinks you might have opened this toure [1] better.
Oh, hideous! I cannot suffer it! D'ye see 40
how't sits?

ELIZA. Well enough, cousin, if dressing be your
aversion.

OLIV. 'Tis so: and for variety of rich clothes,
they are more my aversion. 45

LET. Ay, 'tis because your ladyship wears 'em
too long; for indeed a gown, like a gallant, grows
one's aversion, by having too much of it.

OLIV. Insatiable creature! I'll be sworn I have
had this not above three days, cousin, and 50
within this month have made some six more.

ELIZA. Then your aversion to 'em is not altogether so great.

OLIV. Alas! 'tis for my woman only I wear 'em,
cousin. 55

LET. If it be for me only, madam, pray do not
wear 'em.

ELIZA. But what d'ye think of visits — balls — ?

OLIV. Oh, I detest 'em!

ELIZA. Of plays? 60

OLIV. I abominate 'em; filthy, obscene, hideous
things!

ELIZA. What say you to masquerading in the
winter, and Hyde Park in the summer?

OLIV. Insipid pleasures I taste not. 65

ELIZA. Nay, if you are for more solid pleasure,
what think you of a rich young husband?

OLIV. Oh, horrid! marriage! what a pleasure you
have found out! I nauseate it of all things.

LET. But what does your ladyship think then 70
of a liberal, handsome, young lover?

OLIV. A handsome young fellow, you impudent!
Begone, out of my sight! Name a handsome young
fellow to me! foh! a hideous, handsome, young
fellow I abominate. (*Spits.*) 75

ELIZA. Indeed! But let's see — will nothing
please you? what d'ye think of the court?

OLIV. How? the court! the court, cousin! my
aversion, my aversion, my aversion of all aversions!

ELIZA. How? the court! where — 80

OLIV. Where sincerity is a quality as out of fashion, and as unprosperous, as bashfulness: I could not
laugh at a quibble, though it were a fat privy-
counsellor's; nor praise a lord's ill verses, though I
were myself the subject; nor an old lady's young 85
looks, though I were her woman; nor sit to a vain
young simile-maker, though he flattered me. In
short, I could not gloat [2] upon a man when he comes
into a room, and laugh at him when he goes out: I
cannot rail at the absent, to flatter the standers- 90
by; I —

ELIZA. Well, but railing now is so common, that

'tis no more malice, but the fashion; and the absent
think they are no more the worse for being railed at,
than the present think they're the better for be- 95
ing flattered; and for the court —

OLIV. Nay, do not defend the court; for you'll
make me rail at it, like a trusting citizen's widow.

ELIZA. Or like a Holborn [3] lady, who could not
get into the last ball, or was out of countenance 100
in the drawing-room [4] the last Sunday of her appearance there; for none rail at the court but those who
cannot get into it, or else who are ridiculous when
they are there; and I shall suspect you were laughed
at when you were last there, or would be a maid 105
of honor.

OLIV. I a maid of honor! To be a maid of honor
were yet of all things my aversion.

ELIZA. In what sense am I to understand you?
But, in fine, by the word aversion, I'm sure you 110
dissemble; for I never knew woman yet that used it
who did not. Come, our tongues belie our hearts
more than our pocket-glasses do our faces; but methinks we ought to leave off dissembling, since 'tis
grown of no use to us; for all wise observers un- 115
derstand us now-a-days, as they do dreams, alma-
nacs, and Dutch gazettes,[5] by the contrary: and a
man no more believes a woman, when she says she
has an aversion for him, than when she says she'll
cry out. 120

OLIV. Oh, filthy! hideous! Peace, cousin! or your
discourse will be my aversion; and you may believe
me.

ELIZA. Yes; for if anything be a woman's aversion, 'tis plain dealing from another woman: 125
and perhaps that's your quarrel to the world, for that
will talk, as your woman says.

OLIV. Talk not of me, sure; for what men do I
converse with? what visits do I admit?

Enter Boy.

BOY. Here's the gentleman to wait upon you, 130
madam.

OLIV. On me! you little, unthinking fop, d'ye
know what you say?

BOY. Yes, madam, 'tis the gentleman that comes
every day to you, who — 135

OLIV. Hold your peace, you heedless little animal,
and get you gone. *Exit Boy.*

This country boy, cousin, takes my dancing-
master, tailor, or the spruce milliner, for visitors.

LET. No, madam; 'tis Mr. Novel, I'm sure, 140
by his talking so loud: I know his voice too, madam.

---

[3] Holborn was an unfashionable part of town; cf. *The Man of
Mode*, III. iii. 307.

[4] At court.

[5] The Dutch reports of success in the wars, naturally discredited in England.

---

[1] A crescent front of false hair.　　[2] Gaze admiringly upon.

66] Q4Q6W1 *pleasures.*　　87] W1 *smile-maker.*　　95] Q1 *they are.*　　111] W1 om. *that.*

OLIV. You know nothing, you buffle-headed,[1] stupid creature, you; you would make my cousin believe I receive visits. But if it be Mr. — what did you call him? 145

LET. Mr. Novel, madam; he that —

OLIV. Hold your peace, I'll hear no more of him; but if it be your Mr. — (I can't think of his name again) I suppose he has followed my cousin hither. 150

ELIZA. No, cousin, I will not rob you of the honor of the visit: 'tis to you, cousin, for I know him not.

OLIV. Nor did I ever hear of him before, upon my honor, cousin; besides, han't I told you, that visits, and the business of visits, flattery, and detraction, are my aversion? D'ye think then I would 155 admit such a coxcomb as he is? who, rather than not rail, will rail at the dead, whom none speak ill of; and, rather than not flatter, will flatter the poets of the age, whom none will flatter; who affects 160 novelty as much as the fashion, and is as fantastical as changeable, and as well known as the fashion; who likes nothing but what is new, nay, would choose to have his friend, or his title, a new one. In fine, he is my aversion. 165

ELIZA. I find you do know him, cousin; at least, have heard of him.

OLIV. Yes, now I remember, I have heard of him.

ELIZA. Well; but since he is such a coxcomb, for heaven's sake, let him not come up. — Tell him, 170 Mrs. Lettice, your lady is not within.

OLIV. No, Lettice, tell him my cousin is here, and that he may come up; for, notwithstanding I detest the sight of him, you may like his conversation; and though I would use him scurvily, I will not be 175 rude to you in my own lodging; since he has followed you hither, let him come up, I say.

ELIZA. Very fine! Pray let him go to the devil, I say, for me: I know him not, nor desire it. Send him away, Mrs. Lettice. 180

OLIV. Upon my word, she shan't: I must disobey your commands, to comply with your desires. — Call him up, Lettice.

ELIZA. Nay, I'll swear she shall not stir on that errand. (*Holds* LETTICE.) 185

OLIV. Well then, I'll call him myself for you, since you will have it so. (*Calls out at the door.*) Mr. Novel, sir, sir!

Enter NOVEL.

NOV. Madam, I beg your pardon; perhaps you were busy: I did not think you had company 190 with you.

ELIZA (*aside*). Yet he comes to me, cousin!

OLIV. Chairs there!

(*They sit.*) [*Exit* LETTICE.]

[1] Heavy-witted.

148] WI *cannot.*

NOV. Well, but, madam, d'ye know whence I come now? 195

OLIV. From some melancholy place, I warrant, sir, since they have lost your good company.

ELIZA. So!

NOV. From a place where they have treated me at dinner with so much civility and kindness, a 200 pox on 'em! that I could hardly get away to you, dear madam.

OLIV. You have a way with you so new and obliging, sir!

ELIZA (*apart to* OLIVIA). You hate flattery, 205 cousin!

NOV. Nay, faith, madam, d'ye think my way new? Then you are obliging, madam. I must confess, I hate imitation, to do anything like other people: all that know me do me the honor to 210 say I am an original, faith; but, as I was saying, madam, I have been treated today with all the ceremony and kindness imaginable at my Lady Autum's; but the nauseous old woman at the upper end of her table — 215

OLIV. Revives the old Grecian custom, of serving in a death's head with their banquets.

NOV. Ha, ha! fine, just, i'faith; nay, and new. 'Tis like eating with the ghost in *The Libertine*:[2] she would frighten a man from her dinner, with her 220 hollow invitations, and spoil one's stomach —

OLIV. To meat, or women. I detest her hollow, cherry cheeks; she looks like an old coach new painted, affecting an unseemly smugness, whilst she is ready to drop in pieces. 225

ELIZA (*apart to* OLIVIA). You hate detraction, I see, cousin!

NOV. But the silly old fury, whilst she affects to look like a woman of this age, talks —

OLIV. Like one of the last, and as passion- 230 ately as an old courtier who has outlived his office.

NOV. Yes, madam; but pray let me give you her character. Then she never counts her age by the years, but —

OLIV. By the masques she has lived to see. 235

NOV. Nay then, madam, I see you think a little harmless railing too great a pleasure for any but yourself, and therefore I've done.

OLIV. Nay, faith, you shall tell me who you had there at dinner. 240

NOV. If you would hear me, madam.

OLIV. Most patiently; speak, sir.

NOV. Then, we had her daughter —

OLIV. Ay, her daughter, the very disgrace to good clothes, which she always wears but to heighten 245 her deformity, not mend it; for she is still most

[2] By Thomas Shadwell: the incident referred to occurs in Act IV, sc. iv.

splendidly, gallantly ugly, and looks like an ill piece of daubing in a rich frame.

Nov. So! But have you done with her, madam? And can you spare her to me a little now?   250

Oliv. Ay, ay, sir.

Nov. Then, she is like —

Oliv. She is, you'd say, like a city bride, the greater fortune, but not the greater beauty, for her dress.   255

Nov. Well: yet have you done, madam? Then she —

Oliv. Then she bestows as unfortunately on her face all the graces in fashion, as the languishing eye, the hanging or pouting lip; but as the fool is   260 never more provoking than when he aims at wit, the ill-favored of our sex are never more nauseous than when they would be beauties, adding to their natural deformity the artificial ugliness of affectation.

Eliza. So, cousin, I find one may have a   265 collection of all one's acquaintances' pictures as well at your house as at Mr. Lely's; only the difference is, there we find 'em much handsomer than they are, and like; here, much uglier, and like: and you are the first of the profession of picture-drawing I ever   270 knew without flattery.

Oliv. I draw after the life; do nobody wrong, cousin.

Eliza. No, you hate flattery and detraction!

Oliv. But, Mr. Novel, who had you besides   275 at dinner?

Nov. Nay, the devil take me if I tell you, unless you will allow me the privilege of railing in my turn. But, now I think on't, the women ought to be your province, as the men are mine: and you must   280 know, we had him whom —

Oliv. Him, whom —

Nov. What, invading me already? And giving the character, before you know the man?

Eliza. No, that is not fair, though it be usual.   285

Oliv. I beg your pardon, Mr. Novel; pray go on.

Nov. Then, I say, we had that familiar coxcomb who is at home wheresoe'er he comes.

Oliv. Ay, that fool —

Nov. Nay then, madam, your servant; I'm   290 gone. Taking a fool out of one's mouth is worse than taking the bread out of one's mouth.

Oliv. I've done; your pardon, Mr. Novel; pray proceed.

Nov. I say, the rogue, that he may be the   295 only wit in company, will let nobody else talk, and —

Oliv. Ay, those fops who love to talk all themselves are of all things my aversion.

Nov. Then you'll let me speak, madam, sure. The rogue, I say, will force his jest upon you;   300 and I hate a jest that's forced upon a man, as much as a glass.

Eliza. Why, I hope, sir, he does not expect a man of your temperance in jesting should do him reason?   305

Nov. What, interruption from this side too! I must [then] —   (Offers to rise. Olivia holds him.)

Oliv. No, sir. — You must know, cousin, that fop he means, though he talks only to be commended, will not give you leave to do't.   310

Nov. But, madam —

Oliv. He a wit! Hang him, he's only an adopter of straggling jests and fatherless lampoons, by the credit of which he eats at good tables, and so, like the barren beggar-woman, lives by borrowed   315 children.

Nov. Madam —

Oliv. And never was author of anything but his news; but that is still all his own.

Nov. Madam, pray —   320

Oliv. An eternal babbler; and makes no more use of his ears, than a man that sits at a play by his mistress, or in fop-corner:[1] he's, in fine, a base detracting fellow, and is my aversion. — But who else prithee, Mr. Novel, was there with you? Nay, you   325 shan't stir.

Nov. I beg your pardon, madam; I cannot stay in any place where I'm not allowed a little Christian liberty of railing.

Oliv. Nay, prithee, Mr. Novel, stay; and   330 though you should rail at me, I would hear you with patience. Prithee, who else was there with you?

Nov. Your servant, madam!

Oliv. Nay, prithee tell us, Mr. Novel, prithee do.

Nov. We had nobody else.   335

Oliv. Nay, faith, I know you had. Come, my Lord Plausible was there too, who is, cousin, a —

Eliza. You need not tell me what he is, cousin; for I know him to be a civil, good-natured, harmless gentleman, that speaks well of all the world,   340 and is always in good humor; and —

Oliv. Hold, cousin, hold! I hate detraction, but I must tell you, cousin, his civility is cowardice, his good-nature want of wit; and has neither courage or sense to rail: and for his being always in humor,   345 'tis because he is never dissatisfied with himself: in fine, he is my aversion, and I never admit his visits beyond my hall.

Nov. No, he visit you! Damn him, cringing, grinning rogue! if I should see him coming up   350 to you, I would make bold to kick him down again. — Ha! —

Enter my Lord Plausible.

My dear lord, your most humble servant!
    (*Rises and salutes* Plausible, *and kisses him.*)

[1] That part of the pit in which the fops gathered: probably the side-box.

279] Q4 *woman.*   291] W1 *the fool.*   307] Q3Q4Q6 *the;* Q1W1 *then.*
313] Q4 *strangling.*   344–45] Q6 *nor sense.*

ELIZA (*aside*). So! I find kissing and railing succeed each other with the angry men as well as 355 with the angry women; and their quarrels are like love-quarrels, since absence is the only cause of them; for as soon as the man appears again, they are over.

L. PLAUS. Your most faithful, humble servant, generous Mr. Novel; and, madam, I am your 360 eternal slave, and kiss your fair hands; which I had done sooner, according to your commands, but —

OLIV. No excuses, my lord.

ELIZA (*apart*). What, you sent for him then, cousin? 365

NOV. (*aside*). Ha! invited!

OLIV. I know you must divide yourself, for your good company is too general a good to be ingrossed by any particular friend.

L. PLAUS. O Lord, madam, my company! 370 your most obliged, faithful, humble servant! But I could have brought you good company indeed, for I parted at your door with two of the worthiest, bravest men —

OLIV. Who were they, my lord? 375

NOV. Who do you call the worthiest, bravest men, pray?

L. PLAUS. Oh, the wisest, bravest gentlemen! men of such honor and virtue! of such good qualities! ah — 380

ELIZA (*aside*). This is a coxcomb that speaks ill of all people a different way, and libels everybody with dull praise, and commonly in the wrong place, so makes his panegyrics abusive lampoons.

OLIV. But pray let me know who they were. 385

L. PLAUS. Ah! such patterns of heroic virtue! such —

NOV. Well, but who the devil were they?

L. PLAUS. The honor of our nation! the glory of our age! Ah, I could dwell a twelvemonth on 390 their praise, which indeed I might spare by telling their names: Sir John Current and Sir Richard Court-Title.

NOV. Court-Title! Ha, ha!

OLIV. And Sir John Current! Why will you 395 keep such a wretch company, my lord?

L. PLAUS. O madam, seriously you are a little too severe; for he is a man of unquestioned reputation in everything.

OLIV. Yes, because he endeavors only with 400 the women to pass for a man of courage, and with the bullies for a wit; with the wits for a man of business, and with the men of business for a favorite at court; and at court for good City security.[1]

NOV. And for Sir Richard, he — 405

L. PLAUS. He loves your choice, picked company, persons that —

OLIV. He loves a lord indeed; but —

NOV. Pray, dear madam, let me have but a bold stroke or two at his picture. He loves a lord, 410 as you say, though —

OLIV. Though he borrowed his money, and ne'er paid him again.

NOV. And would bespeak a place three days before at the back-end of a lord's coach to Hyde 415 Park.

L. PLAUS. Nay, i'faith, i'faith, you are both too severe.

OLIV. Then to show yet more his passion for quality, he makes love to that fulsome coach- 420 load of honor, my Lady Goodly, for he is always at her lodging.

L. PLAUS. Because it is the conventicle gallant, the meeting-house of all the fair ladies and glorious superfine beauties of the town. 425

NOV. Very fine ladies! there's first —

OLIV. Her honor, as fat as an hostess.

L. PLAUS. She is something plump indeed, a goodly, comely, graceful person.

NOV. Then there's my Lady Frances — 430 what d'ye call 'er? — as ugly —

OLIV. As a citizen's lawfully begotten daughter.

L. PLAUS. She has wit in abundance, and the handsomest heel, elbow, and tip of an ear you ever saw. 435

NOV. Heel and elbow! ha, ha! And there's my Lady Betty, you know —

OLIV. As sluttish and slatternly as an Irish woman bred in France.

L. PLAUS. Ah, all she has hangs with a loose 440 air, indeed, and becoming negligence.

ELIZA. You see all faults with lover's eyes, I find, my lord.

L. PLAUS. Ah, madam, your most obliged, faithful, humble servant to command! — But you 445 can say nothing, sure, against the superfine mistress —

OLIV. I know who you mean. She is as censorious and detracting a jade as a superannuated sinner.

L. PLAUS. She has a smart way of raillery, 450 'tis confessed.

NOV. And then, for Mrs. Grideline [2] —

L. PLAUS. She, I'm sure, is —

OLIV. One that never spoke ill of anybody, 'tis confessed; for she is as silent in conversation as 455 a country lover, and no better company than a clock, or a weatherglass: for if she sounds, 'tis but once an

---

[1] One whose bond would be acceptable in the City (the commercial district).

[2] Gridelin means pale purple or gray-violet. Morgan suggests that the name betokens demureness.

358] Q4 *mam.*   376] Q1 *braviest.*   421] W1 *he's.*
431] W1 *her.*   452] W1 om. comma.

hour, to put you in mind of the time of day, or tell you 'twill be cold or hot, rain or snow.

L. PLAUS. Ah, poor creature! she's extremely   460 good and modest.

NOV. And for Mrs. Bridlechin, she's —

OLIV. As proud as a churchman's wife.

L. PLAUS. She's a woman of great spirit and honor, and will not make herself cheap, 'tis true. 465

NOV. Then Mrs. Hoyden, that calls all people by their surnames, and is —

OLIV. As familiar a duck —

NOV. As an actress in the tiring room. There I was once beforehand with you, madam.   470

L. PLAUS. Mrs. Hoyden! a poor, affable, good-natured soul! But the divine Mrs. Trifle comes thither too: sure, her beauty, virtue, and conduct you can say nothing to.

OLIV. No?   475

NOV. No? — Pray let me speak, madam.

OLIV. First, can any one be called beautiful that squints?

L. PLAUS. Her eyes languish a little, I own.

NOV. Languish! ha, ha!   480

OLIV. Languish! Then, for her conduct, she was seen at *The Country Wife*[1] after the first day. There's for you, my lord.

L. PLAUS. But, madam, she was not seen to use her fan all the play long, turn aside her head, or 485 by a conscious blush discover more guilt than modesty.

OLIV. Very fine! Then you think a woman modest that sees the hideous *Country Wife* without blushing or publishing her detestation of it? 490 D'ye hear him, cousin?

ELIZA. Yes, and am, I must confess, something of his opinion, and think that as an over-captious fool at a play, by endeavoring to show the author's want of wit, exposes his own to more censure, 495 so may a lady call her own modesty in question, by publicly cavilling with the poet's; for all those grimaces of honor and artificial modesty disparage a woman's real virtue as much as the use of white and red does the natural complexion, and you 500 must use very, very little, if you would have it thought your own.

OLIV. Then you would have a woman of honor with passive looks, ears, and tongue undergo all the hideous obscenity she hears at nasty plays? 505

ELIZA. Truly, I think a woman betrays her want of modesty by showing it publicly in a playhouse, as much as a man does his want of courage by a quarrel there; for the truly modest and stout say least, and are least exceptious, especially in public. 510

[1] This earlier play by Wycherley had aroused wide protest even in his free-spoken day.

OLIV. Oh, hideous! Cousin, this cannot be your opinion; but you are one of those who have the confidence to pardon the filthy play.

ELIZA. Why, what is there of ill in't, say you?

OLIV. Oh, fie! fie! fie! would you put me to 515 the blush anew? call all the blood into my face again? But to satisfy you then; first, the clandestine obscenity in the very name of Horner.

ELIZA. Truly, 'tis so hidden, I cannot find it out, I confess.   520

OLIV. Oh, horrid! Does not it give you the rank conception or image of a goat, a town-bull, or a satyr? nay, what is yet a filthier image than all the rest, that of an eunuch?

ELIZA. What then? I can think of a goat, a 525 bull, or satyr, without any hurt.

OLIV. Ay; but, cousin, one cannot stop there.

ELIZA. I can, cousin.

OLIV. Oh, no! for when you have those filthy creatures in your head once, the next thing you 530 think, is what they do; as their defiling of honest men's beds and couches, rapes upon sleeping and waking country virgins, under hedges, and on haycocks; nay, further —

ELIZA. Nay, no farther, cousin. We have 535 enough of your comment on the play, which will make me more ashamed than the play itself.

OLIV. Oh, believe me, 'tis a filthy play, and you may take my word for a filthy play as soon as another's; but the filthiest thing in that play, or 540 any other play, is —

ELIZA. Pray keep it to yourself, if it be so.

OLIV. No, faith, you shall know it; I'm resolved to make you out of love with the play. I say, the lewdest, filthiest thing is his china; nay, I will 545 never forgive the beastly author his china; he has quite taken away the reputation of poor china itself, and sullied the most innocent and pretty furniture of a lady's chamber, insomuch that I was fain to break all my defiled vessels. You see I have 550 none left; nor you, I hope.

ELIZA. You'll pardon me; I cannot think the worse of my china for that of the playhouse.

OLIV. Why, you will not keep any now, sure! 'Tis now as unfit an ornament for a lady's 555 chamber as the pictures that come from Italy and other hot countries, as appears by their nudities, which I always cover, or scratch out, whereso'er I find 'em. But china! out upon't, filthy china! nasty, debauched china!   560

ELIZA. All this will not put me out of conceit with china, nor the play, which is acted today, or another of the same beastly author's, as you call him, which I'll go see.

OLIV. You will not, sure! nay, you sha' not 565

458] Q1W1 *or to tell.*   475] Q1Q3Q4Q6W1 *No!*   476] Q1Q3Q4Q6W1 *No!*   493] Q1W1 *over-conscious.*
521] Q1Q6W1 *it not.*   522] Q4Q6 *or town-bull.*   526] W1 *or a satyr.*   534] Q1 *farther.*
546] Q6W1 *never forget.*   558] Q4Q6 om. *I.*   558] Q4Q6 *search out.*

venture your reputation by going, and mine by leaving me alone with two men here: nay, you'll disoblige me forever, if —   (*Pulls her back.*)

ELIZA. I stay; — your servant!   *Exit* ELIZA.

OLIV. Well — but, my lord, though you jus- 570 tify everybody, you cannot in earnest uphold so beastly a writer, whose ink is so smutty, as one may say.

L. PLAUS. Faith, I dare swear the poor man did not think to disoblige the ladies by any amor- 575 ous, soft, passionate, luscious saying in his play.

OLIV. Foy, my lord! But what think you, Mr. Novel, of the play? though I know you are a friend to all that are new.

NOV. Faith, madam, I must confess the new 580 plays would not be the worse for my advice, but I could never get the silly rogues, the poets, to mind what I say; but I'll tell you what counsel I gave the surly fool you speak of.

OLIV. What was't?   585

NOV. Faith, to put his play into rithme, for rithme, you know, often makes mystical nonsense pass with the critics for wit, and a double-meaning saying with the ladies for soft, tender, and moving passion. But now I talk of passion, I saw 590 your old lover this morning — Captain —

(*Whispers.*)

Enter CAPTAIN MANLY, FREEMAN, *and* FIDELIA *standing behind.*

OLIV. Whom? — nay, you need not whisper.

MAN. We are luckily got hither unobserved! — How! in a close conversation with these supple rascals, the outcasts of sempstresses' shops!   595

FREE. Faith, pardon her, captain, that, since she could no longer be entertained with your manly bluntness and honest love, she takes up with the pert chat and commonplace flattery of these flutter-ing parrots of the town, apes and echoes of 600 men only.

MAN. Do not you, sir, play the echo too, mock me, dally with my own words, and show yourself as impertinent as they are.

FREE. Nay, captain —   605

FID. Nay, lieutenant, do not excuse her; me-thinks she looks very kindly upon 'em both, and seems to be pleased with what that fool there says to her.

MAN. You lie, sir! and hold your peace, that 610 I may not be provoked to give you a worse reply.

OLIV. Manly returned, d'ye say! And is he safe?

NOV. My lord saw him too. — Hark you, my lord.   (*Whispers to* PLAUSIBLE.)

MAN. (*aside*). She yet seems concerned for 615 my safety, and perhaps they are admitted now here

but for their news of me; for intelligence indeed is the common passport of nauseous fools when they go their round of good tables and houses.

OLIV. I heard of his fighting only, without 620 particulars, and confess I always loved his brutal courage, because it made me hope it might rid me of his more brutal love.

MAN. (*aside*). What's that?

OLIV. But is he at last returned, d'ye say, 625 unhurt?

NOV. Ay, faith, without doing his business; for the rogue has been these two years pretending to a wooden leg, which he would take from fortune as kindly as the staff of a marshal of France, and 630 rather read his name in a gazette —

OLIV. Than in the entail of a good estate.

MAN. (*aside*). So!

NOV. I have an ambition, I must confess, of losing my heart before such a fair enemy as 635 yourself, madam; but that silly rogues should be ambitious of losing their arms, and —

OLIV. Looking like a pair of compasses.

NOV. But he has no use of his arms but to set 'em on kimbow,[1] for he never pulls off his hat, at 640 least not to me, I'm sure; for you must know, madam, he has a fanatical hatred to good company: he can't abide me.

L. PLAUS. Oh, be not so severe to him, as to say he hates good company; for I assure you he has 645 a great respect, esteem, and kindness for me.

MAN. [*aside*]. That kind, civil rogue has spoken yet ten thousand times worse of me than t'other.

OLIV. Well, if he be returned, Mr. Novel, then shall I be pestered again with his boist'rous 650 sea-love, have my alcove smell like a cabin, my chamber perfumed with his tarpaulin Branden-burgh,[2] and near volleys of brandy sighs, enough to make a fog in one's room. Foh! I hate a lover that smells like Thames Street![3]   655

MAN. (*aside*). I can bear no longer, and need hear no more. — [*To* OLIVIA.] But since you have these two pulvillio[4] boxes, these essence-bottles, this pair of musk-cats here, I hope I may venture to come yet nearer you.   660

OLIV. Overheard us, then?

NOV. (*aside*). I hope he heard me not.

L. PLAUS. Most noble and heroic captain, your most obliged, faithful, humble servant!

NOV. Dear tar, thy humble servant!   665

MAN. Away! — Madam —

OLIV. (*thrusts* NOVEL *and* LORD PLAUSIBLE *on*

---

[1] Akimbo.
[2] Tarred-canvas morning-gown.
[3] The river-front.
[4] Scented powder.

each side). Nay, I think I have fitted you ¹ for list'ning.

MAN. You have fitted me for believing you 670 could not be fickle, though you were young; could not dissemble love, though 'twas your interest; nor be vain, though you were handsome; nor break your promise, though to a parting lover; nor abuse your best friend, though you had wit: but I take 675 not your contempt of me worse than your esteem or civility for these things here, though you know 'em.

NOV. Things!

L. PLAUS. Let the captain rally a little.

MAN. Yes, things! Canst thou be angry, 680 thou thing?   (*Coming up to* NOVEL.)

NOV. No, since my lord says you speak in raillery; for though your sea-raillery be something rough, yet, I confess, we use one another [too] as bad every day at Locket's,² and never quarrel for the 685 matter.

L. PLAUS. Nay, noble captain, be not angry with him; a word with you, I beseech you —
                          (*Whispers to* MANLY.)

OLIV. (*aside).* Well, we women, like the rest of the cheats of the world, when our cullies or credi- 690 tors have found us out, and will or can trust no longer, pay debts and satisfy obligations with a quarrel, the kindest present a man can make to his mistress, when he can make no more presents: for oftentimes in love, as at cards, we are forced to 695 play foul only to give over the game, and use our lovers like the cards, when we can get no more by 'em — throw 'em up in a pet, upon the first dispute.

MAN. My lord, all that you have made me know by your whispering which I knew not before, is, 700 that you have a stinking breath; there's a secret for your secret.

L. PLAUS. Pshaw! pshaw!

MAN. But, madam, tell me, pray, what was't about this spark could take you? Was it the 705 merit of his fashionable impudence, the briskness of his noise, the wit of his laugh, his judgment, or fancy in his garniture? or was it a well-trimmed glove, or the scent of it, that charmed you?

NOV. Very well, sir; 'gad these sea-captains 710 make nothing of dressing. But let me tell you, sir, a man by his dress, as much as by anything, shows his wit and judgment, nay, and his courage too.

FREE. How his courage, Mr. Novel?

NOV. Why, for example, by red breeches, 715 tucked-up hair or peruke, a greasy broad belt, and now-a-days a short sword.

MAN. Thy courage will appear more by thy belt than thy sword, I dare swear. — Then, madam, for

this gentle piece of courtesy, this man of tame 720 honor, what could you find in him? Was it his languishing affected tone? his mannerly look? his second-hand flattery, the refuse of the playhouse tiring-rooms? or his slavish obsequiousness in watching at the door of your box at the playhouse, 725 for your hand to your chair? or his jaunty way of playing with your fan? or was it the gunpowder spot ³ on his hand, or the jewel in his ear, that purchased your heart?

OLIV. Good jealous captain, no more of 730 your —

L. PLAUS. No, let him go on, madam, for perhaps he may make you laugh, and I would contribute to your pleasure any way.

MAN. Gentle rogue!   735

OLIV. No, noble captain, you cannot, sure, think anything could take me more than that heroic title of yours, captain; for you know we women love honor inordinately.

NOV. Ha, ha! faith, she is with thee, bully, 740 for thy raillery.

MAN. (*aside to* NOVEL). Faith, so shall I be with you, no-bully, for your grinning.

OLIV. Then, that noble lion-like mien of yours, that soldier-like, weather-beaten complexion, 745 and that manly roughness of your voice; how can they otherwise than charm us women, who hate effeminacy!

NOV. Ha, ha! faith I can't hold from laughing.

MAN. (*aside to* NOVEL). Nor shall I from 750 kicking anon.

OLIV. And then, that captain-like carelessness in your dress, but especially your scarf; 'twas just such another, only a little higher tied; made me in love with my tailor as he passed by my window 755 the last training-day; ⁴ for we women adore a martial man, and you have nothing wanting to make you more one, or more agreeable, but a wooden leg.

L. PLAUS. Nay, i'faith, there your ladyship was a wag, and it was fine, just, and well rallied. 760

NOV. Ay, ay, madam, with you ladies too, martial men must needs be very killing.

MAN. Peace, you Bartholomew Fair buffoons! ⁵ — and be not you vain that these laugh on your side, for they will laugh at their own dull jests; 765 but no more of 'em, for I will only suffer now this lady to be witty and merry.

OLIV. You would not have your panegyric interrupted. I go on then to your humor. Is there

---

³ A beauty-spot, tattooed with gunpowder.
⁴ Day on which the militia is called out for review.
⁵ Bartholomew Fair, held annually about St. Bartholomew's Day (August 24) in West Smithfield, something more than a quarter of a mile north of St. Paul's Cathedral. It was noted for farcical theatrical performances and puppet-shows.

---

¹ Dealt with you fitly.
² Locket's ordinary, a fashionable tavern in Charing Cross.

anything more agreeable than the pretty sul- 770
lenness of that? than the greatness of your courage?
which most of all appears in your spirit of contradiction, for you dare give all mankind the lie; and your
opinion is your only mistress, for you renounce that
too, when it becomes another man's. 775

Nov. Ha, ha! I cannot hold, I must laugh at
thee, tar, faith!

L. Plaus. And i'faith, dear captain, I beg your
pardon, and leave to laugh at you too, though I protest I mean you no hurt; but when a lady 780
rallies, a stander-by must be complaisant, and do
her reason in laughing. Ha, ha!

Man. Why, you impudent, pitiful wretches, you
presume, sure, upon your effeminacy to urge me; for
you are in all things so like women, that you 785
may think it in me a kind of cowardice to beat you.

Oliv. No hectoring, good captain!

Man. Or, perhaps, you think this lady's presence
secures you; but have a care, she has talked herself
out of all the respect I had for her, and by 790
using me ill before you has given me a privilege of
using you so before her: but if you would preserve
your respect to her, and not be beaten before her,
go, begone immediately!

Nov. 'Begone!' what? 795

L. Plaus. Nay, worthy, noble, generous, captain —

Man. Begone, I say!

Nov. 'Begone' again! to us 'begone!'

Man. No chattering, baboons; instantly be- 800
gone, or —

(Manly *puts 'em out of the room:* Novel
struts, Plausible *cringes.*)

Nov. Well, madam, we'll go make the cards ready
in your bedchamber: sure you will not stay long
with him. *Exeunt* Plausible, Novel.

Oliv. Turn hither your rage, good Cap- 805
tain Swagger-huff, and be saucy with your mistress,
like a true captain; but be civil to your rivals and
betters, and do not threaten anything but me here,
no, not so much as my windows, nor do not think
yourself in the lodgings of one of your sub- 810
urb mistresses beyond the Tower.[1]

Man. Do not give me cause to think so; for those
less infamous women part with their lovers, just as
you did from me, with unforced vows of constancy
and floods of willing tears; but the same winds 815
bear away their lovers and their vows: and for their
grief, if the credulous, unexpected fools return, they
find new comforters, fresh cullies, such as I found
here. The mercenary love of those women too
suffers shipwreck with their gallants' fortunes; 820
now you have heard chance has used me scurvily,

therefore you do too. Well, persevere in your ingratitude, falsehood, and disdain; have constancy
in something, and I promise you to be as just to your
real scorn as I was to your feigned love, and 825
henceforward will despise, contemn, hate, loathe, and
detest you most faithfully.

Enter Lettice.

Oliv. Get the ombre cards ready in the next
room, Lettice, and —
(*Whispers to* Lettice.) [*Exit* Lettice.]

Free. Bravely resolved, captain! 830

Fid. And you'll be sure to keep your word, I hope,
sir.

Man. I hope so too.

Fid. Do you but hope it, sir? If you are not as
good as your word, 'twill be the first time you 835
ever bragged, sure.

Man. She has restored my reason with my heart.

Free. But, now you talk of restoring, captain,
there are other things which, next to one's heart, one
would not part with; I mean your jewels and 840
money, which it seems she has, sir.

Man. What's that to you, sir?

Free. Pardon me, whatsoever is yours, I have
a share in't, I'm sure, which I will not lose for asking,
though you may be too generous or too angry 845
now to do't yourself.

Fid. Nay, then I'll make bold to make my claim
too. (*Both going towards* Olivia.)

Man. Hold, you impertinent, officious fops!
(*Aside.*) How have I been deceived! 850

Free. Madam, there are certain appurtenances
to a lover's heart, called jewels, which always go
along with it.

Fid. And which, with lovers, have no value in
themselves, but from the heart they come 855
with. Our captain's, madam, it seems you scorn to
keep, and much more will those worthless things
without it, I am confident.

Oliv. A gentleman so well made as you are may
be confident — us easy women could not deny 860
you anything you ask, if 'twere for yourself; but,
since 'tis for another, I beg your leave to give him
my answer. — (*Aside.*) An agreeable young fellow
this! — and would not be my aversion! — (*Aside to*
Manly.) Captain, your young friend here 865
has a very persuading face, I confess; yet you might
have asked me yourself for those trifles you left with
me, which (hark you a little, for I dare trust you
with the secret: you are a man of so much honor, I'm
sure) — I say, then, not expecting your return, 870
or hoping ever to see you again, I have delivered
your jewels to —

Man. Whom?

Oliv. My husband.

---

[1] Living east of the Tower of London.

MAN. Your husband!   875

OLIV. Ay, my husband; for, since you could leave me, I am lately and privately married to one, who is a man of so much honor and experience in the world, that I dare not ask him for your jewels again, to restore 'em to you, lest he should conclude 880 you never would have parted with 'em to me on any other score but the exchange of my honor: which rather than you'd let me lose, you'd lose, I'm sure, yourself those trifles of yours.

MAN. Triumphant impudence! but married 885 too!

OLIV. Oh, speak not so loud! my servants know it not: I am married; there's no resisting one's destiny or love, you know.

MAN. Why, did you love him too?   890

OLIV. Most passionately; nay, love him now, though I have married him, and he me: which mutual love I hope you are too good, too generous a man to disturb, by any future claim, or visits to me. 'Tis true, he is now absent in the country, but 895 returns shortly; therefore I beg of you, for your own ease and quiet, and my honor, you will never see me more.

MAN. I wish I never had seen you.

OLIV. But if you should ever have anything 900 to say to me hereafter, let that young gentleman there be your messenger.

MAN. You would be kinder to him; I find he should be welcome.

OLIV. Alas, his youth would keep my hus-   905 band from suspicions, and his visits from scandal; for we women may have pity for such as he, but no love: and I already think you do not well to spirit him away to sea; and the sea is already but too rich with the spoils of the shore.   910

MAN (aside). True, perfect woman! If I could say anything more injurious to her now, I would, for I could outrail a bilked whore, or a kicked coward; but, now I think on't, that were rather to discover my love than hatred; and I must not talk, for   915 something I must do.

OLIV. (aside). I think I have given him enough of me now, never to be troubled with him again.

Enter LETTICE.

Well, Lettice, are the cards and all ready within? I come, then. — Captain, I beg your pardon: 920 you will not make one at ombre?

MAN. No, madam, but I'll wish you a little good luck before you go.

OLIV. No, if you would have me thrive, curse me; for that you'll do heartily, I suppose.   925

MAN. Then, if you will have it so, may all the curses light upon you, women ought to fear, and you

deserve! First, may the curse of loving play attend your sordid covetousness, and fortune cheat you, by trusting to her, as you have cheated me; the 930 curse of pride, or a good reputation, fall on your lust; the curse of affectation on your beauty; the curse of your husband's company on your pleasures; and the curse of your gallant's disappointments in his absence; and the curse of scorn, jealousy, or 935 despair on your love; and then the curse of loving on!

OLIV. And, to requite all your curses, I will only return you your last; may the curse of loving me still fall upon your proud, hard heart, that could be so cruel to me in these horrid curses! but heaven 940 forgive you!   *Exit OLIVIA.*

MAN. Hell and the devil reward thee!

FREE. Well, you see now, mistresses, like friends, are lost by letting 'em handle your money; and most women are such kind of witches, who can 945 have no power over a man, unless you give 'em money; but when once they have got any from you, they never leave you till they have all. Therefore I never dare give a woman a farthing.

MAN. Well, there is yet this comfort by 950 losing one's money with one's mistress, a man is out of danger of getting another; of being made prize again by love, who, like a pirate, takes you by spreading false colors: but when once you have run your ship aground, the treacherous picaroon loofs,[1] so 955 by your ruin you save yourself from slavery at least.

Enter Boy.

BOY. Mrs. Lettice, here's Madam Blackacre come to wait upon her honor.

                        [*Exeunt LETTICE and Boy.*]

MAN. D'ye hear that? Let us be gone be- 960 fore she comes; for henceforward I'll avoid the whole damned sex for ever, and woman as a sinking ship.

                        Exeunt MANLY and FIDELIA.

FREE. And I'll stay, to revenge on her your quarrel to the sex; for out of love to her jointure, and hatred to business, I would marry her, to make an 965 end of her thousand suits, and my thousand engagements, to the comfort of two unfortunate sorts of people, my plaintiffs and her defendants, my creditors and her adversaries.

Enter WIDOW BLACKACRE, led in by MAJOR OLDFOX, and JERRY BLACKACRE following, laden with green bags.

WID. 'Tis an arrant sea-ruffian, but I am 970 glad I met with him at last, to serve him again, major, for the last service was not good in law. — Boy, duck, Jerry, where is my paper of memorandums?

---

[1] The treacherous pirate luffs (changes his course).

Give me, child! so.   Where is my cousin Olivia, now, my kind relation?   975

FREE. Here is one that would be your kind relation, madam.

WID. What mean you, sir?

FREE. Why, faith, to be short, to marry you, widow.   980

WID. Is not this the wild, rude person we saw at Captain Manly's?

JER. Ay, forsooth, an't please.

WID. What would you? what are you?   Marry me!   985

FREE. Ay, faith; for I am a younger brother, and you are a widow.

WID. You are an impertinent person — and go about your business!

FREE. I have none, but to marry thee, wid-   990 ow.

WID. But I have other business, I'd have you to know.

FREE. But you have no business a-nights, widow; and I'll make you pleasanter business than   995 any you have: for a-nights, I assure you, I am a man of great business; for the business —

WID. Go! I'm sure you're an idle fellow.

FREE. Try me but, widow, and employ me as you find my abilities and industry.   1000

OLD. Pray be civil to the lady, Mr. —— she's a person of quality, a person that is no person —

FREE. Yes, but she's a person that is a widow. Be you mannerly to her, because you are to pretend only to be her squire, to arm her to her   1005 lawyer's chambers; but I will be impudent and bawdy, for she must love and marry me.

WID. Marry come up, you saucy, familiar Jack! You think, with us widows, 'tis no more than up and ride. Gad forgive me! now-a-days, every   1010 idle, young, hectoring, roaring companion, with a pair of turned red breeches and a broad back, thinks to carry away any widow of the best degree; but I'd have you to know, sir, all widows are not got, like places at court, by impudence and   1015 importunity only.

OLD. No, no, soft, soft! you are a young man, and not fit —

FREE. For a widow?   Yes, sure, old man, the fitter.   1020

OLD. Go to, go to! if others had not laid in their claims before you —

FREE. Not you, I hope.

OLD. Why not I, sir?   Sure I am a much more proportionable match for her than you, sir; I,   1025 who am an elder brother, of a comfortable fortune, and of equal years with her.

WID. How's that?   You unmannerly person, I'd have you to know, I was born but in *Ann' undec'*

Caroli prim.' [1]   1030

OLD. Your pardon, lady, your pardon; be not offended with your very servant. — But I say, sir, you are a beggarly younger brother, twenty years younger than her, without any land or stock, but your great stock of impudence: therefore what   1035 pretension can you have to her?

FREE. You have made it for me: first, because I am a younger brother.

WID. Why, is that a sufficient plea to a relict? How appears it, sir? by what foolish custom?   1040

FREE. By custom time out of mind only.   Then, sir, because I have nothing to keep me after her death, I am the likelier to take care of her life.   And for my being twenty years younger than her, and having a sufficient stock of impudence, I leave it   1045 to her whether they will be valid exceptions to me in her widow's law or equity.

OLD. Well, she has been so long in chancery, that I'll stand to her equity and decree between us. — (*Aside to* WIDOW BLACKACRE.)   Come,   1050 lady, pray snap up this young snap [2] at first, or we shall be troubled with him; give him a city-widow's answer, that is, with all the ill-breeding imaginable. Come, madam.

WID. Well then, to make an end of this   1055 foolish wooing, for nothing interrupts business more: first, for you, major —

OLD. You declare in my favor, then?

FREE. What, direct the court! — (*To* JERRY.) Come, young lawyer, thou sha't be a coun-   1060 sel for me.

JER. Gad, I shall betray your cause then, as well as an older lawyer; never stir.

WID. First, I say, for you, major, my walking hospital of an ancient foundation, thou bag of   1065 mummy, that wouldst fall asunder, if 'twere not for thy cerecloths —

OLD. How, lady?

FREE. Ha, ha! —

JER. Hey, brave mother! use all suitors   1070 thus, for my sake.

WID. Thou withered, hobbling, distorted cripple; nay, thou art a cripple all over: wouldst thou make me the staff of thy age, the crutch of thy decrepidness? Me —   1075

FREE. Well said, widow!   Faith, thou wouldst make a man love thee now, without dissembling.

WID. Thou senseless, impertinent, quibbling, drivelling, feeble, paralytic, impotent, fumbling, frigid nincompoop!   1080

---

[1] The eleventh year of Charles I, i.e., 1635–36. If true, this would make the Widow Blackacre about thirty in the supposed year of the action; but since Jerry is over twenty-one (as we learn eventually), her statement is an obvious and comic piece of vanity.   [2] Speak sharply to this young swindler.

JER. Hey, brave mother, for calling of names, i'fac!

WID. Wouldst thou make a [caudle-maker],[1] a nurse of me? Can't you be bedrid without a bed-fellow? Won't your swan-skins,[2] furs, flan- 1085 nels, and the scorched trencher[3] keep you warm there? Would you have me your Scotch warming-pan,[4] with a pox to you? Me —

OLD. O heavens!

FREE. I told you I should be thought the 1090 fitter man, major.

JER. Ay, you old fobus,[5] and you would have been my guardian, would you, to have taken care of my estate, that half of't should never come to me, by let-ting long leases at pepper-corn rents?[6] 1095

WID. If I would have married an old man, 'tis well known I might have married an earl, nay, what's more, a judge, and been covered the winter nights with the lamb-skins,[7] which I prefer to the ermines of nobles: and dost thou think I would wrong 1100 my poor minor there for you?

FREE. Your minor is a chopping[8] minor, God bless him!　　(Strokes JERRY on the head.)

OLD. Your minor may be a major of horse or foot, for his bigness; and it seems you will have the 1105 cheating of your minor to yourself.

WID. Pray, sir, bear witness: cheat my minor! I'll bring my action of the case for the slander.

FREE. Nay, I would bear false witness for thee now, widow, since you have done me justice, 1110 and have thought me the fitter man for you.

WID. Fair and softly, sir, 'tis my minor's case, more than my own; and I must do him justice now on you.

FREE. How?　　　　　　　　　　　1115
OLD. So then.

WID. You are, first, I warrant, some renegado from the inns of court and the law; and thou'lt come to suffer for't by the law, that is, be hanged.

JER. Not about your neck, forsooth, I hope. 1120

FREE. But, madam —

OLD. Hear the court.

WID. Thou art some debauched, drunken, lewd, hectoring, gaming companion,[9] and want'st some widow's old gold to nick upon;[10] but I thank 1125 you, sir, that's for my lawyers.

---

[1] A caudle is a medicinal warm drink.
[2] A kind of fine flannel.
[3] A heated platter, used to warm a bed.
[4] A slang term for a wench.
[5] A derogatory epithet of uncertain meaning.
[6] When land was leased free it was customary to fix a nominal rent of a pepper-corn, in order that the lease might be good in law.
[7] Judges wore robes furred with lamb-skin.
[8] Lusty.　　　[9] Fellow.　　　[10] Gamble with.

FREE. Faith, we should ne'er quarrel about that, for guineas would serve my turn.[11] But, widow —

WID. Thou art a foul-mouthed boaster of thy lust, a mere braggadocio of thy strength for wine 1130 and women, and wilt belie thyself more than thou dost women, and art every way a base deceiver of women; and would deceive me too, would you?

FREE. Nay, faith, widow, this is judging without seeing the evidence.　　　　　　　　1135

WID. I say, you are a worn-out whore-master at five-and-twenty, both in body and fortune; and cannot be trusted by the common wenches of the town, lest you should not pay 'em; nor by the wives of the town lest you should pay 'em: so you 1140 want women, and would have me your bawd to procure 'em for you.

FREE. Faith, if you had any good acquaintance, widow, 'twould be civilly done of thee; for I am just come from sea.　　　　　　　　　　1145

WID. I mean, you would have me keep you, that you might turn keeper; for poor widows are only used like bawds by you: you go to church with us, but to get other women to lie with. In fine, you are a cheating, chousing[12] spendthrift, and 1150 having sold your own annuity, would waste my jointure.

JER. And make havoc of our estate personal, and all our old gilt plate; I should soon be picking up all our mortgaged apostle-spoons,[13] bowls, and 1155 beakers, out of most of the ale-houses betwixt Hercules' Pillars and the Boatswain in Wapping;[14] nay, and you'd be scouring[15] amongst my trees, and make 'em knock down one another, like routed reel-ing watchmen at midnight. Would you so, 1160 bully?

FREE. Nay, prithee, widow, hear me.

WID. No, sir! I'd have you to know, thou pitiful, paltry, lath-backed fellow, if I would have married a young man, 'tis well known I could have 1165 had any young heir in Norfolk, nay, the hopefull'st young man this day at the King's Bench bar; I that am a relict and executrix of known plentiful assets and parts, who understand myself and the law. And would you have me under covert-baron[16] 1170 again? No, sir, no covert-baron for me.

FREE. But, dear widow, hear me. I value you only, not your jointure.

---

[11] Freeman contrasts guineas, first coined in 1662, with old gold.　　　[12] Swindling.
[13] Spoons the handles of which end in figures of the apostles.
[14] Two taverns in opposite corners of London; one near Hyde Park Corner, the other some distance east of the Tower of London.
[15] Roistering.
[16] Law-French for a married woman (who could not maintain actions at law).

1083] Q3 candle-maker; Q1Q4Q6W1 caudle-maker.　　1129] Q4Q6W1 foul-mouth.　　1131] Q6W1 will belie.
1158] Q4Q6 would be.

WID. Nay, sir, hold there; I know your love to a widow is covetousness of her jointure: and 1175 a widow, a little stricken in years, with a good jointure, is like an old mansion-house in a good purchase, never valued, but take one, take t'other: and perhaps, when you are in possession, you'd neglect it, let it drop to the ground, for want of neces- 1180 sary repairs or expenses upon't.

FREE. No, widow, one would be sure to keep all tight, when one is to forfeit one's lease by dilapidation.

WID. Fie! fie! I neglect my business with 1185 this foolish discourse of love. Jerry, child, let me see the list of the jury: I'm sure my cousin Olivia has some relations amongst 'em. But where is she?

FREE. Nay, widow, but hear me one word only.

WID. Nay, sir, no more, pray; I will no 1190 more hearken again to your foolish love-motions, than to offers of arbitration.

Exeunt WIDOW BLACKACRE *and* JERRY.

FREE. Well, I'll follow thee yet; for he that has a pretension at court, or to a widow, must never give over for a little ill-usage.   1195

OLD. Therefore I'll get her by assiduity, patience, and long-sufferings, which you will not undergo; for you idle young fellows leave off love when it comes to be business; and industry gets more women than love.   1200

FREE. Ay, industry, the fool's and old man's merit; but I'll be industrious too, and make a business on't, and get her by law, wrangling, and contests, and not by sufferings: and, because you are no dangerous rival, I'll give thee counsel, major: 1205

If you litigious widow e'er would gain,
Sigh not to her, but by the law complain;
To her, as to a bawd, defendant sue
With statutes, and make justice pimp for you.

Exeunt.

ACT III

SCENE I

Westminster Hall.

Enter MANLY *and* FREEMAN, *two Sailors behind.*

MAN. I hate this place, worse than a man that has inherited a chancery suit: I wish I were well out on't again.

FREE. Why, you need not be afraid of this place: for a man without money needs no more fear a 5 crowd of lawyers than a crowd of pickpockets.

MAN. This, the reverend of the law would have thought the palace or residence of Justice; but, if it be, she lives here with the state of a Turkish emperor,

rarely seen; and besieged rather than defended 10 by her numerous black guard [1] here.

FREE. Methinks 'tis like one of their own halls in Christmas time, whither from all parts fools bring their money, to try by the dice (not the worst judges) whether it shall be their own or no: [2] 15 but after a tedious fretting and wrangling they drop away all their money on both sides, and, finding neither the better, at last, go emptily and lovingly away together to the tavern, joining their curses against the young lawyer's box, that sweeps all, 20 like the old ones.

MAN. Spoken like a revelling Christmas lawyer.

FREE. Yes, I was one, I confess, but was fain to leave the law, out of conscience, and fall to making false musters: [3] rather chose to cheat the king 25 than his subjects; plunder, rather than take fees.

MAN. Well, a plague and a purse-famine light on the law, and that female limb of it who dragged me hither today! But prithee, go see if, in that crowd of daggled [4] gowns there (*pointing to a crowd of* 30 *lawyers at the end of the stage*), thou canst find her.

Exit FREEMAN.

Manet MANLY.

How hard it is to be an hypocrite!
At least to me, who am but newly so.
I thought it once a kind of knavery,
Nay, cowardice, to hide one's faults; but now 35
The common frailty, love, becomes my shame.
He must not know I love th' ungrateful still,
Lest he contemn me more than she; for I,
It seems, can undergo a woman's scorn,
But not a man's —   40

Enter to him FIDELIA.

FID. Sir, good sir, generous captain.

MAN. Prithee, kind impertinence, leave me. Why should'st thou follow me, flatter my generosity now, since thou know'st I have no money left? If I had it, I'd give it thee, to buy my quiet.   45

FID. I never followed yet, sir, reward or fame, but you alone; nor do I now beg anything but leave to share your miseries. You should not be a niggard of 'em, since, methinks, you have enough to spare. Let me follow you now, because you hate me, as 50 you have often said.

MAN. I ever hated a coward's company, I must confess.

---

[1] The lawyers wore black robes. Manly makes a double pun, referring both to the dark-skinned guard of the Sultan and to 'blackguard' in its common meaning.
[2] During the revels held between Christmas and Twelfth Night gambling was permitted in the Inns of Court.
[3] Army officers sometimes carried the names of non-existent soldiers on their muster-rolls, and appropriated the pay allotted to them.   [4] Spattered.

1183] Q6 *right.*   ACT III. 25] Q4Q6W1 *chuse.*   37] W1 *the ungrateful.*

Fid. Let me follow you till I am none, then; for you, I'm sure, will through such worlds of 55 dangers, that I shall be inured to 'em; nay, I shall be afraid of your anger more than danger, and so turn valiant out of fear.   Dear captain, do not cast me off till you have tried me once more: do not, do not go to sea again without me.   60

Man. Thou to sea! to court, thou fool! remember the advice I gave thee: thou art a handsome spaniel, and canst fawn naturally: go, busk about,[1] and run thyself into the next great man's lobby; first fawn upon the slaves without, and then run into the 65 lady's bedchamber; thou mayst be admitted, at last, to tumble her bed: go, seek, I say, and lose me; for I am not able to keep thee; I have not bread for myself.

Fid. Therefore I will not go, because then I 70 may help and serve you.

Man. Thou!

Fid. I warrant you, sir; for, at worst, I could beg or steal for you.

Man. Nay, more bragging!   Dost thou not 75 know there's venturing your life in stealing?   Go, prithee, away: thou art as hard to shake off as that flattering, effeminating mischief, love.

Fid. Love did you name?   Why, you are not so miserable as to be yet in love, sure?   80

Man. No, no, prithee away, begone, or — (aside) I had almost discovered my love and shame; well, if I had? — that thing could not think the worse of me — or if he did? — no — yes, he shall know it — he shall — but then I must never leave him, for 85 they are such secrets that make parasites and pimps lords of their masters; for any slavery or tyranny is easier than love's. — [To Fidelia.]   Come hither. Since thou art so forward to serve me, hast thou but resolution enough to endure the torture of a 90 secret? for such, to some, is insupportable.

Fid. I would keep it as safe as if your dear, precious life depended on't.

Man. Damn your dearness!   It concerns more than my life — my honor.   95

Fid. Doubt it not, sir.

Man. And do not discover it by too much fear of discovering it; but have a great care you let not Freeman find it out.

Fid. I warrant you, sir.   I am already all joy 100 with the hopes of your commands, and shall be all wings in the execution of 'em: speak quickly, sir.

Man. You said you would beg for me.

Fid. I did, sir.

Man. Then you shall beg for me.   105

Fid. With all my heart, sir.

Man. That is, pimp for me.

Fid. How, sir?

[1] Seek about (a nautical phrase).

Man. D'ye start!   Think'st thou, thou couldst do me any other service?   Come, no dissem- 110 bling honor: I know you can do it handsomely; thou wert made for't.   You have lost your time with me at sea; you must recover it.

Fid. Do not, sir, beget yourself more reasons for your aversion to me, and make my obedience to 115 you a fault; I am the unfittest in the world to do you such a service.

Man. Your cunning arguing against it shows but how fit you are for it.   No more dissembling; here, I say, you must go use it for me to Olivia.   120

Fid. To her, sir?

Man. Go flatter, lie, kneel, promise, anything to get her for me: I cannot live unless I have her. Didst thou not say thou wouldst do anything to save my life?   And she said you had a persuading 125 face.

Fid. But did you not say, sir, your honor was dearer to you than your life?   And would you have me contribute to the loss of that, and carry love from you to the most infamous, most false, and —   130

Man. And most beautiful! —   (Sighs aside.)

Fid. Most ungrateful woman that ever lived; for sure she must be so, that could desert you so soon, use you so basely, and so lately too: do not, do not forget it, sir, and think —   135

Man. No, I will not forget it, but think of revenge: I will lie with her out of revenge.   Go, begone, and prevail for me, or never see me more.

Fid. You scorned her last night.

Man. I know not what I did last night; I dis- 140 sembled last night.

Fid. Heavens!

Man. Begone, I say, and bring me love or com- pliance back, or hopes at least, or I'll never see thy face again, by —   145

Fid. Oh, do not swear, sir! first hear me.

Man. I am impatient: away! you'll find me here till twelve.   (Turns away.)

Fid. Sir —

Man. Not one word, no insinuating argu- 150 ment more, or soothing persuasion; you'll have need of all your rhetoric with her: go strive to alter her, not me; begone.   Exit Manly at the end of the stage.

Manet Fidelia.

Fid. Should I discover to him now my sex, And lay before him his strange cruelty,   155 'Twould but incense it more. — No, 'tis not time. For his love must I then betray my own? Were ever love or chance, till now, severe? Or shifting women posed with such a task? Forced to beg that which kills her, if obtained, 160 And give away her lover not to lose him!

Exit Fidelia.

Enter WIDOW BLACKACRE *in the middle of half-a-
dozen lawyers, whispered to by a fellow in black;*
JERRY BLACKACRE *following the crowd.*

WID. Offer me a reference,[1] you saucy companion,
you! d'ye know who you speak to? Art thou a
solicitor in chancery, and offer a reference? A
pretty fellow! Mr. Serjeant Ploddon, here's a 165
fellow has the impudence to offer me a reference.

SERJ. PLOD. Who's that has the impudence to
offer a reference within these walls?

WID. Nay, for a splitter of causes to do't!

SERJ. PLOD. No, madam; to a lady learned 170
in the law, as you are, the offer of a reference were
to impose upon you.

WID. No, no, never fear me for a reference, Mr.
Serjeant. But come, have you not forgot your
brief? Are you sure you shan't make the mis- 175
take of — hark you — (*Whispers.*) Go then, go to
your court of Common Pleas, and say one thing over
and over again: you do it so naturally, you'll never
be suspected for protracting time.

SERJ. PLOD. Come, I know the course of the 180
court, and your business. *Exit* SERJEANT PLODDON.

WID. Let's see, Jerry, where are my minutes?
Come, Mr. Quaint, pray go talk a great deal for me
in Chancery; let your words be easy, and your sense
hard; my cause requires it: branch it bravely,[2] 185
and deck my cause with flowers, that the snake may
lie hidden. Go, go, and be sure you remember the
decree of my Lord Chancellor, *tricesimo quart'* of the
Queen.[3]

QUAINT. I will, as I see cause, extenuate [4] 190
or amplify matter of fact; baffle truth with impudence; answer exceptions with questions, though
never so impertinent; for reasons give 'em words;
for law and equity, tropes and figures; and so relax
and enervate the sinews of their argument with 195
the oil of my eloquence. But when my lungs can
reason no longer, and not being able to say anything
more for our cause, say everything of our adversary,
whose reputation, though never so clear and evident
in the eye of the world, yet with sharp invec- 200
tives —

WID. Alias, Belin'sgate.[5]

QUAINT. With poignant and sour invectives, I
say, I will deface, wipe out, and obliterate his fair
reputation, even as a record with the juice of 205

---

[1] A reference of a suit to a master in chancery might lead to
a settlement without the opportunity for an argument in open
court: such an outcome would deprive the widow of her
pleasure.

[2] Be diffuse.

[3] In the thirty-fourth year of the Queen (Elizabeth), i.e.,
1591–92.

[4] Draw out.

[5] Billingsgate; coarse, personal abuse.

lemons; and tell such a story (for the truth on't is, all
that we can do for our client in Chancery is telling
a story), a fine story, a long story, such a story —

WID. Go, save thy breath for the cause; talk at
the bar, Mr. Quaint. You are so copiously 210
fluent, you can weary any one's ears sooner than
your own tongue. Go, weary our adversaries'
counsel, and the court; go, thou art a fine-spoken
person: adad, I shall make thy wife jealous of me, if
you can but court the court into a decree for 215
us. Go, get you gone, remember — (*Whispers.*)
                                      Exit QUAINT.

Come, Mr. Blunder, pray bawl soundly for me, at
the King's Bench; bluster, sputter, question, cavil;
but be sure your argument be intricate enough to
confound the court, and then you do my busi- 220
ness. Talk what you will, but be sure your tongue
never stand still; for your own noise will secure your
sense from censure: 'tis like coughing or hemming
when one has got the belly-ache, which stifles the
unmannerly noise. Go, dear rogue, and suc- 225
ceed; and I'll invite thee, ere it be long, to more
soused [6] venison.

BLUND. I'll warrant you, after your verdict your
judgment shall not be arrested upon if's and and's.[7]
                                      [*Exit.*]

WID. Come, Mr. Petulant, let me give you 230
some new instructions for our cause in the Exchequer. Are the barons sate?

PET. Yes, no; may be they are, may be they are
not: what know I? what care I?

WID. Heyday! I wish you would but snap 235
up the counsel on t'other side anon at the bar as
much, and have a little more patience with me, that
I might instruct you a little better.

PET. You instruct me! What is my brief for,
mistress? 240

WID. Ay, but you seldom read your brief but at
the bar, if you do it then.

PET. Perhaps I do, perhaps I don't, and perhaps
'tis time enough: pray hold yourself contented,
mistress. 245

WID. Nay, if you go there too, I will not be contented, sir; though you, I see, will lose my cause for
want of speaking, I wo' not: you shall hear me, and
shall be instructed. Let's see your brief.

PET. Send your solicitor to me. Instructed 250
by a woman! I'd have you to know, I do not wear
a bar-gown —

WID. By a woman! And I'd have you to know
I am no common woman, but a woman conversant
in the laws of the land, as well as yourself, 255
though I have no bar-gown.

---

[6] Pickled.

[7] If's (in this sense generally written 'an's').

PET. Go to, go to, mistress, you are impertinent, and there's your brief for you: instruct me!

(Flings her breviate at her.)

WID. Impertinent to me, you saucy Jack, you! You return my breviate, but where's my fee?　260 You'll be sure to keep that, and scan that so well, that if there chance to be but a brass half-crown in't, one's sure to hear on't again: would you would but look on your breviate half so narrowly! But pray give me my fee too, as well as my brief.　265

PET. Mistress, that's without precedent. When did a counsel ever return his fee, pray? And you are impertinent, and ignorant to demand it.

WID. Impertinent again, and ignorant, to me! Gadsbodikins, you puny upstart in the law, to　270 use me so! you green-bag carrier, you murderer of unfortunate causes, the clerk's ink is scarce off of your fingers — you that newly come from lamp-blacking the judges' shoes, and are not fit to wipe mine; you call me impertinent and ignorant!　275 I would give thee a cuff on the ear, sitting the courts,[1] if I were ignorant. Marry gep,[2] if it had not been for me, thou hadst been yet but a hearing counsel[3] at the bar.　　　*Exit* PETULANT.

Enter MR. BUTTONGOWN, *crossing the stage in haste.*

Mr. Buttongown, Mr. Buttongown, whither so　280 fast? what, won't you stay till we are heard?

BUT. I cannot, Mrs. Blackacre, I must be at the Council; my lord's cause stays there for me.

WID. And mine suffers here.

BUT. I cannot help it.　　　285

WID. I'm undone.

BUT. What's that to me?

WID. Consider the five-pound fee, if not my cause: that was something to you.

BUT. Away, away! pray be not so trouble-　290 some, mistress, I must be gone.

WID. Nay, but consider a little: I am your old client, my lord but a new one; or let him be what he will, he will hardly be a better client to you than myself. I hope you believe I shall be in law as　295 long as I live; therefore am no despicable client. Well, but go to your lord; I know you expect he should make you a judge one day; but I hope his promise to you will prove a true lord's promise.

---

[1] While the courts are in session. To commit an assault at such a time within the environs of a court was to subject oneself to severe penalties.

[2] Go along with you! (a phrase commonly addressed to a horse).

[3] A lawyer entitled to appear in interlocutory hearings, but not to plead before the full court; or, perhaps, an assistant counsel who listens to a trial and makes suggestions, but does not speak.

But that he might be sure to fail you, I wish　300 you had his bond for't.

BUT. But what! will you be thus impertinent, mistress?

WID. Nay, I beseech you, sir, stay; if it be but to tell me my lord's case; come, in short —　305

BUT. Nay, then —　　　*Exit* BUTTONGOWN.

WID. Well, Jerry, observe, child, and lay it up for hereafter: these are those lawyers who, by being in all causes, are in none; therefore if you would have 'em for you, let your adversary fee 'em; for he　310 may chance to depend upon 'em, and so, in being against thee, they'll be for thee.

JER. Ay, mother, they put me in mind of the unconscionable wooers of widows, who undertake briskly their matrimonial business for their　315 money; but when they have got it once, let [who] will drudge for them. Therefore have a care of 'em, forsooth: there's advice for your advice.

WID. Well said, boy. — Come, Mr. Splitcause, pray go see when my cause in Chancery comes　320 on; and go speak with Mr. Quillit in the King's Bench, and Mr. Quirk in the Common Pleas, and see how our matters go there.

Enter MAJOR OLDFOX.

OLD. Lady, a good and propitious morning to you; and may all your causes go as well as if I　325 myself were judge of 'em!

WID. Sir, excuse me; I am busy, and cannot answer compliments in Westminster Hall. — Go, Mr. Splitcause, and come to me again, to that book-seller's; there I'll stay for you, that you may be　330 sure to find me.

OLD. No, sir, come to the other bookseller's. — I'll attend your ladyship thither.

　　　Exit SPLITCAUSE.

WID. Why to the other?

OLD. Because he is my bookseller, lady.　335

WID. What, to sell you lozenges for your catarrh? or medicines for your corns? What else can a major deal with a bookseller for?

OLD. Lady, he prints for me.

WID. Why, are you an author?　　　340

OLD. Of some few essays; deign you, lady, to peruse 'em. — *(Aside.)* She is a woman of parts, and I must win her by showing mine.

The Bookseller's Boy [comes forward].

BOY. Will you see [Culpeper], mistress? *Aristotle's Problems*? *The Complete Midwife*?[4]　345

---

[4] Nicholas Culpeper, author of *The English Physician*, an enormously popular family handbook on medicine. The remaining two books were works erroneously ascribed to Aristotle.

WID. No; let's see Dalton, [Hughes, Sheppard], Wingate.[1]

BOY. We have no law books.

WID. No? you are a pretty bookseller then.

OLD. Come, have you e'er a one of my essays 350 left?

BOY. Yes, sir, we have enough, and shall always have 'em.

OLD. How so?

BOY. Why, they are good, steady, lasting 355 ware.

OLD. Nay, I hope they will live; let's see. — Be pleased, madam, to peruse the poor endeavors of my pen; [for I have a pen,] though I say it, that —

(*Gives her a book.*)

JER. Pray let me see *St. George for Christen-* 360 *dom* or *The Seven Champions of England*.[2]

WID. No, no; give him *The Young Clerk's Guide*.[3] — What, we shall have you read yourself into a humor of rambling, and fighting, and studying military discipline, and wearing red breeches! 365

OLD. Nay, if you talk of military discipline, show him my *Treatise of the Art Military*.

WID. Hold; I would as willingly he should read a play.

JER. Oh, pray, forsooth, mother, let me have 370 a play!

WID. No, sirrah; there are young students of the law enough spoiled already by plays; they would make you in love with your laundress, or, what's worse, some queen of the stage that was a 375 laundress; and so turn keeper before you are of age. (*Several crossing the stage.*) But stay, Jerry, is not that Mr. What-d'ye-call-him, that goes there, he that offered to sell me a suit in chancery for five hundred pound, for a hundred down, and only 380 paying the clerk's fees?

JER. Ay, forsooth, 'tis he.

WID. Then stay here, and have a care of the bags, whilst I follow him: have a care of the bags, I say.

JER. And do you have a care, forsooth, of the 385 statute against champerty,[4] I say.

Exit WIDOW BLACKACRE.

Enter FREEMAN *to them.*

FREE. (*aside*). So, there's a limb of my widow, which was wont to be inseparable from her: she

can't be far. — [*To* JERRY.] How now, my pretty son-in-law that shall be, where's my widow? 390

JER. My mother, but not your widow, will be forthcoming presently.

FREE. Your servant, major! What, are you buying furniture for a little sleeping closet, which you miscall a study? For you do only by your 395 books, as by your wenches, bind 'em up neatly and make 'em fine, for other people to use 'em; and your bookseller is properly your upholsterer, for he furnishes your room, rather than your head.

OLD. Well, well, good sea-lieutenant, study 400 you your compass; that's more than your head can deal with. — (*Aside.*) I will go find out the widow, to keep her out of his sight, or he'll board her, whilst I am treating a peace.   *Exit* OLDFOX.

Manent FREEMAN, JERRY.

JER. [*to the Bookseller's Boy*]. Nay, prithee, 405 friend, now let me have but *The Seven Champions*: you shall trust me no longer than till my mother's Mr. Splitcause comes; for I hope he'll lend me wherewithal to pay for't.

FREE. Lend thee! here, I'll pay him. Do 410 you want money, squire? I'm sorry a man of your estate should want money.

JER. Nay, my mother will ne'er let me be at age: and till then, she says —

FREE. At age! why, you are at age already 415 to have spent an estate, man: there are younger than you have kept their women this three years, have had half a dozen claps, and lost as many thousand pounds at play.

JER. Ay, they are happy sparks! Nay, I 420 know some of my schoolfellows who, when we were at school, were two years younger than me, but now, I know not how, are grown men before me, and go where they will, and look to themselves; but my curmudgeonly mother won't allow me where- 425 withal to be a man of myself with.

FREE. Why, there 'tis; I knew your mother was in fault. Ask but your schoolfellows what they did to be men of themselves.

JER. Why, I know they went to law with 430 their mothers; for they say, there's no good to be done upon a widow mother, till one goes to law with her; but mine is as plaguy a lawyer as any's of our inn. Then would she marry too, and cut down my trees: now, I should hate, man, to have my 435 father's wife kissed and slapped, and t'other thing too (you know what I mean) by another man; and our trees are the purest, tall, even, shady twigs, by my fa —

FREE. Come, squire, let your mother and 440

---

[1] Michael Dalton, William Hughes, William Sheppard, Edmund Wingate, all seventeenth-century writers upon the law.

[2] Jerry has here confused the titles of two pieces of popular literature.

[3] A manual for young lawyers, by Sir Richard Hutton.

[4] An illegal bargain to pay the expenses of a legal action in which one has no real interest, in return for a share of the sum recovered.

346] Q1Q3Q4Q6W1 *Hughs, Shepherd.*   359] Q1W1 *pen; for I have a pen, though;* Q3Q4Q6 om. *for I have a pen.*
367] Q3Q4Q6 Art of Military; Q1W1 Art Military.   377] Q4Q6 *is it not.*   417] Q1 *these three.*
428] Q5Q6W1 *in fault;* Q1Q3 *in the fault.*

your trees fall as she pleases, rather than wear this gown and carry green bags all thy life, and be pointed at for a tony.[1] But you shall be able to deal with her yet the common way; thou shalt make false love to some lawyer's daughter, whose father, upon   445 the hopes of thy marrying her, shall lend thee money and law to preserve thy estate and trees; and thy mother is so ugly nobody will have her, if she cannot cut down thy trees.

JER. Nay, if I had but anybody to stand by   450 me I am as stomachful as another.

FREE. That will I: I'll not see any hopeful young gentleman abused.

BOY (aside). By any but yourself.

JER. The truth on't is, mine's as arrant a   455 widow-mother to her poor child as any's in England. She won't so much as let one have sixpence in one's pocket to see a motion,[2] or the dancing of the ropes,[3] or —

FREE. Come, you shan't want money;   460 there's gold for you.

JER. O Lord, sir, two guineas! D'ye lend me this? Is there no trick in't? Well, sir, I'll give you my bond for security.

FREE. No, no; thou hast given me thy face   465 for security: anybody would swear thou dost not look like a cheat. You shall have what you will of me; and if your mother will not be kinder to you, come to me, who will.

JER. (aside). By my fa — he's a curious   470 fine gentleman! — But will you stand by one?

FREE. If you can be resolute.

JER. Can be resolved! Gad, if she gives me but a cross word, I'll leave her tonight and come to you. But now I have got money, I'll go to Jack-of-   475 all-Trades, at t'other end of the Hall, and buy the neatest, purest things —

FREE. [aside]. And I'll follow the great boy, and my blow at his mother: steal away the calf, and the cow will follow you.   480

Exit JERRY, *followed by* FREEMAN.

Enter, on the other side, MANLY, WIDOW BLACKACRE, *and* OLDFOX.

MAN. Damn your cause! can't you lose it without me? which you are like enough to do, if it be, as you say, an honest one: I will suffer no longer for't.

WID. Nay, captain, I tell you, you are my prime witness; and the cause is just now coming on,   485 Mr. Splitcause tells me. Lord, methinks you should take a pleasure in walking here, as half you see now do; for they have no business here, I assure you.

[1] Fool.   [2] Puppet-show.
[3] I.e., upon the tight-rope.

MAN. Yes; but I'll assure you then, their business is to persecute me; but d'ye think I'll stay   490 any longer, to have a rogue, because he knows my name, pluck me aside and whisper a news-book secret [4] to me with a stinking breath? A second come piping angry from the court, and sputter in my face his tedious complaints against it?   495 A third law-coxcomb, because he saw me once at a reader's dinner,[5] come and put me a long law case, to make a discovery of his indefatigable dulness and my wearied patience? A fourth, a most barbarous civil rogue, who will keep a man half an hour in   500 the crowd with a bowed body, and a hat off, acting the reformed sign of the Salutation tavern,[6] to hear his bountiful professions of service and friendship, whilst he cares not if I were damned, and I am wishing him hanged out of my way? — I'd as soon   505 run the gauntlet, as walk t'other turn.

Enter to them JERRY BLACKACRE *without his bags, but laden with trinkets, which he endeavors to hide from his mother, and followed at a distance by* FREEMAN.

WID. Oh, are you come, sir? But where have you been, you ass? and how come you thus laden?

JER. Look here, forsooth, mother; now here's a duck, here's a boar-cat,[7] and here's an owl.   510
(Making a noise with catcalls and other such like instruments.)

WID. Yes, there is an owl, sir.

OLD. He's an ungracious bird indeed.

WID. But go, thou trangame,[8] and carry back those trangames, which thou hast stolen or purloined; for nobody would trust a minor in   515 Westminster Hall, sure.

JER. Hold yourself contented, forsooth: I have these commodities by a fair bargain and sale; and there stands my witness, and creditor.

WID. How's that? What, sir, d'ye think to   520 get the mother by giving the child a rattle? — But where are my bags, my writings, you rascal?

JER. (aside). O law! where are they indeed!

WID. How, sirrah? speak, come —

MAN. (apart to [FREEMAN]). You can tell   525 her, Freeman, I suppose.

[4] A secret which has been gleaned from a newspaper, i.e., no secret at all.
[5] Readers, or lecturers, at the Inns of Court paid for their honorable office by dispensing lavish hospitality during the term of their lectures.
[6] The original sign was a picture of the Annunciation. This was changed several times. The tavern (a famous one) was in Billingsgate.
[7] Tom-cat.
[8] Paltry toy.

446] Q6 (copy used by Churchill) *thy hopes.*   466] Q4Q6 *and any body.*
508] Q4Q6W1 *came.*   (A misprint in Churchill's edition assigns these variants to line 497.)
525] Q1Q3Q4Q6W1 (*apart to him*).   525] Q6 *Who can.*

FREE. (*apart to him*). 'Tis true, I made one of your salt-water sharks steal 'em whilst he was eagerly choosing his commodities, as he calls 'em, in order to my design upon his mother.   530

WID. Won't you speak? Where were you, I say, you son of a — an unfortunate woman? — Oh, major, I'm undone! They are all that concern my estate, my jointure, my husband's deed of gift, my evidences for all my suits now depending!   535 What will become of them?

FREE. (*aside*). I'm glad to hear this. — [*Aloud.*] They'll be safe, I warrant you, madam.

WID. Oh, where? where? Come, you villain, along with me, and show me where.   540

Exeunt WIDOW BLACKACRE, JERRY, OLDFOX.

Manent MANLY, FREEMAN.

MAN. Thou hast taken the right way to get a widow, by making her great boy rebel; for when nothing will make a widow marry, she'll do't to cross her children. But canst thou in earnest marry this harpy, this volume of shrivelled blurred parch-   545 ments and law, this attorney's desk?

FREE. Ay, ay, I'll marry and live honestly: that is, give my creditors, not her, due benevolence — pay my debts.

MAN. Thy creditors, you see, are not so bar-   550 barous as to put thee in prison; and wilt thou commit thyself to a noisome dungeon for thy life? which is the only satisfaction thou canst give thy creditors by this match.

FREE. Why, is not she rich?   555

MAN. Ay, but he that marries a widow for her money will find himself as much mistaken as the widow that marries a young fellow for due benevolence, as you call it.

FREE. Why, d'ye think I shan't deserve   560 wages? I'll drudge faithfully.

MAN. I tell thee again, he that is the slave in the mine has the least propriety in the ore: you may dig, and dig; but if thou wouldst have her money, rather get to be her trustee than her husband; for a   565 true widow will make over her estate to anybody, and cheat herself, rather than be cheated by her children or a second husband.

Enter to them JERRY, *running in a fright*.

JER. O law! I'm undone, I'm undone! my mother will kill me. You said you'd stand by   570 one.

FREE. So I will, my brave squire, I warrant thee.

JER. Ay, but I dare not stay till she comes, for she's as furious, now she has lost her writings, as a bitch when she has lost her puppies.   575

MAN. The comparison's handsome.

JER. Oh, she's here!

Enter WIDOW BLACKACRE *and* OLDFOX.

FREE. (*to the Sailor*). Take him, Jack, and make haste with him to your master's lodging; and be sure you keep him up till I come.   580

[*Exeunt*] JERRY *and Sailor*.

WID. Oh, my dear writings! Where's this heathen rogue, my minor?

FREE. Gone to drown or hang himself.

WID. No, I know him too well; he'll ne'er be *felo de se* [1] that way: but he may go and choose a   585 guardian of his own head, and so be *felo de ses biens*; [2] for he has not yet chosen one.

FREE. (*aside*). Say you so? And he shan't want one.

WID. But, now I think on't, 'tis you, sir,   590 have put this cheat upon me; for there is a saying, 'Take hold of a maid by her smock, and a widow by her writings, and they cannot get from you.' But I'll play fast and loose with you yet, if there be law; and my minor and writings are not forth-   595 coming, I'll bring my action of detinue or trover. [3] But first, I'll try to find out this guardianless, graceless villain. — Will you jog, major?

MAN. If you have lost your evidence, I hope your causes cannot go on, and I may be gone?   600

WID. Oh, no; stay but a making-water while, as one may say, and I'll be with you again.

Exeunt WIDOW BLACKACRE *and* OLDFOX.

Manent MANLY, FREEMAN.

FREE. Well, sure I am the first man that ever began a love-intrigue in Westminster Hall.

MAN. No, sure; for the love to a widow gen-   605 erally begins here: and as the widow's cause goes against the heir or executors, the jointure-rivals commence their suit to the widow.

FREE. Well, but how, pray, have you passed your time here, since I was forced to leave you   610 alone? You have had a great deal of patience.

MAN. Is this a place to be alone, or have patience in? But I have had patience indeed, for I have drawn upon me, since I came, but three quarrels and two lawsuits.   615

FREE. Nay, faith, you are too cursed [4] to be let loose in the world; you should be tied up again in your sea-kennel, called a ship. But how could you quarrel here?

---

[1] A suicide (murderer of himself).

[2] A coinage by the widow out of law-Latin and law-French, meaning 'a murderer of his estate.'

[3] The former action was a method of recovering personal property lawfully obtained but unlawfully withheld; the latter a method of recovering damages for things wrongfully withheld. For once the widow's law is at fault; her proper action to recover her papers would have been replevin.

[4] Quarrelsome, perverse.

MAN. How could I refrain? A lawyer 620 talked peremptorily and saucily to me, and as good as gave me the lie.

FREE. They do it so often to one another at the bar, that they make no bones on't elsewhere.

MAN. However, I gave him a cuff on the ear; 625 whereupon he jogs two men, whose backs were turned to us (for they were reading at a bookseller's) to witness I struck him, sitting the courts; which office they so readily promised that I called 'em rascals and knights of the post. One of 'em 630 presently calls two other absent witnesses, who were coming towards us at a distance; whilst the other, with a whisper, desires to know my name, that he might have satisfaction by way of challenge, as t'other by way of writ; but if it were not rather 635 to direct his brother's writ, than his own challenge: there, you see, is one of my quarrels, and two of my lawsuits.

FREE. So! — and the other two?

MAN. For advising a poet to leave off writing 640 and turn lawyer, because he is dull and impudent, and says or writes nothing now but by precedent.

FREE. And the third quarrel?

MAN. For giving more sincere advice to a handsome, well-dressed young fellow (who asked it 645 too) not to marry a wench that he loved and I had lain with.

FREE. Nay, if you will be giving your sincere advice to lovers and poets you will not fail of quarrels. 650

MAN. Or if I stay in this place, for I see more quarrels crowding upon me. Let's be gone, and avoid 'em.

Enter NOVEL *at a distance, coming towards them.*

A plague on him, that sneer is ominous to us; he is coming upon us, and we shall not be rid of him. 655

NOV. Dear bully, don't look so grum [1] upon me; you told me just now, you had forgiven me a little harmless raillery upon wooden legs last night.

MAN. Yes, yes, pray begone, I am talking of business. 660

NOV. Can't I hear it? I love thee, and will be faithful, and always —

MAN. Impertinent! 'Tis business that concerns Freeman only.

NOV. Well, I love Freeman too, and would 665 not divulge his secret: prithee speak, prithee, I must —

MAN. Prithee let me be rid of thee; I must be rid of thee.

NOV. Faith, thou canst hardly, I love thee 670 so. Come, I must know the business.

[1] Sour, morose.

MAN. (*aside*). So, I have it now. — [*Aloud.*] Why, if you needs will know it, he has a quarrel, and his adversary bids him bring two friends with him: now, I am one, and we are thinking who 675 we shall have for a third.

(*Several crossing the stage.*)

NOV. A pox, there goes a fellow owes me an hundred pound, and goes out of town to-morrow: I'll speak with him, and come to you presently.

Exit NOVEL.

MAN. No, but you won't. 680

FREE. You are dextrously rid of him.

Enter OLDFOX.

MAN. To what purpose, since here comes another as impertinent? I know by his grin he is bound hither.

OLD. Your servant, worthy, noble captain. 685 Well, I have left the widow, because she carried me from your company: for, faith, captain, I must needs tell thee thou art the only officer in England, who was not an Edgehill officer,[2] that I care for.

MAN. I'm sorry for't. 690

OLD. Why, wouldst thou have me love them?

MAN. Anybody, rather than me.

OLD. What! you are modest, I see; therefore, too, I love thee.

MAN. No, I am not modest, but love to 695 brag myself, and can't patiently hear you fight over the last civil war; therefore, go look out the fellow I saw just now here, that walks with his stockings and his sword out at heels, and let him tell you the history of that scar on his cheek, to give you 700 occasion to show yours, got in the field at Bloomsbury,[3] not that of Edgehill. Go to him, poor fellow, he is fasting, and has not yet the happiness this morning to stink of brandy and tobacco: go, give him some to hear you; I am busy. 705

OLD. Well, ygad, I love thee now, boy, for thy surliness: thou art no tame captain, I see, that will suffer —

MAN. An old fox.

OLD. All that shan't make me angry: I con- 710 sider thou art peevish, and fretting at some ill success at law. Prithee, tell me what ill luck you have met with here.

MAN. You.

OLD. Do I look like the picture of ill luck? 715 Gadsnouns,[4] I love thee more and more; and shall I tell thee what made me love thee first?

[2] An officer (on the king's side) in the first battle of the Civil War, at Edge Hill, Warwickshire, in 1642.

[3] The fields north of Montagu House and Southampton House in Bloomsbury (behind the present British Museum) were favorite duelling-grounds.

[4] Probably a corruption of 'God's wounds.'

640] Q6 *For desiring.* 680] Q1 *wo'not.* 698–99] W1 *his sword and stockings.*
702] Q6 *at Edgehill.* 710–11] W1 *consider that thou.*

MAN. Do, that I may be rid of that damned quality and thee.

OLD. 'Twas thy wearing that broad sword 720 there.

MAN. Here, Freeman, let's change: I'll never wear it more.

OLD. How! you won't, sure. Prithee, don't look like one of our holiday captains now-a-days, 725 with a bodkin by your side, your martinet rogues.[1]

MAN. (aside). Oh, then there's hopes. — [Aloud.] What, d'ye find fault with martinet? Let me tell you, sir, 'tis the best exercise in the world; the most ready, most easy, most graceful exercise that 730 ever was used, and the most —

OLD. Nay, nay, sir, no more, sir; your servant! if you praise martinet once, I have done with you, sir. — Martinet! martinet! —   Exit OLDFOX.

FREE. Nay, you have made him leave you 735 as willingly as ever he did an enemy; for he was truly for the king and parliament: for the parliament, in their list; and for the king, in cheating 'em of their pay, and never hurting the king's party in the field.

Enter a Lawyer towards them.

MAN. A pox! this way; here's a lawyer I 740 know threat'ning us with another greeting.

LAW. Sir, sir, your very servant! I was afraid you had forgotten me.

MAN. I was not afraid you had forgotten me.

LAW. No, sir; we lawyers have pretty 745 good memories.

MAN. You ought to have, by your wits.

LAW. Oh, you are a merry gentleman, sir; I remember you were merry when I was last in your company.   750

MAN. I was never merry in thy company, Mr. Lawyer, sure.

LAW. Why, I'm sure you joked upon me, and shammed me all night long.

MAN. 'Shammed'! prithee, what barbarous 755 law-term is that?

LAW. Shamming! Why, don't you know that? 'tis all our way of wit, sir.

MAN. I am glad I do not know it then. Shamming! What does he mean by't, Freeman! 760

FREE. Shamming is telling you an insipid dull lie with a dull face, which the sly wag the author only laughs at himself; and making himself believe 'tis a good jest, puts the sham only upon himself.

MAN. So, your lawyer's jest, I find, like his 765 practice, has more knavery than wit in't. I should make the worst shammer in England: I must always

deal ingeniously,[2] as I will with you, Mr. Lawyer, and advise you to be seen rather with attorneys and solicitors, than such fellows as I am; they will 770 credit your practice more.

LAW. No, sir, your company's an honor to me.

MAN. No, faith; go thy ways, there goes an attorney; leave me for him; let it be never said a lawyer's civility did him hurt.   775

LAW. No, worthy, honored sir; I'll not leave you for any attorney, sure.

MAN. Unless he had a fee in his hand.

LAW. Have you any business here, sir? Try me: I'd serve you sooner than any attorney breath- 780 ing.

MAN. Business! — (Aside.) So, I have thought of a sure way. — [Aloud.] Yes, faith, I have a little business.

LAW. Have you so, sir? in what court, sir? 785 what is't, sir? Tell me but how I may serve you, and I'll do't, sir, and take it for as great an honor —

MAN. Faith, 'tis for a poor orphan of a sea officer of mine, that has no money; but if it could be followed *in forma pauperis*,[3] and when the leg- 790 acy's recovered —

LAW. *Forma pauperis*, sir!

MAN. Ay, sir.   (Several crossing the stage.)

LAW. Mr. Bumblecase, Mr. Bumblecase! a word with you. — Sir, I beg your pardon at pres- 795 ent; I have a little business —

MAN. Which is not *in forma pauperis*.

                                        Exit Lawyer.

FREE. So, you have now found a way to be rid of people without quarrelling.

Enter Alderman.

MAN. But here's a city rogue will stick 800 as hard upon us, as if I owed him money.

ALD. Captain, noble sir, I am yours heartily, d'ye see; why should you avoid your old friends?

MAN. And why should you follow me? I owe you nothing.   805

ALD. Out of my hearty respects to you; for there is not a man in England —

MAN. Thou wouldst save from hanging, with the expense of a shilling only.

ALD. Nay, nay, but, captain, you are like 810 enough to tell me —

MAN. Truth, which you won't care to hear; therefore you had better go talk with somebody else.

ALD. No, I know nobody can inform me better of some young wit, or spendthrift, that has a 815

---

[1] Young officers who approved of the infantry drill instituted by General Martinet, a contemporary French drill-master.

[2] Ingenuously.

[3] In the form of a pauper; a legal action by which a poor person might have legal redress without the payment of a fee.

724] Q1 *wo'not.*   726] W1 *you martinet.*   768] Q6W1 *as well with.*   773] Q1W1 *go this way.*
774] W1 *never be.*

good dipped seat [1] and estate in Middlesex, Hertford-shire, Essex, or Kent; any of these would serve my turn: now, if you knew of such an one, and would but help —

MAN. You to finish his ruin. 820

ALD. I'faith, you should have a snip [2] —

MAN. Of your nose, you thirty-in-the-hundred rascal; [3] would you make me your squire setter, [4] your bawd for manors? (*Takes him by the nose.*)

ALD. Oh! 825

FREE. Hold, or here will be your third law-suit.

ALD. Gads precious, you hectoring person you, are you wild? I meant you no hurt, sir: I begin to think, as things go, land-security best, and have, for a convenient mortgage, some ten, fifteen, or 830 twenty thousand pound by me.

MAN. Then go lay it out upon an hospital, and take a mortgage of heaven, according to your city custom; for you think, by laying out a little money, to hook in that too hereafter: do, I say, and 835 keep the poor you've made by taking forfeitures, that heaven may not take yours.

ALD. No, to keep the cripples you make this war; this war spoils our trade.

MAN. Damn your trade! 'tis the better 840 for't.

ALD. What, will you speak against our trade?

MAN. And dare you speak against the war, our trade?

ALD. (*aside*). Well, he may be a convoy of 845 ships I am concerned in. — [*Aloud.*] Come, captain, I will have a fair correspondency with you, [5] say what you will.

MAN. Then prithee begone.

ALD. No, faith; prithee, captain, let's go 850 drink a dish of laced coffee, [6] and talk of the times: come, I'll treat you; nay, you shall go, for I have no business here.

MAN. But I have.

ALD. To pick up a man to give thee a 855 dinner? Come, I'll do thy business for thee.

MAN. Faith, now I think on't, so you may, as well as any man; for 'tis to pick up a man to be bound with me, to one who expects city security, for —

ALD. Nay, then your servant, captain! business must be done. 860

MAN. Ay, if it can; but hark you, alderman, with-out you —

ALD. Business, sir, I say, must be done; (*several*

crossing the stage*) and there's an officer of the 865 treasury I have an affair with —

Exit Alderman.

MAN. You see now what the mighty friendship of the world is; what all ceremony, embraces, and plen-tiful professions come to: you are no more to believe a professing friend than a threat'ning enemy; 870 and as no man hurts you, that tells you he'll do you a mischief, no man, you see, is your servant, who says he is so. Why the devil, then, should a man be troubled with the flattery of knaves, if he be not a fool or cully; or with the fondness of fools, 875 if he be not a knave or cheat?

FREE. Only for his pleasure; for there is some in laughing at fools and disappointing knaves.

MAN. That's a pleasure, I think, would cost you too dear, as well as marrying your widow to 880 disappoint her; but, for my part, I have no pleasure by 'em but in despising 'em, wheresoe'er I meet 'em; and then the pleasure of hoping so to be rid of 'em. But now my comfort is, I am not worth a shilling in the world, which all the world shall 885 know; and then I'm sure I shall have none of 'em come near me.

FREE. A very pretty comfort, which I think you pay too dear for. But is the twenty pound gone since the morning? 890

MAN. To my boat's crew. Would you have the poor, honest, brave fellows want?

FREE. Rather than you or I.

MAN. Why, art thou without money? thou who art a friend to everybody? 895

FREE. I ventured my last stake upon the squire to nick him of [7] his mother, and cannot help you to a dinner, unless you will go dine with my lord —

MAN. No, 'no; the ordinary is too dear 900 for me, where flattery must pay for my dinner: I am no herald, or poet.

FREE. We'll go then to the bishop's —

MAN. There you must flatter the old philosophy: I cannot renounce my reason for a dinner. 905

FREE. Why, then let's go to your alderman's.

MAN. Hang him, rogue! that were not to dine; for he makes you drunk with lees of sack before dinner, to take away your stomach: and there you must call usury and extortion God's blessing, or 910 the honest turning of the penny; hear him brag of the leather breeches in which he trotted first to town, and make a greater noise with his money in his parlor, than his cashiers do in his counting-house, without hopes of borrowing a shilling. 915

FREE. Ay, a pox on't! 'tis like dining with the great gamesters; and when they fall to their com-

[1] Mortgaged residence.
[2] Share.
[3] Lender of money at thirty per cent.
[4] Spy upon the landed gentry. A 'setter,' in thieves' slang, is the man who finds out what victims are worth robbing.
[5] Be on good terms with you.
[6] Coffee mixed with spirits.

[7] Lure him from.

mon dessert, see the heaps of gold drawn on all hands, without going to twelve.[1] Let us go to my Lady Goodly's.   920

MAN. There, to flatter her looks, you must mistake her grandchildren for her own; praise her cook, that she may rail at him; and feed her dogs, not yourself.

FREE. What d'ye think of eating with your 925 lawyer, then?

MAN. Eat with him! damn him! To hear him employ his barbarous eloquence in a reading upon the two-and-thirty good bits in a shoulder of veal,[2] and be forced yourself to praise the cold bribe- 930 pie that stinks, and drink law-French wine as rough and harsh as his law-French. A pox on him! I'd rather dine in the Temple-rounds[3] or walks, with the knights without noses,[4] or the knights of the post, who are honester fellows, and better company. 935 But let us home and try our fortune; for I'll stay no longer here for your damned widow.

FREE. Well, let us go home then; for I must go for my damned widow, and look after my new damned charge. Three or four hundred years 940 ago a man might have dined in this hall.[5]

MAN. But now the lawyer only here is fed; And, bully-like, by quarrels gets his bread.

                                                 Exeunt.

ACT IV

SCENE I

MANLY'S *lodging.*

Enter MANLY *and* FIDELIA.

MAN. Well, there's success in thy face. Hast thou prevailed? say.

FID. As I could wish, sir.

MAN. So; I told thee what thou wert fit for, and thou wouldst not believe me. Come, thank me 5 for bringing thee acquainted with thy genius. Well, thou hast mollified her heart for me?

FID. No, sir, not so; but what's better.

MAN. How? what's better!

FID. I shall harden your heart against her. 10

MAN. Have a care, sir; my heart is too much in earnest to be fooled with, and my desire at heighth, and needs no delays to incite it. What, you are too

[1] Apparently gambling slang, but the meaning is obscure: if 'twelve' is a cant term for a pair of dice, the phrase may mean 'without handling the dice.'

[2] An old commonplace.

[3] The confines of the Temple.

[4] The recumbent statues of the old Knights Templar in the Temple Church had become badly dilapidated.

[5] It had been built for a banqueting-hall by William II in 1097.

good a pimp already, and know how to endear pleasure by withholding it? But leave off your 15 page's bawdy-house tricks, sir, and tell me, will she be kind?

FID. Kinder than you could wish, sir.

MAN. So, then: well, prithee, what said she?

FID. She said —   20

MAN. What? thou'rt so tedious: speak comfort to me; what?

FID. That of all things you are her aversion.

MAN. How!

FID. That she would sooner take a bedfellow 25 out of an hospital, and diseases, into her arms, than you.

MAN. What?

FID. That she would rather trust her honor with a dissolute debauched hector, nay worse, with a 30 finical baffled[6] coward, all over loathsome with affectation of the fine gentleman.

MAN. What's all this you say?

FID. Nay, that my offers of your love to her were more offensive than when parents woo their 35 virgin-daughters to the enjoyment of riches only; and that you were in all circumstances as nauseous to her as a husband on compulsion.

MAN. Hold! I understand you not.

FID. (*aside*). So, 'twill work, I see.   40

MAN. Did not you tell me —

FID. She called you ten thousand ruffians.

MAN. Hold, I say.

FID. Brutes —

MAN. Hold.   45

FID. Sea-monsters —

MAN. Damn your intelligence! Hear me a little now.

FID. Nay, surly coward she called you too.

MAN. Won't you hold yet? Hold, or —   50

FID. Nay, sir, pardon me; I could not but tell you she had the baseness, the injustice, to call you coward, sir; coward, coward, sir.

MAN. Not yet? —

FID. I've done. Coward, sir.   55

MAN. Did not you say she was kinder than I could wish her?

FID. Yes, sir.

MAN. How then? — Oh! — I understand you now. At first she appeared in rage and disdain, 60 the truest sign of a coming woman; but at last you prevailed, it seems: did you not?

FID. Yes, sir.

MAN. So then, let's know that only; come, prithee, without delays. I'll kiss thee for that 65 news beforehand.

[6] Degraded.

FID. (aside). So; the kiss, I'm sure, is welcome to me, whatsoe'er the news will be to you.

MAN. Come, speak, my dear volunteer.

FID. (aside). How welcome were that kind 70 word too, if it were not for another woman's sake!

MAN. What, won't you speak? You prevailed for me at last, you say?

FID. No, sir.

MAN. No more of your fooling, sir: it will not 75 agree with my impatience or temper.

FID. Then not to fool you, sir, I spoke to her for you, but prevailed for myself; she would not hear me when I spoke in your behalf, but bid me say what I would in my own, though she gave me 80 no occasion, she was so coming, and so was kinder, sir, than you could wish; which I was only afraid to let you know, without some warning.

MAN. How's this? Young man, you are of a lying age; but I must hear you out, and if — 85

FID. I would not abuse you, and cannot wrong her by any report of her, she is so wicked.

MAN. How, wicked! had she the impudence, at the second sight of you only —

FID. Impudence, sir! oh, she has impudence 90 enough to put a court out of countenance, and debauch a stews.

MAN. Why, what said she?

FID. Her tongue, I confess, was silent; but her speaking eyes gloated such things, more im- 95 modest and lascivious than ravishers can act, or women under a confinement think.

MAN. I know there are whose eyes reflect more obscenity than the glasses in alcoves; but there are others who use a little art with their looks, to 100 make 'em seem more beautiful, not more loving; which vain young fellows like you are apt to interpret in their own favor, and to the lady's wrong.

FID. Seldom, sir. Pray, have you a care of gloating eyes; for he that loves to gaze upon 'em will 105 find at last a thousand fools and cuckolds in 'em instead of Cupids.

MAN. Very well, sir. But what, you had only eye-kindness from Olivia?

FID. I tell you again, sir, no woman sticks 110 there; eye-promises of love they only keep; nay, they are contracts which make you sure of 'em. In short, sir, she, seeing me with shame and amazement dumb, unactive, and resistless, threw her twisting arms about my neck, and smothered me with 115 a thousand tasteless kisses: believe me, sir, they were so to me.

MAN. Why did you not avoid 'em then?

FID. I fenced with her eager arms, as you did with the grapples of the enemy's fireship, and 120 nothing but cutting 'em off could have freed me.

MAN. Damned, damned woman, that could be so false and infamous! And damned, damned heart of mine, that cannot yet be false, though so infamous! What easy, tame, suffering, trampled things 125 does that little god of talking cowards make of us! but —

FID. (aside). So! it works, I find, as I expected.

MAN. But she was false to me before; she told me so herself, and yet I could not quite believe 130 it; but she was, so that her second falseness is a favor to me, not an injury, in revenging me upon the man that wronged me first of her love. Her love! — a whore's, a witch's love! — But what, did she not kiss well, sir? — I'm sure I thought her lips — 135 but I must not think of 'em more — but yet they are such I could still kiss — grow to — and then tear off with my teeth, grind 'em into mammocks,[1] and spit 'em into her cuckold's face.

FID. (aside). Poor man, how uneasy he is! I 140 have hardly the heart to give him so much pain, though withal I give him a cure, and to myself new life.

MAN. But what, her kisses sure could not but warm you into desire at last, or a compliance 145 with hers at least?

FID. Nay, more, I confess —

MAN. What more? speak.

FID. All you could fear had passed between us, if I could have been made to wrong you, sir, in 150 that nature.

MAN. Could have been made! you lie, you did.

FID. Indeed, sir, 'twas impossible for me; besides, we were interrupted by a visit; but I confess, she would not let me stir, till I promised to return 155 to her again within this hour, as soon as it should be dark, by which time she would dispose of her visit, and her servants, and herself, for my reception: which I was fain to promise, to get from her.

MAN. Ha! 160

FID. But if ever I go near her again, may you, sir, think me as false to you, as she is; hate and renounce me, as you ought to do her, and, I hope, will do now.

MAN. Well, but now I think on't, you shall keep your word with your lady. What, a young 165 fellow, and fail the first, nay, so tempting an assignation!

FID. How, sir?

MAN. I say, you shall go to her when 'tis dark, and shall not disappoint her. 170

FID. I, sir! I should disappoint her more by going; for —

MAN. How so?

FID. Her impudence and injustice to you will make me disappoint her love, loathe her. 175

[1] Shapeless pieces.

MAN. Come, you have my leave; and if you disgust [1] her, I'll go with you, and act love, whilst you shall talk it only.

FID. You, sir! nay, then I'll never go near her. You act love, sir! You must but act it indeed, 180 after all I have said to you. Think of your honor, sir — love! —

MAN. Well, call it revenge, and that is honorable: I'll be revenged on her; and thou shalt be my second.

FID. Not in a base action, sir, when you are 185 your own enemy. Oh, go not near her, sir; for heaven's sake, for your own, think not of it!

MAN. How concerned you are! I thought I should catch you. What, you are my rival at last, and are in love with her yourself; and have 190 spoken ill of her out of your love to her, not me; and therefore would not have me go to her!

FID. Heaven witness for me, 'tis because I love you only, I would not have you go to her.

MAN. Come, come, the more I think on't, 195 the more I'm satisfied you do love her: those kisses, young man, I knew were irresistible; 'tis certain.

FID. There is nothing certain in the world, sir, but my truth and your courage.

MAN. Your servant, sir! Besides, false 200 and ungrateful as she has been to me, and though I may believe her hatred to me great as you report it, yet I cannot think you are so soon and at that rate beloved by her, though you may endeavor it.

FID. Nay, if that be all, and you doubt it 205 still, sir, I will conduct you to her; and unseen, your ears shall judge of her falseness, and my truth to you, if that will satisfy you.

MAN. Yes, there is some satisfaction in being quite out of doubt; because 'tis that alone 210 withholds us from the pleasure of revenge.

FID. Revenge! What revenge can you have, sir? Disdain is best revenged by scorn; and faithless love, by the loving another and making her happy with the other's losings: which, if I might advise — 215

Enter FREEMAN.

MAN. Not a word more.

FREE. What, are you talking of love yet, captain? I thought you had done with't.

MAN. Why, what did you hear me say?

FREE. Something imperfectly of love, I 220 think.

MAN. I was only wondering why fools, rascals, and desertless wretches should still have the better of men of merit with all women, as much as with their own common mistress, Fortune. 225

FREE. Because most women, like Fortune, are blind, seem to do all things in jest, and take pleasure

in extravagant actions; their love deserves neither thanks or blame, for they cannot help it: 'tis all sympathy; therefore the noisy, the finical, the 230 talkative, the cowardly, and effeminate have the better of the brave, the reasonable, and man of honor; for they have no more reason in their love, or kindness, than Fortune herself.

MAN. Yes, they have their reason. First, 235 honor in a man they fear too much to love; and sense in a lover upbraids their want of it; and they hate anything that disturbs their admiration of themselves; but they are of that vain number who had rather show their false generosity, in giving 240 away profusely to worthless flatterers, than in paying just debts. And, in short, all women, like Fortune (as you say) and rewards, are lost by too much meriting.

FID. All women, sir! sure there are some who 245 have no other quarrel to a lover's merit but that it begets their despair of him.

MAN. Thou art young enough to be credulous; but we —

Enter first Sailor.

1ST SAIL. Here are now below the scolding 250 daggled gentlewoman and that Major Old — Old — fop, I think you call him.

FREE. Oldfox: — prithee bid 'em come up, — with your leave, captain, for now I can talk with her upon the square, if I shall not disturb you. 255
[Exit Sailor.]

MAN. No; for I'll be gone. Come, volunteer.

FREE. Nay, pray stay; the scene between us will not be so tedious to you as you think; besides, you shall see how I have rigged my squire out with the remains of my shipwracked wardrobe; he is 260 under your sea valet-de-chambre's hands, and by this time dressed, and will be worth your seeing. Stay, and I'll fetch my fool.

MAN. No; you know I cannot easily laugh; besides, my volunteer and I have business abroad. 265
Exeunt MANLY, FIDELIA *on one side;* FREEMAN *on t'other.*

Enter MAJOR OLDFOX *and* WIDOW BLACKACRE.

WID. What, nobody here! Did not the fellow say he was within?

OLD. Yes, lady; and he may be perhaps a little busy at present; but if you think the time long till he comes, *(unfolding papers)* I'll read you here 270 some of the fruits of my leisure, the overflowings of my fancy and pen. — *(Aside.)* To value me right, she must know my parts. — *[Aloud.]* Come —

WID. No, no; I have reading work enough of my own in my bag, I thank you. 275

---
[1] Have no taste for her.

OLD. Ay, law, madam; but here is a poem, in blank verse, which I think a handsome declaration of one's passion.

WID. Oh, if you talk of declarations,[1] I'll show you one of the prettiest penned things, which 280 I mended too myself, you must know.

OLD. Nay, lady, if you have used yourself so much to the reading of harsh law that you hate smooth poetry, here is a character for you, of —

WID. A character! Nay, then I'll show you 285 my bill in chancery here, that gives you such a character of my adversary, makes him as black —

OLD. Pshaw! away, away, lady! But if you think the character too long, here is an epigram, not above twenty lines, upon a cruel lady, who decreed 290 her servant should hang himself, to demonstrate his passion.

WID. Decreed! if you talk of decreeing, I have such a decree here, drawn by the finest clerk —

OLD. O lady, lady, all interruption, and no 295 sense between us, as if we were lawyers at the bar! But I had forgot, Apollo and Littleton[2] never lodge in a head together. If you hate verses, I'll give you a cast[3] of my politics in prose: 'tis a letter to a friend in the country, which is now the way of all such 300 sober, solid persons as myself, when they have a mind to publish their disgust to the times; though perhaps, between you and I, they have no friend in the country. And sure a politic, serious person may as well have a feigned friend in the country to 305 write to, as well as an idle poet a feigned mistress to write to. And so here's my *Letter to a Friend* (or no friend) *in the Country, concerning the late Conjuncture of Affairs, in relation to Coffee-houses; or the Coffeeman's Case*.[4] 310

WID. Nay, if your letter have a case in't, 'tis something; but first I'll read you a letter of mine, to a friend in the country, called a letter of attorney.[5]

Enter to them FREEMAN, *and* JERRY BLACKACRE *in an old gaudy suit and red breeches of* FREEMAN'S.

OLD. (*aside*). What, interruption still! Oh, the plague of interruption! worse to an author than 315 the plague of critics.

WID. What's this I see? Jerry Blackacre, my minor, in red breeches! What, hast thou left the modest, seemly garb of gown and cap for this? and have I lost all my good Inns of Chancery breed- 320 ing upon thee, then? and thou wilt go a-breeding thy-

self from our Inn of Chancery and Westminster Hall, at coffee-houses and ordinaries,[6] play-houses, tennis-courts, and bawdy-houses?

JER. Ay, ay, what then? perhaps I will; but 325 what's that to you? here's my guardian and tutor now, forsooth, that I am out of your huckster's hands.

WID. How? thou hast not chosen him for thy guardian yet? 330

JER. No, but he has chosen me for his charge, and that's all one; and I'll do anything he'll have me, and go all the world over with him: to ordinaries and bawdy-houses, or anywhere else.

WID. To ordinaries and bawdy-houses! have 335 a care, minor, thou wilt infeeble there thy estate and body: do not go to ordinaries and bawdy-houses, good Jerry.

JER. Why, how come you to know any ill by bawdy-houses? You never had any hurt by 340 'em, had you, forsooth? Pray hold yourself contented; if I do go where money and wenches are to be had, you may thank yourself; for you used me so unnaturally, you would never let me have a penny to go abroad with, nor so much as come near the 345 garret where your maidens lay; nay, you would not so much as let me play at hotcockles[7] with 'em, nor have any recreation with 'em, though one should have kissed you behind, you were so unnatural a mother, so you were. 350

FREE. Ay, a very unnatural mother, faith, squire.

WID. But, Jerry, consider thou art yet but a minor; however, if thou wilt go home with me again, and be a good child, thou shalt see —

FREE. Madam, I must have a better care of 355 my heir under age than so; I would sooner trust him alone with a stale waiting-woman and a parson, than with his widow-mother and her lover or lawyer.

WID. Why, thou villain! part mother and minor! rob me of my child and my writings! but thou 360 shalt find there's law; and as in the case of ravishment of guard — Westminster the Second.[8]

OLD. Young gentleman, squire, pray be ruled by your mother and your friends.

JER. Yes, I'll be ruled by my friends, there- 365 fore not by my mother, so I won't: I'll choose him for my guardian till I am of age; nay, maybe, for as long as I live.

WID. Wilt thou so, thou wretch? and when thou'rt of age, thou wilt sign, seal, and deliver 370 too, wilt thou?

---

[1] In the legal sense — statements of claim.

[2] Sir Thomas de Littleton (d. 1481), author of a classic work on land tenures.

[3] Sample.

[4] Apparently a reference to one of several occasions on which the government closed the coffee-houses as centers of disaffection.

[5] A document authorizing one person to act for another.

[6] Eating-houses.

[7] A game in which a blindfolded player, being struck by one of the others, guesses who struck him.

[8] The Second Statute of Westminster, chapter 35 (1285) provided a remedy against the abduction of a ward (*ravishment de gard*).

JER. Yes, marry will I, if you go there too.

WID. Oh, do not squeeze wax,¹ son; rather go to ordinaries and bawdy-houses than squeeze wax. If thou dost that, farewell the goodly manor of 375 Blackacre, with all its woods, underwoods, and appurtenances whatever! Oh, oh! (*Weeps.*)

FREE. Come, madam, in short, you see I am resolved to have a share in the estate, yours or your son's; if I cannot get you, I'll keep him, who is 380 less coy, you find; but if you would have your son again you must take me too. Peace or war? love or law? You see my hostage is in my hand: I'm in possession.

WID. Nay, if one of us must be ruined, e'en 385 let it be him. By my body, a good one! Did you ever know yet a widow marry or not marry for the sake of her child? I'd have you to know, sir, I shall be hard enough for you both yet, without marrying you: if Jerry won't be ruled by me — what say 390 you, booby, will you be ruled? speak.

JER. Let one alone, can't you?

WID. Wilt thou choose him for guardian, whom I refuse for husband?

JER. Ay, to choose, I thank you. 395

WID. And are all my hopes frustrated? Shall I never hear thee put cases again to John the butler, or our vicar? never see thee amble the circuit with the judges, and hear thee, in our town-hall, louder than the crier? 400

JER. No, for I have taken my leave of lawyering and pettifogging.

WID. Pettifogging! thou profane villain, hast thou so? Pettifogging! — then you shall take your leave of me, and your estate too; thou shalt be an 405 alien to me and it forever. Pettifogging!

JER. Oh, but if you go there too, mother, we have the deed and settlements, I thank you: would you cheat me of my estate, i'fac?

WID. No, no, I will not cheat your little 410 brother Bob; for thou wert not born in wedlock.

FREE. How's that?

JER. How? What quirk has she got in her head now?

WID. I say thou canst not, shalt not inherit 415 the Blackacres' estate.

JER. Why? Why, forsooth? What d'ye mean, if you go there too?

WID. Thou art but my base ² child, and according to the law, canst not inherit it. Nay, thou art 420 not so much as bastard eigne.³

JER. What, what? Am I then the son of a whore, mother?

WID. The law says —

FREE. Madam, we know what the law says, 425 but have a care what you say. Do not let your passion to ruin your son ruin your reputation.

WID. Hang reputation, sir! am not I a widow? have no husband, nor intend to have any? Nor would you, I suppose, now have me for a wife. 430 So I think now I'm revenged on my son and you, without marrying, as I told you.

FREE. But consider, madam.

JER. What, have you no shame left in you, mother? 435

WID. (*aside to* OLDFOX). Wonder not at it, major. 'Tis often the poor pressed widow's case, to give up her honor to save her jointure, and seem to be a light woman, rather than marry: as some young men, they say, pretend to have the filthy disease, and lose 440 their credit with most women, to avoid the importunities of some.

FREE. But one word with you, madam.

WID. No, no, sir. Come, major, let us make haste now to the Prerogative Court.⁴ 445

OLD. But, lady, if what you say be true, will you stigmatise your reputation on record? and if it be not true, how will you prove it?

WID. Pshaw! I can prove anything; and for my reputation, know, major, a wise woman will 450 no more value her reputation in disinheriting a rebellious son of a good estate, than she would in getting him, to inherit an estate.

Exeunt WIDOW BLACKACRE *and* OLDFOX.

FREE. Madam! — We must not let her go so, squire. 455

JER. Nay, the devil can't stop her, though, if she has a mind to't. But come, bully guardian, we'll go and advise with three attorneys, two proctors,⁵ two solicitors, and a shrewd man of White-friars,⁶ neither attorney, proctor, or solicitor, 460 but as pure a pimp to the law as any of 'em; and sure all they will be hard enough for her, for I fear, bully guardian, you are too good a joker to have any law in your head.

FREE. Thou'rt in the right on't, squire; I 465 understand no law, especially that against bastards, since I'm sure the custom is against that law, and more people get estates by being so, than lose 'em.

Exeunt.

---

¹ I.e., by impressing it with a seal.
² Illegitimate.
³ Elder bastard — a legal term for an illegitimate child whose parents had subsequently married each other and had a child born in wedlock.

⁴ The archbishop's court for the trial of cases concerning wills.
⁵ Lawyers practising in the ecclesiastical courts.
⁶ The disreputable district called Alsatia was in Whitefriars. It still had the privilege of sanctuary, and consequently harbored all kinds of ne'er-do-wells.

[Scene II]

The scene changes to Olivia's *lodging.*

Enter Lord Plausible *and Boy with a candle.*

L. Plaus. Little gentleman, your most obedient, faithful, humble servant! Where, I beseech you, is that divine person, your noble lady?

Boy. Gone out, my lord; but commanded me to give you this letter.　　　(*Gives him a letter.*)　5

Enter to him Novel.

L. Plaus. (*aside*). Which he must not observe.
　　　　　　　　　　　　　　(*Puts it up.*)

Nov. Hey, boy, where is thy lady?

Boy. Gone out, sir; but I must beg a word with you.　　　*Gives him a letter, and exit.*

Nov. For me? So.— (*Puts up the letter.*)　10 Servant, servant, my lord! you see the lady knew of your coming, for she is gone out.

L. Plaus. Sir, I humbly beseech you not to censure the lady's good breeding: she has reason to use more liberty with me than with any other　15 man.

Nov. How, viscount, how?

L. Plaus. Nay, I humbly beseech you, be not in choler; where there is most love, there may be most freedom.　20

Nov. Nay, then 'tis time to come to an *éclaircissement*[1] with you, and to tell you, you must think no more of this lady's love.

L. Plaus. Why, under correction, dear sir?

Nov. There are reasons, reasons, viscount.　25

L. Plaus. What, I beseech you, noble sir?

Nov. Prithee, prithee, be not impertinent, my lord; some of you lords are such conceited, well-assured, impertinent rogues.

L. Plaus. And you noble wits are so full of　30 shamming and drolling, one knows not where to have you seriously.

Nov. Well, you shall find me in bed with this lady one of these days.

L. Plaus. Nay, I beseech you, spare the　35 lady's honor; for hers and mine will be all one shortly.

Nov. Prithee, my lord, be not an ass. Dost thou think to get her from me? I have had such good encouragements —

L. Plaus. I have not been thought unworthy　40 of 'em.

Nov. What, not like mine! Come to an *éclaircissement*, as I said.

L. Plaus. Why, seriously then, she has told me 'Viscountess' sounded prettily.　45

Nov. And me, that Novel was a name she would sooner change hers for than for any title in England.

L. Plaus. She has commended the softness and respectfulness of my behavior.

Nov. She has praised the briskness of my　50 raillery, of all things, man.

L. Plaus. The sleepiness of my eyes she liked.

Nov. Sleepiness! dulness, dulness. But the fierceness of mine she adored.

L. Plaus. The brightness of my hair she　55 liked.

Nov. The brightness! no, the greasiness, I warrant. But the blackness and lustre of mine she admires.

L. Plaus. The gentleness of my smile.　60

Nov. The subtilty of my leer.

L. Plaus. The clearness of my complexion.

Nov. The redness of my lips.

L. Plaus. The whiteness of my teeth.

Nov. My jaunty way of picking them.　65

L. Plaus. The sweetness of my breath.

Nov. Ha, ha!— Nay, then she abused you, 'tis plain; for you know what Manly said: the sweetness of your pulvillio she might mean; but for your breath! ha, ha, ha! Your breath is such, man, that　70 nothing but tobacco can perfume, and your complexion nothing could mend but the small-pox.

L. Plaus. Well, sir, you may please to be merry; but, to put you out of all doubt, sir, she has received some jewels from me of value.　75

Nov. And presents from me, besides what I presented her jauntily, by way of ombre, of three or four hundred pound value, which I'm sure are the earnest-pence for our love-bargain.

L. Plaus. Nay, then, sir, with your favor,　80 and to make an end of all your hopes, look you there, sir, she has writ to me —

Nov. How! how! well, well, and so she has to me; look you there — (*Deliver to each other their letters.*)

L. Plaus. What's here?　85

Nov. How's this? (*Reads out.*)

— 'My dear lord, — You'll excuse me for breaking my word with you, since 'twas to oblige, not offend you; for I am only gone abroad but to disappoint Novel, and meet you in the drawing-room, where　90 I expect you with as much impatience as when I used to suffer Novel's visits — the most impertinent fop that ever affected the name of a wit: therefore not capable, I hope, to give you jealousy; for, for your sake alone, you saw I renounced an old　95 lover, and will do all the world. Burn the letter, but lay up the kindness of it in your heart, with your
　　　　　　　　　　　　　　Olivia.'

Very fine! but pray let's see mine.

L. Plaus. I understand it not; but sure she　100 cannot think so of me.

Nov. (*reads the other letter*). Humh! ha!— 'meet — for your sake' — umh — 'quitted an old lover —

---

[1] Clarification, understanding.

world — burn — in your heart, with your Olivia.'
Just the same, the names only altered.   105

L. PLAUS. Surely there must be some mistake, or
somebody has abused her and us.

NOV. Yes, you are abused, no doubt on't, my
lord; but I'll to Whitehall, and see.

L. PLAUS. And I, where I shall find you are   110
abused.

NOV. Where, if it be so, for our comfort, we cannot
fail of meeting with fellow-sufferers enough; for, as
Freeman said of another, she stands in the drawing-
room, like the glass, ready for all comers, to set   115
their gallantry by her: and, like the glass too, lets
no man go from her unsatisfied with himself.

Exeunt ambo.

Enter OLIVIA *and Boy.*

OLIV. Both here, and just gone?

BOY. Yes, madam.

OLIV. But are you sure neither saw you   120
deliver the other a letter?

BOY. Yes, yes, madam, I am very sure.

OLIV. Go then to the Old Exchange, to Westminster, Holborn,[1] and all the other places I told
you of; I shall not need you these two hours: 125
begone, and take the candle with you, and be sure
you leave word again below, I am gone out, to all
that ask.

BOY. Yes, madam.   *Exit.*

OLIV. And my new lover will not ask, I'm   130
sure; he has his lesson, and cannot miss me here,
though in the dark, which I have purposely designed,
as a remedy against my blushing gallant's modesty;
for young lovers, like gamecocks, are made bolder
by being kept without light.   135

Enter her husband VERNISH, *as from a journey.*

VER. (*softly*). Where is she? Darkness everywhere!

OLIV. What! come before your time? My soul!
my life! your haste has augmented your kindness;
and let me thank you for it thus, and thus —   140
(*embracing and kissing him*). And though, my soul,
the little time since you left me has seemed an age to
my impatience, sure it is yet but seven —

VER. How! who's that you expected after seven?

OLIV. (*aside*). Ha! my husband returned!   145
and have I been throwing away so many kind kisses
on my husband, and wronged my lover already?

VER. Speak, I say, who was't you expected after
seven?

OLIV. (*aside*). What shall I say? — oh! —   150
[*Aloud.*] Why 'tis but seven days, is it, dearest, since

you went out of town? and I expected you not so
soon.

VER. No, sure, 'tis but five days since I left you.

OLIV. Pardon my impatience, dearest, I   155
thought 'em seven at least.

VER. Nay, then —

OLIV. But, my life, you shall never stay half so
long from me again; you shan't indeed, by this kiss
you shan't.   160

VER. No, no; but why alone in the dark?

OLIV. Blame not my melancholy in your absence.
But, my soul, since you went, I have strange news
to tell you: Manly is returned.

VER. Manly returned! Fortune forbid!   165

OLIV. Met with the Dutch in the channel, fought,
sunk his ship, and all he carried with him. He was
here with me yesterday.

VER. And did you own our marriage to him?

OLIV. I told him I was married to put an   170
end to his love and my trouble; but to whom is yet
a secret kept from him and all the world. And I
have used him so scurvily, his great spirit will ne'er
return to reason it farther with me: I have sent him
to sea again, I warrant.   175

VER. 'Twas bravely done. And sure he will now
hate the shore more than ever, after so great a disappointment. Be you sure only to keep a while our
great secret, till he be gone; in the mean time, I'll
lead the easy, honest fool by the nose, as I used   180
to do; and whilst he stays, rail with him at thee; and
when he's gone, laugh with thee at him. But have
you his cabinet of jewels safe? Part not with a seed-
pearl to him, to keep him from starving.

OLIV. Nor from hanging.   185

VER. He cannot recover 'em, and, I think, will
scorn to beg 'em again.

OLIV. But, my life, have you taken the thousand
guineas he left in my name out of the goldsmith's
hands?   190

VER. Ay, ay; they are removed to another goldsmith's.

OLIV. Ay, but, my soul, you had best have a care
he find not where the money is; for his present wants,
as I'm informed, are such as will make him in-   195
quisitive enough.

VER. You say true, and he knows the man too;
but I'll remove it tomorrow.

OLIV. Tomorrow! Oh, do not stay till tomorrow;
go tonight, immediately.   200

VER. Now I think on't, you advise well, and I will
go presently.

OLIV. Presently! instantly! I will not let you
stay a jot.

VER. I will then, though I return not home   205
till twelve.

OLIV. Nay, though not till morning, with all my

---

[1] These three places are widely separated: the 'Old Exchange'
was the Royal Exchange in Cornhill.

145] Q1W1 om. (*aside*).   194] W1 *you find.*

heart: go, dearest; I am impatient till you are gone.
(*Thrusts him out.*) — So, I have at once now brought
about those two grateful businesses which all　210
prudent women do together, secured money and
pleasure; and now all interruptions of the last are
removed. Go, husband, and come up, friend; just
the buckets in the well; the absence of one brings the
other; but I hope, like them too, they will not　215
meet in the way, justle, and clash together.

Enter FIDELIA, *and* MANLY, *treading softly and
staying behind at some distance.*

So, are you come? (but not the husband-bucket, I
hope, again). — (*Softly.*) Who's there? my dearest?

FID. My life —

OLIV. Right, right. — Where are thy lips?　220
Here, take the dumb and best welcomes, kisses and
embraces; 'tis not a time for idle words. In a duel of
love, as in others, parleying shows basely. Come,
we are alone, and now the word is only satisfaction,
and defend not thyself.　225

MAN. (*aside*). How's this? Wuh, she makes love
like a devil in a play; and in this darkness, which
conceals her angel's face, if I were apt to be afraid,
I should think her a devil.

OLIV. (FIDELIA *avoiding her*). What, you　230
traverse ground, young gentleman!

FID. I take breath only.

MAN. (*aside*). Good heavens! how was I deceived!

OLIV. Nay, you are a coward; what, are you
afraid of the fierceness of my love?　235

FID. Yes, madam, lest its violence might presage
its change; and I must needs be afraid you would
leave me quickly, who could desert so brave a gentleman as Manly.

OLIV. Oh, name not his name! for in a time　240
of stol'n joys, as this is, the filthy name of husband
were not a more allaying sound.

MAN. (*aside*). There's some comfort yet.

FID. But did you not love him?

OLIV. Never. How could you think it?　245

FID. Because he thought it, who is a man of that
sense, nice discerning, and diffidency, that I should
think it hard to deceive him.

OLIV. No; he that distrusts most the world, trusts
most to himself, and is but the more easily　250
deceived because he thinks he can't be deceived: his
cunning is like the coward's sword, by which he is
oft'ner worsted than defended.

FID. Yet, sure, you used no common art to deceive him.　255

OLIV. I knew he loved his own singular morose-
ness so well as to dote upon any copy of it; wherefore
I feigned an hatred to the world too, that he might

love me in earnest: but, if it had been hard to deceive
him, I'm sure 'twere much harder to love him.　260
A dogged, ill-mannered —

FID. (*aside to* MANLY). D'ye hear her, sir? pray,
hear her.

OLIV. Surly, untractable, snarling brute! he! a
masty [1] dog were as fit a thing to make a gal-　265
lant of.

MAN. (*aside*). Ay, a goat or monkey were fitter for
thee.

FID. I must confess, for my part, though my rival,
I cannot but say he has a manly handsomeness　270
in's face and mien.

OLIV. So has a Saracen in the sign. [2]

FID. Is proper, and well-made.

OLIV. As a drayman.

FID. Has wit.　275

OLIV. He rails at all mankind.

FID. And undoubted courage.

OLIV. Like the hangman's; can murder a man
when his hands are tied. He has cruelty indeed,
which is no more courage, than his railing is　280
wit.

MAN. (*aside*). Thus women, and men like women,
are too hard for us, when they think we do not hear
'em: and reputation, like other mistresses, is never
true to a man in his absence.　285

FID. He is —

OLIV. Prithee, no more of him; I thought I had
satisfied you enough before, that he could never be
a rival for you to apprehend; and you need not be
more assured of my aversion to him but by the　290
last testimony of my love to you; which I am ready
to give you. Come, my soul, this way —

(*Pulls* FIDELIA.)

FID. But, madam, what could make you dissemble love to him, when 'twas so hard a thing for
you, and flatter his love to you?　295

OLIV. That which makes all the world flatter
and dissemble, 'twas his money: I had a real passion
for that. Yet I loved not that so well as for it to
take him; for, as soon as I had his money, I hastened
his departure, like a wife, who, when she has　300
made the most of a dying husband's breath, pulls
away the pillow.

MAN. [*aside*]. Damned money! its master's potent
rival still; and like a saucy pimp, corrupts, itself, the
mistress it procures for us.　305

OLIV. But I did not think with you, my life, to
pass my time in talking. Come hither, come; yet
stay, till I have locked a door in the other room, that
may chance to let us in some interruption; which

---

[1] Mastiff.

[2] I.e., of the Saracen's Head tavern, in what is now Holborn
Viaduct.

reciting poets or losing gamesters fear not more 310
than I at this time do.   *Exit* OLIVIA.

FID. Well, I hope you are now satisfied, sir, and
will be gone, to think of your revenge?

MAN. No, I am not satisfied, and must stay to be
revenged.   315

FID. How, sir? You'll use no violence to her, I
hope, and forfeit your own life, to take away hers?
That were no revenge.

MAN. No, no, you need not fear: my revenge
shall only be upon her honor, not her life.   320

FID. How, sir? her honor? O heavens! consider,
sir, she has no honor. D'ye call that revenge? Can
you think of such a thing? But reflect, sir, how she
hates and loathes you.

MAN. Yes, so much she hates me, that it 325
would be a revenge sufficient to make her accessary
to my pleasure, and then let her know it.

FID. No, sir, no; to be revenged on her now, were
to disappoint her. Pray, sir, let us be gone.
          (*Pulls* MANLY.)

MAN. Hold off! What, you are my rival 330
then! and therefore you shall stay, and keep the door
for me, whilst I go in for you; but when I'm gone, if
you dare to stir off from this very board, or breathe
the least murmuring accent, I'll cut her throat first;
and if you love her, you will not venture her 335
life. Nay, then I'll cut your throat too; and I know
you love your own life at least.

FID. But, sir, good sir!

MAN. Not a word more, lest I begin my revenge
on her by killing you.   340

FID. But are you sure 'tis revenge that makes
you do this? how can it be?

MAN. Whist![1]

FID. 'Tis a strange revenge, indeed.

MAN. If you make me stay, I shall keep my 345
word, and begin with you. No more!

Exit MANLY, *at the same door* OLIVIA *went.*

Manet FIDELIA.

FID. O heav'ns! is there not punishment enough
In loving well, if you will have't a crime,
But you must add fresh torments daily to't,
And punish us like peevish rivals still,   350
Because we fain would find a heaven here?
But did there never any love like me,
That, untried tortures, you must find me out?
Others, at worst, you force to kill themselves;
But I must be self-murdress of my love,   355
Yet will not grant me pow'r to end my life,
My cruel life; for when a lover's hopes
Are dead and gone, life is unmerciful.
          (*Sits down and weeps.*)

[1] Hush!

Enter MANLY *to her.*

MAN. (*aside*). I have thought better on't; I must
not discover myself now; I am without wit- 360
nesses; for if I barely should publish it, she would
deny it with as much impudence as she would act it
again with this young fellow here. — Where are you?

FID. Here — oh — now I suppose we may be
gone.   365

MAN. I will, but not you; you must stay and act
the second part of a lover, that is, talk kindness to
her.

FID. Not I, sir.

MAN. No disputing, sir, you must; 'tis neces- 370
sary to my design of coming again tomorrow night.

FID. What, can you come again then hither?

MAN. Yes; and you must make the appointment,
and an apology for your leaving her so soon; for I
have said not a word to her; but have kept your 375
counsel, as I expect you should do mine. Do this
faithfully, and I promise you here, you shall run my
fortune still, and we will never part as long as we
live; but if you do not do it, expect not to live.

FID. 'Tis hard, sir, but such a consideration 380
will make it easier; you won't forget your promise,
sir?

MAN. No, by heav'ns! But I hear her coming.
          Exit.

Enter OLIVIA *to* FIDELIA.

OLIV. Where is my life? Run from me already!
You do not love me, dearest; nay, you are angry 385
with me, for you would not so much as speak a kind
word to me within: what was the reason?

FID. I was transported too much.

OLIV. That's kind; but come, my soul, what make
you here? Let us go in again; we may be sur- 390
prised in this room, 'tis so near the stairs.

FID. No, we shall hear the better here, if anybody
should come up.

OLIV. Nay, I assure you, we shall be secure
enough within: come, come —   395

FID. I am sick, and troubled with a sudden
dizziness; cannot stir yet.

OLIV. Come, I have spirits within.

FID. Oh! — don't you hear a noise, madam?

OLIV. No, no, there is none; come, come.   400
          (*Pulls her.*)

FID. Indeed there is; and I love you so much, I
must have a care of your honor, if you wo' not, and
go; but to come to you tomorrow night, if you please.

OLIV. With all my soul; but you must not go yet;
come, prithee.   405

FID. Oh! — I am now sicker, and am afraid of one
of my fits.

OLIV. What fits?

FID. Of the falling sickness; and I lie generally an hour in a trance: therefore pray consider your 410 honor for the sake of my love, and let me go, that I may return to you often.

OLIV But will you be sure then to come tomorrow night?

FID. Yes. 415

OLIV. Swear.

FID. By our past kindness!

OLIV. Well, go your ways then, if you will, you naughty creature you. *Exit* FIDELIA. These young lovers, with their fears and 420 modesty, make themselves as bad as old ones to us; and I apprehend their bashfulness more than their tattling.

FIDELIA *returns.*

FID. O madam, we're undone! There was a gentleman upon the stairs, coming up with a 425 candle, which made me retire. Look you, here he comes!

Enter VERNISH, *and his Man with a light.*

OLIV. How, my husband! Oh, undone indeed! This way. *Exit.*

VER. Ha! You shall not escape me so, sir. 430 *(Stops* FIDELIA.*)*

FID. *(aside).* O heav'ns! more fears, plagues, and torments yet in store!

VER. Come, sir, I guess what your business was here; but this must be your business now. Draw! *(Draws.)*

FID. Sir — 435

VER. No expostulations; I shall not care to hear of't. Draw!

FID. Good sir!

VER. How, you rascal! not courage to draw, yet durst do me the greatest injury in the world? 440 Thy cowardice shall not save thy life. *(Offers to run at* FIDELIA.*)*

FID. Oh, hold, sir, and send but your servant down, and I'll satisfy you, sir, I could not injure you as you imagine.

VER. Leave the light and begone. — 445 *Exit Servant.* Now, quickly, sir, what you've to say, or —

FID. I am a woman, sir, a very unfortunate woman.

VER. How! a very handsome woman, I'm sure then: here are witnesses of't too, I confess — 450 *(Pulls off her peruke and feels her breasts.)* *(Aside.)* Well, I'm glad to find the tables turned, my wife in more danger of cuckolding than I was.

FID. Now, sir, I hope you are so much a man of

honor as to let me go, now I have satisfied you, 455 sir.

VER. When you have satisfied me, madam, I will.

FID. I hope, sir, you are too much a gentleman to urge those secrets from a woman which concern her honor. You may guess my misfortune to 460 be love by my disguise; but a pair of breeches could not wrong you, sir.

VER. I may believe love has changed your outside, which could not wrong me; but why did my wife run away? 465

FID. I know not, sir; perhaps because she would not be forced to discover me to you, or to guide me from your suspicions, that you might not discover me yourself; which ungentlemanlike curiosity I hope you will cease to have, and let me go. 470

VER. Well, madam, if I must not know who you are, 'twill suffice for me only to know certainly what you are: which you must not deny me. Come, there is a bed within, the proper [rack] for lovers; and if you are a woman, there you can keep no se- 475 crets; you'll tell me there all unasked. Come. *(Pulls her.)*

FID. Oh! what d'ye mean? Help! oh! —

VER. I'll show you; but 'tis in vain to cry out: no one dares help you, for I am lord here.

FID. Tyrant here! — But if you are master 480 of this house, which I have taken for a sanctuary, do not violate it yourself.

VER. No, I'll preserve you here, and nothing shall hurt you, and will be as true to you as your disguise; but you must trust me then. Come, come. 485

FID. Oh! oh! rather than you shall drag me to a [deed] so horrid and so shameful, I'll die here a thousand deaths. — But you do not look like a ravisher, sir.

VER. Nor you like one would put me to't; 490 but if you will —

FID. Oh! oh! help! help! —

Enter Servant.

VER. You saucy rascal, how durst you come in, when you heard a woman squeak? That should have been your cue to shut the door. 495

SERV. I come, sir, to let you know, the alderman coming home immediately after you were at his house, has sent his cashier with the money, according to your note.

VER. Damn his money! Money never came 500 to any, sure, unseasonably, till now. Bid him stay.

SERV. He says, he cannot a moment.

VER. Receive it you then.

SERV. He says, he must have your receipt for it: — he is in haste, for I hear him coming up, sir. 505

430] Q1 *scape.*   431] Q6W1 *heavens.*   431] W1 *fear.*   446] W1 *what have you to.*
474] Q3Q4Q6 *racks;* Q1W1 *rack.*   486] Q6W1 *should.*   487] Q1Q3Q4Q6W1 *death;* Hunt *deed.*
493] Q4 *dost.*

VER. Damn him! Help me in here then with this dishonorer of my family.

FID. Oh! oh!

SERV. You say she is a woman, sir.

VER. No matter, sir: must you prate?   510

FID. O heav'ns! is there —

> (*They thrust her in, and lock the door.*)

VER. Stay there, my prisoner; you have a short reprieve.

I'll fetch the gold, and that she can't resist,
For with a full hand 'tis we ravish best.   515

> *Exeunt.*

ACT V

SCENE I

ELIZA's *lodging.*

Enter OLIVIA *and* ELIZA.

OLIV. Ah, cousin, nothing troubles me, but that I have given the malicious world its revenge, and reason now to talk as freely of me as I used to do of it.

ELIZA. Faith, then, let not that trouble you; for, to be plain, cousin, the world cannot talk worse   5 of you than it did before.

OLIV. How, cousin? I'd have you to know, before this *faux pas*, this trip of mine, the world could not talk of me.

ELIZA. Only that you mind other people's   10 actions so much that you take no care of your own, but to hide 'em; that, like a thief, because you know yourself most guilty, you impeach your fellow-criminals first, to clear yourself.

OLIV. O wicked world!   15

ELIZA. That you pretend an aversion to all man-kind in public, only that their wives and mistresses may not be jealous, and hinder you of their conversation in private.

OLIV. Base world!   20

ELIZA. That abroad you fasten quarrels upon innocent men for talking of you, only to bring 'em to ask you pardon at home, and to become dear friends with them, who were hardly your acquaintance before.   25

OLIV. Abominable world!

ELIZA. That you condemn the obscenity of modern plays, only that you may not be censured for never missing the most obscene of the old ones.

OLIV. Damned world!   30

ELIZA. That you deface the nudities of pictures and little statues only because they are not real.

OLIV. Oh, fie, fie, fie! hideous, hideous, cousin! the obscenity of their censures makes me blush!

ELIZA. The truth of 'em, the naughty world   35 would say now.

Enter LETTICE *hastily.*

LET. O madam! here is that gentleman coming up who now you say is my master.

OLIV. O cousin! whither shall I run? protect me, or —   40

> (OLIVIA *runs away, and stands at a distance.*)

Enter VERNISH.

VER. Nay, nay, come —

OLIV. O sir, forgive me!

VER. Yes, yes, I can forgive you being alone in the dark with a woman in man's clothes; but have a care of a man in woman's clothes.   45

OLIV. (*aside*). What does he mean? he dissembles, only to get me into his power: or has my dear friend made him believe he was a woman? My husband may be deceived by him, but I'm sure I was not.

VER. Come, come, you need not have lain   50 out of your house for this; but perhaps you were afraid, when I was warm with suspicions, you must have discovered who she was: and prithee may I not know it?

OLIV. She was — (*Aside.*) I hope he has been   55 deceived: and since my lover has played the card, I must not renounce.[1]

VER. Come, what's the matter with thee? If I must not know who she is, I'm satisfied without. Come hither.   60

OLIV. Sure you do know her; she has told you herself, I suppose.

VER. No, I might have known her better, but that I was interrupted by the goldsmith you know, and was forced to lock her into your chamber, to   65 keep her from his sight; but, when I returned, I found she was got away by tying the window-curtains to the balcony, by which she slid down into the street; for, you must know, I jested with her, and made her believe I'd ravish her, which she   70 apprehended, it seems, in earnest.

OLIV. And she got from you?

VER. Yes.

OLIV. And is quite gone?

VER. Yes.   75

OLIV. I'm glad on't — otherwise you had ravished her, sir? But how dar'st you go so far as to make her believe you would ravish her? let me understand that, sir. What! there's guilt in your face, you blush too; nay, then you did ravish her, you   80 did, you base fellow! What, ravish a woman in the first month of our marriage! 'Tis a double injury to me, thou base, ungrateful man! wrong my bed already, villain! I could tear out those false eyes, barbarous, unworthy wretch!   85

ELIZA. So, so! —

---

[1] Fail to follow suit.

VER. Prithee hear, my dear.

OLIV. I will never hear you, my plague, my torment!

VER. I swear — prithee, hear me.　　90

OLIV. I have heard already too many of your false oaths and vows, especially your last in the church. O wicked man! and wretched woman that I was! I wish I had then sunk down into a grave, rather than to have given you my hand, to be led to your　95 loathsome bed. Oh — oh —　　(*Seems to weep.*)

VER. So, very fine! just a marriage-quarrel! which, though it generally begins by the wife's fault, yet, in the conclusion, it becomes the husband's; and whosoever offends at first, he only is sure to　100 ask pardon at last. My dear —

OLIV. My devil!

VER. Come, prithee be appeased, and go home; I have bespoken our supper betimes: for I could not eat till I found you. Go, I'll give you all kind　105 of satisfactions; and one, which uses to be a reconciling one, two hundred of those guineas I received last night, to do what you will with.

OLIV. What, would you pay me for being your bawd?　　110

VER. Nay, prithee no more; go, and I'll throughly satisfy you when I come home; and then, too, we will have a fit of laughter at Manly, whom I am going to find at the Cock in Bow Street, where, I hear, he dined. Go, dearest, go home.　　115

ELIZA (*aside*). A very pretty turn, indeed, this!

VER. Now, cousin, since by my wife I have that honor and privilege of calling you so, I have something to beg of you too, which is, not to take notice of our marriage to any whatever yet a while,　120 for some reasons very important to me; and next, that you will do my wife the honor to go home with her; and me the favor, to use that power you have with her, in our reconcilement.

ELIZA. That, I dare promise, sir, will be no　125 hard matter. Your servant!　　*Exit* VERNISH.
Well, cousin, this, I confess, was reasonable hypocrisy; you were the better for't.

OLIVE. What hypocrisy?

ELIZA. Why, this last deceit of your husband　130 was lawful, since in your own defence.

OLIV. What deceit? I'd have you to know I never deceived my husband.

ELIZA. You do not understand me, sure; I say, this was an honest come-off, and a good one;　135 but 'twas a sign your gallant had had enough of your conversation, since he could so dext'rously cheat your husband in passing for a woman.

OLIV. What d'ye mean, once more, with my gallant, and passing for a woman?　　140

ELIZA. What do you mean? You see your husband took him for a woman.

OLIV. Whom?

ELIZA. Heyday! Why, the man he found you with, for whom last night you were so much　145 afraid; and who you told me —

OLIV. Lord, you rave, sure!

ELIZA. Why, did not you tell me last night —

OLIV. I know not what I might tell you last night in a fright.　　150

ELIZA. Ay, what was that fright for? for a woman? besides, were you not afraid to see your husband just now? I warrant, only for having been found with a woman! Nay, did you not just now, too, own your false step, or trip, as you called it?　155 which was with a woman too! Fie, this fooling is so insipid, 'tis offensive!

OLIV. And fooling with my honor will be more offensive. Did you not hear my husband say he found me with a woman in man's clothes? and　160 d'ye think he does not know a man from a woman?

ELIZA. Not so well, I'm sure, as you do; therefore I'd rather take your word.

OLIV. What, you grow scurrilous, and are, I find, more censorious than the world! I must have　165 a care of you, I see.

ELIZA. No, you need not fear yet; I'll keep your secret.

OLIV. My secret! I'd have you to know, I have no need of confidents,[1] though you value your-　170 self upon being a good one.

ELIZA. O admirable confidence! You show more in denying your wickedness, than other people in glorying in't.

OLIV. 'Confidence,' to me! to me such lan-　175 guage! nay, then I'll never see your face again. — (*Aside.*) I'll quarrel with her, that people may never believe I was in her power, but take for malice all the truth she may speak against me. — Lettice, where are you? Let us be gone from this censorious,　180 ill woman.

ELIZA (*aside*). Nay, thou shalt stay a little, to damn thyself quite. — One word first, pray, madam; can you swear that whom your husband found you with —　　185

OLIV. Swear! ay, that whosoever 'twas that stole up, unknown, into my room, when 'twas dark, I know not, whether man or woman, by heav'ns! by all that's good, or may I never more have joys here, or in the other world! Nay, may I eternally —　190

ELIZA. Be damned. So, so, you are damned enough already by your oaths; and I enough confirmed; and now you may please to be gone. Yet take this advice with you, in this plain-dealing age, to leave off forswearing yourself; for when　195 people hardly think the better of a woman for her

---

[1] Confidants. Eliza plays on the word in her next speech.

real modesty, why should you put that great constraint upon yourself to feign it?

OLIV. Oh, hideous, hideous advice! Let us go out of the hearing of it. She will spoil us, Lettice. 200

Exeunt OLIVIA *and* LETTICE *at one door,* ELIZA *at t'other.*

[SCENE II]

The scene changes to the Cock in Bow Street.
A table and bottles.

MANLY *and* FIDELIA.

MAN. How! saved her honor by making her husband believe you were a woman! 'Twas well, but hard enough to do, sure.

FID. We were interrupted before he could contradict me. 5

MAN. But can't you tell me, d'ye say, what kind of man he was?

FID. I was so frightened, I confess, I can give no other account of him but that he was pretty tall, round-faced, and one, I'm sure, I ne'er had 10 seen before.

MAN. But she, you say, made you swear to return tonight?

FID. But I have since sworn, never to go near her again; for the husband would murder me, or 15 worse, if he caught me again.

MAN. No, I'll go with you, and defend you tonight, and then I'll swear, too, never to go near her again.

FID. Nay, indeed, sir, I will not go, to be 20 accessary to your death too. Besides, what should you go again, sir, for?

MAN. No disputing, or advice, sir; you have reason to know I am unalterable. Go, therefore, presently, and write her a note, to enquire if 25 her assignation with you holds; and if not to be at her own house, where else; and be importunate to gain admittance to her tonight. Let your messenger, ere he deliver your letter, enquire first if her husband be gone out. Go, 'tis now almost six of the 30 clock; I expect you back here before seven, with leave to see her then. Go, do this dextrously, and expect the performance of my last night's promise, never to part with you.

FID. Ay, sir; but will you be sure to remem- 35 ber that?

MAN. Did I ever break my word? Go, no more replies, or doubts.   *Exit* FIDELIA.

Enter FREEMAN *to* MANLY.

Where hast thou been?

FREE. In the next room, with my Lord 40 Plausible and Novel.

MAN. Ay, we came hither, because 'twas a private house; but with thee indeed no house can be private, for thou hast that pretty quality of the familiar fops of the town, who, in an eating-house, always 45 keep company with all people in't but those they came with.

FREE. I went into their room, but to keep them, and my own fool the squire, out of your room; but you shall be peevish now, because you have no 50 money. But why the devil won't you write to those we were speaking of? since your modesty, or your spirit, will not suffer you to speak to 'em, to lend you money, why won't you try 'em at last that way?

MAN. Because I know 'em already, and can 55 bear want better than denials, nay, than obligations.

FREE. Deny you! they cannot. All of 'em have been your intimate friends.

MAN. No, they have been people only I have obliged particularly. 60

FREE. Very well; therefore you ought to go to 'em the rather, sure.

MAN. No, no. Those you have obliged most, most certainly avoid you, when you can oblige 'em no longer; and they take your visits like so many 65 duns: friends, like mistresses, are avoided for obligations past.

FREE. Pshaw! but most of 'em are your relations, men of great fortune and honor.

MAN. Yes; but relations have so much honor 70 as to think poverty taints the blood, and disown their wanting kindred; believing, I suppose, that as riches at first makes a gentleman, the want of 'em degrades him. But damn 'em! now I am poor, I'll anticipate their contempt, and disown them. 75

FREE. But you have many a female acquaintance whom you have been liberal to, who may have a heart to refund to you a little, if you would ask it: they are not all Olivias.

MAN. Damn thee! how couldst thou think of 80 such a thing? I would as soon rob my footman of his wages. Besides 'twere in vain too; for a wench is like a box in an ordinary, receives all people's money easily, but there is no getting, nay, shaking any out again; and he that fills it is surest never to keep 85 the key.

FREE. Well, but noble captain, would you make me believe that you, who know half the town, have so many friends, and have obliged so many, can't borrow fifty or an hundred pound? 90

MAN. Why, noble lieutenant, you who know all the town, and call all you know friends, methinks should not wonder at it, since you find ingratitude too· for how many lords' families (though descended from blacksmiths or tinkers) hast thou called 95 great and illustrious? how many ill tables [called]

4] Q4Q6 *are interrupted.*   17] Q6W1 *I will go.*   37] Q4Q6 *never.*   73] Q6 *make.*   74] Q1 *I'm.*

83] Q4Q6 *receive.*   85] Q1W1 *sure.*   96] Q1Q3Q4Q6W1 *call.*

good eating? how many noisy coxcombs wits? how many pert, cocking[1] cowards stout? how many tawdry, affected rogues well-dressed? how many perukes admired? and how many ill verses 100 applauded? and yet canst not borrow a shilling. Dost thou expect I, who always spoke truth, should?

FREE. Nay, now you think you have paid me; but hark you, captain, I have heard of a thing called grinning honor,[2] but never of starving honor. 105

MAN. Well, but it has been the fate of some brave men: and if they wo'not give me a ship again, I can go starve anywhere, with a musket on my shoulder.

FREE. Give you a ship! why, you will not solicit it. 110

MAN. If I have not solicited it by my services, I know no other way.

FREE. Your servant, sir! nay, then I'm satisfied, I must solicit my widow the closer, and run the desperate fortune of matrimony on shore. *Exit.* 115

Enter, to MANLY, VERNISH.

MAN. How! — Nay, here is a friend indeed; and he that has him in his arms can know no wants.

(*Embraces* VERNISH.)

VER. Dear sir! and he that is in your arms is secure from all fears whatever: nay, our nation is secure by your defeat at sea, and the Dutch 120 that fought against you have proved enemies to themselves only, in bringing you back to us.

MAN. Fie, fie! this from a friend? and yet from any other 'twere unsufferable: I thought I should never have taken anything ill from you. 125

VER. A friend's privilege is to speak his mind, though it be taken ill.

MAN. But your tongue need not tell me you think too well of me; I have found it from your heart, which spoke in actions, your unalterable heart. 130 But Olivia is false, my friend, which I suppose is no news to you.

VER. (*aside*). He's in the right on't.

MAN. But couldst thou not keep her true to me?

VER. Not for my heart, sir. 135

MAN. But could you not perceive it at all before I went? Could she so deceive us both?

VER. I must confess, the first time I knew it was three days after your departure, when she received the money you had left in Lombard Street in 140 her name; and her tears did not hinder her, it seems, from counting that. You would trust her with all, like a true generous lover.

MAN. And she, like a mean, jilting —

VER. Trait'rous — 145

MAN. Base —

VER. Damned —

MAN. Covetous —

VER. Mercenary whore. — (*Aside.*) I can hardly hold from laughing. 150

MAN. Ay, a mercenary whore indeed, for she made me pay her before I lay with her.

VER. How! — Why, have you lain with her?

MAN. Ay, ay.

VER. Nay, she deserves you should report it 155 at least, though you have not.

MAN. Report it! by heav'n, 'tis true!

VER. How! sure not.

MAN. I do not use to lie, nor you to doubt me.

VER. When? 160

MAN. Last night, about seven or eight of the clock.

VER. Ha! — (*Aside.*) Now I remember, I thought she spake as if she expected some other rather than me. A confounded whore, indeed! 165

MAN. But what, thou wonderest at it! nay, you seem to be angry too.

VER. I cannot but be enraged against her, for her usage of you: damned, infamous, common jade!

MAN. Nay, her cuckold, who first cuckolded 170 me in my money, shall not laugh all himself; we will do him reason, shan't we?

VER. Ay, ay.

MAN. But thou dost not, for so great a friend, take pleasure enough in your friend's revenge, 175 methinks.

VER. Yes, yes; I'm glad to know it, since you have lain with her.

MAN. Thou canst not tell me who that rascal, her cuckold, is? 180

VER. No.

MAN. She would keep it from you, I suppose.

VER. Yes, yes.

MAN. Thou wouldst laugh, if thou knewest but all the circumstances of my having her. Come, 185 I'll tell thee.

VER. Damn her! I care not to hear any more of her.

MAN. Faith, thou shalt. You must know —

Enter FREEMAN *backwards, endeavoring to keep out* NOVEL, LORD PLAUSIBLE, JERRY, *and* OLDFOX, *who all press in upon him.*

FREE. I tell you, he has a wench with him, 190 and would be private.

MAN. Damn 'em! a man can't open a bottle in these eating-houses, but presently you have these impudent, intruding, buzzing flies and insects in your glass. — Well, I'll tell thee all anon. In 195 the mean time, prithee, go to her, but not from me,

---

[1] Swaggering (either from cocking the hat jauntily, or from strutting like a cock).

[2] The grimace of a man slain in honorable combat; cf. Falstaff's 'I like not such grinning honor as Sir Walter hath.' (*I Henry IV*, V. iii. 61, 62).

and try if you can get her to lend me but an hundred pound of my money, to supply my present wants; for I suppose there is no recovering any of it by law.

VER. Not any; think not of it; or by this   200 way neither.

MAN. Go try, at least.

VER. I'll go; but I can satisfy you beforehand 'twill be to no purpose. You'll no more find a re-funding wench —   205

MAN. Than a refunding lawyer; indeed their fees alike scarce ever return. However, try her; put it to her.

VER. Ay, ay, I'll try her, put it to her home with a vengeance.   *Exit* VERNISH.   210

Manent cæteri.

NOV. Nay, you shall be our judge, Manly. — Come, major, I'll speak it to your teeth; if people provoke me to say bitter things to their faces, they must take what follows; though, like my Lord Plau-sible, I'd rather do't civilly behind their   215 backs.

MAN. Nay, thou art a dangerous rogue, I've heard, behind a man's back.

L. PLAUS. You wrong him sure, noble captain; he would do a man no more harm behind his   220 back than to his face.

FREE. I am of my lord's mind.

MAN. Yes, a fool, like a coward, is the more to be feared behind a man's back, more than a witty man; for, as a coward is more bloody than a brave   225 man, a fool is more malicious than a man of wit.

NOV. A fool, tar, — a fool! nay, thou art a brave sea-judge of wit! a fool! Prithee, when did you ever find me want something to say, as you do often?

MAN. Nay, I confess thou art always talk-   230 ing, roaring, or making a noise; that I'll say for thee.

NOV. Well, and is talking a sign of a fool?

MAN. Yes, always talking, especially too if it be loud and fast, is the sign of a fool.

NOV. Pshaw! talking is like fencing, the   235 quicker the better; run 'em down, run 'em down, no matter for parrying; push on still, sa, sa, sa! no matter whether you argue in form; push in, guard or no.

MAN. Or hit or no; I think thou always   240 talk'st without thinking, Novel.

NOV. Ay, ay; studied play's [1] the worse, to follow the allegory, as the old pedant says.

OLD. A young fop!

MAN. I ever thought the man of most wit   245 had been like him of most money, who has no vanity in showing it everywhere, whilst the beggarly pusher

of his fortune has all he has about him still, only to show.

NOV. Well, sir, and makes a very pretty   250 show in the world, let me tell you; nay, a better than your close hunks. [2] A pox! give ready money in play: what care I for a man's reputation? what are we the better for your substantial, thrifty curmud-geon in wit, sir?   255

OLD. Thou art a profuse young rogue indeed.

NOV. So much for talking, which I think I have proved a mark of wit; and so is railing, roaring, and making a noise; for railing is satire, you know; and roaring and making a noise, humor.   260

Enter to them FIDELIA, *taking* MANLY *aside, and showing him a paper.*

FID. The hour is betwixt seven and eight ex-actly: 'tis now half an hour after six.

MAN. Well, go then to the Piazza, [3] and wait for me; as soon as it is quite dark, I'll be with you. I must stay here yet a while for my friend.   265

Exit FIDELIA.

But is railing satire, Novel?

FREE. And roaring and making a noise, humor?

NOV. What, won't you confess there's humor in roaring and making a noise?

FREE. No.   270

NOV. Nor in cutting napkins and hangings?

MAN. No, sure.

NOV. Dull fops!

OLD. O rogue, rogue, insipid rogue! — Nay, gentlemen, allow him those things for wit, for   275 his parts lie only that way.

NOV. Peace, old fool! I wonder not at thee; but that young fellows should be so dull as to say there's no humor in making a noise and breaking windows! I tell you, there's wit and humor too in both;   280 and a wit is as well known by his frolic, as by his simile.

OLD. Pure rogue! there's your modern wit for you! Wit and humor in breaking of windows! There's mischief, if you will, but no wit, or   285 humor.

NOV. Prithee, prithee, peace, old fool! I tell you, where there is mischief, there's wit. Don't we esteem the monkey a wit amongst beasts, only because he's mischievous? And let me tell you,   290 as good-nature is a sign of a fool, being mischievous is a sign of wit.

OLD. O rogue, rogue! pretend to be a wit, by doing mischief and railing!

NOV. Why, thou, old fool, hast no other   295

[2] Miser.
[3] The Great Piazza on the north side of Covent Garden.

[1] Sword-play's.

pretence to the name of a wit, but by railing at new plays!

OLD. Thou, by railing at that facetious, noble way of wit, quibbling!

NOV. Thou callest thy dulness gravity; and   300
thy dozing, thinking.

OLD. You, sir, your dulness, spleen; and you talk much, and say nothing.

NOV. Thou readest much, and understand'st nothing, sir.   305

OLD. You laugh loud and break no jest.

NOV. You rail, and nobody hangs himself; and thou hast nothing of the satire but in thy face.

OLD. And you have no jest but your face, sir.

NOV. Thou art an illiterate pedant.   310

OLD. Thou art a fool with a bad memory.

MAN. Come, a pox on you both! you have done like wits now; for you wits, when you quarrel, never give over till you prove one another fools.

NOV. And you fools have never any occasion   315
of laughing at us wits but when we quarrel. There-fore, let us be friends, Oldfox.

MAN. They are such wits as thou art, who make the name of a wit as scandalous as that of bully and signify a loud-laughing, talking, incorrigible   320
coxcomb, as bully a roaring, hardened coward.

FREE. And would have his noise and laughter pass for wit, as t'other his huffing and blust'ring for courage.

Enter VERNISH.

MAN. Gentlemen, with your leave, here is   325
one I would speak with, and I have nothing to say to you.   *Puts 'em out of the room.*

Manent MANLY, VERNISH.

VER. I told you 'twas in vain to think of getting money out of her: she says, if a shilling would do't, she would not save you from starving or hang-   330
ing or, what you would think worse, begging or flatter-ing; and rails so at you, one would not think you had lain with her.

MAN. O friend, never trust for that matter a woman's railing; for she is no less a dissembler   335
in her hatred than her love; and as her fondness of her husband is a sign he's a cuckold, her railing at an-other man is a sign she lies with him.

VER. (*aside*). He's in the right on't: I know not what to trust to.   340

MAN. But you did not take any notice of it to her, I hope?

VER. (*aside*). So! Sure he is afraid I should have disproved him by an enquiry of her: all may be well yet.   345

MAN. What hast thou in thy head that makes thee seem so unquiet?

VER. Only this base, impudent woman's false-ness; I cannot put her out of my head.

MAN. O my dear friend, be not you too sen-   350
sible of my wrongs, for then I shall feel 'em too with more pain, and think 'em unsufferable. Damn her, her money, and that ill-natured whore, too, Fortune herself! But if thou wouldst ease a little my present trouble, prithee go borrow me somewhere else   355
some money: I can trouble thee.

VER. You trouble me, indeed, most sensibly, when you command me anything I cannot do. I have lately lost a great deal of money at play, more than I can yet pay; so that not only my money,   360
but my credit too is gone, and know not where to borrow; but could rob a church for you. — (*Aside.*) Yet would rather end your wants by cutting your throat.

MAN. Nay, then I doubly feel my poverty,   365
since I'm incapable of supplying thee.

(*Embraces him.*)

VER. But, methinks, she that granted you the last favor (as they call it) should not deny you any-thing —

NOVEL *looks in.*

NOV. Hey, tarpaulin, have you done?   370
[*He*] *retires again.*

VER. I understand not that point of kindness, I confess.

MAN. No, thou dost not understand it, and I have not time to let you know all now; for these fools, you see, will interrupt us; but anon, at   375
supper, we'll laugh at leisure together at Olivia's cuckold, who took a young fellow, that goes between his wife and me, for a woman.

VER. Ha!

MAN. Senseless, easy rascal! 'twas no won-   380
der she chose him for a husband; but she thought him, I thank her, fitter than me for that blind, bear-ing [1] office.

VER. (*aside*). I could not be deceived in that long woman's hair tied up behind, nor those infal-   385
lible proofs, her pouting, swelling breasts: I have handled too many, sure, not to know 'em.

MAN. What, you wonder the fellow could be such a blind coxcomb?

VER. Yes, yes —   390

NOVEL *looks in again.*

NOV. Nay, prithee, come to us, Manly. Gad, all the fine things one says in their company are lost without thee.

MAN. Away, fop! I'm busy yet.

[NOVEL] *retires.*

_____
[1] Passive, enduring.

You see we cannot talk here at our ease; be-   395
sides, I must be gone immediately, in order to meeting with Olivia again tonight.

VER. Tonight! it cannot be, sure —

MAN. I had an appointment just now from her.

VER. For what time?   400

MAN. At half an hour after seven precisely.

VER. Don't you apprehend the husband?

MAN. He! snivelling gull! he a thing to be feared!
a husband! the tamest of creatures!

VER. (*aside*). Very fine!   405

MAN. But, prithee, in the mean time, go try to
get me some money. Though thou art too modest
to borrow for thyself, thou canst do anything for
me, I know. Go, for I must be gone to Olivia.
Go, and meet me here, anon. — Freeman,   410
where are you?   *Exit* MANLY.

Manet VERNISH.

VER. Ay, I'll meet with you, I warrant, but it
shall be at Olivia's. Sure, it cannot be: she denies it
so calmly, and with that honest, modest assurance,
it can't be true — and he does not use to lie —   415
but belying a woman when she won't be kind is the
only lie a brave man will least scruple. But then
the woman in man's clothes, whom he calls a man! —
Well, but by her breasts I know her to be a woman —
but then again, his appointment from her, to   420
meet with him tonight! I am distracted more with
doubt than jealousy. Well, I have no way to disa-
buse or revenge myself but by going home immediately, putting on a riding-suit, and pretending
to my wife the same business which carried me   425
out of town last requires me again to go post to Oxford tonight. Then, if the appointment he boasts
of be true, it's sure to hold; and I shall have an
opportunity either of clearing her, or revenging
myself on both. Perhaps she is his wench, of   430
an old date, and I am his cully, whilst I think him
mine; and he has seemed to make his wench rich only
that I might take her off his hands: or if he has
but lately lain with her, he must needs discover by
her my treachery to him, which I'm sure he   435
will revenge with my death, and which I must prevent with his, if it were only but for fear of his too
just reproaches; for I must confess, I never had till
now any excuse, but that of int'rest, for doing ill to
him.   *Exit* VERNISH.   440

Re-enter MANLY *and* FREEMAN.

MAN. Come hither; only, I say, be sure you mistake not the time; you know the house exactly where
Olivia lodges; 'tis just hard by.

FREE. Yes, yes.

MAN. Well then, bring 'em all, I say, thither,   445

and all you know that may be then in the house;
for the more witnesses I have of her infamy, the
greater will be my revenge: and be sure you come
straight up to her chamber without more ado. Here,
take the watch; you see 'tis above a quarter   450
past seven; be there in half an hour exactly.

FREE. You need not doubt my diligence or dexterity; I am an old scourer,[1] and can naturally beat
up a wench's quarters that won't be civil. Shan't
we break her windows too?   455

MAN. No, no; be punctual only.   *Exeunt ambo.*

Enter WIDOW BLACKACRE, *and two Knights of
the Post; a Waiter with wine.*

WID. Sweetheart, are you sure the door was shut
close, that none of those roysters saw us come in?

WAIT. Yes, mistress; and you shall have a privater
room above, instantly.   *Exit Waiter.*   460

WID. You are safe enough, gentlemen; for I have
been private in this house ere now, upon other
occasions, when I was something younger. Come,
gentlemen; in short, I leave my business to your care
and fidelity: and so, here's to you.   465

1 KNIGHT. We were ungrateful rogues if we
should not be honest to you; for we have had a great
deal of your money.

WID. And you have done me many a good job
for't; and so, here's to you again.   470

2 KNIGHT. Why, we have been perjured but six
times for you.

1 KNIGHT. Forged but four deeds, with your
husband's last deed of gift.

2 KNIGHT. And but three wills.   475

1 KNIGHT. And counterfeited hands and seals
to some six bonds; I think that's all, brother.

WID. Ay, that's all, gentlemen; and so, here's to
you again.

2 KNIGHT. Nay, 'twould do one's heart good   480
to be forsworn for you: you have a conscience in
your ways, and pay us well.

1 KNIGHT. You are in the right on't, brother; one
would be damned for her with all one's heart.

2 KNIGHT. But there are rogues, who make   485
us forsworn for 'em; and when we come to be paid,
they'll be forsworn too, and not pay us our wages,
which they promised with oaths sufficient.

1 KNIGHT. Ay, a great lawyer that shall be nameless bilked me too.   490

WID. That was hard, methinks, that a lawyer
should use gentlemen witnesses no better.

2 KNIGHT. A lawyer! d'ye wonder a lawyer should
do't? I was bilked by a reverend divine, that

---

[1] A member of a gang of lawless blades who, like the Mohocks of later times, terrified the town by their nightly outrages.

preaches twice on Sundays, and prays half an　495
hour still before dinner.

WID. How! a conscientious divine, and not pay
people for damning themselves! Sure then, for all his
talking, he does not believe damnation. But come,
to our business. Pray be sure to imitate ex-　500
actly the flourish at the end of this name.

(Pulls out a deed or two.)

1 KNIGHT. Oh, he's the best in England at untang-
ling a flourish, madam.

WID. And let not the seal be a jot bigger: observe
well the dash too, at the end of this name.　505

2 KNIGHT. I warrant you, madam.

WID. Well, these and many other shifts, poor
widows are put to sometimes; for everybody would
be riding a widow, as they say, and breaking into her
jointure. They think marrying a widow an　510
easy business, like leaping the hedge where another
has gone over before; a widow is a mere gap, a gap
with them.

Enter to them MAJOR OLDFOX, *with two Waiters.
The Knights of the Post huddle up the writings.*

What, he here! Go then, go, my hearts, you have
your instructions. *Exeunt Knights of the Post.*　515

OLD. Come, madam, to be plain with you, I'll
be fobbed off no longer. — (*Aside.*) I'll bind her
and gag her but she shall hear me. — [*To the Waiters.*]
Look you, friends, there's the money I promised you;
and now do you what you promised me: here　520
are my garters, and here's a gag. — [*To the* WIDOW
BLACKACRE.] You shall be acquainted with my parts,
lady, you shall.

WID. Acquainted with your parts! A rape! a
rape! — What, will you ravish me?　525

*The Waiters tie her to the chair, and gag her,
and exeunt.*

OLD. Yes, lady, I will ravish you; but it shall be
through the ear, lady, the ear only, with my well-
penned acrostics.

Enter to them FREEMAN, JERRY BLACKACRE, *three
Bailiffs, a Constable, and his Assistants, with the
two Knights of the Post.*

What, shall I never read my things undisturbed
again?　530

JER. O law! my mother bound hand and foot,
and gaping as if she rose before her time to-day!

FREE. What means this, Oldfox? — But I'll release you from him; you shall be no man's prisoner
but mine. — Bailiffs, execute your writ.　535

(FREEMAN *unties her.*)

OLD. Nay, then I'll be gone, for fear of being
bail, and paying her debts, without being her
husband.　　　*Exit* OLDFOX.

1ST BAIL. [*to the* WIDOW BLACKACRE]. We arrest

you in the king's name, at the suit of Mr. Free-　540
man, guardian to Jeremiah Blackacre, Esquire, in
an action of ten thousand pounds.

WID. How, how! in a choke-bail action![1] What,
and the pen-and-ink gentlemen taken too! — Have
you confessed, you rogues?　545

1ST KNIGHT. We needed not to confess; for the
bailiffs dodged [2] us hither to the very door, and
overheard all that you and we said.

WID. Undone, undone then! no man was ever too
hard for me till now. O Jerry, child, wilt thou　550
vex again the womb that bore thee?

JER. Ay, for bearing me before wedlock, as you
say. But I'll teach you to call a Blackacre a bastard,
though you were never so much my mother.

WID. (*aside*). Well, I'm undone! not one　555
trick left? no law-meush [3] imaginable? — (*To* FREE-
MAN.) Cruel sir, a word with you, I pray.

FREE. In vain, madam; for you have no other
way to release yourself, but by the bonds of matrimony.　560

WID. How, sir, how! that were but to sue out
an habeas corpus for a removal from one prison to
another. Matrimony!

FREE. Well, bailiffs, away with her.

WID. Oh, stay, sir! can you be so cruel as to　565
bring me under covert-baron again, and put it out of
my power to sue in my own name? Matrimony to
a woman [is] worse than excommunication, in de-
priving her of the benefit of the law; and I would
rather be deprived of life. But hark you, sir,　570
I am contented you should hold and enjoy my person
by lease or patent, but not by the spiritual patent
called a licence; that is, to have the privileges of
a husband without the dominion; that is, *durante
beneplacito*: [4] in consideration of which I will,　575
out of my jointure, secure you an annuity of three
hundred pounds a year, and pay your debts; and
that's all you younger brothers desire to marry a
widow for, I'm sure.

FREE. Well, widow, if —　580

JER. What! I hope, bully guardian, you are not
making agreements without me?

FREE. No, no. First, widow, you must say no
more that he is the son of a whore; have a care of
that. And then, he must have a settled exhibi-　585
tion [5] of forty pounds a year, and a nag of assizes,[6]
kept by you, but not upon the common; and have
free ingress, egress, and regress to and from your
maids' garret.

WID. Well, I can grant all that too　590

---

[1] In arrests for serious offenses, and in civil cases where large
sums were involved, bail was not allowed.
[2] Dogged.　　　[3] Gap in the law.
[4] During good pleasure.　　　[5] Fixed allowance.
[6] Horse of standard quality.

JER. Ay, ay, fair words butter no cabbage; but guardian, make her sign, sign and seal; for otherwise, if you knew her as well as I, you would not trust her word for a farthing.

FREE. I warrant thee, squire. — Well, wid- 595 ow, since thou art so generous, I will be generous too; and if you'll secure me four hundred pound a year, but during your life, and pay my debts, not above a thousand pound, I'll bate you your person, to dispose of as you please.   600

WID. Have a care, sir, a settlement without a consideration is void in the law: you must do something for't.

FREE. Prithee, then let the settlement on me be called alimony, and the consideration, our sep- 605 aration. Come; my lawyer, with writings ready drawn, is within, and in haste. Come.

WID. But what! no other kind of consideration, Mr. Freeman? Well, a widow, I see, is a kind of a sinecure, by custom of which the unconscion- 610 able incumbent enjoys the profits without any duty, but does that still elsewhere.   *Exeunt omnes.*

[SCENE III]

The scene changes to Olivia's lodging.

Enter OLIVIA with a candle in her hand.

OLIV. So, I am now prepared once more for my timorous young lover's reception. My husband is gone; and go thou out too, thou next interrupter of love. — (*Puts out the candle.*) Kind darkness, that frees us lovers from scandal and bashfulness, from 5 the censure of our gallants and the world! — So, are you there?

Enter to OLIVIA, FIDELIA, followed softly by MANLY.

Come, my dear punctual lover, there is not such another in the world; thou hast beauty and youth to please a wife; address and wit, to amuse[1] and 10 fool a husband; nay, thou hast all things to be wished in a lover, but your fits. I hope, my dear, you won't have one tonight; and that you may not, I'll lock the door, though there be no need of it but to lock out your fits; for my husband is just gone out of 15 town again. Come, where are you?

                    (*Goes to the door and locks it.*)

MAN. (*aside*). Well, thou hast impudence enough to give me fits too, and make revenge itself impotent, hinder me from making thee yet more infamous, if it can be.   20

OLIV. Come, come, my soul, come.

FID. Presently, my dear; we have time enough, sure.

OLIV. How? time enough! True lovers can no
[1] Beguile.

more think they ever have time enough than 25 love enough. You shall stay with me all night; but that is but a lover's moment. Come.

FID. But won't you let me give you and myself the satisfaction of telling you how I abused your husband last night?   30

OLIV. Not when you can give me, and yourself too, the satisfaction of abusing him again tonight. Come.

FID. Let me but tell you how your husband —

OLIV. Oh, name not his, or Manly's more 35 loathsome name, if you love me! I forbid 'em last night: and you know I mentioned my husband but once, and he came. No talking, pray; 'twas ominous to us. — (*A noise at the door.*) You make me fancy a noise at the door already, but I'm resolved not 40 to be interrupted. Where are you? Come, for rather than lose my dear expectation now, though my husband were at the door, and the bloody ruffian Manly here in the room, with all his awful insolence, I would give myself to this dear hand, to be led 45 away to heavens of joys which none but thou canst give. — (*The noise at the door increases.*) But what's this noise at the door? So, I told you what talking would come to. Ha! — O heavens, my husband's voice! —   (OLIVIA *listens at the door.*) 50

MAN. (*aside*). Freeman is come too soon.

OLIV. Oh, 'tis he! — Then here's the happiest minute lost that ever bashful boy or trifling woman fooled away! I'm undone! my husband's reconcilement too was false, as my joy all delusion. But 55 come this way, here's a back door.

                    Exit, and returns.

The officious jade has locked us in, instead of locking others out; but let us then escape your way, by the balcony; and whilst you pull down the curtains I'll fetch from my closet what next will best secure 60 our escape. I have left my key in the door, and 'twill not suddenly be broke open.   *Exit.*

           (*A noise as it were people forcing the door.*)

MAN. Stir not, yet fear nothing.

FID. Nothing but your life, sir.

MAN. We shall now know this happy man 65 she calls husband.

OLIVIA re-enters.

OLIV. Oh, where are you? What, idle with fear? Come, I'll tie the curtains, if you will hold. Here, take this cabinet and purse, for it is thine, if we escape; — (MANLY *takes from her the cabinet and* 70 *purse*) — therefore let us make haste.

                    Exit OLIVIA.

MAN. 'Tis mine indeed now again, and it shall never escape more from me, to you at least.

           (*The door broken open, enter* VERNISH *alone,*

with a dark-lantern and a sword, running at
MANLY, *who draws, puts by the thrust, and
defends himself, whilst* FIDELIA *runs at*
VERNISH *behind.*)

VER. (*with a low voice*). So, there I'm right, sure —
MAN. (*softly*). Sword and dark-lantern, 75
villain, are some odds; but —
VER. (*with a low voice*). Odds! I'm sure I find
more odds than I expected. What, has my insatiable two seconds at once? but —

   (*Whilst they fight,* OLIVIA *re-enters, tying two
   curtains together.*)

OLIV. Where are you now? — What, is he 80
entered then, and are they fighting? — Oh, do not
kill one that can make no defence! — (MANLY
throws VERNISH *down and disarms him.*) How! but
I think he has the better on't. Here's his scarf,
'tis he. — So, keep him down still: I hope thou 85
hast no hurt, my dearest?   (*Embracing* MANLY.)

Enter to them FREEMAN, LORD PLAUSIBLE, NOVEL,
   JERRY BLACKACRE, *and the* WIDOW BLACKACRE,
   lighted in by the two Sailors with torches.

Ha! — what? — Manly! and have I been thus concerned for him, embracing him? and has he his jewels
again too? What means this? Oh, 'tis too sure,
as well as my shame! which I'll go hide for ever. 90
   (*Offers to go out;* MANLY *stops her.*)
MAN. No, my dearest; after so much kindness as
has passed between us, I cannot part with you yet —
Freeman, let nobody stir out of the room; for notwithstanding your lights, we are yet in the dark, till
this gentleman please to turn his face. — (*Pulls* 95
VERNISH *by the sleeve.*) How! Vernish! art thou
the happy man then? Thou! thou! speak, I say!
but thy guilty silence tells me all. — Well, I shall
not upbraid thee, for my wonder is striking me as
dumb as thy shame has made thee. But what? 100
my little volunteer hurt, and fainting!
FID. My wound, sir, is but a slight one in my arm;
'tis only my fear of your danger, sir, not yet well
over.
MAN. But what's here? More strange 105
things! — (*Observing* FIDELIA'S *hair untied behind,
and without a peruke, which she lost in the scuffle.*)
What means this long woman's hair? — and face,
now all of it appears, too beautiful for a man; which
I still thought womanish indeed! What, you 110
have not deceived me too, my little volunteer?
OLIV. (*aside*). Me she has, I'm sure.
MAN. Speak!

      Enter ELIZA *and* LETTICE.

ELIZA. What, cousin, I am brought hither by

your woman, I suppose, to be a witness of the 115
second vindication of your honor?
OLIV. Insulting is not generous. You might
spare me: I have you.
ELIZA. Have a care, cousin, you'll confess anon
too much; and I would not have your secrets. 120
MAN. (*to* FIDELIA). Come, your blushes answer
me sufficiently, and you have been my volunteer in
love.
FID. I must confess I needed no compulsion to
follow you all the world over, which I at- 125
tempted in this habit, partly out of shame to own my
love to you, and fear of a greater shame, your refusal
of it; for I knew of your engagement to this lady and
the constancy of your nature, which nothing could
have altered but herself. 130
MAN. Dear madam, I desired you to bring me out
of confusion, and you have given me more. I know
not what to speak to you, or how to look upon you;
the sense of my rough, hard, and ill usage of you
(though chiefly your own fault) gives me more 135
pain now 'tis over than you had when you suffered
it: and if my heart, the refusal of such a woman,
(*pointing to* OLIVIA) were not a sacrifice to profane
your love, and a greater wrong to you than ever yet
I did you, I would beg of you to receive it, 140
though you used it as she had done; for though it
deserved not from her the treatment she gave it, it
does from you.
FID. Then it has had punishment sufficient from
her already, and needs no more from me; and, I 145
must confess, I would not be the only cause of making you break your last night's oath to me, of never
parting with me; if you do not forget or repent it.
MAN. Then take for ever my heart, and this with
it; (*gives her the cabinet*) for 'twas given to you 150
before, and my heart was before your due; I only beg
leave to dispose of these few. — Here, madam, I
never yet left my wench unpaid.
   (*Takes some of the jewels, and offers 'em to
   OLIVIA; she strikes 'em down;* PLAUSIBLE
   and NOVEL *take 'em up.*)
OLIV. So it seems, by giving her the cabinet.
L. PLAUS. These pendants appertain to your 155
most faithful, humble servant.
NOV. And this locket is mine — my earnest for
love, which she never paid: therefore my own again.
WID. By what law, sir, pray? — Cousin Olivia,
a word. What, do they make a seizure on 160
your goods and chattels, *vi et armis?*[1] Make your
demand, I say, and bring your trover, bring your
trover. I'll follow the law for you.

[1] With force and weapons (a legal term used in complaining
of an assault).

---

90 s.d.] Q4Q6W1 out, and *MANLY.*
108–9] Q6 *hair! and face, now... appears too;* W1 *hair, and face! Now... appears too.*   128] Q4Q6 *know.*
144–45] W1 *for her.*   155] Q4Q6 *The pendants.*   161–62] Q6 *you demand.*

OLIV. And I my revenge.   *Exit* OLIVIA.

MAN. (*to* VERNISH). But 'tis, my friend, in   165
your consideration most that I would have returned
part of your [wife's] portion, for 'twere hard to take all
from thee, since thou hast paid so dear for't, in being
such a rascal. Yet thy wife is a fortune without a
portion; and thou art a man of that extraor-   170
dinary merit in villainy, the world and fortune can
never desert thee, though I do; therefore be not
melancholy. Fare you well, sir.

Exit VERNISH *doggedly.*

Now, madam, (*turning to* FIDELIA) I beg your pardon
for lessening the present I made you; but my   175
heart can never be lessened. This, I confess, was too
small for you before, for you deserve the Indian
world; and I would now go thither, out of covetousness for your sake only.

FID. (*pulling* MANLY *from the company*).   180
Your heart, sir, is a present of that value, I can never
make any return to't; but I can give you back such a
present as this, which I got by the loss of my father,
a gentleman of the north, of no mean extraction,
whose only child I was; therefore left me in the   185
present possession of two thousand pounds a year,
which I left, with multitudes of pretenders, to follow
you, sir; having in several public places seen you,
and observed your actions thoroughly, with admiration, when you were too much in love to take   190
notice of mine, which yet was but too visible. The

name of my family is Grey, my other, Fidelia. The
rest of my story you shall know when I have fewer
auditors.

MAN. Nay, now, madam, you have taken   195
from me all power of making you any compliment on
my part; for I was going to tell you, that for your sake
only I would quit the unknown pleasure of a retirement; and rather stay in this ill world of ours still,
though odious to me, than give you more frights   200
again at sea, and make again too great a venture
there, in you alone. But if I should tell you now
all this, and that your virtue (since greater than I
thought any was in the world) had now reconciled
me to't, my friend here would say, 'tis your   205
estate that has made me friends with the world.

FREE. I must confess I should; for I think most of
our quarrels to the world are just such as we have
to a handsome woman: only because we cannot enjoy
her as we would do.   210

MAN. Nay, if thou art a plain dealer too, give me
thy hand; for now I'll say, I am thy friend indeed;
and for your two sakes, though I have been so lately
deceived in friends of both sexes,

I will believe there are now in the world   215
Good-natured friends, who are not prostitutes,
And handsome women worthy to be friends;
Yet, for my sake, let no one e'er confide
In tears, or oaths, in love, or friend untried.

Exeunt omnes.

167] Q1Q3Q4 *wives;* Q6W1 *wife's.*   213] Q4Q6 om. *two.*   219] Q4Q6 *In years.*

EPILOGUE

To you, the judges learnèd in stage-laws,
Our poet now, by me, submits his cause;
For with young judges, such as most of you,
The men by women best their bus'ness do:
And, truth on't is, if you did not sit here,   5
To keep for us a term throughout the year,
We could not live by'r tongues; nay, but for you,
Our chamber-practice would be little too.
And 'tis not only the stage-practiser
Who by your meeting gets her living here;   10
For as in Hall of Westminster
Sleek sempstress vents amidst the courts her ware;
So, while we bawl, and you in judgment sit,
The visor-mask sells linen too i' th' pit.
Oh, many of your friends, besides us here,   15
Do live by putting off their several ware.
Here's daily done the great affair o' th' nation;
Let love and us then ne'er have long-vacation.
But hold! like other pleaders I have done
Not my poor client's bus'ness, but my own.   20
Spare me a word, then, now for him.   First know,
Squires of the long robe, he does humbly show
He has a just right in abusing you,
Because he is a brother-Templar too:
For at the bar you rally one another;   25
Nay, 'fool' and 'knave' is swallowed from a brother:
If not the poet here, the Templar spare,
And maul him when you catch him at the bar.
From you, our common modish censurers,
Your favor, not your judgment, 'tis he fears: 30
Of all loves begs you then to rail, find fault; ⎫
For plays, like women, by the world are thought, ⎬
When you speak kindly of 'em, very naught. ⎭

26] Q1W1 *And fool.*

The Relapse; or, Virtue in Danger

BY SIR JOHN VANBRUGH

To Ber.] But before I go, one Glaſs of Nectar more to Drink her Health.

Ber. Stand off, or I ſhall hate you, by Heavens.

Lov. Kiſſing her.] In matters of Love, a Woman's Oath is no more to be minded than a Man's.

Ber. Um ——

Enter Worthy.

Wor. Ha! What's here? my old Miſtreſs, and ſo cloſe, I faith? I wou'd not ſpoil her ſport for the Univerſe [*He retires.*

Ber. O Ged —— Now do I pray to Heaven,

                        [*Exit* Loveleſs *running.*

With all my Heart and Soul, that the Devil
In Hell may take me, if ever——I was better pleas'd in
My Life——This Man has bewitch'd me, that's certain.
Sighing.] Well, I am Condemn'd ; but thanks to Heaven I feel
My ſelf each Moment more and more prepar'd for my
Execution. Nay, to that degree, I don't perceive I have
The leaſt fear of Dying. No, I find, let the——
Executioner be but a Man, and there's nothing will
Suffer with more Reſolution than a Woman.
Well, I never had but one Intrigue yet :
But I confeſs I long to have another.
Pray Heaven it end as the firſt did tho',
That we may both grow weary at a time,
For 'tis a Melancholy thing for Lovers to out-live one another.

Enter Worthy.

Wor. aſide.] This Diſcovery's a lucky one, I hope to make a happy uſe on't.

That Gentlewoman there is no Fool ; ſo I ſhall be able to make her underſtand her Intereſt.

To Ber.] Your Servant Madam, I need not ask you how you do, you have got ſo good a Colour.

Ber. No better than I us'd to have I ſuppoſe ?

Wor. A little more Blood in your Cheeks.

Ber. The Weather's hot.

                H   *Wor.*

A PAGE FROM THE FIRST QUARTO, 1697, OF *THE RELAPSE, OR, VIRTUE IN DANGER*
Berinthia's long prose speech (Act III, Scene ii) is printed in the semblance of verse

THE PREFACE

To GO about to excuse half the defects this abortive brat is come into the world with, would be to provoke the town with a long useless preface, when 'tis, I doubt, sufficiently soured already by a tedious play.

I do therefore (with all the humility of a repenting sinner) confess, it wants every thing — but length; and in that, I hope, the severest critic will be pleased to acknowledge I have not been wanting. But my modesty will sure atone for every thing, when the world shall know it is so great, I am even to this day insensible of those two shining graces in the play (which some part of the town is pleased to compliment me with) blasphemy and bawdy.

For my part, I cannot find 'em out: if there was any obscene expressions upon the stage, here they are in the print; for I have dealt fairly, I have not sunk a syllable that could (though by racking of mysteries) be ranged under that head; and yet I believe with a steady faith, there is not one woman of a real reputation in town, but when she has read it impartially over in her closet, will find it so innocent, she'll think it no affront to her prayer-book to lay it upon the same shelf. So to them (with all manner of deference) I entirely refer my cause; and I'm confident they'll justify me against those pretenders to good manners, who, at the same time, have so little respect for the ladies, they would extract a bawdy jest from an ejaculation, to put 'em out of countenance. But I expect to have these well-bred persons always my enemies, since I'm sure I shall never write any thing lewd enough to make 'em my friends.

As for the saints (your thorough-paced ones, I mean, with screwed faces and wry mouths) I despair of them; for they are friends to nobody. They love nothing but their altars and themselves. They have too much zeal to have any charity; they make debauches in piety, as sinners do in wine, and are as quarrelsome in their religion as other people are in their drink: so I hope nobody will mind what they say. But if any man (with flat plod shoes, a little band, greasy hair, and a dirty face, who is wiser than I, at the expense of being forty years older) happens to be offended at a story of a cock and a bull, and a priest and a bull-dog, I beg his pardon with all my heart; which, I hope, I shall obtain, by eating my words, and making this public recantation. I do therefore, for his satisfaction, acknowledge I lied when I said they never quit their hold; for in that little time I have lived in the world, I thank God I have seen 'em forced to 't more than once; but next time I'll speak with more caution and truth, and only say, they have very good teeth.

If I have offended any honest gentleman of the town whose friendship or good word is worth the having, I am very sorry for it; I hope they'll correct me as gently as they can, when they consider I have had no other design, in running a very great risk, than to divert (if possible) some part of their spleen, in spite of their wives and their taxes.

One word more about the bawdy, and I have done. I own, the first night this thing was acted some indecencies had like to have happened; but 'twas not my fault.

The fine gentleman of the play,[1] drinking his mistress's health in Nantes brandy, from six in the morning to the time he waddled on upon the stage in the evening, had toasted himself up to such a pitch of vigor, I confess I once gave Amanda for gone, and I am since (with all due respect to Mrs. Rogers [2]) very sorry she scaped; for I am confident a certain lady (let no one take it to herself that's handsome) who highly blames the play, for the barrenness of the conclusion, would then have allowed it a very natural close.

[1] Powell, who played the part of Worthy.   [2] The Amanda of the original production.

8] P *them*.   8] P *there were*.   15, 16, 25] P *them*.   25] Q2P *to it*.

PROLOGUE

Spoken by Miss Cross.[1]

Ladies, this play in too much haste was writ,
To be o'ercharged with either plot or wit;
'Twas got, conceived, and born in six weeks space,
And wit, you know, 's as slow in growth — as grace.
Sure it can ne'er be ripened to your taste;   5
I doubt 'twill prove our author bred too fast:
For mark 'em well, who with the Muses marry,
They rarely do conceive, but they miscarry.
'Tis the hard fate of those wh'are big with rhyme,
Still to be brought to bed before their time.   10
Of our late poets, Nature few has made;
The greatest part — are only so by trade.
Still want of something brings the scribbling fit; ⎫
For want of money some of 'em have writ,   ⎬
And others do't, you see — for want of wit.   ⎭   15
Honor, they fancy, summons 'em to write,   ⎫
So out they lug [2] in wresty [3] Nature's spite, ⎬
As some of you spruce beaux do — when you fight.   ⎭
Yet let the ebb of wit be ne'er so low,   ⎫
Some glimpse of it a man may hope to show,   ⎬   20
Upon a theme so ample — as a beau.   ⎭
So, howsoe'er true courage may decay,   ⎫
Perhaps there's not one smock-face [4] here today, ⎬
But's bold as Cæsar — to attack a play.   ⎭
Nay, what's yet more, with an undaunted face,   ⎫   25
To do the thing with more heroic grace,   ⎬
'Tis six to four y'attack the strongest place.   ⎭
You are such Hotspurs [5] in this kind of venture,
Where there's no breach, just there you needs must enter.
But be advised.   30
E'en give the hero and the critic o'er,[6]   ⎫
For Nature sent you on another score;   ⎬
She formed her beau for nothing but her whore.   ⎭

---

[1] In the part of Miss Hoyden.
[2] Draw (their pens).   The term is commonly used with the meaning 'draw a sword.'
[3] A variant form of restive, used here in the relatively uncommon sense of 'dull, sluggish.'
[4] Effeminate man.
[5] Referring to the hot-headed and 'very valiant rebel' in *King Henry IV*, Part I.
[6] Give up attempting to be heroes and critics.

18] Q2 *you, spruce beaux, do.*
33] Q1Q2P and various later editions print a second prologue, spoken on the third night, which is omitted from this edition.

DRAMATIS PERSONÆ

MEN.

Sir NOVELTY FASHION, newly created Lord
   FOPPINGTON
YOUNG [THOMAS] FASHION, his brother
[EDWARD] LOVELESS, husband to Amanda
[WILLIAM] WORTHY, a gentleman of the town
Sir TUNBELLY CLUMSEY, a country gentleman
Sir JOHN FRIENDLY, his neighbor
COUPLER, a matchmaker
[ROGER] BULL, chaplain to Sir Tunbelly
SERRINGE,[1] a surgeon
LORY, servant to Young Fashion
[TUGG, a waterman]
[LA VÉROLE,[2] valet to Lord Foppington]
[A] shoemaker

[A] tailor
[MEND-LEGS, a hosier]
[FORETOP, a] periwig-maker
[Page, servants, etc.]

WOMEN.

AMANDA, wife to Loveless
BERINTHIA, her cousin, a young widow
Miss HOYDEN, a great fortune, daughter to Sir
   Tunbelly
Nurse, her gouvernante [3]
[Mrs. CALLICOE, a sempstress]
[ABIGAIL, maid to Berinthia]
[Maid to Amanda]

[1] An obsolete spelling of 'syringe.'   [2] I.e., the pox.
[3] The word means either 'governess' or 'housekeeper'; the nurse appears to have served in both capacities.

d.p.] Q1Q2 not infrequently have *Lovelace* in the text.
d.p.] Q1Q2P and other early editions read, after '*LORY*,' *Shoemaker, Taylor, Perriwig-maker, &c.*

THE RELAPSE;

OR,

VIRTUE IN DANGER:

[By Sir John Vanbrugh:]

Being the Sequel of

[LOVE'S LAST SHIFT; OR]

THE FOOL IN FASHION

[By Colley Cibber]

ACT I

Scene I

[*A room in* Loveless's *country house.*]

Enter Loveless, *reading.*

Lov. How true is that philosophy which says
Our heaven is seated in our minds!
Through all the roving pleasures of my youth,
(Where nights and days seemed all consumed in joy,
Where the false face of luxury displayed such
    charms   5
As might have shaken the most holy hermit,
And made him totter at his altar)
I never knew one moment's peace like this.
Here — in this little soft retreat,
My thoughts unbent from all the cares of life,   10
Content with fortune,
Eased from the grating duties of dependence,
From envy free, ambition under foot,
The raging flame of wild destructive lust
Reduced to a warm pleasing fire of lawful love, 15
My life glides on, and all is well within.

Enter Amanda.

Lov. (*meeting her kindly*). How does the happy
    cause of my content, my dear Amanda?
You find me musing on my happy state,
And full of grateful thoughts to heaven, and you.
  Aman. Those grateful offerings heaven can't re-
    ceive   20
With more delight than I do:
Would I could share with it as well
The dispensations of its bliss,
That I might search its choicest favors out,
And shower 'em on your head for ever.   25

Lov. The largest boons that heaven thinks fit to
    grant
To things it has decreed shall crawl on earth,
Are in the gift of women formed like you.
Perhaps, when time shall be no more,
When the aspiring soul shall take its flight,   30
And drop this pond'rous lump of clay behind it,
It may have appetites we know not of,
And pleasures as refined as its desires ——
But till that day of knowledge shall instruct me,
The utmost blessing that my thought can
    reach, (*taking her in his arms*)   35
Is folded in my arms, and rooted in my heart.
  Aman. There let it grow for ever.
  Lov. Well said, Amanda — let it be for ever —
Would heaven grant that ——
  Aman.   'Twere all the heaven I'd ask.
But we are clad in black mortality,   40
And the dark curtain of eternal night
At last must drop between us.
  Lov.   It must:
That mournful separation we must see.
A bitter pill it is to all;
But doubles its ungrateful taste,   45
When lovers are to swallow it.
  Aman. Perhaps that pain may only be my lot,
You possibly may be exempted from it;
Men find out softer ways to quench their fires.
  Lov. Can you then doubt my constancy,
    Amanda?   50
You'll find 'tis built upon a steady basis —
The rock of reason now supports my love,
On which it stands so fixed,
The rudest hurricane of wild desire
Would, like the breath of a soft slumb'ring babe, 55
Pass by, and never shake it.

4] Q2P *seem.*   28] Q2P *woman.*   40–42] Q1Q2P print as two lines, the first ending with *curtain.*
42] Q1Q2P prefix *It must* to line following.   43–44] Q1Q2P print as one line.
43] Q1Q2P print the first four words at the end of the preceding line.

AMAN. Yet still 'tis safer to avoid the storm;
The strongest vessels, if they put to sea,
May possibly be lost.
Would I could keep you here in this calm port for
    ever! 60
Forgive the weakness of a woman,
I am uneasy at your going to stay so long in town;
I know its false insinuating pleasures;
I know the force of its delusions;
I know the strength of its attacks; 65
I know the weak defence of nature;
I know you are a man — and I — a wife.
    LOV. You know then all that needs [1] to give you rest,
For wife's the strongest claim that you can urge.
When you would plead your title to my heart, 70
On this you may depend; therefore be calm,
Banish your fears, for they are traitors to your peace;
Beware of 'em: they are insinuating busy things
That gossip to and fro,
And do a world of mischief where they come: 75
But you shall soon be mistress of 'em all,
I'll aid you with such arms for their destruction,
They never shall erect their heads again.
You know the business is indispensible,
That obliges me to go for London, 80
And you have no reason, that I know of,
To believe I'm glad of the occasion:
For my honest conscience is my witness,
I have found a due succession of such charms
In my retirement here with you, 85
I have never thrown one roving thought that way;
But since, against my will, I'm dragged once more
To that uneasy theatre of noise,
I am resolved to make such use on't,
As shall convince you 'tis an old cast mistress, 90
Who has been so lavish of her favors,
She's now grown bankrupt of her charms,
And has not one allurement left to move me.
    AMAN. Her bow, I do believe, is grown so weak,
Her arrows (at this distance) cannot hurt you, 95
But in approaching 'em you give 'em strength:
The dart that has not far to fly will put
The best of armor to a dangerous trial.
    LOV. That trial past, and y'are at ease for ever;
When you have seen the helmet proved, 100
You'll apprehend no more for him that wears it:
Therefore to put a lasting period to your fears,
I am resolved, this once, to launch into temptation.
I'll give you an essay of all my virtues:
My former boon companions of the bottle 105

Shall fairly try what charms are left in wine:
I'll take my place amongst 'em, they shall hem me in,
Sing praises to their god, and drink his glory;
Turn wild enthusiasts for his sake, and beasts to do
    him honor:
Whilst I, a stubborn atheist, sullenly look on, 110
Without one reverend glass to his divinity.
That for my temperance: then for my constancy ——
    AMAN. Ay, there take heed.
    LOV.   Indeed the danger's small.
    AMAN. And yet my fears are great.
    LOV.   Why are you so timorous?
    AMAN. Because you are so bold. 115
    LOV. My courage should disperse your apprehen-
    sions.
    AMAN. My apprehensions should alarm your
    courage.
    LOV. Fy, fy, Amanda, it is not kind thus to dis-
    trust me.
    AMAN. And yet my fears are founded on my love.
    LOV. Your love then is not founded as it
    ought; 120
For if you can believe 'tis possible
I should again relapse to my past follies,[2]
I must appear to you a thing
Of such an undigested composition,
That but to think of me with inclination 125
Would be a weakness in your taste
Your virtue scarce could answer.
    AMAN. 'Twould be a weakness in my tongue,
My prudence could not answer,
If I should press you farther with my fears; 130
I'll therefore trouble you no longer with 'em.
    LOV. Nor shall they trouble you much longer,
A little time shall show you they were groundless;
This winter shall be the fiery trial of my virtue,
Which, when it once has past, 135
You'll be convinced 'twas of no false allay;
There all your cares will end.
    AMAN.   Pray heaven they may!
    Exeunt hand in hand.

SCENE [II]

Whitehall.[3]

Enter YOUNG FASHION, LORY, *and Waterman.*

Y. FAS. Come, pay the waterman, and take the
portmantle.

[2] In Cibber's play, to which this is a sequel, Loveless had
deserted Amanda; the action of the play showed how, after ten
years' absence, he was won back by her.

[3] Not the modern street of that name, but the district sur-

---

[1] Is necessary.

63] Q2 *'tis false.*   73] P *them.*
79–82] Q1Q2P print as three lines, ending with *obliges, I,* and *occasion.*   In Q1 *knew,* although it begins a line, is not capitalized.
82] Q2P *believe that I'm.*   83] Q1 *witness.*   97] Q1Q2P prefix *Will put* to line following.
107] Q1Q2P print as two lines.   107] P *them.*   109] Q1Q2P print as two lines.
110] Q1Q2P print as two lines.   112] Q1Q2P print as two lines.   113] Q1P print as two lines.
114] Q1P print as two lines.

Lo. Faith, sir, I think the waterman had as good take the portmantle and pay himself.

Y. Fas. Why, sure there's something left in't! 5

Lo. But a solitary old waistcoat, upon honor, sir.

Y. Fas. Why, what's become of the blue coat, sirrah?

Lo. Sir, 'twas eaten at Gravesend;[1] the reckoning came to thirty shillings, and your privy-purse 10 was worth but two half-crowns.

Y. Fas. 'Tis very well.

Wat. Pray, master, will you please to dispatch me?

Y. Fas. Ay, here a — canst thou change me a 15 guinea?

Lo. (*aside*). Good!

Wat. Change a guinea, master! Ha, ha, your honor's pleased to compliment.

Y. Fas. I'gad I don't know how I shall pay 20 thee then, for I have nothing but gold about me.

Lo. (*aside*). Hum, hum.

Y. Fas. What dost thou expect, friend?

Wat. Why, master, so far against wind and tide is richly worth half a piece.[2] 25

Y. Fas. Why, faith, I think thou art a good conscionable fellow. I'gad, I begin to have so good an opinion of thy honesty, I care not if I leave my portmantle with thee, till I send thee thy money.

Wat. Ha! God bless your honor; I should 30 be as willing to trust you, master, but that you are, as a man may say, a stranger to me, and these are nimble times. There are a great many sharpers stirring. (*Taking up the portmantle.*) Well, master, when your worship sends the money, your port- 35 mantle shall be forthcoming; my name's Tugg, my wife keeps a brandy-shop in Drab Alley at Wapping.[3]

Y. Fas. Very well; I'll send for't tomorrow.

Exit Waterman.

Lo. So! Now, sir, I hope you'll own yourself a happy man; you have outlived all your cares. 40

Y. Fas. How so, sir?

Lo. Why you have nothing left to take care of.

Y. Fas. Yes, sirrah, I have myself and you to take care of still.

Lo. Sir, if you could but prevail with some- 45 body else to do that for you, I fancy we might both fare the better for't.

Y. Fas. Why, if thou canst tell me where to apply myself, I have at present so little money, and so

much humility about me, I don't know but I 50 may follow a fool's advice.

Lo. Why then, sir, your fool advises you to lay aside all animosity and apply to Sir Novelty, your elder brother.

Y. Fas. Damn my elder brother! 55

Lo. With all my heart; but get him to redeem your annuity, however.

Y. Fas. My annuity! 'Sdeath, he's such a dog, he would not give his powder-puff to redeem my soul.

Lo. Look you, sir, you must wheedle him, or 60 you must starve.

Y. Fas. Look you, sir, I will neither wheedle him nor starve.

Lo. Why? What will you do then?

Y. Fas. I'll go into the army. 65

Lo. You can't take the oaths; you are a Jacobite.

Y. Fas. Thou may'st as well say I can't take orders because I'm an atheist.

Lo. Sir, I ask your pardon; I find I did not know the strength of your conscience so well as I did 70 the weakness of your purse.

Y. Fas. Methinks, sir, a person of your experience should have known that the strength of the conscience proceeds from the weakness of the purse.

Lo. Sir, I am very glad to find you have a 75 conscience able to take care of us, let it proceed from what it will; but I desire you'll please to consider that the army alone will be but a scanty maintenance for a person of your generosity (at least as rents[4] now are paid); I shall see you stand in damnable 80 need of some auxiliary guineas for [your *menus*] *plaisirs*;[5] I will therefore turn fool once more for your service, and advise you to go directly to your brother.

Y. Fas. Art thou then so impregnable a 85 blockhead, to believe he'll help me with a farthing?

Lo. Not if you treat him *de haut en bas*, as you use to do.

Y. Fas. Why, how would'st have me treat him?

Lo. Like a trout — tickle him.[6] 90

Y. Fas. I can't flatter.

Lo. Can you starve?

Y. Fas. Yes.

Lo. I can't; good-by t'ye, sir —— *Going.*

Y. Fas. Stay, thou wilt distract me. What 95 would'st thou have me say to him?

Lo. Say nothing to him: apply yourself to his favorites; speak to his periwig, his cravat, his feather, his snuff-box, and when you are well with them ——

---

rounding the royal palace, which stretched from the modern Whitehall down to the Thames. This scene presumably takes place on the river bank.

[1] Travelers from France commonly came overland from Dover to Gravesend, and thence (twenty-eight miles) by barge on the Thames to London.

[2] Half a guinea.

[3] A riverside district on the Thames, just east of London; much frequented by sailors.

[4] Revenues, not necessarily from land; in this case, apparently a commissioned officer's pay.

[5] Amusements.

[6] To catch a trout by tickling the fisherman places his hand under the trout's belly and rubs it gently; the fish gradually moves backward until it is caught by the gills.

6] Q2P *upon my honor.*   35] Q1 *money. Your.*   81] Q1 *you* menu; Q2P *your* menu.

desire him to lend you a thousand pounds. 100
I'll engage you prosper.

Y. Fas. 'Sdeath and Furies! why was that coxcomb thrust into the world before me? O Fortune
— Fortune — thou art a bitch, by Gad!

Exeunt.

Scene [III]

A dressing-room.

Enter Lord Foppington *in his night-gown.*[1]

L. Fop. Page!

Enter Page.

Page. Sir.

L. Fop. 'Sir!' Pray, sir, do me the favor to teach
your tongue the title the king has thought fit to
honor me with.   5

Page. I ask your lordship's pardon, my lord.

L. Fop. Oh, you can pronounce the word, then;
I thought it would have choked you. D'ye hear?

Page. My lord.

L. Fop. Call La Vérole; I would dress —   10
Exit Page.

(*Solus.*) Well, 'tis an unspeakable pleasure to be a
man of quality —— strike me dumb! —— 'My
lord!' —— 'Your lordship!' —— 'My Lord Foppington!' —— *Ah! c'est quelque chose de beau, que le
diable m'emporte.*[2] Why, the ladies were ready 15
to puke at me, whilst I had nothing but Sir Navelty
to recommend me to 'em. Sure, whilst I was but
a knight, I was a very nauseous fellow. Well, 'tis
ten thousand pawnd well given —— stap my
vitals ——   20

Enter La Vérole.

[L. V.] Me Lord, de shoemaker, de tailor, de hosier, de sempstress, de barber, be all ready, if your
lordship please to be dress.

L. Fop. 'Tis well; admit 'em.

L. V. *Hey, messieurs, entrez.*   25

Enter Tailor, etc.

L. Fop. So, gentlemen, I hope you have all taken
pains to show yourselves masters in your professions.

Tai. I think I may presume to say, sir ——

L. V. 'My lord' —— you clawn, you!

Tai. Why, is he made a lord? —— My lord,   30
I ask your lordship's pardon, my lord; I hope, my
lord, your lordship will please to own, I have brought
your lordship as accomplished a suit of clothes as
ever peer of England trode the stage in,[3] my lord:

[1] Dressing-gown.
[2] Ah! that's something fine, devil take me.
[3] Gentlemen often sat on the stage at this time.

will your lordship please to try 'em now?   35

L. Fop. Ay, but let my people dispose the glasses
so, that I may see myself before and behind; for
I love to see myself all raund ——

Whilst he puts on his clothes, enter Young Fashion
and Lory.

Y. Fas. Hey-dey, what the devil have we here?
Sure my gentleman's grown a favorite at Court, 40
he has got so many people at his levee.

Lo. Sir, these people come in order to make him
a favorite at Court; they are to establish him with
the ladies.

Y. Fas. Good God! to what an ebb of taste 45
are women fallen, that it should be in the power of
a laced coat to recommend a gallant to 'em ——

Lo. Sir, tailors and periwig-makers are now become the bawds of the nation: 'tis they debauch all
the women.   50

Y. Fas. Thou sayest true; for there's that fop
now, has not by nature wherewithal to move a cook-
maid, and by that time these fellows have done with
him, i'gad, he shall melt down a countess. But now
for my reception: I'll engage it shall be as cold a 55
one, as a courtier's to his friend, who comes to put
him in mind of his promise.

L. Fop. (*to his tailor*). Death and eternal tartures!
Sir, I say the packet's too high by a foot.

Tai. My lord, if it had been an inch lower it 60
would not have held your lordship's pocket-handkerchief.

L. Fop. Rat my pocket-handkerchief! Have not
I a page to carry it? You may make him a packet
up to his chin a purpose for it; but I will not have 65
mine come so near my face.

Tai. 'Tis not for me to dispute your lordship's
fancy.

Y. Fas. (*to* Lory). His lordship! Lory, did you
observe that?   70

Lo. Yes, sir; I always thought 'twould end there.
Now, I hope, you'll have a little more respect for him.

Y. Fas. Respect! Damn him for a coxcomb;
now has he ruined his estate to buy a title, that he
may be a fool of the first rate. But let's accost 75
him. (*To* Lord Foppington.) Brother, I'm your
humble servant.

L. Fop. O Lard, Tam; I did not expect you in
England: brother, I am glad to see you. —— (*Turning to his tailor.*) Look you, sir, I shall never be 80
reconciled to this nauseous packet; therefore pray
get me another suit with all manner of expedition,
for this is my eternal aversion. Mrs. Callicoe, are
not you of my mind?

Sem. Oh, directly, my lord; it can never be 85
too low —

3] Q1 *Sir, Pray Sir do;* Q2P *Sir; Pray, Sir, do.*   10] Q2P *Varole* (throughout the scene).   23] Q2P om. *be.*
34] Q2P *trod.*

L. Fop. You are positively in the right on't, for the packet becomes no part of the body but the knee.
[Exit Tailor.]

Sem. I hope your lordship is pleased with your steenkirk.[1]   90

L. Fop. In love with it, stap my vitals. Bring your bill, you shall be paid tomorrow —

Sem. I humbly thank your honor.
Exit Sempstress.

L. Fop. Hark thee, shoemaker, these shoes a'n't ugly, but they don't fit me.   95

Shoe. My lord, my thinks they fit you very well.

L. Fop. They hurt me just below the instep.

Shoe. *(feeling his foot).* My lord, they don't hurt you there.

L. Fop. I tell thee, they pinch me execrably.   100

Shoe. My lord, if they pinch you, I'll be bound to be hanged, that's all.

L. Fop. Why, wilt thou undertake to persuade me I cannot feel?

Shoe. Your lordship may please to feel what   195 you think fit, but that shoe does not hurt you; I think I understand my trade.

L. Fop. Now by all that's great and powerful, thou art an incomprehensible coxcomb; but thou makest good shoes, and so I'll bear with thee.   110

Shoe. My lord, I have worked for half the people of quality in town these twenty years; and 'twere very hard I should not know when a shoe hurts and when it don't.

L. Fop. Well, prithee begone about thy busi-   115 ness.   *Exit Shoemaker.*
(To the Hosier.) Mr. Mend-legs, a word with you; the calves of these stockings are thickened a little too much. They make my legs look like a chairman's ——   120

Mend. My lord, my thinks they look mighty well.

L. Fop. Ay, but you are not so good a judge of these things as I am; I have studied 'em all my life; therefore pray let the next be the thickness of a crawnpiece less. —— *(Aside.)* If the town   125 takes notice my legs are fallen away, 'twill be attributed to the violence of some new intrigue.
[Exit Hosier.]
(To the Periwig-maker.) Come, Mr. Foretop, let me see what you have done, and then the fatigue of the marning will be over.   130

Foretop. My lord, I have done what I defy any prince in Europe t' out-do; I have made you a periwig so long, and so full of hair, it will serve you for hat and cloak in all weathers.

L. Fop. Then thou hast made me thy friend   135 to eternity: come, comb it out.

[1] A neck-cloth with long laced ends.

Y. Fas. Well, Lory, what do'st think on't? A very friendly reception from a brother after three years' absence!

Lo. Why, sir, it's your own fault: we sel-   140 dom care for those that don't love what we love; if you would creep into his heart, you must enter into his pleasures. Here have you stood ever since you came in, and have not commended any one thing that belongs to him.   145

Y. Fas. Nor never shall, whilst they belong to a coxcomb.

Lo. Then, sir, you must be content to pick a hungry bone.

Y. Fas. No, sir, I'll crack it, and get to the   150 marrow before I have done.

L. Fop. Gad's curse! Mr. Foretop, you don't intend to put this upon me for a full periwig?

Fore. Not a full one, my lord? I don't know what your lordship may please to call a full   155 one, but I have crammed twenty ounces of hair into it.

L. Fop. What it may be by weight, sir, I shall not dispute; but by tale,[2] there are not nine hairs on a side.   160

Fore. O Lord! O Lord! O Lord! Why, as Gad shall judge me, your honor's side-face is reduced to the tip of your nose.

L. Fop. My side-face may be in eclipse for aught I know; but I'm sure my full-face is like the   165 full-moon.

Fore. *(rubbing his eyes).* Heaven bless my eyesight! Sure I look through the wrong end of the perspective, for by my faith, an't please your honor, the broadest place I see in your face does not   170 seem to me to be two inches diameter.

L. Fop. If it did, it would be just two inches too broad; far a periwig to a man should be like a mask to a woman: nothing should be seen but his eyes.

Fore. My lord, I have done; if you please   175 to have more hair in your wig, I'll put it in.

L. Fop. Passitively, yes.

Fore. Shall I take it back now, my lord?

L. Fop. No: I'll wear it today, though it show such a manstrous pair of cheeks: stop my vitals,   180 I shall be taken for a trumpeter.   *Exit Foretop.*

Y. Fas. Now your people of business are gone, brother, I hope I may obtain a quarter of an hour's audience of you.

L. Fop. Faith, Tam, I must beg you'll ex-   185 cuse me at this time, for I must away to the House of Lards immediately; my Lady Teaser's case is to come on today, and I would not be absent for the salvation of mankind. — Hey, page! is the coach at the door?

[2] By count.

87] P *passitively.*   112–113] P *'tis very.*   123] Q2P *those things.*   130] Q2P *morning.*
132] Q2P *to outdo.*   133–134] Q2P *for a hat.*   140] Q2P *'tis.*   143] Q2P *you have stood.*
146] Q2P *while.*   164] Q2P *in an eclipse.*   172] P *just be.*   173] Q2P *for.*   180] Q2 *monstrous.*

PAGE. Yes, my lord.   190

L. FOP. You'll excuse me, brother.   *Going.*

Y. FAS. Shall you be back at dinner?

L. FOP. As Gad shall jidge me, I can't tell; for 'tis passible I may dine with some of aur House at Lacket's.[1]   195

Y. FAS. Shall I meet you there? for I must needs talk with you.

L. FOP. That, I'm afraid, mayn't be so praper; far the lards I commonly eat with are people of a nice conversation; and you know, Tam, your   200 education has been a little at large: but if you'll stay here, you'll find a family dinner. — Hey, fellow! What is there for dinner? — There's beef: I suppose my brother will eat beef. Dear Tam, I'm glad to see thee in England, stap my vitals.   205

Exit with his equipage.[2]

Y. FAS. Hell and Furies, is this to be borne?

LO. Faith, sir, I could almost have given him a knock o' th' pate myself.

Y. FAS. 'Tis enough; I will now show thee the excess of my passion by being very calm.   210 Come, Lory, lay your loggerhead to mine, and in cool blood let us contrive his destruction.

LO. Here comes a head, sir, would contrive it better than us both, if he would but join in the confederacy.   215

Enter COUPLER.

Y. FAS. By this light, old Coupler alive still! Why, how now, matchmaker, art thou here still to plague the world with matrimony? You old bawd, how have you the impudence to be hobbling out of your grave twenty years after you are rotten!   220

COUP. When you begin to rot, sirrah, you'll go off like a pippin; one winter will send you to the devil. What mischief brings you home again? Ha! you young lascivious rogue, you! let me put my hand in your bosom, sirrah.   225

Y. FAS. Stand off, old Sodom.

COUP. Nay, prithee, now, don't be so coy.

Y. FAS. Keep your hands to yourself, you old dog, you, or I'll wring your nose off.

COUP. Hast thou then been a year in Italy,   230 and brought home a fool at last? By my conscience, the young fellows of this age profit no more by their going abroad than they do by their going to church. Sirrah, sirrah, if you are not hanged before you come to my years, you'll know a cock from a hen.   235 But come, I'm still a friend to thy person, though I have a contempt of thy understanding; and therefore I would willingly know thy condition, that I

[1] Locket's: a fashionable tavern in Charing Cross.
[2] Retinue.

may see whether thou stand'st in need of my assistance; for widows swarm, my boy, the town's in-   240 fected with 'em.

Y. FAS. I stand in need of anybody's assistance that will help me to cut my elder brother's throat, without the risk of being hanged for him.

COUP. I'gad, sirrah, I could help thee to do   245 him almost as good a turn, without the danger of being burnt in the hand for't.

Y. FAS. Sayest thou so, old Satan? Show me but that, and my soul is thine.

COUP. Pox o' thy soul! give me thy warm   250 body, sirrah; I shall have a substantial title to't when I tell thee my project.

Y. FAS. Out with it then, dear dad, and take possession as soon as thou wilt.

COUP. Sayest thou so, my Hephestion?[3]   255 Why, then, thus lies the scene — but hold! who's that? if we are heard we are undone.

Y. FAS. What, have you forgot Lory?

COUP. Who? trusty Lory, is it thee?

LO. At your service, sir.   260

COUP. Give me thy hand, old boy; i'gad, I did not know thee again; but I remember thy honesty, though I did not thy face; I think thou hadst like to have been hanged once or twice for thy master.

LO. Sir, I was very near once having that   265 honor.

COUP. Well, live and hope; don't be discouraged; eat with him, and drink with him, and do what he bids thee, and it may be thy reward at last as well as another's. (*To* YOUNG FASHION.) Well, sir,   270 you must know I have done you the kindness to make up a match for your brother.

Y. FAS. Sir, I am very much beholding to you, truly.

COUP. You may be, sirrah, before the   275 wedding-day yet; the lady is a great heiress; fifteen hundred pounds a year, and a great bag of money; the match is concluded, the writings are drawn, and the pipkin's to be cracked in a fortnight. Now you must know, stripling (with respect to your   280 mother), your brother's the son of a whore.

Y. FAS. Good!

COUP. He has given me a bond of a thousand pounds for helping him to this fortune, and has promised me as much more in ready money   285 upon the day of marriage, which, I understand by a friend, he ne'er designs to pay me. If therefore you will be a generous young dog, and secure me five thousand pounds, I'll be a covetous old rogue, and help you to the lady.   290

Y. FAS. I'gad, if thou canst bring this about, I'll

[3] The intimate companion of Alexander the Great.

193] Q2 *God.*   194] Q2 *our.*   199] P *are a people.*   209] P *show you.*
221-225] Q1Q2 print as five lines of verse.   224-225] P *into your.*   239] Q2P *standest.*   248] P *Say'st.*
273] P om. *Sir.*   273] Q2P *beholden.*

have thy statue cast in brass. But don't you dote, you old pander, you, when you talk at this rate?

COUP. That your youthful parts shall judge of. This plump partridge that I tell you of lives in 295 the country, fifty miles off, with her honored parents, in a lonely old house which nobody comes near; she never goes abroad, nor sees company at home; to prevent all misfortunes, she has her breeding within doors: the parson of the parish teaches her to 300 play on the bass-viol, the clerk to sing, her nurse to dress, and her father to dance. In short, nobody can give you admittance there but I; nor can I do it any other way, than by making you pass for your brother. 305

Y. FAS. And how the devil wilt thou do that?

COUP. Without the devil's aid, I warrant thee. Thy brother's face not one of the family ever saw; the whole business has been managed by me, and all the letters go through my hands: the last that 310 was writ to Sir Tunbelly Clumsey (for that's the old gentleman's name) was to tell him, his lordship would be down in a fortnight to consummate. Now you shall go away immediately, pretend you writ that letter only to have the romantic 315 pleasure of surprising your mistress, fall desperately in love as soon as you see her; make that your plea for marrying her immediately, and when the fatigue of the wedding-night's over you shall send me a swinging purse of gold, you dog, you. 320

Y. FAS. I'gad, old dad, I'll put my hand in thy bosom now.

COUP. Ah, you young hot lusty thief, let me muzzle you —— (*kissing*) —— sirrah, let me muzzle you. 325

Y. FAS. (*aside*). Psha, the old lecher ——

COUP. Well, I'll warrant thou hast not a farthing of money in thy pocket now, no; one may see it in thy face ——

Y. FAS. Not a souse,[1] by Jupiter. 330

COUP. Must I advance then? well, sirrah, be at my lodgings in half an hour, and I'll see what may be done; we'll sign and seal, and eat a pullet, and when I have given thee some farther instructions, thou sha't hoist sail and be gone. (*Kissing*.) T'other 335 buss, and so adieu.

Y. FAS. Um, psha.

COUP. Ah, you young warm dog, you; what a delicious night will the bride have on't!

Exit COUPLER.

Y. FAS. So, Lory: Providence, thou seest 340 at last, takes care of men of merit: we are in a fair way to be great people.

LO. Ay, sir, if the devil don't step between the cup and the lip, as he uses to do.

[1] Sou.

Y. FAS. Why, faith, he has played me many 345 a damned trick to spoil my fortune, and, i'gad, I'm almost afraid he's at work about it again now; but if I should tell thee how, thou'dst wonder at me.

LO. Indeed, sir, I should not.

Y. FAS. How dost know? 350

LO. Because, sir, I have wondered at you so often, I can wonder at you no more.

Y. FAS. No? what wouldst thou say if a qualm of conscience should spoil my design?

LO. I would eat my words, and wonder more 355 than ever.

Y. FAS. Why, faith, Lory, though I am a young rake-hell, and have played many a roguish trick, this is so full-grown a cheat, I find I must take pains to come up to't; I have scruples. 360

LO. They are strong symptoms of death; if you find they increase, pray, sir, make your will.

Y. FAS. No, my conscience shan't starve me, neither. But thus far I will harken to it, before I execute this project. I'll try my brother to the 365 bottom; I'll speak to him with the temper of a philosopher; my reasons (though they press him home) shall yet be clothed with so much modesty, not one of all the truths they urge shall be so naked to offend his sight: if he has yet so much 370 humanity about him as to assist me (though with a moderate aid) I'll drop my project at his feet, and show him I can — do for him much more than what I ask he'd do for me. This one conclusive trial of him I resolve to make. 375

Succeed or no, still victory's my lot;
If I subdue his heart, 'tis well; if not,
I shall subdue my conscience to my plot.

Exeunt.

ACT II

SCENE I

[LOVELESS's *lodgings in London.*]

Enter LOVELESS *and* AMANDA.

LOV. How do you like these lodgings, my dear? For my part, I am so well pleased with 'em, I shall hardly remove whilst we stay in town, if you are satisfied.

AMAN. I am satisfied with everything that 5 pleases you; else I had not come to town at all.

LOV. Oh, a little of the noise and bustle of the world sweetens the pleasures of retreat: we shall find the charms of our retirement doubled, when we return to it. 10

AMAN. That pleasing prospect will be my chiefest entertainment, whilst (much against my will) I am obliged to stand surrounded with these

empty pleasures which 'tis so much the fashion to
be fond of. 15

Lov. I own most of 'em are indeed but empty; nay,
so empty, that one would wonder by what magic
power they act, when they induce us to be vicious
for their sakes. Yet some there are we may speak
kindlier of: there are delights, of which a 20
private life is destitute, which may divert an honest man, and be a harmless entertainment to a virtuous woman. The conversation of the town is one;
and truly (with some small allowances) the plays,
I think, may be esteemed another. 25

Aman. The plays, I must confess, have some small
charms, and would have more, would they restrain
that loose, obscene encouragement to vice which
shocks, if not the virtue of some women, at least
the modesty of all. 30

Lov. But till that reformation can be made I
would not leave the wholesome corn for some intruding tares that grow amongst it. Doubtless the
moral of a well-wrought scene is of prevailing
force — last night there happened one that 35
moved me strangely.

Aman. Pray, what was that?

Lov. Why, 'twas about — but 'tis not worth
repeating.

Aman. Yes, pray let me know it. 40

Lov. No, I think 'tis as well let alone.

Aman. Nay, now you make me have a mind to
know.

Lov. 'Twas a foolish thing: you'd perhaps grow
jealous should I tell it you, though without cause, 45
heaven knows.

Aman. I shall begin to think I have a cause, if
you persist in making it a secret.

Lov. I'll then convince you you have none, by making it no longer so. Know then, I happened 50
in the play to find my very character, only with
the addition of a relapse, which struck me so, I put
a sudden stop to a most harmless entertainment
which till then diverted me between the acts. 'Twas
to admire the workmanship of Nature in the face 55
of a young lady that sate some distance from me,
she was so exquisitely handsome.

Aman. 'So exquisitely handsome!'

Lov. Why do you repeat my words, my dear?

Aman. Because you seemed to speak 'em 60
with such pleasure, I thought I might oblige you
with their echo.

Lov. Then you are alarmed, Amanda?

Aman. It is my duty to be so, when you are in
danger. 65

Lov. You are too quick in apprehending for me;
all will be well when you have heard me out. I do
confess I gazed upon her, nay, eagerly I gazed upon
her.

Aman. Eagerly? That's with desire. 70

Lov. No, I desired her not: I viewed her with a
world of admiration, but not one glance of love.

Aman. Take heed of trusting to such nice distinctions.

Lov. I did take heed; for, observing in the 75
play that he who seemed to represent me there was,
by an accident like this, unwarily surprized into a net
in which he lay a poor entangled slave, and brought
a train of mischiefs on his head, I snatched my eyes
away; they pleaded hard for leave to look again, 80
but I grew absolute, and they obeyed.

Aman. Were they the only things that were inquisitive? Had I been in your place, my tongue, I
fancy, had been curious, too: I should have asked
her name, and where she lived (yet still without 85
design). Who was she, pray?

Lov. Indeed I cannot tell.

Aman. You will not tell.

Lov. By all that's sacred, then, I did not ask.

Aman. Nor do you know what company was 90
with her?

Lov. I do not.

Aman. Then I am calm again.

Lov. Why were you disturbed?

Aman. Had I then no cause? 95

Lov. None, certainly.

Aman. I thought I had.

Lov. But you thought wrong, Amanda; for turn
the case, and let it be your story. Should you come
home, and tell me you had seen a handsome 100
man, should I grow jealous because you had eyes?

Aman. But should I tell you he were exquisitely
so; that I had gazed on him with admiration; that
I had looked with eager eyes upon him; should you
not think 'twere possible I might go one step 105
farther, and enquire his name?

Lov. (aside). She has reason on her side: I have
talked too much; but I must turn it off another
way. (To Amanda.) Will you then make no difference, Amanda, between the language of our 110
sex and yours? There is a modesty restrains your
tongues which makes you speak by halves when
you commend; but roving flattery gives a loose to
ours, which makes us still speak double what we
think: you should not therefore in so strict a 115
sense take what I said to her advantage.

Aman. Those flights of flattery, sir, are to our
faces only: when women once are out of hearing,
you are as modest in your commendations as we
are. But I shan't put you to the trouble of 120
farther excuses; if you please, this business shall rest
here. Only give me leave to wish, both for your
peace and mine, that you may never meet this
miracle of beauty more.

Lov. I am content. 125

16] Q2P *them.*　　　45] P *without a cause.*　　　56] P *sat.*　　　60] P *them.*　　　70] Q2P *Eagerly!*
80] Q2 om. *to look.*　　　86] Q2 *she, I pray?*　　　106] Q2P *further.*　　　121] Q2 *further.*

Enter Servant.

SERV. Madam, there's a young lady at the door in a chair, desires to know whether your ladyship sees company. I think her name is Berinthia.

AMAN. O dear! 'tis a relation I have not seen these five years. — Pray her to walk in.   130

Exit Servant.

(*To* LOVELESS.) Here's another beauty for you. She was young when I saw her last; but I hear she's grown extremely handsome.

LOV. Don't you be jealous now, for I shall gaze upon her too.   135

Enter BERINTHIA.

LOV. (*aside*). Ha! By heavens, the very woman!

BER. (*saluting* AMANDA). Dear Amanda, I did not expect to meet with you in town.

AMAN. Sweet cousin, I'm overjoyed to see you. (*To* LOVELESS.) Mr. Loveless, here's a rela-   140 tion and a friend of mine I desire you'll be better acquainted with.

LOV. (*saluting* BERINTHIA). If my wife never desires a harder thing, madam, her request will be easily granted.   145

BER. (*to* AMANDA). I think, madam, I ought to wish you joy.

AMAN. Joy! Upon what?

BER. Upon your marriage: you were a widow when I saw you last.[1]   150

LOV. You ought rather, madam, to wish me joy upon that, since I am the only gainer.

BER. If she has got so good a husband as the world reports, she has gained enough to expect the compliments of her friends upon it.   155

LOV. [If] the world is so favorable to me, to allow I deserve that title, I hope 'tis so just to my wife to own I derive it from her.

BER. Sir, it is so just to you both, to own you are, and deserve to be, the happiest pair that   160 live in it.

LOV. I'm afraid we shall lose that character, madam, whenever you happen to change your condition.

Enter Servant.

SER. Sir, my Lord Foppington presents his   165 humble service to you, and desires to know how you do. He but just now heard you were in town. He's at the next door; and if it be not inconvenient, he'll come and wait upon you.

LOV. Lord Foppington! I know him not.   170

BER. Not his dignity, perhaps, but you do his

person. 'Tis Sir Novelty; he has bought a barony, in order to marry a great fortune: his patent[2] has not been passed eight-and-forty hours, and he has already sent how-do-ye's[3] to all the town, to   175 make 'em acquainted with his title.

LOV. Give my service to his lordship, and let him know I am proud of the honor he intends me.

Exit [Servant].

Sure this addition of quality must have so improved [this] coxcomb, he can't but be very good   180 company for a quarter of an hour.

AMAN. Now it moves my pity more than my mirth, to see a man whom nature has made no fool, be so very industrious to pass for an ass.

LOV. No, there you are wrong, Amanda; you   185 should never bestow your pity upon those who take pains for your contempt. Pity those whom nature abuses, but never those who abuse nature.

BER. Besides, the town would be robbed of one of its chief diversions, if it should become a crime   190 to laugh at a fool.

AMAN. I could never yet perceive the town inclined to part with any of its diversions for the sake of their being crimes; but I have seen it very fond of some I think had little else to recommend   195 'em.

BER. I doubt, Amanda, you are grown its enemy, you speak with so much warmth against it.

AMAN. I must confess I am not much its friend.   200

BER. Then give me leave to make you mine, by not engaging in its quarrel.

AMAN. You have many stronger claims than that, Berinthia, whenever you think fit to plead your title.   205

LOV. You have done well to engage a second, my dear; for here comes one will be apt to call you to an account for your country principles.

Enter LORD FOPPINGTON.

L. FOP. (*to* LOVELESS). Sir, I am your most humble servant.   210

LOV. I wish you joy, my lord.

L. FOP. O Lard, sir! —— madam, your ladyship's welcome to tawn.

AMAN. I wish your lordship joy.

L. FOP. O heavens, madam! ——   215

LOV. My lord, this young lady is a relation of my [wife's].

L. FOP. (*saluting her*). The beautifullest race of people upon earth, rat me. Dear Loveless, I am overjoyed to see you have braught your fam-   220

---

[1] In Cibber's play Amanda wore mourning during Loveless's absence.

[2] The royal writ conferring the title.

[3] Messages of greeting.

129–130] P *this five*   155] P *compliment.*   156] Q1 *I the;* Q2 *Ay, the;* P *If the.*   162] Q2 *loose.*
174] Q2P *passed above eight-and-forty.*   178 s.d.] Q1Q2P om. Servant.   180] Q1Q2P *his coxcomb.*
190] Q2P *chiefest.*   212] P *Laird.*   217] Q1Q2 *wives;* P *wife's.*   220] Q2P *brought.*

ily to tawn again: I am, stap my vitals — (aside) far
I design to lie with your wife. (To AMANDA.) Far
Gad's sake, madam, haw has your ladyship been
able to subsist thus long under the fatigue of a
country life?   225

AMAN. My life has been very far from that, my
lord; it has been a very quiet one.

L. FOP. Why, that's the fatigue I speak of,
madam, for 'tis impossible to be quiet, without
thinking: now thinking is to me the greatest   230
fatigue in the world.

AMAN. Does not your lordship love reading, then?

L. FOP. Oh, passionately, madam —— but I
never think of what I read.

BER. Why, can your lordship read without   235
thinking?

L. FOP. O Laid —— can your ladyship pray
without devotion — madam?

AMAN. Well, I must own I think books the best
entertainment in the world.   240

L. FOP. I am so much of your ladyship's mind,
madam, that I have a private gallery, where I walk
sometimes, is furnished with nothing but books and
looking-glasses. Madam, I have gilded 'em, and
ranged 'em so prettily, before Gad, it is the   245
most entertaining thing in the world to walk and
look upon 'em.

AMAN. Nay, I love a neat library too; but 'tis, I
think, the inside of the book should recommend it
most to us.   250

L. FOP. That, I must confess, I am nat altogether
so fand of. Far to mind the inside of a book is to
entertain one's self with the forced product of another man's brain. Naw I think a man of quality
and breeding may be much better diverted with   255
the natural sprauts of his own. But to say the truth,
madam, let a man love reading never so well, when
once he comes to know this tawn he finds so many
better ways of passing the four-and-twenty hours,
that 'twere ten thousand pities he should con-   260
sume his time in that. Far example, madam, my
life; my life, madam, is a perpetual stream of pleasure, that glides through such a variety of entertainments, I believe the wisest of our ancestors never
had the least conception of any of 'em. I rise,   265
madam, about ten a'clock. I don't rise sooner,
because 'tis the worst thing in the world for the
complexion; nat that I pretend to be a beau, but
a man must endeavour to look wholesome, lest he
makes so nauseous a figure in the side-bax, the   270
ladies should be compelled to turn their eyes upon
the play. So at ten a'clack, I say, I rise. Naw, if

I find 'tis a good day, I resalve to take a turn in the
park, and see the fine women; so huddle on my
clothes, and get dressed by one. If it be nasty   275
weather, I take a turn in the chocolate-hause, where,
as you walk, madam, you have the prettiest prospect
in the world; you have looking-glasses all round
you. —— But I'm afraid I tire the company.

BER. Not at all. Pray go on.   280

L. FOP. Why then, ladies, from thence I go to
dinner at Lacket's, where you are so nicely and
delicately served that, stap my vitals, they shall
compose you a dish no bigger than a saucer, shall
come to fifty shillings. Between eating my   285
dinner, and washing my mauth, ladies, I spend my
time till I go to the play, where, till nine a'clack, I
entertain myself with looking upon the company;
and usually dispose of one hour more in leading 'em
aut. So there's twelve of the four-and-twenty   290
pretty well over. The other twelve, madam, are
disposed of in two articles: in the first four I toast
myself drunk, and in t'other eight I sleep myself
sober again. Thus, ladies, you see my life is an
eternal raund O of delights.   295

LOV. 'Tis a heavenly one, indeed.

AMAN. But I thought, my lord, you beaux spent
a great deal of your time in intrigues: you have
given us no account of them yet.

L. FOP. (aside). Soh! she would enquire into   300
my amours —— that's jealousy —— she begins to be
in love with me. (To AMANDA.) Why, madam — as
to time for my intrigues, I usually make detachments
of it from my other pleasures, according to the exi-
gency. Far your ladyship may please to take   305
notice, that those who intrigue with women of
quality have rarely occasion far above half an hour
at a time: people of that rank being under those
decorums, they can seldom give you a langer view
than will just serve to shoot 'em flying. So   310
that the course of my other pleasures is not very
much interrupted by my amours.

LOV. But your lordship now is become a pillar
of the state; you must attend the weighty affairs of
the nation.   315

L. FOP. Sir —— as to weighty affairs —— I leave
them to weighty heads. I never intend mine shall
be a burthen to my body.

LOV. Oh, but you'll find the House will expect
your attendance.   320

L. FOP. Sir, you'll find the House will compound
for my appearance.

LOV. But your friends will take it ill if you don't
attend their particular causes.

221–222] Q2P for I.   244] P them.   249] Q2P a book.   251] Q2P not.   255] P om. better.
259] Q2P passing away the.   272] Q2P a'clock.   273] P find it.   276] P chocolate-house.
282] P Lacket's, and there you.   283–284] P can compose.   286] Q2P mouth.   287] P a'clock.
289] Q2P them.   295] Q2P round.   297] P But, my lord, you beaux spend.   299] Q2 'em.
307] Q2P for.   309] P larger.   318] P burden.

L. Fop. Not, sir, if I come time enough 325
to give 'em my particular vote.

Ber. But pray, my lord, how do you dispose of
yourself on Sundays? for that, methinks, is a day
should hang wretchedly upon your hands.

L. Fop. Why, faith, madam —— Sunday 330
—— is a vile day, I must confess. I intend to move
for leave to bring in a bill, that the players may work
upon it, as well as the hackney coaches. Though
this I must say for the Government, it leaves us the
churches to entertain us —— but then again, 335
they begin so abominable early, a man must rise by
candle-light to get dressed by the psalm.

Ber. Pray, which church does your lordship most
oblige with your presence?

L. Fop. Oh, St. James's, madam —— there's 340
much the best company.

Aman. Is there good preaching too?

L. Fop. Why, faith, madam —— I can't tell.
A man must have very little to do there, that can
give an account of the sermon. 345

Ber. You can give us an account of the ladies, at
least.

L. Fop. Or I deserve to be excommunicated.
There is my Lady Tattle, my Lady Prate, my Lady
Titter, my Lady Leer, my Lady Giggle, and 350
my Lady Grin. These sit in the front of the boxes,
and all church-time are the prettiest company in the
world, stap my vitals. (*To* Amanda.) Mayn't we
hope for the honor to see your ladyship added to
our society, madam? 355

Aman. Alas, my lord, I am the worst company in
the world at church: I'm apt to mind the prayers, or
the sermon, or ——

L. Fop. One is indeed strangely apt at church
to mind what one should not do. But I hope, 360
madam, at one time or other, I shall have the
honor to lead your ladyship to your coach there.
(*Aside.*) Methinks she seems strangely pleased
with everything I say to her. 'Tis a vast pleasure to receive encouragement from a woman 365
before her husband's face —— I have a good mind
to pursue my conquest, and speak the thing plainly
to her at once. —— I'gad, I'll do 't, and that in so
cavalier a manner, she shall be surprised at it. ——
Ladies, I'll take my leave; I'm afraid I begin 370
to grow troublesome with the length of my visit.

Aman. Your lordship's too entertaining to grow
troublesome anywhere.

L. Fop. (*aside*). That now was as much as if she
had said 'Pray lie with me.' I'll let her see I'm 375
quick of apprehension. (*To* Amanda.) O Lard,
madam, I had like to have forgot a secret I must
needs tell your ladyship. (*To* Loveless.) Ned,
you must not be so jealous now as to listen.

Lov. Not I, my lord; I am too fashionable 380
a husband to pry into the secrets of my wife.

L. Fop. (*to* Amanda, *squeezing her hand*). I am in
love with you to desperation, strike me speechless.

Aman. (*giving him a box o' th' ear*). Then thus
I return your passion —— an impudent fool! 385

L. Fop. Gad's curse, madam, I'm a peer of the
realm.

Lov. Hey; what the devil! do you affront my wife,
sir? Nay, then ——

(*They draw and fight. The women run shriek-*
ing for help.)

Aman. Ah! What has my folly done? Help! 390
Murder, help! Part 'em, for heaven's sake!

L. Fop. (*falling back, and leaning upon his sword*).
Ah —— quite through the body —— stap my vitals.

Enter Servants.

Lov. (*running to him*). I hope I han't killed the
fool, however. —— [Bear][1] him up! —— 395
Where's your wound?

L. Fop. Just through the guts.

Lov. Call a surgeon there: unbutton him quickly.

L. Fop. Ay, pray make haste. [*Exit Servant.*]

Lov. This mischief you may thank yourself 400
for.

L. Fop. I may so——love's the devil indeed, Ned.

Enter Serringe *and Servant.*

Serv. Here's Mr. Serringe, sir, was just going by
the door.

L. Fop. He's the welcom'st man alive. 405

Ser. Stand by, stand by, stand by. Pray, gentlemen, stand by. Lord have mercy upon us! did you
never see a man run through the body before? Pray
stand by.

L. Fop. Ah, Mr. Serringe—I'm a dead man. 410

Ser. A dead man, and I by —— I should laugh to
see that, i'gad.

Lov. Prithee don't stand prating, but look upon
his wound.

Ser. Why, what if I won't look upon his 415
wound this hour, sir?

Lov. Why, then he'll bleed to death, sir.

Ser. Why, then I'll fetch him to life again, sir.

Lov. 'Slife, he's run through the guts, I tell
thee. 420

Ser. Would he were run through the heart:
I should get the more credit by his cure. Now I
hope you're satisfied? —— Come, now let me come
at him; now let me come at him. (*Viewing his*

[1] It is just possible that the reading of the quartos (*Bare*) is
correct, and that the meaning is 'Lay bare his wound.' Cf.
Loveless's next speech. But I can find no other instance of the
phrase 'bare up' in this sense.

wound.) Oons, what a gash is here! —— Why, 425
sir, a man may drive a coach and six horses into
your body.

L. Fop. Ho! ——

Ser. Why, what the devil! have you run the gentleman through with a scythe? (*Aside*.) A 430
little prick between the skin and the ribs, that's all.

Lov. Let me see his wound.

Ser. Then you shall dress it, sir; for if anybody
looks upon it, I won't.

Lov. Why, thou art the veriest coxcomb I 435
ever saw.

Ser. Sir, I am not master of my trade for nothing.

L. Fop. Surgeon!

Ser. Well, sir?

L. Fop. Is there any hopes?   440

Ser. Hopes? —— I can't tell. —— What are you
willing to give for your cure?

L. Fop. Five hundred paunds with pleasure.

Ser. Why, then perhaps there may be hopes. But
we must avoid farther delay. Here, help the 445
gentleman into a chair, and carry him to my house
presently: that's the properest place — (*aside*) to
bubble him out of his money. —— Come, a chair, a
chair quickly —— there, in with him.

(*They put him into a chair*.)

L. Fop. Dear Loveless —— adieu. If I die 450
—— I forgive thee; and if I live —— I hope thou'lt
do as much by me. I'm very sorry you and I should
quarrel; but I hope here's an end on't, for if you are
satisfied —— I am.

Lov. I shall hardly think it worth my prose- 455
cuting any farther, so you may be at rest, sir.

L. Fop. Thou art a generous fellow, strike me
dumb. (*Aside*.) But thou hast an impertinent
wife, stap my vitals.

Ser. So, carry him off, carry him off; we 460
shall have him prate himself into a fever by and by;
carry him off.

Exit Serringe *with* Lord Foppington.

Aman. Now on my knees, my dear, let me ask
your pardon for my indiscretion: my own I never
shall obtain.   465

Lov. Oh, there's no harm done: you served him
well.

Aman. He did indeed deserve it. But I tremble
to think how dear my indiscreet resentment might
have cost you.   470

Lov. Oh, no matter; never trouble yourself about
that.

Ber. For heaven's sake, what was't he did to you?

Aman. Oh, nothing; he only squeezed me kindly
by the hand, and frankly offered me a cox- 475
comb's heart. I know I was [to]¹ blame to resent

¹ The reading 'too blame' in Q1 has been defended, but this

it as I did, since nothing but a quarrel could ensue.
But the fool so surprised me with his insolence, I
was not mistress of my fingers.

Ber. Now I dare swear he thinks you had 480
'em at great command, they obeyed you so readily.

Enter Worthy.

Wor. Save you, save you, good people; I'm glad
to find you all alive; I met a wounded peer carrying
off. For heaven's sake, what was the matter?

Lov. Oh, a trifle: he would have lain with my 485
wife before my face, so she obliged him with a box o'
the ear, and I run him through the body: that was all.

Wor. Bagatelle on all sides. But, pray, madam,
how long has this noble lord been an humble servant of yours?   490

Aman. This is the first I have heard on't. So I
suppose 'tis his quality, more than his love, has
brought him into this adventure. He thinks his
title an authentic passport to every woman's heart,
below the degree of a peeress.   495

Wor. He's coxcomb enough to think anything.
But I would not have you brought into trouble for
him: I hope there's no danger of his life?

Lov. None at all: he's fallen into the hands of a
roguish surgeon, I perceive designs to frighten 500
a little money out of him. But I saw his wound —
'tis nothing; he may go to the play tonight if he
pleases.

Wor. I am glad you have corrected him without
farther mischief. And now, sir, if these ladies 505
have no farther service for you, you'll oblige me if you
can go to the place I spoke to you of t'other day.

Lov. With all my heart. (*Aside*.) Though I
could wish, methinks, to stay and gaze a little longer
on that creature. Good gods! how beautiful 510
she is! —— but what have I to do with beauty?
I have already had my portion, and must not
covet more. (*To* Worthy.) Come, sir, when you
please.

Wor. Ladies, your servant.   515

Aman. Mr. Loveless, pray one word with you
before you go.

Lov. (*to* Worthy). I'll overtake you, sir. (*Exit*
Worthy.) [*Aside to* Amanda.] What would my
dear?   520

Aman. Only a woman's foolish question; how do
you like my cousin here?

Lov. Jealous already, Amanda?

Aman. Not at all; I ask you for another reason.

Lov. (*aside*). Whate'er her reason be, I must 525
not tell her true. (*To* Amanda.) Why, I confess
she's handsome. But you must not think I slight

erroneous phrase was uncommon after 1600, and the assumption of a misprint here seems reasonable.

445] Q2P *further.*   451] Q2P *thou wilt.*   452] Q2P *I am.*   456] Q2P *further.*
476] Q1 *too blame*; Q2P *to blame.*   500] P *surgeon, who I.*

your kinswoman if I own to you, of all the women who may claim that character she is the last would triumph in my heart.   530

AMAN. I'm satisfied.

LOV. Now tell me why you asked.

AMAN. At night I will. Adieu.

LOV. (*kissing her*). I'm yours.   *Exit* LOVELESS.

[AMAN.] (*aside*). I'm glad to find he does not 535 like her; for I have a great mind to persuade her to come and live with me. (*To* BERINTHIA.) Now, dear Berinthia, let me enquire a little into your affairs: for I do assure you, I am enough your friend to interest myself in everything that concerns you.   540

BER. You formerly have given me such proofs on't, I should be very much to blame to doubt it. I am sorry I have no secrets to trust you with, that I might convince you how entire a confidence I durst repose in you.   545

AMAN. Why, is it possible, that one so young and beautiful as you should live and have no secrets?

BER. What secrets do you mean?

AMAN. Lovers.

BER. Oh, twenty; but not one secret one 550 amongst 'em. Lovers in this age have too much honor to do anything underhand; they do all aboveboard.

AMAN. That, now, methinks, would make me hate a man.   555

BER. But the women of the town are of another mind: for by this means a lady may, with the expense of a few coquet glances, lead twenty fools about in a string for two or three years together. Whereas, if she should allow 'em greater fa- 560 vors, and oblige 'em to secrecy, she would not keep one of 'em a fortnight.

AMAN. There's something indeed in that to satisfy the vanity of a woman, but I can't comprehend how the men find their account in it.   565

BER. Their entertainment, I must confess, is a riddle to me. For there's very few of 'em ever get farther than a bow and an ogle. I have half a score for my share, who follow me all over the town; and at the play, the park, and the church do (with 570 their eyes) say the violent'st things to me —— but I never hear any more of 'em.

AMAN. What can be the reason of that?

BER. One reason is, they don't know how to go farther. They have had so little practice, 575 they don't understand the trade. But besides their ignorance, you must know there is not one of my half-score lovers but what follows half a score mistresses. Now their affections, being divided amongst so many, are not strong enough for 580 any one to make 'em pursue her to the purpose.

Like a young puppy in a warren, they have a flirt at all, and catch none.

AMAN. Yet they seem to have a torrent of love to dispose of.   585

BER. They have so: but 'tis like the rivers of a modern philosopher whose works, though a woman, I have read: it sets out with a violent stream, splits in a thousand branches, and is all lost in the sands.   590

AMAN. But do you think this river of love runs all its course without doing any mischief? Do you think it overflows nothing?

BER. Oh yes; 'tis true, it never breaks into anybody's ground that has the least fence about it; 595 but it overflows all the commons that lie in its way. And this is the utmost achievement of those dreadful champions in the field of love — the beaux.

AMAN. But prithee, Berinthia, instruct me a little farther, for I'm so great a novice, I am almost 600 ashamed on't. My husband's leaving me whilst I was young and fond threw me into that depth of discontent, that ever since I have led so private and recluse a life, my ignorance is scarce conceivable. I therefore fain would be instructed; not, 605 heaven knows, that what you call intrigues have any charms for me: my love and principles are too well fixed. The practic part of all unlawful love is ——

BER. Oh, 'tis abominable: but for the speculative — that we must all confess is entertaining. 610 The conversation of all the virtuous women in the town turns upon that and new clothes.

AMAN. Pray be so just then to me, to believe, 'tis with a world of innocency I would enquire whether you think those women we call women of 615 reputation do really 'scape all other men, as they do those shadows of 'em, the beaux.

BER. Oh no, Amanda; there are a sort of men make dreadful work amongst 'em: men that may be called the beaux' antipathy, for they agree 620 in nothing but walking upon two legs.

These have brains: the beau has none.

These are in love with their mistress: the beau with himself.

They take care of her reputation: he's in- 625 dustrious to destroy it.

They are decent: he's a fop.

They are sound: he's rotten.

They are men: he's an ass.

AMAN. If this be their character, I fancy 630 we had here e'en now a pattern of 'em both.

BER. His lordship and Mr. Worthy?

AMAN. The same.

BER. As for the lord, he's eminently so: and for the other, I can assure you there's not a man in 635

535] Q1 om. *AMAN.*   567] Q2P *them.*   586] P *river.*   587–588] Q1Q2P (*whose works ... have read*).
600] P *for I am.*   600] Q2P *I'm almost.*
622–629] Q1 prints each phrase, not each sentence, as a separate line.

town who has a better interest with the women that are worth having an interest with. But 'tis all private: he's like a back-stair minister at Court, who, whilst the reputed favorites are sauntering in the bed-chamber, is ruling the roast in the closet. 640

AMAN. He answers then the opinion I had ever of him. Heavens! what a difference there is between him and that vain, nauseous fop, Sir Novelty! (*Taking her hand.*) I must acquaint you with a secret, cousin. 'Tis not that fool alone 645 has talked to me of love: Worthy has been tampering too: 'tis true, he has done't in vain: not all his charms or art have power to shake me. My love, my duty, and my virtue are such faithful guards, I need not fear my heart should e'er betray me. 650 But what I wonder at is this: I find I did not start at his proposal, as when it came from one whom I contemned. I therefore mention his attempt, that I may learn from you whence it proceeds that vice, which cannot change its nature, should 655 so far change at least its shape as that the self-same crime, proposed from one, shall seem a monster gaping at your ruin, when from another it shall look so kind as though it were your friend, and never meant to harm you. Whence, 660 think you, can this difference proceed? For 'tis not love, heaven knows.

BER. Oh, no. I would not for the world believe it were. But possibly, should there a dreadful sentence pass upon you to undergo the rage of 665 both their passions, the pain you'd apprehend from one might seem so trivial to the other, the danger would not quite so much alarm you.

AMAN. Fy, fy, Berinthia! You would indeed alarm me, could you incline me to a thought 670 that all the merit of mankind combined could shake that tender love I bear my husband. No, he sits triumphant in my heart, and nothing can dethrone him.

BER. But should he abdicate again, do you 675 think you should preserve the vacant throne ten tedious winters more, in hopes of his return?

AMAN. Indeed I think I should. Though I confess, after those obligations he has to me, should he abandon me once more, my heart would 680 grow extremely urgent with me to root him thence, and cast him out forever.

BER. Were I that thing they call a slighted wife, somebody should run the risk of being that thing they call — a husband. 685

AMAN. Oh fy, Berinthia! No revenge should ever be taken against a husband: but to wrong his bed is a vengeance, which of all vengeance ——

BER. Is the sweetest — ha, ha, ha! Don't I talk madly? 690

AMAN. Madly indeed.

BER. Yet I'm very innocent.

AMAN. That I dare swear you are. I know how to make allowances for your humor: you were always very entertaining company; but I find since 695 marriage and widowhood have shown you the world a little, you are very much improved.

BER. (*aside*). Alackaday, there has gone more than that to improve me, if she knew all.

AMAN. For heaven's sake, Berinthia, tell me 700 what way I shall take to persuade you to come and live with me.

BER. Why, one way in the world there is —— and but one.

AMAN. Pray which is that? 705

BER. It is to assure me — I shall be very welcome.

AMAN. If that be all, you shall e'en lie here tonight.

BER. Tonight?

AMAN. Yes, tonight.

BER. Why, the people where I lodge will 710 think me mad.

AMAN. Let 'em think what they please.

BER. Say you so, Amanda? Why then they shall think what they please: for I'm a young widow, and I care not what anybody thinks. Ah, 715 Amanda, it's a delicious thing to be a young widow.

AMAN. You'll hardly make me think so.

BER. Phu, because you are in love with your husband: but that is not every woman's case.

AMAN. I hope 'twas yours, at least. 720

BER. Mine, say ye? Now have I a great mind to tell you a lie, but I should do it so awkwardly you'd find me out.

AMAN. Then e'en speak the truth.

BER. Shall I? —— Then after all, I did love 725 him, Amanda —— as a nun does penance.

AMAN. Why did not you refuse to marry him, then?

BER. Because my mother would have whipped me. 730

AMAN. How did you live together?

BER. Like man and wife — asunder;
He loved the country, I the town:
He hawks and hounds, I coaches and equipage: 735
He eating and drinking, I carding and playing:
He the sound of a horn, I the squeak of a fiddle.
We were dull company at table, worse abed.
Whenever we met, we gave one another the spleen.
And never agreed but once, which was about lying alone. 740

AMAN. But tell me one thing truly and sincerely.

BER. What's that?

AMAN. Notwithstanding all these jars, did not his death at last —— extremely trouble you? 745

BER. Oh, yes: not that my present pangs were so very violent, but the after-pains were intoler-

---

647] P *done it.*   653] Q2P *this attempt.*   666] Q2P *you apprehend.*   721] P *I have.*

able. I was forced to wear a beastly wídow's band [1] a twelve-month for't.

AMAN. Women, I find, have different incli-   750
nations.

BER. Women, I find, keep different company. When your husband ran away from you, if you had fallen into some of my acquaintance, 'twould have saved you many a tear. But you go   755
and live with a grandmother, a bishop, and an old nurse, which was enough to make any woman break her heart for her husband. Pray, Amanda, if ever you are a widow again, keep yourself so, as I do.

AMAN. Why, do you then resolve you'll   760
never marry?

BER. Oh, no; I resolve I will.

AMAN. How so?

BER. That I never may.

AMAN. You banter me.   765

BER. Indeed I don't. But I consider I'm a woman, and form my resolutions accordingly.

AMAN. Well, my opinion is, form what resolution you will, matrimony will be the end on't.

BER. Faith it won't.   770

AMAN. How do you know?

BER. I'm sure on't.

AMAN. Why, do you think 'tis impossible for you to fall in love?

BER. No.   775

AMAN. Nay, but to grow so passionately fond, that nothing but the man you love can give you rest?

BER. Well, what then?

AMAN. Why, then you'll marry him.   780

BER. How do you know that?

AMAN. Why, what can you do else?

BER. Nothing — but sit and cry.

AMAN. Psha!

BER. Ah, poor Amanda, you have led a   785
country life: but if you'll consult the widows of this town, they'll tell you you should never take a lease of a house you can hire for a quarter's warning.

Exeunt.

ACT III

[SCENE I]

[LORD FOPPINGTON's *lodgings.*]

Enter LORD FOPPINGTON *and Servant.*

L. FOP. Hey, fellow, let the coach come to the door.

SERV. Will your lordship venture so soon to expose yourself to the weather?

L. FOP. Sir, I will venture as soon as I can to   5
expose myself to the ladies: though give me my

[1] Lace head-band.

cloak, however, for in that side-box, what between the air that comes in at the door on one side, and the intolerable warmth of the masks [2] on t'other, a man gets so many heats and colds, 'twould destroy   10
the canstitution of a harse.

SERV. (*putting on his cloak*). I wish your lordship would please to keep house a little longer; I'm afraid your honor does not well consider your wound.

L. FOP. My wound? — I would not be in   15
eclipse another day, though I had as many wounds in my guts as I have had in my heart.

Enter YOUNG FASHION.

Y. FAS. Brother, your servant: how do you find yourself today?

L. FOP. So well, that I have ardered my   20
coach to the door: so there's no great danger of death this baut, Tam.

Y. FAS. I'm very glad of it.

L. FOP. (*aside*). That I believe's a lie. —— Prithee, Tam, tell me one thing: did nat your   25
heart cut a caper up to your mauth, when you heard I was run through the bady?

Y. FAS. Why do you think it should?

L. FOP. Because I remember mine did so, when I heard my father was shat through the head.   30

Y. FAS. It then did very ill.

L. FOP. Prithee, why so?

Y. FAS. Because he used you very well.

L. FOP. Well? —— naw strike me dumb, he starved me. He has let me want a thousand   35
women for want of a thousand paund.

Y. FAS. Then he hindered you from making a great many ill bargains, for I think no woman is worth money, that will take money.

L. FOP. If I were a younger brother, I should   40
think so too.

Y. FAS. Why, is it possible you can value a woman that's to be bought?

L. FOP. Prithee, why not as well as a pad-nag? [3]

Y. FAS. Because a woman has a heart to dis-   45
pose of; a horse has none.

L. FOP. Look you, Tam, of all things that belang to a woman, I have an aversion to her heart; far when once a woman has given you her heart —— you can never get rid of the rest of her bady.   50

Y. FAS. This is strange doctrine. But pray, in your amours how is it with your own heart?

L. FOP. Why, my heart in my amours —— is like my heart aut of my amours: *à la glace.* [4] My bady, Tam, is a watch, and my heart is the pendulum   55
to it; whilst the finger runs raund to every hour in the circle, that still beats the same time.

[2] Masked women.   [3] An easy-going saddle horse.
[4] Like ice.

Y. FAS. Then you are seldom much in love?

L. FOP. Never, stap my vitals.

Y. FAS. Why then did you make all this 60 bustle about Amanda?

L. FOP. Because she was a woman of an insolent virtue, and I thought myself [piqued] in honor to debauch her.

Y. FAS. Very well. (*Aside.*) Here's a rare 65 fellow for you, to have the spending of five thousand pounds a year. But now for my business with him. (*To* LORD FOPPINGTON.) Brother, though I know to talk to you of business (especially of money) is a theme not quite so entertaining to you as that 70 of the ladies, my necessities are such, I hope you'll have patience to hear me.

L. FOP. The greatness of your necessities, Tam, is the worst argument in the world far your being patiently heard. I do believe you are going to 75 make me a very good speech, but, strike me dumb, it has the worst beginning of any speech I have heard this twelvemonth.

Y. FAS. I'm very sorry you think so.

L. FOP. I do believe thau art. But come, 80 let's know thy affair quickly; far 'tis a new play, and I shall be so rumpled and squeezed with pressing through the crawd to get to my servant, the women will think I have lain all night in my clothes.

Y. FAS. Why then (that I may not be the 85 author of so great a misfortune) my case in a word is this: the necessary expenses of my travels have so much exceeded the wretched income of my annuity that I have been forced to mortgage it for five hundred pounds, which is spent; so that unless you 90 are so kind to assist me in redeeming it, I know no remedy but to go take a purse.

L. FOP. Why, faith, Tam —— to give you my sense of the thing, I do think taking a purse the best remedy in the world; for if you succeed, you are 95 relieved that way; if you are taken —— you are relieved t'other.

Y. FAS. I'm glad to see you are in so pleasant a humor; I hope I shall find the effects on't.

L. FOP. Why, do you then really think it a 100 reasonable thing I should give you five hundred paunds?

Y. FAS. I do not ask it as a due, brother; I am willing to receive it as a favor.

L. FOP. Thau art willing to receive it any 105 haw, strike me speechless. But these are damned times to give money in: taxes are so great, repairs so exorbitant, tenants such rogues, and periwigs so dear, that the devil take me, I am reduced to that extremity in my cash, I have been forced to 110 retrench in that one article of sweet pawder, till I have braught it dawn to five guineas a manth.

Naw Judge, Tam, whether I can spare you five hundred paunds?

Y. FAS. If you can't, I must starve, that's all. 115 (*Aside.*) Damn him!

L. FOP. All I can say is, you should have been a better husband.[1]

Y. FAS. 'Oons, if you can't live upon five thousand a year, how do you think I should do't 120 upon two hundred?

L. FOP. Don't be in a passion, Tam, far passion is the most unbecoming thing in the world —— to the face. Look you, I don't love to say anything to you to make you melancholy; but upon this 125 occasion I must take leave to put you in mind that a running horse does require more attendance than a coach-horse. Nature has made some difference 'twixt you and I.

Y. FAS. Yes, she has made you older. 130 (*Aside.*) Pox take her!

L. FOP. That is nat all, Tam.

Y. FAS. Why, what is there else?

L. FOP. (*looking first upon himself, then upon his brother*). Ask the ladies. 135

Y. FAS. Why, thou essence bottle, thou muskcat, dost thou then think thou hast any advantage over me but what fortune has given thee?

L. FOP. I do —— stap my vitals.

Y. FAS. Now, by all that's great and power- 140 ful, thou art the prince of coxcombs.

L. FOP. Sir —— I am praud of being at the head of so prevailing a party.

Y. FAS. Will nothing then provoke thee? —— Draw, coward! 145

L. FOP. Look you, Tam, you know I have always taken you for a mighty dull fellow, and here is one of the foolishest plats broke out that I have seen a long time. Your paverty makes your life so burthensome to you, you would provoke me to a quarrel, in 150 hopes either to slip through my lungs into my estate, or to get yourself run through the guts, to put an end to your pain. But I will disappoint you in both your designs; far with the temper of a philasapher, and the discretion of a statesman —— I will go 155 to the play with my sword in my scabbard.

Exit LORD FOPPINGTON.

Y. FAS. So! Farewell, snuff-box. And now, conscience, I defy thee. Lory!

Enter LORY.

LO. Sir.

Y. FAS. Here's rare news, Lory; his lordship 160 has given me a pill has purged off all my scruples.

LO. Then my heart's at ease again: for I have been in a lamentable fright, sir, ever since your con-

[1] Manager.

63] Q1 *pickt*; Q2 *prickt*; P *piqued*.   80] P *thou*.   81] P *for*.

92] P om. *go*.   110] P *farced*.   149] P *burdensome*.

science had the impudence to intrude into your
company.   165

Y. FAS. Be at peace, it will come there no more:
my brother has given it a wring by the nose, and
I have kicked it down stairs. So run away to the
inn; get the horses ready quickly, and bring 'em to
old Coupler's, without a moment's delay.   170

LO. Then, sir, you are going straight about the
fortune?

Y. FAS. I am: away! fly, Lory!

LO. The happiest day I ever saw. I'm upon the
wing already.   *Exeunt several ways.*   175

SCENE [II]

A garden [adjoining LOVELESS's *lodgings].*

Enter LOVELESS *and Servant.*

LOV. Is my wife within?

SERV. No, sir, she has been gone out this half hour.

LOV. 'Tis well; leave me.

(*Solus.*) Sure, fate has yet some business to be done,
Before Amanda's heart and mine must rest;   5
Else why, amongst those legions of her sex,
Which throng the world,
Should she pick out for her companion
The only one on earth
Whom nature has endowed for her undoing?   10
'Undoing' was't I said? —— Who shall undo her?
Is not her empire fixed? Am I not hers?
Did she not rescue me, a grov'ling slave?
When, chained and bound by that black tyrant,
    Vice,
I labored in his vilest drudgery,   15
Did she not ransom me, and set me free?
Nay, more: when by my follies sunk
To a poor tattered, despicable beggar,
Did she not lift me up to envied fortune?
Give me herself, and all that she possessed? —   20
Without a thought of more return,
Than what a poor repenting heart might make her.
Han't she done this? And if she has,
Am I not strongly bound to love her for it?
To love her! — Why, do I not love her then?   25
By earth and heaven, I do!
Nay, I have demonstration that I do:
For I would sacrifice my life to serve her.
Yet hold: —— if laying down my life
Be demonstration of my love,   30
What is't I feel in favor of Berinthia?
For should she be in danger, methinks, I could
    incline
To risk it for her service too; and yet I do not love
    her.

How then subsists my proof? — Oh, I have found it
    out.
What I would do for one is demonstration of my
    love;   35
And if I'd do as much for t'other,
[It] there is demonstration of my friendship.
    Ay —̣
It must be so. I find I'm very much her friend.
Yet let me ask myself one puzzling question more:
Whence springs this mighty friendship all at
    once?   40
For our acquaintance is of later date.
Now friendship's said to be a plant of tedious
    growth,
Its root composed of tender fibres,
Nice in their taste, cautious in spreading,
Checked with the least corruption in the soil;   45
Long ere it take, and longer still ere it appear to do
    so.
Whilst mine is in a moment shot so high,
And fixed so fast, it seems beyond the power
Of storms to shake it. I doubt it thrives too fast.
                                           (*Musing.*)

Enter BERINTHIA.

Ha! she here! Nay, then,   50
Take heed, my heart, for there are dangers towards.

BER. What makes you look so thoughtful, sir?
I hope you are not ill.

LOV. I was debating, madam, whether I was so or
not; and that was it which made me look so   55
thoughtful.

BER. Is it then so hard a matter to decide? I
thought all people had been acquainted with their
own bodies, though few people know their own
minds.   60

LOV. What if the distemper, I suspect, be in the
mind?

BER. Why, then I'll undertake to prescribe you a
cure.

LOV. Alas, you undertake you know not   65
what.

BER. So far at least then allow me to be a physician.

LOV. Nay, I'll allow you so yet farther: for I have
reason to believe, should I put myself into your   70
hands, you would increase my distemper.

BER. Perhaps I might have reasons from the
college [1] not to be too quick in your cure; but 'tis
possible I might find ways to give you often ease, sir.

LOV. Were I but sure of that, I'd quickly   75
lay my case before you.

[1] Professional (medical) reasons. The college Berinthia alludes to is the College (i.e. society) of Physicians.

169] P *them.*   13] P *groveling slave.*   15] P *drudgery?*   34] Q1Q2P print as two lines.
36–38] Q1Q2P print as prose.   37] Q1Q2 *if there;* P *it there.*   41] P *of a later.*
42–51] Q1Q2P print as prose.

BER. [Whether] you are sure of it or no, what risk do you run in trying?

LOV. Oh, a very great one.

BER. How?   80

LOV. You might betray my distemper to my wife.

BER. And so lose all my practice.

LOV. Will you then keep my secret?

BER. I will, if it don't burst me.

LOV. Swear.   85

BER. I do.

LOV. By what?

BER. By woman.

LOV. That's swearing by my deity. Do it by your own, or I shan't believe you.   90

BER. By man, then.

LOV. I'm satisfied. Now hear my symptoms, And give me your advice. The first were these: When 'twas my chance to see you at the play, A random glance you threw, at first alarmed me; 95
I could not turn my eyes from whence the danger came:
I gazed upon you, till you shot again,
And then my fears came on me.
My heart began to pant, my limbs to tremble,
My blood grew thin, my pulse beat quick,   100
My eyes grew hot and dim, and all the frame
Of nature shook with apprehension.
'Tis true, some small recruits of resolution
My manhood brought to my assistance,
And by their help I made a stand a while,   105
But found at last your arrows flew so thick,
They could not fail to pierce me; so left the field,
And fled for shelter to Amanda's arms.
What think you of these symptoms, pray?

BER. Feverish, every one of 'em.   110
But what relief, pray, did your wife afford you?

LOV. Why, instantly she let me blood,
Which for the present much assuaged my flame.
But when I saw you, out it burst again,
And raged with greater fury than before.   115
Nay, since you now appear, 'tis so encreased
That in a moment, if you do not help me,
I shall, whilst you look on, consume to ashes.

(Taking hold of her hand.)

BER. (breaking from him). O Lard, let me go: 'tis the plague, and we shall all be infected.   120

LOV. (catching her in his arms, and kissing her). Then we'll die together, my charming angel.

BER. O Ged — the devil's in you.
Lord, let me go, here's somebody coming.

Enter Servant.

SERV. Sir, my lady's come home, and desires   125
to speak with you: she's in her chamber.

LOV. Tell her I'm coming.   Exit Servant.
(To BERINTHIA.) But before I go, one glass of nectar more to drink her health.

BER. Stand off, or I shall hate you, by heav-   130
ens.

LOV. (kissing her). In matters of love, a woman's oath is no more to be minded than a man's.

BER. Um ——

Enter WORTHY.

WOR. Ha! What's here? my old mistress,   135
and so close, i'faith? I would not spoil her sport for the universe.   He retires.

BER. O Ged —— Now do I pray to heaven, (exit LOVELESS running) with all my heart and soul, that the devil in hell may take me, if ever ——   140
I was better pleased in my life —— this man has bewitched me, that's certain. (Sighing.) Well, I am condemned, but, thanks to heaven, I feel myself each moment more and more prepared for my exe-cution — nay, to that degree, I don't perceive   145
I have the least fear of dying. No, I find, let the —— executioner be but a man, and there's nothing will suffer with more resolution than a woman. Well, I never had but one intrigue yet: but I confess I long to have another. Pray heaven it end as   150
the first did, though, that we may both grow weary at a time; for 'tis a melancholy thing for lovers to outlive one another.

Enter WORTHY.

WOR. (aside). This discovery's a lucky one; I hope to make a happy use on't. That gentlewoman   155
there is no fool, so I shall be able to make her under-stand her interest. (To BERINTHIA.) Your servant, madam; I need not ask you how you do, you have got so good a color.

BER. No better than I used to have, I sup-   160
pose?

WOR. A little more blood in your cheeks.

BER. The weather's hot.

WOR. If it were not, a woman may have a color.

BER. What do you mean by that?   165

WOR. Nothing.

BER. Why do you smile then?

WOR. Because the weather's hot.

BER. You'll never leave roguing, I see that.

WOR. (putting his finger to his nose). You'll   170
never leave —— I see that.

BER. Well, I can't imagine what you drive at. Pray tell me what you mean?

WOR. Do you tell me; it's the same thing.

BER. I can't.   175

WOR. Guess!

BER. I shall guess wrong.

77] Q1Q2 *Whither*; P *Whether*.   92, 93] Q1Q2P print as prose.   107] Q1Q2P print as two lines.
112-118] Q1Q2P print as prose.   138-153] Q1Q2 print as verse, the lines ending with *heaven, devil, pleased in, certain, feel, for my, have, let the, will, woman, yet, another, though, time, another.*
160-161] Q2P *suppose*.   174] Q1Q2 *Do you tell me it's the same thing?*; P *Do you tell me, it's the same thing*.

Wor. Indeed you won't.

Ber. Psha! either tell, or let it alone.

Wor. Nay, rather than let it alone, I will 180 tell. But first I must put you in mind that, after what has past 'twixt you and I, very few things ought to be secrets between us.

Ber. Why, what secrets do we hide? I know of none. 185

Wor. Yes, there are two; one I have hid from you, and t'other you would hide from me. You are fond of Loveless, which I have discovered; and I am fond of his wife ——

Ber. Which I have discovered. 190

Wor. Very well, now I confess your discovery to be true: what do you say to mine?

Ber. Why, I confess —— I would swear 'twere false, if I thought you were fool enough to believe me. 195

Wor. Now am I almost in love with you again. Nay, I don't know but I might be quite so, had I made one short campaign with Amanda. Therefore, if you find 'twould tickle your vanity to bring me down once more to your lure, e'en help me 200 quickly to dispatch her business, that I may have nothing else to do but to apply myself to yours.

Ber. Do you then think, sir, I am old enough to be a bawd?

Wor. No, but I think you are wise enough 205 to ——

Ber. To do what?

Wor. To hoodwink Amanda with a gallant, that she mayn't see who is her husband's mistress.

Ber. (aside). He has reason: the hint's a 210 good one.

Wor. Well, madam, what think you on't?

Ber. I think you are so much a deeper politician in these affairs than I am, that I ought to have a very great regard to your advice. 215

Wor. Then give me leave to put you in mind that the most easy, safe, and pleasant situation for your own amour is the house in which you now are, provided you keep Amanda from any sort of suspicion: that the way to do that, is to engage her in an 220 intrigue of her own, making yourself her confident: and the way to bring her to intrigue, is to make her jealous of her husband in a wrong place; which the more you foment, the less you'll be suspected. This is my scheme, in short; which if you follow as 225 you should do (my dear Berinthia) we may all four pass the winter very pleasantly.

Ber. Well, I could be glad to have nobody's sins to answer for but my own. But where there is a necessity —— 230

Wor. Right [1] as you say; where there is a neces-
[1] Exactly.

sity, a Christian is bound to help his neighbor. So, good Berinthia, lose no time, but let us begin the dance as fast as we can.

Ber. Not till the fiddles are in tune, pray, 235 sir. Your lady's strings will be very apt to fly, I can tell you that, if they are wound up too hastily. But if you'll have patience to screw 'em to their pitch by degrees, I don't doubt but she may endure to be played upon. 240

Wor. Ay, and will make admirable music, too, or I'm mistaken. But have you had no private closet discourse with her yet about males and females, and so forth, which may give you hopes in her constitution; for I know her morals are the 245 devil against us.

Ber. I have had so much discourse with her, that I believe were she once cured of her fondness to her husband, the fortress of her virtue would not be so impregnable as she fancies. 250

Wor. What? she runs, I'll warrant you, into that common mistake of fond wives, who conclude themselves virtuous because they can refuse a man they don't like when they have got one they do.

Ber. True, and therefore I think 'tis a pre- 255 sumptuous thing in a woman to assume the name of virtuous till she has heartily hated her husband and been soundly in love with somebody else —— whom if she has withstood — then — much good may it do her! 260

Wor. Well, so much for her virtue. Now, one word of her inclinations, and every one to their post. What opinion do you find she has of me?

Ber. What you could wish; she thinks you handsome and discreet. 265

Wor. Good! that's thinking half seas over. One tide more brings us into port.

Ber. Perhaps it may, though still remember, there's a difficult bar to pass.

Wor. I know there is, but I don't question 270 I shall get well over it, by the help of such a pilot.

Ber. You may depend upon your pilot, she'll do the best she can; so weigh anchor, and be gone as soon as you please.

Wor. I'm under sail already. Adieu. 275
                                   Exit Worthy.

Ber. *Bon voyage.* (*Sola.*) So, here's fine work. What a business have I undertaken! I'm a very pretty gentlewoman, truly; but there was no avoiding it: he'd have ruined me if I had refused him. Besides, faith, I begin to fancy there may be as 280 much pleasure in carrying on another body's intrigue as one's own. This at least is certain, it exercises almost all the entertaining faculties of a woman: for there's employment for hypocrisy, invention, deceit, flattery, mischief, and lying. 285

Enter AMANDA, *her Woman following her.*

WOM. If you please, madam, only to say, [whether] you'll have me buy 'em or not.

AMAN. Yes, no, go fiddle! I care not what you do. Prithee leave me.

WOM. I have done.   *Exit Woman.* 290

BER. What in the name of Jove's the matter with you?

AMAN. The matter, Berinthia! I'm almost mad, I'm plagued to death.

BER. Who is it that plagues you?   295

AMAN. Who do you think should plague a wife, but her husband?

BER. O ho, is it come to that? We shall have you wish yourself a widow by and by.

AMAN. Would I were anything but what I 300 am! A base ungrateful man, after what I have done for him, to use me thus!

BER. What! he has been ogling now, I'll warrant you?

AMAN. Yes, he has been ogling.   305

BER. And so you are jealous? Is that all?

AMAN. That all! Is jealousy then nothing?

BER. It should be nothing, if I were in your case.

AMAN. Why, what would you do?

BER. I'd cure myself.   310

AMAN. How?

BER. Let blood in the fond vein: care as little for my husband as he did for me.

AMAN. That would not stop his course.

BER. Nor nothing else, when the wind's in 315 the warm corner. Look you, Amanda, you may build castles in the air, and fume, and fret, and grow thin and lean and pale and ugly, if you please. But I tell you, no man worth having is true to his wife, or can be true to his wife, or ever was, or ever will 320 be so.

AMAN. Do you then really think he's false to me? for I did but suspect him.

BER. Think so? I know he's so.

AMAN. Is it possible? Pray tell me what 325 you know.

BER. Don't press me then to name names, for that I have sworn I won't do.

AMAN. Well, I won't; but let me know all you can without perjury.   330

BER. I'll let you know enough to prevent any wise woman's dying of the pip; and I hope you'll pluck up your spirits, and show, upon occasion, you can be as good a wife as the best of 'em.

AMAN. Well, what a woman can do I'll en- 335 deavor.

BER. Oh, a woman can do a great deal, if once she sets her mind to it. Therefore pray don't stand trifling any longer, and teasing yourself with this

and that, and your love and your virtue, and 340 I know not what. But resolve to hold up your head, get a tiptoe, and look over 'em all; for to my certain knowledge your husband is a-pickering [1] elsewhere.

AMAN. You are sure on't?

BER. Positively; he fell in love at the play. 345

AMAN. Right, the very same; do you know the ugly thing?

BER. Yes, I know her well enough; but she's no such an ugly thing, neither.

AMAN. Is she very handsome?   350

BER. Truly, I think so.

AMAN. Hey ho!

BER. What do you sigh for now?

AMAN. Oh, my heart!

BER. (*aside*). Only the pangs of nature! she's 355 in labor of her love; heaven send her a quick delivery; I'm sure she has a good midwife.

AMAN. I'm very ill, I must go to my chamber. Dear Berinthia, don't leave me a moment.

BER. No, don't fear. (*Aside.*) I'll see you 360 safe brought to bed, I'll warrant you.

Exeunt, AMANDA *leaning upon* BERINTHIA.

SCENE [III]

[The gate of] a country house.

Enter YOUNG FASHION *and* LORY.

Y. FAS. So, here's our inheritance, Lory, if we can but get into possession. But methinks the seat of our family looks like Noah's ark, as if the chief part on't were designed for the fowls of the air and the beasts of the field.   5

LO. Pray, sir, don't let your head run upon the orders of building here; get but the heiress, let the devil take the house.

Y. FAS. Get but the house, let the devil take the heiress, I say; at least if she be as old Coupler 10 describes her. But come, we have no time to squander. Knock at the door. (LORY *knocks two or three times.*) What the devil, have they got no ears in this house? Knock harder.

LO. I'gad, sir, this will prove some enchanted 15 castle; we shall have the giant come out by and by with his club, and beat our brains out.

(*Knocks again.*)

Y. FAS. Hush! they come.

[SERV.] (*from within*). Who is there?

LO. Open the door and see: is that your 20 country breeding?

[SERV.] (*within*). Ay, but two words to a bargain: Tummas, is the blunderbuss primed?

Y. FAS. Oons, give 'em good words, Lory; we shall be shot here a fortune-catching.   25

[1] Skirmishing (amorously).

Lo. I'gad, sir, I think y'are in the right on't. —— Ho, Mr. What d'ye-call-um.

(*Servant appears at the window with a blunder-buss.*)

SERV. Weall naw what's yare business?

Y. FAS. Nothing, sir, but to wait upon Sir Tunbelly, with your leave.   30

SERV. To weat upon Sir Tunbelly? Why, you'll find that's just as Sir Tunbelly pleases.

Y. FAS. But will you do me the favor, sir, to know whether Sir Tunbelly pleases or not?

SERV. Why, look you, do you see, with good 35 words much may be done. —— Ralph, go thy weas, and ask Sir Tunbelly if he pleases to be waited upon. And, dost hear? call to nurse, that she may lock up Miss Hoyden before the geats open.

Y. FAS. D'ye hear that, Lory?   40

Lo. Ay, sir, I'm afraid we shall find a difficult job on't. Pray heaven that old rogue Coupler han't sent us to fetch milk out of the gunroom!

Y. FAS. I'll warrant thee all will go well: see, the door opens.   45

Enter SIR TUNBELLY, *with his Servants armed with guns, clubs, pitchforks, scythes, etc.*

Lo. (*running behind his master*). O Lord, O Lord, O Lord, we are both dead men!

Y. FAS. Take heed, fool; thy fear will ruin us.

Lo. My fear, sir — 'sdeath, sir, I fear nothing. (*Aside.*) Would I were well up to the chin in 50 a horsepond!

SIR TUN. Who is it here has any business with me?

Y. FAS. Sir, 'tis I, if your name be Sir Tunbelly Clumsey.

SIR TUN. Sir, my name is Sir Tunbelly 55 Clumsey, [whether] you have any business with me or not. So you see I am not ashamed of my name — nor my face, neither.

Y. FAS. Sir, you have no cause, that I know of.

SIR TUN. Sir, if you have no cause neither, 60 I desire to know who you are; for till I know your name, I shall not ask you to come into my house; and when I know your name — 'tis six to four I don't ask you neither.

Y. FAS. (*giving him a letter*). Sir, I hope you'll 65 find this letter an authentic passport.

SIR TUN. Cod's my life, I ask your lordship's pardon ten thousand times. (*To his Servants.*) Here, run in a-doors quickly: get a Scotch coal fire in the great parlor; set all the Turkey-work chairs 70 in their places; get the great brass candlesticks out, and be sure stick the sockets full of laurel; run! (*Turning to* YOUNG FASHION.) My lord, I ask your lordship's pardon. (*To other Servants.*) And do you hear, run away to nurse, bid her let Miss 75

Hoyden loose again, and if it was not shifting-day,[1] let her put on a clean tucker — quick! (*Exeunt Servants confusedly.*) (*To* YOUNG FASHION.) I hope your honor will excuse the disorder of my family; we are not used to receive men of your 80 lordship's great quality every day; pray, where are your coaches and servants, my lord?

Y. FAS. Sir, that I might give you and your fair daughter a proof how impatient I am to be nearer akin to you, I left my equipage to follow me, and 85 came away post with only one servant.

SIR TUN. Your lordship does me too much honor; it was exposing your person to too much fatigue and danger, I protest it was; but my daughter shall endeavor to make you what amends she can; and 90 though I say it, that should not say it — Hoyden has charms.

Y. FAS. Sir, I am not a stranger to them, though I am to her; common fame has done her justice.

SIR TUN. My lord, I am common fame's very 95 grateful humble servant. My lord — my girl's young: Hoyden is young, my lord; but this I must say for her, what she wants in art, she has by nature; what she wants in experience, she has in breeding; and what's wanting in her age is made good in 100 her constitution. So pray, my lord, walk in; pray, my lord, walk in.

Y. FAS. Sir, I wait upon you.   *Exeunt.*

[SCENE IV]

[MISS HOYDEN'S *chamber within the house.*]

MISS HOYDEN, *sola.*

Sure, never nobody was used as I am. I know well enough what other girls do, for all they think to make a fool of me: it's well I have a husband a coming, or i'cod, I'd marry the baker, I would so. Nobody can knock at the gate, but presently I 5 must be locked up; and here's the young greyhound bitch can run loose about the house all day long, she can; 'tis very well.

NURSE (*without, opening the door*). Miss Hoyden! Miss, Miss, Miss; Miss Hoyden!   10

Enter Nurse.

MISS. Well, what do you make such a noise for, ha? What do you din a body's ears for? Can't one be at quiet for you!

NURSE. What do I din your ears for? Here's one come will din your ears for you.   15

MISS. What care I who's come? I care not a fig who comes, nor who goes, as long as I must be locked up like the ale-cellar.

_____
[1] The day for changing one's clothes.

NURSE. That, miss, is for fear you should be drank before you are ripe. 20

MISS. Oh, don't you trouble your head about that: I'm as ripe as you, though not so mellow.

NURSE. Very well; now have I a good mind to lock you up again, and not let you see my lord to-night. 25

MISS. My lord? Why, is my husband come?

NURSE. Yes, marry is he, and a goodly person too.

MISS (hugging Nurse). O my dear nurse, forgive me this once, and I'll never misuse you again; 30 no, if I do, you shall give me three thumps on the back, and a great pinch by the cheek.

NURSE. Ah, the poor thing, see how it melts; it's as full of good-nature as an egg's full of meat.

MISS. But, my dear nurse, don't lie now; is 35 he come, by your troth?

NURSE. Yes, by my truly, is he.

MISS. O Lord! I'll go put on my laced smock, though I'm whipped till the blood run down my heels for't. *Exit running.* 40

NURSE. Eh —— the Lord succor thee, how thou art delighted! *Exit after her.*

[SCENE V]

[Another room in the house.]

Enter SIR TUNBELLY *and* YOUNG FASHION. *A Servant with wine.*

SIR TUN. My lord, I am proud of the honor to see your lordship within my doors, and I humbly crave leave to bid you welcome in a cup of sack wine.

Y. FAS. Sir, to your daughter's health. 5
(*Drinks.*)

SIR TUN. Ah, poor girl, she'll be scared out of her wits on her wedding night; for, honestly speaking, she does not know a man from a woman, but by his beard, and his britches.

Y. FAS. Sir, I don't doubt but she has a 10 virtuous education, which, with the rest of her merit, makes me long to see her mine. I wish you would dispense with the canonical hour, and let it be this very night.

SIR TUN. Oh, not so soon, neither; that's 15 shooting my girl before you bid her stand. No, give her fair warning: we'll sign and seal to-night if you please, and this day seven-night — let the jade look to her quarters.

Y. FAS. This day sennight? —— Why, what! 20 do you take me for a ghost, sir? 'Slife, sir, I'm made of flesh and blood, and bones and sinews, and can no more live a week without your daughter — (*aside*) than I can live a month with her.

SIR TUN. Oh, I'll warrant you, my hero; 25 young men are hot, I know, but they don't boil over at that rate, neither; besides, my wench's wedding gown is not come home yet.

Y. FAS. Oh, no matter, sir; I'll take her in her shift. (*Aside.*) A pox of this old fellow; he'll 30 delay the business till my damned star finds me out, and discovers me. (*To Sir* TUNBELLY.) Pray, sir, let it be done without ceremony; 'twill save money.

SIR TUN. Money? —— save money when Hoyden's to be married? Udswoons, I'll give my 35 wench a wedding dinner, though I go to grass with the King of Assyria [1] for't; and such a dinner it shall be, as is not to be cooked in the poaching of an egg. Therefore, my noble lord, have a little patience; we'll go and look over our deeds and settlements im- 40 mediately; and as for your bride, though you may be sharp set before she's quite ready, I'll engage for my girl, she stays your stomach at last. *Exeunt.*

ACT IV

[SCENE I]

[A room in SIR TUNBELLY'S *house.]*

Enter MISS HOYDEN *and Nurse.*

NURSE. Well, miss, how do you like your husband that is to be?

MISS. O Lord, nurse, I'm so overjoyed, I can scarce contain myself.

NURSE. Oh, but you must have a care of being 5 too fond, for men nowadays hate a woman that loves 'em.

MISS. Love him? Why, do you think I love him, nurse? I'cod, I would not care if he were hanged, so I were but once married to him. No —— that 10 which pleases me, is to think what work I'll make when I get to London; for when I am a wife and a lady both, nurse, i'cod, I'll flaunt it with the best of 'em.

NURSE. Look, look, if his honor be not coming 15 again to you; now if I were sure you would behave yourself handsomely, and not disgrace me that have brought you up, I'd leave you alone together.

MISS. That's my best nurse: do as you would be done by; trust us together this once, and if I 20 don't show my breeding from the head to the foot of me, may I be twice married, and die a maid!

NURSE. Well, this once I'll venture you; but if you disparage me ——

MISS. Never fear; I'll show him my parts, I'll 25 warrant him. *Exit Nurse.*
(*Sola.*) These old women are so wise when they get

[1] Nebuchadnezzar, King of Babylon, who 'did eat grass as oxen.' Daniel, iv. 33.

a poor girl in their clutches, but ere it be long I shall know what's what, as well as the best of 'em.

Enter YOUNG FASHION.

Y. FAS. Your servant, madam: I'm glad to 30
find you alone, for I have something of importance to speak to you about.

MISS. Sir, —— my lord, I meant —— you may speak to me about what you please; I shall give you a civil answer.   35

Y. FAS. You give me so obliging a one, it encourages me to tell you in few words what I think both for your interest and mine. Your father, I suppose you know, has resolved to make me happy in being your husband, and I hope I may depend 40 upon your consent to perform what he desires.

MISS. Sir, I never disobey my father in any thing but eating of green gooseberries.

Y. FAS. So good a daughter must needs make an admirable wife; I am therefore impatient till you 45 are mine, and hope you will so far consider the violence of my love that you won't have the cruelty to defer my happiness so long as your father designs it.

MISS. Pray, my lord, how long is that?

Y. FAS. Madam, a thousand year — a whole 50 week.

MISS. A week! — why, I shall be an old woman by that time.

Y. FAS. And I an old man, which you'll find a greater misfortune than t'other.   55

MISS. Why, I thought 'twas to be tomorrow morning, as soon as I was up; I'm sure nurse told me so.

Y. FAS. And it shall be tomorrow morning still, if you'll consent.   60

MISS. If I'll consent? Why, I thought I was to obey you as my husband.

Y. FAS. That's when we are married; till then I am to obey you.

MISS. Why then, if we are to take it by turns, 65 it's the same thing: I'll obey you now, and when we are married, you shall obey me.

Y. FAS. With all my heart; but I doubt we must get nurse on our side, or we shall hardly prevail with the chaplain.   70

MISS. No more we shan't, indeed, for he loves her better than he loves his pulpit, and would always be a-preaching to her, by his good will.

Y. FAS. Why then, my dear little bedfellow, if you'll call her hither, we'll try to persuade her 75 presently.

MISS. O Lord, I can tell you a way how to persuade her to any thing.

Y. FAS. How's that?

MISS. Why, tell her she's a wholesome, comely 80 woman — and give her half a crown.

Y. FAS. Nay, if that will do, she shall have half a score of 'em.

MISS. O Gemini! for half that she'd marry you herself: I'll run and call her. *Exit* MISS HOYDEN. 85

Y. FAS. (*solus*). So, matters go swimmingly; this is a rare girl, i'faith; I shall have a fine time on't with her at London. I'm much mistaken if she don't prove a March hare all the year round. What a scamp'ring chase will she make on't, when she finds the 90 whole kennel of beaux at her tail! hey to the park and the play, and the church, and the devil; she'll show 'em sport, I'll warrant 'em. But no matter: she brings an estate will afford me a separate maintenance.   95

Enter MISS HOYDEN *and Nurse.*

Y. FAS. How do you do, good Mistress Nurse; I desired your young lady would give me leave to see you, that I might thank you for your extraordinary care and conduct in her education; pray accept of this small acknowledgement for it at present, 100 and depend upon my farther kindness when I shall be that happy thing, her husband.

NURSE (*aside*). Gold, by makings![1] —— Your honor's goodness is too great: alas! all I can boast of is, I gave her pure good milk, and so your honor 105 would have said, an you had seen how the poor thing sucked it —— Eh, God's blessing on the sweet face on't! how it used to hang at this poor tett, and suck and squeeze, and kick and sprawl it would, till the belly on't was so full it would drop off like a 110 leech.

MISS (*to Nurse, taking her angrily aside*). Pray one word with you; —— prithee, nurse, don't stand ripping up old stories, to make one ashamed before one's love: do you think such a fine proper 115 gentleman as he cares for a fiddlecome[2] tale of a draggle-tailed girl? if you have a mind to make him have a good opinion of a woman, don't tell him what one did then: tell him what one can do now. (*To* YOUNG FASHION.) I hope your honor will ex- 120 cuse my mismanners to whisper before you; it was only to give some orders about the family.

Y. FAS. Oh, everything, madam, is to give way to business; besides, good housewif'ry is a very commendable quality in a young lady.   125

MISS. Pray, sir, are the young ladies good housewives at London town? do they darn their own linen?

Y. FAS. Oh, no; they study how to spend money, not to save it.

[1] A meaningless interjection.
[2] Silly, nonsensical.

MISS. I'cod, I don't know but that may be   130
better sport than t'other; ha, nurse?

Y. FAS. Well, you shall have your choice when
you come there.

MISS. Shall I? —— then by my troth I'll get there
as fast as I can. (*To Nurse.*) His honor desires   135
you'll be so kind as to let us be married tomorrow.

NURSE. Tomorrow, my dear madam?

Y. FAS. Yes, tomorrow, sweet nurse, privately;
young folks, you know, are impatient, and Sir Tunbelly would make us stay a week for a wedding-   140
dinner. Now all things being signed and sealed and
agreed, I fancy there could be no great harm in
practising a scene or two of matrimony in private,
if it were only to give us the better assurance when
we come to play it in public.   145

NURSE. Nay, I must confess stol'n pleasures are
sweet; but if you should be married now, what will
you do when Sir Tunbelly calls for you to be wed?

MISS. Why, then we'll be married again.

NURSE. What, twice, my child?   150

MISS. I'cod, I don't care how often I'm married,
not I.

Y. FAS. Pray, nurse, don't you be against your
young lady's good; for by this means she'll have
the pleasure of two wedding-days.   155

MISS (*to Nurse softly*). And of two wedding-
nights, too, nurse.

NURSE. Well, I'm such a tender-hearted fool, I
find I can refuse nothing; so you shall e'en follow
your own inventions.   160

MISS. Shall I? (*Aside.*) O Lord, I could leap
over the moon.

Y. FAS. Dear nurse, this goodness of yours
shan't go unrewarded; but now you must employ
your power with Mr. Bull, the chaplain, that   165
he may do us his friendly office too, and then we shall
all be happy; do you think you can prevail with him?

NURSE. Prevail with him? —— or he shall never
prevail with me, I can tell him that.

MISS. My lord, she has had him upon the   170
hip this seven year.

Y. FAS. I'm glad to hear it; however, to
strengthen your interest with him, you may let him
know I have several fat livings in my gift, and that
the first that falls shall be in your disposal.   175

NURSE. Nay, then I'll make him marry more
folks than one, I'll promise him.

MISS. Faith, do, nurse, make him marry you too;
I'm sure he'll do 't for a fat living; for he loves eating
more than he loves his Bible; and I have often   180
heard him say a fat living was the best meat in the
world.

NURSE. Ay, and I'll make him commend the sauce
too, or I'll bring his gown to a cassock,[1] I will so.

Y. FAS. Well, nurse, whilst you go and settle   185
matters with him, then your lady and I will go take
a walk in the garden.

NURSE. I'll do your honor's business in the catching up of a garter.   *Exit Nurse.*

Y. FAS. (*giving* [MISS HOYDEN] *his hand*).   190
Come, madam, dare you venture yourself alone
with me?

MISS. Oh dear, yes, sir; I don't think you'll do
any thing to me I need be afraid on.   *Exeunt.*

[SCENE II]

[LOVELESS'S *lodgings.*]

Enter AMANDA *and* BERINTHIA.

A SONG.

I.

'I SMILE at love, and all its arts,'
    The charming Cynthia cried;
'Take heed, for Love has piercing darts,'
    A wounded swain replied.
'Once free and blest as you are now,   5
    I trifled with his charms;
I pointed at his little bow,
    And sported with his arms:
Till urged too far, "Revenge!" he cries,
    A fatal shaft he drew;   10
It took its passage through your eyes,
    And to my heart it flew.

II.

'To tear it thence I tried in vain;
    To strive, I quickly found,
Was only to encrease the pain,   15
    And to enlarge the wound.
Ah! much too well I fear you know
    What pain I'm to endure,
Since what your eyes alone could do,
    Your heart alone can cure.   20
And that (grant heaven I may mistake)
    I doubt[2] is doomed to bear
A burthen for another's sake,
    Who ill rewards its care.'

AMAN. Well, now, Berinthia, I'm at leisure to   25
hear what 'twas you had to say to me.

BER. What I had to say was only to echo the sighs
and groans of a dying lover.

AMAN. Phu, will you never learn to talk in earnest
of anything?   30

BER. Why, this shall be in earnest, if you please;
for my part, I only tell you matter of fact — you may

---

[1] The cassock was worn under the clergyman's gown. Apparently the nurse threatens to tear the gown off the chaplain's
back.
[2] Fear.

148] P *wedded?*   149] P *we will*.   166] P om. *us*.   167] P *be all*.   186] P *go and take*.
190] Q1Q2P *giving her*.   SCENE II. 17] P *well, I fear, you*.   23] P *burden*.

take it which way you like best; but if you'll follow the women of the town, you'll take it both ways; for when a man offers himself to one of them, first 35 she takes him in jest, and then she takes him in earnest.

AMAN. I'm sure there's so much jest and earnest in what you say to me, I scarce know how to take it; but I think you have bewitched me, for I don't 40 find it possible to be angry with you, say what you will.

BER. I'm very glad to hear it, for I have no mind to quarrel with you, for more reasons than I'll brag of; but quarrel or not, smile or frown, I must tell 45 you what I have suffered upon your account.

[AMAN.] Upon my account!

BER. Yes, upon yours; I have been forced to sit still and hear you commended for two hours together, without one compliment to myself; now don't 50 you think a woman had a blessed time of that?

AMAN. Alas! I should have been unconcerned at it; I never knew where the pleasure lay of being praised by the men: but pray who was this that commended me so? 55

BER. One you have a mortal aversion to — Mr. Worthy; he used you like a text, he took you all to pieces, but spoke so learnedly upon every point, one might see the spirit of the church was in him: if you are a woman, you'd have been in an ecstasy to 60 have heard how feelingly he handled your hair, your eyes, your nose, your mouth, your teeth, your tongue, your chin, your neck, and so forth. Thus he preached for an hour, but when he came to use an application, he observed that all these, without a 65 gallant, were nothing. Now consider of what has been said, and heaven give you grace to put it in practice!

AMAN. Alas! Berinthia, did I incline to a gallant (which you know I do not), do you think a man 70 so nice as he could have the least concern for such a plain unpolished thing as I am? It is impossible!

BER. Now have you a great mind to put me upon commending you.

AMAN. Indeed that was not my design. 75

BER. Nay, if it were, it's all one, for I won't do't; I'll leave that to your looking-glass. But to show you I have some good-nature left, I'll commend him, and may be that may do as well.

AMAN. You have a great mind to persuade me 80 I am in love with him.

BER. I have a great mind to persuade you, you don't know what you are in love with.

AMAN. I am sure I am not in love with him, nor never shall be; so let that pass: but you were 85 saying something you would commend him for.

BER. Oh, you'd be glad to hear a good character of him, however.

AMAN. Psha!

BER. 'Psha!' —— Well, 'tis a foolish under- 90 taking for women, in these kind of matters, to pretend to deceive one another — have not I been bred a woman as well as you?

AMAN. What then?

BER. Why, then I understand my trade so 95 well, that whenever I am told of a man I like, I cry, 'Psha!' But that I may spare you the pains of putting me a second time in mind to commend him, I'll proceed, and give you this account of him: that though 'tis possible he may have had women 100 with as good faces as your ladyship's (no discredit to it neither), yet you must know your cautious behavior, with that reserve in your humor, has given him his death's wound; he mortally hates a coquette; he says 'tis impossible to love where we cannot 105 esteem; and that no woman can be esteemed by a man who has sense, if she makes herself cheap in the eye of a fool. That pride to a woman, is as necessary as humility to a divine; and that far-fetched and dear bought is meat for gentlemen as well as for 110 ladies — in short, that every woman who has beauty may set a price upon herself, and that by underselling the market they ruin the trade. This is his doctrine: how do you like it?

AMAN. So well that, since I never intend to 115 have a gallant for myself, if I were to recommend one to a friend, he should be the man.

Enter WORTHY.

Bless me, he's here! pray heaven he did not hear me!

BER. If he did, it won't hurt your reputa- 120 tion; your thoughts are as safe in his heart as in your own.

WOR. I venture in at an unseasonable time of night, ladies; I hope if I am troublesome, you'll use the same freedom in turning me out again. 125

AMAN. I believe it can't be late, for Mr. Loveless is not come home yet, and he usually keeps good hours.

WOR. Madam, I'm afraid he'll transgress a little tonight; for he told me about half an hour ago 130 he was going to sup with some company he doubted would keep him out till three or four o'clock in the morning, and desired I would let my servant acquaint you with it, that you might not expect[1] him: but my fellow's a blunder-head, so, lest he 135 should make some mistake, I thought it my duty to deliver the message myself.

AMAN. I'm very sorry he should give you that trouble, sir: but ——

BER. But since he has, will you give me 140 leave, madam, to keep him to play at ombre with us?

[1] Wait for.

AMAN. Cousin, you know you command my house.

WOR. (*to* BERINTHIA). And, madam, you know you command me, though I'm a very wretched 145 gamester.

BER. Oh, you play well enough to lose your money, and that's all the ladies require; so without any more ceremony let us go into the next room and call for the cards. 150

AMAN. With all my heart.

Exit WORTHY *leading* AMANDA.

BER. (*sola*). Well, how this business will end, heaven knows; but she seems to me to be in as fair a way —— as a boy is to be a rogue, when he's put clerk to an attorney. 155

Exit BERINTHIA.

[SCENE III]

[BERINTHIA'S *chamber*.]

Enter LOVELESS *cautiously in the dark.*

LOV. So, thus far all's well. I'm got into her bed-chamber, and I think nobody has perceived me steal into the house; my wife don't expect me home till four o'clock; so if Berinthia comes to bed by eleven, I shall have a chase of five hours. Let me see, 5 where shall I hide myself? under her bed? No; we shall have her maid searching there for something or other; her closet's a better place, and I have a master key will open it: I'll e'en in there, and attack her just when she comes to her prayers: that's the most 10 likely to prove her critical minute, for then the devil will be there to assist me.

(*He opens the closet, goes in, and shuts the door after him.*)

Enter BERINTHIA *with a candle in her hand.*

BER. Well, sure I am the best-natured woman in the world. I that love cards so well (there is but one thing upon earth I love better) have pretended 15 letters to write, to give my friends —— a *tête-à-tête*; however, I'm innocent, for picquet is the game I set 'em to: at her own peril be it, if she ventures to play with him at any other. But now what shall I do with myself? I don't know how in the world to 20 pass my time; would Loveless were here to *badiner* [1] a little. Well, he's a charming fellow; I don't wonder his wife's so fond of him. What if I should sit down and think of him till I fall asleep, and dream of the Lord knows what? Oh, but then if I should 25 dream we were married, I should be fright'ned out of my wits. (*Seeing a book.*) What's this book? I think I had best go read. Oh, *splénétique!* [2] it's a sermon. Well, I'll go into my closet, and read *The*

[1] Trifle. [2] Depressing.

Plotting Sisters. [3] (*She opens the closet, sees* 30 LOVELESS, *and shrieks out.*) O Lord, a ghost, a ghost, a ghost, a ghost!

Enter LOVELESS, *running to her.*

LOV. Peace, my dear; it's no ghost; take it in your arms —— you'll find 'tis worth a hundred of 'em.

BER. Run in again; here's somebody coming. 35

[*Exit* LOVELESS.]

Enter her Maid.

MAID. Lord, madam, what's the matter?

BER. O heav'ns! I'm almost frighted out of my wits: I thought verily I had seen a ghost, and 'twas nothing but the white curtain, with a black hood pinned up against it; you may be gone again, I 40 am the fearfull'st fool. ——   *Exit Maid.*

Re-enter LOVELESS.

LOV. Is the coast clear?

BER. The coast clear! I suppose you are clear [4] —— you'd never play such a trick as this else.

LOV. I am very well pleased with my trick 45 thus far, and shall be so till I have played it out, if it ben't your fault: where's my wife?

BER. At cards.

LOV. With whom?

BER. With Worthy. 50

LOV. Then we are safe enough.

BER. Are you so? Some husbands would be of another mind, if he were at cards with their wives.

LOV. And they'd be in the right on't too. But I dare trust mine. Besides, I know he's in love in 55 another place, and he's not one of those who court half a dozen at a time.

BER. Nay, the truth on't is, you'd pity him if you saw how uneasy he is at being engaged with us; but 'twas my malice: I fancied he was to meet his 60 mistress somewhere else, so did it to have the pleasure of seeing him fret.

LOV. What says Amanda to my staying abroad so late?

BER. Why, she's as much out of humor as he; 65 I believe they wish one another at the devil.

LOV. Then I'm afraid they'll quarrel at play, and soon throw up the cards; (*offering to pull her into the closet*) therefore, my dear charming angel, let us make a good use of our time. 70

BER. Heavens, what do you mean?

LOV. Pray, what do you think I mean?

BER. I don't know.

LOV. I'll show you.

BER. You may as well tell me. 75

[3] The sub-title of Thomas Durfey's play, *A Fond Husband*.
[4] A cant word for drunk.

Lov. No, that would make you blush worse than t'other.

Ber. Why, do you intend to make me blush?

Lov. Faith, I can't tell that; but if I do, it shall be in the dark.   (*Pulling her.*)   80

Ber. O, heavens! I would not be in the dark with you for all the world.

Lov. I'll try that.   (*Puts out the candles.*)

Ber. O Lord! are you mad? What shall I do for light?   85

Lov. You'll do as well without it.

Ber. Why, one can't find a chair to sit down!

Lov. Come into the closet, madam: there's moonshine upon the couch.

Ber. Nay, never pull, for I will not go.   90

Lov. Then you must be carried. (*Carrying her.*)

Ber. (*very softly*). Help, help, I'm ravished, ruined, undone! O Lord, I shall never be able to bear it.   [*Exeunt.*]

SCENE [IV]

Sir Tunbelly's *house.*

Enter Miss Hoyden, *Nurse,* Young Fashion, *and* Bull.

Y. Fas. This quick dispatch of yours, Mr. Bull, I take so kindly, it shall give you a claim to my favor as long as I live, I do assure you.

Miss. And to mine too, I promise you.

Bull. I must humbly thank your honors, and   5
I hope, since it has been my lot to join you in the holy bands of wedlock, you will so well cultivate the soil which I have craved a blessing on that your children may swarm about you like bees about a honey-comb.   10

Miss. I'cod, with all my heart: the more the merrier, I say; ha, nurse?

Enter Lory, *taking his master hastily aside.*

Lo. One word with you, for heaven's sake.

Y. Fas. What the devil's the matter?

Lo. Sir, your fortune's ruined, and I don't   15
think your life's worth a quarter of an hour's purchase: yonder's your brother arrived with two coaches and six horses, twenty footmen and pages, a coat worth fourscore pound, and a periwig down to his knees: so judge what will become of your   20
lady's heart.

Y. Fas. Death and Furies! 'tis impossible.

Lo. Fiends and spectres, sir! 'tis true.

Y. Fas. Is he in the house yet?

Lo. No, they are capitulating with him at the   25
gate; the porter tells him he's come to run away with Miss Hoyden, and has cocked the blunderbuss at him; your brother swears, Gad damme, they are a parcel of clawns, and he has a good mind to break off

the match; but they have given the word for Sir   30
Tunbelly, so I doubt all will come out presently. Pray, sir, resolve what you'll do this moment, for i'gad they'll maul you.

Y. Fas. Stay a little. —— (*To* Miss Hoyden.) My dear, here's a troublesome business my man   35
tells me of; but don't be frightened, we shall be too hard for the rogue. Here's an impudent fellow at the gate (not knowing I was come hither *incognito*) has taken my name upon him, in hopes to run away with you.   40

Miss. Oh, the brazen-faced varlet! it's well we are married, or may be we might never a been so.

Y. Fas. (*aside*). I'gad, like enough! —— Prithee, dear doctor, run to Sir Tunbelly and stop him from going to the gate before I speak with him.   45

Bull. I fly, my good lord ——   *Exit* Bull.

Nurse. An't please your honor, my lady and I had best lock ourselves up till the danger be over.

Y. Fas. Ay, by all means.

Miss. Not so fast: I won't be locked up any   50
more. I'm married.

Y. Fas. Yes, pray, my dear, do, till we have seized this rascal.

Miss. Nay, if you pray me, I'll do any thing.
          Exeunt Miss Hoyden *and Nurse.*

Y. Fas. Oh! here's Sir Tunbelly coming. ——   55
(*To* Lory.) Hark you, sirrah, things are better than you imagine: the wedding's over.

Lo. The devil it is, sir.

Y. Fas. Not a word, all's safe: but Sir Tunbelly don't know it, nor must not yet; so I am resolved   60
to brazen the business out, and have the pleasure of turning the impostor [1] upon his lordship, which I believe may easily be done.

Enter Sir Tunbelly, *Chaplain and Servants armed.*

Y. Fas. Did you ever hear, sir, of so impudent an undertaking?   65

Sir Tun. Never, by the mass; but we'll tickle him, I'll warrant him.

Y. Fas. They tell me, sir, he has a great many people with him disguised like servants.

Sir Tun. Ay, ay, rogues enough; but I'll soon   70
raise the posse upon 'em.

Y. Fas. Sir, if you'll take my advice, we'll go a shorter way to work; I find, whoever this spark is, he knows nothing of my being privately here; so if you pretend to receive him civilly, he'll enter   75
without suspicion; and as soon as he is within the gate we'll whip up the drawbridge upon his back, let fly the blunderbuss to disperse his crew, and so commit him to goal.[2]

[1] Turning the role of imposter.
[2] An older form of 'gaol' or 'jail.'

SIR TUN. I'gad, your lordship is an ingenious   80
person, and a very great general; but shall we kill
any of 'em, or not?

Y. FAS. No, no, fire over their heads only to
fright 'em; I'll warrant the regiment scours [1] when
the colonel's a prisoner.   85

SIR TUN. Then come along, my boys, and let your
courage be great —— for your danger is but small.
                                          Exeunt.

SCENE [V]

The gate.

Enter LORD FOPPINGTON *and Followers.*

LORD FOP. A pax of these bumkinly people! ——
will they open the gate, or do they desire I should
grow at their moat-side like a willow? (*To the
Porter.*) Hey, fellow — prithee do me the favor, in
as few words as thou canst find to express thyself,   5
to tell me whether thy master will admit me or not,
that I may turn about my coach and be gone.

POR. Here's my master himself now at hand;
he's of age, he'll give you his answer.

Enter SIR TUNBELLY *and Servants.*

SIR TUN. My most noble lord, I crave your   10
pardon for making your honor wait so long; but my
orders to my servants have been to admit no body
without my knowledge, for fear of some attempt
upon my daughter, the times being full of plots and
roguery.   15

LORD FOP. Much caution, I must confess, is a sign
of great wisdom: but, [stap] my vitals, I have got a
cold enough to destroy a porter —— he, hem ——

SIR TUN. I am very sorry for't, indeed, my lord;
but if your lordship please to walk in, we'll help   20
you to some brown sugar-candy. My lord, I'll
show you the way.

LORD FOP. Sir, I follow you with pleasure.
                                          Exeunt.

(*As* LORD FOPPINGTON'S *Servants go to follow
him in, they clap the door against* LA
VÉROLE.)

SERVANTS (*within*). Nay, hold you me there, sir.

LA VÉR. *Jernie die, qu'est ce que veut dire ça?* [2]   25

SIR TUN. (*within*). —— Fire, porter.

PORT. (*fires*). Have among you, my masters!

LA VÉR. *Ah, je suis mort* [3] ——
                         The Servants all run off.

PORT. Not one soldier left, by the mass.

[1] Runs away.
[2] Zounds, what's that he says?
[3] Ah, I am dead!

[SCENE VI]

Scene changes to the hall.

Enter SIR TUNBELLY, *the Chaplain and Servants,
with* LORD FOPPINGTON *disarmed.*

SIR TUN. Come, bring him along, bring him along.

LORD FOP. What the pax do you mean, gentlemen?
is it fair time,[4] that you are all drunk before dinner?

SIR TUN. Drunk, sirrah? Here's an impudent
rogue for you! Drunk or sober, bully, I'm a   5
justice of the peace, and know how to deal with
strollers.

LORD FOP. Strollers!

SIR TUN. Ay, strollers; come, give an account of
yourself; what's your name? where do you live?   10
Do you pay scot and lot? [5]   Are you a Williamite, or
a Jacobite? Come.

LORD FOP. And why dost thou ask me so many
impertinent questions?

SIR TUN. Because I'll make you answer 'em   15
before I have done with you, you rascal you.

LORD FOP. Before Gad, all the answer I can make
thee to 'em, is, that thou art a very extraordinary
old fellow; [stap] my vitals ——

SIR TUN. Nay, if you are for joking with   20
deputy-lieutenants, we'st know how to deal with
you. —— Here, draw a warrant for him immediately.

LORD FOP. A warrant —— what the devil is't
thou wouldst be at, old gentleman?

SIR TUN. I would be at you, sirrah, (if my   25
hands were not tied as a magistrate) and with these
two double fists beat your teeth down your throat,
you dog you.

LORD FOP. And why would'st thou spoil my face
at that rate?   30

SIR TUN. For your design to rob me of my
daughter, villain.

LORD FOP. Rab thee of thy daughter! —— Now
do I begin to believe I am abed and asleep, and that
all this is but a dream. If it be, 'twill be an   35
agreeable surprise enough to waken by and by and
instead of the impertinent company of a nasty
country justice, find myself, perhaps, in the arms of a
woman of quality. (*To* SIR TUNBELLY.) Prithee,
old father, wilt thou give me leave to ask thee   40
one question?

SIR TUN. I can't tell whether I will or not, till I
know what it is.

LORD FOP. Why, then, it is, whether thou didst
not write to my Lord Foppington to come down   45
and marry thy daughter.

SIR TUN. Yes, marry did I, and my Lord Fopping-

[4] I.e., the season of the local fair.
[5] Do you pay taxes?

9 s.d.] P and his servants.   SCENE V. 13] Q2P *attempts.*   17] Q1 *stop.*   25] Q2P om. die.
s.d.] P changes into a hall.   SCENE VI. 19] Q1 *stop.*   21] P *we know.*   34] Q2P *I do.*

ton is come down, and shall marry my daughter before she's a day older.

LORD FOP. Now give me thy hand, dear dad: 50 I thought we should understand one another at last.

SIR TUN. This fellow's mad —— here, bind him hand and foot.   (*They bind him down.*)

LORD FOP. Nay, prithee, knight, leave fooling: thy jest begins to grow dull.   55

SIR TUN. Bind him, I say, he's mad —— bread and water, a dark room, and a whip, may bring him to his senses again.

LORD FOP. (*aside*). I'gad, if I don't waken quickly, by all I can see, this is like to prove one of the 60 most impertinent dreams that ever I dreamt in my life.

Enter MISS HOYDEN *and Nurse.*

MISS (*going up to him*). Is this he that would have run away with me? Fough, how he stinks of sweets! Pray, father, let him be dragged through the 65 horse-pond.

LORD FOP. (*aside*). This must be my wife, by her natural inclination to her husband.

MISS. Pray, father, what do you intend to do with him? hang him?   70

SIR TUN. That at least, child.

NURSE. Ay, and it's e'en too good for him too.

LORD FOP. (*aside*). *Madame la gouvernante*, I presume: hitherto [1] this appears to me to be one of the most extraordinary families that ever man of 75 quality matched into.

SIR TUN. What's become of my lord, daughter?

MISS. He's just coming, sir.

LORD FOP. (*aside*). 'My lord!' —— what does he mean by that, now?   80

Enter YOUNG FASHION *and* LORY.

(*Seeing him.*) Stap my vitals, Tam! —— now the dream's out.

Y. FAS. Is this the fellow, sir, that designed to trick me of your daughter?

SIR TUN. This is he, my lord: how do you like 85 him? Is not he a pretty fellow to get a fortune?

Y. FAS. I find by his dress, he thought your daughter might be taken with a beau.

MISS. O [Gemini]! Is this a beau? let me see him again —— ha! I find a beau is no such ugly 90 thing, neither.

Y. FAS. I'gad, she'll be in love with him presently; I'll e'en have him sent away to goal. (*To* LORD FOPPINGTON.) Sir, though your undertaking shows you are a person of no extraordinary modesty, I 95 suppose you han't confidence enough to expect much favor from me?

LORD FOP. Strike me dumb, Tam, thou art a very impudent fellow.

[1] To the present moment.

NURSE. Look if the varlet has not the front- 100 ery to call his lordship plain Thomas.

BULL. The business is, he would feign himself mad, to avoid going to goal.

LORD FOP. (*aside*). That must be the chaplain, by his unfolding of mysteries.   105

SIR TUN. Come, is the warrant writ?

CLERK. Yes, sir.

SIR TUN. Give me the pen, I'll sign it —— so! —— now, constable, away with him.

LORD FOP. Hold one moment; pray, gentle- 110 men! —— My Lord Foppington, shall I beg one word with your lordship?

NURSE. O ho, it's 'my lord' with him now; see how afflictions will humble folks.

MISS. Pray, my lord, don't let him whisper 115 too close, lest he bite your ear off.

LORD FOP. I am not altogether so hungry as your ladyship is pleased to imagine. (*To* YOUNG FASH- ION.) Look you, Tam, I am sensible I have not been so kind to you as I ought, but I hope you'll for- 120 get what's past, and accept of the five thousand pounds I offer; thou may'st live in extreme splendor with it, stap my vitals.

Y. FAS. It's a much easier matter to prevent a disease than to cure it; a quarter of that sum 125 would have secured your mistress; twice as much won't redeem her.   (*Leaving him.*)

SIR TUN. Well, what says he?

Y. FAS. Only the rascal offered me a bribe to let him go.   130

SIR TUN. Ay, he shall go, with a pox to him. —— Lead on, constable.

LORD FOP. One word more, and I have done.

SIR TUN. Before Gad, thou art an impudent fel- low, to trouble the court at this rate, after thou 135 art condemned; but speak once for all.

LORD FOP. Why then once for all, I have at last luckily called to mind that there is a gentleman of this country, who I believe cannot live far from this place, if he were here, would satisfy you, I am 140 Navelty, Baron of Foppington, with five thousand pounds a year, and that fellow there a rascal not worth a groat.

SIR TUN. Very well; now who is this honest gentle- man you are so well acquainted with? (*To* 145 YOUNG FASHION.) Come, sir, we shall hamper him.

LORD FOP. 'Tis Sir John Friendly.

SIR TUN. So: he lives within half a mile, and came down into the country but last night; this bold-faced fellow thought he had been at London still, and 150 so quoted him; now we shall display him in his colors: I'll send for Sir John immediately. —— Here, fellow, away presently,[2] and desire my neighbor he'll do me the favor to step over, upon an extraordinary occa-

[2] Immediately.

sion; [*exit Servant*] —— and in the meanwhile 155
you had best secure this sharper in the gate-house.

CONST. An't please your worship, he may chance
to give us the slip thence: if I were worthy to advise,
I think the dog-kennel's a surer place.

SIR TUN. With all my heart —— anywhere. 160

LORD FOP. Nay, for heaven's sake, sir, do me the
favor to put me in a clean room, that I mayn't daub
my clothes.

SIR TUN. Oh, when you have married my
daughter, her estate will afford you new ones. 165
—— Away with him.

LORD FOP. A dirty country justice is a barbarous
magistrate, stap my vitals!

Exit Constable with LORD FOPPINGTON.

Y. FAS. (*aside*). I'gad, I must prevent this
knight's coming, or the house will grow soon 170
too hot to hold me. (*To* SIR TUNBELLY.) Sir, I
fancy 'tis not worth while to trouble Sir John upon
this impertinent fellow's desire: I'll send and call the
messenger back ——

SIR TUN. Nay, with all my heart; for to be 175
sure he thought he was far enough off, or the rogue
would never have named him.

Enter Servant.

SERV. Sir, I met Sir John just lighting at the gate;
he's come to wait upon you.

SIR TUN. Nay, then it happens as one could 180
wish.

Y. FAS. (*aside*). The devil it does! —— Lory, you
see how things are: here will be a discovery presently,
and we shall have our brains beat out, for my
brother will be sure to swear he don't know 185
me: therefore run into the stable, take the two first
horses you can light on: I'll slip out at the back door,
and we'll away immediately.

LO. What, and leave your lady, sir?

Y. FAS. There's no danger in that, as long 190
as I have taken possession; I shall know how to
treat with them well enough, if once I am out of
their reach: away, I'll steal after thee.

Exit LORY: his master follows him out at one
door, as SIR JOHN enters at t'other.

Enter SIR JOHN.

SIR TUN. Sir John, you are the welcom'st man
alive; I had just sent a messenger to desire 195
you'd step over, upon a very extraordinary occasion
—— we are all in arms here.

SIR JOHN. How so?

SIR TUN. Why, you must know —— a finical sort
of a tawdry fellow here (I don't know who the 200
devil he is, not I) hearing, I suppose, that the match
was concluded between my Lord Foppington and
my girl Hoyden, comes impudently to the gate, with

a whole pack of rogues in liveries, and would have
passed upon me for his lordship: but what 205
does I? I comes up to him boldly at the head of his
guards, takes him by the throat, strikes up his heels,
binds him hand and foot, dispatches a warrant, and
commits him prisoner to the dog-kennel.

SIR JOHN. So, but how do you know but this 210
was my lord? for I was told he set out from London
the day before me, with a very fine retinue, and intended to come directly hither.

SIR TUN. Why now to show you how many lies
people raise in that damned town, he came 215
two nights ago post, with only one servant, and is
now in the house with me. But you don't know the
cream of the jest yet; this same rogue (that lies
yonder neck and heels among the hounds) thinking
you were out of the country, quotes you for 220
his acquaintance, and said, if you were here, you'd
justify him to be Lord Foppington, and I know not
what.

SIR JOHN. Pray will you let me see him?

SIR TUN. Ay, that you shall presently. —— 225
Here, fetch the prisoner.   *Exit Servant.*

SIR JOHN. I wish there ben't some mistake in this
business; where's my lord? I know him very well.

SIR TUN. He was here just now; —— see for him,
doctor, tell him Sir John is here to wait upon 230
him.   *Exit Chaplain.*

SIR JOHN. I hope, Sir Tunbelly, the young lady
is not married yet.

SIR TUN. No, things won't be ready this week;
but why do you say you hope she is not mar- 235
ried?

SIR JOHN. Some foolish fancies only; perhaps I'm
mistaken.

Re-enter Chaplain.

BULL. Sir, his lordship is just rid out to take the
air. 240

SIR TUN. To take the air! is that his London
breeding, to go take the air when gentlemen come
to visit him?

SIR JOHN. 'Tis possible he might want it: he
might not be well —— some sudden qualm per- 245
haps.

Enter Constable, etc., with LORD FOPPINGTON.

LORD FOP. Stap my vitals, I'll have satisfaction.

SIR JOHN (*running to him*). My dear Lord Foppington!

LORD FOP. Dear Friendly, thou art come 250
in the critical minute, strike me dumb.

SIR JOHN. Why, I little thought I should have
found you in fetters.

LORD FOP. Why truly, the world must do me the
justice to confess I do use to appear a little 255

203] P and with.   227-228] P the business.   252] P thought to have.

more *dégagé:*[1] but this old gentleman, not liking the freedom of my air, has been pleased to skewer down my arms like a rabbit.

SIR TUN. Is it then possible that this should be the true Lord Foppington at last?   260

LORD FOP. Why, what do you see in his face to make you doubt of it? Sir, without presuming to have any extraordinary opinion of my figure, give me leave to tell you, if you had seen as many lords as I have done, you would not think it impos-   265 sible a person of a worse *taille*[2] than mine might be a modern man of quality.

SIR TUN. Unbind him, slaves. —— My lord, I'm struck dumb: I can only beg pardon by signs; but if a sacrifice will appease you, you shall have   270 it. —— Here, pursue this Tartar, bring him back —— away, I say! —— a dog, oons! —— I'll cut off his ears and his tail, I'll draw out all his teeth, pull his skin over his head —— and —— and what shall I do more?   275

SIR JOHN. He does indeed deserve to be made an example of.

LORD FOP. He does deserve to be [*châtré*],[3] stap my vitals.

SIR TUN. May I then hope I have your   280 honor's pardon?

LORD FOP. Sir, we courtiers do nothing without a bribe; that fair young lady might do miracles.

SIR TUN. Hoyden, come hither, Hoyden.

LORD FOP. Hoyden is her name, sir?   285

SIR TUN. Yes, my lord.

LORD FOP. The prettiest name for a song I ever heard.

SIR TUN. My lord —— here's my girl, she's yours; she has a wholesome body and a virtuous   290 mind; she's a woman complete, both in flesh and in spirit; she has a bag of milled crowns, as scarce as they are, and fifteen hundred a year stitched fast to her tail: so go thy ways, Hoyden.

LORD FOP. Sir, I do receive her like a   295 gentleman.

SIR TUN. Then I'm a happy man, I bless heaven, and if your lordship will give me leave, I will, like a good Christian at Christmas, be very drunk by way of thanksgiving. Come, my noble peer, I be-   300 lieve dinner's ready; if your honor pleases to follow me, I'll lead you on to the attack of a venison pasty.   *Exit* SIR TUNBELLY.

LORD FOP. Sir, I wait upon you. —— Will your ladyship do me the favor of your little finger,   305 madam?

MISS. My lord, I'll follow you presently: I have a little business with my nurse.

LORD FOP. Your ladyship's most humble servant. —— Come, Sir John, the ladies have *des affaires.*[4]   310
Exeunt LORD FOPPINGTON *and* SIR JOHN.

MISS. So, nurse, we are finely brought to bed! what shall we do now?

NURSE. Ah, dear miss, we are all undone! Mr. Bull, you were used to help a woman to a remedy.
(Crying.)

BULL. Alack-a-day, but it's past my skill   315 now; I can do nothing.

NURSE. Who would have thought that ever your invention should have been drained so dry?

MISS. Well, I have often thought old folks fools, and now I'm sure they are so; I have found   320 a way myself to secure us all.

NURSE. Dear lady, what's that?

MISS. Why, if you two will be sure to hold your tongues, and not say a word of what's past, I'll e'en marry this lord too.   325

NURSE. What! two husbands, my dear?

MISS. Why you have had three, good nurse; you may hold your tongue.

NURSE. Ay, but not [all together], sweet child.

MISS. Psha, if you had, you'd ne'er a   330 thought much on't.

NURSE. Oh, but 'tis a sin — sweeting.

BULL. Nay, that's my business to speak to, nurse: I do confess, to take two husbands for the satisfaction of the flesh is to commit the sin   335 of exorbitancy, but to do it for the peace of the spirit is no more than to be drunk by way of physic: besides, to prevent a parent's wrath is to avoid the sin of disobedience; for when the parent's angry the child is froward. So that upon the whole mat-   340 ter, I do think, though miss should marry again, she may be saved.

MISS. I'cod, and I will marry again then, and so there's an end of the story.   *Exeunt.*

ACT V

SCENE [I]

London.

Enter COUPLER, YOUNG FASHION, *and* LORY.

COUP. Well, and so Sir John coming in ——?

Y. FAS. And so Sir John coming in, I thought it might be manners in me to go out, which I did, and getting on horseback as fast as I could, rid away as if the devil had been at the rear of me; what has   5 happened since, heav'n knows.

COUP. I'gad, sirrah, I know as well as heaven.

Y. FAS. What do you know?

COUP. That you are a cuckold.

---

[1] At ease.   [2] Figure.   [3] Castrated.   [4] Business.

Y. Fas. The devil I am! by who?   10

Coup. By your brother.

Y. Fas. My brother! which way?

Coup. The old way —— he has lain with your wife.

Y. Fas. Hell and Furies, what dost thou mean?

Coup. I mean plainly; I speak no parable.   15

Y. Fas. Plainly! Thou dost not speak common sense; I cannot understand one word thou say'st.

Coup. You will do soon, youngster. In short, you left your wife a widow, and she married again.

Y. Fas. It's a lie.   20

Coup. —— I'cod, if I were a young fellow, I'd break your head, sirrah.

Y. Fas. Dear dad, don't be angry, for I'm as mad as Tom of Bedlam.

Coup. Then [1] I had fitted you with a wife, you   25 should have kept her.

Y. Fas. But is it possible the young strumpet could play me such a trick?

Coup. A young strumpet, sir —— can play twenty tricks.   30

Y. Fas. But prithee instruct me a little farther; whence comes thy intelligence!

Coup. From your brother, in this letter; there you may read it.

Y. Fas. (reads). 'Dear Coupler, (pulling   35 off his hat) [2] I have only time to tell thee in three lines, or thereabouts, that here has been the devil: that rascal Tam, having stole the letter thou hadst formerly writ for me to bring to Sir Tunbelly, formed a damnable design upon my   40 mistress, and was in a fair way of success when I arrived. But after having suffered some indignities (in which I have all daubed my embroidered coat) I put him to flight. I sent out a party of horse after him, in hopes to have   45 made him my prisoner, which if I had done, I would have qualified him for the seraglio, stap my vitals.

The danger I have thus narrowly 'scaped has made me fortify myself against further at-   50 tempts by ent'ring immediately into an association with the young lady, by which we engage to stand by one another as long as we both shall live.

In short, the papers are sealed and the con-   55 tract is signed, so the business of the lawyer is achevé; [3] but I defer the divine part of the thing till I arrive at London, not being willing to consummate in any other bed but my own.

'Postscript. 'Tis passible I may be in tawn   60 as soon as this letter, for I find the lady is so violently in love with me, I have determined to make her happy with all the dispatch that is practicable, without disardering my coach harses.'   65

So, here's rare work, i'faith!

Lo. I'gad, Miss Hoyden has laid about her bravely.

Coup. I think my country girl has played her part as well as if she had been born and bred in   70 St. James's parish.

Y. Fas. —— That rogue the chaplain!

Lo. And then that jade the nurse, sir.

Y. Fas. And then that drunken sot, Lory, sir, that could not keep himself sober to be a witness   75 to the marriage.

Lo. Sir — with respect — I know very few drunken sots that do keep themselves sober.

Y. Fas. Hold your prating, sirrah, or I'll break your head. Dear Coupler, what's to be done?   80

Coup. Nothing's to be done till the bride and bridegroom come to town.

Y. Fas. Bride and bridegroom? Death and Furies, I can't bear that thou shouldst call 'em so.   85

Coup. Why, what shall I call 'em, dog and cat?

Y. Fas. Not for the world; that sounds more like man and wife than t'other.

Coup. Well, if you'll hear of 'em in no language, we'll leave 'em for the nurse and the chaplain.   90

Y. Fas. The devil and the witch.

Coup. When they come to town ——

Lo. We shall have stormy weather.

Coup. Will you hold your tongues, gentlemen, or not?   95

Lo. Mum.

Coup. I say, when they come we must find what stuff they are made of —— whether the churchman be chiefly composed of the flesh or the spirit; I presume the former —— for as chaplains now go, 'tis   100 probable he eats three pound of beef to the reading of one chapter; this gives him carnal desires: he wants money, preferment, wine, a whore; therefore we must invite him to supper, give him fat capons, sack and sugar, a purse of gold, and a plump   105 sister. Let this be done, and I'll warrant thee, my boy, he speaks truth like an oracle.

Y. Fas. Thou art a profound statesman, I allow it; but how shall we gain the nurse?

Coup. Oh, never fear the nurse, if once you   110 have got the priest, for the devil always rides the hag. Well, there's nothing more to be said of the matter at this time, that I know of; so let us go and enquire if there's any news of our people yet; perhaps they

---

[1] Equivalent to 'when'; an old usage. Perhaps 'When' is the correct reading, but it appears in none of the early editions.

[2] Apparently the meaning is that Coupler pulls off his hat when he hears himself addressed by a lord, even in a letter.

[3] Finished.

---

may be come. But let me tell you one thing by   115
the way, sirrah: I doubt you have been an idle fellow;
if thou hadst behaved thyself as thou shouldst have
done, the girl would never have left thee.   *Exeunt.*

Scene [II]

BERINTHIA'S *apartment.*

Enter her Maid, passing the stage, followed by
WORTHY.

Wor. Hem, Mrs. Abigail, is your mistress to be
spoken with?

Ab. By you, sir, I believe she may.

Wor. Why 'tis by me I would have her spoken
with.   5

Ab. I'll acquaint her, sir.   *Exit* ABIGAIL.

Wor. (*solus*). One lift more I must persuade her to
give me, and then I'm mounted. Well, a young
bawd and a handsome one for my money: 'tis they
do the execution; I'll never go to an old one, but   10
when I have occasion for a witch. Lewdness looks
heavenly to a woman when an angel appears in its
cause, but when a hag is advocate, she thinks it
comes from the devil. An old woman has something
so terrible in her looks, that whilst she is per-   15
suading your mistress to forget she has a soul, she
stares hell and damnation full in her face.

Enter BERINTHIA.

Ber. Well, sir, what news bring you?

Wor. No news, madam: there's a woman going
to cuckold her husband.   20

Ber. Amanda?

Wor. I hope so.

Ber. Speed her well.

Wor. Ay, but there must be a more than a God-
speed, or your charity won't be worth a farthing.   25

Ber. Why, han't I done enough already?

Wor. Not quite.

Ber. What's the matter?

Wor. The lady has a scruple still, which you must
remove.   30

Ber. What's that?

Wor. Her virtue —— she says.

Ber. And do you believe her?

Wor. No, but I believe it's what she takes for her
virtue; it's some relics of lawful love: she is not   35
yet fully satisfied her husband has got another
mistress, which unless I can convince her of, I have
opened the trenches in vain, for the breach must be
wider before I dare storm the town.

Ber. And so I'm to be your engineer?   40

Wor. I'm sure you know best how to manage the
battery.

Ber. What think you of springing a mine? I
have a thought just now come into my head, how to
blow her up at once.   45

Wor. That would be a thought, indeed!

Ber. —— Faith, I'll do't, and thus the execution
of it shall be. We are all invited to my Lord Foppington's tonight to supper; he's come to town with
his bride, and makes a ball, with an entertain-   50
ment of music. Now you must know, my undoer
here, Loveless, says he must needs meet me about
some private business (I don't know what 'tis) before
we go to the company. To which end he has told his
wife one lie, and I have told her another. But   55
to make her amends, I'll go immediately and tell her
a solemn truth.

Wor. What's that?

Ber. Why, I'll tell her, that to my certain knowledge her husband has a rendezvous with his mis-   60
tress this afternoon; and that if she'll give me her
word she'll be satisfied with the discovery without
making any violent inquiry after the woman, I'll
direct her to a place where she shall see 'em meet.
Now, friend, this I fancy may help you to a   65
critical minute. For home she must go again to
dress. You, with your good-breeding, come to wait
upon us to the ball, find her all alone, her spirit en-
flamed against her husband for his treason, and her
flesh in a heat from some contemplations upon   70
the treachery; her blood on a fire, her conscience in
ice; a lover to draw, and the devil to drive —— Ah,
poor Amanda!

Wor. (*kneeling*). Thou angel of light, let me fall
down and adore thee!   75

Ber. Thou minister of darkness, get up again,
for I hate to see the devil at his devotions.

Wor. Well, my incomparable Berinthia —— how
shall I requite you ——?

Ber. Oh, ne'er trouble yourself about that: 80
virtue is its own reward: there's a pleasure in doing
good, which sufficiently pays itself. Adieu.

Wor. Farewell, thou best of women.

Exeunt several ways.

Enter AMANDA, *meeting* BERINTHIA.

Aman. Who was that went from you?

Ber. A friend of yours.   85

Aman. What does he want?

Ber. Something you might spare him, and be
ne'er the poorer.

Aman. I can spare him nothing but my friendship;
my love already's all disposed of: though, I con-   90
fess, to one ungrateful to my bounty.

Ber. Why, there's the mystery: you have been
so bountiful you have cloyed him. Fond wives do
by their husbands as barren wives do by their lap-

26] Q1Q2 *Why han't*; P *Why, han't.*   50] P *maketh.*   62] P *she will.*   64] P *them.*
68] Q1 *ball. Find*; Q2P *ball, find.*

dogs —— cram 'em with sweetmeats till they 95
spoil their stomachs.

AMAN. Alas! Had you but seen how passionately
fond he has been since our last reconciliation, you
would have thought it were impossible he ever should
have breathed an hour without me. 100

BER. Ay, but there you thought wrong again,
Amanda; you should consider that in matters of love
men's eyes are always bigger than their bellies.
They have violent appetites, 'tis true, but they have
soon dined. 105

AMAN. Well; there's nothing upon earth astonishes me more than men's inconstancy.

BER. Now there's nothing upon earth astonishes
me less, when I consider what they and we are
composed of. For nature has made them chil- 110
dren, and us babies.[1] Now, Amanda, how we used
our babies, you may remember. We were mad to
have 'em as soon as we saw 'em; kissed 'em to pieces
as soon as we got 'em; then pulled off their clothes,
saw 'em naked, and so threw 'em away. 115

AMAN. But do you think all men are of this
temper?

BER. All but one.

AMAN. Who is that?

BER. Worthy. 120

AMAN. Why, he's weary of his wife too, you see.

BER. Ay, that's no proof.

AMAN. What can be a greater?

BER. Being weary of his mistress.

AMAN. Don't you think 'twere possible he 125
might give you that too?

BER. Perhaps he might, if he were my gallant;
not if he were yours.

AMAN. Why do you think he should be more constant to me than he would to you? I'm sure 130
I'm not so handsome.

BER. Kissing goes by favor; he likes you best.

AMAN. Suppose he does: that's no demonstration
he would be constant to me.

BER. No, that I'll grant you: but there are 135
other reasons to expect it; for you must know after
all, Amanda, the inconstancy we commonly see in
men of brains does not so much proceed from the uncertainty of their temper as from the misfortunes of
their love. A man sees perhaps a hundred 140
women he likes well enough for an intrigue and away,
but possibly, through the whole course of his life,
does not find above one who is exactly what he could
wish her: now her, 'tis a thousand to one, he never
gets. Either she is not to be had at all (though 145
that seldom happens, you'll say) or he wants those
opportunities that are necessary to gain her. Either

[1] Dolls.

she likes somebody else much better than him or,
uses him like a dog because he likes nobody so well
as her. Still something or other fate claps in 150
the way between them and the woman they are
capable of being fond of: and this makes them wander about from mistress to mistress, like a pilgrim
from town to town, who every night must have a
fresh lodging, and 's in haste to be gone in the 155
morning.

AMAN. 'Tis possible there may be something in
what you say; but what do you infer from it, as to
the man we were talking of?

BER. Why, I infer, that you being the 160
woman in the world the most to his humor, 'tis not
likely he would quit you for one that is less.

AMAN. That is not to be depended upon, for you
see Mr. Loveless does so.

BER. What does Mr. Loveless do? 165

AMAN. Why, he runs after something for variety,
I'm sure he does not like so well as he does me.

BER. That's more than you know, madam.

AMAN. No, I'm sure on't: I'm not very vain,
Berinthia, and yet I'd lay my life, if I could 170
look into his heart, he thinks I deserve to be preferred to a thousand of her.

BER. Don't be too positive in that, neither: a
million to one, but she has the same opinion of you.
What would you give to see her? 175

AMAN. Hang her, dirty trull! though I really believe she's so ugly, she'd cure me of my jealousy.

BER. All the men of sense about town say she's
handsome.

AMAN. They are as often out in those things 180
as any people.

BER. Then I'll give you farther proof —— all the
women about town say she's a fool: now I hope you
are convinced?

AMAN. Whate'er she be, I'm satisfied he 185
does not like her well enough to bestow anything
more than a little outward gallantry upon her.

BER. Outward gallantry? —— (Aside.) I can't
bear this. (To AMANDA.) Don't you think she's a
woman to be fobbed off[2] so. Come, I'm too 190
much your friend to suffer you should be thus grossly
imposed upon by a man who does not deserve the
least part about you, unless he knew how to set a
greater value upon it. Therefore, in one word, to
my certain knowledge he is to meet her; now, 195
within a quarter of an hour, somewhere about that
Babylon of wickedness, Whitehall. And if you'll
give me your word that you'll be content with seeing
her masked in his hand, without pulling her head-
clothes off, I'll step immediately to the person 200

[2] Cheated.

95] P them.   113] P them (thrice).   114] P them.   115] P saw them.   115} Q2P threw them.
119] P Who's.   169] Q2 I am sure.   169] Q2P I am not.   170] P I'll lay.   182] Q2P further.
195] Q2P om. semicolon.

from whom I have my intelligence, and send you word whereabouts you may stand to see 'em meet. My friend and I'll watch 'em from another place, and dodge[1] 'em to their private lodging: but don't you offer to follow 'em, lest you do it awkwardly, 205 and spoil all. I'll come home to you again, as soon as I have [earthed] 'em, and give you an account in what corner of the house the scene of their lewdness lies.

AMAN. If you can do this, Berinthia, he's a 210 villain.

BER. I can't help that: men will be so.

AMAN. Well! I'll follow your directions, for I shall never rest till I know the worst of this matter.

BER. Pray, go immediately, and get your- 215 self ready, then. Put on some of your woman's clothes, a great scarf and a mask, and you shall presently receive orders. (*Calls within.*) Here, who's there? get me a chair quickly.

[*Enter Servant.*]

SERV. There are chairs at the door, madam. 220

BER. 'Tis well; I'm coming. [*Exit Servant.*]

AMAN. But pray, Berinthia, before you go, tell me how I may know this filthy thing, if she should be so forward (as I suppose she will) to come to the rendezvous first; for methinks I would fain 225 view her a little.

BER. Why, she's about my height, and very well shaped.

AMAN. I thought she had been a little crooked?

BER. O no, she's as straight as I am. But 230 we lose time: come away. *Exeunt.*

[SCENE III]

[YOUNG FASHION's *lodgings.*]

Enter YOUNG FASHION, *meeting* LORY.

Y. FAS. Well, will the doctor come?

LO. Sir, I sent a porter to him as you ordered me. He found him with a pipe of tobacco and a great tankard of ale, which he said he would dispatch while I could tell[2] three, and be here. 5

Y. FAS. He does not suspect 'twas I that sent for him?

LO. Not a jot, sir; he divines as little for himself as he does for other folks.

Y. FAS. Will he bring nurse with him? 10

LO. Yes.

Y. FAS. That's well; where's Coupler?

LO. He's half way up the stairs taking breath; he must play his bellows a little before he can get to the top. 15

Enter COUPLER.

Y. FAS. Oh, here he is. Well, old phthisic? The doctor's coming.

COUP. Would the pox had the doctor —— I'm quite out of wind. (*To* LORY.) Set me a chair, sirrah. Ah! (*Sits down. To* YOUNG FASHION.) 20 Why the plague canst not thou lodge upon the ground floor?

Y. FAS. Because I love to lie as near heaven as I can.

COUP. Prithee let heaven alone; ne'er affect 25 tending that way: thy center's downwards.

Y. FAS. That's impossible. I have too much ill luck in this world to be damned in the next.

COUP. Thou art out in thy logic. Thy major is true, but thy minor is false; for thou art the 30 luckiest fellow in the universe.

Y. FAS. Make out that.

COUP. I'll do't: last night the devil ran away with the parson of Fatgoose living.

Y. FAS. If he had run away with the parish 35 too, what's that to me?

COUP. I'll tell thee what it's to thee. This living is worth five hundred pound a year, and the presentation of it is thine, if thou canst prove [thy]self a lawful husband to Miss Hoyden. 40

Y. FAS. Say'st thou so, my protector? then i'cad I shall have a brace of evidences here presently.

COUP. The nurse and the doctor?

Y. FAS. The same: the devil himself won't have interest enough to make 'em withstand it. 45

COUP. That we shall see presently: here they come.

Enter Nurse and Chaplain; they start back, seeing YOUNG FASHION.

NURSE. Ah goodness, Roger, we are betrayed.

Y. FAS. (*laying hold on 'em*). Nay, nay, ne'er flinch for the matter, for I have you safe. Come, 50 to your trials immediately: I have no time to give you copies of your indictment. There sits your judge.

BOTH (*kneeling*). Pray, sir, have compassion on us.

NURSE. I hope, sir, my years will move your 55 pity; I am an aged woman.

COUP. That is a moving argument, indeed.

BULL. I hope, sir, my character will be considered; I am heaven's ambassador.

COUP. (*to* BULL). Are not you a rogue of 60 sanctity?

BULL. Sir, with respect to my function, I do wear a gown.

COUP. Did not you marry this vigorous young fellow to a plump young buxom wench? 65

NURSE (*to* BULL). Don't confess, Roger, unless you are hard put to it, indeed.

COUP. Come, out with't! — Now is he chewing the cud of his roguery, and grinding a lie between his teeth.   70

BULL. Sir —— I cannot positively say —— I say, sir —— positively I cannot say ——

COUP. Come, no equivocation, no Roman turns upon us. Consider thou standest upon Protestant ground, which will slip from under thee like a   75 Tyburn cart;[1] for in this country we have always ten hangmen for one Jesuit.

BULL (*to* YOUNG FASHION). Pray, sir, then will you but permit me to speak one word in private with nurse?   80

Y. FAS. Thou art always for doing something in private with nurse.

COUP. But pray let his betters be served before him for once. I would do something in private with her myself. Lory, take care of this reverend   85 gownman in the next room a little. Retire, priest. (*Exit* LORY *with* BULL.) — Now, virgin, I must put the matter home to you a little: do you think it might not be possible to make you speak truth?

NURSE. Alas! sir, I don't know what you   90 mean by truth.

COUP. Nay, 'tis possible thou may'st be a stranger to it.

Y. FAS. Come, nurse, you and I were better friends when we saw one another last and I still   95 believe you are a very good woman in the bottom. I did deceive you and your young lady, 'tis true, but I always designed to make a very good husband to her, and to be a very good friend to you. And 'tis possible, in the end she might have found   100 herself happier and you richer than ever my brother will make you.

NURSE. Brother! Why, is your worship then his lordship's brother?

Y. FAS. I am; which you should have   105 known, if I durst have stayed to have told you; but I was forced to take horse a little in haste, you know.

NURSE. You were, indeed, sir: poor young man, how he was bound to scour for't. Now won't your worship be angry, if I confess the truth to you: 110 when I found you were a cheat (with respect be it spoken) I verily believed miss had got some pitiful skip-jack[2] varlet or other to her husband, or I had ne'er let her think of marrying again.

COUP. But where was your conscience all   115 this while, woman? Did not that stare in your face with huge saucer-eyes, and a great horn upon the forehead? Did not you think you should be damned for such a sin? Ha?

Y. FAS. Well said, divinity: pass[3] that home   120 upon her.

NURSE. Why, in good truly, sir, I had some fearful thoughts on't, and could never be brought to consent, till Mr. Bull said it was a *peckadilla*,[4] and he'd secure my soul for a tithe-pig.   125

Y. FAS. There was a rogue for you!

COUP. And he shall thrive accordingly: he shall have a good living. Come, honest nurse, I see you have butter in your compound: you can melt. Some compassion you can have of this handsome   130 young fellow.

NURSE. I have, indeed, sir.

Y. FAS. Why, then, I'll tell you what you shall do for me. You know what a warm living here is fallen, and that it must be in the disposal of   135 him who has the disposal of Miss. Now if you and the doctor will agree to prove my marriage, I'll present him to it, upon condition he makes you his bride.

NURSE. Naw the blessing of the Lord follow   140 your good worship both by night and by day! Let him be fetched in by the ears; I'll soon bring his nose to the grindstone.

COUP. (*aside*). Well said, old white-leather.[5] —— Hey; bring in the prisoner there.   145

Enter LORY *with* BULL.

COUP. Come, advance, holy man! Here's your duck, does not think fit to retire with you into the chancel at this time; but she has a proposal to make to you in the face of the congregation. Come, nurse, speak for yourself; you are of age.   150

NURSE. Roger, are not you a wicked man, Roger, to set your strength against a weak woman, and persuade her it was no sin to conceal miss's nuptials? My conscience flies in my face for it, thou priest of Baal; and I find by woful experience, thy ab-   155 solution is not worth an old cassock. Therefore I am resolved to confess the truth to the whole world, though I die a beggar for it. But his worship overflows with his mercy and his bounty: he is not only pleased to forgive us our sins, but designs   160 thou sha't squat thee down in Fatgoose living; and, which is more than all, has prevailed with me to become the wife of thy bosom.

Y. FAS. All this I intend for you, doctor. What you are to do for me, I need not tell you.   165

BULL. Your worship's goodness is unspeakable.

---

[1] The cart which carried the condemned criminal to the gallows.

[2] Trifling, foppish.

[3] Push. (Perhaps 'pass' is a misprint for 'press,' which is the reading of several modern editions.)

[4] The nurse's pronunciation of peccadillo — a trivial fault.

[5] A specially prepared kind of leather, here referred to as a symbol of toughness, or elasticity (of conscience), or both.

74] P *stand'st*.   116] P *stare you in the face*.   163] Q2 om. *of*.

Yet there is one thing seems a point of conscience, and conscience is a tender babe. If I should bind myself, for the sake of this living, to marry nurse, and maintain her afterwards, I doubt it might   170 be looked on as a kind of simony.

COUP. (*rising up*). If it were sacrilege, the living's worth it: therefore no more words, good doctor, but with the parish —— here (*giving Nurse to him*) —— take the parsonage-house. 'Tis true, 'tis a   175 little out of repair; some dilapidations there are to be made good; the windows are broke, the wainscot is warped, the ceilings are peeled, and the walls are cracked; but a little glazing, painting, white-wash, and plaster will make it last thy time.   180

BULL. Well, sir, if it must be so, I shan't contend: what Providence orders, I submit to.

NURSE. And so do I, with all humility.

COUP. Why, that now was spoke like good people: come, my turtle-doves, let us go help this poor   185 pigeon to his wandering mate again; and after institution and induction you shall all go a-cooing together.   *Exeunt.*

[SCENE IV]

[LOVELESS'S *lodgings.*]

Enter AMANDA, *in a scarf, etc., as just returned, her Woman following her.*

AMAN. Prithee, what care I who has been here?

WOM. Madam, 'twas my Lady Bridle and my Lady Tiptoe.

AMAN. My Lady Fiddle and my Lady Faddle. What dost stand troubling me with the visits of a   5 parcel of impertinent women? when they are well seamed with the small-pox they won't be so fond of showing their faces. There are more coquettes about this town ——

WOM. Madam, I suppose they only came to   10 return your ladyship's visit, according to the custom of the world.

AMAN. Would the world were on fire, and you in the middle on't! Begone: leave me. *Exit Woman.*

AMAN. (*sola*). At last I am convinced. My eyes are testimonies of his falsehood.   15
The base, ungrateful, perjured villain ——
Good gods — what slippery stuff are men composed of?
Sure the account of their creation's false,
And 'twas the woman's rib that they were formed of.
But why am I thus angry?   20
This poor relapse should only move my scorn.
'Tis true, the roving flights of his unfinished youth
Had strong [excuses] from the plea of Nature:

Reason had thrown the reins loose on his neck,
And slipt [1] him to unlimited desire.   25
If therefore he went wrong, he had a claim
To my forgiveness, and I did him right.
But since the years of manhood rein him in,
And reason, well digested into thought,
Has pointed out the course he ought to run;   30
If now he strays?
'Twould be as weak and mean in me to pardon,
As it has been in him t'offend. But hold:
'Tis an ill cause indeed, where nothing's to be said for't.
My beauty possibly is in the wane: 35
Perhaps sixteen has greater charms for him:
Yes, there's the secret. But let him know,
My quiver's not entirely emptied yet,
I still have darts, and I can shoot 'em too;
They're not so blunt, but they can enter still;   40
The want's not in my power, but in my will.
Virtue's his friend; or, through another's heart,
I yet could find the way to make his smart.

(*Going off, she meets* WORTHY.)

Ha! He here?
Protect me, heaven, for this looks ominous.   45

WOR. You seem disordered, madam;
I hope there's no misfortune happened to you?

AMAN. None that will long disorder me, I hope.

WOR. Whate'er it be disturbs you, I would
To heaven 'twere in my power to bear the pain   50
Till I were able to remove the cause.

AMAN. I hope ere long it will remove itself.
At least, I have given it warning to be gone.

WOR. Would I durst ask, where 'tis the thorn torments you?
Forgive me if I grow inquisitive;   55
'Tis only with desire to give you ease.

AMAN. Alas! 'tis in a tender part.
It can't be drawn without a world of pain:
Yet out it must;
For it begins to fester in my heart.   60

WOR. If 'tis the sting of unrequited love,
Remove it instantly:
I have a balm will quickly heal the wound.

AMAN. You'll find the undertaking difficult:
The surgeon who already has attempted it   65
Has much tormented me.

WOR.   I'll aid him with a gentler hand —
If you will give me leave.

AMAN.   How soft soe'er the hand may be,
There still is terror in the operation.

WOR. Some few preparatives would make it easy,
Could I persuade you to apply 'em.   70

[1] Released: a hunting term.

188] Q2 om. Exeunt.   SCENE IV. 23] Q1Q2P *excuse.*   26] Q1Q2P prefix *he had a claim* to succeeding line.
31] Q2P *strays.*   33] Q1Q2P print *But hold* as a separate line.
46-191] Q1Q2P print the rest of this scene as prose, except as hereafter noted.
54-56] Q1Q2 print as verse.   59-60] Q1 prints as verse.   61-68] Q1Q2P print as verse.

Make home reflections, madam, on your slighted
    love.
Weigh well the strength and beauty of your charms:
Rouse up that spirit women ought to bear,
And slight your god, if he neglects his angel.
With arms of ice receive his cold embraces,   75
And keep your fire for those who come in flames.
Behold a burning lover at your feet,
His fever raging in his veins.
See how he trembles, how he pants!
See how he glows, how he consumes!   80
Extend the arms of mercy to his aid;
His zeal may give him title to your pity,
Although his merit cannot claim your love.

    AMAN. Of all my feeble sex, sure I must be the
    weakest,
Should I again presume to think on love.   85
(*Sighing.*) Alas! my heart has been too roughly
    treated.

    WOR. 'Twill find the greater bliss in softer usage.

    AMAN. But where's that usage to be found?

    WOR.   'Tis here,
Within this faithful breast; which, if you doubt,
I'll rip it up before your eyes,   90
Lay all its secrets open to your view,
And then you'll see 'twas sound.

    AMAN. With just such honest words as these
The worst of men deceived me.

    WOR.   He therefore merits
All revenge can do; his fault is such,   95
The extent and stretch of vengeance cannot reach
    it.
Oh, make me but your instrument of justice;
You'll find me execute it with such zeal
As shall convince you I abhor the crime.

    AMAN. The rigor of an executioner   100
Has more the face of cruelty than justice,
And he who puts the cord about the wretch's neck
Is seldom known to exceed him in his morals.

    WOR. What proof then can I give you of my truth?

    AMAN. There is on earth but one.

    WOR.   And is that in my power?

    AMAN.   It is.   105
And one that would so thoroughly convince me,
I should be apt to rate your heart so high,
I possibly might purchase it with a part of mine.

    WOR. Then, heav'n, thou art my friend, and I am
    blest;
For if 'tis in my power, my will, I'm sure,   110
Will reach it. No matter what the terms may
    be,
When such a recompense is offered.
Oh, tell me quickly what the proof must be.
What is it will convince you of my love?

    AMAN. I shall believe you love me as you
    ought   115

If from this moment you forbear to ask
Whatever is unfit for me to grant.
— You pause upon it, sir — I doubt, on such hard
    terms
A woman's heart is scarcely worth the having.

    WOR. A heart like yours on any terms is worth
    it;   120
'Twas not on that I paused. But I was thinking
    (*drawing nearer to her*)
Whether some things there may not be
Which women cannot grant without a blush,
And yet which men may take without offense.
(*Taking her hand.*) Your hand, I fancy, may be of
    the number: 125
Oh, pardon me, if I commit a rape
Upon it (*kissing it eagerly*) and thus devour it with
    my kisses!

    AMAN. O heavens! let me go!

    WOR. Never, whilst I have strength to hold you
    here.
(*Forcing her to sit down on a couch.*) My life, my
    soul, my goddess — Oh, forgive me!   130

    AMAN. Oh, whither am I going? Help, heaven,
    or I am lost.

    WOR. Stand neuter, gods, this once I do invoke
    you.

    AMAN. Then save me, virtue, and the glory's
    thine.

    WOR. Nay, never strive!

    AMAN.   I will, and conquer, too.
My forces rally bravely to my aid, (*breaking from
    him*)   135
And thus I gain the day.

    WOR. Then mine as bravely double their attack,
    (*seizing her again*)
And thus I wrest it from you. Nay, struggle not,
For all's in vain: or death or victory,
I am determined.

    AMAN.   And so am I. (*Rushing from him.*) 140
Now keep your distance, or we part for ever.

    WOR. (*offering again*). For heaven's sake —

    AMAN. (*going*).   Nay, then farewell.

    WOR. (*kneeling and holding by her clothes*). Oh,
    stay, and see the magic force of love:
Behold this raging lion at your feet,
Struck dead with fear, and tame as charms can make
    him.   145
What must I do to be forgiven by you?

    AMAN. Repent, and never more offend.

    WOR. Repentance for past crimes is just and easy;
But sin no more's a task too hard for mortals.

    AMAN. Yet those who hope for heaven   150
Must use their best endeavors to perform it.

    WOR. Endeavors we may use; but flesh and blood
Are got in t'other scale, and they are pond'rous
    things.

132] P *once, I.*

AMAN. Whate'er they are, there is a weight in
    resolution
Sufficient for their balance. The soul, I do con-
    fess,   155
Is usually so careless of its charge,
So soft, and so indulgent to desire,
It leaves the reins in the wild hand of Nature,
Who, like a Phaeton, drives the fiery chariot,
And sets the world on flame.   160
Yet still the sovereignty is in the mind,
Whene'er it pleases to exert its force.
Perhaps you may not think it worth your while
To take such mighty pains for my esteem;
But that I leave to you.   165
You see the price I set upon my heart;
Perhaps 'tis dear: but spite of all your art,
You'll find on cheaper terms we ne'er shall part.[1]

                        Exit AMANDA.

WOR. (*solus*). Sure there's divinity about her;
And sh'as dispensed some portion on't to me. 170
For what but now was the wild flame of love,
Or (to dissect that specious term)
The vile, the gross desires of flesh and blood,
Is in a moment turned to adoration.
The coarser appetite of nature's gone,   175
And 'tis, methinks the food of angels I require:
How long this influence may last, heaven knows.
But in this moment of my purity
I could on her own terms accept her heart.
Yes, lovely woman, I can accept it,   180
For now 'tis doubly worth my care.
Your charms are much encreased, since thus adorned.
When truth's extorted from us, then we own
The robe of virtue is a graceful habit.
Could women but our secret counsels scan, 185
Could they but reach the deep reserves of man,
They'd wear it on, that that of love might last;
For when they throw off one, we soon the other cast.
Their sympathy is such ——
The fate of one the other scarce can fly; 190
They live together, and together die.   *Exit.*

[SCENE V]

[LORD FOPPINGTON'S *lodgings.*]

Enter MISS HOYDEN *and Nurse.*

MISS. But is it sure and certain, say you, he's my
lord's own brother?

NURSE. As sure as he's your lawful husband.

MISS. I'cod, if I had known that in time, I don't
know but I might have kept him; for between 5
you and I, nurse, he'd have made a husband worth
two of this I have. But which do you think you
should fancy most, nurse?

NURSE. Why, truly, in my poor fancy, madam,
your first husband is the prettier gentleman. 10

MISS. I don't like my lord's shapes, nurse.

NURSE. Why, in good truly, as a body may say,
he is but a slam.[2]

MISS. What do you think now he puts me in mind
of? Don't you remember a long, loose, sham- 15
bling sort of a horse my father called Washy?

NURSE. As like as two twin brothers.

MISS. I'cod, I have thought so a hundred times:
'faith, I'm tired of him.

NURSE. Indeed, madam, I think you had e'en 20
as good stand to your first bargain.

MISS. Oh, but, nurse, we han't considered the
main thing yet. If I leave my lord, I must leave
'my lady' too: and when I rattle about the streets in
my coach, they'll only say, 'There goes Mistress 25
— Mistress —'. Mistress what? What's this man's
name I have married, nurse?

NURSE. Squire Fashion.

MISS. Squire Fashion, is it? —— Well, Squire ——
that's better than nothing: do you think one 30
could not get him made a knight, nurse?

NURSE. I don't know but one might, madam,
when the king's in a good humor.

MISS. I'cod, that would do rarely. For then he'd
be as good a man as my father, you know. 35

NURSE. By'r Lady, and that's as good as the best
of 'em.

MISS. So 'tis, faith; for then I shall be 'my lady'
and 'your ladyship' at every word; that's all I have
to care for. Ha, nurse! —— but hark you me, one 40
thing more, and then I have done. I'm afraid, if I
change my husband again, I shan't have so much
money to throw about, nurse.

NURSE. Oh, enough's as good as a feast: besides,
madam, one don't know but as much may fall to 45
your share with the younger brother as with the
elder. For though these lords have a power of
wealth, indeed, yet as I have heard say, they give it
all to their sluts and their trulls, who joggle it about
in their coaches, with a murrain to 'em, whilst 50
poor madam sits sighing and wishing, and knotting
and crying, and has not a spare half-crown to buy
her a *Practice of Piety*.[3]

MISS. Oh, but for that, don't deceive yourself,
nurse. For this I must say for my lord, and a — 55
(*snapping her fingers*) for him: he's as free as an open
house at Christmas. For this very morning he told

---

[1] I.e., part after having come to an agreement.

[2] The *O.E.D.* cites this as the sole instance of this word,
and gives the meaning as '? an ill-shaped person.' In Q1 the
word is spelled with a lower-case *fl* ligature: it may be a misprint for 'flam' (cheat), referring to the fact that Lord Foppington's clothes are padded.

[3] A very popular religious manual by Lewis Bayly, Bishop
of Bangor in the early seventeenth century.

166-168] Q1Q2P print as verse.   185-191] Q1Q2P print as verse.

me I should have two hundred a year to buy pins.
Now, nurse, if he gives me two hundred a year to buy
pins, what do you think he'll give me to buy fine   60
petticoats?

NURSE. Ah, my dearest, he deceives thee faully,
and he's no better than a rogue for his pains.   These
Londoners have got a gibberidge with 'em, would
confound a gipsy.   That which they call pin-   65
money is to buy their wives every thing in the
varsal¹ world, dawn to their very shoe-ties: nay, I
have heard folks say that some ladies, if they will
have gallants, as they call 'um, are forced to find
them out of their pin-money too.   70

MISS. Has he serv'd me so, say ye? —— then I'll
be his wife no longer, so that's fixed.   Look, here he
comes, with all the fine folk at 's heels.   I'cod, nurse,
these London ladies will laugh till they crack again,
to see me slip my collar, and run away from my   75
husband.   But, d'ye hear? pray take care of one
thing: when the business comes to break out, be sure
you get between me and my father, for you know his
tricks; he'll knock me down.

NURSE. I'll mind him, ne'er fear, madam.   80

Enter LORD FOPPINGTON, LOVELESS, WORTHY,
    AMANDA, *and* BERINTHIA.

LORD FOP. Ladies and gentlemen, you are all welcome.   (*To* LOVELESS.)   Loveless — that's my
wife; prithee do me the favor to salute her: and dost
hear, (*aside to him*) if thau hast a mind to try thy
fartune, to be revenged of me, I won't take it ill,   85
stap my vitals.

LOV. You need not fear, sir: I'm too fond of my
own wife to have the least inclination to yours.
                (*All salute* MISS HOYDEN.)

LORD FOP. (*aside*).   I'd give a thousand paund he
would make love to her, that he may see she has   90
sense enough to prefer me to him, though his own
wife has not: (*viewing him*) — he's a very beastly
fellow, in my opinion.

MISS (*aside*).   What a power of fine men there are
in this London!   He that kissed me first is a   95
goodly gentleman, I promise you: sure those wives
have a rare time on't, that live here always!

Enter SIR TUNBELLY, *with Musicians, Dancers, etc.*

SIR TUN. Come; come in, good people, come in;
come, tune your fiddles, tune your fiddles.   (*To the
Hautboys.*)   Bag-pipes, make ready there.   100
Come, strike up!   (*Sings.*)

> For this is Hoyden's wedding-day;
> And therefore we keep holy-day,
> And come to be merry.

¹ Universal.

Ha! there's my wench, i'faith: touch and take,   105
I'll warrant her; she'll breed like a tame rabbit.

MISS (*aside*).   I'cod, I think my father's gotten
drunk before supper.

SIR TUN. (*to* LOVELESS *and* WORTHY).   Gentlemen,
you are welcome.   (*Saluting* AMANDA *and*   110
BERINTHIA.)   Ladies, by your leave. —— Ha ——
they bill like turtles.   Udsookers, they set my old
blood afire; I shall cuckold somebody before
morning.

LORD FOP. (*to* SIR TUNBELLY).   Sir, you be-   115
ing master of the entertainment, will you desire the
company to sit?

SIR TUN. Oons, sir, —— I'm the happiest man on
this side the Ganges.

LORD FOP. (*aside*).   This is a mighty unac-   120
countable old fellow.   (*To* SIR TUNBELLY.)   I said,
sir, it would be convenient to ask the company to sit.

SIR TUN. Sit? —— with all my heart. —— Come,
take your places, ladies; take your places, gentlemen:
come, sit down, sit down; a pox of ceremony,   125
take your places.   (*They sit, and the masque begins.*)

DIALOGUE BETWEEN CUPID AND HYMEN.

CUPID.   1.

Thou bane to my empire, thou spring of contest,
Thou source of all discord, thou period to rest;
Instruct me what wretches in bondage can see,
That the aim of their life is still pointed to thee.   130

HYMEN.   2.

Instruct me, thou little impertinent god,
From whence all thy subjects have taken the mode
To grow fond of a change, to whatever it be,
And I'll tell thee why those would be bound, who
    are free.

Chorus.

For change, we're for change, to whatever it be,   135
We are neither contented with freedom nor thee.
   Constancy's an empty sound.
   Heaven and earth and all go round;
   All the works of nature move,
   And the joys of life and love   140
     Are in variety.

CUPID.   3.

Were love the reward of a painstaking life,
Had a husband the art to be fond of his wife,
Were virtue so plenty, a wife could afford,
These very hard times, to be true to her lord;   145
Some specious account might be given of those
Who are tied by the tail, to be led by the nose.

67] Q2 *drawn to*; P *down to.*   69] P *call 'em.*   73] P *folks.*   89] Q1Q2 *give you a*; P *give a.*
89] Q2P *thousand.*   118-119] Q2 *one this.*

4.

But since 'tis the fate of a man and his wife
To consume all their days in contention and
    strife:
Since whatever the bounty of heaven may create
    her,   150
He's morally sure he shall heartily hate her;
I think 'twere much wiser to ramble at large,
And the volleys of love on the herd to discharge.

HYMEN.   5.

Some color of reason thy counsel might bear,
Could a man have no more than his wife to his
    share: 155
Or were I a monarch so cruelly just,
To oblige a poor wife to be true to her trust;
But I have not pretended, for many years past,
By marrying of people, to make 'em grow chaste.

6.

I therefore advise thee to let me go on,   160
Thou'lt find I'm the strength and support of thy
    throne;
For hadst [thou] but eyes, thou wouldst quickly per-
    ceive it,
    How smoothly thy dart
    Slips into the heart
    Of a woman that's wed;   165
    Whilst the shivering maid
Stands trembling, and wishing, but dare not receive
    it.

Chorus.

For change, *etc.*

The masque ended, enter YOUNG FASHION,
    COUPLER, *and* BULL.

SIR TUN. So, very fine, very fine, i'faith; this is
something like a wedding; now if supper were   170
but ready, I'd say a short grace; and if I had such a
bedfellow as Hoyden tonight —— I'd say as short
prayers. (*Seeing* YOUNG FASHION.) How now
—— what have we got here? a ghost? Nay, it must
be so, for his flesh and his blood could never   175
have dared to appear before me. (*To him.*) Ah,
rogue ——!
LORD FOP. Stap my vitals, Tam again.
SIR TUN. My lord, will you cut his throat? or
shall I?   180
LORD FOP. Leave him to me, sir, if you please.
—— Prithee, Tam, be so ingenuous, now, as to tell
me what thy business is here?
Y. FAS. 'Tis with your bride.
LORD FOP. Thau art the impudent'st fellow   185

that nature has yet spawned into the warld, strike
me speechless.
Y. FAS. Why, you know my modesty would have
starved me; I sent it a-begging to you, and you would
not give it a groat.   190
LORD FOP. And dost thau expect by an excess of
assurance to extart a maintenance fram me?
Y. FAS. (*taking* MISS HOYDEN *by the hand*). I do
intend to extort your mistress from you, and that I
hope will prove one.   195
LORD FOP. I ever thaught Newgate or Bedlam [1]
would be his fartune, and naw his fate's decided.
Prithee, Loveless, dost know of ever a mad doctor
hard by?
Y. FAS. There's one at your elbow will cure   200
you presently. (*To* BULL.) Prithee, doctor, take
him in hand quickly.
LORD FOP. Shall I beg the favor of you, sir, to
pull your fingers out of my wife's hand?
Y. FAS. His wife! Look you there; now I   205
hope you are all satisfied he's mad?
LORD FOP. Naw is it not passible far me to
penetrate what species of fally it is thau art driving
at.
SIR TUN. Here, here, here, let me beat out   210
his brains, and that will decide all.
LORD FOP. No, pray, sir, hold: we'll destray him
presently accarding to law.
Y. FAS. (*to* BULL). Nay, then advance, doctor;
come, you are a man of conscience; answer   215
boldly to the questions I shall ask: did not you marry
me to this young lady, before ever that gentleman
there saw her face?
BULL. Since the truth must out, I did.
Y. FAS. Nurse, sweet nurse, were not you a   220
witness to it?
NURSE. Since my conscience bids me speak —
I was.
Y. FAS. (*to* MISS HOYDEN). Madam, am not I
your lawful husband?   225
MISS. Truly I can't tell, but you married me first.
Y. FAS. Now I hope you are all satisfied?
SIR TUN. (*offering to strike him, is held by* LOVE-
LESS *and* WORTHY). Oons and thunder, you lie.
LORD FOP. Pray, sir, be calm: the battle is   230
in disarder, but requires more canduct than courage
to rally our forces. —— Pray, dactar, one word with
you. (*To* BULL *aside.*) Look you, sir, though I will
not presume to calculate your notions of damnation
fram the description you give us of hell, yet   235
since there is at least a passibility you may have a
pitchfark thrust in your backside, methinks it should
not be worth your while to risk your saul in the next

---

[1] Prison or the insane asylum.

162] Q1 *thru*; Q2P *thou.*   163] Q2P *the dart.*   175] Q2P *and blood.*   206] Q2P *mad.*   208] P *thou.*
213] Q2P *according.*

warld for the sake of a beggarly yaunger brather who is nat able to make your bady happy in this.   240

BULL. Alas! my lord, I have no worldly ends; I speak the truth, heaven knows.

LORD FOP. Nay, prithee, never engage heaven in the matter, far, by all I can see, 'tis like to prove a business for the devil.   245

Y. FAS. Come, pray, sir, all above-board: no corrupting of evidences, if you please; this young lady is my lawful wife, and I'll justify it in all the courts of England; so your lordship (who always had a passion for variety) may go seek a new   250 mistress, if you think fit.

LORD FOP. I am struck dumb with his impudence, and cannot passitively tell whether ever I shall speak again or nat.

SIR TUN. Then let me come and examine the   255 business a little: I'll jerk the truth out of 'em presently; here, give me my dog-whip.

Y. FAS. Look you, old gentleman, 'tis in vain to make a noise; if you grow mutinous, I have some friends within call, have swords by their sides   260 above four foot long; therefore be calm, hear the evidence patiently, and when the jury have given their verdict, pass sentence according to law: here's honest Coupler shall be foreman, and ask as many questions as he pleases.   265

COUP. All I have to ask is whether nurse persists in her evidence? The parson, I dare swear, will never flinch from his.

NURSE (to SIR TUNBELLY, kneeling). I hope in heaven your worship will pardon me; I have   270 served you long and faithfully, but in this thing I was over-reached; your worship, however, was deceived as well as I, and if the wedding-dinner had been ready, you had put madam to bed to him with your own hands.   275

SIR TUN. But how durst you do this, without acquainting of me?

NURSE. Alas! if your worship had seen how the poor thing begged, and prayed, and clung, and twined about me, like ivy to an old wall, you   280 would say I, who had suckled it, and swaddled it, and nursed it both wet and dry, must have had a heart of adamant to refuse it.

SIR TUN. Very well!

Y. FAS. Foreman, I expect your verdict.   285

COUP. Ladies and gentlemen, what's your opinions?

ALL. A clear case, a clear case.

COUP. Then, my young folks, I wish you joy.

SIR TUN. (to YOUNG FASHION). Come   290 hither, stripling; if it be true, then, that thou hast married my daughter, prithee tell me who thou art?

Y. FAS. Sir, the best of my condition is, I am your son-in-law; and the worst of it is, I am brother to that noble peer there.   295

SIR TUN. Art thou brother to that noble peer? —— Why then, that noble peer, and thee, and thy wife, and the nurse, and the priest —— may all go and be damned together.   Exit SIR TUNBELLY.

LORD FOP. (aside). Now, for my part, I   300 think the wisest thing a man can do with an aching heart, is to put on a serene countenance, for a philosophical air is the most becoming thing in the world to the face of a person of quality; I will therefore bear my disgrace like a great man, and let   305 the people see I am above an affront. (To YOUNG FASHION.) Dear Tam, since things are thus fallen aut, prithee give me leave to wish thee jay: I do it de bon cœur,[1] strike me dumb: you have married a woman beautiful in her person, charming in her airs,   310 prudent in her canduct, canstant in her inclinations, and of a nice marality, split my windpipe.

Y. FAS. Your lordship may keep up your spirits with your grimace, if you please; I shall support mine with this lady and two thousand pound   315 a year.

(Taking MISS HOYDEN.) Come, madam:
We once again, you see, are man and wife,
And now, perhaps, the bargain's struck for life;
If I mistake, and we should part again,   320
At least you see you may have choice of men:
Nay, should the war at length such havoc make
That lovers should grow scarce, yet for your sake,
Kind heaven always will preserve a beau:
(Pointing to LORD FOPPINGTON).
You'll find his lordship ready to come to.[2]   325

LORD FOP. Her ladyship shall stap my vitals if I do.

[1] Heartily.
[2] To be reconciled.

EPILOGUE

Spoken by Lord Foppington.

Gentlemen and ladies,
These people have regaled you here today
(In my opinion) with a saucy play;
In which the author does presume to show
That coxcomb, *ab origine* — was beau.   5
Truly I think the thing of so much weight, ⎫
That if some sharp chastisement ben't his fate, ⎬
Gad's curse, it may in time destroy the state. ⎭
I hold no one its friend, I must confess,
Who would discauntenance your men of dress.   10
Far, give me leave t'adserve, good clothes are things
Have ever been of great support to kings:
All treasons come fram slovens; it is not
Within the reach of gentle beaux to plat;
They have no gall, no spleen, no teeth, no stings,   15
Of all Gad's creatures, the most harmless things.
Through all recard, no prince was ever slain
By one who had a feather in his brain.
They're men of too refined an education,
To squabble with a court — for a vile dirty nation.   20
I'm very pasitive, you never saw
A through[1] republican a finished beau.
Nor truly shall you very often see
A Jacobite much better dressed than he:
In shart, through all the courts that I have been in,   25
Your men of mischief — still are in faul linen.
Did ever one yet dance the Tyburn jig[2]
With a free air, or a well pawdered wig?
Did ever highway-man yet bid you stand
With a sweet bawdy snuff-bax in his hand;   30
Ar do you ever find they ask your purse
As men of breeding do? — Ladies, Gad's curse,
This author is a dag, and 'tis not fit
You should allow him ev'n one grain of wit.
To which, that his pretence may ne'er be named,   35
My humble motion is —— he may be damned.

[1] Thorough.   [2] Suffer death by hanging.

10] P *you men.*

The Way of the World

BY WILLIAM CONGREVE

THE
Way of the World,
A
COMEDY.

As it is ACTED
AT THE
Theatre in *Lincoln's-Inn-Fields*,
BY
His Majefty's Servants.

Written by Mr. *CONGREVE*.

Audire eſt Operæ pretium, procedere recte
Qui mæchis non vultis ———   Hor. Sat. 2. l. 1.
———*Metuat doti deprenſa.* ———   Ibid.

LONDON:
Printed for *Jacob Tonſon*, within *Gray's-Inn-Gate* next
Gray's-Inn-Lane. 1700.

TITLE-PAGE OF FIRST EDITION, 1700, OF *THE WAY OF THE WORLD*

DEDICATION

To the Right Honorable Ralph, Earl of Mountague, &c.

My Lord,

Whether the world will arraign me of vanity, or not, that I have presumed to dedicate this comedy to your Lordship, I am yet in doubt; though it may be it is some degree of vanity even to doubt of it. One who has at any time had the honor of your Lordship's conversation cannot be supposed to think very meanly of that which he would prefer to your perusal; yet it were to incur the imputation of too much sufficiency, to pretend to such a merit as might abide the test of your Lordship's censure.

Whatever value may be wanting to this play while yet it is mine will be sufficiently made up to it when it is once become your Lordship's; and it is my security, that I cannot have overrated it more by my dedication, than your Lordship will dignify it by your patronage.

That it succeeded on the stage was almost beyond my expectation;[1] for but little of it was prepared for that general taste which seems now to be predominant in the palates of our audience.

Those characters which are meant to be ridiculous* in most of our comedies are of fools so gross that, in my humble opinion, they should rather disturb than divert the well-natured and reflecting part of an audience; they are rather objects of charity than contempt; and instead of moving our mirth, they ought very often to excite our compassion.

This reflection moved me to design some characters, which should appear ridiculous, not so much through a natural folly (which is incorrigible, and therefore not proper for the stage) as through an affected wit; a wit, which at the same time that it is affected, is also false. As there is some difficulty in the formation of a character of this nature, so there is some hazard which attends the progress of its success upon the stage: for many come to a play, so overcharged with criticism, that they very often let fly their censure, when through their rashness they have mistaken their aim. This I had occasion lately to observe: for this play had been acted two or three days, before some of these hasty judges could find the leisure to distinguish betwixt the character of a Witwoud and a Truewit.

I must beg your Lordship's pardon for this digression from the true course of this epistle; but that it may not seem altogether impertinent, I beg that I may plead the occasion of it, in part of that excuse of which I stand in need, for recommending this comedy to your protection. It is only by the countenance of your Lordship, and the *few* so qualified, that such who write with care and pains can hope to be distinguished: for the prostituted name of *poet*[2] promiscuously levels all that bear it.

Terence, the most correct writer in the world, had a Scipio and a Lælius, if not to assist him, at least to support him in his reputation: and notwithstanding his extraordinary merit, it may be their countenance was not more than necessary.

The purity of his style, the delicacy of his turns, and the justness of his characters, were all of them beauties which the greater part of his audience were incapable of tasting; some of the coarsest strokes of Plautus, so severely censured by Horace, were more likely to affect the multitude; such, who come with expectation to laugh out† the last act of a play, and are better entertained with two or three unseasonable jests, than with the artful solution of the *fable*.

As Terence excelled in his performances, so had he great advantages to encourage his undertakings; for he built most on the foundations of Menander: his plots were generally modelled, and his characters ready drawn to his hand. He copied Menander; and Menander had no less light in the formation of his characters, from the observations of Theophrastus, of whom he was a disciple; and Theophrastus, it is known, was not only the disciple, but the immediate successor of Aristotle, the first and greatest judge of poetry. These were great models to design by; and the further advantage which Terence possessed, towards giving his plays the due ornaments of purity of style, and justness of manners, was not less considerable from the freedom of conversation, which was permitted him with Lælius and Scipio, two of the greatest and most polite men of his age. And indeed, the privilege of such a conversation is the only certain means of attaining to the perfection of dialogue.

---

[1] As a matter of fact, the play was a failure at its first performance; cf. the general tone of the dedication and the prologue.
[2] In the older sense (common in the seventeenth century) of "creative writer," without regard to whether the medium were prose or verse.

---

* Q2W1 *ridiculed.*
† W1 *at.*

DEDICATION

If it has happened in any part of this comedy, that I have gained a turn of style, or expression more correct, or at least more corrigible, than in those which I have formerly written, I must, with equal pride and gratitude, ascribe it to the honor of your Lordship's admitting me into your conversation, and that of a society where everybody else was so well worthy of you, in your retirement last summer from the town; for it was immediately after that this comedy was written. If I have failed in my performance, it is only to be regretted, where there were so many, not inferior either to a Scipio or a Lælius, that there should be one wanting equal to the capacity of a Terence.*

If I am not mistaken, poetry is almost the only art which has not yet laid claim to your Lordship's patronage. Architecture, and painting, to the great honor of our country, have flourished under your influence and protection. In the mean time, poetry, the eldest sister of all arts, and parent of most, seems to have resigned her birthright, by having neglected to pay her duty to your Lordship, and by permitting others of a later extraction to prepossess that place in your esteem, to which none can pretend a better title. Poetry, in its nature, is sacred to the good and great; the relation between them is reciprocal, and they are ever propitious to it. It is the privilege of poetry to address to them, and it is their prerogative alone to give it protection.

This received maxim is a general apology for all writers who consecrate their labors to great men: but I could wish at this time, that this address were exempted from the common pretence of all dedications; and that as I can distinguish your Lordship even among the most deserving, so this offering might become remarkable by some particular instance of respect, which should assure your Lordship that I am, with all due sense of your extreme worthiness, and humanity, my Lord, your Lordship's most obedient and most obliged humble servant,

WILL. CONGREVE.

---

* WI *equal in capacity to a Terence.*

PROLOGUE

Spoken by Mr. Betterton.[1]

Of those few fools, who with ill stars are cursed,
Sure scribbling fools, called poets, fare the worst;
For they're a sort of fools which Fortune makes,
And, after she has made 'em fools, forsakes.
With Nature's oafs 'tis quite a diff'rent case,
For Fortune favors all her idiot race;
In her own nest the cuckoo-eggs we find,
O'er which she broods to hatch the changeling kind.
No portion for her own she has to spare,
So much she dotes on her adopted care.   10
 Poets are bubbles, by the town drawn in,
Suffered at first some trifling stakes to win;
But what unequal hazards do they run!
Each time they write they venture all they've won;
The squire that's buttered [2] still is sure to be undone.   15
This author, heretofore, has found your favor,
But pleads no merit from his past behavior.
To build on that might prove a vain presumption,
Should grants to poets made admit resumption;
And in Parnassus he must lose his seat   20
If that be found a forfeited estate.
 He owns, with toil he wrote the following scenes,
But if they're naught ne'er spare him for his pains.
Damn him the more: have no commiseration
For dullness on mature deliberation.   25
He swears he'll not resent one hissed-off scene,
Nor, like those peevish wits, his play maintain,
Who, to assert their sense, your taste arraign.
Some plot we think he has, and some new thought,
Some humor, too, no farce — but that's a fault.   30
Satire, he thinks, you ought not to expect:
For so reformed a town who dares correct?
To please this time has been his sole pretense;
He'll not instruct, lest it should give offense.
Should he by chance a knave or fool expose   35
That hurts none here; sure here are none of those.
In short, our play shall (with your leave to show it)
Give you one instance of a passive poet,
Who to your judgments yields all resignation:
So save or damn, after your own discretion.

---

[1] In the part of Fainall.

[2] Is induced to 'pyramid' his bets. Cf. Addison (*Freeholder* No. 40): 'It is a fine simile in one of Congreve's prologues which compares a writer to a "buttering" gamester, that stakes all his winning upon one cast; so that if he loses the last throw he is sure to be undone.' Congreve, however, uses the verb in the passive mood.

PERSONÆ DRAMATIS

MEN

FAINALL, in love with MRS. MARWOOD

[EDWARD] MIRABELL, in love with MRS. MILLAMANT

[ANTHONY] WITWOUD, } followers of MRS. MILLA-
PETULANT, } MANT

SIR WILFULL WITWOUD, half-brother to WITWOUD, and nephew to LADY WISHFORT

WAITWELL, servant to MIRABELL

WOMEN

LADY WISHFORT, enemy to MIRABELL, for having falsely pretended love to her

MRS. MILLAMANT, a fine lady, niece to LADY WISHFORT, and loves MIRABELL

MRS. MARWOOD, friend to MR. FAINALL, and likes MIRABELL

MRS. [ARABELLA] FAINALL, daughter to LADY WISHFORT, and wife to FAINALL, formerly frienc' to MIRABELL

FOIBLE, woman to LADY WISHFORT

MINCING, woman to MRS. MILLAMANT

[BETTY, servant in a chocolate-house]

[PEG, servant to LADY WISHFORT]

Dancers, Footmen, and Attendants

SCENE: LONDON

The time equal to that of the presentation.[1]

[1] I.e., 'Time, the present.'

THE WAY OF THE WORLD

By WILLIAM CONGREVE.

ACT I

SCENE I

A chocolate-house.

MIRABELL *and* FAINALL, *rising from cards.*
BETTY *waiting.*

MIRA. You are a fortunate man, Mr. Fainall.

FAIN. Have we done?

MIRA. What you please. I'll play on to entertain you.

FAIN. No, I'll give you your revenge another 5 time, when you are not so indifferent; you are thinking of something else now, and play too negligently; the coldness of a losing gamester lessens the pleasure of the winner: I'd no more play with a man that slighted his ill fortune, than I'd make love to a 10 woman who undervalued the loss of her reputation.

MIRA. You have a taste extremely delicate, and are for refining on your pleasures.

FAIN. Prithee, why so reserved? Something has put you out of humor. 15

MIRA. Not at all: I happen to be grave today; and you are gay; that's all.

FAIN. Confess, Millamant and you quarrelled last night, after I left you; my fair cousin has some humors that would tempt the patience of a 20 Stoic. What! some coxcomb came in, and was well received by her, while you were by.

MIRA. Witwoud and Petulant; and what was worse, her aunt, your wife's mother, my evil genius; or to sum up all in her own name, my old Lady 25 Wishfort came in.

FAIN. Oh, there it is then! She has a lasting passion for you, and with reason. What! then my wife was there?

MIRA. Yes, and Mrs. Marwood and three or 30 four more, whom I never saw before; seeing me, they all put on their grave faces, whispered one another, then complained aloud of the vapors, and after fell into a profound silence.

FAIN. They had a mind to be rid of you. 35

MIRA. For which reason I resolved not to stir. At last the good old lady broke through her painful taciturnity, with an invective against long visits. I would not have understood her, but Millamant joining in the argument, I rose and with a con- 40 strained smile told her I thought nothing was so easy as to know when a visit began to be troublesome; she reddened and I withdrew, without expecting [1] her reply.

FAIN. You were to blame to resent what she 45 spoke only in compliance with her aunt.

MIRA. She is more mistress of herself than to be under the necessity of such a resignation.

FAIN. What? though half her fortune depends upon her marrying with my lady's approbation? 50

MIRA. I was then in such a humor, that I should have been better pleased if she had been less discreet.

FAIN. Now I remember, I wonder not they were weary of you; last night was one of their cabal- 55 nights; they have 'em three times a week, and meet by turns, at one another's apartments, where they come together like the coroner's inquest, to sit upon the murdered reputations of the week. You and I are excluded; and it was once proposed that all 60 the male sex should be excepted; but somebody moved that to avoid scandal there might be one man of the community; upon which motion Witwoud and Petulant were enrolled members.

MIRA. And who may have been the foundress 65 of this sect? My Lady Wishfort, I warrant, who publishes her detestation of mankind; and full of the vigor of fifty-five, declares for a friend and ratafia; [2] and let posterity shift for itself, she'll breed no more. 70

FAIN. The discovery of your sham addresses to her, to conceal your love to her niece, has provoked this separation: had you dissembled better, things might have continued in the state of nature.

MIRA. I did as much as man could, with any 75 reasonable conscience; I proceeded to the very last act of flattery with her, and was guilty of a song in her commendation. Nay, I got a friend to put her into a lampoon, and compliment her with the imputation of an affair with a young fellow, which 80 I carried so far, that I told her the malicious town took notice that she was grown fat of a sudden; and when she lay in of a dropsy, persuaded her she was reported to be in labor. The devil's in't, if an old woman is to be flattered further, unless a man 85 should endeavor downright personally to debauch her; and that my virtue forbade me. But for the discovery of that amour, I am indebted to your friend, or your wife's friend, Mrs. Marwood.

---

[1] Awaiting. [2] A variety of brandy.

FAIN. What should provoke her to be your 90
enemy, without she has made you advances, which
you have slighted? Women do not easily forgive
omissions of that nature.

MIRA. She was always civil to me, till of late.
I confess I am not one of those coxcombs who are 95
apt to interpret a woman's good manners to her
prejudice; and think that she who does not refuse
'em everything, can refuse 'em nothing.

FAIN. You are a gallant man, Mirabell; and
though you may have cruelty enough not to 100
satisfy a lady's longing, you have too much generosity not to be tender of her honor. Yet you
speak with an indifference which seems to be affected; and confesses you are conscious of a negligence. 105

MIRA. You pursue the argument with a distrust
that seems to be unaffected, and confesses you are
conscious of a concern for which the lady is more
indebted to you than your wife.

FAIN. Fie, fie, friend, if you grow censorious 110
I must leave you. I'll look upon the gamesters in
the next room.

MIRA. Who are they?

FAIN. Petulant and Witwoud. [*To* BETTY.]
Bring me some chocolate. *Exit.* 115

MIRA. Betty, what says your clock?

BET. Turned of the last canonical hour,[1] sir.

MIRA. How pertinently the jade answers me!
Ha! almost one o'clock! (*Looking on his watch.*)
Oh, y'are come —— 120

Enter a Servant.

Well, is the grand affair over? You have been something tedious.

SERV. Sir, there's such coupling at Pancras,[2] that
they stand behind one another, as 'twere in a
country dance. Ours was the last couple to 125
lead up; and no hopes appearing of dispatch, besides,
the parson growing hoarse, we were afraid his lungs
would have failed before it came to our turn; so we
drove round to Duke's Place; and there they were
riveted in a trice. 130

MIRA. So, so, you are sure they are married.

SERV. Married and bedded, sir: I am witness.

MIRA. Have you the certificate?

SERV. Here it is, sir.

MIRA. Has the tailor brought Waitwell's 135
clothes home, and the new liveries?

[1] Past twelve o'clock. (The canonical hours, during which
marriages might legally be performed, were, at this date, from
eight to twelve in the morning.)
[2] St. Pancras Church, as well as St. James's, Duke's Place,
referred to just below, were two of several places in which
marriages could be celebrated without special license or publication of banns.

SERV. Yes, sir.

MIRA. That's well. Do you go home again, d'ee
hear, and adjourn the consummation till farther
order; bid Waitwell shake his ears, and Dame 140
Partlet[3] rustle up her feathers, and meet me at one
o'clock by Rosamond's Pond;[4] that I may see her
before she returns to her lady; and as you tender[5]
your ears be secret. *Exit Servant.*

Re-enter FAINALL.

FAIN. Joy of your success, Mirabell; you 145
look pleased.

MIRA. Ay; I have been engaged in a matter of
some sort of mirth, which is not yet ripe for discovery. I am glad this is not a cabal-night. I
wonder, Fainall, that you who are married, and 150
of consequence should be discreet, will suffer your
wife to be of such a party.

FAIN. Faith, I am not jealous. Besides, most
who are engaged are women and relations; and for
the men, they are of a kind too contemptible to 155
give scandal.

MIRA. I am of another opinion. The greater the
coxcomb, always the more the scandal: for a woman
who is not a fool, can have but one reason for as-
sociating with a man that is. 160

FAIN. Are you jealous as often as you see Witwoud entertained by Millamant?

MIRA. Of her understanding I am, if not of her
person.

FAIN. You do her wrong; for to give her her 165
due, she has wit.

MIRA. She has beauty enough to make any man
think so, and complaisance enough not to contradict
him who shall tell her so.

FAIN. For a passionate lover, methinks you 170
are a man somewhat too discerning in the failings
of your mistress.

MIRA. And for a discerning man, somewhat too
passionate a lover; for I like her with all her faults;
nay, like her for her faults. Her follies are so 175
natural, or so artful, that they become her; and
those affectations which in another woman would
be odious, serve but to make her more agreeable.
I'll tell thee, Fainall, she once used me with that
insolence, that in revenge I took her to pieces; 180
sifted her and separated her failings; I studied 'em,
and got 'em by rote. The catalogue was so large,
that I was not without hopes, one day or other, to
hate her heartily: to which end I so used myself to
think of 'em, that at length, contrary to my 185
design and expectation, they gave me every hour

[3] The wife of Chantecleer in the tale of the cock and the fox.
[4] A small pond in St. James's Park.
[5] Have regard for.

less and less disturbance; till in a few days it became habitual to me to remember 'em without being displeased. They are now grown as familiar to me as my own frailties; and in all probability in a   190 little time longer I shall like 'em as well.

FAIN. Marry her, marry her; be half as well acquainted with her charms as you are with her defects, and my life on't, you are your own man again.

MIRA. Say you so?   195

FAIN. Ay, ay; I have experience: I have a wife, and so forth.

Enter Messenger.

MESS. Is one Squire Witwoud here?

BET. Yes; what's your business?

MESS. I have a letter for him, from his   200 brother, Sir Wilfull, which I am charged to deliver into his own hands.

BET. He's in the next room, friend — that way.

Exit Messenger.

MIRA. What, is the chief of that noble family in town, Sir Wilfull Witwoud?   205

FAIN. He is expected to-day. Do you know him?

MIRA. I have seen him; he promises to be an extraordinary person; I think you have the honor to be related to him.

FAIN. Yes; he is half-brother to this Wit-   210 woud by a former wife, who was sister to my Lady Wishfort, my wife's mother. If you marry Millamant, you must call cousins too.

MIRA. I had rather be his relation than his acquaintance.   215

FAIN. He comes to town in order to equip himself for travel.

MIRA. For travel! Why the man that I mean is above forty.[1]

FAIN. No matter for that; 'tis for the honor   220 of England, that all Europe should know we have blockheads of all ages.

MIRA. I wonder there is not an act of Parliament to save the credit of the nation, and prohibit the exportation of fools.   225

FAIN. By no means, 'tis better as 'tis; 'tis better to trade with a little loss, than to be quite eaten up, with being overstocked.

MIRA. Pray, are the follies of this knight-errant, and those of the squire his brother, anything   230 related?

FAIN. Not at all; Witwoud grows by the knight, like a medlar grafted on a crab.[2] One will melt in your mouth, and t'other set your teeth on edge; one is all pulp, and the other all core.   235

MIRA. So one will be rotten before he be ripe, and the other will be rotten without ever being ripe at all.

FAIN. Sir Wilfull is an odd mixture of bashfulness and obstinacy. But when he's drunk, he's   240 as loving as the monster in *The Tempest;*[3] and much after the same manner. To give the t'other his due, he has something of good nature, and does not always want wit.

MIRA. Not always; but as often as his mem-   245 ory fails him, and his commonplace of comparisons. He is a fool with a good memory, and some few scraps of other folks' wit. He is one whose conversation can never be approved, yet it is now and then to be endured. He has indeed one good   250 quality, he is not exceptious; for he so passionately affects the reputation of understanding raillery, that he will construe an affront into a jest; and call downright rudeness and ill language, satire and fire.   255

FAIN. If you have a mind to finish his picture, you have an opportunity to do it at full length. Behold the original.

Enter WITWOUD.

WIT. Afford me your compassion, my dears; pity me, Fainall, Mirabell, pity me.   260

MIRA. I do from my soul.

FAIN. Why, what's the matter?

WIT. No letters for me, Betty?

BET. Did not the messenger bring you one but now, sir?   265

WIT. Ay, but no other?

BET. No, sir.

WIT. That's hard, that's very hard; — a messenger, a mule, a beast of burden: he has brought me a letter from the fool my brother, as heavy   270 as a panegyric in a funeral sermon, or a copy of commendatory verses from one poet to another. And what's worse, 'tis as sure a forerunner of the author, as an epistle dedicatory.

MIRA. A fool, and your brother, Witwoud!   275

WIT. Ay, ay, my half-brother. My half-brother he is, no nearer upon honor.

MIRA. Then 'tis possible he may be but half a fool.

WIT. Good, good, Mirabell, *le drôle!*[4] Good,   280 good! — hang him, don't let's talk of him. — Fainall, how does your lady? Gad, I say anything in the world to get this fellow out of my head. I beg pardon that I should ask a man of pleasure, and the

---

[1] The usual time for a young English gentleman to make the 'grand tour' of Europe was immediately after completing his stay at Oxford or Cambridge.

[2] A medlar (a soft, pulpy fruit) grafted on a crabapple.

[3] Probably referring to Caliban's conduct in II. ii.; Summers suggests that the reference is to Sycorax, Caliban's sister, an added character in the revised version of *The Tempest* by Dryden and D'Avenant.

[4] Witty fellow.

town, a question at once so foreign and domes- 285
tic. But I talk like an old maid at a marriage, I
don't know what I say: but she's the best woman in
the world.

FAIN. 'Tis well you don't know what you say, or
else your commendation would go near to make 290
me either vain or jealous.

WIT. No man in town lives well with a wife but
Fainall. Your judgment, Mirabell.

MIRA. You had better step and ask his wife, if you
would be credibly informed.   295

WIT. Mirabell.

MIRA. Ay.

WIT. My dear, I ask ten thousand pardons. —
Gad, I have forgot what I was going to say to you.

MIRA. I thank you heartily, heartily.   300

WIT. No, but prithee excuse me — my memory
is such a memory.

MIRA. Have a care of such apologies, Witwoud;
for I never knew a fool but he affected to complain,
either of the spleen or his memory.   305

FAIN. What have you done with Petulant?

WIT. He's reckoning his money — my money it
was; I have no luck today.

FAIN. You may allow him to win of you at play,
for you are sure to be too hard for him at re- 310
partee: since you monopolize the wit that is between
you, the fortune must be his of course.

MIRA. I don't find that Petulant confesses the
superiority of wit to be your talent, Witwoud.

WIT. Come, come, you are malicious now, 315
and would breed debates. Petulant's my friend,
and a very honest fellow, and a very pretty fellow,
and has a smattering — faith and troth, a pretty
deal of an odd sort of a small wit. Nay, I'll do him
justice. I'm his friend, I won't wrong him, 320
neither. And if he had but any judgment in the
world, he would not be altogether contemptible.
Come, come, don't detract from the merits of my
friend.

FAIN. You don't take your friend to be over- 325
nicely bred.

WIT. No, no, hang him, the rogue has no manners
at all, that I must own — no more breeding than a
bum-baily,[1] that I grant you. 'Tis pity, faith; the
fellow has fire and life.   330

MIRA. What, courage?

WIT. Hum, faith I don't know as to that — I
can't say as to that. Yes, faith, in a controversy
he'll contradict anybody.

MIRA. Though 'twere a man whom he feared, 335
or a woman whom he loved.

WIT. Well, well, he does not always think before
he speaks. We have all our failings; you're too hard

---

[1] A low type of bailiff or sheriff's officer.

upon him, you are, faith. Let me excuse him — I
can defend most of his faults, except one or 340
two; one he has, that's the truth on't, if he were my
brother, I could not acquit him. That, indeed, I
could wish were otherwise.

MIRA. Ay, marry, what's that, Witwoud?

WIT. Oh, pardon me! Expose the infirm- 345
ities of my friend? No, my dear, excuse me there.

FAIN. What! I warrant, he's unsincere, or 'tis
some such trifle.

WIT. No, no, what if he be? 'Tis no matter for
that, his wit will excuse that: a wit should no 350
more be sincere, than a woman constant; one argues
a decay of parts, as t'other of beauty.

MIRA. Maybe you think him too positive?

WIT. No, no, his being positive is an incentive to
argument, and keeps up conversation.   355

FAIN. Too illiterate.

WIT. That! that's his happiness. His want of
learning gives him the more opportunities to show
his natural parts.

MIRA. He wants words.   360

WIT. Ay; but I like him for that now; for his want
of words gives me the pleasure very often to explain
his meaning.

FAIN. He's impudent.

WIT. No, that's not it.   365

MIRA. Vain.

WIT. No.

MIRA. What, he speaks unseasonable truths
sometimes, because he has not wit enough to invent
an evasion!   370

WIT. Truths! Ha, ha, ha! No, no, since you
will have it — I mean, he never speaks truth at all —
that's all. He will lie like a chambermaid, or a
woman of quality's porter. Now that is a fault.

Enter Coachman.

COACH. Is Master Petulant here, mistress? 375

BET. Yes.

COACH. Three gentlewomen in the coach would
speak with him.

FAIN. O brave Petulant, three!

BET. I'll tell him.   380

COACH. You must bring two dishes of chocolate
and a glass of cinnamon-water.

[Exeunt BETTY and Coachman.]

WIT. That should be for two fasting strumpets,
and a bawd troubled with wind. Now you may
know what the three are.   385

MIRA. You are very free with your friend's
acquaintance.

WIT. Ay, ay, friendship without freedom is as
dull as love without enjoyment, or wine without
toasting; but to tell you a secret, these are 390
trulls that he allows coach-hire, and something more

by the week, to call on him once a day at public places.

MIRA. How!

WIT. You shall see he won't go to 'em be- 395 cause there's no more company here to take notice of him. Why, this is nothing to what he used to do; before he found out this way, I have known him call for himself ——

FAIN. Call for himself? What dost thou 400 mean?

WIT. Mean? — why, he would slip you out of this chocolate-house, just when you had been talking to him. As soon as your back was turned — whip he was gone; then trip to his lodging, clap on a 405 hood and scarf, and mask, slap into a hackney-coach, and drive hither to the door again in a trice; where he would send in for himself — that I mean — call for himself, wait for himself, nay and what's more, not finding himself, sometimes leave a letter 410 for himself.

MIRA. I confess this is something extraordinary — I believe he waits for himself now, he is so long a-coming. Oh, I ask his pardon!

Enter PETULANT [*and* BETTY].

BET. Sir, the coach stays. [*Exit.*] 415

PET. Well, well; I come. — 'Sbud,[1] a man had as good be a professed midwife as a professed whore-master, at this rate; to be knocked up and raised at all hours, and in all places! Pox on 'em, I won't come. — D'ee hear, tell 'em I won't come. Let 420 'em snivel and cry their hearts out.

FAIN. You are very cruel, Petulant.

PET. All's one, let it pass — I have a humor to be cruel.

MIRA. I hope they are not persons of con- 425 dition that you use at this rate.

PET. Condition! condition's a dried fig, if I am not in humor. By this hand, if they were your — a — a — your what-d'ee-call-'ems themselves, they must wait or rub off,[2] if I want appetite. 430

MIRA. What-d'ee-call-'ems! What are they, Witwoud?

WIT. Empresses, my dear — by your what-d'ee-call-'ems he means sultana queens.

PET. Ay, Roxolanas.[3] 435

MIRA. Cry you mercy.

FAIN. Witwoud says they are ——

PET. What does he say th'are?

WIT. I — fine ladies, I say.

PET. Pass on, Witwoud. — Hark 'ee, by this 440 light, his relations — two co-heiresses his cousins,

---

[1] A contraction of 'sbodikins, meaning 'God's dear body.'
[2] Go away.
[3] Roxolana is the wife of Solyman the Magnificent in D'Ave-nant's *The Siege of Rhodes.*

and an old aunt, that loves catterwauling better than a conventicle.

WIT. Ha, ha, ha! I had a mind to see how the rogue would come off. Ha, ha, ha! Gad I can't 445 be angry with him, if he said they were my mother and my sisters.

MIRA. No!

WIT. No; the rogue's wit and readiness of in-vention charm me: dear Petulant. 450

[Re-enter BETTY.]

BET. They are gone, sir, in great anger.

PET. Enough, let 'em trundle. Anger helps complexion, saves paint.

FAIN. This continence is all dissembled; this is in order to have something to brag of the next 455 time he makes court to Millamant, and swear he has abandoned the whole sex for her sake.

MIRA. Have you not left off your impudent pre-tensions there yet? I shall cut your throat, some-time or other, Petulant, about that business. 460

PET. Ay, ay, let that pass — there are other throats to be cut ——

MIRA. Meaning mine, sir?

PET. Not I — I mean nobody — I know nothing But there are uncles and nephews in the world 465 — and they may be rivals. What then? All's one for that ——

MIRA. How! Hark 'ee, Petulant, come hither. Explain, or I shall call your interpreter.

PET. Explain! I know nothing. Why you 470 have an uncle, have you not, lately come to town, and lodges by my Lady Wishfort's?

MIRA. True.

PET. Why, that's enough. You and he are not friends; and if he should marry and have a 475 child, you may be disinherited, ha?

MIRA. Where hast thou stumbled upon all this truth?

PET. All's one for that; why, then say I know something. 480

MIRA. Come, thou art an honest fellow, Petulant, and shalt make love to my mistress, thou sha't, faith. What hast thou heard of my uncle?

PET. I? nothing I. If throats are to be cut, let swords clash; snug's the word, I shrug and am 485 silent.

MIRA. O raillery, raillery. Come, I know thou art in the women's secrets. What, you're a cabalist; I know you stayed at Millamant's last night, after I went. Was there any mention made of my 490 uncle, or me? Tell me; if thou hadst but good na-ture equal to thy wit, Petulant, Tony Witwoud, who is now thy competitor in fame, would show as dim by thee as a dead whiting's eye by a pearl of Orient; he would no more be seen by thee,[4] than Mer- 495

---

[4] Beside thee.

cury is by the sun.   Come, I'm sure thou wo't tell me.

PET. If I do, will you grant me common sense then, for the future?

MIRA. Faith, I'll do what I can for thee;   500 and I'll pray that heaven may grant it thee in the meantime.

PET. Well, hark'ee.

[*They converse in dumb-show.*]

FAIN. Petulant and you both will find Mirabell as warm a rival as a lover.   505

WIT. Pshaw, pshaw, that she laughs at Petulant is plain.   And for my part — but that it is almost a fashion to admire her, I should — hark'ee — to tell you a secret, but let it go no further — between friends, I shall never break my heart for her.   510

FAIN. How!

WIT. She's handsome; but she's a sort of an uncertain woman.

FAIN. I thought you had died for her.

WIT. Umh — no ——   515

FAIN. She has wit.

WIT. 'Tis what she will hardly allow anybody else.   Now, demme, I should hate that, if she were as handsome as Cleopatra.   Mirabell is not so sure of her as he thinks for.   520

FAIN. Why do you think so?

WIT. We stayed pretty late there last night, and heard something of an uncle to Mirabell, who is lately come to town, — and is between him and the best part of his estate.   Mirabell and he are   525 at some distance, as my Lady Wishfort has been told; and you know she hates Mirabell, worse than a Quaker hates a parrot, or than a fishmonger hates a hard frost.   Whether this uncle has seen Mrs. Millamant or not, I cannot say; but there were   530 items of such a treaty being in embryo; and if it should come to life, poor Mirabell would be in some sort unfortunately fobbed[1] i'faith.

FAIN. 'Tis impossible Millamant should hearken to it.   535

WIT. Faith, my dear, I can't tell; she's a woman and a kind of a humorist.

MIRA. [*conversing apart with* PETULANT]. And this is the sum of what you could collect last night.

PET. The quintessence.   Maybe Witwoud   540 knows more, he stayed longer.   Besides, they never mind him; they say anything before him.

MIRA. I thought you had been the greatest favorite.

PET. Ay, *tête-à-tête;* but not in public, be-   545 cause I make remarks.

MIRA. Do you?

PET. Ay, ay; pox, I'm malicious, man.   Now, he's soft, you know; they are not in awe of him.   The fellow's well bred, he's what you call a —   550

[1] Imposed upon.

what-d'ee-call-'em.   A fine gentleman, but he's silly withal.

MIRA. I thank you, I know as much as my curi-osity requires. — Fainall, are you for the Mall?[2]

FAIN. Ay, I'll take a turn before dinner.   555

WIT. Ay, we'll all walk in the Park, the ladies talked of being there.

MIRA. I thought you were obliged to watch for your brother Sir Wilfull's arrival.

WIT. No, no, he comes to his aunt's, my   560 Lady Wishfort; pox on him, I shall be troubled with him too; what shall I do with the fool?

PET. Beg him for his estate, that I may beg you afterwards, and so have but one trouble with you both.   565

WIT. O rare Petulant! thou art as quick as a fire in a frosty morning; thou shalt to the Mall with us, and we'll be very severe.

PET. Enough! I'm in a humor to be severe.

MIRA. Are you?   Pray then walk by your-   570 selves — let not us be accessary to your putting the ladies out of countenance, with your senseless rib-aldry, which you roar out aloud as often as they pass by you; and when you have made a handsome woman blush, then you think you have been severe.   575

PET. What, what?   Then let 'em either show their innocence by not understanding what they hear, or else show their discretion by not hearing what they would not be thought to understand.

MIRA. But hast not thou then sense enough   580 to know that thou ought'st to be most ashamed thyself, when thou hast put another out of counte-nance?

PET. Not I, by this hand — I always take blush-ing either for a sign of guilt, or ill breeding.   585

MIRA. I confess you ought to think so.   You are in the right, that you may plead the error of your judgment in defence of your practice.

Where modesty's ill manners, 'tis but fit
That impudence and malice pass for wit.   590

Exeunt.

ACT II

SCENE I

St. James's Park.

Enter MRS. FAINALL *and* MRS. MARWOOD.

MRS. FAIN. Ay, ay, dear Marwood, if we will be happy, we must find the means in ourselves, and among ourselves.   Men are ever in extremes; either doting or averse.   While they are lovers, if they have fire and sense, their jealousies are insup-   5 portable: and when they cease to love, (we ought to think at least) they loathe; they look upon us

[2] In St. James's Park: cf. Witwoud's next speech.

with horror and distaste; they meet us like the ghosts of what we were, and as such, fly from us.

MRS. MAR. True, 'tis an unhappy circum- 10 stance of life, that love should ever die before us; and that the man so often should outlive the lover. But say what you will, 'tis better to be left, than never to have been loved. To pass our youth in dull indifference, to refuse the sweets of life be- 15 cause they once must leave us, is as preposterous as to wish to have been born old, because we one day must be old. For my part, my youth may wear and waste, but it shall never rust in my possession.

MRS. FAIN. Then it seems you dissemble an 20 aversion to mankind, only in compliance with my mother's humor.

MRS. MAR. Certainly. To be free; I have no taste of those insipid dry discourses, with which our sex of force must entertain themselves, apart 25 from men. We may affect endearments to each other, profess eternal friendships, and seem to dote like lovers; but 'tis not in our natures long to perse- vere. Love will resume his empire in our breasts, and every heart, or soon or late, receive and re- 30 admit him as its lawful tyrant.

MRS. FAIN. Bless me, how have I been deceived! Why, you profess a libertine.

MRS. MAR. You see my friendship by my free- dom. Come, be as sincere, acknowledge that 35 your sentiments agree with mine.

MRS. FAIN. Never.

MRS. MAR. You hate mankind.

MRS. FAIN. Heartily, inveterately.

MRS. MAR. Your husband. 40

MRS. FAIN. Most transcendently; ay, though I say it, meritoriously.

MRS. MAR. Give me your hand upon it.

MRS. FAIN. There.

MRS. MAR. I join with you; what I have said 45 has been to try you.

MRS. FAIN. Is it possible? Dost thou hate those vipers, men?

MRS. MAR. I have done hating 'em, and am now come to despise 'em; the next thing I have to 50 do, is eternally to forget 'em.

MRS. FAIN. There spoke the spirit of an Amazon, a Penthesilea.[1]

MRS. MAR. And yet I am thinking sometimes to carry my aversion further. 55

MRS. FAIN. How?

MRS. MAR. Faith, by marrying; if I could but find one that loved me very well, and would be thor- oughly sensible of ill usage, I think I should do my- self the violence of undergoing the ceremony. 60

MRS. FAIN. You would not make him a cuckold?

MRS. MAR. No; but I'd make him believe I did, and that's as bad.

MRS. FAIN. Why, had not you as good do it?

MRS. MAR. Oh, if he should ever discover it, 65 he would then know the worst, and be out of his pain; but I would have him ever to continue upon the rack of fear and jealousy.

MRS. FAIN. Ingenious mischief! Would thou wert married to Mirabell. 70

MRS. MAR. Would I were.

MRS. FAIN. You change color.

MRS. MAR. Because I hate him.

MRS. FAIN. So do I; but I can hear him named. But what reason have you to hate him in par- 75 ticular?

MRS. MAR. I never loved him; he is, and always was, insufferably proud.

MRS. FAIN. By the reason you give for your aversion, one would think it dissembled; for you 80 have laid a fault to his charge, of which his enemies must acquit him.

MRS. MAR. Oh, then it seems you are one of his favorable enemies. Methinks you look a little pale, and now you flush again. 85

MRS. FAIN. Do I? I think I am a little sick o' the sudden.

MRS. MAR. What ails you?

MRS. FAIN. My husband. Don't you see him? He turned short upon me unawares, and has 90 almost overcome me.

Enter FAINALL *and* MIRABELL.

MRS. MAR. Ha, ha, ha! he comes opportunely for you.

MRS. FAIN. For you, for he has brought Mira- bell with him. 95

FAIN. My dear.

MRS. FAIN. My soul.

FAIN. You don't look well today, child.

MRS. FAIN. D'ee think so?

MIRA. He is the only man that does, madam. 100

MRS. FAIN. The only man that would tell me so at least; and the only man from whom I could hear it without mortification.

FAIN. O my dear, I am satisfied of your tender- ness; I know you cannot resent anything from 105 me; especially what is an effect of my concern.

MRS. FAIN. Mr. Mirabell, my mother interrupted you in a pleasant relation last night: I would fain hear it out.

MIRA. The persons concerned in that affair 110 have yet a tolerable reputation. I am afraid Mr. Fainall will be censorious.

MRS. FAIN. He has a humor more prevailing than his curiosity, and will willingly dispense with the hearing of one scandalous story, to avoid giving 115

[1] Queen of the Amazons in the Trojan War.

an occasion to make another by being seen to walk
with his wife.   This way, Mr. Mirabell, and I dare
promise you will oblige us both.

Exeunt MRS. FAINALL *and* MIRABELL.

FAIN. Excellent creature! Well, sure if I should
live to be rid of my wife, I should be a miser-   120
able man.

MRS. MAR. Ay!

FAIN. For having only that one hope, the accomplishment of it, of consequence, must put an
end to all my hopes; and what a wretch is he   125
who must survive his hopes!   Nothing remains
when that day comes, but to sit down and weep like
Alexander, when he wanted other worlds to conquer.

MRS. MAR. Will you not follow 'em?

FAIN. Faith, I think not.   130

MRS. MAR. Pray let us; I have a reason.

FAIN. You are not jealous?

MRS. MAR. Of whom?

FAIN. Of Mirabell.

MRS. MAR. If I am, is it inconsistent with   135
my love to you that I am tender of your honor?

FAIN. You would intimate, then, as if there were
a fellow-feeling between my wife and him.

MRS. MAR. I think she does not hate him to that
degree she would be thought.   140

FAIN. But he, I fear, is too insensible.

MRS. MAR. It may be you are deceived.

FAIN. It may be so. I do now begin to apprehend
it.

MRS. MAR. What?   145

FAIN. That I have been deceived, madam, and
you are false.

MRS. MAR. That I am false! What mean you?

FAIN. To let you know I see through all your
little arts. Come, you both love him; and both   150
have equally dissembled your aversion. Your
mutual jealousies of one another have made you
clash till you have both struck fire. I have seen the
warm confession reddening on your cheeks, and
sparkling from your eyes.   155

MRS. MAR. You do me wrong.

FAIN. I do not. 'Twas for my ease to oversee
and wilfully neglect the gross advances made him
by my wife, that by permitting her to be engaged, I
might continue unsuspected in my pleasures,   160
and take you oftener to my arms in full security.
But could you think, because the nodding husband
would not wake, that e'er the watchful lover slept?

MRS. MAR. And wherewithal can you reproach
me?   165

FAIN. With infidelity, with loving of another,
with love of Mirabell.

MRS. MAR. 'Tis false. I challenge you to show
an instance that can confirm your groundless accusation. I hate him.   170

FAIN. And wherefore do you hate him? He is
insensible, and your resentment follows his neglect.
An instance? The injuries you have done him are
a proof: your interposing in his love. What cause
had you to make discoveries of his pretended   175
passion? To undeceive the credulous aunt, and be
the officious obstacle of his match with Millamant?

MRS. MAR. My obligations to my lady urged me:
I had professed a friendship to her; and could not
see her easy nature so abused by that dis-   180
sembler.

FAIN. What, was it conscience then? Professed
a friendship! Oh, the pious friendships of the
female sex!

MRS. MAR. More tender, more sincere, and   185
more enduring, than all the vain and empty vows
of men, whether professing love to us, or mutual
faith to one another.

FAIN. Ha, ha, ha! you are my wife's friend too.

MRS. MAR. Shame and ingratitude! Do   190
you reproach me? You, you upbraid me! Have I
been false to her, through strict fidelity to you, and
sacrificed my friendship to keep my love inviolate?
And have you the baseness to charge me with the
guilt, unmindful of the merit! To you it   195
should be meritorious, that I have been vicious:
and do you reflect that guilt upon me, which should
lie buried in your bosom?

FAIN. You misinterpret my reproof. I meant
but to remind you of the slight account you   200
once could make of strictest ties, when set in competition with your love to me.

MRS. MAR. 'Tis false, you urged it with deliberate
malice — 'twas spoke in scorn, and I never will
forgive it.   205

FAIN. Your guilt, not your resentment, begets
your rage. If yet you loved, you could forgive a
jealousy: but you are stung to find you are discovered.

MRS. MAR. It shall be all discovered. You   210
too shall be discovered; be sure you shall. I can
but be exposed. If I do it myself I shall prevent [1]
your baseness.

FAIN. Why, what will you do?

MRS. MAR. Disclose it to your wife; own   215
what has passed between us.

FAIN. Frenzy!

MRS. MAR. By all my wrongs I'll do't! — I'll
publish to the world the injuries you have done me,
both in my fame and fortune. With both I   220
trusted you, you bankrupt in honor, as indigent of
wealth!

FAIN. Your fame I have preserved. Your fortune
has been bestowed as the prodigality of your love
would have it, in pleasures which we both have   225

[1] Anticipate.

143] Q2W1 *I do not now.*

shared. Yet, had not you been false, I had e'er this repaid it. 'Tis true. Had you permitted Mirabell with Millamant to have stolen their marriage, my lady had been incensed beyond all means of reconcilement: Millamant had forfeited the moiety 230 of her fortune, which then would have descended to my wife; and wherefore did I marry, but to make lawful prize of a rich widow's wealth, and squander it on love and you?

MRS. MAR. Deceit and frivolous pretence! 235

FAIN. Death, am I not married? What's pretence? Am I not imprisoned, fettered? Have I not a wife? Nay, a wife that was a widow, a young widow, a handsome widow; and would be again a widow, but that I have a heart of proof, and 240 something of a constitution to bustle through the ways of wedlock and this world. Will you yet be reconciled to truth and me?

MRS. MAR. Impossible. Truth and you are inconsistent — I hate you, and shall forever. 245

FAIN. For loving you?

MRS. MAR. I loathe the name of love after such usage; and next to the guilt with which you would asperse me, I scorn you most. Farewell.

FAIN. Nay, we must not part thus. 250

MRS. MAR. Let me go.

FAIN. Come, I'm sorry.

MRS. MAR. I care not — let me go — break my hands, do — I'd leave 'em to get loose.

FAIN. I would not hurt you for the world. 255 Have I no other hold to keep you here?

MRS. MAR. Well, I have deserved it all.

FAIN. You know I love you.

MRS. MAR. Poor dissembling! — Oh, that — well, it is not yet —— 260

FAIN. What? What is it not? What is it not yet? It is not yet too late ——

MRS. MAR. No, it is not yet too late — I have that comfort.

FAIN. It is, to love another. 265

MRS. MAR. But not to loathe, detest, abhor mankind, myself, and the whole treacherous world.

FAIN. Nay, this is extravagance. Come, I ask your pardon — no tears — I was to blame, I could not love you and be easy in my doubts. — 270 Pray forbear — I believe you; I'm convinced I've done you wrong; and any way, every way will make amends; I'll hate my wife yet more, damn her, I'll part with her, rob her of all she's worth, and will retire somewhere, anywhere, to another world. 275 I'll marry thee — be pacified. — 'Sdeath, they come; hide your face, your tears. You have a mask, wear it a moment. This way, this way, be persuaded.   *Exeunt.*

Enter MIRABELL *and* MRS. FAINALL.

MRS. FAIN. They are here yet. 280

MIRA. They are turning into the other walk.

MRS. FAIN. While I only hated my husband, I could bear to see him; but since I have despised him, he's too offensive.

MIRA. Oh, you should hate with prudence. 285

MRS. FAIN. Yes, for I have loved with indiscretion.

MIRA. You should have just so much disgust for your husband as may be sufficient to make you relish your lover. 290

MRS. FAIN. You have been the cause that I have loved without bounds, and would you set limits to that aversion, of which you have been the occasion? Why did you make me marry this man?

MIRA. Why do we daily commit disagree- 295 able and dangerous actions? To save that idol, reputation. If the familiarities of our loves had produced that consequence, of which you were apprehensive, where could you have fixed a father's name with credit, but on a husband? I knew 300 Fainall to be a man lavish of his morals, an interested and professing friend, a false and a designing lover; yet one whose wit and outward fair behavior have gained a reputation with the town, enough to make that woman stand excused, who has suffered 305 herself to be won by his addresses. A better man ought not to have been sacrificed to the occasion; a worse had not answered to the purpose. When you are weary of him, you know your remedy.

MRS. FAIN. I ought to stand in some degree 310 of credit with you, Mirabell.

MIRA. In justice to you, I have made you privy to my whole design, and put it in your power to ruin or advance my fortune.

MRS. FAIN. Whom have you instructed to 315 represent your pretended uncle?

MIRA. Waitwell, my servant.

MRS. FAIN. He is an humble servant to Foible, my mother's woman, and may win her to your interest. 320

MIRA. Care is taken for that. She is won and worn by this time. They were married this morning.

MRS. FAIN. Who?

MIRA. Waitwell and Foible. I would not 325 tempt my servant to betray me by trusting him too far. If your mother, in hopes to ruin me, should consent to marry my pretended uncle, he might, like Mosca in *The Fox*,[1] stand upon terms; so I made him sure beforehand. 330

MRS. FAIN. So, if my poor mother is caught in a contract, you will discover the imposture betimes, and release her by producing a certificate of her gallant's former marriage.

---

[1] In this play by Jonson, Mosca, the servant of the swindler, Volpone, blackmails his master by threats of exposure.

MIRA. Yes, upon condition she consent to 335
my marriage with her niece, and surrender the moiety of her fortune in her possession.

MRS. FAIN. She talked last night of endeavoring
at a match between Millamant and your uncle.

MIRA. That was by Foible's direction, and 340
my instruction, that she might seem to carry it more
privately.

MRS. FAIN. Well, I have an opinion of your success, for I believe my lady will do anything to get a
husband; and when she has this, which you 345
have provided for her, I suppose she will submit to
anything to get rid of him.

MIRA. Yes, I think the good lady would marry
anything that resembled a man, though 'twere no
more than what a butler could pinch out of a 350
napkin.[1]

MRS. FAIN. Female frailty! We must all come
to it, if we live to be old, and feel the craving of a
false appetite when the true is decayed.

MIRA. An old woman's appetite is depraved 355
like that of a girl. 'Tis the green-sickness of a second childhood; and like the faint offer of a latter
spring, serves but to usher in the fall; and withers in
an affected bloom.

MRS. FAIN. Here's your mistress. 360

Enter MRS. MILLAMANT, WITWOUD, *and*
MINCING.

MIRA. Here she comes, i'faith, full sail, with her
fan spread and her streamers out, and a shoal of
fools for tenders. — Ha, no, I cry her mercy!

MRS. FAIN. I see but one poor empty sculler; and
he tows her woman after him. 365

MIRA. You seem to be unattended, madam.
You used to have the *beau monde* throng after you;
and a flock of gay fine perukes hovering round you.

WIT. Like moths about a candle. — I had like to
have lost my comparison for want of breath. 370

MILLA. Oh, I have denied myself airs today. I
have walked as fast through the crowd ——

WIT. As a favorite in disgrace; and with as few
followers.

MILLA. Dear Mr. Witwoud, truce with your 375
similitudes: for I am as sick of 'em ——

WIT. As a physician of a good air. — I cannot
help it, madam, though 'tis against myself.

MILLA. Yet again! Mincing, stand between me
and his wit. 380

WIT. Do, Mrs. Mincing, like a screen before a
great fire. I confess I do blaze today, I am too
bright.

MRS. FAIN. But, dear Millamant, why were you
so long? 385

[1] I.e., as a decoration for a dinner table.

MILLA. Long! Lord, have I not made violent
haste? I have asked every living thing I met for
you; I have enquired after you, as after a new
fashion.

WIT. Madam, truce with your similitudes. 390
No, you met her husband, and did not ask him for
her.

MIRA. By your leave, Witwoud, that were like
enquiring after an old fashion, to ask a husband for
his wife. 395

WIT. Hum, a hit, a hit, a palpable hit, I confess
it.

MRS. FAIN. You were dressed before I came
abroad.

MILLA. Ay, that's true — oh, but then I 400
had — Mincing, what had I? Why was I so long?

MINC. O mem, your la'ship stayed to peruse a
a pecquet of letters.

MILLA. Oh, ay, letters — I had letters — I am
persecuted with letters — I hate letters. No- 405
body knows how to write letters; and yet one has
'em, one does not know why. They serve one to pin
up one's hair.

WIT. Is that the way? Pray, madam, do you
pin up your hair with all your letters? I find 410
I must keep copies.

MILLA. Only with those in verse, Mr. Witwoud.
I never pin up my hair with prose. I fancy one's
hair would not curl if it were pinned up with prose.
I think I tried once, Mincing. 415

MINC. O mem, I shall never forget it.

MILLA. Ay, poor Mincing tift [2] and tift all the
morning.

MINC. Till I had the cremp in my fingers, I'll vow,
mem. And all to no purpose. But when your 420
la'ship pins it up with poetry, it sits so pleasant the
next day as anything, and is so pure and so crips.[3]

WIT. Indeed, so 'crips'?

MINC. You're such a critic, Mr. Witwoud.

MILLA. Mirabell, did not you take excep- 425
tions last night? Oh, ay, and went away. Now I
think on't I'm angry. — No, now I think on't I'm
pleased — for I believe I gave you some pain.

MIRA. Does that please you?

MILLA. Infinitely; I love to give pain. 430

MIRA. You would affect a cruelty which is not
in your nature; your true vanity is in the power of
pleasing.

MILLA. Oh, I ask your pardon for that. One's
cruelty is one's power, and when one parts with 435
one's cruelty, one parts with one's power; and when
one has parted with that, I fancy one's old and ugly.

MIRA. Ay, ay, suffer your cruelty to ruin the ob-

[2] Arranged, dressed [my hair].
[3] A dialectal form of 'crisp.'

ject of your power, to destroy your lover — and then how vain, how lost a thing you'll be! Nay, 'tis 440 true: you are no longer handsome when you've lost your lover; your beauty dies upon the instant: for beauty is the lover's gift; 'tis he bestows your charms — your glass is all a cheat. The ugly and the old, whom the looking-glass mortifies, yet after 445 commendation can be flattered by it, and discover beauties in it: for that reflects our praises, rather than your face.

MILLA. Oh, the vanity of these men! Fainall, d'ee hear him? If they did not commend us, 450 we were not handsome! Now you must know they could not commend one, if one was not handsome. Beauty the lover's gift — Lord, what is a lover, that it can give? Why, one makes lovers as fast as one pleases, and they live as long as one 455 pleases, and they die as soon as one pleases: and then if one pleases, one makes more.

WIT. Very pretty. Why you make no more of making of lovers, madam, than of making so many card-matches.[1] 460

MILLA. One no more owes one's beauty to a lover, than one's wit to an echo: they can but reflect what we look and say; vain empty things if we are silent or unseen, and want a being.

MIRA. Yet, to those two vain empty things, 465 you owe two the greatest pleasures of your life.

MILLA. How so?

MIRA. To your lover you owe the pleasure of hearing yourselves praised; and to an echo the pleasure of hearing yourselves talk. 470

WIT. But I know a lady that loves talking so incessantly, she won't give an echo fair play; she has that everlasting rotation of tongue, that an echo must wait till she dies, before it can catch her last words. 475

MILLA. Oh, fiction! Fainall, let us leave these men.

MIRA. (aside to MRS. FAINALL). Draw off Witwoud.

MRS. FAIN. [aside]. Immediately. — I have 480 a word or two for Mr. Witwoud.

MIRA. I would beg a little private audience too.

Exeunt WITWOUD *and* MRS. FAINALL.

You had the tyranny to deny me last night; though you knew I came to impart a secret to you that concerned my love. 485

MILLA. You saw I was engaged.

MIRA. Unkind. You had the leisure to entertain a herd of fools; things who visit you from their excessive idleness; bestowing on your easiness that time, which is the incumbrance of their lives. 490 How can you find delight in such society? It is im-

possible they should admire you, they are not capable: or if they were, it should be to you as a mortification; for sure to please a fool is some degree of folly. 495

MILLA. I please myself — besides, sometimes to converse with fools is for my health.

MIRA. Your health! Is there a worse disease than the conversation of fools?

MILLA. Yes, the vapors; fools are physic for 500 it, next to asafœtida.

MIRA. You are not in a course of fools?[2]

MILLA. Mirabell, if you persist in this offensive freedom, you'll displease me. I think I must resolve, after all, not to have you. We shan't 505 agree.

MIRA. Not in our physic, it may be.

MILLA. And yet our distemper in all likelihood will be the same; for we shall be sick of one another. I shan't endure to be reprimanded, nor in- 510 structed; 'tis so dull to act always by advice, and so tedious to be told of one's faults — I can't bear it. Well, I won't have you, Mirabell — I'm resolved — I think — you may go — ha, ha, ha! What would you give, that you could help loving me? 515

MIRA. I would give something that you did not know I could not help it.

MILLA. Come, don't look grave then. Well, what do you say to me?

MIRA. I say that a man may as soon make 520 a friend by his wit, or a fortune by his honesty, as win a woman with plain dealing and sincerity.

MILLA. Sententious Mirabell! Prithee, don't look with that violent and inflexible wise face, like Solomon at the dividing of the child in an old 525 tapestry hanging.

MIRA. You are merry, madam, but I would persuade you for one moment to be serious.

MILLA. What, with that face? No, if you keep your countenance, 'tis impossible I should hold 530 mine. Well, after all, there is something very moving in a lovesick face. Ha, ha, ha! — well, I won't laugh, don't be peevish — heigho! Now I'll be melancholy, as melancholy as a watch-light.[3] Well, Mirabell, if ever you will win me, [woo] me 535 now. — Nay, if you are so tedious, fare you well; I see you are walking away.

MIRA. Can you not find in the variety of your disposition one moment ——

MILLA. To hear you tell me that Foible's 540 married, and your plot like to speed? No.

MIRA. But how you came to know it ——

MILLA. Unless by the help of the devil, you can't

---

[1] Pieces of card dipped in melted sulphur.

[2] Playing on the expression 'in a (prescribed) course of physic.'

[3] A night-light.

imagine; unless she should tell me herself. Which of the two it may have been, I will leave you 545 to consider; and when you have done thinking of that, think of me.   *Exit.*

MIRA. I have something more —. Gone! — Think of you! To think of a whirlwind, though 'twere in a whirlwind, were a case of more 550 steady contemplation; a very tranquillity of mind and mansion. A fellow that lives in a windmill, has not a more whimsical dwelling than the heart of a man that is lodged in a woman. There is no point of the compass to which they cannot turn, 555 and by which they are not turned, and by one as well as another; for motion, not method, is their occupation. To know this, and yet continue to be in love, is to be made wise from the dictates of reason, and yet persevere to play the fool by the force 560 of instinct. Oh, here come my pair of turtles! [1] — What, billing so sweetly! Is not Valentine's Day over with you yet?

Enter WAITWELL *and* FOIBLE.

Sirrah Waitwell, why sure you think you were married for your own recreation, and not for 565 my conveniency.

WAIT. Your pardon, sir. With submission, we have indeed been solacing in lawful delights; but still with an eye to business, sir. I have instructed her as well as I could. If she can take your 570 directions as readily as my instructions, sir, your affairs are in a prosperous way.

MIRA. Give you joy, Mrs. Foible.

FOIB. O 'las, sir, I'm so ashamed — I'm afraid my lady has been in a thousand inquietudes 575 for me. But I protest, sir, I made as much haste as I could.

WAIT. That she did indeed, sir. It was my fault that she did not make more.

MIRA. That I believe.   580

FOIB. But I told my lady as you instructed me, sir. That I had a prospect of seeing Sir Rowland, your uncle; and that I would put her ladyship's picture in my pocket to show him; which I'll be sure to say has made him so enamored of her beauty, 585 that he burns with impatience to lie at her ladyship's feet and worship the original.

MIRA. Excellent Foible! Matrimony has made you eloquent in love.

WAIT. I think she has profited, sir. I think 590 so.

FOIB. You have seen Madam Millamant, sir?

MIRA. Yes.

FOIB. I told her, sir, because I did not know that you might find an opportunity; she had so 595 much company last night.

[1] Turtle-doves.

MIRA. Your diligence will merit more. In the meantime ——   (*Gives money.*)

FOIB. O dear sir, your humble servant.

WAIT. Spouse!   600

MIRA. Stand off, sir, not a penny. — Go on and prosper, Foible. The lease shall be made good and the farm stocked, if we succeed.

FOIB. I don't question your generosity, sir: and you need not doubt of success. If you have no 605 more commands, sir, I'll be gone; I'm sure my lady is at her toilet, and can't dress 'till I come. — Oh dear, I'm sure that (*looking out*) was Mrs. Marwood that went by in a mask; if she has seen me with you I'm sure she'll tell my lady. I'll make haste home 610 and prevent [2] her. Your servant, sir. B'w'y, Waitwell.   *Exit* FOIBLE.

WAIT. Sir Rowland, if you please. — The jade's so pert upon her preferment she forgets herself.

MIRA. Come, sir, will you endeavor to for- 615 get yourself — and transform into Sir Rowland.

WAIT. Why, sir, it will be impossible I should remember myself — married, knighted, and attended all in one day! 'Tis enough to make any man forget himself. The difficulty will be 620 how to recover my acquaintance and familiarity with my former self; and fall from my transformation to a reformation into Waitwell. Nay, I shan't be quite the same Waitwell neither — for now I remember me, I am married, and can't be my 625 own man again.

Ay, there's the grief; that's the sad change of life;
To lose my title, and yet keep my wife.   *Exeunt.*

ACT III

SCENE I

A room in LADY WISHFORT'S *house.*

LADY WISHFORT *at her toilet,* PEG *waiting.*

LADY WISH. Merciful,[3] no news of Foible yet?

PEG. No, madam.

LADY WISH. I have no more patience. If I have not fretted myself till I am pale again, there's no veracity in me. Fetch me the red — the red, do 5 you hear, sweetheart? An errant ash color, as I'm a person. Look you how this wench stirs! Why dost thou not fetch me a little red? Didst thou not hear me, mopus? [4]

PEG. The red ratafia does your ladyship 10 mean, or the cherry-brandy?

LADY WISH. Ratafia, fool! No, fool. Not the ratafia, fool — grant me patience! I mean the

[2] Anticipate.   [3] Heaven (or God) understood.
[4] Stupid person.

Spanish paper,[1] idiot, — complexion, darling. Paint, paint, paint, dost thou understand that, change- 15 ling, dangling thy hands like bobbins before thee? Why dost thou not stir, puppet? — thou wooden thing upon wires!

PEG. Lord, madam, your ladyship is so impatient. I cannot come at the paint, madam; Mrs. Foible 20 has locked it up, and carried the key with her.

LADY WISH. A pox take you both! Fetch me the cherry-brandy then. (*Exit* PEG.) I'm as pale and as faint, I look like Mrs. Qualmsick the curate's wife, that's always breeding. — Wench, come, 25 come, wench, what art thou doing, sipping? tasting? Save thee, dost thou not know the bottle?

Enter PEG *with a bottle and china cup.*

PEG. Madam, I was looking for a cup.

LADY WISH. A cup, save thee, and what a cup hast thou brought! Dost thou take me for a 30 fairy, to drink out of an acorn? Why didst thou not bring thy thimble? Hast thou ne'er a brass thimble clinking in thy pocket with a bit of nutmeg?[2] I warrant thee. Come, fill, fill. — So — again. (*One knocks.*) See who that is. — Set down the 35 bottle first. Here, here, under the table. What, wouldst thou go with the bottle in thy hand like a tapster? [*Exit* PEG.] As I'm a person, this wench has lived in an inn upon the road, before she came to me, like Maritornes the Asturian in *Don* 40 *Quixote.*[3] [*Re-enter* PEG.] No Foible yet?

PEG. No, madam, — Mrs. Marwood.

LADY WISH. Oh, Marwood! let her come in. Come in, good Marwood.

Enter MRS. MARWOOD.

MRS. MAR. I'm surprised to find your lady- 45 ship in dishabille at this time of day.

LADY WISH. Foible's a lost thing; has been abroad since morning, and never heard of since.

MRS. MAR. I saw her but now, as I came masked through the Park, in conference with Mirabell. 50

LADY WISH. With Mirabell! You call my blood into my face, with mentioning that traitor. She durst not have the confidence. I sent her to negotiate an affair, in which if I'm detected I'm undone. If that wheedling villain has wrought upon 55 Foible to detect me, I'm ruined. Oh, my dear friend, I'm a wretch of wretches if I'm detected.

MRS. MAR. O madam, you cannot suspect Mrs. Foible's integrity.

LADY WISH. Oh, he carries poison in his 60 tongue that would corrupt integrity itself. If she has given him an opportunity, she has as good as

[1] A cosmetic preparation imported from Spain.
[2] As good-luck charms.　　　[3] Part I, III. ii.

put her integrity into his hands. Ah, dear Marwood, what's integrity to an opportunity? — Hark! I hear her. [*To* PEG.] Go, you thing, and send 65 her in! (*Exit* PEG.) Dear friend, retire into my closet, that I may examine her with more freedom. — You'll pardon me, dear friend, I can make bold with you. — There are books over the chimney — Quarles[4] and Prynne,[5] and *The Short View of* 70 *the Stage,* with Bunyan's works, to entertain you.

Exit MARWOOD.

Enter FOIBLE.

O Foible, where hast thou been? What hast thou been doing?

FOIB. Madam, I have seen the party.

LADY WISH. But what hast thou done? 75

FOIB. Nay, 'tis your ladyship has done, and are to do; I have only promised. But a man so enamored — so transported! Well, here it is, all that is left; all that is not kissed away. Well, if worshipping of pictures be a sin — poor Sir Rowland, I 80 say.

LADY WISH. The miniature has been counted like — but hast thou not betrayed me, Foible? Hast thou not detected me to that faithless Mirabell? What hadst thou to do with him in the Park? 85 Answer me, has he got nothing out of thee?

FOIB. [*aside*]. So, the devil has been beforehand with me: what shall I say? — Alas, madam, could I help it, if I met that confident thing? Was I in fault? If you had heard how he used me, and 90 all upon your ladyship's account, I'm sure you would not suspect my fidelity. Nay, if that had been the worst, I could have borne: but he had a fling at your ladyship too; and then I could not hold, but, i'faith, I gave him his own. 95

LADY WISH. Me? What did the filthy fellow say?

FOIB. O madam, 'tis a shame to say what he said — with his taunts and his fleers,[6] tossing up his nose. 'Humh!' says he, 'what, you are a hatching some plot,' says he, 'you are so early abroad, or cater- 100 ing,' says he, 'ferreting for some disbanded officer, I warrant — half pay is but thin subsistence,' says he. 'Well, what pension does your lady propose? Let me see,' says he; 'what, she must come down pretty deep now: she's superannuated,' says he, 105 'and ——'

LADY WISH. Ods my life, I'll have him — I'll have him murdered. I'll have him poisoned. Where does he eat? I'll marry a drawer to have him

[4] Francis Quarles (1592–1644), author of *Divine Emblems* and other popular religious writings.
[5] William Prynne (1600–1669), Puritan writer; author of numerous pamphlets and books, including *Histrio-Mastix* (1633), an attack on the stage.
[6] Gibes.

poisoned in his wine. I'll send for Robin from 110
Locket's [1] immediately.

FOIB. Poison him? Poisoning's too good for
him. Starve him, madam, starve him; marry Sir
Rowland and get him disinherited. Oh, you would
bless yourself, to hear what he said.   115

LADY WISH. A villain! 'superannuated!'

FOIB. 'Humh!' says he, 'I hear you are laying
designs against me, too,' says he, 'and Mrs. Millamant is to marry my uncle;' — (he does not suspect
a word of your ladyship); — 'but,' says he, 'I'll 120
fit you for that, I warrant you,' says he, 'I'll hamper
you for that,' says he, 'you and your old frippery,[2]
too,' says he, 'I'll handle you ——'

LADY WISH. Audacious villain! handle me! would
he durst! — 'Frippery? old frippery!' Was there 125
ever such a foul-mouthed fellow? I'll be married
tomorrow, I'll be contracted tonight.

FOIB. The sooner the better, madam.

LADY WISH. Will Sir Rowland be here, say'st
thou? When, Foible?   130

FOIB. Incontinently, madam. No new sheriff's
wife expects the return of her husband after knighthood, with that impatience in which Sir Rowland
burns for the dear hour of kissing your ladyship's
hands after dinner.   135

LADY WISH. 'Frippery? superannuated frippery!'
I'll frippery the villain; I'll reduce him to frippery
and rags. A tatterdemalion! — I hope to see him
hung with tatters, like a Long Lane pent-house,[3] or
a gibbet-thief. A slander-mouthed railer: I 140
warrant the spendthrift prodigal's in debt as much
as the million lottery,[4] or the whole court upon a
birthday.[5] I'll spoil his credit with his tailor. Yes,
he shall have my niece with her fortune, he shall.

FOIB. He! I hope to see him lodge in Lud- 145
gate first, and angle into Blackfriars for brass
farthings, with an old mitten.[6]

LADY WISH. Ay, dear Foible; thank thee for that,
dear Foible. He has put me out of all patience.
I shall never recompose my features to receive 150
Sir Rowland with any economy of face. This

wretch has fretted me that I am absolutely decayed.
Look, Foible.

FOIB. Your ladyship has frowned a little too
rashly, indeed, madam. There are some 155
cracks discernible in the white varnish.

LADY WISH. Let me see the glass. — Cracks,
say'st thou? Why, I am arrantly flayed. I look
like an old peeled wall. Thou must repair me,
Foible, before Sir Rowland comes; or I shall 160
never keep up to my picture.

FOIB. I warrant you, madam; a little art once
made your picture like you; and now a little of the
same art must make you like your picture. Your
picture must sit for you, madam.   165

LADY WISH. But art thou sure Sir Rowland will
not fail to come? Or will a not fail when he does
come? Will he be importunate, Foible, and push?
For if he should not be importunate — I shall never
break decorums — I shall die with confusion, 170
if I am forced to advance — oh no, I can never advance — I shall swoon if he should expect advances.
No, I hope Sir Rowland is better bred, than to put a
lady to the necessity of breaking her forms. I
won't be too coy neither. I won't give him 175
despair — but a little disdain is not amiss; a little
scorn is alluring.

FOIB. A little scorn becomes your ladyship.

LADY WISH. Yes, but tenderness becomes me
best — a sort of a dyingness. — You see that 180
picture has a sort of a — ha, Foible? A swimminess
in the eyes. Yes, I'll look so. My niece affects it;
but she wants features. Is Sir Rowland handsome?
Let my toilet be removed — I'll dress above. I'll
receive Sir Rowland here. Is he handsome? 185
Don't answer me. I won't know: I'll be surprised.
I'll be taken by surprise.

FOIB. By storm, madam. Sir Rowland's a brisk
man.

LADY WISH. Is he! Oh, then he'll impor- 190
tune, if he's a brisk man. I shall save decorums if
Sir Rowland importunes. I have a mortal terror at
the apprehension of offending against decorums.
Nothing but importunity can surmount decorums.
Oh, I'm glad he's a brisk man! Let my things 195
be removed, good Foible.   *Exit.*

Enter MRS. FAINALL.

MRS. FAIN. O Foible, I have been in a fright, lest
I should come too late. That devil, Marwood, saw
you in the Park with Mirabell, and I'm afraid will
discover it to my lady.   200

FOIB. Discover what, madam?

MRS. FAIN. Nay, nay, put not on that strange
face. I am privy to the whole design, and know
that Waitwell, to whom thou wert this morning

[1] Presumably a tapster at Locket's, the fashionable tavern in
Charing Cross.

[2] Either 'cast-off garments' or 'tawdry finery'; it is difficult to
say in which sense Mirabell is using the word here, but probably
the former; cf. l. 137 infra.

[3] A stall in Long Lane (where old clothes were sold).

[4] In 1694 the government raised a loan of £1,000,000 by
means of a lottery, the prizes being annuities for sixteen years.
Apparently these annuities were in arrears.

[5] Courtiers were expected to appear in new and expensive
clothes on the sovereign's birthday.

[6] The Fleet Prison in Ludgate, in the district of Blackfriars,
was a common place of confinement for persons arrested for
debt. The inmates of the prison often appealed for charity from
passers-by in the manner suggested by Foible.

married, is to personate Mirabell's uncle, and as　205
such, winning my lady, to involve her in those difficulties from which Mirabell only must release her,
by his making his conditions to have my cousin and
her fortune left to her own disposal.

FOIB. O dear madam, I beg your pardon. It　210
was not my confidence in your ladyship that was
deficient; but I thought the former good correspondence between your ladyship and Mr. Mirabell
might have hindered his communicating this secret.

MRS. FAIN. Dear Foible, forget that.　　215

FOIB. O dear madam, Mr. Mirabell is such a
sweet winning gentleman — but your ladyship is
the pattern of generosity. Sweet lady, to be so
good! Mr. Mirabell cannot choose but be grateful.
I find your ladyship has his heart still. Now,　220
madam, I can safely tell your ladyship our success;
Mrs. Marwood had told my lady, but I warrant I
managed myself. I turned it all for the better. I
told my lady that Mr. Mirabell railed at her. I laid
horrid things to his charge, I'll vow; and my　225
lady is so incensed, that she'll be contracted to Sir
Rowland tonight, she says; I warrant I worked her
up, that he may have her for asking for, as they say
of a Welsh maidenhead.

MRS. FAIN. O rare Foible!　　230

FOIB. Madam, I beg your ladyship to acquaint
Mr. Mirabell of his success. I would be seen as
little as possible to speak to him; besides, I believe
Madam Marwood watches me. She has a month's
mind;[1] but I know Mr. Mirabell can't abide　235
her. (Enter Footman.) John, remove my lady's
toilet. Madam, your servant. My lady is so impatient, I fear she'll come for me, if I stay.

MRS. FAIN. I'll go with you up the back stairs,
lest I should meet her.　　　　Exeunt.　240

Enter MRS. MARWOOD.

MRS. MAR. Indeed, Mrs. Engine,[2] is it thus with
you? Are you become a go-between of this importance? Yes, I shall watch you. Why, this wench is
the passe-partout, a very master-key to everybody's
strong box. My friend Fainall, have you　245
carried it so swimmingly? I thought there was
something in it; but it seems it's over with you.
Your loathing is not from a want of appetite then,
but from a surfeit. Else you could never be so cool
to fall from a principal to be an assistant, to　250
procure for him! A pattern of generosity, that I
confess. Well, Mr. Fainall, you have met with your
match. — O man, man! Woman, woman! The
devil's an ass: if I were a painter, I would draw him
like an idiot, a driveler, with a bib and bells.　255

[1] A strong inclination (toward Mirabell).
[2] Mrs. Trickery.

Man should have his head and horns, and woman the
rest of him. Poor simple fiend! 'Madam Marwood
has a month's mind, but he can't abide her.' —
'Twere better for him you had not been his con-
fessor in that affair, without you could have　260
kept his counsel closer. I shall not prove another
pattern of generosity, and stalk for him, till he takes
his stand to aim at a fortune; he has not obliged me
to that with those excesses of himself; and now I'll
have none of him. Here comes the good lady,　265
panting ripe; with a heart full of hope, and a head
full of care, like any chemist upon the day of projection.[3]

Enter LADY WISHFORT.

LADY WISH. O dear Marwood, what shall I say
for this rude forgetfulness? But my dear　270
friend is all goodness.

MRS. MAR. No apologies, dear madam. I have
been very well entertained.

LADY WISH. As I'm a person, I am in a very
chaos to think I should so forget myself — but　275
I have such an olio[4] of affairs, really I know not
what to do. — (Calls.) Foible! — I expect my nephew Sir Wilfull every moment too. — Why, Foible!
— He means to travel for improvement.

MRS. MAR. Methinks Sir Wilfull should　280
rather think of marrying than travelling at his
years. I hear he is turned of forty.

LADY WISH. Oh, he's in less danger of being
spoiled by his travels. I am against my nephew's
marrying too young. It will be time enough　285
when he comes back, and has acquired discretion
to choose for himself.

MRS. MAR. Methinks Mrs. Millamant and he
would make a very fit match. He may travel afterwards. 'Tis a thing very usual with young　290
gentlemen.

LADY WISH. I promise you I have thought on't
— and since 'tis your judgment, I'll think on't again.
I assure you I will; I value your judgment extremely.
On my word, I'll propose it.　　　295

Enter FOIBLE.

Come, come, Foible — I had forgot my nephew will
be here before dinner. I must make haste.

FOIB. Mr. Witwoud and Mr. Petulant are come
to dine with your ladyship.

LADY WISH. Oh dear, I can't appear till I'm　300
dressed. Dear Marwood, shall I be free with you
again, and beg you to entertain 'em? I'll make all
imaginable haste. Dear friend, excuse me.

　　　Exeunt LADY WISHFORT and FOIBLE.

[3] Projection, in alchemy, was the casting into the crucible of
the element which was to transmute base metal into gold.
[4] Hotch-potch.

Enter MRS. MILLAMANT *and* MINCING.

MILLA. Sure never anything was so unbred as that odious man. — Marwood, your servant. 305

MRS. MAR. You have a color; what's the matter?

MILLA. That horrid fellow, Petulant, has provoked me into a flame. I have broke my fan. — Mincing, lend me yours. — Is not all the powder out of my hair? 310

MRS. MAR. No. What has he done?

MILLA. Nay, he has done nothing; he has only talked. Nay, he has said nothing neither; but he has contradicted everything that has been said. For my part, I thought Witwoud and he would 315 have quarrelled.

MINC. I vow, mem, I thought once they would have fit.

MILLA. Well, 'tis a lamentable thing, I'll swear, that one has not the liberty of choosing one's 320 acquaintance as one does one's clothes.

MRS. MAR. If we had the liberty, we should be as weary of one set of acquaintance, though never so good, as we are of one suit, though never so fine. A fool and a doily stuff [1] would now and then 325 find days of grace, and be worn for variety.

MILLA. I could consent to wear 'em, if they would wear alike; but fools never wear out — they are such *drap-de-Berry* [2] things! — without one could give 'em to one's chambermaid after a day or 330 two.

MRS. MAR. 'Twere better so indeed. Or what think you of the playhouse? A fine gay glossy fool should be given there, like a new masking habit, after the masquerade is over, and we have done 335 with the disguise. For a fool's visit is always a disguise; and never admitted by a woman of wit, but to blind her affair with a lover of sense. If you would but appear barefaced now, and own Mirabell, you might as easily put off Petulant and Wit- 340 woud, as your hood and scarf. And indeed 'tis time, for the town has found it: the secret is grown too big for the pretence. 'Tis like Mrs. Primly's great belly; she may lace it down before, but it burnishes [3] on her hips. Indeed, Millamant, you can no 345 more conceal it, than my Lady Strammel [4] can her face, that goodly face, which in defiance of her Rhenish-wine tea,[5] will not be comprehended in a mask.

MILLA. I'll take my death, Marwood, you 350 are more censorious than a decayed beauty, or a discarded toast. — Mincing, tell the men they may come up. My aunt is not dressing. — Their folly is

[1] A light, cheap woollen cloth.
[2] A heavier woollen cloth.
[3] Grows plump.   [4] Ill-favored person.
[5] Apparently Rhenish wine was supposed to be good both for the figure and the complexion.

less provoking than your malice. 'The town has found it!' (*Exit* MINCING.) What has it 355 found? That Mirabell loves me is no more a secret, than it is a secret that you discovered it to my aunt, or than the reason why you discovered it is a secret.

MRS. MAR. You are nettled. 360

MILLA. You're mistaken. Ridiculous!

MRS. MAR. Indeed, my dear, you'll tear another fan, if you don't mitigate those violent airs.

MILLA. O silly! Ha, ha, ha! I could laugh immoderately. Poor Mirabell! His constancy 365 to me has quite destroyed his complaisance for all the world beside. I swear, I never enjoined it him, to be so coy. If I had the vanity to think he would obey me, I would command him to show more gallantry. 'Tis hardly well bred to be so particu- 370 lar on one hand, and so insensible on the other. But I despair to prevail, and so let him follow his own way. Ha, ha, ha! Pardon me, dear creature, I must laugh, ha, ha, ha! — though I grant you 'tis a little barbarous, ha, ha, ha! 375

MRS. MAR. What pity 'tis, so much fine raillery, and delivered with so significant gesture, should be so unhappily directed to miscarry.

MILLA. [Heh?] Dear creature, I ask your pardon — I swear I did not mind you.[6] 380

MRS. MAR. Mr. Mirabell and you both may think it a thing impossible, when I shall tell him by telling you ——

MILLA. O dear, what? for it is the same thing, if I hear it — ha, ha, ha! 385

MRS. MAR. That I detest him, hate him, madam.

MILLA. O madam, why so do I — and yet the creature loves me, ha, ha, ha! How can one forbear laughing to think of it. I am a sibyl if I am not amazed to think what he can see in me. I'll 390 take my death, I think you are handsomer — and within a year or two as young. If you could but stay for me, I should overtake you — but that cannot be. Well, that thought makes me melancholy. Now I'll be sad. 395

MRS. MAR. Your merry note may be changed sooner than you think.

MILLA. D'ee say so? Then I'm resolved I'll have a song to keep up my spirits.

Enter MINCING.

MINC. The gentlemen stay but to comb, 400 madam, and will wait on you.

MILLA. Desire Mrs. —— that is in the next room to sing the song I would have learnt yesterday. You shall hear it, madam — not that there's any great matter in it — but 'tis agreeable to my 405 humor.

[6] Pay attention to you.

319] Q2W1 *I swear.*   333] Q2W1 *glosly.*   379] Q1Q2W1 *Hœ?*   394] W1 *melancholic.*

SONG

Set by Mr. John Eccles, and sung by Mrs. Hodgson.

I

Love's but the frailty of the mind,
　When 'tis not with ambition joined;
A sickly flame, which if not fed expires;
　And feeding, wastes in self-consuming fires.　　410

II

'Tis not to wound a wanton boy
Or am'rous youth, that gives the joy;
But 'tis the glory to have pierced a swain,
For whom inferior beauties sighed in vain.

III

Then I alone the conquest prize,　　415
　When I insult a rival's eyes:
If there's delight in love, 'tis when I see
That heart which others bleed for, bleed for me.

Enter PETULANT *and* WITWOUD.

MILLA. Is your animosity composed, gentlemen?

WIT. Raillery, raillery, madam; we have no　420
animosity — we hit off a little wit now and then,
but no animosity. The falling out of wits is like
the falling out of lovers. We agree in the main, like
treble and base. Ha, Petulant?

PET. Ay, in the main. But when I have a　425
humor to contradict ——

WIT. Ay, when he has a humor to contradict,
then I contradict too. What, I know my cue.
Then we contradict one another like two battledores;
for contradictions beget one another like Jews.　430

PET. If he says black's black — if I have a humor
to say 'tis blue — let that pass — all's one for that.
If I have a humor to prove it, it must be granted.

WIT. Not positively must — but it may — it
may.　　435

PET. Yes, it positively must, upon proof positive.

WIT. Ay, upon proof positive it must; but upon
proof presumptive it only may. That's a logical
distinction now, madam.

MRS. MAR. I perceive your debates are of　440
importance and very learnedly handled.

PET. Importance is one thing, and learning's
another; but a debate's a debate, that I assert.

WIT. Petulant's an enemy to learning; he relies
altogether on his parts.　　445

PET. No, I'm no enemy to learning; it hurts not
me.

MRS. MAR. That's a sign indeed it's no enemy
to you.

PET. No, no, it's no enemy to anybody, but　450
them that have it.

MILLA. Well, an illiterate man's my aversion.

I wonder at the impudence of any illiterate man, to
offer to make love.

WIT. That I confess I wonder at too.　　455

MILLA. Ah! to marry an ignorant that can hardly
read or write!

PET. Why should a man be ever the further from
being married though he can't read, any more than
he is from being hanged? The ordinary's paid　460
for setting the psalm,[1] and the parish-priest for
reading the ceremony. And for the rest which is to
follow in both cases, a man may do it without book
— so all's one for that.

MILLA. D'ee hear the creature? Lord,　465
here's company, I'll be gone.

Exeunt MILLAMANT *and* MINCING.

WIT. In the name of Bartlemew and his fair,[2]
what have we here?

MRS. MAR. 'Tis your brother, I fancy. Don't
you know him?　　470

WIT. Not I — yes, I think it is he — I've almost
forgot him; I have not seen him since the Revolution.[3]

Enter SIR WILFULL WITWOUD *in a country riding
habit, and Servant to* LADY WISHFORT.

SERV. Sir, my lady's dressing. Here's company,
if you please to walk in, in the meantime.　　475

SIR WIL. Dressing! What, it's but morning here
I warrant with you in London; we should count it
towards afternoon in our parts, down in Shropshire.
Why then belike my aunt han't dined yet — ha,
friend?　　480

SERV. Your aunt, sir?

SIR WIL. My aunt, sir, yes, my aunt, sir, and
your lady, sir; your lady is my aunt, sir. Why,
what, dost thou not know me, friend? Why, then
send somebody here that does. How long hast　485
thou lived with thy lady, fellow, ha?

SERV. A week, sir; longer than anybody in the
house, except my lady's woman.

SIR WIL. Why then belike thou dost not know
thy lady, if thou see'st her, ha, friend?　　490

SERV. Why truly, sir, I cannot safely swear to
her face in a morning, before she is dressed. 'Tis
like I may give a shrewd guess at her by this time.

SIR WIL. Well, prithee try what thou canst do;
if thou canst not guess, enquire her out, dost　495
hear, fellow? And tell her, her nephew, Sir Wilfull
Witwoud, is in the house.

[1] The ordinary (prison chaplain) regularly read a psalm before the execution of a criminal.

[2] The popular fair held in Smithfield about St. Bartholomew's
Day (Aug. 24).

[3] The 'Glorious Revolution' of 1688 which dethroned
James II.

SERV. I shall, sir.

SIR WIL. Hold ye, hear me, friend; a word with you in your ear; prithee who are these gallants?   500

SERV. Really, sir, I can't tell; here come so many here, 'tis hard to know 'em all.   *Exit Servant.*

SIR WIL. Oons,[1] this fellow knows less than a starling; I don't think a' knows his own name.

MRS. MAR. Mr. Witwoud, your brother is   505 not behindhand in forgetfulness — I fancy he has forgot you too.

WIT. I hope so — the devil take him that remembers first, I say.

SIR WIL. Save you, gentlemen and lady.   510

MRS. MAR. For shame, Mr. Witwoud; why won't you speak to him? — And you, sir.

WIT. Petulant, speak.

PET. And you, sir.

SIR WIL. No offence, I hope.   515

[*Salutes* MARWOOD.]

MRS. MAR. No, sure, sir.

WIT. This is a vile dog, I see that already. No offence! Ha, ha, ha! To him; to him, Petulant, smoke him.[2]

PET. It seems as if you had come a journey,   520 sir; hem, hem.   (*Surveying him round.*)

SIR WIL. Very likely, sir, that it may seem so.

PET. No offence, I hope, sir.

WIT. Smoke the boots, the boots, Petulant, the boots; ha, ha, ha!   525

SIR WIL. Maybe not, sir; thereafter as 'tis meant, sir.

PET. Sir, I presume upon the information of your boots.

SIR WIL. Why, 'tis like you may, sir: if you   530 are not satisfied with the information of my boots, sir, if you will step to the stable, you may enquire further of my horse, sir.

PET. Your horse, sir! Your horse is an ass, sir!

SIR WIL. Do you speak by way of offence,   535 sir?

MRS. MAR. The gentleman's merry, that's all, sir. — [*Aside.*] S'life, we shall have a quarrel betwixt an horse and an ass, before they find one another out. — [*Aloud.*] You must not take   540 anything amiss from your friends, sir. You are among your friends here, though it may be you don't know it. If I am not mistaken, you are Sir Wilfull Witwoud.

SIR WIL. Right, lady; I am Sir Wilfull Wit-   545 woud, so I write myself; no offence to anybody, I hope; and nephew to the Lady Wishfort of this mansion.

MRS. MAR. Don't you know this gentleman, sir?   550

SIR WIL. Hum! What, sure 'tis not. — Yea, by'r lady, but 'tis. — 'Sheart, I know not whether 'tis or no. — Yea, but 'tis, by the Wrekin.[3] Brother Anthony! What, Tony, i'faith! What, dost thou not know me? By'r Lady, nor I thee, thou   555 art so becravatted, and so beperiwigged. — 'Sheart, why dost not speak? Art thou o'erjoyed?

WIT. Odso,[4] brother, is it you? Your servant, brother.

SIR WIL. Your servant! Why yours, sir.   560 Your servant again. — 'Sheart, and your friend and servant to that — and a — (*puff*) and a flapdragon [5] for your service, sir, and a hare's foot, and a hare's scut [6] for your service, sir, an you be so cold and so courtly!   565

WIT. No offence, I hope, brother.

SIR WIL. 'Sheart, sir, but there is, and much offence. A pox, is this your Inns o' Court breeding,[7] not to know your friends and your relations, your elders, and your betters?   570

WIT. Why, brother Wilfull of Salop,[8] you may be as short as a Shrewsbury cake,[9] if you please. But I tell you 'tis not modish to know relations in town. You think you're in the country, where great lubberly brothers slabber and kiss one another   575 when they meet, like a call of serjeants.[10] 'Tis not the fashion here; 'tis not indeed, dear brother.

SIR WIL. The fashion's a fool; and you're a fop, dear brother. 'Sheart, I've suspected this. By'r Lady, I conjectured you were a fop, since you   580 began to change the style of your letters, and write in a scrap of paper gilt round the edges, no broader than a *subpœna*. I might expect this when you left off 'Honored Brother,' and 'hoping you are in good health,' and so forth — to begin with a 'Rat   585 me,[11] knight, I'm so sick of a last night's debauch' — Od's heart, and then tell a familiar tale of a cock and a bull, and a whore and a bottle, and so conclude. You could write news before you were out of your time, when you lived with honest Pumple   590 Nose, the attorney of Furnival's Inn. You could intreat to be remembered then to your friends round the Wrekin. We could have gazettes then, and

[1] A contraction of 'God's wounds!'   [2] Banter him.

[3] A high hill near the center of Shropshire. 'All friends round the Wrekin' is the Shropshire toast; cf. ll. 592–593 below.
[4] A variant of 'Godso,' an exclamation of surprise.
[5] A raisin used in the Christmas game of flapdragon or snapdragon; here used as the type of something of little value; cf. 'A fig for him!'
[6] Tail.
[7] The four Inns of Court were the societies in which lawyers were trained, and which had the power to admit to the bar. Furnival's Inn, mentioned below, was one of them.
[8] Shropshire.
[9] A kind of short-bread.
[10] A group of serjeants-at-law (lawyers of a superior rank) who had been raised to that rank at the same time.
[11] Rot me (i.e., 'God rot me').

Dawks's Letter,[1] and the weekly bill,[2] 'till of late
days.   595

PET. 'Slife, Witwoud, were you ever an attorney's
clerk? Of the family of the Furnivals. Ha, ha, ha!

WIT. Ay, ay, but that was for a while. Not long,
not long. Pshaw! I was not in my own power
then. An orphan, and this fellow was my   600
guardian; ay, ay, I was glad to consent to that man
to come to London. He had the disposal of me then.
If I had not agreed to that, I might have been bound
prentice to a felt-maker in Shrewsbury; this fellow
would have bound me to a maker of felts.   605

SIR WIL. 'Sheart, and better than to be bound to
a maker of fops; where, I suppose, you have served
your time and now you may set up for yourself.

MRS. MAR. You intend to travel, sir, as I'm informed.   610

SIR WIL. Belike I may, madam. I may chance
to sail upon the salt seas, if my mind hold.

PET. And the wind serve.

SIR WIL. Serve or not serve, I shan't ask license
of you, sir; nor the weather-cock your com-   615
panion. I direct my discourse to the lady, sir. 'Tis
like my aunt may have told you, madam — yes, I
have settled my concerns, I may say now, and am
minded to see foreign parts. If an how that the
peace holds, whereby, that is, taxes abate.[3]   620

MRS. MAR. I thought you had designed for
France at all adventures.

SIR WIL. I can't tell that; 'tis like I may, and 'tis
like I may not. I am somewhat dainty in making
a resolution, — because when I make it I keep   625
it. I don't stand shill I, shall I, then; if I say't, I'll
do't: but I have thoughts to tarry a small matter in
town, to learn somewhat of your lingo first, before
I cross the seas. I'd gladly have a spice of your
French, as they say, whereby to hold discourse   630
in foreign countries.

MRS. MAR. Here is an academy in town for that
use.

SIR WIL. There is? 'Tis like there may.

MRS. MAR. No doubt you will return very   635
much improved.

WIT. Yes, refined, like a Dutch skipper from a
whale-fishing.[4]

Enter LADY WISHFORT *and* FAINALL.

LADY WISH. Nephew, you are welcome.

SIR WIL. Aunt, your servant.   640

[1] *Dawks's News-letter*, a weekly summary of the news.
[2] Weekly bills of mortality (i.e., lists of deaths) were published by a number of London parishes.
[3] The Peace of Ryswick (1697) had temporarily halted the
war with France, the cost of which had raised English taxes.
[4] The refining of whale-oil, carried on on board ship, impreg-
nated the clothing of the sailors with a strong and lasting odor.

FAIN. Sir Wilfull, your most faithful servant.

SIR WIL. Cousin Fainall, give me your hand.

LADY WISH. Cousin Witwoud, your servant;
Mr. Petulant, your servant. — Nephew, you are
welcome again. Will you drink anything after   645
your journey, nephew, before you eat? Dinner's
almost ready.

SIR WIL. I'm very well, I thank you, aunt —
however, I thank you for your courteous offer.
'Sheart, I was afraid you would have been in   650
the fashion too, and have remembered to have forgot your relations. Here's your Cousin Tony, belike, I mayn't call him brother for fear of offence.

LADY WISH. Oh, he's a rallier, nephew — my
cousin's a wit; and your great wits always   655
rally their best friends to choose. When you have
been abroad, nephew, you'll understand raillery
better. (FAINALL *and* MRS. MARWOOD *talk apart*.)

SIR WIL. Why then let him hold his tongue in the
meantime; and rail when that day comes.   660

Enter MINCING.

MINC. Mem, I come to acquaint your la'ship that
dinner is impatient.

SIR WIL. Impatient? Why then belike it won't
stay till I pull off my boots. Sweetheart, can you
help me to a pair of slippers? My man's with   665
his horses, I warrant.

LADY WISH. Fie, fie, nephew, you would not pull
off your boots here. Go down into the hall —
dinner shall stay for you. — My nephew's a little
unbred, you'll pardon him, madam. — Gentle-   670
men, will you walk? Marwood——

MRS. MAR. I'll follow you, madam, before Sir
Wilfull is ready.

Manent MRS. MARWOOD *and* FAINALL.

FAIN. Why then Foible's a bawd, an errant, rank,
match-making bawd. And I, it seems, am a   675
husband, a rank husband; and my wife a very errant,
rank wife — all in the way of the world. 'Sdeath,
to be an anticipated cuckold, a cuckold in embryo!
Sure I was born with budding antlers like a young
satyr, or a citizen's child.[5] 'Sdeath, to be out-   680
witted, to be out-jilted — out-matrimonied! If I
had kept my speed like a stag, 'twere somewhat, but
to crawl after with my horns like a snail, and [be]
outstripped by my wife — 'tis scurvy wedlock.

MRS. MAR. Then shake it off: you have   685
often wished for an opportunity to part, and now
you have it. But first prevent their plot — the half
of Millamant's fortune is too considerable to be
parted with, to a foe, to Mirabell.

[5] Two stock jokes are here combined — that about the horns
supposed to grow on the forehead of a cuckold, and that concerning the seduction of citizens' wives by courtiers. Cf. the
epilogue to *The London Merchant*, ll. 11–12.

FAIN. Damn him, that had been mine, had 690 you not made that fond discovery — that had been forfeited, had they been married. My wife had added lustre to my horns, by that increase of fortune; I could have worn 'em tipt with gold, though my forehead had been furnished like a deputy- 695 lieutenant's hall.[1]

MRS. MAR. They may prove a cap of maintenance[2] to you still, if you can away with your wife. And she's no worse than when you had her — I dare swear she had given up her game be- 700 fore she was married.

FAIN. Hum! That may be. —— She might throw up her cards; but I'll be hanged if she did not put Pam[3] in her pocket.

MRS. MAR. You married her to keep you; 705 and if you can contrive to have her keep you better than you expected, why should you not keep her longer than you intended?

FAIN. The means, the means!

MRS. MAR. Discover to my lady your wife's 710 conduct; threaten to part with her. My lady loves her, and will come to any composition to save her reputation. Take the opportunity of breaking it, just upon the discovery of this imposture. My lady will be enraged beyond bounds, and sacrifice 715 niece, and fortune, and all at that conjuncture. And let me alone to keep her warm; if she should flag in her part, I will not fail to prompt her.

FAIN. Faith, this has an appearance.

MRS. MAR. I'm sorry I hinted to my lady 720 to endeavor a match between Millamant and Sir Wilfull; that may be an obstacle.

FAIN. Oh, for that matter leave me to manage him; I'll disable him for that; he will drink like a Dane: after dinner, I'll set his hand in.[4]   725

MRS. MAR. Well, how do you stand affected towards your lady?

FAIN. Why, faith, I'm thinking of it. — Let me see — I am married already, so that's over; — my wife has played the jade with me — well, that's 730 over too; — I never loved her, or if I had, why that would have been over too by this time. — Jealous of her I cannot be, for I am certain; so there's an end of jealousy. Weary of her, I am, and shall be — no, there's no end of that; no, no, that were 735 too much to hope. Thus far concerning my repose. Now for my reputation. — As to my own, I married not for it; so that's out of the question. — And as to

my part in my wife's — why, she had parted with hers before; so bringing none to me, she can 740 take none from me; 'tis against all rule of play, that I should lose to one who has not wherewithal to stake.

MRS. MAR. Besides, you forget, marriage is honorable.   745

FAIN. Hum! Faith, and that's well thought on; marriage is honorable, as you say; and if so, wherefore should cuckoldom be a discredit, being derived from so honorable a root?

MRS. MAR. Nay, I know not; if the root be 750 honorable, why not the branches?[5]

FAIN. So, so, why this point's clear. Well, how do we proceed?

MRS. MAR. I will contrive a letter which shall be delivered to my lady at the time when that 755 rascal who is to act Sir Rowland is with her. It shall come as from an unknown hand — for the less I appear to know of the truth, the better I can play the incendiary. Besides, I would not have Foible provoked if I could help it, — because you know 760 she knows some passages. Nay, I expect all will come out — but let the mine be sprung first, and then I care not if I'm discovered.

FAIN. If the worst come to the worst, I'll turn my wife to grass. — I have already a deed of 765 settlement of the best part of her estate, which I wheedled out of her, and that you shall partake at least.

MRS. MAR. I hope you are convinced that I hate Mirabell; now you'll be no more jealous.   770

FAIN. Jealous, no! — by this kiss — let husbands be jealous, but let the lover still believe; or if he doubt, let it be only to endear his pleasure, and prepare the joy that follows, when he proves his mistress true; but let husbands' doubts convert to 775 endless jealousy; or if they have belief, let it corrupt to superstition, and blind credulity. I am single, and will herd no more with 'em. True, I wear the badge, but I'll disown the order. And since I take my leave of 'em, I care not if I leave 'em a 780 common motto to their common crest:

All husbands must, or pain, or shame, endure;
The wise too jealous are, fools too secure. *Exeunt.*

ACT IV

SCENE I

Scene continues.

LADY WISHFORT *and* FOIBLE.

LADY WISH. Is Sir Rowland coming, say'st thou, Foible? and are things in order?

---

[1] I.e., with numerous antlers.

[2] In heraldry a 'cap of maintenance' is a special kind of cap carried before a king or high official: Marwood is here playing on the words.

[3] The jack of clubs, the highest card in the game of loo.

[4] Start him.

[5] Another pun — this time on the branches of a stag's antlers.

702–704] W1 om. *She might . . . pocket.*
770] Q1 *Mirabell. now . . . jealous.* Q2 *Mirabell, now . . . jealous.* W1 *Mirabell now: . . . jealous?*

FOIB. Yes, madam. I have put waxlights in the sconces, and placed the footmen in a row in the hall, in their best liveries, with the coachman and 5 postilion to fill up the equipage.[1]

LADY WISH. Have you pulvilled[2] the coachman and postilion, that they may not stink of the stable, when Sir Rowland comes by?

FOIB. Yes, madam.   10

LADY WISH. And are the dancers and the music ready, that he may be entertained in all points with correspondence to his passion?

FOIB. All is ready, madam.

LADY WISH. And — well — and how do I 15 look, Foible?

FOIB. Most killing well, madam.

LADY WISH. Well, and how shall I receive him? In what figure shall I give his heart the first impression? There is a great deal in the first 20 impression. Shall I sit? — No, I won't sit — I'll walk — ay, I'll walk from the door upon his entrance; and then turn full upon him. — No, that will be too sudden. I'll lie — ay, I'll lie down — I'll receive him in my little dressing-room; there's 25 a couch — yes, yes, I'll give the first impression on a couch. — I won't lie neither, but loll and lean upon one elbow, with one foot a little dangling off, jogging in a thoughtful way — yes — and then as soon as he appears, start, ay, start and be surprised, 30 and rise to meet him in a pretty disorder — yes — oh, nothing is more alluring than a levee from a couch in some confusion. — It shows the foot to advantage, and furnishes with blushes, and recomposing airs beyond comparison. Hark! 35 There's a coach.

FOIB. 'Tis he, madam.

LADY WISH. Oh dear, has my nephew made his addresses to Millamant? I ordered her.

FOIB. Sir Wilfull is set in to[3] drinking, 40 madam, in the parlor.

LADY WISH. Ods my life, I'll send him to her. Call her down, Foible; bring her hither. I'll send him as I go. When they are together, then come to me, Foible, that I may not be too long alone 45 with Sir Rowland.   *Exit.*

Enter MRS. MILLAMANT *and* MRS. FAINALL.

FOIB. Madam, I stayed here, to tell your ladyship that Mr. Mirabell has waited this half-hour for an opportunity to talk with you. Though my lady's orders were to leave you and Sir Wilfull to- 50 gether. Shall I tell Mr. Mirabell that you are at leisure?

MILLA. No — what would the dear man have?

[1] Retinue.
[2] Powdered (with scented powder).
[3] Has set to work at.

I am thoughtful, and would amuse myself, — bid him come another time.   55
(*Repeating and walking about.*)

> There never yet was woman made,
> Nor shall, but to be curst.[4]

That's hard!

MRS. FAIN. You are very fond of Sir John Suckling to-day, Millamant, and the poets. 60

MILLA. [Heh]? Ay, and filthy verses — so I am.

FOIB. Sir Wilfull is coming, madam. Shall I send Mr. Mirabell away?

MILLA. Ay, if you please, Foible, send him away, — or send him hither, — just as you will, dear 65 Foible. — I think I'll see him — Shall I? Ay, let the wretch come. (*Repeating.*)

> Thyrsis, a youth of the inspired train.[5]

Dear Fainall, entertain Sir Wilfull — thou hast philosophy to undergo a fool; thou art married, 70 and hast patience. — I would confer with my own thoughts.

MRS. FAIN. I am obliged to you, that you would make me your proxy in this affair; but I have business of my own.   75

Enter SIR WILFULL.

— O Sir Wilfull, you are come at the critical instant. There's your mistress up to the ears in love and contemplation; pursue your point, now or never.

SIR WIL. Yes; my aunt would have it so, — I would gladly have been encouraged with a bottle 80 or two, because I'm somewhat wary at first, before I am acquainted. — (*This while* MILLAMANT *walks about repeating to herself.*) But I hope, after a time, I shall break my mind — that is, upon further acquaintance. — So for the present, cousin, I'll 85 take my leave — if so be you'll be so kind to make my excuse, I'll return to my company ——

MRS. FAIN. Oh, fie, Sir Wilfull! What, you must not be daunted.

SIR WIL. Daunted! no, that's not it, it is not 90 so much for that — for if so be that I set on't, I'll do't. But only for the present, 'tis sufficient till further acquaintance, that's all — your servant.

MRS. FAIN. Nay, I'll swear you shall never lose so favorable an opportunity, if I can help it. 95 I'll leave you together, and lock the door. *Exit.*

SIR WIL. Nay, nay, cousin, — I have forgot my gloves. What d'ee do? — 'Sheart, a' has locked the door indeed, I think. — Nay, Cousin Fainall, open the door. — Pshaw, what a vixen trick is 100 this? — Nay, now a' has seen me too. — Cousin, I

[4] The opening lines of an untitled poem by Sir John Suckling.
[5] The opening lines of Edmund Waller's *The Story of Phoebus and Daphne, Applied.*

40] Q1Q2 *into*; W1 *in to.*   61] Q1Q2W1 *He?*   79] Q2W1 *will have.*

made bold to pass through as it were — I think this door's inchanted ——

MILLA. (*repeating*).

> I prithee spare me, gentle boy,
> Press me no more for that slight toy, —[1]   105

SIR WIL. Anan?[2] Cousin, your servant.

MILLA. [*repeating*].

> That foolish trifle of a heart ——

Sir Wilfull!

SIR WIL. Yes — your servant. No offence, I hope, cousin.   110

MILLA. (*repeating*).

> I swear it will not do its part,
> Though thou dost thine, employ'st thy power and art.

Natural, easy Suckling!

SIR WIL. Anan? Suckling? No such suckling neither, cousin, nor stripling: I thank heaven, 115 I'm no minor.

MILLA. Ah, rustic, ruder than Gothic![3]

SIR WIL. Well, well, I shall understand your lingo one of these days, cousin; in the meanwhile I must answer in plain English.   120

MILLA. Have you any business with me, Sir Wilfull?

SIR WIL. Not at present, cousin. — Yes, I made bold to see, to come and know if that how you were disposed to fetch a walk this evening, if so be 125 that I might not be troublesome, I would have [sought] a walk with you.

MILLA. A walk? What then?

SIR WIL. Nay, nothing — only for the walk's sake, that's all ——   130

MILLA. I nauseate walking; 'tis a country diversion; I loathe the country and everything that relates to it.

SIR WIL. Indeed! Hah! Look ye, look ye, you do? Nay, 'tis like you may. — Here are choice 135 of pastimes here in town, as plays and the like; that must be confessed indeed.

MILLA. Ah, *l'étourdie!*[4] I hate the town too.

SIR WIL. Dear heart, that's much. — Hah! that you should hate 'em both! Hah! 'tis like you 140 may; there are some can't relish the town, and others can't away with the country, — 'tis like you may be one of those, cousin.

MILLA. Ha, ha, ha! Yes, 'tis like I may. — You have nothing further to say to me?   145

SIR WIL. Not at present, cousin. — 'Tis like

when I have an opportunity to be more private, — I may break my mind in some measure — I conjecture you partly guess. — However, that's as time shall try, — but spare to speak and spare to 150 speed, as they say.

MILLA. If it is of no great importance, Sir Wilfull, you will oblige me to leave me: I have just now a little business ——

SIR WIL. Enough, enough, cousin: yes, yes, 155 all a case. — When you're disposed, when you're disposed. Now's as well as another time; and another time as well as now. All's one for that, — yes, yes, if your concerns call you, there's no haste; it will keep cold as they say. — Cousin, your 160 servant. — I think this door's locked.

MILLA. You may go this way, sir.

SIR WIL. Your servant! then with your leave I'll return to my company.   *Exit.*

MILLA. Ay, ay; ha, ha, ha!   165

> Like Phœbus sung the no less am'rous boy.[5]

Enter MIRABELL.

MIRA.

> Like Daphne she, as lovely and as coy.

Do you lock yourself up from me, to make my search more curious?[6] Or is this pretty artifice contrived, to signify that here the chase must 170 end, and my pursuit be crowned, for you can fly no further?

MILLA. Vanity! No — I'll fly and be followed to the last moment. Though I am upon the very verge of matrimony, I expect you should solicit 175 me as much as if I were wavering at the grate of a monastery, with one foot over the threshold. I'll be solicited to the very last, nay, and afterwards.

MIRA. What, after the last?

MILLA. Oh, I should think I was poor and 180 had nothing to bestow, if I were reduced to an inglorious ease, and freed from the agreeable fatigues of solicitation.

MIRA. But do not you know, that when favors are conferred upon instant and tedious solicita- 185 tion, that they diminish in their value, and that both the giver loses the grace, and the receiver lessens his pleasure?

MILLA. It may be in things of common application; but never sure in love. Oh, I hate a lover 190 that can dare to think he draws a moment's air, independent on the bounty of his mistress. There is not so impudent a thing in nature, as the saucy look of an assured man, confident of success. The pedantic arrogance of a very husband has not 195

---

[1] The five lines spoken by Millamant, with interruptions, constitute the first stanza of an untitled song by Suckling.
[2] An interjection equivalent to 'What do you say?'
[3] At this time equivalent to 'barbarian.'
[4] Ah, the giddy (town)! Some editors emend to '*l'étourdi,*' when the meaning becomes, 'Ah, the fool!'
[5] The third line of the poem by Waller previously quoted by Millamant; Mirabell caps it with the fourth line.
[6] Intricate.

127] Q1Q2W1 *fought.*   174] Q2W1 *moment, though.*

so pragmatical [1] an air. Ah! I'll never marry, unless I am first made sure of my will and pleasure.

MIRA. Would you have 'em both before marriage? Or will you be contented with the first now,
and stay for the other till after grace? [2]　　　200

MILLA. Ah, don't be impertinent. — My dear
liberty, shall I leave thee? My faithful solitude,
my darling contemplation, must I bid you then
adieu? Ay-h, adieu — my morning thoughts,
agreeable wakings, indolent slumbers, all ye　205
douceurs,[3] ye *sommeils du matin*,[4] adieu? — I can't
do't, 'tis more than impossible. Positively, Mirabell, I'll lie abed in a morning as long as I please.

MIRA. Then I'll get up in a morning as early as
I please.　　　210

MILLA. Ah! Idle creature, get up when you
will. — And d'ee hear, I won't be called names after
I'm married; positively I won't be called names.

MIRA. Names!

MILLA. Ay, as wife, spouse, my dear, joy,　215
jewel, love, sweetheart, and the rest of that nauseous
cant, in which men and their wives are so fulsomely
familiar — I shall never bear that. — Good Mirabell, don't let us be familiar or fond, nor kiss before
folks, like my Lady Fadler [5] and Sir Francis: nor　220
go to Hyde Park together the first Sunday in a new
chariot, to provoke eyes and whispers; and then
never to be seen there together again; as if we were
proud of one another the first week, and ashamed
of one another for ever after. Let us never　225
visit together, nor go to a play together, but let us
be very strange [6] and well bred: let us be as strange
as if we had been married a great while; and as well
bred as if we were not married at all.

MIRA. Have you any more conditions to　230
offer? Hitherto your demands are pretty reasonable.

MILLA. Trifles, — as liberty to pay and receive
visits to and from whom I please; to write and receive letters, without interrogatories or wry faces
on your part. To wear what I please; and　235
choose conversation with regard only to my own
taste; to have no obligation upon me to converse
with wits that I don't like, because they are your
acquaintance; or to be intimate with fools, because
they may be your relations. Come to dinner　240
when I please, dine in my dressing-room when I'm
out of humor, without giving a reason. To have
my closet [7] inviolate; to be sole empress of my tea-
table, which you must never presume to approach
without first asking leave. And lastly, wher-　245
ever I am, you shall always knock at the door before

you come in. These articles subscribed, if I continue to endure you a little longer, I may by degrees
dwindle into a wife.

MIRA. Your bill of fare is something ad-　250
vanced [8] in this latter account. Well, have I liberty
to offer conditions — that when you are dwindled
into a wife, I may not be beyond measure enlarged
into a husband?

MILLA. You have free leave; propose your　255
utmost, speak and spare not.

MIRA. I thank you. *Imprimis* then, I covenant
that your acquaintance be general; that you admit
no sworn confident, or intimate of your own sex; no
she-friend to screen her affairs under your　260
countenance, and tempt you to make trial of a
mutual secrecy. No decoy-duck to wheedle you
a 'fop-scrambling' [9] to the play in a mask —
then bring you home in a pretended fright, when
you think you shall be found out — and rail at　265
me for missing the play, and disappointing the frolic
which you had, to pick me up and prove my constancy.

MILLA. Detestable *imprimis!* I go to the play
in a mask!　　　270

MIRA. *Item*, I article,[10] that you continue to like
your own face as long as I shall; and while it passes
current with me, that you endeavor not to new-coin
it. To which end, together with all vizards for the
day, I prohibit all masks for the night, made　275
of oiled-skins and I know not what — hog's bones,
hare's gall, pig-water, and the marrow of a roasted
cat. In short, I forbid all commerce with the
gentlewoman in What-d'ye-call-it Court.[11] *Item*,
I shut my doors against all bawds with baskets,　280
and pennyworths of muslin, china, fans, atlases,[12]
etc. — *Item*, when you shall be breeding ——

MILLA. Ah! name it not.

MIRA. Which may be presumed, with a blessing
on our endeavors ——　　　285

MILLA. Odious endeavors!

MIRA. I denounce against all strait lacing,
squeezing for a shape, till you mould my boy's head
like a sugar-loaf; and instead of a man-child, make
me the father to a crooked billet. Lastly, to　290
the dominion of the tea-table I submit, — but with
proviso, that you exceed not in your province; but
restrain yourself to native and simple tea-table
drinks, as tea, chocolate, and coffee, as likewise to
genuine and authorized tea-table talk — such　295
as mending of fashions, spoiling reputations, railing
at absent friends, and so forth — but that on no
account you encroach upon the men's prerogative,

---

[1] Conceited.
[2] Here referring to the prayer concluding the marriage ceremony.
[3] Indulgences.　　　[4] Morning slumbers.
[5] Fondler.　　　[6] Reserved.　　　[7] Private room.

[8] Somewhat increased.　　　[9] Scrambling for fops.
[10] Stipulate.
[11] Presumably a seller of cosmetics well-known in her day.
[12] A kind of silk-satin.

and presume to drink healths, or toast fellows; for prevention of which I banish all foreign forces, 300 all auxiliaries to the tea-table, as orange-brandy, all aniseed, cinnamon, citron, and Barbadoes waters, together with ratafia and the most noble spirit of clary,[1] — but for cowslip-wine, poppy water, and all dormitives,[2] those I allow. These provisos 305 admitted, in other things I may prove a tractable and complying husband.

MILLA. Oh, horrid provisos! filthy strong waters! I toast fellows, odious men! I hate your odious provisos. 310

MIRA. Then we're agreed. Shall I kiss your hand upon the contract? And here comes one to be a witness to the sealing of the deed.

Enter MRS. FAINALL.

MILLA. Fainall, what shall I do? Shall I have him? I think I must have him. 315

MRS. FAIN. Ay, ay, take him, take him, what should you do?

MILLA. Well then — I'll take my death, I'm in a horrid fright — Fainall, I shall never say it — well — I think — I'll endure you. 320

MRS. FAIN. Fie, fie! have him, have him, and tell him so in plain terms: for I am sure you have a mind to him.

MILLA. Are you? I think I have — and the horrid man looks as if he thought so too. — 325 Well, you ridiculous thing you, I'll have you — I won't be kissed, nor I won't be thanked — here, kiss my hand though. — So, hold your tongue now, and don't say a word.

MRS. FAIN. Mirabell, there's a necessity for 330 your obedience; — you have neither time to talk nor stay. My mother is coming; and in my conscience, if she should see you, would fall into fits, and maybe not recover time enough to return to Sir Rowland, who, as Foible tells me, is in a fair way to suc- 335 ceed. Therefore spare your ecstasies for another occasion, and slip down the backstairs, where Foible waits to consult you.

MILLA. Ay, go, go. In the meantime I suppose you have said something to please me. 340

MIRA. I am all obedience.   Exit MIRABELL.

MRS. FAIN. Yonder Sir Wilfull's drunk; and so noisy that my mother has been forced to leave Sir Rowland to appease him; but he answers her only with singing and drinking. — What they have 345 done by this time I know not; but Petulant and he were upon quarrelling as I came by.

---

[1] Probably Congreve meant 'clary-water,' a mixture of brandy, sugar, clary-flowers, cinnamon, and ambergris, rather than the milder clary, made of wine, honey, and spices.
[2] Sleep-inducing drinks.

MILLA. Well, if Mirabell should not make a good husband, I am a lost thing; — for I find I love him violently. 350

MRS. FAIN. So it seems, when you mind not what's said to you. — If you doubt him, you had best take up with Sir Wilfull.

MILLA. How can you name that superannuated lubber? foh! 355

Enter WITWOUD from drinking.

MRS. FAIN. So, is the fray made up, that you have left 'em?

WIT. Left 'em? I could stay no longer — I have laughed like ten christ'nings — I am tipsy with laughing. — If I had stayed any longer I should 360 have burst, — I must have been let out and pieced in the sides like an unsized camlet.[3] — Yes, yes, the fray is composed; my lady came in like a [nolle] prosequi[4] and stopped their proceedings.

MILLA. What was the dispute? 365

WIT. That's the jest; there was no dispute. They could neither of 'em speak for rage; and so fell a sputt'ring at one another like two roasting apples.

Enter PETULANT drunk.

WIT. Now, Petulant, all's over, all's well. Gad, my head begins to whim it about.[5] — Why 370 dost thou not speak? Thou art both as drunk and as mute as a fish.

PET. Look you, Mrs. Millamant — if you can love me, dear nymph — say it — and that's the conclusion — pass on, or pass off, — that's all. 375

WIT. Thou hast uttered volumes, folios, in less than decimo sexto,[6] my dear Lacedemonian.[7] Sirrah Petulant, thou art an epitomizer of words.

PET. Witwoud — you are an annihilator of sense.

WIT. Thou art a retailer of phrases; and 380 dost deal in remnants of remnants, like a maker of pincushions — thou art in truth (metaphorically speaking) a speaker of shorthand.

PET. Thou art (without a figure) just one half of an ass; and Baldwin[8] yonder, thy half-brother, 385 is the rest. — A gemini[9] of asses split, would make just four of you.

---

[3] Cloth is sized by treating it with a glutinous substance, which, among other things, helps to preserve it. The composition of camlet varied: in this period it was woven from the hair of Angora goats.
[4] A motion in a legal action by which the complaining party abandons his case.
[5] To be dizzy.
[6] A very small size (referring to books); usually written 16mo.
[7] The Spartans were famous for terseness of speech.
[8] Baldwin was the name of the ass in medieval beast epics.
[9] Pair.

328] W1 om. and.   345] W1 they may have.   362] B and MS report unfixed as the reading in some copies of Q1.
363] Q1Q2W1 noli.   364] W1 the proceedings.

WIT. Thou dost bite, my dear mustard seed;[1] kiss me for that.

PET. Stand off — I'll kiss no more males, — 390 I have kissed your twin yonder in a humor of reconciliation, till he (*hiccup*) rises upon my stomach like a radish.

MILLA. Eh! filthy creature! — what was the quarrel? 395

PET. There was no quarrel — there might have been a quarrel.

WIT. If there had been words enow between 'em to have expressed provocation, they had gone together by the ears like a pair of castanets. 400

PET. You were the quarrel.

MILLA. Me!

PET. If I have a humor to quarrel, I can make less matters conclude premises.[2] If you are not handsome, what then, if I have a humor to 405 prove it? — If I shall have my reward, say so; if not, fight for your face the next time yourself. — I'll go sleep.

WIT. Do, wrap thyself up like a woodlouse, and dream revenge — and hear me, if thou canst 410 learn to write by tomorrow morning, pen me a challenge — I'll carry it for thee.

PET. Carry your mistress's monkey a spider, — go flea dogs,[3] and read romances! — I'll go to bed to my maid. *Exit.* 415

MRS. FAIN. He's horridly drunk. — How came you all in this pickle?

WIT. A plot, a plot, to get rid of the knight, — your husband's advice; but he sneaked off.

Enter LADY WISHFORT, *and* SIR WILFULL, *drunk.*

LADY WISH. Out upon't, out upon't, at 420 years of discretion, and comport yourself at this rantipole[4] rate!

SIR WIL. No offence, aunt.

LADY WISH. Offence? As I'm a person, I'm ashamed of you. — Fogh! how you stink of 425 wine! D'ee think my niece will ever endure such a borachio![5] you're an absolute borachio.

SIR WIL. Borachio!

LADY WISH. At a time when you should commence an amour and put your best foot fore- 430 most ——

SIR WIL. 'Sheart, an you grutch me your liquor, make a bill. Give me more drink, and take my purse. (*Sings.*)

Prithee fill me the glass 435
　　Till it laugh in my face,
With ale that is potent and mellow;
　　He that whines for a lass,
　　Is an ignorant ass,
For a bumper has not its fellow. 440

But if you would have me marry my cousin, — say the word, and I'll do't — Wilfull will do't, that's the word — Wilfull will do't, that's my crest — my motto I have forgot.

LADY WISH. My nephew's a little overtaken, 445 cousin — but 'tis with drinking your health. — O' my word you are obliged to him ——

SIR WIL. *In vino veritas*,[6] aunt. — If I drunk your health today, cousin, — I am a borachio. But if you have a mind to be married, say the word, 450 and send for the piper; Wilfull will do't. If not, dust it away,[7] and let's have t'other round. — Tony, 'odsheart, where's Tony. — Tony's an honest fellow, but he spits after a bumper, and that's a fault.

(*Sings.*)

We'll drink and we'll never ha' done, boys, 455
　　Put the glass then around with the sun, boys,
Let Apollo's example invite us;
　　For he's drunk every night,
　　And that makes him so bright,
That he's able next morning to light us. 460

The sun's a good pimple,[8] an honest soaker;[9] he has a cellar at your Antipodes. If I travel, aunt, I touch at your Antipodes. — Your Antipodes are a good rascally sort of topsy-turvy fellows. If I had a bumper, I'd stand upon my head and drink a 465 health to 'em. — A match or no match, cousin with the hard name? — Aunt, Wilfull will do't. If she has her maidenhead, let her look to't; if she has not, let her keep her own counsel in the meantime, and cry out at the nine months' end. 470

MILLA. Your pardon, madam, I can stay no longer — Sir Wilfull grows very powerful. Egh! how he smells! I shall be overcome if I stay. Come, cousin. *Exeunt* MILLAMANT *and* MRS. FAINALL.

LADY WISH. Smells! he would poison a tal- 475 low-chandler and his family. Beastly creature, I know not what to do with him. — Travel, quoth a; ay travel, travel, get thee gone, get thee but far enough, to the Saracens, or the Tartars, or the Turks — for thou art not fit to live in a Christian 480 commonwealth, thou beastly pagan.

SIR WIL. Turks, no; no Turks, aunt: your Turks are infidels, and believe not in the grape. Your Mahometan, your Mussulman, is a dry stinkard — no offence, aunt. My map says that your Turk 485

[1] Probably playing on Petulant's size and the mordant quality of his wit.
[2] Bring matters to a head.
[3] Pick fleas from lap-dogs' coats.
[4] Ill-mannered.
[5] Drunkard.

[6] In wine there is truth; i.e., drunkards speak the truth frankly.
[7] Toss off your drink quickly.
[8] Boon companion.　　[9] Hard drinker.

is not so honest a man as your Christian — I cannot find by the map that your Mufti [1] is orthodox — whereby it is a plain case, that orthodox is a hard word, aunt, and (*hiccup*) Greek for claret.   (*Sings.*)

> To drink is a Christian diversion,   490
> Unknown to the Turk and the Persian:
>   Let Mahometan fools
>   Live by heathenish rules,
> And be damned over tea-cups and coffee.
>   But let British lads sing,   495
>   Crown a health to the king,
> And a fig for your sultan and sophy.[2]

Ah, Tony!

Enter FOIBLE *and whispers* LADY WISHFORT.

LADY WISH. Sir Rowland impatient? Good lack! what shall I do with this beastly tumbril? [3] — 500 Go lie down and sleep, you sot — or as I'm a person, I'll have you bastinadoed with broomsticks. Call up the wenches.   *Exit* FOIBLE.

SIR WIL. Ahey! Wenches, where are the wenches?

LADY WISH. Dear Cousin Witwoud, get him   505 away, and you will bind me to you inviolably. I have an affair of moment that invades me with some precipitation. — You will oblige me to all futurity.

WIT. Come, knight. — Pox on him, I don't know what to say to him. — Will you go to a cock- 510 match?

SIR WIL. With a wench, Tony? Is she a shake-bag, sirrah? Let me bite your cheek for that.

WIT. Horrible! He has a breath like a bagpipe. — Ay, ay; come, will you march, my Salopian? [4]   515

SIR WIL. Lead on, little Tony — I'll follow thee, my Anthony, my Tantony. Sirrah, thou sha't be my Tantony; and I'll be thy pig.[5]

— And a fig for your sultan and sophy.

Exit singing with WITWOUD.

LADY WISH. This will never do. It will   520 never make a match. — At least before he has been abroad.

Enter WAITWELL, *disguised as for* SIR ROWLAND.

Dear Sir Rowland, I am confounded with confusion at the retrospection of my own rudeness, — I have more pardons to ask than the pope distributes   525 in the year of jubilee.[6] But I hope where there is likely to be so near an alliance, we may unbend the

severity of decorum, and dispense with a little ceremony.

WAIT. My impatience, madam, is the effect   530 of my transport; — and till I have the possession of your adorable person, I am tantalized on a rack; and do but hang, madam, on the tenter [7] of expectation

LADY WISH. You have excess of gallantry, Sir Rowland; and press things to a conclusion,   535 with a most prevailing vehemence. — But a day or two for decency of marriage ——

WAIT. For decency of funeral, madam. The delay will break my heart — or if that should fail, I shall be poisoned. My nephew will get an ink- 540 ling of my designs, and poison me, — and I would willingly starve him before I die — I would gladly go out of the world with that satisfaction. That would be some comfort to me, if I could but live so long as to be revenged on that unnatural viper.   545

LADY WISH. Is he so unnatural, say you? Truly I would contribute much both to the saving of your life, and the accomplishment of your revenge. Not that I respect [8] myself, though he has been a perfidious wretch to me.   550

WAIT. Perfidious to you!

LADY WISH. O Sir Rowland, the hours that he has died away at my feet, the tears that he has shed, the oaths that he has sworn, the palpitations that he has felt, the trances, and the tremblings, the ardors   555 and the ecstasies, the kneelings and the risings, the heart-heavings, and the hand-gripings, the pangs and the pathetic regards of his protesting eyes! Oh, no memory can register!

WAIT. What, my rival! is the rebel my rival?   560 a' dies.

LADY WISH. No, don't kill him at once, Sir Rowland; starve him gradually inch by inch.

WAIT. I'll do't. In three weeks he shall be barefoot; in a month out at knees with begging an   565 alms; — he shall starve upward and upward, till he has nothing living but his head, and then go out in a stink like a candle's end upon a save-all.[9]

LADY WISH. Well, Sir Rowland, you have the way, — you are no novice in the labyrinth of   570 love — you have the clue. — But as I am a person, Sir Rowland, you must not attribute my yielding to any sinister appetite, or indigestion of widowhood; nor impute my complacency to any lethargy of continence. I hope you do not think me prone to   575 any iteration of nuptials. ——

WAIT. Far be it from me ——

LADY WISH. If you do, I protest I must recede — or think that I have made a prostitution of decorums,

---

[1] The Grand Mufti — head of the Mohammedan religion in Turkey.
[2] The Shah of Persia.
[3] Heavy cart.
[4] Native of Shropshire.
[5] St. Antony, or Tantony, was the patron of swineherds, and was represented in art as accompanied by a pig.
[6] The year in which this play was produced (1700) was a jubilee year.

[7] Tenter-hook.
[8] Consider, regard.
[9] A contrivance for holding a candle which permits it to burn to the end.

491] W1 *Turk or.*   503] W1 *wenches with broomsticks.*   532] Q2W1 *the rack.*

but in the vehemence of compassion, and to 580
save the life of a person of so much importance ——

WAIT. I esteem it so ——

LADY WISH. Or else you wrong my condescension ——

WAIT. I do not, I do not —— 585

LADY WISH. Indeed you do.

WAIT. I do not, fair shrine of virtue.

LADY WISH. If you think the least scruple of
carnality was an ingredient ——

WAIT. Dear madam, no. You are all cam- 590
phire[1] and frankincense, all chastity and odor.

LADY WISH. Or that ——

Enter FOIBLE.

FOIB. Madam, the dancers are ready, and there's
one with a letter, who must deliver it into your own
hands. 595

LADY WISH. Sir Rowland, will you give me leave?
Think favorably, judge candidly, and conclude you
have found a person who would suffer racks in
honor's cause, dear Sir Rowland, and will wait on you
incessantly. *Exit.* 600

WAIT. Fie, fie! — What a slavery have I under-
gone! Spouse, hast thou any cordial? — I want
spirits.

FOIB. What a washy rogue art thou, to pant thus
for a quarter of an hour's lying and swearing to 605
a fine lady!

WAIT. Oh, she is the antidote to desire. Spouse,
thou wilt fare the worse for't — I shall have no appetite to iteration of nuptials — this eight and forty
hours: — by this hand I'd rather be a chairman 610
in the dog-days — than act Sir Rowland till this
time tomorrow.

Enter LADY WISHFORT *with a letter.*

LADY WISH. Call in the dancers. — Sir Rowland,
we'll sit, if you please, and see the entertainment.
(*Dance.*)

Now with your permission, Sir Rowland, I 615
will peruse my letter — I would open it in your
presence, because I would not make you uneasy.
If it should make you uneasy I would burn it —
speak if it does — but you may see by the superscription it is like a woman's hand. 620

FOIB. (*to him*). By heaven! Mrs. Marwood's, I
know it; — my heart aches — get it from her ——

WAIT. A woman's hand? No, madam, that's no
woman's hand, I see that already. That's somebody whose throat must be cut. 625

LADY WISH. Nay, Sir Rowland, since you give me
a proof of your passion by your jealousy, I promise
you I'll make you a return, by a frank communica-

[1] Used during this period as an antaphrodisiac.

tion. — You shall see it — we'll open it together —
look you here. 630

(*Reads.*) 'Madam, though unknown to you,' —
Look you there, 'tis from nobody that I know — 'I
have that honor for your character, that I think myself obliged to let you know you are abused. He
who pretends to be Sir Rowland is a cheat and 635
a rascal ——' Oh heavens! what's this?

FOIB. [*aside*]. Unfortunate, all's ruined.

WAIT. How, how, let me see, let me see! (*Reading.*) 'A rascal, and disguised and suborned for that
imposture,' — O villainy! O villainy! — 'by 640
the contrivance of ——'

LADY WISH. I shall faint, I shall die, I shall die,
oh!

FOIB. (*to him*). Say 'tis your nephew's hand. —
Quickly, his plot, swear, swear it. 645

WAIT. Here's a villain! Madam, don't you perceive it, don't you see it?

LADY WISH. Too well, too well. I have seen too
much.

WAIT. I told you at first I knew the hand. 650
A woman's hand? The rascal writes a sort of a large
hand, your Roman hand. I saw there was a throat
to be cut presently. If he were my son, as he is my
nephew, I'd pistol him ——

FOIB. O treachery! But you are sure, Sir 655
Rowland, it is his writing?

WAIT. Sure? am I here? do I live? do I love this
pearl of India? I have twenty letters in my pocket
from him, in the same character.

LADY WISH. How! 660

FOIB. Oh, what luck it is, Sir Rowland, that you
were present at this juncture! This was the business
that brought Mr. Mirabell disguised to Madam
Millamant this afternoon. I thought something was
contriving, when he stole by me and would 665
have hid his face.

LADY WISH. How, how! — I heard the villain
was in the house indeed, and now I remember, my
niece went away abruptly, when Sir Wilfull was to
have made his addresses. 670

FOIB. Then, then, madam, Mr. Mirabell waited
for her in her chamber, but I would not tell your
ladyship to discompose you when you were to receive Sir Rowland.

WAIT. Enough, his date is short. 675

FOIB. No, good Sir Rowland, don't incur the law.

WAIT. Law! I care not for law. I can but die,
and 'tis in a good cause — my lady shall be satisfied
of my truth and innocence, though it cost me my
life. 680

LADY WISH. No, dear Sir Rowland, don't fight; if
you should be killed I must never show my face; or
hanged — oh, consider my reputation, Sir Rowland! No, you shan't fight. I'll go in and examine

my niece; I'll make her confess. I conjure 685 you, Sir Rowland, by all your love, not to fight.

WAIT. I am charmed, madam, I obey. But some proof you must let me give you; — I'll go for a black box, which contains the writings of my whole estate, and deliver that into your hands.   690

LADY WISH. Ay, dear Sir Rowland, that will be some comfort; bring the black box.

WAIT. And may I presume to bring a contract to be signed this night? May I hope so far?

LADY WISH. Bring what you will; but come 695 alive, pray come alive. Oh, this is a happy discovery!

WAIT. Dead or alive I'll come — and married we will be in spite of treachery; ay, and get an heir that shall defeat the last remaining glimpse of 700 hope in my abandoned nephew. Come, my buxom widow:

E'er long you shall substantial proof receive
That I'm an arrant [1] knight ——

FOIB. [aside]. Or arrant knave. Exeunt. 705

ACT V

SCENE I

Scene continues.

LADY WISHFORT *and* FOIBLE.

LADY WISH. Out of my house, out of my house, thou viper, thou serpent, that I have fostered! thou bosom traitress, that I raised from nothing! — begone, begone, begone, go, go! — that I took from washing of old gauze and weaving of dead hair,[2] 5 with a bleak blue nose, over a chafing-dish of starved embers, and dining behind a traverse rag, in a shop no bigger than a bird-cage, — go, go, starve again, do, do!

FOIB. Dear madam, I'll beg pardon on my 10 knees.

LADY WISH. Away, out, out, go set up for yourself again! — do, drive a trade, do, with your threepenny worth of small ware, flaunting upon a packthread, under a brandy-seller's bulk,[3] or against 15 a dead wall by a ballad-monger! Go, hang out an old Frisoneer gorget,[4] with a yard of yellow colberteen [5] again! do! an old gnawed mask, two rows of pins, and a child's fiddle; a glass necklace with the beads broken, and a quilted nightcap with one 20 ear! Go, go, drive a trade! — These were your commodities, you treacherous trull, this was your merchandise you dealt in, when I took you into my

house, placed you next myself, and made you governante [6] of my whole family! You have forgot 25 this, have you, now you have feathered your nest?

FOIB. No, no, dear madam. Do but hear me, have but a moment's patience — I'll confess all. Mr. Mirabell seduced me; I am not the first that he has wheedled with his dissembling tongue; your 30 ladyship's own wisdom has been deluded by him, — then how should I, a poor ignorant, defend myself? O madam, if you knew but what he promised me, and how he assured me your ladyship should come to no damage! — Or else the wealth of the Indies 35 should not have bribed me to conspire against so good, so sweet, so kind a lady as you have been to me.

LADY WISH. No damage? What, to betray me, to marry me to a cast servingman; to make me a receptacle, an hospital for a decayed pimp? No 40 damage? O thou frontless [7] impudence, more than a big-bellied actress!

FOIB. Pray, do but hear me, madam; he could not marry your ladyship, madam. — No indeed, his marriage was to have been void in law; for he was 45 married to me first, to secure your ladyship. He could not have bedded your ladyship; for if he had consummated with your ladyship, he must have run the risk of the law, and been put upon his clergy.[8] — Yes indeed, I enquired of the law in that case 50 before I would meddle or make.

LADY WISH. What, then I have been your property, have I? I have been convenient to you, it seems, — while you were catering for Mirabell, I have been broker for you? What, have you 55 made a passive bawd of me? — This exceeds all precedent; I am brought to fine uses, to become a botcher [9] of second-hand marriages between Abigails and Andrews! [10] I'll couple you! Yes, I'll baste you together, you and your Philander! [11] I'll Duke's 60 Place you,[12] as I'm a person. Your turtle is in custody already; you shall coo in the same cage, if there be constable or warrant in the parish.   Exit.

FOIB. Oh, that ever I was born! Oh, that I was ever married! — A bride, ay, I shall be a Bride- 65 well-bride.[13] Oh!

Enter MRS. FAINALL.

MRS. FAIN. Poor Foible, what's the matter?

FOIB. O madam, my lady's gone for a constable; I shall be had to a justice, and put to Bridewell to beat hemp! Poor Waitwell's gone to prison already. 70

[6] Housekeeper.   [7] Shameless.
[8] A criminal, if he could read, might avoid sentence of death for all but atrocious crimes by claiming 'benefit of clergy,' a privilege not limited, at this date, to persons in holy orders.
[9] Mending tailor.   [10] Lady's maids and valets.
[11] Lover.   [12] Cf. I. i. 129.
[13] Bridewell was a prison situated between Ludgate Circus and the Thames.

---

[1] Waitwell uses this word in its earlier sense, 'wandering' (errant): Foible plays on it in its later, opprobrious sense, 'downright.'

[2] I.e., making wigs.   [3] Stall.
[4] Woollen neck-piece.   [5] A kind of lace.

MRS. FAIN. Have a good heart, Foible; Mirabell's gone to give security for him. This is all Marwood's and my husband's doing.

FOIB. Yes, yes; I know it, madam; she was in my lady's closet, and overheard all that you said to 75 me before dinner. She sent the letter to my lady; and that missing effect,[1] Mr. Fainall laid this plot to arrest Waitwell, when he pretended to go for the papers; and in the meantime Mrs. Marwood declared all to my lady. 80

MRS. FAIN. Was there no mention made of me in the letter? — My mother does not suspect my being in the confederacy? I fancy Marwood has not told her, though she has told my husband.

FOIB. Yes, madam; but my lady did not see 85 that part; we stifled the letter before she read so far. Has that mischievous devil told Mr. Fainall of your ladyship then?

MRS. FAIN. Ay, all's out, my affair with Mirabell, everything discovered. This is the last day of 90 our living together, that's my comfort.

FOIB. Indeed, madam, and so 'tis a comfort if you knew all; — he has been even with your ladyship, which I could have told you long enough since, but I love to keep peace and quietness, by my good 95 will: I had rather bring friends together than set 'em at distance. But Mrs. Marwood and he are nearer related than ever their parents thought for.

MRS. FAIN. Say'st thou so, Foible? Canst thou prove this? 100

FOIB. I can take my oath of it, madam, so can Mrs. Mincing; we have had many a fair word from Madam Marwood, to conceal something that passed in our chamber one evening when you were at Hyde Park; — and we were thought to have gone 105 a-walking, but we went up unawares — though we were sworn to secrecy too. Madam Marwood took a book and swore us upon it; but it was but a book of verses and poems. So as long as it was not a Bible oath, we may break it with a safe conscience. 110

MRS. FAIN. This discovery is the most opportune thing I could wish. Now, Mincing?

Enter MINCING.

MINC. My lady would speak with Mrs. Foible, mem. Mr. Mirabell is with her; he has set your spouse at liberty, Mrs. Foible, and would have 115 you hide yourself in my lady's closet, till my old lady's anger is abated. Oh, my old lady is in a perilous passion at something Mr. Fainall has said; he swears, and my old lady cries. There's a fearful hurricane, I vow. He says, mem, how that he'll 120 have my lady's fortune made over to him, or he'll be divorced.

MRS. FAIN. Does your lady and Mirabell know that?

MINC. Yes, mem, they have sent me to see if 125 Sir Wilfull be sober, and to bring him to them. My lady is resolved to have him, I think, rather than lose such a vast sum as six thousand pound. Oh, come, Mrs. Foible, I hear my old lady.

MRS. FAIN. Foible, you must tell Mincing 130 that she must prepare to vouch when I call her.

FOIB. Yes, yes, madam.

MINC. Oh, yes, mem, I'll vouch anything for your ladyship's service, be what it will.

Exeunt MINCING *and* FOIBLE.

Enter LADY WISHFORT *and* MRS. MARWOOD.

LADY WISH. Oh, my dear friend, how can I 135 enumerate the benefits that I have received from your goodness? To you I owe the timely discovery of the false vows of Mirabell; to you the detection of the impostor Sir Rowland. And now you are become an intercessor with my son-in-law, to save 140 the honor of my house, and compound for the frailties of my daughter. Well, friend, you are enough to reconcile me to the bad world, or else I would retire to deserts and solitudes; and feed harmless sheep by groves and purling streams. Dear Marwood, 145 let us leave the world, and retire by ourselves and be shepherdesses.

MRS. MAR. Let us first dispatch the affair in hand, madam. We shall have leisure to think of retirement afterwards. — Here is one who is con- 150 cerned in the treaty.

LADY WISH. O daughter, daughter, is it possible thou shouldst be my child, bone of my bone, and flesh of my flesh, and as I may say, another me, and yet transgress the most minute particle of 155 severe virtue? Is it possible you should lean aside to iniquity, who have been cast in the direct mold of virtue? I have not only been a mold but a pattern for you, and a model for you, after you were brought into the world. 160

MRS. FAIN. I don't understand your ladyship.

LADY WISH. Not understand? Why, have you not been naught?[2] Have you not been sophisticated?[3] Not understand? Here I am ruined to compound for your caprices and your cuckold- 165 oms. I must pawn my plate and my jewels, and ruin my niece, and all little enough ——

MRS. FAIN. I am wronged and abused, and so are you. 'Tis a false accusation, as false as hell, as false as your friend there, ay, or your friend's friend, 170 my false husband.

MRS. MAR. My friend, Mrs. Fainall? Your husband my friend! what do you mean?

---

[1] Failing of its purpose.

[2] Immoral. [3] Corrupted.

109] W1 om. *verses and.*　　109] Q2W1 *So long as.*　　138] W1 *to you I owe the detection.*

MRS. FAIN. I know what I mean, madam, and so do you; and so shall the world at a time con- 175 venient.

MRS. MAR. I am sorry to see you so passionate, madam. More temper[1] would look more like innocence. But I have done. I am sorry my zeal to serve your ladyship and family should admit of 180 misconstruction, or make me liable to affronts. You will pardon me, madam, if I meddle no more with an affair in which I am not personally concerned.

LADY WISH. O dear friend, I am so ashamed that you should meet with such returns! — [To 185 MRS. FAINALL.] You ought to ask pardon on your knees, ungrateful creature! she deserves more from you, than all your life can accomplish. — [To MRS. MARWOOD.] Oh, don't leave me destitute in this perplexity! — no, stick to me, my good genius. 190

MRS. FAIN. I tell you, madam, you're abused. — Stick to you? ay, like a leech, to suck your best blood — she'll drop off when she's full. Madam, you sha' not pawn a bodkin, nor part with a brass counter in composition for me. I defy 'em all. 195 Let 'em prove their aspersions: I know my own innocence, and dare stand by[2] a trial.   *Exit.*

LADY WISH. Why, if she should be innocent, if she should be wronged after all, ha? I don't know what to think, — and I promise you, her edu- 200 cation has been unexceptionable — I may say it; for I chiefly made it my own care to initiate her very infancy in the rudiments of virtue, and to impress upon her tender years a young odium and aversion to the very sight of men; — ay, friend, she would 205 ha' shrieked if she had but seen a man, till she was in her teens. As I'm a person, 'tis true. She was never suffered to play with a male-child, though but in coats; nay, her very babies[3] were of the feminine gender. Oh, she never looked a man in the 210 face but her own father, or the chaplain, and him we made a shift to put upon her for a woman, by the help of his long garments, and his sleek face, till she was going in her fifteen.

MRS. MAR. 'Twas much she should be de- 215 ceived so long.

LADY WISH. I warrant you, or she would never have borne to have been catechised by him; and have heard his long lectures against singing and dancing, and such debaucheries; and going to 220 filthy plays, and profane music-meetings, where the lewd trebles squeek nothing but bawdy, and the bases roar blasphemy. Oh, she would have swooned at the sight or name of an obscene play-book — and can I think, after all this, that my daughter can 225 be naught? What, a whore? And thought it ex-

communication to set her foot within the door of a play-house! O my dear friend, I can't believe it, no, no! As she says, let him prove it, let him prove it!

MRS. MAR. Prove it, madam? What, and 230 have your name prostituted in a public court! yours and your daughter's reputation worried at the bar by a pack of bawling lawyers? To be ushered in with an 'Oyez' of scandal; and have your case opened by an old fumbling lecher in a quoif[4] like a man 235 midwife, to bring your daughter's infamy to light; to be a theme for legal punsters, and quibblers by the statute; and become a jest, against a rule of court, where there is no precedent for a jest in any record, not even in Doomsday Book; to discompose the 240 gravity of the bench, and provoke naughty interrogatories in more naughty law Latin; while the good judge, tickled with the proceeding, simpers under a grey beard, and fidges[5] off and on his cushion as if he had swallowed cantharides,[6] or sat upon 245 cowitch![7]

LADY WISH. Oh, 'tis very hard!

MRS. MAR. And then to have my young revellers of the Temple take notes, like 'prentices at a conventicle;[8] and after, talk it all over again in 250 Commons, or before drawers in an eating-house.

LADY WISH. Worse and worse!

MRS. MAR. Nay, this is nothing; if it would end here, 'twere well. But it must after this be consigned by the shorthand writers to the public press; 255 and from thence be transferred to the hands, nay, into the throats and lungs of hawkers, with voices more licentious than the loud flounder-man's, or the woman that cries grey-pease; and this you must hear till you are stunned; nay, you must hear noth- 260 ing else for some days.

LADY WISH. Oh, 'tis insupportable. No, no, dear friend, make it up, make it up; ay, ay, I'll compound. I'll give up all, myself and my all, my niece and her all, — anything, everything for composition. 265

MRS. MAR. Nay, madam, I advise nothing; I only lay before you, as a friend, the inconveniencies which perhaps you have overseen. Here comes Mr. Fainall. If he will be satisfied to huddle up all in silence, I shall be glad. You must think I would rather 270 congratulate than condole with you.

Enter FAINALL.

LADY WISH. Ay, ay, I do not doubt it, dear Marwood; no, no, I do not doubt it.

---

[1] Equanimity.   [2] Undergo.   [3] Dolls.

[4] A white head-dress worn by a serjeant-at-law.
[5] Moves about restlessly.   [6] An aphrodisiac.
[7] Cowage, a tropical plant, the pods of which are covered with stinging hairs.
[8] Dissenting tradesmen sometimes catechised their apprentices on the subject-matter of sermons, to which they were required to listen.

194] Q2W1 *shan't.*   197] W1 *stand a trial.*   228] W1 om. *my.*   234] Q2W1 *O yes.*
244] W1 *figes.*   245] Q2W1 *sate.*   250] W1 om. *all.*   258–259] W1 om. *or the woman … pease.*

FAIN. Well, madam; I have suffered myself to be overcome by the importunity of this lady your 275 friend; and am content you shall enjoy your own proper estate during life, on condition you oblige yourself never to marry, under such penalty as I think convenient.

LADY WISH. Never to marry? 280

FAIN. No more Sir Rowlands; — the next imposture may not be so timely detected.

MRS. MAR. That condition, I dare answer, my lady will consent to, without difficulty; she has already but too much experienced the perfidiousness of 285 men. Besides, madam, when we retire to our pastoral solitude we shall bid adieu to all other thoughts.

LADY WISH. Ay, that's true; but in case of necessity, as of health, or some such emergency ——

FAIN. Oh, if you are prescribed marriage, 290 you shall be considered; I will only reserve to myself the power to choose for you. If your physic be wholesome, it matters not who is your apothecary. Next, my wife shall settle on me the remainder of her fortune, not made over already, and for her 295 maintenance depend entirely on my discretion.

LADY WISH. This is most inhumanly savage; exceeding the barbarity of a Muscovite husband.

FAIN. I learned it from his Czarish majesty's retinue,[1] in a winter evening's conference over 300 brandy and pepper, amongst other secrets of matrimony and policy, as they are at present practised in the northern hemisphere. But this must be agreed unto, and that positively. Lastly, I will be endowed, in right of my wife, with that six thousand 305 pound, which is the moiety of Mrs. Millamant's fortune in your possession; and which she has forfeited (as will appear by the last will and testament of your deceased husband, Sir Jonathan Wishfort) by her disobedience in contracting herself against your 310 consent or knowledge; and by refusing the offered match with Sir Wilfull Witwoud, which you, like a careful aunt, had provided for her.

LADY WISH. My nephew was *non compos*,[2] and could not make his addresses. 315

FAIN. I come to make demands, — I'll hear no objections.

LADY WISH. You will grant me time to consider?

FAIN. Yes, while the instrument is drawing, to which you must set your hand till more suffi- 320 cient deeds can be perfected: which I will take care shall be done with all possible speed. In the meanwhile, I will go for the said instrument, and till my return you may balance this matter in your own discretion. *Exit* FAINALL. 325

LADY WISH. This insolence is beyond all precedent, all parallel; must I be subject to this merciless villain?

---
[1] Peter the Great had visited England in 1698.
[2] Not in his right mind.

MRS. MAR. 'Tis severe indeed, madam, that you should smart for your daughter's wantonness. 330

LADY WISH. 'Twas against my consent that she married this barbarian, but she would have him, though her year [3] was not out. — Ah! her first husband, my son Languish, would not have carried it [4] thus. Well, that was my choice, this is hers; 335 she is matched now with a witness.[5] I shall be mad, dear friend, — is there no comfort for me? Must I live to be confiscated at this rebel-rate? [6] — Here come two more of my Egyptian plagues, [7] too. 340

Enter MILLAMANT *and* SIR WILFULL.

SIR WIL. Aunt, your servant.

LADY WISH. Out, caterpillar,[8] call not me aunt! I know thee not!

SIR WIL. I confess I have been a little in disguise,[9] as they say, — 'sheart! and I'm sorry for't. 345 What would you have? I hope I committed no offence, aunt — and if I did I am willing to make satisfaction; and what can a man say fairer? If I have broke anything, I'll pay for't, an it cost a pound. And so let that content for what's past, and 350 make no more words. For what's to come, to pleasure you I'm willing to marry my cousin. So pray let's all be friends; she and I are agreed upon the matter before a witness.

LADY WISH. How's this, dear niece? Have I 355 any comfort? Can this be true?

MILLA. I am content to be a sacrifice to your repose, madam; and to convince you that I had no hand in the plot, as you were misinformed, I have laid my commands on Mirabell to come in per- 360 son, and be a witness that I give my hand to this flower of knighthood; and for the contract that passed between Mirabell and me, I have obliged him to make a resignation of it in your ladyship's presence; he is without, and waits your leave for ad- 365 mittance.

LADY WISH. Well, I'll swear I am something revived at this testimony of your obedience; but I cannot admit that traitor; — I fear I cannot fortify myself to support his appearance. He is as terrible 370 to me as a Gorgon; if I see him, I fear I shall turn to stone, petrify incessantly.

MILLA. If you disoblige him, he may resent your refusal, and insist upon the contract still. Then, 'tis the last time he will be offensive to you. 375

LADY WISH. Are you sure it will be the last time?

---
[3] Her first year of widowhood.
[4] Behaved. [5] Without a doubt.
[6] I.e., as completely as the property of rebels is confiscated.
[7] Alluding to the ten plagues visited upon Pharaoh: Ex. iii-xii.
[8] Apparently used here merely as an opprobrious name, not in the sense of 'rapacious person.'
[9] A polite periphrasis for 'drunk.'

— If I were sure of that — shall I never see him again?

MILLA. Sir Wilfull, you and he are to travel together, are you not?   380

SIR WIL. 'Sheart, the gentleman's a civil gentleman, aunt, let him come in; why, we are sworn brothers and fellow-travellers. We are to be Pylades and Orestes,[1] he and I. He is to be my interpreter in foreign parts. He has been over-seas once already; and with proviso that I marry my cousin, will cross 'em once again, only to bear me company. — 'Sheart, I'll call him in; — an I set on't once, he shall come in; and see who'll hinder him.   *Exit*.

MRS. MAR. [*aside*]. This is precious fooling,   390 if it would pass; but I'll know the bottom of it.

LADY WISH. O dear Marwood, you are not going?

MAR. Not far, madam; I'll return immediately.
    Exit.

Re-enter SIR WILFULL *and* MIRABELL.

SIR WIL. Look up, man, I'll stand by you; 'sbud, an she do frown, she can't kill you; — besides   395 — hark'ee, she dare not frown desperately, because her face is none of her own; 'sheart, an she should, her forehead would wrinkle like the coat of a cream-cheese; but mum for that, fellow-traveller.

MIRA. If a deep sense of the many injuries I   400 have offered to so good a lady, with a sincere remorse, and a hearty contrition, can but obtain the least glance of compassion, I am too happy. — Ah, madam, there was a time — but let it be forgotten — I confess I have deservedly forfeited the high   405 place I once held, of sighing at your feet; nay, kill me not, by turning from me in disdain — I come not to plead for favor, — nay, not for pardon; I am a suppliant only for your pity — I am going where I never shall behold you more ——   410

SIR WIL. How, fellow-traveller! You shall go by yourself then.

MIRA. Let me be pitied first; and afterwards forgotten — I ask no more.

SIR WIL. By'r Lady, a very reasonable request, and will cost you nothing, aunt. Come,   415 come, forgive and forget, aunt; why you must, an you are a Christian.

MIRA. Consider, madam, in reality you could not receive much prejudice; it was an innocent device; though I confess it had a face of guiltiness, it   420 was at most an artifice which love contrived — and errors which love produces have ever been accounted venial. At least think it is punishment enough, that I have lost what in my heart I hold most dear,   425 that to your cruel indignation I have offered up this

beauty, and with her my peace and quiet; nay, all my hopes of future comfort.

SIR WIL. An he does not move me, would I might never be o' the quorum![2] — an it were not as   430 good a deed as to drink, to give her to him again, I would I might never take shipping! — Aunt, if you don't forgive quickly, I shall melt, I can tell you that. My contract went no further than a little mouth glue,[3] and that's hardly dry; — one doleful sigh   435 more from my fellow-traveller and 'tis dissolved.

LADY WISH. Well, nephew, upon your account. — Ah, he has a false insinuating tongue! — Well, sir, I will stifle my just resentment at my nephew's request. I will endeavor what I can to forget —   440 but on proviso that you resign the contract with my niece immediately.

MIRA. It is in writing and with papers of concern; but I have sent my servant for it, and will deliver it to you, with all acknowledgments for your   445 transcendent goodness.

LADY WISH. (*apart*). Oh, he has witchcraft in his eyes and tongue! When I did not see him, I could have bribed a villain to his assassination; but his appearance rakes the embers which have so long   450 lain smothered in my breast.

Enter FAINALL *and* MRS. MARWOOD.

FAIN. Your date of deliberation, madam, is expired. Here is the instrument; are you prepared to sign?

LADY WISH. If I were prepared, I am not   455 impowered. My niece exerts a lawful claim, having matched herself by my direction to Sir Wilfull.

FAIN. That sham is too gross to pass on me, though 'tis imposed on you, madam.

MILLA. Sir, I have given my consent.   460

MIRA. And, sir, I have resigned my pretensions.

SIR WIL. And, sir, I assert my right; and will maintain it in defiance of you, sir, and of your instrument. 'Sheart, an you talk of an instrument, sir, I have an old fox[4] by my thigh shall hack your   465 instrument of ram vellum[5] to shreds, sir! It shall not be sufficient for a mittimus[6] or a tailor's measure; therefore, withdraw your instrument, sir, or by'r Lady I shall draw mine.

LADY WISH. Hold, nephew, hold!   470

MILLA. Good Sir Wilfull, respite your valor!

FAIN. Indeed? Are you provided of a guard, with your single beefeater there? But I'm prepared for you; and insist upon my first proposal. You shall submit your own estate to my management,   475

---

[1] Types of loyal friendship. Pylades accompanied Orestes on the long journey during which he was pursued by the Furies.

[2] A member of the bench of magistrates.
[3] An oral promise.
[4] Sword.
[5] Legal document, written on parchment.
[6] A warrant of arrest.

---

and absolutely make over my wife's to my sole use, as pursuant to the purport and tenor of this other covenant. — I suppose, madam, your consent is not requisite in this case; nor, Mr. Mirabell, your resig- 480 nation; nor, Sir Wilfull, your right. You may draw your fox if you please, sir, and make a bear-garden flourish somewhere else; for here it will not avail. This, my Lady Wishfort, must be subscribed, or your darling daughter's turned adrift, like a leaky 485 hulk to sink or swim, as she and the current of this lewd town can agree.

LADY WISH. Is there no means, no remedy, to stop my ruin? Ungrateful wretch! dost thou not owe thy being, thy subsistence, to my daughter's fortune?

FAIN. I'll answer you when I have the rest of 490 it in my possession.

MIRA. But that you would not accept of a rem-edy from my hands — I own I have not deserved you should owe any obligation to me; or else perhaps I could advise —— 495

LADY WISH. Oh, what? what? to save me and my child from ruin, from want, I'll forgive all that's past; nay, I'll consent to anything to come, to be delivered from this tyranny.

MIRA. Ay, madam; but that is too late, my 500 reward is intercepted. You have disposed of her, who only could have made me a compensation for all my services; — but be it as it may, I am resolved I'll serve you — you shall not be wronged in this savage manner! 505

LADY WISH. How! Dear Mr. Mirabell, can you be so generous at last! But it is not possible. Hark'ee, I'll break my nephew's match, you shall have my niece yet, and all her fortune, if you can but save me from this imminent danger. 510

MIRA. Will you? I take you at your word. I ask no more. I must have leave for two criminals to appear.

LADY WISH. Ay, ay, anybody, anybody!

MIRA. Foible is one, and a penitent. 515

Enter MRS. FAINALL, FOIBLE, *and* MINCING.

MRS. MAR. (*to* FAINALL). Oh, my shame! these corrupt things are bought and brought hither to expose me.

(MIRABELL *and* LADY WISHFORT *go to* MRS. FAINALL *and* FOIBLE.)

FAIN. If it must all come out, why let 'em know it; 'tis but the *way of the world*. That shall not 520 urge me to relinquish or abate one tittle of my terms; no, I will insist the more.

FOIB. Yes, indeed, madam, I'll take my Bible oath of it.

MINC. And so will I, mem. 525

LADY WISH. O Marwood, Marwood, art thou false? my friend deceive me? Hast thou been a wicked accomplice with that profligate man?

MRS. MAR. Have you so much ingratitude and injustice, to give credit against your friend, to 530 the aspersions of two such mercenary trulls?

MINC. Mercenary, mem? I scorn your words. 'Tis true we found you and Mr. Fainall in the blue garret; by the same token, you swore us to secrecy upon Messalinas's poems.[1] Mercenary? No, 535 if we would have been mercenary, we should have held our tongues; you would have bribed us suffi-ciently.

FAIN. Go, you are an insignificant thing! — Well, what are you the better for this! Is this Mr. 540 Mirabell's expedient? I'll be put off no longer. — You thing that was a wife, shall smart for this! I will not leave thee wherewithal to hide thy shame; your body shall be naked as your reputation.

MRS. FAIN. I despise you, and defy your 545 malice! You have aspersed me wrongfully — I have proved your falsehood. Go you and your treacher-ous — I will not name it — but starve together — perish!

FAIN. Not while you are worth a groat, in- 550 deed, my dear. Madam, I'll be fooled no longer.

LADY WISH. Ah, Mr. Mirabell, this is small com-fort, the detection of this affair.

MIRA. Oh, in good time. Your leave for the other offender and penitent to appear, madam. 555

Enter WAITWELL *with a box of writings.*

LADY WISH. O Sir Rowland! — Well, rascal!

WAIT. What your ladyship pleases. I have brought the black box at last, madam.

MIRA. Give it me. Madam, you remember your promise. 560

LADY WISH. Ay, dear sir.

MIRA. Where are the gentlemen?

WAIT. At hand, sir, rubbing their eyes — just risen from sleep.

FAIN. 'Sdeath, what's this to me? I'll not 565 wait your private concerns.

Enter PETULANT *and* WITWOUD.

PET. How now? what's the matter? whose hand's out?

WIT. Hey day! what, are you all got together, like players at the end of the last act? 570

MIRA. You may remember, gentlemen, I once re-quested your hands as witnesses to a certain parch-ment.

[1] Probably Mincing's happy malapropism for *Miscellaneous Poems*, a common title for collections of verse at this time. Messalina was the notoriously profligate wife of the Roman emperor Claudius.

WIT. Ay, I do, my hand I remember — Petulant set his mark.   575

MIRA. You wrong him, his name is fairly written, as shall appear. — You do not remember, gentlemen, anything of what that parchment contained?

(*Undoing the box.*)

WIT. No.

PET. Not I. I writ, I read nothing.   580

MIRA. Very well, now you shall know. — Madam, your promise.

LADY WISH. Ay, ay, sir, upon my honor.

MIRA. Mr. Fainall, it is now time that you should know that your lady, while she was at her own 585 disposal, and before you had by your insinuations wheedled her out of a pretended settlement of the greatest part of her fortune ——

FAIN. Sir! pretended!

MIRA. Yes, sir. I say that this lady while a 590 widow, having, it seems, received some cautions respecting your inconstancy and tyranny of temper, which from her own partial opinion and fondness of you she could never have suspected — she did, I say, by the wholesome advice of friends and of 595 sages learned in the laws of this land, deliver this same as her act and deed to me in trust, and to the uses within mentioned. You may read if you please (*holding out the parchment*) — though perhaps what is inscribed on the back may serve your 600 occasions.

FAIN. Very likely, sir. What's here? Damnation! (*Reads.*) 'A deed of conveyance of the whole estate real of Arabella Languish, widow, in trust to Edward Mirabell.' — Confusion!   605

MIRA. Even so, sir; 'tis the *way of the world*, sir — of the widows of the world. I suppose this deed may bear an elder date than what you have obtained from your lady.

FAIN. Perfidious fiend! then thus I'll be re- 610 venged. ——   (*Offers to run at* MRS. FAINALL.)

SIR WIL. Hold, sir! now you may make your bear-garden flourish somewhere else, sir.

FAIN. Mirabell, you shall hear of this, sir, be sure you shall. — Let me pass, oaf.   *Exit.* 615

MRS. FAIN. [*to* MRS. MARWOOD]. Madam, you seem to stifle your resentment. You had better give it vent.

MRS. MAR. Yes, it shall have vent — and to your confusion, or I'll perish in the attempt. *Exit.* 620

LADY WISH. O daughter, daughter! 'tis plain thou hast inherited thy mother's prudence.

MRS. FAIN. Thank Mr. Mirabell, a cautious friend, to whose advice all is owing.

LADY WISH. Well, Mr. Mirabell, you have 625 kept your promise — and I must perform mine. — First, I pardon for your sake Sir Rowland there and

Foible; — the next thing is to break the matter to my nephew — and how to do that ——

MIRA. For that, madam, give yourself no 630 trouble; let me have your consent. Sir Wilfull is my friend; he has had compassion upon lovers, and generously engaged a volunteer in this action, for our service, and now designs to prosecute his travels.

SIR WIL. 'Sheart, aunt, I have no mind to 635 marry. My cousin's a fine lady, and the gentleman loves her and she loves him, and they deserve one another; my resolution is to see foreign parts — I have set' on't — and when I'm set on't, I must do't. And if these two gentlemen would travel too, I 640 think they may be spared.

PET. For my part, I say little — I think things are best off or on.[1]

WIT. I' gad, I understand nothing of the matter; I'm in a maze yet, like a dog in a dancing- 645 school.

LADY WISH. Well, sir, take her, and with her all the joy I can give you.

MILLA. Why does not the man take me? Would you have me give myself to you over again?   650

MIRA. Ay, and over and over again; for I would have you as often as possibly I can. (*Kisses her hand.*) Well, heaven grant I love you not too well, that's all my fear.

SIR WIL. 'Sheart, you'll have him time 655 enough to toy after you're married; or if you will toy now, let us have a dance in the mean time, that we who are not lovers may have some other employment besides looking on.

MIRA. With all my heart, dear Sir Wilfull. 660 What shall we do for music?

FOIB. O sir, some that were provided for Sir Rowland's entertainment are yet within call. (*A dance.*)

LADY WISH. As I am a person, I can hold out no longer; I have wasted my spirits so today al- 665 ready, that I am ready to sink under the fatigue; and I cannot but have some fears upon me yet, that my son Fainall will pursue some desperate course.

MIRA. Madam, disquiet not yourself on that account; to my knowledge his circumstances are 670 such, he must of force comply. For my part, I will contribute all that in me lies to a reunion; in the mean time, madam (*to* MRS. FAINALL), let me before these witnesses restore to you this deed of trust. It may be a means, well managed, to make you 675 live easily together.

From hence let those be warned, who mean to wed;
Lest mutual falsehood stain the bridal-bed:
For each deceiver to his cost may find,
That marriage frauds too oft are paid in kind.   680

Exeunt omnes.

[1] Either one way or the other.

600] WI *is written on.*   651] Q2WI om. *for.*   655] WI om. *him.*

EPILOGUE

SPOKEN BY MRS. BRACEGIRDLE.[1]

AFTER our epilogue this crowd dismisses,
[I'm] thinking how this play'll be pulled to pieces.
But pray consider, ere you doom its fall,
How hard a thing 'twould be, to please you all.
There are some critics so with spleen diseased,   5
They scarcely come inclining to be pleased:
And sure he must have more than mortal skill,
Who pleases any one against his will.
Then, all bad poets we are sure are foes,
And how their number's swelled the town well knows: 10
In shoals, I've marked 'em judging in the pit; ⎫
Though they're on no pretence for judgment fit, ⎬
But that they have been damned for want of wit. ⎭
Since when, they by their own offences taught,
Set up for spies on plays and finding fault.   15
Others there are whose malice we'd prevent; ⎫
Such who watch plays with scurrilous intent ⎬
To mark out who by characters are meant. ⎭
And though no perfect likeness they can trace;
Yet each pretends to know the copied face.   20
These with false glosses feed their own ill-nature,
And turn to libel what was meant a satire.
May such malicious fops this fortune find,
To think themselves alone the fools designed:
If any are so arrogantly vain, ⎫   25
To think they singly can support a scene, ⎬
And furnish fool enough to entertain. ⎭
For well the learn'd and the judicious know, ⎫
That satire scorns to stoop so meanly low, ⎬
As any one abstracted[2] fop to show. ⎭   30
For, as when painters form a matchless face,
They from each fair one catch some different grace,
And shining features in one portrait blend,
To which no single beauty must pretend;
So poets oft do in one piece expose   35
Whole *belles assemblées*[3] of coquettes and beaux.

---

[1] In the part of Millamant.   [2] Separate.   [3] Fashionable gatherings.

2] Q1 *In*; Q2W1 *I'm*.

The Beaux' Stratagem

BY GEORGE FARQUHAR

AN
EPILOGUE,

Defign'd to be fpoke in the Beaux Stratagem.

IF to our Play Your Judgment can't be kind,
  Let its expiring Author Pity find.
Survey his mournful Cafe with melting Eyes,
Nor let the Bard be dam'd before he dies.
Forbear you Fair on his laft Scene to frown,
But his true Exit with a Plaudit Crown;
Then fhall the dying Poet ceafe to Fear,
The dreadful Knell, while your Applaufe he hears.
At Leuctra fo, the Conqu'ring Theban dy'd,
Claim'd his Friend's Praifes, but their Tears deny'd:
Pleas'd in the Pangs of Death he greatly Thought
Conqueft with lofs of Life but cheaply bought.
The Difference this, the Greek was one wou'd fight
As brave, tho' not fo gay as Serjeant Kite;
Ye Sons of Will's what's that to thofe who write?
To Thebes alone the Grecian ow'd his Bays,
You may the Bard above the Hero raife,
Since yours is greater than Athenian Praife.

Dramatis

EPILOGUE, FORESHADOWING FARQUHAR'S DEATH, WHICH CLOSELY FOLLOWED THE PRODUCTION OF
HIS FINAL MASTERPIECE
From the first undated quarto, 1707

PROLOGUE

Spoken by Mr. Wilks [1]

When strife disturbs, or sloth corrupts an age,
Keen satire is the business of the stage.
When the Plain Dealer [2] writ, he lashed those crimes
Which then infested most — the modish times:
But now, when faction sleeps and sloth is fled,   5
And all our youth in active fields are bred; [3]
When through Great Britain's fair extensive round,
The trumps of fame the notes of Union [4] sound;
When Anna's sceptre points the laws their course,
And her example gives her precepts force: 10
There scarce is room for satire; all our lays
Must be, or songs of triumph, or of praise.
But as in grounds best cultivated, tares
And poppies rise among the golden ears;
Our products so, fit for the field or school,   15
Must mix with nature's favorite plant — a fool:
A weed that has to twenty summers ran,
Shoots up in stalk, and vegetates to man.
Simpling [5] our author goes from field to field,
And culls such fools as may diversion yield;   20
And, thanks to nature, there's no want of those,
For, rain or shine, the thriving coxcomb grows.
Follies tonight we show ne'er lashed before,
Yet such as nature shows you every hour;
Nor can the pictures give a just offence,   25
For fools are made for jests to men of sense.

[1] In the part of Archer.
[2] Wycherley is here referred to by the title of his best-known play.
[3] The War of the Spanish Succession had been in progress for more than five years.
[4] The union of England and Scotland was finally brought about in 1707.
[5] Gathering medicinal herbs.

24] C e'ry.

DRAMATIS PERSONÆ

MEN

[THOMAS] AIMWELL, } two gentlemen of broken
[FRANCIS] ARCHER, } fortune, the first as master,
} and the second as servant.

COUNT BELLAIR, a French officer, prisoner at Lichfield.

SULLEN, a country blockhead, brutal to his wife.

[SIR CHARLES] FREEMAN, a gentleman from London.

FOIGARD, a priest, chaplain to the French officers.

GIBBET, a highwayman.

HOUNSLOW, } his companions.
BAGSHOT, }

BONNIFACE, landlord of the inn.

SCRUB, servant to MR. SULLEN.

WOMEN

LADY BOUNTIFUL, an old, civil country gentlewoman,
that cures all her neighbors of all distempers, and
foolishly fond of her son, SULLEN.

DORINDA, LADY BOUNTIFUL's daughter.

MRS. SULLEN, her daughter-in-law.

GIPSEY, maid to the ladies.

CHERRY, the landlord's daughter in the inn.

SCENE, LICHFIELD.

---

d.p.] *Bountiful* is sometimes spelled *Bountyful* in the text.

THE BEAUX' STRATAGEM

By GEORGE FARQUHAR

ACT I

SCENE I

Scene, an inn.

Enter BONIFACE, *running.*

BON. Chamberlain![1] maid! Cherry! daughter Cherry! all asleep? all dead?

Enter CHERRY, *running.*

CHER. Here, here! why d'ye bawl so, father? d'ye think we have no ears?

BON. You deserve to have none, you young 5 minx! The company of the Warrington [2] coach has stood in the hall this hour, and nobody to show them to their chambers.

CHER. And let 'em wait farther; there's neither red-coat in the coach, nor footman behind it. 10

BON. But they threaten to go to another inn tonight.

CHER. That they dare not, for fear the coachman should overturn them tomorrow. — Coming! coming! — Here's the London coach arrived. 15

Enter several people with trunks, bandboxes, and other luggage, and cross the stage.

BON. Welcome, ladies!

CHER. Very welcome, gentlemen! — Chamberlain, show the *Lion* and the *Rose*.[3]

Exit with the company.

Enter AIMWELL *in riding-habit,* ARCHER *as footman carrying a portmantle.*

BON. This way, this way, gentlemen!

AIM. [*to* ARCHER]. Set down the things; go to 20 the stable, and see my horses well rubbed.

ARCH. I shall, sir. *Exit.*

AIM. You're my landlord, I suppose?

BON. Yes, sir, I'm old Will Boniface, pretty well known upon this road, as the saying is. 25

AIM. O Mr. Boniface, your servant!

BON. O sir! — What will your honor please to drink, as the saying is?

AIM. I have heard your town of Lichfield much famed for ale; I think I'll taste that. 30

BON. Sir, I have now in my cellar ten tun of the best ale in Staffordshire; 'tis smooth as oil, sweet as milk, clear as amber, and strong as brandy; and will be just fourteen year old the fifth day of next March, old style.[4] 35

AIM. You're very exact, I find, in the age of your ale.

BON. As punctual, sir, as I am in the age of my children. I'll show you such ale! — Here, tapster, broach number 1706,[5] as the saying is. — Sir, 40 you shall taste my *Anno Domini*. I have lived in Lichfield, man and boy, above eight-and-fifty years, and, I believe, have not consumed eight-and-fifty ounces of meat.

AIM. At a meal, you mean, if one may guess 45 your sense by your bulk.

BON. Not in my life, sir. I have fed purely upon ale; I have eat my ale, drank my ale, and I always sleep upon ale.

Enter Tapster with a bottle and glass.

Now, sir, you shall see! — (*Filling it out.*) Your 50 worship's health. — Ha! delicious, delicious! — fancy it burgundy, only fancy it, and 'tis worth ten shillings a quart.

AIM. (*drinks*). 'Tis confounded strong!

BON. Strong! It must be so, or how should 55 we be strong that drink it?

AIM. And have you lived so long upon this ale, landlord?

BON. Eight-and-fifty years, upon my credit, sir; but it killed my wife, poor woman, as the saying 60 is.

AIM. How came that to pass?

BON. I don't know how, sir; she would not let the ale take its natural course, sir; she was for qualifying it every now and then with a dram,[6] as the say- 65 ing is; and an honest gentleman that came this way from Ireland made her a present of a dozen bottles of usquebaugh [7] — but the poor woman was never well after. But, howe'er, I was obliged to the gentleman, you know. 70

---

[4] During the first half of the eighteenth century the English calendar was eleven days behind that of western Europe, which had adopted the 'new style' in 1582.

[5] By this transparent 'code number' and the phrase '*Anno Domini*' Boniface refers to the ale brewed in the preceding autumn (of 1706), which he proposes to palm off on the travellers in place of the fourteen-year-old ale of which he has boasted.

[6] I.e., of spirituous liquor. [7] Whiskey.

---

[1] The servant in charge of the bed-chambers.

[2] A town about sixty miles north of Lichfield, on the road to Preston and Lancaster.

[3] Rooms in inns were known by names, not numbers.

AIM. Why, was it the usquebaugh that killed her?

BON. My Lady Bountiful said so. She, good lady, did what could be done; she cured her of three tympanies,[1] but the fourth carried her off. But she's happy, and I'm contented, as the saying is.   75

AIM. Who's that Lady Bountiful you mentioned?

BON. Ods my life, sir, we'll drink her health. — (Drinks.) My Lady Bountiful is one of the best of women. Her last husband, Sir Charles Bountiful, left her worth a thousand pound a year;   80 and, I believe, she lays out one-half on't in charitable uses for the good of her neighbors; she cures rheumatisms, ruptures, and broken shins in men; green-sickness,[2] obstructions, and fits of the mother[3] in women; the king's evil,[4] chincough,[5] and   85 chilblains in children: in short, she has cured more people in and about Lichfield within ten years than the doctors have killed in twenty; and that's a bold word.

AIM. Has the lady been any other way useful   90 in her generation?

BON. Yes, sir; she has a daughter by Sir Charles, the finest woman in all our country, and the greatest fortune. She has a son too, by her first husband, Squire Sullen, who married a fine lady from   95 London t'other day; if you please, sir, we'll drink his health.

AIM. What sort of a man is he?

BON. Why, sir, the man's well enough; says little, thinks less, and does — nothing at all, faith.   100 But he's a man of a great estate, and values nobody.

AIM. A sportsman, I suppose?

BON. Yes, sir, he's a man of pleasure; he plays at whisk[6] and smokes his pipe eight and forty hours together sometimes.   105

AIM. And married, you say?

BON. Ay, and to a curious woman, sir. — But he's a — he wants it here, sir.

(Pointing to his forehead.)

AIM. He has it there, you mean.[7]

BON. That's none of my business; he's my   110 landlord, and so a man, you know, would not — But — icod, he's no better than — Sir, my humble service to you. — (Drinks.) Though I value not a farthing what he can do to me; I pay him his rent at quarter-day;[8] I have a good running-trade; I   115 have but one daughter, and I can give her — but no matter for that.

AIM. You're very happy, Mr. Bonniface; pray, what other company have you in town?

BON. A power of fine ladies; and then we   120 have the French officers.[9]

AIM. Oh, that's right, you have a good many of those gentlemen. Pray, how do you like their company?

BON. So well, as the saying is, that I could   125 wish we had as many more of 'em; they're full of money, and pay double for everything they have: they know, sir, that we paid good round taxes for the taking of 'em, and so they are willing to reimburse us a little. One of 'em lodges in my house.   130

Enter ARCHER.

ARCH. Landlord, there are some French gentlemen below that ask for you.

BON. I'll wait on 'em — (To ARCHER.) Does your master stay long in town, as the saying is?

ARCH. I can't tell, as the saying is.   135

BON. Come from London?

ARCH. No.

BON. Going to London, mayhap?

ARCH. No.

BON. [aside]. An odd fellow this. — [To   140 AIMWELL.] I beg your worship's pardon, I'll wait on you in half a minute.   *Exit.*

AIM. The coast's clear, I see. — Now, my dear Archer, welcome to Lichfield!

ARCH. I thank thee, my dear brother in   145 iniquity.

AIM. Iniquity! prithee, leave canting; you need not change your style with your dress.

ARCH. Don't mistake me, Aimwell, for 'tis still my maxim, that there is no scandal like rags, nor   150 any crime so shameful as poverty.

AIM. The world confesses it every day in its practice, though men won't own it for their opinion. Who did that worthy lord, my brother, single out of the side-box[10] to sup with him t'other night?   155

ARCH. Jack Handicraft, a handsome, well-dressed, mannerly, sharping rogue, who keeps the best company in town.

AIM. Right! And, pray, who married my lady Manslaughter t'other day, the great fortune?   160

ARCH. Why, Nick Marrabone,[11] a professed pick-

---

[1] Tumors.   [2] An anemic disease of adolescence.

[3] Hysteria.   [4] Scrofula.

[5] Whooping-cough.   [6] Whist.

[7] Bonniface meant that the squire was not very intelligent; Aimwell twists his remark to imply that the squire bears the 'horns' of a cuckold on his forehead.

[8] There were four recognized days for the payment of rent; in March, June, September and December.

[9] Officers captured during the War of the Spanish Succession were liberated on parole in various parts of England.

[10] The side-box at the theatre was a favorite place for the beaux.

[11] A corruption of 'Marylebone,' the name of a district on the northern edge of London which was a fashionable gaming center. Bowling, in which there had been a revival of interest in 1706, was one of the games which served as a basis for wagering; see Lady Mary Wortley Montagu's *The Basset-table*, ll. 99–100:

At the Groom-Porter's battered bullies play,
Some dukes at Mary-bone bowl time away.

101] C om. *a.*

pocket, and a good bowler; but he makes a handsome figure, and rides in his coach, that he formerly used to ride behind.

AIM. But did you observe poor Jack Generous in the Park [1] last week?　　165

ARCH. Yes, with his autumnal periwig, shading his melancholy face, his coat older than anything but its fashion, with one hand idle in his pocket, and with the other picking his useless teeth; and 170 though the Mall was crowded with company, yet was poor Jack as single and solitary as a lion in a desert.

AIM. And as much avoided, for no crime upon earth but the want of money.　　175

ARCH. And that's enough. Men must not be poor; idleness is the root of all evil; the world's wide enough, let 'em bustle. Fortune has taken the weak under her protection, but men of sense are left to their industry.　　180

AIM. Upon which topic we proceed, and, I think, luckily hitherto. Would not any man swear now that I am a man of quality, and you my servant, when if our intrinsic value were known ——

ARCH. Come, come, we are the men of in- 185 trinsic value who can strike our fortunes out of ourselves, whose worth is independent of accidents in life, or revolutions in government; we have heads to get money, and hearts to spend it.

AIM. As to our hearts, I grant ye, they are as 190 willing tits [2] as any within twenty degrees; but I can have no great opinion of our heads from the service they have done us hitherto, unless it be that they have brought us from London hither to Lichfield, made me a lord, and you my servant.　　195

ARCH. That's more than you could expect already. But what money have we left?

AIM. But two hundred pound.

ARCH. And our horses, clothes, rings, etc. — Why, we have very good fortunes now for moderate 200 people; and let me tell you, besides, that this two hundred pound, with the experience that we are now masters of, is a better estate than the ten [thousand] we have spent. Our friends, indeed, began to suspect that our pockets were low; but we came off 205 with flying colors, showed no signs of want either in word or deed.

AIM. Ay, and our going to Brussels was a good pretence enough for our sudden disappearing; and, I warrant you, our friends imagine that we are 210 gone a-volunteering.

ARCH. Why, faith, if this prospect fails, it must e'en come to that. I am for venturing one of the

hundreds, if you will, upon this knight-errantry; but, in case it should fail, we'll reserve the 215 t'other to carry us to some counterscarp, where we may die, as we lived, in a blaze.

AIM. With all my heart; and we have lived justly, Archer; we can't say that we have spent our fortunes, but that we have enjoyed 'em.　　220

ARCH. Right! So much pleasure for so much money; we have had our pennyworths, and, had I millions, I would go to the same market again. O London! London! Well, we have had our share, and let us be thankful; past pleasures, for 225 aught I know, are best, such as we are sure of: those to come may disappoint us.

AIM. It has often grieved the heart of me to see how some inhuman wretches murther their kind fortunes; those that, by sacrificing all to one ap- 230 petite, shall starve all the rest. You shall have some that live only in their palates, and in their sense of tasting shall drown the other four. Others are only epicures in appearances, such who shall starve their nights to make a figure a-days, 235 and famish their own to feed the eyes of others: a contrary sort confine their pleasures to the dark, and contract their specious acres to the circuit of a muff-string.

ARCH. Right! But they find the Indies [3] in 240 that spot where they consume 'em, and I think your kind keepers [4] have much the best on't; for they indulge the most senses by one expense: there's the seeing, hearing, and feeling, amply gratified; and, some philosophers will tell you that from such a 245 commerce there arises a sixth sense, that gives infinitely more pleasure than the other five put together.

AIM. And to pass to the other extremity, of all keepers I think those the worst that keep their money.　　250

ARCH. Those are the most miserable wights in being; they destroy the rights of nature, and disappoint the blessings of Providence. Give me a man that keeps his five senses keen and bright as his sword, that has 'em always drawn out in their 255 just order and strength, with his reason as commander at the head of 'em; that detaches 'em by turns upon whatever party of pleasure agreeably offers, and commands 'em to retreat upon the least appearance of disadvantage or danger! For 260 my part, I can stick to my bottle while my wine, my company, and my reason holds good; I can be charmed with Sappho's singing without falling in love with her face; I love hunting, but would not, like Actæon,[5] be eaten up by my own dogs; I 265

---

[1] The reference to the Mall in Archer's next speech shows that St. James's Park is meant here.
[2] Horses.

[3] The source of their delights.　　[4] Of mistresses.
[5] Actæon, who surprised Artemis bathing, was turned to a stag and torn to pieces by his dogs.

201–204] Q1 *besides thousand, . . . the ten we*; C om. *besides* and *thousand*.

love a fine house, but let another keep it; and just so I love a fine woman.

AIM. In that last particular you have the better of me.

ARCH. Ay, you're such an amorous puppy, 270 that I'm afraid you'll spoil our sport; you can't counterfeit the passion without feeling it.

AIM. Though the whining part be out of doors in town, 'tis still in force with the country ladies; and let me tell you, Frank, the fool in that 275 passion shall outdo the knave at any time.

ARCH. Well, I won't dispute it now; you command for the day, and so I submit. — At Nottingham, you know, I am to be master.

AIM. And at Lincoln, I again. 280

ARCH. Then, at Norwich I mount, which, I think, shall be our last stage; for, if we fail there, we'll imbark for Holland, bid adieu to Venus, and welcome Mars.

AIM. A match! 285

Enter BONNIFACE.

Mum!

BON. What will your worship please to have for supper?

AIM. What have you got?

BON. Sir, we have a delicate piece of beef 290 in the pot, and a pig at the fire.

AIM. Good supper-meat, I must confess. — I can't eat beef, landlord.

ARCH. And I hate pig.

AIM. Hold your prating, sirrah! do you 295 know who you are?

BON. Please to bespeak something else; I have everything in the house.

AIM. Have you any veal?

BON. Veal! Sir, we had a delicate loin of veal 300 on Wednesday last.

AIM. Have you got any fish or wildfowl?

BON. As for fish, truly, sir, we are an inland town, and indifferently provided with fish, that's the truth on't; and then for wildfowl — we have a 305 delicate couple of rabbits.

AIM. Get me the rabbits fricasseed.

BON. Fricasseed! Lard, sir, they'll eat much better smothered with onions.

ARCH. Pshaw! Damn your onions! 310

AIM. Again, sirrah! — Well, landlord, what you please. But hold, I have a small charge [1] of money, and your house is so full of strangers, that I believe it may be safer in your custody than mine; for when this fellow of mine gets drunk, he minds noth- 315 ing. — Here, sirrah, reach me the strong-box.

ARCH. Yes, sir. — (*Aside.*) This will give us a reputation.   (*Brings the box.*)

[1] Burden, amount.

AIM. Here, landlord; the locks are sealed down both for your security and mine; it holds some- 320 what above two hundred pound; if you doubt it, I'll count it to you after supper; but be sure you lay it where I may have it at a minute's warning; for my affairs are a little dubious at present; perhaps I may be gone in half an hour, perhaps I may be 325 your guest till the best part of that be spent; and pray order your ostler to keep my horses always saddled. But one thing above the rest I must beg, that you would let this fellow have none of your *Anno Domini*, as you call it; for he's the most in- 330 sufferable sot. — Here, sirrah, light me to my chamber.   *Exit, lighted by* ARCHER.

BON. Cherry! Daughter Cherry!

Enter CHERRY.

CHER. D'ye call, father?

BON. Ay, child, you must lay by this box 335 for the gentleman; 'tis full of money.

CHER. Money! all that money! Why, sure, father, the gentleman comes to be chosen parliament-man. Who is he?

BON. I don't know what to make of him; 340 he talks of keeping his horses ready saddled, and of going perhaps at a minute's warning, or of staying perhaps till the best part of this be spent.

CHER. Ay, ten to one, father, he's a highwayman.

BON. A highwayman! Upon my life, girl, 345 you have hit it, and this box is some new-purchased booty. — Now, could we find him out, the money were ours.

CHER. He don't belong to our gang?

BON. What horses have they? 350

CHER. The master rides upon a black.

BON. A black! ten to one the man upon the black mare; and since he don't belong to our fraternity, we may betray him with a safe conscience. I don't think it lawful to harbor any rogues but 355 my own. Look ye, child, as the saying is, we must go cunningly to work; proofs we must have. The gentleman's servant loves drink, — I'll ply him that way; and ten to one loves a wench, — you must work him t'other way. 360

CHER. Father, would you have me give my secret for his?

BON. Consider, child, there's two hundred pound to boot. — (*Ringing without.*) Coming! coming! — Child, mind your business.   [*Exit.*] 365

CHER. What a rogue is my father! My father! I deny it. My mother was a good, generous, free-hearted woman, and I can't tell how far her good nature might have extended for the good of her children. This landlord of mine, for I think I can 370 call him no more, would betray his guest, and debauch his daughter into the bargain — by a footman, too!

Enter ARCHER.

ARCH. What footman, pray, mistress, is so happy as to be the subject of your contemplation? 375

CHER. Whoever he is, friend, he'll be but little the better for't.

ARCH. I hope so, for I'm sure you did not think of me.

CHER. Suppose I had? 380

ARCH. Why, then you're but even with me; for the minute I came in, I was a-considering in what manner I should make love to you.

CHER. Love to me, friend!

ARCH. Yes, child. 385

CHER. Child! manners! If you kept a little more distance, friend, it would become you much better.

ARCH. Distance! Good-night, saucebox. (*Going.*)

CHER. [*aside*]. A pretty fellow! I like his pride. — [*Aloud.*] Sir, pray, sir, you see, sir, (ARCHER *returns*) I have the credit to be intrusted with your master's fortune here, which sets me a degree above his footman; I hope, sir, you an't affronted?

ARCH. Let me look you full in the face, and 395 I'll tell you whether you can affront me or no. — 'Sdeath, child, you have a pair of delicate eyes, and you don't know what to do with 'em!

CHER. Why, sir, don't I see everybody?

ARCH. Ay, but if some women had 'em, 400 they would kill everybody. Prithee, instruct me, I would fain make love to you, but I don't know what to say.

CHER. Why, did you never make love to anybody before? 405

ARCH. Never to a person of your figure, I can assure you, madam; my addresses have been always confined to people within my own sphere; I never aspired so high before. (*A song.*)

But you look so bright, 410
And are dressed so tight,
[That a man would swear you're right,
As arm was e'er laid over.
Such an air
You freely wear 415
To ensnare,
As makes each guest a lover!

Since then, my dear, I'm your guest,
Prithee give me of the best
Of what is ready dressed: 420
Since then, my dear, etc.]

CHER. (*aside*). What can I think of this man? — Will you give me that song, sir?

ARCH. Ay, my dear, take it while 'tis warm. — (*Kisses her.*) Death and fire! her lips are 425 honeycombs.

CHER. And I wish there had been bees too, to have stung you for your impudence.

ARCH. There's a swarm of Cupids, my little Venus, that has done the business much better. 430

CHER. (*aside*). This fellow is misbegotten as well as I. — What's your name, sir?

ARCH. (*aside*). Name! igad, I have forgot it. — [*Aloud.*] Oh! Martin.

CHER. Where were you born? 435

ARCH. In St. Martin's parish.

CHER. What was your father?

ARCH. St. Martin's parish.

CHER. Then, friend, good-night.

ARCH. I hope not. 440

CHER. You may depend upon't.

ARCH. Upon what?

CHER. That you're very impudent.

ARCH. That you're very handsome.

CHER. That you're a footman. 445

ARCH. That you're an angel.

CHER. I shall be rude.

ARCH. So shall I.

CHER. Let go my hand.

ARCH. Give me a kiss. (*Kisses her.*) (*Call* 450 *without.*) Cherry! Cherry!

CHER. I'm-m — my father calls; you plaguy devil, how durst you stop my breath so? Offer to follow me one step, if you dare. *Exit.*

ARCH. A fair challenge, by this light! This 455 is a pretty fair opening of an adventure; but we are knight-errants, and so Fortune be our guide. *Exit.*

ACT II

SCENE [I]

A gallery in LADY BOUNTIFUL's *house.*

MRS. SULLEN *and* DORINDA, *meeting.*

DOR. Morrow, my dear sister; are you for church this morning?

MRS. SUL. Anywhere to pray; for heaven alone can help me. But I think, Dorinda, there's no form of prayer in the liturgy against bad husbands. 5

DOR. But there's a form of law in Doctors-Commons;[1] and I swear, sister Sullen, rather than see you thus continually discontented, I would advise you to apply to that: for besides the part that I bear in your vexatious broils, as being sister to 10 the husband, and friend to the wife, your example

[1] The London society of lawyers learned in the civil law and entitled, among other things, to plead cases of separation or divorce in the ecclesiastical courts.

412–421] QɪC om. bracketed passage, which is here supplied from the seventh edition of the *Dramatic Works*, 1736.
452] *I'm*. ACT II. 11–12] C *examples give*.

gives me such an impression of matrimony, that I shall be apt to condemn my person to a long vacation all its life. But supposing, madam, that you brought it to a case of separation, what can you 15 urge against your husband? My brother is, first, the most constant man alive.

MRS. SUL. The most constant husband, I grant ye.

DOR. He never sleeps from you.

MRS. SUL. No, he always sleeps with me.   20

DOR. He allows you a maintenance suitable to your quality.

MRS. SUL. A maintenance! Do you take me, madam, for an hospital child,[1] that I must sit down, and bless my benefactors for meat, drink, and 25 clothes? As I take it, madam, I brought your brother ten thousand pounds, out of which I might expect some pretty things, called pleasures.

DOR. You share in all the pleasures that the country affords.   30

MRS. SUL. Country pleasures! Racks and torments! dost think, child, that my limbs were made for leaping of ditches, and clamb'ring over stiles? or that my parents, wisely foreseeing my future happiness in country pleasures, had early instructed 35 me in the rural accomplishments of drinking fat [2] ale, playing at whisk, and smoking tobacco with my husband? or of spreading of plasters, brewing of diet-drinks, and stilling [3] rosemary-water, with the good old gentlewoman, my mother-in-law?   40

DOR. I'm sorry, madam, that it is not more in our power to divert you; I could wish, indeed, that our entertainments were a little more polite, or your taste a little less refined. But, pray, madam, how came the poets and philosophers, that labored 45 so much in hunting after pleasure, to place it at last in a country life?

MRS. SUL. Because they wanted money, child, to find out the pleasures of the town. Did you ever see a poet or philosopher worth ten thousand 50 pound? If you can show me such a man, I'll lay you fifty pound you'll find him somewhere within the weekly bills.[4] Not that I disapprove rural pleasures, as the poets have painted them; in their landscape, every Phyllis has her Corydon, every murmur- 55 ing stream, and every flow'ry mead, gives fresh alarms to love. — Besides, you'll find that their couples were never married. — But yonder I see my Corydon, and a sweet swain it is, heaven knows! Come, Dorinda, don't be angry, he's my hus- 60 band, and your brother; and, between both, is he not a sad brute?

[1] Inmate of an orphan asylum.
[2] Full-bodied.
[3] Distilling.
[4] Within the limits of the London parishes for which weekly bills of mortality (lists of deaths) were published.

DOR. I have nothing to say to your part of him — you're the best judge.

MRS. SUL. O sister, sister! if ever you marry, 65 beware of a sullen, silent sot, one that's always musing, but never thinks. There's some diversion in a talking blockhead; and since a woman must wear chains, I would have the pleasure of hearing 'em rattle a little. Now you shall see, but take 70 this by the way. He came home this morning at his usual hour of four, wakened me out of a sweet dream of something else, by tumbling over the tea-table, which he broke all to pieces; after his man and he had rolled about the room, like sick pas- 75 sengers in a storm, he comes flounce into bed, dead as a salmon into a fishmonger's basket; his feet cold as ice, his breath hot as a furnace, and his hands and his face as greasy as his flannel night-cap. O matrimony! He tosses up the clothes with a bar- 80 barous swing over his shoulders, disorders the whole economy of my bed, leaves me half naked, and my whole night's comfort is the tuneable serenade of that wakeful nightingale, his nose! Oh, the pleasure of counting the melancholy clock by a 85 snoring husband! — But now, sister, you shall see how handsomely, being a well-bred man, he will beg my pardon.

Enter SULLEN.

SUL. My head aches consumedly.

MRS. SUL. Will you be pleased, my dear, to 90 drink tea with us this morning? It may do your head good.

SUL. No.

DOR. Coffee, brother?

SUL. Pshaw!   95

MRS. SUL. Will you please to dress, and go to church with me? The air may help you.

SUL. Scrub!

Enter SCRUB.

SCRUB. Sir.

SUL. What day o' th' week is this?   100

SCRUB. Sunday, an't please your worship.

SUL. Sunday! Bring me a dram; and d'ye hear, set out the venison-pasty, and a tankard of strong beer upon the hall-table; I'll go to breakfast. (*Going.*)

DOR. Stay, stay, brother, you shan't get off 105 so; you were very naught [5] last night, and must make your wife reparation; come, come, brother, won't you ask pardon?

SUL. For what?

DOR. For being drunk last night.   110

SUL. I can afford it, can't I?

MRS. SUL. But I can't, sir.

SUL. Then you may let it alone.

[5] Naughty.

MRS. SUL. But I must tell you, sir, that this is not to be borne.   115

SUL. I'm glad on't.

MRS. SUL. What is the reason, sir, that you use me thus inhumanely?

SUL. Scrub!

SCRUB. Sir.   120

SUL. Get things ready to shave my head.

Exit [followed by SCRUB].

MRS. SUL. Have a care of coming near his temples, Scrub, for fear you meet something there that may turn the edge of your razor. — Inveterate stupidity! did you ever know so hard, so ob- 125 stinate a spleen as his? O sister, sister! I shall never ha' good of the beast till I get him to town: London, dear London, is the place for managing and breaking a husband.

DOR. And has not a husband the same op- 130 portunities there for humbling a wife?

MRS. SUL. No, no, child, 'tis a standing maxim in conjugal discipline, that when a man would enslave his wife, he hurries her into the country; and when a lady would be arbitrary with her hus- 135 band, she wheedles her booby up to town. A man dare not play the tyrant in London, because there are so many examples to encourage the subject to rebel. O Dorinda, Dorinda! a fine woman may do anything in London: o' my conscience, she may 140 raise an army of forty thousand men.

DOR. I fancy, sister, you have a mind to be trying your power that way here in Lichfield; you have drawn the French count to your colors already.

MRS. SUL. The French are a people that 145 can't live without their gallantries.

DOR. And some English that I know, sister, are not averse to such amusements.

MRS. SUL. Well, sister, since the truth must out, it may do as well now as hereafter; I think one 150 way to rouse my lethargic, sottish husband is to give him a rival. Security begets negligence in all people, and men must be alarmed to make 'em alert in their duty: women are like pictures, of no value in the hands of a fool, till he hears men of sense bid 155 high for the purchase.

DOR. This might do, sister, if my brother's understanding were to be convinced into a passion for you; but I fancy there's a natural aversion of his side; and I fancy, sister, that you don't come 160 much behind him, if you dealt fairly.

MRS. SUL. I own it, we are united contradictions, fire and water. But I could be contented, with a great many other wives, to humor the censorious mob, and give the world an appearance of living 165 well with my husband, could I bring him but to dissemble a little kindness to keep me in countenance.

DOR. But how do you know, sister, but that, instead of rousing your husband by this artifice to a counterfeit kindness, he should awake in a real 170 fury?

MRS. SUL. Let him: if I can't entice him to the one, I would provoke him to the other.

DOR. But how must I behave myself between ye?

MRS. SUL. You must assist me.   175

DOR. What, against my own brother!

MRS. SUL. He's but half a brother, and I'm your entire friend. If I go a step beyond the bounds of honor, leave me; till then, I expect you should go along with me in everything; while I trust my 180 honor in your hands, you may trust your brother's in mine. The count is to dine here today.

DOR. 'Tis a strange thing, sister, that I can't like that man.

MRS. SUL. You like nothing; your time is 185 not come: love and death have their fatalities, and strike home one time or other. You'll pay for all one day, I warrant ye. But come, my lady's tea is ready, and 'tis almost church time.   *Exeunt.*

SCENE [II]

The inn.

Enter AIMWELL *dressed, and* ARCHER.

AIM. And was she the daughter of the house?

ARCH. The landlord is so blind as to think so; but I dare swear she has better blood in her veins.

AIM. Why dost think so?

ARCH. Because the baggage has a pert *je ne* 5 *sais quoi;* [1] she reads plays, keeps a monkey, and is troubled with vapors.

AIM. By which discoveries I guess that you know more of her.

ARCH. Not yet, faith; the lady gives herself 10 airs; forsooth, nothing under a gentleman!

AIM. Let me take her in hand.

ARCH. Say one word more o' that, and I'll declare myself, spoil your sport there, and everywhere else; look ye, Aimwell, every man in his own sphere. 15

AIM. Right; and therefore you must pimp for your master.

ARCH. In the usual forms, good sir, after I have served myself. — But to our business. You are so well dressed, Tom, and make so handsome a 20 figure, that I fancy you may do execution in a country church; the exterior part strikes first, and you're in the right to make that impression favorable.

AIM. There's something in that which may turn to advantage. The appearance of a stranger in 25 a country church draws as many gazers as a blazing-star; no sooner he comes into the cathedral, but a train of whispers runs buzzing round the congregation in a moment: 'Who is he? Whence comes he? Do you know him?' Then I sir, tips me the 30 verger with half a crown; he pockets the simony,

[1] An inexpressible something.

and inducts me into the best pew in the church. I pull out my snuff-box, turn myself round, bow to the bishop, or the dean, if he be the commanding officer; single out a beauty, rivet both my eyes to hers, 35 set my nose a-bleeding by the strength of imagination, and show the whole church my concern by my endeavoring to hide it; after the sermon, the whole town gives me to her for a lover, and by persuading the lady that I am a-dying for her, the tables are 40 turned, and she in good earnest falls in love with me.

ARCH. There's nothing in this, Tom, without a precedent; but instead of riveting your eyes to a beauty, try to fix 'em upon a fortune; that's our business at present.   45

AIM. Pshaw! no woman can be a beauty without a fortune. Let me alone, for I am a marksman.

ARCH. Tom!

AIM. Ay.

ARCH. When were you at church before, pray? 50

AIM. Um — I was there at the coronation.[1]

ARCH. And how can you expect a blessing by going to church now?

AIM. Blessing! nay, Frank, I ask but for a wife.
                                                   Exit.

ARCH. Truly, the man is not very unreasona- 55 ble in his demands.   *Exit at the opposite door.*

Enter BONNIFACE *and* CHERRY.

BON. Well, daughter, as the saying is, have you brought Martin to confess?

CHER. Pray, father, don't put me upon getting anything out of a man; I'm but young, you 60 know, father, and I don't understand wheedling.

BON. Young! why, you jade, as the saying is, can any woman wheedle that is not young? Your mother was useless at five and twenty. Not wheedle! would you make your mother a whore, 65 and me a cuckold, as the saying is? I tell you his silence confesses it, and his master spends his money so freely, and is so much a gentleman every manner of way, that he must be a highwayman.

Enter GIBBET, *in a cloak.*

GIB. Landlord, landlord, is the coast clear? 70

BON. O Mr. Gibbet, what's the news?

GIB. No matter, ask no questions, all fair and honorable. — Here, my dear Cherry. (*Gives her a bag.*) Two hundred sterling pounds, as good as any that ever hanged or saved a rogue; lay 'em by 75 with the rest; and here — three wedding or mourning rings, 'tis much the same, you know. — Here, two silver-hilted swords; I took those from fellows that never show any part of their swords but the hilts. Here is a diamond necklace which the lady hid 80

[1] I.e., of Queen Anne, five years earlier.

in the privatest place in the coach, but I found it out. This gold watch I took from a pawnbroker's wife; it was left in her hands by a person of quality — there's the arms upon the case.

CHER. But who had you the money from? 85

GIB. Ah! poor woman! I pitied her; from a poor lady just eloped from her husband. She had made up her cargo, and was bound for Ireland, as hard as she could drive; she told me of her husband's barbarous usage, and so I left her half a crown. 90 But I had almost forgot, my dear Cherry, I have a present for you.

CHER. What is't?

GIB. A pot of ceruse,[2] my child, that I took out of a lady's under-pocket.   95

CHER. What! Mr. Gibbet, do you think that I paint?

GIB. Why, you jade, your betters do; I'm sure the lady that I took it from had a coronet upon her handkerchief. Here, take my cloak, and go, 100 secure the premises.

CHER. I will secure 'em.   *Exit.*

BON. But, hark ye, where's Hounslow and Bagshot?

GIB. They'll be here tonight.   105

BON. D'ye know of any other gentlemen o' the pad[3] on this road?

GIB. No.

BON. I fancy that I have two that lodge in the house just now.   110

GIB. The devil! How d'ye smoke[4] 'em?

BON. Why, the one is gone to church.

GIB. That's suspicious, I must confess.

BON. And the other is now in his master's chamber; he pretends to be servant to the other. 115 We'll call him out and pump him a little.

GIB. With all my heart.

BON. [*calls.*] Mr. Martin! Mr. Martin!

Enter MARTIN, *combing a periwig and singing.*

GIB. The roads are consumed deep; I'm as dirty as Old Brentford at Christmas.[5] — A good 120 pretty fellow that. — Whose servant are you, friend?

ARCH. My master's.

GIB. Really?

ARCH. Really.

GIB. That's much. — [*Aside to* BONNIFACE.] 125 The fellow has been at the bar by his evasions. — But pray, sir, what is your master's name?

ARCH. *Tall, all dall!* (*Sings and combs the periwig.*) This is the most obstinate curl ——

[2] A cosmetic compounded from white lead.
[3] Highwaymen.
[4] Come to suspect.
[5] A proverbially muddy town and a proverbially muddy time of year are combined here.

72–73] Q1 (BM copy, according to Morgan) om. *all . . . Here,.*   103] C *hark'e.*

GIB. I ask you his name.　　　　　　　　130

ARCH. Name, sir — *tall, all dall!* — I never asked him his name in my life. — *Tall, all dall!*

BON. [*aside to* GIBBET]. What think you now?

GIB. [*aside to* BONNIFACE]. Plain, plain; he talks now as if he were before a judge. — But pray,　135 friend, which way does your master travel?

ARCH. A-horseback.

GIB. [*aside*]. Very well again, an old offender, right. — But I mean, does he go upwards or downwards?　　　　　　　　140

ARCH. Downwards, I fear, sir. — *Tall, all!*

GIB. I'm afraid my fate will be a contrary way.

BON. Ha, ha, ha! Mr. Martin, you're very arch. This gentleman is only travelling towards Chester, and would be glad of your company, that's all.　145 — Come, Captain, you'll stay tonight, I suppose? I'll show you a chamber. Come, Captain.

GIB. Farewell, friend!

ARCH. Captain, your servant. [*Exeunt* BONNI-FACE *and* GIBBET.] — Captain! a pretty fel-　150 low! 'Sdeath, I wonder that the officers of the army don't conspire to beat all scoundrels in red but their own.

Enter CHERRY.

CHER. (*aside*). Gone! and Martin here! I hope he did not listen; I would have the merit of the　155 discovery all my own, because I would oblige him to love me. — Mr. Martin, who was that man with my father?

ARCH. Some recruiting sergeant, or whipped-out [1] trooper, I suppose.　　　　　　　　160

CHER. [*aside*]. All's safe, I find.

ARCH. Come, my dear, have you conned over the catechise I taught you last night?

CHER. Come, question me.

ARCH. What is love?　　　　　　　　165

CHER. Love is I know not what, it comes I know not how, and goes I know not when.

ARCH. Very well, an apt scholar. — (*Chucks her under the chin.*) Where does love enter?

CHER. Into the eyes.　　　　　　　　170

ARCH. And where go out?

CHER. I won't tell ye.

ARCH. What are [the] objects of that passion?

CHER. Youth, beauty, and clean linen.

ARCH. The reason?　　　　　　　　175

CHER. The two first are fashionable in nature, and the third at court.

ARCH. That's my dear. — What are the signs and tokens of that passion?

CHER. A stealing look, a stammering tongue,　180

---

[1] Soldiers, for certain offenses, were flogged out of the army.

words improbable, designs impossible, and actions impracticable.

ARCH. That's my good child, kiss me. — What must a lover do to obtain his mistress?

CHER. He must adore the person that dis-　185 dains him, he must bribe the chambermaid that betrays him, and court the footman that laughs at him. — He must, he must ——

ARCH. Nay, child, I must whip you if you don't. mind your lesson; he must treat his ——　190

CHER. Oh, ay! — he must treat his enemies with respect, his friends with indifference, and all the world with contempt; he must suffer much, and fear more; he must desire much, and hope little; in short, he must embrace his ruin, and throw　195 himself away.

ARCH. Had ever man so hopeful a pupil as mine! — Come, my dear, why is Love called a riddle?

CHER. Because, being blind, he leads those that see, and, though a child, he governs a man.　200

ARCH. Mighty well! — And why is Love pictured blind?

CHER. Because the painters out of the weakness or privilege of their art chose to hide those eyes that they could not draw.　　　　　　　　205

ARCH. That's my dear little scholar, kiss me again. — And why should Love, that's a child, govern a man?

CHER. Because that a child is the end of love.

ARCH. And so ends love's catechism. — And　210 now, my dear, we'll go in and make my master's bed.

CHER. Hold, hold, Mr. Martin! You have taken a great deal of pains to instruct me, and what d'ye think I have learnt by it?

ARCH. What?　　　　　　　　215

CHER. That your discourse and your habit are contradictions, and it would be nonsense in me to believe you a footman any longer.

ARCH. 'Oons, what a witch it is!

CHER. Depend upon this, sir, nothing in this　220 garb shall ever tempt me; for, though I was born to servitude, I hate it. Own your condition, swear you love me, and then ——

ARCH. And then we shall go make the bed?

CHER. Yes.　　　　　　　　225

ARCH. You must know, then, that I am born a gentleman, my education was liberal; but I went to London a younger brother, fell into the hands of sharpers, who stripped me of my money; my friends disowned me, and now my necessity　230 brings me to what you see.

CHER. Then take my hand — promise to marry me before you sleep, and I'll make you master of two thousand pound.

ARCH. How!　　　　　　　　235

CHER. Two thousand pound that I have this minute in my own custody; so, throw off your livery this instant, and I'll go find a parson.

ARCH. What said you? A parson!

CHER. What! do you scruple?   240

ARCH. Scruple! no, no, but — Two thousand pound, you say?

CHER. And better.

ARCH. [aside]. 'Sdeath, what shall I do? — [Aloud.] But hark'ee, child, what need you 245 make me master of yourself and money, when you may have the same pleasure out of me, and still keep your fortune in your hands?

CHER. Then you won't marry me?

ARCH. I would marry you, but ——   250

CHER. O sweet sir, I'm your humble servant! you're fairly caught: would you persuade me that any gentleman who could bear the scandal of wearing a livery would refuse two thousand pound, let the condition be what it would? No, no, sir. 255 But I hope you'll pardon the freedom I have taken, since it was only to inform myself of the respect that I ought to pay you.   (Going.)

ARCH. [aside]. Fairly bit, by Jupiter! — Hold! hold! And have you actually two thousand 260 pound?

CHER. Sir, I have my secrets as well as you; when you please to be more open, I shall be more free, and be assured that I have discoveries that will match yours, be what they will — in the meanwhile, 265 be satisfied that no discovery I make shall ever hurt you; but beware of my father!   [Exit.]

ARCH. So! we're like to have as many adventures in our inn as Don Quixote had in his.[1] Let me see — two thousand pound! If the wench would 270 promise to die when the money were spent, igad, one would marry her; but the fortune may go off in a year or two, and the wife may live — Lord knows how long. Then an innkeeper's daughter! ay, that's the devil — there my pride brings me off.   275

For whatsoe'er the sages charge on pride,
The angels' fall, and twenty faults beside,
On earth, I'm sure, 'mong us of mortal calling,
Pride saves man oft, and woman too, from falling.
                                        Exit.

ACT III

[SCENE I

The gallery in LADY BOUNTIFUL'S *house.*]

Enter MRS. SULLEN, DORINDA.

MRS. SUL. Ha, ha, ha! my dear sister, let me embrace thee: now we are friends indeed; for I shall have a secret of yours as a pledge for mine — now

[1] See *Don Quixote*, III. ii–iii.

you'll be good for something; I shall have you conversable [2] in the subjects of the sex.   5

DOR. But do you think that I am so weak as to fall in love with a fellow at first sight?

MRS. SUL. Pshaw! now you spoil all; why should not we be as free in our friendships as the men? I warrant you the gentleman has got to his confi- 10 dent already, has avowed his passion, toasted your health, called you ten thousand angels, has run over your lips, eyes, neck, shape, air, and everything, in a description that warms their mirth to a second enjoyment.   15

DOR. Your hand, sister, I an't well.

MRS. SUL. So — she's breeding already! — Come, child, up with it — hem a little — so — now tell me, don't you like the gentleman that we saw at church just now?   20

DOR. The man's well enough.

MRS. SUL. Well enough! is he not a demigod, a Narcissus, a star, the man i' the moon?

DOR. O sister, I'm extremely ill!

MRS. SUL. Shall I send to your mother, child, 25 for a little of her cephalic plaster [3] to put to the soles of your feet, or shall I send to the gentleman for something for you? — Come, unlace your stays, unbosom yourself — the man is perfectly a pretty fellow; I saw him when he first came into church. 30

DOR. I saw him too, sister, and with an air that shone, methought, like rays about his person.

MRS. SUL. Well said, up with it!

DOR. No forward coquet behavior, no airs to set him off, no studied nor artful posture — 35 but Nature did it all ——

MRS. SUL. Better and better! One touch more — come!

DOR. But then his looks — did you observe his eyes?   40

MRS. SUL. Yes, yes, I did. — His eyes, well, what of his eyes?

DOR. Sprightly, but not wand'ring; they seemed to view, but never gazed on anything but me. — And then his looks so humble were, and yet so noble, 45 that they aimed to tell me that he could with pride die at my feet, though he scorned slavery anywhere else.

MRS. SUL. The physic works purely![4] — How d'ye find yourself now, my dear?   50

DOR. Hem! much better, my dear. — Oh, here comes our Mercury!

Enter SCRUB.

Well, Scrub, what news of the gentleman?

SCRUB. Madam, I have brought you a packet of news.   55

[2] Disposed to converse.
[3] A remedy for diseases of the head.   [4] Finely.

DOR. Open it quickly, come.

SCRUB. In the first place I enquired who the gentleman was; they told me he was a stranger. Secondly, I asked what the gentleman was; they answered and said, that they never saw him before. 60
Thirdly, I enquired what countryman he was; they replied, 'twas more than they knew. Fourthly, I demanded whence he came; their answer was, they could not tell. And, fifthly, I asked whither he went; and they replied, they knew nothing of the mat- 65
ter, — and this is all I could learn.

MRS. SUL. But what do the people say? Can't they guess?

SCRUB. Why, some think he's a spy, some guess he's a mountebank, some say one thing, some an- 70
other; but for my own part, I believe he's a Jesuit.

DOR. A Jesuit. Why a Jesuit?

SCRUB. Because he keeps his horses always ready saddled, and his footman talks French.

MRS. SUL. His footman! 75

SCRUB. Ay, he and the count's footman were gabbering French like two intriguing ducks in a millpond; and I believe they talked of me, for they laughed consumedly.

DOR. What sort of livery has the footman? 80

SCRUB. Livery! Lord, madam, I took him for a captain, he's so bedizened with lace! And then he has tops to his shoes, up to his mid leg, a silverheaded cane dangling at his knuckles; he carries his hands in his pockets just so — (walks in the 85
French air) — and has a fine long periwig tied up in a bag. Lord, madam, he's clear another sort of man than I!

MRS. SUL. That may easily be. — But what shall we do now, sister? 90

DOR. I have it. This fellow has a world of simplicity, and some cunning; the first hides the latter by abundance. — Scrub!

SCRUB. Madam!

DOR. We have a great mind to know who this 95
gentleman is, only for our satisfaction.

SCRUB. Yes, madam, it would be a satisfaction, no doubt.

DOR. You must go and get acquainted with his footman, and invite him hither to drink a bottle 100
of your ale, because you're butler today.

SCRUB. Yes, madam, I am butler every Sunday.

MRS. SUL. O brave, sister! O' my conscience, you understand the mathematics already — 'tis the best plot in the world: your mother, you know, will 105
be gone to church, my spouse will be got to the alehouse with his scoundrels, and the house will be our own — so we drop in by accident, and ask the fellow some questions ourselves. In the country, you know, any stranger is company, and we're glad 110
to take up with the butler in a country-dance, and happy if he'll do us the favor.

SCRUB. Oh! Madam, you wrong me! I never refused your ladyship the favor in my life.

Enter GIPSEY.

GIP. Ladies, dinner's upon table. 115

DOR. Scrub, we'll excuse your waiting — go where we ordered you.

SCRUB. I shall. *Exeunt.*

[SCENE II]

Scene changes to the inn.

Enter AIMWELL *and* ARCHER.

ARCH. Well, Tom, I find you're a marksman.

AIM. A marksman! who so blind could be, as not discern a swan among the ravens?

ARCH. Well, but hark'ee, Aimwell —

AIM. Aimwell! Call me Oroondates, Cesario, 5
Amadis, [1] all that romance can in a lover paint, and then I'll answer. O Archer! I read her thousands in her looks, she looked like Ceres in her harvest: corn, wine, and oil, milk and honey, gardens, groves, and purling streams played on her plen- 10
teous face.

ARCH. Her face! her pocket, you mean; the corn, wine, and oil lies there. In short, she has ten thousand pound, that's the English on't.

AIM. Her eyes —— 15

ARCH. Are demi-cannons, to be sure; so I won't stand their battery. *(Going.)*

AIM. Pray excuse me; my passion must have vent.

ARCH. Passion! what a plague, d'ee think these romantic airs will do our business? Were my 20
temper as extravagant as yours, my adventures have something more romantic by half.

AIM. Your adventures!

ARCH. Yes;

The nymph that with her twice ten hundred pounds, 25
With brazen engine [2] hot, and quoif [3] clear starched,
Can fire the guest in warming of the bed ——

There's a touch of sublime Milton for you, and the subject but an innkeeper's daughter! I can play with a girl as an angler does with his fish; he 30
keeps it at the end of his line, runs it up the stream, and down the stream, till at last he brings it to hand, tickles [4] the trout, and so whips it into his basket.

Enter BONNIFACE.

BON. Mr. Martin, as the saying is — yonder's an honest fellow below, my Lady Bountiful's but- 35
ler, who begs the honor that you would go home with him and see his cellar.

---

[1] Well-known heroes of romance.
[2] Warming-pan.   [3] Cap.
[4] Trout were 'tickled' by stroking them gently until they were quiet enough to permit the fisherman to close his hand upon them.

ARCH. Do my *baise-mains* [1] to the gentleman, and tell him I will do myself the honor to wait on him immediately.   *Exit* BONNIFACE. 40

AIM. What do I hear?

Soft Orpheus play, and fair Toftida [2] sing!

ARCH. Pshaw! damn your raptures! I tell you, here's a pump going to be put into the vessel, and the ship will get into harbor, my life on't. You 45 say there's another lady very handsome there?

AIM. Yes, faith.

ARCH. I am in love with her already.

AIM. Can't you give me a bill upon Cherry in the mean time? 50

ARCH. No, no, friend, all her corn, wine, and oil is ingrossed [3] to my market. — And once more I warn you to keep your anchorage clear of mine; for if you fall foul of me, by this light you shall go to the bottom! What! make prize of my little frigate, 55 while I am upon the cruise for you!

AIM. Well, well, I won't.   *Exit* ARCHER.

Enter BONNIFACE.

Landlord, have you any tolerable company in the house? I don't care for dining alone.

BON. Yes, sir, there's a captain below, as the 60 saying is, that arrived about an hour ago.

AIM. Gentlemen of his coat are welcome everywhere; will you make him a compliment from me, and tell him I should be glad of his company?

BON. Who shall I tell him, sir, would —— 65

AIM. [*aside*]. Ha! that stroke was well thrown in! —[*Aloud.*] I'm only a traveller like himself, and would be glad of his company, that's all.

BON. I obey your commands, as the saying is.
                              Exit.

Enter ARCHER.

ARCH. 'Sdeath! I had forgot; what title will 70 you give yourself?

AIM. My brother's, to be sure; he would never give me anything else, so I'll make bold with his honor this bout. — You know the rest of your cue.

ARCH. Ay, ay.   [*Exit.*] 75

Enter GIBBET.

GIB. Sir, I'm yours.

AIM. 'Tis more than I deserve, sir, for I don't know you.

GIB. I don't wonder at that, sir, for you never saw me before — (*aside*) I hope. 80

AIM. And pray, sir, how came I by the honor of seeing you now?

¹ Hand-kissings: the phrase is equivalent to 'Pay my respects.'
² Katherine Tofts, a famous contemporary soprano.
³ Bought up, monopolized.

GIB. Sir, I scorn to intrude upon any gentleman — but my landlord ——

AIM. O sir, I ask your pardon! You're the 85 captain he told me of?

GIB. At your service, sir.

AIM. What regiment, may I be so bold?

GIB. A marching regiment, sir, an old corps.

AIM. (*aside*). Very old, if your coat be regi- 90 mental. — [*Aloud.*] You have served abroad, sir?

GIB. Yes, sir — in the plantations; [4] 'twas my lot to be sent into the worst service. I would have quitted it indeed, but a man of honor, you know — besides, 'twas for the good of my country that 95 I should be abroad. Anything for the good of one's country — I'm a Roman for that.

AIM. (*aside*). One of the first, [5] I'll lay my life. — You found the West Indies very hot, sir?

GIB. Ay, sir, too hot for me. 100

AIM. Pray, sir, han't I seen your face at Will's coffee-house?

GIB. Yes, sir, and at White's [6] too.

AIM. And where is your company now, captain?

GIB. They an't come yet. 105

AIM. Why, d'ye expect 'em here?

GIB. They'll be here tonight, sir.

AIM. Which way do they march?

GIB. Across the country. — [*Aside.*] The devil's in't, if I han't said enough to encourage him to 110 declare; but I'm afraid he's not right; I must tack about.

AIM. Is your company to quarter in Lichfield?

GIB. In this house, sir.

AIM. What! all? 115

GIB. My company's but thin, ha, ha, ha! we are but three, ha, ha, ha!

AIM. You're merry, sir.

GIB. Ay, sir, you must excuse me, sir; I understand the world, especially the art of travelling; 120 I don't care, sir, for answering questions directly upon the road — for I generally ride with a charge [7] about me.

AIM. (*aside*). Three or four, I believe.

GIB. I am credibly informed that there are 125 highwaymen upon this quarter; not, sir, that I could suspect a gentleman of your figure — but truly, sir, I have got such a way of evasion upon the road, that I don't care for speaking truth to any man.

⁴ The audience is to understand that Gibbet's 'service' in the colonies was not as a soldier, but as a felon sentenced to transportation.
⁵ Gibbet's reference was to the Roman virtue of patriotism; Aimwell's aside, presumably, to the pillaging of Italy by the early Romans under Æneas.
⁶ Will's coffee house was the resort of literary men, White's of gamblers.
⁷ In the sense of 'sum of money'; Aimwell puns upon the word in the sense of loads of powder and shot for a pistol.

AIM. Your caution may be necessary. — 130
Then I presume you're no captain?

GIB. Not I, sir; captain is a good travelling name,
and so I take it; it stops a great many foolish inquir-
ies that are generally made about gentlemen that
travel; it gives a man an air of something, and 135
makes the drawers obedient: — and thus far I am a
captain, and no farther.

AIM. And pray, sir, what is your true profession?

GIB. O sir, you must excuse me! — Upon my
word, sir, I don't think it safe to tell you. 140

AIM. Ha, ha, ha! upon my word, I commend you.

Enter BONNIFACE.

Well, Mr. Bonniface, what's the news?

BON. There's another gentleman below, as the
saying is, that hearing you were but two, would be
glad to make the third man, if you would give 145
him leave.

AIM. What is he?

BON. A clergyman, as the saying is.

AIM. A clergyman! Is he really a clergyman? or
is it only his travelling name, as my friend the 150
captain has it?

BON. O sir, he's a priest, and chaplain to the
French officers in town.

AIM. Is he a Frenchman?

BON. Yes, sir, born at Brussels. 155

GIB. A Frenchman, and a priest! I won't be
seen in his company, sir; I have a value for my reputation, sir.

AIM. Nay, but, captain, since we are by ourselves
— Can he speak English, landlord? 160

BON. Very well, sir; you may know him, as the
saying is, to be a foreigner by his accent, and that's
all.

AIM. Then he has been in England before?

BON. Never, sir; but he's a master of lan- 165
guages, as the saying is — he talks Latin — it does
me good to hear him talk Latin.

AIM. Then you understand Latin, Mr. Bonniface?

BON. Not I, sir, as the saying is; but he talks 170
it so very fast, that I'm sure it must be good.

AIM. Pray, desire him to walk up.

BON. Here he is, as the saying is.

Enter FOIGARD.

FOI. Save you, gentlemens, both.

AIM. [aside]. A Frenchman! — [To FOIGARD.] 175
Sir, your most humble servant.

FOI. Och, dear joy,[1] I am your most faithful
shervant, and yours alsho.

GIB. Doctor, you talk very good English, but you
have a mighty twang of the foreigner. 180

FOI. My English is very vel for the vords, but we

---

foreigners, you know, cannot bring our tongues about
the pronunciation so soon.

AIM. (aside). A foreigner! a downright Teague,[2]
by this light! — Were you born in France, 185
doctor?

FOI. I was educated in France, but I was borned
at Brussels; I am a subject of the King of Spain, joy.

GIB. What King of Spain, sir? speak!

FOI. Upon my shoul, joy, I cannot tell you 190
as yet.[3]

AIM. Nay, captain, that was too hard upon the
doctor; he's a stranger.

FOI. Oh, let him alone, dear joy; I am of a nation
that is not easily put out of countenance. 195

AIM. Come, gentlemen, I'll end the dispute. —
Here, landlord, is dinner ready?

BON. Upon the table, as the saying is.

AIM. Gentlemen — pray — that door —

FOI. No, no, fait, the captain must lead. 200

AIM. No, doctor, the church is our guide.

GIB. Ay, ay, so it is.   Exit foremost, they follow.

[SCENE III]

*Scene changes to a gallery in LADY BOUNTIFUL'S
house.*

*Enter ARCHER and SCRUB singing, and hugging one
another, SCRUB with a tankard in his hand,
GIPSEY listening at a distance.*

SCRUB. *Tall, all dall!* — Come, my dear boy, let's
have that song once more.

ARCH. No, no, we shall disturb the family. — But
will you be sure to keep the secret?

SCRUB. Pho! upon my honor, as I'm a gentle- 5
man.

ARCH. 'Tis enough. — You must know, then, that
my master is the Lord Viscount Aimwell; he fought
a duel t'other day in London, wounded his man so
dangerously that he thinks fit to withdraw till he 10
hears whether the gentleman's wounds be mortal or
not. He never was in this part of England before, so
he chose to retire to this place, that's all.

GIP. [aside]. And that's enough for me.   Exit.

SCRUB. And where were you when your 15
master fought?

ARCH. We never know of our masters' quarrels.

SCRUB. No? If our masters in the country here
receive a challenge, the first thing they do is to tell
their wives; the wife tells the servants, the ser- 20
vants alarm the tenants, and in half an hour you shall
have the whole county in arms.

ARCH. To hinder two men from doing what they
have no mind for. — But if you should chance to
talk now of my business? 25

---

[2] Irishman.
[3] The War of the Spanish Succession had not yet settled this
question.

[1] A common term of friendly address among the Irish.

SCRUB. Talk! ay, sir, had I not learned the knack of holding my tongue, I had never lived so long in a great family.

ARCH. Ay, ay, to be sure there are secrets in all families. 30

SCRUB. Secrets! ay; — but I'll say no more. — Come, sit down, we'll make an end of our tankard: here ——

ARCH. With all my heart; who knows but you and I may come to be better acquainted, eh? — 35 Here's your ladies' healths; you have three, I think, and to be sure there must be secrets among 'em. [*Drinks.*]

SCRUB. Secrets! ay, friend. I wish I had a friend —

ARCH. Am not I your friend? Come, you and I will be sworn brothers. 40

SCRUB. Shall we?

ARCH. From this minute. — Give me a kiss — and now, brother Scrub ——

SCRUB. And now, brother Martin, I will tell you a secret that will make your hair stand on end. 45 You must know that I am consumedly in love.

ARCH. That's a terrible secret, that's the truth on't.

SCRUB. That jade, Gipsey, that was with us just now in the cellar, is the arrantest whore that ever wore a petticoat; and I'm dying for love of her. 50

ARCH. Ha, ha, ha! — Are you in love with her person or her virtue, brother Scrub?

SCRUB. I should like virtue best, because it is more durable than beauty; for virtue holds good with some women long and many a day after they 55 have lost it.

ARCH. In the country, I grant ye, where no woman's virtue is lost, till a bastard be found.

SCRUB. Ay, could I bring her to a bastard, I should have her all to myself; but I dare not put 60 it upon that lay,[1] for fear of being sent for a soldier.— Pray, brother, how do you gentlemen in London like that same Pressing Act?[2]

ARCH. Very ill, brother Scrub; 'tis the worst that ever was made for us. Formerly I remember the 65 good days, when we could dun our masters for our wages, and if they refused to pay us, we could have a warrant to carry 'em before a justice; but now if we talk of eating, they have a warrant for us, and carry us before three justices. 70

SCRUB. And to be sure we go, if we talk of eating; for the justices won't give their own servants a bad example. Now this is my misfortune — I dare not speak in the house, while that jade Gipsey dings[3] about like a fury — once I had the better end of 75 the staff.

[1] I dare not take that line.
[2] The act authorizing the impressment of men into the military service, passed two or three years earlier.
[3] Flings.

ARCH. And how comes the change now?

SCRUB. Why, the mother of all this mischief is a priest.

ARCH. A priest! 80

SCRUB. Ay, a damned son of a whore of Babylon, that came over hither to say grace to the French officers, and eat up our provisions. There's not a day goes over his head without dinner or supper in this house. 85

ARCH. How came he so familiar in the family?

SCRUB. Because he speaks English as if he had lived here all his life; and tells lies as if he had been a traveller from his cradle.

ARCH. And this priest, I'm afraid, has con- 90 verted the affections of your Gipsey.

SCRUB. Converted! ay, and perverted, my dear friend: for I'm afraid he has made her a whore and a papist! — But this is not all; there's the French count and Mrs. Sullen, they're in the confeder- 95 acy, and for some private ends of their own, to be sure.

ARCH. A very hopeful family yours, brother Scrub! I suppose the maiden lady has her lover too.

SCRUB. Not that I know. She's the best on 'em, that's the truth on't. But they take care to 100 prevent my curiosity, by giving me so much business, that I'm a perfect slave. What d'ye think is my place in this family?

ARCH. Butler, I suppose.

SCRUB. Ah, Lord help you! — I'll tell you. — 105 Of a Monday I drive the coach; of a Tuesday I drive the plough; on Wednesday I follow the hounds; a-Thursday I dun the tenants; on Friday I go to market; on Saturday I draw warrants; and a-Sunday I draw beer. 110

ARCH. Ha, ha, ha! if variety be a pleasure in life, you have enough on't, my dear brother. — But what ladies are those?

[SCRUB.] Ours, ours; that upon the right hand is Mrs. Sullen, and the other is Mrs. Dorinda. — 115 Don't mind 'em; sit still, man.

Enter MRS. SULLEN *and* DORINDA.

MRS. SUL. I have heard my brother talk of my Lord Aimwell; but they say that his brother is the finer gentleman.

DOR. That's impossible, sister. 120

MRS. SUL. He's vastly rich, but very close, they say.

DOR. No matter for that; if I can creep into his heart, I'll open his breast, I warrant him. I have heard say, that people may be guessed at by the 125 behavior of their servants; I could wish we might talk to that fellow.

MRS. SUL. So do I; for I think he's a very pretty fellow. Come this way, I'll throw out a lure for him presently. 130

(*They walk a turn towards the opposite side of the stage.*)

ARCH. [*aside*]. Corn, wine, and oil indeed! But, I think, the wife has the greatest plenty of flesh and blood; she should be my choice. — Ah, a, say you so! — (MRS. SULLEN *drops her glove,* ARCHER *runs, takes it up, and gives it to her.*) Madam — your lady- 135 ship's glove.

MRS. SUL. O sir, I thank you! — [*To* DORINDA.] What a handsome bow the fellow has!

DOR. Bow! why, I have known several footmen come down from London set up here for danc- 140 ing-masters, and carry off the best fortunes in the country.

ARCH. (*aside*). That project, for aught I know, had been better than ours. — Brother Scrub, why don't you introduce me?   145

SCRUB. Ladies, this is the strange gentleman's servant that you see at church today; I understood he came from London, and so I invited him to the cellar, that he might show me the newest flourish in whetting my knives.   150

DOR. And I hope you have made much of him?

ARCH. Oh yes, madam, but the strength of your ladyship's liquor is a little too potent for the consti- tution of your humble servant.

MRS. SUL. What, then you don't usually 155 drink ale?

ARCH. No, madam; my constant drink is tea, or a little wine and water. 'Tis prescribed me by the physician for a remedy against the spleen.

SCRUB. O la! O la! a footman have the 160 spleen!

MRS. SUL. I thought that distemper had been only proper to people of quality.

ARCH. Madam, like all other fashions it wears out, and so descends to their servants; though 165 in a great many of us I believe it proceeds from some melancholy particles in the blood, occasioned by the stagnation of wages.

DOR. [*aside to* MRS. SULLEN]. How affectedly the fellow talks! — How long, pray, have you 170 served your present master?

ARCH. Not long; my life has been mostly spent in the service of the ladies.

MRS. SUL. And pray, which service do you like best?   175

ARCH. Madam, the ladies pay best; the honor of serving them is sufficient wages; there is a charm in their looks that delivers a pleasure with their com- mands, and gives our duty the wings of inclination.

MRS. SUL. [*aside*]. The flight was above the 180 pitch of a livery. — And, sir, would not you be satis- fied to serve a lady again?

ARCH. As a groom of the chamber, madam, but not as a footman.

MRS. SUL. I suppose you served as footman 185 before.

ARCH. For that reason I would not serve in that post again; for my memory is too weak for the load of messages that the ladies lay upon their servants in London. My Lady Howd'ye, the last mis- 190 tress I served, called me up one morning, and told me, 'Martin, go to my Lady Allnight with my humble service; tell her I was to wait on her ladyship yes- terday, and left word with Mrs. Rebecca, that the preliminaries of the affair she knows of are 195 stopped till we know the concurrence of the person that I know of, for which there are circumstances wanting which we shall accommodate at the old place; but that in the meantime there is a person about her ladyship that, from several hints and 200 surmises, was accessary at a certain time to the dis- appointments that naturally attend things, that to her knowledge are of more importance ——'

MRS. SUL., DOR. Ha, ha, ha! where are you going, sir?   205

ARCH. Why, I han't half done! — The whole howd'ye was about half an hour long; so I happened to misplace two syllables, and was turned off, and rendered incapable.

DOR. [*aside*]. The pleasantest fellow, sister, 210 I ever saw! — But, friend, if your master be married, I presume you still serve a lady.

ARCH. No, madam, I take care never to come into a married family; the commands of the master and mistress are always so contrary, that 'tis impos- 215 sible to please both.

DOR. (*aside*). There's a main point gained. My lord is not married, I find.

MRS. SUL. But I wonder, friend, that in so many good services you had not a better provision 220 made for you.

ARCH. I don't know how, madam. I had a lieu- tenancy offered me three or four times; but that is not bread, madam — I live much better as I do.

SCRUB. Madam, he sings rarely. — I was 225 thought to do pretty well here in the country till he came; but alack a day, I'm nothing to my brother Martin!

DOR. Does he? — Pray, sir, will you oblige us with a song?   230

ARCH. Are you for passion or humor?

SCRUB. Oh la! he has the purest ballad about a trifle ——

MRS. SUL. A trifle! pray, sir, let's have it.

ARCH. I'm ashamed to offer you a trifle, 235 madam; but since you command me —

(*Sings to the tune of Sir Simon the King.*)

A trifling song you shall hear,
Begun with a trifle and ended,

133] C *Ay, ay, say.*   215] C *too contrary.*   232] Q1C *Oh le.*

[All trifling people draw near,
And I shall be nobly attended.   240

Were it not for trifles a few,
That lately have come into play;
The men would want something to do,
And the women want something to say.

What makes men trifle in dressing?   245
Because the ladies (they know)
Admire, by often possessing,
That eminent trifle, a beau.

When the lover his moments has trifled,
The trifle of trifles to gain,   250
No sooner the virgin is rifled,
But a trifle shall part 'em again.

What mortal man would be able
At White's half an hour to sit?
Or who could bear a tea-table,   255
Without talking of trifles for wit?

The court is from trifles secure,
Gold keys[1] are no trifles, we see;
White rods[2] are no trifles, I'm sure,
Whatever their bearers may be.   260

But if you will go to the place,
Where trifles abundantly breed,
The levee will show you his Grace
Makes promises trifles indeed.

A coach with six footmen behind,   265
I count neither trifle nor sin:
But, ye gods! how oft do we find
A scandalous trifle within?

A flask of champagne, people think it
A trifle, or something as bad: 270
But if you'll contrive how to drink it,
You'll find it no trifle, egad!

A parson's a trifle at sea,
A widow's a trifle in sorrow;
A peace is a trifle today,   275
Who knows what may happen tomorrow?

A black coat a trifle may cloak,
Or to hide [it], the red may endeavor:
But if once the army is broke,
We shall have more trifles than ever.   280

The stage is a trifle, they say,
The reason, pray carry along,
Because at ev'ry new play,
The house they with trifles so throng.

---

[1] Symbols of office of the groom of the stole and the mistress of the robes.
[2] Symbols of office of high-ranking cabinet ministers.

But with people's malice to trifle,   285
And to set us all on a foot:
The author of this is a trifle,
And his song is a trifle to boot.]

MRS. SUL. Very well, sir, we're obliged to you. —
Something for a pair of gloves.   290
                    (Offering him money.)
ARCH. I humbly beg leave to be excused: my master, madam, pays me; nor dare I take money from any other hand, without injuring his honor, and disobeying his commands.   Exit [with SCRUB].
DOR. This is surprising! Did you ever see so   295
pretty a well-bred fellow?
MRS. SUL. The devil take him for wearing that livery!
DOR. I fancy, sister, he may be some gentleman, a friend of my lord's, that his lordship has   300
pitched upon for his courage, fidelity, and discretion, to bear him company in this dress, and who, ten to one, was his second too.
MRS. SUL. It is so, it must be so, and it shall be so! — for I like him.   305
DOR. What! better than the count?
MRS. SUL. The count happened to be the most agreeable man upon the place; and so I chose him to serve me in my design upon my husband. — But I should like this fellow better in a design upon   310
myself.
DOR. But now, sister, for an interview with this lord and this gentleman; how shall we bring that about?
MRS. SUL. Patience! You country ladies   315
give no quarter if once you be entered.[3] — Would you prevent[4] their desires, and give the fellows no wishing-time? — Look ye, Dorinda, if my Lord Aimwell loves you or deserves you, he'll find a way to see you, and there we must leave it. My   320
business comes now upon the tapis. — Have you prepared your brother?
DOR. Yes, yes.
MRS. SUL. And how did he relish it?
DOR. He said little, mumbled something to   325
himself, promised to be guided by me — but here he comes.

Enter SULLEN.

SUL. What singing was that I heard just now?
MRS. SUL. The singing in your head, my dear; you complained of it all day.   330
SUL. You're impertinent.
MRS. SUL. I was ever so, since I became one flesh with you.

---

[3] Engaged in action.   [4] Anticipate.

239–288] Q1C om. bracketed passage.   It is here supplied from the seventh edition of the *Dramatic Works*, 1736, where the entire song is printed after the epilogue.
278] 1736 *in.*

Sul. One flesh! rather two carcasses joined unnaturally together.   335

Mrs. Sul. Or rather a living soul coupled to a dead body.

Dor. So, this is fine encouragement for me!

Sul. Yes, my wife shows you what you must do.

Mrs. Sul. And my husband shows you what 340 you must suffer.

Sul. 'Sdeath, why can't you be silent?

Mrs. Sul. 'Sdeath, why can't you talk?

Sul. Do you talk to any purpose?

Mrs. Sul. Do you think to any purpose?   345

Sul. Sister, hark ye! (*Whispers.*) [*Aloud.*] I shan't be home till it be late.   *Exit.*

Mrs. Sul. What did he whisper to ye?

Dor. That he would go round the back way, come into the closet, and listen as I directed him. 350 But let me beg you once more, dear sister, to drop this project; for as I told you before, instead of awaking him to kindness, you may provoke him to a rage; and then who knows how far his brutality may carry him?   355

Mrs. Sul. I'm provided to receive him, I warrant you. But here comes the count — vanish!

Exit Dorinda.

Enter Count Bellair.

Don't you wonder, monsieur le count, that I was not at church this afternoon?

Count Bel. I more wonder, madam, that 360 you go dere at all, or how you dare to lift those eyes to heaven that are guilty of so much killing.

Mrs. Sul. If heaven, sir, has given to my eyes with the power of killing the virtue of making a cure, I hope the one may atone for the other. 365

Count Bel. Oh, largely, madam. Would your ladyship be as ready to apply the remedy as to give the wound? Consider, madam, I am doubly a prisoner — first to the arms of your general, then to your more conquering eyes. My first chains 370 are easy — there a ransom may redeem me; but from your fetters I never shall get free.

Mrs. Sul. Alas, sir! why should you complain to me of your captivity, who am in chains myself? You know, sir, that I am bound, nay, most be-tied 375 up in that particular that might give you ease: I am like you, a prisoner of war — of war, indeed! I have given my parole of honor; would you break yours to gain your liberty?

Count Bel. Most certainly I would, were I 380 a prisoner among the Turks; dis is your case: you're a slave, madam, slave to the worst of Turks, a husband.

Mrs. Sul. There lies my foible, I confess; no fortifications, no courage, conduct, nor vigi- 385

lancy can pretend to defend a place where the cruelty of the governor forces the garrison to mutiny.

Count Bel. And where de besieger is resolved to die before de place. — Here will I fix (*kneels*) — with tears, vows, and prayers assault your heart, 390 and never rise till you surrender; or if I must storm — Love and St. Michael! — And so I begin the attack. —

Mrs. Sul. Stand off! — (*Aside.*) Sure he hears me not! And I could almost wish he — did 395 not! The fellow makes love very prettily. — [*Aloud.*] But, sir, why should you put such a value upon my person, when you see it despised by one that knows it so much better?

Count Bel. He knows it not, though he 400 possesses it; if he but knew the value of the jewel he is master of, he would always wear it next his heart, and sleep with it in his arms.

Mrs. Sul. But since he throws me unregarded from him —— 405

Count Bel. And one that knows your value well comes by and takes you up, is it not justice?

(*Goes to lay hold of her.*)

Enter Sullen *with his sword drawn.*

Sul. Hold, villain, hold!

Mrs. Sul. (*presenting a pistol*). Do you hold!

Sul. What! murther your husband, to de- 410 fend your bully!

Mrs. Sul. Bully! for shame, Mr. Sullen. Bullies wear long swords, the gentleman has none; he's a prisoner, you know. — I was aware of your outrage, and prepared this to receive your violence; and, 415 if occasion were, to preserve myself against the force of this other gentleman.

Count Bel. O madam, your eyes be bettre firearms than your pistol; they nevre miss.

Sul. What! court my wife to my face! 420

Mrs. Sul. Pray, Mr. Sullen, put up; suspend your fury for a minute.

Sul. To give you time to invent an excuse!

Mrs. Sul. I need none.

Sul. No, for I heard every syllable of your 425 discourse.

Count Bel. Ah! and begar, I tink de dialogue was vera pretty.

Mrs. Sul. Then I suppose, sir, you heard something of your own barbarity? 430

Sul. Barbarity! 'Oons, what does the [woman] call barbarity? Do I ever meddle with you?

Mrs. Sul. No.

Sul. As for you, sir, I shall take another time.

Count Bel. Ah, begar, and so must I. 435

Sul. Look'ee, madam, don't think that my anger proceeds from any concern I have for your honor, but for my own, and if you can contrive any way of being a whore without making me a cuckold, do it and welcome. 440

Mrs. Sul. Sir, I thank you kindly; you would allow me the sin but rob me of the pleasure. — No, no, I'm resolved never to venture upon the crime without the satisfaction of seeing you punished for't.

Sul. Then will you grant me this, my dear? 445 Let anybody else do you the favor but that Frenchman, for I mortally hate his whole generation. *Exit.*

Count Bel. Ah, sir, that be ungrateful, for begar, I love some of yours. — Madam ——

(*Approaching her.*)

Mrs. Sul. No, sir. — 450

Count Bel. No, sir! — Garzoon, madam, I am not your husband!

Mrs. Sul. 'Tis time to undeceive you, sir. I believed your addresses to me were no more than an amusement, and I hope you will think the same 455 of my complaisance; and to convince you that you ought, you must know that I brought you hither only to make you instrumental in setting me right with my husband, for he was planted to listen by my appointment. 460

Count Bel. By your appointment?

Mrs. Sul. Certainly.

Count Bel. And so, madam, while I was telling twenty stories to part you from your husband, begar, I was bringing you together all the while? 465

Mrs. Sul. I ask your pardon, sir, but I hope this will give you a taste of the virtue of the English ladies.

Count Bel. Begar, madam, your virtue be vera great, but garzoon, your honeste be vera little.

Enter Dorinda.

Mrs. Sul. Nay, now, you're angry, sir. 470

Count Bel. Angry! — *Fair Dorinda.* (*Sings 'Dorinda,' the opera tune, and addresses to* Dorinda.) Madam, when your ladyship want a fool, send for me. *Fair Dorinda, Revenge, etc.*[1] *Exit.*

Mrs. Sul. There goes the true humor of his 475 nation — resentment with good manners, and the height of anger in a song! — Well, sister, you must be judge, for you have heard the trial.

Dor. And I bring in my brother guilty.

Mrs. Sul. But I must bear the punishment. 480 'Tis hard, sister.

Dor. I own it; but you must have patience.

Mrs. Sul. Patience! the cant of custom — Providence sends no evil without a remedy — should I

[1] Stonehill suggests that the count combines snatches from Buononcini's opera *Camilla* (1706), with libretto by Stampiglio, translated by MacSwiney. In the first act Lavinia sings an air, 'Fair Dorinda, happy, happy, happy may'st thou ever be': in the second act an air sung by Camilla begins, 'Revenge, revenge I summon.'

lie groaning under a yoke I can shake off, I 485 were accessary to my ruin, and my patience were no better than self-murder.

Dor. But how can you shake off the yoke? Your divisions[2] don't come within the reach of the law for a divorce. 490

Mrs. Sul. Law! what law can search into the remote abyss of nature? what evidence can prove the unaccountable disaffections of wedlock? Can a jury sum up the endless aversions that are rooted in our souls, or can a bench give judgment upon an- 495 tipathies?

Dor. They never pretended, sister; they never meddle, but in case of uncleanness.

Mrs. Sul. Uncleanness! O sister! casual violation is a transient injury, and may possibly be 500 repaired, but can radical hatreds be ever reconciled? — No, no, sister, nature is the first lawgiver, and when she has set tempers opposite, not all the golden links of wedlock nor iron manacles of law can keep 'um fast. 505

Wedlock we own ordained by heaven's decree,
But such as heaven ordained it first to be —
Concurring tempers in the man and wife
As mutual helps to draw the load of life.
View all the works of Providence above, 510
The stars with harmony and concord move;
View all the works of Providence below, ⎫
The fire, the water, earth, and air, we know, ⎬
All in one plant agree to make it grow. ⎭
Must man, the chiefest work of art divine, 515
Be doomed in endless discord to repine?
No, we should injure heaven by that surmise;
Omnipotence is just, were man but wise.

ACT IV

[SCENE I]

Scene continues.

Enter Mrs. Sullen.

Mrs. Sul. Were I born an humble Turk, where women have no soul nor property, there I must sit contented. But in England, a country whose women are its glory, must women be abused? where women rule, must women be enslaved? nay, cheated into 5 slavery, mocked by a promise of comfortable society into a wilderness of solitude? I dare not keep the thought about me. — Oh, here comes something to divert me.

Enter a Country Woman.

Wom. I come, an't please your ladyships — 10 you're my Lady Bountiful, an't ye?

Mrs. Sul. Well, good woman, go on.

[2] Disagreements.

Wom. I have come seventeen long mail to have a cure for my husband's sore leg.

Mrs. Sul. Your husband! what, woman, 15 cure your husband!

Wom. Ay, poor man, for his sore leg won't let him stir from home.

Mrs. Sul. There, I confess, you have given me a reason. Well, good woman, I'll tell you what 20 you must do. You must lay your husband's leg upon a table, and with a chopping-knife you must lay it open as broad as you can; then you must take out the bone, and beat the flesh soundly with a rolling-pin; then take salt, pepper, cloves, mace, and 25 ginger, some sweet herbs, and season it very well; then roll it up like brawn, and put it into the oven for two hours.

Wom. Heavens reward your ladyship! — I have two little babies too that are piteous bad with 30 the graips, an't please ye.

Mrs. Sul. Put a little pepper and salt in their bellies, good woman.

Enter LADY BOUNTIFUL.

I beg your ladyship's pardon for taking your business out of your hands; I have been a-tampering 35 here a little with one of your patients.

Lady Boun. Come, good woman, don't mind this mad creature; I am the person that you want, I suppose. What would you have, woman?

Mrs. Sul. She wants something for her hus- 40 band's sore leg.

Lady Boun. What's the matter with his leg, goody?

Wom. It come first, as one might say, with a sort of dizziness in his foot, then he had a kind of a 45 laziness in his joints, and then his leg broke out, and then it swelled, and then it closed again, and then it broke out again, and then it festered, and then it grew better, and then it grew worse again.

Mrs. Sul. Ha, ha, ha! 50

Lady Boun. How can you be merry with the misfortunes of other people?

Mrs. Sul. Because my own make me sad, madam.

Lady Boun. The worst reason in the world, daughter; your own misfortunes should teach 55 you to pity others.

Mrs. Sul. But the woman's misfortunes and mine are nothing alike; her husband is sick, and mine, alas! is in health.

Lady Boun. What! would you wish your hus- 60 band sick?

Mrs. Sul. Not of a sore leg, of all things.

Lady Boun. Well, good woman, go to the pantry, get your bellyful of victuals, then I'll give you a receipt of diet-drink for your husband. — But 65 d'ye hear, goody, you must not let your husband move too much.

Wom. No, no, madam, the poor man's inclinable enough to lie still. *Exit.*

Lady Boun. Well, daughter Sullen, though 70 you laugh, I have done miracles about the country here with my receipts.

Mrs. Sul. Miracles indeed, if they have cured anybody; but I believe, madam, the patient's faith goes farther toward the miracle than your pre- 75 scription.

Lady Boun. Fancy helps in some cases; but there's your husband, who has as little fancy as anybody; I brought him from death's door.

Mrs. Sul. I suppose, madam, you made him 80 drink plentifully of ass's milk.

Enter DORINDA, *runs to* MRS. SULLEN.

Dor. News, dear sister! news! news!

Enter ARCHER, *running.*

Arch. Where, where is my Lady Bountiful? — Pray, which is the old lady of you three?

Lady Boun. I am. 85

Arch. O madam, the fame of your ladyship's charity, goodness, benevolence, skill, and ability, have drawn me hither to implore your ladyship's help in behalf of my unfortunate master, who is this moment breathing his last. 90

Lady Boun. Your master! where is he?

Arch. At your gate, madam. Drawn by the appearance of your handsome house to view it nearer, and walking up the avenue within five paces of the court-yard, he was taken ill of a sudden with a 95 sort of I know not what, but down he fell, and there he lies.

Lady Boun. Here, Scrub! Gipsey! all run, get my easy chair down stairs, put the gentleman in it, and bring him in quickly, quickly! 100

Arch. Heaven will reward your ladyship for this charitable act.

Lady Boun. Is your master used to these fits?

Arch. O yes, madam, frequently — I have known him have five or six of a night. 105

Lady Boun. What's his name?

Arch. Lord, madam, he's a-dying! a minute's care or neglect may save or destroy his life!

Lady Boun. Ah, poor gentleman! Come, friend, show me the way; I'll see him brought in my- 110 self. *Exit with* ARCHER.

Dor. O sister, my heart flutters about strangely! I can hardly forbear running to his assistance.

Mrs. Sul. And I'll lay my life he deserves your assistance more than he wants it; did not I tell 115 you that my lord would find a way to come at you? Love's his distemper, and you must be the physician; put on all your charms, summon all your fire into your eyes, plant the whole artillery of your looks against his breast, and down with him. 120

DOR. O sister! I'm but a young gunner; I shall be afraid to shoot, for fear the piece should recoil and hurt myself.

MRS. SUL. Never fear, you shall see me shoot before you, if you will.   125

DOR. No, no, dear sister; you have missed your mark so unfortunately, that I shan't care for being instructed by you.

Enter AIMWELL *in a chair carried by* ARCHER *and* SCRUB; LADY BOUNTIFUL [*and*] GIPSEY. AIM-WELL *counterfeiting a swoon.*

LADY BOUN. Here, here, let's see the hartshorn drops. — Gipsey, a glass of fair [1] water! His fit's very strong. — Bless me, how his hands are clinched!   130

ARCH. For shame, ladies, what d'ye do? why don't you help us? — (*To* DORINDA.) Pray, madam, take his hand and open it, if you can, whilst I hold his head.   (DORINDA *takes his hand.*)   135

DOR. Poor gentleman! — Oh! — he has got my hand within his, and squeezes it unmercifully ——

LADY BOUN. 'Tis the violence of his convulsion, child.   140

ARCH. Oh, madam, he's perfectly possessed in these cases — he'll bite if you don't have a care.

DOR. Oh, my hand! my hand!

LADY BOUN. What's the matter with the foolish girl? I have got this hand open, you see, with a great deal of ease.   145

ARCH. Ay, but, madam, your daughter's hand is somewhat warmer than your ladyship's, and the heat of it draws the force of the spirits that way.

MRS. SUL. I find, friend, you're very learned in these sorts of fits.   150

ARCH. 'Tis no wonder, madam, for I'm often troubled with them myself; I find myself extremely ill at this minute.   (*Looking hard at* MRS. SULLEN.)

MRS. SUL. (*aside*). I fancy I could find a way to cure you.   155

LADY BOUN. His fit holds him very long.

ARCH. Longer than usual, madam. — Pray, young lady, open his breast, and give him air.

LADY BOUN. Where did his illness take him first, pray?   160

ARCH. Today at church, madam.

LADY BOUN. In what manner was he taken?

ARCH. Very strangely, my lady. He was of a sudden touched with something in his eyes, which, at the first, he only felt, but could not tell whether 'twas pain or pleasure.   165

LADY BOUN. Wind, nothing but wind!

ARCH. By soft degrees it grew and mounted to his brain, — there his fancy caught it; there formed it so beautiful, and dressed it up in such gay, pleasing colors, that his transported appetite seized the fair   170

[1] Pure.

idea, and straight conveyed it to his heart. That hospitable seat of life sent all its sanguine spirits forth to meet, and opened all its sluicy gates to take the stranger in.   175

LADY BOUN. Your master should never go without a bottle to smell to. — Oh — he recovers! The lavender-water — some feathers to burn under his nose — Hungary-water [2] to rub his temples. — Oh, he comes to himself! — Hem a little, sir, hem. — Gipsey! bring the cordial-water.   180

(AIMWELL *seems to awake in amaze.*)

DOR. How d'ye, sir?

AIM. Where am I?   (*Rising.*)

Sure I have passed the gulf of silent death,   185
And now I land on the Elysian shore! —
Behold the goddess of those happy plains,
Fair Proserpine — let me adore thy bright divinity.

(*Kneels to* DORINDA, *and kisses her hand.*)

MRS. SUL. So, so, so! I knew where the fit would end!   190

AIM. Eurydice perhaps —

How could thy Orpheus keep his word,
And not look back upon thee?
No treasure but thyself could sure have bribed him
To look one minute off thee.   195

LADY BOUN. Delirious, poor gentleman!

ARCH. Very delirious, madam, very delirious.

AIM. Martin's voice, I think.

ARCH. Yes, my lord. — How does your lordship?

LADY BOUN. Lord! did you mind that, girls?   200

AIM. Where am I?

ARCH. In very good hands, sir. — You were taken just now with one of your old fits, under the trees, just by this good lady's house; her ladyship had you taken in, and has miraculously brought you to yourself, as you see.   205

AIM. I am so confounded with shame, madam, that I can now only beg pardon — and refer my acknowledgments for your ladyship's care till an opportunity offers of making some amends. — I dare be no longer troublesome. — Martin! give two guineas to the servants.   (*Going.*)   210

DOR. Sir, you may catch cold by going so soon into the air; you don't look, sir, as if you were perfectly recovered.   215

(*Here* ARCHER *talks to* LADY BOUNTIFUL *in dumb show.*)

AIM. That I shall never be, madam; my present illness is so rooted that I must expect to carry it to my grave.

MRS. SUL. Don't despair, sir; I have known several in your distemper shake it off with a fort-night's physic.   220

LADY BOUN. Come, sir, your servant has been telling me that you're apt to relapse if you go into

[2] A mixture of spirit of wine and rosemary flowers.

the air. — Your good manners shan't get the better of ours — you shall sit down again, sir. —   225 Come, sir, we don't mind ceremonies in the country — here, sir, my service t'ye. You shall taste my water; 'tis a cordial I can assure you, and of my own making — drink it off, sir. — (AIMWELL *drinks*.) And how d'ye find yourself now, sir?   230

AIM. Somewhat better — though very faint still.

LADY BOUN. Ay, ay, people are always faint after these fits. — Come, girls, you shall show the gentleman the house. — 'Tis but an old family building, sir; but you had better walk about and cool by   235 degrees, than venture immediately into the air. You'll find some tolerable pictures. — Dorinda, show the gentleman the way. I must go to the poor woman below.   *Exit.*

DOR. This way, sir.   240

AIM. Ladies, shall I beg leave for my servant to wait on you, for he understands pictures very well?

MRS. SUL. Sir, we understand originals[1] as well as he does pictures, so he may come along.

Exeunt DORINDA, MRS. SULLEN, AIMWELL, ARCHER. AIMWELL *leads* DORINDA.

Enter FOIGARD *and* SCRUB, *meeting.*

FOI. Save you, Master Scrub!   245

SCRUB. Sir, I won't be saved your way — I hate a priest, I abhor the French, and I defy the devil. Sir, I'm a bold Briton, and will spill the last drop of my blood to keep out popery and slavery.

FOI. Master Scrub, you would put me down   250 in politics, and so I would be speaking with Mrs. Shipsey.

SCRUB. Good Mr. Priest, you can't speak with her; she's sick, sir, she's gone abroad, sir, she's — dead two months ago, sir.   255

Enter GIPSEY.

GIP. How now, impudence! how dare you talk so saucily to the doctor? — Pray, sir, don't take it ill; for the common people of England are not so civil to strangers, as —

SCRUB. You lie! you lie! 'Tis the common   260 people that are civilest to strangers.

GIP. Sirrah, I have a good mind to — get you out, I say!

SCRUB. I won't.

GIP. You won't, sauce-box! — Pray, doctor,   265 what is the captain's name that came to your inn last night?

SCRUB [*aside*]. The captain! Ah, the devil, there she hampers me again; — the captain has me on one side, and the priest on t'other: — so between   270

the gown and the sword, I have a fine time on't. — But *cedunt arma togæ*.[2]   (*Going.*)

GIP. What, sirrah, won't you march?

SCRUB. No, my dear, I won't march — but I'll walk. — [*Aside.*] And I'll make bold to listen   275 a little too.   (*Goes behind the side-scene and listens.*)

GIP. Indeed, doctor, the count has been barbarously treated, that's the truth on't.

FOI. Ah, Mrs. Gipsey, upon my shoul, now, gra,[3] his complainings would mollify the marrow in   280 your bones, and move the bowels of your commiseration! He veeps, and he dances, and he fistles, and he swears, and he laughs, and he stamps, and he sings: in conclusion, joy, he's afflicted *à la française*, and a stranger would not know whider to cry or   285 to laugh with him.

GIP. What would you have me do, doctor?

FOI. Noting, joy, but only hide the count in Mrs. Sullen's closet when it is dark.

GIP. Nothing! is that nothing? It would be   290 both a sin and a shame, doctor.

FOI. Here is twenty louis d'ors, joy, for your shame; and I will give you an absolution for the shin.

GIP. But won't that money look like a bribe?

FOI. Dat is according as you shall tauk it.—   295 If you receive the money beforehand, 'twill be *logicè*, a bribe; but if you stay till afterwards, 'twill be only a gratification.[4]

GIP. Well, doctor, I'll take it *logicè*. — But what must I do with my conscience, sir?   300

FOI. Leave dat wid me, joy; I am your priest, gra; and your conscience is under my hands.

GIP. But should I put the count into the closet——

FOI. Vel, is dere any shin for a man's being in a closhet? One may go to prayers in a closhet.   305

GIP. But if the lady should come into her chamber, and go to bed?

FOI. Vel, and is dere any shin in going to bed, joy?

GIP. Ay, but if the parties should meet, doctor?

FOI. Vel den — the parties must be responsi-   310 ble. — Do you be after putting the count in the closhet; and leave the shins wid themselves. — I will come with the count to instruct you in your chamber.

GIP. Well, doctor, your religion is so pure! — Methinks I'm so easy after an absolution, and   315 can sin afresh with so much security, that I'm resolved to die a martyr to't. — Here's the key of the garden door, come in the back way when 'tis late, I'll be ready to receive you; but don't so much as whisper, only take hold of my hand; I'll lead   320 you, and do you lead the count, and follow me.

Exeunt.

---

[1] A pun on the word 'original' in its meaning of an odd or eccentric person.

[2] 'Let arms yield to the gown.' (Cicero, *De Officiis*, I. 22.)

[3] Dear.

[4] I.e., a gratuity.

284] Q1 C *francois.*

Enter SCRUB.

SCRUB. What witchcraft now have these two imps of the devil been a-hatching here? — There's twenty louis-d'ors; I heard that, and saw the purse. But I must give room to my betters.   [*Exit.*] 325

Enter AIMWELL, *leading* DORINDA, *and making love in dumb show;* MRS. SULLEN *and* ARCHER.

MRS. SUL. (*to* ARCHER). Pray, sir, how d'ye like that piece?

ARCH. Oh, 'tis Leda! You find, madam, how Jupiter comes disguised to make love ——

MRS. SUL. But what think you there of 330 Alexander's battles?

ARCH. We only want a Le Brun,[1] madam, to draw greater battles, and a greater general of our own.[2] The Danube,[3] madam, would make a greater figure in a picture than the Granicus;[4] and we have 335 our Ramillies to match their Arbela.[5]

MRS. SUL. Pray, sir, what head is that in the corner there?

ARCH. O madam, 'tis poor Ovid in his exile.

MRS. SUL. What was he banished for?   340

ARCH. His ambitious love, madam. — (*Bowing.*) His misfortune touches me.

MRS. SUL. Was he successful in his amours?

ARCH. There he has left us in the dark. He was too much a gentleman to tell.   345

MRS. SUL. If he were secret, I pity him.

ARCH. And if he were successful, I envy him.

MRS. SUL. How d'ye like that Venus over the chimney?

ARCH. Venus! I protest, madam, I took it 350 for your picture; but now I look again, 'tis not handsome enough.

MRS. SUL. Oh, what a charm is flattery! If you would see my picture, there it is, over that cabinet. — How d'ye like it?   355

ARCH. I must admire anything, madam, that has the least resemblance of you. — But, methinks, madam — (*He looks at the picture and* MRS. SULLEN *three or four times, by turns.*) Pray, madam, who drew it?   360

MRS. SUL. A famous hand, sir.

Here AIMWELL *and* DORINDA *go off.*

[1] Charles Le Brun (1619–1690), court painter of Louis XIV; painter of murals, at Versailles and elsewhere, celebrating the deeds of his patron. He had also executed a series of murals depicting the exploits of Alexander the Great.

[2] The Duke of Marlborough.

[3] Blenheim, scene of the great victory (1704) of the English and the Austrians over the French and the Bavarians, was on the Danube.

[4] A river in Asia Minor which was the scene of Alexander the Great's overwhelming defeat of the Persians in 334 B.C.

[5] The first-named battle (1706) was a victory of the Allies over the French; the second (331 B.C.) one in which Alexander defeated Darius.

407] C om *and.*

ARCH. A famous hand, madam! — Your eyes, indeed, are featured there; but where's the sparkling moisture, shining fluid, in which they swim? The picture, indeed, has your dimples; but where's 365 the swarm of killing Cupids that should ambush there? the lips too are figured out; but where's the carnation dew, the pouting ripeness, that tempts the taste in the original?

MRS. SUL. [*aside*]. Had it been my lot to 370 have matched with such a man!

ARCH. Your breasts too—presumptuous man!— what, paint heaven! — Apropos, madam, in the very next picture is Salmoneus, that was struck dead with lightning, for offering to imitate Jove's thun- 375 der; I hope you served the painter so, madam?

MRS. SUL. Had my eyes the power of thunder, they should employ their lightning better.

ARCH. There's the finest bed in that room, madam! I suppose 'tis your ladyship's bed- 380 chamber.

MRS. SUL. And what then, sir?

ARCH. I think the quilt is the richest that ever I saw. — I can't at this distance, madam, distinguish the figures of the embroidery; will you give 385 me leave, madam? —   [*Goes toward the door.*]

MRS. SUL. [*aside*]. The devil take his impudence! — Sure, if I gave him an opportunity, he durst not offer it? — I have a great mind to try. — (*Going; returns.*) 'Sdeath, what am I doing? — And 390 alone, too! — Sister! sister!   (*Runs out.*)

ARCH. I'll follow her close —
For where a Frenchman durst attempt to storm,
A Briton sure may well the work perform.
                                        (*Going.*)

Enter SCRUB.

SCRUB. Martin! brother Martin!   395

ARCH. O brother Scrub, I beg your pardon, I was not a-going; here's a guinea my master ordered you.

SCRUB. A guinea! hi, hi, hi! a guinea! eh — by this light it is a guinea! But I suppose you 400 expect one and twenty shillings in change.

ARCH. Not at all; I have another for Gipsey.

SCRUB. A guinea for her! Faggot and fire for the witch! — Sir, give me that guinea, and I'll discover a plot.   405

ARCH. A plot!

SCRUB. Ay, sir, a plot, and a horrid plot! — First, it must be a plot, because there's a woman in't; secondly, it must be a plot, because there's a priest in't; thirdly, it must be a plot, because there's 410 French gold in't; and fourthly, it must be a plot, because I don't know what to make on't.

ARCH. Nor anybody else, I'm afraid, brother Scrub.

SCRUB. Truly, I'm afraid so too; for where 415 there's a priest and a woman, there's always a mystery and a riddle. This I know, that here has been the doctor with a temptation in one hand and an absolution in the other; and Gipsey has sold herself to the devil; I saw the price paid down, 420 my eyes shall take their oath on't.

ARCH. And is all this bustle about Gipsey?

SCRUB. That's not all; I could hear but a word here and there; but I remember they mentioned a count, a closet, a back door, and a key. 425

ARCH. The count! — Did you hear nothing of Mrs. Sullen?

SCRUB. I did hear some word that sounded that way; but whether it was Sullen or Dorinda, I could not distinguish. 430

ARCH. You have told this matter to nobody, brother?

SCRUB. Told! No, sir, I thank you for that; I'm resolved never to speak one word *pro* nor *con*, till we have a peace. 435

ARCH. You're i' the right, brother Scrub; here's a treaty afoot between the count and the lady: the priest and the chambermaid are the plenipotentiaries. — It shall go hard but I find a way to be included in the treaty. — Where's the doctor now? 440

SCRUB. He and Gipsey are this moment devouring my lady's marmalade in the closet.

AIM. (*from without*). Martin! Martin!

ARCH. I come, sir, I come.

SCRUB. But you forget the other guinea, 445 brother Martin.

ARCH. Here, I give it with all my heart.

SCRUB. And I take it with all my soul. — Icod, I'll spoil your plotting, Mrs. Gipsey! and if you should set the captain upon me, these two 450 guineas will buy me off. [*Exeunt severally.*]

Enter MRS. SULLEN *and* DORINDA, *meeting.*

MRS. SUL. Well, sister!

DOR. And well, sister!

MRS. SUL. What's become of my lord?

DOR. What's become of his servant? 455

MRS. SUL. Servant! he's a prettier fellow, and a finer gentleman by fifty degrees than his master.

DOR. O' my conscience, I fancy you could beg that fellow at the gallows-foot! [1]

MRS. SUL. O' my conscience I could, pro- 460 vided I could put a friend of yours in his room.

DOR. You desired me, sister, to leave you, when you transgressed the bounds of honor.

MRS. SUL. Thou dear censorious country girl!

[1] Occasionally a criminal condemned to death was reprieved upon the offer by a respectable woman to marry him if his life were spared. For an interesting instance of this custom see Narcissus Luttrell's diary for November, 1687.

what dost mean? You can't think of the man 465 without the bedfellow, I find.

DOR. I don't find anything unnatural in that thought; while the mind is conversant with flesh and blood, it must conform to the humors of the company. 470

MRS. SUL. How a little love and good company improves a woman! why, child, you begin to live — you never spoke before.

DOR. Because I was never spoke to. — My lord has told me that I have more wit and beauty 475 than any of my sex; and truly I begin to think the man is sincere.

MRS. SUL. You're in the right, Dorinda; pride is the life of a woman, and flattery is our daily bread; and she's a fool that won't believe a man there, 480 as much as she that believes him in anything else. — But I'll lay you a guinea that I had finer things said to me than you had.

DOR. Done! — What did your fellow say to ye?

MRS. SUL. My fellow took the picture of 485 Venus for mine.

DOR. But my lover took me for Venus herself.

MRS. SUL. Common cant! Had my spark called me a Venus directly, I should have believed him a footman in good earnest. 490

DOR. But my lover was upon his knees to me.

MRS. SUL. And mine was upon his tiptoes to me.

DOR. Mine vowed to die for me.

MRS. SUL. Mine swore to die with me.

DOR. Mine spoke the softest moving things. 495

MRS. SUL. Mine had his moving things too.

DOR. Mine kissed my hand ten thousand times.

MRS. SUL. Mine has all that pleasure to come.

DOR. Mine offered marriage.

MRS. SUL. O Lard! D'ye call that a moving 500 thing?

DOR. The sharpest arrow in his quiver, my dear sister! — Why, my ten thousand pounds may lie brooding here this seven years, and hatch nothing at last but some ill-natured clown like yours. 505 Whereas, if I marry my Lord Aimwell, there will be title, place, and precedence, the Park, the play, and the drawing-room, splendor, equipage, noise, and flambeaux. — 'Hey, my Lady Aimwell's servants there! — Lights, lights to the stairs! — My 510 Lady Aimwell's coach put forward! — Stand by, make room for her ladyship!' — Are not these things moving? — What! melancholy of a sudden?

MRS. SUL. Happy, happy sister! your angel has been watchful for your happiness, whilst mine 515 has slept regardless of his charge. — Long smiling years of circling joys for you, but not one hour for me! (*Weeps.*)

DOR. Come, my dear, we'll talk of something else.

MRS. SUL. O Dorinda! I own myself a 520

woman, full of my sex, a gentle, generous soul — easy
and yielding to soft desires; a spacious heart, where
Love and all his train might lodge. And must the
fair apartment of my breast be made a stable for a
brute to lie in?   525

Dor. Meaning your husband, I suppose?

Mrs. Sul. Husband! no, — even husband is too
soft a name for him. — But, come, I expect my
brother here tonight or tomorrow; he was abroad
when my father married me; perhaps he'll find   530
a way to make me easy.

Dor. Will you promise not to make yourself easy
in the meantime with my lord's friend?

Mrs. Sul. You mistake me, sister. It happens
with us as among the men, the greatest talkers   535
are the greatest cowards; and there's a reason for it;
those spirits evaporate in prattle, which might do
more mischief if they took another course. —Though,
to confess the truth, I do love that fellow; — and if I
met him dressed as he should be, and I un-   540
dressed as I should be — look ye, sister, I have no
supernatural gifts — I can't swear I could resist the
temptation; though I can safely promise to avoid it;
and that's as much as the best of us can do.

Exeunt Mrs. Sullen *and* Dorinda.

[Scene II]

[*The inn.*]

Enter Aimwell *and* Archer, *laughing.*

Arch. And the awkward kindness of the good
motherly old gentlewoman——

Aim. And the coming easiness of the young one —
'Sdeath, 'tis pity to deceive her!

Arch. Nay, if you adhere to those principles,   5
stop where you are.

Aim. I can't stop; for I love her to distraction.

Arch. 'Sdeath, if you love her a hair's breadth
beyond discretion, you must go no farther.

Aim. Well, well, anything to deliver us from   10
sauntering away our idle evenings at White's, Tom's,
or Will's,[1] and be stinted to bear looking at our old
acquaintance, the cards, because our impotent
pockets can't afford us a guinea for the mercenary
drabs.   15

Arch. Or be obliged to some purse-proud coxcomb for a scandalous bottle, where we must not
pretend to our share of the discourse, because we
can't pay our club[2] o' th' reckoning. Damn it, I had
rather sponge upon Morris,[3] and sup upon a   20
dish of bohea[4] scored behind the door!

---

[1] Fashionable London coffee-houses.
[2] Share.
[3] Presumably the owner of Morris's coffee-house in Essex
Street, the Strand.
[4] A kind of black tea.

Aim. And there expose our want of sense by talking criticisms, as we should our want of money by
railing at the government.

Arch. Or be obliged to sneak into the side-   25
box, and between both houses steal two acts of a
play,[5] and because we han't money to see the other
three, we come away discontented, and damn the
whole five.

Aim. And ten thousand such rascally tricks—   30
had we outlived our fortunes among our acquaintance. — But now——

Arch. Ay, now is the time to prevent all this. —
Strike while the iron is hot. — This priest is the
luckiest part of our adventure; he shall marry   35
you, and pimp for me.

Aim. But I should not like a woman that can be
so fond of a Frenchman.

Arch. Alas, sir! Necessity has no law. The lady
may be in distress; perhaps she has a confounded   40
husband, and her revenge may carry her farther than
her love. — Igad, I have so good an opinion of her,
and of myself, that I begin to fancy strange things;
and we must say this for the honor of our women,
and indeed of ourselves, that they do stick to   45
their men as they do to their *Magna Charta*. If the
plot lies as I suspect, I must put on the gentleman.
— But here comes the doctor. — I shall be ready.

Exit.

Enter Foigard.

Foi. Sauve you, noble friend.

Aim. O sir, your servant! Pray, doctor, may   50
I crave your name?

Foi. Fat naam is upon me? My naam is Foigard,
joy.

Aim. Foigard! a very good name for a clergyman.[6]
Pray, Doctor Foigard, were you ever in Ire-   55
land?

Foi. Ireland! no, joy. Fat sort of plaace is dat
saam Ireland? Dey say de people are catched dere
when dey are young.

Aim. And some of 'em when they're old — as   60
for example. — (*Takes* Foigard *by the shoulder.*) Sir,
I arrest you as a traitor against the government;
you're a subject of England, and this morning showed
me a commission, by which you served as chaplain
in the French army. This is death by our law,   65
and your reverence must hang for't.

Foi. Upon my shoul, noble friend, dis is strange
news you tell me! Fader Foigard a subject of England! de son of a burgomaster of Brussels a subject of England! ubooboo[7]——   70

---

[5] The box-keeper collected the money for the performance
after the second act.
[6] It means 'defender of the faith.'
[7] Supposed to be a typical Irish interjection.

AIM. The son of a bog-trotter in Ireland! Sir, your tongue will condemn you before any bench in the kingdom.

FOI. And is my tongue all your evidensh, joy?

AIM. That's enough.   75

FOI. No, no, joy, for I vil never spake English no more.

AIM. Sir, I have other evidence. — Here, Martin!

Enter ARCHER.

You know this fellow?

ARCH. (*in a brogue*). Saave you, my dear cus-   80
sen, how does your health?

FOI. (*aside*). Ah! upon my shoul dere is my countryman, and his brogue will hang mine. — [*To* AIMWELL.] *Mynheer, Ick wet neat watt hey zacht.* [*To* ARCHER.] *Ick universton ewe neat, sacramant!*[1]   85

AIM. Altering your language won't do, sir; this fellow knows your person, and will swear to your face.

FOI. Faace! fey, is dear a brogue upon my faash too?

ARCH. Upon my soulvation dere ish, joy! —   90
But cussen Mackshane, vil you not put a remembrance upon me?

FOI. (*aside*). Mackshane! by St. Paatrick, dat is [my] naame, shure enough!

AIM. [*aside to* ARCHER]. I fancy, Archer, you   95
have it.

FOI. The devil hang you, joy! By fat acquaintance are you my cussen?

ARCH. Oh, de devil hang yourshelf, joy! You know we were little boys togeder upon de   100
school, and your foster-moder's son was married upon my nurse's chister, joy, and so we are Irish cussens.

FOI. De devil taak the relation! Vel, joy, and fat school was it?   105

ARCH. I tinks it vas — aay — 'twas Tipperary.

FOI. No, no, joy; it vas Kilkenny.

AIM. That's enough for us — self-confession. Come, sir, we must deliver you into the hands of the next magistrate.   110

ARCH. He sends you to gaol, you're tried next assizes, and away you go swing into purgatory.

FOI. And is it so wid you, cussen?

ARCH. It vil be sho wid you, cussen, if you don't immediately confess the secret between you   115
and Mrs. Gipsey. — Look'ee, sir, the gallows or the secret, take your choice.

FOI. The gallows! Upon my shoul I hate that saam gallow, for it is a diseash dat is fatal to our family. — Vel, den, dere is nothing, shentlemens,   120

but Mrs. Shullen would spaak wid the count in her chamber at midnight, and dere is no haarm, joy, for I am to conduct the count to the plash, myshelf.

ARCH. As I guessed. — Have you communicated the matter to the count?   125

FOI. I have not sheen him since.

ARCH. Right again! Why then, doctor — you shall conduct me to the lady instead of the count.

FOI. Fat, my cussen to the lady! Upon my shoul, gra, dat is too much upon the brogue.   130

ARCH. Come, come, doctor; consider we have got a rope about your neck, and if you offer to squeak, we'll stop your windpipe, most certainly. We shall have another job for you in a day or two, I hope.

AIM. Here's company coming this way; let's   135
into my chamber, and there concert our affairs farther.

ARCH. Come, my dear cussen, come along. *Exeunt.*

Enter BONNIFACE, HOUNSLOW, *and* BAGSHOT *at one door,* GIBBET *at the opposite.*

GIB. Well, gentlemen, 'tis a fine night for our enterprise.   140

HOUN. Dark as hell.

BAG. And blows like the devil; our landlord here has showed us the window where we must break in, and tells us the plate stands in the wainscot cupboard in the parlor.   145

BON. Ay, ay, Mr. Bagshot, as the saying is, knives and forks, and cups and cans, and tumblers and tankards. There's one tankard, as the saying is, that's near upon as big as me; it was a present to the squire from his godmother, and smells of nut-   150
meg and toast like an East India ship.

HOUN. Then you say we must divide at the stairhead?

BON. Yes, Mr. Hounslow, as the saying is. — At one end of that gallery lies my Lady Bountiful   155
and her daughter, and at the other Mrs. Sullen. — As for the squire ——

GIB. He's safe enough, I have fairly entered[2] him, and he's more than half seas over already. But such a parcel of scoundrels are got about him   160
now, that, igad, I was ashamed to be seen in their company.

BON. 'Tis now twelve, as the saying is — Gentlemen, you must set out at one.

GIB. Hounslow, do you and Bagshot see our   165
arms fixed, and I'll come to you presently.

HOUN., BAG. We will.   *Exeunt.*

GIB. Well, my dear Bonny, you assure me that Scrub is a coward.

BON. A chicken, as the saying is. — You'll   170
have no creature to deal with but the ladies.

[1] Foigard's speech, in 'Flemish' of his own invention, appears to mean, 'Sir, I don't know what he says. — I don't understand you, egad!'

[2] Started.

GIB. And I can assure you, friend, there's a great deal of address and good manners in robbing a lady; I am the most a gentleman that way that ever travelled the road. — But, my dear Bonny, this 175 prize will be a galleon, a Vigo business.[1] — I warrant you we shall bring off three or four thousand pound.

BON. In plate, jewels, and money, as the saying is, you may.   180

GIB. Why then, Tyburn,[2] I defy thee! I'll get up to town, sell off my horse and arms, buy myself some pretty employment in the household,[3] and be as snug and as honest as any courtier of 'um all.

BON. And what think you then of my daugh- 185 ter Cherry for a wife?

GIB. Look'ee, my dear Bonny — Cherry 'is the goddess I adore,' as the song goes; but it is a maxim that man and wife should never have it in their power to hang one another; for if they should, the 190 Lord have mercy on 'um both!   *Exeunt.*

ACT V

[SCENE I]

Scene continues.

(Knocking without.)

Enter BONNIFACE.

BON. Coming! Coming! — A coach and six foaming horses at this time o' night! Some great man, as the saying is, for he scorns to travel with other people.

Enter SIR CHARLES FREEMAN.

SIR CHAS. What, fellow! a public house, and 5 abed when other people sleep?

BON. Sir, I an't abed, as the saying is.

SIR CHAS. Is Mr. Sullen's family abed, think'ee?

BON. All but the squire himself, sir, as the saying is; he's in the house.   10

SIR CHAS. What company has he?

BON. Why, sir, there's the constable, Mr. Gage the exciseman, the hunchbacked barber, and two or three other gentlemen.

SIR CHAS. [*aside*]. I find my sister's letters 15 gave me the true picture of her spouse.

Enter SULLEN, *drunk.*

BON. Sir, here's the squire.

SUL. The puppies left me asleep. — Sir!

---

[1] Referring to the capture or sinking of the Spanish treasure-ships by the allied fleet, in Vigo harbor, in northwestern Spain, in 1702.

[2] The site of the gallows in London.

[3] The royal household, the Court.

SIR CHAS. Well, sir.

SUL. Sir, I'm an unfortunate man — I have 20 three thousand pound a year, and I can't get a man to drink a cup of ale with me.

SIR CHAS. That's very hard.

SUL. Ay, sir; and unless you have pity upon me, and smoke one pipe with me, I must e'en go 25 home to my wife, and I had rather go [to] the devil by half.

SIR CHAS. But I presume, sir, you won't see your wife tonight; she'll be gone to bed — you don't use to lie with your wife in that pickle?   30

SUL. What! not lie with my wife! Why, sir, do you take me for an atheist or a rake?

SIR CHAS. If you hate her, sir, I think you had better lie from her.

SUL. I think so too, friend. — But I'm a jus- 35 tice of peace, and must do nothing against the law.

SIR CHAS. Law! As I take it, Mr. Justice, nobody observes law for law's sake, only for the good of those for whom it was made.

SUL. But if the law orders me to send you to 40 goal,[4] you must lie there, my friend.

SIR CHAS. Not unless I commit a crime to deserve it.

SUL. A crime? 'Oons, an't I married?

SIR CHAS. Nay, sir, if you call marriage a 45 crime, you must disown it for a law.

SUL. Eh! — I must be acquainted with you, sir. — But, sir, I should be very glad to know the truth of this matter.

SIR CHAS. Truth, sir, is a profound sea, and 50 few there be that dare wade deep enough to find out the bottom on't. Besides, sir, I'm afraid the line of your understanding mayn't be long enough.

SUL. Look'ee, sir, I have nothing to say to your sea of truth, but if a good parcel of land can 55 intitle a man to a little truth, I have as much as any he in the country.

BON. I never heard your worship, as the saying is, talk so much before.

SUL. Because I never met with a man that I 60 liked before.

BON. Pray, sir, as the saying is, let me ask you one question: are not man and wife one flesh?

SIR CHAS. You and your wife, Mr. Guts, may be one flesh, because ye are nothing else; — but 65 rational creatures have minds that must be united.

SUL. Minds!

SIR CHAS. Ay, minds, sir; don't you think that the mind takes place of[5] the body?

SUL. In some people.   70

---

[4] An old spelling of 'gaol.'

[5] Takes precedence of.

184] C *'em.*   191] C *'em.*   ACT V. 26] QI om. *to*; C as in text.
41] C (BM copy, according to Morgan) *gaol.*

SIR CHAS. Then the interest of the master must be consulted before that of his servant.

SUL. Sir, you shall dine with me tomorrow! — 'Oons, I always thought that we were naturally one.

SIR CHAS. Sir, I know that my two hands are   75 naturally one, because they love one another, kiss one another, help one another in all the actions of life; but I could not say so much if they were always at cuffs.

SUL. Then 'tis plain that we are two.   80

SIR CHAS. Why don't you part with her, sir?

SUL. Will you take her, sir?

SIR CHAS. With all my heart.

SUL. You shall have her tomorrow morning, and a venison-pasty into the bargain.   85

SIR CHAS. You'll let me have her fortune too?

SUL. Fortune! Why, sir, I have no quarrel at her fortune. I only hate the woman, sir, and none but the woman shall go.

SIR CHAS. But her fortune, sir ——   90

SUL. Can you play at whisk, sir?

SIR CHAS. No, truly, sir.

SUL. Nor at all-fours?[1]

SIR CHAS. Neither!

SUL. (aside). 'Oons! where was this man   95 bred? — [Aloud.] Burn me, sir! I can't go home; 'tis but two o'clock.

SIR CHAS. For half an hour, sir, if you please. But you must consider 'tis late.

SUL. Late! that's the reason I can't go to   100 bed. — Come, sir!   Exeunt.

Enter CHERRY, runs across the stage and knocks at AIMWELL'S chamber door. Enter AIMWELL in his nightcap and gown.

AIM. What's the matter? You tremble, child; you're frighted.

CHER. No wonder, sir. — But, in short, sir, this very minute a gang of rogues are gone to rob   105 my Lady Bountiful's house.

AIM. How!

CHER. I dogged 'em to the very door, and left 'em breaking in.

AIM. Have you alarmed anybody else with   110 the news?

CHER. No, no, sir, I wanted to have discovered the whole plot, and twenty other things, to your man Martin; but I have searched the whole house, and can't find him. Where is he?   115

AIM. No matter, child, will you guide me immediately to the house?

CHER. With all my heart, sir; my Lady Bountiful is my godmother, and I love Mrs. Dorinda so well ——   120

AIM. Dorinda! The name inspires me, the glory

[1] A two-handed card-game.

and the danger shall be all my own. — Come, my life, let me but get my sword.   Exeunt.

[SCENE II]

Scene changes to a bedchamber in LADY BOUNTIFUL'S *house.*

Enter MRS. SULLEN, DORINDA *undressed; a table and lights.*

DOR. 'Tis very late, sister. No news of your spouse yet?

MRS. SUL. No, I'm condemned to be alone till towards four, and then perhaps I may be executed with his company.   5

DOR. Well, my dear, I'll leave you to your rest; you'll go directly to bed, I suppose?

MRS. SUL. I don't know what to do. — Heigh-ho!

DOR. That's a desiring sigh, sister.

MRS. SUL. This is a languishing hour, sister.   10

DOR. And might prove a critical minute, if the pretty fellow were here.

MRS. SUL. Here! What, in my bedchamber at two o'clock o' th' morning, I undressed, the family asleep, my hated husband abroad, and my lovely   15 fellow at my feet! — O 'gad, sister!

DOR. Thoughts are free, sister, and them I allow you. — So, my dear, good night.

MRS. SUL. A good rest to my dear Dorinda! — [Exit DORINDA.] Thoughts free! are they so?   20 Why, then suppose him here, dressed like a youthful, gay, and burning bridegroom, (here ARCHER *steals out of the closet*) with tongue enchanting, eyes bewitching, knees imploring. — (*Turns a little o' one side and sees* ARCHER *in the posture she describes.*)   25 — Ah! — (*Shrieks, and runs to the other side of the stage.*) Have my thoughts raised a spirit? — What are you, sir, a man or a devil?

ARCH. (*rising*). A man, a man, madam.

MRS. SUL. How shall I be sure of it?   30

ARCH. Madam, I'll give you demonstration this minute.   (*Takes her hand.*)

MRS. SUL. What, sir! do you intend to be rude?

ARCH. Yes, madam, if you please.

MRS. SUL. In the name of wonder, whence   35 came ye?

ARCH. From the skies, madam — I'm a Jupiter in love, and you shall be my Alcmena.[2]

MRS. SUL. How came you in?

ARCH. I flew in at the window, madam; your   40 cousin Cupid lent me his wings, and your sister Venus opened the casement.

MRS. SUL. I'm struck dumb with admiration!

ARCH. And I — with wonder!   (*Looks passionately at her.*)

MRS. SUL. What will become of me?   45

[2] The mother of Hercules by Zeus, who assumed the form of her husband.

ARCH. How beautiful she looks! — The teeming, jolly spring smiles in her blooming face, and when she was conceived, her mother smelt to roses, looked on lilies —

Lilies unfold their white, their fragrant charms,   50
When the warm sun thus darts into their arms.

(*Runs to her.*)

MRS. SUL. (*shrieks*). Ah!

ARCH. 'Oons, madam, what d'ye mean? you'll raise the house.

MRS. SUL. Sir, I'll wake the dead before I   55
bear this! — What! approach me with the freedoms of a keeper! I'm glad on't, your impudence has cured me.

ARCH. If this be impudence — (*kneels*) I leave to your partial self; no panting pilgrim, after a   60
tedious, painful voyage, e'er bowed before his saint with more devotion.

MRS. SUL. (*aside*). Now, now, I'm ruined if he kneels! — Rise, thou prostrate engineer, not all thy undermining skill shall reach my heart. Rise,   65
and know I am a woman without my sex; I can love to all the tenderness of wishes, sighs, and tears — but go no farther. Still, to convince you that I'm more than woman, I can speak my frailty, confess my weakness even for you — but ——   70

ARCH. (*going to lay hold on her*). For me!

MRS. SUL. Hold, sir! build not upon that; for my most mortal hatred follows if you disobey what I command you now. Leave me this minute. — (*Aside.*) If he denies, I'm lost.   75

ARCH. Then you'll promise ——

MRS. SUL. Anything another time.

ARCH. When shall I come?

MRS. SUL. Tomorrow when you will.

ARCH. Your lips must seal the promise.   80

MRS. SUL. Pshaw!

ARCH. They must! they must! — (*Kisses her.*) Raptures and paradise! — And why not now, my angel? the time, the place, silence, and secrecy, all conspire. And the now conscious stars have   85
preordained this moment for my happiness.

(*Takes her in [his] arms.*)

MRS. SUL. You will not! cannot, sure!

ARCH. If the sun rides fast, and disappoints not mortals of tomorrow's dawn, this night shall crown my joys.   90

MRS. SUL. My sex's pride assist me!

ARCH. My sex's strength help me!

MRS. SUL. You shall kill me first!

ARCH. I'll die with you.   (*Carrying her off.*)

MRS. SUL. Thieves! thieves! murther! —   95

Enter SCRUB *in his breeches, and one shoe.*

SCRUB. Thieves! thieves! murther! popery!

ARCH. Ha! the very timorous stag will kill in rutting time.   (*Draws, and offers to stab* SCRUB.)

SCRUB (*kneeling*). Oh pray, sir, spare all I have, and take my life!   100

MRS. SUL. (*holding* ARCHER'S *hand*). What does the fellow mean?

SCRUB. O madam, down upon your knees, your marrow-bones! — He's one of 'um.

ARCH. Of whom?   105

SCRUB. One of the rogues — I beg your pardon, sir, one of the honest gentlemen that just now are broke into the house.

ARCH. How!

MRS. SUL. I hope you did not come to rob   110
me?

ARCH. Indeed I did, madam, but I would have taken nothing but what you might ha' spared; but your crying 'Thieves' has waked this dreaming fool, and so he takes 'em for granted.   115

SCRUB. Granted! 'tis granted, sir; take all we have.

MRS. SUL. The fellow looks as if he were broke out of Bedlam.

SCRUB. 'Oons, madam, they're broke into the house with fire and sword; I saw them, heard   120
them; they'll be here this minute.

ARCH. What, thieves?

SCRUB. Under favor, sir, I think so.

MRS. SUL. What shall we do, sir?

ARCH. Madam, I wish your ladyship a good   125
night.

MRS. SUL. Will you leave me?

ARCH. Leave you! Lord, madam, did not you command me to be gone just now, upon pain of your immortal hatred?   130

MRS. SUL. Nay, but pray, sir ——

(*Takes hold of him.*)

ARCH. Ha, ha, ha! now comes my turn to be ravished. You see now, madam, you must use men one way or other; but take this by the way, good madam, that none but a fool will give you the   135
benefit of his courage, unless you'll take his love along with it. — How are they armed, friend?

SCRUB. With sword and pistol, sir.

ARCH. Hush! — I see a dark lanthorn coming through the gallery. — Madam, be assured I   140
will protect you, or lose my life.

MRS. SUL. Your life! No, sir, they can rob me of nothing that I value half so much; therefore, now, sir, let me intreat you to be gone.

ARCH. No, madam, I'll consult my own   145
safety for the sake of yours; I'll work by stratagem. Have you courage enough to stand the appearance of 'em?

MRS. SUL. Yes, yes, since I have 'scaped your hands, I can face anything.   150

ARCH. Come hither, brother Scrub! don't you know me?

86 s.d.] Q1 her arms; C as in text.   107] C om. *sir*.

SCRUB. Eh! my dear brother, let me kiss thee.
(*Kisses* ARCHER.)
ARCH. This way — here ——
(ARCHER *and* SCRUB *hide behind the bed*.)

Enter GIBBET, *with a dark lanthorn in one hand, and a pistol in t'other.*

GIB. Ay, ay, this is the chamber, and the　155
lady alone.
MRS. SUL. Who are you, sir? what would you
have? d'ye come to rob me?
GIB. Rob you! Alack-a-day, madam, I'm only
a younger brother,[1] madam; and so, madam, if　160
you make a noise, I'll shoot you through the head;
but don't be afraid, madam. — (*Laying his lanthorn
and pistol upon the table.*) These rings, madam —
don't be concerned, madam, I have a profound
respect for you, madam; your keys, madam —　165
don't be frighted, madam, I'm the most of a gentleman. — (*Searching her pockets.*) This necklace,
madam — I never was rude to a lady; — I have a
veneration — for this necklace ——
(*Here* ARCHER, *having come round and seized
the [pistol], takes* GIBBET *by the collar, trips
up his heels, and claps the pistol to his breast.*)
ARCH. Hold, profane villain, and take the　170
reward of thy sacrilege!
GIB. Oh! pray, sir, don't kill me; I an't prepared.
ARCH. How many is there of 'em, Scrub?
SCRUB. Five-and-forty, sir.
ARCH. Then I must kill the villain, to have　175
him out of the way.
GIB. Hold, hold, sir, we are but three, upon my
honor.
ARCH. Scrub, will you undertake to secure
him?　180
SCRUB. Not I, sir; kill him, kill him!
ARCH. Run to Gipsey's chamber, there you'll find
the doctor; bring him hither presently. — (*Exit*
SCRUB, *running*.) Come, rogue, if you have a short
prayer, say it.　185
GIB. Sir, I have no prayer at all; the government
has provided a chaplain to say prayers for us on
these occasions.
MRS. SUL. Pray, sir, don't kill him. You fright
me as much as him.　190
ARCH. The dog shall die, madam, for being the
occasion of my disappointment. — Sirrah, this moment is your last.
GIB. Sir, I'll give you two hundred pound to spare
my life.　195

----

[1] A jesting reference to the fact that under the laws of
primogeniture younger brothers had to make their living by
any means that offered. Gibbet pretends to the rank of
gentleman.

ARCH. Have you no more, rascal?
GIB. Yes, sir, I can command four hundred, but
I must reserve two of 'em to save my life at the
sessions.

Enter SCRUB *and* FOIGARD.

ARCH. Here, doctor, I suppose Scrub and　200
you between you may manage him. — Lay hold of
him, doctor.　　　(FOIGARD *lays hold of* GIBBET.)
GIB. What! turned over to the priest already! —
Look ye, doctor, you come before your time; I an't
condemned yet, I thank ye.　205
FOI. Come, my dear joy, I vill secure your body
and your shoul too; I vill make you a good Catholic,
and give you an absolution.
GIB. Absolution! can you procure me a pardon,
doctor?　210
FOI. No, joy.
GIB. Then you and your absolution may go to
the devil!
ARCH. Convey him into the cellar; there bind
him. Take the pistol, and if he offers to resist,　215
shoot him through the head — and come back to us
with all the speed you can.
SCRUB. Ay, ay; come, doctor, do you hold him
fast, and I'll guard him.
[*Exit* FOIGARD *and* SCRUB *with* GIBBET.]
MRS. SUL. But how came the doctor ——　220
ARCH. In short, madam — (*shrieking without*).
'Sdeath! the rogues are at work with the other ladies.
I'm vexed I parted with the pistol; but I must fly to
their assistance. Will you stay here, madam, or
venture yourself with me?　225
MRS. SUL. Oh, with you, dear sir, with you.
Takes him by the arm and exeunt.

[SCENE III]

*Scene changes to another apartment in the same
house.*

Enter HOUNSLOW *dragging in* LADY BOUNTIFUL, *and*
BAGSHOT *hauling in* DORINDA; *the rogues with
swords drawn.*

[BAG.] Come, come, your jewels, mistress!
[HOUN.] Your keys, your keys, old gentlewoman!

Enter AIMWELL *and* CHERRY.

AIM. Turn this way, villains! I durst engage
an army in such a cause.　　　(*He engages 'em both.*)
DOR. O madam, had I but a sword to help　5
the brave man!
LADY BOUN. There's three or four hanging up in
the hall; but they won't draw. I'll go fetch one,
however.　　　　　　　　　　　　　　　　*Exit.*

Enter ARCHER *and* MRS. SULLEN.

ARCH. Hold, hold, my lord! every man his   10
bird, pray.

> (*They engage man to man; the rogues are
> thrown and disarmed.*)

CHER. [*aside*]. What! the rogues taken! then
they'll impeach my father; I must give him timely
notice.   *Runs out.*

ARCH. Shall we kill the rogues?   15

AIM. No, no, we'll bind them.

ARCH. Ay, ay. — (*To* MRS. SULLEN, *who stands
by him.*) Here, madam, lend me your garter.

MRS. SUL. (*aside*). The devil's in this fellow! he
fights, loves, and banters, all in a breath. —   20
[*Aloud.*] Here's a cord that the rogues brought
with 'em, I suppose.

ARCH. Right, right, the rogue's destiny, a rope
to hang himself. — Come, my lord. — This is but a
scandalous sort of an office (*binding the rogues*   25
together) if our adventures should end in this sort of
hangman-work; but I hope there is something in
prospect that ——

Enter SCRUB.

Well, Scrub, have you secured your Tartar?

SCRUB. Yes, sir; I left the priest and him   30
disputing about religion.

AIM. And pray carry these gentlemen to reap the
benefit of the controversy.

> *Delivers the prisoners to* SCRUB, *who leads
> 'em out.*

MRS. SUL. Pray, sister, how came my lord here?

DOR. And pray, how came the gentleman   35
here?

MRS. SUL. I'll tell you the greatest piece of
villainy ——   (*They talk in dumb show.*)

AIM. I fancy, Archer, you have been more successful in your adventures than the house-   40
breakers.

ARCH. No matter for my adventure, yours is the
principal. Press her this minute to marry you —
now while she's hurried between the palpitation of
her fear and the joy of her deliverance, now   45
while the tide of her spirits are at high-flood. Throw
yourself at her feet, speak some romantic nonsense
or other — address her like Alexander in the height
of his victory, confound her senses, bear down her
reason, and away with her. The priest is in   50
the cellar and dare not refuse to do the work.

Enter LADY BOUNTIFUL.

AIM. But how shall I get off without being observed?

ARCH. You a lover, and not find a way to get off!
— Let me see ——   55

AIM. You bleed, Archer.

ARCH. 'Sdeath, I'm glad on't; this wound will do

the business. — I'll amuse the old lady and Mrs.
Sullen about dressing my wound, while you carry off
Dorinda.   60

LADY BOUN. Gentlemen, could we understand
how you would be gratified for the services ——

ARCH. Come, come, my lady, this is no time for
compliments; I'm wounded, madam.

LADY BOUN., MRS. SUL. How! wounded!   65

DOR. [*to* AIMWELL]. I hope, sir, you have received
no hurt?

AIM. None but what you may cure ——
> (*Makes love in dumb show.*)

LADY BOUN. Let me see your arm, sir. — I must
have some powder-sugar to stop the blood. —   70
O me! an ugly gash, upon my word, sir! You must
go into bed.

ARCH. Ay, my lady, a bed would do very well. —
(*To* MRS. SULLEN.) Madam, will you do me the
favor to conduct me to a chamber.   75

LADY BOUN. Do, do, daughter — while I get the
lint and the probe and the plaster ready.

> *Runs out one way;* AIMWELL *carries off*
> DORINDA *another.*

ARCH. Come, madam, why don't you obey your
mother's commands?

MRS. SUL. How can you, after what is passed,   80
have the confidence to ask me?

ARCH. And if you go to that, how can you, after
what is passed, have the confidence to deny me?
Was not this blood shed in your defence, and my
life exposed for your protection? Look ye,   85
madam, I'm none of your romantic fools, that fight
giants and monsters for nothing; my valor is downright Swiss;[1] I'm a soldier of fortune, and must be
paid.

MRS. SUL. 'Tis ungenerous in you, sir, to   90
upbraid me with your services!

ARCH. 'Tis ungenerous in you, madam, not to
reward 'em.

MRS. SUL. How! at the expense of my honor?

ARCH. Honor! can honor consist with in-   95
gratitude? If you would deal like a woman of
honor, do like a man of honor. D'ye think I would
deny you in such a case?

Enter a Servant.

SERV. Madam, my lady ordered me to tell you
that your brother is below at the gate. [*Exit.*]   100

MRS. SUL. My brother! Heavens be praised! —
Sir, he shall thank you for your services; he has it in
his power.

ARCH. Who is your brother, madam?

MRS. SUL. Sir Charles Freeman. You'll   105
excuse me, sir; I must go and receive him. [*Exit.*]

ARCH. Sir Charles Freeman! 'Sdeath and hell!

---

[1] The Swiss were famed for their services as mercenaries in
the armies of foreign nations.

my old acquaintance. Now unless Aimwell has made good use of his time, all our fair machine goes souse into the sea like the Eddystone.[1] *Exit.* 110

[SCENE IV]

Scene changes to the gallery in the same house.

Enter AIMWELL *and* DORINDA.

DOR. Well, well, my lord, you have conquered; your late generous action will, I hope, plead for my easy yielding; though I must own, your lordship had a friend in the fort before.

AIM. The sweets of Hybla[2] dwell upon her 5 tongue! — Here, doctor ——

Enter FOIGARD, *with a book.*

FOI. Are you prepared, boat?

DOR. I'm ready. But first, my lord, one word. I have a frightful example of a hasty marriage in my own family; when I reflect upon't, it shocks me. 10 Pray, my lord, consider a little ——

AIM. Consider! Do you doubt my honor or my love?

DOR. Neither. I do believe you equally just as brave; and were your whole sex drawn out for 15 me to choose, I should not cast a look upon the multitude if you were absent. But, my lord, I'm a woman; colors, concealments may hide a thousand faults in me — therefore know me better first. I hardly dare affirm I know myself in anything 20 except my love.

AIM. (*aside*). Such goodness who could injure! I find myself unequal to the task of villain; she has gained my soul, and made it honest like her own. I cannot, cannot hurt her. — Doctor, retire. — 25 (*Exit* FOIGARD.) Madam, behold your lover and your proselyte, and judge of my passion by my conversion! I'm all a lie, nor dare I give a fiction to your arms; I'm all counterfeit, except my passion.

DOR. Forbid it, heaven! a counterfeit! 30

AIM. I am no lord, but a poor needy man, come with a mean, a scandalous design to prey upon your fortune. But the beauties of your mind and person have so won me from myself that, like a trusty servant, I prefer the interest of my mistress to 35 my own.

DOR. Sure I have had the dream of some poor mariner, a sleepy image of a welcome port, and wake involved in storms! — Pray, sir, who are you?

AIM. Brother to the man whose title I 40 usurped, but stranger to his honor or his fortune.

DOR. Matchless honesty! — Once I was proud,

sir, of your wealth and title, but now am prouder that you want it; now I can show my love was justly levelled, and had no aim but love. — Doctor, 45 come in.

Enter FOIGARD *at one door,* GIPSEY *at another, who whispers* DORINDA.

[*To* FOIGARD.] Your pardon, sir, we sha'not [want] you now. — [*To* AIMWELL.] Sir, you must excuse me. I'll wait on you presently. *Exit with* GIPSEY.

FOI. Upon my shoul, now, dis is foolish. 50
Exit.

AIM. Gone! and bid the priest depart! — It has an ominous look.

Enter ARCHER.

ARCH. Courage, Tom! Shall I wish you joy?

AIM. No.

ARCH. 'Oons, man, what ha' you been doing? 55

AIM. O Archer! my honesty, I fear, has ruined me.

ARCH. How?

AIM. I have discovered myself.

ARCH. Discovered! and without my consent? What! have I embarked my small remains in the 60 same bottom with yours, and you dispose of all without my partnership?

AIM. O Archer! I own my fault.

ARCH. After conviction — 'tis then too late for pardon. You may remember, Mr. Aimwell, 65 that you proposed this folly — as you begun, so end it. Henceforth I'll hunt my fortune single. So farewell!

AIM. Stay, my dear Archer, but a minute.

ARCH. Stay! what, to be despised, exposed, 70 and laughed at! No, I would sooner change conditions with the worst of the rogues we just now bound, than bear one scornful smile from the proud knight that once I treated as my equal.

AIM. What knight? 75

ARCH. Sir Charles Freeman, brother to the lady that I had almost — but no matter for that; 'tis a cursed night's work, and so I leave you to make the best on't. (*Going.*)

AIM. Freeman! — One word, Archer. Still 80 I have hopes; methought she received my confession with pleasure.

ARCH. 'Sdeath! who doubts it?

AIM. She consented after to the match; and still I dare believe she will be just. 85

ARCH. To herself, I warrant her, as you should have been.

AIM. By all my hopes, she comes, and smiling comes!

Enter DORINDA, *mighty gay.*

DOR. Come, my dear lord — I fly with im- 90

---

[1] The 'great storm' of 1703 destroyed the first Eddystone lighthouse, an engineering marvel of its day.

[2] Mt. Hybla, in Sicily, was famous for its honey.

47-48] Q1C *Your pardon, sir, we sha'not; won't you now, sir? you must.*

patience to your arms.   The minutes of my absence was a tedious year.   Where's this tedious priest?

Enter FOIGARD.

ARCH.   'Oons, a brave girl!

DOR.   I suppose, my lord, this gentleman is privy to our affairs?   95

ARCH.   Yes, yes, madam, I'm to be your father.

DOR.   Come, priest, do your office.

ARCH.   Make haste, make haste, couple 'em any way. — (*Takes* AIMWELL's *hand.*)   Come, madam, I'm to give you ——   100

DOR.   My mind's altered; I won't.

ARCH.   Eh! —

AIM.   I'm confounded!

FOI.   Upon my shoul, and sho is myshelf.

ARCH.   What's the matter now, madam?   105

DOR.   Look ye, sir, one generous action deserves another.   This gentleman's honor obliged him to hide nothing from me; my justice engages me to conceal nothing from him.   In short, sir, you are the person that you thought you counterfeited;   110 you are the true Lord Viscount Aimwell, and I wish your lordship joy. — Now, priest, you may be gone; if my lord is pleased now with the match, let his lordship marry me in the face of the world.

AIM., ARCH.   What does she mean?   115

DOR.   Here's a witness for my truth.

Enter SIR CHARLES FREEMAN *and* MRS. SULLEN.

SIR CHAS.   My dear Lord Aimwell, I wish you joy.

AIM.   Of what?

SIR CHAS.   Of your honor and estate.   Your brother died the day before I left London; and   120 all your friends have writ after you to Brussels; among the rest I did myself the honor.

ARCH.   Hark ye, sir knight, don't you banter now?

SIR CHAS.   'Tis truth, upon my honor.

AIM.   Thanks to the pregnant stars that   125 formed this accident!

ARCH.   Thanks to the womb of time that brought it forth! — away with it!

AIM.   Thanks to my guardian angel that led me to the prize!   (*Taking* DORINDA's *hand.*)   130

ARCH.   And double thanks to the noble Sir Charles Freeman. — My Lord, I wish you joy. — My Lady, I wish you joy. — Igad, Sir Freeman, you're the honestest fellow living! — 'Sdeath, I'm grown strange airy upon this matter! — My   135 lord, how d'ye? — A word, my lord; don't you remember something of a previous agreement, that entitles me to the moiety of this lady's fortune, which, I think, will amount to five thousand pound?

AIM.   Not a penny, Archer; you would ha'   140 cut my throat just now, because I would not deceive this lady.

ARCH.   Ay, and I'll cut your throat again, if you should deceive her now.

AIM.   That's what I expected; and to end the   145 dispute, the lady's fortune is ten thousand pound; we'll divide stakes: take the ten thousand pound or the lady.

DOR.   How! is your lordship so indifferent?

ARCH.   No, no, no, madam! his lordship   150 knows very well that I'll take the money; I leave you to his lordship, and so we're both provided for.

Enter COUNT BELLAIR.

COUNT BEL.   *Mesdames et messieurs,* I am your servant trice humble!   I hear you be rob here.

AIM.   The ladies have been in some danger,   155 sir.

COUNT BEL.   And, begar, our inn be rob too!

AIM.   Our inn! by whom?

COUNT BEL.   By the landlord, begar!   Garzoon, he has rob himself and run away!   160

ARCH.   Robbed himself!

COUNT BEL.   Ay, begar, and me too of a hundre pound.

ARCH.   A hundred pound?

COUNT BEL.   Yes, that I owed him.   165

AIM.   Our money's gone, Frank.

ARCH.   Rot the money! my wench is gone. — [*To* COUNT BELLAIR.]   *Savez-vous quelque chose de Mademoiselle Cherry?* [1]

(*Enter a Fellow with a strong-box and a letter.*)

FELL.   Is there one Martin here?   170

ARCH.   Ay, ay — who wants him?

FELL.   I have a box here and letter for him.

ARCH.   (*taking the box*).   Ha, ha, ha! what's here? Legerdemain! — By this light, my lord, our money again! — But this unfolds the riddle. — (*Open-*   175 *ing the letter, reads*) Hum, hum, hum! — Oh, 'tis for the public good, and must be communicated to the company.   [*Reads.*]

MR. MARTIN,

My father being afraid of an impeach-   180 ment by the rogues that are taken tonight, is gone off; but if you can procure him a pardon, he will make great discoveries that may be useful to the country.   Could I have met you instead of your master tonight, I would   185 have delivered myself into your hands, with a sum that much exceeds that in your strong-box, which I have sent you, with an assurance to my dear Martin that I shall ever be his most faithful friend till death.   190

CHERRY BONNIFACE.

---

[1]   Do you know anything about Miss Cherry?

There's a billet-doux for you! As for the father, I think he ought to be encouraged; and for the daughter — pray, my lord, persuade your bride to take her into her service instead of Gipsey.   195

AIM. I can assure you, madam, your deliverance was owing to her discovery.

DOR. Your command, my lord, will do without the obligation. I'll take care of her.

SIR CHAS. This good company meets op-   200
portunely in favor of a design I have in behalf of my unfortunate sister. I intend to part her from her husband — gentlemen, will you assist me?

ARCH. Assist you! 'Sdeath, who would not?

COUNT BEL. Assist! Garzoon, we all assest!   205

Enter SULLEN.

SUL. What's all this? — They tell me, spouse, that you had like to have been robbed.

MRS. SUL. Truly, spouse, I was pretty near it — had not these two gentlemen interposed.

SUL. How came these gentlemen here?   210

MRS. SUL. That's his way of returning thanks, you must know.

COUNT BEL. Garzoon, the question be apropos for all dat.

SIR CHAS. You promised last night, sir, that   215
you would deliver your lady to me this morning.

SUL. Humph!

ARCH. Humph! what do you mean by humph? Sir, you shall deliver her! — in short, sir, we have saved you and your family; and if you are not   220
civil, we'll unbind the rogues, join with 'um, and set fire to your house. — What does the man mean? not part with his wife!

COUNT BEL. Ay, garzoon, de man no understan common justice.   225

MRS. SUL. Hold, gentlemen, all things here must move by consent; compulsion would spoil us. Let my dear and I talk the matter over, and you shall judge it between us.

SUL. Let me know first who are to be our   230
judges. — Pray, sir, who are you?

SIR CHAS. I am Sir Charles Freeman, come to take away your wife.

SUL. And you, good sir?

AIM. [Thomas], Viscount Aimwell, come to   235
take away your sister.

SUL. And you, pray, sir?

ARCH. Francis Archer, esquire, come ——

SUL. To take away my mother, I hope. — Gentlemen, you're heartily welcome; I never   240
met with three more obliging people since I was born! — And now, my dear, if you please, you shall have the first word.

ARCH. And the last, for five pound!

MRS. SUL. Spouse!   245

SUL. Rib!

MRS. SUL. How long have we been married?

SUL. By the almanac, fourteen months — but by my account, fourteen years.

MRS. SUL. 'Tis thereabout by my reckoning.   250

COUNT BEL. Garzoon, their account will agree.

MRS. SUL. Pray, spouse, what did you marry for?

SUL. To get an heir to my estate.

SIR CHAS. And have you succeeded?

SUL. No.   255

ARCH. The condition fails of his side. — Pray, madam, what did you marry for?

MRS. SUL. To support the weakness of my sex by the strength of his, and to enjoy the pleasures of an agreeable society.   260

SIR CHAS. Are your expectations answered?

MRS. SUL. No.

COUNT BEL. A clear case! a clear case!

SIR CHAS. What are the bars to your mutual contentment?   265

MRS. SUL. In the first place, I can't drink ale with him.

SUL. Nor can I drink tea with her.

MRS. SUL. I can't hunt with you.

SUL. Nor can I dance with you.   270

MRS. SUL. I hate cocking and racing.

SUL. And I abhor ombre and piquet.

MRS. SUL. Your silence is intolerable.

SUL. Your prating is worse.

MRS. SUL. Have we not been a perpetual of-   275
fence to each other? a gnawing vulture at the heart?

SUL. A frightful goblin to the sight?

MRS. SUL. A porcupine to the feeling?

SUL. Perpetual wormwood to the taste?

MRS. SUL. Is there on earth a thing we could   280
agree in?

SUL. Yes — to part.

MRS. SUL. With all my heart.

SUL. Your hand.

MRS. SUL. Here.   285

SUL. These hands joined us, these shall part us. Away!

MRS. SUL. North.

SUL. South.

MRS. SUL. East.   290

SUL. West — far as the poles asunder.

COUNT BEL. Begar, the ceremony be vera pretty!

SIR CHAS. Now, Mr. Sullen, there wants only my sister's fortune to make us easy.

SUL. Sir Charles, you love your sister, and I   295
love her fortune; every one to his fancy.

ARCH. Then you won't refund —

SUL. Not a stiver.

ARCH. Then I find, madam, you must e'en go to your prison again.   300

COUNT BEL. What is the portion?

SIR CHAS. Ten thousand pound, sir.

COUNT BEL. Garzoon, I'll pay it, and she shall go home wid me.

ARCH. Ha, ha, ha! French all over. — Do 305 you know, sir, what ten thousand pound English is?

COUNT BEL. No, begar, not *justement*.[1]

ARCH. Why, sir, 'tis a hundred thousand livres.

COUNT BEL. A hundre tousand livres! Ah, garzoon! me canno' do't; your beauties and 310 their fortunes are both too much for me.

ARCH. Then I will. — This night's adventure has proved strangely lucky to us all — for Captain Gibbet in his walk had made bold, Mr. Sullen, with your study and escritoire, and had taken out 315 all the writings of your estate, all the articles of marriage with his lady, bills, bonds, leases, receipts to an infinite value. I took 'em from him, and I deliver them to Sir Charles.

(*Gives him a parcel of papers and parchments.*)

SUL. How, my writings! — my head aches 320 consumedly. — Well, gentlemen, you shall have her fortune, but I can't talk. If you have a mind, Sir Charles, to be merry, and celebrate my sister's wedding and my divorce, you may command my house — but my head aches consumedly. — 325 Scrub, bring me a dram.

ARCH. (*to* MRS. SULLEN). Madam, there's a country dance to the trifle that I sung today; your hand, and we'll lead it up. (*Here a dance.*)

ARCH. 'Twould be hard to guess which of 330 these parties is the better pleased, the couple joined, or the couple parted; the one rejoicing in hopes of an untasted happiness, and the other in their deliverance from an experienced misery.

Both happy in their several states we find, 335
Those parted by consent, and those conjoined.
Consent, if mutual, saves the lawyer's fee —
Consent is law enough to set you free.

AN EPILOGUE

DESIGNED TO BE SPOKE IN 'THE BEAUX' STRATAGEM.'

IF to our play your judgment can't be kind,
Let its expiring author pity find:[2]
Survey his mournful case with melting eyes,
Nor let the bard be damned before he dies.
Forbear, you fair, on his last scene to frown,   5
But his true exit with a plaudit crown;
Then shall the dying poet cease to fear
The dreadful knell, while your applause he hears.
At Leuctra so the conqu'ring Theban died,[3]
Claimed his friends' praises, but their tears denied: 10
Pleased in the pangs of death he greatly thought
Conquest with loss of life but cheaply bought.
The difference this, the Greek was one would fight, ⎫
As brave, though not so gay, as Sergeant Kite;[4]   ⎬
Ye sons of Will's, what's that to those who write? ⎭   15
To Thebes alone the Grecian owed his bays, ⎫
You may the bard above the hero raise,   ⎬
Since yours is greater than Athenian praise.   ⎭

---

[1] Exactly.   [2] Farquhar lay on his death-bed when *The Beaux' Stratagem* was produced.
[3] Epaminondas actually died at the battle of Mantineia, nine years after his victory over the Spartans at Leuctra.
[4] The recruiting officer in Farquhar's play of the same name.

309–310] Q1C *A garzoon.*

JEREMY COLLIER'S ATTACK ON THE STAGE

As THE seventeenth century neared its close, the growing, but hitherto somewhat desultory, forces of protest against the license of the Restoration stage were marshalled for direct attack by a Nonconformist parson, Jeremy Collier. In March, 1698, the publication of his *Short View of the Immorality and Profaneness of the English Stage* was the declaration of open and vindictive warfare. Even during the early years when the reopened theatres catered to Cavalier audiences contemptuous of Puritan restraint, playwrights and playgoers had at times acknowledged the excesses committed in the name of liberty. The death of the 'Merry Monarch' brought no sudden changes in the fashions which the Comedy of Manners mirrored. But when the Revolution of 1688 deposed James II and brought William and Mary to the throne, the way of the Court world was pointed at least towards greater outward decorum, if not to purer morals. The gradual return of the middle classes to larger influence in the social life which the London theatre could not keep exclusively aristocratic helped to strengthen tendencies to reform. The pendulum which, during the dramatic interregnum, had swung to the extreme of constraint, and during the Restoration, to the extreme of license, was now naturally swinging back once more.

The turning tendencies of the times are already evident in the years that preceded Jeremy Collier's attack. A contemporary reference, dated January 8, 1692, is suggestive: 'His Majesty yesterday checked a young lord for swearing within his hearing; telling him the Court should give good examples, and reformation should begin there first, and then others would follow.' The founding that very year of a Society for the Reformation of Manners, soon followed by other similar societies, showed that the contagious influence of the Court was no longer that of the days of Charles II, when 'All, by the King's example, lived and loved.' In 1695 Sir Richard Blackmore prefaced his moral epic, *Prince Arthur*, with a diatribe against the license of Dryden and other stage poets. In January, 1696, Colley Cibber's *Love's Last Shift*, though its epilogue confessed to the audience that 'Four acts for your coarse palates was designed,' reclaimed the libertine husband in the final act with a foreshadowing of the moralized sentimental comedy of the coming century.

Nevertheless, when Jeremy Collier in 1698 delivered his first philippic against the theatre, Restoration comedy, free and flagrant, held the center of the stage. Congreve and Vanbrugh, new leaders of the comic stage, were already firmly established in popular favor. So far from accepting the fifth-act conversion of Colley Cibber's libertine, Vanbrugh had promptly raised the curtain again in his sequel, *The Relapse, or Virtue in Danger* (December, 1696), not merely to demonstrate the inevitable relapse of Cibber's Loveless, but to impel even the constant wife, Amanda, towards a fifth act of desperate and all but fatal temptation. It is significant that Jeremy Collier presently selected *The Relapse* for special attack in closing one of his most vigorous chapters.

A Short View of the Immorality and Profaneness of the English Stage is divided into six long chapters. The first five carry the brunt of direct attack upon the contemporary stage. The sixth chapter, on 'The Opinion of Paganism, of the Church, and State concerning the Stage,' is a pretentious and prolix appendix which ranges far afield and loses its vital objectives in the mass of objections turned against the theatre itself rather than against immediate abuses on the English stage. Even the earlier chapters which center attack on Restoration comedy often fail to differentiate between moral and artistic issues, and waste time on trivialities. Collier's bludgeon fell indiscriminately on violations of virtue or of the dramatic unities. At times, in belaboring comic dialogue, he mistook persiflage for profanity. But if he lacked subtlety, he had the strength of his convictions and the relentless zeal of the reformer. His rough and ready assault on the licentiousness of the stage prevailed by force without need of strategy.

Collier's attack was timely. It was his good fortune to voice what many had increasingly felt. The *Short View* reflected as well as aroused public opinion. The strength of its main position was directly attested by the dramatists attacked. Vanbrugh and Congreve rallied uneasily in self-defence only to be reattacked by Collier in his *Defence of the Short View*, published in November, 1698. Dryden, the veteran of the Restoration stage, more tolerantly admitted the force, despite the extravagance, of Collier's main indictment. At the turn of the century and thereafter in the pamphlet warfare that protracted itself for several decades (1698–1726), Jeremy Collier remained the central figure in the general struggle that is still known as the 'Collier Controversy.'

G. H. N.

REFERENCE WORKS

1914. Nettleton, George H. *English Drama of the Restoration and Eighteenth Century.* [Especially chapter IX.]

1924. Krutch, Joseph W. *Comedy and Conscience after the Restoration.* New York. Columbia University Press. [Especially chapters V–VI, and bibliography (pp. 264–270).]

1937. Anthony, Sister Rose. *The Jeremy Collier Stage Controversy* 1698–1726. Milwaukee. Marquette University Press. [A full-volume study, with extensive bibliography (pp. 301–318).]

A Short View of the Immorality and Profaneness of the English Stage

BY JEREMY COLLIER

A SHORT

VIEW

OF THE

Immorality, and Profaneß

OF THE

𝕰𝖓𝖌𝖑𝖎𝖘𝖍 𝕾𝖙𝖆𝖌𝖊,

TOGETHER

With the Senfe of Antiquity
upon this Argument,

By *JEREMY COLLIER*, M. A.

London, Printed for S. Keble at the *Turk's-Head*
in *Fleetftreet*, R. Sare at *Gray's-Inn-Gate*,
and H. Hindmarth againft the *Exchange* in
Cornhil. 1698.

A SHORT VIEW OF THE IMMORALITY AND PROFANENESS OF THE ENGLISH STAGE, TOGETHER WITH THE SENSE OF ANTIQUITY UPON THIS ARGUMENT

By JEREMY COLLIER

[The Introduction, and the early parts of Chapter I]

THE INTRODUCTION

The business of plays is to recommend virtue, and discountenance vice; to show the uncertainty of human greatness, the sudden turns of fate, and the unhappy conclusions of violence and injustice: 'tis to expose the singularities of pride and fancy, to make folly and falsehood contemptible, and to bring everything that is ill under infamy and neglect. This design has been oddly pursued by the English stage. Our poets write with a different view, and are gone into another interest. 'Tis true, were their intentions fair, they might be serviceable to this purpose. They have in a great measure the springs of thought and inclination in their power. Show, music, action, and rhetoric, are moving entertainments; and, rightly employed, would be very significant. But force and motion are things indifferent, and the use lies chiefly in the application. These advantages are now in the enemies' hand, and under a very dangerous management. Like cannon seized, they are pointed the wrong way, and by the strength of the defence the mischief is made the greater. That this complaint is not unreasonable I shall endeavor to prove by showing the misbehavior of the stage with respect to morality and religion. Their liberties in the following particulars are intolerable — viz. their smuttiness of expression; their swearing, profaneness, and lewd application of Scripture; their abuse of the clergy; their making their top characters libertines, and giving them success in their debauchery. This charge, with some other irregularities, I shall make good against the stage, and show both the novelty and scandal of the practice. And first, I shall begin with the rankness and indecency of their language.

CHAPTER I

THE IMMODESTY OF THE STAGE

In treating this head, I hope the reader does not expect that I should set down chapter and page, and give him the citations at length. To do this would be a very unacceptable and foreign employment.

Indeed the passages, many of them, are in no condition to be handled: he that is desirous to see these flowers let him do it in their own soil: 'tis my business rather to kill the root than transplant it. But that the poets may not complain of injustice, I shall point to the infection at a distance, and refer in general to play and person.

Now among the curiosities of this kind we may reckon Mrs. Pinchwife, Horner, and Lady Fidget in the *Country Wife*; Widow Blackacre and Olivia in the *Plain Dealer*. These, though not all the exceptionable characters, are the most remarkable. I'm sorry the author should stoop his wit thus low, and use his understanding so unkindly. Some people appear coarse and slovenly out of poverty: they can't well go to the charge of sense. They are offensive, like beggars, for want of necessaries. But this is none of the *Plain Dealer's* case; he can afford his muse a better dress when he pleases. But then the rule is, where the motive is the less, the fault is the greater. To proceed. Jacinta, Elvira, Dalinda, and Lady Plyant, in the *Mock Astrologer*, *Spanish Friar*, *Love Triumphant* and *Double Dealer*, forget themselves extremely: and almost all the characters in the *Old Bachelor* are foul and nauseous. *Love for Love* and the *Relapse* strike sometimes upon this sand, and so likewise does *Don Sebastian*.

I don't pretend to have read the stage through, neither am I particular to my utmost. Here is quoting enough unless 'twere better: besides, I may have occasion to mention somewhat of this kind afterwards. But from what has been hinted already, the reader may be over furnished. Here is a large collection of debauchery; such pieces are rarely to be met with: 'tis sometimes painted at length too, and appears in great variety of progress and practice. It wears almost all sorts of dresses to engage the fancy, and fasten upon the memory, and keep up the charm from languishing. Sometimes you have it in image and description; sometimes by way of allusion; sometimes in disguise; and sometimes without it. And what can be the meaning of such a representation, unless it be to tincture the audience, to extinguish shame, and make lewdness a diversion? This is the natural consequence, and therefore one would think 'twas the intention too. Such licentious discourse tends to no point but to stain the imagination, to awaken folly, and to weaken the defences of virtue. It was upon the account of these disorders that Plato banished poets his *Commonwealth*: and one of the fathers calls poetry *vinum dæmonum*, an intoxicating draught, made up by the Devil's dispensatory.

I grant the abuse of a thing is no argument against the use of it. However, young people, particularly, should not entertain themselves with a lewd picture; especially when 'tis drawn by a masterly hand. For such a liberty may probably raise those passions which can neither be discharged without trouble, nor satisfied without a crime: 'tis not safe for a man to trust his virtue too far, for fear it should give him the slip! But the danger of such an entertainment is but part of the objection: 'tis all scandal and meanness into the bargain: it does in effect degrade human nature, sinks reason into appetite, and breaks down the distinctions between man and beast. Goats and monkeys, if they could speak, would express their brutality in such language as this.

To argue the matter more at large. Smuttiness is a fault in behavior as well as in religion. 'Tis a very coarse diversion, the entertainment of those who are generally least both in sense and station. The looser part of the mob have no true relish of decency and honor, and want education and thought, to furnish out a genteel conversation. Barrenness of fancy makes them often take up with those scandalous liberties. A vicious imagination may blot a great deal of paper at this rate with ease enough: and 'tis possible convenience may sometimes invite to the expedient. The modern poets seem to use smut as the old ones did machines, to relieve a fainting invention. When Pegasus is jaded, and would stand still, he is apt, like other tits, to run into every puddle.

Obscenity in any company is a rustic uncreditable talent; but among women 'tis particularly rude. Such talk would be very affrontive in conversation, and not endured by any lady of reputation. Whence then comes it to pass that those liberties which disoblige so much in conversation should entertain upon the stage? Do the women leave all the regards to decency and conscience behind them when they come to the play-house? Or does the place transform their inclinations, and turn their former aversions into pleasure? Or were their pretences to sobriety elsewhere nothing but hypocrisy and grimace? Such suppositions as these are all satire and invective: they are rude imputations upon the whole sex. To treat the ladies with such stuff is no better than taking their money to abuse them.

It supposes their imagination vicious, and their memories ill-furnished: that they are practised in the language of the stews, and pleased with the scenes of brutishness, when at the same time the customs of education, and the laws of decency, are so very cautious and reserved in regard to women — I say, so very reserved — that 'tis almost a fault for them to understand they are ill-used. They can't discover their disgust without disadvantage, nor blush without disservice to their modesty. To appear with any skill in such cant, looks as if they had fallen upon ill conversation; or managed their curiosity amiss. In a word, he that treats the ladies with such discourse must conclude either that they like it, or they do not. To suppose the first, is a gross reflection upon their virtue. And as for the latter case, it entertains them with their own aversion; which is ill nature, and ill manners enough, in all conscience. And in this particular, custom and conscience, the forms of breeding, and the maxims of religion are on the same side. In other instances vice is often too fashionable; but here a man can't be a sinner, without being a clown.

In this respect the stage is faulty to a scandalous degree of nauseousness and aggravation. For

1st. The poets make women speak smuttily. Of this the places before mentioned are sufficient evidence: and, if there was occasion, they might be multiplied to a much greater number: indeed the comedies are seldom clear of these blemishes: and sometimes you have them in tragedy. For instance: *The Orphan's* Monimia[1] makes a very improper description; and the royal Leonora, in the *Spanish Friar*, runs a strange length in the history of love, p. 50. And do princesses use to make their reports with such fulsome freedoms? Certainly this Leonora was the first queen of her family. Such raptures are too lascivious for Joan of Naples. Are these the tender things Mr. Dryden says the ladies call on him for? I suppose he means the ladies that are too modest to show their faces in the pit. This entertainment can be fairly designed for none but such. Indeed it hits their palate exactly. It regales their lewdness, graces their character, and keeps up their spirits for their vocation. Now, to bring women under such misbehavior is violence to their native modesty, and a mispresentation of their sex. For modesty, as Mr. Rapin[2] observes, is the character of women. To represent them without this quality is to make monsters of them, and throw them out of their kind. Euripides, who was no negligent observer of human nature, is always careful of this decorum. Thus Phaedra,[3] when possessed with an

---

[1] The heroine of Otway's play, *The Orphan*. Collier's 1698 text reads 'The *Orphans Monimia*.'
[2] In his *Reflections upon Aristotle*.
[3] In the *Hippolitus*.

infamous passion, takes all imaginable pains to conceal it. She is as regular and reserved in her language as the most virtuous matron. 'Tis true, the force of shame and desire, the scandal of satisfying, and the difficulty of parting with her inclinations, disorder her to distraction. However, her frenzy is not lewd; she keeps her modesty even after she has lost her wits. Had Shakespeare secured this point for his young virgin Ophelia, the play had been better contrived. Since he was resolved to drown the lady like a kitten, he should have set her a-swimming a little sooner. To keep her alive only to sully her reputation, and discover the rankness of her breath, was very cruel. But it may be said the freedoms of distraction go for nothing, a fever has no faults, and a man *non compos* may kill without murder. It may be so: but then such people ought to be kept in dark rooms and without company. To show them, or let them loose, is somewhat unreasonable. But after all, the modern stage seems to depend upon this expedient. Women are sometimes represented silly, and sometimes mad, to enlarge their liberty, and screen their impudence from censure: this politic contrivance we have in Marcella, Hoyden, and Miss Prue.[1] However, it amounts to this confession; that women when they have their understandings about them ought to converse otherwise. In fine; modesty is the distinguishing virtue of that sex, and serves both for ornament and defence: modesty was designed by Providence as a guard to virtue; and that it might be always at hand, 'tis wrought into the mechanism of the body. 'Tis likewise proportioned to the occasions of life, and strongest in youth when passion is so too. 'Tis a quality as true to innocence as the senses are to health; whatever is ungrateful to the first is prejudicial to the latter. The enemy no sooner approaches but the blood rises in opposition, and looks defiance

[1] In Durfey's *Don Quixote*, Vanbrugh's *Relapse*, and Congreve's *Love for Love*.

to an indecency. It supplies the room of reasoning, and collection: intuitive knowledge can scarcely make a quicker impression; and what then can be a surer guide to the unexperienced? It teaches by sudden instinct and aversion; this is both a ready and a powerful method of instruction. The tumult of the blood and spirits, and the uneasiness of the sensation, are of singular use. They serve to awaken reason, and prevent surprise. Thus the distinctions of good and evil are refreshed, and the temptation kept at proper distance.

2dly. They represent their single ladies, and persons of condition, under these disorders of liberty. This makes the irregularity still more monstrous and a greater contradiction to nature and probability: but rather than not be vicious, they will venture to spoil a character. This mismanagement we have partly seen already. Jacinta and Belinda[2] are farther proof. And the *Double Dealer* is particularly remarkable. There are but four ladies in this play, and three of the biggest of them are whores. A great compliment to quality to tell them there is not above a quarter of them honest! This was not the Roman breeding, Terence and Plautus his strumpets[3] were little people; but of this more hereafter.

3dly. They have oftentimes not so much as the poor refuge of a double meaning to fly to. So that you are under a necessity either of taking ribaldry or nonsense. And when the sentence has two handles, the worst is generally turned to the audience. The matter is so contrived that the smut and scum of the thought rises uppermost; and, like a picture drawn to sight, looks always upon the company.

4ly. And which is still more extraordinary: the Prologues, and Epilogues are sometimes scandalous to the last degree. I shall discover them for once, and let them stand like rocks in the margin.

[2] In Dryden's *Mock Astrologer* and Congreve's *Old Bachelor*.
[3] I.e., 'The strumpets of Terence and of Plautus.'

Eighteenth-Century Drama

EARLY EIGHTEENTH–CENTURY DRAMA (1700–1730)

SENTIMENTAL COMEDY

THE transition from the Restoration comedy of manners to moralized and sentimental comedy was so gradual that it is impossible to set any date at which one style decayed and the other gained the ascendency. A glance at the dates of the examples chosen to illustrate the two styles in this anthology shows that the periods overlap each other, and in fact the overlapping was even greater than these dates suggest. Moralized comedy is generally said to have begun with Colley Cibber's *Love's Last Shift* (1696): on the other hand, Mrs. Centlivre, who certainly belongs to the Restoration school, flourished between 1700 and 1722. One might go still farther and point out that Gay's *Beggar's Opera* (1728), although it is usually assigned to a separate category because of its musical character, was really an offshoot of the older comedy, as was his earlier play, *Three Hours after Marriage*, written in 1717 in conjunction with Pope and Arbuthnot. But it may safely be said that the trend, after the publication of Collier's *Short View*, was definitely in the direction of moralized and sentimental comedy.

COLLEY CIBBER (1671–1757) was not only an author, but an actor and a theatrical manager as well. During a turbulent career he had a hand in many enterprises, and attempted (without much success) to write both lyrical verse and biography. His appointment as poet-laureate, in 1730, brought a storm of abuse from contemporary writers: in 1742, after years of bickering with Pope, he was made the hero of the fourth book of the *Dunciad*, and subsequently of the entire poem. He wrote some thirty plays, mostly comedies, among which *Love's Last Shift* and *The Careless Husband* (1704), both classed as sentimental, are the best known. His move toward a less licentious mode of writing was experimental, and some of his later comedies are closer to the Restoration mode. *Love's Last Shift* did not altogether break with the older way of writing: some of its scenes, especially those connected with the sub-plots, would have pleased the public of Etherege. But the main business of the play is to tell the story of an errant husband who, after a ten years' absence, is recaptured by a faithful wife through a device that is reminiscent of Helena's in *All's Well that Ends Well*. The sympathetic treatment of the wife's misfortunes gives the sentimental tone, but the absence of any severe reprehension of the husband's conduct undoubtedly displeased the moralists. Much the same thing might be said of *The Careless Husband*, in which the faithful wife's strategy consists of a steadfast refusal to upbraid her husband for his infidelities, although she manages to let him know, in an indirect manner, that she is aware of them. Here, though the repentant husband, Sir Charles Easy, confesses his faults more *in extenso* than did his counterpart in the earlier play, one cannot help feeling that his reform is due less to a sense of guilt than to admiration for his wife's behavior, and that Lady Easy's gratitude is a little too fulsome.

Sir RICHARD STEELE (1672–1729) carried sentimental comedy a step farther by emphasizing the moral purpose of his plays. Of his four comedies, three (*The Funeral*, 1701; *The Lying Lover*, 1703; *The Tender Husband*, 1705) belong to his earlier career, and one (*The Conscious Lovers*, 1722) to his later: between the two periods of dramatic composition fell the most important part of his literary work, the periodical essays, of which the most famous appeared in the *Tatler* (1709–1710) and the *Spectator* (1711–1712). *The Funeral* is in many ways Steele's best comedy. It is evident that its author subscribed to the theory that the business of comedy is to attack the lesser faults of humanity with the weapon of ridicule. That Steele was on the side of the reformers of the drama was evidenced not by moralizing, but by the almost complete absence of indecency from both the action and the dialogue.   Steele's stand on this matter is made clear in his attack on Etherege (*Spectator* No. 65), and his sincerity is evinced in another essay (*Spectator* No. 51) in which he accepted a rebuke from a correspondent and, as a result, altered a passage in *The Funeral* which to the playgoers of the day must have seemed mild indeed.   In *The Lying Lover* Steele went one step further and introduced the moralizing element quite openly.   In the preface to the play he observed:

> . . . it is the general complaint of the more learned and virtuous amongst us that the English stage has extremely offended . . . I thought therefore it would be an honest ambition to attempt a comedy which might be no improper entertainment in a Christian commonwealth.   In order to this, the spark of this play is introduced with as much agility and life as he brought with him from France, and as much humor as I could bestow upon him in England . . . he makes false love, gets drunk, and kills his man, but in the fifth act awakes from his debauch with the compunction and remorse which is suitable to a man's finding himself in a goal [1] for the death of his friend, without his knowing why. The anguish he there expresses, and the mutual sorrow between an only child and a tender father in that distress are, perhaps, an injury to the rules of comedy, but I am sure they are a justice to those of morality: and passages of such a nature being so frequently applauded on the stage, it is high time we should no longer draw occasions of mirth from those images which the religion of our country tells us we ought to tremble at with horror.

The mixture of comedy and sentiment was continued in both of the later plays, and in the preface to each Steele proclaimed his moral purpose: in *The Conscious Lovers*, indeed, he averred that 'the whole was writ for the sake of the scene of the fourth act, wherein Mr. Bevil evades the quarrel with his friend.'   The passage discussing the function of comedy which immediately follows this shows, when it is compared with the excerpt which has been quoted from the preface to *The Lying Lover*, how far Steele had altered his position in nineteen years.

The increasing divergence in purpose between the two schools of comic writing was inevitably fatal.   It might be said that comedy was divided by a sort of judgment of Solomon, one party laying hold upon the purpose (to correct manners) and the other upon the means (ridicule).   The first of these parties drew to it the more capable dramatic writers of the early eighteenth century; the other group drifted into the composition of farces.

A. E. C.

[1] Jail.

REFERENCE WORKS

1914. Nettleton, George H.   *English Drama of the Restoration and Eighteenth Century*.   New York and London.   [Chapter IX, with Bibliographical Notes.]

1924. Krutch, Joseph Wood.   *Comedy and Conscience after the Restoration*.   New York.

1925. Bateson, F. W.   *English Comic Drama, 1700–1750*.   Oxford.

1925. Bernbaum, Ernest.   *The Drama of Sensibility*.   Cambridge [Massachusetts].

1929. Nicoll, Allardyce.   *A History of Early Eighteenth Century Drama*.   Oxford.   [Chapter III.]

The Careless Husband

BY COLLEY CIBBER

THE
Careleſs Husband.

A
COMEDY.

As it is ACTED at the

THEATRE ROYAL,

BY

Her MAJESTY's Servants.

Written by *C. CIBBER*.

Yet none Sir Fopling Him, or Him can call,
He's Knight o' th' Shire, and Repreſents you all.
Qui Capit, Ille Facit.

LONDON,

Printed *for* William Davis, *at the* Black Bull, *over-againſt the* Royal Exchange *in* Cornhill, 1705.

TITLE-PAGE OF FIRST EDITION, 1705, OF *THE CARELESS HUSBAND*

THE PROLOGUE

Of all the various vices of the age,
And shoals of fools exposed upon the stage,
How few are lashed, that call for satire's rage!
What can you think, to see our plays so full
Of madmen, coxcombs, and the driveling fool;   5
Of cits, of sharpers, rakes and roaring bullies,
Of cheats, of cuckolds, aldermen and cullies? [1]
Would not one swear, 'twere taken for a rule,
That satire's rod in the dramatic school
Was only meant for the incorrigible fool?   10
As if too vice and folly were confined
To the vile scum alone of human kind,
Creatures a muse should scorn; such abject trash
Deserve not satire's but the hangman's lash.
Wretches so far shut out from sense of shame,   15
Newgate or Bedlam [2] only should reclaim;
For satire ne'er was meant to make wild monsters tame.
No, sirs,——
    We rather think the persons fit for plays,
Are they whose birth and education says   20
They've every help that should improve mankind,
Yet still live slaves to a vile tainted mind;
Such as in wit are often seen t'abound,
And yet have some weak part, where folly's found:
For follies sprout like weeds, highest in fruitful ground.   25
And 'tis observed, the garden of the mind
To no infestive weed's so much inclined,
As the rank pride, that some from affectation find.
A folly too well known to make its court
With most success among the better sort.   30
Such are the persons we today provide,
And Nature's fools for once are laid aside.
This is the ground on which our play we build;
But in the structure must to judgment yield:
And where the poet fails in art or care,   35
We beg your wonted mercy to the player.

[1] Dupes.   [2] The prison and the insane asylum.

The dedication, to John, Duke of Argyle, is omitted.   22] Q1 (some copies, according to Habbema) *like slaves*.

DRAMATIS PERSONÆ

MEN	WOMEN
LORD MORELOVE	LADY BETTY MODISH
LORD FOPPINGTON	LADY EASY
SIR CHARLES EASY	LADY GRAVEAIRS
	MRS. EDGING, *Woman to* LADY EASY

SCENE — WINDSOR.[1]

[1] Some twenty miles west of London; the seat of one of the most famous royal castles, and at this period frequented by fashionable society while the court was in residence there.

QQ *The Persons.*   QQ om. *MEN* and *WOMEN.*   QQ *The Scene.*

Lud. Du Guernier inv. et Sculp.

FRONTISPIECE OF THE SEVENTH EDITION, 1731, OF *THE CARELESS HUSBAND*
The discovery by Lady Easy of her husband and her
maid 'asleep in two easy chairs.' (Act v, scene v.)

THE CARELESS HUSBAND

BY COLLEY CIBBER

ACT I

SCENE I

Scene, SIR CHARLES EASY'S *lodgings.*

Enter LADY EASY *alone.*

L. EA. Was ever woman's spirit, by an injurious husband, broke like mine? A vile, licentious man! must he bring home his follies too? Wrong me with my very servant! Oh, how tedious a relief is patience! and yet in my condition 'tis the only 5 remedy, for to reproach him with my wrongs is taking on myself the means of a redress, bidding defiance to his falsehood, and naturally but provokes him to undo me. Th' uneasy thought of my continual jealousy may tease him to a fixed aver- 10 sion, and hitherto, though he neglects, I cannot think he hates me. — It must be so: since I want power to please him, he never shall upbraid me with an attempt of making him uneasy —— My eyes and tongue shall yet be blind and silent to my 15 wrongs, nor would I have him think my virtue could suspect him, till by some gross apparent proof of his misdoing he forces me to see — and to forgive it.

Enter EDGING *hastily.*

EDG. Oh, madam!

L. EA. What's the matter? 20

EDG. I have the strangest thing to show your ladyship — such a discovery ——

L. EA. You are resolved to make it without much ceremony, I find. What's the business, pray?

EDG. The business, madam! I have not pa- 25 tience to tell you — I am out of breath at the very thoughts on't — I shall not be able to speak this half hour.

L. EA. Not to the purpose, I believe; but methinks you talk impertinently with a great deal of ease. 30

EDG. Nay, madam, perhaps not so impertinent as your ladyship thinks: there's that will speak to the purpose, I am sure — a base man!

(Gives a letter.)

L. EA. What's this — an open letter? Whence comes it? 35

EDG. Nay, read it, madam, you'll soon guess —— if these are the tricks of husbands, keep me a maid still, say I.

L. EA. *(looking on the superscription, aside).* 'To Sir Charles Easy!' Ha! Too well I know this 40 hateful hand. Oh, my heart! but I must veil my jealousy, which 'tis not fit this creature should suppose I am acquainted with. — This direction is to your master: how came you by it?

EDG. Why, madam, as my master was lying 45 down, after he came in from hunting, he sent me into his dressing-room to fetch his snuff-box out of his waistcoat-pocket, and so, as I was searching for the box, madam, there I found this wicked letter from a mistress, which I had no sooner read but, I de- 50 clare it, my very blood rose at him again: methought I could have torn him and her to pieces.

L. EA. *(aside).* Intolerable! This odious thing's jealous of him herself, and wants me to join with her in a revenge upon him. Sure I am fallen indeed! 55 But 'twere to make me lower yet, to let her think I understand her.

EDG. Nay, pray, madam, read it; you'll be out of patience at it.

L. EA. You are bold, mistress; has my indul- 60 gence [or] your master's good humor flattered you into the assurance of reading his letters? — a liberty I never gave myself. Here — lay it where you had it immediately: should he know of your sauciness, 'twould not be my favor could protect you. 65

Exit LADY EASY.

EDG. Your favor! Marry come up! Sure I don't depend upon your favor! — 'tis not come to that, I hope. Poor creature — don't you think I am my master's mistress for nothing: you shall find, madam, I won't be snapped up as I have been. 70 Not but it vexes me to think she should not be as uneasy as I. I am sure he's a base man to me, and I could cry my eyes out that she should not think him as bad to her every jot. If I am wronged, sure she may very well expect it, that is but his wife. A 75 conceited thing! — she need not be so easy neither — I am as handsome as she, I hope. Here's my master — I'll try whether I am to be huffed by her or no.

(Walks behind.)

Enter SIR CHARLES EASY.

SIR CHA. So! the day is come again. Life but rises to another stage, and the same dull journey 80 is before us. How like children do we judge of happiness! When I was stinted in my fortune almost everything was a pleasure to me, because, most things then being out of my reach, I had always the pleasure of hoping for 'em; now Fortune's in my 85 hand she's as insipid as an old acquaintance. It's mighty silly, faith. Just the same thing by my wife too; I am told she's extremely handsome — nay, and I have heard a great many people say she is certainly the best woman in the world. Why, I don't 90 know but she may, yet I could never find that her person or good qualities gave me any concern. In my eye the woman has no more charms than my mother.

EDG. Hum! — he takes no notice of me yet; 95 I'll let him see I can take as little notice of him. (*She walks by him gravely; he turns her about and holds her; she struggles.*) Pray, sir!

SIR CHA. A pretty pert air, that —— I'll humor it. What's the matter, child? Are you not 100 well? Kiss me, hussy.

EDG. No, the deuce fetch me if I do.

SIR CHA. Has anything put thee out of humor, love?

EDG. No, sir, 'tis not worth my being out of 105 humor at — though if ever you have anything to say to me again I'll be burned.

SIR CHA. Somebody has belied me to thee.

EDG. No, sir, 'tis you have belied yourself to me. Did not I ask you, when you first made a fool 110 of me, if you would be always constant to me, and did not you say I might be sure you would? And here, instead of that, you are going on in your old intrigue with my Lady Graveairs ——

SIR CHA. So! 115

EDG. Beside, don't you suffer my lady to huff me every day as if I were her dog, or had no more concern with you? I declare I won't bear it, and she shan't think to huff me — for aught I know I am as agreeable as she, and though she dares not take 120 any notice of your baseness to her, you shan't think to use me so — and so pray take your nasty letter — I know the hand well enough — for my part I won't stay in the family to be abused at this rate; I that have refused lords and dukes for your sake: I'd 125 have you to know, sir, I have had as many blue and green ribbons [1] after me, for aught I know, as would have made me a Falbala apron. [2]

SIR CHA. 'My Lady Graveairs!' 'my nasty letter!' and 'I won't stay in the family!' —— 130 Death! I'm in a pretty condition. What an unlimited privilege has this jade got from being a whore!

---

[1] Blue and green ribbons were parts of the insignia of the orders of the Garter and the Thistle, respectively.

[2] An apron with flounces.

EDG. I suppose, sir, you think to use everybody as you do your wife. 135

SIR CHA. My wife, ha! Come hither, Mrs. Edging; hark you, drab! (*Seizing her by the shoulder.*)

EDG. Oh!

SIR CHA. When you speak of my wife, you are to say 'your lady,' and you are never to speak of 140 your lady to me in any regard of her being my wife — for look you, child, you are not *her* strumpet but *mine*, therefore I only give you leave to be saucy with me; in the next place, you are never to suppose there is any such person as my Lady Graveairs; 145 and lastly, my pretty one, how came you by this letter?

EDG. It's no matter, perhaps.

SIR CHA. Ay, but if you should not tell me quickly, how are you sure I won't take a great 150 piece of flesh out of your shoulder? — my dear!
(*Shakes her.*)

EDG. O lud! o lud! I will tell you, sir.

SIR CHA. Quickly, then. (*Again.*)

EDG. Oh! I took it out of your pocket, sir.

SIR CHA. When? 155

EDG. Oh! this morning, when you sent me for your snuff-box.

SIR CHA. And your ladyship's pretty curiosity has looked it over, I presume! — ha. (*Again.*)

EDG. O lud! dear sir, don't be angry — 160 indeed I'll never touch one again.

SIR CHA. I don't believe you will, and I'll tell you how you shall be sure you never will.

EDG. Yes, sir.

SIR CHA. By steadfastly believing that the 165 next time you offer it you will have your pretty white neck twisted behind you.

EDG. (*curtsying*). Yes, sir.

SIR CHA. And you will be sure to remember everything I have said to you? 170

EDG. Yes, sir.

SIR CHA. And now, child, I was not angry with your person, but your follies, which, since I find you are a little sensible of — don't be wholly discouraged — for I believe I — I shall have occasion for 175 you again ——

EDG. Yes, sir.

SIR CHA. In the meantime let me hear no more of your lady, child.

EDG. No, sir. 180

SIR CHA. Here she comes: begone.

EDG. Yes, sir. —— Oh! I was never so frightened in my life. *Exit.*

SIR CHA. So! good discipline makes good soldiers. It often puzzles me to think, from my own care- 185 lessness and my wife's continual good humor, whether she really knows anything of the strength of my forces. I'll sift her a little.

Enter LADY EASY.

My dear, how do you do? You are dressed very
early today; are you going out?   190

L. EA. Only to church, my dear.

SIR CHA. Is it so late then?

L. EA. The bell has just rung.

SIR CHA. Well, child, how does Windsor air agree
with you? Do you find yourself any better 195
yet? or have you a mind to go to London again?

L. EA. No, indeed, my dear; the air's so very
pleasant that if it were a place of less company I
could be content to end my days here.

SIR CHA. Prithee, my dear, what sort of   200
company would most please you?

L. EA. When business would permit it, yours; and
in your absence a sincere friend that were truly happy in an honest husband, to sit a cheerful hour and
talk in mutual praise of our condition.   205

SIR CHA. Are you then really very happy, my
dear?

L. EA. (*smiling on him*). Why should you question it?

SIR CHA. Because I fancy I am not so good   210
to you as I should be.

L. EA. Pshah!

SIR CHA. Nay, the deuce take me if I don't really
confess myself so bad, that I have often wondered
how any woman of your sense, rank, and per- 215
son could think it worth her while to have so many
useless good qualities.

L. EA. Fie, my dear!

SIR CHA. By my soul, I'm serious.

L. EA. I can't boast of my good qualities,   220
nor if I could, do I believe you think 'em useless.

SIR CHA. Nay, I submit to you, don't you find
'em so? Do you perceive that I am one tittle the
better husband for your being so good a wife?

L. EA. Pshah! you jest with me.   225

SIR CHA. Upon my life, I don't. Tell me truly,
was you never jealous of me?

L. EA. Did I ever give you any sign of it?

SIR CHA. Um — that's true — but do you really
think I never gave you occasion?   230

L. EA. That's an odd question — but suppose
you had?

SIR CHA. Why then, what good has your virtue
done you, since all the good qualities of it could not
keep me to yourself?   235

L. EA. What occasion have you given me to suppose I have not kept you to myself?

SIR CHA. I given you occasion —— Fie! my dear
— you may be sure I — I — look you, that is not
the thing, but still a — [*aside*] death! what a 240
blunder have I made! — [*aloud*] a — still, I say,
madam, you shan't make me believe you have never

been jealous of me; not that you ever had any real
cause, but I know women of your principles have
more pride than those that have no principles 245
at all; and where there is pride there must be some
jealousy — so that if you are jealous, my dear, you
know you wrong me, and ——

L. EA. Why then upon my word, my dear, I don't
know that ever I wronged you that way in my 250
life.

SIR CHA. But suppose I had given you a real
cause to be jealous, how would you do then?

L. EA. It must be a very substantial one that
makes me jealous.   255

SIR CHA. Say it were a substantial one; suppose
now I were well with a woman of your own acquaintance that, under pretence of frequent visits to
you, should only come to carry on an affair with
me — suppose now my Lady Graveairs and I 260
were great ——?

L. EA. (*aside*). Would I could not suppose it.

SIR CHA. (*aside*). If I come off here I believe I am
pretty safe. —— Suppose, I say, my lady and I were
so very familiar that not only yourself, but 265
half the town should see it?

L. EA. Then I should cry myself sick in some dark
closet, and forget my tears when you spoke kindly
to me.

SIR CHA. (*aside*). The most convenient piece 270
of virtue, sure, that ever wife was mistress of.

L. EA. But pray, my dear, did you ever think
that I had any ill thoughts of my Lady Graveairs?

SIR CHA. Oh fie! child — only you know she and I
used to be a little free sometimes, so I had a 275
mind to see if you thought there was any harm in
it: but since I find you very easy, I think myself
obliged to tell you that upon my soul, my dear, I have
so little regard to her person, that the deuce take me
if I would not as soon have an affair with thy 280
own woman.

L. EA. Indeed, my dear, I should as soon suspect
you with one as t'other.

SIR CHA. Poor dear — shouldst thou? — give me
a kiss!   285

L. EA. Pshah! you don't care to kiss me.

SIR CHA. By my soul, I do — I wish I may die
if I don't think you a very fine woman.

L. EA. I only wish you would think me a good
wife. ([SIR CHARLES] *kisses her*.) But pray, 290
my dear, what has made you so strangely inquisitive?

SIR CHA. Inquisitive — why — a — I don't
know — one's always saying one foolish thing or
another — *Toll le roll. (Sings and talks.)* My dear,
what! are we never to have any ball here? 295
Toll le roll. I fancy I could recover my dancing
again, if I would but practise. *Toll loll loll.*

L. EA. [*aside*]. This excess of carelessness to me

226] QQ *SIR CHA. I don't really — Tell.*   252] DD om. *you.*   292] QQ *a — nay I.*

excuses half his vices: if I can make him once think
seriously — time yet may be my friend.   300

Enter a Servant.

SERV. Sir, my Lord Morelove gives his service ——
SIR CHA. Lord Morelove! where is he?
SERV. At the chocolate-house; he called me to
him as I went by and bid me tell your honor   305
he'll wait upon you presently.
L. EA. I thought you had not expected him here
again this season, my dear.
SIR CHA. I thought so too, but you see there's no
depending upon the resolution of a man that's   310
in love.
L. EA. Is there a chair?
SERV. Yes, madam.   *Exit Servant.*
L. EA. I suppose Lady Betty Modish has drawn
him hither.   315
SIR CHA. Ay, poor soul, for all his bravery, I am
afraid so.
L. EA. Well, my dear, I han't time to ask my lord
how he does now; you'll excuse me to him, but I
hope you'll make him dine with us.   320
SIR CHA. I'll ask him. If you see Lady Betty at
prayers make her dine too, but don't take any notice of my lord's being in town.
L. EA. Very well! if I should not meet her there,
I'll call at her lodgings.   325
SIR CHA. Do so.
L. EA. My dear, your servant.
SIR CHA. My dear, I'm yours. (*Exit* LADY EASY.)
Well! one way or other this woman will certainly
bring about her business with me at last; for   330
though she can't make me happy in her own person,
she lets me be so intolerably easy with the women
that can that she has at least brought me into a fair
way of being as weary of them too.

Enter Servant and LORD MORELOVE.

SERV. Sir, my lord's come.   335
L. MO. Dear Charles!
SIR CHA. My dear lord! this is an happiness un-
dreamt of. I little thought to have seen you at
Windsor again this season: I concluded of course that
books and solitude had secured you till winter.   340
L. MO. Nay, I did not think of coming myself,
but I found myself not very well in London, so I
thought — a — little hunting, and this air ——
SIR CHA. Ha! ha! ha!
L. MO. What do you laugh at?   345
SIR CHA. Only because you should not go on with
your story: if you did but see how sillily a man
fumbles for an excuse when he's a little ashamed of

being in love, you would not wonder what I laugh
at, ha! ha!   350
L. MO. Thou art a very happy fellow — nothing
touches thee — always easy. Then you conclude
I follow Lady Betty again?
SIR CHA. Yes, faith, do I: and to make you easy,
my lord, I cannot see why a man that can ride   355
fifty miles after a poor stag should be ashamed of
running twenty in chase of a fine woman that, in all
probability, will make him so much the better sport,
too.   (*Embracing.*)
L. MO. Dear Charles, don't flatter my dis-   360
temper; I own I still follow her. Do you think her
charms have power to excuse me to the world?
SIR CHA. Ay! ay! a fine woman's an excuse for
anything; and the scandal of being her jest is a jest
itself; we are all forced to be their fools before   365
we can be their favorites.
L. MO. You are willing to give me hope, but I
can't believe she has the least degree of inclination
for me.
SIR CHA. I don't know that — I'm sure her   370
pride likes you, and that's generally your fine lady's
darling passion.
L. MO. Do you suppose if I could grow indifferent
it would touch her?
SIR CHA. Sting her to the heart. Will you   375
take my advice?
L. MO. I have no relief but that; had I not thee
now and then to talk an hour, my life were insupportable.
SIR CHA. I am sorry for that, my lord, but   380
mind what I say to you. But hold! first let me
know the particulars of your late quarrel with her.
L. MO. Why, about three weeks ago, when I was
last here at Windsor, she had for some days treated
me with a little more reserve, and another with   385
more freedom, than I found myself easy at.
SIR CHA. Who was that other?
L. MO. One of my Lord Foppington's gang, the
pert coxcomb that's just come to a small estate and
a great periwig — he that sings himself among   390
the women — what d'ye call him? — he won't
speak to a commoner when a lord's in company —
you always see him with a cane dangling at his button, his breast open, no gloves, one eye tucked under
his hat, and a tooth-pick —— Startup, that's   395
his name.
SIR CHA. Oh! I have met him in a visit — but
pray go on.
L. MO. So, disputing with her about the conduct
of women, I took the liberty to tell her how far   400
I thought she erred in hers; she told me I was rude,
and that she would never believe any man could love

301] DD om. *my.*   326] QQ *Do so.* Re-enter the Servant.   347] DD *silly.*
364–366] QQ om. all of speech after *anything.*   367] QQ *L. Mo. You take a great deal of pains to give.*
370] QQ *I am.*   378–379] Q1 *we insupportable.*   382] QQ om. *late.*   392] QQ *to a gentleman.*

a woman that thought her in the wrong in anything she had a mind to, at least if he dared to tell her so. This provoked me into her whole character,   405 with as much spite and civil malice as I have seen her bestow upon a woman of true beauty when the men first toasted her; so, in the middle of my wisdom, she told me she desired to be alone, that I would take my odious proud heart along with me and   410 trouble her no more.   I — bowed very low, and, as I left the room, vowed I never would, and that my proud heart should never be humbled by the outside of a fine woman.   About an hour after I whipped into my chaise for London, and have never seen   415 her since.

SIR CHA.   Very well, and how did you find your proud heart by that time you got to Hounslow? [1]

L. MO.   I am almost ashamed to tell you — I found her so much in the right that I cursed my   420 pride for contradicting her at all, and began to think, according to her maxim, that no woman could be in the wrong to a man that she had in her power.

SIR CHA.   Ha! ha!   Well, I'll tell you what you shall do.   You can see her without trembling,   425 I hope.

L. MO.   Not if she receives me well.

SIR CHA.   If she receives you well, you will have no occasion for what I am going to say to you. First, you shall dine with her.   430

L. MO.   How? where? when?

SIR CHA.   Here! here! at two o'clock.

L. MO.   Dear Charles!

SIR CHA.   My wife's gone to invite her.   When you see her first, be neither too humble nor too   435 stubborn; let her see by the ease in your behavior you are still pleased in being near her while she is upon reasonable terms with you.   This will either open the door of an *éclaircissement*,[2] or quite shut it against you — and if she is still resolved to keep   440 you out ——

L. MO.   Nay, if she insults me then, perhaps I may recover pride enough to rally her by an over-acted submission.

SIR CHA.   Why, you improve, my lord; this   445 is the very thing I was going to propose to you.

L. MO.   Was it, faith!   Hark you, dare you stand by me?

SIR CHA.   Dare I! ay, to my last drop of assurance, against all the insolent airs of the proudest   450 beauty in Christendom.

L. MO.   Nay, then defiance to her!   We two —! Thou hast inspired me; I find myself as valiant as a flattered coward.

SIR CHA.   Courage, my lord — I'll warrant   455 we beat her.

---

[1] Hounslow is about halfway between Windsor and London.
[2] Explanation.

L. MO.   My blood stirs at the very thought on't; I long to be engaged.

SIR CHA.   She'll certainly give ground when she once sees you are thoroughly provoked.   460

L. MO.   Dear Charles, thou art a friend indeed.

Enter a Servant.

SERV.   Sir, my Lord Foppington gives his service, and if your honor's at leisure, he'll wait on you as soon as he's dressed.

L. MO.   Lord Foppington! is he in town?   465

SIR CHA.   Yes — I heard last night he was come. —— Give my service to his lordship, and tell him I shall be glad he'll do me the honor of his company here at dinner.   (*Exit Servant.*)   We may have occasion for him in our design upon Lady Betty.   470

L. MO.   What use can we make of him?

SIR CHA.   We'll see when he comes; at least there's no danger in him — not but I suppose you know he's your rival.

L. MO.   Pshah! a coxcomb.   475

SIR CHA.   Nay, don't despise him, neither — he's able to give you advice; for though he's in love with the same woman, yet to him she has not charms enough to give a minute's pain.

L. MO.   Prithee, what sense has he of love?   480

SIR CHA.   Faith, very near as much as a man of sense ought to have.   I grant you he knows not how to value a woman truly deserving, but he has a pretty just esteem for most ladies about town.

L. MO.   — That he follows, I grant you —   485 for he seldom visits any of extraordinary reputation.

SIR CHA.   Have a care — I have seen him at Lady Betty Modish's.

L. MO.   To be laughed at.

SIR CHA.   Don't be too confident of that: the   490 women now begin to laugh *with* him, not *at* him, for he really sometimes rallies his own humor with so much ease and pleasantry that a great many women begin to think he has no follies at all, and those he has have been as much owing to his   495 youth and a great estate as want of natural wit. 'Tis true, he's often a bubble to his pleasures, but he has always been wisely vain enough to keep himself from being too much the ladies' humble servant in love.   500

L. MO.   There indeed I almost envy him.

SIR CHA.   The easiness of his opinion upon the sex will go near to pique you.   We must have him.

L. MO.   As you please — but what shall we do with ourselves till dinner?   505

SIR CHA.   What think you of a party at piquet?

L. MO.   Oh, you are too hard for me.

SIR CHA.   Fie! fie! what, when you play with his grace?

L. Mo. Upon my soul, he gives me three 510 points.

Sir Cha. Does he? why then you shall give me but two. — Here, fellow, get cards. — *Allons.*

Exeunt.

ACT II

Scene I

The scene, Lady Betty Modish's *lodgings.*

Enter Lady Betty *and* Lady Easy, *meeting.*

L. Bet. Oh, my dear! I am overjoyed to see you. I am strangely happy today; I have just received my new scarf from London, and you are most critically [1] come to give me your opinion of it.

L. Ea. Oh, your servant, madam! I am a very 5 indifferent judge, you know. What, is it with sleeves?

L. Bet. Oh, 'tis impossible to tell you what it is. 'Tis all extravagance both in mode and fancy; my dear, I believe there's six thousand yards of 10 edging in it — then such an enchanting slope from the elbow —— something so new, so lively, so noble, so coquet and charming —— but you shall see it, my dear ——

L. Ea. Indeed I won't, my dear; I am re- 15 solved to mortify you for being so wrongly fond of a trifle.

L. Bet. Nay, now, my dear, you are ill-natured.

L. Ea. Why truly, I'm half angry to see a woman of your sense so warmly concerned in the care of 20 her outside; for when we have taken our best pains about it, 'tis the beauty of the mind alone that gives us lasting value.

L. Bet. Ah, my dear, my dear! you have been a married woman to a fine purpose indeed, that 25 know so little of the taste of mankind. Take my word, a new fashion upon a fine woman is often a greater proof of her value than you are aware of.

L. Ea. That I can't comprehend; for you see among the men nothing's more ridiculous than 30 a new fashion: those of the first sense are always the last that come into 'em.

L. Bet. That is because the only merit of a man is his sense, but doubtless the greatest value of a woman is her beauty; an homely woman at the head of a 35 fashion would not be allowed in it by the men, and consequently not followed by the women, so that to be successful in one's fancy is an evident sign of one's being admired, and I always take admiration for the best proof of beauty; and beauty certainly is the 40 source of power, as power in all creatures is the heighth of happiness.

[1] Opportunely.

L. Ea. At this rate you had rather be thought beautiful than good.

L. Bet. As I had rather command than obey. 45 The wisest homely woman can't make a man of sense of a fool, but the veriest fool of a beauty shall make an ass of a statesman —— so that, in short, I can't see a woman of spirit has any business in this world but to dress —— and make the men like her. 50

L. Ea. Do you suppose this is a principle the men of sense will admire you for?

L. Bet. I do suppose that when I suffer any man to like my person he shan't dare to find fault with my principle. 55

L. Ea. But men of sense are not so easily humbled.

L. Bet. The easiest of any: one has ten thousand times the trouble with a coxcomb.

L. Ea. Nay, that may be, for I have seen you throw away more good humor in hopes of a 60 *tendresse* [2] from my Lord Foppington, who loves all women alike, than would have made my Lord Morelove perfectly happy, who loves only you.

L. Bet. The men of sense, my dear, make the best fools in the world; their sincerity and good 65 breeding throws 'em so entirely into one's power, and gives one such an agreeable thirst of using 'em ill, to show that power —— 'tis impossible not to quench it.

L. Ea. But methinks my Lord Morelove's manner to you might move any woman to a kinder 70 sense of his merit.

L. Bet. Ay! but would it not be hard, my dear, for a poor weak woman to have a man of his quality and reputation in her power, and not let the world see him there? Would any creature sit new- 75 dressed all day in her closet? Could you bear to have a sweet-fancied suit and never show it at the play or the drawing-room?

L. Ea. But one would not ride in it, methinks, or harass it out when there's no occasion. 80

L. Bet. Pooh! my Lord Morelove's a mere Indian damask [3] —— one can't wear him out; o' my conscience, I must give him to my woman at last; I begin to be known by him. Had not I best leave him off, my dear? For (poor soul) I believe I have 85 a little fretted him of late.

L. Ea. Now, 'tis to me amazing, how a man of his spirit can bear to be used like a dog for four or five years together —— but nothing's a wonder in love. Yet pray, when you found you could not like 90 him at first, why did you ever encourage him?

L. Bet. Why, what would you have one do? for my part, I could no more choose a man by my eye,

[2] Display of affection.
[3] Damask, originally a silk cloth of elaborate design, made in Damascus, was later copied in other countries and in cheaper fabrics, such as wool and cotton.

19] QQ *I am.*　　　43] QQDD *would rather.*　　　44] QQ *good?*　　　74 QQ *not to let.*　　　79] QQDD *in't.*

than a shoe; one must draw 'em on a little to see if
they are right to one's foot.   95

L. Ea. But I'd no more fool on with a man I could
not like than I'd wear a shoe that pinched me.

L. Bet. Ay, but then a poor wretch tells one he'll
widen 'em or do anything, and is so civil and silly
that one does not know how to turn such a trifle   100
as a pair of shoes or an heart upon a fellow's hands
again.

L. Ea. Well! I confess you are very happily distinguished among most women of fortune, to have a
man of my Lord Morelove's sense and quality   105
so long and honorably in love with you, for nowadays
one hardly ever hears of such a thing as a man of
quality in love with the woman he would marry.
To be in love now is only having a design upon a
woman, a modish way of declaring war against   110
her virtue, which they generally attack first by toasting up her vanity.

L. Bet. Ay, but the world knows that is not the
case between my lord and me.

L. Ea. Therefore I think you happy.   115

L. Bet. Now I don't see it; I'll swear I'm better
pleased to know there are a great many foolish fellows of quality that take occasion to toast me frequently.

L. Ea. I vow I should not thank any gentle-   120
man for toasting me, and I have often wondered how
a woman of your spirit could bear a great many
other freedoms I have seen some men take with you.

L. Bet. As how, my dear? come, prithee be free
with me; for you must know I love dearly to   125
hear my faults. Who is't you have observed to be
too free with me?

L. Ea. Why, there's my Lord Foppington; could
any woman but you bear to see him with a respectful fleer stare full in her face, draw up his breath   130
and cry, 'Gad! you're handsome'?

L. Bet. My dear, fine fruit will have flies about it;
but, poor things, they do it no harm, for, if you observe, people are generally most apt to choose that
that the flies have been busy with —— ha! ha!   135

L. Ea. Thou art a strange, giddy creature.

L. Bet. That may be from so much circulation of
thought, my dear.

L. Ea. But my Lord Foppington's married, and
one would not fool with him for his lady's sake;   140
it may make her uneasy and ——

L. Bet. Poor creature, her pride indeed makes her
carry it off without taking any notice of it to me,
though I know she hates me in her heart, and I can't
endure malicious people, so I used to dine there   145
once a week, purely to give her disorder; if you had
but seen, when my lord and I fooled a little — the
creature looked so ugly.

L. Ea. But I should not think my reputation safe;
my Lord Foppington's a man that talks often   150
of his amours, but seldom speaks of favors that are
refused him.

L. Bet. Pshah! will anything a man says make a
woman less agreeable? Will his talking spoil one's
complexion, or put one's hair out of order? —   155
and for reputation, look you, my dear, take it for a
rule, that as amongst the lower rank of people no
woman wants beauty that has fortune, so amongst
people of fortune no woman wants virtue that has
beauty: but an estate and beauty joined is of an   160
unlimited, nay, a power pontifical — makes one not
only absolute, but infallible. A fine woman's never
in the wrong, or if we were, 'tis not the strength
of a poor creature's reason that can unfetter him.
Oh, how I love to hear a wretch curse himself   165
for loving on, or now and then coming out with
a ——

> Yet, for the plague of human race,
> This devil has an angel's face.

L. Ea. At this rate I don't see you allow   170
reputation to be at all essential to a fine woman.

L. Bet. Just as much as honor to a great man.
Power always is above scandal: don't you hear people
say the King of France owes most of his conquests
to breaking his word? and would not the con-   175
federates [1] have a fine time on't if they were only to
go to war with reproaches? Indeed, my dear, that
jewel reputation is a very fanciful business; one shall
not see an homely creature in town but wears it in
her mouth as monstrously as the Indians do   180
bobs [2] at their lips, and it really becomes 'em just alike.

L. Ea. Have a care, my dear, of trusting too far to
power alone, for nothing is more ridiculous than the
fall of pride, and woman's pride at best may be suspected to be more a distrust than a real con-   185
tempt of mankind. For when we have said all we can,
a deserving husband is certainly our best happiness,
and I don't question but my Lord Morelove's merit,
in a little time, will make you think so too; for whatever airs you give yourself to the world, I am   190
sure your heart don't want good nature.

L. Bet. You are mistaken: I am very ill-natured,
though your good humor won't let you see it.

L. Ea. Then to give me a proof on't, let me see
you refuse to go immediately and dine with me,   195
after I have promised Sir Charles to bring you.

L. Bet. Pray don't ask me.

L. Ea. Why?

L. Bet. Because, to let you see I hate good nature,

---

[1] The allies in the War of the Spanish Succession — England,
Holland, and the Emperor.
[2] Pendants.

134] QQ *are always most.*   160] DD *are of.*   161] DD *make.*   181] DD *them.*
182-183] QQ *of being too eagerly fond of power: for.*

I'll go without asking, that you mayn't have   200
the malice to say I did you a favor.

L. EA. Thou art a mad creature.

Exeunt arm in arm.

[SCENE II]

The scene changes to SIR CHARLES's *lodgings.*

LORD MORELOVE *and* SIR CHARLES *at piquet.*

SIR CHA. Come, my lord, one single game for the
tout,[1] and so have done.

L. MO. No, hang 'em, I have enough of 'em: ill
cards are the dullest company in the world. How
much is it?   5

SIR CHA. Three parties.[2]

L. MO. Fifteen pound —— very well.

(*While* LORD MORELOVE *counts out his money,
a Servant gives* SIR CHARLES *a letter, which he
reads to himself.*)

SIR CHA. (*to the Servant*). Give my service; say I
have company dines with me: if I have time, I'll call
there in the afternoon — ha! ha! ha!   10

Exit Servant.

L. MO. What's the matter? (*Paying the money.*)
There!

SIR CHA. The old affair — my Lady Graveairs.

L. MO. Oh! prithee, how does that go on?

SIR CHA. As agreeably as a chancery suit, for   15
now it's come to the intolerable plague of my not
being able to get rid on't, as you may see.

(*Giving the letter.*)

L. MO. (*reads*). 'Your behavior since I came to
Windsor has convinced me of your villainy without
my being surprised or angry at it: I desire you   20
would let me see you at my lodgings immediately,
where I shall have a better opportunity to convince
you that I never can, or positively will be as I have
been, Yours,' etc. A very whimsical letter! faith,
I think she has hard luck with you. If a man   25
were obliged to have a mistress, her person and condition seem to be cut out for the ease of a lover, for
she's a young, handsome, wild, well-jointured widow.
But what's your quarrel?

SIR CHA. Nothing — she sees the coolness   30
happens to be first on my side, and her business with
me now, I suppose, is to convince me how heartily
she's vexed that she was not beforehand with me.

L. MO. Her pride and your indifference must occasion a pleasant scene, sure; what do you intend   35
to do?

SIR CHA. Treat her with a cool, familiar air, till I
pique her to forbid me her sight, and then take her
at her word.

L. MO. Very gallant and provoking.   40

Enter a Servant.

SERV. Sir, my Lord Foppington.   *Exit.*

SIR CHA. Oh! now, my lord, if you have a mind
to be let into the mystery of making love without
pain, here's one that's a master of the art, and shall
declaim to you ——   45

Enter LORD FOPPINGTON.

My dear Lord Foppington!

L. FOP. My dear agreeable! *Que je t'embrasse!
Pardi! Il y a cent ans que je ne t'ai vu.*[3] — My lord,
I am your lordship's most obedient humble serv-
ant.   50

L. MO. My lord, I kiss your hands. I hope we
shall have you here some time; you seem to have laid
in a stock of health to be in at the diversions of the
place. You look extremely well.

L. FOP. To see one's friends look so may eas-   55
ily give a *vermeil*[4] to one's complexion.

SIR CHA. Lovers in hope, my lord, always have a
visible *brillant*[5] in their eyes and air.

L. FOP. What dost thou mean, Charles!

SIR CHA. Come, come, confess what really   60
brought you to Windsor, now you have no business
there.

L. FOP. Why two hours, and six of the best nags
in Christendom, or the devil drive me.

L. MO. You make haste, my lord.   65

L. FOP. My lord, I always fly when I pursue. But
they are well kept indeed: I love to have creatures go
as I bid 'em. You have seen 'em, Charles, but so has
all the world: Foppington's long-tails are known in
every road in England.   70

SIR CHA. Well, my lord, but how came they to
bring you this road? You don't use to take these
irregular jaunts without some design in your head of
having more than nothing to do.

L. FOP. Pshah! pox! prithee, Charles, thou   75
know'st I am a fellow *sans conséquence,*[6] be where
I will.

SIR CHA. Nay, nay, this is too much among friends,
my lord. Come, come, we must have it: your real
business here?   80

---

[1] To give an opportunity for a complete victory.
[2] Games.

[3] Let me kiss thee. By Jove, it's a hundred years since I
saw thee last.
[4] Rosiness.   [5] Sparkle.   [6] Aimless.

202 s.d.] QQ om. arm in arm.   SCENE II. 11–12] QQ om. (Paying the money). *There!*   14] QQ *go forward? — here —*
22–23] QQ *to satisfy you.*   24] QQ om. etc.   28] QQ *well-jointed.*   31] QQ *of my side.*
41] QQ *Foppington's come.*   53] QQ *in stock.*   55] QQDD *so, my lord, nay.*
60] QQ *come, my lord, confess.*   61–62] QQ *business here.*   75] QQ *Pshah! prithee pox! Charles.*
78–79] QQ *Nay, nay, we must have it — come, come, your real.*

L. Fop. Why then, *entre nous*, there is a certain *fille de joie* about the court here that loves winning at cards better than all the fine things I have been able to say to her, so I have brought an odd thousand [pound] bill in my pocket that I design *tête-a-tête* 85 to play off with her at piquet, or so; and now the business is out.

Sir Cha. Ah! and a very good business, too, my lord.

L. Fop. If it be well done, Charles. 90

Sir Cha. That's as you manage your cards, my lord.

L. Mo. This must be a woman of consequence, by the value you set upon her favors.

Sir Cha. Oh, nothing's above the price of a 95 fine woman.

L. Fop. Nay, look you, gentlemen, the price may not happen to be altogether so high, neither, for I fancy I know enough of the game to make it but an even bet I get her for nothing. 100

L. Mo. How so, my lord?

L. Fop. Because, if she happen to lose a good sum to me, I shall buy her with her own money.

L. Mo. That's new, I confess.

L. Fop. You know, Charles, 'tis not impos- 105 sible but I may be five hundred pound deep with her: then bills may fall short, and the devil's in't if I want assurance to ask her to pay me some way or other.

Sir Cha. And a man must be a churl indeed, 110 that won't take a lady's personal security — ha! ha! ha!

L. Fop. Heh! heh! heh! thou art a devil, Charles.

L. Mo. (*aside*). Death! how happy is this cox-comb! 115

L. Fop. But to tell you the truth, gentlemen, I had another pressing temptation that brought me hither, which was — my wife.

L. Mo. That's kind, indeed. My lady has been here this month: she'll be glad to see you. 120

L. Fop. That I don't know, for I design this after-noon to send her to London.

L. Mo. What! the same day you come, my lord? — that would be cruel.

L. Fop. Ay, but it will be mighty conven- 125 ient, for she is positively of no manner of use in my amours.

L. Mo. That's your fault: the town thinks her a very deserving woman.

L. Fop. If she were a woman of the town, 130 perhaps I should think so too; but she happens to be my wife, and when a wife is once given to deserve

more than her husband's inclinations can pay, in my mind she has no merit at all.

L. Mo. She's extremely well bred, and of a 135 very prudent conduct.

L. Fop. Um — ay — the woman's proud enough.

L. Mo. Add to this, all the world allows her hand-some.

L. Fop. The world's extremely civil, my 140 lord; and I should take it as a favor done to me if they could find an expedient to unmarry the poor woman from the only man in the world that can't think her handsome.

L. Mo. I believe there are a great many in 145 the world that are sorry 'tis not in their power to unmarry her.

L. Fop. I am a great many in the world's very humble servant, and whenever they find 'tis in their power, their high and mighty wisdoms may 150 command me at a quarter of an hour's warning.

L. Mo. Pray, my lord, what did you marry for?

L. Fop. To pay my debts at play, and disinherit my younger brother.

L. Mo. But there are some things due to a 155 wife.

L. Fop. And there are some debts I don't care to pay — to both which I plead husband and my lord.

L. Mo. If I should do so, I should expect to have my own coach stopped in the street, and to 160 meet my wife with the windows up in a hackney.

L. Fop. Then would I put in bail, and order a separate maintenance.

L. Mo. So pay double the sum of the debt, and be married for nothing. 165

L. Fop. Now I think deferring a dun and getting rid of one's wife are two the most agreeable sweets in the liberties of an English subject.

L. Mo. If I were married, I would as soon part from my estate, as my wife. 170

L. Fop. Now I would not, sunburn me if I would.

L. Mo. Death! But since you are thus indiffer-ent, my lord, why would you needs marry a woman of so much merit? Could not you have laid out your spleen upon some ill-natured shrew that wanted 175 the plague of an ill husband, and have let her alone to some plain, honest man of quality that would have deserved her?

L. Fop. Why, faith, my lord, that might have been considered; but I really grew so passionately 180 fond of her fortune that, curse catch me, I was quite blind to the rest of her good qualities: for to tell you the truth, if it had been possible the old putt of a peer could have tossed me in t'other five thousand

85] Q2PDD om. *pound.*   93] QQ *of some consequence.*   95] QQ *Sir Cha. Pshah! nothing's.*

98] QQ *for, all this while, I.*   100] QQ *bet, that I.*   102] QQ *happens.*   120] QQ *this fortnight.*

133] QQ *husband can.*   138] QQ *And to this.*   140] QQ *very civil.*

172] QQ *Death! my lord, but.*   172–173] QQ *indifferent, why.*   180] QQ om. *so.*

183] QQ *it were possible.*   184–185] QQ *toss'd her into t'other five thousand pound for 'em.*

for 'em, by my consent she should have relin- 185 quished her merit and virtues to any of her younger sisters.

Sir Cha. Ay, ay, my lord, virtues in a wife are good for nothing but to make her proud, and put the world in mind of her husband's faults.   190

L. Fop. Right, Charles! and strike me blind, but the women of virtue are now grown such idiots in love, they expect of a man, just as they do of a coach-horse, that one's appetite, like t'other's flesh, should increase by feeding.   195

Sir Cha. Right, my lord! and don't consider that *toujours chapons bouillés*¹ will never do with an English stomach.

L. Fop. Ha! ha! ha! To tell you the truth, Charles, I have known so much of that sort of   200 eating that I now think, for an hearty meal no wild-fowl in Europe is comparable to a joint of Banstead mutton.²

L. Mo. How do you mean?

L. Fop. Why, that for my part, I had rather   205 have a plain slice of my wife's woman than my guts full of e'er an ortolan³ duchess in Christendom.

L. Mo. But I thought, my lord, your chief busi-ness now at Windsor had been your design upon a woman of quality.   210

L. Fop. That's true, my lord; though I don't think your fine lady the best dish myself, yet a man of quality can't be without such things at his table.

L. Mo. Oh! then you only desire the reputation of an affair with her?   215

L. Fop. I think the reputation is the most inviting part of an amour with most women of quality.

L. Mo. Why so, my lord?

L. Fop. Why, who the devil would run through all the degrees of form and ceremony that lead one   220 up to the last favor, if it were not for the reputation of understanding the nearest way to get over the difficulty?

L. Mo. But, my lord, does not the reputation of your being so general an undertaker frighten   225 the women from engaging with you? for they say no man can love but one at a time.

L. Fop. That's just one more than ever I came up to, for [stap] my breath if ever I loved one in my life.

L. Mo. How do you get 'em, then?   230

L. Fop. Why, sometimes as they get other people; I dress, and let 'em get me; or, if that won't do, as I got my title, I buy 'em.

L. Mo. But how can you, that profess indiffer-ence, think it worth your while to come so often   235 up to the price of a woman of quality?

L. Fop. Because you must know, my lord, that most of them begin now to come down to reason; I mean those that are to be had, for some die fools. But with the wiser sort 'tis not of late so very   240 expensive; now and then a *partie carrée*,⁴ a jaunt or two in a hack to an Indian house,⁵ a little china, an odd thing for a gown, or so, and in three days after you meet her at the conveniency of trying it [on] *chez Madamoiselle D'Épingle*.⁶   245

Sir Cha. Ay, ay, my lord, and when you are there, you know, what between a little chat, a dish of tea, madamoiselle's good humor, and a *petit chanson*⁷ or two, the devil's in't if a man can't fool away the time till he sees how it looks upon her by candle-   250 light.

L. Fop. Heh! heh! well said, Charles! Igad, I fancy thee and I have unlaced many a reputation there— your great lady is as soon undressed as her woman.

L. Mo. I could never find it so — the shame   255 or scandal of a repulse always made me afraid of attempting a woman of condition.

Sir. Cha. Ha! ha! Igad, my lord, you deserve to be ill used; your modesty's enough to spoil any woman in the world: but my lord and I under-   260 stand the sex a little better; we see plainly that women are only cold. as some men are brave, from the modesty or fear of those that attack 'em.

L. Fop. Right, Charles! — a man should no more give up his heart to a woman than his sword to   265 a bully; they are both as insolent as the devil after it.

Sir Cha. (*aside to* Lord Morelove). How do you like that, my lord?

L. Mo. Faith, I envy him. —— But, my lord, sup-pose your inclination should stumble upon a   270 woman truly virtuous, would not a severe repulse from such an one put you strangely out of counte-nance?

L. Fop. Not at all, my lord, for if a man don't mind a box o' the ear in a fair struggle with a   275 fresh country girl, why the deuce should he be con-cerned at an impertinent frown for an attack upon a woman of quality?

L. Mo. Then you have no notion of a lady's cruelty?   280

L. Fop. Ha! ha! let me blood, if I think there's a greater jest in nature. I am ready to crack my guts

¹ Always boiled capon; i.e., a monotonous diet.
² Banstead (now Epsom) Downs, near London, was a center for sheep-raising.
³ A small bird of delicate flavor, regarded as a luxury.
⁴ A party of two men and two women.
⁵ A shop for the sale of Indian wares.
⁶ At Madam Pin's (a 'label' name for a dress-maker).
⁷ Little song.

208] QQ om. *chief.*   214–215] QQ *of having an affair.*
224] QQ *my lord, since the world sees you make so little of the difficulty, does not.*   225] QQ *being too general.*
229] QQ *stap*; PDD *stop.*   232] QQDD *them.*   238] QQ *'em.*   244] QQ *trying it on*; PDD om. *on.*
250–251] QQ *candle-light, ha! ha!*   254] QQ *woman, ha! ha!*   271] QQ *a formal repulse.*
275] QQ *on the ear.*   276] QQ *why the devil.*

with laughing to see a senseless flirt, because the creature happens to have a little pride that she calls
virtue about her, give herself all the insolent   285
airs of resentment and disdain to an honest fellow
that all the while does not care three pinches of snuff
if she and her virtue were to run with their last
favors through the first regiment of guards — ha! ha!
it puts me in mind of an affair of mine, so im-   290
pertinent ——

L. Mo. Oh, that's impossible, my lord! — pray
let's hear it.

L. Fop. Why, I happened once to be very well in
a certain man of quality's family, and his wife   295
liked me.

L. Mo. How do you know she liked you?

L. Fop. Why, from the very moment I told her I
liked her she never durst trust herself at the end of a
room with me.   300

L. Mo. That might be her not liking you.

L. Fop. My lord, women of quality don't use to
speak the thing plain; but to satisfy you I did not
want encouragement, I never came there in my life
but she did immediately smile and borrow my   305
snuff-box.

L. Mo. She liked your snuff at least. Well, but
how did she use you?

L. Fop. By all that's infamous, she jilted me.

L. Mo. How! Jilt you?   310

L. Fop. Ay, death's curse! she jilted me.

L. Mo. Pray let's hear.

L. Fop. For when I was pretty well convinced she
had a mind to me, I one day made her a hint of an
appointment: upon which, with an insolent   315
frown in her face (that made her look as ugly as the
devil) she told me that if ever I came thither again
her lord should know that she had forbidden me the
house before. Did you ever hear of such a slut?

Sir Cha. Intolerable!   320

L. Mo. But how did her answer agree with you?

L. Fop. Oh, passionately well, for I stared full in
her face and burst out a-laughing, at which she
turned upon her heel, gave a crack with her fan like a
coach-whip, and bridled out of the room with   325
the air and complexion of an incensed turkey-cock.

(A Servant whispers Sir Charles.)

L. Mo. What did you then?

L. Fop. I — looked after her, gaped, threw up the
sash, and fell a-singing out of the window — so that
you see, my lord, while a man is not in love,   330
there's no great affliction in missing one's way to a
woman.

Sir Cha. Ay, ay, you talk this very well, my lord;
but now let's see how you dare behave yourself upon

action; dinner's served, and the ladies stay for   335
us: there's one within has been too hard for as brisk
a man as yourself.

L. Mo. I guess who you mean. — Have a care, my
lord: she'll prove your courage for you.

L. Fop. Will she! then she's an undone crea-   340
ture. For let me tell you, gentlemen, courage is the
whole mystery of making love, and of more use than
conduct is in war; for the bravest fellow in Europe
may beat his brains out against the stubborn walls
of a town — but ——   345

  Women, born to be controlled,
  Stoop to the forward and the bold.   *Exeunt.*

ACT III

Scene I

The scene continues.

Enter Lord Morelove *and* Sir Charles.

L. Mo. So! Did not I bear up bravely?

Sir Cha. Admirably! with the best bred insolence
in nature! You insulted like a woman of quality
when her country-bred husband's jealous of her in
the wrong place.   5

L. Mo. Ha! ha! Did you observe, when I first came
into the room, how carelessly she brushed her eyes
over me, and when the company saluted me, stood
all the while with her face to the window? ha! ha!

Sir Cha. What astonished airs she gave her-   10
self when you asked her what made her so grave
upon her old friends.

L. Mo. And whenever I offered anything in talk,
what affected care she took to direct her observations of it to a third person.   15

Sir Cha. I observed she did not eat above the
rump of a pigeon all dinner time.

L. Mo. And how she colored when I told her her
ladyship had lost her stomach!

Sir Cha. If you keep your temper she's un-   20
done.

L. Mo. Provided she sticks to her pride, I believe
I may.

Sir Cha. Ah! never fear her; I warrant, in the
humor she is in she would as soon part with her   25
sense of feeling.

L. Mo. Well! what's to be done next?

Sir Cha. Only observe her motions; for by her
behavior at dinner I am sure she designs to gall you
with my Lord Foppington; if so, you must even   30
stand her fire, and then play my Lady Graveairs
upon her, whom I'll immediately pique and prepare
for your purpose.

294] QQ *to be well.*   299-300] QQ *of the room.*   303] QQ *satisfy you, that I.*
304-305] QQ *life, that she did not immediately.*   319] QQ *before, ha! ha!*   322] QQ om. *Oh.*
323] QQ *busted.*   324] DD *heel, and gave.*   336] QQ *within, that has.*   338] QQ *I know whom.*
342] QQ *mystery of love.*

L. Mo. I understand you — the properest woman in the world, too, for she'll certainly encourage 35 the least offer from me, in hopes of revenging her slights upon you.

Sir Cha. Right! and the very encouragement she gives you, at the same time will give me a pretence to widen the breach of my quarrel to her. 40

L. Mo. Besides, Charles, I own I am fond of any attempt that will forward a misunderstanding there, for your lady's sake: a woman so truly good in her nature ought to have something more from a man than bare occasions to prove her goodness. 45

Sir Cha. Why then, upon honor, my lord, to give you proof that I am positively the best husband in the world, my wife — never yet found me out.

L. Mo. That may be her being the best wife in the world: she, may be, won't find you out. 50

Sir Cha. Nay, if she won't tell a man of his faults when she sees 'em, how the deuce should he mend 'em? But however, you see I am going to leave 'em off as fast as I can.

L. Mo. Being tired of a woman is indeed a 55 pretty tolerable assurance of a man's not designing to fool on with her. —— Here she comes, and, if I don't mistake, brimful of reproaches. You can't take her in a better time —— I'll leave you.

Enter Lady Graveairs.

Your ladyship's most humble servant! is the 60 company broke up, pray?

L. Gra. No, my lord, they are just talking of basset;[1] my Lord Foppington has a mind to tally, if your lordship would encourage the table.

L. Mo. O madam, with all my heart! But 65 Sir Charles, I know, is hard to be got to it; I'll leave your ladyship to prevail with him.

Exit Lord Morelove.

(Sir Charles *and* Lady Graveairs *salute coldly, and trifle some time before they speak.*)

L. Gra. Sir Charles, I sent you a note this morning ——

Sir Cha. Yes, madam, but there were some 70 passages I did not expect from your ladyship; you seemed to tax me with things that ——

L. Gra. Look you, sir, 'tis not at all material whether I taxed you with anything or no: I don't in the least desire to hear you clear yourself; upon 75 my word, you may be very easy as to that matter; for my part, I am mighty well satisfied things are as they are; all I have to say to you is that you need not give yourself the trouble to call at my lodgings this

[1] A card game for five persons, popular with gamblers.

afternoon, if you should have time, as you were 80 pleased to send me word — and so your servant, sir! — that's all. (*Going.*)

Sir Cha. Hold, madam.

L. Gra. Look you, Sir Charles, 'tis not your calling me back that will signify anything, I can 85 assure you.

Sir Cha. Why this extraordinary haste, madam?

L. Gra. In short, Sir Charles, I have taken a great many things from you of late that you know I have often told you I would positively bear no longer: 90 but I see things are in vain, and the more people strive to oblige people, the less they are thanked for't. And since there must be an end of one's ridiculousness one time or other, I don't see any time so proper as the present, and therefore, sir, I desire you 95 would think of things accordingly — your servant!

(*Going: he holds her.*)

Sir Cha. Nay, madam, let's start fair, however; you ought at least to stay till I am as ready as your ladyship, and then — if we must part ——

(*Affectedly.*)

Adieu, ye silent grots and shady groves,   100
Ye soft amusements of our growing loves!
Adieu, ye whispered sighs that fanned the fire,
And all the thrilling joys of young desire!

L. Gra. Oh, mighty well, sir! I am very glad we are at last come to a right understanding, the 105 only way I have long wished for; not but I'd have you to know I see your design through all your painted ease of resignation; I know you would give your soul to make me uneasy now.

Sir Cha. Oh fie, madam!—upon my word, I 110 would not make you uneasy if it were in my power.

L. Gra. O dear sir, you need not take such care, upon my word; you'll find I can part with you without the least disorder —— I'll try, at least; and so once more, and forever, sir, your servant! Not 115 but you must give me leave to tell you, as my last thought of you, too, that I do think — you are a villain. *Exit hastily.*

Sir Cha. (*bowing low*). Oh, your very humble servant, madam! —— What a charming qual- 120 ity is a woman's pride, that's strong enough to refuse a man her favors, when he's weary of 'em — ah!

Lady Graveairs *returns.*

L. Gra. Look you, Sir Charles, don't presume upon the easiness of my temper: for to convince you that I am positively in earnest in this matter, 125 I desire you would let me have what letters you have had of mine since you came to Windsor, and I expect

36–37] QQ *her late slights.*   46–47] QQ *give you a proof.*   62] QQ *they were just.*
77–78] QQ *satisfied, that things . . . all that I.*   78] QQ om. *not.*
95–96] Q1 *you would things*; Q2 *you'd dispose things*; DD *you'd think of things.*   96] QQ om. stage direction.
98–99] QQ *till I have got it in my head too, and*; DD *till I'm as ready as your ladyship, and.*   100] QQ *you silent.*
102] QQ *the whisper'd.*   107–108] QQ *all this painted.*   108–109] QQ *you'd give your eyes*; DD *you'd give your soul.*

you'll return the rest, as I will yours, as soon as we come to London.

SIR CHA. Upon my faith, madam, I never 130 keep any; I always put snuff in 'em, and so they wear out.

L. GRA. Sir Charles, I must have 'em, for positively I won't stir without 'em.

SIR CHA. (*aside*). Ha! Then I must be civil, 135 I see. —— Perhaps, madam, I have no mind to part with them — or you.

L. GRA. Look you, sir, all those sort of things are in vain, now there's an end of everything between us. If you say you won't give 'em, I must 140 even get 'em as well as I can.

SIR CHA. (*aside*). Ha! that won't do then, I find.

L. GRA. Who's there? Mrs. Edging? —— Your keeping a letter, sir, won't keep me, I'll assure you.

Enter EDGING.

EDG. Did your ladyship call me, madam?   145

L. GRA. Ay, child, pray do me the favor to fetch my scarf out of the dining-room.

EDG. Yes, madam ——

SIR CHA. (*aside*). Oh! then there's hope again.

EDG. (*aside*). Ha! she looks as if my mas- 150 ter had quarreled with her; I hope she's going away in a huff — she shan't stay for her scarf, I warrant her. This is pure.[1]   *Exit smiling.*

L. GRA. Pray, Sir Charles, before I go, give me leave now, after all, to ask you — why you 155 have used me thus?

SIR CHA. What is't you call usage, madam?

L. GRA. Why then, since you will have it, how comes it you have been so grossly careless and neglectful of me of late? Only tell me seriously 160 wherein I have deserved this.

SIR CHA. Why then, seriously, madam ——

Re-enter EDGING *with a scarf.*

We are interrupted.

EDG. Here's your ladyship's scarf, madam.

L. GRA. Thank you, Mrs. Edging —— Oh 165 law! pray will you let somebody get me a chair to the door?

EDG. [*aside*]. Humh! she might have told me that before, if she had been in such haste to go.   *Exit.*

L. GRA. Now, sir.   170

SIR CHA. Then seriously, I say, I am of late grown so very lazy in my pleasures that I had rather lose a woman than go through the plague and trouble of having or keeping her; and to be free, I have found

[1] Excellent.

so much even in my acquaintance with you, 175 whom I confess to be a mistress in the art of pleasing, that I am from henceforth resolved to follow no pleasure that rises above the degree of amusement — and that woman that expects I should make her my business, why — like my business, is then in a 180 fair way of being forgot. When once she comes to reproach me with vows, and usage, and stuff, I had as lief hear her talk of bills, bonds and ejectments; her passion becomes as troublesome as a law suit, and I would as soon converse with my solicitor. In 185 short, I shall never care sixpence for any woman that won't be obedient.

L. GRA. I'll swear, sir, you have a very free way of treating people; I am glad I am so well acquainted with your principles, however. And you'd 190 have me obedient?

SIR CHA. Why not? my wife's so, and I think she has as much pretence to be proud as your ladyship.

L. GRA. Lard! is there no chair to be had, I wonder?   195

Enter EDGING.

EDG. Here's a chair, madam.

L. GRA. 'Tis very well, Mrs. Edging — pray will you let somebody get me a glass of fair[2] water?

EDG. [*aside*]. Humh! her huff's almost over, I suppose. I see he is a villain still.   *Exit.* 200

L. GRA. Well, that was the prettiest fancy about obedience, sure, that ever was! Certainly a woman of condition must be infinitely happy under the dominion of so generous a lover! But how came you to forget kicking and whipping all this while? 205 methinks you should not have left so fashionable an article out of your scheme of government.

SIR CHA. Um! — no, there's too much trouble in that, though I have known 'em of admirable use in the reformation of some humorsome gentlewomen. 210

L. GRA. But one thing more and I have done. Pray, what degree of spirit must the lady have that is to make herself happy under so much freedom, order and tranquility?

SIR CHA. Oh, she must at least have as 215 much spirit as your ladyship, or she'd give me no pleasure in breaking it.

L. GRA. No, that would be troublesome. You had better take one that's broken to your hand — there are such souls to be hired, I believe — things 220 that will rub your temples in an evening till you fall fast asleep in their laps — creatures, too, that think their wages their reward; I fancy, at last that will

[2] Pure.

135] QQ om. (aside).   141] DD *e'en.*   142] QQ om. (aside).   144] Q1 *keeping letter;* Q2 *keeping-letter.*
147] QQ *my hood and scarf.*   149] QQ om. (aside).   153] QQ Exit. After some pause Lady Graveairs speaks.
157] QQDD *is it.*   161] QQ *deserved it.*   162 s.d.] QQ om. with a scarf.
168–169] QQ *that at first, if.*   171] QQ *Why then.*   177–178] QQ *no diversion that rises;* DD *no pleasure that arises.*
178] QQ *of an amusement.*   199] QQ *Hah! her.*   200] QQDD *he's.*
218] QQ *Oh! that . . . troublesome — No, you.*

be the best method for the lazy passion of a married man that has outlived his any other sense of gratification. 225

SIR CHA. Look you, madam, I have loved you very well a great while: now you would have me love you better and longer, which is not in my power to do; and I don't think there's any plague upon 230 earth like a dun that comes for more money than one's ever likely to be able to pay.

L. GRA. A dun! do you take me for a dun, sir? do I come a-dunning to you?   (*Walks in an heat.*)

SIR CHA. H'st! don't expose yourself — 235 here's company.

L. GRA. I care not — a dun! You shall see, sir, I can revenge an affront, though I despise the wretch that offers it. A dun! Oh! I could die with laughing at the fancy.   *Exit.* 240

SIR CHA. So! she's in admirable order. Here comes my lord, and, I'm afraid, in the very nick of his occasion for her.

Enter LORD MORELOVE.

L. MO. Oh, Charles! Undone again! all's lost and ruined.   245

SIR CHA. What's the matter now?

L. MO. I have been playing the fool yonder even to contempt; my senseless jealousy has confessed a weakness I never shall forgive myself. She has insulted on it to that degree, too — I can't bear 250 the thought —— O Charles! this devil still is mistress of my heart, and I could dash my brains to think how grossly too I have let her know it.

SIR CHA. Ah! how it would tickle her if she saw you in this condition: ha! ha! ha!   255

L. MO. Prithee don't torture me: think of some present ease, or I shall burst.

SIR CHA. Well, well, let's hear, pray! — what has she done to you? ha! ha!

L. MO. Why, ever since I left you she treated 260 me with so much coolness and ill nature, and that thing of a lord with so much laughing ease, such an acquainted, such a spiteful familiarity, that at the last she saw and triumphed in my uneasiness.

SIR CHA. Well! and so you left the room in a 265 pet? ha!

L. MO. Oh, worse, worse still! for at last, with half shame and anger in my looks, I thrust myself between my lord and her, pressed her by the hand, and, in a whisper, trembling, begged her, in pity of 270 herself and me, to show her good humor only where she knew it was truly valued; at which she broke from me with a cold smile, sat her down by the peer,

whispered him, and burst into a loud laughter in my face.   275

SIR CHA. Ha! ha! then would I have given fifty pound to have seen your face. Why, what, in the name of common sense, had you to do with humility? Will you never have enough on't? Death! 'twas setting a lighted match to gunpowder to blow 280 yourself up.

L. MO. I see my folly now, Charles — but what shall I do with the small remains of life that she has left me?

SIR CHA. (*in a whining tone*). Oh, throw it 285 at her feet, by all means, put on your tragedy face, catch fast hold of her petticoat, whip out your handkerchief, and in point-blank verse desire her one way or other to make an end of the business.

L. MO. What a fool dost thou make me!   290

SIR CHA. I only show you as you come out of her hands, my lord.

L. MO. How contemptibly have I behaved myself!

SIR CHA. That's according as you bear her behavior.   295

L. MO. Bear it! no! I thank thee, Charles; thou hast waked me now, and if I bear it ——! What have you done with my Lady Graveairs?

SIR CHA. Your business, I believe — she's ready for you; she's just gone downstairs, and if you 300 don't make haste after her, I expect her back again with a knife or a pistol, presently.

L. MO. I'll go this minute.

SIR CHA. No, stay a little, here comes my lord: we'll see what we can get out of him first.   305

L. MO. Methinks I now could laugh at her.

Enter LORD FOPPINGTON.

L. FOP. Nay, prithee, Sir Charles, let's have a little of thee — we have been so *chagrin* [1] without thee that, stap my breath, the ladies are gone half asleep to church for want of thy company.   310

SIR CHA. That's hard indeed, while your lordship was among 'em. Is Lady Betty gone too?

L. FOP. She was just upon the wing; but I caught her by the snuff-box, and she pretends to stay to see if I'll give it her again, or no.   315

L. MO. (*aside to* SIR CHARLES). Death! 'tis that I gave her, and the only present she ever would receive from me. Ask him how he came by it.

SIR CHA. Prithee don't be uneasy. —— Did she give it you, my lord?   320

L. FOP. Faith, Charles, I can't say she did, or she did not, but we were playing the fool, and I took

[1] Dull.

227] QQ *madam, I have told you that reproaches will never do your business with me: I have loved.*   235] QQ *S't!*
253] QQ *I've.*   256–257] QQ *some remedy for present.*   249] QQ om. *ha! ha!*   260] QQ *she has treated.*
261] QQ *ill humor.*   263–264] QQ *that she at last saw.*   266] QQ om. *ha!*
268–269] QQ *before my lord, pressed.*   273] Q1 *sate.*   283] QQDD om. *small.*
285] QQ om. (in a whining tone).   288] Q1 *handkercher.*   290] QQ *L. MO.* (smiling).
309] D9 *stop.*   315] QQ om. *her.*

it — *à la* — pshah!　I can't tell thee in French, neither, but Horace touches it to a nicety — 'twas *pignus direptum male pertinaci.*[1]　　325

L. Mo. [*aside*]. So! but I must bear it. — If your lordship has a mind to the box, I'll stand by you in the keeping of it.

L. Fop. My lord, I am passionately obliged to you, but I am afraid I can't answer your hazard-　330 ing so much of the lady's favor.

L. Mo. Not at all, my lord: 'tis possible I may not have the same regard to her frown that your lordship has.

L. Fop. (*aside*). That's a bite,[2] I'm sure —　335 he'd give a joint of his little finger to be as well with her as I am. —— But here she comes.　Charles, stand by me!　Must not a man be a vain coxcomb, now, to think this creature followed one?

Sir Cha. Nothing so plain, my lord.　　340

L. Fop. Flattering devil!

Enter Lady Betty.

L. Bet. Pshah! my Lord Foppington!　Prithee don't play the fool, now, but give me my snuff-box. Sir Charles, help me to take it from him!

Sir Cha. You know I hate trouble, madam.　345

L. Bet. Pooh! you'll make me stay till prayers are half over now.

L. Fop. If you'll promise me not to go to church I'll give it you.

L. Bet. I'll promise nothing at all, for posi-　350 tively I will have it.　　(*Struggles with him.*)

L. Fop. Then comparatively I won't part with it — ha! ha!
　　　　　　　　　　　(*Struggling with her.*)

L. Bet. Oh, you devil! you have killed my arm! Oh!　Well — if you'll let me have it, I'll give　355 you a better.

L. Mo. (*aside to* Sir Charles). O Charles! that has a view of distant kindness in it.

L. Fop. Nay, now I keep it superlatively; I find there's a secret value in it.　　360

L. Bet. Oh, dismal! upon my word, I am only ashamed to give it you.　Do you think I would offer such an odious-fancied thing to anybody I had the least value for?

Sir Cha. (*aside to* Lord Morelove). Now　365 it comes a little nearer, methinks it does not seem to be any kindness at all.

L. Fop. Why, really, madam, upon second view, it has not extremely the mode of a lady's utensil; are you sure it never held anything but snuff?　370

[1] 'A pledge snatched from one who is not altogether unyielding' (*Odes,* I. ix. 23, 24).
[2] An untruth.

L. Bet. Oh! you monster!

L. Fop. Nay, I only ask because it seems to me to have very much the air and fancy of Monsieur Smoakandsot's tobacco-box.

L. Mo. [*aside to* Sir Charles]. I can bear no　375 more.

Sir Cha. Why, don't, then; I'll step into the company, and return to your relief immediately.
　　　　　　　　　　　　　　　Exit.

L. Mo. (*to* Lady Betty). Come, madam, will your ladyship give me leave to end the difference?　380 Since the slightness of the thing may let you bestow it without any mark of favor, shall I beg it of your ladyship?

L. Bet. Oh, my lord, nobody sooner! — I beg you give it my lord.　　385

　　(*Looking earnestly on* Lord Foppington, *who*
　　　smiling gives it to Lord Morelove, *and then*
　　　bows gravely to her.)

L. Mo. Only to have the honor of restoring it to your lordship; and if there be any other trifle of mine your lordship has a fancy to, though it were a mistress, I don't know any person in the world that has so good a claim to my resignation.　　390

L. Fop. O my lord, this generosity will distract me.

L. Mo. My lord, I do you but common justice; but from your conversation, I had never known the true value of the sex: you positively understand　395 'em the best of any man breathing, therefore I think every one of common prudence ought to resign to you.

L. Fop. Then positively your lordship's the most obliging person in the world, for I'm sure your judgment can never like any woman that is not the　400 finest creature in the universe.
　　　　　　　　　　(*Bowing to* Lady Betty.)

L. Mo. Oh!　Your lordship does me too much honor; I have the worst judgment in the world: no man has been more deceived in it.

L. Fop. Then your lordship, I presume, has　405 been apt to choose in a mask, or by candle-light.

L. Mo. In a mask indeed, my lord, and of all masks the most dangerous.

L. Fop. Pray, what's that, my lord?

L. Mo. A bare face.　　410

L. Fop. Your lordship will pardon me, if I don't so readily comprehend how a woman's bare face can hide her face.

L. Mo. It often hides her heart, my lord, and therefore I think it sometimes a more danger-　415 ous mask than a piece of velvet: that's rather a mark than a disguise of an ill woman.　But the

---

330] DD *cannot.*　　335–336] QQ *That's bite, I'm sure — I know he'd give;* DD *That's a bite, I am sure — he'd give.*
340] QQ Sir Cha. *Oh! Nothing.*　　344] QQ *from him.*　(Goes to L. Fop.).　　351] DD *Struggling.*
353] QQ om. *ha! ha!*　　353] DD *Struggles.*　　355] QQ *Well seriously.*　　378] QQ *relief, when there's occasion.*
385 s.d.] QQ *Looking very earnestly upon.*　　396] QQ *breathing, and therefore.*　　412] DD *really comprehend.*
415] QQ om. *sometimes.*

mischiefs skulking behind a beauteous form give no warning: they are always sure, fatal, and innumerable.   420

L. Bet. Oh, barbarous aspersion! My Lord Foppington, have you nothing to say for the poor women?

L. Fop. I must confess, madam, nothing of this nature ever happened in my course of amours: 425 I always judge the beauteous form of a woman to be the most agreeable part of her composition, and when once a lady does me the honor to toss that into my arms, I think myself obliged in good nature not to quarrel about the rest of her equipage.   430

L. Bet. Why, ay, my lord, there's some good humor in that, now.

L. Mo. He's happy in a plain English stomach, madam. I could recommend a dish that's perfectly to your lordship's gust,[1] where beauty is the   435 only sauce to it.

L. Bet. So!

L. Fop. My lord, when my wine's right, I never care it should be zested.[2]

L. Mo. I know some ladies would thank you   440 for that opinion.

L. Bet. My Lord Morelove's really grown such a churl to the women, I don't only think he is not, but can't conceive how he ever could be in love.

L. Mo. (smiling). Upon my word, madam,   445 I once thought I was.

L. Bet. Fie! fie! how could you think so? I fancy, now, you had only a mind to domineer over some poor creature, and so you thought you were in love, ha! ha!   450

L. Mo. The lady I loved, madam, grew so unfortunate in her conduct that she at last brought me to treat her with the same indifference and civility as I now pay your ladyship.

L. Bet. And ten to one, just at that time she   455 never thought you such tolerable company.

L. Mo. (mimicking her). That I can't say, madam, for at that time she grew so affected, there was no judging of her thoughts at all.

L. Bet. What! and so you left the poor   460 lady? Oh, you inconstant creature!

L. Mo. No, madam, to have loved her on had been inconstancy, for she was never two hours together the same woman.

(Lady Betty and Lord Morelove seem to talk.)

L. Fop. (aside). Ha! ha! ha! I see he has a   465

mind to abuse her, so I'll e'en give him an opportunity of doing his business with her at once forever.
—— My lord, I perceive your lordship's going to be good company to the lady, and for her sake I don't think it good manners in me to disturb you.   470

Enter Sir Charles.

Sir Cha. My Lord Foppington ——

L. Fop. O Charles! I was just wanting thee. Hark thee! — I have three thousand secrets for thee — I have made such discoveries — to tell thee all in one word, Morelove's as jealous of me   475 as the devil; heh! heh! heh!

Sir Cha. Is't possible? has she given him any occasion?

L. Fop. Only rallied him to death upon my account; she told me within, just now, she'd use   480 him like a dog, and begged me to draw off for an opportunity.

Sir Cha. Oh! Keep in [3] while the scent lies, and she's your own, my lord.

L. Fop. I can't tell that, Charles, but I'm   485 sure she's fairly unharbored,[4] and when I once throw off my inclinations I usually follow 'em till the game has enough on't; and between thee and I she's pretty well blown, too; she can't stand long, I believe, for curse catch me if I have not rid down   490 half a thousand pound after her already.

Sir Cha. What do you mean?

L. Fop. I have lost five hundred to her at piquet since dinner.

Sir Cha. You are a fortunate man, faith;   495 you are resolved not to be thrown out,[5] I see.

L. Fop. Hang it! what should a man come out for, if he does not keep up to the sport?

Sir Cha. Well pushed,[6] my lord.

L. Fop. Tayo! [7] Have at her!   500

Sir Cha. Down, down, my lord! — ah, 'ware hanches! [8]

L. Fop. Ay, Charles! (*Embracing him.*) Prithee let's observe a little: there's a foolish cur, now I have run her to a stand, has a mind to be at her by   505 himself, and thou shalt see she won't stir out of her way for him.   (*They stand aside.*)

L. Mo. Ha! ha! Your ladyship's very grave of a sudden; you look as if your lover had insolently recovered his common senses.   510

---

[1] Taste.
[2] Treated in a manner to make it more sparkling.

[3] The figures of speech in this and the next nine speeches are borrowed from the hunting field.
[4] Driven from cover.
[5] Thrown out of the hunt by losing the scent.
[6] Pressed forward.
[7] Tallyho!   [8] Beware of being bitten.

428] QQ *when a lady once does.*   429] QQ *oblig'd in honor not.*   437] QQ La. Bet. (Aside). *So!*
439] QQ *zested; a fine woman, like a fine oyster, needs no sauce but her own.*   456] QQ *company, ha! ha!*
457] QQ (Mimicking her manner).   465–466] QQ *Ha! ha! ha! he has a mind to abuse her, I find; so.*
466] QQDD *ev'n.*   470] QQ *disturb it.*   476] QQ *heh! heh! ha!*   486] QQD8 *once I.*
503] QQDD *Ah! Charles.*

L. Bet. And your lordship is so very gay and unlike yourself, one would swear you were just come from the pleasure of making your mistress afraid of you.

L. Mo. No, faith, quite contrary: for do you 515 know, madam, I have just found out that upon your account I have made myself one of the most ridiculous puppies upon the face of the earth —— I have, upon my faith! — nay, and so extravagantly such — ha! ha! ha! — that it's at last become 520 a jest even to myself, and I can't help laughing at it for the soul of me; ha! ha! ha!

L. Bet. (aside). I want to cure him of that laugh, now. —— My lord, since you are so generous, I'll tell you another secret: do you know, too, that 525 I still find, spite of all your great wisdom and my contemptible qualities, as you are pleased now and then to call 'em — do you know, I say, that I see under all this, you still love me with the same helpless passion; and can your vast foresight imagine I 530 won't use you accordingly for these extraordinary airs you are pleased to give yourself?

L. Mo. Oh, by all means, madam! 'tis fit you should, and I expect it, whenever it is in your power. (Aside.) Confusion! 535

L. Bet. My lord, you have talked to me this half hour without confessing pain: (pauses, and affects to gape) — only remember it!

L. Mo. Hell and tortures!

L. Bet. What did you say, my lord? 540

L. Mo. Fire and furies!

L. Bet. [aside]. Ha! ha! he's disordered; now I am easy. —— My Lord Foppington, have you a mind to your revenge at piquet?

L. Fop. I have always a mind to an oppor- 545 tunity of entertaining your ladyship, madam.

(Lady Betty coquets with Lord Foppington.)

L. Mo. O Charles! the insolence of this woman might furnish out a thousand devils.

Sir Cha. And your temper is enough to furnish out a thousand such women. Come away — I 550 have business for you upon the terrace.

L. Mo. Let me but speak one word to her.

Sir Cha. Not a syllable — the tongue's a weapon you'll always have the worst at, for I see you have no guard, and she carries a devilish edge. 555

L. Bet. My lord, don't let anything I have said frighten you away, for if you have the least inclination to stay and rail you know the old conditions; 'tis but your asking me pardon next day, and you may give your passion any liberty you think fit. 560

L. Mo. Daggers and death!

Sir Cha. Are you mad?

L. Mo. Let me speak to her now, or I shall burst.

Sir Cha. Upon condition you'll speak no more of her to me, my lord, do as you please. 565

L. Mo. Prithee pardon me! — I know not what to do.

Sir Cha. Come along — I'll set you to work, I warrant you. Nay, nay, none of your parting ogles! Will you go? 570

L. Mo. Yes — and I hope for ever.

Exit Sir Charles *pulling away* Lord Morelove.

L. Fop. Ha! ha! ha! Did ever mortal monster set up for a lover with such unfortunate qualifications?

L. Bet. Indeed, my Lord Morelove has 575 something strangely singular in his manner.

L. Fop. I thought I should have burst to see the creature pretend to rally, and give himself the airs of one of us. But run me through, madam! your ladyship pushed like a fencing-master; that 580 last thrust was a *coup de grâce*, I believe: I am afraid his honor will hardly meet your ladyship in haste again.

L. Bet. Not unless his second, Sir Charles, keeps him better in practice, perhaps. (Aside.) 585 Well, the humor of this creature has done me signal service today; I must keep it up for fear of a second engagement.

L. Fop. Never was poor wit so foiled at his own weapon, sure. 590

L. Bet. Wit! Had he ever any pretence to it?

L. Fop. Ha! ha! he has not much in love, I think, though he wears the reputation of a very pretty young fellow among some sort of people; but strike me stupid, if ever I could discover com- 595 mon sense in all the progress of his amours: he expects a woman should like him for endeavoring to convince her that she has not one good quality belonging to the whole composition of her soul and body.

L. Bet. That, I suppose, is only in a modest 600 hope that she'll mend her faults to qualify herself for his vast merit, ha! ha!

L. Fop. (aside). Poor Morelove! I see she can't endure him.

L. Bet. Or if one really had all those faults, 605 he does not consider that sincerity in love is as much out of fashion as sweet snuff; nobody takes it now.

L. Fop. Oh, no mortal, madam, unless it be here and there a squire that's making his lawful 610 court to the cherry-cheek charms of my Lord Bishop's great fat daughter in the country.

L. Bet. (throwing her hand carelessly upon his). Oh, what a surfeiting couple has he put together!

L. Fop. (aside). Fond of me, by all that's ten- 615

522] QQ om. *ha! ha! ha!*   523] QQ (disdainfully and aside).   528] DD *them.*   530] QQ *imagine, that I.*
546 s.d.] QQ om. s.d.   547] QQ om. *O.*   556] QQDD *I've.*   578] QQ *railery.*   581] QQDD *I'm.*
585] QQ om. (Aside).

der! Poor fool, I'll give thee ease immediately. ——
But, madam, you were pleased just now to offer me
my revenge at piquet. Now, here's nobody within,
and I think we can't make use of a better opportunity.

L. Bet. Oh, no! not now, my lord; I have a   620
favor I would fain beg of you first.

L. Fop. But time, madam, is very precious in this
place, and I shall not easily forgive myself if I don't
take him by the forelock.

L. Bet. But I have a great mind to have   625
a little more sport with my Lord Morelove first, and
would fain beg your assistance.

L. Fop. Oh, with all my heart! — (aside) and,
upon second thoughts, I don't know but piquing a
rival in public may be as good sport as being   630
well with a mistress in private: for, after all, the
pleasure of a fine woman is like that of her own virtue, not so much in the thing as the reputation of
having it. —— Well, madam, but how can I serve
you in this affair?   635

L. Bet. Why, methought, as my Lord Morelove
went out, he showed a stern resentment in his look
that seemed to threaten me with rebellion and downright defiance. Now I have a great fancy that you
and I should follow him to the terrace and   640
laugh at his resolution before he has time to put it
in practice.

L. Fop. And so punish his fault before he commits
it — ha! ha! ha!

L. Bet. Nay, we won't give him time, if his   645
courage should fail, to repent it.

L. Fop. Ha! ha! ha! let me blood, if I don't long
to be at it! ha! ha!

L. Bet. Oh, 'twill be such diversion to see him bite
his lips and broil within, only with seeing us   650
ready to split our sides in laughing at nothing,
ha! ha!

L. Fop. (aside). Ha! ha! I see the creature does
really like me. — And then, madam, to hear him
hum a broken piece of a tune in affectation   655
of his not minding us — 'twill be so foolish when we
know he loves us to death all the while, ha! ha!

L. Bet. And if at last his sage mouth should open
in surly contradiction of our humor, then will we, in
pure opposition to his, immediately fall foul   660
upon everything that is not gallant and fashionable;
constancy shall be the mark of age and ugliness, virtue a jest; we'll rally discretion out of doors, lay
gravity at our feet, and only love, free love, disorder,
liberty and pleasure be our standing principles.   665

L. Fop. Madam, you transport me: for if ever
I was obliged to nature for any one tolerable
qualification, 'twas positively the talent of being
exuberantly pleasant upon this subject. I am im-

patient — my fancy's upon the wing already   670
— let's fly to him.

L. Bet. No, no; stay till I am just got out: our
going together won't be so proper.

L. Fop. As your ladyship pleases, madam. But
when this affair is over, you won't forget that   675
I have a certain revenge due.

L. Bet. Ay! ay! after supper I am for you. Nay,
you shan't stir a step, my lord.

L. Fop. (seeing her to the door). Only to tell you,
you have fixed me yours to the last existence   680
of my soul's eternal entity.

L. Bet. Oh, your servant!   Exit.

L. Fop. Ha! ha! stark mad for me, by all that's
handsome! Poor Morelove! that a fellow who has
ever been abroad should think a woman of her   685
spirit is to be taken as the confederates do towns, by
a regular siege, when so many of the French successes
might have shown him the surest way is to whisper
the governor. How can a coxcomb give himself
the fatigue of bombarding a woman's under-   690
standing, when he may with so much ease make a
friend of her constitution? I'll see if I can show
him a little French play with Lady Betty. Let me
see — ay, I'll make an end of it the old way — get
her into piquet at her own lodgings, not mind   695
one tittle of my play, give her every game before
she's half up, that she may judge the strength of
my inclination by my haste of losing up to her price;
then of a sudden, with a familiar leer, cry 'Rat piquet!'
— sweep counters, cards and money all upon   700
the floor, et donc — l'affaire est faite.[1]   Exit.

ACT IV

Scene I

Scene, the Castle terrace.

Enter Lady Betty *and* Lady Easy.

L. Ea. My dear, you really talk to me as if I were
your lover, and not your friend; or else I am so dull
that by all you've said I can't make the least guess
at your real thoughts. Can you be serious for a
moment?   5

L. Bet. Not easily, but I would do more to oblige
you.

L. Ea. Then pray deal ingenuously, and tell me
without reserve, are you sure you don't love my
Lord Morelove?   10

L. Bet. Then seriously — I think not: but because I won't be positive, you shall judge by the
worst of my symptoms. First, I own I like his con-

[1] And then — the business is done.

622] QQ *at this.*   634] QQ *But how, madam, can.*   646] QQ *fail to.*   647] QQ *Ha! ha! let.*   672] QQ *No, stay.*
700] QQ om. *all.*   Act iv. s.d.] QQ The scene the Terrace.   s.d.] QQ Enter Lady Easy *and* Lady Betty.
8] QQ *ingeniously.*

versation; his person has neither fault nor beauty — well enough; I don't remember I ever secretly   15 wished myself married to him, or — that I ever seriously resolved against it.

L. EA. Well, so far you are tolerably safe. But come, as to his manner of [addressing] to you, what effect has that had?   20

L. BET. I am not a little pleased to observe few men follow a woman with the same fatigue and spirit that he does me; am more pleased when he lets me use him ill; and if ever I have a favorable thought of him, 'tis when I see he can't bear that usage.   25

L. EA. Have a care! that last is a dangerous symptom: he pleases your pride, I find.

L. BET. Oh! perfectly: in that — I own no mortal ever can come up to him.

L. EA. But now, my dear, now comes the   30 main point — jealousy! are you sure you have never been touched with it? Tell me that with a safe conscience, and then I pronounce you clear.

L. BET. Nay, then I defy him, for positively I was never jealous in my life.   35

L. EA. How, madam! have you never been stirred enough to think a woman strangely forward for being a little familiar in talk with him? Or are you sure his gallantry to another never gave you the least disorder? Were you never, upon no acci-   40 dent, in an apprehension of losing him?

L. BET. Hah! Why, madam — bless me! — wh — wh — why sure, you don't call this jealousy, my dear?

L. EA. Nay, nay, that is not the business.   45 Have you ever felt anything of this nature, madam?

L. BET. Lord! don't be so hasty, my dear — anything of this nature —— O lud! I swear I don't like it. Dear creature, bring me off here, for I am half frighted out of my wits.   50

L. EA. Nay, if you can rally upon't, your wound is not over deep, I'm afraid.

L. BET. Well, that's comfortably said, however.

L. EA. But come, to the point! — how far have you been jealous?   55

L. BET. Why — Oh, bless me! He gave the music one night to my Lady Languish [1] here upon the terrace, and, though she and I were very good friends, I remember I could not speak to her in a week for 't — Oh!   60

L. EA. Nay, now you may laugh if you can, for take my word, the marks are upon you. But come, what else?

L. BET. Oh, nothing else, upon my word, my dear.

L. EA. Well, one word more, and then I give   65

[1] Hired the orchestra to perform in her honor, and directed it to play whatever she desired.

sentence. Suppose you were heartily convinced that he actually followed another woman?

L. BET. But, pray, my dear, what occasion is there to suppose any such thing at all?

L. EA. Guilty, upon my honor!   70

L. BET. Pshah! I defy him to say that ever I owned any inclination for him.

L. EA. No, but you have given him terrible leave to guess it.

L. BET. If ever you see us meet again you'll   75 have but little reason to think so, I can assure you.

L. EA. That I shall see presently, for here comes Sir Charles, and I am sure my lord can't be far off.

Enter SIR CHARLES.

SIR CHA. Servant, Lady Betty! — my dear, how do you do?   80

L. EA. At your service, my dear! But pray, what have you done with my Lord Morelove?

L. BET. Ay, Sir Charles, pray, how does your pupil do? Have you any hopes of him? Is he docible?

SIR CHA. Well, madam, to confess your tri-   85 umph over me, as well as him, I own my hopes of him are lost. I offered what I could to his instruction, but — he's incorrigibly yours, and undone — and the news, I presume, does not displease your ladyship.   90

L. BET. Fie, fie, Sir Charles! you disparage your friend: I am afraid you don't take pains with him.

SIR CHA. Ha! I fancy, Lady Betty, your good nature won't let you sleep a-nights. Don't you love dearly to hurt people?   95

L. BET. Oh, your servant! then, without a jest, the man is so unfortunate in his want of patience that let me die if I don't often pity him.

SIR CHA. Ha! strange goodness! — Oh, that I were your lover for a month or two!   100

L. BET. What then?

SIR CHA. I would make that pretty heart's blood of yours ache in a fortnight.

L. BET. Hugh! I should hate you: your assurance would make your address intolerable.   105

SIR CHA. I believe it would, for I'd never address to you at all.

L. BET. (*hitting him with her fan*). Oh, you clown, you!

SIR CHA. Why, what to do? to feed a dis-   110 eased pride, that's eternally breaking out in the affectation of an ill nature that — in my conscience I believe is but affectation.

L. BET. You, nor your friend have no great reason to complain of my fondness, I believe. Ha!   115 ha! ha!

SIR CHA. (*looking earnestly on her*). Thou insolent

19] P *addressings*; QQDD *addressing*.   21] QQ *LA. BET. Humh!* (Smiling.) *I am.*   40] QQ *Was you.*
42] Q1 *Hay!*   49] QQ om. *for.*   65–66] QQ *I proceed to sentence.*   73] QQ om. *No.*
99] QQ om. *Ha!*   104] QQ *Auh!*   114] QQ *friends.*

creature! How can you make a jest of a man whose whole life's but one continued torment from your want of common gratitude?   120

L. BET. Torment! for my part, I really believe him as easy as you are.

SIR CHA. Poor, intolerable affectation! You know the contrary, you know him blindly yours, you know your power, and the whole pleasure of   125 your life's the poor and low abuse of it.

L. BET. Pray, how do I abuse it? — if I have any power.

SIR CHA. You drive him to extremes that make him mad, then punish him for acting against   130 his reason. You've almost turned his brain; his common judgment fails him; he's now, at this very moment, driven by his despair upon a project, in hopes to free him from your power, that I am sensible (and so must any one be that has his sense)   135 of course must ruin him with you forever. I almost blush to think of it, yet your unreasonable disdain has forced him to it, and should he now suspect I offered but a hint of it to you, as in contempt of his design, I know he'd call my life to answer it.   140 But I have no regard to men in madness: I rather choose for once to trust in your good nature, in hopes the man, whom your unwary beauty had made miserable, your generosity would scorn to make ridiculous.   145

L. BET. Sir Charles, you charge me very home:[1] I never had it in my inclination to make anything ridiculous that did not deserve it. Pray, what is this business you think so extravagant in him?

Sir CHA. Something so absurdly rash and   150 bold, you'll hardly forgive ev'n me that tell it you.

L. BET. Oh fie! If it be a fault, Sir Charles, I shall consider it as *his*, not *yours*. Pray, what is it?

L. EA. I long to know, methinks.

SIR CHA. You may be sure he did not want[2]   155 my dissuasions from it.

L. BET. Let's hear it.

SIR CHA. Why, this man, whom I have known to love you with such excess of generous desire, whom I have heard in his ecstatic praises on your   160 beauty talk till from the soft heat of his distilling thoughts the tears have fallen ——

L. BET. (*blushing*). Oh, Sir Charles ——

SIR CHA. Nay, grudge not, since 'tis past, to hear what was (though you contemned it) once his   165 merit. But now I own that merit ought to be forgotten.

L. BET. Pray, sir, be plain.

SIR CHA. This man, I say, whose unhappy passion has so ill succeeded with you, at last has for-   170

feited all his hopes (into which, pardon me, I confess my friendship had lately flattered him) his hopes of ev'n deserving now your lowest pity or regard.

L. BET. You amaze me — for I can't suppose his utmost malice dares assault my reputation —   175 and what ——

SIR CHA. No, but he maliciously presumes the world will do it for him; and indeed, he has taken no unlikely means to make them busy with their tongues, for he is this moment upon the open   180 terrace in the highest public gallantry with my Lady Graveairs. And to convince the world and me, he said, he was not that tame lover we fancied him, he'd venture to give her the music tonight: nay, I heard him, before my face, speak to one of the haut-   185 boys [3] to engage the rest, and desired they would all take their directions only from my Lady Graveairs.

L. BET. My Lady Graveairs! truly, I think my lord's very much in the right on't: for my part, Sir Charles, I don't see anything in this that's so   190 very ridiculous, nor indeed that ought to make me think either the better or worse of him for't.

SIR CHA. Pshah! Pshah! Madam, you and I know 'tis not in his power to renounce you; this is but the poor disguise of a resenting passion   195 vainly ruffled to a storm, which the least gentle look from you can reconcile at will and laugh into a calm again.

L. BET. Indeed, Sir Charles, I shan't give myself that trouble, I believe.   200

SIR CHA. So I told him, madam. 'Are not all your complaints,' said I, 'already owing to her pride, and can you suppose this public defiance of it (which you know you can't make good, too) won't incense her more against you?' 'That's what I'd   205 have,' said he, starting wildly: 'I care not what becomes of me, so I but live to see her piqued at it.'

L. BET. (*disordered*). Upon my word, I fancy my lord will find himself mistaken —— I shan't be piqued, I believe — I must first have a value for   210 the thing I lose before it piques me. 'Piqued'! ha! ha! ha!

SIR CHA. Madam, you've said the very thing I urged to him. 'I know her temper so well,' said I, 'that though she doted on you, if you once   215 stood out against her she'd sooner burst than show the least motion of uneasiness.'

L. BET. I can assure you, Sir Charles, my lord won't find himself deceived in your opinion. 'Piqued'!   220

SIR CHA. (*aside*). She has it!

L. EA. Alas, poor woman! how little do our passions make us!

---

[1] Accuse me very directly.   [2] Lack.   [3] One of the oboes (i.e., oboe-players).

L. BET. Not but I would advise him to have a little regard to my reputation in this business: 225 I would have him take heed of publicly affronting me.

SIR CHA. Right, madam, that's what I strictly warned him of; for among friends, whenever the world sees him follow another woman, the 230 malicious tea-tables will be very apt to be free with your ladyship.

L. BET. I'd have him consider that, methinks.

SIR CHA. But alas, madam! 'tis not in his power to think with reason; his mad resentment has 235 destroyed even his principles of common honesty. He considers nothing but a senseless, proud revenge, which in this fit of lunacy 'tis impossible that either threats or danger can dissuade him from.

L. BET. What! does he defy me, threaten 240 me? — then he shall see that I have passions, too, and know as well as he to stir my heart 'gainst any pride that dares insult me. Does he suppose I fear him? Fear the little malice of a slighted passion that my own scorn has stung into a despised re- 245 sentment! Fear him! Oh! it provokes me to think he dares have such a thought.

L. EA. Dear creature, don't disorder yourself so.

L. BET. (walking disordered). Let me but live to see him once more within my power, and I'll 250 forgive the rest of fortune.

[L. EA.] (aside). Well! certainly I am very ill-natured, for though I see this news has disturbed my friend, I can't help being pleased with any hopes of my Lady Graveairs being otherwise disposed 255 of. —— My dear, I am afraid you have provoked her a little too far.

SIR CHA. Oh, not at all. You shall see — I'll sweeten her, and she'll cool like a dish of tea.

L. BET. I may see him with his complaining 260 face again ——

SIR CHA. I am sorry, madam, you so wrongly judge of what I've told you; I was in hopes to have stirred your pity, not your anger; I little thought your generosity would punish him for faults 265 which you yourself resolved he should commit. Yonder he comes, and all the world with him. Might I advise you, madam, you should not resent this thing at all — I would not so much as stay to see him in his fault; nay, I'd be the last that 270 heard of it: nothing can sting him more, or so justly punish his folly, as your utter neglect of it.

L. EA. Come, dear creature, be persuaded, and go home with me; it will show more indifference to avoid him. 275

L. BET. No, madam, I'll oblige his vanity for

once, and stay to let him see how strangely he has piqued me.

SIR CHA. (aside). Oh, not at all to speak of; you had as good part with a little of that pride of 280 yours, or I shall yet make it a very troublesome companion to you.

(Goes from them and whispers LORD MORE-LOVE.)

Enter LORD FOPPINGTON; a little after, LORD MORELOVE, LADY GRAVEAIRS, and other ladies.

L. FOP. Ladies, your servant! — Oh, we have wanted you beyond reparation — such diversion!

L. BET. Well, my lord! have you seen my 285 Lord Morelove?

L. FOP. Seen him! — ha! ha! ha! — oh, I have such things to tell you, madam — you'll die ——

L. BET. Oh, pray let's hear 'em; I was never in a better humor to receive them. 290

L. FOP. Hark you!   (They whisper.)

L. MO. (to SIR CHARLES). So, she's engaged already.

SIR CHA. So much the better; make but a just advantage of my success, and she's undone. 295

L. FOP. } Ha! ha! ha!
L. BET. }

SIR CHA. You see already what ridiculous pains she's taking to stir your jealousy and cover her own.

L. FOP. } Ha! ha! ha!   300
L. BET. }

L. MO. Oh, never fear me, for upon my word, it now appears ridiculous ev'n to me.

SIR CHA. And hark you —!

(Whispers LORD MORELOVE.)

L. BET. And so the widow was as full of airs as his lordship?   305

SIR CHA. (aside). Only observe that, and 'tis impossible you can fail.

L. MO. Dear Charles, you have convinced me, and I thank you.

L. GRA. My Lord Morelove! What! do you 310 leave us?

L. MO. Ten thousand pardons, madam, I was but just ——

L. GRA. Nay, nay, no excuses, my lord, so you will but let us have you again.   315

SIR CHA. (aside to LADY GRAVEAIRS). I see you have good humor, madam, when you like your company.

L. GRA. And you, I see, for all your mighty thirst of dominion, could stoop to be obedient, if one 320 thought it worth one's while to make you so.

236] QQDD ev'n.   238] DD his fit.   239] QQ dangers.   245] QQ stung to a.   247] DD dare.
252] P L. BET. Well.   258] QQ Pshah! not.   269] DD the thing.   274] QQDD indeed it will.
274] QQ indifferent.   s.d.] QQ and a little.   287] QQ om. oh.   289] QQ let's have 'em, for I.
302] DD even.   304] QQ Ha! ha! and so.   319] DD And you see.   321] QQ so ha! ha!

SIR CHA. (*aside*). Ha! Power would make her an admirable tyrant.

L. EA. (*aside, observing* SIR CHARLES *and* LADY GRAVEAIRS). So! there's another couple have 325 quarreled too, I find. Those airs to my Lord Morelove look as if designed to recover Sir Charles into jealousy. I'll endeavor to join the company, and it may be that will let me into the secret. —— My Lord Foppington, I vow this is very uncomplaisant, 330 to engross so agreeable a part of the company to yourself.

SIR CHA. Nay, my lord, that is not fair, indeed, to enter into secrets among friends. — Ladies, what say you? I think we ought to declare against it. 335

LADIES. Oh, no secrets, no secrets!

L. BET. Well, ladies, I ought only to ask your pardon: my lord's excusable, for I would haul him into a corner.

L. FOP. I swear it's very hard [though]! I 340 observe two people of extreme condition can no sooner grow particular, but the multitude of both sexes are immediately up, and think their properties invaded ——

L. BET. Odious multitude! 345

L. FOP. Perish the *canaille*!

L. GRA. Oh, my lord! we women have all reason to be jealous of Lady Betty Modish's power.

L. MO. (*to* LADY BETTY). As the men, madam, all have of my Lord Foppington; beside, favorites 350 of great merit discourage those of an inferior class for their prince's service: he has already lost you one of your retinue, madam.

L. BET. Not at all, my lord, he has only made room for another: one must sometimes make 355 vacancies, or there could be no preferments.

L. FOP. Ha! ha! Ladies' favors, my lord, like places at court, are not always held for life, you know.

L. BET. No, indeed! if they were, the poor, 360 fine women would be all used like their wives, and no more minded than the business of the nation.

L. EA. Have a care, madam: an undeserving favorite has been the ruin of many a prince's empire.

L. FOP. Ha! ha! Upon my soul, Lady 365 Betty, we must grow more discreet, for positively, if we go on at this rate we shall have the world throw you under the scandal of constancy, and I shall have all the swords of condition at my throat for a monopolist. 370

L. MO. Oh, there's no great fear of that, my lord: though the men of sense give it over, there will be always some idle fellows vain enough to believe their merit may succeed as well as your lordship's.

L. BET. Or if they should not, my lord, cast [1] 375

[1] Rejected.

lovers, you know, need not fear being long out of employment while there are so many well-disposed people in the world. There are generally neglected wives, stale maids, or charitable widows always ready to relieve the necessities of a disappointed 380 passion — and, by the way, hark you, Sir Charles!

L. MO. (*aside*). So! she's stirred, I see, for all her pains to hide it: she would hardly have glanced an affront at a woman she was not piqued at.

L. GRA. (*aside*). That wit was thrown at me, 385 I suppose; but I'll return it.

L. BET. (*softly to* SIR CHARLES). Pray, how came you all this while to trust your mistress so easily?

SIR CHA. One is not so apt, madam, to be alarmed at the liberties of an old acquaintance as per- 390 haps your ladyship ought to be at the resentment of an hard-used, honorable lover.

L. BET. Suppose I were alarmed, how does that make you easy?

SIR CHA. Come, come, be wise at last; my 395 trusting them together may easily convince you that (as I told you before) I know his addresses to her are only outward, and 'twill be your fault now if you let him go on till the world thinks him in earnest, and a thousand busy tongues are set upon 400 malicious enquiries into your reputation.

L. BET. Why, Sir Charles, do you suppose while he behaves himself as he does that I won't convince him of my indifference?

SIR CHA. But hear me, madam ——! 405

L. GRA. (*aside*). The air of that whisper looks as if the lady had a mind to be making her peace again; and 'tis possible his worship's being so busy in the matter too may proceed as much from his jealousy of my lord with me as friendship to her — at 410 least I fancy so: therefore I'm resolved to keep her still piqued and prevent it, though it be only to gall him. —— Sir Charles, that is not fair, to take a privilege you just now declared against in my Lord Foppington. 415

L. MO. Well observed, madam.

L. GRA. Beside, it looks so affected to whisper when everybody guesses the secret.

L. MO. Ha! ha! ha!

L. BET. Oh, madam, your pardon in partic- 420 ular! But 'tis possible you may be mistaken: the secrets of people that have any regard to their actions are not so soon guessed as theirs that have made a confident of the whole town.

L. FOP. Ha! ha! ha! 425

L. GRA. A *coquette*, in her affected airs of disdain to a revolted lover, I'm afraid must exceed your ladyship in prudence, not to let the world see at the same time she'd give her eyes to make her peace with him. Ha! ha! 430

L. Mo. Ha! ha! ha!

L. Bet. 'Twould be a mortification indeed if it were in the power of a fading widow's charms to prevent it; and the man must be miserably reduced, sure, that could bear to live buried in woollen,[1] 435 or take up with the motherly comforts of a swan-skin [2] petticoat. Ha! ha!

L. Fop. Ha! ha! ha!

L. Gra. Widows, it seems, are not so squeamish to their interest: they know their own minds 440 and take the man they like, though it happens to be one that a froward, vain girl has disobliged and is pining to be friends with.

L. Mo. Nay, though it happens to be one that confesses he once was fond of a piece of folly 445 and afterwards ashamed on't.

L. Bet. Nay, my lord, there's no standing against two of you.

L. Fop. No, faith, that's odds at tennis, my lord. Not but, if your ladyship pleases, I'll endeavor 450 to keep your back-hand a little [3] — though upon my soul you may safely set me up at the line,[4] for knock me down if ever I saw a rest [5] of wit better played than that last in my life. —— What say you, madam? — shall we engage? 455

L. Bet. As you please, my lord.

L. Fop. Ha! ha! ha! *Allons! Tout de bon, jouez, mi lor!* [6]

L. Mo. Oh, pardon me, sir! I shall never think myself in anything a match for the lady. 460

L. Fop. To you, madam.

L. Bet. That's much, my lord, when the world knows you have been so many years teasing me to play the fool with you.

L. Fop. Ah! *Bien joué!* [7] Ha! ha! ha! 465

L. Mo. At that game I confess your ladyship has chosen a much properer person to improve your hand with.

L. Fop. To me, madam. —— My lord, I presume whoever the lady thinks fit to play the fool 470 with will at least be able to give as much envy as the wise person that had not wit enough to keep well with her when he was so.

L. Gra. Oh, my lord! both parties must needs be greatly happy, for I dare swear neither will 475 have any rivals to disturb 'em.

L. Mo. Ha! ha!

[1] A law passed in the reign of Charles II, intended to assist England's wool industry, required that all bodies be buried in woollen. The well-to-do commonly broke the law and paid the fine, which in effect became a tax.   [2] Canton flannel.

[3] Help you by playing strokes that come to your backhand. In this and the following seven speeches the figures are drawn from the game of court (or royal) tennis.

[4] Place me near the net (where a partner is of little use, but is out of the way of a partner who is a skilful player).

[5] Rally, exchange of strokes.

[6] Come! in earnest, play, my lord.   [7] Well-played.

L. Bet. None that will disturb 'em, I dare swear.

L. Fop. Ha! ha! ha!

L. Mo. }

L. Gra. } Ha! ha! ha!   480

L. Bet. }

Sir Cha. I don't know, gentlefolks — but you are all in extreme good humor, methinks; I hope there's none of it affected.

L. Ea. (*aside*). I should be loth to answer for any but my Lord Foppington. 485

L. Bet. Mine is not, I'll swear.

L. Mo. Nor mine, I'm sure.

L. Gra. Mine's sincere, depend upon't.

L. Fop. And may the eternal frowns of the whole sex doubly demme if mine is not. 490

L. Ea. Well, good people, I am mighty glad to hear it. You have all performed extremely well, but if you please you shall ev'n give over your wit now, while it is well.

L. Bet. (*to herself*). Now I see his humor 495 I'll stand it out, if I were sure to die for't.

Sir Cha. (*aside to* Lady Betty). You should not have proceeded so far with my Lord Foppington after what I had told you.

L. Bet. Pray, Sir Charles, give me leave to 500 understand myself a little.

Sir Cha. Your pardon, madam! I thought a right understanding would have been for both your interests and reputation.

L. Bet. For his, perhaps. 505

Sir Cha. Nay, then, madam, it's time for me to take care of my friend.

L. Bet. I never in the least doubted your friendship to him in anything that was to show yourself my enemy. 510

Sir Cha. Since I see, madam, you have so ungrateful a sense of my Lord Morelove's merit and my service, I shall never be ashamed of using my power henceforth to keep him entirely out of your ladyship's. 515

L. Bet. (*to herself*). Was ever anything so insolent! I could find in my heart to run the hazard of a downright compliance, if it were only to convince him that my power, perhaps, is not inferior to his.

L. Ea. My Lord Foppington, I think you 520 generally lead the company upon these occasions. Pray, will you think of some prettier sort of diversion for us than parties and whispers?

L. Fop. What say you, ladies? — shall we step and see what's done at the basset-table? 525

L. Bet. With all my heart! Lady Easy ——

L. Ea. I think 'tis the best thing we can do, and because we won't part tonight, you shall all sup where you dined. —— What say you, my lord?

L. Mo. Your ladyship may be sure of me, 530 madam.

L. Fop. Ay! ay! we'll all come.

L. Ea. Then pray let's change parties a little. My Lord Foppington, you shall squire me.

L. Fop. Oh! you do me honor, madam.   535

L. Bet. My Lord Morelove, pray let me speak with you.

L. Mo. Me, madam?

L. Bet. If you please, my lord.

L. Mo. (aside). Ha! that look shot through   540 me! what can this mean?

L. Bet. This is no proper place to tell you what it is, but there is one thing I'd fain be truly answered in: I suppose you'll be at my Lady Easy's by and by, and if you'll give me leave there ——   545

L. Mo. If you please to do me that honor, madam, I shall certainly be there.

L. Bet. That's all, my lord.

L. Mo. Is not your ladyship for walking?

L. Bet. If your lordship dares venture with   550 me.

L. Mo. (taking her hand). Oh, madam! (Aside.) How my heart dances; what heavenly music's in her voice, when softened into kindness.

L. Bet. (aside). Ha! his hand trembles —   555 Sir Charles may be mistaken.

L. Fop. My Lady Graveairs, you won't let Sir Charles leave us?

L. Gra. No, my lord, we'll follow you. (To Sir Charles.) Stay a little.   560

Sir Cha. I thought your ladyship designed to follow 'em.

L. Gra. Perhaps I'd speak with you.

Sir Cha. But, madam, consider we shall certainly be observed.   565

L. Gra. Lord, sir! If you think it such a favor ——!   Exit hastily.

Sir Cha.

  Is she gone? Let her go; [faith, boys, I care not;
  I'll not sue after her, I dare not, I dare not.][1]

Exit singing.

ACT V

Scene I

The scene continues.

Enter Sir Charles *and* Lord Morelove.

Sir Cha. Come a little this way! — my Lady Graveairs had an eye upon me as I stole off, and I'm apprehensive will make use of any opportunity to talk with me.

[1] The first two lines of an anonymous song, *The Careless Swain*. It is printed in full in *Westminster Drollery* (Part I), 1671.

L. Mo. Oh, we are pretty safe here. Well,   5 you were speaking of Lady Betty.

Sir Cha. Ay, my lord — I say, notwithstanding all this sudden change of her behavior, I would not have you yet be too secure of her, for, between you and I, since, as I told you, I have professed my-   10 self an open enemy to her power with you, 'tis not impossible but this new air of good humor may very much proceed from a little woman's pride of convincing me you are not yet out of her power.

L. Mo. Not unlikely: but still, can we make   15 no advantage of it?

Sir Cha. That's what I have been thinking of. Look you! — death! my Lady Graveairs!

L. Mo. Ha! She will have audience, I find.

Sir Cha. There's no avoiding her. The truth   20 is, I have owed her a little good nature a great while — I see there is but one way of getting rid of her —— I must ev'n appoint her a day of payment at last. If you'll step into my lodgings, my lord, I'll just give her an answer and be with you in a moment.   25

L. Mo. Very well, I'll stay there for you.

Exit Lord Morelove.

Enter Lady Graveairs *on the other side.*

L. Gra. Sir Charles!

Sir Cha. Come, come, no more of these reproachful looks! You'll find, madam, I have deserved better of you than your jealousy imagines. Is   30 it a fault to be tender of your reputation? — fie! fie! This may be a proper time to talk, and of my contriving, too — you see I just now shook off my Lord Morelove on purpose.

L. Gra. May I believe you?   35

Sir Cha. Still doubting my fidelity, and mistaking my discretion for want of good nature.

L. Gra. Don't think me troublesome — for I confess 'tis death to think of parting with you. Since the world sees, for you I have neglected   40 friends and reputation, have stood the little insults of disdainful prudes that envied me, perhaps, your friendship, have borne the freezing looks of near and general acquaintance — since this is so, don't let 'em ridicule me, too, and say my foolish vanity un-   45 did me; don't let 'em point at me as a cast mistress.

Sir Cha. You wrong me to suppose the thought; you'll have better of me when we meet. When shall you be at leisure?

L. Gra. I confess I would see you once again;   50 if what I have more to say prove ineffectual, perhaps it may convince me then 'tis my interest to part with you. Can you come tonight?

Sir Cha. You know we have company, and I'm afraid they'll stay too late. Can't it be before   55 supper? What's o'clock now?

L. Gra. It's almost six.

Sir Cha. At seven, then, be sure of me; till when I'd have you go back to the ladies to avoid suspicion, and about that time — have the vapors.　　60

L. Gra. May I depend upon you?　　　*Exit.*

Sir Cha. Depend on everything! — A very troublesome business this — send me once fairly rid on't, if ever I'm caught in an *honorable* affair again ——! A debt, now, that a little ready civility 65 and away would satisfy, a man might bear with, but to have a rent-charge upon one's good nature, with an unconscionable long scroll of arrears, too, that would eat out the profits of the best estate in Christendom — ah! intolerable! Well, I'll even 70 to my lord and shake off the thoughts on't.　　*Exit.*

Enter Lady Betty *and* Lady Easy.

L. Bet. I observe, my dear, you have usually this great fortune at play; it were enough to make one suspect your good luck with an husband.

L. Ea. Truly, I don't complain of my fortune 75 either way.

L. Bet. Prithee tell me — you are often advising me to it — are there those real comfortable advantages in marriage that our old aunts and grandmothers would persuade us of?　　80

L. Ea. Upon my word, if I had the worst husband in the world I should still think so.

L. Bet. Ay, but then the hazard of not having a good one, my dear.

L. Ea. You may have a good one, I dare say, 85 if you don't give airs till you spoil him.

L. Bet. Can there be the same dear, full delight in giving ease, as pain? Oh, my dear! the thought of parting with one's power is insupportable.

L. Ea. And the keeping it till it dwindles into 90 no power at all is most ruefully foolish.

L. Bet. But still, to marry before one's heartily in love ——

L. Ea. Is not half so formidable a calamity. But if I have any eyes, my dear, you'll run no great 95 hazard of that in venturing upon my Lord Morelove. You don't know, perhaps, that within this half hour the tone of your voice is strangely softened to him, ha! ha! ha!

L. Bet. My dear, you are positively, one or 100 other, the most censorious creature in the world, and so I see it's in vain to talk with you. Pray, will you go back to the company?

L. Ea. Ah! Poor Lady Betty!　　　*Exeunt.*

[SCENE II]

The scene changes to Sir Charles's *lodgings.*

Enter Sir Charles *and* Lord Morelove.

L. Mo. Charles! you have transported me; you have made my part in the scene so very easy, too. 'tis impossible I should fail in it.

Sir Cha. That's what I considered, for now the more you throw yourself into her power, the 5 more I shall be able to force her into yours.

L. Mo. After all (begging the ladies' pardon) your fine women, like bullies, are only stout where they know their men: a man of an honest courage may fright 'em into anything! Well, I am fully in- 10 structed, and will about it instantly. Won't you go along with me?

Sir Cha. That may not be so proper: besides, I have a little business upon my hands.

L. Mo. Oh, your servant, sir! — Good bye to 15 you! — you shan't stir.

Sir Cha. My lord, your servant!

Exit Lord Morelove.

So! now to dispose of myself till 'tis time to think of my Lady Graveairs. — Umph! — I have no great maw to that business, methinks — I don't find 20 myself in humor enough to come up to the civil things that are usually expected in the making up of an old quarrel. (Edging *crosses the stage.*) There goes a warmer temptation by half. —— Ha! into my wife's bedchamber, too! I question if the 25 jade has any great business there; I have a fancy she has only a mind to be taking the opportunity of nobody's being at home to make her peace with me. Let me see — ay, I shall have time enough to go to her ladyship afterwards — besides, I want a lit- 30 tle sleep, I find. Your young fops may talk of their women of quality, but to me, now, there's a strange agreeable convenience in a creature one is not obliged to say much to upon these occasions.　　(*Going.*)

Enter Edging.

Edg. Did you call me, sir?　　　35

Sir Cha. (*aside*). Ha! all's right. —— Yes, madam, I did call you.　　　(*Sits down.*)

Edg. What would you please to have, sir?

Sir Cha. Have! why, I would have you grow a good girl and know when you are well used, 40 hussy.

Edg. Sir, I don't complain of anything, not I.

Sir Cha. Well, don't be uneasy — I am not angry with you now. Come and kiss me.

Edg. Lard, sir!　　　45

Sir Cha. Don't be a fool, now — come hither.

Edg. Pshah!　　　(*Goes to him.*)

Sir Cha. No wry faces — so — sit down. I won't have you look grave, neither. Let me see you smile, you jade, you.　　　50

Edg. Ha! ha!　　　(*Laughs and blushes.*)

Sir Cha. Ah, you melting rogue!

Edg. Come, don't you be at your tricks, now!

83] QQ *of having.*　　　99] QQ *ha! ha! ha! ha!*　　　104] QQ *Betty.* L. Bet. *Pshah!* Exeunt.
Scene ii. 8] DD *stout when.*　　13] QQ *beside.*　　26] QQ *a great fancy.*　　30] QQ *beside.*　　37] QQ He *sits down.*

Lard! can't you sit still and talk with one? I am sure there's ten times more love in that, and fifty 55 times the satisfaction, people may say what they will.

SIR CHA. Well! now you're good you shall have your own way. I am going to lie down in the next room, and, since you love a little chat, come and throw my night-gown over me, and you shall 60 talk me to sleep.   *Exit* SIR CHARLES.

EDG. Yes, sir. —— For all his way, I see he likes me still.   *Exit after him.*

[SCENE III]

The scene changes to the terrace.

Enter LADY BETTY, LADY EASY, *and* LORD MORELOVE.

L. MO. Nay, madam, there you are too severe upon him, for baiting now and then a little vanity, my Lord Foppington does not want wit sometimes to make him a very tolerable woman's man.

L. BET. But such eternal vanity grows tire- 5 some.

L. EA. Come, if he were not so loose in his morals, vanity, methinks, might easily be excused, consider-ing how much 'tis in fashion. For pray observe, what's half the conversation of most of the fine 10 young people about town but a perpetual affectation of appearing foremost in the knowledge of manners, new modes, and scandal? and in that I don't see any-body comes up to him.

L. MO. Nor I, indeed — and here he comes. 15 [*To* LADY BETTY.] Pray, madam, let's have a little more of him; nobody shows him to more advantage than your ladyship.

L. BET. Nay, with all my heart; you'll second me, my lord.   20

L. MO. Upon occasion, madam.

L. EA. (*aside, and smiling to* LORD MORELOVE). Engaging upon parties, my lord?

Enter LORD FOPPINGTON.

L. FOP. So, ladies! what's the affair now?

L. BET. Why, you were, my lord; I was allow- 25 ing you a great many good qualities, but Lady Easy says you are a perfect hypocrite, and that whatever airs you give yourself to the women, she's confident you value no woman in the world equal to your own lady.   30

L. FOP. You see, madam, how I am scandalized upon your account. But it's so natural for a prude to be malicious when a man endeavors to be well with anybody but herself: did you never observe she was piqued at that before? Ha! ha!   35

L. BET. I'll swear you are a provoking creature.

L. FOP. Let's be more familiar upon't and give her disorder: ha! ha!

L. BET. Ha! ha! ha!

L. FOP. Stap my breath, but Lady Easy is an 40 admirable discoverer. Marriage is indeed a pro-digious security of one's inclination: a man's likely to take a world of pains in an employment where he can't be turned out for his idleness.

L. BET. I vow, my lord, that's vastly generous 45 to all the fine women; you are for giving 'em a despotic power in love, I see, to reward and punish as they think fit.

L. FOP. Ha! ha! Right, madam! what signifies beauty without power? And a fine woman when 50 she's married makes as ridiculous a figure as a beaten general marching out of a garrison.

L. EA. I'm afraid, Lady Betty, the greatest danger in your use of power would be from a too heedless liberality; you would more mind the 55 man than his merit.

L. FOP. (*to* LADY BETTY). Piqued again, by all that's fretful! Well, certainly to give envy is a pleasure inexpressible.

L. BET. Ha! ha! ha!   60

L. EA. (*aside to* LORD MORELOVE). Does not she show him well, my lord?

L. MO. (*to* LADY EASY). Perfectly, and me too to myself, for now I almost blush to think I ever was uneasy at him.   65

L. FOP. Lady Easy, I ask ten thousand pardons! I'm afraid I am rude all this while.

L. EA. Oh, not at all, my lord: you are always good company when you please: not but in some things, indeed, you are apt to be like other fine gentle- 70 men, a little too loose in your principles.

L. FOP. O madam! never to the offence of the ladies; I agree in any community with them; nobody is a more constant churchman, when the fine women are there.   75

L. EA. Oh fie, my lord! you ought not to go for their sakes at all. And I wonder you, that are for being such a good husband of your virtues, are not afraid of bringing your prudence into a lampoon or a play.   80

L. BET. Lampoons and plays, madam, are only things to be laughed at.

L. MO. Plays now, indeed, we need not be so much afraid of, for since the late short-sighted view of 'em[1] vice may go on and prosper; the stage 85 dares hardly show a vicious person speaking like him-self, for fear of being called profane for exposing him.

L. EA. 'Tis hard, indeed, when people won't dis-tinguish between what's meant for contempt and what for example.   90

[1] I.e., Collier's *Short View.*

8] DD *be easily.*   16] P (some copies, according to Habbema) om. *madam.*   46] DD *them.*
60] DD *Ha! ha!*   63] DD om. *too.*   66] QQ *Ha! ha! Lady Easy.*   83] QQDD *one need.*

L. Fop. Od so! Ladies, the court's coming home, I see; shall not we make our bows?

L. Bet. Oh, by all means!

L. Ea. Lady Betty, I must leave you, for I'm obliged to write letters, and I know you won't 95
give me time after supper.

L. Bet. Well, my dear, I'll make a short visit and be with you.   *Exit* Lady Easy.
Pray, what's become of my Lady Graveairs!

L. Mo. Oh, I believe she's gone home, 100
madam; she seemed not to be very well.

L. Fop. And where's Sir Charles, my lord?

L. Mo. I left him at his own lodgings.

L. Bet. He's upon some ramble, I'm afraid.

L. Fop. Nay, as for that matter, a man may 105
ramble at home sometimes. But here come the chaises; we must make a little more haste, madam.
        Exeunt.

[Scene IV]

The scene changes to Sir Charles's *lodgings.*

Enter Lady Easy *and a Servant.*

L. Ea. Is your master come home?

Serv. Yes, madam.

L. Ea. Where is he?

Serv. I believe, madam, he's laid down to sleep.

L. Ea. Where's Edging? Bid her get me some 5
wax and paper — stay! it's no matter, now I think on't — there's some above upon my toilet.
        Exeunt severally.

[Scene V]

The scene opens, and discovers Sir Charles *without his periwig, and* Edging *by him, both asleep in two easy chairs.*

Then enter Lady Easy, *who starts and trembles some time, unable to speak.*

L. Ea. Ha!
Protect me, virtue, patience, reason!
Teach me to bear this killing sight, or let
Me think my dreaming senses are deceived!
For sure a sight like this might raise the arm 5
Of duty, even to the breast of love. At least
I'll throw this vizor of my patience off,
Now wake him in his guilt,
And barefaced front him with my wrongs.
I'll talk to him till he blushes, nay till he —— 10
Frowns on me, perhaps — and then
I'm lost again. The ease of a few tears
Is all that's left to me ——
And duty, too, forbids me to insult,

Where I have vowed obedience. Perhaps 15
The fault's in me, and nature has not formed
Me with the thousand little requisites
That warm the heart to love.
Somewhere there is a fault:
But heav'n best knows what both of us deserve. 20
Ha! bareheaded, and in so sound a sleep!
Who knows, while thus exposed to th' unwholesome air,
But heav'n, offended, may o'ertake his crime,
And, in some languishing distemper, leave him
A severe example of its violated laws. 25
Forbid it mercy, and forbid it love!
This may prevent it.
        (*Takes a steinkirk* [1] *off her neck, and lays it gently on his head.*)
And if he should wake offended at my too busy care, let my heart-breaking patience, duty, and my fond affection plead my pardon.   *Exit.* 30
        (*After she has been out some time, a bell rings;* Edging *wakes, and stirs* Sir Charles.)

Edg. Oh!

Sir Cha. How now! what's the matter?

Edg. Oh, bless my soul! my lady's come home.

Sir Cha. Go! go then!   (*Bell rings.*)

Edg. O lud! My head's in such a condition, 35
too. [*Runs to the glass.*] I am coming, madam — Oh lud! here's no powder neither — here, madam! *Exit.*

Sir Cha. How now! (*Feeling the steinkirk upon his head*). What's this? How came it here? (*Puts on his wig.*) Did not I see my wife wear this today? 40
—— Death! she can't have been here, sure! It could not be jealousy that brought her home — for my coming was accidental — so too, I fear, might hers. How careless have I been! — not to secure the door neither! — 'twas foolish. It must be 45
so: she certainly has seen me here sleeping with her woman. If so, how low an hypocrite to her must that sight have proved me! — the thought has made me despicable ev'n to myself. How mean a vice is lying! and how often have these empty pleasures 50
lulled my honor and my conscience to a lethargy, while I grossly have abused her, poorly skulking behind a thousand falsehoods! Now I reflect, this has not been the first of her discoveries. How contemptible a figure must I have made to her! A crowd 55
of recollected circumstances confirm me now, she has been long acquainted with my follies, and yet with what amazing prudence has she borne the secret pangs of injured love, and wore an everlasting smile

---

[1] A neckcloth, of a style imported from France and named after a French victory over the English in 1692.

92] QQ *we go make.*   100] QQ om. *Oh!*   Scene iv. 7] QQDD *on it.*   Scene v. s.d.] QQ *And then enter.*
15] DD *When I.*   22] QQ *the unwholesome.*   23–27] QQ print these lines as prose.   25] QQ *of his.*
s.d.] QQ *her steinkirk from her neck.*   s.d.] QQ *over his head.*   29] Q2 *and fond.*
s.d.] QQ *rings; at which the maid waking starts, and stirs.*   36] QQ apply s.d. to Sir Charles.
39–40] QQ om. stage direction.   56] DD *confirms.*

to me! This asks a little thinking—something 60
should be done. I'll see her instantly, and be resolved from her behavior. *Exit.*

[SCENE VI]

The scene changes to another room.

Enter LADY EASY *and* EDGING.

L. EA. Where have you been, Edging?

EDG. Been, madam! I—I—I—I came as soon
as I heard you ring, madam.

L. EA. (*aside*). How guilt confounds her! but she's
below my thought. — Fetch my last new scarf 5
hither — I have a mind to alter it a little — make
haste!

EDG. Yes, madam. —— [*Aside.*] I see she does
not suspect anything. *Exit.*

L. EA. (*sitting down*). Heigh ho! I had forgot 10
— but I'm unfit for writing now. 'Twas an hard
conflict — yet it's a joy to think it over, a secret
pride to tell my heart my conduct has been just.
How low are vicious minds, that offer injuries: how
much superior innocence that bears 'em! Still, 15
there's a pleasure even in the melancholy of a quiet
conscience. Away, my fears! it is not yet impossible — for while his humane nature is not quite
shook off, I ought not to despair.

Re-enter EDGING *with a scarf.*

EDG. Here's the scarf, madam. 20

L. EA. So, sit down there and — let me see —
here, rip off all that silver!

EDG. Indeed, I always thought it would become
your ladyship better without it. But now suppose,
madam, you carried another row of gold round 25
the scollops, and then you take and lay this silver
plain all along the gathers, and your ladyship will
perfectly see it will give the thing ten thousand times
another air.

L. EA. Prithee don't be impertinent: do as I 30
bid you!

EDG. Nay, madam, with all my heart; your ladyship may do as you please.

L. EA. (*aside*). This creature grows so confident,
and I dare not part with her, lest he should think 35
it jealousy.

Enter SIR CHARLES.

SIR CHA. So, my dear! What, at work! How
are you employed, pray?

L. EA. I was thinking to alter this scarf here.

SIR CHA. What's amiss? methinks it's very 40
pretty.

EDG. Yes, sir, it's pretty enough, for that matter,
but my lady has a mind it should be proper, too.

SIR CHA. Indeed!

L. EA. I fancy plain gold and black would 45
become me better.

SIR CHA. That's a grave thought, my dear.

EDG. Oh, dear sir, not at all! my lady's much in
the right; I am sure, as it is, it's fit for nothing but a
girl. 50

SIR CHA. Leave the room!

EDG. Lard, sir! I can't stir, I must stay to ——

SIR CHA. (*angrily*). Go!

EDG. (*throwing down the work hastily and crying
aside*). If ever I speak to him again I'll be 55
burned. *Exit* EDGING.

SIR CHA. Sit still, my dear, — I came to talk with
you, and — which you well may wonder at — what
I have to say is of importance, too, but 'tis in order
to my hereafter always talking kindly to you. 60

L. EA. Your words were never disobliging, nor
can I charge you with a look that ever had the appearance of unkind.

SIR CHA. The perpetual spring of your good humor lets me draw no merit from what I have ap- 65
peared to be, which makes me curious now to know
your thoughts of what I really am: and never having
asked you this before, it puzzles me; nor can I (my
strange negligence considered) reconcile to reason
your first thoughts of venturing upon marriage 70
with me.

L. EA. I never thought it such an hazard.

SIR CHA. How could a woman of your restraint
in principles, sedateness, sense, and tender disposition, propose to see an happy life with one 75
(now I reflect) that hardly took an hour's pains ev'n
before marriage, to appear but what I am? — a loose,
unheeding wretch, absent in all I do, civil, and as
often rude without design, unseasonably thoughtful, easy to a fault, and, in my best of praise, 80
but carelessly good-natured. How shall I reconcile
your temper with having made so strange a choice?

L. EA. Your own words may answer you — your
having never seemed to be but what you really were;
and through that carelessness of temper there 85
still shone forth to me an undesigning honesty I always doubted of in smoother faces. Thus, while I
saw you took least pains to win me, you pleased and
wooed me most: nay, I have often thought that such
a temper could never be deliberately unkind, or, 90
at the worst, I knew that errors from want of thinking might be borne, at least when probably one moment's serious thought would end 'em. These were
my worst of fears, and these, when weighed by growing love against my solid hopes, were nothing. 95

SIR CHA. My dear, your understanding startles
me, and justly calls my own in question. I blush to

2] QQ *I-I-I-came.* 4] QQDD om. (aside). 17] QQ *my tears.* 26] QQ *these scollops.*
43] QQ *had a mind.* 54] QQ *the scarf hastily.* 68–69] QQ (*that strange.* 72] DD *a hazard.*
78] DD *unheeded.* 89] DD *I have thought.*

think I've worn so bright a jewel in my bosom and till this hour have scarce been curious once to look upon its lustre.　　　　　100

L. Ea. You set too high a value on the common qualities of an easy wife.

Sir Cha. Virtues, like benefits, are double, when concealed: and I confess I yet suspect you of an higher value far than I have spoke you.　　105

L. Ea. I understand you not.

Sir Cha. I'll speak more plainly to you. Be free and tell me — where did you leave this handkerchief?

L. Ea. Hah!　　　　　110

Sir Cha. What is't you start at? You hear the question.

L. Ea. What shall I say? my fears confound me.

Sir Cha. Be not concerned, my dear: be easy in the truth, and tell me.　　　　　115

L. Ea. I cannot speak — and I could wish you'd not oblige me to it — 'tis the only thing I ever yet refused you — and though I want a reason for my will, let me not answer you.

Sir Cha. Your will then be a reason, and　120 since I see you are so generously tender of reproaching me, 'tis fit I should be easy in my gratitude, and make what ought to be my shame my joy; let me be therefore pleased to tell you now, your wondrous conduct has waked me to a sense of your dis-　125 quiet past, and resolution never to disturb it more. And (not that I offer it as a merit, but yet in blind compliance to my will) let me beg you would immediately discharge your woman.

L. Ea. Alas! I think not of her. (Weeping.)　130 Oh, my dear! distract me not with this excess of goodness.

Sir Cha. Nay, praise me not, lest I reflect how little I have deserved it. I see you are in pain to give me this confusion; come, I will not shock　135 your softness by my untimely blush for what is past, but rather soothe you to a pleasure at my sense of joy for my recovered happiness to come. Give then to my new-born love what name you please, it cannot, shall not be too kind — oh, it cannot be　140 too soft for what my soul swells up with emulation to deserve. Receive me then entire at last, and take what yet no woman ever truly had, my conquered heart.

L. Ea. Oh, the soft treasure! Oh, the dear re-　145 ward of long desiring love! — now I am blest indeed to see you kind without th' expense of pain in being so, to make you mine with easiness. Thus, thus to have you mine is something more than happiness, 'tis double life, and madness of abounding　150 joy. But 'twas a pain intolerable to give you a confusion.

Sir Cha. Oh, thou engaging virtue! But I'm too

slow in doing justice to thy love: I know thy softness will refuse me, but remember I insist　155 upon it — let thy woman be discharged this minute.

L. Ea. No, my dear, think me not so low in faith, to fear that, after what you've said, 'twill ever be in her power to do me future injury. When I can conveniently provide for her I'll think on't: but to　160 discharge her now might let her guess at the occasion, and methinks I would have all our differences, like our endearments, be equally a secret to our servants.

Sir Cha. Still my superior every way! — be it as you have better thought. Well, my dear, now　165 I'll confess a thing that was not in your power to accuse me of; to be short, I own this creature is not the only one I have been to blame with.

L. Ea. I know she is not, and was always less concerned to find it so, for constancy in errors　170 might have been fatal to me.

Sir Cha. (surprised). What is't you know, my dear?

L. Ea. Come, I am not afraid to accuse you now — my Lady Graveairs. Your carelessness, my　175 dear, let all the world know it, and it would have been hard indeed had it been only to me a secret.

Sir Cha. My dear, I'll ask no more questions, for fear of being more ridiculous: I do confess I thought my discretion there had been a mas-　180 terpiece. How contemptible must I have looked all this while!

L. Ea. You shan't say so.

Sir Cha. Well, to let you see I had some shame as well as nature in me, I had writ this to my　185 Lady Graveairs, upon my first discovering that you knew I had wronged you: read it.

L. Ea. (reads). 'Something has happened that prevents the visit I intended you, and I could gladly wish you never would reproach me if I tell you　190 'tis utterly inconvenient that I should ever see you more.' This, indeed, was more than I had merited.

Enter Servant.

Sir Cha. Who's there? Here — step with this to my Lady Graveairs.

(*Seals the letter and gives it to the Servant.*)

Serv. Yes, sir. —— Madam, my Lady　195 Betty's come.

L. Ea. I'll wait on her.

Sir Cha. My dear, I'm thinking there may be other things my negligence may have wronged you in; but be assured, as I discover 'em all shall be　200 corrected. Is there any part or circumstance in your fortune that I can change or yet make easier to you?

L. Ea. None, my dear; your good nature never stinted me in that, and now, methinks, I have less occasion there than ever.　　　　　205

Re-enter Servant.

SERV. Sir, my Lord Morelove's come.

SIR CHA. I am coming. —— I think I told you of the design we had laid against Lady Betty.

L. EA. You did, and I should be pleased to be myself concerned in it.   210

SIR CHA. I believe we may employ you: I know he waits me with impatience. But, my dear, won't you think me tasteless to the joy you've given me, to suffer at this time any concern but you t'employ my thoughts?   215

L. EA. Seasons must be obeyed; and since I know your friend's happiness depending, I could not taste my own should you neglect it.

SIR CHA. Thou easy sweetness! —— Oh, what a waste on thy neglected love has my unthink- 220 ing brain committed! But time and future thrift of tenderness shall yet repair it all: the hours will come when this soft gliding stream that swells my heart uninterrupted shall renew its course,

And like the ocean after ebb, shall move   225
With constant force of due returning love.

Exeunt.

[SCENE VII]

The scene changes to another room.

And then re-enter LADY EASY *and* LADY BETTY.

L. BET. You have been in tears, my dear, and yet you look pleased too.

L. EA. You'll pardon me if I can't let you into circumstances, but be satisfied Sir Charles has made me happy ev'n to a pain of joy.   5

L. BET. Indeed, I am truly glad of it, though I am sorry to find that anyone who has generosity enough to do you justice should, unprovoked, be so great an enemy to me.

L. EA. Sir Charles your enemy!   10

L. BET. My dear, you'll pardon me if I always thought him so. But now I am convinced of it.

L. EA. In what, pray? I can't think you'll find him so.

L. BET. Oh, madam! it has been his whole 15 business of late to make an utter breach between my Lord Morelove and me.

L. EA. That may be owing to your usage of my lord: perhaps he thought it would not disoblige you: I am confident you are mistaken in him.   20

L. BET. Oh, I don't use to be out in things of this nature; I can see well enough. But I shall be able to tell you more when I have talked with my lord.

L. EA. Here he comes, and because you shall talk with him — no excuses! — for positively I'll 25 leave you together.

L. BET. Indeed, my dear, I desire you would stay, then; for I know you think now that I have a mind to — to ——

L. EA. To — to — ha! ha! ha!   *(Going.)* 30

L. BET. Well! remember this!

Enter LORD MORELOVE.

L. MO. I hope I don't fright you away, madam.

L. EA. Not at all, my lord, but I must beg your pardon for a moment; I'll wait upon you immediately.

Exit.

L. BET. My Lady Easy gone?   35

L. MO. Perhaps, madam, in friendship to you; she thinks I may have deserved the coldness you of late have shown me, and was willing to give you this opportunity to convince me you have not done it without just grounds and reason.   40

L. BET. *(aside).* How handsomely does he reproach me! But I can't bear that he should think I know it. —— My lord, whatever has passed between you and me, I dare swear that could not be her thoughts at this time, for when two people have appeared 45 professed enemies she can't but think one will as little care to give as t'other to receive a justification of their actions.

L. MO. Passion, indeed, often does repented injuries on both sides, but I don't remember in 50 my heat of error I ever yet professed myself your enemy.

L. BET. My lord, I shall be very free with you — I confess I do think now I have not a greater enemy in the world.   55

L. MO. If having long loved you, to my own disquiet, be injurious, I am contented then to stand the foremost of your enemies.

L. BET. Oh, my lord, there's no great fear of your being my enemy that way, I dare say.   60

L. MO. There's no other way my heart can bear to offend you now, and I foresee in that it will persist to my undoing.

L. BET. Fie, fie, my lord! we know where your heart is well enough.   65

L. MO. My conduct has indeed deserved this scorn, and therefore 'tis but just I should submit to your resentment, and beg (though I am assured in vain) for pardon. *(Kneels.)*

Enter SIR CHARLES.

SIR CHA. How, my lord!   70

*(*LORD MORELOVE *rises.)*

L. BET. *(aside).* Ha! He here? This was unlucky.

L. MO. *(to* LADY BETTY*).* Oh, pity my confusion!

SIR CHA. I am sorry to see you can so soon forget

212] DD *waits for me.*   SCENE VII. 1] QQDD *You've.*   2] D8 *look'd.*   3] QQ *can't yet let.*
6] DD *Indeed, I'm.*   23] QQ *lord, ha! ha! ha!*   25] QQDD *I will.*   34] QQ om. Exit.
44] QQ *thought.*   49–50 DD *repeated injuries.*   61] QQ *There is.*   68] QQDD *I'm*

yourself; methinks the insults you have borne 75
from that lady, by this time, should have warned
you into a disgust of her regardless principles.

L. Mo. Hold, Sir Charles! While you and I are
friends I desire you would speak with honor of this
lady. 'Tis sufficient I have no complaint against 80
her, and ——

L. Bet. My lord, I beg you would resent this thing
no farther. An injury like this is better punished
with our contempt; apparent malice only should be
laughed at. 85

Sir Cha. Ha! ha! the old recourse! offers of any
hopes to delude him from his resentment, and then,
as the Grand Monarch did with Cavalier,[1] you are
sure to keep your word with him.

L. Bet. Sir Charles, to let you know how far 90
I am above your little spleen — [to Lord Morelove]
my lord, your hand from this hour!

Sir Cha. Pshah! Pshah! All design! all pique!
mere artifice and disappointed woman.

L. Bet. Look you, sir, not that I doubt my 95
lord's opinion of me, yet ——

Sir Cha. Look you, madam! in short, your word
has been too often taken to let you make up quarrels,
as you used to do, with a soft look and a fair promise
you never intended to keep. 100

L. Bet. Was ever such an insolence? he won't give
me leave to speak.

L. Mo. Sir Charles!

L. Bet. No, pray, my lord, have patience! and
since his malice seems to grow particular, I dare 105
his worst, and urge him to the proof on't. Pray, sir,
wherein can you charge me with breach of promise to
my lord?

Sir Cha. Death! you won't deny it? How often,
to piece up a quarrel, have you appointed him 110
to visit you alone? and though you have promised to
see no other company the whole day, when he has
come, he has found you among the laugh of noisy
fops, coquettes, and coxcombs, dissolutely gay, while
your full eyes ran o'er with transport of their 115
flattery and your own vain power of pleasing? How
often, I say, have you been known to throw away at
least four hours of your good humor upon such
wretches, and, the minute they were gone, grew only
dull to him, sunk into a distasteful spleen, com- 120
plained you had talked yourself into the headache,
and then indulged upon the dear delight of seeing
him in pain: and by that time you had stretched and
gaped him heartily out of patience, of a sudden most

importunately remember you had out-sate 125
your appointment with my Lady Fiddle-faddle, and
immediately order your coach to the park?

L. Bet. Yet, sir, have you done?

Sir Cha. No — though this might serve to show
the nature of your principles. But the noble 130
conquest you have gained at last over defeated sense
of reputation, too, has made your fame immortal.

L. Mo. How, sir?

L. Bet. My reputation?

Sir Cha. Ay, madam, your reputation. — 135
My lord, if I advance a falsehood, then resent it! —
I say, your reputation — 't has been your life's whole
pride of late to be the common toast of every public
table, vain even in the infamous addresses of a married man, my Lord Foppington; let that be 140
reconciled with reputation, I'll now shake hands with
shame and bow me to the low contempt which you
deserve from him. Not but I suppose you'll yet
endeavor to recover him: now you find ill usage in
danger of losing your conquest, 'tis possible 145
you'll stop at nothing to preserve it.

L. Bet. Sir Charles ——

(*Walks disordered, and he after her.*)

Sir Cha. I know your vanity is so voracious 'twill
ev'n wound itself to feed itself — offer him a blank,
perhaps, to fill up with hopes of what nature he 150
pleases, and part with even your pride to keep him.

L. Bet. (*bursting into tears*). Sir Charles, I have
not deserved this of you.

Sir Cha. Ah! true woman! Drop him a soft,
dissembling tear, and then his just resentment 155
must be hushed of course.

L. Mo. [*aside*]. O Charles! I can bear no more;
those tears are too reproaching.

Sir Cha. (*aside*). Hist! for your life! (*And then
aloud.*) My lord, if you believe her, you're un- 160
done; the very next sight of my Lord Foppington
would make her yet forswear all that she can promise.

L. Bet. My Lord Foppington! Is that the mighty
crime that must condemn me, then? You know I
used him but as a tool of my resentment, which 165
you yourself, by a pretended friendship to us both,
most artfully provoked me to ——

L. Mo. Hold, I conjure you, madam! I want not
this conviction.

L. Bet. Send for him this minute, and you 170
and he shall both be witnesses of the contempt and
detestation I have for any forward hopes his vanity
may have given him or your malice would insinuate.

Sir Cha. Death! you would as soon eat fire, as
soon part with your luxurious taste of folly, as 175
dare to own the half of this before his face, or any one,
that would make you blush to deny it to. —— Here
comes my wife; now you shall see. Ha! and my
Lord Foppington with her! —— Now, now, we shall

---

[1] During the year 1704 Louis XIV had persuaded Jean
Cavalier, leader of the rebel Camisards, to make peace in return
for a commission in the French army and a large sum of money.
When the Camisards deserted Cavalier because of this treachery, as they regarded it, Louis XIV was reported to be preparing to imprison Cavalier.

75] DD *insult*.　　84] DD *should only*.　　123] QQ om. *had*.　　125] QQDD *importantly*.　　179] QQDD *her — now we shall*.

see this mighty proof of your sincerity. —— 180
Now, my lord, you'll have a warning, sure, and
henceforth know me for your friend indeed.

Enter Lady Easy *and* Lord Foppington.

L. Ea. In tears, my dear? what's the matter?

L. Bet. Oh, my dear! all I told you's true: Sir
Charles has shown himself so [inveterately] my   185
enemy that if I believed I deserved but half his hate
'twould make me hate myself.

L. Fop. Hark you, Charles! prithee what is this
business?

Sir Cha. Why, yours, my lord, for aught I   190
know: I have made such a breach betwixt 'em — I
can't promise much for the courage of a woman, but
if hers holds, I am sure it's wide enough; you may
enter ten abreast, my lord.

L. Fop. Say'st thou so, Charles? then I hold [1]   195
six to four I am the first man in the town.

L. Ea. Sure, there must be some mistake in this;
I hope he has not made my lord your enemy.

L. Bet. I know not what he has done.

L. Mo. Far be that thought! Alas! I am too   200
much in fear myself that what I have this day committed, advised by his mistaken friendship, may
have done my love irreparable prejudice.

L. Bet. No, my lord: since I perceive his little
arts have not prevailed upon your good nature   205
to my prejudice, I am bound in gratitude, in duty to
myself and to the confession you have made, my
lord, to acknowledge now I have been to blame too.

L. Mo. Ha! is't possible? can you own so much?
Oh, my transported heart!   210

L. Bet. He says I have taken pleasure in seeing
you uneasy — I own it — but 'twas when that uneasiness, I thought, proceeded from your love; and
if you did love — 'twill not be much to pardon it.

L. Mo. Oh, let my soul, thus bending to your   215
power, adore this soft descending goodness.

L. Bet. And since the giddy woman's slights I
have shown you too often have been made public,
'tis fit at last the amends and reparation should be
so: therefore, what I offered to Sir Charles, I   220
now repeat before this company, my utter detestation of any past or future gallantry that has or shall
be offered me to your uneasiness.

L. Mo. Oh, be less generous, or teach me to deserve it. —— Now blush, Sir Charles, at your   225
injurious accusation.

L. Fop. (*aside*). Hah! *Pardi, voila quelque chose
d'extraordinaire.*[2]

L. Bet. As for my Lord Foppington, I owe him
thanks for having been so friendly an instru-   230

---

ment of our reconciliation; for though in the little
outward gallantry I received from him I did not immediately trust him with my design in it, yet I have
a better opinion of his understanding than to suppose
he could mistake it.   235

L. Fop. I am struck dumb with [the] deliberation
of her assurance, and do not positively remember
that the *nonchalance* of my temper ever had so bright
an occasion to show itself before.

L. Bet. My lord, I hope you'll pardon the   240
freedom I have taken with you.

L. Fop. Oh, madam, don't be under the confusion
of an apology upon my account; for in cases of this
nature I am never disappointed but when I find a
lady of the same mind two hours together.   245
Madam, I have lost a thousand fine women in my
time, but never had the ill manners to be out of
humor with anyone for refusing me since I was born.

L. Bet. My lord, that's a very prudent temper.

L. Fop. Madam, to convince you that I am   250
in an universal peace with mankind, since you own I
have so far contributed to your happiness, give me
leave to have the honor of completing it by joining
your hand where you have already offered up your
inclination.   255

L. Bet. My lord, that's a favor I can't refuse you.

L. Mo. Generous indeed, my lord.

(Lord Foppington *joins their hands.*)

L. Fop. And stap my breath if ever I was better
pleased since my first entrance into human nature.

Sir Cha. How now, my lord! What! throw   260
up the cards before you have lost the game?

L. Fop. Look you, Charles, 'tis true I did design to
have played with her alone: but he that will keep
well with the ladies must sometimes be content to
make one at a pool with 'em: and since I know   265
I must engage her in my turn, I don't see any great
odds in letting him take the first game with her.

Sir Cha. Wisely considered, my lord.

L. Bet. And now, Sir Charles ——

Sir Cha. And now, madam, I'll save you the   270
trouble of a long speech, and, in one word, confess
that everything I have done in regard to you this day
was purely artificial. I saw there was no way to
secure you to my Lord Morelove but by alarming
your pride with the danger of losing him, and   275
since the success must have by this time convinced
you that in love nothing is more ridiculous than an
over-acted aversion, I am sure you won't take it ill
if we at last congratulate your good nature by heartily laughing at the fright we had put you in.   280
Ha! ha! ha!

L. Ea. Ha! ha! ha!

L. Bet. Why — well, I declare it now, I hate you
worse than ever.

---

[1] Wager.
[2] By Jove, there's something extraordinary.

SIR CHA. Ha! ha! ha! And was it afraid 285
they would take its love from it? Poor Lady Betty!
ha! ha!

L. EA. My dear, I beg your pardon, but 'tis impossible not to laugh when one's so heartily pleased.

L. FOP. Really, madam, I am afraid the 290
good humor of the company will draw me into your
displeasure too; but if I were to expire this moment,
my last breath would positively go out in a laugh.
Ha! ha! ha!

L. BET. Nay, I have deserved it all, that's 295
the truth on't — [to LORD MORELOVE] but I hope,
my lord, you were not in this design against me.

L. MO. As a proof, madam, I am inclined never to
deceive you more — I do confess I had my share in't.

L. BET. You do, my lord! — then I declare 300
'twas a design, one or other, the best carried on that
ever I knew in my life; and (to my shame I own it)
for aught I know the only thing that could have prevailed upon my temper. 'Twas a foolish pride, that
has cost me many a bitten lip to support it. 305
I wish we don't both repent, my lord.

L. MO. Don't you repent without me, and we
never shall.

SIR CHA. Well, madam, now the worst that the
world can say of your past conduct is that my 310
lord had constancy and you have tried it.

Enter a Servant to LORD MORELOVE.

SERV. My lord, Mr. Le Fevre's below, and desires
to know what time your lordship will please to have
the music begin.

L. MO. Sir Charles, what say you? Will you 315
give me leave to bring 'em hither?

SIR CHA. As the ladies think fit, my lord.

L. BET. Oh, by all means! 'twill be better here,
unless we could have the terrace to ourselves.

L. MO. Then pray desire 'em to come all 320
hither immediately.

SERV. Yes, my lord.　　　　　　　*Exit Servant.*

Enter LADY GRAVEAIRS.

SIR CHA. Lady Graveairs!

L. GRA. Yes! you may well start! but don't suppose
I am now come like a poor tame fool to upbraid 325
your guilt, but, if I could, to blast you with a look.

SIR CHA. Come, come, you have sense — don't expose yourself; you are unhappy, and I own myself the
cause. The only satisfaction I can offer you is to protest no new engagement takes me from you, 330
but a sincere reflection of the long neglect and injuries I've done the best of wives, for whose amends
and only sake I must part with you and all the inconvenient pleasures of my life.

L. GRA. Have you, then, fallen into the low 335
contempt of exposing me, and to your wife, too?

SIR CHA. 'Twas impossible, without it, I could
ever be sincere in my conversion.

L. GRA. Despicable!

SIR CHA. Do not think so — for my sake I 340
know she'll not reproach you, nor by her carriage
ever let the world perceive you've wronged her. ——
My dear ——

L. EA. Lady Graveairs, I hope you'll sup with us?

L. GRA. I can't refuse so much good com- 345
pany, madam.

SIR CHA. You see the worst of her resentment;
in the mean time don't endeavor to be her friend,
and she'll never be your enemy.

L. GRA. I am unfortunate — 'tis what my 350
folly has deserved, and I submit to it.

L. MO. So! here's the music.

L. EA. Come, ladies, shall we sit?

(After the music, a song.)

　　Sabina with an angel's face,
　　　By love ordained for joy, 355
　　Seems of the sirens' cruel race,
　　　To charm and then destroy:

　　With all the arts of look and dress
　　　She fans the fatal fire;
　　Through pride, mistaken oft for grace, 360
　　　She bids the swain expire.

　　The god of love, enraged to see
　　　The nymph defy his flame,
　　Pronounced this merciless decree
　　　Against the haughty dame; 365

　　'Let age with double speed o'ertake her,
　　　Let love the room of pride supply;
　　And when the lovers all forsake her
　　　A spotless virgin let her die.'

(SIR CHARLES comes forward with LADY EASY.)

SIR CHA. Now, my dear, I find my happiness 370
grow fast upon me; in all my past experience of the
sex, I found even among the better sort so much of
folly, pride, malice, passion, and irresolute desire that
I concluded thee but of the foremost rank, and therefore scarce worthy my concern; but thou hast 375
stirred me with so severe a proof of thy exalted virtue, it gives me wonder equal to my love. If then
the unkindly thought of what I have been hereafter
should intrude upon thy growing quiet, let this reflection teach thee to be easy: 380
　　Thy wrongs, when greatest, most thy virtue proved,
　　And from that virtue found, I blushed, and truly
　　　loved.　　　　　　　　　　　*Exeunt.*

286] DD *take away its.*　　291] DD om. *good.*　　305] QQ *bitter.*　　324] DD *Ye! you.*

327] QQ *you yet have.*　　333] QQDD *I now must.*　　364] DD *his merciless.*　　382] QQ om. *Exeunt.*

THE EPILOGUE

Conquest and freedom are at length our own,[1] ⎞
False fears of slavery no more are shown; ⎬
Nor dread of paying tribute to a foreign throne. ⎠

All stations now the fruits of conquest share, ⎞
Except (if small with great things may compare) ⎬ 5
Th' opprest condition of the lab'ring player. ⎠

We're still in fears (as you of late from France)
Of the despotic power of song, and dance:

For while subscription like a tyrant reigns, ⎞
Nature's neglected, and the stage in chains, ⎬ 10
And English actors slaves to swell the Frenchman's gains. ⎠

Like Æsop's crow, the poor outwitted stage,
That lived on wholesome plays i'th' latter age,
Deluded once to sing, ev'n justly served,
Let fall her cheese to the fox's mouth and starved: 15

Oh, that your judgment, as your courage has ⎞
Your fame extended, would assert our cause, ⎬
That nothing English might submit to foreign laws. ⎠

If we but live to see that joyful day, ⎞
Then of the English stage, revived, we may, ⎬ 20
As of your honor now, with proper application, say. ⎠

So when the Gallic Fox by fraud of peace
Had lulled the British Lion into ease,

And saw that sleep composed his couchant head, ⎞
He bids him wake and see himself betrayed ⎬ 25
In toils of treacherous politics around him laid: ⎠

Shows him how one close hour of Gallic thought
Retook those towns for which he years had fought.

At this th' indignant savage[2] rolls his fiery eyes,
Dauntless, though blushing at the base surprise. 30

Pauses awhile — but finds delays are vain: ⎞
Compelled to fight, he shakes his shaggy mane, ⎬
He grinds his dreadful fangs, and stalks to Blenheim's plain. ⎠

There, with erected crest and horrid roar, ⎞
He, furious, plunges on through streams of gore, ⎬ 35
And dyes with false Bavarian blood the purple Danube's shore. ⎠

In one pushed battle frees the destined slaves;
Revives old English honor, and an empire saves.

FINIS

[1] The year 1704 had been a memorably successful one for the allied armies of England, Holland and the Emperor, with the battle of Blenheim as a climax.
[2] Wild beast.

The Conscious Lovers

BY SIR RICHARD STEELE

THE
Conscious Lovers.

ACT I. SCENE I.

SCENE, *Sir* John Bevil's *House.*

Enter Sir John Bevil, *and* Humphrey.

Sir JOHN BEVIL.

AVE you order'd that I should not be interrupted while I am dressing?

Humph. Yes, Sir: I believ'd you had something of Moment to say to me.

Sir J. Bev. Let me see, *Humphrey*; I think it is now full forty Years since I first took thee, to be about my Self.

Humph. I thank you, Sir, it has been an easy forty Years; and I have pass'd 'em without much Sickness, Care, or Labour.

Sir J. Bev. Thou hast a brave Constitution; you are a Year or two older than I am, Sirrah.

B   *Humph.*

THE PREFACE

Tᴴɪs comedy has been received with universal acceptance, for it was in every part excellently performed; and there needs no other applause of the actors but that they excelled according to the dignity and difficulty of the character they represented. But this great favor done to the work in acting renders the expectation still the greater from the author, to keep up the spirit in the representation of the closet,[1] or any other circumstance of the reader, whether alone or in company: to which I can only say that it must be remembered a play is to be seen, and is made to be represented with the advantage of action, nor can appear but with half the spirit without it. For the greatest effect of a play in reading is to excite the reader to go see it; and when he does so, it is then a play has the effect of example and precept.

The chief design of this was to be an innocent performance, and the audience have abundantly showed how ready they are to support what is visibly intended that way. Nor do I make any difficulty to acknowledge that the whole was writ for the sake of the scene of the fourth act, wherein Mr. Bevil evades the quarrel with his friend, and hope it may have some effect upon the Goths and Vandals that frequent the theatres, or a more polite audience may supply their absence.

But this incident, and the case of the father and daughter, are esteemed by some people no subjects of comedy; but I cannot be of their mind, for anything that has its foundation in happiness and success must be allowed to be the object of comedy; and sure it must be an improvement of it to introduce a joy too exquisite for laughter, that can have no spring but in delight, which is the case of this young lady. I must, therefore, contend that the tears which were shed on that occasion flowed from reason and good sense, and that men ought not to be laughed at for weeping till we are come to a more clear notion of what is to be imputed to the hardness of the head and the softness of the heart; and I think it was very politely said of Mr. Wilks,[2] to one who told him there was a general [3] weeping for Indiana, 'I'll warrant he'll fight ne'er the worse for that.' To be apt to give way to the impressions of humanity is the excellence of a right disposition and the natural working of a well-turned spirit. But as I have suffered by critics who are got no farther than to enquire whether they ought to be pleased or not, I would willingly find them properer matter for their employment, and revive here a song which was omitted for want of a performer, and designed for the entertainment of Indiana. Signor Carbonelli,[4] instead of it, played on the fiddle, and it is for want of a singer that such advantageous things are said of an instrument which were designed for a voice. The song is the distress of a love-sick maid, and may be a fit entertainment for some small critics to examine whether the passion is just or the distress male or female.

I

From place to place forlorn I go,
　　With downcast eyes a silent shade;
Forbidden to declare my woe;
　　To speak, till spoken to, afraid.

II

My inward pangs, my secret grief,
　　My soft, consenting looks betray.
He loves, but gives me no relief;
　　Why speaks not he who may?

It remains to say a word concerning Terence,[5] and I am extremely surprised to find what **Mr. Cibber** told me * prove a truth — that what I valued myself so much upon — the translation of him — should be

---

[1] Private study.
[2] The actor who took the part of Myrtle in the first production.
[3] General Charles Churchill.
[4] An Italian violinist recently come to England.
[5] The play was partly based on the *Andria* of Terence, especially in the first two acts.

---

* Z om. *me.*

imputed to me as a reproach. Mr. Cibber's zeal for the work, his care and application in instructing the actors and altering the disposition of the scenes, when I was, through sickness, unable to cultivate such things myself, has been a very obliging favor and friendship to me. For this reason I was very hardly persuaded to throw away Terence's celebrated funeral,[1] and take only the bare authority of the young man's character; and how I have worked it into an Englishman, and made use of the same circumstances of discovering a daughter when we least hoped for one, is humbly submitted to the learned reader.

[1] *Andria*, Act I.

PROLOGUE

By Mr. Welsted [1]

Spoken by Mr. Wilks [2]

To win your hearts and to secure your praise,
The comic-writers strive by various ways;
By subtle stratagems they act their game,
And leave untried no avenue to fame.
One writes the spouse a beating from his wife, 5
And says each stroke was copied from the life.
Some fix all wit and humor in grimace,
And make a livelihood of Pinkey's [3] face.
Here one gay show and costly habits tries,
Confiding to the judgment of your eyes; 10
Another smuts his scene (a cunning shaver),
Sure of the rakes' and of the wenches' favor.
Oft have these arts prevailed, and, one may guess,
If practised o'er again, would find success.
But the bold sage — the poet of to-night — 15
By new and desp'rate rules resolved to write;
Fain would he give more just applauses rise,
And please by wit that scorns the aids of vice.
The praise he seeks from worthier motives springs,
Such praise as praise to those that give it brings. 20
Your aid, most humbly sought, then, Britons, lend,
And lib'ral mirth like lib'ral men defend.
No more let ribaldry, with licence writ,
Usurp the name of eloquence or wit;
No more let lawless farce uncensured go, 25
The lewd dull gleanings of a Smithfield show. [4]
'Tis yours with breeding to refine the age,
To chasten wit, and moralize the stage.
Ye modest, wise and good, ye fair, ye brave,
To-night the champion of your virtues save; 30
Redeem from long contempt the comic name,
And judge politely for your country's fame.

[1] Leonard Welsted, a minor author and a friend of Steele.
[2] In the part of Myrtle.
[3] William Pinkethman, a celebrated comedian: cf. Pope's *Epistle to Augustus*, ll. 292–3.
[4] Bartholomew Fair, held in Smithfield during late August and early September, was notorious for its licentious 'drolls' or farces, in which actors from the regular theatres frequently took part.

DRAMATIS PERSONÆ

MEN

SIR JOHN BEVIL

MR. SEALAND

[JOHN] BEVIL JUNIOR, *in love with* INDIANA

[CHARLES] MYRTLE, *in love with* LUCINDA

CIMBERTON, *a coxcomb*

HUMPHR[E]Y, *an old servant to* SIR JOHN

TOM, *servant to* BEVIL JUNIOR.

DANIEL, *a country boy, servant to* INDIANA

WOMEN

MRS. SEALAND, *second wife to* SEALAND

ISABELLA, *sister to* SEALAND.

INDIANA, SEALAND'S *daughter by his first wife*

LUCINDA, SEALAND'S *daughter by his second wife*

PHILLIS, *maid to* LUCINDA

SCENE: LONDON

---

d.p.] Humphrey's name is usually so spelled in the text; in the dramatis personæ, however, it is spelled Humphry.

THE CONSCIOUS [1] LOVERS

A Comedy by Sir RICHARD STEELE

Illud genus narrationis quod in personis positum est, debet habere sermonis festivitatem, animorum dissimilitudinem, gravitatem, lenitatem, spem, metum, suspicionem, desiderium, dissimulationem, misericordiam, rerum varietates, fortunæ commutationem, insperatum incommodum, subitam lætitiam, jucundum exitum rerum. Cic. Rhetor ad Herenn. Lib. 1.[2]

ACT I

SCENE I

Scene, Sir John Bevil's *house.*

Enter Sir John Bevil *and* Humphrey.

Sir J. Bev. Have you ordered that I should not be interrupted while I am dressing?

Humph. Yes, sir; I believed you had something of moment to say to me.

Sir J. Bev. Let me see, Humphrey; I think it 5 is now full forty years since I first took thee to be about myself.

Humph. I thank you, sir; it has been an easy forty years, and I have passed 'em without much sickness, care, or labor. 10

Sir J. Bev. Thou hast a brave constitution; you are a year or two older than I am, sirrah.

Humph. You have ever been of that mind, sir.

Sir J. Bev. You knave, you know it; I took thee for thy gravity and sobriety, in my wild 15 years.

Humph. Ah, sir! our manners were formed from our different fortunes, not our different age. Wealth gave a loose to your youth, and poverty put a restraint upon mine. 20

Sir J. Bev. Well, Humphrey, you know I have been a kind master to you; I have used you, for the ingenuous nature I observed in you from the beginning, more like an humble friend than a servant.

Humph. I humbly beg you'll be so tender of 25 me as to explain your commands, sir, without any farther preparation.

Sir J. Bev. I'll tell thee, then. In the first place, this wedding of my son's, in all probability — (shut the door!) — will never be at all. 30

Humph. How, sir! not be at all? For what reason is it carried on in appearance?

Sir J. Bev. Honest Humphrey, have patience, and I'll tell thee all in order. I have myself, in some part of my life, lived, indeed, with freedom, but, 35

I hope, without reproach. Now, I thought liberty would be as little injurious to my son; therefore, as soon as he grew towards man, I indulged him in living after his own manner: I knew not how, otherwise, to judge of his inclination; for what can be con- 40 cluded from a behavior under restraint and fear? But what charms me above all expression is that my son has never, in the least action, the most distant hint or word, valued himself upon that great estate of his mother's, which, according to our marriage 45 settlement, he has had ever since he came to age.

Humph. No, sir; on the contrary, he seems afraid of appearing to enjoy it before you or any belonging to you. He is as dependent and resigned to your will as if he had not a farthing but what must 50 come from your immediate bounty. You have ever acted like a good and generous father, and he like an obedient and grateful son.

Sir J. Bev. Nay, his carriage is so easy to all with whom he converses, that he is never assuming, 55 never prefers himself to others, nor ever is guilty of that rough sincerity which a man is not called to and certainly disobliges most of his acquaintance. To be short, Humphrey, his reputation was so fair in the world, that old Sealand, the great India mer- 60 chant, has offered his only daughter and sole heiress to that vast estate of his, as a wife for him. You may be sure I made no difficulties; the match was agreed on, and this very day named for the wedding.

Humph. What hinders the proceeding? 65

Sir J. Bev. Don't interrupt me. You know I was last Thursday at the masquerade; my son, you may remember, soon found us out. He knew his grandfather's habit, which I then wore; and though it was the mode in the last age, yet the maskers, you 70 know, followed us as if we had been the most monstrous figures in that whole assembly.

Humph. I remember, indeed, a young man of quality, in the habit of a clown,[3] that was particularly troublesome. 75

Sir J. Bev. Right; he was too much what he seemed to be. You remember how impertinently he followed and teased us, and would know who we were.

---

[1] Conscientious.

[2] 'The kind of story that is told by stage-characters should have gaiety of speech, variety of personalities, energy, smoothness, hope, fear, suspicion, desire, dissembling, compassion, diversity of circumstances, reversal of fortune, unexpected trouble, sudden joy, and a happy outcome.'

[3] Country laborer.

HUMPH. (*aside*). I know he has a mind to 80
come into that particular.[1]

SIR J. BEV. Ay, he followed us till the gentleman
who led the lady in the Indian mantle presented that
gay creature to the rustic, and bid him (like Cymon
in the fable) [2] grow polite by falling in love, and 85
let that worthy old gentleman alone — meaning me.
The clown was not reformed, but rudely persisted,
and offered to force off my mask; with that the
gentleman, throwing off his own, appeared to be my
son, and, in his concern for me, tore off that of 90
the nobleman. At this they seized each other, the
company called the guards, and in the surprise the
lady swooned away, upon which my son quitted his
adversary, and had now no care but of the lady,
when, raising her in his arms, 'Art thou gone,' 95
cried he, 'forever? — forbid it, heaven!' She revives at his known voice, and with the most familiar,
though modest, gesture, hangs in safety over his
shoulder weeping, but wept as in the arms of one before whom she could give herself a loose, were 100
she not under observation. While she hides her face
in his neck, he carefully conveys her from the company.

HUMPH. I have observed this accident has dwelt
upon you very strongly. 105

SIR J. BEV. Her uncommon air, her noble modesty, the dignity of her person, and the occasion
itself, drew the whole assembly together; and I soon
heard it buzzed about, she was the adopted daughter
of a famous sea-officer who had served in 110
France. Now this unexpected and public discovery
of my son's so deep concern for her ——

HUMPH. Was what, I suppose, alarmed Mr. Sealand, in behalf of his daughter, to break off the
match? 115

SIR J. BEV. You are right. He came to me yesterday and said he thought himself disengaged from the
bargain, being credibly informed my son was already
married, or worse, to the lady at the masquerade.
I palliated matters, and insisted on our agree- 120
ment; but we parted with little less than a direct
breach between us.

HUMPH. Well, sir; and what notice have you
taken of all this to my young master?

SIR J. BEV. That's what I wanted to debate 125
with you. I have said nothing to him yet. But
look you, Humphrey — if there is so much in this
amour of his that he denies upon my summons to
marry, I have cause enough to be offended; and then
by my insisting upon his marrying today I 130
shall know how far he is engaged to this lady in
masquerade, and from thence only shall be able to

take my measures. In the mean time I would have
you find out how far that rogue, his man, is let into
his secret. He, I know, will play tricks as much 135
to cross me, as to serve his master.

HUMPH. Why do you think so of him, sir? I believe he is no worse than I was for you at your son's
age.

SIR J. BEV. I see it in the rascal's looks. But 140
I have dwelt on these things too long; I'll go to my
son immediately, and while I'm gone, your part is
to convince his rogue Tom that I am in earnest.
I'll leave him to you.   *Exit* SIR JOHN BEVIL.

HUMPH. Well, though this father and son 145
live as well together as possible, yet their fear of giving each other pain is attended with constant mutual
uneasiness. I'm sure I have enough to do to be
honest and yet keep well with them both. But they
know I love 'em, and that makes the task less 150
painful, however. — Oh, here's the prince of poor
coxcombs, the representative of all the better fed
than taught. — Ho! ho! Tom, whither so gay and so
airy this morning?

Enter TOM, *singing.*

TOM. Sir, we servants of single gentlemen 155
are another kind of people than you domestic ordinary drudges that do business; we are raised above
you. The pleasures of board-wages, tavern dinners,
and many a clear gain — vails [3] — alas! you never
heard or dreamt of. 160

HUMPH. Thou hast follies and vices enough for a
man of ten thousand a year, though 'tis but as
t'other day that I sent for you to town to put you
into Mr. Sealand's family, that you might learn a
little before I put you to my young master, who 165
is too gentle for training such a rude thing as you
were into proper obedience. You then pulled off
your hat to everyone you met in the street, like a
bashful great awkward cub as you were. But your
great oaken cudgel, when you were a booby, 170
became you much better than that dangling stick at
your button, now you are a fop. That's fit for
nothing, except it hangs there to be ready for your
master's hand when you are impertinent.

TOM. Uncle Humphrey, you know my mas- 175
ter scorns to strike his servants. You talk as if the
world was now just as it was when my old master
and you were in your youth — when you went to
dinner because it was so much o'clock, when the
great blow [4] was given in the hall at the pantry 180
door, and all the family came out of their holes in
such strange dresses and formal faces as you see in
the pictures in our long gallery in the country.

HUMPH. Why, you wild rogue!

---

[1] To enter upon a discussion of that incident.
[2] The first story of the fifth day of Boccaccio's *Decamerone.*

[3] Tips.   [4] I.e., upon the dinner-gong.

TOM. You could not fall to your dinner till a 185
formal fellow in a black gown said something over
the meat, as if the cook had not made it ready
enough.

HUMPH. Sirrah, who do you prate after? Despising men of sacred characters! I hope you 190
never heard my good young master talk so like a
profligate.

TOM. Sir, I say you put upon me,[1] when I first
came to town, about being orderly, and the doctrine
of wearing shams [2] to make linen last clean a 195
fortnight, keeping my clothes fresh, and wearing a
frock within doors.

HUMPH. Sirrah, I gave you those lessons because
I supposed at that time your master and you might
have dined at home every day and cost you 200
nothing; then you might have made a good family
servant. But the gang you have frequented since
at chocolate houses and taverns, in a continual round
of noise and extravagance ——

TOM. I don't know what you heavy inmates 205
call noise and extravagance; but we gentlemen, who
are well fed and cut a figure, sir, think it a fine life,
and that we must be very pretty fellows who are
kept only to be looked at.

HUMPH. Very well, sir! I hope the fashion 210
of being lewd and extravagant, despising of decency
and order, is almost at an end, since it is arrived at
persons of your quality.

TOM. Master Humphrey, ha! ha! you were an unhappy lad to be sent up to town in such queer 215
days as you were. Why, now, sir, the lackeys are
the men of pleasure of the age, the top gamesters;
and many a laced coat [3] about town have had their
education in our parti-colored regiment. We are
false lovers; have a taste of music, poetry, 220
billet-doux, dress, politics; ruin damsels; and when
we are weary of this lewd town and have a mind to
take up,[4] whip into our masters' wigs and linen, and
marry fortunes.

HUMPH. Hey-day! 225

TOM. Nay, sir, our order is carried up to the highest dignities and distinctions; step but into the
Painted Chamber,[5] and by our titles you'd take us all
for men of quality. Then, again, come down to the
Court of Requests,[5] and you see us all laying 230
our broken heads together for the good of the nation;
and though we never carry a question *nemine contradicente*,[6] yet this I can say with a safe conscience

(and I wish every gentleman of our cloth could lay
his hand upon his heart and say the same), that 235
I never took so much as a single mug of beer for my
vote in all my life.

HUMPH. Sirrah, there is no enduring your extravagance; I'll hear you prate no longer. I wanted
to see you to enquire how things go with your 240
master, as far as you understand them. I suppose
he knows he is to be married today.

TOM. Ay, sir, he knows it, and is dressed as gay
as the sun; but, between you and I, my dear, he has
a very heavy heart under all that gaiety. As 245
soon as he was dressed I retired, but overheard him
sigh in the most heavy manner. He walked thought-
fully to and fro in the room, then went into his
closet; when he came out he gave me this for his
mistress, whose maid, you know — 250

HUMPH. Is passionately fond of your fine person.

TOM. The poor fool is so tender, and loves to hear
me talk of the world, and the plays, operas and
ridottos [7] for the winter, the parks and Belsize [8] for
our summer diversions; and 'Lard!' says she, 255
'you are so wild! — but you have a world of humor.'

HUMPH. Coxcomb! Well, but why don't you
run with your master's letter to Mrs. Lucinda, as he
ordered you?

TOM. Because Mrs. Lucinda is not so easily 260
come at as you think for.

HUMPH. Not easily come at? Why, sirrah, are
not her father and my old master agreed that she
and Mr. Bevil are to be one flesh before tomorrow
morning? 265

TOM. It's no matter for that; her mother, it seems,
Mrs. Sealand, has not agreed to it, and you must
know, Mr. Humphrey, that in that family the grey
mare is the better horse.

HUMPH. What dost thou mean? 270

TOM. In one word, Mrs. Sealand pretends to have
a will of her own, and has provided a relation of hers,
a stiff, starched philosopher and a wise fool, for her
daughter; for which reason, for these ten days past
she has suffered no message nor letter from my 275
master to come near her.

HUMPH. And where had you this intelligence?

TOM. From a foolish, fond soul that can keep
nothing from me — one that will deliver this letter
too, if she is rightly managed. 280

HUMPH. What! her pretty handmaid, Mrs. Phillis?

TOM. Even she, sir; this is the very hour, you
know, she usually comes hither, under a pretence of
a visit to your housekeeper, forsooth, but in reality
to have a glance at — 285

---

[1] Imposed upon me.   [2] False shirt-fronts.
[3] Gentleman.   [4] Reform.
[5] Presumably taverns close to these institutions, and named
after them. Servants often met at such places and assumed
the names and characters of their masters in burlesque. See
Spectator No. 88, by Steele.
[6] Unanimously.

[7] Entertainments consisting of music followed by dancing.
[8] Belsize House, in Hampstead, a fashionable pleasure-
garden.

HUMPH. Your sweet face, I warrant you.

TOM. Nothing else in nature; you must know, I love to fret and play with the little wanton —

HUMPH. 'Play with the little wanton!' What will this world come to! 290

TOM. I met her this morning in a new manteau [1] and petticoat not a bit the worse for her lady's wearing, and she has always new thoughts and new airs with new clothes. Then, she never fails to steal some glance or gesture from every visitant at 295 their house, and is, indeed, the whole town of coquettes at second-hand. — But here she comes; in one motion she speaks and describes herself better than all the words in the world can.

HUMPH. Then I hope, dear sir, when your 300 own affair is over, you will be so good as to mind your master's with her.

TOM. Dear Humphrey, you know my master is my friend, and those are people I never forget.

HUMPH. Sauciness itself! but I'll leave you 305 to do your best for him. *Exit.*

Enter PHILLIS.

PHIL. Oh, Mr. Thomas, is Mrs. Sugarkey at home? Lard! one is almost ashamed to pass along the streets. The town is quite empty, and nobody of fashion left in it; and the ordinary people do 310 so stare to see anything dressed like a woman of condition, as it were, on the same floor with them, pass by! Alas! alas! it is a sad thing to walk. O Fortune! Fortune!

TOM. What! a sad thing to walk? Why, 315 Madam Phillis, do you wish yourself lame?

PHIL. No, Mr. Tom, but I wish I were generally carried in a coach or chair, and of a fortune neither to stand nor go, but to totter, or slide, to be short-sighted, or stare, to fleer in the face, to look dis- 320 tant, to observe, to overlook, yet all become me; and if I was rich, I could twire [2] and loll as well as the best of them. O Tom! Tom! is it not a pity that you should be so great a coxcomb, and I so great a coquette, and yet be such poor devils as we are? 325

TOM. Mrs. Phillis, I am your humble servant for that —

PHIL. Yes, Mr. Thomas, I know how much you are my humble servant, and know what you said to Mrs. Judy, upon seeing her in one of her lady's 330 cast [3] manteaus — that any one would have thought her the lady, and that she had ordered the other to wear it till it sat easy, for now only it was becoming — to my lady it was only a covering, to Mrs. Judy it was a habit. This you said, after somebody 335 or other. O Tom! Tom! thou art as false and as base as the best gentleman of them all; but, you

wretch, talk to me no more on the old odious subject — don't, I say.

TOM (*in a submissive tone, retiring*). I know 340 not how to resist your commands, madam.

PHIL. Commands about parting are grown mighty easy to you of late.

TOM (*aside*). Oh, I have her; I have nettled and put her into the right temper to be wrought 345 upon and set a-prating. — Why, truly, to be plain with you, Mrs. Phillis, I can take little comfort of late in frequenting your house.

PHIL. Pray, Mr. Thomas, what is it all of a sudden offends your nicety at our house? 350

TOM. I don't care to speak particulars, but I dislike the whole.

PHIL. I thank you, sir, I am a part of that whole.

TOM. Mistake me not, good Phillis.

PHIL. Good Phillis! Saucy enough. But 355 however —

TOM. I say, it is that thou art a part which gives me pain for the disposition of the whole. You must know, madam, to be serious, I am a man, at the bottom, of prodigious nice honor. You are too 360 much exposed to company at your house. To be plain, I don't like so many, that would be your mistress's lovers, whispering to you.

PHIL. Don't think to put that upon me.[4] You say this because I wrung you to the heart when 365 I touched your guilty conscience about Judy.

TOM. Ah, Phillis! Phillis! if you but knew my heart!

PHIL. I know too much on't.

TOM. Nay, then, poor Crispo's [5] fate and 370 mine are one. Therefore give me leave to say, or sing at least, as he does upon the same occasion —
(*Sings.*)

Se vedete, etc.[6]

PHIL. What, do you think I'm to be fobbed off with a song? I don't question but you have sung the same to Mrs. Judy too. 375

TOM. Don't disparage your charms, good Phillis, with jealousy of so worthless an object; besides, she is a poor hussy, and if you doubt the sincerity of my love, you will allow me true to my interest. You are a fortune, Phillis — 380

PHIL. What would the fop be at now? In good time, indeed, you shall be setting up for a fortune!

TOM. Dear Mrs. Phillis, you have such a spirit that we shall never be dull in marriage when we come together. But I tell you, you are a for- 385 tune, and you have an estate in my hands.
(*He pulls out a purse; she eyes it.*)

---

[1] A loose upper garment.   [2] Leer.   [3] Discarded.

[4] To deceive me by that story.
[5] In Buononcini's opera of the same name.
[6] The aria begins, 'If you see my thoughts, just gods, defend the innocence of my heart.'

PHIL. What pretence have I to what is in your hands, Mr. Tom?

TOM. As thus: there are hours, you know, when a lady is neither pleased or displeased, neither 390 sick or well; when she lolls or loiters; when she's without desires — from having more of everything than she knows what to do with.

PHIL. Well, what then?

TOM. — When she has not life enough to 395 keep her bright eyes quite open, to look at her own dear image in the glass.

PHIL. Explain thyself, and don't be so fond of thy own prating.

TOM. There are also prosperous and good- 400 natured moments, as when a knot or a patch is happily fixed, when the complexion particularly flourishes.

PHIL. Well, what then? I have not patience!

TOM. Why, then — or on the like occasions 405 — we servants who have skill to know how to time business see when such a pretty folded thing as this (shows a letter) may be presented, laid, or dropped, as best suits the present humor. And, madam, because it is a long, wearisome journey to run 410 through all the several stages of a lady's temper, my master, who is the most reasonable man in the world, presents you this to bear your charges [1] on the road.

(Gives her the purse.)

PHIL. Now you think me a corrupt hussy.

TOM. Oh, fie! I only think you'll take the 415 letter.

PHIL. Nay, I know you do, but I know my own innocence; I take it for my mistress's sake.

TOM. I know it, my pretty one, I know it.

PHIL. Yes, I say, I do it because I would not 420 have my mistress deluded by one who gives no proof of his passion; but I'll talk more of this as you see me on my way home. No, Tom, I assure thee I take this trash of thy master's, not for the value of the thing, but as it convinces me he has a true re- 425 spect for my mistress. I remember a verse to the purpose —
They may be false who languish and complain,
But they who part with money never feign. *Exeunt.*

SCENE II

BEVIL JUNIOR'S *lodgings.*

BEVIL JUNIOR, *reading.*

BEV. JUN. These moral writers practise virtue after death. This charming vision of Mirza! [2] Such an author consulted in a morning sets the spirit for the vicissitudes of the day better than the glass does a man's person. But what a day have I to go 5 through! to put on an easy look with an aching heart. If this lady my father urges me to marry should not refuse me, my dilemma is insupportable. But why should I fear it? Is not she in equal distress with me? Has not the letter I have sent her this 10 morning confessed my inclination to another? Nay, have I not moral assurances of her engagements, too, to my friend Myrtle? It's impossible but she must give in to it: for sure, to be denied is a favor any man may pretend to. It must be so. Well, then, 15 with the assurance of being rejected, I think I may confidently say to my father I am ready to marry her. Then let me resolve upon — what I am not very good at, though it is — an honest dissimulation.

Enter TOM.

TOM. Sir John Bevil, sir, is in the next room. 20

BEV. JUN. Dunce! Why did not you bring him in?

TOM. I told him, sir, you were in your closet.

BEV. JUN. I thought you had known, sir, it was my duty to see my father anywhere.

(*Going himself to the door.*)

TOM (*aside*). The devil's in my master! he 25 has always more wit than I have.

BEV. JUN. (*introducing* SIR JOHN). Sir, you are the most gallant, the most complaisant of all parents. Sure, 'tis not a compliment to say these lodgings are yours. Why would you not walk in, sir? 30

SIR J. BEV. I was loth to interrupt you unseasonably on your wedding-day.

BEV. JUN. One to whom I am beholden for my birthday might have used less ceremony.

SIR J. BEV. Well, son, I have intelligence you 35 have writ to your mistress this morning. It would please my curiosity to know the contents of a wedding-day letter, for courtship must then be over.

BEV. JUN. I assure you, sir, there was no insolence in it upon the prospect of such a vast fortune's 40 being added to our family, but much acknowledgment of the lady's greater desert.

SIR J. BEV. But, dear Jack, are you in earnest in all this? And will you really marry her?

BEV. JUN. Did I ever disobey any command 45 of yours, sir? — nay, any inclination that I saw you bent upon?

SIR J. BEV. Why, I can't say you have, son; but methinks in this whole business you have not been so warm as I could have wished you. You 50 have visited her, it's true, but you have not been particular.[3] Everyone knows you can say and do as handsome things as any man, but you have done nothing but lived in the general — been complaisant only. 55

BEV. JUN. As I am ever prepared to marry if you

---

[1] Pay your expenses.
[2] A paper by Addison in the 159th number of the *Spectator.*
[3] Especially attentive.

bid me, so I am ready to let it alone if you will have me.

HUMPHREY *enters, unobserved.*

SIR J. BEV. Look you there now! Why, what am I to think of this so absolute and so indiffer- 60 ent a resignation?

BEV. JUN. Think? that I am still your son, sir. Sir, you have been married, and I have not. And you have, sir, found the inconvenience there is when a man weds with too much love in his head. I 65 have been told, sir, that at the time you married, you made a mighty bustle on the occasion. There was challenging and fighting, scaling walls, locking up the lady, and the gallant under an arrest for fear of killing all his rivals. Now, sir, I suppose you, 70 having found the ill consequences of these strong passions and prejudices in preference of one woman to another, in case of a man's becoming a widower —

SIR J. BEV. How is this?

BEV. JUN. I say, sir, experience has made you 75 wiser in your care of me; for, sir, since you lost my dear mother your time has been so heavy, so lonely, and so tasteless, that you are so good as to guard me against the like unhappiness, by marrying me prudentially by way of bargain and sale. For as 80 you well judge, a woman that is espoused for a fortune is yet a better bargain if she dies; for then a man still enjoys what he did marry, the money, and is disencumbered of what he did not marry, the woman.

SIR J. BEV. But pray, sir, do you think 85 Lucinda, then, a woman of such little merit?

BEV. JUN. Pardon me, sir, I don't carry it so far neither. I am rather afraid I shall like her too well; she has, for one of her fortune, a great many needless and superfluous good qualities.   90

SIR J. BEV. I am afraid, son, there's something I don't see yet — something that's smothered under all this raillery.

BEV. JUN. Not in the least, sir. If the lady is dressed and ready, you see I am. I suppose the 95 lawyers are ready too.

HUMPH. (*aside*). This may grow warm if I don't interpose. — Sir, Mr. Sealand is at the coffee-house, and has sent to speak with you.

SIR J. BEV. Oh, that's well! Then I warrant 100 the lawyers are ready. Son, you'll be in the way,[1] you say —

BEV. JUN. If you please, sir, I'll take a chair, and go to Mr. Sealand's, where the young lady and I will wait your leisure.   105

SIR J. BEV. By no means. The old fellow will be so vain if he sees —

BEV. JUN. Ay; but the young lady, sir, will think me so indifferent —

[1] Near at hand.

HUMPH. (*aside to* BEVIL JUNIOR). Ay, there 110 you are right; press your readiness to go to the bride — he won't let you.

BEV. JUN. (*aside to* HUMPHREY). Are you sure of that?

HUMPH. (*aside*). How he likes being pre- 115 vented!

SIR J. BEV. (*looking on his watch*). No, no. You are an hour or two too early.

BEV. JUN. You'll allow me, sir, to think it too late to visit a beautiful, virtuous young woman, 120 in the pride and bloom of life, ready to give herself to my arms; and to place her happiness or misery, for the future, in being agreeable or displeasing to me, is a — Call a chair!

SIR J. BEV. No, no, no, dear Jack! this Sea- 125 land is a moody old fellow. There's no dealing with some people but by managing with indifference. We must leave to him the conduct of this day: it is the last of his commanding his daughter.

BEV. JUN. Sir, he can't take it ill that I am 130 impatient to be hers.

SIR J. BEV. Pray, let me govern in this matter; you can't tell how humorsome old fellows are. There's no offering reason to some of 'em, especially when they are rich. — (*Aside.*) If my son 135 should see him before I've brought old Sealand into better temper the match would be impracticable.

HUMPH. Pray, sir, let me beg you to let Mr. Bevil go. — (*Aside to* SIR JOHN.) See whether he will or not. — (*Then to* BEVIL JUNIOR.) Pray, sir, 140 command yourself; since you see my master is positive, it is better you should not go.

BEV. JUN. My father commands me as to the object of my affections, but I hope he will not as to the warmth and height of them.   145

SIR J. BEV. [*aside*]. So! I must even leave things as I found them, and in the meantime, at least, keep old Sealand out of his sight. — Well, son, I'll go myself and take orders in your affair. You'll be in the way, I suppose, if I send to you. I'll leave 150 your old friend with you. — [*Aside.*] Humphrey, don't let him stir, d'ye hear? — Your servant, your servant!   *Exit* SIR JOHN BEVIL.

HUMPH. I have a sad time on't, sir, between you and my master. I see you are unwilling, and 155 I know his violent inclinations for the match. — [*Aside.*] I must betray neither and yet deceive you both, for your common good. — Heaven grant a good end of this matter! But there is a lady, sir, that gives your father much trouble and sor- 160 row. — You'll pardon me.

BEV. JUN. Humphrey, I know thou art a friend to both, and in that confidence I dare tell thee — that lady is a woman of honor and virtue. You may assure yourself I never will marry without 165

100] Y *That's.*   108] Z *Ah — but.*

my father's consent. But give me leave to say, too, this declaration does not come up to [1] a promise that I will take whomsoever he pleases.

HUMPH. Come, sir, I wholly understand you. You would engage my services to free you from this 170 woman whom my master intends you, to make way in time for the woman you have really a mind to.

BEV. JUN. Honest Humphrey, you have always been an useful friend to my father and myself; I beg you, continue your good offices, and don't let 175 us come to the necessity of a dispute; for, if we should dispute, I must either part with more than life, or lose the best of fathers.

HUMPH. My dear master, were I but worthy to know this secret that so near concerns you, my 180 life, my all should be engaged to serve you. This, sir, I dare promise, that I am sure I will and can be secret. Your trust, at worst, but leaves you where you were; and if I cannot serve you, I will at once be plain and tell you so. 185

BEV. JUN. That's all I ask. Thou hast made it now my interest to trust thee. Be patient, then, and hear the story of my heart.

HUMPH. I am all attention, sir.

BEV. JUN. You may remember, Humphrey, 190 that in my last travels my father grew uneasy at my making so long a stay at Toulon.

HUMPH. I remember it; he was apprehensive some woman had laid hold of you.

BEV. JUN. His fears were just, for there I 195 first saw this lady. She is of English birth: her father's name was Danvers — a younger brother of an ancient family, and originally an eminent merchant of Bristol, who, upon repeated misfortunes, was reduced to go privately to the Indies. In this 200 retreat Providence again grew favorable to his industry, and in six years' time restored him to his former fortunes. On this he sent directions over that his wife and little family should follow him to the Indies. His wife, impatient to obey such 205 welcome orders, would not wait the leisure of a convoy, but took the first occasion of a single ship, and, with her husband's sister only, and this daughter, then scarce seven years old, undertook the fatal voyage — for here, poor creature, she lost her 210 liberty and life: she and her family, with all they had, were unfortunately taken by a privateer from Toulon. Being thus made a prisoner, though as such not ill-treated, yet the fright, the shock, and cruel disappointment seized with such violence 215 upon her unhealthy frame, she sickened, pined, and died at sea.

HUMPH. Poor soul! Oh, the helpless infant!

BEV. JUN. Her sister yet survived, and had the care of her. The captain, too, proved to have 220 humanity, and became a father to her; for having himself married an English woman, and being childless, he brought home into Toulon this her little country-woman, presenting her, with all her dead mother's movables of value, to his wife, to be 225 educated as his own adopted daughter.

HUMPH. Fortune here seemed again to smile on her.

BEV. JUN. Only to make her frowns more terrible; for in his height of fortune this captain, too, her 230 benefactor, unfortunately was killed at sea, and dying intestate, his estate fell wholly to an advocate, his brother, who, coming soon to take possession, there found, among his other riches, this blooming virgin at his mercy. 235

HUMPH. He durst not, sure, abuse his power!

BEV. JUN. No wonder if his pampered blood was fired at the sight of her — in short, he loved. But when all arts and gentle means had failed to move, he offered, too, his menaces in vain, denouncing 240 vengeance on her cruelty, demanding her to account for all her maintenance from her childhood, seized on her little fortune as his own inheritance, and was dragging her by violence to prison, when Providence at the instant interposed, and sent me, by mir- 245 acle, to relieve her.

HUMPH. 'Twas Providence, indeed. But pray, sir, after all this trouble how came this lady at last to England?

BEV. JUN. The disappointed advocate, find- 250 ing she had so unexpected a support, on cooler thoughts descended to a composition, which I, without her knowledge, secretly discharged.

HUMPH. That generous concealment made the obligation double. 255

BEV. JUN. Having thus obtained her liberty, I prevailed, not without some difficulty, to see her safe to England, where no sooner arrived but my father, jealous of my being imprudently engaged, immediately proposed this other fatal match that 260 hangs upon my quiet.[2]

HUMPH. I find, sir, you are irrecoverably fixed upon this lady.

BEV. JUN. As my vital life dwells in my heart; and yet you see what I do to please my father: 265 walk in this pageantry of dress, this splendid covering of sorrow. But, Humphrey, you have your lesson.

HUMPH. Now, sir, I have but one material question — 270

BEV. JUN. Ask it freely.

HUMPH. Is it, then, your own passion for this secret lady, or hers for you, that gives you this

---

[1] Amount to.

[2] Disturbs my peace.

aversion to the match your father has proposed you?

BEV. JUN. I shall appear, Humphrey, more 275 romantic in my answer than in all the rest of my story; for though I dote on her to death, and have no little reason to believe she has the same thoughts for me, yet in all my acquaintance and utmost privacies with her I never once directly told her 280 that I loved.

HUMPH. How was it possible to avoid it?

BEV. JUN. My tender obligations to my father have laid so inviolable a restraint upon my conduct that till I have his consent to speak I am deter- 285 mined, on that subject, to be dumb forever.

HUMPH. Well, sir, to your praise be it spoken, you are certainly the most unfashionable lover in Great Britain.

Enter TOM.

TOM. Sir, Mr. Myrtle's at the next door, and, 290 if you are at leisure, will be glad to wait on you.

BEV. JUN. Whenever he pleases. — Hold, Tom! did you receive no answer to my letter?

TOM. Sir, I was desired to call again, for I was told her mother would not let her be out of her 295 sight. But about an hour hence, Mrs. Lettice said, I should certainly have one.

BEV. JUN. Very well.

HUMPH. Sir, I will take another opportunity: in the meantime, I only think it proper to tell you 300 that, from a secret I know, you may appear to your father as forward as you please to marry Lucinda, without the least hazard of its coming to a conclusion. Sir, your most obedient servant!

BEV. JUN. Honest Humphrey, continue but 305 my friend in this exigence and you shall always find me yours. *Exit* HUMPHREY. [*Aside.*] I long to hear how my letter has succeeded with Lucinda — but I think it cannot fail, for at worst, were it possible she could take it ill, her 310 resentment of my indifference may as probably occasion a delay as her taking it right. Poor Myrtle, what terrors must he be in all this while? Since he knows she is offered to me and refused to him there is no conversing or taking any measures with 315 him for his own service. But I ought to bear with my friend, and use him as one in adversity:

All his disquiets by my own I prove;
The greatest grief's perplexity in love. *Exeunt.*

ACT II

SCENE I

Scene continues.

Enter BEVIL JUNIOR *and* TOM.

TOM. Sir, Mr. Myrtle.

BEV. JUN. Very well — do you step again, and wait for an answer to my letter. [*Exit* TOM.]

Enter MYRTLE.

BEV. JUN. Well, Charles, why so much care in thy countenance? Is there anything in this world 5 deserves it? — You, who used to be so gay, so open, so vacant![1]

MYRT. I think we have of late changed complexions. You, who used to be much the graver man, are now all air in your behavior. But the cause 10 of my concern may, for aught I know, be the same object that gives you all this satisfaction. In a word, I am told that you are this very day — and your dress confirms me in it — to be married to Lucinda. 15

BEV. JUN. You are not misinformed. — Nay, put not on the terrors of a rival till you hear me out. I shall disoblige the best of fathers if I don't seem ready to marry Lucinda; and you know I have ever told you you might make use of my secret resolu- 20 tion never to marry her, for your own service, as you please. But I am now driven to the extremity of immediately refusing or complying unless you help me to escape the match.

MYRT. Escape? Sir, neither her merit or her 25 fortune are below your acceptance. Escaping do you call it?

BEV. JUN. Dear sir, do you wish I should desire the match?

MYRT. No, but such is my humorous[2] and 30 sickly state of mind since it has been able to relish nothing but Lucinda, that though I must owe my happiness to your aversion to this marriage, I can't bear to hear her spoken of with levity or unconcern.

BEV. JUN. Pardon me, sir; I shall transgress 35 that way no more. She has understanding, beauty, shape, complexion, wit —

MYRT. Nay, dear Bevil, don't speak of her as if you loved her, neither.

BEV. JUN. Why, then, to give you ease at 40 once, though I allow Lucinda to have good sense, wit, beauty, and virtue, I know another in whom these qualities appear to me more amiable than in her.

MYRT. There you spoke like a reasonable and 45 good-natured friend. When you acknowledge her merit and own your prepossession for another, at once you gratify my fondness and cure my jealousy.

BEV. JUN. But all this while you take no notice, you have no apprehension, of another man that 50 has twice the fortune of either of us.

MYRT. Cimberton! Hang him, a formal, philosophical, pedantic coxcomb! for the sot, with all these crude notions of divers things, under the direction of great vanity and very little judgment, shows his 55 strongest bias is avarice — which is so predominant in him that he will examine the limbs of his mistress

[1] Disengaged from toil or business.
[2] Unhealthy, captious.

with the caution of a jockey, and pays no more compliment to her personal charms than if she were a mere breeding animal.   60

BEV. JUN. Are you sure that is not affected? I have known some women sooner set on fire by that sort of negligence than by —

MYRT. No, no! hang him, the rogue has no art; it is pure, simple insolence and stupidity.   65

BEV. JUN. Yet with all this, I don't take him for a fool.

MYRT. I own the man is not a natural;[1] he has a very quick sense, though very slow understanding. He says, indeed, many things that want only the 70 circumstances of time and place to be very just and agreeable.

BEV. JUN. Well, you may be sure of me if you can disappoint him; but my intelligence says the mother has actually sent for the conveyancer to draw   75 articles for his marriage with Lucinda, though those for mine with her are, by her father's order, ready for signing. But it seems she has not thought fit to consult either him or his daughter in the matter.

MYRT. Pshaw! a poor, troublesome woman.   80 Neither Lucinda nor her father will ever be brought to comply with it; besides, I am sure Cimberton can make no settlement upon her without the concurrence of his great-uncle, Sir Geoffry, in the west.

BEV. JUN. Well, sir, and I can tell you that's 85 the very point that is now laid before her counsel, to know whether a firm settlement can be made without this uncle's actual joining in it. Now pray consider, sir, when my affair with Lucinda comes — as it soon must — to an open rupture, how are you   90 sure that Cimberton's fortune may not then tempt her father, too, to hear his proposals?

MYRT. There you are right, indeed; that must be provided against. Do you know who are her counsel?

BEV. JUN. Yes, for your service I have found 95 out that, too: they are Sergeant Bramble and old Target — by the way, they are neither of 'em known in the family. Now, I was thinking why you might not put a couple of false counsel upon her to delay and confound matters a little; besides, it may   100 probably let you into the bottom of her whole design against you.

MYRT. As how, pray?

BEV. JUN. Why can't you slip on a black wig and a gown, and be old Bramble yourself?   105

MYRT. Ha! I don't dislike it. — But what shall I do for a brother in the case?

BEV. JUN. What think you of my fellow Tom? The rogue's intelligent, and is a good mimic. All his part will be but to stutter heartily, for that's   110 old Target's case. Nay, it would be an immoral thing to mock him, were it not that his impertinence is the occasion of its breaking out to that degree.

[1] An idiot.

The conduct of the scene will chiefly lie upon you.

MYRT. I like it of all things. If you'll send 115 Tom to my chambers I will give him full instructions. This will certainly give me occasion to raise difficulties, to puzzle or confound her project for a while at least.

BEV. JUN. I'll warrant you success. So far 120 we are right, then. And now, Charles, your apprehension of my marrying her is all you have to get over.

MYRT. Dear Bevil, though I know you are my friend, yet when I abstract myself from my   125 own interest in the thing, I know no objection she can make to you or you to her, and therefore hope —

BEV. JUN. Dear Myrtle, I am as much obliged to you for the cause of your suspicion as I am offended at the effect; but be assured, I am taking meas-   130 ures for your certain security, and that all things with regard to me will end in your entire satisfaction.

MYRT. Well, I'll promise you to be as easy and as confident as I can, though I cannot but remember that I have more than life at stake on your fi-   135 delity.   (Going.)

BEV. JUN. Then depend upon it, you have no chance against you.

MYRT. Nay, no ceremony — you know I must be going.   Exit MYRTLE.   140

BEV. JUN. Well! This is another instance of the perplexities which arise, too, in faithful friendship. We must often in this life go on in our good offices even under the displeasure of those to whom we do them, in compassion to their weaknesses 145 and mistakes. — But all this while poor Indiana is tortured with the doubt of me. She has no support or comfort but in my fidelity, yet sees me daily pressed to marriage with another. How painful, in such a crisis, must be every hour she thinks on   150 me! I'll let her see at least my conduct to her is not changed. I'll take this opportunity to visit her; for though the religious vow I have made to my father restrains me from ever marrying without his approbation, yet that confines me not from   155 seeing a virtuous woman that is the pure delight of my eyes and the guiltless joy of my heart. But the best condition of human life is but a gentler misery.

To hope for perfect happiness is vain,
And love has ever its allays[2] of pain.   Exit.   160

[SCENE II]

Enter ISABELLA *and* INDIANA *in her own lodgings.*

ISAB. Yes, I say 'tis artifice, dear child: I say to thee again and again, 'tis all skill and management.

IND. Will you persuade me there can be an ill design in supporting me in the condition of a woman of quality — attended, dressed, and lodged like   5

[2] Admixtures, alloys.

one — in my appearance abroad and my furniture at home, every way in the most sumptuous manner — and he that does it has an artifice, a design in it?

ISAB. Yes, yes.

IND. And all this without so much as explain- 10 ing to me that all about me comes from him!

ISAB. Ay, ay, the more for that. That keeps the title to all you have the more in him.

IND. The more in him! He scorns the thought —

ISAB. Then he — he — he — 15

IND. Well, be not so eager. If he is an ill man, let us look into his stratagems. Here is another of them. (*Showing a letter.*) Here's two hundred and fifty pound in bank notes, with these words: 'To pay for the set of dressing-plate which will be 20 brought home to-morrow.' Why, dear aunt, now here's another piece of skill for you, which I own I cannot comprehend, and it is with a bleeding heart I hear you say anything to the disadvantage of Mr. Bevil. When he is present I look upon him as 25 one to whom I owe my life and the support of it — then, again, as the man who loves me with sincerity and honor. When his eyes are cast another way and I dare survey him, my heart is painfully divided between shame and love. Oh! could I tell you — 30

ISAB. Ah! you need not; I imagine all this for you.

IND. This is my state of mind in his presence, and when he is absent, you are ever dinning my ears with notions of the arts of men — that his hidden bounty, his respectful conduct, his careful provision for 35 me, after his preserving me from utmost misery, are certain signs he means nothing but to make I know not what of me.

ISAB. Oh! You have a sweet opinion of him, truly. 40

IND. I have, when I am with him, ten thousand things, besides my sex's natural decency and shame, to suppress my heart, that yearns to thank, to praise, to say it loves him. I say, thus it is with me while I see him; and in his absence I am enter- 45 tained with nothing but your endeavors to tear this amiable image from my heart and in its stead to place a base dissembler, an artful invader of my happiness, my innocence, my honor.

ISAB. Ah, poor soul! has not his plot taken? 50 don't you die for him? has not the way he has taken been the most proper with you? Oh! ho! He has sense, and has judged the thing right.

IND. Go on, then, since nothing can answer you; say what you will of him. Heigh! ho! 55

ISAB. Heigh! ho! indeed. It is better to say so, as you are now, than as many others are. There are, among the destroyers of women, the gentle, the generous, the mild, the affable, the humble, who all, soon after their success in their designs, turn to 60 the contrary of those characters. I will own to you,

Mr. Bevil carries his hypocrisy the best of any man living, but still he is a man, and therefore a hypocrite. They have usurped an exemption from shame for any baseness, any cruelty towards us. They 65 embrace without love; they make vows without conscience of obligation; they are partners, nay, seducers to the crime wherein they pretend to be less guilty.

IND. (*aside*). That's truly observed. — But 70 what's all this to Bevil?

ISAB. This it is to Bevil and all mankind. Trust not those who will think the worse of you for your confidence in them — serpents who lie in wait for doves. Won't you be on your guard against 75 those who would betray you? Won't you doubt those who would contemn you for believing 'em? Take it from me, fair and natural dealing is to invite injuries; 'tis bleating to escape wolves who would devour you! Such is the world — (*aside*) and 80 such (since the behavior of one man to myself) have I believed all the rest of the sex.

IND. I will not doubt the truth of Bevil; I will not doubt it. He has not spoke it by an organ that is given to lying; his eyes are all that have ever 85 told me that he was mine. I know his virtue, I know his filial piety, and ought to trust his management with a father to whom he has uncommon obligations. What have I to be concerned for? my lesson is very short. If he takes me forever, my purpose of 90 life is only to please him. If he leaves me (which heaven avert), I know he'll do it nobly, and I shall have nothing to do but to learn to die, after worse than death has happened to me.

ISAB. Ay, do! persist in your credulity! 95 Flatter yourself that a man of his figure and fortune will make himself the jest of the town, and marry a handsome beggar for love.

IND. The town! I must tell you, madam, the fools that laugh at Mr. Bevil will but make 100 themselves more ridiculous. His actions are the result of thinking, and he has sense enough to make even virtue fashionable.

ISAB. O' my conscience, he has turned her head! — Come, come, if he were the honest fool you 105 take him for, why has he kept you here these three weeks without sending you to Bristol in search of your father, your family, and your relations?

IND. I am convinced he still designs it, and that nothing keeps him here but the necessity of not 110 coming to a breach with his father in regard to the match he has proposed him. Beside, has he not writ to Bristol? and has not he advice that my father has not been heard of there almost these twenty years? 115

ISAB. All sham — mere evasion; he is afraid if he should carry you thither, your honest relations may take you out of his hands and so blow up all his wicked hopes at once.

IND. Wicked hopes! did I ever give him any 120 such?

ISAB. Has he ever given you any honest ones? Can you say, in your conscience, he has ever once offered to marry you?

IND. No; but by his behavior I am con- 125 vinced he will offer it the moment 'tis in his power, or consistent with his honor, to make such a promise good to me.

ISAB. His honor!

IND. I will rely upon it; therefore desire you 130 will not make my life uneasy by these ungrateful jealousies of one to whom I am, and wish to be, obliged, for from his integrity alone I have resolved to hope for happiness.

ISAB. Nay, I have done my duty; if you 135 won't see, at your peril be it!

IND. Let it be. — This is his hour of visiting me.

ISAB. (apart). Oh, to be sure, keep up your form; don't see him in a bed-chamber! This is pure [1] prudence, when she is liable, wherever he meets 140 her, to be conveyed where'er he pleases.

IND. All the rest of my life is but waiting till he comes. I live only when I'm with him.   Exit.

ISAB. Well, go thy ways, thou wilful innocent! I once had almost as much love for a man who 145 poorly left me to marry an estate — and I am now, against my will, what they call an old maid — but I will not let the peevishness of that condition grow upon me; only keep up the suspicion of it, to prevent this creature's being any other than a virgin, 150 except upon proper terms.   Exit.

Re-enter INDIANA, *speaking to a Servant.*

IND. Desire Mr. Bevil to walk in. — Design! impossible! A base, designing mind could never think of what he hourly puts in practice. And yet, since the late rumor of his marriage, he seems more 155 reserved than formerly; he sends in, too, before he sees me, to know if I am at leisure — such new respect may cover coldness in the heart. It certainly makes me thoughtful. I'll know the worst at once; I'll lay such fair occasions in his way that it 160 shall be impossible to avoid an explanation, for these doubts are insupportable.— But see, he comes and clears them all.

Enter BEVIL JUNIOR.

BEV. JUN. Madam, your most obedient! I am afraid I broke in upon your rest last night; 165 'twas very late before we parted, but 'twas your own fault: I never saw you in such agreeable humor.

IND. I am extremely glad we were both pleased, for I thought I never saw you better company.

[1] Admirable.

BEV. JUN. Me, madam! you rally; I said 170 very little.

IND. But I am afraid you heard me say a great deal; and, when a woman is in the talking vein, the most agreeable thing a man can do, you know, is to have patience to hear her.   175

BEV. JUN. Then it's pity, madam, you should ever be silent, that we might be always agreeable to one another.

IND. If I had your talent or power to make my actions speak for me, I might indeed be silent, 180 and yet pretend to something more than the agreeable.

BEV. JUN. If I might be vain of anything in my power, madam, 'tis that my understanding from all your sex has marked you out as the most de- 185 serving object of my esteem.

IND. Should I think I deserve this, 'twere enough to make my vanity forfeit the very esteem you offer me.

BEV. JUN. How so, madam?   190

IND. Because esteem is the result of reason, and to deserve it from good sense, the height of human glory. Nay, I had rather a man of honor should pay me that, than all the homage of a sincere and humble love.   195

BEV. JUN. You certainly distinguish right, madam; love often kindles from external merit only —

IND. But esteem arises from a higher source — the merit of the soul.

BEV. JUN. True — and great souls only can 200 deserve it.

(Bowing respectfully.)

IND. Now I think they are greater still that can so charitably part with it.

BEV. JUN. Now, madam, you make me vain, since the utmost pride and pleasure of my life 205 is that I esteem you — as I ought.

IND. (aside). As he ought! still more perplexing! He neither saves nor kills my hope.

BEV. JUN. But, madam, we grow grave, methinks. Let's find some other subject. Pray, how did 210 you like the opera last night?

IND. First give me leave to thank you for my tickets.

BEV. JUN. Oh, your servant, madam! But pray tell me; you, now, who are never partial to the 215 fashion, I fancy, must be the properest judge of a mighty dispute among the ladies — that is, whether *Crispo* or *Griselda* [2] is the more agreeable entertainment.

IND. With submission, now, I cannot be a 220 proper judge of this question.

BEV. JUN. How so, madam?

[2] Undoubtedly the opera by Buononcini (1722), although another *Griselda*, with music by Alessandro Scarlatti, was produced in 1721.

IND. Because I find I have a partiality for one of them.

BEV. JUN. Pray, which is that? 225

IND. I do not know — there's something in that rural cottage of Griselda, her forlorn condition, her poverty, her solitude, her resignation, her innocent slumbers, and that lulling 'Dolce sógno' ¹ that's sung over her; it had an effect upon me that — 230 in short, I never was so well deceived at any of them.

BEV. JUN. Oh! Now, then, I can account for the dispute. Griselda, it seems, is the distress of an injured, innocent woman; Crispo, that only of 235 a man in the same condition: therefore the men are mostly concerned for Crispo, and, by a natural indulgence, both sexes for Griselda.

IND. So that judgment, you think, ought to be for one, though fancy and complaisance have 240 got ground for the other. Well, I believe you will never give me leave to dispute with you on any subject, for I own Crispo has its charms for me too, though in the main all the pleasure the best opera gives us is but mere sensation. Methinks it's 245 pity the mind can't have a little more share in the entertainment. The music's certainly fine, but, in my thoughts, there's none of your composers come up to old Shakespeare and Otway.

BEV. JUN. How, madam! Why, if a wom- 250 an of your sense were to say this in the drawing-room —

Enter a Servant.

SERV. Sir, here's Signor Carbonelli says he waits your commands in the next room.

BEV. JUN. Apropos! You were saying yes- 255 terday, madam, you had a mind to hear him; will you give him leave to entertain you now?

IND. By all means. — Desire the gentleman to walk in. *Exit Servant.*

BEV. JUN. I fancy you will find something 260 in this hand that is uncommon.

IND. You are always finding ways, Mr. Bevil, to make life seem less tedious to me.

*Enter Music Master.*²

When the gentleman pleases.

(*After a sonata* ³ *is played,* BEVIL *waits on the Master to the door, etc.*)

BEV. JUN. You smile, madam, to see me so 265 complaisant to one whom I pay for his visit. Now I own I think it is not enough barely to pay those whose talents are superior to our own (I mean such

¹ 'Sweet dream.' The aria beginning with these words is sung by Gualtiero (Walter) in the eighth scene of the second act of Buononcini's *Griselda*.
² See Steele's preface.
³ In the old sense of a composition for an instrument, as distinguished from one for the voice.

talents as would become our condition, if we had them): methinks we ought to do something 270 more than barely gratify them for what they do at our command only because their fortune is below us.

IND. You say I smile. I assure you it was a smile of approbation; for indeed, I cannot but think it the distinguishing part of a gentleman to make 275 his superiority of fortune as easy to his inferiors as he can. — (*Aside.*) Now once more to try him. — I was saying just now, I believed you would never let me dispute with you, and I daresay it will always be so. However, I must have your opinion upon 280 a subject which created a debate between my aunt and me just before you came hither. She would needs have it that no man ever does any extraordinary kindness or service for a woman but for his own sake. 285

BEV. JUN. Well, madam! Indeed, I can't but be of her mind.

IND. What, though he should maintain and support her, without demanding anything of her on her part? 290

BEV. JUN. Why, madam, is making an expense in the service of a valuable woman (for such I must suppose her), though she should never do him any favor — nay, though she should never know who did her such service — such a mighty heroic 295 business?

IND. Certainly! I should think he must be a man of an uncommon mould.

BEV. JUN. Dear madam, why so? 'tis but, at best, a better taste in expense. To bestow upon 300 one whom he may think one of the ornaments of the whole creation; to be conscious that from his superfluity an innocent, a virtuous spirit is supported above the temptations and sorrows of life; that he sees satisfaction, health, and gladness 305 in her countenance, while he enjoys the happiness of seeing her (as that I will suppose too, or he must be too abstracted, too insensible) — I say, if he is allowed to delight in that prospect, alas, what mighty matter is there in all this? 310

IND. No mighty matter in so disinterested a friendship!

BEV. JUN. Disinterested! I can't think him so. Your hero, madam, is no more than what every gentleman ought to be and I believe very many 315 are. He is only one who takes more delight in reflections than in sensations. He is more pleased with thinking than eating; that's the utmost you can say of him. Why, madam, a greater expense than all this men lay out upon an unnecessary 320 stable of horses.

IND. Can you be sincere in what you say?

BEV. JUN. You may depend upon it, if you know any such man, he does not love dogs inordinately.

IND. No, that he does not. 325

BEV. JUN. Nor cards, nor dice.

IND. No.

BEV. JUN. Nor bottle companions.

IND. No.

BEV. JUN. Nor loose women.   330

IND. No, I'm sure he does not.

BEV. JUN. Take my word, then, if your admired hero is not liable to any of these kind of demands, there's no such pre-eminence in this as you imagine. Nay, this way of expense you speak of is what   335 exalts and raises him that has a taste for it; and, at the same time, his delight is incapable of satiety, disgust, or penitence.

IND. But still I insist, his having no private interest in the action makes it prodigious, al-   340 most incredible.

BEV. JUN. Dear madam, I never knew you more mistaken. Why, who can be more an usurer than he who lays out his money in such valuable purchases? If pleasure be worth purchasing, how great a   345 pleasure is it, to him who has a true taste of life, to ease an aching heart, to see the [human] countenance lighted up into smiles of joy, on the receipt of a bit of ore which is superfluous and otherwise useless in a man's own pocket? What could a man do   350 better with his cash? This is the effect of an humane disposition where there is only a general tie of nature and common necessity. What then must it be when we serve an object of merit, of admiration!

IND. Well! the more you argue against it,   355 the more I shall admire the generosity.

BEV. JUN. Nay, nay! — then, madam, 'tis time to fly, after a declaration that my opinion strengthens my adversary's argument. I had best hasten to my appointment with Mr. Myrtle, and be gone   360 while we are friends and — before things are brought to an extremity.   *Exit carelessly.*

Enter ISABELLA.

ISAB. Well, madam, what think you of him now, pray?

IND. I protest, I begin to fear he is wholly   365 disinterested in what he does for me. On my heart, he has no other view but the mere pleasure of doing it, and has neither good or bad designs upon me.

ISAB. Ah! dear niece! don't be in fear of both! I'll warrant you, you will know time enough   370 that he is not indifferent.

IND. You please me when you tell me so, for if he has any wishes towards me I know he will not pursue them but with honor.

ISAB. I wish I were as confident of one as   375 t'other. I saw the respectful downcast of his eye when you catched him gazing at you during the music. He, I warrant, was surprised, as if he had

been taken stealing your watch. Oh, the undissembled, guilty look!   380

IND. But did you observe any such thing, really? I thought he looked most charmingly graceful! How engaging is modesty in a man when one knows there is a great mind within! So tender a confusion! and yet, in other respects, so much himself,   385 so collected, so dauntless, so determined!

ISAB. Ah, niece! there is a sort of bashfulness which is the best engine[1] to carry on a shameless purpose: some men's modesty serves their wickedness, as hypocrisy gains the respect due to pi-   390 ety. But I will own to you, there is one hopeful symptom, if there could be such a thing as a disinterested lover. But it's all a perplexity — till — till — till —

IND. Till what?   395

ISAB. Till I know whether Mr. Myrtle and Mr. Bevil are really friends or foes. And that I will be convinced of before I sleep, for you shall not be deceived.

IND. I'm sure I never shall if your fears can   400 guard me. In the mean time I'll wrap myself up in the integrity of my own heart, nor dare to doubt of his.

As conscious honor all his actions steers,
So conscious innocence dispels my fears.   405
Exeunt.

ACT III

SCENE I

Scene, SEALAND'S *house.*

Enter TOM, *meeting* PHILLIS.

TOM. Well, Phillis! — what! with a face as if you had never seen me before? — [*Aside.*] What a work have I to do now? She has seen some new visitant at their house, whose airs she has catched, and is resolved to practise them upon me. Number-   5 less are the changes she'll dance through before she'll answer this plain question, videlicet, 'Have you delivered my master's letter to your lady?' Nay, I know her too well to ask an account of it in an ordinary way; I'll be in my airs as well as she. —   10 (*Looking steadfastly at her.*) Well, madam, as unhappy as you are at present pleased to make me, I would not, in the general, be any other than what I am; I would not be a bit wiser, a bit richer, a bit taller, a bit shorter than I am at this instant.   15

PHIL. Did ever anybody doubt, Master Thomas, but that you were extremely satisfied with your sweet self?

TOM. I am, indeed. The thing I have least reason

[1] Trick, device.

to be satisfied with is my fortune, and I am glad   20
of my poverty.   Perhaps if I were rich I should overlook the finest woman in the world, that wants nothing but riches to be thought so.

PHIL. (*aside*). How prettily was that said! But
I'll have a great deal more before I'll say one   25
word.

TOM. I should, perhaps, have been stupidly above
her, had I not been her equal, and by not being her
equal, never had opportunity of being her slave.   I
am my master's servant for hire—I am my   30
mistress's from choice, would she but approve my
passion.

PHIL. I think it's the first time I ever heard you
speak of it with any sense of the anguish, if you really
do suffer any.   35

TOM. Ah, Phillis! can you doubt, after what you
have seen?

PHIL. I know not what I have seen, nor what I
have heard.   But since I'm at leisure, you may tell
me when you fell in love with me, how you fell   40
in love with me, and what you have suffered or are
ready to suffer for me.

TOM (*aside*). Oh, the unmerciful jade! when I'm
in haste about my master's letter.   But I must go
through it. — Ah! too well I remember when,   45
and how, and on what occasion I was first surprised.
It was on the first of April, one thousand seven hundred and fifteen, I came into Mr. Sealand's service; I
was then a hobbledehoy, and you a pretty little tight[1]
girl, a favorite handmaid of the housekeeper.   50
At that time we neither of us knew what was in us.
I remember I was ordered to get out of the window,
one pair of stairs,[2] to rub the sashes clean; the person employed on the inner side was your charming
self, whom I had never seen before.   55

PHIL. I think I remember the silly accident.
What made ye, you oaf, ready to fall down into the
street?

TOM. You know not, I warrant you! — you could
not guess what surprised me!   You took no de-   60
light when you immediately grew wanton in your conquest, and put your lips close and breathed upon the
glass! and when my lips approached, a dirty cloth
you rubbed against my face, and hid your beauteous
form.   When I again drew near, you spit, and   65
rubbed, and smiled at my undoing.

PHIL. What silly thoughts you men have!

TOM. We were Pyramus and Thisbe — but ten
times harder was my fate.   Pyramus could peep only
through a wall; I saw her — saw my Thisbe in all   70
her beauty, but as much kept from her as if a hundred walls between — for there was more; there was
her will against me.   Would she but yet relent! O

[1] Trim, neat.
[2] On the second (*anglice* first) floor of the house.

Phillis! Phillis! shorten my torment and declare you
pity me.   75

PHIL. I believe it's very sufferable; the pain is
not so exquisite but that you may bear it a little
longer.

TOM. Oh, my charming Phillis! if all depended on
my fair one's will I could with glory suffer: but,   80
dearest creature, consider our miserable state!

PHIL. How!   Miserable!

TOM. We are miserable to be in love and under the
command of others than those we love — with that
generous passion in the heart, to be sent to and   85
fro on errands, called, checked, and rated for the
meanest trifles.   O Phillis! you don't know how
many china cups and glasses my passion for you has
made me break.   You have broke my fortune as well
as my heart.   90

PHIL. Well, Mr. Thomas, I cannot but own to
you that I believe your master writes and you speak
the best of any men in the world.   Never was woman
so well pleased with a letter as my young lady was
with his, and this is an answer to it.   95
                              (*Gives him a letter.*)

TOM. This was well done, my dearest.   Consider,
we must strike out some pretty livelihood for ourselves by closing their affairs.   It will be nothing for
them to give us a little being of our own, some
small tenement, out of their large possessions.   100
Whatever they give us, 'twill be more than what
they keep for themselves.   One acre with Phillis
would be worth a whole county without her.

PHIL. Oh, could I but believe you!

TOM. If not the utterance, believe the touch   105
of my lips.   (*Kisses her.*)

PHIL. There's no contradicting you; how closely
you argue, Tom!

TOM. And will closer, in due time.   But I must
hasten with this letter, to hasten towards the   110
possession of you.   Then, Phillis, consider how I must
be revenged — look to it — of all your skittishness,
shy looks, and at best but coy compliances.

PHIL. O Tom! you grow wanton and sensual, as my
lady calls it; I must not endure it.   Oh! foh!   115
you are a man — an odious, filthy male creature!
You should behave, if you had a right sense or were a
man of sense, like Mr. Cimberton, with distance and
indifference, or — let me see — some other becoming
hard word — with seeming in — in — inadver-   120
tency, and not rush on one as if you were seizing a
prey. — But hush! the ladies are coming. — [Good]
Tom, don't kiss me above once, and be gone.   Lard,
we have been fooling and toying, and not considered
the main business of our masters and mistresses.   125

TOM. Why, their business is to be fooling and
toying as soon as the parchments are ready.

PHIL.   Well remembered! — parchments!   My

lady, to my knowledge, is preparing writings between her coxcomb cousin, Cimberton, and my mis- 130 tress, though my master has an eye to the parchments already prepared between your master, Mr. Bevil, and my mistress; and, I believe, my mistress herself has signed and sealed, in her heart, to Mr. Myrtle. — Did I not bid you kiss me but once, 135 and be gone? But I know you won't be satisfied.

TOM (*kissing her hand*). No, you smooth creature, how should I?

PHIL. Well, since you are so humble, or so cool, as to ravish my hand only, I'll take my leave 140 of you like a great lady, and you a man of quality. (*They salute¹ formally.*)

TOM. Pox of all this state!
(*Offers to kiss her more closely.*)

PHIL. No, prithee, Tom, mind your business! We must follow that interest which will take, but endeavor at that which will be most for us and 145 we like most. Oh, here's my young mistress! (TOM *taps her neck behind, and kisses his fingers.*) Go, ye liquorish² fool! *Exit* TOM.

Enter LUCINDA.

LUC. Who was that you was hurrying away?

PHIL. One that I had no mind to part with. 150

LUC. Why did you turn him away then?

PHIL. For your ladyship's service — to carry your ladyship's letter to his master. I could hardly get the rogue away.

LUC. Why, has he so little love for his mas- 155 ter?

PHIL. No; but he has so much love for his mistress.

LUC. But I thought I heard him kiss you. Why do you suffer that? 160

PHIL. Why, madam, we vulgar take it to be a sign of love. We servants, we poor people, that have nothing but our persons to bestow or treat for, are forced to deal and bargain by way of sample, and therefore, as we have no parchments or wax nec- 165 essary in our agreements, we squeeze with our hands and seal with our lips to ratify vows and promises.

LUC. But can't you trust one another without such earnest³ down?

PHIL. We don't think it safe, any more than 170 you gentry, to come together without deeds executed.

LUC. Thou art a pert, merry hussy.

PHIL. I wish, madam, your lover and you were as happy as Tom and your servant are.

LUC. You grow impertinent. 175

PHIL. I have done, madam; and I won't ask you what you intend to do with Mr. Myrtle, what your father will do with Mr. Bevil, nor what you all, especially my lady, mean by admitting Mr. Cimberton as particularly here as if he were married to you 180

already — nay, you are married actually as far as people of quality are.

LUC. How's that?

PHIL. You have different beds in the same house.

LUC. Pshaw! I have a very great value for 185 Mr. Bevil, but have absolutely put an end to his pretensions in the letter I gave you for him. But my father, in his heart, still has a mind to him, were it not for this woman they talk of; and I am apt to imagine he is married to her, or never designs 190 to marry at all.

PHIL. Then Mr. Myrtle —

LUC. He had my parents' leave to apply to me, and by that has won me and my affections; who is to have this body of mine without 'em, it seems, is 195 nothing to me. My mother says it's indecent for me to let my thoughts stray about the person of my husband; nay, she says a maid, rigidly virtuous, though she may have been where her lover was a thousand times, should not have made observa- 200 tions enough to know him from another man when she sees him in a third place.

PHIL. That is more than the severity of a nun, for not to see when one may is hardly possible; not to see when one can't is very easy. At this rate, 205 madam, there are a great many whom you have not seen who —

LUC. Mamma says the first time you see your husband should be at that instant he is made so, when your father, with the help of the minis- 210 ter, gives you to him; then you are to see him, then you are to observe and take notice of him, because then you are to obey him.

PHIL. But does not my lady remember you are to love as well as obey? 215

LUC. To love is a passion, 'tis a desire, and we must have no desires. Oh! I cannot endure the reflection. With what insensibility on my part, with what more than patience, have I been exposed and offered to some awkward booby or other in 220 every county of Great Britain!

PHIL. Indeed, madam, I wonder I never heard you speak of it before with this indignation.

LUC. Every corner of the land has presented me with a wealthy coxcomb. As fast as one treaty 225 has gone off, another has come on, till my name and person have been the tittle-tattle of the whole town. What is this world come to? No shame left — to be bartered for like the beasts of the fields, and that in such an instance as coming together to an en- 230 tire familiarity and union of soul and body! Oh! and this without being so much as well-wishers to each other, but for increase of fortune.

PHIL. But madam, all these vexations will end very soon in one for all. Mr. Cimberton is 235 your mother's kinsman, and three hundred years an older gentleman than any lover you ever had; for

---

¹ Kiss.　　　² Greedy, lecherous.　　　³ Partial payment.

which reason, with that of his prodigious large estate, she is resolved on him, and has sent to consult the lawyers accordingly — nay, has (whether 240 you know it or no) been in treaty with Sir Geoffry, who, to join in the settlement, has accepted of a sum to do it, and is every moment expected in town for that purpose.

Luc. How do you get all this intelligence? 245

Phil. By an art I have, I thank my stars, beyond all the waiting-maids in Great Britain — the art of list'ning, madam, for your ladyship's service.

Luc. I shall soon know as much as you do. Leave me, leave me, Phillis; begone! Here, here! 250 I'll turn you out. My mother says I must not converse with my servants, though I must converse with no one else.   *Exit* Phillis.
How unhappy we are who are born to great fortunes! No one looks at us with indifference, 255 or acts towards us on the foot of plain dealing; yet by all I have been heretofore offered to or treated for I have been used with the most agreeable of all abuses — flattery. But now, by this phlegmatic fool I am used as nothing, or a mere thing. He, for- 260 sooth, is too wise, too learned, to have any regard to desires, and I know not what the learned oaf calls sentiments of love and passion. — Here he comes with my mother. It's much if he looks at me, or if he does, takes no more notice of me than of any 265 other movable in the room.

Enter Mrs. Sealand *and* Mr. Cimberton.

Mrs. Seal. How do I admire this noble, this learned taste of yours, and the worthy regard you have to our own ancient and honorable house, in consulting a means to keep the blood as pure 270 and as regularly descended as may be.

Cimb. Why, really, madam, the young women of this age are treated with discourses of such a tendency, and their imaginations so bewildered in flesh and blood, that a man of reason can't talk to be 275 understood. They have no ideas of happiness but what are more gross than the gratification of hunger and thirst.

Luc. (*aside*). With how much reflection he is a coxcomb!   280

Cimb. And in truth, madam, I have considered it as a most brutal custom that persons of the first character in the world should go as ordinarily and with as little shame to bed as to dinner with one another. They proceed to the propagation of 285 the species as openly as to the preservation of the individual.

Luc. (*aside*). She that willingly goes to bed to thee must have no shame, I'm sure.

Mrs. Seal. O cousin Cimberton! cousin 290 Cimberton! how abstracted, how refined is your sense of things! But indeed, it is too true there is noth-

ing so ordinary as to say, in the best governed families, 'My master and lady are gone to bed'; one does not know but it might have been said of one's 295 self!   (*Hiding her face with her fan.*)

Cimb. Lycurgus, madam, instituted otherwise; among the Lacedæmonians the whole female world was pregnant, but none but the mothers themselves knew by whom. Their meetings were secret, 300 and the amorous congress always by stealth, and no such professed doings between the sexes as are tolerated among us under the audacious word 'marriage.'

Mrs. Seal. Oh, had I lived in those days 305 and been a matron of Sparta! one might with less indecency have had ten children, according to that modest institution, than one under the confusion of our modern, barefaced manner!

Luc. (*aside*). And yet, poor woman, she has 310 gone through the whole ceremony, and here I stand a melancholy proof of it.

Mrs. Seal. We will talk then of business. That girl walking about the room there is to be your wife. She has, I confess, no ideas, no sentiments, that 315 speak her born of a thinking mother.

Cimb. I have observed her; her lively look, free air, and disengaged countenance speak her very —

Luc. Very what?

Cimb. If you please, madam — to set her 320 a little that way.

Mrs. Seal. Lucinda, say nothing to him; you are not a match for him. When you are married, you may speak to such a husband when you're spoken to. But I am disposing of you above your- 325 self every way.

Cimb. Madam, you cannot but observe the inconveniences I expose myself to, in hopes that your ladyship will be the consort of my better part.[1] As for the young woman, she is rather an impedi- 330 ment than a help to a man of letters and speculation. Madam, there is no reflection, no philosophy, can at all times subdue the sensitive life, but the animal shall sometimes carry away the man. Ha! ay, the vermilion of her lips —   335

Luc. Pray, don't talk of me thus.

Cimb. The pretty enough — pant of her bosom —

Luc. Sir! — Madam, don't you hear him?

Cimb. Her forward chest —

Luc. Intolerable!   340

Cimb. High health —

Luc. The grave, easy impudence of him!

Cimb. Proud heart —

Luc. Stupid coxcomb!

Cimb. I say, madam, her impatience while 345 we are looking at her, throws out all attractions — her arms — her neck — what a spring in her step!

---

[1] I.e., my intellectual companion.

Luc. Don't you run me over thus, you strange unaccountable!

Cimb. What an elasticity in her veins and 350 arteries!

Luc. I have no veins, no arteries.

Mrs. Seal. O child, hear him! he talks finely! He's a scholar; he knows what you have.

Cimb. The speaking invitation of her shape, 355 the gathering of herself up, and the indignation you see in the pretty little thing. Now, I am considering her, on this occasion, but as one that is to be pregnant.

Luc. (aside). The familiar, learned, unsea- 360 sonable puppy!

Cimb. And pregnant undoubtedly she will be yearly. I fear I shan't, for many years, have discretion enough to give her one fallow season.

Luc. Monster! there's no bearing it. The 365 hideous sot! there's no enduring it, to be thus surveyed like a steed at sale.

Cimb. At sale! She's very illiterate — but she's very well limbed too. Turn her in; I see what she is.
　　　　　　　　　　　Exit Lucinda, in a rage.

Mrs. Seal. Go, you creature! I am ashamed 370 of you.

Cimb. No harm done. — You know, madam, the better sort of people, as I observed to you, treat by their lawyers of weddings (adjusting himself at the glass) — and the woman in the bargain, like 375 the mansion-house in the sale of the estate, is thrown in — and what that is, whether good or bad, is not at all considered.

Mrs. Seal. I grant it, and therefore make no demand for her youth and beauty, and every 380 other accomplishment, as the common world think 'em, because she is not polite.

Cimb. Madam, I know your exalted understanding, abstracted as it is from vulgar prejudices, will not be offended when I declare to you, I 385 marry to have an heir to my estate, and not to beget a colony or a plantation.[1] This young woman's beauty and constitution will demand provision for a tenth child at least.

Mrs. Seal (aside). With all that wit and 390 learning, how considerate! What an economist! — Sir, I cannot make her any other than she is, or say she is much better than the other young women of this age, or fit for much besides being a mother; but I have given directions for the marriage settle- 395 ments, and Sir Geoffry Cimberton's counsel is to meet ours here at this hour, concerning this joining in the deed which, when executed, makes you capable of settling what is due to Lucinda's fortune. Herself, as I told you, I say nothing of. 400

Cimb. No, no, no, indeed, madam, it is not usual;

and I must depend upon my own reflection and philosophy not to overstock my family.

Mrs. Seal. I cannot help her, cousin Cimberton, but she is, for aught I see, as well[2] as the 405 daughter of anybody else.

Cimb. That is very true, madam.

Enter a Servant, who whispers Mrs. Sealand.

Mrs. Seal. The lawyers are come, and now we are to hear what they have resolved as to the point whether it's necessary that Sir Geoffry should 410 join in the settlement, as being what they call in the remainder. But, good cousin, you must have patience with 'em. These lawyers, I am told, are of a different kind; one is what they call a chamber counsel, the other a pleader. The convey- 415 ancer is slow, from an imperfection in his speech, and therefore shunned the bar, but extremely passionate and impatient of contradiction. The other is as warm as he, but has a tongue so voluble, and a head so conceited, he will suffer nobody to 420 speak but himself.

Cimb. You mean old Sergeant Target and Counsellor Bramble? I have heard of 'em.

Mrs. Seal. The same. — Show in the gentlemen.
　　　　　　　　　　　　　　　Exit Servant.

Re-enter Servant, introducing Myrtle and
Tom disguised as Bramble and Target.

Mrs. Seal. Gentlemen, this is the party 425 concerned, Mr. Cimberton; and I hope you have considered of the matter.

Tar. Yes, madam, we have agreed that it must be by indent — dent — dent — dent —

Bram. Yes, madam, Mr. Sergeant and my- 430 self have agreed, as he is pleased to inform you, that it must be an indenture tripartite, and tripartite let it be, for Sir Geoffry must needs be a party; old Cimberton, in the year 1619, says, in that ancient roll in Mr. Sergeant's hands, as, recourse thereto 435 being had, will more at large appear —

Tar. Yes, and by the deeds in your hands, it appears that —

Bram. Mr. Sergeant, I beg of you to make no inferences upon what is in our custody, but 440 speak to the titles in your own deeds. I shall not show that deed till my client is in town.

Cimb. You know best your own methods.

Mrs. Seal. The single question is whether the entail is such that my cousin, Sir Geoffry, is 445 necessary in this affair?

Bram. Yes, as to the lordship of Tretriplet, but not as to the messuage of Grimgribber.

Tar. I say that Gr — Gr — that Gr — Gr — Grimgribber, Grimgribber is in us; that is to 450

---

[1] A synonym for colony.

[2] Good.

say, the remainder thereof, as well as that of Tr —
Tr — triplet.

BRAM. You go upon the deed of Sir Ralph, made
in the middle of the last century, precedent to that in
which old Cimberton made over the remainder,   455
and made it pass to the heirs general, by which your
client comes in; and I question whether the remainder even of Tretriplet is in him.   But we are willing
to waive that, and give him a valuable consideration.
But we shall not purchase what is in us for-   460
ever, as Grimgribber is, at the rate as we guard against
the contingent of Mr. Cimberton having no son.
Then we know Sir Geoffry is the first of the collateral
male line in this family, yet —

TAR. Sir, Gr — Gr — ber is —   465

BRAM. I apprehend you very well, and your argument might be of force, and we would be inclined
to hear that in all its parts.   But, sir, I see very
plainly what you are going into.   I tell you, it is as
probable a contingent that Sir Geoffry may die   470
before Mr. Cimberton, as that he may outlive him.

TAR. Sir, we are not ripe for that yet, but I must
say —

BRAM. Sir, I allow you the whole extent of that
argument; but that will go no farther than as   475
to the claimants under old Cimberton.   I am of opinion that according to the instruction of Sir Ralph
he could not dock the entail and then create a new
estate for the heirs general.

TAR. Sir, I have not patience to be told   480
that, when Gr — Gr — ber —

BRAM. I will allow it you, Mr. Sergeant; but there
must be the word 'heirs for ever,' to make such an
estate as you pretend.

CIMB. I must be impartial, though you are   485
counsel for my side of the question.   Were it not that
you are so good as to allow him what he has not said,
I should think it very hard you should answer him
without hearing him.   But, gentlemen, I believe you
have both considered this matter and are firm   490
in your different opinions.   'Twere better, therefore,
you proceeded according to the particular sense of
each of you and gave your thoughts distinctly in
writing.   And do you see, sirs, pray let me have a
copy of what you say, in English.   495

BRAM. Why, what is all we have been saying?
In English! — Oh! but I forgot myself; you're a wit.
But, however, to please you, sir, you shall have it
in as plain terms as the law will admit of.

CIMB. But I would have it, sir, without de-   500
lay.

BRAM. That, sir, the law will not admit of.   The
courts are sitting at Westminster, and I am this moment obliged to be at every one of them, and 'twould
be wrong if I should not be in the Hall to at-   505
tend one of 'em at least; the rest would take it ill else.
Therefore I must leave what I have said to Mr. Ser-

geant's consideration, and I will digest his arguments
on my part, and you shall hear from me again, sir.

                                        Exit BRAMBLE.

TAR. Agreed, agreed.   510

CIMB. Mr. Bramble is very quick; he parted a
little abruptly.

TAR. He could not bear my argument; I pinched
him to the quick about that Gr — Gr — ber.

MRS. SEAL. I saw that, for he durst not so   515
much as hear you.   I shall send to you, Mr. Sergeant,
as soon as Sir Geoffry comes to town, and then I hope
all may be adjusted.

TAR. I shall be at my chambers at my usual hours.

                                        Exit.

CIMB. Madam, if you please, I'll now attend   520
you to the tea table, where I shall hear from your
ladyship reason and good sense, after all this law
and gibberish.

MRS. SEAL. 'Tis a wonderful thing, sir, that men
of professions do not study to talk the sub-   525
stance of what they have to say in the language of the
rest of the world.   Sure, they'd find their account [1] in it.

CIMB. They might, perhaps, madam, with people
of your good sense; but with the generality 'twould
never do.   The vulgar would have no respect   530
for truth and knowledge if they were exposed to
naked view.

Truth is too simple, of all art bereaved:
Since the world will — why, let it be deceived.

                                        Exeunt.

ACT IV

SCENE I

Scene, BEVIL JUNIOR'S *lodgings.*

BEVIL JUNIOR, *with a letter in his hand,*
                    followed by TOM.

TOM. Upon my life, sir, I know nothing of the matter.   I never opened my lips to Mr. Myrtle about
anything of your honor's letter to Madam Lucinda.

BEV. JUN. What's the fool in such a fright for?
I don't suppose you did.   What I would know is,   5
whether Mr. Myrtle showed any suspicion, or asked
you any questions, to lead you to say casually that
you had carried any such letter for me this morning.

TOM. Why, sir, if he did ask me any questions,
how could I help it?   10

BEV. JUN. I don't say you could, oaf!   I am not
questioning you, but him.   What did he say to you?

TOM. Why, sir, when I came to his chambers, to
be dressed for the lawyer's part your honor was
pleased to put me upon, he asked me if I had   15
been at Mr. Sealand's this morning.   So I told him,
sir, I often went thither — because, sir, if I had not

[1] Profit.

said that, he might have thought there was something more in my going now than at another time.

BEV. JUN. Very well! — (*Aside*.) The fel-   20
low's caution, I find, has given him this jealousy. —
Did he ask you no other questions?

TOM. Yes, sir; now I remember as we came away
in the hackney coach from Mr. Sealand's, 'Tom,'
says he, 'as I came in to your master this morn-   25
ing, he bade you go for an answer to a letter he had
sent. Pray, did you bring him any?' says he. 'Ah!'
says I, 'sir, your honor is pleased to joke with me;
you have a mind to know whether I can keep a
secret or no?'   30

BEV. JUN. And so, by showing him you could,
you told him you had one?

TOM (*confused*). Sir ——

BEV. JUN. [*aside*]. What mean actions does jealousy make a man stoop to! How poorly has he   35
used art [1] with a servant to make him betray his
master! — Well, and when did he give you this letter
for me?

TOM. Sir, he writ it before he pulled off his lawyer's
gown, at his own chambers.   40

BEV. JUN. Very well; and what did he say when
you brought him my answer to it?

TOM. He looked a little out of humor, sir, and said
it was very well.

BEV. JUN. I knew he would be grave upon't.   45
— Wait without.

TOM. Humh! 'gad, I don't like this; I am afraid
we are all in the wrong box here.   *Exit* TOM.

BEV. JUN. I put on a serenity while my fellow was
present; but I have never been more thoroughly   50
disturbed. This hot man! to write me a challenge,
on supposed artificial dealing, when I professed myself his friend! I can live contented without glory,
but I cannot suffer shame. What's to be done? But
first let me consider Lucinda's letter again.   55
                                          (*Reads*.)
'Sir,
   I hope it is consistent with the laws a woman
ought to impose upon herself, to acknowledge that
your manner of declining a treaty of marriage in
our family, and desiring the refusal may come   60
from me, has something more engaging in it than
the courtship of him who, I fear, will fall to my
lot, except your friend exerts himself for our common safety and happiness. I have reasons for
desiring Mr. Myrtle may not know of this let-   65
ter till hereafter, and am your most obliged humble
servant,
                                    Lucinda Sealand.'
Well, but the postscript ——   (*Reads*.)
   'I won't, upon second thoughts, hide any-   70

thing from you. But my reason for concealing
this is, that Mr. Myrtle has a jealousy in his temper which gives me some terrors; but my esteem
for him inclines me to hope that only an ill effect
which sometimes accompanies a tender love,   75
and what may be cured by a careful and un-
blameable conduct.'
Thus has this lady made me her friend and confident, and put herself, in a kind, under my protection. I cannot tell him immediately the purport   80
of her letter, except I could cure him of the violent
and untractable passion of jealousy, and so serve him
and her, by disobeying her in the article of secrecy,
more than I should by complying with her directions. — But then this duelling, which custom   85
has imposed upon every man who would live with
reputation and honor in the world — how must I
preserve myself from imputations there? He'll, forsooth, call it or think it fear, if I explain without
fighting. — But his letter — I'll read it again —   90
'Sir,
   You have used me basely in corresponding
and carrying on a treaty where you told me you
were indifferent. I have changed my sword since
I saw you, which advertisement [2] I thought   95
proper to send you against the next meeting between you and the injured
                                    Charles Myrtle.'

Enter TOM.

TOM. Mr. Myrtle, sir. Would your honor please
to see him?   100

BEV. JUN. Why, you stupid creature! Let Mr.
Myrtle wait at my lodgings! Show him up.
                                          Exit TOM.
Well, I am resolved upon my carriage to him. He
is in love, and in every circumstance of life a little distrustful, which I must allow for — but here he is.   105

Enter TOM, *introducing* MYRTLE.

Sir, I am extremely obliged to you for this honor. —
[*To* TOM.] But, sir, you, with your very discerning
face, leave the room.   *Exit* TOM.
Well, Mr. Myrtle, your commands with me?

MYRT. The time, the place, our long ac-   110
quaintance, and many other circumstances which
affect me on this occasion, oblige me, without farther
ceremony or conference, to desire you would not only,
as you already have, acknowledge the receipt of my
letter, but also comply with the request in it.   115
I must have farther notice taken of my message than
these half lines — 'I have yours — I shall be at home.'

BEV. JUN. Sir, I own I have received a letter from
you in a very unusual style; but as I design every-

[1] Trickery.   [2] Notice.

thing in this matter shall be your own action,   120
your own seeking, I shall understand nothing but
what you are pleased to confirm face to face, and I
have already forgot the contents of your epistle.

MYRT. This cool manner is very agreeable to the
abuse you have already made of my simplicity   125
and frankness, and I see your moderation tends to
your own advantage and not mine — to your own
safety, not consideration of your friend.

BEV. JUN. My own safety, Mr. Myrtle?

MYRT. Your own safety, Mr. Bevil.   130

BEV. JUN. Look you, Mr. Myrtle, there's no dis-
guising that I understand what you would be at; but,
sir, you know I have often dared to disapprove of the
decisions a tyrant custom has introduced, to the
breach of all laws, both divine and human.   135

MYRT. Mr. Bevil, Mr. Bevil, it would be a good
first principle in those who have so tender a conscience that way, to have as much abhorrence of
doing injuries as —

BEV. JUN. As what?   140

MYRT. As fear of answering for 'em.

BEV. JUN. As fear of answering for 'em! But that
apprehension is just or blameable according to the object of that fear. I have often told you, in confidence
of heart, I abhorred the daring to offend the   145
Author of life, and rushing into His presence — I say,
by the very same act, to commit the crime against
Him, and immediately to urge on to His tribunal.

MYRT. Mr. Bevil, I must tell you, this coolness,
this gravity, this show of conscience, shall   150
never cheat me of my mistress. You have, indeed,
the best excuse for life — the hopes of possessing Lucinda. But consider, sir, I have as much reason to be
weary of it, if I am to lose her; and my first attempt
to recover her shall be to let her see the daunt-   155
less man who is to be her guardian and protector.

BEV. JUN. Sir, show me but the least glimpse of
argument, that I am authorized by my own hand to
vindicate any lawless insult of this nature, and I will
show thee, to chastise thee hardly deserves the   160
name of courage — slight, inconsiderate man! There
is, Mr. Myrtle, no such terror in quick anger; and you
shall, you know not why, be cool, as you have, you
know not why, been warm.

MYRT. Is the woman one loves so little an   165
occasion of anger? You, perhaps, who know not
what it is to love — who have your ready, your com-
modious, your foreign trinket for your loose
hours, and from your fortune, your specious outward carriage, and other lucky circumstances,   170
as easy a way to the possession of a woman of honor
— you know nothing of what it is to be alarmed, to
be distracted with anxiety and terror of losing more
than life. Your marriage, happy man, goes on like
common business, and in the interim you have   175

your rambling captive, your Indian princess, for your
soft moments of dalliance — your convenient, your
ready Indiana.

BEV. JUN. You have touched me beyond the patience of a man, and I'm excusable, in the guard   180
of innocence (or from the infirmity of human nature,
which can bear no more), to accept your invitation
and observe your letter. Sir, I'll attend you.

Enter TOM.

TOM. Did you call, sir? I thought you did; I heard
you speak aloud.   185

BEV. JUN. Yes; go call a coach!

TOM. Sir — master — Mr. Myrtle — friends —
gentlemen — what d'ye mean? I am but a servant,
or —

BEV. JUN. Call a coach!   *Exit* TOM.   190
(*A long pause, walking sullenly by each
other.*)

[BEV. JUN.] (*aside*). Shall I (though provoked to the
uttermost) recover myself at the entrance of a third
person, and that my servant, too, and not have respect enough to all I have ever been receiving from
infancy, the obligation to the best of fathers, to   195
an unhappy virgin too, whose life depends on mine?
(*Shutting the door — to* MYRTLE.) I have, thank
heaven, had time to recollect myself, and shall not,
for fear of what such a rash man as you think of me,
keep longer unexplained the false appearances   200
under which your infirmity of temper makes you
suffer, when perhaps too much regard to a false point
of honor makes me prolong that suffering.

MYRT. I am sure Mr. Bevil cannot doubt but I
had rather have satisfaction from his innocence   205
than his sword.

BEV. JUN. Why, then, would you ask it first that
way?

MYRT. Consider, you kept your temper yourself no longer than till I spoke to the disad-   210
vantage of her you loved.

BEV. JUN. True; but let me tell you, I have saved
you from the most exquisite distress, even though
you had succeeded in the dispute. I know you so well
that I am sure to have found this letter about   215
a man you had killed would have been worse than
death to yourself. — Read it. — (*Aside.*) When he
is thoroughly mortified and shame has got the better
of jealousy, when he has seen himself throughly,
he will deserve to be assisted towards obtain-   220
ing Lucinda.

MYRT. [*aside*]. With what a superiority has he
turned the injury on me, as the aggressor! I begin
to fear I have been too far transported. — 'A treaty
in our family —' is not that saying too much?   225
I shall relapse. — But I find (on the postscript)
'something like jealousy.' With what face can I see

219] YZ *thoroughly*.

my benefactor, my advocate, whom I have treated like a betrayer? — Oh! Bevil, with what words shall I — 　　　　　　　　　　　　　　　　　230

BEV. JUN. There needs none; to convince is much more than to conquer.

MYRT. But can you —

BEV. JUN. You have o'erpaid the inquietude you gave me, in the change I see in you towards　235 me. Alas! what machines are we! Thy face is altered to that of another man — to that of my companion, my friend.

MYRT. That I could be such a precipitant wretch!　　　　　　　　　　　　　　　　　240

BEV. JUN. Pray, no more!

MYRT. Let me reflect how many friends have died by the hands of friends, for want of temper; and you must give me leave to say again and again how much I am beholden to that superior spirit you have　245 subdued me with. What had become of one of us, or perhaps both, had you been as weak as I was, and as incapable of reason!

BEV. JUN. I congratulate to us both the escape from ourselves, and hope the memory of it will　250 make us dearer friends than ever.

MYRT. Dear Bevil, your friendly conduct has convinced me that there is nothing manly but what is conducted by reason and agreeable to the practice of virtue and justice. And yet how many have　255 been sacrificed to that idol, the unreasonable opinion of men! Nay, they are so ridiculous, in it, that they often use their swords against each other with dissembled anger and real fear.

Betrayed by honor and compelled by shame,　260
They hazard being to preserve a name:
Nor dare enquire into the dread mistake,
Till plunged in sad eternity they wake.　*Exeunt.*

SCENE [II]

St. James's Park.

Enter SIR JOHN BEVIL *and* MR. SEALAND.

SIR J. BEV. Give me leave, however, Mr. Sealand, as we are upon a treaty for uniting our families, to mention only the business of an ancient house. Genealogy and descent are to be of some consideration in an affair of this sort.　　　　　　　　5

MR. SEAL. Genealogy and descent! Sir, there has been in our family a very large one. There was Galfrid the father of Edward, the father of Ptolemey, the father of Crassus, the father of Earl Richard, the father of Henry the Marquis, the father of Duke　10 John —

SIR J. BEV. What, do you rave, Mr. Sealand? — all these great names in your family?

MR. SEAL. These? Yes, sir. I have heard my father name 'em all, and more.　　　　　　15

SIR J. BEV. Ay, sir? and did he say they were all in your family?

MR. SEAL. Yes, sir, he kept 'em all. He was the greatest cocker[1] in England. He said Duke John won him many battles, and never lost one.　　20

SIR J. BEV. Oh, sir, your servant! you are laughing at my laying any stress upon descent; but I must tell you, sir, I never knew anyone but he that wanted that advantage turn it into ridicule.

MR. SEAL. And I never knew anyone who　25 had many better advantages put that into his account. But, Sir John, value yourself as you please upon your ancient house, I am to talk freely of everything you are pleased to put into your bill of rates on this occasion. Yet, sir, I have made no objec-　30 tions to your son's family. 'Tis his morals that I doubt.

SIR J. BEV. Sir, I can't help saying that what might injure a citizen's credit may be no stain to a gentleman's honor.　　　　　　　　　　　35

MR. SEAL. Sir John, the honor of a gentleman is liable to be tainted by as small a matter as the credit of a trader. We are talking of a marriage, and in such a case the father of a young woman will not think it an addition to the honor or credit of her　40 lover that he is a keeper —

SIR J. BEV. Mr. Sealand, don't take upon you to spoil my son's marriage with any woman else.

MR. SEAL. Sir John, let him apply to any woman else, and have as many mistresses as he pleases.　45

SIR J. BEV. My son, sir, is a discreet and sober gentleman.

MR. SEAL. Sir, I never saw a man that wenched soberly and discreetly that ever left it off; the decency observed in the practice hides, even from the　50 sinner, the iniquity of it. They pursue it, not that their appetites hurry 'em away, but, I warrant you, because 'tis their opinion they may do it.

SIR J. BEV. Were what you suspect a truth — do you design to keep your daughter a virgin till　55 you find a man unblemished that way?

MR. SEAL. Sir, as much a cit[2] as you take me for, I know the town and the world: and give me leave to say that we merchants are a species of gentry that have grown into the world this last century, and　60 are as honorable, and almost as useful, as you landed folks that have always thought yourselves so much above us; for your trading, forsooth, is extended no farther than a load of hay or a fat ox. You are pleasant people, indeed, because you are generally　65 bred up to be lazy; therefore, I warrant you, industry is dishonorable.

SIR J. BEV. Be not offended, sir; let us go back to our point.

MR. SEAL. Oh, not at all offended! but I don't　70

---

[1] Cockfighter.

[2] Citizen, merchant, member of the London middle class.

love to leave any part of the account unclosed; look you, Sir John, comparisons are odious, and more particularly so on occasions of this kind, when we are projecting races that are to be made out of both sides of the comparisons.   75

Sir J. Bev. But my son, sir, is, in the eye of the world, a gentleman of merit.

Mr. Seal. I own to you, I think him so. But, Sir John, I am a man exercised and experienced in chances and disasters. I lost, in my earlier 80 years, a very fine wife, and with her a poor little infant. This makes me, perhaps, overcautious to preserve the second bounty of providence to me, and be as careful as I can of this child. You'll pardon me; my poor girl, sir, is as valuable to me as 85 your boasted son to you.

Sir J. Bev. Why, that's one very good reason, Mr. Sealand, why I wish my son had her.

Mr. Seal. There is nothing but this strange lady here, this *incognita*, that can be objected to him. 90 Here and there a man falls in love with an artful creature, and gives up all the motives of life to that one passion.

Sir J. Bev. A man of my son's understanding cannot be supposed to be one of them.   95

Mr. Seal. Very wise men have been so enslaved, and when a man marries with one of them upon his hands, whether moved from the demand of the world or slighter reasons, such a husband soils [1] with his wife for a month perhaps — then 'Good b'w'ye, 100 madam!' — the show's over. Ah! John Dryden points out such a husband to a hair, where he says, —

And while abroad so prodigal the dolt is,
Poor spouse at home as ragged as a colt is.[2]

Now, in plain terms, sir, I shall not care to 105 have my poor girl turned a-grazing, and that must be the case when —

Sir J. Bev. But pray consider, sir, my son —

Mr. Seal. Look you, sir, I'll make the matter short. This unknown lady, as I told you, is all 110 the objection I have to him; but, one way or other, he is, or has been, certainly engaged to her. I am therefore resolved this very afternoon to visit her. Now, from her behavior or appearance I shall soon be let into what I may fear or hope for.   115

Sir J. Bev. Sir, I am very confident there can be nothing enquired into, relating to my son, that will not, upon being understood, turn to his advantage.

Mr. Seal. I hope that as sincerely as you believe it. Sir John Bevil, when I am satisfied in this 120 great point, if your son's conduct answers the character you give him, I shall wish your alliance more than that of any gentleman in Great Britain — and so, your servant!   *Exit.*

[1] Cohabits with.
[2] Misquoted from Dryden's prologue to Southerne's *Disappointment.*

Sir J. Bev. He is gone in a way but barely 125 civil; but his great wealth, and the merit of his only child, the heiress of it, are not to be lost for a little peevishness.

Enter Humphrey.

Oh, Humphrey! you are come in a seasonable minute. I want to talk to thee, and to tell thee 130 that my head and heart are on the rack about my son.

Humph. Sir, you may trust his discretion; I am sure you may.

Sir J. Bev. Why, I do believe I may, and yet I'm in a thousand fears when I lay this vast wealth 135 before me; when I consider his prepossessions, either generous to a folly in an honorable love, or abandoned past redemption in a vicious one — and, from the one or the other, his insensibility to the fairest prospect towards doubling our estate. A father 140 who knows how useful wealth is, and how necessary, even to those who despise it — I say a father, Humphrey, a father cannot bear it.

Humph. Be not transported, sir; you will grow incapable of taking any resolution in your 145 perplexity.

Sir J. Bev. Yet, as angry as I am with him, I would not have him surprised in anything. This mercantile, rough man may go grossly into the examination of this matter, and talk to the gentle- 150 woman so as to —

Humph. No, I hope, not in an abrupt manner.

Sir J. Bev. No, I hope not! Why, dost thou know anything of her, or of him — or of anything of it, or all of it?   155

Humph. My dear master, I know so much that I told him this very day you had reason to be secretly out of humor about her.

Sir J. Bev. Did you go so far? Well, what said he to that?   160

Humph. His words were, looking upon me steadfastly: 'Humphrey,' says he, 'that woman is a woman of honor.'

Sir J. Bev. How! Do you think he is married to her, or designs to marry her?   165

Humph. I can say nothing to the latter, but he says he can marry no one without your consent while you are living.

Sir J. Bev. If he said so much, I know he scorns to break his word with me.   170

Humph. I am sure of that.

Sir J. Bev. You are sure of that. Well, that's some comfort. Then I have nothing to do but to see the bottom of this matter during this present ruffle.[3] — O Humphrey —   175

Humph. You are not ill, I hope, sir.

Sir J. Bev. Yes, a man is very ill that's in a very ill humor. To be a father is to be in care for one

[3] Annoyance.

whom you oftener disoblige than please by that very care. Oh, that sons could know the duty to a 180 father before they themselves are fathers! But perhaps you'll say now that I am one of the happiest fathers in the world; but I assure you, that of the very happiest is not a condition to be envied.

HUMPH. Sir, your pain arises, not from the 185 thing itself, but your particular sense of it. You are overfond — nay, give me leave to say you are unjustly apprehensive from your fondness. My master Bevil never disobliged you, and he will — I know he will — do everything you ought to expect. 190

SIR J. BEV. He won't take all this money with this girl. For aught I know, he will, forsooth, have so much moderation as to think he ought not to force his liking for any consideration.

HUMPH. He is to marry her, not you; he is 195 to live with her, not you, sir.

SIR J. BEV. I know not what to think. But I know nothing can be more miserable than to be in this doubt. Follow me; I must come to some resolution. *Exeunt.* 200

SCENE [III]

BEVIL JUNIOR'S *lodgings.*

Enter TOM *and* PHILLIS.

TOM. Well, madam, if you must speak with Mr. Myrtle, you shall; he is now with my master in the library.

PHIL. But you must leave me alone with him, for he can't make me a present, nor I so handsomely 5 take anything from him, before you. It would not be decent.

TOM. It will be very decent, indeed, for me to retire and leave my mistress with another man!

PHIL. He is a gentleman and will treat one 10 properly.

TOM. I believe so; but, however, I won't be far off, and therefore will venture to trust you. I'll call him to you. *Exit* TOM.

PHIL. What a deal of pother and sputter here 15 is between my mistress and Mr. Myrtle from mere punctilio! I could, any hour of the day, get her to her lover, and would do it — but she, forsooth, will allow no plot to get [to] him; but, if he can come to her, I know she would be glad of it. I must, 20 therefore, do her an acceptable violence and surprise her into his arms. I am sure I go by the best rule [1] imaginable; if she were my maid, I should think her the best servant in the world for doing so by me.

Enter MYRTLE *and* TOM.

Oh, sir! You and Mr. Bevil are fine gentle- 25 men to let a lady remain under such difficulties as my poor mistress, and no attempt to set her at liberty or

[1] I.e., the Golden Rule.

release her from the danger of being instantly married to Cimberton.

MYRT. Tom has been telling — but what is 30 to be done?

PHIL. What is to be done? — when a man can't come at his mistress! Why, can't you fire our house, or the next house to us, to make us run out, and you take us? 35

MYRT. How, Mrs. Phillis!

PHIL. Ay; let me see that rogue deny to fire a house, make a riot, or any other little thing, when there were no other way to come at me!

TOM. I am obliged to you, madam! 40

PHIL. Why, don't we hear every day of people's hanging themselves for love, and won't they venture the hazard of being hanged for love? Oh! were I a man —

MYRT. What manly thing would you have 45 me undertake, according to your ladyship's notion of a man?

PHIL. Only be at once what, one time or other, you may be, and wish to be, or must be.

MYRT. Dear girl, talk plainly to me, and 50 consider I, in my condition, can't be in very good humor. You say, to be at once what I must be.

PHIL. Ay, ay — I mean no more than to be an old man; I saw you do it very well at the masquerade. In a word, old Sir Geoffry Cimberton is every 55 hour expected in town to join in the deeds and settlements for marrying Mr. Cimberton. He is half blind, half lame, half deaf, half dumb — though as to his passions and desires he is as warm and ridiculous as when in the heat of youth. 60

TOM. Come, to the business, and don't keep the gentleman in suspense for the pleasure of being courted, as you serve me.

PHIL. I saw you at the masquerade act such a one to perfection. Go and put on that very habit, 65 and come to our house as Sir Geoffry. There is not one there but myself knows his person; I was born in the parish where he is lord of the manor.[2] I have seen him often and often at church in the country. Do not hesitate, but come thither; they will 70 think you bring a certain security against Mr. Myrtle, and you bring Mr. Myrtle! Leave the rest to me. I leave this with you, and expect — they don't, I told you, know you; they think you out of town, which you had as good be for ever if you lose this op- 75 portunity. I must be gone; I know I am wanted at home.

MYRT. My dear Phillis!

(*Catches and kisses her, and gives her money.*)

PHIL. O fie! my kisses are not my own; you have committed violence; but I'll carry 'em to the 80 right owner. (TOM *kisses her.* — *To* TOM.) Come,

[2] The chief landholder, and hence the most important personage.

see me downstairs, and leave the lover to think of his last game for the prize. *Exeunt* TOM *and* PHILLIS.

MYRT. I think I will instantly attempt this wild expedient. The extravagance of it will make 85 me less suspected, and it will give me opportunity to assert my own right to Lucinda, without whom I cannot live. But I am so mortified at this conduct of mine towards poor Bevil. He must think meanly of me — I know not how to reassume myself and 90 be in spirit enough for such an adventure as this. Yet I must attempt it, if it be only to be near Lucinda under her present perplexities; and sure —

The next delight to transport with the fair,
Is to relieve her in her hours of care. *Exit.* 95

ACT V

SCENE I

Scene, SEALAND'S *house.*

Enter PHILLIS, *with lights, before* MYRTLE, *disguised like old* SIR GEOFFRY, *supported by* MRS. SEALAND, LUCINDA, *and* CIMBERTON.

MRS. SEAL. Now I have seen you thus far, Sir Geoffry, will you excuse me a moment while I give my necessary orders for your accommodation?
Exit MRS. SEALAND.

MYRT. I have not seen you, cousin Cimberton, since you were ten years old; and as it is incum- 5 bent on you to keep up our name and family, I shall, upon very reasonable terms, join with you in a settlement to that purpose. Though I must tell you, cousin, this is the first merchant that has married into our house. 10

LUC. (*aside*). Deuce on 'em! Am I a merchant because my father is?

MYRT. But is he directly a trader at this time?

CIMB. There's no hiding the disgrace, sir; he trades to all parts of the world. 15

MYRT. We never had one of our family before who descended from persons that did anything.

CIMB. Sir, since it is a girl that they have, I am, for the honor of my family, willing to take it in again, and to sink her into our name, and no harm done. 20

MYRT. 'Tis prudently and generously resolved. — Is this the young thing?

CIMB. Yes, sir.

PHIL. [*aside to* LUCINDA]. Good madam, don't be out of humor, but let them run to the utmost of 25 their extravagance — hear them out.

MYRT. Can't I see her nearer? My eyes are but weak.

PHIL. [*still aside*]. Beside, I am sure the uncle has something worth your notice. I'll take care to 30 get off the young one, and leave you to observe what

may be wrought out of the old one for your good.
Exit.

CIMB. Madam, this old gentleman, your great-uncle, desires to be introduced to you and to see you nearer. — Approach, sir. 35

MYRT. By your leave, young lady. (*Puts on spectacles.*) — Cousin Cimberton! She has exactly that sort of neck and bosom for which my sister Gertrude was so much admired in the year sixty-one, before the French dresses first discovered any- 40 thing in women below the chin.

LUC. (*aside*). What a very odd situation am I in!— though I cannot but be diverted at the extravagance of their humors, equally unsuitable to their age. — Chin, quotha! I don't believe my passionate 45 lover there knows whether I have one or not. Ha! ha!

MYRT. Madam, I would not willingly offend, but I have a better glass —— (*Pulls out a large one.*)

Enter PHILLIS *to* CIMBERTON.

PHIL. Sir, my lady desires to show the apartment to you that she intends for Sir Geoffry. 50

CIMB. Well, sir, by that time you have sufficiently gazed and sunned yourself in the beauties of my spouse there, I will wait on you again.
Exeunt CIMBERTON *and* PHILLIS.

MYRT. Were it not, madam, that I might be troublesome, there is something of importance, 55 though we are alone, which I would say more safe from being heard.

LUC. [*aside*]. There is something in this old fellow, methinks, that raises my curiosity.

MYRT. To be free, madam, I as heartily con- 60 temn this kinsman of mine as you do, and am sorry to see so much beauty and merit devoted by your parents to so insensible a possessor.

LUC. Surprising! — I hope, then, sir, you will not contribute to the wrong you are so generous as to 65 pity, whatever may be the interest of your family.

MYRT. This hand of mine shall never be employed to sign anything against your good and happiness.

LUC. I am sorry, sir, it is not in my power to make you proper acknowledgments, but there is a 70 gentleman in the world whose gratitude will, I am sure, be worthy of the favor.

MYRT. All the thanks I desire, madam, are in your power to give.

LUC. Name them, and command them. 75

MYRT. Only, madam, that the first time you are alone with your lover you will with open arms receive him.

LUC. As willingly as his heart could wish it.

MYRT. Thus, then, he claims your promise. — 80 O Lucinda!

LUC. Oh! a cheat! a cheat! a cheat!

94] XX-Y *transport, with*; YZ *transport with.*

MYRT. Hush! 'tis I, 'tis I, your lover — Myrtle himself, madam.

LUC. Oh, bless me! what a rashness and 85 folly to surprise me so! — but hush! — my mother.

Enter MRS. SEALAND, CIMBERTON, *and* PHILLIS.

MRS. SEAL. How now! what's the matter?

LUC. O madam! as soon as you left the room my uncle fell into a sudden fit, and — and — so I cried out for help to support him and conduct him 90 to his chamber.

MRS. SEAL. That was kindly done. — Alas, sir! how do you find yourself?

MYRT. Never was taken in so odd a way in my life — pray, lead me!   Oh! I was talking here 95 — pray carry me — to my cousin Cimberton's young lady —

MRS. SEAL (*aside*). My cousin Cimberton's young lady! How zealous he is, even in his extremity, for the match! — a right [1] Cimberton!   100

(CIMBERTON *and* LUCINDA *lead him as one in pain, etc.*)

CIMB. Pox! Uncle, you will pull my ear off.

LUC. Pray, uncle! you will squeeze me to death.

MRS. SEAL. No matter, no matter — he knows not what he does. — Come, sir, shall I help you out?

MYRT. By no means! I'll trouble nobody 105 but my young cousins here.   *They lead him off.*

PHIL. But pray, madam, does your ladyship intend that Mr. Cimberton shall really marry my young mistress at last? I don't think he likes her.

MRS. SEAL. That's not material. Men of 110 his speculation are above desires. But be it as it may, now I have given old Sir Geoffry the trouble of coming up to sign and seal, with what countenance can I be off?

PHIL. As well as with twenty others, madam. 115 It is the glory and honor of a great fortune to live in continual treaties, and still to break off. It looks great, madam.

MRS. SEAL. True, Phillis — yet to return our blood again into the Cimbertons' is an honor 120 not to be rejected. — But were not you saying that Sir John Bevil's creature, Humphrey, has been with Mr. Sealand?

PHIL. Yes, madam; I overheard them agree that Mr. Sealand should go himself and visit this un- 125 known lady that Mr. Bevil is so great with; and if he found nothing there to fright him, that Mr. Bevil should still marry my young mistress.

MRS. SEAL. How! nay, then, he shall find she is my daughter as well as his. I'll follow him 130 this instant and take the whole family along with me. The disputed power of disposing of my own daughter

shall be at an end this very night.   I'll live no longer in anxiety for a little hussy that hurts my appearance wherever I carry her, and for whose sake I seem 135 to be [not] at all regarded, and that in the best of my days.

PHIL. Indeed, madam, if she were married, your ladyship might very well be taken for Mr. Sealand's daughter.   140

MRS. SEAL. Nay, when the chit has not been with me, I have heard the men say as much. I'll no longer cut off the greatest pleasure of a woman's life — the shining in assemblies — by her forward antici- pation of the respect that's due to her superior; 145 she shall down to Cimberton Hall — she shall — she shall!

PHIL. I hope, madam, I shall stay with your ladyship.

MRS. SEAL. Thou shalt, Phillis, and I'll place 150 thee then more about me. But order chairs immedi- ately — I'll be gone this minute.   *Exeunt.*

SCENE [II]

Charing Cross.

Enter MR. SEALAND *and* HUMPHREY.

MR. SEAL. I am very glad, Mr. Humphrey, that you agree with me that it is for our common good I should look thoroughly into this matter.

HUMPH. I am, indeed, of that opinion; for there is no artifice, nothing concealed, in our family, 5 which ought in justice to be known. I need not de- sire you, sir, to treat the lady with care and respect.

MR. SEAL. Master Humphrey, I shall not be rude, though I design to be a little abrupt and come into the matter at once, to see how she will bear upon 10 a surprise.

HUMPH. That's the door, sir; I wish you success.— (*While* HUMPHREY *speaks* [*aside*], SEALAND *consults his table book.*[2])   I am less concerned what happens there because I hear Mr. Myrtle is well lodged as 15 old Sir Geoffry; so I am willing to let this gentleman employ himself here, to give them time at home; for I am sure 'tis necessary for the quiet of our family Lucinda were disposed of out of it, since Mr. Bevil's inclination is so much otherwise engaged. *Exit.* 20

MR. SEAL. I think this is the door. (*Knocks.*) I'll carry this matter with an air of authority, to enquire, though I make an errand to begin discourse. (*Knocks again, and enter a Foot-boy.*)   So, young man! is your lady within?   25

BOY. Alack, sir! I am but a country boy — I dan't know whether she is or noa; but an you'll stay a bit, I'll goa and ask the gentlewoman that's with her.

MR. SEAL. Why, sirrah, though you are a 30 country boy, you can see, can't you? You know whether she is at home, when you see her, don't you?

BOY. Nay, nay, I'm not such a country lad neither, master, to think she's at home because I see her. I have been in town but a month, and I 35 lost one place already for believing my own eyes.

MR. SEAL. Why, sirrah! have you learnt to lie already?

BOY. Ah, master! things that are lies in the country are not lies at London — I begin to know 40 my business a little better than so. But an you please to walk in, I'll call a gentlewoman to you that can tell you for certain — she can make bold to ask my lady herself.

MR. SEAL. Oh! then she is within, I find, 45 though you dare not say so.

BOY. Nay, nay! that's neither here nor there: what's matter whether she is within or no, if she has not a mind to see anybody?

MR. SEAL. I can't tell, sirrah, whether you are 50 arch or simple; but, however, get me a direct answer, and here's a shilling for you.

BOY. Will you please to walk in; I'll see what I can do for you.

MR. SEAL. I see you will be fit for your busi- 55 ness in time, child. But I expect to meet with nothing but extraordinaries in such a house.

BOY. Such a house! Sir, you han't seen it yet. Pray walk in.

MR. SEAL. Sir, I'll wait upon you. *Exeunt.* 60

SCENE [III]

INDIANA'S *house.*

Enter ISABELLA.

ISAB. What anxiety do I feel for this poor creature! What will be the end of her? Such a languishing, unreserved passion for a man that at last must certainly leave or ruin her — and perhaps both! Then the aggravation of the distress is, that she does 5 not believe he will — not but, I must own, if they are both what they would seem, they are made for one another as much as Adam and Eve were, for there is no other of their kind but themselves.

Enter BOY.

So, Daniel! what news with you? 10

BOY. Madam, there's a gentleman below would speak with my lady.

ISAB. Sirrah, don't you know Mr. Bevil yet?

BOY. Madam, 'tis not the gentleman who comes every day, and asks for you, and won't go in till 15 he knows whether you are with her or no.

ISAB. Ha! that's a particular I did not know be-

fore. — Well, be it who it will, let him come up to me.

Exit Boy, and re-enters with MR. SEALAND; ISABELLA *looks amazed.*

MR. SEAL. Madam, I can't blame your being a little surprised to see a perfect stranger make a 20 visit, and —

ISAB. I am indeed surprised! — [*Aside.*] I see he does not know me.

MR. SEAL. You are very prettily lodged here, madam; in troth, you seem to have everything 25 in plenty. — (*Aside, and looking about.*) A thousand a year, I warrant you, upon this pretty nest of rooms and the dainty one within them.

ISAB. (*apart*). Twenty years, it seems, have less effect in the alteration of a man of thirty than of 30 a girl of fourteen — he's almost still the same. But alas! I find by other men, as well as himself, I am not what I was. As soon as he spoke I was convinced 'twas he. How shall I contain my surprise and satisfaction! He must not know me yet. 35

MR. SEAL. Madam, I hope I don't give you any disturbance, but there is a young lady here with whom I have a particular business to discourse, and I hope she will admit me to that favor.

ISAB. Why, sir, have you had any notice con- 40 cerning her? I wonder who could give it you.

MR. SEAL. That, madam, is fit only to be communicated to herself.

ISAB. Well, sir, you shall see her. — [*Aside.*] I find he knows nothing yet, nor shall from me. 45 I am resolved I will observe this interlude, this sport of nature and of fortune. — You shall see her presently, sir, for now I am as a mother, and will trust her with you. *Exit.*

MR. SEAL. As a mother! right; that's the old 50 phrase for one of those commode [1] ladies, who lend out beauty for hire to young gentlemen that have pressing occasions. But here comes the precious lady herself. In troth, a very sightly woman!

Enter INDIANA.

IND. I am told, sir, you have some affair that 55 requires your speaking with me.

MR. SEAL. Yes, madam: there came to my hands a bill drawn by Mr. Bevil, which is payable tomorrow, and he, in the intercourse of business, sent it to me, who have cash of his, and desired me to send a 60 servant with it; but I have made bold to bring you the money myself.

IND. Sir, was that necessary?

MR. SEAL. No, madam; but, to be free with you, the fame of your beauty and the regard which 65 Mr. Bevil is a little too well known to have for you excited my curiosity.

IND. Too well known to have for me! Your sober

[1] Accommodating.

appearance, sir, which my friend described, made me expect no rudeness, or absurdity, at least. — 70 Who's there? — Sir, if you pay the money to a servant 'twill be as well.

MR. SEAL. Pray, madam, be not offended. I came hither on an innocent, nay, a virtuous design; and if you will have patience to hear me it may be as 75 useful to you, as you are in a friendship with Mr. Bevil, as to my only daughter, whom I was this day disposing of.

IND. You make me hope, sir, I have mistaken you. I am composed again; be free, say on — (aside) 80 what I am afraid to hear.

MR. SEAL. I feared, indeed, an unwarranted passion here, but I did not think it was in abuse of so worthy an object, so accomplished a lady as your sense and mien bespeak. But the youth of our 85 age care not what merit and virtue they bring to shame, so they gratify —

IND. Sir, you are going into very great errors; but as you are pleased to say you see something in me that has changed at least the color of your sus- 90 picions, so has your appearance altered mine, and made me earnestly attentive to what has any way concerned you to enquire into my affairs and character.

MR. SEAL. [aside]. How sensibly, with what 95 an air she talks!

IND. Good sir, be seated, and tell me tenderly — keep all your suspicions concerning me alive, that you may in a proper and prepared way — acquaint me why the care of your daughter obliges a per- 100 son of your seeming worth and fortune to be thus inquisitive about a wretched, helpless, friendless — (weeping). But I beg your pardon: though I am an orphan, your child is not; and your concern for her, it seems, has brought you hither. I'll be com- 105 posed; pray go on, sir.

MR. SEAL. How could Mr. Bevil be such a monster, to injure such a woman?

IND. No, sir, you wrong him; he has not injured me; my support is from his bounty. 110

MR. SEAL. Bounty! when gluttons give high prices for delicates, they are prodigious bountiful!

IND. Still, still you will persist in that error. But my own fears tell me all. You are the gentleman, I suppose, for whose happy daughter he is de- 115 signed a husband by his good father, and he has, perhaps, consented to the overture. He was here this morning, dressed beyond his usual plainness — nay, most sumptuously — and he is to be, perhaps, this night a bridegroom. 120

MR. SEAL. I own he was intended such; but, madam, on your account, I have determined to defer my daughter's marriage till I am satisfied from your own mouth of what nature are the obligations you are under to him. 125

IND. His actions, sir, his eyes, have only made me think he designed to make me the partner of his heart. The goodness and gentleness of his demeanor made me misinterpret all. 'Twas my own hope, my own passion, that deluded me; he never made 130 one amorous advance to me. His large heart and bestowing hand have only helped the miserable; nor know I why, but from his mere delight in virtue, that I have been his care, the object on which to indulge and please himself with pouring favors. 135

MR. SEAL. Madam, I know not why it is, but I, as well as you, am methinks afraid of entering into the matter I came about; but 'tis the same thing as if we had talked never so distinctly — he ne'er shall have a daughter of mine. 140

IND. If you say this from what you think of me, you wrong yourself and him. Let not me, miserable though I may be, do injury to my benefactor. No, sir, my treatment ought rather to reconcile you to his virtues. If to bestow without a prospect of 145 return; if to delight in supporting what might, perhaps, be thought an object of desire, with no other view than to be her guard against those who would not be so disinterested — if these actions, sir, can in a careful parent's eye commend him to a daugh- 150 ter, give yours, sir — give her to my honest, generous Bevil! What have I to do but sigh and weep, to rave, run wild, a lunatic in chains, or, hid in darkness, mutter in distracted starts and broken accents my strange, strange story! 155

MR. SEAL. Take comfort, madam.

IND. All my comfort must be to expostulate in madness, to relieve with frenzy my despair, and shrieking to demand of fate, 'Why — why was I born to such variety of sorrows?' 160

MR. SEAL. If I have been the least occasion —

IND. No, 'twas heaven's high will I should be such — to be plundered in my cradle! tossed on the seas! and even there an infant captive! to lose my mother, hear but of my father! to be adopted! 165 lose my adopter! then plunged again in worse calamities!

MR. SEAL. An infant captive!

IND. Yet then to find the most charming of mankind, once more to set me free from what I 170 thought the last distress; to load me with his services, his bounties and his favors; to support my very life in a way that stole, at the same time, my very soul itself from me!

MR. SEAL. And has young Bevil been this 175 worthy man?

IND. Yet then, again, this very man to take another, without leaving me the right, the pretence, of easing my fond heart with tears! For, oh! I can't reproach him, though the same hand that raised 180 me to this height now throws me down the precipice.

MR. SEAL. Dear lady! Oh, yet one moment's patience! my heart grows full with your affliction. But yet there's something in your story that —

IND. My portion here is bitterness and sor- 185 row.

MR. SEAL. Do not think so. Pray answer me: does Bevil know your name and family?

IND. Alas, too well! Oh, could I be any other thing than what I am! I'll tear away all traces 190 of my former self, my little ornaments, the remains of my first state, the hints of what I ought to have been —

(*In her disorder she throws away a bracelet, which* SEALAND *takes up, and looks earnestly on it.*)

MR. SEAL. Ha! what's this? My eyes are not deceived! It is, it is the same! the very bracelet 195 which I bequeathed my wife at our last mournful parting!

IND. What said you, sir? Your wife! Whither does my fancy carry me? What means this unfelt motion at my heart? And yet, again my for- 200 tune but deludes me; for if I err not, sir, your name is Sealand, but my lost father's name was —

MR. SEAL. Danvers — was it not?

IND. What new amazement! That is, indeed, my family. 205

MR. SEAL. Know, then, when my misfortunes drove me to the Indies, for reasons too tedious now to mention, I changed my name of Danvers into Sealand.

Enter ISABELLA.

ISAB. If yet there wants an explanation of 210 your wonder, examine well this face: yours, sir, I well remember. Gaze on, and read in me your sister, Isabella.

MR. SEAL. My sister!

ISAB. But here's a claim more tender yet — 215 your Indiana, sir, your long-lost daughter.

MR. SEAL. O my child! my child!

IND. All-gracious heaven! Is it possible? Do I embrace my father?

MR. SEAL. And do I hold thee? — These pas- 220 sions are too strong for utterance. Rise, rise, my child, and give my tears their way. — O my sister! (*Embracing her.*)

ISAB. Now, dearest niece, my groundless fears, my painful cares no more shall vex thee. If I have wronged thy noble lover with too hard suspi- 225 cions, my just concern for thee, I hope, will plead my pardon.

MR. SEAL. Oh, make him, then, the full amends, and be yourself the messenger of joy. Fly this instant! tell him all these wondrous turns of 230 Providence in his favor! Tell him I have now a daughter to bestow which he no longer will decline; that this day he still shall be a bridegroom; nor shall

a fortune, the merit which his father seeks, be wanting; tell him the reward of all his virtues waits 235 on his acceptance. *Exit* ISABELLA.

— My dearest Indiana! (*Turns and embraces her.*)

IND. Have I then, at last, a father's sanction on my love? — his bounteous hand to give, and make my heart a present worthy of Bevil's generosity? 240

MR. SEAL. O my child! how are our sorrows past o'erpaid by such a meeting! Though I have lost so many years of soft paternal dalliance with thee, yet, in one day to find thee thus, and thus bestow thee in such perfect happiness, is ample, ample repara- 245 tion. — And yet again, the merit of thy lover —

IND. Oh, had I spirits left to tell you of his actions! — how strongly filial duty has suppressed his love, and how concealment still has doubled all his obligations — the pride, the joy of his alliance, 250 sir, would warm your heart, as he has conquered mine.

MR. SEAL. How laudable is love when born of virtue! I burn to embrace him —

IND. See, sir, my aunt already has succeeded, and brought him to your wishes. 255

Enter ISABELLA, *with* SIR JOHN BEVIL, BEVIL JUNIOR, MRS. SEALAND, CIMBERTON, MYRTLE *and* LUCINDA.

SIR J. BEV. (*entering*). Where, where's this scene of wonder? Mr. Sealand, I congratulate, on this occasion, our mutual happiness. Your good sister, sir, has, with the story of your daughter's fortune, filled us with surprise and joy. Now all ex- 260 ceptions are removed; my son has now avowed his love, and turned all former jealousies and doubts to approbation; and, I am told, your goodness has consented to reward him.

MR. SEAL. If, sir, a fortune equal to his 265 father's hopes can make this object worthy his acceptance.

BEV. JUN. I hear your mention, sir, of fortune, with pleasure only as it may prove the means to reconcile the best of fathers to my love. Let 270 him be provident, but let me be happy. — (*Embracing* INDIANA.) My ever-destined, my acknowledged wife!

IND. Wife! Oh, my ever loved! my lord! my master! 275

SIR J. BEV. I congratulate myself, as well as you, that I had a son who could, under such disadvantages, discover your great merit.

MR. SEAL. O Sir John! how vain, how weak is human prudence! What care, what foresight, 280 what imagination could contrive such blest events to make our children happy as Providence in one short hour has laid before us?

CIMB. (*to* MRS. SEALAND). I am afraid, madam, Mr. Sealand is a little too busy for our affair: 285 if you please, we'll take another opportunity.

MRS. SEAL. Let us have patience, sir.

CIMB. But we make Sir Geoffry wait, madam.

MYRT. O sir, I am not in haste.

(*During this* BEVIL JUNIOR *presents* LUCINDA *to* INDIANA.)

MR. SEAL. But here — here's our general 290 benefactor! Excellent young man, that could be at once a lover to her beauty and a parent to her virtue.

BEV. JUN. If you think that an obligation, sir, give me leave to overpay myself, in the only instance that can now add to my felicity, by begging you to 295 bestow this lady on Mr. Myrtle.

MR. SEAL. She is his without reserve; I beg he may be sent for. — Mr. Cimberton, notwithstanding you never had my consent, yet there is, since I last saw you, another objection to your marriage 300 with my daughter.

CIMB. I hope, sir, your lady has concealed nothing from me?

MR. SEAL. Troth, sir, nothing but what was concealed from myself — another daughter, who 305 has an undoubted title to half my estate.

CIMB. How, Mr. Sealand! Why then, if half Mrs. Lucinda's fortune is gone, you can't say that any of my estate is settled upon her. I was in treaty for the whole, but if that is not to be come at, to be 310 sure there can be no bargain. Sir, I have nothing to do but to take my leave of your good lady, my cousin, and beg pardon for the trouble I have given this old gentleman.

MYRT. That you have, Mr. Cimberton, with 315 all my heart. (*Discovers himself.*)

OMN. Mr. Myrtle!

MYRT. And I beg pardon of the whole company that I assumed the person of Sir Geoffry, only to be present at the danger of this lady's being dis- 320 posed of, and in her utmost exigence to assert my right to her; which, if her parents will ratify, as they once favored my pretensions, no abatement of fortune shall lessen her value to me.

LUC. Generous man! 325

MR. SEAL. If, sir, you can overlook the injury of being in treaty with one who as meanly left her as you have generously asserted your right in her, she is yours.

LUC. Mr. Myrtle, though you have ever had 330 my heart, yet now I find I love you more because I bring you less.

MYRT. We have much more than we want, and I am glad any event has contributed to the discovery of our real inclinations to each other. 335

MRS. SEAL. (*aside*). Well! However, I'm glad the girl's disposed of, any way.

BEV. JUN. Myrtle, no longer rivals now, but brothers!

MYRT. Dear Bevil, you are born to triumph 340 over me. But now our competition ceases; I rejoice in the preëminence of your virtue, and your alliance adds charms to Lucinda.

SIR J. BEV. Now, ladies and gentlemen, you have set the world a fair example. Your happiness 345 is owing to your constancy and merit, and the several difficulties you have struggled with evidently show —

Whate'er the generous mind itself denies,
The secret care of Providence supplies. *Exeunt.*

EPILOGUE

By Mr. Welsted

Intended to be spoken by Indiana

Our author, whom intreaties cannot move,
Spite of the dear coquetry that you love,
Swears he'll not frustrate (so he plainly means),
By a loose epilogue, his decent scenes.
Is it not, sirs, hard fate I meet today,   5
To keep me rigid [1] still beyond the play?
And yet I'm saved a world of pains that way.
I now can look, I now can move at ease,
Nor need I torture these poor limbs to please,
Nor with the hand or foot attempt surprise,   10
Nor wrest my features, nor fatigue my eyes.
Bless me! what freakish gambols have I played!
What motions tried, and wanton looks betrayed!
Out of pure kindness all, to over-rule
The threatened hiss, and screen some scribbling fool.   15
With more respect I'm entertained tonight:
Our author thinks I can with ease delight.
My artless looks while modest graces arm,
He says I need but to appear, and charm.
A wife so formed, by these examples bred,   20
Pours joy and gladness 'round the marriage bed;
Soft source of comfort, kind relief from care,
And 'tis her least perfection to be fair.
The nymph with Indiana's worth who vies,
A nation will behold with Bevil's eyes.   25

---

[1] Strictly moral, strait-laced.

BLANK–VERSE TRAGEDY

TRAGEDY during the early decades of the eighteenth century was an extension, in a weakened form, of later Restoration tragedy. It attracted the attention and efforts of several major writers and of many minor ones, but unfortunately neither major nor minor authors, with one exception, displayed any natural bent for dramatic composition. Moreover, as the period progressed, the moralizing and sentimentalizing forces which had begun to influence the comedy of the period made headway also in the tragedy, and with less opposition, since both tendencies were already present in later Restoration tragedy. The unities and other neo-classical 'rules' were generally assumed as the basis of dramatic writing, but in practice they were frequently slighted even by those who purported to do them honor. This state of affairs may have been furthered to some extent by the increasing homage given to Shakespeare, and to the doctrine, expressed by Dryden in the *Essay of Dramatic Poesy*, and echoed by later writers, which permitted English playwrights certain liberties that were in accord with the national temperament. The natural anti-French feeling which resulted from the War of the Spanish Succession, and which found expression in many prologues and epilogues, may also have tended to weaken the French authority. Had any English writer appeared with a new and positive theory of drama, something of importance might have been accomplished: but as no such writer did make his appearance, English tragedy merely drifted.

Among the best-known writers of tragedy between 1700 and 1730 were (in roughly chronological order) Dennis, Rowe, Addison, Young, and Thomson. Of these five only Rowe could have survived in literary history on the merits of his tragedies: Dennis is now remembered as a critic, Addison as an essayist, and Young and Thomson as poets.

There has been some misunderstanding about the relationship of JOSEPH ADDISON (1672–1719) and of his famous play, *Cato*, to the dramatic history of his time. His friend and literary executor, Thomas Tickell, gives us some important information about its composition:

> The tragedy of *Cato* appeared in public in the year 1713, when the greatest part of the last act was added by the author of the foregoing, which he had kept by him for many years. He took up a design of writing a play upon this subject, when he was young at the University [Oxford], and even attempted something in it there, though not a line as it now stands. The work was performed by him in his travels, and retouched in England, without any formed resolutions of bringing it upon the stage, till his friends of the first quality and distinction prevailed with him to put the last finishing to it, at a time when they thought the doctrine of liberty very seasonable.

According to this account, then, the play was conceived before 1699, and largely written between 1699 and 1703, while Addison was still under academic influences, and before he had had any great contact with the literary world of London. It is possible to detect in *Cato* classical, as well as neo-classical influences: in particular, there seem to be traces of the direct influence of Seneca, as well as of the indirect influence through the French tradition. *Cato* seems to have been originally designed as closet drama: it has the coldness, the rhetoric, the didacticism, the lack of dramatic movement, even the political allusions of the Roman author.

The play was (and still is) generally held up as a model of 'regular' tragedy. The unities of time and place are observed, indeed — the latter to an extent that brings about some ludicrous situations — but the more important unity of action is violated by the introduction of a sub-plot, intended to supply the 'love interest,' which is attached to the main theme by the slenderest of threads. Moreover, while the death of Marcus and the suicide of Cato take place off-stage, the killing of Sempronius is accomplished in full view of the audience, although in actual performance it must have been unconvincing, and would therefore have fallen under the ban of both the strict neo-classicists and those who approved of the liberties allowed by Dryden. Most of the play's departures from the 'rules' are found in the first four acts: they suggest that even in his early days Addison was not a partisan of the rigid neo-classical school. On the whole, one suspects that Voltaire's praise of Addison as 'the first English writer who composed a regular tragedy and infused a spirit of elegance through every part of it' was at least partly motivated by a desire to encourage the English to continue in the French tradition, especially as he elsewhere deprecated the love plot in *Cato*, and advised writers to imitate Addison's excellences only.

Cato, then, largely represents Addison's taste at the turn of the century. There are indications that his taste had altered ten years later. He was disinclined to finish the piece; he even asked John Hughes to write the fifth act, when completion of the play was urged upon him; and when he did take up the task himself, he disposed of it with significant brevity. His papers on tragedy (*Spectator* Nos. 39, 40, 44) adopt many of the classical rules, but they deal with so many of the specific problems that arise in connection with *Cato* that they suggest special pleading on the part of the author, whose play was apparently well-known to his friends, although he seems not to have contemplated either producing or publishing it in 1711, when these essays were written. Against these papers discussing classical tragedy should be set *Spectators* Nos. 160 and 592, which exhibit great admiration for Shakespeare, and praise natural genius, unhampered by rules, as being at least as acceptable as 'regular' genius. Apparently Addison admired both schools of tragedy: his own liking for order, his academic training, his desire to defend his own youthful work and to praise the classical plays of some of his friends (e.g., Ambrose Philips, author of *The Distrest Mother*), all led him in one direction, and no doubt he should be placed among the supporters of the classical tradition: on the other hand, circumstances have conspired to make him appear more of a classicist than he actually was in his maturer years.

It is difficult to estimate the influence of *Cato*. The play was translated into several foreign languages; it was performed frequently; it was generally spoken of with admiration for at least half a century, although there were a few persons (among them Dennis and Fielding) who were not impressed. There are, however, no plays which can be said with certainty to have been modelled upon *Cato*. On the other hand, the tendency of dramatists to imitate Shakespeare was quite clear. The heightened interest in his plays was attested by the appearance of three editions within the space of twenty-five years (Rowe's, 1709; Pope's, 1725; Theobald's, 1734). This last editor carried his admiration so far as to write a play, *Double Falsehood*, which he attempted to palm off as Shakespeare's.

NICHOLAS ROWE (1674–1718) was not only the first critical editor of Shakespeare: he was also the eighteenth-century dramatist who best succeeded in imitating his master. His earlier plays show the influences of both the neo-classical school and the Elizabethan drama. His *Fair Penitent* (1703), a reworking of *The Fatal Dowry* of Massinger and Field, is still remembered for the character of 'gay' Lothario. Throughout his career he submitted to certain rules of the day: in particular, he simplified his casts and his action. But *Jane Shore* (1714) was a professed imitation of Shakespeare's style, and had in its subject matter some kinship with *Richard III*. It is characterized by a naturalness and a lack of bombast which are refreshing. Rowe does not venture to include a sub-plot, either comic or tragic, and thus he gains unity of action: the other two unities, however, are disregarded, or at least very liberally interpreted. The blank verse, while it does not often rise to poetic heights, is handled with more ease than was usual in Rowe's day, and shows surprisingly little influence of the cadences of the heroic couplet. Unfortunately Rowe's restraint comes perilously near to a lack of force. His characters are often pathetic, but seldom great, and consequently they fall below tragic stature. Judged either as an original play or as an imitation of Shakespeare,

Jane Shore cannot be said to equal Dryden's *All for Love* or Otway's *Venice Preserved*. That it has, nevertheless, a good claim to be called the best English tragedy written during the first half of the eighteenth century is an indication of the decline that had taken place.

A. E. C.

REFERENCE WORKS

1914. Nettleton, George H. *English Drama of the Restoration and Eighteenth Century.* New York and London. [Chapter X, with Bibliographical Notes.]

1929. Dobrée, Bonamy. *Restoration Tragedy, 1660–1720.* Oxford.

1929. Nicoll, Allardyce. *A History of Early Eighteenth Century Drama.* Cambridge [England]. [Chapter II.]

1934. Green, Clarence C. *The Neo-Classic Theory of Tragedy in the Eighteenth Century.* Cambridge [Massachusetts].

Cato

BY JOSEPH ADDISON

ACT V. SCENE I.

Cato *folus, fitting in a thoughtful Pofture:* In his Hand Plato's *Book on the Immortality of the Soul.* A drawn Sword *on the Table by him.*

IT muft be fo—*Plato,* thou reafon'ft well! ——
Elfe whence this pleafing Hope, this fond Defire,
This Longing after Immortality?
Or whence this fecret Dread, and inward Horror,
Of falling into Nought? Why fhrinks the Soul
Back on her felf, and ftartles at Deftruction?
'Tis the Divinity that ftir's within us;
'Tis Heav'n its felf, that point's out an Hereafter,
And intimate's Eternity to Man.
Eternity! thou pleafing, dreadful, Thought!
Through what Variety of untry'd Being,
Through what new Scenes and Changes muft we pafs!
The wide, th' unbounded Profpect, lie's before me;
But Shadows, Clouds, and Darknefs, reft upon it.
Here will I hold. If there's a Pow'r above us,
(And that there is all Nature cries aloud
Through all her Works) He muft delight in Virtue;
And that which he delights in muft be happy.
But when! or where!---This World was made for *Cæfar.*
I'm weary of Conjectures——This muft end 'em.
　　　　　　　[*Laying his Hand on his Sword.*

Thus

OPENING OF CATO'S SOLILOQUY, FIRST QUARTO, 1713

PROLOGUE

By Mr. Pope

Spoken by Mr. Wilks [1]

To wake the soul by tender strokes of art,
To raise the genius and to mend the heart,
To make mankind in conscious virtue bold,
Live o'er each scene and be what they behold; —
For this the tragic muse first trod the stage,   5
Commanding tears to stream through every age;
Tyrants no more their savage nature kept,
And foes to virtue wondered how they wept.
Our author shuns by vulgar springs to move
The hero's glory or the virgin's love;   10
In pitying love, we but our weakness show,
And wild ambition well deserves its woe.
Here tears shall flow from a more gen'rous cause,
Such tears as patriots shed for dying laws.
He bids your breasts with ancient ardor rise,   15
And calls forth Roman drops from British eyes.
Virtue confessed in human shape he draws,
What Plato thought, and godlike Cato was:
No common object to your sight displays,
But — what with pleasure heav'n itself surveys —   20
A brave man struggling in the storms of fate,
And greatly falling with a falling state!
While Cato gives his little senate laws, [2]
What bosom beats not in his country's cause?
Who sees him act, but envies ev'ry deed?   25
Who hears him groan, and does not wish to bleed?
Ev'n when proud Cæsar, 'midst triumphal cars,
The spoils of nations, and the pomp of wars,
Ignobly vain and impotently great,
Showed Rome her Cato's figure drawn in state;   30
As her dead father's rev'rend image past,
The pomp was darkened and the day o'ercast,
The triumph ceased — tears gushed from every eye,
The world's great victor past unheeded by;
Her last good man dejected Rome adored,   35
And honored Cæsar's less than Cato's sword.
Britons, attend: be worth like this approved,
And show you have the virtue to be moved.
With honest scorn the first famed Cato viewed
Rome learning arts from Greece, whom she subdued.   40
Our scene precariously subsists too long
On French translation and Italian song.
Dare to have sense yourselves; assert the stage,
Be justly warmed with your own native rage.
Such plays alone should please a British ear,   45
As Cato's self had not disdained to hear.

---

[1] In the part of Juba.
[2] Pope repeated this line, slightly altered in form, in his famous portrait of Atticus (Addison), *Epistle to Dr. Arbuthnot,* l. 209.

DRAMATIS PERSONÆ

MEN

CATO.

LUCIUS, *a Senator.*

SEMPRONIUS, *a Senator.*

JUBA, *Prince of Numidia.*

SYPHAX, *General of the Numidians.*

PORTIUS, } *Sons of* CATO.
MARCUS, }

DECIUS, *Ambassador from Cæsar.*

Mutineers, Guards, etc.

WOMEN

MARCIA, *Daughter to* CATO.   LUCIA, *Daughter to* LUCIUS.

SCENE — A LARGE HALL IN THE GOVERNOR'S PALACE OF UTICA.

[TIME — 46 B.C.]

CATO

By JOSEPH ADDISON

ACT I

SCENE I

PORTIUS, MARCUS.

POR. The dawn is overcast, the morning low'rs,
And heavily in clouds brings on the day,
The great, th' important day, big with the fate
Of Cato and of Rome. Our father's death
Would fill up all the guilt of civil war   5
And close the scene of blood. Already Cæsar
Has ravaged more than half the globe, and sees
Mankind grown thin by his destructive sword:
Should he go further, numbers would be wanting
To form new battles and support his crimes.   10
Ye gods, what havoc does ambition make
Among your works!
MAR.   Thy steady temper, Portius,
Can look on guilt, rebellion, fraud, and Cæsar,
In the calm lights of mild philosophy;
I'm tortured, ev'n to madness, when I think   15
On the proud victor: ev'ry time he's named
Pharsalia rises to my view — I see
Th' insulting tyrant prancing o'er the field
Strowed with Rome's citizens, and drenched in
        slaughter,
His horse's hoofs wet with patrician blood.   20
O Portius! is there not some chosen curse,
Some hidden thunder in the stores of heav'n,
Red with uncommon wrath, to blast the man
Who owes his greatness to his country's ruin?
POR. Believe me, Marcus, 'tis an impious great-
        ness,   25
And mixed with too much horror to be envied.
How does the lustre of our father's actions,
Through the dark cloud of ills that cover him,
Break out, and burn with more triumphant bright-
        ness!
His suff'rings shine, and spread a glory round
        him;   30
Greatly unfortunate, he fights the cause
Of honor, virtue, liberty, and Rome.
His sword ne'er fell but on the guilty head;
Oppression, tyranny, and power usurped,
Draw all the vengeance of his arm upon 'em.   35
MAR. Who knows not this? But what can Cato
        do
Against a world, a base, degenerate world

That courts the yoke, and bows the neck to Cæsar?
Pent up in Utica he vainly forms
A poor epitome of Roman greatness,   40
And, covered with Numidian guards, directs
A feeble army and an empty senate,
Remnants of mighty battles fought in vain.
By heav'ns, such virtues, joined with such success,
Distract my very soul: our father's fortune   45
Would almost tempt us to renounce his precepts.
POR. Remember what our father oft has told us:
The ways of heav'n are dark and intricate,
Puzzled in mazes and perplext with errors;
Our understanding traces 'em in vain,   50
Lost and bewildered in the fruitless search,
Nor sees with how much art the windings run,
Nor where the regular confusion ends.
MAR. These are suggestions of a mind at ease:
O Portius! didst thou taste but half the griefs   55
That wring my soul, thou couldst not talk thus
        calmly.
Passion unpitied and successless love
Plant daggers in my heart, and aggravate
My other griefs. Were but my Lucia kind! —
POR. (aside). Thou seest not that thy brother is
        thy rival;   60
But I must hide it, for I know thy temper.
— Now, Marcus, now, thy virtue's on the proof:
Put forth thy utmost strength, work ev'ry nerve,
And call up all thy father in thy soul:
To quell the tyrant love, and guard thy heart   65
On this weak side, where most our nature fails,
Would be a conquest worthy Cato's son.
MAR. Portius, the counsel which I cannot take,
Instead of healing, but upbraids my weakness.
Bid me for honor plunge into a war   70
Of thickest foes, and rush on certain death,
Then shalt thou see that Marcus is not slow
To follow glory and confess his father.
Love is not to be reasoned down, or lost
In high ambition and a thirst of greatness;   75
'Tis second life, it grows into the soul,
Warms ev'ry vein, and beats in ev'ry pulse,
I feel it here: my resolution melts —
POR. Behold young Juba, the Numidian prince!
With how much care he forms himself to glory,   80
And breaks the fierceness of his native temper
To copy out our father's bright example.
He loves our sister Marcia, greatly loves her,

His eyes, his looks, his actions all betray it:
But still the smothered fondness burns within
 him.   85
When most it swells and labors for a vent,
Then sense of honor and desire of fame
Drive the big passion back into his heart.
What! shall an African, shall Juba's heir
Reproach great Cato's son, and show the world 90
A virtue wanting in a Roman soul?
 MAR. Portius, no more! your words leave stings
  behind 'em.
Whene'er did Juba, or did Portius show
A virtue that has cast me at a distance,
And thrown me out in the pursuits of honor? 95
 POR. Marcus, I know thy generous temper well;
Fling but th' appearance of dishonor on it,
It straight takes fire, and mounts into a blaze.
 MAR. A brother's suff'rings claim a brother's pity.
 POR. Heav'n knows I pity thee: behold my
  eyes   100
Ev'n whilst I speak. — Do they not swim in tears?
Were but my heart as naked to thy view,
Marcus would see it bleed in his behalf.
 MAR. Why then dost treat me with rebukes,
  instead
Of kind, condoling cares and friendly sorrow? 105
 POR. O Marcus! did I know the way to ease
Thy troubled heart, and mitigate thy pains,
Marcus, believe me, I could die to do it.
 MAR. Thou best of brothers, and thou best of
  friends!
Pardon a weak, distempered soul, that swells 110
With sudden gusts, and sinks as soon in calms,
The sport of passions — but Sempronius comes:
He must not find this softness hanging on me.
            [*Exeunt.*]

SCENE II

[*Enter* SEMPRONIUS.]

 SEM. (*solus*). Conspiracies no sooner should be
  formed
Than executed. What means Portius here?
I like not that cold youth. I must dissemble,
And speak a language foreign to my heart.

   SEMPRONIUS, PORTIUS.

 Good-morrow, Portius! let us once embrace, 5
Once more embrace, whilst yet we both are free.
Tomorrow should we thus express our friendship,
Each might receive a slave into his arms:
This sun, perhaps, this morning sun's the last
That e'er shall rise on Roman liberty. 10
 POR. My father has this morning called together
To this poor hall his little Roman senate

(The leavings of Pharsalia) to consult
If yet he can oppose the mighty torrent
That bears down Rome, and all her gods, before
 it,   15
Or must at length give up the world to Cæsar.
 SEM. Not all the pomp and majesty of Rome
Can raise her senate more than Cato's presence.
His virtues render our assembly awful,
They strike with something like religious fear, 20
And make ev'n Cæsar tremble at the head
Of armies flushed with conquest: O my Portius,
Could I but call that wondrous man my father,
Would but thy sister Marcia be propitious
To thy friend's vows, I might be blessed indeed! 25
 POR. Alas! Sempronius, wouldst thou talk of love
To Marcia, whilst her father's life's in danger?
Thou might'st as well court the pale trembling vestal,
When she beholds the holy flame expiring.
 SEM. The more I see the wonders of thy race, 30
The more I'm charmed. Thou must take heed, my
  Portius!
The world has all its eyes on Cato's son.
Thy father's merit sets thee up to view,
And shows thee in the fairest point of light,
To make thy virtues or thy faults conspicuous. 35
 POR. Well dost thou seem to check my ling'ring
  here
On this important hour! — I'll straight away,
And while the fathers of the senate meet
In close debate to weigh th' events of war,
I'll animate the [soldiers'] drooping courage, 40
With love of freedom, and contempt of life.
I'll thunder in their ears their country's cause,
And try to rouse up all that's Roman in 'em.
'Tis not in mortals to command success,
But we'll do more, Sempronius; we'll deserve it. 45
            Exit.
 SEM. (*solus*). Curse on the stripling! how he apes
  his sire!
Ambitiously sententious! — but I wonder
Old Syphax comes not; his Numidian genius
Is well disposed to mischief, were he prompt
And eager on it; but he must be spurred, 50
And every moment quickened to the course.
Cato has used me ill: he has refused
His daughter Marcia to my ardent vows.
Besides, his baffled arms and ruined cause
Are bars to my ambition. Cæsar's favor, 55
That show'rs down greatness on his friends, will
  raise me
To Rome's first honors. If I give up Cato,
I claim in my reward his captive daughter.
But Syphax comes! —

87] Q1 (Harv. copy) Q2Q3Q4Q5Q6D7D8W *The sense.*
113 s.d.] Q1Q2Q3Q4Q5Q6D7D8W Exit. W prints next four lines as an aside, and places SEMPRONIUS, PORTIUS at the beginning of scene.   SCENE II. 40] Q1Q2Q3Q4Q5Q6D7D8W *soldier's.*

SCENE III

SYPHAX, SEMPRONIUS.

SYPH.   Sempronius, all is ready;
I've sounded my Numidians, man by man,
And find 'em ripe for a revolt: they all
Complain aloud of Cato's discipline,
And wait but the command to change their
    master.   5
SEM. Believe me, Syphax, there's no time to waste;
Ev'n whilst we speak, our conqueror comes on,
And gathers ground upon us ev'ry moment.
Alas! thou know'st not Cæsar's active soul,
With what a dreadful course he rushes on   10
From war to war: in vain has nature formed
Mountains and oceans to oppose his passage;
He bounds o'er all, victorious in his march,
The Alps and Pyreneans sink before him;
Through winds and waves and storms he works
    his way,   15
Impatient for the battle: one day more
Will set the victor thund'ring at our gates.
But tell me, hast thou yet drawn o'er young Juba?
That still would recommend thee more to Cæsar,
And challenge better terms.
SYPH.   Alas, he's lost,   20
He's lost, Sempronius; all his thoughts are full
Of Cato's virtues: — but I'll try once more
(For every instant I expect him here)
If yet I can subdue those stubborn principles
Of faith, of honor, and I know not what,   25
That have corrupted his Numidian temper,
And struck th' infection into all his soul.
SEM. Be sure to press upon him ev'ry motive.
Juba's surrender, since his father's death,
Would give up Afric into Cæsar's hands,   30
And make him lord of half the burning zone.
SYPH. But is it true, Sempronius, that your senate
Is called together? Gods! thou must be cautious!
Cato has piercing eyes, and will discern
Our frauds, unless they're covered thick with art. 35
SEM. Let me alone, good Syphax: I'll conceal
My thoughts in passion ('tis the surest way);
I'll bellow out for Rome and for my country,
And mouth at Cæsar till I shake the senate.
Your cold hypocrisy's a stale device,   40
A worn-out trick: wouldst thou be thought in earnest?
Clothe thy feigned zeal in rage, in fire, in fury!
SYPH. In troth, thou'rt able to instruct grey hairs,
And teach the wily African deceit!
SEM. Once more, be sure to try thy skill on
    Juba.   45
Meanwhile I'll hasten to my Roman soldiers,
Inflame the mutiny, and underhand
Blow up their discontents, till they break out
Unlooked for, and discharge themselves on Cato.

Remember, Syphax, we must work in haste: 50
Oh, think what anxious moments pass between
The birth of plots and their last fatal periods.
Oh! 'tis a dreadful interval of time,
Filled up with horror all, and big with death!
Destruction hangs on ev'ry word we speak,   55
On ev'ry thought, till the concluding stroke
Determines all, and closes our design.   *Exit.*
SYPH. (*solus*). I'll try if yet I can reduce to reason
This headstrong youth, and make him spurn at Cato.
The time is short, Cæsar comes rushing on us — 60
But hold! young Juba sees me, and approaches.

SCENE IV

JUBA, SYPHAX.

JUBA. Syphax, I joy to meet thee thus alone.
I have observed of late thy looks are fall'n,
O'ercast with gloomy cares and discontent;
Then tell me, Syphax, I conjure thee, tell me,
What are the thoughts that knit thy brow in
    frowns,   5
And turn thine eye thus coldly on thy prince?
SYPH. 'Tis not my talent to conceal my thoughts,
Nor carry smiles and sunshine in my face,
When discontent sits heavy at my heart.
I have not yet so much the Roman in me.   10
JUBA. Why dost thou cast out such ungen'rous
    terms
Against the lords and sov'reigns of the world?
Dost thou not see mankind fall down before 'em,
And own the force of their superior virtue?
Is there a nation in the wilds of Afric,   15
Amidst our barren rocks and burning sands,
That does not tremble at the Roman name?
SYPH. Gods! where's the worth that sets this
    people up
Above your own Numidia's tawny sons!
Do they with tougher sinews bend the bow?   20
Or flies the javelin swifter to its mark,
Launched from the vigor of a Roman arm?
Who like our active African instructs
The fiery steed, and trains him to his hand?
Or guides in troops th' embattled elephant,   25
Loaden with war? these, these are arts, my prince,
In which your Zama [1] does not stoop to Rome.
JUBA. These all are virtues of a meaner rank,
Perfections that are placed in bones and nerves.
A Roman soul is bent on higher views: 30
To civilize the rude, unpolished world,
And lay it under the restraint of laws;
To make man mild and sociable to man;
To cultivate the wild, licentious savage

[1] A town in northern Africa, famous as the scene of the decisive defeat of Hannibal by Scipio. Addison seems to have thought it the capital city of Numidia.

With wisdom, discipline, and lib'ral arts —   35
Th' embellishments of life; virtues like these
Make human nature shine, reform the soul,
And break our fierce barbarians into men.
    Syph. Patience, kind heav'ns! — excuse an old
       man's warmth.
What are these wondrous civilizing arts,   40
This Roman polish, and this smooth behavior,
That render man thus tractable and tame?
Are they not only to disguise our passions,
To set our looks at variance with our thoughts,
To check the starts and sallies of the soul,   45
And break off all its commerce with the tongue;
In short, to change us into other creatures
Than what our nature and the gods designed us?
    Juba. To strike thee dumb, turn up thy eyes to
       Cato!
There may'st thou see to what a godlike height   50
The Roman virtues lift up mortal man.
While good, and just, and anxious for his friends,
He's still severely bent against himself;
Renouncing sleep, and rest, and food, and ease,
He strives with thirst and hunger, toil and heat; 55
And when his fortune sets before him all
The pomps and pleasures that his soul can wish,
His rigid virtue will accept of none.
    Syph. Believe me, prince, there's not an African
That traverses our vast Numidian deserts   60
In quest of prey, and lives upon his bow,
But better practises these boasted virtues.
Coarse are his meals, the fortune of the chase;
Amidst the running stream he slakes his thirst,
Toils all the day, and at th' approach of night   65
On the first friendly bank he throws him down,
Or rests his head upon a rock till morn:
Then rises fresh, pursues his wonted game,
And if the following day he chance to find
A new repast, or an untasted spring,   70
Blesses his stars, and thinks it luxury.
    Juba. Thy prejudices, Syphax, won't discern
What virtues grow from ignorance and choice,
Nor how the hero differs from the brute.
But grant that others could with equal glory   75
Look down on pleasures, and the baits of sense;
Where shall we find the man that bears affliction,
Great and majestic in his griefs, like Cato?
Heav'ns, with what strength, what steadiness of
       mind,
He triumphs in the midst of all his sufferings!   80
How does he rise against a load of woes,
And thank the gods that throw the weight upon him!
    Syph. 'Tis pride, rank pride, and haughtiness of
      soul:
I think the Romans call it stoicism.
Had not your royal father thought so highly   85
Of Roman virtue, and of Cato's cause,

He had not fall'n by a slave's hand inglorious;
Nor would his slaughtered army now have lain
On Afric's sands, disfigured with their wounds,
To gorge the wolves and vultures of Numidia.   90
    Juba. Why dost thou call my sorrows up afresh?
My father's name brings tears into my eyes.
    Syph. Oh, that you'd profit by your father's ills!
    Juba. What wouldst thou have me do?
    Syph.   Abandon Cato.
    Juba. Syphax, I should be more than twice an
      orphan   95
By such a loss.
    Syph.   Ay, there's the tie that binds you!
You long to call him father. Marcia's charms
Work in your heart unseen, and plead for Cato.
No wonder you are deaf to all I say.
    Juba. Syphax, your zeal becomes importu-
      nate;   100
I've hitherto permitted it to rave,
And talk at large; but learn to keep it in,
Lest it should take more freedom than I'll give it.
    Syph. Sir, your great father never used me thus.
Alas! he's dead! but can you e'er forget   105
The tender sorrows, and the pangs of nature,
The fond embraces, and repeated blessings,
Which you drew from him in your last farewell?
Still must I cherish the dear, sad remembrance,
At once to torture and to please my soul.   110
The good old king, at parting, wrung my hand,
(His eyes brimful of tears) then sighing cried,
'Prithee, be careful of my son!' — his grief
Swelled up so high, he could not utter more.
    Juba. Alas, thy story melts away my soul.   115
That best of fathers! how shall I discharge
The gratitude and duty which I owe him!
    Syph. By laying up his counsels in your heart.
    Juba. His counsels bade me yield to thy directions:
Then, Syphax, chide me in severest terms,   120
Vent all thy passion, and I'll stand its shock,
Calm and unruffled as a summer sea,
When not a breath of wind flies o'er its surface.
    Syph. Alas, my prince, I'd guide you to your
      safety.
    Juba. I do believe thou wouldst: but tell me
      how.   125
    Syph. Fly from the fate that follows Cæsar's foes.
    Juba. My father scorned to do 't.
    Syph.   And therefore died.
    Juba. Better to die ten thousand thousand deaths,
Than wound my honor.
    Syph.   Rather say, your love.
    Juba. Syphax, I've promised to preserve my
      temper.   130
Why wilt thou urge me to confess a flame
I long have stifled, and would fain conceal?
    Syph. Believe me, prince, 'tis hard to conquer love,

87] D7D8W *hand, inglorious.*   133] D7D8W *though hard.*

But easy to divert and break its force:
Absence might cure it, or a second mistress   135
Light up another flame, and put out this.
The glowing dames of Zama's royal court
Have faces flushed with more exalted charms,
The sun, that rolls his chariot o'er their heads,
Works up more fire and color in their cheeks: 140
Were you with these, my prince, you'd soon forget
The pale, unripened beauties of the north.
   JUBA. 'Tis not a set of features, or complexion,
The tincture of a skin, that I admire.
Beauty soon grows familiar to the lover,   145
Fades in his eye, and palls upon the sense.
The virtuous Marcia tow'rs above her sex:
True, she is fair, (oh, how divinely fair!),
But still the lovely maid improves her charms
With inward greatness, unaffected wisdom,   150
And sanctity of manners.   Cato's soul
Shines out in everything she acts or speaks,
While winning mildness and attractive smiles
Dwell in her looks, and with becoming grace
Soften the rigor of her father's virtues.   155
   SYPH. How does your tongue grow wanton in her
    praise!
But on my knees I beg you would consider —

Enter MARCIA *and* LUCIA.

   JUBA. Hah! Syphax, is't not she? — she moves
    this way:
And with her Lucia, Lucius's fair daughter.
My heart beats thick — I prithee, Syphax, leave
    me.   160
   SYPH. [*aside*]. Ten thousand curses fasten on 'em
    both!
Now will this woman, with a single glance,
Undo what I've been lab'ring all this while.   *Exit.*

[SCENE V]

JUBA, MARCIA, LUCIA.

   JUBA. Hail, charming maid!   How does thy
    beauty smooth
The face of war, and make ev'n horror smile!
At sight of thee my heart shakes off its sorrows;
I feel a dawn of joy break in upon me,
And for a while forget th' approach of Cæsar.   5
   MAR. I should be grieved, young prince, to think
    my presence
Unbent your thoughts, and slackened 'em to arms,
While, warm with slaughter, our victorious foe
Threatens aloud, and calls you to the field.
   JUBA. O Marcia, let me hope thy kind con-
    cerns   10
And gentle wishes follow me to battle!

The thought will give new vigor to my arm,
Add strength and weight to my descending sword,
And drive it in a tempest on the foe.
   MAR. My prayers and wishes always shall
    attend   15
The friends of Rome, the glorious cause of virtue,
And men approved of by the gods and Cato.
   JUBA. That Juba may deserve thy pious cares,
I'll gaze forever on thy godlike father,
Transplanting, one by one, into my life,   20
His bright perfections, till I shine like him.
   MAR. My father never, at a time like this,
Would lay out his great soul in words, and waste
Such precious moments.
   JUBA.   Thy reproofs are just,
Thou virtuous maid; I'll hasten to my troops,   25
And fire their languid souls with Cato's virtue;
If e'er I lead them to the field, when all
The war shall stand ranged in its just array
And dreadful pomp, then will I think on thee!
O lovely maid, then will I think on thee!   30
And, in the shock of charging hosts, remember
What glorious deeds should grace the man who hopes
For Marcia's love.   *Exit.*

[SCENE VI]

   LUC.   Marcia, you're too severe:
How could you chide the young good-natured prince,
And drive him from you with so stern an air,
A prince that loves and dotes on you to death?
   MAR. 'Tis therefore, Lucia, that I chide him
    from me.   5
His air, his voice, his looks, and honest soul
Speak all so movingly in his behalf.
I dare not trust myself to hear him talk.
   LUC. Why will you fight against so sweet a passion,
And steel your heart to such a world of charms? 10
   MAR. How, Lucia, wouldst thou have me sink away
In pleasing dreams, and lose myself in love,
When ev'ry moment Cato's life's at stake?
Cæsar comes armed with terror and revenge,
And aims his thunder at my father's head.   15
Should not the sad occasion swallow up
My other cares, and draw them all into it?
   LUC. Why have not I this constancy of mind,
Who have so many griefs to try its force?
Sure, nature formed me of her softest mould,   20
Enfeebled all my soul with tender passions,
And sunk me ev'n below my own weak sex:
Pity and love, by turns, oppress my heart.
   MAR. Lucia, disburthen all thy cares on me,
And let me share thy most retired distress;   25
Tell me who raises up this conflict in thee?

134] D7D8W *'Tis easy.*   157 s.d.] W om. Enter *MARCIA and LUCIA.*
s.d.] Q1Q2Q3Q4Q5Q6 om. *SCENE V.* The indications of scenes, from this point forward, do not appear in the quartos. They
are supplied from D7D8W.   Minor differences due to this fact are not noted hereafter.

Luc. I need not blush to name them, when I tell
    thee
They're Marcia's brothers, and the sons of Cato.
    Mar. They both behold thee with their sister's
    eyes,
And often have revealed their passion to me.   30
But tell me whose address thou favor'st most;
I long to know, and yet I dread to hear it.
    Luc. Which is it Marcia wishes for?
    Mar.   For neither —
And yet for both; — the youths have equal share
In Marcia's wishes, and divide their sister: 35
But tell me, which of them is Lucia's choice?
    Luc. Marcia, they both are high in my esteem,
But in my love — why wilt thou make me name him?
Thou know'st it is a blind and foolish passion,
Pleased and disgusted with it knows not what —   40
    Mar. O Lucia, I'm perplexed; oh, tell me which
I must hereafter call my happy brother.
    Luc. Suppose 'twere Portius, could you blame my
    choice?
O Portius, thou hast stol'n away my soul!
With what a graceful tenderness he loves!   45
And breathes the softest, the sincerest vows!
Complacency,[1] and truth, and manly sweetness
Dwell ever on his tongue, and smooth his thoughts.
Marcus is over-warm: his fond complaints
Have so much earnestness and passion in them,   50
I hear him with a secret kind of dread,
And tremble at his vehemence of temper.
    Mar. Alas, poor youth! how canst thou throw
    him from thee?
Lucia, thou know'st not half the love he bears thee;
Whene'er he speaks of thee, his heart's in flames.   55
He sends out all his soul in ev'ry word,
And thinks, and talks, and looks like one transported.
Unhappy youth! how will thy coldness raise
Tempests and storms in his afflicted bosom!
I dread the consequence.
    Luc.   You seem to plead   60
Against your brother Portius.
    Mar.   Heaven forbid!
Had Portius been the unsuccessful lover,
The same compassion would have fall'n on him.
    Luc. Was ever virgin love distressed like mine!
Portius himself oft falls in tears before me,   65
As if he mourned his rival's ill success,
Then bids me hide the motions of my heart,
Nor show which way it turns. So much he fears
The sad effects that it would have on Marcus.
    Mar. He knows too well how easily he's fired,   70
And would not plunge his brother in despair,
But waits for happier times, and kinder moments.
    Luc. Alas! too late I find myself involved

In endless griefs, and labyrinths of woe,
Born to afflict my Marcia's family,   75
And sow dissension in the hearts of brothers.
Tormenting thought! it cuts into my soul.
    Mar. Let us not, Lucia, aggravate our sorrows,
But to the gods permit th' event[2] of things.
Our lives, discolored with our present woes,   80
May still grow bright, and smile with happier hours.
So the pure limpid stream, when foul with stains
Of rushing torrents and descending rains,
Works itself clear, and as it runs, refines;
Till, by degrees, the floating mirror shines,   85
Reflects each flow'r that on the border grows,
And a new heav'n in its fair bosom shows.   *Exeunt.*

ACT II

SCENE I

THE SENATE.[3]

    Sem. Rome still survives in this assembled senate!
Let us remember we are Cato's friends,
And act like men who claim that glorious title.
    Luc. Cato will soon be here, and open to us
Th' occasion of our meeting. Hark! he comes!   5
                  (*A sound of trumpets.*)
May all the guardian gods of Rome direct him!

              Enter Cato.

    Cato. Fathers, we once again are met in council.
Cæsar's approach has summoned us together,
And Rome attends her fate from our resolves:
How shall we treat this bold, aspiring man?   10
Success still follows him and backs his crimes;
Pharsalia gave him Rome; Egypt has since
Received his yoke, and the whole Nile is Cæsar's.
Why should I mention Juba's overthrow,
And Scipio's death? Numidia's burning sands   15
Still smoke with blood. 'Tis time we should decree
What course to take. Our foe advances on us,
And envies us ev'n Libya's sultry deserts.
Fathers, pronounce your thoughts: are they still fixt
To hold it out, and fight it to the last?   20
Or are your hearts subdued at length, and wrought
By time and ill success to a submission?
Sempronius, speak.
    Sem.   My voice is still for war.
Gods, can a Roman senate long debate
Which of the two to choose, slav'ry or death!   25
No, let us rise at once, gird on our swords,
And, at the head of our remaining troops,
Attack the foe, break through the thick array
Of his thronged legions, and charge home upon him.

[2] Outcome.
[3] This means the members of the senate, not the senate
chamber. There is no change of scene throughout the play.

[1] Complaisance, courtesy.

51] D7D8W *kind of horror.*   81] W *grow white.*

Perhaps some arm, more lucky than the rest,　30
May reach his heart, and free the world from
　　bondage.
Rise, fathers, rise! 'tis Rome demands your help;
Rise, and revenge her slaughtered citizens,
Or share their fate! the corps [1] of half her senate
Manure the fields of Thessaly, while we　35
Sit here, delib'rating in cold debates,
If we should sacrifice our lives to honor,
Or wear them out in servitude and chains.
Rouse up, for shame! our brothers of Pharsalia
Point at their wounds, and cry aloud, 'To
　　battle!'　40
Great Pompey's shade complains that we are slow,
And Scipio's ghost walks unrevenged amongst us!
　　CATO. Let not a torrent of impetuous zeal
Transport thee thus beyond the bounds of reason:
True fortitude is seen in great exploits,　45
That justice warrants, and that wisdom guides;
All else is tow'ring frenzy and distraction.
Are not the lives of those who draw the sword
In Rome's defence intrusted to our care?
Should we thus lead them to a field of slaughter,　50
Might not th' impartial world with reason say
We lavished at our deaths the blood of thousands,
To grace our fall, and make our ruin glorious?
Lucius, we next would know what's your opinion.
　　LUC. My thoughts, I must confess, are turned on
　　peace.　55
Already have our quarrels filled the world
With widows and with orphans: Scythia mourns
Our guilty wars, and earth's remotest regions
Lie half unpeopled by the feuds of Rome:
'Tis time to sheathe the sword, and spare man-
　　kind.　60
It is not Cæsar, but the gods, my fathers,
The gods declare against us, and repel
Our vain attempts.　To urge the foe to battle,
(Prompted by blind revenge and wild despair)
Were to refuse th' awards of Providence,　65
And not to rest in heav'n's determination.
Already have we shown our love to Rome,
Now let us show submission to the gods.
We took up arms, not to revenge ourselves,
But free the commonwealth; when this end fails,　70
Arms have no further use: our country's cause,
That drew our swords, now wrests 'em from our
　　hands,
And bids us not delight in Roman blood,
Unprofitably shed; what men could do
Is done already: heav'n and earth will witness,　75
If Rome must fall, that we are innocent.
　　SEM. (aside to CATO). This smooth discourse and
　　mild behavior oft

[1] Corpses.

Conceal a traitor — something whispers me
All is not right — Cato, beware of Lucius.
　　CATO. Let us appear nor rash nor diffident:　80
Immoderate valor swells into a fault,
And fear, admitted into public councils,
Betrays like treason.　Let us shun 'em both.
Fathers, I cannot see that our affairs
Are grown thus desp'rate.　We have bulwarks
　　round us;　85
Within our walls are troops enured to toil
In Afric's heats, and seasoned to the sun;
Numidia's spacious kingdom lies behind us,
Ready to rise at its young prince's call.
While there is hope, do not distrust the gods;　90
But wait at least till Cæsar's near approach
Force us to yield.　'Twill never be too late
To sue for chains and own a conqueror.
Why should Rome fall a moment ere her time?
No, let us draw her term of freedom out　95
In its full length, and spin it to the last,
So shall we gain still one day's liberty;
And let me perish, but in Cato's judgment,
A day, an hour, of virtuous liberty
Is worth a whole eternity in bondage.　100

Enter MARCUS.

　　MAR. Fathers, this moment, as I watched the
　　gates,
Lodged on my post, a herald is arrived
From Cæsar's camp, and with him comes old Decius,
The Roman knight; he carries in his looks
Impatience, and demands to speak with Cato.　105
　　CATO. By your permission, fathers, bid him enter.
　　　　　　　　　　　　　　　　　　Exit MARCUS.
Decius was once my friend, but other prospects
Have loosed those ties, and bound him fast to Cæsar.
His message may determine our resolves.

[SCENE II]

Enter DECIUS.

　　DEC. Cæsar sends health to Cato.
　　CATO.　　　　　　　　　　Could he send it
To Cato's slaughtered friends, it would be welcome.
Are not your orders to address the senate?
　　DEC. My business is with Cato: Cæsar sees
The straits to which you're driv'n; and, as he
　　knows　5
Cato's high worth, is anxious for his life.
　　CATO. My life is grafted on the fate of Rome:
Would he save Cato?　Bid him spare his country.
Tell your dictator this, and tell him, Cato
Disdains a life which he has pow'r to offer.　10
　　DEC. Rome and her senators submit to Cæsar;
Her gen'rals and her consuls are no more,

Who checked his conquests, and denied his triumphs.
Why will not Cato be this Cæsar's friend?

CATO. Those very reasons thou hast urged forbid
it. 15

DEC. Cato, I've orders to expostulate
And reason with you, as from friend to friend:
Think on the storm that gathers o'er your head,
And threatens ev'ry hour to burst upon it;
Still may you stand high in your country's
honors, 20
Do but comply, and make your peace with Cæsar.
Rome will rejoice, and cast its eyes on Cato,
As on the second of mankind.

CATO. No more!
I must not think of life on such conditions.

DEC. Cæsar is well acquainted with your vir-
tues, 25
And therefore sets this value on your life:
Let him but know the price of Cato's friendship,
And name your terms.

CATO. Bid him disband his legions;
Restore the commonwealth to liberty,
Submit his actions to the public censure, 30
And stand the judgment of a Roman senate:
Bid him do this, and Cato is his friend.

DEC. Cato, the world talks loudly of your wisdom —

CATO. Nay more, though Cato's voice was ne'er
employed
To clear the guilty, and to varnish crimes, 35
Myself will mount the rostrum in his favor,
And strive to gain his pardon from the people.

DEC. A style like this becomes a conqueror.

CATO. Decius, a style like this becomes a Roman.

DEC. What is a Roman, that is Cæsar's foe? 40

CATO. Greater than Cæsar, he's a friend to virtue.

DEC. Consider, Cato, you're in Utica,
And at the head of your own little senate;
You don't now thunder in the Capitol,
With all the mouths of Rome to second you. 45

CATO. Let him consider that who drives us hither:
'Tis Cæsar's sword has made Rome's senate little,
And thinn'd its ranks. Alas! thy dazzled eye
Beholds this man in a false glaring light,
Which conquest and success have thrown upon
him; 50
Didst thou but view him right, thou'dst see him black
With murder, treason, sacrilege, and crimes
That strike my soul with horror but to name 'em.
I know thou look'st on me, as on a wretch
Beset with ills, and covered with misfortunes; 55
But, by the gods I swear, millions of worlds
Should never buy me to be like that Cæsar.

DEC. Does Cato send this answer back to Cæsar,
For all his gen'rous cares, and proffered friendship?

CATO. His cares for me are insolent and vain: 60

Presumptuous man! the gods take care of Cato.
Would Cæsar show the greatness of his soul,
Bid him employ his care for these my friends,
And make good use of his ill-gotten power,
By shelt'ring men much better than himself. 65

DEC. Your high unconquered heart makes you
forget
That you're a man. You rush on your destruction.
But I have done. When I relate hereafter
The tale of this unhappy embassy,
All Rome will be in tears. Exit DECIUS.

[SCENE III]

SEM. Cato, we thank thee.
The mighty genius of immortal Rome
Speaks in thy voice, thy soul breathes liberty:
Cæsar will shrink to hear the words thou utter'st,
And shudder in the midst of all his conquests. 5

LUC. The senate owns its gratitude to Cato,
Who with so great a soul consults its safety,
And guards our lives, while he neglects his own.

SEM. Sempronius gives no thanks on this account.
Lucius seems fond of life; but what is life? 10
'Tis not to stalk about, and draw fresh air
From time to time, or gaze upon the sun;
'Tis to be free. When liberty is gone,
Life grows insipid, and has lost its relish.
Oh, could my dying hand but lodge a sword 15
In Cæsar's bosom, and revenge my country,
By heav'ns, I could enjoy the pangs of death,
And smile in agony.

LUC. Others perhaps
May serve their country with as warm a zeal,
Though 'tis not kindled into so much rage. 20

SEM. This sober conduct is a mighty virtue
In lukewarm patriots.

CATO. Come! no more, Sempronius!
All here are friends to Rome, and to each other.
Let us not weaken still the weaker side
By our divisions.

SEM. Cato, my resentments 25
Are sacrificed to Rome — I stand reproved.

CATO. Fathers, 'tis time you come to a resolve.

LUC. Cato, we all go into your opinion,
Cæsar's behavior has convinced the senate
We ought to hold it out till terms arrive. 30

SEM. We ought to hold it out till death; but, Cato,
My private voice is drowned amid the senate's.

CATO. Then let us rise, my friends, and strive
to fill
This little interval, this pause of life,
(While yet our liberty and fates are doubtful) 35
With resolution, friendship, Roman bravery,
And all the virtues we can crowd into it;
That heav'n may say, it ought to be prolonged.

Fathers, farewell!   The young Numidian prince
Comes forward, and expects to know our counsels.   *Exeunt Senators.*   40

[SCENE IV]

Enter JUBA.

CATO.   Juba, the Roman senate has resolved,
Till time give better prospects, still to keep
The sword unsheathed, and turn its edge on Cæsar.

JUBA.   The resolution fits a Roman senate.
But, Cato, lend me for a while thy patience,   5
And condescend to hear a young man speak.
My father, when some days before his death
He ordered me to march for Utica,
(Alas! I thought not then his death so near)
Wept o'er me, pressed me in his aged arms,   10
And, as his griefs gave way, 'My son,' said he,
'Whatever fortune shall befall thy father,
Be Cato's friend; he'll train thee up to great
And virtuous deeds: do but observe him well,
Thou'lt shun misfortunes, or thou'lt learn to bear
  'em.'   15

CATO.   Juba, thy father was a worthy prince,
And merited, alas! a better fate;
But heav'n thought otherwise.

JUBA.   My father's fate,
In spite of all the fortitude that shines
Before my face, in Cato's great example,   20
Subdues my soul, and fills my eyes with tears.

CATO.   It is an honest sorrow, and becomes thee.

JUBA.   My father drew respect from foreign climes:
The kings of Afric sought him for their friend;
Kings far remote, that rule, as fame reports,   25
Behind the hidden sources of the Nile,
In distant worlds, on t'other side the sun:
Oft have their black ambassadors appeared,
Loaden with gifts, and filled the courts of Zama.

CATO.   I am no stranger to thy father's greatness.   30

JUBA.   I would not boast the greatness of my father,
But point out new alliances to Cato.
Had we not better leave this Utica,
To arm Numidia in our cause, and court
Th' assistance of my father's pow'rful friends?   35
Did they know Cato, our remotest kings
Would pour embattled multitudes about him;
Their swarthy hosts would darken all our plains,
Doubling the native horror of the war,
And making death more grim.

CATO.   And canst thou think   40
Cato will fly before the sword of Cæsar?
Reduced, like Hannibal, to seek relief
From court to court, and wander up and down,
A vagabond in Afric!

JUBA.   Cato, perhaps

I'm too officious, but my forward cares   45
Would fain preserve a life of so much value.
My heart is wounded, when I see such virtue
Afflicted by the weight of such misfortunes.

CATO.   Thy nobleness of soul obliges me.
But know, young prince, that valor soars above   50
What the world calls misfortune and affliction.
These are not ills; else would they never fall
On heav'n's first fav'rites, and the best of men:
The gods, in bounty, work up storms about us,
That give mankind occasion to exert   55
Their hidden strength, and throw out into practice
Virtues that shun the day, and lie concealed
In the smooth seasons and the calms of life.

JUBA.   I'm charmed whene'er thou talk'st!   I
  pant for virtue
And all my soul endeavors at perfection.   60

CATO.   Dost thou love watchings, abstinence, and
  toil,
Laborious virtues all? learn them from Cato:
Success and fortune must thou learn from Cæsar.

JUBA.   The best good fortune that can fall on Juba,
The whole success at which my heart aspires,   65
Depends on Cato.

CATO.   What does Juba say?
Thy words confound me.

JUBA.   I would fain retract them,
Give 'em me back again.   They aimed at nothing.

CATO.   Tell me thy wish, young prince; make not
  my ear
A stranger to thy thoughts.

JUBA.   Oh! they're extravagant;   70
Still let me hide them.

CATO.   What can Juba ask
That Cato will refuse?

JUBA.   I fear to name it.
Marcia — inherits all her father's virtues.

CATO.   What wouldst thou say?

JUBA.   Cato, thou hast a daughter.

CATO.   Adieu, young prince; I would not hear a
  word   75
Should lessen thee in my esteem: remember
The hand of fate is over us, and heav'n
Exacts severity from all our thoughts:
It is not now a time to talk of aught
But chains or conquest, liberty or death.   *Exit.*   80

[SCENE V]

Enter SYPHAX.

SYPH.   How's this, my prince, what! covered with
  confusion?
You look as if yon stern philosopher
Had just now chid you.

JUBA.   Syphax, I'm undone!

SYPH.   I know it well.

JUBA   Cato thinks meanly of me.
SYPH. And so will all mankind.
JUBA.   I've opened to him 5
The weakness of my soul, my love for Marcia.
SYPH. Cato's a proper person to entrust
A love-tale with!
JUBA.   Oh! I could pierce my heart,
My foolish heart! was ever wretch like Juba?
SYPH. Alas! my prince, how are you changed of
        late!   10
I've known young Juba rise before the sun,
To beat the thicket where the tiger slept,
Or seek the lion in his dreadful haunts:
How did the color mount into your cheeks,
When first you roused him to the chase! I've seen
        you,   15
Ev'n in the Libyan dog-days, hunt him down,
Then charge him close, provoke him to the rage
Of fangs and claws, and stooping from your horse
Rivet the panting savage to the ground.
JUBA. Prithee, no more!
SYPH.   How would the old king smile 20
To see you weigh the paws, when tipped with gold,
And throw the shaggy spoils about your shoulders!
JUBA. Syphax, this old man's talk (though honey
        flowed
In ev'ry word) would now lose all its sweetness.
Cato's displeased, and Marcia lost forever!   25
SYPH. Young prince, I yet could give you good
        advice.
Marcia might still be yours.
JUBA.   What say'st thou, Syphax?
By heav'ns, thou turn'st me all into attention.
SYPH. Marcia might still be yours.
JUBA.   As how, dear Syphax?
SYPH. Juba   commands   Numidia's   hardy
        troops,   30
Mounted on steeds, unused to the restraint
Of curbs or bits, and fleeter than the winds:
Give but the word, we'll snatch this damsel up
And bear her off.
JUBA.   Can such dishonest thoughts
Rise up in man! wouldst thou seduce my youth 35
To do an act that would destroy my honor?
SYPH. Gods! I could tear my beard to hear you
        talk!
Honor's a fine imaginary notion,
That draws in raw and unexperienced men
To real mischiefs, while they hunt a shadow.   40
JUBA. Wouldst thou degrade thy prince into a
        ruffian?
SYPH. The boasted ancestors of these great men,
Whose virtues you admire, were all such ruffians.
This dread of nations, this almighty Rome,
That comprehends in her wide empire's bounds 45
All under heaven, was founded on a rape.
Your Scipios, Cæsars, Pompeys, and your Catos,

(These gods on earth) are all the spurious brood
Of violated maids, of ravished Sabines.
JUBA. Syphax, I fear that hoary head of thine 50
Abounds too much in our Numidian wiles.
SYPH. Indeed, my prince, you want to know the
        world;
You have not read mankind; your youth admires
The throes and swellings of a Roman soul,
Cato's bold flights, th' extravagance of virtue. 55
JUBA. If knowledge of the world makes man
        perfidious,
May Juba ever live in ignorance!
SYPH. Go, go, you're young.
JUBA.   Gods! must I tamely bear
This arrogance unanswered? thou'rt a traitor,
A false old traitor.
SYPH. (aside).   I have gone too far.   60
JUBA. Cato shall know the baseness of thy soul.
SYPH. (aside). I must appease this storm, or perish
        in it.
— Young prince, behold these locks that are grown
        white
Beneath a helmet in your father's battles.
JUBA. Those locks shall ne'er protect thy inso-
        lence.   65
SYPH. Must one rash word, th' infirmity of age,
Throw down the merit of my better years?
This the reward of a whole life of service!
(Aside.) Curse on the boy! how steadily he hears me!
JUBA. Is it because the throne of my fore-
        fathers   70
Still stands unfilled, and that Numidia's crown
Hangs doubtful yet, whose head it shall enclose,
Thou thus presumest to treat thy prince with scorn?
SYPH. Why will you rive my heart with such
        expressions?
Does not old Syphax follow you to war?   75
What are his aims? why does he load with darts
His trembling hand, and crush beneath a casque
His wrinkled brows? what is it he aspires to?
Is it not this, to shed the slow remains,
His last poor ebb of blood, in your defense?   80
JUBA. Syphax, no more! I would not hear you
        talk.
SYPH. Not hear me talk! what, when my faith to
        Juba,
My royal master's son, is called in question?
My prince may strike me dead, and I'll be dumb:
But whilst I live, I must not hold my tongue, 85
And languish out old age in his displeasure.
JUBA. Thou know'st the way too well into my
        heart,
I do believe thee loyal to thy prince.
SYPH. What greater instance can I give? I've
        offered
To do an action which my soul abhors,   90
And gain you whom you love at any price.

JUBA. Was this thy motive? I have been too
　　hasty.
SYPH. And 'tis for this my prince has called me
　　traitor.
JUBA. Sure thou mistakest; I did not call thee so.
SYPH. You did indeed, my prince, you called me
　　traitor:　　　　　　　　　　　　　　　　95
Nay, further, threatened you'd complain to Cato.
Of what, my prince, would you complain to Cato?
That Syphax loves you, and would sacrifice
His life, nay, more, his honor in your service.
　　JUBA. Syphax, I know thou lov'st me, but
　　　　indeed　　　　　　　　　　　　　　100
Thy zeal for Juba carried thee too far.
Honor's a sacred tie, the law of kings,
The noble mind's distinguishing perfection,
That aids and strengthens virtue where it meets her,
And imitates her actions, where she is not:　　105
It ought not to be sported with.
　　SYPH.　　　　　　　　　　　By heav'ns,
I'm ravished when you talk thus, though you chide
　　me!
Alas! I've hitherto been used to think
A blind, officious zeal to serve my king
The ruling principle that ought to burn　　　110
And quench all others in a subject's heart.
Happy the people, who preserve their honor
By the same duties that oblige their prince!
　　JUBA. Syphax, thou now begin'st to speak thyself.
Numidia's grown a scorn among the nations　　115
For breach of public vows. Our Punic faith
Is infamous, and branded to a proverb.
Syphax, we'll join our cares, to purge away
Our country's crimes, and clear her reputation.
　　SYPH. Believe me, prince, you make old Syphax
　　　　weep　　　　　　　　　　　　　　120
To hear you talk — but 'tis with tears of joy.
If e'er your father's crown adorn your brows,
Numidia will be blest by Cato's lectures.[1]
　　JUBA. Syphax, thy hand! we'll mutually forget
The warmth of youth, and frowardness of age:　125
Thy prince esteems thy worth, and loves thy person.
If e'er the scepter comes into my hand,
Syphax shall stand the second in my kingdom.
　　SYPH. Why will you overwhelm my age with
　　　　kindness?
My joy grows burdensome, I shan't support it.　130
　　JUBA. Syphax, farewell, I'll hence, and try to find
Some blest occasion that may set me right
In Cato's thoughts. I'd rather have that man
Approve my deeds, than worlds for my admirers.
　　　　　　　　　　　　　　　　　　Exit.
SYPH. (solus). Young men soon give, and soon
　　forget affronts;　　　　　　　　　　135
Old age is slow in both — 'A false old traitor!'
Those words, rash boy, may chance to cost thee dear.

　　　[1] Counsels, examples.

My heart had still some foolish fondness for thee:
But hence! 'tis gone: I give it to the winds:
Cæsar, I'm wholly thine —　　　　　　　140

[SCENE VI]

Enter SEMPRONIUS.

SYPH.　　　　　　　　　All hail, Sempronius!
Well, Cato's senate is resolved to wait
The fury of a siege before it yields.
　　SEM. Syphax, we both were on the verge of fate:
Lucius declared for peace, and terms were offered　5
To Cato by a messenger from Cæsar.
Should they submit, ere our designs are ripe,
We both must perish in the common wreck,
Lost in a gen'ral, undistinguished ruin.
　　SYPH. But how stands Cato?
　　SEM.　　　　　　Thou hast seen Mount Atlas:　10
While storms and tempests thunder on its brows,
And oceans break their billows at its feet,
It stands unmoved, and glories in its height.
Such is that haughty man; his towering soul,
'Midst all the shocks and injuries of fortune,　　15
Rises superior, and looks down on Cæsar.
　　SYPH. But what's this messenger?
　　SEM.　　　　　　　　　　I've practised with him,
And found a means to let the victor know
That Syphax and Sempronius are his friends.
But let me now examine in my turn:　　　　20
Is Juba fixt?
　　SYPH.　　　Yes — but it is to Cato.
I've tried the force of every reason on him,
Soothed and caressed, been angry, soothed again,
Laid safety, life, and int'rest in his sight,
But all are vain, he scorns them all for Cato.　　25
　　SEM. Come, 'tis no matter, we shall do without
　　　　him.
He'll make a pretty figure in a triumph,
And serve to trip before the victor's chariot.
Syphax, I now may hope thou hast forsook
Thy Juba's cause, and wishest Marcia mine.　　30
　　SYPH. May she be thine as fast as thou wouldst
　　　　have her!
　　SEM. Syphax, I love that woman; though I curse
Her and myself, yet, spite of me, I love her.
　　SYPH. Make Cato sure, and give up Utica,
Cæsar will ne'er refuse thee such a trifle.　　35
But are thy troops prepared for a revolt?
Does the sedition catch from man to man,
And run among their ranks?
　　SEM.　　　　　　　　All, all is ready.
The factious leaders are our friends, that spread
Murmurs and discontents among the soldiers.　40
They count their toilsome marches, long fatigues,
Unusual fastings, and will bear no more
This medley of philosophy and war.
Within an hour they'll storm the senate-house.

Syph. Meanwhile I'll draw up my Numidian
    troops   45
Within the square, to exercise their arms,
And, as I see occasion, favor thee.
I laugh to think how your unshaken Cato
Will look aghast, while unforeseen destruction
Pours in upon him thus from every side.   50
So, where our wide Numidian wastes extend,
Sudden, th' impetuous hurricanes descend,
Wheel through the air, in circling eddies play,
Tear up the sands, and sweep whole plains away.
The helpless traveller, with wild surprise, ⎫ 55
Sees the dry desert all around him rise, ⎬
And smothered in the dusty whirlwind dies. ⎭

                        Exeunt.

ACT III

SCENE I

MARCUS *and* PORTIUS.

Mar. Thanks to my stars, I have not ranged about
The wilds of life, ere I could find a friend;
Nature first pointed out my Portius to me,
And early taught me, by her secret force,
To love thy person, ere I knew thy merit; 5
Till, what was instinct, grew up into friendship.
   Por. Marcus, the friendships of the world are oft
Confed'racies in vice, or leagues of pleasure;
Ours has severest virtue for its basis,
And such a friendship ends not but with life. 10
   Mar. Portius, thou know'st my soul in all its
    weakness;
Then prithee spare me on its tender side,
Indulge me but in love, my other passions
Shall rise and fall by virtue's nicest rules.
   Por. When love's well-timed, 'tis not a fault to
    love. 15
The strong, the brave, the virtuous, and the wise
Sink in the soft captivity together.
I would not urge thee to dismiss thy passion,
(I know 'twere vain) but to suppress its force,
Till better times may make it look more graceful. 20
   Mar. Alas! thou talk'st like one who never felt
Th' impatient throbs and longings of a soul
That pants and reaches after distant good.
A lover does not live by vulgar time:
Believe me, Portius, in my Lucia's absence 25
Life hangs upon me, and becomes a burden;
And yet, when I behold the charming maid,
I'm ten times more undone; while hope, and fear,
And grief, and rage, and love, rise up at once,
And with variety of pain distract me. 30
   Por. What can thy Portius do to give thee help?
   Mar. Portius, thou oft enjoy'st the fair one's
    presence:
Then undertake my cause, and plead it to her

With all the strength and heats of eloquence
Fraternal love and friendship can inspire. 35
Tell her thy brother languishes to death,
And fades away, and withers in his bloom;
That he forgets his sleep, and loathes his food,
That youth, and health, and war, are joyless to him.
Describe his anxious days and restless nights, 40
And all the torments that thou seest me suffer.
   Por. Marcus, I beg thee give me not an office
That suits with me so ill. Thou know'st my temper.
   Mar. Wilt thou behold me sinking in my woes?
And wilt thou not reach out a friendly arm, 45
To raise me from amidst this plunge of sorrows?
   Por. Marcus, thou canst not ask what I'd refuse.
But here, believe me, I've a thousand reasons —
   Mar. I know thou'lt say my passion's out of
    season;
That Cato's great example and misfortunes 50
Should both conspire to drive it from my thoughts.
But what's all this to one who loves like me!
Oh, Portius, Portius, from my soul I wish
Thou didst but know thyself what 'tis to love!
Then wouldst thou pity and assist thy brother. 55
   Por. (*aside*). What should I do? If I disclose my
    passion,
Our friendship's at an end: if I conceal it,
The world will call me false to a friend and brother.
   Mar. But see where Lucia, at her wonted hour,
Amid the cool of yon high marble arch, 60
Enjoys the noon-day breeze! observe her, Portius!
That face, that shape, those eyes, that heav'n of
    beauty!
Observe her well, and blame me, if thou canst.
   Por. She sees us, and advances —
   Mar.   I'll withdraw,
And leave you for a while. Remember, Portius, 65
Thy brother's life depends upon thy tongue. *Exit.*

[SCENE II]

Enter LUCIA.

Luc. Did not I see your brother Marcus here?
Why did he fly the place, and shun my presence?
   Por. Oh, Lucia, language is too faint to show
His rage of love; it preys upon his life;
He pines, he sickens, he despairs, he dies: 5
His passions and his virtues lie confused,
And mixt together in so wild a tumult,
That the whole man is quite disfigured in him.
Heav'ns! would one think 'twere possible for love
To make such ravage in a noble soul! 10
O Lucia, I'm distrest! my heart bleeds for him;
Ev'n now, while thus I stand blest in thy presence,
A secret damp of grief comes o'er my thoughts,
And I'm unhappy, though thou smilest upon me.
   Luc. How wilt thou guard thy honor in the
    shock

Of love and friendship! think betimes, my Portius,
Think how the nuptial tie, that might ensure
Our mutual bliss, would raise to such a height
Thy brother's griefs, as might perhaps destroy him.
   Por. Alas, poor youth! what dost thou think, my
     Lucia?   20
His gen'rous, open, undesigning heart
Has begged his rival to solicit for him.
Then do not strike him dead with a denial,
But hold him up in life, and cheer his soul
With the faint glimm'ring of a doubtful hope: 25
Perhaps, when we have passed these gloomy hours,
And weathered out the storm that beats upon us —
   Luc. No, Portius, no! I see thy sister's tears,
Thy father's anguish, and thy brother's death,
In the pursuit of our ill-fated loves.   30
And, Portius, here I swear, to heaven I swear,
To heav'n, and all the pow'rs that judge mankind,
Never to mix my plighted hands with thine,
While such a cloud of mischiefs hangs about us,
But to forget our loves, and drive thee out   35
From all my thoughts, as far — as I am able.
   Por. What hast thou said! I'm thunderstruck! —
     recall
Those hasty words, or I am lost forever.
   Luc. Has not the vow already passed my lips?
The gods have heard it, and 'tis sealed in
     heav'n.   40
May all the vengeance that was ever poured
On perjured heads o'erwhelm me, if I break it!
   Por. (after a pause). Fixt in astonishment, I gaze
     upon thee;
Like one just blasted by a stroke from heav'n,
Who pants for breath, and stiffens, yet alive,   45
In dreadful looks — a monument of wrath!
   Luc. At length I've acted my severest part,
I feel the woman breaking in upon me,
And melt about my heart! my tears will flow.
But oh, I'll think no more! the hand of fate   50
Has torn thee from me, and I must forget thee.
   Por. Hard-hearted, cruel maid!
   Luc.   Oh, stop those sounds,
Those killing sounds! why dost thou frown upon me?
My blood runs cold, my heart forgets to heave,
And life itself goes out at thy displeasure.   55
The gods forbid us to indulge our loves,
But oh! I cannot bear thy hate and live!
   Por. Talk not of love, thou never knew'st its force,
I've been deluded, led into a dream
Of fancied bliss. O Lucia, cruel maid!   60
Thy dreadful vow, loaden with death, still sounds
In my stunned ears. What shall I say or do?
Quick, let us part! perdition's in thy presence,
And horror dwells about thee! — hah, she faints!
Wretch that I am! what has my rashness done!   65
Lucia, thou injured innocence! thou best

And loveli'st of thy sex! awake, my Lucia,
Or Portius rushes on his sword to join thee.
— Her imprecations reach not to the tomb,
They shut not out society in death —   70
But, hah, she moves! life wanders up and down
Through all her face, and lights up ev'ry charm.
   Luc. O Portius, was this well! — to frown on her
That lives upon thy smiles! to call in doubt
The faith of one expiring at thy feet,   75
That loves thee more than ever woman loved!
— What do I say? my half-recovered sense
Forgets the vow in which my soul is bound.
Destruction stands betwixt us! we must part.
   Por. Name not the word, my frighted thoughts
     run back,   80
And startle into madness at the sound.
   Luc. What wouldst thou have me do? consider
     well
The train of ills our love would draw behind it.
Think, Portius, think, thou seest thy dying brother
Stabbed at his heart, and all besmeared with
     blood,   85
Storming at heav'n and thee! thy awful sire
Sternly demands the cause, th' accursèd cause,
That robs him of his son! poor Marcia trembles,
Then tears her hair, and frantic in her griefs
Calls out on Lucia! What could Lucia answer? 90
Or how stand up in such a scene of sorrow?
   Por. To my confusion and eternal grief,
I must approve the sentence that destroys me.
The mist that hung about my mind clears up;
And now, athwart the terrors that thy vow   95
Has planted round thee, thou appear'st more fair,
More amiable, and risest in thy charms.
Loveli'st of women! heav'n is in thy soul,
Beauty and virtue shine for ever round thee,
Bright'ning each other! thou art all divine!   100
   Luc. Portius, no more! thy words shoot through
     my heart,
Melt my resolves, and turn me all to love.
Why are those tears of fondness in thy eyes?
Why heaves thy heart? Why swells thy soul with
     sorrow?
It softens me too much — farewell, my Portius,   105
Farewell, though death is in the word, forever.
   Por. Stay, Lucia, stay! what dost thou say?
     Forever?
   Luc. Have I not sworn? if, Portius, thy success
Must throw thy brother on his fate, farewell —
Oh, how shall I repeat the word? — forever!   110
   Por. Thus o'er the dying lamp th' unsteady flame
Hangs quiv'ring on a point, leaps off by fits,
And falls again, as loth to quit its hold.
Thou must not go, my soul still hovers o'er thee,
And can't get loose.
   Luc.   If the firm Portius shake 115

43] W om. (after a pause).

To hear of parting, think what Lucia suffers!

POR. 'Tis true; unruffled and serene I've met
The common accidents of life, but here
Such an unlooked-for storm of ills falls on me,
It beats down all my strength. I cannot bear
   it.   120
We must not part.

LUC.   What dost thou say? not part?
Hast thou forgot the vow that I have made?
Are there not heav'ns, and gods, and thunder o'er us?
— But see! thy brother Marcus bends this way!
I sicken at the sight. Once more, farewell,   125
Farewell, and know thou wrong'st me, if thou
   think'st
Ever was love, or ever grief, like mine.   *Exit.*

[SCENE III]

Enter MARCUS.

MAR. Portius, what hopes? how stands she? am I
   doomed
To life or death?

POR.   What wouldst thou have me say?

MAR. What means this pensive posture? thou
   appear'st
Like one amazed and terrified.

POR.   I've reason.

MAR. Thy downcast looks and thy disordered
   thoughts   5
Tell me my fate. I ask not the success
My cause has found.

POR.   I'm grieved I undertook it.

MAR. What! does the barb'rous maid insult my
   heart,
My aching heart! and triumph in my pains?
That I could cast her from my thoughts for ever!   10

POR. Away! you're too suspicious in your griefs;
Lucia, though sworn never to think of love,
Compassionates your pains, and pities you!

MAR. Compassionates my pains, and pities me!
What is compassion when 'tis void of love?   15
Fool that I was to choose so cold a friend
To urge my cause! compassionate my pains!
Prithee what art, what rhetoric didst thou use
To gain this mighty boon? She pities me!
To one that asks the warm return of love,   20
Compassion's cruelty, 'tis scorn, 'tis death —

POR. Marcus, no more! have I deserved this
   treatment?

MAR. What have I said! O Portius, oh, forgive me!
A soul exasp'rated in ills falls out
With ev'rything, its friend, its self — but, hah!   25
What means that shout, big with the sounds of war?
What new alarm?

POR.   A second, louder yet,
Swells in the winds, and comes more full upon us.

MAR. Oh, for some glorious cause to fall in battle!
Lucia, thou hast undone me! thy disdain   30
Has broke my heart: 'tis death must give me ease.

POR. Quick, let us hence; who knows if Cato's life
Stand sure? O Marcus, I am warmed; my heart
Leaps at the trumpet's voice, and burns for glory.
                                                  Exeunt.

[SCENE IV]

Enter SEMPRONIUS *with the Leaders of the mutiny.*

SEM. At length the winds are raised, the storm
   blows high,
Be it your care, my friends, to keep it up
In its full fury, and direct it right,
Till it has spent itself on Cato's head.
Meanwhile I'll herd among his friends, and seem   5
One of the number, that whate'er arrive,
My friends and fellow soldiers may be safe. [*Exit.*]

FIRST LEAD. We all are safe, Sempronius is our
   friend,
Sempronius is as brave a man as Cato.
But, hark! he enters. Bear up boldly to him;   10
Be sure you beat him down, and bind him fast.
This day will end our toils, and give us rest;
Fear nothing, for Sempronius is our friend.

[SCENE V]

Enter CATO, SEMPRONIUS, LUCIUS, PORTIUS, *and*
MARCUS.

CATO. Where are these bold, intrepid sons of war,
That greatly turn their backs upon the foe,
And to their general send a brave defiance?

SEM. (*aside*). Curse on their dastard souls, they
   stand astonished!

CATO. Perfidious men! and will you thus dis-
   honor   5
Your past exploits, and sully all your wars?
Do you confess 'twas not a zeal for Rome,
Nor love of liberty, nor thirst of honor,
Drew you thus far; but hopes to share the spoil
Of conquered towns and plundered provinces?   10
Fired with such motives you do well to join
With Cato's foes, and follow Cæsar's banners.
Why did I scape the invenomed aspic's rage,
And all the fiery monsters of the desert,
To see this day? why could not Cato fall   15
Without your guilt? Behold, ungrateful men,
Behold my bosom naked to your swords,
And let the man that's injured strike the blow.
Which of you all suspects that he is wronged,
Or thinks he suffers greater ills than Cato?   20
Am I distinguished from you but by toils,
Superior toils, and heavier weight of cares?
Painful pre-eminence!

SCENE IV. 7] Q1Q2Q3Q4W om. Exit; Q5Q6D7D8 supply it.   SCENE V. 16] Q5 om. comma.

Sem. (*aside*).   By heav'ns, they droop!
Confusion to the villains! all is lost.
 Cato. Have you forgotten Libya's burning
  waste,   25
Its barren rocks, parched earth, and hills of sand,
Its tainted air, and all its broods of poison?
Who was the first to explore th' untrodden path,
When life was hazarded in every step?
Or, fainting in the long, laborious march, 30
When on the banks of an unlooked-for stream
You sunk the river with repeated draughts,
Who was the last in all your host that thirsted?
 Sem. If some penurious source by chance ap-
  peared,
Scanty of waters, when you scooped it dry, 35
And offered the full helmet up to Cato,
Did he not dash th' untasted moisture from him?
Did he not lead you through the mid-day sun,
And clouds of dust? did not his temples glow
In the same sultry winds and scorching heats? 40
 Cato. Hence, worthless men! hence! and com-
  plain to Cæsar
You could not undergo the toils of war,
Nor bear the hardships that your leader bore.
 Luc. See, Cato, see th' unhappy men! they weep!
Fear, and remorse, and sorrow for their crime, 45
Appear in ev'ry look, and plead for mercy.
 Cato. Learn to be honest men, give up your
  leaders,
And pardon shall descend on all the rest.
 Sem. Cato, commit these wretches to my care.
First, let 'em each be broken on the rack, 50
Then, with what life remains, impaled and left
To writhe at leisure round the bloody stake.
There let 'em hang, and taint the southern wind.
The partners of their crime will learn obedience,
When they look up and see their fellow-traitors 55
Stuck on a fork, and black'ning in the sun.
 Luc. Sempronius, why, why wilt thou urge the
  fate
Of wretched men?
 Sem.   How! wouldst thou clear rebellion?
Lucius (good man) pities the poor offenders,
That would inbrue their hands in Cato's blood. 60
 Cato. Forbear, Sempronius! — see they suffer
  death,
But in their deaths remember they are men.
Strain not the laws to make their tortures grievous.
Lucius, the base, degenerate age requires
Severity, and justice in its rigor;   65
This awes an impious, bold, offending world,
Commands obedience, and gives force to laws.
When by just vengeance guilty mortals perish,
The gods behold their punishment with pleasure,
And lay th' uplifted thunderbolt aside. 70
 Sem. Cato, I execute thy will with pleasure,
 Cato. Meanwhile we'll sacrifice to liberty.

Remember, O my friends, the laws, the rights,
The generous plan of power delivered down,
From age to age, by your renowned forefathers, 75
(So dearly bought, the price of so much blood)
Oh, let it never perish in your hands!
But piously transmit it to your children.
Do thou, great Liberty, inspire our souls,
And make our lives in thy possession happy, 80
Or our deaths glorious in thy just defense.
       Exeunt Cato, *etc.*

[Scene VI]

Sempronius *and the Leaders of the mutiny.*

 1st Lead. Sempronius, you have acted like your-
  self,
One would have thought you had been half in earnest.
 Sem. Villain, stand off! base, grov'lling, worthless
  wretches,
Mongrels in faction, poor faint-hearted traitors!
 2d Lead. Nay, now you carry it too far, Sem-
  pronius: 5
Throw off the mask, there are none here but friends.
 Sem. Know, villains, when such paltry slaves
  presume
To mix in treason, if the plot succeeds,
They're thrown neglected by: but if it fails,
They're sure to die like dogs, as you shall do. 10
      [*Calls to Guards without.*]
Here, take these factious monsters, drag 'em forth
To sudden death.

     Enter Guards.

 1st Lead.   Nay, since it comes to this —
 Sem. Dispatch 'em quick, but first pluck out their
  tongues,
Lest with their dying breath they sow sedition.
    Exeunt Guards with the Leaders.

[Scene VII]

Enter Syphax.

 Syph. Our first design, my friend, has proved
  abortive;
Still there remains an after-game to play:
My troops are mounted; their Numidian steeds
Snuff up the wind, and long to scour the desert:
Let but Sempronius head us in our flight, 5
We'll force the gate where Marcus keeps his guard,
And hew down all that would oppose our passage.
A day will bring us into Cæsar's camp.
 Sem. Confusion! I have failed of half my purpose:
Marcia, the charming Marcia's left behind! 10
 Syph. How! will Sempronius turn a woman's
  slave?
 Sem. Think not thy friend can ever feel the soft
Unmanly warmth and tenderness of love.

Syphax, I long to clasp that haughty maid,
And bend her stubborn virtue to my passion: 15
When I have gone thus far, I'd cast her off.

SYPH. Well said! that's spoken like thyself, Sem-
pronius.
What hinders then, but that thou find her out,
And hurry her away by manly force?

SEM. But how to gain admission? for access   20
Is given to none but Juba and her brothers.

SYPH. Thou shalt have Juba's dress and Juba's
guards:
The doors will open, when Numidia's prince
Seems to appear before the slaves that watch them.

SEM. Heav'ns, what a thought is there! Marcia's
my own!   25
How will my bosom swell with anxious joy,
When I behold her struggling in my arms,
With glowing beauty and disordered charms,
While fear and anger, with alternate grace,
Pant in her breast, and vary in her face!   30
So Pluto, seized of[1] Proserpine, conveyed
To hell's tremendous gloom th' affrighted maid,
There grimly smiled, pleased with the beauteous
prize,
Nor envied Jove his sunshine and his skies. [*Exeunt.*]

ACT IV

SCENE I

LUCIA *and* MARCIA.

LUC. Now tell me, Marcia, tell me from thy soul,
If thou believ'st 'tis possible for woman
To suffer greater ills than Lucia suffers?

MAR. O Lucia, Lucia, might my big-swoln heart
Vent all its griefs, and give a loose to sorrow: 5
Marcia could answer thee in sighs, keep pace
With all thy woes, and count out tear for tear.

LUC. I know thou'rt doomed, alike, to be beloved
By Juba and thy father's friend, Sempronius;
But which of these has power to charm like Por-
tius?   10

MAR. Still must I beg thee not to name Sem-
pronius?
Lucia, I like not that loud, boist'rous man;
Juba to all the bravery of a hero
Adds softest love, and more than female sweetness;
Juba might make the proudest of our sex,   15
Any of womankind, but Marcia, happy.

LUC. And why not Marcia? come, you strive in
vain
To hide your thoughts from one who knows too well
The inward glowings of a heart in love.

MAR. While Cato lives, his daughter has no
right   20

[1] *Possessed of.*

To love or hate, but as his choice directs.

LUC. But should this father give you to Sempronius?

MAR. I dare not think he will: but if he should —
Why wilt thou add to all the griefs I suffer
Imaginary ills, and fancied tortures?   25
I hear the sound of feet! they march this way!
Let us retire, and try if we can drown
Each softer thought in sense of present danger.
When love once pleads admission to our hearts,
(In spite of all the virtue we can boast)   30
The woman that deliberates is lost.   *Exeunt.*

[SCENE II]

Enter SEMPRONIUS, *dressed like* JUBA, *with Numidian
Guards.*

SEM. The deer is lodged. I've tracked her to
her covert.
Be sure you mind the word, and when I give it,
Rush in at once, and seize upon your prey.
Let not her cries or tears have force to move you.
— How will the young Numidian rave, to see   5
His mistress lost! if aught could glad my soul,
Beyond th' enjoyment of so bright a prize,
'Twould be to torture that young gay barbarian.
— But, hark, what noise! death to my hopes! 'tis he,
'Tis Juba's self! there is but one way left —   10
He must be murdered, and a passage cut
Through those his guards — Hah! dastards, do you
tremble!
Or act like men, or by yon azure heav'n —

Enter JUBA.

JUBA. What do I see? who's this that dare usurp
The guards and habits of Numidia's prince?   15

SEM. One that was born to scourge thy arrogance,
Presumptuous youth!

JUBA.   What can this mean? Sempronius!

SEM. My sword shall answer thee. Have at thy
heart.

JUBA. Nay, then beware thy own, proud, bar-
b'rous man!
(SEMPRONIUS *falls. His Guards surrender.*)

SEM. Curse on my stars! am I then doomed to
fall   20
By a boy's hand, disfigured in a vile
Numidian dress, and for a worthless woman?
Gods, I'm distracted! this my close of life!
Oh, for a peal of thunder that would make
Earth, sea, and air, and heav'n, and Cato
tremble!   (*Dies.*)   25

JUBA. With what a spring his furious soul broke
loose.
And left the limbs still quiv'ring on the ground!
Hence let us carry off those slaves to Cato,

That we may there at length unravel all
This dark design, this mystery of fate.　30
　　　　　Exit JUBA, *with Prisoners, etc.*

[SCENE III]

Enter LUCIA *and* MARCIA.

Luc. Sure 'twas the clash of swords; my troubled heart
Is so cast down, and sunk amidst its sorrows,
It throbs with fear and aches at every sound.
O Marcia, should thy brothers for my sake! —
I die away with horror at the thought.　5
　　MAR. See, Lucia, see! here's blood! here's blood and murder!
Hah, a Numidian! heav'ns preserve the prince!
The face lies muffled up within the garment.
But hah! death to my sight, a diadem,
And purple robes! O gods! 'tis he, 'tis he!　10
Juba, the loveliest youth that ever warmed
A virgin's heart, Juba lies dead before us!
　　Luc. Now, Marcia, now call up to thy assistance
Thy wonted strength and constancy of mind;
Thou canst not put it to a greater trial.　15
　　MAR. Lucia, look there, and wonder at my patience.
Have I not cause to rave, and beat my breast,
To rend my heart with grief, and run distracted?
　　Luc. What can I think or say to give thee comfort?
　　MAR. Talk not of comfort, 'tis for lighter ills:　20
Behold a sight that strikes all comfort dead.

Enter JUBA, *list'ning.*

I will indulge my sorrows, and give way
To all the pangs and fury of despair:
That man, that best of men, deserved it from me.
　　JUBA. What do I hear! and was the false Sempronius　25
That best of men? Oh, had I fall'n like him,
And could have thus been mourned, I had been happy!
　　Luc. Here will I stand, companion in thy woes,
And help thee with my tears! when I behold
A loss like thine, I half forget my own.　30
　　MAR. 'Tis not in fate to ease my tortured breast.
This empty world, to me a joyless desert,
Has nothing left to make poor Marcia happy.
　　JUBA. I'm on the rack! was he so near her heart?
　　MAR. Oh! he was all made up of love and charms,　35
Whatever maid could wish or man admire:
Delight of ev'ry eye! when he appeared,
A secret pleasure gladdened all that saw him;
But when he talked, the proudest Roman blushed

To hear his virtues, and old age grew wise.　40
　　JUBA. I shall run mad —
　　MAR.　　　　　　O Juba! Juba! Juba!
　　JUBA. What means that voice? did she not call on Juba?
　　MAR. Why do I think on what he was! he's dead!
He's dead, and never knew how much I loved him.
Lucia, who knows but his poor bleeding heart,　45
Amidst its agonies, remembered Marcia,
And the last words he uttered called me cruel!
Alas! he knew not, hapless youth, he knew not
Marcia's whole soul was full of love and Juba.
　　JUBA. Where am I? do I live! or am indeed　50
What Marcia thinks! all is Elysium round me!
　　MAR. Ye dear remains of the most loved of men!
Nor modesty nor virtue here forbid
A last embrace, while thus —
　　JUBA [*throwing himself before her*]. See, Marcia, see,
The happy Juba lives! he lives to catch　55
That dear embrace, and to return it too
With mutual warmth and eagerness of love.
　　MAR. With pleasure and amaze, I stand transported!
Sure 'tis a dream! dead and alive at once!
If thou art Juba, who lies there?
　　JUBA.　　　　　　A wretch,　60
Disguised like Juba, on a curst design.
The tale is long, nor have I heard it out;
Thy father knows it all. I could not bear
To leave thee in the neighborhood of death,
But flew, in all the haste of love, to find thee;　65
I found thee weeping, and confess, this once
Am [rapt] [1] with joy to see my Marcia's tears.
　　MAR. I've been surprised in an unguarded hour,
But must not now go back: the love, that lay
Half smothered in my breast, has broke through all　70
Its weak restraints, and burns in its full lustre;
I cannot, if I would, conceal it from thee.
　　JUBA. I'm lost in ecstasy! and dost thou love,
Thou charming maid?
　　MAR.　　　　　　And dost thou live to ask it?
　　JUBA. This, this is life indeed! life worth preserving,　75
Such life as Juba never felt till now!
　　MAR. Believe me, prince, before I thought thee dead,
I did not know myself how much I loved thee.
　　JUBA. O fortunate mistake!
　　MAR.　　　　　　O happy Marcia!
　　JUBA. My joy! my best beloved! my only wish!　80
How shall I speak the transport of my soul?

---

[1] Transported.

MAR. Lucia, thy arm! oh, let me rest upon it! —
The vital blood, that had forsook my heart,
Returns again in such tumultuous tides,
It quite o'ercomes me. Lead to my apart-
ment. —   85
O prince! I blush to think what I have said,
But fate has wrested the confession from me;
Go on, and prosper in the paths of honor,
Thy virtue will excuse my passion for thee,
And make the gods propitious to our love.   90

                          Exeunt MARCIA *and* LUCIA.

JUBA. I am so blest, I fear 'tis all a dream.
Fortune, thou now hast made amends for all
Thy past unkindness. I absolve my stars.
What though Numidia add her conquered towns
And provinces to swell the victor's triumph!   95
Juba will never at his fate repine;
Let Cæsar have the world, if Marcia's mine. *Exit.*

[SCENE IV]

(A march at a distance.)

Enter CATO *and* LUCIUS.

LUC. I stand astonished! what, the bold Sem-
              pronius!
That still broke foremost through the crowd of
              patriots,
As with a hurricane of zeal transported,
And virtuous ev'n to madness —
CATO.   Trust me, Lucius,
Our civil discords have produced such crimes,   5
Such monstrous crimes, I am surprised at nothing.
— O Lucius! I am sick of this bad world!
The daylight and the sun grow painful to me.

Enter PORTIUS.

But see where Portius comes! What means this
              haste?
Why are thy looks thus changed?
POR.   My heart is grieved.   10
I bring such news as will afflict my father.
CATO. Has Cæsar shed more Roman blood?
POR.   Not so.
The traitor Syphax, as within the square
He exercised his troops, the signal given,
Flew off at once with his Numidian horse   15
To the south gate, where Marcus holds the watch.
I saw, and called to stop him, but in vain,
He tossed his arm aloft, and proudly told me,
He would not stay and perish like Sempronius.
CATO. Perfidious men! but haste, my son, and
              see   20
Thy brother Marcus acts a Roman's part.

                                  Exit PORTIUS.

— Lucius, the torrent bears too hard upon me:

Justice gives way to force: the conquered world
Is Cæsar's: Cato has no business in it.
LUC. While pride, oppression, and injustice
              reign,   25
The world will still demand her Cato's presence.
In pity to mankind, submit to Cæsar,
And reconcile thy mighty soul to life.
CATO. Would Lucius have me live to swell the
              number
Of Cæsar's slaves, or by a base submission   30
Give up the cause of Rome, and own a tyrant?
LUC. The victor never will impose on Cato
Ungen'rous terms. His enemies confess
The virtues of humanity are Cæsar's.
CATO. Curse on his virtues! they've undone his
              country.   35
Such popular humanity is treason —
But see young Juba! the good youth appears
Full of the guilt of his perfidious subjects.
LUC. Alas! poor prince! his fate deserves com-
              passion.

Enter JUBA.

JUBA. I blush and am confounded to appear   40
Before thy presence, Cato.
CATO.   What's thy crime?
JUBA. I'm a Numidian.
CATO.   And a brave one too.
Thou hast a Roman soul.
JUBA.   Hast thou not heard
Of my false countrymen?
CATO.   Alas! young prince,
Falsehood and fraud shoot up in every soil,   45
The product of all climes — Rome has its Cæsars.
JUBA. 'Tis generous thus to comfort the distressed.
CATO. 'Tis just to give applause where 'tis de-
              served;
Thy virtue, prince, has stood the test of fortune,
Like purest gold, that, tortured in the furnace,   50
Comes out more bright, and brings forth all its
              weight.
JUBA. What shall I answer thee? my ravished
              heart
O'erflows with secret joy: I'd rather gain
Thy praise, O Cato, than Numidia's empire.

Enter PORTIUS *hastily.*

POR. Misfortune on misfortune! grief on grief! 55
My brother Marcus —
CATO.   Hah! what has he done?
Has he forsook his post? has he giv'n way?
Did he look tamely on, and let 'em pass?
POR. Scarce had I left my father, but I met him
Borne on the shields of his surviving soldiers,   60
Breathless and pale, and covered o'er with wounds.
Long, at the head of his few faithful friends,

He stood the shock of a whole host of foes.
Till, obstinately brave, and bent on death,
Oppressed with multitudes, he greatly fell.   65
   CATO. I'm satisfied.
   POR.   Nor did he fall before
His sword had pierced through the false heart of
   Syphax.
Yonder he lies.   I saw the hoary traitor
Grin in the pangs of death, and bite the ground.
   CATO. Thanks to the gods! my boy has done his
   duty.   70
— Portius, when I am dead, be sure thou place
His urn near mine.
   POR.   Long may they keep asunder.
   LUC. O Cato! arm thy soul with all its patience;
See where the corpse of thy dead son approaches!
The citizens and senators, alarmed,   75
Have gathered round it, and attend it weeping.
   CATO (*meeting the corpse*). Welcome, my son! here
   lay him down, my friends,
Full in my sight, that I may view at leisure
The bloody corse, and count those glorious wounds.
How beautiful is death, when earned by virtue! 80
Who would not be that youth? what pity is it
That we can die but once to serve our country!
Why sits this sadness on your brows, my friends?
I should have blushed if Cato's house had stood
Secure, and flourished in a civil war.   85
— Portius, behold thy brother, and remember
Thy life is not thy own, when Rome demands it.
   JUBA (*aside*). Was ever man like this!
   CATO.   Alas! my friends!
Why mourn you thus? let not a private loss
Afflict your hearts. 'Tis Rome requires our
   tears,   90
The mistress of the world, the seat of empire,
The nurse of heroes, the delight of gods,
That humbled the proud tyrants of the earth,
And set the nations free, Rome is no more.
O liberty! O virtue! O my country!   95
   JUBA (*aside*). Behold that upright man! Rome
   fills his eyes
With tears, that flowed not o'er his own dead son.
   CATO. Whate'er the Roman virtue has subdued,
The sun's whole course, the day and year, are
   Cæsar's.
For him the self-devoted Decii died,   100
The Fabii fell, and the great Scipios conquered;
Ev'n Pompey fought for Cæsar. Oh! my friends!
How is the toil of fate, the work of ages,
The Roman empire fall'n! O curst ambition!
Fall'n into Cæsar's hands! Our great fore-
   fathers   105
Had left him nought to conquer but his country.
   JUBA. While Cato lives, Cæsar will blush to see

Mankind enslaved, and be ashamed of empire.
   CATO. Cæsar ashamed! has not he seen Pharsalia?
   LUC. Cato, 'tis time thou save thyself and us. 110
   CATO. Lose not a thought on me; I'm out of
   danger.
Heav'n will not leave me in the victor's hand.
Cæsar shall never say, 'I've conquered Cato.'
But, oh! my friends, your safety fills my heart
With anxious thoughts: a thousand secret ter-
   rors   115
Rise in my soul: how shall I save my friends!
'Tis now, O Cæsar, I begin to fear thee.
   LUC. Cæsar has mercy, if we ask it of him.
   CATO. Then ask it, I conjure you! let him know
Whate'er was done against him, Cato did it.   120
Add, if you please, that I request it of him,
That I myself, with tears, request it of him,
The virtue of my friends may pass unpunished.
— Juba, my heart is troubled for thy sake.
Should I advise thee to regain Numidia,   125
Or seek the conqueror? —
   JUBA.   If I forsake thee
Whilst I have life, may heav'n abandon Juba!
   CATO. Thy virtues, prince, if I foresee aright,
Will one day make thee great; at Rome, hereafter,
'Twill be no crime to have been Cato's friend. 130
Portius, draw near! my son, thou oft hast seen
Thy sire engaged in a corrupted state,
Wrestling with vice and faction: now thou seest me
Spent, overpowered, despairing of success;
Let me advise thee to retreat betimes   135
To thy paternal seat, the Sabine field,
Where the great Censor[1] toiled with his own hands,
And all our frugal ancestors were blessed
In humble virtues and a rural life.
There live retired, pray for the peace of Rome: 140
Content thyself to be obscurely good.
When vice prevails, and impious men bear sway,
The post of honor is a private station.
   POR. I hope my father does not recommend
A life to Portius that he scorns himself.   145
   CATO. Farewell, my friends! if there be any of you
That dares not trust the victor's clemency,
Know, there are ships prepared by my command,
(Their sails already op'ning to the winds)
That shall convey you to the wished-for port.   150
Is there aught else, my friends, I can do for you?
The conqueror draws near.   Once more farewell!
If e'er we meet hereafter, we shall meet
In happier climes, and on a safer shore,
Where Cæsar never shall approach us more.   155
      (*Pointing to the body of his dead son.*)
There the brave youth, with love of virtue fired,
Who greatly in his country's cause expired,
  [1] The elder Cato.

113] D7D8W *I conquered.*   122] W om. the entire line.   147] D7D8W *Who dare not.*
155 s.d.] D7D8W om. the body of.

Shall know he conquered.　The firm patriot there
(Who made the welfare of mankind his care,
Though still by faction, vice, and fortune
　　　　crossed)　　　　　　　　　　　　　　160
Shall find the gen'rous labor was not lost. [*Exeunt.*]

ACT V

SCENE I

CATO *solus, sitting in a thoughtful posture: in his hand*
　Plato's book on the immortality of the soul.　A
　drawn sword on the table by him.

　[CATO.] It must be so — Plato, thou reason'st
　　　well! —
Else whence this pleasing hope, this fond desire,
This longing after immortality?
Or whence this secret dread, and inward horror,
Of falling into nought? why shrinks the soul　　5
Back on herself, and startles at destruction?
'Tis the divinity that stirs within us;
'Tis heav'n itself, that points out an hereafter,
And intimates eternity to man.
Eternity! thou pleasing, dreadful thought!　　10
Through what variety of untried being,
Through what new scenes and changes must we
　　　pass!
The wide, th' unbounded prospect, lies before me;
But shadows, clouds, and darkness, rest upon it.
Here will I hold.　If there's a pow'r above us,　15
(And that there is all Nature cries aloud
Through all her works) he must delight in virtue:
And that which he delights in must be happy.
But when! or where! — This world was made for
　　　Cæsar.
I'm weary of conjectures — this must end 'em.　20
　　　　(*Laying his hand on his sword.*)
Thus am I doubly armed: my death and life,
My bane and antidote, are both before me:
This in a moment brings me to an end;
But this informs me I shall never die.
The soul, secured in her existence, smiles　　25
At the drawn dagger, and defies its point.
The stars shall fade away, the sun himself
Grow dim with age, and nature sink in years;
But thou shalt flourish in immortal youth,
Unhurt amidst the wars of elements,　　　　30
The wrecks of matter, and the crush of worlds.
　　What means this heaviness that hangs upon
　　　me?
This lethargy that creeps through all my senses?
Nature, oppressed and harassed out with care,
Sinks down to rest.　This once I'll favor her,　35
That my awakened soul may take her flight,
Renewed in all her strength, and fresh with life,
An off'ring fit for heav'n.　Let guilt or fear

Disturb man's rest: Cato knows neither of 'em,
Indiff'rent in his choice to sleep or die.　　　40

[SCENE II]

Enter PORTIUS.

　CATO. But, hah! how's this, my son? why this
　　　intrusion?
Were not my orders that I would be private?
Why am I disobeyed?
　POR.　　　　　　　Alas! my father!
What means this sword, this instrument of death?
Let me convey it hence!
　CATO.　　　　　　Rash youth, forbear!　5
　POR. Oh, let the pray'rs, th' entreaties of your
　　　friends,
Their tears, their common danger, wrest it from
　　　you.
　CATO. Wouldst thou betray me? wouldst thou
　　　give me up
A slave, a captive, into Cæsar's hands?
Retire, and learn obedience to a father,　　　10
Or know, young man! —
　[POR.　　　　　　Look not thus sternly on me;
You know I'd rather die than disobey you.
　CATO. 'Tis well! again I'm master of myself.
Now, Cæsar, let thy troops beset our gates,
And bar each avenue, thy gathering fleets　　15
O'erspread the sea, and stop up every port;
Cato shall open to himself a passage,
And mock thy hopes —]
　POR.　　　　　　O sir! forgive your son,
Whose grief hangs heavy on him!　O my father!
How am I sure it is not the last time　　　　20
I e'er shall call you so? be not displeased,
Oh, be not angry with me whilst I weep,
And, in the anguish of my heart beseech you
To quit the dreadful purpose of your soul!
　CATO. Thou hast been ever good and dutiful.　25
　　　　　　　　　(*Embracing him.*)
Weep not, my son.　All will be well again.
The righteous gods, whom I have sought to please,
Will succor Cato, and preserve his children.
　POR. Your words give comfort to my drooping
　　　heart.
　CATO. Portius, thou may'st rely upon my con-
　　　duct.　　　　　　　　　　　　　　30
Thy father will not act what misbecomes him.
But go, my son, and see if aught be wanting
Among thy father's friends; see them embarked;
And tell me if the winds and seas befriend them.
My soul is quite weighed down with care, and
　　　asks　　　　　　　　　　　　　　35
The soft refreshment of a moment's sleep.　*Exit.*
　POR. My thoughts are more at ease, my heart
　　　revives.

159, 160] Q1Q2Q3Q4Q5Q6D7D8W *care*) ... *crost.*　　SCENE II. 11–18] Q1Q2 and some copies of Q3 om. bracketed passage.

[SCENE III]

Enter MARCIA.

POR. O Marcia, O my sister, still there's hope!
Our father will not cast away a life
So needful to us all, and to his country.
He is retired to rest, and seems to cherish
Thoughts full of peace.   He has dispatched me
        hence   5
With orders that bespeak a mind composed,
And studious for the safety of his friends.
Marcia, take care that none disturb his slumbers.
                                        Exit.

MAR. O ye immortal powers, that guard the good,
Watch round his couch, and soften his repose,   10
Banish his sorrows, and becalm his soul
With easy dreams; remember all his virtues!
And show mankind that goodness is your care.

[SCENE IV]

Enter LUCIA.

LUC. Where is your father, Marcia, where is Cato?
MAR. Lucia, speak low, he is retired to rest.
Lucia, I feel a gently-dawning hope
Rise in my soul.   We shall be happy still.
LUC. Alas! I tremble when I think on Cato,   5
In every view, in every thought I tremble!
Cato is stern, and awful as a god;
He knows not how to wink at human frailty,
Or pardon weakness that he never felt.
MAR. Though stern and awful to the foes of
        Rome,   10
He is all goodness, Lucia, always mild,
Compassionate, and gentle to his friends.
Filled with domestic tenderness, the best,
The kindest father! I have ever found him
Easy, and good, and bounteous to my wishes.   15
LUC. 'Tis his consent alone can make us blest.
Marcia, we both are equally involved
In the same intricate, perplexed distress.
The cruel hand of fate, that has destroyed
Thy brother Marcus, whom we both lament —   20
MAR. And ever shall lament, unhappy youth!
LUC. Has set my soul at large, and now I stand
Loose of my vow.   But who knows Cato's thoughts?
Who knows how yet he may dispose of Portius,
Or how he has determined of thyself?   25
MAR. Let him but live! commit the rest to heav'n.

Enter LUCIUS.

LUCIUS. Sweet are the slumbers of the virtuous
        man!
O Marcia, I have seen thy godlike father:
Some pow'r invisible supports his soul,

And bears it up in all its wonted greatness.   30
A kind refreshing sleep is fall'n upon him:
I saw him stretched at ease, his fancy lost
In pleasing dreams: as I drew near his couch,
He smiled, and cried, 'Cæsar, thou canst not hurt
        me.'
MAR. His mind still labors with some dreadful
        thought.   35
LUCIUS. Lucia, why all this grief, these floods of
        sorrow?
Dry up thy tears, my child, we all are safe
While Cato lives — his presence will protect us.

Enter JUBA.

JUBA. Lucius, the horsemen are returned from
        viewing
The number, strength, and posture of our foes,   40
Who now encamp within a short hour's march.
On the high point of yon bright western tower
We ken them from afar; the setting sun
Plays on their shining arms and burnished helmets,
And covers all the field with gleams of fire.   45
LUCIUS. Marcia, 'tis time we should awake thy
        father.
Cæsar is still disposed to give us terms,
And waits at distance till he hears from Cato.

Enter PORTIUS.

Portius, thy looks speak somewhat of importance,
What tidings dost thou bring? methinks I see   50
Unusual gladness sparkling in thy eyes.
POR. As I was hasting to the port, where now
My father's friends, impatient for a passage,
Accuse the ling'ring winds, a sail arrived
From Pompey's son, who through the realms of
        Spain   55
Calls out for vengeance on his father's death,
And rouses the whole nation up to arms.
Were Cato at their head, once more might Rome
Assert her rights and claim her liberty.
But, hark! what means that groan!   Oh, give me
        way,   60
And let me fly into my father's presence.   [*Exit.*]
LUCIUS. Cato, amidst his slumbers, thinks on
        Rome,
And in the wild disorder of his soul
Mourns o'er his country, — Hah! a second groan! —
Heav'n guard us all —
MAR.   Alas! 'tis not the voice   65
Of one who sleeps! 'tis agonizing pain,
'Tis death is in that sound —

Re-enter PORTIUS.

POR.   Oh sight of woe!
O Marcia, what we feared is come to pass!

8 s.d.] W om. **Exit.**   9] Q3Q4Q5Q6D7D8W *guard the just.*
SCENE IV. 61] Q1Q2Q3Q4Q5Q6W om. Exit; D7D8 supply it.

Cato is fall'n upon his sword —
    Lucius.   O Portius,
Hide all the horrors of thy mournful tale,   70
And let us guess the rest.
    Por.   I've raised him up,
And placed him in his chair, where, pale and faint,
He gasps for breath, and, as his life flows from him,
Demands to see his friends. His weeping servants,
Obsequious to his orders, bear him hither.   75
        (*The back scene opens and discovers* Cato.)
    Mar. O heaven, assist me in this dreadful hour
To pay the last sad duties to my father.
    Juba. These are thy triumphs, thy exploits, O
      Cæsar!
    Lucius. Now is Rome fall'n indeed!
        (Cato *brought forward in his chair.*)
    Cato.   Here set me down —
Portius, come near me — are my friends em-
    barked?   80
Can anything be thought of for their service?
Whilst I yet live, let me not live in vain.
— O Lucius, art thou here? — thou art too good! —
Let this our friendship live between our children;
Make Portius happy in thy daughter Lucia.   85
Alas! poor man, he weeps! — Marcia, my daugh-
    ter —
— Oh, bend me forward! — Juba loves thee, Marcia.
A senator of Rome, while Rome survived,

Would not have matched his daughter with a king,
But Cæsar's arms have thrown down all distinc-
    tion;   90
Whoe'er is brave and virtuous, is a Roman. —
— I'm sick to death — Oh, when shall I get loose
From this vain world, th' abode of guilt and sorrow!
— And yet methinks a beam of light breaks in
On my departing soul. Alas! I fear   95
I've been too hasty! O ye powers that search
The heart of man, and weigh his inmost thoughts,
If I have done amiss, impute it not! —
The best may err, but you are good, and — oh!
           (*Dies.*)
    Lucius. There fled the greatest soul that ever
    warmed   100
A Roman breast. O Cato! O my friend!
Thy will shall be religiously observed.
But let us bear this awful corpse to Cæsar,
And lay it in his sight, that it may stand
A fence betwixt us and the victor's wrath;   105
Cato, though dead, shall still protect his friends.
From hence, let fierce contending nations know
What dire effects from civil discord flow.
'Tis this that shakes our country with alarms,
And gives up Rome a prey to Roman arms,   110
Produces fraud, and cruelty, and strife,
And robs the guilty world of Cato's life.
                 Exeunt omnes.

74] W *his servants weeping.*
112] This line was written by Pope: Addison's original line was, *And oh! 'twas this that ended Cato's life.*
112] W om. Exeunt omnes.

EPILOGUE

By Dr. Garth [1]

Spoken by Mrs. Porter [2]

What odd fantastic things we women do! }
Who would not listen when young lovers woo? }
But die a maid, yet have the choice of two! }
Ladies are often cruel to their cost;
To give you pain, themselves they punish most.   5
Vows of virginity should well be weighed;
Too oft they're cancelled, though in convents made.
Would you revenge such rash resolves — you may: }
Be spiteful — and believe the thing we say; }
We hate you when you're easily said nay.   10
How needless, if you knew us, were your fears!
Let love have eyes, and beauty will have ears.
Our hearts are formed, as you yourselves would choose,
Too proud to ask, too humble to refuse:
We give to merit, and to wealth we sell;   15
He sighs with most success that settles well.
The woes of wedlock with the joys we mix;
'Tis best repenting in a coach and six.
Blame not our conduct, since we but pursue
Those lively lessons we have learned from you: 20
Your breasts no more the fire of beauty warms,
But wicked wealth usurps the power of charms;
What pains to get the gaudy thing you hate,
To swell in show, and be a wretch in state!
At plays you ogle, at the Ring [3] you bow;   25
Even churches are no sanctuaries now:
There, golden idols all your vows receive,
She is no goddess that has nought to give.
Oh, may once more the happy age appear,
When words were artless, and the thoughts sincere;   30
When gold and grandeur were unenvied things,
And courts less coveted than groves and springs.
Love then shall only mourn when truth complains,
And constancy feel transport in its chains.
Sighs with success their own soft anguish tell,   35
And eyes shall utter what the lips conceal:
Virtue again to its bright station climb,
And beauty fear no enemy but time,
The fair shall listen to desert alone,
And every Lucia find a Cato's son.   40

[1] Whig physician and minor poet; best known for his burlesque poem, *The Dispensary.*
[2] In the part of Lucia.   [3] A promenade in Hyde Park.

The Tragedy of Jane Shore

BY NICHOLAS ROWE

[1]

THE
TRAGEDY
OF
Jane Shore.

ACT I. SCENE I.

SCENE the *Tower*.

Enter the Duke of Glofter, *Sir* Richard Ratcliffe, *and* Catesby.

Gloft. THUS far Succefs attends upon our Councils,
And each Event has anfwer'd to my Wifh ;
The Queen and all her upftart Race are quell'd ;
Dorfet is banifh'd, and her Brother *Rivers* ;
'Ere this lies fhorter by the Head at *Pomfret.*
The Nobles have with joint Concurrence nam'd me
Protector of the Realm : My Brother's Children,
Young *Edward* and the little *York*, are lodg'd

B   Here,

PROLOGUE

SPOKEN BY MR. WILKS [1]

Tonight, if you have brought your good old taste,
We'll treat you with a downright English feast —
A tale which, told long since in homely wise,
Hath never failed of melting gentle eyes.
Let no nice sir despise our hapless dame   5
Because recording ballads chaunt her name;
Those venerable ancient song-enditers
Soared many a pitch above our modern writers:
They caterwauled in no romantic ditty,
Sighing for Phyllis's, or Chloe's pity.   10
Justly they drew the fair, and spoke her plain,
And sung her by her Christ'an name — 'twas Jane.
Our numbers may be more refined than those,
But what we've gained in verse, we've lost in prose.
Their words no shuffling, double-meaning knew,   15
Their speech was homely, but their hearts were true.
In such an age, immortal Shakespeare wrote,
By no quaint rules nor hampering critics taught;
With rough, majestic force he moved the heart,
And strength and nature made amends for art.   20
Our humble author does his steps pursue;
He owns he had the mighty bard in view,
And in these scenes has made it more his care
To rouse the passions than to charm the ear.
Yet for those gentle beaux who love the chime,   25
The ends of acts still jingle into rhime.
The ladies, too, he hopes, will not complain;⎫
Here are some subjects for a softer strain — ⎬
A nymph forsaken, and a perjured swain. ⎭
What most he fears is, lest the dames should frown,⎫   30
The dames of wit and pleasure about town, ⎬
To see our picture drawn unlike their own. ⎭
But lest that error should provoke to fury
The hospitable hundreds of Old Drury,
He bid me say, in our Jane Shore's defence,   ⎫   35
She doled about the charitable pence,   ⎬
Built hospitals, turned saint, and died long since.⎭
For her example, whatsoe'er we make it,
They have their choice to let alone or take it:
Though few, as I conceive, will think it meet   40
To weep so sorely for a sin so sweet;
Or mourn and mortify the pleasant sense,
To rise in tragedy two ages hence.

---

[1] In the part of Dumont.

The dedication, to the Duke of Queensberry, is omitted.   4] Q1 *Have.*

DRAMATIS PERSONÆ

MEN

DUKE OF GLOSTER.
LORD HASTINGS.
[WILLIAM] CATESBY.
SIR RICHARD RATCLIFFE.

BELLMOUR.
DUMONT [WILLIAM SHORE *in disguise*].
[EARL OF DERBY].

WOMEN

ALICIA.
JANE SHORE.

Several Lords of the Council, Guards, and Attendants.

SCENE: LONDON

[TIME: JUNE, 1483]

THE TRAGEDY OF JANE SHORE

WRITTEN IN IMITATION OF SHAKESPEARE'S STYLE

BY NICHOLAS ROWE

... Conjux ubi pristinus illi
Respondet curis.   VIRG.[1]

ACT I

SCENE I

The Tower.

Enter the DUKE OF GLOSTER, SIR RICHARD
RATCLIFFE, AND CATESBY.

GLOST. Thus far success attends upon our coun-
    cils,
And each event has answered to my wish;
The queen [2] and all her upstart race are quelled;
Dorset [3] is banished, and her brother Rivers [4]
Ere this lies shorter by the head at Pomfret.   5
The nobles have with joint concurrence named me
Protector of the realm. My brother's children,
Young Edward and the little York, are lodged
Here, safe within the Tower. How say you, sirs,
Does not this business wear a lucky face?   10
The scepter and the golden wreath of royalty
Seem hung within my reach.
  RAT.   Then take 'em to you
And wear them long and worthily; you are
The last remaining male of princely York:
(For Edward's boys, the state esteems not of
   'em)   15
And therefore on your sovereignty and rule
The commonweal does her dependence make,
And leans upon your highness' able hand.
  CAT. And yet tomorrow does the council meet
To fix a day for Edward's coronation: 20
Who can expound this riddle?
  GLOST.   That can I.
Those lords are each one my approved, good friends.
Of special trust and nearness to my bosom:
And howsoever busy they may seem,
And diligent to bustle in the state,   25
Their zeal goes on no farther than we lead,

---

[1] 'Where her former husband responds to her sorrows.'
                        (*Æneid*, vi. 473, 474.)
[2] Elizabeth Woodville, widow of Edward IV and mother of
Edward V.
[3] Thomas Gray, Marquis of Dorset, son of Elizabeth Woodville by her first marriage.
[4] Anthony Woodville, Earl Rivers.

And at our bidding stays.
  CAT.   Yet there is one,
And he amongst the foremost in his power,
Of whom I wish your highness were assured:
For me — perhaps it is my nature's fault —   30
[I] own, I doubt of his inclining, much.
  GLOST. I guess the man at whom your words
       would point:
Hastings —
  CAT.   The same.
  GLOST.   He bears me great good will.
  CAT. 'Tis true, to you, as to the Lord Protector
And Gloster's duke, he bows with lowly service: 35
But were he bid to cry, 'God save King Richard,'
Then tell me in what terms he would reply.
Believe me, I have proved the man and found him
I know he bears a most religious reverence
To his dead master Edward's royal memory,   40
And whither that may lead him is most plain;
Yet more — one of that stubborn sort he is
Who, if they once grow fond of an opinion,
They call it honor, honesty, and faith,
And sooner part with life than let it go.   45
  GLOST. And yet, this tough, impracticable heart
Is governed by a dainty-fingered girl.
Such flaws are found in the most worthy natures;
A laughing, toying, wheedling, whimpering she
Shall make him amble on a gossip's message,   50
And take the distaff with a hand as patient
As e'er did Hercules.
  RAT.   The fair Alicia,[5]
Of noble birth and exquisite of feature,
Has held him long a vassal to her beauty.
  CAT. I fear he fails in his allegiance there;   55
Or my intelligence is false, or else
The dame has been too lavish of her feast,
And fed him 'till he loathes.
  GLOST.   No more; he comes.

Enter LORD HASTINGS.

  L. HAST. Health and the happiness of many days
Attend upon your grace.

---

[5] There is no historical warrant for this character in the play.

18] Q1 *highness's.*   31] D2 om. *I* (dropped type).

GLOST.   My good Lord Chamberlain! 60
W'are much beholden to your gentle friendship.

L. HAST. My lord, I come an humble suitor to
you.

GLOST. In right good time! Speak out your
pleasure freely.

L. HAST. I am to move your highness in behalf
Of Shore's unhappy wife.

GLOST.   Say you? of Shore? 65

L. HAST. Once a bright star that held her place
on high:
The first and fairest of our English dames
While royal Edward held the sovereign rule.
Now sunk in grief, and pining with despair,
Her waning form no longer shall incite   70
Envy in woman, or desire in man.
She never sees the sun but through her tears,
And wakes to sigh the livelong night away.

GLOST. Marry! the times are badly changed with
her
From Edward's days to these.   Then all was jol-
lity,   75
Feasting and mirth, light wantonness and laughter,
Piping and playing, minstrelsy and masquing,
Till life fled from us like an idle dream,
A show of mommery without a meaning.
My brother — rest and pardon to his soul! —   80
Is gone to his account; for this his minion,
The revel-rout is done. — But you were speaking
Concerning her. — I have been told that you
Are frequent in your visitation to her.

L. HAST. No farther, my good lord, than friendly
pity   85
And tender-hearted charity allow.

GLOST. Go to! I did not mean to chide you for
it.
For, sooth to say, I hold it noble in you
To cherish the distressed. — On with your tale.

L. HAST. Thus is it, gracious sir, that certain
officers,   90
Using the warrant of your mighty name,
With insolence unjust and lawless power
Have seized upon the lands which late she held
By grant from her great master Edward's bounty.

GLOST. Somewhat of this, but slightly, have I
heard;   95
And though some counsellors of forward zeal,
Some of most ceremonious sanctity
And bearded wisdom, often have provoked
The hand of justice to fall heavy on her,
Yet still in kind compassion of her weakness   100
And tender memory of Edward's love,
I have withheld the merciless, stern law
From doing outrage on her helpless beauty.

L. HAST. Good heav'n, who renders mercy back
for mercy,

With open-handed bounty shall repay you·   105
This gentle deed shall fairly be set foremost,
To screen the wild escapes of lawless passion
And the long train of frailties flesh is heir to.

GLOST. Thus far, the voice of pity pleaded
only;
Our farther and more full extent of grace   110
Is given to your request.   Let her attend,
And to ourself deliver up her griefs.
She shall be heard with patience, and each wrong
At full redressed.   But I have other news
Which much import us both, for still my for-
tunes   115
Go hand in hand with yours; our common foes,
The queen's relations, our new-fangled gentry,
Have fall'n [1] their haughty crests. — That for your
privacy.   *Exeunt.*

SCENE II

An apartment in JANE SHORE'S *house.*

Enter BELLMOUR *and* DUMONT.

BELL. How she has lived, you've heard my tale
already;
The rest, your own attendance in her family,
Where I have found the means this day to place you,
And nearer observation best will tell you.
See! with what sad and sober cheer she comes. 5

Enter JANE SHORE.

Sure, or I read her visage much amiss,
Or grief besets her hard. — Save you, fair lady,
The blessings of the cheerful morn be on you,
And greet your beauty with its opening sweets.

J. SH. My gentle neighbor! your good wishes
still   10
Pursue my hapless fortunes.   Ah! good Bellmour,
How few, like thee, enquire the wretched out,
And court the offices of soft humanity;
Like thee, reserve their raiment for the naked,
Reach out their bread to feed the crying orphan, 15
Or mix their pitying tears with those that weep!
Thy praise deserves a better tongue than mine
To speak and bless thy name.   Is this the gentleman
Whose friendly service you commended to me?

BELL. Madam! it is.

J. SH. *(aside).*   A venerable aspect!   20
Age sits with decent grace upon his visage,
And worthily becomes his silver locks;
He wears the marks of many years well spent,
Of virtue, truth well tried, and wise experience;
A friend like this would suit my sorrows well.   25
(To DUMONT.) Fortune, I fear me, sir, has meant
you ill,
Who pays your merit with that scanty pittance
Which my poor hand and humble roof can give.

    [1] Have let fall.

But to supply those golden vantages
Which elsewhere you might find, expect to meet   30
A just regard and value for your worth,
The welcome of a friend, and the free partnership
Of all that little good the world allows me.
    Dum. You overrate me much, and all my answer
Must be my future truth; let that speak for me   35
And make up my deserving.
    J. Sh.   Are you of England?
    Dum. No, gracious lady, Flanders claims my birth;
At Antwerp has my constant biding been,
Where sometimes I have known more plenteous days
Than those which now my failing age affords.   40
    J. Sh. Alas! at Antwerp! (*Weeping.*) — Oh, for-
      give my tears!
They fall for my offences — and must fall
Long, long ere they shall wash my stains away.
You knew perhaps — oh grief! oh shame! — my
    husband.
    Dum. I knew him well — but stay this flood of
    anguish;   45
The senseless grave feels not your pious sorrows.
Three years and more are past since I was bid,
With many of our common friends, to wait him
To his last peaceful mansion. I attended,
Sprinkled his clay-cold corse with holy drops,   50
According to our church's reverend rite,
And saw him laid, in hallowed ground, to rest.
    J. Sh. Oh! that my soul had known no joy but
    him;
That I had lived within his guiltless arms,
And dying slept in innocence beside him!   55
But now his honest dust abhors the fellowship,
And scorns to mix with mine.

Enter a Servant.

    Serv.   The lady Alicia
Attends your leisure.
    J. Sh.   Say I wish to see her.
                         Exit Servant.
Please, gentle sir, one moment to retire.
I'll wait you on the instant, and inform you   60
Of each unhappy circumstance in which
Your friendly aid and counsel much may stead me.
              Exeunt Bellmour *and* Dumont.

Enter Alicia.

    Alic. Still, my fair friend, still shall I find you
    thus?
Still shall these sighs heave after one another,
These trickling drops chase one another still,   65
As if the posting [1] messengers of grief
Could overtake the hours fled far away,
And make old time come back?
    J. Sh.   No, my Alicia,
Heaven and its saints be witness to my thoughts,
    [1] Hastening.

There is no hour of all my life o'erpast,   70
That I could wish should take its turn again.
    Alic. And yet some of those days my friend has
    known;
Some of those years might pass for golden ones —
At least if womankind can judge of happiness.
What could we wish, we who delight in empire,   75
Whose beauty is our sovereign good, and gives us
Our reasons to rebel and power to reign —
What could we more than to behold a monarch,
Lovely, renowned, a conqueror, and young,
Bound in our chains, and sighing at our feet?   80
    J. Sh. 'Tis true, the royal Edward was a wonder,
The goodly pride of all our English youth;
He was the very joy of all that saw him,
Formed to delight, to love, and to persuade.
Impassive spirits and angelic natures   85
Might have been charmed, like yielding human
    weakness,
Stooped from their heav'n and listened to his talking.
But what had I to do with kings and courts?
My humble lot had cast me far beneath him;
And that he was the first of all mankind,   90
The bravest and most lovely, was my curse.
    Alic. Sure, something more than fortune joined
    your loves;
Nor could his greatness, and his gracious form,
Be elsewhere matched so well, as to the sweetness
And beauty of my friend.
    J. Sh.   Name him no more: 95
He was the bane and ruin of my peace.
This anguish and these tears, these are the legacies
His fatal love has left me. Thou wilt see me;
Believe me, my Alicia, thou wilt see me,
Ere yet a few short days pass o'er my head,   100
Abandoned to the very utmost wretchedness.
The hand of pow'r has seized almost the whole
Of what was left for needy life's support;
Shortly thou wilt behold me poor, and kneeling
Before thy charitable door for bread.   105
    Alic. Joy of my life, my dearest Shore, forbear
To wound my heart with thy foreboding sorrows.
Raise thy sad soul to better hopes than these;
Lift up thy eyes and let 'em shine once more,
Bright as the morning sun above the mists.   110
Exert thy charms, seek out the stern Protector,
And soothe his savage temper with thy beauty.
Spite of his deadly, unrelenting nature,
He shall be moved to pity and redress thee.
    J. Sh. My form, alas! has long forgot to
    please.   115
The scene of beauty and delight is changed:
No roses bloom upon my fading cheek,
Nor laughing graces wanton in my eyes;
But haggard grief, lean-looking, sallow care,
And pining discontent, a rueful train,   120
Dwell on my brow, all hideous and forlorn.

One only shadow of a hope is left me;
The noble-minded Hastings, of his goodness,
Has kindly underta'en to be my advocate,
And move my humble suit to angry Gloster.   125

ALIC. Does Hastings undertake to plead your
    cause?
But wherefore should he not?   Hastings has eyes;
The gentle lord has a right tender heart,
Melting and easy, yielding to impression,
And catching the soft flame from each new
    beauty.   130
But yours shall charm him long.

J. SH.   Away, you flatterer!
Nor charge his generous meaning with a weakness
Which his great soul and virtue must disdain.
Too much of love thy hapless friend has proved;
Too many giddy, foolish hours are gone,   135
And in fantastic measures danced away:
May the remaining few know only friendship.
So thou, my dearest, truest, best Alicia,
Vouchsafe to lodge me in thy gentle heart
A partner there; I will give up mankind,   140
Forget the transports of encreasing passion,
And all the pangs we feel for its decay.

ALIC. (embracing). Live! live and reign forever in
    my bosom;
Safe and unrivalled there possess thy own;
And you, ye brightest of the stars above,   145
Ye saints that once were women here below,
Be witness of the truth, the holy friendship,
Which here to this my other self I vow.
If I not hold her nearer to my soul,
Than ev'ry other joy the world can give,   150
Let poverty, deformity and shame,
Distraction and despair seize me on earth;
Let not my faithless ghost have peace hereafter,
Nor taste the bliss of your celestial fellowship.

J. SH. Yes, thou art true, and only thou art
    true;   155
Therefore these jewels, once the lavish bounty
Of royal Edward's love, I trust to thee.

               (Giving a casket.)
Receive this all that I can call my own,
And let it rest unknown and safe with thee:
That if the state's injustice should oppress me,   160
Strip me of all, and turn me out a wanderer,
My wretchedness may find relief from thee,
And shelter from the storm.

ALIC.   My all is thine;
One common hazard shall attend us both,
And both be fortunate or both be wretched.   165
But let thy fearful, doubting heart be still;
The saints and angels have thee in their charge,
And all things shall be well.   Think not, the good,
The gentle deeds of mercy thou hast done
Shall die forgotten all; the poor, the pris'ner,   170
The fatherless, the friendless, and the widow,

Who daily own the bounty of thy hand,
Shall cry to heav'n, and pull a blessing on thee;
Ev'n man — the merciless insulter, man —
Man, who rejoices in our sex's weakness,   175
Shall pity thee, and with unwonted goodness,
Forget thy failings and record thy praise.

J. SH. Why should I think that man will do for me
What yet he never did for wretches like me?
Mark by what partial justice we are judged;   180
Such is the fate unhappy women find,
And such the curse entailed upon our kind,
That man, the lawless libertine, may rove
Free and unquestioned through the wilds of love;
While woman, sense and nature's easy fool,   185
If poor, weak woman swerve from virtue's rule,
If, strongly charmed, she leave the thorny way,
And in the softer paths of pleasure stray;
Ruin ensues, reproach and endless shame,
And one false step entirely damns her fame.   190
In vain with tears the loss she may deplore, ⎫
In vain look back to what she was before; ⎬
She sets, like stars that fall, to rise no more. ⎭

                          Exeunt.

ACT II

SCENE I

Scene continues.

Enter ALICIA, *speaking to* JANE SHORE *as
entering.*

ALIC. No farther, gentle friend; good angels
    guard you,
And spread their gracious wings about your slum-
    bers.
— The drowsy night grows on the world, and now
The busy craftsman and o'er-labored hind
Forget the travail of the day in sleep.   5
Care only wakes, and moping Pensiveness;
With meagre, discontented looks they sit,
And watch the wasting of the midnight taper.
Such vigils must I keep; so wakes my soul,
Restless and self-tormented!   O false Hastings!   10
Thou hast destroyed my peace.   (*Knocking without.*)
                    What noise is that?
What visitor is this who with bold freedom
Breaks in upon the peaceful night and rest
With such a rude approach?

Enter a Servant.

SERV.   One from the court;
Lord Hastings (as I think) demands my lady.   15

ALIC. Hastings!   Be still my heart, and try to
    meet him
With his own arts — with falsehood. — But he
    comes.

Enter LORD HASTINGS.   *Speaks to a Servant at entering.*

L. HAST. Dismiss my train and wait alone
without.

[*Aside.*] Alicia here! Unfortunate encounter!
But be it as it may.

ALIC.   When humbly, thus,   20
The great descend to visit the afflicted;
When thus unmindful of their rest, they come
To soothe the sorrows of the midnight mourner;
Comfort comes with them, like the golden sun,
Dispels the sullen shades with her sweet influ-
ence,   25
And cheers the melancholy house of care.

L. HAST. 'Tis true, I would not overrate a
courtesy,
Nor let the coldness of delay hang on it
To nip and blast its favor like a frost;
But rather chose, at this late hour, to come,   30
That your fair friend may know I have prevailed:
The Lord Protector has received her suit,
And means to show her grace.

ALIC.   My friend! my lord!

L. HAST. Yes, lady, yours: none has a right more
ample
To task my power than you.

ALIC.   I want the words   35
To pay you back a compliment so courtly;
But my heart guesses at the friendly meaning,
And wo' not die your debtor.

L. HAST.   'Tis well, madam.
But I would see your friend.

ALIC.   O thou false lord!
I would be mistress of my heaving heart,   40
Stifle this rising rage, and learn from thee
To dress my face in easy, dull indifference.
But 'two'not be; my wrongs will tear their way,
And rush at once upon thee.

L. HAST.   Are you wise?
Have you the use of reason? Do you wake?   45
What means this raving — this transporting passion?

ALIC. O thou cool traitor! thou insulting tyrant!
Dost thou behold my poor distracted heart,
Thus rent with agonizing love and rage,
And ask me what it means? Art thou not false?   50
Am I not scorned, forsaken, and abandoned —
Left, like a common wretch, to shame and infamy;
Giv'n up to be the sport of villains' tongues,
Of laughing parasites, and lewd buffoons;
And all because my soul has doted on thee   55
With love, with truth, and tenderness unutterable?

L. HAST. Are these the proofs of tenderness and
love?
These endless quarrels, discontents, and jealousies;
These never-ceasing wailings and complainings;

These furious starts, these whirlwinds of the
soul,   60
Which every other moment rise to madness?

ALIC. What proof, alas! have I not given of love?
What have I not abandoned to thy arms?
Have I not set at nought my noble birth,
A spotless fame and an unblemished race,   65
The peace of innocence and pride of virtue?
My prodigality has giv'n thee all;
And now I've nothing left me to bestow;
You hate the wretched bankrupt you have made.

L. HAST. Why am I thus pursued from place to
place,   70
Kept in the view, and crossed at every turn?
In vain I fly, and like a hunted deer
Scud o'er the lawns and hasten to the covert;
Ere I can reach my safety, you o'ertake me
With the swift malice of some keen reproach,   75
And drive the wingèd shaft deep in my heart.

ALIC. Hither you fly, and here you seek repose;
Spite of the poor deceit, your arts are known,
Your pious, charitable, midnight visits.

L. HAST. If you are wise and prize your peace of
mind,   80
Yet take the friendly counsel of my love;
Believe me true, nor listen to your jealousy;
Let not that devil which undoes your sex,
That cursed curiosity, seduce you
To hunt for needless secrets which, neglected,   85
Shall never hurt your quiet, but once known,
Shall sit upon your heart, pinch it with pain,
And banish the sweet sleep forever from you.
Go to! — be yet advised, —

ALIC.   Dost thou in scorn
Preach patience to my rage? and bid me tamely   90
Sit like a poor, contented idiot down,
Nor dare to think thou'st wronged me? — ruin seize
thee,
And swift perdition overtake thy treachery!
Have I the least remaining cause to doubt?
Hast thou endeavored once to hide thy false-
hood?   95
To hide it, might have spoke some little tenderness,
And shown thee half unwilling to undo me.
But thou disdain'st the weakness of humanity;
Thy words and all thy actions have confessed it.
Ev'n now thy eyes avow it, now they speak,   100
And insolently own the glorious villainy.

L. HAST. Well then, I own my heart has broke
your chains.
Patient I bore the painful bondage long:
At length my generous love disdains your tyranny;
The bitterness and stings of taunting jealousy,   105
Vexatious days, and jarring joyless nights,
Have driv'n him forth to seek some safer shelter,
Where he may rest his weary wings in peace.

ALIC. You triumph! do! And with gigantic pride
Defy impending vengeance. Heav'n shall wink;   110
No more his arm shall roll the dreadful thunder,
Nor send his light'nings forth. No more his justice
Shall visit the presuming sons of men,
But perjury, like thine, shall dwell in safety.

L. HAST. Whate'er my fate decrees for me here-
    after,   115
Be present to me now, my better angel!
Preserve me from the storm which threatens now,
And if I have beyond atonement sinned,
Let any other kind of plague o'ertake me,
So I escape the fury of that tongue.   120

ALIC. Thy pray'r is heard — I go; — but know,
    proud lord,
Howe'er thou scorn'st the weakness of my sex,
This feeble hand may find the means to reach thee,
Howe'er sublime in pow'r and greatness placed,
With royal favor guarded round and graced;   125
On eagle's wings my rage shall urge her flight,
And hurl thee headlong from thy topmost height;
Then like thy fate, superior will I sit,
And view thee fall'n and grov'ling at my feet;
See thy last breath with indignation go,   130
And tread thee sinking to the shades below.
                                    Exit ALICIA.

L. HAST. How fierce a fiend is passion. With
    what wildness,
What tyranny untamed, it reigns in woman.
Unhappy sex! whose easy, yielding temper
Gives way to every appetite alike;   135
Each gust of inclination, uncontrolled,
Sweeps through their souls and sets 'em in an up-
    roar;
Each motion of the heart rises to fury,
And love in their weak bosoms is a rage
As terrible as hate and as destructive.   140
So the wind roars o'er the wide fenceless ocean,
And heaves the billows of the boiling deep,
Alike from north, from south, from east, from west;
With equal force the tempest blows by turns
From every corner of the seaman's compass.   145
But soft ye now — for here comes one disclaims
Strife and her wrangling train. Of equal elements,
Without one jarring atom, was she formed,
And gentleness and joy make up her being.

Enter JANE SHORE.

— Forgive me, fair one, if officious friendship   150
Intrudes on your repose, and comes thus late
To greet you with the tidings of success.
The princely Gloster has vouchsafed you hearing;
Tomorrow he expects you at the court.
There plead your cause with never failing
    beauty;   155

Speak all your griefs and find a full redress.

J. SH. (kneeling). Thus humbly let your lowly
    servant bend;
Thus let me bow my grateful knee to earth,
And bless your noble nature for this goodness.

L. HAST. Rise, gentle dame. You wrong my
    meaning much;   160
Think me not guilty of a thought so vain,
To sell my courtesy for thanks like these.

J. SH. 'Tis true, your bounty is beyond my
    speaking;
But though my mouth be dumb, my heart shall
    thank you;
And when it melts before the throne of mercy, 165
Mourning and bleeding for my past offences,
My fervent soul shall breathe one prayer for you,
If prayers of such a wretch are heard on high,
That heav'n will pay you back when most you need
The grace and goodness you have shown to me.   170

L. HAST. If there be aught of merit in my service,
Impute it there where most 'tis due, to love;
Be kind, my gentle mistress, to my wishes,
And satisfy my panting heart with beauty.

J. SH. Alas! my lord —

L. HAST.   Why bend thy eyes to earth?   175
Wherefore these looks of heaviness and sorrow?
Why breathes that sigh, my love? And wherefore
    falls
This trickling show'r of tears to stain thy sweetness?

J. SH. If pity dwells within your noble breast,
(As sure it does) oh, speak not to me thus!   180

L. HAST. Can I behold thee and not speak of love?
Ev'n now, thus sadly as thou stand'st before me,
Thus desolate, dejected, and forlorn,
Thy softness steals upon my yielding senses
Till my soul faints and sickens with desire.   185
How canst thou give this motion to my heart,
And bid my tongue be still?

J. SH.   Cast round your eyes
Upon the highborn beauties of the court;
Behold, like opening roses, where they bloom,
Sweet to the sense, unsullied all, and spotless. 190
There choose some worthy partner of your heart,
To fill your arms and bless your virtuous bed,
Nor turn your eyes this way, where sin and misery,
Like loathsome weeds, have overrun the soil,
And the destroyer shame has laid all waste.   195

L. HAST. What means this peevish, this fantastic
    change?
Where is thy wonted pleasantness of face?
Thy wonted graces, and thy dimpled smiles?
Where hast thou lost thy wit and sportive mirth,
That cheerful heart, which used to dance for-
    ever,   200
And cast a day of gladness all around thee?

129] Q1 groveling.   132] Q1 friend.   138] Hart reports their heart as reading of one copy of D2.
143] Q1 and west.   172] Q1 there, where most is due to love.   178] Q1 teats.

J. Sh. Yes, I will own I merit the reproach,
And for those foolish days of wanton pride
My soul is justly humbled to the dust.
All tongues, like yours, are licensed to upbraid
me,　　　　　　　　　　　　　　　　205
Still to repeat my guilt, to urge my infamy,
And treat me like that abject thing I have been.
Yet let the saints be witness to this truth,
That now, though late, I look with horror back,
That I detest my wretched self, and curse　　210
My past polluted life. All-judging heav'n,
Who knows my crimes, has seen my sorrow for them.
　　L. Hast. No more of this dull stuff. 'Tis time
　　　　enough
To whine and mortify thyself with penance
When the decaying sense is palled with pleas-
　　ure,　　　　　　　　　　　　　　215
And weary nature tires in her last stage.
Then weep and tell thy beads, when alt'ring rheums
Have stained the lustre of thy starry eyes,
And failing palsies shake thy withered hand.
The present moments claim more generous use;　220
Thy beauty, night, and solitude reproach me
For having talked thus long. Come, let me press
　　thee, (laying hold on her)
Pant on thy bosom, sink into thy arms,
And lose myself in the luxurious fold.
　　J. Sh. Never! By those chaste lights above, I
　　　　swear,　　　　　　　　　　　225
My soul shall never know pollution more!
(Kneeling.) Forbear, my lord! Here let me rather
　　die;
Let quick destruction overtake me here,
And end my sorrows and my shame forever.
　　L. Hast. Away with this perverseness — 'tis too
　　　　much.　　　　　　　　　　　　230
(Striving.) Nay, if you strive — 'tis monstrous
　　affectation.
　　J. Sh. Retire! I beg you, leave me —
　　L. Hast.　　　　　　Thus to coy it! —
With one who knows you, too!
　　J. Sh.　　　　　　　　For mercy's sake —
　　L. Hast. Ungrateful woman! is it thus you pay
My services?
　　J. Sh.　　　　　Abandon me to ruin　　235
Rather than urge me —
　　L. Hast. (pulling her). This way to your chamber;
There if you struggle —
　　J. Sh. (crying out).　　Help! O gracious heaven!
Help! Save me! Help!

　　　　　Enter Dumont; he interposes.

　　Dum.　　　　　My lord! for honor's sake —
　　L. Hast. Hah! What art thou? — Begone!
　　Dum.　　　　　　　　My duty calls me
To my attendance on my mistress here.　　240

　　J. Sh. For pity let me go!
　　L. Hast.　　　　　Avaunt! base groom —
At distance wait and know thy office better.
　　Dum. Forego your hold, my lord! 'tis most un-
　　　　manly,
This violence —
　　L. Hast.　　　Avoid the room this moment,
Or I will tread thy soul out.
　　Dum.　　　　　　　No, my lord —　245
The common ties of manhood call me now,
And bid me thus stand up in the defence
Of an oppressed, unhappy, helpless woman.
　　L. Hast. And dost thou know me? Slave!
　　Dum.　　　　　　　Yes, thou proud lord!
I know thee well; know thee with each advan-
　　tage　　　　　　　　　　　　250
Which wealth, or power, or noble birth can give thee.
I know thee, too, for one who stains those honors,
And blots a long illustrious line of ancestry,
By poorly daring thus to wrong a woman.
　　L. Hast. 'Tis wondrous well! I see, my saint-
　　　　like dame,　　　　　　　　255
You stand provided of your braves and ruffians
To man your cause, and bluster in your brothel.
　　Dum. Take back the foul reproach, unmannered
　　　　railer,
Nor urge my rage too far, lest thou shouldst find
I have as daring spirits in my blood　　　260
As thou or any of thy race e'er boasted.
And though no gaudy titles graced my birth —
Titles, the servile courtier's lean reward,
Sometimes the pay of virtue, but more oft
The hire which greatness gives to slaves and syco-
　　phants —　　　　　　　　　　265
Yet heav'n, that made me honest, made me more
Than ever king did when he made a lord.
　　L. Hast. Insolent villain! Henceforth let this
　　　　teach thee (draws and strikes him)
The distance 'twixt a peasant and a prince.
　　Dum. Nay then, my lord! (Drawing.) Learn you
　　　　by this how well　　　　　　270
An arm resolved can guard its master's life.
　　　　　　　　　　　　　(They fight.)
　　J. Sh. Oh, my distracting fears! hold, for sweet
　　　　heav'n!
　　　　(They fight; Dumont disarms Lord Has-
　　　　tings.)
　　L. Hast. Confusion! baffled by a base-born hind!
　　Dum. Now, haughty sir, where is our difference
　　　　now?
Your life is in my hand, and did not honor,　275
The gentleness of blood, and inborn virtue
(Howe'er unworthy I may seem to you)
Plead in my bosom, I should take the forfeit.
But wear your sword again, and know, a lord
Opposed against a man is but a man.　　280

L. Hast. Curse on my failing hand! Your better
    fortune
Has giv'n you vantage o'er me; but perhaps
Your triumph may be bought with dear repentance.
                       Exit.

J. Sh. Alas! what have you done! Know you
    the pow'r,
The mightiness that waits upon this lord?   285

Dum. Fear not, my worthiest mistress; 'tis a cause
In which heav'n's guard shall wait you. Oh, pursue,
Pursue the sacred counsels of your soul
Which urge you on to virtue; let not danger,
Nor the encumb'ring world, make faint your pur-
    pose!   290
Assisting angels shall conduct your steps,
Bring you to bliss, and crown your end with peace.

J. Sh. Oh, that my head were laid, my sad eyes
    closed,
And my cold corse wound in my shroud to rest;
My painful heart will never cease to beat,   295
Will never know a moment's peace till then.

Dum. Would you be happy? Leave this fatal
    place,
Fly from the court's pernicious neighborhood,
Where innocence is shamed, and blushing modesty
Is made the scorner's jest; where hate, deceit,   300
And deadly ruin, wear the masks of beauty,
And draw deluded fools with shows of pleasure.

J. Sh. Where should I fly, thus helpless and for-
    lorn,
Of friends and all the means of life bereft?

Dum. Bellmour, whose friendly care still wakes
    to serve you,   305
Has found you out a little peaceful refuge.
Far from the court and the tumultuous city,
Within an ancient forest's ample verge,
There stands a lonely but a healthful dwelling,
Built for convenience and the use of life.   310
Around it fallows, meads, and pastures fair,
A little garden, and a limpid brook,
By nature's own contrivance, seem disposed —
No neighbors but a few poor simple clowns,
Honest and true, with a well-meaning priest.   315
No faction, or domestic fury's rage,
Did e'er disturb the quiet of that place
When the contending nobles shook the land
With York and Lancaster's disputed sway.
Your virtue, there, may find a safe retreat   320
From the insulting pow'rs of wicked greatness.

J. Sh. Can there be so much happiness in store!
A cell like that is all my hopes aspire to.
Haste then, and thither let us wing our flight,
Ere the clouds gather and the wintry sky   325
Descends in storms to intercept our passage.

Dum. Will you then go? You glad my very soul.
Banish your fears, cast all your cares on me;

Plenty, and ease, and peace of mind shall wait you,
And make your latter days of life most happy.   330
O lady! — but I must not, cannot tell you
How anxious I have been for all your dangers,
And how my heart rejoices at your safety.
So when the spring renews the flow'ry field,
And warns the pregnant nightingale to build,   335
She seeks the safest shelter of the wood,
Where she may trust her little tuneful brood,
Where no rude swains her shady cell may know,
No serpents climb, nor blasting winds may blow;
Fond of the chosen place, she views it o'er,   340
Sits there and wanders through the grove no more.
Warbling she charms it each returning night,
And loves it with a mother's dear delight. *Exeunt.*

ACT III

Scene I

The Court.

Enter Alicia *with a paper.*

Alic. This paper to the great Protector's hand
With care and secrecy must be conveyed;
His bold ambition now avows its aim,
To pluck the crown from Edward's infant brow
And fix it on his own. I know he holds   5
My faithless Hastings adverse to his hopes
And much devoted to the orphan king;
On that I build. This paper meets his doubts,
And marks my hated rival as the cause
Of Hastings' zeal for his dead master's sons.   10
O jealousy! Thou bane of pleasing friendship,
Thou worst invader of our tender bosoms;
How does thy rancor poison all our softness,
And turn our gentle natures into bitterness!
— See where she comes! Once my heart's dearest
    blessing,   15
Now my changed eyes are blasted with her beauty,
Loathe that known face, and sicken to behold her.

Enter Jane Shore.

J. Sh. Now whither shall I fly to find relief?
What charitable hand will aid me now?
Will stay my failing steps, support my ruins,   20
And heal my wounded mind with balmy comfort?
O my Alicia!

Alic.   What new grief is this?
What unforeseen misfortune has surprised thee,
That racks thy tender heart thus?

J. Sh.   O Dumont!

Alic. Say! What of him?

J. Sh.   That friendly, honest man,   25
Whom Bellmour brought of late to my assistance;
On whose kind cares, whose diligence and faith,
My surest trust was built, this very morn

307] Q1 *tumultous.*

Was seized on by the cruel hand of pow'r,
Forced from my house, and borne away to
   prison.   30
  ALIC. To prison, said you! Can you guess the
   cause?
  J. SH. Too well, I fear. His bold defence of me
Has drawn the vengeance of Lord Hastings on him.
  ALIC. Lord Hastings! ha!
  J. SH.   Some fitter time must tell thee
The tale of my hard hap. Upon the present   35
Hang all my poor, my last remaining hopes.
Within this paper is my suit contained;
Here, as the princely Gloster passes forth,
I wait to give it on my humble knees,
And move him for redress.
   (She gives the paper to ALICIA, *who opens and*
     seems to read it.)
  ALIC. *(aside).*   Now for a wile   40
To sting my thoughtless rival to the heart,
To blast her fatal beauties, and divide her
Forever from my perjured Hastings' eyes.
The wanderer may then look back to me,
And turn to his forsaken home again.   45
   (Pulling out the other paper.)
Their fashions are the same; it cannot fail.
  J. SH. But see, the great Protector comes this way,
Attended by a train of waiting courtiers.
Give me the paper, friend.
  ALIC. *(aside).*   For love and vengeance!
   (She gives her the other paper.)

Enter the DUKE OF GLOSTER, SIR RICHARD RAT-
  CLIFFE, CATESBY, *Courtiers, and other Attend-*
  ants.

  J. SH. *(kneeling).* O noble Gloster, turn thy
   gracious eye,   50
Incline thy pitying ear to my complaint!
A poor, undone, forsaken, helpless woman
Intreats a little bread for charity,
To feed her wants and save her life from perishing.
  GLOST. *(receiving the paper, and raising her).* Arise,
   fair dame, and dry your watery eyes.   55
Beshrew me, but 'twere pity of his heart
That could refuse a boon to such a suitress.
Y'have got a noble friend to be your advocate;
A worthy and right gentle lord he is,
And to his trust most true. This present now   60
Some matters of the state detain our leisure;
Those once dispatched, we'll call for you anon
And give your griefs redress. Go to! be comforted.
  J. SH. Good heaven repay your highness for this
   pity,
And show'r down blessings on your princely
   head.   65
Come, my Alicia, reach thy friendly arm,
And help me to support this feeble frame

That nodding totters with oppressive woe,
And sinks beneath its load.
       Exeunt JANE SHORE *and* ALICIA.
  GLOST. Now, by my hollidame!   70
Heavy of heart she seems, and sore afflicted.
But thus it is when rude calamity
Lays its strong gripe upon these mincing minions;
The dainty gew-gaw forms dissolve at once,
And shiver at the shock. What says her paper? 75
         (Seeming to read.)
Ha! What is this? Come nearer, Ratcliffe! —
   Catesby!
Mark the contents, and then divine the meaning.
         (He reads.)
'Wonder not, princely Gloster, at the notice
This paper brings you from a friend unknown.
Lord Hastings is inclined to call you master,   80
And kneel to Richard, as to England's king;
But Shore's bewitching wife misleads his heart,
And draws his service to King Edward's sons.
Drive her away, you break the charm that holds him,
And he, and all his powers, attend on you.'   85
  RAT. 'Tis wonderful!
  CAT.   The means by which it came
Yet stranger too!
  GLOST.   You saw it given but now.
  RAT. She could not know the purport.
  GLOST.   No, 'tis plain —
She knows it not; it levels at her life;
Should she presume to prate of such high mat-
   ters —   90
The meddling harlot! — dear she should abide[1] it.
  CAT. What hand soe'er it comes from, be assured,
It means your highness well —
  GLOST.   Upon the instant
Lord Hastings will be here. This morn I mean
To prove him to the quick; then if he flinch   95
No more but this, away with him at once;
He must be mine or nothing. — But he comes!
Draw nearer this way and observe me well.
         (They whisper.)

       Enter LORD HASTINGS.

  L. HAST. *[aside].* This foolish woman hangs about
   my heart,
Lingers and wanders in my fancy still;   100
This coyness is put on, 'tis art and cunning,
And worn to urge desire; I must possess her;
The groom who lift his saucy hand against me,
Ere this is humbled and repents his daring.
Perhaps ev'n she may profit by th' example,   105
And teach her beauty not to scorn my pow'r.
  GLOST. This do, and wait me ere the council sits.
       Exeunt RATCLIFFE *and* CATESBY.
— My lord, y'are well encountered; here has been
    [1] Properly 'abye' ('pay for').

63] Q1D2 *Go too!*

A fair petitioner this morning with us.
Believe me, she has won me much to pity her.   110
Alas! her gentle nature was not made
To buffet with adversity.   I told her
How worthily her cause you had befriended,
How much for your good sake we meant to do,
That you had spoke and all things should be
    well.   115
L. HAST.   Your highness binds me ever to your
    service.
    GLOST.   You know your friendship is most potent
    with us,
And shares our power.   But of this enough,
For we have other matters for your ear.
The state is out of tune; distracting fears   120
And jealous doubts jar in our public councils;
Amidst the wealthy city murmurs rise,
Lewd railings and reproach on those that rule,
With open scorn of government; hence credit
And public trust 'twixt man and man are broke.   125
The golden streams of commerce are withheld,
Which fed the wants of needy hinds and artizans,
Who therefore curse the great and threat rebellion.
    L. HAST.   The resty [1] knaves are overrun with ease,
As plenty ever is the nurse of faction.   130
If in good days, like these, the headstrong herd
Grow madly wanton and repine, it is
Because the reins of power are held too slack,
And reverend authority of late
Has worn a face of mercy more than justice.   135
    GLOST.   Beshrew my heart! but you have well
        divined
The source of these disorders.   Who can wonder
If riot and misrule o'erturn the realm
When the crown sits upon a baby brow?
Plainly to speak, hence comes the general cry   140
And sum of all complaint: ''Twill ne'er be well
With England' (thus they talk) 'while children
    govern.'
    L. HAST.   'Tis true the king is young; but what of
        that?
We feel no want of Edward's riper years
While Gloster's valor and most princely wisdom   145
So well supply our infant sovereign's place —
His youth's support, and guardian of his throne.
    GLOST.   The council (much I'm bound to thank
        'em for it)
Have placed a pageant scepter in my hand,
Barren of pow'r, and subject to control,   150
Scorned by my foes, and useless to my friends.
O worthy lord! were mine the rule indeed,
I think I should not suffer rank offence
At large to lord it in the commonweal.
    [1] Restive.

Nor would the realm be rent by discord thus,   155
Thus fear and doubt betwixt disputed titles.
    L. HAST.   Of this I am to learn, as not supposing
A doubt like this —
    GLOST.   Ay, marry, but there is —
And that of much concern.   Have you not heard
How, on a late occasion, Doctor Shaw [2]   160
Has moved the people much about the lawfulness
Of Edward's issue,[3] by right grave authority
Of learning and religion plainly proving
A bastard scion never should be grafted
Upon a royal stock? from thence, at full   165
Discoursing on my brother's former contract
To lady Elizabeth Lucy,[4] long before
His jolly match with that same buxom widow,
The queen he left behind him —
    L. HAST.   Ill befall
Such meddling priests, who kindle up confusion,   170
And vex the quiet world with their vain scruples!
By heav'n, 'tis done in perfect spite to peace,
[As if they feared their trade were at an end
If laymen should agree.]   Did not the king,
Our royal master Edward, in concurrence   175
With his estates assembled, well determine
What course the sovereign rule should take hence-
    forward?
When shall the deadly hate of faction cease;
When shall our long divided land have rest,
If every peevish, moody malcontent   180
Shall set the senseless rabble in an uproar,
Fright them with dangers, and perplex their brains
Each day with some fantastic, giddy change?
    GLOST.   [What if the same estates, the Lords and
        Commons,
Should alter —
    L. HAST.   What?
    GLOST.   The order of succession.]   185
    L. HAST.   Curse on the innovating hand attempts
        it!
Remember him, the villain, righteous heaven,
In thy great day of vengeance!   Blast the traitor
And his pernicious counsels; who for wealth,
For pow'r, the pride of greatness or revenge,   190
Would plunge his native land in civil wars.
    GLOST.   You go too far, my lord.
    L. HAST.   Your highness' pardon —
Have we so soon forgot those days of ruin,

[2] Doctor Ralph Shaw, a popular preacher.
[3] The means of 'moving the people' was a sermon preached
at Paul's Cross, in the precincts of the cathedral, a favorite place
for haranguing the citizens.
[4] This lady absolved Edward of having been contracted to
her.   Subsequently Parliament, at Richard's instigation, alleged that Edward had had a pre-contract with Lady Eleanor
Butler, daughter of the Earl of Shrewsbury.

169] Q1 *I'll befall.*   173–174] Passage in brackets supplied from P.
184–185] Passage in brackets supplied from P; Q1D2D3W1 GLOS. *What if some patriot for the public good | Should vary from
your scheme, new mold the state?*
                                                    192] Q1 *highness's.*

When York and Lancaster drew forth the battles;
When, like a matron butchered by her sons,   195
And cast beside some common way a spectacle
Of horror and affright to passers-by,
Our groaning country bled at every vein;
When murders, rapes, and massacres prevailed;
When churches, palaces, and cities blazed;   200
When insolence and barbarism triumphed,
And swept away distinction? Peasants trod
Upon the necks of nobles. Low were laid
The reverend crosier and the holy mitre,
And desolation covered all the land.   205
Who can remember this, and not, like me,
Here vow to sheath a dagger in his heart
Whose damned ambition would renew those horrors,
And set, once more, that scene of blood before us?
  GLOST. How now! So hot!
  L. HAST.   So brave, and so resolved.   210
  GLOST. Is then our friendship of so little moment
That you could arm your hand against my life?
  L. HAST. I hope your highness does not think I
  meant it;
No, heaven forefend that e'er your princely person
Should come within the scope of my resent-
  ment.   215
  GLOST. O noble Hastings! nay, I must embrace
  you!   (*Embraces him.*)
By holy Paul! y'are a right honest man;
The time is full of danger and distrust,
And warns us to be wary. Hold me not
Too apt for jealousy and light surmise   220
If, when I meant to lodge you next my heart,
I put your truth to trial. Keep your loyalty,
And live your king and country's best support:
For me, I ask no more than honor gives —
To think me yours, and rank me with your
  friends.   225
  L. HAST. Accept what thanks a grateful heart
  should pay.
O princely Gloster! judge me not ungentle,
Of manners rude, and insolent of speech
If, when the public safety is in question,
My zeal flows warm and eager from my tongue.   230
  GLOST. Enough of this: to deal in wordy compli-
  ment
Is much against the plainness of my nature.
I judge you by myself, a clear true spirit,
And as such once more join you to my bosom.
                    [*Embraces him.*]
— Farewell, and be my friend.   *Exit* GLOSTER.
  L. HAST.   I am not read,   235
Not skilled and practised in the arts of greatness,
To kindle thus, and give a scope to passion.
The duke is surely noble; but he touched me
Ev'n on the tend'rest point, the master-string
That makes most harmony or discord to me.   240

I own the glorious subject fires my breast,
And my soul's darling passion stands confessed —
Beyond or love's or friendship's sacred band,
Beyond myself I prize my native land.
On this foundation would I build my fame,   245
And emulate the Greek and Roman name;
Think England's peace bought cheaply with my
  blood,
And die with pleasure for my country's good. *Exit.*

ACT IV

[SCENE I]

Scene continues.

Enter DUKE OF GLOSTER, RATCLIFFE, *and*
CATESBY.

  GLOST. This was the sum of all, that he would
  brook
No alteration in the present state.
Marry! at last, the testy gentleman
Was almost moved to bid us bold defiance;
But there I dropped the argument, and changing   5
The first design and purport of my speech,
I praised his good affection to young Edward,
And left him to believe my thoughts like his.
Proceed we then to this fore-mentioned matter
As nothing bound or trusting to his friendship.   10
  RAT. Ill does it thus befall. I could have wished
This lord had stood with us. His friends are wealthy,
Thereto, his own possessions large and mighty;
The vassals and dependants on his power
Firm in adherence, ready, bold, and many.   15
His name had been of 'vantage to your highness,
And stood our present purpose much in stead.
  GLOST. This wayward and perverse declining
  from us
Has warranted at full the friendly notice
Which we this morn received. I hold it certain,   20
This puling, whining harlot rules his reason,
And prompts his zeal for Edward's bastard brood.
  CAT. If she have such dominion o'er his heart,
And turn it at her will, you rule her fate
And should, by inference and apt deduction,   25
Be arbiter of his. Is not her bread,
The very means immediate to her being,
The bounty of your hand? Why does she live
If not to yield obedience to your pleasure,
To speak, to act, to think as you command?   30
  RAT. Let her instruct her tongue to bear your
  message,
Teach every grace to smile in your behalf
And her deluding eyes to gloat for you;
His ductile reason will be wound about,
Be led and turned again, say and unsay,   35
Receive the yoke, and yield exact obedience.

GLOST. Your counsel likes me well; it shall be
  followed.
She waits without, attending on her suit;
Go, call her in, and leave us here alone.

       Exeunt RATCLIFFE *and* CATESBY.

How poor a thing is he, how worthy scorn,   40
Who leaves the guidance of imperial manhood
To such a paltry piece of stuff as this is —
A moppet made of prettiness and pride,
That oft'ner does her giddy fancies change
Than glittering dew-drops in the sun do colors.   45
Now shame upon it! Was our reason given
For such a use — to be thus puffed about
Like a dry leaf, an idle straw, a feather,
The sport of every whiffling blast that blows?
Beshrew my heart, but it is wond'rous strange;   50
Sure, there is something more than witchcraft in
  them
That masters ev'n the wisest of us all.

       Enter JANE SHORE.

— Oh! you are come most fitly. We have pondered
On this your grievance: and though some there are —
Nay, and those great ones too — who would en-
  force   55
The rigor of our power to afflict you
And bear a heavy hand, yet fear not you.
We've ta'en you to our favor; our protection
Shall stand between, and shield you from mishap.
  J. SH. The blessings of a heart with anguish
    broken   60
And rescued from despair attend your highness!
Alas! my gracious lord! what have I done
To kindle such relentless wrath against me?
If in the days of all my past offences,
When most my heart was lifted with delight,   65
If I withheld my morsel from the hungry,
Forgot the widows' want, and orphans' cry;
If I have known a good I have not shared,
Nor called the poor to take his portion with me,
Let my worst enemies stand forth and now   70
Deny the succor which I gave not then.
  GLOST. Marry, there are, though I believe them
    not,
Who say you meddle in affairs of state;
That you presume to prattle, like a busybody,
Give your advice, and teach the lords o'th' coun-
  cil   75
What fits the order of the commonweal.
  J. SH. Oh, that the busy world at least in this
Would take example from a wretch like me!
None then would waste their hours in foreign
  thoughts,
Forget themselves and what concerns their
  peace,   80
To tread the mazes of fantastic Falsehood,

To haunt her idle sounds and flying tales
Through all the giddy, noisy courts of rumor:
Malicious slander never would have leisure
To search with prying eyes for faults abroad,   85
If all, like me, considered their own hearts,
And wept the sorrows which they found at home.
  GLOST. Go to! I know your power, and though
    I trust not
To every breath of fame, I'm not to learn
That Hastings is professed your loving vassal.   90
But fair befall your beauty; use it wisely,
And may it stand your fortunes much in stead,
Give back your forfeit land with large encrease,
And place you high in safety and in honor.
Nay, I could point a way, the which pursuing,   95
You shall not only bring yourself advantage,
But give the realm much worthy cause to thank you.
  J. SH. Oh! where or how? — Can my unworthy
    hand
Become an instrument of good to any?
Instruct your lowly slave, and let me fly   100
To yield obedience to your dread command.
  GLOST. Why, that's well said. Thus then; ob-
    serve me well.
The state, for many high and potent reasons,
Deeming my brother Edward's sons unfit
For the imperial weight of England's crown —   105
  J. SH. (*aside*). Alas! for pity.
  GLOST.   Therefore have resolved
To set aside their unavailing infancy,
And vest the sovereign rule in abler hands.
This, though of great importance to the public,
Hastings, for very peevishness and spleen,   110
Does stubbornly oppose.
  J. SH.   Does he? Does Hastings?
  GLOST. Ay, Hastings.
  J. SH. Reward him for the noble deed, just
    heavens!
For this one action guard him and distinguish him
With signal mercies, and with great deliverance.   115
Save him from wrong, adversity and shame;
Let never-fading honors flourish round him,
And consecrate his name even to time's end;
Let him know nothing else but good on earth,
And everlasting blessedness hereafter.   120
  GLOST. How now!
  J. SH. The poor, forsaken, royal little ones!
Shall they be left a prey to savage power?
Can they lift up their harmless hands in vain,
Or cry to heaven for help and not be heard?   125
Impossible! O gallant, generous Hastings,
Go on, pursue! Assert the sacred cause;
Stand forth, thou proxy of all-ruling Providence,
And save the friendless infants from oppression.
Saints shall assist thee with prevailing prayers,   130
And warring angels combat on thy side.

130] Q1 *The saints.*

GLOST. You're passing rich in this same heav'nly
speech,
And spend it at your pleasure.   Nay, but mark me!
My favor is not bought with words like these.
Go to! — you'll teach your tongue another tale.   135
 J. SH. No, though the royal Edward has undone
me,
He was my king, my gracious master still.
He loved me too; though 'twas a guilty flame
And fatal to my peace, yet still he loved me:
With fondness, and with tenderness he doted,   140
Dwelt in my eyes, and lived but in my smiles.
And can I — oh, my heart abhors the thought —
Stand by and see his children robbed of right?
 GLOST. Dare not, ev'n for thy soul, to thwart me
further;
None of your arts, your feigning, and your fool-
ery,   145
Your dainty, squeamish coying it, to me!
Go — to your lord, your paramour, begone!
Lisp in his ear, hang wanton on his neck,
And play your monkey gambols over to him.
You know my purpose; look that you pursue it,   150
And make him yield obedience to my will.
Do it — or woe upon thy harlot's head!
 J. SH. Oh, that my tongue had ev'ry grace of
speech,
Great and commanding as the breath of kings,
Sweet as the poet's numbers, and prevailing   155
As soft persuasion to a love-sick maid;
That I had art and eloquence divine
To pay my duty to my master's ashes,
And plead till death the cause of injured innocence!
 GLOST. Ha! dost thou brave me, minion?   Dost
thou know   160
How vile, how very a wretch, my pow'r can make
thee?
That I can let loose fear, distress, and famine,
To hunt thy heels like hell-hounds through the
world?
That I can place thee in such abject state
As help shall never find thee — where repining   165
Thou shalt sit down and gnaw the earth for anguish,
Groan to the pitiless winds without return,
Howl like the midnight wolf amidst the desert,
And curse thy life in bitterness of misery?
 J. SH. Let me be branded for the public scorn,   170
Turned forth and driven to wander like a vagabond;
Be friendless and forsaken, seek my bread
Upon the barren, wild, and desolate waste,
Feed on my sighs, and drink my falling tears,
Ere I consent to teach my lips injustice,   175
Or wrong the orphan who has none to save him.
 GLOST. 'Tis well — we'll try the temper of your
heart.
—What ho!   Who waits without?

Enter RATCLIFFE, CATESBY, *and Attendants.*
 RAT.   Your highness' pleasure.—
 GLOST. Go, some of you, and turn this strumpet
forth!
Spurn her into the street; there let her perish   180
And rot upon a dunghill.   Through the city
See it proclaimed that none, on pain of death,
Presume to give her comfort, food, or harbor.
Who ministers the smallest comfort, dies.
Her house, her costly furniture and wealth,   185
The purchase of her loose, luxurious life,
We seize on, for the profit of the state.
—Away!   Begone!
 J. SH.   O thou most righteous judge —
Humbly, behold, I bow myself to thee,
And own thy justice in this hard decree: 190
No longer then my ripe offences spare,
But what I merit, let me learn to bear.
Yet since 'tis all my wretchedness can give,
For my past crimes my forfeit life receive;
No pity for my sufferings here I crave,   195
And only hope forgiveness in the grave.
     Exit JANE SHORE *guarded by* CATESBY *and
         others.*
 GLOST. (*to* RATCLIFFE). So much for this.   Your
project's at an end:
This idle toy, this hilding,[1] scorns my power,
And sets us all at nought.   See that a guard
Be ready at my call —
 RAT.   The council waits   200
Upon your highness' leisure.
 GLOST.   Bid 'em enter.

Enter the DUKE OF BUCKINGHAM, EARL OF DERBY,
    BISHOP OF ELY, LORD HASTINGS *and others, as
    to the council.   The* DUKE OF GLOSTER *takes his
    place at the upper end; then the rest sit.*
 DER. In happy time are we assembled here,
To point the day and fix the solemn pomp
For placing England's crown with all due rites
Upon our sovereign Edward's youthful brow.   205
 L. HAST. Some busy, meddling knaves 'tis said
there are,
As such will still be prating, who presume
To carp and cavil at his royal right.
Therefore I hold it fitting, with the soonest
T'appoint the order of the coronation;   210
So to approve our duty to the king,
And stay the babbling of such vain gainsayers.
 DER. (*to* GLOSTER). We all attend to know your
highness' pleasure
 GLOST. My lords! a set of worthy men you are,
Prudent and just, and careful for the state.   215
Therefore, to your most grave determination,
I yield myself in all things, and demand
 [1] Paltry person.

132] Q1 *heavenly.*

What punishment your wisdom shall think meet
T'inflict upon those damnable contrivers
Who shall with potions, charms, and witching
    drugs,   220
Practice against our person and our life.
   L. Hast. So much I hold the king your highness'
    debtor,
So precious are you to the commonweal,
That I presume, not only for myself,
But in behalf of these my noble brothers,   225
To say, whoe'er they be, they merit death.
   Glost. Then judge yourselves; convince your
    eyes of truth.   (*Pulling up his sleeve.*)
Behold my arm thus blasted, dry and withered;
Shrunk like a foul abortion, and decayed,
Like some untimely product of the seasons;   230
Robbed of its properties of strength and office.
This is the sorcery of Edward's wife,
Who in conjunction with that harlot Shore
And other like confederate midnight hags,
By force of potent spells, of bloody characters, 235
And conjurations horrible to hear,
Call fiends and spectres from the yawning deep,
And set the ministers of hell at work
To torture and despoil me of my life.
   L. Hast. If they have done this deed —
   Glost.   If they have done it! 240
Talk'st thou to me of if's, audacious traitor?
Thou art that strumpet witch's chief abettor,
The patron and complotter of her mischiefs,
And joined in this contrivance for my death.
Nay, start not, lords. — What ho! a guard there,
    sirs!   245

             Enter Guard.

Lord Hastings, I arrest thee of high treason!
— Seize him, and bear him instantly away;
He sha' not live an hour.   By holy Paul!
I will not dine before his head be brought me!
Ratcliffe, stay you and see that it be done.   250
The rest that love me, rise and follow me.
    Exeunt Gloster *and Lords following. Ma-*
    nent Lord Hastings, Ratcliffe, *and Guard.*
   L. Hast. What! and no more but this — how! to
    the scaffold?
O gentle Ratcliffe, tell me; do I hold thee?
Or if I dream, what shall I do to wake,
To break, to struggle through this dread con-
    fusion?   255
For surely death itself is not so painful
As is this sudden horror and surprise.
   Rat. You heard; the duke's commands to me
    were absolute.
Therefore, my lord, address you to your shrift
With all good speed you may.   Summon your
    courage,   260

And be yourself; for you must die this instant.
   L. Hast. Yes, Ratcliffe, I will take thy friendly
    counsel,
And die as a man should.   'Tis somewhat hard
To call my scattered spirits home at once;
But since what must be, must be — let neces-
    sity   265
Supply the place of time and preparation,
And arm me for the blow.   'Tis but to die;
'Tis but to venture on that common hazard
Which many a time in battle I have run;
'Tis but to do what, at that very moment,   270
In many nations of the peopled earth,
A thousand and a thousand shall do with me;
'Tis but to close my eyes and shut out daylight —
To view no more the wicked ways of men,
No longer to behold the tyrant Gloster,   275
And be a weeping witness of the woes,
The desolation, slaughter, and calamities,
Which he shall bring on this unhappy land.

             Enter Alicia.

   Alic. Stand off! and let me pass — I will, I must
Catch him once more in these despairing arms,   280
And hold him to my heart. — O Hastings, Hastings!
   L. Hast. Alas! why com'st thou at this dreadful
    moment,
To fill me with new terrors, new distractions;
To turn me wild with thy distempered rage,
And shock the peace of my departing soul?   285
Away!   I prithee, leave me!
   Alic.   Stop a minute —
Till my full griefs find passage.   Oh, the tyrant!
Perdition fall on Gloster's head and mine.
   L. Hast. What means thy frantic grief?
   Alic.   I cannot speak —
But I have murdered thee. — Oh, I could tell
    thee —!   290
   L. Hast. Speak, and give ease to thy conflicting
    passions.
Be quick, nor keep me longer in suspense;
Time presses, and a thousand crowding thoughts
Break in at once.   This way and that they snatch,
They tear my hurried soul.   All claim attention, 295
And yet not one is heard.   Oh, speak and leave me,
For I have business would employ an age,
And but a minute's time to get it done in.
   Alic. That, that's my grief — 'tis I that urge
    thee on,
Thus haunt thee to the toil,[1] sweep thee from
    earth,   300
And drive thee down this precipice of fate.
   L. Hast. Thy reason is grown wild.   Could thy
    weak hand
Bring on this mighty ruin?   If it could,

   [1] Snare.

2—] Q1 *highness's.*   290] Q1 *I would tell.*   300] Q1 *hunt.*

What have I done so grievous to thy soul,
So deadly, so beyond the reach of pardon,   305
That nothing but my life can make atonement?

ALIC. Thy cruel scorn had stung me to the heart,
And set my burning bosom all in flames.
Raving and mad I flew to my revenge,
And writ I know not what — told the Protector, 310
That Shore's detested wife by wiles had won thee
To plot against his greatness.   He believed it
(Oh, dire event of my pernicious counsel!),
And while I meant destruction on her head,
H' has turned it all on thine.

L. HAST.   Accursèd jealousy!   315
O merciless, wild, and unforgiving fiend!
Blindfold it runs to undistinguished mischief,
And murders all it meets.   Curst be its rage,
For there is none so deadly; doubly curst
Be all those easy fools who give it harbor,   320
Who turn a monster loose among mankind,
Fiercer than famine, war, or spotted pestilence,
Baneful as death and horrible as hell.

ALIC. If thou wilt curse, curse rather thine own
    falsehood;
Curse the lewd maxims of thy perjured sex,   325
Which taught thee first to laugh at faith and justice,
To scorn the solemn sanctity of oaths,
And make a jest of a poor woman's ruin;
Curse thy proud heart, and thy insulting tongue
That raised this fatal fury in my soul   330
And urged my vengeance to undo us both.

L. HAST. Oh, thou inhuman! turn thy eyes away.
And blast me not with their destructive beams.
Why should I curse thee with my dying breath?
Begone! and let me sigh it out in peace.   335

ALIC. Canst thou — O cruel Hastings — leave
    me thus?
Hear me, I beg thee — I conjure thee, hear me!
While with an agonizing heart, I swear
By all the pangs I feel, by all the sorrows,
The terrors and despair thy loss shall give me, 340
My hate was on my rival bent alone.
Oh! had I once divined, false as thou art,
A danger to thy life, I would have died,
I would have met it for thee, and made bare
My ready, faithful breast to save thee from it.   345

L. HAST. Now mark! and tremble at heaven's just
    award.
While thy insatiate wrath and fell revenge
Pursued the innocence which never wronged thee,
Behold! the mischief falls on thee and me.
Remorse and heaviness of heart shall wait thee, 350
And everlasting anguish be thy potion;
For me, the snares of death are wound about me,
And now, in one poor moment, I am gone.
Oh, if thou hast one tender thought remaining,

Fly to thy closet, fall upon thy knee,   355
And recommend my parting soul to mercy!

ALIC. (kneeling). Oh, yet, before I go forever
    from thee,
Turn thee in gentleness and pity to me,
And in compassion of my strong affliction,
Say, is it possible you can forgive   360
The fatal rashness of ungoverned love?
For oh, 'tis certain, if I had not loved thee
Beyond my peace, my reason, fame, and life,
Desired to death, and doted to distraction,
This day of horror never should have known us. 365

L. HAST. (raising her). Oh, rise, and let me hush
    thy stormy sorrows!
Assuage thy tears, for I will chide no more,
No more upbraid thee, thou unhappy fair one.
I see the hand of heav'n is armed against me,
And, in mysterious providence, decrees   370
To punish me by thy mistaking hand.
Most righteous doom! for, oh, while I behold thee,
Thy wrongs rise up in terrible array,
And charge thy ruin on me — thy fair fame,
Thy spotless beauty, innocence, and youth,   375
Dishonored, blasted, and betrayed by me!

ALIC. And does thy heart relent for my undoing?
Oh, that inhuman Gloster could be moved
But half so easily as I can pardon!

L. HAST. Here, then, exchange we mutually
    forgiveness.   380
So may the guilt of all my broken vows,
My perjuries to thee, be all forgotten,
As here my soul acquits thee of my death,
As here I part without one angry thought;
As here I leave thee with the softest tenderness, 385
Mourning the chance of our disastrous loves,
And begging heav'n to bless and to support thee.

RAT. My lord, dispatch; the duke has sent to
    chide me
For loitering in my duty.

L. HAST.   I obey.

ALIC. Insatiate, savage, monster!   Is a mo-
    ment   390
So tedious to thy malice?   Oh, repay him,
Thou great Avenger; give him blood for blood!
Guilt haunt him! fiends pursue him! lightnings blast
    him!
Some horrid, cursèd kind of death o'ertake him,
Sudden, and in the fullness of his sins!   395
That he may know how terrible it is
To want that moment he denies thee now.

L. HAST. 'Tis all in vain, this rage that tears
    thy bosom;
Like a poor bird that flutters in its cage,
Thou beat'st thyself to death.   Retire, I beg
    thee;   400

316] Q1 *forgiving*.   385] Q1 om. *thee.*
390] Q1D2 capitalize *savage*, indicating that it is to be construed as a noun.

To see thee thus, thou know'st not how it wounds
    me;
Thy agonies are added to my own,
And make the burden more than I can bear.
Farewell! Good angels visit thy afflictions
And bring thee peace and comfort from above! 405
   ALIC. Oh, stab me to the heart, some pitying
    hand —
Now strike me dead —!
   L. HAST.   One thing I had forgot:
I charge thee by our present common miseries,
By our past loves, if yet they have a name,
By all thy hopes of peace here and hereafter, 410
Let not the rancor of thy hate pursue
The innocence of thy unhappy friend.
Thou know'st who 'tis I mean; oh, shouldst thou
    wrong her,
Just heav'n shall double all thy woes upon thee,
And make 'em know no end. Remember this 415
As the last warning of a dying man.
Farewell forever! (*The Guards carry* HASTINGS *off.*)
   ALIC.   Forever! Oh, forever!
Oh, who can bear to be a wretch forever!
My rival too! His last thoughts hung on her,
And, as he parted, left a blessing for her. 420
Shall she be blest, and I be curst, forever?
No! Since her fatal beauty was the cause
Of all my suff'rings, let her share my pains;
Let her, like me, of ev'ry joy forlorn,
Devote [1] the hour when such a wretch was born: 425
Like me to deserts and to darkness run,
Abhor the day, and curse the golden sun;
Cast ev'ry good, and ev'ry hope behind;
Detest the works of nature, loathe mankind;
Like me, with cries distracted fill the air, ⎱
Tear her poor bosom, rend her frantic hair, ⎰ 430
And prove the torments of the last despair. ⎰

                               Exit.

ACT V

SCENE I

The street.

Enter BELLMOUR *and* DUMONT, *or* SHORE.

   SH. You saw her then?
   BELL.   I met her, as returning
In solemn penance from the public cross.
Before her, certain rascal officers,
Slaves in authority, the knaves of justice,
Proclaimed the tyrant Gloster's cruel orders. 5
On either side her marched an ill-looked priest,
Who with severe, with horrid, haggard eyes,
Did ever and anon by turns upbraid her,
And thunder in her trembling ear damnation.
   [1] Curse.

Around her, numberless the rabble flowed, 10
Should'ring each other, crowding for a view,
Gaping and gazing, taunting and reviling;
Some pitying, but those, alas! how few!
The most, such iron hearts we are, and such
The base barbarity of human kind,   15
With insolence and lewd reproach pursued her,
Hooting and railing, and with villainous hands
Gathering the filth from out the common ways,
To hurl upon her head.
   SH.   Inhuman dogs!
How did she bear it?
   BELL.   With the gentlest patience. 20
Submissive, sad, and lowly was her look;
A burning taper in her hand she bore,
And on her shoulders, carelessly confused,
With loose neglect her lovely tresses hung;
Upon her cheek a faintish flush was spread; 25
Feeble she seemed, and sorely smit with pain,
While barefoot as she trod the flinty pavement,
Her footsteps all along were marked with blood.
Yet silent still she passed and unrepining;
Her streaming eyes bent ever on the earth, 30
Except when in some bitter pang of sorrow
To heav'n she seemed in fervent zeal to raise,
And beg that mercy man denied her here.
   SH. When was this piteous sight?
   BELL.   These last two days.
You know my care was wholly bent on you, 35
To find the happy means of your deliverance,
Which but for Hastings' death I had not gained.
During that time, although I have not seen her,
Yet divers trusty messengers I've sent,
To wait about and watch a fit convenience 40
To give her some relief; but all in vain.
A churlish guard attends upon her steps,
Who menace those with death that bring her com-
    fort
And drive all succor from her.
   SH.   Let 'em threaten.
Let proud oppression prove its fiercest malice; 45
So heav'n befriend my soul, as here I vow
To give her help and share one fortune with her.
   BELL. Mean you to see her thus, in your own
    form?
   SH. I do.
   BELL.   And have you thought upon the
    consequence?
   SH. What is there I should fear?
   BELL.   Have you examined 50
Into your inmost heart, and tried at leisure
The several secret springs that move the passions?
Has Mercy fixed her empire there so sure,
That Wrath and Vengeance never may return?
Can you resume a husband's name, and bid 55
That wakeful dragon, fierce resentment, sleep?

32] Sutherland reports *raise them* as the reading of one copy of D2.

Sh. Why dost thou search so deep, and urge my
    memory
To conjure up my wrongs to life again?
I have long labored to forget myself,
To think on all time, backward, like a space   60
Idle and void, where nothing e'er had being.
But thou hast peopled it again; Revenge
And Jealousy renew their horrid forms,
Shoot all their fires, and drive me to distraction.

Bell. Far be the thought from me! my care was
    only   65
To arm you for the meeting. Better were it
Never to see her than to let that name
Recall forgotten rage, and make the husband
Destroy the generous pity of Dumont.

Sh. Oh! thou hast set my busy brain at work,   70
And now she musters up a train of images
Which to preserve my peace I had cast aside
And sunk in deep oblivion — Oh, that form!
That angel-face on which my dotage hung!
How I have gazed upon her, till my soul   75
With very eagerness went forth towards her,
And issued at my eyes. Was there a gem
Which the sun ripens in the Indian mine,
Or the rich bosom of the ocean yields,
What was there art could make, or wealth could
    buy,   80
Which I have left unsought to deck her beauty?
What could her king do more? — And yet she fled.

Bell. Away with that sad fancy.

Sh.   Oh, that day!
The thought of it must live forever with me.
I met her, Bellmour, when the royal spoiler   85
Bore her in triumph from my widowed home!
Within his chariot by his side she sate
And listened to his talk with downward looks;
Till sudden, as she chanced aside to glance,
Her eyes encountered mine. — Oh, then, my
    friend!   90
Oh, who can [paint] my grief and her amazement!
As at the stroke of death, twice turned she pale,
And twice a burning crimson blushed all o'er her;
Then, with a shriek heart-wounding, loud she cried,
While down her cheeks two gushing torrents
    ran   95
Fast falling on her hands, which thus she wrung.
Moved at her grief, the tyrant ravisher,
With courteous action wooed her oft to turn;
Earnest he seemed to plead, but all in vain;
Ev'n to the last she bent her sight towards me,   100
And followed me — till I had lost myself.

Bell. Alas, for pity! Oh, those speaking tears!
Could they be false? Did she not suffer with you?
For though the king by force possessed her person,
Her unconsenting heart dwelt still with you.   105

If all her former woes were not enough,
Look on her now; behold her where she wanders,
Hunted to death, distressed on every side,
With no one hand to help; and tell me, then,
If ever misery were known like hers.   110

Sh. And can she bear it? Can that delicate frame
Endure the beating of a storm so rude?
Can she, for whom the various seasons changed
To court her appetite and crown her board,
For whom the foreign vintages were pressed,   115
For whom the merchant spread his silken stores,
Can she —
Intreat for bread, and want the needful raiment
To wrap her shivering bosom from the weather?
When she was mine, no care came ever nigh her.   120
I thought the gentlest breeze that wakes the spring
Too rough to breathe upon her. Cheerfulness
Danced all the day before her, and at night
Soft slumbers waited on her downy pillow.
Now sad and shelterless, perhaps, she lies   125
Where piercing winds blow sharp, and the chill rain
Drops from some pent-house on her wretched head,
Drenches her locks, and kills her with the cold.
It is too much. Hence with her past offences;
They are atoned at full. Why stay we then?   130
Oh! let us haste, my friend, and find her out.

Bell. Somewhere about this quarter of the town,
I hear the poor, abandoned creature lingers.
Her guard, though set with strictest watch to keep
All food and friendship from her, yet permit her   135
To wander in the streets, there choose her bed,
And rest her head on what cold stone she pleases.

Sh. Here let us then divide, each in his round
To search her sorrows out. Whose hap it is
First to behold her, this way let him lead   140
Her fainting steps, and meet we here together.
                        Exeunt.

Enter Jane Shore, *her hair hanging loose on her*
    shoulders, and barefooted.

J. Sh. Yet, yet endure, nor murmur, O my soul!
For are not thy transgressions great and numberless?
Do they not cover thee, like rising floods,
And press thee like a weight of waters down?   145
Does not the hand of righteousness afflict thee;
And who shall plead against it? Who shall say
To pow'r almighty, 'Thou hast done enough:'
Or bid his dreadful rod of vengeance stay?
Wait then with patience till the circling hours   150
Shall bring the time of thy appointed rest
And lay thee down in death. The hireling thus
With labor drudges out the painful day,
And often looks with long expecting eyes
To see the shadows rise and be dismissed.   155
And hark! methinks the roar that late pursued me

87] Q1 *he sate.*   91] Q1D2 *point.* The earliest edition I have found with the correct reading is the 1766 *Works.*
94] Q1D2 *skriek.*

Sinks like the murmurs of a falling wind,
And softens into silence. Does revenge
And malice then grow weary, and forsake me?
My guard, too, that observed me still so close, 160
Tire in the task of their inhuman office,
And loiter far behind. Alas, I faint;
My spirits fail at once. — This is the door
Of my Alicia — blessèd opportunity!
I'll steal a little succor from her goodness 165
Now, while no eye observes me.
                    (*She knocks at the door.*)

Enter a Servant.

                          Is your lady —
My gentle friend, at home? Oh, bring me to her.
                              (*Going in.*)
    SERV. (*putting her back*). Hold, mistress, whither
        would you?
    J. SH.   Do you not know me?
    SERV. I know you well, and know my orders too.
You must not enter here.
    J. SH.   Tell my Alicia, 170
'Tis I would see her.
    SERV.   She is ill at ease
And will admit no visitor.
    J. SH.   But tell her
'Tis I, her friend, the partner of her heart,
Wait at the door and beg —
    SERV.   'Tis all in vain.
Go hence, and howl to those that will regard
    you.   *Shuts the door, and exit.* 175
    J. SH. It was not always thus; the time has been
When this unfriendly door that bars my passage,
Flew wide, and almost leaped from off its hinges
To give me entrance here; when this good house
Has poured forth all its dwellers to receive me; 180
When my approach has made a little holy-day,
And ev'ry face was dressed in smiles to meet me.
But now 'tis otherwise, and those who blessed me
Now curse me to my face. Why should I wander —
Stray further on, for I can die ev'n here! 185
                    (*She sits down at the door.*)

Enter ALICIA in disorder, two Servants following.

    ALIC. What wretch art thou whose misery and
        baseness
Hangs on my door; whose hateful whine of woe
Breaks in upon my sorrows, and distracts
My jarring senses with thy beggar's cry?
    J. SH. A very beggar, and a wretch indeed; 190
One driv'n by strong calamity to seek
For succor here; one perishing for want,
Whose hunger has not tasted food these three days;
And humbly asks, for charity's dear sake,
A draught of water and a little bread. 195
    ALIC. And dost thou come to me, to me for bread?
I know thee not. Go, hunt for it abroad,

Where wanton hands upon the earth have scattered
    it,
Or cast it on the waters. — Mark the eagle
And hungry vulture, where they wind the prey; 200
Watch where the ravens of the valley feed,
And seek thy food with them — I know thee not.
    J. SH. And yet there was a time when my Alicia
Has thought unhappy Shore her dearest blessing,
And mourned that livelong day she passed without
    me; 205
When, paired like turtles, we were still together;
When often as we prattled arm in arm,
Inclining fondly to me, she has sworn
She loved me more than all the world beside.
    ALIC. Ha! say'st thou! — let me look upon thee
        well. 210
'Tis true — I know thee now. A mischief on thee!
Thou art that fatal fair, that cursèd she,
That set my brain a madding. Thou hast robbed
    me;
Thou hast undone me. — Murder! Oh, my Has-
    tings!
— See, his pale, bloody head shoots glaring by
    me! 215
Give him me back again, thou soft deluder,
Thou beauteous witch —
    J. SH.   Alas, I never wronged you!
Oh, then be good to me; have pity on me!
Thou never knew'st the bitterness of want,
And mayst thou never know it. Oh, bestow 220
Some poor remain, the voiding of thy table,
A morsel to support my famished soul.
    ALIC. Avaunt! and come not near me —
    J. SH.   To thy hand
I trusted all — gave my whole store to thee.
Nor do I ask it back; allow me but 225
The smallest pittance, give me but to eat,
Least I fall down and perish here before thee.
    ALIC. Nay, tell not me! Where is thy king, thy
        Edward,
And all the smiling, cringing train of courtiers
That bent the knee before thee?
    J. SH.   Oh, for mercy! 230
    ALIC. Mercy? I know it not — for I am miser-
        able.
I'll give thee Misery, for here she dwells.
This is her house, where the sun never dawns;
The bird of night sits screaming o'er the roof,
Grim spectres sweep along the horrid gloom, 235
And nought is heard but wailings and lamentings.
Hark! something cracks above! — It shakes, it tot-
    ters!
And see, the nodding ruin falls to crush me!
'Tis fall'n, 'tis here! I feel it on my brain!
    1 SERV. This sight disorders her.
    2 SERV.   Retire, dear lady, 240
And leave this woman —

ALIC.   Let her take my counsel!
Why shouldst thou be a wretch? Stab, tear thy
    heart,
And rid thyself of this detested being;
I wo'not linger long behind thee here.
A waving flood of bluish fire swells o'er me;   245
And now 'tis out, and I am drowned in blood.
— Ha! what art thou, thou horrid headless trunk?
It is my Hastings! — See, he wafts me on!
— Away! I go! I fly! I follow thee.
— But come not thou with mischief-making
    beauty   250
To interpose between us; look not on him;
Give thy fond arts and thy delusions o'er,
For thou shalt never, never part us more.
                (She runs off, her Servants following.)
    J. SH. Alas! she raves; her brain, I fear, is turned.
In mercy look upon her, gracious heaven,   255
Nor visit her for any wrong to me.
Sure, I am near upon my journey's end;
My head runs round, my eyes begin to fail,
And dancing shadows swim before my sight.
I can no more. *(Lies down.)* Receive me, thou
    cold earth;   260
Thou common parent, take me to thy bosom,
And let me rest with thee.

                Enter BELLMOUR.

    BELL.   Upon the ground!
Thy miseries can never lay thee lower.
— Look up, thou poor afflicted one — thou mourner,
Whom none has comforted! Where are thy
    friends,   265
The dear companions of thy joyful days,
Whose hearts thy warm prosperity made glad,
Whose arms were taught to grow like ivy round
    thee,
And bind thee to their bosoms? 'Thus with thee,
Thus let us live, and let us die,' they said,   270
'For sure thou art the sister of our loves,
And nothing shall divide us.' — Now where are
    they?
    J. SH. Ah! Bellmour, where indeed! they stand
    aloof,
And view my desolation from afar;
When they pass by, they shake their heads in
    scorn   275
And cry, 'Behold the harlot and her end!'
And yet thy goodness turns aside to pity me!
Alas! there may be danger; get thee gone!
Let me not pull a ruin on thy head!
Leave me to die alone, for I am fall'n   280
Never to rise, and all relief is vain.
    BELL. Yet raise thy drooping head, for I am come
To chase away despair. Behold, where yonder
That honest man, that faithful, brave Dumont,
Is hasting to thy aid! —

    J. SH. *(raising herself and looking about).* Dumont?
    Ha! where?   285
Then heav'n has heard my pray'r; his very name
Renews the springs of life and cheers my soul.
Has he then 'scaped the snare?
    BELL.   He has: but see —
He comes, unlike to that Dumont you knew,
For now he wears your better angel's form,   290
And comes to visit you with peace and pardon.

                Enter SHORE.

    J. SH. Speak — tell me! Which is he? And
    oh! what would
This dreadful vision! See, it comes upon me —
It is my husband — ah!   *(She swoons.)*
    SH.   She faints! Support her;
Sustain her head while I infuse this cordial   295
Into her dying lips — from spicy drugs,
Rich herbs, and flow'rs the potent juice is drawn;
With wondrous force it strikes the lazy spirits,
Drives 'em around, and wakens life anew.
    BELL. Her weakness could not bear the strong
    surprise.   300
— But see, she stirs! and the returning blood
Faintly begins to blush again, and kindle
Upon her ashy cheek —
    SH. *(raising her up).* So — gently raise her —
    J. SH. Ha! what art thou? — Bellmour!
    BELL.   How fare you, lady?
    J. SH. My heart is thrilled with horror —
    BELL.   Be of courage —   305
Your husband lives! 'Tis he, my worthiest friend —
    J. SH. Still art thou there? — still dost thou
    hover round me?
Oh, save me, Bellmour, from his angry shade!
    BELL. 'Tis he himself! — he lives! — look up —
    J. SH.   I dare not!
Oh, that my eyes could shut him out forever —   310
    SH. Am I so hateful then, so deadly to thee,
To blast thy eyes with horror? Since I'm grown
A burthen to the world, myself, and thee,
Would I had ne'er survived to see thee more.
    J. SH. Oh, thou most injured! Dost thou live,
    indeed?   315
Fall then, ye mountains, on my guilty head;
Hide me, ye rocks, within your secret caverns;
Cast thy black veil upon my shame, O night,
And shield me with thy sable wing forever!
    SH. Why dost thou turn away? — why tremble
    thus?   320
Why thus indulge thy fears, and in despair,
Abandon thy distracted soul to horror?
Cast every black and guilty thought behind thee,
And let 'em never vex thy quiet more.
My arms, my heart are open to receive thee,   325
To bring thee back to thy forsaken home
With tender joy, with fond, forgiving love,

And all the longings of my first desires.

J. SH. No, arm thy brow with vengeance, and
    appear
The minister of heav'n's enquiring justice;   330
Array thyself all terrible for judgment,
Wrath in thy eyes, and thunder in thy voice;
Pronounce my sentence, and if yet there be
A woe I have not felt, inflict it on me.

SH. The measure of thy sorrows is complete, 335
And I am come to snatch thee from injustice.
The hand of pow'r no more shall crush thy weakness,
Nor proud oppression grind thy humble soul.

J. SH. Art thou not risen by miracle from death?
Thy shroud is fall'n from off thee, and the grave 340
Was bid to give thee up, that thou might'st come
The messenger of grace and goodness to me,
To seal my peace and bless me ere I go.
Oh, let me then fall down beneath thy feet
And weep my gratitude forever there;   345
Give me your drops, ye soft-descending rains,
Give me your streams, ye never-ceasing springs,
That my sad eyes may still supply my duty,
And feed an everlasting flood of sorrow.

SH. Waste not thy feeble spirits. I have long 350
Beheld, unknown, thy mourning and repentance;
Therefore my heart has set aside the past,
And holds thee white as unoffending innocence;
Therefore, in spite of cruel Gloster's rage,
Soon as my friend had broke my prison doors, 355
I flew to thy assistance. Let us haste
Now, while occasion seems to smile upon us,
Forsake this place of shame and find a shelter.

J. SH. What shall I say to you? But I obey —
SH. Lean on my arm —

J. SH.   Alas! I am wondrous faint: 360
But that's not strange; I have not eat these three
    days.

SH. Oh, merciless! Look here, my love, I've
    brought thee
Some rich conserves.

J. SH.   How can you be so good?
But you were ever thus; I well remember
With what fond care, what diligence of love, 365
You lavished out your wealth to buy me pleasures,
Preventing [1] every wish. Have you forgot
The costly string of pearl you brought me home
And tied about my neck? — How could I leave you?

SH. Taste some of this, or this —
J. SH.   You're strangely altered — 370
Say, gentle Bellmour, is he not? How pale
Your visage is become! Your eyes are hollow;
Nay, you are wrinkled too. Alas the day!
My wretchedness has cost you many a tear
And many a bitter pang since last we parted. 375

SH. No more of that — thou talk'st but dost not
    eat.

[1] Anticipating.

J. SH. My feeble jaws forget their common office,
My tasteless tongue cleaves to the clammy roof,
And now a gen'ral loathing grows upon me.
Oh, I am sick at heart! —   [She swoons.]
SH.   Thou murd'rous sorrow! 380
Wo't thou still drink her blood, pursue her still?
Must she then die? Oh, my poor penitent,
Speak peace to thy sad heart. — She hears me not;
Grief masters ev'ry sense. Help me to hold her —

Enter CATESBY, *with a Guard.* [2]

CAT. Seize on 'em both, as traitors to the
    state. 385
BELL. What means this violence?
    (*Guard lay hold on* SHORE *and* BELLMOUR.)
CAT.   Have we not found you,
In scorn of the Protector's strict command,
Assisting this base woman and abetting
Her infamy?
SH.   Infamy on thy head!
Thou tool of power, thou pander to authority! 390
I tell thee, knave, thou know'st of none so virtuous,
And she that bore thee was an Ethiop to her!

CAT. You'll answer this at full. — Away with 'em.
SH. Is charity grown treason to your court?
What honest man would live beneath such rul-
    ers? 395
I am content that we shall die together.

CAT. Convey the men to prison; but for her,
Leave her to hunt her fortune as she may.

J. SH. I will not part with him! — For me — for
    me!
Oh, must he die for me?
    (*Following him as he is carried off. She falls.*)
SH.   Inhuman villains! 400
    (*Breaks from the Guard.*)
Stand off! the agonies of death are on her —
She pulls, she gripes me hard with her cold hand.

J. SH. Was this blow wanting to complete my
    ruin?
Oh, let him go, ye ministers of terror;
He shall offend no more, for I will die 405
And yield obedience to your cruel master.
Tarry a little, but a little longer,
And take my last breath with you.
SH.   O my love! —
Why have I lived to see this bitter moment,
This grief by far surpassing all my former! 410
Why dost thou fix thy dying eyes upon me
With such an earnest, such a piteous look,
As if thy heart were full of some sad meaning
Thou couldst not speak! —

J. SH.   Forgive me! — but forgive me!
SH. Be witness for me, ye celestial host, 415
Such mercy and such pardon as my soul
Accords to thee, and begs of heav'n to show thee,

[2] Used here as a collective noun.

May such befall me at my latest hour,
And make my portion blest or curst forever.
   J. Sh. Then all is well, and I shall sleep in
     peace.   420
'Tis very dark, and I have lost you now.
Was there not something I would have bequeathed
     you?
But I have nothing left me to bestow —
Nothing but one sad sigh. Oh, mercy, heav'n!
                     (*Dies.*)
   Bell. There fled the soul,   425
And left her load of misery behind.
   Sh. Oh, my heart's treasure! Is this pale, sad
     visage
All that remains of thee? Are these dead eyes
The light that cheer my soul? Oh, heavy hour!

But I will fix my trembling lips to thine   430
Till I am cold and senseless quite, as thou art.
What, must we part then? —
         (*To the Guards taking him away.*)
                  Will you?
                  (*Kissing her.*)
               — Fare thee well!
— Now execute your tyrant's will, and lead me
To bonds or death; 'tis equally indifferent.   435
   Bell. Let those who view this sad example know
What fate attends the broken marriage vow;
And teach their children in succeeding times,
No common vengeance waits upon these crimes,
When such severe repentance could not save,   440
From want, from shame, and an untimely grave.
                       Exeunt.

EPILOGUE

SPOKEN BY MRS. OLDFIELD [1]

Ye modest matrons all, ye virtuous wives,
Who lead with horrid husbands decent lives,
You who, for all you are in such a taking
To see your spouses drinking, gaming, raking,
Yet make a conscience still of cuckold-making; 5
What can we say your pardon to obtain?
This matter here was proved against poor Jane:
She never once denied it, but in short,
Whimpered, and cried, 'Sweet sir — I'm sorry for't.'
'Twas well she met a kind, good-natured soul, 10
We are not all so easy to control.
I fancy one might find in this good town
Some would ha' told the gentleman his own;
Have answered smart, 'To what do you pretend,
Blockhead? — As if I mustn't see a friend! 15
Tell me of hackney-coaches — jaunts to th' City!
Where should I buy my china? — Faith, I'll fit ye! —'
Our wife was of a milder, meeker spirit:
You! — lords and masters! — was not that some merit?
Don't you allow it to be virtuous bearing, 20
When we submit thus to your domineering?
Well, peace be with her; she did wrong most surely,
But so do many more who look demurely:
Nor should our mourning madam weep alone,
There are more ways of wickedness than one. 25
If the reforming stage should fall to shaming
Ill-nature, pride, hypocrisy, and gaming,
The poets frequently might move compassion,
And with she-tragedies o'errun the nation.
Then judge the fair offender, with good nature; 30
And let your fellow-feeling curb your satire.
What if our neighbors have some little failing;
Must we needs fall to damning and to railing?
For her excuse, too, be it understood,
That if the woman was not quite so good, 35
Her lover was a king; she, flesh and blood.
And since she has dearly paid the sinful score,
Be kind at last, and pity poor Jane Shore.

In the part of Jane Shore.

BALLAD OPERA

OPERA in England was partly a natural development of the Elizabethan masque and partly the result of the caution of D'Avenant, who, desiring to revive the theater in spite of the Commonwealth's ban, produced *The Siege of Rhodes* (1656) as a piece 'made a representation by the art of prospective in scenes, and the story sung in recitative music.' Throughout the Restoration English opera was a familiar, although not a dominating feature of the dramatic world, provoking only occasional grumbles from the adherents of the spoken drama. Various English authors, including Dryden, tried their hands in this form of art. In 1705, however, an uproar was caused by the production of two Italian operas: *Arsinoë*, translated from the Italian and set to new music by an English composer, Thomas Clayton, at Drury Lane; and *Camilla*, with the original music by Buononcini, and with the text partly in Italian and partly in English, at the Haymarket. English authors and actors who saw themselves thus supplanted by foreigners were indignant, and they were promptly supported by almost the entire body of critics. The novelty and artificiality of the Italian style attracted the upper classes, however, and the new entertainment survived, with varying fortunes, all attempts to drive it from the stage. Attacks were made upon it in periodicals (notably the *Spectator*), in pamphlets, in burlesques (the earliest, apparently, being Richard Estcourt's *Prunella*, 1708), and by means of competitive English operas, among which may be mentioned Addison's unsuccessful *Rosamund* (1706). Händel and Buononcini, at first strong props of Italian opera, eventually settled in England and composed music for English texts, a turn of events which served to moderate the storm of adverse criticism, since English composers were not so vocal in their protests against foreign competition as were English authors. Even so, there was enough patriotic discontent with 'outlandish' art and artists to provide a receptive audience for the greatest of all the counterblasts against the intruders — *The Beggar's Opera*.

JOHN GAY (1685–1732) had, during his early days of authorship, written a good deal of verse, the basis of his early reputation, some prose, and several works in dramatic form, none of them very successful. In some of these music had been used, and one (*Acis and Galatea*), which is alleged by two centuries of tradition to have been written by him in the early 1720's, is an operatic text which was eventually set to music by Händel and performed in the year of Gay's death. *The Beggar's Opera* grew out of several convergent ideas, of which the antipathy to Italian opera was but one: an even more cogent one was the satirizing of the court circle by comparing it with the underworld. The germ of the opera seems to have been Swift's suggestion that Gay should write a series of Newgate pastorals, carrying on the burlesque of the pastoral tradition which he had so skilfully begun in *The Shepherd's Week*. The most original thing about *The Beggar's Opera* was the author's use of well-known English ballad airs for the large majority of his songs: by this device he guaranteed the popularity of his piece on the musical side, and at the same time enlisted the national prejudices of his audience and struck a blow at foreign opera.

The Beggar's Opera was phenomenally successful. It had sixty-two performances between January 29 and June 19, 1728, of which thirty-two were consecutive. It quickly became the talk of the fashionable world; pictures of its scenes and characters decorated screens, fans, and playing-cards; the actors were lionized; and both the author and the manager, John Rich, profited handsomely. The popular *bon mot* had it that the opera had made Gay rich and Rich gay. The latter deserved his good fortune: he had taken up the play after Cibber had rejected it, and he had the pleasure of seeing it advance his theater, Lincoln's Inn Fields, to unquestioned predominance. The success of the opera in 1728 was continued through the following season, during which there were fifty-nine performances at Lincoln's Inn Fields, including sixteen by a company of children. In the mean time the play was being given in the provinces and in Ireland.

The enthusiasm for *The Beggar's Opera* naturally begot imitations. Two other ballad operas by different authors were brought on the stage before the end of 1728. Twelve (not counting Gay's *Polly*) were produced or published in the following year, and the number of new imitations continued at a fairly steady rate thereafter until 1733, in the course of which year there were no fewer than twenty-two new ballad operas, among them Gay's posthumous *Achilles*. During the next ten years the number of new productions declined gradually, but sporadic examples appeared in the latter half of the century, and there are clear indications of the influence of ballad opera upon the English comic opera of later times.

None of the imitations of *The Beggar's Opera* approached it in popularity, although among the authors who attempted the form were Cibber, Fielding, and Lillo. This may be partly accounted for by the fact that Gay, the first in the field, had the advantage of novelty, and had, moreover, chosen the best of the available tunes. His imitators had either to use less catchy airs or to repeat those which, by association, were now regarded as belonging to the original opera. It is interesting to note that not all the ballad operas followed their prototype in adhering to the Restoration school of comedy: several of them belong to the sentimental tradition, among them Gay's *Polly*, the sequel to *The Beggar's Opera*. In this continuation Polly follows Macheath to the West Indies, to which he has been transported as a punishment for his crimes. He there disguises himself as a Negro, gathers about him a gang of European outlaws, and embarks upon a career of piracy against the English traders and their allies, the Indians. Polly, escaping in boy's clothes from the unwelcome attentions of one of the traders, falls into the hands of the pirates, but is rescued by a young Indian chief. Macheath is finally captured and executed, Polly learning his identity just too late to save him. There is a good deal of Gay's witty dialogue, but there is also much moralizing by the Indians upon the corruption of European civilization: 'European,' in their mouths, is the worst of insults. The young Indian chief, Cawwawkee, is the hero: he is an excellent example of the eighteenth century's conception of the 'noble savage.' At the end of the opera the audience is given to understand that he will be rewarded for his virtue with the hand of Polly.

Polly would probably not have been as successful as *The Beggar's Opera*, but the opportunity of proving this was not given. Walpole, the prime minister, enraged at hostile political references in the earlier work, ordered the lord chamberlain not to license the production of the sequel — whether in a spirit of revenge or because of the political satire in *Polly* is not quite clear. However, Gay printed the play, the sales of which were certainly increased by the lord chamberlain's ban upon the performance. The opera was not played until 1777. Gay's final opera, *Achilles*, was brought upon the stage in 1733 for eighteen performances, but the general opinion of contemporary critics seems to have been that it was supported by the reputation of its author, who had died shortly after the completion of the text. Gay was therefore spared the disappointment of learning that he had been unable to follow up his first success.

A. E. C.

REFERENCE WORKS

1913. Pearce, Charles E. *'Polly Peachum' . . . and 'The Beggar's Opera.'*
1923. Schultz, William E. *Gay's 'Beggar's Opera.'* New Haven.
1928. Dent, Edward J. *The Foundation of English Opera.* Cambridge [England].
1929. Nicoll, Allardyce. *A History of Early Eighteenth Century Drama, 1700–1750.* Cambridge [England]. [Chapter IV.]
1937. Gagey, Edmond M. *Ballad Opera.* New York.

The Beggar's Opera

BY JOHN GAY

THE BEGGAR'S OPERA

DRAMATIS PERSONÆ[1]

MEN		WOMEN	
PEACHUM		MRS. PEACHUM.	
LOCKIT.		POLLY PEACHUM.	
MACHEATH.		LUCY LOCKIT.	
FILCH.		DIANA TRAPES.	
JEMMY TWITCHER,		MRS. COAXER,	
CROOK-FINGERED JACK,		DOLLY TRULL,	
WAT DREARY,		MRS. VIXEN,	
ROBIN OF BAGSHOT,	MACHEATH's *Gang.*	BETTY DOXY,	*Women of the Town.*
NIMMING NED,		JENNY DIVER,	
HARRY PADINGTON,		MRS. SLAMMEKIN,	
MATT OF THE MINT,		SUKY TAWDRY,	
BEN BUDGE,		MOLLY BRAZEN,	
BEGGAR.			
PLAYER.			

Constables, Drawer, Turnkey, etc.

INTRODUCTION

BEGGAR, PLAYER

BEG. If poverty be a title to poetry, I am sure nobody can dispute mine. I own myself of the company of beggars; and I make one at their weekly festivals at St. Giles's.[2] I have a small yearly salary for my catches, and am welcome to a dinner there whenever I please, which is more than most poets can say.

PLAY. As we live by the Muses, 'tis but gratitude in us to encourage poetical merit wherever we find it. The Muses, contrary to all other ladies, pay no distinction to dress, and never partially mistake the pertness of embroidery for wit, nor the modesty of want for dulness. Be the author who he will, we push his play as far as it will go. So (though you are in want) I wish you success heartily.

BEG. This piece I own was originally writ for the celebrating the marriage of James Chanter and Moll Lay, two most excellent ballad-singers. I have introduced the similes that are in all your celebrated operas: the swallow, the moth, the bee, the ship, the flower, etc. Besides, I have a prison-scene, which the ladies always reckon charmingly pathetic. As to the parts, I have observed such a nice impartiality to our two ladies, that it is impossible for either of them to take offence.[3] I hope I may be forgiven, that I have not made my opera throughout unnatural, like those in vogue; for I have no recitative; excepting this, as I have consented to have neither prologue nor epilogue, it must be allowed an opera in all its forms. The piece indeed hath been heretofore frequently represented by ourselves in our great room at St. Giles's, so that I cannot too often acknowledge your charity in bringing it now on the stage.

PLAY. But I see 'tis time for us to withdraw; the actors are preparing to begin. — Play away the overture. *Exeunt.*

---

[1] Most of the names given to the characters are 'label' names, based largely upon the canting language of the underworld. Peachum (to 'peach' is to inform against one's accomplices) probably represents Jonathan Wild, a notorious 'thief-taker' of the period, who was the head of a band of criminals, some of whom he occasionally betrayed to the police for pay. He had been executed in 1725 for acting as a receiver of stolen goods. 'Macheath' ('son of the heath') alludes to the fact that the open heaths surrounding London were the favorite haunts of the highwaymen who halted and robbed stage-coaches. A 'twitcher' is a pick-pocket. Bagshot is the name of one of the heaths, lying to the west of London, on the road to Winchester and Salisbury. 'Nimming' means stealing. Paddington and the Mint were disreputable districts of London, the latter, south of the Thames, being especially famous because it preserved until the reign of George I the characteristics of a medieval sanctuary, in which the officers of the law could not arrest persons for debt. A 'budge' is a sneak-thief. 'Trapes' and 'slammekin' are synonyms for a slovenly woman; 'trull' and 'doxy' for a prostitute. A 'diver' is a pickpocket. The other names are self-explanatory.

[2] The parish of St. Giles-in-the-Fields, near Holborn, was largely inhabited by poor persons and beggars.

[3] There had been frequent quarrels about precedence among the Italian opera-singers in London, especially the leading sopranos.

OUVERTURE in SCORE

Compos'd by Dr. *PEPUSCH*.

By JOHN GAY

ACT I

SCENE I

Peachum's house.

PEACHUM *sitting at a table with a large book of accounts before him.*

AIR I. *An old woman clothed in gray.*

Through all the employments of life,
    Each neighbor abuses his brother;
Whore and rogue they call husband and wife:
    All professions be-rogue one another.
The priest calls the lawyer a cheat,   5
    The lawyer be-knaves the divine;
And the statesman, because he's so great,
    Thinks his trade as honest as mine.

A lawyer is an honest employment; so is mine.
Like me, too, he acts in a double capacity, both   10
against rogues and for 'em; for 'tis but fitting that
we should protect and encourage cheats, since we
live by 'em.

SCENE II

PEACHUM, FILCH.

FILCH. Sir, Black Moll hath sent word her trial
comes on in the afternoon, and she hopes you will
order matters so as to bring her off.

PEACH. Why, she may plead her belly[1] at worst;
to my knowledge she hath taken care of that   5
security. But as the wench is very active and industrious, you may satisfy her that I'll soften the
evidence.

[1] It was against the law to execute a woman who was with
child.

FILCH. Tom Gagg, sir, is found guilty.

PEACH. A lazy dog! When I took him the   10
time before, I told him what he would come to if he
did not mend his hand. This is death without reprieve. I may venture to book him. (*Writes.*)
'For Tom Gagg, forty pounds.' Let Betty Sly know
that I'll save her from transportation,[2] for I can   15
get more by her staying in England.

FILCH. Betty hath brought more goods into our
lock[3] to-year,[4] than any five of the gang; and in
truth, 'tis a pity to lose so good a customer.

PEACH. If none of the gang take her off,[5] she   20
may, in the common course of business, live a twelve-
month longer. I love to let women scape. A good
sportsman always lets the hen partridges fly, because
the breed of the game depends upon them. Besides,
here the law allows us no reward; there is noth-   25
ing to be got by the death of women — except our
wives.

FILCH. Without dispute, she is a fine woman!
'Twas to her I was obliged for my education, and
(to say a bold word) she hath trained up more   30
young fellows to the business than the gaming-table.

PEACH. Truly, Filch, thy observation is right.
We and the surgeons are more beholden to women
than all the professions besides.

[2] I.e., to the colonies — a frequent punishment.
[3] A cant word, signifying a warehouse where stolen goods are
deposited. (Gay's note to III. iii. 16.)
[4] This year.
[5] Remove her (either by killing her or by betraying her to
the authorities).

AIR II. *The bonny gray-eyed morn, etc.*

FILCH. 'Tis woman that seduces all mankind, 35
By her we first were taught the wheedling arts;
Her very eyes can cheat; when most she's kind,
She tricks us of our money with our hearts.
For her, like wolves by night we roam for prey,
And practise ev'ry fraud to bribe her charms; 40
For suits of love, like law, are won by pay,
And beauty must be fee'd into our arms.

PEACH. But make haste to Newgate,[1] boy, and let
my friends know what I intend; for I love to make
them easy one way or other. 45

FILCH. When a gentleman is long kept in suspense, penitence may break his spirit ever after.
Besides, certainty gives a man a good air upon his
trial, and makes him risk another without fear or
scruple. But I'll away, for 'tis a pleasure to be 50
the messenger of comfort to friends in affliction.

SCENE III

PEACHUM.

PEACH. But 'tis now high time to look about me
for a decent execution against next sessions.[2] I hate
a lazy rogue, by whom one can get nothing till he is
hanged. (*Reading.*) 'A register of the gang.
Crook-fingered Jack.' A year and a half in the 5
service. Let me see how much the stock owes to his
industry; one, two, three, four, five gold watches,
and seven silver ones. A mighty clean-handed fellow! Sixteen snuff-boxes, five of them of true gold.
Six dozen of handkerchiefs, four silver-hilted 10
swords, half a dozen of shirts, three tie-periwigs, and
a piece of broadcloth. Considering these are only
the fruits of his leisure hours, I don't know a prettier
fellow, for no man alive hath a more engaging presence of mind upon the road. 'Wat Dreary, alias 15
Brown Will' — an irregular dog, who hath an underhand way of disposing of his goods. I'll try him
only for a sessions or two longer upon his good behavior. 'Harry Padington' — a poor petty-larceny
rascal, without the least genius; that fellow, 20
though he were to live these six months, will never
come to the gallows with any credit. 'Slippery
Sam' — he goes off the next sessions, for the villain
hath the impudence to have views of following his
trade as a tailor, which he calls an honest em- 25
ployment. 'Matt of the Mint' — listed[3] not above
a month ago, a promising sturdy fellow, and diligent
in his way: somewhat too bold and hasty, and may
raise good contributions on the public, if he does not
cut himself short by murder. 'Tom Tipple' — 30

[1] The chief prison of London, situated in the street of the same name.
[2] In anticipation of the next session of the criminal court.
[3] Enlisted.

a guzzling soaking sot, who is always too drunk to
stand himself, or to make others stand. A cart[4] is
absolutely necessary for him. 'Robin of Bagshot,
alias Gorgon, alias Bluff Bob, alias Carbuncle, alias
Bob Booty —'[5] 35

SCENE IV

PEACHUM, MRS. PEACHUM.

MRS. PEACH. What of Bob Booty, husband? I
hope nothing bad hath betided him? You know,
my dear, he's a favorite customer of mine. 'Twas
he made me a present of this ring.

PEACH. I have set his name down in the black- 5
list, that's all, my dear; he spends his life among
women, and as soon as his money is gone, one or
other of the ladies will hang him for the reward, and
there's forty pound lost to us forever.

MRS. PEACH. You know, my dear, I never 10
meddle in matters of death; I always leave those
affairs to you. Women indeed are bitter bad judges
in these cases, for they are so partial to the brave,
that they think every man handsome who is going
to the camp or the gallows. 15

AIR III. Cold and raw, &c.

AIR III. *Cold and raw, etc.*

If any wench Venus's girdle wear,
    Though she be never so ugly;
Lilies and roses will quickly appear,
    And her face look wond'rous smugly.
Beneath the left ear so fit but a cord, 20
    (A rope so charming a zone is!)
The youth in his cart hath the air of a lord,
    And we cry, 'There dies an Adonis!'

But really, husband, you should not be too hard-
hearted, for you never had a finer, braver set of 25
men than at present. We have not had a murder

[4] I.e., a hangman's cart.
[5] These names were understood by the audience to refer to Robert Walpole.

among them all, these seven months. And truly, my dear, that is a great blessing.

PEACH. What a dickens is the woman always a-whimp'ring about murder for? No gentleman 30 is ever looked upon the worse for killing a man in his own defence; and if business cannot be carried on without it, what would you have a gentleman do?

MRS. PEACH. If I am in the wrong, my dear, you must excuse me, for nobody can help the frailty 35 of an over-scrupulous conscience.

PEACH. Murder is as fashionable a crime as a man can be guilty of. How many fine gentlemen have we in Newgate every year, purely upon that article? If they have wherewithal to persuade the jury to 40 bring it in manslaughter, what are they the worse for it? So, my dear, have done upon this subject. Was Captain Macheath here this morning, for the bank-notes he left with you last week?

MRS. PEACH. Yes, my dear; and though the 45 bank hath stopped payment, he was so cheerful and so agreeable! Sure there is not a finer gentleman upon the road than the captain! If he comes from Bagshot at any reasonable hour he hath promised to make one this evening with Polly and me, and 50 Bob Booty, at a party of quadrille.[1] Pray, my dear, is the captain rich?

PEACH. The captain keeps too good company ever to grow rich. Marybone and the chocolate-houses[2] are his undoing. The man that proposes to get 55 money by play should have the education of a fine gentleman, and be trained up to it from his youth.

MRS. PEACH. Really, I am sorry upon Polly's account the captain hath not more discretion. What business hath he to keep company with lords and 60 gentlemen? he should leave them to prey upon one another.

PEACH. 'Upon Polly's account!' What, a plague, does the woman mean? — 'Upon Polly's account!'

MRS. PEACH. Captain Macheath is very fond 65 of the girl.

PEACH. And what then?

MRS. PEACH. If I have any skill in the ways of women, I am sure Polly thinks him a very pretty man. 70

PEACH. And what then? You would not be so mad to have the wench marry him! Gamesters and highwaymen are generally very good to their whores, but they are very devils to their wives.

MRS. PEACH. But if Polly should be in love, 75 how should we help her, or how can she help herself? Poor girl, I am in the utmost concern about her.

[1] A four-handed card-game.
[2] Marybone, a district on the northwestern edge of London, was the center for gambling on the game of bowling; the choco-late-houses, especially White's, were the places for gambling with cards and dice.

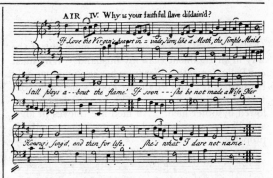

AIR IV. *Why is your faithful slave disdained?*

If love the virgin's heart invade,
How, like a moth, the simple maid
    Still plays about the flame!   80
If soon she be not made a wife,
Her honor's singed, and then for life
She's — what I dare not name.

PEACH. Look ye, wife. A handsome wench in our way of business is as profitable as at the bar 85 of a Temple coffee-house,[3] who looks upon it as her livelihood to grant every liberty but one. You see I would indulge the girl as far as prudently we can. In anything but marriage! After that, my dear, how shall we be safe? Are we not then in her 90 husband's power? For a husband hath the absolute power over all a wife's secrets but her own. If the girl had the discretion of a court lady, who can have a dozen young fellows at her ear without complying with one, I should not matter it;[4] but Polly is 95 tinder, and a spark will at once set her on a flame. Married! If the wench does not know her own profit, sure she knows her own pleasure better than to make herself a property! My daughter to me should be, like a court lady to a minister of state, a key to 100 the whole gang. Married! if the affair is not already done, I'll terrify her from it, by the example of our neighbors.

MRS. PEACH. Mayhap, my dear, you may injure the girl. She loves to imitate the fine ladies, 105 and she may only allow the captain liberties in the view of interest.

PEACH. But 'tis your duty, my dear, to warn the girl against her ruin, and to instruct her how to make the most of her beauty. I'll go to her this 110 moment, and sift[5] her. In the mean time, wife, rip out the coronets and marks of these dozen of cambric handkerchiefs, for I can dispose of them this after-noon to a chap[6] in the City.[7]

[3] A coffee-house near the inns-of-court.
[4] Mind it.
[5] Question.
[6] Purchaser.
[7] The older part of London, within the ancient walls.

SCENE V

MRS. PEACHUM.

MRS. PEACH. Never was a man more out of the way in an argument than my husband! Why must our Polly, forsooth, differ from her sex, and love only her husband? And why must Polly's marriage, contrary to all observation, make her the less followed by other men? All men are thieves in love, and like a woman the better for being another's property.

AIR V. *Of all the simple things we do, etc.*

A maid is like the golden [ore],
    Which hath guineas intrinsical in't   10
Whose worth is never known, before
    It is tried and impressed in the mint.
A wife's like a guinea in gold,
    Stamped with the name of her spouse;
Now here, now there; is bought, or is sold;   15
    And is current in every house.

SCENE VI

MRS. PEACHUM, FILCH.

MRS. PEACH. Come hither, Filch. — I am as fond of this child as though my mind misgave me he were my own. He hath as fine a hand at picking a pocket as a woman, and is as nimble-fingered as a juggler. If an unlucky session does not cut the rope of thy 5 life, I pronounce, boy, thou wilt be a great man in history. Where was your post last night, my boy?

FILCH. I plied at the opera, madam; and considering 'twas neither dark nor rainy, so that there was no great hurry in getting chairs and coaches, 10 made a tolerable hand on't. These seven handkerchiefs, madam.

MRS. PEACH. Colored ones, I see. They are of sure sale from our warehouse at Redriff [1] among the seamen.   15

[1] The corrupted pronunciation of Rotherhithe, a district including the London docks.

FILCH. And this snuff-box.

MRS. PEACH. Set in gold! A pretty encouragement this to a young beginner.

FILCH. I had a fair tug at a charming gold watch. Pox take the tailors for making the fobs so deep 20 and narrow! It stuck by the way, and I was forced to make my escape under a coach. Really, madam, I fear I shall be cut off in the flower of my youth, so that every now and then (since I was pumped) [2] I have thoughts of taking up [3] and going to sea. 25

MRS. PEACH. You should go to Hockley in the Hole [4] and to Marybone, child, to learn valor. These are the schools that have bred so many brave men. I thought, boy, by this time thou hadst lost fear as well as shame. Poor lad! how little does he 30 know as yet of the Old Bailey! [5] For the first fact [6] I'll insure thee from being hanged; and going to sea, Filch, will come time enough upon a sentence of transportation. But now, since you have nothing better to do, ev'n go to your book, and learn 35 your catechism; for really a man makes but an ill figure in the ordinary's paper, [7] who cannot give a satisfactory answer to his questions. But, hark you, my lad. Don't tell me a lie; for you know I hate a liar. Do you know of anything that hath passed 40 between Captain Macheath and our Polly?

FILCH. I beg you, madam, don't ask me; for I must either tell a lie to you or to Miss Polly; for I promised her I would not tell.

MRS. PEACH. But when the honor of our fam- 45 ily is concerned —

FILCH. I shall lead a sad life with Miss Polly, if ever she come to know that I told you. Besides, I would not willingly forfeit my own honor by betraying anybody.   50

MRS. PEACH. Yonder comes my husband and Polly. Come, Filch, you shall go with me into my own room, and tell me the whole story. I'll give thee a glass of a most delicious cordial that I keep for my own drinking.   55

SCENE VII

PEACHUM, POLLY.

POLLY. I know as well as any of the fine ladies how to make the most of myself and of my man too. A woman knows how to be mercenary, though she hath never been in a court or at an assembly. We have it in our natures, papa. If I allow Captain 5

[2] Pickpockets were sometimes ducked under a pump when caught by citizens.
[3] Altering my way of life.
[4] A rough quarter on the northern edge of London, best known for its bear-garden.
[5] The chief criminal court, situated next to Newgate Prison.
[6] Crime.
[7] The report of the prison chaplain, who prepared criminals for execution.

Macheath some trifling liberties, I have this watch
and other visible marks of his favor to show for it.
A girl who cannot grant some things, and refuse what
is most material, will make but a poor hand of her
beauty, and soon be thrown upon the common.   10

AIR VI. *What shall I do to show how much I love her?*

Virgins are like the fair flower in its lustre,
　　Which in the garden enamels the ground;
Near it the bees in play flutter and cluster,
　　And gaudy butterflies frolic around.
But, when once plucked, 'tis no longer alluring,   15
　　To Covent Garden [1] 'tis sent, (as yet sweet),
There fades, and shrinks, and grows past all enduring,
　　Rots, stinks, and dies, and is trod under feet.

PEACH. You know, Polly, I am not against your
toying and trifling with a customer in the way   20
of business, or to get out a secret, or so.   But if I
find out that you have played the fool and are married, you jade you, I'll cut your throat, hussy. Now
you know my mind.

SCENE VIII

PEACHUM, POLLY, MRS. PEACHUM.

[1] The site of a market for flowers and vegetables; also a haunt
of prostitutes.

1] O1 om. *have.*

AIR VII. *Oh, London is a fine town.*

MRS. PEACHUM (*in a very great passion*).

Our Polly is a sad slut! nor heeds what we have
　　taught her.
I wonder any man alive will ever rear a daughter!
For she must have both hoods and gowns, and hoops
　　to swell her pride,
With scarfs and stays, and gloves and lace; and she
　　will have men beside;
And when she's dressed with care and cost, all-
　　tempting, fine and gay,   5
As men should serve a cowcumber, she flings herself
　　away.
　　Our Polly is a sad slut, etc.

You baggage, you hussy! you inconsiderate jade! had
you been hanged, it would not have vexed me, for
that might have been your misfortune; but to   10
do such a mad thing by choice! — The wench is
married, husband.

PEACH. Married! The captain is a bold man, and
will risk anything for money; to be sure he believes
her a fortune. — Do you think your mother   15
and I should have lived comfortably so long together,
if ever we had been married? Baggage!

MRS. PEACH. I knew she was always a proud slut;
and now the wench hath played the fool and married, because forsooth she would do like the   20
gentry. Can you support the expense of a husband,
hussy, in gaming, drinking and whoring? have you
money enough to carry on the daily quarrels of man
and wife about who shall squander most? There are
not many husbands and wives who can bear the   25
charges of plaguing one another in a handsome way.
If you must be married, could you introduce nobody
into our family but a highwayman? Why, thou foolish jade, thou wilt be as ill used, and as much neglected, as if thou hadst married a lord!   30

PEACH. Let not your anger, my dear, break
through the rules of decency, for the captain looks
upon himself in the military capacity, as a gentleman
by his profession. Besides what he hath already, I
know he is in a fair way of getting, or of dying;   35
and both these ways, let me tell you, are most excellent

chances for a wife. — Tell me, hussy, are you ruined or no?

MRS. PEACH. With Polly's fortune, she might very well have gone off to a person of distinction. 40 — Yes, that you might, you pouting slut!

PEACH. What, is the wench dumb? Speak, or I'll make you plead by squeezing out an answer from you.[1] Are you really bound wife to him, or are you only upon liking? (*Pinches her.*) 45

POLLY (*screaming*). Oh!

MRS. PEACH. How the mother is to be pitied who hath handsome daughters! Locks, bolts, bars, and lectures of morality are nothing to them; they break through them all. They have as much 50 pleasure in cheating a father and mother as in cheating at cards.

PEACH. Why, Polly, I shall soon know if you are married, by Macheath's keeping from our house.

AIR VIII. *Grim king of the ghosts, etc.*

POLLY. Can love be controlled by advice? 55
    Will Cupid our mothers obey?
Though my heart were as frozen as ice,
    At his flame 'twould have melted away.
When he kissed me so closely he pressed,
    'Twas so sweet that I must have complied: 60
So I thought it both safest and best
    To marry, for fear you should chide.

MRS. PEACH. Then all the hopes of our family are gone for ever and ever!

PEACH. And Macheath may hang his father 65 and mother-in-law, in hope to get into their daughter's fortune.

POLLY. I did not marry him (as 'tis the fashion) coolly and deliberately for honor or money. But, I love him. 70

MRS. PEACH. Love him! worse and worse! I thought the girl had been better bred. O husband,

[1] Accused criminals who refused to plead either guilty or not guilty were sometimes forced to do so by being pressed under heavy weights.

husband! her folly makes me mad! my head swims! I'm distracted! I can't support myself — oh!
(*Faints.*)

PEACH. See, wench, to what a condition you 75 have reduced your poor mother! a glass of cordial, this instant. How the poor woman takes it to heart! (POLLY *goes out and returns with it.*) Ah, hussy, now this is the only comfort your mother has left!

POLLY. Give her another glass, sir; my mama 80 drinks double the quantity whenever she is out of order. — This, you see, fetches her.

MRS. PEACH. The girl shows such a readiness, and so much concern, that I could almost find in my heart to forgive her. 85

AIR IX. *O Jenny, O Jenny, where hast thou been?*

O Polly, you might have toyed and kissed;
    By keeping men off, you keep them on.
POLLY. But he so teased me,
    And he so pleased me,
What I did, you must have done. 90

MRS. PEACH. Not with a highwayman. — You sorry slut!

PEACH. A word with you, wife. [*Aside to* MRS. PEACHUM.] 'Tis no new thing for a wench to take a man without consent of parents. You know 'tis 95 the frailty of woman, my dear.

MRS. PEACH. Yes, indeed, the sex is frail. But the first time a woman is frail, she should be somewhat nice, methinks, for then or never is the time to make her fortune. After that, she hath 100 nothing to do but to guard herself from being found out, and she may do what she pleases.

PEACH. Make yourself a little easy; I have a thought shall soon set all matters again to rights. — Why so melancholy, Polly? since what is done 105 cannot be undone, we must all endeavor to make the best of it.

MRS. PEACH. Well, Polly; as far as one woman can forgive another, I forgive thee. Your father is too fond of you, hussy. 110

POLLY. Then all my sorrows are at an end.

MRS. PEACH. A mighty likely speech, in troth, for a wench who is just married!

AIR X. *Thomas, I cannot, etc.*

POLLY. I, like a ship in storms, was tossed;
　　Yet afraid to put in to land;　　115
　For seized in the port the vessel's lost,
　Whose treasure is contraband.
　　The waves are laid,
　　My duty's paid,
　Oh joy beyond expression!　　120
　　Thus, safe ashore,
　　I ask no more,
　My all is in my possession.

PEACH. I hear customers in t'other room.　Go, talk with 'em, Polly; but come to us again, as　125 soon as they are gone. — But, hark ye, child, if 'tis the gentleman who was here yesterday about the repeating watch, say, you believe we can't get intelligence of it till tomorrow.　For I lent it to Suky Straddle, to make a figure with it tonight at a　130 tavern in Drury Lane.　If t'other gentleman calls for the silver-hilted sword, you know Beetle-browed Jemmy hath it on, and he doth not come from Tunbridge till Tuesday night, so that it cannot be had till then.　　135

SCENE IX

PEACHUM, MRS. PEACHUM.

PEACH. Dear wife, be a little pacified.　Don't let your passion run away with your senses.　Polly, I grant you, hath done a rash thing.

MRS. PEACH. If she had had only an intrigue with the fellow, why the very best families have ex-　5 cused and huddled up a frailty of that sort.　'Tis marriage, husband, that makes it a blemish.

PEACH. But money, wife, is the true fuller's earth for reputations: there is not a spot or a stain but what it can take out.　A rich rogue now-a-days is fit　10 company for any gentleman; and the world, my dear, hath not such a contempt for roguery as you imagine. I tell you, wife, I can make this match turn to our advantage.

MRS. PEACH. I am very sensible, husband,　15 that Captain Macheath is worth money, but I am in doubt whether he hath not two or three wives already, and then if he should die in a session or two, Polly's dower would come into dispute.

PEACH. That, indeed, is a point which ought　20 to be considered.

AIR XI. *A soldier and a sailor.*

A fox may steal your hens, sir,
A whore your health and pence, sir,
Your daughter rob your chest, sir,
Your wife may steal your rest, sir,　　25
　A thief your goods and plate.
But this is all but picking,
With rest, pence, chest, and chicken;
It ever was decreed, sir,
If lawyer's hand is fee'd, sir,　　30
　He steals your whole estate.

The lawyers are bitter enemies to those in our way. They don't care that anybody should get a clandestine livelihood but themselves.

SCENE X

MRS. PEACHUM, PEACHUM, POLLY.

POLLY. 'Twas only Nimming Ned.　He brought in a damask window-curtain, a hoop-petticoat, a pair of silver candlesticks, a periwig, and one silk stocking, from the fire that happened last night.

PEACH. There is not a fellow that is cleverer in　5 his way, and saves more goods out of the fire than Ned.　But now, Polly, to your affair; for matters must not be left as they are.　You are married then, it seems?

POLLY. Yes, sir.　　**10**

PEACH. And how do you propose to live, child?

POLLY. Like other women, sir, upon the industry of my husband.

MRS. PEACH. What, is the wench turned fool? A highwayman's wife, like a soldier's, hath as little 15 of his pay as of his company.

PEACH. And had not you the common views of a gentlewoman in your marriage, Polly?

POLLY. I don't know what you mean, sir.

PEACH. Of a jointure, and of being a widow. 20

POLLY. But I love him, sir: how then could I have thoughts of parting with him?

PEACH. Parting with him! Why, that is the whole scheme and intention of all marriage articles. The comfortable estate of widowhood is the only 25 hope that keeps up a wife's spirits. Where is the woman who would scruple to be a wife, if she had it in her power to be a widow whenever she pleased? If you have any views of this sort, Polly, I shall think the match not so very unreasonable. 30

POLLY. How I dread to hear your advice! Yet I must beg you to explain yourself.

PEACH. Secure what he hath got, have him peached the next sessions, and then at once you are made a rich widow. 35

POLLY. What, murder the man I love! The blood runs cold at my heart with the very thought of it.

PEACH. Fie, Polly! What hath murder to do in the affair? Since the thing sooner or later must happen, I dare say the captain himself would like 40 that we should get the reward for his death sooner than a stranger. Why, Polly, the captain knows that as 'tis his employment to rob, so 'tis ours to take robbers; every man in his business. So that there is no malice in the case. 45

MRS. PEACH. Ay, husband, now you have nicked the matter.[1] To have him peached is the only thing could ever make me forgive her.

AIR XII. *Now ponder well, ye parents dear.*

POLLY. Oh, ponder well! be not severe;
    So save a wretched wife! 50
For on the rope that hangs my dear
    Depends poor Polly's life.

MRS. PEACH. But your duty to your parents,

[1] Hit the mark.

hussy, obliges you to hang him. What would many a wife give for such an opportunity! 55

POLLY. What is a jointure, what is widowhood to me? I know my heart. I cannot survive him.

AIR XIII. *Le printemps rappelle aux armes.*

The turtle[2] thus with plaintive crying,
    Her lover dying,
The turtle thus with plaintive crying, 60
    Laments her dove.
Down she drops, quite spent with sighing,
    Paired in death, as paired in love.

Thus, sir, it will happen to your poor Polly.

MRS. PEACH. What, is the fool in love in 65 earnest then? I hate thee for being particular.[3] Why, wench, thou art a shame to thy very sex.

POLLY. But hear me, mother! If you ever loved —

MRS. PEACH. Those cursed play-books she 70 reads have been her ruin. One word more, hussy, and I shall knock your brains out, if you have any.

PEACH. Keep out of the way, Polly, for fear of mischief, and consider of what is proposed to you.

MRS. PEACH. Away, hussy. Hang your hus- 75 band, and be dutiful.

SCENE XI

MRS. PEACHUM, PEACHUM.

POLLY *listening.*

MRS. PEACH. The thing, husband, must and shall be done. For the sake of intelligence we must take other measures, and have him peached the next session without her consent. If she will not know her duty, we know ours. 5

PEACH. But really, my dear, it grieves one's heart to take off a great man. When I consider his personal bravery, his fine stratagem, how much we have already got by him, and how much more we may get, methinks I can't find in my heart to 10 have a hand in his death. I wish you could have made Polly undertake it.

[2] Turtle-dove.   [3] Fastidious.

MRS. PEACH. But in a case of necessity — our own lives are in danger.

PEACH. Then, indeed, we must comply with 15 the customs of the world, and make gratitude give way to interest. He shall be taken off.

MRS. PEACH. I'll undertake to manage Polly.

PEACH. And I'll prepare matters for the Old Bailey. 20

SCENE XII

POLLY.

Now I'm a wretch, indeed. Methinks I see him already in the cart, sweeter and more lovely than the nosegay in his hand![1] — I hear the crowd extolling his resolution and intrepidity! — What volleys of sighs are sent from the windows of Holborn,[2] that 5 so comely a youth should be brought to disgrace! — I see him at the tree! The whole circle are in tears! — even butchers weep! — Jack Ketch[3] himself hesitates to perform his duty, and would be glad to lose his fee by a reprieve. What then will become 10 of Polly? As yet I may inform him of their design, and aid him in his escape. It shall be so. But then he flies, absents himself, and I bar myself from his dear, dear conversation! that too will distract me. If he keep out of the way, my papa and mama 15 may in time relent, and we may be happy. If he stays, he is hanged, and then he is lost forever! He intended to lie concealed in my room, till the dusk of the evening. If they are abroad, I'll this instant let him out, lest some accident should prevent him. 20

Exit, and returns.

SCENE XIII

POLLY, MACHEATH.

AIR XIV. Pretty Parrot, say.

[1] A condemned criminal, on his way to the gallows, carried a nosegay.

[2] A street leading from Newgate toward the gallows at Tyburn.

[3] A generic name for executioners, after the headsman who became notorious at the time of Monmouth's Rebellion.

AIR XIV. *Pretty Parrot, say, etc.*

MACH.	Pretty Polly, say,
	When I was away,
	Did your fancy never stray
	To some newer lover?
POLLY.	Without disguise, 5
	Heaving sighs,
	Doting eyes,
	My constant heart discover.
	Fondly let me loll!
MACH.	O pretty, pretty Poll. 10

POLLY. And are *you* as fond as ever, my dear?

MACH. Suspect my honor, my courage, suspect anything but my love. May my pistols miss fire, and my mare slip her shoulder while I am pursued, if I ever forsake thee! 15

POLLY. Nay, my dear, I have no reason to doubt you, for I find in the romance you lent me, none of the great heroes were ever false in love.

AIR XV. *Pray, fair one, be kind.*

MACH.	My heart was so free,
	It roved like the bee, 20
	Till Polly my passion requited;
	I sipped each flower,
	I changed ev'ry hour,
	But here ev'ry flower is united.

POLLY. Were you sentenced to transporta- 25 tion, sure, my dear, you could not leave me behind you — could you?

MACH. Is there any power, any force that could tear me from thee? You might sooner tear a pension out of the hands of a courtier, a fee from a 30 lawyer, a pretty woman from a looking glass, or any woman from quadrille. But to tear me from thee is impossible!

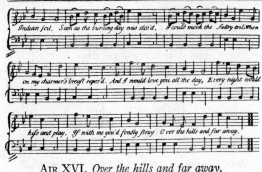

AIR XVI. *Over the hills and far away.*

Were I laid on Greenland's coast,
   And in my arms embraced my lass: 35
Warm amidst eternal frost,
   Too soon the half year's night would pass.
POLLY. Were I sold on Indian soil,
   Soon as the burning day was closed,
I could mock the sultry toil,   40
   When on my charmer's breast reposed.
MACH. And I would love you all the day,
POLLY. Every night would kiss and play,
MACH. If with me you'd fondly stray
POLLY. Over the hills and far away.   45

POLLY. Yes, I would go with thee. But oh! —
how shall I speak it? I must be torn from thee. We
must part.
MACH. How! Part!
POLLY. We must, we must. My papa and   50
mama are set against thy life. They now, even now
are in search after thee. They are preparing evidence against thee. Thy life depends upon a moment.

AIR XVII. *Gin thou wert mine awn thing.*

Oh, what pain it is to part!
   Can I leave thee, can I leave thee?   55
Oh, what pain it is to part!
   Can thy Polly ever leave thee?
But lest death my love should thwart,
   And bring thee to the fatal cart,

Thus I tear thee from my bleeding heart! 60
   Fly hence, and let me leave thee.
One kiss and then — one kiss — begone — farewell.
   MACH. My hand, my heart, my dear, is so riveted
to thine, that I cannot unloose my hold.
   POLLY. But my papa may intercept thee, 65
and then I should lose the very glimmering of hope. A
few weeks, perhaps, may reconcile us all. Shall thy
Polly hear from thee?
   MACH. Must I then go?
   POLLY. And will not absence change your love? 70
   MACH. If you doubt it, let me stay — and be
hanged.
   POLLY. Oh, how I fear! how I tremble! — Go —
but when safety will give you leave, you will be sure
to see me again; for till then Polly is wretched. 75

AIR XVIII. *Oh, the broom, etc.*

(*Parting, and looking back at each other with
fondness; he at one door, she at the other.*)
MACH. The miser thus a shilling sees,
   Which he's obliged to pay,
With sighs resigns it by degrees,
   And fears 'tis gone for aye.
POLLY. The boy, thus, when his sparrow's
      flown, 80
   The bird in silence eyes;
But soon as out of sight 'tis gone,
   Whines, whimpers, sobs and cries.
            [*Exeunt.*]

ACT II

SCENE I

A tavern near Newgate.

JEMMY TWITCHER, CROOK-FINGERED JACK, WAT
   DREARY, ROBIN OF BAGSHOT, NIMMING NED,
   HENRY PADINGTON, MATT OF THE MINT, BEN

BUDGE, *and the rest of the gang, at the table, with wine, brandy and tobacco.*

BEN. But pr'ythee, Matt, what is become of thy brother Tom? I have not seen him since my return from transportation.

MATT. Poor brother Tom had an accident this time twelve-month, and so clever a made fellow 5 he was, that I could not save him from those flaying rascals the surgeons; and now, poor man, he is among the otamys [1] at Surgeons' Hall.

BEN. So it seems, his time was come.

JEM. But the present time is ours, and no- 10 body alive hath more. Why are the laws levelled at us? Are we more dishonest than the rest of mankind? What we win, gentlemen, is our own by the law of arms and the right of conquest.

CROOK. Where shall we find such another set 15 of practical philosophers, who to a man are above the fear of death?

WAT. Sound men, and true!

ROBIN. Of tried courage, and indefatigable industry! 20

NED. Who is there here that would not die for his friend?

HARRY. Who is there here that would betray him for his interest?

MATT. Show me a gang of courtiers that can 25 say as much.

BEN. We are for a just partition of the world, for every man hath a right to enjoy life.

MATT. We retrench the superfluities of mankind. The world is avaricious, and I hate avarice. A 30 covetous fellow, like a jackdaw, steals what he was never made to enjoy, for the sake of hiding it. These are the robbers of mankind, for money was made for the free-hearted and generous; and where is the injury of taking from another what he hath not 35 the heart to make use of?

JEM. Our several stations for the day are fixed. Good luck attend us all. Fill the glasses.

AIR XIX. *Fill ev'ry glass, etc.*

MATT. Fill ev'ry glass, for wine inspires us,
And fires us, 40
With courage, love and joy.

[1] For 'atomies' — anatomized bodies or skeletons.

Women and wine should life employ.
Is there aught else on earth desirous?
CHORUS. Fill ev'ry glass, etc.

SCENE II

To them enter MACHEATH.

MACH. Gentlemen, well met. My heart hath been with you this hour; but an unexpected affair hath detained me. No ceremony, I beg you.

MATT. We were just breaking up to go upon duty. Am I to have the honor of taking the air with 5 you, sir, this evening upon the heath? I drink a dram now and then with the stage-coachmen in the way of friendship and intelligence, and I know that about this time there will be passengers upon the western road [2] who are worth speaking with. 10

MACH. I was to have been of that party — but —

MATT. But what, sir?

MACH. Is there any man who suspects my courage?

MATT. We have all been witnesses of it.

MACH. My honor and truth to the gang? 15

MATT. I'll be answerable for it.

MACH. In the division of our booty, have I ever shown the least marks of avarice or injustice?

MATT. By these questions something seems to have ruffled you. Are any of us suspected? 20

MACH. I have a fixed confidence, gentlemen, in you all, as men of honor, and as such I value and respect you. Peachum is a man that is useful to us.

MATT. Is he about to play us any foul play? I'll shoot him through the head. 25

MACH. I beg you, gentlemen, act with conduct and discretion. A pistol is your last resort.

MATT. He knows nothing of this meeting.

MACH. Business cannot go on without him. He is a man who knows the world, and is a necessary 30 agent to us. We have had a slight difference, and till it is accommodated I shall be obliged to keep out of his way. Any private dispute of mine shall be of no ill consequence to my friends. You must continue to act under his direction, for the moment we break 35 loose from him, our gang is ruined.

MATT. As a bawd to a whore, I grant you, he is to us of great convenience.

MACH. Make him believe I have quitted the gang, which I can never do but with life. At our pri- 40 vate quarters I will continue to meet you. A week or so will probably reconcile us.

MATT. Your instructions shall be observed. 'Tis now high time for us to repair to our several duties; so till the evening at our quarters in Moorfields [3] 45 we bid you farewell.

[2] The road through Bagshot Heath; cf. 'Robin of Bagshot.'
[3] A district outside Moorgate, on the northeastern edge of London, frequented by the lower classes.

MACH. I shall wish myself with you.   Success attend you!   (*Sits down melancholy at the table.*)

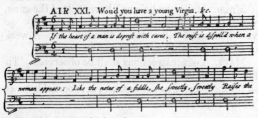

AIR XX. *March in Rinaldo,[1] with drums and trumpets.*

MATT. Let us take the road.

> Hark! I hear the sound of coaches!   50
> The hour of attack approaches,
> To your arms, brave boys, and load!
> See the ball I hold!
> Let the chymists toil like asses,
> Our fire their fire surpasses,   55
> And turns all our lead to gold.

The gang, ranged in the front of the stage, load their pistols, and stick them under their girdles; then go off singing the first part in chorus.

SCENE III

MACHEATH, *Drawer*.

MACH. What a fool is a fond wench!   Polly is most confoundedly bit.   I love the sex.   And a man who loves money might as well be contented with one guinea, as I with one woman.   The town perhaps hath been as much obliged to me, for re-   5 cruiting it with free-hearted ladies, as to any recruiting officer in the army.   If it were not for us and the other gentlemen of the sword, Drury Lane[2] would be uninhabited.

AIR XXI. *Would you have a young virgin, etc.*

> If the heart of a man is depressed with cares,   10
> The mist is dispelled when a woman appears;
>   Like the notes of a fiddle, she sweetly, sweetly
> Raises the spirits, and charms our ears.
>   Roses and lilies her cheeks disclose,
>   But her ripe lips are more sweet than those,   15
>   Press her,
>   Caress her
>   With blisses,
>   Her kisses
> Dissolve us in pleasure, and soft repose.   20

I must have women.   There is nothing unbends the mind like them.   Money is not so strong a cordial for the time. — Drawer!   (*Enter Drawer.*)   Is the porter gone for all the ladies, according to my directions?

DRAW. I expect him back every minute.   25 But you know, sir, you sent him as far as Hockley in the Hole for three of the ladies, for one in Vinegar Yard, and for the rest of them somewhere about Lewkner's Lane.[3]   Sure some of them are below, for I hear the bar bell.   As they come I will show   30 them up. — Coming! coming!

SCENE IV

MACHEATH, MRS. COAXER, DOLLY TRULL, MRS. VIXEN, BETTY DOXY, JENNY DIVER, MRS. SLAMMEKIN, SUKY TAWDRY, *and* MOLLY BRAZEN.

MACH. Dear Mrs. Coaxer, you are welcome.   You look charmingly today.   I hope you don't want the repairs of quality, and lay on paint. — Dolly Trull! kiss me, you slut; are you as amorous as ever, hussy?   You are always so taken up with stealing hearts,   5 that you don't allow yourself time to steal anything else.   Ah Dolly, thou wilt ever be a coquette. — Mrs. Vixen, I'm yours; I always loved a woman of wit and spirit; they make charming mistresses, but plaguy wives. — Betty Doxy! come hither,   10 hussy.   Do you drink as hard as ever?   You had

---

[1] An opera by Händel (1711).
[2] A street close to Covent Garden, well-known as a resort for prostitutes.

[3] The two last-named streets, near St. Giles's Church and Drury Lane, respectively, were both quarters of ill-repute, like Hockley in the Hole.

52] Q (in engraved music) *T'your arms.*

better stick to good wholesome beer; for in troth, Betty, strong waters will in time ruin your constitution. You should leave those to your betters. — What! and my pretty Jenny Diver too! As 15 prim and demure as ever! There is not any prude, though ever so high bred, hath a more sanctified look, with a more mischievous heart. Ah! thou art a dear artful hypocrite. — Mrs. Slammekin! as careless and genteel as ever! all you fine ladies, who know 20 your own beauty, affect an undress. — But see, here's Suky Tawdry come to contradict what I was saying. Everything she gets one way, she lays out upon her back. Why, Suky, you must keep at least a dozen tally-men.[1] — Molly Brazen! (*She* 25 *kisses him.*) That's well done. I love a free-hearted wench. Thou hast a most agreeable assurance, girl, and art as willing as a turtle. But hark! I hear music. The harper is at the door. 'If music be the food of love, play on.'[2] Ere you seat yourselves, 30 ladies, what think you of a dance? — Come in. (*Enter Harper.*) Play the French tune, that Mrs. Slammekin was so fond of.

(*A dance à la ronde in the French manner; near the end of it this song and chorus.*)

AIR XXII. *Cotillon.*

Youth's the season made for joys,
　　Love is then our duty; 35
She alone who that employs,
　　Well deserves her beauty.
　　　　Let's be gay,
　　　　While we may,

Beauty's a flower, despised in decay. 40
　　Youth's the season, etc.

Let us drink and sport today,
　　Ours is not tomorrow.
Love with youth flies swift away,
　　Age is nought but sorrow. 45
　　　　Dance and sing,
　　　　Time's on the wing,
Life never knows the return of spring.
CHORUS. Let us drink, etc.

MACH. Now, pray ladies, take your places. — 50 Here, fellow. (*Pays the Harper.*) Bid the drawer bring us more wine. (*Exit Harper.*) If any of the ladies choose gin, I hope they will be so free to call for it.

JENNY. You look as if you meant me. Wine 55 is strong enough for me. Indeed, sir, I never drink strong waters, but when I have the colic.

MACH. Just the excuse of the fine ladies! Why, a lady of quality is never without the colic. — I hope, Mrs. Coaxer, you have had good success of late 60 in your visits among the mercers.

COAX. We have so many interlopers! — yet, with industry, one may still have a little picking. I carried a silver-flowered lutestring[2] and a piece of black padesoy to Mr. Peachum's lock but last week. 65

VIX. There's Molly Brazen hath the ogle of a rattlesnake. She riveted a linen-draper's eye so fast upon her, that he was nicked[3] of three pieces of cambric before he could look off.

BRAZ. O dear madam! But sure nothing 70 can come up to your handling of laces! And then you have such a sweet deluding tongue! To cheat a man is nothing; but the woman must have fine parts indeed who cheats a woman!

VIX. Lace, madam, lies in a small compass, 75 and is of easy conveyance. But you are apt, madam, to think too well of your friends.

COAX. If any woman hath more art than another, to be sure, 'tis Jenny Diver. Though her fellow be never so agreeable, she can pick his pocket as 80 coolly as if money were her only pleasure. Now that is a command of the passions uncommon in a woman!

JENNY. I never go to the tavern with a man, but in the view of business. I have other hours, and other sort of men for my pleasure. But had I 85 your address, madam ——

MACH. Have done with your compliments, ladies; and drink about. — You are not so fond of me, Jenny, as you used to be.

JENNY. 'Tis not convenient, sir, to show my 90 fondness among so many rivals. 'Tis your own choice, and not the warmth of my inclination that will determine you.

---

[1] Merchants who sell goods on credit.
[2] The opening line of *Twelfth Night.*

[2] A silk fabric, as is padesoy.
[3] Cheated.

AIR XXIII. *All in a misty morning.*

Before the barn-door crowing,
  The cock by hens attended,   95
His eyes around him throwing,
  Stands for a while suspended.
Then one he singles from the crew,
  And cheers the happy hen;
With how do you do, and how do you do, 100
  And how do you do again.

MACH. Ah Jenny! thou art a dear slut.

TRULL. Pray, madam, were you ever in keeping?

TAWD. I hope, madam, I han't been so long upon
the town, but I have met with some good for- 105
tune as well as my neighbors.

TRULL. Pardon me, madam, I meant no harm by
the question; 'twas only in the way of conversation.

TAWD. Indeed, madam, if I had not been a fool, I
might have lived very handsomely with my last 110
friend. But upon his missing five guineas, he turned
me off. Now I never suspected he had counted them.

SLAM. Who do you look upon, madam, as your
best sort of keepers?

TRULL. That, madam, is thereafter as they 115
be.

SLAM. I, madam, was once kept by a Jew; and
bating their religion, to women they are a good sort
of people.

TAWD. Now for my part, I own I like an old 120
fellow; for we always make them pay for what they
can't do.

VIX. A spruce prentice, let me tell you, ladies, is
no ill thing: they bleed freely. I have sent at least
two or three dozen of them in my time to the 125
plantations.

JENNY. But to be sure, sir, with so much good
fortune as you have had upon the road, you must be
grown immensely rich.

MACH. The road, indeed, hath done me jus- 130
tice, but the gaming-table hath been my ruin.

**AIR XXIV. *When once I lay with another man's
wife.***

JENNY. The gamesters and lawyers are jugglers
alike,
  If they meddle, your all is in danger:
Like gypsies, if once they can finger a souse,[1]
Your pockets they pick, and they pilfer your
  house,   135
And give your estate to a stranger.

A man of courage should never put anything to the
risk but his life. (*She takes up his pistol.*) These are
the tools of a man of honor. Cards and dice are only
fit for cowardly cheats, who prey upon their 140
friends.   (*TAWDRY takes up the other [pistol].*)

TAWD. This, sir, is fitter for your hand. Besides
your loss of money, 'tis a loss to the ladies. Gaming
takes you off from women. How fond could I be of
you! but before company, 'tis ill-bred. 145

MACH. Wanton hussies!

JENNY. I must and will have a kiss to give my
wine a zest.

  (*They take him about the neck, and make signs
  to PEACHUM and Constables, who rush in
  upon him.*)

SCENE V

To them, PEACHUM *and Constables.*

PEACH. I seize you, sir, as my prisoner.

MACH. Was this well done, Jenny? — Women are
decoy ducks; who can trust them! Beasts, jades,
jilts, harpies, furies, whores!

PEACH. Your case, Mr. Macheath, is not par- 5
ticular. The greatest heroes have been ruined by
women. But, to do them justice, I must own they
are a pretty sort of creatures, if we could trust them.
You must now, sir, take your leave of the ladies, and
if they have a mind to make you a visit, they will 10
be sure to find you at home. The gentleman, ladies,
lodges in Newgate. Constables, wait upon the captain to his lodgings.

---

[1] Lay hands on a sou.

100-101] Q (in engraved music) *d'you do and how d'you do And how d'you do.*   137-138] O1 om. *A man . . . life.*

all kinds of ill. *I shall find no such Furies as these are.*

AIR XXV. *When first I laid siege to my Chloris.*

MACH. At the tree [1] I shall suffer with pleasure,
At the tree I shall suffer with pleasure.　　15
　　Let me go where I will,
　　In all kinds of ill,
I shall find no such furies as these are.

PEACH. Ladies, I'll take care the reckoning shall
be discharged.　　20

Exit MACHEATH, *guarded, with* PEACHUM *and
Constables.*

SCENE VI

The Women remain.

VIX. Look ye, Mrs. Jenny, though Mr. Peachum
may have made a private bargain with you and Suky
Tawdry for betraying the captain, as we were all
assisting, we ought all to share alike.

COAX. I think Mr. Peachum, after so long an　　5
acquaintance, might have trusted me as well as
Jenny Diver.

SLAM. I am sure at least three men of his hanging,
and in a year's time too (if he did me justice) should
be set down to my account.　　10

TRULL. Mrs. Slammekin, that is not fair. For
you know one of them was taken in bed with me.

JENNY. As far as a bowl of punch or a treat, I
believe Mrs. Suky will join with me. As for anything else, ladies, you cannot in conscience ex-　　15
pect it.

SLAM. [*inviting* TRULL *to precede her in leaving the
room*]. Dear madam ——

TRULL. I would not for the world ——
SLAM. 'Tis impossible for me ——　　20
TRULL. As I hope to be saved, madam ——
SLAM. Nay, then I must stay here all night.
TRULL. Since you command me.

Exeunt with great ceremony.

SCENE VII

Newgate.

LOCKIT, *Turnkeys,* MACHEATH, *Constables.*

LOCK. Noble captain, you are welcome. You
have not been a lodger of mine this year and half.
You know the custom, sir. Garnish,[2] captain, garnish. [*To Turnkey.*] Hand me down those fetters
there.　　5

MACH. Those, Mr. Lockit, seem to be the heaviest
of the whole set! With your leave, I should like the
further pair better.

---

[1] Gallows.
[2] A gratuity exacted from a new prisoner for the benefit of
older prisoners and the jailor.

LOCK. Look ye, captain, we know what is fittest
for our prisoners. When a gentleman uses me　　10
with civility, I always do the best I can to please
him. — Hand them down, I say. — We have them
of all prices, from one guinea to ten, and 'tis fitting
every gentleman should please himself.

MACH. I understand you, sir. (*Gives money.*)　　15
The fees here are so many, and so exorbitant, that
few fortunes can bear the expense of getting off handsomely, or of dying like a gentleman.

LOCK. Those, I see, will fit the captain better.
Take down the further pair. — Do but examine　　20
them, sir — never was better work. How genteelly
they are made! They will fit as easy as a glove, and
the nicest man in England might not be ashamed to
wear them. (*He puts on the chains.*) If I had the
best gentleman in the land in my custody I could　　25
not equip him more handsomely. And so, sir — I
now leave you to your private meditations.

SCENE VIII

MACHEATH.

AIR XXVI. Courtiers, Courtiers, think it no harm.

*Man may escape from rope and gun; Nay, some have out-liv'd the
Doctor's pill: Who takes a woman must be undone, that Basi-lisk is
sure to kill. The Fly that sips treacle is lost in the sweets, so
he that tastes Woman, Woman, Woman, he that tastes Woman, ruin meets.*

AIR XXVI. *Courtiers, courtiers, think it no harm.*

Man may escape from rope and gun;
　　Nay, some have out-lived the doctor's pill;
Who takes a woman must be undone,
　　That basilisk is sure to kill.
The fly that sips treacle is lost in the sweets,　　5
　　So he that tastes woman, woman, woman,
He that tastes woman, ruin meets.

To what a woeful plight have I brought myself!
Here must I (all day long, till I am hanged) be confined to hear the reproaches of a wench who lays　　10
her ruin at my door. I am in the custody of her
father, and to be sure, if he knows of the matter I shall
have a fine time on't betwixt this and my execution. — But I promised the wench marriage. —
What signifies a promise to a woman? does not　　15
man in marriage itself promise a hundred things that
he never means to perform? Do all we can, women

will believe us; for they look upon a promise as an excuse for following their own inclinations. — But here comes Lucy, and I cannot get from her. 20 Would I were deaf!

SCENE IX

MACHEATH, LUCY.

LUCY. You base man, you, how can you look me in the face after what hath passed between us? See here, perfidious wretch, how I am forced to bear about the load of infamy you have laid upon me — O Macheath! thou hast robbed me of my quiet — 5 to see thee tortured would give me pleasure.

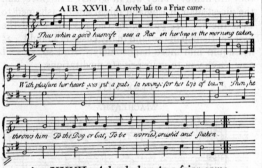

AIR XXVII. *A lovely lass to a friar came.*

Thus when a good huswife sees a rat
  In her trap in the morning taken,
With pleasure her heart goes pit-a-pat
  In revenge for her loss of bacon.   10
    Then she throws him
    To the dog or cat,
  To be worried, crushed and shaken.

MACH. Have you no bowels, no tenderness, my dear Lucy, to see a husband in these circum- 15 stances?

LUCY. A husband!

MACH. In every respect but the form, and that, my dear, may be said over us at any time. Friends should not insist upon ceremonies. From a 20 man of honor, his word is as good as his bond.

LUCY. 'Tis the pleasure of all you fine men to insult the women you have ruined.

AIR XXVIII. *'Twas when the sea was roaring.*

How cruel are the traitors,
  Who lie and swear in jest,   25
To cheat unguarded creatures
  Of virtue, fame, and rest!
Whoever steals a shilling
  Through shame the guilt conceals;
In love the perjured villain   30
  With boasts the theft reveals.

MACH. The very first opportunity, my dear (have but patience) you shall be my wife in whatever manner you please.

LUCY. Insinuating monster! And so you 35 think I know nothing of the affair of Miss Polly Peachum. — I could tear thy eyes out!

MACH. Sure, Lucy, you can't be such a fool as to be jealous of Polly!

LUCY. Are you not married to her, you brute, 40 you?

MACH. Married! Very good! The wench gives it out only to vex thee, and to ruin me in thy good opinion. 'Tis true I go to the house; I chat with the girl, I kiss her, I say a thousand things to 45 her (as all gentlemen do) that mean nothing, to divert myself; and now the silly jade hath set it about that I am married to her, to let me know what she would be at. Indeed, my dear Lucy, these vio- lent passions may be of ill consequence to a 50 woman in your condition.

LUCY. Come, come, captain, for all your assur- ance, you know that Miss Polly hath put it out of your power to do me the justice you promised me.

MACH. A jealous woman believes everything 55 her passion suggests. To convince you of my sin- cerity, if we can find the ordinary, I shall have no scruples of making you my wife; and I know the con- sequence of having two at a time.

LUCY. That you are only to be hanged, and 60 so get rid of them both.

MACH. I am ready, my dear Lucy, to give you satisfaction — if you think there is any in marriage. What can a man of honor say more?

LUCY. So then it seems, you are not married 65 to Miss Polly.

MACH. You know, Lucy, the girl is prodigiously conceited. No man can say a civil thing to her, but (like other fine ladies) her vanity makes her think he's her own for ever and ever. 70

AIR XXIX. *The sun had loosed his weary teams.*

The first time at the looking-glass
  The mother sets her daughter,
The image strikes the smiling lass
  With self-love ever after.
Each time she looks, she, fonder grown,   75
  Thinks ev'ry charm grows stronger.
But alas, vain maid, all eyes but your own
  Can see you are not younger.

When women consider their own beauties, they are
all alike unreasonable in their demands; for they   80
expect their lovers should like them as long as they
like themselves.

Lucy. Yonder is my father — perhaps this way
we may light upon the ordinary, who shall try if you
will be as good as your word. For I long to be   85
made an honest woman.

SCENE X

PEACHUM, LOCKIT *with an account-book.*

Lock. In this last affair, brother Peachum, we are
agreed. You have consented to go halves in
Macheath.

Peach. We shall never fall out about an execution. But as to that article, pray how stands our   5
last year's account?

Lock. If you will run your eye over it, you'll find
'tis fair and clearly stated.

Peach. This long arrear of the government is
very hard upon us! Can it be expected that we   10
should hang our acquaintance for nothing, when our
betters will hardly save theirs without being paid for
it? Unless the people in employment pay better,
I promise them for the future, I shall let other
rogues live besides their own.   15

Lock. Perhaps, brother, they are afraid these
matters may be carried too far. We are treated too
by them with contempt, as if our profession were not
reputable.

Peach. In one respect, indeed, our employ-   20
ment may be reckoned dishonest, because, like great
statesmen, we encourage those who betray their
friends.

Lock. Such language, brother, anywhere else
might turn to your prejudice. Learn to be   25
more guarded, I beg you.

AIR XXX. *How happy are we, etc.*

When you censure the age,
  Be cautious and sage,
Lest the courtiers offended should be.
  If you mention vice or bribe,   30
    'Tis so pat to all the tribe;
  Each cries — 'That was levelled at me.'

Peach. Here's poor Ned Clincher's[1] name, I see.
Sure, brother Lockit, there was a little unfair proceeding in Ned's case; for he told me in the   35
condemned hold, that for value received, you had
promised him a session or two longer without moles-
tation.

Lock. Mr. Peachum, — this is the first time my
honor was ever called in question.   40

Peach. Business is at an end — if once we act dis-
honorably.

Lock. Who accuses me?

Peach. You are warm, brother.

Lock. He that attacks my honor, attacks my   45
livelihood. And this usage — sir — is not to be
borne.

Peach. Since you provoke me to speak, I must
tell you too, that Mrs. Coaxer charges you with
defrauding her of her information-money, for   50
the apprehending of Curl-pated Hugh. Indeed, indeed, brother, we must punctually pay our spies, or
we shall have no information.

Lock. Is this language to me, sirrah — who have
saved you from the gallows, sirrah?   55
       (*Collaring each other.*)

Peach. If I am hanged, it shall be for ridding the
world of an arrant rascal.

Lock. This hand shall do the office of the halter
you deserve, and throttle you — you dog!

Peach. Brother, brother — we are both in   60
the wrong — we shall be both losers in the dispute —
for you know we have it in our power to hang each
other. You should not be so passionate.

Lock. Nor you so provoking.

Peach. 'Tis our mutual interest; 'tis for the   65
interest of the world we should agree. If I said any-

---

[1] 'Clinch' is thieves' slang for a prison cell, especially for the
'condemned hold,' reserved for prisoners sentenced to death.

thing, brother, to the prejudice of your character, I ask pardon.

LOCK. Brother Peachum — I can forgive as well as resent.   Give me your hand.   Suspicion does   70 not become a friend.

PEACH. I only meant to give you occasion to justify yourself.   But I must now step home, for I expect the gentleman about this snuff-box, that Filch nimmed two nights ago in the park.   I ap-   75 pointed him at this hour.

SCENE XI

LOCKIT, LUCY.

LOCK. Whence come you, hussy!

LUCY. My tears might answer that question.

LOCK. You have then been whimpering and fondling, like a spaniel, over the fellow that hath abused you.   5

LUCY. One can't help love; one can't cure it.   'Tis not in my power to obey you, and hate him.

LOCK. Learn to bear your husband's death like a reasonable woman.   'Tis not the fashion, now-a-days, so much as to affect sorrow upon these oc-   10 casions.   No woman would ever marry, if she had not the chance of mortality for a release.   Act like a woman of spirit, hussy, and thank your father for what he is doing.

AIR XXXI. *Of a noble race was Shenkin.*

[LUCY.] Is then his fate decreed, sir?   15
    Such a man can I think of quitting?
    When first we met, so moves me yet,
    Oh, see how my heart is splitting!

LOCK. Look ye, Lucy — there is no saving him. — So, I think, you must ev'n do like other widows   20 — buy yourself weeds, and be cheerful.

AIR XXXII.

AIR XXXII.[1]

You'll think, [ere] many days ensue,
    This sentence not severe;
I hang your husband, child, 'tis true,
    But with him hang your care.   25
    Twang dang dillo dee.

Like a good wife, go moan over your dying husband. That, child, is your duty — consider, girl, you can't have the man and the money too — so make yourself as easy as you can by getting all you can   30 from him.

SCENE XII

LUCY, MACHEATH.

LUCY. Though the ordinary was out of the way today, I hope, my dear, you will, upon the first opportunity, quiet my scruples.   Oh, sir! — my father's hard heart is not to be softened, and I am in the utmost despair.   5

MACH. But if I could raise a small sum — would not twenty guineas, think you, move him?   Of all the arguments in the way of business, the perquisite is the most prevailing.   Your father's perquisites for the escape of prisoners must amount to a con-   10 siderable sum in the year.   Money well timed and properly applied will do anything.

AIR XXXIII. *London ladies.*

If you at an office solicit your due,
    And would not have matters neglected;
You must quicken the clerk with the perquisite too,   15
    To do what his duty directed.

[1] This air and Air XXXVII are the only two in the opera without names.

Or would you the frowns of a lady prevent,
  She too has this palpable failing,
The perquisite softens her into consent;
  That reason with all is prevailing.   20

LUCY. What love or money can do shall be done:
for all my comfort depends upon your safety.

SCENE XIII

LUCY, MACHEATH, POLLY.

POLLY. Where is my dear husband? — Was a rope
ever intended for this neck! Oh, let me throw my
arms about it, and throttle thee with love! — Why
dost thou turn away from me? — 'Tis thy Polly —
'tis thy wife.   5

MACH. Was ever such an unfortunate rascal as
I am!

LUCY. Was there ever such another villain!

POLLY. O Macheath! was it for this we parted?
Taken! imprisoned! tried! hanged! — cruel re-   10
flection! I'll stay with thee till death — no force
shall tear thy dear wife from thee now. — What
means my love? — not one kind word! not one kind
look! think what thy Polly suffers to see thee in this
condition.   15

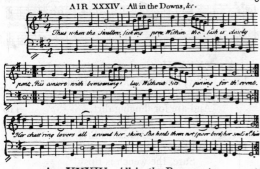

AIR XXXIV. *All in the Downs,* etc.

AIR XXXIV. *All in the Downs, etc.*

Thus when the swallow, seeking prey,
  Within the sash is closely pent,
His consort, with bemoaning lay,
  Without sits pining for th' event.
Her chatt'ring lovers all around her skim;   20
She heeds them not (poor bird!) — her soul's with
    him.

MACH. (*aside*). I must disown her. [*To* LUCY.]
The wench is distracted.

LUCY. Am I then bilked of my virtue? Can I
have no reparation? Sure, men were born to lie,   25
and women to believe them. O villain! villain!

POLLY. Am I not thy wife? Thy neglect of me,
thy aversion to me, too severely proves it. Look on
me. Tell me, am I not thy wife?

LUCY. Perfidious wretch!   30

POLLY. Barbarous husband!

LUCY. Hadst thou been hanged five months ago,
I had been happy.

POLLY. And I too. If you had been kind to me
till death, it would not have vexed me — and   35
that's no very unreasonable request (though from a
wife), to a man who hath not above seven or eight
days to live.

LUCY. Art thou then married to another? Hast
thou two wives, monster?   40

MACH. If women's tongues can cease for an
answer — hear me.

LUCY. I won't. Flesh and blood can't bear my
usage.

POLLY. Shall I not claim my own? Justice   45
bids me speak.

AIR XXXV. *Have you heard of a frolicsome ditty?*

MACH. How happy could I be with either,
      Were t'other dear charmer away!
    But while you thus tease me together,
      To neither a word will I say: 50
    But tol de rol, etc.

POLLY. Sure, my dear, there ought to be some
preference shown to a wife! At least she may claim
the appearance of it. He must be distracted with
his misfortunes, or he could not use me thus!   55

LUCY. O villain, villain! thou hast deceived me —
I could even inform against thee with pleasure. Not
a prude wishes more heartily to have facts against
her intimate acquaintance, than I now wish to have
facts against thee. I would have her satisfac-   60
tion, and they should all out.

AIR XXXVI. *Irish trot.*

POLLY. I'm bubbled.[1]
LUCY. —— I'm bubbled.
POLLY. Oh, how I am troubled!
LUCY. Bamboozled, and bit!

[1] Cheated.

POLY. —— My distresses are doubled.

LUCY. When you come to the tree, should the hangman refuse, 65
These fingers, with pleasure, could fasten the noose.

POLLY. I'm bubbled, etc.

MACH. Be pacified, my dear Lucy — this is all a fetch[1] of Polly's to make me desperate with you in case I get off. If I am hanged, she would fain 70 have the credit of being thought my widow.—Really, Polly, this is no time for a dispute of this sort; for whenever you are talking of marriage, I am thinking of hanging.

POLLY. And hast thou the heart to persist in 75 disowning me?

MACH. And hast thou the heart to persist in persuading me that I am married? Why, Polly, dost thou seek to aggravate my misfortunes?

LUCY. Really, Miss Peachum, you but ex- 80 pose yourself. Besides, 'tis barbarous in you to worry a gentleman in his circumstances.

AIR XXXVII.

POLLY.   Cease your funning,
          Force or cunning
Never shall my heart trapan.[2]   85
          All these sallies
          Are but malice
To seduce my constant man.
          'Tis most certain,
          By their flirting,   90
Women oft have envy shown;
          Pleased, to ruin
          Others' wooing;
Never happy in their own!

POLLY. Decency, madam, methinks, might 95 teach you to behave yourself with some reserve with the husband, while his wife is present.

MACH. But, seriously, Polly, this is carrying the joke a little too far.

[1] Trick.   [2] Beguile.

LUCY. If you are determined, madam, to 100 raise a disturbance in the prison, I shall be obliged to send for the turnkey to show you the door. I am sorry, madam, you force me to be so ill-bred.

POLLY. Give me leave to tell you, madam, these forward airs don't become you in the least, 105 madam. And my duty, madam, obliges me to stay with my husband, madam.

AIR XXXVIII. *Good-morrow, gossip Joan.*

LUCY.   Why, how now, Madam Flirt?
              If you thus must chatter;
         And are for flinging dirt,   110
              Let's try who best can spatter!
                   Madam Flirt!
POLLY.   Why, how now, saucy jade;
              Sure, the wench is tipsy!
         (*To him.*) How can you see me made 115
              The scoff of such a gipsy?
                   (*To her.*) Saucy jade!

SCENE XIV

LUCY, MACHEATH, POLLY, PEACHUM.

PEACH. Where's my wench? — Ah, hussy! hussy! Come you home, you slut; and when your fellow is hanged, hang yourself, to make your family some amends.

POLLY. Dear, dear father, do not tear me from 5 him — I must speak; I have more to say to him. — Oh! twist thy fetters about me, that he may not haul me from thee!

PEACH. Sure all women are alike! If ever they commit the folly, they are sure to commit an- 10 other by exposing themselves. — Away — not a word more — you are my prisoner now, hussy.

AIR XXXIX. *Irish howl.*

POLLY. No power on earth can e'er divide
    The knot that sacred love hath tied.
  When parents draw against our mind, 15
    The true-love's knot they faster bind.
  [Ho ho ra in ambora,
    Ho an ho derry,
    Hi an hi derry,
    Hoo, hoo, derry, derry, derry, 20
    Derry ambora.]

(*Holding* MACHEATH, PEACHUM *pulling her.*)

SCENE XV

LUCY, MACHEATH.

MACH. I am naturally compassionate, wife, so that I could not use the wench as she deserved; which made you at first suspect there was something in what she said.

LUCY. Indeed, my dear, I was strangely 5 puzzled.

MACH. If that had been the case, her father would never have brought me into this circumstance. No, Lucy, I had rather die than be false to thee.

LUCY. How happy am I if you say this from 10 your heart! For I love thee so, that I could sooner bear to see thee hanged than in the arms of another.

MACH. But couldst thou bear to see me hanged?

LUCY. O Macheath, I can never live to see that day. 15

MACH. You see, Lucy, in the account of love you are in my debt, and you must now be convinced that I rather choose to die than be another's. Make me, if possible, love thee more, and let me owe my life to thee — if you refuse to assist me, Peachum and 20 your father will immediately put me beyond all means of escape.

LUCY. My father, I know, hath been drinking hard with the prisoners, and I fancy he is now taking his nap in his own room. If I can procure the 25 keys, shall I go off with thee, my dear?

MACH. If we are together, 'twill be impossible to lie concealed. As soon as the search begins to be a little cool, I will send to thee — till then my heart is thy prisoner. 30

LUCY. Come then, my dear husband — owe thy life to me — and though you love me not, be grateful — But that Polly runs in my head strangely.

MACH. A moment of time may make us unhappy forever. 35

AIR XL. *The lass of Patie's mill.*

LUCY. I like the fox shall grieve,
    Whose mate hath left her side,
    Whom hounds, from morn to eve,
    Chase o'er the country wide.
  Where can my lover hide? 40
    Where cheat the wary pack?
  If love be not his guide,
    He never will come back!   [*Exeunt.*]

ACT III

SCENE I

Newgate.

LOCKIT, LUCY.

LOCK. To be sure, wench, you must have been aiding and abetting to help him to this escape.

LUCY. Sir, here hath been Peachum and his daughter Polly, and to be sure they know the ways of Newgate as well as if they had been born and 5 bred in the place all their lives. Why must all your suspicion light upon me?

LOCK. Lucy, Lucy, I will have none of these shuffling answers.

LUCY. Well then — if I know anything of 10 him I wish I may be burnt!

AIR XXXIX] Q (in engraved music) *AIR XXX.* How happy are we, etc.
17–21] O1O2Q *Oh, oh ray, oh amborah* — *Oh, oh, etc.*; bracketed passage supplied from Q (engraved music).
SCENE XV. 41] O1 (and some copies of O2) *weary pack.*

Lock. Keep your temper, Lucy, or I shall pronounce you guilty.

Lucy. Keep yours, sir. I do wish I may be burnt. I do! — and what can I say more to convince 15 you?

Lock. Did he tip handsomely? How much did he come down with? Come, hussy, don't cheat your father, and I shall not be angry with you. Perhaps you have made a better bargain with 20 him than I could have done. How much, my good girl?

Lucy. You know, sir, I am fond of him, and would have given money to have kept him with me.

Lock. Ah, Lucy! thy education might have 25 put thee more upon thy guard; for a girl in the bar of an ale-house is always besieged.

Lucy. Dear sir, mention not my education — for 'twas to that I owe my ruin.

Air XLI. *If love's a sweet passion, etc.*

When young at the bar you first taught me to
　　score,　　　　　　　　　　　　　　　　　30
And bid me be free of my lips, and no more;
I was kissed by the parson, the squire, and the sot.
When the guest was departed, the kiss was forgot.
But his kiss was so sweet, and so closely he pressed,
That I languished and pined till I granted the
　　rest.　　　　　　　　　　　　　　　　　35

If you can forgive me, sir, I will make a fair confession, for to be sure, he hath been a most barbarous villain to me.

Lock. And so you have let him escape, hussy — have you?　　　　　　　　　　　　　　　　40

Lucy. When a woman loves, a kind look, a tender word can persuade her to anything — and I could ask no other bribe.

Lock. Thou wilt always be a vulgar slut, Lucy. If you would not be looked upon as a fool, you 45 should never do anything but upon the foot of interest. Those that act otherwise are their own bubbles.

Lucy. But love, sir, is a misfortune that may happen to the most discreet woman, and in love 50 we are all fools alike. Notwithstanding all he swore, I am now fully convinced that Polly Peachum is actually his wife. Did I let him escape (fool that I was!) to go to her? Polly will wheedle herself into his money, and then Peachum will hang him, 55 and cheat us both.

Lock. So I am to be ruined, because, forsooth, you must be in love! — a very pretty excuse!

Lucy. I could murder that impudent happy strumpet: I gave him his life, and that creature 60 enjoys the sweets of it. Ungrateful Macheath!

Air XLII. *South-sea ballad.*

My love is all madness and folly,
　　Alone I lie,
　　Toss, tumble, and cry,
What a happy creature is Polly!　　　　　　65
　　Was e'er such a wretch as I!
With rage I redden like scarlet,
That my dear inconstant varlet,
　　Stark blind to my charms,
　　Is lost in the arms　　　　　　　　　　70
Of that jilt, that inveigling harlot!
　　Stark blind to my charms,
　　Is lost in the arms
Of that jilt, that inveigling harlot!
This, this my resentment alarms.　　　　　75

Lock. And so, after all this mischief, I must stay here to be entertained with your caterwauling, Mistress Puss! Out of my sight, wanton strumpet! you shall fast and mortify yourself into reason, with now and then a little handsome discipline to bring 80 you to your senses. Go!

SCENE II

LOCKIT.

Peachum then intends to outwit me in this affair; but I'll be even with him. The dog is leaky in his liquor, so I'll ply him that way, get the secret from him, and turn this affair to my own advantage. Lions, wolves, and vultures don't live together in 5 herds, droves or flocks. Of all animals of prey, man is the only sociable one. Every one of us preys upon his neighbor, and yet we herd together. Peachum is my companion, my friend: according to the custom of the world, indeed, he may quote thousands of 10 precedents for cheating me — and shall not I make use of the privilege of friendship to make him a return?

AIR XLIII. *Packington's Pound.*

AIR XLIII. *Packington's pound.*

Thus gamesters united in friendship are found,
Though they know that their industry all is a
    cheat; 15
They flock to their prey at the dice-box's sound,
And join to promote one another's deceit.
    But if by mishap
    They fail of a chap,
To keep in their hands, they each other entrap. 20
Like pikes, lank with hunger, who miss of their ends,
They bite their companions, and prey on their friends.

Now, Peachum, you and I, like honest tradesmen, are to have a fair trial which of us two can overreach the other. Lucy! (*Enter* LUCY.) Are there 25 any of Peachum's people now in the house?

LUCY. Filch, sir, is drinking a quartern [1] of strong waters in the next room with Black Moll.

LOCK. Bid him come to me.

SCENE III

LOCKIT, FILCH.

LOCK. Why, boy, thou lookest as if thou wert half starved; like a shotten herring.[2]

FILCH. One had need have the constitution of a horse to go thorough the business. Since the favorite child-getter was disabled by a mishap, I have 5 picked up a little money by helping the ladies to a pregnancy against their being called down to sentence. But if a man cannot get an honest livelihood any easier way, I am sure 'tis what I can't undertake for another session. 10

LOCK. Truly, if that great man should tip off,[3] 'twould be an irreparable loss. The vigor and prowess of a knight-errant never saved half the ladies in distress that he hath done. But, boy, canst thou tell me where thy master is to be found? 15

FILCH. At his lock, sir, at the Crooked Billet.

LOCK. Very well. I have nothing more with you. (*Exit* FILCH.) I'll go to him there, for I have many important affairs to settle with him; and in the way of those transactions I'll artfully get into his 20 secret. So that Macheath shall not remain a day longer out of my clutches. [*Exit.*]

SCENE IV

A gaming-house.

MACHEATH *in a fine tarnished coat*, BEN BUDGE, MATT OF THE MINT.

MACH. I am sorry, gentlemen, the road was so barren of money. When my friends are in difficulties, I am always glad that my fortune can be serviceable to them. (*Gives them money.*) You see, gentlemen, I am not a mere court friend, who professes 5 everything and will do nothing.

AIR XLIV. Lillibulero.

[1] Gill. [2] A herring that has spawned. [3] Die.

AIR XLIV. *Lillibullero.*

The modes of the court so common are grown
  That a true friend can hardly be met;
Friendship for interest is but a loan,
  Which they let out for what they can get.   10
    'Tis true, you find
    Some friends so kind,
Who will give you good counsel themselves to defend.
    In sorrowful ditty,
    They promise, they pity,   15
But shift you, for money, from friend to friend.

But we, gentlemen, have still honor enough to break
through the corruptions of the world. And while I
can serve you, you may command me.

BEN. It grieves my heart that so generous a   20
man should be involved in such difficulties as oblige
him to live with such ill company, and herd with
gamesters.

MATT. See the partiality of mankind! One man
may steal a horse, better than another look over   25
a hedge. Of all mechanics, of all servile handicrafts-
men, a gamester is the vilest. But yet, as many of
the quality are of the profession, he is admitted
amongst the politest company. I wonder we are
not more respected.   30

MACH. There will be deep play tonight at Marybone and consequently money may be picked up
upon the road. Meet me there, and I'll give you the
hint who is worth setting.[1]

MATT. The fellow with a brown coat with   35
a narrow gold binding, I am told, is never without
money.

MACH. What do you mean, Matt? Sure you will
not think of meddling with him! He's a good honest
kind of a fellow, and one of us.   40

BEN. To be sure, sir, we will put ourselves under
your direction.

MACH. Have an eye upon the money-lenders. A
rouleau[2] or two would prove a pretty sort of an
expedition. I hate extortion.   45

MATT. Those rouleaus are very pretty things. I
hate your bank bills — there is such a hazard in putting them off.

_____
[1] Making a set at.   [2] A roll of gold coins.

MACH. There is a certain man of distinction
who in his time hath nicked me out of a great   50
deal of the ready.[3] He is in my cash,[4] Ben; I'll point
him out to you this evening, and you shall draw
upon him for the debt. — The company are met; I
hear the dice-box in the other room. So, gentlemen,
your servant! You'll meet me at Marybone.   55
[*Exeunt.*]

SCENE V

PEACHUM'S *lock.*

A table with wine, brandy, pipes and tobacco.

PEACHUM, LOCKIT.

LOCK. The coronation account,[5] brother Peachum,
is of so intricate a nature that I believe it will never
be settled.

PEACH. It consists, indeed, of a great variety of
articles. It was worth to our people, in fees, of   5
different kinds, above ten instalments.[6] This is part
of the account, brother, that lies open before us.

LOCK. A lady's tail[7] of rich brocade — that, I see,
is disposed of.

PEACH. To Mrs. Diana Trapes, the tally-   10
woman, and she will make a good hand on't in shoes
and slippers, to trick out young ladies, upon their
going into keeping.

LOCK. But I don't see any article of the jewels.

PEACH. Those are so well known that they   15
must be sent abroad. You'll find them entered under
the article of exportation. As for the snuff-boxes,
watches, swords, etc., I thought it best to enter them
under their several heads.

LOCK. Seven and twenty women's pockets[8]   20
complete, with the several things therein contained;
all sealed, numbered, and entered.

PEACH. But, brother, it is impossible for us now
to enter upon this affair. We should have the whole
day before us. Besides, the account of the last   25
half-year's plate is in a book by itself, which lies at
the other office.

LOCK. Bring us then more liquor. Today shall
be for pleasure — tomorrow for business. — Ah
brother, those daughters of ours are two slippery   30
hussies. Keep a watchful eye upon Polly, and
Macheath in a day or two shall be our own again.

AIR XLV. Down in the North Country.

_____
[3] Money.   [4] Indebted to me.
[5] The crowds at the coronation of George II, about three
months before the opera was first produced, had provided the
usual harvest for pickpockets.
[6] I.e., installations of the lord mayor. These annual ceremonies were beloved by the masses.
[7] Train.   [8] Purses.

AIR XLV. *Down in the North Country.*

LOCK. What gudgeons are we men!
  Ev'ry woman's easy prey,
  Though we have felt the hook, again 35
  We bite and they betray.

The bird that hath been trapped,
  When he hears his calling mate,
  To her he flies, again he's clapped
  Within the wiry grate. 40

PEACH. But what signifies catching the bird, if
your daughter Lucy will set open the door of the
cage?

LOCK. If men were answerable for the follies and
frailties of their wives and daughters, no friends 45
could keep a good correspondence [1] together for two
days. This is unkind of you, brother; for among
good friends, what they say or do goes for nothing.

Enter a Servant.

SERV. Sir, here's Mrs. Diana Trapes wants to
speak with you. 50

PEACH. Shall we admit her, brother Lockit?

LOCK. By all means — she's a good customer, and
a fine-spoken woman — and a woman who drinks
and talks so freely will enliven the conversation.

PEACH. Desire her to walk in. *Exit Servant.* 55

SCENE VI

PEACHUM, LOCKIT, MRS. TRAPES.

PEACH. Dear Mrs. Dye, your servant! — one may
know by your kiss that your gin is excellent.

TRAPES. I was always very curious [2] in my liquors.

LOCK. There is no perfumed breath like it. I have
been long acquainted with the flavor of those 5
lips — han't I, Mrs. Dye?

TRAPES. Fill it up. I take as large draughts of
liquor as I did of love. I hate a flincher in either.

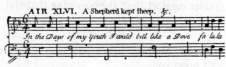

AIR XLVI. A Shepherd kept sheep. &c.

In the Days of my youth I could bill like a Dove fa la la

[1] Agreement, friendship.   [2] Fastidious.

AIR XLVI. *A shepherd kept sheep, etc.*

In the days of my youth I could bill like a dove,
  fa, la, la, etc.
Like a sparrow at all times was ready for love,
  fa, la, la, etc. 10
The life of all mortals in kissing should pass
Lip to lip while we're young — then the lip to the
  glass, fa, la, etc.

But now, Mr. Peachum, to our business. If you
have blacks of any kind, brought in of late: manteaus
— velvet scarfs — petticoats — let it be what it 15
will — I am your chap — for all my ladies are very
fond of mourning.

PEACH. Why, look ye, Mrs. Dye — you deal so
hard with us, that we can afford to give the gentlemen, who venture their lives for the goods, little 20
or nothing.

TRAPES. The hard times oblige me to go very near
in my dealing.[3] To be sure, of late years I have been
a great sufferer by the parliament. Three thousand
pounds would hardly make me amends. The act 25
for destroying the Mint [4] was a severe cut upon our
business — 'till then, if a customer stepped out of the
way — we knew where to have her. No doubt you
know Mrs. Coaxer — there's a wench now (till to-
day) with a good suit of clothes of mine upon her 30
back, and I could never set eyes upon her for three

[3] Deal parsimoniously.
[4] The Mint, a district in Southwark, was anciently a refuge
for debtors, who could not be arrested within its limits. This
privilege had recently been abolished by law.

months together. — Since the act too against imprisonment for small sums my loss there too hath been very considerable; and it must be so, when a lady can borrow a handsome petticoat, or a clean 35 gown, and I not have the least hank [1] upon her! And, o' my conscience, now-a-days most ladies take a delight in cheating, when they can do it with safety.

PEACH. Madam, you had a handsome gold watch of us t'other day for seven guineas. Consider- 40 ing we must have our profit — to a gentleman upon the road, a gold watch will be scarce worth the taking.

TRAPES. Consider, Mr. Peachum, that watch was remarkable and not of very safe sale. If you have any black velvet scarfs — they are a handsome 45 winter wear, and take with most gentlemen who deal with my customers. 'Tis I that put the ladies upon a good foot. 'Tis not youth or beauty that fixes their price. The gentlemen always pay according to their dress, from half a crown to two guineas; and yet 50 those hussies make nothing of bilking of me. Then, too, allowing for accidents. I have eleven fine customers now down under the surgeon's hands; what with fees and other expenses, there are great goings-out, and no comings-in, and not a farthing to pay 55 for at least a month's clothing. We run great risks — great risks indeed.

PEACH. As I remember, you said something just now of Mrs. Coaxer.

TRAPES. Yes, sir. To be sure, I stripped her 60 of a suit of my own clothes about two hours ago, and have left her as she should be, in her shift, with a lover of hers, at my house. She called him up stairs, as he was going to Marybone in a hackney coach. And I hope, for her own sake and mine, she will 65 persuade the captain to redeem her, for the captain is very generous to the ladies.

LOCK. What captain?

TRAPES. He thought I did not know him. An intimate acquaintance of yours, Mr. Peachum 70 — only Captain Macheath — as fine as a lord.

PEACH. Tomorrow, dear Mrs. Dye, you shall set your own price upon any of the goods you like. We have at least half a dozen velvet scarfs, and all at your service. Will you give me leave to make 75 you a present of this suit of nightclothes for your own wearing? But are you sure it is Captain Macheath?

TRAPES. Though he thinks I have forgot him; nobody knows him better. I have taken a great deal of the captain's money in my time at 80 second-hand, for he always loved to have his ladies well dressed.

PEACH. Mr. Lockit and I have a little business with the captain — you understand me — and we will satisfy you for Mrs. Coaxer's debt. 85

LOCK. Depend upon it — we will deal like men of honor.

[1] Hold.

TRAPES. I don't enquire after your affairs — so whatever happens, I wash my hands on't. It hath always been my maxim, that one friend should 90 assist another. But if you please, I'll take one of the scarfs home with me: 'tis always good to have something in hand. [Exeunt.]

SCENE VII

Newgate.

LUCY.

Jealousy, rage, love and fear are at once tearing me to pieces. How I am weatherbeaten and shattered with distresses!

AIR XLVII. *One evening, having lost my way.*

I'm like a skiff on the ocean tossed,
　　Now high, now low, with each billow borne, 5
With her rudder broke, and her anchor lost,
　　Deserted and all forlorn.
While thus I lie rolling and tossing all night,
That Polly lies sporting on seas of delight!
　　Revenge, revenge, revenge, 10
Shall appease my restless sprite.

I have the ratsbane ready. I run no risk, for I can lay her death upon the gin, and so many die of that naturally that I shall never be called in question. But say I were to be hanged — I never 15 could be hanged for anything that would give me greater comfort than the poisoning that slut.

Enter FILCH.

FILCH. Madam, here's our Miss Polly come to wait upon you.

LUCY. Show her in. 20

SCENE VIII

LUCY, POLLY.

LUCY. Dear madam, your servant. I hope you will pardon my passion, when I was so happy to see you last. I was so overrun with the spleen,[1] that I was perfectly out of myself. And really, when one hath the spleen everything is to be excused by a 5 friend.

AIR XLVIII. *Now Roger, I'll tell thee, because thou'rt my son.*

When a wife's in her pout,
  (As she's sometimes, no doubt),
The good husband, as meek as a lamb,
  Her vapors to still,   10
  First grants her her will,
And the quieting draught is a dram.
Poor man! And the quieting draught is a dram.

— I wish all our quarrels might have so comfortable a reconciliation.   15

POLLY. I have no excuse for my own behavior, madam, but my misfortunes. And really, madam, I suffer too upon your account.

LUCY. But, Miss Polly — in the way of friendship, will you give me leave to propose a glass of 20 cordial to you?

POLLY. Strong waters are apt to give me the headache — I hope, madam, you will excuse me.

LUCY. Not the greatest lady in the land could have better in her closet, for her own private drinking. 25 You seem mighty low in spirits, my dear.

POLLY. I am sorry, madam, my health will not allow me to accept of your offer. I should not have left you in the rude manner I did when we met last, madam, had not my papa hauled me away so un- 30 expectedly. I was indeed somewhat provoked, and perhaps might use some expressions that were disrespectful. But really, madam, the captain treated me with so much contempt and cruelty that I deserved your pity, rather than your resentment. 35

LUCY. But since his escape no doubt all matters

are made up again. Ah Polly! Polly! 'tis I am the unhappy wife, and he loves you as if you were only his mistress.

POLLY. Sure, madam, you cannot think me so 40 happy as to be the object of your jealousy. A man is always afraid of a woman who loves him too well — so that I must expect to be neglected and avoided.

LUCY. Then our cases, my dear Polly, are exactly alike. Both of us, indeed, have been too fond. 45

AIR XLIX. *Oh, Bessy Bell, etc.*

POLLY. A curse attends that woman's love,
  Who always would be pleasing.
LUCY. The pertness of the billing dove,
  Like tickling, is but teasing.
POLLY. What then in love can woman do?   50
LUCY. If we grow fond they shun us.
POLLY. And when we fly them, they pursue.
LUCY. But leave us when they've won us.

LUCY. Love is so very whimsical in both sexes, that it is impossible to be lasting. But my heart 55 is particular,[2] and contradicts my own observation.

POLLY. But really, Mistress Lucy, by his last behavior, I think I ought to envy you. When I was forced from him, he did not show the least tenderness. But perhaps he hath a heart not capable of it. 60

AIR L. *Would fate to me Belinda give.*

Among the men, coquets we find,
Who court by turns all womankind;
And we grant all their hearts desired,
When they are flattered and admired.

The coquets of both sexes are self-lovers, and 65
that is a love no other whatever can dispossess. I
fear, my dear Lucy, our husband is one of those.

LUCY. Away with these melancholy reflections;
indeed, my dear Polly, we are both of us a cup too
low. Let me prevail upon you to accept of my 70
offer.

AIR LI. *Come, sweet lass.*

Come, sweet lass,
Let's banish sorrow
Till tomorrow;
Come, sweet lass, 75
Let's take a chirping [1] glass.
Wine can clear
The vapors of despair;
And make us light as air;
Then drink, and banish care. 80

I can't bear, child, to see you in such low spirits.
And I must persuade you to what I know will do
you good. (*Aside.*) I shall now soon be even with
the hypocritical strumpet.

SCENE IX

POLLY.

POLLY. All this wheedling of Lucy cannot be for
nothing. At this time, too, when I know she hates
me! The dissembling of a woman is always the
forerunner of mischief. By pouring strong waters
down my throat, she thinks to pump some 5
secrets out of me. I'll be upon my guard, and won't
taste a drop of her liquor, I'm resolved.

SCENE X

LUCY, *with strong waters.* POLLY.

LUCY. Come, Miss Polly.

[1] Cheering.

POLLY. Indeed, child, you have given yourself
trouble to no purpose. You must, my dear, excuse
me.

LUCY. Really, Miss Polly, you are so squeam- 5
ishly affected about taking a cup of strong waters as
a lady before company. I vow, Polly, I shall take it
monstrously ill if you refuse me. Brandy and men
(though women love them never so well) are always
taken by us with some reluctance — unless 'tis 10
in private.

POLLY. I protest, madam, it goes against me. —
What do I see! Macheath again in custody! Now
every glimmering of happiness is lost.

(*Drops the glass of liquor on the ground.*)

LUCY [*aside*]. Since things are thus, I'm glad 15
the wench hath escaped: for by this event 'tis plain
she was not happy enough to deserve to be poisoned.

SCENE XI

LOCKIT, MACHEATH, PEACHUM, LUCY, POLLY.

LOCK. Set your heart to rest, captain. You have
neither the chance of love or money for another
escape, for you are ordered to be called down upon
your trial immediately.

PEACH. Away, hussies! This is not a time for 5
a man to be hampered with his wives. You see, the
gentleman is in chains already.

LUCY. O husband, husband, my heart longed to
see thee; but to see thee thus distracts me!

POLLY. Will not my dear husband look upon 10
his Polly? Why hadst thou not flown to me for
protection? with me thou hadst been safe.

AIR LII. *The last time I went o'er the moor.*

POLLY. Hither, dear husband, turn your eyes.
LUCY. Bestow one glance to cheer me.
POLLY. Think, with that look, thy Polly dies. 15
LUCY. Oh, shun me not — but hear me.

POLLY. 'Tis Polly sues.

LUCY.   — 'Tis Lucy speaks.

POLLY. Is thus true love requited?

LUCY. My heart is bursting.

POLLY.   — Mine too breaks.

LUCY. Must I —

POLLY.   — Must I be slighted?   20

MACH. What would you have me say, ladies? You see, this affair will soon be at an end, without my disobliging either of you.

PEACH. But the settling this point, captain, might prevent a law suit between your two widows.   25

AIR LIII. *Tom Tinker's my true love, etc.*

MACH. Which way shall I turn me? how can I decide?

Wives, the day of our death, are as fond as a bride.
One wife is too much for most husbands to hear,
But two at a time there's no mortal can bear.
This way, and that way, and which way I will,   30
What would comfort the one, t'other wife would take ill.

POLLY. But if his own misfortunes have made him insensible to mine, a father sure will be more compassionate. — Dear, dear sir, sink the material evidence, and bring him off at his trial — Polly   35 upon her knees begs it of you.

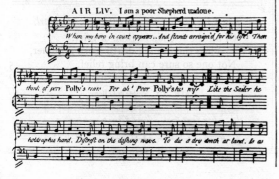

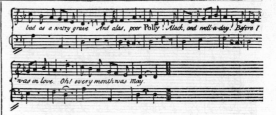

AIR LIV. *I am a poor shepherd undone.*

When my hero in court appears,
    And stands arraigned for his life;
Then think of poor Polly's tears;
    For ah! poor Polly's his wife.   40
Like the sailor he holds up his hand,
    Distressed on the dashing wave.
To die a dry death at land,
    Is as bad as a wat'ry grave.
And alas, poor Polly;   45
    Alack, and well-a-day!
Before I was in love,
    Oh! every month was May!

LUCY. If Peachum's heart is hardened, sure you, sir, will have more compassion on a daughter.   50 I know the evidence is in your power.   How then can you be a tyrant to me?   (*Kneeling.*)

AIR LV. *Ianthe the lovely, etc.*

When he holds up his hand arraigned for his life,
Oh think of your daughter, and think I'm his wife!
What are cannons, or bombs, or clashing of swords?   55
For death is more certain by witnesses' words.
Then nail up their lips; that dread thunder allay;
And each month of my life will hereafter be May.

LOCK. Macheath's time is come, Lucy.   We know

our own affairs, therefore let us have no more 60
whimpering or whining.

AIR LVI. *A cobbler there was, etc.*

Ourselves, like the great, to secure a retreat,
    When matters require it, must give up our gang:
        And good reason why,
        Or, instead of the fry,   65
        Ev'n Peachum and I,
Like poor petty rascals, might hang, hang;
Like poor petty rascals might hang.

PEACH. Set your heart at rest, Polly. Your husband is to die today. Therefore, if you are not 70
already provided, 'tis high time to look about for
another. There's comfort for you, you slut.

LOCK. We are ready, sir, to conduct you to the
Old Bailey.

AIR LVII. *Bonny Dundee.*

MACH. The charge is prepared; the lawyers are
met,   75

The judges all ranged (a terrible show!)
I go, undismayed — for death is a debt,
    A debt on demand. So, take what I owe.
Then farewell, my love — dear charmers, adieu!
Contented I die — 'tis the better for you.   80
    Here ends all dispute the rest of our lives,
    For this way at once I please all my wives.
Now, gentlemen, I am ready to attend you.

SCENE XII

LUCY, POLLY, FILCH.

POLLY. Follow them, Filch, to the court. And
when the trial is over, bring me a particular account
of his behavior, and of everything that happened.
You'll find me here with Miss Lucy.   *Exit* FILCH.
But why is all this music?   5

LUCY. The prisoners whose trials are put off till
next session are diverting themselves.

POLLY. Sure there is nothing so charming as music!
I'm fond of it to distraction! — But alas! now, all
mirth seems an insult upon my affliction. — Let   10
us retire, my dear Lucy, and indulge our sorrows.
The noisy crew, you see, are coming upon us. *Exeunt.*
    A dance of prisoners in chains, etc.

SCENE XIII

The condemned hold.

MACHEATH, *in a melancholy posture.*

AIR LVIII. *Happy groves.*

O cruel, cruel, cruel case!
Must I suffer this disgrace?

AIR LIX. *Of all the girls that are so smart.*

Of all the friends in time of grief,
    When threat'ning death looks grimmer,
Not one so sure can bring relief,   5
    As this best friend, a brimmer.   (*Drinks.*)

AIR LX. *Britons, strike home.*

Since I must swing, — I scorn, I scorn to wince or
whine. (*Rises.*)

AIR LXI. *Chevy Chase.*

But now again my spirits sink;
I'll raise them high with wine.
(*Drinks a glass of wine.*)

AIR LXII. *To old Sir Simon the King.*

But valor the stronger grows, 10
The stronger liquor we're drinking.
And how can we feel our woes,
When we've lost the trouble of thinking?
(*Drinks.*)

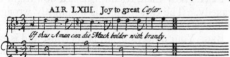

AIR LXIII. *Joy to great Cæsar.*

If thus — a man can die
Much bolder with brandy. 15
(*Pours out a bumper of brandy.*)

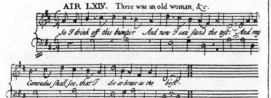

AIR LXIV. *There was an old woman, etc.*

So I drink off this bumper. — And now I can stand
the test.
And my comrades shall see that I die as brave as
the best. (*Drinks.*)

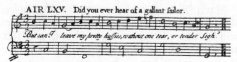

AIR LXV. *Did you ever hear of a gallant sailor?*

But can I leave my pretty hussies,
Without one tear, or tender sigh?

AIR LXVI. *Why are mine eyes still flowing?*

Their eyes, their lips, their busses, 20
Recall my love. — Ah, must I die?

AIR LXVII. *Greensleeves.*

Since laws were made for ev'ry degree,
To curb vice in others, as well as me,
I wonder we han't better company,
Upon Tyburn tree! 25
But gold from law can take out the sting;
And if rich men like us were to swing,
'Twould thin the land, such numbers to string
Upon Tyburn tree!

[*Enter Jailor.*]

JAILOR. Some friends of yours, captain, de- 30
sire to be admitted. I leave you together.

SCENE XIV

MACHEATH, BEN BUDGE, MATT OF THE MINT.

MACH. For my having broke prison, you see,
gentlemen, I am ordered immediate execution. The
sheriff's officers, I believe, are now at the door. That
Jemmy Twitcher should peach me, I own surprised
me! 'Tis a plain proof that the world is all alike, 5
and that even our gang can no more trust one another than other people. Therefore, I beg you,

gentlemen, look well to yourselves, for in all probability you may live some months longer.

MATT. We are heartily sorry, captain, for 10
your misfortune. But 'tis what we must all come to.

MACH. Peachum and Lockit, you know, are infamous scoundrels. Their lives are as much in your
power, as yours are in theirs. Remember your dying
friend! — 'tis my last request. Bring those vil- 15
lains to the gallows before you, and I am satisfied.

MATT. We'll do't.

[Re-enter Jailor.]

JAILOR. Miss Polly and Miss Lucy intreat a word
with you.

MACH. Gentlemen, adieu. 20

SCENE XV

LUCY, MACHEATH, POLLY.

MACH. My dear Lucy — my dear Polly — whatsoever hath passed between us is now at an end. If
you are fond of marrying again, the best advice I can
give you is to ship yourselves off for the West Indies,
where you'll have a fair chance of getting a hus- 5
band apiece; or by good luck, two or three, as you
like best.

POLLY. How can I support this sight!

LUCY. There is nothing moves one so much as a
great man in distress. 10

AIR LXVIII. *All you that must take a leap, etc.*
LUCY. Would I might be hanged!
POLLY.   — And I would so too!
LUCY. To be hanged with you —
POLLY.   — My dear, with you.
MACH. Oh, leave me to thought! I fear! I doubt!
I tremble! I droop! — See, my courage is out.

(Turns up the empty bottle.)

POLLY. No token of love?
MACH.   — See, my courage is out. 15

(Turns up the empty pot.)

LUCY. No token of love?
POLLY.   — Adieu!
LUCY.   — Farewell!
MACH. But hark! I hear the toll of the bell!
CHORUS. Tol de rol lol, etc.

[Re-enter Jailor.]

JAILOR. Four women more, captain, with a child
apiece! See, here they come. 20

Enter Women and Children.

MACH. What — four wives more! — This is too
much. — Here — tell the sheriff's officers I am
ready.   *Exit* MACHEATH *guarded.*

SCENE XVI

To them enter PLAYER *and* BEGGAR.

PLAY. But, honest friend, I hope you don't intend
that Macheath shall be really executed.

BEG. Most certainly, sir. To make the piece
perfect, I was for doing strict poetical justice.
Macheath is to be hanged; and for the other 5
personages of the drama, the audience must have
supposed they were all either hanged or transported.

PLAY. Why then, friend, this is a downright deep
tragedy. The catastrophe is manifestly wrong, for
an opera must end happily. 10

BEG. Your objection, sir, is very just and is easily
removed. For you must allow that in this kind of
drama 'tis no matter how absurdly things are brought
about. — So — you rabble there — run and cry a
reprieve! — let the prisoner be brought back to 15
his wives in triumph.

PLAY. All this we must do, to comply with the
taste of the town.

BEG. Through the whole piece you may observe
such a similitude of manners in high and low life, 20
that it is difficult to determine whether (in the fashionable vices) the fine gentlemen imitate the gentlemen of the road, or the gentlemen of the road the fine
gentlemen. Had the play remained as I at first intended, it would have carried a most excellent 25
moral. 'Twould have shown that the lower sort of
people have their vices in a degree as well as the rich;
and that they are punished for them.

SCENE XVII

To them MACHEATH, *with rabble, etc.*

MACH. So it seems, I am not left to my choice, but
must have a wife at last. — Look ye, my dears, we
will have no controversy now. Let us give this day
to mirth, and I am sure she who thinks herself my
wife will testify her joy by a dance. 5

ALL. Come, a dance — a dance.

MACH. Ladies, I hope you will give me leave to present a partner to each of you. And (if I may without offence) for this time, I take Polly for mine. (*To* POLLY.) And for life, you slut, — for 10 we were really married. As for the rest — but at present keep your own secret. (*A dance.*)

AIR LXIX. *Lumps of pudding, etc.*

Thus I stand like the Turk, with his doxies around;
From all sides their glances his passion confound:
For black, brown, and fair, his inconstancy
    burns, 15
And the different beauties subdue him by turns:
Each calls forth her charms, to provoke his desires:
Though willing to all, with but one he retires.
But think of this maxim, and put off your sorrow,
The wretch of today may be happy tomorrow. 20
    CHORUS. But think of this maxim, etc.

                     [*Exeunt.*]

19] Q (in engraved music) *all sorrow.*

MID–EIGHTEENTH–CENTURY DRAMA
(1730–1770)

No two of the plays chosen to illustrate English drama in the middle of the eighteenth century can profitably be discussed together. This fact is an index of the lack of integration which is evident in the period, during which some of the older trends were followed without producing plays of great distinction, and some new experiments were attempted without perfecting the types which they initiated. Several circumstances combined to discourage the writing of either high comedy or great tragedy. One of these was the increasingly strict supervision of the theatre by the government. Another was the rise of the English novel, which absorbed the energies of several writers of whom some, at least, might otherwise have turned their attention to the drama. But perhaps most important of all was the attitude of the public. The stage, indeed, was probably more popular than ever before, but it was the actor rather than the playwright who was the center of interest. Cibber, Macklin, Peg Woffington, Garrick and others made for themselves names which have not been forgotten after two centuries. But the audiences apparently cared little whether the pieces these actors performed were new plays of no great merit, or old plays, good or mediocre. There was, consequently, no external stimulus to urge a dramatic writer to excel.

Five plays of different types have been chosen to illustrate this 'Garrick era' of the English stage. No generalization can be made which will apply to all five: it will be best to consider each in its chronological order, for want of any more significant arrangement.

HENRY FIELDING (1707–1754), whose reputation now rests upon his novels, especially *Joseph Andrews* and *Tom Jones*, began his literary career as a dramatist and continued it as a journalist. He was descended from a well-to-do county family, but was forced by financial reverses to make his own way from his twenty-first year. He began by turning out farces to supply the popular demand, wrote a few longer comedies, and even attempted some adaptations from Molière. He also worked the vein of political satire which Gay had tapped in *The Beggar's Opera*, at first attacking general corruption in politics, but later concentrating his fire upon the administration of Walpole. This course had important effects upon both his own career and the history of the British theatre, for Walpole, irritated by constant criticism, and dissatisfied with the extent of the government's control over the stage, finally brought about the passage of the Licensing Act of 1737. This law gave statutory authority to the Lord Chamberlain's power of forbidding any theatrical production whenever he chose to do so, without providing any machinery for appeals from his decisions. This extraordinary power, which still exists, not only halted Fielding's theatrical career but has been the cause of endless difficulties for later British dramatists.

The play of Fielding's which is included in this collection, however, falls within the classifications of neither farce nor political satire; it is a dramatic burlesque, the first notable successor to *The Rehearsal*. All that it is necessary to say of the type has already been said in connection with Buckingham's play; this particular specimen shows that many of the faults of the heroic drama and ranting tragedy still survived to be criticized, and that Fielding was an adept at satire even in his early twenties. The burlesque was first produced in 1730, as *Tom Thumb*, and upon its success was lengthened from two to three acts and brought out anew in 1731, under the name of *The Tragedy of Tragedies*. It proved a welcome novelty in the familiar field of *The Rehearsal*, which, with revisions, had held the stage since its first appearance nearly sixty years earlier, and, like it, remained in the repertories of the London theatres until both burlesques yielded pride of place to Sheridan's *Critic* in 1779.

GEORGE LILLO (1693–1739), son of a jeweller in the 'City,' and himself in the trade, wrote his most famous play almost at the outset of his career: *The London Merchant* had been preceded from his pen only by a not very successful ballad opera. There had been a few attempts during the Elizabethan period to write tragedies based upon middle-class life (such as *A Yorkshire Tragedy* and *A Woman Killed with Kindness*), and in a certain sense Otway and Rowe had continued the type. But *The London Merchant* differed from these plays in at least two respects: it was written throughout in prose (although the cadences of blank verse often crept in, especially in the more impassioned moments), and it was almost militant in its pride in the middle class. Some traces of this class feeling can be found in certain Elizabethan comedies; and in the early eighteenth century Addison and Steele, among others, had spoken up for the mercantile community, not only in their periodicals, but in such comedies as *The Conscious Lovers*, where Mr. Sealand certainly does not come off second-best in his discussion of the subject with Sir John Bevil. Lillo did not hesitate to draw upon an old ballad for his plot and characters, although he knew that such a procedure would be condemned as 'low' by the fastidious. Unfortunately the use of prose does not make the dialogue of the play more natural, as it was intended to do, and the constant moralizing detracts greatly from the naturalness of most of the characters. It would probably distress Lillo to know that according to the consensus of modern critical opinion Millwood is by far his finest creation, and her defense of herself is the most moving speech in the tragedy.

The great success of the play (it was acted for twenty nights or more in its first summer season, and remained a stock piece even into the nineteenth century) showed that the dramatist, like the author in other fields, would for the future have to take into account the tastes of others than the courtiers and the highly educated. The immediate effect of the play upon English drama, however, was not very great. Lillo himself wrote no other tragedy in prose, though he did write one other 'domestic tragedy' in blank verse. In the small number of English plays which imitated *The London Merchant* only Edward Moore's *The Gamester* stands out. Lillo's influence on the continent was more striking: George Barnwell's tragic fate was rehearsed in Dutch, French, and German, and had a marked effect upon such important writers as Diderot and Lessing. When the romantic movement gained strength with the beginning of the nineteenth century the theory that the lower ranks of society provided material fit for tragedy finally gained a more secure foothold.

DAVID GARRICK (1717–1779), like Colley Cibber, combined the careers of actor, manager (of Drury Lane), and playwright. Aside from his adaptations of Shakespeare and his collaboration with Colman in *The Clandestine Marriage*, his most important compositions were a number of farces, ranging from *The Lying Valet* (1741) at the very beginning of his connection with the theatre to *Bon Ton* (1775) at the end. Even before Garrick's time the custom of providing an after-piece, usually quite out of key with the main play, had become well established: music, pantomimes, burlesques, or amorphous creations called 'entertainments' were often employed, to an extent that caused complaints that they were usurping the center of the stage. Pope's well-known description of conditions in the theatre in the early 1730's (*Epistle to Arbuthnot*, ll. 302–337), while perhaps somewhat heightened, had a foundation of fact. The farces, usually two acts in length, were certainly not the most objectionable of after-pieces; the best of them were comedies quite capable of standing upon their own merits. Garrick's good sense of 'theatre,' his eye for the ridiculous, and his knack of writing natural dialogue made him extremely successful in this field. His closest rivals were Samuel Foote, Arthur Murphy, and James Townley, the latter the author of what is perhaps the best-remembered of the eighteenth-century farces, *High Life below Stairs* (1759). Foote, who was a remarkably versatile mimic, devoted much of his time to ridiculing persons of little importance even in their day, and of no interest to later times. A few of his pieces, however, are general rather than particular satires, and in the best of them, such as *The Minor* (1760) and *The Maid of Bath* (1771), he is quite on a par with Garrick. The latter play has the adventitious interest of being based on incidents in the early life of Elizabeth Linley, the concert singer, who eventually became the wife of Richard Brinsley Sheridan.

JOHN HOME (1722–1808), a Scots Presbyterian minister, is now recalled only for his first tragedy, *Douglas*, which, after rejection by Garrick, was produced in Edinburgh in 1756 and, upon its proving to be a success, in London in 1757 by Rich at Covent Garden. The play had been written in Scotland before Home had had any significant contact with the theatrical world of London, and it was therefore hailed by the Scots as a triumph for their national drama. Like *The London Merchant*, it is founded upon a ballad, but the likeness ends here. The persons of the tragedy are of high rank, the atmosphere is romantic, and the medium is blank verse, which is rather declamatory in many places. Home was much more influenced by Shakespeare, with whom he was frequently compared by his admiring countrymen, than by any eighteenth-century author, and *Douglas* stands apart from the English drama of its day. It was moderately successful on the London stage, and remained in the repertory a long time. Home was never able to repeat his triumph, although he had five other plays produced.

GEORGE COLMAN, the elder (1732–1794), a nephew of the Earl of Bath, alienated his uncle, on whom his prospects depended, by preferring the theatre to the law. His first play, an after-piece called *Polly Honeycombe*, was produced anonymously in 1760; in the following year came his best comedy, *The Jealous Wife*, written in the old comic tradition. Colman acknowledged debts to several sources for this play, chiefly to Fielding's novel, *Tom Jones*, from which he borrowed a number of characters and incidents. Mrs. Oakly (the jealous wife), her husband, and their domestic difficulties are, however, Colman's own contributions to the play. *The Clandestine Marriage* (1766), which Colman wrote in collaboration with Garrick, has some traces of sentimentality, but on the whole may be classed as 'laughing comedy.' These two plays, together with revivals of Elizabethan and Restoration comedies, did much to preserve the comic spirit on the English stage through the middle of the eighteenth century. Of the numerous other plays which Colman wrote or adapted none is of great importance.

A. E. C.

REFERENCE WORKS

1914. Nettleton, George H. *English Drama of the Restoration and Eighteenth Century.* New York and London. [Chapters XII–XV, with Bibliographical Notes.]

1925. Bateson, F. W. *English Comic Drama, 1700–1750.* Oxford. [Chapter VII.]

1925. Bernbaum, Ernest. *The Drama of Sensibility.* Cambridge [Massachusetts]. [Chapter VIII.]

1927. Nicoll, Allardyce. *A History of Late Eighteenth Century Drama, 1750–1800.* Cambridge [England]. [Chapters II, III.]

1929. Nicoll, Allardyce. *A History of Early Eighteenth Century Drama, 1700–1750.* Cambridge [England]. [Chapters II, IV.]

1936. Smith, Dane F. *Plays about the Theatre in England.* Oxford.

Tom Thumb (The Tragedy of Tragedies; or, The Life and Death of Tom Thumb the Great)

BY HENRY FIELDING

Dramatis Personæ.

MEN.

King Arthur,   Mr. Mullart.
Tom Thumb,   Miss Jones.
Lord Grizzle,   Mr. Jones.
Mr. Noodle,   Mr. Marshall.
Mr. Doodle,   Mr. Reynolds.
1 Physician,   Mr. Hallam.
2 Physician,   Mr. Dove.

WOMEN.

Queen Dollalolla,   Mrs. Mullart.
Princess Huncamunca,   Mrs. Jones.
Cleora.
Mustacha.
Slaves, &c.

Dramatis Personæ.

King *Arthur*, A passionate sort of King, Husband to Queen *Dollalolla*, of whom he stands a little in Fear; Father to *Huncamunca*, whom he is very fond of; and in Love with *Glumdalca*.   Mr. *Mullart*.

Tom Thumb the Great, A little Hero with a great Soul, something violent in his Temper, which is a little abated by his Love for *Huncamunca*.   Young *Verhuych*.

Ghost of *Gaffar Thumb*, A whimsical sort of Ghost.   Mr. *Lacy*.

Lord *Grizzle*, Extremely zealous for the Liberty of the Subject, very cholerick in his Temper, and in Love with *Huncamunca*.   Mr. *Jones*.

Merlin, A Conjurer, and in some sort Father to *Tom Thumb*.   Mr. *Hallam*.

Noodle, } Courtiers in Place, and consequently
Doodle, } of that Party that is uppermost.   Mr. *Reynolds*.   Mr. *Wathan*.

Foodle, A Courtier that is out of Place, and consequently of that Party that is undermost.   Mr. *Ayres*.

Bailiff, and } Of the Party of the Plaintiff.
Follower, }   Mr. *Peterson*.   Mr. *Hicks*.

Parson, Of the Side of the Church.   Mr. *Watson*.

WOMEN.

Queen *Dollalolla*, Wife to King *Arthur*, and Mother to *Huncamunca*, a Woman entirely faultless, saving that she is a little given to Drink; a little too much a *Virago* towards her Husband, and in Love with *Tom Thumb*.   Mrs. *Mullart*.

The Princess *Huncamunca*, Daughter to their Majesties King *Arthur* and Queen *Dollalolla*, of a very sweet, gentle, and amorous Disposition, equally in Love with Lord *Grizzle* and *Tom Thumb*, and desirous to be married to them both.   Mrs. *Jones*.

Glumdalca, of the Giants, a Captive Queen, belov'd by the King, but in Love with *Tom Thumb*.   Mrs. *Dove*.

Cleora, } Maids of Honour, in } *Noodle*.
Mustacha, } Love with } *Doodle*.

Courtiers, Guards, Rebels, Drums, Trumpets, Thunder and Lightning.

SCENE *the Court of King Arthur, and a Plain thereabouts*.

TOM

H. SCRIBLERUS SECUNDUS

HIS PREFACE

The town hath seldom been more divided in its opinion than concerning the merit of the following scenes. Whilst some publicly affirmed that no author could produce so fine a piece but Mr. P[ope], others have with as much vehemence insisted that no one could write anything so bad but Mr. F[ielding].

Nor can we wonder at this dissension about its merit, when the learned world have not unanimously decided even the very nature of this tragedy. For though most of the universities in Europe have honored it with the name of *egregium et maximi pretii opus, tragœdiis tam antiquis quam novis longe anteponendum*; [1] nay, Dr. B[entley] hath pronounced, *Citius Mœvii Æneadem quam Scribleri istius tragœdiam hanc crediderim, cujus auctorem Senecam ipsum tradidisse haud dubitarim*; [2] and the great Professor Burman [3] hath styled *Tom Thumb, Heroum omnium tragicorum facile principem*. [4] Nay, though it hath, among other languages, been translated into Dutch, and celebrated with great applause at Amsterdam (where burlesque never came) by the title of *Mynheer Vander Thumb*, the burgomasters receiving it with that reverent and silent attention which becometh an audience at a deep tragedy: notwithstanding all this, there have not been wanting some who have represented these scenes in a ludicrous light; and Mr. D[ennis] [5] hath been heard to say with some concern, that he wondered a tragical and Christian nation would permit a representation on its theatre so visibly designed to ridicule and extirpate everything that is great and solemn among us.

This learned critic and his followers were led into so great an error by that surreptitious and piratical copy which stole last year [6] into the world — with what injustice and prejudice to our author, I hope will be acknowledged by everyone who shall happily peruse this genuine and original copy. Nor can I help remarking, to the great praise of our author, that, however imperfect the former was, still did even that faint resemblance of the true *Tom Thumb* contain sufficient beauties to give it a run of upwards of forty nights, to the politest audiences. But, notwithstanding that applause which it received from all the best judges, it was as severely censured by some few bad ones and, I believe, rather maliciously than ignorantly reported to have been intended a burlesque on the loftiest parts of tragedy and designed to banish what we generally call *fine things* from the stage.

Now, if I can set my country right in an affair of this importance, I shall lightly esteem any labor which it may cost. And this I the rather undertake; first, as it is indeed in some measure incumbent on me to vindicate myself from that surreptitious copy before mentioned, published by some ill-meaning people under my name; secondly, as knowing myself more capable of doing justice to our author than any other man, as I have given myself more pains to arrive at a thorough understanding of this little piece, having for ten years together read nothing else; in which time I think I may modestly presume, with the help of my English dictionary, to comprehend all the meanings of every word in it.

But should any error of my pen awaken Clariss. Bentleium [7] to enlighten the world with his annotations on our author, I shall not think that the least reward or happiness arising to me from these my endeavors.

I shall waive at present what hath caused such feuds in the learned world, whether this piece was originally written by Shakespeare, though certainly that, were it true, must add a considerable share to its merit, especially with such as are so generous as to buy and to commend what they never read, from an implicit faith in the author only — a faith which our age abounds in as much as it can be called deficient in any other.

Let it suffice that the *Tragedy of Tragedies, or, The Life and Death of Tom Thumb*, was written in the reign of Queen Elizabeth. Nor can the objection be made by Mr. D[ennis] that the tragedy must then have been antecedent to the history, have any weight, when we consider that though the *History of Tom Thumb*, printed by and for Edward M[idwinte]r, at the Looking-Glass [8] on London Bridge, be of a later date; still must we suppose this history to have been transcribed from some other, unless we suppose the writer thereof to be

[1] 'A distinguished and most valuable work, vastly to be preferred alike to ancient and to modern tragedies.'
[2] 'More readily should I believe that Mævius wrote the *Æneid* than that this Scriblerus of yours wrote this tragedy, the author of which, I have no doubt, Seneca himself recorded.'
[3] A learned Latin scholar of Amsterdam.
[4] 'Easily the first of all tragic heroes.'
[5] English essayist and dramatist, whom Fielding frequently hits in his 'Annotations.'
[6] Referring to the two-act 1730 version of *Tom Thumb*.
[7] 'The most illustrious Bentley,' the leading English classical scholar already cited by Fielding (line 7).
[8] Midwinter's shop. Midwinter and Curll (cited below) were London printers and publishers.

inspired, a gift very faintly contended for by the writers of our age. As to this history's not bearing the stamp of second, third, or fourth edition, I see but little in that objection, editions being very uncertain lights to judge of books by; and perhaps Mr. M[idwinte]r may have joined twenty editions in one, as Mr. C[url]l hath ere now divided one into twenty.

Nor doth the other argument, drawn from the little care our author hath taken to keep up to the letter of the history, carry any greater force. Are there not instances of plays wherein the history is so perverted that we can know the heroes whom they celebrate by no other marks than their names? Nay, do we not find the same character placed by different poets in such different lights that we can discover not the least sameness or even likeness in the features? The Sophonisba of Mairet [1] and of Lee [2] is a tender, passionate, amorous mistress of Massinissa. Corneille [3] and Mr. Thomson [4] give her no other passion but the love of her country, and make her as cool in her affection to Massinissa as to Syphax. In the two latter she resembles the character of Queen Elizabeth; in the two former, she is the picture of Mary, Queen of Scotland. In short, the one Sophonisba is as different from the other as the Brutus [5] of Voltaire is from the Marius, Jun. [6] of Otway, or as the Minerva is from the Venus of the ancients.

Let us now proceed to a regular examination of the tragedy before us, in which I shall treat separately of the fable, the moral, the characters, the sentiments, and the diction. And first of the *fable*, which I take to be the most simple imaginable, and, to use the words of an eminent author,[7] 'One, regular, and uniform, not charged with a multiplicity of incidents, and yet affording several revolutions of fortune; by which the passions may be excited, varied, and driven to their full tumult of emotion.' Nor is the action of this tragedy less great than uniform. The spring of all is the love of Tom Thumb for Huncamunca, which causeth the quarrel between their majesties in the first act; the passion of Lord Grizzle in the second; the rebellion, fall of Lord Grizzle and Glumdalca, devouring of Tom Thumb by the cow, and that bloody catastrophe, in the third.

Nor is the *moral* of this excellent tragedy less noble than the *fable*: it teaches these two instructive lessons, viz.: that human happiness is exceeding transient, and that death is the certain end of all men; the former whereof is inculcated by the fatal end of Tom Thumb, the latter by that of all the other personages.

The *characters* are, I think, sufficiently described in the *Dramatis Personæ*, and I believe we shall find few plays where greater care is taken to maintain them throughout and to preserve in every speech that characteristic mark which distinguishes them from each other. 'But,' says Mr. D[ennis], 'how well does the character of Tom Thumb, whom we must call the hero of this tragedy — if it hath any hero — agree with the precepts of Aristotle,[8] who defineth tragedy to be the imitation of a short but perfect action containing a just greatness in itself, etc.? What greatness can be in a fellow whom history relateth to have been no higher than a span?' This gentleman seemeth to think, with Sergeant Kite,[9] that the greatness of a man's soul is in proportion to that of his body, the contrary of which is affirmed by our English physiognomical [10] writers. Besides, if I understand Aristotle right, he speaketh only of the greatness of the action, and not of the person.

As for the *sentiments* and *diction*, which now only remain to be spoken to: I thought I could afford them no stronger justification than by producing parallel passages out of the best of our English writers. Whether this sameness of thought and expression which I have quoted from them proceeded from an agreement in their way of thinking, or whether they have borrowed from our author, I leave the reader to determine. I shall adventure to affirm this of the sentiments of our author, that they are generally the most familiar which I have ever met with and at the same time delivered with the highest dignity of phrase; which brings me to speak of his *diction*. Here I shall only beg one postulatum, viz.: that the greatest perfection of the language of a tragedy is, that it is not to be understood; which granted (as I think it must be), it will necessarily follow that the only way to avoid this is by being too high or too low for the understanding, which will comprehend everything within its reach. These two extremities of style Mr. Dryden [11] illustrates by the familiar image of two inns, which I shall term the aërial and the subterrestrial.

Horace goes farther, and showeth when it is proper to call at one of these inns, and when at the other:

> *Telephus et Peleus, cum pauper et exsul uterque,*
> *Projicit ampullas et sesquipedalia verba.*[12]

---

[1] Mairet's *Sophonisbe* (1634).   [2] Lee's *Sophonisba* (acted 1675, printed 1676).   [3] Corneille's *Sophonisbe* (1663).
[4] Thomson's *The Tragedy of Sophonisba* (1730).   [5] Voltaire's *Brutus* (acted 1730, printed 1731).
[6] Otway's *Caius Marius* (printed 1680).   [7] James Thomson, preface to *The Tragedy of Sophonisba* (1730).
[8] In his *Poetics*.   [9] In Farquhar's *Recruiting Officer* (1706).
[10] See Hillhouse, p. 153, for discussion of variant spellings in different editions.
[11] In his essay *Of Heroic Plays*, prefixed to *The Conquest of Granada*.
[12] 'Both Telephus and Peleus, when in poverty and exile, reject bombast and sesquipedalian words.'

That he approveth of the *sesquipedalia verba* is plain; for had not Telephus and Peleus used this sort of diction in prosperity, they could not have dropped it in adversity. The aërial inn, therefore, says Horace, is proper only to be frequented by princes and other great men in the highest affluence of fortune; the subterrestrial is appointed for the entertainment of the poorer sort of people only, whom Horace advises *dolere sermone pedestri;* [1] the true meaning of both which citations is, that bombast is the proper language for joy and doggerel for grief, the latter of which is literally implied in the *sermo pedestris* as the former is in the *sesquipedalia verba.*

Cicero recommendeth the former of these. *Quid est tam furiosum vel tragicum quam verborum sonitus inanis, nullâ subjectâ sententiâ neque scientiâ.* [2] What can be so proper for tragedy as a set of big-sounding words, so contrived together as to convey no meaning? — which I shall one day or other prove to be the sublime of Longinus. Ovid declareth absolutely for the latter inn: *Omne genus scripti gravitate tragœdia vincit.* [3] Tragedy hath of all writings the greatest share in the bathos, which is the profound of Scriblerus.

I shall not presume to determine which of these two styles be properer for tragedy. It sufficeth that our author excelleth in both. He is very rarely within sight through the whole play, either rising higher than the eye of your understanding can soar or sinking lower than it careth to stoop. But here it may perhaps be observed that I have given more frequent instances of authors who have imitated him in the sublime than in the contrary. To which I answer: First, bombast being properly a redundancy of genius, instances of this nature occur in poets whose names do no more honor to our author than the writers in the doggerel which proceeds from a cool, calm, weighty way of thinking — instances whereof are most frequently to be found in authors of a lower class; secondly, that the works of such authors are difficultly found at all; thirdly, that it is a very hard task to read them, in order to extract these flowers from them; and lastly, it is very often difficult to transplant them at all, they being like some flowers of a very nice nature which will flourish in no soil but their own. For it is easy to transcribe a thought, but not the want of one. The *Earl of Essex,* [4] for instance, is a little garden of choice rarities whence you can scarce transplant one line so as to preserve its original beauty. This must account to the reader for his missing the names of several of his acquaintance, which he had certainly found there had I ever read their works; for which, if I have not a just esteem, I can at least say with Cicero, *Quae non contemno, quippe quae nunquam legerim.* [5] However, that the reader may meet with due satisfaction in this point, I have a young commentator from the University who is reading over all the modern tragedies, at five shillings a dozen, and collecting all that they have stole from our author, which shall shortly be added as an appendix to this work.

[1] 'To voice grief in prosaic language.'
[2] Fielding's loose translation of a sentence in Cicero's *De Oratore* follows immediately.
[3] 'In point of dignity, tragedy surpasses all other forms of writing.'
[4] This play of John Banks is specifically burlesqued by Fielding.
[5] 'I do not despise these things, for I have never read them.'

DRAMATIS PERSONÆ

MEN

KING ARTHUR, *a passionate sort of king, husband to* QUEEN DOLLALLOLLA, *of whom he stands a little in fear; father to* HUNCAMUNCA, *whom he is very fond of; and in love with* GLUMDALCA.

TOM THUMB THE GREAT, *a little hero with a great soul, something violent in his temper, which is a little abated by his love for* HUNCAMUNCA.

GHOST OF GAFFER THUMB, *a whimsical sort of Ghost.*

LORD GRIZZLE, *extremely zealous for the liberty of the subject, very choleric in his temper, and in love with* HUNCAMUNCA.

MERLIN, *a conjurer, and in some sort father to* TOM THUMB.

NOODLE, ⎱ *courtiers in place, and consequently of that*
DOODLE, ⎰ *party that is uppermost.*

FOODLE, *a courtier that is out of place, and consequently of that party that is undermost.*

BAILIFF *and* ⎱ *of the party of the plaintiff.*
FOLLOWER, ⎰

PARSON, *of the side of the church.*

WOMEN

QUEEN DOLLALLOLLA, *wife to* KING ARTHUR, *and mother to* HUNCAMUNCA, *a woman entirely faultless, saving that she is a little given to drink, a little too much a virago towards her husband, and in love with* TOM THUMB.

THE PRINCESS HUNCAMUNCA, *daughter to their Majesties* KING ARTHUR *and* QUEEN DOLLALLOLLA, *of a very sweet, gentle, and amorous disposition, equally in love with* LORD GRIZZLE *and* TOM THUMB, *and desirous to be married to them both.*

GLUMDALCA, *of the giants, a captive queen, beloved by the king, but in love with* TOM THUMB.

CLEORA ⎱ *maids of honor,* ⎱ NOODLE.
MUSTACHA ⎰ *in love with* ⎰ DOODLE.

Courtiers, Guards, Rebels, Drums, Trumpets, Thunder and Lightning.

SCENE. — THE COURT OF KING ARTHUR, AND A PLAIN THEREABOUTS.

THE TRAGEDY OF TRAGEDIES;

OR,

THE LIFE AND DEATH OF TOM THUMB THE GREAT

With the Annotations of

H. SCRIBLERUS SECUNDUS *

[HENRY FIELDING]

ACT I

SCENE I

The Palace.

DOODLE, NOODLE.

DOOD. Sure such a [1] day as this was never seen!
The sun himself, on this auspicious day,
Shines like a beau in a new birthday suit:
This down the seams embroidered, that the beams.
All nature wears one universal grin. 5

NOOD. This day, O Mr. Doodle, is a day
Indeed! — a day [2] we never saw before.

[1] Corneille recommends some very remarkable day, wherein
to fix the action of a tragedy. This the best of our tragical
writers have understood to mean a day remarkable for the
serenity of the sky, or what we generally call a fine summer's
day: so that, according to this their exposition, the same months
are proper for tragedy which are proper for pastoral. Most of
our celebrated English tragedies, as *Cato* [ADDISON], *Mariamne*
[FENTON], *Tamerlane* [ROWE], &c., begin with their observations on the morning. Lee seems to have come the nearest to
this beautiful description of our author's:

> The morning dawns with an unwonted crimson,
> The flowers all odorous seem, the garden birds
> Sing louder, and the laughing sun ascends
> The gaudy earth with an unusual brightness:
> All nature smiles. *Cæs[ar] Borg[ia]* [LEE].

Massinissa, in the new *Sophonisba* [THOMSON], is also a favorite
of the sun:

> — The sun too seems
> As conscious of my joy, with broader eye
> To look abroad the world, and all things smile
> Like Sophonisba.

Memnon, in the *Persian Princess* [THEOBALD], makes the
sun decline rising, that he may not peep on objects which would
profane his brightness:

> — The morning rises slow,
> And all those ruddy streaks that used to paint
> The day's approach are lost in clouds, as if
> The horrors of the night had sent 'em back,
> To warn the sun he should not leave the sea,
> To peep, &c.

[2] This line is highly conformable to the beautiful simplicity

The mighty [3] Thomas Thumb victorious comes;
Millions of giants crowd his chariot wheels,
[4] Giants! to whom the giants in Guildhall † 10
of the ancients. It hath been copied by almost every modern.

> Not to be is not to be in woe.
> *State of Innocence* [DRYDEN].
> Love is not sin but where 'tis sinful love.
> *Don Sebastian* [DRYDEN].
> Nature is nature, Lælius.
> *Sophonisba* [THOMSON].
> Men are but men, we did not make ourselves.
> *Revenge* [YOUNG].

[3] Dr. B[entle]y reads, The mighty Tall-mast Thumb. Mr.
D[enni]s, The mighty Thumping Thumb. Mr. T[heobal]d
reads, Thundering. I think Thomas more agreeable to the
great simplicity so apparent in our author.

[4] That learned historian Mr. S[almo]n, in the third number
of his criticism on our author, takes great pains to explode this
passage. 'It is,' says he, 'difficult to guess what giants are here
meant, unless the giant Despair in the *Pilgrim's Progress*, or
the giant Greatness in the *Royal Villain* [sub-title of Theobald's
Persian Princess]; for I have heard of no other sort of giants in
the reign of King Arthur.' Petrus Burmannus [Dutch scholar]
makes three Tom Thumbs, one whereof he supposes to have
been the same whom the Greeks called Hercules, and
that by these giants are to be understood the Centaurs slain by
that hero. Another Tom Thumb he contends to have been no
other than the Hermes Trismegistus of the ancients. The
third Tom Thumb he places under the reign of King Arthur;
to which third Tom Thumb, says he, the actions of the other
two were attributed. Now, though I know that this opinion is
supported by an assertion of Justus Lipsius [Belgian scholar]
'*Thomam illum Thumbum non alium quam Herculem fuisse satis
constat*,' yet shall I venture to oppose one line of Mr. Midwinter
[see *Preface*] against them all:

> In Arthur's court Tom Thumb did live.

'But then,' says Dr. B[entle]y, 'if we place Tom Thumb in
the court of King Arthur, it will be proper to place that court
out of Britain, where no giants were ever heard of.' Spenser,
in his *Fairy Queen*, is of another opinion, where, describing
Albion, he says,

> — Far within a savage nation dwelt
> Of hideous giants.

And in the same canto:

> Then Elfar, with two brethren giants had,
> The one of which had two heads —
> The other three.

Risum teneatis, amici. ['Restrain your laughter, friends.']

* Henry Fielding had used this pseudonym, without the 'H.,'
in *The Author's Farce* (1730) and in the second and third editions of *Tom Thumb* (1730). 'Secundus' recognizes Pope's
prior use of 'Scriblerus.'

† Tall wooden images of Gog and Magog, set up in Guildhall in 1708.

ftn. 3] 1751 (fourth) ed. reads *Thumbing* for *Thumping*.

Are infant dwarfs. They frown, and foam, and roar,
While Thumb, regardless of their noise, rides on.
So some cock-sparrow in a farmer's yard,
Hops at the head of an huge flock of turkeys.

DOOD. When Goody Thumb first brought this
    Thomas forth,   15
The Genius of our land triumphant reigned;
Then, then, O Arthur! did thy Genius reign.

NOOD. They tell me it is [5] whispered in the books
Of all our sages, that this mighty hero,
By Merlin's art begot, hath not a bone   20
Within his skin, but is a lump of gristle.

DOOD. Then 'tis a gristle of no mortal kind;
Some god, my Noodle, stept into the place
Of Gaffer Thumb, and more than [6] half begot
This mighty Tom.

NOOD.   [7] — Sure he was sent express   25
From heav'n to be the pillar of our state.
Though small his body be, so very small
A chairman's leg is more than twice as large,
Yet is his soul like any mountain big;
And as a mountain once brought forth a mouse,   30
[8] So doth this mouse contain a mighty mountain.

DOOD. Mountain indeed! So terrible his name,
[9] The giant nurses frighten children with it,
And cry Tom Thumb is come, and if you are
Naughty, will surely take the child away.   35

---

[5] 'To whisper in books,' says Mr. D[enni]s, 'is errant [arrant] nonsense.' I am afraid this learned man does not sufficiently understand the extensive meaning of the word whisper. If he had rightly understood what is meant by the 'senses whisp'ring the soul,' in the *Persian Princess* [THEOBALD], or what 'whisp'-ring like winds' is in *Aurengzebe* [DRYDEN], or like thunder in another author, he would have understood this. Emmeline [heroine of *King Arthur*] in Dryden sees a voice, but she was born blind, which is an excuse Panthea cannot plead in *Cyrus* [BANKS], who hears a sight:
    —— Your description will surpass
All fiction, painting, or dumb show of horror,
That ever ears yet heard, or eyes beheld.
When Mr. D[enni]s understands these, he will understand whispering in books.

[6] — Some ruffian stept into his father's place,
And more than half begot him.
           Mary Q[ueen] of Scots [BANKS].

[7] — For Ulamar seems sent express from heaven,
To civilize this rugged Indian clime.
           Liberty Asserted [DENNIS].

[8] '*Omne majus continet in se minus, sed minus non in se majus continere potest*,' ['The greater ever contains the less, but the less cannot contain the greater'] says Scaliger in *Thumbo*. — I suppose he would have cavilled at these beautiful lines in the *Earl of Essex* [BANKS]:
    —— Thy most inveterate soul,
That looks through the foul prison of thy body.
And at those of Dryden:
    The palace is without too well designed;
    Conduct me in, for I will view thy mind.
           Aurengzebe [DRYDEN].

[9] Mr. Banks hath copied this almost verbatim:
It was enough to say, here's Essex come,
And nurses stilled their children with the fright.
           E[arl] of Essex [BANKS].

NOOD. But hark! [10] these trumpets speak the
    king's approach.

DOOD. He comes most luckily for my petition.
           (*Flourish.*)

SCENE II

KING, QUEEN, GRIZZLE, NOODLE, DOODLE, FOODLE.

KING. [11] Let nothing but a face of joy appear;
The man who frowns this day shall lose his head,
That he may have no face to frown withal.
Smile, Dollallolla! — Ha! what wrinkled sorrow
[12] Hangs, sits, lies, frowns upon thy knitted brow?   5
Whence flow those tears fast down thy blubbered
    cheeks,
Like a swoln gutter, gushing through the streets?

QUEEN. [13] Excess of joy, my lord, I've heard folks
    say,
Gives tears as certain as excess of grief.

KING. If it be so, let all men cry for joy,   10
[14] Till my whole court be drownèd with their tears;

---

[10] The trumpet in a tragedy is generally as much as to say *Enter King*, which makes Mr. Banks, in one of his plays, call it 'the trumpet's formal sound.'

[11] Phraortes, in the *Captives* [GAY], seems to have been acquainted with King Arthur:
Proclaim a festival for seven days' space,
Let the court shine in all its pomp and lustre,
Let all our streets resound with shouts of joy;
Let music's care-dispelling voice be heard;
The sumptuous banquet and the flowing goblet
Shall warm the cheek and fill the heart with gladness.
Astarbe shall sit mistress of the feast.

[12] Repentance frowns on thy contracted brow.
           Sophonisba [THOMSON].
Hung on his clouded brow, I marked despair.
           Ibid.
    —— A sullen gloom
Scowls on his brow.   *Busiris* [YOUNG].

[13] Plato is of this opinion, and so is Mr. Banks:
Behold these tears sprung from fresh pain and joy.
           E[arl] of Essex [BANKS].

[14] These floods are very frequent in the tragic authors:
Near to some murmuring brook I'll lay me down,
Whose waters, if they should too shallow flow,
My tears shall swell them up till I will drown.
           LEE'S *Sophonisba*.
Pouring forth tears at such a lavish rate,
That were the world on fire they might have drowned
The wrath of heav'n, and quenched the mighty ruin.
           Mithridates [LEE].
One author changes the waters of grief to those of joy:
    —— These tears, that sprung from tides of grief,
Are now augmented to a flood of joy.
           Cyrus the Great [BANKS].
Another:
Turns all the streams of heat, and makes them flow
In pity's channel.   *Royal Villain* [THEOBALD].
One drowns himself:
    —— Pity like a torrent pours me down,
Now I am drowning all within a deluge.
           Anna Bullen [BANKS].
Cyrus drowns the whole world:
Our swelling grief
Shall melt into a deluge, and the world
Shall drown in tears.   *Cyrus the Great* [BANKS].

Nay, till they overflow my utmost land,
And leave me nothing but the sea to rule.

DOOD. My liege, I a petition have here got.

KING. Petition me no petitions, sir, to-day; 15
Let other hours be set apart for business.
To-day it is our pleasure to be [15] drunk,
And this our queen shall be as drunk as we.

QUEEN. (Though I already [16] half seas over am)
If the capacious goblet overflow 20
With arrack * punch — 'fore George! I'll see it out:
Of rum, and brandy, I'll not taste a drop.

KING. Though rack, in punch, eight shillings be a
    quart,
And rum and brandy be no more than six,
Rather than quarrel you shall have your will. 25
                  (*Trumpets.*)
But, ha! the warrior comes — the great Tom
    Thumb —
The little hero, giant-killing boy,
Preserver of my kingdom, is arrived.

SCENE III

TOM THUMB *to them, with Officers, Prisoners,*
and Attendants.

KING. [17] Oh! welcome most, most welcome to my
    arms.
What gratitude can thank away the debt
Your valor lays upon me?

QUEEN (*aside*). ——— [18] Oh! ye gods!

THUMB. When I'm not thanked at all, I'm
    thanked enough;

[15] An expression vastly beneath the dignity of tragedy, says
Mr. D[enni]s, yet we find the word he cavils at in the mouth of
Mithridates less properly used, and applied to a more terrible
idea:
    I would be drunk with death.
                  Mithrid[ates] [LEE].
The author of the new *Sophonisba* [THOMSON] taketh hold of
this monosyllable, and uses it pretty much to the same purpose:
    The Carthaginian sword with Roman blood
    Was drunk.
I would ask Mr. D[enni]s which gives him the best idea, a
drunken king, or a drunken sword?
Mr. Tate dresses up King Arthur's resolution in heroics:
    Merry, my lord, o' th' captain's humor right,
    I am resolved to be dead drunk to-night.
Lee also uses this charming word:
    Love's the drunkenness of the mind.
                  Gloriana [LEE].
[16] Dryden hath borrowed this, and applied it improperly:
    I'm half seas o'er in death.
                 Cleom[enes] [DRYDEN].
[17] This figure is in great use among the tragedians:
    'Tis therefore, therefore 'tis.
                  Victim [JOHNSON].
    I long, repent, repent, and long again.
                 Busiris [YOUNG].
[18] A tragical exclamation.

---

* Native spirituous liquor (an Eastern term).

[19] I've done my duty, and I've done no more. 5

QUEEN (*aside*). Was ever such a godlike creature
    seen?

KING. Thy modesty's a [20] candle to thy merit,
It shines itself, and shows thy merit too.
But say, my boy, where didst thou leave the giants?

THUMB. My liege, without the castle gates they
    stand, 10
The castle gates too low for their admittance.

KING. What look they like?

THUMB. Like nothing but themselves.

QUEEN (*aside*). [21] And sure thou art like nothing
    but thyself.

KING. Enough! the vast idea fills my soul. 15
I see them — yes, I see them now before me:
The monstrous, ugly, barb'rous sons of whores.
But ha! what form majestic strikes our eyes?
[22] So perfect, that it seems to have been drawn
By all the gods in council: so fair she is, 20
That surely at her birth the council paused,
And then at length cried out, 'This is a woman!'

THUMB. Then were the gods mistaken — she is
    not
A woman, but a giantess — whom we,
[23] With much ado, have made a shift to haul 25
Within the town: [24] for she is by a foot

[19] This line is copied verbatim in the *Captives* [GAY].
[20] We find a candlestick for this candle in two celebrated
authors: —
    —— Each star withdraws
    His golden head, and burns within the socket.
                  Nero [LEE].
    A soul grown old and sunk into the socket.
                 Sebastian [DRYDEN].
[21] This simile occurs very frequently among the dramatic
writers of both kinds.
[22] Mr. Lee hath stolen this thought from our author:
    — This perfect face, drawn by the gods in council,
    Which they were long a making.
           Lu[cius] Jun[ius] Brut[us] [LEE].
    —— At his birth the heavenly council paused,
    And then at last cried out, 'This is a man!'
Dryden hath improved this hint to the utmost perfection:
    So perfect, that the very gods who formed you, wondered
    At their own skill, and cried, 'A lucky hit
    Has mended our design!' Their envy hindered,
    Or you had been immortal, and a pattern,
    When heaven would work for ostentation sake,
    To copy out again.   *All for Love* [DRYDEN].
Banks prefers the works of Michael Angelo to that of the gods:
    A pattern for the gods to make a man by,
    Or Michael Angelo to form a statue.
[23] It is impossible, says Mr. W— [Welsted? Warburton?]
sufficiently to admire this natural easy line.
[24] This tragedy, which in most points resembles the ancients,
differs from them in this — that it assigns the same honor to
lowness of stature which they did to height. The gods and
heroes in Homer and Virgil are continually described higher
by the head than their followers, the contrary of which is observed by our author. In short, to exceed on either side is
equally admirable, and a man of three foot is as wonderful a
sight as a man of nine.

Shorter than all her subject giants were.

GLUM. We yesterday were both a queen and wife,
One hundred thousand giants owned our sway,
Twenty whereof were married to ourself.   30

QUEEN. Oh! happy state of giantism — where husbands
Like mushrooms grow, whilst hapless we are forced
To be content, nay, happy thought, with one.

GLUM. But then to lose them all in one black day,
That the same sun which, rising, saw me wife   35
To twenty giants, setting, should behold
Me widowed of them all. — 25 My worn-out heart,
That ship, leaks fast, and the great heavy lading,
My soul, will quickly sink.

QUEEN.   Madam, believe
I view your sorrows with a woman's eye;   40
But learn to bear them with what strength you may,
To-morrow we will have our grenadiers
Drawn out before you, and you then shall choose
What husbands you think fit.

GLUM.   26 Madam, I am
Your most obedient and most humble servant.   45

KING. Think, mighty princess, think this court your own,
Nor think the landlord me, this house my inn;
Call for whate'er you will, you'll nothing pay.
27 I feel a sudden pain within my breast,
Nor know I whether it arise from love   50
Or only the wind-colic. Time must show.
O Thumb! what do we to thy valor owe!
Ask some reward, great as we can bestow.

THUMB. 28 I ask not kingdoms, I can conquer those;
I ask not money, money I've enough;   55
For what I've done, and what I mean to do,
For giants slain, and giants yet unborn,
Which I will slay — if this be called a debt,
Take my receipt in full: I ask but this, —
29 To sun myself in Huncamunca's eyes.   60

KING. Prodigious bold request.

QUEEN (aside).   — 30 Be still, my soul.

25 My blood leaks fast, and the great heavy lading
My soul will quickly sink.   Mithrid[ates] [LEE].
My soul is like a ship.   Injured Love [TATE].
26 This well-bred line seems to be copied in the Persian Princess [THEOBALD]:
        To be your humblest and most faithful slave.
27 This doubt of the king puts me in mind of a passage in the Captives [GAY], where the noise of feet is mistaken for the rustling of leaves.
        —— Methinks I hear
        The sound of feet:
        No; 'twas the wind that shook yon cypress boughs.
28 Mr. Dryden seems to have had this passage in his eye in the first page of Love Triumphant. [Fielding's mistake; the passage parodied is in The Indian Queen, I. i. 30–36.]
29 Don Carlos, in the Revenge [YOUNG], suns himself in the charms of his mistress:
        While in the lustre of her charms I lay.
30 A tragical phrase much in use.

THUMB. 31 My heart is at the threshold of your mouth,
And waits its answer there. — Oh! do not frown.
I've tried, to reason's tune, to tune my soul,
But love did overwind and crack the string.   65
Though Jove in thunder had cried out, YOU SHAN'T,
I should have loved her still — for oh, strange fate!
Then when I loved her least, I loved her most!

KING. It is resolved — the princess is your own.

THUMB. Oh! 32 happy, happy, happy, happy Thumb!   70

QUEEN. Consider, sir; reward your soldier's merit,
But give not Huncamunca to Tom Thumb.

KING. Tom Thumb! Odzooks! my wide-extended realm
Knows not a name so glorious as Tom Thumb.
Let Macedonia Alexander boast,   75
Let Rome her Cæsars and her Scipios show,
Her Messieurs France, let Holland boast Mynheers,
Ireland her O's, her Macs let Scotland boast,
Let England boast no other than Tom Thumb.

QUEEN. Though greater yet his boasted merit was,   80
He shall not have my daughter, that is pos'.*

KING. Ha! sayest thou, Dollallolla?

QUEEN.   —— I say he shan't.

KING. 33 Then by our royal self we swear you lie.

QUEEN. 34 Who, but a dog, who, but a dog
Would use me as thou dost? Me, who have lain   85
35 These twenty years so loving by thy side!
But I will be revenged. I'll hang myself.
Then tremble all who did this match persuade,

31 This speech hath been taken to pieces by several tragical authors, who seem to have rifled it, and shared its beauties among them.
        My soul waits at the portal of thy breast,
        To ravish from thy lips the welcome news.
                Anna Bullen [BANKS].
        My soul stands list'ning at my ears.
                Cyrus the Great [BANKS].
        Love to his tune my jarring heart would bring,
        But reason overwinds, and cracks the string.
                D[uke] of Guise [DRYDEN and LEE].
        —— I should have loved,
        Though Jove, in muttering thunder, had forbid it.
                New Sophonisba [THOMSON].
        And when it (my heart) wild resolves to love no more,
        Then is the triumph of excessive love.   Ibidem.
32 Massinissa is one-fourth less happy than Tom Thumb:
        Oh! happy, happy, happy! New Sophonisba.
33 No, by myself.   Anna Bullen [BANKS].
34 —— Who caused
        This dreadful revolution in my fate.
        Ulamar. Who, but a dog — who, but a dog?
                Liberty Asserted [DENNIS].
35 —— A bride,
        Who twenty years lay loving by your side.
                [Anna Bullen] [BANKS].

* Positive.

³⁶ For, riding on a cat, from high I'll fall,
And squirt down royal vengeance on you all.   90

FOOD. ³⁷ Her majesty the queen is in a passion.

KING. ³⁸ Be she, or be she not, I'll to the girl
And pave thy way, O Thumb. — Now by ourself,
We were indeed a pretty king of clouts
To truckle to her will. — For when by force   95
Or art the wife her husband overreaches,
Give him the petticoat, and her the breeches.

THUMB. ³⁹ Whisper ye winds, that Huncamunca's
    mine!
Echoes repeat, that Huncamunca's mine!
The dreadful business of the war is o'er,   100
And beauty, heav'nly beauty! crowns my toils!
I've thrown the bloody garment now aside,
And hymeneal sweets invite my bride.

So when some chimney-sweeper all the day
Hath through dark paths pursued the sooty way, 105
At night, to wash his hands and face he flies,
And in his t'other shirt with his Brickdusta lies.

SCENE IV

GRIZZLE solus.

[GRIZZLE.] ⁴⁰ Where art thou, Grizzle? where are
    now thy glories?
Where are the drums that waken thee to honor?
Greatness is a laced coat from Monmouth-street,*
Which fortune lends us for a day to wear,
To-morrow puts it on another's back.   5
The spiteful sun but yesterday surveyed
His rival high as Saint Paul's cupola;
Now may he see me as Fleet-ditch laid low.

SCENE V

QUEEN, GRIZZLE.

QUEEN. ⁴¹ Teach me to scold, prodigious-minded
    Grizzle.
Mountain of treason, ugly as the devil,
Teach this confounded hateful mouth of mine

---

³⁶ For, borne upon a cloud, from high I'll fall,
    And rain down royal vengeance on you all.
                        Albion Queens [BANKS].
³⁷ An information very like this we have in the *Tragedy of
Love* [BANKS], where, Cyrus having stormed in the most violent
manner, Cyaxares observes very calmly,
        Why, nephew Cyrus — you are moved.
³⁸ 'Tis in your choice:
        Love me, or love me not.
                        Conquest of Granada.
[Hillhouse notes that this speech is not in Dryden's play.]
³⁹ There is not one beauty in this charming speech but hath
been borrowed by almost every tragic writer.
⁴⁰ Mr. Banks has (I wish I could not say too servilely) imitated this of Grizzle in his *Earl of Essex:*
        Where art thou, Essex, &c.
⁴¹ The Countess of Nottingham, in the *Earl of Essex* [BANKS],
is apparently acquainted with Dollallolla.

---

* Known for its old clothes dealers.

To spout forth words malicious as thyself,
Words which might shame all Billingsgate to
    speak.   5

GRIZ. Far be it from my pride to think my tongue
Your royal lips can in that art instruct,
Wherein you so excel. But may I ask,
Without offence, wherefore my queen would scold?

QUEEN. Wherefore? Oh! blood and thunder!
    ha'n't you heard   10
(What ev'ry corner of the court resounds)
That little Thumb will be a great man made?

GRIZ. I heard it, I confess — for who, alas!
⁴² Can always stop his ears? — But would my teeth,
By grinding knives, had first been set on edge! 15

QUEEN. Would I had heard, at the still noon of
    night,
The hallaloo of fire in every street!
Odsbobs! I have a mind to hang myself,
To think I should a grandmother be made
By such a rascal! — Sure the king forgets   20
When in a pudding, by his mother put,
The bastard, by a tinker, on a stile
Was dropped. — O, good lord Grizzle! can I bear
To see him from a pudding mount the throne?
Or can, oh can, my Huncamunca bear   25
To take a pudding's offspring to her arms?

GRIZ. O horror! horror! horror! cease, my queen.
⁴³ Thy voice, like twenty screech-owls, wracks my
    brain.

QUEEN. Then rouse thy spirit — we may yet
    prevent
This hated match.

GRIZ. —— We will; ⁴⁴ not fate itself,   30
Should it conspire with Thomas Thumb, should
    cause it.
I'll swim through seas; I'll ride upon the clouds;
I'll dig the earth; I'll blow out every fire;
I'll rave; I'll rant; I'll rise; I'll rush; I'll roar;   ⎫
Fierce as the man whom ⁴⁵ smiling dolphins bore ⎬ 35
From the prosaic to poetic shore.   ⎭
I'll tear the scoundrel into twenty pieces.

QUEEN. Oh, no! prevent the match, but hurt
    him not;
For, though I would not have him have my daughter,

---

⁴² Grizzle was not probably possessed of that glue of which
Mr. Banks speaks in his *Cyrus*:
        I'll glue my ears to ev'ry word.
⁴³ Screech-owls, dark ravens, and amphibious monsters,
        Are screaming in that voice. *Mary Q[ueen] of Scots* [BANKS].
⁴⁴ The reader may see all the beauties of this speech in a late
ode, called the *Naval Lyric* [by Edward Young, published April,
1730].
⁴⁵ This epithet to a dolphin doth not give one so clear an idea
as were to be wished; a smiling fish seeming a little more difficult to be imagined than a flying fish. Mr. Dryden is of
opinion that smiling is the property of reason, and that no
irrational creature can smile:
        Smiles not allowed to beasts from reason move.
                        State of Innocence [DRYDEN].

Yet can we kill the man that killed the giants?   40

GRIZ. I tell you, madam, it was all a trick;
He made the giants first, and then he killed them;
As fox-hunters bring foxes to the wood,
And then with hounds they drive them out again.

QUEEN. How! have you seen no giants? Are
there not   45
Now, in the yard, ten thousand proper giants?

GRIZ. [46] Indeed I cannot positively tell,
But firmly do believe there is not one.

QUEEN. Hence! from my sight! thou traitor, hie
away;
By all my stars! thou enviest Tom Thumb.   50
Go, sirrah! go,[47] hie away! hie! — thou art
A setting dog: begone!

GRIZ.   Madam, I go.
Tom Thumb shall feel the vengeance you have
raised.
So, when two dogs are fighting in the streets,
With a third dog one of the two dogs meets,   55
With angry teeth he bites him to the bone,
And this dog smarts for what that dog had done.

SCENE VI

QUEEN sola.

[QUEEN.] And whither shall I go? — Alack a day!
I love Tom Thumb — but must not tell him so;
For what's a woman, when her virtue's gone?
A coat without its lace; wig out of buckle;
A stocking with a hole in't — I can't live   5
Without my virtue, or without Tom Thumb.
[48] Then let me weigh them in two equal scales;
In this scale put my virtue, that, Tom Thumb.
Alas! Tom Thumb is heavier than my virtue.
But hold! — perhaps I may be left a widow: 10
This match prevented, then Tom Thumb is mine:

[46] These lines are written in the same key with those in the
Earl of Essex [BANKS]:
> Why, say'st thou so? I love thee well, indeed
> I do, and thou shalt find by this, 'tis true.

Or with this in *Cyrus* [BANKS]:
> The most heroic mind that ever was.

And with above half of the modern tragedies.

[47] Aristotle, in that excellent work of his which is very justly
styled his masterpiece, earnestly recommends using the terms
of art, however coarse or even indecent they may be.   Mr.
Tate is of the same opinion.
> *Bru.* Do not, like young hawks, fetch a course about:
>   Your game flies fair.
> *Fra.* Do not fear it.
>   He answers you in your hawking phrase.
>   *Injured Love* [TATE].

I think these two great authorities are sufficient to justify
Dollallolla in the use of the phrase, 'Hie away, hie!' when in
the same line she says she is speaking to a setting dog.

[48] We meet with such another pair of scales in Dryden's
King Arthur:
> Arthur and Oswald, and their different fates,
> Are weighing now within the scales of heav'n.

Also in *Sebastian* [DRYDEN]:
> This hour my lot is weighing in the scales.

In that dear hope I will forget my pain.
So, when some wench to Tothill-Bridewell's *
sent,
With beating hemp and flogging she's content;
She hopes in time to ease her present pain,   15
At length is free, and walks the streets again.

ACT II

SCENE I

The street.

BAILIFF, FOLLOWER.

BAIL. Come on, my trusty follower, come on;
This day discharge thy duty, and at night
A double mug of beer, and beer shall glad thee.
Stand here by me, this way must Noodle pass.

FOL. No more, no more, O bailiff! every word   5
Inspires my soul with virtue. — Oh! I long
To meet the enemy in the street — and nab him;
To lay arresting hands upon his back,
And drag him trembling to the sponging-house.

BAIL. There when I have him, I will sponge upon
him.   10
[49] Oh! glorious thought! by the sun, moon, and stars,
I will enjoy it, though it be in thought!
Yes, yes, my follower, I will enjoy it.

FOL. Enjoy it then some other time, for now
Our prey approaches.   15

BAIL. Let us retire.

SCENE II

TOM THUMB, NOODLE, BAILIFF, FOLLOWER.

THUMB. Trust me, my Noodle, I am wondrous
sick;
For, though I love the gentle Huncamunca,
Yet at the thought of marriage I grow pale;
For, oh! [50] but swear thou'lt keep it ever secret,
I will unfold a tale will make thee stare.   5

NOOD. I swear by lovely Huncamunca's charms

THUMB. Then know — [51] my grandmamma hath
often said,

[49] Mr. Rowe is generally imagined to have taken some hints
from this scene in his character of Bajazet [in *Tamerlane*]; but
as he, of all the tragic writers, bears the least resemblance to
our author in his diction, I am unwilling to imagine he would
condescend to copy him in this particular.

[50] This method of surprising an audience, by raising their
expectation to the highest pitch, and then baulking it, hath
been practised with great success by most of our tragical authors.

[51] Almeyda, in *Sebastian* [DRYDEN], is in the same distress:
> Sometimes methinks I hear the groan of ghosts,
> Thin hollow sounds and lamentable screams;
> Then, like a dying echo from afar,
> My mother's voice that cries, 'Wed not, Almeyda;
> Forewarned, Almeyda, marriage is thy crime.'

---

* A London jail where disorderly women were punished by
being forced to beat hemp.

'Tom Thumb, beware of marriage.'

NOOD.   Sir, I blush
To think a warrior, great in arms as you,
Should be affrighted by his grandmamma.   10
Can an old woman's empty dreams deter
The blooming hero from the virgin's arms?
Think of the joy that will your soul alarm,
When in her fond embraces clasped you lie,
While on her panting breast, dissolved in bliss,   15
You pour out all Tom Thumb in every kiss.

    THUMB. Oh! Noodle, thou hast fired my eager
      soul;
Spite of my grandmother she shall be mine;
I'll hug, caress, I'll eat her up with love.
Whole days, and nights, and years shall be too
    short   20
For our enjoyment; every sun shall rise
52 Blushing to see us in our bed together.

    NOOD. O, sir! this purpose of your soul pursue.
    BAIL. O, sir! I have an action against you.
    NOOD. At whose suit is it?   25
    BAIL. At your tailor's, sir.
Your tailor put this warrant in my hands,
And I arrest you, sir, at his commands.

    THUMB. Ha! dogs! Arrest my friend before my
      face!
Think you Tom Thumb will suffer this disgrace?   30
But let vain cowards threaten by their word,
Tom Thumb shall show his anger by his sword.
                (Kills the Bailiff and his Follower.)

    BAIL. Oh, I am slain!
    FOL.   I am murdered also
And to the shades, the dismal shades below,
My bailiff's faithful follower I go.   35

    NOOD. 53 Go then to hell, like rascals as you are,
And give our service to the bailiffs there.

    THUMB. Thus perish all the bailiffs in the land,
Till debtors at noon-day shall walk the streets,
And no one fear a bailiff or his writ.   40

---

52 'As very well he may, if he hath any modesty in him,'
says Mr. D[enni]s. The author of *Busiris* is extremely zealous
to prevent the sun's blushing at any indecent object; and therefore on all such occasions he addresses himself to the sun, and
desires him to keep out of the way.
    Rise never more, O sun! let night prevail,
    Eternal darkness close the world's wide scene.
                        Busiris [YOUNG].
    Sun, hide thy face, and put the world in mourning.
                               Ibid.
Mr. Banks makes the sun perform the office of Hymen, and
therefore not likely to be disgusted at such a sight:
    The sun sets forth like a gay brideman with you.
                  Mary Q[ueen] of Scots [BANKS].
53 Nourmahal sends the same message to heaven:
    For I would have you, when you upwards move,
    Speak kindly of us to our friends above.
                    Aurengzebe [DRYDEN].
We find another 'to hell,' in the *Persian Princess* [THEOBALD]:
    Villain, get thee down
    To hell, and tell them that the fray's begun.

SCENE III

The Princess Huncamunca's apartment. —

HUNCAMUNCA, CLEORA, MUSTACHA.

HUNC. 54 Give me some music — see that it be sad.

    CLEORA *sings.*

[I]

Cupid, ease a love-sick maid,
Bring thy quiver to her aid;
With equal ardor wound the swain:
Beauty should never sigh in vain.   5

II

Let him feel the pleasing smart,
Drive thy arrow through his heart;
When one you wound, you then destroy;
When both you kill, you kill with joy.

    HUNC. 55 O Tom Thumb! Tom Thumb! where-
    fore art thou Tom Thumb?   10
Why hadst thou not been born of royal race?
Why had not mighty Bantam been thy father?
Or else the King of Brentford, Old or New? *

    MUST. I am surprised that your Highness can
give yourself a moment's uneasiness about that   15
little insignificant fellow,56 Tom Thumb the Great —
one properer for a plaything than a husband. —
Were he my husband, his horns should be as long as
his body. — If you had fallen in love with a grenadier, I should not have wondered at it. — If you   20
had fallen in love with something; but to fall in love
with nothing!

    HUNC. Cease, my Mustacha, on thy duty cease.
The zephyr, when in flow'ry vales it plays,
Is not so soft, so sweet as Thummy's breath.   25
The dove is not so gentle to its mate.

    MUST. The dove is every bit as proper for a
husband. — Alas! madam, there's not a beau about
the court looks so little like a man. He is a perfect butterfly, a thing without substance, and   30
almost without shadow too.

    HUNC. This rudeness is unseasonable: desist;
Or I shall think this railing comes from love.
Tom Thumb's a creature of that charming form,
That no one can abuse, unless they love him.   35

    MUST. Madam, the king.

---

54 Anthony gives the same command in the same words.
                       [*All for Love.* DRYDEN].
55 Oh! Marius, Marius, wherefore art thou Marius?
                          Otway's Marius.
56 Nothing is more common than these seeming contradictions; such as,
                Haughty weakness.   *Victim* [JOHNSON].
                Great small world.
                   Noah's Flood [ECCLESTONE].

* The Two Kings of Brentford are burlesqued in *The Rehearsal.*

SCENE IV

KING, HUNCAMUNCA.

KING. Let all but Huncamunca leave the room.
Exeunt CLEORA *and* MUSTACHA.
Daughter, I have observed of late some grief
Unusual in your countenance — your eyes
[57] That, like two open windows, used to show
The lovely beauty of the rooms within,   5
Have now two blinds before them. — What is the cause?
Say, have you not enough of meat and drink?
We've giv'n strict orders not to have you stinted.

HUNC. Alas! my lord, I value not myself
That once I eat two fowls and half a pig;   10
[58] Small is that praise! but oh! a maid may want
What she can neither eat nor drink.

KING.   What's that?

HUNC. O [59] spare my blushes; but I mean a husband.

KING. If that be all, I have provided one,
A husband great in arms, whose warlike sword   15
Streams with the yellow blood of slaughtered giants,
Whose name in Terra Incognita is known,
Whose valor, wisdom, virtue make a noise
Great as the kettle-drums of twenty armies.

HUNC. Whom does my royal father mean?

KING.   Tom Thumb.   20

HUNC. Is it possible?

KING.   Ha! the window-blinds are gone;

---

[57] Lee hath improved this metaphor:
　　Dost thou not view joy peeping from my eyes,
　　The casements opened wide to gaze on thee,
　　So Rome's glad citizens to windows rise,
　　When they some young triumpher fain would see.
　　　　　　　　　　　Gloriana [LEE].

[58] Almahide hath the same contempt for these appetites:
　　To eat and drink can no perfection be.
　　　　　　　　Conquest of Granada [DRYDEN].
The Earl of Essex is of a different opinion, and seems to place the chief happiness of a general therein:
　　Were but commanders half so well rewarded,
　　Then they might eat.   BANKS's *Earl of Essex*.
But, if we may believe one who knows more than either, the devil himself, we shall find eating to be an affair of more moment than is generally imagined:
　　Gods are immortal only by their food.
　　　　　　Lucifer, in the *State of Innocence* [DRYDEN].

[59] 'This expression is enough of itself,' says Mr. D[enni]s, 'utterly to destroy the character of Huncamunca!' Yet we find a woman of no abandoned character in Dryden adventuring farther, and thus excusing herself:
　　To speak our wishes first, forbid it pride,
　　Forbid it modesty; true, they forbid it,
　　But Nature does not. When we are athirst,
　　Or hungry, will imperious Nature stay,
　　Nor eat, nor drink, before 'tis bid fall on?
　　　　　　　　　　Cleomenes [DRYDEN].
Cassandra speaks before she is asked: Huncamunca afterwards. Cassandra speaks her wishes to her lover: Huncamunca only to her father.

---

[60] A country-dance of joy is in your face;
Your eyes spit fire, your cheeks grow red as **beef**.

HUNC. Oh, there's a magic-music in that sound,
Enough to turn me into beef indeed!   25
Yes, I will own, since licensed by your word,
I'll own Tom Thumb the cause of all my grief.
For him I've sighed, I've wept, I've gnawed my sheets.

KING. Oh! thou shalt gnaw thy tender sheets no more;
A husband thou shalt have to mumble now.   30

HUNC. Oh! happy sound! henceforth let no one tell
That Huncamunca shall lead apes in hell.*
Oh! I am overjoyed!

KING.   I see thou art.
[61] Joy lightens in thy eyes, and thunders from thy brows;
Transports, like lightning, dart along thy soul,   35
As small-shot through a hedge.

HUNC.   Oh! say not small.

KING. This happy news shall on our tongue ride post,
Ourself we bear the happy news to Thumb.
Yet think not, daughter, that your powerful charms
Must still detain the hero from his arms;   40
Various his duty, various his delight;
Now is his turn to kiss, and now to fight;
And now to kiss again. So, mighty [62] Jove,
When with excessive thund'ring tired above,
Comes down to earth, and takes a bit — and then   45
Flies to his trade of thund'ring back again.

SCENE V

GRIZZLE, HUNCAMUNCA.

[63] GRIZ. Oh! Huncamunca, Huncamunca, oh!

---

[60] Her eyes resistless magic bear;
　　Angels, I see, and gods are dancing there.
　　　　　　　　　　LEE's *Sophonisba*.

[61] Mr. Dennis, in that excellent tragedy called *Liberty Asserted*, which is thought to have given so great a stroke to the late French king, hath frequent imitations of this beautiful speech of King Arthur:
　　Conquest light'ning in his eyes, and thund'ring in his arm.
　　Joy lightened in her eyes.
　　Joys like lightning dart along my soul.

[62] Jove, with excessive thund'ring tired above,
　　Comes down for ease, enjoys a nymph, and then
　　Mounts dreadful, and to thund'ring goes again.
　　　　　　　　　　Gloriana [LEE].

[63] This beautiful line, which ought, says Mr. W— [Welsted? Warburton?], to be written in gold, is imitated in the *New Sophonisba* [THOMSON]:
　　Oh! Sophonisba, Sophonisba, oh!
　　Oh! Narva, Narva, oh!
The author of a song called *Duke upon Duke* hath improved it:
　　Alas! O Nick! O Nick, alas!
Where, by the help of a little false spelling, you have two meanings in the repeated words.

---

* The proverbial fate of one who dies an old maid.

Thy pouting breasts, like kettle-drums of brass,
Beat everlasting loud alarms of joy;
As bright as brass they are, and oh, as hard.
Oh! Huncamunca, Huncamunca, oh! 5

HUNC. Ha! dost thou know me, princess as I am,
[64] That thus of me you dare to make your game?

GRIZ. Oh! Huncamunca, well I know that you
A princess are, and a king's daughter, too;
But love no meanness scorns, no grandeur fears; ⎫ 10
Love often lords into the cellar bears, ⎬
And bids the sturdy porter come up stairs. ⎭
For what's too high for love, or what's too low?
Oh! Huncamunca, Huncamunca, oh!

HUNC. But, granting all you say of love were
true, 15
My love, alas! is to another due!
In vain to me a suitoring you come,
For I'm already promised to Tom Thumb.

GRIZ. And can my princess such a durgen * wed?
One fitter for your pocket than your bed! 20
Advised by me, the worthless baby shun,
Or you will ne'er be brought to bed of one.
Oh, take me to thy arms, and never flinch,
Who am a man, by Jupiter! ev'ry inch.
[65] Then, while in joys together lost we lie, 25
I'll press thy soul while gods stand wishing by.

HUNC. If, sir, what you insinuate you prove,
All obstacles of promise you remove;
For all engagements to a man must fall,
Whene'er that man is proved no man at all. 30

GRIZ. Oh! let him seek some dwarf, some fairy
miss,
Where no joint-stool must lift him to the kiss.
But, by the stars and glory! you appear
Much fitter for a Prussian grenadier;
One globe alone on Atlas' shoulders rests, 35
Two globes are less than Huncamunca's breasts;
The milky way is not so white, that's flat,
And sure thy breasts are full as large as that.

HUNC. Oh, sir, so strong your eloquence I find,
It is impossible to be unkind. 40

GRIZ. Ah! speak that o'er again; and let the
[66] sound
From one pole to another pole rebound;
The earth and sky each be a battledore,

---

[64] Edith, in the *Bloody Brother* [FLETCHER], speaks to her
lover in the same familiar language:
    Your grace is full of game.
[65] Traverse the glittering chambers of the sky,
    Borne on a cloud in view of fate I'll lie,
    And press her soul while gods stand wishing by.
        Hannibal [LEE].
[66] Let the four winds from distant corners meet,
    And on their wings first bear it into France;
    Then back again to Edina's† proud walls,
    Till victim to the sound th' aspiring city falls.
        Albion Queens [BANKS].

---

* Dwarf. † Edinburgh's.

And keep the sound, that shuttlecock, up an hour!
To Doctors-Commons * for a license I, 45
Swift as an arrow from a bow, will fly.

HUNC. Oh, no! lest some disaster we should meet,
'Twere better to be married at the Fleet.†

GRIZ. Forbid it, all ye powers, a princess should
By that vile place contaminate her blood; 50
My quick return shall to my charmer prove
I travel on the [67] post-horses of love.

HUNC. Those post-horses to me will seem too slow
Though they should fly swift as the gods, when they
Ride on behind that post-boy, Opportunity. 55

SCENE VI

TOM THUMB, HUNCAMUNCA.

THUMB. Where is my princess? where's my
Huncamunca?
Where are those eyes, those cardmatches of love,
That [68] light up all with love my waxen soul?
Where is that face with artful nature made
[69] In the same moulds where Venus' self was cast? 5

---

[67] I do not remember any metaphors so frequent in the tragic
poets as those borrowed from riding post:
    The gods and opportunity ride post.
        Hannibal [LEE].
    —— Let's rush together,
    For death rides post:
        Duke of Guise [LEE, but in his *Cæsar Borgia*].
    Destruction gallops to thy murder post.
        Gloriana [LEE].
[68] This image, too, very often occurs:
    —— Bright as when thy eye
    First lighted up our loves. *Aurengzebe* [DRYDEN].
    'Tis not a crown alone lights up my name.
        Busiris [YOUNG].
[69] There is great dissension among the poets concerning the
method of making man. One tells his mistress that the mould
she was made in being lost, heaven cannot form such another.
Lucifer, in Dryden, gives a merry description of his own formation:
    Whom heaven, neglecting, made and scarce designed,
    But threw me in for number to the rest.
        State of Innocence [DRYDEN]
In one place, the same poet supposes man to be made of metal:
        I was formed
    Of that coarse metal which, when she was made,
    The gods threw by for rubbish.
        All for Love [DRYDEN].
In another, of dough:
    When the gods moulded up the paste of man,
    Some of their clay was left upon their hands,
    And so they made Egyptians. *Cleomenes* [DRYDEN].
In another, of clay:
    —— Rubbish of remaining clay.
        Sebastian [DRYDEN].
One makes the soul of wax:
    Her waxen soul begins to melt apace.
        Anna Bullen [BANKS].
Another of flint:
    Sure our two souls have somewhere been acquainted
    In former beings, or, struck out together,
    One spark to Afric flew, and one to Portugal.
        Sebastian [DRYDEN].

---

* Where marriage licenses could be procured.
† Where secret marriages could be arranged.

HUNC. 70 Oh! what is music to the ear that's deaf,
Or a goose-pie to him that has no taste?
What are these praises now to me, since I
Am promised to another?

THUMB.   Ha! promised?

HUNC. Too sure; 'tis written in the book of
fate.   10

THUMB. 71 Then I will tear away the leaf
Wherein it's writ; or, if fate won't allow
So large a gap within its journal-book,
I'll blot it out at least.

SCENE VII

GLUMDALCA, TOM THUMB, HUNCAMUNCA.

GLUM. 72 I need not ask if you are Huncamunca,
Your brandy-nose proclaims —

HUNC.   I am a princess;
Nor need I ask who you are.

GLUM.   A giantess;
The queen of those who made and unmade queens.

HUNC. The man whose chief ambition is to be 5
My sweetheart hath destroyed these mighty giants.

GLUM. Your sweetheart? Dost thou think the
man who once
Hath worn my easy chains will e'er wear thine?

HUNC. Well may your chains be easy, since, if
fame
Says true, they have been tried on twenty husbands.   10

73 The glove or boot, so many times pulled on,

To omit the great quantities of iron, brazen, and leaden souls
which are so plenty in modern authors — I cannot omit the
dress of a soul as we find it in Dryden:
        Souls shirted but with air.   *King Arthur.*
Nor can I pass by a particular sort of soul in a particular sort
of description in the *New Sophonisba* [THOMSON]:
        Ye mysterious powers,
        —— Whether through your gloomy depths I wander,
        Or on the mountains walk, give me the calm,
        The steady smiling soul, where wisdom sheds
        Eternal sunshine, and eternal joy.
70 This line Mr. Banks has plundered entire in his *Anna
Bullen.*
71 Good heaven! the book of fate before me lay,
        But to tear out the journal of that day.
        Or, if the order of the world below
        Will not the gap of one whole day allow,
        Give me that minute when she made her vow.
                        Conquest of Granada [DRYDEN].
72 I know some of the commentators have imagined that Mr.
Dryden, in the altercative scene between Cleopatra and Octavia [*All for Love,* Act III], a scene which Mr. Addison inveighs
against with great bitterness [in *The Guardian,* no. 110], is much
beholden to our author. How just this their observation is I
will not presume to determine.
73 'A cobbling poet indeed,' says Mr. D[ennis]; and yet I believe we may find as monstrous images in the tragic authors: I'll
put down one:
Untie your folded thoughts, and let them dangle loose as a
        bride's hair.   *Injured Love* [TATE].
Which line seems to have as much title to a milliner's shop as
our author's to a shoemaker's.

May well sit easy on the hand or foot.

GLUM. I glory in the number, and when I
Sit poorly down, like thee, content with one,
Heaven change this face for one as bad as thine. 15

HUNC. Let me see nearer what this beauty is
That captivates the heart of men by scores.
                    (*Holds a candle to her face.*)
Oh! heaven, thou art as ugly as the devil.

GLUM. You'd give the best of shoes within your
shop
To be but half so handsome.

HUNC.   Since you come 20
74 To that, I'll put my beauty to the test:
Tom Thumb, I'm yours, if you with me will go.

GLUM. Oh! stay, Tom Thumb, and you alone
shall fill
That bed where twenty giants used to lie.

THUMB. In the balcony that o'erhangs the
stage,   25
I've seen a whore two 'prentices engage;
One half-a-crown does in his fingers hold,
The other shows a little piece of gold;
She the half-guinea wisely does purloin,
And leaves the larger and the baser coin.   30

GLUM. Left, scorned, and loathed for such a chit
as this;
75 I feel the storm that's rising in my mind,
Tempests and whirlwinds rise, and roll, and roar.
I'm all within a hurricane, as if
76 The world's four winds were pent within my
carcase.   35
77 Confusion, horror, murder, guts, and death!

SCENE VIII

KING, GLUMDALCA.

KING. 78 Sure never was so sad a king as I!
79 My life is worn as ragged as a coat
A beggar wears; a prince should put it off.

74 Mr. L— [Lee? Lyttelton?] takes occasion in this place to
commend the great care of our author to preserve the metre of
blank verse, in which Shakespeare, Jonson, and Fletcher were
so notoriously negligent; and the moderns, in imitation of our
author, so laudably observant:
                        Then does
        Your majesty believe that he can be
        A traitor?   *Earl of Essex* [BANKS].
Every page of *Sophonisba* [THOMSON] gives us instances of this
excellence.
75 Love mounts and rolls about my stormy mind.
                        Aurengzebe [DRYDEN].
        Tempests and whirlwinds through my bosom move.
                        Cleom[enes] [DRYDEN].
76 With such a furious tempest on his brow,
        As if the world's four winds were pent within
        His blustering carcase.   *Anna Bullen* [BANKS].
77 *Verba Tragica.*
78 This speech hath been terribly mauled by the poet.
79 —— My life is worn to rags,
        Not worth a prince's wearing.
                        Love Triumph[ant] [DRYDEN].

[30] To love a captive and a giantess!
Oh love! oh love! how great a king art thou! 5
My tongue's thy trumpet, and thou trumpetest,
Unknown to me, within me. [81] Oh, Glumdalca!
Heaven thee designed a giantess to make,
But an angelic soul was shuffled in.
[82] I am a multitude of walking griefs, 10
And only on her lips the balm is found
[83] To spread a plaster that might cure them all.
GLUM. What do I hear?
KING.   What do I see?
GLUM.   Oh!
KING.   Ah!
[84] GLUM. Ah! wretched queen!
KING.   Oh! wretched king!
[85] GLUM.   Ah!
KING.   Oh!

SCENE IX

TOM THUMB, HUNCAMUNCA, PARSON.

PAR. Happy's the wooing that's not long a-doing;
For, if I guess aright, Tom Thumb this night
Shall give a being to a new Tom Thumb.
THUMB. It shall be my endeavor so to do.
HUNC. Oh! fie upon you, sir, you make me
    blush. 5

[80] Must I beg the pity of my slave?
  Must a king beg? But love's a greater king,
  A tyrant, nay, a devil, that possesses me.
  He tunes the organ of my voice and speaks,
  Unknown to me, within me.   Sebastian [DRYDEN].
[81] When thou wert formed heaven did a man begin;
  But a brute soul by chance was shuffled in.
                    Aurengzebe [DRYDEN].
[82] —— I am a multitude
  Of walking griefs.
     New Sophonisba [But not in THOMSON's play].
[83] I will take thy scorpion blood,
  And lay it to my grief till I have ease.
                    Anna Bullen [BANKS].
[84] Our author, who everywhere shows his great penetration
into human nature, here outdoes himself: where a less judicious
poet would have raised a long scene of whining love, he, who
understood the passions better, and that so violent an affection
as this must be too big for utterance, chooses rather to send
his characters off in this sullen and doleful manner, in which
admirable conduct he is imitated by the author [MALLET] of
the justly celebrated Eurydice. Dr. Young seems to point at
this violence of passions:
           —— Passion chokes
  Their words, and they're the statues of despair.
And Seneca tells us, 'Curæ leves loquuntur, ingentes stupent.'
['Light cares speak out; the weighty have no words.'] The
story of the Egyptian king in Herodotus is too well known to
need to be inserted; I refer the more curious reader to the excellent Montaigne, who hath written an essay [Essais, I, 2] on
this subject.
[85] To part is death. ——
  ———— ———— ———— ———— ———— 'Tis death to part.
  ———— ———— ———— ———— ———— ———— Ah!
  ———— ———— ———— ———— ———— ———— Oh!
Don Carlos [OTWAY, but passage is in GAY, What D'ye Call It,
I. ii].

THUMB. It is the virgin's sign, and suits you well:
[86] I know not where, nor how, nor what I am;
[87] I'm so transported, I have lost myself.
HUNC. Forbid it, all ye stars, for you're so small,
That were you lost, you'd find yourself no more. 10
So the unhappy sempstress once, they say,
Her needle in a pottle, lost, of hay;
In vain she looked, and looked, and made her moan,
For ah, the needle was forever gone.
PAR. Long may they live, and love, and propa-
    gate, 15
Till the whole land be peopled with Tom Thumbs!
[88] So, when the Cheshire cheese a maggot breeds,
Another and another still succeeds:
By thousands and ten thousands they increase,
Till one continued maggot fills the rotten cheese. 20

[86] Nor know I whether
  What am I, who, or where.
                    Busiris [YOUNG].
  I was I know not what, and am I know not how.
                    Gloriana [LEE].
[87] To understand sufficiently the beauty of this passage, it
will be necessary that we comprehend every man to contain
two selfs. I shall not attempt to prove this from philosophy,
which the poets make so plainly evident.
One runs away from the other:
    —— Let me demand your majesty,
  Why fly you from yourself?
              Duke of Guise [DRYDEN and LEE].
In a second, one self is a guardian to the other:
  Leave me the care of me.
             Conquest of Granada [DRYDEN].
Again:
  Myself am to myself less near.
                    Ibid.
In the same, the first self is proud of the second:
  I myself am proud of me.
           State of Innocence [DRYDEN].
In a third, distrustful of him:
  Fain I would tell, but whisper it in mine ear,
  That none besides might hear, nay, not myself.
             Earl of Essex [BANKS].
In a fourth, honors him:
  I honor Rome,
  And honor too myself.
             Sophonisba [THOMSON].
In a fifth, at variance with him:
  Leave me not thus at variance with myself.
             Busiris [YOUNG].
Again, in a sixth:
  I find myself divided from myself.
             Medea [JOHNSON].
  She seemed the sad effigies of herself.
         [Albion Queens] Banks.
  Assist me, Zulema, if thou wouldst be
  The friend thou seemest, assist me against me.
Albion Queens [But this reference belongs above with Banks.
The present couplet is from The Conquest of Granada, Part I,
Act II. Hillhouse notes the misprint, but it still persists.]
From all which it appears that there are two selfs; and there-
fore Tom Thumb's losing himself is no such solecism as it hath
been represented by men rather ambitious of criticising than
qualified to criticise.
[88] Mr. F[ielding] imagines this parson to have been a Welsh
one, from his simile.

SCENE X

NOODLE, and then GRIZZLE.

NOOD. [89] Sure, Nature means to break her solid chain,
Or else unfix the world, and in a rage
To hurl it from its axletree and hinges;
All things are so confused, the king's in love,
The queen is drunk, the princess married is.   5
GRIZ. Oh, Noodle! Hast thou Huncamunca seen?
NOOD. I've seen a thousand sights this day, where none
Are by the wonderful bitch herself outdone.
The king, the queen, and all the court, are sights.
GRIZ. [90] D—n your delay, you trifler! are you drunk, ha?   10
I will not hear one word but Huncamunca.
NOOD. By this time she is married to Tom Thumb.
GRIZ. [91] My Huncamunca!
NOOD. Your Huncamunca,
Tom Thumb's Huncamunca, every man's Huncamunca.   15
GRIZ. If this be true, all womankind are damned.
NOOD. If it be not, may I be so myself.
GRIZ. See where she comes! I'll not believe a word
Against that face, upon whose [92] ample brow
Sits innocence with majesty enthroned.   20

GRIZZLE, HUNCAMUNCA.

GRIZ. Where has my Huncamunca been? See here
The license in my hand!
HUNC.   Alas! Tom Thumb.
GRIZ. Why dost thou mention him?
HUNC.   Ah, me! Tom Thumb.
GRIZ. What means my lovely Huncamunca?
HUNC.   Hum!
GRIZ. Oh! speak.
HUNC.   Hum!
GRIZ.   Ha! your every word is hum.   25
[93] You force me still to answer you, Tom Thumb.

[89] Our author hath been plundered here, according to custom:
  Great Nature, break thy chain that links together
  The fabric of the world, and make a chaos
  Like that within my soul.   *Love Triumphant* [DRYDEN].
  —— Startle Nature, unfix the globe,
  And hurl it from its axletree and hinges.
            Albion Queens [BANKS].
  The tott'ring earth seems sliding off its props.
            [*The Persian Princess*, THEOBALD].
[90] D—n your delay, ye torturers, proceed;
  I will not hear one word but Almahide.
            Conq[uest] of Granada [DRYDEN].
[91] Mr. Dryden hath imitated this in *All for Love* [Act IV].
[92] This Miltonic style abounds in the *New Sophonisba*
[THOMSON]:
  —— And on her ample brow
  Sat majesty.
[93] Your ev'ry answer still so ends in that,
  You force me still to answer you Morat.
            Aurengzebe [DRYDEN].

[94] Tom Thumb, Tom Thumb, Tom Thumb — you love the name;
Tom Thumb — I'm on the rack — I'm in a flame.
So pleasing is that sound, that, were you dumb,
You still would find a voice to cry, 'Tom Thumb.'   30
HUNC. Oh! be not hasty to proclaim my doom!
My ample heart for more than one has room:
A maid like me heaven formed at least for two —
[95] I married him, and now I'll marry you.
GRIZ. Ha! dost thou own thy falsehood to my face?   35
Think'st thou that I will share thy husband's place?
Since to that office one cannot suffice,
And since you scorn to dine one single dish on,
Go, get your husband put into commission.
Commissioners to discharge (ye gods! it fine is)   40
The duty of a husband to your Highness.
Yet think not long I will my rival bear,
Or unrevenged the slighted willow wear;
The gloomy, brooding tempest, now confined
Within the hollow caverns of my mind,   45
In dreadful whirl shall roll along the coasts,
Shall thin the land of all the men it boasts,
[96] And cram up ev'ry chink of hell with ghosts.
[97] So have I seen, in some dark winter's day,
A sudden storm rush down the sky's highway,   50
Sweep through the streets with terrible ding-dong,
Gush through the spouts, and wash whole crowds along.
The crowded shops the thronging vermin screen,
Together cram the dirty and the clean,
And not one shoe-boy in the street is seen.   55
HUNC. Oh, fatal rashness! should his fury slay

[94] Morat, Morat, Morat! you love the name.
            Aurengzebe.
[95] 'Here is a sentiment for the virtuous Huncamunca!' says Mr. D[enni]s. And yet, with the leave of this great man, the virtuous Panthea, in *Cyrus*, hath an heart every whit as ample:
  For two I must confess are gods to me,
  Which is my Abradatus first, and thee.
            Cyrus the Great [BANKS].
Nor is the lady in *Love Triumphant* [DRYDEN] more reserved, though not so intelligible:
  I am so divided,
  That I grieve most for both, and love both most.
[96] A ridiculous supposition to any one who considers the great and extensive largeness of hell, says a commentator; but not so to those who consider the great expansion of immaterial substance. Mr. Banks makes one soul to be so expanded that heaven could not contain it:
  The heavens are all too narrow for her soul.
            Virtue Betrayed [BANKS].
The *Persian Princess* [THEOBALD] hath a passage not unlike the author of this:
  We will send such shoals of murdered slaves,
  Shall glut hell's empty regions.
This threatens to fill hell, even though it were empty: Lord Grizzle, only to fill up the chinks, supposing the rest already full.
[97] Mr. Addison is generally thought to have had this simile in his eye when he wrote that beautiful one at the end of the third act of his *Cato*.

My hapless bridegroom on his wedding-day,
I, who this morn of two chose which to wed,
May go again this night alone to bed.
98 So have I seen some wild unsettled fool, 60
Who had her choice of this and that joint-stool,
To give the preference to either loth,
And fondly coveting to sit on both,
While the two stools her sitting-part confound,
Between 'em both fall squat upon the ground. 65

ACT III

SCENE I

KING ARTHUR'S *palace.*

99 GHOST (*solus*). Hail! ye black horrors of mid-
night's midnoon!
Ye fairies, goblins, bats, and screech-owls, hail!
And, oh! ye mortal watchmen, whose hoarse throats
Th' immortal ghosts' dread croakings counterfeit,
All hail! — Ye dancing phantoms, who, by day, 5

98 This beautiful simile is founded on a proverb which does
honor to the English language:
Between two stools the breech falls to the ground.
I am not so well pleased with any written remains of the
ancients as with those little aphorisms which verbal tradition
hath delivered down to us under the title of proverbs. It were
to be wished that, instead of filling their pages with the fabulous
theology of the pagans, our modern poets would think it worth
their while to enrich their works with the proverbial sayings
of their ancestors. Mr. Dryden hath chronicled one in heroic:
Two *ifs* scarce make one possibility.
                                    Conquest of Granada [DRYDEN].
My Lord Bacon is of opinion that, whatever is known of arts
and sciences might be proved to have lurked in the Proverbs of
Solomon. I am of the same opinion in relation to those above
mentioned; at least I am confident that a more perfect system
of ethics, as well as economy, might be compiled out of them
than is at present extant, either in the works of the ancient
philosophers, or those more valuable, as more voluminous ones
of the modern divines.
99 Of all the particulars in which the modern stage falls short
of the ancient, there is none so much to be lamented as the
great scarcity of ghosts in the latter. Whence this proceeds I
will not presume to determine. Some are of opinion that the
moderns are unequal to that sublime language which a ghost
ought to speak. One says, ludicrously, that ghosts are out of
fashion; another, that they are properer for comedy; forgetting,
I suppose, that Aristotle hath told us that a ghost is the soul of
tragedy; for so I render the ψυχὴ ὁ μῦθος τῆς τραγωδίας which
M. Dacier [French critic], amongst others, hath mistaken; I
suppose misled by not understanding the *fabula* of the Latins,
which signifies a ghost as well as a fable.
Te premet nox, fabulæque manes.   *Hor*[ace].
['Night presses down on thee, and the storied shades.']
Of all the ghosts that have ever appeared on the stage, a very
learned and judicious foreign critic gives the preference to this
of our author. These are his words, speaking of this tragedy:
— *Nec quidquam in illâ admirabilius quàm phasma quoddam hor-
rendum, quod omnibus aliis spectris, quibuscum scatet Angelorum
tragædia, longè* (*pace D—ysii V. Doctiss. dixerim*) *prætulerim.*
['Nor is there in that tragedy anything more admirable than a
certain horrifying ghost which I should far prefer to all other
ghosts in which English tragedy abounds — speaking with due
respect to the most learned man Dionysius.' (? Dennis)]

Are some condemned to fast, some feast in fire,
Now play in churchyards, skipping o'er the graves,
To the 100 loud music of the silent bell,
All hail!

SCENE II

KING *and* GHOST.

KING. What noise is this? What villain dares,
At this dread hour, with feet and voice profane,
Disturb our royal walls?
GHOST.   One who defies
Thy empty power to hurt him; 101 one who dares
Walk in thy bedchamber.
KING.   Presumptuous slave! 5
Thou diest.
GHOST.   Threaten others with that word:
102 I am a ghost, and am already dead.
KING. Ye stars! 'tis well. Were thy last hour to
come,
This moment had been it; 103 yet by thy shroud
I'll pull thee backward, squeeze thee to a bladder, 10
Till thou dost groan thy nothingness away.
Thou flyest! 'Tis well.   (*Ghost retires.*)
104 I thought what was the courage of a ghost!
Yet, dare not, on thy life — Why say I that,
Since life thou hast not? — Dare not walk again 15
Within these walls, on pain of the Red Sea.
For, if henceforth I ever find thee here,
As sure, sure as a gun, I'll have thee laid —
GHOST. Were the Red Sea a sea of Holland's
gin,

100 We have already given instances of this figure.
101 Almanzor reasons in the same manner:
                            —— A ghost I'll be;
        And from a ghost, you know, no place is free.
                                    Conq[uest] of Granada [DRYDEN].
102 'The man who writ this wretched pun,' says Mr. D[ennis],
'would have picked your pocket:' which he proceeds to show
not only bad in itself, but doubly so on so solemn an occasion.
And yet, in that excellent play of *Liberty Asserted* [DENNIS], we
find something very much resembling a pun in the mouth of a
mistress, who is parting with the lover she is fond of:
    Ul. Oh, mortal woe! one kiss, and then farewell.
    Irene. The gods have given to others to fare well.
        O! miserably must Irene fare.
Agamemnon, in the *Victim* [JOHNSON], is full as facetious on
the most solemn occasion — that of sacrificing his daughter:
        Yes, daughter, yes; you will assist the priest;
        Yes, you must offer up your — vows for Greece.
103 I'll pull thee backwards by thy shroud to light,
        Or else I'll squeeze thee, like a bladder, there,
        And make thee groan thyself away to air.
                                    Conquest of Granada [DRYDEN].
Snatch me, ye gods, this moment into nothing.
                                    Cyrus the Great [BANKS].
104 So, art thou gone? Thou canst no conquest boast:
    I thought what was the courage of a ghost.
                                    Conquest of Granada [DRYDEN].
King Arthur seems to be as brave a fellow as Almanzor, who
says most heroically,
                In spite of ghosts I'll on.

The liquor (when alive) whose very smell   20
I did detest, did loathe — yet, for the sake
Of Thomas Thumb, I would be laid therein.
    KING. Ha! said you?
    GHOST.   Yes, my liege, I said Tom Thumb,
Whose father's ghost I am — once not unknown
To mighty Arthur. But, I see, 'tis true,   25
The dearest friend, when dead, we all forget.
    KING. 'Tis he — it is the honest Gaffer Thumb.
Oh! let me press thee in my eager arms,
Thou best of ghosts! thou something more than
    ghost!
    GHOST. Would I were something more, that we
    again   30
Might feel each other in the warm embrace.
But now I have th' advantage of my king,
[105] For I feel thee, whilst thou dost not feel me.
    KING. But say, [106] thou dearest air, oh! say what
    dread,
Important business sends thee back to earth?   35
    GHOST. Oh! then prepare to hear — which but
    to hear
Is full enough to send thy spirit hence.
Thy subjects up in arms, by Grizzle led,
Will, ere the rosy-fingered morn shall ope
The shutters of the sky, before the gate   40
Of this thy royal palace, swarming spread.
[107] So have I seen the bees in clusters swarm,
So have I seen the stars in frosty nights,
So have I seen the sand in windy days,
So have I seen the ghosts on Pluto's shore,   45
So have I seen the flowers in spring arise,
So have I seen the leaves in autumn fall,
So have I seen the fruits in summer smile,
So have I seen the snow in winter frown.
    KING. D—n all thou'st seen! dost thou, beneath
    the shape   50
Of Gaffer Thumb, come hither to abuse me
With similes, to keep me on the rack?
Hence — or, by all the torments of thy hell,
[108] I'll run thee through the body, though thou'st
    none.

[105] The ghost of Lausaria, in *Cyrus*, is a plain copy of this, and is therefore worth reading:
    Ah, Cyrus!
    Thou may'st as well grasp water, or fleet air,
    As think of touching my immortal shade.
                  Cyrus the Great [BANKS].
[106] Thou better part of heavenly air.
                  Conquest of Granada [DRYDEN].
[107] 'A string of similes,' says one, 'proper to be hung up in the cabinet of a prince.'
[108] This passage [DRYDEN, *King Arthur*, II. ii] hath been understood several different ways by the commentators. For my part, I find it difficult to understand it at all. Mr. Dryden says:
    I've heard something how two bodies meet,
    But how two souls join I know not.
So that, till the body of a spirit be better understood, it will be difficult to understand how it is possible to run him through it.

    GHOST. Arthur, beware! I must this moment
    hence,   55
Not frighted by your voice, but by the cocks!
Arthur beware, beware, beware, beware!
Strive to avert thy yet impending fate;
For, if thou'rt killed to-day,
To-morrow all thy care will come too late.   60

SCENE III

KING *solus*.

    KING. Oh! stay, and leave me not uncertain thus!
And whilst thou tellest me what's like my fate,
Oh! teach me how I may avert it too!
Curst be the man who first a simile made!
Curst ev'ry bard who writes! — So have I seen   5
Those whose comparisons are just and true,
And those who liken things not like at all.
The devil is happy that the whole creation
Can furnish out no simile to his fortune.

SCENE IV

KING, QUEEN.

    QUEEN. What is the cause, my Arthur, that you
    steal
Thus silently from Dollallolla's breast?
Why dost thou leave me in the [109] dark alone,
When well thou know'st I am afraid of sprites?
    KING. Oh, Dollallolla! do not blame my love!   5
I hoped the fumes of last night's punch had laid
Thy lovely eyelids fast. — But, oh! I find
There is no power in drams to quiet wives;
Each morn, as the returning sun, they wake,
And shine upon their husbands.
    QUEEN.   Think, oh think!   10
What a surprise it must be to the sun,
Rising, to find the vanished world away.
What less can be the wretched wife's surprise
When, stretching out her arms to fold thee fast,
She folds her useless bolster in her arms.   15
[110] Think, think, on that. — Oh! think, think well
    on that!
I do remember also to have read
[111] In Dryden's *Ovid's Metamorphoses*,
That Jove in form inanimate did lie
With beauteous Danaë: and, trust me, love,   20
[112] I feared the bolster might have been a Jove.

[109] Cydaria is of the same fearful temper with Dollallolla.
    I never durst in darkness be alone.
                Ind[ian] Emp[eror] [DRYDEN].
[110] Think well of this, think that, think every way.
                Sophonisba [THOMSON].
[111] These quotations are more usual in the comic than in the tragic writers.
[112] 'This distress,' says Mr. D[ennis], 'I must allow to be extremely beautiful, and tends to heighten the virtuous character of Dollallolla, who is so exceeding delicate, that she is in the highest apprehension from the inanimate embrace of a bolster. An example worthy of imitation from all our writers of tragedy.'

KING. Come to my arms, most virtuous of thy sex;
O, Dollallolla! were all wives like thee,
So many husbands never had worn horns.
Should Huncamunca of thy worth partake, 25
Tom Thumb indeed were blest. — Oh, fatal name!
For didst thou know one quarter what I know,
Then wouldst thou know — Alas! what thou
    wouldst know!
QUEEN. What can I gather hence? Why dost
    thou speak
Like men who carry raree-shows about? 30
'Now you shall see, gentlemen, what you shall see.'
O, tell me more, or thou hast told too much.

SCENE V

KING, QUEEN, NOODLE.

NOOD. Long life attend your majesties serene,
Great Arthur, king, and Dollallolla, queen!
Lord Grizzle, with a bold rebellious crowd,
Advances to the palace, threat'ning loud,
Unless the princess be delivered straight, } 5
And the victorious Thumb, without his pate, }
They are resolved to batter down the gate. }

SCENE VI

KING, QUEEN, HUNCAMUNCA, NOODLE.

KING. See where the princess comes! Where is
    Tom Thumb?
HUNC. Oh! sir, about an hour and half ago
He sallied out to encounter with the foe,
And swore, unless his fate had him misled, }
From Grizzle's shoulders to cut off his head, } 5
And serve't up with your chocolate in bed. }
KING. 'Tis well, I found one devil told us both.
Come, Dollallolla, Huncamunca, come;
Within we'll wait for the victorious Thumb;
In peace and safety we secure may stay, 10
While to his arm we trust the bloody fray;
Though men and giants should conspire with gods,
113 He is alone equal to all these odds.
QUEEN. He is, indeed, 114 a helmet to us all;

---

113   'Credat Judæus Appella,
                    Non ego,'
says Mr. D[ennis]. 'For, passing over the absurdity of being
equal to odds, can we possibly suppose a little insignificant
fellow — I say again, a little insignificant fellow — able to vie
with a strength which all the Samsons and Herculeses of
antiquity would be unable to encounter?' I shall refer this
incredulous critic to Mr. Dryden's defence of his Almanzor;
and, lest that should not satisfy him, I shall quote a few lines
from the speech of a much braver fellow than Almanzor, Mr.
Johnson's Achilles:
    Though human race rise in embattled hosts,
    To force her from my arms — Oh! son of Atreus!
    By that immortal pow'r, whose deathless spirit
    Informs this earth, I will oppose them all.
                                    Victim [JOHNSON].
114 'I have heard of being supported by a staff,' says Mr.
D[ennis], 'but never of being supported by an helmet.' I be-

While he supports, we need not fear to fall; 15
His arm dispatches all things to our wish,
And serves up every foe's head in a dish.
Void is the mistress of the house of care,
While the good cook presents the bill of fare;
Whether the cod, that northern king of fish, 20
Or duck, or goose, or pig, adorn the dish,
No fears the number of her guests afford,
But at her hour she sees the dinner on the board.

SCENE VII

A plain.

LORD GRIZZLE, FOODLE, and Rebels.

GRIZ. Thus far our arms with victory are
    crowned;
For, though we have not fought, yet we have found
115 No enemy to fight withal.
FOOD.   Yet I,
Methinks, would willingly avoid this day,
116 This first of April, to engage our foes. 5
GRIZ. This day, of all the days of th' year, I'd
    choose,
For on this day my grandmother was born.
Gods! I will make Tom Thumb an April-fool;
117 Will teach his wit an errand it ne'er knew,
And send it post to the Elysian shades. 10
FOOD. I'm glad to find our army is so stout,
Nor does it move my wonder less than joy.
GRIZ. 118 What friends we have, and how we came
    so strong,
I'll softly tell you as we march along.

---

lieve he never heard of sailing with wings, which he may read
in no less a poet than Mr. Dryden:
        Unless we borrow wings, and sail through air.
            Love Triumphant [DRYDEN, but in King Arthur].
        What will he say to a kneeling valley?
            —— I'll stand
        Like a safe valley, that low bends the knee
        To some aspiring mountain.   Injured Love [TATE].
I am ashamed of so ignorant a carper, who doth not know that
an epithet in tragedy is very often no other than an expletive.
Do not we read in the New Sophonisba [THOMSON] of 'grinding
chains, blue plagues, white occasions, and blue serenity?'
Nay, 'tis not the adjective only, but sometimes half a sentence
is put by way of expletive, as, 'Beauty pointed high with spirit,'
in the same play; and, 'In the lap of blessing, to be most curst,'
in the Revenge [YOUNG].
115 A victory like that of Almanzor:
        Almanzor is victorious without fight.
                    Conq[uest] of Granada [DRYDEN].
116 Well have we chose an happy day for fight;
        For every man, in course of time, has found
        Some days are lucky, some unfortunate.
                    K[ing] Arthur [DRYDEN].
117 We read of such another in Lee:
        Teach his rude wit a flight she never made,
        And send her post to the Elysian shade.
                    Gloriana [LEE].
118 These lines are copied verbatim in the Indian Emperor.
                    [DRYDEN].

SCENE VIII

Thunder and Lightning.

TOM THUMB, GLUMDALCA, *cum suis.*

THUMB. Oh, Noodle! hast thou seen a day like this?
[119] The unborn thunder rumbles o'er our heads,
[120] As if the gods meant to unhinge the world;
And heaven and earth in wild confusion hurl;
Yet will I boldly tread the tott'ring ball.   5
MERL. [*without*].   Tom Thumb!
THUMB.   What voice is this I hear?
MERL. [*without*].   Tom Thumb!
THUMB. Again it calls.
MERL. [*without*].   Tom Thumb!
GLUM.   It calls again.
THUMB. Appear, whoe'er thou art; I fear thee not.
MERL. [*appearing*]. Thou hast no cause to fear, I
am thy friend,
Merlin by name, a conjurer by trade,   10
And to my art thou dost thy being owe.
THUMB. How!
MERL. Hear then the mystic getting of Tom
Thumb.
[121] His father was a ploughman plain,
    His mother milked the cow;   15
And yet the way to get a son
    This couple knew not how.
Until such time the good old man
    To learnèd Merlin goes,
And there to him, in great distress,   20
    In secret manner shows;
How in his heart he wished to have
    A child, in time to come,
To be his heir, though it may be
    No bigger than his thumb: 25
Of which old Merlin was foretold
    That he his wish should have;
And so a son of stature small
    The charmer to him gave.
Thou'st heard the past, look up and see the fu-
ture.   30
THUMB. [122] Lost in amazement's gulf, my senses
sink;
See there, Glumdalca, see another [123] me!

[119] Unborn thunder rolling in a cloud.
    Conq[uest] of Gran[ada] [DRYDEN].
[120] Were heaven and earth in wild confusion hurled,
Should the rash gods unhinge the rolling world,
Undaunted would I tread the tottering ball,
Crushed, but unconquered, in the dreadful fall.
    Female Warrior [HOPKINS].
[121] See the *History of Tom Thumb*, page 2.
[122] Amazement swallows up my sense,
And in th' impetuous whirl of circling fate
Drinks down my reason.
    Pers[ian] Princess [THEOBALD].
[123]   I have outfaced myself.
What! am I two? Is there another me?
    K[ing] Arthur [DRYDEN].

GLUM. O sight of horror! see, you are devoured
By the expanded jaws of a red cow.
MERL. Let not these sights deter thy noble
mind,   35
[124] For, lo! a sight more glorious courts thy eyes.
See from afar a theatre arise;
There ages, yet unborn, shall tribute pay
To the heroic actions of this day:
Then buskin tragedy at length shall choose   40
Thy name the best supporter of her muse.
THUMB. Enough: let every warlike music sound.
We fall contented, if we fall renown'd.

SCENE IX

LORD GRIZZLE, FOODLE, *Rebels, on one side;*
TOM THUMB, GLUMDALCA, *on the other.*

FOOD. At length the enemy advances nigh,
[125] I hear them with my ear, and see them with my
eye.
GRIZ. Draw all your swords: for liberty we fight,
[126] And liberty the mustard is of life.
THUMB. Are you the man whom men famed
    Grizzle name?   5
GRIZ. [127] Are you the much more famed Tom
    Thumb?
THUMB.   The same.
GRIZ. Come on; our worth upon ourselves we'll
    prove;
For liberty I fight.
THUMB.   And I for love.
[*A bloody engagement between the two armies
    here; drums beating, trumpets sounding,
    thunder and lightning. — They fight off and
    on several times. Some fall. GRIZZLE and
    GLUMDALCA remain.*]
GLUM. Turn, coward, turn; nor from a woman fly.
GRIZ. Away — thou art too ignoble for my arm.   10
GLUM. Have at thy heart.

[124] The character of Merlin is wonderful throughout, but
most so in this prophetic part. We find several of these proph-
ecies in the tragic authors, who frequently take this opportunity
to pay a compliment to their country, and sometimes to their
prince. None but our author (who seems to have detested the
least appearance of flattery) would have passed by such an
opportunity of being a political prophet.
[125] I saw the villain, Myron; with these eyes I saw him.
    Busiris [YOUNG].
In both which places it is intimated that it is sometimes possible to see with other eyes than your own.
[126] 'This mustard,' says Mr. D[ennis], 'is enough to turn
one's stomach. I would be glad to know what idea the author
had in his head when he wrote it.' This will be, I believe, best
explained by a line of Mr. Dennis:
    And gave him liberty, the salt of life.
    Liberty Asserted [DENNIS].
The understanding that can digest the one will not rise at the
other.
[127] *Han.* Are you the chief whom men famed Scipio call?
    Scip. Are you the much more famous Hannibal?
    Hannib[al] [LEE].

GRIZ.   Nay, then I thrust at thine.
GLUM. You push too well; you've run me
    through the guts.
And I am dead.
GRIZ.   Then there's an end of one.
THUMB. When thou art dead, then there's an end
    of two,
128 Villain.   15
GRIZ. Tom Thumb!
THUMB. Rebel!
GRIZ. Tom Thumb!
THUMB. Hell!
GRIZ. Huncamunca!   20
THUMB. Thou hast it there.
GRIZ. Too sure I feel it.
THUMB. To hell then, like a rebel as you are,
And give my service to the rebels there.
GRIZ. Triumph not, Thumb, nor think thou shalt
    enjoy   25
Thy Huncamunca undisturbed; I'll send
129 My ghost to fetch her to the other world;
130 It shall but bait at heaven, and then return.
131 But, ha! I feel death rumbling in my brains.
132 Some kinder sprite knocks softly at my soul,   30
And gently whispers it to haste away.
I come, I come, most willingly I come.
133 So, when some city wife, for country air,
To Hampstead or to Highgate does repair,
Her to make haste her husband does implore,   35
And cries, 'My dear, the coach is at the door:'
With equal wish, desirous to be gone,
She gets into the coach, and then she cries — 'Drive
    on!'

128 Dr. Young seems to have copied this engagement in his
Busiris:
    Myr. Villain!
    Mem. Myron!
    Myr. Rebel!
    Mem. Myron!
    Myr. Hell!
    Mem. Mandane!
129 This last speech of my Lord Grizzle hath been of great
service to our poets:
            I'll hold it fast
    As life, and when life's gone I'll hold this last;
    And if thou tak'st it from me when I'm slain,
    I'll send my ghost, and fetch it back again.
                        Conquest of Granada [DRYDEN].
130   My soul should with such speed obey,
        It should not bait at heaven to stop its way.
    Lee seems to have had this last in his eye:
        'Twas not my purpose, sir, to tarry there;
        I would but go to heaven to take the air.
                            Gloriana [LEE].
131   A rising vapor rumbling in my brains.
                        Cleomenes [DRYDEN].
132   Some kind sprite knocks softly at my soul,
        To tell me fate's at hand.   [*Sebastian*, DRYDEN].
133 Mr. Dryden seems to have had this simile in his eye, when
he says,
    My soul is packing up, and just on wing.
                        Conquest of Granada [DRYDEN].

THUMB. With those last words 134 he vomited his
    soul,
Which, 135 like whipt cream, the devil will swallow
    down.   40
Bear off the body, and cut off the head,
Which I will to the king in triumph lug.
Rebellion's dead, and now I'll go to breakfast.

SCENE X

KING, QUEEN, HUNCAMUNCA, *Courtiers.*

KING. Open the prisons, set the wretched free,
And bid our treasurer disburse six pounds
To pay their debts. — Let no one weep to-day.
Come, Dollallolla; 136 curse that odious name!
It is so long, it asks an hour to speak it.   5
By heavens! I'll change it into Doll, or Loll,
Or any other civil monosyllable,
That will not tire my tongue. — Come, sit thee down.
Here seated, let us view the dancers' sports;
Bid 'em advance. This is the wedding-day   10
Of Princess Huncamunca and Tom Thumb;
Tom Thumb! who wins two victories 137 to-day,
And this way marches, bearing Grizzle's head.

A dance here.

NOOD. Oh! monstrous, dreadful, terrible, Oh! Oh!
Deaf be my ears, for ever blind my eyes!   15
Dumb be my tongue! feet lame! all senses lost!
138 Howl wolves, grunt bears, hiss snakes, shriek
    all ye ghosts!
KING. What does the blockhead mean?
NOOD.   I mean, my liege,
139 Only to grace my tale with decent horror.
Whilst from my garret, twice two stories high,   20
I looked abroad into the streets below,
I saw Tom Thumb attended by the mob;
Twice twenty shoe-boys, twice two dozen links,
Chairmen and porters, hackney-coachmen, whores;
Aloft he bore the grizzly head of Grizzle;   25
When of a sudden through the streets there came

134   And in a purple vomit poured his soul.
                            Cleomenes [DRYDEN].
135   The devil swallows vulgar souls
            Like whipt cream.   *Sebastian* [DRYDEN].
136   How I could curse my name of Ptolemy!
        It is so long, it asks an hour to write it.
        By heav'n! I'll change it into Jove or Mars!
        Or any other civil monosyllable,
        That will not tire my hand.   *Cleomenes* [DRYDEN].
137 Here is a visible conjunction of two days in one, by which
our author may have either intended an emblem of a wedding,
or to insinuate that men in the honey-moon are apt to imagine
time shorter than it is. It brings into my mind a passage in
the comedy called *The Coffee-House Politician* [FIELDING]:
        We will celebrate this day at my house to-morrow.
138 These beautiful phrases are all to be found in one single
speech of *King Arthur, or The British Worthy* [DRYDEN].
139   I was but teaching him to grace his tale
        With decent horror.   *Cleomenes* [DRYDEN].

A cow, of larger than the usual size,
And in a moment — guess, oh! guess the rest! —
And in a moment swallowed up Tom Thumb.

KING. Shut up again the prisons, bid my treas-
urer   30
Not give three farthings out — hang all the culprits,
Guilty or not — no matter — Ravish virgins;
Go bid the schoolmasters whip all their boys!
Let lawyers, parsons, and physicians loose
To rob, impose on, and to kill the world.   35

NOOD. Her majesty the queen is in a swoon.

QUEEN. Not so much in a swoon but I have still
Strength to reward the messenger of ill news.
                                    (Kills NOODLE.)

NOOD. O! I am slain.

CLE. My lover's killed, I will revenge him so.   40
                                    (Kills the QUEEN.)

HUNC. My mamma killed! vile murderess, beware.
                                    (Kills CLEORA.)

DOOD. This for an old grudge to thy heart.
                                    (Kills HUNCAMUNCA.)

MUST. And this
I drive to thine, O Doodle! for a new one.
                                    (Kills DOODLE.)

KING. Ha! murderess vile, take that.   45
                                    (Kills MUSTACHA.)

140 And take thou this.   (Kills himself, and falls.)

140   We may say with Dryden,
       Death did at length so many slain forget,
       And left the tale, and took them by the great.
                                    [Conquest of Granada].

So when the child, whom nurse from danger guards,
Sends Jack for mustard with a pack of cards,
Kings, queens, and knaves, throw one another down,
Till the whole pack lies scattered and o'er-
thrown;   50
So all our pack upon the floor is cast,
And all I boast is — that I fall the last.   (Dies.)

I know of no tragedy which comes nearer to this charming and
bloody catastrophe than *Cleomenes* [DRYDEN], where the curtain
covers five principal characters dead on the stage. These lines
too —

    I asked no questions then, of who killed who?
    The bodies tell the story as they lie —

seem to have belonged more properly to this scene of our author;
nor can I help imagining they were originally his. *The Rival
Ladies* [DRYDEN], too, seem beholden to this scene:

    We're now a chain of lovers linked in death;
    Julia goes first, Gonsalvo hangs on her,
    And Angelina hangs upon Gonsalvo,
    As I on Angelina.

No scene, I believe, ever received greater honors than this. It
was applauded by several encores, a word very unusual in
tragedy. And it was very difficult for the actors to escape
without a second slaughter. This I take to be a lively assurance of that fierce spirit of liberty which remains among us,
and which Mr. Dryden, in his *Essay on Dramatic Poetry*, hath
observed: 'Whether custom,' says he, 'hath so insinuated itself into our countrymen, or nature hath so formed them to
fierceness, I know not; but they will scarcely suffer combats
and other objects of horror to be taken from them.' And
indeed I am for having them encouraged in this martial disposition: nor do I believe our victories over the French have
been owing to anything more than to those bloody spectacles
daily exhibited in our tragedies, of which the French stage is
so entirely clear.

The London Merchant;

or, The History of George Barnwell

BY GEORGE LILLO

SCENE X.

(To them.)   Keeper.

Keep. The Officers attend you, Sir.——— Mrs. *Millwood* is already summon'd.

Barn. Tell 'em I'm ready.———And now, my Friend, farewell, [*Embracing.*] Support and comfort the beſt you can this Mourning Fair.———No more.——Forget not to pray for me, — [*Turning to Maria*] would you, bright Excellence, permit me the Honour of a chaſte Embrace, ——— the laſt Happineſs this World cou'd give were mine, [*She enclines towards him; they embrace.*] Exalted Goodneſs! ——— O turn your Eyes from Earth, and me, to Heaven, ———where Virtue, like yours, is ever heard. ——— Pray for the Peace of my departing Soul.———Early my Race of Wickedneſs began, and ſoon has reach'd the Summet: ——— E'er Nature has finiſh'd her Work, and ſtamp'd me Man,——juſt at the Time that others begin to ſtray,——my Courſe is finiſh'd; tho' ſhort my Span of Life, and few my Days; yet count my Crimes for Years, and I have liv'd whole Ages.——Juſtice and Mercy are in Heaven the ſame: Its utmoſt Severity is Mercy to the whole, ———thereby to cure Man's Folly and Preſumption, which elſe wou'd render even infinite Mercy vain and ineffeＣtual. —— Thus Juſtice, in Compaſſion to Mankind, cuts off a Wretch like me, by one ſuch Example to ſecure Thouſands from future Ruin.

If any Youth, like you,——in future Times,
Shall mourn my Fate,——tho' he abhor my Crimes;
Or tender Maid, like you,——my Tale ſhall hear,
And to my Sorrows give a pitying Tear:
To each ſuch melting Eye, and throbbing Heart,
Would gracious Heaven this Benefit impart,
Never to know my Guilt,——nor feel my Pain,
Then muſt you own, you ought not to complain;
Since you nor weep,——nor ſhall I die in vain.

SCENE

BARNWELL'S LAST SCENE (ACT V, SCENE X), AS IT APPEARS IN THE FIRST EDITION, 1731, OF *THE LONDON MERCHANT*

[DEDICATION]

To Sir John Eyles, Baronet, Member of Parliament for, and Alderman of the City of London, and Sub-Governor of the South Sea Company

Sir,

If tragic poetry be, as Mr. Dryden has somewhere said,[1] the most excellent and most useful kind of writing, the more extensively useful the moral of any tragedy is, the more excellent that piece must be of its kind.

I hope I shall not be thought to insinuate that this, to which I have presumed to prefix your name, is such; that depends on its fitness to answer the end of tragedy, the exciting of the passions in order to the correcting such of them as are criminal, either in their nature, or through their excess. Whether the following scenes do this in any tolerable degree, is, with the deference that becomes one who would not be thought vain, submitted to your candid and impartial judgment.

What I would infer is this, I think, evident truth; that tragedy is so far from losing its dignity by being accommodated to the circumstances of the generality of mankind that it is more truly august in proportion to the extent of its influence and the numbers that are properly affected by it, as it is more truly great to be the instrument of good to many who stand in need of our assistance, than to a very small part of that number.

If princes, etc. were alone liable to misfortunes arising from vice or weakness in themselves or others, there would be good reason for confining the characters in tragedy to those of superior rank; but, since the contrary is evident, nothing can be more reasonable than to proportion the remedy to the disease.

I am far from denying that tragedies, founded on any instructive and extraordinary events in history, or well-invented fables, where the persons introduced are of the highest rank, are without their use, even to the bulk of the audience. The strong contrast between a Tamerlane and a Bajazet[2] may have its weight with an unsteady people, and contribute to the fixing of them in the interest of a prince of the character of the former, when, through their own levity or the arts of designing men, they are rendered factious and uneasy, though they have the highest reason to be satisfied. The sentiments and example of a Cato may inspire his spectators with a just sense of the value of liberty, when they see that honest patriot prefer death to an obligation from a tyrant who would sacrifice the constitution of his country and the liberties of mankind, to his ambition or revenge. I have attempted, indeed, to enlarge the province of the graver kind of poetry, and should be glad to see it carried on by some abler hand. Plays founded on moral tales in private life may be of admirable use, by carrying conviction to the mind with such irresistible force as to engage all the faculties and powers of the soul in the cause of virtue, by stifling vice in its first principles. They who imagine this to be too much to be attributed to tragedy, must be strangers to the energy of that noble species of poetry. Shakespeare, who has given such amazing proofs of his genius, in that as well as in comedy, in his *Hamlet* has the following lines:

> Had he the motive and the cause for passion
> That I have, he would drown the stage with tears
> And cleave the general ear with horrid speech;
> Make mad the guilty, and appall the free;
> Confound the ign'rant, and amaze indeed
> The very faculty of eyes and ears.[3]

And farther, in the same speech:

> I've heard that guilty creatures at a play
> Have, by the very cunning of the scene,
> Been so struck to the soul, that presently
> They have proclaimed their malefactions.

---

[1] This exact statement has not been found in Dryden's works.

[2] The spelling of the names indicates that Lillo is referring to Nicholas Rowe's play, *Tamerlane*, in which Tamerlane is a benevolent monarch and Bajazet a tyrant.

[3] This quotation and the two following are taken, with some inaccuracies, from *Hamlet*, II. ii, 595–642.

O7 om. the dedication.
19] O1O2 *a well-invented fable.*

12] O1O2MD4D5D6O7 *by it. As it.*
20] O1 (some copies) *contract.*

Prodigious! yet strictly just.   But I shan't take up your valuable time with my remarks; only give me leave just to observe, that he seems so firmly persuaded of the power of a well-wrote piece to produce the effect here ascribed to it, as to make Hamlet venture his soul on the event, and rather trust that than a messenger from the other world, though it assumed, as he expresses it, his noble father's form, and assured him that it was his spirit.   'I'll have,' says Hamlet, 'grounds more relative.

> . . . The play's the thing,
> Wherein I'll catch the conscience of the king.'

Such plays are the best answers to them who deny the lawfulness of the stage.

Considering the novelty of this attempt, I thought it would be expected from me to say something in its excuse; and I was unwilling to lose the opportunity of saying something of the usefulness of tragedy in general, and what may be reasonably expected from the farther improvement of this excellent kind of poetry.

Sir, I hope you will not think I have said too much of an art, a mean specimen of which I am ambitious enough to recommend to your favor and protection.   A mind conscious of superior worth as much despises flattery as it is above it.   Had I found in myself an inclination to so contemptible a vice, I should not have chose Sir John Eyles for my patron.   And indeed the best-writ panegyric, though strictly true, must place you in a light much inferior to that in which you have long been fixed by the love and esteem of your fellow citizens, whose choice of you for one of their representatives in Parliament has sufficiently declared their sense of your merit.   Nor hath the knowledge of your worth been confined to the City.[1]   The proprietors in the South Sea Company, in which are included numbers of persons as considerable for their rank, fortune, and understanding as any in the kingdom, gave the greatest proof of their confidence in your capacity and probity when they chose you sub-governor of their company at a time when their affairs were in the utmost confusion and their properties in the greatest danger.[2]   Neither is the Court insensible of your importance. I shall not therefore attempt a character [3] so well known nor pretend to add anything to a reputation so well established.

Whatever others may think of a dedication wherein there is so much said of other things, and so little of the person to whom it is addressed, I have reason to believe that you will the more easily pardon it on that very account.

I am, sir,

Your most obedient

Humble servant,

George Lillo.

ADVERTISEMENT

The scene added in this fifth edition is, with some variation, in the original copy, but by the advice of some friends it was left out in the representation, and is now published by the advice of others: which are in the right I shall not pretend to determine.   There are amongst both, gentlemen whose judgment I prefer to my own.   As this play succeeded on the stage without it, I should not, perhaps, have published it but to distinguish this edition from the incorrect, pirated ones which the town swarms,[4] to the great prejudice of the proprietors of the copy, as well as to all the fair traders, who scorn to encourage such unjust practices.

I could not but reproach myself with ingratitude should I neglect this opportunity of confessing my obligations and returning my thanks to the public in general for their favorable reception of this piece. I am very sensible how much I owe to their indulgence, and wish I may be able by any future performance, if any should appear, to deserve the continuance of their favor.

[1] The old city within the walls — the financial center of London.
[2] Eyles was appointed sub-governor on Jan. 31, 1721, in the general reorganization following the disastrous panic of 1720, the 'South Sea Year.'
[3] Attempt the description of a character.
[4] Apparently in the rare sense, 'breeds swarms of.'

66] O1 *Nor is.*   67] O1O2MD4 *attempt your character, nor.*

PROLOGUE

Spoken by Mr. Cibber, Jun.[1]

The Tragic Muse, sublime, delights to show
Princes distrest and scenes of royal woe;
In awful pomp, majestic, to relate
The fall of nations or some hero's fate:
That sceptered chiefs may by example know   5
The strange vicissitude of things below;
What dangers on security attend;
How pride and cruelty in ruin end;
Hence Providence supreme to know, and own
Humanity adds glory to a throne.   10
   In ev'ry former age and foreign tongue
With native grandeur thus the goddess sung.
Upon our stage, indeed, with wished success,
You've sometimes seen her in a humbler dress —
Great only in distress.   When she complains   15
In Southerne's, Rowe's, or Otway's moving strains,
The brillant drops that fall from each bright eye
The absent pomp with brighter gems supply.
Forgive us then, if we attempt to show,
In artless strains, a tale of private woe.   20
A London 'prentice ruined, is our theme,
Drawn from the famed old song that bears his name.
We hope your taste is not so high to scorn
A [moral] tale, esteemed ere you were born;
Which, for a century of rolling years,   25
Has filled a thousand thousand eyes with tears.
If thoughtless youth to warn, and shame the age
From vice destructive, well becomes the stage;
If this example innocence insure,
Prevent our guilt, or by reflection cure;   30
If Millwood's dreadful crimes and sad despair
Commend the virtue of the good and fair:
Though art be wanting, and our numbers fail,
Indulge the attempt, in justice to the tale!

[1] In the part of George Barnwell.

Heading] O1O2MD4 *Spoke.*   14] D6O7 *an humbler.*   24] O1O2MD4D6O7 *moral;* D5 *mortal.*
29] O1 *innocence secure.*   30] O1 (some copies) *Prevents.*   31] O1 *dreadful guilt.*
34] O1O2MD4 *th' attempt.*

DRAMATIS PERSONÆ

Men.

THOROWGOOD
BARNWELL, *uncle to* GEORGE
GEORGE BARNWELL
TRUEMAN
BLUNT

Women.

MARIA [THOROWGOOD]
MILLWOOD
LUCY

Officers with their Attendants, Keeper, and Footmen.

SCENE: LONDON, AND AN ADJACENT VILLAGE

[TIME: ABOUT 1587]

THE LONDON MERCHANT;

OR,

THE HISTORY OF GEORGE BARNWELL

BY GEORGE LILLO

Learn to be wise from others' harm,
And you shall do full well.
Old Ballad of The Lady's Fall.

ACT I

SCENE I

A room in THOROWGOOD'S *house.*

Enter THOROWGOOD *and* TRUEMAN.

TR. Sir, the packet from Genoa is arrived.

(Gives letters.)

THOR. Heav'n be praised! The storm that threatened our royal mistress, pure religion, liberty and laws, is for a time diverted: the haughty and revengeful Spaniard, disappointed of the loan on 5
which he depended from Genoa, must now attend the slow return of wealth from his new world to supply his empty coffers ere he can execute his purposed invasion of our happy island; by which means time is gained to make such preparations on our part as 10
may, heav'n concurring, prevent his malice, or turn the meditated mischief on himself.

TR. He must be insensible, indeed, who is not affected when the safety of his country is concerned. Sir, may I know by what means — if I am too 15
bold —

THOR. Your curiosity is laudable. And I gratify it with the greater pleasure, because from thence you may learn how honest merchants, as such, may sometimes contribute to the safety of their coun- 20
try, as they do at all times to its happiness; that if hereafter you should be tempted to any action that has the appearance of vice or meanness in it, upon reflecting upon the dignity of our profession you may, with honest scorn, reject whatever is unworthy 25
of it.

TR. Should Barnwell, or I, who have the benefit of your example, by our ill conduct bring any imputation on that honorable name, we must be left without excuse. 30

THOR. You compliment, young man. (TRUEMAN *bows respectfully.*) Nay, I'm not offended. As the name of merchant never degrades the gentleman, so by no means does it exclude him; only take heed not to purchase the character of complaisant at 35
the expense of your sincerity. But to answer your question. The bank of Genoa had agreed, at excessive interest and on good security, to advance the King of Spain a sum of money sufficient to equip his vast Armado; of which our peerless Elizabeth 40
(more than in name the mother of her people) being well informed, sent Walsingham, her wise and faithful secretary, to consult the merchants of this loyal city, who all agreed to direct their several agents to influence, if possible, the Genoese to break their 45
contract with the Spanish court. 'Tis done; the state and bank of Genoa, having maturely weighed and rightly judged of their true interest, prefer the friendship of the merchants of London to that of a monarch who proudly styles himself King of 50
both Indies.[1]

TR. Happy success of prudent councils! What an expense of blood and treasure is here saved! Excellent queen! Oh, how unlike those princes who make the danger of foreign enemies a pretence to op- 55
press their subjects by taxes great and grievous to be borne.

THOR. Not so our gracious queen, whose richest exchequer is her people's love, as their happiness her greatest glory. 60

TR. On these terms to defend us is to make our protection a benefit worthy her who confers it, and well worth our acceptance. — Sir, have you any commands for me at this time?

THOR. Only look carefully over the files to 65
see whether there are any tradesmen's bills unpaid; if there are, send and discharge 'em. We must not let artificers lose their time, so useful to the public and their families, in unnecessary attendance.

Exit TRUEMAN.

[1] There appears to be no historical foundation for this incident. Lillo may be repeating a tradition current in the 'City.'

---

s.d.] O1O2 om. *Enter.* Throughout the play O1 and O2 follow the French system of scene division. Variants due merely to this fact are not noted hereafter. 24] O1 *reflecting on.*
54] O1 *unlike to former princes, who made.* 65] O1 *Only to look.* 67] O1 *and if there are, to send.*

Enter MARIA.

— Well, Maria, have you given orders for the   70
entertainment?   I would have it in some measure
worthy the guests.   Let there be plenty, and of the
best, that the courtiers may at least commend our
hospitality.

MA. Sir, I have endeavored not to wrong your   75
well-known generosity by an ill-timed parsimony.

THOR. Nay, 'twas a needless caution; I have no
cause to doubt your prudence.

MA. Sir, I find myself unfit for conversation; I
should but increase the number of the company   80
without adding to their satisfaction.

THOR. Nay, my child, this melancholy must not
be indulged.

MA. Company will but increase it.   I wish you
would dispense with [1] my absence; solitude best   85
suits my present temper.

THOR. You are not insensible that it is chiefly
on your account these noble lords do me the honor
so frequently to grace my board; should you be
absent, the disappointment may make them   90
repent their condescension and think their labor lost.

MA. He that shall think his time or honor lost in
visiting you can set no real value on your daughter's
company, whose only merit is that she is yours. The
man of quality who chooses to converse with a   95
gentleman and merchant of your worth and character may confer honor by so doing, but he loses none.

THOR. Come, come, Maria; I need not tell you
that a young gentleman may prefer your conversation to mine, yet intend me no disrespect   100
at all; for, though he may lose no honor in my company, 'tis very natural for him to expect more pleasure in yours.   I remember the time when the company of the greatest and wisest man in the kingdom
would have been insipid and tiresome to me if it   105
had deprived me of an opportunity of enjoying your
mother's.

MA. Yours no doubt was as agreeable to her, for
generous minds know no pleasure in society but
where 'tis mutual.   110

THOR. Thou know'st I have no heir, no child but
thee; the fruits of many years' successful industry
must all be thine.   Now, it would give me pleasure
great as my love to see on whom you would bestow
it.   I am daily solicited by men of the greatest   115
rank and merit for leave to address you, but I have
hitherto declined it, in hopes that by observation I
should learn which way your inclination tends; for,
as I know love to be essential to happiness in the
marriage state, I had rather my approbation   120
should confirm your choice than direct it.

MA. What can I say?   How shall I answer as I
ought this tenderness, so uncommon even in the best
of parents?   But you are without example; yet had
you been less indulgent, I had been most   125
wretched.   That I look on the crowd of courtiers
that visit here with equal esteem but equal indifference, you have observed, and I must needs confess;
yet had you asserted your authority, and insisted on
a parent's right to be obeyed, I had submitted,   130
and to my duty sacrificed my peace.

THOR. From your perfect obedience in every other
instance I feared as much, and therefore would leave
you without a bias in an affair wherein your happiness is so immediately concerned.   135

MA. Whether from a want of that just ambition
that would become your daughter, or from some
other cause, I know not, but I find high birth and
titles don't recommend the man who owns them to
my affections.   140

THOR. I would not that they should, unless his
merit recommends him more.   A noble birth and
fortune, though they make not a bad man good,
yet they are a real advantage to a worthy one, and
place his virtues in the fairest light.   145

MA. I cannot answer for my inclinations, but they
shall ever be submitted to your wisdom and authority; and, as you will not compel me to marry where I
cannot love, love shall never make me act contrary
to my duty.   Sir, have I your permission to   150
retire?

THOR. I'll see you to your chamber.   *Exeunt.*

SCENE II

A room in MILLWOOD'S *house.*

MILLWOOD *at her toilet.* LUCY, *waiting.*

MILL. How do I look today, Lucy?

LUCY. Oh, killingly, madam!   A little more red,
and you'll be irresistible!   But why this more than
ordinary care of your dress and complexion?   What
new conquest are you aiming at?   5

MILL. A conquest would be new indeed!

LUCY. Not to you, who make 'em every day, —
but to me — well! 'tis what I'm never to expect, unfortunate as I am.   But your wit and beauty —

MILL. First made me a wretch, and still con-   10
tinue me so.   Men, however generous or sincere to
one another, are all selfish hypocrites in their affairs
with us.   We are no otherwise esteemed or regarded
by them but as we contribute to their satisfaction.

LUCY. You are certainly, madam, on the   15
wrong side in this argument.   Is not the expense all
theirs?   And I am sure it is our own fault if we ha'n't
our share of the pleasure.

MILL. We are but slaves to men.

[1] Put up with.

73] O1O2 *courtiers, though they should deny us citizens politeness, may.*   79] O1 *conversation at present, I.*
149] O1O2 *love, so love.*   s.d.] O1 om. *at her toilet.*   17] O1O2 *hav'n't.*

LUCY. Nay, 'tis they that are slaves most   20
certainly; for we lay them under contribution.

MILL. Slaves have no property — no, not even in
themselves. All is the victor's.

LUCY. You are strangely arbitrary in your principles, madam.   25

MILL. I would have my conquests complete, like
those of the Spaniards in the New World, who first
plundered the natives of all the wealth they had, and
then condemned the wretches to the mines for life
to work for more.   30

LUCY. Well, I shall never approve of your scheme
of government; I should think it much more politic,
as well as just, to find my subjects an easier employment.

MILL. It's a general maxim among the know-   35
ing part of mankind, that a woman without virtue,
like a man without honor or honesty, is capable of
any action, though never so vile; and yet what pains
will they not take, what arts not use, to seduce us
from our innocence, and make us contemptible   40
and wicked, even in their own opinions! Then is
it not just, the villains, to their cost, should find us
so? But guilt makes them suspicious, and keeps
them on their guard; therefore we can take advantage only of the young and innocent part of the   45
sex, who, having never injured women, apprehend no
injury from them.

LUCY. Ay, they must be young indeed.

MILL. Such a one, I think, I have found. As I've
passed through the City, I have often observed   50
him, receiving and paying considerable sums of
money; from thence I conclude he is employed in
affairs of consequence.

LUCY. Is he handsome?

MILL. Ay, ay, the stripling is well made and   55
has a good face.

LUCY. About —

MILL. Eighteen.

LUCY. Innocent, handsome, and about eighteen.
You'll be vastly happy. Why, if you manage   60
well, you may keep him to yourself these two or
three years.

MILL. If I manage well, I shall have done with
him much sooner. Having long had a design on
him, and meeting him yesterday, I made a full   65
stop, and, gazing wishfully on his face, asked him his
name. He blushed, and bowing very low, answered:
'George Barnwell.' I begged his pardon for the
freedom I had taken, and told him that he was the
person I had long wished to see, and to whom I   70
had an affair of importance to communicate at a
proper time and place. He named a tavern; I talked

of honor and reputation, and invited him to my
house. He swallowed the bait, promised to come,
and this is the time I expect him. (Knocking   75
at the door.) Somebody knocks; — d'ye hear; I am
at home to nobody today but him.   Exit LUCY.
— Less affairs must give way to those of more consequence, and I am strangely mistaken if this does
not prove of great importance to me and him   80
too, before I have done with him. Now, after what
manner shall I receive him? Let me consider —
what manner of person am I to receive? He is
young, innocent, and bashful; therefore I must take
care not to put him out of countenance at first.   85
But then, if I have any skill in physiognomy, he is
amorous, and, with a little assistance, will soon get
the better of his modesty. — I'll e'en trust to Nature,
who does wonders in these matters. If to seem what
one is not, in order to be the better liked for   90
what one really is; if to speak one thing, and mean
the direct contrary, be art in a woman — I know
nothing of nature.

Enter BARNWELL, *bowing very low.* LUCY *at a
distance.*

MILL. Sir! the surprise and joy —

BARN. Madam —   95

MILL. (*advancing*). This is such a favor —

BARN. Pardon me, madam —

MILL. (*still advances*). So unhoped for — (BARN-
WELL *salutes her, and retires in confusion*) — to see
you here. Excuse the confusion —   100

BARN. I fear I am too bold.

MILL. Alas, sir! I may justly apprehend you
think me so. Please, sir, to sit. — I am as much at
a loss how to receive this honor as I ought, as I am
surprised at your goodness in conferring it.   105

BARN. I thought you had expected me — I
promised to come.

MILL. That is the more surprising; few men are
such religious observers of their word.

BARN. All who are honest are.   110

MILL. To one another. But we simple women
are seldom thought of consequence enough to gain
a place in your remembrance.

(*Laying her hand on his, as by accident.*)

BARN. (*aside*). Her disorder is so great, she don't
perceive she has laid her hand on mine. Heav-   115
ens! how she trembles! What can this mean?

MILL. The interest I have in all that relates to you
(the reason of which you shall know hereafter), ex-
cites my curiosity; and, were I sure you would pardon
my presumption, I should desire to know your   120
real sentiments on a very particular subject.

55–56] O1 om. *and has a good face.*   64–65] O1O2MD4 *sooner, having . . . on him; and.*
85] O1O2 *to shock him at first.*   88] O1O2 om. *e'en.*
102–103] O1O2 *Alas, sir! All my apprehensions proceed from my fears of your thinking me so.*
111] O1O2 *silly women.*   115–116] O1O2MD4 *Heaven.*   121] O1O2 *particular affair.*

BARN. Madam, you may command my poor thoughts on any subject; I have none that I would conceal.

MILL. You'll think me bold. 125

BARN. No, indeed.

MILL. What then are your thoughts of love?

BARN. If you mean the love of women, I have not thought of it at all. My youth and circumstances make such thoughts improper in me yet. But 130 if you mean the general love we owe to mankind, I think no one has more of it in his temper than myself. I don't know that person in the world whose happiness I don't wish and wouldn't promote, were it in my power. In an especial manner I love 135 my uncle and my master, but, above all, my friend.

MILL. You have a friend then whom you love?

BARN. As he does me, sincerely.

MILL. He is, no doubt, often blessed with your company and conversation. 140

BARN. We live in one house, and both serve the same worthy merchant.

MILL. Happy, happy youth! Whoe'er thou art, I envy thee, and so must all who see and know this youth. What have I lost, by being formed a 145 woman! I hate my sex — myself. Had I been a man, I might, perhaps, have been as happy in your friendship, as he who now enjoys it; but, as it is — oh!

BARN. (aside). I never observed women be- 150 fore, or this is sure the most beautiful of her sex! — You seem disordered, madam! May I know the cause?

MILL. Do not ask me. I can never speak it, whatever is the cause. I wish for things impossible. I would be a servant, bound to the same master, 155 to live in one house with you.

BARN. (aside). How strange, and yet how kind, her words and actions are! And the effect they have on me is as strange. I feel desires I never knew before. I must be gone, while I have power to go. 160 — Madam, I humbly take my leave.

MILL. You will not, sure, leave me so soon!

BARN. Indeed, I must.

MILL. You cannot be so cruel! I have prepared a poor supper, at which I promised myself 165 your company.

BARN. I am sorry I must refuse the honor that you designed me, but my duty to my master calls me hence. I never yet neglected his service; he is so gentle, and so good a master, that, should I 170 wrong him, though he might forgive me, I never should forgive myself.

MILL. Am I refused, by the first man, the second favor I ever stooped to ask? Go then, thou proud, hard-hearted youth! But know, you are the 175

only man that could be found who would let me sue twice for greater favors.

BARN. [aside]. What shall I do! How shall I go or stay!

MILL. Yet do not, do not, leave me! I with 180 my sex's pride would meet your scorn, but when I look upon you — when I behold those eyes — oh! spare my tongue, and let my blushes — (this flood of tears to that will force its way) declare — what woman's modesty should hide. 185

BARN. [aside]. Oh, heavens! she loves me, worthless as I am; her looks, her words, her flowing tears confess it. And can I leave her, then? Oh, never, never! — Madam, dry up your tears! You shall command me always; I will stay here forever, 190 if you'd have me.

LUCY (aside). So! she has wheedled him out of his virtue of obedience already, and will strip him of all the rest, one after another, till she has left him as few as her ladyship or myself. 195

MILL. Now you are kind, indeed; but I mean not to detain you always. I would have you shake off all slavish obedience to your master, but you may serve him still.

LUCY (aside). 'Serve him still'! Ay, or he'll 200 have no opportunity of fingering his cash, and then he'll not serve your end, I'll be sworn.

Enter BLUNT.

BLUNT. Madam, supper's on the table.

MILL. Come, sir, you'll excuse all defects. My thoughts were too much employed on my 205 guest to observe the entertainment.

Exeunt MILLWOOD *and* BARNWELL.

BLUNT. [What! is] all this preparation, this elegant supper, variety of wines, and music, for the entertainment of that young fellow?

LUCY. So it seems. 210

BLUNT. What! is our mistress turned fool at last? She's in love with him, I suppose.

LUCY. I suppose not; but she designs to make him in love with her if she can.

BLUNT. What will she get by that? He 215 seems under age, and can't be supposed to have much money.

LUCY. But his master has, and that's the same thing, as she'll manage it.

BLUNT. I don't like this fooling with a hand- 220 some young fellow; while she's endeavoring to ensnare him, she may be caught herself.

LUCY. Nay, were she like me, that would certainly be the consequence, for I confess, there is something in youth and innocence that moves me might- 225 ily.

129] O1O2 *it all.*   141] O1 *house together.*   155–156] O1O2 *master as you are, to.*
180] O1 *I wish.*   183–184] O1 *blushes speak. This flood of tears to that will force their way, and declare.*
189] O1 *those tears.*   207] O1 *What is all*; O2MD4D5D6O7 *What's all.*   211] O1O2MD4D5D6O7 *What is our.*

BLUNT. Yes, so does the smoothness and plumpness of a partridge move a mighty desire in the hawk to be the destruction of it.

LUCY. Why, birds are their prey, as men are 230 ours — though, as you observed, we are sometimes caught ourselves; but that, I dare say, will never be the case with our mistress.

BLUNT. I wish it may prove so, for you know we all depend upon her. Should she trifle away her 235 time with a young fellow that there's nothing to be got by, we must all starve.

LUCY. There's no danger of that, for I am sure she has no view in this affair but interest.

BLUNT. Well, and what hopes are there of 240 success in that?

LUCY. The most promising that can be. 'Tis true, the youth has his scruples; but she'll soon teach him to answer them by stifling his conscience. Oh, the lad is in a hopeful way, depend upon't. 245
Exeunt.

Scene draws and discovers BARNWELL *and* MILL-WOOD *at supper. An entertainment of music and singing. After which they come forward.*

BARN. What can I answer? All that I know is, that you are fair and I am miserable.

MILL. We are both so, and yet the fault is in ourselves.

BARN. To ease our present anguish by plung- 250 ing into guilt is to buy a moment's pleasure with an age of pain.

MILL. I should have thought the joys of love as lasting as they are great; if ours prove otherwise, 'tis your inconstancy must make them so. 255

BARN. The law of heaven will not be reversed, and that requires us to govern our passions.

MILL. To give us sense of beauty and desires, and yet forbid us to taste and be happy, is cruelty to nature. Have we passions only to torment 260 us?

BARN. To hear you talk, though in the cause of vice; to gaze upon your beauty, press your hand, and see your snow-white bosom heave and fall, en- flames my wishes: my pulse beats high; my 265 senses all are in a hurry, and I am on the rack of wild desire. Yet, for a moment's guilty pleasure, shall I lose my innocence, my peace of mind, and hopes of solid happiness?

MILL. Chimeras all! Come on with me and prove 270 No joys like woman kind, no heav'n like love.

BARN. I would not, yet must on. — Reluctant thus, the merchant quits his ease, And trusts to rocks, and sands, and stormy seas;

In hopes some unknown golden coast to find, 275 Commits himself, though doubtful, to the wind; Longs much for joys to come, yet mourns those left behind.

Exeunt.

ACT II

SCENE I

A room in Thorowgood's house.

Enter BARNWELL.

BARN. How strange are all things round me! Like some thief, who treads forbidden ground and fain would lurk unseen, fearful I enter each apartment of this well-known house. To guilty love, as if that were too little, already have I added breach of 5 trust. — A thief! — Can I know myself that wretched thing, and look my honest friend and in- jured master in the face? Though hypocrisy may a while conceal my guilt, at length it will be known, and public shame and ruin must ensue. In the 10 meantime, what must be my life? Ever to speak a language foreign to my heart; hourly to add to the number of my crimes in order to conceal 'em! Sure, such was the condition of the grand apostate,[1] when first he lost his purity; like me, disconsolate he 15 wandered, and, while yet in heaven, bore all his future hell about him.

Enter TRUEMAN.

TR. Barnwell! Oh, how I rejoice to see you safe! so will our master and his gentle daughter, who during your absence often enquired after you. 20

BARN. (*aside*). Would he were gone! His officious love will pry into the secrets of my soul.

TR. Unless you knew the pain the whole family has felt on your account, you can't conceive how much you are beloved. But why thus cold and 25 silent? When my heart is full of joy for your return, why do you turn away? why thus avoid me? what have I done? how am I altered since you saw me last? Or rather, what have you done? and why are you thus changed, for I am still the same. 30

BARN. (*aside*). What have I done, indeed!

TR. Not speak! — nor look upon me!

BARN. (*aside*). By my face he will discover all I would conceal; methinks already I begin to hate him.

TR. I cannot bear this usage from a friend — 35 one whom till now I ever found so loving — whom yet I love, though this unkindness strikes at the root of friendship, and might destroy it in any breast but mine.

[1] Lucifer.

---

s.d.] O1O2 *BARNWELL and* MILLWOOD *at an entertainment.*   259] D6O7 *is a cruelty.*   271] O1 *nor heav'n.*
272] O1O2 *yet I must.*   ACT II. 2-3] om. *and . . . unseen.*   4-5] O1O2 *that was.*

BARN. (*turning to him*). I am not well. Sleep 40
has been a stranger to these eyes since you beheld
them last.

TR. Heavy they look indeed, and swoll'n with
tears; now they o'erflow; rightly did my sympathizing heart forbode last night, when thou wast 45
absent, something fatal to our peace.

BARN. Your friendship engages you too far. My
troubles, whate'er they are, are mine alone; you have
no interest in them, nor ought your concern for me
give you a moment's pain. 50

TR. You speak as if you knew of friendship
nothing but the name. Before I saw your grief I
felt it. Since we parted last I have slept no more
than you, but pensive in my chamber sat alone and
spent the tedious night in wishes for your safety 55
and return; e'en now, though ignorant of the cause,
your sorrow wounds me to the heart.

BARN. 'Twill not be always thus. Friendship and
all engagements cease, as circumstances and occasions vary; and, since you once may hate me, 60
perhaps it might be better for us both that now you
loved me less.

TR. Sure, I but dream! Without a cause would
Barnwell use me thus? Ungenerous and ungrateful
youth, farewell! I shall endeavor to follow 65
your advice. (*Going.*) [*Aside.*] Yet stay; perhaps
I am too rash, and angry when the cause demands
compassion. Some unforeseen calamity may have
befall'n him, too great to bear.

BARN. [*aside*]. What part am I reduced to 70
act! 'Tis vile and base to move his temper thus —
the best of friends and men!

TR. I am to blame; prithee, forgive me, Barnwell!
Try to compose your ruffled mind, and let me know
the cause that thus transports you from your- 75
self. My friendly counsel may restore your peace.

BARN. All that is possible for man to do for man,
your generous friendship may effect; but here even
that's in vain.

TR. Something dreadful is laboring in your 80
breast. Oh, give it vent, and let me share your
grief; 'twill ease your pain, should it admit no cure,
and make it lighter by the part I bear.

BARN. Vain supposition! My woes increase by
being observed; should the cause be known, they 85
would exceed all bounds.

TR. So well I know thy honest heart, guilt cannot
harbor there.

BARN. (*aside*). Oh, torture insupportable!

TR. Then why am I excluded? Have I a 90
thought I would conceal from you?

BARN. If still you urge me on this hated subject,
I'll never enter more beneath this roof nor see your
face again.

TR. 'Tis strange. But I have done, say but 95
you hate me not!

BARN. Hate you! I am not that monster yet.

TR. Shall our friendship still continue?

BARN. It's a blessing I never was worthy of, yet
now must stand on terms, and but upon con- 100
ditions can confirm it.

TR. What are they?

BARN. Never hereafter, though you should
wonder at my conduct, desire to know more than I
am willing to reveal. 105

TR. 'Tis hard; but upon any conditions, I must
be your friend.

BARN. Then, as much as one lost to himself can
be another's, I am yours.   (*Embracing.*)

TR. Be ever so, and may heav'n restore 110
your peace!

BARN. Will yesterday return? We have heard
the glorious sun, that till then incessant rolled, once
stopped his rapid course, and once went back: the
dead have risen, and parched rocks poured 115
forth a liquid stream to quench a people's thirst: the
sea divided and formed walls of water, while a whole
nation passed in safety through its sandy bosom:
hungry lions have refused their prey, and men unhurt have walked amidst consuming flames;[1] 120
but never yet did time, once past, return.

TR. Though the continued chain of time has never
once been broke, nor ever will, but uninterrupted
must keep on its course, till lost in eternity it ends
there where it first begun; yet, as heaven can 125
repair whatever evils time can bring upon us, we
ought never to despair. But business requires our attendance — business, the youth's best preservative
from ill, as idleness his worst of snares. Will you
go with me? 130

BARN. I'll take a little time to reflect on what has
passed, and follow you.   *Exit* TRUEMAN.
— I might have trusted Trueman and engaged him
to apply to my uncle to repair the wrong I have done
my master — but what of Millwood? must I ex- 135
pose her too? Ungenerous and base! Then heav'n
requires it not. But heaven requires that I forsake
her. What! never see her more! Does heaven require that? I hope I may see her, and heaven not be
offended. Presumptuous hope — dearly al- 140
ready have I proved my frailty; should I once more
tempt heav'n, I may be left to fall never to rise again.
Yet shall I leave her, forever leave her, and not let
her know the cause? — she who loves me with such
a boundless passion. Can cruelty be duty? I 145
judge of what she then must feel by what I now

[1] The miracles referred to in this speech are described in
Jos. 10.12–14; 2 Kn. 20.9–11; 1 Kn. 17.17–24; Ex. 17.5–7; Ex.
14.21–31; Dan. 6.16–23; Dan. 3.19–27.

49–50] D607 *for me to give.*   126–127] O1 *us, he who trusts heav'n ought.*
133–134] O1 *Trueman to have applied to my uncle to have repaired;* O2 *Trueman, who would apply to my uncle to repair.*

endure. The love of life and fear of shame, opposed by inclination strong as death or shame, like wind and tide in raging conflict met, when neither can prevail, keep me in doubt. How then can I de- 150 termine?

Enter THOROWGOOD.

THOR. Without a cause assigned, or notice given, to absent yourself last night was a fault, young man, and I came to chide you for it, but hope I am prevented.[1] That modest blush, the confusion so 155 visible in your face, speak grief and shame. When we have offended heaven, it requires no more; and shall man, who needs himself to be forgiven, be harder to appease? If my pardon or love be of moment to your peace, look up, secure of both.   160

BARN. (*aside*). This goodness has o'ercome me. — O sir! you know not the nature and extent of my offence, and I should abuse your mistaken bounty to receive it. Though I had rather die than speak my shame; though racks could not have forced the 165 guilty secret from my breast, your kindness has.

THOR. Enough, enough; whate'er it be, this concern shows you're convinced, and I am satisfied. (*Aside.*) How painful is the sense of guilt to an ingenuous mind — some youthful folly which it 170 were prudent not to enquire into. When we consider the frail condition of humanity, it may raise our pity, not our wonder, that youth should go astray when reason, weak at the best opposed to inclination, scarce formed and wholly unassisted by experi- 175 ence, faintly contends, or willingly becomes the slave of sense. The state of youth is much to be deplored, and the more so because they see it not, being then to danger most exposed when they are least prepared for their defence.   180

BARN. It will be known, and you recall your pardon and abhor me.

THOR. I never will. Yet be upon your guard in this gay, thoughtless season of your life; when the sense of pleasure's quick and passion high, the 185 voluptuous appetites raging and fierce demand the strongest curb; take heed of a relapse. When vice becomes habitual, the very power of leaving it is lost.

BARN. Hear me on my knees confess —

THOR. Not a syllable more upon this subject; 190 it were not mercy, but cruelty, to hear what must give you such torment to reveal.

BARN. This generosity amazes and distracts me.

THOR. This remorse makes thee dearer to me than if thou hadst never offended. Whatever is 195 your fault, of this I'm certain; 'twas harder for you

[1] Anticipated.

to offend than me to pardon.   *Exit* THOROWGOOD.

BARN. Villain! villain! villain! basely to wrong so excellent a man! Should I again return to folly? — detested thought! — But what of Millwood 200 then? — Why, I renounce her — I give her up. — The struggle's over and virtue has prevailed. Reason may convince, but gratitude compels. This unlooked-for generosity has saved me from destruction.   (*Going.*) 205

Enter a Footman.

FOOT. Sir, two ladies from your uncle in the country desire to see you.

BARN. (*aside*). Who should they be? — Tell them I'll wait upon 'em.   *Exit Footman.* — Methinks I dread to see 'em. Now every- 210 thing alarms me. Guilt, what a coward hast thou made me!   [*Exit.*]

SCENE II

Another room in THOROWGOOD'S *house.*

MILLWOOD *and* LUCY *discovered.*

Enter Footman.

FOOT. Ladies, he'll wait upon you immediately.

MILL. 'Tis very well. I thank you.

Exit Footman.

Enter BARNWELL.

BARN. [*aside*]. Confusion! — Millwood!

MILL. That angry look tells me that here I'm an unwelcome guest. I feared as much — the un- 5 happy are so everywhere.

BARN. Will nothing but my utter ruin content you?

MILL. Unkind and cruel! Lost myself, your happiness is now my only care.   10

BARN. How did you gain admission?

MILL. Saying we were desired by your uncle to visit and deliver a message to you, we were received by the family without suspicion, and with much respect conducted here.   15

BARN. Why did you come at all?

MILL. I never shall trouble you more; I'm come to take my leave forever. Such is the malice of my fate. I go hopeless, despairing ever to return. This hour is all I have left. One short hour is all I 20 have to bestow on love and you, for whom I thought the longest life too short.

BARN. Then we are met to part forever?

MILL. It must be so. Yet think not that time or absence shall ever put a period to my grief or 25

164] O1 *receive 'em.*   169] O1 om. (Aside).   174] O1 *best when opposed.*   178] O1 *not, they being.*
183] O1 *will; so heav'n confirm to me the pardon of my offences.* *Yet.*   184] O1 *life; now when.*
189] O1 *me then on.*   190] O1 *I will not hear a.*   210–212] O1O2 transpose the last two sentences.
SCENE II. 15] O1O2 *directed here.*   20] O1O2MD4 *left me.*   25] O1 *ever shall.*

make me love you less: though I must leave you, yet condemn me not!

BARN. Condemn you? No, I approve your resolution and rejoice to hear it; 'tis just, 'tis necessary. I have well weighed, and found it so.   30

LUCY (*aside*). I'm afraid the young man has more sense than she thought he had.

BARN. Before you came, I had determined never to see you more.

MILL. (*aside*). Confusion!   35

LUCY (*aside*). Ay! we are all out! This is a turn so unexpected that I shall make nothing of my part; they must e'en play the scene betwixt themselves.

MILL. 'Twas some relief to think, though absent, you would love me still; but to find, though   40 Fortune had been indulgent, that you, more cruel and inconstant, had resolved to cast me off — this, as I never could expect, I have not learnt to bear.

BARN. I am sorry to hear you blame in me a resolution that so well becomes us both.   45

MILL. I have reason for what I do, but you have none.

BARN. Can we want a reason for parting, who have so many to wish we never had met?

MILL. Look on me, Barnwell! Am I de-   50 formed or old, that satiety so soon succeeds enjoyment? Nay, look again; am I not she whom yesterday you thought the fairest and the kindest of her sex? whose hand, trembling with ecstasy, you pressed and moulded thus, while on my eyes you gazed   55 with such delight, as if desire increased by being fed?

BARN. No more! let me repent my former follies, if possible, without rememb'ring what they were.

MILL. Why?

BARN. Such is my frailty that 'tis dangerous.   60

MILL. Where is the danger, since we are to part?

BARN. The thought of that already is too painful.

MILL. If it be painful to part, then I may hope at least you do not hate me?

BARN. No — no — I never said I did. — O   65 my heart! —

MILL. Perhaps you pity me?

BARN. I do — I do — indeed, I do.

MILL. You'll think upon me?

BARN. Doubt it not, while I can think at all!   70

MILL. You may judge an embrace at parting too great a favor — though it would be the last? (*He draws back.*) A look shall then suffice — farewell, forever.   *Exeunt* MILLWOOD *and* LUCY.

BARN. If to resolve to suffer be to conquer, I   75 have conquered. Painful victory!

Re-enter MILLWOOD *and* LUCY.

MILL. One thing I had forgot; I never must return to my own house again. This I thought proper to

let you know, lest your mind should change and you should seek in vain to find me there. Forgive   80 me this second intrusion; I only came to give you this caution, and that perhaps was needless.

BARN. I hope it was; yet it is kind, and I must thank you for it.

MILL. (*to* LUCY). My friend, your arm. —   85 Now I am gone forever.   (*Going.*)

BARN. One thing more: sure, there's no danger in my knowing where you go? If you think otherwise —

MILL. (*weeping*). Alas!   90

LUCY (*aside*). We are right, I find; that's my cue. — Ah, dear sir, she's going she knows not whither; but go she must.

BARN. Humanity obliges me to wish you well. Why will you thus expose yourself to needless   95 troubles?

LUCY. Nay, there's no help for it. She must quit the town immediately, and the kingdom as soon as possible; it was no small matter, you may be sure, that could make her resolve to leave you.   100

MILL. No more, my friend, since he for whose dear sake alone I suffer, and am content to suffer, is kind and pities me. Whene'er I wander through [wilds] and deserts, benighted and forlorn, that thought shall give me comfort.   105

BARN. For my sake? Oh, tell me how! which way am I so cursed as to bring such ruin on thee?

MILL. No matter; I am contented with my lot.

BARN. Leave me not in this incertainty!

MILL. I have said too much.   110

BARN. How, how am I the cause of your undoing?

MILL. To know it will but increase your troubles.

BARN. My troubles can't be greater than they are.

LUCY. Well, well, sir, if she won't satisfy you, I will.   115

BARN. I am bound to you beyond expression.

MILL. Remember, sir, that I desired you not to hear it.

BARN. Begin, and ease my racking expectation!

LUCY. Why, you must know, my lady here   120 was an only child; but her parents, dying while she was young, left her and her fortune (no inconsiderable one, I assure you) to the care of a gentleman who has a good estate of his own.

MILL. Ay, ay, the barbarous man is rich   125 enough — but what are riches when compared to love?

LUCY. For a while he performed the office of a faithful guardian, settled her in a house, hired her servants — but you have seen in what manner   130 she lived; so I need say no more of that.

MILL. How I shall live hereafter, heaven knows!

LUCY. All things went on as one could wish till,

some time ago, his wife dying, he fell violently in love with his charge, and would fain have married 135 her. Now, the man is neither old nor ugly, but a good, personable sort of a man; but I don't know how it was, she could never endure him. In short, her ill usage so provoked him, that he brought in an account of his executorship, wherein he makes her 140 debtor to him.

MILL. A trifle in itself, but more than enough to ruin me, whom, by his unjust account, he had stripped of all before.

LUCY. Now, she having neither money nor 145 friend, except me, who am as unfortunate as herself, he compelled her to pass his account, and give bond for the sum he demanded, but still provided handsomely for her and continued his courtship till, being informed by his spies (truly I suspect 150 some in her own family) that you were entertained at her house and stayed with her all night, he came this morning raving and storming like a madman; talks no more of marriage — so there's no hopes of making up matters that way — but vows her 155 ruin unless she'll allow him the same favor that he supposes she granted you.

BARN. Must she be ruined or find her refuge in another's arms?

MILL. He gave me but an hour to resolve in. 160 That's happily spent with you — and now I go.

BARN. To be exposed to all the rigors of the various seasons, the summer's parching heat, and winter's cold; unhoused to wander friendless through the unhospitable world, in misery and want, 165 attended with fear and danger, and pursued by malice and revenge — wouldst thou endure all this for me, and can I do nothing, nothing to prevent it?

LUCY. 'Tis really a pity there can be no way found out. 170

BARN. [aside]. Oh, where are all my resolutions now? Like early vapors, or the morning dew, chased by the sun's warm beams, they're vanished and lost, as though they had never been.

LUCY. Now, I advised her, sir, to comply 175 with the gentleman; that would not only put an end to her troubles, but make her fortune at once.

BARN. Tormenting fiend, away! I had rather perish, nay, see her perish, than have her saved by him; I will myself prevent her ruin, though with 180 my own. A moment's patience; I'll return immediately. *Exit* BARNWELL.

LUCY. 'Twas well you came, or by what I can perceive you had lost him.

MILL. That, I must confess, was a danger I 185 did not foresee. I was only afraid he should have come without money. You know a house of entertainment like mine is not kept without expense.

LUCY. That's very true. But then, you should be reasonable in your demands; 'tis pity to dis- 190 courage a young man.

MILL. Leave that to me.

Re-enter BARNWELL *with a bag of money.*

BARN. What am I about to do? Now you, who boast your reason all-sufficient, suppose yourselves in my condition, and determine for me whether 195 it's right to let her suffer for my faults, or, by this small addition to my guilt, prevent the ill effects of what is past.

LUCY (aside). These young sinners think everything in the ways of wickedness so strange. 200 But I could tell him that this is nothing but what's very common; for one vice as naturally begets another, as a father a son. But he'll find out that himself, if he lives long enough.

BARN. Here, take this, and with it purchase 205 your deliverance; return to your house, and live in peace and safety.

MILL. So I may hope to see you there again.

BARN. Answer me not, but fly — lest, in the agonies of my remorse, I take again what is not 210 mine to give, and abandon thee to want and misery!

MILL. Say but you'll come!

BARN. You are my fate, my heaven, or my hell. Only leave me now; dispose of me hereafter as you please. *Exeunt* MILLWOOD *and* LUCY. 215 What have I done! Were my resolutions founded on reason and sincerely made, why then has heaven suffered me to fall? I sought not the occasion; and if my heart deceives me not, compassion and generosity were my motives. Is virtue inconsistent 220 with itself, or are vice and virtue only empty names? Or do they depend on accidents, beyond our power to produce or to prevent — wherein we have no part, and yet must be determined by the event? But why should I attempt to reason? All is confu- 225 sion, horror, and remorse. I find I am lost, cast down from all my late erected hopes, and plunged again in guilt, yet scarce know how or why:

Such undistinguished horrors make my brain,
Like hell, the seat of darkness and of pain. 230
Exit.

ACT III

SCENE I

A room in THOROWGOOD'S *house.*

Enter THOROWGOOD *and* TRUEMAN.

THOR. Methinks I would not have you only learn the method of merchandise and practise it hereafter,

---

143] O1 *this unjust.*   188] O1 *kept with nothing.*   192] O1 om. Millwood's speech.
s.d.] O1O2 om. with a bag of money.   199] O1O2 om. (Aside).   208] D4 *again —*; O7 *again?*   209] O1 *least.*
228] D3 (according to Morgan) *known.*   231 s.d.] O1 om. Exit.   ACT III. s.d.] O1O2 om. A room ... house.

merely as a means of getting wealth; 'twill be well worth your pains to study it as a science, to see how it is founded in reason and the nature of things; 5 how it promotes humanity, as it has opened and yet keeps up an intercourse between nations far remote from one another in situation, customs and religion; promoting arts, industry, peace and plenty; by mutual benefits diffusing mutual love from pole 10 to pole.

TR. Something of this I have considered, and hope, by your assistance, to extend my thoughts much farther. I have observed those countries where trade is promoted and encouraged do not make 15 discoveries to destroy, but to improve, mankind; by love and friendship to tame the fierce and polish the most savage; to teach them the advantages of honest traffic by taking from them, with their own consent, their useless superfluities, and giving them in 20 return what, from their ignorance in manual arts, their situation, or some other accident, they stand in need of.

THOR. 'Tis justly observed. The populous East, luxuriant, abounds with glittering gems, bright 25 pearls, aromatic spices, and health-restoring drugs. The late found western world's rich earth glows with unnumbered veins of gold and silver ore. On every climate and on every country heaven has bestowed some good peculiar to itself. It is the industri- 30 ous merchant's business to collect the various blessings of each soil and climate, and, with the product of the whole, to enrich his native country. — Well! I have examined your accounts. They are not only just, as I have always found them, but regularly 35 kept and fairly entered. I commend your diligence. Method in business is the surest guide. He who neglects it frequently stumbles, and always wanders perplexed, uncertain, and in danger. Are Barnwell's accounts ready for my inspection? He 40 does not use to be the last on these occasions.

TR. Upon receiving your orders he retired, I thought, in some confusion. If you please, I'll go and hasten him. I hope he hasn't been guilty of any neglect. 45

THOR. I'm now going to the Exchange; let him know, at my return I expect to find him ready.
Exeunt.

Enter MARIA *with a book; sits and reads.*

MARIA. How forcible is truth! The weakest mind, inspired with love of that, fixed and collected in itself, with indifference beholds the united force 50 of earth and hell opposing. Such souls are raised above the sense of pain, or so supported that they regard it not. The martyr cheaply purchases his heaven: small are his sufferings, great is his reward.

Not so the wretch who combats love with duty, 55 when the mind, weakened and dissolved by the soft passion, feeble and hopeless, opposes its own desires. What is an hour, a day, a year of pain, to a whole life of tortures such as these?

Enter TRUEMAN.

TR. O Barnwell! O my friend, how art thou 60 fallen!

MA. Ha! Barnwell! What of him? Speak! — say, what of Barnwell!

TR. 'Tis not to be concealed. I've news to tell of him that will afflict your generous father, 65 yourself, and all who know him.

MA. Defend us, heaven!

TR. I cannot speak it. See there.
(Gives a letter. MARIA *reads.)*
'Trueman,
  I know my absence will surprise my honored 70 master and yourself, and the more when you shall understand that the reason of my withdrawing, is my having embezzled part of the cash with which I was entrusted. After this, 'tis needless to inform you that I intend never to 75 return again. Though this might have been known by examining my accounts, yet, to prevent that unnecessary trouble, and to cut off all fruitless expectations of my return, I have left this from the lost 80
                    George Barnwell.'

TR. Lost indeed! Yet how he should be guilty of what he there charges himself withal, raises my wonder equal to my grief. Never had youth a higher sense of virtue. Justly he thought, and as he 85 thought he practised; never was life more regular than his — an understanding uncommon at his years — an open, generous manliness of temper — his manners easy, unaffected, and engaging.

MA. This and much more you might have 90 said with truth. He was the delight of every eye and joy of every heart that knew him.

TR. Since such he was, and was my friend, can I support his loss? See! the fairest and happiest maid this wealthy city boasts, kindly condescends to 95 weep for thy unhappy fate, poor ruined Barnwell!

MA. Trueman, do you think a soul so delicate as his, so sensible of shame, can e'er submit to live a slave to vice?

TR. Never, never! So well I know him, I'm 100 sure this act of his, so contrary to his nature, must have been caused by some unavoidable necessity.

MA. Is there no means yet to preserve him?

TR. Oh, that there were! But few men recover reputation lost — a merchant, never. Nor 105 would he, I fear, though I should find him, ever be brought to look his injured master in the face.

MA. I fear as much — and therefore would never have my father know it.

TR. That's impossible.   110

MA. What's the sum?

TR. 'Tis considerable. I've marked it here, to show it, with the letter, to your father, at his return.

MA. If I should supply the money, could you so dispose of that, and the account, as to conceal 115 this unhappy mismanagement from my father?

TR. Nothing more easy. But can you intend it? Will you save a helpless wretch from ruin? Oh! 'twere an act worthy such exalted virtue as Maria's. Sure, heaven in mercy to my friend inspired the 120 generous thought!

MA. Doubt not but I would purchase so great a happiness at a much dearer price: — but how shall he be found?

TR. Trust to my diligence for that. In the 125 meantime, I'll conceal his absence from your father, or find such excuses for it that the real cause shall never be suspected.

MA. In attempting to save from shame one whom we hope may yet return to virtue, to heaven 130 and you, the only witnesses of this action, I appeal, whether I do anything misbecoming my sex and character.

TR. Earth must approve the deed, and heaven, I doubt not, will reward it.   135

MA. If heaven succeeds it, I am well rewarded. A virgin's fame is sullied by suspicion's lightest breath; and therefore as this must be a secret from my father and the world, for Barnwell's sake, for mine, let it be so to him!   *Exeunt.* 140

SCENE II

[*A room in* MILLWOOD'S *house.*]

Enter LUCY *and* BLUNT.

LUCY. Well! what do you think of Millwood's conduct now?

BLUNT. I own it is surprising; I don't know which to admire most, her feigned or his real passion — though I have sometimes been afraid that her 5 avarice would discover her. But his youth and want of experience make it the easier to impose on him.

LUCY. No, it is his love. To do him justice, notwithstanding his youth, he don't want understanding; but you men are much easier imposed on in 10 these affairs than your vanity will allow you to believe. Let me see the wisest of you all as much

in love with me as Barnwell is with Millwood, and I'll engage to make as great a fool of him.

BLUNT. And all circumstances considered, to 15 make as much money of him too?

LUCY. I can't answer for that. Her artifice in making him rob his master at first, and the various stratagems by which she has obliged him to continue that course, astonish even me, who know 20 her so well.

BLUNT. But then you are to consider that the money was his master's.

LUCY. There was the difficulty of it. Had it been his own, it had been nothing. Were the world 25 his, she might have it for a smile. But those golden days are done; he's ruined, and Millwood's hopes of farther profits there are at an end.

BLUNT. That's no more than we all expected.

LUCY. Being called by his master to make up 30 his accounts, he was forced to quit his house and service, and wisely flies to Millwood for relief and entertainment.

BLUNT. I have not heard of this before! How did she receive him?   35

LUCY. As you would expect. She wondered what he meant; was astonished at his impudence; and, with an air of modesty peculiar to herself, swore so heartily that she never saw him before, that she put me out of countenance.   40

BLUNT. That's much, indeed! But how did Barnwell behave?

LUCY. He grieved, and, at length, enraged at this barbarous treatment, was preparing to be gone; when, making toward the door, he showed a sum 45 of money which he had brought from his master's — the last he's ever like to have from thence.

BLUNT. But then Millwood?

LUCY. Ay, she, with her usual address, returned to her old arts of lying, swearing, and dissem- 50 bling — hung on his neck, wept, and swore 'twas meant in jest, till the amorous youth melted into tears, threw the money into her lap, and swore he had rather die than think her false.

BLUNT. Strange infatuation!   55

LUCY. But what followed was stranger still. As doubts and fears, followed by reconcilement, ever increase love where the passion is sincere, so in him it caused so wild a transport of excessive fondness, such joy, such grief, such pleasure, and such an- 60 guish, that nature in him seemed sinking with the weight, and the charmed soul disposed to quit his breast for hers. Just then, when every passion with lawless anarchy prevailed, and reason was in the rag-

---

131] O1O2 *the judges of.*   132] O1 *I have done anything.*   136] O1 *succeed.*   137] O1O2 *slightest.*
SCENE II. s.d.] O1O2 *MILLWOOD'S* house; MD4O7 A room in *MILLWOOD'S* house; D5D6 Another room in *THOROWGOOD'S* house.
19–20] O1O2 *continue in that.*   45] O1O2 *and, making.*   45] D6O7 *towards.*   45] O1O2 *door, showed.*
45–46] O1 *a bag of money, which he had stolen from his master.*   51] O1O2MD4 *neck, and wept.*
52] O1 *the easy fool, melted;* O2MD4 *the amorous youth, melted.*

ing tempest lost, the cruel, artful Millwood pre- 65
vailed upon the wretched youth to promise — what I
tremble but to think on.

BLUNT. I am amazed! What can it be?

LUCY. You will be more so, to hear it is to attempt
the life of his nearest relation and best benefac- 70
tor —

BLUNT. His uncle! whom we have often heard him
speak of as a gentleman of a large estate and fair
character in the country where he lives.

LUCY. The same. She was no sooner pos- 75
sessed of the last dear purchase of his ruin, but her
avarice, insatiate as the grave, demanded this horrid
sacrifice. Barnwell's near relation and unsuspected
virtue must give too easy means to seize the good
man's treasure, whose blood must seal the dread- 80
ful secret and prevent the terrors of her guilty fears.

BLUNT. Is it possible she could persuade him to do
an act like that? He is, by nature, honest, grateful,
compassionate, and generous; and though his love
and her artful persuasions have wrought him to 85
practise what he most abhors, yet we all can witness
for him with what reluctance he has still complied!
So many tears he shed o'er each offence, as might, if
possible, sanctify theft, and make a merit of a crime.

LUCY. 'Tis true, at the naming the murder of 90
his uncle he started into rage, and, breaking from her
arms, where she till then had held him with well-
dissembled love and false endearments, called her
'cruel, monster, devil,' and told her she was born for
his destruction. She thought it not for her pur- 95
pose to meet his rage with rage, but affected a most
passionate fit of grief — railed at her fate and cursed
her wayward stars, that still her wants should force
her to press him to act such deeds as she must needs
abhor as well as he: but told him necessity had 100
no law, and love no bounds; that therefore he never
truly loved, but meant, in her necessity, to forsake
her; then kneeled, and swore that since, by his refusal, he had given her cause to doubt his love, she
never would see him more, unless, to prove it 105
true, he robbed his uncle to supply her wants, and
murdered him to keep it from discovery.

BLUNT. I am astonished! What said he?

LUCY. Speechless he stood; but in his face you
might have read that various passions tore his 110
very soul. Oft he, in anguish, threw his eyes towards
heaven, and then as often bent their beams on her;
then wept and groaned, and beat his troubled breast.
At length, with horror, not to be expressed, he cried:
'Thou cursed fair! have I not given dreadful 115
proofs of love? What drew me from my youthful
innocence, to stain my then unspotted soul, but love?
What caused me to rob my worthy gentle master,

but cursed love? What makes me now a fugitive
from his service, loathed by myself, and scorned 120
by all the world, but love? What fills my eyes with
tears, my soul with torture never felt on this side
death before? Why, love, love, love! And why,
above all, do I resolve (for,' tearing his hair, he cried,
'I do resolve) to kill my uncle?' 125

BLUNT. Was she not moved? It makes me weep
to hear the sad relation.

LUCY. Yes — with joy, that she had gained her
point. She gave him no time to cool, but urged him
to attempt it instantly. He's now gone; if he 130
performs it and escapes, there's more money for her;
if not, he'll ne'er return, and then she's fairly rid of
him.

BLUNT. 'Tis time the world were rid of such a
monster. 135

LUCY. If we don't do our endeavors to prevent
this murder, we are as bad as she.

BLUNT. I'm afraid it is too late.

LUCY. Perhaps not. — Her barbarity to Barnwell
makes me hate her. We have run too great a 140
length with her already. I did not think her or
myself so wicked as I find, upon reflection, we are.

BLUNT. 'Tis true, we have all been too much so.
But there is something so horrid in murder, that all
other crimes seem nothing when compared to 145
that. I would not be involved in the guilt of that
for all the world.

LUCY. Nor I, heaven knows; therefore, let us clear
ourselves by doing all that is in our power to prevent
it. I have just thought of a way that, to me, 150
seems probable. Will you join with me to detect
this curs'd design?

BLUNT. With all my heart. He who knows of a
murder intended to be committed and does not discover it, in the eye of the law and reason is a 155
murderer.

LUCY. Let us lose no time; I'll acquaint you with
the particulars as we go.   *Exeunt.*

SCENE III

A walk at some distance from a country seat.

Enter BARNWELL.

BARN. A dismal gloom obscures the face of day;
either the sun has slipped behind a cloud, or journeys
down the west of heaven with more than common
speed, to avoid the sight of what I'm doomed to act.
Since I set forth on this accursed design, where'er 5
I tread, methinks, the solid earth trembles beneath
my feet. Yonder limpid stream, whose hoary fall
has made a natural cascade, as I passed by, in doleful
accents seemed to murmur 'Murder.' The earth,

77] O1 *demands.*   94] O1 *cruel monster.*   113] O1 om. *troubled.*   118] O1 om. *worthy.*
120] D6O7 *himself.*   134] O1O2MD4 *was rid.*   140] O1 *We've.*
153] O1 *heart. How else shall I clear myself? He.*   SCENE III. 4] D6O7 *I am.*

the air, and water, seemed concerned — but　10
that's not strange; the world is punished, and nature
feels a shock when Providence permits a good man's
fall! Just heaven! Then what should I be? — for
him that was my father's only brother, and since his
death has been to me a father, who took me up　15
an infant, and an orphan; reared me with tenderest
care, and still indulged me with most paternal fondness. Yet here I stand avowed his destined murderer. I stiffen with horror at my own impiety.
'Tis yet unperformed. What if I quit my bloody　20
purpose, and fly the place! (*Going, then stops.*) But
[whither], oh whither, shall I fly? My master's once
friendly doors are ever shut against me; and without
money Millwood will never see me more, and life is
not to be endured without her. She's got such　25
firm possession of my heart, and governs there with
such despotic sway — ay, there's the cause of all
my sin and sorrow! 'Tis more than love; 'tis the
fever of the soul and madness of desire. In vain does
nature, reason, conscience, all oppose it; the im-　30
petuous passion bears down all before it, and drives
me on to lust, to theft, and murder. O conscience!
feeble guide to virtue, thou only show'st us when we
go astray, but wantest power to stop us in our course.
— Ha, in yonder shady walk I see my uncle.　35
He's alone. Now for my disguise! (*Plucks out a
vizor.*) This is his hour of private meditation. Thus
daily he prepares his soul for heaven — whilst I —
but what have I to do with heaven? Ha! No
struggles, conscience!　40
Hence, hence, remorse, and ev'ry thought that's
good:
The storm that lust began must end in blood.

(*Puts on the vizor, draws a pistol and exit.*)

SCENE IV

A close walk in a wood.

Enter UNCLE.

UN. If I were superstitious, I should fear some
danger lurked unseen, or death were nigh. A heavy
melancholy clouds my spirits; my imagination is
filled with gashly forms of dreary graves and bodies
changed by death, when the pale, lengthened　5
visage [1] attracts each weeping eye, and fills the musing soul, at once, with grief and horror, pity and
aversion. I will indulge the thought. The wise man
prepares himself for death by making it familiar to
his mind. When strong reflections hold the　10

[1] I.e., of the corpse awaiting burial.

mirror near, and the living in the dead behold their
future selves, how does each inordinate passion and
desire cease, or sicken at the view! The mind scarce
moves; the blood, curdling and chilled, creeps slowly
through the veins — fixed, still, and motionless　15
we stand — so like the solemn object of our thoughts,
we are almost at present — what we must be hereafter, till curiosity awakes the soul and sets it on
inquiry.

Enter GEORGE BARNWELL *at a distance.*

— O Death, thou strange mysterious power,　20
seen every day, yet never understood but by the in-
communicative dead, what art thou? The extensive
mind of man, that with a thought circles the earth's
vast globe, sinks to the center, or ascends above the
stars; that worlds exotic finds, or thinks it finds　25
— thy thick clouds attempts to pass in vain: lost and
bewildered in the horrid gloom, defeated she [2] returns
more doubtful than before, of nothing certain — but
of labor lost.

(*During this speech,* BARNWELL *sometimes
presents the pistol and draws it back again.*)

BARN. (*throwing down the pistol*). Oh, 'tis im-　30
possible!

(*Uncle starts and attempts to draw his sword.*)

UN. A man so near me, armed and masked!

BARN. Nay, then there's no retreat.

(*Plucks a poniard from his bosom, and stabs
him.*)

UN. Oh! I am slain! All-gracious heaven, regard the prayer of thy dying servant! Bless,　35
with the choicest blessings, my dearest nephew; forgive my murderer, and take my fleeting soul to endless mercy!

(BARNWELL *throws off his mask, runs to him,
and, kneeling by him, raises and chafes him.*)

BARN. Expiring saint! O murdered, martyred
uncle! Lift up your dying eyes, and view your　40
nephew in your murderer! Oh, do not look so tenderly upon me! Let indignation lighten from your
eyes, and blast me ere you die! — By heaven, he
weeps in pity of my woes. Tears, — tears, for blood!
The murdered, in the agonies of death, weeps for　45
his murderer. — Oh, speak your pious purpose —
pronounce my pardon then — and take me with you!
— He would, but cannot. — Oh, why, with such fond
affection, do you press my murdering hand? — What!
will you kiss me? (BARNWELL *kisses his uncle,*　50

[2] The antecedent of 'she,' as well as of the preceding 'it,' is
'the mind of man.'

10] O1O2 *seem.*　　12] O1O2 *the shock.*　　　22] O1O2MD4 *whether, O whether;* D5 *whether, O whither.*
33] O1O2MD4 *virtue, who only shows.*　　　34] O1O2MD4 *but wants the power.*　　　SCENE IV. 1] O1O2MD4 *was.*
4] O7 *ghastly.*　　6] O1O2 *attracks;* MD4 *attacks.*　　16] O1 om. *we stand, so.*　　16–17] O1 *thoughts. We.*
25] O1 *world's.*　　29 s.d.] O1O2 *again; at last he drops it,* at which his uncle starts, and draws his sword.
30 s.d.] O1O2 om. (throwing . . . pistol).　　31 s.d.] O1O2 om. (Uncle . . . sword).　　36] O1O2 *thy choicest.*
37[1] D3 (according to Morgan) *take away my.*　　50–51] O1O2MD4 (Kisses him.) UNCLE. (Groans and dies.)

who groans and dies.) Life, that hovered on his lips
but till he had sealed my pardon, in that kiss expired.
He's gone forever — and oh! I follow. (*Swoons
away upon his uncle's dead body.*) — Do I still live to
press the suffering bosom of the earth? Do I still   55
breathe, and taint with my infectious breath the
wholesome air? Let heaven from its high throne,
in justice or in mercy, now look down on that dear
murdered saint and me the murderer, and, if his
vengeance spares, let pity strike and end my   60
wretched being! — Murder the worst of crimes, and
parricide the worst of murders, and this the worst of
parricides! Cain, who stands on record from the
birth of time, and must to its last final period, as accursed, slew a brother favored above him. De-   65
tested Nero by another's hand dispatched a mother
that he feared and hated. But I, with my own hand,
have murdered a brother, mother, father, and a friend
most loving and beloved. This execrable act of
mine's without a parallel. Oh, may it ever stand   70
alone — the last of murders, as it is the worst!

The rich man thus, in torment and despair,
Preferred his vain but charitable prayer.[1]
The fool, his own soul lost, would fain be wise
For others' good; but heaven his suit denies.   75
By laws and means well known we stand or fall,
And one eternal rule remains for all.   [*Exit.*]

ACT IV

SCENE I

A room in THOROWGOOD'S *house.*

Enter MARIA.

MA. How falsely do they judge who censure or
applaud, as we're afflicted or rewarded here! I
know I am unhappy, yet cannot charge myself with
any crime more than the common frailties of our
kind, that should provoke just heaven to mark   5
me out for sufferings so uncommon and severe.
Falsely to accuse ourselves, heaven must abhor; then
it is just and right that innocence should suffer, for
heaven must be just in all its ways. Perhaps by that
we are kept from moral evils much worse than   10
penal, or more improved in virtue; or may not the
lesser ills that we sustain be made the means of
greater good to others? Might all the joyless days
and sleepless nights that I have passed but purchase
peace for thee,   15

Thou dear, dear cause of all my grief and pain,
Small were the loss, and infinite the gain;
Though to the grave in secret love I pine,
So life and fame and happiness were thine.

[1] Luke 16.19-31.

Enter TRUEMAN.

— What news of Barnwell?   20

TR. None. I have sought him with the greatest
diligence, but all in vain.

MA. Does my father yet suspect the cause of his
absence?

TR. All appeared so just and fair to him, it is   25
not possible he ever should; but his absence will no
longer be concealed. Your father's wise; and, though
he seems to hearken to the friendly excuses I would
make for Barnwell, yet I am afraid he regards 'em
only as such, without suffering them to influence   30
his judgment.

MA. How does the unhappy youth defeat all our
designs to serve him! Yet I can never repent what
we have done. Should he return, 'twill make his
reconciliation with my father easier, and pre-   35
serve him from future reproach from a malicious, unforgiving world.

Enter THOROWGOOD *and* LUCY.

THOR. This woman here has given me a sad, and
(bating some circumstances) too probable account of
Barnwell's defection.   40

LUCY. I am sorry, sir, that my frank confession of
my former unhappy course of life should cause you
to suspect my truth on this occasion.

THOR. It is not that; your confession has in it all
the appearance of truth. (*To them.*) Among   45
many other particulars, she informs me that Barnwell has been influenced to break his trust, and wrong
me at several times of considerable sums of money;
now, as I know this to be false, I would fain doubt
the whole of her relation, too dreadful to be will-   50
ingly believed.

MA. Sir, your pardon; I find myself on a sudden
so indisposed that I must retire. — (*Aside.*) Providence opposes all attempts to save him. Poor ruined
Barnwell! Wretched, lost Maria!   55

Exit MARIA.

THOR. How am I distressed on every side! Pity
for that unhappy youth, fear for the life of a much
valued friend — and then my child, the only joy and
hope of my declining life! Her melancholy increases
hourly, and gives me painful apprehensions   60
of her loss. O Trueman! this person informs me
that your friend, at the instigation of an impious
woman, is gone to rob and murder his venerable
uncle.

TR. Oh, execrable deed! I am blasted with   65
the horror of the thought.

LUCY. This delay may ruin all.

THOR. What to do or think I know not. That he

51–52] O1 om. *Life . . . expired.*   52] Ward's reading of *sigh* instead of *kiss* in D4 is incorrect.
ACT IV. s.d.] O1O2 om. A room . . . house.   9–10] O1O2MD4 *that they are.*   12] O1O2MD4 *that they sustain.*
12] O1 om. *made.*   23] O1 *Doth.*   23–24] O1 *his absenting himself.*

ever wronged me, I know is false; the rest may be so too — there's all my hope. 70

TR. Trust not to that; rather suppose all true than lose a moment's time: even now the horrid deed may be a doing — dreadful imagination! — or it may be done, and we be vainly debating on the means to prevent what is already past. 75

THOR. [aside]. This earnestness convinces me that he knows more than he has yet discovered. — What ho! without there! who waits?

Enter a Servant.

— Order the groom to saddle the swiftest horse and prepare to set out with speed! An affair of life 80 and death demands his diligence. *Exit Servant.*
—[*To* LUCY.] For you, whose behavior on this occasion I have no time to commend as it deserves, I must engage your farther assistance. Return and observe this Millwood till I come. I have your 85 directions, and will follow you as soon as possible.
Exit LUCY.
— Trueman, you, I am sure, will not be idle on this occasion. *Exit* THOROWGOOD.

TR. He only who is a friend can judge of my distress. *Exit.* 90

SCENE II

MILLWOOD'S *house.*

Enter MILLWOOD.

MILL. I wish I knew the event[1] of his design; the attempt without success would ruin him. — Well! what have I to apprehend from that? I fear too much. The mischief being only intended, his friends, in pity of his youth, turn all their rage on me. I 5 should have thought of that before. Suppose the deed done: then, and then only, I shall be secure. Or what if he returns without attempting it at all?

Enter BARNWELL, *bloody.*

But he is here, and I have done him wrong; his bloody hands show he has done the deed, but 10 show he wants the prudence to conceal it.

BARN. Where shall I hide me? [whither] shall I fly to avoid the swift, unerring hand of Justice?

MILL. Dismiss your fears. Though thousands had pursued you to the door, yet being entered 15 here, you are safe as innocence. I have such a cavern, by art so cunningly contrived, that the piercing eyes of Jealousy and Revenge may search in vain, nor find the entrance to the safe retreat. There will I hide you if any danger's near. 20

BARN. Oh, hide me — from myself if it be pos-
¹ Outcome.

sible; for while I bear my conscience in my bosom, though I were hid where man's eye never saw nor light e'er dawned, 'twere all in vain. For oh! that inmate — that impartial judge, will try, convict, 25 and sentence me for murder, and execute me with never-ending torments. Behold these hands all crimsoned o'er with my dear uncle's blood! Here's a sight to make a statue start with horror, or turn a living man into a statue. 30

MILL. Ridiculous! Then it seems you are afraid of your own shadow, or, what's less than a shadow, your conscience.

BARN. Though to man unknown I did the accursed act, what can we hide from heaven's all- 35 seeing eye?

MILL. No more of this stuff! What advantage have you made of his death? or what advantage may yet be made of it? Did you secure the keys of his treasure — those no doubt were about him. 40 What gold, what jewels, or what else of value have you brought me?

BARN. Think you I added sacrilege to murder? Oh! had you seen him as his life flowed from him in a crimson flood, and heard him praying for me by 45 the double name of nephew and of murderer! (alas, alas! he knew not then that his nephew was his murderer) how would you have wished, as I did, though you had a thousand years of life to come, to have given them all to have lengthened his one hour! 50 But, being dead, I fled the sight of what my hands had done, nor could I, to have gained the empire of the world, have violated, by theft, his sacred corpse.

MILL. Whining, preposterous, canting villain, to murder your uncle, rob him of life, nature's first, 55 last, dear prerogative, after which there's no injury — then fear to take what he no longer wanted, and bring to me your penury and guilt! Do you think I'll hazard my reputation — nay, my life, to entertain you? 60

BARN. O Millwood! this from thee! — but I have done; if you hate me, if you wish me dead, then are you happy — for oh! 'tis sure my grief will quickly end me.

MILL. (aside). In his madness he will discover[2] 65 all and involve me in his ruin. We are on a precipice from whence there's no retreat for both — then to preserve myself. (*Pauses.*) There is no other way, — 'tis dreadful; but reflection comes too late when danger's pressing — and there's no room for 70 choice. It must be done. (*Rings a bell.*)

Enter a Servant.

— Fetch me an officer, and seize this villain: he has
² Reveal.

74] O1O2MD4 we are.   80] O1 prepare himself to.   87] O1O2MD4 would not.
SCENE II. 12] O1O2MD4D5 whether; D6O7 whither.   14] O1 those fears.   24] O1 om. oh!
35-36] O1 heav'n's omniscient eye.   65] O1O2 om. (Aside).   71] O1O2 done. (Stamps.)

confessed himself a murderer; should I let him escape,
I justly might be thought as bad as he.

Exit Servant.

BARN. O Millwood! sure you do not, cannot 75
mean it. Stop the messenger! — upon my knees I
beg you'd call him back! 'Tis fit I die indeed, but
not by you. I will this instant deliver myself into
the hands of justice, indeed I will; for death is all I
wish. But thy ingratitude so tears my wounded 80
soul, 'tis worse ten thousand times than death with
torture.

MILL. Call it what you will, I am willing to live,
and live secure — which nothing but your death can
warrant. 85

BARN. If there be a pitch of wickedness that seats
the author beyond the reach of vengeance, you must
be secure. But what remains for me but a dismal
dungeon, hard-galling fetters, an awful trial, and an
ignominious death — justly to fall unpitied and 90
abhorred? — after death to be suspended between
heaven and earth, a dreadful spectacle, the warning
and horror of a gaping crowd? This I could bear —
nay, wish not to avoid, had it but come from any
hand but thine. 95

Enter BLUNT, Officer and Attendants.

MILL. Heaven defend me! Conceal a murderer?
Here, sir; take this youth into your custody. I accuse him of murder, and will appear to make good
my charge. (They seize him.)

BARN. To whom, of what, or how shall I 100
complain? I'll not accuse her: the hand of heav'n
is in it, and this the punishment of lust and parricide.
Yet heav'n, that justly cuts me off, still suffers her to
live, perhaps to punish others. Tremendous mercy!
so fiends are cursed with immortality, to be the 105
executioners of heaven. —

Be warned, ye youths, who see my sad despair,
Avoid lewd women, false as they are fair;
By reason guided, honest joys pursue; ⎫
The fair, to honor and to virtue true, ⎬ 110
Just to herself, will ne'er be false to you. ⎭
By my example learn to shun my fate;
(How wretched is the man who's wise too late!)
Ere innocence, and fame, and life, be lost,
Here purchase wisdom cheaply, at my cost! 115

Exeunt BARNWELL, Officer and Attendants.

MILL. Where's Lucy? Why is she absent at such
a time?

BLUNT. Would I had been so too. Lucy will soon
be here, and, I hope, to thy confusion, thou devil!

MILL. Insolent! This to me? 120

BLUNT. The worst that we know of the devil is

that he first seduces to sin and then betrays to
punishment. Exit BLUNT.

MILL. They disapprove of my conduct then, and
mean to take this opportunity to set up for 125
themselves. My ruin is resolved. I see my danger,
but scorn both it and them; I was not born to fall by
such weak instruments. (Going.)

Enter THOROWGOOD.

THOR. Where is the scandal of her own sex and
curse of ours? 130

MILL. What means this insolence? Who do you
seek?

THOR. Millwood.

MILL. Well, you have found her then. I am
Millwood. 135

THOR. Then you are the most impious wretch that
e'er the sun beheld.

MILL. From your appearance I should have expected wisdom and moderation, but your manners
belie your aspect. What is your business here? 140
I know you not.

THOR. Hereafter you may know me better; I am
Barnwell's master.

MILL. Then you are master to a villain — which,
I think, is not much to your credit. 145

THOR. Had he been as much above thy arts as my
credit [1] is superior to thy malice, I need not have
blushed to own him.

MILL. My arts? I don't understand you, sir. If
he has done amiss, what's that to me? Was 150
he my servant, or yours? You should have taught
him better.

THOR. Why should I wonder to find such uncommon impudence in one arrived to such a height of
wickedness? When innocence is banished, 155
modesty soon follows. — Know, sorceress, I'm not ignorant of any of thy arts by which you first deceived
the unwary youth: I know how, step by step, you've
led him on, reluctant and unwilling, from crime to
crime, to this last horrid act, which you con- 160
trived and, by your cursed wiles, even forced him to
commit.

MILL. (aside). Ha! Lucy has got the advantage and accused me first. Unless I can turn the accusation and fix it upon her and Blunt, I am 165
lost.

THOR. Had I known your cruel design sooner, it
had been prevented. To see you punished as the
law directs is all that now remains. Poor satisfaction! for he, innocent as he is, compared to 170
you, must suffer too. But heaven, who knows our

<hr>

[1] Reputation for trustworthiness.

<hr>

75] O1O2 thou dost.   77] O1O2M you call.   89–90] O1O2MD4 and ignominious.
118–119] O1O2 too, thou devil.   124] O1 om. then.   129] O1O2M this scandal.
147–148] O1O2 need not blush.   157] O1O2 your arts; MD4 the arts.
162] O1 commit, and then betrayed him.   163–164] O1 advantage of me, and.

frame and graciously distinguishes between frailty and presumption, will make a difference, though man cannot, who sees not the heart, but only judges by the outward action.   175

MILL. I find, sir, we are both unhappy in our servants. I was surprised at such ill treatment, without cause, from a gentleman of your appearance, and therefore too hastily returned it; for which I ask your pardon. I now perceive you have been so   180 far imposed on as to think me engaged in a former correspondence with your servant, and, some way or other, accessary to his undoing.

THOR. I charge you as the cause, the sole cause, of all his guilt and all his suffering — of all he   185 now endures, and must endure, till a violent and shameful death shall put a dreadful period to his life and miseries together.

MILL. 'Tis very strange! but who's secure from scandal and detraction? So far from contrib-   190 uting to his ruin, I never spoke to him till since that fatal accident, which I lament as much as you. 'Tis true, I have a servant, on whose account he has of late frequented my house; if she has abused my good opinion of her, am I to blame? Hasn't   195 Barnwell done the same by you?

THOR. I hear you; pray, go on!

MILL. I have been informed he had a violent passion for her, and she for him; but till now I always thought it innocent; I know her poor, and   200 given to expensive pleasures: now who can tell but she may have influenced the amorous youth to commit this murder, to supply her extravagancies? It must be so. I now recollect a thousand circumstances that confirm it. I'll have her and a manserv-   205 ant that I suspect as an accomplice, secured immediately. I hope, sir, you will lay aside your ill-grounded suspicions of me, and join to punish the real contrivers of this bloody deed.   (Offers to go.)

THOR. Madam, you pass not this way; I   210 see your design, but shall protect them from your malice.

MILL. I hope you will not use your influence, and the credit of your name, to screen such guilty wretches. Consider, sir, the wickedness of per-   215 suading a thoughtless youth to such a crime!

THOR. I do — and of betraying him when it was done.

MILL. That which you call betraying him, may convince you of my innocence. She who loves   220 him, though she contrived the murder, would never have delivered him into the hands of justice, as I, struck with horror at his crimes, have done.

THOR. [aside]. How should an unexperienced youth escape her snares? The powerful magic of her   225

wit and form might betray the wisest to simple dotage, and fire the blood that age had froze long since. Even I, that with just prejudice came prepared, had, by her artful story, been deceived, but that my strong conviction of her guilt makes even a doubt im-   230 possible. — Those whom subtilely you would accuse, you know are your accusers; and (which proves unanswerably their innocence and your guilt) they accused you before the deed was done, and did all that was in their power to prevent it.   235

MILL. Sir, you are very hard to be convinced; but I have such a proof which, when produced, will silence all objections.   Exit MILLWOOD.

Enter LUCY, TRUEMAN, BLUNT, *Officers, etc.*

LUCY. Gentlemen, pray place yourselves, some on one side of that door, and some on the other;   240 watch her entrance, and act as your prudence shall direct you. — (*To* THOROWGOOD.) This way! and note her behavior. I have observed her; she's driven to the last extremity, and is forming some desperate resolution. I guess at her design.   245

Re-enter MILLWOOD *with a pistol.* TRUEMAN *secures her.*

TR. Here thy power of doing mischief ends, deceitful, cruel, bloody woman!

MILL. Fool, hypocrite, villain — man! Thou canst not call me that.

TR. To call thee woman were to wrong thy   250 sex, thou devil!

MILL. That imaginary being is an emblem of thy cursed sex collected — a mirror, wherein each particular man may see his own likeness and that of all mankind.   255

TR. Think not by aggravating the faults of others to extenuate thy own, of which the abuse of such uncommon perfections of mind and body is not the least!

MILL. If such I had, well may I curse your   260 barbarous sex, who robbed me of 'em ere I knew their worth; then left me, too late, to count their value by their loss. Another and another spoiler came, and all my gain was poverty and reproach. My soul disdained, and yet disdains, depend-   265 ence and contempt. Riches, no matter by what means obtained, I saw, secured the worst of men from both. I found it therefore necessary to be rich, and to that end I summoned all my arts. You call 'em wicked; be it so! They were such as my   270 conversation with your sex had furnished me withal.

THOR. Sure, none but the worst of men conversed with thee.

MILL. Men of all degrees and all professions I have

178] O1 om. *without cause.*   178–179] O1 *appearance, without cause, and.*   199] O1O2 om. *till now.*
222] D3 (according to Morgan) *hand.*   223] O1O2 *with the horror of his.*   232] O1O2MD4 *what proves.*
235] O1O2MD4 *to have prevented it.*   250–251] O1O2M *the sex.*   256] O1O2 *fault.*

known, yet found no difference but in their sev- 275
eral capacities; all were alike wicked to the utmost of
their power.   In pride, contention, avarice, cruelty
and revenge, the reverend priesthood were my unerring guides.   From suburb-magistrates, who live by
ruined reputations,[1] as the unhospitable na- 280
tives of Cornwall do by shipwrecks,[2] I learned that
to charge my innocent neighbors with my crimes,
was to merit their protection; for to screen the guilty
is the less scandalous when many are suspected,
and detraction, like darkness and death, black- 285
ens all objects and levels all distinction.   Such are
your venal magistrates, who favor none but such
as, by their office, they are sworn to punish.   With
them, not to be guilty is the worst of crimes, and
large fees privately paid are every needful 290
virtue.

THOR.   Your practice has sufficiently discovered
your contempt of laws, both human and divine; no
wonder then that you should hate the officers of
both.   295

MILL.   I know you and I hate you all.   I expect
no mercy and I ask for none; I followed my inclinations, and that the best of you do every day.   All
actions seem alike natural and indifferent to man
and beast, who devour, or are devoured, as 300
they meet with others weaker or stronger than themselves.

THOR.   What pity it is, a mind so comprehensive,
daring, and inquisitive, should be a stranger to religion's sweet and powerful charms!   305

MILL.   I am not fool enough to be an atheist,
though I have known enough of men's hypocrisy to
make a thousand simple women so.   Whatever religion is in itself, as practised by mankind it has
caused the evils you say it was designed to cure. 310
War, plague, and famine, has not destroyed so many
of the human race as this pretended piety has done,
and with such barbarous cruelty, as if the only way
to honor heaven were to turn the present world
into hell.   315

THOR.   Truth is truth, though from an enemy and
spoke in malice.   You bloody, blind, and superstitious bigots, how will you answer this?

MILL.   What are your laws, of which you make
your boast, but the fool's wisdom and the 320

[1] Magistrates in the environs of London, i.e., outside the
'City,' had no regular salary, but subsisted upon their fees;
many of them therefore encouraged vice in order to increase
their profits.

[2] During the eighteenth century the practice of plundering
shipwrecked vessels became increasingly common, especially
in Cornwall, in the Highlands of Scotland, and on the western
coast of Ireland.

coward's valor — the instrument and screen of all
your villainies, by which you punish in others what
you act yourselves, or would have acted had you
been in their circumstances?   The judge who condemns the poor man for being a thief had been 325
a thief himself had he been poor.   Thus you go on
deceiving and being deceived, harassing, plaguing,
and destroying one another: but women are your
universal prey.

Women, by whom you are, the source of joy,   330
With cruel arts you labor to destroy;
A thousand ways our ruin you pursue,
Yet blame in us those arts first taught by you.
O may, from hence, each violated maid,
By flatt'ring, faithless, barb'rous man betrayed, 335
When robbed of innocence and virgin fame,
From your destruction raise a nobler name;
To right their sex's wrongs devote their mind,
And future Millwoods prove, to plague mankind!
                                                [*Exeunt.*]

ACT V

SCENE I

A room in a prison.

Enter THOROWGOOD, BLUNT *and* LUCY.

THOR.   I have recommended to Barnwell a reverend divine, whose judgment and integrity I am well
acquainted with: nor has Millwood been neglected,
but she, unhappy woman, still obstinate, refuses his
assistance.   5

LUCY.   This pious charity to the afflicted well
becomes your character; yet pardon me, sir, if I
wonder you were not at their trial.

THOR.   I knew it was impossible to save him, and I
and my family bear so great a part in his distress, 10
that to have been present would but have aggravated
our sorrows without relieving his.

BLUNT.   It was mournful, indeed.   Barnwell's
youth and modest deportment, as he passed, drew
tears from every eye.   When placed at the bar 15
and arraigned before the reverend judges, with many
tears and interrupting sobs he confessed and aggravated his offences, without accusing or once reflecting on Millwood, the shameless author of his ruin —
who, dauntless and unconcerned, stood by his 20
side, viewing with visible pride and contempt the
vast assembly, who all with sympathizing sorrow
wept for the wretched youth.   Millwood, when
called upon to answer, loudly insisted upon her innocence, and made an artful and a bold defence; 25
but, finding all in vain, the impartial jury and the

290] O1O2MD4 *is every.*
296–297] *I hate you all!   I know you, and expect no mercy; nay, I ask for none; I have done nothing that I am sorry for.   I have
followed;* O2 as in text, except *none; and I followed.*   298] O1O2M *does.*   299] O1 *actions are.*
305] O1 *but powerful.*   311] D6O7 *have not destroyed.*   11] O1O2MD4 om. *but.*

learned bench concurring to find her guilty, how did she curse herself, poor Barnwell, us, her judges, all mankind! But what could that avail? she was condemned, and is this day to suffer with him.　　30

THOR. The time draws on; I am going to visit Barnwell, as you are Millwood.

LUCY. We have not wronged her, yet I dread this interview. She's proud, impatient, wrathful, and unforgiving. To be the branded instruments of　35 vengeance, to suffer in her shame and sympathise with her in all she suffers, is the tribute we must pay for our former ill-spent lives and long confederacy with her in wickedness.

THOR. Happy for you it ended when it did!　40 What you have done against Millwood, I know proceeded from a just abhorrence of her crimes, free from interest, malice, or revenge. Proselytes to virtue should be encouraged. Pursue your purposed reformation, and know me hereafter for your　45 friend.

LUCY. This is a blessing as unhoped for as unmerited; but heaven, that snatched us from impending ruin, sure intends you as its instrument to secure us from apostasy.　　50

THOR. With gratitude to impute your deliverance to heaven, is just. Many, less virtuously disposed than Barnwell was, have never fallen in the manner he has done; may not such owe their safety rather to Providence than to themselves? With pity and　55 compassion let us judge him! Great were his faults, but strong was the temptation. Let his ruin learn [1] us diffidence, humanity, and circumspection; for we, who wonder at his fate — perhaps, had we like him been tried, like him we had fallen too. *Exeunt.*　60

SCENE II

A dungeon. A table and lamp.

BARNWELL, *reading. Enter* THOROWGOOD *at a distance.*

THOR. There see the bitter fruits of passion's detested reign and sensual appetite indulged — severe reflections, penitence, and tears.

BARN. My honored, injured master, whose goodness has covered me a thousand times with　5 shame, forgive this last unwilling disrespect! indeed, I saw you not.

THOR. 'Tis well; I hope you were better employed in viewing of yourself. Your journey's long, your time for preparation almost spent. I sent a rev-　10 erend divine to teach you to improve it, and should be glad to hear of his success.

BARN. The word of truth, which he recommended

[1] Teach.

for my constant companion in this my sad retirement, has at length removed the doubts I　15 labored under. From thence I've learned the infinite extent of heavenly mercy; that my offences, though great, are not unpardonable; and that 'tis not my interest only, but my duty, to believe and to rejoice in that hope: so shall heaven receive the glory,　20 and future penitents the profit of my example.

THOR. Proceed!

BARN. 'Tis wonderful that words should charm despair, speak peace and pardon to a murderer's conscience; but truth and mercy flow in every　25 sentence, attended with force and energy divine. How shall I describe my present state of mind? I hope in doubt, and trembling I rejoice; I feel my grief increase, even as my fears give way. Joy and gratitude now supply more tears than the horror　30 and anguish of despair before.

THOR. These are the genuine signs of true repentance, the only preparatory,[2] the certain way to everlasting peace. — Oh, the joy it gives to see a soul formed and prepared for heaven! For this the　35 faithful minister devotes himself to meditation, abstinence, and prayer, shunning the vain delights of sensual joys, and daily dies that others may live forever. For this he turns the sacred volumes o'er, and spends his life in painful search of truth.　40 The love of riches and the lust of power, he looks upon with just contempt and detestation, who only counts for wealth the souls he wins, and whose highest ambition is to serve mankind. If the reward of all his pains be to preserve one soul from wander-　45 ing, or turn one from the error of his ways, how does he then rejoice, and own his little labors overpaid!

BARN. What do I owe for all your generous kindness? But though I cannot, heaven can and will reward you.　　50

THOR. To see thee thus is joy too great for words. Farewell! heaven strengthen thee! Farewell!

BARN. O sir, there's something I would say if my sad, swelling heart would give me leave.　55

THOR. Give it vent a while and try.

BARN. I had a friend — 'tis true I am unworthy, yet methinks your generous example might persuade — could I not see him once before I go from whence there's no return?　　60

THOR. He's coming, and as much thy friend as ever. (*Aside.*) But I'll not anticipate his sorrow; too soon he'll see the sad effect of his contagious ruin. This torrent of domestic misery bears too hard upon me; I must retire to indulge a weakness I find　65

[2] The capitalizing of this word in the early texts shows that it is to be construed as a noun.

44] O1O2 *proposed.*　　SCENE II. s.d.] O1 om. *at a distance.*　　1] O1O2 *See there.*
22] O1 THOR. *Go on. How happy am I who live to see this?*　　33] *preparatory certain.*　　41-42] O1O2M *looks on.*
54] O1 *could say.*

impossible to overcome. — Much loved, and much lamented youth, farewell! Heaven strengthen thee! Eternally farewell!

BARN. The best of masters and of men, farewell! While I live, let me not want your prayers! 70

THOR. Thou shalt not: thy peace being made with heaven, death's already vanquished; bear a little longer the pains that attend this transitory life, and cease from pain forever.   *Exit* THOROWGOOD.

BARN. Perhaps I shall. I find a power within 75 that bears my soul above the fears of death, and, spite of conscious shame and guilt, gives me a taste of pleasure more than mortal.

Enter TRUEMAN *and Keeper.*

KEEP. Sir, there's the prisoner.   *Exit Keeper.*

BARN. Trueman — my friend, whom I so 80 wished to see! yet now he's here I dare not look upon him. (*Weeps.*)

TR. O Barnwell! Barnwell!

BARN. Mercy, mercy, gracious heaven! For death, but not for this, I was prepared.   85

TR. What have I suffered since I saw you last! What pain hath absence given me! But oh! to see thee thus!

BARN. I know it is dreadful! I feel the anguish of thy generous soul — but I was born to murder 90 all who love me. (*Both weep.*)

TR. I came not to reproach you; I thought to bring you comfort. But I'm deceived, for I have none to give. I came to share thy sorrow, but cannot bear my own.   95

BARN. My sense of guilt, indeed, you cannot know: 'tis what the good and innocent, like you, can ne'er conceive. But other griefs at present I have none but what I feel for you. In your sorrow I read you love me still; but yet methinks 'tis strange, 100 when I consider what I am.

TR. No more of that! I can remember nothing but thy virtues, thy honest, tender friendship, our former happy state, and present misery. — Oh, had you trusted me when first the fair seducer 105 tempted you, all might have been prevented.

BARN. Alas, thou know'st not what a wretch I've been! Breach of friendship was my first and least offence: so far was I lost to goodness, so devoted to the author of my ruin, that, had she insisted on 110 my murdering thee, I think — I should have done it.

TR. Prithee, aggravate thy faults no more!

BARN. I think I should! — thus good and generous as you are, I should have murdered you!

TR. We have not yet embraced, and may 115 be interrupted. Come to my arms!

BARN. Never! never will I taste such joys on earth; never will I so soothe my just remorse. Are these honest arms and faithful bosom fit to embrace and to support a murderer? These iron fetters 120 only shall clasp, and flinty pavement bear me (*throwing himself on the ground*) — even these too good for such a bloody monster.

TR. Shall fortune sever those whom friendship joined? Thy miseries cannot lay thee so low 125 but love will find thee. Here will we offer to stern calamity, this place the altar, and ourselves the sacrifice! Our mutual groans shall echo to each other through the dreary vault; our sighs shall number the moments as they pass, and mingling 130 tears communicate such anguish as words were never made to express.

BARN. Then be it so! (*Rising.*) Since you propose an intercourse of woe, pour all your griefs into my breast, and in exchange take mine! 135 (*Embracing.*) Where's now the anguish that you promised? You've taken mine and make me no return. Sure, peace and comfort dwell within these arms, and sorrow can't approach me while I'm here! This too is the work of heaven, which, having 140 before spoke peace and pardon to me, now sends thee to confirm it. Oh, take, take some of the joy that overflows my breast!

TR. I do, I do. Almighty Power, how hast thou made us capable to bear, at once, the ex- 145 tremes of pleasure and of pain!

Enter Keeper.

KEEP. Sir!

TR. I come.   *Exit Keeper.*

BARN. Must you leave me? Death would soon have parted us forever.   150

TR. O my Barnwell, there's yet another task behind; again your heart must bleed for others' woes.

BARN. To meet and part with you, I thought was all I had to do on earth! What is there more 155 for me to do or suffer?

TR. I dread to tell thee; yet it must be known! — Maria —

BARN. Our master's fair and virtuous daughter?

TR. The same.   160

BARN. No misfortune, I hope, has reached that lovely maid! Preserve her, heaven, from every ill, to show mankind that goodness is your care!

TR. Thy, thy misfortunes, my unhappy friend, have reached her. Whatever you and I have 165 felt, and more, if more be possible, she feels for you.

BARN. (*aside*). I know he doth abhor a lie and would not trifle with his dying friend. This is, indeed, the bitterness of death!

75] O1 om. *Perhaps I shall.*   85] O1O2MD4 *was I.*   87] O1O2M *has.*   119] O1O2MD4 *those honest.*
126] O1 *thee.* (Lies down by him.) *Upon this rugged couch then let us lie, for well it suits our most deplorable condition.   Here.*
127] O1O2 *this earth the.*   133] O1 om. (Rising.)   140] O1O2 *heaven, who.*   144] O1O2MD4 *have you.*

TR. You must remember, for we all ob-　170
served it, for some time past a heavy melancholy
weighed her down. Disconsolate she seemed, and
pined and languished from a cause unknown till,
hearing of your dreadful fate, the long stifled flame
blazed out: she wept, she wrung her hands, and　175
tore her hair, and in the transport of her grief discovered her own lost state whilst she lamented yours.

BARN. Will all the pain I feel restore thy ease,
lovely, unhappy maid? (*Weeping.*) Why did you
not let me die and never know it?　180

TR. It was impossible; she makes no secret of her
passion for you, and is determined to see you ere
you die. She waits for me to introduce her.
　　　　　　　　　　　　　　　　Exit TRUEMAN.

BARN. Vain, busy thoughts, be still! What avails
it to think on what I might have been? I now　185
am — what I've made myself.

Enter TRUEMAN *with* MARIA.

TR. Madam, reluctant I lead you to this dismal
scene. This is the seat of misery and guilt. Here
awful justice reserves [1] her public victims. This is
the entrance to shameful death.　190

MA. To this sad place, then no improper guest,
the abandoned, lost Maria brings despair — and
see the subject and the cause of all this world of
woe! Silent and motionless he stands, as if his soul
had quitted her abode and the lifeless form　195
alone was left behind — yet that so perfect that
beauty and death, ever at enmity, now seem united
there.

BARN. I groan but murmur not. Just heaven, I
am your own; do with me what you please.　200

MA. Why are your streaming eyes still fixed
below, as though thou'dst give the greedy earth
thy sorrows and rob me of my due? Were happiness within your power, you should bestow it
where you pleased; but in your misery I must　205
and will partake!

BARN. Oh! say not so, but fly, abhor, and leave
me to my fate! Consider what you are — how vast
your fortune, and how bright your fame; have pity
on your youth, your beauty, and unequalled　210
virtue, for which so many noble peers have sighed
in vain! Bless with your charms some honorable
lord! adorn with your beauty and by your example
improve the English court, that justly claims such
merit; so shall I quickly be to you — as though　215
I had never been.

MA. When I forget you, I must be so, indeed.
Reason, choice, virtue, all forbid it. Let women
like Millwood, if there are more such women, smile
in prosperity and in adversity forsake! Be it　220

[1] Sets apart.

the pride of virtue to repair, or to partake, the ruin
such have made.

TR. Lovely, ill-fated maid! Was there ever such
generous distress before? How must this pierce his
grateful heart, and aggravate his woes!　225

BARN. Ere I knew guilt or shame, when fortune
smiled, and when my youthful hopes were at the
highest — if then to have raised my thoughts to
you had been presumption in me, never to have been
pardoned, think how much beneath yourself　230
you condescend, to regard me now!

MA. Let her blush who, preferring love, invades
the freedom of your sex's choice, and meanly sues in
hopes of a return! Your inevitable fate hath rendered hope impossible as vain. Then why should　235
I fear to avow a passion so just and so disinterested?

TR. If any should take occasion from Millwood's
crimes to libel the best and fairest part of the creation, here let them see their error! The most distant
hopes of such a tender passion from so bright a　240
maid might add to the happiness of the most happy,
and make the greatest proud. Yet here 'tis lavished
in vain: though by the rich present the generous
donor is undone, he on whom it is bestowed receives
no benefit.　245

BARN. So the aromatic spices of the East, which
all the living covet and esteem, are, with unavailing kindness, wasted on the dead.

MA. Yes, fruitless is my love, and unavailing all
my sighs and tears. Can they save thee from　250
approaching death — from such a death? Oh, terrible idea! What is her misery and distress, who
sees the first, last object of her love, for whom alone
she'd live — for whom she'd die a thousand, thousand deaths, if it were possible — expiring in　255
her arms? Yet she is happy when compared to
me. Were millions of worlds mine, I'd gladly give
them in exchange for her condition. The most consummate woe is light to mine. The last of curses to
other miserable maids is all I ask for my relief,　260
and that's denied me.

TR. Time and reflection cure all ills.

MA. All but this; his dreadful catastrophe, virtue
herself abhors. To give a holiday to suburb slaves,[2]
and passing [3] entertain the savage herd who,　265
elbowing each other for a sight, pursue and press
upon him like his fate! A mind with piety and resolution armed may smile on death. But public igno-
miny, everlasting shame, — shame, the death of
souls — to die a thousand times, and yet sur-　270
vive even death itself, in never-dying infamy — is
this to be endured? Can I, who live in him, and

[2] In the sixteenth and seventeenth centuries the environs
of London were chiefly inhabited by the less reputable classes.
[3] Dying.

177] D7 *while.*　　179–180] O1 *didn't;* O2M *did not you.*　　219] O1O2MD4 *there be more.*　　232] O1 *professing.*
260] O1 om. *for my relief.*　　261] O7 *that denied.*

must, each hour of my devoted[1] life, feel all these woes renewed — can I endure this?

TR. Grief has so impaired her spirits, she 275 pants as in the agonies of death.

BARN. Preserve her, heaven, and restore her peace; nor let her death be added to my crimes! (*Bell tolls.*) I am summoned to my fate.

Enter Keeper and Officers.

KEEP. Sir, the officers attend you; Mill- 280 wood is already summoned.

BARN. Tell 'em I'm ready. — And now, my friend, farewell! (*Embracing.*) Support and comfort the best you can this mourning fair. No more! Forget not to pray for me! — (*Turning to* MARIA.) 285 Would you, bright excellence, permit me the honor of a chaste embrace, the last happiness this world could give were mine. (*She inclines toward him; they embrace.*) Exalted goodness! Oh, turn your eyes from earth and me to heaven, where virtue 290 like yours is ever heard. Pray for the peace of my departing soul! Early my race of wickedness began, and soon reached the summit. Ere nature has finished her work and stamped me man — just at the time that others begin to stray — my course 295 is finished. Though short my span of life, and few my days, yet count my crimes for years, and I have lived whole ages. Thus justice, in compassion to mankind, cuts off a wretch like me, by one such example to secure thousands from future ruin. 300 Justice and mercy are in heaven the same: its utmost severity is mercy to the whole, thereby to cure man's folly and presumption, which else would render even infinite mercy vain and ineffectual.

If any youth, like you, in future times,   305
Shall mourn my fate, though he abhor my crimes;
Or tender maid, like you, my tale shall hear,
And to my sorrows give a pitying tear;
To each such melting eye and throbbing heart
Would gracious heaven this benefit impart —   310
Never to know my guilt nor feel my pain.
Then must you own, you ought not to complain;
Since you nor weep, nor shall I die, in vain.

Exeunt BARNWELL *and Officers* [*and* TRUEMAN
and MARIA].

SCENE THE LAST

The place of execution. The gallows and ladders at the farther end of the stage. A crowd of spectators.

BLUNT *and* LUCY.

LUCY. Heavens! What a throng!

[1] Accursed.

BLUNT. How terrible is death when thus prepared!

LUCY. Support them, heaven; thou only canst support them; all other help is vain.

OFFICER (*within*). Make way there; make 5 way, and give the prisoners room!

LUCY. They are here; observe them well. How humble and composed young Barnwell seems! But Millwood looks wild, ruffled with passion, confounded and amazed.   10

Enter BARNWELL, MILLWOOD, *Officers and Executioner.*

BARN. See, Millwood, see, our journey's at an end. Life, like a tale that's told, is past away; that short, but dark and unknown passage, death, is all the space 'tween us and endless joys, or woes eternal.   15

MILL. Is this the end of all my flattering hopes? Were youth and beauty given me for a curse, and wisdom only to insure my ruin? They were, they were. Heaven, thou hast done thy worst. Or if thou hast in store some untried plague, some- 20 what that's worse than shame, despair and death, unpitied death, confirmed despair and soul-confounding shame — something that men and angels can't describe, and only fiends, who bear it, can conceive — now, pour it now on this devoted[2] 25 head, that I may feel the worst thou canst inflict and bid defiance to thy utmost power.

BARN. Yet ere we pass the dreadful gulf of death, yet ere you're plunged in everlasting woe, oh, bend your stubborn knees and harder heart, humbly 30 to deprecate the wrath divine. Who knows but heaven, in your dying moments, may bestow that grace and mercy which your life despised?

MILL. Why name you mercy to a wretch like me? Mercy's beyond my hope, almost beyond 35 my wish. I can't repent, nor ask to be forgiven.

BARN. Oh, think what 'tis to be for ever, ever miserable; nor with vain pride oppose a power that's able to destroy you.

MILL. That will destroy me: I feel it will. A 40 deluge of wrath is pouring on my soul. Chains, darkness, wheels, racks, sharp stinging scorpions, molten lead, and seas of sulphur are light to what I feel.

BARN. Oh, add not to your vast account de- 45 spair — a sin more injurious to heaven than all you've yet committed.

MILL. Oh! I have sinned beyond the reach of mercy.

BARN. Oh, say not so: 'tis blasphemy to think 50

[2] Doomed.

275] O1O2 om. *so.*   278] O1 (some copies) *crime.*   280] O1 *The officers attend you, sir.*
280–281] O1 *Mrs. Milwood is already;* D3 (according to Morgan) *Millwood already.*   293] O1O2 *soon has reached.*
298–304] O1 transposes these two sentences.
SCENE THE LAST] O1O2MD4 omit this scene down to the entrance of Trueman. Instead the previous scene continues, Blunt and Lucy entering to Trueman and Maria.   3] O7 *can.*   s.d.] O7 *Executioners.*   24] D6 *friends·*

it. As yon bright roof is higher than the earth, so and much more does heaven's goodness pass our apprehension. Oh, what created being shall presume to circumscribe mercy, that knows no bounds?

MILL. This yields no hope. Though mercy 55 may be boundless, yet 'tis free: and I was doomed, before the world began, to endless pains, and thou to joys eternal.

BARN. O gracious heaven! extend thy pity to her: let thy rich mercy flow in plenteous streams to 60 chase her fears and heal her wounded soul.

MILL. It will not be. Your prayers are lost in air, or else returned perhaps with double blessings to your bosom; but me they help not.

BARN. Yet hear me, Millwood! 65

MILL. Away! I will not hear thee: I tell thee, youth, I am by heaven devoted a dreadful instance of its power to punish. (BARNWELL *seems to pray*.) If thou wilt pray, pray for thyself, not me. — How doth his fervent soul mount with his words, and 70 both ascend to heaven! that heaven, whose gates are shut with adamantine bars against my prayers, had I the will to pray. I cannot bear it — sure, 'tis the worst of torments to behold others enjoy that bliss that we must never taste. 75

OFFICER. The utmost limit of your time's expired.

MILL. Incompassed with horror, whither must I go? I would not live — nor die. That I could cease to be! — or ne'er had been!

BARN. Since peace and comfort are denied 80

her here, may she find mercy where she least expects it, and this be all her hell. From our example may all be taught to fly the first approach of vice; but, if o'ertaken

By strong temptation, weakness, or surprise, 85
Lament their guilt, and by repentance rise;
Th' impenitent alone die unforgiven;
To sin's like man, and to forgive like heaven.

[BARNWELL *and* MILLWOOD *are conducted toward the gallows.*]

Enter TRUEMAN.

LUCY. Heart-breaking sight! O wretched, wretched Millwood! 90

TR. How is she disposed to meet her fate?

BLUNT. Who can describe unutterable woe?

LUCY. She goes to death encompassed with horror — loathing life, and yet afraid to die; no tongue can tell her anguish and despair. 95

TR. Heaven be better to her than her fears! may she prove a warning to others, a monument of mercy in herself!

LUCY. Oh, sorrow insupportable! break, break, my heart! 100

TR. In vain
With bleeding hearts and weeping eyes we show
A human, gen'rous sense of others' woe,
Unless we mark what drew their ruin on,
And, by avoiding that — prevent our own. 105

[*Exeunt.*]

51] D6 *you bright.*   91] O1O2MD4 *TR. You came from her, then; how.*   92] O1 *unalterable.*

EPILOGUE

WRITTEN BY COLLEY CIBBER, ESQ., POET LAUREATE, AND SPOKEN BY MRS. CIBBER [1]

Since fate has robbed me of the hapless youth
For whom my heart had hoarded up its truth,
By all the laws of love and honor, now
I'm free again to choose — and one of you.

But soft — with caution first I'll round me peep;   5
Maids, in my case, should look before they leap.
Here's choice enough, of various sorts and hue,
The cit, the wit, the rake cocked up in cue,[2]
The fair, spruce mercer, and the tawny Jew.

Suppose I search the sober gallery — no,   10
There's none but prentices — and cuckolds all a-row;
And these, I doubt, are those that make 'em so.

(Pointing to the boxes.)

'Tis very well, enjoy the jest! But you,
Fine, powdered sparks — nay, I'm told 'tis true —
Your happy spouses — can make cuckolds too.   15

'Twixt you and them, the diff'rence this perhaps:
The cit's ashamed whene'er his duck he traps;
But you, when madam's tripping, let her fall,
Cock up your hats, and take no shame at all.

What if some favored poet I could meet,   20
Whose love would lay his laurels at my feet?
No; painted passion real love abhors:[3]
His flame would prove the suit of creditors.[4]

Not to detain you, then, with longer pause,
In short, my heart to this conclusion draws: 25
I yield it to the hand that's loudest in applause.

---

[1] In the part of Maria.   [2] With his hair spruced up in a queue.   [3] 'Love' is the subject of this clause.
[4] Would prove to be no more disinterested than the pleas of creditors.

HEADING] O1 om. *Poet Laureat.*   HEADING] O1 *SPOKE.*   1] O1 (some copies) *hopeless.*   24] D6O7 *Nor to.*

The Lying Valet

BY DAVID GARRICK

THE
LYING VALET.

ACT I. SCENE I.

GAYLESS's *Lodgings.*

Enter GAYLESS *and* SHARP.

SHARP.

OW, Sir! ſhall you be married To-morrow? Eh, I'm afraid you joke with your poor humble Servant.

Gay. I tell thee, *Sharp*, laſt Night *Meliſſa* conſented, and fixed to-morrow for the happy Day.

B   *Sharp.*

DRAMATIS PERSONÆ

MEN	WOMEN
[TIMOTHY] SHARP, *the lying valet*	MELISSA
[CHARLES] GAYLESS	KITTY PRY
JUSTICE GUTTLE	Mrs. GADABOUT
BEAU TRIPPIT	Mrs. TRIPPIT
DICK	[PRISSY, *Mrs.* GADABOUT's *daughter*]
[*Servants*]	[*A niece of Mrs.* GADABOUT's]

d.p.] Or reverses order of first two names.   d.p.] The name 'Trippit' is frequently spelled 'Trippet' in the text.

THE LYING VALET

By DAVID GARRICK

ACT I

SCENE I

GAYLESS' *lodgings.*

Enter GAYLESS *and* SHARP.

SHARP. How, sir! shall you be married tomorrow? Eh, I'm afraid you joke with your poor humble servant.

GAY. I tell thee, Sharp, last night Melissa consented, and fixed tomorrow for the happy day.   5

SHARP. 'Twas well she did, sir, or it might have been a dreadful one for us in our present condition: all your money spent; your movables sold; your honor almost ruined, and your humble servant almost starved; we could not possibly have stood   10 it two days longer. But if this young lady will marry you and relieve us, o' my conscience, I'll turn friend to the sex, rail no more at matrimony, but curse the whores, and think of a wife myself.

GAY. And yet, Sharp, when I think how I   15 have imposed upon her, I am almost resolved to throw myself at her feet, tell her the real situation of my affairs, ask her pardon, and implore her pity.

SHARP. After marriage, with all my heart, sir; but don't let your conscience and honor so far get   20 the better of your poverty and good sense, as to rely on so great uncertainties as a fine lady's mercy and good-nature.

GAY. I know her generous temper, and am almost persuaded to rely upon it: what, because I am   25 poor, shall I abandon my honor?

SHARP. Yes, you must, sir, or abandon me: so pray, discharge one of us; for eat I must, and speedily too: and you know very well that that honor of yours will neither introduce you to a great man's   30 table, nor get me credit for a single beefsteak.

GAY. What can I do?

SHARP. Nothing while honor sticks in your throat: do gulp, master, and down with it.

GAY. Prithee leave me to my thoughts.   35

SHARP. Leave you! No, not in such bad company, I'll assure you! why, you must certainly be a very great philosopher, sir, to moralize and declaim so charmingly, as you do, about honor and conscience, when your doors are beset with bailiffs,   40 and not one single guinea in your pocket to bribe the villains.

GAY. Don't be witty, and give your advice, sirrah!

SHARP. Do you be wise, and take it, sir.   45 But to be serious, you certainly have spent your fortune, and outlived your credit, as your pockets and my belly can testify: your father has disowned you; all your friends forsook you, except myself, who am starving with you. Now, sir, if you   50 marry this young lady, who as yet, thank heaven, knows nothing of your misfortunes, and by that means procure a better fortune than that you squandered away, make a good husband, and turn economist, you still may be happy, may still be Sir   55 William's heir, and the lady too no loser by the bargain; there's reason and argument, sir.

GAY. 'Twas with that prospect I first made love to her; and though my fortune has been ill spent, I have, at least, purchased discretion with it.   60

SHARP. Pray then convince me of that, sir, and make no more objections to the marriage. You see I am reduced to my waistcoat already; and when necessity has undressed me from top to toe, she must begin with you; and then we shall be forced to   65 keep house[1] and die by inches. Look you, sir, if you won't resolve to take my advice, while you have one coat to your back, I must e'en take to my heels while I have strength to run, and something to cover me: so, sir, wishing you much comfort and consola-   70 tion with your bare conscience, I am your most obedient and half-starved friend and servant.

(Going.)

GAY. Hold, Sharp, you won't leave me.

SHARP. I must eat, sir; by my honor and appetite I must!   75

GAY. Well then, I am resolved to favor the cheat, and as I shall quite change my former course of life, happy may be the consequences; at least of this I am sure —

SHARP. That you can't be worse than you are   80 at present.   *(A knocking without.)*

GAY. Who's there?

SHARP. Some of your former good friends, who favored you with money at fifty per cent, and helped you to spend it; and are now become   85 daily mementoes to you of the folly of trusting rogues, following whores, and laughing at my advice.

GAY. Cease your impertinence! to the door! If

[1] Remain indoors.

38] D8 om. *very.*   47] D8 *you credit.*   48] D8 om. *my.*   55] D8 *you you still.*

they are duns, tell 'em my marriage is now certainly fixed, and persuade 'em still to forbear a few 90 days longer, and keep my circumstances a secret for their sakes as well as my own.

SHARP. Oh, never fear it, sir: they still have so much friendship for you, not to desire your ruin to their own disadvantage.   95

GAY. And do you hear, Sharp, if it should be anybody from Melissa, say I am not at home, lest the bad appearance we make here should make 'em suspect something to our disadvantage.

SHARP. I'll obey you, sir; — but I am afraid 100 they will easily discover the consumptive situation of our affairs by my chopfallen countenance.
                                        Exit SHARP.

GAY. These very rascals who are now continually dunning and persecuting me were the very persons who led me to my ruin, partook of my pros- 105 perity, and professed the greatest friendship.

SHARP (*without*). Upon my word, Mrs. Kitty, my master's not at home.

KITTY (*without*). Look'ee, Sharp, I must and will see him!   110

GAY. Ha, what do I hear? Melissa's maid! what has brought her here? my poverty has made her my enemy too — she is certainly come with no good intent — no friendship there, without fees — she's coming up stairs. — What must I do? — I'll 115 get into this closet and listen.   *Exit* GAYLESS.

Enter SHARP *and* KITTY.

KITTY. I must know where he is, and will know too, Mr. Impertinence!

SHARP (*aside*). Not of me you won't. — He's not within, I tell you, Mrs. Kitty; I don't know 120 myself: do you think I can conjure?

KITTY. But I know you will lie abominably; therefore don't trifle with me. I come from my mistress Melissa; you know, I suppose, what's to be done tomorrow morning?   125

SHARP. Ay, and tomorrow night too, girl!

KITTY (*aside*). Not if I can help it. — But come, where is your master? for see him I must.

SHARP. Pray, Mrs. Kitty, what's your opinion of this match between my master and your mis- 130 tress?

KITTY. Why, I have no opinion of it at all; and yet most of our wants will be relieved by it too: for instance now, your master will get a fortune, that's what I'm afraid he wants; my mistress will get 135 a husband, that's what she has wanted for some time; you will have the pleasure of my conversation, and I an opportunity of breaking your head for your impertinence.

SHARP. Madam, I'm your most humble 140 servant! but I'll tell you what, Mrs. Kitty, I am

positively against the match; for, was I a man of my master's fortune —

KITTY. You'd marry if you could and mend it. Ha, ha, ha! Pray, Sharp, where does your 145 master's estate lie!

GAY (*aside*). Oh, the devil! what a question was there!

SHARP. Lie, lie! why it lies — faith, I can't name any particular place, it lies in so many: his 150 effects are divided, some here, some there; his steward hardly knows himself.

KITTY. Scattered, scattered, I suppose. But hark'ee, Sharp, what's become of your furniture? You seem to be a little bare here at present. 155

GAY (*aside*). What, has she found out that too?

SHARP. Why, you must know, as soon as the wedding was fixed, my master ordered me to remove his goods into a friend's house, to make room for a ball which he designs to give here the day after 160 the marriage.

KITTY. The luckiest thing in the world! for my mistress designs to have a ball and entertainment here tonight before the marriage; and that's my business with your master.   165

SHARP (*aside*). The devil it is!

KITTY. She'll not have it public; she designs to invite only eight or ten couple of friends.

SHARP. No more?

KITTY. No more: and she ordered me to de- 170 sire your master not to make a great entertainment.

SHARP. Oh, never fear —

KITTY. Ten or a dozen little nice things, with some fruit, I believe, will be enough in all conscience.

SHARP (*aside*). Oh, curse your conscience! 175

KITTY. And what do you think I have done of my own head.

SHARP. What?

KITTY. I have invited all my Lord Stately's serv- ants to come and see you, and have a dance 180 in the kitchen: won't your master be surprised!

SHARP. Much so indeed!

KITTY. Well, be quick and find out your master, and make what haste you can with your prepara- tions: you have no time to lose. — Prithee, 185 Sharp, what's the matter with you? I have not seen you for some time, and you seem to look a little thin.

SHARP (*aside*). Oh, my unfortunate face! — I'm in pure [1] good health, thank you, Mrs. Kitty; 190 and I'll assure you, I have a very good stomach, never better in all my life, and I am as full of vigor, hussy!   (*Offers to kiss her.*)

KITTY. What, with that face! well, bye, bye. (*Going.*) — Oh, Sharp, what ill-looking fellows 195

[1] Excellent.

---

are those, were standing about your door when I came in? They want your master too, I suppose.

SHARP. Hum! yes, they are waiting for him. — They are some of his tenants out of the country that want to pay him some money. 200

KITTY. Tenants! what, do you let his tenants stand in the street?

SHARP. They choose it; as they seldom come to town, they are willing to see as much of it as they can, when they do; they are raw, ignorant, honest people. 205

KITTY. Well, I must run home, farewell! — But do you hear? Get something substantial for us in the kitchen — a ham, a turkey, or what you will — we'll be very merry; and, be sure remove the 210 tables and chairs away there too, that we may have room to dance: I can't bear to be confined in my French dances; tal, lal, lal. (*Dancing.*) Well, adieu! Without any compliment, I shall die if I don't see you soon. *Exit* KITTY. 215

SHARP. And without any compliment, I pray heaven you may!

Enter GAYLESS.

(*They look for some time sorrowful at each other.*)

GAY. O Sharp!

SHARP. O master!

GAY. We are certainly undone! 220

SHARP. That's no news to me.

GAY. Eight or ten couple of dancers — ten or a dozen little nice dishes, with some fruit — my Lord Stately's servants, ham and turkey!

SHARP. Say no more, the very sound creates 225 an appetite: and I am sure of late I have had no occasion for whetters and provocatives.

GAY. Cursed misfortune! what can we do?

SHARP. Hang ourselves; I see no other remedy; except you have a receipt to give a ball and a 230 supper without meat or music.

GAY. Melissa has certainly heard of my bad circumstances, and has invented this scheme to distress me, and break off the match.

SHARP. I don't believe it, sir; begging your 235 pardon.

GAY. No? why did her maid then make so strict an enquiry into my fortune and affairs?

SHARP. For two very substantial reasons: the first, to satisfy a curiosity, natural to her as a 240 woman; the second, to have the pleasure of my conversation, very natural to her as a woman of taste and understanding.

GAY. Prithee be more serious: is not our all at stake? 245

SHARP. Yes, sir: and yet that all of ours is of so

little consequence, that a man, with a very small share of philosophy may part from it without much pain or uneasiness. However, sir, I'll convince you in half an hour, that Mrs. Melissa knows noth- 250 ing of your circumstances, and I'll tell you what too, sir, she shan't be here tonight, and yet you shall marry her tomorrow morning.

GAY. How, how, dear Sharp!

SHARP. 'Tis here, here, sir! warm, warm, 255 and delays will cool it; therefore I'll away to her, and do you be as merry as love and poverty will permit you.

Would you succeed, a faithful friend depute,
Whose head can plan, and front can execute.
I am the man, and I hope you neither dispute my 260
friendship or qualification.

GAY. Indeed I don't. Prithee be gone.

SHARP. I fly.   *Exeunt.*

SCENE [II]

MELISSA'S *lodgings.*

Enter MELISSA *and* KITTY.

MEL. You surprise me, Kitty! the master not at home! the man in confusion! no furniture in the house! and ill-looking fellows about the doors! 'Tis all a riddle.

KITTY. But very easy to be explained. 5

MEL. Prithee explain it then, nor keep me longer in suspense.

KITTY. The affair is this, madam: Mr. Gayless is over head and ears in debt; you are over head and ears in love; you'll marry him tomorrow, the 10 next day, your whole fortune goes to his creditors, and you and your children are to live comfortably upon the remainder.

MEL. I cannot think him base.

KITTY. But I know they are all base — you 15 are very young, and very ignorant of the sex; I am young too, but have more experience: you never was in love before; I have been in love with an hundred, and tried 'em all; and know 'em to be a parcel of barbarous, perjured, deluding, be- 20 witching devils.

MEL. The low wretches you have had to do with may answer the character you give 'em; but Mr. Gayless —

KITTY. Is a man, madam. 25

MEL. I hope so, Kitty, or I would have nothing to do with him.

KITTY. With all my heart — I have given you my sentiments upon the occasion, and shall leave you to your own inclinations. 30

MEL. Oh, madam, I am much obliged to you for your great condescension, ha, ha, ha! However, I have so great a regard for your opinion, that had I certain proofs of his villainy —

KITTY. Of his poverty you may have a hun- 35 dred: I am sure I have had none to the contrary.

MEL. (*aside*). Oh, there the shoe pinches.

KITTY. Nay, so far from giving me the usual perquisites of my place, he has not so much as kept me in temper with little endearing civilities; and 40 one might reasonably expect when a man is deficient in one way, that he should make it up in another. (*Knocking without.*)

MEL. See who's at the door. (*Exit* KITTY.) — I must be cautious how I hearken too much to 45 this girl; her bad opinion of Mr. Gayless seems to arise from his disregard of her.

Enter SHARP *and* KITTY.

So, Sharp; have you found your master? will things be ready for the ball and entertainment?

SHARP. To your wishes, madam. I have 50 just now bespoke the music and supper, and wait now for your ladyship's farther commands.

MEL. My compliments to your master, and let him know I and my company will be with him by six; we design to drink tea, and play at cards, 55 before we dance.

KITTY (*aside*). So shall I and my company, Mr. Sharp.

SHARP. Mighty well, madam!

MEL. Prithee, Sharp, what makes you come 60 without your coat? 'Tis too cool to go so airy, sure.

KITTY. Mr. Sharp, madam, is of a very hot constitution, ha, ha, ha!

SHARP. If it had been ever so cool I have had enough to warm me since I came from home, I'm 65 sure; but no matter for that. (*Sighing.*)

MEL. What d'ye mean?

SHARP. Pray don't ask me, madam; I beseech you don't: let us change the subject.

KITTY. Insist upon knowing it, madam — 70 (*aside*) my curiosity must be satisfied, or I shall burst.

MEL. I do insist upon knowing — on pain of my displeasure, tell me!

SHARP. If my master should know — I must 75 not tell you, madam, indeed.

MEL. I promise you, upon my honor, he never shall.

SHARP [*indicating* KITTY]. But can your ladyship insure secrecy from that quarter? 80

KITTY. Yes, Mr. Jackanapes, for anything you can say.

MEL. I'll engage for her.

SHARP. Why then, in short, madam — I cannot tell you. 85

MEL. Don't trifle with me.

SHARP. Then since you will have it, madam, — I lost my coat in defence of your reputation.

MEL. In defence of my reputation!

SHARP. I will assure you, madam, I've suf- 90 fered very much in defence of it; which is more than I would have done for my own.

MEL. Prithee explain.

SHARP. In short, madam, you was seen, about a month ago, to make a visit to my master alone. 95

MEL. Alone! my servant was with me.

SHARP. What, Mrs. Kitty? So much the worse; for she was looked upon as my property; and I was brought in guilty as well as you and my master.

KITTY. What, your property, jackanapes! 100

MEL. What is all this?

SHARP. Why, madam, as I came out but now to make preparations for you and your company tonight, Mrs. Pryabout, the attorney's wife at next door, calls to me: 'Hark'ee fellow!' says she, 105 'Do you and your modest master know that my husband shall indict your house, at the next parish meeting, for a nuisance?'

MEL. A nuisance!

SHARP. I said so: — 'A nuisance! I believe 110 none in the neighborhood live with more decency and regularity than I and my master,' as is really the case. 'Decency and regularity!' cries she, with a sneer, — 'why, sirrah, does not my window look into your master's bed chamber? And did not 115 he bring in a certain lady, such a day?' — describing you, madam. 'And did not I see —'

MEL. See! oh scandalous! what?

SHARP. Modesty requires my silence.

MEL. Did not you contradict her? 120

SHARP. Contradict her! why, I told her I was sure she lied: 'For, zounds!' said I, — for I could not help swearing, — 'I am so well convinced of the lady's and my master's prudence, that, I am sure, had they a mind to amuse themselves they 125 would certainly have drawn the window-curtains.'

MEL. What, did you say nothing else? Did not you convince her of her error and impertinence?

SHARP. She swore to such things, that I could do nothing but swear and call names: upon 130 which out bolts her husband upon me, with a fine taper crab [1] in his hand and fell upon me with such violence, that, being half delirious, I made a full confession.

MEL. A full confession! what did you con- 135 fess?

SHARP. That my master loved fornication; that you had no aversion to it; that Mrs. Kitty was a bawd, and your humble servant a pimp.

KITTY. A bawd! a bawd! do I look like a 140 bawd, madam?

[1] A cudgel made of wood from a crab tree.

SHARP. And so, madam, in the scuffle, my coat was torn to pieces as well as your reputation.

MEL. And so you joined to make me infamous!

SHARP. For heaven's sake, madam, what 145 could I do? his proofs fell so thick upon me, as witness my head, (*showing his head plastered*) that I would have given up all the maidenheads in the kingdom, rather than have my brains beat to a jelly.

MEL. Very well! — but I'll be revenged! — 150 and did not you tell your master this?

SHARP. Tell him! No, madam; had I told him, his love is so violent for you, that he would certainly have murdered half the attornies in town by this time.　　　　　　　　　　　　　　　　155

MEL. Very well! but I'm resolved not to go to your master's tonight.

SHARP (*aside*). Heavens and my impudence be praised.

KITTY. Why not, madam? If you are not 160 guilty, face your accusers.

SHARP (*aside*). Oh, the devil! ruined again! — To be sure, face 'em by all means, madam — they can but be abusive, and break the windows a little: — besides, madam, I have thought of a way to 165 make this affair quite diverting to you — I have a fine blunderbuss charged with half a hundred slugs, and my master has a delicate large Swiss broad sword; and between us, madam, we shall so pepper and slice 'em, that you will die with laughing. 170

MEL. What, at murder?

KITTY. Don't fear, madam, there will be no murder if Sharp's concerned.

SHARP. Murder, madam! 'Tis self-defence; besides, in these sort of skirmishes, there are 175 never more than two or three killed: for, supposing they bring the whole body of militia upon us, down but with a brace of them, and away fly the rest of the covey.

MEL. Persuade me never so much, I won't 180 go; that's my resolution.

KITTY. Why then, I'll tell you what, madam; since you are resolved not to go to the supper, suppose the supper was to come to you: 'tis great pity such great preparations as Mr. Sharp has made 185 should be thrown away.

SHARP. So it is, as you say, Mistress Kitty. But I can immediately run back and unbespeak what I have ordered; 'tis soon done.

MEL. But then what excuse can I send to 190 your master? He'll be very uneasy at my not coming.

SHARP. Oh terribly so! — but I have it — I'll tell him you are very much out of order — that you were suddenly taken with the vapors or 195 qualms; or what you please, madam.

MEL. I'll leave it to you, Sharp, to make my apology; and there's half a guinea for you to help your invention.

SHARP (*aside*). Half a guinea! — 'Tis so 200 long since I had anything to do with money, that I scarcely know the current coin of my own country. O Sharp, what talents hast thou! to secure thy master; deceive his mistress; out-lie her chambermaid; and yet be paid for thy honesty? But 205 my joy will discover me. — Madam, you have eternally fixed Timothy Sharp your most obedient humble servant! — [*Aside.*] Oh, the delights of impudence and a good understanding! 　*Exit* SHARP.

KITTY. Ha, ha, ha! was there ever such a 210 lying varlet? with his slugs and his broad swords; his attorneys and broken heads, and nonsense! well, madam, are you satisfied now? do you want more proofs?

MEL. Of your modesty I do: but I find, you 215 are resolved to give me none.

KITTY. Madam?

MEL. I see through your little mean artifice: you are endeavoring to lessen Mr. Gayless in my opinion, because he has not paid you for services he had 220 no occasion for.

KITTY. Pay me, madam! I am sure I have very little occasion to be angry with Mr. Gayless for not paying me, when, I believe, 'tis his general practice.

MEL. 'Tis false! he's a gentleman and a 225 man of honor, and you are —

KITTY (*curtsying*). Not in love, I thank heaven!

MEL. You are a fool.

KITTY. I have been in love; but I am much wiser now.　　　　　　　　　　　　　　　　　230

MEL. Hold your tongue, impertinence!

KITTY (*aside*). That's the severest thing she has said yet.

MEL. Leave me.

KITTY. Oh this love, this love is the devil! 235
　　　　　　　　　　　　　　　　　　Exit KITTY.

MEL. We discover our weaknesses to our servants, make them our confidents, put 'em upon an equality with us, and so they become our advisers — Sharp's behavior, though I seemed to disregard it, makes me tremble with apprehensions; and though 240 I have pretended to be angry with Kitty for her advice, I think it of too much consequence to be neglected.

Enter KITTY.

KITTY. May I speak, madam?

MEL. Don't be a fool. What do you want? 245

KITTY. There is a servant just come out of the country says he belongs to Sir William Gayless, and

---

178] D8 om. *but.*　　　204–205] W1 *his chambermaid.*　　　227] D8 om. *I.*　　　237] W1 *confidants.*
237] D8 *upon equality;* W1 *on an equality.*

has got a letter for you from his master, upon very urgent business.

MEL. Sir William Gayless! What can this 250 mean? where is the man?

KITTY. In the little parlor, madam.

MEL. I'll go to him — my heart flutters strangely.
Exit MELISSA.

KITTY. O woman, woman, foolish woman! she'll certainly have this Gayless: nay, were she as 255 well convinced of his poverty as I am, she'd have him. A strong dose of love is worse than one of ratafia;[1] when it once gets into our heads, it trips up our heels, and then good night to discretion. Here is she going to throw away fifteen thousand 260 pounds; upon what? faith, little better than nothing — he's a man, and that's all — and heaven knows mere man is but small consolation.

Be this advice pursued by each fond maid,
Ne'er slight the substance for an empty shade: 265
Rich, weighty sparks alone should please and charm
    ye:
For should spouse cool, his gold will always warm ye.

ACT II

[SCENE I]

[GAYLESS' *lodgings*.]

Enter GAYLESS *and* SHARP.

GAY. Prithee be serious, Sharp. Hast thou really succeeded?

SHARP. To our wishes, sir. In short, I have managed the business with such skill and dexterity, that neither your circumstances nor my veracity are 5 suspected.

GAY. But how hast thou excused me from the ball and entertainment?

SHARP. Beyond expectation, sir. But in that particular I was obliged to have recourse to 10 truth, and declare the real situation of your affairs. I told her we had so long disused ourselves to dressing either dinners or suppers, that I was afraid we should be but awkward in our preparations. In short, sir, — at that instant a cursed gnawing 15 seized my stomach, that I could not help telling her that both you and myself seldom make a good meal now-a-days once in a quarter of a year.

GAY. Hell and confusion, have you betrayed me, villain? Did you not tell me this moment, she 20 did not in the least suspect my circumstances?

SHARP. No more she did, sir, till I told her.

GAY. Very well; and was this your skill and dexterity?

SHARP. I was going to tell you; but you won't 25

[1] Brandy.

hear reason; my melancholy face and piteous narration had such an effect upon her generous bowels, that she freely forgives all that's past.

GAY. Does she, Sharp?

SHARP. Yes; and desires never to see your 30 face again; and, as a farther consideration for so doing, she has sent you half a guinea.
(Shows the money.)

GAY. What do you mean?

SHARP. To spend it, spend it, sir; and regale.

GAY. Villain, you have undone me! 35

SHARP. What, by bringing you money, when you are not worth a farthing in the whole world? Well, well, then to make you happy again, I'll keep it myself; and wish somebody would take it in their head to load me with such misfortunes. 40
(Puts up the money.)

GAY. Do you laugh at me, rascal!

SHARP. Who deserves more to be laughed at! ha, ha, ha! Never for the future, sir, dispute the success of my negotiations, when even you, who know me so well, can't help swallowing my hook. 45 Why, sir, I could have played with you backwards and forwards at the end of my line, till I had put your senses into such a fermentation, that you should not have known in an hour's time, whether you was a fish or a man. 50

GAY. Why, what is all this you have been telling me?

SHARP. A downright lie from beginning to end.

GAY. And have you really excused me to her?

SHARP. No, sir; but I have got this half 55 guinea to make her excuses to you; and, instead of a confederacy between you and me to deceive her, she thinks she has brought me over to put the deceit upon you.

GAY. Thou excellent fellow! 60

SHARP. Don't lose time, but slip out of the house immediately; the back way, I believe, will be the safest for you, and to her as fast as you can; pretend vast surprise and concern, that her indisposition has debarred you the pleasure of her company here 65 tonight: you need know no more, away!

GAY. But what shall we do, Sharp? here's her maid again.

SHARP. The devil she is — I wish I could poison her; for I'm sure, while she lives, I can never 70 prosper.

Enter KITTY.

KITTY. Your door was open, so I did not stand upon ceremony.

GAY. I am sorry to hear your mistress is taken so suddenly. 75

KITTY. Vapors, vapors only, sir, a few matrimonial omens, that's all; but I suppose Mr. Sharp has made her excuses.

GAY. And tells me I can't have the pleasure of her company, tonight. I had made a small 80 preparation; but 'tis no matter: Sharp shall go to the rest of the company; and let 'em know 'tis put off.

KITTY. Not for the world, sir; my mistress was sensible you must have provided for her, and 85 the rest of the company; so is she resolved, though she can't, the other ladies and gentlemen shall partake of your entertainment; she's very good-natured.

SHARP. I had better run, and let 'em know 90 'tis deferred. *(Going.)*

KITTY *(stopping him).* I have been with 'em already, and told 'em my mistress insists upon their coming, and they have all promised to be here; so, pray, don't be under any apprehensions, that 95 your preparations will be thrown away.

GAY. But as I can't have her company, Mrs. Kitty, 'twill be a greater pleasure to me, and a greater compliment to her, to defer our mirth; besides I can't enjoy anything at present, and 100 she not partake of it.

KITTY. Oh, no, to be sure; but what can I do? My mistress will have it so, and Mrs. Gadabout and the rest of the company will be here in a few minutes; there are two or three coachfuls of 'em. 105

SHARP [*aside*]. Then my master must be ruined in spite of my parts.

GAY *(aside to* SHARP). 'Tis all over, Sharp.

SHARP. I know it, sir.

GAY. I shall go distracted; what shall I do? 110

SHARP. Why, sir, as our rooms are a little out of furniture at present, take 'em into the captain's that lodges here, and set 'em down to cards; if he should come in the mean time, I'll excuse you to him.

KITTY [*aside*]. I have disconcerted their 115 affairs, I find; I'll have some sport with 'em. — Pray, Mr. Gayless, don't order too many things; they only make you a friendly visit; the more ceremony, you know, the less welcome. Pray, sir, let me intreat you not to be profuse. If I can be 120 of service, pray command me; my mistress has sent me on purpose; while Mr. Sharp is doing the business without doors, I may be employed within; *(to* SHARP) if you'll lend me the keys of your sideboard I'll dispose of your plate to the best 125 advantage. *(Knocking.)*

SHARP. Thank you, Mrs. Kitty; but it is disposed of already. *(Knocking at the door.)*

KITTY. Bless me, the company's come! I'll go to the door and conduct 'em into your presence. 130

Exit KITTY.

SHARP. If you'd conduct 'em into a horse-pond,

and wait of 'em there yourself, we should be more obliged to you.

GAY. I can never support this!

SHARP. Rouse your spirits and put on an 135 air of gaiety, and I don't despair of bringing you off yet.

GAY. Your words have done it effectually.

Enter MRS. GADABOUT, *her Daughter and Niece,* MR. GUTTLE, MR. TRIPPIT *and* MRS. TRIPPIT.

GAD. Ah, my dear, Mr. Gayless! *(Kisses him.)*

GAY. My dear widow! *(Kisses her.)* 140

GAD. We are come to give you joy, Mr. Gayless.

SHARP *(aside).* You never was more mistaken in your life.

GAD. I have brought some company here, I believe, is not so well known to you, and I protest 145 I have been all about the town to get the little I have — Prissy, my dear — Mr. Gayless, my daughter.

GAY. And as handsome as her mother; you must have a husband shortly, my dear.

PRIS. I'll assure you I don't despair, sir. 150

GAD. My niece, too.

GAY. I know by her eyes she belongs to you, widow.

GAD. Mr. Guttle, sir, Mr. Gayless; Mr. Gayless, Justice Guttle. 155

GAY [*aside*]. Oh, destruction! one of the quorum.[1]

GUT. Hem, though I had not the honor of any personal knowledge of you, yet at the instigation of Mrs. Gadabout I have, without any previous acquaintance with you, throwed aside all cere- 160 mony to let you know that I joy to hear the solemnization of your nuptials is so near at hand.

GAY. Sir, though I cannot answer you with the same elocution, however, sir, I thank you with the same sincerity. 165

GAD. Mr. and Mrs. Trippit, sir, the properest lady in the world for your purpose, for she'll dance for four and twenty hours together.

TRIP. My dear Charles, I am very angry with you, faith; so near marriage and not let me 170 know, 'twas barbarous; you thought, I suppose, I should rally you upon it; but dear Mrs. Trippit here has long ago eradicated all my anti-matrimonial principles.

MRS. TRIP. I eradicate! fie, Mr. Trippit, 175 don't be so obscene.

KITTY. Pray, ladies, walk into the next room; Mr. Sharp can't lay his cloth till you are set down to cards.

GAD. One thing I had quite forgot; Mr. Gay- 180 less, my nephew who you never saw will be in town from France presently, so I left word to send him here immediately to make one.

[1] The body of justices of the peace.

GAY. You do me honor, madam.

SHARP. Do the ladies choose cards or the 185
supper first?

GAY. [aside]. Supper! what does the fellow mean?

GUT. Oh, the supper by all means, for I have eat
nothing to signify since dinner.

SHARP (aside). Nor I, since last Monday 190
was a fortnight.

GAY. Pray, ladies, walk into the next room:
Sharp, get things ready for supper, and call the
music.

SHARP. Well said, master. 195

GAY. Without ceremony, ladies.

Exeunt ladies [and GAYLESS].

KITTY [aside]. I'll to my mistress, and let her
know everything is ready for her appearance.

Exit KITTY.

GUTTLE *and* SHARP.

GUT. Pray Mr. What's-your-name, don't be long
with supper; but hark'ee, what can I do in 200
the meantime? Suppose you get me a pipe and
some good wine; I'll try to divert myself that way
till supper's ready.

SHARP. Or suppose, sir, you was to take a nap
till then, there's a very easy couch in that 205
closet.

GUT. The best thing in the world. I'll take your
advice, but be sure to wake me when supper is
ready. *Exit* GUTTLE.

SHARP. Pray heav'n you may not wake till 210
then — what a fine situation my master is in at
present! I have promised him my assistance, but
his affairs are in so desperate a way, that I am afraid
'tis out of all my skill to recover 'em. Well, fools
have fortune, says an old proverb, and a very 215
true one it is, for my master and I are two of the most
unfortunate mortals in the creation.

Enter GAYLESS.

GAY. Well, Sharp, I have set 'em down to cards,
and now what have you to propose?

SHARP. I have one scheme left which in all 220
probability may succeed. The good citizen, over-
loaded with his last meal, is taking a nap in that
closet, in order to get him an appetite for yours.
Suppose, sir, we should make him treat us.

GAY. I don't understand you. 225

SHARP. I'll pick his pocket, and provide us a supper with the booty.

GAY. Monstrous! for without considering the
villainy of it, the danger of waking him makes it
impracticable! 230

SHARP. If he wakes, I'll smother him, and lay his

death to indigestion — a very common death among
the justices.

GAY. Prithee be serious, we have no time to lose;
can you invent nothing to drive 'em out of 235
the house?

SHARP. I can fire it.

GAY. Shame and confusion so perplex me, I cannot give myself a moment's thought.

SHARP. I have it; did not Mrs. Gadabout 240
say her nephew would be here?

GAY. She did.

SHARP. Say no more, but [in to] your company; if
I don't send 'em out of the house for the night, I'll
at least frighten their stomachs away; and if 245
this stratagem fails, I'll relinquish politics, and
think my understanding no better than my neighbors'.

GAY. How shall I reward thee, Sharp?

SHARP. By your silence and obedience; 250
away to your company, sir. *Exit* GAYLESS.
Now, dear madam Fortune, for once, open your
eyes, and behold a poor unfortunate man of parts
addressing you; now is your time to convince your
foes you are not that blind whimsical whore 255
they take you for; but let 'em see by your assisting
me, that men of sense, as well as fools, are sometimes intitled to your favor and protection. — So
much for prayer, now for a great noise and a lie.

(*Goes aside and cries out.*)

Help, help, master; help, gentlemen, ladies; 260
murder, fire, brimstone; help, help, help!

Enter Mr. GAYLESS, [MR. TRIPPET,] *and the ladies,
with cards in their hands, and* SHARP *enters running, and meets 'em.*

GAY. What's the matter?

SHARP. Matter, sir! if you don't run this minute
with that gentleman, this lady's nephew will be
murdered; I am sure 'twas he; he was set upon 265
the corner of the street, by four; he has killed two,
and if you don't make haste, he'll be either murdered or took to prison.

GAD. For heaven's sake, gentlemen, run to his
assistance. (*Aside.*) How I tremble for 270
Melissa; this frolic of hers may be fatal.

GAY. Draw, sir, and follow me.

[*Exeunt*] GAYLESS *and* GADABOUT.

TRIP. Not I; I don't care to run myself into
needless quarrels; I have suffered too much formerly
by flying into passions; besides I have pawned 275
my honor to Mrs. Trippit, never to draw my sword
again; and in her present condition, to break my
word might have fatal consequences.

SHARP. Pray, sir, don't excuse yourself, the young
gentleman may be murdered by this time. 280

185] D8 om. *the.*   210] O6W1 *heaven.*   214] W1 *it is out of my.*   243] O1O2 *into;* O6D8W1 *in to.*

256] D8 *them.*   259] D8 *and lie.*   261 s.d.] D8W1 them.   272 s.d.] O1O2O6D8W1 Exit.

TRIP. Then my assistance will be of no service to him; however — I'll go to oblige you, and look on at a distance.

MRS. TRIP. I shall certainly faint, Mr. Trippit, if you draw.   285

Enter GUTTLE, *disordered, as from sleep.*

GUT. What noise and confusion is this?

SHARP. Sir, there's a man murdered in the street.

GUT. Is that all — zounds, I was afraid you had throwed the supper down — a plague of your noise — I shan't recover my stomach this half hour.   290

Enter GAYLESS *and* GADABOUT, *with* MELISSA *in boy's clothes, dressed in the French manner.*

GAD. Well, but my dear Jemmy, you are not hurt, sure?

MEL. A little with riding post only.

GAD. Mr. Sharp alarmed us all with an account of your being set upon by four men; that you   295 had killed two, and was attacking the other when he came away, and when we met you at the door, we were running to your rescue.

MEL. I had a small rencounter with half a dozen villains; but finding me resolute, they were wise   300 enough to take to their heels; I believe I scrat [1] some of 'em.   (*Laying her hand to her sword.*)

SHARP (*aside*). His vanity has saved my credit. I have a thought come into my head may prove to our advantage, provided monsieur's ignorance   305 bears any proportion to his impudence.

GAD. Now my fright's over, let me introduce you, my dear, to Mr. Gayless; sir, this is my nephew.

GAY. (*saluting her*).   Sir, I shall be proud of your friendship.   310

MEL. I don't doubt but we shall be better acquainted in a little time.

GUT. Pray, sir, what news in France?

MEL. Faith, sir, very little that I know of in the political way; I had no time to spend among   315 the politicians. I was —

GAY. Among the ladies, I suppose.

MEL. Too much, indeed. Faith, I have not philosophy enough to resist their solicitations; (*to* GAYLESS *aside*) you take me.   320

GAY. (*aside to* SHARP). Yes, to be a most incorrigible fop; 'sdeath, this puppy's impertinence is an addition to my misery.

MEL. (*aside to* GADABOUT). Poor Gayless, to what shifts is he reduced? I cannot bear to   325 see him much longer in this condition; I shall discover myself.

GAD. Not before the end of the play; besides, the

more his pain now, the greater his pleasure when relieved from it.   330

TRIP. Shall we return to our cards? I have a *sans prendre* [2] here, and must insist you play it out.

LADIES. With all my heart.

MEL. *Allons donc.*

(*As the company goes out,* SHARP *pulls* ME-
LISSA *by the sleeve.*)

SHARP. Sir, sir, shall I beg leave to speak   335 with you? Pray, did you find a bank-note in your way hither?

MEL. What, between here and Dover do you mean?

SHARP. No, sir, within twenty or thirty   340 yards of this house.

MEL. You are drunk, fellow.

SHARP. I am undone, sir; but not drunk, I'll assure you.

MEL. What is all this?   345

SHARP. I'll tell you, sir: a little while ago my master sent me out to change a note of twenty pounds; but I, unfortunately hearing a noise in the street of, 'damme, sir,' and clashing of swords, and 'rascal,' and 'murder'; I runs up to the place,   350 and saw four men upon one; and having heard you was a mettlesome young gentleman, I immediately concluded it must be you; so ran back to call my master, and when I went to look for the note to change it, I found it gone, either stole or lost;   355 and if I don't get the money immediately, I shall certainly be turned out of my place, and lose my character.

MEL. (*aside*). I shall laugh in his face. — Oh, I'll speak to your master about it, and he will for-   360 give you at my intercession.

SHARP. Ah, sir! you don't know my master.

MEL. I'm very little acquainted with him; but I have heard he's a very good-natured man.

SHARP. I have heard so too, but I have felt   365 it otherwise; he has so much good-nature, that, if I could compound for one broken head a day, I should think myself very well off.

MEL. Are you serious, friend?

SHARP. Look'ee, sir, I take you for a man   370 of honor; there is something in your face that is generous, open, and masculine; you don't look like a foppish, effeminate tell-tale; so I'll venture to trust you. — See here, sir — (*shows his head*) these are the effects of my master's good-nature.   375

MEL. (*aside*). Matchless impudence! — Why do you live with him then after such usage?

SHARP. He's worth a great deal of money, and

[2] A hand so good that the player might contract to take a majority of the tricks without the assistance of a partner.

[1] Scratched.

when he's drunk, which is commonly once a day, he's very free, and will give me anything; 380 but I design to leave him when he's married, for all that.

MEL. Is he going to be married then?

SHARP. Tomorrow, sir, and between you and I, he'll meet with his match, both for humor and 385 something else too.

MEL. What, she drinks too?

SHARP. Damnably, sir; but mum. — You must know this entertainment was designed for madam tonight; but she got so very gay after dinner, 390 that she could not walk out of her own house; so her maid, who was half gone too, came here with an excuse, that Mrs. Melissa had got the vapors, and so she had indeed violently; here, here, sir.

(*Pointing to his head.*)

MEL. (*aside*). This is scarcely to be borne. 395 — Melissa! I have heard of her; they say she's very whimsical.

SHARP. A very [1] woman, and [2] please your honor, and between you and I, none of the mildest or wisest of her sex — but to return, sir, to the twenty 400 pounds.

MEL. I am surprised you who have got so much money in his service, should be at a loss for twenty pounds, to save your bones at this juncture.

SHARP. I have put all my money out at in- 405 terest; I never keep above five pounds by me; and if your honor would lend me the other fifteen, and take my note for it.   (*Knocking.*)

MEL. Somebody's at the door.

SHARP. I can give very good security.   410
(*Knocking.*)

MEL. Don't let the people wait, Mr. —

SHARP. Ten pounds will do.   (*Knocking.*)

MEL. *Allez-vous-en!* [3]

SHARP. Five, sir.   (*Knocking.*)

MEL. *Je ne puis pas.* [4]   415

SHARP [*aside*]. '*Je ne puis pas.*' I find we shan't understand one another, I do but lose time; and, if I had any thought, I might have known young fops return from their travels generally with as little money as improvement.   *Exit* SHARP. 420

MEL. Ha, ha, ha, what lies doth this fellow invent, and what rogueries does he commit for his master's service? There never sure was a more faithful servant to his master, or a greater rogue to the rest of mankind; but here he comes 425 again; the plot thickens; I'll in and observe Gayless.

Exit MELISSA.

[1] True.
[2] 'And' is a corruption of 'an't' or 'an it' = 'if it.'
[3] Go!
[4] I cannot.

Enter SHARP *before several persons with dishes in their hands, and a Cook, drunk.*

SHARP (*aside*). Fortune, I thank thee: the most lucky accident! — This way, gentlemen, this way.

COOK. I am afraid I have mistook the house. Is this Mr. Treatwell's?   430

SHARP. The same, the same: what, don't you know me?

COOK. Know you! — Are you sure there was a supper bespoke here?

SHARP. Yes: upon my honor, Mr. Cook, the 435 company is in the next room, and must have gone without, had not you brought it. I'll draw in a table. I see you have brought a cloth with you; but you need not have done that, for we have a very good stock of linen — (*aside*) at the pawn- 440 broker's.

(*Exit, and returns immediately, drawing in a table.*) Come, come my boys, be quick, the company began to be very uneasy; but I knew my old friend Lickspit here would not fail us.

COOK. Lick-spit! I am no friend of yours; 445 so I desire less familiarity: Lick-spit too!

Enter GAYLESS, *and stares.*

GAY. What is all this?

SHARP (*aside to* GAYLESS). Sir, if the sight of the supper is offensive, I can easily have it removed.

GAY. Prithee explain thyself, Sharp.   450

SHARP. Some of our neighbors, I suppose, have bespoke this supper; but the cook has drank away his memory, forgot the house, and brought it here; however, sir, if you dislike it, I'll tell him of his mistake, and send him about his business. 455

GAY. Hold, hold, necessity obliges me against my inclination to favor the cheat, and feast at my neighbor's expense.

COOK. Hark you, friend, is that [your] master?

SHARP. Ay, and the best master in the world. 460

COOK. I'll speak to him then. — Sir, I have according to your commands, dressed as genteel a supper as my art and your price would admit of.

SHARP (*aside to* GAYLESS). Good again, sir, 'tis paid for.   465

GAY. I don't in the least question your abilities, Mr. Cook, and I am obliged to you for your care.

COOK. Sir, you are a gentleman, — and if you would but look over the bill and approve it, (*pulls out a bill*) you will over and above return the 470 obligation.

SHARP [*aside*]. Oh, the devil!

GAY. (*looking on a bill*). Very well, I'll send my man to pay you tomorrow.

COOK. I'll spare him that trouble, and take 475

it with me, sir — I never work but for ready money.

GAY. Hah?

SHARP (*aside*). Then you won't have our custom.
— My master is busy now, friend; do you think he
won't pay you? 480

COOK. No matter what I think; either my meat
or my money.

SHARP. 'Twill be very ill-convenient for him to
pay you tonight.

COOK. Then I'm afraid it will be ill-conven- 485
ient to pay me tomorrow, so d'ye hear —

Enter MELISSA.

GAY. Prithee be advised! 'sdeath, I shall be discovered!   (*Takes the Cook aside.*)

MEL. (*to* SHARP). What's the matter?

SHARP. The cook has not quite answered my 490
master's expectations about the supper, sir, and he's
a little angry at him, that's all.

MEL. Come, come, Mr. Gayless, don't be uneasy; a bachelor cannot be supposed to have things
in the utmost regularity; we don't expect it. 495

COOK. But I do expect it, and will have it.

MEL. What does that drunken fool say?

COOK. That I will have my money, and I won't
stay till tomorrow — and, and —

SHARP (*runs and stops his mouth*). Hold, 500
hold, what are you doing? are you mad?

MEL. What do you stop the man's breath for?

SHARP. Sir, he was going to call you names. —
Don't be abusive, cook; the gentleman is a man of
honor, and said nothing to you; pray be paci- 505
fied; you are in liquor.

COOK. I will have my —

SHARP (*holding, still*). Why, I tell you, fool, you
mistake the gentleman; he is a friend of my master's, and has not said a word to you. — Pray, 510
good sir, go into the next room; the fellow's drunk,
and takes you for another. — You'll repent this
when you are sober, friend. — Pray, sir, don't stay
to hear his impertinence.

GAY. Pray, sir, walk in — he's below your 515
anger.

MEL. Damn the rascal! What does he mean by
affronting me! Let the scoundrel go; I'll polish his
brutality, I warrant you: here's the best reformer of
manners in the universe. (*Draws his sword.*) 520
Let him go, I say.

SHARP. So, so you have done finely, now. — Get
away as fast as you can: he's the most courageous
mettlesome man in all England. Why, if his passion
was up he could eat you. — Make your escape, 525
you fool!

COOK. I won't. Eat me! he'll find me damned
hard of digestion though —

SHARP. Prithee come here; let me speak with you.
          (*They walk aside.*)

Enter KITTY.

KITTY. Gad's me, is supper on the table 530
already? Sir, pray defer it for a few moments; my
mistress is much better, and will be here immediately.

GAY. Will she indeed! bless me — I did not
expect — but however — Sharp?

KITTY (*aside to* MELISSA). What success, 535
madam?

MEL. As we could wish, girl — but he is in such
pain and perplexity I can't hold it out much longer.

KITTY. Ay, that not holding out is the ruin of
half our sex. 540

SHARP. I have pacified the cook, and if you can
but borrow twenty pieces of that young prig, all
may go well yet; you may succeed though I could
not: remember what I told you — about it straight,
sir — 545

GAY. (*to* MELISSA). Sir, sir, I beg to speak a
word with you; my servant, sir, tells me he has had
the misfortune, sir, to lose a note of mine of twenty
pounds, which I sent him to receive — and the
bankers' shops being shut up, and having very 550
little cash by me, I should be much obliged to you
if you would favor me with twenty pieces till to-
morrow.

MEL. Oh, sir, with all my heart (*taking out her
purse*), and as I have a small favor to beg of 555
you, sir, the obligation will be mutual.

GAY. How may I oblige you, sir?

MEL. You are to be married, I hear, to Melissa.

GAY. Tomorrow, sir.

MEL. Then you'll oblige me, sir, by never 560
seeing her again.

GAY. Do you call this a small favor, sir!

MEL. A mere trifle, sir — breaking of contracts,
suing for divorces, committing adultery, and such
like, are all reckoned trifles now-a-days; and 565
smart young fellows, like you and myself, Gayless,
should never be out of fashion.

GAY. But pray, sir, how are you concerned in
this affair!

MEL. Oh, sir, you must know I have a very 570
great regard for Melissa, and, indeed, she for me;
and, by the by, I have a most despicable opinion of
you; for *entre nous*, I take you, Charles, to be a
very great scoundrel.

GAY. Sir! 575

MEL. Nay, don't look fierce, sir! and give yourself
airs — damme, sir, I shall be through your body
else in the snapping of a finger.

GAY. I'll be as quick as you, villain!
          (*Draws and makes at* MELISSA.)

507] W1 *I shall have.*   524] W1 *mettlesome young man.*   532] W1 om. *much.*

KITTY. Hold, hold, murder! you'll kill my 580
mistress — the young gentleman, I mean.

GAY. Ah! her mistress!   (*Drops his sword.*)

SHARP. How! Melissa! nay, then drive away
cart. All's over now.

Enter all the company laughing.

GAD. What, Mr. Gayless, engaging with 585
Melissa before your time. Ah, ah, ah!

KITTY (*to* SHARP). Your humble servant, good
Mr. Politician. — This is, gentlemen and ladies, the
most celebrated and ingenious Timothy Sharp,
schemer general, and redoubted squire to the 590
most renowned and fortunate adventurer Charles
Gayless, knight of the woeful countenance: ha, ha,
ha! Oh, that dismal face and more dismal head of
yours.   (*Strikes* SHARP *upon the head.*)

SHARP. 'Tis cruel in you to disturb a man 595
in his last agonies.

MEL. Now, Mr. Gayless! — what, not a word!
you are sensible I can be no stranger to your misfortunes, and I might reasonably expect an excuse for
your ill treatment of me.   600

GAY. No, madam, silence is my only refuge; for
to endeavor to vindicate my crimes would show a
greater want of virtue than even the commission
of 'em.

MEL. Oh, Gayless! 'twas poor to impose 605
upon a woman, and one that loved you too.

GAY. Oh, most unpardonable; but my necessities —

SHARP. And mine, madam, were not to be
matched, I'm sure, o' this side starving.   610

MEL. [*aside*]. His tears have softened me at
once. — Your necessities, Mr. Gayless, with such
real contrition, are too powerful motives not to
affect the breast already prejudiced in your favor —
you have suffered too much already for your 615
extravagance; and as I take part in your sufferings,
'tis easing myself to relieve you: know, therefore,
all that's past I freely forgive.

GAY. You cannot mean it, sure: I am lost in
wonder.   620

MEL. Prepare yourself for more wonder — you
have another friend in masquerade here: Mr. Cook,
pray throw aside your drunkenness, and make your
sober appearance — don't you know that face, sir?

COOK. Ay, master, what, have you forgot 625
your friend Dick, as you used to call me?

GAY. More wonder indeed! don't you live with
my father?

MEL. Just after your hopeful servant there had
left me, comes this man from Sir William with 630
a letter to me; upon which (being by that wholly
convinced of your necessitous condition) I invented,

by the help of Kitty and Mrs. Gadabout, this little
plot, in which your friend Dick there has acted
miracles, resolving to tease you a little, that 635
you might have a greater relish for a happy turn in
your affairs. Now, sir, read that letter, and complete your joy.

GAY. (*reads*).

'Madam, I am father to the unfortunate 640
young man, who, I hear by a friend of mine (that
by my desire, has been a continual spy upon him)
is making his addresses to you: if he is so happy as
to make himself agreeable to you (whose character
I am charmed with) I shall own him with joy 645
for my son, and forget his former follies. I am,

   Madam,

      Your most humble servant,

         William Gayless.

P. S. I will be soon in town myself to 650
congratulate his reformation and marriage.'

O Melissa, this is too much; thus let me show my
thanks and gratitude, (*kneeling; she raises him*) for
here 'tis only due.

SHARP. A reprieve! a reprieve! a reprieve! 655

KITTY [*to* GAYLESS]. I have been, sir, a most
bitter enemy to you; but since you are likely to be
a little more conversant with cash than you have
been, I am now, with the greatest sincerity, your
most obedient friend and humble servant. And 660
I hope, sir, all former enmity will be forgotten.

GAY. Oh, Mrs. Pry, I have been too much indulged with forgiveness myself not to forgive lesser
offences in other people.

SHARP. Well then, madam, since my master 665
has vouchsafed pardon to your handmaid Kitty, I
hope you'll not deny it to his footman Timothy.

MEL. Pardon! for what?

SHARP. Only for telling you about ten thousand
lies, madam, and, among the rest, insinuating 670
that your ladyship would —

MEL. I understand you; and can forgive any
thing, Sharp, that was designed for the service of
your master; and if Pry and you will follow our
example, I'll give her a small fortune as a re- 675
ward for both your fidelities.

SHARP. I fancy, madam, 'twould be better to half
the small fortune between us, and keep us both
single: for as we shall live in the same house, in all
probability we may taste the comforts of mat- 680
rimony, and not be troubled with its inconveniences; what say you, Kitty?

KITTY. Do you hear, Sharp, before you talk of
the comforts of matrimony, taste the comforts of a
good dinner, and recover your flesh a little, 685
do, puppy.

SHARP. The devil backs her, that's certain; and I am no match for her at any weapon.

MEL. And now, Mr. Gayless, to show I have not provided for you by halves, let the music pre- 690
pare themselves, and, with the approbation of the company, we'll have a dance.

ALL. By all means, a dance.

GUT. By all means a dance — after supper though — 695

SHARP. Oh, pray, sir, have supper first, or, I'm sure, I shan't live till the dance is finished.

GAY. Behold, Melissa, as sincere a convert as ever truth and beauty made. The wild impetuous sallies of my youth are now blown over, and 700
a most pleasing calm of perfect happiness succeeds. Thus Ætna's flames the verdant earth consume, But milder heat makes drooping nature bloom: So virtuous love affords us springing joy, Whilst vicious passions, as they burn, destroy. 705

692] D8 *well have.*

EPILOGUE

SPOKEN BY MR. GARRICK[1]

That I'm a lying rogue, you all agree:
And yet look round the world, and you will see
How many more, my betters, lie as fast as me.
Against this vice we all are ever railing,
And yet, so tempting is it, so prevailing, 5
You'll find but few without this useful failing.
Lady or Abigail,[2] my lord or Will,
The lie goes round, and the ball's never still.
My lies were harmless, told to show my parts;
And not like those, when tongues belie their hearts. 10
In all professions you will find this flaw;
And in the gravest too, in physic and in law.
The gouty sergeant cries, with formal pause,
'Your plea is good, my friend, don't starve the cause.'
But when my lord decrees for t'other side, 15
Your costs of suit convince you — that he lied.
A doctor comes with formal wig and face,
First feels your pulse, then thinks, and knows your case.
'Your fever's slight, not dang'rous, I assure you,
Keep warm, and *repetatur haustus*,[3] sir, will cure you.' 20
Around the bed, next day, his friends are crying:
The patient dies, the doctor's paid for lying.
The poet, willing to secure the pit,
Gives out, his play has humor, taste and wit:
The cause comes on, and, while the judges try, 25
Each groan and catcall gives the bard the lie.
Now let us ask, pray, what the ladies do:
They too will fib a little *entre nous*,
'Lord!' says the prude (her face behind her fan)
'How can our sex have any joy in man? 30
As for my part, the best could ne'er deceive me,
And were the race extinct 'twould never grieve me:
Their sight is odious, but their touch — O Gad!
The thought of that's enough to drive one mad.'
Thus rails at man the squeamish Lady Dainty. 35
Yet weds, at fifty-five, a rake of twenty.
In short, a beau's intrigues, a lover's sighs,
The courtier's promise, the rich widow's cries,
And patriot's zeal, are seldom more than lies.
Sometimes you'll see a man belie his nation, 40
Nor to his country show the least relation.
For instance now —
A cleanly Dutchman, or a Frenchman grave,
A sober German, or a Spaniard brave,
An Englishman a coward or a slave. 45
Mine, though a fibbing, was an honest art:
I served my master, played a faithful part:
Rank me not therefore 'mong the lying crew,
For, though my tongue was false, my heart was true.

---

[1] In the part of Sharp.   [2] A generic name for a maid-servant.
[3] 'Let the draught be repeated,' a phrase employed in medical prescriptions; here loosely used to mean 'repeated draughts.'

Epilogue] O1 om. entire epilogue.   7] D8 *Abigal.*   20] D8 repititur.

Douglas

BY JOHN HOME

DOUGLAS:

A

TRAGEDY.

As it is ACTED at the

THEATRE-ROYAL

IN

COVENT-GARDEN.

Non ego fum vates, fed prifci confcius ævi.

EDINBURGH:

Printed for G. HAMILTON & J. BALFOUR, W. GRAY & W. PETER.
M,DCC,LVII.

[Price One Shilling Sixpence.]

THE FIRST EDINBURGH EDITION, 1757, WITHOUT THE AUTHOR'S NAME, OF *DOUGLAS: A TRAGEDY*

PROLOGUE

Spoken at Edinburgh

In days of classic fame, when Persia's lord [1]
Opposed his millions to the Grecian sword,
Flourished the state of Athens; small her store,
Rugged her soil, and rocky was her shore,
Like Caledonia's: yet she gained a name   5
That stands unrivalled in the rolls of fame.
    Such proud pre-eminence not valor gave,
(For who than Sparta's dauntless sons more brave?)
But learning, and the love of every art,
That Virgin Pallas and the Muse impart.   10
    Above the rest the Tragic Muse admired
Each Attic breast, with noblest passions fired.
In peace their poets with their heroes shared
Glory, the hero's and the bard's reward.
The Tragic Muse each glorious record kept,   15
And, o'er the kings she conquered, Athens wept. [2]
    Here let me cease, impatient for the scene;
To you I need not praise the Tragic Queen:
Oft has this audience soft compassion shown
To woes of heroes, heroes not their own.   20
This night our scenes no common tear demand:
He comes, the hero of your native land!
Douglas, a name through all the world renowned,
A name that rouses like the trumpet's sound!
Oft have your fathers, prodigal of life,   25
A Douglas followed through the bloody strife;
Hosts have been known at that dread time to yield
And, Douglas dead, his name hath won the field.
    Listen attentive to the various tale,
    Mark if the author's kindred feelings fail;   30
    Swayed by alternate hopes, alternate fears,
    He waits the test of your congenial tears.
    If they shall flow, back to the Muse he flies,
    And bids your heroes in succession rise;
    Collects the wand'ring warriors as they roam,   35
    Douglas assures them of a welcome-home.

[1] Xerxes.   [2] 'See the *Persai* of Æschylus.' [Note in the original Edinburgh and London Editions.]

PROLOGUE

SPOKEN [AT LONDON] BY MR. SPARKS [1]

In ancient times, when Britain's trade was arms,
And the loved music of her youth, alarms;
A god-like race sustained fair England's fame:
Who has not heard of gallant Percy's name?
Ay, and of Douglas?   Such illustrious foes   5
In rival Rome and Carthage never rose!
From age to age bright shone the British fire,
And every hero was a hero's sire.
When powerful fate decreed one warrior's doom,
Up sprung the phœnix from his parent's tomb.   10
But whilst these generous rivals fought and fell,
These generous rivals loved each other well:
Though many a bloody field was lost and won,
Nothing in hate, in honor all was done.
When Percy, wronged, defied his prince or peers,   15
Fast came the Douglas, with his Scottish spears;
And, when proud Douglas made his king his foe,
For Douglas, Percy bent his English bow.
Expelled their native homes by adverse fate,
They knocked alternate at each other's gate: 20
Then blazed the castle, at the midnight hour,
For him whose arms had shook its firmest tow'r.

This night a Douglas your protection claims;
A wife! a mother!   Pity's softest names:
The story of her woes indulgent hear,   25
And grant your suppliant all she begs, a tear.
In confidence she begs; and hopes to find
Each English breast, like noble Percy's, kind.

[1] The Old Norval of the London cast.

4] EL *Piercy's*; M *Percy's*.　　　12] E *those*; LDBM *these*.　　　16] M *First*.

DRAMATIS PERSONÆ

[MEN]

LORD RANDOLPH
GLENALVON
[YOUNG] NORVAL, *Douglas* [1]
STRANGER [OLD NORVAL] [2]
Servants

WOMEN

MATILDA, LADY RANDOLPH
ANNA [*her confidante*]

[SCENE — LORD RANDOLPH'S CASTLE IN THE WEST OF SCOTLAND.]

[TIME, ABOUT THE MIDDLE OF THE TWELFTH CENTURY.]

---

[1] The stress on concealed identity involves some confusion in the text. The hero, designated as *Young Man* in stage direction at his first entrance (II. 5–6), is called *The Stranger* until he reveals himself as NORVAL (i.e. YOUNG NORVAL). Throughout Act V he is called DOUGLAS, since his true identity has been established in Act IV.

[2] Textual difficulties multiply in the general use of the term, *Stranger*, for characters as yet unidentified. *A Stranger*, in the opening stage direction in Act II is the *servant* of YOUNG NORVAL (see II. 4–5 and 69–70). As indicated above, YOUNG NORVAL himself is the chief *Stranger* in Act II. In Act III, OLD NORVAL, designated as the STRANGER in the *Dramatis Personæ*, and in the stage direction (III. 224), is otherwise called the *Prisoner*. In Act V, stage directions call him OLD NORVAL, but speech directions read simply NORVAL, as DOUGLAS is now substituted for [YOUNG] NORVAL.

DOUGLAS

By JOHN HOME

ACT I

The court of a castle surrounded with woods.

Enter LADY RANDOLPH.

[LADY R.] Ye woods and wilds, whose melan-
  choly gloom
Accords with my soul's sadness, and draws forth
The voice of sorrow from my bursting heart,
Farewell a while: I will not leave you long;
For in your shades I deem some spirit dwells,   5
Who from the chiding stream, or groaning oak,
Still hears and answers to Matilda's moan.
O Douglas! Douglas! if departed ghosts
Are e'er permitted to review this world,
Within the circle of that wood thou art,   10
And with the passion of immortals hear'st
My lamentation: hear'st thy wretched wife
Weep for her husband slain, her infant lost.
My brother's timeless [1] death I seem to mourn,
Who perished with thee on this fatal day.   15
To thee I lift my voice; to thee address
The plaint which mortal ear has never heard.
O disregard me not; though I am called
Another's now, my heart is wholly thine.
Incapable of change, affection lies   20
Buried, my Douglas, in thy bloody grave. —
But Randolph comes, whom fate has made my lord,
To chide my anguish, and defraud the dead.

Enter LORD RANDOLPH.

[LORD R.] Again these weeds of woe! Say, dost
  thou well
To feed a passion which consumes thy life?   25
The living claim some duty; vainly thou
Bestow'st thy cares upon the silent dead.

LADY R. Silent, alas! is he for whom I mourn:
Childless, without memorial of his name,
He only now in my remembrance lives.   30
«This fatal day stirs my time-settled sorrow —
Troubles afresh the fountain of my heart.»

LORD R. «When was it pure of sadness! These
  black weeds
Express the wonted color of thy mind,
Forever dark and dismal. Seven long years   35
Are passed, since we were joined by sacred ties:
Clouds, all the while, have hung upon thy brow,
Nor broke, nor parted by one gleam of joy.»

[1] Untimely.

Time, that wears out the trace of deepest anguish,
«As the sea smooths the prints made in the
  sand,»   40
Has passed o'er thee in vain.

«LADY R.   If time to come
Should prove as ineffectual, yet, my lord,
Thou canst not blame me. When our Scottish
  youth
Vied with each other for my luckless love,
Oft I besought them, I implored them all   45
Not to assail me with my father's aid,
Nor blend their better destiny with mine.
For melancholy had congealed my blood,
And froze affection in my chilly breast.
At last my sire, roused with the base attempt   50
To force me from him, which thou rend'redst vain,
To his own daughter bowed his hoary head,
Besought me to commiserate his age,
And vowed he should not, could not, die in peace,
Unless he saw me wedded, and secured   55
From violence and outrage. Then, my lord!
In my extreme distress I called on thee,
Thee I bespake, professed my strong desire
To lead a single, solitary life,
And begged thy nobleness, not to demand   60
Her for a wife whose heart was dead to love.
How thou persisted'st after this, thou know'st,
And must confess that I am not unjust,
Nor more to thee than to myself injurious.»

LORD R. «That I confess; yet ever must regret   65
The grief I cannot cure.» Would thou wert not
Composed of grief and tenderness alone,
«But hadst a spark of other passions in thee,
Pride, anger, vanity, the strong desire
Of admiration, dear to womankind;   70
These might contend with, and allay thy grief,
As meeting tides and currents smooth our firth.[2]»

«LADY R. To such a cause the human mind oft
  owes
Its transient calm, a calm I envy not.»

LORD R. Sure thou art not the daughter of Sir
  Malcolm: 75
Strong was his rage, eternal his resentment:
For when thy brother fell, he smiled to hear
That Douglas' son in the same field was slain.

LADY R. Oh! rake not up the ashes of my fathers:
Implacable resentment was their crime,   80

[2] The Firth of Forth.

31–38] Here, and subsequently, guillemets « » indicate passages omitted in L and D.   72] M *frith.*

And grievous has the expiation been.
Contending with the Douglas, gallant lives
Of either house were lost; my ancestors
Compelled, at last, to leave their ancient seat
On Tiviot's [1] pleasant banks; and now, of them   85
No heir is left. Had they not been so stern,
I had not been the last of all my race.

LORD R. Thy grief wrests to its purposes my
     words.
I never asked of thee that ardent love,
Which in the breasts of fancy's children burns.   90
Decent affection and complacent kindness
Were all I wished for; but I wished in vain.
Hence with the less regret my eyes behold
The storm of war that gathers o'er this land:
If I should perish by the Danish sword,   95
Matilda would not shed one tear the more.

LADY R. Thou dost not think so: woeful as I am,
I love thy merit, and esteem thy virtues.
But whither go'st thou now?

LORD R.   Straight to the camp,
Where every warrior on the tip-toe stands   100
Of expectation, and impatient asks
Each who arrives, if he is come to tell
The Danes are landed.

LADY R.   O! may adverse winds,
Far from the coast of Scotland, drive their fleet!
And every soldier of both hosts return   105
In peace and safety to his pleasant home!

LORD R. Thou speak'st a woman's, hear a war-
     rior's wish:
Right from their native land, the stormy north,
May the wind blow, till every keel is fixed
Immovable in Caledonia's strand!   110
Then shall our foes repent their bold invasion,
And roving armies shun the fatal shore.

LADY R. War I detest: but war with foreign foes,
Whose manners, language, and whose looks are
     strange,
Is not so horrid, nor to me so hateful,   115
As that which with our neighbors oft we wage.
A river here, there an ideal line,
By fancy drawn, divides the sister kingdoms.
On each side dwells a people similar,
As twins are to each other; valiant both;   120
Both for their valor famous through the world.
Yet will they not unite their kindred arms,
And, if they must have war, wage distant war,
But with each other fight in cruel conflict.
Gallant in strife, and noble in their ire,   125
The battle is their pastime. They go forth
Gay in the morning, as to summer sport;
When ev'ning comes, the glory of the morn,
The youthful warrior, is a clod of clay.
Thus fall the prime of either hapless land;   130
And such the fruit of Scotch and English wars.

     [1] The river Teviot.

LORD R. I'll hear no more: this melody would
     make
A soldier drop his sword, and doff his arms,
Sit down and weep the conquests he has made;
Yea, (like a monk), sing rest and peace in
     heav'n   135
To souls of warriors in his battles slain.
Lady, farewell: I leave thee not alone;
Yonder comes one whose love makes duty light.
                             Exit.

Enter ANNA.

ANNA. Forgive the rashness of your Anna's love:
Urged by affection, I have thus presumed   140
To interrupt your solitary thoughts;
And warn you of the hours that you neglect,
And lose in sadness.

LADY R.   So to lose my hours
Is all the use I wish to make of time.

ANNA. To blame thee, lady, suits not with my
     state: 145
But sure I am, since death first preyed on man,
Never did sister thus a brother mourn.
What had your sorrows been if you had lost,
In early youth, the husband of your heart?

LADY R. Oh!   150

ANNA. Have I distressed you with officious love,
And ill-timed mention of your brother's fate?
Forgive me, lady: humble though I am,
The mind I bear partakes not of my fortune:
So fervently I love you, that to dry   155
These piteous tears, I'd throw my life away.

LADY R. What power directed thy unconscious
     tongue
To speak as thou hast done? to name —

ANNA.   I know not:
But since my words have made my mistress tremble,
I will speak so no more; but silent mix   160
My tears with hers.

LADY R.   No, thou shalt not be silent.
I'll trust thy faithful love, and thou shalt be
Henceforth th' instructed partner of my woes.
But what avails it? Can thy feeble pity
Roll back the flood of never-ebbing time?   165
Compel the earth and ocean to give up
Their dead alive?

ANNA.   What means my noble mistress?

LADY R. Didst thou not ask what had my sor-
     rows been?
If I in early youth had lost a husband? —
In the cold bosom of the earth is lodged,   170
Mangled with wounds, the husband of my youth;
And in some cavern of the ocean lies
My child and his. —

ANNA.   O! lady, most revered!
The tale wrapt up in your amazing words
Deign to unfold.

LADY R.   Alas! an ancient feud,   175
Hereditary evil, was the source
Of my misfortunes.   Ruling fate decreed
That my brave brother should in battle save
The life of Douglas' son, our house's foe:
The youthful warriors vowed eternal friendship.   180
To see the vaunted sister of his friend
Impatient, Douglas to Balarmo came,
Under a borrowed name. — My heart he gained;
Nor did I long refuse the hand he begged:
My brother's presence authorized our marriage.   185
Three weeks, three little weeks, with wings of down,
Had o'er us flown, when my loved lord was called
To fight his father's battles; and with him,
In spite of all my tears, did Malcolm go.
Scarce were they gone, when my stern sire was
     told   190
That the false stranger was Lord Douglas' son.
Frantic with rage, the baron drew his sword,
And questioned me.   Alone, forsaken, faint,
Kneeling beneath his sword, falt'ring, I took
An oath equivocal, that I ne'er would   195
Wed one of Douglas' name.   Sincerity,
Thou first of virtues, let no mortal leave
Thy onward path! although the earth should gape,
And from the gulf of hell destruction cry,
To take dissimulation's winding way.   200
     ANNA.   Alas! how few of woman's fearful kind
Durst own a truth so hardy!
     LADY R.   The first truth
Is easiest to avow.   This moral learn,
This precious moral, from my tragic tale. —
In a few days the dreadful tidings came   205
That Douglas and my brother both were slain.
My lord! my life! my husband! — Mighty God!
What had I done to merit such affliction?
     ANNA.   My dearest lady! many a tale of tears
I've listened to; but never did I hear   210
A tale so sad as this.
     LADY R.   In the first days
Of my distracting grief, I found myself —
As women wish to be who love their lords.
But who durst tell my father?   The good priest
Who joined our hands, my brother's ancient
     tutor,   215
With his loved Malcolm, in the battle fell:
They two alone were privy to the marriage.
On silence and concealment I resolved,
Till time should make my father's fortune mine.
That very night on which my son was born,   220
My nurse, the only confidante I had,
Set out with him to reach her sister's house:
But nurse, nor infant, have I ever seen,
Or heard of, Anna, since that fatal hour.
My murdered child! — had thy fond mother
     feared   225

The loss of thee, she had loud fame defied,
Despised her father's rage, her father's grief,
And wandered with thee through the scorning world.
     ANNA.   Not seen nor heard of! then perhaps he
     lives.
     LADY R.   No.   It was dark December: wind and
     rain   230
Had beat all night.   Across the Carron [1] lay
The destined road; and in its swelling flood
My faithful servant perished with my child.
O hapless son! of a most hapless sire! —
But they are both at rest; and I alone   235
Dwell in this world of woe, condemned to walk,
Like a guilt-troubled ghost, my painful rounds:
Nor has despiteful fate permitted me
The comfort of a solitary sorrow.
Though dead to love, I was compelled to wed   240
Randolph, who snatched me from a villain's arms;
And Randolph now possesses the domains,
That by Sir Malcolm's death on me devolved —
Domains that should to Douglas' son have giv'n
A baron's title, and a baron's power.   245
Such were my soothing thoughts, while I bewailed
The slaughtered father of a son unborn.
And when that son came, like a ray from heav'n,
Which shines and disappears; alas! my child!
How long did thy fond mother grasp the hope   250
Of having thee, she knew not how, restored.
Year after year hath worn her hope away;
But left still undiminished her desire.
     ANNA.   The hand that spins th' uneven thread of
     life
May smooth the length that's yet to come of
     yours.   255
     LADY R.   Not in this world: I have considered well
Its various evils, and on whom they fall.
Alas! how oft does goodness wound itself,
And sweet affection prove the spring of woe!
O! had I died when my loved husband fell!   260
Had some good angel op'd to me the book
Of Providence, and let me read my life,
My heart had broke, when I beheld the sum
Of ills, which one by one I have endured.
     ANNA.   That God whose ministers good angels
     are,   265
Hath shut the book, in mercy to mankind.
But we must leave this theme: Glenalvon comes:
I saw him bend on you his thoughtful eyes,
And hitherwards he slowly stalks his way.
     LADY R.   I will avoid him.   An ungracious
     person   270
Is doubly irksome in an hour like this.
     ANNA.   Why speaks my lady thus of Randolph's
     heir?

[1] The river Carron, which flows into the Firth of Forth.

221] EL *confident*; M *confidante*.   269] M *hitherward*.

LADY R. Because he's not the heir of Randolph's
    virtues,
Subtle and shrewd, he offers to mankind
An artificial image of himself;   275
And he with ease can vary to the taste
Of different men its features. Self-denied,
And master of his appetites he seems:
But his fierce nature, like a fox chained up,
Watches to seize unseen the wished-for prey.   280
Never were vice and virtue poised so ill,
As in Glenalvon's unrelenting mind.
Yet is he brave and politic in war,
And stands aloft in these unruly times.
Why I describe him thus I'll tell hereafter: 285
Stay and detain him till I reach the castle.
                         Exit LADY RANDOLPH.
    ANNA. O happiness! where art thou to be found?
I see thou dwellest not with birth and beauty,
Though graced with grandeur, and in wealth arrayed:
Nor dost thou, it would seem, with virtue dwell;   290
Else had this gentle lady missed thee not.

              Enter GLENALVON.

    GLEN. What dost thou muse on, meditating maid?
Like some entranced and visionary seer,
On earth thou stand'st, thy thoughts ascend to
    heaven.
    ANNA. Would that I were, e'en as thou say'st, a
    seer,   295
To have my doubts by heav'nly vision cleared!
    GLEN. What dost thou doubt of? what hast thou
    to do
With subjects intricate? Thy youth, thy beauty,
Cannot be questioned: think of these good gifts;
And then thy contemplations will be pleasing.   300
    ANNA. Let women view yon monument of woe,
Then boast of beauty: who so fair as she?
But I must follow: this revolving day
Awakes the memory of her ancient woes.
                              Exit ANNA.

             GLENALVON *solus.*

[GLEN.] So! — Lady Randolph shuns me; by and
    by   305
I'll woo her as the lion woos his brides.
The deed's a-doing now, that makes me lord
Of these rich valleys, and a chief of power.
The season is most apt; my sounding steps
Will not be heard amidst the din of arms.   310
Randolph has lived too long: his better fate
Had the ascendant once, and kept me down:
When I had seized the dame, by chance he came,
Rescued, and had the lady for his labor.
I 'scaped unknown: a slender consolation!   315
Heaven is my witness that I do not love
To sow in peril, and let others reap
The jocund harvest. Yet I am not safe:

By love, or something like it, stung, inflamed,
Madly I blabbed my passion to his wife,   320
And she has threatened to acquaint him of it.
The way of woman's will I do not know:
But well I know the baron's wrath is deadly.
I will not live in fear: the man I dread
Is as a Dane to me; ay, and the man   325
Who stands betwixt me and my chief desire.
No bar but he; she has no kinsman near;
No brother in his sister's quarrel bold;
And for the righteous cause, a stranger's cause,
I know no chief that will defy Glenalvon.   [*Exit.*]

                  ACT II

        A court, etc. [*as before*].

Enter Servants and a STRANGER [1] *at one door, and*
    LADY RANDOLPH *and* ANNA *at another.*

    LADY R. What means this clamor? Stranger,
    speak secure;
Hast thou been wronged? Have these rude men
    presumed
To vex the weary traveller on his way?
    FIRST SERV. By us no stranger ever suffered
    wrong:
This man with outcry wild has called us forth;   5
So sore afraid he cannot speak his fears.

Enter LORD RANDOLPH *and* [*a*] *Young Man,*[2] *with
    their swords drawn and bloody.*

    LADY R. Not vain the stranger's fears! — How
    fares my lord?
    LORD R. That it fares well, thanks to this gallant
    youth,
Whose valor saved me from a wretched death! —
As down the winding dale I walked alone,   10
At the cross way four armèd men attacked me —
Rovers, I judge, from the licentious camp —
Who would have quickly laid Lord Randolph low,
Had not this brave and generous stranger come,
Like my good angel, in the hour of fate,   15
And, mocking danger, made my foes his own.
They turned upon him: but his active arm
Struck to the ground, from whence they rose no more,
The fiercest two; the others fled amain,
And left him master of the bloody field.   20
Speak, Lady Randolph: upon beauty's tongue
Dwell accents pleasing to the brave and bold.
Speak, noble dame, and thank him for thy lord.
    LADY R. My lord, I cannot speak what now I feel.
My heart o'erflows with gratitude to heav'n;   25
And to this noble youth, who, all unknown
To you and yours, deliberated not,

    [1] The 'Stranger's' servant to whom his master later refers
(ll. 69–70).
    [2] The 'Stranger,' as the text continues to call him until he
discloses his name.

Nor paused at peril, but humanely brave
Fought on your side, against such fearful odds.
Have you yet learned of him whom we should
    thank?   30
Whom call the savior of Lord Randolph's life?

    LORD R. I asked that question, and he answered
    not:
But I must know who my deliverer is.
                          (*To the* STRANGER.)
    STRANGER. A low-born man, of parentage obscure,
Who nought can boast but his desire to be   35
A soldier, and to gain a name in arms.

    LORD R. Whoe'er thou art, thy spirit is ennobled
By the great King of Kings! Thou art ordained
And stamped a hero by the sovereign hand
Of Nature! Blush not, flower of modesty,   40
As well as valor, to declare thy birth.

    STRANGER. My name is Norval: on the Grampian
    hills,[1]
My father feeds his flocks; a frugal swain,
Whose constant cares were to increase his store,
And keep his only son, myself, at home.   45
For I had heard of battles, and I longed
To follow to the field some warlike lord:
And heaven soon granted what my sire denied.
This moon which rose last night, round as my shield,
Had not yet filled her horns, when, by her light,   50
A band of fierce barbarians, from the hills,
Rushed like a torrent down upon the vale,
Sweeping our flocks and herds. The shepherds fled
For safety, and for succor. I alone,
With bended bow, and quiver full of arrows,   55
Hovered about the enemy, and marked
The road he took, then hasted to my friends;
Whom, with a troop of fifty chosen men,
I met advancing. The pursuit I led,
Till we o'ertook the spoil-encumbered foe.   60
We fought and conquered. Ere a sword was drawn,
An arrow from my bow had pierced their chief,
Who wore that day the arms which now I wear.
Returning home in triumph, I disdained
The shepherd's slothful life: and having heard   65
That our good king had summoned his bold peers
To lead their warriors to the Carron side,
I left my father's house, and took with me
A chosen servant to conduct my steps; —
Yon trembling coward, who forsook his master.   70
Journeying with this intent, I passed these towers,
And, heaven-directed, came this day to do
The happy deed that gilds my humble name.

    LORD R. He is as wise as brave. Was ever tale
With such a gallant modesty rehearsed?   75
My brave deliverer! thou shalt enter now
A nobler list, and in a monarch's sight
Contend with princes for the prize of fame.

    [1] Mountains that range across central Scotland.

I will present thee to our Scottish king,
Whose valiant spirit ever valor loved. —   80
Ha, my Matilda! wherefore starts that tear?

    LADY R. I cannot say: for various affections,
And strangely mingled, in my bosom swell;
Yet each of them may well command a tear.
I joy that thou art safe; and I admire   85
Him and his fortunes who hath wrought thy safety;
«Yea, as my mind predicts, with thine his own.»
Obscure and friendless, he the army sought,
Bent upon peril, in the range of death
Resolved to hunt for fame, and with his sword   90
To gain distinction which his birth denied.
In this attempt unknown he might have perished,
And gained, with all his valor, but oblivion.
Now, graced by thee, his virtue serves no more
Beneath despair. The soldier now of hope   95
He stands conspicuous; fame and great renown
Are brought within the compass of his sword.
On this my mind reflected, whilst you spoke,
And blessed the wonder-working Lord of heaven.

    LORD R. Pious and grateful ever are thy
    thoughts!   100
My deeds shall follow where thou point'st the way.
Next to myself, and equal to Glenalvon,
In honor and command shall Norval be.

    NORVAL. I know not how to thank you. Rude I am
In speech and manners: never till this hour   105
Stood I in such a presence: yet, my lord,
There's something in my breast, which makes me
    bold
To say that Norval ne'er will shame thy favor.

    LADY R. I will be sworn thou wilt not. Thou
    shalt be
My knight; and ever, as thou didst to-day,   110
With happy valor guard the life of Randolph.

    LORD R. Well hast thou spoke. Let me forbid
    reply.   (*To* NORVAL.)
We are thy debtors still; thy high desert
O'ertops our gratitude. I must proceed,
As was at first intended, to the camp.   115
Some of my train, I see, are speeding hither,
Impatient, doubtless, of their lord's delay.
Go with me, Norval, and thine eyes shall see
The chosen warriors of thy native land,
Who languish for the fight, and beat the air   120
With brandished swords.

    NORVAL.   Let us begone, my lord.

    LORD R. (*to* LADY RANDOLPH).
About the time that the declining sun
Shall his broad orbit o'er yon hills suspend,
Expect us to return. This night once more
Within these walls I rest; my tent I pitch   125
To-morrow in the field. Prepare the feast.
Free is his heart who for his country fights:
He in the eve of battle may resign

57] M *hasten'd*.   85] LDB *and admire*.   87] LDB omit entire line.   123] M *broad orb o'er yonder hills*.

Himself to social pleasure; sweetest then,
When danger to a soldier's soul endears   130
The human joy that never may return.

    Exeunt [LORD] RANDOLPH *and* NORVAL [*and
    Servants*].

        LADY RANDOLPH *and* ANNA.

LADY R. His parting words have struck a fatal
    truth.
O Douglas! Douglas! tender was the time
When we two parted, ne'er to meet again!
How many years of anguish and despair   135
Has heav'n annexed to those swift-passing hours
Of love and fondness! Then my bosom's flame,
Oft, as blown back by the rude breath of fear,
Returned, and with redoubled ardor blazed.

  ANNA. May gracious heav'n pour the sweet balm
    of peace   140
Into the wounds that fester in your breast!
For earthly consolation cannot cure them.

  LADY R. One only cure can heav'n itself bestow —
A grave — that bed in which the weary rest.
Wretch that I am! Alas! why am I so?   145
At every happy parent I repine!
How blest the mother of yon gallant Norval!
She for a living husband bore her pains,
And heard him bless her when a man was born:
She nursed her smiling infant on her breast;   150
Tended the child, and reared the pleasing boy:
She, with affection's triumph, saw the youth
In grace and comeliness surpass his peers:
Whilst I to a dead husband bore a son,
And to the roaring waters gave my child.   155

  ANNA. Alas, alas! why will you thus resume
Your grief afresh? I thought that gallant youth
Would for a while have won you from your woe.
On him intent you gazèd, with a look
Much more delighted than your pensive eye   160
Has deigned on other objects to bestow.

  LADY R. Delighted, say'st thou? Oh! even there
    mine eye
Found fuel for my life-consuming sorrow.
I thought, that had the son of Douglas lived,
He might have been like this young gallant
    stranger,   165
And paired with him in features and in shape;
In all endowments, as in years, I deem,
My boy with blooming Norval might have numbered.
Whilst thus I mused, a spark from fancy fell
On my sad heart, and kindled up a fondness   170
For this young stranger, wand'ring from his home,
And like an orphan cast upon my care.
I will protect thee (said I to myself),
With all my power, and grace with all my favor.

  ANNA. Sure heav'n will bless so gen'rous a
    resolve.   175

You must, my noble dame, exert your power:
You must awake: devices will be framed,
And arrows pointed at the breast of Norval.

  LADY R. Glenalvon's false and crafty head will
    work
Against a rival in his kinsman's love,   180
If I deter him not: I only can.
Bold as he is, Glenalvon will beware
How he pulls down the fabric that I raise.
I'll be the artist of young Norval's fortune.
'Tis pleasing to admire! most apt was I   185
To this affection in my better days;
Though now I seem to you shrunk up, retired
Within the narrow compass of my woe.
Have you not sometimes seen an early flower
Open its bud, and spread its silken leaves,   190
To catch sweet airs, and odors to bestow;
Then, by the keen blast nipt, pull in its leaves,
And, though still living, die to scent and beauty?
Emblem of me: affliction, like a storm,
Hath killed the forward blossom of my heart.   195

        Enter GLENALVON.

  GLEN. Where is my dearest kinsman, noble Ran-
    dolph?

  LADY R. Have you not heard, Glenalvon, of the
    base —

  GLEN. I have: and that the villains may not
    'scape,
With a strong band I have begirt the wood.
If they lurk there, alive they shall be taken,   200
And torture force from them th' important secret,
Whether some foe of Randolph hired their swords,
Or if —

  LADY R. That care becomes a kinsman's love. —
I have a counsel for Glenalvon's ear.   *Exit* ANNA.

  GLEN. To him your counsels always are com-
    mands.   205

  LADY R. I have not found so: thou art known to
    me.

  GLEN. Known!

  LADY R.   And most certain is my cause of
    knowledge.

  GLEN. What do you know? By the most blessèd
    cross,
You much amaze me. No created being,
Yourself except, durst thus accost Glenalvon.   210

  LADY R. Is guilt so bold! and dost thou make a
    merit
Of thy pretended meekness! This to me,
Who, with a gentleness which duty blames,
Have hitherto concealed what, if divulged,
Would make thee nothing; or, what's worse than
    that,   215
An outcast beggar, and unpitied too!
For mortals shudder at a crime like thine.

132] LD begin Scene II here.   175] E *generous*: L *gen'rous*.   195] M *blossoms*.   209] LDB *created thing*.

GLEN. Thy virtue awes me. First of womankind!
Permit me yet to say, that the fond [1] man
Whom love transports beyond strict virtue's
    bounds, 220
If he is brought by love to misery,
In fortune ruined, as in mind forlorn,
Unpitied cannot be. Pity's the alms
Which on such beggars freely is bestowed:
For mortals know that love is still their lord, 225
And o'er their vain resolves advances still,
As fire, when kindled by our shepherds, moves
Through the dry heath before the fanning wind.

LADY R. Reserve these accents for some other ear.
To love's apology I listen not. 230
Mark thou my words; for it is meet thou should'st.
His brave deliverer Randolph here retains.
Perhaps his presence may not please thee well:
But, at thy peril, practise aught against him:
Let not thy jealousy attempt to shake 235
And loosen the good root he has in Randolph;
Whose favorites I know thou hast supplanted.
Thou look'st at me, as if thou fain would'st pry
Into my heart. 'Tis open as my speech.
I give this early caution, and put on 240
The curb, before thy temper breaks away.
The friendless stranger my protection claims:
His friend I am, and be not thou his foe. *Exit.*

Manet GLENALVON.

GLEN. Child that I was, to start at my own
    shadow,
And be the shallow fool of coward conscience! 245
I am not what I have been; what I should be.
The darts of destiny have almost pierced
My marble heart. Had I one grain of faith
In holy legends, and religious tales,
I should conclude there was an arm above 250
That fought against me, and malignant turned;
To catch myself, the subtle snare I set.
Why, rape and murder are not simple means!
Th' imperfect rape to Randolph gave a spouse;
And the intended murder introduced 255
A favorite to hide the sun from me;
And, worst of all, a rival. Burning hell!
This were thy center, if I thought she loved him!
'Tis certain she contemns me; nay, commands me,
And waves the flag of her displeasure o'er me, 260
In his behalf. And shall I thus be braved?
Curbed, as she calls it, by dame chastity?
Infernal fiends, if any fiends there are
More fierce than hate, ambition, and revenge,
Rise up and fill my bosom with your fires, 265
And policy remorseless! Chance may spoil
A single aim; but perseverance must
Prosper at last. For chance and fate are words:

[1] Foolish.

Persistive wisdom is the fate of man.
Darkly a project peers upon my mind, 270
Like the red moon when rising in the east,
Crossed and divided by strange-colored clouds.
I'll seek the slave who came with Norval hither,
And for his cowardice was spurned from him.
I've known a follower's rankled bosom breed 275
Venom most fatal to his heedless lord. *Exit.*

ACT III

A court, etc., as before.

Enter ANNA.

ANNA. Thy vassals, Grief! great Nature's order
    break,
And change the noon-tide to the midnight hour.
Whilst Lady Randolph sleeps, I will walk forth,
And taste the air that breathes on yonder bank.
Sweet may her slumbers be! Ye ministers 5
Of gracious heaven who love the human race,
Angels and seraphs who delight in goodness,
Forsake your skies, and to her couch descend!
There from her fancy chase those dismal forms
That haunt her waking; her sad spirit charm 10
With images celestial, such as please
The blest above upon their golden beds.

Enter Servant.

SERV. One of the vile assassins is secured.
We found the villain lurking in the wood:
With dreadful imprecations he denies 15
All knowledge of the crime. But this is not
His first essay: these jewels were concealed
In the most secret places of his garment;
Belike the spoils of some that he has murdered.

ANNA. Let me look on them! Ha! here is a
    heart, 20
The chosen crest of Douglas' valiant name!
These are no vulgar [2] jewels. — Guard the wretch.
    Exit ANNA.

Enter Servants with a PRISONER.

PRISONER. I know no more than does the child
    unborn
Of what you charge me with.

FIRST SERV.   You say so, sir!
But torture soon shall make you speak the truth. 25
Behold, the lady of Lord Randolph comes:
Prepare yourself to meet her just revenge.

Enter LADY RANDOLPH *and* ANNA.

ANNA. Summon your utmost fortitude, before
You speak with him. Your dignity, your fame,
Are now at stake. Think of the fatal secret, 30

[2] Common.

Which in a moment from your lips may fly.

LADY R. Thou shalt behold me, with a desperate heart,

Hear how my infant perished. See, he kneels.

(The PRISONER kneels.)

PRIS. Heav'n bless that countenance, so sweet and mild!

A judge like thee makes innocence more bold. 35

O save me, lady! from these cruel men,

Who have attacked and seized me; who accuse

Me of intended murder. As I hope

For mercy at the judgment-seat of God,

The tender lamb, that never nipped the grass, 40

Is not more innocent than I of murder.

LADY R. Of this man's guilt what proof can ye produce?

FIRST SERV. We found him lurking in the hollow glynn.[1]

When viewed and called upon, amazed he fled.

We overtook him, and inquired from whence 45

And what he was: he said, he came from far,

And was upon his journey to the camp.

Not satisfied with this, we searched his clothes,

And found these jewels, whose rich value plead

Most powerfully against him. Hard he seems, 50

And old in villainy. Permit us try

His stubbornness against the torture's force.

PRIS. O gentle lady! by your lord's dear life,

Which these weak hands, I swear, did ne'er assail;

And by your children's welfare, spare my age! 55

Let not the iron tear my ancient joints,

And my grey hairs bring to the grave with pain.

LADY R. Account for these: thine own they cannot be:

For these, I say: be steadfast to the truth;

Detected falsehood is most certain death. 60

(ANNA removes the Servants and returns.)

PRIS. Alas! I'm sore beset! let never man,

For sake of lucre, sin against his soul!

Eternal justice is in this most just!

I, guiltless now, must former guilt reveal.

LADY R. O! Anna, hear! — Once more I charge thee speak 65

The truth direct: for these to me foretell

And certify a part of thy narration;

With which, if the remainder tallies not,

An instant and a dreadful death abides thee.

PRIS. Then, thus adjured, I'll speak to you as just 70

As if you were the minister of heaven,

Sent down to search the secret sins of men.

Some eighteen years ago, I rented land

Of brave Sir Malcolm, then Balarmo's lord;

But falling to decay, his servants seized 75

All that I had, and then turned me and mine

(Four helpless infants and their weeping mother)

Out to the mercy of the winter winds.

A little hovel by the river's side

Received us: there hard labor, and the skill 80

In fishing, which was formerly my sport,

Supported life. Whilst thus we poorly lived,

One stormy night, as I remember well,

The wind and rain beat hard upon our roof:

Red came the river down, and loud and oft 85

The angry spirit of the water shrieked.[2]

At the dead hour of night was heard the cry

Of one in jeopardy. I rose, and ran

To where the circling eddy of a pool,

Beneath the ford, used oft to bring within 90

My reach whatever floating thing the stream

Had caught. The voice was ceased; the person lost:

But looking sad and earnest on the waters,

By the moon's light I saw, whirled round and round,

A basket: soon I drew it to the bank, 95

And nestled curious [3] there an infant lay.

LADY R. Was he alive?

PRIS. He was.

LADY R. Inhuman that thou art!

How could'st thou kill what waves and tempests spared?

PRIS. I am not so inhuman.

LADY R. Didst thou not?

ANNA. My noble mistress, you are moved too much: 100

This man has not the aspect of stern murder;

Let him go on, and you, I hope, will hear

Good tidings of your kinsman's long lost child.

PRIS. The needy man who has known better days,

One whom distress has spited [4] at the world, 105

Is he whom tempting fiends would pitch upon

To do such deeds as make the prosperous men

Lift up their hands, and wonder who could do them.

And such a man was I — a man declined,

Who saw no end of black adversity: 110

Yet, for the wealth of kingdoms, I would not

Have touched that infant with a hand of harm.

LADY R. Ha! dost thou say so? Then perhaps he lives!

PRIS. Not many days ago he was alive.

LADY R. O God of heav'n! Did he then die so lately? 115

PRIS. I did not say he died; I hope he lives.

Not many days ago these eyes beheld

Him, flourishing in youth, and health, and beauty.

LADY R. Where is he now?

PRIS. Alas! I know not where.

[1] Glen (*N.E.D.* cites this passage).

[2] The 'water sprite' or 'kelpie,' as a prophet of disaster or death by drowning, is familiar in the popular lore and literature of Scotland.

[3] Carefully.   [4] Filled with spite.

LADY R. O fate! I fear thee still. Thou riddler,
    speak   120
Direct and clear; else I will search thy soul.
  ANNA. Permit me, ever honored! Keen im-
    patience,
Though hard to be restrained, defeats itself. —
Pursue thy story with a faithful tongue,
To the last hour that thou didst keep the child. 125
  PRIS. Fear not my faith, though I must speak
    my shame.
Within the cradle, where the infant lay,
Was stowed a mighty store of gold and jewels;
Tempted by which, we did resolve to hide,
From all the world, this wonderful event,   130
And like a peasant breed the noble child.
That none might mark the change of our estate,
We left the country, travelled to the north,
Bought flocks and herds, and gradually brought forth
Our secret wealth. But God's all-seeing eye   135
Beheld our avarice, and smote us sore:
For one by one all our own children died,
And he, the stranger, sole remained the heir
Of what indeed was his.   Fain then would I,
Who with a father's fondness loved the boy,   140
Have trusted him, now in the dawn of youth,
With his own secret: but my anxious wife,
Foreboding evil, never would consent.
Meanwhile the stripling grew in years and beauty;
And, as we oft observed, he bore himself,   145
Not as the offspring of our cottage blood;
For nature will break out: mild with the mild,
But with the froward he was fierce as fire,
And night and day he talked of war and arms.
I set myself against his warlike bent;   150
But all in vain: for when a desperate band
Of robbers from the savage mountains came —
  LADY R. Eternal Providence! What is thy
    name?
  PRIS. My name is Norval; and my name he bears.
  LADY R. 'Tis he; 'tis he himself! It is my
    son!   155
O sovereign mercy! 'Twas my child I saw!
No wonder, Anna, that my bosom burned.
  ANNA. Just are your transports: ne'er was woman's
    heart
Proved with such fierce extremes. High-fated dame!
But yet remember that you are beheld   160
By servile eyes; your gestures may be seen
Impassioned strange;[1] perhaps your words o'erheard.
  LADY R. Well dost thou counsel, Anna. Heaven
    bestow
On me that wisdom which my state requires!
  ANNA. The moments of deliberation pass,   165
And soon you must resolve. This useful man
Must be dismissed in safety, ere my lord

    [1] I.e. to be strangely impassioned.

Shall with his brave deliverer return.
  PRIS. If I, amidst astonishment and fear,
Have of your words and gestures rightly judged, 170
Thou art the daughter of my ancient master;
The child I rescued from the flood is thine.
  LADY R. With thee dissimulation now were vain.
I am indeed the daughter of Sir Malcolm;
The child thou rescued'st from the flood is mine. 175
  PRIS. Blest be the hour that made me a poor man!
My poverty hath saved my master's house!
  LADY R. Thy words surprise me: sure thou dost
    not feign!
The tear stands in thine eye: such love from thee
Sir Malcolm's house deserved not; if aright   180
Thou told'st the story of thy own distress.
  PRIS. Sir Malcolm of our barons was the flower;
The fastest friend, the best, the kindest master;
But ah! he knew not of my sad estate.
After that battle, where his gallant son,   185
Your own brave brother, fell, the good old lord
Grew desperate and reckless of the world;
And never, as he erst was wont, went forth
To overlook the conduct of his servants.
By them I was thrust out, and them I blame: 190
May heav'n so judge me as I judged my master!
And God so love me as I love his race!
  LADY R. His race shall yet reward thee. On
    thy faith
Depends the fate of thy loved master's house.
Rememb'rest thou a little lonely hut,   195
That like a holy hermitage appears
Among the clifts of Carron?
  PRIS.   I remember
The cottage of the clifts.
  LADY R.   'Tis that I mean:
There dwells a man of venerable age,
Who in my father's service spent his youth: 200
Tell him I sent thee, and with him remain,
Till I shall call upon thee to declare,
Before the king and nobles, what thou now
To me hast told. No more but this, and thou
Shalt live in honor all thy future days: 205
Thy son so long shall call thee father still,
And all the land shall bless the man who saved
The son of Douglas, and Sir Malcolm's heir.
Remember well my words: if thou should'st meet
Him whom thou call'st thy son, still call him so; 210
And mention nothing of his nobler father.
  PRIS. Fear not that I shall mar so fair an harvest,
By putting in my sickle ere 'tis ripe.
Why did I leave my home and ancient dame?
To find the youth, to tell him all I knew,   215
And make him wear these jewels in his arms,
Which might, I thought, be challenged, and so bring
To light the secret of his noble birth.
    (LADY RANDOLPH goes *towards the Servants.*)

183] L *the best and kindest master.*   197, 198] M *clifts.*

LADY R. This man is not th' assassin you sus-
pected,
Though chance combined some likelihoods against
him. 220
He is the faithful bearer of the jewels
To their right owner, whom in haste he seeks.
'Tis meet that you should put him on his way,
Since your mistaken zeal hath dragged him hither.

Exeunt STRANGER [1] *and Servants.*

LADY R. My faithful Anna! dost thou share my
joy? 225
I know thou dost. Unparalleled event!
Reaching from heav'n to earth, Jehovah's arm
Snatched from the waves, and brings to me my son!
Judge of the widow, and the orphan's father!
Accept a widow's and a mother's thanks 230
For such a gift! — What does my Anna think
Of the young eaglet of a valiant nest?
How soon he gazed on bright and burning arms,
Spurned the low dunghill where his fate had thrown
him,
And towered up to the region of his sire! 235

ANNA. How fondly did your eyes devour the boy!
Mysterious nature, with the unseen cord
Of powerful instinct, drew you to your own.

LADY R. The ready story of his birth believed
Suppressed my fancy quite; nor did he owe 240
To any likeness my so sudden favor:
But now I long to see his face again,
Examine every feature, and find out
The lineaments of Douglas, or my own.
But most of all I long to let him know 245
Who his true parents are, to clasp his neck,
And tell him all the story of his father.

ANNA. With wary caution you must bear yourself
In public, lest your tenderness break forth,
And in observers stir conjectures strange. 250
For, if a cherub in the shape of woman
Should walk this world, yet defamation would,
Like a vile cur, bark at the angel's train —
To-day the baron started at your tears.

LADY R. He did so, Anna! Well thy mistress
knows 255
If the least circumstance, mote of offence,
Should touch the baron's eye, his sight would be
With jealousy disordered. But the more
It does behove me instant to declare
The birth of Douglas, and assert his rights. 260
This night I purpose with my son to meet,
Reveal the secret, and consult with him:
For wise he is, or my fond judgment errs.
As he does now, so looked his noble father,

Arrayed in nature's ease: his mien, his speech, 265
Were sweetly simple, and full oft deceived
Those trivial mortals who seem always wise.
But, when the matter matched his mighty mind,
Up rose the hero: on his piercing eye
Sat observation: on each glance of thought 270
Decision followed, as the thunderbolt
Pursues the flash.

ANNA. That demon haunts you still:
Behold Glenalvon.

LADY R. Now I shun him not.
This day I braved him in behalf of Norval;
Perhaps too far: at least my nicer [2] fears 275
For Douglas thus interpret.

Enter GLENALVON.

GLEN. Noble dame!
The hov'ring Dane at last his men hath landed —
No band of pirates, but a mighty host,
That come to settle where their valor conquers;
To win a country, or to lose themselves. 280

LADY R. But whence comes this intelligence,
Glenalvon?

GLEN. A nimble courier sent from yonder camp
To hasten up the chieftains of the north,
Informed me, as he passed, that the fierce Dane
Had on the eastern coast of Lothian landed, 285
Near to that place where the sea-rock immense,
Amazing Bass, looks o'er a fertile land.[3]

LADY R. Then must this western army march
to join
The warlike troops that guard Edina's [4] tow'rs.

GLEN. Beyond all question. If impairing time 290
Has not effaced the image of a place
Once perfect in my breast, there is a wild
Which lies to westward of that mighty rock,
And seems by nature formèd for the camp
Of water-wafted armies, whose chief strength 295
Lies in firm foot, unflanked with warlike horse.
If martial skill directs the Danish lords,
There inaccessible their army lies
To our swift-scow'ring horse; the bloody field
Must man to man, and foot to foot, be fought. 300

LADY R. How many mothers shall bewail their
sons!
How many widows weep their husbands slain!
Ye dames of Denmark! ev'n for you I feel,
Who, sadly sitting on the sea-beat shore,
Long look for lords that never shall return. 305

---

[1] The 'Prisoner,' now released, and henceforth identified as
'Old Norval.' The term 'Stranger' is somewhat confusingly
applied to both Norvals while appearing *incognito*.

[2] Subtler.

[3] Sir Walter Scott quotes ll. 286–287, in recalling Home's
appointment in 1746 as 'minister of Athelstaneford, in East
Lothian, a locality which he has not forgotten in his celebrated
tragedy.' (Tunney edition, p. 88.) Bass Rock lies near the
mouth of the Firth of Forth, off its southern shore.

[4] Edinburgh's.

GLEN. Oft has th' unconquered Caledonian sword
Widowed the north.   The children of the slain
Come, as I hope, to meet their fathers' fate.
The monster war, with her infernal brood,
Loud yelling fury, and life-ending pain,   310
Are objects suited to Glenalvon's soul.
Scorn is more grievous than the pains of death:
Reproach more piercing than the pointed sword.

    LADY R. I scorn thee not, but when I ought to
      scorn;
Nor e'er reproach, but when insulted virtue   315
Against audacious vice asserts herself.
I own thy worth, Glenalvon; none more apt
Than I to praise thine eminence in arms,
And be the echo of thy martial fame.
No longer vainly feed a guilty passion: 320
Go and pursue a lawful mistress, Glory.
Upon the Danish crests redeem thy fault,
And let thy valor be the shield of Randolph.

    GLEN. One instant stay, and hear an altered man.
When beauty pleads for virtue, vice abashed   325
Flies its own colors, and goes o'er to virtue.
I am your convert; time will show how truly:
Yet one immediate proof I mean to give.
That youth, for whom your ardent zeal to-day
Somewhat too haughtily defied your slave,   330
Amidst the shock of armies I'll defend,
And turn death from him with a guardian arm.
Sedate by use, my bosom maddens not
At the tumultuous uproar of the field.

    LADY R. Act thus, Glenalvon, and I am thy
      friend: 335
But that's thy least reward.   Believe me, sir,
The truly generous is the truly wise;
And he who loves not others lives unblest.
                Exit LADY RANDOLPH.

          GLENALVON *solus*.

[GLEN.] Amen! and virtue is its own reward! —
I think that I have hit the very tone   340
In which she loves to speak.   Honeyed assent,
How pleasing art thou to the taste of man,
And woman also!   Flattery direct
Rarely disgusts.   They little know mankind
Who doubt its operation: 'tis my key,   345
And opes the wicket of the human heart.
How far I have succeeded now, I know not:
Yet I incline to think her stormy virtue
Is lulled awhile.   'Tis her alone I fear:
Whilst she and Randolph live, and live in faith   350
And amity, uncertain is my tenure.
Fate o'er my head suspends disgrace and death,
By that weak hair, a peevish female's will.
I am not idle: but the ebbs and flows
Of fortune's tide cannot be calculated.   355
That slave of Norval's I have found most apt:

I showed him gold, and he has pawned his soul
To say and swear whatever I suggest.
Norval, I'm told, has that alluring look,
'Twixt man and woman, which I have observed   360
To charm the nicer [1] and fantastic dames,
Who are, like Lady Randolph, full of virtue.
In raising Randolph's jealousy, I may
But point him to the truth.   He seldom errs,
Who thinks the worst he can of womankind.   365
                        [*Exit.*]

ACT IV

[*A court, etc., as before.*]

Flourish of trumpets.

Enter LORD RANDOLPH *attended.*

    LORD R. Summon an hundred horse, by break of
      day,
To wait our pleasure at the castle gate.

Enter LADY RANDOLPH.

    LADY R. Alas! my lord! I've heard unwelcome
      news;
The Danes are landed.

    LORD R.   Ay, no inroad this
Of the Northumbrian, bent to take a spoil: 5
No sportive war, no tournament essay
Of some young knight resolved to break a spear,
And stain with hostile blood his maiden arms.
The Danes are landed: we must beat them back,
Or live the slaves of Denmark.

    LADY R.   Dreadful times! 10

    LORD R. The fenceless [2] villages are all forsaken;
The trembling mothers, and their children, lodged
In wall-girt towers and castles, whilst the men
Retire indignant.   Yet, like broken waves,
They but retire more awful to return.   15

    LADY R. Immense, as fame reports, the Danish
      host!

    LORD R. Were it as numerous as loud fame reports,
An army knit like ours would pierce it through:
Brothers, that shrink not from each other's side,
And fond companions, fill our warlike files: 20
For his dear offspring, and the wife he loves,
The husband and the fearless father arm.
In vulgar breasts heroic ardor burns,
And the poor peasant mates [3] his daring lord.

    LADY R. Men's minds are tempered, like their
      swords, for war;   25
Lovers of danger, on destruction's brink
They joy to rear erect their daring forms.
Hence, early graves; hence, the lone widow's life;
And the sad mother's grief-embittered age. —

[1] More fastidious.   [2] Defenceless.
[3] Rivals, matches.

342] M *pleasant.*   ACT IV. 13] LD *well-girt.*   (Here, as elsewhere, D depends on L, not on E.)

Where is our gallant guest?

LORD R.   Down in the vale   30
I left him, managing a fiery steed,
Whose stubbornness had foiled the strength and skill
Of every rider. But behold! he comes,
In earnest conversation with Glenalvon.

Enter NORVAL *and* GLENALVON.

Glenalvon! with the lark arise; go forth,   35
And lead my troops that lie in yonder vale:
Private I travel to the royal camp:
Norval, thou goest with me. But say, young man!
Where didst thou learn so to discourse of war,
And in such terms as I o'erheard to-day?   40
War is no village science, nor its phrase
A language taught amongst the shepherd swains.

NORVAL. Small is the skill my lord delights to
        praise
In him he favors. — Hear from whence it came.
Beneath a mountain's brow, the most remote   45
And inaccessible by shepherds trod,
In a deep cave, dug by no mortal hand,
A hermit lived, a melancholy man,
Who was the wonder of our wand'ring swains.
Austere and lonely, cruel to himself,   50
Did they report him; the cold earth his bed,
Water his drink, his food the shepherd's alms.
I went to see him, and my heart was touched
With rev'rence and with pity. Mild he spake,
And, ent'ring on discourse, such stories told   55
As made me oft revisit his sad cell.
For he had been a soldier in his youth;
And fought in famous battles, when the peers
Of Europe, by the bold Godfredo [1] led,
Against th' usurping infidel displayed   60
The cross of Christ, and won the Holy Land.
Pleased with my admiration, and the fire
His speech struck from me, the old man would shake
His years away, and act his young encounters:
Then, having showed his wounds, he'd sit him   65
        down,
And all the live-long day discourse of war.
To help my fancy, in the smooth green turf
He cut the figures of the marshalled hosts;
Described the motion, and explained the use
Of the deep column, and the lengthened line,   70
The square, the crescent, and the phalanx firm.
For all that Saracen or Christian knew
Of war's vast art, was to this hermit known.

LORD R. Why did this soldier in a desert hide
Those qualities that should have graced a camp?   75

---

[1] This reference to the French Crusader Godfrey de Bouillon,
a leader in the First Crusade (1096–1099), seems, as H. J.
Tunney suggests, to place the action of *Douglas* 'as about the
middle of the twelfth century.'

NORVAL. That too at last I learned. Unhappy
        man!
Returning homewards by Messina's port,
Loaded with wealth and honors bravely won,
A rude and boist'rous captain of the sea
Fastened a quarrel on him. Fierce they fought: 80
The stranger fell, and with his dying breath
Declared his name and lineage. 'Mighty God!'
The soldier cried, 'My brother! Oh! my brother!'

LADY R. His brother!

NORVAL.   Yes; of the same parents born,
His only brother. They exchanged forgiveness: 85
And happy, in my mind, was he that died:
For many deaths has the survivor suffered.
In the wild desert on a rock he sits,
Or on some nameless stream's untrodden banks,
And ruminates all day his dreadful fate.   90
At times, alas! not in his perfect mind,
Holds dialogues with his loved brother's ghost
And oft each night forsakes his sullen couch
To make sad orisons for him he slew.

LADY R. To what mysterious woes are mortals
        born!   95
In this dire tragedy, were there no more
Unhappy persons? Did the parents live?

NORVAL. No; they were dead: kind heav'n had
        closed their eyes
Before their son had shed his brother's blood.

LORD R. Hard is his fate; for he was not to
        blame!   100
There is a destiny in this strange world,
Which oft decrees an undeservèd doom:
Let schoolmen tell us why. — From whence these
        sounds?   (*Trumpets at a distance.*)

Enter an Officer.

OFF. My lord, the trumpets of the troops of Lorn: [2]
The valiant leader hails the noble Randolph.   105

LORD R. Mine ancient guest! Does he the
        warriors lead?
Has Denmark roused the brave old knight to arms?

OFF. No; worn with warfare, he resigns the sword.
His eldest hope, the valiant John of Lorn,
Now leads his kindred bands.

LORD R.   Glenalvon, go,   110
With hospitality's most strong request
Entreat the chief.   *Exit* GLENALVON.

OFF.   My lord, requests are vain.
He urges on, impatient of delay,
Stung with the tidings of the foe's approach.

LORD R. May victory sit on the warrior's
        plume!   115

---

[2] 'As the historical John of Lorn fought with Bruce in 1309,
Home apparently hoped the audience would telescope history,
or else assume that some progenitor of the famous John of
Lorn would be understood.' (MacMillan-Jones edition.)

54] LD *reverence and pity.*   74, 88] E *desart.*   105] LD *Their valiant.*   112] E *Intreat.*

Bravest of men! his flocks and herds are safe;
Remote from war's alarms his pastures lie.
By mountains inaccessible secured:
Yet foremost he into the plain descends,
Eager to bleed in battles not his own.   120
Such were the heroes of the ancient world —
Contemners they of indolence and gain,
But still, for love of glory and of arms,
Prone to encounter peril, and to lift
Against each strong antagonist the spear.   125
I'll go and press the hero to my breast.
             Exit [LORD] RANDOLPH [*with the Officer*].

        Mane[*n*]*t* LADY RANDOLPH *and* NORVAL.

LADY R. The soldier's loftiness, the pride and
        pomp
Investing awful war, Norval, I see,
Transport thy youthful mind.
NORVAL.   Ah! should they not?
Blest be the hour I left my father's house!   130
I might have been a shepherd all my days,
And stole obscurely to a peasant's grave.
Now, if I live, with mighty chiefs I stand;
And, if I fall, with noble dust I lie.
LADY R. There is a gen'rous spirit in thy
        breast,   135
That could have well sustained a prouder fortune.
This way with me; under yon spreading beech,
Unseen, unheard, by human eye or ear,
I will amaze thee with a wondrous tale.
NORVAL. Let there be danger, lady, with the
        secret,   140
That I may hug it to my grateful heart,
And prove my faith. Command my sword, my life:
These are the sole possessions of poor Norval.
LADY R. Know'st thou these gems?
NORVAL.   Durst I believe mine eyes,
I'd say I knew them, and they were my father's.   145
LADY R. Thy father's, say'st thou? Ah! they
        were thy father's!
NORVAL. I saw them once and curiously inquired
Of both my parents whence such splendor came;
But I was checked and more could never learn.
LADY R. Then learn of me, thou art not Norval's
        son.   150
NORVAL. Not Norval's son!
LADY R.   Nor of a shepherd sprung.
NORVAL. Lady, who am I then?
LADY R.   Noble thou art;
For noble was thy sire!
NORVAL.   I will believe —
O! tell me farther! Say, who was my father?
LADY R. Douglas!
NORVAL.   Lord Douglas whom to-day I
        saw?   155
LADY R. His younger brother.

NORVAL.   And in yonder camp?
LADY R. Alas!
NORVAL.   You make me tremble — Sighs
        and tears! —
Lives my brave father?
LADY R.   Ah! too brave indeed!
He fell in battle ere thyself was born.
NORVAL. Ah me, unhappy! ere I saw the
        light?   160
But does my mother live? I may conclude,
From my own fate, her portion has been sorrow.
LADY R. She lives; but wastes her life in constant
        woe,
Weeping her husband slain, her infant lost.
NORVAL. You that are skilled so well in the
        sad story   165
Of my unhappy parents, and with tears
Bewail their destiny, now have compassion
Upon the offspring of the friends you loved.
O! tell me who, and where my mother is!
Oppressed by a base world, perhaps she bends   170
Beneath the weight of other ills than grief;
And, desolate, implores of heav'n the aid
Her son should give. It is, it must be so —
Your countenance confesses that she's wretched.
O! tell me her condition! Can the sword —   175
Who shall resist me in a parent's cause?
LADY R. Thy virtue ends her woe. — My son!
        my son!
I am thy mother, and the wife of Douglas!
                      (*Falls upon his neck.*)
NORVAL. O heav'n and earth, how wondrous is
        my fate!
Art thou my mother? Ever let me kneel!   180
LADY R. Image of Douglas! Fruit of fatal love!
All that I owe thy sire, I pay to thee.
NORVAL. Respect and admiration still possess me,
Checking the love and fondness of a son.
Yet I was filial to my humble parents.   185
But did my sire surpass the rest of men,
As thou excellest all of womankind?
LADY R. Arise, my son! In me thou dost behold
The poor remains of beauty once admired:
The autumn of my days is come already;   190
For sorrow made my summer haste away.
Yet in my prime I equalled not thy father:
His eyes were like the eagle's, yet sometimes
Liker the dove's; and, as he pleased, he won
All hearts with softness, or with spirit awed.   195
NORVAL. How did he fall? Sure 'twas a bloody
        field
When Douglas died. O! I have much to ask.
LADY R. Hereafter thou shalt hear the lengthened
        tale
Of all thy father's and thy mother's woes.
At present this: thou art the rightful heir   200

126 s.d.] D *Manent*; EL *Manet*.   177] M *woes*.

Of yonder castle, and the wide domains
Which now Lord Randolph, as my husband, holds.
But thou shalt not be wronged; I have the power
To right thee still: before the king I'll kneel,
And call Lord Douglas to protect his blood.　205
　　NORVAL. The blood of Douglas will protect itself.
　　LADY R. But we shall need both friends and favor,
　　　　boy,
To wrest thy lands and lordship from the gripe
Of Randolph and his kinsman. Yet I think
My tale will move each gentle heart to pity,　210
My life incline the virtuous to believe.
　　NORVAL. To be the son of Douglas is to me
Inheritance enough. Declare my birth,
And in the field I'll seek for fame and fortune.
　　LADY R. Thou dost not know what perils and
　　　　injustice　215
Await the poor man's valor. O! my son!
The noblest blood in all the land's abashed,
Having no lackey but pale poverty.
Too long hast thou been thus attended, Douglas!
Too long hast thou been deemed a peasant's
　　　　child.　220
The wanton heir of some inglorious chief
Perhaps has scorned thee, in the youthful sports,
Whilst thy indignant spirit swelled in vain!
Such contumely thou no more shalt bear:
But how I purpose to redress thy wrongs　225
Must be hereafter told. Prudence directs
That we should part before yon chiefs return.
Retire, and from thy rustic follower's hand
Receive a billet, which thy mother's care,
Anxious to see thee, dictated before　230
This casual opportunity arose
Of private conference. Its purport mark;
For as I there appoint we meet again.
Leave me, my son! and frame thy manners still
To Norval's, not to noble Douglas' state.　235
　　NORVAL. I will remember. Where is Norval now,
That good old man?
　　LADY R.　　　　At hand concealed he lies,
An useful witness. But beware, my son,
Of yon Glenalvon; in his guilty breast
Resides a villain's shrewdness, ever prone　240
To false conjecture. He hath grieved my heart.
　　NORVAL. Has he, indeed? Then let yon false
　　　　Glenalvon
Beware of me.　　　　　　　　Exit DOUGLAS.
　　　　Manet LADY RANDOLPH.
　　LADY R.　　There burst the smothered flame! —
O! thou all righteous and eternal King!
Who father of the fatherless art called,　245
Protect my son! — Thy inspiration, Lord!
Hath filled his bosom with that sacred fire,
Which in the breast of his forefathers burned:

Set him on high, like them, that he may shine
The star and glory of his native land!　250
Then let the minister of death descend,
And bear my willing spirit to its place.
Yonder they come. — How do bad women find
Unchanging aspects to conceal their guilt?
When I, by reason and by justice urged,　255
Full hardly can dissemble with these men
In nature's pious cause?

　　　　Enter LORD RANDOLPH and GLENALVON.

　　LORD R.　　　　　　Yon gallant chief,
Of arms enamoured, all repose disclaims.
　　LADY R. Be not, my lord, by his example swayed:
Arrange the business of to-morrow now,　260
And, when you enter, speak of war no more.
　　　　　　　　　　　　Exit LADY RANDOLPH.

　　　　Manent LORD RANDOLPH and GLENALVON.

　　LORD R. 'Tis so, by heav'n! her mien, her voice,
　　　　her eye,
And her impatience to be gone, confirm it.
　　GLEN. He parted from her now: behind the mount,
Amongst the trees, I saw him glide along.　265
　　LORD R. For sad, sequestered virtue she's re-
　　　　nowned!
　　GLEN. Most true, my lord.
　　LORD R.　　　　　Yet this distinguished dame
Invites a youth, the acquaintance of a day,
Alone to meet her at the midnight hour.
This assignation, (shows a letter) the assassin
　　　　freed,　270
Her manifest affection for the youth,
Might breed suspicion in a husband's brain,
Whose gentle consort all for love had wedded;
Much more in mine. Matilda never loved me.
Let no man, after me, a woman wed,　275
Whose heart he knows he has not; though she brings
A mine of gold, a kingdom for her dowry;
For let her seem, like the night's shadowy queen,
Cold and contemplative — he cannot trust her:
She may, she will, bring shame and sorrow on
　　　　him;　280
The worst of sorrows, and the worst of shames!
　　GLEN. Yield not, my lord, to such afflicting
　　　　thoughts;
But let the spirit of an husband sleep,
Till your own senses make a sure conclusion.
This billet must to blooming Norval go:　285
At the next turn awaits my trusty spy;
I'll give it him refitted for his master.
In the close thicket take your secret stand;
The moon shines bright, and your own eyes may
　　　　judge
Of their behavior.
　　LORD R.　　　　Thou dost counsel well.　290

217] M of all.

GLEN. Permit me now to make one slight essay.
Of all the trophies which vain mortals boast,
By wit, by valor, or by wisdom won,
The first and fairest, in a young man's eye,
Is woman's captive heart. Successful love   295
With glorious fumes intoxicates the mind;
And the proud conqueror in triumph moves,
Air-borne, exalted above vulgar men.
   LORD R. And what avails this maxim?
   GLEN.   Much, my lord,
Withdraw a little: I'll accost young Norval,   300
And with ironical derisive counsel
Explore his spirit. If he is no more
Than humble Norval, by thy favor raised,
Brave as he is, he'll shrink astonished from me:
But if he be the fav'rite of the fair,   305
Loved by the first of Caledonia's dames,
He'll turn upon me, as the lion turns
Upon the hunter's spear.
   LORD R.   'Tis shrewdly thought.
   GLEN. When we grow loud, draw near. But
     let my lord
His rising wrath restrain.   *Exit* RANDOLPH.

Manet GLENALVON.

   GLEN.   'Tis strange, by heav'n!   310
That she should run full tilt her fond career,
To one so little known. She, too, that seemed
Pure as the winter stream, when ice embossed
Whitens its course. Even I did think her chaste,
Whose charity exceeds not. Precious sex!   315
Whose deeds lascivious pass Glenalvon's thoughts!

NORVAL *appears.*

His port I love; he's in a proper mood
To chide the thunder, if at him it roared. —
Has Norval seen the troops?
   NORVAL.   The setting sun
With yellow radiance lightened all the vale;   320
And as the warriors moved, each polished helm,
Corslet, or spear, glanced back his gilded beams.
The hill they climbed, and halting at its top,
Of more than mortal size, tow'ring, they seemed
An host angelic, clad in burning arms.   325
   GLEN. Thou talk'st it well; no leader of our host,
In sounds more lofty, speaks of glorious war.
   NORVAL. If I shall e'er acquire a leader's name,
My speech will be less ardent. Novelty
Now prompts my tongue, and youthful admira-
     tion   330
Vents itself freely; since no part is mine
Of praise pertaining to the great in arms.
   GLEN. You wrong yourself, brave sir; your martial
     deeds
Have ranked you with the great: but mark me,
     Norval;

Lord Randolph's favor now exalts your youth   335
Above his veterans of famous service.
Let me, who know these soldiers, counsel you.
Give them all honor; seem not to command;
Else they will scarcely brook your late sprung power,
Which nor alliance props, nor birth adorns.   340
   NORVAL. Sir, I have been accustomed all my days
To hear and speak the plain and simple truth:
And though I have been told that there are men
Who borrow friendship's tongue to speak their scorn,
Yet in such language I am little skilled.   345
Therefore I thank Glenalvon for his counsel,
Although it sounded harshly. Why remind
Me of my birth obscure? Why slur my power
With such contemptuous terms?
   GLEN.   I did not mean
To gall your pride, which now I see is great.   350
   NORVAL. My pride!
   GLEN.   Suppress it as you wish to prosper.
Your pride's excessive. Yet, for Randolph's sake,
I will not leave you to its rash direction.
If thus you swell, and frown at high-born men,
Will high-born men endure a shepherd's scorn?   355
   NORVAL. A shepherd's scorn!
   GLEN.   Yes, if you presume
To bend on soldiers these disdainful eyes,
As if you took the measure of their minds,
And said in secret, 'You're no match for me,'
What will become of you?
   NORVAL (*aside*).   If this were told! —   360
Hast thou no fears for thy presumptuous self?
   GLEN. Ha! Dost thou threaten me?
   NORVAL.   Didst thou not hear?
   GLEN. Unwillingly I did; a nobler foe
Had not been questioned thus. But such as thee —
   NORVAL. Whom dost thou think me?
   GLEN.   Norval.
   NORVAL.   So I am —   365
And who is Norval in Glenalvon's eyes?
   GLEN. A peasant's son, a wand'ring beggar-boy;
At best no more, even if he speaks the truth.
   NORVAL. False as thou art, dost thou suspect my
     truth?
   GLEN. Thy truth! Thou'rt all a lie; and false as
     hell   370
Is the vain-glorious tale thou told'st to Randolph.
   NORVAL. If I were chained, unarmed, and bed-rid
     old,
Perhaps I should revile. But as I am,
I have no tongue to rail. The humble Norval
Is of a race who strive not but with deeds.   375
Did I not fear to freeze thy shallow valor,
And make thee sink too soon beneath my sword,
I'd tell thee — what thou art. I know thee well.
   GLEN. Dost thou not know Glenalvon, born to
     command

298] EL *air-born;* M *air-borne.*

Ten thousand slaves like thee?

NORVAL.   Villain, no more: 380
Draw and defend thy life.   I did design
To have defied thee in another cause:
But heaven accelerates its vengeance on thee.
Now for my own and Lady Randolph's wrongs.

Enter LORD RANDOLPH.

LORD R. Hold, I command you both.   The man
    that stirs 385
Makes me his foe.

NORVAL.   Another voice than thine
That threat had vainly sounded, noble Randolph.

GLEN. Hear him, my lord; he's wondrous con-
    descending!
Mark the humility of shepherd Norval!

NORVAL. Now you may scoff in safety.

                (Sheathes his sword.)

LORD R.   Speak not thus, 390
Taunting each other; but unfold to me
The cause of quarrel, then I judge betwixt you.

NORVAL. Nay, my good lord, though I revere you
    much,
My cause I plead not, nor demand your judgment.
I blush to speak; I will not, cannot speak 395
Th' opprobrious words that I from him have borne.
To the liege-lord of my dear native land
I owe a subject's homage; but ev'n him
And his high arbitration I'd reject.
Within my bosom reigns another lord; 400
Honor, sole judge and umpire of itself.
If my free speech offend you, noble Randolph,
Revoke your favors, and let Norval go
Hence as he came, alone, but not dishonored.

LORD R. Thus far I'll mediate with impartial
    voice: 405
The ancient foe of Caledonia's land
Now waves his banners o'er her frighted fields.
Suspend your purpose, till your country's arms
Repel the bold invader; then decide
The private quarrel.

GLEN.   I agree to this. 410

NORVAL. And I.

Enter Servant.

SERV.   The banquet waits.

LORD R.   We come.

      Exit [LORD] RANDOLPH [*with Servant*].

GLEN.   Norval,
Let not our variance mar the social hour,
Nor wrong the hospitality of Randolph.
Nor frowning anger, nor yet wrinkled hate,
Shall stain my countenance. Smooth thou thy 415
    brow;
Nor let our strife disturb the gentle dame.

NORVAL. Think not so lightly, sir, of my resentment:

When we contend again, our strife is mortal.

                    [*Exeunt.*]

ACT V

The wood.

Enter DOUGLAS.[1]

DOUGLAS. This is the place, the center of the
    grove;
Here stands the oak, the monarch of the wood.
How sweet and solemn is this midnight scene!
The silver moon, unclouded, holds her way
Through skies where I could count each little
    star. 5
The fanning west wind scarcely stirs the leaves;
The river, rushing o'er its pebbled bed,
Imposes silence with a stilly sound.
In such a place as this, at such an hour,
If ancestry can be in aught believed,[2] 10
Descending spirits have conversed with man,
And told the secrets of the world unknown.

Enter OLD NORVAL.

OLD NORVAL. 'Tis he.   But what if he should
    chide me hence?
His just reproach I fear.

        (DOUGLAS *turns and sees him.*)
                    Forgive, forgive!
Can'st thou forgive the man, the selfish man, 15
Who bred Sir Malcolm's heir a shepherd's son?

DOUGLAS. Kneel not to me: thou art my father
    still:
Thy wished-for presence now completes my joy.
Welcome to me, my fortunes thou shalt share,
And ever honored with thy Douglas live. 20

OLD NORVAL. And dost thou call me father? O
    my son!
I think that I could die to make amends
For the great wrong I did thee. 'Twas my crime
Which in the wilderness so long concealed
The blossom of thy youth.

DOUGLAS.   Not worse the fruit, 25
That in the wilderness the blossom blowed.
Amongst the shepherds, in the humble cote,
I learned some lessons, which I'll not forget
When I inhabit yonder lofty towers.
I, who was once a swain, will ever prove 30
The poor man's friend; and, when my vassals bow,
Norval shall smooth the crested pride of Douglas.

OLD NORVAL. Let me but live to see thine exalta-
    tion!
Yet grievous are my fears. O leave this place,
And those unfriendly towers.

   [1] Henceforth Young Norval is designated as Douglas.
   [2] 'If we can give any credence to ancient legend (or, primitive belief).'

398] E *even*; LD *ev'n*.   411] M *Exit with Servant*.   ACT V. 27] M *cot*.

DOUGLAS.   Why should I leave them?   35
OLD NORVAL. Lord Randolph and his kinsman
    seek your life.
DOUGLAS. How know'st thou that?
OLD NORVAL.   I will inform you how.
When evening came, I left the secret place
Appointed for me by your mother's care,
And fondly trod in each accustomed path   40
That to the castle leads.   Whilst thus I ranged,
I was alarmed with unexpected sounds
Of earnest voices.   On the persons came;
Unseen I lurked, and overheard them name
Each other as they talked, Lord Randolph this,   45
And that Glenalvon: still of you they spoke,
And of the lady: threat'ning was their speech,
Though but imperfectly my ear could hear it.
'Twas strange, they said, a wonderful discov'ry;
And ever and anon they vowed revenge.   50
DOUGLAS. Revenge! for what?
OLD NORVAL.   For being what you are,
Sir Malcolm's heir: how else have you offended?
When they were gone, I hied me to my cottage
And there sat musing how I best might find
Means to inform you of their wicked purpose.   55
But I could think of none: at last, perplexed,
I issued forth, encompassing the tower
With many a weary step and wishful look.
Now Providence hath brought you to my sight,
Let not your too courageous spirit scorn   60
The caution which I give.
DOUGLAS.   I scorn it not.
My mother warned me of Glenalvon's baseness:
But I will not suspect the noble Randolph.
In our encounter with the vile assassins,
I marked his brave demeanor: him I'll trust.   65
OLD NORVAL. I fear you will, too far.
DOUGLAS.   Here in this place,
I wait my mother's coming.   She shall know
What thou hast told: her counsel I will follow:
And cautious ever are a mother's counsels.
You must depart; your presence may prevent   70
Our interview.
OLD NORVAL. My blessing rest upon thee!
O may heav'n's hand, which saved thee from the
    wave,
And from the sword of foes, be near thee still;
Turning mischance, if aught hangs o'er thy head,
All upon mine!   *Exit* OLD NORVAL.
DOUGLAS.   He loves me like a parent;   75
And must not, shall not, lose the son he loves,
Although his son has found a nobler father.
Eventful day! how hast thou changed my state!
Once on the cold and winter shaded side
Of a bleak hill, mischance had rooted me,   80
Never to thrive, child of another soil:
Transplanted now to the gay sunny vale,

Like the green thorn of May my fortune flowers.
Ye glorious stars! high heav'n's resplendent host!
To whom I oft have of my lot complained,   85
Hear and record my soul's unaltered wish!
Dead or alive, let me but be renowned!
May heav'n inspire some fierce gigantic Dane,
To give a bold defiance to our host!
Before he speaks it out I will accept;   90
Like Douglas conquer, or like Douglas die.

Enter LADY RANDOLPH.

LADY R. My son!   I heard a voice —
DOUGLAS.   — The voice was mine.
LADY R. Didst thou complain aloud to Nature's
    ear,
That thus in dusky shades, at midnight hours,
By stealth the mother and the son should meet?   95
    (*Embracing him.*)
DOUGLAS. No; on this happy day, this better
    birthday,
My thoughts and words are all of hope and joy.
LADY R. Sad fear and melancholy still divide
The empire of my breast with hope and joy.
Now hear what I advise.
DOUGLAS.   First, let me tell   100
What may the tenor of your counsel change.
LADY R. My heart forbodes some evil!
DOUGLAS.   'Tis not good. —
At eve, unseen by Randolph and Glenalvon,
The good old Norval in the grove o'erheard
Their conversation: oft they mentioned me   105
With dreadful threat'nings; you they sometimes
    named.
'Twas strange, they said, a wonderful discov'ry;
And ever and anon they vowed revenge.
LADY R. Defend us, gracious God! we are be-
    trayed!
They have found out the secret of thy birth;   110
It must be so.   That is the great discovery.
Sir Malcolm's heir is come to claim his own;
And he will be revenged.   Perhaps even now,
Armed and prepared for murder, they but wait
A darker and more silent hour, to break   115
Into the chamber where they think thou sleep'st.
This moment, this, heav'n hath ordained to save
    thee!
Fly to the camp, my son!
DOUGLAS.   And leave you here?
No: to the castle let us go together,
Call up the ancient servants of your house,   120
Who in their youth did eat your father's bread.
Then tell them loudly that I am your son.
If in the breasts of men one spark remains
Of sacred love, fidelity, or pity,
Some in your cause will arm.   I ask but few   125
To drive those spoilers from my father's house.

113] LDM *they* for *he.*

LADY R. O Nature, Nature! what can check thy
    force?
Thou genuine offspring of the daring Douglas!
But rush not on destruction: save thyself,
And I am safe.   To me they mean no harm.   130
Thy stay but risks thy precious life in vain.
That winding path conducts thee to the river.
Cross where thou seest a broad and beaten way,
Which running eastward leads thee to the camp.
Instant demand admittance to Lord Douglas.   135
Show him these jewels which his brother wore.
Thy look, thy voice, will make him feel the truth,
Which I by certain proof will soon confirm.
    DOUGLAS. I yield me and obey: but yet my heart
Bleeds at this parting.   Something bids me
    stay,   140
And guard a mother's life.   Oft have I read
Of wondrous deeds by one bold arm achieved.
Our foes are two: no more: let me go forth,
And see if any shield can guard Glenalvon.
    LADY R. If thou regard'st thy mother, or
    rever'st   145
Thy father's mem'ry, think of this no more.
One thing I have to say before we part:
Long wert thou lost; and thou art found, my
    child,
In a most fearful season.   War and battle
I have great cause to dread.   Too well I see   150
Which way the current of thy temper sets:
To-day I've found thee.   Oh! my long-lost hope!
If thou to giddy valor giv'st the rein,
To-morrow I may lose my son forever.
The love of thee, before thou saw'st the light,   155
Sustained my life when thy brave father fell.
If thou shalt fall, I have nor love nor hope
In this waste world!   My son, remember me!
    DOUGLAS. What shall I say?   How can I give
    you comfort?
The God of battles of my life dispose   160
As may be best for you! for whose dear sake
I will not bear myself as I resolved.
But yet consider, (as no vulgar name
That which I boast sounds amongst martial men,)
How will inglorious caution suit my claim?   165
The post of fate unshrinking I maintain.
My country's foes must witness who I am.
On the invaders' heads I'll prove my birth,
Till friends and foes confess the genuine strain.
If in this strife I fall, blame not your son,   170
Who, if he lives not honored, must not live
    LADY R. I will not utter what my bosom feels.
Too well I love that valor which I warn.
Farewell, my son! my counsels are but vain;
                    (Embracing.)

And as high heav'n hath willed it, all must be.   175
               ([They are about to] separate).
Gaze not on me, thou wilt mistake the path;
I'll point it out again.

Just as they are separating, enter from the wood
    LORD RANDOLPH *and* GLENALVON.
    LORD R.   Not in her presence.
    [*Exeunt, at different sides,* DOUGLAS *and*
    LADY RANDOLPH.]
Now —
    GLEN. I'm prepared.
    LORD R.   No: I command thee stay.
I go alone: it never shall be said
That I took odds to combat mortal man.   180
The noblest vengeance is the most complete.
               Exit LORD RANDOLPH.
    (GLENALVON *makes some steps to the same side*
    of the stage, listens and speaks.)
    GLEN. Demons of death, come, settle on my sword,
And to a double slaughter guide it home!
The lover and the husband both must die.
        (LORD RANDOLPH *behind the scenes.*)
    LORD R. Draw, villain! draw.
    DOUGLAS.   Assail me not, Lord Randolph!   185
Not as thou lov'st thyself.   (*Clashing of swords.*)
    GLEN.   Now is the time. (*Running out.*)

Enter LADY RANDOLPH *at the opposite side of the*
    stage, faint and breathless.
    LADY R. Lord Randolph, hear me; all shall be
    thine own:
But spare! oh, spare my son!

    Enter DOUGLAS *with a sword in each hand.*
    DOUGLAS.   My mother's voice!
I can protect thee still.
    LADY R.   He lives, he lives!
For this, for this to heaven eternal praise!   190
But sure I saw thee fall.
    DOUGLAS.   It was Glenalvon.
Just as my arm had mastered Randolph's sword,
The villain came behind me; but I slew him.
    LADY R. Behind thee!   Ah, thou'rt wounded!
    O my child,
How pale thou look'st!   And shall I lose thee
    now?   195
    DOUGLAS. Do not despair: I feel a little faintness;
I hope it will not last.   (*Leans upon his sword.*)
    LADY R.   There is no hope!
And we must part! the hand of death is on thee!
O my belovèd child!   O Douglas, Douglas!
        [DOUGLAS *growing more and more faint.*]
    DOUGLAS. Too soon we part; I have not long been
    Douglas.   200

150] L omits *I* before *have.*   164] EL have period after *men*; M has comma.
175 s.d.] EL *separate*; M *They are about to separate.*   177] M supplies stage direction after 'Not in her presence.'
199] E lacks, but both L and D have, the stage direction.

O destiny! hardly thou deal'st with me:
Clouded and hid, a stranger to myself,
In low and poor obscurity I lived.

LADY R. Has heav'n preserved thee for an end
　　like this?

DOUGLAS. O had I fall'n as my brave fathers
　　fell,   205
Turning with great effórt the tide of battle!
Like them I should have smiled and welcomed
　　death.
But thus to perish by a villain's hand!
Cut off from nature's and from glory's course,
Which never mortal was so fond to run.   210

LADY R. Hear, justice! hear! stretch thy aveng-
　　ing arm.   (DOUGLAS falls.)

DOUGLAS. Unknown I die; no tongue shall speak
　　of me. —
Some noble spirits, judging by themselves,
May yet conjecture what I might have proved,
And think life only wanting to my fame: 215
But who shall comfort thee?

LADY R.   Despair! despair!

DOUGLAS. O had it pleased high heaven to let
　　me live
A little while! — My eyes that gaze on thee
Grow dim apace! my mother! — O! my mother!
　　　　　　　　　　　　　　　　　　　(Dies.)

Enter LORD RANDOLPH *and* ANNA.

LORD R. Thy words, the words of truth, have
　　pierced my heart.   220
I am the stain of knighthood and of arms.
Oh! if my brave deliverer survives
The traitor's sword —

ANNA.   Alas! look there, my lord.

LORD R. The mother and her son! How curst
　　I am!
Was I the cause? No: I was not the cause.   225
Yon matchless villain did seduce my soul
To frantic jealousy.

ANNA.   My lady lives:
The agony of grief hath but suppressed
A while her powers.

LORD R.   But my deliverer's dead!
The world did once esteem Lord Randolph
　　well —   230
Sincere of heart, for spotless honor famed:
And, in my early days, glory I gained
Beneath the holy banner of the cross.
Now, past the noon of life, shame comes upon me;
Reproach, and infamy, and public hate,   235
Are near at hand: for all mankind will think
That Randolph basely stabbed Sir Malcolm's heir.
　　　　　　　　　　　　　(LADY RANDOLPH *recovering*.)

LADY R. Where am I now? still in this wretched
　　world!
Grief cannot break a heart so hard as mine.
My youth was worn in anguish; but youth's
　　strength,   240
With hope's assistance, bore the brunt of sorrow,
And trained me on to be the object, now,
On which Omnipotence displays itself,
Making a spectacle, a tale of me,
To awe its vassal, man.

LORD R.   O misery!   245
Amidst thy raging grief I must proclaim
My innocence.

LADY R. Thy innocence!

LORD R.   My guilt
Is innocence, compared with what thou think'st it.

LADY R. Of thee I think not: what have I to do
With thee, or anything? My son! my son!   250
My beautiful! my brave! how proud was I
Of thee, and of thy valor! My fond heart
O'erflowed this day with transport, when I thought
Of growing old amidst a race of thine,
Who might make up to me their father's child-
　　hood,   255
And bear my brother's and my husband's name:
Now all my hopes are dead! A little while
Was I a wife! a mother not so long!
What am I now? — I know. — But I shall be
That only whilst I please; for such a son   260
And such a husband make a woman bold.
　　　　　　　　　　　　　　　　(Runs out.)

LORD R. Follow her, Anna: I myself would
　　follow,
But in this rage she must abhor my presence.
　　　　　　　　　　　　　　　　　　Exit ANNA.

Enter OLD NORVAL.

[OLD] NORVAL. I hear the voice of woe; heaven
　　guard my child!

LORD R. Already is the idle gaping crowd,   265
The spiteful vulgar, come to gaze on Randolph.
Begone!

[OLD] NORVAL. I fear thee not. I will not go.
Here I'll remain. I'm an accomplice, lord,
With thee in murder. Yes, my sins did help
To crush down to the ground this lovely plant.   270
O noblest youth that ever yet was born!
Sweetest and best, gentlest and bravest spirit
That ever blessed the world! Wretch that I am,
Who saw that noble spirit swell and rise
Above the narrow limits that confined it,   275
Yet never was by all thy virtues won
To do thee justice, and reveal the secret,
Which, timely known, had raised thee far above

205] EL *fallen*; M *fall'n*.　　　　206] E *great effort*; LD *fatal arm*; M *effort great*.
211] L *are these the fruits of virtue?* for *stretch . . . arm*.　　219] LD omit final *O! my mother!*
239] E has comma, after *mine*; L has period.　　264] LD *heard*.

The villain's snare! Oh! I am punished now!
These are the hairs that should have strewed the
          ground,   280
And not the locks of Douglas.

(*Tears his hair, and throws himself upon the
          body of* DOUGLAS.)

LORD R. I know thee now: thy boldness I for-
          give;
My crest is fall'n. For thee I will appoint
A place of rest, if grief will let thee rest.
I will reward, although I cannot punish.   285
Curst, curst Glenalvon, he escaped too well,
Though slain and baffled [1] by the hand he hated.
Foaming with rage and fury to the last,
Cursing his conqueror the felon died.

Enter ANNA.

ANNA. My lord! my lord!
LORD R.   Speak: I can hear of horror.   290
ANNA. Horror indeed!
LORD R.   Matilda? —
ANNA.   Is no more.
She ran, she flew like lightning up the hill,
Nor halted till the precipice she gained,
Beneath whose low'ring top the river falls,

[1] Disgraced.

Engulfed in rifted rocks: thither she came,   295
As fearless as the eagle lights upon it,
And headlong down —
LORD R.   'Twas I! alas! 'twas I
That filled her breast with fury; drove her down
The precipice of death! Wretch that I am!
ANNA. O had you seen her last despairing
          look!   300
Upon the brink she stood, and cast her eyes
Down on the deep: then lifting up her head
And her white hands to heaven, seeming to say,
'Why am I forced to this?' she plunged herself
Into the empty air.
LORD R.   I will not vent,   305
In vain complaints, the passion of my soul.
Peace in this world I never can enjoy.
These wounds the gratitude of Randolph gave.
They speak aloud, and with the voice of fate
Denounce my doom. I am resolved. I'll go   310
Straight to the battle, where the man that makes
Me turn aside must threaten worse than death. —
Thou, faithful to thy mistress, take this ring,
Full warrant of my power. Let every rite
With cost and pomp upon their funerals wait: 315
For Randolph hopes he never shall return.

[*Exeunt.*]

281] LDM conclude the stage direction, *throws himself upon the ground.*   295] ELM *Ingulph'd.*

EPILOGUE [1]

An epilogue I asked; but not one word
Our bard will write.   He vows 'tis most absurd
With comic wit to contradict the strain
Of tragedy, and make your sorrows vain.
Sadly he says, that pity is the best,
The noblest passion of the human breast:
For when its sacred streams the heart o'erflow,
In gushes pleasure with the tide of woe;
And when its waves retire, like those of Nile,
They leave behind them such a golden soil,   10
That there the virtues without culture grow,
There the sweet blossoms of affection blow.
These were his words: — void of delusive art
I felt them; for he spoke them from his heart
Nor will I now attempt, with witty folly,   15
To chase away celestial melancholy.

[1] E includes the epilogue: L adds, 'Spoken by Mr. BARRY.'   Barry, the Young Norval of the London cast, may have written the epilogue which he spoke.

The Jealous Wife

BY GEORGE COLMAN, THE ELDER

ADVERTISEMENT.

THE Ufe that has been made in this Comedy of *Fielding's* admirable Novel of *Tom Jones*, muft be obvious to the moft ordinary Reader. Some Hints have alfo been taken from the Account of Mr. and Mrs. *Freeman*, in N°. 212, and N°. 216, of the *Spectator*; and the fhort Scene of *Charles's* Intoxication, at the End of the Third Act, is partly an Imitation of the Behaviour of *Syrus*, much in the fame Circumftances, in the *Adelphi* of *Terence*. There are alfo fome Traces of the Character of the Jealous Wife, in one of the latter Papers of the *Connoiffeur*.

It would be unjuft, indeed, to omit mentioning my Obligations to Mr. *Garrick*. To his Infpection the Comedy was fubmitted in its firft rude State; and to my Care and Attention to follow his Advice in many Particulars, relating both to the Fable and Characters, I know that I am much indebted for the Reception which this Piece has met with from the Publick.

Dra-

PROLOGUE

Written by Mr. Lloyd,[1]

And Spoken by Mr. Garrick.[2]

The Jealous Wife! a Comedy! Poor man!
A charming subject, but a wretched plan!
His skittish wit, o'erleaping the due bound,
Commits flat trespass upon tragic ground.
Quarrels, upbraidings, jealousies, and spleen,   5
Grow too familiar in the comic scene.
Tinge but the language with heroic chime,
'Tis passion, pathos, character, sublime!
What round big words had swelled the pompous scene,
A king the husband, and the wife a queen!   10
Then might Distraction rend her graceful hair,
See sightless forms, and scream, and gape, and stare.
Drawcansir[3] Death had raged without control,
Here the drawn dagger, there the poisoned bowl.
What eyes had streamed at all the whining woe!   15
What hands had thundered at each *ha!* and *oh!*
 But peace! the gentle Prologue custom sends,
Like drum and sergeant, to beat up for friends.
At vice and folly, each a lawful game,
Our author flies, but with no *partial* aim.   20
He read the manners, open as they lie
In Nature's volume to the general eye.
Books too he read, nor blushed to use their store —
He does but what his betters did before.
Shakespeare has done it, and the Grecian stage   25
Caught truth of character from Homer's page.
 If in his scenes an honest skill is shown,
And borrowing little, much appears his own;
If what a master's happy pencil drew
He brings more forward in dramatic view;   30
To your decision he submits his cause,
Secure of candor, anxious for applause.
 But if, all rude, his artless scenes deface
The simple beauties which he meant to grace;
If, an invader upon others' land,   35
He spoil and plunder with a robber's hand;
Do justice on him! — as on fools before —
And give to *blockheads* past one *blockhead* more.

---

[1] Robert Lloyd (1733–1764), poet, dramatist, and friend of Colman.
[2] David Garrick (1717–1779), appeared as Mr. Oakly in the opening performance.
[3] Drawcansir, in *The Rehearsal*, 'kills 'em all on both sides.'

DRAMATIS PERSONÆ

OAKLY   JOHN
MAJOR OAKLY   TOM
CHARLES   *Servant to* LADY FREELOVE
RUSSET
SIR HARRY BEAGLE   MRS. OAKLY
LORD TRINKET   LADY FREELOVE
CAPTAIN O'CUTTER   HARRIOT
PARIS   TOILET
WILLIAM   *Chambermaid*

THE JEALOUS WIFE

By GEORGE COLMAN, The Elder

ACT I

Scene [I]

A room in OAKLY'S *house.* *Noise heard within.*

MRS. OAKLY (*within*). Don't tell me! I know it is so. It's monstrous, and I will not bear it.

OAKLY (*within*). But, my dear!

MRS. OAK. [*within*]. Nay, nay, *etc.*

(*Squabbling within.*)

Enter MRS. OAKLY, *with a letter,* OAKLY *following.*

MRS. OAK. Say what you will, Mr. Oakly, 5 you shall never persuade me but this is some filthy intrigue of yours.

OAK. I can assure you, my love —

MRS. OAK. Your love! Don't I know your — Tell me, I say, this instant, every circumstance 10 relating to this letter.

OAK. How can I tell you, when you will not so much as let me see it?

MRS. OAK. Look you, Mr. Oakly, this usage is not to be borne. You take a pleasure in 15 abusing my tenderness and soft disposition. To be perpetually running over the whole town, nay, the whole kingdom too, in pursuit of your amours! Did not I discover that you were great with Mademoiselle, my own woman? Did not you con- 20 tract a shameful familiarity with Mrs. Freeman? Did not I detect your intrigue with Lady Wealthy? Were not you —

OAK. Ooons, madam, the Grand Turk himself has not half so many mistresses! You throw 25 me out of all patience. Do I know anybody but our common friends? Am I visited by anybody that does not visit you? Do I ever go out, unless you go with me? And am I not as constantly by your side as if I was tied to your apron strings? 30

MRS. OAK. Go, go, you are a false man. Have not I found you out a thousand times? And have I not this moment a letter in my hand, which convinces me of your baseness? Let me know the whole affair, or I will — 35

OAK. Let you know! — Let me know what you would have of me. You stop my letter before it comes to my hands, and then expect that I should know the contents of it.

MRS. OAK. Heaven be praised! I stopped 40 it. I suspected some of these doings for some time

past. But the letter informs me who she is, and I'll be revenged on her sufficiently. O, you base man, you!

OAK. I beg, my dear, that you would mod- 45 erate your passion! Show me the letter, and I'll convince you of my innocence.

MRS. OAK. Innocence! abominable! innocence! But I am not to be made such a fool. I am convinced of your perfidy, and very sure that — 50

OAK. 'Sdeath and fire! your passion hurries you out of your senses. Will you hear me?

MRS. OAK. No, you are a base man, and I will not hear you.

OAK. Why then, my dear, since you will 55 neither talk reasonably yourself, nor listen to reason from me, I shall take my leave till you are in a better humor. So, your servant! (*Going.*)

MRS. OAK. Ay, go, you cruel man! Go to your mistresses, and leave your poor wife to her 60 miseries. How unfortunate a woman am I! I could die with vexation.

(*Throwing herself into a chair.*)

OAK. There it is. Now dare not I stir a step further. If I offer to go, she is in one of her fits in an instant. Never, sure, was woman at once 65 of so violent and so delicate a constitution! What shall I say to soothe her? — Nay, never make thyself so uneasy, my dear. Come, come, you know I love you. Nay, nay, you shall be convinced.

MRS. OAK. I know you hate me; and that 70 your unkindness and barbarity will be the death of me. (*Whining.*)

OAK. Do not vex yourself at this rate. I love you most passionately. Indeed I do. This must be some mistake. 75

MRS. OAK. O, I am an unhappy woman!

(*Weeping.*)

OAK. Dry up thy tears, my love, and be comforted! — You will find that I am not to blame in this matter. Come, let me see this letter. Nay, you shall not deny me. (*Taking the letter.*) 80

MRS. OAK. There! take it! You know the hand, I am sure.

OAK. (*reading*). 'To CHARLES OAKLY, ESQ.' — Hand! 'Tis a clerk-like hand, indeed! A good round text! and was certainly never penned 85 by a fair lady.

MRS. OAK. Ay, laugh at me, do!

OAK. Forgive me, my love, I did not mean to laugh at thee. But what says the letter? —

(Reading.)

Daughter eloped — You must be privy to 90 *it — scandalous — dishonorable — satisfaction — revenge — um, um, um — injured father,*

Henry Russet.

MRS. OAK. *(rising).* Well, sir, you see I have detected you. Tell me this instant where she 95 is concealed.

OAK. So, so, so! This hurts me — I am shocked.

(To himself.)

MRS. OAK. What! are you confounded with your guilt? Have I caught you at last?

OAK. O that wicked Charles! To decoy a 100 young lady from her parents in the country! The profligacy of the young fellows of this age is abominable. *(To himself.)*

MRS. OAK. *(half aside and musing).* Charles! — Let me see! — Charles! — No! impossible! 105 This is all a trick.

OAK. He has certainly ruined this poor lady.

(To himself.)

MRS. OAK. Art! art! all art! There's a sudden turn now! You have a ready wit for intrigue, I find.

OAK. Such an abandoned action! I wish I 110 had never had the care of him. *(To himself.)*

MRS. OAK. Mighty fine, Mr. Oakly! — Go on, sir, go on! I see what you mean. Your assurance provokes me beyond your very falsehood itself. So you imagine, sir, that this affected concern, 115 this flimsy pretence about Charles, is to bring you off. Matchless confidence! But I am armed against everything. I am prepared for all your dark schemes. I am aware of all your low stratagems.

OAK. See there now! Was ever anything so 120 provoking? To persevere in your ridiculous — For heaven's sake, my dear, don't distract me. When you see my mind thus agitated and uneasy, that a young fellow, whom his dying father, my own brother, committed to my care, should be 125 guilty of such enormous wickedness; I say, when you are witness of my distress on this occasion, how can you be weak enough, and cruel enough to —

MRS. OAK. Prodigiously well, sir! You do it very well. Nay, keep it up, carry it on, 130 there's nothing like going through with it. O you artful creature! But, sir, I am not to be so easily satisfied. — I do not believe a syllable of all this. Give me the letter. *(Snatching the letter.)* You shall sorely repent this vile business, for I am 135 resolved that I will know the bottom of it. *Exit.*

OAKLY *solus.*

OAK. This is beyond all patience. Provoking woman! Her absurd suspicions interpret every-

thing the wrong way. She delights to make me wretched, because she sees I am attached to 140 her; and converts my tenderness and affection into the instruments of my own torture. But this ungracious boy! In how many troubles will he involve his own and this lady's family! I never imagined that he was of such abandoned principles. — 145 O, here he comes!

Enter MAJOR OAKLY, *and* CHARLES.

CHAR. Good-morrow, sir!

MAJ. Good-morrow, brother, good-morrow! What! you have been at the old work, I find. I heard you — ding-dong! i'faith! She has 150 rung a noble peal in your ears. But how now? Why, sure, you've had a remarkable warm bout on't. You seem more ruffled than usual.

OAK. I am indeed, brother! thanks to that young gentleman there. Have a care, Charles! you 155 may be called to a severe account for this. The honor of a family, sir, is no such light matter.

CHAR. Sir!

MAJ. Hey-day! What, has a curtain-lecture produced a lecture of morality? What is all 160 this?

OAK. To a profligate mind, perhaps, these things may appear agreeable in the beginning. But don't you tremble at the consequences?

CHAR. I see, sir, that you are displeased 165 with me, but I am quite at a loss how to guess at the occasion.

OAK. Tell me, sir! where is Miss Harriot Russet?

CHAR. Miss Harriot Russet! Sir, explain.

OAK. Have not you decoyed her from her 170 father?

CHAR. I! decoyed her! decoyed my Harriot! I would sooner die than do her the least injury. What can this mean?

MAJ. I believe the young dog has been at 175 her, after all.

OAK. I was in hopes, Charles, you had better principles. But there is a letter just come from her father —

CHAR. A letter! what letter? dear sir, give 180 it me. Some intelligence of my Harriot, Major! The letter, sir, the letter this moment, for heaven's sake!

OAK. If this warmth, Charles, tends to prove your innocence — 185

CHAR. Dear sir, excuse me. I'll prove anything. Let me but see this letter, and I'll —

OAK. Let you see it? I could hardly get a sight of it myself. Mrs. Oakly has it.

CHAR. Has she got it? Major, I'll be with 190 you again directly. *Exit hastily.*

MAJ. Hey-day! the devil's in the boy! What a

fiery set of people! By my troth, I think the whole family is made up of nothing but combustibles.

Oak. I like this emotion. It looks well. It 195 may serve, too, to convince my wife of the folly of her suspicions. Would to heaven I could quiet them forever!

Maj. Why, pray now, my dear naughty brother, what heinous offence have you committed this 200 morning? What new cause of suspicion? You have been asking one of the maids to mend your ruffle, I suppose; or have been hanging your head out of the window, when a pretty young woman has passed by; or — 205

Oak. How can you trifle with my distresses, Major? Did not I tell you it was about a letter?

Maj. A letter! hum! a suspicious circumstance, to be sure! What, and the seal a true-lover's knot now, ha? or an heart transfixed with darts; or 210 possibly the wax bore the industrious impression of a thimble; or perhaps, the folds were lovingly connected by a wafer, pricked with a pin, and the direction written in a vile scrawl, and not a word spelled as it should be. Ha, ha, ha! 215

Oak. Pho, brother! whatever it was, the letter, you find, was for Charles, not for me. This outrageous jealousy is the devil.

Maj. Mere matrimonial blessings and domestic comfort, brother! Jealousy is a certain sign of 220 love.

Oak. Love! It is this very love that hath made us both so miserable. Her love for me hath confined me to my house, like a state prisoner, without the liberty of seeing my friends, or the use of 225 pen, ink, and paper; while my love for her has made such a fool of me, that I have never had the spirit to contradict her.

Maj. Ay, ay, there you've hit it: Mrs. Oakly would make an excellent wife, if you did but 230 know how to manage her.

Oak. You are a rare fellow, indeed, to talk of managing a wife. A debauched bachelor, a rattle-brained rioting fellow, who have picked up your commonplace notions of women in bagnios, 235 taverns, and the camp; whose most refined commerce with the sex has been in order to delude country girls at your quarters, or to besiege the virtue of abigails, milliners, or mantuamakers' prentices. 240

Maj. So much the better! so much the better! Women are all alike in the main, brother; high or low, married or single, quality or no quality. I have found them so, from a duchess down to a milkmaid.

Oak. Your savage notions are ridiculous. 245 What do you know of a husband's feelings? You, who comprise all your qualities in your *honor*, as you call it! Dead to all sentiments of delicacy,

and incapable of any but the grossest attachments to women! This is your boasted refinement, 250 your thorough knowledge of the world! while, with regard to women, one poor train of thinking, one narrow set of ideas, like the uniform of the regiment, serves the whole corps.

Maj. Very fine, brother! there's common- 255 place for you, with a vengeance. Henceforth, expect no quarter from me. I tell you again and again, I know the sex better than you do. They all love to give themselves airs, and to have power. Every woman is a tyrant at the bottom. But 260 they could never make a fool of me. No, no! no woman should ever domineer over me, let her be mistress or wife.

Oak. Single men can be no judges in these cases. They must happen in all families. But when 265 things are driven to extremities — to see a woman in uneasiness — a woman one loves too — one's wife — who can withstand it? You neither speak nor think like a man that has loved, and been married, Major. 270

Maj. I wish I could hear a married man speak my language. I'm a bachelor, it's true; but I am no bad judge of your case, for all that. I know yours and Mrs. Oakly's disposition to a hair. She is all impetuosity and fire; a very magazine of 275 touchwood and gunpowder. You are hot enough too upon occasion, but then it's over in an instant. In comes love and conjugal affection, as you call it; that is, mere folly and weakness; and you draw off your forces, just when you should pursue 280 the attack, and follow your advantage. Have at her with spirit, and the day's your own, brother!

Oak. I tell you, brother, you mistake the matter. Sulkiness, fits, tears! these, and such as these, are the things which make a feeling man uneasy. 285 Her passion and violence have not half such an effect on me.

Maj. Why, then, you may be sure, she'll play that upon you which she finds does most execution. But you must be proof against everything. If 290 she's furious, set passion against passion; if you find her at her tricks, play off art against art, and foil her at her own weapons. That's your game, brother!

Oak. Why, what would you have me do? 295

Maj. Do as you please for one month, whether she like it or not; and I'll answer for it, she will consent you shall do as you please all her life after.

Oak. This is fine talking. You do not consider the difficulty that — 300

Maj. You must overcome all difficulties. Assert your right boldly, man! give your own orders to servants, and see they observe them; read your own letters, and never let her have a sight of them; make

---

your own appointments, and never be per- 305
suaded to break them; see what company you like;
go out when you please; return when you please;
and don't suffer yourself to be called to account
where you have been. In short, do but show yourself a man of spirit, leave off whining about 310
love and tenderness, and nonsense, and the business
is done, brother!

OAK. I believe you're in the right, Major! I see
you're in the right. I'll do't, I'll certainly do't.
But then it hurts me to the soul, to think what 315
uneasiness I shall give her. The first opening of
my design will throw her into fits, and the pursuit
of it, perhaps, may be fatal.

MAJ. Fits! ha, ha, ha! I'll engage to cure her
of her fits. Nobody understands hysterical 320
cases better than I do. Besides, my sister's symptoms are not very dangerous. Did you ever hear
of her falling into a fit, when you were not by?
Was she ever found in convulsions in her closet?
No, no! these fits, the more care you take of 325
them, the more you will increase the distemper.
Let them alone, and they will wear themselves out,
I warrant you.

OAK. True; very true; you're certainly in the
right. I'll follow your advice. Where do you 330
dine to-day? I'll order the coach, and go with you.

MAJ. O brave! keep up this spirit, and you're
made forever.

OAK. You shall see now, Major! Who's there?
(*Enter Servant.*) Order the coach directly. 335
I shall dine out to-day.

SERV. The coach, sir? now, sir?

OAK. Ay, now, immediately.

SERV. Now, sir? The — the — coach, sir? That
is — my mistress — 340

OAK. Sirrah, do as you're bid. Bid them put to
this instant.

SERV. Ye — yes, sir; yes, sir.   *Exit.*

OAK. Well, where shall we dine?

MAJ. At the St. Alban's, or where you will. 345
This is excellent, if you do but hold it.

OAK. I will have my own way, I am determined.

MAJ. That's right.

OAK. I am steel.

MAJ. Bravo!   350

OAK. Adamant.

MAJ. Bravissimo!

OAK. Just what you'd have me.

MAJ. Why, that's well said. But *will* you do it?

OAK. I will.   355

MAJ. You won't.

OAK. I will. I'll be a fool to her no longer. But
hark ye, Major! My hat and sword lie in my study.
I'll go and steal them out, while she is busy talking
with Charles.   360

MAJ. Steal them! for shame! Prithee take them

boldly, call for them, make them bring them to you
here, and go out with spirit, in the face of your
whole family!

OAK. No, no; you are wrong. Let her rave 365
after I am gone, and when I return, you know, I
shall exert myself with more propriety, after this
open affront to her authority.

MAJ. Well, take your own way.

OAK. Ay, ay; let me manage it, let me 370
manage it.   *Exit.*

MAJOR OAKLY *solus.*

MAJ. Manage it! ay, to be sure, you're a rare
manager! It is dangerous, they say, to meddle
between man and wife. I am no great favorite of
Mrs. Oakly's already; and in a week's time I 375
expect to have the door shut in my teeth.

Enter CHARLES.

How now, Charles, what news?

CHAR. Ruined and undone! She's gone, uncle!
My Harriot's lost forever!

MAJ. Gone off with a man? I thought so; 380
they are all alike.

CHAR. O, no! fled to avoid that hateful match
with Sir Harry Beagle.

MAJ. Faith, a girl of spirit! Joy, Charles! I
give you joy! She is your own, my boy! A 385
fool and a great estate! devilish strong temptations!

CHAR. A wretch! I was sure she would never
think of him.

MAJ. No, to be sure! commend me to your
modesty! Refuse five thousand a year, and a 390
baronet, for pretty Mr. Charles Oakly! It is true,
indeed, that the looby has not a single idea in his
head, besides a hound, a hunter, a five-barred gate,
and a horse-race: but then he's rich, and that will
qualify his absurdities. Money is a wonder- 395
ful improver of the understanding. But whence
comes all this intelligence?

CHAR. In an angry letter from her father. How
miserable I am! If I had not offended my Harriot,
much offended her, by that foolish riot and 400
drinking at your house in the country, she would
certainly at such a time have taken refuge in my
arms.

MAJ. A very agreeable refuge for a young lady,
to be sure, and extremely decent!   405

CHAR. I am all uneasiness. Did not she tell
me that she trembled at the thoughts of having
trusted her affections with a man of such a wild
disposition? What a heap of extravagancies was
I guilty of!   410

MAJ. Extravagancies with a witness! Ah, you
silly young dog, you would ruin yourself with her
father, in spite of all I could do. There you sat, as
drunk as a lord, telling the old gentleman the whole

affair, and swearing you would drive Sir Harry 415
Beagle out of the country, though I kept winking
and nodding, pulling you by the sleeve, and kicking
your shins under the table, in hopes of stopping
you; but all to no purpose.

CHAR. What distress may she be in at this 420
instant! alone and defenceless! where, where can
she be?

MAJ. What relations or friends has she in town?

CHAR. Relation! Let me see: faith, I have it.
If she is in town, ten to one but she is at her 425
aunt's Lady Freelove's. I'll go thither immediately.

MAJ. Lady Freelove's! Hold, hold, Charles!
do you know her ladyship?

CHAR. Not much; but I'll break through 430
all forms, to get to my Harriot.

MAJ. I do know her ladyship.

CHAR. Well, and what do you know of her?

MAJ. O, nothing! Her ladyship is a woman of
the world, that's all. She'll introduce Harriot 435
to the best company.

CHAR. What do you mean?

MAJ. Yes, yes, I would trust a wife, or a daughter,
or a mistress, with Lady Freelove, to be sure! I
tell you what, Charles! you're a good boy, but 440
you don't know the world. Women are fifty times
oftener ruined by their acquaintance with each
other than by their attachment to men. One
thorough-paced lady will train up a thousand
novices. That Lady Freelove is an arrant — 445
By the bye, did not she, last summer, make formal
proposals to Harriot's father from Lord Trinket?

CHAR. Yes; but they were received with the
utmost contempt. The old gentleman, it seems,
hates a lord, and he told her so in plain terms. 450

MAJ. Such an aversion to the nobility may not
run in the blood. The girl, I warrant you, has no
objection. However, if she's there, watch her
narrowly, Charles! Lady Freelove is as mischievous as a monkey, and as cunning too. Have a 455
care of her; I say, have a care of her.

CHAR. If she's there, I'll have her out of the
house within this half hour, or set fire to it.

MAJ. Nay, now you're too violent. Stay a moment, and we'll consider what's best to be 460
done.

Re-enter OAKLY.

OAK. Come, is the coach ready? Let us be gone.
Does Charles go with us?

CHAR. I go with you! What can I do? I am so
vexed and distracted, and so many thoughts 465
crowd in upon me, I don't know what way to turn
myself.

MRS. OAK. (*within*). The coach! Dines out!
Where is your master?

OAK. Zoun[d]s, brother, here she is! 470

Enter MRS. OAKLY.

MRS. OAK. Pray, Mr. Oakly, what is the matter
you cannot dine at home to-day?

OAK. Don't be uneasy, my dear! I have a little
business to settle with my brother; so I am only just
going to dinner with him and Charles to the 475
tavern.

MRS. OAK. Why cannot you settle your business
here as well as at a tavern? But it is some of your
ladies' business, I suppose, and so you must get rid
of my company. This is chiefly your fault, 480
Major Oakly.

MAJ. Lord, sister, what signifies it, whether a
man dines at home or abroad? (*Coolly.*)

MRS. OAK. It signifies a great deal, sir! and I
don't choose — 485

MAJ. Pho! let him go, my dear sister, let him go!
he will be ten times better company when he comes
back. I tell you what, sister: you sit at home till
you are quite tired of one another, and then you
grow cross, and fall out. If you would but part 490
a little now and then, you might meet again in
good humor.

MRS. OAK. I beg, Major Oakly, that you would
trouble yourself about your own affairs; and let me
tell you, sir, that I — 495

OAK. Nay, do not put thyself into a passion with
the Major, my dear! It is not his fault; and I shall
come back to thee very soon.

MRS. OAK. Come back! why need you go out?
I know well enough when you mean to de- 500
ceive me; for then there is always a pretence of dining with Sir John, or my Lord, or somebody; but
when you tell me that you are going to a tavern,
it's such a barefaced affront —

OAK. This is so strange now! Why, my 505
dear, I shall only just —

MRS. OAK. Only just go after the lady in the letter, I suppose.

OAK. Well, well, I won't go then. Will that convince you? I'll stay with you, my dear. Will 510
that satisfy you?

MAJ. For shame! hold out, if you are a man.
(*Apart to* OAKLY.)

OAK. She has been so much vexed }
this morning already, I must hu- } (*Apart*
mor her a little now. } *between* 515

MAJ. Fie, fie! go out, or you're } OAKLY
undone. } *and the*

OAK. You see it's impossible. } MAJOR.)

(*To* MRS. OAKLY.) I'll dine at home with thee,
my love. 520

514] O1O2 *Aside*; O3O4 *Apart.*

MRS. OAK. Ay, ay, pray do, sir! Dine at a tavern indeed!   (*Going.*)

OAK. (*returning*). You may depend on me another time, Major.

MAJ. Steel! adamant! ah!   525

MRS. OAK. (*returning*). Mr. Oakly!

OAK. O, my dear!   *Exeunt.*

Manent MAJOR OAKLY *and* CHARLES.

MAJ. Ha, ha, ha! there's a picture of resolution. There goes a philosopher for you! Ha, Charles!

CHAR. O, uncle! I have no spirits to laugh   530
now.

MAJ. So! I have a fine time on't, between you and my brother. Will you meet me to dinner at the St. Alban's, by four? We'll drink her health, and think of this affair.   535

CHAR. Don't depend on me: I shall be running all over the town, in pursuit of my Harriot. I have been considering what you have said; but at all events I'll go directly to Lady Freelove's. If I find her not there, which way I shall direct myself,   540
heaven knows.

MAJ. Hark ye, Charles! if you meet with her, you may be at a loss. Bring her to my house: I have a snug room, and —

CHAR. Pho! prithee, uncle, don't trifle with   545
me now.

MAJ. Well, seriously then, my house is at your service.

CHAR. I thank you. But I must be gone.

MAJ. Ay, ay, bring her to my house, and   550
we'll settle the whole affair for you. You shall clap her into a post-chaise, take the chaplain of our regiment along with you, wheel her down to Scotland, and when you come back, send to settle her fortune with her father. That's the modern art of   555
making love, Charles!   *Exeunt.*

ACT II

SCENE [I]

A room in the Bull and Gate Inn.

Enter SIR HARRY BEAGLE *and* TOM.

SIR H. Ten guineas a mare, and a crown the man; ha, Tom?

TOM. Yes, your honor.

SIR H. And are you sure, Tom, that there is no flaw in his blood?   5

TOM. He's as good a thing, sir, and as little beholden to the ground, as any horse that ever went over the turf upon four legs. Why, here's his whole pedigree, your honor.

SIR H. Is it attested?   10

TOM. Very well attested: it is signed by Jack Spur, and my Lord Startall.   (*Giving the pedigree.*)

SIR H. Let me see.   (*Reading.*)

Tom-come-tickle-me was got out of the famous Tantwivy mare, by Sir Aaron Driver's   15
chestnut horse White Stockings. White Stockings, his dam, was got by Lord Hedge's South Barb, full sister to the Proserpine filly, and his sire Tom Jones; his grandam was the Irish Duchess, and his grandsire 'Squire Sportly's   20
Trajan; his great-grandam, and great-great-grandam, were Newmarket Peggy and Black Moll; and his great-grandsire, and great-great-grandsire, were Sir Ralph Whip's Regulus, and the famous Prince Anamaboo.   25

his

John X Spur,

mark.

STARTALL.

TOM. All fine horses, and won everything!   30
A foal out of your honor's Bald-faced Venus, by this horse, would beat the world.

SIR H. Well then, we'll think on't. But pox on't, Tom, I have certainly knocked up my little roan gelding, in this damned wild-goose chase   35
of threescore miles an end.

TOM. He's deadly blown, to be sure, your honor; and I am afraid we are upon a wrong scent after all. Madam Harriot certainly took across the country, instead of coming on to London.   40

SIR H. No, no, we traced her all the way up. But d'ye hear, Tom, look out among the stables and repositories here in town, for a smart road nag, and a strong horse to carry a portmanteau.

TOM. Sir Roger Turf's horses are to be sold: 45
I'll see if there's ever a tight thing there. But I suppose, sir, you would have one somewhat stronger than Snip: I do not think he's quite enough of a horse for your honor.

SIR H. Not enough of a horse! Snip's a   50
powerful gelding, master of two stone more than my weight. If Snip stands sound, I would not take a hundred guineas for him. Poor Snip! go into the stable, Tom; see they give him a warm mash, and look at his heels and his eyes. But   55
where's Mr. Russet all this while?

TOM. I left the squire at breakfast on a cold pigeon-pie, and enquiring after Madam Harriot in the kitchen. I'll let him know your honor would be glad to see him here.   60

SIR H. Ay, do. But hark ye, Tom, be sure you take care of Snip.

TOM. I'll warrant, your honor.

SIR H. I'll be down in the stables myself by and by.   *Exit* TOM.   65

525] OO *Steel and adamant!*   528] O1 *Ha! ha! ha! ha!*   528] O1O2 *the;* O3O4 *a.*   ACT II. 2] O1O2 *hey.*
3] O1O2 *sir:* O3O4 *your Honor.*   17] O1O2 omit *got;* O3O4 *was got.*   44] OO *portmantua.*

SIR HARRY *solus.*

Let me see — Out of the famous Tantwivy by White Stockings; White Stockings, his dam, full sister to the Proserpine filly, and his sire — Pox on't, how unlucky it is, that this damned accident should happen in the Newmarket week! Ten 70 to one I lose my match with Lord Choakjade, by not riding myself; and I shall have no opportunity to hedge my bets neither. What a damned piece of work have I made on't! I have knocked up poor Snip, shall lose my match, and as to Harriot, 75 why, the odds are that I lose my match there too. A skittish young tit! If I once get her tight in hand, I'll make her wince for it. Her estate joined to my own, I would have the finest stud and the noblest kennel in the whole country. But here 80 comes her father, puffing and blowing like a broken-winded horse up hill.

Enter RUSSET.

RUS. Well, Sir Harry, have you heard anything of her?

SIR H. Yes, I have been asking Tom about 85 her, and he says you may have her for five hundred guineas.

RUS. Five hundred guineas! how d'ye mean? where is she? which way did she take?

SIR H. Why, first she went to Epsom, then to 90 Lincoln, then to Nottingham, and now she is at York.

RUS. Impossible! she could not go over half the ground in the time. What the devil are you talking of? 95

SIR H. Of the mare you were just now saying you wanted to buy.

RUS. The devil take the mare! who would think of her, when I am mad about an affair of so much more consequence? 100

SIR H. You seemed mad about her a little while ago. She's a fine mare; a thing of shape and blood.

RUS. Damn her blood! Harriot! my dear provoking Harriot! where can she be? Have you got any intelligence of her? 105

SIR H. No, faith, not I. We seem to be quite thrown out here. But, however, I have ordered Tom to try if he can hear anything of her among the ostlers.

RUS. Why don't you enquire after her your- 110 self? Why don't you run up and down the whole town after her? T'other young rascal knows where she is, I warrant you. What a plague it is to have a daughter! when one loves her to distraction, and has toiled and labored to make her happy, the 115 ungrateful slut will sooner go to hell her own way. But she *shall* have him: I will make her happy, if I break her heart for it. A provoking gipsy! to run

away, and torment her poor father, that doats on her! I'll never see her face again. Sir Harry, 120 how can we get any intelligence of her? Why don't you speak? Why don't you tell me? Zoun[d]s, you seem as indifferent as if you did not care a farthing about her!

SIR H. Indifferent! you may well call me 125 indifferent. This damned chase after her will cost me a thousand. If it had not been for her, I would not have been off the course this week, to have saved the lives of my whole family. I'll hold you six to two that — 130

RUS. Zoun[d]s, hold your tongue, or talk more to the purpose! I swear, she is too good for you: you don't deserve such a wife. A fine, dear, sweet, lovely, charming girl! She'll break my heart. How shall I find her out? Do, prithee, Sir Harry, 135 my dear honest friend, consider how we may discover where she is fled to.

SIR H. Suppose you put an advertisement into the newspapers, describing her marks, her age, her height, and where she strayed from. I re- 140 covered a bay mare once by that method.

RUS. Advertise her! What! describe my daughter, and expose her in the public papers, with a reward for bringing her home, like horses, stolen or strayed! — Recovered a bay mare! — The 145 devil's in the fellow! He thinks of nothing but racers, and bay mares, and stallions. 'Sdeath! I wish your ——

SIR H. I wish Harriot was fairly pounded.[1] It would save us both a great deal of trouble. 150

RUS. Which way shall I turn myself? I am half distracted. If I go to that young dog's house, he has certainly conveyed her somewhere out of my reach. If she does not send to me to-day, I'll give her up forever. Perhaps, though, she may 155 have met with some accident, and has nobody to assist her. No, she is certainly with that young rascal. I wish she was dead, and I was dead. I'll blow young Oakly's brains out.

Enter TOM.

SIR H. Well Tom, how is poor Snip? 160

TOM. A little better, sir, after his warm mash. But Lady, the pointing bitch that followed you all the way, is deadly foot-sore.

RUS. Damn Snip and Lady! Have you heard anything of Harriot? 165

TOM. Why, I came on purpose to let my master and your honor know, that John Ostler says as how just such a lady, as I told him Madam Harriot was, came here in a four-wheel chaise, and was fetched away soon after by a fine lady in a chariot. 170

RUS. Did she come alone?

[1] Impounded, shut up in a pound.

Tom. Quite alone — only a servant-maid, please your honor.

Rus. And what part of the town did they go to? 175

Tom. John Ostler says as how, they bid the coachman drive to Grosvenor Square.

Sir H. Soho! puss! yoic[k]s![1]

Rus. She is certainly gone to that young rogue. He has got his aunt to fetch her from hence. 180 Or else she is with her own aunt, Lady Freelove. They both live in that part of the town. I'll go to his house; and, in the meanwhile, Sir Harry, you shall step to Lady Freelove's. We'll find her, I warrant you. I'll teach my young mistress to be 185 gadding. She shall marry you to-night. Come along, Sir Harry, come along! We won't lose a minute. Come along!

Sir H. Soho! hark forward! wind 'em and cross 'em! hark forward! yoic[k]s! yoic[k]s! *Exeunt.* 190

[Scene II]

Scene changes to Oakly's.

Mrs. Oakly *sola.*

Mrs. Oak. After all, that letter was certainly intended for my husband. I see plain enough they are all in a plot against me: my husband intriguing, the Major working him up to affront me, Charles owning his letters, and so playing into each 5 other's hands. They think me a fool, I find; but I'll be too much for them yet. I have desired to speak with Mr. Oakly, and expect him here immediately. His temper is naturally open, and if he thinks my anger abated, and my suspicions laid 10 asleep, he will certainly betray himself by his behavior. I'll assume an air of good humor, pretend to believe the fine story they have trumped up, throw him off his guard, and so draw the secret out of him. Here he comes. How hard it is to dis- 15 semble one's anger! O, I could rate him soundly! But I'll keep down my indignation at present, though it chokes me.

Enter Oakly.

O, my dear! I am very glad to see you. Pray sit down. (*They sit.*) I longed to see you. It 20 seemed an age till I had an opportunity of talking over the silly affair that happened this morning.

(*Mildly.*)

Oak. Why really, my dear —

Mrs. Oak. Nay, don't look so grave now. Come, it's all over. Charles and you have cleared up 25 matters. I am satisfied.

Oak. Indeed! I rejoice to hear it. You make me happy beyond my expectation. This disposi-

[1] An old fox-hunting cry, raised when the quarry is sighted.

tion will insure our felicity. Do but lay aside your cruel, unjust suspicion, and we should never 30 have the least difference.

Mrs. Oak. Indeed I begin to think so. I'll endeavor to get the better of it. And really sometimes it is very ridiculous. My uneasiness this morning, for instance! ha, ha, ha! to be so much 35 alarmed about that idle letter, which turned out quite another thing at last. Was not I very angry with you? ha, ha, ha! (*Affecting a laugh.*)

Oak. Don't mention it. Let us both forget it. Your present cheerfulness makes amends for 40 everything.

Mrs. Oak. I am apt to be too violent: I love you too well to be quite easy about you. (*Fondly.*) Well; no matter. What is become of Charles?

Oak. Poor fellow! he is on the wing, ram- 45 bling all over the town in pursuit of this young lady.

Mrs. Oak. Where is he gone, pray?

Oak. First of all, I believe, to some of her relations.

Mrs. Oak. Relations! who are they? where do they live? 50

Oak. There is an aunt of hers lives just in the neighborhood — Lady Freelove.

Mrs. Oak. Lady Freelove! O, ho! gone to Lady Freelove's, is he? And do you think he will hear anything of her? 55

Oak. I don't know; but I hope so, with all my soul.

Mrs. Oak. Hope! with all your soul! Do you hope so? (*Alarmed.*)

Oak. Hope so! Ye-yes. Why, don't you hope so? (*Surprised.*) 60

Mrs. Oak. Well! Yes, (*recovering*) O, ay, to be sure. I hope it of all things. You know, my dear, it must give me great satisfaction, as well as yourself, to see Charles well settled.

Oak. I should think so; and really I don't 65 know where he can be settled so well. She is a most deserving young woman, I assure you.

Mrs. Oak. You are well acquainted with her then?

Oak. To be sure, my dear; after seeing her so 70 often last summer at the Major's house in the country, and at her father's.

Mrs. Oak. So often!

Oak. O, ay, very often — Charles took care of that — almost every day. 75

Mrs. Oak. Indeed! But, pray — a — a — a — I say, — a — a (*Confused.*)

Oak. What do you say, my dear?

Mrs. Oak. I say — a — a — (*Stammering.*) Is she handsome? 80

Oak. Prodigiously handsome indeed.

Mrs. Oak. Prodigiously handsome! And is she reckoned a sensible girl?

Oak. A very sensible, modest, agreeable young lady as ever I knew. You would be ex- 85 tremely fond of her, I am sure. You can't imagine how happy I was in her company. Poor Charles! she soon made a conquest of him, and no wonder. She has so many elegant accomplishments! such an infinite fund of cheerfulness, and good 90 humor! Why, she's the darling of the whole country.

MRS. OAK. Lord! you seem quite in raptures about her.

OAK. Raptures! not at all. I was only telling you the young lady's character. I thought you 95 would be glad to find that Charles had made so sensible a choice, and was so likely to be happy.

MRS. OAK. O, Charles! True, as you say, Charles will be mighty happy.

OAK. Don't you think so?   100

MRS. OAK. I am convinced of it. Poor Charles! I am much concerned for him. He must be very uneasy about her. I was thinking whether we could be of any service to him in this affair.

OAK. Were you, my love? that is very good 105 of you. Why, to be sure, we must endeavor to assist him. Let me see! how can we manage it? Gad, I have hit it! The luckiest thought! and it will be of great service to Charles.

MRS. OAK. Well, what is it? (Eagerly.) 110 You know I would do anything to serve Charles, and oblige you.   (Mildly.)

OAK. That is so kind! Lord, my dear, if you would but always consider things in this proper light, and continue this amiable temper, we 115 should be the happiest people —

MRS. OAK. I believe so. But what's your proposal?

OAK. I am sure you'll like it. Charles, you know, may perhaps be so lucky as to meet with this 120 lady.

MRS. OAK. True.

OAK. Now I was thinking, that he might, with your leave, my dear —

MRS. OAK. Well?   125

OAK. Bring her home here.

MRS. OAK. How!

OAK. Yes, bring her home here, my dear! It will make poor Charles's mind quite easy; and you may take her under your protection, till her 130 father comes to town.

MRS. OAK. Amazing! this is even beyond my expectation.

OAK. Why, what —

MRS. OAK. Was there ever such assurance! 135 Take her under my protection! What! would you keep her under my nose?

OAK. Nay, I never conceived — I thought you would have approved —

MRS. OAK. What! make me your con- 140 venient woman? no place but my own house to serve your purposes?

OAK. Lord, this is the strangest misapprehension! I am quite astonished.

MRS. OAK. Astonished! Yes; confused, de- 145 tected, betrayed by your vain confidence of imposing on me. Why, sure you imagine me an idiot, a driveller. Charles, indeed! Yes, Charles is a fine excuse for you. The letter this morning, the letter, Mr. Oakly!   150

OAK. The letter! why, sure that —

MRS. OAK. Is sufficiently explained. You have made it very clear to me. Now I am convinced, I have no doubt of your perfidy. But I thank you for some hints you have given me, and you may 155 be sure I shall make use of them. Nor will I rest till I have full conviction, and overwhelm you with the strongest proofs of your baseness towards me.

OAK. Nay, but —   160

MRS. OAK. Go, go! I have no doubt of your falsehood. Away!   Exit.

OAKLY solus.

[OAK.] Was there ever anything like this? Such unaccountable behavior! Angry I don't know why! jealous of I know not what! pretending to be 165 satisfied merely to draw me in, and then creating imaginary proofs out of an innocent conversation! Hints! hints I have given her! What can she mean?

[Enter] TOILET crossing the stage.

Toilet! where are you going?   170

TOIL. To order the porter to let in no company to my lady to-day. She won't see a single soul, sir.
                                                 Exit.

OAK. What an unhappy woman! Now will she sit all day, feeding on her suspicions, till she has convinced herself of the truth of them.   175

[Enter] JOHN crossing the stage.

Well, sir, what's your business?

JOHN. Going to order the chariot, sir. My lady's going out immediately.   Exit.

OAK. Going out! what is all this? But every way she makes me miserable. Wild and ungovern- 180 able as the sea or the wind! made up of storms and tempests! I can't bear it; and, one way or other, I will put an end to it.   Exit.

SCENE [III]

LADY FREELOVE'S.

Enter LADY FREELOVE with a card. Servant following.

L. FREE. (reading as she enters). 'And will take the liberty of waiting on her ladyship en cavalier, as he comes from the *manège*.'[1] Does anybody wait that brought this card?

SERV. Lord Trinket's servant is in the hall, 5 madam.

L. FREE. My compliments, and I shall be glad to see his lordship. Where is Miss Russet?

SERV. In her own chamber, madam.

L. FREE. What is she doing?   10

SERV. Writing, I believe, madam.

L. FREE. O, ridiculous! Scribbling to that Oakly, I suppose. (*Apart.*) Let her know I should be glad of her company here.   *Exit Servant.*

LADY FREELOVE *sola.*

It is a mighty troublesome thing to manage a 15 simple girl, that knows nothing of the world. Harriot, like all other girls, is foolishly fond of this young fellow of her own choosing; her first love; that is to say, the first man that is particularly civil, and the first air of consequence which a young 20 lady gives herself. Poor silly soul! But Oakly must not have her, positively. A match with Lord Trinket will add to the dignity of the family. I must bring her into it. I will throw her into his way as often as possible, and leave him to make his 25 party good as fast as he can. But here she comes.

Enter HARRIOT.

Well, Harriot, still in the pouts? Nay, prithee, my dear little runaway girl, be more cheerful! Your everlasting melancholy puts one into the vapors.[2]

HAR. Dear madam, excuse me. How can I 30 be cheerful in my present situation? I know my father's temper so well, that I am sure this step of mine must almost distract him. I sometimes wish that I had remained in the country, let what would have been the consequence.   35

L. FREE. Why, it is a naughty child, that's certain; but it need not be so uneasy about papa, as you know that I wrote by last night's post, to acquaint him that his little lost sheep was safe, and that you are ready to obey his commands in 40 every particular, except marrying that oaf, Sir Harry Beagle. Lord! Lord! what a difference there is between a country and town education! Why, a London lass would have jumped out of a window into a gallant's arms, and, without 45 thinking of her father, unless it were to have drawn a few bills on him, been an hundred miles off in nine or ten hours, and perhaps out of the kingdom in twenty-four.

HAR. I fear I have already been too precipi- 50 tate. I tremble for the consequences.

L. FREE. I swear, child, you are a downright

<hr>

[1] Riding-school.
[2] An eighteenth-century term for 'the blues'; melancholia.

prude. Your way of talking gives me the spleen;[3] so full of affection, and duty, and virtue, 'tis just like a funeral sermon. And, yet, pretty soul! 55 it can love. Well, I wonder at your taste; a sneaking simple gentleman! without a title! and when, to my knowledge, you might have a man of quality to-morrow.

HAR. Perhaps so. Your ladyship must ex- 60 cuse me, but many a man of quality would make me miserable.

L. FREE. Indeed, my dear, these antediluvian notions will never do now-a-days; and, at the same time too, those little wicked eyes of yours speak 65 a very different language. Indeed you have fine eyes, child; and they have made fine work with Lord Trinket.

HAR. Lord Trinket!   (*Contemptuously.*)

L. FREE. Yes, Lord Trinket. You know it 70 as well as I do; and yet, you ill-natured thing, you will not vouchsafe him a single smile. But you must give the poor soul a little encouragement; prithee do.

HAR. Indeed I can't, madam; for of all man- 75 kind Lord Trinket is my aversion.

L. FREE. Why so, child? He is counted a well-bred, sensible, young fellow; and the women all think him handsome.

HAR. Yes, he is just polite enough to be able 80 to be very unmannerly with a great deal of good breeding, is just handsome enough to make him most excessively vain of his person, and has just reflection enough to finish him for a coxcomb; qualifications which are all very common among 85 those whom your ladyship calls men of quality.

L. FREE. A satirist, too! Indeed, my dear, this affectation fits very awkwardly upon you. There will be a superiority in the behavior of persons of fashion.   90

HAR. A superiority, indeed! for his lordship always behaves with so much insolent familiarity that I should almost imagine he was soliciting me for other favors, rather than to pass my whole life with him.   95

L. FREE. Innocent freedoms, child, which every fine woman expects to be taken with her, as an acknowledgment of her beauty.

HAR. They are freedoms which, I think, no innocent woman can allow.   100

L. FREE. Romantic to the last degree! Why, you are in the country still, Harriot!

Enter Servant.

SERV. My Lord Trinket, madam.   *Exit.*

L. FREE. I swear now I have a good mind to tell him all you have said.   105

<hr>

[3] A term kindred to 'the vapors.'

<hr>

26] O1O2 *But here comes the girl*; O3O4 *But here she comes.*   54] O1O2 *its*; O3O4 *'tis.*

Enter LORD TRINKET, *in boots, &c. as from the
riding-house.*

Your lordship's most obedient humble servant.

L. TRINK. Your ladyship does me too much honor.
Here I am, *en bottine*, as you see; just come from the
manège. Miss Russet, I am your slave. I declare
it makes me quite happy to find you together.　110
'Pon honor, ma'am (*to* HARRIOT), I begin to conceive great hopes of you: and as for you, Lady
Freelove, I cannot sufficiently commend your assiduity with your fair pupil. She was before possessed of every grace that Nature could be-　115
stow on her, and nobody is so well qualified as your
ladyship, to give her the *bon ton*.

HAR. Compliment and contempt all in a breath!
My lord, I am obliged to you. But, waving my
acknowledgments, give me leave to ask your　120
lordship, whether Nature and the *bon ton* (as you
call it) are so different, that we must give up one
in order to obtain the other?

L. TRINK. Totally opposite, madam. The chief
aim of the *bon ton* is to render persons of　125
family different from the vulgar, for whom indeed
Nature serves very well. For this reason it has, at
various times, been ungenteel to see, to hear, to
walk, to be in good health, and to have twenty other
horrible perfections of Nature. Nature indeed　130
may do very well sometimes. It made *you*, for instance, and it then made something very lovely; and
if you suffer us of quality to give you the *ton*, you
would be absolutely divine. But now — me —
madam — me — Nature never made such a　135
thing as me.

HAR. Why, indeed, I think your lordship has very
few obligations to her.

L. TRINK. Then you really think it's all my own?
I declare now that is a mighty genteel compli-　140
ment. Nay, if you begin to flatter already, you improve apace. 'Pon honor, Lady Freelove, I believe
we shall make something of her at last.

L. FREE. No doubt on't. It is in your lordship's
power to make her a complete woman of fashion　145
at once.

L. TRINK. Hum! Why, ay —

HAR. Your lordship must excuse me. I am of a
very tasteless disposition. I shall never bear to be
carried out of Nature.　150

L. FREE. You are out of Nature now, Harriot!
I am sure no woman but yourself ever objected
to being carried among persons of quality. Would
you believe it, my lord? here has she been a whole
week in town, and would never suffer me to in-　155
troduce her to a rout, an assembly, a concert, or even
to court, or to the opera; nay, would hardly so much
as mix with a living soul that has visited me.

L. TRINK. No wonder, madam, you do not adopt
the manners of persons of fashion, when you　160
will not even honor them with your company. Were
you to make one in our little *coteries*, we should soon
make you sick of the boors and bumpkins of the
horrid country. By the bye, I met a monster at
the riding-house this morning, who gave me　165
some intelligence that will surprise you, concerning
your family.

HAR. What intelligence?

L. FREE. Who was this monster, as your lordship calls him? A curiosity, I dare say.　170

L. TRINK. This monster, madam, was formerly
my head groom, and had the care of all my running horses; but growing most abominably surly and
extravagant, as you know all those fellows do, I
turned him off; and ever since my brother　175
Slouch Trinket has had the care of my stud, rides
all my principal matches himself, and —

HAR. Dear my lord, don't talk of your groom and
your brother, but tell me the news. Do you know
anything of my father?　180

L. TRINK. Your father, madam, is now in town.
This fellow, you must know, is now groom to
Sir Harry Beagle, your sweet rural swain, and informed me, that his master and your father were
running all over the town in quest of you; and　185
that he himself had orders to enquire after you; for
which reason, I suppose, he came to the riding-house
stables to look after a horse, thinking it, to be sure,
a very likely place to meet you. Your father perhaps is gone to see you at the Tower, or at　190
Westminster Abbey, which is all the idea he has of
London; and your faithful lover is probably cheap-
ening[1] a hunter, and drinking strong beer, at the
Horse and Jockey in Smithfield.

L. FREE. The whole set admirably disposed　195
of!

HAR. Did not your lordship inform him where
I was?

L. TRINK. Not I, 'pon honor, madam. That I
left to their own ingenuity to discover.　200

L. FREE. And pray, my lord, where in this town
have this polite company bestowed themselves?

L. TRINK. They lodge, madam, of all places in the
world, at the Bull and Gate Inn in Holborn.

L. FREE. Ha, ha, ha! the Bull and Gate!　205
incomparable! What, have they brought any hay
or cattle to town?

L. TRINK. Very well, Lady Freelove, very well,
indeed! There they are, like so many graziers; and
there, it seems, they have learnt that this lady　210
is certainly in London.

HAR. Do, dear madam, send a card directly to

---

[1] Bargaining for.

my father, informing him where I am, and that your ladyship would be glad to see him here. For my part, I dare not venture into his presence, 215 till you have in some measure pacified him; but, for heaven's sake, desire him not to bring that wretched fellow along with him.

L. TRINK. Wretched fellow! O ho! *courage,* milor[d] Trinket! (*Aside.*) 220

L. FREE. I'll send immediately. Who's there?

Enter Servant.

SERV. (*apart to* LADY FREELOVE). Sir Harry Beagle is below, madam.

L. FREE. (*apart to Servant*). I am not at home. Have they let him in? 225

SERV. Yes, madam.

L. FREE. How abominably unlucky this is! Well, then show him into my dressing-room. I will come to him there. *Exit Servant.*

L. TRINK. Lady Freelove! no engagement, I 230 hope. We won't part with you, 'pon honor.

L. FREE. The worst engagement in the world; a pair of musty old prudes! Lady Formal and Miss Prate.

L. TRINK. O, the beldams! as nauseous as 235 ipecacuanha, 'pon honor.

L. FREE. Lud! lud! what shall I do with them? Why do these foolish women come troubling me now? I must wait on them in the dressing-room; and you must excuse the card, Harriot, till they 240 are gone. I'll dispatch them as soon as I can; but heaven knows when I shall get rid of them, for they are both everlasting gossips; though the words come from her ladyship one by one, like drops from a still, while the other tiresome woman overwhelms 245 us with a flood of impertinence. Harriot, you'll entertain his lordship till I return. *Exit.*

L. TRINK. [*aside*]. Gone! 'Egad, my affairs here begin to grow very critical. The father in town! lover in town! surrounded by enemies! What 250 shall I do? I have nothing for it but a *coup de main!* (*To* HARRIOT.) 'Pon honor, I am not sorry for the coming in of these old tabbies, and am much obliged to her ladyship for leaving us such an agreeable *tête-à-tête.* 255

HAR. Your lordship will find me extremely bad company.

L. TRINK. Not in the least, my dear! We'll entertain ourselves one way or other, I'll warrant you. 'Egad! I think it a mighty good opportunity 260 to establish a better acquaintance with you.

HAR. I don't understand you.

L. TRINK. No? why then I'll speak plainer.

(*Pausing, and looking her full in the face.*) You are an amazing fine creature, 'pon honor. 265

《HAR. Sir! — How!

《L. TRINK. O, ma'am, I'll show you how.》

HAR. If this be your lordship's polite conversation, I shall leave you to amuse yourself in soliloquy. (*Going.*) 270

L. TRINK. No, no, no, madam, that must not be. (*Stopping her.*) This place, my passion, the opportunity, all conspire 《to make me happy, and you must not deny me.》

HAR. How, sir! you don't intend to do me 275 any violence.

L. TRINK. 'Pon honor, ma'am, it will be doing great violence to myself, if I do not. You must excuse me. (*Struggling with her.*)

HAR. Help! help! murder! help! 280

L. TRINK. Your yelping will signify nothing; nobody will come. (*Struggling.*)

HAR. For heaven's sake! Sir! my lord!
(*Noise within.*)

L. TRINK. Pox on't, what noise? Then I must be quick. (*Still struggling.*) 285

HAR. Murder! help! help!

Enter CHARLES, *hastily.*

CHAR. What do I hear? my Harriot's voice calling for help? Ha! (*Seeing them.*) Is it possible? Turn, ruffian! I'll find you employment. (*Drawing.*)

L. TRINK. You are a most impertinent 290 scoundrel, and I'll whip you through the lungs, 'pon honor.

(*They fight,* HARRIOT *runs out screaming* Help! &c. *Then*)

Enter LADY FREELOVE, SIR HARRY BEAGLE, *and Servants.*

L. FREE. How's this? swords drawn in my house! Part them! (*They are parted.*) This is the most impudent thing! 295

L. TRINK. Well, rascal, I shall find a time; I know you, sir!

CHAR. The sooner the better. I know your lordship too.

SIR H. I'faith, madam. (*To* LADY FREE- 300 LOVE.) We had like to have been in at the death.

L. FREE. What is all this? Pray, sir, what is the meaning of your coming hither to raise this disturbance? Do you take my house for a brothel? (*To* CHARLES.) 305

CHAR. Not I, indeed, madam! but I believe his lordship does.

L. TRINK. Impudent scoundrel!

L. FREE. Your conversation, sir, is as insolent

248–252] O1 omits Gone — coup de main; O2 begins [To HARRIOT]: 'Pon honor, gone, and omits 'Pon honor in line 252.
265] O1 a damned fine piece; O2O3O4 an amazing fine creature.
266–267; 273–274] Passages in guillemets 《   》 are included in O1 and D.   272] O1 that chamber for my passion.

as your behavior. Who are you? What 310
brought you here?

CHAR. I am one, madam, always ready to draw
my sword in defence of innocence in distress, and
more especially in the cause of that lady I delivered
from his lordship's fury; in search of whom I 315
troubled your ladyship's house.

L. FREE. Her lover, I suppose? or what?

CHAR. At your ladyship's service; though not
quite so violent in my passion as his lordship there.

L. TRINK. Impertinent rascal! 320

L. FREE. You shall be made to repent of this
insolence.

L. TRINK. Your ladyship may leave that to me.

CHAR. Ha, ha!

SIR H. But pray what is become of the lady 325
all this while? Why, Lady Freelove, you told me
she was not here, and, i'faith, I was just drawing
off another way, if I had not heard the view-hollow.[1]

L. FREE. You shall see her immediately, sir.
Who's there? 330

Enter Servant.

Where is Miss Russet?

SERV. Gone out, madam.

L. FREE. Gone out! where?

SERV. I don't know, madam. But she ran down
the back stairs crying for help, crossed the 335
servants' hall in tears, and took a chair at the door.

L. FREE. Blockheads! to let her go out in a chair
alone! Go and enquire after her immediately.

Exit Servant.

SIR H. Gone! what a pox had I just run her down,
and is the little puss stole away at last? 340

L. FREE. (*to* SIR HARRY). Sir, if you will walk in
with his lordship and me, perhaps you may hear
some tidings of her; though it is most probable
she may be gone to her father. I don't know any
other friend she has in town. 345

CHAR. I am heartily glad she is gone. She is safer
anywhere than in this house.

L. FREE. Mighty well, sir! My lord, Sir Harry,
I attend you.

L. TRINK. You shall hear from me, sir! 350
　　　　　　　　　　　　　　(*To* CHARLES.)

CHAR. Very well, my lord!

SIR H. Stole away! pox on't! stole away.

Exeunt SIR HARRY *and* LORD TRINKET.

Manent CHARLES *and* LADY FREELOVE.

L. FREE. Before I follow the company, give me
leave to tell you, sir, that your behavior here has
been so extraordinary — 355

[1] Huntsman's shout on seeing the fox break cover; view-halloo.

CHAR. My treatment here, madam, has indeed
been very extraordinary.

L. FREE. Indeed! Well; no matter. Permit me
to acquaint you, sir that there lies your way out, and
that the greatest favor you can do me is to 360
leave the house immediately.

CHAR. That your ladyship may depend on.
Since you have put Miss Russet to flight, you may
be sure of not being troubled with my company.
I'll after her immediately. I can't rest till I 365
know what is become of her.

L. FREE. If she has any regard for her reputation,
she'll never put herself into such hands as yours.

CHAR. O, madam, there can be no doubt of her
regard to that, by her leaving your ladyship. 370

《L. FREE. Insolent monster!

《CHAR. Poor lady!

《L. FREE. Begone this moment.

《CHAR. Immediately — My dear Harriot! Would
I could have spoken with her! — But she was 375
in danger, and I delivered her. — That's comfort
still — and yet —》

L. FREE. Leave my house!

CHAR. Directly. A charming house! and a
charming lady of the house too! ha! ha! 380

L. FREE. Vulgar fellow!

CHAR. Fine lady!　　　　　　　*Exeunt severally.*

ACT III

SCENE [I]

LADY FREELOVE'S.

Enter LADY FREELOVE, *and* LORD TRINKET.

L. TRINK. *Doucement, doucement,* my dear Lady
Freelove! excuse me! I meant no harm, 'pon honor.

L. FREE. Indeed, indeed, my Lord Trinket, this
is absolutely intolerable. What! to offer rudeness
to a young lady in my house! What will the 5
world say of it?

L. TRINK. Just what the world pleases. It does
not signify a doit what they say. However, I ask
pardon; but, 'egad, I thought it was the best way.

L. FREE. For shame, for shame, my lord! I 10
am quite hurt at your want of discretion.

《L. TRINK. 'Pon honor, now, I am always for
taking them by a *coup de main.* I never knew it
fail before.》

L. FREE. Leave the whole conduct of this 15
affair to me, or I'll have done with it at once. How
strangely you have acted! There I went out of the
way on purpose to serve you, by keeping off that
looby Sir Harry Beagle, and preventing him or her
father from seeing the girl, till we had some 20

chance of managing her ourselves, and then you chose to make a disturbance, and spoiled all.

L. TRINK. Devil take Sir Harry, and t'other scoundrel too! That they should come driving hither just at so critical an instant! and that the 25 wild little thing should take wing, and fly away the Lord knows whither!

L. FREE. Ay! and there again you were indiscreet past redemption. To let her know that her father was in town, and where he was to be 30 found too! For there I am confident she must be gone, as she is not acquainted with one creature in London.

L. TRINK. Why, a father is in these cases the *pis-aller,*[1] I must confess. 'Pon honor, Lady 35 Freelove, I can scarce believe this obstinate girl a relation of yours. Such narrow notions! I'll swear, there is less trouble in getting ten women of the *première volée,*[2] than in conquering the scruples of a silly girl in that style of life.   40

L. FREE. Come, come, my lord, a truce with your reflections on my niece! Let us consider what is best to be done.

L. TRINK. E'en just what your ladyship thinks proper. For my part, I am entirely *dérangé.*   45

L. FREE. Will you submit to be governed by me then?

L. TRINK. I'll be all obedience: your ladyship's slave, 'pon honor.

L. FREE. Why then, as this is rather an ugly 50 affair in regard to me, as well as your lordship, and may make some noise, I think it absolutely necessary, merely to save appearances, that you should wait on her father, palliate matters as well as you can, and make a formal repetition of your pro- 55 posal of marriage.

L. TRINK. Your ladyship is perfectly in the right. You are quite *au fait* of the affair. It shall be done immediately; and then your reputation will be safe, and my conduct justified to all the 60 world. But should the old rustic continue as stubborn as his daughter, your ladyship, I hope, has no objections to my being a little *rusé;*[3] for I must have her, 'pon honor.

L. FREE. Not in the least.   65

L. TRINK. Or if a good opportunity should offer, and the girl should be still untractable —

L. FREE. Do what you will; I wash my hands of it; she's out of my care now, you know. But you must beware of your rivals. One, you know, is 70 in the house with her, and the other will lose no opportunities of getting to her.

L. TRINK. As to the fighting gentleman, I shall

cut out work for him in his own way. I'll send him a *petit billet* to-morrow morning, and then there 75 can be no great difficulty in outwitting her bumpkin father, and the baronet.

Enter Servant.

SERV. Captain O'Cutter to wait on your ladyship.

L. FREE. O the hideous fellow! The Irish sailorman, for whom I prevailed on your lordship to 80 get the post of a regulating captain.[4] I suppose he is come to load me with his odious thanks. I won't be troubled with him now.

L. TRINK. Let him in, by all means. He is the best creature to laugh at in nature. He is a 85 perfect sea-monster, and always looks and talks as if he was upon deck. Besides, a thought strikes me; he may be of use.

L. FREE. Well, send the creature up then.

Exit Servant.

But what fine thought is this?   90

L. TRINK. A *coup de maître,* 'pon honor! I intend — but hush! here the porpoise comes.

Enter CAPTAIN O'CUTTER.

L. FREE. Captain, your humble servant! I am very glad to see you.

O'CUT. I am much obloged to you, my lady! 95 Upon my conscience, the wind favors me at all points. I have no sooner got under way to tank your ladyship, but I have borne down upon my noble friend his lordship too. I hope your lordship's well.

L. TRINK. Very well, I thank you, captain. 100 But you seem to be hurt in the service. What is the meaning of that patch over your right eye?

O'CUT. Some advanced wages from my new post, my lord! This pressing[5] is hot work, though it entitles us to no smart-money.[6]   105

L. FREE. And pray in what perilous adventure did you get that scar, captain?

O'CUT. Quite out of my ilement, indeed, my lady! I got it in an engagement by land. A day or two ago I spied tree stout fellows, belonging 110 to a marchant-man. They made down Wapping. I immediately gave my lads the signal to chase, and we bore down right upon them. They tacked, and lay to. We gave them a tundering broadside, which they resaved like men; and one of them 115 made use of small arms, which carried off the weadermost corner of Ned Gage's hat; so I immediately stood in with him, and raked him, but resaved a wound on my starboord eye, from the stock of the pistol. However, we took them all, and they 120

---

[1] Last resource.   [2] High rank.   [3] Sly, designing.

[4] Officer superintending the raising of seamen.
[5] Impressing for naval service.
[6] Compensation for injuries incurred on duty.

now lie under the hatches, with fifty more, a-boord a tinder off the Tower.

L. TRINK. Well done, noble captain! But, however, you will soon have better employment; for I think the next step to your present post is 125 commonly a ship.

O'CUT. The sooner the better, my lord. Honest Terence O'Cutter shall never flinch, I'll warrant you; and has had as much seen-sarvice as any man in the navy. 130

L. TRINK. You may depend on my good offices, captain. But in the meantime it is in your power to do me a favor.

O'CUT. A favor, my lord! Your lordship does me honor. I would go round the world, from one 135 ind to the other, by day or by night, to sarve your lordship, or my good lady here.

L. TRINK. Dear madam, the luckiest thought in nature. (*Apart to* LADY FREELOVE.) The favor I have to ask of you, captain, need not carry 140 you so far out of your way. The whole affair is, that there are a couple of impudent fellows at an inn in Holborn, who have affronted me, and you would oblige me infinitely, by pressing them into his Majesty's service. 145

L. FREE. Now I understand you. Admirable! (*Apart to* LORD TRINKET.)

O'CUT. With all my heart, my lord, and tank you too, fait. But, by the bye, I hope they are not housekeepers, or freemen of the city. There's the devil to pay in meddling with them; they 150 bodder one so about liberty and property and stuff. It was but t'other day that Jack Trowser was carried before my lord-mayor, and lost above a twelve-month's pay, for nothing at all — at all.

L. TRINK. I'll take care you shall be brought 155 into no trouble. These fellows were formerly my grooms. If you'll call on me in the morning, I'll go with you to the place.

O'CUT. I'll be with your lordship, and bring with me four or five as pretty boys as you'd 160 wish to clap your two lucking eyes upon of a summer's day.

L. TRINK. I am much obliged to you. But, captain, I have another little favor to beg of you.

O'CUT. Upon my shoul, and I'll do it. 165

L. TRINK. What, before you know it?

O'CUT. Fore and aft, my lord.

L. TRINK. A gentleman has offended me in a point of honor.

O'CUT. Cut his troat. 170

L. TRINK. Will you carry him a letter from me?

O'CUT. Indeed and I will; and I'll take you in tow too, and you shall engage him yard-arm and yard-arm.

L. TRINK. Why then, captain, you'll come 175 a little earlier to-morrow morning than you proposed, that you may attend him with my *billet*, before you proceed on the other affair.

O'CUT. Never fear it, my lord! Your servant! My ladyship, your humble servant! 180

L. FREE. Captain, yours! Pray give my service to my friend Mrs. O'Cutter. How does she do?

O'CUT. I tank your ladyship's axing: the dear crature is purely tight and well.

L. TRINK. How many children have you, 185 captain?

O'CUT. Four, and please your lordship, and another upon the stocks.

L. TRINK. When it is launched, I hope to be at the christening. I'll stand godfather, captain. 190

O'CUT. Your lordship's very good.

L. TRINK. Well, you'll come to-morrow.

O'CUT. O, I'll not fail, my lord! Little Terence O'Cutter never fails, fait, when a troat is to be cut.

Exit.

L. FREE. Ha, ha, ha! But sure you don't 195 intend to ship off both her father and her country lover for the Indies?

L. TRINK. O no! only let them contemplate the inside of a ship for a day or two.

L. FREE. Well, but after all, my lord, this 200 is a very bold undertaking. I don't think you'll be able to put it in practice.

L. TRINK. Nothing so easy, 'pon honor. To press a gentleman, a man of quality, one of us, would not be so easy, I grant you. But these fellows, 205 you know, have not half so decent an appearance as one of my footmen; and from their behavior, conversation, and dress, it is very possible to mistake them for grooms and ostlers.

L. FREE. There may be something in that, 210 indeed. But what use do you propose to make of this stratagem?

L. TRINK. Every use in nature. This artifice must at least take them out of the way for some time; and in the meanwhile measures may be 215 concerted to carry off the girl.

Enter Servant.

SERV. Mrs. Oakly, madam, is at the door, in her chariot, and desires to have the honor of speaking to your ladyship on particular business.

L. TRINK. Mrs. Oakly! What can that 220 jealous-pated woman want with you?

L. FREE. No matter what. I hate her mortally. Let her in. *Exit Servant.*

L. TRINK. What wind blows her hither?

L. FREE. A wind that must blow us some 225 good.

L. Trink. How? I was amazed you chose to see her.

L. Free. How can you be so slow of apprehension? She comes, you may be sure, on some 230 occasion relating to this girl; in order to assist young Oakly perhaps, to soothe me, and gain intelligence, and so forward the match; but I'll forbid the banns, I warrant you. Whatever she wants, I'll draw some sweet mischief out of it. But away, 235 away! I think I hear her. Slip down the back-stairs — or — stay — now I think on't, go out this way; meet her, and be sure to make her a very respectful bow, as you go out.

L. Trink. Hush! here she is. 240

Enter Mrs. Oakly.

Lord Trinket *bows, and exit.*

Mrs. Oak. I beg pardon for giving your ladyship this trouble.

L. Free. I am always glad of the honor of seeing Mrs. Oakly.

Mrs. Oak. There is a letter, madam, just 245 come from the country, which has occasioned some alarm in our family. It comes from Mr. Russet.

L. Free. Mr. Russet!

Mrs. Oak. Yes, from Mr. Russet, madam; and is chiefly concerning his daughter. As she has 250 the honor of being related to your ladyship, I took the liberty of waiting on you.

L. Free. She is indeed, as you say, madam, a relation of mine; but after what has happened, I scarce know how to acknowledge her. 255

Mrs. Oak. Has she been so much to blame, then?

L. Free. So much, madam! Only judge for yourself. Though she had been so indiscreet, not to say indecent in her conduct, as to elope from her 260 father, I was in hopes to have hushed up that matter, for the honor of our family. But she has run away from me too, madam; went off in the most abrupt manner, not an hour ago.

Mrs. Oak. You surprise me. Indeed her father, by his letter, seems apprehensive of the worst 265 consequences. But does your ladyship imagine any harm has happened?

L. Free. I can't tell; I hope not; but, indeed, she is a strange girl. You know, madam, young women can't be too cautious in their conduct. She is, 270 I am sorry to declare it, a very dangerous person to take into a family.

Mrs. Oak. Indeed! (*Alarmed.*)

L. Free. If I was to say all I know!

Mrs. Oak. Why, sure, your ladyship knows 275 of nothing that has been carried on clandestinely between her and Mr. Oakly! (*In disorder.*)

L. Free. Mr. Oakly!

Mrs. Oak. Mr. Oakly! no, not Mr. Oakly —

that is, not my husband: I don't mean him — 280 not him — but his nephew, young Mr. Oakly.

L. Free. Jealous of her husband! So, so! now I know my game. (*Aside.*)

Mrs. Oak. But pray, madam, give me leave to ask, was there anything very particular in her 285 conduct, while she was in your ladyship's house?

L. Free. Why, really, considering she was here scarce a week, her behavior was rather mysterious. Letters and messages, to and fro, between her and I don't know who. I suppose you know that 290 Mr. Oakly's nephew has been here, madam.

Mrs. Oak. I was not sure of it. Has he been to wait on your ladyship already on this occasion?

L. Free. To wait on me! The expression is much too polite for the nature of his visit. My 295 Lord Trinket, the nobleman whom you met as you came in, had, you must know, madam, some thoughts of my niece; and as it would have been an advantageous match, I was glad of it: but I believe after what he has been witness to this morn- 300 ing, he will drop all thoughts of it.

Mrs. Oak. I am sorry that any relation of mine should so far forget himself —

L. Free. It's no matter; his behavior indeed, as well as the young lady's, was pretty extraor- 305 dinary. And yet, after all, I don't believe *he* is the object of her affections.

Mrs. Oak. Ha! (*Much alarmed.*)

L. Free. She has certainly an attachment somewhere, a strong one; but his lordship, who was 310 present all the time, was convinced, as well as myself, that Mrs. Oakly's nephew was rather a convenient friend, a kind of go-between, than a lover. Bless me, madam, you change color! You seem uneasy! What's the matter? 315

Mrs. Oak. Nothing — madam — nothing! A little shocked that my husband should behave so.

L. Free. Your husband, madam!

Mrs. Oak. His nephew, I mean. His unpardonable rudeness! But I am not well: I am sorry 320 I have given your ladyship so much trouble; I'll take my leave.

L. Free. I declare, madam, you frighten me. Your being so visibly affected makes me quite uneasy: I hope I have not said anything — I 325 really don't believe your husband is in fault. Men, to be sure, allow themselves strange liberties. But I think, nay I am sure, it cannot be so. It is impossible. Don't let what I have said, have any effect on you. 330

Mrs. Oak. No, it has not — I have no idea of such a thing. Your ladyship's most obedient! (*Going, returns.*) But sure, madam, you have not heard, or don't know anything —

L. Free. Come, come, Mrs. Oakly, I see 335

how it is, and it would not be kind to say all I know.
I dare not tell you what I have heard.   Only be on
your guard: there can be no harm in that.   Do you
be against giving the girl any countenance, and see
what effect it has.   340

MRS. OAK. I will.   I am much obliged — But
does it appear to your ladyship, then, that Mr.
Oakly —

L. FREE. No, not at all.   Nothing in't, I dare say.
I would not create uneasiness in a family: but 345
I am a woman myself, have been married, and can't
help feeling for you.   But don't be uneasy; there's
nothing in't, I dare say.

MRS. OAK. I think so.   Your ladyship's humble
servant.   350

L. FREE. Your servant, madam.   Pray don't be
alarmed; I must insist on your not making yourself
uneasy.

MRS. OAK. Not at all alarmed; not in the least
uneasy.   Your most obedient.   *Exit.* 355

L. FREE. Ha, ha, ha!   There she goes, brimful
of anger and jealousy, to vent it all on her husband.
Mercy on the poor man!

Enter LORD TRINKET.

Bless me, my lord!   I thought you were gone.

L. TRINK. Only into the next room.   My 360
curiosity would not let me stir a step further.   I
heard it all, and was never more diverted in my life,
'pon honor.   Ha, ha, ha!

L. FREE. How the silly creature took it!   Ha,
ha, ha!   365

L. TRINK. Ha, ha, ha!   My dear Lady Freelove, you have a deal of ingenuity, a deal of *esprit,*
'pon honor.

L. FREE. A little shell thrown into the enemy's
works, that's all.   370

BOTH. Ha, ha, ha, ha!

L. FREE. But I must leave you.   I have twenty
visits to pay.   You'll let me know how you succeed
in your secret expedition.

L. TRINK. That you may depend on.   375

L. FREE. Remember then that to-morrow morning I expect to see you.   At present your lordship
will excuse me.   Who's there? (*Calling to the
Servants.*) Send Epingle into my dressing-room.
                                                         Exit.

LORD TRINKET solus.

L. TRINK. So!   If O'Cutter and his myr- 380
midons are alert, I think I can't fail of success; and
then *prenez garde,* mademoiselle Harriot!   This is
one of the drollest circumstances in nature.   Here is
my Lady Freelove, a woman of sense, a woman that
knows the world too, assisting me in this de- 385
sign.   I never knew her ladyship so much out.

How, in the name of wonder, can she imagine that a
man of quality, or any man else, 'egad, would marry
a fine girl, after — Not I, 'pon honor.   No, no!
when I have had the *entamure,*[1] let who will 390
take the rest of the loaf.   *Exit.*

[SCENE II]

Scene changes to MR. OAKLY'S.

Enter HARRIOT, *following a Servant.*

HAR. Not at home! are you sure that Mrs. Oakly
is not at home, sir?

SERV. She is just gone out, madam.

HAR. I have something of consequence — If you
will give me leave, sir, I will wait till she returns.   5

SERV. You would not see her, if you did, madam.
She has given positive orders not to be interrupted
with any company to-day.

HAR. Sure, sir, if you were to let her know that I
had particular business —   10

SERV. I should not dare to trouble her, indeed,
madam.

HAR. How unfortunate this is!   What can I do?
Pray, sir, can I see *Mr.* Oakly then?

SERV. Yes, madam: I'll acquaint my master, 15
if you please.

HAR. Pray do, sir.

SERV. Will you favor me with your name,
madam?

HAR. Be pleased, sir, to let him know that a 20
lady desires to speak with him.

SERV. I shall, madam.   *Exit Servant.*

HARRIOT sola.

[HAR.] I wish I could have seen Mrs. Oakly!
What an unhappy situation am I reduced to!   What
will the world say of me? and yet what could I 25
do?   To remain at Lady Freelove's was impossible.
Charles, I must own, has this very day revived much
of my tenderness for him; and yet I dread the wildness of his disposition.   I must now, however, solicit
Mr. Oakly's protection; a circumstance (all 30
things considered) rather disagreeable to a delicate
mind, and which nothing, but the absolute necessity
of it, could excuse.   Good heavens, what a multitude of difficulties and distresses am I thrown into,
by my father's obstinate perseverance to force 35
me into a marriage which my soul abhors!

Enter OAKLY.

OAK. (*at entering*). Where is this lady? (*Seeing
her.*) Bless me, Miss Russet, is it you? — (*Aside.*)
Was ever anything so unlucky? [*Aloud.*] Is it possible, madam, that I see you here?   40

---

[1] First cut.

HAR. It is too true, sir! and the occasion on which I am now to trouble you, is so much in need of an apology, that —

OAK. Pray make none, madam! — If my wife should return before I get her out of the house 45 again!   (*Aside.*)

HAR. I dare say, sir, you are not quite a stranger to the attachment your nephew has professed to me.

OAK. I am not, madam! I hope Charles has not been guilty of any baseness toward you. If he 50 has, I'll never see his face again.

HAR. I have no cause to accuse him. But —

OAK. But what, madam? Pray be quick! — The very person in the world I would not have seen!
(*Aside.*)

HAR. You seem uneasy, sir.   55

OAK. No, nothing at all. Pray go on, madam.

HAR. I am at present, sir, through a concurrence of strange accidents, in a very unfortunate situation; and do not know what will become of me, without your assistance.   60

OAK. I'll do everything in my power to serve you. I know of your leaving your father, by a letter we have had from him. Pray let me know the rest of your story.

HAR. My story, sir, is very short. When I 65 left my father's, I came immediately to London, and took refuge with a relation, where, instead of meeting with the protection I expected, I was alarmed with the most infamous designs upon my honor. It is not an hour ago since your nephew rescued me from 70 the attempts of a villain. I tremble to think that I left him actually engaged in a duel.

OAK. He is very safe. He has just sent home the chariot from the St. Alban's tavern, where he dines to-day. But what are your commands for me, 75 madam?

HAR. I am heartily glad to hear of his safety. The favor, sir, I would now request of you is, that you will suffer me to remain for a few days in your house.

OAK. Madam!   80

HAR. And that, in the meantime, you will use your utmost endeavors to reconcile me to my father, without his forcing me into a marriage with Sir Harry Beagle.

OAK. This is the most perplexing situation! 85 Why did not Charles take care to bestow you properly?

HAR. It is most probable, sir, that I should not have consented to such a measure myself. The world is but too apt to censure, even without a 90 cause: and if you are so kind as to admit me into your house, I must desire you not to consider Mr. Oakly in any other light than as your nephew; as, in my present circumstances, I have particular objections to it.   95

OAK. What an unlucky circumstance! Upon my soul, madam, I would do anything to serve you; but being in my house creates a difficulty that —

HAR. I hope, sir, you do not doubt the truth of what I have told you.   100

OAK. I religiously believe every tittle of it, madam; but I have particular family considerations, that —

HAR. Sure, sir, you cannot suspect me to be base enough to form any connections in your family, 105 contrary to your inclinations, while I am living in your house.

OAK. Such connections, madam, would do me and all my family great honor. I never dreamed of any scruples on that account. What can I do? 110 Let me see — let me see — suppose — (*Pausing.*)

Enter MRS. OAKLY *behind, in a capuchin,[1] tippet, &c.*

MRS. OAK. I am sure I heard the voice of a woman conversing with my husband. Ha! (*Seeing* HARRIOT.) It is so, indeed! Let me contain myself! I'll listen.   115

HAR. I see, sir, you are not inclined to serve me. Good heavens, what am I reserved to? Why, why did I leave my father's house, to expose myself to greater distresses?   (*Ready to weep.*)

OAK. I would do anything for your sake; in- 120 deed I would. So, pray be comforted; and I'll think of some proper place to bestow you in.

MRS. OAK. So, so!

HAR. What place can be so proper as your own house?   125

OAK. My dear madam, I — I —

MRS. OAK. My *dear* madam! mighty well!

OAK. Hush! hark! what noise? No, nothing But I'll be plain with you, madam; we may be interrupted. The family consideration I hinted at, 130 is nothing else than my wife. She is a little unhappy in her temper, madam; and if you were to be admitted into the house, I don't know what might be the consequence.

MRS. OAK. Very fine!   135

HAR. My behavior, sir —

OAK. My dear life, it would be impossible for you to behave in such a manner as not to give her suspicion.

HAR. But if your nephew, sir, took every- 140 thing upon himself —

OAK. Still that would not do, madam. Why, this very morning, when the letter came from your father, though I positively denied any knowledge of it, and Charles owned it, yet it was almost im- 145 possible to pacify her.

MRS. OAK. The letter! How have I been bubbled?[2]

HAR. What shall I do? What will become of me?

---

[1] Cloak and hood (like a friar's).   [2] Deceived.

OAK. Why, look ye, my dear madam, since 150
my wife is so strong an objection, it is absolutely impossible for me to take you into the house. Nay, if
I had not known she was gone out, just before you
came, I should be uneasy at your being here even
now. So we must manage as well as we can: 155
I'll take a private lodging for you a little way off,
unknown to Charles or my wife, or anybody; and if
Mrs. Oakly should discover it at last, why the whole
matter will light upon Charles, you know.

MRS. OAK. Upon Charles! 160

HAR. How unhappy is my situation! (*Weeping.*)
I am ruined forever.

OAK. Ruined! not at all. Such a thing as this
has happened to many a young lady before you, and
all has been well again. Keep up your spirits! 165
I'll contrive, if I possibly can, to visit you every day.

MRS. OAK. (*advancing*). Will you so? O, Mr.
Oakly! have I discovered you at last? I'll visit you,
indeed. And you, my *dear* madam, I'll —

HAR. Madam, I don't understand — 170

MRS. OAK. I understand the whole affair, and
have understood it for some time past. You shall
have a private lodging, miss! It is the fittest place
for you, I believe. How dare you look me in the
face? 175

OAK. For heaven's sake, my love, don't be so
violent. You are quite wrong in this affair; you
don't know who you are talking to. That lady is a
person of fashion.

MRS. OAK. Fine fashion, indeed! To seduce 180
other women's husbands!

HAR. Dear madam, how can you imagine —

OAK. I tell you, my dear, this is the young lady
that Charles —

MRS. OAK. Mighty well! But that won't 185
do, sir! Did not I hear you lay the whole intrigue
together? Did not I hear your fine plot of throwing
all the blame upon Charles?

OAK. Nay, be cool a moment. You must know,
my dear, that the letter which came this 190
morning, related to this lady.

MRS. OAK. I know it.

OAK. And since that, it seems, Charles has been
so fortunate as to —

MRS. OAK. O, you deceitful man! that trick 195
is too stale to pass again with me. It is plain now
what you meant by your proposing to take her into
the house this morning. But the gentlewoman
could introduce herself, I see.

OAK. Fie, fie, my dear! she came on purpose 200
to enquire for you.

MRS. OAK. For me! Better and better! Did
not she watch her opportunity, and come to you just
as I went out? But I am obliged to you for your
visit, madam. It is sufficiently paid. Pray, 205
don't let me detain you.

OAK. For shame, for shame, Mrs. Oakly! How
can you be so absurd? Is this proper behavior to a
lady of her character!

MRS. OAK. I have heard her character. Go, 210
my fine runaway madam! Now you've eloped from
your father, and run away from your aunt, go! You
shan't stay here, I promise you.

OAK. Prithee, be quiet. You don't know what
you are doing. She shall stay. 215

OAK. She sha'n't stay a minute.

OAK. She shall stay a minute, an hour, a day, a
week, a month, a year! 'Sdeath, madam, she shall
stay forever, if I choose it.

MRS. OAK. How! 220

HAR. For heaven's sake, sir, let me go. I am
frighted to death.

OAK. Don't be afraid, madam! She shall stay, I
insist upon it.

RUSSET (*within*). I tell you, sir, I will go up. 225
I am sure that the lady is here, and nothing shall
hinder me.

HAR. O, my father, my father! (*Faints away.*)

OAK. See! she faints. (*Catching her.*) Ring the
bell! Who's there? 230

MRS. OAK. What, take her in your arms too! I
have no patience.

Enter RUSSET *and Servants.*

RUS. Where is this — Ha! fainting! (*Running to
her.*) O, my dear Harriot! my child! my child!

OAK. Your coming so abruptly shocked her 235
spirits. But she revives. How do you, madam?

HAR. (*to* RUSSET). O, sir!

RUS. O, my dear girl! how could you run away
from your father, that loves you with such fondness!
But I was sure I should find you here. 240

MRS. OAK. There, there! Sure he should find her
here! Did not I tell you so? Are not you a wicked
man, to carry on such base underhand doings, with a
gentleman's daughter?

RUS. Let me tell you, sir, whatever you may 245
think of the matter, I shall not easily put up with
this behavior. How durst you encourage my daughter to an elopement, and receive her in your house?

MRS. OAK. There, mind that! The thing is as
plain as the light. 250

OAK. I tell you, you misunderstand —

RUS. Look you, Mr. Oakly, I shall expect satis-
faction from your family for so gross an affront.
Zounds, sir, I am not to be used ill by any man in
England! 255

HAR. My dear sir, I can assure you —

RUS. Hold your tongue, girl! You'll put me in a
passion.

OAK. Sir, this is all a mistake.

RUS. A mistake! Did not I find her in your 260
house?

OAK. Upon my soul, she has not been in the house above —

MRS. OAK. Did not I hear you say you would take her a lodging? a private lodging?   265

OAK. Yes; but that —

RUS. Has not this affair been carried on a long time, in spite of my teeth?

OAK. Sir, I never troubled myself —

MRS. OAK. Never troubled yourself! Did   270 not you insist on her staying in the house, whether I would or not?

OAK. No.

RUS. Did not you send to meet her, when she came to town?   275

OAK. No.

MRS. OAK. Did not you deceive me about the letter this morning?

OAK. No, no, no. I tell you, no.

MRS. OAK. Yes, yes, yes. I tell you, yes.   280

RUS. Sha'n't I believe my own eyes?

MRS. OAK. Sha'n't I believe my own ears?

OAK. I tell you, you are both deceived.

RUS. Zounds, sir, I'll have satisfaction.

MRS. OAK. I'll stop these fine doings, I war-   285 rant you.

OAK. 'Sdeath, you will not let me speak! And you are both alike, I think. I wish you were married to one another, with all my heart.

MRS. OAK. Mighty well! mighty well!   290

RUS. I shall soon find a time to talk with you.

OAK. Find a time to talk! You have talked enough now for all your lives.

MRS. OAK. Very fine! Come along, sir! Leave that lady with her father. Now she is in the   295 properest hands.   *Exit.*

OAK. I wish I could leave you in his hands. (*Going, returns.*) I shall follow you, madam! One word with you, sir! The height of your passion, and Mrs. Oakly's strange misapprehension of this   300 whole affair, makes it impossible to explain matters to you at present. I will do it when you please, and how you please.   *Exit.*

Manent RUSSET *and* HARRIOT.

RUS. Yes, yes; I'll have satisfaction. — So, madam! I have found you at last. You have   305 made a fine confusion here.

HAR. I have, indeed, been the innocent cause of a great deal of confusion.

RUS. Innocent! What business had you to be running hither after —   310

HAR. My dear sir, you misunderstand the whole affair. I have not been in this house half an hour.

RUS. Zounds, girl, don't put me in a passion! You know I love you; but a lie puts me in a passion! But come along; we'll leave this house directly.   315 (CHARLES *singing without.*) Heyday! what now?

After a noise without, enter CHARLES, *drunk.*

CHAR. *But my wine neither nurses nor babies can bring,*
   And a big-bellied bottle's a mighty good thing. (*Singing.*)

What's here, a woman? Harriot! Impossible! My dearest, sweetest Harriot! I have been   320 looking all over the town for you, and at last, when I was tired — and weary — and disappointed — why then the honest Major and I sat down together, to drink your health in pint bumpers.
                    (*Running up to her.*)

RUS. Stand off! How dare you take any lib-   325 erties with my daughter before me? Zounds, sir, I'll be the death of you!

CHAR. Ha, 'squire Russet too! You jolly old cock, how do you? But, Harriot! my dear girl! (*Taking hold of her.*) My life, my soul, my —   330

RUS. Let her go, sir! Come away, Harriot! Leave him this instant, or I'll tear you asunder.
                    (*Pulling her.*)

HAR. There needs no violence to tear me from a man who could disguise himself in such a gross man-ner, at a time when he knew I was in the utmost   335 distress. (*Disengages herself, and exit with* RUSSET.)

CHARLES *solus.*

[CHAR.] Only hear me, sir! madam! My dear Harriot! Mr. Russet! Gone! She's gone; and 'egad in very ill humor, and in very bad company! I'll go after her. But hold! I shall only   340 make it worse, as I did, now I recollect, once before. How the devil came they here? Who would have thought of finding her in my own house? My dear turns round with conjectures. I believe I am drunk, very drunk; so 'egad, I'll e'en go and sleep   345 myself sober, and then enquire the meaning of all this. *For, I love Sue, and Sue loves me, &c.*
                    Exit singing.

ACT IV

SCENE [I]

OAKLY'S.

Enter MRS. OAKLY *and* MAJOR OAKLY.

MAJ. Well, well! but, sister!

MRS. OAK. I will know the truth of this matter. Why can't you tell me the whole story?

MAJ. I'll tell you nothing. There's nothing to tell. You know the truth already. Besides,   5 what have I to do with it? Suppose there was a dis-turbance yesterday, what's that to me? Was I here? It's no business of mine.

MRS. OAK. Then why do you study to make it so?

Am I not well assured that this mischief com- 10
menced at your house in the country? And now you
are carrying it on in town.

Maj. This is always the case in family squabbles.
My brother has put you out of humor, and you
choose to vent your spleen upon me. 15

Mrs. Oak. Because I know that you are the occasion of his ill usage. Mr. Oakly never behaved in
such a manner before.

Maj. I! am I the occasion of it?

Mrs. Oak. Yes, you. I am sure on't. 20

Maj. I am glad on't with all my heart.

Mrs. Oak. Indeed!

Maj. Ay, indeed; and you are the more obliged to
me. Come, come, sister, it's time you should reflect
a little. My brother is become a public jest; 25
and by and by, if this foolish affair gets wind, the
whole family will be the subject of town-talk.

Mrs. Oak. And well it may, when you take so
much pains to expose us. The little disquiets and
uneasinesses of other families are kept secret; 30
but here quarrels are fomented, and afterwards industriously made public. And you, sir, you have
done all this. You are my greatest enemy!

Maj. Your truest friend, sister.

Mrs. Oak. But it's no wonder. You have 35
no feelings of humanity, no sense of domestic happiness, no idea of tenderness or attachment to any
woman.

Maj. No idea of plague and disquiet! No, no!
And yet I can love a woman, for all that, heart- 40
ily; as you say, tenderly. But then I always choose
a woman should show a little love for me too.

Mrs. Oak. Cruel insinuation! But I defy your
malice! Mr. Oakly can have no doubt of my affection for him. 45

Maj. Nor I neither! and yet your affection, such
as it is, has all the evil properties of aversion. You
absolutely kill him with kindness. Why, what a life
he leads! He serves for nothing but a mere whet-
stone of your ill humor. 50

Mrs. Oak. Pray now, sir —

Maj. The violence of your temper makes his house
uncomfortable to him, poisons his meals, and breaks
his rest.

Mrs. Oak. I beg, Major Oakly, that — 55

Maj. This it is to have a wife that dotes upon one!
The least trifle kindles your suspicion; you take fire
in an instant, and set the whole family in a blaze.

Mrs. Oak. This is beyond all patience. No, sir,
'tis you are the incendiary; you are the cause of 60
— I can't bear such — (Ready to weep.) From this
instant, sir, I forbid you my house. However Mr.
Oakly may treat me himself, I'll never be made the
sport of all his insolent relations. Exit.

Major Oakly solus.

[Maj.] Yes, yes, I knew I should be turned 65
out of doors. There she goes; back again to my
brother directly. Poor gentleman! 'Slife, if he was
but half the man that I am, I'd engage to keep her
going to and fro all day, like a shuttlecock.

Enter Charles.

What, Charles! 70

Char. O, Major! have you heard of what happened after I left you yesterday?

Maj. Heard! Yes, yes; I have heard it plain
enough. But, poor Charles! Ha, ha, ha, ha!
What a scene of confusion! I would give the 75
world to have been there.

Char. And I would give the world to have been
anywhere else. Cursed fortune!

Maj. To come in so opportunely at the tail of an
adventure! Was not your mistress mighty glad 80
to see you? You were very fond of her, I dare say.

Char. I am upon the rack. Who can tell what
rudeness I might offer her? I can remember nothing! I deserve to lose her. To make myself a beast!
and at such a time too! O, fool, fool, fool! 85

Maj. Prithee, be quiet, Charles! Never vex yourself about nothing; this will all be made up the first
time you see her.

Char. I should dread to see her! And yet the not
knowing where she is, distracts me. Her father 90
may force her to marry Sir Harry Beagle immediately.

Maj. Not he, I promise you. She'd run plum[b]
into your arms first, in spite of her father's teeth.

Char. But then her father's violence, and 95
the mildness of her disposition —

Maj. Mildness! ridiculous! Trust to the spirit of
the sex in her. I warrant you, like all the rest, she'll
have perverseness enough not to do as her father
would have her. 100

Char. Well, well! But then my behavior to her;
to expose myself in such a condition to her again!
the very occasion of our former quarrel!

Maj. Quarrel! ha, ha, ha! What signifies a quarrel with a mistress? Why, the whole affair of 105
making love, as they call it, is nothing but quarrelling
and making it up again. They quarrel o'purpose to
kiss and be friends.

Char. Then, indeed, things seemed to be taking a
fortunate turn. To renew our difference at 110
such a time! just when I had some reason to hope for
a reconciliation. May wine be my poison, if ever
I am drunk again!

Maj. Ay, ay, so every man says the next morning.

Char. Where, where can she be? Her father 115
would hardly have carried her back to Lady Free-

love's, and he has no house in town himself, nor Sir Harry. I don't know what to think. I'll go in search of her, though I don't know where to direct myself.   120

Enter Servant.

SERV. A gentleman, sir, that calls himself Captain O'Cutter, desires to speak with you.

CHAR. Don't trouble me! I'll see nobody: I'm not at home!

SERV. The gentleman says he has very par- 125 ticular business, and he must see you.

CHAR. *What's* his name? *Who* did you say?

SERV. Captain O'Cutter, sir.

CHAR. Captain O'Cutter! I never heard of him before. Do you know anything of him, Major? 130

MAJ. Not I. But you hear he has particular business. I'll leave the room.

CHAR. He can have no business that need be a secret to you. Desire the captain to walk up.

Exit Servant.

What would I give if this unknown captain 135 were to prove a messenger from my Harriot!

Enter CAPTAIN O'CUTTER.

O'CUT. Jontlemen, your sarvant! Is either of your names Charles Oakly, Esq.

CHAR. Charles Oakly, sir, is my name, if you have any business with it.   140

O'CUT. Avast, avast, my dear! I have a little business with your name; but as I was to let nobody know it, I can't mention it, till you clear the decks, fait.   (*Pointing to the* MAJOR.)

CHAR. This gentleman, sir, is my most inti- 145 mate friend, and anything that concerns me may be mentioned before him.

O'CUT. Oh, if he's your friend, my dear, we may do all above-board. It's only about your deciding a deferance with my Lord Trinket. He wants 150 to show you a little warm work; and as I was steering this way, he desired me to fetch you this letter.

(*Giving a letter.*)

MAJ. How, sir, a challenge?

O'CUT. Yes, fait, a challenge. I am to be his lordship's second; and if you are fond of a hot 155 birth, and will come along with that jontleman, we'll all go to it together, and make a little line of battle ahead of our own, my dear!

CHAR. (*reading*). Ha! what's this? This may be useful.   (*Aside.*) 160

MAJ. Sir, I am infinitely obliged to you! A rare fellow this! (*Aside.*) Yes, yes, I'll meet all the good company: I'll be there in my waistcoat and pumps,

and take a morning's breathing with you. Are you very fond of fighting, sir?   165

O'CUT. Indeed and I am. I love it better than salt beef or biscuit. I love it better than grog.

MAJ. But pray, sir, how are you interested in this difference? Do you know what it is about?

O'CUT. Oh, the devil burn me, not I. What 170 signifies what it's about, you know, so we do but tilt a little?

MAJ. What! fight and not know for what?

O'CUT. Whan the signal's out for engaging, what signifies talking?   175

MAJ. I fancy, sir, a duel is a common breakfast with you. I'll warrant now, you have been engaged in many such affairs.

O'CUT. Upon my shoul, and I have; sea or land, it's all one to little Terence O'Cutter. 180 When I was last in Dublin, I fought one jontleman for cheating me out of a tousand pounds; I fought two of the Mermaid's crew about Sally Macguire; tree about politics; and one about the playhouse in Smock-Alley.[1] But, upon my fait, since I am 185 in England, I have done nothing at all, at all!

CHAR. This is lucky! but my transport will discover me. (*Aside.*) Will you be so kind, sir, (*To* O'CUTTER) as to make my compliments to his lordship, and assure him that I shall do myself the 190 honor of waiting on him.

O'CUT. Indeed, and I will. Arrah, my dear, won't you come too?   (*To* MAJOR OAKLY.)

MAJ. Depend upon't. We'll go through the whole exercise; Carte, tierce, and segoon,[2] captain! 195

CHAR. Now to get my intelligence. (*Aside.*) I think the time, sir, his lordship appoints, in his letter, is — a —

O'CUT. You say right — six o'clock.

CHAR. And the place — a — a — is — I 200 think, behind Montague-House?[3]

O'CUT. No, my dear! avast! by the ring in Hyde-Park, fait. I settled it there myself, for fare of interruption.

CHAR. True, as you say, the ring in Hyde- 205 Park: I had forgot. Very well, I'll not fail you, sir.

O'CUT. Devil burn me, nor I. Upon my shoul, little Terence O'Cutter will see fair play, or he'll know the rason. And so, my dear, your sarvant.

Exit.

MAJ. Ha, ha, ha! what a fellow! He loves 210 fighting, like a game-cock.

CHAR. O, uncle! the luckiest thing in the world!

MAJ. What, to have the chance of being run through the body! I desire no such good fortune.

---

[1] In Dublin.   [2] Terms in fencing.
[3] In London.

136] OO *was*.   137] O1O2 *servant*; O3O4 *sarvant*.
167] OO omit *I love . . . grog.*   174] OO *When*.
209] O1 *Servant*; O3O4 *sarvant*.

152] O1 *bring*; O2O3O4 *fetch*.
186] OO *noting*.

CHAR. Wish me joy, wish me joy! I have 215
found her; my dear girl, my Harriot! She is at an
inn in Holborn, Major!

MAJ. Ay! how do you know?

CHAR. Why this dear, delightful, charming, blundering captain has delivered me a wrong letter. 220

MAJ. A wrong letter!

CHAR. Yes, a letter from Lord Trinket to Lady
Freelove.

MAJ. The devil! What are the contents?

CHAR. The news I told you just now, that 225
she's at an inn in Holborn: and, besides, an excuse
from my lord, for not waiting on her ladyship this
morning, according to his promise, as he shall be
entirely taken up with his design upon Harriot.

MAJ. So, so! a plot between the lord and the 230
lady.

CHAR. What his plot is I don't know, but I shall
beg leave to be made a party in it. So perhaps his
lordship and I may meet, and *decide* our *deferance*,
as the captain calls it, before to-morrow morn- 235
ing. There! read, read, man!　　(*Giving the letter.*)

MAJ. (*reading*). Um — um — um — very fine!
And what do you propose doing?

CHAR. To go thither immediately.

MAJ. Then you shall take me with you. 240
Who knows what his lordship's designs may be? I
begin to suspect foul play.

CHAR. No, no; pray mind your own business. If
I find there is any need of your assistance, I'll send
for you. 245

MAJ. You'll manage this affair like a boy now —
go on rashly, with noise and bustle, and fury, and get
yourself into another scrape.

CHAR. No, no; let me alone; I'll go *incog.*; leave
my chariot at some distance; proceed pru- 250
dently, and take care of myself, I warrant you. I
did not imagine that I should ever rejoice at receiving
a challenge; but this is the most fortunate accident
that could possibly have happened. B'ye, b'ye,
uncle!　　*Exit hastily.* 255

MAJOR OAKLY *solus.*

[MAJ.] I don't half approve this; and yet I can
hardly suspect his lordship of any very deep designs
neither. Charles may easily outwit him. Hark ye,
William!　　(*As seeing a servant at some distance.*)

Enter Servant.

SERV. Sir! 260

MAJ. Where's my brother?

SERV. In his study, alone, sir!

MAJ. And how is he, William?

SERV. Pretty well, I believe, sir.

MAJ. Ay, ay, but is he in good humor, or — 265

SERV. I never meddle in family affairs, not I, sir.
　　Exit.

MAJOR OAKLY *solus.*

[MAJ.] Well said, William! No bad hint for me,
perhaps! What a strange world we live in! No two
people in it love one another better than my brother
and sister, and yet the bitterest enemies could 270
not torment each other more heartily. Ah, if he had
but half my spirit! And yet he don't want it neither.
But I know his temper: he pieces out the matter with
maxims, and scraps of philosophy, and odds and ends
of sentences: 'I must live in peace' — 275
'Patience is the best remedy' — 'anything for a
quiet life' — and so on! However, yesterday, to
give him his due, he behaved like a man. Keep it
up, brother! keep it up! or it's all over with you.
Since mischief is on foot, I'll e'en set it forwards 280
on all sides. I'll in to him directly, read him one of
my morning-lectures, and persuade him, if I possibly
can, to go out with me immediately; or work him up
to some open act of rebellion against the sovereign
authority of his lady-wife. Zounds, brother, 285
rant, and roar, and rave, and turn the house out of
the window. If I was a husband! 'Sdeath, what a
pity it is that nobody knows how to manage a wife,
but a bachelor.　　*Exit.*

[SCENE II]

Scene changes to the Bull and Gate Inn.

HARRIOT *sola.*

[HAR.] What will become of me? My father is
enraged, and deaf to all remonstrances; and here I
am to remain, by his positive orders, to receive this
booby baronet's odious addresses. Among all my
distresses, I must confess that Charles's be- 5
havior yesterday is not the least. So wild! so given
up to excesses! And yet, I am ashamed to own it
even to myself, I love him; and death itself shall not
prevail on me to give my hand to Sir Harry. But
here he comes! What shall I do with him? 10

Enter SIR HARRY BEAGLE.

SIR HAR. Your servant, miss! What, not speak?
Bashful mayhap; why then I will. Look'e, miss, I
am a man of few words. What signifies haggling?
It looks just like a dealer. What d'ye think of me
for a husband? I am a tight young fellow — 15
sound wind and limb — free from all natural blemishes, rum all over, damme.

HAR. Sir, I don't understand you. Speak English,
and I'll give you an answer.

SIR H. English! why so I do, and good plain 20
English too. What d'ye think of me for a husband?

That's English, e'nt it? I know none of your French lingo, none of your *parlyvoos*, not I. What d'ye think of me for a husband? The 'squire says you shall marry me.   25

HAR. What shall I say to him? I had best be civil. (*Aside.*) I think, sir, you deserve a much better wife, and beg —

SIR H. Better! No, no, though you're so knowing, I'm not to be taken in so. You're a fine 30 thing: your points are all good.

HAR. Sir Harry! sincerity is above all ceremony. Excuse me, if I declare, I never will be your wife, and if you have a real regard for me, and my happiness, you will give up all pretension to me. Shall I 35 beseech you, sir, to persuade my father not to urge a marriage, to which I am determined never to consent?

SIR H. Ha! how! what! be off! Why, it's a match, miss! it's done and done on both sides.

HAR. For heaven's sake, sir, withdraw your 40 claim to me. I never can be prevailed on — indeed I can't.

SIR H. What, make a match and then draw stakes! That's doing of nothing — Play or pay, all the world over.   45

HAR. Let me prevail on you, sir! I am determined not to marry you, at all events.

SIR H. But your father's determined you shall, miss! so the odds are on my side. I am not quite sure of my horse, but I have the rider hollow. 50

HAR. Your horse, sir! — d'ye take me for — but I forgive you. I beseech you come into my proposal. It will be better for us both in the end.

SIR H. I can't be off.

HAR. Let me entreat you.   55

SIR H. I tell you, it's unpossible.

HAR. Pray, pray do, sir.

SIR H. I can't, damme.

HAR. I beseech you.

SIR H. (*Whistles.*)   60

HAR. How! laughed at?

SIR H. *Will you marry me, dear Ally, Ally Croker?* [1]
                                         (*Singing.*)

HAR. Marry you? I had rather be married to a slave, a wretch — You!   (*Walks about.*)

SIR H. A fine going thing. She has a deal of 65 foot, treads well upon her pasterns, goes above her ground —

HAR. Peace, wretch! do you talk to me as if I were your horse.

SIR H. Horse! why not speak of my horse! 70 If your fine ladies had half as many good qualities, they would be much better bargains.

HAR. And if their wretches of husbands liked them half so well as they do their horses, they would lead better lives.   75

[1] A popular Irish song.

SIR H. Mayhap so: but what signifies talking to you? The 'squire shall know your tricks! he'll doctor you! I'll go and talk to him.

HAR. Go anywhere, so that you go from me.

SIR H. He'll break you in! If you won't go 80 in a snaffle, you must be put in a curb. He'll break you, damme!   *Exit.*

HARRIOT *sola.*

[HAR.] A wretch! But I was to blame to suffer his brutal behavior to ruffle my temper. I could expect nothing else from him, and he is below 85 my anger. How much trouble has this odious fellow caused both to me and my poor father! I never disobeyed him before, and my denial now makes him quite unhappy. In anything else I would be all submission; and even now, while I dread his 90 rage, my heart bleeds for his uneasiness. I wish I could resolve to obey him!

Enter RUSSET.

RUS. Are not you a sad girl! a perverse, stubborn, obstinate —

HAR. My dear sir —   95

RUS. Look ye, Harriot, don't speak. You'll put me in a passion. Will you have him? Answer me that. Why don't the girl speak? Will you have him?

HAR. Dearest sir, there is nothing in the 100 world else —

RUS. Why there! there! look ye there! Zounds, you shall have him! hussy, you shall have him! you shall marry him to-night! Did not you promise to receive him civilly? How came you to affront 105 him?

HAR. Sir, I did receive him very civilly; but his behavior was so insolent and insupportable —

RUS. Insolent! zounds, I'll blow his brains out. Insolent to my dear Harriot! a rogue! a villain! 110 a scoundrel! I'll — but it's a lie! I know it's a lie! He durst not behave insolent. Will you have him? Answer me that. Will you have him? Zounds, you shall have him!

HAR. If you have any love for me, sir —   115

RUS. Love for you! You know I love you; you know your poor fond father dotes on you to madness: I would not force you, if I did not love you. Don't I want you to be happy? But I know what you would have: you want young Oakly, a rake- 120 helly, drunken —

HAR. Release me from Sir Harry, and if I ever marry against your consent, renounce me forever.

RUS. I *will* renounce you, unless you'll have Sir Harry.   125

HAR. Consider, my dear sir, you'll make me miserable. I would die to please you, but cannot prostitute my hand to a man my heart abhors. Absolve me from this hard command, and in everything else it will be happiness to obey you.   130

Rus. You'll break my heart, Harriot, you'll break my heart. Make you miserable! don't I want to make you happy? Is not he the richest man in the county? That will make you happy. Don't all the pale-faced girls in the country long to get him?   135 and yet you are so perverse, and wayward, and stubborn — Zounds, you shall have him!

Har. For heaven's sake, sir —

Rus. Hold your tongue, Harriot! I'll hear none of your nonsense. You shall have him, I tell   140 you, you shall have him! He shall marry you this very night. I'll go for a license and a parson immediately. Zounds, why do I stand arguing with you? An't I your father? Have not I a right to dispose of you? You shall have him!   145

Har. Sir!

Rus. I won't hear a word. You shall have him!
Exit.

Harriot *sola.*

[Har.] Sir! hear me! but one word! He will not hear me, and is gone to prepare for this odious marriage. I will die before I consent to it. 'You   150 *shall* have him!' Oh, that fathers would enforce their commands by better arguments! And yet I pity him, while he afflicts me. He upbraided me with Charles's wildness and intemperance; alas! but too justly! I see that he is wedded to his excesses;   155 and I ought to conquer an affection for him which will only serve to make me unhappy.

Enter CHARLES *in a frock, &c.*

Ha! what do I see?   (*Screaming.*)

Char. Peace, my love! my dear life, make no noise! I have been hovering about the house   160 this hour. I just now saw your father and Sir Harry go out, and have seized this precious opportunity to throw myself at your feet.

Har. You have given yourself, sir, a great deal of needless trouble. I did not expect or hope for   165 the favor of such a visit.

Char. O, my dear Harriot, your words and looks cut me to the soul! You can't imagine what I suffer, and have suffered, since last night. And yet I have in some fond moments flattered myself that the   170 service I was so fortunate as to do you at Lady Freelove's would plead a little in my favor.

Har. You may remember, sir, that you took a very early opportunity of cancelling that obligation.

Char. I do remember it with shame and de-   175 spair. But may I perish, if my joy at having delivered you from a villain, was not the cause! My transport more than half intoxicated me, and wine made an easy conquest over me. I tremble to think

lest I should have behaved in such a manner   180 as you cannot pardon.

Har. Whether I pardon you or no, sir, is a matter of mighty little consequence.

Char. O, my Harriot! upbraid me, reproach me, do anything but look and talk with that air of   185 coldness and indifference. Must I lose you for one offence, when my soul dotes on you, when I love you to distraction!

Har. Did it appear like love, your conduct yesterday? to lose yourself in riot, when I was   190 exposed to the greatest distresses!

Char. I feel, I feel my shame, and own it.

Har. You confess that you don't know in what manner you behaved. Ought not I to tremble at the very thoughts of a man devoted to a vice which   195 renders him no longer a judge or master of his own conduct?

Char. Abandon me, if ever I am guilty of it again. O, Harriot! I am distracted with ten thousand fears and apprehensions of losing you forever.   200 The chambermaid, whom I bribed to admit me to you, told me that when the two gentlemen went out they talked of a license. What am I to think? Is it possible that you can resign yourself to Sir Harry Beagle? (*Harriot pauses.*) Can you then   205 consent to give your hand to another? No; let me once more deliver you. Let us seize this lucky moment! My chariot stands at the corner of the next street. Let me gently force you, while their absence allows it, and convey you from the brutal vio-   210 lence of a constrained marriage.

Har. I will wait the event,[1] be it what it may. O, Charles, I am too much inclined — They shan't force me to marry Sir Harry. But your behavior! Not half an hour ago, my father reproached me   215 with the looseness of your character.   (*Weeping.*)

Char. I see my folly, and am ashamed of it. You have reclaimed me, Harriot! On my soul, you have. If all women were as attentive as yourself to the morals of their lovers, a libertine would be an   220 uncommon character. But let me persuade you to leave this place, while you may. Major Oakly will receive us at his house with pleasure. I am shocked at the thoughts of what your stay here may reserve you to.   225

Har. No; I am determined to remain. To leave my father again, to go off openly with a man, of whose libertine character he has himself so lately been a witness, would justify his anger, and impeach my reputation.   230

Char. Fool! fool! How unhappy have I made myself! Consider, my Harriot, the peculiarity of your situation; besides, I have reason to fear other designs against you.

---

[1] Outcome.

HAR. From other designs I can be nowhere 235
so secure as with my father.

CHAR. Time flies. Let me persuade you!

HAR. I am resolved to stay here.

CHAR. You distract me. For heaven's sake —

HAR. I will not think of it. 240

CHAR. Consider, my angel!

HAR. I do consider, that your conduct has made
it absolutely improper for me to trust myself to
your care.

CHAR. My conduct! Vexation! 'Sdeath! 245
But then, my dear Harriot, the danger you are in,
the necessity —

Enter CHAMBERMAID.

CHAMB. Oh law, ma'am! such a terrible accident!
As sure as I am here, there's a press-gang has seized
the two gemmin, and is carrying them away, 250
thof so be one an'em says as how he's a knight and
baronight, and that t'other's a 'squire and a housekeeper.

HAR. Seized by a press-gang! Impossible.

CHAR. Oh, now the design comes out. But 255
I'll balk his lordship.

CHAMB. Lack-a-dasy, ma'am, what can we do?
There is master, and John Ostler, and Bootcatcher,
all gone a'ter 'em. There is such an uproar as never
was! *Exit.* 260

HAR. If I thought this was your contrivance,
sir, I would never speak to you again.

CHAR. I would sooner die than be guilty of it.
This is Lord Trinket's doing, I am sure. I knew he
had some scheme in agitation, by a letter I 265
intercepted this morning.

HAR. Ah! *(Screams.)*

CHAR. Ha! here he comes! Nay, then, it's plain
enough. Don't be frighted, my love! I'll protect
you. But now I must desire you to follow 270
my directions.

Enter LORD TRINKET.

L. TRINK. Now, madam! Pox on't, he here again!
Nay, then! *(Drawing.)* Come, sir! You're unarmed, I see. Give up the lady: give her up, I say;
or I am through you in a twinkling. 275

(Going to make a pass at CHARLES.*)*

CHAR. Keep your distance, my lord! I have
arms. *(Producing a pistol.)* If you come a foot
nearer, you have a brace of balls through your
lordship's head.

L. TRINK. How? what's this? pistols! 280

CHAR. At your lordship's service. Sword and
pistol, my lord! Those, you know, are our weapons. If this misses, I have the fellow to't in my
pocket. Don't be frighted, madam! His lordship
has removed your friends and relations, but 285

he will take great care of you. Shall I leave you
with him?

HAR. Cruel Charles! You know I *must* go with
you now.

CHAR. A little away from the door, if your 290
lordship pleases. *(Waving his hand.)*

L. TRINK. Sir! 'Sdeath! Madam!

CHAR. A little more round, my lord! *(Waving.)*

L. TRINK. But, sir! Mr. Oakly.

CHAR. I have no leisure to talk with your 295
lordship now. A little more that way, if you please.
(Waving.) You know where I live. If you have any
commands for Miss Russet, you will hear of her too
at my house. Nay, keep back, my lord! *(Presenting.)* Your lordship's most obedient humble 300
servant! *Exit with* HARRIOT.

Manet LORD TRINKET.

*(Looking after him, and pausing for a short
time.)*

[L. TRINK.] I cut a mighty ridiculous figure here,
'pon honor. So, I have been concerting this deep
scheme merely to serve him. Oh, the devil take such
intrigues, and all silly country girls, that can 305
give up a man of quality and figure, for a fellow
that nobody knows! *Exit.*

ACT V

SCENE [I]

LADY FREELOVE'S.

Enter LORD TRINKET, LADY FREELOVE *with a letter,
and* CAPTAIN O'CUTTER.

L. TRINK. Was ever anything so unfortunate?
Pox on't, captain, how could you make such a strange
blunder?

O'CUT. I never tought of a blunder. I was to
daliver two letters, and if I gave them one 5
a-piece I tought it was all one, fait.

L. FREE. And so, my lord, the ingenious captain
gave the letter intended for me to young Oakly, and
here he has brought me a challenge.

L. TRINK. Ridiculous! Never was anything 10
so *mal-à-propos*. Did not you read the direction,
captain?

O'CUT. Who, me! Devil burn me, not I. I never
rade at all.

L. TRINK. 'Sdeath, how provoking! When I 15
had secured the servants, and got all the people
out of the way; when everything was *en train*!

L. FREE. Nay, never despair, my lord! Things
have happened unluckily, to be sure; and yet, I
think I could hit upon a method to set every- 20
thing right again.

267] OO omit *Ah!*   21] OO *to right.*

L. Trink. How, how, my dear Lady Freelove, how?

L. Free. Suppose, then, your lordship was to go and deliver these country gentlemen from their 25 confinement; make them believe it was a plot of young Oakly's to carry off my niece; and so make a merit of your own services with the father.

L. Trink. Admirable! I'll about it immediately.　　　　　　　　　　　30

O'Cut. Has your lordship any occasion for my sarvice, in this expedition?

L. Trink. Oh, no. Only release me these people, and then keep out of the way, dear captain!

O'Cut. With all my heart, fait! But you are 35 all wrong. This will not signify a brass farding. If you would let me alone, I would give him a salt eel, I warrant you. But, upon my credit, there's nothing to be done without a little tilting.　　*Exit.*

L. Free. Ha, ha! poor captain!　　　　40

L. Trink. But where shall I carry them, when I have delivered them?

L. Free. To Mr. Oakly's, by all means. You may be sure my niece is there.

L. Trink. To Mr. Oakly's! Why, does your 45 ladyship consider, 'tis going directly into the fire of the enemy? Throwing the *démenti*[1] full in their teeth?

L. Free. So much the better. Face your enemies: nay, you shall outface them too. Why, 50 where's the difference between truths and untruths, if you do but stick close to the point? Falsehood would scarce ever be detected, if we had confidence enough to support it.

L. Trink. Nay, I don't want *bronze*[2] upon 55 occasion: but, to go amongst a whole troop of people, sure to contradict every word I say, is so dangerous —

L. Free. To leave Russet alone amongst them would be ten times more dangerous. You may 60 be sure that Oakly's will be the first place he will go to after his daughter; where, if you don't accompany him, he will be open to all their suggestions. They'll be all in one story, and nobody there to contradict them: and then their dull truth would triumph; 65 which must not be. No, no; positively, my lord, you must battle it out.

L. Trink. Well! I'll go, 'pon honor; and, if I could depend on your ladyship, as a *corps de reserve* —

L. Free. I'll certainly meet you there. 70 Tush! my lord, there's nothing in it. It's hard, indeed, if two persons of condition can't bear themselves out against such trumpery folks as the family of the Oaklys.

[1] Lie.
[2] Impudence (cf. 'brass').

L. Trink. Odious low people! But I lose 75 time. I must after the captain. And so, till we meet at Mr. Oakly's, I kiss your ladyship's hands. You won't fail me?

L. Free. You may depend on me.

　　　　　　　　　　Exit Lord Trinket.

Lady Freelove *sola.*

[L. Free.] So, here is fine work! This artful 80 little hussy has been too much for us all. Well! what's to be done? Why, when a woman of fashion gets into a scrape, nothing but a fashionable assurance can get her out of it again. I'll e'en go boldly to Mr. Oakly's, as I have promised; and, if it 85 appears practicable, I will forward Lord Trinket's match; but if I find that matters have taken another turn, his lordship must excuse me. In that case, I'll fairly drop him, seem a perfect stranger to all his intentions, and give my visit an air of congratu- 90 lation to my niece and any other husband which fortune, her wise father, or her ridiculous self, may have provided for her.　　　　　　　*Exit.*

Scene [II]

Scene changes to Mrs. Oakly's *dressing-room.*
Mrs. Oakly *sola.*

[Mrs. Oak.] This is worse and worse! He never held me so much in contempt before. To go out without so much as speaking to me, or taking the least notice! I am obliged to the Major for this. How could he take him out? and how could Mr. 5 Oakly go with him?

Enter Toilet.

Mrs. Oak. Well, Toilet!

Toil. My master is not come back yet, ma'am.

Mrs. Oak. Where is he gone?

Toil. I don't know, I can assure your lady- 10 ship.

Mrs. Oak. Why don't you know? You know nothing! But I warrant, you know well enough, if you would tell. You shall never persuade me but you knew of Mr. Oakly's going out to-day. 15

Toil. I wish I may die, ma'am, upon my honor, and I protest to your ladyship, I knew nothing in the world of the matter, no more than the child unborn. There is Mr. Paris, my master's gentleman, knows —　　　　　　　　　　　20

Mrs. Oak. What does he know?

Toil. That I know nothing at all of the matter.

Mrs. Oak. Where is Paris? What is he doing?

Toil. He is in my master's room, ma'am.

Mrs. Oak. Bid him come here.　　　25

Toil. Yes, ma'am.　　　　　　*Exit.*

MRS. OAK. He is certainly gone after this young flirt. His confidence, and the Major's insolence, provoke me beyond expression.

Re-enter TOILET *with* PARIS.

Where's your master?   30

PAR. *Il est sorti.*

MRS. OAK. Where is he gone?

PAR. Ah, madame! *Je n'en sais rien.* I know nothing of it.

MRS. OAK. Nobody knows anything. Why 35 did not you tell me he was going out?

PAR. I dress him; *Je ne m'en soucie pas plus.* He go where he will; I have no bisness wis it.

MRS. OAK. Yes, you should have told me; that was your business: and if you don't mind your 40 business better, you sha'n't stay here, I can tell you, sir.

PAR. *Voilà quelque chose d'extraordinaire!*

MRS. OAK. Don't stand jabbering and shrugging your shoulders; but go, and enquire — go — 45 and bring me word where he is gone.

PAR. I don't know vat I am do: I'll ask-a Jean.

MRS. OAK. Bid John come here.

PAR. *De tout mon coeur. Jean! ici! Jean!* Speak mi ladi!   *Exit.* 50

MRS. OAK. Impudent fellow! his insolent gravity and indifference are insupportable. Toilet!

TOIL. Ma'am.

MRS. OAK. Where's John? Why don't he come? Why do you stand with your hands before you? 55 Why don't you fetch him?

TOIL. Yes, ma'am: I'll go this minute. Oh! here! John! my lady wants you.

Enter JOHN.

MRS. OAK. Where's your master?

JOHN. Gone out, madam.   60

MRS. OAK. Why did not you go with him?

JOHN. Because he went out in the Major's chariot, madam.

MRS. OAK. Where did they go to?

JOHN. To the Major's, I suppose, madam.   65

MRS. OAK. Suppose! Don't you know?

JOHN. I believe so; but can't tell for certain, indeed, madam.

MRS. OAK. Believe! and suppose! and don't know! and can't tell! You are all fools! Go about 70 your business! (JOHN *going.*) Come here! (*Returns.*) Go to the Major's — No; it does not signify. Go along! (JOHN *going.*) Yes, hark ye! (*Returns.*) Go to the Major's, and see if your master is there.   75

JOHN. Give your compliments, madam?

MRS. OAK. My compliments, blockhead! Get along! (JOHN *going.*) Come hither! (*Returns.*)

Can't you go to the Major's, and bring me word if Mr. Oakly is there, without taking any further 80 notice?

JOHN. Yes, ma'am!

MRS. OAK. Well! why don't you go, then? And make haste back. And, d'ye hear? John!

(JOHN, *going, returns.*)

JOHN. Madam.   85

MRS. OAK. Nothing at all: go along! (JOHN *goes.*) How uneasy Mr. Oakly makes me! — Hark ye! John!   (JOHN *returns.*)

JOHN. Madam.

MRS. OAK. Send the porter here.   90

JOHN. Yes, madam.   *Exit* JOHN.

TOIL. So! she's in a rare humor! I shall have a fine time on't. (*Aside.*) — Will your ladyship choose to dress?

MRS. OAK. Prithee, creature, don't tease me 95 with your fiddle-faddle stuff: I have a thousand things to think of. Where is the porter? Why has not that booby sent him? What is the meaning —

Re-enter JOHN.

JOHN. Madam, my master is this moment returned with Major Oakly, and my young mas- 100 ter, and the lady that was here yesterday.

MRS. OAK. Very well. (*Exit* JOHN.) Returned! Yes, truly, he is returned; and in a very extraordinary manner. This is setting me at open defiance. But I'll go down, and show them I have too 105 much spirit to endure such usage. (*Going.*) Or, stay; I'll not go amongst his company; I'll go out. Toilet!

TOIL. Ma'am.

MRS. OAK. Order the coach; I'll go out. 110 (TOILET *going.*) Toilet! stay! I'll e'en go down to them. No. Toilet!

TOIL. Ma'am.

MRS. OAK. Order me a boiled chicken: I'll not go down to dinner. I'll dine in my own room; 115 and sup there: I'll not see his face these three days.

Exeunt.

SCENE [III]

Scene changes to another room.

Enter OAKLY, MAJOR OAKLY, CHARLES, *and* HARRIOT.

CHAR. My dear Harriot, do not make yourself so uneasy.

HAR. Alas! I have too much cause for my uneasiness. Who knows what that vile lord has done with my father?   5

OAK. Be comforted, madam. We shall soon hear of Mr. Russet; and all will be well, I dare say.

HAR. You are too good to me, sir! But, I can

assure you, I am not a little concerned on your
account, as well as my own; and, if I did not   10
flatter myself with the hopes of explaining everything to Mrs. Oakly's satisfaction, I should never
forgive myself for having disturbed the peace of
such a worthy family.

MAJ. Don't mind that, madam; they'll be   15
very good friends again. This is nothing among
married people. 'Sdeath, here she is! No; it's only
Mrs. Toilet.

Enter TOILET.

OAK. Well, Toilet, what now? (TOILET *whispers.*) Not well? can't come down to dinner?   20
wants to see me above? Hark ye, brother; what
shall I do?

MAJ. If you go, you're undone.

HAR. Go, sir! go to Mrs. Oakly. Indeed you had
better.   25

MAJ. 'Sdeath, brother, don't budge a foot! This
is all fractiousness and ill humor.

OAK. No; I'll not go. Tell her I have company,
and we shall be glad to see her here. *Exit* TOILET.

MAJ. That's right.   30

OAK. Suppose I go, and watch how she proceeds.

MAJ. What d'ye mean? You would not go to
her! Are you mad?

OAK. By no means go to her: I only want to know
how she takes it. I'll lie *perdu*[1] in my study, and   35
observe her motions.

MAJ. I don't like this pitiful ambuscade-work;
this bush-fighting. Why can't you stay here? Ay,
ay! I know how it will be. She'll come bounce
in upon you, with a torrent of anger and pas-   40
sion, or, if necessary, a whole flood of tears, and
carry all before her at once.

OAK. You shall find that you're mistaken, Major.
Don't imagine, because I wish not to be void of
humanity, that I am destitute of resolution.   45
Now I am convinced I'm in the right, I'll support
that right with ten times your steadiness.

MAJ. You talk this well, brother!

OAK. I'll *do* it well, brother!

MAJ. If you don't, you're undone.   50

OAK. Never fear, never fear!   *Exit.*

MAJ. Well, Charles!

CHAR. I can't bear to see my Harriot so uneasy.
I'll go immediately in quest of Mr. Russet. Perhaps I may learn at the inn, where his lord-   55
ship's ruffians have carried him.

RUS. (*without*). Here? yes, yes; I know she's
here, well enough. Come along, Sir Harry, come
along.

HAR. He's here! my father! I know his   60
voice. Where is Mr. Oakly? Oh, now, good sir,

[1] Hidden.

(*to the* MAJOR) do but pacify him, and you'll be a
friend indeed.

Enter RUSSET, LORD TRINKET, *and* SIR HARRY
BEAGLE.

L. TRINK. There, sir! I told you it was so.

RUS. Ay, ay, it is too plain. Oh, you provok-   65
ing slut! Elopement after elopement! and, at last,
to have your father carried off by violence! to endanger my life! Zounds, I am so angry, I dare not
trust myself within reach of you!

CHAR. I can assure you, sir, that your   70
daughter is entirely —

RUS. You assure me? You are the fellow that
has perverted her mind; that has set my own child
against me!

CHAR. If you will but hear me, sir —   75

RUS. I won't hear a word you say! I'll have
my daughter. I won't hear a word!

MAJ. Nay, Mr. Russet, hear reason. If you will
but have patience —

RUS. I'll have no patience. I'll have my   80
daughter; and she shall marry Sir Harry to-night.

L. TRINK. That is dealing rather too much *en
cavalier* with me, Mr. Russet, 'pon honor. You take
no notice of my pretensions, though my rank and
family —   85

RUS. What care I for rank and family! I don't
want to make my daughter a rantipole[2] woman of
quality. I'll give her to whom I please. Take her
away, Sir Harry! She shall marry you to-night.

HAR. For heaven's sake, sir, hear me but a   90
moment.

RUS. Hold your tongue, girl! Take her away,
Sir Harry, take her away.

CHAR. It must not be.

MAJ. Only three words, Mr. Russet —   95

RUS. Why don't the booby take her!

SIR H. Hold hard! hold hard! You are all on a
wrong scent. Hold hard! I say, hold hard! Hark
ye, squire Russet.

RUS. Well! what now?   100

SIR H. It was proposed, you know, to match me
with Miss Harriot; but she can't take kindly to
me. When one has made a bad bet, it is best to
hedge off, you know; and so I have e'en swopped
her with Lord Trinket here for his brown horse   105
Nabob, that he bought of Lord Whistle-Jacket, for
fifteen hundred guineas.

RUS. Swopped her? Swopped my daughter for
a horse? Zounds, sir, what d'ye mean?

SIR HAR. Mean? why I mean to be off, to be   110
sure! It won't do; I tell you, it won't do; first of
all, I knocked up myself and my horses, when they

[2] Rakish.

took for London; and now I have been stewed aboard a tender: I have wasted three stone at least. If I could have rid my match, it would not have 115 grieved me. And so, as I said before, I have swopped her for Nabob.

Rus. The devil take Nabob, and yourself, and Lord Trinket, and —

L. Trink. *Pardon! je vous demande pardon*, 120 *monsieur* Russet, 'pon honor!

Rus. Death and the devil! I shall go distracted. My daughter plotting against me! the —

Maj. Come, Mr. Russet, I am your man, after all. Give me but a moment's hearing, and I'll 125 engage to make peace between you and your daughter, and throw the blame where it ought to fall most deservedly.

Sir H. Ay, ay, that's right. Put the saddle on the right horse, my buck! 130

Rus. Well, sir! what d'ye say? Speak! I don't know what to do!

Maj. I'll speak the truth, let who will be offended by it: I have proof presumptive and positive for you, Mr. Russet. From his lordship's behavior 135 at Lady Freelove's, when my nephew rescued her, we may fairly conclude that he would stick at no measures to carry his point: there's proof presumptive. But, sir, we can give you proof positive too; proof under his lordship's own hand, that 140 he, likewise, was the contriver of the gross affront that has just been offered you.

Rus. Hey! how!

L. Trink. Every syllable romance, 'pon honor.

Maj. Gospel, every word on't. 145

Char. This letter will convince you, sir. In consequence of what happened at Lady Freelove's, his lordship thought fit to send me a challenge; but the messenger blundered, and gave me this letter instead of it. (*Giving the letter.*) I have the case which 150 enclosed it in my pocket.

L. Trink. Forgery, from beginning to end, 'pon honor.

Maj. Truth, upon *my* honor. But read, Mr. Russet; read and be convinced. 155

Rus. Let me see — let me see — (*Reading.*) — Um um — um — um — so! so! — um — um — um — Damnation! — '*Wish me success — obedient slave — Trinket.*' — Fire and fury! How dare you do this? 160

L. Trink. When you are cool, Mr. Russet, I will explain this matter to you.

Rus. Cool? 'Sdeath and hell! I'll never be cool again! I'll be revenged! So my Harriot, my dear girl, is innocent at last! Say so, Harriot; 165 tell me you are innocent. (*Embracing her.*)

Har. I am, indeed, sir! and happy beyond expression at your being convinced of it.

Rus. I am glad on't — I am glad on't — I believe you, Harriot! You were always a good girl. 170

Maj. So she is, an excellent girl! worth a regiment of such lords and baronets! Come, sir, finish everything handsomely at once. Come, Charles will have a handsome fortune.

Rus. Marry! she durst not do it. 175

Maj. Consider, sir, they have long been fond of each other; old acquaintance — faithful lovers — turtles — and may be very happy.

Rus. Well, well; since things are so — I love my girl — Hark ye, young Oakly, if you don't make 180 her a good husband, you'll break my heart, you rogue.

Maj. I'll cut his throat, if he don't.

Char. Do not doubt it, sir! my Harriot has reformed me altogether. 185

Rus. Has she? Why then — there — heaven bless you both — there — now there's an end on't.

Sir Har. So, my lord, you and I are both distanced — a hollow thing, damme.

L. Trink. *N'importe.* 190

Sir Har. (*aside*). Now this stake is drawn, my lord may be for hedging off, mayhap. Ecod! I'll go to Jack Speed's, and secure Nabob, and be out of town in an hour. Soho! Lady Freelove! yoic[k]s! *Exit.* 195

Enter Lady Freelove.

L. Free. My dear Miss Russet, you'll excuse —

Char. Mrs. Oakly, at your ladyship's service.

L. Free. Married?

Har. Not yet, madam; but my father has been so good as to give his consent. 200

L. Free. I protest, I am prodigiously glad of it. My dear, I give you joy! and you, Mr. Oakly! I wish you joy, Mr. Russet, and all the good company! for I think they are most of them parties concerned. 205

Maj. How easy, impudent, and familiar! (*Aside.*)

L. Free. Lord Trinket here too! I vow I did not see your lordship before.

L. Trink. Your ladyship's most obedient slave. (*Bowing.*)

L. Free. You seem grave, my lord! Come, 210 come, I know there has been some difference between you and Mr. Oakly. You must give me leave to be a mediator in this affair.

L. Trink. Here has been a small *fracas*, to be sure, madam! We are all blown, 'pon honor. 215

L. Free. Blown! What do you mean, my lord?

L. Trink. Nay, your ladyship knows that I never mind these things, and I know that they never discompose your ladyship. But things have happened a little *en travers*: the little billet that I 220 sent your ladyship has fallen into the hands of that

---

124] OO *Come, come.*   170] OO *was.*   183] OO omit Major's speech.

gentleman (*pointing to* CHARLES); and so, there has been a little *brouillerie*¹ about it; that's all.

L. FREE. You talk to me, my lord, in a very extraordinary style. If you have been 225 guilty of any misbehavior, I am sorry for it; but your ill conduct can fasten no imputation on me. Miss Russet will justify me sufficiently.

MAJ. Had not your ladyship better appeal to my friend Charles here? The letter, Charles! 230 out with it this instant!

CHAR. Yes, I have the credentials of her ladyship's integrity in my pocket. Mr. Russet, the letter you read a little while ago was inclosed in this cover; which also I now think it my duty 235 to put into your hands.

RUS. (*reading*). '*To the Right Honourable Lady Freelove.*' 'Sdeath and hell! and now I recollect, the letter itself was pieced with scraps of French, and *madam*, and *your ladyship*. Fire and fury! 240 Madam, how came you to use me so? I am obliged to you then, for the insult that has been offered me.

L. FREE. What is all this? Your obligations to me, Mr. Russet, are of a nature that —

RUS. Fine obligations! I dare say I am 245 partly obliged to you too for the attempt on my daughter by that thing of a lord yonder, at your house. Zounds, madam, these are injuries never to be forgiven! They are the grossest affronts to me and my family — All the world shall know 250 them! Zounds! I'll —

L. FREE. Mercy on me! how boisterous are these country gentlemen! Why really, Mr. Russet, you rave like a man in Bedlam; I'm afraid you'll beat me: and then you swear most abominably! 255 How can you be so vulgar? I see the meaning of this low malice: but the reputations of women of quality are not so easily impeached; my rank places me above the scandal of little people, and I shall meet such petty insolence with the greatest ease 260 and tranquillity. But you and your simple girl will be the sufferers: I had some thoughts of introducing her into the first company; but now, madam, I shall neither receive nor return your visits, and will entirely withdraw my protection from the ordi- 265 nary part of the family.   *Exit.*

RUS. Zounds! what impudence! That's worse than all the rest.

L. TRINK. Fine presence of mind, faith! the true French *nonchalance*. But, good folks, why 270 such a deal of rout² and *tapage*³ about nothing at all? If mademoiselle Harriot had rather be Mrs. Oakly than Lady Trinket — why — I wish her joy, that's all. Mr. Russet, I wish you joy of your son-in-law — Mr. Oakly, I wish you joy of 275 the lady — and you, madam, (*to* HARRIOT) of the

gentleman — And, in short, I wish you all joy of one another, 'pon honor.   *Exit.*

RUS. There's a fine fellow of a lord now! The devil's in your London folks of the first fash- 280 ion, as you call them. They will rob you of your estate, debauch your daughter, or lie with your wife; and all, as if they were doing you a favor — 'pon honor!   (*Bell rings violently.*)

MAJ. Hey! what now?   285

Enter OAKLY.

OAK. D'ye hear, Major, d'ye hear?

MAJ. Zounds! what a clatter! She'll pull down all the bells in the house.

OAK. My observations since I left you have con-firmed my resolution. I see plainly that her 290 good humor, and her ill humor, her smiles, her tears, and her fits, are all calculated to play upon me.

MAJ. Did not I always tell you so? It's the way with them all: they will be rough, and smooth, and hot, and cold, and all in a breath: anything to 295 get the better of us.

OAK. She is in all moods at present, I promise you. I am at once angry and ashamed of her; and yet she is so ridiculous I can't help laughing at her. There has she been in her chamber, fuming and 300 fretting, and dispatching a messenger to me every two minutes; servant after servant — Now she insists on my coming to her — now again she writes a note to entreat — then Toilet is sent to let me know that she is ill — absolutely dying — then, 305 the very next minute, she'll never see my face again — she'll go out of the house directly. (*Bell rings.*) Again! Now the storm rises.

MAJ. It will soon drive this way then. Now, brother, prove yourself a man. You have 310 gone too far to retreat.

OAK. Retreat! retreat! No, no! I'll preserve the advantage I have gained, I am determined.

MAJ. Ay, ay! keep your ground! fear nothing! up with your noble heart! Good discipline makes 315 good soldiers. Stick close to my advice, and you may stand buff⁴ to a tigress.

OAK. Here she is, by heavens. Now, brother!

MAJ. And now, brother! now, or never!

Enter MRS. OAKLY.

MRS. OAK. I think, Mr. Oakly, you might 320 have had humanity enough to have come to see how I did. You have taken your leave, I suppose, of all tenderness and affection! But I'll be calm; I'll not throw myself into a passion. You want to drive me out of your house; I see what you aim at, and 325 will be aforehand with you. Let me keep my tem-per! I'll send for a chair, and leave the house this instant.

¹ Misunderstanding.
² Noise.   ³ Racket.
⁴ Firm.

OAK. True, my love! I knew you would not think of dining in your own chamber alone, 330 when I had company below. You shall sit at the head of the table, as you ought, to be sure, as you say, and make my friends welcome.

MRS. OAK. Excellent raillery! Look ye, Mr. Oakly, I see the meaning of all this affected 335 coolness and indifference!

OAK. My dear, consider where you are!

MRS. OAK. You would be glad, I find, to get me out of your house, and have all your flirts about you.

OAK. Before all this company! Fie! 340

MRS. OAK. But I'll disappoint you; for I shall remain in it to support my due authority. As for you, Major Oakly —

MAJ. Heyday! what have I done?

MRS. OAK. I think you might find better em- 345 ployment than to create divisions between married people! And you, sir —

OAK. Nay, but, my dear!

MRS. OAK. Might have more sense, as well as tenderness, than to give ear to such idle stuff. 350

OAK. Lord! Lord!

MRS. OAK. You and your wise counsellor there, I suppose, think to carry all your points with me.

OAK. Was ever anything —

MRS. OAK. But it won't do, sir! You shall 355 find that I will have my own way, and that I will govern my own family.

OAK. You had better learn to govern yourself, by half. Your passion makes you ridiculous. Did ever anybody see so much fury and violence? Af- 360 fronting your best friends, breaking my peace, and disconcerting your own temper! And all for what? For nothing. 'Sdeath, madam, at these years you ought to know better!

MRS. OAK. At these years! very fine! Am 365 I to be talked to in this manner?

OAK. Talked to! why not? You have talked to me long enough; almost talked me to death; and I have taken it all, in hopes of making you quiet: but all in vain; for the more one bears, the worse 370 you are. Patience, I find, is all thrown away upon you; and henceforward, come what may, I am resolved to be master of my own house.

MRS. OAK. So, so! master indeed! Yes, sir, and you'll take care to have mistresses enough too, 375 I warrant you.

OAK. Perhaps I may; but they shall be quiet ones, I assure you.

MRS. OAK. Indeed! And do you think I am such a tame fool as to sit quietly and bear all this? 380 You shall know, sir, that I will resent this behavior! You shall find that I have a spirit —

OAK. Of the devil.

MRS. OAK. Intolerable! You shall find then that I will exert that spirit. I am sure I have need 385

of it. As soon as the house is once cleared again, I'll shut my doors against all company. You sha'n't see a single soul for this month.

OAK. 'Sdeath, madam, madam, but I will. I'll keep open house for a year; I'll send cards to 390 the whole town; *Mr.* Oakly's rout [1]! All the world will come; and I'll go among the world too: I'll be mewed up no longer.

MRS. OAK. Provoking insolence! This is not to be endured. Look ye, Mr. Oakly — 395

OAK. And look ye, Mrs. Oakly, I will have my own way.

MRS. OAK. Nay then, let me tell you, sir —

OAK. And let me tell you, madam, I will not be crossed; I won't be made a fool! 400

MRS. OAK. Why, you won't let me speak!

OAK. Because you don't speak as you ought. Madam, madam, you sha'n't look, nor walk, nor talk, nor think, but as I please!

MRS. OAK. Was there ever such a monster? 405 I can bear this no longer. (*Bursts into tears.*) Oh, you vile man! I see through your design. You cruel, barbarous, unhuman — Such usage to your poor wife! You'll be the death of her.

OAK. She sha'n't be the death of me, I am 410 determined.

MRS. OAK. That it should ever come to this! To be contradicted — (*sobbing*) — insulted — abused — hated — 'tis too much — my heart will burst with — oh — oh — (*Falls into a fit.*) 415

(HARRIOT, CHARLES, &c. run to her assistance.)

OAK. (*interposing*). Let her alone.

HAR. Sir, Mrs. Oakly —

CHAR. For heaven's sake, sir! she will be —

OAK. Let her alone, I say; I won't have her touched; let her alone! If her passions throw 420 her into fits, let the strength of them carry her through them.

HAR. Pray, my dear sir, let us assist her! She may —

OAK. I don't care. You sha'n't touch her — 425 Let her bear them patiently. She'll learn to behave better another time. Let her alone, I say.

MRS. OAK. (*rising*). Oh, you monster! you villain! you base man! Would you let me die for want of help? would you? 430

OAK. Bless me, madam, your fit is very violent! Take care of yourself.

MRS. OAK. Despised! ridiculed! But I'll be revenged! You shall see, sir —

OAK. *Tol-de-rol lol-de-rol lol-de-rol lol.* (*Singing.*) 435

MRS. OAK. What, am I made a jest of? exposed to all the world? If there's law or justice —

OAK. *Tol-de-rol lol-de-rol lol-de-rol lol.* (*Singing.*)

[1] Fashionable assembly.

Mrs. Oak. I shall burst with anger! Have a care, sir! you may repent this. Scorned and made   440 ridiculous! No power on earth shall hinder my revenge. (*Going*.)

Har. (*interposing*). Stay, madam!

Mrs. Oak. Let me go. I cannot bear this place.

Har. Let me beseech you, madam.   445

Oak. What does the girl mean? ⎫

Maj. Courage, brother! You have ⎬ (*Apart*.) done wonders.

Oak. I think she'll have no more fits. ⎭

Har. Stay, madam! pray stay! but one mo-   450 ment. I have been a painful witness of your uneasiness, and in great part the innocent occasion of it. Give me leave then —

Mrs. Oak. I did not expect, indeed, to have found you here again. But, however —   455

Har. I see the agitation of your mind, and it makes me miserable. Suffer me to tell you the real truth. I can explain everything to your satisfaction.

Mrs. Oak. May be so; I cannot argue with   460 you.

Char. Pray, madam, hear her — for my sake — for your own — dear madam!

Mrs. Oak. Well, well; proceed.

Oak. I shall relapse; I cannot bear to ⎫   465 see her so uneasy.   ⎬ (*Apart*.)

Maj. Hush, hush!   ⎭

Har. I understand, madam, that your first alarm was occasioned by a letter from my father to your nephew.   470

Rus. I was in a bloody passion to be sure, madam! The letter was not over civil, I believe; I did not know but the young rogue had ruined my girl. But it's all over now, and so —

Mrs. Oak. You were here yesterday, sir?   475

Rus. Yes, I came after Harriot. I thought I should find my young madam with my young sir, here.

Mrs. Oak. With Charles, did you say, sir?

Rus. Ay, with Charles, madam. The young   480 rogue has been fond of her a long time, and she of him, it seems.

Mrs. Oak. I fear I have been to blame.
                                    (*Aside*.)

Rus. I ask pardon, madam, for the disturbance I made in your house.   485

Har. And the abrupt manner in which I came into it demands a thousand apologies: but the occasion must be my excuse.

Mrs. Oak. How have I been mistaken! (*Aside*.)

But did not I overhear you and Mr. Oakly —   490
                            (*To* Harriot.)

Har. Dear madam, you had but a partial hearing of our conversation. It related entirely to this gentleman.

Char. To put it beyond doubt, madam, Mr. Russet and my guardian have consented to our   495 marriage; and we are in hopes that you will not withhold your approbation.

Mrs. Oak. I have no further doubt; I see you are innocent, and it was cruel to suspect you. You have taken a load of anguish off my mind; and   500 yet your kind interposition comes too late; Mr. Oakly's love for me is entirely destroyed. (*Weeping*.)

Oak. I must go to her! ⎫
                       ⎬ (*Apart*.)
Maj. Not yet, not yet! ⎭

Har. Do not disturb yourself with such ap-   505 prehensions; I am sure Mr. Oakly loves you most affectionately.

Oak. I can hold no longer. (*Going to her*.) My affection for you, madam, is as warm as ever; nothing can ever extinguish it. My constrained   510 behavior cut me to the soul; for, within these few hours, it has been all constrained; and it was with the utmost difficulty that I was able to support it.

Mrs. Oak. O, Mr. Oakly, how have I ex-   515 posed myself! What low arts has my jealousy induced me to practise! I see my folly, and fear that you can never forgive me.

Oak. Forgive you! you are too good, my love! forgive you! can you forgive me? This change   520 transports me. Brother! Mr. Russet! Charles! Harriot! give me joy! I am the happiest man in the world.

Maj. Joy, much joy to you both! though, by the bye, you are not a little obliged to me for   525 it. Did not I tell you I would cure all the disorders in your family? I beg pardon, sister, for taking the liberty to prescribe for you. My medicines have been somewhat rough, I believe, but they have had an admirable effect, and so don't   530 be angry with your physician.

Mrs. Oak. I am indeed obliged to you, and I feel —

Oak. Nay, my dear, no more of this. All that's past must be utterly forgotten.   535

Mrs. Oak. I have not merited this kindness; but it shall hereafter be my study to deserve it. Away with all idle jealousies! and, since my suspicions have hitherto been groundless, I am resolved for the future never to suspect at all.   540

EPILOGUE

SPOKEN BY MRS. CLIVE. [1]

Ladies! I've had a squabble with the poet —
About his characters — and you shall know it.
'Young man,' said I, 'restrain your saucy satire!
My part's ridiculous — false — out of nature.
Fine draughts indeed of ladies! sure you hate 'em!   5
Why, sir! — My part is *scandalum magnatum*.' [2]
'Lord, ma'am,' said he, 'to copy life my trade is,
And poets ever have made free with ladies!
One Simon — the deuce take such names as these! —
A hard Greek name — O — ay — Simonides [3] —   10
He showed — our freaks, this whim and that desire,
Rose first from earth, sea, air, nay, some from fire;
Or that we owe our persons, minds, and features
To birds, forsooth, and filthy four-legg'd creatures.
'The dame, of manners various, temper fickle,   15
Now all for pleasure, now the conventicle!
Who prays, then raves, now calm, now all commotion,
Rises, another Venus, from the ocean.
'Constant at every sale, the curious fair,
Who longs for Dresden, and old China ware;   20
Who dotes on pagods, [4] and gives up vile man
For niddle-noddle figures from Japan;
Critic in jars and josses, [5] shows her birth
Drawn, like the brittle ware itself, from earth.
'The flaunting she, so stately, rich and vain,   25
Who gains her conquests by her length of train;
While all her vanity is under sail,
Sweeps, a proud peacock, with a gaudy tail.
'Husband and wife, with *sweets!* and *dears!* and *loves!*
What are they, but a pair of cooing doves?   30
But seized with spleen, fits, humors, and all that,
Your dove and turtle turn to dog and cat.
'The gossip, prude, old maid, coquette, and trapes, [6]
Are parrots, foxes, magpies, wasps, and apes:
But she, with ev'ry charm of form and mind,   35
Oh! she's — sweet soul — the phoenix of her kind.
«The phoenix of her kind! upon my word,
He's a sly wretch — pray — is there such a bird?' »
This his apology! — 'Tis rank abuse —
A fresh affront, instead of an excuse!   40
His own sex rather such description suits:
Why don't he draw *their* characters — the brutes!
Ay, let him paint those ugly monsters, *men!*
Meantime — mend we our lives — he'll mend his pen.

---

[1] Catharine ('Kitty') Clive (1711–1785) appeared as Lady Freelove in the first performance.
[2] A law term for slander of high personages.
[3] A Greek poet (circ. 660 B.C.), who satirized women by comparing them to various animals.
[4] Pagodas.
[5] Chinese idols.
[6] Sluttish woman (cf. the character of Diana Trapes in *The Beggar's Opera*).

37–38] O1D include; O2O3O4 omit the couplet.

LATER EIGHTEENTH–CENTURY DRAMA

(1770–1780)

SENTIMENTAL VERSUS LAUGHING COMEDY

THE persistent influence of sentimentalism on eighteenth-century drama is conspicuous in the Garrick era. Especially during the last decade of David Garrick's leadership of the Drury Lane Theatre, sentimental comedy found fullest expression and encountered strongest opposition. From Colley Cibber and Richard Steele, succeeding playwrights had inherited the general type of sentimental comedy exemplified in *The Careless Husband* and *The Conscious Lovers*, and had further exploited moralized sentimentality in dramatic theme and diction. Of the later exponents of this prevalent type of sentimental comedy, two are outstanding — Hugh Kelly and Richard Cumberland. Kelly's *False Delicacy* (1768) and Cumberland's *The West Indian* (1771) are excellent examples of the popular dramatic mode.

HUGH KELLY (1739–1777), son of a Dublin tavern-keeper who had early apprenticed him as a staymaker, came to London in 1760 to try his hand at literature. For some years he lived the life of a literary hack, and among varied ventures gained some experience as theatrical critic and attracted the notice of David Garrick. With Garrick's encouragement he wrote his first comedy, *False Delicacy*, produced at Drury Lane on January 23, 1768. Fortified with prologue and epilogue by Garrick, and further profiting from the manager's theatrical experience and prestige, *False Delicacy* caught immediately the popular fancy for sentimental comedy and won for Kelly instant and extravagant favor. Six days later, the belated offering at Covent Garden of Oliver Goldsmith's first comedy, *The Good-Natured Man*, found the force of its novel challenge blunted by Kelly's triumph already achieved under Garrick's guidance at Drury Lane. For the time being, victory seemed to rest with the popular favorite, and the advent of another sentimental dramatist, Richard Cumberland, further strengthened the cause.

RICHARD CUMBERLAND (1732–1811), born in the master's lodge at Trinity College, Cambridge, schooled at Westminster, graduated at Cambridge with mathematical honors, and early elected to a fellowship at Trinity College, held various posts under Lord Halifax and seemed headed for further political advancement. Disappointed, however, by his failure to secure a coveted under-secretaryship when Lord Halifax became Secretary of State, Cumberland entered seriously on the career of dramatist to which his early interest and some actual experimentation in playwriting naturally inclined him. His first regular and considerably successful comedy, *The Brothers* (1769), was followed by his most popular sentimental comedy, *The West Indian* (1771). Though the earlier comedy had been staged at Covent Garden Theatre, Garrick, susceptible to the personal flattery included in its epilogue, took up Cumberland and secured for *The West Indian* a theatrical triumph at Drury Lane. It ran for twenty-eight nights, sold rapidly in various editions, and established Cumberland as a popular playwright and well-known figure in London literary circles. Henceforth he shared with Hugh Kelly the leadership in sentimental drama, and presently bore with him the brunt of the insurgent attack already launched by Oliver Goldsmith and soon to be powerfully supported by Richard Brinsley Sheridan.

False Delicacy and *The West Indian* are alike 'genteel' comedies, in which the delicate distresses of sentimental lovers are showered with a wealth of moral aphorisms all along the path that leads to the assured rewards of virtue. *False Delicacy* points its 'principal moral' with the parting conclusion that 'those who generously labor for the happiness of others, will, sooner or later, arrive at happiness themselves.' In an earlier speech of his final act, Kelly makes one of his characters, Winworth, the mouthpiece of the whole group of sentimental dramatists in declaring that 'the stage should be a school of morality.' *False Delicacy*, to be sure, relieves its sentimentality and sermon-izing with touches of truer comedy, as in characters like Cecil and Mrs. Harley who disdain the compunctions of false delicacy and the nice excesses of 'refined sentiment.' But, in the main, Kelly's insistent purpose is to justify the ways of sentimental comedy and to school his audience in the lessons of didactic morality.

In *The West Indian*, Cumberland bestows on the sentimental hero 'a heart beaming with benevo-lence, an animated nature, fallible indeed, but not incorrigible.' Young Belcour's hazard of new fortunes in London is comfortably assured by his possession of a vast West Indian fortune left to him as a supposed foundling in Jamaica. His prosperous path is turned luckily to the home of the merchant Stockwell, in reality his long-lost father. The hero's benevolent heart, after due chastening of his 'fallible, but not incorrigible,' impulses, is united with the virtuous Louisa's at the altar of sentiment. In the secondary plot virtuous love is again triumphant, and its material rewards conveniently provided by the opportune disclosure of the secret of a missing will. Within the obviously artificial frame-work of sentimental comedy, and with a group of characters designed to suit its conventions of plot and dialogue, Cumberland contrived to fulfil remarkably the demands of the theatre and of an audience attuned to his key.

The rise of sentimental comedy to full height in *False Delicacy* and *The West Indian* quickened, instead of quelled, opposition. OLIVER GOLDSMITH (1728–1774) had long ago, as critic, taken deci-sive stand against those who sought to shackle the free spirit of comedy. As early as 1759, in *The Present State of Polite Learning*, he had inveighed against 'the power of one single monosyllable' to brand as 'low' whatever exceeded the limits imposed by 'genteel' conventions. 'Does the poet paint the absurdities of the vulgar; then he is *low*; does he exaggerate the features of folly, to render it more thoroughly ridiculous, he is then very *low*. In short, they have proscribed the comic or satirical muse from every walk but high life.' How heavily this proscription continued to weigh is made manifest in Goldsmith's preface to *The Good-Natured Man* (1768), the militant declaration of his dramatic creed. 'When I undertook to write a comedy, I confess I was strongly prepossessed in favor of the poets of the last age, and strove to imitate them. The term, *genteel comedy*, was then unknown amongst us, and little more was desired by an audience than nature and humor in whatever walks of life they were most conspicuous.' Seeking 'to delineate character' as his 'prin-cipal aim,' and 'sensible that, in pursuing humor, it will sometimes lead us into the recesses of the mean,' Goldsmith was 'even tempted to look for it in the master of a spunging-house; but in deference to the public taste, grown of late, perhaps, too delicate, the scene of the bailiffs was re-trenched in the representation.' Against the false delicacy which forbade comedy to bring matter so vulgarian betwixt the wind and its gentility, Goldsmith appealed to 'the reader in his closet,' by restoring the scene in print. Hopeful 'that too much refinement will not banish humor and character from ours, as it has already done from the French theatre,' he reminds his countrymen that 'French comedy is now become so very elevated and sentimental that it has not only ban-ished humor and *Molière* from the stage, but it has banished all spectators too.'

The immediate victory of *False Delicacy* over *The Good-Natured Man*, in January, 1768, and the further success of Cumberland's *The West Indian*, in 1771, halted, but failed to defeat, Goldsmith's settled campaign against sentimental comedy. Rallying his full forces for final attack on the entrenched foe, he first redefined the critical issues. The new year of 1773 opened with his chal-lenging *Essay on the Theatre; or, A Comparison between Laughing and Sentimental Comedy* (here reprinted in full, pp. 759–763). It puts the question unequivocally: 'Which deserves the preference, — the weeping sentimental comedy so much in fashion at present, or the laughing, and even low comedy, which seems to have been last exhibited by Vanbrugh and Cibber?' To that question Goldsmith himself presently gave most decisive answer with the production, on March 15, 1773, of *She Stoops to Conquer*.

Obstacles, local as well as general, had threatened. The faint-hearted manager of Covent Garden, George Colman, had dallied and despaired. In dedicating his play to his generous supporter, Dr. Johnson, Goldsmith permitted himself a pointed reference to Colman: 'The undertaking a comedy not merely sentimental, was very dangerous; and Mr. Colman, who saw this piece in its various stages, always thought it so.' Some of the actors shared the manager's misgivings and objected to their rôles. Dr. Johnson, however, staunchly supported Goldsmith's play and on the opening night led the laughter and applause. The cause of 'laughing, and even low comedy' was vindicated decisively. Goldsmith had stooped to conquer false delicacy.

Even Horace Walpole, patrician defender of the faith in 'genteel comedy,' had to admit that Goldsmith's play had 'succeeded prodigiously.' It was in vain that he branded its humor as 'low,' its characters as 'very low,' and the play itself as 'the lowest of all farces.' In the lowly setting of an alehouse room (I. ii), the several 'shabby fellows' who applaud Tony Lumpkin's song had become mocking instruments for Goldsmith's harping on the warfare of the words 'low' and 'genteel.' 'The power of one single monosyllable' could no longer 'damn anything's that's *low*.' Over the genteel prejudices that had rejected the bailiffs' scene from his earlier comedy, Goldsmith had at last triumphed gloriously.

The death of Oliver Goldsmith a year later, in 1774, did not eclipse the gaiety of comedy. In January, 1775, the cause of laughing comedy was assured by the advent of a new leader, RICHARD BRINSLEY SHERIDAN (1751–1816). Goldsmith's ultimate victory in the theatre had come to him late in life and in a field which he had long left untried. Sheridan was but twenty-three when *The Rivals* appeared on the stage of Covent Garden Theatre. The story of its initial failure on January 17, 1775, of its immediate withdrawal for revision, and of its quick success on January 28, assured by radical improvements of text and acting, is familiar stage-history. In the author's *Prologue, Spoken on the Tenth Night*, Sheridan directly challenged 'the goddess of the woful countenance — the sentimental Muse,' defending true comedy from the didactic intrusions, and tragedy from the 'dire encroachments,' of sentimental drama. In *The Rivals*, the heroine of sentimental comedy is delightfully satirized in the person of Lydia Languish, whose romantic impulses are fed on the sentimental novels of the circulating library. In the 'sentimental swearing' of Bob Acres and in Mrs. Malaprop's 'nice derangement of epitaphs' Sheridan gives full play to 'humors' of speech, while 'humors' of character are zestfully underscored in the names bestowed on many of the *dramatis personæ*. In some of the Julia-Faulkland passages which genteel critics found quite to their taste, and in occasional lapses, as in Julia's closing speech, into artificial diction Sheridan is not untouched by the sentimentalism against which he was mainly in revolt. But prologue and play together attest his essential creed and practice. Recognizing the bad eminence which sentimental comedy had attained, he deliberately set face against its tyranny of tears and moral maxims. Goldsmith's protest against 'weeping sentimental comedy' reverberates in Sheridan's defiance of 'the goddess of the woful countenance — the sentimental Muse.'

Sheridan followed *The Rivals* with a brief farce, *St. Patrick's Day* (May 2, 1775) and an opera, *The Duenna* (November 21, 1775), whose instant and prolonged popularity rivalled that of *The Beggar's Opera* half a century earlier. His success had been established at Covent Garden, and these 'two best comedies of his age' sufficed to assure Dr. Johnson's favor and Sheridan's election, in 1777, to the Literary Club. In June, 1776, however, a new way opened with David Garrick's retirement from his long leadership in the theatre. As Garrick's successor as manager of Drury Lane Theatre, Sheridan had henceforth at direct disposal his own stage.

In his first season, Sheridan recognized popular demand for a new play from the author-manager, but delayed full response. On February 24, 1777, his adaptation of Vanbrugh's Restoration comedy, *The Relapse*, revised and expurgated under the title, *A Trip to Scarborough*, temporized with the situation. Late in the season, however, on May 8, 1777, the utmost popular expectations were exceeded in the triumph of *The School for Scandal*. Abandoning the constraint of revising and reforming the text and ethics of a given Restoration play, Sheridan now recalled the spirit, but not the letter, of the Restoration comedy of manners. With wit of dialogue that vied with Congreve's, and with superior craftsmanship, Sheridan recaptured the way of the world of fashion. Once more the *beau monde* peopled the stage, and comedy regained the weapon of wit. In Sheridan's hands it cut quick through sentimental tissue. The moral maxims of sentimental drama were exposed to the thrust of satire in their transfer from the mouths of the virtuous to the lip-service of the hypocrite Joseph Surface, the 'man of sentiment.' 'Again our young Don Quixote takes the road,' declared Garrick in the prologue which he wrote for his successor at Drury Lane, 'And seeks this hydra, Scandal, in his den.' Sheridan, indeed, had found in his scandal-mongers a fit theme for satirical comedy. Though, as in *The Rivals*, his critical stand against the 'Sentimental Muse' continued firm, his creative instinct had again impelled him far beyond the limits of merely destructive warfare. Not content with dethroning 'the goddess of the woful countenance,' Sheridan set in her place the true 'Figure of Comedy.'

On October 30, 1779, Sheridan gave to his Drury Lane stage another masterpiece, *The Critic; or, A Tragedy Rehearsed*. Though first performed as an after-piece to *Hamlet*, and limited accordingly to three acts, and though abandoning the higher comedy of manners for the lesser form of dramatic burlesque, *The Critic* revealed anew Sheridan's mastery of dramatic art. Following the general type of dramatic burlesque established for the Restoration age in *The Rehearsal*, and for the earlier eighteenth century in *Tom Thumb*, but depending far less on parody of precise speeches or of specific scenes from a multitude of contemporary plays, Sheridan raised his burlesque of the theatrical fashions of his day into satire of perennial absurdities of drama and of the enveloping world of the theatre. Though he took Richard Cumberland as immediate target, he created in Sir Fretful Plagiary, within the confines of a single scene of the opening act, a character surpassing the exigencies of personal caricature. Though one of Hugh Kelly's cardinal maxims is taken from *False Delicacy* and mockingly put in the mouth of Sneer — 'the theatre, in proper hands, might certainly be made the school of morality' — the opening dialogue of Dangle and Sneer prevailingly satirizes the general absurdities of the whole school of sentimental dramatists. Though the opening act is full of allusions to the immediate political situation, and the 'Tragedy Rehearsed,' *The Spanish Armada*, is pointedly linked with the Spanish invasion imminently threatened in the fall of 1779, Sheridan's dialogue is sustained throughout with sheer wit worthy of the 'Comic Muse.' The constant popularity of *The Critic* with later generations of playgoers mainly unfamiliar with the local allusions of Sheridan's text proves his power to raise the most ephemeral of dramatic forms from contemporary burlesque to enduring satire.

Within the half-decade from *The Rivals* (January, 1775) to *The Critic* (October, 1779) Sheridan had become ruler of Drury Lane Theatre and the foremost dramatist of his age. At twenty-eight he had fulfilled the measure of his prodigal powers in the theatre. *The Critic* virtually concludes his brief and brilliant period of original dramatic creation. It conveniently marks also the end of a decade of English drama which, closely viewed, centers in the conflict between sentimental and laughing comedy. Broadly viewed, the decade from 1770 to 1780 is supremely significant in its permanent creative achievement. Independent of temporary circumstances and local influences, *She Stoops to Conquer*, *The Rivals*, and *The School for Scandal* stand as the enduring contribution of the eighteenth century to English comedy. In its lesser but adjacent field, *The Critic* shares with them the continuity and vitality of their historic tradition and contribution to the modern

English stage. In the work of Goldsmith and Sheridan, the long course of English dramatic development from 1660 to 1780 here reviewed is richly fulfilled.

G. H. N.

REFERENCE WORKS

1903. Dobson, Austin. *The Good Natur'd Man and She Stoops to Conquer.* (*Belles-Lettres Series.*) Boston [U.S.A.] and London. [*Introduction.*]

1906. Nettleton, George H. *The Major Dramas of Richard Brinsley Sheridan.* (*Athenæum Press Series.*) Boston.

1913. *Cambridge History of English Literature*, Vol. X. Cambridge. [Chapter IV, by George H. Nettleton; Chapter IX, by Austin Dobson.]

1914. Nettleton, George H. *English Drama of the Restoration and Eighteenth Century.* New York. [Chapters XVI, XVII, XVIII.]

1915. Bernbaum, Ernest. *The Drama of Sensibility.* Boston [U.S.A.] and London. [Chapters XII–XIII.]

1927. Nicoll, Allardyce. *A History of Late Eighteenth Century Drama 1750–1800.*

1931. Nettleton, George H. *Sheridan et la Comédie de Mœurs.* Paris.

The West Indian

BY RICHARD CUMBERLAND

THE
WEST INDIAN:
A
COMEDY.

As it is Performed at the

THEATRE ROYAL

IN

DRURY-LANE

(Quis novus hic Hofpes?)

A NEW EDITION.

LONDON:
Printed for W. GRIFFIN, at GARRICK'S HEAD,
in Catherine Street Strand.
MDCCLXXI.

ENGRAVED TITLE-PAGE OF THE REVISED ('NEW') EDITION, 1771, OF *THE WEST INDIAN*

PROLOGUE

Spoken by Mr. Reddish [1]

Critics, hark forward! noble game and new;
A fine West Indian started full in view:
Hot as the soil, the clime, which gave him birth,
You'll run him on a burning scent to earth;
Yet don't devour him in his hiding place;   5
Bag him, he'll serve you for another chase;
For sure that country has no feeble claim,
Which swells your commerce, and supports your fame.
And in this humble sketch, we hope you'll find
Some emanations of a noble mind;   10
Some little touches, which, though void of art,
May find perhaps their way into the heart.
Another hero your excuse implores,
Sent by your sister kingdom to your shores;
Doomed by religion's too severe command,   15
To fight for bread against his native land:
A brave, unthinking, animated rogue,
With here and there a touch upon the brogue;
Laugh, but despise him not, for on his lip
His errors lie; his heart can never trip.   20
Others there are — but may we not prevail
To let the gentry tell their own plain tale?
Shall they come in?   They'll please you, if they can;
If not, condemn the bard — but spare the *man*.
For speak, think, act, or write in angry times,   25
A wish to please is made the worst of crimes;
Dire slander now with black envenomed dart,
Stands ever armed to stab you to the heart.
    Rouse, Britons, rouse, for honor of your isle,
Your old good humor; and be seen to smile.   30
You say we write not like our fathers — true,
Nor were our fathers half so strict as you,
Damned not each error of the poet's pen,
But judging man, remembered they were men.
Awed into silence by the times' abuse,   35
Sleeps many a wise, and many a witty muse;
We that for mere experiment come out,
Are but the light-armed rangers on the scout:
High on Parnassus' lofty summit stands
The immortal camp; there lie the chosen bands!   40
But give fair quarter to us puny elves,
The giants then will sally forth themselves;
With wit's sharp weapons vindicate the age,
And drive ev'n *Arthur's* [2] magic from the *stage*.

---

[1] Samuel Reddish (1735–1785) acted at Drury Lane, 1767–1777.
[2] Garrick's revival of Dryden's *King Arthur* during the Drury Lane season of 1770–1771 had popularized it with playgoers.

DRAMATIS PERSONÆ

MEN	WOMEN
STOCKWELL	LADY RUSPORT
BELCOUR	CHARLOTTE RUSPORT
CAPTAIN DUDLEY	LOUISA, *daughter to* DUDLEY
CHARLES DUDLEY	MRS. FULMER
MAJOR O'FLAHERTY	LUCY
STUKELY	*Housekeeper belonging to* STOCKWELL
FULMER	
VARLAND	
Servant to STOCKWELL	

Clerks belonging to STOCKWELL; *servants, sailors, negroes, &c.*

SCENE — LONDON.

THE WEST INDIAN

By RICHARD CUMBERLAND

ACT I

SCENE I

A merchant's compting-house.[1]

*In an inner room, set off by glass doors, are discovered
several clerks, employed at their desks. A writing
table in the front room.* STOCKWELL *is discovered
reading a letter;* STUKELY *comes gently out of the
back room, and observes him some time before
he speaks.*

STUKELY. He seems disordered: something in
that letter; and I'm afraid of an unpleasant sort.
He has many ventures of great account at sea; a
ship richly freighted for Barcelona; another for
Lisbon; and others expected from Cadiz of still 5
greater value. Besides these, I know he has many
deep concerns in foreign bottoms, and underwritings
to a vast amount. I'll accost him. Sir! Mr.
Stockwell!

STOCKWELL. Stukely! — Well, have you 10
shipped the cloths?

STUKELY. I have, sir; here's the bill of lading, and
copy of the invoice: the assortments are all compared: Mr. Traffick will give you the policy upon
'Change. 15

STOCK. 'Tis very well; lay these papers by; and
no more of business for a while. Shut the door,
Stukely; I have had long proof of your friendship
and fidelity to me; a matter of most intimate concern
lies on my mind, and 'twill be a sensible relief 20
to unbosom myself to you; I have just now been
informed of the arrival of the young West Indian,
I have so long been expecting; you know who
I mean.

STUKELY. Yes, sir; Mr. Belcour, the young 25
gentleman, who inherited old Belcour's great estates
in Jamaica.

STOCK. Hush, not so loud; come a little nearer
this way. This Belcour is now in London; part of
his baggage is already arrived; and I expect him 30
every minute. Is it to be wondered at, if his coming
throws me into some agitation, when I tell you,
Stukely, he is my son?

STUKELY. Your son!

STOCK. Yes, sir, my only son; early in life I 35
accompanied his grandfather to Jamaica as his clerk;
he had an only daughter, somewhat older than

myself; the mother of this gentleman: it was my
chance (call it good or ill) to engage her affections:
and, as the inferiority of my condition made it 40
hopeless to expect her father's consent, her fondness
provided an expedient, and we were privately
married; the issue of that concealed engagement is,
as I have told you, this Belcour.

STUKELY. That event, surely, discovered 45
your connection.

STOCK. You shall hear. Not many days after
our marriage old Belcour set out for England; and,
during his abode here, my wife was, with great
secrecy, delivered of this son. Fruitful in expe- 50
dients to disguise her situation, without parting
from her infant, she contrived to have it laid and
received at her door as a foundling. After some
time her father returned, having left me here; in
one of those favorable moments that decide 55
the fortunes of prosperous men, this child was
introduced; from that instant, he treated him as
his own, gave him his name, and brought him up
in his family.

STUKELY. And did you never reveal this 60
secret, either to old Belcour, or your son?

STOCK. Never.

STUKELY. Therein you surprise me; a merchant
of your eminence, and a member of the British
parliament, might surely aspire, without offence, 65
to the daughter of a planter. In this case too,
natural affection would prompt to a discovery.

STOCK. Your remark is obvious; nor could I have
persisted in this painful silence, but in obedience
to the dying injunctions of a beloved wife. The 70
letter you found me reading conveyed those injunctions to me; it was dictated in her last illness, and
almost in the article of death (you'll spare me the
recital of it); she there conjures me, in terms as
solemn as they are affecting, never to reveal 75
the secret of our marriage, or withdraw my son,
while her father survived.

STUKELY. But on what motives did your unhappy
lady found these injunctions?

STOCK. Principally, I believe, from appre- 80
hension on my account, lest old Belcour, on whom
at her decease I wholly depended, should withdraw
his protection: in part from consideration of his
repose, as well knowing the discovery would deeply
affect his spirit, which was haughty, vehement, 85
and unforgiving: and lastly, in regard to the interest

---

[1] Counting-house.

of her infant, whom he had warmly adopted; and
for whom, in case of a discovery, everything was to
be dreaded from his resentment.   And, indeed,
though the alteration in my condition might   90
have justified me in discovering myself, yet I always
thought my son safer in trusting to the caprice than
to the justice of his grandfather.   My judgment
has not suffered by the event; old Belcour is dead,
and has bequeathed his whole estate to him we   95
are speaking of.

STUKELY. Now then you are not longer bound to
secrecy.

STOCK. True: but before I publicly reveal myself,
I could wish to make some experiment of my   100
son's disposition: this can only be done by letting
his spirit take its course without restraint; by these
means, I think I shall discover much more of his
real character under the title of his merchant, than
I should under that of his father.   105

SCENE II

*A Sailor enters, ushering in several black Servants,
carrying portmanteaus, trunks, &c.*

SAILOR. Save your honor! is your name Stockwell,
pray?

STOCK. It is.

SAILOR. Part of my master Belcour's baggage
an't please you; there's another cargo not far   5
astern of us; and the coxswain has got charge of the
dumb creatures.

STOCK. Prithee, friend, what dumb creatures do
you speak of; has Mr. Belcour brought over a
collection of wild beasts?   10

SAILOR. No, Lord love him; no, not he: let me see;
there's two green monkeys, a pair of grey parrots,
a Jamaica sow and pigs, and a Mangrove[1] dog;
that's all.

STOCK. Is that all?   15

SAILOR. Yes, your honor; yes, that's all; bless
his heart; 'a might have brought over the whole
island if he would; 'a didn't leave a dry eye in it.

STOCK. Indeed! Stukely, show 'em where to
bestow their baggage. Follow that gentleman.   20

SAILOR. Come, bear a hand, my lads, bear a hand.
Exit with STUKELY *and Servants.*

STOCK. If the principal tallies with his purveyors,
he must be a singular spectacle in this place: he has
a friend, however, in this seafaring fellow; 'tis no
bad prognostic of a man's heart, when his ship-   25
mates give him a good word.   *Exit.*

[1] Here, 'Jamaican' or 'West Indian.'

SCENE III

*Scene changes to a drawing-room.   A Servant dis-
covered setting the chairs by, &c.   A Woman
Servant enters to him.*

HOUSEKEEPER. Why, what a fuss does our good
master put himself in about this West Indian: see
what a bill of fare I've been forced to draw out:
seven and nine, I'll assure you, and only a family
dinner as he calls it: why if my Lord Mayor   5
was expected, there couldn't be a greater to-do
about him.

SERV. I wish to my heart you had but seen the
loads of trunks, boxes, and portmanteaus he has
sent hither. An ambassador's baggage, with all   10
the smuggled goods of his family, does not exceed it.

HOUSEK. A fine pickle he'll put the house into:
had he been master's own son, and a Christian
Englishman, there could not be more rout[2] than
there is about this Creolian, as they call 'em.   15

SERV. No matter for that; he's very rich, and
that's sufficient. They say he has rum and sugar
enough belonging to him, to make all the water
in the Thames into punch. But I see my master's
coming.   *Exeunt.*   20

SCENE IV

STOCKWELL *enters, followed by a Servant.*

STOCK. Where is Mr. Belcour? Who brought
this note from him?

SERV. A waiter from the London Tavern, sir;
he says the young gentleman is just dressed, and
will be with you directly.   5

STOCK. Show him in when he arrives.

SERV. I shall, sir. — (*Aside.*) I'll have a peep
at him first, however; I've a great mind to see this
outlandish spark. The sailor fellow says he'll make
rare doings amongst us.   10

STOCK. You need not wait; leave me.
Exit Servant.

Let me see. (*Reads.*)
*Sir,
I write to you under the hands of the hairdresser;
as soon as I have made myself decent, and   15
slipped on some fresh clothes, I will have the honor
of paying you my devoirs.
Yours,
Belcour.*

He writes at his ease; for he's unconscious to   20
whom his letter is addressed, but what a palpitation
does it throw my heart into; a father's heart! 'Tis
an affecting interview; when my eyes meet a son,

[2] Ado.

whom yet they never saw, where shall I find constancy to support it? Should he resemble his 25 mother, I am overthrown. All the letters I have had from him (for I industriously drew him into a correspondence with me) bespeak him of quick and ready understanding. All the reports I ever received give me favorable impressions of his 30 character; wild, perhaps, as the manner of his country is, but, I trust, not frantic or unprincipled.

SCENE V

Servant enters.

SERV. Sir, the foreign gentleman is come.

[*Enter*] *another Servant.*

[SECOND] SERV. Mr. Belcour.

BELCOUR *enters.*

STOCK. Mr. Belcour, I'm rejoiced to see you; you're welcome to England.

BEL. I thank you heartily, good Mr. Stock- 5 well; you and I have long conversed at a distance; now we are met; and the pleasure this meeting gives me amply compensates for the perils I have run through in accomplishing it.

STOCK. What perils, Mr. Belcour? I could 10 not have thought you would have met a bad passage at this time o'year.

BEL. Nor did we: courier-like, we came posting to your shores, upon the pinions of the swiftest gales that ever blew; 'tis upon English ground all 15 my difficulties have arisen; 'tis the passage from the riverside I complain of.

STOCK. Ay, indeed! What obstructions can you have met between this and the riverside?

BEL. Innumerable! Your town's as full of 20 defiles as the Island of Corsica; and, I believe, they are as obstinately defended: so much hurry, bustle, and confusion, on your quays; so many sugar-casks, porter-butts, and common council-men, in your streets; that, unless a man marched with 25 artillery in his front, 'tis more than the labor of a Hercules can effect to make any tolerable way through your town.

STOCK. I am sorry you have been so incommoded.

BEL. Why, faith, 'twas all my own fault; ac- 30 customed to a land of slaves, and out of patience with the whole tribe of custom-house extortioners, boatmen, tide-waiters,[1] and water-bailiffs,[2] that beset me on all sides, worse than a swarm of mosquitoes, I proceeded a little too roughly to brush 35 them away with my rattan; the sturdy rogues took

[1] Customs officers who awaited the arrival of ships (with the tide).

[2] Custom-house officers who searched ships.

this in dudgeon, and beginning to rebel, the mob chose different sides, and a furious scuffle ensued; in the course of which, my person and apparel suffered so much, that I was obliged to step into 40 the first tavern to refit, before I could make my approaches in any decent trim.

STOCK. (*aside*). All without is as I wish; dear Nature add the rest, and I am happy. — Well, Mr. Belcour, 'tis a rough sample you have had of my 45 countrymen's spirit; but, I trust, you'll not think the worse of them for it.

BEL. Not at all, not at all; I like 'em the better; was I only a visitor, I might, perhaps, wish them a little more tractable; but, as a fellow subject, 50 and a sharer in their freedom, I applaud their spirit, though I feel the effects of it in every bone in my skin.

STOCK. (*aside*). That's well; I like that well. How gladly I could fall upon his neck, and own 55 myself his father.

BEL. Well, Mr. Stockwell, for the first time in my life, here am I in England; at the fountain head of pleasure, in the land of beauty, of arts, and elegancies. My happy stars have given me a good 60 estate, and the conspiring winds have blown me hither to spend it.

STOCK. To use, not to waste it, I should hope; to treat it, Mr. Belcour, not as a vassal, over whom you have a wanton and despotic power, but as 65 a subject, which you are bound to govern with a temperate and restrained authority.

BEL. True, sir; most truly said; mine's a commission, not a right: I am the offspring of distress, and every child of sorrow is my brother; while 70 I have hands to hold, therefore, I will hold them open to mankind: but, sir, my passions are my masters; they take me where they will; and oftentimes they leave to reason and to virtue nothing but my wishes and my sighs. 75

STOCK. Come, come, the man who can accuse corrects himself.

BEL. Ah! that's an office I am weary of: I wish a friend would take it up: I would to heaven you had leisure for the employ; but, did you drive a trade 80 to the four corners of the world, you would not find the task so toilsome as to keep me free from faults.

STOCK. Well, I am not discouraged; this candor tells me I should not have the fault of self- 85 conceit to combat; that, at least, is not amongst the number.

BEL. No; if I knew that man on earth who thought more humbly of me than I do of myself, I would take up his opinion and forego my own. 90

STOCK. And, was I to choose a pupil, it should be one of your complexion; so if you'll come along with me, we'll agree upon your admission, and enter on a course of lectures directly.

BEL. With all my heart. *Exeunt.* 95

SCENE VI

Scene changes to a room in LADY RUSPORT'S *house.*

LADY RUSPORT *and* CHARLOTTE.

LADY RUSPORT. Miss Rusport, I desire to hear no more of Captain Dudley and his destitute family: not a shilling of mine shall ever cross the hands of any of them: because my sister chose to marry a beggar, am I bound to support him and his 5 posterity?

CHARLOTTE. I think you are.

LADY R. You think I am; and pray where do you find the law that tells you so?

CHARLOTTE. I am not proficient enough to 10 quote chapter and verse; but I take charity to be a main clause in the great statute of Christianity.

LADY R. I say charity, indeed! And pray, miss, are you sure that it is charity, pure charity, which moves you to plead for Captain Dudley? 15 Amongst all your pity, do you find no spice of a certain anti-spiritual passion, called love? Don't mistake yourself, you are no saint, child, believe me; and, I am apt to think the distresses of old Dudley, and of his daughter into the bargain, 20 would never break your heart, if there was not a certain young fellow of two and twenty in the case; who, by the happy recommendation of a good person, and the brilliant appointments of an ensigncy, will, if I am not mistaken, cozen you out of a 25 fortune of twice twenty thousand pounds, as soon as ever you are of age to bestow it upon him.

CHARLOTTE. A nephew of your ladyship's can never want any other recommendation with me; and, if my partiality for Charles Dudley is ac- 30 quitted by the rest of the world, I hope Lady Rusport will not condemn me for it.

LADY R. I condemn you! I thank heaven, Miss Rusport, I am no ways responsible for your conduct; nor is it any concern of mine how you dispose 35 of yourself; you are not my daughter; and, when I married your father, poor Sir Stephen Rusport, I found you a forward spoiled miss of fourteen far above being instructed by me.

CHARLOTTE. Perhaps your ladyship calls this 40 instruction.

LADY R. You're strangely pert; but 'tis no wonder: your mother, I'm told, was a fine lady; and according to the modern style of education you was brought up. It was not so in my 45 young days; there was then some decorum in the world, some subordination, as the great Locke expresses it. Oh! 'twas an edifying sight, to see the regular deportment observed in our family: no giggling, no gossiping was going on there; my 50 good father, Sir Oliver Roundhead, never was seen to laugh himself, nor ever allowed it in his children.

CHARLOTTE. Ay; those were happy times, indeed.

LADY R. But, in this forward age, we have coquettes in the egg-shell, and philosophers in 55 the cradle; girls of fifteen that lead the fashion in new caps and new opinions, that have their sentiments and their sensations, and the idle fops encourage 'em in it. O' my conscience, I wonder what it is the men can see in such babies. 60

CHARLOTTE. True, madam; but all men do not overlook the maturer beauties of your ladyship's age, witness your admirer Major Dennis O'Flaherty; there's an example of some discernment; I declare to you, when your ladyship is by, the Major 65 takes no more notice of me than if I was part of the furniture of your chamber.

LADY R. The Major, child, has travelled through various kingdoms and climates, and has more enlarged notions of female merit than falls to 70 the lot of an English home-bred lover; in most other countries, no woman on your side forty would ever be named in a polite circle.

CHARLOTTE. Right, madam; I've been told that in Vienna they have coquettes upon crutches 75 and Venuses in their grand clima[c]teric; a lover there celebrates the wrinkles, not the dimples, in his mistress's face. The Major, I think, has served in the imperial army.

LADY R. Are you piqued, my young madam? 80 Had my sister Louisa yielded to the addresses of one of Major O'Flaherty's person and appearance, she would have had some excuse: but to run away, as she did, at the age of sixteen too, with a man of old Dudley's sort — 85

CHARLOTTE. Was, in my opinion, the most venial trespass that ever girl of sixteen committed; of a noble family, an engaging person, strict honor, and sound understanding, what accomplishment was there wanting in Captain Dudley, 90 but that which the prodigality of his ancestors had deprived him of?

LADY R. They left him as much as he deserves; hasn't the old man captain's half-pay? And is not the son an ensign? 95

CHARLOTTE. An ensign! Alas, poor Charles! Would to heaven he knew what my heart feels and suffers for his sake.

Servant enters.

SERV. Ensign Dudley to wait upon your ladyship. 100

SCENE VI.　12] R *mean* for *main* (a bad misprint).
81] O1DB *now yielded*; O2O3N omit *now*.

63] R *admired* for *admirer* (probably another misprint).

LADY R. Who! Dudley! What can have brought him to town?

CHARLOTTE. Dear madam, 'tis Charles Dudley, 'tis your nephew.

LADY R. Nephew! I renounce him as my　105 nephew; Sir Oliver renounced him as his grandson: wasn't he son of the eldest daughter, and only male descendant of Sir Oliver; and didn't he cut him off with a shilling? Didn't the poor dear good man leave his whole fortune to me, except a　110 small annuity to my maiden sister, who spoiled her constitution with nursing him? And, depend upon it, not a penny of that fortune shall ever be disposed of otherwise than according to the will of the donor.　115

CHARLES DUDLEY *enters.*

So, young man, whence come you? What brings you to town?

CHARLES. If there is any offence in my coming to town, your ladyship is in some degree responsible for it, for part of my errand was to pay my　120 duty here.

LADY R. I hope you have some better excuse than all this.

CHARLES. 'Tis true, madam, I have other motives; but, if I consider my trouble repaid by　125 the pleasure I now enjoy, I should hope my aunt would not think my company the less welcome for the value I set upon hers.

LADY R. Coxcomb! And where is your father, child; and your sister? Are they in town too?　130

CHARLES. They are.

LADY R. Ridiculous! I don't know what people do in London, who have no money to spend in it.

CHARLOTTE. Dear madam, speak more kindly to your nephew; how can you oppress a youth　135 of his sensibility?

LADY R. Miss Rusport, I insist upon your retiring to your apartment; when I want your advice I'll send to you.　　　*Exit* CHARLOTTE. So you have put on a red coat too, as well as　140 your father; 'tis plain what value you set upon the good advice Sir Oliver used to give you; how often has he cautioned you against the army?

CHARLES. Had it pleased my grandfather to enable me to have obeyed his caution, I would　145 have done it; but you well know how destitute I am; and 'tis not to be wondered at if I prefer the service of my king to that of any other master.

LADY R. Well, well, take your own course; 'tis no concern of mine: you never consulted me.　150

CHARLES. I frequently wrote to your ladyship, but could obtain no answer; and, since my grandfather's death, this is the first opportunity I have had of waiting upon you.

LADY R. I must desire you not to mention　155 the death of that dear good man in my hearing, my spirits cannot support it.

CHARLES. I shall obey you; permit me to say, that, as that event has richly supplied you with the materials of bounty, the distresses of my　160 family can furnish you with objects of it.

LADY R. The distresses of your family, child, are quite out of the question at present; had Sir Oliver been pleased to consider them, I should have been well content; but he has absolutely taken no　165 notice of you in his will, and that to me must and shall be a law. Tell your father and your sister I totally disapprove of their coming up to town.

CHARLES. Must I tell my father that, before your ladyship knows the motive that brought him　170 hither? Allured by the offer of exchanging for a commission on full pay, the veteran, after thirty years' service, prepares to encounter the fatal heats of Senegambia; but wants a small supply to equip him for the expedition.　175

Servant enters.

SERV. Major O'Flaherty to wait upon your ladyship.

MAJOR *enters.*

MAJOR. Spare your speeches, young man, don't you think her ladyship can take my word for that? I hope, madam, 'tis evidence enough of my　180 being present, when I've the honor of telling you so myself.

LADY R. Major O'Flaherty, I am rejoiced to see you. Nephew Dudley, you perceive I'm engaged.　185

CHARLES. I shall not intrude upon your ladyship's more agreeable engagements. I presume I have my answer.

LADY R. Your answer, child! What answer can you possibly expect; or how can your romantic　190 father suppose that I am to abet him in all his idle and extravagant undertakings? Come, Major, let me show you the way into my dressing-room; and let us leave this young adventurer to his meditation.　　　*Exit.*　195

O'FLAHERTY. I follow you, my lady. Young gentleman, your obedient! [*Aside.*] Upon my conscience, as fine a young fellow as I would wish to clap my eyes on: he might have answered my salute, however,— well, let it pass; Fortune, perhaps,　200 frowns upon the poor lad; she's a damned slippery lady, and very apt to jilt us poor fellows, that wear cockades in our hats. Fare-thee-well, honey, who-ever thou art.

CHARLES. So much for the virtues of a puri-　205 tan; out upon it, her heart is flint; yet that woman,

---

116] R *came*; all 1771 eds. *come* (R alters needlessly).　　194-195] O1DB *meditations*; O2O3N *meditation*.

that aunt of mine, without one worthy particle in
her composition, would, I dare be sworn, as soon
set her foot in a pest-house, as in a play-house.
                                                (*Going.*)

MISS RUSPORT *enters to him.*

CHARLOTTE. Stop, stay a little, Charles, 210
whither are you going in such haste?

CHARLES. Madam! Miss Rusport! what are
your commands?

CHARLOTTE. Why so reserved? We had used
to answer to no other names than those of 215
Charles and Charlotte.

CHARLES. What ails you? you've been weeping.

CHARLOTTE. No, no; or if I have — your eyes
are full too; but I have a thousand things to say
to you: before you go, tell me, I conjure you, 220
where you are to be found; here give me your
direction; write it upon the back of this visiting-
ticket — Have you a pencil?

CHARLES. I have: but why should you desire to find
us out? 'tis a poor little inconvenient place; 225
my sister has no apartment fit to receive you in.

Servant enters.

SERV. Madam, my lady desires your company
directly.

CHARLOTTE. I am coming — well, have you wrote
it? Give it me. O Charles! either you do 230
not, or you will not, understand me.

                                        Exeunt severally.

ACT II

SCENE I

A room in FULMER'S *house.*

FULMER *and* MRS. FULMER.

MRS. FULMER. Why, how you sit, musing and
moping, sighing and desponding! I'm ashamed of
you, Mr. Fulmer: is this the country you described
to me, a second Eldorado, rivers of gold and rocks
of diamonds? You found me in a pretty snug re- 5
tired way of life at Bo[u]logne, out of the noise and
bustle of the world, and wholly at my ease; you,
indeed, was upon the wing, with a fiery persecution
at your back: but, like a true son of Loyola, you
had then a thousand ingenious devices to repair 10
your fortune; and this your native country was to be
the scene of your performances: fool that I was, to
be inveigled into it by you; but thank heaven, our
partnership is revocable: I am not your wedded
wife, praised be my stars! for what have we got, 15
whom have we gulled but ourselves? which of all
your trains has taken fire? even this poor expedient
of your bookseller's shop seems abandoned, for if a

chance customer drops in, who is there, pray, to
help him to what he wants?   20

FULMER. Patty, you know it is not upon slight
grounds that I despair; there had used to be a
livelihood to be picked up in this country, both for
the honest and dishonest; I have tried each walk,
and am likely to starve at last: there is not a 25
point to which the wit and faculty of man can turn,
that I have not set mine to; but in vain, I am beat
through every quarter of the compass.

MRS. F. Ah! common efforts all: strike me a
master-stroke, Mr. Fulmer, if you wish to make 30
any figure in this country.

FULMER. But where, how, and what? I have
blustered for prerogative; I have bellowed for freedom; I have offered to serve my country; I have
engaged to betray it; a master-stroke, truly; 35
why, I have talked treason, writ treason, and if a man
can't live by that he can live by nothing. Here I
set up as a bookseller; why, men left off reading;
and if I was to turn butcher, I believe o' my conscience they'd leave off eating.   40

CAPTAIN DUDLEY *crosses the stage.*

MRS. F. Why there now's your lodger, old Captain Dudley, as he calls himself; there's no flint
without fire; something might be struck out of him,
if you'd the wit to find the way.

FULMER. Hang him, an old dry-skinned cur- 45
mudgeon; you may as well think to get truth out of
a courtier, or candor out of a critic: I can make
nothing of him; besides, he's poor, and therefore
not for our purpose.

MRS. F. The more fool he! Would any man 50
be poor that had such a prodigy in his possession?

FULMER. His daughter, you mean; she is indeed
uncommonly beautiful.

MRS. F. Beautiful! Why she need only be seen
to have the first men in the kingdom at her 55
feet. Egad, I wish I had the leasing of her beauty;
what would some of our young nabobs give — ?

FULMER. Hush; here comes the Captain; good
girl, leave us to ourselves, and let me try what I
can make of him.   60

MRS. F. Captain, truly; i' faith I'd have a regiment, had I such a daughter, before I was three
months older.   *Exit.*

SCENE II

CAPTAIN DUDLEY *enters to him.*

FULMER. Captain Dudley, good morning to you.

DUDLEY. Mr. Fulmer, I have borrowed a book
from your shop; 'tis the sixth volume of my deceased friend Tristram:[1] he is a flattering writer to

[1] The sixth volume of Sterne's *Tristram Shandy* appeared in
1762.

ACT II. SCENE I. 6] N *Bologne*; but *Boulogne* in IV. i. 16.

us poor soldiers; and the divine story of Le Fever, 5
which makes part of this book,[1] in my opinion of it,
does honor not to its author only, but to human
nature.

FULMER. He is an author I keep in the way of
trade, but one I never relished; he is much too 10
loose and profligate for my taste.

DUDLEY. That's being too severe: I hold him to
be a moralist in the noblest sense; he plays indeed
with the fancy, and sometimes perhaps too wantonly;
but while he thus designedly marks his main 15
attack, he comes at once upon the heart; refines,
amends it, softens it; beats down each selfish barrier
from about it, and opens every sluice of pity and
benevolence.

FULMER. We of the Catholic persuasion are 20
not much bound to him. — Well, sir, I shall not
oppose your opinion; a favorite author is like a
favorite mistress; and there you know, Captain, no
man likes to have his taste arraigned.

DUDLEY. Upon my word, sir, I don't know 25
what a man likes in that case; 'tis an experiment I
never made.

FULMER. Sir! — Are you serious?

DUDLEY. 'Tis of little consequence whether you
think so.   30

FULMER (aside). What a formal old prig it is!
— [Aloud.] I apprehend you, sir; you speak with
caution; are you married?

DUDLEY. I have been.

FULMER. And this young lady, which accom- 35
panies you —

DUDLEY. Passes for my daughter.

FULMER (aside). Passes for his daughter! humph
— [Aloud.] She is exceedingly beautiful, finely
accomplished, of a most enchanting shape and 40
air.

DUDLEY. You are much too partial; she has the
greatest defect a woman can have.

FULMER. How so, pray?

DUDLEY. She has no fortune.   45

FULMER. Rather say that you have none; and
that's a sore defect in one of your years, Captain
Dudley: you've served, no doubt?

DUDLEY (aside). Familiar coxcomb! But I'll
humor him.   50

FULMER (aside). A close old fox! But I'll un-
kennel him.

DUDLEY. Above thirty years I've been in the
service, Mr. Fulmer.

FULMER. I guessed as much; I laid it at no 55
less: why 'tis a wearisome time; 'tis an apprentice-
ship to a profession, fit only for a patriarch. But
preferment must be closely followed: you never
could have been so far behindhand in the chase,

[1] Chapters VI–XIII.

unless you had palpably mistaken your way. 60
You'll pardon me, but I begin to perceive you have
lived in the world, not with it.

DUDLEY. It may be so; and you perhaps can
give me better counsel. I'm now soliciting a favor;
an exchange to a company on full pay; nothing 65
more; and yet I meet a thousand bars to that;
though, without boasting, I should think the certificate of services, which I sent in, might have purchased that indulgence to me.

FULMER. Who thinks or cares about 'em? 70
Certificate of services, indeed! Send in a certificate of your fair daughter; carry her in your hand
with you.

DUDLEY. What! Who! My daughter! Carry
my daughter; well, and what then?   75

FULMER. Why then your fortune's made, that's
all.

DUDLEY. I understand you: and this you call
knowledge of the world? Despicable knowledge;
but, sirrah, I will have you know — 80
                          (Threatening him.)

FULMER. Help! Who's within? Would you
strike me, sir; would you lift up your hand against
a man in his own house?

DUDLEY. In a church, if he dare insult the poverty of a man of honor.   85

FULMER. Have a care what you do; remember
there is such a thing in law as an assault and battery;
ay, and such trifling forms as warrants and indict-
ments.

DUDLEY. Go, sir; you are too mean for my 90
resentment: 'tis that, and not the law, protects you.
Hence!

FULMER (aside). An old, absurd, incorrigible
blockhead! I'll be revenged of him.   Exit.

SCENE III

YOUNG DUDLEY enters to him.

CHARLES. What is the matter, sir? Sure I heard
an outcry as I entered the house.

DUDLEY. Not unlikely; our landlord and his wife
are forever wrangling. — Did you find your aunt
Dudley at home?   5

CHARLES. I did.

DUDLEY. And what was your reception?

CHARLES. Cold as our poverty and her pride
could make it.

DUDLEY. You told her the pressing occasion 10
I had for a small supply to equip me for this exchange; has she granted me the relief I asked?

CHARLES. Alas! Sir, she has peremptorily refused
it.

DUDLEY. That's hard; that's hard, indeed! 15
My petition was for a small sum; she has refused it,

you say: well, be it so; I must not complain. Did you see the broker about the insurance of my life?

CHARLES. There again I am the messenger of ill news; I can raise no money, so fatal is the climate: 20 alas! that ever my father should be sent to perish in such a place!

SCENE IV

MISS DUDLEY *enters hastily.*

DUDLEY. Louisa, what's the matter? you seem frighted.

LOUISA. I am, indeed: coming from Miss Rusport's, I met a young gentleman in the streets, who has beset me in the strangest manner. 5

CHARLES. Insufferable! Was he rude to you?

LOUISA. I cannot say he was absolutely rude to me, but he was very importunate to speak to me, and once or twice attempted to lift up my hat: he followed me to the corner of the street, and there 10 I gave him the slip.

DUDLEY. You must walk no more in the streets, child, without me or your brother.

LOUISA. O Charles! Miss Rusport desires to see you directly; Lady Rusport is gone out, and she 15 has something particular to say to you.

CHARLES. Have you any commands for me, sir?

DUDLEY. None, my dear; by all means wait upon Miss Rusport. Come, Louisa, I shall desire you to go up to your chamber, and compose yourself. 20
Exeunt.

SCENE V

BELCOUR *enters, after peeping in at the door.*

BEL. Not a soul, as I'm alive. Why, what an odd sort of a house is this! Confound the little jilt, she has fairly given me the slip. A plague upon this London, I shall have no luck in it: such a crowd, and such a hurry, and such a number of 5 shops, and one so like the other, that whether the wench turned into this house or the next, or whether she went up stairs or down stairs, (for there's a world above and a world below, it seems) I declare, I know no more than if I was in the Blue Moun- 10 tains.[1] In the name of all the devils at once, why did she run away? If every handsome girl I meet in this town is to lead me such a wild goose chase, I had better have stayed in the torrid zone: I shall be wasted to the size of a sugar cane: what shall 15 I do? Give the chase up: hang it, that's cowardly: shall I, a true-born son of Phœbus, suffer this little nimble-footed Daphne to escape me? — 'Forbid it honor, and forbid it love.'[2] Hush! hush! here she comes! Oh! the devil! What tawdry thing 20 have we got here?

[1] In eastern Jamaica.   [2] Cf. *The Careless Husband*, V. iv. 26.

MRS. FULMER *enters to him.*

MRS. FULMER. Your humble servant, sir.

BEL. Your humble servant, madam.

MRS. F. A fine summer's day, sir.

BEL. Yes, ma'am, and so cool, that if the cal- 25 endar didn't call it July, I should swear it was January.

MRS. F. Sir!

BEL. Madam!

MRS. F. Do you wish to speak to Mr. Fulmer, 30 sir?

BEL. Mr. Fulmer, madam? I haven't the honor of knowing such a person.

MRS. F. No, I'll be sworn, have you not; thou art much too pretty a fellow, and too much 35 of a gentleman to be an author thyself, or to have anything to say to those that are so. 'Tis the Captain, I suppose, you are waiting for.

BEL. I rather suspect it is the Captain's wife.

MRS. F. The Captain has no wife, sir. 40

BEL. No wife? I'm heartily sorry for it; for then she's his mistress; and that I take to be the more desperate case of the two: pray, madam, wasn't there a lady just now turned into your house? 'Twas with her I wished to speak. 45

MRS. F. What sort of a lady, pray?

BEL. One of the loveliest sort my eyes ever beheld; young, tall, fresh, fair; in short, a goddess.

MRS. F. Nay, but dear, dear sir, now I'm sure you flatter; for 'twas me you followed into the 50 shop door this minute.

BEL. You! No, no, take my word for it, it was not you, madam.

MRS. F. But what is it you laugh at?

BEL. Upon my soul, I ask your pardon; but it 55 was not you, believe me; be assured it wasn't.

MRS. F. Well, sir, I shall not contend for the honor of being noticed by you; I hope you think you wouldn't have been the first man that noticed me in the streets; however, this I'm positive of, 60 that no living woman but myself has entered these doors this morning.

BEL. Why then I'm mistaken in the house, that's all; for 'tis not humanly possible I can be so far out in the lady. (*Going.*) 65

MRS. F. Coxcomb! But hold — a thought occurs; as sure as can be he has seen Miss Dudley. A word with you, young gentleman; come back.

BEL. Well, what's your pleasure?

MRS. F. You seem greatly captivated with 70 this young lady; are you apt to fall in love thus at first sight?

BEL. Oh, yes: 'tis the only way I can ever fall in love; any man may tumble into a pit by surprise, none but a fool would walk into one by choice. 75

Mrs. F. You are a hasty lover it seems; have you spirit to be a generous one? They that will please the eye mustn't spare the purse.

Bel. Try me; put me to the proof; bring me to an interview with the dear girl that has thus 80 captivated me, and see whether I have spirit to be grateful.

Mrs. F. But how, pray, am I to know the girl you have set your heart on?

Bel. By an undescribable grace, that ac- 85 companies every look and action that falls from her: there can be but one such woman in the world, and nobody can mistake that one.

Mrs. F. Well, if I should stumble upon this angel in my walks, where am I to find you? 90 What's your name?

Bel. Upon my soul, I can't tell you my name.

Mrs. F. Not tell me! Why so?

Bel. Because I don't know what it is myself; as yet I have no name. 95

Mrs. F. No name!

Bel. None; a friend, indeed, lent me his; but he forbade me to use it on any unworthy occasion.

Mrs. F. But where is your place of abode?

Bel. I have none; I never slept a night in 100 England in my life.

Mrs. F. Hey-day!

SCENE VI

FULMER enters.

Fulmer. A fine case, truly, in a free country; a pretty pass things are come to, if a man is to be assaulted in his own house.

Mrs. F. Who has assaulted you, my dear?

Fulmer. Who! why this Captain Drawcansir,[1] 5 this old Dudley, my lodger; but I'll unlodge him; I'll unharbor him, I warrant.

Mrs. F. Hush! Hush! Hold your tongue, man; pocket the affront and be quiet; I've a scheme on foot will pay you a hundred beatings. Why 10 you surprise me, Mr. Fulmer; Captain Dudley assault you! Impossible.

Fulmer. Nay, I can't call it an absolute assault; but he threatened me.

Mrs. F. Oh, was that all? I thought how it 15 would turn out — a likely thing, truly, for a person of his obliging compassionate turn: no, no, poor Captain Dudley, he has sorrows and distresses enough of his own to employ his spirits, without setting them against other people. Make it 20 up as fast as you can: watch this gentleman out; follow him wherever he goes; and bring me word

[1] The vainglorious hero of Buckingham's burlesque, *The Rehearsal*.

who and what he is; be sure you don't lose sight of him; I've other business in hand.   *Exit.*

Bel. Pray, sir, what sorrows and distresses 25 have befallen this old gentleman you speak of?

Fulmer. Poverty, disappointments, and all the distresses attendant thereupon: sorrow enough of all conscience: I soon found how it was with him by his way of living, low enough of all reason; but what 30 I overheard this morning put it out of all doubt.

Bel. What did you overhear this morning?

Fulmer. Why, it seems he wants to join his regiment, and has been beating the town over to raise a little money for that purpose upon his 35 pay; but the climate, I find, where he is going is so unhealthy that nobody can be found to lend him any.

Bel. Why then your town is a damned good-for-nothing town; and I wish I had never come 40 into it.

Fulmer. That's what I say, sir; the hard-heartedness of some folks is unaccountable. There's an old Lady Rusport, a near relation of this gentleman's; she lives hard by here, opposite to 45 Stockwell's, the great merchant; he sent to her a begging, but to no purpose; though she is as rich as a Jew, she would not furnish him with a farthing.

Bel. Is the Captain at home?

Fulmer. He is upstairs, sir. 50

Bel. Will you take the trouble to desire him to step hither? I want to speak to him.

Fulmer. I'll send him to you directly. — I don't know what to make of this young man; but, if I live, I will find him out, or know the reason 55 why.   *Exit.*

Bel. I've lost the girl it seems; that's clear: she was the first object of my pursuit; but the case of this poor officer touches me; and, after all, there may be as much true delight in rescuing a fellow 60 creature from distress, as there would be in plunging one into it — But let me see; it's a point that must be managed with some delicacy — Apropos! there's pen and ink — I've struck upon a method that will do. (*Writes.*) Ay, ay, this is the very thing; 65 'twas devilish lucky I happened to have these bills about me. There, there, fare you well; I'm glad to be rid of you; you stood a chance of being worse applied, I can tell you.

(*Encloses and seals the paper.*)

SCENE VII

FULMER brings in DUDLEY.

Fulmer. That's the gentleman, sir. I shall make bold, however, to lend an ear.

Dudley. Have you any commands for me, sir?

Bel. Your name is Dudley, sir — ?

DUDLEY. It is.   5

BEL. You command a company, I think, Captain Dudley?

DUDLEY. I did: I am now upon half-pay.

BEL. You've served some time?

DUDLEY. A pretty many years; long enough   10
to see some people of more merit, and better interest than myself, made general officers.

BEL. Their merit I may have some doubt of; their interest I can readily give credit to; there is little promotion to be looked for in your profes-   15
sion, I believe, without friends, Captain?

DUDLEY. I believe so too. Have you any other business with me, may I ask?

BEL. Your patience for a moment. I was informed you was about to join your regiment   20
in distant quarters abroad.

DUDLEY. I have been soliciting an exchange to a company on full-pay, quartered at James's Fort, in Senegambia; but, I'm afraid, I must drop the undertaking.   25

BEL. Why so, pray?

DUDLEY. Why so, sir? 'Tis a home question for a perfect stranger to put; there is something very particular in all this.

BEL. If it is not impertinent, sir, allow me   30
to ask you what reason you have for despairing of success.

DUDLEY. Why really, sir, mine is an obvious reason for a soldier to have — want of money; simply that.   35

BEL. May I beg to know the sum you have occasion for?

DUDLEY. Truly, sir, I cannot exactly tell you on a sudden; nor is it, I suppose, of any great consequence to you to be informed; but I should   40
guess, in the gross, that two hundred pounds would serve.

BEL. And do you find a difficulty in raising that sum upon your pay? 'Tis done every day.

DUDLEY. The nature of the climate makes it   45
difficult; I can get no one to insure my life.

BEL. Oh! that's a circumstance may make for you, as well as against: in short, Captain Dudley, it so happens, that I can command the sum of two hundred pounds: seek no farther; I'll accom-   50
modate you with it upon easy terms.

DUDLEY. Sir! do I understand you rightly? — I beg your pardon; but am I to believe that you are in earnest?

BEL. What is your surprise? Is it an un-   55
common thing for a gentleman to speak truth; or is it incredible that one fellow creature should assist another?

DUDLEY. I ask your pardon — May I beg to know to whom? Do you propose this in the   60
way of business?

BEL. Entirely: I have no other business on earth.

DUDLEY. Indeed! you are not a broker, I'm persuaded.

BEL. I am not.   65

DUDLEY. Nor an army agent, I think?

BEL. I hope you will not think the worse of me for being neither; in short, sir, if you will peruse this paper, it will explain to you who I am, and upon what terms I act; while you read it, I will step   70
home, and fetch the money; and we will conclude the bargain without loss of time. In the meanwhile, good day to you.   *Exit hastily.*

DUDLEY. Humph! there's something very odd in all this — let me see what we've got here —   75
This paper is to tell me who he is, and what are his terms: in the name of wonder, why has he sealed it! Hey-day! what's here? Two bank notes, of a hundred each! I can't comprehend what this means. Hold; here's a writing; perhaps that will show   80
me. 'Accept this trifle; pursue your fortune, and prosper.' — Am I in a dream? Is this a reality?

SCENE VIII
Enter MAJOR O'FLAHERTY.

MAJOR. Save you, my dear! Is it you now that are Captain Dudley, I would ask? — Whuh! What's the hurry the man's in? If 'tis the lad that run out of the shop you would overtake, you might as well stay where you are, by my soul, he's as   5
nimble as a Croat, you are a full hour's march in his rear — Ay, faith, you may as well turn back, and give over the pursuit; well, Captain Dudley, if that's your name, there's a letter for you. Read man, read it; and I'll have a word with you, after   10
you've done.

DUDLEY. More miracles on foot! So, so, from Lady Rusport.

O'FLAHERTY. You're right, it is from her ladyship.

DUDLEY. Well, sir, I have cast my eye over it;   15
'tis short and peremptory; are you acquainted with the contents?

O'FLAHERTY. Not at all, my dear, not at all.

DUDLEY. Have you any message from Lady Rusport?   20

O'FLAHERTY. Not a syllable, honey; only when you've digested the letter, I've a little bit of a message to deliver you from myself.

DUDLEY. And may I beg to know who yourself is?

O'FLAHERTY. Dennis O'Flaherty, at your   25
service; a poor major of grenadiers, nothing better.

DUDLEY. So much for your name and title, sir; now be so good to favor me with your message.

O'FLAHERTY. Why, then, Captain, I must tell you I have promised Lady Rusport you shall do   30
whatever it is she bids you to do in that letter there.

DUDLEY. Ay, indeed; have you undertaken so

much, Major, without knowing either what she commands, or what I can perform?

O'FLAHERTY. That's your concern, my dear, 35 not mine; I must keep my word you know.

DUDLEY. Or else, I suppose, you and I must measure swords.

O'FLAHERTY. Upon my soul, you've hit it.

DUDLEY. That would hardly answer to either 40 of us; you and I have, probably, had enough of fighting in our time before now.

O'FLAHERTY. Faith and troth, Master Dudley, you may say that; 'tis thirty years, come the time, that I have followed the trade, and in a pretty 45 many countries — Let me see — In the war before last I served in the Irish Brigade, d'ye see; there, after bringing off the French monarch, I left his service, with a British bullet in my body, and this ribband in my button-hole. Last war I followed 50 the fortunes of the German eagle, in the corps of grenadiers; there I had my bellyful of fighting, and a plentiful scarcity of everything else. After six and twenty engagements, great and small, I went off with this gash on my skull, and a kiss of 55 the Empress Queen's sweet hand (heaven bless it!) for my pains: since the peace, my dear, I took a little turn with the Confederates there in Poland — but such another set of madcaps! — by the Lord Harry, I never knew what it was they were scuffling 60 about.

DUDLEY. Well, Major, I won't add another action to the list, you shall keep your promise with Lady Rusport; she requires me to leave London; I shall go in a few days, and you may take what 65 credit you please from my compliance.

O'FLAHERTY. Give me your hand, my dear boy, this will make her my own; when that's the case, we shall be brothers, you know, and we'll share her fortune between us. 70

DUDLEY. No so, Major; the man who marries Lady Rusport will have a fair title to her whole fortune without division. But, I hope, your expectations of prevailing are founded upon good reasons.

O'FLAHERTY. Upon the best grounds in the 75 world; first, I think she will comply, because she is a woman; secondly, I am persuaded she won't hold out long, because she's a widow; and thirdly, I make sure of her, because I've married five wives (en militaire, Captain), and never failed yet; 80 and, for what I know, they're all alive and merry at this very hour.

DUDLEY. Well, sir, go on and prosper; if you can inspire Lady Rusport with half your charity, I shall think you deserve all her fortune; at present, I 85 must beg your excuse: good morning to you. Exit.

O'FLAHERTY. A good sensible man, and very

much a soldier; I did not care if I was better acquainted with him: but 'tis an awkward kind of a country for that; the English, I observe, are 90 close friends, but distant acquaintance. I suspect the old lady has not been over generous to poor Dudley: I shall give her a little touch about that; upon my soul I know but one excuse a person can have for giving nothing, and that is, like myself, 95 having nothing to give.   Exit.

SCENE IX

Scene changes to LADY RUSPORT'S *house.*
A dressing-room.

MISS RUSPORT *and* LUCY.

CHARLOTTE. Well, Lucy, you've dislodged the old lady at last; but methought you was a tedious time about it.

LUCY. A tedious time indeed; I think they who have least to spare, contrive to throw the most 5 away; I thought I should never have got her out of the house.

CHARLOTTE. Why, she's as deliberate in canvassing every article of her dress, as an ambassador would be in settling the preliminaries of a treaty. 10

LUCY. There was a new hood and handkerchief, that had come express from Holborn Hill on the occasion, that took as much time in adjusting —

CHARLOTTE. As they did in making, and she was as vain of them as an old maid of a young lover. 15

LUCY. Or a young lover of himself. Then, madam, this being a visit of great ceremony to a person of distinction, at the West end of the town, the old state chariot was dragged forth on the occasion, with strict charges to dress out the 20 box with the leopard-skin hammer-cloth.[1]

CHARLOTTE. Yes, and to hang the false tails on the miserable stumps of the old crawling cattle. Well, well, pray heaven the crazy affair don't break down again with her! at least till she gets to her 25 journey's end. — But where's Charles Dudley? Run down, dear girl, and be ready to let him in; I think he's as long in coming, as she was in going.

LUCY. Why, indeed, madam, you seem the more alert of the two, I must say.   Exit. 30

CHARLOTTE. Now the deuce take the girl for putting that notion into my head; I'm sadly afraid Dudley does not like me; so much encouragement as I have given him to declare himself, I never could get a word from him on the subject! This 35 may be very honorable, but upon my life it's very provoking. By the way, I wonder how I look to-day. Oh! shockingly, hideously pale! like a witch! This

[1] Cloth covering the driver's box in a state coach.

is the old lady's glass; and she has left some of her wrinkles on it. How frightfully have I put 40 on my cap! all awry! and my hair dressed so unbecomingly! Altogether, I'm a most complete fright.

SCENE X

CHARLES DUDLEY *comes in unobserved.*

CHARLES. That I deny.

CHARLOTTE. Ah!

CHARLES. Quarrelling with your glass, cousin? Make it up; make it up and be friends; it cannot compliment you more than by reflecting you as 5 you are.

CHARLOTTE. Well, I vow, my dear Charles, that is delightfully said, and deserves my very best curtesy: your flattery, like a rich jewel, has a value not only from its superior lustre, but from its 10 extraordinary scarceness; I verily think this is the only civil speech you ever directed to my person in your life.

CHARLES. And I ought to ask pardon of your good sense for having done it now.   15

CHARLOTTE. Nay, now you relapse again: don't you know, if you keep well with a woman on the great score of beauty, she'll never quarrel with you on the trifling article of good sense? But anything serves to fill up a dull yawning hour 20 with an insipid cousin; you have brighter moments, and warmer spirits, for the dear girl of your heart.

CHARLES. Oh! fie upon you, fie upon you.

CHARLOTTE. You blush, and the reason is apparent, you are a novice at hypocrisy; but no 25 practice can make a visit of ceremony pass for a visit of choice: love is ever before its time, friendship is apt to lag a little after it: pray, Charles, did you make any extraordinary haste hither?

CHARLES. By your question, I see you acquit 30 me of the impertinence of being in love.

CHARLOTTE. But why impertinence? Why the impertinence of being in love? You have one language for me, Charles, and another for the woman of your affection.   35

CHARLES. You are mistaken; the woman of my affection shall never hear any other language from me than what I use to you.

CHARLOTTE. I am afraid, then, you'll never make yourself understood by her.   40

CHARLES. It is not fit I should; there is no need of love to make me miserable; 'tis wretchedness enough to be a beggar.

CHARLOTTE. A beggar do you call yourself! O Charles, Charles, rich in every merit and accom- 45 plishment, whom may you not aspire to? And why think you so unworthily of our sex, as to conclude there is not one to be found with sense to discern your virtue, and generosity to reward it?

CHARLES. You distress me, I must beg to 50 hear no more.

CHARLOTTE. Well, I can be silent — Thus does he always serve me, whenever I am about to disclose myself to him.

CHARLES. Why do you not banish me and 55 my misfortunes forever from your thoughts?

CHARLOTTE. Ay, wherefore do I not, since you never allowed me a place in yours? But go, sir, I have no right to stay you; go where your heart directs you, go to the happy, the distinguished 60 fair one.

CHARLES. Now, by all that's good, you do me wrong: there is no such fair one for me to go to, nor have I an acquaintance amongst the sex, your-self excepted, which answers to that description. 65

CHARLOTTE. Indeed!

CHARLES. In very truth: there then let us drop the subject. May you be happy though I never can!

CHARLOTTE. O, Charles! give me your hand; if I have offended you, I ask you pardon; you have 70 been long acquainted with my temper, and know how to bear with its infirmities.

CHARLES. Thus, my dear Charlotte, let us seal our reconciliation. (*Kissing her hand.*) Bear with thy infirmities! By heaven, I know not any one 75 failing in thy whole composition, except that of too great a partiality for an undeserving man.

CHARLOTTE. And you are now taking the very course to augment that failing. A thought strikes me: I have a commission that you must abso- 80 lutely execute for me; I have immediate occasion for the sum of two hundred pounds; you know my fortune is shut up till I am of age; take this paltry box (it contains my earrings, and some other baubles I have no use for), carry it to our op- 85 posite neighbor, Mr. Stockwell (I don't know where else to apply), leave it as a deposit in his hands, and beg him to accommodate me with the sum.

CHARLES. Dear Charlotte, what are you about to do? How can you possibly want two hun- 90 dred pounds?

CHARLOTTE. How can I possibly do without it, you mean? Doesn't every lady want two hundred pounds? Perhaps I have lost it at play; perhaps I mean to win as much to it; perhaps I want it for 95 two hundred different uses.

CHARLES. Pooh! pooh! all this is nothing; don't I know you never play?

CHARLOTTE. You mistake; I have a spirit to set not only this trifle, but my whole fortune, upon 100 a stake; therefore make no wry faces, but do as I bid you: you will find Mr. Stockwell a very honor-able gentleman.

SCENE IX. 42] R *unbecoming.*   SCENE X. 64*] R *among.*

LUCY *enters in haste.*

LUCY. Dear madam, as I live, here comes the old lady in a hackney-coach.　　　　105

CHARLOTTE. The old chariot has given her a second tumble: away with you; you know your way out without meeting her; take the box, and do as I desire you.

CHARLES. I must not dispute your orders.　110 Farewell!　　　*Exeunt* CHARLES *and* CHARLOTTE.

SCENE XI

LADY RUSPORT *enters, leaning on* MAJOR O'FLAHERTY'S *arm.*

O'FLAHERTY. Rest yourself upon my arm, never spare it; 'tis strong enough: it has stood harder service than you can put it to.

LUCY. Mercy upon me, what is the matter; I am frightened out of my wits: has your ladyship had　5 an accident?

LADY R. O Lucy! the most untoward one in nature; I know not how I shall repair it.

O'FLAHERTY. Never go about to repair it, my lady; ev'n build a new one; 'twas but a crazy　10 piece of business at best.

LUCY. Bless me, is the old chariot broke down with you again?

LADY R. Broke, child? I don't know what might have been broke, if, by great good for-　15 tune, this obliging gentleman had not been at hand to assist me.

LUCY. Dear madam, let me run and fetch you a cup of the cordial drops.

LADY R. Do, Lucy. [*Exit* LUCY.] Alas! sir, ever　20 since I lost my husband, my poor nerves have been shook to pieces; there hangs his beloved picture; that precious relic, and a plentiful jointure, is all that remains to console me for the best of men.

O'FLAHERTY. Let me see; i' faith a comely　25 personage: by his fur cloak I suppose he was in the Russian service, and by the gold chain round his neck, I should guess he had been honored with the order of St. Catharine.

LADY R. No, no; he meddled with no St.　30 Catharines: that's the habit he wore in his mayor-alty — Sir Stephen was Lord Mayor of London; but he is gone, and has left me a poor, weak, solitary widow behind him.

O'FLAHERTY. By all means, then, take a　35 strong, able, hearty man to repair his loss: if such a plain fellow as one Dennis O'Flaherty can please you, I think I may venture to say, without any disparagement to the gentleman in the fur gown there —　　　　40

LADY R. What are you going to say? Don't shock my ears with any comparison, I desire.

O'FLAHERTY. Not I, by my soul; I don't believe there's any comparison in the case. [*Re-enter* LUCY.]

LADY R. Oh, are you come? Give me the　45 drops; I'm all in a flutter.

O'FLAHERTY. Hark'ee, sweetheart, what are those same drops? Have you any more left in the bottle? I didn't care if I took a little sip of them myself.

LUCY. Oh! sir, they are called the cordial　50 restorative elixir, or the nervous golden drops; they are only for ladies' cases.

O'FLAHERTY. Yes, yes, my dear, there are gentlemen as well as ladies that stand in need of those same golden drops; they'd suit my case to a tittle.　55

LADY R. Well, Major, did you give old Dudley my letter, and will the silly man do as I bid him, and be gone?

O'FLAHERTY. You are obeyed; he's on his march.

LADY R. That's well; you have managed this　60 matter to perfection; I didn't think he would have been so easily prevailed upon.

O'FLAHERTY. At the first word; no difficulty in life; 'twas the very thing he was determined to do, before I came; I never met a more obliging　65 gentleman.

LADY R. Well, 'tis no matter; so I am but rid of him, and his distresses: would you believe it, Major O'Flaherty, it was but this morning he sent a-begging to me for money to fit him out upon some wild-　70 goose expedition to the coast of Africa, I know not where.

O'FLAHERTY. Well, you sent him what he wanted?

LADY R. I sent him, what he deserved, a　75 flat refusal.

O'FLAHERTY. You refused him!

LADY R. Most undoubtedly.

O'FLAHERTY. You sent him nothing!

LADY R. Not a shilling.　　　　80

O'FLAHERTY. Good morning to you — Your servant —　　　　(*Going.*)

LADY R. Hey-day! What ails the man? Where are you going?

O'FLAHERTY. Out of your house, before the　85 roof falls on my head — to poor Dudley, to share the little modicum that thirty years' hard service has left me; I wish it was more for his sake.

LADY R. Very well, sir; take your course; I shan't attempt to stop you; I shall survive it; it　90 will not break my heart if I never see you more.

O'FLAHERTY. Break your heart! No, o' my conscience, will it not. — You preach, and you pray, and you turn up your eyes, and all the while you're as hard-hearted as a hyena — A hyena, truly!　95 By my soul there isn't in the whole creation so savage an animal as a human creature without pity.　　　　*Exit.*

LADY R. A hyena, truly! Where did the fellow

blunder upon that word? Now the deuce 100
take him for using it, and the macaronies[1] for
inventing it.

ACT III

SCENE I

A room in STOCKWELL'S *house.*

STOCKWELL *and* BELCOUR.

STOCK. Gratify me so far, however, Mr. Belcour,
as to see Miss Rusport; carry her the sum she wants,
and return the poor girl her box of diamonds, which
Dudley left in my hands; you know what to say
on the occasion better than I do; that part of 5
your commission I leave to your own discretion, and
you may season it with what gallantry you think fit.

BEL. You could not have pitched upon a greater
bungler at gallantry than myself, if you had rum-
maged every company in the city, and the whole 10
court of aldermen into the bargain: part of your
errand, however, I will do; but whether it shall be
with an ill grace, or a good one, depends upon the
caprice of a moment, the humor of the lady, the
mode of our meeting, and a thousand undefin- 15
able small circumstances that nevertheless determine
us upon all the great occasions of life.

STOCK. I persuade myself you will find Miss
Rusport an ingenuous, worthy, animated girl.

BEL. Why, I like her the better, as a woman; 20
but name her not to me, as a wife! No, if ever I
marry, it must be a staid, sober, considerate damsel,
with blood in her veins as cold as a turtle's; quick
of scent as a vulture when danger's in the wind,
wary and sharp-sighted as a hawk when 25
treachery is on foot: with such a companion at my
elbow, forever whispering in my ear — 'Have a
care of this man, he's a cheat; don't go near that
woman, she's a flirt; over head there's a scaffold,
under foot there's a well'; oh! sir, such a woman 30
might lead me up and down this great city without
difficulty or danger; but with a girl of Miss Rusport's
complexion, heaven and earth! Sir, we should
be duped, undone, and distracted, in a fortnight.

STOCK. Ha! ha! ha! Why you are become 35
wondrous circumspect of a sudden, pupil; and if
you can find such a prudent damsel as you describe,
you have my consent — only beware how you choose;
discretion is not the reigning quality amongst the
fine ladies of the present time; and I think in 40
Miss Rusport's particular I have given you no
bad counsel.

BEL. Well, well, if you'll fetch me the jewels,
I believe I can undertake to carry them to her;

[1] Dandies of the period.

but as for the money, I'll have nothing to do 45
with that; Dudley would be your fittest ambassador
on that occasion; and, if I mistake not, the most
agreeable to the lady.

STOCK. Why, indeed, from what I know of the
matter, it may not improbably be destined to 50
find its way into his pockets.   *Exit.*

BEL. Then depend upon it these are not the
only trinkets she means to dedicate to Captain
Dudley. As for me, Stockwell indeed wants me
to marry; but till I can get this bewitching girl, 55
this incognita, out of my head, I can never think
of any other woman.

Servant enters, and delivers a letter.

Hey-day! Where can I have picked up a correspondent already? 'Tis a most execrable manuscript — Let me see — Martha Fulmer — Who 60
is Martha Fulmer? Pshaw! I won't be at the
trouble of deciphering her damned pothooks. Hold,
hold, hold! What have we got here?

Dear Sir,
I've discovered the lady you was so much 65
smitten with, and can procure you an interview with
her; if you can be as generous to a pretty girl as you
was to a paltry old captain — (How did she find
that out!) *— you need not despair: come to me im-*
mediately; the lady is now in my house, and 70
expects you.
                                        Yours,
                                        Martha Fulmer.

O thou dear, lovely, and enchanting paper, which I
was about to tear into a thousand scraps, 75
devoutly I entreat thy pardon: I have slighted thy
contents, which are delicious; slandered thy characters, which are divine; and all the atonement I
can make is implicitly to obey thy mandates.

STOCKWELL returns.

STOCK. Mr. Belcour, here are the jewels; this 80
letter encloses bills for the money; and, if you will
deliver it to Miss Rusport, you'll have no farther
trouble on that score.

BEL. Ah, sir! the letter which I've been reading
disqualifies me for delivering the letter which 85
you have been writing: I have other game on foot;
the loveliest girl my eyes ever feasted upon is
started in view, and the world cannot now divert
me from pursuing her.

STOCK. Hey-day! What has turned you 90
thus on a sudden?

BEL. A woman: one that can turn, and overturn
me and my tottering resolutions every way she
will. Oh, sir, if this is folly in me, you must rail

19] O1O2O3 *ingenuous*; DBN *ingenions*. (Cf. *ingenuous heart* in IV. viii. 31.)

at Nature: you must chide the sun, that was　95
vertical at my birth, and would not wink upon my
nakedness, but swaddled me in the broadest, hottest
glare of his meridian beams.

STOCK.　Mere rhapsody; mere childish rhapsody;
the libertine's familiar plea — Nature made　100
us, 'tis true, but we are the responsible creators of
our own faults and follies.

BEL.　Sir!

STOCK.　Slave of every face you meet, some hussy
has inveigled you, some handsome profligate　105
(the town is full of them); and, when once fairly
bankrupt in constitution, as well as fortune, Nature
no longer serves as your excuse for being vicious,
necessity, perhaps, will stand your friend, and
you'll reform.　　　　　　　　　　　　　110

BEL.　You are severe.

STOCK.　It fits me to be so — it well becomes a
father — I would say a friend. — [Aside.]　How
strangely I forget myself — How difficult it is to
counterfeit indifference, and put a mask upon　115
the heart — I've struck him hard; he reddens.

BEL.　How could you tempt me so? Had you not
inadvertently dropped the name of father, I fear
our friendship, short as it has been, would scarce
have held me — But even your mistake I　120
reverence — Give me your hand — 'tis over.

STOCK.　Generous young man — let me embrace
you — How shall I hide my tears? I have been
to blame; because I bore you the affection of a
father, I rashly took up the authority of one.　125
I ask your pardon — pursue your course; I have
no right to stop it — What would you have me do
with these things?

BEL.　This, if I might advise; carry the money
to Miss Rusport immediately; never let gener-　130
osity wait for its materials; that part of the business presses.　Give me the jewels; I'll find an
opportunity of delivering them into her hands;
and your visit may pave the way for my reception.

　　　　　　　　　　　　　　　　　　　Exit.

STOCK.　Be it so: good morning to you.—Fare-　135
well advice!　Away goes he upon the wing for pleasure.　What various passions he awakens in me!　He
pains, yet pleases me; affrights, offends, yet grows
upon my heart.　His very failings set him off —
forever trespassing, forever atoning, I almost　140
think he would not be so perfect, were he free from
fault: I must dissemble longer; and yet how painful
the experiment! — Even now he's gone upon some
wild adventure; and who can tell what mischief may
befall him!　O Nature, what it is to be a　145
father!　Just such a thoughtless headlong thing
was I, when I beguiled his mother into love.

　　　　　　　　　　　　　　　　　　　Exit.

SCENE II

Scene changes to FULMER'S *house.*

FULMER *and his* WIFE.

FULMER.　I tell you, Patty, you are a fool to
think of bringing him and Miss Dudley together;
'twill ruin everything, and blow your whole scheme
up to the moon at once.

MRS. F.　Why, sure, Mr. Fulmer, I may be　5
allowed to rear a chicken of my own hatching, as
they say.　Who first sprung the thought but I,
pray?　Who first contrived the plot?　Who proposed
the letter, but I, I?

FULMER.　And who dogged the gentleman　10
home?　Who found out his name, fortune, connection, that he was a West Indian, fresh landed, and
full of cash; a gull to our heart's content; a hot-
brained, headlong spark, that would run into our
trap, like a wheat-ear under a turf?　　　　15

MRS. F.　Hark! he's come: disappear, **march;** and
leave the field open to my machinations.

　　　　　　　　　　　　　　　　　Exit FULMER.

SCENE III

BELCOUR *enters to her.*

BEL.　O, thou dear minister to my happiness, let
me embrace thee!　Why thou art my polar star,
my propitious constellation, by which I navigate
my impatient bark into the port of pleasure and
delight.　　　　　　　　　　　　　　　　5

MRS. F.　Oh, you men are sly creatures!　Do
you remember now, you cruel, what you said to me
this morning?

BEL.　All a jest, a frolic; never think on't, bury
it forever in oblivion; thou! why thou are all　10
over nectar and ambrosia, powder of pearl and odour
of roses; thou hast the youth of Hebe, the beauty
of Venus, and the pen of Sappho; but in the name of
all that's lovely, where's the lady?　I expected to
find her with you.　　　　　　　　　　　15

MRS. F.　No doubt you did, and these raptures
were designed for her, but where have you loitered?
the lady's gone, you are too late; girls of her sort
are not to be kept waiting like negro slaves in your
sugar plantations.　　　　　　　　　　20

BEL.　Gone; whither is she gone? tell me that I
may follow her.

MRS. F.　Hold, hold, not so fast, young gentleman,
this is a case of some delicacy; should Captain
Dudley know that I introduced you to his　25
daughter, he is a man of such scrupulous honor —

BEL.　What do you tell me! is she daughter to
the old gentleman I met here this morning?

MRS. F.　The same; him you was so generous to.

BEL. There's an end of the matter then at 30 once; it shall never be said of me, that I took advantage of the father's necessities to trepan the daughter.   (*Going*.)

MRS. F. [*aside*]. So, so, I've made a wrong cast, he's one of your conscientious sinners I find, 35 but I won't lose him thus — Ha! ha! ha!

BEL. What is it you laugh at?

MRS. F. Your absolute inexperience: have you lived so very little time in this country, as not to know that between young people of equal ages, 40 the term of sister often is a cover for that of mistress? This young lady is, in that sense of the word, sister to young Dudley, and consequently daughter to my old lodger.

BEL. Indeed! are you serious?   45

MRS. F. Can you doubt it? I must have been pretty well assured of that before I invited you hither.

BEL. That's true; she cannot be a woman of honor, and Dudley is an unconscionable young 50 rogue to think of keeping one fine girl in pay, by raising contributions on another; he shall therefore give her up; she is a dear, bewitching, mischievous, little devil; and he shall positively give her up.

MRS. F. Ay, now the freak has taken you 55 again; I say give her up; there's one way, indeed, and certain of success.

BEL. What's that?

MRS. F. Outbid him, never dream of outblus- tering him; buy out his lease of possession, and 60 leave her to manage his ejectment.

BEL. Is she so venal? Never fear me then, when beauty is the purchase, I shan't think much of the price.

MRS. F. All things, then, will be made easy 65 enough; let me see; some little genteel present to begin with: what have you got about you? Ay, search; I can bestow it to advantage, there's no time to be lost.

BEL. Hang it, confound it; a plague upon't, 70 say I! I haven't a guinea left in my pocket; I parted from my whole stock here this morning, and have forgot to supply myself since.

MRS. F. Mighty well; let it pass then; there's an end; think no more of the lady, that's all.   75

BEL. Distraction! think no more of her? let me only step home and provide myself, I'll be back with you in an instant.

MRS. F. Pooh, pooh! that's a wretched shift: have you nothing of value about you? Mon- 80 ey's a coarse slovenly vehicle, fit only to bribe elec- tors in a borough; there are more graceful ways of purchasing a lady's favors; rings, trinkets, jewels!

BEL. Jewels! Gadso, I protest I had forgot: I have a case of jewels; but they won't do, I must not 85

part from them; no, no, they are appropriated; they are none of my own.

MRS. F. Let me see, let me see! Ay, now, this were something like: pretty creatures, how they sparkle! these would ensure success.   90

BEL. Indeed!

MRS. F. These would make her your own forever.

BEL. Then the deuce take 'em for belonging to another person; I could find in my heart to give 'em the girl, and swear I've lost them.   95

MRS. F. Ay, do, say they were stolen out of your pocket.

BEL. No, hang it, that's dishonorable; here, give me the paltry things, I'll write you an order on my merchant for double their value.   100

MRS. F. An order! No; order for me no orders upon merchants, with their value received and three days' grace; their noting, protesting, and en- dorsing, and all their counting-house formalities; I'll have nothing to do with them; leave your 105 diamonds with me, and give your order for the value of them to the owner: the money would be as good as the trinkets, I warrant you.

BEL. Hey! how! I never thought of that; but a breach of trust; 'tis impossible; I never can con- 110 sent, therefore, give me the jewels back again.

MRS. F. Take 'em; I am now to tell you the lady is in this house.

BEL. In this house?

MRS. F. Yes, sir, in this very house; but 115 what of that? you have got what you like better; your toys, your trinkets, go, go. Oh! you're a man of a notable spirit, are you not?

BEL. Provoking creature! Bring me to the sight of the dear girl, and dispose of me as you 120 think fit.

MRS. F. And of the diamonds too?

BEL. Damn 'em, I would there was not such a bauble in nature! But come, come, dispatch; if I had the throne of Delhi I should give it to her. 125

MRS. F. Swear to me then that you will keep within bounds, remember she passes for the sister of young Dudley. Oh! if you come to your flights, and your rhapsodies, she'll be off in an instant.

BEL. Never fear me.   130

MRS. F. You must expect to hear her talk of her father, as she calls him, and her brother, and your bounty to her family.

BEL. Ay, ay, never mind what she talks of, only bring her.   135

MRS. F. You'll be prepared upon that head?

BEL. I shall be prepared, never fear; away with you.

MRS. F. But hold, I had forgot: not a word of the diamonds; leave that matter to my 140 management.

101-102] D *No order for me; no orders upon merchants*; O1O2O3N punctuate as above.

BEL. Hell and vexation! Get out of the room, or I shall run distracted.   *Exit* MRS. FULMER. Of a certain, Belcour, thou art born to be the fool of woman: sure no man sins with so much 145 repentance, or repents with so little amendment, as I do. I cannot give away another person's property, honor forbids me; and I positively cannot give up the girl; love, passion, constitution, everything protests against that. How shall 150 I decide? I cannot bring myself to break a trust, and I am not at present in the humor to balk my inclinations. Is there no middle way? Let me consider — There is, there is: my good genius has presented me with one; apt, obvious, honor- 155 able: the girl shall not go without her baubles, I'll not go without the girl, Miss Rusport shan't lose her diamonds, I'll save Dudley from destruction, and every party shall be a gainer by the project.

SCENE IV

MRS. FULMER *introducing* MISS DUDLEY.

MRS. F. Miss Dudley, this is the worthy gentleman you wish to see; this is Mr. Belcour.

LOUISA (*aside*). As I live, the very man that beset me in the streets.

BEL. (*aside*). An angel, by this light! Oh I 5 am gone past all retrieving!

LOUISA. Mrs. Fulmer, sir, informs me you are the gentleman from whom my father has received such civilities.

BEL. Oh! never name 'em.   10

LOUISA. Pardon me, Mr. Belcour, they must be both named and remembered; and if my father was here —

BEL. I am much better pleased with his representative.   15

LOUISA. That title is my brother's, sir; I have no claim to it.

BEL. I believe it.

LOUISA. But as neither he nor my father were fortunate enough to be at home, I could not 20 resist the opportunity —

BEL. Nor I neither, by my soul, madam: let us improve it, therefore. I am in love with you to distraction; I was charmed at the first glance; I attempted to accost you; you fled; I followed; 25 but was defeated of an interview; at length I have obtained one, and seize the opportunity of casting my person and my fortune at your feet.

LOUISA. You astonish me! Are you in your senses, or do you make a jest of my misfortunes? 30 Do you ground pretences on your generosity, or do you make a practice of this folly with every woman you meet?

BEL. Upon my life, no: as you are the handsomest woman I ever met, so you are the first to whom 35 I ever made the like professions: as for my generosity, madam, I must refer you on that score to this good lady, who I believe has something to offer in my behalf.

LOUISA. Don't build upon that, sir; I must 40 have better proofs of your generosity than the mere divestment of a little superfluous dross, before I can credit the sincerity of professions so abruptly delivered.   *Exit hastily.*

BEL. Oh! ye gods and goddesses, how her 45 anger animates her beauty!   (*Going out.*)

MRS. F. Stay, sir; if you stir a step after her, I renounce your interest forever; why you'll ruin everything.

BEL. Well, I must have her, cost what it will: 50 I see she understands her own value though; a little superfluous dross, truly! She must have better proofs of my generosity.

MRS. F. 'Tis exactly as I told you; your money she calls dross; she's too proud to stain her 55 fingers with your coin; bait your hook well with jewels; try that experiment, and she's your own.

BEL. Take 'em; let 'em go; lay 'em at her feet; I must get out of the scrape as I can; my propensity is irresistible: there! you have 'em; they are 60 yours; they are hers; but remember they are a trust; I commit them to her keeping till I can buy 'em off with something she shall think much more valuable; now tell me when shall I meet her?

MRS. F. How can I tell that? Don't you see 65 what an alarm you have put her into? Oh, you're a rare one! But go your ways for this while; leave her to my management, and come to me at seven this evening; but remember not to bring empty pockets with you — Ha! ha! ha!   70
          Exeunt severally.

SCENE V

LADY RUSPORT'S *house.*

MISS RUSPORT *enters, followed by a Servant.*

CHARLOTTE. Desire Mr. Stockwell to walk in.
          Exit Servant.

STOCKWELL *enters.*

STOCK. Madam, your most obedient servant: I am honored with your commands, by Captain Dudley; and have brought the money with me as you directed: I understand the sum you have 5 occasion for is two hundred pounds.

CHARLOTTE. It is, sir; I am quite confounded at your taking this trouble upon yourself, Mr. Stockwell.

STOCK. There is a bank-note, madam, to the 10

amount: your jewels are in safe hands, and will be delivered to you directly. If I had been happy in being better known to you, I should have hoped you would not have thought it necessary to place a deposit in my hands for so trifling a sum as 15 you have now required me to supply you with.

CHARLOTTE. The baubles I sent you may very well be spared; and, as they are the only security, in my present situation, I can give you, I could wish you would retain them in your hands: when I 20 am of age (which, if I live a few months, I shall be), I will replace your favor, with thanks.

STOCK. It is obvious, Miss Rusport, that your charms will suffer no impeachment by the absence of these superficial ornaments; but they should 25 be seen in the suite of a woman of fashion, not as creditors to whom you are indebted for your appearance, but as subservient attendants, which help to make up your equipage.

CHARLOTTE. Mr. Stockwell is determined not 30 to wrong the confidence I reposed in his politeness.

STOCK. I have only to request, madam, that you will allow Mr. Belcour, a young gentleman in whose happiness I particularly interest myself, to have the honor of delivering you the box of 35 jewels.

CHARLOTTE. Most gladly; any friend of yours cannot fail of being welcome here.

STOCK. I flatter myself you will not find him totally undeserving your good opinion; an ed- 40 ucation, not of the strictest kind, and strong animal spirits, are apt sometimes to betray him into youthful irregularities; but an high principle of honor, and an uncommon benevolence, in the eye of candor, will, I hope, atone for any faults, by which these 45 good qualities are not impaired.

CHARLOTTE. I dare say Mr. Belcour's behavior wants no apology: we've no right to be over strict in canvassing the morals of a common acquaintance.

STOCK. I wish it may be my happiness to see 50 Mr. Belcour in the list, not of your common, but particular acquaintance, of your friends, Miss Rusport — I dare not be more explicit.

CHARLOTTE. Nor need you, Mr. Stockwell: I shall be studious to deserve his friendship; and, 55 though I have long since unalterably placed my affections on another, I trust, I have not left myself insensible to the merits of Mr. Belcour; and hope that neither you nor he will, for that reason, think me less worthy your good opinion and regards. 60

STOCK. Miss Rusport, I sincerely wish you happy: I have no doubt you have placed your affection on a deserving man; and I have no right to combat your choice.   *Exit.*

CHARLOTTE. How honorable is that behavior! 65 Now, if Charles was here, I should be happy. The

old lady is so fond of her new Irish acquaintance, that I have the whole house at my disposal.

Exit CHARLOTTE.

SCENE VI

BELCOUR *enters, preceded by a Servant.*

SERV. I ask your honor's pardon; I thought my young lady was here: who shall I inform her would speak to her?

BEL. Belcour is my name, sir; and pray beg your lady to put herself in no hurry on my account; 5 for I'd sooner see the devil than see her face.

Exit Servant.

In the name of all that's mischievous, why did Stockwell drive me hither in such haste? A pretty figure, truly, I shall make: an ambassador without credentials. Blockhead that I was to 10 charge myself with her diamonds; officious, meddling puppy! Now they are irretrievably gone: that suspicious jade Fulmer wouldn't part even with a sight of them, though I would have ransomed 'em at twice their value. Now must I trust to my 15 poor wits to bring me off: a lamentable dependance. Fortune be my helper! Here comes the girl — if she is noble minded, as she is said to be, she will forgive me; if not, 'tis a lost cause; for I have not thought of one word in my excuse.   20

SCENE VII

CHARLOTTE *enters.*

CHARLOTTE. Mr. Belcour, I'm proud to see you: your friend, Mr. Stockwell, prepared me to expect this honor; and I am happy in the opportunity of being known to you.

BEL. (*aside*). A fine girl, by my soul! Now 5 what a cursed hang-dog do I look like!

CHARLOTTE. You are newly arrived in this country, sir?

BEL. Just landed, madam; just set ashore, with a large cargo of Muscovado[1] sugars, rum- 10 puncheons,[2] mahogany-slabs, wet sweetmeats, and green paroquets.[3]

CHARLOTTE. May I ask you how you like London, sir?

BEL. To admiration: I think the town and 15 the town's-folk are exactly suited; 'tis a great, rich, overgrown, noisy, tumultuous place: the whole morning is a bustle to get money, and the whole afternoon is a hurry to spend it.

CHARLOTTE. Are these all the observations 20 you have made?

BEL. No, madam; I have observed the women are very captivating, and the men very soon caught.

[1] Raw, unrefined.   [2] Casks of rum.
[3] Small parrots.

CHARLOTTE. Ay, indeed! Whence do you draw that conclusion? 25

BEL. From infallible guides; the first remark I collect from what I now see, the second from what I now feel.

CHARLOTTE. Oh, the deuce take you! But to waive this subject; I believe, sir, this was a 30 visit of business, not compliment; was it not?

BEL. Ay; now comes on my execution.

CHARLOTTE. You have some foolish trinkets of mine, Mr. Belcour; haven't you?

BEL. No, in truth; (aside) they are gone in 35 search of a trinket, still more foolish than themselves.

CHARLOTTE. Some diamonds I mean, sir; Mr. Stockwell informed me you was charged with 'em.

BEL. Oh, yes, madam; but I have the most treacherous memory in life — Here they are! 40 Pray put them up; they're all right; you need not examine 'em. (Gives a box.)

CHARLOTTE. Hey-day! right, sir! Why these are not my diamonds; these are quite different; and, as it should seem, of much greater value. 45

BEL. Upon my life I'm glad on't; for then I hope you value 'em more than your own.

CHARLOTTE. As a purchaser I should, but not as an owner; you mistake, these belong to somebody else. 50

BEL. 'Tis yours, I'm afraid, that belong to somebody else.

CHARLOTTE. What is it you mean? I must insist upon your taking 'em back again.

BEL. Pray, madam, don't do that; I shall in- 55 fallibly lose them; I have the worst luck with diamonds of any man living.

CHARLOTTE. That you might well say, was you to give me these in the place of mine; but pray, sir, what is the reason of all this? Why have you 60 changed the jewels? and where have you disposed of mine?

BEL. Miss Rusport, I cannot invent a lie for my life; and, if it was to save it, I couldn't tell one: I am an idle, dissipated, unthinking fellow, not 65 worth your notice: in short, I am a West Indian; and you must try me according to the charter of my colony, not by a jury of English spinsters: the truth is, I've given away your jewels; caught with a pair of sparkling eyes, whose lustre blinded theirs, 70 I served your property, as I should my own, and lavished it away; let me not totally despair of your forgiveness; I frequently do wrong, but never with impunity; if your displeasure is added to my own, my punishment will be too severe. When I parted 75 from the jewels, I had not the honor of knowing their owner.

CHARLOTTE. Mr. Belcour, your sincerity charms me, I enter at once into your character, and I make

all the allowances for it you can desire. I take 80 your jewels for the present, because I know there is no other way of reconciling you to yourself; but, if I give way to your spirit in one point, you must yield to mine in another; remember I will not keep more than the value of my own jewels: there is 85 no need to be pillaged by more than one woman at a time, sir.

BEL. Now may every blessing that can crown your virtues, and reward your beauty, be showered upon you; may you meet admiration without 90 envy, love without jealousy: and old age without malady; may the man of your heart be ever constant, and you never meet a less penitent, or less grateful offender than myself.

Servant enters and delivers a letter.

CHARLOTTE. Does your letter require such 95 haste?

SERV. I was bade to give it into your own hands, madam.

CHARLOTTE. From Charles Dudley, I see — have I your permission? Good heaven, what do I 100 read: Mr. Belcour you are concerned in this —

Dear Charlotte; in the midst of our distress, Providence has cast a benefactor in our way, after the most unexpected manner: a young West Indian, rich, and with a warmth of heart peculiar to 105 his climate, has rescued my father from his troubles, satisfied his wants, and enabled him to accomplish his exchange: when I relate to you the manner in which this was done, you will be charmed; I can only now add, that it was by chance we found 110 out that his name is Belcour, and that he is a friend of Mr. Stockwell's. I lose not a moment's time in making you acquainted with this fortunate event, for reasons which delicacy obliges me to suppress; but, perhaps, if you have not received the 115 money on your jewels, you will not think it necessary now to do it. I have the honor to be,

　　　Dear Madam,
　　　　　Most faithfully yours,
　　　　　　　Charles Dudley. 120

Is this your doing, sir? Never was generosity so worthily exerted.

BEL. Or so greatly overpaid.

CHARLOTTE. After what you have now done for this noble, but indigent, family, let me not 125 scruple to unfold the whole situation of my heart to you. Know then, sir, (and don't think the worse of me for the frankness of my declaration) that such is my attachment to the son of that worthy officer whom you relieved, that the moment 130 I am of age, and in possession of my fortune, I should hold myself the happiest of women to share it with young Dudley.

08| O1O2O3 *truth*; N *the truth*.

BEL. Say you so, madam! then let me perish if I don't love and reverence you above all woman- 135 kind; and if such is your generous resolution, never wait till you're of age; life is too short, pleasure too fugitive; the soul grows narrower every hour; I'll equip you for your escape; I'll convoy you to the man of your heart, and away with you then to 140 the first hospitable parson that will take you in.

CHARLOTTE. O blessed be the torrid zone forever, whose rapid vegetation quickens nature into such benignity! These latitudes are made for politics and philosophy; friendship has no root in 145 this soil. But had I spirit to accept your offer, which is not improbable, wouldn't it be a mortifying thing, for a fond girl to find herself mistaken, and sent back to her home, like a vagrant; and such, for what I know, might be my case. 150

BEL. Then he ought to be proscribed the society of mankind forever — Ay, ay, 'tis the sham sister makes him thus indifferent; 'twill be a meritorious office to take that girl out of the way.

SCENE VIII

Servant enters.

SERV. Miss Dudley to wait on you, madam.

BEL. Who?

SERV. Miss Dudley.

CHARLOTTE. What's the matter, Mr. Belcour? Are you frighted at the name of a pretty girl? 5 'Tis the sister of him we were speaking of — pray admit her.

BEL. The sister! — So, so; he has imposed upon her too — this is an extraordinary visit, truly. Upon my soul, the assurance of some folks is not to be 10 accounted for.

CHARLOTTE. I insist upon your not running away; you'll be charmed with Louisa Dudley.

BEL. Oh, yes, I am charmed with her.

CHARLOTTE. You've seen her then, have you? 15

BEL. Yes, yes, I've seen her.

CHARLOTTE. Well, isn't she a delightful girl?

BEL. Very delightful.

CHARLOTTE. Why, you answer as if you was in a court of justice. O'my conscience! I be- 20 lieve you are caught; I've a notion she has tricked you out of your heart.

BEL. I believe she has, and you out of your jewels; for, to tell you the truth, she's the very person I gave 'em to. 25

CHARLOTTE. You gave her my jewels! Louisa Dudley my jewels? admirable! inimitable! Oh, the sly little jade! but hush, here she comes; I don't know how I shall keep my countenance.

LOUISA *enters.*

My dear, I'm rejoiced to see you; how d'ye do? 30 I beg leave to introduce Mr. Belcour, a very worthy friend of mine; I believe, Louisa, you have seen him before.

LOUISA. I have met the gentleman.

CHARLOTTE. You have met the gentleman; 35 well, sir, and you have met the lady; in short, you have met each other; why then don't you speak to each other? How you both stand! tongue-tied, and fixed as statues — Ha, ha, ha! Why you'll fall asleep by and by. 40

LOUISA. Fie upon you; fie upon you; is this fair?

BEL. (*aside*). Upon my soul, I never looked so like a fool in my life; the assurance of that girl puts me quite down.

CHARLOTTE. Sir — Mr. Belcour — Was it 45 your pleasure to advance anything? Not a syllable. Come, Louisa, women's wit, they say, is never at a loss — Nor you neither? Speechless both — Why you was merry enough before this lady came in.

LOUISA. I am sorry I have been any inter- 50 ruption to your happiness, sir.

BEL. Madam.

CHARLOTTE. Madam! Is that all you can say? But come, my dear girl, I won't tease you. Apropos! I must show you what a present this dumb 55 gentleman has made me; are not these handsome diamonds?

LOUISA. Yes, indeed, they seem very fine; but I am no judge of these things.

CHARLOTTE. Oh, you wicked little hypocrite, 60 you are no judge of these things, Louisa; you have no diamonds, not you.

LOUISA. You know I haven't, Miss Rusport: you know those things are infinitely above my reach.

CHARLOTTE. Ha! ha! ha! 65

BEL. [*aside*]. She does tell a lie with an admirable countenance, that's true enough.

LOUISA. What ails you, Charlotte. What impertinence have I been guilty of that you should find it necessary to humble me at such a rate? If you 70 are happy, long may you be so; but, surely, it can be no addition to it to make me miserable.

CHARLOTTE. So serious! there must be some mystery in this — Mr. Belcour will you leave us together? You see I treat you with all the fa- 75 miliarity of an old acquaintance already.

BEL. Oh, by all means; pray command me. Miss Rusport, I'm your most obedient! By your condescension in accepting those poor trifles, I am under eternal obligations to you. — To you, 80 Miss Dudley, I shall not offer a word on that subject: you despise finery; you have a soul above it; I adore your spirit; I was rather unprepared for meeting you here; but I shall hope for an opportunity of making myself better known to you.   *Exit.* 85

SCENE IX

CHARLOTTE *and* LOUISA.

CHARLOTTE. Louisa Dudley, you surprise me; I never saw you act thus before: can't you bear a little innocent raillery before the man of your heart?

LOUISA. The man of my heart, madam? Be assured I never was so visionary to aspire to any 5 man whom Miss Rusport honors with her choice.

CHARLOTTE. My choice, my dear! Why we are playing at cross purposes: how entered it into your head that Mr. Belcour was the man of my choice?

LOUISA. Why didn't he present you with those 10 diamonds?

CHARLOTTE. Well; perhaps he did — and pray, Louisa, have you no diamonds?

LOUISA. I diamonds truly! Who should give me diamonds? 15

CHARLOTTE. Who, but this very gentleman. Apropos! here comes your brother —

SCENE X

CHARLES *enters.*

[CHARLOTTE.] I insist upon referring our dispute to him: your sister and I, Charles, have a quarrel; Belcour, the hero of your letter, has just left us — somehow or other, Louisa's bright eyes have caught him; and the poor fellow's fallen desperately in 5 love with her — (don't interrupt me, hussy) — Well, that's excusable enough, you'll say; but the jet [1] of the story is, that this hair-brained spark, who does nothing like other people, has given her the very identical jewels which you pledged for me to 10 Mr. Stockwell; and will you believe that this little demure slut made up a face, and squeezed out three or four hypocritical tears, because I rallied her about it?

CHARLES. I'm all astonishment! Louisa, tell 15 me without reserve, has Mr. Belcour given you any diamonds?

LOUISA. None, upon my honor.

CHARLES. Has he made any professions to you?

LOUISA. He has, but altogether in a style so 20 whimsical and capricious, that the best which can be said of them is to tell you that they seemed more the result of good spirits than good manners.

CHARLOTTE. Ay, ay, now the murder's out; he's in love with her, and she has no very great dis- 25 like to him; trust to my observation, Charles, for that: as to the diamonds, there's some mistake about them, and you must clear it up: three minutes' conversation with him will put everything in a

[1] Gist.

right train; go, go, Charles, 'tis a brother's busi- 30 ness; about it instantly; ten to one you'll find him over the way at Mr. Stockwell's.

CHARLES. I confess I'm impatient to have the case cleared up; I'll take your advice, and find him out: good-bye to you. 35

CHARLOTTE. Your servant; my life upon it you'll find Belcour a man of honor. Come, Louisa, let us adjourn to my dressing-room; I've a little private business to transact with you, before the old lady comes up to tea, and interrupts us. 40

ACT IV

SCENE I

FULMER'S *house.*

FULMER *and* MRS. FULMER.

FULMER. Patty, wasn't Mr. Belcour with you?

MRS. F. He was, and is now shut up in my chamber, in high expectation of an interview with Miss Dudley; she's at present with her brother, and 'twas with some difficulty I persuaded my hot- 5 headed spark to wait 'till he has left her.

FULMER. Well, child, and what then?

MRS. F. Why then, Mr. Fulmer, I think it will be time for you and me to steal a march, and be gone. 10

FULMER. So this is all the fruit of your ingenious project; a shameful overthrow, or a sudden flight.

MRS. F. Why, my project was a mere impromptu, and can at worst but quicken our departure a few days; you know we had fairly outlived our credit 15 here, and a trip to Boulogne is no ways unseasonable. Nay, never droop, man — Hark! hark! here's enough to bear charges.   (*Showing a purse.*)

FULMER. Let me see, let me see: this weighs well; this is of the right sort: why your West Indian 20 bled freely.

MRS. F. But that's not all: look here! Here are the sparklers! (*Showing the jewels.*) Now what d'ye think of my performances? Heh! a foolish scheme, isn't it? — a silly woman — ? 25

FULMER. Thou art a Judith, a Joan of Arc, and I'll march under thy banners, girl, to the world's end: come, let's begone; I've little to regret; my creditors may share the old books amongst them, they'll have occasion for philosophy to sup- 30 port their loss; they'll find enough upon my shelves: the world is my library; I read mankind — Now, Patty, lead the way.

MRS. F. Adieu, Belcour!   *Exeunt.*

SCENE II

CHARLES DUDLEY *and* LOUISA.

CHARLES. Well, Louisa, I confess the force of what you say: I accept Miss Rusport's bounty, and,

when you see my generous Charlotte, tell her — but
have a care, there is a selfishness even in gratitude,
when it is too profuse; to be overthankful for any   5
one favor, is in effect to lay out for another; the
best return I could make my benefactress would be
never to see her more.

LOUISA. I understand you.

CHARLES. We that are poor, Louisa, should   10
be cautious; for this reason, I would guard you
against Belcour; at least till I can unravel the mystery of Miss Rusport's diamonds; I was disappointed of finding him at Mr. Stockwell's, and am
now going in search of him again: he may in-   15
tend honorably, but I confess to you I am staggered;
think no more of him, therefore, for the present:
of this be sure, while I have life, and you have
honor, I will protect you, or perish in your defence.

Exit.

LOUISA. Think of him no more! Well, I'll   20
obey; but if a wand'ring uninvited thought should
creep by chance into my bosom, must I not give the
harmless wretch a shelter? Oh! yes; the great
artificer of the human heart knows every thread he
wove into its fabric, nor puts his work to harder   25
uses than it was made to bear: my wishes then, my
guiltless ones, I mean, are free. How fast they spring
within me at that sentence! Down, down, ye busy
creatures! Whither would you carry me? Ah!
there is one amongst you, a forward, new in-   30
truder, that, in the likeness of an offending, generous
man, grows into favor with my heart. Fie, fie
upon it! Belcour pursues, insults me: yet such is
the fatality of my condition, that what should rouse
resentment, only calls up love.   35

SCENE III

BELCOUR *enters to her.*

BEL. Alone, by all that's happy!

LOUISA. Ah!

BEL. Oh! shriek not, start not, stir not, loveliest
creature! but let me kneel, and gaze upon your
beauties.   5

LOUISA. Sir, Mr. Belcour, rise! What is it you do?

BEL. See, I obey you; mould me as you will, behold your ready servant! New to your country,
ignorant of your manners, habits, and desires, I put
myself into your hands for instruction; make   10
me only such as you can like yourself, and I shall be
happy.

LOUISA. I must not hear this, Mr. Belcour; go;
should he that parted from me but this minute now
return, I tremble for the consequence.   15

BEL. Fear nothing; let him come: I love you,
madam; he'll find it hard to make me unsay that.

LOUISA. You terrify me; your impetuous temper

frightens me; you know my situation; it is not
generous to pursue me thus.   20

BEL. True; I do know your situation, your real
one, Miss Dudley, and am resolved to snatch you
from it; 'twill be a meritorious act; the old Captain
shall rejoice; Miss Rusport shall be made happy;
and even he, even your beloved brother, with   25
whose resentment you threaten me, shall in the end
applaud and thank me. Come, thou'rt a dear enchanting girl, and I'm determined not to live a
minute longer without thee.

LOUISA. Hold, are you mad? I see you are   30
a bold, assuming man, and know not where to stop.

BEL. Who that beholds such beauty can? By
heaven, you put my blood into a flame. Provoking
girl! is it within the stretch of my fortune to content you? What is it you can further ask that I   35
am not ready to grant?

LOUISA. Yes, with the same facility that you bestowed upon me Miss Rusport's diamonds. For
shame! for shame! was that a manly story?

BEL. So! so! these devilish diamonds meet me   40
everywhere — Let me perish if I meant you any
harm. Oh! I could tear my tongue out for saying
a word about the matter.

LOUISA. Go to her then, and contradict it; till
that is done, my reputation is at stake.   45

BEL. [*aside*]. Her reputation! Now she has got
upon that, she'll go on forever. — What is there I
will not do for your sake? I will go to Miss Rusport.

LOUISA. Do so; restore her own jewels to her,
which I suppose you kept back for the purpose of   50
presenting others to her of a greater value; but for
the future, Mr. Belcour, when you would do a
gallant action to that lady, don't let it be at my
expense.

BEL. I see where she points: she is willing   55
enough to give up Miss Rusport's diamonds, now
she finds she shall be a gainer by the exchange.
Be it so! 'tis what I wished — Well, madam, I will
return Miss Rusport her own jewels, and you shall
have others of tenfold their value.   60

LOUISA. No, sir, you err most widely; it is my
good opinion, not my vanity, which you must bribe.

BEL. [*aside*]. Why, what the devil would she have
now? — Miss Dudley, it is my wish to obey and
please you, but I have some apprehension that   65
we mistake each other.

LOUISA. I think we do: tell me, then, in few
words, what it is you aim at.

BEL. In few words, then, and in plain honesty, I
must tell you, so entirely am I captivated with   70
you, that had you but been such as it would have
become me to have called my wife, I had been happy
in knowing you by that name; as it is, you are
welcome to partake my fortune, give me in return

your person, give me pleasure, give me love; 75
free, disencumbered, antimatrimonial love.

LOUISA. Stand off, and let me never see you more.

BEL. Hold, hold, thou dear, tormenting, tantalizing girl! Upon my knees I swear you shall not stir till you've consented to my bliss. 80

LOUISA. Unhand me, sir: O Charles! protect me, rescue me, redress me. *Exit.*

SCENE IV

CHARLES DUDLEY *enters.*

CHARLES. How's this? Rise, villain, and defend yourself.

BEL. Villain!

CHARLES. The man who wrongs that lady is a villain — Draw! 5

BEL. Never fear me, young gentleman; brand me for a coward, if I balk you.

CHARLES. Yet hold! Let me not be too hasty: your name, I think, is Belcour?

BEL. Well, sir. 10

CHARLES. How is it, Mr. Belcour, you have done this mean, unmanly wrong; beneath the mask of generosity to give this fatal stab to our domestic peace? You might have had my thanks, my blessing; take my defiance now. 'Tis Dudley speaks 15 to you, the brother, the protector of that injured lady.

BEL. The brother? Give yourself a truer title.

CHARLES. What is't you mean?

BEL. Come, come, I know both her and 20 you: I found you, sir (but how or why I know not), in the good graces of Miss Rusport — (yes, color at the name!) — I gave you no disturbance there, never broke in upon you in that rich and plenteous quarter; but, when I could have blasted all your projects 25 with a word, spared you, in foolish pity spared you, nor roused her from the fond credulity in which your artifice had lulled her.

CHARLES. No, sir, nor boasted to her of the splendid present you had made my poor Louisa; 30 the diamonds, Mr. Belcour; how was that? What can you plead to that arraignment?

BEL. You question me too late; the name of Belcour and of villain never met before: had you enquired of me before you uttered that rash 35 word, you might have saved yourself or me a mortal error: now, sir, I neither give nor take an explanation; so, come on! ⌞ (*They fight.*)

SCENE V

LOUISA, *and afterwards* O'FLAHERTY.

LOUISA. Hold, hold, for heaven's sake hold! Charles! Mr. Belcour! Help! Sir, sir, make haste, they'll murder one another.

O'FLAHERTY. Hell and confusion! What's all

this uproar for? Can't you leave off cutting 5 one another's throats, and mind what the poor girl says to you? You've done a notable thing, haven't you, both, to put her into such a flurry? I think, o' my conscience, she's the most frighted of the three. 10

CHARLES. Dear Louisa, recollect yourself; why did you interfere? 'Tis in your cause.

BEL. [*aside*]. Now could I kill him for caressing her.

O'FLAHERTY. O sir, your most obedient! 15 You are the gentleman I had the honor of meeting here before; you was then running off at full speed like a Calmuck,[1] now you are tilting and driving like a Bedlamite[2] with this lad here, that seems as mad as yourself. 'Tis pity but your country 20 had a little more employment for you both.

BEL. Mr. Dudley, when you've recovered the lady, you know where I am to be found. *Exit.*

O'FLAHERTY. Well then, can't you stay where you are, and that will save the trouble of looking 25 after you? Yon volatile fellow thinks to give a man the meeting by getting out of his way: by my soul 'tis a roundabout method that of his. But I think he called you Dudley: hark'ee, young man, are you son of my friend the old Captain? 30

CHARLES. I am. Help me to convey this lady to her chamber, and I shall be more at leisure to answer your questions.

O'FLAHERTY. Ay, will I: come along, pretty one; if you've had wrong done you, young man, you 35 need look no further for a second; Dennis O'Flaherty's your man for that; but never draw your sword before a woman, Dudley; damn it, never while you live draw your sword before a woman.
Exeunt.

SCENE VI

LADY RUSPORT'S *house.*

LADY RUSPORT *and Servant.*

SERV. An elderly gentleman, who says his name is Varland, desires leave to wait on your ladyship.

LADY R. Show him in; the very man I wish to see: Varland; he was Sir Oliver's solicitor, and privy to all his affairs; he brings some good tidings; 5 some fresh mortgage, or another bond come to light; they start up every day.

VARLAND *enters.*

Mr. Varland, I'm glad to see you; you're heartily welcome, honest Mr. Varland; you and I haven't met since our late irreparable loss: how have 10 you passed your time this age?

VAR. Truly, my lady, ill enough: I thought I must have followed good Sir Oliver.

---
[1] Rover.   [2] Lunatic.

LADY R. Alack-a-day, poor man! Well, Mr. Varland, you find me here overwhelmed with 15 trouble and fatigue; torn to pieces with a multiplicity of affairs; a great fortune poured upon me unsought for and unexpected: 'twas my good father's will and pleasure it should be so, and I must submit.

VAR. Your ladyship inherits under a will 20 made in the year Forty-five, immediately after Captain Dudley's marriage with your sister.

LADY R. I do so, Mr. Varland; I do so.

VAR. I well remember it; I engrossed every syllable; but I am surprised to find your lady- 25 ship set so little store by this vast accession.

LADY R. Why you know, Mr. Varland, I am a moderate woman; I had enough before; a small matter satisfies me; and Sir Stephen Rusport (heaven be his portion!) took care I shouldn't 30 want that.

VAR. Very true; very true, he did so; and I am overjoyed at finding your ladyship in this disposition; for, truth to say, I was not without apprehension the news I have to communicate would 35 have been of some prejudice to your ladyship's tranquility.

LADY R. News, sir! What news have you for me?

VAR. Nay, nothing to alarm you; a trifle, in your present way of thinking: I have a will of Sir 40 Oliver's you have never seen.

LADY R. A will! Impossible! How came you by it, pray?

VAR. I drew it up, at his command, in his last illness: it will save you a world of trouble: it 45 gives his whole estate from you to his grandson, Charles Dudley.

LADY R. To Dudley? His estate to Charles Dudley? I can't support it! I shall faint! You've killed me, you vile man! I never shall survive it! 50

VAR. Look'ee there now: I protest, I thought you would have rejoiced at being clear of the incumbrance.

LADY R. 'Tis false; 'tis all a forgery, concerted between you and Dudley; why else did I never 55 hear of it before?

VAR. Have patience, my lady, and I'll tell you. By Sir Oliver's direction, I was to deliver this will into no hands but his grandson Dudley's: the young gentleman happened to be then in Scotland; 60 I was dispatched thither in search of him; the hurry and fatigue of my journey brought on a fever by the way, which confined me in extreme danger for several days; upon my recovery, I pursued my journey, found young Dudley had left Scotland 65 in the interim, and am now directed hither; where, as soon as I can find him, doubtless, I shall discharge my conscience, and fulfil my commission.

LADY R. Dudley then, as yet, knows nothing of this will?   70

VAR. Nothing; that secret rests with me.

LADY R. (aside). A thought occurs: by this fellow's talking of his conscience, I should guess it was upon sale. — [Aloud.] Come, Mr. Varland, if 'tis as you say, I must submit. I was somewhat 75 flurried at first, and forgot myself; I ask your pardon: this is no place to talk of business; step with me into my room; we will there compare the will, and resolve accordingly. — [Aside.] Oh! would your fever had you, and I had your paper.   80

Exeunt.

SCENE VII

MISS RUSPORT, CHARLES, *and* O'FLAHERTY.

CHARLOTTE. So, so! My lady and her lawyer have retired to close confabulation: now, Major, if you are the generous man I take you for, grant me one favor.

O'FLAHERTY. Faith will I, and not think much 5 of my generosity neither; for, though it may not be in my power to do the favor you ask, look you, it can never be in my heart to refuse it.

CHARLES (aside). Could this man's tongue do justice to his thoughts, how eloquent would he 10 be!

CHARLOTTE. Plant yourself then in that room: keep guard, for a few moments, upon the enemy's motions, in the chamber beyond; and, if they should attempt a sally, stop their march a moment, till 15 your friend here can make good his retreat down the back-stairs.

O'FLAHERTY. A word to the wise! I'm an old campaigner; make the best use of your time; and trust me for tying the old cat up to the picket. 20

CHARLOTTE. Hush! hush! not so loud.

CHARLES. 'Tis the office of a sentinel, Major, you have undertaken, rather than that of a field-officer.

O'FLAHERTY. 'Tis the office of a friend, my dear boy; and, therefore, no disgrace to a general. *Exit.* 25

SCENE VIII

CHARLES *and* CHARLOTTE.

CHARLOTTE. Well, Charles, will you commit yourself to me for a few minutes?

CHARLES. Most readily; and let me, before one goes by, tender you the only payment I can ever make for your abundant generosity.   5

CHARLOTTE. Hold, hold! so vile a thing as money must not come between us. What shall I say! O Charles! O Dudley! What difficulties have you thrown upon me! Familiarly as we have lived, I shrink at what I'm doing; and, anxiously as I 10 have sought this opportunity, my fears almost persuade me to abandon it.

CHARLES. You alarm me!

CHARLOTTE. Your looks and actions have been so

distant, and at this moment are so deterring, 15 that, was it not for the hope that delicacy, and not disgust, inspires this conduct in you, I should sink with shame and apprehension; but time presses; and I must speak; and plainly too — Was you now in possession of your grandfather's estate, as justly 20 you ought to be, and, was you inclined to seek a companion for life, should you, or should you not, in that case, honor your unworthy Charlotte with your choice?

CHARLES. My unworthy Charlotte! So 25 judge me heaven, there is not a circumstance on earth so valuable as your happiness, so dear to me as your person: but to bring poverty, disgrace, reproach from friends, ridicule from all the world upon a generous benefactress; thievishly to steal into 30 an open, unreserved, ingenuous heart, O Charlotte! dear, unhappy girl, it is not to be done.

CHARLOTTE. Nay, now you rate too highly the poor advantages fortune alone has given me over you: how otherwise could we bring our merits 35 to any balance? Come, my dear Charles, I have enough; make that enough still more by sharing it with me: sole heiress of my father's fortune, a short time will put it in my disposal; in the meanwhile you will be sent to join your regiment; let us prevent 40 a separation, by setting out this very night for that happy country where marriage still is free: carry me this moment to Belcour's lodgings.

CHARLES. Belcour's? — (Aside.) The name is ominous; there's murder in it: bloody inexora- 45 ble honor!

CHARLOTTE. D'ye pause? Put me into his hands, while you provide the means for our escape: he is the most generous, the most honorable of men.

CHARLES. Honorable! most honorable! 50

CHARLOTTE. Can you doubt it? Do you demur? Have you forgot your letter? Why, Belcour 'twas that prompted me to this proposal, that promised to supply the means, that nobly offered his unasked assistance — 55

O'FLAHERTY *enters hastily.*

O'FLAHERTY. Run, run, for holy St. Antony's sake, to horse and away! The conference is broke up, and the old lady advances upon a full Piedmontese trot, within pistol-shot of your encampment.

CHARLOTTE. Here, here, down the back- 60 stairs! O, Charles, remember me!

CHARLES. Farewell! Now, now I feel myself a coward. *Exit.*

CHARLOTTE. What does he mean?

O'FLAHERTY. Ask no questions, but begone! 65 [*Exit* CHARLOTTE.] She has cooled the lad's courage, and wonders he feels like a coward. There's a damned deal of mischief brewing between this hyena and her lawyer: egad I'll step behind this screen and listen:

a good soldier must sometimes fight in ambush 70 as well as open field. (*Retires.*)

SCENE IX

LADY RUSPORT *and* VARLAND.

LADY R. Sure I heard somebody. Hark! No; only the servants going down the back-stairs. Well, Mr. Varland, I think then we are agreed; you'll take my money; and your conscience no longer stands in your way. 5

VAR. Your father was my benefactor; his will ought to be sacred; but, if I commit it to the flames, how will he be the wiser? Dudley, 'tis true, has done me no harm; but five thousand pounds will do me much good; so, in short, madam, I take your 10 offer; I will confer with my clerk, who witnessed the will; and to-morrow morning put it into your hands, upon condition you put five thousand good pounds into mine.

LADY R. 'Tis a bargain: I'll be ready for you: 15 farewell. *Exit.*

VAR. Let me consider — Five thousand pounds prompt payment for destroying this scrap of paper, not worth five farthings; 'tis a fortune easily earned; yes, and 'tis another man's fortune easily thrown 20 away: 'tis a good round sum to be paid down at once for a bribe, but 'tis a damned rogue's trick in me to take it.

O'FLAHERTY (*aside*). So, so! this fellow speaks truth to himself, though he lies to other people 25 — but hush!

VAR. 'Tis breaking the trust of my benefactor: that's a foul crime, but he's dead, and can never reproach me with it: and 'tis robbing young Dudley of his lawful patrimony, that's a hard case, but 30 he's alive and knows nothing of the matter.

O'FLAHERTY (*aside*). These lawyers are so used to bring off the rogueries of others, that they are never without an excuse for their own.

VAR. Were I assured now that Dudley would 35 give me half the money for producing this will, that Lady Rusport does for concealing it, I would deal with him, and be an honest man at half price; I wish every gentleman of my profession could lay his hand on his heart and say the same thing. 40

O'FLAHERTY. A bargain, old gentleman! Nay, never start, nor stare, you wasn't afraid of your own conscience, never be afraid of me.

VAR. Of you, sir; who are you, pray?

O'FLAHERTY. I'll tell you who I am: you seem 45 to wish to be honest, but want the heart to set about it; now I am the very man in the world to make you so; for if you do not give me up that paper this very instant, by the soul of me, fellow, I will not leave one whole bone in your skin that shan't be 50 broken.

VAR. What right have you, pray, to take this paper from me?

O'FLAHERTY. What right have you, pray, to keep it from young Dudley? I don't know what it 55 contains, but I am apt to think it will be safer in my hands than in yours; therefore give it me without more words, and save yourself a beating: do now, you had best.

VAR. Well, sir, I may as well make a grace of 60 necessity. There! I have acquitted my conscience, at the expense of five thousand pounds.

O'FLAHERTY. Five thousand pounds! Mercy upon me! When there are such temptations in the law, can we wonder if some of the corps are a 65 disgrace to it?

VAR. Well, you have got the paper; if you are an honest man, give it to Charles Dudley.

O'FLAHERTY. An honest man! look at me, friend, I am a soldier, this is not the livery of a knave; 70 I am an Irishman, honey; mine is not the country of dishonor. Now, sirrah, begone; if you enter these doors, or give Lady Rusport the least item of what has passed, I will cut off both your ears, and rob the pillory of its due.   75

VAR. I wish I was once fairly out of his sight
                                              Exeunt.

SCENE X

A room in STOCKWELL'S *house.*

STOCK. I must disclose myself to Belcour; this noble instance of his generosity, which old Dudley has been relating, allies me to him at once; concealment becomes too painful; I shall be proud to own him for my son — But see, he's here.   5

BELCOUR *enters and throws himself on a sofa.*

BEL. O my curst tropical constitution! Would to heaven I had been dropped upon the snows of Lapland, and never felt the blessed influence of the sun, so I had never burnt with these inflammatory passions!   10

STOCK. So, so, you seem disordered, Mr. Belcour.

BEL. Disordered, sir! why did I ever quit the soil in which I grew; what evil planet drew me from that warm sunny region, where naked nature walks without disguise, into this cold contriving artificial 15 country?

STOCK. Come, sir, you've met a rascal; what o' that? general conclusions are illiberal.

BEL. No, sir, I've met reflection by the way; I've come from folly, noise, and fury, and met a 20 silent monitor — Well, well, a villain! 'twas not to be pardoned — pray never mind me, sir.

STOCK. Alas! my heart bleeds for him.

BEL. And yet, I might have heard him: now

plague upon that blundering Irishman for com- 25 ing in as he did; the hurry of the deed might palliate the event: deliberate execution has less to plead — Mr. Stockwell, I am bad company to you.

STOCK. Oh, sir; make no excuse. I think you have not found me forward to pry into the 30 secrets of your pleasures and pursuits; 'tis not my disposition; but there are times when want of curiosity would be want of friendship.

BEL. Ah, sir, mine is a case wherein you and I shall never think alike; the punctilious rules, by 35 which I am bound, are not to be found in your ledgers, nor will pass current in the compting-house of a trader.

STOCK. 'Tis very well, sir; if you think I can render you any service; it may be worth your 40 trial to confide in me; if not, your secret is safer in your own bosom.

BEL. That sentiment demands my confidence: pray, sit down by me. You must know, I have an affair of honor on my hands with young Dudley; 45 and though I put up with no man's insult, yet I wish to take away no man's life.

STOCK. I know the young man, and am apprised of your generosity to his father; what can have bred a quarrel between you?   50

BEL. A foolish passion on my side, and a haughty provocation on his. There is a girl, Mr. Stockwell, whom I have unfortunately seen, of most uncommon beauty; she has withal an air of so much natural modesty, that had I not had good assurance of 55 her being an attainable wanton, I declare I should as soon have thought of attempting the chastity of Diana.

Servant enters.

STOCK. Hey-day, do you interrupt us?

SERV. Sir, there's an Irish gentleman will 60 take no denial; he says he must see Mr. Belcour directly, upon business of the last consequence.

BEL. Admit him; 'tis the Irish officer that parted us, and brings me young Dudley's challenge; I should have made a long story of it, and he'll 65 tell you in three words.

O'FLAHERTY enters.

O'FLAHERTY. Save you, my dear; and you, sir! I have a little bit of a word in private for you.

BEL. Pray deliver your commands; this gentleman is my intimate friend.   70

O'FLAHERTY. Why then, Ensign Dudley will be glad to measure swords with you, yonder at the London Tavern, in Bishopsgate-Street, at nine o'clock — you know the place.

BEL. I do; and shall observe the appointment. 75

O'FLAHERTY. Will you be of the party, sir? We shall want a fourth hand.

STOCK. Savage as the custom is, I close with your proposal, and though I am not fully informed of the occasion of your quarrel, I shall rely on Mr. Bel- 80 cour's honor for the justice of it; and willingly stake my life in his defence.

O'FLAHERTY. Sir, you're a gentleman of honor, and I shall be glad of being better known to you — But hark'ee, Belcour, I had like to have forgot 85 part of my errand: there is the money you gave old Dudley; you may tell it over, faith; 'tis a receipt in full; now the lad can put you to death with a safe conscience, and when he has done that job for you, let it be a warning how you attempt the sister 90 of a man of honor.

BEL. The sister?

O'FLAHERTY. Ay, the sister; 'tis English, is it not? Or Irish; 'tis all one; you understand me, his sister, or Louisa Dudley, that's her name I think, call 95 her which you will: by St. Patrick, 'tis a foolish piece of a business, Belcour, to go about to take away a poor girl's virtue from her, when there are so many to be met in this town, who have disposed of theirs to your hands.   *Exit.* 100

STOCK. Why, I am thunderstruck! what is it you have done, and what is the shocking business in which I have engaged? If I understood him right, 'tis the sister of young Dudley you've been attempt- ing; you talked to me of a professed wanton; 105 the girl he speaks of has beauty enough indeed to inflame your desires, but she has honor, innocence, and simplicity to awe the most licentious passion; if you have done that, Mr. Belcour, I renounce you, I abandon you, I forswear all fellowship or 110 friendship with you forever.

BEL. Have patience for a moment; we do indeed speak of the same person, but she is not innocent, she is not young Dudley's sister.

STOCK. Astonishing! who told you this? 115

BEL. The woman where she lodges; the person who put me on the pursuit and contrived our meetings.

STOCK. What woman? What person?

BEL. Fulmer her name is: I warrant you I 120 did not proceed without good grounds.

STOCK. Fulmer, Fulmer? Who waits? (*A Serv- ant enters.*) Send Mr. Stukely hither directly; I begin to see my way into this dark transaction: Mr. Belcour, Mr. Belcour, you are no match for 125 the cunning and contrivances of this intriguing town.

STUKELY *enters.*

Prithee, Stukely, what is the name of the woman and her husband, who were stopped upon suspicion

of selling stolen diamonds at our next-door 130 neighbor's, the jeweller?

STUKELY. Fulmer.

STOCK. So!

BEL. Can you procure me a sight of those dia- monds?   135

STUKELY. They are now in my hand; I was desired to show them to Mr. Stockwell.

STOCK. Give 'em to me: what do I see? As I live, the very diamonds Miss Rusport sent hither, and which I entrusted to you to return.   140

BEL. Yes, but I betrayed that trust, and gave 'em Mrs. Fulmer to present to Miss Dudley.

STOCK. With a view no doubt to bribe her to compliance.

BEL. I own it.   145

STOCK. For shame, for shame! and 'twas this woman's intelligence you relied upon for Miss Dudley's character?

BEL. I thought she knew her; by heaven, I would have died sooner than have insulted a woman of 150 virtue, or a man of honor.

STOCK. I think you would, but mark the danger of licentious courses; you are betrayed, robbed, abused, and but for this providential discovery in a fair way of being sent out of the world with 155 all your follies on your head — Dear Stukely, go to my neighbor, tell him I have an owner for the jewels, and beg him to carry the people under custody to the London Tavern, and wait for me there.

Exit STUKELY.

I fear the law does not provide a punishment to 160 reach the villainy of these people; but how in the name of wonder could you take anything on the word of such an informer?

BEL. Because I had not lived long enough in your country to know how few informers' words are 165 to be taken: persuaded however as I was of Miss Dudley's guilt, I must own to you I was staggered with the appearance of such innocence, especially when I saw her admitted into Miss Rusport's com- pany.   170

STOCK. Good heaven! did you meet her at Miss Rusport's, and could you doubt her being a woman of reputation?

BEL. By you perhaps such a mistake could not have been made, but in a perfect stranger, I 175 hope it is venial: I did not know what artifices young Dudley might have used to conceal her character; I did not know what disgrace attended the detection of it.

STOCK. I see it was a trap laid for you, which 180 you have narrowly escaped; you addressed a woman of honor with all the loose incense of a profane ad- mirer, and you have drawn upon you the resentment of a man of honor who thinks himself bound to pro-

---

125] O1O2O3N *your* for *you* (a persistent misprint).   140] O1O2O3N *intrusted.*

tect her. Well, sir, you must atone for this   185
mistake.

BEL. To the lady the most penitent submission I
can make is justly due, but in the execution of an
act of justice it never shall be said my soul was
swayed by the least particle of fear: I have re-   190
ceived a challenge from her brother; now though I
would give my fortune, almost my life itself, to
purchase her happiness, yet I cannot abate her one
scruple of my honor; I have been branded with the
name of villain.   195

STOCK. Ay, sir, you mistook her character and he
mistook yours; error begets error.

BEL. Villain, Mr. Stockwell, is a harsh word.

STOCK. It is a harsh word, and should be unsaid.

BEL. Come, come, it shall be unsaid.   200

STOCK. Or else what follows? why the sword is
drawn and to heal the wrongs you have done to the
reputation of the sister, you make an honorable
amends by murdering the brother.

BEL. Murdering!   205

STOCK. 'Tis thus religion writes and speaks the
word; in the vocabulary of modern honor there is
no such term — But come, I don't despair of satisfying the one without alarming the other; that done,
I have a discovery to unfold that you will then,   210
I hope, be fitted to receive.

ACT V

SCENE I

The London Tavern.

O'FLAHERTY, STOCKWELL, CHARLES, *and* BELCOUR.

O'FLAHERTY. Gentlemen, well met! you understand each other's minds, and as I see you have
brought nothing but your swords, you may set to
without any further ceremony.

STOCK. You will not find us backward in any   5
worthy cause; but before we proceed any further, I
would ask this young gentleman, whether he has
any explanation to require of Mr. Belcour.

CHARLES. Of Mr. Belcour none; his actions speak
for themselves: but to you, sir, I would fain pro-   10
pose one question.

STOCK. Name it.

CHARLES. How is it, Mr. Stockwell, that I meet
a man of your character on this ground?

STOCK. I will answer you directly, and my   15
answer shall not displease you. I come hither in
defence of the reputation of Miss Dudley, to redress
the injuries of an innocent young lady.

O'FLAHERTY. By my soul the man knows he's
to fight, only he mistakes which side he's to be of.   20

STOCK. You are about to draw your sword to
refute a charge against your sister's honor; you
would do well, if there were no better means within

reach; but the proofs of her innocence are lodged in
our bosoms, and if we fall, you destroy the evi-   25
dence that most effectually can clear her fame.

CHARLES. How's that, sir?

STOCK. This gentleman could best explain it to
you, but you have given him an undeserved name
that seals his lips against you: I am not under   30
the same inhibition, and if your anger can keep cool
for a few minutes, I desire I may call in two witnesses, who will solve all difficulties at once. Here,
waiter! bring those people in that are without.

O'FLAHERTY. Out upon it, what need is there   35
for so much talking about the matter; can't you
settle your differences first, and dispute about 'em
afterwards?

FULMER *and* MRS. FULMER *brought in.*

CHARLES. Fulmer and his wife in custody?

STOCK. Yes, sir, these are your honest land-   40
lord and landlady, now in custody for defrauding
this gentleman of certain diamonds intended to
have been presented to your sister. Be so good,
Mrs. Fulmer, to inform the company why you so
grossly scandalized the reputation of an innocent   45
lady, by persuading Mr. Belcour that Miss Dudley
was not the sister, but the mistress, of this gentleman.

MRS. F. Sir, I don't know what right you have
to question me, and I shall not answer till I see
occasion.   50

STOCK. Had you been as silent heretofore, madam,
it would have saved you some trouble; but we don't
want your confession. This letter, which you wrote
to Mr. Belcour, will explain your design; and these
diamonds, which of right belong to Miss Rus-   55
port, will confirm your guilt: the law, Mrs. Fulmer,
will make you speak, though I can't. Constable,
take charge of your prisoners.

FULMER. Hold a moment: Mr. Stockwell, you
are a gentleman that knows the world, and a   60
member of parliament; we shall not attempt to impose upon you; we know we are open to the law,
and we know the utmost it can do against us. Mr.
Belcour has been ill used to be sure, and so has
Miss Dudley; and, for my own part, I always   65
condemned the plot as a very foolish plot, but it was
a child of Mrs. Fulmer's brain, and she would not
be put out of conceit with it.

MRS. F. You are a very foolish man, Mr. Fulmer,
so prithee hold your tongue.   70

FULMER. Therefore, as I was saying, if you send
her to Bridewell, it won't be amiss; and if you give
her a little wholesome discipline, she may be the
better for that too: but for me, Mr. Stockwell, who
am a man of letters, I must beseech you, sir,   75
not to bring any disgrace upon my profession.

STOCK. 'Tis you, Mr. Fulmer, not I, that disgrace
your profession, therefore begone, nor expect that

I will betray the interests of mankind so far as to show favor to such incendiaries. Take 'em 80 away; I blush to think such wretches should have the power to set two honest men at variance.

Exeunt FULMER, *etc.*

CHARLES. Mr. Belcour, we have mistaken each other; let us exchange forgiveness. I am convinced you intended no affront to my sister, and I ask 85 your pardon for the expression I was betrayed into.

BEL. 'Tis enough, sir; the error began on my side, and was Miss Dudley here, I would be the first to atone.

STOCK. Let us all adjourn to my house, and 90 conclude the evening like friends: you will find a little entertainment ready for you; and, if I am not mistaken, Miss Dudley and her father will make part of our company. Come, Major, do you consent? 95

O'FLAHERTY. Most readily, Mr. Stockwell; a quarrel well made up is better than a victory hardly earned. Give me your hand, Belcour; o' my conscience you are too honest for the country you live in. And now, my dear lad, since peace is con- 100 cluded on all sides, I have a discovery to make to you, which you must find out for yourself, for deuce take me if I rightly comprehend it, only that your aunt Rusport is in a conspiracy against you, and a vile rogue of a lawyer, whose name I forget, at 105 the bottom of it.

CHARLES. What conspiracy? Dear Major, recollect yourself.

O'FLAHERTY. By my soul, I've no faculty at recollecting myself; but I've a paper some- 110 where about me, that will tell you more of the matter than I can. When I get to the merchant's, I will endeavor to find it.

CHARLES. Well, it must be in your own way; but I confess you have thoroughly roused my curi- 115 osity.

Exeunt.

SCENE II

STOCKWELL'S *house.*

CAPTAIN DUDLEY, LOUISA, *and* STUKELY.

DUDLEY. And are those wretches, Fulmer and his wife, in safe custody?

STUKELY. They are in good hands; I accompanied them to the Tavern, where your son was to be, and then went in search of you. You may 5 be sure Mr. Stockwell will enforce the law against them as far as it will go.

DUDLEY. What mischief might their cursed machinations have produced, but for this timely discovery! 10

LOUISA. Still I am terrified; I tremble with apprehension lest Mr. Belcour's impetuosity and Charles's spirit should not wait for an explanation,

but drive them both to extremes, before the mistake can be unravelled. 15

STUKELY. Mr. Stockwell is with them, madam, and you have nothing to fear; you cannot suppose he would ask you hither for any other purpose, but to celebrate their reconciliation and to receive Mr. Belcour's atonement. 20

DUDLEY. No, no, Louisa, Mr. Stockwell's honor and discretion guard us against all danger or offence; he well knows we will endure no imputation on the honor of our family, and he certainly has invited us to receive satisfaction on that score in an 25 amicable way.

LOUISA. Would to heaven they were returned!

STUKELY. You may expect them every minute; and see, madam, agreeable to your wish, they are here. *Exit.* 30

SCENE III

CHARLES *enters, and afterwards* STOCKWELL *and* O'FLAHERTY.

LOUISA. O Charles, O brother, how could you serve me so, how could you tell me you was going to Lady Rusport's and then set out with a design of fighting Mr. Belcour? But where is he; where is your antagonist? 5

STOCK. Captain, I am proud to see you, and you, Miss Dudley, do me particular honor. We have been adjusting, sir, a very extraordinary and dangerous mistake, which I take for granted my friend Stukely has explained to you. 10

DUDLEY. He has; I have too good an opinion of Mr. Belcour to believe he could be guilty of a designed affront to an innocent girl, and I am much too well acquainted with your character to suppose you could abet him in such design; I have 15 no doubt therefore all things will be set to rights in very few words when we have the pleasure of seeing Mr. Belcour.

STOCK. He has only stepped into the comptinghouse and will wait upon you directly. You 20 will not be over strict, madam, in weighing Mr. Belcour's conduct to the minutest scruple; his manners, passions, and opinions are not as yet assimilated to this climate; he comes amongst you a new character, an inhabitant of a new world, and 25 both hospitality as well as pity recommend him to our indulgence.

SCENE IV

BELCOUR *enters, bows to* MISS DUDLEY.

BEL. I am happy and ashamed to see you; no man in his senses would offend you; I forfeited mine and erred against the light of the sun, when I overlooked your virtues; but your beauty was predom-

inant and hid them from my sight; I now per- 5
ceive I was the dupe of a most improbable report,
and humbly entreat your pardon.

LOUISA. Think no more of it; 'twas a mistake.

BEL. My life has been composed of little else;
'twas founded in mystery and has continued 10
in error: I was once given to hope, Mr. Stockwell,
that you was to have delivered me from these difficulties, but either I do not deserve your confidence,
or I was deceived in my expectations.

STOCK. When this lady has confirmed your 15
pardon, I shall hold you deserving of my confidence.

LOUISA. That was granted the moment it was
asked.

BEL. To prove my title to his confidence honor
me so far with yours as to allow me a few min- 20
utes' conversation in private with you.

(She turns to her father.)

DUDLEY. By all means, Louisa; come, Mr. Stockwell, let us go into another room.

CHARLES. And now, Major O'Flaherty, I claim
your promise of a sight of the paper that is to 25
unravel this conspiracy of my aunt Rusport's: I
think I have waited with great patience.

O'FLAHERTY. I have been endeavoring to call
to mind what it was I overheard; I've got the paper
and will give you the best account I can of the 30
whole transaction.   *Exeunt.*

SCENE V

BELCOUR *and* LOUISA.

BEL. Miss Dudley, I have solicited this audience
to repeat to you my penitence and confusion. How
shall I atone? What reparation can I make to you
and virtue?

LOUISA. To me there's nothing due, nor any- 5
thing demanded of you but your more favorable
opinion for the future, if you should chance to think
of me. Upon the part of virtue I'm not empowered
to speak, but if hereafter, as you range through life,
you should surprise her in the person of some 10
wretched female, poor as myself and not so well protected, enforce not your advantage, complete not
your licentious triumph, but raise her, rescue her
from shame and sorrow, and reconcile her to herself
again.   15

BEL. I will, I will; by bearing your idea ever
present in my thoughts, virtue shall keep an advocate within me; but tell me, loveliest, when you
pardon the offence, can you, all perfect as you are,
approve of the offender? As I now cease to 20
view you in that false light I lately did, can you, and
in the fulness of your bounty will you, cease also to
reflect upon the libertine addresses I have paid you,
and look upon me as your reformed, your rational
admirer?   25

LOUISA. Are sudden reformations apt to last; and
how can I be sure the first fair face you meet will not
ensnare affections so unsteady, and that I shall not
lose you lightly as I gained you?

BEL. Because though you conquered me by 30
surprise, I have no inclination to rebel; because since
the first moment that I saw you, every instant has
improved you in my eyes, because by principle as
well as passion I am unalterably yours, in short
there are ten thousand causes for my love to you; 35
would to heaven I could plant one in your soft bosom
that might move you to return it!

LOUISA. Nay, Mr. Belcour. —

BEL. I know I am not worthy your regard; I know
I'm tainted with a thousand faults, sick of a 40
thousand follies, but there's a healing virtue in your
eyes that makes recovery certain; I cannot be a villain in your arms.

LOUISA. That you can never be; whomever you
shall honor with your choice, my life upon't, 45
that woman will be happy; it is not from suspicion
that I hesitate, it is from honor; 'tis the severity of
my condition, it is the world that never will interpret
fairly in our case.

BEL. Oh, what am I, and who in this wide 50
world concerns himself for such a nameless, such a
friendless thing as I am? I see, Miss Dudley, I've
not yet obtained your pardon.

LOUISA. Nay, that you are in full possession of.

BEL. Oh, seal it with your hand then, loveliest 55
of women, confirm it with your heart; make me honorably happy, and crown your penitent not with
your pardon only, but your love.

LOUISA. My love! —

BEL. By heaven, my soul is conquered with 60
your virtues more than my eyes are ravished with
your beauty. Oh, may this soft, this sensitive alarm
be happy, be auspicious! Doubt not, deliberate not,
delay not. If happiness be the end of life, why do
we slip a moment?   65

SCENE VI

O'FLAHERTY *enters, and afterwards* DUDLEY *and* CHARLES *with* STOCKWELL.

O'FLAHERTY. Joy, joy, joy! sing, dance, leap,
laugh for joy! Ha' done making love and fall down
on your knees to every saint in the calendar, for
they're all on your side and honest St. Patrick at the
head of them.   5

CHARLES. O Louisa, such an event! by the luckiest
chance in life we have discovered a will of my grandfather's made in his last illness, by which he cuts off
my Aunt Rusport with a small annuity, and leaves
me heir to his whole estate, with a fortune of 10
fifteen thousand pounds to yourself.

LOUISA. What is it you tell me? *(To her father.)*

O sir, instruct me to support this unexpected turn of fortune.

DUDLEY. Name not fortune; 'tis the work of 15 Providence, 'tis the justice of heaven that would not suffer innocence to be oppressed, nor your base aunt to prosper in her cruelty and cunning.

A Servant whispers BELCOUR, *and he goes out.*

O'FLAHERTY. You shall pardon me, Captain Dudley, but you must not overlook St. Patrick 20 neither, for by my soul if he had not put it into my head to slip behind the screen when your righteous aunt and the lawyer were plotting together, I don't see how you would ever have come at the paper there, that Master Stockwell is reading. 25

DUDLEY. True my good friend, you are the father of this discovery, but how did you contrive to get this will from the lawyer?

O'FLAHERTY. By force, my dear, the only way of getting anything from a lawyer's clutches. 30

STOCK. Well, Major, when he brings his action of assault and battery against you, the least Dudley can do is to defend you with the weapons you have put into his hands.

CHARLES. That I am bound to do, and after 35 the happiness I shall have in sheltering a father's age from the vicissitudes of life, my next delight will be in offering you an asylum in the bosom of your country.

O'FLAHERTY. And upon my soul, my dear, 40 'tis high time I was there, for 'tis now thirty long years since I sat foot in my native country, and by the power of St. Patrick I swear I think it's worth all the rest of the world put together.

DUDLEY. Ay, Major, much about that time 45 have I been beating the round of service, and 'twere well for us both to give over; we have stood many a tough gale and abundance of hard blows, but Charles shall lay us up in a little private, but safe, harbor, where we'll rest from our labors, and peace- 50 fully wind up the remainder of our days.

O'FLAHERTY. Agreed, and you may take it as a proof of my esteem, young man, that Major O'Flaherty accepts a favor at your hands, for by heaven I'd sooner starve than say I thank you 55 to the man I despise. But I believe you are an honest lad, and I'm glad you've trounced the old cat, for on my conscience I believe I must otherwise have married her myself to have let you in for a share of her fortune. 60

STOCK. Hey-day, what's become of Belcour?

LOUISA. One of your servants called him out just now and seemingly on some earnest occasion.

STOCK. I hope, Miss Dudley, he has atoned to you as a gentleman ought. 65

LOUISA. Mr. Belcour, sir, will always do what a gentleman ought, and in my case I fear only you will think he has done too much.

STOCK. (*aside*). What has he done; and what can be too much? Pray heaven, it may be as I wish! 70

DUDLEY. Let us hear it, child.

LOUISA. With confusion for my own unworthiness, I confess to you he has offered me —

STOCK. Himself.

LOUISA. 'Tis true. 75

STOCK. Then I am happy; all my doubts, my cares are over, and I may own him for my son. — Why these are joyful tidings: come, my good friend, assist me in disposing your lovely daughter to accept this returning prodigal; he is no unprincipled, no 80 hardened libertine; his love for you and virtue is the same.

DUDLEY. 'Twere vile ingratitude in me to doubt his merit — What says my child?

O'FLAHERTY. Begging your pardon now, 'tis 85 a frivolous sort of a question, that of yours; for you may see plainly enough by the young lady's looks, that she says a great deal, though she speaks never a word.

CHARLES. Well, sister, I believe the Major has 90 fairly interpreted the state of your heart.

LOUISA. I own it; and what must that heart be, which love, honor, and beneficence like Mr. Belcour's can make no impression on?

STOCK. I thank you. What happiness has 95 this hour brought to pass!

O'FLAHERTY. Why don't we all sit down to supper then and make a night on't.

STOCK. Hold, here comes Belcour.

SCENE VII

BELCOUR *introducing* MISS RUSPORT.

BEL. Mr. Dudley, here is a fair refugee, who properly comes under your protection; she is equipped for Scotland, but your good fortune, which I have related to her, seems inclined to save you both the journey — Nay, madam, never go back; you are 5 amongst friends.

CHARLES. Charlotte!

CHARLOTTE. The same; that fond officious girl, that haunts you everywhere; that persecuting spirit — 10

CHARLES. Say rather, that protecting angel; such you have been to me.

CHARLOTTE. O Charles, you have an honest, but proud heart.

CHARLES. Nay, chide me not, dear Charlotte. 15

BEL. Seal up her lips then; she is an adorable girl; her arms are open to you; and love and happiness are ready to receive you.

CHARLES. Thus then I claim my dear, my destined wife. 20

(*Embracing her.*)

Scene VIII

Lady Rusport *enters.*

LADY R. Hey-day! mighty fine! wife truly! mighty well! kissing, embracing — did ever anything equal this? Why you shameless hussy! — But I won't condescend to waste a word upon you. — You, sir, you, Mr. Stockwell, you fine, sanctified, fair- 5 dealing man of conscience, is this the principle you trade upon? Is this your neighborly system, to keep a house of reception for runaway daughters, and young beggarly fortune-hunters?

O'FLAHERTY. Be advised now, and don't put 10 yourself in such a passion; we were all very happy till you came.

LADY R. Stand away, sir; haven't I a reason to be in a passion?

O'FLAHERTY. Indeed, honey, and you have, 15 if you knew all.

LADY R. Come, madam, I have found out your haunts; dispose yourself to return home with me: young man, let me never see you within my doors again: Mr. Stockwell, I shall report your be- 20 havior, depend on it.

STOCK. Hold, madam, I cannot consent to lose Miss Rusport's company this evening, and I am persuaded you won't insist upon it; 'tis an unmotherly action to interrupt your daughter's happi- 25 ness in this manner, believe me it is.

LADY R. Her happiness truly; upon my word! and I suppose it's an unmotherly action to interrupt her ruin; for what but ruin must it be to marry a beggar? (*To* CAPTAIN DUDLEY.) I think my 30 sister had a proof of that, sir, when she made choice of you.

DUDLEY. Don't be too lavish of your spirits, Lady Rusport.

O'FLAHERTY. By my soul you'll have occasion 35 for a sip of the cordial elixir by and by.

STOCK. It don't appear to me, madam, that Mr. Dudley can be called a beggar.

LADY R. But it appears to me, Mr. Stockwell; I am apt to think a pair of colors cannot furnish 40 settlement quite sufficient for the heiress of Sir Stephen Rusport.

CHARLOTTE. But a good estate in aid of a commission may do something.

LADY R. A good estate, truly! where should 45 he get a good estate pray?

STOCK. Why suppose now a worthy old gentleman on his death-bed should have taken it in mind to leave him one —

LADY R. Hah! what's that you say? 50

O'FLAHERTY. O ho! you begin to smell a plot, do you?

STOCK. Suppose there should be a paper in the world that runs thus — 'I do hereby give and bequeath all my estates, real and personal, to 55 Charles Dudley, son of my late daughter Louisa, &c. &c. &c.'

LADY R. Why I am thunderstruck! by what contrivance, what villainy did you get possession of that paper? 60

STOCK. There was no villainy, madam, in getting possession of it; the crime was in concealing it, none in bringing it to light.

LADY R. Oh, that cursed lawyer, Varland!

O'FLAHERTY. You may say that, faith, he is 65 a cursed lawyer, and a cursed piece of work I had to get the paper from him; your ladyship now was to have paid him five thousand pounds for it, I forced him to give it me of his own accord for nothing at all, at all. 70

LADY R. Is it you that have done this? Am I foiled by your blundering contrivances, after all?

O'FLAHERTY. 'Twas a blunder, faith, but as natural a one as if I'd made it o' purpose.

CHARLES. Come, let us not oppress the fallen; 75 do right even now, and you shall have no cause to complain.

LADY R. Am I become an object of your pity then? Insufferable! confusion light amongst you! marry and be wretched: let me never see you more. 80
Exit.

CHARLOTTE. She is outrageous; I suffer for her, and blush to see her thus exposed.

CHARLES. Come, Charlotte, don't let this angry woman disturb our happiness: we will save her in spite of herself; your father's memory shall not 85 be stained by the discredit of his second choice.

CHARLOTTE. I trust implicitly to your discretion, and am in all things yours.

BEL. Now, lovely but obdurate, does not this example soften? 90

LOUISA. What can you ask for more? Accept my hand, accept my willing heart.

BEL. O bliss inutterable! brother, father, friend, and you the author of this general joy —

O'FLAHERTY. Blessing of St. Patrick upon us 95 all! 'tis a night of wonderful and surprising ups and downs: I wish we were all fairly set down to supper, and there was an end on't.

STOCK. Hold for a moment! I have yet one word to interpose — Entitled by my friendship to a 100 voice in your disposal, I have approved your match; there yet remains a father's consent to be obtained.

BEL. Have I a father?

STOCK. You have a father: did not I tell you I had a discovery to make? Compose yourself: you 105 have a father, who observes, who knows, who loves you.

BEL. Keep me no longer in suspense; my heart is

softened for the affecting discovery, and nature fits me to receive his blessing.   110

STOCK. I am your father.

BEL. My father? Do I live?

STOCK. I am your father.

BEL. It is too much; my happiness o'erpowers me; to gain a friend and find a father is too much;   115 I blush to think how little I deserve you.

(They embrace.)

DUDLEY. See, children, how many new relations spring from this night's unforeseen events, to endear us to each other.

O'FLAHERTY. O' my conscience, I think we   120 shall be all related by and by.

STOCK. How happily has this evening concluded, and yet how threat'ning was its approach! let us repair to the supper room, where I will unfold to you every circumstance of my mysterious   125 story. Yes, Belcour, I have watched you with a patient, but enquiring eye, and I have discovered through the veil of some irregularities, a heart beaming with benevolence, an animated nature, fallible indeed, but not incorrigible; and your election   130 of this excellent young lady makes me glory in acknowledging you to be my son.

BEL. I thank you, and in my turn glory in the father I have gained: sensibly impressed with gratitude for such extraordinary dispensations, I   135 beseech you, amiable Louisa, for the time to come, whenever you perceive me deviating into error or offence, bring only to my mind the Providence of this night, and I will turn to reason and obey.

END OF THE PLAY.

EPILOGUE

Written by D. G.,[1] Esq.

Spoken by Mrs. Abington[2]

N.B. The lines in italics are to be spoken in a catechise[3] tone.

Confess, good folks, has not Miss Rusport shown,
Strange whims for Seventeen Hundred Seventy-one?
What, pawn her jewels! — there's a precious plan!
To extricate from want a brave *old* man;
And fall in love with poverty and honor;   5
A girl of fortune, fashion! — Fie upon her.
But do not think we females of the stage,
So dead to the refinements of the age,
That we agree with our old-fashioned poet:
I am point-blank against him, and I'll show it: 10
And that my tongue may more politely run,
Make me a lady — Lady Blabington.
Now, with a rank and title to be free, ⎫
I'll make a catechism — and you shall see, ⎬
What is the *veritable Baume de Vie:*[4] ⎭   15
As I change place, I stand for that, or this,
My Lady questions first — then answers Miss.
              (*She speaks as my Lady.*)
'Come, tell me, child, what were our modes and dress,
In those strange times of that old fright Queen Bess?' —
And now for Miss —
              (*She changes place, and speaks for Miss.*)
              When Bess was England's queen,   20
Ladies were dismal beings, seldom seen;
They rose betimes, and breakfasted as soon
On beef and beer, then studied Greek till noon;
Unpainted cheeks with blush of health did glow, ⎫
Beruffed and fardingaled from top to toe, ⎬   25
Nor necks, nor ankles would they ever show. ⎭
Learnt Greek! — (*Laughs.*) — Our outside head takes half a day;
Have we much time to dress the *inside*, pray?
No heads dressed *à la Grecque*; the ancients quote,
There may be learning in a *papillote*:[5]   30
Cards are *our* classics; and I, Lady B., ⎫
In learning will not yield to any she, ⎬
Of the late founded *female* university. ⎭
But now for Lady Blab —
              (*Speaks as my Lady.*)
              'Tell me, Miss Nancy,
What sports and what employments did they fancy?'   35
              (*Speaks as Miss.*)
The vulgar creatures seldom left their houses,
But taught their children, worked, and loved their spouses;

---

[1] David Garrick (1717–1779) produced *The West Indian* at Drury Lane.
[2] Mrs. Frances [Barton] Abington (1737–1815) appeared as Charlotte Rusport.
[3] Suiting the 'catechism' in the Epilogue.   [4] Balm of Life.   [5] Curl-paper.

The use of cards at Christmas only knew,
They played for little, and their games were few,
One-and-thirty, Put, All-fours, and Lantera Loo; [1]   40
They bore a race of mortals stout and bony,
And never heard the name of Macaroni. —
                    (Speaks as my Lady.)
'Oh brava, brava! that's my pretty dear —
Now let a modern, modish fair appear;
No more of these old dowdy maids and wives,   45
Tell how superior beings pass their lives.' —
                    (Speaks as Miss.)
Till noon they sleep, from noon till night they dress,
From night till morn they game it more or less,
Next night the same sweet course of joy run o'er, ⎫
Then the night after as the night before,   ⎬   50
And the night after that, encore, encore! —   ⎭
                    (She comes forward.)
Thus with our cards we *shuffle* off all sorrow,
To-morrow, and to-morrow, and to-morrow!
We *deal apace*, from youth unto our prime,
To the last moment of our *tabby*-time;   55
And all our yesterdays, from rout and drum,
Have lighted fools with empty pockets home.
Thus do our lives with rapture roll away,
Not with the nonsense of our author's play;
This is true life — true spirit — give it praise;   60
Don't snarl and sigh for good Queen Bess's days:
For all you look so sour, and bend the brow,
You all rejoice with me, you're living now.

[1] Old games of cards.

An Essay on the Theatre; or, A Comparison Between Laughing and Sentimental Comedy

BY OLIVER GOLDSMITH

AN ESSAY ON THE THEATRE;

OR,

A COMPARISON BETWEEN LAUGHING AND SENTIMENTAL COMEDY

BY OLIVER GOLDSMITH

(Westminster Magazine, for December, 1772) [1]

THE theatre, like all other amusements, has its fashions and its prejudices: and when satiated with its excellence, mankind begin to mistake change for improvement. For some years tragedy was the reigning entertainment; but of late it has entirely given way to comedy, and our best efforts are now exerted in these lighter kinds of composition. The pompous train, the swelling phrase, and the unnatural rant, are displaced for that natural portrait of human folly and frailty, of which all are judges, because all have sat for the picture.

But as in describing nature it is presented with a double face, either of mirth or sadness, our modern writers find themselves at a loss which chiefly to copy from; and it is now debated, whether the exhibition of human distress is likely to afford the mind more entertainment than that of human absurdity?

Comedy is defined by Aristotle to be a picture of the frailties of the lower part of mankind, to distinguish it from tragedy, which is an exhibition of the misfortunes of the great. When comedy, therefore, ascends to produce the characters of princes or generals upon the stage, it is out of its walks, since low life and middle life are entirely its object. The principal question, therefore, is, whether, in describing low or middle life, an exhibition of its follies be not preferable to a detail of its calamities? Or, in other words, which deserves the preference, — the weeping sentimental comedy so much in fashion at present, or the laughing, and even low comedy, which seems to have been last exhibited by Vanbrugh and Cibber?

If we apply to authorities, all the great masters in the dramatic art have but one opinion. Their rule is, that as tragedy displays the calamities of the great, so comedy should excite our laughter by ridiculously exhibiting the follies of the lower part of mankind. Boileau, one of the best modern critics, asserts, that comedy will not admit of tragic distress: —

'Le comique, ennemi des soupirs et des pleurs,
N'admet point dans ses vers de tragiques douleurs.' [2]

Nor is this rule without the strongest foundation in nature, as the distresses of the mean by no means affect us so strongly as the calamities of the great. When tragedy exhibits to us some great man fallen from his height, and struggling with want and adversity, we feel his situation in the same manner as we suppose he himself must feel, and our pity is increased in proportion to the height from which he fell. On the contrary, we do not so strongly sympathise with one born in humbler circumstances, and encountering accidental distress: so that while we melt for Belisarius,[3] we scarcely give halfpence to the beggar who accosts us in the street. The one has our pity; the

---

[1] For detailed explanation of date, see Textual Notes, p. 947.
[2] *L'Art Poétique*, chant III. 'Comedy, enemy of sighs and tears, by no means admits of tragic distress in its lines.'
[3] The story ran that Belisarius, once the illustrious Byzantine general of the sixth century, became in old age a blind beggar, asking food from door to door.

other our contempt. Distress, therefore, is the proper object of tragedy, since the great excite our pity by their fall; but not equally so of comedy, since the actors employed in it are originally so mean, that they sink but little by their fall.

Since the first origin of the stage, tragedy and comedy have run in distinct channels, and never till of late encroached upon the provinces of each other. Terence, who seems to have made the nearest approaches, always judiciously stops short before he comes to the downright pathetic; and yet he is even reproached by Cæsar for wanting the *vis comica*. All the other comic writers of antiquity aim only at rendering folly or vice ridiculous, but never exalt their characters into buskined pomp, or make what Voltaire humorously calls *a tradesman's tragedy*.

Yet notwithstanding this weight of authority, and the universal practice of former ages, a new species of dramatic composition has been introduced, under the name of *sentimental* comedy, in which the virtues of private life are exhibited, rather than the vices exposed; and the distresses rather than the faults of mankind make our interest in the piece. These comedies have had of late great success, perhaps from their novelty, and also from their flattering every man in his favorite foible. In these plays almost all the characters are good, and exceedingly generous; they are lavish enough of their *tin* money on the stage; and though they want humor, have abundance of sentiment and feeling. If they happen to have faults or foibles, the spectator is taught, not only to pardon, but to applaud them, in consideration of the goodness of their hearts; so that folly, instead of being ridiculed, is commended, and the comedy aims at touching our passions without the power of being truly pathetic. In this manner we are likely to lose one great source of entertainment on the stage; for while the comic poet is invading the province of the tragic muse, he leaves her lovely sister quite neglected. Of this, however, he is no way solicitous, as he measures his fame by his profits.

But it will be said, that the theatre is formed to amuse mankind, and that it matters little, if this end be answered, by what means it is obtained. If mankind find delight in weeping at comedy, it would be cruel to abridge them in that or any other innocent pleasure. If those pieces are denied the name of comedies, yet call them by any other name and, if they are delightful, they are good. Their success, it will be said, is a mark of their merit, and it is only abridging our happiness to deny us an inlet to amusement.

These objections, however, are rather specious than solid. It is true, that amusement is a great object of the theatre, and it will be allowed that these sentimental pieces do often amuse us; but the question is, whether the true comedy would not amuse us more? The question is, whether a character supported throughout a piece, with its ridicule still attending, would not give us more delight than this species of bastard tragedy, which only is applauded because it is new?

A friend of mine, who was sitting unmoved at one of these sentimental pieces, was asked how he could be so indifferent? 'Why, truly,' says he, 'as the hero is but a tradesman, it is indifferent to me whether he be turned out of his counting-house on Fish Street Hill, since he will still have enough left to open shop in St. Giles's.'

The other objection is as ill-grounded; for though we should give these pieces another name, it will not mend their efficacy. It will continue a kind of *mulish* production, with all the defects of its opposite parents, and marked with sterility. If we are permitted to make comedy weep, we have an equal right to make tragedy laugh, and to set down in blank verse the jests and repartees of all the attendants in a funeral procession.

But there is one argument in favor of sentimental comedy, which will keep it on the stage, in spite of all that can be said against it. It is, of all others, the most easily written. Those abilities that can hammer out a novel are fully sufficient for the production of a sentimental comedy. It is only sufficient to raise the characters a little; to deck out the hero with a riband, or give the heroine a title; then to put an insipid dialogue, without character or humor, into their mouths, give them mighty good hearts, very fine clothes, furnish a new set of scenes, make a pathetic scene or two, with a sprinkling of tender melancholy conversation through the whole, and there is no doubt but all the ladies will cry, and all the gentlemen applaud.

Humor at present seems to be departing from the stage, and it will soon happen that our comic players will have nothing left for it but a fine coat and a song. It depends upon the audience whether they will actually drive those poor merry creatures from the stage, or sit at a play as gloomy as at the Tabernacle.[1] It is not easy to recover an art when once lost; and it will be but a just punishment, that when, by our being too fastidious, we have banished humor from the stage, we should ourselves be deprived of the art of laughing.

[1] Whitefield's Tabernacle in London, where George Whitefield (1714–1770), founder of the Calvinistic Methodists, had preached.

She Stoops to Conquer;

or, The Mistakes of a Night

BY OLIVER GOLDSMITH

To SAMUEL JOHNSON, L.L D.

Dear Sir,

BY inscribing this slight performance to you, I do not mean so much to compliment you as myself. It may do me some honour to inform the public, that I have lived many years in intimacy with you. It may serve the interests of mankind also to inform them, that the greatest wit may be found in a character, without impairing the most unaffected piety.

I have, particularly, reason to thank you for your partiality to this performance. The undertaking a comedy, not merely sentimental, was very dangerous; and Mr. Colman, who saw this piece in its various stages, always thought it so. However I ventured to trust it to the public; and though it was necessarily delayed till late in the season, I have every reason to be grateful.

I am, Dear Sir,

Your most sincere friend,

And admirer,

OLIVER GOLDSMITH.

GOLDSMITH'S DEDICATION TO DR. JOHNSON OF THE FIRST EDITION, 1773, OF SHE STOOPS TO CONQUER

PROLOGUE

By David Garrick, Esq.[1]

Enter Mr. Woodward,[2]
Dressed in black, and holding a handkerchief to his eyes.

Excuse me, sirs, I pray — I can't yet speak —
I'm crying now — and have been all the week!
'Tis not alone this mourning suit, good masters;
I've that within — for which there are no plasters!
Pray would you know the reason why I'm crying?   5
The Comic Muse, long sick, is now a-dying!
And if she goes, my tears will never stop;
For, as a play'r, I can't squeeze out one drop:
I am undone, that's all — shall lose my bread —
I'd rather, but that's nothing — lose my head.   10
When the sweet maid is laid upon the bier,
Shuter and *I* shall be chief mourners here.
To *her* a mawkish drab of spurious breed,
Who deals in *sentimentals,* will succeed!
Poor *Ned* [3] and *I* are dead to all intents,   15
We can as soon speak *Greek* as *sentiments!*
Both nervous grown, to keep our spirits up,
We now and then take down a hearty cup.
What shall we do? — If Comedy forsake us!
They'll turn us out, and no one else will take us, —   20
But why can't I be moral? — Let me try —
My heart thus pressing — fixed my face and eye —
With a sententious look, that nothing means,
(Faces are blocks in sentimental scenes)
Thus I begin — *All is not gold that glitters,*   25
Pleasure seems sweet, but proves a glass of bitters.
When ign'rance enters, folly is at hand;
Learning is better far than house and land.
Let not your virtue trip, who trips may stumble,
And virtue is not virtue, if she tumble.   30
    I give it up — morals won't do for me;
To make you laugh, I must play tragedy.
One hope remains — hearing the maid was ill,
A *doctor* comes this night to show his skill.
To cheer her heart, and give your muscles motion,   35
He, in *five draughts* prepared, presents a potion:
A kind of magic charm — for, be assured,
If you will *swallow* it, the maid is cured:
But desp'rate the Doctor, and her case is,
If you reject the dose, and make wry faces!   40
This truth he boasts, will boast it while he lives,
No *pois'nous drugs* are mixed in what he gives.
Should he succeed, you'll give him his degree;
If not, within he will receive no fee!
The college *you,* must his pretensions back,   45
Pronounce him *regular,* or dub him *quack.*

---

[1] David Garrick, who, in 1768, had offset Goldsmith's first 'low' comedy, *The Good-Natured Man*, at Covent Garden, by running Hugh Kelly's sentimental comedy, *False Delicacy*, at Drury Lane, here espouses the cause of Goldsmith and his 'laughing, and even low comedy.'

[2] The Covent Garden actor who later was the Captain Absolute of *The Rivals*. Woodward does not appear in the original cast of *She Stoops to Conquer*.

[3] 'Ned' Shuter, the popular comedian, as Croaker and Hardcastle in Goldsmith's two comedies, contributed much to their success.

DRAMATIS PERSONÆ

<table>
<tr><td>Men</td><td>Women</td></tr>
<tr><td>Sir Charles Marlow</td><td>Mrs. Hardcastle</td></tr>
<tr><td>Young [Charles] Marlow (his Son)</td><td>Miss [Kate] Hardcastle</td></tr>
<tr><td>[Richard] Hardcastle</td><td>Miss [Constance] Neville</td></tr>
<tr><td>[George] Hastings</td><td>Maid</td></tr>
<tr><td>Tony Lumpkin</td><td></td></tr>
<tr><td>Diggory</td><td></td></tr>
</table>

Landlords, Servants, &c., &c.

SHE STOOPS TO CONQUER;

OR,

THE MISTAKES OF A NIGHT *

By OLIVER GOLDSMITH

ACT I

SCENE [I]

A chamber in an old-fashioned house.

Enter MRS. HARDCASTLE *and* MR. HARDCASTLE.

MRS. HARD. I vow, Mr. Hardcastle, you're very particular. Is there a creature in the whole country, but ourselves, that does not take a trip to town now and then, to rub off the rust a little? There's the two Miss Hoggs, and our neighbor, Mrs. Grigsby, 5 go to take a month's polishing every winter.

HARD. Ay, and bring back vanity and affectation to last them the whole year. I wonder why London cannot keep its own fools at home. In my time, the follies of the town crept slowly among us, but 10 now they travel faster than a stage-coach. Its fopperies come down, not only as inside passengers, but in the very basket.[1]

MRS. HARD. Ay, *your* times were fine times indeed; you have been telling us of *them* for many 15 a long year. Here we live in an old rumbling[2] mansion, that looks for all the world like an inn, but that we never see company. Our best visitors are old Mrs. Oddfish, the curate's wife, and little Cripplegate, the lame dancing-master: and all our 20 entertainment your old stories of Prince Eugene[3] and the Duke of Marlborough. I hate such old-fashioned trumpery.

HARD. And I love it. I love everything that's old: old friends, old times, old manners, old books, 25 old wine; and, I believe, Dorothy, (*taking her hand*) you'll own I have been pretty fond of an old wife.

MRS. HARD. Lord, Mr. Hardcastle, you're forever at your Dorothy's and your old wife's. You may be a Darby, but I'll be no Joan,[4] I promise you. 30 I'm not so old as you'd make me, by more than one good year. Add twenty to twenty, and make money of that.

HARD. Let me see; twenty added to twenty — makes just fifty and seven. 35

MRS. HARD. It's false, Mr. Hardcastle: I was but twenty when I was brought to bed of Tony, that I had by Mr. Lumpkin, my first husband; and he's not come to years of discretion yet.

HARD. Nor ever will, I dare answer for him. 40 Ay, you have taught *him* finely!

MRS. HARD. No matter. Tony Lumpkin has a good fortune. My son is not to live by his learning. I don't think a boy wants much learning to spend fifteen hundred a year. 45

HARD. Learning, quotha! A mere composition of tricks and mischief!

MRS. HARD. Humor, my dear; nothing but humor. Come, Mr. Hardcastle, you must allow the boy a little humor. 50

HARD. I'd sooner allow him a horse-pond! If burning the footmen's shoes, frighting the maids, and worrying the kittens, be humor, he has it. It was but yesterday he fastened my wig to the back of my chair, and when I went to make a bow, I popped 55 my bald head in Mrs. Frizzle's face.

MRS. HARD. And am I to blame? The poor boy was always too sickly to do any good. A school would be his death. When he comes to be a little stronger, who knows what a year or two's Latin 60 may do for him?

HARD. Latin for him! A cat and fiddle! No, no, the alehouse and the stable are the only schools he'll ever go to.

MRS. HARD. Well, we must not snub the poor 65 boy now, for I believe we shan't have him long among us. Anybody that looks in his face may see he's consumptive.

HARD. Ay, if growing too fat be one of the symptoms. 70

MRS. HARD. He coughs sometimes.

HARD. Yes, when his liquor goes the wrong way.

MRS. HARD. I'm actually afraid of his lungs.

HARD. And truly, so am I; for he sometimes whoops like a speaking-trumpet — (TONY *hal-* 75 *looing behind the scenes*) — O, there he goes — a very consumptive figure, truly!

---

[1] Outside compartment at back of stage-coach.

[2] Perhaps a misprint for *rambling*. (See textual footnote below.)

[3] Marlborough's ally at Blenheim.

[4] 'The Happy Old Couple' of eighteenth-century ballad and tradition.

---

* The main title adapts Dryden's 'But kneels to conquer, and yet stoops to rise.' The sub-title retains one of several suggested names.

16] OO *rumbling*; Larpent MS. *rambling*. (Modern editions usually follow the consensus of the five octavos of 1773; M prefers *rambling*.)

Enter TONY, *crossing the stage.*

MRS. HARD. Tony, where are you going, my charmer? Won't you give papa and I a little of your company, lovee?   80

TONY. I'm in haste, mother, I cannot stay.

MRS. HARD. You shan't venture out this raw evening, my dear: you look most shockingly.

TONY. I can't stay, I tell you. 'The Three Pigeons' expects me down every moment. There's some   85 fun going forward.

HARD. Ay; the alehouse, the old place: I thought so.

MRS. HARD. A low, paltry set of fellows.

TONY. Not so low, neither. There's Dick   90 Muggins, the exciseman; Jack Slang, the horse-doctor; little Aminadab, that grinds the music-box; and Tom Twist, that spins the pewter platter.

MRS. HARD. Pray, my dear, disappoint them for one night at least.   95

TONY. As for disappointing *them*, I should not so much mind; but I can't abide to disappoint *myself*.

MRS. HARD. (*detaining him*). You shan't go.

TONY. I will, I tell you.

MRS. HARD. I say you shan't.   100

TONY. We'll see which is strongest, you or I.

Exit, hauling her out.

HARDCASTLE *solus.*

HARD. Ay, there goes a pair that only spoil each other. But is not the whole age in a combination to drive sense and discretion out of doors? There's my pretty darling, Kate; the fashions of the   105 times have almost infected her too. By living a year or two in town, she is as fond of gauze, and French frippery, as the best of them.

Enter MISS HARDCASTLE.

Blessings on my pretty innocence! Dressed out as usual, my Kate. Goodness! what a quantity   110 of superfluous silk has[t] thou got about thee, girl! I could never teach the fools of this age that the indigent world could be clothed out of the trimmings of the vain.

MISS HARD. You know our agreement, sir.   115 You allow me the morning to receive and pay visits, and to dress in my own manner; and in the evening, I put on my housewife's dress to please you.

HARD. Well, remember, I insist on the terms of our agreement; and, by the bye, I believe I shall   120 have occasion to try your obedience this very evening.

MISS HARD. I protest, sir, I don't comprehend your meaning.

HARD. Then, to be plain with you, Kate, I expect the young gentleman I have chosen to be your   125 husband from town this very day. I have his father's letter, in which he informs me his son is set out, and that he intends to follow himself shortly after.

MISS HARD. Indeed! I wish I had known   130 something of this before. Bless me, how shall I behave? It's a thousand to one I shan't like him; our meeting will be so formal, and so like a thing of business, that I shall find no room for friendship or esteem.   135

HARD. Depend upon it, child, I'll never control your choice; but Mr. Marlow, whom I have pitched upon, is the son of my old friend, Sir Charles Marlow, of whom you have heard me talk so often. The young gentleman has been bred a scholar, and   140 is designed for an employment in the service of his country. I am told he's a man of an excellent understanding.

MISS HARD. Is he?

HARD. Very generous.   145

MISS HARD. I believe I shall like him.

HARD. Young and brave.

MISS HARD. I'm sure I shall like him.

HARD. And very handsome.

MISS HARD. My dear papa, say no more,   150 (*kissing his hand*) he's mine, I'll have him!

HARD. And, to crown all, Kate, he's one of the most bashful and reserved young fellows in all the world.

MISS HARD. Eh! you have frozen me to   155 death again. That word 'reserved' has undone all the rest of his accomplishments. A reserved lover, it is said, always makes a suspicious husband.

HARD. On the contrary, modesty seldom resides in a breast that is not enriched with nobler vir-   160 tues. It was the very feature in his character that first struck me.

MISS HARD. He must have more striking features to catch me, I promise you. However, if he be so young, so handsome, and so everything, as you   165 mention, I believe he'll do still. I think I'll have him.

HARD. Ay, Kate, but there is still an obstacle. It's more than an even wager he may not have *you*.

MISS HARD. My dear papa, why will you mortify one so? — Well, if he refuses, instead of   170 breaking my heart at his indifference, I'll only break my glass for its flattery, set my cap to some new fashion, and look out for some less difficult admirer.

HARD. Bravely resolved! In the meantime, I'll go prepare the servants for his reception; as we   175 seldom see company, they want as much training as a company of recruits the first day's muster. *Exit.*

MISS HARDCASTLE *sola.*

MISS HARD. Lud, this news of papa's puts me all in a flutter. 'Young, handsome'; these he put last, but I put them foremost. 'Sensible, good-   180 natured'; I like all that. But then, 'reserved,' and

---

'sheepish'; that's much against him. Yet, can't he be cured of his timidity by being taught to be proud of his wife? Yes, and can't I — But I vow I'm disposing of the husband, before I have secured 185 the lover.

Enter Miss Neville.

Miss Hard. I'm glad you're come, Neville, my dear. Tell me, Constance, how do I look this evening? Is there anything whimsical about me? Is it one of my well-looking days, child? Am I in 190 face to-day?

Miss Nev. Perfectly, my dear. Yet, now I look again — bless me! — sure, no accident has happened among the canary birds or the gold-fishes? Has your brother or the cat been meddling? Or has the 195 last novel been too moving?

Miss Hard. No; nothing of all this. I have been threatened — I can scarce get it out — I have been threatened with a lover.

Miss Nev. And his name — 200

Miss Hard. Is Marlow.

Miss Nev. Indeed!

Miss Hard. The son of Sir Charles Marlow.

Miss Nev. As I live, the most intimate friend of Mr. Hastings, *my* admirer. They are never 205 asunder. I believe you must have seen him when we lived in town.

Miss Hard. Never.

Miss Nev. He's a very singular character, I assure you. Among women of reputation and 210 virtue, he is the modestest man alive; but his acquaintance give him a very different character among creatures of another stamp: you understand me.

Miss Hard. An odd character, indeed! I shall never be able to manage him. What shall I 215 do? Pshaw, think no more of him, but trust to occurrences for success. But how goes on your own affair, my dear? Has my mother been courting you for my brother Tony, as usual?

Miss Nev. I have just come from one of 220 our agreeable *tête-à-têtes*. She has been saying a hundred tender things, and setting off her pretty monster as the very pink of perfection.

Miss Hard. And her partiality is such that she actually thinks him so. A fortune like yours 225 is no small temptation. Besides, as she has the sole management of it, I'm not surprised to see her unwilling to let it go out of the family.

Miss Nev. A fortune like mine, which chiefly consists in jewels, is no such mighty tempta- 230 tion. But at any rate, if my dear Hastings be but constant, I make no doubt to be too hard for her at last. However, I let her suppose that I am in love with her son; and she never once dreams that my affections are fixed upon another. 235

Miss Hard. My good brother holds out stoutly. I could almost love him for hating you so.

Miss Nev. It is a good-natured creature at bottom, and I'm sure would wish to see me married to anybody but himself. But my aunt's bell rings 240 for our afternoon's walk round the improvements. *Allons.* Courage is necessary, as our affairs are critical.

Miss Hard. Would it were bedtime, and all were well.[1] *Exeunt.* 245

Scene [II]

An alehouse room.

Several shabby fellows with punch and tobacco. Tony *at the head of the table, a little higher than the rest: a mallet in his hand.*

Omnes. Hurrea, hurrea, hurrea, bravo!

First Fellow. Now, gentlemen, silence for a song. The Squire is going to knock himself down[2] for a song.

Omnes. Ay, a song, a song. 5

Tony. Then I'll sing you, gentlemen, a song I made upon this alehouse, 'The Three Pigeons.'

Song

Let schoolmasters puzzle their brain,
　　With grammar, and nonsense, and learning;
Good liquor, I stoutly maintain, 10
　　Gives *genus* a better discerning.
Let them brag of their heathenish gods,
　　Their Lethes, their Styxes, and Stygians;
Their Quis, and their Quæs, and their Quods,
　　They're all but a parcel of pigeons.[3] 15
　　　　Toroddle, toroddle, toroll!

When Methodist preachers come down,
　　A-preaching that drinking is sinful,
I'll wager the rascals a crown,
　　They always preach best with a skinful. 20
But when you come down with your pence,
　　For a slice of their scurvy religion,
I'll leave it to all men of sense,
　　But you, my good friend, are the pigeon.
　　　　Toroddle, toroddle, toroll! 25

Then come, put the jorum[4] about,
　　And let us be merry and clever,
Our hearts and our liquors are stout,
　　Here's the Three Jolly Pigeons forever.
Let some cry up woodcock or hare, 30
　　Your bustards, your ducks, and your widgeons;
But of all the birds in the air,
　　Here's a health to the Three Jolly Pigeons.
　　　　Toroddle, toroddle, toroll!

---

[1] Cf. Falstaff's phrase, *I Henry IV*, V. i. 125.
[2] 'Call upon himself.' Tony, mallet in hand, presides as chairman.
[3] Simpletons, dupes.　　[4] Drinking-bowl.

24] OO *But you*; some modern editions alter to *That you.*

OMNES. Bravo, bravo!   35

FIRST FELLOW. The Squire has got spunk in him.

SECOND FEL. I loves to hear him sing, bekeays he never gives us nothing that's *low*.

THIRD FEL. O, damn anything that's *low*, I cannot bear it!   40

FOURTH FEL. The genteel thing is the genteel thing at any time; if so be that a gentleman bees in a concatenation accordingly.

THIRD FEL. I like the maxum of it, Master Muggins. What, though I am obligated to dance a   45 bear, a man may be a gentleman for all that. May this be my poison, if my bear ever dances but to the very genteelest of tunes: *Water Parted*,[1] or the minuet in *Ariadne*.[2]

SECOND FEL. What a pity it is the Squire is   50 not come to his own. It would be well for all the publicans within ten miles round of him.

TONY. Ecod, and so it would, Master Slang. I'd then show what it was to keep choice of company.

SECOND FEL. O, he takes after his own father   55 for that. To be sure, old Squire Lumpkin was the finest gentleman I ever set my eyes on. For winding the straight horn, or beating a thicket for a hare, or a wench, he never had his fellow. It was a saying in the place, that he kept the best horses, dogs, and   60 girls, in the whole county.

TONY. Ecod, and when I'm of age I'll be no bastard, I promise you. I have been thinking of Bet Bouncer and the miller's gray mare to begin with. But come, my boys, drink about and be merry,   65 for you pay no reckoning. Well, Stingo, what's the matter?

Enter Landlord.

LAND. There be two gentlemen in a post-chaise at the door. They have lost their way upo' the forest; and they are talking something about Mr.   70 Hardcastle.

TONY. As sure as can be, one of them must be the gentleman that's coming down to court my sister. Do they seem to be Londoners?

LAND. I believe they may. They look   75 woundily [3] like Frenchmen.

TONY. Then desire them to step this way, and I'll set them right in a twinkling. (*Exit Landlord.*) Gentlemen, as they mayn't be good enough company for you, step down for a moment, and I'll be with   80 you in the squeezing of a lemon.   *Exeunt mob.*

TONY *solus.*

TONY. Father-in-law has been calling me whelp, and hound, this half year. Now, if I pleased, I could be so revenged upon the old grumbletonian. But

then I'm afraid, — afraid of what! I shall soon   85 be worth fifteen hundred a year, and let him frighten me out of *that* if he can.

Enter Landlord, conducting MARLOW *and* HASTINGS.

MARL. What a tedious, uncomfortable day have we had of it! We were told it was but forty miles across the country, and we have come above   90 threescore!

HAST. And all, Marlow, from that unaccountable reserve of yours, that would not let us enquire more frequently on the way.

MARL. I own, Hastings, I am unwilling to lay   95 myself under an obligation to everyone I meet, and often stand the chance of an unmannerly answer.

HAST. At present, however, we are not likely to receive any answer.

TONY. No offence, gentlemen. But I'm told   100 you have been enquiring for one Mr. Hardcastle, in [these] parts. Do you know what part of the country you are in?

HAST. Not in the least, sir, but should thank you for information.   105

TONY. Nor the way you came?

HAST. No, sir; but if you can inform us —

TONY. Why, gentlemen, if you know neither the road you are going, nor where you are, nor the road you came, the first thing I have to inform you   110 is, that — you have lost your way.

MARL. We wanted no ghost to tell us that.[4]

TONY. Pray, gentlemen, may I be so bold as to ask the place from whence you came?

MARL. That's not necessary towards direct-   115 ing us where we are to go.

TONY. No offence; but question for question is all fair, you know. — Pray, gentlemen, is not this same Hardcastle a cross-grained, old-fashioned, whimsical fellow, with an ugly face, a daughter, and a   120 pretty son?

HAST. We have not seen the gentleman, but he has the family you mention.

TONY. The daughter, a tall, trapesing, trolloping, talkative maypole — the son, a pretty, well-   125 bred, agreeable youth, that everybody is fond of!

MARL. Our information differs in this. The daughter is said to be well-bred, and beautiful; the son, an awkward booby, reared up and spoiled at his mother's apron-string.   130

TONY. He-he-hem — Then, gentlemen, all I have to tell you is, that you won't reach Mr. Hardcastle's house this night, I believe.

HAST. Unfortunate!

TONY. It's a damned long, dark, boggy,   135 dirty, dangerous way. Stingo, tell the gentlemen

---

[1] Song in Arne's opera, *Artaxerxes*, 1762.
[2] Händel's opera, 1734.   [3] Exceedingly.

[4] Cf. Horatio's phrase, *Hamlet*, I. v. 125.

42] OO *time. If so.*   61] D *country for county* (possibly a misprint).   102] OO *those.*

the way to Mr. Hardcastle's; (*winking upon the Landlord*) Mr. Hardcastle's, of Quagmire Marsh, you understand me.

LAND. Master Hardcastle's! Lack-a-daisy, 140 my masters, you're come a deadly deal wrong! When you came to the bottom of the hill, you should have crossed down Squash-lane.

MARL. Cross down Squash-lane!

LAND. Then you were to keep straight for- 145 ward, till you came to four roads.

MARL. Come to where four roads meet!

TONY. Ay; but you must be sure to take only one of them.

MARL. O sir, you're facetious. 150

TONY. Then, keeping to the right, you are to go sideways till you come upon Crack-skull Common: there you must look sharp for the track of the wheel, and go forward, till you come to farmer Murrain's barn. Coming to the farmer's barn, you are to 155 turn to the right, and then to the left, and then to the right about again, till you find out the old mill —

MARL. Zounds, man! we could as soon find out the longitude![1]

HAST. What's to be done, Marlow? 160

MARL. This house promises but a poor reception; though perhaps the landlord can accommodate us.

LAND. Alack, master, we have but one spare bed in the whole house.

TONY. And to my knowledge, that's taken 165 up by three lodgers already. (*After a pause, in which the rest seem disconcerted.*) I have hit it. Don't you think, Stingo, our landlady could accommodate the gentlemen by the fireside, with — three chairs and a bolster? 170

HAST. I hate sleeping by the fireside.

MARL. And I detest your three chairs and a bolster.

TONY. You do, do you? — then, let me see — what — if you go on a mile further, to the 175 Buck's Head; the old Buck's Head on the hill, one of the best inns in the whole county?

HAST. O ho! so we have escaped an adventure for this night, however.

LAND. (*apart to* TONY). Sure, you ben't send- 180 ing them to your father's as an inn, be you?

TONY. Mum, you fool you. Let *them* find that out. (*To them.*) You have only to keep on straight forward, till you come to a large old house by the roadside. You'll see a pair of large horns over 185 the door. That's the sign. Drive up the yard, and call stoutly about you.

---

[1] An Act of 1713 offered rewards totalling £20,000 for close determination of a ship's longitude. Not until June, 1773, did the winner, John Harrison, receive payment in full, after various partial early awards.

HAST. Sir, we are obliged to you. The servants can't miss the way?

TONY. No, no: but I tell you, though, the 190 landlord is rich, and going to leave off business; so he wants to be thought a gentleman, saving your presence, he! he! he! He'll be for giving you his company; and, ecod, if you mind him, he'll persuade you that his mother was an alderman, and his aunt 195 a justice of peace.

LAND. A troublesome old blade, to be sure; but 'a keeps as good wines and beds as any in the whole country.

MARL. Well, if he supplies us with these, we 200 shall want no further connection. We are to turn to the right, did you say?

TONY. No, no; straight forward. I'll just step myself, and show you a piece of the way. (*To the Landlord.*) Mum! 205

LAND. Ah, bless your heart, for a sweet, pleasant — damned mischievous son of a whore. *Exeunt.*

ACT II

SCENE [I]

An old-fashioned house.

Enter HARDCASTLE, *followed by three or four awkward Servants.*

HARD. Well, I hope you're perfect in the table exercise I have been teaching you these three days. You all know your posts and your places, and can show that you have been used to good company, without ever stirring from home. 5

OMNES. Ay, ay.

HARD. When company comes, you are not to pop out and stare, and then run in again, like frighted rabbits in a warren.

OMNES. No, no. 10

HARD. You, Diggory, whom I have taken from the barn, are to make a show at the side-table; and you, Roger, whom I have advanced from the plough, are to place yourself behind *my* chair. But you're not to stand so, with your hands in your pockets. 15 Take your hands from your pockets, Roger; and from your head, you blockhead, you. See how Diggory carries his hands. They're a little too stiff, indeed, but that's no great matter.

DIGG. Ay, mind how I hold them. I learned 20 to hold my hands this way, when I was upon drill for the militia. And so being upon drill —

HARD. You must not be so talkative, Diggory. You must be all attention to the guests. You must hear us talk, and not think of talking; you must 25 see us drink, and not think of drinking; you must see us eat, and not think of eating.

DIGG. By the laws, your worship, that's parfectly unpossible. Whenever Diggory sees yeating going forward, ecod, he's always wishing for a mouth- 30 ful himself.

HARD. Blockhead! Is not a bellyful in the kitchen as good as a bellyful in the parlor? Stay your stomach with that reflection.

DIGG. Ecod, I thank your worship, I'll make 35 a shift to stay my stomach with a slice of cold beef in the pantry.

HARD. Diggory, you are too talkative. Then, if I happen to say a good thing, or tell a good story at table, you must not all burst out a-laughing, as if 40 you made part of the company.

DIGG. Then, ecod, your worship must not tell the story of Ould Grouse in the gun-room: I can't help laughing at that — he! he! he! — for the soul of me. We have laughed at that these twenty years — 45 ha! ha! ha!

HARD. Ha! ha! ha! The story is a good one. Well, honest Diggory, you may laugh at that — but still remember to be attentive. Suppose one of the company should call for a glass of wine, how will 50 you behave? A glass of wine, sir, if you please. (*To* DIGGORY.) — Eh, why don't you move?

DIGG. Ecod, your worship, I never have courage till I see the eatables and drinkables brought upo' the table, and then I'm as bauld as a lion. 55

HARD. What, will nobody move?

FIRST SERV. I'm not to leave this pleace.

SECOND SERV. I'm sure it's no pleace of mine.

THIRD SERV. Nor mine, for sartain.

DIGG. Wauns,[1] and I'm sure it canna be 60 mine.

HARD. You numskulls! and so while, like your betters, you are quarrelling for places, the guests must be starved. O you dunces! I find I must begin all over again. — But don't I hear a coach 65 drive into the yard? To your posts, you blockheads! I'll go in the meantime, and give my old friend's son a hearty reception at the gate. *Exit* HARDCASTLE.

DIGG. By the elevens,[2] my pleace is quite gone out my head! 70

ROGER. I know that my pleace is to be everywhere.

FIRST SERV. Where the devil is mine?

SECOND SERV. My pleace is to be nowhere at all; and so I'ze go about my business.

Exeunt Servants, running about as if frighted, different ways.

Enter Servant [ROGER] [3] *with candles, showing in* MARLOW *and* HASTINGS.

SERV. Welcome, gentlemen, very welcome. 75 This way.

[1] A corruption of 'swounds' ('God's wounds').
[2] A phrase 'of uncertain origin' (*N.E.D.*).
[3] See l. 318, below.

HAST. After the disappointments of the day, welcome once more, Charles, to the comforts of a clean room and a good fire. Upon my word, a very well-looking house; antique but creditable. 80

MARL. The usual fate of a large mansion. Having first ruined the master by good housekeeping, it at last comes to levy contributions as an inn.

HAST. As you say, we passengers are to be taxed to pay all these fineries. I have often seen a 85 good sideboard, or a marble chimney-piece, though not actually put in the bill, enflame a reckoning confoundedly.

MARL. Travellers, George, must pay in all places. The only difference is that, in good inns, you 90 pay dearly for luxuries; in bad inns, you are fleeced and starved.

HAST. You have lived pretty much among them. In truth, I have been often surprised that you, who have seen so much of the world, with your nat- 95 ural good sense, and your many opportunities, could never yet acquire a requisite share of assurance.

MARL. The Englishman's malady. But tell me, George, where could I have learned that assurance you talk of? My life has been chiefly spent in a 100 college, or an inn, in seclusion from that lovely part of the creation that chiefly teach men confidence. I don't know that I was ever familiarly acquainted with a single modest woman — except my mother. But among females of another class, you 105 know —

HAST. Ay, among them you are impudent enough, of all conscience.

MARL. They are of *us*, you know.

HAST. But in the company of women of 110 reputation I never saw such an idiot, such a trembler; you look for all the world as if you wanted an opportunity of stealing out of the room.

MARL. Why, man, that's because I *do* want to steal out of the room. Faith, I have often formed 115 a resolution to break the ice, and rattle away at any rate. But I don't know how, a single glance from a pair of fine eyes has totally overset my resolution. An impudent fellow may counterfeit modesty, but I'll be hanged if a modest man can ever 120 counterfeit impudence.

HAST. If you could but say half the fine things to them that I have heard you lavish upon the bar-maid of an inn, or even a college bed-maker —

MARL. Why, George, I can't say fine things 125 to them. They freeze, they petrify me. They may talk of a comet, or a burning mountain, or some such bagatelle; but to me a modest woman, dressed out in all her finery, is the most tremendous object of the whole creation. 130

HAST. Ha! ha! ha! At this rate, man, how can you ever expect to marry?

MARL. Never; unless, as among kings and princes,

my bride were to be courted by proxy. If, indeed, like an Eastern bridegroom, one were to be 135 introduced to a wife he never saw before, it might be endured. But to go through all the terrors of a formal courtship, together with the episode of aunts, grandmothers, and cousins, and at last to blurt out the broad, staring question of, *Madam, will you* 140 *marry me?* No, no, that's a strain much above me, I assure you.

HAST. I pity you. But how do you intend behaving to the lady you are come down to visit at the request of your father? 145

MARL. As I behave to all other ladies. Bow very low; answer yes, or no, to all her demands — But for the rest, I don't think I shall venture to look in her face till I see my father's again.

HAST. I'm surprised that one who is so 150 warm a friend can be so cool a lover.

MARL. To be explicit, my dear Hastings, my chief inducement down was to be instrumental in forwarding your happiness, not my own. Miss Neville loves you; the family don't know you; as my friend, 155 you are sure of a reception; and let honor do the rest.

HAST. My dear Marlow! But I'll suppress the emotion. Were I a wretch, meanly seeking to carry off a fortune, you should be the last man in the 160 world I would apply to for assistance. But Miss Neville's person is all I ask, and that is mine, both from her deceased father's consent, and her own inclination.

MARL. Happy man! you have talents and art 165 to captivate any woman. I'm doomed to adore the sex, and yet to converse with the only part of it I despise. This stammer in my address, and this awkward, prepossessing [1] visage of mine, can never permit me to soar above the reach of a milliner's 170 'prentice, or one of the duchesses of Drury Lane.[2] Pshaw! this fellow here to interrupt us.

Enter HARDCASTLE.

HARD. Gentlemen, once more you are heartily welcome. Which is Mr. Marlow? Sir, you're heartily welcome. It's not my way, you see, to re- 175 ceive my friends with my back to the fire. I like to give them a hearty reception, in the old style, at my gate. I like to see their horses and trunks taken care of.

MARL. (*aside*). He has got our names from 180 the servants already. (*To him.*) We approve your caution and hospitality, sir. (*To* HASTINGS.) I

[1] Causing prejudice. Modern editions often alter OO to read *unprepossessing.*
[2] Women of the town.

have been thinking, George, of changing our travelling dresses in the morning. I am grown confoundedly ashamed of mine. 185

HARD. I beg, Mr. Marlow, you'll use no ceremony in this house.

HAST. I fancy, [Charles], you're right: the first blow is half the battle. I intend opening the campaign with the white and gold. 190

HARD. Mr. Marlow — Mr. Hastings — gentlemen — pray be under no constraint in this house. This is Liberty-Hall, gentlemen. You may do just as you please here.

MARL. Yet, George, if we open the cam- 195 paign too fiercely at first, we may want ammunition before it is over. I think to reserve the embroidery to secure a retreat.

HARD. Your talking of a retreat, Mr. Marlow, puts me in mind of the Duke of Marlborough, when 200 we went to besiege Denain.[3] He first summoned the garrison —

MARL. Don't you think the *ventre d'or* waistcoat will do with the plain brown?

HARD. He first summoned the garrison, 205 which might consist of about five thousand men —

HAST. I think not: brown and yellow mix but very poorly.

HARD. I say, gentlemen, as I was telling you, he summoned the garrison, which might consist of 210 about five thousand men —

MARL. The girls like finery.

HARD. Which might consist of about five thousand men, well appointed with stores, ammunition, and other implements of war. 'Now,' says the 215 Duke of Marlborough to George Brooks, that stood next to him — you must have heard of George Brooks — 'I'll pawn my dukedom,' says he, 'but I take that garrison without spilling a drop of blood.' So — 220

MARL. What, my good friend, if you gave us a glass of punch in the meantime; it would help us to carry on the siege with vigor.

HARD. Punch, sir! (*Aside.*) This is the most unaccountable kind of modesty I ever met with! 225

MARL. Yes, sir, punch! A glass of warm punch, after our journey, will be comfortable. This is Liberty-Hall, you know.

HARD. Here's cup, sir.

MARL. (*aside*). So this fellow, in his Liberty- 230 Hall, will only let us have just what he pleases.

HARD. (*taking the cup*). I hope you'll find it to your mind. I have prepared it with my own hands, and I believe you'll own the ingredients are toler-

[3] Here the French defeated the Allies in 1712.

able. Will you be so good as to pledge me, 235 sir? Here, Mr. Marlow, here is to our better acquaintance.   (*Drinks.*)

MARL. (*aside*). A very impudent fellow this! But he's a character, and I'll humor him a little. Sir, my service to you.   (*Drinks.*) 240

HAST. (*aside*). I see this fellow wants to give us his company, and forgets that he's an innkeeper before he has learned to be a gentleman.

MARL. From the excellence of your cup, my old friend, I suppose you have a good deal of busi- 245 ness in this part of the country. Warm work, now and then, at elections, I suppose.

HARD. No, sir, I have long given that work over. Since our betters have hit upon the expedient of electing each other, there's no business *for us* 250 *that sell ale.*

HAST. So, then, you have no turn for politics, I find.

HARD. Not in the least. There was a time, indeed, I fretted myself about the mistakes of 255 government, like other people; but finding myself every day grow more angry, and the government growing no better, I left it to mend itself. Since that, I no more trouble my head about Hyder Ally, or Ally Cawn,[1] than about *Ally Croaker.*[2] Sir, my 260 service to you.

HAST. So that with eating above stairs, and drinking below, with receiving your friends within, and amusing them without, you lead a good, pleasant, bustling life of it.   265

HARD. I do stir about a great deal, that's certain. Half the differences of the parish are adjusted in this very parlor.

MARL. (*after drinking*). And you have an argument in your cup, old gentleman, better than any in 270 Westminster Hall.[3]

HARD. Ay, young gentleman, that, and a little philosophy.

MARL. (*aside*). Well, this is the first time I ever heard of an innkeeper's philosophy.   275

HAST. So, then, like an experienced general, you attack them on every quarter. If you find their reason manageable, you attack it with your philosophy; if you find they have no reason, you attack them with this. Here's your health, my phi- 280 losopher.   (*Drinks.*)

HARD. Good, very good, thank you; ha! ha! Your generalship puts me in mind of Prince Eugene, when he fought the Turks at the battle of Belgrade.[4] You shall hear —   285

[1] Hyder Ali and Ali Khan were Indian potentates of the period.
[2] A popular Irish song.
[3] Seat of Law Courts in Goldsmith's day.
[4] Prince Eugene's victory in 1717.

MARL. Instead of the battle of Belgrade, I believe it's almost time to talk about supper. What has your philosophy got in the house for supper?

HARD. For supper, sir! (*Aside.*) Was ever such a request to a man in his own house!   290

MARL. Yes, sir, supper, sir; I begin to feel an appetite. I shall make devilish work to-night in the larder, I promise you.

HARD. (*aside*). Such a brazen dog sure never my eyes beheld. (*To him.*) Why, really, sir, as 295 for supper, I can't well tell. My Dorothy and the cook-maid settle these things between them. I leave these kind of things entirely to them.

MARL. You do, do you?

HARD. Entirely. By the bye, I believe they 300 are in actual consultation upon what's for supper this moment in the kitchen.

MARL. Then I beg they'll admit *me* as one of their privy council. It's a way I have got. When I travel, I always choose to regulate my own supper. 305 Let the cook be called. No offence, I hope, sir.

HARD. Oh no, sir, none in the least; yet I don't know how: our Bridget, the cook-maid, is not very communicative upon these occasions. Should we send for her, she might scold us all out of the 310 house.

HAST. Let's see your list of the larder, then. I ask it as a favor. I always match my appetite to my bill of fare.

MARL. (*to* HARDCASTLE, *who looks at them with* 315 *surprise*). Sir, he's very right, and it's my way, too.

HARD. Sir, you have a right to command here. Here, Roger, bring us the bill of fare for to-night's supper; I believe it's drawn out.   [*Exit* ROGER.] Your manner, Mr. Hastings, puts me in mind 320 of my uncle, Colonel Wallop. It was a saying of his, that no man was sure of his supper till he had eaten it.

HAST. (*aside*). All upon the high ropes! His uncle a colonel! We shall soon hear of his mother being a justice of peace. [*Re-enter* ROGER.] 325 But let's hear the bill of fare.

MARL. (*perusing*). What's here? For the first course; for the second course; for the dessert. The devil, sir, do you think we have brought down the whole Joiners' Company, or the Corporation of 330 Bedford, to eat up such a supper? Two or three little things, clean and comfortable, will do.

HAST. But let's hear it.

MARL. (*reading*). For the first course, at the top, a pig, and pruin [5] sauce.   335

HAST. Damn your pig, I say!

MARL. And damn your pruin sauce, say I!

HARD. And yet, gentlemen, to men that are hungry, pig with pruin sauce is very good eating.

[5] Prune.

MARL. At the bottom, a calf's tongue and 340 brains.

HAST. Let your brains be knocked out, my good sir; I don't like them.

MARL. Or you may clap them on a plate by themselves. I do. 345

HARD. (*aside*). Their impudence confounds me. (*To them.*) Gentlemen, you are my guests; make what alterations you please. Is there anything else you wish to retrench or alter, gentlemen?

MARL. Item: a pork pie, a boiled rabbit and 350 sausages, a florentine,¹ a shaking pudding, and a dish of tiff — taff — taffety cream!²

HAST. Confound your made dishes! I shall be as much at a loss in this house as at a green and yellow dinner at the French Ambassador's table.³ 355 I'm for plain eating.

HARD. I'm sorry, gentlemen, that I have nothing you like; but if there be anything you have a particular fancy to —

MARL. Why, really, sir, your bill of fare is 360 so exquisite, that any one part of it is full as good as another. Send us what you please. So much for supper. And now to see that our beds are aired, and properly taken care of.

HARD. I entreat you'll leave all that to me. 365 You shall not stir a step.

MARL. Leave that to you! I protest, sir, you must excuse me; I always look to these things myself.

HARD. I must insist, sir, you'll make yourself easy on that head. 370

MARL. You see I'm resolved on it. (*Aside.*) A very troublesome fellow this, as ever I met with.

HARD. Well, sir, I'm resolved at least to attend you. (*Aside.*) This may be modern modesty, but I never saw anything look so like old-fashioned 375 impudence. *Exeunt* MARLOW *and* HARDCASTLE.

HASTINGS *solus.*

HAST. So I find this fellow's civilities begin to grow troublesome. But who can be angry at those assiduities which are meant to please him? Ha! what do I see? Miss Neville, by all that's 380 happy!

Enter MISS NEVILLE.

MISS NEV. My dear Hastings! To what unexpected good fortune, to what accident, am I to ascribe this happy meeting?

HAST. Rather let me ask the same question, 385 as I could never have hoped to meet my dearest Constance at an inn.

MISS NEV. An inn! sure you mistake! My aunt,

my guardian, lives here. What could induce you to think this house an inn? 390

HAST. My friend, Mr. Marlow, with whom I came down, and I, have been sent here as to an inn, I assure you. A young fellow, whom we accidentally met at a house hard by, directed us hither.

MISS NEV. Certainly it must be one of my 395 hopeful cousin's tricks, of whom you have heard me talk so often; ha! ha! ha! ha!

HAST. He whom your aunt intends for you? He of whom I have such just apprehensions?

MISS NEV. You have nothing to fear from 400 him, I assure you. You'd adore him if you knew how heartily he despises me. My aunt knows it too, and has undertaken to court me for him, and actually begins to think she has made a conquest.

HAST. Thou dear dissembler! You must 405 know, my Constance, I have just seized this happy opportunity of my friend's visit here to get admittance into the family. The horses that carried us down are now fatigued with their journey, but they'll soon be refreshed; and then, if my dearest girl 410 will trust in her faithful Hastings, we shall soon be landed in France, where even among slaves the laws of marriage are respected.⁴

MISS NEV. I have often told you that, though ready to obey you, I yet should leave my little 415 fortune behind with reluctance. The greatest part of it was left me by my uncle, the India director, and chiefly consists in jewels. I have been for some time persuading my aunt to let me wear them. I fancy I'm very near succeeding. The instant 420 they are put into my possession, you shall find me ready to make them and myself yours.

HAST. Perish the baubles! Your person is all I desire. In the meantime, my friend Marlow must not be let into his mistake. I know the strange 425 reserve of his temper is such that, if abruptly informed of it, he would instantly quit the house before our plan was ripe for execution.

MISS NEV. But how shall we keep him in the deception? Miss Hardcastle is just returned 430 from walking; what if we still continue to deceive him? — This, this way — (*They confer.*)

Enter MARLOW.

MARL. The assiduities of these good people tease me beyond bearing. My host seems to think it ill manners to leave me alone, and so he claps not 435 only himself but his old-fashioned wife on my back. They talk of coming to sup with us too; and then, I suppose, we are to run the gauntlet through all the rest of the family. — What have we got here?

HAST. My dear Charles! Let me congratu- 440 late you! — The most fortunate accident! — Who do you think is just alighted?

---

¹ A 'made dish' of baked meat pastry.
² Velvet cream.
³ A hit at the extravagant style and disappointing substance of the French diplomatic dinners.
⁴ A hit at the restrictive Royal Marriage Act of 1772.

MARL. Cannot guess.

HAST. Our mistresses, boy, Miss Hardcastle and Miss Neville. Give me leave to introduce Miss 445 Constance Neville to your acquaintance. Happening to dine in the neighborhood, they called, on their return to take fresh horses, here. Miss Hardcastle has just stepped into the next room, and will be back in an instant. Wasn't it lucky? eh!   450

MARL. (aside). I have just been mortified enough of all conscience, and here comes something to complete my embarrassment.

HAST. Well! but wasn't it the most fortunate thing in the world?   455

MARL. Oh! yes. Very fortunate — a most joyful encounter — But our dresses, George, you know, are in disorder — What if we should postpone the happiness till to-morrow? — to-morrow at her own house — It will be every bit as convenient —   460 and rather more respectful — To-morrow let it be.
                                        (Offering to go.)

HAST. By no means, sir. Your ceremony will displease her. The disorder of your dress will show the ardor of your impatience. Besides, she knows you are in the house, and will permit you to see her.   465

MARL. O! the devil! how shall I support it? Hem! hem! Hastings, you must not go. You are to assist me, you know. I shall be confoundedly ridiculous. Yet, hang it, I'll take courage! Hem!

HAST. Pshaw, man! it's but the first plunge,   470 and all's over! She's but a woman, you know.

MARL. And of all women, she that I dread most to encounter!

Enter MISS HARDCASTLE, *as returned from walking, a bonnet, &c.*

HAST. (introducing them). Miss Hardcastle, Mr. Marlow; I'm proud of bringing two persons of   475 such merit together, that only want to know, to esteem each other.

MISS HARD. (aside). Now for meeting my modest gentleman with a demure face, and quite in his own manner. (After a pause, in which he appears   480 very uneasy and disconcerted.) I'm glad of your safe arrival, sir — I'm told you had some accidents by the way.

MARL. Only a few, madam. Yes, we had some. Yes, madam, a good many accidents, but   485 should be sorry — madam — or rather glad of any accidents — that are so agreeably concluded. Hem!

HAST. (to him). You never spoke better in your whole life. Keep it up, and I'll insure you the victory.   490

MISS HARD. I'm afraid you flatter, sir. You that have seen so much of the finest company can find little entertainment in an obscure corner of the country.

MARL. (gathering courage). I have lived,   495 indeed, in the world, madam; but I have kept very little company. I have been but an observer upon life, madam, while others were enjoying it.

MISS NEV. But that, I am told, is the way to enjoy it at last.   500

HAST. (to him). Cicero never spoke better. Once more, and you are confirmed in assurance forever.

MARL. (to him). Hem! stand by me then, and when I'm down, throw in a word or two to set me up again.   505

MISS HARD. An observer, like you, upon life, were, I fear, disagreeably employed, since you must have had much more to censure than to approve.

MARL. Pardon me, madam. I was always willing to be amused. The folly of most people is   510 rather an object of mirth than uneasiness.

HAST. (to him). Bravo, bravo. Never spoke so well in your whole life. Well, Miss Hardcastle, I see that you and Mr. Marlow are going to be very good company. I believe our being here will but   515 embarrass the interview.

MARL. Not in the least, Mr. Hastings. We like your company of all things. (To him.) Zounds, George, sure you won't go? How can you leave us?

HAST. Our presence will but spoil conver-   520 sation, so we'll retire to the next room. (To him.) You don't consider, man, that we are to manage a little tête-à-tête of our own.

                Exeunt [HASTINGS *with* MISS NEVILLE].

MISS HARD. (after a pause). But you have not been wholly an observer, I presume, sir. The   525 ladies, I should hope, have employed some part of your addresses.

MARL. (relapsing into timidity). Pardon me, madam, I — I — I — as yet have studied — only — to — deserve them.   530

MISS HARD. And that, some say, is the very worst way to obtain them.

MARL. Perhaps so, madam. But I love to converse only with the more grave and sensible part of the sex. — But I'm afraid I grow tiresome.   535

MISS HARD. Not at all, sir; there is nothing I like so much as grave conversation myself; I could hear it forever. Indeed I have often been surprised how a man of *sentiment* could ever admire those light, airy pleasures, where nothing reaches the heart.   540

MARL. It's — a disease — of the mind, madam. In the variety of tastes there must be some who, wanting a relish — for — um – a – um —

MISS HARD. I understand you, sir. There must be some who, wanting a relish for refined pleasures,   545 pretend to despise what they are incapable of tasting.

MARL. My meaning, madam, but infinitely better expressed. And I can't help observing — a —

MISS HARD. (aside). Who could ever suppose this fellow impudent upon some occasions! (To   550 him.) You were going to observe, sir, —

MARL. I was observing, madam — I protest, madam, I forget what I was going to observe.

MISS HARD. (aside). I vow and so do I. (To him.) You were observing, sir, that in this age of 555 hypocrisy — something about hypocrisy, sir.

MARL. Yes, madam. In this age of hypocrisy there are few who upon strict enquiry do not — a — a — a —

MISS HARD. I understand you perfectly, sir. 560

MARL. (aside). Egad! and that's more than I do myself.

MISS HARD. You mean that in this hypocritical age there are few who do not condemn in public what they practise in private; and think they pay 565 every debt to virtue when they praise it.

MARL. True, madam; those who have most virtue in their mouths have least of it in their bosoms. But I'm sure I tire you, madam.

MISS HARD. Not in the least, sir; there's 570 something so agreeable and spirited in your manner, such life and force — pray, sir, go on.

MARL. Yes, madam, I was saying — that there are some occasions — when a total want of courage, madam, destroys all the — and puts us — 575 upon — a — a — a —

MISS HARD. I agree with you entirely; a want of courage upon some occasions assumes the appearance of ignorance, and betrays us when we most want to excel. I beg you'll proceed. 580

MARL. Yes, madam. Morally speaking, madam — But I see Miss Neville expecting us in the next room. I would not intrude for the world.

MISS HARD. I protest, sir, I never was more agreeably entertained in all my life. Pray go on. 585

MARL. Yes, madam. I was — But she beckons us to join her. Madam, shall I do myself the honor to attend you?

MISS HARD. Well, then, I'll follow.

MARL. (aside). This pretty smooth dialogue 590 has done for me. Exit.

MISS HARDCASTLE sola.

MISS HARD. Ha! ha! ha! Was there ever such a sober, sentimental interview? I'm certain he scarce looked in my face the whole time. Yet the fellow, but for his unaccountable bashfulness, is pretty 595 well, too. He has good sense, but then so buried in his fears, that it fatigues one more than ignorance. If I could teach him a little confidence, it would be doing somebody that I know of a piece of service. But who is that somebody? — that, faith, is 600 a question I can scarce answer. Exit.

Enter TONY *and* MISS NEVILLE, *followed by* MRS. HARDCASTLE *and* HASTINGS.

TONY. What do you follow me for, cousin Con? I wonder you're not ashamed to be so very engaging.

MISS NEV. I hope, cousin, one may speak to one's own relations, and not be to blame. 605

TONY. Ay, but I know what sort of a relation you want to make me, though; but it won't do. I tell you, cousin Con, it won't do; so I beg you'll keep your distance. I want no nearer relationship.

(*She follows, coquetting him to the back scene.*)

MRS. HARD. Well, I vow, Mr. Hastings, you 610 are very entertaining. There's nothing in the world I love to talk of so much as London, and the fashions, though I was never there myself.

HAST. Never there! You amaze me! From your air and manner, I concluded you had been 615 bred all your life either at Ranelagh, St. James's, or Tower Wharf.[1]

MRS. HARD. O! sir, you're only pleased to say so. We country persons can have no manner at all. I'm in love with the town, and that serves to raise 620 me above some of our neighboring rustics; but who can have a manner, that has never seen the Pantheon, the Grotto Gardens, the Borough, and such places, where the nobility chiefly resort? All I can do is to enjoy London at second-hand. I take care to 625 know every *tête-à-tête* from the *Scandalous Magazine*,[2] and have all the fashions, as they come out, in a letter from the two Miss Rickets of Crooked Lane. Pray, how do you like this head, Mr. Hastings?

HAST. Extremely elegant and *degagée*, upon 630 my word, madam. Your *friseur* is a Frenchman, I suppose?

MRS. HARD. I protest, I dressed it myself from a print in the *Ladies' Memorandum-book* for the last year. 635

HAST. Indeed! Such a head in a side-box, at the playhouse, would draw as many gazers as my Lady May'ress at a City Ball.

MRS. HARD. I vow, since inoculation began,[3] there is no such thing to be seen as a plain woman; so 640 one must dress a little particular or one may escape in the crowd.

HAST. But that can never be your case, madam, in any dress. (*Bowing.*)

MRS. HARD. Yet, what signifies *my* dressing, 645 when I have such a piece of antiquity by my side as Mr. Hardcastle? All I can say will never argue down a single button from his clothes. I have often wanted him to throw off his great flaxen wig, and where he was bald to plaster it over, like my 650 Lord Pately, with powder.

HAST. You are right, madam; for, as among the ladies there are none ugly, so among the men there are none old.

[1] Here, and in Mrs. Hardcastle's rejoinder, fashionable and vulgar London resorts are amusingly intermingled.

[2] *The Town and Country Magazine*, notorious for its *Tête-à-Tête* sketches of society scandals.

[3] Introduced into England by Lady Mary Wortley Montagu after her return from Turkey in 1718.

MRS. HARD. But what do you think his 655
answer was? Why, with his usual Gothic[1] vivacity,
he said I only wanted him to throw off his wig to
convert it into a *tête*[2] for my own wearing.

HAST. Intolerable! At your age you may wear
what you please, and it must become you.   660

MRS. HARD. Pray, Mr. Hastings, what do you
take to be the most fashionable age about town?

HAST. Some time ago forty was all the mode; but
I'm told the ladies intend to bring up fifty for the
ensuing winter.   665

MRS. HARD. Seriously? Then I shall be too
young for the fashion.

HAST. No lady begins now to put on jewels till
she's past forty. For instance, Miss there, in a polite
circle, would be considered as a child, as a mere   670
maker of samplers.

MRS. HARD. And yet, Mrs.[3] Niece thinks herself
as much a woman, and is as fond of jewels, as the
oldest of us all.

HAST. Your niece, is she? And that young   675
gentleman, — a brother of yours, I should presume?

MRS. HARD. My son, sir. They are contracted to
each other. Observe their little sports. They fall
in and out ten times a day, as if they were man   680
and wife already. (*To them.*) Well, Tony, child,
what soft things are you saying to your cousin Constance this evening?

TONY. I have been saying no soft things; but that
it's very hard to be followed about so. Ecod! 685
I've not a place in the house now that's left to myself
but the stable.

MRS. HARD. Never mind him, Con, my dear.
He's in another story behind your back.

MISS NEV. There's something generous in   690
my cousin's manner. He falls out before faces, to
be forgiven in private.

TONY. That's a damned confounded — crack.[4]

MRS. HARD. Ah, he's a sly one! Don't you think
they're like each other about the mouth, Mr.   695
Hastings? The Blenkinsop mouth to a T. They're
of a size, too. Back to back, my pretties, that Mr.
Hastings may see you. Come, Tony.

TONY. You had as good not make me, I tell you.
(*Measuring.*)

MISS NEV. O lud! he has almost cracked my   700
head.

MRS. HARD. O the monster! For shame, Tony.
You a man, and behave so!

TONY. If I'm a man, let me have my fortin.
Ecod, I'll not be made a fool of no longer.   705

MRS. HARD. Is this, ungrateful boy, all that I'm

to get for the pains I have taken in your education?
I that have rocked you in your cradle, and fed that
pretty mouth with a spoon! Did not I work that
waistcoat to make you genteel? Did not I pre-   710
scribe for you every day, and weep while the receipt
was operating?

TONY. Ecod! you had reason to weep, for you
have been dosing me ever since I was born. I have
gone through every receipt in *The Complete*   715
Huswife[5] ten times over; and you have thoughts of
coursing me through *Quincy*[6] next spring. But,
ecod! I tell you, I'll not be made a fool of no longer.

MRS. HARD. Wasn't it all for your good, viper?
Wasn't it all for your good?   720

TONY. I wish you'd let me and my good alone,
then. Snubbing this way when I'm in spirits! If
I'm to have any good, let it come of itself; not to
keep dinging it, dinging it into one so.

MRS. HARD. That's false; I never see you   725
when you're in spirits. No, Tony, you then go to
the alehouse or kennel. I'm never to be delighted
with your agreeable wild notes, unfeeling monster!

TONY. Ecod! mamma, your own notes are the
wildest of the two.   730

MRS. HARD. Was ever the like? But I see he
wants to break my heart, I see he does.

HAST. Dear madam, permit me to lecture the
young gentleman a little. I'm certain I can persuade
him to his duty.   735

MRS. HARD. Well! I must retire. Come, Constance, my love. You see, Mr. Hastings, the wretchedness of my situation. Was ever poor woman
so plagued with a dear, sweet, pretty, provoking,
undutiful boy?   740

Exeunt MRS. HARDCASTLE *and* MISS NEVILLE.

HASTINGS, TONY.

TONY (*singing*). *There was a young man riding by,
and fain would have his will. Rang do didlo dee.* —
Don't mind her. Let her cry. It's the comfort of
her heart. I have seen her and sister cry over a book
for an hour together, and they said they liked   745
the book the better the more it made them cry.

HAST. Then you're no friend to the ladies, I find,
my pretty young gentleman?

TONY. That's as I find 'um.

HAST. Not to her of your mother's choos-   750
ing, I dare answer? And yet she appears to me a
pretty, well-tempered girl.

TONY. That's because you don't know her as well
as I. Ecod! I know every inch about her; and
there's not a more bitter, cantankerous toad   755
in all Christendom.

---

[1] Barbarous, uncouth.   [2] Fashionable lady's wig.
[3] The abbreviation could then be applied to an unmarried
woman.
[4] Lie.

[5] *The Compleat Housewife: or Accomplished Gentlewoman's
Companion,* a popular cook-book (1729 and other editions).
[6] Dr. John Quincy's *Complete English Dispensatory* (1721;
14th edition, 1772).

HAST. (*aside*). Pretty encouragement, this, for a lover!

TONY. I have seen her since the height of that. She has as many tricks as a hare in a thicket, 760 or a colt the first day's breaking.

HAST. To me she appears sensible and silent.

TONY. Ay, before company. But when she's with her playmates, she's as loud as a hog in a gate.

HAST. But there is a meek modesty about 765 her that charms me.

TONY. Yes, but curb her never so little, she kicks up, and you're flung in a ditch.

HAST. Well, but you must allow her a little beauty. — Yes, you must allow her some beauty. 770

TONY. Bandbox! She's all a made-up thing, mun. Ah! could you but see Bet Bouncer of these parts, you might then talk of beauty. Ecod! she has two eyes as black as sloes, and cheeks as broad and red as a pulpit cushion. She'd make two 775 of she.

HAST. Well, what say you to a friend that would take this bitter bargain off your hands?

TONY. Anon![1]

HAST. Would you thank him that would take 780 Miss Neville, and leave you to happiness and your dear Betsy?

TONY. Ay; but where is there such a friend, for who would take *her*?

HAST. I am he. If you but assist me, I'll 785 engage to whip her off to France, and you shall never hear more of her.

TONY. Assist you! Ecod, I will, to the last drop of my blood. I'll clap a pair of horses to your chaise that shall trundle you off in a twinkling, and 790 may be get you a part of her fortin besides, in jewels, that you little dream of.

HAST. My dear Squire, this looks like a lad of spirit.

TONY. Come along then, and you shall see 795 more of my spirit before you have done with me.

(*Singing.*)

> *We are the boys*
> *That fears no noise*
> *Where the thundering cannons roar.*
>   *Exeunt.*

ACT III

[SCENE I]

[*The house.*]

Enter HARDCASTLE *solus.*

HARD. What could my old friend Sir Charles mean by recommending his son as the modestest young man in town? To me he appears the most impudent

[1] 'How?' — 'What do you say?'

piece of brass that ever spoke with a tongue. He has taken possession of the easy chair by the 5 fireside already. He took off his boots in the parlor, and desired me to see them taken care of. I'm desirous to know how his impudence affects my daughter. — She will certainly be shocked at it.

Enter MISS HARDCASTLE, *plainly dressed.*

HARD. Well, my Kate, I see you have changed 10 your dress, as I bid you; and yet, I believe, there was no great occasion.

MISS HARD. I find such a pleasure, sir, in obeying your commands, that I take care to observe them without ever debating their propriety. 15

HARD. And yet, Kate, I sometimes give you some cause, particularly when I recommended my *modest* gentleman to you as a lover to-day.

MISS HARD. You taught me to expect something extraordinary, and I find the original exceeds 20 the description.

HARD. I was never so surprised in my life! He has quite confounded all my faculties!

MISS HARD. I never saw anything like it: and a man of the world, too! 25

HARD. Ay, he learned it all abroad — what a fool was I, to think a young man could learn modesty by travelling. He might as soon learn wit at a masquerade.

MISS HARD. It seems all natural to him. 30

HARD. A good deal assisted by bad company and a French dancing-master.

MISS HARD. Sure, you mistake, papa. A French dancing-master could never have taught him that timid look — that awkward address — that 35 bashful manner.

HARD. Whose look, whose manner, child?

MISS HARD. Mr. Marlow's: his *mauvaise honte*, his timidity, struck me at the first sight.

HARD. Then your first sight deceived you; 40 for I think him one of the most brazen first sights that ever astonished my senses.

MISS HARD. Sure, sir, you rally! I never saw any one so modest.

HARD. And can you be serious! I never saw 45 such a bouncing, swaggering puppy since I was born. Bully Dawson[2] was but a fool to him.

MISS HARD. Surprising! He met me with a respectful bow, a stammering voice, and a look fixed on the ground. 50

HARD. He met me with a loud voice, a lordly air, and a familiarity that made my blood freeze again.

MISS HARD. He treated me with diffidence and respect; censured the manners of the age; admired the prudence of girls that never laughed; tired 55 me with apologies for being tiresome; then left the

[2] A Whitefriars ruffian (cf. *Spectator*, No. 2).

room with a bow, and 'Madam, I would not for the world detain you.'

HARD. He spoke to me as if he knew me all his life before; asked twenty questions, and never 60 waited for an answer; interrupted my best remarks with some silly pun; and when I was in my best story of the Duke of Marlborough and Prince Eugene, he asked if I had not a good hand at making punch. Yes, Kate, he asked your father if he was a 65 maker of punch!

MISS HARD. One of us must certainly be mistaken.

HARD. If he be what he has shown himself, I'm determined he shall never have my consent.

MISS HARD. And if he be the sullen thing I 70 take him, he shall never have mine.

HARD. In one thing then we are agreed — to reject him.

MISS HARD. Yes — but upon conditions. For if you should find him less impudent, and I 75 more presuming; if you find him more respectful, and I more importunate — I don't know — the fellow is well enough for a man — Certainly we don't meet many such at a horse-race in the country.

HARD. If we should find him so — But that's 80 impossible. The first appearance has done my business. I'm seldom deceived in that.

MISS HARD. And yet there may be many good qualities under that first appearance.

HARD. Ay, when a girl finds a fellow's out- 85 side to her taste, she then sets about guessing the rest of his furniture. With her, a smooth face stands for good sense, and a genteel figure for every virtue.

MISS HARD. I hope, sir, a conversation begun with a compliment to my good sense won't end with 90 a sneer at my understanding?

HARD. Pardon me, Kate. But if young Mr. Brazen can find the art of reconciling contradictions, he may please us both, perhaps.

MISS HARD. And as one of us must be mis- 95 taken, what if we go to make further discoveries?

HARD. Agreed. But depend on't I'm in the right.

MISS HARD. And depend on't I'm not much in the wrong.   *Exeunt.*

Enter TONY, *running in with a casket.*

TONY. Ecod! I have got them. Here they 100 are. My cousin Con's necklaces, bobs¹ and all. My mother shan't cheat the poor souls out of their fortin neither. O! my genus, is that you?

Enter HASTINGS.

HAST. My dear friend, how have you managed with your mother? I hope you have amused 105 her with pretending love for your cousin, and that you are willing to be reconciled at last? Our horses

¹ Pendants.

will be refreshed in a short time, and we shall soon be ready to set off.

TONY. And here's something to bear your 110 charges by the way (*giving the casket*) — your sweetheart's jewels. Keep them, and hang those, I say, that would rob you of one of them!

HAST. But how have you procured them from your mother?   115

TONY. Ask me no questions, and I'll tell you no fibs. I procured them by the rule of thumb. If I had not a key to every drawer in mother's bureau, how could I go to the alehouse so often as I do? An honest man may rob himself of his own at any 120 time.

HAST. Thousands do it every day. But to be plain with you; Miss Neville is endeavoring to procure them from her aunt this very instant. If she succeeds, it will be the most delicate way, at 125 least, of obtaining them.

TONY. Well, keep them, till you know how it will be. But I know how it will be well enough; she'd as soon part with the only sound tooth in her head.

HAST. But I dread the effects of her resent- 130 ment, when she finds she has lost them.

TONY. Never you mind her resentment; leave *me* to manage that. I don't value her resentment the bounce of a cracker. Zounds! here they are! Morrice!² Prance!   *Exit* HASTINGS. 135

TONY, MRS. HARDCASTLE, MISS NEVILLE.

MRS. HARD. Indeed, Constance, you amaze me. Such a girl as you want jewels? It will be time enough for jewels, my dear, twenty years hence, when your beauty begins to want repairs.

MISS NEV. But what will repair beauty at 140 forty, will certainly improve it at twenty, madam.

MRS. HARD. Yours, my dear, can admit of none. That natural blush is beyond a thousand ornaments. Besides, child, jewels are quite out at present. Don't you see half the ladies of our acquaintance, my 145 Lady Kill-day-light, and Mrs. Crump, and the rest of them, carry their jewels to town, and bring nothing but paste and marcasites³ back?

MISS NEV. But who knows, madam, but somebody that shall be nameless would like me best 150 with all my little finery about me?

MRS. HARD. Consult your glass, my dear, and then see if, with such a pair of eyes, you want any better sparklers. What do you think, Tony, my dear? Does your cousin Con want any jewels, 155 in your eyes, to set off her beauty?

TONY. That's as thereafter may be.

MISS NEV. My dear aunt, if you knew how it would oblige me.

MRS. HARD. A parcel of old-fashioned rose 160

² 'Decamp!' (slang).   ³ Common mineral ornaments.

and table-cut things.[1] They would make you look like the court of King Solomon at a puppet-show. Besides, I believe I can't readily come at them. They may be missing, for aught I know to the contrary.   165

TONY (*apart to* MRS. HARDCASTLE). Then why don't you tell her so at once, as she's so longing for them? Tell her they're lost. It's the only way to quiet her. Say they're lost, and call me to bear witness.

MRS. HARD. (*apart to* TONY). You know, my   170 dear, I'm only keeping them for you. So if I say they're gone, you'll bear me witness, will you? He! he! he!

TONY. Never fear me. Ecod! I'll say I saw them taken out with my own eyes.   175

MISS NEV. I desire them but for a day, madam, just to be permitted to show them as relics, and then they may be locked up again.

MRS. HARD. To be plain with you, my dear Constance, if I could find them you should have   180 them. They're missing, I assure you. Lost, for aught I know; but we must have patience, wherever they are.

MISS NEV. I'll not believe it; this is but a shallow pretence to deny me. I know they're too val-   185 uable to be so slightly kept, and as you are to answer for the loss —

MRS. HARD. Don't be alarmed, Constance. If they be lost, I must restore an equivalent. But my son knows they are missing, and not to be found.   190

TONY. That I can bear witness to. They are missing, and not to be found, I'll take my oath on't.

MRS. HARD. You must learn resignation, my dear; for though we lose our fortune, yet we should not lose our patience. See me, how calm I am.   195

MISS NEV. Ay, people are generally calm at the misfortunes of others.

MRS. HARD. Now, I wonder a girl of your good sense should waste a thought upon such trumpery. We shall soon find them; and in the meantime   200 you shall make use of my garnets till your jewels be found.

MISS NEV. I detest garnets!

MRS. HARD. The most becoming things in the world to set off a clear complexion. You have   205 often seen how well they look upon me. You *shall* have them.   *Exit.*

MISS NEV. I dislike them of all things. You shan't stir. — Was ever anything so provoking — to mislay my own jewels, and force me to wear her   210 trumpery?

TONY. Don't be a fool. If she gives you the garnets take what you can get. The jewels are your own already. I have stolen them out of her bureau, and she does not know it. Fly to your spark,   215

[1] Jewelry with stones cut flat (as compared with the many facets of a 'rose' jewel).

he'll tell you more of the matter. Leave me to manage *her.*

MISS NEV. My dear cousin!

TONY. Vanish. She's here, and has missed them already. [*Exit* MISS NEVILLE.] Zounds! how   220 she fidgets and spits about like a Catherine wheel.[2]

Enter MRS. HARDCASTLE.

MRS. HARD. Confusion! thieves! robbers! We are cheated, plundered, broke open, undone!

TONY. What's the matter, what's the matter, mamma? I hope nothing has happened to any   225 of the good family?

MRS. HARD. We are robbed. My bureau has been broke open, the jewels taken' out, and I'm undone!

TONY. Oh! is that all? Ha! ha! ha! By   230 the laws, I never saw it better acted in my life. Ecod, I thought you was ruined in earnest, ha, ha, ha!

MRS. HARD. Why, boy, I *am* ruined in earnest. My bureau has been broke open, and all taken away.

TONY. Stick to that; ha, ha, ha! stick to that.   235 I'll bear witness, you know, call me to bear witness.

MRS. HARD. I tell you, Tony, by all that's precious, the jewels are gone, and I shall be ruined forever.

TONY. Sure I know they're gone, and I am   240 to say so.

MRS. HARD. My dearest Tony, but hear me. They're gone, I say.

TONY. By the laws, mamma, you make me for to laugh, ha! ha! I know who took them well   245 enough, ha! ha! ha!

MRS. HARD. Was there ever such a blockhead, that can't tell the difference between jest and earnest? I can tell you I'm not in jest, booby.

TONY. That's right, that's right! You must   250 be in a bitter passion, and then nobody will suspect either of us. I'll bear witness that they are gone.

MRS. HARD. Was there ever such a cross-grained brute, that won't hear me? Can you bear witness that you're no better than a fool? Was ever   255 poor woman so beset with fools on one hand, and thieves on the other?

TONY. I can bear witness to that.

MRS. HARD. Bear witness again, you blockhead, you, and I'll turn you out of the room directly.   260 My poor niece, what will become of *her!* Do you laugh, you unfeeling brute, as if you enjoyed my distress?

TONY. I can bear witness to that.

MRS. HARD. Do you insult me, monster?   265 I'll teach you to vex your mother, I will!

TONY. I can bear witness to that.

(*He runs off, she follows him.*)

[2] Pin-wheel, fireworks.

Enter MISS HARDCASTLE *and Maid.*

MISS HARD. What an unaccountable creature is that brother of mine, to send them to the house as an inn! ha! ha! I don't wonder at his impudence. 270

MAID. But what is more, madam, the young gentleman, as you passed by in your present dress, asked me if you were the bar-maid. He mistook you for the bar-maid, madam!

MISS HARD. Did he? Then, as I live, I'm re- 275 solved to keep up the delusion. Tell me, Pimple, how do you like my present dress? Don't you think I look something like Cherry in *The Beaux' Stratagem?* [1]

MAID. It's the dress, madam, that every lady wears in the country, but when she visits or re- 280 ceives company.

MISS HARD. And are you sure he does not remember my face or person?

MAID. Certain of it.

MISS HARD. I vow I thought so; for though 285 we spoke for some time together, yet his fears were such that he never once looked up during the interview. Indeed, if he had, my bonnet would have kept him from seeing me.

MAID. But what do you hope from keeping 290 him in his mistake?

MISS HARD. In the first place, I shall be *seen*, and that is no small advantage to a girl who brings her face to market. Then I shall perhaps make an acquaintance, and that's no small victory gained 295 over one who never addresses any but the wildest of her sex. But my chief aim is to take my gentleman off his guard, and, like an invisible champion of romance, examine the giant's force before I offer to combat. 300

MAID. But are you sure you can act your part, and disguise your voice so that he may mistake that, as he has already mistaken your person?

MISS HARD. Never fear me. I think I have got the true bar cant. — Did your honor call? — Attend 305 the Lion [2] there. — Pipes and tobacco for the Angel. [2] — The Lamb [2] has been outrageous this half hour!

MAID. It will do, madam. But he's here.

Exit Maid.

Enter MARLOW.

MARL. What a bawling in every part of the house; I have scarce a moment's repose. If I go to the 310 best room, there I find my host and his story. If I fly to the gallery, there we have my hostess with her curtesy down to the ground. I have at last got a moment to myself, and now for recollection.

(Walks and muses.)

MISS HARD. Did you call, sir? Did your 315 honor call?

MARL. *(musing).* As for Miss Hardcastle, she's too grave and sentimental for me.

[1] The landlord's daughter in Farquhar's play.
[2] Names of inn-rooms.

MISS HARD. Did your honor call?

(She still places herself before him, he turning away.)

MARL. No, child. *(Musing.)* Besides, 320 from the glimpse I had of her, I think she squints.

MISS HARD. I'm sure, sir, I heard the bell ring.

MARL. No, no. *(Musing.)* I have pleased my father, however, by coming down, and I'll tomorrow please myself by returning. 325

(Taking out his tablets and perusing.)

MISS HARD. Perhaps the other gentleman called, sir?

MARL. I tell you, no.

MISS HARD. I should be glad to know, sir. We have such a parcel of servants. 330

MARL. No, no, I tell you. *(Looks full in her face.)* Yes, child, I think I did call. I wanted — I wanted — I vow, child, you are vastly handsome.

MISS HARD. O la, sir, you'll make one ashamed.

MARL. Never saw a more sprightly, malicious 335 eye. Yes, yes, my dear, I did call. Have you got any of your — a — what d'ye call it, in the house?

MISS HARD. No, sir, we have been out of that these ten days.

MARL. One may call in this house, I find, to 340 very little purpose. Suppose I should call for a taste, just by way of trial, of the nectar of your lips; perhaps I might be disappointed in that too.

MISS HARD. Nectar! nectar! That's a liquor there's no call for in these parts. French, I sup- 345 pose. We keep no French wines here, sir.

MARL. Of true English growth, I assure you.

MISS HARD. Then it's odd I should not know it. We brew all sorts of wines in this house, and I have lived here these eighteen years. 350

MARL. Eighteen years! Why, one would think, child, you kept the bar before you were born. How old are you?

MISS HARD. O! sir, I must not tell my age. They say women and music should never be dated. 355

MARL. To guess at this distance, you can't be much above forty. *(Approaching.)* Yet nearer, I don't think so much. *(Approaching.)* By coming close to some women, they look younger still; but when we come very close indeed — 360

(Attempting to kiss her.)

MISS HARD. Pray, sir, keep your distance. One would think you wanted to know one's age as they do horses, by mark of mouth.

MARL. I protest, child, you use me extremely ill. If you keep me at this distance, how is it pos- 365 sible you and I can be ever acquainted?

MISS HARD. And who wants to be acquainted with you? I want no such acquaintance, not I. I'm sure you did not treat Miss Hardcastle, that was here a while ago, in this obstropalous manner. I'll 370 warrant me, before her you looked dashed, and kept bowing to the ground, and talked, for all the world, as if you was before a justice of peace.

MARL. (*aside*). Egad, she has hit it, sure enough. (*To her.*) In awe of her, child? Ha! ha! 375 ha! A mere awkward, squinting thing! No, no. I find you don't know me. I laughed and rallied her a little; but I was unwilling to be too severe. No, I could not be too severe, *curse me!*

MISS HARD. O! then, sir, you are a favorite, 380 I find, among the ladies!

MARL. Yes, my dear, a great favorite. And yet, hang me, I don't see what they find in me to follow. At the Ladies' Club in town,[1] I'm called their agreeable Rattle. Rattle, child, is not my real 385 name, but one I'm known by. My name is Solomons. Mr. Solomons, my dear, at your service.

(*Offering to salute her.*)

MISS HARD. Hold, sir, you are introducing me to your club, not to yourself. And you're so great a favorite there, you say? 390

MARL. Yes, my dear. There's Mrs. Mantrap, Lady Betty Blackleg, the Countess of Sligo, Mrs. Langhorns, old Miss Biddy Buckskin,[2] and your humble servant, keep up the spirit of the place.

MISS HARD. Then it's a very merry place, 395 I suppose?

MARL. Yes, as merry as cards, suppers, wine, and old women can make us.

MISS HARD. And their agreeable Rattle, ha! ha! ha! 400

MARL. (*aside*). Egad! I don't quite like this chit. She looks knowing, methinks. You laugh, child?

MISS HARD. I can't but laugh to think what time they all have for minding their work or their family.

MARL. (*aside*). All's well; she don't laugh 405 at me. (*To her.*) Do *you* ever work, child?

MISS HARD. Ay, sure. There's not a screen or a quilt in the whole house but what can bear witness to that.

MARL. Odso! then you must show me your 410 embroidery. I embroider and draw patterns myself a little. If you want a judge of your work you must apply to me. (*Seizing her hand.*)

Enter HARDCASTLE, *who stands in surprise.*

MISS HARD. Ay, but the colors don't look well by candlelight. You shall see all in the morning. 415 (*Struggling.*)

MARL. And why not now, my angel? Such beauty

[1] The 'Female Coterie,' a fashionable London club in Albemarle Street.

[2] A pointed reference to Miss Rachael Lloyd, a prominent member of the 'Ladies' Club in town,' was toned down by altering 'Miss Rachael Buckskin' [Larpent MS. reading] to 'Miss Biddy Buckskin' in the first printed edition. (See Morgan, p. 977, footnotes.)

fires beyond the power of resistance. — Pshaw! the father here! My old luck: I never nicked seven that I did not throw ames ace three times following.[3]

Exit MARLOW.

HARD. So, madam! So I find *this* is your 420 *modest* lover. This is your humble admirer that kept his eyes fixed on the ground, and only adored at humble distance. Kate, Kate, art thou not ashamed to deceive your father so?

MISS HARD. Never trust me, dear papa, 425 but he's still the modest man I first took him for; you'll be convinced of it as well as I.

HARD. By the hand of my body, I believe his impudence is infectious! Didn't I see him seize your hand? Didn't I see him haul you about like 430 a milkmaid? And now you talk of his respect and his modesty, forsooth!

MISS HARD. But if I shortly convince you of his modesty, that he has only the faults that will pass off with time, and the virtues that will im- 435 prove with age, I hope you'll forgive him.

HARD. The girl would actually make one run mad! I tell you I'll not be convinced. I am convinced. He has scarcely been three hours in the house, and he has already encroached on all 440 my prerogatives. You may like his impudence, and call it modesty. But my son-in-law, madam, must have very different qualifications.

MISS HARD. Sir, I ask but this night to convince you. 445

HARD. You shall not have half the time, for I have thoughts of turning him out this very hour.

MISS HARD. Give me that hour, then, and I hope to satisfy you.

HARD. Well, an hour let it be then. But 450 I'll have no trifling with your father. All fair and open, do you mind me?

MISS HARD. I hope, sir, you have ever found that I considered your commands as my pride; for your kindness is such, that my duty as yet has 455 been inclination. *Exeunt.*

ACT IV

[SCENE I]

[*The house.*]

Enter HASTINGS *and* MISS NEVILLE.

HAST. You surprise me! Sir Charles Marlow expected here this night? Where have you had your information?

MISS NEV. You may depend upon it. I just saw

[3] 'I never had good luck without having the worst possible luck on top of it.' (Marlow's terms refer to winning and losing throws of the dice.)

his letter to Mr. Hardcastle, in which he tells him 5
he intends setting out a few hours after his son.

HAST. Then, my Constance, all must be completed before he arrives. He knows me; and should
he find me here, would discover my name, and perhaps my designs, to the rest of the family. 10

MISS NEV. The jewels, I hope, are safe?

HAST. Yes, yes. I have sent them to Marlow,
who keeps the keys of our baggage. In the meantime, I'll go to prepare matters for our elopement.
I have had the Squire's promise of a fresh pair of 15
horses; and, if I should not see him again, will write
him further directions. *Exit.*

MISS NEV. Well, success attend you! In the
meantime, I'll go amuse my aunt with the old pretence of a violent passion for my cousin. *Exit.* 20

Enter MARLOW, *followed by a Servant.*

MARL. I wonder what Hastings could mean by
sending me so valuable a thing as a casket to keep
for him, when he knows the only place I have is the
seat of a post-coach at an inn-door. Have you
deposited the casket with the landlady, as I or- 25
dered you? Have you put it into her own hands?

SERV. Yes, your honor.

MARL. She said she'd keep it safe, did she?

SERV. Yes; she said she'd keep it safe enough; she
asked me how I came by it; and she said she had 30
a great mind to make me give an account of myself.
Exit Servant.

MARL. Ha! ha! ha! They're safe, however. What
an unaccountable set of beings have we got amongst!
This little bar-maid, though, runs in my head most
strangely, and drives out the absurdities of all 35
the rest of the family. She's mine, she must be mine,
or I'm greatly mistaken.

Enter HASTINGS.

HAST. Bless me! I quite forgot to tell her that I
intended to prepare at the bottom of the garden.
Marlow here, and in spirits too! 40

MARL. Give me joy, George! Crown me, shadow
me with laurels! Well, George, after all, we modest
fellows don't want for success among the women.

HAST. Some women, you mean. But what success has your honor's modesty been crowned 45
with now, that it grows so insolent upon us?

MARL. Didn't you see the tempting, brisk, lovely
little thing that runs about the house with a bunch
of keys to its girdle?

HAST. Well, and what then? 50

MARL. She's mine, you rogue, you. Such fire,
such motion, such eyes, such lips — but, egad! she
would not let me kiss them though.

HAST. But are you so sure, so very sure of her?

MARL. Why, man, she talked of showing me 55
her work above-stairs, and I am to improve the
pattern.

HAST. But how can *you*, Charles, go about to rob
a woman of her honor?

MARL. Pshaw! pshaw! We all know the 60
honor of the bar-maid of an inn. I don't intend to
rob her, take my word for it; there's nothing in this
house I shan't honestly *pay* for.

HAST. I believe the girl has virtue.

MARL. And if she has, I should be the last 65
man in the world that would attempt to corrupt it.

HAST. You have taken care, I hope, of the casket
I sent you to lock up? It's in safety?

MARL. Yes, yes; it's safe enough. I have taken
care of it. But how could you think the seat of 70
a post-coach at an inn-door a place of safety? Ah!
numskull! I have taken better precautions for you
than you did for yourself — I have —

HAST. What?

MARL. I have sent it to the landlady to keep 75
for you.

HAST. To the landlady!

MARL. The landlady.

HAST. You did!

MARL. I did! She's to be answerable for its 80
forthcoming, you know.

HAST. Yes, she'll bring it forth, with a witness.

MARL. Wasn't I right? I believe you'll allow
that I acted prudently upon this occasion?

HAST. (*aside*). He must not see my uneasiness. 85

MARL. You seem a little disconcerted, though, methinks. Sure nothing has happened?

HAST. No, nothing. Never was in better spirits
in all my life. And so you left it with the landlady,
who, no doubt, very readily undertook the 90
charge.

MARL. Rather too readily. For she not only kept
the casket, but, through her great precaution, was
going to keep the messenger too. Ha! ha! ha!

HAST. He! he! he! They're safe, however. 95

MARL. As a guinea in a miser's purse.

HAST. (*aside*). So now all hopes of fortune are at
an end, and we must set off without it. (*To him.*)
Well, Charles, I'll leave you to your meditations on
the pretty bar-maid, and he! he! he! may you be 100
as successful for yourself as you have been for me.
Exit.

MARL. Thank ye, George! I ask no more. Ha!
ha! ha!

Enter HARDCASTLE.

HARD. I no longer know my own house. It's
turned all topsy-turvy. His servants have got 105
drunk already. I'll bear it no longer, and yet, from
my respect for his father, I'll be calm. (*To him.*)

62] OO a comma follows *for it.*

Mr. Marlow, your servant. I'm your very humble servant. *(Bowing low.)*

MARL. Sir, your humble servant. *(Aside.)* 110 What's to be the wonder now?

HARD. I believe, sir, you must be sensible, sir, that no man alive ought to be more welcome than your father's son, sir. I hope you think so?

MARL. I do from my soul, sir. I don't want 115 much entreaty. I generally make my father's son welcome wherever he goes.

HARD. I believe you do, from my soul, sir. But though I say nothing to your own conduct, that of your servants is insufferable. Their manner of 120 drinking is setting a very bad example in this house, I assure you.

MARL. I protest, my very good sir, that's no fault of mine. If they don't drink as they ought, *they* are to blame. I ordered them not to spare the 125 cellar. I did, I assure you. *(To the side-scene.)* Here, let one of my servants come up. *(To him.)* My positive directions were, that as I did not drink myself, they should make up for my deficiencies below. 130

HARD. Then they had your orders for what they do? I'm satisfied!

MARL. They had, I assure you. You shall hear from one of themselves.

Enter Servant [JEREMY], *drunk.*

MARL. You, Jeremy! Come forward, sirrah! 135 What were my orders? Were you not told to drink freely, and call for what you thought fit, for the good of the house?

HARD. *(aside).* I begin to lose my patience.

JEREMY. Please your honor, liberty and 140 Fleet Street[1] forever! Though I'm but a servant, I'm as good as another man. I'll drink for no man before supper, sir, damme! Good liquor will sit upon a good supper, but a good supper will not sit upon — hiccup — upon my conscience, sir. *Exit.* 145

MARL. You see, my old friend, the fellow is as drunk as he can possibly be. I don't know what you'd have more, unless you'd have the poor devil soused in a beer-barrel.

HARD. Zounds! he'll drive me distracted, if I 150 contain myself any longer. Mr. Marlow — sir! I have submitted to your insolence for more than four hours, and I see no likelihood of its coming to an end. I'm now resolved to be master here, sir, and I desire that you and your drunken pack may leave my 155 house directly.

MARL. Leave your house! — Sure you jest, my good friend? What, when I am doing what I can to please you!

HARD. I tell you, sir, you don't please me; 160 so I desire you'll leave my house.

MARL. Sure you cannot be serious? At this time of night, and such a night? You only mean to banter me.

HARD. I tell you, sir, I'm serious; and now 165 that my passions are roused, I say this house is mine, sir; this house is mine, and I command you to leave it directly.

MARL. Ha! ha! ha! A puddle in a storm. I shan't stir a step, I assure you. *(In a serious* 170 *tone.)* This your house, fellow! It's my house. This is my house. Mine, while I choose to stay. What right have you to bid me leave this house, sir? I never met with such impudence, curse me, never in my whole life before. 175

HARD. Nor I, confound me if ever I did! To come to my house, to call for what he likes, to turn me out of my own chair, to insult the family, to order his servants to get drunk, and then to tell me, *This house is mine, sir!* By all that's impudent, it makes 180 me laugh. Ha! ha! ha! Pray, sir, *(bantering)* as you take the house, what think you of taking the rest of the furniture? There's a pair of silver candlesticks, and there's a fire-screen, and here's a pair of brazen-nosed bellows; perhaps you may take a 185 fancy to them?

MARL. Bring me your bill, sir; bring me your bill, and let's make no more words about it.

HARD. There are a set of prints, too. What think you of *The Rake's Progress*[2] for your own apart- 190 ment?

MARL. Bring me your bill, I say; and I'll leave you and your infernal house directly.

HARD. Then there's a mahogany table that you may see your face in. 195

MARL. My bill, I say.

HARD. I had forgot the great chair, for your own particular slumbers, after a hearty meal.

MARL. Zounds! bring me my bill, I say, and let's hear no more on't. 200

HARD. Young man, young man, from your father's letter to me, I was taught to expect a well-bred, modest man as a visitor here, but now I find him no better than a coxcomb and a bully; but he will be down here presently, and shall hear more of it. 205
Exit.

MARL. How's this! Sure I have not mistaken the house! Everything looks like an inn; the servants cry 'Coming'; the attendance is awkward; the barmaid, too, to attend us. But she's here, and will further inform me. Whither so fast, child? 210 A word with you.

---

[1] Known for its convivial taverns.

[2] Hogarth's series issued in 1735.

Enter MISS HARDCASTLE.

MISS HARD. Let it be short, then. I'm in a hurry. (*Aside.*) I believe he begins to find out his mistake. But it's too soon quite to undeceive him.

MARL. Pray, child, answer me one question. 215 What are you, and what may your business in this house be?

MISS HARD. A relation of the family, sir.

MARL. What! a poor relation?

MISS HARD. Yes, sir. A poor relation ap- 220 pointed to keep the keys, and to see that the guests want nothing in my power to give them.

MARL. That is, you act as the bar-maid of this inn.

MISS HARD. Inn! O law! — What brought that into your head? One of the best families in 225 the county keep an inn! Ha! ha! ha! old Mr. Hardcastle's house an inn!

MARL. Mr. Hardcastle's house! Is this house Mr. Hardcastle's, child?

MISS HARD. Ay, sure. Whose else should it 230 be?

MARL. So, then, all's out, and I have been damnably imposed on. O, confound my stupid head, I shall be laughed at over the whole town. I shall be stuck up in caricatura in all the print-shops — 235 the *Dullissimo Macaroni.*[1] To mistake this house of all others for an inn, and my father's old friend for an innkeeper! What a swaggering puppy must he take me for! What a silly puppy do I find myself! There again, may I be hanged, my dear, but I 240 mistook you for the bar-maid.

MISS HARD. Dear me! dear me! I'm sure there's nothing in my *behavour*[2] to put me upon a level with one of that stamp.

MARL. Nothing, my dear, nothing. But I 245 was in for a list of blunders, and could not help making you a subscriber. My stupidity saw everything the wrong way. I mistook your assiduity for assurance, and your simplicity for allurement. But it's over — this house I no more show *my* face in. 250

MISS HARD. I hope, sir, I have done nothing to disoblige you. I'm sure I should be sorry to affront any gentleman who has been so polite, and said so many civil things to me. I'm sure I should be sorry (*pretending to cry*) if he left the family upon my 255 account. I'm sure I should be sorry people said anything amiss, since I have no fortune but my character.

MARL. (*aside*). By heaven, she weeps! This is the first mark of tenderness I ever had from a 260 modest woman, and it touches me. (*To her.*) Ex-

[1] An allusion to current prints caricaturing London fops.

[2] Miss Hardcastle has put aside 'the true bar cant,' but retains the vulgarian accent of a supposed servant. (See textual footnote.)

cuse me, my lovely girl, you are the only part of the family I leave with reluctance. But to be plain with you, the difference of our birth, fortune, and education, make an honorable connection impossible; 265 and I can never harbor a thought of seducing simplicity that trusted in my honor, or bringing ruin upon one whose only fault was being too lovely.

MISS HARD. (*aside*). Generous man! I now begin to admire him. (*To him.*) But I'm sure my 270 family is as good as Miss Hardcastle's, and though I'm poor, that's no great misfortune to a contented mind, and, until this moment, I never thought that it was bad to want fortune.

MARL. And why now, my pretty simplicity? 275

MISS HARD. Because it puts me at a distance from one that, if I had a thousand pound, I would give it all to.

MARL. (*aside*). This simplicity bewitches me, so that if I stay I'm undone. I must make one 280 bold effort, and leave her. (*To her.*) Your partiality in my favor, my dear, touches me most sensibly, and were I to live for myself alone, I could easily fix my choice. But I owe too much to the opinion of the world, too much to the authority of a 285 father, so that — I can scarcely speak it — it affects me! Farewell. *Exit.*

MISS HARD. I never knew half his merit till now. He shall not go if I have power or art to detain him. I'll still preserve the character in which I *stooped* 290 *to conquer*, but will undeceive my papa, who, perhaps, may laugh him out of his resolution. *Exit.*

Enter TONY *and* MISS NEVILLE.

TONY. Ay, you may steal for yourselves the next time. I have done my duty. She has got the jewels again, that's a sure thing; but she believes it 295 was all a mistake of the servants.

MISS NEV. But, my dear cousin, sure you won't forsake us in this distress? If she in the least suspects that I am going off, I shall certainly be locked up, or sent to my aunt Pedigree's, which is ten 300 times worse.

TONY. To be sure, aunts of all kinds are damned bad things. But what can I do? I have got you a pair of horses that will fly like Whistlejacket;[3] and I'm sure you can't say but I have courted you 305 nicely before her face. Here she comes; we must court a bit or two more, for fear she should suspect us. (*They retire, and seem to fondle.*)

Enter MRS. HARDCASTLE.

MRS. HARD. Well, I was greatly fluttered, to be sure. But my son tells me it was all a mistake of the servants. I shan't be easy, however, till they 310

[3] A famous race-horse.

are fairly married, and then let her keep her own fortune. But what do I see! Fondling together, as I'm alive. I never saw Tony so sprightly before. Ah! have I caught you, my pretty doves? What, billing, exchanging stolen glances, and broken 315 murmurs! Ah!

TONY. As for murmurs, mother, we grumble a little now and then, to be sure. But there's no love lost between us.

MRS. HARD. A mere sprinkling, Tony, upon 320 the flame, only to make it burn brighter.

MISS NEV. Cousin Tony promises to give us more of his company at home. Indeed, he shan't leave us any more. It won't leave us, cousin Tony, will it?

TONY. O! it's a pretty creature. No, I'd 325 sooner leave my horse in a pound, than leave you when you smile upon one so. Your laugh makes you so becoming.

MISS NEV. Agreeable cousin! Who can help admiring that natural humor, that pleasant, 330 broad, red, thoughtless (*patting his cheek*) — ah! it's a bold face!

MRS. HARD. Pretty innocence.

TONY. I'm sure I always loved cousin Con's hazel eyes, and her pretty long fingers, that she 335 twists this way and that, over the haspicholls,[1] like a parcel of bobbins.

MRS. HARD. Ah! he would charm the bird from the tree. I was never so happy before. My boy takes after his father, poor Mr. Lumpkin, ex- 340 actly. The jewels, my dear Con, shall be yours incontinently. You shall have them. Isn't he a sweet boy, my dear. You shall be married to-morrow, and we'll put off the rest of his education, like Dr. Drowsy's sermons, to a fitter opportunity. 345

Enter DIGGORY.

DIGG. Where's the Squire? I have got a letter for your worship.

TONY. Give it to my mamma. She reads all my letters first.

DIGG. I had orders to deliver it into your own 350 hands.

TONY. Who does it come from?

DIGG. Your worship mun ask that o' the letter itself. [*Exit* DIGGORY.]

TONY. I could wish to know, though. 355
(*Turning the letter, and gazing on it.*)

MISS NEV. (*aside*). Undone, undone! A letter to him from Hastings. I know the hand. If my aunt sees it, we are ruined forever. I'll keep her employed a little if I can. (*To* MRS. HARDCASTLE.) But I have not told you, madam, of my cousin's 360 smart answer just now to Mr. Marlow. We so laughed — you must know, madam — this way a little, for he must not hear us. (*They confer.*)

[1] Harpsichord.

TONY (*still gazing*). A damned cramp piece of penmanship as ever I saw in my life. I can read 365 your print-hand very well. But here there are such handles, and shanks, and dashes, that one can scarce tell the head from the tail. *To Anthony Lumpkin, Esquire.* It's very odd, I can read the outside of my letters, where my own name is, well enough. 370 But when I come to open it, it's all — buzz. That's hard, very hard; for the inside of the letter is always the cream of the correspondence.

MRS. HARD. Ha! ha! ha! Very well, very well. And so my son was too hard for the philosopher. 375

MISS NEV. Yes, madam; but you must hear the rest, madam. A little more this way, or he may hear us. You'll hear how he puzzled him again.

MRS. HARD. He seems strangely puzzled now himself, methinks. 380

TONY (*still gazing*). A damned up-and-down hand, as if it was disguised in liquor. (*Reading.*) *Dear Sir,* — Ay, that's that. Then there's an *M*, and a *T*, and an *S*, but whether the next be an *izzard*[2] or an *R*, confound me, I cannot tell! 385

MRS. HARD. What's that, my dear? Can I give you any assistance?

MISS NEV. Pray, aunt, let me read it. Nobody reads a cramp hand better than I. (*Twitching the letter from her.*) Do you know who it is from? 390

TONY. Can't tell, except from Dick Ginger, the feeder.[3]

MISS NEV. Ay, so it is. (*Pretending to read.*) DEAR SQUIRE, Hoping that you're in health, as I am at this present. The gentlemen of the Shake- 395 bag[4] club has cut the gentlemen of Goose-green quite out of feather. The odds — um — odd battle — um — long fighting — um — here, here, it's all about cocks, and fighting; it's of no consequence; here, put it up, put it up. 400
(*Thrusting the crumpled letter upon him.*)

TONY. But I tell you, miss, it's of all the consequence in the world! I would not lose the rest of it for a guinea. Here, mother, do you make it out. Of no consequence!
(*Giving* MRS. HARDCASTLE *the letter.*)

MRS. HARD. How's this? (*Reads.*) 405
Dear Squire, I'm now waiting for Miss Neville with a post-chaise and pair, at the bottom of the garden, but I find my horses yet unable to perform the journey. I expect you'll assist us with a pair of fresh horses, as you promised. Dispatch is necessary, as the hag 410 *— ay, the hag — your mother, will otherwise suspect us. Yours, Hastings.*
Grant me patience. I shall run distracted! My rage chokes me.

MISS NEV. I hope, madam, you'll suspend 415 your resentment for a few moments, and not impute

[2] The letter Z.　　　[3] Trainer of game-cocks.
[4] Shake-bag is a large game-cock.

to me any impertinence, or sinister design that belongs to another.

MRS. HARD. (*curtseying very low*). Fine spoken, madam, you are most miraculously polite and 420 engaging, and quite the very pink of courtesy and circumspection, madam. (*Changing her tone.*) And you, you great ill-fashioned oaf, with scarce sense enough to keep your mouth shut — were you too joined against me? But I'll defeat all your 425 plots in a moment. As for you, madam, since you have got a pair of fresh horses ready, it would be cruel to disappoint them. So, if you please, instead of running away with your spark, prepare, this very moment, to run off with *me*. Your old aunt 430 Pedigree will keep you secure, I'll warrant me. You, too, sir, may mount your horse, and guard us upon the way. Here, Thomas, Roger, Diggory! I'll show you that I wish you better than you do yourselves.
                                                            Exit.

MISS NEV. So now I'm completely ruined. 435

TONY. Ay, that's a sure thing.

MISS NEV. What better could be expected from being connected with such a stupid fool, — and after all the nods and signs I made him!

TONY. By the laws, miss, it was your own 440 cleverness, and not my stupidity, that did your business. You were so nice and so busy with your Shake-bags and Goose-greens that I thought you could never be making believe.

Enter HASTINGS.

HAST. So, sir, I find by my servant that you 445 have shown my letter, and betrayed us. Was this well done, young gentleman?

TONY. Here's another. Ask miss, there, who betrayed you. Ecod! it was her doing, not mine.

Enter MARLOW.

MARL. So I have been finely used here 450 among you. Rendered contemptible, driven into ill-manners, despised, insulted, laughed at.

TONY. Here's another. We shall have old Bedlam broke loose presently.

MISS NEV. And there, sir, is the gentleman 455 to whom we all owe every obligation.

MARL. What can I say to him, a mere boy, an idiot, whose ignorance and age are a protection!

HAST. A poor contemptible booby, that would but disgrace correction. 460

MISS NEV. Yet with cunning and malice enough to make himself merry with all our embarrassments.

HAST. An insensible cub.

MARL. Replete with tricks and mischief.

TONY. Baw! damme, but I'll fight you both, 465 one after the other, — with baskets.[1]

[1] Single-sticks with basket hilts.

MARL. As for him, he's below resentment. But your conduct, Mr. Hastings, requires an explanation. You knew of my mistakes, yet would not undeceive me. 470

HAST. Tortured as I am with my own disappointments, is this a time for explanations? It is not friendly, Mr. Marlow.

MARL. But, sir —

MISS NEV. Mr. Marlow, we never kept on 475 your mistake, till it was too late to undeceive you. Be pacified.

Enter Servant.

SERV. My mistress desires you'll get ready immediately, madam. The horses are putting to. Your hat and things are in the next room. We are 480 to go thirty miles before morning.   *Exit Servant.*

MISS NEV. Well, well, I'll come presently.

MARL. (*to* HASTINGS). Was it well done, sir, to assist in rendering me ridiculous? To hang me out for the scorn of all my acquaintance? Depend 485 upon it, sir, I shall expect an explanation.

HAST. Was it well done, sir, if you're upon that subject, to deliver what I entrusted to yourself, to the care of another, sir?

MISS NEV. Mr. Hastings! Mr. Marlow! 490 Why will you increase my distress by this groundless dispute? I implore, I entreat you —

Enter Servant.

SERV. Your cloak, madam. My mistress is impatient.

MISS NEV. I come. [*Exit Servant.*] Pray, 495 be pacified. If I leave you thus, I shall die with apprehension.

Enter Servant.

SERV. Your fan, muff, and gloves, madam. The horses are waiting.   [*Exit Servant.*]

MISS NEV. O, Mr. Marlow! if you knew 500 what a scene of constraint and ill-nature lies before me, I'm sure it would convert your resentment into pity.

MARL. I'm so distracted with a variety of passions, that I don't know what I do. Forgive me, 505 madam. George, forgive me. You know my hasty temper, and should not exasperate it.

HAST. The torture of my situation is my only excuse.

MISS NEV. Well, my dear Hastings, if you 510 have that esteem for me that I think, that I am sure you have, your constancy for three years will but increase the happiness of our future connection. If —

MRS. HARD. (*within*). Miss Neville! Con- 515 stance! why, Constance, I say!

MISS NEV. I'm coming! Well, constancy. Remember, constancy is the word.　　　　*Exit.*

HAST. My heart! How can I support this! To be so near happiness, and such happiness!　　520

MARL. (*to* TONY). You see now, young gentleman, the effects of your folly. What might be amusement to you is here disappointment, and even distress.

TONY (*from a reverie*). Ecod, I have hit it. It's here! Your hands. Yours, and yours, my　525 poor Sulky. My boots there, ho! Meet me two hours hence at the bottom of the garden; and if you don't find Tony Lumpkin a more good-natured fellow than you thought for, I'll give you leave to take my best horse, and Bet Bouncer into the bar-　530 gain. Come along. My boots, ho!　　　　*Exeunt.*

ACT V

[SCENE I]

Scene continues. [*The house.*]

Enter HASTINGS *and Servant.*

HAST. You saw the old lady and Miss Neville drive off, you say?

SERV. Yes, your honor. They went off in a post-coach, and the young Squire went on horseback. They're thirty miles off by this time.　　5

HAST. Then all my hopes are over.

SERV. Yes, sir. Old Sir Charles is arrived. He and the old gentleman of the house have been laughing at Mr. Marlow's mistake this half hour. They are coming this way.　　　　[*Exit.*]　10

HAST. Then I must not be seen. So now to my fruitless appointment at the bottom of the garden. This is about the time.　　　　*Exit.*

Enter SIR CHARLES MARLOW *and* HARDCASTLE.

HARD. Ha! ha! ha! The peremptory tone in which he sent forth his sublime commands!　15

SIR CHAS. And the reserve with which I suppose he treated all your advances.

HARD. And yet he might have seen something in me above a common innkeeper, too.

SIR CHAS. Yes, Dick, but he mistook you for　20 an uncommon innkeeper, ha! ha! ha!

HARD. Well, I'm in too good spirits to think of anything but joy. Yes, my dear friend, this union of our families will make our personal friendships hereditary; and though my daughter's fortune is　25 but small —

SIR CHAS. Why, Dick, will you talk of fortune to *me?* My son is possessed of more than a competence already, and can want nothing but a good and virtuous girl to share his happiness and increase it.　30 If they like each other, as you say they do —

HARD. *If*, man! I tell you they *do* like each other. My daughter as good as told me so.

SIR CHAS. But girls are apt to flatter themselves, you know.　　35

HARD. I saw him grasp her hand in the warmest manner myself; and here he comes to put you out of your *ifs*, I warrant him.

Enter MARLOW.

MARL. I come, sir, once more, to ask pardon for my strange conduct. I can scarce reflect on my　40 insolence without confusion.

HARD. Tut, boy, a trifle. You take it too gravely. An hour or two's laughing with my daughter will set all to rights again. She'll never like you the worse for it.　　45

MARL. Sir, I shall be always proud of her approbation.

HARD. Approbation is but a cold word, Mr. Marlow; if I am not deceived, you have something more than approbation thereabouts. You take　50 me?

MARL. Really, sir, I have not that happiness.

HARD. Come, boy, I'm an old fellow, and know what's what as well as you that are younger. I know what has passed between you; but mum.　55

MARL. Sure, sir, nothing has passed between us but the most profound respect on my side, and the most distant reserve on hers. You don't think, sir, that my impudence has been passed upon all the rest of the family?　　60

HARD. Impudence! No, I don't say that — not quite impudence — though girls like to be played with, and rumpled a little, too, sometimes. But she has told no tales, I assure you.

MARL. I never gave her the slightest cause.　65

HARD. Well, well, I like modesty in its place well enough; but this is over-acting, young gentleman. You *may* be open. Your father and I will like you the better for it.

MARL. May I die, sir, if I ever —　　70

HARD. I tell you she don't dislike you; and as I am sure you like her —

MARL. Dear sir — I protest, sir —

HARD. I see no reason why you should not be joined as fast as the parson can tie you.　　75

MARL. But hear me, sir —

HARD. Your father approves the match; I admire it; every moment's delay will be doing mischief; so —

MARL. But why won't you hear me? By all that's just and true, I never gave Miss Hardcastle the　80 slightest mark of my attachment, or even the most distant hint to suspect me of affection. We had but one interview, and that was formal, modest, and uninteresting.

HARD. (*aside*). This fellow's formal, modest 85 impudence is beyond bearing.

SIR CHAS. And you never grasped her hand, or made any protestations!

MARL. As heaven is my witness, I came down in obedience to your commands. I saw the lady 90 without emotion, and parted without reluctance. I hope you'll exact no further proofs of my duty, nor prevent me from leaving a house in which I suffer so many mortifications. *Exit.*

SIR CHAS. I'm astonished at the air of sincer- 95 ity with which he parted.

HARD. And I'm astonished at the deliberate intrepidity of his assurance.

SIR CHAS. I dare pledge my life and honor upon his truth. 100

HARD. Here comes my daughter, and I would stake my happiness upon her veracity.

Enter MISS HARDCASTLE.

HARD. Kate, come hither, child. Answer us sincerely, and without reserve; has Mr. Marlow made you any professions of love and affection? 105

MISS HARD. The question is very abrupt, sir. But since you require unreserved sincerity, I think he has.

HARD. (*to* SIR CHARLES). You see.

SIR CHAS. And pray, madam, have you and 110 my son had more than one interview?

MISS HARD. Yes, sir, several.

HARD. (*to* SIR CHARLES). You see.

SIR CHAS. But did he profess any attachment?

MISS HARD. A lasting one. 115

SIR CHAS. Did he talk of love?

MISS HARD. Much, sir.

SIR CHAS. Amazing! And all this formally?

MISS HARD. Formally.

HARD. Now, my friend, I hope you are satis- 120 fied.

SIR CHAS. And how did he behave, madam?

MISS HARD. As most professed admirers do — said some civil things of my face, talked much of his want of merit, and the greatness of mine; men- 125 tioned his heart, gave a short tragedy speech, and ended with pretended rapture.

SIR CHAS. Now I'm perfectly convinced, indeed. I know his conversation among women to be modest and submissive. This forward, canting, rant- 130 ing manner by no means describes him, and I am confident he never sat for the picture.

MISS HARD. Then what, sir, if I should convince you to your face of my sincerity? If you and my papa, in about half an hour, will place your- 135 selves behind that screen, you shall hear him declare his passion to me in person.

SIR CHAS. Agreed. And if I find him what you describe, all my happiness in him must have an end.
Exit.

MISS HARD. And if you don't find him what 140 I describe — I fear my happiness must never have a beginning. *Exeunt.*

[SCENE II]

Scene changes to the back of the garden.

Enter HASTINGS.

HAST. What an idiot am I, to wait here for a fellow who probably takes a delight in mortifying me. He never intended to be punctual, and I'll wait no longer. What do I see? It is he, and perhaps with news of my Constance. 5

Enter TONY, *booted and spattered.*

HAST. My honest Squire! I now find you a man of your word. This looks like friendship.

TONY. Ay, I'm your friend, and the best friend you have in the world, if you knew but all. This riding by night, by the bye, is cursedly tiresome. 10 It has shook me worse than the basket of a stage-coach.

HAST. But how? where did you leave your fellow travellers? Are they in safety? Are they housed?

TONY. Five and twenty miles in two hours 15 and a half is no such bad driving. The poor beasts have smoked for it: rabbit [1] me, but I'd rather ride forty miles after a fox, than ten with such *varment*.

HAST. Well, but where have you left the ladies? I die with impatience. 20

TONY. Left them! Why, where should I leave them but where I found them?

HAST. This is a riddle.

TONY. Riddle me this, then. What's that goes round the house, and round the house, and never 25 touches the house?

HAST. I'm still astray.

TONY. Why, that's it, mon. I have led them astray. By jingo, there's not a pond or slough within five miles of the place but they can tell 30 the taste of.

HAST. Ha! ha! ha! I understand; you took them in a round, while they supposed themselves going forward. And so you have at last brought them home again. 35

TONY. You shall hear. I first took them down Feather-bed Lane, where we stuck fast in the mud. I then rattled them crack over the stones of Up-and-down Hill. I then introduced them to the gibbet on Heavy-tree Heath; and from that, with a cir- 40 cumbendibus, I fairly lodged them in the horse-pond at the bottom of the garden.

[1] A slang interjection. (Fr. *rabattre*, humble.)

17] OO *Rabbet.*

HAST. But no accident, I hope?

TONY. No, no; only mother is confoundedly frightened. She thinks herself forty miles off. 45 She's sick of the journey, and the cattle can scarce crawl. So if your own horses be ready, you may whip off with Cousin, and I'll be bound that no soul here can budge a foot to follow you.

HAST. My dear friend, how can I be grateful? 50

TONY. Ay, now it's 'dear friend,' 'noble Squire.' Just now, it was all 'idiot,' 'cub,' and 'run me through the guts.' Damn *your* way of fighting, I say. After we take a knock in this part of the country, we kiss and be friends. But if you had run 55 me through the guts, then I should be dead, and you might go kiss the hangman.

HAST. The rebuke is just. But I must hasten to relieve Miss Neville; if you keep the old lady employed, I promise to take care of the young one. 60

TONY. Never fear me. Here she comes. Vanish!
Exit HASTINGS.
She's got from the pond, and draggled up to the waist like a mermaid.

Enter MRS. HARDCASTLE.

MRS. HARD. Oh, Tony, I'm killed! Shook! Battered to death! I shall never survive it. 65 That last jolt that laid us against the quickset hedge has done my business.

TONY. Alack, mama, it was all your own fault. You would be for running away by night, without knowing one inch of the way. 70

MRS. HARD. I wish we were at home again. I never met so many accidents in so short a journey. Drenched in the mud, overturned in a ditch, stuck fast in a slough, jolted to a jelly, and at last to lose our way! Whereabouts do you think we are, 75 Tony?

TONY. By my guess we should be upon Crackskull Common, about forty miles from home.

MRS. HARD. O lud! O lud! The most notorious spot in all the country. We only want a rob- 80 bery to make a complete night on't.

TONY. Don't be afraid, mama, don't be afraid. Two of the five that kept here [1] are hanged, and the other three may not find us. Don't be afraid. Is that a man that's galloping behind us? No, it's 85 only a tree. Don't be afraid.

MRS. HARD. The fright will certainly kill me.

TONY. Do you see anything like a black hat moving behind the thicket?

MRS. HARD. O death! 90

TONY. No, it's only a cow. Don't be afraid, mama, don't be afraid.

MRS. HARD. As I'm alive, Tony, I see a man coming towards us. Ah! I'm sure on't. If he perceives us, we are undone. 95

TONY (*aside*). Father-in-law, by all that's unlucky, come to take one of his night walks. (*To her.*) Ah, it's a highwayman, with pistils [2] as long as my arm. A damned ill-looking fellow.

MRS. HARD. Good heaven defend us! He 100 approaches.

TONY. Do you hide yourself in that thicket, and leave me to manage him. If there be any danger, I'll cough and cry hem. When I cough be sure to keep close. 105
(MRS. HARDCASTLE *hides behind a tree in the back scene.*)

Enter HARDCASTLE.

HARD. I'm mistaken, or I heard voices of people in want of help. Oh, Tony, is that you? I did not expect you so soon back. Are your mother and her charge in safety?

TONY. Very safe, sir, at my aunt Pedigree's. 110 Hem.

MRS. HARD. (*from behind*). Ah, death! I find there's danger.

HARD. Forty miles in three hours; sure that's too much, my youngster. 115

TONY. Stout horses and willing minds make short journeys, as they say. Hem.

MRS. HARD. (*from behind*). Sure he'll do the dear boy no harm.

HARD. But I heard a voice here; I should be 120 glad to know from whence it came?

TONY. It was I, sir, talking to myself, sir. I was saying that forty miles in four hours was very good going. Hem. As to be sure it was. Hem. I have got a sort of cold by being out in the air. 125 We'll go in, if you please. Hem.

HARD. But if you talked to yourself, you did not answer yourself. I am certain I heard two voices, and am resolved (*raising his voice*) to find the other out. 130

MRS. HARD. (*from behind*). Oh! he's coming to find me out. Oh!

TONY. What need you go, sir, if I tell you? Hem. I'll lay down my life for the truth — hem — I'll tell you all, sir. (*Detaining him.*) 135

HARD. I tell you I will not be detained. I insist on seeing. It's in vain to expect I'll believe you.

MRS. HARD. (*running forward from behind*). O lud! he'll murder my poor boy, my darling! Here, good gentleman, whet your rage upon me. Take my 140 money, my life, but spare that young gentleman, spare my child, if you have any mercy.

[1] Frequented this spot.

[2] Usually normalized to 'pistols,' but perhaps meant to suit Tony's lingo.

61] OO stage direction after *young one* (l. 60).　　98] OO *pistils*; many modern editions *pistols*.

HARD. My wife, as I'm a Christian! From whence can she come, or what does she mean?

MRS. HARD. (*kneeling*). Take compassion on 145 us, good Mr. Highwayman. Take our money, our watches, all we have, but spare our lives. We will never bring you to justice, indeed we won't, good Mr. Highwayman.

HARD. I believe the woman's out of her 150 senses. What, Dorothy, don't you know *me?*

MRS. HARD. Mr. Hardcastle, as I'm alive! My fears blinded me. But who, my dear, could have expected to meet you here, in this frightful place, so far from home? What has brought you to fol- 155 low us?

HARD. Sure, Dorothy, you have not lost your wits? So far from home, when you are within forty yards of your own door! (*To him.*) This is one of your old tricks, you graceless rogue, you! (*To* 160 *her.*) Don't you know the gate, and the mulberry tree; and don't you remember the horse-pond, my dear?

MRS. HARD. Yes, I shall remember the horse-pond as long as I live; I have caught my death in it. 165 (*To* TONY.) And is it to you, you graceless varlet, I owe all this? I'll teach you to abuse your mother, I will.

TONY. Ecod, mother, all the parish says you have spoiled me, so you may take the fruits on't. 170

MRS. HARD. I'll spoil you, I will.

Follows him off the stage. Ex[eunt.]

HARD. There's morality, however, in his reply.
Exit.

Enter HASTINGS *and* MISS NEVILLE.

HAST. My dear Constance, why will you deliberate thus? If we delay a moment, all is lost forever. Pluck up a little resolution, and we shall soon 175 be out of the reach of her malignity.

MISS NEV. I find it impossible. My spirits are so sunk with the agitations I have suffered, that I am unable to face any new danger. Two or three years' patience will at last crown us with happiness. 180

HAST. Such a tedious delay is worse than inconstancy. Let us fly, my charmer. Let us date our happiness from this very moment. Perish fortune. Love and content will increase what we possess beyond a monarch's revenue. Let me prevail. 185

MISS NEV. No, Mr. Hastings, no. Prudence once more comes to my relief, and I will obey its dictates. In the moment of passion, fortune may be despised, but it ever produces a lasting repentance. I'm resolved to apply to Mr. Hardcastle's compassion 190 and justice for redress.

HAST. But though he had the will, he has not the power to relieve you.

MISS NEV. But he has influence, and upon that I am resolved to rely. 195

HAST. I have no hopes. But since you persist, I must reluctantly obey you. *Exeunt.*

[SCENE III]

Scene changes. [The house.]

Enter SIR CHARLES *and* MISS HARDCASTLE.

SIR CHAS. What a situation am I in! If what you say appears, I shall then find a guilty son. If what he says be true, I shall then lose one that, of all others, I most wished for a daughter.

MISS HARD. I am proud of your approbation, 5 and to show I merit it, if you place yourselves as I directed, you shall hear his explicit declaration. But he comes.

SIR CHAS. I'll to your father, and keep him to the appointment. *Exit* SIR CHARLES. 10

Enter MARLOW.

MARL. Though prepared for setting out, I come once more to take leave, nor did I, till this moment, know the pain I feel in the separation.

MISS HARD. (*in her own natural manner*). I believe these sufferings cannot be very great, sir, which 15 you can so easily remove. A day or two longer, perhaps, might lessen your uneasiness, by showing the little value of what you now think proper to regret.

MARL. (*aside*). This girl every moment improves upon me. (*To her.*) It must not be, madam. I 20 have already trifled too long with my heart. My very pride begins to submit to my passion. The disparity of education and fortune, the anger of a parent, and the contempt of my equals begin to lose their weight; and nothing can restore me to 25 myself but this painful effort of resolution.

MISS HARD. Then go, sir; I'll urge nothing more to detain you. Though my family be as good as hers you came down to visit, and my education, I hope, not inferior, what are these advantages 30 without equal affluence? I must remain contented with the slight approbation of imputed merit; I must have only the mockery of your addresses, while all your serious aims are fixed on fortune.

Enter HARDCASTLE *and* SIR CHARLES *from behind*.

SIR CHAS. Here, behind this screen. 35

HARD. Ay, ay, make no noise. I'll engage my Kate covers him with confusion at last.

MARL. By heavens, madam, fortune was ever my smallest consideration. Your beauty at first caught my eye; for who could see that without 40 emotion? But every moment that I converse with you, steals in some new grace, heightens the picture, and gives it stronger expression. What at first seemed rustic plainness, now appears refined simplicity. What seemed forward assurance, now 45 strikes me as the result of courageous innocence and conscious virtue.

SIR CHAS. What can it mean? He amazes me!

HARD. I told you how it would be. Hush!

MARL. I am now determined to stay, madam, 50 and I have too good an opinion of my father's discernment, when he sees you, to doubt his approbation.

MISS HARD. No, Mr. Marlow, I will not, cannot detain you. Do you think I could suffer a connection in which there is the smallest room for re- 55 pentance? Do you think I would take the mean advantage of a transient passion, to load you with confusion? Do you think I could ever relish that happiness which was acquired by lessening yours?

MARL. By all that's good, I can have no hap- 60 piness but what's in your power to grant me. Nor shall I ever feel repentance but in not having seen your merits before. I will stay, even contrary to your wishes; and though you should persist to shun me, I will make my respectful assiduities atone 65 for the levity of my past conduct.

MISS HARD. Sir, I must entreat you'll desist. As our acquaintance began, so let it end, in indifference. I might have given an hour or two to levity; but seriously, Mr. Marlow, do you think I could ever 70 submit to a connection where I must appear mercenary, and you imprudent? Do you think I could ever catch at the confident addresses of a secure admirer?

MARL. (kneeling). Does this look like security? Does this look like confidence? No, madam, 75 every moment that shows me your merit, only serves to increase my diffidence and confusion. Here let me continue —

SIR CHAS. I can hold it no longer. Charles, Charles, how hast thou deceived me! Is this 80 your indifference, your uninteresting conversation!

HARD. Your cold contempt! your formal interview! What have you to say now?

MARL. That I'm all amazement! What can it mean? 85

HARD. It means that you can say and unsay things at pleasure; that you can address a lady in private, and deny it in public; that you have one story for us, and another for my daughter.

MARL. Daughter! — this lady your daughter! 90

HARD. Yes, sir, my only daughter — my Kate; whose else should she be?

MARL. Oh, the devil!

MISS HARD. Yes, sir, that very identical tall, squinting lady you were pleased to take me for 95 (curtseying); she that you addressed as the mild, modest, sentimental man of gravity, and the bold,

forward, agreeable Rattle of the Ladies' Club. Ha! ha! ha!

MARL. Zounds, there's no bearing this; it's 100 worse than death!

MISS HARD. In which of your characters, sir, will you give us leave to address you? As the faltering gentleman, with looks on the ground, that speaks just to be heard, and hates hypocrisy; or the loud, 105 confident creature, that keeps it up with Mrs. Mantrap, and old Miss Biddy Buckskin, till three in the morning? Ha! ha! ha!

MARL. O, curse on my noisy head! I never attempted to be impudent yet, that I was not 110 taken down. I must be gone.

HARD. By the hand of my body, but you shall not. I see it was all a mistake, and I am rejoiced to find it. You shall not, sir, I tell you. I know she'll forgive you. Won't you forgive him, Kate? We'll 115 all forgive you. Take courage, man.

(*They retire, she tormenting him, to the back scene.*)

Enter MRS. HARDCASTLE [*and*] TONY.

MRS. HARD. So, so, they're gone off. Let them go, I care not.

HARD. Who gone?

MRS. HARD. My dutiful niece and her gentle- 120 man, Mr. Hastings, from town. He who came down with our modest visitor here.

SIR CHAS. Who, my honest George Hastings! As worthy a fellow as lives, and the girl could not have made a more prudent choice. 125

HARD. Then, by the hand of my body, I'm proud of the connection.

MRS. HARD. Well, if he has taken away the lady, he has not taken her fortune; that remains in this family to console us for her loss. 130

HARD. Sure, Dorothy, you would not be so mercenary?

MRS. HARD. Ay, that's my affair, not yours.

[HARD.] But you know if your son, when of age, refuses to marry his cousin, her whole fortune 135 is then at her own disposal.

[MRS. HARD.] Ay, but he's not of age, and she has not thought proper to wait for his refusal.

Enter HASTINGS *and* MISS NEVILLE.

MRS. HARD. (*aside*). What, returned so soon? I begin not to like it. 140

HAST. (*to* HARDCASTLE). For my late attempt to fly off with your niece, let my present confusion be my punishment. We are now come back, to appeal from your justice to your humanity. By her father's consent, I first paid her my addresses, and our 145 passions were first founded in duty.

134–138] OO give *But you ... disposal* to Mrs. Hardcastle, and *Ay, but he's ... refusal* to Mr. Hardcastle. Modern editions usually correct as above.

MISS NEV. Since his death, I have been obliged to stoop to dissimulation to avoid oppression. In an hour of levity, I was ready even to give up my fortune to secure my choice. But I'm now recov-   150 ered from the delusion, and hope from your tenderness what is denied me from a nearer connection.

MRS. HARD. Pshaw, pshaw! this is all but the whining end of a modern novel.

HARD. Be it what it will, I'm glad they're   155 come back to reclaim their due. Come hither, Tony, boy. Do you refuse this lady's hand whom I now offer you?

TONY. What signifies my refusing? You know I can't refuse her till I'm of age, father.   160

HARD. While I thought concealing your age, boy, was likely to conduce to your improvement, I concurred with your mother's desire to keep it secret. But since I find she turns it to a wrong use, I must now declare, you have been of age this three   165 months.

TONY. Of age! Am I of age, father?

HARD. Above three months.

TONY. Then you'll see the first use I'll make of my liberty. (*Taking* MISS NEVILLE'S *hand*.) Wit-   170 ness all men, by these presents, that I, Anthony Lumpkin, Esquire, of BLANK place, refuse you, Constantia Neville, spinster, of no place at all, for my true and lawful wife. So Constance Neville may marry whom she pleases, and Tony Lumpkin is   175 his own man again!

SIR CHAS. O brave Squire!

HAST. My worthy friend!

MRS. HARD. My undutiful offspring.

MARL. Joy, my dear George, I give you   180 joy sincerely. And could I prevail upon my little tyrant here to be less arbitrary, I should be the happiest man alive, if you would return me the favor.

HAST. (*to* MISS HARDCASTLE). Come, madam, you are now driven to the very last scene of all your   185 contrivances. I know you like him, I'm sure he loves you, and you must and shall have him.

HARD. (*joining their hands*). And I say so, too. And, Mr. Marlow, if she makes as good a wife as she has a daughter, I don't believe you'll ever re-   190 pent your bargain. So now to supper; to-morrow we shall gather all the poor of the parish about us, and the Mistakes of the Night shall be crowned with a merry morning; so, boy, take her; and as you have been mistaken in the mistress, my wish is, that   195 you may never be mistaken in the wife.

EPILOGUE

By Dr. Goldsmith

[Spoken by Mrs. Bulkley in the Character of Miss Hardcastle.]

Well, having stooped to conquer with success,
And gained a husband without aid from dress,
Still as a bar-maid, I could wish it too,
As I have conquered him to conquer you:
And let me say, for all your resolution,   5
That pretty bar-maids have done execution.
Our life is all a play, composed to please;
'We have our exits and our entrances.'
The first act shows the simple country maid,
Harmless and young, of ev'rything afraid;   10
Blushes when hired, and with unmeaning action,
'I hopes as how to give you satisfaction.'
Her second act displays a livelier scene, —
Th' unblushing bar-maid of a country inn,
Who whisks about the house, at market caters,   15
Talks loud, coquets the guests, and scolds the waiters.
Next the scene shifts to town, and there she soars,
The chop-house toast of ogling connoisseurs.
On Squires and Cits she there displays her arts,
And on the gridiron broils her lovers' hearts —   20
And as she smiles, her triumphs to complete,
E'en Common Councilmen forget to eat.
The fourth act shows her wedded to the Squire,
And Madam now begins to hold it higher;
Pretends to taste, at Operas cried *caro!*   25
And quits her *Nancy Dawson* [1] for *Che Faro:* [2]
Doats upon dancing, and in all her pride,
Swims round the room, the Heinel [3] of Cheapside;
Ogles and leers, with artificial skill,
Till, having lost in age the power to kill,   30
She sits all night at cards, and ogles at spadille. [4]
Such, through our lives, th' eventful history —
The fifth and last act still remains for me:
The bar-maid now for your protection prays,
Turns female barrister, and pleads for Bayes. [5]   35

---

[1] A popular song, named after the actress who had danced into fame to its tune in a revival of *The Beggar's Opera* in 1759.
[2] In Glück's opera, *Orfeo*, 1764.
[3] A foreign danseuse who had recently become a London favorite.
[4] The leading trump in ombre.
[5] 'The author' (cf. Bayes in *The Rehearsal*).

22] OO *Even.*

EPILOGUE *

To be Spoken in the Character of Tony Lumpkin

By J. Cradock,[1] Esq.

Well — now all's ended — and my comrades gone,
Pray what becomes of *mother's nonly*[2] *son?*
A hopeful blade! — in town I'll fix my station,
And try to make a bluster in the nation.
As for my cousin Neville, I renounce her,   5
Off, in a crack, I'll carry big Bet Bouncer.
   Why should not I in the great world appear?
I soon shall have a thousand pounds a year;
No matter what a man may here inherit,
In London — 'gad, they've some regard to spirit.   10
I see the horses prancing up the streets,
And big Bet Bouncer bobs to all she meets;
Then hoikes to jigs and pastimes ev'ry night —
Not to the plays — they say it a'n't polite;
To Sadler's Wells, perhaps, or operas go,   15
And once, by chance, to the roratorio.
Thus here and there, forever up and down,
We'll set the fashions, too, to half the town;
And then at auctions — money ne'er regard —
Buy pictures, like the great, ten pounds a yard;   20
Zounds! we shall make these London gentry say,
We know what's damned genteel, as well as they.

* This came too late to be spoken.

---

[1] Joseph Cradock [OO *Craddock*] (1742–1826), Goldsmith's friend, whose tragedy, *Zobeide*, had appeared in 1771.
[2] Tony's lingo, not a misprint.   He continues to speak in 'character.'

The Rivals

BY RICHARD BRINSLEY SHERIDAN

THE
RIVALS,
a
COMEDY.

as it is PERFORM'D at the

Theatre Royal in Covent Garden.

— The Third Edition. —

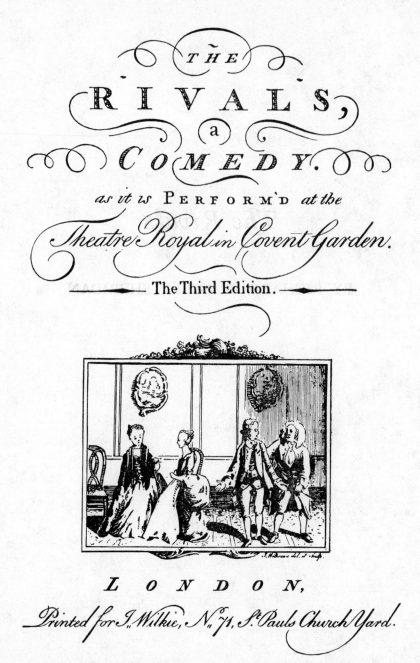

LONDON,

Printed for J. Wilkie, N⁰ 71, S.t Pauls Church Yard.

TITLE WITH ILLUSTRATION (ACT IV, SCENE II) OF *THE RIVALS*, THIRD OCTAVO EDITION, 1776
Main title-page bears author's name, the date, and designation as 'The Third Edition Corrected.'

PROLOGUE

By the Author

Spoken by Mr. Woodward and Mr. Quick[1]

Enter Serjeant-at-Law and Attorney following and giving a paper.

SERJ. What's here! a vile cramp hand! I cannot see
Without my spectacles.
    ATT. [*aside*].   He means his fee.
Nay, Mr. Serjeant, good sir, try again. (*Gives money.*)
    SERJ. The scrawl improves. (*More.*) O come, 'tis pretty plain.
«How's this? The poet's brief *again!*[2] O ho!   5
Cast, I suppose?
    ATT.   O pardon me — no — no —
We found the court, o'erlooking stricter laws,
Indulgent to the *merits* of the cause;
By *judges* mild, unused to harsh denial,
A rule was granted for *another trial.*   10
    SERJ. Then heark'ee, *Dibble*, did you *mend* your *pleadings?*
Errors, no few, we've *found* in our *proceedings.*
    ATT. Come, courage, sir, we did *amend* our *plea*,[3]
Hence your *new brief*, and this *refreshing fee.*»
Some sons of Phœbus — in the courts we meet.   15
    SERJ. And fifty sons of Phœbus in the Fleet![4]
    ATT. Nor pleads he worse, who with a decent sprig
Of bays adorns his legal waste of wig.
    SERJ. Full-bottomed heroes thus, on signs, unfurl
A leaf of laurel — in a grove of curl!   20
Yet tell your client, that, in adverse days,
This wig is warmer than a bush of bays.
    ATT. Do you, then, sir, my client's place supply,
Profuse of robe, and prodigal of tie ——
Do you, with all those blushing pow'rs of face,   25
And wonted bashful hesitating grace,
Rise in the court, and flourish on the case.   *Exit.*
    SERJ. [*addressing the audience*]. For practice, then, suppose — this brief will show it, —
Me, Serjeant *Woodward*, — counsel for the poet.
Used to the ground — I know 'tis hard to deal   30
With this dread *court*, from whence there's *no appeal;*
No *tricking* here, to blunt the edge of *law*,
Or, damned in *equity* — escape by *flaw:*

---

[1] Woodward appeared as Captain Absolute and Quick as Bob Acres in the original cast.
[2] Referring to the revision of the play after its initial failure and temporary withdrawal. See 'The Initial Failure and Final Triumph of *The Rivals*,' in *The Major Dramas of Richard Brinsley Sheridan* (N), Introduction, lxiv–lxviii.
[3] Revise our play.   [4] Poets in the debtors' (Fleet) prison.

5–14] O1 and O2 read as above; O3 revises thus:

    Hey! how's this? — *Dibble!* — sure it cannot be!
    A poet's brief! A poet and a fee!
      Att. Yea, sir! — though *you* without reward, I know,
    Would gladly plead the Muses' cause — (*Serj.*) So-So!
    And if the fee offends — your wrath should fall
    On me — (*Serj.*) Dear Dibble, no offence at all —

29] O1O2 *Council*; O3–O6 *Counsel.*

But *judgment* given — *your sentence* must remain;
— No *writ of error* lies — to *Drury Lane!* [1]   35
   Yet, when so kind you seem — 'tis past dispute
We gain some favor, if not *costs of suit.*
No spleen is here!   I see no hoarded fury;
— I think I never faced a milder jury!
Sad else our plight! — where frowns are transportation,   40
A hiss the gallows, — and a groan, damnation!
But such the public candor, without fear
My client waives all *right of challenge* here.
No newsman [2] from *our* session is dismissed,
Nor wit nor critic *we* scratch off the list;   45
His faults can never hurt another's ease,
His crime at worst — a *bad attempt* to please:
Thus, all respecting, he appeals to all,
And by the general voice will *stand* or *fall.*

[1] No appeal from the verdict of Covent Garden Theatre can be made to the rival Drury Lane Theatre.
[2] Reporter.

PROLOGUE

BY THE AUTHOR

SPOKEN ON THE TENTH NIGHT, BY MRS. BULKLEY[1]

Granted our cause, our suit and trial o'er,
The worthy serjeant[2] need appear no more:
In pleasing I a different client choose;
He served the poet — I would serve the Muse:
Like him, I'll try to merit your applause,   5
A female counsel in a female's cause.

    Look on this form,*— where Humor, quaint and sly,
Dimples the cheek, and points the beaming eye;
Where gay Invention seems to boast its wiles
In amorous hint, and half-triumphant smiles;   10
While her light masks or covers Satire's strokes,
All hides the conscious blush her wit provokes.
Look on her well — does she seem formed to teach?
Should you *expect* to hear this lady preach?
Is grey experience suited to her youth?   15
Do solemn sentiments become that mouth?
Bid her be grave, those lips should rebel prove
To every theme that slanders mirth or love.

    Yet, thus adorned with every graceful art
To charm the fancy and yet reach the heart ——   20
Must we displace her, and instead advance
The goddess of the woful countenance —
The sentimental Muse? — Her emblems view,
The Pilgrim's Progress, and a sprig of rue!
View her — too chaste to look like flesh and blood —   25
Primly portrayed on emblematic wood!
There, fixed in usurpation, should she stand,
She'll snatch the dagger from her sister's hand:
And having made her votaries *weep a flood*,
Good heav'n! she'll end her comedies in blood —   30
Bid Harry Woodward [CAPTAIN ABSOLUTE] break poor Dunstal's [DAVID] crown!
Imprison Quick [ACRES], and knock Ned Shuter [SIR ANTHONY ABSOLUTE] down;
While sad Barsanti [LYDIA LANGUISH], weeping o'er the scene,
Shall stab herself — or poison Mrs. Green [MRS. MALAPROP].

    Such dire encroachments to prevent in time,   35
Demands the critic's voice — the poet's rhyme.
Can our light scenes add strength to holy laws?
Such puny patronage but hurts the cause:
Fair Virtue scorns our feeble aid to ask;
And moral Truth disdains the trickster's mask.   40
For here their fav'rite stands,† whose brow — severe
And sad — claims Youth's respect, and Pity's tear;
Who, when oppressed by foes her worth creates,
Can point a poniard at the guilt she hates.

---

* *Pointing to the Figure of* COMEDY [in Covent Garden Theatre].
† *Pointing to* TRAGEDY [the opposite 'Figure' in Covent Garden Theatre].
[1] The Julia of the original cast of *The Rivals*.   [2] The Serjeant-at-Law of the previous Prologue.

PROLOGUE SPOKEN ON THE TENTH NIGHT] In O3 but not in O1 and O2.

DRAMATIS PERSONÆ

MEN   WOMEN

MEN	WOMEN
SIR ANTHONY ABSOLUTE	MRS. MALAPROP
CAPT. ABSOLUTE	LYDIA LANGUISH
FAULKLAND	JULIA
ACRES	LUCY
SIR LUCIUS O'TRIGGER	
FAG	
DAVID	
COACHMAN	

Maid, Boy, Servants, &c.

SCENE — BATH

TIME OF ACTION, WITHIN ONE DAY

s.d.] OI *Time of Action, Five Hours.*

THE RIVALS

By RICHARD BRINSLEY SHERIDAN

ACT I

SCENE I

A street in Bath.

Coachman crosses the stage. — Enter FAG, *looking after him.*

FAG. What! — Thomas! — Sure, 'tis he? — What! — Thomas! — Thomas!

COACH. Hey! — Odd's life![1] — Mr. Fag! — give us your hand, my old fellow-servant.

FAG. Excuse my glove, Thomas: — I'm 5 dev'lish glad to see you, my lad: why, my prince of charioteers, you look as hearty! — but who the deuce thought of seeing you in Bath!

COACH. Sure, Master, Madam Julia, Harry, Mrs. Kate, and the postilion be all come! 10

FAG. Indeed!

COACH. Aye! Master thought another fit of the gout was coming to make him a visit: — so he'd a mind to gi't the slip, and whip! we were all off at an hour's warning. 15

FAG. Aye, aye! hasty in everything, or it would not be Sir Anthony Absolute!

COACH. But tell us, Mr. Fag, how does young master? Odd! Sir Anthony will stare to see the Captain here! 20

FAG. I do not serve Captain Absolute now. —

COACH. Why sure!

FAG. At present I am employed by Ensign Beverley.

COACH. I doubt, Mr. Fag, you ha'n't changed 25 for the better.

FAG. I have not changed, Thomas.

COACH. No! why, didn't you say you had left young master?

FAG. No. — Well, honest Thomas, I must 30 puzzle you no farther: — briefly then — Captain Absolute and Ensign Beverley are one and the same person.

COACH. The devil they are!

FAG. So it is indeed, Thomas; and the *En-* 35 *sign*-half of my master being on guard at present — the *Captain* has nothing to do with me.

COACH. So, so! — What, this is some freak, I war-

rant! — Do tell us, Mr. Fag, the meaning o't — you know I ha' trusted you. 40

FAG. You'll be secret, Thomas?

COACH. As a coach-horse.

FAG. Why then the cause of all this is — LOVE, — Love, Thomas, who (as you may get read to you) has been a masquerader ever since the days of Ju- 45 piter.

COACH. Aye, aye; — I guessed there was a lady in the case: — but pray, why does your master pass only for *Ensign?* — Now if he had shammed *General*, indeed —— 50

FAG. Ah! Thomas, there lies the mystery o' the matter. — Hark'ee, Thomas, my master is in love with a lady of a very singular taste: a lady who likes him better as a *half-pay Ensign* than if she knew he was son and heir to Sir Anthony Absolute, a 55 baronet of three thousand a-year!

COACH. That is an odd taste indeed! — but has she got the stuff, Mr. Fag? is she rich, hey?

FAG. Rich! — why, I believe she owns half the stocks! — Z—ds![2] Thomas, she could pay the 60 national debt as easily as I could my washerwoman! — She has a lap-dog that eats out of gold, — she feeds her parrot with small pearls, — and all her thread-papers[3] are made of bank-notes!

COACH. Bravo! — Faith! — Odd! I warrant 65 she has a set of thousands[4] at least. But does she draw kindly with the Captain?

FAG. As fond as pigeons.

COACH. May one hear her name?

FAG. Miss Lydia Languish. — But there is an 70 old tough aunt in the way; — though, by the by — she has never seen my master — for he got acquainted with Miss while on a visit in Gloucestershire.

COACH. Well — I wish they were once har- 75 nessed together in matrimony. — But pray, Mr. Fag, what kind of a place is this Bath? — I ha' heard a deal of it — here's a mort[5] o' merry-making — hey?

FAG. Pretty well, Thomas, pretty well — 'tis a good lounge.[6] «Though at present we are, like 80

---

[1] A corruption of 'God's life.'

[2] Zounds, a corruption of 'God's wounds.'
[3] Papers for rolling up skeins of thread.
[4] A team of six horses worth thousands of pounds.
[5] Provincial expression for 'a great deal.'
[6] Resort for idlers.

56] O1 *baronet with.*   61] O1 *easy.*

80–86] Here, and subsequently, guillemets « » indicate passages included in O1 and O2 but omitted in O3 ('The Third Edition Corrected').

other great assemblies, divided into parties — High-roomians and Low-roomians;[1] however, for my part, I have resolved to stand neuter; and so I told Bob Brush at our last committee.

«Coach. But what do the folks do here? 85

«Fag. Oh! there are little amusements enough. —» In the morning we go to the Pump-room (though neither my master nor I drink the waters); after breakfast we saunter on the Parades, or play a game at billiards; at night we dance: but d—n the 90 place, I'm tired of it: their regular hours stupefy me — not a fiddle nor a card after eleven! — However, Mr. Faulkland's gentleman[2] and I keep it up a little in private parties; — I'll introduce you there, Thomas — you'll like him much. 95

Coach. Sure I know Mr. Du-Peigne — you know his master is to marry Madam Julia.

Fag. I had forgot. — But Thomas, you must pol-ish a little — indeed you must. — Here now — this wig! what the devil do you do with a wig, 100 Thomas? — none of the London whips of any degree of *ton*[3] wear *wigs* now.

Coach. More's the pity! more's the pity, I say — Odd's life! when I heard how the lawyers and doctors had took to their own hair, I thought how 105 'twould go next: — Odd rabbit it![4] when the fashion had got foot on the Bar, I guessed 'twould mount to the Box! — But 'tis all out of character, believe me, Mr. Fag: and look'ee, I'll never gi' up mine — the lawyers and doctors may do as they will. 110

Fag. Well, Thomas, we'll not quarrel about that.

Coach. Why, bless you, the gentlemen of they professions ben't all of a mind — for in our village now, tho'ff[5] *Jack Gauge*, the *exciseman*, has ta'en to his carrots,[6] there's little Dick, the farrier, 115 swears he'll never forsake his *bob*,[7] tho' all the college should appear with their own heads!

Fag. Indeed! well said, Dick! But hold — mark! mark! Thomas.

Coach. Zooks![8] 'tis the Captain! — Is 120 that the lady with him?

Fag. No! no! that is Madam Lucy — my mas-ter's mistress's maid. — They lodge at that house — but I must after him to tell him the news.

Coach. Odd! he's giving her money! — 125 Well, Mr. Fag——

Fag. Good-bye, Thomas. — I have an appoint-ment in Gyde's Porch[9] this evening at eight; meet me there, and we'll make a little party.

Exeunt severally.

Scene II

A dressing-room in Mrs. Malaprop's *lodgings.*

Lydia *sitting on a sofa, with a book in her hand.* — Lucy, *as just returned from a message.*

Lucy. Indeed, ma'am, I traversed half the town in search of it: — I don't believe there's a circulating library in Bath I ha'n't been at.

Lyd. And could not you get *The Reward of Constancy?*[10] 5

Lucy. No, indeed, ma'am.

Lyd. Nor *The Fatal Connection?*

Lucy. No, indeed, ma'am.

Lyd. Nor *The Mistakes of the Heart?*

Lucy. Ma'am, as ill-luck would have it, Mr. 10 Bull[11] said Miss Sukey Saunter had just fetched it away.

Lyd. Heigh-ho! — Did you inquire for *The Deli-cate Distress?* —

Lucy. Or *The Memoirs of Lady Woodford?* 15 Yes, indeed, ma'am. — I asked everywhere for it; and I might have brought it from Mr. Frederick's,[12] but Lady Slattern Lounger, who had just sent it home, had so soiled and dog's-eared it, it wa'n't fit for a Christian to read. 20

Lyd. Heigh-ho! — Yes, I always know when Lady Slattern has been before me. — She has a most ob-serving thumb; and I believe cherishes her nails for the convenience of making marginal notes. — Well, child, what *have* you brought me? 25

Lucy. Oh! here, ma'am. (*Taking books from under her cloak, and from her pockets.*) This is *The Gordian Knot*, — and this *Peregrine Pickle*. Here are *The Tears of Sensibility* and *Humphry Clinker*. This is *The Memoirs of a Lady of Quality, written* 30 *by herself*, — and here the second volume of *The Sentimental Journey*.

Lyd. Heigh-ho! — What are those books by the glass?

Lucy. The great one is only *The Whole Duty* 35 *of Man* — where I press a few blonds,[13] ma'am.

Lyd. Very well — give me the *sal volatile*.

Lucy. Is it in a blue cover, ma'am?

---

[1] The 'Upper' and 'Lower Rooms' of fashionable Bath assemblies.
[2] Valet.
[3] Fashion (*bon ton*).
[4] 'God confound it,' used merely as a mild expletive.
[5] Though.
[6] Natural head of reddish-yellow hair.
[7] Wig.
[8] 'Gadzooks,' a corrupt form of interjection.

[9] 'The Lower Rooms... kept by Mr. Gyde.'
[10] See 'The Books of Lydia Languish's Circulating Library,' in *The Major Dramas of Richard Brinsley Sheridan* (N), Intro-duction, lxviii–lxxvii, for full accounts of these popular novels of the day.
[11] A Bath bookseller.
[12] Another Bath bookseller.
[13] A special form of silk lace.

1] O1 *transferr'd.*

Lyd. My smelling bottle, you simpleton!

Lucy. Oh, the drops! — Here, ma'am.　　40

«Lyd. No note, Lucy?

«Lucy. No, indeed, ma'am — but I have seen a certain person ——

«Lyd. What, my Beverley! — Well, Lucy?

«Lucy. O ma'am! he looks so desponding and　45 melancholic!»

Lyd. Hold! — here's some one coming — quick! see who it is.　　　　　　　　　　*Exit* Lucy.

Surely I heard my cousin Julia's voice!

Re-enter Lucy.

Lucy. Lud! ma'am, here is Miss Melville.　50

Lyd. Is it possible! ——

Enter Julia.

Lyd. My dearest Julia, how delighted am I! — (*Embrace.*) How unexpected was this happiness!

Jul. True, Lydia — and our pleasure is the greater; — but what has been the matter? —　55 you were denied to me at first!

Lyd. Ah! Julia, I have a thousand things to tell you! — but first inform me what has conjured you to Bath? — Is Sir Anthony here?

Jul. He is — we are arrived within this hour　60 — and I suppose he will be here to wait on Mrs. Malaprop as soon as he is dressed.

Lyd. Then, before we are interrupted, let me impart to you some of my distress! — I know your gentle nature will sympathize with me,　65 though your prudence may condemn me! — My letters have informed you of my whole connection with Beverley; — but I have lost him, Julia! — my aunt has discovered our intercourse by a note she intercepted, and has confined me ever since! — Yet,　70 would you believe it? she has fallen absolutely in love with a tall Irish baronet she met one night since we have been here, at Lady Macshuffle's rout.

Jul. You jest, Lydia!

Lyd. No, upon my word. — She really carries　75 on a kind of correspondence with him, under a feigned name though, till she chooses to be known to him; — but it is a *Delia* or a *Celia*, I assure you.

Jul. Then surely she is now more indulgent to her niece.　　　　　　　　　　　　　　80

Lyd. Quite the contrary. Since she has discovered her own frailty she is become more suspicious of mine. Then I must inform you of another plague! — That odious Acres is to be in Bath to-day; so that I protest I shall be teased out of all spirits!　85

Jul. Come, come, Lydia, hope the best. — Sir Anthony shall use his interest with Mrs. Malaprop.

Lyd. But you have not heard the worst. Unfortunately I had quarrelled with my poor Beverley just before my aunt made the discovery, and I　90 have not seen him since to make it up.

Jul. What was his offence?

Lyd. Nothing at all! — But, I don't know how it was, as often as we had been together we had never had a quarrel! — And, somehow, I was afraid he　95 would never give me an opportunity. — So last Thursday I wrote a letter to myself to inform myself that Beverley was at that time paying his addresses to another woman. — I signed it *your friend unknown*, showed it to Beverley, charged him with　100 his falsehood, put myself in a violent passion, and vowed I'd never see him more.

Jul. And you let him depart so, and have not seen him since?

Lyd. 'Twas the next day my aunt found the　105 matter out. I intended only to have teased him three days and a half, and now I've lost him forever!

Jul. If he is as deserving and sincere as you have represented him to me, he will never give you up so. Yet consider, Lydia, you tell me he is but an　110 ensign, and you have thirty thousand pounds!

Lyd. But you know I lose most of my fortune if I marry without my aunt's consent, till of age; and that is what I have determined to do ever since I knew the penalty. — Nor could I love the man　115 who would wish to wait a day for the alternative.

Jul. Nay, this is caprice!

Lyd. What, does Julia tax me with caprice? — I thought her lover Faulkland had enured her to it.

Jul. I do not love even *his* faults.　　　　120

Lyd. But a-propos — you have sent to him, I suppose?

Jul. Not yet, upon my word — nor has he the least idea of my being in Bath. — Sir Anthony's resolution was so sudden I could not inform him　125 of it.

Lyd. Well, Julia, you are your own mistress (though under the protection of Sir Anthony), yet have you for this long year been a slave to the caprice, the whim, the jealousy of this ungrate-　130 ful Faulkland, who will ever delay assuming the right of a husband, while you suffer him to be equally imperious as a lover.

Jul. Nay, you are wrong entirely. — We were contracted before my father's death. — That,　135 and some consequent embarrassments, have delayed what I know to be my Faulkland's most ardent wish. — He is too generous to trifle on such a point. — And for his character, you wrong him there too. — No, Lydia, he is too proud, too noble to be jealous;　140 if he is captious, 'tis without dissembling; if fretful, without rudeness. — Unused to the fopperies of love, he is negligent of the little duties expected from a lover — but being unhackneyed in the passion, his

---

47] O1 *Hold Lucy!*　　75] O1 *absolutely* for *really.*　　129] O1 *the slave.*　　135] O1 italicizes *That.*

142] O1 *foppery.*

affection is ardent and sincere; and as it en- 145
grosses his whole soul, he expects every thought and
emotion of his mistress to move in unison with his. —
Yet, though his pride calls for this full return — his
humility makes him undervalue those qualities in
him which would entitle him to it; and not feel- 150
ing why he should be loved to the degree he wishes,
he still suspects that he is not loved enough. — This
temper, I must own, has cost me many unhappy
hours; but I have learned to think myself his debtor
for those imperfections which arise from the 155
ardor of his attachment.

Lyd. Well, I cannot blame you for defending him.
— But tell me candidly, Julia, had he never saved
your life, do you think you should have been attached
to him as you are? — Believe me, the rude blast 160
that overset your boat was a prosperous gale of love
to him.

Jul. Gratitude may have strengthened my attachment to Mr. Faulkland, but I loved him before
he had preserved me; yet surely that alone were 165
an obligation sufficient —

Lyd. Obligation! — Why, a water-spaniel would
have done as much. — Well, I should never think of
giving my heart to a man because he could swim!

Jul. Come, Lydia, you are too inconsiderate. 170

Lyd. Nay, I do but jest. — What's here?

Enter Lucy in a hurry.

Lucy. O ma'am, here is Sir Anthony Absolute
just come home with your aunt.

Lyd. They'll not come here. — Lucy, do you
watch.   Exit Lucy. 175

Jul. Yet I must go. — Sir Anthony does not
know I am here, and if we meet, he'll detain me, to
show me the town. — I'll take another opportunity
of paying my respects to Mrs. Malaprop, when she
shall treat me, as long as she chooses, with her 180
select words so ingeniously misapplied, without being
mispronounced.

Re-enter Lucy.

Lucy. O Lud! ma'am, they are both coming up
stairs.

Lyd. Well, I'll not detain you, coz. — Adieu, 185
my dear Julia. I'm sure you are in haste to send to
Faulkland. — There — through my room you'll find
another stair-case.

Jul. Adieu. —— (Embrace.)   Exit Julia.

Lyd. Here, my dear Lucy, hide these books. 190
— Quick, quick! — Fling Peregrine Pickle under the
toilet — throw Roderick Random into the closet —
put The Innocent Adultery into The Whole Duty of
Man — thrust Lord Aimworth under the sofa — cram
Ovid behind the bolster — there — put The 195
Man of Feeling into your pocket — so, so, — now lay

Mrs. Chapone in sight, and leave Fordyce's Sermons
open on the table.

Lucy. O burn it, ma'am! the hair-dresser has torn
away as far as Proper Pride. 200

Lyd. Never mind — open at Sobriety. — Fling me
Lord Chesterfield's Letters. — Now for 'em.

Enter Mrs. Malaprop, and Sir Anthony Absolute.

Mrs. Mal. There, Sir Anthony, there sits the deliberate simpleton, who wants to disgrace her family,
and lavish herself on a fellow not worth a 205
shilling!

Lyd. Madam, I thought you once ——

Mrs. Mal. You thought, miss! — I don't know
any business you have to think at all. — Thought
does not become a young woman. But the 210
point we would request of you is, that you will promise to forget this fellow — to illiterate him, I say,
quite from your memory.

Lyd. Ah! madam! our memories are independent
of our wills. — It is not so easy to forget. 215

Mrs. Mal. But I say it is, miss; there is nothing
on earth so easy as to forget, if a person chooses to set
about it. — I'm sure I have as much forgot your poor
dear uncle as if he had never existed — and I thought
it my duty so to do; and let me tell you, Lydia, 220
these violent memories don't become a young woman.

Sir Anth. Why sure she won't pretend to remember what she's ordered not! — aye, this comes of her
reading!

Lyd. What crime, madam, have I committed 225
to be treated thus?

Mrs. Mal. Now don't attempt to extirpate yourself from the matter; you know I have proof con-
trovertible of it. — But tell me, will you promise to
do as you're bid? — Will you take a husband of 230
your friend's choosing?

Lyd. Madam, I must tell you plainly, that had I
no preference for any one else, the choice you have
made would be my aversion.

Mrs. Mal. What business have you, miss, 235
with preference and aversion? They don't become a
young woman; and you ought to know, that as both
always wear off, 'tis safest in matrimony to begin with
a little aversion. I am sure I hated your poor dear
uncle before marriage as if he'd been a black-a- 240
moor — and yet, miss, you are sensible what a wife
I made! — and when it pleased heav'n to release me
from him, 'tis unknown what tears I shed! — But
suppose we were going to give you another choice, will
you promise us to give up this Beverley? 245

Lyd. Could I belie my thoughts so far as to give
that promise, my actions would certainly as far belie
my words.

145] O1 love for affection.   150] O1 should.   156] O1 love for attachment.   210–211] O1 woman; the point.   231] O1 friends.

MRS. MAL. Take yourself to your room. — You are fit company for nothing but your own ill-humors.

LYD. Willingly, ma'am — I cannot change for the worse.   *Exit* LYDIA.

MRS. MAL. There's a little intricate hussy for you!

SIR ANTH. It is not to be wondered at, ma'am — all this is the natural consequence of teaching girls to read. — Had I a thousand daughters, by heaven! I'd as soon have them taught the black art as their alphabet!

MRS. MAL. Nay, nay, Sir Anthony, you are an absolute misanthropy.

SIR ANTH. In my way hither, Mrs. Malaprop, I observed your niece's maid coming forth from a circulating library! — She had a book in each hand — they were half-bound volumes, with marble covers! — From that moment I guessed how full of duty I should see her mistress!

MRS. MAL. Those are vile places, indeed!

SIR ANTH. Madam, a circulating library in a town is as an ever-green tree of diabolical knowledge! — It blossoms through the year! — And depend on it, Mrs. Malaprop, that they who are so fond of handling the leaves, will long for the fruit at last.

«MRS. MAL. Well, but Sir Anthony, your wife, Lady Absolute, was fond of books.

«SIR ANTH. Aye — and injury sufficient they were to her, madam. — But were I to choose another helpmate, the extent of her erudition should consist in her knowing her simple letters, without their mischievous combinations; — and the summit of her science be — her ability to count as far as twenty. — The first, Mrs. Malaprop, would enable her to work A. A. upon my linen; — and the latter would be quite sufficient to prevent her giving me a shirt No. 1 and a stock No. 2.»

MRS. MAL. Fie, fie, Sir Anthony, you surely speak laconically!

SIR ANTH. Why, Mrs. Malaprop, in moderation, now, what would you have a woman know?

MRS. MAL. Observe me, Sir Anthony. — I would by no means wish a daughter of mine to be a progeny of learning; I don't think so much learning becomes a young woman; for instance — I would never let her meddle with Greek, or Hebrew, or Algebra, or Simony, or Fluxions, or Paradoxes, or such inflammatory branches of learning — neither would it be necessary for her to handle any of your mathematical, astronomical, diabolical instruments; — but, Sir Anthony, I would send her, at nine years old, to a boarding-school, in order to learn a little ingenuity and artifice. — Then, sir, she should have a supercilious knowledge in accounts; — and as she grew up, I would have her instructed in geometry, that she might know something of the contagious countries; — but above all, Sir Anthony, she should be mistress of orthodoxy, that she might not mis-spell, and mis-pronounce words so shamefully as girls usually do; and likewise that she might reprehend the true meaning of what she is saying. — This, Sir Anthony, is what I would have a woman know; — and I don't think there is a superstitious article in it.

SIR ANTH. Well, well, Mrs. Malaprop, I will dispute the point no further with you; though I must confess that you are a truly moderate and polite arguer, for almost every third word you say is on my side of the question. — But, Mrs. Malaprop, to the more important point in debate, — you say you have no objection to my proposal.

MRS. MAL. None, I assure you. — I am under no positive engagement with Mr. Acres, and as Lydia is so obstinate against him, perhaps your son may have better success.

SIR ANTH. Well, madam, I will write for the boy directly. — He knows not a syllable of this yet, though I have for some time had the proposal in my head. He is at present with his regiment.

MRS. MAL. We have never seen your son, Sir Anthony; but I hope no objection on his side.

SIR ANTH. Objection! — let him object if he dare! — No, no, Mrs. Malaprop, Jack knows that the least demur puts me in a frenzy directly. My process was always very simple — in their younger days, 'twas 'Jack do this'; — if he demurred — I knocked him down — and if he grumbled at that — I always sent him out of the room.

MRS. MAL. Aye, and the properest way, o' my conscience! — nothing is so conciliating to young people as severity. — Well, Sir Anthony, I shall give Mr. Acres his discharge, and prepare Lydia to receive your son's invocations; — and I hope you will represent *her* to the Captain as an object not altogether illegible.

SIR ANTH. Madam, I will handle the subject prudently. — Well, I must leave you — and let me beg you, Mrs. Malaprop, to enforce this matter roundly to the girl; — take my advice — keep a tight hand — if she rejects this proposal — clap her under lock and key: — and if you were just to let the servants forget to bring her dinner for three or four days, you can't conceive how she'd come about!   *Exit* SIR ANTHONY.

MRS. MAL. Well, at any rate I shall be glad to get her from under my intuition. — She has somehow discovered my partiality for Sir Lucius O'Trigger — sure, Lucy can't have betrayed me! — No, the girl is such a simpleton, I should have made her confess it. — Lucy! — Lucy! — (*Calls.*) Had she been one of your artificial ones, I should never have trusted her.

Enter LUCY.

LUCY. Did you call, ma'am?

MRS. MAL. Yes, girl. — Did you see Sir Lucius while you was out?

LUCY. No, indeed, ma'am, not a glimpse of him.

MRS. MAL. You are sure, Lucy, that you 365 never mentioned ——

LUCY. O Gemini! I'd sooner cut my tongue out.

MRS. MAL. Well, don't let your simplicity be imposed on.

LUCY. No, ma'am.   370

MRS. MAL. So, come to me presently, and I'll give you another letter to Sir Lucius; — but mind, Lucy — if ever you betray what you are intrusted with — (unless it be other people's secrets to me) you forfeit my malevolence forever: — and your being a 375 simpleton shall be no excuse for your locality.

Exit MRS. MALAPROP.

LUCY. Ha! ha! ha! — So, my dear *simplicity*, let me give you a little respite — (*altering her manner*) — let girls in my station be as fond as they please of appearing expert, and knowing in their trusts — com- 380 mend me to a mask of *silliness*, and a pair of sharp eyes for my own interest under it! — Let me see to what account have I turned my *simplicity* lately — [*Looks at a paper*]. For *abetting Miss Lydia Languish in a design of running away with an Ensign!* — 385 *in money* — *sundry times* — *twelve pound twelve* — *gowns, five* — *hats, ruffles, caps, &c., &c.* — *numberless!* — *From the said Ensign, within this last month, six guineas and a half.* — About a quarter's pay! — Item, *from Mrs. Malaprop, for betraying the* 390 *young people to her* — when I found matters were likely to be discovered — *two guineas, and a black paduasoy.* — Item, *from Mr. Acres, for carrying divers letters* — which I never delivered — *two guineas, and a pair of buckles.* — Item, *from* 395 *Sir Lucius O'Trigger* — *three crowns* — *two gold pocket-pieces* — *and a silver snuff-box!* — Well done, *simplicity!* — Yet I was forced to make my Hibernian believe that he was corresponding, not with the *aunt*, but with the *niece:* for, though not over rich, I 400 found he had too much pride and delicacy to sacrifice the feelings of a gentleman to the necessities of his fortune.   *Exit.*

ACT II

SCENE I

CAPTAIN ABSOLUTE'S *lodgings.*

CAPTAIN ABSOLUTE *and* FAG.

FAG. Sir, while I was there Sir Anthony came in: I told him you had sent me to inquire after his health, and to know if he was at leisure to see you.

ABS. And what did he say on hearing I was at Bath?   5

FAG. Sir, in my life I never saw an elderly gentleman more astonished! He started back two or three paces, rapped out a dozen interjectoral oaths, and asked what the devil had brought you here!

ABS. Well, sir, and what did you say?   10

FAG. O, I lied, sir — I forget the precise lie; but you may depend on't, he got no truth from me. Yet, with submission, for fear of blunders in future, I should be glad to fix what *has* brought us to Bath, in order that we may lie a little consistently. — Sir 15 Anthony's servants were curious, sir, very curious indeed.

ABS. You have said nothing to them ——?

FAG. O, not a word, sir — not a word. — Mr. Thomas, indeed, the coachman (whom I take to 20 be the discreetest of whips) ——

ABS. 'Sdeath! — you rascal! you have not trusted him!

FAG. O, *no*, sir! — no — no — not a syllable, upon my veracity! — He was, indeed, a little inquis- 25 itive; but I was sly, sir — devilish sly! — My master (said I), honest Thomas (you know, sir, one says *honest* to one's inferiors), is come to Bath to *recruit* — Yes, sir — I said, *to recruit* — and whether for men, money, or constitution, you know, sir, is nothing 30 to him, nor any one else.

ABS. Well — *recruit* — will do — let it be so ——

FAG. O, sir, recruit will do surprisingly — indeed, to give the thing an air, I told Thomas that your Honor had already enlisted five disbanded chair- 35 men,[1] seven minority waiters,[2] and thirteen billiard markers.

ABS. You blockhead, never say more than is necessary.

FAG. I beg pardon, sir — I beg pardon — 40 But, with submission, a lie is nothing unless one supports it. — Sir, whenever I draw on my invention for a good current lie, I always forge *indorsements*, as well as the bill.

ABS. Well, take care you don't hurt your 45 credit by offering too much security. — Is Mr. Faulkland returned?

FAG. He is above, sir, changing his dress.

ABS. Can you tell whether he has been informed of Sir Anthony's and Miss Melville's arrival? 50

FAG. I fancy not, sir; he has seen no one since he came in, but his gentleman, who was with him at Bristol. — I think, sir, I hear Mr. Faulkland coming down ——

ABS. Go tell him I am here.   55

[1] Sedan-chair bearers.

[2] Extra hands only occasionally employed (waiters out of work).

383] O1 *I have.*   11] O1 *forgot.*

FAG. Yes, sir — (*going*). I beg pardon, sir, but should Sir Anthony call, you will do me the favor to remember that we are *recruiting*, if you please.

ABS. Well, well.

FAG. And in tenderness to my character, if 60 your Honor could bring in the chairmen and waiters, I shall esteem it as an obligation; — for though I never scruple a lie to serve my master, yet it *hurts* one's conscience to be found out.   *Exit.*

ABS. Now for my whimsical friend — if he 65 does not know that his mistress is here, I'll tease him a little before I tell him ——

Enter FAULKLAND.

Faulkland, you're welcome to Bath again; you are punctual in your return.

FAULK. Yes; I had nothing to detain me 70 when I had finished the business I went on. Well, what news since I left you? How stand matters between you and Lydia?

ABS. Faith, much as they were; I have not seen her since our quarrel; however, I expect to be 75 recalled every hour.

FAULK. Why don't you persuade her to go off with you at once?

ABS. What, and lose two-thirds of her fortune? You forget that, my friend. — No, no, I could 80 have brought her to that long ago.

FAULK. Nay then, you trifle too long — if you are sure of *her*, propose to the aunt *in your own character*, and write to Sir Anthony for his consent.

ABS. Softly, softly, for though I am con- 85 vinced my little Lydia would elope with me as Ensign Beverley, yet am I by no means certain that she would take me with the impediment of our friends' consent, a regular humdrum wedding, and the reversion of a good fortune on my side; no, no, I 90 must prepare her gradually for the discovery, and make myself necessary to her, before I risk it. — Well, but Faulkland, you'll dine with us to-day at the hotel?

FAULK. Indeed, I cannot: I am not in spirits 95 to be of such a party.

ABS. By heavens! I shall forswear your company. You are the most teasing, captious, incorrigible lover! — Do love like a man!

FAULK. I own I am unfit for company.   100

ABS. Am not *I* a lover; aye, and a romantic one too? Yet do I carry everywhere with me such a confounded farrago of doubts, fears, hopes, wishes, and all the flimsy furniture of a country miss's brain!

FAULK. Ah! Jack, your heart and soul are 105 not, like mine, fixed immutably on one only object. — You throw for a large stake, but losing — you could stake, and throw again: — but I have set my sum

of happiness on this cast, and not to succeed were to be stripped of all.   110

ABS. But, for heaven's sake! what grounds for apprehension can your whimsical brain conjure up at present? «Has Julia missed writing this last post? or was her last too tender, or too cool; or too grave, or too gay; or ——   115

«FAULK. Nay, nay, Jack.

«ABS. Why, her love — her honor — her prudence, you cannot doubt.

FAULK. «O! upon my soul, I never have; — but» what grounds for apprehension did you say? 120 Heavens! are there not a thousand! I fear for her spirits — her health — her life. — My absence may fret her; her anxiety for my return, her fears for me, may oppress her gentle temper. And for her health — does not every hour bring me cause to be 125 alarmed? If it rains, some shower may even then have chilled her delicate frame! — If the wind be keen, some rude blast may have affected her! The heat of noon, the dews of the evening, may endanger the life of her, for whom only I value mine. O! 130 Jack, when delicate and feeling souls are separated, there is not a feature in the sky, not a movement of the elements, not an aspiration of the breeze, but hints some cause for a lover's apprehension!

ABS. Aye, but we may choose whether we 135 will take the hint or not. — So then, Faulkland, if you were convinced that Julia were well and in spirits, you would be entirely content?

FAULK. I should be happy beyond measure — I am anxious only for that.   140

ABS. Then to cure your anxiety at once — Miss Melville is in perfect health, and is at this moment in Bath!

FAULK. Nay, Jack — don't trifle with me.

ABS. She is arrived here with my father 145 within this hour.

FAULK. Can you be serious?

ABS. I thought you knew Sir Anthony better than to be surprised at a sudden whim of this kind. — Seriously then, it is as I tell you — upon my 150 honor.

FAULK. My dear friend! — Hollo, Du-Peigne! my hat — my dear Jack — now nothing on earth can give me a moment's uneasiness.

Enter FAG.

FAG. Sir, Mr. Acres just arrived is below. 155

ABS. Stay, Faulkland, this Acres lives within a mile of Sir Anthony, and he shall tell you how your mistress has been ever since you left her. — Fag, show the gentleman up.   *Exit* FAG.

FAULK. What, is he much acquainted in the 160 family?

136] O1 *no. — Well then.*   137] O1 *Julia was.*
153–154] O1 italicizes *now … uneasiness.*

140] O1 *I'm*; O3 *I'am*; O5O6 *I am*

ABS. O, very intimate. I insist on your not going: besides, his character will divert you.

FAULK. Well, I should like to ask him a few questions.   165

ABS. He is likewise a rival of mine — that is of my *other self's*, for he does not think his friend Captain Absolute ever saw the lady in question; — and it is ridiculous enough to hear him complain to me of *one Beverley*, a concealed skulking rival, who —— 170

FAULK. Hush! — He's here.

Enter ACRES.

ACRES. Hah! my dear friend, noble captain, and honest Jack, how dost thou? Just arrived, faith, as you see. — Sir, your humble servant. Warm work on the roads, Jack! — Odds whips and wheels! 175 I've travelled like a comet, with a tail of dust all the way as long as the Mall.

ABS. Ah! Bob, you are indeed an eccentric planet, but we know your attraction hither. — Give me leave to introduce Mr. Faulkland to you; Mr. 180 Faulkland, Mr. Acres.

ACRES. Sir, I am most heartily glad to see you: sir, I solicit your connections. — Hey, Jack, — what, — this is Mr. Faulkland, who ——?

ABS. Aye, Bob, Miss Melville's Mr. Faulk- 185 land.

ACRES. Od'so! she and your father can be but just arrived before me — I suppose you have seen them. — Ah! Mr. Faulkland, you are indeed a happy man.

FAULK. I have not seen Miss Melville yet, 190 sir. — I hope she enjoyed full health and spirits in Devonshire?

ACRES. Never knew her better in my life, sir — never better. — Odd's blushes and blooms! she has been as healthy as the German Spa.   195

FAULK. Indeed! — I did hear that she had been a little indisposed.

ACRES. False, false, sir — only said to vex you: quite the reverse, I assure you.

FAULK. There, Jack, you see she has the ad- 200 vantage of me; I had almost fretted myself ill.

ABS. Now are you angry with your mistress for not having been sick.

FAULK. No, no, you misunderstand me: — yet surely a little trifling indisposition is not an un- 205 natural consequence of absence from those we love. — Now confess — isn't there something unkind in this violent, robust, unfeeling health?

ABS. O, it was very unkind of her to be well in your absence, to be sure!   210

ACRES. Good apartments, Jack.

FAULK. Well, sir, but you were saying that Miss Melville has been so *exceedingly* well — what, then she has been merry and gay, I suppose? — Always in spirits — hey?   215

ACRES. Merry! Odds crickets! she has been the belle and spirit of the company wherever she has been — so lively and entertaining! so full of wit and humor!

FAULK. There, Jack, there! — O, by my 220 soul! there is an innate levity in woman, that nothing can overcome. — What! happy, and I away!

ABS. Have done: — how foolish this is! Just now you were only apprehensive for your mistress's *spirits*.   225

FAULK. Why, Jack, have I been the joy and spirit of the company?

ABS. No, indeed, you have not.

FAULK. Have I been lively and entertaining?

ABS. O, upon my word, I acquit you.   230

FAULK. Have I been full of wit and humor?

ABS. No, faith; to do you justice, you have been confoundedly stupid indeed.

ACRES. What's the matter with the gentleman?

ABS. He is only expressing his great satisfac- 235 tion at hearing that Julia has been so well and happy — that's all — hey, Faulkland?

FAULK. Oh! I am rejoiced to hear it — yes, yes, she has a *happy* disposition!

ACRES. That she has indeed. — Then she is 240 so accomplished — so sweet a voice — so expert at her harpsichord — such a mistress of flat and sharp, squallante, rumblante, and quiverante! — there was this time month — Odds minnums and crotchets![1] how she did chirrup at Mrs. Piano's concert! 245

FAULK. There again, what say you to this? You see she has been all mirth and song — not a thought of me!

ABS. Pho! man, is not music the food of love?

FAULK. Well, well, it may be so. — Pray, 250 Mr. —— what's his d—d name? Do you remember what songs Miss Melville sung?

ACRES. Not I, indeed.

ABS. Stay now, they were some pretty, melancholy, purling-stream airs, I warrant; perhaps 255 you may recollect; — did she sing — '*When absent from my soul's delight'*?[2]

ACRES. No, that wa'n't it.

ABS. Or — '*Go, gentle gales'*? —— '*Go, gentle gales!*'   (*Sings.*) 260

ACRES. O no! nothing like it. — Odds! now I recollect one of them — '*My heart's my own, my will is free.*'   (*Sings.*)

FAULK. Fool! fool that I am! to fix all my happiness on such a trifler! 'Sdeath! to make herself 265 the pipe and ballad-monger of a circle! to soothe her light heart with catches and glees! — What can you say to this, sir?

[1] Half and quarter notes.
[2] On these songs, see Notes in N, pp. 280–281.

175] O1 *Odds, whips.*   233] O1 *confounded.*   261] O1 *Odds slips?* for *Odds!*

ABS. Why, that I should be glad to hear my mistress had been so merry, *sir.*   270

FAULK. Nay, nay, nay — I am not sorry that she has been happy — no, no, I am glad of that — I would not have had her sad or sick — yet surely a sympathetic heart would have shown itself even in the choice of a song — she might have been   275 temperately healthy, and, somehow, plaintively gay; — but she has been dancing too, I doubt not!

ACRES. What does the gentleman say about dancing?

ABS. He says the lady we speak of dances as   280 well as she sings.

ACRES. Aye, truly, does she — there was at our last race-ball ——

FAULK. Hell and the devil! There! there! — I told you so! I told you so! Oh! she thrives   285 in my absence! — Dancing! — but her whole feelings have been in opposition with mine! — I have been anxious, silent, pensive, sedentary — my days have been hours of care, my nights of watchfulness. — She has been all Health! Spirit! Laugh!   290 Song! Dance! — Oh! d—n'd, d—n'd levity!

ABS. For heaven's sake! Faulkland, don't expose yourself so. — Suppose she has danced, what then? — Does not the ceremony of society often oblige ——

FAULK. Well, well, I'll contain myself. —   295 Perhaps, as you say — for form sake. — What, Mr. Acres, you were praising Miss Melville's manner of dancing a *minuet* — hey?

ACRES. O I dare insure her for that — but what I was going to speak of was her *country dancing:*   300 — Odds swimmings! she has such an air with her! —

FAULK. Now disappointment on her! — Defend this, Absolute, why don't you defend this? — Country-dances! jiggs, and reels! Am I to blame now? A minuet I could have forgiven — I should not   305 have minded that — I say I should not have regarded a minuet — but *country-dances!* Z——ds! had she made one in a cotillion — I believe I could have forgiven even that — but to be monkey-led for a night! — to run the gauntlet through a string   310 of amorous palming puppies! — to show paces like a managed filly! — O Jack, there never can be but *one* man in the world whom a truly modest and delicate woman ought to pair with in a *country-dance*; and even then, the rest of the couples should be   315 her great uncles and aunts!

ABS. Aye, to be sure! — grand-fathers and grandmothers!

FAULK. If there be but one vicious mind in the set, 'twill spread like a contagion — the action of   320 their pulse beats to the lascivious movement of the jigg — their quivering, warm-breathed sighs impregnate the very air — the atmosphere becomes electrical to love, and each amorous spark darts through

every link of the chain! — I must leave you —   325 I own I am somewhat flurried — and that confounded looby has perceived it.   (*Going.*)

《ABS. Aye, aye, you are in a hurry to throw yourself at Julia's feet.

《FAULK. I'm not in a humor to be trifled   330 with — I shall see her only to upbraid her. (*Going.*)》

ABS. Nay, but stay, Faulkland, and thank Mr. Acres for his good news.

FAULK. D—n his news!   *Exit* FAULKLAND.

ABS. Ha! ha! ha! Poor Faulkland! Five   335 minutes since — 'nothing on earth could give him a moment's uneasiness!'

ACRES. The gentleman wa'n't angry at my praising his mistress, was he?

ABS. A little jealous, I believe, Bob.   340

ACRES. You don't say so? Ha! ha! jealous of me? — that's a good joke.

ABS. There's nothing strange in that, Bob: let me tell you, that sprightly grace and insinuating manner of yours will do some mischief among the girls   345 here.

ACRES. Ah! you joke — ha! ha! — mischief — ha! ha! But you know I am not my own property; my dear Lydia has forestalled me. — She could never abide me in the country, because I used to dress   350 so badly — but odds frogs and tambours! I shan't take matters so here — now ancient madam has no voice in it. — I'll make my old clothes know who's master. — I shall straightway cashier the hunting-frock — and render my leather breeches inca-   355 pable. — My hair has been in training some time.

ABS. Indeed!

ACRES. Aye — and tho'ff the side-curls are a little restive, my hind-part takes to it very kindly.

ABS. O, you'll polish, I doubt not.   360

ACRES. Absolutely I propose so. — Then if I can find out this Ensign Beverley, odds triggers and flints! I'll make him know the difference o't.

ABS. Spoke like a man — but pray, Bob, I observe you have got an odd kind of a new method   365 of swearing ——

ACRES. Ha! ha! you've taken notice of it? — 'Tis genteel, isn't it? — I didn't invent it myself, though; but a commander in our militia — a great scholar, I assure you — says that there is no meaning in   370 the common oaths, and that nothing but their antiquity makes them respectable; — because, he says, the ancients would never stick to an oath or two, but would say, by Jove! or by Bacchus! or by Mars! or by Venus! or by Pallas! according to the senti-   375 ment; — so that to swear with propriety, says my little major, the 'oath should be an echo to the sense'; and this we call the *oath referential*, or *sentimental swearing* — ha! ha! 'tis genteel, isn't it?

ABS. Very genteel, and very new, indeed   380

308] O1 *Cotillon.*   347 s.d.] O1 misprints *Abs.* for *Acres.*   368] O1 omits *it* after *isn't.*

— and I dare say will supplant all other figures of imprecation.

ACRES. Aye, aye, the best terms will grow obsolete. — Damns have had their day.

Enter FAG.

FAG. Sir, there is a gentleman below desires 385
to see you. — Shall I show him into the parlor?

ABS. Aye — you may.

ACRES. Well, I must be gone ——

ABS. Stay; who is it, Fag?

FAG. Your father, sir.   390

ABS. You puppy, why didn't you show him up
directly?   *Exit* FAG.

ACRES. You have business with Sir Anthony. — I
expect a message from Mrs. Malaprop at my lodgings. — I have sent also to my dear friend, Sir 395
Lucius O'Trigger. — Adieu, Jack! We must meet at
night, when you shall give me a dozen bumpers to
little Lydia.

ABS. That I will, with all my heart. *Exit* ACRES.

ABS. Now for a parental lecture. — I hope 400
he has heard nothing of the business that has brought
me here. — I wish the gout had held him fast in
Devonshire, with all my soul!

Enter SIR ANTHONY.

ABS. Sir, I am delighted to see you here; and looking so well! — Your sudden arrival at Bath 405
made me apprehensive for your health.

SIR ANTH. Very apprehensive, I dare say, Jack. —
What, you are recruiting here, hey?

ABS. Yes, sir, I am on duty.

SIR ANTH. Well, Jack, I am glad to see you, 410
though I did not expect it, for I was going to write to
you on a little matter of business. — Jack, I have
been considering that I grow old and infirm, and shall
probably not trouble you long.

ABS. Pardon me, sir, I never saw you look 415
more strong and hearty; and I pray frequently that
you may continue so.

SIR ANTH. I hope your prayers may be heard with
all my heart. Well then, Jack, I have been considering that I am so strong and hearty, I may con- 420
tinue to plague you a long time. — Now, Jack, I am
sensible that the income of your commission, and
what I have hitherto allowed you, is but a small
pittance for a lad of your spirit.

ABS. Sir, you are very good.   425

SIR ANTH. And it is my wish, while yet I live, to
have my boy make some figure in the world. — I
have resolved, therefore, to fix you at once in a
noble independence.

ABS. Sir, your kindness overpowers me — 430
such generosity makes the gratitude of reason more
lively than the sensations even of filial affection.

SIR ANTH. I am glad you are so sensible of my attention — and you shall be master of a large estate
in a few weeks.   435

ABS. Let my future life, sir, speak my gratitude:
I cannot express the sense I have of your munificence. —— Yet, sir, I presume you would not wish
me to quit the army?

SIR ANTH. O, that shall be as your wife 440
chooses.

ABS. My wife, sir!

SIR ANTH. Aye, aye, — settle that between you —
settle that between you.

ABS. A *wife*, sir, did you say?   445

SIR ANTH. Aye, a wife — why; did not I mention
her before?

ABS. Not a word of her, sir.

SIR ANTH. Odd so! — I mus'n't forget *her*, though.
— Yes, Jack, the independence I was talking of 450
is by a marriage — the fortune is saddled with a wife
— but I suppose that makes no difference.

ABS. Sir! sir! — you amaze me!

SIR ANTH. Why, what the devil's the matter with
the fool? Just now you were all gratitude and 455
duty.

ABS. I was, sir, — you talked to me of independence and a fortune, but not a word of a wife.

SIR ANTH. Why — what difference does that
make? Odds life, sir! if you have the estate, 460
you must take it with the live stock on it, as it
stands.

ABS. If my happiness is to be the price, I must beg
leave to decline the purchase. — Pray, sir, who is
the lady?   465

SIR ANTH. What's that to you, sir? — Come, give
me your promise to love, and to marry her directly.

ABS. Sure, sir, this is not very reasonable, to summon my affections for a lady I know nothing of!

SIR ANTH. I am sure, sir, 'tis more unreason- 470
able in you to *object* to a lady you know nothing of.

ABS. Then, sir, I must tell you plainly that my inclinations are fixed on another.

«SIR ANTH. They are, are they? Well, that's lucky
— because you will have more merit in your 475
obedience to me.»

«ABS. Sir,» my heart is engaged to an angel.

SIR ANTH. Then pray let it send an excuse. ——
It is very sorry — but *business* prevents its waiting
on her.   480

ABS. But my vows are pledged to her.

SIR ANTH. Let her foreclose, Jack; let her foreclose; they are not worth redeeming: besides, you
have the angel's vows in exchange, I suppose; so
there can be no loss there.   485

ABS. You must excuse me, sir, if I tell you, once
for all, that in this point I cannot obey you.

SIR ANTH. Hark'ee, Jack; — I have heard you for

384] O1 D—ns.   396–397] O1 *at night — Odds bottles and glasses! you* ...   448] O1 *of it.*   454] O1 *d——l's.*

some time with patience — I have been cool — quite cool; — but take care — you know I am com-   490 pliance itself — when I am not thwarted; — no one more easily led — when I have my own way; — but don't put me in a frenzy.

ABS. Sir, I must repeat it — in this I cannot obey you.   495

SIR ANTH. Now, d—n me! if ever I call you *Jack* again while I live!

ABS. Nay, sir, but hear me.

SIR ANTH. Sir, I won't hear a word — not a word! not one word! so give me your promise by a   500 nod — and I'll tell you what, Jack — I mean, you dog — if you don't, by ——

ABS. What, sir, promise to link myself to some mass of ugliness! to ——

SIR ANTH. Z——ds! sirrah! the lady shall   505 be as ugly as I choose: she shall have a hump on each shoulder; she shall be as crooked as the Crescent; her one eye shall roll like the Bull's in Cox's Museum[1] — she shall have a skin like a mummy, and the beard of a Jew — she shall be all this, sirrah!   510 — yet I'll make you ogle her all day, and sit up all night to write sonnets on her beauty.

ABS. This is reason and moderation indeed!

SIR ANTH. None of your sneering, puppy! no grinning, jackanapes!   515

ABS. Indeed, sir, I never was in a worse humor for mirth in my life.

SIR ANTH. 'Tis false, sir! I know you are laughing in your sleeve: I know you'll grin when I am gone, sirrah!   520

ABS. Sir, I hope I know my duty better.

SIR ANTH. None of your passion, sir! none of your violence! if you please. — It won't do with me, I promise you.

ABS. Indeed, sir, I never was cooler in my   525 life.

SIR ANTH. 'Tis a confounded lie! — I know you are in a passion in your heart; I know you are, you hypocritical young dog! But it won't do.

ABS. Nay, sir, upon my word.   530

SIR ANTH. So you will fly out! Can't you be cool, like me? What the devil good can *passion* do! — *Passion* is of no service, you impudent, insolent, overbearing reprobate! — There you sneer again! — don't provoke me! — But you rely upon the mildness   535 of my temper — you do, you dog! you play upon the meekness of my disposition! Yet take care — the patience of a saint may be overcome at last! — but mark! I give you six hours and a half to consider of this: if you then agree, without any condition,   540 to do everything on earth that I choose, why — con-

found you! I may in time forgive you —— If not, z——ds! don't enter the same hemisphere with me! don't dare to breathe the same air, or use the same light with me; but get an atmosphere and a sun   545 of your own! I'll strip you of your commission; I'll lodge a five-and-threepence[2] in the hands of trustees, and you shall live on the interest. — I'll disown you, I'll disinherit you, I'll unget you! and — d—n me, if ever I call you Jack again!   550

Exit SIR ANTHONY.

ABSOLUTE *solus.*

ABS. Mild, gentle, considerate father — I kiss your hands. — What a tender method of giving his opinion in these matters Sir Anthony has! I dare not trust him with the truth. — I wonder what old wealthy hag it is that he wants to bestow on me!   555 — yet he married himself for love! and was in his youth a bold intriguer, and a gay companion!

Enter FAG.

FAG. Assuredly, sir, our father is wrath to a degree; he comes down stairs eight or ten steps at a time — muttering, growling, and thumping the   560 bannisters all the way: I, and the cook's dog, stand bowing at the door — rap! he gives me a stroke on the head with his cane; bids me carry that to my master; then kicking the poor turnspit into the area, d—ns us all for a puppy triumvirate! — Upon   565 my credit, sir, were I in your place, and found my father such very bad company, I should certainly drop his acquaintance.

ABS. Cease your impertinence, sir, at present. — Did you come in for nothing more? — Stand   570 out of the way!   *Pushes him aside, and exit.*

FAG *solus.*

FAG. Soh! Sir Anthony trims[3] my master. He is afraid to reply to his father — then vents his spleen on poor Fag! — When one is vexed by one person, to revenge one's self on another who   575 happens to come in the way — is the vilest injustice! Ah! it shows the worst temper — the basest ——

Enter Errand-Boy.

BOY. Mr. Fag! Mr. Fag! your master calls you.

FAG. Well, you little, dirty puppy, you need not bawl so! — The meanest disposition! the ——   580

BOY. Quick, quick, Mr. Fag!

FAG. *Quick, quick,* you impudent jackanapes! am I to be commanded by you too? you little, impertinent, insolent, kitchen-bred ——

Exit, kicking and beating him.

---

[1] A 'Curious Bull' was one of many valuable mechanical curiosities exhibited by James Cox in 1773–1774 in Spring Gardens.

[2] A quarter-guinea.
[3] Scolds.

Scene II

The North Parade.

Enter Lucy.

Lucy. So — I shall have another rival to add to my mistress's list — Captain Absolute. —— However, I shall not enter his name till my purse has received notice in form. Poor Acres is dismissed! — Well, I have done him a last friendly office in letting him know that Beverley was here before him. — Sir Lucius is generally more punctual when he expects to hear from his *dear Dalia*, as he calls her: — I wonder he's not here! — I have a little scruple of conscience from this deceit; though I should not   10 be paid so well, if my hero knew that *Delia* was near fifty, and her own mistress. «I could not have thought he would have been so nice, when there's a golden egg in the case, as to care whether he has it from a pullet or an old hen!»   15

Enter Sir Lucius O'Trigger.

Sir Luc. Hah! my little embassadress — upon my conscience, I have been looking for you; I have been on the South Parade this half-hour.

Lucy (*speaking simply*). O gemini! and I have been waiting for your worship here on the North.   20

Sir Luc. Faith! — may be that was the reason we did not meet; and it is very comical, too, how you could go out and I not see you — for I was only taking a nap at the Parade Coffee-house, and I chose the *window* on purpose that I might not miss you.   25

Lucy. My stars! Now I'd wager a sixpence I went by while you were asleep.

Sir Luc. Sure enough it must have been so — and I never dreamt it was so late, till I waked. Well, but my little girl, have you got nothing for me?   30

Lucy. Yes, but I have: — I've got a letter for you in my pocket.

Sir Luc. O faith! I guessed you weren't come empty-handed — well — let me see what the dear creature says.   35

Lucy. There, Sir Lucius.   (*Gives him a letter.*)

Sir Luc. (*reads*). *Sir — there is often a sudden incentive impulse in love, that has a greater induction than years of domestic combination: such was the commotion I felt at the first superfluous view of Sir Lucius*   40 *O'Trigger.* — Very pretty, upon my word. — «*As my motive is interested, you may be assured my love shall never be miscellaneous.* Very well.» *Female punctuation forbids me to say more; yet let me add, that it will give me joy infallible to find Sir Lucius worthy the*   45 *last criterion of my affections.* — «*Yours, while meretricious —*» Delia. Upon my conscience! Lucy, your lady is a great mistress of language. — Faith, she's quite the queen of the dictionary! — for the

devil a word dare refuse coming at her call —   50 though one would think it was quite out of hearing.

Lucy. Aye, sir, a lady of her experience ——

Sir Luc. Experience! what, at seventeen?

Lucy. O true, sir — but then she reads so — my stars! how she will read off-hand!   55

Sir Luc. Faith, she must be very deep read to write this way — though she is rather an arbitrary writer too — for here are a great many poor words pressed into the service of this note, that would get their *habeas corpus* from any court in Christen-   60 dom. «However, when affection guides the pen, Lucy, he must be a brute who finds fault with the style.»

Lucy. Ah! Sir Lucius, if you were to hear how she talks of you!   65

Sir Luc. O tell her I'll make her the best husband in the world, and Lady O'Trigger into the bargain! — But we must get the old gentlewoman's consent — and do everything fairly.

Lucy. Nay, Sir Lucius, I thought you wa'n't   70 rich enough to be so nice! [1]

Sir Luc. Upon my word, young woman, you have hit it: — I am so poor that I can't afford to do a dirty action. — If I did not want money I'd steal your mistress and her fortune with a great deal of   75 pleasure. — However, my pretty girl (*gives her money*), here's a little something to buy you a ribband; and meet me in the evening, and I'll give you an answer to this. So, hussy, take a kiss beforehand to put you in mind.   (*Kisses her.*)   80

Lucy. O lud! Sir Lucius — I never seed such a gemman! My lady won't like you if you're so impudent.

Sir Luc. Faith she will, Lucy —— That same —— pho! what's the name of it? — *Modesty!* —— is a   85 quality in a lover more praised by the women than liked; so, if your mistress asks you whether Sir Lucius ever gave you a kiss, tell her *fifty* — my dear.

Lucy. What, would you have me tell her a lie?

Sir Luc. Ah, then, you baggage! I'll make it   90 a truth presently.

Lucy. For shame now; here is some one coming.

Sir Luc. O faith, I'll quiet your conscience.

Sees Fag. — *Exit, humming a tune.*

Enter Fag.

Fag. So, so, ma'am. I humbly beg pardon.

Lucy. O lud! — now, Mr. Fag — you flurry   95 one so.

Fag. Come, come, Lucy, here's no one by — so a little less simplicity, with a grain or two more sincerity, if you please. —— You play false with us, madam. — I saw you give the baronet a letter.   100

[1] Scrupulous.

— My master shall know this — and if he don't call him out — I will.

Lucy. Ha! ha! ha! you gentlemen's gentlemen are so hasty. — That letter was from Mrs. Malaprop, 105 simpleton. — She is taken with Sir Lucius's address.

Fag. How! what tastes some people have! — Why, I suppose I have walked by her window an hundred times. —— But what says our young lady? Any message to my master?   110

Lucy. Sad news, Mr. Fag! — A worse rival than Acres! — Sir Anthony Absolute has proposed his son.

Fag. What, Captain Absolute?

Lucy. Even so. — I overheard it all.

Fag. Ha! ha! ha! — very good, faith. —   115 Good-bye, Lucy, I must away with this news.

Lucy. Well — you may laugh — but it is true, I assure you. (*Going.*) But — Mr. Fag — tell your master not to be cast down by this.

Fag. O, he'll be so disconsolate!   120

Lucy. And charge him not to think of quarrelling with young Absolute.

Fag. Never fear! — never fear!

Lucy. Be sure — bid him keep up his spirits.

Fag. We will — we will. *Exeunt severally.* 125

ACT III

Scene I

The North Parade.

Enter Absolute.

Abs. 'Tis just as Fag told me, indeed. — Whimsical enough, faith! My father wants to *force* me to marry the very girl I am plotting to run away with! — He must not know of my connection with her yet awhile. — He has too summary a method of pro- 5 ceeding in these matters — «and Lydia shall not yet lose her hopes of an elopement.» However, I'll read my recantation instantly. — My conversion is something sudden, indeed — but I can assure him it is very *sincere*. —— So, so — here he comes. 10 — He looks plaguy gruff.   (*Steps aside.*)

Enter Sir Anthony.

[Sir Anth.] No — I'll die sooner than forgive him. — *Die*, did I say? I'll live these fifty years to plague him. — At our last meeting, his impudence had almost put me out of temper. — An ob- 15 stinate, passionate, self-willed boy! — Who can he take after? This is my return for getting him before all his brothers and sisters! — for putting him, at twelve years old, into a marching regiment, and allowing him fifty pounds a-year, beside his pay 20 ever since! — But I have done with him; — he's any-body's son for me. — I never will see him more, — never — never — never — never!

Abs. Now for a penitential face.

Sir Anth. Fellow, get out of my way.   25

Abs. Sir, you see a penitent before you.

Sir Anth. I see an impudent scoundrel before me.

Abs. A sincere penitent. — I am come, sir, to acknowledge my error, and to submit entirely to your will.   30

Sir Anth. What's that?

Abs. I have been revolving, and reflecting, and considering on your past goodness, and kindness, and condescension to me.

Sir Anth. Well, sir?   35

Abs. I have been likewise weighing and balancing what you were pleased to mention concerning duty, and obedience, and authority.

Sir Anth. Well, puppy?

Abs. Why then, sir, the result of my reflec- 40 tions is — a resolution to sacrifice every inclination of my own to your satisfaction.

Sir Anth. Why, now you talk sense — absolute sense — I never heard anything more sensible in my life. —— Confound you, you shall be *Jack* 45 again!

Abs. I am happy in the appellation.

Sir Anth. Why then, Jack, my dear Jack, I will now inform you — who the lady really is. — Nothing but your passion and violence, you silly 50 fellow, prevented my telling you at first. Prepare, Jack, for wonder and rapture! — prepare! —— What think you of Miss Lydia Languish?

Abs. Languish! What, the Languishes of Worcestershire?   55

Sir Anth. Worcestershire! No. Did you never meet Mrs. Malaprop and her niece, Miss Languish, who came into our country just before you were last ordered to your regiment?

Abs. Malaprop! Languish! I don't remem- 60 ber ever to have heard the names before. Yet, stay — I think I do recollect something. —— *Languish! Languish!* She squints, don't she? — A little, red-haired girl?

Sir Anth. Squints? — A red-haired girl! — 65 Z——ds, no!

Abs. Then I must have forgot; it can't be the same person.

Sir Anth. Jack! Jack! what think you of blooming, love-breathing seventeen?   70

Abs. As to that, sir, I am quite indifferent. — If I can please you in the matter, 'tis all I desire.

Sir Anth. Nay, but Jack, such eyes! such eyes! so innocently wild! so bashfully irresolute! Not a glance but speaks and kindles some thought of 75 love! Then, Jack, her cheeks! her cheeks, Jack! so deeply blushing at the insinuations of her tell-tale eyes! Then, Jack, her lips! — O Jack, lips smiling at their own discretion; and if not smiling, more sweetly pouting; more lovely in sullenness!   80

ABS. [aside]. That's she, indeed. — Well done, old gentleman!

SIR ANTH. Then, Jack, her neck! — O Jack! Jack!

ABS. And which is to be mine, sir, the niece or the aunt?   85

SIR ANTH. Why, you unfeeling, insensible puppy, I despise you! When I was of your age, such a description would have made me fly like a rocket! The *aunt*, indeed! — Odds life! when I ran away with your mother, I would not have touched   90 anything old or ugly to gain an empire.

ABS. Not to please your father, sir?

SIR ANTH. To please my father! —— Z——ds! not to please —— O, my father! — Oddso! — yes — yes! if my father, indeed, had desired — 95 that's quite another matter. — Though he wa'n't the indulgent father that I am, Jack.

ABS. I dare say not, sir.

SIR ANTH. But, Jack, you are not sorry to find your mistress is so beautiful?   100

ABS. Sir, I repeat it; if I please you in this affair, 'tis all I desire. Not that I think a woman the worse for being handsome; but, sir, if you please to recollect, you before hinted something about a hump or two, one eye, and a few more graces of that 105 kind. — Now, without being very nice, I own I should rather choose a wife of mine to have the usual number of limbs, and a limited quantity of back: and though *one* eye may be very agreeable, yet as the prejudice has always run in favor of *two*, 110 I would not wish to affect a singularity in that article.

SIR ANTH. What a phlegmatic sot it is! Why, sirrah, you're an anchorite! — a vile, insensible stock. — You a soldier! — you're a walking block, fit only to dust the company's regimentals on! 115 — Odds life! I've a great mind to marry the girl myself!

ABS. I am entirely at your disposal, sir; if you should think of addressing Miss Languish yourself, I suppose you would have me marry the *aunt;* 120 or if you should change your mind, and take the old lady — 'tis the same to me — I'll marry the *niece.*

SIR ANTH. Upon my word, Jack, thou'rt either a very great hypocrite, or —— but come, I know your indifference on such a subject must be all a lie 125 — I'm sure it must — come, now — damn your demure face! — come, confess, Jack — you have been lying — ha'n't you? «You have been lying, hey? I'll never forgive you, if you ha'n't: — so now, own, my dear Jack,» you have been play- 130

ing the hypocrite, hey? — I'll never forgive you if you ha'n't been lying and playing the hypocrite.

ABS. I'm sorry, sir, that the respect and duty which I bear to you should be so mistaken.

SIR ANTH. Hang your respect and duty! 135 But come along with me, I'll write a note to Mrs. Malaprop, and you shall visit the lady directly.

«ABS. Where does she lodge, sir?

«SIR ANTH. What a dull question! — Only on the Grove [1] here.   140

«ABS. O! then I can call on her in my way to the coffee-house.

«SIR ANTH. In your way to the coffee-house! You'll set your heart down in your way to the coffee-house, hey? Ah! you leaden-nerved, wooden- 145 hearted dolt! But come along, you shall see her directly;» her eyes shall be the Promethean torch to you — come along. I'll never forgive you if you don't come back stark mad with rapture and impatience. — If you don't, egad, I'll marry the 150 girl myself!   *Exeunt.*

SCENE II

JULIA's *dressing-room.*

FAULKLAND *solus.*

FAULK. They told me Julia would return directly; I wonder she is not yet come! — How mean does this captious, unsatisfied temper of mine appear to my cooler judgment! Yet I know not that I indulge it in any other point: — but on this one subject,   5 and to this one subject, whom I think I love beyond my life, I am ever ungenerously fretful, and madly capricious! — I am conscious of it — yet I cannot correct myself! What tender, honest joy sparkled in her eyes when we met! — How delicate was   10 the warmth of her expressions! — I was ashamed to appear less happy — though I had come resolved to wear a face of coolness and upbraiding. Sir Anthony's presence prevented my proposed expostulations: — yet I must be satisfied that she has 15 not been so *very* happy in my absence. — She is coming! — Yes! — I know the nimbleness of her tread when she thinks her impatient Faulkland counts the moments of her stay.

Enter JULIA.

JUL. I had not hoped to see you again so soon. 20

FAULK. Could I, Julia, be contented with my first welcome — restrained as we were by the presence of a third person?

[1] The fashionable 'Orange Grove,' named after the Prince of Orange.

---

101 s.d.] O1 misprints *Sir Anth.* for *Abs.*
115] O1 corrects in *Errata* the misprint *regiment* for *regimentals* in its main text.
119] O1 corrects in *Errata* the misprint *Anguish* for *Languish* in its main text.   121] O1 misprints *you're* for *your.*
126] O1 *d—n.*   SCENE II. 2] O1 omits *I* before *wonder.*   6] O1 *object* for *subject.*

JUL. O Faulkland, when your kindness can make me thus happy, let me not think that I discov- 25 ered something of coldness in your first salutation.

FAULK. 'Twas but your fancy, Julia. — I *was* rejoiced to see you — to see you in such health. — Sure I had no cause for coldness?

JUL. Nay then, I see you have taken some- 30 thing ill. — You must not conceal from me what it is.

FAULK. Well then — shall I own to you — «but you will despise me, Julia — nay, I despise myself for it. —— Yet I *will* own,» that my joy at hearing of your health and arrival here, by your neigh- 35 bor Acres, was somewhat damped by his dwelling much on the high spirits you had enjoyed in Devonshire — on your mirth — your singing — dancing, and I know not what! — For such is my temper, Julia, that I should regard every mirthful mo- 40 ment in your absence as a treason to constancy. — The mutual tear that steals down the cheek of parting lovers is a compact that no smile shall live there till they meet again.

JUL. Must I never cease to tax my Faulkland 45 with this teasing minute caprice? — Can the idle reports of a silly boor weigh in your breast against my tried affection?

FAULK. They have no weight with me, Julia: no, no — I am happy if you have been so — yet 50 only say that you did not sing with *mirth* — say that you *thought* of Faulkland in the dance.

JUL. I never can be happy in your absence. — If I wear a countenance of content, it is to show that my mind holds no doubt of my Faulkland's 55 truth. —— If I seemed sad — it were to make malice triumph, and say that I had fixed my heart on one who left me to lament his roving, and my own credulity. — Believe me, Faulkland, I mean not to upbraid you when I say that I have often 60 dressed sorrow in smiles, lest my friends should guess whose unkindness had caused my tears.

FAULK. You were ever all goodness to me. — O, I am a brute when I but admit a doubt of your true constancy! 65

JUL. If ever, without such cause from you, as I will not suppose possible, you find my affections veering but a point, may I become a proverbial scoff for levity and base ingratitude.

FAULK. Ah! Julia, that last word is grating 70 to me. I would I had no title to your *gratitude!* Search your heart, Julia; perhaps what you have mistaken for love, is but the warm effusion of a too thankful heart!

JUL. For what quality must I love you? 75

FAULK. For no quality! To regard me for any quality of mind or understanding were only to *esteem* me. And for person — I have often wished myself deformed, to be convinced that I owed no obligation *there* for any part of your affection. 8c

JUL. Where Nature has bestowed a show of nice attention in the features of a man, he should laugh at it as misplaced. I have seen men who in *this* vain article perhaps might rank above you; but my heart has never asked my eyes if it were so or not. 85

FAULK. Now this is not well from *you*, Julia. — I despise person in a man. — Yet if you loved me as I wish, though I were an Æthiop, you'd think none so fair.

JUL. I see you are determined to be unkind. 90 — The *contract* which my poor father bound us in gives you more than a lover's privilege.

FAULK. Again, Julia, you raise ideas that feed and justify my doubts. — I would not have been more free — no — I am proud of my restraint. 95 —— Yet — yet — perhaps your high respect alone for this solemn compact has fettered your inclinations, which else had made a worthier choice. — How shall I be sure, had you remained unbound in thought and promise, that I should still have 100 been the object of your persevering love?

JUL. Then try me now. — Let us be free as strangers as to what is past: — *my* heart will not feel more liberty!

FAULK. There now! so hasty, Julia! so anx- 105 ious to be free! — If your love for me were fixed and ardent, you would not lo[o]se your hold, even though I wished it!

JUL. O, you torture me to the heart! — I cannot bear it. 110

FAULK. I do not mean to distress you. — If I loved you less I should never give you an uneasy moment. — But hear me. — All my fretful doubts arise from this — Women are not used to weigh, and separate the motives of their affections: — 115 the cold dictates of prudence, gratitude, or filial duty, may sometimes be mistaken for the pleadings of the heart. —— I would not boast — yet let me say that I have neither age, person, or character to found dislike on; — my fortune such as few 120 ladies could be charged with *indiscretion* in the match. — O Julia! when *Love* receives such countenance from *Prudence*, nice minds will be suspicious of its *birth*.

JUL. I know not whither your insinuations 125 would tend: — but as they seem pressing to insult me — I will spare you the regret of having done so. — I have given you no cause for this!   *Exit in tears*.

FAULK. In tears! Stay, Julia: stay but for a moment. —— The door is fastened! — Julia! 130 — my soul — but for one moment: — I hear her

---

26] O3 *something . . . salutation*; O1 *more coolness in your first salutation than my long-hoarded joy could have presaged.*
36] O1 *something*.   70] O1 italicizes *last*.   98] O1 *made worthier*.   107] O1 *loose*; O3–O6 *lose.*
126] O1 omits *but* before *as*.

sobbing! — 'Sdeath! what a brute am I to use her thus! Yet stay! — Aye — she is coming now. — How little resolution there is in woman! — How a few soft words can turn them! —— No, faith! 135 — she is *not* coming either! —— Why, Julia — my love — say but that you forgive me — come but to tell me that. — Now, this is being *too* resentful. — Stay! she *is* coming too — I thought she would — no *steadiness* in anything! her going away must 140 have been a mere trick then. — She sha'n't see that I was hurt by it. — I'll affect indifference. — (*Hums a tune: then listens.*) —— No — Z—ds! she's *not* coming! — nor don't intend it, I suppose. — This is not *steadiness*, but *obstinacy!* Yet I deserve it. 145 — What, after so long an absence to quarrel with her tenderness! — 'twas barbarous and unmanly! — I should be ashamed to see her now. — I'll wait till her just resentment is abated — and when I distress her so again, may I lose her forever! and be 150 linked instead to some antique virago, whose gnawing passions, and long-hoarded spleen shall make me curse my folly half the day, and all the night!

Exit.

Scene III

Mrs. Malaprop's *lodgings.*

Mrs. Malaprop, *with a letter in her hand, and* Captain Absolute.

Mrs. Mal. Your being Sir Anthony's son, Captain, would itself be a sufficient accommodation; — but from the ingenuity of your appearance, I am convinced you deserve the character here given of you.

Abs. Permit me to say, madam, that as I 5 never yet have had the pleasure of seeing Miss Languish, my principal inducement in this affair at present is the honor of being allied to Mrs. Malaprop; of whose intellectual accomplishments, elegant manners, and unaffected learning, no tongue is 10 silent.

Mrs. Mal. Sir, you do me infinite honor! — I beg, Captain, you'll be seated. — (*Sit*) — Ah! few gentlemen now-a-days know how to value the ineffectual qualities in a woman! — few think how a little 15 knowledge becomes a gentlewoman! Men have no sense now but for the worthless flower of beauty!

Abs. It is but too true, indeed, ma'am. — Yet I fear our ladies should share the blame — they think our admiration of *beauty* so great, that 20 *knowledge* in *them* would be superfluous. Thus, like garden-trees, they seldom show fruit till time has robbed them of the more specious blossom. — Few, like Mrs. Malaprop and the orange-tree, are rich in both at once! 25

Mrs. Mal. Sir — you overpower me with good-

breeding. — He is the very pine-apple of politeness! — You are not ignorant, Captain, that this giddy girl has somehow contrived to fix her affections on a beggarly, strolling, eaves-dropping Ensign, 30 whom none of us have seen, and nobody knows anything of.

Abs. O, I have heard the silly affair before. — I'm not at all prejudiced against her on *that* account.

Mrs. Mal. You are very good, and very con- 35 siderate, Captain. — I am sure I have done everything in my power since I exploded the affair! Long ago I laid my positive conjunctions on her never to think on the fellow again; — I have since laid Sir Anthony's preposition before her; — 40 but, I'm sorry to say, she seems resolved to decline every particle that I enjoin her.

Abs. It must be very distressing, indeed, ma'am.

Mrs. Mal. Oh! it gives me the hydrostatics to such a degree! — I thought she had persisted 45 from corresponding with him; but behold this very day I have interceded another letter from the fellow! I believe I have it in my pocket.

Abs. (*aside*). O the devil! my last note.

Mrs. Mal. Aye, here it is. 50

Abs. (*aside*). Aye, my note, indeed! O the little traitress Lucy.

Mrs. Mal. There, perhaps you may know the writing. (*Gives him the letter.*)

Abs. I think I have seen the hand before — 55 yes, I *certainly must* have seen this hand before: ——

Mrs. Mal. Nay, but read it, Captain.

Abs. (*reads*). '*My soul's idol, my adored Lydia!*' — Very tender, indeed!

Mrs. Mal. Tender! aye, and profane, too, 60 o' my conscience!

Abs. '*I am excessively alarmed at the intelligence you send me, the more so as my new rival*' ——

Mrs. Mal. That's *you*, sir.

Abs. '*has universally the character of being an* 65 *accomplished gentleman, and a man of honor.*' —— Well, that's handsome enough.

Mrs. Mal. O, the fellow had some design in writing so.

Abs. That he had, I'll answer for him, ma'am. 70

Mrs. Mal. But go on, sir — you'll see presently.

Abs. '*As for the old weather-beaten she-dragon who guards you*' — Who can he mean by that?

Mrs. Mal. *Me!* Sir — *me!* — he means *me!* There — what do you think now? — But go on 75 a little further.

Abs. Impudent scoundrel! — '*it shall go hard but I will elude her vigilance, as I am told that the same ridiculous vanity which makes her dress up her coarse features, and deck her dull chat with hard words* 80 *which she don't understand*' ——

MRS. MAL. There, sir! an attack upon my language! What do you think of that? — an aspersion upon my parts of speech! Was ever such a brute! Sure if I reprehend anything in this world, it is 85 the use of my oracular tongue, and a nice derangement of epitaphs!

ABS. He deserves to be hanged and quartered! Let me see — 'same ridiculous vanity' —

MRS. MAL. You need not read it again, sir. 90

ABS. I beg pardon, ma'am —— 'does also lay her open to the grossest deceptions from flattery and pretended admiration' — an impudent coxcomb! —— 'so that I have a scheme to see you shortly with the old harridan's consent, and even to make her a go- 95 between in our interviews.' — Was ever such assurance!

MRS. MAL. Did you ever hear anything like it? He'll elude my vigilance, will he? — Yes, yes! ha! ha! He's very likely to enter these doors! — We'll 100 try who can plot best!

ABS. So we will, ma'am — so we will. Ha! ha! ha! A conceited puppy, ha! ha! ha! —— Well, but Mrs. Malaprop, as the girl seems so infatuated by this fellow, suppose you were to wink at her 105 corresponding with him for a little time — let her even plot an elopement with him — then do you connive at her escape — while I, just in the nick,[1] will have the fellow laid by the heels, and fairly contrive to carry her off in his stead. 110

MRS. MAL. I am delighted with the scheme; never was anything better perpetrated!

ABS. But, pray, could not I see the lady for a few minutes now? — I should like to try her temper a little. 115

MRS. MAL. Why, I don't know — I doubt she is not prepared for a visit of this kind. — There is a decorum in these matters.

ABS. O Lord! she won't mind me — only tell her Beverley —— 120

MRS. MAL. Sir! ——

ABS. (aside). Gently, good tongue.

MRS. MAL. What did you say of Beverley?

ABS. O, I was going to propose that you should tell her, by way of jest, that it was Beverley 125 who was below — she'd come down fast enough then — ha! ha! ha!

MRS. MAL. 'Twould be a trick she well deserves. — Besides, you know the fellow tells her he'll get my consent to see her — ha! ha! — Let him if 130 he can, I say again. — Lydia, come down here! (Calling.) — He'll make me a go-between in their interviews! — ha! ha! — Come down, I say, Lydia! — I don't wonder at your laughing, ha! ha! ha! — his impudence is truly ridiculous. 135

[1] 'The nick of time.'

ABS. 'Tis very ridiculous, upon my soul, ma'am, ha! ha! ha!

MRS. MAL. The little hussy won't hear. — Well, I'll go and tell her at once who it is. — She shall know that Captain Absolute is come to wait 140 on her. — And I'll make her behave as becomes a young woman.

ABS. As you please, ma'am.

MRS. MAL. For the present, Captain, your servant. — Ah! you've not done laughing yet, I 145 see — elude my vigilance! — yes, yes, ha! ha! ha!

Exit.

ABS. Ha! ha! ha! one would think now I might throw off all disguise at once, and seize my prize with security — but such is Lydia's caprice that to undeceive were probably to lose her. — I'll see 150 whether she knows me.

(Walks aside, and seems engaged in looking at the pictures.)

Enter LYDIA.

LYD. What a scene am I now to go through! Surely nothing can be more dreadful than to be obliged to listen to the loathsome addresses of a stranger to one's heart. — I have heard of girls 155 persecuted as I am, who have appealed in behalf of their favored lover to the generosity of his rival: suppose I were to try it — there stands the hated rival — an officer too! — but O, how unlike my Beverley! — I wonder he don't begin — Truly he seems a 160 very negligent wooer! — Quite at his ease, upon my word! — I'll speak first. — [Aloud.] Mr. Absolute.

ABS. Madam.   (Turns round.)

LYD. O heav'ns! Beverley!

ABS. Hush! — hush, my life! — Softly! Be 165 not surprised.

LYD. I am so astonished! and so terrified! and so overjoyed! — For heav'n's sake! how came you here?

ABS. Briefly — I have deceived your aunt. 170 — I was informed that my new rival was to visit here this evening, and contriving to have him kept away, have passed myself on her for Captain Absolute.

LYD. O, charming! — And she really takes you for young Absolute? 175

ABS. O, she's convinced of it.

LYD. Ha! ha! ha! I can't forbear laughing to think how her sagacity is overreached!

ABS. But we trifle with our precious moments — such another opportunity may not occur — 180 then let me now conjure my kind, my condescending angel, to fix the time when I may rescue her from undeserved persecution, and with a licensed warmth plead for my reward.

LYD. Will you then, Beverley, consent to 185

forfeit that portion of my paltry wealth? — that burden on the wings of love?

Abs. O, come to me — rich only thus — in loveliness. — Bring no portion to me but thy love — 'twill be generous in you, Lydia — for well you 190 know, it is the only dower your poor Beverley can repay.

Lyd. How persuasive are his words! — how charming will poverty be with him!

Abs. Ah! my soul, what a life will we then 195 live! Love shall be our idol and support! We will worship him with a monastic strictness; abjuring all worldly toys, to center every thought and action there. — Proud of calamity, we will enjoy the wreck of wealth; while the surrounding gloom of ad- 200 versity shall make the flame of our pure love show doubly bright. — By heav'ns! I would fling all goods of fortune from me with a prodigal hand to enjoy the scene where I might clasp my Lydia to my bosom, and say, the world affords no smile to 205 me — but here. (*Embracing her.*) —— (*Aside.*) If she holds out now the devil is in it!

Lyd. Now could I fly with him to the Antipodes! but my persecution is not yet come to a crisis.

Enter Mrs. Malaprop, *listening.*

Mrs. Mal. (*aside*). I am impatient to know 210 how the little hussy deports herself.

Abs. So pensive, Lydia! — is then your warmth abated?

Mrs. Mal. [*aside*]. *Warmth abated!* — So! she has been in a passion, I suppose. 215

Lyd. No — nor never can while I have life.

Mrs. Mal. [*aside*]. An ill-tempered little devil! — She'll be *in a passion all her life* — will she?

Lyd. Think not the idle threats of my ridiculous aunt can ever have any weight with me. 220

Mrs. Mal. [*aside*]. Very dutiful, upon my word!

Lyd. Let her choice be *Captain Absolute*, but Beverley is mine.

Mrs. Mal. [*aside*]. I am astonished at her assurance! — *to his face* — *this is to his face!* 225

Abs. Thus then let me enforce my suit.

(*Kneeling.*)

Mrs. Mal. [*aside*]. Aye — poor young man! — down on his knees entreating for pity! — I can contain no longer. — [*Aloud.*] Why, thou vixen! — I have overheard you. 230

Abs. (*aside*). O, confound her vigilance!

Mrs. Mal. Captain Absolute — I know not how to apologize for her shocking rudeness.

Abs. (*aside*). So — all's safe, I find. — [*Aloud.*]

I have hopes, madam, that time will bring the 235 young lady ——

Mrs. Mal. O, there's nothing to be hoped for from her! She's as headstrong as an allegory on the banks of Nile.

Lyd. Nay, madam, what do you charge me 240 with now?

Mrs. Mal. Why, thou unblushing rebel — didn't you tell this gentleman to his face that you loved another better? — didn't you say you never would be his? 245

Lyd. No, madam — I did not.

Mrs. Mal. Good heav'ns! what assurance! — Lydia, Lydia, you ought to know that lying don't become a young woman! — Didn't you boast that Beverley — that stroller Beverley — possessed 250 your heart? — Tell me that, I say.

Lyd. 'Tis true, ma'am, and none but Beverley ——

Mrs. Mal. Hold — hold, Assurance! — you shall not be so rude.

Abs. Nay, pray Mrs. Malaprop, don't stop 255 the young lady's speech: — she's very welcome to talk thus — it does not hurt *me* in the least, I assure you.

Mrs. Mal. You are *too* good, Captain — *too* amiably patient — but come with me, miss. — 260 Let us see you again soon, Captain. — Remember what we have fixed.

Abs. I shall, ma'am.

Mrs. Mal. Come, take a graceful leave of the gentleman. 265

Lyd. May every blessing wait on my Beverley, my loved Bev ——

Mrs. Mal. Hussy! I'll choke the word in your throat! — come along — come along.

Exeunt severally, Beverley [Absolute] *kissing his hand to* Lydia — Mrs. Malaprop *stopping her from speaking.*

Scene IV

Acres's *lodgings.*

Acres *and* David.

Acres *as just dressed.*

Acres. Indeed, David — do you think I become it so?

Dav. You are quite another creature, believe me, master, by the Mass! an'[1] we've any luck we shall see the Devon monkeyrony[2] in all the print-shops 5 in Bath!

Acres. Dress *does* make a difference, David.

[1] If.   [2] David's corruption of 'macaroni.'

187] O1 *burthen.*   210] O1 *I'm.*   225] O1 omits *is.*   229] O1 *Why, huzzy! huzzy!*
269 s.d.] O1–O6 Beverley for Absolute.
Scene iv. s.d.] O1O2 Scene v (inadvertently retaining here the Larpent MS. numbering, though the printed text has merged the first two scenes of the MS. into Scene i).

DAV. 'Tis all in all, I think. — Difference! why, an' you were to go now to Clod-Hall, I am certain the old lady wouldn't know you: Master Butler 10 wouldn't believe his own eyes, and Mrs. Pickle would cry, 'Lard presarve me!' — our dairy-maid would come giggling to the door, and I warrant Dolly Tester, your Honor's favorite, would blush like my waistcoat. — Oons! I'll hold a gallon, 15 there a'n't a dog in the house but would bark, and question whether *Phyllis* would wag a hair of her tail!

ACRES. Aye, David, there's nothing like *polishing.*

DAV. So I says of your Honor's boots; but the boy never heeds me! 20

ACRES. But, David, has Mr. De-la-Grace been here? I must rub up my balancing, and chasing, and boring.[1]

DAV. I'll call again, sir.

ACRES. Do — and see if there are any letters 25 for me at the post-office.

DAV. I will. — By the Mass, I can't help looking at your head! — If I hadn't been by at the cooking, I wish I may die if I should have known the dish again myself! *Exit.* 30

ACRES *comes forward, practising a dancing step.*

ACRES. Sink, slide — coupee! — Confound the first inventors of cotillons! say I — they are as bad as algebra to us country gentlemen. — I can walk a minuet easy enough when I'm forced! — and I have been accounted a good stick in a country-dance. 35 — Odds jigs and tabors! — I never valued your cross-over to couple — figure in — right and left — and I'd foot it with e'er a captain in the county! — But these outlandish heathen Allemandes[2] and Cotillons are quite beyond me! — I shall never 40 prosper at 'em, that's sure. — Mine are true-born English legs — they don't understand their curst French lingo! — their *pas* this, and *pas* that, and *pas* t'other! — D—n me! my feet don't like to be called paws! No, 'tis certain I have most anti-Galli- 45 can toes!

Enter Servant.

SERV. Here is Sir Lucius O'Trigger to wait on you, sir.

ACRES. Show him in.

Enter SIR LUCIUS.

SIR LUC. Mr. Acres, I am delighted to em- 50 brace you.

ACRES. My dear Sir Lucius, I kiss your hands.

[1] Terms of dancing (cf. Fr. '*balancer, chasser, faire des pas de Bourrée*').
[2] German dances.

SIR LUC. Pray, my friend, what has brought you so suddenly to Bath?

ACRES. Faith! I have followed Cupid's 55 Jack-a-Lantern, and find myself in a quagmire at last. — In short, I have been very ill-used, Sir Lucius. — I don't choose to mention names, but look on me as on a very ill-used gentleman.

SIR LUC. Pray, what is the case? — I ask no 60 names.

ACRES. Mark me, Sir Lucius, I fall as deep as need be in love with a young lady — her friends take my part — I follow her to Bath — send word of my ar- rival, and receive answer that the lady is to be 65 otherwise disposed of. — This, Sir Lucius, I call being ill-used.

SIR LUC. Very ill, upon my conscience. — Pray, can you divine the cause of it?

ACRES. Why, there's the matter: she has 70 another lover, one *Beverley*, who, I am told, is now in Bath. — Odds slanders and lies! he must be at the bottom of it.

SIR LUC. A rival in the case, is there? — And you think he has supplanted you unfairly? 75

ACRES. Unfairly! — to be sure he has. — He never could have done it fairly.

SIR LUC. Then sure you know what is to be done!

ACRES. Not I, upon my soul!

SIR LUC. We wear no swords here, but you 80 understand me.

ACRES. What! fight him?

SIR LUC. Aye, to be sure: what can I mean else?

ACRES. But he has given me no provocation.

SIR LUC. Now, I think he has given you the 85 greatest provocation in the world. — Can a man commit a more heinous offence against another than to fall in love with the same woman? O, by my soul, it is the most unpardonable breach of friendship!

ACRES. Breach of friendship! Aye, aye; but 90 I have no acquaintance with this man. I never saw him in my life.

SIR LUC. That's no argument at all — he has the less right then to take such a liberty.

ACRES. 'Gad, that's true. — I grow full of 95 anger, Sir Lucius! — I fire apace! Odds hilts and blades! I find a man may have a deal of valor in him and not know it! But couldn't I contrive to have a little right of my side?

SIR LUC. What the devil signifies *right* when 100 your *honor* is concerned? Do you think *Achilles*, or my little *Alexander the Great* ever inquired where the right lay? No, by my soul, they drew their broad- swords, and left the lazy sons of peace to settle the justice of it. 105

ACRES. Your words are a grenadier's march to my

17] O3 spells *Phillis* here, but *Phyllis* IV. i. 82. 37] O1 *two* for *to.* 62] O1 *falls.*
71] O1 italicizes *one* instead of *Beverley.* 76] O1 italicizes *Unfairly!*
90] O1 italicizes *friendship.* 100] O1 *d—l.*

heart! I believe courage must be catching! — I certainly do feel a kind of valor rising, as it were — a kind of courage, as I may say. —— Odds flints, pans, and triggers! I'll challenge him directly. 110

SIR LUC. Ah, my little friend! if we had *Blunderbuss-Hall* here — I could show you a range of ancestry, in the O'Trigger line, that would furnish the New Room,[1] every one of whom had killed his man! — For though the mansion-house and dirty 115 acres have slipt through my fingers, I thank heav'n our honor, and the family-pictures, are as fresh as ever.

ACRES. O Sir Lucius! I have had ancestors too! every man of 'em colonel or captain in the 120 militia! — Odds balls and barrels! say no more — I'm braced for it — «my nerves are become catgut! my sinews wire! and my heart pinchbeck!»[2] The thunder of your words has soured the milk of human kindness in my breast! —— Z—ds! as the man 125 in the play says, 'I could do such deeds!'[3]

SIR LUC. Come, come, there must be no passion at all in the case — these things should always be done civilly.

ACRES. I must be in a passion, Sir Lucius — 130 I must be in a rage. — Dear Sir Lucius, let me be in a rage, if you love me. — Come, here's pen and paper. (*Sits down to write.*) I would the ink were red! — Indite, I say, indite! — How shall I begin? Odds bullets and blades! I'll write a good *bold* 135 *hand*, however.

SIR LUC. Pray compose yourself.

ACRES. Come — now, shall I begin with an oath? Do, Sir Lucius, let me begin with a damme.

SIR LUC. Pho! pho! do the thing *decently* 140 and like a Christian. Begin now, — '*Sir*' ——

ACRES. That's too civil by half.

SIR LUC. '*To prevent the confusion that might arise*' —

ACRES [*writing*]. Well —— 145

SIR LUC. '*From our both addressing the same lady*' ——

ACRES. Aye — there's the reason — [*writing*] '*same lady*' — Well ——

SIR LUC. '*I shall expect the honor of your* 150 *company*' ——

ACRES. Z——ds! I'm not asking him to dinner.

SIR LUC. Pray be easy.

ACRES. Well then [*writing*] — '*honor of your company*' —— 155

SIR LUC. '*To settle our pretensions*' —

ACRES [*writing*]. Well ——

SIR LUC. Let me see — aye, *King's-Mead-Fields* will do — '*In King's-Mead-Fields.*'

[1] The new Assembly rooms, opened in 1771.
[2] A cheap metal alloy, named after its inventor, Pinchbeck.
[3] Acres faintly recalls Lear's 'I will do such things' (II. iv.).

116] O1 *I thank God.*

ACRES. So that's done. — Well, I'll fold it 160 up presently; my own crest — a hand and dagger shall be the seal.

SIR LUC. You see now, this little explanation will put a stop at once to all confusion or misunderstanding that might arise between you. 165

ACRES. Aye, we fight to prevent any misunderstanding.

SIR LUC. Now, I'll leave you to fix your own time. — Take my advice, and you'll decide it this evening if you can; then let the worst come of it, 'twill 170 be off your mind to-morrow.

ACRES. Very true.

SIR LUC. So I shall see nothing more of you, unless it be by letter, till the evening. — I would do myself the honor to carry your message; but, to tell 175 you a secret, I believe I shall have just such another affair on my own hands. There is a gay captain here, who put a jest on me lately at the expense of my country, and I only want to fall in with the gentleman, to call him out. 180

ACRES. By my valor, I should like to see you fight first! Odds life! I should like to see you kill him, if it was only to get a little lesson.

SIR LUC. I shall be very proud of instructing you. — Well for the present — but remember now, 185 when you meet your antagonist, do everything in a mild and agreeable manner. — Let your courage be as keen, but at the same time as polished, as your sword.   *Exeunt severally.*

ACT IV

SCENE I

ACRES's *lodgings.*

ACRES *and* DAVID.

DAV. Then, by the Mass, sir! I would do no such thing — ne'er a Sir Lucius O'Trigger in the kingdom should make me fight, when I wa'n't so minded. Oons! what will the old lady say when she hears o't! 5

ACRES. Ah! David, if you had heard Sir Lucius! — Odds sparks and flames! he would have roused your valor.

DAV. Not he, indeed. I hates such bloodthirsty cormorants. Look'ee, master, if you'd wanted 10 a bout at boxing, quarter-staff, or short-staff, I should never be the man to bid you cry off: but for your curst sharps and snaps,[3] I never knew any good come of 'em.

ACRES. But my *honor*, David, my *honor!* I 15 must be very careful of my honor.

DAV. Aye, by the Mass! and I would be very

[3] Sharp duelling swords and pistols.

careful of it; and I think in return my *honor* couldn't do less than to be very careful of *me*.

ACRES. Odds blades! David, no gentleman 20 will ever risk the loss of his honor!

DAV. I say then, it would be but civil in *honor* never to risk the loss of a *gentleman*. — Look'ee, master, this *honor* seems to me to be a marvellous false friend; aye, truly, a very courtier-like 25 servant. — Put the case, I was a gentleman (which, thank God, no one can say of me); well — my honor makes me quarrel with another gentleman of my acquaintance. — So — we fight. (Pleasant enough that.) Boh! — I kill him — (the more's my 30 luck). Now, pray who gets the profit of it? — Why, my *honor*. — But put the case that he kills me! — by the Mass! I go to the worms, and my honor whips over to my enemy!

ACRES. No, David — in that case! — Odds 35 crowns and laurels! your honor follows you to the grave.

DAV. Now, that's just the place where I could make a shift to do without it.

ACRES. Z——ds, David, you're a coward! 40 — It doesn't become my valor to listen to you. — What, shall I disgrace my ancestors? — Think of that, David — think what it would be to disgrace my ancestors!

DAV. Under favor, the surest way of not 45 disgracing them is to keep as long as you can out of their company. Look'ee now, master, to go to them in such haste — with an ounce of lead in your brains — I should think might as well be let alone. Our ancestors are very good kind of 50 folks; but they are the last people I should choose to have a visiting acquaintance with.

ACRES. But David, now, you don't think there is such very, very, *very* great danger, hey? — Odds life! people often fight without any mischief 55 done!

DAV. By the Mass, I think 'tis ten to one against you! — Oons! here to meet some lion-headed fellow, I warrant, with his d—n'd double-barrelled swords, and cut-and-thrust pistols! Lord bless 60 us! it makes me tremble to think o't. — Those be such desperate bloody-minded weapons! Well, I never could abide 'em! — from a child I never could fancy 'em! — I suppose there a'n't so merciless a beast in the world as your loaded pistol! 65

ACRES. Z—ds! I *won't* be afraid! — Odds fire and fury! you shan't make me afraid! — Here is the challenge, and I have sent for my dear friend Jack Absolute to carry it for me.

DAV. Aye, i' the name of mischief, let *him* 70 be the messenger. — For my part, I wouldn't lend a hand to it for the best horse in your stable. By the Mass! it don't look like another letter! It is, as I may say, a designing and malicious-looking letter! — and I warrant smells of gunpowder, like a sol- 75 dier's pouch! — Oons! I wouldn't swear it mayn't go off!

ACRES. Out, you poltroon! — You ha'n't the valor of a grasshopper.

DAV. Well, I say no more — 'twill be sad 80 news, to be sure, at Clod-Hall! — but I ha' done. — How Phyllis will howl when she hears of it! — Aye, poor bitch, she little thinks what shooting her master's going after! — And I warrant old Crop, who has carried your Honor, field and road, 85 these ten years, will curse the hour he was born.

(*Whimpering.*)

ACRES. It won't do, David — I am determined to fight — so get along, you coward, while I'm in the mind.

Enter Servant.

SERV. Captain Absolute, sir. 90

ACRES. O! show him up.   *Exit Servant.*

DAV. Well, heaven send we be all alive this time to-morrow.

ACRES. What's that! — Don't provoke me, David! 95

DAV. Good bye, master.   (*Whimpering.*)

ACRES. Get along, you cowardly, dastardly, croaking raven.   *Exit* DAVID.

Enter ABSOLUTE.

ABS. What's the matter, Bob?

ACRES. A vile, sheep-hearted blockhead! — 100 If I hadn't the valor of St. George and the dragon to boot ——

ABS. But what did you want with me, Bob?

ACRES. O! — There ——

(*Gives him the challenge.*)

ABS. 'To Ensign Beverley.' (*Aside.*) So — 105 what's going on now? [*Aloud.*] Well, what's this?

ACRES. A challenge!

ABS. Indeed! — Why, you won't fight him, will you, Bob?

ACRES. 'Egad, but I will, Jack. — Sir Lucius 110 has wrought me to it. He has left me full of rage — and I'll fight this evening, that so much good passion mayn't be wasted.

ABS. But what have I to do with this?

ACRES. Why, as I think you know some- 115 thing of this fellow, I want you to find him out for me, and give him this mortal *defiance*.

ABS. Well, give it to me, and trust me he gets it.

ACRES. Thank you, my dear friend, my 120 dear Jack; but it is giving you a great deal of trouble.

ABS. Not in the least — I beg you won't mention it. — No trouble in the world, I assure you.

ACRES. You are very kind. — What it is to   125
have a friend! — You couldn't be my second — could
you, Jack?

ABS. Why no, Bob — not in *this* affair — it would
not be quite so proper.

ACRES. Well then, I must get my friend Sir   130
Lucius. I shall have your good wishes, however,
Jack.

ABS. Whenever he meets you, believe me.

Enter Servant.

SERV. Sir Anthony Absolute is below, inquiring
for the Captain.   135

ABS. I'll come instantly. — Well, my little hero,
success attend you.   (*Going.*)

ACRES. Stay — stay, Jack. — If Beverley should
ask you what kind of a man your friend Acres is,
do tell him I am a devil of a fellow — will   140
you, Jack?

ABS. To be sure I shall. — I'll say you are a
determined dog — hey, Bob?

ACRES. Aye, do, do — and if that frightens him,
'egad, perhaps he mayn't come. So tell him   145
I generally kill a man a week — will you, Jack?

ABS. I will, I will; I'll say you are called in the
country '*Fighting Bob!*'

ACRES. Right, right — 'tis all to prevent mischief;
for I don't want to take his life if I clear my   150
honor.

ABS. No! — that's very kind of you.

ACRES. Why, you don't wish me to kill him —
do you, Jack?

ABS. No, upon my soul, I do not. — But a   155
devil of a fellow, hey?   (*Going.*)

ACRES. True, true — but stay — stay, Jack —
you may add that you never saw me in such a rage
before — a most devouring rage!

ABS. I will, I will.   160

ACRES. Remember, Jack — a determined dog!

ABS. Aye, aye, '*Fighting Bob!*'   *Exeunt severally.*

SCENE II

MRS. MALAPROP'S *lodgings.*

MRS. MALAPROP *and* LYDIA.

MRS. MAL. Why, thou perverse one! — tell me
what you can object to him? — Isn't he a handsome
man? — tell me that. — A genteel man? a pretty
figure of a man?

LYD. (*aside*). She little thinks whom she is   5
praising! — [*Aloud.*] So is Beverley, ma'am.

MRS. MAL. No caparisons, miss, if you please! —
Caparisons don't become a young woman. — No!
Captain Absolute is indeed a fine gentleman!

LYD. (*aside*). Aye, the Captain Absolute *you*   10
have seen.

MRS. MAL. Then he's *so* well bred; — *so* full of
alacrity, and adulation! — and has *so much* to say
for himself: — in such good language, too! — His
physiognomy so grammatical! — Then his pres-   15
ence is so noble! — I protest, when I saw him,
I thought of what Hamlet says in the play:[1] —
'Hesperian curls! — the front of *Job* himself! — An
eye, like *March*, to threaten at command! — A
station, like Harry Mercury, new' — something   20
about kissing — on a hill — however, the similitude
struck me directly.

LYD. (*aside*). How enraged she'll be presently
when she discovers her mistake!

Enter Servant.

SERV. Sir Anthony and Captain Absolute   25
are below, ma'am.

MRS. MAL. Show them up here.   *Exit Servant.*
Now, Lydia, I insist on your behaving as becomes
a young woman. — Show your good breeding at
least, though you have forgot your duty.   30

LYD. Madam, I have told you my resolution; —
I shall not only give him no encouragement, but I
won't even speak to, or look at him.

(*Flings herself into a chair, with her face from
the door.*)

Enter SIR ANTHONY *and* ABSOLUTE.

SIR ANTH. Here we are, Mrs. Malaprop, come
to mitigate the frowns of unrelenting beauty —   35
and difficulty enough I had to bring this fellow. —
I don't know what's the matter; but if I hadn't
held him by force, he'd have given me the slip.

MRS. MAL. You have infinite trouble, Sir
Anthony, in the affair. I am ashamed for the   40
cause! — (*Aside to her.*) Lydia, Lydia, rise, I beseech you! — pay your respects!

SIR ANTH. I hope, madam, that Miss Languish
has reflected on the worth of this gentleman, and
the regard due to her aunt's choice, and *my*   45
alliance. — (*Aside to him.*) Now, Jack, speak to her!

ABS. (*aside*). What the d—l shall I do! — [*Aloud.*]
You see, sir, she won't even look at me whilst you
are here. — I knew she wouldn't! — I told you so. —
Let me entreat you, sir, to leave us together!   50

(ABSOLUTE *seems to expostulate with his
father.*)

LYD. (*aside*). I wonder I ha'n't heard my aunt
exclaim yet! Sure she can't have looked at him! —
Perhaps their regimentals are alike, and she is
something blind.

SIR ANTH. I say, sir, I won't stir a foot yet!   55

MRS. MAL. I am sorry to say, Sir Anthony, that

[1] Mrs. Malaprop's 'nice derangement' of *Hamlet*, III. iv.
56–59.

130] O1 *must fix on my.*

my affluence over my niece is very small. — (*Aside to her.*) Turn round, Lydia, I blush for you!

SIR ANTH. May I not flatter myself that Miss Languish will assign what cause of dislike she 60 can have to my son! — Why don't you begin, Jack? — (*Aside to him.*) Speak, you puppy — speak!

MRS. MAL. It is impossible, Sir Anthony, she can have any. — She will not *say* she has. — (*Aside to her.*) Answer, hussy! why don't you answer? 65

SIR ANTH. Then, madam, I trust that a childish and hasty predilection will be no bar to Jack's happiness. — (*Aside to him.*) Z—ds! sirrah! why don't you speak?

LYD. (*aside*). I think my lover seems as lit- 70 tle inclined to conversation as myself. — How strangely blind my aunt must be!

ABS. Hem! hem! — madam — hem! — (ABSOLUTE *attempts to speak, then returns to* SIR ANTHONY.) — Faith! sir, I am so confounded! — and so — 75 so — confused! — I told you I should be so, sir, — I knew it. — The — the — tremor of my passion entirely takes away my presence of mind.

SIR ANTH. But it don't take away your voice, fool, does it? — Go up, and speak to her directly! 80
(ABSOLUTE *makes signs to* MRS. MALAPROP *to leave them together.*)

MRS. MAL. Sir Anthony, shall we leave them together? — (*Aside to her.*) Ah! you stubborn little vixen!

SIR ANTH. Not yet, ma'am, not yet! — (*Aside to him.*) What the d—l are you at? Unlock your 85 jaws, sirrah, or ——
(ABSOLUTE *draws near* LYDIA.)

ABS. (*aside*). Now heav'n send she may be too sullen to look round! — I must disguise my voice. — (*Speaks in a low hoarse tone.*) —— Will not Miss Languish lend an ear to the mild accents of 90 true love? — Will not ——

SIR ANTH. What the d—l ails the fellow? — Why don't you speak out? — not stand croaking like a frog in a quinsy!

ABS. The — the — excess of my awe, and 95 my — my — my modesty quite choke me!

SIR ANTH. Ah! your *modesty* again! — I'll tell you what, Jack, if you don't speak out directly, and glibly, too, I shall be in such a rage! — Mrs. Malaprop, I wish the lady would favor us with 100 something more than a side-front!
(MRS. MALAPROP *seems to chide* LYDIA.)

ABS. So! — All will out I see!
(*Goes up to* LYDIA, *speaks softly.*)
Be not surprised, my Lydia; suppress all surprise at present.

LYD. (*aside*). Heav'ns! 'tis Beverley's voice! — 105 Sure he can't have imposed on Sir Anthony, too! — (*Looks round by degrees, then starts up.*)

Is this possible! — my Beverley! — how can this be? — my Beverley?

ABS. (*aside*). Ah! 'tis all over.

SIR ANTH. Beverley! — the devil! — Bev- 110 erley! — What can the girl mean? — This is my son, Jack Absolute!

MRS. MAL. For shame, hussy! for shame! — your head runs so on that fellow that you have him always in your eyes! — Beg Captain Absolute's 115 pardon directly.

LYD. I see no Captain Absolute, but my loved Beverley!

SIR ANTH. Z—ds! the girl's mad! — her brain's turned by reading! 120

MRS. MAL. O' my conscience, I believe so! — What do you mean by Beverley, hussy? — You saw Captain Absolute before to-day; there he is — your husband that shall be.

LYD. With all my soul, ma'am. — When I 125 refuse my Beverley ——

SIR ANTH. O! she's as mad as Bedlam! — Or has this fellow been playing us a rogue's trick! — Come here, sirrah! — who the d—l are you?

ABS. Faith, sir, I am not quite clear my- 130 self; but I'll endeavor to recollect.

SIR ANTH. Are you my son, or not? — answer for your mother, you dog, if you won't for me.

MRS. MAL. Aye, sir, who are you? O mercy! I begin to suspect! —— 135

ABS. (*aside*). Ye Powers of Impudence befriend me! — [*Aloud.*] Sir Anthony, most assuredly I am your wife's son; and that I sincerely believe myself to be *yours* also, I hope my duty has always shown. — Mrs. Malaprop, I am your most respectful 140 admirer — and shall be proud to add *affectionate nephew.* — I need not tell my Lydia, that she sees her faithful Beverley, who, knowing the singular generosity of her temper, assumed that name, and a station which has proved a test of the most 145 disinterested love, which he now hopes to enjoy in a more elevated character.

LYD. (*sullenly*). So! — there will be no elopement after all!

SIR ANTH. Upon my soul, Jack, thou art a 150 very impudent fellow! to do you justice, I think I never saw a piece of more consummate assurance!

ABS. O you flatter me, sir — you compliment — 'tis my *modesty* you know, sir — my *modesty* that has stood in my way. 155

SIR ANTH. Well, I am glad you are not the dull, insensible varlet you pretended to be, however! — I'm glad you have made a fool of your father, you dog — I am. —— So this was your *penitence*, your *duty*, and *obedience!* — I thought it was d—n'd sud- 160 den! — You *never heard their names before*, not you! — *What!* The *Languishes of Worcestershire*, hey?

— *if you could please me in the affair, 'twas all you desired!* — Ah! you dissembling villain! — What! — (*pointing to* Lydia) *she squints, don't she?* 165 — *a little red-haired girl!* — hey? — Why, you hypocritical young rascal! — I wonder you a'n't ashamed to hold up your head!

Abs. 'Tis with difficulty, sir. — I *am* confused — very much confused, as you must perceive. 170

Mrs. Mal. O Lud! Sir Anthony! — a new light breaks in upon me! — Hey! how! what! Captain, did *you* write the letters then? — What! — am I to thank *you* for the elegant compilation of '*an old weather-beaten she-dragon*' — hey? — O mercy! 175 was it *you* that reflected on my parts of speech?

Abs. Dear sir! my modesty will be overpowered at last, if you don't assist me. — I shall certainly not be able to stand it!

Sir Anth. Come, come, Mrs. Malaprop, we 180 must forget and forgive. — Odds life! matters have taken so clever a turn all of a sudden, that I could find in my heart to be so good-humored! and so gallant! — hey! Mrs. Malaprop!

Mrs. Mal. Well, Sir Anthony, since *you* 185 desire it, we will not anticipate the past; — so mind, young people — our retrospection will now be all to the future.

Sir Anth. Come, we must leave them together; Mrs. Malaprop, they long to fly into each 190 other's arms, I warrant! [*Aside.*] — Jack — isn't the *cheek* as I said, hey? — and the eye, you rogue! — and the lip — hey? — Come, Mrs. Malaprop, we'll not disturb their tenderness — theirs is the time of life for happiness! —— '*Youth's the season made for* 195 *joy*'[1] — (*Sings.*) — hey! — Odds life! I'm in such spirits, — I don't know what I couldn't do! — Permit me, ma'am — (*Gives his hand to* Mrs. Malaprop.) (*Sings.*) Tol-de-rol! — 'gad, I should like a little fooling myself — Tol-de rol! de-rol! 200

    Exit singing, and handing Mrs. Malaprop.
    (Lydia *sits sullenly in her chair.*)

Abs. (*aside*). So much thought bodes me no good. — [*Aloud.*] So grave, Lydia!

Lyd. Sir!

Abs. (*aside*). So! — egad! I thought as much! — That d—n'd monosyllable has froze me! — 205 [*Aloud.*] What, Lydia, now that we are as happy in our friends' consent, as in our mutual vows ——

Lyd. (*peevishly*). Friends' consent, indeed!

Abs. Come, come, we must lay aside some of our romance — a little *wealth* and *comfort* may 210 be endured after all. And for your fortune, the lawyers shall make such settlements as ——

Lyd. Lawyers! — I *hate* lawyers!

Abs. Nay then, we will not wait for their linger-

[1] From Gay's *Beggar's Opera*, II. iv.

ing forms, but instantly procure the license, 215 and ——

Lyd. The *license!* — I *hate* license!

Abs. O my love! be not so unkind! — Thus let me intreat —— (*Kneeling.*)

Lyd. Pshaw! — what signifies kneeling 220 when you know I *must* have you?

Abs. (*rising*). Nay, madam, there shall be no constraint upon your inclinations, I promise you. — If I have lost your *heart*, — I resign the rest. — (*Aside.*) 'Gad, I must try what a little 225 *spirit* will do.

Lyd. (*rising*). Then, sir, let me tell you, the interest you had there was acquired by a mean, unmanly imposition, and deserves the punishment of fraud. — What, you have been treating *me* 230 like a *child!* — humoring my romance! and laughing, I suppose, at your success!

Abs. You wrong me, Lydia, you wrong me. — Only hear ——

Lyd. So, while *I* fondly imagined we were 235 deceiving my relations, and flattered myself that I should outwit and incense them *all* — behold! my hopes are to be crushed at once, by my aunt's consent and approbation! — and *I* am *myself* the only dupe at last!   (*Walking about in heat.*) 240

«Abs. Nay, but hear me ——

«Lyd. No, sir, you could not think that such paltry artifices could please me, when the mask was thrown off! — But I suppose since your tricks have made you secure of my *fortune*, you are 245 little solicitous about my *affections*.» But here, sir, here is the picture — Beverley's picture! (*taking a miniature from her bosom*) which I have worn, night and day, in spite of threats and entreaties! — There, sir (*flings it to him*) — and be assured 250 I throw the original from my heart as easily!

Abs. Nay, nay, ma'am, we will not differ as to that. — Here (*taking out a picture*), here is Miss Lydia Languish. — What a difference! — Aye, *there* is the heav'nly assenting smile that first gave 255 soul and spirit to my hopes! — those are the lips which sealed a vow, as yet scarce dry in Cupid's calendar! — and *there*, the *half* resentful blush that *would* have checked the ardor of my thanks. — Well, all that's past! — all over indeed! — There, 260 madam — in *beauty*, that copy is not equal to you, but in my mind its merit over the original, in being still the same, is such — that — I cannot find in my heart to *part with* it.   (*Puts it up again.*)

Lyd. (*softening*). 'Tis *your own* doing, sir. 265 — I — I — I suppose you are perfectly satisfied.

Abs. O, most certainly — sure now this is much better than being in love! — ha! ha! ha! — there's some spirit in *this!* — What signifies breaking some scores of solemn promises, «half an hundred 270 vows, under one's hand, with the marks of a dozen or two angels to witness!» all that's of no consequence, you know. — To be sure, people will say that Miss didn't know her own mind — but never mind that: — or perhaps they may be ill- 275 natured enough to hint that the gentleman grew tired of the lady and forsook her — but don't let that fret you.

LYD. There's no bearing his insolence.

(Bursts into tears.)

Enter MRS. MALAPROP *and* SIR ANTHONY.

MRS. MAL. *(entering)*. Come, we must in- 280 terrupt your billing and cooing a while.

LYD. *This* is *worse* than your treachery and deceit, you base ingrate!   *(Sobbing.)*

SIR ANTH. What the devil's the matter now! — Z—ds! Mrs. Malaprop, this is the *oddest billing* 285 and *cooing* I ever heard! — But what the deuce is the meaning of it? — I'm quite astonished!

ABS. Ask the lady, sir.

MRS. MAL. O mercy! — I'm quite analysed, for my part! — Why, Lydia, what is the reason 290 of this?

LYD. Ask the *gentleman*, ma'am.

SIR ANTH. Z—ds! I shall be in a frenzy! — Why, Jack, you are not come out to be any one else, are you?   295

MRS. MAL. Aye, sir, there's no more *trick*, is there? — You are not like Cerberus, *three* gentlemen at once, are you?

ABS. You'll not let me speak. — I say the *lady* can account for *this* much better than I can. 300

LYD. Ma'am, you once commanded me never to think of Beverley again — *there* is the man — I now obey you: — for, from this moment, I renounce him forever.   *Exit* LYDIA.

MRS. MAL. O mercy! and miracles! what a 305 turn here is! — Why sure, Captain, you haven't behaved disrespectfully to my niece?

SIR ANTH. Ha! ha! ha! — ha! ha! ha! — now I see it — ha! ha! ha! — now I see it — you have been too lively, Jack.   310

ABS. Nay, sir, upon my word ——

SIR ANTH. Come, no lying, Jack — I'm sure 'twas so.

MRS. MAL. O Lud! Sir Anthony! — O fie, Captain!   315

ABS. Upon my soul, ma'am ——

SIR ANTH. Come, no excuses, Jack; — why, your father, you rogue, was so before you: — the blood of the Absolutes was always impatient. — Ha! ha! ha!

poor little Lydia! — why, you've frightened 320 her, you dog, you have.

ABS. By all that's good, sir ——

SIR ANTH. Z—ds! say no more, I tell you. — Mrs. Malaprop shall make your peace. — You must make his peace, Mrs. Malaprop; — you must tell 325 her 'tis Jack's way — tell her 'tis all our ways — it runs in the blood of our family! — Come, away, Jack — ha! ha! ha! Mrs. Malaprop — a young villain!   *(Pushes him out.)*

MRS. MAL. O! Sir Anthony! — O fie, Cap- 330 tain!   *Exeunt severally.*

SCENE III

The North Parade.

Enter SIR LUCIUS O'TRIGGER.

SIR LUC. I wonder where this Captain Absolute hides himself. — Upon my conscience! — these officers are always in one's way in love-affairs: — I remember I might have married Lady Dorothy Carmine, if it had not been for a little rogue of a 5 major, who ran away with her before she could get a sight of me! — And I wonder too what it is the ladies can see in them to be so fond of them — unless it be a touch of the old serpent in 'em, that makes the little creatures be caught, like 10 vipers, with a bit of red cloth. — Hah! — isn't this the Captain coming? — faith it is! — There is a probability of succeeding about that fellow that is mighty provoking! — Who the devil is he talking to?   *(Steps aside.)*

Enter CAPTAIN ABSOLUTE.

ABS. To what fine purpose I have been plot- 15 ting! A noble reward for all my schemes, upon my soul! — A little gypsy! — I did not think her romance could have made her so d—n'd absurd either. — 'Sdeath, I never was in a worse humor in my life! — I could cut my own throat, or any 20 other person's, with the greatest pleasure in the world!

SIR LUC. O, faith! I'm in the luck of it — I never could have found him in a sweeter temper for my purpose — to be sure I'm just come in the 25 nick! Now to enter into conversation with him, and so quarrel genteelly. *(SIR LUCIUS goes up to* ABSOLUTE.) —— With regard to that matter, Captain, I must beg leave to differ in opinion with you.

ABS. Upon my word then, you must be a 30 very subtle disputant: — because, sir, I happened just then to be giving no opinion at all.

SIR LUC. That's no reason. — For give me leave

294] O1 *Jack, you scoundrel.*   327] O1 *Come, get on.*   329 s.d.] O1 *Pushing.*
SCENE III. s.d.] O1–O6 SCENE IV (as in III. iv, the Larpent MS. numbering is carelessly kept, though SCENE II of the MS. has been dropped).

to tell you, a man may *think* an untruth as well as *speak* one. 35

ABS. Very true, sir, but if a man never utters his thoughts I should think they *might* stand a *chance* of escaping controversy.

SIR LUC. Then, sir, you differ in opinion with me, which amounts to the same thing. 40

ABS. Hark'ee, Sir Lucius, — if I had not before known you to be a gentleman, upon my soul, I should not have discovered it at this interview: — for what you can drive at, unless you mean to quarrel with me, I cannot conceive! 45

SIR LUC. I humbly thank you, sir, for the quickness of your apprehension. — (*Bowing.*) — You have named the very thing I would be at.

ABS. Very well, sir — I shall certainly not balk your inclinations — but I should be glad you 50 would please to explain your motives.

SIR LUC. Pray, sir, be easy — the quarrel is a very pretty quarrel as it stands — we should only spoil it by trying to explain it. — However, your memory is very short — or you could not have 55 forgot an affront you passed on me within this week. — So no more, but name your time and place.

ABS. Well, sir, since you are so bent on it, the sooner the better; — let it be this evening — here, by the Spring-Gardens.[1] — We shall scarcely be 60 interrupted.

SIR LUC. Faith! that same interruption in affairs of this nature shows very great ill-breeding. — I don't know what's the reason, but in England, if a thing of this kind gets wind, people make such a 65 pother that a gentleman can never fight in peace and quietness. — However, if it's the same to you, Captain, I should take it as a particular kindness if you'd let us meet in King's-Mead-Fields, as a little business will call me there about six o'clock, and 70 I may dispatch both matters at once.

ABS. 'Tis the same to me exactly. — A little after six, then, we will discuss this matter more seriously.

SIR LUC. If you please, sir, there will be very pretty small-sword light, though it won't do for 75 a long shot. — So that matter's settled! and my mind's at ease! *Exit* SIR LUCIUS.

Enter FAULKLAND, *meeting* ABSOLUTE.

ABS. Well met. — I was going to look for you. — O, Faulkland! all the dæmons of spite and disappointment have conspired against me! I'm so 80 vexed that if I had not the prospect of a resource in being knocked on the head by and by, I should scarce have spirits to tell you the cause.

FAULK. What can you mean? — Has Lydia changed her mind? — I should have thought 85 her duty and inclination would now have pointed to the same object.

[1] A favorite Bath resort for evening parties.

ABS. Aye, just as the eyes do of a person who squints: — when her *love-eye* was fixed on *me* — t'other — her *eye* of *duty*, was finely obliqued: 90 — but when duty bid her point *that* the same way — off t'other turned on a swivel, and secured its retreat with a frown!

FAULK. But what's the resource you ——

ABS. O, to wind up the whole, a good-95 natured Irishman here has — (*mimicking* SIR LUCIUS) — begged leave to have the pleasure of cutting my throat — and I mean to indulge him — that's all.

FAULK. Prithee, be serious. 100

ABS. 'Tis fact, upon my soul. — Sir Lucius O'Trigger — you know him by sight — for some affront, which I am sure I never intended, has obliged me to meet him this evening at six o'clock: 'tis on that account I wished to see you — you 105 must go with me.

FAULK. Nay, there must be some mistake, sure. — Sir Lucius shall explain himself — and I dare say matters may be accommodated: — but this evening, did you say? — I wish it had been 110 any other time.

ABS. Why? — there will be light enough: — there will (as Sir Lucius says) 'be very pretty small-sword light, though it won't do for a long shot.' — Confound his long shots! 115

FAULK. But I am myself a good deal ruffled by a difference I have had with Julia — my vile tormenting temper has made me treat her so cruelly that I shall not be myself till we are reconciled.

ABS. By heav'ns, Faulkland, you don't de-120 serve her.

Enter Servant, gives FAULKLAND *a letter.*

FAULK. O Jack! this is from Julia. — I dread to open it. — I fear it may be to take a last leave — perhaps to bid me return her letters — and restore —— O! how I suffer for my folly! 125

ABS. Here — let me see. (*Takes the letter and opens it.*) Aye, a final sentence indeed! — 'tis all over with you, faith!

FAULK. Nay, Jack — don't keep me in suspense.

ABS. Hear then. — '*As I am convinced that* 130 *my dear* FAULKLAND'S *own reflections have already upbraided him for his last unkindness to me, I will not add a word on the subject.* — *I wish to speak with you as soon as possible.* — *Yours ever and truly,* JULIA.' — There's stubbornness and resentment for you! 135 (*Gives him the letter.*) Why, man, you don't seem one whit happier at this.

FAULK. O, yes, I am — but — but ——

ABS. Confound your *buts.* — You never hear anything that would make another man bless him-140 self, but you immediately d—n it with a *but.*

FAULK. Now, Jack, as you are my friend, own

honestly — don't you think there is something forward — something indelicate in this haste to forgive? — Women should never sue for reconcil-　145
iation: — *that* should *always* come from us. — *They*
should retain their coldness till *wooed* to kindness —
and their *pardon*, like their *love*, should 'not unsought be won.' [1]

ABS. I have not patience to listen to you:　150
— thou'rt incorrigible! — so say no more on the
subject. — I must go to settle a few matters. — Let
me see you before six — remember — at my lodgings. — A poor industrious devil like me, who have
toiled, and drudged, and plotted to gain my　155
ends, and am at last disappointed by other people's
folly — may in pity be allowed to swear and grumble
a little; — but a captious sceptic in love, — a slave
to fretfulness and whim — who has no difficulties
but of *his own* creating — is a subject more　160
fit for ridicule than compassion!　　*Exit* ABSOLUTE.

FAULK. I feel his reproaches! — yet I would not
change this too exquisite nicety for the gross content
with which *he* tramples on the thorns of love. — His
engaging me in this duel has started an idea　165
in my head, which I will instantly pursue. — I'll use
it as the touchstone of Julia's sincerity and disinter-
estedness. — If her love prove pure and sterling ore
— my name will rest on it with honor! — and once
I've stamped it there, I lay aside my doubts　170
forever: — but if the dross of selfishness, the
allay [2] of pride predominate — 'twill be best to
leave her as a toy for some less cautious fool to sigh
for.　　　　　　　　　　　　　　*Exit* FAULKLAND.

ACT V

SCENE I

JULIA'S *dressing-room.*

JULIA *sola.*

[JUL.] How this message has alarmed me! What
dreadful accident can he mean! why such charge to
be alone? — O Faulkland! — how many unhappy
moments! — how many tears have you cost me!

Enter FAULKLAND [*muffled up in a riding-coat*].

JUL. What means this? — why this caution,　5
Faulkland?

FAULK. Alas! Julia, I am come to take a long
farewell.

JUL. Heav'ns! what do you mean?

FAULK. You see before you a wretch, whose　10
life is forfeited. — Nay, start not! — the infirmity
of my temper has drawn all this misery on me. — I
left you fretful and passionate — an untoward accident drew me into a quarrel — the event is, that

[1] From *Paradise Lost*, viii, 503.　　　　[2] Alloy.

I must fly this kingdom instantly. — O Julia,　15
had I been so fortunate as to have called you mine entirely before this mischance had fallen on me, I should
not so deeply dread my banishment!　《But no
more of that — your heart and promise were given
to one happy in friends, character, and station!　20
they are not bound to wait upon a solitary, guilty
exile.》

JUL. My soul is oppressed with sorrow at the
nature of your misfortune: had these adverse circumstances arisen from a less fatal cause, I　25
should have felt strong comfort in the thought that
I could *now* chase from your bosom every doubt of
the warm sincerity of my love. — My heart has long
known no other guardian. — I now entrust my person to your honor — we will fly together. —　30
When safe from pursuit, my father's will may be
fulfilled — and I receive a legal claim to be the partner of your sorrows, and tenderest comforter. Then
on the bosom of your wedded Julia, you may lull
your keen regret to slumbering; while virtuous　35
love, with a cherub's hand, shall smooth the brow
of upbraiding thought, and pluck the thorn from
compunction.

FAULK. O Julia! I am bankrupt in gratitude!
But the time is so pressing, it calls on you for so　40
hasty a resolution — would you not wish some hours
to weigh the advantages you forego, and what little
compensation poor Faulkland can make you beside
his solitary love?

JUL. I ask not a moment. — No, Faulkland, I　45
have loved you for yourself: and if I now, more than
ever, prize the solemn engagement which so long has
pledged us to each other, it is because it leaves no
room for hard aspersions on my fame, and puts the
seal of duty to an act of love. — But let us not　50
linger. — Perhaps this delay ——

FAULK. 'Twill be better I should not venture out
again till dark. — Yet am I grieved to think what
numberless distresses will press heavy on your gentle
disposition!　　　　　　　　　　　　　　　55

JUL. Perhaps your fortune may be forfeited by
this unhappy act. — I know not whether 'tis so —
but sure that alone can never make us unhappy. —
The little I have will be sufficient to *support* us; and
exile never should be splendid.　　　　　　　60

FAULK. Aye, but in such an abject state of life,
my wounded pride perhaps may increase the natural
fretfulness of my temper, till I become a rude, morose
companion, beyond your patience to endure. Perhaps the recollection of a deed my conscience　65
cannot justify may haunt me in such gloomy and
unsocial fits, that I shall hate the tenderness that
would relieve me, break from your arms, and quarrel
with your fondness!

JUL. If your thoughts should assume so un-　70

4 s.d.] O1 *muffled ... Riding-coat*; O3 omits.

happy a bent, you will the more want some mild and affectionate spirit to watch over and console you: — one who, by bearing *your* infirmities with gentleness and resignation, may teach you *so* to bear the evils of your fortune.   75

FAULK. Julia, I have proved you to the quick! and with this useless device I throw away all my doubts. How shall I plead to be forgiven this last unworthy effect of my restless, unsatisfied disposition?

JUL. Has no such disaster happened as you 80 related?

FAULK. I am ashamed to own that it was all pretended; yet in pity, Julia, do not kill me with resenting a fault which never can be repeated: but sealing, this once, my pardon, let me to-morrow, 85 in the face of heaven, receive my future guide and monitress, and expiate my past folly by years of tender adoration.

JUL. Hold, Faulkland! — That you are free from a crime which I before feared to name, heaven 90 knows how sincerely I rejoice! — These are tears of thankfulness for that! But that your cruel doubts should have urged you to an imposition that has wrung my heart, gives me now a pang more keen than I can express!   95

FAULK. By heav'ns! Julia ——

JUL. Yet hear me. — My father loved you, Faulkland! and you preserved the life that tender parent gave me; in his presence I pledged my hand —*joyfully* pledged it — where before I had 100 given my heart. When, soon after, I lost that parent, it seemed to me that Providence had, in Faulkland, shown me whither to transfer without a pause my grateful duty, as well as my affection: hence I have been content to bear from you 105 what pride and delicacy would have forbid me from another. — I will not upbraid you by repeating how you have trifled with my sincerity. ——

FAULK. I confess it all! yet hear ——

JUL. After such a year of trial — I might 110 have flattered myself that I should not have been insulted with a new probation of my sincerity, as cruel as unnecessary! «A trick of such a nature as to show me plainly that when I thought you loved me best, you even then regarded me as a mean 115 dissembler; an artful, prudent hypocrite.

«FAULK. Never! never!»

JUL. I now see it is not in your nature to be content or confident in love. With this conviction — I never will be yours. While I had hopes that 120 my persevering attention and unreproaching kindness might in time reform your temper, I should have been happy to have gained a dearer influence over you; but I will not furnish you with a licensed power to keep alive an incorrigible fault, at the ex- 125 pense of one who never would contend with you.

FAULK. Nay, but Julia, by my soul and honor, if after this ——

JUL. But one word more. — As my faith has once been given to you, I never will barter it with 130 another. — I shall pray for your happiness with the truest sincerity; and the dearest blessing I can ask of heaven to send you will be to charm you from that unhappy temper which alone has prevented the performance of our solemn engagement. — All 135 I request of *you* is that you will yourself reflect upon this infirmity, and when you number up the many true delights it has deprived you of — let it not be your *least* regret that it lost you the love of one — who would have followed you in beggary 140 through the world!   *Exit.*

FAULK. She's gone! — forever! — There was an awful resolution in her manner, that riveted me to my place. — O fool! — dolt! — barbarian! — Curst as I am with more imperfections than my 145 fellow-wretches, kind Fortune sent a heaven-gifted cherub to my aid, and, like a ruffian, I have driven her from my side! — I must now haste to my appointment. — Well, my mind is tuned for such a scene. — I shall wish only to become a principal 150 in it, and reverse the tale my cursed folly put me upon forging here. — O love! — tormentor! — fiend! whose influence, like the moon's, acting on men of dull souls, makes idiots of them, but meeting subtler spirits, betrays their course, and urges sensibil- 155 ity to madness!   *Exit.*

Enter Maid and LYDIA.

MAID. My mistress, ma'am, I know, was here just now — perhaps she is only in the next room.
                                                                     Exit Maid.

LYD. Heigh-ho! — Though he has used me so, this fellow runs strangely in my head. I be- 160 lieve one lecture from my grave cousin will make me recall him.

Enter JULIA.

LYD. O Julia, I am come to you with such an appetite for consolation. — Lud! child, what's the matter with you? — You have been crying! — 165 I'll be hanged if that Faulkland has not been tormenting you!

JUL. You mistake the cause of my uneasiness. Something *has* flurried me a little. — Nothing that you can guess at. — (*Aside.*) I would not ac- 170 cuse Faulkland to a sister!

LYD. Ah! whatever vexations you may have, I can assure you mine surpass them. — You know who Beverley proves to be?

JUL. I will now own to you, Lydia, that Mr. 175 Faulkland had before informed me of the whole affair. Had young Absolute been the person you took

---

76] O1 *O Julia.*   87] O1 *expiate*: O3 misprints *expatiate.*

him for, I should not have accepted your confidence
on the subject without a serious endeavor to counteract your caprice.   180

LYD. So, then, I see I have been deceived by everyone! — But I don't care — I'll never have him.

JUL. Nay, Lydia ——

LYD. Why, is it not provoking? when I thought
we were coming to the prettiest distress imagi-   185
nable, to find myself made a mere Smithfield[1] bargain of at last! — There had I projected one of the
most sentimental elopements! — so becoming a disguise! — so amiable a ladder of ropes! — Conscious
moon — four horses — Scotch parson — with   190
such surprise to Mrs. Malaprop — and such paragraphs in the newspapers! — O, I shall die with
disappointment!

JUL. I don't wonder at it!

LYD. Now — sad reverse! — what have I   195
to expect, but, after a deal of flimsy preparation,
with a bishop's license, and my aunt's blessing, to go
simpering up to the altar; or perhaps be cried three
times in a country-church, and have an unmannerly
fat clerk ask the consent of every butcher in   200
the parish to join John Absolute and Lydia Languish,
spinster! O, that I should live to hear myself called
spinster!

JUL. Melancholy, indeed!

LYD. How mortifying to remember the dear   205
delicious shifts I used to be put to, to gain half a
minute's conversation with this fellow! — How often
have I stole forth in the coldest night in January,
and found him in the garden, stuck like a dripping
statue! — There would he kneel to me in the   210
snow, and sneeze and cough so pathetically! he
shivering with cold, and I with apprehension! and
while the freezing blast numbed our joints, how
warmly would he press me to pity his flame, and
glow with mutual ardor! — Ah, Julia, that was   215
something like being in love!

JUL. If I were in spirits, Lydia, I should chide you
only by laughing heartily at you: but it suits more
the situation of my mind, at present, earnestly to
entreat you not to let a man, who loves you   220
with sincerity, suffer that unhappiness from your
caprice, which I know too well caprice can inflict.

LYD. O Lud! what has brought my aunt here?

Enter MRS. MALAPROP, FAG, *and* DAVID.

MRS. MAL. So! so! here's fine work! — here's fine
suicide, paracide, and simulation going on in   225
the fields! and Sir Anthony not to be found to prevent the antistrophe!

JUL. For heaven's sake, madam, what's the meaning of this?

MRS. MAL. That gentleman can tell you —   230
'twas he enveloped the affair to me.

LYD. (*to* FAG). Do, sir, will you, inform us.

FAG. Ma'am, I should hold myself very deficient
in every requisite that forms the man of breeding if
I delayed a moment to give all the information   235
in my power to a lady so deeply interested in the
affair as you are.

LYD. But quick! quick, sir!

FAG. True, ma'am, as you say, one should be
quick in divulging matters of this nature; for   240
should we be tedious, perhaps while we are flourishing on the subject, two or three lives may be lost!

LYD. O patience! — Do, ma'am, for heaven's sake!
tell us what is the matter!

MRS. MAL. Why, murder's the matter!   245
slaughter's the matter! killing's the matter! — but
he can tell you the perpendiculars.

LYD. Then, prithee, sir, be brief.

FAG. Why then, ma'am — as to murder — I cannot take upon me to say — and as to slaughter,   250
or man-slaughter, that will be as the jury finds it.

LYD. But who, sir — who are engaged in this?

FAG. Faith, ma'am, one is a young gentleman
whom I should be very sorry anything was to happen
to — a very pretty behaved gentleman! —   255
We have lived much together, and always on terms.

LYD. But who is this? who! who! who!

FAG. My master, ma'am — my master — I
speak of my master.

LYD. Heavens! What, Captain Absolute!   260

MRS. MAL. O, to be sure, you are frightened now!

JUL. But who are with him, sir?

FAG. As to the rest, ma'am, this gentleman can
inform you better than I.

JUL. (*to* DAVID). Do speak, friend.   265

DAV. Look'ee, my lady — by the Mass! there's
mischief going on. — Folks don't use to meet for
amusement with fire-arms, fire-locks, fire-engines,
fire-screens, fire-office, and the devil knows what
other crackers beside! — This, my lady, I say,   270
has an angry favor.

JUL. But who is there beside Captain Absolute,
friend?

DAV. My poor master — under favor, for mentioning him first. — You know me, my lady   275
— I am David — and my master, of course, is, or
was, Squire Acres. — Then comes Squire Faulkland.

JUL. Do, ma'am, let us instantly endeavor to
prevent mischief.

MRS. MAL. O fie — it would be very inele-   280
gant in us: — we should only participate things.

DAV. Ah! do, Mrs. Aunt, save a few lives. —
They are desperately given, believe me. — Above
all, there is that bloodthirsty Philistine, Sir Lucius
O'Trigger.   285

MRS. MAL. Sir Lucius O'Trigger! — O mercy! have they drawn poor little dear Sir Lucius into the scrape? — Why, how you stand, girl! you have no more feeling than one of the Derbyshire putre-factions! [1]   290

LYD. What are we to do, madam?

MRS. MAL. Why, fly with the utmost felicity, to be sure, to prevent mischief. — Here, friend — you can show us the place?

FAG. If you please, ma'am, I will conduct   295 you. — David, do you look for Sir Anthony.
                                        Exit DAVID.

MRS. MAL. Come, girls! — this gentleman will exhort us. — Come, sir, you're our envoy — lead the way, and we'll precede.

FAG. Not a step before the ladies for the   300 world!

MRS. MAL. You're sure you know the spot?

FAG. I think I can find it, ma'am; and one good thing is we shall hear the report of the pistols as we draw near, so we can't well miss them: never   305 fear, ma'am, never fear.   *Exeunt, he talking.*

SCENE II

South Parade.

Enter ABSOLUTE, *putting his sword under his great-coat.*

ABS. A sword seen in the streets of Bath [2] would raise as great an alarm as a mad-dog. How provok-ing this is in Faulkland! — never punctual! I shall be obliged to go without him at last. — O, the devil! here's Sir Anthony! —— How shall I escape him?   5
(*Muffles up his face, and takes a circle to go off.*)

Enter SIR ANTHONY.

SIR ANTH. How one may be deceived at a little distance! Only that I see he don't know me, I could have sworn that was Jack! — Hey! — 'Gad's life! it is. — Why, Jack! — what are you afraid of? — hey! — sure I'm right. — Why, Jack! — Jack   10 Absolute!   (*Goes up to him.*)

ABS. Really, sir, you have the advantage of me: — I don't remember ever to have had the honor —— my name is Saunderson, at your service.

SIR ANTH. Sir, I beg your pardon — I took   15 you — hey! — why, z—ds! it is —— stay —— (*Looks up to his face.*) — So, so — your humble servant, Mr. Saunderson! — Why, you scoundrel, what tricks are you after now?

ABS. O! a joke, sir, a joke! — I came here on   20 purpose to look for you, sir.

SIR ANTH. You did! Well, I am glad you were so

---

[1] Petrifactions.
[2] Beau Nash had enforced stringent laws against duelling.

lucky: — but what are you muffled up so for? — what's this for? — hey?

ABS. 'Tis cool, sir; isn't it? — rather chilly,   25 somehow: — but I shall be late — I have a particu-lar engagement.

SIR ANTH. Stay. — Why, I thought you were looking for me? — Pray, Jack, where is't you are going?   30

ABS. Going, sir!

SIR ANTH. Aye — where are you going?

ABS. Where am I going?

SIR ANTH. You unmannerly puppy!

ABS. I was going, sir, to — to — to — to   35 Lydia — sir, to Lydia — to make matters up if I could; — and I was looking for you, sir, to — to ——

SIR ANTH. To go with you, I suppose. — Well, come along.

ABS. O! z—ds! no, sir, not for the world! —   40 I wished to meet with you, sir, — to — to — to —— You find it cool, I'm sure, sir — you'd better not stay out.

SIR ANTH. Cool! — not at all. — Well, Jack — and what will you say to Lydia?   45

ABS. O, sir, beg her pardon, humor her — promise and vow: — but I detain you, sir — consider the cold air on your gout.

SIR ANTH. O, not at all! — not at all! — I'm in no hurry. — Ah! Jack, you youngsters, when   50 once you are wounded here — (*Putting his hand to* ABSOLUTE'S *breast.*) Hey! what the deuce have you got here?

ABS. Nothing, sir — nothing.

SIR ANTH. What's this? — here's something   55 d—d hard!

ABS. O, trinkets, sir! trinkets — a bauble for Lydia!

SIR ANTH. Nay, let me see your taste. (*Pulls his coat open, the sword falls.*) Trinkets! — a   60 bauble for Lydia! — z—ds! sirrah, you are not go-ing to cut her throat, are you?

ABS. Ha! ha! ha! — I thought it would divert you, sir; though I didn't mean to tell you till afterwards.

SIR ANTH. You didn't? — Yes, this is a very   65 diverting trinket, truly!

ABS. Sir, I'll explain to you. — You know, sir, Lydia is romantic — dev'lish romantic, and very absurd of course. — Now, sir, I intend, if she refuses to forgive me — to unsheathe this sword —   70 and swear — I'll fall upon its point, and expire at her feet!

SIR ANTH. Fall upon a fiddle-stick's end! — why, I suppose it is the very thing that would please her. — Get along, you fool. —   75

ABS. Well, sir, you shall hear of my success — you shall hear. — 'O Lydia! — forgive me, or this pointed steel' — says I.

SIR ANTH. 'O, booby! stab away and welcome' — says she. — Get along! — and d—n your 80 trinkets!   *Exit* ABSOLUTE.

Enter DAVID, *running.*

DAV. Stop him! Stop him! Murder! Thief! Fire! — Stop fire! Stop fire! — O! Sir Anthony — call! call! bid 'em stop! Murder! Fire!

SIR ANTH. Fire! Murder! Where?   85

DAV. Oons! he's out of sight! and I'm out of breath, for my part! O, Sir Anthony, why didn't you stop him? why didn't you stop him?

SIR ANTH. Z—ds! the fellow's mad! — Stop whom? Stop Jack?   90

DAV. Aye, the Captain, Sir! — there's murder and slaughter —

SIR ANTH. Murder!

DAV. Aye, please you, Sir Anthony, there's all kinds of murder, all sorts of slaughter to be 95 seen in the fields: there's fighting going on, sir — bloody sword-and-gun fighting!

SIR ANTH. Who are going to fight, dunce?

DAV. Everybody that I know of, Sir Anthony: — everybody is going to fight; my poor master, 100 Sir Lucius O'Trigger, your son, the Captain —

SIR ANTH. O, the dog! — I see his tricks. — Do you know the place?

DAV. King's-Mead-Fields.

SIR ANTH. You know the way?   105

DAV. Not an inch; — but I'll call the mayor — aldermen — constables — church-wardens — and beadles — we can't be too many to part them.

SIR ANTH. Come along — give me your shoulder! we'll get assistance as we go. — The lying vil- 110 lain! — Well, I shall be in such a frenzy! — So — this was the history of his trinkets! I'll bauble him!   *Exeunt.*

SCENE III

King's-Mead-Fields.

SIR LUCIUS *and* ACRES, *with pistols.*

ACRES. By my valor! then, Sir Lucius, forty yards is a good distance. — Odds levels and aims! — I say it is a good distance.

SIR LUC. Is it for muskets or small field-pieces? Upon my conscience, Mr. Acres, you must leave 5 those things to me. — Stay now — I'll show you. — (*Measures paces along the stage.*) There now, that is a very pretty distance — a pretty gentleman's distance.

ACRES. Z—ds! we might as well fight in a 10 sentry-box! — I tell you, Sir Lucius, the farther he is off, the cooler I shall take my aim.

SIR LUC. Faith! then I suppose you would aim at him best of all if he was out of sight!

ACRES. No, Sir Lucius — but I should think 15 forty, or eight and thirty yards —

SIR LUC. Pho! pho! nonsense! Three or four feet between the mouths of your pistols is as good as a mile.

ACRES. Odds bullets, no! — By my valor! 20 there is no merit in killing him so near: — do, my dear Sir Lucius, let me bring him down at a long shot: — a long shot, Sir Lucius, if you love me!

SIR LUC. Well — the gentleman's friend and I must settle that. — But tell me now, Mr. Acres, 25 in case of an accident, is there any little will or commission I could execute for you?

ACRES. I am much obliged to you, Sir Lucius — but I don't understand —

SIR LUC. Why, you may think there's no be- 30 ing shot at without a little risk — and if an unlucky bullet should carry a *quietus* with it — I say it will be no time then to be bothering you about family matters.

ACRES. A *quietus!*   35

SIR LUC. For instance, now — if that should be the case — would you choose to be pickled and sent home? — or would it be the same to you to lie here in the Abbey? — I'm told there is very snug lying in the Abbey.   40

ACRES. Pickled! — Snug lying in the Abbey! — Odds tremors! Sir Lucius, don't talk so!

SIR LUC. I suppose, Mr. Acres, you never were engaged in an affair of this kind before?

ACRES. No, Sir Lucius, never before.   45

SIR LUC. Ah! that's a pity! — there's nothing like being used to a thing. — Pray now, how would you receive the gentleman's shot?

ACRES. Odds files! — I've practised that. — There, Sir Lucius — there (*puts himself in an* 50 *attitude*) — a side-front, hey? — Odd! I'll make myself small enough: — I'll stand edge-ways.

SIR LUC. Now — you're quite out — for if you stand so when I take my aim — (*Levelling at him.*)

ACRES. Z—ds! Sir Lucius — are you sure it is 55 not cocked?

SIR LUC. Never fear.

ACRES. But — but — you don't know — it may go off of its own head!

SIR LUC. Pho! be easy. — Well, now if I hit 60 you in the body, my bullet has a double chance — for if it misses a vital part on your right side — 'twill be very hard if it don't succeed on the left!

ACRES. A vital part! «O, my poor vitals!»

SIR LUC. But, there — fix yourself so. — 65 (*Placing him.*) Let him see the broad side of your full front — there — now a ball or two may pass clean through your body, and never do any harm at all.

ACRES. Clean through me! — a ball or two clean through me!   70

SIR LUC. Aye — may they — and it is much the genteelest attitude into the bargain.

ACRES. Look'ee! Sir Lucius — I'd just as lieve be shot in an awkward posture as a genteel one — so, by my valor! I will stand edge-ways.   75

SIR LUC. (looking at his watch). Sure they don't mean to disappoint us. — Hah? — No, faith — I think I see them coming.

ACRES. Hey! — what! — coming! ——

SIR LUC. Aye. — Who are those yonder get-   80 ting over the stile?

ACRES. There are two of them indeed! — well — let them come — hey, Sir Lucius? we — we — we — we — won't run. —

SIR LUC. Run!   85

ACRES. No — I say — we won't run, by my valor!

SIR LUC. What the devil's the matter with you?

ACRES. Nothing — nothing — my dear friend — my dear Sir Lucius — but — I — I — I don't feel quite so bold, somehow — as I did.   90

SIR. LUC. O fie! — consider your honor.

ACRES. Aye — true — my honor — Do, Sir Lucius, edge in a word or two every now and then about my honor.

SIR LUC. (looking). Well, here they're coming.   95

ACRES. Sir Lucius — if I wa'n't with you, I should almost think I was afraid. — If my valor should leave me! — Valor will come and go.

SIR LUC. Then, pray, keep it fast while you have it.   100

ACRES. Sir Lucius — I doubt it is going — yes — my valor is certainly going! — it is sneaking off! — I feel it oozing out as it were at the palms of my hands!

SIR LUC. Your honor — your honor. — Here they are.   105

ACRES. O mercy! — now — that I were safe at Clod-Hall! or could be shot before I was aware!

Enter FAULKLAND and ABSOLUTE.

SIR LUC. Gentlemen, your most obedient — hah! — what — Captain Absolute! — So, I suppose, sir, you are come here, just like myself — to do a   110 kind office, first for your friend — then to proceed to business on your own account.

ACRES. What, Jack! — my dear Jack! — my dear friend!

ABS. Hark'ee, Bob, Beverley's at hand.   115

SIR LUC. Well, Mr. Acres — I don't blame your saluting the gentleman civilly. — So, Mr. Beverley (to FAULKLAND), if you'll choose your weapons, the Captain and I will measure the ground.

FAULK. My weapons, sir!   120

ACRES. Odds life! Sir Lucius, I'm not going to fight Mr. Faulkland; these are my particular friends.

SIR LUC. What, sir, did not you come here to fight Mr. Acres?

FAULK. Not I, upon my word, sir.   125

SIR LUC. Well, now, that's mighty provoking! But I hope, Mr. Faulkland, as there are three of us come on purpose for the game — you won't be so cantankerous as to spoil the party by sitting out.

ABS. O pray, Faulkland, fight to oblige Sir   130 Lucius.

FAULK. Nay, if Mr. Acres is so bent on the matter ——

ACRES. No, no, Mr. Faulkland — I'll bear my disappointment like a Christian. — Look'ee,   135 Sir Lucius, there's no occasion at all for me to fight; and if it is the same to you, I'd as lieve let it alone.

SIR LUC. Observe me, Mr. Acres — I must not be trifled with. You have certainly challenged somebody — and you came here to fight him. —   140 Now, if that gentleman is willing to represent him — I can't see, for my soul, why it isn't just the same thing.

ACRES. Why no, Sir Lucius — I tell you, 'tis one Beverley I've challenged — a fellow, you   145 see, that dare not show his face! If he were here, I'd make him give up his pretensions directly! ——

ABS. Hold, Bob — let me set you right. — There is no such man as Beverley in the case. — The person who assumed that name is before you;   150 and as his pretensions are the same in both characters, he is ready to support them in whatever way you please.

SIR LUC. Well, this is lucky! — Now you have an opportunity ——   155

ACRES. What, quarrel with my dear friend Jack Absolute? — not if he were fifty Beverleys! Z—ds! Sir Lucius, you would not have me be so unnatural.

SIR LUC. Upon my conscience, Mr. Acres, your valor has oozed away with a vengeance!   160

ACRES. Not in the least! Odds backs and abettors! I'll be your second with all my heart — and if you should get a quietus, you may command me entirely. I'll get you a snug lying in the Abbey here; or pickle you, and send you over to Blunder-   165 buss-hall, or anything of the kind, with the greatest pleasure.

SIR LUC. Pho! pho! you are little better than a coward.

ACRES. Mind, gentlemen, he calls me a   170 coward; coward was the word, by my valor!

SIR LUC. Well, sir?

ACRES. Look'ee, Sir Lucius, 'tisn't that I mind the word coward — Coward may be said in joke. — But if you had called me a poltroon, odds   175 daggers and balls! ——

SIR LUC. Well, sir?

ACRES. —— I should have thought you a very ill-bred man.

SIR LUC. Pho! you are beneath my notice.   180

93] O1 hedge.   144] O1 Z—ds, Sir Lucius.   166] O1 any of.

ABS. Nay, Sir Lucius, you can't have a better second than my friend Acres. — He is a most *determined dog* — called in the country, *Fighting Bob.* — He generally *kills a man a week*; don't you, Bob?

ACRES. Aye — at home!   185

SIR LUC. Well then, Captain, 'tis we must begin. — So come out, my little counsellor (*draws his sword*), and ask the gentleman, whether he will resign the lady without forcing you to proceed against him.   190

ABS. Come on then, sir; (*draws*) since you won't let it be an amicable suit, here's *my reply.*

Enter SIR ANTHONY, DAVID, *and the Women.*

DAV. Knock 'em all down, sweet Sir Anthony; knock down my master in particular — and bind his hands over to their good behavior!   195

SIR ANTH. Put up, Jack, put up, or I shall be in a frenzy. — How came you in a duel, sir?

ABS. Faith, sir, that gentleman can tell you better than I; 'twas he called on me, and you know, sir, I serve his Majesty.   200

SIR ANTH. Here's a pretty fellow! I catch him going to cut a man's throat, and he tells me he serves his Majesty! — Zounds! sirrah, then how durst you draw the King's sword against one of his subjects?

ABS. Sir, I tell you! That gentleman called   205 me out, without explaining his reasons.

SIR ANTH. Gad! sir, how came you to call my son out, without explaining your reasons?

SIR LUC. Your son, sir, insulted me in a manner which my honor could not brook.   210

SIR ANTH. Zounds! Jack, how durst you insult the gentleman in a manner which his honor could not brook?

MRS. MAL. Come, come, let's have no honor before ladies — Captain Absolute, come here —   215 How could you intimidate us so? — Here's Lydia has been terrified to death for you.

ABS. For fear I should be killed, or escape, ma'am?

MRS. MAL. Nay, no delusions to the past — Lydia is convinced; — speak, child.   220

SIR LUC. With your leave, ma'am, I must put in a word here — I believe I could interpret the young lady's silence — Now mark ——

LYD. What is it you mean, sir?

SIR LUC. Come, come, Delia, we must be   225 serious now — this is no time for trifling.

LYD. 'Tis true, sir; and your reproof bids me offer this gentleman my hand, and solicit the return of his affections.

ABS. O! my little angel, say you so? — Sir   230 Lucius — I perceive there must be some mistake here. — With regard to the affront which you affirm I have given you — I can only say that it could not have been intentional. — And as you must be

convinced that I should not fear to support a   235 real injury — you shall now see that I am not ashamed to atone for an inadvertency. — I ask your pardon. — But for this lady, while honored with her approbation, I will support my claim against any man whatever.   240

SIR ANTH. Well said, Jack! and I'll stand by you, my boy.

ACRES. Mind, I give up all my claim — I make no pretensions to anything in the world — and if I can't get a wife without fighting for her, by my   245 valor! I'll live a bachelor.

SIR LUC. Captain, give me your hand — an affront handsomely acknowledged becomes an obligation — and as for the lady — if she chooses to deny her own handwriting here ——   250
(*Takes out letters.*)

MRS. MAL. O, he will dissolve my mystery! — Sir Lucius, perhaps there's some mistake — perhaps, I can illuminate ——

SIR LUC. Pray, old gentlewoman, don't interfere where you have no business. — Miss Languish,   255 are you my Delia, or not?

LYD. Indeed, Sir Lucius, I am not.
(LYDIA *and* ABSOLUTE *walk aside.*)

MRS. MAL. Sir Lucius O'Trigger — ungrateful as you are — I own the soft impeachment — pardon my blushes, I am Delia.   260

SIR LUC. You Delia! — pho! pho! be easy.

MRS. MAL. Why, thou barbarous Vandyke! — those letters are mine. — When you are more sensible of my benignity — perhaps I may be brought to encourage your addresses.   265

SIR LUC. Mrs. Malaprop, I am extremely sensible of your condescension; and whether you or Lucy have put this trick upon me, I am equally beholden to you. — And to show you I'm not ungrateful — Captain Absolute! since you have taken that   270 lady from me, I'll give you my Delia into the bargain.

ABS. I am much obliged to you, Sir Lucius; but here's our friend, Fighting Bob, unprovided for.

SIR LUC. Hah! little Valor — here, will you make your fortune?   275

ACRES. Odds wrinkles! No. — But give me your hand, Sir Lucius; forget and forgive; but if ever I give you a chance of *pickling* me again, say Bob Acres is a dunce, that's all.

SIR ANTH. Come, Mrs. Malaprop, don't be   280 cast down — you are in your bloom yet.

MRS. MAL. O Sir Anthony! — men are all barbarians —— (*All retire but* JULIA *and* FAULKLAND.)

JUL. [*aside*]. He seems dejected and unhappy — not sullen. — There was some foundation,   285 however, for the tale he told me. — O woman! how true should be your judgment, when your resolution is so weak!

---

250 s.d.] O1 *Taking.*   251] O1 *desolve*; O3 *disolve*; O5O6 *dissolve.*   276] O1 *us.*

FAULK. Julia! — how can I sue for what I so little deserve? I dare not presume — yet 290 Hope is the child of Penitence.

JUL. Oh! Faulkland, you have not been more faulty in your unkind treatment of me than I am now in wanting inclination to resent it. As my heart honestly bids me place my weakness to the 295 account of love, I should be ungenerous not to admit the same plea for yours.

FAULK. Now I shall be blest indeed!

(SIR ANTHONY *comes forward.*)

SIR ANTH. What's going on here? — So you have been quarrelling too, I warrant. — Come, 300 Julia, I never interfered before; but let me have a hand in the matter at last. — All the faults I have ever seen in my friend Faulkland seemed to proceed from what he calls the *delicacy* and *warmth* of his affection for you. — There, marry him directly, 305 Julia; you'll find he'll mend surprisingly!

(*The rest come forward.*)

SIR LUC. Come now, I hope there is no dissatisfied person but what is content; for as I have been disappointed myself, it will be very hard if I have not the satisfaction of seeing other people succeed 310 better ——

ACRES. You are right, Sir Lucius. — So, Jack, I wish you joy — Mr. Faulkland the same. — Ladies, — come now, to show you I'm neither vexed nor angry, odds tabors and pipes! I'll order the 315 fiddles in half an hour to the New Rooms — and I insist on your all meeting me there.

SIR ANTH. Gad! sir, I like your spirit; and at night we single lads will drink a health to the young couples, and a husband to Mrs. Malaprop.   320

FAULK. Our partners are stolen from us, Jack — I hope to be congratulated by each other — *yours* for having checked in time the errors of an ill-directed imagination, which might have betrayed an innocent heart; and *mine*, for having, by 325 her gentleness and candor, reformed the unhappy temper of one who by it made wretched whom he loved most, and tortured the heart he ought to have adored.

ABS. Well, [Faulkland,] we have both tasted 330 the bitters, as well as the sweets, of love — with this difference only, that *you* always prepared the bitter cup for yourself, while *I* ——

LYD. Was always obliged to *me* for it, hey, Mr. Modesty? —— But come, no more of that — 335 our happiness is now as unalloyed as general.

JUL. Then let us study to preserve it so; and while Hope pictures to us a flattering scene of future Bliss, let us deny its pencil those colors which are too bright to be lasting. — When Hearts deserving 340 Happiness would unite their fortunes, Virtue would crown them with an unfading garland of modest, hurtless flowers; but ill-judging Passion will force the gaudier Rose into the wreath, whose thorn offends them, when its leaves are dropt!   345

Exeunt omnes.

317] O1 *you.*   322, 325] O1 does not italicize *yours* and *mine.*   330] O1O3 *Jack;* Larpent MS. *Faulkland* (cf. also II. 1).
336] O1O3 *unallay'd.*   341] O1 *fortune.*

EPILOGUE

By the Author

Spoken by Mrs. Bulkley

Ladies, for *you* — I heard our poet say —
He'd try to coax some *moral* from his play:
'One moral's plain' — cried I — 'without more fuss;
'Man's social happiness all rests on us —
'Through all the drama — whether damned or not —   5
'*Love* gilds the *scene*, and *women* guide the *plot*.
'From ev'ry rank — obedience is our due —
'D'ye doubt? — The world's great stage shall prove it true.'

 The cit[1] — well skilled to shun domestic strife —
Will sup abroad; — but first — he'll ask his *wife:*   10
John Trot, his friend — for once, will do the same,
But then — he'll just '*step home to tell my dame.*' —

 The *surly 'Squire* — at noon resolves to rule,
And half the day — zounds! madam is a fool!
Convinced at night — the vanquished victor says,   15
'Ah! Kate! *you women have such coaxing ways!*' —

 The *jolly toper* chides each tardy blade, —
Till reeling Bacchus calls on love for aid:
Then with each toast, he sees fair bumpers swim,
And kisses Chloe on the sparkling brim!   20

 Nay, I have heard that statesmen — great and wise —
Will *sometimes* counsel with a lady's eyes;
The servile suitors — watch her various face, ⎫
She smiles preferment — or she frowns disgrace, ⎬
Curtsies a pension here — there nods a place. ⎭ 25

 Nor with less awe, in scenes of humbler life,
Is *viewed* the *mistress*, or is *heard* the *wife*.
The poorest peasant of the poorest soil,
The child of poverty, and heir to toil —
Early from radiant love's impartial light,   30
Steals one small spark, to cheer his world of night:
Dear spark! — that oft through winter's chilling woes,
Is all the warmth his little cottage knows!

 The wand'ring *tar* — who not for *years* has pressed
The widowed partner of his *day* of rest —   35
On the cold deck — far from her arms removed —
Still hums the ditty which his Susan loved:
And while around the cadence rude is blown,
The boatswain whistles in a softer tone.

---

[1] Citizen.

5] O1 *d—n'd*.

The *soldier*, fairly proud of wounds and toil,   40
Pants for the *triumph* of his Nancy's smile;
But ere the battle, should he list' her cries,
The lover trembles — and the hero dies!
That heart, by war and honor steeled to fear,
Droops on a sigh, and sickens at a tear!   45

But ye more cautious — ye nice judging few,
Who give to beauty only beauty's due,
Though friends to love — *ye* view with deep regret
Our conquests marred — and triumphs incomplete,
'Till polished Wit more lasting charms disclose,   50
And Judgment fix the darts which Beauty throws!
— In female breasts did Sense and Merit rule,
The lover's mind would ask no other school;
Shamed into sense — the scholars of our eyes,
Our Beaux from *gallantry* would soon be wise;   55
Would gladly light, their homage to improve,
The Lamp of Knowledge at the Torch of Love!

49] Or *our triumphs.*

The School for Scandal

BY RICHARD BRINSLEY SHERIDAN

The

To Mrs Crewe
from the Author

School for Scandal

A

Comedy

R B Sheridan

TITLE-PAGE OF THE 'MS. COPY' PRESENTED 'TO MRS. CREWE'
The author's inscription and his textual revisions are in Sheridan's handwriting.
Riggs Memorial Library, Georgetown University.

A PORTRAIT;

Addressed to Mrs. Crewe, with the Comedy of The School for Scandal [1]

By R. B. SHERIDAN, Esq.

Tell me, ye prim adepts in Scandal's school,
Who rail by precept, and detract by rule,
Lives there no character, so tried, so known,
So decked with grace, and so unlike your own,
That even you assist her fame to raise,   5
Approve by envy, and by silence praise!
Attend! — a model shall attract your view —
Daughters of calumny, I summon you!
You shall decide if this a portrait prove,
Or fond creation of the Muse and Love.   10
Attend, ye virgin critics, shrewd and sage,
Ye matron censors of this childish age,
Whose peering eye and wrinkled front declare
A fixed antipathy to young and fair;
By cunning, cautious; or by nature, cold,   15
In maiden madness, virulently bold!
Attend, ye skilled to coin the precious tale,
Creating proof, where innuendos fail!
Whose practised memories, cruelly exact,
Omit no circumstance, except the fact! —   20
Attend, all ye who boast, — or old or young, —
The living libel of a slanderous tongue!
So shall my theme as far contrasted be,
As saints by fiends or hymns by calumny.
Come, gentle Amoret (for 'neath that name [2]   25
In worthier verse is sung thy beauty's fame),
Come — for but thee who seeks the Muse? and while
Celestial blushes check thy conscious smile,
With timid grace and hesitating eye,
The perfect model which I boast supply: —   30
Vain Muse! couldst thou the humblest sketch create
Of her, or slightest charm couldst imitate —
Could thy blest strain in kindred colors trace
The faintest wonder of her form and face —
Poets would study the immortal line,   35
And Reynolds [3] own *his* art subdued by thine;
That art, which well might added lustre give
To nature's best and heaven's superlative:
On Granby's [4] cheek might bid new glories rise,
Or point a purer beam from Devon's [5] eyes!   40

[1] Sheridan's dedicatory verses to Mrs. Crewe, according to his own subsequent account, 'were sent with a MS. copy of the play finely bound' [the Crewe MS. copy, with the author's handwritten corrections]. They early circulated in manuscript, as Horace Walpole attests in a letter of October 8, 1777, but his hope that 'they will not long retain their MS.-hood' proved idle. An undated letter of Sheridan, written late in life to his second wife, was prompted by their unauthorized appearance, 'incorrectly printed,' in a 'newspaper professing to *publish* for the *first time* some verses of mine to Mrs. (now Lady) Crewe.' After Sheridan's death, they were included in the Murray (1821) edition of Sheridan's *Works* (II, 3–7) in the form thereafter habitually accepted.

[2] Fox had extolled Mrs. Crewe as *Amoret* in verses printed at Walpole's Strawberry Hill Press in 1775.

[3] Sir Joshua Reynolds (1723–1792) had portrayed Mrs. Sheridan as St. Cecilia in 1775.

[4] Mary Isabella, Marchioness of Granby, later Duchess of Rutland.   [5] Georgiana, Duchess of Devonshire.

Hard is the task to shape that beauty's praise,
Whose judgment scorns the homage flattery pays?
But praising Amoret we cannot err,
No tongue o'ervalues heaven, or flatters her!
Yet she by fate's perverseness — she alone   45
Would doubt our truth, nor deem such praise her own!
Adorning fashion, unadorned by dress,
Simple from taste, and not from carelessness;
Discreet in gesture, in deportment mild,
Not stiff with prudence, nor uncouthly wild: 50
No state has Amoret; no studied mien;
She frowns no *goddess*, and she moves no *queen*,
The softer charm that in her manner lies
Is framed to captivate, yet not surprise;
It justly suits th' expression of her face, —   55
'Tis less than dignity, and more than grace!
On her pure cheek the native hue is such,
That, formed by heaven to be admired so much,
The hand divine, with a less partial care,
Might well have fixed a fainter crimson there,   60
And bade the gentle inmate of her breast —
Inshrinèd Modesty — supply the rest.
But who the peril of her lips shall paint?
Strip them of smiles — still, still all words are faint!
But moving Love himself appears to teach   65
Their action, though denied to rule her speech;
And thou who seest her speak, and dost not hear,
Mourn not her distant accents 'scape thine ear;
Viewing those lips, thou still may'st make pretense
To judge of what she says, and swear 'tis sense: 70
Clothed with such grace, with such expression fraught,
They move in meaning, and they pause in thought!
But dost thou farther watch, with charmed surprise,
The mild irresolution of her eyes,
Curious to mark how frequent they repose,   75
In brief eclipse and momentary close —
Ah! seest thou not an ambushed Cupid there,
Too tim'rous of his charge, with jealous care
Veils and unveils those beams of heav'nly light,
Too full, too fatal else, for mortal sight?   80
Nor yet, such pleasing vengeance fond to meet,
In pard'ning dimples hope a safe retreat.
What though her peaceful breast should ne'er allow
Subduing frowns to arm her altered brow,
By Love, I swear, and by his gentle wiles,   85
More fatal still the mercy of her smiles!
Thus lovely, thus adorned, possessing all
Of bright or fair that can to woman fall,
The height of vanity might well be thought
Prerogative in her, and Nature's fault.   90
Yet gentle Amoret, in mind supreme
As well as charms, rejects the vainer theme;
And, half mistrustful of her beauty's store,
She barbs with wit those darts too keen before: —
Read in all knowledge that her sex should reach,   95
Though Greville,[1] or the Muse, should deign to teach,

[1] Mrs. Fulke Greville, mother of Mrs. Crewe. Sheridan dedicated *The Critic* 'To Mrs. Greville' (see p. 880).

Fond to improve, nor tim'rous to discern
How far it is a woman's grace to learn;
In Millar's [1] dialect she would not prove
Apollo's priestess, but Apollo's love,   100
Graced by those signs which truth delights to own,
The timid blush, and mild submitted tone:
Whate'er she says, though sense appear throughout,
Displays the tender hue of female doubt;
Decked with that charm, how lovely wit appears,   105
How graceful *science*, when that robe she wears!
Such too her talents, and her bent of mind,
As speak a sprightly heart by thought refined:
A taste for mirth, by contemplation schooled,
A turn for ridicule, by candor ruled,   110
A scorn of folly, which she tries to hide;
An awe of talent, which she owns with pride!
   Peace, idle Muse! no more thy strain prolong,
But yield a theme, thy warmest praises wrong;
Just to her merit, though thou canst not raise   115
Thy feeble verse, behold th' acknowledged praise
Has spread conviction through the envious train,
And cast a fatal gloom o'er Scandal's reign!
And lo! each pallid hag, with blistered tongue,
Mutters assent to all thy zeal has sung —   120
Owns all the colors just — the outline true:
Thee my inspirer, and my *model* — CREWE!

[1] Lady Miller (Millar), an eighteenth-century Mrs. Leo Hunter, whose literary 'assemblies' near Bath were notorious.

PROLOGUE

SPOKEN BY MR. KING [1]

WRITTEN BY D. GARRICK, ESQ.*

A School for Scandal! tell me, I beseech you,
Needs there a school this modish art to teach you?
No need of lessons now, the knowing think —
We might as well be taught to eat and drink.
Caused by a dearth of scandal, should the vapors   5
Distress our fair ones — let 'em read the papers;
Their pow'rful mixtures such disorders hit;
Crave what they will, there's *quantum sufficit*.[2]
   'Lord!' cries my Lady Wormwood (who loves tattle,
And puts much salt and pepper in her prattle),   10
Just ris'n at noon, all night at cards when threshing
Strong tea and scandal — 'Bless me, how refreshing!
Give me the papers, Lisp — how bold and free! (*Sips.*)
Last night Lord L—— (sips) was caught with Lady D——
For aching heads what charming sal volatile! (*Sips.*)   15
If Mrs. B—— will still continue flirting,
We hope she'll DRAW, *or we'll* UNDRAW *the curtain.*
Fine satire, poz [3] — in public all abuse it,
But, by ourselves (*sips*), our praise we can't refuse it.
Now, Lisp, read *you* — there, at that dash and star.' [4]   20
'Yes, ma'am. — *A certain Lord had best beware,*
Who lives not twenty miles from Grosv'nor Square;
For should he Lady W—— find willing,
WORMWOOD *is bitter*' —— 'Oh! that's me! the villain!
Throw it behind the fire, and never more   25
Let that vile paper come within my door.' —
   Thus at our friends we laugh, who feel the dart;
To reach our feelings, we ourselves must smart.
Is our young bard so young, to think that he
Can stop the full spring-tide of calumny?   30
Knows he the world so little, and its trade?
Alas! the devil is sooner raised than laid.
So strong, so swift, the monster there's no gagging:
Cut Scandal's head off — still the tongue is wagging.
Proud of your smiles once lavishly bestow'd,   35
Again your young Don Quixote [5] takes the road:
To show his gratitude, he draws his pen,
And seeks this hydra, Scandal, in his den.
For your applause all perils he would through —
He'll fight — that's *write* — a cavalliero true,   40
Till every drop of blood — that's *ink* — is spilt for you.

---

[1] Thomas King, the original Sir Peter Teazle.   [2] Plenty.   [3] Positively.
[4] A frequent method of veiled reference to the names of those involved in fashionable intrigues. See the early allusion to the
Têtes-à-Têtes in the *Town and Country Magazine* (*S. for S.*, I. i.).
[5] Sheridan had first ridiculed the sentimental drama and novel in *The Rivals*.

PROLOGUE] 'Written by D. Garrick Esq!' is in Sheridan's own handwriting on the Crewe MS. copy (C).
11–12] C begins quotation-marks at *Just ris'n.*   27–41] C indents these lines.   36] C *your;* M *our.*

DRAMATIS PERSONÆ

MEN

SIR PETER TEAZLE	*Mr. King*
SIR OLIVER SURFACE	*Mr. Yates*
JOSEPH SURFACE	*Mr. Palmer*
CHARLES SURFACE	*Mr. Smith*
CRABTREE	*Mr. Parsons*
SIR BENJAMIN BACKBITE	*Mr. Dodd*
ROWLEY	*Mr. Aickin*
TRIP	*Mr. LaMash*
MOSES	*Mr. Baddeley*
SNAKE	*Mr. Packer*
CARELESS	*Mr. Farren*

and other Companions to CHARLES [SURFACE],
Servants, etc.

WOMEN

LADY TEAZLE	*Mrs. Abington*
MARIA	*Miss P. Hopkins*
LADY SNEERWELL	*Miss Sherry*
MRS. CANDOUR	*Miss Pope*

[SCENE — LONDON]

DRAMATIS PERSONÆ] The Crewe MS. is here followed both in the order of characters and in indication of actors' names. The cast is that of the original production in May, 1777. The part of Sir Toby Bumper appears neither in the *Dram. Pers.* nor in the heading of the scene (III. iii) in which he figures as one of the 'other Companions to CHARLES.' Originally, his song was given to Careless (Rae text), and later (in the Crewe MS.) provision for its transfer was made by introducing Sir Toby Bumper into the text. The rôle was early taken by Mr. Gaudry but, as here indicated, the stress was on the song and not on the nominal character-part that served the turn. Neither the Crewe MS. nor Sheridan in correcting it specified Sir Toby in the *Dram. Pers.* (For M.'s change to Sir Harry, see text, III. iii.)

THE SCHOOL FOR SCANDAL

By RICHARD BRINSLEY SHERIDAN

ACT I

SCENE I

[LADY SNEERWELL'S *house.*]

LADY SNEERWELL *at the dressing-table —*
SNAKE *drinking chocolate.*

LADY SNEER. The paragraphs, you say, Mr. Snake,
were all inserted?

SNAKE. They were, madam, and as I copied them
myself in a feigned hand, there can be no suspicion
whence they came.   5

LADY SNEER. Did you circulate the reports of
Lady *Brittle's* intrigue with Captain *Boastall?*

SNAKE. That is in as fine a train as your ladyship
could wish, — in the common course of things, I
think it must reach Mrs. *Clackit's* ears within   10
four-and-twenty hours; and then, you know, the
business is as good as done.

LADY SNEER. Why, truly, Mrs. *Clackit* has a very
pretty talent, and a great deal of industry.

SNAKE. True, madam, and has been tolerably   15
successful in her day: — to my knowledge, she has
been the cause of six matches being broken off, and
three sons being disinherited, of four forced elopements, as many close confinements, nine separate
maintenances, and two divorces; — nay, I have   20
more than once traced her causing a *Tête-à-Tête* in the
Town and Country Magazine,[1] when the parties perhaps had never seen each other's faces before in the
course of their lives.

LADY SNEER. She certainly has talents, but   25
her manner is gross.

SNAKE. 'Tis very true, — she generally designs
well, has a free tongue, and a bold invention; but her
coloring is too dark, and her outline often extravagant. She wants that *delicacy* of *hint,* and *mel-*   30
lowness of *sneer,* which distinguish your ladyship's
scandal.

LADY SNEER. Ah! you are partial, Snake.

[1] Since 1769, this magazine had published monthly sketches
of fashionable intrigues. (See N, pp. 289–290, and R, II, 14–15.)

SNAKE. Not in the least; everybody allows that
Lady *Sneerwell* can do more with a *word* or a *look*   35
than many can with the most labored detail, even
when they happen to have a little truth on their side
to support it.

LADY SNEER. Yes, my dear Snake; and I am no
hypocrite to deny the satisfaction I reap from the   40
success of my efforts. Wounded myself, in the early
part of my life, by the envenomed tongue of slander,
I confess I have since known no pleasure equal to the
reducing others to the level of my own injured
reputation.   45

SNAKE. Nothing can be more natural. But, Lady
Sneerwell, there is one affair in which you have lately
employed me, wherein, I confess, I am at a loss to
guess your motives.

LADY SNEER. I conceive you mean with re-   50
spect to my neighbor, Sir Peter Teazle, and his
family?

SNAKE. I do; here are two young men, to whom
Sir Peter has acted as a kind of guardian since their
father's death; the elder possessing the most   55
amiable character, and universally well spoken of;
the youngest, the most dissipated and extravagant
young fellow in the kingdom, without friends or character, — the former an avowed admirer of your ladyship, and apparently your favorite; the latter at-   60
tached to Maria, Sir Peter's ward, and confessedly
beloved by her. Now, on the face of these circumstances, it is utterly unaccountable to me, why you,
the widow of a city knight, with a good jointure,
should not close with the passion of a man of   65
such character and expectations as Mr. *Surface;* and
more so why you should be so uncommonly earnest
to destroy the mutual attachment subsisting between
his brother *Charles* and *Maria.*

LADY SNEER. Then, at once to unravel this   70
mystery, I must inform you that love has no share
whatever in the intercourse between Mr. *Surface*
and me.

SNAKE. No!

LADY SNEER. His real attachment is to *Maria,*   75

6] CD *reports*; SMR *report.*   8] CSD *That is*; MR *That's.*   17] D *broke* (a misprint).
18] CSD *sons being disinherited*; MR *sons disinherited.*   19] CSD *as many*; MR *and as many.*
23] CSD *faces*; MR *face.*   29] CSD *outline*; MR *outlines.*   30] CSD *hint*; MR *tint.*
31] C *distinguish*; SDMR *distinguishes.*   33] CSD *Ah! you are*; MR *You are.*
44–45] CSMR *injured reputation*; D *reputation.*
47] CSEMR *have lately*; D omits *lately.* (Moore's first emendation [E] of D restores the omitted word.)
55] CS *elder*; DMR *eldest.*   68] CSEMR *attachment subsisting*; D omits *subsisting.* (Moore's second emendation.)

or her fortune; but, finding in his brother a favored rival, he has been obliged to mask his pretensions, and profit by my assistance.

SNAKE. Yet still I am more puzzled why you should interest yourself in his success.   80

LADY SNEER. Heav'ns! how dull you are! Cannot you surmise the weakness which I hitherto, through shame, have concealed even from *you*? Must I confess that *Charles* — that libertine, that extravagant, that bankrupt in fortune and repu- 85 tation — that he it is for whom I am thus anxious and malicious, and to gain whom I would sacrifice everything?

SNAKE. Now, indeed, your conduct appears consistent; but how came you and Mr. *Surface* so 90 confidential?

LADY SNEER. For our mutual interest. I have found him out a long time since — I know him to be artful, selfish, and malicious — in short, a sentimental knave.   95

SNAKE. Yet, Sir Peter vows he has not his equal in England — and, above all, he praises him as a man of sentiment.

LADY SNEER. True; and with the assistance of his sentiment and hypocrisy he has brought him 100 [Sir Peter] entirely into his interest with regard to *Maria*.

Enter Servant.

SERV. Mr. Surface.

LADY SNEER. Show him up.   *Exit Servant.* He generally calls about this time. I don't 105 wonder at people's giving him to me for a lover.

Enter JOSEPH SURFACE.

JOS. SURF. My dear Lady Sneerwell, how do you do to-day? Mr. Snake, your most obedient.

LADY SNEER. Snake has just been arraigning me on our mutual attachment, but I have informed 110 him of our real views; you know how useful he has been to us; and, believe me, the confidence is not ill placed.

JOS. SURF. Madam, it is impossible for me to suspect a man of Mr. *Snake's* sensibility and dis- 115 cernment.

LADY SNEER. Well, well, no compliments now; —

but tell me when you saw your mistress, *Maria* — or, what is more material to me, your brother.

JOS. SURF. I have not seen either since I left 120 you; but I can inform you that they never meet. Some of your stories have taken a good effect on Maria.

LADY SNEER. Ah, my dear Snake! the merit of this belongs to you. But do your brother's dis- 125 tresses increase?

JOS. SURF. Every hour; — I am told he has had another execution in the house yesterday; in short, his dissipation and extravagance exceed any thing I ever heard of.   130

LADY SNEER. Poor Charles!

JOS. SURF. True, madam; — notwithstanding his vices, one can't help feeling for him. — Aye, poor Charles! I'm sure I wish it was in *my* power to be of any essential service to him. — For the man 135 who does not share in the distresses of a brother, even though merited by his own misconduct, de- serves ——

LADY SNEER. O lud! you are going to be moral, and forget that you are among friends.   140

JOS. SURF. Egad, that's true! — I'll keep that sentiment till I see Sir Peter. However, it is certainly a charity to rescue Maria from such a libertine, who, if he is to be reclaimed, can be so only by a person of your ladyship's superior accomplish- 145 ments and understanding.

SNAKE. I believe, Lady Sneerwell, here's company coming, — I'll go and copy the letter I mentioned to you. — Mr. Surface, your most obedient.

Exit SNAKE.

JOS. SURF. Sir, your very devoted. — Lady 150 Sneerwell, I am very sorry you have put any further confidence in that fellow.

LADY SNEER. Why so?

JOS. SURF. I have lately detected him in frequent conference with old *Rowley*, who was formerly 155 my father's steward, and has never, you know, been a friend of mine.

LADY SNEER. And do you think he would betray us?

JOS. SURF. Nothing more likely: take my 160 word for't, Lady Sneerwell, that fellow hasn't virtue enough to be faithful even to his own villainy. — Hah! Maria!

76] CSEMR *finding in*; D *finding*.   81] CSD *Heav'ns! how dull*; MR *How dull*.   86] CSD *I am*; MR *I'm*.

95] DM add (after *knave*) *while with Sir Peter, and indeed with all his acquaintance, he passes for a* [*youthful* (M)] *miracle of prudence, good sense, and benevolence*. CSE omit; R brackets.

96] CS *Yet, Sir Peter*; D *Nay, Sir Peter*; MR *Yes; yet Sir Peter*.   100] CSD *him*; MR *Sir Peter*.

102] DM add (after *Maria*) *while poor Charles has no friend in the house, though I fear he has a powerful one in Maria's heart, against whom we must direct our schemes*. CSE omit; R brackets.

105-106] M omits *He generally . . . lover*. R brackets; CSD include.   109] CSD *arraigning*; MR *rallying*.

122] CDMR *good*; S *great*.   129] CSMR *any thing*; D *every thing*.   130] CSD *I ever*; MR *I have ever*.

133] CSM *can't*; DR *cannot*.   133] CSDR *Aye*; M omits *Aye*.   134] R adds *indeed* after *Charles*.

134] CMR *I'm*; SD *I am*.   134] CSD *was*; MR *were*.   144-145] CSEMR *a person*; D *one*.

151] CSD *further*; MR *farther*.   161] CSMR *for't*; D *for it*.   161] CSMR *hasn't*; D *has not*.

162] CSEMR *faithful*; D *faithful or constant*.   163] CD *Hah* (S *ha*); MR *Ah*.

Enter MARIA.

LADY SNEER. Maria, my dear, how do you do? — What's the matter?   165

MARIA. Oh! there is that disagreeable lover of mine, Sir *Benjamin Backbite*, has just called at my guardian's, with his odious uncle, *Crabtree*; so I slipped out, and run hither to avoid them.

LADY SNEER. Is that all?   170

JOS. SURF. If my brother *Charles* had been of the party, ma'am, perhaps you would not have been so much alarmed.

LADY SNEER. Nay, now you are severe; for I dare swear the truth of the matter is, Maria heard   175 *you* were here; — but, my dear, what has Sir Benjamin done, that you should avoid him so?

MARIA. Oh, he has done nothing — but 'tis for what he has said, — his conversation is a perpetual libel on all his acquaintance.   180

JOS. SURF. Aye, and the worst of it is, there is no advantage in not knowing him; for he'll abuse a stranger just as soon as his best friend — and his uncle's as bad.

LADY SNEER. Nay, but we should make al-   185 lowance; Sir Benjamin is a wit and a poet.

MARIA. For my part, I own, madam, wit loses its respect with me, when I see it in company with malice. — What do you think, Mr. Surface?

JOS. SURF. Certainly, madam; to smile at the   190 jest which plants a thorn in another's breast is to become a principal in the mischief.

LADY SNEER. Pshaw! there's no possibility of being witty without a little ill nature: the malice of a good thing is the barb that makes it stick. —   195 What's your opinion, Mr. Surface?

JOS. SURF. To be sure, madam, that conversation, where the spirit of raillery is suppressed, will ever appear tedious and insipid.

MARIA. Well, I'll not debate how far scandal   200 may be allowable; but in a man, I am sure, it is always contemptible. — We have pride, envy, rivalship, and a thousand motives to depreciate each other; but the male slanderer must have the cowardice of a woman before he can traduce one.   205

Enter Servant.

SERV. Madam, Mrs. Candour is below, and, if your ladyship's at leisure, will leave her carriage.

LADY SNEER. Beg her to walk in. [*Exit Servant.*] Now Maria, however here is a character to your

taste; for, though Mrs. Candour is a little talk-   210 ative, everybody allows her to be the best-natured and best sort of woman.

MARIA. Yes, with a very gross affectation of good nature and benevolence, she does more mischief than the direct malice of old Crabtree.   215

JOS. SURF. I'faith 'tis very true, Lady Sneerwell; whenever I hear the current running against the characters of my friends, I never think them in such danger as when Candour undertakes their defence.

LADY SNEER. Hush! — here she is!   220

Enter MRS. CANDOUR.

MRS. CAN. My dear Lady Sneerwell, how have you been this century? — Mr. Surface, what news do you hear? — though indeed it is no matter, for I think one hears nothing else but scandal.

JOS. SURF. Just so, indeed, madam.   225

MRS. CAN. Ah, Maria! child, — what, is the whole affair off between you and Charles? His extravagance, I presume — the town talks of nothing else.

MARIA. I am very sorry, ma'am, the town   230 has so little to do.

MRS. CAN. True, true, child: but there is no stopping people's tongues. — I own I was hurt to hear it, as indeed I was to learn, from the same quarter, that your guardian, Sir Peter, and Lady Teazle have   235 not agreed lately so well as could be wished.

MARIA. 'Tis strangely impertinent for people to busy themselves so.

MRS. CAN. Very true, child, but what's to be done? People will talk — there's no preventing   240 it. — Why, it was but yesterday I was told that Miss Gadabout had eloped with Sir Filigree Flirt. — But, Lord! there's no minding what one hears — though, to be sure, I had this from very good authority.

MARIA. Such reports are highly scandalous.   245

MRS. CAN. So they are, child — shameful, shameful! But the world is so censorious, no character escapes. — Lord, now who would have suspected your friend, Miss Prim, of an indiscretion? Yet such is the ill-nature of people, that they say her uncle   250 stopped her last week, just as she was stepping into the York Diligence with her dancing-master.

MARIA. I'll answer for't there are no grounds for the report.

MRS. CAN. Oh, no foundation in the world, I   255 dare swear; no more, probably, than for the story

166] CSM *there is*; DR *there's*.   169] CS *run*; DMR *ran*.   172] CS *ma'am*; DMR *madam*.
177] CSD *should*; MR *would*. SER omit *so*.   184] CSM *uncle's*; DR *uncle is*.
194] CSEMR *the malice*; D omits *the*.   195] D *barb which*.   203] CSEM *motives*; DR *little motives*.
209] CSD *however*; MR omit *however*.   213] CSM *Yes*; DR *Yet*.
216] CSD *'tis very true*; M *that's true*; R *'tis true*.   225] M *ma'am* for *madam*.
226] CSDR *Ah!*; M *Oh*.   226] CSEMR *what*; D omits *what* (E emends D, on the authority of C).
231] CSER *has*; D *have*; M *town is not better employed*.   232] CD *there is*; SMR *there's*.
234] CSD *indeed I*; MR *I indeed*.   236] CSD *so*; MR *as*.
245] D adds to Maria's speech, *I'm sure such reports are* —; E deletes, on the authority of C.

circulated last month, of Mrs. Festino's affair with Colonel Cassino; — though, to be sure, that matter was never rightly cleared up.

Jos. Surf. The license of invention some 260 people take is monstrous indeed.

Maria. 'Tis so. — But, in my opinion, those who report such things are equally culpable.

Mrs. Can. To be sure they are; tale-bearers are as bad as the tale-makers — 'tis an old observa- 265 tion, and a very true one — but what's to be done, as I said before? how will you prevent people from talking? — To-day, Mrs. Clackit assured me Mr. and Mrs. Honeymoon were at last become mere man and wife, like the rest of their acquaintances. — 270 She likewise hinted that a certain widow, in the next street, had got rid of her dropsy and recovered her shape in a most surprising manner. And at the same time Miss Tattle, who was by, affirmed that Lord Buffalo had discovered his lady at a house of no 275 extraordinary fame — and that Sir Harry Bouquet and Tom Saunter were to measure swords on a simi- lar provocation. But, Lord, do you think I would report these things! No, no! tale-bearers, as I said before, are just as bad as tale-makers. 280

Jos. Surf. Ah! Mrs. Candour, if everybody had your forbearance and good nature!

Mrs. Can. I confess, Mr. Surface, I cannot bear to hear people attacked behind their backs, and when ugly circumstances come out against one's ac- 285 quaintance I own I always love to think the best. — By the bye, I hope it is not true that your brother is absolutely ruined?

Jos. Surf. I am afraid his circumstances are very bad indeed, ma'am. 290

Mrs. Can. Ah! — I heard so — but you must tell him to keep up his spirits — everybody almost is in the same way! Lord Spindle, Sir Thomas Splint, Captain Quinze, and Mr. Nickit — all up, I hear, within this week; so, if Charles is undone, he'll 295 find half his acquaintances ruined too — and that, you know, is a consolation.

Jos. Surf. Doubtless, ma'am — a very great one.

Enter Servant.

Serv. Mr. Crabtree and Sir Benjamin Backbite.
Exit Servant.

Lady Sneer. So, Maria, you see your lover 300 pursues you; positively you shan't escape.

Enter Crabtree and Sir Benjamin Backbite.

Crab. Lady Sneerwell, I kiss your hands. Mrs.

Candour, I don't believe you are acquainted with my nephew, Sir Benjamin Backbite? Egad, ma'am, he has a pretty wit, and is a pretty poet too; 305 isn't he, Lady Sneerwell?

Sir Ben. O fie, uncle!

Crab. Nay, egad it's true — I'll back him at a rebus or a charade against the best rhymer in the kingdom. Has your ladyship heard the epi- 310 gram he wrote last week on Lady Frizzle's feather catching fire? — Do, Benjamin, repeat it — or the charade you made last night extempore at Mrs. Drowzie's conversazione. — Come now; your *first* is the name of a fish, your *second* a great naval 315 commander, and ——

Sir Ben. Uncle, now — prithee ——

Crab. I'faith, ma'am, 'twould surprise you to hear how ready he is at these things.

Lady Sneer. I wonder, Sir Benjamin, you 320 never publish anything.

Sir Ben. To say truth, ma'am, 'tis very vulgar to print; and, as my little productions are mostly satires and lampoons on particular people, I find they cir- culate more by giving copies in confidence to the 325 friends of the parties — however, I have some love elegies, which, when favored with this lady's smiles, I mean to give to the public.

Crab. 'Fore heav'n, ma'am, they'll immortalize you! — you'll be handed down to posterity like 330 Petrarch's Laura, or Waller's Sacharissa.[1]

Sir Ben. Yes, madam, I think you will like them, when you shall see them on a beautiful quarto page, where a neat rivulet of text shall murmur through a meadow of margin. 'Fore gad, they will be the 335 most elegant things of their kind!

Crab. But, ladies, that's true — have you heard the news?

Mrs. Can. What, sir, do you mean the report of —

Crab. No, ma'am, that's not it. — Miss 340 Nicely is going to be married to her own footman.

Mrs. Can. Impossible!

Crab. Ask Sir Benjamin.

Sir Ben. 'Tis very true, ma'am — everything is fixed, and the wedding liveries bespoke. 345

Crab. Yes — and they *do* say there were pressing reasons for it.

Lady Sneer. Why, I *have* heard something of this before.

Mrs. Can. It can't be — and I wonder any 350 one should believe such a story of so prudent a lady as Miss Nicely.

[1] Edmund Waller's poetical name for Lady Dorothy Sidney.

265] D *as tale-makers*.   270] CS *their acquaintances*; D *her acquaintance*; MR *their acquaintance*.
275] D omits *at*.   280] CSD *tale-makers*; MR *the tale-makers*.   285–286] CSD *one's*; MR *our* (D *acquaintances*).
287] CS *it is*; DMR *'tis*.   292–293] D omits *everybody ... Lord Spindle*; CSEMR include.   294] D misprints *Quinzes*.
295] D *he will* for *he'll*.   299] D omits *Exit Servant*.   302] CSD *hands*; MR *hand*.   308] D *'tis* for *it's*.
308] CSD *I'll back*; MR *I back*.   315] CSEMR *a fish*; D *the fish*.
319] CSD *at these things*; M *at all these fine sort of things*; R *at all these things*.   328] CSD *give to the*; MR *give the*.
330] CSD *you'll*; MR *you will*.   344] D misprints *every* for *very*; E, following C, corrects.

SIR BEN. O lud! ma'am, that's the very reason 'twas believed at once. She has always been so *cautious* and so *reserved*, that everybody was 355 sure there was some reason for it at bottom.

MRS. CAN. Why, to be sure, a tale of scandal is as fatal to the credit of a prudent lady of her stamp as a fever is generally to those of the strongest constitutions; but there is a sort of 360 puny, sickly reputation that is always ailing, yet will outlive the robuster characters of a hundred prudes.

SIR BEN. True, madam, there are valetudinarians in reputation as well as constitution, who, being 365 conscious of their weak part, avoid the least breath of air, and supply their want of stamina by care and circumspection.

MRS. CAN. Well, but this may be all a mistake. You know, Sir Benjamin, very trifling circum- 370 stances often give rise to the most injurious tales.

CRAB. That they do, I'll be sworn, ma'am. Did you ever hear how Miss Piper came to lose her lover and her character last summer at Tunbridge? — Sir Benjamin, you remember it? 375

SIR BEN. Oh, to be sure! — the most whimsical circumstance —

LADY SNEER. How was it, pray?

CRAB. Why, one evening, at Mrs. Ponto's as- sembly, the conversation happened to turn on 380 the difficulty of breeding Nova Scotia sheep in this country. Says a young lady in company, 'I have known instances of it; for Miss Letitia Piper, a first cousin of mine, had a Nova Scotia sheep that pro- duced her twins.' 'What!' cries the old Dowa- 385 ger Lady Dundizzy (who you know is as deaf as a post), 'has Miss Piper had twins?' This mistake, as you may imagine, threw the whole company into a fit of laughing. However, 'twas the next morning everywhere reported, and in a few days be- 390 lieved by the whole town, that Miss Letitia Piper had actually been brought to bed of a fine boy and a girl — and in less than a week there were people who could name the father, and the farm-house where the babies were put out to nurse! 395

LADY SNEER. Strange, indeed!

CRAB. Matter of fact, I assure you. — O lud! Mr. Surface, pray is it true that your uncle, Sir Oliver, is coming home?

JOS. SURF. Not that I know of, indeed, sir. 400

CRAB. He has been in the East Indias a long time. You can scarcely remember him, I believe. — Sad

comfort, whenever he returns, to hear how your brother has gone on!

JOS. SURF. Charles has been imprudent, sir, 405 to be sure; but I hope no busy people have already prejudiced Sir Oliver against him, — he may re- form.

SIR BEN. To be sure he may — for my part I never believed him to be so utterly void of prin- 410 ciple as people say — and though he has lost all his friends, I am told nobody is better spoken of by the Jews.

CRAB. That's true, egad, nephew. If the old Jewry were a ward, I believe Charles would 415 be an alderman; no man more popular there, 'fore gad! I hear he pays as many annuities as the Irish tontine;[1] and that, whenever he's sick, they have prayers for the recovery of his health in the Syna- gogue. 420

SIR BEN. Yet no man lives in greater splendor. — They tell me, when he entertains his friends, he can sit down to dinner with a dozen of his own securities; have a score [of] tradesmen waiting in the antechamber, and an officer behind every 425 guest's chair.

JOS. SURF. This may be entertainment to you, gentlemen, but you pay very little regard to the feelings of a brother.

MARIA. Their malice is intolerable! — 430 Lady Sneerwell, I must wish you a good morning — I'm not very well.   *Exit* MARIA.

MRS. CAN. O dear! she changes color very much!

LADY SNEER. Do, Mrs. Candour, follow 435 her — she may want assistance.

MRS. CAN. That I will, with all my soul, ma'am. — Poor dear girl! who knows what her situation may be!   *Exit* MRS. CANDOUR.

LADY SNEER. 'Twas nothing but that she 440 could not bear to hear Charles reflected on, not- withstanding their difference.

SIR BEN. The young lady's *penchant* is obvious.

CRAB. But, Benjamin, you mustn't give up the pursuit for that; follow her, and put her into 445 good humor. Repeat her some of your own verses. — Come, I'll assist you.

SIR BEN. Mr. Surface, I did not mean to hurt

[1] In 1773 and thereafter, the Irish parliament raised con- siderable revenues by selling life annuities to subscribers. The 'tontine' plan took its name from the inventor, Tonti, an Italian banker.   (See N, pp. 290–291.)

381] CSDR *the difficulty of breeding*; M *the breeding*.   382] CSEMR *young lady*; D omits *young*.
385–386] CS *old Dowager Lady Dundizzy*; D omits *old*; R *Lady Dowager Dundizzy*.
389] CSER *laughing*; DM *laughter*.   389] CSEM *morning*; DR *day*.   395] CSDR *put out*; M *put*.
401] C *Indias*; SDMR *Indies*.   415] Sheridan apparently corrects *was* (?) to *were*.
416–417] CS punctuate *there, 'foregad I hear*.   418] CS *he's*; DMR *he is*.
419–420] CSD *in the Synagogue*; MR *in all the synagogues*.   423] CSD *can*; MR *will*. S reads *can set down with*.
424] CS *score*; DMR *score of*.   424] D omits *waiting*; E, following C, inserts.   424–425] S *in his* for *in the*.
438] CSEMR *girl*; D *creature*.   444] CSD *mustn't*; MR *must not*.

you; but depend upon't your brother is utterly undone. *(Going.)* * 450

CRAB. O lud, aye! undone as ever man was — can't raise a guinea. *(Going.)* *

SIR BEN. And everything sold, I'm told, that was movable. *(Going.)* *

CRAB. I have seen one that was at his 455 house — not a thing left but some empty bottles that were overlooked, and the family pictures, which I believe are framed in the wainscot. *(Going.)* *

SIR BEN. And I am very sorry to hear also some bad stories against him. *(Going.)* 460

CRAB. Oh, he has done many mean things, that's certain. *(Going.)*

SIR BEN. But, however, as he's your brother —— *(Going.)*

CRAB. We'll tell you all, another opportunity.

Exeunt CRABTREE *and* SIR BENJAMIN.

LADY SNEER. Ha, ha! ha! 'tis very hard for 465 them to leave a subject they have not quite run down.

JOS. SURF. And I believe the abuse was no more acceptable to your ladyship than to Maria.

LADY SNEER. I doubt [1] her affections are 470 farther engaged than we imagined; but the family are to be here this evening, so you may as well dine where you are, and we shall have an opportunity of observing farther; — in the meantime, I'll go and plot mischief, and you shall study sentiments. 475

Exeunt.

SCENE II

SIR PETER TEAZLE'S *house.*

Enter SIR PETER.

SIR PET. When an old bachelor takes a young wife, what is he to expect? — 'Tis now six months since Lady Teazle made me the happiest of men — and I have been the miserablest dog ever since that ever committed wedlock! We tift a little going 5 to church, and came to a quarrel before the bells were done ringing. I was more than once nearly choked with gall during the honeymoon, and had lost all comfort in life before my friends had done wishing me joy! Yet I chose with caution — 10

[1] Suspect.

a girl bred wholly in the country, who never knew luxury beyond one silk gown, nor dissipation above the annual gala of a race ball. Yet now she plays her part in all the extravagant fopperies of the fashion and the town, with as ready a grace as 15 if she had never seen a bush nor a grass-plat out of Grosvenor Square! I am sneered at by my old acquaintance — paragraphed in the newspapers. She dissipates my fortune, and contradicts all my humors; yet the worst of it is, I doubt I love 20 her, or I should never bear all this. However, I'll never be weak enough to own it.

Enter ROWLEY.

ROW. Oh! Sir Peter, your servant, — how is it with you, sir?

SIR PET. Very bad, Master Rowley, very 25 bad; — I meet with nothing but crosses and vexations.

ROW. What can have happened to trouble you since yesterday?

SIR PET. A good question to a married man! 30

ROW. Nay, I'm sure your lady, Sir Peter, can't be the cause of your uneasiness.

SIR PET. Why, has anyone told you she was dead?

ROW. Come, come, Sir Peter, you love her, notwithstanding your tempers don't exactly agree. 35

SIR PET. But the fault is entirely hers, Master Rowley. I am, myself, the sweetest-tempered man alive, and hate a teasing temper — and so I tell her a hundred times a day.

ROW. Indeed! 40

SIR PET. Aye; and what is very extraordinary, in all our disputes she is always in the wrong! But Lady Sneerwell, and the set she meets at her house, encourage the perverseness of her disposition. Then, to complete my vexations, Maria, my ward, 45 whom I ought to have the power of a father over, is determined to turn rebel too, and absolutely refuses the man whom I have long resolved on for her husband; — meaning, I suppose, to bestow herself on his profligate brother. 50

ROW. You know, Sir Peter, I have always taken the liberty to differ with you on the subject of these two young gentlemen. I only wish you may not be deceived in your opinion of the elder. For

449] CS *upon't*; DMR *on't.*

450] The four stage directions marked * are added by Sheridan in his own handwriting. The later s.d. are in the copyist's handwriting. S confirms C.

453] M *wainscots* for *wainscot.*   459] CSD *I am*; MR *I'm.*   459] CSD *to hear also*; MR *also, to hear.*

465] CSD *Ha! ha! ha!*; MR *Ha! ha!*   468] CSEMR *the*; D *their.*   468] CDM *no*; SER *not.*

469] CSER *than to*; DM *than.*   471] D *further* for *farther* (and again in this speech).

471] CSD *imagined*; MR *imagine.*   475] CSD *sentiments*; MR *sentiment.*

SCENE II. 1] CSD *takes*; MR *marries.*   4] CSD *miserablest*; MR *most miserable.*

4-5] CSER *that ever committed wedlock*; DM omit.   6] CSDR *came to a quarrel*; M *fairly quarrelled.*

7] CSD *were done*; MR *had done.*   7-8] CDMR *nearly choked*; SE omit *nearly.*

17-18] CSD *my old acquaintance*; MR *all my acquaintance.*   18] CSD — *paragraphed*; MR *and paragraphed.*

31] CSM *your lady, Sir Peter*; DR *Sir Peter, your lady.*   33] CSEMR *any one*; D *any body.*   39] D *an* for *a.*

45] CS *vexations*; DMR *vexation.*

Charles, my life on't! he will retrieve his errors   55
yet. Their worthy father, once my honored master,
was, at his years, nearly as wild a spark; yet, when
he died, he did not leave a more benevolent heart
to lament his loss.

SIR PET. You are wrong, Master Rowley.   60
On their father's death, you know, I acted as a
kind of guardian to them both, till their uncle Sir
Oliver's Eastern liberality gave them an early independence; of course, no person could have more
opportunities of judging of their hearts, and I   65
was never mistaken in my life. Joseph is indeed a
model for the young men of the age. He is a man
of sentiment, and acts up to the sentiments he
professes; but, for the other, take my word for't,
if he had any grains of virtue by descent, he   70
has dissipated them with the rest of his inheritance.
Ah! my old friend, Sir Oliver, will be deeply mortified when he finds how part of his bounty has been
misapplied.

Row. I am sorry to find you so violent against   75
the young man, because this may be the most
critical period of his fortune. I came hither with
news that will surprise you.

SIR PET. What! let me hear.

Row. Sir Oliver *is* arrived, and at this mo-   80
ment in town.

SIR PET. How! you astonish me! I thought you
did not expect him this month.

Row. I did not; but his passage has been
remarkably quick.   85

SIR PET. Egad, I shall rejoice to see my old friend,
— 'tis sixteen years since we met — we have had
many a day together; but does he still enjoin us not
to inform his nephews of his arrival?

Row. Most strictly. He means, before it is   90
known, to make some trial of their dispositions.

SIR PET. Ah! There needs no art to discover
their merits — however, he shall have his way; but,
pray, does he know I am married?

Row. Yes, and will soon wish you joy.   95

SIR PET. What, as we drink health to a friend in
a consumption! Ah, Oliver will laugh at me —
we used to rail at matrimony together — but he
has been steady to his text. Well, he must be at
my house, though — I'll instantly give orders   100
for his reception. But, Master Rowley, don't drop
a word that Lady Teazle and I ever disagree.

Row. By no means.

SIR PET. For I should never be able to stand
Noll's jokes; so I'd have him think, Lord for-   105
give me! that we are a very happy couple.

Row. I understand you — but then you must

be very careful not to differ while he's in the house
with you.

SIR PET. Egad, and so we must — and   110
that's impossible. Ah! Master Rowley, when an
old bachelor marries a young wife, he deserves —
no — the crime carries the punishment along with
it.   *Exeunt.*

End of Act 1st.

ACT II

SCENE I

SIR PETER TEAZLE'S *house.*

Enter SIR PETER *and* LADY TEAZLE.

SIR PET. Lady Teazle, Lady Teazle, I'll not bear
it!

LADY TEAZ. Sir Peter, Sir Peter, you may bear
it or not, as you please; but I ought to have my
own way in everything, and what's more, I *will*   5
too. — What! though I was educated in the country,
I know very well that women of fashion in London
are accountable to nobody after they are married.

SIR PET. Very well, ma'am, very well, — so a
husband is to have no influence, no authority?   10

LADY TEAZ. Authority! No, to be sure — if you
wanted authority over me, you should have adopted
me, and not married me; I am sure you were old
enough.

SIR PET. Old enough! — aye, there it is! —   15
Well, well, Lady Teazle, though my life may be
made unhappy by your temper, I'll not be ruined
by your extravagance.

LADY TEAZ. My extravagance! I'm sure I'm not
more extravagant than a woman of fashion   20
ought to be.

SIR PET. No, no, madam, you shall throw away
no more sums on such unmeaning luxury. 'Slife!
to spend as much to furnish your dressing-room
with flowers in winter as would suffice to turn   25
the Pantheon [1] into a greenhouse, and give a *fête
champêtre* [2] at Christmas!

LADY TEAZ. Lord, Sir Peter, am I to blame
because flowers are dear in cold weather? You
should find fault with the climate, and not with   30
me. For my part, I am sure I wish it was spring
all the year round, and that roses grew under
one's feet!

SIR PET. Oons! madam — if you had been born
to this, I shouldn't wonder at your talking thus.   35

[1] A fashionable concert-hall in Oxford Street.
[2] An open-air festival.

57] CSEMR *yet*; D *but*.   63] M omits *Eastern*.   70] CSD *grains*; MR *grain*.   71] CSD *them*; MR *it*.
88] CSEMR *us*; D *me*.   99] CSD *be at*; M *be soon at*; R *lie at* (which he terms 'the obvious emendation').
102] CSEMR *ever*; D omits.   104] D *shall* for *should*.   108] CSD *he's*; MR *he is*.   113] CSDR *the*; M *its*.
ACT II] Hereafter the detailed collations, as given in Act I, are replaced by selective textual notes. See Appendix.

— But you forget what your situation was when I married you.

LADY TEAZ. No, no, I don't; 'twas a very disagreeable one, or I should never have married *you*.

SIR PET. Yes, yes, madam, you were then 40 in somewhat an humbler style — the daughter of a plain country squire. Recollect, Lady Teazle, when I saw you first, sitting at your tambour,[1] in a pretty figured linen gown, with a bunch of keys by your side, your hair combed smooth over a roll, and 45 your apartment hung round with fruits in worsted, of your own working.

LADY TEAZ. O, yes! I remember it very well, and a curious life I led — my daily occupation to inspect the dairy, superintend the poultry, 50 make extracts from the family receipt-book, and comb my aunt Deborah's lap-dog.

SIR PET. Yes, yes, ma'am, 'twas so indeed.

LADY TEAZ. And then, you know, my evening amusements! To draw patterns for ruffles, 55 which I had not the materials to make; to play Pope Joan[2] with the curate; to read a novel to my aunt; or to be stuck down to an old spinet to strum my father to sleep after a fox-chase.

SIR PET. I am glad you have so good a 60 memory. Yes, madam, these were the recreations I took you from; but now you must have your coach — *vis-à-vis* — and three powdered footmen before your chair and, in summer, a pair of white cats[3] to draw you to Kensington Gardens. — 65 No recollection, I suppose, when you were content to ride double, behind the butler, on a docked coach-horse?

LADY TEAZ. No — I swear I never did that — I deny the butler and the coach-horse. 70

SIR PET. This, madam, was your situation — and what have I not done for you? I have made you a woman of fashion, of fortune, of rank — in short, I have made you my wife.

LADY TEAZ. Well, then, and there is but one 75 thing more you can make me to add to the obligation — and that is ——

SIR PET. My widow, I suppose?

LADY TEAZ. Hem! hem!

SIR PET. Thank you, madam — but don't 80 flatter yourself; for though your ill-conduct may disturb my peace, it shall never break my heart, I promise you: however, I am equally obliged to you for the hint.

LADY TEAZ. Then why will you endeavor 85 to make yourself so disagreeable to me, and thwart me in every little elegant expense?

SIR PET. 'Slife, madam, I say, had you any of these elegant expenses when you married me?

LADY TEAZ. Lud, Sir Peter! would you have 90 me be out of the fashion?

SIR PET. The fashion, indeed! what had you to do with the fashion before you married me?

LADY TEAZ. For my part, I should think you would like to have your wife thought a woman 95 of taste.

SIR PET. Aye — there again — taste! Zounds! madam, you had no taste when you married *me*!

LADY TEAZ. That's very true, indeed, Sir Peter! and, *after* having married you, I am sure I 100 should never pretend to taste again! But now, Sir Peter, if we have finished our daily jangle, I presume I may go to my engagement of [at] Lady Sneerwell's?

SIR PET. Aye — there's another precious 105 circumstance! — a charming set of acquaintance you have made there!

LADY TEAZ. Nay, Sir Peter, they are people of rank and fortune, and remarkably tenacious of reputation. 110

SIR PET. Yes, egad, they are tenacious of reputation with a vengeance; for they don't choose anybody should have a character but themselves! Such a crew! Ah! many a wretch has rid on a hurdle[4] who has done less mischief than those utterers 115 of forged tales, coiners of scandal, — and clippers of reputation.

LADY TEAZ. What! would you restrain the freedom of speech?

SIR PET. Oh! they have made you just as bad 120 as any one of the society.

LADY TEAZ. Why, I believe I do bear a part with a tolerable grace. But I vow I have no malice against the people I abuse; when I say an ill-natured thing, 'tis out of pure good humor — 125 and I take it for granted they deal exactly in the same manner with me. But, Sir Peter, you know you promised to come to Lady Sneerwell's too.

SIR PET. Well, well, I'll call in just to look after my own character. 130

LADY TEAZ. Then, indeed, you must make haste after me or you'll be too late. — So good-bye to ye.

Exit LADY TEAZLE.

SIR PET. So — I have gained much by my intended expostulations! Yet with what a charming air she contradicts everything I say, and how 135 pleasingly she shows her contempt of my authority!

---

[1] Embroidery-frame. [2] An old-fashioned game of cards.
[3] Ponies (Rae text reads *cobs*).

[4] Rough cart on which criminals were taken to the place of execution. 'Hurdles, with four, five, six wretches convicted of counterfeiting or mutilating the money of the realm, were dragged month after month up Holborn Hill.' (See N, p. 291.)

100-101] CSER *I am sure . . . again*; DM omit *I am sure* and add (after *again*) *I allow*. D agrees with the original copyist's reading in the Crewe MS., but Sheridan, in his own handwriting, added *I am sure* and deleted *I allow*. Moore, *Life of Sheridan*, pp. 190-191, has a long footnote precisely confirming every detail of Sheridan's own revision of this particular passage in the Crewe MS.

Well, though I can't make her love me, there is a great satisfaction in quarrelling with her; and I think she never appears to such advantage as when she's doing everything in her power to plague 140 me.   *Exit.*

SCENE II

LADY SNEERWELL'S.

LADY SNEERWELL, MRS. CANDOUR, CRABTREE, SIR BENJAMIN BACKBITE, *and* JOSEPH SURFACE.

LADY SNEER. Nay, positively, we will hear it.

JOS. SURF. Yes, yes, the epigram, by all means.

SIR BEN. Plague on't, uncle! 'tis mere nonsense.

CRAB. No, no; 'fore gad, very clever for an extempore! 5

SIR BEN. But, ladies, — you must know, that one day last week, as Lady Betty Curricle was taking the dust in Hyde Park, in a sort of duodecimo [1] phaëton, she desired me to write some verses on 10 her ponies; upon which, I took out my pocket-book, and in one moment produced the following:

'Sure never were seen two such beautiful ponies!
Other horses are clowns, and these macaronies!
Nay, to give 'em this title I'm sure isn't wrong — 15
Their legs are so slim, and their tails are so long.'

CRAB. There, ladies — done in the smack of a whip, and on horseback too!

JOS. SURF. A very Phœbus, mounted — indeed, Sir Benjamin. 20

SIR BEN. O dear sir — trifles — trifles.

Enter LADY TEAZLE *and* MARIA.

MRS. CAN. I must have a copy.

LADY SNEER. Lady Teazle, I hope we shall see Sir Peter.

LADY TEAZ. I believe he'll wait on your lady- 25 ship presently.

LADY SNEER. Maria, my love, you look grave. Come, you shall sit down to cards with Mr. Surface.

MARIA. I take very little pleasure in cards — however, I'll do as your ladyship pleases. 30

LADY TEAZ. [*aside*]. I am surprised Mr. Surface should sit down with *her*. — I thought he would have embraced this opportunity of speaking to me before Sir Peter came.

MRS. CAN. Now, I'll die but you are so scan- 35 dalous, I'll forswear your society.

[1] Diminutive.

LADY TEAZ. What's the matter, Mrs. Candour?

MRS. CAN. They'll not allow our friend Miss Vermilion to be handsome.

LADY SNEER. Oh, surely, she's a pretty woman. 40

CRAB. I am very glad you think so, ma'am.

MRS. CAN. She has a charming fresh color.

LADY TEAZ. Yes, when it is fresh put on.

MRS. CAN. O fie! I'll swear her color is natural — I have seen it come and go. 45

LADY TEAZ. I dare swear you have, ma'am — it goes of a night, and comes again in the morning.

MRS. CAN. Ha! ha! ha! how I hate to hear you talk so! But surely, now, her sister *is*, or *was*, very handsome. 50

CRAB. Who? Mrs. Evergreen? — O Lord! she's six-and-fifty if she's an hour!

MRS. CAN. Now positively you wrong her; fifty-two or fifty-three is the utmost — and I don't think she looks more. 55

SIR BEN. Ah! there is no judging by her looks, unless one could see her face.

LADY SNEER. Well, well, if Mrs. Evergreen *does* take some pains to repair the ravages of time, you must allow she effects it with great ingenuity; 60 and surely that's better than the careless manner in which the widow Ochre caulks her wrinkles.

SIR BEN. Nay, now, Lady Sneerwell, you are severe upon the widow. Come, come, it is not that she paints so ill — but, when she has 65 finished her face, she joins it on so badly to her neck, that she looks like a mended statue, in which the connoisseur may see at once that the head's modern, though the trunk's antique!

CRAB. Ha! ha! ha! Well said, nephew! 70

MRS. CAN. Ha! ha! ha! Well, you make me laugh, but I vow I hate you for't. — What do you think of Miss Simper?

SIR BEN. Why, she has very pretty teeth.

LADY TEAZ. Yes; and on that account, when 75 she is neither speaking nor laughing (which very seldom happens), she never absolutely shuts her mouth, but leaves it always on a jar, as it were.

MRS. CAN. How can you be so ill-natured?

LADY TEAZ. Nay, I allow even that's better 80 than the pains Mrs. Prim takes to conceal her losses in front. She draws her mouth till it positively resembles the aperture of a poor's-box,[2] and all her words appear to slide out edgeways.

[2] Referring to the narrow slit in the top of the church contribution-box for the poor of the parish.

28] CSER *cards*; DM *piquet*. (Sheridan's handwritten emendation on the Crewe MS. Moore's emendation of D precisely confirms).

43–47] In the Rae text the successive speeches of Lady Teazle, Mrs. Candour, and Lady Teazle are allocated to Crab., Lady Teaz., and Crab., and followed by a reply of Sir Ben.: '*True, uncle, it not only comes and goes but what's more egad her maid can fetch and carry it —*' C drops this speech and allocates the preceding ones as given above. SD both follow C. M allocates speeches as in C and D, but restores the dropped speech, altering *uncle* to *ma'am* to adjust the reply.

47] D alters to *goes off at night*, but *goes of a night* is the reading alike in Sheridan's early MS. (Rae) and in C and S.

LADY SNEER. Very well, Lady Teazle; I see 85
you can be a little severe.

LADY TEAZ. In defence of a friend it is but
justice; — but here comes Sir Peter to spoil our
pleasantry.

Enter SIR PETER TEAZLE.

SIR PET. Ladies, your most obedient — Mercy 90
on me, here is the whole set! a character dead at
every word, I suppose.   (*Aside.*) *

MRS. CAN. I am rejoiced you are come, Sir Peter.
They have been *so* censorious. They will allow
good qualities to nobody — not even good na- 95
ture to our friend Mrs. Pursy.

LADY TEAZ. What, the fat dowager who was
at Mrs. Codille's last night?

MRS. CAN. Nay, her bulk is her misfortune; and,
when she takes such pains to get rid of it, you 100
ought not to reflect on her.

LADY SNEER. That's very true, indeed.

LADY TEAZ. Yes, I know she almost lives on
acids and small whey; laces herself by pulleys;
and often, in the hottest noon of summer, you 105
may see her on a little squat pony, with her hair
platted up behind like a drummer's, and puffing
round the Ring[1] on a full trot.

MRS. CAN. I thank you, Lady Teazle, for defending her.   110

SIR PET. Yes, a good defence, truly.

MRS. CAN. But Sir Benjamin is as censorious as
Miss Sallow.

CRAB. Yes, and she is a curious being to pretend
to be censorious! — an awkward gawky, with- 115
out any one good point under heaven.

MRS. CAN. Positively you shall not be so very
severe. Miss Sallow is a relation of mine by marriage, and, as for her person, great allowance is to
be made; for, let me tell you, a woman labors 120
under many disadvantages who tries to pass for a
girl at six-and-thirty.

LADY SNEER. Though, surely, she is handsome still
— and for the weakness in her eyes, considering
how much she reads by candle-light, it is not 125
to be wondered at.

MRS. CAN. True; and then as to her manner,
upon my word I think it is particularly graceful,
considering she never had the least education; for
you know her mother was a Welch milliner, 130
and her father a sugar-baker at Bristol.

SIR BEN. Ah! you are both of you too good-
natured!

[1] The fashionable drive originally laid out in Hyde Park by
Charles II.

SIR PET. Yes, damned good-natured! This their
own relation! mercy on me!   (*Aside.*) * 135

SIR BEN. And Mrs. Candour is of so moral a turn
she can sit for an hour to hear Lady Stucco talk
sentiment.

LADY TEAZ. Nay, I vow Lady Stucco is very
well with the dessert after dinner; for she's 140
just like the French fruit one cracks for mottoes
— made up of paint and proverb.

MRS. CAN. Well, I never will join in ridiculing
a friend; and so I constantly tell my cousin Ogle,
and you all know what pretensions she has to 145
be critical in beauty.

CRAB. Oh, to be sure! she has herself the oddest
countenance that ever was seen; 'tis a collection of
features from all the different countries of the
globe.   150

SIR BEN. So she has, indeed — an Irish front!

CRAB. Caledonian locks!

SIR BEN. Dutch nose!

CRAB. Austrian lip!

SIR BEN. Complexion of a Spaniard!   155

CRAB. And teeth *à la Chinoise!*

SIR BEN. In short, her face resembles a *table
d'hôte* at Spa — where no two guests are of a
nation ——

CRAB. Or a congress at the close of a 160
general war — wherein all the members, even to
her eyes, appear to have a different interest, and her
nose and chin are the only parties likely to join issue.

MRS. CAN. Ha! ha! ha!

SIR PET. Mercy on my life! — a person they 165
dine with twice a week!   (*Aside.*) *

[LADY SNEER. Go — go — you are a couple of
provoking toads.]

MRS. CAN. Nay, but I vow you shall not carry
the laugh off so — for give me leave to say, 170
that Mrs. Ogle ——

SIR PET. Madam, madam, I beg your pardon
— there's no stopping these good gentlemen's
tongues. But when I tell *you*, Mrs. Candour, that
the lady they are abusing is a particular friend 175
of mine — I hope you'll not take her part.

LADY SNEER. Well said, Sir Peter! but you are a
cruel creature — too phlegmatic yourself for a jest,
and too peevish to allow wit on others.

SIR PET. Ah, madam, true wit is more nearly 180
allied to good nature than your ladyship is aware of.

LADY TEAZ. True, Sir Peter; I believe they are
so near akin that they can never be united.

SIR BEN. Or rather, madam, suppose them man
and wife, because one so seldom sees them to- 185
gether.

92] Sheridan adds in C the stage direction marked * and S retains it.   135] Sheridan adds s.d., retained in S.
138] C read originally *sentiments*, corrected (seemingly by Sheridan) to *sentiment*. S retains *sentiment*.
166] Sheridan adds s.d., retained in S.
167-168] This speech in Sheridan's early MS. (Rae) is retained in MR, but omitted in CSD.

LADY TEAZ. But Sir Peter is such an enemy to scandal, I believe he would have it put down by parliament.

SIR PET. 'Fore heaven, madam, if they 190 were to consider the sporting with reputation of as much importance as poaching on manors, and pass *An Act for the Preservation of Fame*, I believe many would thank them for the bill.

LADY SNEER. O lud! Sir Peter; would you 195 deprive us of our privileges?

SIR PET. Aye, madam; and then no person should be permitted to kill characters or run down reputations, but qualified old maids and disappointed widows.   200

LADY SNEER. Go, you monster!

MRS. CAN. But sure you would not be quite so severe on those who only report what they hear.

SIR PET. Yes, madam, I would have law merchant[1] for them too; and in all cases of slan- 205 der currency, whenever the drawer of the lie was not to be found, the injured parties should have a right to come on any of the indorsers.

CRAB. Well, for my part, I believe there never was a scandalous tale without some founda- 210 tion.

LADY SNEER. Come, ladies, shall we sit down to cards in the next room?

Enter Servant and whispers SIR PETER.

SIR PET. I'll be with them directly. — [*Exit Servant.*] I'll get away unperceived. [*Aside.*] 215

LADY SNEER. Sir Peter, you are not leaving us?

SIR PET. Your ladyship must excuse me; I'm called away by particular business — but I leave my character behind me.   *Exit SIR PETER.* 220

SIR BEN. Well certainly, Lady Teazle, that lord of yours is a strange being; I could tell you some stories of him would make you laugh heartily, if he wasn't your husband.

LADY TEAZ. O pray don't mind that — 225 come, do let's hear them.

(*They join the rest of the company, all talking as they are going into the next room.*)

JOS. SURF. (*rising with MARIA*).* Maria, I see you have no satisfaction in this society.

MARIA. How is it possible I should? If to raise malicious smiles at the infirmities and mis- 230 fortunes of those who have never injured us be the province of wit or humor, heaven grant me a double portion of dulness!

JOS. SURF. Yet they appear more ill-natured than they are; they have no malice at heart.   235

MARIA. Then is their conduct still more contempt-

[1] Mercantile law.

ible; for, in my opinion, nothing could excuse the intemperance of their tongues but a natural and ungovernable bitterness of mind.

JOS. SURF. But can you, Maria, feel thus 240 for others, and be unkind to me alone? Is hope to be denied the tenderest passion?

MARIA. Why will you distress me by renewing this subject?

JOS. SURF. Ah, Maria! you would not 245 treat me thus, and oppose your guardian, Sir Peter's will, but that I see that profligate *Charles* is still a favored rival.

MARIA. Ungenerously urged! But, whatever my sentiments of that unfortunate young man 250 are, be assured I shall not feel more bound to give him up, because his distresses have lost him the regard even of a brother.

(LADY TEAZLE *returns*)*

JOS. SURF. Nay, but, Maria, do not leave me with a frown — by all that's honest, I swear 255 —— Gad's life, here's Lady Teazle. (*Aside.*) * — You must not — no, you shall not — for, though I have the greatest regard for Lady Teazle ——

MARIA. Lady Teazle!

JOS. SURF. Yet were Sir Peter to suspect —— 260

LADY TEAZ. (*coming forward*). What's this, pray? Do you take her for me? — Child, you are wanted in the next room. —   *Exit MARIA.* What is all this, pray?

JOS. SURF. Oh, the most unlucky circum- 265 stance in nature! Maria has somehow suspected the tender concern I have for your happiness, and threatened to acquaint Sir Peter with her suspicions, and I was just endeavoring to reason with her when you came.   270

LADY TEAZ. Indeed! but you seemed to adopt a very tender mode of reasoning — do you *usually* argue on your knees?

JOS. SURF. Oh, she's a child — and I thought a little bombast —— but, Lady Teazle, when 275 are you to give me your judgment on my library, as you promised?

LADY TEAZ. No, no, — I begin to think it would be imprudent, and you know I admit you as a lover no further than *fashion* requires.   280

JOS. SURF. True — a mere Platonic cicisbeo,[2] what every London wife is *entitled* to.

LADY TEAZ. Certainly, one must not be out of the fashion; however, I have so many of my country prejudices left, that, though Sir Peter's ill humor 285 may vex me ever so, it never shall provoke me to ——

JOS. SURF. The only revenge in your power. Well, I applaud your moderation.

[2] Gallant to a married woman.

227] Sheridan adds s.d., retained in S.   253] Sheridan interpolates s.d., retained in S.
256] Sheridan interpolates s.d., retained in S.   282] Sheridan interpolates *London* before *wife*. S retains *London.*

LADY TEAZ. Go — you are an insinuating wretch! But we shall be missed — let us join the 290 company.

JOS. SURF. But we had best not return together.

LADY TEAZ. Well, don't stay — for Maria shan't come to hear any more of your *reasoning*, I promise you. *Exit* LADY TEAZLE. 295

JOS. SURF. A curious dilemma, truly, my politics have run me into! I wanted, at first, only to ingratiate myself with Lady Teazle, that she might not be my enemy with Maria; and I have, I don't know how, become her serious lover. Sincerely 300 I begin to wish I had never made such a point of gaining so *very good* a character, for it has led me into so many cursed rogueries that I doubt I shall be exposed at last. *Exit.*

SCENE III

SIR PETER'S.

Enter SIR OLIVER SURFACE *and* ROWLEY.

SIR OLIV. Ha! ha! ha! and so my old friend is married, hey? — a young wife out of the country. — Ha! ha! ha! — that he should have stood bluff [1] to old bachelor so long, and sink into a husband at last!

ROW. But you must not rally him on the sub- 5 ject, Sir Oliver; 'tis a tender point, I assure you, though he has been married only seven months.

SIR OLIV. Then he has been just half a year on the stool of repentance! — Poor Peter! But you say he has entirely given up Charles — never sees him, 10 hey?

ROW. His prejudice against him is astonishing, and I am sure greatly increased by a jealousy of him with Lady Teazle, which he has been industriously led into by a scandalous society in the neighbor- 15 hood, who have contributed not a little to Charles's ill name; whereas the truth is, I believe, if the lady is partial to either of them, his brother is the favorite.

SIR OLIV. Aye, — I know there are a set of malicious, prating, prudent gossips, both male and 20 female, who murder characters to kill time, and will rob a young fellow of his good name before he has years to know the value of it, — but I am not to be prejudiced against my nephew by such, I promise you! No, no; — if Charles has done nothing 25 false or mean, I shall compound for his extravagance.

ROW. Then, my life on't, you will reclaim him. — Ah, sir, it gives me new life to find that *your* heart is not turned against him, and that the son of my good old master has one friend, however, left. 30

SIR OLIV. What! shall I forget, Master Rowley, when I was at his years myself? Egad, my brother and I were neither of us very *prudent* youths — and

[1] Steadfast.

59] Sheridan supplies s.d., retained in S.

yet, I believe, you have not seen many better men than your old master was? 35

ROW. Sir, 'tis this reflection gives me assurance that Charles may yet be a credit to his family. — But here comes Sir Peter.

SIR OLIV. Egad, so he does! — Mercy on me, he's greatly altered, and seems to have a settled mar- 40 ried look! One may read husband in his face at this distance!

Enter SIR PETER TEAZLE.

SIR PET. Hah! Sir Oliver — my old friend! Welcome to England a thousand times!

SIR OLIV. Thank you, thank you, Sir Peter! 45 and i'faith I am glad to find you well, believe me!

SIR PET. Ah! 'tis a long time since we met — sixteen years, I doubt, Sir Oliver, and many a cross accident in the time.

SIR OLIV. Aye, I have had my share — but, 50 what! I find you are married, hey, my old boy? — Well, well, it can't be helped — and so I wish you joy with all my heart!

SIR PET. Thank you, thank you, Sir Oliver. — Yes, I have entered into the happy state — but we'll 55 not talk of that now.

SIR OLIV. True, true, Sir Peter; old friends should not begin on grievances at first meeting. No, no, no.

ROW. (*to* SIR OLIVER).* Take care, pray, sir.

SIR OLIV. Well, so one of my nephews is a 60 wild rogue, hey?

SIR PET. Wild! Ah! my old friend, I grieve for your disappointment there — he's a lost young man, indeed; however, his brother will make you amends; *Joseph* is, indeed, what a youth should be — 65 everybody in the world speaks well of him.

SIR OLIV. I am sorry to hear it — he has too good a character to be an honest fellow. — Everybody speaks well of him! Psha! then he has bowed as low to knaves and fools as to the honest dignity of 70 genius or virtue.

SIR PET. What, Sir Oliver! do you blame him for not making enemies?

SIR OLIV. Yes, if he has merit enough to deserve them. 75

SIR PET. Well, well — you'll be convinced when you know him. 'Tis edification to hear him converse — he professes the noblest sentiments.

SIR OLIV. Ah, plague of his sentiments! If he salutes me with a scrap of morality in his 80 mouth, I shall be sick directly. But, however, don't mistake me, Sir Peter; I don't mean to defend Charles's errors — but, before I form my judgment of either of them, I intend to make a trial of their hearts — and my friend Rowley and I have 85 planned something for the purpose.

Row. And Sir Peter shall own for once he has been mistaken.

Sir Pet. Oh, my life on Joseph's honor!

Sir Oliv. Well, come, give us a bottle of 90 good wine, and we'll drink the lad's health, and tell you our scheme.

Sir Pet. *Allons*, then!

Sir Oliv. And don't, Sir Peter, be so severe against your old friend's son. Odds my life! I am not 95 sorry that he has run out of the course a little; for my part, I hate to see prudence clinging to the green succors of youth; 'tis like ivy round a sapling, and spoils the growth of the tree. *Exeunt.*

End of Act the Second.

ACT III

Scene I

Sir Peter's.

Sir Peter Teazle, Sir Oliver Surface, *and* Rowley.

Sir Pet. Well, then — we will see this fellow first, and have our wine afterwards. But how is this, Master Rowley? I don't see the jet [1] of your scheme.

Row. Why, sir, this Mr. Stanley, whom I was speaking of, is nearly related to them, by their 5 mother; he was once a merchant in Dublin, but has been ruined by a series of undeserved misfortunes. He has applied, by letter, since his confinement, both to Mr. *Surface* and *Charles*—from the former he has received nothing but evasive promises of future 10 service, while Charles has done all that his extravagance has left him power to do; and he is, at this time, endeavoring to raise a sum of money, part of which, in the midst of his own distresses, I know he intends for the service of poor Stanley. 15

Sir Oliv. Ah! he is my brother's son.

Sir Pet. Well, but how is Sir Oliver personally to ——

Row. Why, sir, I will inform Charles and his brother that Stanley has obtained permission to 20 apply in person to his friends, and, as they have neither of them ever seen him, let Sir Oliver assume his character, and he will have a fair opportunity of judging at least of the benevolence of their dispositions; and believe me, sir, you will find in the 25 youngest brother one who, in the midst of folly and

[1] Point, gist.

dissipation, has still, as our immortal bard expresses it, —

'a tear for pity, and a hand
Open as day, for melting charity.' [2]   30

Sir Pet. Psha! What signifies his having an open hand or purse either, when he has nothing left to give? Well, well, make the trial, if you please; but where is the fellow whom you brought for Sir Oliver to examine, relative to Charles's affairs?   35

Row. Below, waiting his commands, and no one can give him better intelligence. — This, Sir Oliver, is a friendly Jew, who, to do him justice, has done everything in his power to bring your nephew to a proper sense of his extravagance.   40

Sir Pet. Pray let us have him in.

Row. Desire Mr. Moses to walk upstairs.

Sir Pet. But why should you suppose he will speak the truth?

Row. Oh, I have convinced him that he has 45 no chance of recovering certain sums advanced to Charles but through the bounty of Sir Oliver, who he knows is arrived; so that you may depend on his fidelity to his [own] interest. I have also another evidence in my power, one Snake, whom I have de- 50 tected in a matter little short of forgery, and shall shortly produce to remove some of *your* prejudices, Sir Peter, relative to Charles and Lady Teazle.

Sir Pet. I have heard too much on that subject.

Row. Here comes the honest Israelite.   55

Enter Moses.

— This is Sir Oliver.

Sir Oliv. Sir, I understand you have lately had great dealings with my nephew Charles.

Mos. Yes, Sir Oliver — I have done all I could for him, but he was ruined before he came to me for 60 assistance.

Sir Oliv. That was unlucky, truly — for you have had no opportunity of showing your talents.

Mos. None at all — I hadn't the pleasure of knowing his distresses — till he was some thousands 65 worse than nothing.

Sir Oliv. Unfortunate, indeed! But I suppose you have done all in your power for him, honest Moses?

Mos. Yes, he knows that. This very evening 70 I was to have brought him a gentleman from the city, who doesn't know him, and will, I believe, advance him some money.

[2] From *Henry IV, Part II*, IV. iv. 31–32. (Quoted correctly, but not transcribed as verse.)

91] CS *the Lad's health*; D *your Lady's good health*; M *the lads' health*; R *your lady's health.*
98] CSM *succours*; Rae text *juices*; R *suckers.*
14] Sheridan corrects *all his distresses* (C) to *his own distresses.* S follows the corrected reading.
30] C read originally *the day* (as in Rae), but *the* is crossed out in correction. S follows the correction.
43] In C the word (? *Pray*) before *why* is heavily blotted out, presumably by Sheridan, to avoid repetition of *pray* in line 41.
49] D *his own interest.* In C the word (? *own*) before *interest* is heavily blotted out (? by Sheridan). S follows the corrected text of C, reading *his interest.*

SIR PET. What, one Charles has never had money from before?   75

MOS. Yes; Mr. Premium, of Crutched Friars [1] — formerly a broker.

SIR PET. Egad, Sir Oliver, a thought strikes me! — Charles, you say, doesn't know Mr. Premium?

MOS. Not at all.   80

SIR PET. Now then, Sir Oliver, you may have a better opportunity of satisfying yourself than by an old romancing tale of a poor relation; — go with my friend Moses, and represent Mr. *Premium*, and then, I'll answer for't, you will see your nephew in all   85 his glory.

SIR OLIV. Egad, I like this idea better than the other, and I may visit *Joseph* afterwards, as old *Stanley*.

SIR PET. True — so you may.   90

ROW. Well, this is taking Charles rather at a disadvantage, to be sure. However, Moses — you understand Sir Peter, and will be faithful?

MOS. You may depend upon me, — this is near the time I was to have gone.   95

SIR OLIV. I'll accompany you as soon as you please, Moses; but hold! I have forgot one thing — how the plague shall I be able to pass for a Jew?

MOS. There's no need — the principal is Christian.

SIR OLIV. Is he? — I'm sorry to hear it —   100 but, then again, an't I rather too smartly dressed to look like a money-lender?

SIR PET. Not at all; 'twould not be out of character, if you went in your own carriage — would it, Moses?   105

MOS. Not in the least.

SIR OLIV. Well, but how must I talk? there's certainly some cant of usury, and mode of treating, that I ought to know.

SIR PET. Oh, there's not much to learn — the   110 great point, as I take it, is to be exorbitant enough in your demands — hey, Moses?

MOS. Yes, that's a very great point.

SIR OLIV. I'll answer for't I'll not be wanting in that. I'll ask him eight or ten per cent on the   115 loan, at least.

MOS. If you ask him no more than that, you'll be discovered immediately.

SIR OLIV. Hey! what the plague! how much then?

MOS. That depends upon the circum-   120 stances. If he appears not very anxious for the supply, you should require only forty or fifty per cent; but if you find him in great distress, and want the moneys very bad — you may ask double.

SIR PET. A good honest trade you're learn-   125 ing, Sir Oliver!

SIR OLIV. Truly I think so — and not unprofitable.

MOS. Then, you know, you haven't the moneys

yourself, but are forced to borrow them for him of a friend.   130

SIR OLIV. Oh! I borrow it of a friend, do I?

MOS. Yes, and your friend is an unconscionable dog, but you can't help it.

SIR OLIV. My friend is an unconscionable dog, is he?   135

MOS. Yes, and he himself has not the moneys by him — but is forced to sell stock at a great loss.

SIR OLIV. He is forced to sell stock, is he, at a great loss, is he? Well, that's very kind of him.

SIR PET. I'faith, Sir Oliver — Mr. Premium,   140 I mean — you'll soon be master of the trade. But, Moses! wouldn't you have him run out a little against the Annuity Bill? [2] That would be in character, I should think.

MOS. Very much.   145

ROW. And lament that a young man now must be at years of discretion before he is suffered to ruin himself?

MOS. Aye, great pity!

SIR PET. And abuse the public for allowing   150 merit to an act whose only object is to snatch misfortune and imprudence from the rapacious relief of usury, and give the minor a chance of inheriting his estate without being undone by coming into possession.   155

SIR OLIV. So, so — Moses shall give me further instructions as we go together.

SIR PET. You will not have much time, for your nephew lives hard by.

SIR OLIV. Oh, never fear! my tutor appears so   160 able, that though Charles lived in the next street, it must be my own fault if I am not a complete rogue before I turn the corner.

Exeunt SIR OLIVER *and* MOSES.

SIR PET. So now I think Sir Oliver will be convinced; — you are partial, Rowley, and would   165 have prepared Charles for the other plot.

ROW. No, upon my word, Sir Peter.

SIR PET. Well, go bring me this Snake, and I'll hear what he has to say presently. — I see Maria, and want to speak with her. — *Exit* ROWLEY.   170 I should be glad to be convinced my suspicions of Lady Teazle and Charles were unjust. I have never yet opened my mind on this subject to my friend *Joseph* — I'm determined I will do it — *he* will give me his opinion sincerely.   175

Enter MARIA.

So, child, has Mr. Surface returned with you?

MARIA. No, sir — he was engaged.

SIR PET. Well, Maria, do you not reflect, the more

[1] A street, not far from the Tower of London, named from an old Convent of Crossed or Crouched Friars.

[2] The Annuity Bill, presented in the House of Commons April 29, 1777, and passed in May (after the first performance of *The S. for S.*) was aimed to safeguard minors against grantors of life annuities. (See N, p. 293.)

you converse with that amiable young man, what return his partiality for you deserves?   180

MARIA. Indeed, Sir Peter, your frequent importunity on this subject distresses me extremely — you compel me to declare, that I know no man who has ever paid me a particular attention whom I would not prefer to Mr. Surface.   185

SIR PET. So — here's perverseness! No, no, Maria, 'tis Charles only whom you would prefer — 'tis evident his vices and follies have won your heart.

MARIA. This is unkind, sir — you know I 190 have obeyed you in neither seeing nor corresponding with him; I have heard enough to convince me that he is unworthy my regard. Yet I cannot think it culpable, if, while my understanding severely condemns his vices, my heart suggests some pity 195 for his distresses.

SIR PET. Well, well, pity him as much as you please, but give your heart and hand to a worthier object.

MARIA. Never to his brother!   200

SIR PET. Go, perverse and obstinate! But take care, madam; you have never yet known what the authority of a guardian is — don't compel me to inform you of it.

MARIA. I can only say, you shall not have 205 *just* reason. 'Tis true, by my father's will, I am for a short period bound to regard you as his substitute, but must cease to think you so, when you would compel me to be miserable.   *Exit* MARIA.

SIR PET. Was ever man so crossed as I am! 210 everything conspiring to fret me! — I had not been involved in matrimony a fortnight, before her father, a hale and hearty man, died — on purpose, I believe, for the pleasure of plaguing me with the care of his daughter. But here comes my helpmate! 215 She appears in great good humor. How happy I should be if I could tease her into loving me, though but a little!

Enter LADY TEAZLE.

LADY TEAZ. Lud! Sir Peter, I hope you haven't been quarrelling with Maria — it isn't using 220 me well to be ill humored when I am not by.

SIR PET. Ah, Lady Teazle, you might have the power to make me good humored at all times.

LADY TEAZ. I am sure I wish I had — for I want you to be in charming sweet temper at this mo- 225 ment. Do be good humored now, and let me have two hundred pounds, will you?

SIR PET. Two hundred pounds! what, an't I to be in a good humor without paying for it! But speak to me thus, and i'faith there's nothing I could 230 refuse you. You shall have it; but seal me a bond for the repayment.

LADY TEAZ. O, no — there — my note of hand will do as well.

SIR PET. (*kissing her hand*).* And you shall 235 no longer reproach me with not giving you an independent settlement, — I mean shortly to surprise you; but shall we always live thus, hey?

LADY TEAZ. If you please. I'm sure I don't care how soon we leave off quarrelling, provided 240 you'll own *you* were tired first.

SIR PET. Well — then let our future contest be, who shall be most obliging.

LADY TEAZ. I assure you, Sir Peter, good nature becomes you. You look now as you did be- 245 fore we were married! — when you used to walk with me under the elms, and tell me stories of what a gallant you were in your youth, and chuck me under the chin, you would, and ask me if I thought I could love an old fellow, who would deny me 250 nothing — didn't you?

SIR PET. Yes, yes, and you were as kind and attentive.

LADY TEAZ. Aye, so I was, and would always take your part, when my acquaintance used to 255 abuse you, and turn you into ridicule.

SIR PET. Indeed!

LADY TEAZ. Aye, and when my cousin Sophy has called you a stiff, peevish old bachelor, and laughed at me for thinking of marrying one 260 who might be my father, I have always defended you — and said, I didn't think you so ugly by any means, and that I dared say you'd make a very good sort of a husband.

SIR PET. And you prophesied right — and 265 we shall certainly now be the happiest couple ——

LADY TEAZ. And never differ again!

SIR PET. No, never! — though at the same time, indeed, my dear Lady Teazle, you must watch your temper very narrowly; for in all our 270 little quarrels, my dear, if you recollect, my love, you always began first.

LADY TEAZ. I beg your pardon, my dear Sir Peter: indeed, you always gave the provocation.

SIR PET. Now, see, my angel! take care — 275 *contradicting* isn't the way to keep friends.

LADY TEAZ. Then, don't *you* begin it, my love!

SIR PET. There, now! you — you are going on — you don't perceive, my life, that you are just doing the very thing which you know always makes 280 me angry.

LADY TEAZ. Nay, you know if you will be angry without any reason ——

SIR PET. There now! you want to quarrel again.   285

LADY TEAZ. No, I am sure I don't — but, if you will be so peevish ——

SIR PET. There now! who begins first?

235] Sheridan supplies the s.d., retained in S.

LADY TEAZ. Why, you, to be sure. I said nothing — but there's no bearing your temper. 290

SIR PET. No, no, madam, the fault's in your own temper.

LADY TEAZ. Aye, you are just what my cousin Sophy said you would be.

SIR PET. Your cousin Sophy is a forward, 295 impertinent gipsy.

LADY TEAZ. You are a great bear, I'm sure, to abuse my relations.

SIR PET. Now may all the plagues of marriage be doubled on me, if ever I try to be friends 300 with you any more!

LADY TEAZ. So much the better.

SIR PET. No, no, madam; 'tis evident you never cared a pin for me, and I was a madman to marry you — a pert, rural coquette, that had refused 305 half the honest squires in the neighborhood!

LADY TEAZ. And I am sure I was a fool to marry you — an old dangling bachelor, who was single at fifty, only because he never could meet with any one who would have him. 310

SIR PET. Aye, aye, madam; but you were pleased enough to listen to me — *you* never had such an offer before.

LADY TEAZ. No! didn't I refuse Sir Twivy Tarrier, who everybody said would have been 315 a better match — for his estate is just as good as yours — and he has broke his neck since we have been married.

SIR PET. I have done with you, madam! You are an unfeeling, ungrateful — but there's an end 320 of everything. I believe you capable of anything that's bad. Yes, madam, I now believe the reports relative to you and Charles, madam — yes, madam, you and Charles — are not without grounds ——

LADY TEAZ. Take care, Sir Peter! you had 325 better not insinuate any such thing! I'll not be suspected with*out cause*, I promise you.

SIR PET. Very well, madam! very well! a separate maintenance as soon as you please. Yes, madam, or a divorce! I'll make an example of my- 330 self for the benefit of all old bachelors. Let us separate, madam.

LADY TEAZ. Agreed! agreed! And now, my dear Sir Peter, we are of a mind once more, we may be the *happiest couple*, and *never differ again*, 335 you know: ha! ha! Well, you are going to be in a passion, I see, and I shall only interrupt you — so, bye! bye!   *Exit.*

SIR PET. Plagues and tortures! can't I make her angry neither? Oh, I am the miserablest fel- 340 low! But I'll not bear her presuming to keep her temper — no! she may break my heart, but she shan't keep her temper.   *Exit.*

SCENE II

CHARLES'S *house.*

Enter TRIP, MOSES, *and* SIR OLIVER SURFACE.

TRIP. Here, Master Moses! if you'll stay a moment, I'll try whether — what's the gentleman's name?

SIR OLIV. Mr. Moses, what *is* my name?

                                            (*Aside.*)*

MOS. Mr. Premium.   5

TRIP. Premium — very well.

                              Exit TRIP, *taking snuff.*

SIR OLIV. To judge by the servants, one wouldn't believe the master was ruined. But what! — sure, this was my brother's house?

MOS. Yes, sir; Mr. Charles bought it of Mr. 10 Joseph, with the furniture, pictures, &c., just as the old gentleman left it — Sir Peter thought it a great piece of extravagance in him.

SIR OLIV. In my mind, the other's economy in *selling* it to him was more reprehensible by half. 15

Re-enter TRIP.

TRIP. My master says you must wait, gentlemen; he has company, and can't speak with you yet.

SIR OLIV. If he knew *who* it was wanted to see him, perhaps he wouldn't have sent such a message?   20

TRIP. Yes, yes, sir; he knows *you* are here — I didn't forget little Premium — no, no, no.

SIR OLIV. Very well — and I pray, sir, what may be your name?

TRIP. Trip, sir — my name is Trip, at your 25 service.

SIR OLIV. Well, then, Mr. Trip, you have a pleasant sort of a place here, I guess.

TRIP. Why, yes — here are three or four of us pass our time agreeably enough; but then our 30 wages are sometimes a little in arrear — and not very great either — but fifty pounds a year, and find our own bags and bouquets.[1]

SIR OLIV. [*aside*]. Bags and bouquets! halters and bastinadoes!   35

TRIP. But *à propos*, Moses, have you been able to get me that little bill discounted?

SIR OLIV. [*aside*]. Wants to raise money, too! — mercy on me! Has his distresses, I warrant, like a lord, — and affects creditors and duns.   40

MOS. 'Twas not to be done, indeed, Mr. Trip.

                                    (*Gives the note.*)

TRIP. Good lack, you surprise me! My friend *Brush* has indorsed it, and I thought when he put his mark on the back of a bill 'twas as good as cash.   45

[1] Footman's trappings. The back-hair of the bag-wig was enclosed in an ornamental bag.

Mos. No, 'twouldn't do.

Trip. A small sum — but twenty pounds. Hark'ee, Moses, do you think you couldn't get it me by way of annuity?

Sir Oliv. [*aside*]. An annuity! ha! ha! ha! a 50 footman raise money by way of annuity! Well done, luxury, egad!

Mos. But you must insure your place.

Trip. Oh, with all my heart! I'll insure my place, and my life too, if you please. 55

Sir Oliv. [*aside*]. It's more than I would your neck.

Trip. But then, Moses, it must be done before this d—d register [1] takes place — one wouldn't like to have one's name made public, you know.

Mos. No, certainly. But is there nothing 60 you could deposit?

Trip. Why, nothing capital of my master's wardrobe has dropped lately; but I could give you a mortgage on some of his winter clothes, with equity of redemption before November — or you 65 shall have the reversion of the French velvet, or a post-obit [2] on the blue and silver; — these, I should think, Moses, with a few pair of point ruffles, as a collateral security — hey, my little fellow?

Mos. Well, well.   (*Bell rings*.)* 70

Trip. Gad, I heard the bell! I believe, gentlemen, I can now introduce you. Don't forget the annuity, little Moses! This way, gentlemen, insure my place, you know.

Sir Oliv. [*aside*]. If the man be a shadow of 75 his master, this is the temple of dissipation indeed!
                                        Exeunt.

Scene III

Charles [Surface], Careless, &c., &c.
at a table with wine, &c.

Chas. Surf. 'Fore heaven, 'tis true! — there's the great degeneracy of the age. Many of our acquaintance have taste, spirit, and politeness; but, plague on't, they won't drink.

Care. It is so, indeed, Charles! they give in 5 to all the substantial luxuries of the table, and abstain from nothing but wine and wit.

Chas. Surf. Oh, certainly society suffers by it intolerably! for now, instead of the social spirit of raillery that used to mantle over a glass of bright 10

Burgundy, their conversation is become just like the Spa-water they drink, which has all the pertness and flatulence of champagne, without its spirit or flavor.

1 Gent. But what are *they* to do who love play better than wine? 15

Care. True! there's Harry diets himself for gaming, and is now under a hazard regimen.[3]

Chas. Surf. Then he'll have the worst of it. What! you wouldn't train a horse for the course by keeping him from corn! For my part, egad, I 20 am now never so successful as when I am a little merry — let me throw on a bottle of champagne, and I never lose — at least I never feel my losses, which is exactly the same thing.

2 Gent. Aye, that I believe. 25

Chas. Surf. And, then, what man can pretend to be a believer in love, who is an abjurer of wine? 'Tis the test by which the lover knows his own heart. Fill a dozen bumpers to a dozen beauties, and she that floats at top is the maid that has bewitched you. 30

Care. Now then, Charles, be honest, and give us your real favorite.

Chas. Surf. Why, I have withheld her only in compassion to you. If I toast her, you must give a round of her peers — which is impossible — on 35 earth.

Care. Oh, then we'll find some canonised vestals or heathen goddesses that will do, I warrant!

Chas. Surf. Here then, bumpers, you rogues! bumpers! Maria! Maria —   (*Drink*.)* 40

1 Gent. Maria who?

Chas. Surf. O, damn the surname! — 'tis too formal to be registered in Love's calendar — but now, Sir Toby Bumper, beware — we must have beauty superlative. 45

Care. Nay, never study, Sir Toby: we'll stand to the toast, though your mistress should want an eye — and you know you have a song will excuse you.

Sir Toby. Egad, so I have! and I'll give him the song instead of the lady.   [*Sings*.] 50

Song and Chorus
Here's to the maiden of bashful fifteen;
    Here's to the widow of fifty;
Here's to the flaunting extravagant quean,
    And here's to the housewife that's thrifty.

Chorus.   Let the toast pass — 55
            Drink to the lass —
I'll warrant she'll prove an excuse for the glass.

3 'Keeps in strict training for gambling.'

---

1 Another reference to the Annuity Bill of 1777, proposed on April 29, and passed in May. It provided 'for registering the Grants of Life Annuities.' (See N, p. 293.)
2 Future claim.

70] Sheridan adds s.d.
Scene III. 8–13] This speech, in Sheridan's early (Rae) text a continuation of Careless's speech (ll. 5–7) was definitely transferred in C to Charles Surface. M, nevertheless, assigns it to Careless.
16] M *Sir Harry* for *Harry*, evidently in anticipation of M's later textual changes (ll. 44, 46, 49 ff.) whereby *Sir Toby Bumper* is transformed into *Sir Harry Bumper*.
40] Sheridan adds s.d.   41] M transfers this speech to *Sir Harry B*[*umper*].
49–50] M allocates this speech to *Sir Harry B*[*umper*], and has *Harry* for *Toby* in lines 44 and 46. CSD unite in calling the character *Sir Toby* (not *Harry*) *Bumper*.

Here's to the charmer whose dimples we prize;
 Now to the maid who has none, sir;
Here's to the girl with a pair of blue eyes,   60
 And here's to the nymph with but one, sir.
Chorus. Let the toast pass, &c.

Here's to the maid with a bosom of snow:
 Now to *her* that's as brown as a berry:
Here's to the wife with a face full of woe,   65
 And now for the damsel that's merry.
Chorus. Let the toast pass, &c.

For let 'em be clumsy, or let 'em be slim,
 Young or ancient, I care not a feather:
So fill a pint bumper quite up to the brim,   70
 — And let us e'en toast 'em **together.**
Chorus. Let the toast pass, &c.

ALL. Bravo! Bravo!

Enter TRIP, *and whispers* CHARLES SURFACE.

CHAS. SURF. Gentlemen, you must excuse me a
little. — Careless, take the chair, will you?   75
CARE. Nay, prithee, Charles, what now? This is
one of your peerless beauties, I suppose, has dropped
in by chance?
CHAS. SURF. No, faith! To tell you the truth,
'tis a Jew and a broker, who are come by ap-   80
pointment.
CARE. Oh, damn it! let's have the Jew in —
1 GENT. Aye, and the broker too, by all means.
2 GENT. Yes, yes, the Jew and the broker.
CHAS. SURF. Egad, with all my heart! — Trip,   85
bid the gentlemen walk in. —   [*Exit* TRIP.]
Though there's one of them a stranger, I can tell you.
CARE. Charles, let us give them some generous
Burgundy, and perhaps they'll grow conscientious.
CHAS. SURF. Oh, hang 'em, no! wine does but   90
draw forth a man's *natural* qualities; and to make
them drink would only be to whet their knavery.

Enter TRIP, SIR OLIVER SURFACE, *and* MOSES.

CHAS. SURF. So, honest Moses; walk in, pray, Mr.
Premium — that's the gentleman's name, isn't it,
Moses?   95
MOS. Yes, sir.
CHAS. SURF. Set chairs, Trip. — Sit down, Mr.
Premium. — Glasses, Trip. — Sit down, Moses. —
Come, Mr. Premium, I'll give you a sentiment; here's
'Success to usury!' — Moses, fill the gentleman   100
a bumper.
MOS. Success to usury!
CARE. Right, Moses — usury is prudence and in-
dustry, and deserves to succeed.
SIR OLIV. Then here's — All the success it   105
deserves!
CARE. No, no, that won't do! Mr. Premium, you

have demurred to the toast, and must drink it in a
pint bumper.
1 GENT. A pint bumper, at least.   110
MOS. Oh, pray, sir, consider — Mr. Premium's
a gentleman.
CARE. And therefore loves good wine.
2 GENT. Give Moses a quart glass — this is
mutiny, and a high contempt of the chair.   115
CARE. Here, now for't! I'll see justice done, to
the last drop of my bottle.
SIR OLIV. Nay, pray, gentlemen — I did not expect this usage.
CHAS. SURF. No, hang it, Careless, you   120
shan't; Mr. Premium's a stranger.
SIR OLIV. [*aside*]. Odd! I wish I was well out of
this company.
CARE. Plague on 'em then! if they won't drink,
we'll not sit down with 'em. Come, Harry, the   125
dice are in the next room. — Charles, you'll join
us — when you have finished your business with these
gentlemen?
CHAS. SURF. I will! I will! — *Exeunt* [*Gentlemen*].
Careless!   130
CARE. [*returning*]. Well!
CHAS. SURF. Perhaps I may want *you.*
CARE. Oh, you know I am always ready — word,
note, or bond, 'tis all the same to me.   *Exit.*
MOS. Sir, this is Mr. Premium, a gentleman   135
of the strictest honor and secrecy; and always performs what he undertakes. Mr. Premium, this
is ——
CHAS. SURF. Pshaw! have done! Sir, my friend
Moses is a very honest fellow, but a little slow   140
at expression; he'll be an hour giving us our titles.
Mr. Premium, the plain state of the matter is this —
I am an extravagant young fellow who want[s] money
to borrow; you I take to be a prudent old fellow, who
ha[s] got money to lend. I am blockhead   145
enough to give fifty per cent sooner than not have it;
and you, I presume, are rogue enough to take a hundred if you could get it. Now, sir, you see we are
acquainted at once, and may proceed to business
without farther ceremony.   150
SIR OLIV. Exceeding frank, upon my word. I see,
sir, you are not a man of many compliments.
CHAS. SURF. Oh, no, sir! plain dealing in business
I always think best.
SIR OLIV. Sir, I like you the better for't.   155
However, you are mistaken in one thing — I have
no money to lend, but I believe I could procure some
of a friend; but then he's an unconscionable dog —
isn't he, Moses? And must sell stock to accommodate you — mustn't he, Moses?   160
MOS. Yes, indeed! You know I always speak
the truth, and scorn to tell a lie!

129] CS *Exeunt*; D *Exeunt Sir Toby, and Gent.*   143] D emends to *wants*; CS *want.*
145] D emends to *has*; CS *have.*

CHAS. SURF. Right! People that expect truth generally do. But these are trifles, Mr. Premium. What! I know money isn't to be bought without paying for't! 165

SIR OLIV. Well, but what security could you give? You have no land, I suppose?

CHAS. SURF. Not a mole-hill, nor a twig, but what's in beau-pots [1] out at the window! 170

SIR OLIV. Nor any stock, I presume?

CHAS. SURF. Nothing but live stock — and that's only a few pointers and ponies. But pray, Mr. Premium, are you acquainted at all with any of my connections? 175

SIR OLIV. Why, to say truth, I am.

CHAS. SURF. Then you must know that I have a devilish rich uncle in the East Indies, Sir *Oliver Surface,* from whom I have the greatest expectations.

SIR OLIV. That you have a wealthy uncle, I 180 have heard — but how your expectations will turn out is more, I believe, than you can tell.

CHAS. SURF. Oh, no! — there can be no doubt — they tell me I'm a prodigious favorite — and that he talks of leaving me everything. 185

SIR OLIV. Indeed! this is the first I've heard on't.

CHAS. SURF. Yes, yes, 'tis just so. — Moses knows 'tis true; don't you, Moses?

MOS. Oh, yes! I'll swear to't.

SIR OLIV. [aside]. Egad, they'll persuade me 190 presently I'm at Bengal.

CHAS. SURF. Now I propose, Mr. Premium, if it's agreeable to you, a post-obit on Sir Oliver's life; though at the same time the old fellow has been so liberal to me that I give you my word I should 195 be very sorry to hear anything had happened to him.

SIR OLIV. Not more than *I* should, I assure you. But the bond you mention happens to be just the worst security you could offer me — for I might live to a hundred and never recover the principal. 200

CHAS. SURF. Oh, yes, you would! — the moment Sir Oliver dies, you know, you'd come on me for the money.

SIR OLIV. Then I believe I should be the most unwelcome dun you ever had in your life. 205

CHAS. SURF. What! I suppose you are afraid now that Sir Oliver is too good a life?

SIR OLIV. No, indeed I am not — though I have heard he is as hale and healthy as any man of his years in Christendom. 210

CHAS. SURF. There again you are misinformed. No, no, the climate has hurt him considerably, poor uncle Oliver. Yes, he breaks apace, I'm told — and so much altered lately that his nearest relations don't know him. 215

SIR OLIV. No! Ha! ha! ha! so much altered lately

[1] Large ornamental flower-pots.

that his relations don't know him! Ha! ha! ha! that's droll, egad — ha! ha! ha!

CHAS. SURF. Ha! ha! — you're glad to hear that, little Premium. 220

SIR OLIV. No, no, I'm not.

CHAS. SURF. Yes, yes, you are — ha! ha! ha! — you know that mends your chance.

SIR OLIV. But I'm told Sir Oliver is coming over — nay, some say he is actually arrived. 225

CHAS. SURF. Pshaw! sure I must know better than you whether he's come or not. No, no, rely on't, he is at this moment at Calcutta, isn't he, Moses?

MOS. Oh, yes, certainly.

SIR OLIV. Very true, as you say, you must 230 know better than I, though I have it from pretty good authority — haven't I, Moses?

MOS. Yes, most undoubted!

SIR OLIV. But, sir, as I understand you want a few hundreds immediately, is there nothing you 235 would dispose of?

CHAS. SURF. How do you mean?

SIR OLIV. For instance, now — I have heard — that your father left behind him a great quantity of massy old plate. 240

CHAS. SURF. O lud! that's gone long ago — Moses can tell you how better than I can.

SIR OLIV. Good lack! all the family race-cups and corporation-bowls! (*Aside.*) * — Then it was also supposed that his library was one of the most 245 valuable and complete.

CHAS. SURF. Yes, yes, so it was — vastly too much so for a private gentleman — for my part, I was always of a communicative disposition, so I thought it a shame to keep so much knowledge to 250 myself.

SIR OLIV. [aside]. Mercy on me! learning that had run in the family like an heirloom! — [*Aloud.*] Pray, what are become of the books?

CHAS. SURF. You must inquire of the auc- 255 tioneer, Master Premium, for I don't believe even Moses can direct you there.

MOS. I never meddle with books.

SIR OLIV. So, so, nothing of the family property left, I suppose? 260

CHAS. SURF. Not much, indeed; unless you have a mind to the family pictures. I have got a room full of ancestors above — and if you have a taste for old paintings, egad, you shall have 'em a bargain!

SIR OLIV. Hey! and the devil! sure, you 265 wouldn't sell your forefathers, would you?

CHAS. SURF. Every man of 'em, to the best bidder.

SIR OLIV. What! your great-uncles and aunts?

CHAS. SURF. Aye, and my great-grandfathers and grandmothers too. 270

SIR OLIV. Now I give him up! — (*Aside.*) * —

190] S supplies s.d., lacking in C.   244] Sheridan interpolates s.d., retained in S.
271] Sheridan interpolates s.d., retained in S.

What the plague, have you no bowels for your own kindred? Odd's life! do you take me for Shylock in the play, that you would raise money of me on your own flesh and blood?   275

CHAS. SURF. Nay, my little broker, don't be angry: what need *you* care, if you have your money's worth?

SIR OLIV. Well, I'll be the purchaser — I think I can dispose of the family. — [*Aside*.] Oh,   280 I'll never forgive him this! never!

Enter CARELESS.

CARE. Come, Charles, what keeps you?

CHAS. SURF. I can't come yet. I'faith! we are going to have a sale above — here's little Premium will buy all my ancestors!   285

CARE. Oh, burn your ancestors!

CHAS. SURF. No, he may do that afterwards, if he pleases. Stay, Careless, we want you; egad, you shall be auctioneer — so come along with us.

CARE. Oh, have with you, if that's the case.   290 — I can handle a hammer as well as a dice box!

SIR OLIV. Oh, the profligates!

CHAS. SURF. Come, Moses, you shall be appraiser, if we want one. — Gad's life, little Premium, you don't seem to like the business.   295

SIR OLIV. Oh, yes, I do, vastly! Ha! ha! yes, yes, I think it a rare joke to sell one's family by auction — ha! ha! — [*Aside*.] Oh, the prodigal!

CHAS. SURF. To be sure! when a man wants money, where the plague should he get assistance, if   300 he can't make free with his own relations? *Exeunt.*

End of the third Act.

ACT IV

SCENE I

Picture-room at CHARLES'S.

Enter CHARLES SURFACE, SIR OLIVER SURFACE, MOSES, *and* CARELESS.

CHAS. SURF. Walk in, gentlemen, pray walk in! — here they are, the family of the Surfaces, up to the Conquest.

SIR OLIV. And, in my opinion, a goodly collection.

CHAS. SURF. Aye, aye, these are done in true   5 spirit of portrait-painting — no volunteer grace or expression — not like the works of your modern Raphael, who gives you the strongest resemblance, yet contrives to make your own portrait independent of you; so that you may sink the original and 10

not hurt the picture. No, no; the merit of these is the inveterate likeness — all stiff and awkward as the originals, and like nothing in human nature beside!

SIR OLIV. Ah! we shall never see such figures 15 of men again.

CHAS. SURF. I hope not. Well, you see, Master Premium, what a domestic character I am — here I sit of an evening surrounded by my family. But come, get to your pulpit, Mr. Auctioneer —   20 here's an old gouty chair of my grandfather's will answer the purpose.

CARE. Aye, aye, this will do. But, Charles, I have ne'er a hammer; and what's an auctioneer without his hammer?   25

CHAS. SURF. Egad, that's true. What parchment have we here? (*Takes down a roll.*)* 'Richard, heir to Thomas' — our genealogy in full. Here, Careless, you shall have no common bit of mahogany — here's the family tree for you, you 30 rogue — this shall be your hammer, and now you may knock down my ancestors with their own pedigree.

SIR OLIV. [*aside*]. What an unnatural rogue! — an *ex post facto* parricide!   35

CARE. Yes, yes, here's a list of your generation indeed; — faith, Charles, this is the most convenient thing you could have found for the business, for 'twill serve not only as a hammer, but a catalogue into the bargain. — But come, begin — A-going, a-going, 40 a-going!

CHAS. SURF. Bravo, Careless! Well, here's my great uncle, Sir Richard Raviline, a marvellous good general in his day, I assure you. He served in all the Duke of Marlborough's wars, and got that 45 cut over his eye at the battle of Malplaquet.[1] What say you, Mr. Premium? look at him — there's a hero for you! not cut out of his feathers, as your modern clipped captains are, but enveloped in wig and regimentals, as a general should be. What 50 do you bid?

MOS. Mr. Premium would have you speak.

CHAS. SURF. Why, then, he shall have him for ten pounds, and I am sure that's not dear for a staff-officer.   55

SIR OLIV. Heaven deliver me! his famous uncle Richard for ten pounds! — Very well, sir, I take him at that.

CHAS. SURF. Careless, knock down my uncle Richard. — Here, now, is a maiden sister of his, 60

[1] On September 11, 1709.

280] Sheridan inks out a word (? *canvass*) after *family*. S follows C, *dispose of the family.*

301] D concludes the act with an added speech (not in either C or S): SIR OLIV. *I'll never forgive him! never! never!* This curtain-speech, echoing Sir Oliver's earlier words, is a bit of stage play often followed in stage productions.

6] In C *Voluntier* is apparently corrected (? by Sheridan) to *Volunteer* (the dot of the copyist's *i* apparently showing, despite a deleting dash, and the stem of the *i* being altered to *e*). D *volunteer*; M *volontier*; some later editions *volontière* (*grace*).

27] Sheridan inserts s.d.   48] Sheridan adds *for you* after *hero.*

my great-aunt Deborah, done by Kneller,[1] thought
to be in his best manner, and a very formidable likeness. There she is, you see, a shepherdess feeding
her flock. You shall have her for five pounds ten —
the sheep are worth the money.   65

Sir Oliv. Ah! poor Deborah! a woman who set
such a value on herself! — Five pound ten — she's
mine.

Chas. Surf. Knock down my aunt Deborah!
Here, now, are two that were a sort of cousins 70
of theirs. — You see, Moses, these pictures were done
some time ago, when beaux wore wigs, and the
ladies wore their own hair.

Sir Oliv. Yes, truly, head-dresses appear to have
been a little lower in those days.   75

Chas. Surf. Well, take that couple for the same.

Mos. 'Tis [a] good bargain.

Chas. Surf. Careless! — This, now, is a grandfather of my mother's, a learned judge, well known
on the western circuit. — What do you rate him 80
at, Moses?

Mos. Four guineas.

Chas. Surf. Four guineas! Gad's life, you don't
bid me the price of his wig. — Mr. Premium, *you*
have more respect for the woolsack;[2] do let us 85
knock his lordship down at fifteen.

Sir Oliv. By all means.

Care. Gone!

Chas. Surf. And there are two brothers of his,
William and Walter Blunt, Esquires, both 90
members of Parliament, and noted speakers; and,
what's very extraordinary, I believe this is the first
time they were ever bought and sold.

Sir Oliv. That's very extraordinary, indeed!
I'll take them at your own price, for the honor 95
of Parliament.

Care. Well said, little Premium! I'll knock 'em
down at forty.

Chas. Surf. Here's a jolly fellow — I don't know
what relation, but he was mayor of Man- 100
chester; take him at eight pounds.

Sir Oliv. No, no — six will do for the mayor.

Chas. Surf. Come, make it guineas, and I'll
throw you the two aldermen there into the bargain.

Sir Oliv. They're mine.   105

Chas. Surf. Careless, knock down the mayor
and aldermen. But, plague on't! we shall be all day
retailing in this manner; do let us deal wholesale —
what say you, little Premium? Give me three hundred pounds for the rest of the family in the 110
lump.

[1] Sir Godfrey Kneller (1648–1723), who painted many portraits of English sovereigns and nobles.
[2] 'For lawyers.' The reference to the Lord Chancellor's
seat on the Woolsack in the House of Lords is here meant as
the symbol of the profession of law.

Care. Aye, aye, that will be the best way.

Sir Oliv. Well, well, anything to accommodate
you; they are mine. But there is one portrait which
you have always passed over.   115

Care. What, that ill-looking little fellow over
the settee?

Sir Oliv. Yes, sir, I mean that; though I don't
think him so ill-looking a little fellow, by any means.

Chas. Surf. What, that? Oh, that's my 120
uncle Oliver! 'Twas done before he went to India.

Care. Your uncle Oliver! Gad, then you'll
never be friends, Charles. That, now, to me, is as
stern a looking rogue as ever I saw — an unforgiving
eye, and a damned disinheriting countenance! 125
an inveterate knave, depend on't. Don't you think
so, little Premium?

Sir Oliv. Upon my soul, sir, I do not; I think it is
as honest a looking face as any in the room, dead or
alive. But I suppose your uncle Oliver goes 130
with the rest of the lumber?

Chas. Surf. No, hang it! I'll not part with poor
Noll. The old fellow has been very good to me, and,
egad, I'll keep his picture while I've a room to put
it in.   135

Sir Oliv. The rogue's my nephew after all!
(*Aside*.) * — But, sir, I have somehow taken a
fancy to that picture.

Chas. Surf. I'm sorry for't, for you certainly will
not have it. Oons! haven't you got enough 140
of 'em?

Sir Oliv. I forgive him everything! (*Aside*.) * —
But, sir, when I take a whim in my head, I don't
value money. I'll give you as much for that as for
all the rest.   145

Chas. Surf. Don't tease me, master broker; I
tell you I'll not part with it, and there's an end on't.

Sir Oliv. How like his father the dog is! —
(*Aloud*.) * Well, well, I have done. — I did not perceive it before, but I think I never saw such a 150
resemblance. — Well, sir — here is a draught for
your sum.

Chas. Surf. Why, 'tis for eight hundred pounds!

Sir Oliv. You will not let Sir Oliver go?

Chas. Surf. Zounds! no! I tell you, once 155
more.

Sir Oliv. Then never mind the difference; we'll
balance another time. But give me your hand on
the bargain; you are an honest fellow, Charles — I
beg pardon, sir, for being so free. — Come, 160
Moses.

Chas. Surf. Egad, this is a whimsical old fellow!
— but hark'ee, Premium, you'll prepare lodgings
for these gentlemen.

Sir Oliv. Yes, yes, I'll send for them in a 165
day or two.

Chas. Surf. But hold — do now — send a genteel conveyance for them, for, I assure you, they were most of them used to ride in their own carriages.

SIR OLIV. I will, I will, for all but — Oliver. 170

CHAS. SURF. Aye, all but the little honest nabob.

SIR OLIV. You're fixed on that?

CHAS. SURF. Peremptorily.

SIR OLIV. A dear extravagant rogue! — Good day! — Come, Moses, — Let me hear now 175 who dares call him profligate!

Exeunt SIR OLIVER *and* MOSES.

CARE. Why, this is the oddest genius of the sort I ever saw!

CHAS. SURF. Egad, he's the prince of brokers, I think. I wonder how the devil Moses got 180 acquainted with so honest a fellow. — Ha! here's Rowley. — Do, Careless, say I'll join the company in a moment.

CARE. I will — but don't let that old blockhead persuade you to squander any of that money 185 on old musty debts, or any such nonsense; for tradesmen, Charles, are the most exorbitant fellows!

CHAS. SURF. Very true, and paying them is only encouraging them.

CARE. Nothing else. 190

CHAS. SURF. Aye, aye, never fear. — *Exit* CARELESS. So! this was an odd old fellow, indeed! Let me see, two-thirds of this is mine by right — five hundred and thirty pounds. 'Fore heaven! I find one's ancestors are more valuable relations 195 than I took 'em for! — Ladies and gentlemen, your most obedient and very grateful humble servant.

Enter ROWLEY.

Ha! old Rowley! egad, you are just come in time to take leave of your old acquaintance.

ROW. Yes, I heard they were going. But I 200 wonder you can have such spirits under so many distresses.

CHAS. SURF. Why, there's the point — my distresses are so many, that I can't afford to part with my spirits; but I shall be rich and splenetic, all 205 in good time. However, I suppose you are surprised that I am not more sorrowful at parting with so many near relations; to be sure, 'tis very affecting; but, rot 'em, you see they never move a muscle, so why should I? 210

ROW. There's no making you serious a moment.

CHAS. SURF. Yes, faith: I am so now. Here, my honest Rowley, here, get me this changed, and take a hundred pounds of it immediately to old Stanley. 215

ROW. A hundred pounds! Consider only ——

CHAS. SURF. Gad's life, don't talk about it! poor Stanley's wants are pressing, and, if you don't make haste, we shall have some one call that has a better right to the money. 220

ROW. Ah! there's the point! I never will cease dunning you with the old proverb ——

CHAS. SURF. 'Be *just* before you're *generous*,' hey! — Why, so I would if I could; but Justice is an old lame hobbling beldame, and I can't get her to 225 keep pace with Generosity, for the soul of me.

ROW. Yet, Charles, believe me, one hour's reflection ——

CHAS. SURF. Aye, aye, it's all very true; but, hark'ee, Rowley, while I have, by heaven I'll 230 give — so, damn your economy! and now for hazard.

Exit.

SCENE II

The parlor.

Enter SIR OLIVER SURFACE *and* MOSES.

MOS. Well, sir, I think, as Sir Peter said, you have seen Mr. Charles in high glory; 'tis great pity he's so extravagant.

SIR OLIV. True, but he wouldn't sell my picture.

MOS. And loves wine and women so much. 5

SIR OLIV. But he wouldn't sell my picture!

MOS. And game[s] so deep.

SIR OLIV. But he wouldn't sell my picture. Oh, here's Rowley.

Enter ROWLEY.

ROW. So, Sir Oliver, I find you have made a 10 purchase ——

SIR OLIV. Yes, yes, our young rake has parted with his ancestors like old tapestry.

ROW. And here has he commissioned me to redeliver you part of the purchase-money — I 15 mean, though, in your necessitous character of old *Stanley*.

MOS. Ah! there is the pity of all: he is so damned charitable.

ROW. And I left a hosier and two tailors in 20 the hall, who, I'm sure, won't be paid, and this hundred would satisfy 'em.

SIR OLIV. Well, well, I'll pay his debts — and his benevolence too; but now I am no more a broker, and you shall introduce me to the elder brother as 25 old Stanley.

ROW. Not yet awhile; Sir Peter, I know, means to call there about this time.

171] The insertion of *honest* is a correction (? by Sheridan).
176] Sheridan corrects *who calls* to *who dares call.* In s.d. *Exit* is corrected to *Exeunt.*
213] In the MS. *directly* (after *chang'd*) is crossed out (? by Sheridan, in view of *immediately* in the next line).
218–219] Sheridan interpolates *if you don't make haste.*
7] C *game*; D *games.*

Enter TRIP.

TRIP. O gentlemen, I beg pardon for not showing
you out; this way — Moses, a word.　　30
Exeunt TRIP *and* MOSES.

SIR OLIV. There's a fellow for you! Would you
believe it, that puppy intercepted the Jew on our
coming, and wanted to raise money before he got to
his master!

ROW. Indeed!　　35

SIR OLIV. Yes, they are now planning an annuity
business. Ah, Master Rowley, in my days, servants
were content with the follies of their masters, when
they were worn a little threadbare — but now they
have their vices, like their birthday clothes,[1]　40
with the gloss on.　　*Exeunt.*

SCENE III

A library [*in* JOSEPH SURFACE'S *house.*]

JOSEPH SURFACE *and Servant.*

JOS. SURF. No letter from Lady Teazle?

SERV. No, sir.

JOS. SURF. [*aside*]. I am surprised she hasn't
sent, if she is prevented from coming. Sir Peter
certainly does not suspect me. Yet I wish I　5
may not lose the heiress, through the scrape I have
drawn myself in with the wife; however, Charles's
imprudence and bad character are great points in
my favor.　　(*Knocking.*)

SERV. Sir, I believe that must be Lady Teazle.　10

JOS. SURF. Hold! See whether it is or not, before
you go to the door — I have a particular message
for you, if it should be my brother.

SERV. 'Tis her ladyship, sir; she always leaves her
chair at the milliner's in the next street.　　15

JOS. SURF. Stay, stay — draw that screen before
the window — that will do; — my opposite neighbor
is a maiden lady of so curious a temper. — (*Servant
draws the screen, and exit.*) I have a difficult hand
to play in this affair. Lady Teazle has lately　20
suspected my views on Maria; but she must by no
means be let into that secret, — at least, not till
I have her more in my power.

Enter LADY TEAZLE.

LADY TEAZ. What, sentiment in soliloquy! Have
you been very impatient now? O lud! don't　25
pretend to look grave. I vow I couldn't come before.

JOS. SURF. O madam, punctuality is a species of
constancy, a very unfashionable quality in a lady.

LADY TEAZ. Upon my word, you ought to pity
me. Do you know that Sir Peter is grown so ill-　30

[1] Ceremonial dress for the King's Birthday celebrations.

tempered to me of late, and so jealous of *Charles*
too — that's the best of the story, isn't it?

JOS. SURF. (*aside*). I am glad my scandalous
friends keep that up.

LADY TEAZ. I am sure I wish he would let　35
Maria marry him, and then perhaps he would be
convinced; don't you, Mr. Surface?

JOS. SURF. (*aside*). Indeed I do not. — Oh,
certainly I do! for then my dear Lady Teazle would
also be convinced how wrong her suspicions　40
were of my having any design on the silly girl.

LADY TEAZ. Well, well, I'm inclined to believe
you. But isn't it provoking, to have the most
ill-natured things said to one? And there's my
friend Lady Sneerwell has circulated I don't　45
know how many scandalous tales of me! and all
without any foundation, too — that's what vexes
me.

JOS. SURF. Aye, madam, to be sure, that *is*
the provoking circumstance — without founda-　50
tion! yes, yes, there's the mortification, indeed; for,
when a scandalous story is believed against one,
there certainly is no comfort like the consciousness
of having deserved it.

LADY TEAZ. No, to be sure — then I'd forgive　55
their malice; but to attack me, who am really so
innocent, and who never say an ill-natured thing
of anybody — that is, of any friend — and then
Sir Peter, too, to have him so peevish, and so
suspicious, when I know the integrity of my　60
own heart — indeed 'tis monstrous!

JOS. SURF. But, my dear Lady Teazle, 'tis your
own fault if you suffer it. When a husband entertains a groundless suspicion of his wife, and withdraws his confidence from her, the original com-　65
pact is broke, and she owes it to the honor of her
sex to endeavor to outwit him.

LADY TEAZ. Indeed! So that, if he suspects me
without cause, it follows that the best way of
curing his jealousy is to give him reason for't?　70

JOS. SURF. Undoubtedly — for your husband
should never be deceived in you: and in that case
it becomes *you* to be frail in compliment to *his*
discernment.

LADY TEAZ. To be sure, what you say is very　75
reasonable, and when the consciousness of my
own innocence ——

JOS. SURF. Ah, my dear madam, there is the
great mistake; 'tis this very conscious innocence
that is of the greatest prejudice to you. What　80
is it makes you negligent of forms, and careless of
the world's opinion? why, the *consciousness* of your
innocence. What makes you thoughtless in your
conduct, and apt to run into a thousand little
imprudences? why, the *consciousness* of your　85

innocence. What makes you impatient of Sir Peter's temper and outrageous at his suspicions? why, the *consciousness* of your own innocence!

LADY TEAZ. 'Tis very true!

JOS. SURF. Now, my dear Lady Teazle, if you 90 would but once make a trifling *faux pas*, you can't conceive how cautious you would grow — and how ready to humor and agree with your husband.

LADY TEAZ. Do you think so?

JOS. SURF. Oh, I'm sure on't; and then you 95 would find all scandal would cease at once, for — in short, your character at present is like a person in a plethora, absolutely dying of too much health.

LADY TEAZ. So, so; then I perceive your prescription is, that I must sin in my own defence, and 100 part with my virtue to preserve my reputation?

JOS. SURF. Exactly so, upon my credit, ma'am.

LADY TEAZ. Well, certainly this is the oddest doctrine, and the newest receipt for avoiding calumny?   105

JOS. SURF. An infallible one, believe me. *Prudence*, like *experience*, must be paid for.

LADY TEAZ. Why, if my understanding were once convinced ——

JOS. SURF. Oh, certainly, madam, your 110 understanding *should* be convinced. Yes, yes — heaven forbid I should persuade you to do anything you *thought* wrong. No, no, I have too much honor to desire it.

LADY TEAZ. Don't you think we may as 115 well leave honor out of the argument?

JOS. SURF. Ah, the ill effects of your country education, I see, still remain with you.

LADY TEAZ. I doubt they do, indeed; and I will fairly own to you, that if I could be persuaded 120 to do wrong, it would be by Sir Peter's ill-usage sooner than your honorable logic, after all.

JOS. SURF. Then, by this hand, which he is unworthy of ——   [*Taking her hand.*]

Re-enter Servant.

'Sdeath, you blockhead — what do you want? 125

SERV. I beg pardon, sir, but I thought you wouldn't choose Sir Peter to come up without announcing him.

JOS. SURF. Sir Peter! — Oons — the devil!

LADY TEAZ. Sir Peter! O lud! I'm ruined! 130 I'm ruined!

SERV. Sir, 'twasn't I let him in.

LADY TEAZ. Oh! I'm undone! What will become of me, now, Mr. Logic? — Oh! mercy, he's on the stairs — I'll get behind here — and if ever I'm 135 so imprudent again —— (*Goes behind the screen.*)

JOS. SURF. Give me that book.

(*Sits down. Servant pretends to adjust his hair.*)

Enter SIR PETER TEAZLE.

SIR PET. Aye, ever improving himself! — Mr. Surface, Mr. Surface ——

JOS. SURF. Oh, my dear Sir Peter, I beg your 140 pardon. (*Gaping, and throws away the book.*) I have been dozing over a stupid book. Well, I am much obliged to you for this call. You haven't been here, I believe, since I fitted up this room. Books, you know, are the only things I am a coxcomb in. 145

SIR PET. 'Tis very neat indeed. Well, well, that's proper; and you make even your screen a source of knowledge — hung, I perceive, with maps.

JOS. SURF. Oh, yes, I find great use in that screen.

SIR PET. I dare say you must — certainly — 150 when you want to find anything in a hurry.

JOS. SURF. [*aside*]. Aye, or to hide anything in a hurry either.

SIR PET. Well, I have a little private business ——

JOS. SURF. You needn't stay. (*To Servant.*)* 155

SERV. No, sir.   *Exit.*

JOS. SURF. Here's a chair, Sir Peter — I beg ——

SIR PET. Well, now we are alone, there is a subject, my dear friend, on which I wish to unburden my mind to you — a point of the 160 greatest moment to my peace: in short, my good friend, Lady Teazle's conduct of late has made me extremely unhappy.

JOS. SURF. Indeed! I am very sorry to hear it.

SIR PET. Yes, 'tis but too plain she has not 165 the least regard for me; but, what's worse, I have pretty good authority to suspect she must have formed an attachment to another.

JOS. SURF. You astonish me!

SIR PET. Yes! and, between ourselves, I 170 think I have discovered the person.

JOS. SURF. How! you alarm me exceedingly.

SIR PET. Aye, my dear friend, I knew you would sympathize with me!

JOS. SURF. Yes, believe me, Sir Peter, such 175 a discovery would hurt me just as much as it would you.

SIR PET. I am convinced of it. — Ah! it is a happiness to have a friend whom one can trust even with one's family secrets. But have you no 180 guess who I mean?

JOS. SURF. I haven't the most distant idea. It can't be Sir Benjamin Backbite!

SIR PET. O, no! What say you to Charles?

JOS. SURF. My brother! impossible! 185

SIR PET. Ah, my dear friend, the goodness of your own heart misleads you — you judge of others by yourself.

JOS. SURF. Certainly, Sir Peter, the heart that is conscious of its own integrity is ever slow to 190 credit another's treachery.

100] Sheridan corrects *your own* to *my own*.   155] Sheridan adds s.d.
169] *Indeed*, before *you astonish* is deleted, apparently by Sheridan.

SIR PET. True; but your brother has no sentiment — you never hear him talk so.

JOS. SURF. Yet I can't but think Lady Teazle
herself has too much principle ——   195

SIR PET. Aye; but what's her principle against
the flattery of a handsome, lively young fellow?

JOS. SURF. That's very true.

SIR PET. And then, you know, the difference of
our ages makes it very improbable that she   200
should have any great affection for me; and if she
were to be frail, and I were to make it public, why
the town would only laugh at me, the foolish old
bachelor who had married a girl.

JOS. SURF. That's true, to be sure — they   205
would laugh.

SIR PET. Laugh! aye, and make ballads, and
paragraphs, and the devil knows what of me.

JOS. SURF. No, you must never make it public.

SIR PET. But then again — that the nephew   210
of my old friend, Sir Oliver, should be the person
to attempt such a wrong, hurts me more nearly.

JOS. SURF. Aye, there's the point. When ingratitude barbs the dart of injury, the wound has
double danger in it.   215

SIR PET. Aye — I, that was, in a manner, left
his guardian — in whose house he had been so
often entertained — who never in my life denied
him — my advice!

JOS. SURF. Oh, 'tis not to be credited! There   220
may be a man capable of such baseness, to be sure;
but, for my part, till you can give me positive proofs,
I cannot but doubt it. However, if it should be
proved on him, he is no longer a brother of mine!
I disclaim kindred with him — for the man   225
who can break through the laws of hospitality,
and attempt the wife of his friend, deserves to be
branded as the pest of society.

SIR PET. What a difference there is between you!
What noble sentiments!   230

JOS. SURF. Yet I cannot suspect Lady Teazle's
honor.

SIR PET. I am sure I wish to think well of
her, and to remove all ground of quarrel between
us. She has lately reproached me more than   235
once with having made no settlement on her; and,
in our last quarrel, she almost hinted that she
should not break her heart if I was dead. Now,
as we seem to differ in our ideas of expense, I
have resolved she shall be her own mistress   240
in that respect for the future; and, if I *were* to
die, she shall find that I have not been inattentive to her interest while living. Here, my friend,
are the drafts of two deeds, which I wish to have
your opinion on. By one, she will enjoy   245
eight hundred a year independent while I live;

and, by the other, the bulk of my fortune after my
death.

JOS. SURF. This conduct, Sir Peter, is indeed
truly generous. — (*Aside.*) I wish it may not   250
corrupt my pupil.

SIR PET. Yes, I am determined she shall have no
cause to complain, though I would not have her
acquainted with the latter instance of my affection
yet awhile.   255

JOS. SURF. Nor I, if I could help it.   (*Aside.*) *

SIR PET. And now, my dear friend, if you please,
we will talk over the situation of your hopes with
Maria.

JOS. SURF. (*softly*). No, no, Sir Peter; an-   260
other time, if you please.

SIR PET. I am sensibly chagrined at the little
progress you seem to make in her affection.

JOS SURF. I beg you will not mention it. What
are my disappointments when your happiness   265
is in debate! (*Softly.*) — 'Sdeath, I shall be ruined
every way!   (*Aside.*) *

SIR PET. And though you are so averse to my
acquainting Lady Teazle with your passion, I am
sure she's not your enemy in the affair.   270

JOS. SURF. Pray, Sir Peter, now oblige me. I am
really too much affected by the subject we have
been speaking on to bestow a thought on my own
concerns. The man who is entrusted with his
friend's distresses can never ——   275

Enter Servant.

Well, sir?

SERV. Your brother, sir, is speaking to a gentleman in the street, and says he knows you are within.

JOS. SURF. 'Sdeath, blockhead — I'm not within
— I'm out for the day.   280

SIR PET. Stay — hold — a thought has struck
me — you shall be at home.

JOS. SURF. Well, well, let him up. — *Exit Servant.*
He'll interrupt Sir Peter — however —

SIR PET. Now, my good friend, oblige me, I   285
entreat you. Before Charles comes, let me conceal
myself somewhere; then do you tax him on the
point we have been talking on, and his answers may
satisfy me at once.

JOS. SURF. O, fie, Sir Peter! would you   290
have me join in so mean a trick? — to trepan my
brother to?

SIR PET. Nay, you tell me you are *sure* he is
innocent; if so, you do him the greatest service by
giving him an opportunity to clear himself,   295
and you will set my heart at rest. Come, you shall
not refuse me; here, behind the screen will be (*Goes
to the screen*) * — Hey! what the devil! there seems to

256] Sheridan adds s.d.   267] Sheridan apparently adds s.d. (*aside*).   292] Sheridan corrects *too* to *to.*
298] Sheridan interpolates s.d.

be *one* listener here already — I'll swear I saw a petticoat!   300

Jos. Surf. Ha! ha! ha! Well, this is ridiculous enough. I'll tell you, Sir Peter, though I hold a man of intrigue to be a most despicable character, yet you know, it doesn't follow that one is to be an absolute Joseph either! Hark'ee! 'tis a little 305 French milliner, a silly rogue that plagues me — and having some character — on your coming, she ran behind the screen.

Sir Pet. Ah, you rogue! — But, egad, she has overheard all I have been saying of my wife. 310

Jos. Surf. Oh, 'twill never go any further, you may depend on't!

Sir Pet. No! then, i'faith, let her hear it out. — Here's a closet will do as well.

Jos. Surf. Well, go in then.   315

Sir Pet. Sly rogue! sly rogue!

(Goes into the closet.)

Jos. Surf. A very narrow escape, indeed! and a curious situation I'm in, to part man and wife in this manner.

Lady Teaz. (*peeping from the screen*).* 320 Couldn't I steal off?

Jos. Surf. Keep close, my angel!

Sir Pet. (*peeping out*). Joseph, tax him home.

Jos. Surf. Back, my dear friend!

Lady Teaz. (*peeping*). Couldn't you lock 325 Sir Peter in?

Jos. Surf. Be still, my life!

Sir Pet. (*peeping*).* You're sure the little milliner won't blab?

Jos. Surf. In, in, my dear Sir Peter! — 330 'Fore gad, I wish I had a key to the door.

Enter CHARLES SURFACE.

Chas. Surf. Hollo! brother, what has been the matter? Your fellow would not let me up at first. What! have you had a Jew or a wench with you?   335

Jos. Surf. Neither, brother, I assure you.

Chas. Surf. But what has made Sir Peter steal off? I thought he had been with you.

Jos. Surf. He was, brother; but, hearing *you* were coming, he did not choose to stay.   340

Chas. Surf. What! was the old gentleman afraid I wanted to borrow money of him!

Jos. Surf. No, sir: but I am sorry to find, Charles, that you have lately given that worthy man grounds for great uneasiness.   345

Chas. Surf. Yes, they tell me I do that to a great many worthy men. But how so, pray?

Jos. Surf. To be plain with you, brother, he thinks you are endeavoring to gain Lady Teazle's affections from him.   350

Chas. Surf. Who, I? O lud! not I, upon my word. — Ha! ha! ha! so the old fellow has found out that he has got a young wife, has he? — or, what's worse, has her ladyship discovered that she has an old husband?   355

Jos. Surf. This is no subject to jest on, brother. — He who can laugh ——

Chas. Surf. True, true, as you were going to say — then, seriously, I never had the least idea of what you charge me with, upon my honor.   360

Jos. Surf. Well, it will give Sir Peter great satisfaction to hear this. (*Aloud.*)

Chas. Surf. To be sure, I once thought the lady seemed to have taken a fancy to me; but, upon my soul, I never gave her the least encourage- 365 ment. Besides, you know my attachment to Maria.

Jos. Surf. But sure, brother, even if Lady Teazle had betrayed the fondest partiality for you ——

Chas. Surf. Why, look'ee, Joseph, I hope I shall never deliberately do a dishonorable ac- 370 tion — but if a pretty woman were purposely to throw herself in my way — and that pretty woman married to a man old enough to be her father ——

Jos. Surf. Well!

Chas. Surf. Why, I believe I should be 375 obliged to borrow a little of your morality, that's all. — But, brother, do you know now that you surprise me exceedingly, by naming *me* with Lady Teazle; for, faith, I alway[s] understood *you* were her favorite.   380

Jos. Surf. Oh, for shame, Charles! This retort is foolish.

Chas. Surf. Nay, I swear I have seen you exchange such significant glances ——

Jos. Surf. Nay, nay, sir, this is no jest —— 385

Chas. Surf. Egad, I'm serious! Don't you remember — one day, when I called here ——

Jos. Surf. Nay, prithee, Charles ——

Chas. Surf. And found you together ——

Jos. Surf. Zounds, sir, I insist —— 390

Chas. Surf. And another time, when your servant ——

Jos. Surf. Brother, brother, a word with you! — (*Aside.*) Gad, I must stop him.

Chas. Surf. Informed me, I say, that —— 395

Jos. Surf. Hush! I beg your pardon, but Sir Peter has overheard all we have been saying — I knew you would clear yourself, or I should not have consented.

Chas. Surf. How, Sir Peter! Where is he? 400

Jos. Surf. Softly, there! (*Points to the closet.*)

Chas. Surf. Oh, 'fore heaven, I'll have him out. — Sir Peter, come forth!

Jos. Surf. No, no ——

Chas. Surf. I say, Sir Peter, come into 405

320] Sheridan supplies s.d.   328] Sheridan supplies s.d.
371] *Was* is corrected to *were*, apparently by Sheridan.

court. — (*Pulls in* SIR PETER.) What! my old guardian! — What — turn inquisitor, and take evidence, incog.?

SIR PET. Give me your hand, Charles — I believe I have suspected you wrongfully — 410 but you mustn't be angry with Joseph — 'twas my plan!

CHAS. SURF. Indeed!

SIR PET. But I acquit you. I promise you I don't think near so ill of you as I did. What 415 I have heard has given me great satisfaction.

CHAS. SURF. Egad, then, 'twas lucky you didn't hear any more. Wasn't it, Joseph?
　　　　　　　　　　　　　　　　(*Half aside.*)*

SIR PET. Ah! you would have retorted on him.

CHAS. SURF. Aye, aye, that was a joke. 420

SIR PET. Yes, yes, I know his honor too well.

CHAS. SURF. But you might as well have suspected him as me in this matter, for all that. Mightn't he, Joseph?　　　　　　(*Half aside.*)*

SIR PET. Well, well, I believe you. 425

JOS. SURF. Would they were both out of the room!

SIR PET. And in future, perhaps, we may not be such strangers.

Enter Servant who whispers JOSEPH SURFACE.

JOS. SURF. Lady Sneerwell! — stop her by 430 all means — (*Exit Servant.*)* Gentlemen — I beg pardon — I must wait on you downstairs — here's a person come on particular business.

CHAS. SURF. Well, you can see him in another room. Sir Peter and I haven't met a long time, 435 and I have something to say to him.

JOS. SURF. They must not be left together. — I'll send Lady Sneerwell away, and return directly. — (*Aside.*)* Sir Peter, not a word of the French milliner.　　　　　*Exit* JOSEPH SURFACE. 440

SIR PET. Oh! not for the world! — Ah, Charles, if you associated more with your brother, one might indeed hope for your reformation. He is a man of sentiment. — Well, there is nothing in the world so noble as a man of sentiment! 445

CHAS. SURF. Pshaw! he is too moral by half, and so apprehensive of his good name, as he calls it, that I suppose he would as soon let a priest into his house as a girl.

SIR PET. No, no, — come, come, — you 450 wrong him. No, no, Joseph is no rake, but he is not such a saint in that respect either, — I have a great mind to tell him — we should have a laugh! (*Aside.*)*

CHAS. SURF. Oh, hang him! he's a very anchorite, a young hermit! 455

SIR PET. Hark'ee — you must not abuse him; he may chance to hear of it again, I promise you.

CHAS. SURF. Why, you won't tell him?

SIR PET. No — but — this way. — [*Aside.*] Egad, I'll tell him. — Hark'ee, have you a 460 mind to have a good laugh at Joseph?

CHAS. SURF. I should like it of all things.

SIR PET. Then, i'faith, we will! — I'll be quit with him for discovering me. (*Aside.*)* — He had a girl with him when I called. 465

CHAS. SURF. What! Joseph? you jest.

SIR PET. Hush! — a little — French milliner — and the best of the jest is — she's in the room now.

CHAS. SURF. The devil she is!

SIR PET. Hush! I tell you. 470
　　　　　　　　　　(*Points* [*to the screen*].)

CHAS. SURF. Behind the screen! 'Slife, let's unveil her!

SIR PET. No, no, he's coming: — you shan't, indeed!

CHAS. SURF. Oh, egad, we'll have a peep at 475 the little milliner!

SIR PET. Not for the world! — Joseph will never forgive me.

CHAS. SURF. I'll stand by you ——

SIR PET. (*struggling with Charles*).* Odds, 480 here he is!

JOSEPH SURFACE *enters just as* CHARLES *throws down the screen.*

CHAS. SURF. Lady Teazle, by all that's wonderful!

SIR PET. Lady Teazle, by all that's horrible!

CHAS. SURF. Sir Peter, this is one of the 485 smartest French milliners I ever saw. Egad, you seem all to have been diverting yourselves here at hide and seek — and I don't see who is out of the secret. Shall I beg your ladyship to inform me? — Not a word! — Brother, will you please to ex- 490 plain this matter? What! Morality dumb too! — Sir Peter, though I *found* you in the dark, perhaps you are not so now! All mute! Well — though *I* can make nothing of the affair, I suppose you perfectly understand one another; so I'll leave you to 495 yourselves. — (*Going.*) Brother, I'm sorry to find you *have given that worthy man so much uneasiness.* — Sir Peter! there's nothing *in the world* so *noble as a man of sentiment!*
　　　　　　　　　　　　　　　　Exit CHARLES.
　([*They*] *stand for some time looking at each other.*)

418] Sheridan adds s.d.　　　424] Sheridan adds s.d.

430–431] Sheridan interpolates *Lady Sneerwell! — stop her by all means — (ex. Serv.).*

438–439] Sheridan alters *send this man* to *send Lady Sneerwell*, and interpolates s.d. (*Aside*) after *directly.*

453, 464] Sheridan adds s.d.　　　　484] DM *damnable.* Sheridan's early MS. (Rae text) and CS alike read *horrible.*

491] Sheridan emends by striking out *is* before *Morality*, and alters the question mark after *dumb too* to an exclamation mark.

Jos. Surf. Sir Peter — notwithstanding I 500
confess that appearances are against me — if you
will afford me your patience — I make no doubt
but I shall explain everything to your satisfaction.

Sir Pet. If you please —

Jos. Surf. The fact is, sir, that Lady Teazle, 505
knowing my pretensions to your ward Maria — I
say, sir, Lady Teazle, being apprehensive of the
jealousy of your temper — and knowing my friendship to the family — she, sir, I say — called here
— in order that — I might explain those pre- 510
tensions — but on your coming — being apprehensive
— as I said — of your jealousy — she withdrew —
and this, you may depend on't is the whole truth of
the matter.

Sir Pet. A very clear account, upon my 515
word; and I dare swear the lady will vouch for
every article of it.

Lady Teaz. (coming forward).* For not one word
of it, Sir Peter!

Sir Pet. How! don't you think it worth 520
while to agree in the lie?

Lady Teaz. There is not one syllable of truth
in what that gentleman has told you.

Sir Pet. I believe you, upon my soul, ma'am!

Jos. Surf. (aside). 'Sdeath, madam, will 525
you betray me?

Lady Teaz. Good Mr. Hypocrite, by your leave,
I will speak for myself.

Sir Pet. Aye, let her alone, sir; you'll find she'll
make out a better story than you, without 530
prompting.

Lady Teaz. Hear me, Sir Peter! — I came here
on no matter relating to your ward, and even ignorant of this gentleman's pretensions to her — but
I came, seduced by his insidious arguments, 535
at least to listen to his pretended passion, if not
to sacrifice your honor to his baseness.

Sir Pet. Now, I believe, the truth is coming,
indeed!

Jos. Surf. The woman's mad! 540

Lady Teaz. No, sir; she has recovered her senses,
and your own arts have furnished her with the
means. — Sir Peter, I do not expect you to credit
me — but the tenderness you expressed for me,
when I am sure you could not think I was a 545
witness to it, has penetrated to my heart, and had I
left the place without the shame of this discovery,
my future life should have spoke[n] the sincerity of
my gratitude. As for that smooth-tongue hypocrite,
who would have seduced the wife of his too 550
credulous friend, while he affected honorable addresses to his ward — I behold him now in a light so
truly despicable, that I shall never again respect
myself for having listened to him. Exit.

Jos. Surf. Nothwithstanding all this, Sir 555
Peter, heaven knows ——

Sir Pet. That you are a villain! — and so I leave
you to your conscience.

Jos. Surf. You are too rash, Sir Peter; you
shall hear me. The man who shuts out con- 560
viction by refusing to ——

Sir Pet. Oh! —

Exeunt, Joseph Surface *following and speaking.*

End of Act 4th.

ACT V

Scene I

The library [*in* Joseph Surface's *house.*]

Enter Joseph Surface *and Servant.*

Jos. Surf. Mr. Stanley! why should you think I
would see him? you *must* know he comes to ask
something.

Serv. Sir, I should not have let him in, but that
Mr. Rowley came to the door with him. 5

Jos. Surf. Pshaw! blockhead! to suppose that I
should *now* be in a temper to receive visits from poor
relations! — Well, why don't you show the fellow up?

Serv. I will, sir. — Why, sir, it was not my fault
that Sir Peter discovered my lady —— 10

Jos. Surf. Go, fool! *Exit Servant.*
Sure, Fortune never played a man of my policy such
a trick before! My character with Sir Peter, my
hopes with Maria, destroyed in a moment! I'm in a
rare humor to listen to other people's distresses! 15
I shan't be able to bestow even a benevolent sentiment on Stanley. — So! here he comes, and Rowley
with him. I must try to recover myself — and put
a little charity into my face, however. *Exit.*

Enter Sir Oliver Surface *and* Rowley.

Sir Oliv. What! does he avoid us? That was 20
he, was it not?

Row. It was, sir — but I doubt you are come a
little too abruptly — his nerves are so weak, that the
sight of a poor relation may be too much for him. —
I should have gone first to break you to him. 25

Sir Oliv. A plague of his nerves! — Yet this is
he whom Sir Peter extols as a man of the most benevolent way of thinking!

Row. As to his way of thinking, I cannot pretend
to decide; for, to do him justice, he appears to 30
have as much speculative benevolence as any private
gentleman in the kingdom, though he is seldom so
sensual as to indulge himself in the exercise of it.

Sir Oliv. Yet has a string of charitable sentiments, I suppose, at his fingers' ends! 35

Row. Or, rather, at his tongue's end, Sir Oliver;

505] Sheridan interpolates *sir* before *Lady Teazle.*
546] Sheridan emends *that had* to *and had.*
518] Sheridan supplies s.d.
562] Sheridan alters *Exit* to *Exeunt*, and adds the final speech of Sir Peter.

for I believe there is no sentiment he has more faith in than that 'Charity begins at home.'

SIR OLIV. And his, I presume, is of that domestic sort which never stirs abroad at all.   40

ROW. I doubt you'll find it so; — but he's coming — I mustn't seem to interrupt you; and you know, immediately as you leave him, I come in to announce your arrival in your real character.

SIR OLIV. True; and afterwards you'll meet   45 me at Sir Peter's.

ROW. Without losing a moment.   *Exit* ROWLEY.

SIR OLIV. So! I don't like the complaisance of his features.

Re-enter JOSEPH SURFACE.

JOS. SURF. Sir, I beg you ten thousand par-   50 dons for keeping you a moment waiting — Mr. Stanley, I presume.

SIR OLIV. At your service.

JOS. SURF. Sir, I beg you will do me the honor to sit down — I entreat you, sir.   55

SIR OLIV. Dear sir — there's no occasion. — Too civil by half!   (*Aside.*)

JOS. SURF. I have not the pleasure of knowing you, Mr. Stanley; but I am extremely happy to see you look so well.   You were nearly related to my   60 mother, I think, Mr. Stanley?

SIR OLIV. I was, sir — so nearly that my present poverty, I fear, may do discredit to her wealthy children — else I should not have presumed to trouble you.   65

JOS. SURF. Dear sir, there needs no apology: he that is in distress, though a stranger, has a right to claim kindred with the wealthy; — I am sure I wish *I* was one of that class, and had it in my power to offer you even a small relief.   70

SIR OLIV. If your uncle, Sir Oliver, were here, I should have a friend.

JOS. SURF. I wish he were, sir, with all my heart: you should not want an advocate with him, believe me, sir.   75

SIR OLIV. I should not *need* one — my distresses would recommend me; but I imagined his bounty had enabled *you* to become the agent of his charity.

JOS. SURF. My dear sir, you were strangely misinformed.   Sir Oliver is a worthy man, a very   80 worthy sort of man; but — avarice, Mr. Stanley, is the vice of age.   I will tell you, my good sir, in confidence, what he has done for me has been a mere nothing; though people, I know, have thought otherwise, and, for my part, I never chose to contra-   85 dict the report.

SIR OLIV. What! has he never transmitted you bullion! rupees!¹ pagodas!²

¹ Silver coins of India, then valued at two shillings.
² Gold coins of India, then valued at eight shillings.

JOS. SURF. O dear sir, nothing of the kind!   No, no; a few presents now and then — china —   90 shawls — Congo tea — avadavats,³ and India[n] crackers⁴ — little more, believe me.

SIR OLIV. [*aside*].   Here's gratitude for twelve thousand pounds! — Avadavats and Indian crackers!

JOS. SURF. Then, my dear sir, you have heard,   95 I doubt not, of the extravagance of my brother; there are very few would credit what I have done for that unfortunate young man.

SIR OLIV. Not I, for one!   (*Aside.*) *

JOS. SURF. The sums I have lent him!   In-   100 deed I have been exceedingly to blame — it was an amiable weakness: however, I don't pretend to defend it — and now I feel it doubly culpable, since it has deprived me of the pleasure of serving *you*, Mr. Stanley, as my heart dictates.   105

SIR OLIV. [*aside*].   Dissembler! — Then, sir, you cannot assist me?

JOS. SURF. At present, it grieves me to say, I cannot; but, whenever I have the ability, you may depend upon hearing from me.   110

SIR OLIV. I am extremely sorry ——

JOS. SURF. Not more than I am, believe me; to pity, without the power to relieve, is still more painful than to ask and be denied.

SIR OLIV. Kind sir, your most obedient hum-   115 ble servant.

JOS. SURF. You leave me deeply affected, Mr. Stanley. — William, be ready to open the door.

SIR OLIV. O dear sir, no ceremony.

JOS. SURF. Your very obedient.   120

SIR OLIV. Sir, your most obsequious.

JOS. SURF. You may depend upon hearing from me, whenever I can be of service.

SIR OLIV. Sweet sir, you are too good.

JOS. SURF. In the meantime I wish you   125 health and spirits.

SIR OLIV. Your ever grateful and perpetual humble servant.

JOS. SURF. Sir, yours as sincerely.

SIR OLIV. Now I am satisfied!   *Exit.*   130

JOS. SURF. (*solus*).   This is one bad effect of a good character; it invites applications from the unfortunate, and there needs no small degree of address to gain the reputation of benevolence without incurring the expense.   The silver ore of pure   135 charity is an expensive article in the catalogue of a man's good qualities; whereas the sentimental French plate I use instead of it makes just as good a show, and pays no tax.

Enter ROWLEY.

ROW. Mr. Surface, your servant — I was ap-   140

³ Small singing-birds of India, having red and black plumage.
⁴ Fire-crackers with colored wrappers.

57] S.d. may have been added by Sheridan.   73] *Was* in the MS. is altered (? by Sheridan) to *were*.   99] Sheridan adds s.d.

prehensive of interrupting you — though my business demands immediate attention — as this note will inform you.

Jos. Surf. Always happy to see Mr. Rowley. — (*Reads.*)* How! '*Oliver — Surface!*' — My 145 uncle arrived!

Row. He is, indeed — we have just parted — quite well, after a speedy voyage, and impatient to embrace his worthy nephew.

Jos. Surf. I am astonished! — William! 150 stop Mr. Stanley, if he's not gone.

Row. Oh! he's out of reach, I believe.

Jos. Surf. Why didn't you let me know this when you came in together?

Row. I thought you had particular business. 155 But I must be gone to inform your brother, and appoint him here to meet his uncle. He will be with you in a quarter of an hour.

Jos. Surf. So he says. Well, I am strangely overjoyed at his coming. — (*Aside.*) Never, to be 160 sure, was anything so damned unlucky!

Row. You will be delighted to see how well he looks.

Jos. Surf. Oh! I'm rejoiced to hear it. — (*Aside.*) Just at this time! 165

Row. I'll tell him how impatiently you expect him.

Jos. Surf. Do, do; pray give my best duty and affection. Indeed, I cannot express the sensations I feel at the thought of seeing him. — [*Exit* 170 Rowley.] Certainly his coming just at this time is the cruellest piece of ill fortune.   *Exit.*

Scene II

At Sir Peter's.

Enter Mrs. Candour *and Maid.*

Maid. Indeed, ma'am, my lady will see nobody at present.

Mrs. Can. Did you tell her it was her friend Mrs. Candour?

Maid. Yes, madam; but she begs you will 5 excuse her.

Mrs. Can. Do go again; I shall be glad to see her, if it be only for a moment, for I am sure she must be in great distress. —   *Exit Maid.*
Dear heart, how provoking! I'm not mistress 10 of half the circumstances! We shall have the whole affair in the newspapers, with the names of the parties at length, before I have dropped the story at a dozen houses.

Enter Sir Benjamin Backbite.

O dear Sir Benjamin! you have heard, I sup- 15 pose ——

Sir Ben. Of Lady Teazle and Mr. Surface ——

Mrs. Can. And Sir Peter's discovery ——

Sir Ben. Oh, the strangest piece of business, to be sure! 20

Mrs. Can. Well, I never was so surprised in my life. I am so sorry for all parties, indeed I am.

Sir Ben. Now, I don't pity Sir Peter at all — he was so extravagantly partial to Mr. Surface.

Mrs. Can. Mr. Surface! Why, 'twas with 25 Charles Lady Teazle was detected.

Sir Ben. No such thing — Mr. Surface is the gallant.

Mrs. Can. No, no — Charles is the man. 'Twas Mr. Surface brought Sir Peter on purpose to dis- 30 cover them.

Sir Ben. I tell you I have it from one ——

Mrs. Can. And I have it from one ——

Sir Ben. Who had it from one, who had it ——

Mrs. Can. From one immediately —— But 35 here's Lady Sneerwell; perhaps she knows the whole affair.

Enter Lady Sneerwell.

Lady Sneer. So, my dear Mrs. Candour, here's a sad affair of our friend Lady Teazle!

Mrs. Can. Aye, my dear friend, who could 40 have thought it ——

Lady Sneer. Well, there's no trusting appearances; though, indeed, she was always too lively for me.

Mrs. Can. To be sure, her manners were a 45 little too free — but she was very young!

Lady Sneer. And had, indeed, some good qualities.

Mrs. Can. So she had, indeed. But have you heard the particulars? 50

Lady Sneer. No; but everybody says that Mr. Surface ——

Sir Ben. Aye, there, I told you — Mr. Surface was the man.

Mrs. Can. No, no, indeed — the assignation 55 was with Charles.

Lady Sneer. With Charles! You alarm me, Mrs. Candour.

Mrs. Can. Yes, yes, he was the lover. Mr. Surface — do him justice — was only the in- 60 former.

Sir Ben. Well, I'll not dispute with you, Mrs. Candour; but, be it which it may, I hope that Sir Peter's wound will not ——

Mrs. Can. Sir Peter's wound! Oh, mercy! 65 I didn't hear a word of their fighting.

Lady Sneer. Nor I, a syllable.

Sir Ben. No! what, no mention of the duel?

Mrs. Can. Not a word.

145] Sheridan interpolates s.d.   161] The MS. adds a second (*aside*) after *unlucky!*
Scene II. 22] Sheridan adds *I am* after *indeed.*   39] Sheridan adds *Lady* before *Teazle.*

SIR BEN. O Lord — yes, yes — they fought   70
before they left the room.

LADY SNEER. Pray let us hear.

MRS. CAN. Aye, do oblige us with the duel.

SIR BEN. 'Sir,' says Sir Peter — immediately
after the discovery — 'you are a most ungrate-   75
ful fellow.'

MRS. CAN. Aye, to Charles ——

SIR BEN. No, no — to Mr. Surface — 'a most
ungrateful fellow; and old as I am, sir,' says he, 'I
insist on immediate satisfaction.'   80

MRS. CAN. Aye, that must have been to Charles;
for 'tis very unlikely Mr. Surface should go to fight
in his house.

SIR BEN. 'Gad's life, ma'am, not at all — 'giving
me immediate satisfaction.' — On this, madam,   85
Lady Teazle, seeing Sir Peter in such danger, ran out
of the room in strong hysterics, and Charles after her,
calling out for hartshorn and water! Then, madam,
they began to fight with swords ——

Enter CRABTREE.

CRAB. With pistols, nephew — I have it from   90
undoubted authority.

MRS. CAN. O Mr. Crabtree, then it is all true!

CRAB. Too true, indeed, ma'am, and Sir Peter's
dangerously wounded ——

SIR BEN. By a thrust of in *seconde*[1] quite   95
through his left side ——

CRAB. By a bullet lodged in the thorax.

MRS. CAN. Mercy on me! Poor Sir Peter!

CRAB. Yes, ma'am — though Charles would have
avoided the matter, if he could.   100

MRS. CAN. I knew Charles was the person.

SIR BEN. Oh, my uncle, I see, knows nothing of
the matter.

CRAB. But Sir Peter taxed him with the basest ingratitude ——   105

SIR BEN. That I told you, you know.

CRAB. Do, nephew, let me speak! — and insisted
on an immediate ——

SIR BEN. Just as I said.

CRAB. Odds life, nephew, allow others to   110
know something too! A pair of pistols lay on the
bureau (for Mr. Surface, it seems, had come the
night before late from Salt-Hill, where he had been
to see the Montem[2] with a friend, who has a son at
Eton), so, unluckily, the pistols were left   115
charged.

SIR BEN. I heard nothing of this.

[1] A term in fencing.
[2] It was formerly the custom of Eton school boys to go to
Salt-Hill (*processus ad montem*) every third year on Whit-
Tuesday, and levy *salt-money* from the onlookers at the ceremony. (See N, p. 296.)

CRAB. Sir Peter forced Charles to take one, and
they fired, it seems, pretty nearly together. Charles's
shot took place, as I told you, and Sir Peter's   120
missed; but, what is very extraordinary, the ball
struck against a little bronze Pliny that stood over
the chimney-piece, grazed out of the window at a
right angle, and wounded the postman, who was
just coming to the door with a double letter   125
from Northamptonshire.

SIR BEN. My uncle's account is more circumstan-
tial, I must confess; but I believe mine is the true
one, for all that.

LADY SNEER. [*aside*]. I am more interested   130
in this affair than they imagine, and must have better
information.   *Exit* LADY SNEERWELL.*

SIR BEN. (*after a pause looking at each other*).* Ah!
Lady Sneerwell's alarm is very easily accounted for.

CRAB. Yes, yes, they certainly *do* say — but   135
that's neither here nor there.

MRS. CAN. But, pray, where is Sir Peter at present?

CRAB. Oh! they brought him home, and he is now
in the house, though the servants are ordered to deny
it.   140

MRS. CAN. I believe so, and Lady Teazle, I suppose, attending him.

CRAB. Yes, yes; I saw one of the faculty enter just
before me.

SIR BEN. Hey! who comes here?   145

CRAB. Oh, this is he — the physician, depend on't.

MRS. CAN. Oh, certainly! it must be the physician; and now we shall know.

Enter SIR OLIVER SURFACE.

CRAB. Well, doctor, what hopes?

MRS. CAN. Aye, doctor, how's your patient?   150

SIR BEN. Now, doctor, isn't it a wound with a
small-sword?

CRAB. A bullet lodged in the thorax, for a hundred!

SIR OLIV. Doctor! a wound with a small-sword!
and a bullet in the thorax? — Oons! are you   155
mad, good people?

SIR BEN. Perhaps, sir, you are not a doctor?

SIR OLIV. Truly, I am to thank you for my degree,
if I am.

CRAB. Only a friend of Sir Peter's, then, I   160
presume. But, sir, you must have heard of this
accident?

SIR OLIV. Not a word!

CRAB. Not of his being dangerously wounded?

SIR OLIV. The devil he is!   165

SIR BEN. Run through the body ——

CRAB. Shot in the breast ——

SIR BEN. By one Mr. Surface ——

CRAB. Aye, the younger.

SIR OLIV. Hey! what the plague! you seem   170

95] The MS. is apparently corrected to *secónde* (with an accent on the second syllable).
132] Sheridan's s.d. reads: '(*ex. Lady Sneer.*).'   133] Sheridan inserts s.d.

to differ strangely in your accounts — however, you agree that Sir Peter is dangerously wounded.

SIR BEN. Oh, yes, we agree there.

CRAB. Yes, yes, I believe there can be no doubt of that.   175

SIR OLIV. Then, upon my word, for a person in that situation, he is the most imprudent man alive — for here he comes, walking as if nothing at all were the matter.

Enter SIR PETER TEAZLE.

Odds heart, Sir Peter! you are come in good   180
time, I promise you; for we had just *given you over*.

SIR BEN. Egad, uncle, this is the most sudden recovery!

SIR OLIV. Why, man! what do you do out of bed with a small-sword through your body, and a   185
bullet lodged in your thorax?

SIR PET. A small-sword and a bullet?

SIR OLIV. Aye; these gentlemen would have killed you without law or physic, and wanted to dub me a doctor — to make me an accomplice.   190

SIR PET. Why, what is all this?

SIR BEN. We rejoice, Sir Peter, that the story of the duel is not true, and are sincerely sorry for your other misfortunes.

SIR PET. So, so; all over the town already.   195
                                                                              (*Aside.*)*

CRAB. Though, Sir Peter, you were certainly vastly to blame to marry at all, at your years.

SIR PET. Sir, what business is that of yours?

MRS. CAN. Though, indeed, as Sir Peter made so good a husband, he's very much to be pitied.   200

SIR PET. Plague on your pity, ma'am! I desire none of it.

SIR BEN. However, Sir Peter, you must not mind the laughing and jests you will meet with on this occasion.   205

SIR PET. Sir, I desire to be master in my own house.

CRAB. 'Tis no uncommon case, that's one comfort.

SIR PET. I insist on being left to myself: without ceremony, I insist on your leaving my house   210
directly!

MRS. CAN. Well, well, we are going; and depend on't, we'll make the best report of you we can.

SIR PET. Leave my house!

CRAB. And tell how hardly you have been   215
treated.

SIR PET. Leave my house!

SIR BEN. And how patiently you bear it.

SIR PET. Fiends! vipers! furies! Oh! that their own venom would choke them!   220

Exeunt MRS. CANDOUR, SIR BENJAMIN BACK-BITE, CRABTREE, &c.

SIR OLIV. They are very provoking indeed, Sir Peter.

Enter ROWLEY.

ROW. I heard high words — what has ruffled you, Sir Peter?

SIR PET. Pshaw! what signifies asking? Do   225
I ever pass a day without my vexations?

SIR OLIV. Well, I'm not inquisitive — I come only to tell you that I have seen both my nephews in the manner we proposed.

SIR PET. A precious couple they are!   230

ROW. Yes, and Sir Oliver is convinced that your judgment was right, Sir Peter.

SIR OLIV. Yes, I find *Joseph* is indeed the man, after all.

ROW. Yes, as Sir Peter says, he's a man of   235
sentiment.

SIR OLIV. And acts up to the sentiments he professes.

ROW. It certainly is edification to hear him talk.

SIR OLIV. Oh, he's a model for the young   240
men of the age! But how's this, Sir Peter? you don't join in your friend Joseph's praise, as I expected.

SIR PET. Sir Oliver, we live in a damned wicked world, and the fewer we praise the better.

ROW. What! do *you* say so, Sir Peter, who   245
were never mistaken in your life?

SIR PET. Pshaw! plague on you both! I see by your sneering you have heard the whole affair. I shall go mad among you!

ROW. Then, to fret you no longer, Sir Peter,   250
we are indeed acquainted with it all. I met Lady Teazle coming from Mr. Surface's, so humbled that she deigned to request me to be her advocate with you.

SIR PET. And does Sir Oliver know all too?   255

SIR OLIV. Every circumstance.

SIR PET. What, of the closet — and the screen, hey?

SIR OLIV. Yes, yes, and the little French milliner. Oh, I have been vastly diverted with the story!   260
ha! ha!

SIR PET. 'Twas very pleasant.

SIR OLIV. I never laughed more in my life, I assure you: ha! ha!

SIR PET. O, vastly diverting! ha! ha!   265

ROW. To be sure, Joseph with his sentiments! ha! ha!

SIR PET. Yes, yes, his sentiments! ha! ha! A hypocritical villain!

SIR OLIV. Aye, and that rogue Charles to   270
pull Sir Peter out of the closet: ha! ha!

SIR PET. Ha! ha! 'twas devilish entertaining, to be sure!

174] In the MS. *doubt* is a correction (? by Sheridan) from *redoubt*.   178] Sheridan emends *was* to *were*.
195] Sheridan adds s.d.   204] In the MS. *the* is altered (? by Sheridan) to *this*.   220] Sheridan alters *Exit* to *Exeunt*.

SIR OLIV. Ha! ha! Egad, Sir Peter, I should like to have seen your face when the screen was 275 thrown down: ha! ha!

SIR PET. Yes, yes, my face when the screen was thrown down: ha! ha! Oh, I must never show my head again!

SIR OLIV. But come, come, it isn't fair to 280 laugh at you neither, my old friend — though, upon my soul, I can't help it.

SIR PET. Oh, pray don't restrain your mirth on my account — it does not hurt me at all! I laugh at the whole affair myself. Yes, yes, I think being a 285 standing jest for all one's acquaintances a very happy situation. O yes, and then of a morning to read the paragraphs about Mr. S——, Lady T——, and Sir P——, will be so entertaining!

ROW. Without affectation, Sir Peter, you 290 may despise the ridicule of fools. But I see Lady Teazle going towards the next room; I am sure you must desire a reconciliation as earnestly as she does.

SIR OLIV. Perhaps my being here prevents her coming to you. Well, I'll leave honest Rowley 295 to mediate between you; but he must bring you all presently to Mr. Surface's, where I am now returning, if not to reclaim a libertine, at least to expose hypocrisy.

SIR PET. Ah! I'll be present at your discov- 300 ering yourself there with all my heart — though 'tis a vile unlucky place for discoveries!

ROW. We'll follow. [Exit SIR OLIVER SURFACE.]

SIR PET. She is not coming here, you see, Rowley.

ROW. No, but she has left the door of that 305 room open, you perceive. See, she is in tears!

SIR PET. Certainly a little mortification appears very becoming in a wife! Don't you think it will do her good to let her pine a little?

ROW. Oh, this is ungenerous in you! 310

SIR PET. Well, I know not what to think. You remember, Rowley, the letter I found of hers, evidently intended for Charles!

ROW. A mere forgery, Sir Peter! laid in your way on purpose. This is one of the points which I 315 intend Snake shall give you conviction on.

SIR PET. I wish I were once satisfied of that. She looks this way. What a remarkably elegant turn of the head she has! Rowley, I'll go to her.

ROW. Certainly. 320

SIR PET. Though, when it is known that we are reconciled, people will laugh at me ten times more!

ROW. Let them laugh, and retort their malice only by showing them you are happy in spite of it.

SIR PET. I'faith, so I will! and, if I'm not 325 mistaken, we may yet be the happiest couple in the country.

ROW. Nay, Sir Peter — he who once lays aside suspicion ——

SIR PET. Hold, my dear Rowley! if you have 330 any regard for me, never let me hear you utter anything like a sentiment — I have had enough of them to serve me the rest of my life. *Exeunt.*

SCENE III

The library [*in* JOSEPH SURFACE'S *house*].

JOSEPH SURFACE *and* LADY SNEERWELL.

LADY SNEER. Impossible! Will not Sir Peter immediately be reconciled to Charles, and of consequence no longer oppose his union with Maria? The thought is distraction to me!

JOS. SURF. Can passion furnish a remedy? 5

LADY SNEER. No, nor cunning either. Oh, I was a fool, an idiot, to league with such a blunderer!

JOS. SURF. Sure, Lady Sneerwell, *I* am the greatest sufferer; yet you see I bear the accident with calmness. 10

LADY SNEER. Because the disappointment doesn't reach your *heart*; your *interest* only attached you to Maria. Had you felt for *her* what *I* have for that ungrateful libertine, neither your temper nor hypocrisy could prevent your showing the sharp- 15 ness of your vexation.

JOS. SURF. But why should your reproaches fall on *me* for this disappointment?

LADY SNEER. Are you not the cause of it? What had you to do to bate in your pursuit of Maria 20 to pervert Lady Teazle by the way? Had you not a sufficient field for your roguery in blinding Sir Peter, and supplanting your brother? I hate such an avarice of crimes; 'tis an unfair monopoly, and never prospers. 25

JOS. SURF. Well, I admit I have been to blame. I confess I deviated from the direct road of wrong, but I don't think we're so totally defeated neither.

LADY SNEER. No!

JOS. SURF. You tell me you have made a 30 trial of Snake since we met, and that you still believe him faithful to us ——

LADY SNEER. I do believe so.

JOS. SURF. And that he has undertaken, should it be necessary, to swear and prove that Charles 35 is at this time contracted by vows and honor to your ladyship — which some of his former letters to you will serve to support?

LADY SNEER. This, indeed, might have assisted.

JOS. SURF. Come, come; it is not too late 40 yet. — [*Knocking at the door.*] But hark! this is probably my uncle, Sir Oliver: retire to that room; we'll consult farther when he's gone.

330] Sheridan emends *Mr. Rowley* to *my dear Rowley.*
SCENE III] S.d. reads actually *Scene the Last.*
21] MS. emendation *pervert* (? from *prevent*) seems Sheridan's correction.

333] S.d. reads actually *Exit Sir Peter & Rowley.*

LADY SNEER. Well! but if *he* should find you out too —   45

Jos. SURF. Oh, I have no fear of that. Sir Peter will hold his tongue for his own credit['s] sake — and you may depend on't I shall soon discover Sir Oliver's weak side!

LADY SNEER. I have no diffidence of your   50 abilities — only be constant to one roguery at a time.   *Exit.*

Jos. SURF. I will, I will! So! 'tis confounded hard, after such bad fortune, to be baited by one's confederate in evil. Well, at all events, my   55 character is so much better than Charles's, that I certainly — hey! — what! — this is not *Sir Oliver*, but old *Stanley* again! Plague on't! that he should return to tease me just now! We shall have Sir Oliver come and find him here — and ——   60

Enter SIR OLIVER SURFACE.

Gad's life, Mr. Stanley, why have you come back to plague me just at this time? You must not stay now, upon my word.

SIR OLIV. Sir, I hear your uncle Oliver is expected here, and though he has been so penurious to   65 *you*, I'll try what he'll do for *me*.

Jos. SURF. Sir, 'tis impossible for you to stay now, so I must beg —— Come any other time, and I promise you, you shall be assisted.

SIR OLIV. No: Sir Oliver and I must be ac-   70 quainted.

Jos. SURF. Zounds, sir! then I insist on your quit- ting the room directly.

SIR OLIV. Nay, sir!

Jos. SURF. Sir, I insist on't! — Here, William!   75 show this gentleman out. Since you compel me, sir — not one moment — this is such insolence!
                                        (*Going to push him out.*)

Enter CHARLES SURFACE.

CHAS. SURF. Heyday! what's the matter now? What the devil, have you got hold of my little broker here? Zounds, brother, don't hurt little Pre-   80 mium. What's the matter, my little fellow?

Jos. SURF. So! he has been with you, too, has he?

CHAS. SURF. To be sure he has! Why, 'tis as honest a little —— But sure, Joseph, you have not been borrowing money too, have you?   85

Jos. SURF. Borrowing! no! But, brother, you know here we expect Sir Oliver every ——

CHAS. SURF. O gad, that's true! Noll mustn't find the little broker here, to be sure.

Jos. SURF. Yet, Mr. *Stanley* insists ——   90

CHAS. SURF. Stanley! why his name is *Premium*.

Jos. SURF. No, no, *Stanley*.

CHAS. SURF. No, no, *Premium*.

Jos. SURF. Well, no matter which — but ——

CHAS. SURF. Aye, aye, Stanley or Premium,   95 'tis the same thing, as you say; for I suppose he goes by half [a] hundred names, besides A.B.'s[1] at the coffee-houses.

Jos. SURF. Death! here's Sir Oliver at the door. (*Knocking again.*)* Now I beg, Mr. Stan-   100 ley ——

CHAS. SURF. Aye, and I beg, Mr. Premium ——

SIR OLIV. Gentlemen ——

Jos. SURF. Sir, by heaven you shall go!

CHAS. SURF. Aye, out with him, certainly.   105

SIR OLIV. This violence ——

Jos. SURF. 'Tis your own fault.

CHAS. SURF. Out with him, to be sure.
                                        (*Both forcing* SIR OLIVER *out.*)

Enter SIR PETER *and* LADY TEAZLE, MARIA, *and* ROWLEY.

SIR PET. My old friend, Sir Oliver — hey! What in the name of wonder! — Here are dutiful   110 nephews! — assault their uncle at the first visit!

LADY TEAZ. Indeed, Sir Oliver, 'twas well we came in to rescue you.

Row. Truly it was; for I perceive, Sir Oliver, the character of old Stanley was no protection to   115 you.

SIR OLIV. Nor of Premium either: the necessities of the *former* could not extort a shilling from *that* be- nevolent gentleman; and now, egad, I stood a chance of faring worse than my ancestors, and being   120 knocked down without being bid for.
                          (*After a pause,* JOSEPH *and* CHARLES *turning to each other.*)*

Jos. SURF. Charles!

CHAS. SURF. Joseph!

Jos. SURF. 'Tis now complete!

CHAS. SURF. Very!   125

SIR OLIV. Sir Peter, my friend, and Rowley too — look on that elder nephew of mine. You know what he has already received from my bounty; and you know also how gladly I would have regarded half my fortune as held in trust for him — judge, then,   130 my disappointment in discovering him to be desti- tute of truth — charity — and gratitude!

SIR PET. Sir Oliver, I should be more surprised at this declaration, if I had not myself found him selfish, treacherous, and hypocritical!   135

LADY TEAZ. And if the gentleman pleads not guilty to these, pray let him call *me* to his character.

SIR PET. Then, I believe, we need add no more. —

[1] A reference to appointments at the coffee-houses made under concealed names.

97–98] Sheridan alters *A.B.* and *coffee-house* to plural forms.   100] Sheridan emends s.d. (*knock*) to (*knocking again*).
102] MS. emendation (? by Sheridan) deletes the second *aye* in *Aye, aye*.   122] Sheridan adds the long s.d.
134] MS. emendation (? by Sheridan) deletes *to be* before *selfish*.

If he knows himself, he will consider it as the most perfect punishment that he is known to the 140 world.

CHAS. SURF. (*aside*).* If they talk this way to *Honesty*, what will they say to *me*, by and be?

(SIR PETER, LADY TEAZLE, *and* MARIA *retire*.)

SIR OLIV. As for that prodigal, his brother, there —— 145

CHAS. SURF. (*aside*).* Aye, now comes my turn: the damned family pictures will ruin me!

JOS. SURF. Sir Oliver! — uncle! — will you honor me with a hearing?

CHAS. SURF. (*aside*).* Now if Joseph would 150 make one of his long speeches, I might recollect myself a little.

SIR OLIV. [*to* JOSEPH SURFACE]. I suppose you would undertake to justify yourself entirely?

JOS. SURF. I trust I could. 155

SIR OLIV. Pshaw! — Well, sir! and *you* (*to* CHARLES) * could justify yourself too, I suppose?

CHAS. SURF. Not that I know of, Sir Oliver.

SIR OLIV. What! — Little Premium has been let too much into the secret, I presume? 160

CHAS. SURF. True, sir; but they were family secrets, and should never be mentioned again, you know.

ROW. Come, Sir Oliver, I know you cannot speak of Charles's follies with anger.

SIR OLIV. Odd's heart, no more I can — nor 165 with gravity either. Sir Peter, do you know the rogue bargained with me for all his ancestors — sold me judges and generals by the foot — and maiden aunts as cheap as broken china.

CHAS. SURF. To be sure, Sir Oliver, I did 170 make a little free with the family canvas, that's the truth on't. My ancestors may certainly rise in evidence against me, there's no denying it; but believe me sincere when I tell you — and upon my soul I would not say it if I was not — that if I do not 175 appear mortified at the exposure of my follies, it is because I feel at this moment the warmest satisfaction in seeing you, my liberal benefactor.

SIR OLIV. Charles, I believe you. Give me your hand again; the ill-looking little fellow over the 180 settee has made your peace.

CHAS. SURF. Then, sir, my gratitude to the original is still increased.

LADY TEAZ. (*pointing to* MARIA).* Yet, I believe, Sir Oliver, here is one whom Charles is 185 still more anxious to be reconciled to.

SIR OLIV. Oh, I have heard of his attachment there; and, with the young lady's pardon, if I construe right — that blush ——

SIR PET. Well, child, speak your sentiments. 190

MARIA. Sir, I have little to say, but that I shall rejoice to hear that he is happy; for me, whatever claim I had to his affection, I willingly resign it to one who has a better title.

CHAS. SURF. How, Maria! 195

SIR PET. Heyday! what's the mystery now? While he appeared an incorrigible rake, you would give your hand to no one else; and now that he is likely to reform, I warrant you won't have him.

MARIA. His own heart — and Lady Sneer- 200 well know the cause.

CHAS. SURF. Lady Sneerwell!

JOS. SURF. Brother, it is with great concern I am obliged to speak on this point, but my regard to justice compels me, and Lady Sneerwell's in- 205 juries can no longer be concealed. (*Goes to the door.*)

Enter LADY SNEERWELL.

SIR PET. So! another French milliner! — Egad, he has one in every room in the house, I suppose!

LADY SNEER. Ungrateful Charles! Well may you be surprised, and feel for the indelicate situa- 210 tion which your perfidy has forced me into.

CHAS. SURF. Pray, uncle, is this another plot of yours? For, as I have life, I don't understand it.

JOS. SURF. I believe, sir, there is but the evidence of one person more necessary to make it ex- 215 tremely clear.

SIR PET. And that person, I imagine, is Mr. Snake. — Rowley, you were perfectly right to bring him with us, and pray let him appear.

ROW. Walk in, Mr. Snake. 220

Enter SNAKE.

I thought his testimony might be wanted; however, it happens unluckily, that he comes to confront Lady Sneerwell, and not to support her.

LADY SNEER. Villain! Treacherous to me at last! (*Aside.*)* — Speak, fellow, have *you* too con- 225 spired against me?

SNAKE. I beg your ladyship ten thousand pardons: you paid me extremely liberally for the lie in question; but I have unfortunately been offered double to speak the truth. 230

SIR PET. Plot and counterplot, egad — I wish your ladyship joy of the success of your negotiation.

LADY SNEER. The torments of shame and disappointment on you all!

LADY TEAZ. Hold, Lady Sneerwell — before 235 you go, let me thank you for the trouble you and that gentleman have taken, in writing letters to me from Charles, and answering them yourself; and let me also request you to make my respects to the Scandal-

---

142, 146, 150] Sheridan adds thrice the s.d. (*aside*), as indicated.　　　156] Sheridan interpolates s.d.

184] Sheridan adds s.d.　　　193] MS. emendation (? by Sheridan) inserts *it* after *resign*.

201] MS. emendation alters *knows* to *know*.　　　205] Sheridan emends *obliges* to *compells* (sic).

225] Sheridan interpolates s.d., and apparently made the deletion of *A* before *Villain!* which is conspicuous in the MS.

ous College, of which you are president, and 240
inform them, that Lady Teazle, licentiate, begs leave
to return the diploma they granted her, as she leaves
off practice, and kills characters no longer

LADY SNEER. You too, madam! — provoking —
insolent! May your husband live these fifty 245
years! *Exit.*

SIR PET. Oons! what a fury!

LADY TEAZ. A malicious creature, indeed!

SIR PET. Hey! not for her last wish?

LADY TEAZ. Oh, no! 250

SIR OLIV. Well, sir, and what have you to say now?

JOS. SURF. Sir, I am so confounded, to find that
Lady *Sneerwell* could be guilty of suborning Mr.
Snake in this manner, to impose on us all, that I
know not what to say; however, lest her re- 255
vengeful spirit should prompt her to injure my
brother, I had certainly better follow her directly.
Exit.

SIR PET. Moral to the last drop!

SIR OLIV. Aye, and marry her, Joseph, if you can.
— Oil and vinegar, egad! you'll do very well 260
together.

ROW. I believe we have no more occasion for Mr.
Snake at present.

SNAKE. Before I go, I beg pardon once for all, for
whatever uneasiness I have been the humble 265
instrument of causing to the parties present.

SIR PET. Well, well, you have made atonement by
a good deed at last.

SNAKE. But I must request of the company, that
it shall never be known. 270

SIR PET. Hey! what the plague! are you ashamed
of having done a right thing once in your life?

SNAKE. Ah, sir, — consider I live by the badness
of my character — I have nothing but my infamy to
depend on! and, if it were once known that I 275
had been betrayed into an honest action, I should lose
every friend I have in the world.

SIR OLIV. Well, well — we'll not traduce you by
saying anything in your praise, never fear.
Exit SNAKE.

SIR PET. There's a precious rogue! yet that 280
fellow is a writer and a critic!

LADY TEAZ. See, Sir Oliver, there needs no persuasion now to reconcile your nephew and Maria.
(CHARLES *and* MARIA *apart.*) *

SIR OLIV. Aye, aye, that's as it should be, and,
egad, we'll have the wedding to-morrow morn- 285
ing.

CHAS. SURF. Thank you, my dear uncle.

SIR PET. What, you rogue! don't you ask the girl's
consent first?

CHAS. SURF. Oh, I have done that a long 290
time — above a minute ago — and she has looked yes.

MARIA. For shame, Charles! — I protest, Sir
Peter, there has not been a word ——

SIR OLIV. Well, then, the fewer the better — may
your love for each other never know abatement. 295

SIR PET. And may you live as happily together as
Lady Teazle and I — intend to do!

CHAS. SURF. Rowley, my old friend, I am sure
you congratulate me; and I suspect that I owe you
much. 300

SIR OLIV. You do, indeed, Charles.

ROW. If my efforts to serve you had not succeeded
you would have been in my debt for the attempt —
but deserve to be happy — and you overpay me.

SIR PET. Aye, honest Rowley always said 305
you would reform.

CHAS. SURF. Why as to reforming, Sir Peter, I'll
make no promises, and that I take to be a proof that
I intend to set about it. — But here shall be my
monitor — my gentle guide. — Ah! can I leave 310
the virtuous path those eyes illumine?

> Though thou, dear maid, shouldst wa[i]ve thy
> *beauty's* sway,
> Thou still must rule, because I *will* obey:
> An humbled fugitive from Folly view,
> No sanctuary near but *Love* and — YOU; 315
> (*To the audience.*)
> *You* can, indeed, each anxious fear remove,
> For even *Scandal* dies, if *you* approve.
> *Finis.*

283] Sheridan supplies s.d. 291] Sheridan inserts *above* before *a minute ago.*
312] The MS. reads *wave* for *waive.*

EPILOGUE

Written by G. Colman,[1] Esq.

Spoken by Mrs. Abington [2]

I, who was late so volatile and gay,
Like a trade-wind must now blow all one way,
Bend all my cares, my studies, and my vows,
To one old rusty weathercock — my spouse!
So wills our virtuous bard — the motley Bayes [3] 5
Of crying epilogues and laughing plays!
   Old bachelors, who marry smart young wives,
Learn from our play to regulate your lives:
Each bring his dear to town, all faults upon her —
London will prove the very source of honor. 10
Plunged fairly in, like a cold bath it serves,
When principles relax, to brace the nerves.
   Such is my case; — and yet I might deplore
That the gay dream of dissipation's o'er;
And say, ye fair, was ever lively wife, 15
Born with a genius for the highest life,
Like me untimely blasted in her bloom,
Like me condemned to such a dismal doom?
Save money — when I just knew how to waste it!
Leave London — just as I began to taste it! 20
Must I then watch the early crowing cock,
The melancholy ticking of a clock;
In the lone rustic hall for ever pounded,
With dogs, cats, rats, and squalling brats surrounded?
With humble curates can I now retire, 25
(While good Sir Peter boozes with the squire,)
And at backgammon mortify my soul,
That pants for loo,[4] or flutters at a vole? [5]
Seven's the main! [6]   Dear sound! — that must expire,
Lost at hot cockles,[7] round a Christmas fire! 30
The transient hour of fashion too soon spent,
Farewell the tranquil mind, farewell content! [8]
Farewell the plumèd head, the cushioned tête,
That takes the cushion from its proper seat!
That spirit-stirring drum! [9] — card drums I mean, 35
Spadille [10] — odd trick — pam [11] — basto [12] — king and queen!
And you, ye knockers, that, with brazen throat,
The welcome visitors' approach denote;

---

[1] George Colman, author of *The Jealous Wife*.   [2] The original Lady Teazle.
[3] Poet, dramatist (from Bayes in *The Rehearsal*).   [4] A favorite eighteenth-century game of cards.
[5] Winning all the tricks.   [6] In hazard, the caster of the dice 'called his *main*' by naming a number from five to nine.
[7] 'A play in which one kneels, and covering his eyes lays his head in another's lap and guesses who struck him.' (Strutt, *Sports and Pastimes*.)
[8] Lines 32–42 parody Othello's soliloquy, III. iii. 347–357.   [9] Fashionable card-party.
[10] The ace of spades.   (See Pope, *The Rape of the Lock*, Canto iii.)   [11] The knave of clubs.   [12] The ace of clubs.

HEADING] Sheridan adds, after *Epilogue*, 'written by G. Colman, Esqr.'
HEADING] M *Spoken by* Lady Teazle; R *Spoken by Mrs.* Abington *in the character of* Lady Teazle.
21] M indents *Must I*, but does not indent l. 7 and l. 13.   The present text follows the Crewe MS.

Farewell! all quality of high renown,
Pride, pomp, and circumstance of glorious town!   40
Farewell! your revels I partake no more,
And Lady Teazle's occupation's o'er!
All this I told our bard — he smiled, and said 'twas clear,
I ought to play deep tragedy next year.
Meanwhile he drew wise morals from his play,   45
And in these solemn periods stalked away: —
'Blest were the fair like you; her faults who stopped,
And closed her follies when the curtain dropped!
No more in vice or error to engage,
Or play the fool at large on life's great stage.'   50

The Critic; or, a Tragedy Rehearsed

BY RICHARD BRINSLEY SHERIDAN

THE CRITIC

OR

A Tragedy Rehearsed

A Dramatic Piece

in three ACTS

as it is performed at the

THEATRE ROYAL in DRURY LANE

By

Richard Brinsley Sheridan Esq.

LONDON.

Printed for T. Becket, Adelphi, Strand,

MDCCLXXXI.

ENGRAVED TITLE OF THE FIRST EDITION, 1781, OF *THE CRITIC*
Dyce copy in the Victoria and Albert Museum, South Kensington.

[DEDICATION]

To Mrs. Greville [1]

Madam,

In requesting your permission to address the following pages to you, which, as they aim themselves to be critical, require every protection and allowance that approving taste or friendly prejudice can give them, I yet ventured to mention no other motive than the gratification of private friendship and esteem. Had I suggested a hope that your implied approbation would give a sanction to their defects, your particular reserve, and dislike to the reputation of critical taste, as well as of poetical talent, would have made you refuse the protection of your name to such a purpose. However, I am not so ungrateful as now to attempt to combat this disposition in you. I shall not here presume to argue that the present state of poetry claims and expects every assistance that taste and example can afford it: nor endeavor to prove that a fastidious concealment of the most elegant productions of judgment and fancy is an ill return for the possession of those endowments. — Continue to deceive yourself in the idea that you are known only to be eminently admired and regarded for the valuable qualities that attach private friendships, and the graceful talents that adorn conversation. Enough of what you have written has stolen into full public notice to answer my purpose; and you will, perhaps, be the only person, conversant in elegant literature, who shall read this address and not perceive that by publishing your particular approbation of the following drama, I have a more interested object than to boast the true respect and regard with which

I have the honor to be,

    Madam,

        Your very sincere,

        And obedient humble servant,

            R. B. Sheridan.

[1] Wife of Fulke Greville, and mother of Mrs. Crewe to whom Sheridan had inscribed his dedicatory poem sent with a MS. copy (Crewe MS.) of *The School for Scandal*.

PROLOGUE

By the Honorable Richard Fitzpatrick [1]

The sister Muses,[2] whom these realms obey,
Who o'er the drama hold divided sway,
Sometimes, by evil counsellors, 'tis said,
Like earth-born potentates have been misled:
In those gay days of wickedness and wit,   5
When Villiers criticised what Dryden writ,[3]
The Tragic Queen, to please a tasteless crowd,
Had learned to bellow, rant, and roar so loud,
That frightened Nature, her best friend before,
The blust'ring beldam's company forswore.   10
Her Comic Sister, who had wit, 'tis true,
With all her merits, had her failings too;
And would sometimes in mirthful moments use
A style too flippant for a well-bred Muse.
Then female modesty abashed began   15
To seek the friendly refuge of the fan;
Awhile behind that slight entrenchment stood,
Till driv'n from thence, she left the stage for good.
In our more pious, and far chaster times,
These sure no longer are the Muse's crimes!   20
But some complain that, former faults to shun,
The reformation to extremes has run.
The frantic hero's wild delirium past,
Now insipidity succeeds bombast;
So slow Melpomene's cold numbers creep,   25
Here dullness seems her drowsy court to keep,
And we are scarce awake, whilst you are fast asleep.
Thalia, once so ill-behaved and rude,
Reformed, is now become an arrant prude,
Retailing nightly to the yawning pit   30
The purest morals, undefiled by wit!
Our author offers, in these motley scenes,
A slight remonstrance to the drama's queens:
Nor let the goddesses be over nice;[4]
Free-spoken subjects give the best advice.   35
Although not quite a novice in his trade,
His cause to-night requires no common aid.
To this, a friendly, just, and pow'rful court,
I come ambassador to beg support.
Can he undaunted brave the critic's rage?   40
In civil broils with brother bards engage?
Hold forth their errors to the public eye,
Nay more, e'en newspapers themselves defy?
Say, must his single arm encounter all?
By numbers vanquished, e'en the brave may fall;   45
And though no leader should success distrust,
Whose troops are willing, and whose cause is just;
To bid such hosts of angry foes defiance,
His chief dependence must be, YOUR ALLIANCE.

[1] Wit, soldier, man of fashion, close friend of Charles James Fox. In 1778, he had returned to London after military service in America.

[2] Melpomene, 'the Tragic Queen' (l. 7), and Thalia, 'her Comic Sister' (l. 11).

[3] See Buckingham's burlesque, *The Rehearsal*.   [4] Scrupulous.

DRAMATIS PERSONÆ

DANGLE
SNEER
SIR FRETFUL PLAGIARY
SIGNOR PASTICCIO RITORNELLO
Interpreter
Under Prompter
AND
PUFF
MRS. DANGLE
Italian Girls

CHARACTERS OF THE TRAGEDY

LORD BURLEIGH
GOVERNOR OF TILBURY FORT
EARL OF LEICESTER
SIR WALTER RALEIGH
SIR CHRISTOPHER HATTON
MASTER OF THE HORSE
BEEFEATER
Justice
Son
Constable
THAMES
AND
DON FEROLO WHISKERANDOS

1st Niece
2d Niece
Justice's Lady
Confidante
AND
TILBURINA

Guards, Constables, Servants, Chorus, Rivers, Attendants, &c. &c.

[SCENE — LONDON]

[TIME: 1779]

THE CRITIC;

OR,

A TRAGEDY REHEARSED

ACT I

SCENE I

MR. *and* MRS. DANGLE *at breakfast, and reading newspapers.*

DANGLE (*reading*). *Brutus to Lord North.*[1] — *Letter the second on the State of the Army.* — Pshaw! *To the first L— dash D of the A— dash Y.*[2] — *Genuine Extract of a Letter from St. Kitt's.*[3] — *Coxheath Intelligence.*[4] — 'It is now confidently asserted that Sir 5 Charles Hardy.'[5] — Pshaw! — Nothing but about the fleet and the nation! — and I hate all politics but theatrical politics. — Where's the *Morning Chronicle?*

MRS. DANGLE. Yes, that's your gazette.

DANGLE. So, here we have it. — '*Theatrical in-* 10 *telligence extraordinary.* — We hear there is a new tragedy in rehearsal at Drury Lane Theatre, called the SPANISH ARMADA, said to be written by Mr. Puff, a gentleman well known in the theatrical world; if we may allow ourselves to give credit to the report 15 of the performers, who, truth to say, are in general but indifferent judges, this piece abounds with the most striking and received beauties of modern composition.' — So! I am very glad my friend Puff's tragedy is in such forwardness. — Mrs. Dangle, my dear, 20 you will be very glad to hear that Puff's tragedy —

MRS. D. Lord, Mr. Dangle, why will you plague me about such nonsense? — Now the plays are begun I shall have no peace. — Isn't it sufficient to make yourself ridiculous by your passion for the the- 25 atre, without continually teasing me to join you? Why can't you ride your hobby-horse without desiring to place me on a pillion behind you, Mr. Dangle?

DANGLE. Nay, my dear, I was only going to read — 30

MRS. D. No, no; you will never read anything that's worth listening to: — you hate to hear about your country; there are letters every day with Roman signatures, demonstrating the certainty of an invasion, and proving that the nation is utterly 35 undone. — But you never will read anything to entertain one.

DANGLE. What has a woman to do with politics, Mrs. Dangle?

MRS. D. And what have you to do with the 40 theatre, Mr. Dangle? Why should you affect the character of a critic? I have no patience with you! — haven't you made yourself the jest of all your acquaintance by your interference in matters where you have no business? Are not you called a 45 theatrical quidnunc,[6] and a mock Mæcenas[7] to second-hand authors?

DANGLE. True; my power with the managers is pretty notorious; but is it no credit to have applications from all quarters for my interest? — From 50 lords to recommend fiddlers, from ladies to get boxes, from authors to get answers, and from actors to get engagements?

MRS. D. Yes, truly; you have contrived to get a share in all the plague and trouble of theatri- 55 cal property, without the profit, or even the credit of the abuse that attends it.

DANGLE. I am sure, Mrs. Dangle, you are no loser by it, however; *you* have all the advantages of it: — mightn't you, last winter, have had the reading 60 of the new pantomime a fortnight previous to its performance? And doesn't Mr. Fosbrook let you take places for a play before it is advertised, and set you down for a box for every new piece through the season? And didn't my friend, Mr. Smatter, 65 dedicate his last farce to you at my particular request, Mrs. Dangle?

MRS. D. Yes; but wasn't the farce damned, Mr. Dangle? And to be sure it is extremely pleasant to have one's house made the motley rendezvous of 70 all the lackeys of literature — the very high 'change of trading authors and jobbing critics! — Yes, my drawing-room is an absolute register-office for candidate actors, and poets without character; — then to be continually alarmed with misses and 75 ma'ams piping hysteric changes on Juliets and Dorindas,[8] Pollys[9] and Ophelias; and the very furniture trembling at the probatory starts and unprovoked rants of would-be Richards and Hamlets! — And

---

[1] First Lord of the Treasury.

[2] First Lord of the Admiralty, John Montagu, Fourth Earl of Sandwich.

[3] St. Christopher, in the West Indies, where the English and French fleets were opposed.

[4] In July, 1779, the militia had been largely assembled at Coxheath camp, near Maidstone.

[5] Admiral of the Channel Fleet.

[6] Newsmonger.   [7] Patron.

[8] Dorinda in *The Beaux' Stratagem.*

[9] Polly Peachum in *The Beggar's Opera.*

what is worse than all, now that the manager 80
has monopolized the Opera-House,[1] haven't we the
signors and signoras calling here, sliding their smooth
semibreves, and gargling glib divisions in their outlandish throats — with foreign emissaries and French
spies, for aught I know, disguised like fiddlers 85
and figure dancers!

DANGLE. Mercy! Mrs. Dangle!

MRS. D. And to employ yourself so idly at such an
alarming crisis as this, too — when, if you had the
least spirit, you would have been at the head of 90
the Westminster associations[2] — or trailing a volunteer pike in the Artillery Ground! — But you —
o'my conscience, I believe if the French were landed
to-morrow, your first inquiry would be, whether they
had brought a theatrical troop with them. 95

DANGLE. Mrs. Dangle, it does not signify — I say
the stage is 'the mirror of nature,' and the actors are
'the abstract and brief chronicles of the time':[3] —
and pray what can a man of sense study better? —
Besides, you will not easily persuade me that 100
there is no credit or importance in being at the head
of a band of critics, who take upon them to decide
for the whole town, whose opinion and patronage all
writers solicit, and whose recommendation no manager dares refuse. 105

MRS. D. Ridiculous! — Both managers and authors of the least merit laugh at your pretensions. —
The *public* is their *critic* — without whose fair approbation they know no play can rest on the stage, and
with whose applause they welcome such attacks 110
as yours, and laugh at the malice of them, where
they can't at the wit.

DANGLE. Very well, madam — very well.

Enter Servant.

SERV. Mr. Sneer, sir, to wait on you.

DANGLE. Oh, show Mr. Sneer up. 115

Exit Servant.

Plague on't! now we must appear loving and affectionate, or Sneer will hitch us into a story.

MRS. D. With all my heart; you can't be more
ridiculous than you are.

DANGLE. You are enough to provoke — 120

Enter MR. SNEER.

Ha! my dear Sneer, I am vastly glad to see you.
My dear, here's Mr. Sneer.

MRS. D. Good morning to you, sir.

DANGLE. Mrs. Dangle and I have been diverting
ourselves with the papers. — Pray, Sneer, won't 125
you go to Drury Lane Theatre the first night of
Puff's tragedy?

SNEER. Yes; but I suppose one sha'n't be able to
get in, for on the first night of a new piece they always fill the house with orders to support it. 130
But here, Dangle, I have brought you two pieces, one
of which you must exert yourself to make the managers accept, I can tell you that; for 'tis written by a
person of consequence.

DANGLE. So! now my plagues are beginning! 135

SNEER. Aye, I am glad of it, for now you'll be
happy. Why, my dear Dangle, it is a pleasure to see
how you enjoy your volunteer fatigue, and your
solicited solicitations.

DANGLE. It's a great trouble — yet, egad, 140
it's pleasant too. — Why, sometimes of a morning, I
have a dozen people call on me at breakfast-time,
whose faces I never saw before, nor ever desire to see
again.

SNEER. That must be very pleasant, indeed! 145

DANGLE. And not a week but I receive fifty letters, and not a line in them about any business of my
own.

SNEER. An amusing correspondence!

DANGLE (*reading*). '*Bursts into tears, and* 150
exit.' What, is this a tragedy?

SNEER. No, that's a genteel comedy, not a translation — only *taken from the French*; it is written in a
style which they have lately tried to run down — the
true sentimental, and nothing ridiculous in it 155
from the beginning to the end.

MRS. D. Well, if they had kept to that, I should
not have been such an enemy to the stage; there was
some edification to be got from those pieces, Mr.
Sneer! 160

SNEER. I am quite of your opinion, Mrs. Dangle;
the theatre, in proper hands, might certainly be made
the school of morality;[4] but now, I am sorry to say
it, people seem to go there principally for their entertainment! 165

MRS. D. It would have been more to the credit
of the managers to have kept it in the other line.

SNEER. Undoubtedly, madam; and hereafter, perhaps, to have had it recorded that, in the midst of a
luxurious and dissipated age, they preserved 170
two houses in the capital where the conversation was
always moral, at least, if not entertaining!

DANGLE. Now, egad, I think the worst alteration
is in the nicety of the audience. — No *double entendre*,
no smart innuendo admitted; even Vanbrugh 175
and Congreve obliged to undergo a bungling reformation![5]

SNEER. Yes, and our prudery in this respect is just
on a par with the artificial bashfulness of a courtesan,

---

[1] In 1779, *Coalition, a Farce Founded on Facts,* satirized
Sheridan's theatrical 'monopoly,' supported by interchange of
actors between Drury Lane and Covent Garden theatres.
[2] Volunteer militia.   [3] *Hamlet,* III. ii. 26, and II. ii. 555.

[4] A hit at sentimental comedy, whose doctrine is expressed in
the next to last speech of Hugh Kelly's *False Delicacy* (1768):
'The stage should be a school of morality.'
[5] In *A Trip to Scarborough* (1777) Sheridan had revised
Vanbrugh's *The Relapse.*

who increases the blush upon her cheek in an 180
exact proportion to the diminution of her modesty.

DANGLE. Sneer can't even give the public a good
word! — [*Opening the second manuscript.*] But what
have we here? — This seems a very odd —

SNEER. Oh, that's a comedy on a very new 185
plan — replete with wit and mirth, yet of a most
serious moral! You see it is called *The Reformed
Housebreaker*; where, by the mere force of humor,
housebreaking is put into so ridiculous a light that,
if the piece has its proper run, I have no doubt 190
but that bolts and bars will be entirely useless by the
end of the season.

DANGLE. Egad, this is new indeed!

SNEER. Yes; it is written by a particular friend of
mine who has discovered that the follies and 195
foibles of society are subjects unworthy the notice
of the Comic Muse, who should be taught to stoop
only at the greater vices and blacker crimes of
humanity — gibbeting capital offences in five acts,
and pillorying petty larcenies in two. — In 200
short, his idea is to dramatize the penal laws and
make the stage a court of ease to the Old Bailey.[1]

DANGLE. It is truly moral.

Enter Servant.

SERV. Sir Fretful Plagiary, sir.

DANGLE. Beg him to walk up. 205
Exit Servant.

Now, Mrs. Dangle, Sir Fretful Plagiary is an author
to your own taste.

MRS. D. I confess he is a favorite of mine, because
everybody else abuses him.

SNEER. Very much to the credit of your 210
charity, madam, if not of your judgment.

DANGLE. But, egad, he allows no merit to any
author but himself, that's the truth on't — though
he's my friend.

SNEER. Never. — He is as envious as an 215
old maid verging on the desperation of six-and-thirty:
and then the insidious humility with which he seduces you to give a free opinion on any of his works,
can be exceeded only by the petulant arrogance with
which he is sure to reject your observations. 220

DANGLE. Very true, egad — though he's my friend.

SNEER. Then his affected contempt of all newspaper strictures; though, at the same time, he is the
sorest man alive, and shrinks like scorched parchment from the fiery ordeal of true criticism: yet 225
is he so covetous of popularity, that he had rather be
abused than not mentioned at all.

DANGLE. There's no denying it — though he is
my friend.

SNEER. You have read the tragedy he has 230
just finished, haven't you?

DANGLE. O yes; he sent it to me yesterday.

SNEER. Well, and you think it execrable, don't
you?

DANGLE. Why, between ourselves, egad, I 235
must own — though he's my friend — that it is one
of the most — (*aside*). He's here — [*aloud*] finished
and most admirable perform —

SIR FRETFUL (*without*). Mr. Sneer with him, did
you say? 240

Enter SIR FRETFUL PLAGIARY.

DANGLE. Ah, my dear friend! — Egad, we were
just speaking of your tragedy. — Admirable, Sir
Fretful, admirable!

SNEER. You never did anything beyond it, Sir
Fretful — never in your life. 245

SIR FRET. You make me extremely happy; — for
without a compliment, my dear Sneer, there isn't a
man in the world whose judgment I value as I do
yours — and Mr. Dangle's.

MRS. D. They are only laughing at you, Sir 250
Fretful; for it was but just now that —

DANGLE. Mrs. Dangle! — Ah, Sir Fretful, you
know Mrs. Dangle. — My friend Sneer was rallying
just now — He knows how she admires you, and —

SIR FRET. O Lord, I am sure Mr. Sneer has 255
more taste and sincerity than to — (*aside*) A
damned double-faced fellow!

DANGLE. Yes, yes, — Sneer will jest — but a
better humored —

SIR FRET. Oh, I know. 260

DANGLE. He has a ready turn for ridicule — his
wit costs him nothing.

SIR FRET. No, egad, — (*aside*) or I should wonder
how he came by it.

MRS. D. Because his jest is always at the 265
expense of his friend.

DANGLE. But, Sir Fretful, have you sent your
play to the managers yet? — or can I be of any
service to you?

SIR FRET. No, no, I thank you; I believe the 270
piece had sufficient recommendation with it. — I
thank you, though. — I sent it to the manager of
Covent Garden Theatre this morning.

SNEER. I should have thought, now, that it might
have been cast (as the actors call it) better at 275
Drury Lane.

SIR FRET. O lud! no — never send a play there
while I live — harkee! (*Whispers* SNEER.)

SNEER. *Writes himself!*[2] — I know he does ——

SIR FRET. I say nothing — I take away from 280
no man's merit — am hurt at no man's good fortune — I say nothing. — But this I will say —
through all my knowledge of life I have observed —
that there is not a passion so strongly rooted in the
human heart as envy! 285

---

[1] The central criminal court of London.

[2] Sheridan, manager of Drury Lane Theatre.

SNEER. I believe you have reason for what you say, indeed.

SIR FRET. Besides — I can tell you it is not always so safe to leave a play in the hands of those who write themselves. 290

SNEER. What, they may steal from them, hey, my dear Plagiary?

SIR FRET. Steal! — to be sure they may; and, egad, serve your best thoughts as gipsies do stolen children, disfigure them to make 'em pass for 295 their own.[1]

SNEER. But your present work is a sacrifice to Melpomene, and *he*, you know, never ——

SIR FRET. That's no security. — A dext'rous plagiarist may do anything. — Why, sir, for 300 aught I know, he might take out some of the best things in my tragedy, and put them into his own comedy.

SNEER. That might be done, I dare be sworn.

SIR FRET. And then, if such a person gives 305 you the least hint or assistance, he is devilish apt to take the merit of the whole —

DANGLE. If it succeeds.

SIR FRET. Aye, — but with regard to this piece, I think I can hit that gentleman, for I can safely 310 swear he never read it.

SNEER. I'll tell you how you may hurt him more.

SIR FRET. How?

SNEER. Swear he wrote it.

SIR FRET. Plague on't now, Sneer, I shall 315 take it ill. — I believe you want to take away my character as an author.

SNEER. Then I am sure you ought to be very much obliged to me.

SIR FRET. Hey! — sir! —— 320

DANGLE. Oh, you know, he never means what he says.

SIR FRET. Sincerely then — you do like the piece?

SNEER. Wonderfully!

SIR FRET. But come now, there must be 325 something that you think might be mended, hey? — Mr. Dangle, has nothing struck you?

DANGLE. Why, faith, it is but an ungracious thing, for the most part, to ——

SIR FRET. With most authors it is just so, in- 330 deed; they are in general strangely tenacious! — But, for my part, I am never so well pleased as when a judicious critic points out any defect to me; for what is the purpose of showing a work to a friend if you don't mean to profit by his opinion? 335

SNEER. Very true. — Why then, though I seri- ously admire the piece upon the whole, yet there is one small objection, which, if you'll give me leave, I'll mention.

[1] Cf. Churchill's lines:
'Still pilfers wretched plans, and makes them worse,
Like gipsies, lest the stolen brat be known,
Defacing first, then claiming for his own.'

SIR FRET. Sir, you can't oblige me more. 340

SNEER. I think it wants incident.

SIR FRET. Good God! you surprise me! — wants incident!

SNEER. Yes; I own I think the incidents are too few. 345

SIR FRET. Good God! — Believe me, Mr. Sneer, there is no person for whose judgment I have a more implicit deference. — But I protest to you, Mr. Sneer, I am only apprehensive that the incidents are too crowded. — My dear Dangle, how does it 350 strike you?

DANGLE. Really I can't agree with my friend Sneer. — I think the plot quite sufficient; and the four first acts by many degrees the best I ever read or saw in my life. If I might venture to sug- 355 gest anything, it is that the interest rather falls off in the fifth.

SIR FRET. Rises, I believe you mean, sir.

DANGLE. No, I don't, upon my word.

SIR FRET. Yes, yes, you do, upon my soul — 360 it certainly don't fall off, I assure you. — No, no; it don't fall off.

DANGLE. Now, Mrs. Dangle, didn't you say it struck you in the same light?

MRS. D. No, indeed, I did not — I did not 365 see a fault in any part of the play, from the begin- ning to the end.

SIR FRET. Upon my soul, the women are the best judges after all!

MRS. D. Or, if I made any objection, I am 370 sure it was to nothing in the piece, but that I was afraid it was, on the whole, a little too long.

SIR FRET. Pray, madam, do you speak as to dura- tion of time, or do you mean that the story is tedi- ously spun out? 375

MRS. D. O lud! no. — I speak only with reference to the usual length of acting plays.

SIR FRET. Then I am very happy — very happy indeed, — because the play is a short play — a re- markably short play. — I should not venture 380 to differ with a lady on a point of taste; but, on these occasions, the watch, you know, is the critic.

MRS. D. Then, I suppose, it must have been Mr. Dangle's drawling manner of reading it to me.

SIR FRET. Oh, if Mr. Dangle read it! that's 385 quite another affair! — But I assure you, Mrs. Dangle, the first evening you can spare me three hours and a half, I'll undertake to read you the whole from beginning to end, with the prologue and epi- logue, and allow time for the music between the 390 acts.

MRS. D. I hope to see it on the stage next.

DANGLE. Well, Sir Fretful, I wish you may be able to get rid as easily of the newspaper criticisms as you do of ours. 395

SIR FRET. The *newspapers*! — Sir, they are the most villainous — licentious — abominable — infernal — Not that I ever read them — No — I make it a rule never to look into a newspaper.

DANGLE. You are quite right — for it cer-   400
tainly must hurt an author of delicate feelings to see the liberties they take.

SIR FRET. No! quite the contrary; — their abuse is, in fact, the best panegyric — I like it of all things. — An author's reputation is only in danger   405
from their support.

SNEER. Why, that's true — and that attack, now, on you the other day ——

SIR FRET. What? where?

DANGLE. Aye, you mean in a paper of   410
Thursday; it was completely ill-natured, to be sure.

SIR FRET. Oh, so much the better. — Ha! ha! ha! — I wouldn't have it otherwise.

DANGLE. Certainly it is only to be laughed at; for ——   415

SIR FRET. You don't happen to recollect what the fellow said, do you?

SNEER. Pray, Dangle — Sir Fretful seems a little anxious ——

SIR FRET. O lud, no! — anxious? — not I —   420
not the least. — I — But one may as well hear, you know.

DANGLE. Sneer, do *you* recollect? — (*Aside.*) Make out something.

SNEER (*To* DANGLE). I will. — Yes, yes,   425
I remember perfectly.

SIR FRET. Well, and pray now — not that it sig-nifies — what might the gentleman say?

SNEER. Why, he roundly asserts that you have not the slightest invention or original genius   430
whatever; though you are the greatest traducer of all other authors living.

SIR FRET. Ha! ha! ha! — very good!

SNEER. That as to *comedy*, you have not one idea of your own, he believes, even in your common-   435
place-book — where stray jokes and pilfered witti-cisms are kept with as much method as the ledger of the Lost-and-Stolen Office.

SIR FRET. Ha! ha! ha! — very pleasant!

SNEER. Nay, that you are so unlucky as not   440
to have the skill even to *steal* with taste; but that you glean from the refuse of obscure volumes, where more judicious plagiarists have been before you; so that the body of your work is a composition of dregs and sediments — like a bad tavern's worst   445
wine.

SIR FRET. Ha! ha!

SNEER. In your more serious efforts, he says, your bombast would be less intolerable if the thoughts were ever suited to the expression; but the   450
homeliness of the sentiment stares through the fan-tastic encumbrance of its fine language, like a clown in one of the new uniforms!

SIR FRET. Ha! ha!

SNEER. That your occasional tropes and   455
flowers suit the general coarseness of your style, as tambour sprigs[1] would a ground of linsey-woolsey; while your imitations of Shakespeare resemble the mimicry of Falstaff's page, and are about as near the standard of the original.   460

SIR FRET. Ha! —

SNEER. In short, that even the finest passages you steal are of no service to you; for the poverty of your own language prevents their assimilating, so that they lie on the surface like lumps of marl   465
on a barren moor, encumbering what it is not in their power to fertilize!

SIR FRET. (*after great agitation*). — Now, another person would be vexed at this.

SNEER. Oh! but I wouldn't have told you,   470
only to divert you.

SIR FRET. I know it — I *am* diverted — Ha! ha! ha! — not the least invention! — Ha! ha! ha! very good! — very good!

SNEER. Yes — no genius! Ha! ha! ha!   475

DANGLE. A severe rogue! Ha! ha! ha! But you are quite right, Sir Fretful, never to read such non-sense.

SIR FRET. To be sure — for if there is anything to one's praise, it is a foolish vanity to be gratified   480
at it; and if it is abuse, — why, one is always sure to hear of it from one damned good-natured friend or another!

Enter Servant.

SERV. Sir, there is an Italian gentleman, with a French interpreter, and three young ladies, and   485
a dozen musicians, who say they are sent by Lady Rondeau and Mrs. Fuge.

DANGLE. Gadso! they come by appointment. Dear Mrs. Dangle, do let them know I'll see them directly.   490

MRS. D. You know, Mr. Dangle, I sha'n't under-stand a word they say.

DANGLE. But you hear there's an interpreter.

MRS. D. Well, I'll try to endure their complais-ance till you come.   *Exit.*   495

SERV. And Mr. Puff, sir, has sent word that the last rehearsal is to be this morning, and that he'll call on you presently.

DANGLE. That's true — I shall certainly be at home.   *Exit Servant.*   500
— Now, Sir Fretful, if you have a mind to have jus-tice done you in the way of answer — egad, Mr. Puff's your man.

SIR FRET. Pshaw! Sir, why should I wish to have it answered when I tell you I am pleased at   505
it?

DANGLE. True, I had forgot that. — But I hope you are not fretted at what Mr. Sneer —

[1] Embroidered ornaments.

SIR FRET. Zounds! no, Mr. Dangle; don't I tell you these things never fret me in the least? 510

DANGLE. Nay, I only thought —

SIR FRET. — And let me tell you, Mr. Dangle, 'tis damned affronting in you to suppose that I am hurt, when I tell you I am not.

SNEER. But why so warm, Sir Fretful? 515

SIR FRET. Gad's life! Mr. Sneer, you are as absurd as Dangle. How often must I repeat it to you, that nothing can vex me but your supposing it possible for me to mind the damned nonsense you have been repeating to me! — And let me tell 520 you, if you continue to believe this, you must mean to insult me, gentlemen — and then your disrespect will affect me no more than the newspaper criticisms — and I shall treat it — with exactly the same calm indifference and philosophic contempt — and 525 so your servant. *Exit.*

SNEER. Ha! ha! ha! Poor Sir Fretful! Now will he go and vent his philosophy in anonymous abuse of all modern critics and authors. — But, Dangle, you must get your friend Puff to take me to 530 the rehearsal of his tragedy.

DANGLE. I'll answer for't, he'll thank you for desiring it. But come and help me to judge of this musical family; they are recommended by people of consequence, I assure you. 535

SNEER. I am at your disposal the whole morning — but I thought you had been a decided critic in music as well as in literature.

DANGLE. So I am — but I have a bad ear. I'faith, Sneer, though, I am afraid we were a 540 little too severe on Sir Fretful — though he is my friend.

SNEER. Why, 'tis certain that unnecessarily to mortify the vanity of any writer is a cruelty which mere dullness never can deserve; but where a 545 base and personal malignity usurps the place of literary emulation, the aggressor deserves neither quarter nor pity.

DANGLE. That's true, egad! — though he's my friend! 550

SCENE II

A drawing-room, harpsichord, &c. Italian family, French Interpreter, MRS. DANGLE, and Servants discovered.

INTERPRETER. Je dis, madame, j'ai l'honneur to *introduce* et de vous demander votre protection pour le Signor Pasticcio Ritornello et pour sa charmante famille.

SIGNOR PASTICCIO. Ah! Vosignoria, noi vi 5 preghiamo di favoritevi colla vostra protezione.

1ST DAUGHTER. Vosignoria fatevi questi grazzie.

2D DAUGHTER. Si, signora.

INTERP. Madame — *me interpret.* — C'est à dire

— in English — qu'ils vous prient de leur faire 10 l'honneur —

MRS. D. — I say again, gentlemen, I don't understand a word you say.

SIGNOR PAST. Questo signore spiegheró —

INTERP. Oui — *me interpret.* — Nous avons 15 les lettres de recommendation pour Monsieur Dangle de —

MRS. D. — Upon my word, sir, I don't understand you.

SIGNOR PAST. La Contessa Rondeau e nostra 20 padrona.

3D DAUGH. Si, padre, et mi Ladi Fuge.

INTERP. Oh! — *me interpret.* — Madame, ils disent — in English — qu'ils ont l'honneur d'être protégés de ces dames. — *You understand?* 25

MRS. D. No, sir, — no understand!

Enter DANGLE and SNEER.

INTERP. Ah, voici Monsieur Dangle!

ALL ITALIANS. A! Signor Dangle!

MRS. D. Mr. Dangle, here are two very civil gentlemen trying to make themselves under- 30 stood, and I don't know which is the interpreter.

DANGLE. Eh, bien!

INTERP. Monsieur Dangle, le grand bruit ⎫
de vos talents pour la critique, et de votre ⎪
intérêt avec Messieurs les Directeurs à tous 35 ⎬ *(Speaking together)*
les théâtres — ⎪
SIGNOR PAST. Vosignoria siete si famoso par ⎪
la vostra conoscensa, e vostra interessa colla ⎪
le Direttore da — ⎭

DANGLE. Egad, I think the interpreter is the 40 hardest to be understood of the two!

SNEER. Why I thought, Dangle, you had been an admirable linguist!

DANGLE. So I am, if they would not talk so damned fast. 45

SNEER. Well, I'll explain that — the less time we lose in hearing them the better — for that, I suppose, is what they are brought here for.

(SNEER *speaks to* SIGNOR PASTICCIO. *They sing trios, etc.,* DANGLE *beating out of time.)*

Servant enters and whispers DANGLE.

DANGLE. Show him up. *Exit Servant.*
Bravo! admirable! bravissimo! admirablissimo! 50 — Ah! Sneer! where will you find such as these voices in England?

SNEER. Not easily.

DANGLE. But Puff is coming. Signor and little Signora's — obligatissimo! — Sposa Signora 55 Danglena — Mrs. Dangle, shall I beg you to offer them some refreshments, and take their address in the next room.

Exit MRS. DANGLE with the Italians and Interpreter ceremoniously.

3] O₁ *Patticcio Retornello.* 24] O₁ *d'etre proteges de ces Demes;* M *d'être protégés de ces dames.* 35] O₁ *interesi;* M *intérêt.*

Re-enter Servant.

SERV. Mr. Puff, sir!

DANGLE. My dear Puff!   60

Enter PUFF.

PUFF. My dear Dangle, how is it with you?

DANGLE. Mr. Sneer, give me leave to introduce Mr. Puff to you.

PUFF. Mr. Sneer is this? — Sir, he is a gentleman whom I have long panted for the honor of know-   65 ing — a gentleman whose critical talents and transcendent judgment —

SNEER. Dear sir —

DANGLE. Nay, don't be modest, Sneer; my friend Puff only talks to you in the style of his profes-   70 sion.

SNEER. His profession!

PUFF. Yes, sir; I make no secret of the trade I follow — among friends and brother authors, Dangle knows I love to be frank on the subject, and to   75 advertise myself *vivâ voce*. — I am, sir, a Practitioner in Panegyric, or, to speak more plainly, a Professor of the Art of Puffing, at your service — or anybody else's.

SNEER. Sir, you are very obliging! — I be-   80 lieve, Mr. Puff, I have often admired your talents in the daily prints.

PUFF. Yes, sir, I flatter myself I do as much business in that way as any six of the fraternity in town. — Devilish hard work all the summer — Friend   85 Dangle — never worked harder! — But, harkee, — the winter managers were a little sore, I believe.

DANGLE. No — I believe they took it all in good part.

PUFF. Aye! — then that must have been   90 affectation in them; for, egad, there were some of the attacks which there was no laughing at!

SNEER. Aye, the humorous ones. — But I should think, Mr. Puff, that authors would in general be able to do this sort of work for themselves.   95

PUFF. Why, yes — but in a clumsy way. — Besides, we look on that as an encroachment, and so take the opposite side. — I dare say, now, you conceive half the very civil paragraphs and advertisements you see to be written by the parties con-   100 cerned, or their friends? — No such thing — nine out of ten manufactured by me in the way of business.

SNEER. Indeed! —

PUFF. Even the auctioneers now — the auctioneers, I say — though the rogues have lately   105 got some credit for their language — not an article of the merit theirs! — take them out of their pulpits, and they are as dull as catalogues! — No, sir; 'twas I first enriched their style — 'twas I first taught them to crowd their advertisements with panegyrical   110 superlatives, each epithet rising above the other, like the bidders in their own auction-rooms! — From

me they learned to inlay their phraseology with variegated chips of exotic metaphor: by *me*, too, their inventive faculties were called forth. —⸤Yes, sir,   115 by *me* they were instructed to clothe ideal walls with gratuitous fruits — to insinuate obsequious rivulets into visionary groves — to teach courteous shrubs to nod their approbation of the grateful soil! or on emergencies to raise upstart oaks where there   120 never had been an acorn; to create a delightful vicinage without the assistance of a neighbor; or fix the temple of Hygeia [1] in the fens of Lincolnshire!

DANGLE. I am sure you have done them infinite service; for now, when a gentleman is ruined,   125 he parts with his house with some credit.

SNEER. Service! — if they had any gratitude they would erect a statue to him; they would figure him as a presiding Mercury, the god of traffic and fiction, [2] with a hammer in his hand instead of a cadu-   130 ceus. — But pray, Mr. Puff, what first put you on exercising your talents in this way?

PUFF. Egad, sir, sheer necessity — the proper parent of an art so nearly allied to invention: you must know, Mr. Sneer, that from the first time   135 I tried my hand at an advertisement, my success was such that, for some time after, I led a most extraordinary life indeed!

SNEER. How, pray?

PUFF. Sir, I supported myself two years en-   140 tirely by my misfortunes.

SNEER. By your misfortunes?

PUFF. Yes, sir, assisted by long sickness and other occasional disorders; and a very comfortable living I had of it.   145

SNEER. From sickness and misfortunes! — You practised as a doctor and an attorney at once?

PUFF. No, egad; both maladies and miseries were my own.

SNEER. Hey! — what the plague!   150

DANGLE. 'Tis true, i'faith.

PUFF. Harkee! — By advertisements — 'To the charitable and humane!' and 'to those whom Providence hath blessed with affluence!'

SNEER. Oh, — I understand you.   155

PUFF. And, in truth, I deserved what I got; for I suppose never man went through such a series of calamities in the same space of time! — Sir, I was five times made a bankrupt, and reduced from a state of affluence by a train of unavoidable mis-   160 fortunes. Then, sir, though a very industrious tradesman, I was twice burnt out, and lost my little all both times! — I lived upon those fires a month. — I soon after was confined by a most excruciating disorder, and lost the use of my limbs! — That   165 told very well; for I had the case strongly attested, and went about to collect the subscriptions myself.

[1] Goddess of health.

[2] Mercury, patron of travellers and god of liars.

DANGLE. Egad, I believe that was when you first called on me.

PUFF. In November last? — O no! — I was 170 at that time a close prisoner in the Marshalsea,[1] for a debt benevolently contracted to serve a friend! — I was afterwards twice tapped for a dropsy, which declined into a very profitable consumption! — I was reduced to — O no — then, I became 175 a widow with six helpless children, — after having had eleven husbands pressed,[2] and being left every time eight months gone with child, and without money to get me into an hospital!

SNEER. And you bore all with patience, I 180 make no doubt?

PUFF. Why, yes, though I made some occasional attempts at *felo de se*;[3] but as I did not find those *rash actions* answer, I left off killing myself very soon. — Well, sir, — at last, what with bank- 185 ruptcies, fires, gouts, dropsies, imprisonments, and other valuable calamities, having got together a pretty handsome sum, I determined to quit a business which had always gone rather against my conscience, and in a more liberal way still to indulge 190 my talents for fiction and embellishment, through my favorite channels of diurnal communication — and so, sir, you have my history.

SNEER. Most obligingly communicative, indeed; and your confession, if published, might cer- 195 tainly serve the cause of true charity, by rescuing the most useful channels of appeal to benevolence from the cant of imposition. — But surely, Mr. Puff, there is no great *mystery* in your present profession?

PUFF. Mystery! Sir, I will take upon me 200 to say the matter was never scientifically treated, nor reduced to rule before.

SNEER. Reduced to rule!

PUFF. O lud, sir, you are very ignorant, I am afraid. — Yes, sir, *Puffing* is of various sorts — 205 the principal are, the *puff direct* — the *puff preliminary* — the *puff collateral* — the *puff collusive* — and the *puff oblique*, or *puff* by *implication*. These all assume, as circumstances require, the various forms of Letter to the Editor, Occasional An- 210 ecdote, Impartial Critique, Observation from Correspondent, or Advertisement from the Party.

SNEER. The puff direct, I can conceive —

PUFF. O yes, that's simple enough, — for instance, a new comedy or farce is to be produced at one 215 of the theatres (though by the bye they don't bring out half what they ought to do) — the author, suppose Mr. Smatter, or Mr. Dapper — or any particular friend of mine — very well; the day before it is to be performed, I write an account of the man- 220 ner in which it was received — I have the plot from

the author, and only add — 'characters strongly drawn' — 'highly colored' — 'hand of a master' — 'fund of genuine humor' — 'mine of invention' — 'neat dialogue' — 'Attic salt!' Then for the 225 performance — 'Mr. Dodd was astonishingly great in the character of Sir Harry';[4] 'that universal and judicious actor, Mr. Palmer, perhaps never appeared to more advantage than in the Colonel';[5] — 'but it is not in the power of language to do justice 230 to Mr. King![6] — indeed he more than merited those repeated bursts of applause which he drew from a most brilliant and judicious audience.' As to the scenery — 'the miraculous powers of Mr. De Loutherbourg's[7] pencil are universally acknowl- 235 edged. — In short, we are at a loss which to admire most, the unrivalled genius of the author, the great attention and liberality of the managers, the wonderful abilities of the painter, or the incredible exertions of all the performers.' 240

SNEER. That's pretty well indeed, sir.

PUFF. Oh, cool — quite cool — to what I sometimes do.

SNEER. And do you think there are any who are influenced by this? 245

PUFF. O lud, yes, sir. — The number of those who go through [undergo (M)] the fatigue of judging for themselves is very small indeed.

SNEER. Well, sir, — the *puff preliminary*?

PUFF. O that, sir, does well in the form of a 250 *caution*. In a matter of gallantry now — Sir Flimsy Gossimer wishes to be well with Lady Fanny Fete. He applies to me — I open trenches for him with a paragraph in the *Morning Post*. — 'It is recommended to the beautiful and accomplished 255 Lady F four stars F dash E to be on her guard against that dangerous character, Sir F dash G; who, however pleasing and insinuating his manners may be, is certainly not remarkable for the *constancy of his attachments*!' — in italics. Here, you see, Sir 260 Flimsy Gossimer is introduced to the particular notice of Lady Fanny, who perhaps never thought of him before — she finds herself publicly cautioned to avoid him, which naturally makes her desirous of seeing him; — the observation of their ac- 265 quaintance causes a pretty kind of mutual embarrassment; this produces a sort of sympathy of interest, which, if Sir Flimsy is unable to improve effectually, he at least gains the credit of having their names mentioned together, by a particular set, and 270 in a particular way — which nine times out of ten is the full accomplishment of modern gallantry.

[4] Dodd, the original Dangle, had created the part of Sir Harry Bouquet in (?) Tickell's *The Camp* (1778).

[5] Palmer, the original Sneer, appeared as Colonel Lambert in Bickerstaffe's *The Hypocrite*, November 11, 1779.

[6] King, the original Puff.

[7] Scenic designer at Drury Lane Theatre. He designed the scenery for *The Critic*.

[1] Debtors' prison in London.

[2] 'Impressed into naval service.'

[3] Law term for 'suicide.'

DANGLE. Egad, Sneer, you will be quite an adept in the business.

PUFF. Now, sir, the *puff collateral* is much 275 used as an appendage to advertisements, and may take the form of anecdote. 'Yesterday, as the celebrated George Bon-Mot was sauntering down St. James's Street, he met the lively Lady Mary Myrtle coming out of the Park: — "Good God, Lady 280 Mary, I'm surprised to meet you in a white jacket, — for I expected never to have seen you but in a full-trimmed uniform and a light horseman's cap!" — "Heavens, George, where could you have learned that?" — "Why," replied the wit, "I just saw 285 a print of you in a new publication called the *Camp Magazine* — which, by the bye, is a devilish clever thing, and is sold at No. 3, on the right hand of the way, two doors from the printing-office, the corner of Ivy Lane, Paternoster Row, price only one 290 shilling!"'

SNEER. Very ingenious indeed!

PUFF. But the *puff collusive* is the newest of any; for it acts in the disguise of determined hostility. — It is much used by bold booksellers and enter- 295 prising poets. — 'An indignant correspondent observes, that the new poem called *Beelzebub's Cotillion, or Proserpine's Fête Champêtre*, is one of the most unjustifiable performances he ever read! The severity with which certain characters are handled 300 is quite shocking! and as there are many descriptions in it too warmly colored for female delicacy, the shameful avidity with which this piece is bought by all people of fashion is a reproach on the taste of the times, and a disgrace to the delicacy of the 305 age.' Here you see, the two strongest inducements are held forth: — first, that nobody ought to read it; and, secondly, that everybody buys it; on the strength of which the publisher boldly prints the tenth edition, before he had sold ten of the 310 first; and then establishes it by threatening himself with the pillory, or absolutely indicting himself for *scan. mag.*[1]

DANGLE. Ha! ha! ha! — 'gad, I know it is so.

PUFF. As to the *puff oblique*, or *puff by impli-* 315 *cation*, it is too various and extensive to be illustrated by an instance. It attracts in titles and presumes in patents; it lurks in the *limitation* of a subscription, and invites in the assurance of crowd and incommodation at public places; it delights to draw forth 320 concealed merit, with a most disinterested assiduity; and sometimes wears a countenance of smiling censure and tender reproach. — It has a wonderful memory for parliamentary debates, and will often give the whole speech of a favored member with 325 the most flattering accuracy. But, above all, it is a great dealer in reports and suppositions. — It has the earliest intelligence of intended preferments that

will reflect *honor* on the *patrons*, and embryo promotions of modest gentlemen — who know noth- 330 ing of the matter themselves. It can hint a ribband for implied services, in the air of a common report; and with the carelessness of a casual paragraph, suggest officers into commands, to which they have no pretension but their wishes. This, sir, is the 335 last principal class in the *art of puffing* — an art which I hope you will now agree with me is of the highest dignity, yielding a tablature of benevolence and public spirit; befriending equally trade, gallantry, criticism, and politics: — the applause of genius — 340 the register of charity — the triumph of heroism — the self-defence of contractors — the fame of orators — and the gazette of ministers!

SNEER. Sir, I am completely a convert both to the importance and ingenuity of your profession; 345 and now, sir, there is but one thing which can possibly increase my respect for you, and that is, your permitting me to be present this morning at the rehearsal of your new trage —

PUFF. Hush, for heaven's sake! — *My* trag- 350 edy! — Egad, Dangle, I take this very ill — you know how apprehensive I am of being known to be the author.

DANGLE. I'faith, I would not have told — but it's in the papers, and your name at length — 355 in the *Morning Chronicle*.

PUFF. Ah! those damned editors never can keep a secret! — Well, Mr. Sneer, no doubt you will do me great honor — I shall be infinitely happy — highly flattered — 360

DANGLE. I believe it must be near the time — shall we go together?

PUFF. No; it will not be yet this hour, for they are always late at that theatre: besides, I must meet you there, for I have some little matters here to 365 send to the papers, and a few paragraphs to scribble before I go. — (*Looking at memorandums.*) — Here is 'a Conscientious Baker, on the subject of the Army Bread'; and 'a Detester of visible Brick-work, in favor of the new-invented Stucco' — both in 370 the style of Junius,[2] and promised for to-morrow. The Thames navigation, too, is at a stand. 'Misomud,' or 'Anti-shoal,' must go to work again directly. — Here too are some political memorandums, I see; aye — To take Paul Jones, and get the 375 Indiamen[3] out of the Shannon — reinforce Byron[4] — compel the Dutch to — so! — I must do that in the evening papers, or reserve it for the *Morning Herald*; for I know that I have undertaken to-morrow, besides, to establish the unanimity of the fleet 380

---

[1] Slander of dignitaries (*scandalum magnatum*).

[2] *Letters of Junius*, which had appeared in *The Public Advertiser* (1768–1772).

[3] Merchantmen.

[4] Vice-Admiral Byron, who had opposed the French fleet in the West Indies, in July, 1779.

in the *Public Advertiser*, and to shoot Charles Fox in the *Morning Post.* — So, egad, I ha'n't a moment to lose!

DANGLE. Well! — we'll meet in the green-room.

Exeunt severally.

ACT II

SCENE I

The Theatre.

Enter DANGLE, PUFF, *and* SNEER, *as before the curtain.*

PUFF. No, no, sir; what Shakespeare says of *actors* may be better applied to the purpose of *plays; they* ought to be 'the abstract and brief chronicles of the time.' Therefore, when history, and particularly the history of our own country, furnishes 5 anything like a case in point, to the time in which an author writes, if he knows his own interest, he will take advantage of it: so, sir, I call my tragedy *The Spanish Armada*; and have laid the scene before Tilbury Fort.[1]   10

SNEER. A most happy thought, certainly!

DANGLE. Egad, it was — I told you so. — But pray now, I don't understand how you have contrived to introduce any love into it.

PUFF. Love! — Oh, nothing so easy; for it is 15 a received point among poets, that where history gives you a good heroic outline for a play, you may fill up with a little love at your own discretion: in doing which, nine times out of ten, you only make up a deficiency in the private history of the times. 20 Now, I rather think I have done this with some success.

SNEER. No scandal about Queen Elizabeth, I hope?

PUFF. O lud! no, no. — I only suppose the 25 governor of Tilbury Fort's daughter to be in love with the son of the Spanish admiral.

SNEER. Oh, is that all!

DANGLE. Excellent, i'faith! I see it at once. — But won't this appear rather improbable?   30

PUFF. To be sure it will — but, what the plague! a play is not to show occurrences that happen every day, but things just so strange, that though they never *did*, they *might* happen.

SNEER. Certainly nothing is unnatural that 35 is not physically impossible.

PUFF. Very true; and for that matter Don Ferolo Whiskerandos — for that's the lover's name — might have been over here in the train of the Spanish ambassador; or Tilburina, for that is the lady's 40

name, might have been in love with him from having heard his character, or seen his picture; or from knowing that he was the last man in the world she ought to be in love with — or for any other good female reason. — However, sir, the fact is, that 45 though she is but a knight's daughter, egad! she is in love like any princess!

DANGLE. Poor young lady! I feel for her already! for I can conceive how great the conflict must be between her passion and her duty — her love for 50 her country, and her love for Don Ferolo Whiskerandos!

PUFF. Oh, amazing! — her poor susceptible heart is swayed to and fro, by contending passions, like —

Enter Under Prompter.

UNDER PROMPTER. Sir, the scene is set and 55 everything is ready to begin, if you please.

PUFF. Egad, then we'll lose no time.

UNDER PROMP. Though, I believe, sir, you will find it very short, for all the performers have profited by the kind permission you granted them.   60

PUFF. Hey! what?

UNDER PROMP. You know, sir, you gave them leave to cut out or omit whatever they found heavy or unnecessary to the plot, and I must own they have taken very liberal advantage of your indul- 65 gence.

PUFF. Well, well! — They are in general very good judges, and I know I am luxuriant. — Now, Mr. Hopkins,[2] as soon as you please.

UNDER PROMP. (*to the Music*). Gentlemen, 70 will you play a few bars of something, just to —

PUFF. Aye, that's right, — for as we have the scenes and dresses, egad, we'll go to't as if it was the first night's performance; — but you need not mind stopping between the acts. —   75

Exit Under Prompter.

(*Orchestra play. Then the bell rings.*)

Soh! stand clear, gentlemen. — Now you know there will be a cry of 'down! down! — hats off! — silence!' — Then up curtain, and let us see what our painters have done for us.

SCENE II

The curtain rises and discovers Tilbury Fort. Two Sentinels asleep.

DANGLE. Tilbury Fort! — very fine indeed!

PUFF. Now, what do you think I open with?

SNEER. Faith, I can't guess —

PUFF. A clock. — Hark! — (*Clock strikes.*) — I open with a clock striking, to beget an awful at- 5 tention in the audience — it also marks the time, which is four o'clock in the morning, and saves a

---

[1] At the mouth of the river Thames. Here Queen Elizabeth assembled her troops at the time of the Armada (1588).

[2] Prompter of the Drury Lane Theatre.

4] O1 *times.*   38] O1 *Wiskerandos* in this scene but *Whiskerandos* in *Dramatis Personae* and III. i.

description of the rising sun, and a great deal about gilding the eastern hemisphere.

DANGLE. But, pray, are the sentinels to be asleep? 10

PUFF. Fast as watchmen.

SNEER. Isn't that odd, though, at such an alarming crisis?

PUFF. To be sure it is, — but smaller things 15 must give way to a striking scene at the opening; that's a rule. — And the case is, that two great men are coming to this very spot to begin the piece; now, it is not to be supposed they would open their lips, if these fellows were watching them; so, egad, I 20 must either have sent them off their posts or set them asleep.

SNEER. Oh, that accounts for it! — But tell us, who are these coming? —

PUFF. These are they — Sir Walter Raleigh 25 and Sir Christopher Hatton.[1] You'll know Sir Christopher by his turning out his toes — famous, you know, for his dancing. I like to preserve all the little traits of character. — Now attend.

Enter SIR WALTER RALEIGH *and* SIR CHRISTOPHER HATTON.

SIR CHRISTOPHER HATTON. True, gallant Raleigh! — 30

DANGLE. What, they had been talking before?

PUFF. O, yes; all the way as they came along. — (*To the Actors.*) I beg pardon, gentlemen, but these are particular friends of mine, whose remarks may be of great service to us. — (*To* SNEER *and* 35 DANGLE.) Don't mind interrupting them whenever anything strikes you.

SIR CHRIST. True, gallant Raleigh!
But O, thou champion of thy country's fame,
There *is* a question which I yet must ask; 40
A question which I never asked before —
What mean these mighty armaments?
This general muster? and this throng of chiefs?

SNEER. Pray, Mr. Puff, how came Sir Christopher Hatton never to ask that question before? 45

PUFF. What, before the play began? — how the plague could he?

DANGLE. That's true, i'faith!

PUFF. But you will hear what he thinks of the matter. 50

SIR CHRIST. Alas! my noble friend, when I behold
Yon tented plains in martial symmetry
Arrayed; when I count o'er yon glittering lines
Of crested warriors, where the proud steeds neigh,
And valor-breathing trumpet's shrill appeal, 55
Responsive vibrate on my list'ning ear;
When virgin majesty herself I view,
Like her protecting Pallas, veiled in steel,

With graceful confidence exhort to arms![2]
When briefly all I hear or see bears stamp 60
Of martial vigilance and stern defence,
I cannot but surmise — forgive, my friend,
If the conjecture's rash — I cannot but
Surmise — the State some danger apprehends!

SNEER. A very cautious conjecture that. 65

PUFF. Yes, that's his character — not to give an opinion but on secure grounds. — Now then!

SIR WALTER RALEIGH. O most accomplished Christopher —

PUFF. He calls him by his Christian name, to show that they are on the most familiar terms. 70

SIR WALTER. O most accomplished Christopher, I find
Thy stanch sagacity still tracks the future
In the fresh print of the o'ertaken past.

PUFF. Figurative!

SIR WALTER. Thy fears are just.

SIR CHRIST.   But where?
    whence? when? and what 75
The danger is — methinks I fain would learn.

SIR WALTER. You know, my friend, scarce two revolving suns,
And three revolving moons, have closed their course,
Since haughty Philip,[3] in despite of peace,
With hostile hand hath struck at England's trade. 80

SIR CHRIST. I know it well.

SIR WALTER. Philip, you know, is proud Iberia's king.

SIR CHRIST. He is.

SIR WALTER.   — His subjects in base bigotry
And Catholic oppression held, — while we,
You know, the Protestant persuasion hold. 85

SIR CHRIST. We do.

SIR WALTER. You know, beside, his boasted armament,
The famed Armada, by the Pope baptized,
With purpose to invade these realms —

SIR CHRIST.   — Is sailed;
Our last advices so report. 90

SIR WALTER. While the Iberian admiral's chief hope,
His darling son —

SIR CHRIST.   Ferolo Whiskerandos hight —

SIR WALTER. The same — by chance a pris'ner hath been ta'en,
And in this fort of Tilbury —

SIR CHRIST.   — Is now

Confined; — 'tis true, and oft from yon tall turret's top 95
I've marked the youthful Spaniard's haughty mien
Unconquered, though in chains.

SIR WALTER.   You also know —

DANGLE. Mr. Puff, as he *knows* all this, why does Sir Walter go on telling him?

PUFF. But the audience are not supposed to 100 know anything of the matter, are they?

---

[1] Appointed Lord Chancellor in April, 1587. In February he had warned the House of Commons of the dangers of a Spanish invasion.

[2] In August, 1588, the 'Virgin Queen,' donned in armor and mounted on a war-horse, had reviewed her troops at Tilbury Fort, exhorting them to arms with the words: 'I know that I have but the body of a weak and feeble woman; but I have the heart of a king, and of a king of England too!'

[3] Philip II of Spain.

SNEER. True; but I think you manage ill, for there certainly appears no reason why Sir Walter should be so communicative.

PUFF. 'Fore gad, now, that is one of the most 105 ungrateful observations I ever heard — for the less inducement he has to tell all this, the more, I think, you ought to be obliged to him; for I am sure you'd know nothing of the matter without it.

DANGLE. That's very true, upon my word. 110

PUFF. But you will find he was *not* going on.

SIR CHRIST. Enough, enough! — 'tis plain — and I no more
Am in amazement lost! —

PUFF. Here, now you see, Sir Christopher did not in fact ask any one question for his own infor- 115 mation.

SNEER. No, indeed: — his has been a most disinterested curiosity!

DANGLE. Really, I find, we are very much obliged to them both. 120

PUFF. To be sure you are. — Now then for the commander-in-chief, the Earl of Leicester, who, you know, was no favorite but of the Queen's. — [*To the Players.*] We left off — 'in amazement lost!'

SIR CHRIST. Am in amazement lost — 125
But see where noble Leicester comes! supreme
In honors and command.

SIR WALTER.   And yet, methinks,
At such a time, so perilous, so feared,
That staff might well become an abler grasp.

SIR CHRIST. And so, by heav'n! think I; but soft, he's here! 130

PUFF. Aye, they envy him.

SNEER. But who are these with him?

PUFF. Oh! very valiant knights; one is the governor of the fort, the other the Master of the Horse. — And now, I think, you shall hear some better 135 language: I was obliged to be plain and intelligible in the first scene, because there was so much matter of fact in it; but now, i'faith, you have trope, figure, and metaphor, as plenty as noun-substantives.

Enter Earl of LEICESTER, *the Governor, and others.*

LEICESTER. How's this, my friends! is't thus your new-fledged zeal 140
And plumèd valor moulds in roosted sloth?
Why dimly glimmers that heroic flame,
Whose redd'ning blaze, by patriot spirit fed,
Should be the beacon of a kindling realm?
Can the quick current of a patriot heart 145
Thus stagnate in a cold and weedy converse,
Or freeze in tideless inactivity!
No! rather let the fountain of your valor
Spring through each stream of enterprise,
Each petty channel of conducive daring, 150
Till the full torrent of your foaming wrath
O'erwhelm the flats of sunk hostility!

PUFF. There it is — followed up!

SIR WALTER. No more! the fresh'ning breath of thy rebuke
Hath filled the swelling canvas of our souls! 155
And thus, though fate should cut the cable of
                                  (*All take hands*)
Our topmost hopes, in friendship's closing line
We'll grapple with despair, and if we fall,
We'll fall in Glory's wake!

LEICEST. There spoke Old England's genius! 160
Then, are we all resolved?

ALL. We are — all resolved.

LEICEST. To conquer — or be free?

ALL. To conquer, or be free.

LEICEST. All? 165

ALL. All.

DANGLE. *Nem. con.*,[1] egad!

PUFF. O yes, where they *do* agree on the stage, their unanimity is wonderful!

LEICEST. Then, let's embrace—and now—[*kneels*]. 170

SNEER. What the plague, is he going to pray?

PUFF. Yes; hush! — in great emergencies there is nothing like a prayer!

LEICEST. O mighty Mars!

DANGLE. But why should he pray to *Mars*? 175

PUFF. Hush!

LEICEST. If in thy homage bred,
Each point of discipline I've still observed;
Nor but by due promotion, and the right
Of service, to the rank of major-general 180
Have ris'n; assist thy votary now!

GOVERN. Yet do not rise, — hear me!

MASTER OF HORSE. And me!

KNIGHT. And me!

SIR WALTER. And me! 185

SIR CHRIST. And me!

PUFF. Now, pray all together.

ALL. Behold thy votaries submissive beg,
That thou wilt deign to grant them all they ask;
Assist them to accomplish all their ends, 190
And sanctify whatever means they use
To gain them!

SNEER. A very orthodox quintetto!

PUFF. Vastly well, gentlemen. — Is that well managed or not? Have you such a prayer as that 195 on the stage?

SNEER. Not exactly.

LEICEST. (*to* PUFF). But, sir, you haven't settled how we are to get off here.

PUFF. You could not go off kneeling, could 200 you?

SIR WALTER (*to* PUFF). O no, sir! impossible!

PUFF. It would have a good effect, i'faith, if you could! — '*exeunt praying!*' — Yes, and would vary the established mode of springing off with a 205 glance at the pit.

[1] *Nemine contradicente,* 'unanimously.'

105] O1 *For, egad now*; M *Fore gad.*

SNEER. O never mind; so as you get them off, I'll answer for it the audience won't care how.

PUFF. Well, then, repeat the last line standing, and go off the old way.   210

ALL. And sanctify whatever means we use
To gain them.   *Exeunt.*

DANGLE. Bravo! a fine exit.

SNEER. Well, really, Mr. Puff —

PUFF. Stay a moment.   215
                    (*The Sentinels get up.*)

1ST SENT. All this shall to Lord Burleigh's[1] ear.

2D SENT. 'Tis meet it should.   *Exeunt Sentinels.*

DANGLE. Hey! — why, I thought those fellows had been asleep!

PUFF. Only a pretence; there's the art of it.   220
They were spies of Lord Burleigh's.

SNEER. But isn't it odd they were never taken notice of, not even by the commander-in-chief?

PUFF. O lud, sir, if people who want to listen, or   225
overhear, were not always connived at in a tragedy, there would be no carrying on any plot in the world.

DANGLE. That's certain!

PUFF. But take care, my dear Dangle; the morn-   230
ing gun is going to fire.   (*Cannon fires.*)

DANGLE. Well, that will have a fine effect.

PUFF. I think so, and helps to realize the scene.
— (*Cannon twice.*) — What the plague! — *three*
morning guns? — There never is but one! — Aye, this   235
is always the way at the theatre; give these fellows a good thing, and they never know when to have
done with it. — You have no more cannon to fire?

PROMPTER (*from within*). No, sir.

PUFF. Now, then, for soft music.

SNEER. Pray, what's that for?   240

PUFF. It shows that Tilburina is coming; nothing introduces you a heroine like soft music. — Here she comes.

DANGLE. And her confidante, I suppose?

PUFF. To be sure. Here they are — incon-   245
solable to the minuet in *Ariadne.*[2]   (*Soft music.*)

Enter TILBURINA *and Confidante.*

TILBURINA. Now has the whispering breath of gentle
            morn
Bade Nature's voice and Nature's beauty rise;
While orient Phœbus, with unborrowed hues,
Clothes the waked loveliness which all night slept   250
In heav'nly drapery! Darkness is fled.
Now flowers unfold their beauties to the sun,
And, blushing, kiss the beam he sends to wake them —
The striped carnation and the guarded rose,
The vulgar wallflow'r and smart gillyflower,   255

---

[1] William Cecil (1520–1598) created Baron of Burghley in 1571, and in the next year Lord High Treasurer of England.
[2] An Italian opera, music by Handel, first produced in London in 1734. (See N, p. 311.)

211–212] O1 prints as one line; M prints as above.

The polyanthus mean — the dapper daisy,
Sweet William, and sweet marjoram, — and all
The tribe of single and of double pinks!
Now, too, the feathered warblers tune their notes
Around, and charm the list'ning grove. The lark!   260
The linnet! chaffinch! bullfinch! goldfinch! green-
            finch!
— But O to me no joy can they afford!
Nor rose, nor wallflow'r, nor smart gillyflower,
Nor polyanthus mean, nor dapper daisy,
Nor William sweet, nor marjoram — nor lark,   265
Linnet, nor all the finches of the grove!

PUFF. Your white handkerchief, madam —

TILB. I thought, sir, I wasn't to use that till 'heart-rending woe.'

PUFF. O yes, madam, at 'the finches of the   270
grove,' if you please.

TILB.   Nor lark,
Linnet, nor all the finches of the grove!   (*Weeps.*)

PUFF. Vastly well, madam!

DANGLE. Vastly well, indeed!   275

TILB. For, O too sure, heart-rending woe is now
The lot of wretched Tilburina!

DANGLE. Oh! — 'tis too much.

SNEER. Oh! — it is, indeed.

CON. Be comforted, sweet lady; for who knows   280
But heav'n has yet some milk-white day in store?

TILB. Alas! my gentle Nora,
Thy tender youth as yet hath never mourned
Love's fatal dart. Else wouldst thou know that when
The soul is sunk in comfortless despair   285
It cannot taste of merriment.

DANGLE. That's certain.

CON. But see where your stern father comes:
It is not meet that he should find you thus.

PUFF. Hey, what the plague! — what a cut   290
is here! — why, what is become of the description of her first meeting with Don Whiskerandos? his gal-lant behavior in the sea fight, and the simile of the canary bird?

TILB. Indeed, sir, you'll find they will not   295
be missed.

PUFF. Very well — very well!

TILB. The cue, ma'am, if you please.

CON. It is not meet that he should find you thus.

TILB. Thou counsel'st right; but 'tis no easy task   300
For barefaced grief to wear a mask of joy.

Enter Governor.

GOVERNOR. How's this! — in tears? — O Tilburina,
            shame!
Is this a time for maudling tenderness,
And Cupid's baby woes? — hast thou not heard
That haughty Spain's Pope-consecrated fleet   305
Advances to our shores, while England's fate,
Like a clipped guinea, trembles in the scale!

TILB. Then is the crisis of *my* fate at hand!
I see the fleet's approach — I see —

PUFF. Now, pray, gentlemen, mind. This 310
is one of the most useful figures we tragedy writers
have by which a hero or heroine, in consideration of
their being often obliged to overlook things that *are*
on the stage, is allowed to hear and see a number of
things that are not. 315

SNEER. Yes; a kind of poetical second-sight!

PUFF. Yes. — Now then, madam.

TILB. I see their decks
Are cleared! — I see the signal made!
The line is formed! — a cable's length asunder! — 320
I see the frigates stationed in the rear;
And now, I hear the thunder of the guns!
I hear the victor's shouts! — I also hear
The vanquished groan! — and now 'tis smoke — and
now
I see the loose sails shiver in the wind! 325
I see — I see — what soon you'll see —

Gov. Hold, daughter! peace! this love hath turned thy
brain:
The Spanish fleet thou *canst* not see — because
— It is not yet in sight!

DANGLE. Egad, though, the governor seems 330
to make no allowance for this poetical figure you
talk of.

PUFF. No, a plain matter-of-fact man — that's
his character.

TILB. But will you then refuse his offer? 335
Gov. I must — I will — I can — I ought — I do.
TILB. Think what a noble price.
Gov. No more — you urge in vain.
TILB. His liberty is all he asks.

SNEER. All *who* asks, Mr. Puff? Who is — 340
PUFF. Egad, sir, I can't tell. — Here has been
such cutting and slashing, I don't know where they
have got to myself.

TILB. Indeed, sir, you will find it will connect
very well. 345

— And your reward secure.

PUFF. Oh, if they hadn't been so devilish free with
their cutting here, you would have found that Don
Whiskerandos has been tampering for his liberty,
and has persuaded Tilburina to make this pro- 350
posal to her father; and now, pray, observe the con-
ciseness with which the argument is conducted.
Egad, the *pro* and *con* goes as smart as hits in a
fencing-match. It is, indeed, a sort of small-
sword logic, which we have borrowed from 355
the French.

TILB. A retreat in Spain!
Gov. Outlawry here!
TILB. Your daughter's prayer!
Gov. Your father's oath! 360
TILB. My lover!
Gov. My country!
TILB. Tilburina!
Gov. England!
TILB. A title! 365

Gov. Honor!
TILB. A pension!
Gov. Conscience!
TILB. A thousand pounds!
Gov. Hah! thou hast touched me nearly! 370

PUFF. There, you see — she threw in 'Tilburina.'
Quick, parry carte [1] with 'England'! — Hah! thrust
in tierce 'a title'! — parried by 'honor.' Hah! 'a
pension' over the arm! — put by by 'conscience.'
Then flankonade with 'a thousand pounds' — 375
and a palpable hit, egad! [2]

TILB. Canst thou —
Reject the *suppliant*, and the *daughter* too?
Gov. No more; I would not hear thee plead in vain:
The *father* softens — but the *governor* 380
Is fixed! *Exit.*

DANGLE. Aye, that antithesis of persons is a
most established figure.

TILB. 'Tis well, — hence then, fond hopes, — fond
passion, hence;
Duty, behold I am all over thine — 385
WHISK. (*without*). Where is my love — my —
TILB. Ha!
WHISK. (*entering*). My beauteous enemy —

PUFF. O dear ma'am, you must start a great deal
more than that; consider, you had just deter- 390
mined in favor of duty — when, in a moment, the
sound of his voice revives your passion — over-
throws your resolution — destroys your obedience.
— If you don't express all that in your start, you
do nothing at all. 395
TILB. Well, we'll try again!
DANGLE. Speaking from within has always a
fine effect.
SNEER. Very.

WHISK. My conquering Tilburina! How! is't thus 400
We meet? why are thy looks averse? what means
That falling tear — that frown of boding woe?
Hah! now indeed I am a prisoner!
Yes, now I feel the galling weight of these
Disgraceful chains — which, cruel Tilburina! 405
Thy doting captive gloried in before. —
But thou art false, and Whiskerandos is undone!
TILB. O no! how little dost thou know thy Tilburina!
WHISK. Art thou then true? — Begone cares, doubts,
and fears!
I make you all a present to the winds; 410
And if the winds reject you — try the waves.

PUFF. The wind, you know, is the established
receiver of all stolen sighs and cast-off griefs and
apprehensions.

TILB. Yet must we part! — stern duty seals our 415
doom: Though here I call yon conscious clouds to witness,

---

[1] Puff uses various terms in fencing.

[2] Since *The Critic* was first produced as an after-piece to
Hamlet, Sheridan's reference to Osric's famous phrase (*Hamlet*,
V. ii. 295) was a 'palpable hit' to the *first night* audience.

Could I pursue the bias of my soul,
All friends, all right of parents, I'd disclaim,
And thou, my Whiskerandos, shouldst be father
And mother, brother, cousin, uncle, aunt,　　420
And friend to me!

WHISK. O matchless excellence! — and must we part?
Well, if — we must — we must; and in that case,
The less is said the better.

PUFF. Hey day! here's a cut! — What, are　　425
all the mutual protestations out?

TILB. Now, pray, sir, don't interrupt us just
here; you ruin our feelings.

PUFF. *Your* feelings! — but zounds, *my* feelings, ma'am!　　430

SNEER. No; pray, don't interrupt them.

WHISK. One last embrace. —

TILB. Now, — farewell, forever.

WHISK. Forever!

TILB. Aye, forever.　　(*Going.*)　435

PUFF. 'Sdeath and fury! — Gad's life! — sir! madam! if you go out without the parting look,
you might as well dance out — Here, here!

CON. But pray, sir, how am *I* to get off here?

PUFF. *You,* pshaw! what the devil signifies　440
how *you* get off! edge away at the top,[1] or where
you will — (*Pushes the Confidante off.*) Now, ma'am,
you see —

TILB. We understand you, sir.

　　　　　Aye, forever.　　　　445
BOTH. Oh — h!　　*Turning back, and exeunt.*
　　　　　　　　　　　(*Scene closes.*)

DANGLE. Oh, charming!

PUFF. Hey! — 'tis pretty well, I believe: you see
I don't attempt to strike out anything new — but
I take it I improve on the established modes.　　450

SNEER. You do, indeed. But, pray, is not Queen
Elizabeth to appear?

PUFF. No, not once — but she is to be talked of
forever, so that, egad, you'll think a hundred times
that she is on the point of coming in.　　455

SNEER. Hang it, I think it's a pity to keep *her*
in the green-room all the night.

PUFF. O no, that always has a fine effect — it
keeps up expectation.

DANGLE. But are we not to have a battle?　460

PUFF. Yes, yes, you will have a battle at last;
but, egad, it's not to be by land, but by sea — and
that is the only quite new thing in the piece.

DANGLE. What, Drake at the Armada, hey?

PUFF. Yes, i'faith — fire-ships and all; then　465
we shall end with the procession. — Hey! that will
do, I think!

SNEER. No doubt on't.

PUFF. Come, we must not lose time; so now for
the *under-plot.*　　470

SNEER. What the plague, have you another plot?

PUFF. O Lord, yes; ever while you live have two
plots to your tragedy. — The grand point in managing them is only to let your under-plot have as
little connection with your main plot as possi-　475
ble. — I flatter myself nothing can be more distinct
than mine; for as in my chief plot the characters
are all great people, I have laid my under-plot in
low life; and as the former is to end in deep distress,
I make the other end as happy as a farce. —　480
Now, Mr. Hopkins, as soon as you please.

Enter Under Prompter.

UNDER PROMPTER. Sir, the carpenter says it is
impossible you can go to the park scene yet.

PUFF. The park scene! No — I mean the description scene here, in the wood.　　485

UND. PROMP. Sir, the performers have cut it out.

PUFF. Cut it out!

UND. PROMP. Yes, sir.

PUFF. What! the whole account of Queen Elizabeth?　　490

UND. PROMP. Yes, sir.

PUFF. And the description of her horse and sidesaddle?

UND. PROMP. Yes, sir.

PUFF. So, so; this is very fine, indeed! Mr.　495
Hopkins, how the plague could you suffer this?

HOPKINS (*from within*). Sir, indeed the pruning-knife —

PUFF. The pruning-knife — zounds! — the axe!
Why, here has been such lopping and topping,　500
I sha'n't have the bare trunk of my play left presently. — Very well, sir — the performers must do as
they please; but, upon my soul, I'll print it every
word.

SNEER. That I would, indeed.　　505

PUFF. Very well, sir — then we must go on. —
Zounds! I would not have parted with the description of the horse! — Well, sir, go on. — Sir, it was
one of the finest and most labored things. — Very
well, sir; let them go on — there you had him　510
and his accoutrements from the bit to the crupper.
— Very well, sir; we must go to the park scene.

UND. PROMP. Sir, there is the point: the carpenters say that unless there is some business put
in here before the drop, they sha'n't have time　515
to clear away the fort, or sink Gravesend and the
river.

PUFF. So! this is a pretty dilemma, truly! —
Gentlemen, you must excuse me — these fellows
will never be ready unless I go and look after　520
them myself.

SNEER. O dear sir, these little things will happen.

PUFF. To cut out this scene! — but I'll print it
— egad, I'll print it every word!　*Exeunt.*　525

---

[1] At the back of the stage.

ACT III

SCENE I

Before the curtain.

Enter PUFF, SNEER, *and* DANGLE.

PUFF. Well, we are ready; — now then for the justices.

Curtain rises — Justices, Constables, &c. discovered.

SNEER. This, I suppose, is a sort of senate scene.

PUFF. To be sure — there has not been one 5 yet.

DANGLE. It is the under-plot, isn't it?

PUFF. Yes. — What, gentlemen, do you mean to go at once to the discovery scene?

JUSTICE. If you please, sir. 10

PUFF. Oh, very well. — Harkee, I don't choose to say anything more — but, i'faith, they have mangled my play in a most shocking manner.

DANGLE. It's a great pity!

PUFF. Now, then, Mr. Justice, if you 15 please.

JUSTICE. Are all the volunteers without?

CONSTABLE.   They are.
Some ten in fetters, and some twenty drunk.

JUST. Attends the youth whose most opprobrious fame
And clear convicted crimes have stamped him soldier? 20

CONST. He waits your pleasure; eager to repay
The blest reprieve that sends him to the fields
Of glory, there to raise his branded hand
In honor's cause.

JUST.   'Tis well — 'tis justice arms him!
O! may he now defend his country's laws 25
With half the spirit he has broke them all!
If 'tis your worship's pleasure, bid him enter.

CONST. I fly, the herald of your will. *Exit Constable.*

PUFF. Quick, sir!

SNEER. But, Mr. Puff, I think not only the 30
Justice but the clown seems to talk in as high a style as the first hero among them.

PUFF. Heaven forbid they should not, in a free country! — Sir, I am not for making slavish distinctions, and giving all the fine language to the 35 upper sort of people.

DANGLE. That's very noble in you, indeed.

Enter Justice's Lady.

PUFF. Now pray mark this scene.[1]

LADY. Forgive this interruption, good my love;
But as I just now passed a pris'ner youth, 40
Whom rude hands hither lead, strange bodings seized
My fluttering heart, and to myself I said,
And if our *Tom* had lived, he'd surely been
This stripling's height!

---

[1] In the burlesque 'recognition scene' which follows, Sheridan seems to have had Home's *Douglas* (1756) especially in mind. (See N, Introduction, civ–cv; also pp. 311 and 330.)

JUST. Ha! sure some powerful sympathy directs 45
Us both —

Enter Son and Constable.

What is thy name?

SON. My name's *Tom Jenkins* — alias have I none —
Though orphaned, and without a friend!

JUST. Thy parents?

SON. My father dwelt in Rochester — and was, 50
As I have heard — a fishmonger — no more.

PUFF. What, sir, do you leave out the account of your birth, parentage, and education?

SON. They have settled it so, sir, here.

PUFF. Oh! oh! 55

LADY. How loudly Nature whispers to my heart!
Had he no other name?

SON.   I've seen a bill
Of his signed *Tomkins*, creditor.

JUST. This does indeed confirm each circumstance
The gipsy told! — Prepare! 60

SON. I do.

JUST. No orphan, nor without a friend art thou —
I am thy father; *here's* thy mother; *there*
Thy uncle — this thy first cousin, and those
Are all your near relations! 65

MOTHER. O ecstasy of bliss!

SON. O most unlooked for happiness!

JUST. O wonderful event!

(They faint alternately in each other's arms.)

PUFF. There, you see relationship, like murder, will out. 70

JUST. Now let's revive — else were this joy too much!
But come — and we'll unfold the rest within;
And thou, my boy, must needs want rest and food.
Hence may each orphan hope, as chance directs,
To find a father — where he least expects! 75
Exeunt.

PUFF. What do you think of that?

DANGLE. One of the finest discovery scenes I ever saw. — Why, this under-plot would have made a tragedy itself.

SNEER. Aye, or a comedy either. 80

PUFF. And keeps quite clear, you see, of the other.

Enter Scenemen, taking away the seats.

PUFF. The scene remains, does it?

SCENEMAN. Yes, sir.

PUFF. You are to leave one chair, you know. —
But it is always awkward, in a tragedy, to have 85
you fellows coming in in your playhouse liveries to remove things — I wish that could be managed better. — So now for my mysterious yeoman.

Enter a Beefeater.[1]

BEEFEATER. Perdition catch my soul, but *I* do love thee.

SNEER. Haven't I heard that line before? 90

PUFF. No, I fancy not — Where, pray?

---

[1] Yeoman of the Guard.

DANGLE. Yes, I think there is something like it in *Othello*.[1]

PUFF. Gad! now you put me in mind on't, I believe there is — but that's of no consequence 95 — all that can be said is, that two people happened to hit on the same thought — and Shakespeare made use of it first, that's all.

SNEER. Very true.

PUFF. Now, sir, your soliloquy — but speak 100 more to the pit, if you please — the soliloquy always to the pit — that's a rule.

BEEF. Though hopeless love finds comfort in despair,
It never can endure a rival's bliss!
But soft — I am observed.   *Exit Beefeater.* 105

DANGLE. That's a very short soliloquy.

PUFF. Yes — but it would have been a great deal longer if he had not been observed.

SNEER. A most sentimental Beefeater that, Mr. Puff.   110

PUFF. Harkee — I would not have you be too sure that he *is* a Beefeater.

SNEER. What, a hero in disguise?

PUFF. No matter — I only give you a hint. — But now for my principal character. — Here he 115 comes — *Lord Burleigh* in person! Pray, gentlemen, step this way — softly — I only hope the Lord High Treasurer is perfect — if he is but perfect!

Enter BURLEIGH; *goes slowly to a chair, and sits.*

SNEER. Mr. Puff!

PUFF. Hush! vastly well, sir! vastly well! a 120 most interesting gravity!

DANGLE. What, isn't he to speak at all?

PUFF. Egad, I thought you'd ask me that — yes, it is a very likely thing — that a minister in his situation, with the whole affairs of the nation on 125 his head, should have time to talk! — but hush! or you'll put him out.

SNEER. Put him out! how the plague can that be, if he's not going to say anything?

PUFF. There's a reason! — why, his part is 130 to *think*; and how the plague do you imagine he can *think* if you keep talking?

DANGLE. That's very true, upon my word!

BURLEIGH *comes forward, shakes his head, and exit.*

SNEER. He is very perfect, indeed. — Now, pray, what did he mean by that?   135

PUFF. You don't take it?

SNEER. No, I don't, upon my soul.

PUFF. Why, by that shake of the head he gave you to understand that even though they had more justice in their cause and wisdom in their 140 measures — yet, if there was not a greater spirit shown on the part of the people, the country would

at last fall a sacrifice to the hostile ambition of the Spanish monarchy.

SNEER. The devil! — did he mean all that 145 by shaking his head?

PUFF. Every word of it — if he shook his head as I taught him.

DANGLE. Ah! there certainly is a vast deal to be done on the stage by dumb show, and expres- 150 sion of face; and a judicious author knows how much he may trust to it.

SNEER. Oh, here are some of our old acquaintance.

Enter HATTON *and* RALEIGH.

SIR CHRIST. *My* niece, and *your* niece too!
By heav'n, there's witchcraft in't; he could not else 155
Have gained their hearts. — But see, where they approach —
Some horrid purpose low'ring on their brows!

SIR WALTER RALEIGH. Let us withdraw and mark them.   *(They withdraw.)*

SNEER. What is all this?   160

PUFF. Ah! here has been more pruning! — but the fact is, these two young ladies are also in love with Don Whiskerandos. — Now, gentlemen, this scene goes entirely for what we call *situation* and *stage effect*, by which the greatest applause may 165 be obtained without the assistance of language, sentiment, or character: pray, mark!

Enter the Two Nieces.

1ST NIECE. Ellena here!
She is his scorn as much as I — that is
Some comfort still!   170

PUFF. O dear madam, you are not to say that to her face! — *aside*, ma'am, *aside*. — The whole scene is to be *aside*.

1ST NIECE *(aside)*. She is his scorn as much as I —
that is
Some comfort still!   175

2D NIECE *(aside)*. I know he prizes not Pollina's love;
But Tilburina lords it o'er his heart.

1ST NIECE *(aside)*. But see the proud destroyer of my
peace.
Revenge is all the good I've left.

2D NIECE *(aside)*. He comes, the false disturber of
my quiet.   180
Now, vengeance, do thy worst. —

Enter WHISKERANDOS.

[WHISK.] O hateful liberty — if thus in vain
I seek my Tilburina!

BOTH NIECES. And ever shalt!

(Sir CHRISTOPHER *and* SIR WALTER *come forward.)*

[BOTH UNCLES]. Hold! we will avenge you. 185

WHISK. Hold *you* — or see your nieces bleed!

(The two Nieces draw their two daggers to strike
WHISKERANDOS; *the two Uncles at the instant,*
with their two swords drawn, catch their two
Nieces' arms and turn the points of their swords
to WHISKERANDOS, *who immediately draws two*
daggers and holds them to the two Nieces' bosoms.)

PUFF. There's situation for you! there's an heroic group! — You see the ladies can't stab Whiskerandos — he durst not strike them for fear of their uncles — the uncles durst not kill him because of their nieces — I have them all at a deadlock! — for every one of them is afraid to let go first.   190

SNEER. Why, then, they must stand there forever.

PUFF. So they would, if I hadn't a very fine contrivance for't. — Now mind —   195

Enter Beefeater, with his halberd.

[BEEF.] In the Queen's name I charge you all to drop Your swords and daggers!
(*They drop their swords and daggers.*)

SNEER. That is a contrivance, indeed!

PUFF. Aye — in the Queen's name.

SIR CHRIST. Come, niece!   200
SIR WALTER. Come, niece! *Exeunt with the two Nieces.*

WHISK. What's he who bids us thus renounce our guard?

BEEF. Thou must do more — renounce thy love!

WHISK. Thou liest — base Beefeater!

BEEF.   Ha! hell! the lie! By heav'n thou'st roused the lion in my heart!   205 Off, yeoman's habit! — base disguise! off! off!
(*Discovers himself, by throwing off his upper dress, and appearing in a very fine waistcoat.*)
Am I a Beefeater now? Or beams my crest as terrible as when In Biscay's Bay I took thy captive sloop?

PUFF. There, egad! he comes out to be the   210 very captain of the privateer who had taken Whiskerandos prisoner — and was himself an old lover of Tilburina's.

DANGLE. Admirably managed, indeed.

PUFF. Now, stand out of their way.   215

WHISK. I thank thee, Fortune! that hast thus bestowed A weapon to chastise this insolent.
(*Takes up one of the swords.*)

BEEF. I take thy challenge, Spaniard, and I thank Thee, Fortune, too! —   (*Takes up the other sword.*)

DANGLE. That's excellently contrived! —   220 it seems as if the two uncles had left their swords on purpose for them.

PUFF. No, egad, they could not help leaving them.

WHISK. Vengeance and Tilburina!

BEEF.   Exactly so —
(*They fight — and after the usual number of wounds given, WHISKERANDOS falls.*)

WHISK. O cursèd parry! — that last thrust in tierce   225 Was fatal — Captain, thou hast fencèd well! And Whiskerandos quits this bustling scene For all eter —

BEEF. — nity — he would have added,[1] but stern Death Cut short his being, and the noun at once!

PUFF. Oh, my dear sir, you are too slow; now   230 mind me. — Sir, shall I trouble you to die again?

WHISK. And Whiskerandos quits this bustling scene For all eter —

BEEF.   — nity — he would have added —

PUFF. No, sir — that's not it — once more, if you please.   235

WHISK. I wish, sir, you would practise this without me — I can't stay dying here all night.

PUFF. Very well; we'll go over it by and by. — I must humor these gentlemen!
Exit WHISKERANDOS.

BEEF. Farewell, brave Spaniard! and when next —   240

PUFF. Dear sir, you needn't speak that speech, as the body has walked off.

BEEF. That's true, sir — then I'll join the fleet.

PUFF. If you please.   *Exit Beefeater.*
Now who comes on?   245

Enter Governor, with his hair properly disordered.

GOV. A hemisphere of evil planets reign! And every planet sheds contagious frenzy! My Spanish prisoner is slain! my daughter, Meeting the dead corse borne along, has gone Distract!   (*A loud flourish of trumpets.*)
          But hark! I am summoned to the fort —   250 Perhaps the fleets have met! amazing crisis! O Tilburina! from thy agèd father's beard Thou'st plucked the few brown hairs which time had left.
Exit Governor.

SNEER. Poor gentleman!

PUFF. Yes — and no one to blame but his   255 daughter!

DANGLE. And the planets —

PUFF. True. — Now enter Tilburina!

SNEER. Egad, the business comes on quick here.

PUFF. Yes, sir — now she comes in stark   260 mad in white satin.

SNEER. Why in white satin?

PUFF. O Lord, sir — when a heroine goes mad, she always goes into white satin — don't she, Dangle?   265

DANGLE. Always — it's a rule.

PUFF. Yes — here it is — (*looking at the book*) 'Enter Tilburina stark mad in white satin, and her confidante stark mad in white linen.'

Enter TILBURINA and Confidante, mad, according to custom.

SNEER. But what the deuce! is the confi-   270 dante to be mad too?

PUFF. To be sure she is; the confidante is always to do whatever her mistress does — weep when she weeps, smile when she smiles, go mad when she goes mad. — Now, madam confidante — but —   275 keep your madness in the background, if you please.

---

[1] The interrupted dying speech recalls Hotspur's (*Henry IV, Part I*, V. iv. 86–87): *Hotspur.* And food — [*Dies*]. *Prince.* For worms, brave Percy. (For a less familiar parallel see R, II, 186–187.)

TILB. The wind whistles — the moon rises — see,
They have killed my squirrel in his cage!
Is this a grasshopper? — Ha! no; it is my
Whiskerandos — you shall not keep him —   280
I know you have him in your pocket —
An oyster may be crossed in love! — Who says
A whale's a bird? — Ha! did you call, my love?
— He's here! He's there! — He's everywhere!
Ah me! He's nowhere!   *Exit* TILBURINA. 285

PUFF. There, do you ever desire to see anybody
madder than that?

SNEER. Never, while I live!

PUFF. You observed how she mangled the metre?

DANGLE. Yes — egad, it was the first thing 290
made me suspect she was out of her senses.

SNEER. And pray what becomes of her?

PUFF. She is gone to throw herself into the sea,
to be sure — and that brings us at once to the scene
of action, and so to my catastrophe — my sea- 295
fight, I mean.

SNEER. What, you bring that in at last?

PUFF. Yes, yes — you know my play is *called* the
Spanish Armada; otherwise, egad, I have no occasion for the battle at all. — Now then for my 300
magnificence! — my battle! — my noise! — and my
procession! — You are all ready?

PROMPT. (*within*). Yes, sir.

PUFF. Is the Thames dressed?

Enter THAMES, *with two Attendants.*

THAMES. Here I am, sir.   305

PUFF. Very well indeed. — See, gentlemen,
there's a river for you! — This is blending a little
of the masque with my tragedy — a new fancy, you
know — and very useful in my case; for as there
must be a procession, I suppose Thames and all 310
his tributary rivers to compliment Britannia with
a fête in honor of the victory.

SNEER. But, pray, who are these gentlemen in
green with him?

PUFF. Those? — those are his banks. 315

SNEER. His banks?

PUFF. Yes, one crowned with alders, and the
other with a villa! — you take the allusions? —
But hey! what the plague! you have got both your
banks on one side — Here, sir, come round — 320
Ever while you live, Thames, go between your
banks. (*Bell rings.*) There, soh! now for't. —
Stand aside, my dear friends! — away, Thames!

Exit THAMES *between his banks.*
(*Flourish of drums, trumpets, cannon, &c. &c.
Scene changes to the sea — the fleets engage
— the music plays 'Britons strike home.' —
Spanish fleet destroyed by fireships, &c. —
English fleet advances — music plays 'Rule,
Britannia.' — The procession of all the
English rivers, and their tributaries, with
their emblems, &c. begins with Handel's
water music;* [1] *ends with a chorus, to the
march in 'Judas Maccabœus.'* [2] *— During
this scene* PUFF *directs and applauds everything — then*)

PUFF. Well, pretty well — but not quite perfect —
so, ladies and gentlemen, if you please, we'll re- 325
hearse this piece again to-morrow.

CURTAIN DROPS

[1] First performed on the Thames, in 1715, in honor of
George I.
[2] Handel's oratorio, first performed in London, in 1747.

Textual Notes

PREFATORY NOTE

THE plays in this collection fall within the chronological limits set in *English Drama of the Restoration and Eighteenth Century (1642–1780)* by George H. Nettleton. To simplify references to this and to other closely related works by the same author the following abbreviations will be used:

Drama. English Drama of the Restoration and Eighteenth Century (1642–1780). The Macmillan Company, New York, 1914.

D & S. The Drama and the Stage [Eighteenth Century], chapter IV in volume X (1913) of the *Cambridge History of English Literature.* Cambridge University Press.

Camb. Bibl. Bibliography to this chapter (*D & S*) in volume X of the *Cambridge History of English Literature,* pp. 425–446.

N. The Major Dramas of Richard Brinsley Sheridan. [*The Rivals, The School for Scandal, The Critic.*] Edited in the *Athenæum Press Series.* Ginn and Company, Boston, 1906.

In the present study it seems natural to utilize freely, but needless to reproduce in detail, materials available in these works. The main interrelations may be briefly noted. This present volume holds to *Drama* and to *D & S*, within its briefer range, the relation of a series of illustrative texts; conversely, those critical histories of the development of English drama supply to the present work detailed background. *Drama, Camb. Bibl.,* and *N* together present a very considerable range of bibliographical material, general and special, with especial reference to the history and criticism of drama. In the present work the bibliographical material primarily concerns the actual printed texts of the plays. Though thus mainly distinct in content and aim, this volume has, in one instance, a closer relationship. The three Sheridan plays were included in *N* in 1906, but subsequent discoveries of new materials and texts — notably the Crewe manuscript of *The School for Scandal* here presented for the first time — have carried the present textual studies beyond obstacles of mere repetition. In general, then, the various interrelated works here summarized supplement rather than duplicate the present volume.

NOTE ON BIBLIOGRAPHIES

The bibliographies that precede the textual notes on individual plays are selective, not inclusive. They aim principally to clarify the subsequent discussions of editions that appeared in the given author's lifetime, and of some significant later reprints and critical editions. Frequently they considerably enlarge general bibliographical data or deepen the bases of special investigation, but they make no attempt to list fully the multitude of reprints of popular plays. Bibliographies and discussions seek rather to disengage from the mass of materials those that have proved especially pertinent and to set them duly into the composite history of textual development.

As an aid to special study, early and rare editions are largely located in five representative libraries, British and American — the British Museum, Bodleian, University of Cambridge, Harvard, and Yale Libraries — which have provided the main bases of the present textual investigations. In various cases, references are included to copies of editions in other libraries that have served individual editorial purposes. Asterisks indicate the basic text adopted, and also the copies mainly used in collation of various editions of a given play. The following abbreviations are used in references to various libraries:

B.M.	British Museum, London.
Bib. Nat.	Bibliothèque Nationale, Paris.
Bod.	Bodleian Library, Oxford.
Camb.	Cambridge [England] University Library.
Colum.	Columbia University Library, New York City.
Harv.	Harvard College Library, Cambridge, Mass.
Hunt.	Huntington Library, San Marino, Cal.
L.C.	Library of Congress, Washington, D.C.
Newb.	Newberry Library, Chicago.
N.U.	Northwestern University Library, Evanston, Ill.
N.Y.P.L.	New York Public Library, New York City.
U. of C.	University of Chicago Library.
Vict.	Victoria and Albert Museum, South Kensington, London.
Yale.	Yale University Library, New Haven, Conn.

COLLECTIONS OF RESTORATION AND
EIGHTEENTH–CENTURY DRAMA

(a) Eighteenth-Century Collections

In 1744, Robert Dodsley published in twelve volumes his *Select Collection of Old Plays*, widely representing pre-Restoration drama. His conspicuous success in the early fields of English drama encouraged kindred ventures in the fields of Restoration and eighteenth-century drama. In 1750, there was 'Printed for H. Scheurleer, Junior, at the Hague,' a ten-volume work entitled *A Select Collection of the Best Modern English Plays. Selected from the Best Authors*. This is confined to English dramas from the Restoration to 1750, and stands virtually as a sequel to Dodsley's work. Collections of these later dramas, varying considerably in scope and content but recognizing alike the widening demands of the play-reading public, began to multiply. In the latter half of the eighteenth century, London and Edinburgh notably, and Dublin in some degree, became influential centers for the publication and distribution of these general collections. (See *Camb. Bibl.*, pp. 440–441, 'Contemporary and Early Collections of Plays.') Early Edinburgh publications, such as *A Select Collection of English Plays* (1755) and *A Select Collection of Farces, As Acted at London and Edinburgh* (1762), reflect Dodsley's influence in more than title. These early compilers were mainly content to collect and to select plays, and to take their texts as they found them. Some of them sought to supply general comment on the playwrights and plays, as in the twelve-volume Edinburgh collection of 1768 entitled *The Theatre: or, Select Works of the British Dramatic Poets . . . To which are prefixed, the Lives of these celebrated Writers, and Strictures on Most of the Plays*. Some London editions, like *The English Theatre* (1765) and the subsequent *New English Theatre*, stressed *the most valuable plays which have been acted on the London Stage*, while *Bell's British Theatre* carried to impressive lengths the extensive possibilities of serial publication. But the texts of the plays were assembled habitually from the most convenient sources, without special scrutiny. The enterprise of publishers and the popular taste of uncritical readers were the controlling factors. The conception of the editorial function hardly ranged beyond general selection and compilation. The unnamed compilers remained assistants as obscure as the compositors. Broadly viewed, publisher and public initiated and determined the character and content of these eighteenth-century collections.

(b) Nineteenth-Century Collections

With the turn of the century the number and variety of these general collections increased rapidly, and there were growing signs of more than perfunctory fulfilment of the editor's task. In contrast with many colorless predecessors, Mrs. Inchbald imparted to her editorial work considerable vigor and individuality. In the twenty-five volumes of her *British Theatre; or, A Collection of Plays . . . with biographical and critical remarks* (1808), she turned her long experience as actress, dramatist, and novelist to fresh account as dramatic commentator and editor. Her practical knowledge of the theatre and her often lively and provocative critical comments stimulated a personal interest which she was quick to capitalize in her *Collection of Farces and other Afterpieces* (7 vols., 1809) and her *Modern Theatre* (10 vols., 1811). These lesser works show merely a ready compiler, but they helped to emphasize her name in her newly acquired rôle of editor. Another well-known name in the theatrical world, that of the comedian, William Oxberry, was later familiarly associated with *Oxberry's New English Drama*, a serial publication in a score of volumes (1818–25). In the forty-three volumes of *Cumberland's British Theatre* (1826, etc.) the publisher, John Cumberland, overshadowed the editor, George Daniel, whose accompanying 'Remarks, Biographical and Critical,' were somewhat elusively signed 'D —— G.' In collections ranging in character from purely impersonal publication to such individual impress as that of Mrs. Inchbald's *British Theatre*, the editorial function was variously interpreted. (For further illustrations, see *Camb. Bibl.*, p. 441.) So far as any common tendency is discernible, it was towards brief biographies of the playwrights and comments on the selected plays.

In these popular collections editors cared little, and publishers still less, for strict authority and accuracy of text. The demands of rapid publication, the frequent lack of original editions, the indifference of uncritical readers, and the meagre knowledge of the editors themselves combined to militate against careful comparison and choice of texts. Eighteenth-century editors of Shakespeare had made progress in textual study, and Isaac Reed, in 1780, in restudying Dodsley's *Select Collection of Old Plays* had sought to better the casual methods of the original editor in his revised edition, 'Corrected and collated with the old copies.' But such hints of deference to earlier English drama were not applied to Restoration and later plays commonly current. Moreover, in these popular collections, Shakespeare himself often appeared in the perverted texts familiar to the later English stage, while many acting texts of Restoration and eighteenth-century plays altered the authentic original versions. Often, to be sure, editors indicated by inverted commas passages cut in stage representation, but their frequent reliance on variant prompt-copies was an added source of textual changes and irregularities. Still another factor in textual alterations was the expurgation or modification of passages deemed objectionable. For convenient illustration in a stock play constantly reprinted, the varying treatment of the 'Nicky-Nacky' scenes in Otway's *Venice Preserved* may serve.   Besides such conscious changes, the silent debasements of text in successive careless reprints — sometimes, as in the case of the Dryden quartos, already evident in the author's lifetime — added yet another factor of unreliability to many of the current editions of early plays which the editors of these popular collections unhesitatingly adopted.   Exposed to such common dangers, these collections have textual defects differing in degree rather than in kind.   In given cases, as in some of Oxberry's or Cumberland's better texts, they still serve special purposes of textual comparison, and comprehensively the collections aid study of acting texts, prompters' copies, and the development of stage business and directions.   But, at least within the limits of present study, no one of them has been found to offer a series of independently trustworthy texts.

In this broad review, it is convenient to differentiate between pre-Victorian and Victorian general collections.   In contrast with the earlier period (*Camb. Bibl.* terminates its special list in 1830), the long Victorian period is markedly unproductive.   In 1832, John Genest published at Bath, in ten volumes, his remarkable work, under the modest title, *Some Account of the English Stage, from the Restoration in 1660 to 1830*.   But his extraordinary contribution to detailed theatrical history was not followed by any comparable critical or textual study of the full range of English drama or of its characteristic types and examples throughout these periods.   As the survivals on the London stage of Restoration and eighteenth-century English dramas inevitably diminished in number and frequency, retention of their texts in the popular collections became less considerable.   Serial collections like Lacy's, running to a hundred volumes, or French's, with its multifarious separate texts, lost the earlier sense of historical proportion and perspective and of selective quality, and stressed the more immediate output of playwrights and the prevalent acting texts.   For present purposes, indeed, Leigh Hunt's assembling, in 1840, of *The Dramatic Works of Wycherley, Congreve, Vanbrugh, and Farquhar*, though confined to the Restoration period, and virtually to the comedy of manners, has more pertinence.   This very edition, the peg on which Macaulay hung his famous arraignment of the immorality of Restoration comedy, suggests, however, a powerful element in the Victorian attitude.   Lapses of morality as well as of time militated against inclusion of Restoration comedy, at least in its original texts, in general play-collections designed for the Victorian public. Another factor that lessened the earlier collective interest in Restoration and eighteenth-century drama was the breaking of the close monopoly long maintained by the Patent Theatres, attended by the disintegrating forces of nondescript popular playhouses and audiences.   The ephemeral character of most of the current theatrical plays and spectacles and the dearth of genuine dramatists weakened the prestige of the theatre and its historical tradition.

Throughout the Victorian era, conditions remained generally unfavorable to scholarly, as well as to popular, interest in the historical development of English drama since the Restoration.   Special aspects or authors attracted critical attention, and there were encouraging instances of a growing respect for textual study of early editions.   For random illustration may be taken the reprint, in Arber's series, of *The Rehearsal* in the text of the first quarto (with some references to other editions and with extensive annotation from Briscoe's *Key* of 1704), Saintsbury's revision of Scott's edition of Dryden, and a few volumes of individual Restoration dramatists included in the *Mermaid Series*.   But there were no general collections broadly representative of Restoration and eighteenth-century drama in authentic texts. The status of scholarly investigation of English dramatic history at the close of the century is best shown by Dr. Adolphus W. Ward's outstanding revision, in 1899, of his *History of English Dramatic Literature to the death of Queen Anne*, which gave in the long final chapter of the third volume the most considerable critical study then available of English drama since 1660.   This important chapter on 'The Later Stuart Drama' included the Queen Anne period, but principally exposed the artistic and moral shortcomings of Restoration drama, much of which it regarded as 'all but consigned to oblivion by the judgment of posterity.'   Though thus largely sustaining the popular verdict of censure and rejection, the enlarged chapter in reality offered broader bases for further investigation of Restoration drama and suggested the need of extending to eighteenth-century drama comprehensive study of its historical development.

(c) Twentieth-Century Collections

At the outset of this century, Doctor Ward's 'New and Revised Edition' (1899) of his *History of English Dramatic Literature* was generally recognized as the central authority and influence.   Under his guidance as General Editor of the *Cambridge History of English Literature*, the account of eighteenth-century drama was extended in *D & S* (1913) through the advent of Hugh Kelly and Richard Cumberland, and in *Drama* (1914) — where dedication and preface attest Doctor Ward's continued influence — through the period of Goldsmith and Sheridan.   In *Camb. Bibl.* (1913) the section most directly related to the present work is that which assembled 'Contemporary and Early Collections of Plays' (pp. 440–441), while *Drama* set the chronological limits here observed and studied the dramatic developments and types here exemplified.

Of various signs of growing attention to the historical development of Restoration and eighteenth-century drama, that which is here most pertinent is the rise of a new series of general collections of plays wholly or mainly representative of the periods already defined (1642–1780).   In their similar chronological range, carefully limited selection of typical plays, emphasis on historical sequence and perspective, and regard for accuracy and authenticity of text, they are clearly differentiated from the popular collections previously reviewed.   After the long intervention of the Victorian age with its disintegrating influences, this new series of collections regains the general chronological range and many of the stock plays included in some of the later eighteenth-century general collections, but in evident distinction from them and their nineteenth-century successors, the successive anthologies from 1914 onwards may be conveniently grouped as the scholarly collections of typical Restoration and eighteenth-century dramas.

The scope and contents of these scholarly collections are severally shown in the following list which includes only those published since *Drama* (1914) and confined, save for minor variants noted, within its chronological limits.

Tupper, 1914. *Representative English Dramas from Dryden to Sheridan.* Edited by Frederick Tupper and James W.
   Tupper. New York [12 plays]. — 1934. Revised edition with six added plays.

Stevens, 1923. *Types of English Drama, 1660–1780.* Edited by David Harrison Stevens. Boston, etc. [22 plays].

Moses, 1929. *British Plays from the Restoration to 1820.* Edited, with introductions and bibliographies, by Montrose
   J. Moses. 2 vols. Boston. [17 plays from Dryden to Sheridan and Shelley's *The Cenci*.] [Also 'Students Edition' in one vol., 1929.]

MJ., 1931. *Plays of the Restoration and Eighteenth Century as they were acted at the Theatres-Royal by Their Majesties'
   Servants.* Edited by Dougald MacMillan and Howard Mumford Jones. New York. [Also London edition,
   1931.] [23 plays from D'Avenant to Sheridan and Thompson's *The Stranger* (1798); Wycherley's *The Plain
   Dealer* subsequently added.]

Mod., 1933. *Twelve Famous Plays of the Restoration and Eighteenth Century.* Introduction by Cecil A. Moore. *The
   Modern Library Series.* New York.

Morgan, 1935. *English Plays 1660–1820.* Edited by A. E. Morgan. New York and London. [22 plays from Dryden
   to Sheridan, and Reynolds' *The Dramatist* (first London edition, 1793), Morton's *Speed the Plough* (1800), and
   Buckstone's *Luke the Labourer* (acted in 1826).]

In all these scholarly editions the emphasis is either exclusively or predominantly on the period from 1660 to 1780,
on dramatists from Dryden to Sheridan. The earliest play included in any of them is D'Avenant's *The Siege of Rhodes,
Part I*, produced in its earliest version in 1656. Two of the collections add single plays, and one collection adds three
plays, subsequent to 1780, but without essentially altering the main bases of selection. All of these collections have
helpful introductions, most of them annotate considerably the separate plays, and one (*Morgan*) — where 'the general
textual principle has been to rely on the first printed edition' — collates other texts extensively. The uncollated anthologies mainly follow this same general textual principle, though *Tom Thumb*, whenever included, appears in Fielding's later three-act revision, and *The Rehearsal* is found variously, in its original printed text and in the author's
recognized revision in the third quarto. For details of textual methods the several editions should be consulted individually, but here the central interest lies in the striking recent development of the whole group of scholarly collections
which have notably furthered comprehensive study of English drama of the Restoration and eighteenth century.

G. H. N.

EDITORIAL PRINCIPLES AND METHODS

The first question that confronts the modern editor of Restoration and eighteenth-century plays is the choice of text; the next is the method of typography. In recent anthologies, the usual textual principle has been to depend on the first printed edition. In special cases, as in *The Rehearsal* or in *Tom Thumb*, later editions conspicuously revised by the author have sometimes been adopted as the preferred texts, but such exceptions have been relatively few. In the present volume, the ultimate choice of text rests on study of all editions published in the author's lifetime, with especial heed to his own sanctions and revisions. Subsequent sections dealing separately with the various plays consider the individual problems and choices involved. These sections, together with the textual footnotes that accompany, page by page, the main texts of the plays, contain much that is pertinent, particularly in matters of detail, to the second editorial question — that of typography. Some general points of method may, however, preferably be reviewed here. In essence, they are aspects of one insistent question — to retain, or not to retain, the original typography of the chosen basic text.

Modern editions of the plays here included range widely from strict reproduction to free modernization of early typography. In general, they divide into two groups according to dominant preference either for the facsimile method or for the modernizing method of reprinting. In the former group may conveniently be included not merely exact reprints but those where minor changes from the precise original — such as disuse of the long *s*, modification of erratic capitals and italics, or correction of misleading misprints — are conceded. Some editions which stress literal fidelity prefer to retain printer's errors and inconsistencies in the main text, though often not in speech and stage directions and like accessories. In general, editions of this first group approximate the original typography, but with divergencies in method and in accuracy which may be observed by close collation with the basic texts reproduced. The second, and by far the larger, group of modern editions prefers to modernize considerably or fully the original typography. Here, the main intent is to free the dramatist's text from early printer's errors and eccentricities and to reprint it in general conformity with modern usage. Of the recent anthologies previously listed those of Montrose J. Moses and A. E. Morgan may be classed in the first group, and the rest in the second group.

Illustration of some of the specific typographical problems presented by early editions used as basic texts in the present anthology may properly preface comment on the general methods adopted to meet them. Etherege's *The Man of Mode; or, Sir Fopling Flutter* is here included as a type of the prose comedy of manners of the Restoration. In the first quarto, however, it bears the semblance of verse drama, for the prose dialogue is printed in lines of quasi-poetic length, heralded with capitals that catch the eye, though they mock the ear that strains for cadence of verse. In so challenging a case, the Morgan anthology frankly abandons its typographical custom and its 'text ignores the method of Q1.' The Moses anthology holds to its habit, but confesses 'great temptation to return the dialogue to the prose form where it belongs.' Modernized editions are, of course, free from this dilemma. The present edition unhesitatingly frees Etherege's prose comedy from its early masquerade as poetic drama.

Otway's *Venice Preserved* presents other typographical problems. The text of the first quarto, the sole edition that appeared in the dramatist's lifetime, bears evidence of hasty and careless printing. The earlier and later portions were set by different compositors, and left without reconciliation of characteristic variants. Misprints, faulty punctuation, and heedless inconsistencies often mar the text and sometimes obscure its meaning. Here again, strict facsimile reproduction would stress printer's errors and eccentricities at the expense of the playwright. The carefully studied Ghosh text, which largely maintains the original typography, finds it advisable to introduce scores of emendations, relegating rejected original readings to corresponding footnotes. The frequency of such changes in an edition where 'corrections have been made very sparingly, and only when the original readings obscure the sense,' emphasizes the need of freeing the essential dramatic text from the impositions of careless printing.

Not merely in individual plays which accentuate special difficulties, but in the general run of Restoration dramatic texts, are typographical irregularities manifold. Apart from actual printers' errors and inadvertencies, free usage in spelling, punctuation, and capitalization tended to lawlessness. Especially in acting texts hurried through the press to catch the quick but uncertain demands of theatrical favor, the chances of error and inconsistency were multiplied. Even when publication was delayed, faulty copy, variant prompt-books, and the indifference of playwright or manager to their correction might remain as adverse factors. Later editions of popular plays range from careful revision by the dramatist to careless reprinting by the publisher. The third edition of *The Rehearsal*, 'with Amendments and large Additions by the Author,' abundantly illustrates both major and minute changes of the original text. The later quartos of Dryden's plays, in their progressive deterioration of text and typography, mainly betray his usual unconcern with the fate of his dramatic texts after they had once achieved publication. Sometimes an author's relation either to initial or to later publication of his play was nominal or negligible. From the first spurious Dublin editions onwards throughout Sheridan's lifetime, no printed text of *The School for Scandal* had the author's sanction, still less his personal correction.

Against such complex backgrounds, the difficulties of consistent adherence to the principle of relying on the first printed edition or to the practice of undeviating fidelity to the original printer stand forth distinctly. The number and variety of concessions made by many modern reprints which mainly prefer such principle and practice are in themselves suggestive. Even when faulty original text and typography are reproduced with unusual accuracy, there remains the larger question whether such fidelity to the printer is not achieved at cost to the playwright. The present Textual Notes and annotations sometimes utilize, as in the case of Dryden's quartos, actual misprints and variants as means to show the successive processes of textual and typographical corruption, but the numerous collations of the present edition have been mainly directed to the recovery of the essential dramatic text and only incidentally to the record of printers' errors and eccentricities. In modernizing the dramatic texts, this anthology of plays has preferred the interests of the student of drama to the special concerns of the professional philologist or investigator of obsolete typography. For such precise purposes, indeed, the only safe substitute for an original printed text is photostatic reproduction.

In following the general usages of modern printing, the editors have sought to observe, and often to restore when obscured in various later reprints, metrical values originally indicated. Thus, metrical elisions or syllabic expansions are preserved in reprinting *indiff'rent, o' th' temple, th' ingenious flatt'ry, Almahida* (used occasionally as an intentional metrical variant for *Almahide*). In the relatively few cases where modern accentuation or typography may invite hesitation as to the original metrical intent, some convenient indications have been supplied (e.g. *triúmph, armèd*), and some early forms (e.g. *blest, curst*) retained. In adopting both modern spelling and typography, this anthology prints *died* for *dy'd, fired* for *fir'd, gored* for *goar'd, spared* for *spar'd, shrieked* for *schriek'd, tamed* for *tam'd, thin-soled shoes* for *thin-sol'd shoos*, etc. Early typography marked habitually in verse and considerably, though often irregularly, in prose, distinctions between the stressed and unstressed *ed* in past tenses and participles which are now generally recognized instinctively. Early poetic texts incessantly marked ordinary elisions with the now generally discarded *'d*, and somewhat confusingly printed *ed* alike in regular and in exceptional cases where it has separate syllabic value — e.g. *pointed, used, needed, formed, trusted, armed*, alike indicate dissyllables (for otherwise, it must be remembered, *us'd, form'd, arm'd*, the normal elided forms, would have been printed). In the rare cases where modern typographical usage may cause question, *ed* as an extra syllable is marked, in the present text, *èd* (*formèd, armèd*). This method safeguards original metrical values, and frees the main text from constant repetition of the once conventional *'d* in the countless opposite instances of normal elision. In many cases (*wou'd, cou'd, shou'd, lay'n* [for *lain*], *it's* [for *its*], *your's, their's*), various early uses of the apostrophe represent practices now needless or discredited. The present texts retain, in prose as well as in verse, elisions that intentionally affect pronunciation (*'em* [for *them*], *gen'rous, lov'st, desp'rate, sputt'ring*), but discard uses of the apostrophe inconsistent with modern practice.

In other matters of typography which concern both prose and verse dramas, modern usages have been followed freely rather than rigidly. The present texts retain some obsolete spellings that affect pronunciation, and some early italics or capitals that emphasize textual points and not merely printers' practices. Punctuation has been modernized somewhat sparingly, with main attention to clarification of the dramatic text, and without attempt to impose strict uniformity in typographical detail throughout the whole range of plays. Convenient, and sometimes necessary, stage directions which are lacking in original texts are supplied in square brackets. References to characters and other details of arrangement in speech and stage directions have been adjusted for like convenience. Photographic reproduction of early specimen pages has admitted some adjustments of scale to the general format of this volume.

G. H. N.

NOTES ON THE INDIVIDUAL PLAYS

THE CONQUEST OF GRANADA, PART I

TEXTS

*Q1. First quarto, 1672. *Yale. Harv. B.M. *Bod. L.C. U. of C. N.Y.P.L.

Q2. Second quarto, 1673. *Yale. Harv. B.M. *Bod. L.C.

Q3. Third quarto, 1678. *Yale. Harv. B.M. *Bod. U. of C. N.Y.P.L.

Q4. Fourth quarto, 1687. *Yale. Harv. B.M. *Bod. *U. of C.

Q5. Fifth quarto, 1695. *Yale. B.M. *Bod. Camb. L.C.

F. Folio, 1701. *The Comedies, Tragedies, and Operas, Written by John Dryden, Esq.; Now first Collected together, and Corrected from the Originals.* 2 vols. [I, 379–422.] *Yale. Harv. B.M. Bod. Camb. L.C.

C. Congreve edition, 1717. *The Dramatick Works of John Dryden, Esq.* Edited by William Congreve. [The long 'Dedication' is signed 'William Congreve,' though his name does not appear on the title-page.] 6 vols. [III, 1–96.]

S. Scott-Saintsbury edition, Edinburgh, 1882. *The Dramatic Works of John Dryden.* Edited by Walter Scott [in 1808], revised and corrected by George Saintsbury. 8 vols. [IV, 1–118.]

N. Noyes edition, Chicago and New York, 1910. *Selected Dramas of John Dryden.* Edited by George R. Noyes. [pp. 1–70.]

T. Tupper edition, New York, 1914. *Representative English Dramas from Dryden to Sheridan.* Edited by Frederick Tupper and James W. Tupper. [pp. 3–38.]

MS. Montague Summers edition, 1932. *Dryden. The Dramatic Works.* Edited by Montague Summers. 6 vols. [III, 1–87.]

M. Morgan edition, New York and London, 1935. *English Plays 1660–1820.* Edited by A. E. Morgan. [pp. 1–52.]

General Note on DRYDEN's *Dramatic Texts and Revisions*

In 1800, in the extensive 'Account of the Life and Writings of John Dryden' which prefaces his edition of Dryden's *Prose Works*, Edmond Malone wrote (I, Part i, 143–144): 'When Dryden issued his several works from the press, he in general seems to have dismissed them from his thoughts, and to have been little solicitous about rendering them more perfect ... To his general negligence in this respect there are, however, several exceptions. The second edition of his *Tyrannick Love* is said in the title page to have been *reviewed* by the author.' Malone instanced also the Preface to the second edition of *The Indian Emperor* as proof of some heed on Dryden's part to typographical revision but also of his confessed lack of leisure to amend 'the more material faults of writing.' The two plays of Dryden included in the present collection — *The Conquest of Granada, Part I*, and *All for Love* — support Malone's main conclusions. Four textual revisions in the fifth act of the former play and possibly one or two in *All for Love* suggest 'author's changes' rather than compositor's corrections, but the first quarto of each play remains the dominant authority.

(Through the courtesy of the editors of *Modern Language Notes*, this Note and the following section on the *Quartos* substantially use an article, published in June, 1935, by the present writer on '*Author's Changes*' in Dryden's *Conquest of Granada, Part I*.)

(a) Quartos

The present text is based on the Bodleian Library and Yale Library copies of Q1. With Q1 were first collated the Bodleian Library and Yale Library copies of Q2. The results were then compared with the Yale Library (and other) copies of the three remaining quartos (Q3, Q4, Q5) printed in Dryden's lifetime. Q1 is decidedly the most important text, but Q2, by reason of various 'author's changes' later discussed, deserves secondary attention. Q1 bears some evidences of haste and error, for it prints after the Epilogue a song marked, '*Misplac'd. Sung at the dance, or* Zambra *in the third Act*,' and in its pagination of the main text repeats the numbers 23 and 24, so that the text of the play has actually 69 instead of 67 pages, as apparently indicated. Q2 transfers the misplaced song to its proper context, has 70 pages of main text, plus Epilogue, and retains the prefatory material of Q1.

In general, Q2 follows Q1 closely, even reproducing some of its misprints. Four passages in Act V, however, which seem authorized alterations rather than compositor's changes, merit especial attention.

(1) Q1   *Benz.*   No, *Ozmyn*, no, it is much less ill
                To leave me than dispute a Fathers will: (V. ii. 67–68)

     Q2   *Benz.*   No, *Ozmyn*, no; 'tis not so great an ill
                  To leave me, as dispute a Fathers Will:

The conscious emendation of Q2 is clearly intended to remedy the metrical defect in the first line of Q1.

    (2) Q1   And, bending to the blast, all pale and dead,
              Hears from within, the wind sing round its head: (V. iii. 131–132)
        Q2   Bends to the blast, all pale, and almost dead
              While the loud Wind sings round its drooping Head.

The conscious emendation of Q2 distinctly revises the entire couplet.

    (3) Q1   When all my joys are gone
              What cause can I for living longer, give,
              But a dull lazy habitude to live?   (V. iii. 245–247)

Q2 eliminates the first short unrhymed line. This seems an intentional excision of an irregular line rather than a compositor's error in dropping a line accidentally.

    (4) Q1   *Almah.*   It was your fault that fire seiz'd all your brest,
                       You should have blown up some, to save the rest.
                       But tis, at worst, but so consum'd by fire
                       As Cities are, that by their falls rise high'r.   (V. iii. 269–272)
        Q2   *Alma.*   Your Heart's, at worst, but so consum'd by fire
                       As Cities are, that by their falls rise high'r.

The emendation of Q2 is obviously designed to eliminate the opening couplet of Q1, for the consequent alteration of the following line shows that the couplet itself was not dropped accidentally by the compositor.

In all four cases Q3 follows Q2, but Q4 reverts to the full original reading of Q1, and is in turn followed by Q5 and F. Thus these four 'author's changes' — definite textual changes, at any rate, sanctioned by higher authority than the mere compositor — are found only in Q2 and Q3, and disappear not merely from the later quartos but from the Folio of 1701.

From the data thus summarized, some important deductions may be made. Compared with the basic text of Q1, only that of Q2 shows evidence of any independent contribution to real revision of text, as distinguished from printer's minor changes of typography. Q3 was evidently printed from Q2, but Q4, in reverting to Q1, re-established the original text. If Dryden had concerned himself with the retention of the 'author's changes' included in Q2 and reproduced in Q3, their omission in Q4 could readily have been rectified in Q5, but there is no evidence of such concern. The sum total of 'author's changes' in Q2 remains, in any case, very small, though Q2 thereby assumes definite significance in textual study. Even the 'several exceptions' in Q2 may be said to prove the rule of 'general negligence' which Malone broadly ascribed to Dryden.

Collation of the other quartos published in Dryden's lifetime amply supports the deductions already drawn as to the dominant authority of Q1 and as to the successive relations of the various quartos. Minor variants in spelling and punctuation are not infrequent, but, with due allowance for accidents and inconsistencies, even misprints seem sometimes significant. Thus, Q3 corrects a misprint — 'I fear [for *hear*] some tread; and fear I am betray'd' (V. i. 68) — made in Q1 and followed in Q2; but Q4, in printing from Q1, reverts to the original misprint *fear*, and is followed by Q5. Similarly, Q3 corrects the punctuation at the end of one line (IV. ii. 194), but Q4 reverts to the punctuation of Q1, and is followed by Q5. The direct dependence of Q5 on Q4 is further evident in the repetition of the Q4 misprint *though* for *thought* (IV. i. 44). The present collations supply and interpret ample additional evidence of the interrelations of the five successive quartos.

(b) *Folio of* 1701

The present collation of the five successive quartos was next compared with the text in the Folio of 1701 (F). On its title-page, the Folio makes misleading claims that Dryden's dramatic works are 'Now first Collected together, and Corrected from the Originals.' The Folio was not published until the year after Dryden's death, but his individual works had already been assembled by Jacob Tonson in convenient separate editions and issued together in a series of volumes with comprehensive title-pages listing their total contents. In 1695, the *Works of Mr. John Dryden* (W) thus assembled Dryden's dramatic works in the first three of its four volumes, in various, usually late, quarto editions of the separate plays, with separate pagination — e.g. *The Wild Gallant*, 1694; *The Conquest of Granada, Part I*, 1695. In Vol. II of the Yale Library copy of W, *All for Love* appears in the edition of 1678 (Q1), but in the copy listed in the *C.H.E.L.* (VIII, 391) it appears in the edition of 1696 (Q3). The inclusion of a 1696 edition in a copy of W (1695) suggests perhaps a belated insertion or the early availability of a forthcoming edition. In any event, W has no independent textual authority, since it merely utilizes indiscriminately convenient editions at hand. The initial claim that the Folio of 1701 is the first collection of Dryden's plays is, however, unwarranted.

The second claim, that the Folio text is 'Corrected from the Originals,' is equally misleading. Both plays here included — *The Conquest of Granada, Part I*, and *All for Love* — are reprinted in F from the latest quartos, Q5 and Q3 respectively, and 'corrections' are made without consultation of the true 'Originals' — the earliest quartos. This practice led frequently to the perpetuation of errors that had crept into the later quartos, and to the introduction of fresh errors, including misprints and conscious, but ill-advised, 'corrections.'

In *The Conquest of Granada, Part I*, the direct dependence of F on Q5 is evident even in the repetition of various misprints occurring only in Q5 — e.g. *mum'd* for *numm'd* (III. 336), *my* for *thy* (III. 508), *insolence* for *innocence* (IV. ii. 240). Elsewhere, and in other ways, the present collations amply illustrate F's habitual reliance on the inferior Q5, and its resort, when textual corrections are deemed necessary, to conjectural emendations instead of the original authority of Q1.

(c) Later Editions

Congreve (C). In 1717, William Congreve, whose early dramatic work Dryden had signally befriended, gratefully acknowledged his debts by editing Dryden's plays in six volumes. Though in *All for Love* Congreve happily reverted to the original text (Q1), he unwisely relied on F for his text of *The Conquest of Granada*. Furthermore, he departed not merely from the quartos but from F in introducing various textual changes, such as inverting 'unmake or make' (I. i. 286), and altering 'be known' (II. i. 109) to 'is known,' and 'not half' (II. i. 146) to 'but half.'

Scott-Saintsbury (S). The undue influence of F as a basic text was persistently maintained by Walter Scott's edition of Dryden's *Dramatic Works*, published in 1808, and eventually revised by George Saintsbury (1882, etc.). In 1904, in the *Mermaid Series* (SM), Saintsbury edited in two volumes Dryden's chief plays, in texts virtually following S. *The Conquest of Granada, Part I*, is in vol. I, 21–117.

Scott himself relied directly on Congreve's text, using the 1735 edition (published six years after Congreve's death), but at times correcting an error or making an independent change. Saintsbury, in turn, mainly followed Scott, thereby continuing various departures by Congreve and by Scott from Dryden's original text. Both Saintsbury editions, S and SM, freely modernize the text and silently maintain or introduce unwarranted variants. They retain, for example, all three of Congreve's specific changes previously instanced, and alter 'long in banishment' (QQF, II. i. 80) to 'in long banishment.' The disturbing process of silently altering the text is further evident in the frequent neglect of elisions and abbreviations originally indicated, and in the substitution of full verbal forms to the detriment of text and meter. The main service of S and SM was to familiarize the general reader with Dryden's plays rather than to maintain Dryden's original text in its integrity.

Noyes (N). In 1910 George R. Noyes signally contributed to scholarly knowledge of Dryden's original texts and editions. His critical edition of *Selected Dramas of Dryden* includes both parts of *The Conquest of Granada* and *All for Love, Marriage à la Mode* and *The Spanish Friar*, and Buckingham's burlesque, *The Rehearsal*. This pioneer work of Professor Noyes has continued influential. His general method was first to collate S 'with the first edition of each play, and next with the Folio, and a record was made of all variants. Then these variants were compared with the readings of the quartos (in which form Dryden's separate plays were always printed) intermediate between the first quarto and the Folio.' In the case of *The Conquest of Granada*, this process led to the sound general conclusion that in Q2 'Dryden seems to have made some trifling changes, which disappeared in the later quartos.' To Professor Noyes, 'it did not seem worth while, however, to collate each line of the second quarto, in order to present a complete list of such changes.' Nevertheless, the present full collation of Q2 with Q1 reveals, as already indicated, four 'author's changes' (N detects variants in two of the cases) which, collectively, help considerably to establish the definite relation of Q2 not merely to Q1 but to each later quarto. The present edition differs considerably from N in basic methods and scope of textual collation, and hence in various findings and interpretations, but its independent results have been helpfully checked with those of N. It has here seemed preferable to omit generally such unwarranted modern alterations as those of S and SM (largely cited in N), and to illustrate rather than to exhaust the variants between F and the quartos. Certain tell-tale misprints have, however, been listed, since their retention or correction sometimes contributes strikingly to the history of the relations of the successive quartos, but full inclusion of minute typographical variants would have needlessly encumbered the present text and notes.

Editors since Noyes have habitually recognized the dominant authority of Q1. Thus the editions here listed as T, MS, and M, all adopt Q1 as the basic text, and MS and M supply pertinent textual collations. The influence of the Folio of 1701, unduly persistent for some two centuries, has eventually yielded to that of the authentic original quarto.

G. H. N.

THE REHEARSAL

Texts

Q1. First quarto, 1672. *Yale. Harv. *B.M. Bod. L.C.

Q2. Second quarto, 1673. *Yale. *Bod. L.C.

*Q3. Third quarto, 1675. 'The Third Edition with Amendments and large Additions by the Author.' *Yale. Harv *B.M. U. of C.

Q4. Fourth quarto, 1683. *Yale. Harv. B.M. *Bod. Camb. U. of C.

Q5. Fifth quarto, 1687. *Yale. *B.M. Bod. Camb. N.Y.P.L.

Q6. Sixth quarto, 1692. *Yale. Harv. B.M. *Camb.

Q7. Seventh quarto, 1701. 'With some [4] Explanatory Notes.' *Yale. Harv. B.M. *Bod. L.C.

Q8. Eighth quarto, 1711. *Yale. Harv.

Key. Samuel Briscoe's *Key*, 1704. *A Key to The Rehearsal, or a Critical View of the Authors, and their Writings, that*

A
KEY
TO THE
REHEARSAL
OR A
CRITICAL VIEW
OF THE
AUTHORS,
AND

Their Writings, that are expos'd in that Celebrated Play:

Written by his Grace GEORGE *late Duke of* Buckingham.

LONDON:
Printed for S. *Briscoe*, 1704.

TITLE-PAGE OF SAMUEL BRISCOE'S *KEY TO THE REHEARSAL*
Harvard Library copy, in Vol. II of *Miscellaneous Works Written by George, Late Duke of Buckingham*, 1705

are expos'd in that Celebrated Play: Written by his Grace George late Duke of Buckingham. London: *Printed for S. Briscoe, 1704.* In vol. II (1705) of Buckingham's, *Miscellaneous Works.* *Harv.

W. Works, 1715. *The Works of his Grace, George Villiers, Late Duke of Buckingham. In Two Volumes . . . The Third Edition with large Additions, adorn'd with Cuts.* London: *Printed for Sam. Briscoe. 1715.* [Both the *Key* and *The Rehearsal* (individually dated 1714) are in vol. II, entitled *The Dramatick Works,* and dated 1715.] *Yale. Harv. *B.M.

A. Arber reprint [of Q1], 1868. *The Rehearsal . . . with illustrations from previous plays.* Edited by Edward Arber in *English Reprints.*

N. Noyes edition, Chicago and New York, 1910. *Selected Dramas of John Dryden, with The Rehearsal by George Villiers, Duke of Buckingham.* Edited by George R. Noyes. [pp. 385–427; Notes, pp. 472–504.]

MS. Montague Summers edition, Stratford-upon-Avon, 1914. *The Rehearsal, by George Villiers, Duke of Buckingham (1625–1687).* Edited by Montague Summers.

(a) *The Earliest Quartos* (Q1, Q2)

The present text is based on British Museum and Yale Library copies of the third quarto (Q3), 1675, 'The third Edition with Amendments and large Additions by the Author.' *The Rehearsal,* first produced on December 7, 1671, was first printed in quarto form, in 1672 (Q1). Prior to production and publication the text evolved gradually through the collaboration of Buckingham and his associates over a considerable period of years. (See p. 5.) Q1 represents the burlesque as it had taken definite acting form during its first Drury Lane season. Q2 (1673) has commonly been dismissed as merely a 'replica' of Q1, and it is, indeed, mainly a page for page and line for line reprint. Nevertheless, careful data as to variants between Q1 and Q2 in the Library of Congress copies, generously supplied by Mr. Parma, Curator of the Rare Book Collection, and amply confirmed by close collation of the Yale Library copies of Q1 and Q2, prove that Q2 contributes not merely typographical betterments but a few actual textual changes. This is significant as evidence of the early beginnings of the process of textual revision usually ascribed wholly to Q3. Thus, typographically, Q2 supplies the running title (missing in Q1) at the top of pages, corrects errors in pagination (the misnumbering, 53, 51, 52), and clarifies (top of p. 28) the stage direction, 'Enter Prince Volscius.' Two definite additions to the text are made: (1) the interpolation of an explanatory phrase — 'that is, the Prologue for the Epilogue, or the Epilogue for the Prologue' (Q2, p. 7); (2) the interpolation of three brief speeches, emphasizing a point of the dialogue (Q2, p. 29: '*Smi.* But pray, Sir, where lies the jest,' etc.).

These two interpolated passages conveniently illustrate both the dangers of too ready acceptance of general appearances of complete uniformity between editions and the helps which even a check of the catch-words at the foot of the page may sometimes supply. In the first of the given cases (p. 7), the added matter made it necessary for the printer of Q2 to carry over the last line of Q1 to his next page, and thus to have 37 (instead of 36) lines on page 8. The altered catch-word on page 7 thus becomes in itself a warning mark. In the second case (p. 29), the printer made his adjustment by lengthening page 30 (38 lines for 36, in Q1), but the altered catch-word on page 29 is again a useful clue. Such methods of interrelating typographical and textual evidence apply to other dramatic texts included in this volume.

(b) *The 'Amended' Quarto* (Q3)

The process of textual revision, of which Q2 gives early hints, was strikingly extended and fulfilled in the third quarto (Q3). The title-page indicates the two main features of this authorized revision, 'with Amendments and large Additions by the Author.' 'Amendments' include many lesser changes of phrase or word. 'Large Additions' include new passages of dialogue, sometimes adding but a few speeches, sometimes interpolating from a dozen to a score of new speeches. The present text conveniently indicates such speeches by prefixing asterisks. These 'large Additions' often notably expand local and personal hits briefly suggested in Q1. Thus an early passing hit at Dryden's alleged relations with the actress, Anne Reeve, is developed in Q3 by the interpolation of anecdote and added comment through nearly a score of consecutive new speeches (I. ii). Other extensive additions expose (as in II. i., II. iv., III. i.) vulnerable points in Dryden's armor, enlarging the use of dramatic parody or personal allusion. Elsewhere briefer additions of two or three speeches point the dialogue or emphasize the action. Doubtless Q3 incorporates various incidental changes that had proved effective on the boards. Burlesque lends itself readily to practical experimentation and to textual changes approved by experience. Throughout the entire play, major and minor changes constantly attest the breadth and the detailed care of the authorized revision published in 1675. The present edition marks major changes by asterisks throughout the main text, and illustrates minor changes by the variants of the first act supplied in textual footnotes.

(c) *The Later Quartos*

The authority of Q3 is accepted by the subsequent quartos. Q4 (1683) and Q5 (1687) maintain that authority throughout Buckingham's lifetime. Their title-pages are somewhat misleading in altering the number of the edition but at the same time retaining Q3's phrasing, 'with Amendments and large Additions by the Author.' The 'Amendments' and 'large Additions' are those of Q3. The author was evidently satisfied with his thorough revision in 1675, and let its printed text stand as final. Though the whole series of eight quartos (1672–1711) has been considerably examined in the complete set of Yale Library copies, variants of the later quartos have rarely been cited, since they lack independent authority.

The title-page of Q7 (1701) reads engagingly, 'With some Explanatory Notes,' but these notes consist merely of four marginal references to plays parodied in *The Rehearsal*. Q8 (1711) simply repeats these references.

(d) Briscoe's 'Key'

The scanty 'Explanatory Notes' of the 1701 quarto are an early hint of the growing need of eighteenth-century readers and playgoers for explanation of local allusions and parodies familiar to Restoration audiences. In 1704, Samuel Briscoe, the publisher, supplied *A Key to the Rehearsal* (fully noted previously), with a list of seventeen plays parodied and with a considerable body of specific references, quotations, and notes. This *Key* was frequently reprinted with editions of the play or of Buckingham's *Works*, and was the essential basis of further critical investigations, notably of Bishop Percy and of Edwin Arber. Percy's long-labored edition of Buckingham's *Works* never achieved final publication, but his work is uniquely preserved in the British Museum in the form of incomplete proof-sheets, assembled in two volumes without printed title. In his 1868 reprint of Q1, Arber largely utilized Briscoe's *Key* and Percy's work, and added other explanatory material.

(e) Recent Critical Editions

Of recent annotated and collated texts of *The Rehearsal* those of George R. Noyes (N), and Montague Summers (MS) have been specially listed. The text of N was based on Q1; that of MS on Q3. N distributes throughout the Notes (pp. 472–504) the main textual additions and some of the other variants of Q3; MS assembles in an Appendix (pp. 153–160) the main textual omissions and many lesser variants of Q1. Both editions thoroughly annotate the text, and MS supplies extensive information as to the history and practices of the Restoration stage.

G. H. N.

ALL FOR LOVE

TEXTS

*Q1. First quarto, 1678. *Yale. Harv. B.M. Bod. L.C. U. of C.

Q2. Second quarto, 1692. *Yale. Harv. B.M. Bod. U. of C.

Q3. Third quarto, 1696. *Yale. Harv. B.M.

F. Folio, 1701. *The Comedies, Tragedies, and Operas, Written by John Dryden, Esq.; Now first Collected together, and Corrected from the Originals.* 2 vols. [*All for Love*, II, 53–106.] *Yale. Harv. B.M. Bod. Camb. L.C.

C. Congreve edition, 1717. *The Dramatick Works of John Dryden, Esq.* Edited by William Congreve. 6 vols. [*All for Love*, IV, 171–272.]

S. Scott-Saintsbury edition, Edinburgh, 1882. *The Dramatic Works of John Dryden.* Edited by Walter Scott [in 1808], revised and corrected by George Saintsbury. 8 vols. [*All for Love*, V, 305–437.]

N. Noyes edition, Chicago and New York, 1910. *Selected Dramas of John Dryden.* Edited by George R. Noyes. [*All for Love*, pp. 221–303.]

Strunk. Strunk edition, Boston and London, 1911. *All for Love and The Spanish Fryar, by John Dryden.* Edited by William Strunk, Jr. *Belles-Lettres Series.*

MS. Montague Summers edition, 1932. *Dryden, The Dramatic Works.* Edited by Montague Summers. 6 vols. [*All for Love*, IV, 165–262.]

M. Morgan edition, New York and London, 1935. *English Plays 1660–1820.* Edited by A. E. Morgan. [*All for Love*, pp. 53–108.]

(a) Quartos

The text is based on a Yale Library copy of Q1. With this have been collated Yale Library copies of Q2 and Q3. Collation of the three quartos published in Dryden's lifetime establishes the dominant authority and superiority of Q1, the generally close adherence to it of Q2, and the habitual dependence of Q3 upon Q2. All quartos contain errors and inconsistencies of spelling and of punctuation, but actual textual difficulties are few. Q2 resets the text of Q1, with minor changes which rarely better, and often debase, the original text. These textual variants seem compositor's changes, though the slight shortening of one speech (IV. 382–383) may be an 'author's change.' Q3 resets the text of Q2, whose alterations, and even misprints, it usually reproduces, to the disregard of Q1. Of the variants between Q3 and Q2 some are surely, and others probably, printer's errors. In general, the three quartos show progressive deterioration of text.

The relation of the successive quartos is strikingly illustrated by this passage (III. 208–210):

> Q1 *Dolla.* As to your equal.
> *Ant.* Well, he's but my equal:
> While I wear this, he never shall be more.
> *Dolla.* I bring Conditions from Him.
>
> Q2 *Dolla.* As to your Equal:
> While I wear this, he never shall be more.
> *Dolla*[.] I bring Conditions from him.
>
> Q3 *Dola.* As to your Equal:
> While I wear this, he never shall be more.
> I bring Conditions from him.

The compositor of Q2, apparently confusing the two short lines ending with the same word (*equal*) in Q1, dropped the entire second line, thereby inadvertently transferring the following line to Dollabella. The compositor of Q3, setting his text from Q2, without reference to Q1, noted the repetition of *Dolla.* in Q2 and eliminated the second *Dolla.*, thereby obscuring, as well as confirming, the initial mistake.

Of many other proofs that Q3 followed Q2 directly, habitually reproducing its changes, for better or for worse, a few examples will suffice. The last line of Act II reads: 'And once triumph o'er Caesar [ere] we die.' Q1 omits *ere*, which Q2 supplies, and Q3 follows, to the obvious betterment of sense and scansion. An amusing misprint in Q2 (IV. 363), whereby Cleopatra is made to have *lawfully*, instead of *lawlessly* (as in Q1), usurped Octavia's 'holy bed,' is reproduced unquestioningly in Q3. Q3, likewise, unhappily follows Q2 in several accidental omissions of short words, thus marring the meter of lines properly given in Q1. The inferiority of Q3 is shown in various independent changes and misprints such as, *go back* for *go not back*, *Roman* for *Romans*, *honour* for *hour*, *will* for *wife*.

None of the three quartos is consistent in spelling or punctuation. Q1, for instance, has *humor, honor, succor, labor'd,* though the *our* spelling in these or in similar words also appears; both *dye* and *dy* are found with but one intervening line of text. All three quartos read *Anthony* in the list of 'Persons Represented,' but Q1 and Q2 prefer *Antony* and Q3 *Anthony,* in the text. Q3 prefers *Dolabella* to the *Dollabella* of Q1 and Q2. Q1, in distinction from Q2 and Q3, has *shipwrack* for *shipwreck, subtile* for *subtle,* and bears, on the whole, evidences of its earlier imprint. Q1 shows considerable care in marking elisions that aid proper scansion, though the later quartos are slightly less scrupulous. In matters of punctuation, Q1 is reasonably clear, despite inconsistencies. Q2 and Q3 make occasional minor betterments, together with some needless or even confusing changes. A noteworthy common characteristic of the punctuation of all the quartos is the frequent use of the colon, which modern usage would often replace by the period, dash, or semicolon.

(b) *Folio of* 1701

The present collation of the three quartos has been compared, chiefly as to verbal variants, but considerably as to other typographical details, with the text of *All for Love* in the Folio of 1701 (F). F did not appear until after Dryden's death, and unfortunately relied on Q3, the poorest of the quartos, without consultation of the original text. In occasional instances, as in the correction of one persistent misprint in QQ (II. 447), F emends helpfully. Textual collation shows, however, how frequently F echoes the errors of Q3 or further debases the text. Even in obviously questionable passages, F fails to consult Q1, or, for that matter, Q2. In a conspicuous early instance (I. 216–227), a misreading of the marginal stage direction, leads F to transfer to Ventidius a dozen lines that clearly belong to Antony. More insidious are minor alterations of text introduced without warning or warrant. In its own day and later, the disturbing influence of F upon the authentic text is evident.

(c) *Later Editions*

Congreve (C). In 1717, William Congreve's text of *All for Love* repeatedly set aside F in favor of the original authentic text. (See for crucial instances, I. 216–227; III. 208; IV. 382–383.) He originated at least one popular emendation (I. 254), but since his readings are mainly significant in confirming the authority of Q1, they are here cited only occasionally.

Scott-Saintsbury (S). In 1808, Walter Scott published his extensive and influential edition of Dryden. Scott used Congreve's edition, but too readily reverted to the guidance of the Folio text of *All for Love.* This unfortunate textual influence was largely maintained in the familiar Scott-Saintsbury edition (S) of Dryden (1882), an extensive revision whose general merits soon established it as the standard edition of Dryden. Its readily accessible dramatic texts early acquired more authority than they now retain. The general tendency of S is to modernize Dryden's text considerably, to discard many verse elisions, colloquial abbreviations, and early, as well as obsolete, spellings of words, and to introduce without warning minor changes both in the order and in the actual use of words. Thus, the opening line of *All for Love* silently changes 'are grown' (QQF) to 'have grown,' the last line of Act II follows Congreve in inverting 'once triumph,' and such other silent changes as 'desires belief' for 'deserves belief' and 'vanquished in a mist' for 'vanish'd in a mist' suggest misreadings of either text or context. Elsewhere, as in the confusion of the speech in the Antony-Ventidius scene already cited, S tends unduly to follow F to the disregard of the original text. In some cases, however, S properly restores readings of Q1.

In 1904, Professor Saintsbury reprinted *All for Love* in his edition of Dryden's chief plays (II, 1–109), in the *Mermaid Series*. The text mainly follows S.

Noyes (N). In 1910, the critical edition of *All for Love*, included by George R. Noyes in his *Selected Dramas of John Dryden, with The Rehearsal*, made outstanding contribution to textual study. The general method of Professor Noyes was to collate S with Q1, then with F, and next to compare the variants thus found with Q2 and Q3. He felt that 'a complete collation of each quarto would have been a mere waste of time,' but such collation may at least be said to confirm fully his main conclusions as to the 'progressive degeneration of the text,' and his judgment in adopting Q1 as his basic text. He suggests (p. 284 ftn.) that one later shortening of a speech was 'possibly by Dryden's own direction,' but in the Preface he says of his textual investigations: 'No sign of author's corrections appeared at any point; the variants were mere printers' errors.' In any case, the retrenchment in question does not seem accidental, and such betterments in Q2 as that of supplying a missing word in the last line of Act II show that not all the variants which Noyes himself records were simply printers' errors. If, however, the present edition differs in details of collation and interpretation, some differences are due to the method of fuller collation of the successive quartos, and some are differences in degree rather than in kind. Thus, greater readiness to credit the inferior quartos with occasional minor betterments is in no wise at variance with decisive recognition of the dominant authority of Q1. The accurate scholarship of N was amply attested by checking with it the completed results of the present independent collation.

Strunk (Strunk). In 1911, William Strunk, Jr., in the *Belles-Lettres Series*, published an important critical edition of *All for Love and The Spanish Fryar*. Professor Strunk's text reproduces the spelling of Q1, modernizes italics, punctuation, and capitalization, and mainly adopts the stage directions of Q2. In method and results, its collations differ somewhat from N. If the general method of collating the successive quartos seems preferable, the actual results seem less assured. The two longest omissions in Q2 and Q3 — the dropped half-line (III. 208) and the shortened speech (IV. 382–383) — are noted by Noyes, but unrecorded by Strunk. The latter does not collate F, but both editors collate Saintsbury's texts (S and SM) and extensively annotate the basic text of the play. The Strunk edition supplies a useful bibliography of texts.

Morgan (M). Since the Noyes and Strunk critical editions, *All for Love* has been reprinted, usually in the basic text of Q1, without detailed collation, in various collections of representative Restoration plays. A noteworthy exception is the extensively collated text included by A. E. Morgan (M) in his *English Plays 1660–1820* (pp. 53–108). Here the text is taken from F, though collated with the quartos, and 'frequently corrected' to Q1, which is recognized as 'on the whole ... the purest text.' The very frequency of these necessary corrections, the infrequency of F's betterments even of the deteriorated text of Q3, and F's unlucky ignorance of the earlier quartos may, indeed, be amply demonstrated from M's own given collations. Thus M's nominal adherence to F hardly constitutes a genuine exception to the sound practice of editors since Noyes of recognizing Q1 as their basic text.

G. H. N.

VENICE PRESERVED

TEXTS

(a) Quartos

*Q1. First quarto, 1682. *Yale. Harv. *B.M. *Bod. L.C.

Q2. Second quarto, 1696. *Yale. Harv. *B.M. Camb. L.C.

Q3. Third quarto, 1704. *Yale. Harv. *B.M. Camb.

(b) Works

For editions of Otway's collected *Works*, see Bibliography in Ghosh's edition (listed below as G), I, 81–84.

(c) Critical Editions

N. Noël edition, 1888. *Thomas Otway with an Introduction and Notes.* Edited by Roden Noël. In *Mermaid Series*. [Text somewhat revised and annotated, but not collated.]

C. McClumpha edition, Boston and London, 1908. *The Orphan and Venice Preserved.* Edited by Charles F. McClumpha. In *Belles-Lettres Series*.

S. Summers edition, 1926. *The Complete Works of Thomas Otway.* Edited by Montague Summers. 3 vols. [III, 1–83.]

G. Ghosh edition, Oxford, 1932. *The Works of Thomas Otway, Plays, Poems, and Love-Letters.* Edited by J. C. Ghosh. 2 vols. [II, 197–289.]

M. Morgan edition, 1935. *English Plays 1660–1820.* Edited by A. E. Morgan. [pp. 235–287.]

(a) The Quartos (1682–1704)

The present text is based on British Museum and Yale Library copies of Q1 (1682), the only edition published in Otway's lifetime. Q2 did not appear until 1696, and Q3 not until 1704, long after Otway's death in 1685. They represent the earliest attempts to revise original faulty printing, and they introduce some betterments of text and typography, together with various needless or careless variants. Q2 and Q3 have been collated in Yale Library copies.

The evidences of careless printing begin on the very title-page of Q1 which prints 'THEATR.' The final 'E' is dropped in all early copies personally examined and in the Ashley Library title-page as reproduced in facsimile in the Catalogue. [The title-pages reproduced in the successive editions of Moses (1929), Ghosh (1932), and Morgan (1935) restore the final 'E.'] Some discrepancies in the text of Q1, especially in the spelling of proper names (*Prinli* and *Prin.* for *Priuli* and *Priu.*) result, as has often been noted, from the distribution of the work between two compositors. Typographical flaws in spelling and punctuation are, however, frequent throughout the play, and at times confusing to the reader. Despite such difficulties, Q1 remains the authentic text. Subsequent editions merely record the successive efforts of later publishers and editors to emend initial errors and imperfections.

Q2 and Q3, though without the authority of author's revision, retain interest as showing the early processes of textual alteration and the forms of text current at the turn from the Restoration to the Queen Anne age. Q2 mainly adheres to Q1, but corrects many obvious, and some subtler, misprints (a few illustrations are included incidentally in the textual footnotes), and betters some points of punctuation. On the other hand, it commits independent errors both of careless misprints and of mistaken 'corrections' of text. Q3 is considerably concerned in metrical emendation to regularize the often rough scansion. The present collations indicate, in the frequency of elisions, fairly consistent effort in Q3 towards that end. Such revision, indeed, suggests a hand more attentive than that of the ordinary compositor.

(b) Editions in Otway's Works (1712–1813)

The subsequent appearance of *Venice Preserved* in editions of Otway's *Works* may be briefly noted. As in the case of Dryden's dramatic works, Otway's plays were first assembled by binding together separate quartos of the individual plays and giving them a collective title-page. In 1692 Richard Bentley thus published a one-volume collected edition of Otway's *Works*, containing nine *Tragedies and Comedies*. (Dyce and Bod. copies.) In 1712, Jacob Tonson published, in two volumes, the *Works, consisting of his Plays, Poems, and Love-Letters*, with an account of Otway's life and works. (B.M. copy.) Neither Bentley's edition (which simply utilizes copies of Q1) nor Tonson's text (which mainly, though not wholly, follows Q3) has independent importance. Six other editions of the *Works* attest Otway's constant popularity in the eighteenth century, but make no vital contribution to the text of *Venice Preserved*. In general, they echo the variants of Q3, though slight further changes are here and there ventured.

In the nineteenth century, the two-volume 1812 edition of the *Works* is similarly unimportant. In the following year Thomas Thornton's three-volume edition of the *Works* (T) attempted fuller revision and modernization of the text, effecting some betterments but also taking injudicious and needless liberties. Thornton's 1813 text thereafter exercised definite influence on later editions, though the *Mermaid Series* text (1888), based on it, deviates independently.

(c) Recent Critical Editions

The general character of texts and collations in the four selected twentieth-century editions listed at the head of this section may here be briefly indicated.

(1) McClumpha, 1908 (C). The text, based on Q1, is extensively collated with Q2 and Q3, 'and with nearly all the editions published since 1712, the date of the first collective edition of Otway's plays.' This text retains the spelling, but not the capitalization or italics, of the seventeenth century, and somewhat emends faulty printing and punctuation. (See C, p. 156 and textual footnotes.) This early edition contributed significantly to critical study of the text.

(2) Summers, 1926 (S). The text, it is claimed (III, 263), 'exactly follows' Q1, but Morgan (p. 238) demonstrates that the transcript of the text is unreliable. Considerable collations of text are assembled in 'The Textual Notes' (III, 263–265). S supplies valuable 'Explanatory Notes' (III, 271–287).

(3) Ghosh, 1932 (G). The text is that of Q1, carefully corrected in accordance with the editor's main principles (see I, 89–94), and with specific variants precisely indicated in textual footnotes. 'Corrections have been made very sparingly, and only when the original readings obscure the sense.' That the textual footnotes indicate some 200 specific changes (in addition to the general changes) deemed advisable in thus sparingly editing the text is striking evidence of the initial imperfections of Q1. It should be remembered that, except as indicated, G reproduces closely the original vagaries of spelling and punctuation, and is not a generally 'modernised' text. G gives no textual collations of editions later than Q1, but the detailed Bibliography (I, 75–76, for the quartos of *Venice Preserved*, and 81–84 for Otway's *Works*) is important.

(4) Morgan, 1935 (M). 'The text is designed to follow the first quarto exactly except in a very few places where divergence is noted.' M collates considerably the quartos, the 1712 and 1727 texts in Otway's *Works*, and an earlier *Collection of the Best English Plays*, 'probably printed for T. Johnson in *The Hague* about 1710.' These later collations reflect the general tendency, previously noted in discussion of the whole series of eighteenth-century editions of Otway's *Works*, to follow Q3 rather than Q1.

In the interests of space and simplicity, the present edition limits its recorded textual variants virtually to the quartos. The further simplification in G — the presentation of the original text of Q1 with specific indication of editorial changes — has, indeed, much to commend it. That method certainly emphasizes the central point that only Q1 appeared in Otway's lifetime, and that later editions must base their emendations directly on Q1.

G. H. N.

THE MAN OF MODE

Texts

*Q1. First quarto, 1676. *Yale. *U. of C. Harv. B.M. Bod. Camb.

Q2. Second quarto, 1684. Yale. *U. of C. Harv. B.M.

Q3. Third quarto, 1693. *Harv. B.M.

W. Works, 8°, 1704. (*The Man of Mode* dated 1703.) *N.U. *U. of C. Newb. Yale. Harv. B.M.
Works, 12°, 1715. U. of C. Harv. Camb.
Plays and poems, 12°, 1723. Yale. Harv. U. of C. Newb. B.M.
Duodecimo, 1733. Harv. B.M.
Duodecimo, 1735. Harv. U. of C.
Dramatic works, 12°, 1735. Bod. Camb.
Verity edition, 1888. *The Works of Sir George Etherege.* Edited by A. Wilson Verity.
Brett-Smith edition, 1927. *The Dramatic Works of Sir George Etherege.* Edited by H. F. B. Brett-Smith.
(2 vols.: *The Man of Mode* in vol. 2.)

The present text of *The Man of Mode* is based upon Q1, with which Q2, Q3, and W have been collated. Only the first two editions can be regarded as having any significance. Q2 was the last edition published in Etherege's lifetime, and there is nothing to indicate that any of the later editions incorporate any corrections by him. Q2 itself shows very few changes from Q1, and these few seem to have originated in the printing shop. The apparent carelessness of the author about his work is what might have been expected of a man who adopted the prevailing attitude of the courtier toward his literary productions — that of the elegant amateur who published 'by request of friends.' The spelling, the punctuation, the stage directions, and, indeed, the whole appearance of the quartos are in perfect harmony with this attitude. Under the circumstances it is surprising that there are not many cruces to be dealt with. Those that exist are chiefly due to slipshod punctuation, which has necessitated more than the usual amount of revision in normalizing the text. The almost universal practice of modern editors of printing the play as prose has been followed (cf. pp. 160 and 918). In general only variants which appear in Q2 have been noted.

A. E. C.

THE PLAIN DEALER

Texts

Q1. First quarto, 1677. *Yale. *Harv. B.M. Bod.

Q2. Second quarto, 1677. Camb.

*Q3. Third quarto ('second edition'), 1678. *Yale. *U. of C. Harv. B.M.

Q4. Fourth quarto ('third edition'), 1677. *Harv.

Q5. Fifth quarto ('third edition'), 1681. Camb.

Q6. Sixth quarto ('fourth edition'), 1686. *Yale. *U. of C. Harv. B.M. Bod.

Q7. Seventh quarto ('fifth edition'), 1691. *Yale. Harv. B.M.

Q8. Eighth quarto ('sixth edition'), 1694. B.M.

Q9. Ninth quarto ('seventh edition'), 1700. *Yale. Harv. B.M. Camb.

Q10. Tenth quarto ('sixth edition'), 1709. *Yale. Harv. B.M.

O1. First octavo, 1710. *Harv. B.M. Camb.

O2. Second octavo, undated. B.M.

O3. Third octavo, 1712. B.M. (Used in making up next item.)

W1. Works, 8°, 1713. *N.U. Newb. B.M.
Plays, 12°, 1720. (2 vols.: *The Plain Dealer* in vol. 1.) *Harv. B.M.
Duodecimo, 1727. N.U.
Plays, 12°, 1731. B.M.
Plays, 12°, Dublin, 1733. N.U.
Plays, 12°, 1735. N.U. B.M.
Duodecimo, 1735. U. of C. B.M.
Plays, 12°, 1736. No copy located.
Hunt edition, 1840. *The Dramatic Works of Wycherley, Congreve, Vanbrugh and Farquhar.* Edited by Leigh Hunt.
Ward edition, 1888. *William Wycherley.* Edited by W. C. Ward. *Mermaid Series.*
Churchill edition, 1911. *The Country Wife and The Plain Dealer.* By William Wycherley. Edited by George B. Churchill. *Belles-Lettres Series.*

Summers edition, 1924. *The Complete Works of William Wycherley.* Edited by Montague Summers. (4 vols.: *The Plain Dealer* in vol. 2.)

The confusion in the dating and the designation of the early editions which is evident in the list given above, together with the rarity of copies of Q2 and Q5, has been the cause of much misunderstanding in discussing the text of *The Plain Dealer.* The relation of the early quartos to each other was at length elucidated by Churchill in his admirable edition of *The Country Wife and The Plain Dealer,* in which he also collated fifteen texts of the play. Summers has caused some uncertainty by citing an edition of 1676, without stating where he consulted it, but as he does not mention any edition of 1677 it is possible that he is assigning to Q1 the date of the *imprimatur* which appears upon the title-page.

An edition of *The Plain Dealer* might reasonably be based upon any one of the first three quartos. The first of these has the claim to respect which commonly attaches to first editions. No copy of Q2 has been available to the present editor, who has therefore been compelled to rely for its readings upon the collations in Churchill's edition, which have been found to be extremely reliable with respect to the other quartos. Q2 follows Q1 in the main, but it introduces numerous emendations, of which only two are undoubted errors, while others are clearly improvements. That the hand of the author, or of an unusually intelligent reviser, was at work is best indicated by the substitution of '*per*' for '*Pere*' at I.i.583 — a correction indicating a knowledge of the law that can hardly be credited to an ordinary corrector of the press. Q3 in turn follows Q2 meticulously, even in the reading just referred to, although all subsequent editions, until Churchill's, revert to the original error. Q3 even follows Q2 at II.i.1083 in printing 'candle-maker' instead of 'caudle-maker' — a slip that was caught in setting up Q4. Q3 differs from its model only in changing 'they're' to 'they are' at II.i.95, and in restoring 'she says,' which had been carelessly dropped from Q2, at II.i.119. These two variants are important only as they help to determine the order of printing of the first four quartos.

Carelessness begins with Q4, and thereafter, until O3 (W1) the text gradually deteriorates. One good example of this process occurs in Freeman's last speech in Act III. Q1 reads, 'Well, let us go home, then,' and this is the reading in Q2 and Q3. Q4 misprints, 'Well, let us go come then,' and is followed by Q5. Q6 emends this obvious error without referring to the earlier editions, and reads, 'Well, let us come then,' and the compositor of Q7, not satisfied, substitutes, 'Well, let us, come then.'

From this history O3 (W1) stands apart. Its importance rests upon two facts — it was the last edition to be published in Wycherley's lifetime, and it appears to have been set up with some regard to the text of Q1. It restores so many of the readings of the first edition, at the same time retaining obviously correct emendations from later quartos, that one is led to speculate whether the author, old and ill as he was in 1712, may not have been responsible for the revision. But the haphazard nature of the corrections, and the persistence, especially in the latter part of the play, of obvious errors which had crept in from time to time, dispose of any claim to authority which might be made for this octavo. Probably it was set up from a copy of O2, imperfectly corrected from an early copy of Q1.

Q2 and Q3, then, appear to be the best texts of the play, and as the former was not available the latter was used perforce as the basis of the present text. With it have been collated Q1, Q4, Q6 and W1, and the variants in these editions have been recorded in the textual notes. Several other editions have been compared at important points of the text, but it has not been thought necessary to give the readings of these editions in more than one or two instances.

A. E. C.

THE RELAPSE

Texts

*Q1. First quarto, 1697. *Yale. *U. of C. Newb. Harv. B.M. Bod.
Q2. Second quarto, 1698. *U. of C. Harv. B.M. Camb.
Q3. Third quarto, 1708. *Yale. Harv. B.M. Bod. Camb.
Edition, format unknown, 1709. Noted by Dobrée. No copy located.
Duodecimo, 1711. B.M.
P. Plays, 12°, 1719. *Yale.
Duodecimo, 1727. Harv. Bod.
Plays, 12°, 1730. Yale. B.M.
Plays, 12°, 1734. (2 vols.: *The Relapse* in vol. 1.) Newb. Bod.
Duodecimo, 1735. Yale. Harv. B.M.
Plays, 12°, 1735. (2 vols.: *The Relapse* in vol. 1.) N.U. B.M. Bod.
Hunt edition, 1840. The Dramatic Works of *Wycherley, Congreve, Vanbrugh and Farquhar.* Edited by Leigh Hunt.
Ward edition, 1893. *Sir John Vanbrugh.* Edited by W. C. Ward. (2 vols.: *The Relapse* in vol. 1.)
Swaen edition, 1896. *Sir John Vanbrugh.* Edited by A. E. H. Swaen. *Mermaid Series.*
Dobrée edition, 1927–1928. *The Complete Works of Sir John Vanbrugh.* Plays edited by Bonamy Dobrée, letters edited by Geoffrey Webb. (4 vols.: *The Relapse* in vol. 1.)

The first quarto of *The Relapse* appears to be the only edition possessing any authority. There is no evidence that Vanbrugh corrected any of the subsequent editions, and he never made a general revision of the play. There were four, or possibly five separate editions of the comedy before his death in 1726, as well as one collected edition of the plays; there was also a separate edition in the year following his death. But Vanbrugh's interest in the stage seems to have ended when he sold his share in the Haymarket Theatre in 1708: the only sign of revival was his writing two new scenes for *The Provoked Wife* when that comedy was played in 1725. An examination of the collected edition of 1719 indicates that he did not take advantage of this opportunity of providing accurate texts of his works.

The early editions reveal the not uncommon condition of progressive deterioration of the text, accompanied by occasional corrections of obvious errors in Q1. One or two examples will suffice to show that the author was not keeping his eye on the press. In Q1, La Vérole, when wounded, cries '*Jernie die!*' (IV.v.25). Q2 omits '*die*' and is followed by subsequent editions. More significant is the confusion at V.iii.57–63, where Q2 misplaces one of Bull's speeches, so that Coupler has two successive speeches. P, instead of following Q1, solves the difficulty by leaving Coupler's speeches as in Q2, but combining Bull's speeches. Finally, Q2, Q3 and P do nothing to correct the careless failure to indicate changes of scene which characterizes the latter half of Q1.

In one respect the present edition departs from Q1 — the setting as verse of some passages which appear as prose in the original, and, in one instance, the setting as prose of a passage which Q1 prints as verse. The inconsistency of the practice of the quartos has long been noted, and Leigh Hunt attempted some modifications in 1840; some of these have been adopted in the present edition. Had Q1 been printed throughout as prose there might have been some question as to the propriety of such a re-arrangement; but in view of the obvious fact that Vanbrugh intended his play to be printed partly as verse and partly as prose there seems to be no escape from the editorial duty of revision. Wherever such alterations have been made the line-endings of the early editions have been indicated in the textual notes.

A. E. C.

THE WAY OF THE WORLD

Texts

*Q1. First quarto, 1700. *Yale. *Harv. B.M. Bod. Camb.

Q2. Second quarto, 1706. *U. of C. *Newb. Harv. B.M. Bod. Camb.

W1. Works, 8°, 1710. (3 vols.: *The Way of the World* in vol. 2.) *Yale. Harv. B.M.
    Duodecimo (pirated), [?1711]. B.M.
    Works, 8°, 1717. (The 1710 edition, re-issued with a new title-page.) B.M.
    Duodecimo, 1720. *N.U.
    Works, 8° ('third edition'), date unknown. No copy seen: described by Bateson as the first edition with two added poems.
    Works, 12°, 1719–1720. (2 vols.: *The Way of the World* in vol. 2.) Harv. B.M.
    Sextodecimo, Dublin, 1724. Yale.
    Dramatic works, 16°, Dublin, 1724. Yale.
    Works, 12°, 1725. (3 vols.: *The Way of the World* in vol. 3.) U. of C.
    Works, 12°, 1730. (3 vols.: *The Way of the World* in vol. 3.) U. of C. Newb. B.M.
    Works, 12°, 1730. (A different edition: 3 vols.: *The Way of the World* dated 1735.) Bod.
    Duodecimo ('sixth edition'), 1735. Yale. Harv. B.M. Bod.
    Plays, 12°, 1735. (2 vols.: *The Way of the World* in vol. 2.) Newb.
    Hunt edition, 1840. *The Dramatic Works of Wycherley, Congreve, Vanbrugh and Farquhar.* Edited by Leigh Hunt.
    Ewald edition, 1887. *William Congreve.* Edited by Alexander Charles Ewald. *Mermaid Series.*
    Archer edition, 1912. *William Congreve.* Edited by William Archer.
    Summers edition, 1923. *The Complete Works of William Congreve.* Edited by Montague Summers. (4 vols.: *The Way of the World* in vol. 3.)
    Bateson edition, 1930. *The Works of Congreve.* Edited by F. W. Bateson.

The present text of *The Way of the World* is based on Q1, although there are arguments in favor of W1. The chief of these is a statement in the preface of W1 which, though unsigned, has been generally attributed to Congreve. The pertinent part of this statement reads: 'This edition of them [the plays] therefore, is only recommended as the least faulty impression which has yet been printed: in which care has been taken both to revise the press and to revise and correct many passages in the writing. Notwithstanding which care, it must be confessed, too many errata, in both kinds, still remain; those of the press, are to be reckoned amongst things, which no diligence can prevent.' The following paragraph speaks specifically of the revision of *The Mourning Bride.* Collation of Q1, Q2 and W1 makes it fairly evident that the statement does not apply to *The Way of the World.* Q2 seems to have been set from Q1, and W1 from Q2. In neither case is there a single instance of an undoubted author's emendation; there is, on the contrary, a great deal of evidence of careless or unintelligent alteration, especially in Q2. Mincing's characteristic use of 'e' for 'a,' in order to attain a 'refined' pronunciation, is misunderstood and 'corrected.' Phrases or sentences are omitted, especially where consecutive phrases or sentences begin or end with the same word; apparently the printer, looking off and on his copy, picked up the second occurrence of the word with his eye (II.i.413, 414; III.i.194).

In one instance Q2 introduces a 'not' which entirely confuses the sense of the passage in which it occurs (II.i.146): notwithstanding this fact, the error is repeated in W1 and in several modern editions. The editions later than Q1 which were published in Congreve's lifetime show no signs of having received any attention from him: this is what might have been expected, in view of his increasing blindness in his later years, and of his attitude of elegant superiority toward the stage after the comparative failure of *The Way of the World*.

The textual notes of the present edition give the variants from Q1 which appear in Q2 and W1, except the changes resulting from the fact that W1 employs the French method of scene division. No account has been taken of a second edition of 1700 mentioned by Allardyce Nicoll in his *Restoration Drama*: it may be a variant of Q1, although collation of four copies in America and (by deputy) four in England has not disclosed any important differences.

A. E. C.

THE BEAUX' STRATAGEM

TEXTS

*Q1. First quarto, [1707]. *Yale. *Harv. B.M. Bod.

Q2. Second quarto, [1707]. Professor A. E. Morgan. ?Camb. (undated quarto).
Comedies, 1707. No copy located.
Octavo, 1710. Harv.

C. Comedies, [?1710]. *Huntington Library. Harv. **B.M.**
Works, 8° ('second edition'), [?1711]. Yale.
Comedies, 12° ('third edition'), 1714. Yale. Harv.
Works, 12° ('third edition') [?1714]. (The foregoing with additional material.) Yale. Harv.
Comedies, 12° ('fourth edition'), [?1718]. (2 vols.: *The Beaux' Stratagem* in vol. 2.) Harv.
Works, 12° ('fourth edition'), 1718. (The foregoing, with poems prefixed to vol. 1.) Harv. B.M.
Works, 12° ('fifth edition'), 1721. (2 vols.: *The Beaux' Stratagem* in vol. 2.) U. of C.
Duodecimo, 1724. Yale.
Works, 12° ('sixth edition'), 1728. (2 vols.: *The Beaux' Stratagem* in vol. 2.) N.U. Harv. B.M.
Works, 12° ('sixth edition'), Dublin, 1728. (2 vols.: *The Beaux' Stratagem* in vol. 2.) Yale.
Duodecimo ('seventh edition'), 1730. Yale. B.M.
Works, 12° ('seventh edition'), 1736–1735. (2 vols.: *The Beaux' Stratagem* in vol. 2.) N.U. B.M. Bod.
Works, 12°, 1736. (2 vols.: different from the preceding.) B.M.
Works, 16° ('eighth edition'), 1742. (2 vols.: *The Beaux' Stratagem* in vol. 2.) N.U. Harv. B.M.
Works, 12° ('ninth edition'), 1748. U. of C. B.M.
Hunt edition, 1840. *The Dramatic Works of Wycherley, Congreve, Vanbrugh and Farquhar.* Edited by Leigh Hunt.
Ewald edition, 1892. *The Dramatic Works of George Farquhar.* Edited by Alexander Charles Ewald. (2 vols.: *The Beaux' Stratagem* in vol. 2.) Fitzgibbon edition, 1898. *The Beaux-Stratagem.* Edited by H. Macaulay Fitzgibbon. *The Temple Dramatists.*
Archer edition, 1906. *George Farquhar.* Edited by William Archer. *Mermaid Series.*
Strauss edition, 1914. *The Recruiting Officer and The Beaux' Stratagem.* By George Farquhar. Edited by Louis A. Strauss. *Belles-Lettres Series.*
Stonehill edition, 1930. *The Complete Works of George Farquhar.* Edited by Charles Stonehill. (2 vols.: *The Beaux' Stratagem* in vol. 2.)

Early editions of *The Beaux' Stratagem* appear to be unusually difficult to secure. The present text is based on Q1, with which I have been unable to collate Q2 or the *Comedies* of 1707. Fortunately this is not as serious a difficulty as might at first appear. The play was produced while Farquhar was on his death-bed, so that there was no opportunity for authorized alterations in the original published text, although, if the edition of 1736 may be believed, Farquhar, after the first night's performance, countenanced a radical revision in the dramatic representation — the elimination of Count Bellair. The collations supplied by Stonehill make it clear that the text became progressively less trustworthy after the first quartos. The first scene provides an excellent example of this tendency. In Q1 and Q2 Bonniface, entering, says to Cherry, 'The company of the Warrington coach has stood in the hall this hour, and nobody to show them to their rooms.' To this Cherry replies, 'And let 'em wait farther.' The octavo 1710 alters this to 'And let 'em wait Father': this version, with an added comma after 'wait,' is adopted by the *Comedies* ?1710 and the *Works* ?1711. The variant readings of the *Comedies* ?1710 are recorded in the textual notes to illustrate the deterioration of the text.

A. E. C.

COLLIER

A Short View of the Immorality and Profaneness of the English Stage, together with the Sense of Antiquity upon this Argument. By Jeremy Collier.

TEXTS

The text of the present selections from Jeremy Collier is based on Bodleian Library and Yale Library copies of the first octavo edition (O1) of 1698. With O1 have been collated the other early octavos. Their rapid succession shows the popular demand for Collier's work, but their trifling typographical variants are without significance to the present purpose. The passages here selected give the Introduction in full and the first ten pages (pp. 3–13) of the opening chapter.

Collier Controversy Bibliographies

For convenient references as to the long protracted (1698–1726) Collier Controversy, see (1) the special bibliographical section entitled 'Jeremy Collier and the Controversy concerning the Morality of the Stage,' in *C.H.E.L.*, VIII, 432–434; (2) the 'Bibliography of the Collier Controversy,' in *Comedy and Conscience after the Restoration*, 1924, by Joseph W. Krutch (pp. 264–270); the extensive 'Bibliography' in *The Jeremy Collier Stage Controversy 1698–1726*, 1937, by Sister Rose Anthony (pp. 300–318).

G. H. N.

THE CARELESS HUSBAND

TEXTS

Q1. First quarto, 1705. *Yale. *U. of C. Harv. Bod. Camb.

Q2. Second quarto, 1705. *Yale. *N.U. B.M. Bod. Camb.

First duodecimo, 1710. No copy located.

Quarto ('fifth edition'), 1718. B.M. Bod.

Octavo (pirated), 1721. U. of C.

*P. Plays, 4°, 1721. (2 vols.: *The Careless Husband* in vol. 1.) *Yale. *U. of C. Harv. B.M.

Duodecimo ('sixth edition'), Dublin, 1723. B.M.

D7. Duodecimo ('seventh edition'), 1731. *Yale. B.M.

Duodecimo ('eighth edition'), Dublin, 1733. Yale.

D8. Duodecimo ('eighth edition'), 1734. *A.E.C. *U. of C. Newb.

D9. Duodecimo, 1735. *Yale. *N.U. Harv. B.M. Bod.

Dramatic works, 12°, 1754. (4 vols.: *The Careless Husband* in vol. 1.) Harv.

Senior edition, 1928. *The Life and Times of Colley Cibber.* By F. Dorothy Senior. (*The Careless Husband* in Appendix E.)

Habbema edition, 1928. *An Appreciation of Colley Cibber.* By D. M. E. Habbema. (Reprints *The Careless Husband*.)

The present text of *The Careless Husband* is based upon that printed in the *Plays*, 1721. No important revisions appear to have been made before that time. The preparation of the collected edition, however, seems to have been taken quite seriously by Cibber: at all events, he made extensive alterations in *The Careless Husband*. The fact that the later duodecimos depart from P in many instances might cast some doubt upon the right of P to be regarded as the final authentic version of the text, were it not for the nature of the changes in the duodecimos. These are of two kinds — reversions to the text of Q1, and entirely new variants. The latter group of changes, when examined, proves to consist of slight verbal differences, which are occasionally corrections of misprints in the earlier text, but far more often insignificant variations that denote mere carelessness in type-setting. Not one of the new readings suggests the hand of an author or an editor. What probably occurred was that the prototype of this series (whether D7 or some edition intervening between P and D7) was set up from a copy of Q1 (or an edition based on Q1), which had been imperfectly corrected from P: the text thus produced became the basis for later editions.

The textual notes which follow record variant readings which occur in Q1, Q2, D8 and D9: the latter two are chosen merely as types of the later duodecimos.

A. E. C.

THE CONSCIOUS LOVERS

Texts

```
*X. Octavo, 1723.  *Yale.  *Newb.
X-Y. Octavo, 1723.  *Yale.  *U. of C.  Harv.
 Y. Octavo, 1723.  *Yale.
 Z. Octavo, 1723.  *A.E.C.  *Harv.
    Octavo (pirated), 1723.  B.M.
    Dramatic works, 1723.  *Yale.  U. of C.  B.M.
    Duodecimo ('third edition'), 1730.  Harv.
    Dramatic works, 1732.  B.M.
    Duodecimo, 1735.  Harv.  Camb.
    Dramatic works, 1736.  Bod.
    Duodecimo, 1741.  (Used in making up next volume.)  *A. E. C.  Dramatic works, 12°, [?1741].  *A. E. C.
    Duodecimo, 1747.  U. of C.  Newb.
    Dramatic works, 12°, 1747.  Newb.
    Aitken edition, 1894.  Sir Richard Steele.  Edited by G. A. Aitken.  Mermaid Series.
```

The only editions of *The Conscious Lovers* which appear to have any authority are three octavos which are dated 1723, of which at least one was printed in 1722. These editions seem not to have been distinguished hitherto. They present a problem more interesting to the bibliographer than to the textual critic, since their variations can hardly be said to be of great importance.

The three editions correspond page for page, but none is designated the second or third edition. The problem of deciding which is the earliest is complicated by the fact that, while there seem to be but three settings of type involved, two of these settings occur in at least three combinations, which, for convenience, I shall call X, X-Y, and Y. X and Y differ in twelve of their fourteen formes; X-Y is like X in eleven of these formes, but like Y in the remaining one (inner E). Almost certainly, therefore, X-Y represents an intermediate state of the book, and the problem is to decide between the claims of X and Y.

The four significant variations among these copies are as follows: X 'I'm,' Y 'I am' (I.i.142); X 'Ay, sir,' Y 'Sir' (I.i.243); X 'Oh, that's,' Y 'That's' (I.ii.100); X 'from me,' Y 'from hence' (IV.i.61). This last variation occurs in the inner forme of signature E, and consequently X-Y agrees with Y here, although elsewhere with X. It seems very improbable that these four slight changes are the result of editorial revision. If they are compositors' alterations, the second and third seem to indicate that Y is later than X, since it is more likely that a type-setter would omit 'Ay' and 'Oh' through carelessness than that he would add them if they were not in his copy. On the other hand it is easier to explain a change of 'from hence' to 'from me' than the reverse.

If the textual evidence is conflicting, the bibliographical evidence is a little more helpful. At the foot of C3 recto, the last word of the text is 'but' and the catch-word is 'I.' At the top of the next page the first two words, in X, are 'But I': in Y (correctly) the first word is 'I.' A compositor setting type from manuscript might easily make the error in X; he would have been less likely to do so if he were setting up page for page from printed copy. Another error, in the catchword of A7 verso, seems to point in the same direction.

Lastly there is the evidence of the press-figures. In X five different presses were at work, and frequently the outer and the inner formes of a gathering bear different press-figures. This is usually indicative of a desire for speed in printing. Copies of X-Y show slightly fewer press-figures. The only copy of Y that I have been able to find was, apparently, produced on two presses only, each of which was perfecting its own sheets, since there is never more than one figure in a gathering. It seems clear that Y was printed under conditions calling for less haste.

The interpretation of the foregoing facts depends upon the circumstances under which the octavos were printed. Steele had sold the right to publish *The Conscious Lovers* to Lintot at least as early as March 1, 1722, and Lintot had sold part or all of his rights to Tonson by October 26 of the same year (Nichols, *Literary Anecdotes*, VIII, 303). The plan, apparently, was to withhold publication of the play until the end of the original run at the theatre. But the book was not set up, or at least not completely set up, before the play was at least in rehearsal. This is clear from the fact, referred to in the preface, that the violin solo in the second act was a substitute for a song for which no singer could be found when the comedy was produced. Moreover, the first sheet, including the preface, which refers to happenings at the public performance, and to certain criticisms made of the play after it was acted, must have been set up and printed still later. The play ran for eighteen nights, beginning with November 7, 1722, and publication of the first octavo took place on December 1. Since it must have been impossible to predict the length of the run, however, the printers must have felt hurried. These facts support the theory that X, the edition showing the greatest signs of haste, was the earliest.

Z seems to have been produced from an entirely new setting of type. It follows the variant readings of Y, with one exception, which may be the result of its having been based on a copy of X-Y which employed a still different combination of the two early settings. This circumstance, together with some careless misprints and the fact that the press-figures in Z are even rarer than those in Y, inclines me to the belief that Z is the latest of the authorized octavos of 1723.

The foregoing is the only plausible explanation I have been able to construct which would take care of all the facts. It seems to me that there is a strong probability that X is the first edition. Accordingly I have based the present text of *The Conscious Lovers* on the Yale copy of X, collated with the Yale copies of X-Y and Y, and with my own copy of Z. I have also examined other copies of the octavos, and have compared results with the editions of 1735 and 1741 at important points. Generally only variants in the octavos of 1723 have been recorded in the textual notes.

A. E. C.

CATO

TEXTS

*Q1. First quarto, 1713. *Yale. *Harv. B.M. Bod.

Q2. Second quarto, 1713. *Yale. *Harv. *A.E.C. B.M.

Q3. Third quarto, 1713. *Harv. B.M. Bod.

Q4. Fourth quarto, 1713. *Yale. *Harv. B.M.

Q5. Fifth quarto, 1713. *Yale. Bod.

Q6. Sixth quarto, 1713. *Yale.

D7. First duodecimo, 1713. *Yale. B.M.

D8. Second duodecimo, 1713. *Yale. *U. of C.

Octavo, Dublin, 1713. B.M.

W. Works, 4°, 1721. (4 vols.: *Cato* in vol. 1.) *Yale. *N.U. U. of C. B.M. Camb.

Works, 8°, Dublin, 1722–1723. B.M. Camb.

Duodecimo ('eleventh edition'), 1725. B.M.

Miscellaneous works, 12°, 1726. (3 vols.: *Cato* in vol. 2.) Yale. Newb.

Duodecimo ('twelfth edition'), 1728. Yale.

Works, 4°, 1730. (4 vols.: *Cato* in vol. 1.) Yale.

Duodecimo ('thirteenth edition'), 1733. Bod.

Duodecimo, 1734. B.M.

Duodecimo, 1735. Yale. Newb. B.M.

Miscellaneous works, 12°, 1736. (3 vols.: *Cato* in vol. 2.) Yale. B.M. U. of C.

Duodecimo, 1739. N.U. Camb.

Duodecimo, 1744. Yale.

Miscellaneous works, 12°, 1746. B.M.

Octavo, Glasgow, 1748. B.M.

Hurd edition, 1811. *The Works of the Right Honourable Joseph Addison.* Edited by Richard Hurd. (6 vols.: *Cato* in vol. 1.) Reprinted several times.

Guthkelch edition, 1914. *The Miscellaneous Works of Joseph Addison.* Edited by A. C. Guthkelch. (2 vols.: *Cato* in vol. 1.)

The problems involved in the editing of *Cato* are bibliographical rather than textual. The important texts are the six quartos and the two duodecimos published by Tonson in 1713, and the version printed under Tickell's editorship, in 1721, two years after Addison's death, in the collected edition of the works. The quartos illustrate the danger of taking the word 'edition' literally in connection with English printing, even as late as the eighteenth century. Comparison of numerous copies of the six quartos discloses that in reality there were but two settings of type involved in their production. Copies of the same 'edition' may have pages or formes printed from either of the two settings. For example, the Harvard copy of Q1 differs from the Yale copy in three formes (inner B, inner C, and outer D). The fact that the Harvard copy of Q2 was printed from the same formes as the Harvard copy of Q1 raises a presumption that the variant formes in the Yale copy of Q1 were the earlier, but it would not be safe to state conclusions on this point without an opportunity to examine many more copies than have been available to the present editor. Variations between copies may well extend through the whole series of quartos. The two Tonson duodecimos of 1713, were printed from a single setting of type; they differ only in their title-pages.

Luckily the significant variations between the editions are few. In the quartos the only important differences are in gatherings B and I. The most notable is the insertion in gathering I of seven lines, divided between Portius and Cato, which were omitted from the early copies (Q1, Q2 and some copies of Q3). Neither the sense nor the metre are affected by the omission. It seems certain that the lines were in the original manuscript and were overlooked by the type-setter: the fact that the break comes at the bottom of a page (I1 recto) may be regarded as evidence that the book was being composed in pages, not in long galleys.

The remaining changes are much less striking. In the early setting of gathering B Marcus accuses Portius of speaking 'calmly' instead of 'coldly' (I.i.56), and a little later 'Then' (changed to 'The' in the later setting: I.i.87) provides a more emphatic reading of the text. In the later setting of gathering I 'guard the good' is changed to 'guard the just' (V.iii.9), and 'his weeping servants, obsequious to his orders' becomes 'his servants weeping, obsequious to his orders' (V.iv.74). The first alteration is in the interests of euphony, the second is not; moreover, it introduces a ludicrous ambiguity in the meaning of the passage.

Ten changes are made in the duodecimo editions of 1713. Two seem designed to remove colloquialisms ('them' for "'em": I.iv.13, and 'You are' for 'That you're': II.ii.67); one substitutes 'Or' for 'Nor' (I.iv.8); another 'horror' for 'dread' (I.vi.51); a third 'habit' for 'habits' (IV.ii.15); a fourth 'I' for I've' (IV.iv.113); and a fifth 'Who dare' for 'That dares' (IV.iv.147). 'Your' replaces 'his' in the interests of clarity (II.ii.6), and at another point a passage is improved by a slight shift of emphasis (I.iv.133, 134). The eighth change is one of punctuation (II.ii.62): it alters the construction without improving the sense.

The version of the play in Tickell's edition of the works follows the text of the duodecimos, with two exceptions: the substitution of 'white' for 'bright' (I.vi.81), and the omission of one entire line (IV.iv.122).

In reviewing these changes it is difficult to reach a decision as to the best text. It is true that several of the revisions tend to make the language of the play more formal or more correct. The substitution of 'who' for 'that' recalls the 78th number of the *Spectator* (written, however, by Steele); but if this change was deliberate, it is odd that Addison did not make similar changes elsewhere in the play, e.g., in I.iv.82, I.vi.4, and IV.i.31. Indeed, except possibly in the cases of 'white' for 'bright' and 'just' for 'good,' none of the alterations seems to be clearly an intentional one originating with the author or the editor, and neither change improves the text so much as 'his servants weeping' alters it for the worse. Taking all the evidence together, it seems probable that Addison emended a few readings that happened to come to his attention, but did not note progressive deteriorations in the text which were due to the errors of the printers. Under the circumstances it seems safest to base the present text on the Yale copy of Q1, supplying the added passage in the fifth act from the Harvard copy of Q3. The scene divisions, which are not indicated in the quartos after I.iv, are supplied from D7, but the stage directions of Q1 are retained, subject to the usual normalization.

A. E. C.

JANE SHORE

TEXTS

Q1. First quarto, 1714. *Yale. *U. of C. Newb. Harv. *Huntington Library. B.M. Bod.

*D2. First duodecimo, 1714. *Yale. *U. of C. Harv. B.M.

P.   *Poems on Several Occasions, by N. Rowe, Esq.*, 4°, 1714. (Contains text of two passages suppressed by the Lord Chamberlain: see III, i. 173–174 and 184–185.)

Duodecimo, 1720. *Yale. Bod.

Dramatic works, 12°, 1720. (2 vols.: *Jane Shore* in vol. 2.) *Yale. Harv. Bod.

Sextodecimo, Dublin, 1727. Yale.

Duodecimo, 1728. Bod.

Miscellaneous works, 12°, 1728. (3 vols.: dramatic works in vols. 2–3: *Jane Shore* in vol. 3.) Harv.

Dramatic works, 12°, 1733. (2 vols.: *Jane Shore* in vol. 2.) Yale. Harv. U. of C.

Miscellaneous works, 1733. (The foregoing with a volume of non-dramatic material prefixed.) Yale. Harv. B.M.

Duodecimo, 1733. B.M. Bod. Camb.

Duodecimo, 1735. B.M.

Sextodecimo ('eighth edition'), Dublin, 1735. Yale.

Plays, 16°, 1736. (2 vols.: *Jane Shore* in vol. 2.) Harv. U. of C. Bod. Camb.

Duodecimo, 1736. Harv.

Duodecimo, 1746. U. of C.

Works, 12°, 1747. (2 vols.: *Jane Shore* in vol. 2.) Yale. B.M.

Octavo, Glasgow, 1748. B.M. Bod.

Hart edition, 1907. *The Fair Penitent and Jane Shore*. Edited by Sophie Chantal Hart. *Belles-Lettres Series.*

Sutherland edition, 1929. *Three Plays by Nicholas Rowe*. Edited by J. R. Sutherland.

The two editions of *Jane Shore* in 1714 were the only ones issued in Rowe's lifetime, and examination of them, together with those printed in the years immediately following his death shows that there was no authorized revision thereafter. The second edition has been adopted as the basis of the present text. There are not many differences between it and the first, but those that exist indicate a careful correction of nearly all the slips made in the presumably hasty setting of Q1. Most of these emendations might have been made by an intelligent proof-reader, although the care with which the revision is effected, together with the occasional substitution of contractions in order to improve the metre, may be taken as some evidence that Rowe himself was at work.

In general only the variant readings of Q1 are given in the textual notes. Two brief passages have been supplied from *Poems on Various Occasions, by Nicholas Rowe, Esq.*, published in 1714 by Edmund Curll,* who attempted to increase sales by announcing that the book contained the 'exceptionable passages' from *Jane Shore* which had been suppressed by the Lord Chamberlain before the play was licensed for production. There are two of these passages:

---

* This volume is extremely rare, and I have been unable to locate a copy. The Huntington Library, however, possesses a copy of Q1 in which has been bound an extra leaf containing the two passages. Almost certainly it is a copy of the same leaf as that included in Rowe's *Poems*: at any rate, its text agrees with the passages in the *Poems* as they are printed by J. R. Sutherland in *Three Plays by Nicholas Rowe*.

the first consists of one and a half lines which were cancelled outright, the second of two lines which were rewritten by the author for the approved version of the tragedy. There is every reason to believe that these suppressed passages are authentic. The first of them (III.i.173,174) fits perfectly into the context and completes a half-line which stands without any apparent reason in the printed version of the play. The second (III.i.184,185) expresses far more cogently and clearly the thought of the two lines that have been substituted for it. Both passages, although ostensibly dealing with fifteenth-century affairs, are actually thinly veiled comments on eighteenth-century politics, the first on the Whig clergy's arguments absolving Englishmen from their oaths of loyalty to James II and his son, the second on the Succession Act which barred the Stuarts from the throne. These references were, of course, highly objectionable to the Whig government which had come into power in the summer of 1714, a few months before *Jane Shore* was brought upon the stage. Had Curll been inventing these passages he would almost certainly have made them more extensive.

A. E. C.

THE BEGGAR'S OPERA

TEXTS

O1. First octavo, 1728. *Yale. *Harv. B.M. Bod. Camb.

O2. Second octavo, 1728. *A.E.C. *Yale. *Harv. *U. of C. Newb. B.M.
 Octavo ('third edition'), Dublin, 1728. Harv. B.M.
 Duodecimo ('third edition,' pirated), 1728. Harv. B.M.

*Q. Quarto ('third edition'), 1729. *Yale. *Newb. *Harv. B.M. Bod.
 Octavo ('fourth edition'), Dublin, 1732. Bod.

O3. Third octavo ('third edition'), 1733. *Harv. B.M. Bod.

O4. Fourth octavo ('fourth edition'), 1735. *Harv. Bod.
 Duodecimo ('seventh edition,' pirated), 1737. Harv. Camb.
 Octavo ('fifth edition,'), Dublin, 1740. Harv.

O5. Fifth octavo ('fifth edition,'), 1742. *Yale. *Harv. B.M. Bod.
 Duodecimo ('seventh edition,' pirated), 1745. B.M.
 Octavo ('seventh edition,' pirated), 1746. Harv.

O6. Sixth octavo ('sixth edition'), 1749. *Harv. B.M. Bod.
 Octavo, Glasgow, 1750. Harv.
 Faber edition, 1926. *The Poetical Works of John Gay.* Edited by G. C. Faber.

The bibliography of *The Beggar's Opera* is complicated: the problem of the text is not. The first edition, although it was probably set up in haste, was unusually free from important errors, and the few mistakes it contained were nearly all corrected in the editions which followed in the next year or so. Aside from a few minor variations between copies of O1, which serve to distinguish 'issues,' the significant errors are the omission of 'have' (I.viii.1), the dropping of a sentence (II.iv.137–138) and of Air LVI, and one misprint ('weary' for 'wary,' II.xv.41). The omitted air is found in some copies of O1, with the music printed in the text: the bibliographical evidence tends to show that these copies are the earliest, and that the air was removed from the later issues of O1 for aesthetic reasons. In O2 the music, instead of being printed at the end, as in O1, was interspersed through the text. In Q it was once more relegated to the end of the book, but this time the words of the songs were engraved with the music, as well as being printed in the text. The misprint 'weary' was corrected while O2 was passing through the press: some copies have one reading, some the other. The remaining two errors were also taken care of in O2. One phrase (possibly correctly printed in O1) was altered in O2, and the airs were numbered continuously throughout the play, instead of by acts, as in O1. Q, which seems to have been printed with great care, follows O2.

The absence of the usual progressive deterioration of the text after the first edition is largely due to the fact that the early octavo 'editions' were really issues of one edition. Examination discloses that much, perhaps all, of the text of O2 is printed from the same setting of type as O1, re-arranged to permit the introduction of the music into the letterpress: moreover, the same setting, re-arranged again, seems to have been used in printing O3 and O4. A new setting of type was finally made for O5, published ten years after Gay's death.

The confusion in the numbering of editions, which is evident from the list given above, was chiefly due to the appearance of piracies. J. Watts was the authorized publisher. He numbered his editions in regular order, except for the fact that, after having designated his quarto the third edition, he seems to have left it out of account in numbering the subsequent octavos. In the list of editions above only Watts's have been given distinguishing symbols. There is no evidence that any of the piracies is of any value in establishing the text.

The text printed here is based on Q, the last newly-set edition in Gay's lifetime. This edition, besides its textual correctness, has two special virtues, both connected with the engraving of the words of the songs with the music at the end of the book: as a result of this circumstance it is possible to be certain of the manner in which the words of the songs were fitted to the music, and to recover certain refrains which are merely indicated in the printed text by 'etc.'

A. E. C.

TOM THUMB
(THE TRAGEDY OF TRAGEDIES: OR, THE LIFE AND DEATH OF
TOM THUMB THE GREAT)

TEXTS

(a) 1730 Version (Two Acts)

Tom Thumb. A Tragedy. As it is Acted at the Theatre in the Hay-Market.

(1) First edition, 1730. [Publisher's advertisement dated 'April 24, 1730.'] 'London, Printed: And Sold by J. Roberts in *Warwick-Lane*. 1730.' Half-title reads: '*Tom Thumb. A Tragedy.* [Price Six Pence.]' *Yale. *Harv. *Bod.

(2) Revised edition (with two new scenes in Act II, etc.), 1730.

   (a) First impression. 'Written by *Scriblerus Secundus. Tragicus plerumque dolet Sermone pedestri.* Hor. London, Printed: And Sold by J. Roberts in *Warwick-Lane*. 1730. [Price Six Pence.]' No half-title. *Yale. *Harv. *Camb.

   (b) *Second edition.* The revised edition (as above) but with insertion on title-page, after the quotation from Horace, of a line reading, 'The Second Edition.' *Yale (two copies). *Harv.

   (c) *Third edition.* The revised edition (as above) but with title-page designation as 'The Third Edition.' *Yale. *Harv. *Bod. *Camb.

[There is also a 1730 Dublin edition of *Tom Thumb*. 'As it is Acted at the Theatres in London. Dublin: Printed and Sold by S. Powell.' *B.M.]

(b) 1731 Version (Three Acts)

The Tragedy of Tragedies; or the Life and Death of Tom Thumb the Great. As it is Acted at the Theatre in the Hay-Market. With the Annotations of H. Scriblerus Secundus.

*First Edition. 'London, Printed; And Sold by J. Roberts in *Warwick-Lane*. M DCC XXXI. Price One Shilling.' *Yale. *Harv. *B.M. *Bod. L.C.

[Second edition. 'No edition marked the second,' according to the standard Fielding Bibliography in Wilbur L. Cross, *The History of Henry Fielding*, III, 292.]

Third Edition, 1737. Title-page designates as 'The Third Edition.' *Yale. Harv. B.M. *Bod. L.C.

Fourth edition, 1751. 'The Fourth Edition.' *Yale. Harv. *B.M.

Fifth edition, 1765 [and 1776] 'The Fifth Edition.' *B.M. copy dated 1765; *Yale. copy 1776 ['MDCCLXXVI'].

(c) Critical Editions

L. Lindner edition, Berlin, 1899. *Fielding's Tom Thumb. Mit Einleitung herausgegeben von Felix Lindner.* (No. 4 in *Englische Textbibliothek*.)

H. Hillhouse edition, New Haven (Yale University Press), 1918. *The Tragedy of Tragedies, or, The Life and Death of Tom Thumb the Great* ... Edited by James T. Hillhouse.

(a) Introduction

The text is based on a Yale Library copy of the 1731 version, entitled *The Tragedy of Tragedies; or the Life and Death of Tom Thumb the Great*, which expands the briefer 1730 text of *Tom Thumb, A Tragedy*, from two acts to three and elaborates the burlesque with the mock critical 'Annotations of H. Scriblerus Secundus' [Henry Fielding]. With this 1731 version have been fully compared Yale Library copies of the three editions, all of 1730, of the earlier two-act version. Literally, the 1731 version is the first edition of *The Tragedy of Tragedies*, and the original 1730 version is the first edition of *Tom Thumb*. Since, however, the brief title, *Tom Thumb*, is usually applied alike to both versions, and since the distinction is between two versions of the same play rather than between two separate plays, the present discussion will differentiate by dates (1730 or 1731) instead of by titles. The wide differences between the versions of 1730 and 1731 make it impracticable to incorporate into the present work full textual collation. Indeed, the admirable critical edition of Fielding's play by Professor James T. Hillhouse (*The Tragedy of Tragedies* ..., Yale University Press, 1918) wisely prefers to reprint the two versions separately, collating each, in turn, with its various editions. The present purpose is best served by interpretation and illustration of the chief results of intensive textual study.

(b) The 1730 Version

The first impression (April 24, 1730) of the first edition of the 1730 version is the briefest text of Fielding's play. A perfect copy (like that in the Dickson Fielding Collection in the Yale Library) has the preliminary half-title, and, following the main title, the leaf (*verso* blank) which bears the publisher's advertisement of another Fielding farce: 'April 24, 1730. *This Day is Publish'd*, The AUTHOR'S FARCE; and the PLEASURES of the TOWN,' etc. This advertisement was soon dropped and the original text was revised with extensive additions of a preface, a prologue ('By no Friend of the Author's'), an epilogue ('Sent by an Unknown Hand'), and two new scenes, of the Bailiff and his Follower, at the beginning of Act II. At the end of one scene (II. viii; originally II. vi) this revision added a six-line speech, given to the King, and in the course of the two acts made some fourteen lesser changes in text or stage directions. The main title-page and the page of *Dramatis Personæ* were also revised, but in early copies (as in another Dickson Collection–Yale copy, and in Harvard and Cambridge University Library copies) without indication of a 'new' or 'second' edition. It seems that, as the popular demand exhausted the first edition, and as the expansion of the stage version had already begun with the two new scenes of Act II, the printed version, though still compressed within the original sixteen pages, received careful and authoritative revision. The revised version, at first silently achieved, was soon openly recognized by inserting on the already revised title-page the words, 'The Second Edition.' For the time being, this revision sufficed, for 'The Third Edition,' save for a few trivial variants, is merely a reprint of the second edition.

(c) The 1731 Version

The 1731 version supplies a new preface, ascribed to 'H. Scriblerus Secundus,' expands the main text from two to three acts, and elaborates it with the mock critical 'Annotations of H. Scriblerus Secundus.' Fielding's pseudonym, with its obvious reminder of Pope's earlier use of 'Scriblerus,' appears on the title-page of the second edition of the 1730 version, but without the 'H.' ('Scriblerus Secundus'). The 1731 version adds to the previous *Dramatis Personæ* the Ghost of Tom Thumb's father, Merlin, Foodle, a Parson, and Glumdalca, but drops the two Physicians. It gives for the first time Fielding's highly diverting descriptions of the various characters. Major structural changes in the play do not occur until Act II, for the six scenes of the original Act I are retained, though with considerable textual revision. Act II of the 1731 version opens with the two scenes of the Bailiff and his Follower which were first inserted in the revised edition of the 1730 version, but the first scene is now cut to less than half its original length, though the second is fully retained and is slightly enlarged by one brief inserted speech. Scenes three and four correspond to scenes one and two of the first edition of the 1730 version, but thereafter differences, both structural and textual, are radical. Thus, in the original 1730 version, the third scene of Act II opens with Doodle's 'Oh! fatal news — the great Tom Thumb is dead,' and though the hero's reappearance (Scene v) belies the report for the time being, and scenes intervene where the two Physicians confer, the play is soon shaped towards its fatal conclusion. The 1731 version, on the contrary, begins its fifth scene with the play's most famous line of parody — 'Oh, Huncamunca, Huncamunca, oh!' — and, omitting the scenes of the Physicians and reserving fatalities for a third act, proceeds to develop the 'conflicts' of love.'

When, towards the close of Act III, the greatly expanded version of 1731 approaches the tragic conclusion, it alters the original dénouement in several important particulars. Most conspicuous is the omission of the killing of the Ghost, an incident (in the 1730 version) which, according to Mrs. Lætitia Pilkington's *Memoirs*, was one of the two spectacles in Dean Swift's experience which moved him to laughter. (Mrs. Pilkington speaks inadvertently of 'Tom Thumb's killing the Ghost,' but actually it is Grizzie who kills the Ghost of Tom Thumb.) In the 1731 version, the Ghost is the Ghost of Gaffer Thumb, Tom Thumb's father, and the killing is omitted. The original dénouement undergoes further revision, for the Queen kills Noodle instead of Doodle, Cleora kills the Queen instead of Noodle, and Cleora is killed by Huncamunca instead of by Mustacha — though the net results of the 'solution by massacre' remain essentially the same.

Besides such structural changes as those just instanced, the 1731 version revises the dialogue at will, sometimes retaining whole scenes virtually intact, sometimes inserting new speeches or lines, and cutting or changing others freely. Thus, in both versions, the fourth scene of Act I is a brief soliloquy by Grizzle, but the actual text of the 1731 version is wholly new, whereas the sixth scene, consisting of the Queen's soliloquy, is identical in both versions. Broadly speaking, resemblances between the two versions are closest in the opening act and divergencies most marked when the version of 1731 undertakes the task of expanding the original second act into two acts by the introduction of new characters and episodes, as well as by radical changes of such parts of the earlier material as are still utilized.

The 1731 version established the dominant text of Fielding's play. A later impression of its first edition (Dickson Collection–Yale copy) made a few minor corrections in spelling and punctuation. Subsequent editions show other variants, some of which effect slight betterments, though others are typographical errors. The most vital results of textual study of Fielding's play remain those derived from detailed comparison of the three editions of the 1730 version with the first edition of the 1731 version. This transformation of a brief two-act burlesque into a three-act text, with full paraphernalia of mock critical 'Annotations,' amply illustrates a wide range of processes of revision, varying from minor verbal alterations to major changes in plot and dialogue.

(d) Critical Editions

An early (1899) critical edition of the three-act version, mainly based on the 1762 (second) edition of Fielding's *Works* with supplementary consideration of the 1731 edition, is that of Felix Lindner, *Fielding's Tom Thumb* (L). Though limited by lack of direct familiarity with early editions, this work retains interest.

The outstanding scholarly study is Professor James T. Hillhouse's critical edition (H), published by the Yale University Press in 1918. For detailed textual investigation, his fully collated and annotated texts of both versions, 1730 and 1731, are most important. His bibliography lists not merely editions of Fielding's burlesque but operatic adaptations of his text, notably that of Kane O'Hara.

G. H. N.

PLAYS PARODIED BY FIELDING

(a) Restoration Drama (1660–1700)

BANKS, JOHN (fl. 1682–1696)
    The Albion Queens: or, The Death of Mary, Queen of Scotland. 1704.
      [A later version of *The Island Queens*, 1684.]
    Cyrus the Great: or, The Tragedy of Love. 1696. (Acted Dec. 1695?)
    The Island Queens: or, The Death of Mary, Queen of Scotland. 1684.
      [Unacted — 'being prohibited the Stage.' See *The Albion Queens*.]
    The Unhappy Favorite: or, The Earl of Essex. 1682. (Acted *circ.* Sept. 1681.)
      [Fielding uses the sub-title.]
    Virtue Betrayed: or, Anna Bullen. 1682.
      [Fielding uses the sub-title.]

DRYDEN, JOHN (1631–1700)
    All for Love: or, The World Well Lost. 1678. (Acted Dec. 1677.)
    Aureng-Zebe. 1676. (Acted Nov. 1675.)
    Cleomenes, The Spartan Hero. 1692.
    The Conquest of Granada by the Spaniards. In two parts. 1672. (*Part I*, acted *circ.* Dec. 1670 — *Part II*, acted
      Jan. 1671.)
    [*Almanzor and Almahide: or, The Conquest of Granada.* — Alternative title, as given in heading, *Part I*, p. 1, 1672
      Quarto, and title-page, *Part II*, 1672 Quarto.]
    Don Sebastian, King of Portugal. 1690. (Acted Dec. 1689.)
    The Indian Emperor: or, The Conquest of Mexico by the Spaniards. 1667. (Acted 1665.)
    King Arthur: or, The British Worthy. A dramatic opera. 1691.
    Love Triumphant: or, Nature will Prevail. A tragi-comedy. 1694. (Acted Dec. 1693?)
    The Rival Ladies. A tragi-comedy. 1664.
    The State of Innocence, and Fall of Man. An opera. Written in heroic verse. 1677. [Unacted.]

DRYDEN, JOHN, and LEE, NATHANIEL.
    The Duke of Guise. 1683.
    Œdipus. 1679.

ECCLESTONE, EDWARD (fl. 1679)
    Noah's Flood: or, The Destruction of the World. 1679. [Unacted.]

FLETCHER, JOHN (1579–1625)
    The Tragedy of Rollo, Duke of Normandy. 1640.
      [Fielding uses the current later title, *The Bloody Brother*.
      This Elizabethan play is included since Fielding recognizes its continued currency on the stage.]

HOPKINS, CHARLES (1664?–1700?)
    Friendship Improved: or, The Female Warrior. 1700. (Acted Nov. 1699.)

LEE, NATHANIEL (1648–49?–1692)
    Cæsar Borgia, Son of Pope Alexander the Sixth. 1680. (Acted *circ.* Sept. 1679.)
    Gloriana: or, The Court of Augustus Cæsar. 1676.
    Lucius Junius Brutus, Father of his Country. 1681. (Acted Dec. 1680.)
    Mithridates, King of Pontus. 1678.
    The Rival Queens; or, The Death of Alexander the Great. 1677.
    Sophonisba: or, Hannibal's Overthrow. 1676. (Acted April, 1675.)
    [Fielding's references to 'LEE'S *Sophonisba*' or to *Hannibal* avoid confusion of this play with Thomson's *New
      Sophonisba*, 1730.]
    The Tragedy of Nero, Emperor of Rome. 1675. (Acted May, 1674.)

OTWAY, THOMAS (1652–1685)
  Don Carlos, Prince of Spain. 1676.
  The History and Fall of Caius Marius. 1680. (Acted *circ.* Sept. 1679.)

(b) Eighteenth-Century Tragedies (1700–1731)

ADDISON, JOSEPH (1672–1719)
  Cato. 1713.

DENNIS, JOHN (1657–1734)
  Liberty Asserted. 1704.

FENTON, ELIJAH (1683–1765)
  Mariamne. 1723.

FIELDING, HENRY (1707–1754)
  The Coffee-House Politician. 1730. [Fielding's 'Annotations' playfully include his own 'Comedy.']

GAY, JOHN (1685–1750)
  The Captives. 1724.

JOHNSON, CHARLES (1679–1748)
  The Tragedy of Medæa. 1731. (Acted 1730.)
  The Victim. 1714.

MALLET, DAVID (1705?–1765)
  Eurydice. 1731.

MARTYN, BENJAMIN (1699–1763)
  Timoleon. 1730.

ROWE, NICHOLAS (1674–1718)
  Tamerlane. 1702.

TATE, NAHUM (1652–1715)
  Injured Love: or, The Cruel Husband. 1707.

THEOBALD, LEWIS (1688–1744)
  The Persian Princess: or, The Royal Villain: 1715. (Acted 1708.)

THOMSON, JAMES (1700–1748)
  The Tragedy of Sophonisba. 1730.
  [*The New Sophonisba,* in distinction from Lee's *Sophonisba: or, Hannibal's Overthrow,* 1681.]

YOUNG, EDWARD (1683–1765)
  Busiris, King of Egypt. 1719.
  The Revenge. 1721.

G. H. N.

THE LONDON MERCHANT

TEXTS

O1. First octavo, 1731. *Yale (two copies with variant readings). Harv. B.M.

O2. Second octavo, 1731. *U. of C. B.M.

D3. Third edition, duodecimo, 1731. Professor A. E. Morgan.
  Octavo (pirated), 1731. Professor A. E. Morgan.
  Octavo, Dublin, 1731. Harv.

D4. Fourth edition, duodecimo, 1732. *Yale.
  Duodecimo ('fifth edition,' pirated), 1733. A.E.C. U. of Texas.

*D5. Fifth edition, duodecimo [?1735]. Professor R. H. Griffith.

D6. Sixth edition, duodecimo, 1735. *Yale. Harv. Camb.
  Duodecimo ('eighth edition,' pirated), 1737. L.C.

O7. Seventh edition, octavo, 1740. *Yale. Harv. U. of C. B.M.
  Works, 1740. (Separate plays bound together.) Harv.
  Ward edition, 1906. *The London Merchant . . . and Fatal Curiosity.* Edited by Adolphus William Ward. *Belles-Lettres Series.*

M. Morgan edition, 1935. *English Plays 1660–1820.* Edited by A. E. Morgan [pp. 637–671].

The early authorized editions of *The London Merchant* were all published by Lillo's friend John Gray, who eventually became his literary executor. There were six of these editions preceding Lillo's death in 1739; in 1740 there was a seventh, which was issued both separately and bound up with other plays to form the first collected edition of Lillo's works. The editions show progressive revision by the author, beginning with corrections in copies of O1, made while the book was passing through the press. The four variants that I have found in this edition all occur in the first and the last gatherings, which consist of six and two leaves, respectively, and were almost certainly printed as one gathering and then cut for binding.

O2 contains more changes than any other edition: it is difficult to account for Ward's statement that it differs in only one place from O1. A less extensive revision was made in D3, the text of which, with minor alterations, was followed in D4. The last general revision was made in the fifth edition, from which D6 and O7 differ only in a few places, and then unintentionally. The fifth edition has accordingly been chosen as the basis of the present text, as representing the author's final draft. It is, incidentally, the first to include the 'gallows scene': it is interesting to learn from Lillo's advertisement to the fifth edition that this scene was not a melodramatic afterthought, but a part of the original version, suppressed on the advice of some of his friends.

Two of these editions, D3 and D5, are of special interest, not only because of their intrinsic importance in the development of the text, but because they have not been collated until very recently. The only known copy of D3 appears to be that owned by Professor A. E. Morgan, Principal of University College, Hull, England, who made it the basis of his edition published in 1935. He was unable to find copies of D4, D5 or D6, however, and made little use of O7, except to supply from it the 'gallows scene.' In the textual notes the variant readings of D3 have been recorded on the authority of Professor Morgan: they are indicated by the symbol M.

Professor R. H. Griffith of the University of Texas is the possessor of the apparently unique copy of D5, which he discusses in an article, *Early Editions of Lillo's 'London Merchant,'* published in The University of Texas *Studies in English*, XV, 23–27 (1935). This copy has a cancel title-page bearing the words 'sixth edition,' but it is from another setting of type than that employed for D6, and the 'advertisement' it contains, referring to 'this fifth edition,' identifies it beyond any reasonable doubt. Professor Griffith suggests that the cancel title-page was substituted to avoid confusion with the pirated 'fifth edition' issued in 1733. The genuine fifth edition was advertised for sale at least as early as February 1, 1735, in *The Country Journal*, but in terms that indicate that it had been on sale for some little time: it is impossible at present to say with confidence whether the book was published in 1734 or 1735. Professor Griffith very kindly lent D5 to the editor of the present text, which is the first to take into account the readings of D5 and D6.

A. E. C.

THE LYING VALET

Texts

O1. First octavo, 1742. *Yale. *Newb. B.M.
    Duodecimo, Dublin, 1741. B.M.

*O2. Second octavo, 1743. *Yale. B.M.

O3. Third octavo, 1743. *Harv. B.M.

O6. Octavo ('sixth edition'), 1756. *Yale. B.M.
    Duodecimo ('eighth edition'), Glasgow, 1759. U. of C.

D8. Duodecimo ('eighth edition'), 1761. *Yale.

W1. Dramatic works, 12°, 1768. (3 vols.: *The Lying Valet* in vol. 1.) *Yale. Harv.
    Octavo ('eleventh edition'), 1769. Newb. B.M.
    Dramatic works, 12° ('third edition'), 1774. (2 vols.: *The Lying Valet* in vol. 1.) Yale. Harv. Newb.
    Osborn edition, 1925. *The Lying Valet. A Peep Behind the Curtain; ... Bon Ton; ... Three Farces by David Garrick.* Edited by Louise Brown Osborn.

The text of *The Lying Valet* presents no serious problems. Of the first two editions O2 seems to be the more carefully printed, and it is the first to contain the epilogue: accordingly it has been chosen as the basis of the present text. O6, D8, and W1, which have been thoroughly collated, show no evidences of any revision by the author; each appears to adopt the errors of its predecessors and to add a few of its own. W3 appears to be based on W1 (or W2, which I have not seen): it is, therefore, entitled to no particular respect, although it was the last edition to appear before Garrick's death.

A. E. C.

DOUGLAS

TEXTS

*E. First Edinburgh octavo, 1757. *Yale. Harv. *Bod.

L. First London octavo, 1757. *Yale. Harv. *B.M. Camb. L.C.

D. First Dublin duodecimo, 1757. *Bod.

B. First Belfast duodecimo, 1757. *B.M.
[B2. Second Belfast duodecimo, 1758. *Yale.]

W1. Dramatic Works, 1760. *Harv. *B.M. Camb.

N. 'New' London octavo, 1786. 'A New Edition.' *Yale.

W2. Dramatic Works, Edinburgh, 1798. *Yale.

R. Royal octavo, Edinburgh, 1798. *Yale.

M. Mackenzie edition of *Works*, Edinburgh, 1822. *The Works of John Home, Esq. Now first collected. To which is prefixed, an account of his life and writings.* By Henry Mackenzie. 3 vols. [*Douglas*, I, 287–387.]

T. Tunney edition, Lawrence (Kansas), 1924. *Home's Douglas.* Edited with introduction and notes by Hubert J. Tunney. In the *Bulletin of the University of Kansas, Humanistic Studies*, III, no. 3.

AM. Morgan edition, 1935. *English Plays 1660–1820.* Edited by A. E. Morgan. [pp. 715–747.]

Critical Study

G. *John Home, a study of his Life and Works with special reference to his tragedy of Douglas and the controversies which followed its first representation.* Caldwell, Idaho. (*The Caxton Printers*), 1916. By Alice Edna Gipson.

(a) First Edinburgh and First London Editions

The text is based on Bodleian Library and Yale Library copies of the first Edinburgh edition, 1757 (E). With E were first collated British Museum and Yale Library copies (Yale has four apparently identical copies) of the first London edition, 1757 (L). The first Edinburgh performance of *Douglas* was on December 14, 1756; the first London performance on March 14, 1757. The respective Edinburgh and London editions were in press at the same time, and both were published during the last fortnight of March, 1757. Contemporary newspaper announcements of publication show that L actually anticipated E by some ten days, but such technical priority of publication does not disturb the inherent authority of the prior Edinburgh stage production. E includes both the London and Edinburgh Prologues and casts of characters, and its title-page, like that of L, reads, 'As it is acted at the Theatre-Royal in Covent-Garden' — facts which suggest that publication may have been slightly delayed to profit by the added prestige of London production. E is clearly the basic text, the omissions in L evidently representing 'cuts' made in a slightly abbreviated acting version. L cuts the opening 75 lines of E to less than half their original number, but thereafter the omission of a single line in Act II is the longest variant. In the present edition the passages entirely omitted in L are included within guillemets « » — an arrangement which has the added advantage of making evident the careful matching of half-lines to preserve the metre without verbal alterations of the original text.

Apart from the 'cuts' in the dialogue, L varies from E in omitting the Edinburgh Prologue and in dividing Acts II and III into three scenes each, though there is no shift of place or break in the continuous action. Verbal changes in the dialogue of the play are infrequent and usually unimportant. In Douglas's dying speech, L breaks off the last words which in E round out the full final line. L alters Lady Randolph's outcry, when Douglas falls, from 'Hear, justice! hear! stretch thy avenging arm!' to 'Hear, justice, hear! are these the fruits of virtue?' — a dubious amendment. L alters 'wall-girt towers' to 'well-girt towers,' 'created being' to 'created thing,' 'the best, the kindest master' to 'the best and kindest master,' and admits other minor variants, intentional or accidental, which embarrass rather than support any assumption that L is an 'improved' text. The very infrequency of even trivial variants, indeed, combines with other evidence to attest L's usual deference to the authority of the original text.

Both E and L show considerable attention to metrical scansion, usually, though not invariably, printing *heav'n*, *lov'st, discov'ry, op'd* (for *opened*), *ent'ring*, and many similar words, and observing such elisions as *th' instructed* and *th' uneven*. Scores of such instances predominate over occasional oversights or inconsistencies, and constitute a characteristic metrical feature of the original text which has often been obscured in later reprints by silent substitution of fuller forms of spelling in place of elisions intentionally marked.

(b) Early Irish Editions

The results of collation of L with E have been compared with most of the other editions that appeared before Home's death in 1808, and with many subsequent reprints, both of the full text and of shortened acting versions. After L and E, the earliest edition of *Douglas* is the rare first Dublin edition, 1757 (D), examined in the Bodleian Library copy. Its publication was prompted by Thomas Sheridan's production of Home's play, in May, 1757, at the Smock-Alley

Theatre, Dublin.   The title-page reads *Douglas: a Tragedy.   As it is acted at the Theatres in Great-Britain and Ireland.*
D is of especial interest since it prefixes to the text of the play not merely David Hume's flattering 'Address to the
Author,' but copies of the 'Admonition and Exhortation, by the Rev. Presbytery of Edinburgh' [originally issued
January 5, 1757] and of the 'Declaration, by the Rev. Presbytery of Glasgow' [originally issued February 14, 1757],
thereby further advertising the storm of church protest and controversy which had promptly broken over the head of
the Scotch minister who had dared to turn playwright.   These prefatory sections are included also in the Belfast edition of 1758, examined in the Yale Library copy.   For the text of the play the early Irish editions depend on L, and
lack independent authority.

(c) Scottish and English Editions

Scottish and English editions after 1757 seem naturally to have followed respectively E and L, the former tending to
preserve the full original text, the latter to repeat the initial changes of L and ultimately to make further 'cuts' in the
acting text.   Sometimes, as in the 1798 royal octavo illustrated subscription edition of *Douglas* (R), and in the 1798
edition of Home's *Dramatic Works* (W2), Edinburgh editions indicate by inverted commas the passages 'omitted in
the representation,' but in retaining the full text and in avoiding minor verbal variants of L, they confirm the integrity
of the original text.   The care bestowed on the printing and illustration of R and the special advertisement of the work
in W2 attest its outstanding position among the later editions published in Home's lifetime.

Fourteen years after Home's death, his friend Henry Mackenzie published, with an extensive *Life of Mr. John Home*,
his three-volume edition of Home's *Dramatic Works*, Edinburgh, 1822 (M).   In reprinting *Douglas*, M follows E quite
closely, giving the full text without even indicating acting 'cuts.'   The chief value of M is to maintain the authority
of E, though in matters of punctuation or stage directions it has some points of secondary interest.   Unfortunately, in
modernizing spelling and punctuation, M eliminates many of the original indications of metrical elisions and introduces, intentionally or otherwise, some needless verbal variants — e.g. 'First came' for 'Fast came'; 'blossoms' for
'blossom'; 'I was [for, *I am*] not so inhuman.'

(d) Recent Critical Editions

The 'critical edition' of *Douglas* by Hubert J. Tunney (T), published in 1924 in the University of Kansas *Humanistic
Studies* (III, no. 3) adopts the text of M, collating it with various earlier and later editions, including L but not E.
Some of the later London stage versions included, like Cumberland's [*British Theatre*, vol. I, 1826], abbreviate the text
of L by further silent 'cuts,' show an amusing tendency to censor the Rev. Mr. Home's frequent use of 'God,' by sub-
stitutions such as 'heaven,' 'power,' and 'hand,' and elsewhere commit other blunders of taste or typography.   The
recent Morgan edition (AM) bases its text on E, with which it collates W1 and, in part, L.

The outstanding historical and critical study of Home is Miss Alice Edna Gipson's volume, 1916 (G), entitled *John
Home, a study of his Life and Works, with special reference to his tragedy of Douglas and the controversies which followed its
first representation.*   Though not directly concerned with editing Home's plays, Miss Gipson includes in her account of
the texts of *Douglas* (Chapter III) some important collations.   While not strictly pertinent to immediate textual questions, her chapters (IV and V) dealing with the church controversies and the war of pamphlets precipitated by the
production of *Douglas* are of primary importance to the history and influence of Home's chief drama.   The general
editor of the series in which T is included notes its unfortunate lack of acquaintance with 'the important Gipson dis-
sertation' and supplies accordingly some references to it.   Familiarity with the original text of E and with Miss Gipson's outstanding scholarly work on Home is, indeed, essential to any thorough textual study.

G. H. N.

THE JEALOUS WIFE

TEXTS

O1. First octavo, 1761.   *Yale.   Harv.   *B.M.   *Bod.   Camb.

O2. Second octavo, 1761.   *Yale.   *Harv.   *B.M.   Camb.

D. First Dublin duodecimo, 1761.   *Yale.   Harv.   *Bod.

O3. Third octavo, 1763.   Oxford.   'The Third Edition.'   *Yale.   Harv.   B.M.   *Bod.

O4. Fourth octavo [1764?].   Oxford [undated].   'The Fourth Edition.'   *Yale.   *B.M.   Bod.   L.C.

*W. Works, 1777.   *The Dramatick Works of George Colman.*   4 vols.   [I, 1–149.]   *Yale.   Harv.   *B.M.

(a) The London and Oxford Octavos

The text is based on that in the first of the four volumes of *The Dramatick Works of George Colman*, 1777 (W), the
earliest representative collection of his plays.   With W have been collated the Yale Library (and other) copies of the
first four octavo editions.   Such collation reveals early and continued revision of verbal details and of a few considerable passages of dialogue.   Colman's 'Advertisement' in O1 shows that his 'comedy was submitted in its first rude
state' to David Garrick, manager of Drury Lane Theatre, and was indebted to him 'in many particulars, relating both

to the fable and characters.' Such helpful co-operation between manager and author prior to the production and publication of the play was continued, and the verbal alterations which gradually modify the printed text in the successive octavos doubtless incorporate the joint sanctions of author and producer. Slightly variant copies of O1 in the Yale Library indicate that the process of textual revision began almost immediately. In V. ii. 22, three copies read: 'That I knew nothing about it, till after my Master was gone.' Three other copies shorten to — 'That I knew nothing at all of the matter' — a change confirmed in O2O3O4, and (with a further alteration of 'knew' to 'know') in W.

The more salient modifications of text in the course of its evolution are of four kinds. (1) There is distinct evidence of toning down some passages of action and dialogue in concession to the 'genteel' sensibilities of the period. This strikingly anticipates Goldsmith's experience, a few years later, when 'in deference to the public taste, grown of late, perhaps, too delicate, the scene of the bailiffs was retrenched in the representation' of *The Good-Natured Man*, in 1768. In Colman's scene (II. iii) of Lord Trinket's attempt upon Harriot, O2 considerably retrenches the more vigorous action and more outspoken dialogue of O1.

(2) There is occasional retrenchment of text for dramatic purposes. Thus O3 cuts four speeches in the scene (II. iii) between Charles Oakly and Lady Freelove which concludes the second act. Here, the retrenchment is simply to expedite the dramatic action at the close of the act. Early in Act III, O2 omits one of Lord Trinket's speeches, and in the Epilogue O2 deletes one couplet. In the present edition such omissions are indicated by inclusion within guillemets « » of the passages retrenched.

(3) Distinct attention is given to improving the consistency of dialect, as in the Irish speeches of Captain O'Cutter. O1 has many indications to the actor of Irish pronunciation, but the later octavos and W continue the process of revising the printed text (e.g. III. i.: *oblaged* for *obliged*, *immadiately* for *immediately*, *tinder* for *tender*, *tank* for *thank*).

(4) Verbal details of general dialogue are often revised. The present collations show the frequent agreement of all four octavos (OO) in points ultimately revised in W. Some of these changes are trivial and some are questionable improvements, but throughout the play W shows evidence of careful revision of text and typography.

(b) The First Dublin Edition

The first Dublin edition (D) is the 1761 duodecimo which reprints without independent authority the London text of O1. Collation of D with the London and Oxford octavos shows its virtual identity with O1, and the consequent absence of the retrenchments and revisions inaugurated with O2 and extended in O3. D is therefore not separately cited in the variant readings listed in the textual footnotes of this edition.

(c) The Dramatic Works (1777)

The four-volume collection of Colman's *Dramatick Works* which appeared in 1777 is a work of substantial importance, carefully prepared and printed. It consolidates the scattered individual plays and confirms their printed texts as progressively established and improved. In the case of *The Jealous Wife*, W represents a text long under direct scrutiny of author and manager. O2 early initiated changes which O3 confirmed and augmented. By 1763, the revision had been mainly accomplished, for O4, the second (undated) Oxford edition is without the importance of the first Oxford revision of 1763 (O3). W confirms the progressive changes that had been incorporated into the successive octavos, and gives evidence of further textual revision and typographical betterment. *The Jealous Wife* is accorded the first position in the opening volume of Colman's *Dramatick Works*, a selected collection of his plays which appeared after Colman had fully established his position as dramatic author and theatrical manager. Its text seems to have satisfied author and public in Colman's own day, and was adopted in Professor Allardyce Nicoll's (uncollated) reprint of *The Jealous Wife* in his collection of *Lesser English Comedies of the Eighteenth Century*. The present collations of the earlier octavos with W supply detailed textual evidence which justifies such choice of text.

Textual study of *The Jealous Wife* throws light on the general processes of revision of a popular play. Its specific retrenchments, though relatively few, show that the original text soon incorporated into itself changes that include not merely ordinary 'cuts' but deliberate revision of the freer dialogue in the scene of Lord Trinket's attempt upon Harriot. This latter early retrenchment is an interesting instance of the constraining influence of the prevalent 'genteel comedy' against which, in the next decade, Goldsmith and Sheridan were in open revolt.

G. H. N.

THE WEST INDIAN
TEXTS

O1. First octavo, 1771. 'By the Author of *The Brothers*,' followed by motto, '*Quis novus hic Hospes?*' *Yale. Harv. B.M. Camb. Colum.

O2. Second octavo, 1771. 'The Second Edition.' *Yale. *Bod. Colum.

O3. Third octavo, 1771. 'The Third Edition.' *Bod.

D. First Dublin duodecimo, 1771. *Yale. Camb.

B. First Belfast duodecimo, 1771. *Bod. Colum.

*N. 'New' [London] edition, 1771. 'A New Edition.' Title-page omits indication of authorship, but retains Latin motto. *Yale. *Bod. Camb. Colum.

R. 'New' edition, reprinted with slight variants, 1792. *Yale. Harv. *B.M.

M. Morgan edition, 1935. *English Plays 1660–1820.* Edited by A. E. Morgan. [pp. 903–946.]

Bibliography

W. Bibliography of Cumberland (pp. 330–347) in *Richard Cumberland: His Life and Dramatic Works*, by Stanley Thomas Williams, New Haven, etc. (*Yale University Press*), 1917.

(a) Editions of 1771

The text is based on Bodleian and Yale Library copies of 'A New Edition' of 1771 (N), 'Printed for W. Griffin,' publisher of the previous London octavos. N revises details of text and typography, but collation of it with O1 shows that the original text was carefully prepared and needed no essential changes. Prior to its first performance, January 19, 1771, *The West Indian* had already been painstakingly revised in accordance with the practical judgment of David Garrick, manager of Drury Lane Theatre. In his letters and personal *Memoirs*, Richard Cumberland testified to his debts, both general and specific, to Garrick. The first entrance of Belcour, for example, was deliberately heightened for stage effect according to the manager's suggestions. 'I entirely adopt your observation on the first scene,' wrote Cumberland to Garrick, 'and have already executed it in a manner that I hope embraces your ideas.' (Quoted in W, p. 69.) Cumberland's sensitiveness to other criticisms is characteristically revealed in the lengthy account in his *Memoirs* (I, 300–306) of certain textual alterations which he introduced in deference to different objections raised by Lord Lyttelton and Nugent Lord Clare.

In his *Memoirs* (I, 298), Cumberland says: 'I sold the copy right to Griffin in Catherine-Street, for 150 *l.* and if he told the truth when he boasted of having vended 12,000 copies, he did not make a bad bargain.' The immediate popularity of *The West Indian* is reflected in the numerous editions of 1771 — three London octavos (O1, O2, O3), and the 'New' [octavo] edition (N), all published by Griffin; and Dublin and Belfast duodecimos derived from them. Collation of all these editions shows that O2 inaugurated a number of minor corrections and betterments which thereafter were confirmed by O3 and N. All told, the variants are relatively few, but N has some justification for its designation as 'A New Edition.' For it there was specially prepared an engraved title-page, and its text was evidently reviewed in the light of betterments already effected and of further conscious emendations. The most interesting emendation is that interpolated in N in brackets in a speech of Major O'Flaherty (II. viii) which was thus made to read: 'I make sure of her, because I've married five wives (*en militaire*, Captain) and never failed yet; and, for what I know, they're all alive and merry at this very hour.' Cumberland's friend, Nugent Lord Clare, had objected that O'Flaherty's 'five wives' were 'four too many for an honest man,' and accordingly Cumberland 'desired Moody [the actor] to manage the matter as well as he could; he put in the qualifier of *en militaire*, and his five wives brought him into no further trouble; all but one were left-handed, and he had German practice for his plea.' (*Memoirs*, I, 306.) This actor's emendation, which first appears in print in N, had Cumberland's continued sanction.

(b) Editions after 1771

Collation of many editions after 1771 has little significance other than as proof of the continuance of a virtually standard text. The term 'New Edition,' which frequently recurs on later title-pages (e.g. 1773, 1775, 1792), echoes N, without voicing independent authority. In the 1792 edition (R), for instance, some variants are certainly misprints, and others are questionable, but habitually it reproduces the text of N. Cumberland died in 1811, fully forty years after the first performance and publication of *The West Indian*. The textual history of his most popular play throughout his long lifetime has, nevertheless, but a single important chapter — that of the initial year, 1771. From the outset, the printed text essentially satisfied author, producer, and publisher. Even between O1 and N the variants have neither the number nor the significance of the textual changes which 'The Third Edition Corrected' of *The Rivals* discloses in comparison with the first edition. Cumberland's own testimony proves that the printed text was not wholly unaltered, but the rarity of later textual changes proves likewise that Garrick's early revision of the manuscript, prior to stage production, had effectually anticipated the actual demands of the theatre. Mrs. Inchbald's late (1808) edition, which conveniently indicates the state of the acting text near the close of Cumberland's long life, has but trivial variants from N.

In the present edition, the textual footnotes show the early establishment of the standard text by collating N with the three previous London octavos of 1771. Textual references to the Irish editions of 1771 and to the later London reprints of the play are incidental, since their contribution is unessential.

The recent Morgan edition (M) carefully reprints the text of O1, but, in collating it less closely with N than with R, seems to ascribe to the latter (1792) various changes already established in N (1771) — and not infrequently in the still earlier editions, O2 and O3, which are not collated in M.

G. H. N.

GOLDSMITH

An Essay on the Theatre;
or, a
Comparison between Laughing and Sentimental Comedy

The text of Goldsmith's *Essay* is based on the British Museum copy of the first volume of *The Westminster Magazine, or The Pantheon of Taste. Containing a View of the History, Politics, Literature, Manners, Gallantry & Fashions of the Year 1773. Vol. I. London.* Goldsmith's unsigned article appears on pp. 4–6 of the first of the monthly issues which comprise Vol. I. The frontispiece is dated 'London, Publish'd Jan[y]. 1st 1773.' The *second* issue, however, is entitled 'For January, 1773,' and includes a 'Monthly Chronicle' running from Dec. 29 to Jan. 28. The *third* issue is similarly entitled 'For February, 1773,' and its 'Monthly Chronicle' runs from Feb. 2 to Feb. 28. The *first* issue, with 'Monthly Chronicle' running from Nov. 30 to Dec. 28, 1772, might therefore be consistently called the issue 'For December, 1772.'

Goldsmith's *Essay* is conveniently reprinted in the *Belles-Lettres* edition (pp. 125–130) of *The Good Natur'd Man and She Stoops to Conquer* (Boston and London, 1903), where the date 'December, 1772' is given in a footnote reference (Introduction, p. xv).

G. H. N.

SHE STOOPS TO CONQUER

Texts
Editions in Goldsmith's Lifetime

O1. First octavo, 1773. *Yale. Harv. *B.M. *Bod.
O2. Second octavo, 1773. *Yale. *Bod. L.C.
O3. Third octavo, 1773. *Yale. Harv. *Bod. Colum.
O4. Fourth octavo, 1773. *Bod. *Harv.
*O5. Fifth octavo, 1773. *Yale. *Harv. *B.M. *Bod. Colum.
D. Dublin duodecimo, 1773. *Yale. Harv. *B.M. Bod.
B. Belfast duodecimo, 1773. *Bod.

[The 1774 Dublin Edition (*Yale) may have appeared before Goldsmith's death.]

Collated Texts

GB. George P. Baker text, Boston and London, 1903. *The Good Natur'd Man and She Stoops to Conquer.* Edited by Austin Dobson. *Text collated by George P. Baker. In the Belles-Lettres Series.*

M. Morgan edition, 1935. *English Plays 1660–1820.* Edited by A. E. Morgan. [pp. 949–992.]

(a) The Editions of 1773
(1) The Five London Octavos

The text is based on the Yale Library copy of the fifth octavo edition (O5), 1773, the last published during Goldsmith's life. With this have been collated the four preceding octavo editions (O1, O2, O3, O4), all of 1773, the first three from Yale Library copies, O4 from the Bodleian Library. All, save O1, bear on the title-page the definite number of the edition. With these have been compared many other copies in British and American collections, public and private. Variants in different issues and copies of O1 and failure to specify the precise copies used have sometimes complicated bibliographical discussions. The present work aims to clarify textual study by collating all five editions that appeared before Goldsmith's death, in copies where the identity of each edition is definitely established.

(2) Variant Copies of O1

Detailed discussion of merely typographical variants in different copies of O1 belongs rather to bibliography than to broader textual interpretation. The valuable bibliographical study (W) of Iolo A. Williams (*Seven XVIIIth Century Bibliographies*, 1924, pp. 153–161) is mainly concerned with variants in titles and half-titles, pagination and page headings, and printer's signatures, catchwords, and devices in different issues and copies of O1, whereas collation of the text of the play itself, through the five successive octavo editions, is mainly concerned with verbal changes in the actual dialogue. The present purpose is sufficiently served by some illustration of certain matters of bibliography. The Yale Library copy of O1 misnumbers p. 65 as 56, and jumps in pagination from 72 to 81, thus having eight pages less than the apparent number — 114 — shown on its last numbered page of text. The British Museum copy, whose numbering of pages of text is consecutive (to 106), transfers the Cradock epilogue to the end, and has other variants, such as the transfer from title-page to half-title of the indication 'Price One Shilling Sixpence,' and the correction to *stores* (p. 24) of the early misprint *stones*, which seem to establish the priority of the Yale copy. W, indeed, concludes that the B.M.

copy is 'the final issue of the first edition,' and that 'there is probably no distinct first issue.'   Data given in W and supplemented from Yale and other copies not therein listed, support the general conclusion that alterations in the course of printing and chance assembling of sheets in different states account for numerous variants in bound copies.   It seems possible, however, in given instances, to determine the relative priority of certain copies.   The Bodleian Library and (Yale) Elizabethan Club copies of O1, for example, when collated with the Yale Library copy, showed by the correction of various textual misprints, the transfer of the Cradock epilogue to the end, and other variants that they were distinctly later in state or issue.   While it is thus readily possible to enlarge the data available in W by examination of other copies of O1 and by collation of typographical variants in the actual text of the play, W amply comprehends and illustrates the complex bibliographical problems involved and wisely declines to dogmatize as to the precise number of different issues or variant states of O1.

(3) *Irish Editions of* 1773

The Dublin text of 1773 (Yale copy) is apparently taken from an early copy of O1.   It reproduces various initial misspellings corrected in O2, locates the Cradock epilogue as in early copies of O1, and has other typographical characteristics of O1.   Like O4 and O5, however, it supplies one word mistakenly omitted in the earlier London octavos, but this seems an unrelated typographical correction.   The Belfast text of 1773 (Bodleian copy) has some betterments not in D, correcting the early misprint *stones* to *stores*, and printing Tony's song (end of Act II) as verse instead of prose, but the present collations cite the Irish editions only incidentally.

(4) O2 *and the Later Octavos*

The excellent text in the *Belles-Lettres* edition (1903) is based on a Harvard Library copy of O5, collated by Professor George Pierce Baker, 'with copies of the first edition, a probable second from Mr. Robert Hoe's library, and a third in the library of Columbia University . . . The third and the fifth editions bear the number on the title-page.'   The second and fourth editions supply the same means of exact identification.   The Yale Library copy of O2 bears on the title-page 'The Second Edition' and the Bodleian Library copy of O4, though lacking part of the title-page, clearly indicates the edition as 'The Four'[th].   The Yale Library copies of O3 and O5 similarly indicate 'The Third Edition' and 'The Fifth Edition.'   Thus all copies used in the present basic collations are definitely identified as to exact edition.   The Bodleian copy of O2 is likewise entitled, 'The Second Edition' and the Harvard Library copy of O4, 'The Fourth Edition.'   With such definite identification of rare copies of O2 and O4, the whole sequence of octavos after O1 is firmly established.

Collation of the Yale copies of O1 and O2 shows that the latter makes various corrections of spelling (e.g. *pity* for *pitty*; *allons* for *alons*; *mauvaise* for *meauvaise*) and of punctuation, and, like the later copies of O1, transfers the Cradock epilogue to the end.   Among other betterments of text, O2 prints as verse the snatch of Tony's song at the end of the second act, an improvement of O1 which has sometimes been credited to O3.   Though not itself typographically perfect, O2 performed a distinct service by consolidating the gains gradually in process in the various stages of O1, and by offering a surer basis for later reprints.   In recent textual study and collation O2 has unfortunately been generally slighted.

The later octavos (O3, O4, O5) are significant chiefly in confirming corrections incorporated in O2 and in showing the substantial integrity of the text throughout the editions preceding Goldsmith's death.   This latter point deserves especial emphasis, for the usual centering of bibliographical discussion on printer's variants in different copies or issues of O1 might arouse misgivings as to the reliability of the actual text of the play itself.   Broadly speaking, full collation of the five successive octavo editions (OO) shows that the dialogue was maintained throughout in consistent integrity.   Emendations are essentially typographical.   O2 of *She Stoops to Conquer* already incorporates most of the minor corrections which make O5 a more verbally accurate text than O1, but some of the original misprints or inaccuracies persist throughout OO, e.g. *those parts* for *these parts* (I. ii. 102); *George* for *Charles* (II. i. 188); *fortune* for Tony's usual *fortin* (III. i. 103).

(b) *Editions after Goldsmith's Death*

Only editions of *She Stoops to Conquer* published in Goldsmith's lifetime are strictly pertinent to the present purpose and textual collations.   For other purposes, bibliographical and historical, many subsequent reprints of the full text or modified acting versions have been considerably studied.   Annotated editions have become increasingly numerous, but critical editions with considerable textual collations have been infrequent.   The *Belles-Lettres Series* critical edition (1903), already cited, made conspicuous contribution to textual study through the work of Professor George P. Baker.   The present edition supports his choice of O5 as basic text and his main conclusions: 'In spite of many typographical faults, the first octavo evidently gave the sense of Goldsmith's play accurately.   The later octavos merely correct faulty type and incorrect spellings.'   It may be noted that full collation of OO shows that the process of accurate typographical revision was not wholly completed in these later editions, and that fuller evidence (e.g. as to the variant forms and copies of O1 and as to O2) alters some points of fact or conjecture, without disturbing the central textual conclusions.

The valuable recent Morgan edition (M), based on O1 (British Museum copy), collates O4 (Worcester College, Oxford, copy) and D, of the editions printed in Goldsmith's lifetime, and a subsequent (1786) edition, and usefully supplies 'a few of the more important' variants of the Larpent MS.   D is noted as 'corrupt,' and it might be added that the 1786 edition is one of various reprints which lack textual authority and sometimes betray careless printing.   The

Larpent MS. of *She Stoops to Conquer*, as compared with the Larpent MS. of Sheridan's *Rivals*, varies relatively little from the first printed edition. Broadly viewed, it shows that Goldsmith's text needed only minor revision before publication, but certain omissions and additions and occasional verbal details may be specifically examined in the variants included in M.

In summary, the present textual collations and comment aim to illustrate sufficiently bibliographical and typographical questions involved, but are mainly concerned with the virtual integrity of the actual text of the play, as maintained throughout the successive editions in Goldsmith's lifetime.

G. H. N.

THE RIVALS

TEXTS

O1. First octavo, 1775. *Yale. Harv. *B.M. Bod. Camb. L.C. Colum.

O2. Second octavo, 1775. *Yale. Harv. *B.M. Colum.

D. First Dublin duodecimo, 1775. *Yale.

*O3. Third octavo, 1776. 'The Third Edition Corrected.' *Yale. Harv. *Vict. (Dyce copy). *B.M.

O4. Fourth octavo, 'The Fourth Edition.' *Harv. *Vict. (Dyce copy).

O5. Fifth octavo, 1791. *Yale. Harv. *B.M. *Bod. *Vict. (Dyce copy). L.C.

O6. Sixth octavo, 1798. *Yale. Harv. Bod. Colum.

M. Murray (Moore) edition, 1821. *The Works of the late Right Honourable Richard Brinsley Sheridan.* 'Advertisement' by Thomas Moore. 2 vols. [I, 1–155.]

N. Nettleton edition, Boston, etc., 1906. *The Major Dramas of Richard Brinsley Sheridan.* Edited by George H. Nettleton. *Athenæum Press Series.*

A. Adams edition, Boston, etc., 1910. *The Rivals.* Edited by Joseph Quincy Adams, Jr. *Riverside Literature Series.*

R. Rhodes edition, Oxford, 1928. [New York, 1929.] *The Plays and Poems of Richard Brinsley Sheridan.* Edited by R. Crompton Rhodes. 3 vols. [I, 1–133.]

AM. Morgan edition, 1935. *English Plays 1660–1820.* Edited by A. E. Morgan. [pp. 993–1049.]

P. Purdy edition, Oxford, 1935. *The Rivals, A Comedy. As it was first Acted at the Theatre-Royal, in Covent-Garden* ... Edited from the Larpent MS. by Richard Little Purdy.

(a) 'The Third Edition Corrected' (O3)

The present text is based on Sheridan's presentation copy to David Garrick of the third octavo edition (O3), 1776, which bears on its title-page the words, 'The Third Edition Corrected.' This copy, inscribed 'David Garrick, Esqr. From The Author,' is in the Dyce Collection in the Library of the Victoria and Albert Museum, South Kensington. One of the two Yale Library copies of O3 lacks the rare half-title, but both agree textually with the Dyce copy and have been constantly used in preparing the present text and collations. In *The Major Dramas of Richard Brinsley Sheridan* (1906), which reprinted the texts of the various Sheridan plays as given by W. Fraser Rae in his *Sheridan's Plays now printed as he wrote them* (1902), I included a collation of Yale Library copies of the first three editions of *The Rivals* (there designated as R1, R2, R3). I have retained the method there adopted of indicating within guillemets《 》various passages cut in O3, though in listing textual variants the change of symbols and the substitution of O3 as the basic text alter superficial appearances. These previous (1906) collations of text proved that the cuts which Rae had ascribed to Wilkie's arbitrary editorial excisions when preparing Sheridan's text, after his death, for the John Murray edition of 1821, had already been made in 'The Third Edition Corrected' of 1776. At that time, however, relying unduly on the Rae text and lacking evidence later acquired as to Sheridan's own revision, I failed to sense the full authority and significance of O3.

In 1928, R. Crompton Rhodes adopted O3 as his basic text, and in his edition of *Sheridan's Plays* (I, 132) gave the following note in his Bibliography: 'This is the first Edition to contain the "Prologue by the Author Spoken on the Tenth Night." The corrections seem to have been Sheridan's: they include the deletion of several passages and many verbal emendations. Nettleton first drew attention to this Edition: it is very rare, especially with the engraved half-title which has a small picture of the characters in Act IV, sc. ii. It is the first edition with Sheridan's name.'

The internal evidence of the 'verbal emendations' which satisfied Rhodes as to their authenticity may be supported by external evidence. The fact that Sheridan personally inscribed to David Garrick a presentation copy of 'The Third Edition Corrected' supports the essential validity of the corrections. Furthermore, *The London Chronicle*, Jan. 14–16, 1777, plainly advertised the publication of 'The Third Edition, corrected by the Author.'

The internal evidence of careful correction of the text is substantial. (1) Every act throughout the play contains judicious cuts, sometimes brief but often extensive, of passages given in O1 and O2. These cuts are clearly planned to shorten the total dialogue and expedite the action. (2) The diction is often bettered by close revision, both in passages considerably cut and in others not appreciably shortened. (3) Precise emendation of individual words (as distinguished from the correction of many misprints in O1) is frequent. Corrections so numerous and so varied as those summarized attest careful and consistent revision of the entire text. The evidence is definite that O3 represents Sheridan's own revision — 'The Third Edition, corrected by the Author.'

(b) The Earlier Octavos (O1 and O2)

The Rivals first appeared in print soon after its initial failure, on January 17, 1775, had been turned into assured success by Sheridan's vigorous revision of his play prior to its second venture on January 28, 1775. (See 'The Initial Failure and Final Triumph of *The Rivals*' in N, Intro. lxiv–lxviii.) *The Morning Chronicle*, Feb. 7–9, 1775, advertised that 'on Saturday next [Feb. 11] will be published ... THE RIVALS, a Comedy: As it is now performing, with universal applause, at the Theatre Royal in Covent Garden.' O1 shows signs of hasty printing. Two obvious misprints, occurring within a few lines of each other, were corrected in the *Errata* inserted on the page preceding the *Dramatis Personæ*, but other errors passed undetected. O2 retains these misprints and even the page of *Errata*, instead of making in the main text the two corrections conspicuously indicated. O2 reads on the title-page, 'The Second Edition,' but as its text is merely a reprint, the present collations simplify by listing only the variants between O1 and O3.

(c) The Later Octavos (O4, O5, O6)

The later octavos confirm the established authority of O3. The Harvard copy of O4 is undated but is clearly designated as 'The Fourth Edition.' (Rhodes, I, 132, gives 1785 as the tentative date of O4.) O4, O5 (1791) and O6 (1798), maintain in virtual integrity the text of O3. Even minor typographical variants are rare, and there are no signs of further 'author's changes' of text. Sheridan's careful revision in O3 is thus further accredited. The present textual footnotes cite the later octavos (O4, O5, O6) only infrequently.

(d) Later Editions

Present limits and purposes do not permit either detailed discussion or bibliographical lists of the many editions of *The Rivals* printed separately or in collections of Sheridan's dramas, or included in general collections of British drama. The successive Sheridan bibliographies of Anderson (appended to Lloyd C. Sanders's *Life of Richard Brinsley Sheridan*, 1890), Nettleton (N, pp. cxi–cxvi), Sichel (*Sheridan*, 1909, II, 445–448), and Rhodes (R, I, 131–133) supply considerable bibliographical material, especially as to the earlier editions, but only the catalogues of the great libraries, British and American, can keep pace even approximately with the constantly enlarging number of modern editions and reprints.

Murray (M). In 1821, five years after Sheridan's death, John Murray published his standard two-volume edition of Sheridan's *Works*. This is prefaced with an apologetic 'Advertisement' by Thomas Moore, dated from Paris, which gives his absence from England as a foremost reason for his failure to furnish the *Life* of Sheridan which was to have accompanied the *Works*, but makes no reference to any editorial responsibility for the published texts of the plays. The Murray edition of 1821 (M) has, however, often been called 'Moore's edition.' M makes no independent contribution to the textual history of *The Rivals*, but its adoption of O3 confirms the continued authority of Sheridan's revised text.

The dominance of O3 as the accepted printed text, established in Sheridan's lifetime and thereafter definitely supported by the influence of Murray's standard edition, long persisted, despite the appearance of various acting versions, usually shortening the text or adding fuller stage directions. The question of whether Sheridan himself can be held responsible for any stage version later than O3 (such as Mrs. Inchbald's acting text of 1808) was debated, pro and con, by F. W. Bateson and R. Crompton Rhodes in the London *Times Literary Supplement*, Nov. 28 and Dec. 19, 1929; Jan. 9 and Jan. 16, 1930. (For an account of 'Mr. Joseph Jefferson's Acting Version of *The Rivals*,' see N, pp. 323–325.) In recent decades, the general tendency of editors of dramatic texts to revert to the earliest editions has been apparent in frequent reprints of O1. In his outstanding critical edition of Sheridan, however, R. Crompton Rhodes adopted O3 and declared that it 'must be regarded as the standard text.' Editorial purposes vary, but the present purpose is best served by similar acceptance, strengthened by evidence unnoted in R, of Sheridan's authentic revision of his own text.

(e) Larpent MS.

Discussion of unpublished dramatic texts, either in author's manuscript or prompter's transcript, exceeds the usual limits of these Textual Notes, but the case of *The Rivals* justifies an exception. The discovery in the Huntington Library and ultimate publication in 1935, by Richard L. Purdy, of the manuscript (Larpent MS.) originally submitted for the Lord Chamberlain's license, Jan. 9, 1775, fully recovers and interprets the text of the play as produced on the night of its initial failure, Jan. 17, 1775. Professor Purdy's admirable critical edition (P) contrasts in parallel columns the texts of the Larpent MS. and O1, and adds the variants of O3. The Introduction is an authoritative initial chapter in the history of *The Rivals* and contributes essentially to understanding both of the late revisions of text and of the ultimate authority of O3.

The extensively collated Morgan text (AM), based on O1, stresses the Larpent MS. variants in careful, though sometimes abbreviated, independent collation. (Both P and AM were in press at the same time.) AM usually lists even minute textual and typographical variants, but merely summarizes the general content of various lengthy passages (e.g. pp. 1019, 1031, 1037, 1047, 1048), where Sheridan's major changes merit close scrutiny.

G. H. N.

THE SCHOOL FOR SCANDAL

Texts

(a) The Crewe MS. Text (1777)

*Sheridan's presentation copy 'To Mrs. Crewe/From The Author./R. B. Sheridan.' Complete manuscript copy of *The School for Scandal* transcribed by a professional copyist and revised by Sheridan. Sheridan's corrections of text and stage directions are in his own handwriting on the manuscript. (In the Riggs Memorial Library, Georgetown University.) This hitherto unpublished Crewe MS. text is the basis of the present edition and textual studies. Sheridan's long dedicatory poem to Mrs. Crewe, written to accompany his presentation copy of the play, has been frequently reprinted. In the Murray edition (II, 3–7) it is entitled A PORTRAIT; *Addressed to Mrs. Crewe, with the Comedy of the School for Scandal, by R. B. Sheridan, Esq.*

(b) The Spurious ('Piratical') Dublin Text

D1. First dated Dublin duodecimo, 1780. 'As it is performed at the Theatres-Royal, in London and Dublin. Dublin: printed in the year, M,DCC,LXXX.' *Yale. *Harv. [*T.L.S.*, Oct. 11, 1934.]

D2. Second Dublin duodecimo, 1781. 'Dublin: printed in the year M.DCC.LXXXI.' *Yale. [*T.L.S.*, Oct. 11, 1934.]

A1. First American [Robert Bell] edition, Philadelphia, 1782. '*The Real and Genuine School for Scandal, A Comedy; Acted with bursts of Applause, at the Theatres in London and Dublin. Written by Brinsley Sheridan, Esquire.*' [Despite title, it reproduces the spurious Dublin text. This text was definitely repudiated in the 1786 Gaine edition (G) listed below.] *Yale. *Lib. Co. of Phil. *Hist. Soc. of Penn. *U. of Penn. [*T.L.S.*, Mar. 28, 1935; Dec. 21, 1935.]

L1. First London [Thomas Cadell] edition, 1783. Title-page follows Bell's (as above), but 'Printed for T. Cadell, in the Strand. M.DCC.LXXXIII.' *B.M. *Bib. Nat. (three copies). [*T.L.S.*, Mar. 28, 1935.]

[N.B. The *undated* edition 'Dublin: Printed for J. Ewling' (*Yale. Harv. *B.M.) long regarded as the first edition, was dated '1799?' by Rhodes, and is now generally discredited as the *editio princeps*. Only editions which I have discussed considerably in *T.L.S.* articles, as indicated above, are here listed. For other editions, see R, II, 164 ff.]

(c) 'Genuine' Editions (to 1821)

G. Gaine edition, New York. 1786. Published by Hugh Gaine, 'From a Manuscript Copy in the possession of John Henry, Esquire, Joint Manager of the American Company [New York], given him by the Author.' [Incorrectly assumed in R, II, 167, to reprint the 'piratical text' which it explicitly repudiates.] *Yale. *L.C. [*T.L.S.*, Dec. 21, 1935.]

D. Dublin, 1799. 'Taken from a correct copy [held in R, II, 161, to be the copy given by Sheridan to his sister, Mrs. Lefanu, for disposal to the Dublin Theatre manager, Ryder], Performed at the Theatres, London and Dublin. Dublin Printed, and sold by the booksellers. 1799.' *Yale.

E. Moore's copy of D, emended in accordance with the Crewe MS. copy. *Royal Irish Academy Library, Dublin.

M. Murray edition, 1821. *The Works of the late Right Honourable Richard Brinsley Sheridan.* Published by John Murray, with 'Advertisement' by Thomas Moore. 2 vols. [II, 1–158.]

(d) Various Critical Editions and Texts

Rae. Rae edition, 1902. *Sheridan's Plays now printed as he wrote them* . . . Edited by W. Fraser Rae. [From Sheridan's early and partly incomplete MS. — the Rae or 'Frampton Court' text.]

N. Nettleton edition, Boston, 1906. *The Major Dramas of Richard Brinsley Sheridan.* Edited by George H. Nettleton. *Athenæum Press Series.* [pp. 105–211; 286–297.] [Rae text.]

W. Webster edition, Boston, 1917. *The School for Scandal.* Collated and edited by Hanson Hart Webster. [With bibliography.] *Riverside College Classics.* [Murray text.]

WR. Williams (and Rhodes) edition, 1926. *The Plays of Richard Brinsley Sheridan.* Edited by Iolo A. Williams. Text of *The School for Scandal* revised by R. Crompton Rhodes. [Mainly based on E.]

J. Jebb edition, Oxford, 1928. *Sheridan's School for Scandal.* Edited by E. M. Jebb. [Text from WR, with a few authorized corrections.]

R. Rhodes edition, Oxford, 1928. [New York, 1929.] *The Plays and Poems of Richard Brinsley Sheridan.* Edited by R. Crompton Rhodes. 3 vols. [II, 1–174.] [Text mainly based on E, with further revision of the earlier Rhodes text in WR.]

(a) Introduction

The School for Scandal presents more formidable textual and bibliographical problems than any other drama included in this volume. It is ironical that the play which is commonly regarded as the most finished product of the comedy of manners, at least in its own period, has invited constant controversy over unauthorized editions and variant texts, and even over the usually simple question of determining what edition was actually the first to appear in print. Within the past decade the very bases of knowledge and critical interpretation have been strikingly altered by discoveries adding important new material and disproving many long accepted assumptions. Here it is possible only to try to clarify certain major aspects of the case, with regard rather to essential facts than to controversial details. That Sheridan was personally responsible for the lack of a definitive London edition of his masterpiece has long been known from Thomas Moore's account in his *Memoirs of the Life of the Right Honourable Richard Brinsley Sheridan* (1825, quarto edition, p. 191):

'It appears singular that, during the life of Mr. Sheridan, no authorized or correct edition of this play should have been published in England. He had, at one time, disposed of the copyright to Mr. Ridgway of Piccadilly, but, after repeated applications from the latter for the manuscript, he was told by Mr. Sheridan, as an excuse for keeping it back, that he had been nineteen years endeavouring to satisfy himself with the style of the School for Scandal, but had not yet succeeded. Mr. Ridgway, upon this, ceased to give him any further trouble on the subject.

'The edition printed in Dublin is, with the exception of a few unimportant omissions and verbal differences, perfectly correct. It appears that, after the success of the comedy in London, he presented a copy of it to his eldest sister, Mrs. Lefanu, to be disposed of, for her own advantage, to the manager of the Dublin Theatre. The sum of a hundred guineas, and free admissions for her family, were the terms upon which Ryder, the manager at that period, purchased from this lady the right of acting the play; and it was from the copy thus procured that the edition afterwards published in Dublin was printed. I have collated this edition with the copy given by Mr. Sheridan to Lady Crewe, (the last, I believe, ever revised by himself,) and find it, with the few exceptions already mentioned, correct throughout.'

Uncertainty as to which one of the many early editions printed in Dublin Thomas Moore had thus declared to be virtually correct disappeared with the discovery by R. Crompton Rhodes, with the assistance of W. J. Lawrence (see *T.L.S.*, Sept. 24, 1925), of the actual copy of the Dublin duodecimo edition of 1799 collated by Moore and annotated in his own handwriting. This copy, 'Presented to the Royal Irish Academy, by Mrs. Thomas Moore, August 28, 1855,' is preserved in the Library of the Royal Irish Academy, Dublin. It contains Moore's explicit statement: 'The MS. copy given by S[heridan] to Mrs. Crewe was evidently revised by himself, and agrees with this printed Copy, except in the few trifling instances marked here in the margin.' Moore's repeated statements as to Sheridan's personal corrections of the Crewe MS. are amply confirmed both in the text and notes of this edition, but he understates the number (actually some 200) of his own marginal corrections and overlooks many variants that he left uncorrected in his printed (1799) copy. That he apparently never knew the details or date (1777) of Sheridan's gift to Mrs. Crewe is not surprising, since he was not born until two years after the production of *The School for Scandal*, and since his work as biographer was not undertaken until after Sheridan's death. Detailed discussion both of the Dublin edition of 1799 (D) and of the emendations (E) in Moore's copy requires some prefatory account of the preceding spurious Dublin text of Sheridan's play.

(b) The First ('Spurious') Dublin Text

It was long assumed that *The School for Scandal* first appeared in print in the undated octavo edition, 'Dublin: Printed for J. Ewling.' This assumption was based on purely conjectural dating — '1778?,' in the British Museum catalogue — '1777?,' in the bibliography by John P. Anderson in the *Life of Richard Brinsley Sheridan* (1890), by Lloyd C. Sanders. Within the past decade, however, the assumed priority of the Ewling edition has been increasingly discredited (see, e.g., M. J. Ryan, in *T.L.S.*, March 22, 1928, and R. Crompton Rhodes, in *The Library*, Dec., 1928, and in R, II, 171). Correspondingly, the first *dated* edition, the rare 1780 Dublin duodecimo (D1), has been advanced and is now generally recognized as the *editio princeps* of the spurious Dublin text. I have elsewhere (*T.L.S.*, Oct. 11, 1934) fully described D1 and summarized the results of collating it with the next Dublin edition — 1781 (D2) — listed by Rhodes (II, 164–165) as seemingly 'the Second Edition.' This collation substantiated his main inferences — necessarily tentative, since he had not 'examined a copy [of D1], for none is to be traced in England' — as to D1 and its general relation to D2. D2 is simply a reprint of D1, differentiated by certain misprints and other minor typographical variants, but without independent textual standing. Collations of many other Dublin editions prior to that of 1799 (D) show the persistent influence of the spurious text of D1. All such 'pirated editions,' Ewling's included, were, of course, printed without Sheridan's sanction and are garbled texts.

(c) The ('Genuine') Dublin Edition of 1799 (Moore's emended copy)

Against this general background, the Dublin edition of 1799 (D) stands out distinctly. The phrasing of the title-page, 'Taken from a correct copy, Performed at the Theatres, London and Dublin,' is not in itself conclusive evidence of an authentic text, for publishers of plays often made misleading claims. But Moore's repeated statements as to the virtual correctness of D and his own use of it for recording his textual emendations (E), to bring it into harmony with the authentic Crewe MS. copy, give it independent endorsement. Moore's emended copy is the basis of the text of the play as revised by R. Crompton Rhodes for *The Plays of Richard Brinsley Sheridan*, edited by Iolo A. Williams, 1926

(WR), and as further revised in Vol. II of *The Plays and Poems of Richard Brinsley Sheridan*, edited by R. Crompton Rhodes, Oxford, 1928; New York, 1929 (R). The text of *Sheridan's School for Scandal*, edited by E. M. Jebb, Oxford, 1928, follows WR, with slight corrections, as authorized. In general, these various recent editions may be grouped as presenting essentially the Rhodes text, which recognizes Sheridan's presentation copy to Mrs. Crewe as the ultimate (but lost or missing) textual authority, and E as the best available means of approximating the original text. (The present textual studies have largely utilized a complete page by page transcript, made during the summer of 1932, by my daughter, Mrs. Gordon S. Haight, in the Library of the Royal Irish Academy, Dublin, of Moore's marginal and other notes in his copy of D. Primarily in collating C and E, and incidentally in checking R, this independent transcript has here been most helpful.)

The very discovery of Moore's emended copy of the Dublin edition of 1799 which gave Mr. Rhodes a valuable secondary means of recovering measurably the Crewe text may, however, have diverted him from further quest of the primary authority — the actual presentation copy itself. His special bibliographical note on 'The Copy sent to Mrs. Crewe' (II, 161) concludes with a subordinate reference to the sale, in 1923, of 'a MS. "To Mrs. Crewe from the Author."' This in itself might well have provided a vital clue to discovery and verification of the long-sought copy, but was dismissed with the passing comment that 'for various reasons fuller particulars are required to establish its authenticity.' Such particulars, ample and precise, are supplied in the next section.

(d) The Crewe MS. Copy

The Crewe MS. copy to which, in 1928, Mr. Rhodes made but guarded reference, since he had neither seen nor traced it, had actually been sold in New York City, April 16, 1923, and had virtually disappeared without entering the main stream of critical research. Textual studies as early as those of Mr. Rhodes (1925-1928) and as recent as others published in 1938 continued without apparent knowledge of its location, if not of its existence. Meantime, while investigating various texts of the play, I was fortunate in discovering the 'missing' copy in the ownership of Mrs. Nicholas J. Brady (the late Mrs. William J. B. Macaulay) and in receiving from her the fullest and freest privileges to study and utilize it. Her personal loan of the copy first provided the essential means of direct verification and protracted collations of it at the Yale Library with other manuscript transcriptions and early editions there available. To her generous co-operation this present work mainly owes its opportunity to recover, for the first time, the most significant, as well as elusive, authentic document in the long-vexed history of the text of *The School for Scandal*.

The Murray text of 1821, and many subsequent reprints, have familiarized even the general reader with Sheridan's dedicatory poem, A PORTRAIT; *Addressed to Mrs. Crewe, with the Comedy of the School for Scandal*. This poem, sent to Mrs. Crewe with a 'finely bound' manuscript copy of the play, was in her hands within a few months after the first production of the play, on May 8, 1777. Sheridan's early presentation to Mrs. Crewe of manuscripts of his play and poem is notably confirmed by an undated letter which, late in life, he wrote to his second wife. (Dated 'about 1812' by Sichel, who gives several extracts from it. For the full text I am indebted to the present owner, Mr. Barton Currie.) Sheridan recounts his surprise at encountering in print, 'at this late date' and in a 'surreptitiously published' and incorrect newspaper version, his verses to Mrs. Crewe that had once linked her name with the triumph of *The School for Scandal*. 'They are inaccurately printed, but on the whole I certainly wrote them and had forgotten them, which is not common with me. . . . They were sent with a M.S. copy of the play finely bound &c. N.B. I was not then 25 — by the way. [A slight slip, for he *was* 'then 25.'] She was then in truth the Handsomest of the set. . . . When I look at these verses Oh! how it reminds me what an ardent romantic Blockhead nature made me!' The past circumstances which Sheridan thus vividly recalled, and made known to the second Mrs. Sheridan, were familiar to the 'set' in which he moved in 1777. By mid-August of that year his verses to Mrs. Crewe had been considerably circulated in manuscript and were thus known to Garrick, Charles Fox, Lord Camden, and others. (See also Horace Walpole's October letter, cited on p. 843, ftn. 1.)

In the century and more since Thomas Moore, in his biography of Sheridan (1825), attested the unique importance of the Crewe MS. of *The School for Scandal*, biographers and editors have repeatedly recognized the value of the 'missing' text of which Moore had spoken from personal knowledge and direct collation.

The authenticity of the copy here studied is firmly established by explicit evidence both internal and external. The title-page bears the inscription, in Sheridan's handwriting, 'To Mrs. Crewe/From The Author,' and is further signed, 'R. B. Sheridan.' The inner cover bears Mrs. Crewe's signature and book-mark. The text of the play is carefully and legibly transcribed in the copyist's hand, and Sheridan's corrections are usually easily differentiated from the occasional copyist's corrections (as of omitted or repeated words) both by his characteristic handwriting and by the different ink he used. In infrequent instances, it is open to question whether a given change (as in the mere crossing out of a word, or a partially blurred alteration) is made by Sheridan or by the copyist. But throughout the play additions, alterations, and excisions which are unmistakably in Sheridan's hand and which occur both in the text and in stage directions, amply attest his personal revision.

Some of Sheridan's corrections of the MS. afford most precise and striking verification of the authenticity of the copy. In Moore's *Life of Sheridan* (1825) occurs an extended footnote (pp. 191-192) to his reference in the main text to 'the copy given by Mr. Sheridan to Lady Crewe (the last, I believe, ever revised by himself).' The full footnote reads: 'Among the corrections in this copy, (which are in his own hand-writing, and but few in number), there is one which shows not only the retentiveness of his memory, but the minute attention which he paid to the structure of his sentences. Lady Teazle, in her scene with Sir Peter in the Second Act, says: "That's very true, indeed, Sir Peter;

and, after having married you, I should never pretend to taste again, I allow." It was thus that the passage stood at first in Lady Crewe's copy, — as it does still, too, in the Dublin edition [1799], and in that given in the Collection of his Works [Murray, 1821]: but in his final revision of this copy, the original reading of the sentence, such as I find it in all his earlier manuscripts, is restored: — "That's very true, indeed, Sir Peter; and, after having married you, I am sure I should never pretend to taste again."' The passage in question (p. 35 of the MS.) shows Sheridan's handwritten corrections of the Crewe copy precisely as Moore, long after Sheridan's death, had meticulously noted them.

Another striking means of confirming the authenticity of the Crewe MS. copy I have found by collating it with a copyist's manuscript (1795) in continuous possession of Sheridan and his descendants until recently. This copy of *The School for Scandal*, now in the Yale Library, is transcribed on paper clearly watermarked '1795.' It remarkably attests the continued maintenance of the Crewe text in full authority, for its few and minor verbal variants are such as usually appear in manuscript transcriptions by different copyists — variants that, even in printed texts, have their counterparts in misprints or other minor typographical differences. This 1795 MS. copy, transmitted through the Sheridan family (and designated as S in the present collations) is actually closer to the original Crewe MS. as revised by Sheridan than is Moore's often meticulous, but sometimes inattentive, revision of the imperfect Dublin edition of 1799 (D). In S, Sheridan's early manuscript corrections and insertions repeatedly appear in the regular text, and the revised Crewe MS. in its totality is followed with unusual precision.

Still another way of confirming the authenticity of the Crewe MS. copy is through Moore's emended copy of D. Moore pronounced D 'perfectly correct' save for the 'few unimportant omissions and verbal differences' which he noted. His 'few' exceptions actually total more than two hundred, in his own handwritten marginal corrections. Furthermore, Mr. Rhodes rightly conjectured (II, 18) that Moore's actual corrections were by no means complete, and that 'he ignored — no doubt as obvious — a number of misprints, verbal transpositions, and the like.' Full collations of C, D, and E (Moore's emended copy of D) reveal that, though Moore's positive emendations closely accord with C, his oversights of inaccuracies in D considerably exceed Mr. Rhodes's lenient conjectures.

Full variants of the many editions and manuscripts collated as bases for the present study cannot here be reproduced, but the present edition offers sufficient illustration of methods and results by listing throughout Act I, textual variants of the following selected manuscripts and editions:

C. The 1777 Crewe MS. copy, as emended by Sheridan in his own handwriting. (Georgetown University Library.)

S. The 1795 MS. transcription, closely confirming C, and regularly incorporating Sheridan's corrections. (Yale Library.)

D. The Dublin edition of 1799, as printed. (Yale Library.)

E. Moore's emended copy of D, confirming C, with his handwritten corrections. (Royal Irish Academy Library, Dublin.)

M. The Murray text of 1821 (and 1823).

R. The Rhodes text of 1928, mainly based on E as a means of recovering approximately the missing original text of C.

In summary, C and S, both fully authentic though not absolutely identical, manuscripts, are in closest textual harmony. E closely corresponds with both C and S in Moore's actual textual emendations, but permits many inaccuracies in D to stand uncorrected. D and M are both 'genuine' (not 'spurious' or 'piratical') printed texts, but D errs frequently in text and typography, as shown both by E and by various collations here supplied. M merits separate consideration.

(e) The Murray Text of 1821 (and 1823)

In 1821, forty-four years after the first production of *The School for Scandal*, John Murray published his influential edition of Sheridan's collected dramatic *Works*. From this, in 1823, he separately reprinted *The School for Scandal*, without textual changes. References (as in R) to the 1823 reprint, or (as in the present edition) to the original 1821 Murray text are thus identical. M is a carefully printed edition, especially in comparison with D, and its text is bettered by inclusion of the majority (about five-eighths) of Moore's 200-odd emendations. It lacks, however, many readings and corrections doubly confirmed by Sheridan and Moore, and often initiates changes unsupported by any known authentic text in manuscript or in print during Sheridan's lifetime. In the absence of any known extant manuscript from which M was printed, various conjectures (e.g., R, II, 162) have been advanced.

Moore's nominal connection with the Murray edition of Sheridan's *Works*, to which he was to have contributed a life of the author, has frequently been misinterpreted. His letters, diary, and apologetic 'Advertisement' in M alike show that his concern was as biographer of Sheridan, not as editor of his dramatic texts. Protracted absence from England delayed the intended biography. When, four years later (1825), Moore's *Life of Sheridan* was eventually published separately, it stressed the final authority of the Crewe MS. of *The School for Scandal*, and even took issue with M for specific textual alteration made 'without authority from any of the manuscript copies.' Full collation of M with E (Moore's emended copy of D) reveals numerous variants which are alien to the assumption that Moore himself edited the text of M. His protracted study of the Sheridan manuscripts, ranging from the earliest tentative fragments to the complete and revised text, enforces his settled judgment in favor of the Crewe MS. text. He adopted it as his own standard in the collation and correction of D, and to it, despite his certain acquaintance with M, he gave his deliberate preference and sanction.

Of the many editions and texts since Sheridan's death, M has remained the most influential, but various acting versions, such as Cumberland's, Lacy's, and French's, show the familiar processes of continued alteration for stage purposes.

(f) The Rae ('Frampton Court') Text

In 1902, W. Fraser Rae, deviated from the long settled custom of reprinting M as the 'received text' by basing his text (Rae) on Sheridan's early handwritten manuscript, then in possession of the Sheridan family at Frampton Court, near Dorchester. The Rae text which I reprinted by permission, in 1906 (N), can here be but briefly considered. The value of this Sheridan manuscript as an early and unquestionably authentic text has been widely recognized since Rae first made it generally accessible. It lacks, however, the end of Act III and the first scene of Act IV, and elsewhere shows the still tentative processes of composition. It belongs in the historical development of the text to an advanced, but not final, stage in the process of composition prior to stage production. The publication of the Rae text attracted wide attention especially at a time when authentic Sheridan manuscripts were virtually unstudied, if not unknown, and when recovery of the Crewe MS. text was not anticipated. The Frampton Court MS. is now owned by Mr. Barton Currie who has generously given me direct use of it, as of other Sheridan material in his collections.

(g) The Rhodes Text

In 1928, R. Crompton Rhodes made his textual and bibliographical study of *The School for Scandal* the central and most extensive contribution of his outstanding critical edition of Sheridan. His main aim was 'to recover the full and genuine text as it was spoken at Drury Lane on the first night under the direction of Richard Brinsley Sheridan.' Recognizing the Crewe text as the ultimate authority, but without direct knowledge of the manuscript itself, he sought to regain it approximately through the secondary means of Moore's emended copy (E) of D. R includes *verbatim* about seven-eighths (M has about five-eighths) of Moore's actual emendations, and reproduces others less exactly, though in several cases departures from E are deliberate. Apart from Moore's emendations, and disregarding the bulk of merely typographical variants between D and M, there remain over 400 textual variants between D and M. In a marked majority (over three-fifths) of these 400-odd variants, R agrees precisely with M, despite the general statement (R, II, 20) that M is 'quite unreliable' and that 'no single reading from it is here accepted without corroborative proof.' The actual Sheridan manuscripts now available show that the text of R deviates still further from C than from E. Though the actual composite text of R falls short of its intent, its emphasis on the authority of the Crewe MS. is sound, and its recovery of Moore's emended copy of D remains a definite aid to textual study.

G. H. N.

THE CRITIC

TEXTS

(a) Thomas Becket's London Octavos (1781–1811)

(Of O1–O6 only copies personally examined and found to have the rare half-title precisely identifying the exact edition are listed. All have the same engraved main title dated '1781,' regardless of differences in actual time of issue. The half-titles of O2–O6 indicate only the number of the given edition, not the year of its publication.)

*O1. First octavo, 1781. *Vict. Half-title: '*The Critic; or, a Tragedy Rehearsed. Price One Shilling and Sixpence.*'

O2. Second octavo, 1781. *Harv. *B.M. Half-title designates 'The Second Edition.'

O3. Third octavo, 1781. *Harv. 'The Third Edition.'

O4. Fourth octavo, 1781. *Harv. *B.M. 'The Fourth Edition.'

O5. Fifth octavo, 1781. *Harv. 'The Fifth Edition.'

O6. Sixth octavo, 1781. *Harv. *N.Y.P.L. 'The Sixth Edition.'

Wm. Watermarked octavo [1795]. Printed on paper watermarked '1795,' with re-engraved main title still retaining the original date '1781,' but signed 'S. J. Neele, Sculpt. Strand.' Main text has 96 (instead of 98) pages. *Yale. B.M. *Bod. Camb.

B. Octavo, 1808. *Colum.

BP. Octavo, 1811. 'Printed for Becket and Porter.' *Yale. (This copy has half-title indicating 'A New Edition. [Price Two Shillings.]'; and final leaf consisting of two pages of T. Becket's book-seller's advertisements.)

(b) Selected Later Editions (after Sheridan's death)

M. Murray (Moore) edition, 1821. *The works of the late Right Honourable Richard Brinsley Sheridan.* 'Advertisement' by Thomas Moore. 2 vols. [II, 205–288.]

Rae. Rae edition, 1902. *Sheridan's Plays now printed as he wrote them.* Edited by W. Fraser Rae.

N. Nettleton edition, Boston, 1906. *The Major Dramas of Richard Brinsley Sheridan.* Edited by George H. Nettleton. *Athenæum Press Series.*

R. Rhodes edition, Oxford, 1928. [New York, 1929.] *The Plays and Poems of Richard Brinsley Sheridan.* 3 vols. [II, 175–263.]

(a) Introduction

Discussion of early editions of *The Critic* may be clarified, at the outset, by differentiating between bibliographical and textual questions. The former are unusually complex; the latter relatively simple. The present choice of text is simplified by the fact that the text first established in print in 1781 (O1) remained unchanged throughout many successive editions issued by the original publisher, Thomas Becket. The first six octavo Becket editions are, from the standpoint of bibliography, distinguishable through the indication of the number of the edition on the half-titles, preserved in rare copies that fortunately retain this conclusive means of precise identification. From the standpoint of purely textual study, these various editions are essentially identical. The significance of the half-titles has long been recognized by Sheridan bibliographers, but the present study definitely locates copies, with the distinguishing half-titles, of all six of these earliest Becket editions. Accordingly it is now possible to satisfy in detail both bibliographical and textual investigation. The present text is based on the Dyce copy of O1 in the Victoria and Albert Museum, South Kensington — one of the few perfect copies with the original half-title. For purposes of collation I have used the remarkable sequence found in the Harvard Library of copies of all five of the subsequent octavos (O2, O3, O4, O5, O6), each with its distinctive half-title.

(b) The Early Becket Editions (1781)

The Critic, first produced on October 30, 1779, at Drury Lane Theatre, did not appear in print until 1781, when Thomas Becket published it with Sheridan's Dedication *To Mrs. Greville.* This Dedication and the internal evidence of careful revision and printing of the text of the play justify the dominant position of O1 among published editions. (For additional evidence of authenticity, see Rhodes, II, 260.) Earlier authentic manuscript texts are (1) the partly incomplete Frampton Court Sheridan manuscript, first printed in 1902 by W. Fraser Rae (Rae), and reprinted in 1906 in my *Sheridan's Major Dramas* (N); (2) the Larpent manuscript in the Huntington Library, the copy submitted for the Lord Chamberlain's license. The former is important for priority and direct authenticity of composition; the latter for text as completed for initial stage production. The delayed publication of O1 permitted the incorporation of many further textual changes sanctioned by practical experience in the theatre. The variants between the so-called Rae text and O1 are fully listed in N, and are not here reproduced. Many of them are minor verbal variants, but some are substantial cuts (as of the Lamplighter scene at the end of Act II) or additions (as at the end of Act III). The Frampton Court manuscript remains the first authentic author's text, but in my early (1906) adherence to Rae's text and preferences, I failed to do justice to the value and validity of the revision of 1781. In the light of later investigation and of the present purpose of stressing the best published text rather than the earliest authentic Sheridan manuscript, I have adopted O1 as the basic text.

In O1, Becket printed *The Critic* with a specially engraved title-page inserted in place of the customary printed main title. In subsequent editions he continued to use this engraved title-page without alteration of the original date '1781.' This practice has been a confusing factor in bibliography. Still more confusing has been the accompanying difficulty inherent in the irregular order of the various leaves of signature A. In a perfect copy (such as the Dyce) of O1, the half-title, printed on A4, (folded back so that, in binding, it became the first leaf of the book) precedes the engraved title, inserted without pagination before the Dedication *To Mrs. Greville* (printed on A). Absence of the half-title in an incomplete copy is thus not readily apparent. In the subsequent editions (O2–O6) only the half-title infallibly indicates the number ('Second,' 'Third,' etc.) of the edition. Hence removal of the half-title from any of these editions gives the semblance of a complete *first* edition which begins with the invariable engraved title ('1781') and thereafter seems to follow the regular sequence of printer's signatures (A, A2) and pagination. The present multiplicity of so-called copies of the first edition is doubtless due in part to careless discarding of the seemingly superfluous printed half-title before the elaborate engraved title-page, and in part to deliberate destruction of the tell-tale half-pages of the numbered editions (O2–O6) so as to give them the appearance of first editions. Sichel (*Sheridan*, II, 452) rightly remarked: 'Without the half-title, it is impossible to distinguish a first edition from a second of this play.' Rhodes, (R, II, 261) who followed him in enumerating six 1781 octavos, added: 'They are to be distinguished by the half-titles, and I have not examined copies with these, since they are usually removed.' The *Catalogue of the Ashley Library* (V, 154–155) gives detailed description, with facsimile of half-title, of the Ashley Library copy of O1. Iolo A. Williams (*Seven XVIII*[th] *Century Bibliographies*, pp. 222–223) explicitly describes the Dyce copy of O1 and gives other pertinent bibliographical data.

(c) Later Becket Editions (1795–1811)

In 1795, Thomas Becket published a new octavo edition which, though sometimes confused with the previous octavos, may readily be distinguished from them. The re-engraved title-page still bears the original date '1781,' but indicates as the engraver — 'S. J. Neele, sculp[t]. Strand.' The edition is printed on paper plainly watermarked '1795.' (In the Yale copy, see, e.g., pp. 53, 65; Bodleian copy, pp. 5, 19, 37, etc.) The main text has 96 (instead of 98) pages, compressing the printing of Act III (from page 81 onwards), but without altering the text verbally.

The Becket text is continued in dated editions — Becket, 1808; Becket and Porter, 1811. The Yale copy of the latter (BP) has the rare half-title, indicating 'A New Edition. [Price Two Shillings.],' and the final leaf consisting of two pages of T. Becket's book-seller's advertisements. Though the foregoing discussions are mainly bibliographical, they are essential in showing that the original Becket text continued during Sheridan's lifetime as the recognized standard of successive printed editions.

(d) Acting Versions

The Becket text of 1781 (O1) maintained its influence in various Becket reprints in Sheridan's lifetime, and thereafter in Murray's (1821) and many later editions. Like the revision (Q3) of *The Rehearsal*, *The Critic* (O1) seems to embody the early changes suggested by actual stage experience in a revision that satisfied author and public as a standard printed edition. Like *The Rehearsal*, *The Critic* was thereafter peculiarly open to those prompter's and actors' changes of text and stage-business which are especially prevalent in the form of dramatic burlesque. Neither Sheridan nor others regarded the text of O1 as static or sacrosanct. Prompt-books, like that of 1782 in the Harvard Library, show how it was early cut or augmented, and printed editions, as early as Dibdin's, in 1814, consciously revise local hits and immediate allusions that had already lost currency. Dibdin's preface frankly recognizes that these 'temporary or local passages . . . have been always varied to suit the times and circumstances of current representation.'

The Critic, originally produced as an after-piece to *Hamlet*, ran in its full three-act form to questionable length. The early acting cuts accepted in the text of O1 were followed eventually by more drastic compression of the original three acts into two. The 1820 Oxberry text and the 1827 text of Cumberland's *British Theatre* (vol. XV) illustrate this major reduction of the extent of text, while their acting gags show considerable freedom in revising the content. The Yale University Dramatic Association acting version, published in New Haven in 1911, is similarly a two-act condensation, but reverts mainly to O1, rejecting the more flagrant changes of text often current in modernizations. (See my Introduction, pp. xi–xii, and text in that 1911 edition.)

Sheridan's Mr. Puff gave his actors 'leave to cut out or omit whatever they found heavy or unnecessary to the plot,' and, as his Under Prompter confessed, they took 'very liberal advantage' of that 'indulgence.' In the light of the history of many acting versions of *The Critic*, Puff's rueful ejaculation, 'The pruning-knife! — zounds! — the axe,' seems to suit not merely Mr. Puff's tragedy, but Sheridan's own burlesque.

G. H. N.